THE

VARIORUM EDITION

of the

Poetry of

JOHN DONNE

VOLUME 3

THE

VARIORUM EDITION

of the

Poetry of

JOHN DONNE

VOLUME 3

GENERAL EDITOR

Gary A. Stringer

ASSOCIATE GENERAL EDITOR

Donald R. Dickson

CHIEF EDITOR OF THE COMMENTARY

Paul A. Parrish

ADVISORY BOARD

Dennis Flynn

Dayton Haskin

M. Thomas Hester

Jeffrey S. Johnson

Albert C. Labriola

Paul A. Parrish

Ted-Larry Pebworth

John R. Roberts

Jeanne Shami

Ernest W. Sullivan, II

COMMENTARY

JEFFREY S. JOHNSON
Principal Co-Volume Commentary Editor

DENNIS FLYNN
Co-Volume Commentary Editor

M. THOMAS HESTER
Co-Volume Commentary Editor

BRIAN BLACKLEY
Contributing Editor

ANNE JAMES
Contributing Editor

PAUL J. STAPLETON
Contributing Editor

JULIE W. YEN
Contributing Editor

TEXTS

DONALD R. DICKSON
Textual Editor

TED-LARRY PEBWORTH
Senior Textual Editor

GARY A. STRINGER
Senior Textual Editor

with assistance from

DENNIS FLYNN
Assistant Textual Editor

TRACY E. McLAWHORN
Assistant Textual Editor

ERNEST W. SULLIVAN, II
Senior Textual Editor

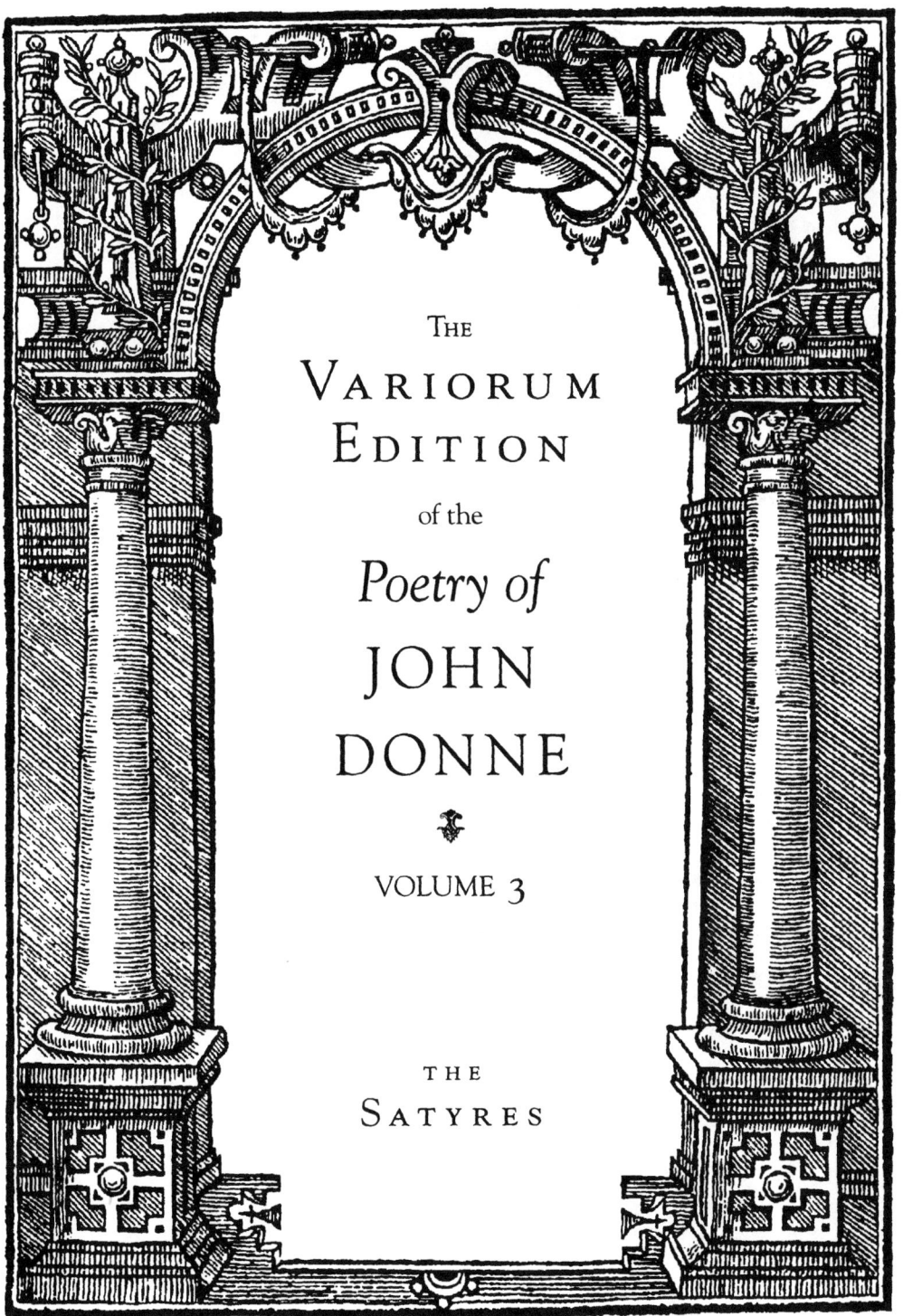

THE
VARIORUM
EDITION
of the
Poetry of
JOHN
DONNE

VOLUME 3

THE
SATYRES

Gary A. Stringer, *General Editor*

Indiana University Press   Bloomington and Indianapolis

The preparation of this volume was made possible in part by grants from the Division of Research Programs of the National Endowment for the Humanities, an independent federal agency. Any views, findings, or recommendations expressed in this publication do not necessarily reflect those of the National Endowment for the Humanities. Work on this volume was also supported by Research Development Funds from the College of Liberal Arts at Texas A&M University and by the David Julian and Virginia Suther Whichard Distinguished Professorship in the Humanities at East Carolina University.

Cataloging information is available from the Library of Congress.

ISBN 978-0-253-01290-6 (cloth)
ISBN 978-0-253-01307-1 (ebook)

2 3 4 5 21 20 19 18 17 16

Dedicated to

CLAUDE

DIANNE AND MALIA

ELEANOR

FLORA AND KAYLA

JAYN

JOHNNY AND JACKIE

LEE

THE MEMORY OF CARL M. STRINGER AND
JANICE WILSON STRINGER PENNY

ROBERT AND TOM

TING-WEI AND SU-O

and

WARREN

CONTENTS

Texts and Apparatuses

THE SATYRES

Commentary

THE SATYRES

Acknowledgments

A great many people and institutions have generously supported the Donne Variorum project since its inception in 1981, not only by providing specific services and financial aid, but also by offering encouragement, advice, and other forms of intangible support. We wish to acknowledge here those friends, colleagues, university administrators, library staffs, research assistants, and granting agencies and foundations that have made the work on this volume possible; and we look forward to recording similar debts as successive volumes proceed to publication.

University Administrators and Programs

We are grateful to the following university administrators and programs for providing financial support, adjusted teaching schedules, equipment and supplies, and staff assistance:

East Carolina University: Department of English; Jeffrey S. Johnson, former Chair, Department of English; Dierdre Mageean, former Vice-Chancellor, Division of Research and Graduate Studies; Alan R. White, former Dean of the Thomas Harriot College of Arts and Sciences.

Northern Illinois University: Department of English.

Texas A&M University: Colleen Cook, former Dean of Libraries; Ben M. Crouch, former Executive Associate Dean, College of Liberal Arts; Richard Furuta, Director, TEES Center for the Study of Digital Libraries; M. Jimmie Killingsworth, former Head, Department of English; Laura C. Mandell, Director, Initiative for Digital Humanities, Media, and Culture; Paul A. Parrish, former Head, Department of English; Steven E. Smith, former Director, Cushing Library and Archives.

Virginia Tech University: Edward S. Diggs Foundation; Joe Eska, Chair, Department of English.

LIBRARIES AND ARCHIVES

We also wish to thank the administrators and staffs of the following libraries and repositories, who have provided indispensable aid and ready access to materials: Aberdeen University Library; Universiteitsbibliotheek, Amsterdam; Bedfordshire Record Office; Bodleian Library; Bradford District Archives; University of British Columbia Library; British Library; Cambridge University Library; Chetham's Library, Manchester; William Andrews Clark Memorial Library; Cook Memorial Library, University of Southern Mississippi; Derbyshire Record Office; East Sussex Record Office; Edinburgh University Library; Ellis Library, University of Missouri; Emmanuel College Library, Cambridge; Fitzwilliam Museum; Cecil H. Green Library, Stanford University; Grosvenor Estate Office; Guildhall Library; Harvard University Libraries; Hertfordshire Record Office; University of Illinois Library; University of Kentucky Library; Leeds Archives Department; Leicestershire Record Office; Lincoln's Inn Library; University of London Library; London Public Record Office; University of Michigan Libraries, Ann Arbor and Dearborn; National Art Library, Victoria and Albert Museum; National Library of Scotland; National Library of Wales; Library of the University of Newcastle upon Tyne; New York Public Library; University of Nottingham Library; University of Pennsylvania Library; Pierpont Morgan Library; Princeton University Library; Rosenbach Museum and Library; Rutgers University Library; John Rylands Library, University of Manchester; St. John's College Library, Cambridge; St. John's College Library, Oxford; St. Paul's Cathedral Library; South African Public Library; University of Texas Library; Texas A&M University Library; Texas Tech University Library; Trinity College Library, Cambridge; Trinity College Library, Dublin; United States Air Force Academy Library; University Research Library, University of California at Los Angeles; Wayne State University Library; Westminster Abbey Library; Library of the University College of North Wales; Yale University Library; University of York Library.

Among librarians and archivists, we wish to express particular gratitude to the following for extraordinary aid in providing information about and access to bibliographical resources: Dr. Mary Ruwell, Head of Special Collections, McDermott Library, United States Air Force Academy, for facilitating access to the Mapletoft volume of the 1633 *Poems*; Mr. John Wells, Department of Manuscripts and University Archives, Cambridge University Library, for guidance in updating citations of materials in Cambridge University Library; Mr. Jo Wisdom, Librarian, St. Paul's Cathedral Library, for an informative conversation on Humphrey Wanley's cataloguing practices; Dr. Heather Wolfe, Curator of Manuscripts and Archivist, Folger Shakespeare Library, for helpful discussion of the Gosse manuscript of "Metempsychosis"; Mr. Peter Young, Archivist, York Minster Historic Collections Team, for providing access to William Mason's commonplace book.

Foundations and Granting Agencies

Although the National Endowment for the Humanities is acknowledged elsewhere in these pages, we wish to reiterate our profound gratitude for the support we have received through the agency's support for Scholarly Editions within the Division of Research Programs. And we appreciate the work of the many anonymous reviewers and panelists who, in reviewing our grant applications over the years, have provided an invaluable critique of our efforts. Without NEH support we could neither have continued this project nor have completed this volume.

Research Assistants

We would particularly like to draw attention to the many and variegated contributions made to this volume and the *Variorum* project generally by former Editorial Assistant Maia Fallesen, who systematically modernized our system of data management and aided greatly in developing the initial phase of *DigitalDonne*, and former Assistant Technology Editor Mary Farrington, who significantly extended the technological development of the project and aided in the construction of the texts and research tools in numerous ways. The manifold contributions of Technology Editor and Assistant Editor Tracy McLawhorn to the completion of this volume are detailed in the Introduction to Volume 3 below.

We also gratefully acknowledge our indebtedness to the late Cameron Purvis, who translated the Donne Variorum Textual Collation program into its current form, and to Carlos Monroy, who wrote the programming for and constructed the digital editions that appear on *DigitalDonne*. For other help in developing digital materials we express gratitude to Neal Audenaert, Stephanie Elmquist, and Tim Weaver.

We would also like to express our gratitude to the following, who as student research assistants at Texas A&M University and East Carolina University aided in the preparation of materials used in this volume and in the development of *DigitalDonne*: Kelley Bradley, Hazel Bright, Meredith Burns, Emma Calow, Cristina Cedillo, Dayoung Chung, Kirsis Concepcion, Olivia Cunningham, Amber Nicole Gardner Drake, Jake Fitzgerald, Marco Garcia, Nazenin L. Naime Gürel, Jacob A. Heil, Annie Jones, Tracey Kniffin, Danielle Lake, Michelle Lampton, Alesha Olesen, Mary Catherine Page, Rocky Patacsil, Laura Perrings, Jessica Scott, Sarah E. Slane, Brittany Swihart, Carly Thompson, Christopher Urban, Beverly Van Note, Paige Vaughan.

Friends and Colleagues

Among those who have rendered this *Variorum* project service over the past ten years, we owe most to Paul A. Parrish, former Head of the Department of English,

Texas A&M University, and to Jeffrey S. Johnson, former Chair of the Department of English, East Carolina University, each of whom at a critical juncture arranged institutional support that enabled the survival of the project.

For supplying translations and other help with items in foreign languages used in the Commentary we are grateful to Dr. James Frankki, the late Grace Hester, Shirley Jones, Dr. Lucjan Mordzak, and Matt Simmons of North Carolina State University and to the late Gustaaf Van Cromphout of Northern Illinois University.

For vetting various sections of the commentary in typescript we thank Heather Dubrow, Dayton Haskin, and Jeanne Shami.

For their several critiques of various parts of the progressing textual work we express appreciation to Joshua Eckhardt, Dennis Flynn, Arnold Hunt, Gregory Kneidel, Steven May, Sean McDowell, Sean Morris, Jeanne Shami, and Daniel Starza Smith.

For photographing pages from William Mason's commonplace book in York Minster Historic Collections we thank Kevin Killeen, and for transcribing Mason's imitation of Donne's first Satyre we thank Daniel Starza Smith.

As always, this project owes more to the support of Mary Ann Stringer than can be recounted or repaid.

CONSULTANTS

Three consultants have contributed immeasurably to our work by providing specialized assistance and expertise. We should like to thank Peter Beal, whose bibliographical contributions to this volume and to Donne studies generally are manifold; Yoshihisa Aizawa, who has continued in his role as general consultant for items of commentary in Japanese; and John R. Roberts, who has continued to serve as the project's principal bibliographer.

SHORT FORMS OF REFERENCE FOR DONNE'S WORKS

(In the interests of convenience and economy, we have used the following short forms throughout the *Variorum* commentary and the textual introductions. These forms are based on traditional headings or numberings except in cases where traditional designations are confusing, imprecise, or nonexistent. Spelling, capitalization, font, and pointing in this list are regularized, and none of these details should be accorded bibliographical or textual significance.)

POEMS

Air	Air and Angels ["Twice or thrice had I loved"]
AltVic	A Letter Written by Sir H. G. and J. D. Alternis Vicibus ["Since every tree begins"]
Amic	Amicissimo et Meritissimo Ben Jonson ["Quod arte ausus es hic tua"]
Anniv	The Anniversary ["All kings and all their favorites"]
Annun	Upon the Annunciation and Passion ["Tamely frail body"]
Antiq	Antiquary ["If in his study"]
Apoth	Apotheosis Ignatij Loyolae ["Qui sacer antefuit"]
Appar	The Apparition ["When by thy scorn"]
AutHook	Ad Autorem ["Non eget Hookerus"]
AutJos	Ad Autorem ["Emendare cupis Joseph"]
Bait	The Bait ["Come live with me"]
BB	To Mr. B.B. ["Is not thy sacred hunger"]
BedfCab	Epitaph on Himself: To the Countess of Bedford ["That I might make your cabinet"]
BedfDead	To the Countess of Bedford: Begun in France ["Though I be dead and buried"]
BedfHon	To the Countess of Bedford ["Honor is so sublime"]
BedfReas	To the Countess of Bedford ["Reason is our soul's left hand"]
BedfRef	To the Countess of Bedford ["You have refined me"]

BedfShe	Elegy to the Lady Bedford ["You that are she"]
BedfTwi	To the Countess of Bedford: On New-Year's Day ["This twilight of two years"]
BedfWrit	To the Countess of Bedford ["To have written then"]
Beggar	A Lame Beggar ["I am unable, yonder beggar cries"]
Blos	The Blossom ["Little thinkest thou"]
BoulNar	Elegy upon the Death of Mrs. Boulstrode ["Language thou art too narrow"]
BoulRec	Elegy on Mrs. Boulstrode ["Death, I recant"]
Break	Break of Day ["'Tis true, 'tis day"]
Broken	The Broken Heart ["He is stark mad"]
Cales	Cales and Guiana ["If you from spoil"]
Calm	The Calm ["Our storm is past"]
Canon	The Canonization ["For God's sake hold your tongue"]
Carey	A Letter to the Lady Carey and Mrs. Essex Rich ["Here where by all"]
CB	To Mr. C. B. ["Thy friend whom thy deserts"]
Christ	A Hymn to Christ at the Author's Last Going into Germany ["In what torn ship soever"]
Citizen	A Tale of a Citizen and his Wife (dubium) ["I sing no harme, goodsooth"]
Commun	Community ["Good we must love"]
Compu	The Computation ["For the first twenty years"]
ConfL	Confined Love ["Some man unworthy"]
Corona	La Corona
Cor1	"Deign at my hands"
Cor2	Annunciation ["Salvation to all that will is nigh"]
Cor3	Nativity ["Immensity cloistered in thy dear womb"]
Cor4	Temple ["With his kind mother who partakes thy woe"]
Cor5	Crucifying ["By miracles exceeding power of man"]
Cor6	Resurrection ["Moist with one drop of thy blood"]
Cor7	Ascension ["Salute the last and everlasting day"]
Coryat	Upon Mr. Thomas Coryat's Crudities ["Oh to what height"]
Cross	The Cross ["Since Christ embraced"]
Curse	The Curse ["Whoever guesses, thinks, or dreams"]
Damp	The Damp ["When I am dead"]
Disinher	Disinherited ["Thy father all from thee"]
Dissol	The Dissolution ["She is dead"]
Dream	The Dream ["Dear love, for nothing less"]
Eclog	Eclogue at the Marriage of the Earl of Somerset ["Unseasonable man, statue of ice"]
Ecst	The Ecstasy ["Where, like a pillow on a bed"]
ED	To E. of D. with Six Holy Sonnets ["See, Sir, how as the sun's"]
EdHerb	To Sir Edward Herbert ["Man is a lump"]
EG	To Mr. E. G. ["Even as lame things"]

EgDD	Epigraph from Death's Duel ["Corporis haec animae"]

Elegies:

ElAnag	The Anagram ["Marry and love thy Flavia"]
ElAut	The Autumnal ["No spring nor summer beauty"]
ElBed	Going to Bed ["Come, Madam, come"]
ElBrac	The Bracelet ["Not that in color it was like thy hair"]
ElChange	Change ["Although thy hand and faith"]
ElComp	The Comparison ["As the sweet sweat of roses in a still"]
ElExpost	The Expostulation ["To make the doubt clear"]
ElFatal	On His Mistress ["By our first strange and fatal interview"]
ElJeal	Jealousy ["Fond woman which would'st have thy husband die"]
ElNat	"Nature's lay idiot"
ElPart	His Parting From Her ["Since she must go"]
ElPerf	The Perfume ["Once and but once found in thy company"]
ElPict	His Picture ["Here take my picture"]
ElProg	Love's Progress ["Whoever loves, if he do not propose"]
ElServe	"Oh, let not me serve so"
ElVar	Variety ["The heavens rejoice in motion"]
ElWar	Love's War ["Till I have peace with thee"]
EpEliz	Epithalamion upon … the Lady Elizabeth ["Hail, Bishop Valentine"]
EpLin	Epithalamion Made at Lincoln's Inn ["The sunbeams in the east"]
EtAD	Epitaph for Ann Donne ["Annae/ Georgii More de filiae"]
EtED	Epitaph for Elizabeth Drury ["Quo pergas, viator"]
EtRD	Epitaph for Robert and Anne Drury ["Roberti Druri/ quo vix alter"]
EtSP	John Donne's Epitaph . . . in St. Paul's Cathedral ["Iohannes Donne/ Sac: Theol: Profess:"]
Expir	The Expiration ["So, so, break off"]
Fare	Farewell to Love ["Whilst yet to prove"]
Father	A Hymn to God the Father ["Wilt thou forgive"]
Faust	Faustinus ["Faustinus keeps his sister"]
Fever	A Fever ["Oh do not die"]
FirAn	The First Anniversary. An Anatomy of the World ["When that rich soul"]
Flea	The Flea ["Mark but this flea"]
Fun	The Funeral ["Whoever comes to shroud me"]
FunEl	A Funeral Elegy ["'Tis lost to trust a tomb"]
Gaz	Translated out of Gazaeus ["God grant thee thine own wish"]
GHerb	To Mr. George Herbert with One of My Seals ["Qui prius assuetus serpentum"]
Goodf	Goodfriday, 1613. Riding Westward ["Let man's soul be a sphere"]
GoodM	The Good Morrow ["I wonder by my troth"]
Ham	An Hymn to the Saints and to the Marquis Hamilton ["Whether that soul which now comes"]

Har	Obsequies upon the Lord Harrington ["Fair soul, which wast not only"]
Harb	The Harbinger to the Progress (by Joseph Hall) ["Two souls move here"]
Heart	"When my heart was mine own"
Henry	Elegy on the Untimely Death of . . . Prince Henry ["Look to me, Faith"]
Hero	Hero and Leander ["Both robbed of air"]
HG	To Sr. Henry Goodyere ["Who makes the past a pattern"]

Holy Sonnets:

HSBatter	"Batter my heart"
HSBlack	"O my black soul"
HSDeath	"Death be not proud"
HSDue	"As due by many titles"
HSLittle	"I am a little world"
HSMade	"Thou hast made me"
HSMin	"If poisonous minerals"
HSPart	"Father part of his double interest"
HSRound	"At the round earth's imagined corners"
HSScene	"This is my play's last scene"
HSShe	"Since she whom I loved"
HSShow	"Show me dear Christ"
HSSighs	"O might those sighs"
HSSouls	"If faithful souls"
HSSpit	"Spit in my face"
HSVex	"O to vex me"
HSWhat	"What if this present"
HSWhy	"Why are we by all creatures"
HSWilt	"Wilt thou love God"
HuntMan	To the Countess of Huntingdon ["Man to God's image"]
HuntUn	To the Countess of Huntingdon ["That unripe side of earth"]
HWHiber	H. W. in Hibernia Belligeranti ["Went you to conquer?"]
HWKiss	To Sir Henry Wotton ["Sir, more than kisses"]
HWNews	To Sir Henry Wotton ["Here's no more news"]
HWVenice	To Sir H. W. at His Going Ambassador to Venice ["After those reverend papers"]

Ignatius, verse from:

IgAver	"Aversa facie Janum referre"
IgFeath	"Feathers or straws swim on the water's face"
IgFlow	"As a flower wet with last night's dew"
IgLark	"The lark by busy and laborious ways"
IgNoise	"With so great noise and horror"
IgOper	"Operoso tramite scandent"

IgPiece	"That the least piece which thence doth fall"
IgPlum	"Aut plumam, aut paleam"
IgQual	"Qualis hesterno madefacta rore"
IgResemb	"Resemble Janus with a diverse face"
IgSport	"My little wandering sportful soul"
IgTanto	"Tanto fragore boatuque"
ILBlest	To Mr. I.L. ["Blest are your north parts"]
ILRoll	To Mr. I.L. ["Of that short roll"]
Image	"Image of her whom I love"
InAA	Inscription in the Album Amicorum of Michael Corvinus ["In propria venit"]
Ind	The Indifferent ["I can love both fair and brown"]
InLI	Inscription in a Bible Presented to Lincoln's Inn ["In Bibliotheca Hospitii"]
Jet	A Jet Ring Sent ["Thou art not so black"]
Jug	The Juggler ["Thou callest me effeminate"]
Julia	Julia (dubium) ["Hearke newes, ô Enuy"]
Klock	Klockius ["Klockius so deeply hath sworn"]
Lam	The Lamentations of Jeremy ["How sits this city"]
Lect	A Lecture upon the Shadow ["Stand still and I will read"]
Leg	The Legacy ["When I died last"]
Liar	The Liar ["Thou in the fields walkest"]
Libro	De Libro Cum Mutuaretur ["Doctissimo Amicissimoque v. D. D. Andrews"]
Licent	A Licentious Person ["Thy sins and hairs"]
Lit	A Litany ["Father of heaven and him"]
LovAlch	Love's Alchemy ["Some that have deeper digged"]
LovDeity	Love's Deity ["I long to talk with some old"]
LovDiet	Love's Diet ["To what a cumbersome unwieldiness"]
LovExch	Love's Exchange ["Love, any devil else but you"]
LovGrow	Love's Growth ["I scarce believe my love to be so pure"]
LovInf	Lovers' Infiniteness ["If yet I have not all thy love"]
LovUsury	Love's Usury ["For every hour that thou wilt spare me"]
Macaron	In Eundem Macaronicon ["Quot, dos haec, linguists"]
Mark	Elegy on the Lady Markham ["Man is the world"]
Martial	Raderus ["Why this man gelded Martial"]
Merc	Mercurius Gallo-Belgicus ["Like Aesop's fellow slaves"]
Mess	The Message ["Send home my long strayed eyes"]
Metem	Metempsychosis ["I sing the progress of a deathless soul"]
MHMary	To the Lady Magdalen Herbert, of St. Mary Magdalen ["Her of your name"]
MHPaper	To Mrs. M. H. ["Mad paper stay"]
NegLov	Negative Love ["I never stooped so low"]
Niobe	Niobe ["By children's birth and death"]
Noct	A Nocturnal upon St. Lucy's Day ["'Tis the year's midnight"]

Triple	The Triple Fool ["I am two fools, I know"]
TWHail	To Mr. T. W. ["All hail sweet poet"]
TWHarsh	To Mr. T. W. ["Haste thee harsh verse"]
TWHence	To Mr. T. W. ["At once from hence"]
TWPreg	To Mr. T. W. ["Pregnant again"]
Twick	Twickenham Garden ["Blasted with sighs and surrounded with tears"]
Under	The Undertaking ["I have done one braver thing"]
ValBook	A Valediction of the Book ["I'll tell thee now"]
ValMourn	A Valediction Forbidding Mourning ["As virtuous men pass mildly away"]
ValName	A Valediction of My Name in the Window ["My name engraved herein"]
ValWeep	A Valediction of Weeping ["Let me pour forth"]
Wall	Fall of a Wall ["Under an undermined and shot-bruised wall"]
Will	The Will ["Before I sigh my last gasp"]
Wing	Sir John Wingfield ["Beyond th'old pillars"]
Witch	Witchcraft by a Picture ["I fix mine eye on thine"]
WomCon	Woman's Constancy ["Now thou has loved me one whole day"]

PROSE WORKS

Biathanatos	Biathanatos, ed. Ernest W. Sullivan, II. Newark: U of Delaware P, 1984.
Devotions	Devotions upon Emergent Occasions, ed. Anthony Raspa. Montreal: McGill-Queen's UP, 1975.
Essays	Essays in Divinity, ed. Evelyn M. Simpson. Oxford: Clarendon, 1952.
Ignatius	Ignatius His Conclave, ed. T. S. Healy, S.J. Oxford: Clarendon, 1969.
Letters	Letters to Severall Persons of Honour (1651). A Facsimile Reproduction with an Introduction by M. Thomas Hester. Delmar, N. Y.: Scholars' Facsimiles & Reprints, 1977.
Paradoxes	Paradoxes and Problems, ed. Helen Peters. Oxford: Clarendon, 1980.
Sermons	The Sermons of John Donne, ed. George R. Potter and Evelyn M. Simpson. 10 vols. Berkeley: U of California P, 1953–62.

Abbreviations Used in the Commentary

Eighteenth- and Nineteenth-Century Periodicals

Ac	*The Academy*. London, 1869–1916.
AR	*The Andover Review*. Boston, 1884–93.
Art	*Artist and Journal of Home Culture*. London, 1880–1902.
Ath	*The Athenaeum*. London, 1828–1921.
Bo	*The Bookman*. London, 1891–1934.
BookR	*Book Reviews*, 1893–1901.
Cit	*The Citizen*. (American Society for Extension of University Teaching) Philadelphia, 1895–98.
EdRev	*The Edinburgh Review*, 1802–1929.
FR	*The Fortnightly Review*. London, 1865–1954.
LEM	*Lowe's Edinburgh Magazine*. Edinburgh, 1846–48.
LitG	*The Literary Gazette*, 1817–62.
LLA	*Littell's Living Age*. Boston, 1844–96.
MPS	*Miscellanies of the Philobiblion Society*, 1856–57.
MR	*The Monthly Review*. London, 1749–1844.
N&Ath	*Nation [and Athenaeum]*. London, 1828–1921.
NewR	*The New Review*, 1889–97.
NMM	*The New Monthly Magazine*. London, 1814–84.
NMMC	*The National Magazine and Monthly Critic*, 1837–38.
NQR	*Notes and Queries for readers and writers, collectors and librarians*. London, 1849–1924.
NR	*The National Review*. London, 1855–64; 1883–1950.
QR	*The Quarterly Review*. London, 1809–1967.
RR	*The Retrospective Review*. London, 1820–28, 1852–54.
SN	*Studies and Notes in Philology and Literature*. Cambridge, MA, 1892–1907.
TB	*Temple Bar*. London, 1860–1906.

Modern Journals

ABR	*American Benedictine Review*
Acc	*Accent*
AION-SG	*Annali Istituto Universitario Orientale, Napoli, Sezione Germanica* (Naples, Italy)
AL	*American Literature*
Anglia	*Anglia: Zeitschrift für Englische Philologie*
ANQ	*ANQ: A Quarterly Journal of Short Articles, Notes, and Reviews*; formerly *American Notes and Queries*
Ant	*Antaios*
Arcadia	*Arcadia: Zeitschrift für Vergleichende Literaturwissenschaft*
ArielE	*ARIEL: A Review of International English Literature* (Calgary, Canada)
ATR	*Anglican Theological Review*
BNYPL	*Bulletin of the New York Public Library*
BookM	*The Bookman* (New York)
BRMMLA	*Bulletin of the Rocky Mountain Modern Language Association*
BSEAA	*Bulletin de la Société d'Etudes Anglo-Américaines des XVIIᵉ et XVIIIᵉ Siècles*
BSUF	*Ball State University Forum*
BuR	*Bucknell Review: A Scholarly Journal of Letters, Arts and Sciences*
BUSE	*Boston University Studies in English*
CE	*College English*
Centrum	*Centrum: Working Papers of the Minnesota Center for Advanced Studies in Language, Style, and Literary Theory*
ChQ	*Church Quarterly*
CIEFLB	*Central Institute of English and Foreign Languages Bulletin*
CL	*Comparative Literature* (Eugene, OR)
CLAJ	*College Language Association Journal*
CLS	*Comparative Literature Studies*
CM	*The Cornhill Magazine*
ContempR	*Contemporary Review*
CP	*Concerning Poetry*
CQ	*The Cambridge Quarterly*
CR	*Critical Review*
Cresset	*Cresset* (Valparaiso, IN)
Criticism	*Criticism: A Quarterly for Literature and the Arts* (Detroit, MI)
CritQ	*Critical Quarterly*
CrSurv	*Critical Survey*
CS	*Cahiers du Sud*
DM	*The Dublin Magazine*
DownR	*Downside Review: A Quarterly of Catholic Thought*
DR	*The Dalhousie Review*
DUS	*Dacca University Studies*

DWB	*Dietsche Warande en Belfort*
EA	*Etudes Anglaises: Grande-Bretagne, Etats-Unis*
E&S	*Essays and Studies* (London)
EIC	*Essays in Criticism: A Quarterly Journal of Literary Criticism* (Oxford)
EIRC	*Explorations in Renaissance Culture*
ELH	*ELH* (formerly *Journal of English Literary History*)
ELLS	*English Literature and Language* (Tokyo)
ELN	*English Language Notes* (Boulder, CO)
ELR	*English Literary Renaissance*
EM	*English Miscellany: A Symposium of History, Literature and the Arts*
EMS	*English Manuscript Studies 1100–1700*
EncL	*Encounter* (London)
EnglRev	*English Review* (Oxford)
EnglStud	*Englische Studien*
ES	*English Studies: A Journal of English Language and Literature* (Lisse, Netherlands)
ESA	*English Studies in Africa: A Journal of the Humanities*
EsFI	*Estudios di filologia inglese*
Expl	*The Explicator*
GHJ	*George Herbert Journal*
GRM	*Germanisch-Romanische Monatsschrift*
HAB	*Humanities Association Review / La Revue de l'Association des Humanités* (formerly *Humanities Association Bulletin*)
Hermathena	*Hermathena: A Dublin University Review*
HLQ	*The Huntington Library Quarterly: A Journal for the History and Interpretation of English and American Civilization*
HudR	*Hudson Review*
IJES	*Indian Journal of English Studies* (Calcutta)
Ins	*Insula* (Supplemento) (Madrid)
Is	*Isis*
ISJR	*Iowa State Journal of Research*
JCP	*Journal of Canadian Poetry*
JDJ	*John Donne Journal: Studies in the Age of Donne*
JEGP	*JEGP: Journal of English and Germanic Philology*
JHI	*Journal of the History of Ideas*
JQ	*Jewish Quarterly*
JRMMRA	*Journal of the Rocky Mountain Medieval and Renaissance Association*
Káñina	*Káñina: Revista de Artes y Letras de la Universidad de Costa Rica*
KR	*Kenyon Review*
KVKEK	*Kroniek van Kunst en Kultur*
L&M	*Literature and Medicine*
Lang&S	*Language and Style: An International Journal*

LeS	*Lingua e Stile: Timestrale di Linguistica e Critica Letteraria* (Bologna)
Lis	*The Listener*
LIT	*Lit: Literature Interpretation Theory*
LitRev	*The Literary Review* (London)
LMer	*The London Mercury*
LWU	*Literatur in Wissenschaft und Unterricht* (Kiel, Germany)
MedHist	*Medical History*
MLN	*MLN* (formerly *Modern Language Notes*)
MLNew	*The Malcom Lowry Review* (formerly *Malcom Lowry Newsletter*)
MLQ	*Modern Language Quarterly*
MLR	*The Modern Language Review*
MLS	*Modern Language Studies*
MP	*Modern Philology: A Journal Devoted to Research in Medieval and Modern Literature*
MR	*The Massachusetts Review: A Quarterly of Literature, Arts and Public Affairs*
N&Q	*Notes and Queries*
NC	*Nineteenth Century*
Neophil	*Neophilologus*
NewQ	*The New Quarterly*
NewW	*The New World*
NLH	*New Literary History*
NM	*Neuphilologische Mitteilungen: Bulletin de la Société Néophilologique / Bulletin of the Modern Language Society*
NStat	*New Statesman*
NWR	*Northwest Review*
NYRB	*The New York Review of Books*
OnsE	*Ons Erfdeel: Algemeen-Nederlands Tweemaandelijks Cultureel Tijdschrift*
Paragone	*Rivista Mensile di Arte Figurativa e Letteratura*
PBA	*Proceedings of the British Academy*
PBSA	*Papers of the Bibliographical Society of America*
PCP	*Pacific Coast Philology*
Person	*Personalist*
PLL	*Papers on Language and Literature: A Journal for Scholars and Critics of Language and Literature*
PLPLS	*Proceedings of the Leeds Philosophical and Literary Society*
PMLA	*PMLA: Publications of the Modern Language Association of America*
PoetryR	*Poetry Review* (London)
PoT	*Poetics Today*
PQ	*Philological Quarterly* (Iowa City, IA)
PURBA	*Panjab University Research Bulletin* (Arts)
QJS	*Quarterly Journal of Speech*

Ren&R	*Renaissance and Reformation / Renaissance et Réforme*
RES	*Review of English Studies: A Quarterly Journal of English Literature and the English Language*
Rev	*Review* (Blacksburg, VA)
RevUnB	*Revue de l'Université de Bruxelles*
RMS	*Renaissance and Modern Studies*
RN	*Renaissance News*
RSH	*Revue des Sciences Humaines*
RSLR	*Rivista di Storia e Letteratura Religiosa*
SAQ	*South Atlantic Quarterly*
SatRLit	*Saturday Review of Literature*
SB	*Studies in Bibliography: Papers of the Bibliographical Society of the University of Virginia*
SCB	*The South Central Bulletin*
SCN	*Seventeenth-Century News*
SCRev	*South Central Review: The Journal of the South Central Modern Language Association*
SEL	*Studies in English Literature, 1500–1900*
SELit	*Studies in English Literature* (Tokyo)
SIcon	*Studies in Iconography*
SLitI	*Studies in Literary Imagination*
SMy	*Studia Mystica*
SoAR	*South Atlantic Review*
SoQ	*The Southern Quarterly: A Journal of the Arts in the South* (Hattiesburg, MS)
SSEng	*Sydney Studies in English*
SP	*Studies in Philology*
SPWVSRA	*Shakespeare and Renaissance Association of West Virginia—Selected Papers* (also known as *Selected Papers from the West Virginia Shakespeare and Renaissance Association*)
SR	*Sewanee Review*
SUSFL	*Studi Urbinati di Storia, Filosofia, e Letteratura*
TEXTiats	*Text: An Interdisciplinary Annual of Textual Studies*
Th	*Theology*
TLS	[London] *Times Literary Supplement*
TNTL	*Tijdschrift voor Nederlandse Taal-en Letterkunde* (Leiden, Netherlands)
Trivium	*Trivium* (Dyfed, Wales)
TSLL	*Texas Studies in Literature and Language: A Journal of the Humanities*
UCPES	*University of California Publications in English Studies*
UR	*The University Review* (Kansas City, MO)
UTQ	*University of Toronto Quarterly*
UWR	*University of Windsor Review* (Windsor, Ontario)
WascanaR	*Wascana Review*

WCR	*West Coast Review*
XUS	*Xavier University Studies: A Journal of Critical and Creative Scholarship* (New Orleans), now called *Xavier Review*
YES	*The Yearbook of English Studies*
YJC	*The Yale Journal of Criticism: Interpretation in the Humanities*

Hebrew Bible

Gen.	Genesis
Exod.	Exodus
Num.	Numbers
Deut.	Deuteronomy
Josh.	Joshua
Judg.	Judges
1 Sam.	1 Samuel
2 Sam.	2 Samuel
1 Chron.	1 Chronicles
Esth.	Esther
Ps.	Psalms
Prov.	Proverbs
Eccles.	Ecclesiastes
Cant.	Canticles (Song of Solomon)
Isa.	Isaiah
Jer.	Jeremiah
Ezek.	Ezekiel
Dan.	Daniel
Hos.	Hosea
Mal.	Malachi
Zech.	Zechariah

New Testament

Matt.	Matthew
Rom.	Romans
1 Cor.	1 Corinthians
2 Cor.	2 Corinthians
Gal.	Galatians
Col.	Colossians
Phil.	Philippians
1 Tim.	1 Timothy
Heb.	Hebrews
1 Pet.	1 Peter
2 Pet.	2 Peter
Rev.	Revelation (Apocalypse)

Shakespeare's Works

Ant.	*Antony and Cleopatra*
AWW	*All's Well That Ends Well*
AYL	*As You Like It*
Cor.	*Coriolanus*
Cym.	*Cymbeline*
Err.	*The Comedy of Errors*
Ham.	Hamlet
1H4	*Henry IV, Part 1*
2H4	*Henry IV, Part 2*
JC	*Julius Caesar*
Jn.	*King John*
LLL	*Love's Labour's Lost*
Lr.	King Lear
Mac.	*Macbeth*
MM	*Measure for Measure*
MND	*A Midsummer Night's Dream*
Oth.	*Othello*
PhT	*The Phoenix and the Turtle*
R2	*Richard II*
Rom.	*Romeo and Juliet*
TGV	*The Two Gentlemen of Verona*
Tmp.	*The Tempest*
TN	*Twelfth Night*
Tro.	*Troilus and Cressida*
Wiv.	*The Merry Wives of Windsor*
WT	*The Winter's Tale*

Other Works

AV	Authorized Version
CYT	The Canon's Yeoman's Tale (*The Canterbury Tales*)
DNB	*Dictionary of National Biography*
FQ	*The Faerie Queene*
Loeb	The Loeb Classical Library, founded by James Loeb
OED	*Oxford English Dictionary*
P.G.	*Patrologia Graeca*, ed. J. P. Migne
P.L.	*Patrologia Latina*, ed. J. P. Migne
Summa	*Summa Theologica* (St. Thomas Aquinas)

Sigla for Textual Sources

Manuscript Sources

(Entries listed as "Beal, *Index*" refer to citations in Peter Beal, comp., *Index of English Literary Manuscripts*; updated and expanded as the online *CELM* [*Catalogue of English Literary Manuscripts 1450–1700*]. <www.celm-ms.org.uk>.)

AF   United States Air Force Academy, Colorado
   AF1   Mapletoft volume (ms. emendations and transcriptions in a copy of A)

AU   Aberdeen University Library
   AU1   Aberdeen ms. 29

B   British Library
   B1   Add. 5956; B2   Add. 10309; B3   Add. 10337 (Elizabeth Rogers's Virginal Book); B4   Add. 15226; B5   Add. 15227; B6   Add. 18044; B7   Add. 18647 (Denbigh ms.); B8   Add. 19268; B9   Add. 21433; B10   Add. 22118; B11   Add. 23229 (Conway Papers); B12   Add. 25303; B13   Add. 25707 (Skipwith ms.); B14   Add. 27407; B15   Add. 28000; B16   Add. 30982 (Leare ms.); B17   Add. 32463; B18   Add. 34324 (Sir Julius Caesar's Papers); B19   Add. 34744 (West Papers XVIII); B20   Add. 44963; B21   Egerton 923; B22   Egerton 2013; B23   Egerton 2230 (Glover ms.); B24   Egerton 2421; B25   Egerton 2725; B26   Harley 3511 (Capell ms.); B27   Harley 3910; B28   Harley 3991 (Rawlinson ms.); B29   Harley 3998; B30   Harley 4064 (Harley Noel ms.); B31   Harley 4888; B32   Harley 4955 (Newcastle ms.); B33   Harley 5110; B34   Harley 5353; B35   Harley 6057; B36   Harley 6383; B37   Harley 6396; B38   Harley 6918; B39   Harley 6931; B40   Lansdowne 740; B41   Lansdowne 878; B42   Lansdowne 984; B43   Sloane 542; B44   Sloane 1792; B45   Sloane 1867; B46   Stowe 961; B47   Stowe 962; B48   *entry canceled*; B49   *entry canceled*; B50   Harley 791; B51   Add. 78423 (formerly siglum OX3)

BD   Bradford District Archives (West Yorkshire Archive Service, Bradford)
   BD1   Hopkinson's M.S.S., Vol. 17; BD2   Hopkinson's M.S.S., Vol. 34; BD3   Spencer-Stanhope Calendar No. 2795 (Bundle 10, No. 34)

BR   Bedfordshire Record Office
BR1   J1583 (St. John ms.)

C   Cambridge University Library
C1   MS Add. 29 (Edward Smyth ms.); C2   MS Add. 5778 (Cambridge Balam ms.); C3   MS Add. 8460 (Mary Browne Commonplace Book); C4   MS Add. 8470 (Edward Hyde ms.); C5   MS Ee. 4. 14 (Moore ms.); C6   MS Ee. 5. 23; C7   Keynes I. 7. 3 (Iosephi Scaligeri [Joseph Scaliger], *OPVS NOVVM DE EMENDATIONE TEMPORVM* (1583), holograph epigram); C8   MS Add. 8467 (Leconfield ms.); C9   MS Add. 8468 (Narcissus Luttrell ms.); C10   Keynes B. 4. 8 (Giles Oldisworth volume [ms. emendations in a copy of C]); C11   MS Add. 8466, Michael Corvinus, "Album Amicorum," holograph inscription; C12   MS Add. 9221

CE   Cambridge University, Emmanuel College Library
CE1   I.3.16 (James 68)

CH   Chester City Record Office
CH1   CR63/2/692/219

CJ   Cambridge University, St. John's College Library
CJ1   S.32 (James 423); CJ2   U.26 (James 548)

CT   Cambridge University, Trinity College Library
CT1   R.3.12 (James 592; Puckering ms.)

DR   Derbyshire Record Office
DR1   D258/28/5i; DR2   D258/31/16; DR3   D258/60/26a

DT   Trinity College Library, Dublin
DT1   877 (formerly G.2.21); DT2   877 (formerly G.2.21, second collection)

EE   Eaton Estate Office, Eccleston
EE1   Personal Papers 2/54

ES   East Sussex Record Office
ES1   RAF/F/13/1

EU   Edinburgh University Library
EU1   D.c.1.69; EU2   Laing III.436; EU3   Laing III.493; EU4   ms. 401 (Halliwell-Phillips Collection)

F   Folger Shakespeare Library
F1   L.b.541 (Loseley); F2   V.a.96; F3   V.a.97; F4   V.a.103 (Thomas Smyth ms.); F5   V.a.124; F6   V.a.125; F7   V.a.162 (Welden ms.); F8   V.a.169; F9   V.a.170; F10   V.a.241 (Gosse ms.); F11   V.a.245; F12   V.a.262; F13   V.a.276; F14   V.a.319; F15   V.a.322; F16   V.a.339; F17   V.a.345 (Curteis ms.); F18   V.b.43; F19   V.b.110; F20   W.a.118; F21   X.d.580 (Rudston ms.,

previously listed as P7)

FM   Fitzwilliam Museum, Cambridge
FM1   Fitzwilliam Virginal Book

H   Harvard University Library
H1   ms. Eng. 626; H2   ms. Eng. 686; H3   ms. Eng. 966.1 (Norton ms. 4502, Carnaby ms.); H4   ms. Eng. 966.3 (Norton ms. 4503); H5   ms. Eng. 966.4 (Norton ms. 4506, Dobell ms.); H6   ms. Eng. 966.5 (Norton ms. 4504, O'Flahertie ms.); H7   ms. Eng. 966.6 (Norton ms. 4500, Stephens ms.); H8   ms. Eng. 966.7 (Norton ms. 4620, Utterson ms.); H9   ms. Eng. 1107(15) (Gell Commonplace Book); H10   William Covell, *A IUST AND TEMPERATE DEFENCE OF THE FIVE BOOKS OF ECCLESIASTICALL POLICIE* . . . (1603), holograph epigram; H11   ms. transcriptions in a copy of A

HH   Henry E. Huntington Library
HH1   EL 6893 (Bridgewater ms.); HH2   HM 116; HH3   HM 172; HH4   HM 198 (Book I, Haslewood-Kingsborough ms.); HH5   HM 198 (Book II, Haslewood-Kingsborough ms.); HH6   HM 41536; HH7   HM 46323

HR   Hertfordshire Record Office
HR1   ms. 19061

IU   University of Illinois Library
IU1   William Leigh Commonplace Book; IU2   ms. 821.08/c737/17 (Joseph Butler Commonplace Book)

LA   Leeds Archives Department (West Yorkshire Archive Service, Leeds)
LA1   MX237

LL   Lincoln's Inn Library, London
LL1   Douai Bible, Vol. 1, holograph inscription

LM   London Metropolitan Archives
LM1   ACC 1360.528 (Clitherow ms.)

LP   London Public Record Office
LP1   State Papers Miscellaneous S.P. 9/51

LR   Leicestershire Record Office
LR1   DG7/Lit.2 (Burley ms.); LR2   DG9/2796

LU   University of London Library
LU1   Cornelius Schrevelius, M. *VALERII MARTIALIS EPIGRAMMATA* . . . (1661), Sir James Astry copy, ms. transcription

MC Chetham's Library, Manchester
MC1   Farmer-Chetham ms. 8012, A.4.15

NP University of Nottingham Library
NP1   Portland ms. Pw V 37 (Welbeck ms.); NP2   Portland ms. Pw V 191;
NP3   Portland ms. Pw V 6

NT University of Newcastle upon Tyne Library
NT1   Bell/White 25

NY New York Public Library
NY1   Arents Collection, Cat. No. S191 (John Cave ms.); NY2   Arents
Collection, Cat. No. S288 (Hugh Barrow ms.); NY3   Berg Collection,
Westmoreland ms.

O   Bodleian Library, Oxford
O1   Add. B.97; O2   Ashmole 36, 37; O3   Ashmole 38; O4   Ashmole 47;
O5   Ashmole 51; O6   Aubrey 6; O7   Aubrey 8; O8   Don.b.9; O9   Don.
c.54; O10   Don.d.58; O11   Douce f.5; O12   Eng. poet. c.9; O13   Eng.
poet. c.50; O14   Eng. poet. c.53; O15   Eng. poet. d.197; O16   Eng. poet.
e.14 (Lawson ms.); O17   Eng. poet. e.37; O18   Eng. poet. e.40; O19   Eng.
poet. e.97; O20   Eng. poet. e.99 (Dowden ms.); O21   Eng. poet. f.9
(Phillipps ms.); O22   Eng. poet. f.25; O23   Eng. poet. f.27; O24   Malone 16;
O25   Malone 19; O26   Malone 23; O27   Music d.238; O28   Music f.575;
O29   Rawlinson poet. 26; O30   Rawlinson poet. 31; O31   Rawlinson poet.
84; O32   Rawlinson poet. 90; O33   Rawlinson poet. 116; O34   Rawlinson
poet. 117 (Wase ms.); O35   Rawlinson poet. 142; O36   Rawlinson poet. 160;
O37   Rawlinson poet. 172; O38   Rawlinson poet. 199; O39   Rawlinson
poet. 212; O40   Rawlinson poet. 214; O41   Sancroft 53; O42   Tanner 465;
O43   Tanner 466; O44   Tanner 876 (ms. emendations in a copy of C);
O45   ms. 1018 (St. Michael's College Library, Tenbury Wells); O46   ms. 1019
(St. Michael's College Library, Tenbury Wells)

OC Oxford University, Corpus Christi College Library
OC1   ms. 327 (Fulman ms.); OC2   ms. 328

OJ Oxford University, St. John's College Library
OJ1   HB4/6.b.5.5 (Nathaniel Crynes volume; ms. emendations in a copy of A)

OQ Oxford University, Queen's College Library
OQ1   ms. 216

OX Oxford University, Christ Church Library
OX1   ms. Music 350; OX2   mss. 736–738; OX3   ms. Evelyn 254 (in
Variorum vols. 2, 6, and 8; identified in subsequently published vols. as B51)

P Private hands
P1 ms. Bedford 26 (Woburn ms. HMC. No. 26), Bedford Estates, London;
P2 Beal, Index, DnJ 1430; P3 Heneage ms.; P4 Frendraught ms. (Thomas
Fraser Duff ms.); P5 Abel Berland volume (ms. emendations in a copy of A,
plus ms.); P6 Sparrow ms.; P7 entry cancelled (see F21)

PM Pierpont Morgan Library, New York
PM1 MA1057 (Holgate ms.)
PT Princeton University Library, Robert H. Taylor Collection
PT1 ms. transcriptions in a copy of 22c; PT2 Beal, Index, DnJ 1431

R Rosenbach Museum and Library, Philadelphia
R1 239/16; R2 239/18; R3 239/22; R4 239/23; R5 239/27; R6 240/7;
R7 243/4.2; R8 1083/15; R9 1083/16 (Bishop ms.); R10 1083/17

RU Rutgers University Library
RU1 FPR 2247, E37

SA South African Public Library, Capetown
SA1 Grey 7 a 29 (formerly 2.a.II)

SN National Library of Scotland
SN1 Advocates' ms. 19.3.4; SN2 2060 (Hawthornden ms. VIII); SN3 2067
(Hawthornden ms. XV); SN4 6504 (Wedderburn ms.); SN5 Advocates' ms.
33.3.19

SP St. Paul's Cathedral Library
SP1 49.B.43; SP2 52.D.14

TA Texas A&M University Library
TA1 Henry White/Alan Haughton volume (ms. emendations in a copy of A)

TM Meisei University, Tokyo
TM1 Crewe ms. (formerly Monckton Milnes ms.)

TT Texas Tech University Library
TT1 PR 1171 D14 (Dalhousie I); TT2 PR 1171 S4 (Dalhousie II); TT3 St.
John Brodrick volume (ms. emendations in a copy of A)

VA Victoria and Albert Museum, Dyce Collection
VA1 Cat. No. 17, ms. 25.F.16 (Neve ms.); VA2 Cat. No. 18, ms. 25.F.17
(Nedham ms.); VA3 Cat. No. 44, ms. 25.F.39 (Todd ms.)

WA Westminster Abbey Library
WA1 ms. 41 (Morley ms.)

WB Library of the University College of North Wales
WB1 ms. 422 (Bangor ms.)

WC William Andrews Clark Memorial Library, Los Angeles
  WC1 S4975M1

WN National Library of Wales
  WN1 Dolau Cothi ms. 6748; WN2 Peniarth 500B; WN3 NLW ms. 5308E
  (Herbert ms.); WN4 NLW ms. 5390D; WN5 NLW ms. 12443A, Part ii;
  WN6 NLW ms. 16852D

Y Yale University Library, James Osborn Collection
  Y1 b62; Y2 b114 (Raphael King ms.); Y3 b148 (Osborn ms.); Y4 b150;
  Y5 b197; Y6 b200; Y7 b205; Y8 f b66; Y9 f b88

PRINTED SOURCES

Citations in parentheses following seventeenth-century publications below are
STC numbers from A. W. Pollard and G. R. Redgrave, eds., *Short-Title Catalogue of
Books Printed in England* . . . 1475–1640, and from Donald Wing et al., eds., *Short-
Title Catalogue of Books Printed in England* . . . 1641–1700. Items listed ambiguously
in the *STC* are further identified by location and shelfmark. Locations of printed
sources are as follows:

AUB	Universiteits-Bibliotheek, Amsterdam
C	Cambridge University Library, Cambridge
CLU–C	William Andrews Clark Memorial Library, Los Angeles, CA
CSmH	Huntington Library, San Marino, CA
CT	Trinity College, Cambridge
CtY	Yale University Library, New Haven, CT
DFo	Folger Shakespeare Library, Washington, DC
ICN	Newberry Library, Chicago, IL
InU	Indiana University Library, Bloomington, IN
IU	University of Illinois Library, Urbana, IL
KyU	University of Kentucky Library, Lexington, KY
L	British Library, London
LG	Guildhall Library, London
LU	London University Library
M	John Rylands Library, University of Manchester
MC	Chetham's Library, Manchester
MH	Harvard University Library, Boston, MA
MiU	University of Michigan Library, Ann Arbor, MI
NjP	Princeton University Library, Princeton, NJ
O	Bodleian Library, Oxford
OCh	Christ Church, Oxford
OJn	St. John's College, Oxford
OWa	Wadham College Library, Oxford

TxAM		Texas A&M University Library, College Station, TX
		(*TxAM1* [Henry White copy of A]; *TxAM2* [Shapiro copy of A])
TxLT		Texas Tech University Library, Lubbock, TX
TxU		University of Texas Library, Austin, TX
WBU		Bangor University Archives and Special Collections, Cathedral Library Collection

Seventeenth-Century Collected Editions/Issues:

A	1633	POEMS (STC 7045)
B	1635	POEMS (STC 7046)
C	1639	POEMS (STC 7047)
D	1649	POEMS (STC D1868)
E	1650	POEMS (STC D1869)
F	1654	POEMS (STC D1870)
G	1669	POEMS (STC D1871)

Selected Modern Editions:

H	1719	Jacob Tonson, ed., *Poems on Several Occasions*, Written by the Reverend John Donne, D. D.
I	1779	John Bell, ed., *The Poetical Works of Dr. John Donne*. Vols. 23–25 of *Bell's Edition: The Poets of Great Britain Complete from Chaucer to Churchill*
J	1793	Robert Anderson, ed., *The Poetical Works of Dr. John Donne*. In vol. 4 of *A Complete Edition of the Poets of Great Britain*
K	1810	Alexander Chalmers, ed., *The Poems of John Donne, D. D.* Vol. 5 of *The Works of the English Poets, from Chaucer to Cowper*
L	1839	Henry Alford, ed., *The Works of John Donne, D. D.*, vol. 6
M	1855	James Russell Lowell, ed., rev. by James Russell Lowell. *The Poetical Works of Dr. John Donne*
N	1872–73	Alexander B. Grosart, ed., *The Complete Poems of John Donne*, 2 vols.
O	1895	[Charles Eliot Norton, ed.], *The Poems of John Donne*, rev. by James Russell Lowell, 2 vols. [The Grolier Club Edition]
P	1896	E. K. Chambers, ed., *The Poems of John Donne*, 2 vols.
Q	1912	H. J. C. Grierson, ed., *The Poems of John Donne*, 2 vols.
R	1923	John Sparrow, ed., with bibliographical note by Geoffrey Keynes, *Devotions upon Emergent Occasions by John Donne*
S	1929	John Hayward, ed., *John Donne, Dean of St. Paul's: Complete Poetry and Selected Prose*
T	1942	Roger Bennett, ed., *The Complete Poems of John Donne*
U	1952	Helen Gardner, ed., *John Donne: The Divine Poems*
V	1956	Theodore Redpath, ed., *The Songs and Sonets of John Donne*
W	1963	Frank Manley, ed., *John Donne: The Anniversaries*
X	1965	Helen Gardner, ed., *John Donne: The Elegies and The Songs and Sonnets*

Y	1967	Wesley Milgate, ed., *John Donne: The Satires, Epigrams, and Verse Letters*
Z	1967	John T. Shawcross, ed., *The Complete Poetry of John Donne*
AA	1971	A. J. Smith, ed., *John Donne: The Complete English Poems*
BB	1978	Wesley Milgate, ed., *John Donne: The Epithalamions, Anniversaries, and Epicedes*
CC	1983	Theodore Redpath, ed., *The Songs and Sonets of John Donne*, 2nd ed.
DD	1985	C. A. Patrides, ed., *The Complete English Poems of John Donne*

Other Seventeenth-Century Sources and Locations:

1	1607	Thomas Dekker, *A KNIGHTS Coniuring* (STC 6508)
2	1607	Thomas Deloney, *Strange Histories* (STC 6567)
3	1607	Ben Jonson, *BEN: IONSON his VOLPONE Or THE FOXE* (STC 14783)
4	1609	Alfonso Ferrabosco, *AYRES* (STC 10827)
5	1609	Joseph Wybarne, *THE NEW AGE OF OLD NAMES* (STC 26055)
6	1611	Thomas Coryat, *CORYATS Crudities* (STC 5808)
7	1611	Thomas Coryat, *THE ODCOMBIAN BANQVET* (STC 5810)
8a	1611	John Donne, *Conclaue Ignati* (STC 7026); b 1611, Continental ed. (L C.110.f.46.); c 1681, in Thomas Barlow, *PAPISMUS* (STC B836); d 1682, in *PAPISMUS* (STC B837)
9a	1611	John Donne, *Ignatius his Conclaue* (STC 7027); b 1626 (STC 7028); c 1634 (STC 7029); d 1635 (STC 7030); e 1652, in *PARADOXES, PROBLEMS, ESSAYES, CHARACTERS* (STC D1866); f 1652, in *PARADOXES, PROBLEMES, ESSAYES, CHARACTERS* (STC D1867)
10	1611	John Donne, Elizabeth Drury Inscription (Hawstead)
11	1612	William Corkine, *THE SECOND BOOKE OF AYRES* (STC 5769)
12a	1613	Josuah Sylvester, *Lachrymæ Lachrymarū* (STC 23578; LU [D.–L.L.] (XVII) Bc [Sylvester] S.R.); b 1613 (STC 23578; DFo STC 23578.2); c 1613 (STC 23578; ICN CASE Y 185. S 9993); d 1613 (STC 23577.5; CtY Ig Sy57 612Ld); e 1613 (STC 23577.5; MC J.1.39); f 1613 (STC 23578; CtY Ig Sy57 612Lc); g 1613 (STC 23578; DFo STC 23578 copy 4); h 1613 (STC 23578; DFo STC 23578 copy 1); i 1613 (STC 23577.5; MH STC 21652 [14455.3517*]); j 1613 (STC 23577.5; M R37802)
13a	1614	Michael Scott, *THE PHILOSOPHERS BANQVET* (STC 22062); b 1633 (STC 22063)
14a	1616	Ben Jonson, *THE WORKES OF Beniamin Jonson* (STC 14751; CSmH 62101); b 1616 (STC 14751; CSmH 62104); c 1616 (STC 14751; TxU Ah J738 +B616a); d 1616 (STC 14752);

e   1640 (STC 14753); f   1640 (STC 14754); g   1692 (STC
J1006)

15   1617   John Donne, Robert Drury Inscription (Hawstead)

16   1617   Henry Fitzgeffrey, *SATYRES: AND SATYRICALL EPIGRAM'S*
(STC 10945)

17a   1618   Henry Fitzgeffrey, *CERTAIN ELEGIES, DONE BY SVNDRIE
Excellent Wits* (STC 10945.3); b   1620 (STC 10945.6)

18a   1619   William Basse, *A HELPE TO DISCOVRSE* (STC 1547);
b   1620 (STC 1548); c   1621 (STC 1549); d   1623 (STC
1549.5); e   1627 (STC 1550); f   1628 (STC 1551); g   1629
(STC 1551.3); h   1630 (STC 1551.5); i   1631 (STC 1551.7);
j   1635 (STC 1552); k   1636 (STC 1553); l   1638 (STC
1554); m   1640 (STC 1554.5); n   1648 (STC E23); o   1654
(STC E24); p   1663 (STC E25); q   1667 (STC E25A);
r   1682 (STC E25B)

19a   1621   William Basse, *A HELPE TO MEMORIE AND DISCOVRSE*
(STC 13051); b   1630 (STC 13051.3)

20a   1624   John Donne, *DEVOTIONS VPON Emergent Occasions* (STC
7033a); b   1624 (STC 7033); c   1624 (STC 7034); d   1626
(STC 7035); e   1627 (STC 7035a); f   1634 (STC 7036);
g   1638 (STC 7037)

21   1631   John Donne, Epitaph (St. Paul's Cathedral)

22a   1632   John Donne, *DEATHS DVELL* (STC 7031); b   1633 (STC
7032); c   1633 (STC 7032a; C Keynes B.5.24); d   1633 (STC
7032a; C Keynes B.5.29)

23a   1633   Henry Holland, *ECCLESIA SANCTI PAVLI ILLVSTRATA*
(STC 13584; L 577.c.4.[2].); b   1633 (STC 13584; LG A.7.6.
no. 2 in 32); c   1634 (STC 13585)

24a   1633   John Stow, *THE SURVEY OF LONDON* (STC 23345);
b   1640 [or later] (STC 23345.5)

25a   1635   John Swan, *SPECVLVM MUNDI* (STC 23516); b   1643
(STC S6238); c   1643 (STC S6238A); d   1665 (STC S6239);
e   1670 (STC S6240); f   1698 (STC S6240A)

26   1635   Katherine Thimelby, *TIXALL LETTERS*, ed. Arthur Clifford
[prints from lost seventeenth-century ms. dated 1635 by Keynes]

27   1640   [John Mennes?], *Wits RECREATIONS* (STC 25870)

28a   1640   Izaak Walton, *THE LIFE AND DEATH OF Dr DONNE*, in
John Donne, *LXXX SERMONS* (STC 7038); b   1658 (STC
W668)

29a   1645   John Gough, *THE ACADEMY OF Complements* (STC
G1401A); b   1646 (STC G1401B); c   1650 (STC G1401C);
d   1650 (STC G1402); e   1654 (STC G1403); f   1658 (STC
G1404); g   1663 (STC G1405); h   1670, *THE Academy OF
COMPLEMENTS Newly Refin'd* (STC G1405B); i   1684

(STC 1406; IU Hill 31 Mr.43 Gen. res.); j   1684 (STC 1406;
O Vet. A3 f. 313)

30   1650   THE MIRROUR OF Complements (STC M2223)

31a   1651   Lucius Cary [Viscount of Falkland], Discourse of
               INFALLIBILITY (STC F317); b   1660 (STC F318)

32a   1653   Francis Beaumont, POEMS (STC B1602); b   1653 (STC
               B1603); c   1660, Francis Beaumont and John Fletcher, POEMS
               (STC B1604)

33a   1653   Samuel Sheppard, MERLINVS ANONYMVS (STC A1588;
               DFo A1588); b   1653 (STC A1588; L E.1348.[1.]); c   1654
               (STC A1589)

34a   1653   Izaak Walton, The Compleat Angler (STC W661); b   1655
               (STC W662); c   1661 (STC W663); d   1664 (STC W664);
               e   1668 (STC W665); f   1676 (STC W666); g   1676,
               Izaak Walton, Charles Cotton, and Robert Venables, THE
               UNIVERSAL ANGLER (STC W674; L C.31.a.7); h   1676,
               Izaak Walton, Charles Cotton, and Robert Venables, THE
               UNIVERSAL ANGLER (STC W674; CSmH 138284)

35   1654   [Robert Chamberlain?], THE HARMONY OF THE MUSES
               (STC C105)

36a   1654   Edmund Gayton, PLEASANT NOTES UPON Don Quixot
               (STC G415; CSmH 148580); b   1654 (STC G415; CSmH
               148581)

37a   1654   Izaak Walton, THE LIFE OF Sir Henry Wotton, in Henry
               Wotton, Reliquiæ Wottonianæ (STC W3649); b   1672 (STC
               W3650); c   1685 (STC W3651)

38   1654   Richard Whitlock, ZΩOTOMIA (STC W2030)

39a   1655   John Cotgrave, WITS INTERPRETER (STC C6370); b   1662
               (STC C6371); c   1671 (STC C6372)

40   1655   Johann Grindal, Aendachtige BEDENCKINGEN (AUB 2328
               F28)

41   1655   Samuel Sheppard, THE MARROVV OF COMPLEMENTS
               (STC M719)

42a   1656   John Mennes, WIT AND DROLLERY (STC W3131); b   1661
               (STC W3132)

43   1656   Abraham Wright, Parnassus Biceps (STC W3686)

44a   1657   Joshua Poole, The English PARNASSUS (STC P2814; ICN
               CASE X 997.69); b   1657 (STC P2814; CSmH 12886);
               c   1677 (STC P2815); d   1678 (STC P2816)

45   1658   William Dugdale, THE HISTORY OF St. PAULS
               CATHEDRAL IN LONDON (STC D2482)

46   1658   Henry Stubbs, DELICIÆ Poetarum ANGLICANORUM IN
               GRÆCVM VERSÆ (STC S6040)

47   1659   John Suckling, THE LAST REMAINS OF St JOHN
               SVCKLING (STC S6130)

		Paul's Church, London. By Izaak Walton. With Some Original Notes, By An Antiquary.
70	1856	John Simeon, MISCELLANIES OF THE Philobiblon Society
71	1893	Sir Edmund Gosse, "The Poetry of John Donne," NewR, 236–47.
72	1899	Sir Edmund Gosse, The Life and Letters of John Donne, vol. 2
73	1958	Sir Geoffrey Keynes, "Dr. Donne and Scaliger," TLS, 21 February: 93, 108.
74	1967	John T. Shawcross, "John Donne and Drummond's Manuscripts," American Notes & Queries 5:104–05.

Variorum siglum	Traditional siglum	Beal siglum	Shelfmark/ call number	Manuscript name
Group I				
B32	H49	Δ 3	Harley 4955	Newcastle
C2	C57	Δ 4	Add. 5778(c)	Cambridge Balam
C8	Lec	Δ 5	Add. 8467	Leconfield
O20	D	Δ 1	Eng. poet. e.99	Dowden
SP1	SP	Δ 6	49.B.43	St. Paul's
Associated with Group I				
B30*	H40	Δ 2	Harley 4064	Harley Noel
Group II				
B7	A18	Δ 7	Add. 18647	Denbigh
CT1	TCC	Δ 13	R.3.12	Puckering
DT1	TCD	Δ 14	877	Dublin (I)
H4	N	Δ 9	Eng. 966.3	Norton
B40	L74	Δ 8	Lansdowne 740	Lansdowne
TT1	none	Δ 11	PR 1171 D14	Dalhousie I
TT2	none	Δ 12	PR 1171 S4	Dalhousie II
WN1**	DC	Δ 10	Dolau Cothi 6748	Dolau Cothi
Group III				
B46	S96	Δ 15	Stowe 961	Stowe I
H5	Dob	Δ 16	Eng. 966.4	Dobell
C9	Lut	Δ 18	Add. 8468	Luttrell
H6	O'F	Δ 17	Eng. 966.5	O'Flahertie
Group IV				
NY3	W	Δ 19	Berg Collection	Westmoreland
Associated with Group III (except HH4, these are listed as Group V in X and BB)				
B13	A25	Δ 21	Add. 25707	Skipwith
H3	Cy	Δ 22	Eng. 966.1	Carnaby
H7	S	Δ 23	Eng. 966.6	Stephens
HH1	B	Δ 24	EL 6893	Bridgewater
HH4	HK1	Δ 25	HM 198, Pt. I	Haslewood-Kingsborough (I)
HH5	HK2	Δ 26	HM 198, Pt. II	Haslewood-Kingsborough (II)
Y2	K or O1	Δ 29	b 114	King
NY1	JC	Δ 27	Cat. No. S 191	John Cave
VA2	D17	Δ 28	Cat. No. 18 [25.F.17]	Nedham
O21	P	Δ 20	Eng. poet. f.9	Phillipps
Y3	O or O2	Δ 30	b 148	Osborn

* First listed with Group I in X

** First listed with Group II in X; reads variously with Groups I and II

Symbols and Abbreviations Used in the Textual Apparatus

(used singly or in combination)

~	base word
^	punctuation mark omitted
→	changed to: A → B = A changed to B
*	obscured letter (the number of asterisks approximating the number of letters obscured)
[...]	conjectured reading
/	line break
|	scribal mark indicating the end of a sentence or section
›...‹	alteration/insertion in the scribal hand
»...«	alteration/insertion in a second hand
<...>	element omitted
{...}	element inserted
app, apps	appearance(s)
cor	corrected state of a press variant
del	deleted
err	reading from errata list
HE	heading
ind	indented, indentation
Keynes	Geoffrey Keynes, A *Bibliography of* . . . *Donne*, 4th ed.
M	margin, marginal
missing	missing because of damage to the artifact
om	omitted
rev.	reversed
SS	subscription
st, sts	stanza(s)
unc	uncorrected state of a press variant
var	variant reading(s)
Σ	all other collated sources
1st	first
2nd	second
3rd	third
4th	fourth

Figures

GENERAL INTRODUCTION

ORIGIN AND PLAN OF THE EDITION

Modern interest in Donne's poetry is amply demonstrated by the appearance of some fourteen major editions of the whole or of parts of the canon in the twentieth century and by the flood of critical and scholarly commentary catalogued in various periodic checklists (including the annual bibliographies published by the Modern Language Association of America, *Studies in Philology*, and the Modern Humanities Research Association) and in a number of specialized reference works. Among these are the four editions of Geoffrey Keynes, *Bibliography of the Works of Dr. John Donne*; Theodore Spencer and Mark Van Doren, *Studies in Metaphysical Poetry: Two Essays and a Bibliography*; Lloyd E. Berry, *A Bibliography of Studies in Metaphysical Poetry, 1939–60*; John R. Roberts, *John Donne: An Annotated Bibliography of Modern Criticism, 1912–67*; A. J. Smith, *John Donne: the Critical Heritage*; and John R. Roberts, *John Donne: An Annotated Bibliography of Modern Criticism, 1968–1978*. In response to the accumulated bulk and the continuing vitality of the critical activity reflected in these works and to a growing conviction within the community of Donne scholars that Donne's text needed to be reedited—a conviction strongly buttressed by the publication in 1980 of Peter Beal's *Index of English Literary Manuscripts*, which identified important manuscript material that none of Donne's editors had ever incorporated—the project to produce this variorum edition was conceived.

After considerable prior discussion about the feasibility and usefulness of such a work, the effort was formally organized in the fall of 1981 when a group of scholars was invited to meet on the Gulf Park campus of the University of Southern Mississippi to define the nature of the task and outline procedures for carrying it out. At that meeting Gary A. Stringer of the University of Southern Mississippi was designated General Editor, and an advisory board comprising the following members was established: William B. Hunter, Jr., University of Houston (Emeritus); Albert C. Labriola, Duquesne University; Paul A. Parrish, Texas A&M University; Ted-Larry Pebworth, University of Michigan-Dearborn; John R. Roberts, University of Missouri; John T. Shawcross, University of Kentucky; and Ernest W. Sullivan, II, Texas Tech University. Later this group was expanded to include M. Thomas Hester, North Carolina State University, and C. A. Patrides, University of Michigan, who sat on the Advisory Board until his death in 1986. In response to evolving organizational and individual purposes, the makeup of the Advisory Board has inevitably changed over the years, but it has been an abiding principle that members would not only help to steer the project, but also actively engage in the editorial work; and the respective contributions of Advisory Board members are noted in the various volumes of the edition, along with those of the other scholars who have participated in various ways. The project has also received widespread support from other individuals and institutions throughout the academic community and from a number of foundations and granting agencies. The contributions of all these supporters are gratefully and specifically acknowledged in the pages of the various volumes.

In accordance with the traditional ways of grouping Donne's works, the edition is organized into volumes, some of multiple parts, as follows:

Volume 1: General Commentary: the Historical Reception of Donne's Poetry
from the Beginnings to the Present
General Textual Introduction and Appendices
Volume 2: Elegies
Volume 3: Satyres, Metempsychosis
Volume 4: Songs and Sonets
Volume 5: Verse Letters
Volume 6: Anniversaries, Epicedes and Obsequies
Volume 7: Divine Poems
Volume 8: Epigrams, Epithalamions, Epitaphs, Inscriptions, Miscellaneous Poems

As this outline indicates, all volumes except the first contain texts and commentary for a set of generically or thematically related poems, and the volumes are numbered in a rough approximation of the order in which the poems were composed. Although this system of numbering may entail a certain amount of bibliographical confusion while the edition is in progress, we trust that upon completion of the entire project this method of ordering the parts will appear rational to bibliographers and critics alike.

THE COMMENTARY

Purpose and Scope

Although the material here presented will undoubtedly lend itself to other uses as well, our fundamental motive in compiling this variorum commentary is to facilitate further understanding of Donne's poems by situating them squarely within the tradition of critical and scholarly discussion that has grown up around them from the poet's own time to the present. This purpose, in turn, has required that we identify and examine all items that properly belong within that tradition. As existing bibliographical aids indicate, the body of commentary on Donne is not only vast, but widely scattered. In his 458-page synopsis of comments on Donne in the Critical Heritage series, for instance, A. J. Smith locates and excerpts 222 items published between 1598 and 1889; and John R. Roberts, in his bibliographies of twentieth-century criticism, lists and annotates well over 2,400 items written on Donne between 1912 and 1978, the second of these registering a trend that now sees the publication of approximately 100 books, articles, and notes on Donne every year. In addition to sheer bulk, as suggested above, the corpus of Donne commentary exhibits two further features that make it difficult to master: much of the material, both that identified in existing bibliographies and that which we have discovered, is dispersed throughout the pages of obscure or inaccessible editions and periodicals, and a good bit of it is written in foreign languages. The result of these circumstances is that scholarly or critical works of our own time frequently fail to align themselves distinctly within the critical tradition, and the continuing interpretive enterprise is marked by repetition and fragmentation.

There has been no previous attempt of this kind. None of the existing editions marshals more than a minute part of the available material, and the bibliographical volumes produced by Smith and Roberts have neither the scope nor the design of a variorum commentary, in addition to leaving entirely uncovered the periods 1890–1911 and 1979–present.[1] This variorum commentary, therefore, will fill a conspicuous gap in the field of Donne studies. In the effort to meet this need, we have defined our task in the broadest chronological and geographical terms. Although bibliographical considerations have dictated that we attempt coverage in each volume only to within three years of the completion of the typescript—and sometimes the gap between cut-off and publication dates is even greater—we have otherwise sought to bring together and synthesize all relevant items from the seventeenth through the twentieth centuries, and we have included material written not only in English, but also in French, German, Dutch, Italian, Spanish, Portuguese, Polish, Czech, and Japanese. Displaying the poems against this evolving, variegated background of critical discourse will, we believe, not only enable a better appreciation of individual works and of Donne's overall poetic achievement, but also provide materials toward an enhanced understanding of the aesthetic and intellectual history of the modern period. In short, the material here gathered will point the way to further research in a number of areas and facilitate the ongoing critical dialogue.

An undertaking like this, of course, is by its very nature conservative, bespeaking respect not only for what Donne has left us, but also for the contributions of those prior critics who have made possible our present understanding. Like those of contemporary critics, of course, the judgments of previous commentators are inevitably conditioned by cultural and personal assumptions about what poetry is (or should be), about how it functions in the world, and about the nature of criticism itself; and the validity of such assumptions tends to appear self-evident to those who hold them, with the frequent result that they are never explicitly stated. While the clarification of such preconceptions is itself a legitimate scholarly aim, we have not attempted in these pages to interpret the criticism nor to examine the various epistemological constructs that have shaped it, but have chosen rather to let each item of commentary

---

[1]Since this introduction was first written, Catherine Phillips has extended Smith's work in *John Donne II: The Critical Heritage* (1996), which adds items up through 1923; and Roberts has added two volumes to his series. All Roberts's volumes, including updates through 2008, are now available online at *DigitalDonne* (http://donnevariorum.tamu.edu).

speak for itself as best it can in the reduced form that it must necessarily take in these volumes. We recognize, of course, that no summary, however carefully prepared, can fully replace the original upon which it is based; indeed, the longer and more complex a given argument is, the less satisfactorily it submits to condensation. The compilation of commentary here offered is thus intended as a guide to, not as a substitute for, the primary works of scholarship that make up the tradition.

Editorial Stance

In attempting this consolidation of the critical heritage we have striven for both completeness and objectivity. Within the historical and linguistic limits noted above, we have sought to gather all published items of commentary and to represent each as accurately and extensively as our format permits. We have, furthermore, presented all these materials without interjecting editorial opinion on their validity or ultimate significance, though we have reduced redundancy in the presentation by fully reporting ideas only upon their first appearance, in some cases briefly tracing the progress of a given observation or line of argument by means of a system of internal cross-referencing. We have added neither glosses nor more general interpretations of our own, and have restricted instances of editorial intrusion (denoted by the abbreviation *ed.* in the text) to the correction of obvious factual error.

Organization of the Material within Volumes

As is customary in a variorum commentary, all material included here is organized chronologically and, when necessary within a given year, alphabetically by author's surname; and each item is aligned as precisely as possible with whichever aspects of the poetry it bears on. Thus, as noted above, Volume 1 traces in general terms the reception of Donne's poetry over the centuries, while the remaining volumes focus on individual genres and groups of poems. We have arranged the commentary in each genre-based volume along a continuum of particularity, beginning with the most general and proceeding to commentary on subsets of poems (where appropriate), commentary on particular poems, and line-by-line notes and glosses.[2] The material at all levels except glosses, moreover, is further organized into topical subunits whenever a common theme or critical concern runs through a number of items. In cases where an individual item of commentary depends specifically upon a previous version of Donne's text, we have included the relevant readings from that version.

Style of Presentation

We have attempted to present the commentary as efficiently and readably as possible. At all levels of organization above Notes and Glosses, the material is invariably summarized in narrative form, as the user is guided through the content by the editor's controlling voice, and the normal conventions of interpreting prose

---

[2]In glosses keyed to specific lines or words, of course, commentators frequently annotate items in surrounding lines as well, and it is not always possible to subdivide such manifold glosses into their component elements without destroying the author's sense. Especially in Notes and Glosses sections of the commentary, therefore, users are advised to examine each entry in the context of those that come before and after in order to ensure full coverage of what has been reported about a particular point.

summary apply. In Notes and Glosses, however, which derive variously both from specific observations abstracted from longer discursive comments and from the brief, telegraphic annotations often employed by editors, we have alternated between the narrative and the dramatic styles as necessary in an attempt to present each bit of material as economically as possible (though we have not intermixed the two modes within the entry for a single author). Following any lemma in the Notes and Glosses, therefore, one commentator's remarks may be rendered dramatically, as though the original author were speaking in his or her own voice, while those of the next may be paraphrased in the editor's voice. The dramatic mode, whether or not any words or phrases in the entry appear in quotation marks, is signaled mechanically by a colon after the bibliographical citation in parentheses, the narrative mode by the absence of a colon. Editorial insertions thus appear in brackets in the dramatic mode and in parentheses in the narrative mode.

Bibliographical Conventions in the Commentary

Works mentioned in the Commentary are cited parenthetically by author and date, and these citations are keyed to a master list of Works Cited in each volume. Since the commentary throughout the *Variorum* is ordered according to a multi-leveled taxonomic system, the author index included in each volume, used in conjunction with the master list of works cited, will provide the further information needed to index the content of the volume.[3] We have used standard nonverbal symbols and short forms of reference insofar as possible, and have derived common scholarly abbreviations, including those for such items as the titles of Shakespeare's plays and books of the Bible, from the current *MLA Style Manual*. For titles of current journals we have used the abbreviations given in the *MLA International Bibliography*, and for early books we have appropriated the short forms of reference standardized by Pollard and Redgrave and by Wing in the *STC*. Lists of abbreviated references to all works cited in the commentary and to Donne's poems and prose works are provided in each volume, and we have standardized all citations of Donne's prose works in the commentary in accordance with the editions specified in the list of Short Forms. Unless otherwise indicated, cross-references pertain to the section of commentary within which they appear.

The Text

Materials and Theory

Ideally stated, the goal of our work on the text is to recover and present exactly what Donne wrote. It is important, however, that we be clear about certain practical and theoretical limits that are imposed upon this goal by the available materials. Apart from about forty prose letters and certain occasional jottings, four inscriptions in the books of friends or acquaintances, and an epitaph on his wife, only a single

---

[3]Beginning with our volume on Donne's elegies in 2000, we have added two further indexes: (1) an index of writers and historical figures mentioned in the commentary and (2) an index of all references to Donne's works in the commentary.

poem—a verse epistle addressed to the Lady Carey and Mrs. Essex Riche—is known to survive in Donne's hand. Of the relatively few poems published before his death in 1631, only for the Anniversaries, in the edition of 1612, and in the first Latin and English editions of *Ignatius* is there any evidence to suggest that the author may have proofread and corrected copy. The remainder of the poems survive only in nonauthorial copies (which amount to well over 4,000 separate transcriptions of individual poems), at indeterminate degrees of remove from holograph and therefore of indeterminate authority. During and immediately following Donne's lifetime these poems, circulating individually or in groups of various sizes and composition, were copied into diaries, commonplace books, miscellanies, and poetic collections that form several distinct strands of scribal transmission; and these strands, in ways impossible to determine exactly, lie behind the print tradition that begins for most of the poems with the publication in 1633 of *Poems, by J. D. with Elegies on the Authors Death* and continues in six additional seventeenth-century collected editions and issues.

The almost total absence of holograph materials or of authorially approved printings renders impossible any attempt to locate textual authority in the author's intentions, as that concept is generally applied in scholarly editing. Indeed, the only "intention" Donne seems to have had for most of his poems in this regard was that they *not be printed at all*. Commenting on the publication of the Anniversaries in a letter to George Garrard from Paris on April 14, 1612, Donne wrote, "I . . . do not pardon my self" for having "descended to print any thing in verse" (*Letters* 238), and when in 1614 he thought himself "brought to a necessity of printing" (*Letters* 196) the poems as a "valediction to the world" before taking holy orders (a necessity he apparently escaped), he sought to borrow from his friend Henry Goodyer an "old book" (*Letters* 197) containing copies of them, thus suggesting that—at least for some of the poems— he had failed even to retain manuscript copies for his own use or reference.

If virtually none of them bears the author's imprimatur, the surviving materials for constructing a text of Donne's poems are nonetheless numerous and diverse. In addition to the seven collected printings issued between 1633 and 1669, they include 239 manuscript sources (nearly 100 of which have been unknown to any of Donne's previous editors); 3 inscriptions on monuments; over 200 seventeenth-century books that collectively contain over 700 copies of individual Donne poems or excerpts (approximately 500 of which have been unknown to Donne's previous editors); and over 20 historically significant editions of all or of parts of the canon from the eigh- teenth century to the present. No one would argue, of course, that all of this material is equally valuable for establishing the text, but all of it, including both corrected and uncorrected states of the seventeenth-century editions (among which we have identified many previously unrecorded press variants), is part of the bibliographical tradition that provides what we currently know of Donne's poems and their textual history. A full description of these textual artifacts and the relations among them is provided in volume 1 of the edition.

The nature of the material described above severely complicates the question of textual authority—not only with respect to the presentation of the individual poems, but also in the matters of how to order the poems within an edition and, to a lesser extent, what works to admit to the canon. No scribal artifact and no pre-twentieth-century edition includes the full complement of what are now generally recognized as authentic poems. While it preserves a general continuity in the texts of individual poems, the tradition represented by the seventeenth-century collected editions shows a gradual expansion and, especially in 1635, rearrangement of the canon, as printers sought to publish increasingly comprehensive and generically rationalized editions; and not until Grosart's edition of 1872–73 do we find a modern editor basing his work extensively on manuscript sources rather than on the print tradition. From Grierson (1912) onward, most of Donne's twentieth-century editors have adopted as copy-text for each poem an early seventeenth-century printing, sometimes emending its details (especially verbal variants) toward manuscript readings, and virtually all modern editions order their contents according to the broad generic divisions introduced in the edition of 1635.

As noted above, we also have adopted the traditional generic divisions as an ordering principle. We have not, however, necessarily followed the majority practice of locating primary textual authority for each poem in an early printing, and we have not practiced the eclecticism that has frequently accompanied such a choice. In accordance with the considerations outlined below, we have selected copy-texts variously from among all the available artifacts, and we have presented them with a minimum of editorial intervention. Both practices require explanation.

We have chosen manuscript copy-texts for many of the poems simply because they seem in fact and in theory more likely to represent the lost originals accurately than do the early printings. As noted above, the exact textual genesis of the early collected editions cannot be ascertained. Although individual poems in some of these editions may have been set from holograph, it is extremely unlikely that even the printer in 1633 possessed authorial copies of more than a few of the poems—and perhaps of none at all. Given the occasional composition, the piecemeal distribution, and the wide circulation of the poems in manuscript—and especially the author's apparent failure to maintain a comprehensive personal archive—it is very hard to imagine that an extensive holograph collection of Donne's poems ever existed, even in the seventeenth century. Indeed, the phrasing of Donne's request for Goodyer's "old book" may suggest that the author himself expected to retrieve transcriptions rather than original copies. Most probable is that the original holographs gradually dropped out of circulation as the poems made the rounds of transmission, and there is thus the virtual certainty that even the earliest editions were set from derivative manuscript collections very much like those that survive.

Whatever their origins, moreover, comparison of the early printings with the surviving scribal manuscripts—or even with the extant holograph verse letter—shows clearly that as texts underwent translation from manuscript to print in the publishing house, they not only suffered some measure of verbal corruption, but also were subjected to institutional conventions of punctuation, spelling, capitalization, and so forth—even in instances when the printer may have been setting from holographs. In thus reflecting the intersection of private scribal or authorial practices with the social norms of commercial printing, the printed text inevitably became a collaborative product that differed in a number of important ways from what Donne had originally set down.[4]

The data clearly show, of course, that the poems were similarly vulnerable to change in the course of scribal transmission. Undoubtedly, many scribes automatically restyled the poems to accord with their own habits of formatting, spelling, capitalization, and punctuation; and some no doubt made conscious verbal "improvements." As they transcribed poems into private collections for their own use or that of patrons, however, the early copyists did not necessarily share the printer's programmatic determination to groom the text into a publicly negotiable, regularized form; and most of the substantive changes they introduced into the text are more likely attributable to carelessness, ignorance, and the general entropy of the transmissional system.

Most of the manuscripts antedate the printed editions, of course, and thus are chronologically closer to the hand of the author. A number of factors, however, seriously restrict any attempt to determine their dates of compilation and thus to construct a comprehensive genealogy of manuscripts. For one thing, many of the manuscripts cannot be dated except in very approximate terms; moreover, an indeterminate number of manuscripts are evidently missing. The greatest limitation on developing a reliable stemma of manuscripts, however, is that virtually all the major manuscript collections, like the printed editions, are composite artifacts containing texts of individual poems drawn from multiple sources, and a given manuscript may thus preserve an early state of one text and a late state of another side by side. In some cases, of course, particular features of content, format, and scribal style point to family relationships among manuscripts and sometimes even reveal direct lines of descent within families. Generally speaking, however, the effort to locate textual authority in a genealogy of manuscripts is doomed to fail.

Given the situation described above, the only remaining alternative is to approach Donne's text on a poem-by-poem basis, examining all copies of each poem and determining insofar as possible its individual history of transmission. As with whole manuscripts, the possibility of missing copies and the intractability of the surviving evidence also make it impossible to construct a complete genealogy for many of the poems. With varying degrees of precision, however, it is possible to identify patterns of variation that lead back to the least corrupted surviving version(s) of a poem and to chart the transmission of its text in a schema of textual relationships. As this procedure implies, of course, the effort to recover Donne's poems necessarily rests partly in the editor's evaluation of the relative semiological integrity of the surviving copies of individual poems. Once this determination has been made, the question then becomes one of how those individual copies shall be edited.

As noted above, most of Donne's twentieth-century editors have created synthetic or eclectic texts, adopting a seventeenth-century printing of each poem as copy-text and generally following that printing's accidentals, while sometimes emending its substantives toward manuscript readings. There are, however, a number of problems with this approach. A major one, in our view, as Charles Moorman has argued in

---

[4]Between the holograph of the 63-line verse letter and the text printed in 1633, for instance, there are 56 differences in punctuation, 63 differences in capitalization, 120 differences in spelling, and 3 differences in wording.

discussing a similar case, is that the practice involves the highly questionable assumption that any modern editor—even one very sensitive, learned, and wise—can reach back over hundreds of years and somehow ascertain what must have been in Donne's mind, root out instances of corruption, and synthetically reconstruct a text reflecting what he actually wrote. Indeed, as Fredson Bowers has pointed out, Greg's rationale of copy-text, the classic formulation of the synthetic principle, was intended to apply in cases in which the variant forms of a work could be assumed to form a single ancestral sequence reaching back to the author's holographs. Clearly, in the case of Donne, whose poems survive in many genealogical strands of indeterminate proximity to each other and to the manuscript originals, an eclectic approach that privileges the early printings offers only a qualified hope of recovering the author's exact words—and even less of recovering his accidentals. Additionally, of course, in cases where an author has revised a work (as Donne did in some instances), an eclectic approach entails the risk of conflating earlier and later states of the text.

Any editor of Donne must, of course, exercise judgment; but there are legitimate differences of opinion about where, how often, and especially at what stage of the editorial process that judgment can most defensibly be exercised. In light of the circumstances described above, we have attempted to identify—by combining bibliographical analysis with such logical criteria as completeness and general semantic coherence—the earliest, least corrupted state of each poem from among the surviving seventeenth-century artifacts or, in the case of poems surviving in multiple authorial versions, the least corrupted state of each version; and once that judgment has been reached, we have edited the text in the conservative manner explained below. The theory underlying our work is thus fundamentally historicist, but balanced by a respect for what we have called the semiological integrity of the individual poem as preserved in an early artifact. We recognize that, except by extreme good fortune, we are not likely to present any nonholographic poem exactly as Donne wrote it, but this approach does allow us to present a text of every poem essentially free of conjecture and anachronistic intervention.

This, then, is the sense in which we mean that we have sought to recover and present exactly what Donne wrote. Our text is a representation of the poem that stands in a metonymic relationship to the lost original, different both in that it may not have the exact wording and pointing of that original and—for texts based on manuscript originals—in that it will be a print exemplum of the copy from which it derives. It is, however, a text that somebody in Donne's own time—the one who had the copy closest to his hand and transcribed it most accurately, if we are lucky—set down as what the author had written. Because it provides an illuminating background for our work and because it is a legitimate scholarly concern in its own right, we have further undertaken to outline the textual history of each poem as fully and as accurately as possible.

Procedures for Choosing and Emending Copy-text

To the ends specified above we have adopted the following procedures for choosing and emending copy-texts and constructing the textual apparatus. First, since most of the texts survive only in nonauthorial copies, we have necessarily examined every surviving seventeenth-century manuscript and multiple copies of seventeenth-century printings.[5] In order to do this, we have entered the texts of all manuscript and early print copies of the poems into computer files and compared the files for each poem by means of the Donne Variorum Collation Program.[6] On the basis of these collations, we have constructed for each poem a schema of textual relationships that accounts, insofar as the evidence permits, for all permutations of the texts in the early artifacts. In order to corroborate the evidence of this analysis, as suggested above, we have independently assessed the evidentiary value of each artifact by determining insofar as possible its date, provenance, and process of compilation and by evaluating all this bibliographical detail in the context of what is known about manuscript transcription and practices of typesetting in the late sixteenth and earlier seventeenth centuries. The copy-text finally chosen is what seems to be the earliest, least-corrupted state of the text as preserved in the best witness among the artifacts in which it appears. Having made this identification, we have corrected obvious errors in the copy-text, emended punctuation when absolutely necessary to prevent misreading, and applied certain print conventions to manuscript copy-texts, but we have not conflated readings from multiple sources. In cases where one or more artifacts preserve a poem in a state so extensively revised or changed as to constitute a new version, we present the successive versions in full and, whenever it seems useful to do so, provide a separate historical collation for each.

In accordance with our determination to represent the copy-text authentically and accurately, we have retained in the *Variorum* texts a number of seventeenth-century orthographical and typographical features and, except for the silent changes specified below, have noted in the apparatus accompanying each poem all emendations to the copy-text. The *Variorum* texts preserve the distinct forms of "i" and "j" and "u" and "v," the ligatured vowels "æ" and "œ," and the fonts of words as they appear in the copy-text. We have, however, expanded brevigraphs, regularized "VV" to "W" and "ff" to "F," and imposed on manuscript copy-texts such print conventions as the consistent capitalization of the first word of each line of poetry. All such emendations, as well as the few editorial corrections deemed necessary, are noted in the lists of emendations. Our only silent emendations of the copy-text are typographical and affect neither spelling nor meaning: we have reduced the long "ſ" to "s," separated such ornamental ligatured consonants as "ſt" and "ct," and regularized inconsistencies of font and the spacing of punctuation.

Because Donne's syntax is often knotty, punctuation itself is frequently interpretive. Recognizing this, we have emended the punctuation of the copy-text very

---

[5] When a seventeenth-century printing is used as copy-text, we have collated at least five copies (or all copies, if fewer than five copies survive); when the copy-text is a manuscript, we have collated at least three copies of all seventeenth-century printings of the poems, except that we have generally collated only one copy if a print source contains only an excerpt from a poem.

[6] We have verified all data files used in the preparation of these texts against original sources, and have compared multiple copies of printed artifacts not only by sight, but also, when it has been possible to bring the requisite materials together, by means of the Lindstrand Comparator or the Hinman Collator. At all stages of transcription and data entry, at least three editors have proofread the work independently, resolving any problems or differences of interpretation in conference. At each stage of production we have taken similar care to verify the accuracy of both text and apparatus.

conservatively, and this principle has resulted in an actual, though not a theoretical, inconsistency. Since printers of the earlier seventeenth century tended to punctuate heavily and grammatically, while many scribes of that period punctuated lightly and rhetorically (sometimes even to the point of regarding the line end as sufficient punctuation in itself), the *Variorum* texts based on printed copy-texts and those based on manuscript copy-texts show markedly different degrees of punctuation. But we think it better to present texts that, in each case, accurately reflect a bibliographically defensible choice of copy-text than to impose consistency of punctuation and with it the possibility of editorial interpretation. Variant seventeenth-century pointing that may affect the sense of a given passage is recorded in the historical collation.

Introductions and Apparatuses

Each poem is provided with a brief textual introduction, and groups of related poems are introduced collectively when it is useful to do so. The introduction to each poem briefly locates the poem in the context of Donne's life or poetic development (when possible) and outlines the seventeenth-century textual history of the poem by grouping the artifacts into families and describing insofar as possible the relationships of those families, as well as noting readings of particular bibliographical or critical interest. It then sketches the treatment of the poem by modern editors and briefly discusses the choice and emendation of the copy-text.

For complete textual information on any poem, of course, readers must consult both the textual introductions and the various parts of the textual apparatus. As suggested above, the textual apparatus may include data drawn from five different classes of material: (1) manuscripts, (2) independent seventeenth-century editions of Donne's poetical works (including seventeenth-century editions of the Anniversaries and collected editions or issues), (3) uncollected seventeenth-century printings of individual poems and excerpts of two or more lines, (4) modern first printings of individual poems, and (5) selected modern editions of Donne's poetical works. In general, the apparatus lists the sigla of source materials in the demonstrable or probable order of the transmission of the text, ordering items within classes alphabetically or numerically as appropriate.

The following categories of information are included in the textual apparatus for each poem, except that in cases where there is nothing to report, the category is omitted:

1. Copy-text and Sources Collated. Lists by sigla the copy-text and the copies and excerpts collated, specifying the folio or page numbers on which the poem or excerpt appears in each artifact, and, in the case of deliberate excerpts, which lines are excerpted.

2. Emendations of the Copy-text. Specifies differences between the copy-text and the *Variorum* text.

3. Historical Collation.

a. Format. Details noteworthy features of the artifacts or transcriptions, including typefaces, paragraphing, patterns of indentation (though not occasional deviations) in stanzaic verse, scribal eccentricities, lines missing in damaged artifacts, and other information affecting text or indicating authorship or provenance.

b. Headings. Lists variant headings (not called "titles," since their authority is uncertain) in seventeenth-century artifacts.

c. Line-by-line collation. Lists all substantive and selected semisubstantive variants (specified below) in seventeenth-century sources, as well as any omissions of words or lines in copies intended to be complete.

d. Subscriptions. Lists all subscriptions in seventeenth-century artifacts.

4. Verbal Variants in Selected Modern Editions. Lists verbal variants in twenty-three historically or bibliographically significant editions from the eighteenth century to the present.[7]

5. Stemma or Schema of Textual Relationships. Charts in schematic form the genealogy of each poem and the relationships of the textual artifacts, denoting definite lines of transmission with arrows, definite associations and family linkages with solid lines, and conjectural lines of relationship with dotted lines.

6. Analyses of Early Printed Copies. Lists copies collated, describes the physical makeup of each, and details press variants.

Reportage of Variants

We have tried to make the list of variants useful to many kinds of readers, from textual scholars and literary historians to critics and metricians. In order to do so, we have reported the following kinds of substantive and semisubstantive variants:

1. All verbal variants in seventeenth-century artifacts, including variant spellings that may be read as different words in context.

2. All nonverbal substantive variants from all seventeenth-century sources, including differences in punctuation that materially affect meaning.[8]

3. All semisubstantive variants from all seventeenth-century sources that may affect either meaning or meter. Included in this category are the capitalization of such words as "Fate," "Nature," and "Heaven"; elided and nonelided vowels and marks of syncope that may affect the number of syllables in a line and therefore meter; and variants of spelling that, in context, may suggest different words or orthographic puns.

4. Variants that illuminate a poem's textual history. This is the broadest and most discretionary category, but an important one nonetheless in that the details it includes clarify the transmission and history of the text. Under this heading are reported verbal variants in modern editions, which are listed separately at the end of the historical collation for each poem.

In reporting the kinds of variants here specified, we intend to provide users with the

---

[7]Over the course of the project, this class of variants has been defined more broadly to include selected substantive and genealogically significant variants in punctuation.

[8]Lists in the historical collations do not record inconsequential variants of punctuation—such as commas separating items in simple compound constructions; neither do they record the absence of nonsubstantive punctuation in corollary copies in cases where the copy-text contains the punctuation necessary for understanding.

data necessary to reconstruct in all essential respects any version of the text of any poem.[9]

Bibliographical Conventions in the Apparatus

The format for entries in the Historical Collation generally follows standard practices of bibliographical notation. Each word or item in the *Variorum* text for which variant readings are reported is presented as a lemma to the left of a right bracket (lemma]) and followed by the variant and a list of sigla for the sources in which the variant appears. Multiple variants and sigla for a given item are presented seriatim and separated by semicolons. When a variant appears in a great number of sources across the spectrum of family groups (and thus conveys no genealogical information about the texts), these sources are collectively denoted by the symbol Σ, and the sigla for artifacts containing the lemmatic reading are listed immediately after the bracket. In the Historical Collation for *ElPerf* 5, for example, the first item appears as follows:

> I,] B32 C2 C8 DT1 H4 NY3 O20 SN4 A–G; ~∧   G.

This entry indicates that the sources B32 through G give the lemmatic reading ("I,"), while the variant ("I" without the following comma) appears in all other sources.

As is shown in the preceding example, a swung dash (~) is used after the bracket to stand for a word in the lemma, and a caret (∧) preceding or following a word or swung dash to the right of the bracket indicates omitted punctuation. When the lemma is a single word and only variants of punctuation are to be reported, the swung dash will thus appear in combination with marks of punctuation and/or carets. For lemmas consisting of multiple words, individual swung dashes are used to the right of the bracket to represent corresponding words in the lemma when the multiword variant can be accurately and economically reported by so doing. Depending on the details of the individual instance, therefore, variants to a multiword lemma may be reported either as a series of swung dashes interspersed with appropriate carets or marks of punctuation or as a combination of words, swung dashes, and punctuation marks. In the Historical Collation for *ElAut*, for instance, the first item reported for line 15 appears as follows:

> Yet lyes not Loue] And her inshrined   CE1; And (heare inshrined)
> O34; ~ is ~ ~   P4; ~ lyeth ~ ~   WN3.

This entry indicates that CE1 and O34 substitute three (differently punctuated) words of their own for those of the lemma, while P4 and WN3 match the lemma except that they substitute respectively "is" and "lyeth" for "lyes." Similarly, the collation for *ElAut* 16 includes the following entry:

> like an] ~ to ~   B25 C9 CE1 DT2 F3 H6 TM1 Y3; ~ ~ old   C4;

---

[9]It should be noted that obvious errors in printed editions, such as "effential" for "essential" and "Beddded" for "Bedded," are not reported in the historical collations except when they result in verbal variants, such as the erroneous "patts" for "parts" (1621 ed. of *SecAn* 233) and the erroneous "close-weaning" for "close-weauing" (1611–25 eds. of *FirAn* 153) or later become the source of error, such as the misprint "ealth" for *health*" (1625 ed. of *FirAn* 91M), which leads to the mistaken emendation "earth" in the subsequent edition of 1633. It should further be noted that in the case of severely damaged or mutilated manuscripts (always so designated in the Format section of the Historical Collation), only fully discernible variants and features that aid in the filiation of manuscripts are reported; no attempt is made to itemize each missing word or feature.

~ a chast   F4 NP1; ~ as ~   H8 HH5 Y2 35; as to ~   O21; (as to ~   O34;
~ a sworne   O36.

This entry indicates that the sources B25 through Y3 read "like to an"; that C4
reads "like an old"; that F4 and NP1 read "like a chast"; that H8 through 35 read
"like as an"; that O21 reads "as to an"; that O34 matches O21, except that it gives
a left parenthesis before "as"; and that O36 reads "like a sworne." As these examples
show, the swung dash is used only when the lemma and the variant are essentially
isomorphic and the correspondences between their respective parts are clear; when
this correlation is not clear, multiword verbal variants are written out in full.

It should be noted that the swung dash does not imply exact identity of spelling,
capitalization, or font between the word it represents and the corresponding word
in the lemma (although the two may in fact be identical), but only that the two are
forms of the same word. For example, the final word of line 8 in "*ELEGIE* on the
untimely Death of the *incomparable Prince*, HENRY" reads as follows in the artifacts:
"*Circumference:*" in 12a–j; "Circumference." in B14, C9, H3, and H6; "Circumfer-
ence" in DT1; "Cyrcumference" in H4; "circumference." in O29, WN1, and A; and
"circumference:" in B through G. Since differences of spelling, font, and capitalization
are not substantive in this case and are thus not reported, these variants are collapsed
into the following synthetic entry in the historical collation:

Circumference:] ~.   B14 C9 H3 H6 O29 WN1 A; ~_∧   DT1 H4.

When the artifacts generally agree in a lengthy variation, but contain minor
differences that need to be reported, we have minimized clutter in the apparatus
by recording such subvariations parenthetically immediately after the siglum of the
source from which they derive. For example, 13a and 13b preserve the variant read-
ings "Wheres now the" and "Where's now the" in the first half of *FirAn* 127. These
variant readings, which differ only in the use of the apostrophe, are reported in the
historical collation as follows:

Where is this] Wheres now the   13a 13b(Where's).

In cases where a reading right of the bracket expresses as a single, synthetic entry
variations of spelling, font, or capitalization that do not affect meaning or meter
(and thus are not reported explicitly), the accidentals of any word that may appear
in the entry are those of the artifact reported first in the sequence unless otherwise
indicated.

Hyphenated constructions within the body of variant readings sometimes pose
particular difficulties of representation. Any hyphenated compound in the reading
text for which variants must be reported invariably appears in the textual apparatus
as a single-item lemma; but hyphenated constructions that appear as variants to
non-hyphenated collocations in the reading text may be divided at the hyphen in
order to promote clarity in the Historical Collation. In a simple sequence of discrete
words, for instance, the *Variorum* text reads *ElPerf* 31 as "The grimm eight foot high
Iron bound Seruing man." Such a diverse array of hyphenated forms appears among
the corollary texts of this line, however, that to keep all such compounds together in
the list of variants would require establishing a single lemma comprising every word
in the line except "The." In order to avoid the plethora of multiword variants that
would thus be produced in the apparatus, we have divided the line into a number of

simpler lemmas and broken compound variants at appropriate points of hyphenation. For instance, the first textual note to the line reads thus:

grimm] ~- B28 B32 B47 C2 C8 CE1 H3 H5 H7 H8 NY1 O16 O20 O21 O34 OC1 SP1 VA2 WN1 A–G.

This entry indicates that while the copy-text gives no hyphen between "grimm" and the following word, the sources B28 through G all read "grimm" and the following word as a hyphenated compound. Unless otherwise noted, the appearance of a hyphen after any variant word in the apparatus thus signals the connection of that word to the one that follows in the source.

As noted above, the Stemma or Schema of Textual Relationships accompanying each poem is designed to outline in broad terms what can be determined of the poem's genealogy. When the evidence is sufficient, we present a traditional stemma outlining in skeletal form the step-by-step transmissional history of the text; in other cases we provide a schema that displays, within the context of full lines, the variants that permit separation of the artifacts into family groups. Accidentals in lines selected for the schema are those of a representative member of the family, and the defining variants are shown in boldface type. Significant intra-family variations are reported parenthetically at the end of each line. Detail reported in the schema is necessarily limited; information enabling the establishment of further genealogical links among copies of the text can be derived from the Historical Collation.

The Editors

INTRODUCTION TO VOLUME 3

GENERAL TEXTUAL INTRODUCTION

The Evolution of Methodology Within the Edition

The Satyres is the fifth of the printed volumes in this *Variorum* series to appear and the first to make a thoroughgoing use of the stemmatological method in its handling of the text. In the first volume published—*"The Anniversaries" and the Epicedes and Obsequies* (vol. 6, 1995)—we faithfully followed the procedures laid out in the general introduction to the series (see pp. li–lxi above). Persuaded that neither a "comprehensive genealogy of manuscripts" nor even a "complete genealogy" of individual poems was possible, we implemented a hybrid editorial approach that, on the basis of shared variant readings, genealogically separated the surviving manuscript witnesses of each poem into major family groups (sporadically distinguishing subfamiles within some of those groups), explained the distinguishing readings in a brief textual introduction, and represented the results of this analysis in a schema of textual relationships, a rudimentary graphic display that depicted each of the major families as the co-equal descendant of the lost holograph of the poem.[1] The copy-text that emerged from this procedure was the witness of each poem judged to embody the text in its "earliest, least-corrupted state," which—in order to avoid the eclecticism that had largely characterized the efforts of our editorial predecessors—we treated as a "best text" and emended/regularized only to the extent of correcting "obvious" verbal errors (scribal slips-of-the-pen and eyeskips, e.g.), emending punctuation "only when absolutely necessary to prevent misreading," and imposing the conventions of print upon manuscript copy-texts. And we proposed to handle authorially revised poems by presenting the "least corrupted state of each version" separately and treating each in this same conservative manner.[2]

Although in that first volume we mentioned the possibility of authorial revision in both *BoulRec* and *BoulNar* (see *DV* 6, pp. 131 and 148, respectively), the first oc-

---

[1] The exception was our schema for the *Anniversaries*, which traced the descent of the texts linearly from their respective first printings through a chronological succession of subsequent seventeenth-century editions.

[2] For a convenient summary of "the alternative editorial models that an editor [of Donne's poems] might choose" (447), see W. Speed Hill, "*The Donne Variorum*: Variations on the Lives of the Author," *HLQ* 62 (3 & 4), 445–54; also available online at http://donnevariorum.tamu.edu.

casion to deal with the question editorially came in our next volume, *The Epigrams, Epithalamions, Epitaphs, Inscriptions, and Miscellaneous Poems* (vol. 8, 1995), published a few months later. In this volume we identified early, intermediate, and late authorial sequences of the epigrams, each recording not only a different number of poems, but also different authorial versions of some of the individual poems. And we printed all three, recognizing that only in so doing could we ensure that each sequence would be readily available for study as a distinct poetic entity.[3] We also, of course, discussed the sequences and the artifacts that contained them in a general textual introduction and in that introduction rendered the data schematically in a comprehensive chart of "Sequences of Epigrams in Seventeenth-Century Artifacts" (see *DV* 8, p. 17). Each printed sequence was based on the manuscript deemed to preserve, on the whole, the cleanest version of the text and emended only in order to repair scribal blunders; and each epigram was accompanied by its own brief textual introduction and—in all cases where this device served to illustrate the variant authorial versions of the poem—by its own individual schema. For two of the three epithalamions we also postulated authorial revision, discussing the successive versions in each poem's textual introduction and depicting this information graphically in a modified version of the schema. Since the revisions in these poems were relatively minor, however, we adhered to stated policy, in each case adopting as copy-text the artifact containing the "best" rendition of the *earliest* text and emending it in the usual conservative manner.

With important modifications and refinements, this procedure carried over into the subsequent volume, *The Elegies* (vol. 2, 2000). Among the volume's 18 poems we identified, with varying degrees of certainty, 7 that had been authorially revised, further describing among them an authorial sequence of 12, which we both discussed and—as previously with the epigrams—illustrated graphically by means of schematic charts in the volume's general textual introduction.[4] Also following the pattern employed for the epigrams, we selected as copy-text for the entire 12-item sequence the artifact judged to preserve the soundest text overall, even though this choice entailed printing the revised—not the "earliest"—version of 2 of the poems,[5] and emended only scribal slips and misleading punctuation and spellings. Four of the remaining 6 poems were among those we judged to have been authorially revised, and of these 4 we printed the revised version in 3 instances and the original in 1, for each of these—as well as the remaining 2—selecting as copy-text the surviving manuscript deemed the least-corrupted and emending it conservatively. Most significantly, while we accompanied most of the poems in the volume with enhanced versions of the

---

[3] A rationale for this method is provided in Ted-Larry Pebworth and Ernest W. Sullivan, II, "Rational Presentation of Multlple Textual Traditions," *Publications of the Bibliographical Society of America* 83 (1989):43–60.

[4] The 7 revised poems included ElBrac, ElPerf, ElJeal, ElAut, ElProg, ElPart, and ElExpost; the sequence of 12 included, in order, ElBrac, ElComp, ElPerf, ElJeal, ElServe, ElNat, ElWar, ElBed, ElChange, ElAnag, ElFatal, and ElPict. See especially "Figure 3: Major Sequences of Elegies in Seventeenth-Century Manuscripts," *DV* 2:lxix.

[5] We justified this intermingling of original and revised texts within the sequence on grounds that "to print the entire sequence from a single, intelligently transcribed source that embodie[d] the set of elegies as the author conceived of it at a given moment is time" was preferable to "construct[ing] a medley of poems from disparate textual traditions" (*DV* 2:xcii).

usual schema, we achieved a breakthrough that we had not imagined at the beginning of the project, managing to develop full stemmas for 2 of the poems (*ElBrac* and *ElPart*) and partial ones for 6 others (*ElComp*, *ElNat*, *ElBed*, *ElChange*, *ElProg*, and *Sappho*).[6] In addition to illustrating the familial relationships discernible among the existing textual artifacts, these devices constituted integral parts of the analysis itself, tracing down a genealogical tree the step-by-step deterioration of the text from the lost holograph (or holographs, in cases involving revision) to its various embodiments in the extant manuscripts and prints, a procedure that entailed positing and naming with Greek letters such missing artifacts as were necessary to populate the full structure (see "On Stemmas and Revision" on pages lxv–lxvi below.) These instruments not only presented a generally more accurate picture of the whole field of textual materials than did the schemas, but also provided two immediate improvements to the editorial procedure: in identifying the exact location of each existing witness on a fully articulated family tree, they placed the selection of the "best" copy-text on a more scientific footing; and—of equal importance—they enabled a more satisfactory, adaptable approach to the process of emendation, especially in instances where the best available choice for copy-text was extremely corrupt and/or remote from the missing holograph. In the language we used to explain the interjection of about two dozen substantive emendations into the "best" surviving text of *ElPart*, the "postulation of a complete stemma…enabled a principled attempt to recover lost authorial readings" (*DV* 2, p. 349), as we emended up the line of transmission toward the readings of the lost holograph.

Despite its implications for the subsequent treatment of texts in the edition, the understanding of the utility of stemmas articulated above was not fully exploited in the volume that followed, *The Holy Sonnets* (vol. 7.1, 2005). In this volume sequencing and revision were again central features, and each was handled primarily according to the precedent established in editing the epigrams. Among the Holy Sonnets we identified and printed (differently constituted) early and late authorial sequences of 12 poems each, also presenting an important intermediate scribal sequence that contained revised versions of 7 of the earlier sonnets and original versions of 4 others that were later incorporated (3 in revised form) into the later sequence. And because of its historical importance, we also printed a typographical facsimile of the editorially confected arrangement of 16 sonnets that first appeared in the second edition of Donne's collected *Poems* (B) in 1635. These sequences and the artifacts containing them were discussed and represented schematically in a series of charts in the general textual introduction, and—in accordance with our evolving commitment to a stemmatological approach—we depicted the relationships among all artifacts containing sequences of the poems in a single comprehensive stemma. Taken together with the detailed transmissional history provided for each sonnet in its textual introduction, the information encoded in this global stemma was deemed sufficiently explanatory that individual stemmas for the poems were unnecessary. That we were not yet prepared

---

[6]In the order listed, these stemmata appear in *DV* 2, pp. 45–46, 365, 56, 131, 172, 203, 306, and 414. As noted in the introduction to the volume, these were the work of Gary A. Stringer (see p. xciv), who—as principal textual editor for volume 7.1—also developed the "Stemma of the Seventeenth-Century Artifacts Containing the Holy Sonnets" in *DV* 7.1, p. lxiv.

to embrace the new method in all its aspects, however, was evident in our general adherence to the original policy of emendation. As with the epigrams, we set each of the 4 sequences from the single artifact preserving the soundest overall text (or, in 2 cases, the only text), and, as usual, we emended each of these texts only to correct scribal pen-slips and—in a few instances—idiosyncratic scribal deviations from the normal lineal reading (i.e., "obvious" errors). For the first and intermediate manuscript sequences this procedure resulted in what we believed to be a verbally sound text; for the late sequence, however, where errors appeared to have been introduced both in the holograph and in the immediate progenitor of the manuscript chosen as copy-text, it left us with a text that we knew to contain a few spurious readings (see DV 7.1, pp. cii–ciii). Had we been willing to impose the emendations implied by the stemmatic knowledge we had developed, these errors might have been corrected.

With the current volume the methodological adaptation described above reaches its final—or, at least, a further—stage. In the introduction that follows, the distribution and sequencing of the poems in this volume are not only explained expositorily, but also—as in the figures accompanying the epigrams, the elegies, and the Holy Sonnets—schematized in diagrammatic charts that stand as important elements of the stemmatological methodology of the volume (see Figures 1 and 2 below). The central instruments of this methodology, however, are the individual stemmas developed for the 5 Satyres and *Metem*, which are included with other material in the poems' textual apparatuses (see Figures 6, 9, 12, 15, 18, and 22 below). And, adopting the procedure first used in the editing of *ElPart*, we here implement a policy of emendation that is commensurate with the stemmatological approach, emending as necessary the copy-text of each poem—whether of an original or a revised version—up the genealogical line toward the readings of the lost holograph. Among the Satyres the number of verbal emendations following from this policy ranges from as few as 3 in the original text of *Sat2* to 23 in the revised text of that poem, the average among the 8 original and revised texts presented below being slightly over 8 per poem. The copy-text of the 520-line *Metem*, for which the only defensible choice is an extremely corrupt offspring of the lost revised holograph (LRH), requires substantive emendation in nearly 70 instances.

On Stemmas and Revision

Like those developed for previous volumes of this edition, the stemmas presented below are concerned with tracing the linguistic provenance of the texts—as opposed to the socio-bibliographical provenance of the artifacts that contain them—and there is no necessary congruence between the one and the other.[7] The precision that can be

---

[7] We first pointed out this distinction in the elegies volume in reconciling the scribal annotation "finishd this 12 of October 1632" on the title page of the O'Flahertie manuscript (H6) with the fact that the texts in the artifact antedate those in some manuscripts transcribed earlier: "...it is important to maintain the distinction between the date or relative evolutionary position of the text as a linguistic structure and the actual chronological relationships of various acts of transcription or of the physical artifacts within which the poems appear" (DV 2:lxxi). Beal makes a similar point: "[artifactual] provenance is not necessarily an indication of textual authority since texts owned even by families personally known to Donne...may actually have been copied at several stages removed from Donne's autographs" (*Index*, p. 247).

achieved in these devices is, of course, limited by the general slipperiness of language itself and by the idiosyncratic peculiarity of the innumerable scribal interventions that inevitably crept into the texts as they were passed from one copyist to another, but the principal historical impediment consists in the gaps left in the transmissional record by the disappearance of an indeterminate number of formerly existing manuscripts. In instances where the evidence points to the quondam existence of such artifacts, as noted above, we have reified them with alphabetically sequenced Greek-character names and identified the particular lections introduced by each into the line of transmission. Each stemma takes the specific shape dictated by the surviving textual evidence for the particular poem whose linguistic evolution it purports to describe—including instances in which the relationships among the artifacts within a given family differ from one poem to the next. As a practical matter, we have applied the principle of parsimony in elaborating each stemma, positing the fewest missing artifacts required to account for the recognizable stages in the text's evolution and marking with dotted lines on the drawings instances in which the nature and/or number of changes suggests that the text was handled by multiple copyists between one identifiable embodiment and the next. Insofar as this expedient is employed (and in light of the other fuzzifying factors noted above), each stemma should be understood as a synecdochic representation of the complete transmissional history that might have been developed had all the evidence survived.

As explained above, we have variously identified authorial revision at both the macro level of the poetic sequence and the micro level of the individual poem in previous volumes of this edition; and in an appendix in the volume containing the Holy Sonnets we articulated the guidelines in terms of which we attempt to distinguish Donne's changes from those of the the various copyists who passed the poems along the channels of manuscript circulation (see *DV* 7.1:111–12). The extent of what we have called revision ranges from the alteration of a mere word or two in individual poems (the replacement of "tollerable Tropique Clyme" with "habitable Tropique Clyme" in *ElAut* 10, e.g.) to the global restructuring involved in the conversion of the early sequence of "Divine Meditations" into the later sequence of "Holy Sonnets."[8] Some of these changes, such as that of "mee thinkes they doe as well" to "Me seemes they do as well" in *Sat4* 184, may be only semi-deliberate or even inadvertent; but—so long as they constitute "genuine alternative[s]" and are not "readily explicable as…scribal misreading[s] or slip[s] of the pen" (two of the criteria itemized in the appendix cited above)—their impact on the meaning of the poem is stemmatically of minor importance. What matters is whether each such variant subsists at the head of a distinct line of transmission and thus marks a separate instance of Donne's having written out or adjusted the text of the poem.

---

[8]These examples conform, respectively, to the "two types of revision" defined in G. Thomas Tanselle, "The Editorial Problem of Final Authorial Intention," *Studies in Bibliography* 29 (1976):167–211: (a) "horizontal revision," which "aims at intensifying, refining, or improving the work as…conceived" at a given point in time; (b) "vertical revision," which "aims at altering the purpose, direction, or character of a work" and thus "moves the work to a different plane" (193).

The Satyres

Dating

Donne's Satyres, especially the first two, have traditionally been numbered among his earliest poems, and such information as there is, both external and internal, identifies the whole set as the product of the 1590s. Actual bibliographical evidence for dating them is both sparse and inconclusive, however, and, for all their topicality, they contain very few precise references linking them to specific historical events. Bibliographically, the solidest piece of evidence pointing to a sixteenth-century date for any of the poems appears in British Library ms. Harley 5110 (B33), which affixes the heading "Jhon Dunne his Satires Anno Domini 1593" to a copy of the first three Satyres, but the exact significance of this date remains uncertain.[9] Moreover, the

---

[9]As recorded in the commentary below, the date in B33—a fascicle of 7 manuscript leaves incorporated into Harley 5110—was first pointed out by J. Payne Collier in 1820, who took it to prove Donne's priority among English satirists; and Collier's discovery was cited by Grosart (N), who—even though he observed that B33's copies of *Sat1* and *Sat2* were written in one hand, *Sat3* in a second hand, occasional emendations and interlinings in a third hand, and the inscription itself in another hand altogether—averred that the manuscript was "unquestionably as early as 1593" and based his texts of the first three Satyres on it (1:2–3). The Grolier Club editors (O) and Chambers (P), without mention of bibliographical details, subsequently also cite the artifact as proof of the poems' early composition, as does Grierson (Q), who states initially that the "earliest date assignable to any of the Satyres is 1593, or more probably 1594–5" (2:100), but—after inconclusively surveying various topical allusions in the poems—concludes that "[the first three Satyres] were probably written between 1594 and 1597" (2:103). Bibliographically, this conclusion is facilitated by Grierson's belief—in which he perhaps follows Grosart (though he remains silent with respect to Grosart's identification of two different hands in the transcriptions of the poems)—that the "handwriting [of the inscription] is not identical with that in which the poems are transcribed" and that it is therefore "impossible to say either when the poems were copied or when the title and date were affixed" (2:100). Following Grierson, Hayward (S) asserts that the 1593 date in B33 "cannot be disregarded" until proved "incorrect" (p. 120), and the only subsequent editor to address the reliability of the inscribed date in B33 is Milgate (Y), who offers a fuller description of the artifact's physical composition and, modifying the description of Grosart, states that a single copyist entered the first two Satyres (including a variant version of *Sat2* 1–6) and the heading for the third, leaving beside this heading a blank sheet upon which a second scribe subsequently began his entry of the text of *Sat3*. In contradistinction to both Grierson and Grosart, however, Milgate asserts that the primary copyist was "possibly" (p. lii) or "probably" (p. 117) the penman of the dated inscription, and this identification corroborates his belief that *Sat1* "almost certainly belongs" to 1593 (p. 117). He thinks the inscription cannot apply, however, to *Sat2*, whose "likely" date of composition he places in 1594, supposing—and in this he follows Grierson—the poem to have been "prompted, in some degree," by the publication of the anonymous sonnet sequence *Zepheria* in that same year (127). Whereas Grierson had tentatively assigned *Sat3* to 1597, Milgate, constructing a circumstantial account of Donne's confessional evolution in the mid 1590s and citing Drummond's statement that the standard arrangement has the Satyres in "number & order" as Donne wrote them (see p. lxxiv below), locates the poem in "1594" (after the composition of *Sat2*) or "1595" (before the composition of *Sat4*) (140).

We also judge that the inscription "Jhon Dunne his Satires / Anno Domini 1593" is written in the hand of the primary scribe, who penned the copies of Satyres 1 and 2 and the heading for *Sat3*, and nothing in our analysis of the physical makeup of the artifact negates the possibility that the inscription was originally meant to apply to the whole of the artifact; indeed, such would be the normal interpretation. Militating against the conclusion that the inscription was actually penned in 1593, however, is that—in the opinion of Steven May—the handwriting of the primary scribe (and, indeed, of the copyist of *Sat3*) seems "very precocious for 1593," more likely to date from "at least a decade later" (private

credibility of the "anno 1594" that William Drummond wrote beside the heading of "Satyre 4" (Sat4) in his copy of Donne's poems (SN3) is undermined by the poem's reference in line 114 to the "losse of Amyens [which Drummond spells 'Amience']" in 1597. Specific topical allusions include those in "Satyre 1" (Sat1) 80–81 to the "wise politique horse" and the "Elephant or Ape," exotic creatures that were "among the sights of the day [earlier 1590s]" (Grierson 2:102), and the phrase "the great Carricks pepper" in "Satyre 5" (Sat5) 85 apparently refers to Raleigh's capture of the Portuguese *Madre de Dios* in 1592; but these allusions, of course, establish only Donne's knowledge of these phenomena, not the dates of their incorporation into the poems. The only references tying any of the Satyres to specific points in time are the above-cited mention of the "losse of Amyens," which places the composition of Sat4 after March of 1597, and Donne's addresses in Sat5 to his "Greatest, and fairest Empress" (l. 28) and to his employer ("You, Sir…whom I /…[haue] leaue to serue" [ll. 31–32]), which locate composition of the poem in the period between Donne's entry into Egerton's service in 1597 and the death of Elizabeth in 1603. These and other possible allusions are extensively discussed by the writers cited in the commentary below.

Circulation and Distribution in Manuscript

Whatever the exact dates of composition of the individual Satyres, before he ever put pen to paper Donne surely recognized that these poems—"writt / in skorne of all" (RWEnvy 7–8), as he characterized the satiric impulse in a sonnet to Rowland Woodward—would prove offensive for their explicit sexuality, their religious heterodoxy, and their unflinching depiction of folly and corruption among the officers and other denizens of the court. And he certainly understood the risks to which authorship of such poems exposed him in a repressive political culture whose increasing nervousness at the outpouring of satirical writing in the 1590s finally culminated in the official ban against the publication of "Satyres or Epigramms" issued jointly by the Archbishop of Canterbury and the Bishop of London in June of 1599.[10] No doubt heightened by the thought that deliberate distribution of these works would now place him in spiritual, if not literal, violation of the law, the apprehensiveness that Donne must always have felt about the Satyres is given explicit voice in the oft-quoted letter accompanying some prose paradoxes that he sent to an unnamed friend in about 1600. In this missive he acknowledges that "to…[his] satyrs there belongs some feare" and, even as he pledges to "acquaint" the recipient with "all" his writings, threatens to share nothing further unless he receives by return letter "an assurance vpō the religion of yʳ frendship yᵗ no coppy shalbee taken for any respect of these or any other my compositions sent to y°." He is, as he understates it, "desirous to hyde them wᵗʰout any over reconing of them or there maker" (LR1, fol. 308v). This and his other attempts to prevent circulation of the poems ultimately failed, of course, but the fear reflected in this letter was belatedly justified 30 years later when, although strict enforcement of the bishops' ban was a thing of the past and

---

correspondence). From this perspective, of course, the inscription, even though penned by the primary scribe, is a mere after-the-fact assertion and the validity of the date impossible to gauge.

[10]See, e.g., Richard A. McCabe, "Elizabethan Satire and the Bishops' Ban of 1599," *The Yearbook of English Studies*, Vol. 11 (1981), pp. 188–93.

Donne had achieved practical sainthood as the recently deceased Dean of St. Paul's, the licenser of the posthumous 1633 *Poems* (A) "excepted" the Satyres until such time as the publisher John Marriot should bring "lawfull authority" (Arber 4:249) to include them, thus instigating a six-weeks delay in the approval process (see Arber 4:261) that forced Marriot to insert the Satyres (with offensive words and lines replaced by long dashes) as the penultimate Donne poems in the volume rather than placing them near the beginning, where they appear in the manuscript that Marriot had presented to the stationers.

No doubt in part because of their controversial subject matter—and despite his efforts to control their dispersal—Donne's Satyres eventually experienced a modest circulation in manuscript during and immediately after his lifetime. Beal (*Index, passim*) dates no artifact containing any of these poems earlier than "early 17th century" (including B33) and assigns all but half a dozen to 1620 or later, but various contemporary references, quotations, and appropriations make clear that, at least to a limited extent, the Satyres were circulating even before the turn of the century. For example, as is discussed in the commentary below, the year before the bishops officially banned the publication of satires and prior to Donne's writing of the aforementioned cautionary letter to his friend, Everard Guilpin's long-acknowledged inclusion of an elaborate adaptation of *Sat1* as "Satyra Quinta" in *Skialethia* (1598, sigs. D4–D7v), which—as Hester (1984) has pointed out—also contains extensive borrowings from *Sat4*, shows that within certain circles access to the poems was possible.[11] Further, in manuscript jottings apparently recorded during the period when he was launching on the new career that eventually led to the publication of *A Poetical Rapsody* (1602 [1st ed.]; 1608 [2nd ed.]), Francis Davison notes among a group of "Papers Lent" that he has loaned "John Dun's Satyres" to his brother Christopher and subsequently, among "Manuscripts to Get," includes "Satyres, Elegies, Epigrams, &c. by John Don," of which he hopes to acquire "some from Eleaz. Hodgson, and Ben Johnson."[12] That Jonson, at least, was a likely source for the Satyres is demonstrated by his penning, in about 1607, the epigram "To Lvcy, Covntesse of Bedford, with M.r Donnes Satyres" to accompany his gift of a set of the poems to the Countess (printed in Jonson, 1616, p. 796); and that by 1609 Joseph Wybarne had seen at least parts of *Sat4* in manuscript is evident from his quotation of lines 18–23a of that poem in *The New Age of Old Names* (siglum 5, pp. 112–13). Donne's wider reputation as a satirist is attested in Thomas Fitzherbert's 1613 "*supplement to the discussion...*," which—even amidst a foreign-published fulmination against the techniques of argument employed in *Pseudo-Martyr*—nevertheless concedes that in his "old occupation of making Satyres"

---

[11] In his "comparatiue discourse" included in *Palladis Tamia* (1598), Francis Meres focuses primarily on published or publicly staged works, but he does note the circulation of Shakespeare's "sugred Sonnets among his priuate friends" (pp. 282), and he is aware that Drayton "is now penning" *Poly-olbion* (p. 281), a work not published until 1612. In this light, Donne's utter absence from Meres's account is difficult to interpret. It may testify to the particular success of Donne's early efforts to "hyde" his works; on the other hand, it may simply indicate the limitations of Meres's knowledge of unpublished work: when he lists the "chiefe" English writers of satire, for example, Meres includes a (very up-to-date) mention of "*the Author of Skialethia*" (p. 284), but is unable to credit Guilpin by name.

[12] Transcribed from Davison's autograph in Harley MS 298, fol. 151 ff., these notes are recorded in Nicolas, vol. 1, pp. xliii–xlv.

Donne "hath some talent" (107); and Thomas Freeman's reference the following year to *Storm*, *Calm*, and "Thy *Satyres* short" in "Epigram 84. *To Iohn Dunne*" (in *Runne, And a great Cast*, sigs. K1v–K2) indicates that by 1614 he had seen a fascicular collection of the satires like those extant in P3, OQ1, and VA1. And in the 1629 issue of *A Help to Discourse* (siglum 18g, p. 116; STC 1551.3), 2 years before the poem's first full printing in A, William Basse includes a manuscript-derived adaptation of lines 3–5 of *Sat5*.

Such sporadic references as those here marshaled point to a continuing, if largely subterranean, traffic in these poems among certain constituencies from the time of their original composition throughout the first three decades of the seventeenth century. The most important evidence of their circulation, of course, consists in the surviving manuscript copies of the poems themselves, a full picture of whose eventual dispersal in seventeenth-century artifacts is presented graphically in Figure 1. Excluding B51 (a 2-line snippet of *Sat3* derived from print) and P1 (an uncollatable series of excerpts of both *Sat2* and *Sat4*), as this figure shows, the surviving seventeenth-century artifacts contain 154 manuscript transcriptions of individual Satyres in 38 compilations, and the remaining copies constitute only a fraction of what must once have existed.[13] Remarkably, given the length of these poems, only 3 of these 154 transcriptions are less than full copies, and all 3 of the partial copies—those in H8 (which lacks lines 61–112 of *Sat1*), NP3 (which lacks lines 55–110 of *Sat3*) and B11 (which lacks lines 1–202 of *Sat4*)—exist in artifacts exhibiting material defects and were apparently, in their original states, complete.[14] Further, 24 of these collections contain all 5 canonical Satyres; and, in light of their genealogical relationships to artifacts that do include the full set, we may infer that the copyists of B32 and TT1, 2 others that have only 4, originally intended and could have expected to record all 5 as well, but through mishap or inadvertence failed to do so (see the further discussion of Group I below). Moreover, as Grierson first observed (2:lxxxii), in its current state B11 consists of all that remains of what appears originally to have been a complete "book" of the Satyres, and NP3, which preserves only the first two Satyres and the first half of *Sat3*, may well have been the same.[15] As is further shown on Figure 1, each of the remaining

---

[13]In addition to the original and revised holographs of the poem, e.g., the stemma for *Sat4* lists 37 extant manuscripts, and the postulation of a further 21 formerly existing copies is necessary to fill out, in even the sparest manner, the genealogical tree for the poem (see Figure 15 below).

For a comparative perspective on the extent of the Satyres' circulation in manuscript see the discussion of the dispersal of the elegies in DV 2:lxi–lxiv, which cites 705 complete or partial copies of the 17 elegies in some 136 manuscripts.

[14]The copy of *Sat1* in H8 breaks off at the bottom of folio 67v with line 60, and *Sat2* begins at the top of folio 68. That the archivist's foliation in the manuscript is continuous suggests that a single leaf containing the remaining 52 lines of *Sat1* was lost prior to binding.

This tally refers to the apparent intentions of the various copyists; the occasional inadvertent omission of a line or brief passage (such as the HH1 scribe's eye-skip omission of *Sat5* 15–18) is noted in the textual apparatuses below.

[15]Along with a useful discussion of the early manuscript circulation of Donne's Satyres, Daniel Starza Smith, "Before (and after) the Miscellany: Reconstructing Donne's Satyres in the Conway Papers," in Eckhardt and Smith (2014), pp. 17–37, examines the provenance and significance of B11 in detail, including a fascinating hypothetical reconstruction of the original form of the artifact.

NP3 is a composite volume of miscellaneous works entered by 5 different copyists. The fascicle containing the fragmentary set of Donne Satyres, all written in the same hand, spans folios 115–119v,

FIGURE 1: COPIES OF SATYRES IN THE 17TH-CENTURY ARTIFACTS*

Source	Sat1	Sat2	Sat3	Sat4	Sat5	"Men Write"	"Sleep, next Society"
B2						•	
B11				•	•		
B13	•	•	•	•	•		
B32	•	•	•	•			
B33	•	•					
B40	•	•	•	•	•		•
B46	•	•		•			
B47	•	•	•	•	•		•
B51			•				
C2	•	•	•	•	•		
C5	•	•					
C8	•	•	•		•		
C9	•	•	•	•	•	•	•
DT1	•	•	•	•	•		•
F21	•	•					
H3	•	•	•	•			
H4	•	•	•	•	•		•
H5	•	•	•	•	•		•
H6	•	•	•	•	•	•	•
H7	•	•	•	•	•		•
H8	•	•	•	•	•	•	•
HH1	•	•	•	•	•	•	•
HH4						•	•
LR1				•			
NP2				•			
NP3	•	•	•				
NY1	•	•	•	•	•		
NY3	•	•	•	•	•		
O3				•			
O16							•
O20	•	•	•	•	•		
O21	•	•	•	•			
OQ1	•	•	•	•	•		
P1		•		•			
P3	•	•	•	•	•		
SN3		•		•			
SN4		•		•			
SP1	•	•	•	•	•		
TT1		•	•	•	•		
VA1	•	•	•	•	•		
VA2	•	•	•	•	•		
Y2	•	•	•	•	•	•	•
Y3	•	•	•	•	•		
A	•	•	•	•	•		
B–F	•	•	•	•	•	•	
G	•	•	•	•	•	•	•

*Excludes post-17th-century mss. IU2 and OJ1 and uncollected printings

FIGURE 2: SEQUENCING AND PLACEMENT OF SATYRES IN THE 17TH-CENTURY MANUSCRIPTS

	Source	Sequencing and Versions					Relation of Storm & Calm	Position of Satyres within Artifact
"Books" of Satyres	B13	4(1)-o	1(2)-o	2(3)-r	3(4)-o	5(5)-o	gwS	in midst of ms.
	OQ1	1(1)-o	2(2)-r	3(3)-o	4(4)-o	5(5)-o	"††	independent unit in composite ms.
	P3	1(1)-o	2(2)-r	3(3)-o	4(4)-o	5(5)-o	"	1st position in ms.
	VA1	1(1)-o	2(2)-r	3(3)-o	4(4)-o	5(5)-o	"	sole contents of ms.
Group III	B46	2(u)*-o	1(u)*-o	4(u)*-o			nia	1st position in ms.
	H5	1(1)-o	5(2)-o	4(4)-o	2(5)-o	3(6)-o	rfS	in midst of ms.
	B47	2(1)-o	1(2)-o	3(3)-o	4(4)-o	5(5)-o	rfS	in midst of ms.
	C9	2(u)**-o	1(2)-o	3(3)-o	4(4)-o	5(5)-o	"	5th position in ms.
	H6	2(u)**-o	1(2)-o	3(3)-o	4(4)-o	5(5)-o	"	in midst of ms.
Associated with Group III	H3	1(u)-o	2(u)-o	4(u)-o	3(4)-o		rfS	6th position in ms.
	O21	2(u)-r	1(1)-o	3(2)-r	5(3)-r²	4(4)-o	rfS	in midst of ms.
	Y3	1(1)-o	3(2)-r	5(3)-r²	4(4)-o	2(u)-r	"	7th position in ms.
	NY1	1(1)-o	2(2)-r	3(3)-o	4(4)-r	5(5)-o	gwS†††	1st position in ms.
	VA2	1(1)-o	2(2)-r	3(3)-o	4(4)-r	5(5)-o	"	" " " "
	HH1	2(u)*-o	1(2)-o	3(3)-o	4(4)-o	5(5)-o	rfS	in midst of ms.
Group IV	NY3	1(1)-r	2(2)-o	3(3)-o	4(4)-r	5(5)-r¹	rfS††††	1st position in ms.
Group I	B32	1(1)-r	2(2)-o	3(3)-o	4(4)-r		rfS	1st position in ms.
	O20	1(1)-r	2(u)-o	3(u)-o	4(u)-r	5(u)-r²	"	" " " "
	SP1	1(1)-r	2(2)-o	3(3)-o	4(4)-r	5(5)-r²	"	" " " " "
Group II	C2	1(1)-r	2(2)-r	3(3)-r	4(4)-r	5(5)-r²	rfS	4th position in ms.
	C8	1(1)-r	2(2)-r	3(3)-r	4(4)-r	5(5)-r²	"	1st position in ms.
	B11†	mis	mis	mis	4(4)-r	5(5)-r²	nia	sole contents of ms.
	DT1	1(u)-r	3(2)-r	4(u)-r	5(u)-r²	2(u)-r	rfS	1st position in ms.
	H4	1(u)-r	3(u)-r	4(u)-r	5(u)-r²	2(u)-r	"	" " " "
	B40	3(u)-r	4(u)-r	5(3)-r²	2(u)-r	1(u)-r	rfS	7th position in ms.
	TT1	3(u)-r	4(u)-r	5(3)-r²	2(u)-r		"	in midst of ms.
Unclassified	B33	1(u)-o	2(2)-o	3(3)-o			nia	sole contents of ms.
	C5	1(1)-o	2(2)-o				gwS	in midst of ms.
	F21	1(1)-r	2(2)-o				nia	1st position in ms.
	H7	1(1)-o	2(2)-o	3(3)-?	4(4)-?	5(5)-o	rfS	1st position in ms.
	H8	1(1)-o	2(2)-r	3(3)-o	4(4)-o	5(5)-o	rfS	in midst of ms.
	LR1	4(u)-o					nia	in midst of ms.
	NP2	4(u)-o					"	sole Donne poem in ms.
	NP3	1(1)-o	2(2)-o	3(3)-o	mis?	mis?	nia	independent unit in composite ms.
	O3	4(u)-r					nia	in midst of ms.
	SN3	4(4)-r	2(2)-o				gwS	in midst of ms.
	SN4	4(4)-r	2(5)-o				"	1st position in ms.
	Y2	1(1)-o	2(2)-o	3(3)-o	4(4)-r	5(5)-o	rfS	1st position in ms.

* = headed "Satyre"
** = section HE "Satyrs" precedes poem
† = B11 is missing Sats1–3 and ll. 1–202 of Sat4
gwS = grouped with Satyres

mis = missing
nia = not in artifact
rfS = remote from Satyres
†† = Curse follows Calm

††† = Lit appears between Sat5 and Storm
†††† = contains Storm on▶

Arabic numerals = conventional number assigned each poem in the 5-poem set
Right-to-left sequence of arabic numerals in each row = order in which the poems appear in the artifact
Arabic numerals in parenthesis = actual number assigned to poem in the artifact (Latin headings are regularized to arabic numerals in this figure; for the literal heading on each manuscript copy, see the Textual Apparatus)
u = unnumbered
o/r following poem number = original/revised version
Normal/boldface font changes = sequence interrupted by other poems

Not listed: partial copies B51 and P1 and post-17th-century mss. IU2 and OJ1

10 Satyres manuscripts records less than a full set, H3 containing 4 of the poems; B33 and B46 containing 3; C5, F21, and the SN3-SN4 pair containing 2; and the LR1-NP2 cognates and O3 containing only a single Satyre.

Organization into Groups in the Manuscripts

The data presented in Figure 1 reappears in Figure 2, augmented and reorganized to display the sequencing and numbering of the poems in the extant seventeenth-century manuscripts, whose sigla are categorized and arranged in descending order in the left-most columns of the chart according to the traditional Griersonian groups as adapted in Beal. Especially when interpreted in light of the transmissional histories represented in the stemmas accompanying the poems—see Figures 6 (Sat1), 9 (Sat2), 12 (Sat3), 15 (Sat4), and 18 (Sat5) elsewhere in this volume—this rearranged data enables a more thorough understanding of the manuscript circulation of these poems and the mechanisms by which the majority of them came to be organized in the standard 5-satire authorial sequence. Combining the information from these divergent sources makes it immediately evident, for example, that lying behind the 28 surviving 5-poem manuscript sequences is a considerably smaller number of originary compilations (in the tallies here provided, B11, B32, NP3, and TT1 are counted with the artifacts containing full, undamaged sets of the Satyres). Beginning at the upper left on Figure 2, these artifacts include (1) the immediate progenitor of the three independent "books" of Satyres (OQ1, VA1, P3) and their cognate B13, designated δ^1 on the stemma for "Satyre 1";[16] (2) the progenitor of the Group-III siblings C9 and H6 and their cognate B47, designated η^2 on the stemma for Sat1; (3) the parent of the siblings O21 and Y3 (Associated with Group III), designated ζ^4 on the Sat1 stemma; (4) the archetype of the Group-Is (B32, O20, SP1), designated δ^3 on the Sat1 stemma; and (5) the archetype of the expanded Group II (C2, C8, B11, DT1, H4, B40, TT1), designated γ^3 on the Sat1 stemma.[17] As is evident, these 19 extant sequences

---

breaking off at the bottom off folio 119v with line 54 of Sat3; folio 120, penned in a different hand, contains the first 26 lines of Herrick's *Oberons Palace* (see Beal, CELM).

[16]Each stemma is an independent construct, and as a matter of editorial policy the Greek-letter name assigned to each missing urtext is determined by that artifact's position on each particular stemma; thus, e.g., the artifact designated δ^1 on the Sat1 stemma is successively labeled ε^2, γ^1, γ^1, and β^1 on the stemmas for Satyres 2–5. In order to simplify the present discussion, however, we here specify only the names assigned to such missing artifacts on the stemma for Sat1.

[17]C2 and C8 ordinarily belong to Group I, but they record Group-II texts of the Satyres; B11, which currently consists entirely of Sat5 and a fragment of Sat4, has no history of association apart from the Satyres.

There can be little doubt that the relationship among B47, C9 and H6 here noted obtains in all 5 of the Satyres, although contamination in B47's text of Sat3 has blurred its genealogy sufficiently that we have left B47 unfiliated on the Sat3 stemma (see the discussion in fn. 1 on p. 102 below). It should also be noted that the stemmas for Sat4 and Sat5 each identify an additional missing artifact—labeled ε^2 and θ, respectively—between the parent of B47 and the parent of the C9-H6 siblings. Despite the intervention of these artifacts, however, the hierarchical relationship of B47 to C9-H6 remains constant across all 5 stemmas, thus confirming η^2's identity as the source of the B47-C9-H6 sequence of Satyres. The ε^2/θ artifact must have occupied a similar place in the line of transmission of all 5 Satyres, but—in accordance with our policy of declining to posit missing manuscripts for which no concrete evidence survives—is not represented on the stemmas for Satyres 1–3.

It perhaps goes without saying that, since each stemma depicts the particular textual genealogy of

descend from only 5 original urtexts; and including the NY1-VA2 parent-child pair in this tally brings the total to 21 full sequences deriving from 6 ancestral collections. That they respectively occupy varying positions on the stemmas of the individual poems makes it impossible to trace either H5, H7, H8, NP3, NY3, or Y2—6 of the remaining manuscripts that contain all 5 poems—to a single superior source text and indicates that each of these copyists compiled his collection independently. And HH1, although the verbal evidence requires that it be located as the otherwise unfiliated direct descendant of the LOH of each poem, similarly manifests the individual effort of a scribe who, in seeking to assemble a full set of Satyres, obtained and recorded them in a nonstandard order (see Figure 2 and the discussion of this artifact below). In the upshot, the surviving—or quasi-surviving—28 collections that preserve all 5 Satyres are ultimately traceable to the efforts of a mere dozen copyists or collectors.

Sequencing in the Manuscripts

Also evident from the information encoded on Figure 2 is that, as might be expected of poems circulating without the author's consent and outside his control, the assembled groups of Satyres appear in a variety of configurations, depending on what individual collectors were able to learn of the number of satires Donne had written and of the sequence in which they were meant to be arranged—and on the collectors' luck in obtaining copies. Among those who had—or claimed—reliable knowledge of these matters was the poet William Drummond, on the flyleaf of whose personal manuscript appears, in a contemporary hand, the inscription "Thirre [These] poems belonginge to Ihon Don Transcribed by William Drummond" (SN3, f. 2). Drummond included Satyres 4 and 2 among the 27 Donne poems in his collection and, in an annotation to his transcription of Sat4, states that "[t]his Satyr (though it here haue the first place because no more was intended to this booke) was indeed the Authors fourth in nomber & order; he hauing wreten fiue in all to which this caution will sufficientlie direct in the rest (f. 14v).[18] Despite his mistaken assignment of Sat4 to 1594 (see above), Drummond's remark has historically been

only a single poem, only those missing artifacts that appear on all 5 stemmas can convey information about the Satyres as a group, including information on sequencing. For example, the urtext labeled η^2 on the stemma for Sat1 is identifiable as a distinct entity that recorded and passed on to its offspring a particular set of poems organized in a particular sequence because it appears (variously named) on every stemma as the ancestor of the same cluster of genealogically related manuscripts (B47, C9, H6). By contrast, the artifact labeled ζ^4, which—on the evidence of the Sat1 stemma alone—would appear to have been a prior source for the set of Satyres in η^2, does not appear on subsequent stemmas and thus cannot be so regarded.

[18]As does the sibling artifact SN4, SN3 records Sat2 after (rather than before) Sat4 (see Figure 2), and Drummond perhaps appended his explanatory gloss in order not only to explain his inclusion of less than a full set of these poems and the anomalous order of the 2 he did include, but also to correct the parent manuscript's mislabeling of Sat2 as "Sat: 5"—the heading it exhibits in SN4. Although their particular thematic concerns may have held a special appeal for him, it seems curious that Drummond should have wished to have Satyres 2 and 4 only, and the fact that of satires the cognate SN4 includes only these 2 suggests that the parent manuscript contained only these and prompts the question whether Drummond actually had access to more of the poems and could have included them had he "intended" to do so. In this connection it should be noted that Milgate—apparently deriving the notion from Grierson (see Q 2:cxxx) and, in our view, implausibly—reads the phrase "belonginge to Ihon Don" in the SN3 inscription to mean "deriv[ing] from copies in Donne's possession," although, partly

accepted as confirmation of the standard 5-poem sequence as Donne's, as it is here (see also, e.g., Milgate, p. 139). And—as is indicated in the rows of numbers beside the manuscript sigla in Figure 2—Drummond's was also the understanding of 9 other copyists, whose efforts eventually resulted in the production of 16 full (or would-be full), conventionally ordered, continuous sequences of the poems. These urtexts and their progeny include—in top-to-bottom order down the chart—(1) the immediate parent of the 3 "books" (which gave rise to OQ1, P3, and VA1), designated ε^1 on the *Sat1* stemma; (2) NY1, which begat VA2; (3) NY3; (4) the Group-I archetype (which engendered B32, O20, and SP1), designated δ^3 on the *Sat1* stemma (see the further discussion of Group I below); (5) the parent of B11, C2, and C8, designated δ^4 on the *Sat1* stemma; and (6) H7, (7) H8, (8) NP3, and (9) Y2. Except for O20, whose scribe numbers only *Sat1* (the others are headed merely "Satyre"), each of these artifacts affixes the correct ordinal number to each poem in its set (see Figure 2).[19]

As the data in Figure 2 further shows, 6 other originary compilations, which eventuated in the penning of 12 further full sets of the poems, were assembled by collectors who—for lack of knowledge or timely access to manuscript material—assembled non-standard (i. e., misordered or discontinuous) collections. These urtexts and their progeny are as follows:

> (a) the lost progenitor of B13 and the parent of the 3 "books" (δ^1 on the *Sat1* stemma). This archetype recorded the poems in the order 4, 1, 2, 3, 5, but numbered them consecutively 1–5, the ordering and numbering repeated in B13. The scribe of the immediate parent of the "books" (ε^1 on the *Sat1* stemma) recognized the misordering and, as noted above, rearranged the poems in the authorial 1–5 sequence, the order in which they appear—and are numbered—in OQ1, P3, and VA1.

> (b) H5. This artifact records the poems in the order 1, 5, 4, 2, 3, but interpolates the non-canonical "Sleep, next society" between *Sat5* and *Sat4*, numbering the 6 poems consecutively 1–6 in Latin.

---

because of the attribution Drummond wrote beside the heading of *Sat2* (see the following), he registers "some doubt" as to whether the claim is true (Y:li).

Beside his heading on *Sat2* ("Satyre 2") Drummond inscribes the attribution "after b. B. coppy." Chambers originally notes this inscription, but misreads it as "C. B." and speculatively identifies it as reference to Christopher Brooke (2:241). Without mentioning Chambers, Grierson subsequently repeats the misreading, declaring it "quite possible" that Brooke is the "Sir" of line 1 to whom the poem is "addressed" (2:111). Finally, Milgate, again misreading Drummond's hand, cites Grierson's "not impossible" suggestion that Brooke is the addressee, but labels the evidence constituted by the inscription "very weak" (128–29).

[19]In either numerals or words (frequently Latin), all but a handful of manuscripts evince numbers on the Satyres they contain (see Figure 2), and only in SN3 and SN4 does that numbering not begin with "1" and continue seriatim. Further, only for 4 artifacts—SN3, SN4, the missing parent of the three "books" (i.e., OQ1, P3, VA1), and the missing parent of the B11-C2-C8 siblings—is there definite evidence that the scribe deliberately followed an externally derived system of numbering and/or ordering rather than automatically numbering the Satyres "1" through "5" as he entered them into his collection. Whether the remaining 5 originary copyists in this list were conscious of following an authorially defined order and numbering thus remains uncertain.

(c) the lost progenitor of B47 and the C9-H6 pair (η^2 on the *Sat1* stemma). This archetype recorded the poems in the order 2, 1, 3, 4, 5, but numbered them consecutively 1–5.

(d) the parent of the O21-Y3 siblings (ζ^4 on the *Sat1* stemma). This collection was assembled piecemeal, Satyres 1, 3, 5, and 4 (numbered consecutively 1–4) appearing together in a continuous run and *Sat2* (unnumbered) standing as a separate item at a distance. The likely reason for *Sat2*'s preceding the others in O21, but following them in Y3, is that the parent manuscript existed as a shuffleable sheaf of loose leaves whose contents were arranged differently when the scribes of O21 and Y3 took their respective copies.

(e) HH1. This artifact records the poems in the order 2, 1, 3, 4, 5, but numbers them consecutively 1–5. In ordering and numbering, HH1 exactly matches B47, C9, and H6, but its location as a direct descendant of the LRH on each successive stemma makes its derivation from the archetype of that subgroup impossible and shows this similarity to be coincidental—the unique instance within the manuscript record of a coincidental replication of a non-standard arrangement of these poems.

(f) the Group-II archetype from which the DT1-H4 parent-child pair and the B40-TT1 siblings derive (γ^3 on the *Sat1* stemma). This archetype recorded all 5 Satyres in a run of 7 poems that included *ElBrac* and the non-canonical "Sleep, next society." Both pairs of descendants record Satyres 3, 4, and 5 in authorial order, but otherwise differ: DT1 passes on to H4 the sequence *Sat1*, *Sat3*, *Sat4*, *Sat5*, "Sleep, next society," *Sat2*, *ElBrac*; B40 records the sequence *Sat3*, *Sat4*, *Sat5*, *Sat2*, *ElBrac*, "Sleep, next society," *Sat1*, while TT1 recapitulates the B40 sequence from *Sat3* through *ElBrac*, but omits "Sleep, next society" and *Sat1*.[20] Although none of these four collections consistently exhibits numbers/headings on the poems (see Figure 2), the repositioning of *Sat2* to follow *Sat5* immediately in the B40-TT1 sequence suggests at least a local attempt on the part of the parental scribe (δ^5 on the *Sat1* stemma) to tighten generic grouping within his collection. The Group-II archetype was also the ultimate source of B11, C2, and C8, whose immediate parent (δ^4 on the *Sat1* stemma) expunged the spurious "Sleep, next society," rearranged the Satyres into the authorial 1–5 order (as did the parent of the 3 "books"), and followed the set with a run of 13 elegies that begins with *ElBrac*, replicating the sequence found in its usual Group-I companions B32, O20, and SP1.

---

[20]The facts that B40's copy of *Sat1* is written in a hand different from that which penned the manuscript's other contents and that the poem is absent from TT1 suggest that *Sat1* was missing from the Group-II archetype when the B40 and TT1 scribes took their copies, but was inserted at the head of the group before the copyist of DT1 took his, *Sat1* being eventually added to the Satyres cluster in B40 by a second scribe. TT1's omission of "Sleep, next society" is likely a simple scribal oversight, although it possibly represents the copyist's conscious rejection of a spurious poem.

The remaining 10 artifacts listed on figure 2 give testimony to the further sporadic circulation of the Satyres in smaller clusters or as single copies and cast further light on the vagaries of the system of manuscript transmission within which these poems subsist. Perhaps the most puzzling in this regard are B46 (which contains 3 of the Satyres, all derived from the LOH) and H3 (which contains 4, also all derived from the LOH). Compiled between 1620 and 1633 according to Beal and originally classified by Grierson as members of Group III, these are among the major Donne manuscripts. The single scribe responsible for each apparently sought to compile as extensive a collection as possible, B46 recording 102 generically diverse canonical poems plus a few by other authors and H3 containing 69 Donne poems in a variety of genres plus a few spurious items. Yet neither scribe managed to obtain the full complement of Satyres, and the ordering and numbering of those that do appear in each collection indicates that neither copyist was aware of the standard numbering and arrangement of these poems (see Figure 2). Among the other artifacts listed on Figure 2, the only one to contain as many as 3 of the poems is B33, which, deriving all its texts from the LOH, consists entirely of Satyres 1–3 and possibly—though by no means certainly—replicates a collection dating from a time in the early 1590s when only these 3 Satyres existed (see footnote 9 above). C5 and F21, which appear in alphabetical order next on the chart, both contain Satyres 1 and 2 (only), but their texts are unrelated (see the stemmas for *Sat1* and *Sat2*, respectively), and—even though each artifact correctly numbers the 2 poems—we cannot know certainly whether either scribe chose to transcribe only these Satyres from a full set or had access to only these 2 (in the case of F21, the latter possibility seems likely; see further remarks on F21 in the discussion of Group I below).[21] Further toward the bottom of Figure 2 appear the siblings LR1 and NP2, which contain *Sat4* only. These manuscripts derive their texts of the poem from a parent that appears at 4 removes down the stemma from the LOH (ε^3) and—in order to introduce itself as an independently circulating single poem—may have borne the title "The Satyre of the courte by M^r. Dune" (as it is subscribed in NP2)—a heading possibly dating ε^3 prior to 1615, when Donne's was made "Doctor." By contrast, the copy of *Sat4* in O3 (an artifact dated "c. 1638" in Beal), which derives from the lost revised holograph of the poem through an indeterminate number of intermediaries, bears a heading that testifies to its considerably later date of inscription: "A Satire against ye Court / wrighten by Docter Donne, In Queene Elizabeths Raigne." As is explained in footnote 18 above, the siblings SN3 and SN4 derive their copies of Satyres 2 and 4 from a common ancestor that, although it seems to have labeled *Sat2* as "Satyre 5" (and thus perhaps points to an even earlier lost progenitor in which all 5 Satyres were present),

---

[21]C5 appears as a direct descendant, through an indeterminate number of intermediaries, of the LOH on the stemma of both *Sat1* and *Sat2*, and the artifact's additional Donne poems include 1 epigram, 13 Songs and Sonnets, 3 verse letters (*Calm*, *Storm*, and *HWNews*), and 9 elegies. By contrast, of Donne poems F21 contains only Satyres 1 and 2, their texts stemming, respectively, from the LRH and the LOH. Citing an early owner's inscription, Beal dates the manuscript "c. 1627–32," and—in light of the other contents of the artifact—conjectures that the collection was originally "compiled principally by a lawyer or law student." Such a collector, of course, might have found Satyres 1 and 2 of particular interest.

apparently contained these 2 Satyres only. The text of *Sat2* in these artifacts derives from the LOH, that of *Sat4* from the LRH.

The Major Manuscript Groups

Reflecting our judgment that Donne revised each of the Satyres in at least minor ways, the stemmas presented below trace the descent of the various manuscripts of the poems either from the lost original holograph (LOH) or from the (or a, in the case of *Sat5*) revised version of it (LRH). Moreover, as has been demonstrated above, a given artifact's position on the stemma may shift from one poem to the next, and such movement can be not only vertical (involving changes in an artifact's relative proximity to the lost holograph), but also lateral (involving changes in which holograph—the original or the revised—an artifact derives from). Attending to both kinds of shifting can not only lead to further understanding of the processes by which individual collections of Satyres came into being (and therefore help to account for the relative soundness of the individual texts within given collections), but also provide insight into the dynamics that determine the larger patterns of circulation observable within the manuscript pool. Drawing on the foregoing discussion and further information embedded in Figure 2, the following numbered sections examine the effects of this position shifting on some of the major manuscripts and groups and on our understanding of them. The bracketed information included in the head of each entry reiterates the authorial and artifactual numbering/ordering of each poem as cited in Figure 2, links each text to either the original or the revised holograph, and notes whether the Satyres are accompanied by *Storm* and/or *Calm*.

1. **B13** [4(1)—LOH, 1(2)—LOH, 2(3)—LRH, 3(4)—LOH, 5(5)—LOH; + *Storm* and *Calm*] and **the "books" (OQ1, P3, and VA1)** [1(1)—LOH, 2(2)—LRH, 3(3)—LOH, 4(4)—LOH, 5(5)—LOH; + *Storm* and *Calm*]. As noted above, these manuscripts derive the Satyres (plus *Storm* and *Calm*) from the artifact designated δ¹ on the *Sat1* stemma. B13 enters *Sat4* first and entitles it "M^r: Dunns first Satire," a title resembling the generic section heading "Mr Iohn Dunnes Satires" that appears above *Sat1* (labeled "Satira 1^a") in OQ1 and that which is incorporated into P3's heading on *Sat1* ("Iohon Donne his Satires / The First").[22] These details suggest that B13's 4-1-2-3-5 sequence, the generic heading attributing the poems to "M^r" Donne (which—like the heading on O3—possibly dates the assembly of δ¹ prior to Donne's receipt of doctorate in 1615), and the association with *Storm* and *Calm* all originated with the ancestral δ¹ and that the normative 1–5 order was introduced by the scribe of ε¹, who also added Donne's given name to the generic heading. Under the Greek-letter name appropriate for each stemma, δ¹ appears variously at 3, 4, 2, 2, and 1 removes from the holograph on the stemmas for Satyres 1–5 respectively, and all its texts derive from the LOH except that of *Sat2*, which derives from the LRH.

Especially when combined with the record of verbal deterioration chronicled in

---

[22]VA1 numbers the poems 1–5, but contains no general generic heading nor mention of Donne. An eighteenth-century owner of the artifact subsequently inscribed a title page for the fascicle: "Poems written about the Year 1616; / and believed to be unprinted; / viz / Five Satires; / A Storme; / and / A Calme. P Neve" (see Beal, *Index*, 254).

the textual introductions to the individual poems below, this stemmatic informa-
tion shows that the presumption of particular authority traditionally accorded these
"books" is unwarranted. Grierson, for instance, found "manuscripts like…[OQ1]
and…[VA1]" of "great importance for the editor" on grounds that they "carry us
back…to the form in which the Satyres circulated before any of the later collections
of Donne's poems were made" and preserve an "older tradition" of the text (2:lxxx);
and he validated this conviction by importing into his A-based text several readings
from B13 and OQ1, including, e.g., the anomalous "He speakes no [for the otherwise
universal *one*] language" in *Sat4* 38 (see the textual introduction to *Sat4* below).
Subsequently Milgate (Y:xlviii), though he adopts almost none of their distinctive
readings, opines that "such 'books' contain a text of the *Satires* in their earliest form,
or at least descending from early copies" (xlvii) and avers that the books (of which
he cites B13, OQ1, and VA1) "contain a version of the Satires which is homoge-
neous and, except to some extent in… [B13], not certainly contaminated" (xlviii).[23]
Grierson, of course, based these conclusions on a knowledge of only about half the
Satyres manuscripts that have now come to light (of the 35 manuscripts of *Sat2*, e.g.,
he cites 17), and Milgate (although he adds 10 to the roster of artifacts known to
Grierson) did not know them all either. And this lack of information obviously hin-
dered these editors' ability to interpret the significance of this group of manuscripts.
Their principal limitation, however, lay in the assumption that artifactual priority
necessarily implied textual authenticity—i.e., in their failure properly to employ the
stemmatic method.[24] Had they done so, they might have achieved the perspective
enabled by the facts marshalled above: that the extant "books" derive from a prior
collection that not only (1) perpetuates textual errors inherited from varying numbers
of genealogical predecessors (from 3 in the most extreme case—that of *Sat2*), but also
(2) introduces numerous substantive errors of its own (over a dozen into the text of
Sat2, e.g.), (3) compiles a mixed collection of texts comprising descendants of both
the LOH and the LRH, and (4) records the Satyres in a non-standard order that
had to be reorganized into the standard arrangement by the copyist of the immediate
parent of the "books," who introduced yet other errors as he did so. From this parent
(5) finally derive OQ1 and—through yet a third missing manuscript—P3 (which
neither Grierson nor Milgate knew) and VA1.[25]

2. Group III: B46 [2(*u*)—LOH, 1(*u*)—LOH, 4(*u*)—LOH; no *Storm* and *Calm*].
H5 [1(1)—LOH, 5(2)—LOH, 4(4)—LOH, 2(5)—LOH, 3(6)—LOH; *Storm* and

[23](a) By "contaminated" Milgate here seems to mean merely "corrupt" rather than "influenced by
a variant textual tradition." (b) As is shown on Figure 2, Milgate's assertion that B13's sequence of
Satyres is "in the accepted order" (xlix) is erroneous; Grierson does not address this question.
    [24]Grierson's brief remarks on OQ1 and VA1 show him grappling with the genealogical relationship
of their texts (2:lxxx), but he thought it "impossible" to construct "a complete genealogy" of manu-
scripts (2:cxi) and did not consider attempting stemmas for individual poems. Milgate actually produces
a rough stemma of the Satyres manuscripts (see p. lxi), but it is incomplete, erroneous in some places,
and insufficiently detailed; and Milgate, like Grierson before him, approached the genealogy of the
Satyres globally rather than poem-by-poem.
    [25]Beginning the count with those introduced by the group's progenitor (ε^2), the cumulative substan-
tive errors registered by B13, OQ1, P3, and VA1 in their text of *Sat2*, e.g., number 25, 35, 52, and 36
respectively.

Calm not associated]. **B47-C9-H6** cluster [2(1)—LOH, 1(2)—LOH, 3(3)—LOH, 4(4)—LOH, 5(5)—LOH; *Storm* and *Calm* not associated]. The membership of Group III has been adjusted repeatedly over the years (Grierson, e.g., originally included B13, HH1, H3, NY1, O21, H7, and NY3 along with H6 and B46 in this group[26]), and the varying sequencing and makeup of the sets of Satyres in the manuscripts here listed reflect the lack of homogeneity that has always been recognized in the group as a whole. All of these artifacts ultimately derive their texts of the Satyres from the LOH of each poem; but none of them presents the poems in the standard order, and all the Satyres texts they record are, to varying degrees, remote from the holograph. B46 contains only Satyres 2, 1, and 4 (all unnumbered), and its texts of these poems stand, respectively, at 2, 7, and 5 removes from the holograph and are correspondingly corrupt, not least because of numerous blunders and interventions initiated by the B46 copyist himself (see the individual textual introductions below). H5 preserves all 5 poems, but—as noted above—in a non-standard arrangement that includes the spurious "Sleep, next society" as its third satire, and its texts exist, respectively, at 7, ?, ?, 4, and 4 removes from the holograph as is shown on the stemmas for Satyres 1–5 below.[27] Evincing the order 2, 1, 3, 4, 5, as is also noted above, the B47-C9-H6 trio ultimately derive from a common progenitor that stands, respectively, at 6, 2, 1, 3, and 2 removes from Donne's original on the stemmas of Satyres 1–5, and the 3 extant artifacts are yet more distant. Among these, the most important is H6, which—as is demonstrated in the textual introductions to the individual Satyres below—significantly influenced the early collected editions, especially that of 1635 (B). The amount of error entailed in the remoteness of his manuscript from the holograph no doubt partly accounts for the readiness of the H6 copyist—who, as we have suggested before, was almost certainly also the compiler of the C9-H6 parent (see *DV* 2:lxx, e.g.)—to "repair" perceived textual defects; and recognizing this tendency together with H6's position on the various stemmas provides a previously unavailable perspective on the trustworthiness of H6 as a source of emendations and, consequently, on the textual integrity of the seventeenth-century prints that reflect its influence.

    3. **H3** [1(*u*)—LOH, 2(*u*)—LOH, 4(*u*)—LOH, 3(4)—LOH; *Storm* and *Calm* not associated]. **O21** [2(*u*)—LRH, 1(1)—LOH, 3(2)—LRH, 5(3)—LRH², 4(4)—LOH; *Storm* and *Calm* not associated]. **Y3** [1(1)—LOH, 3(2)—LRH, 5(3)—LRH², 4(4)—LOH, 2(*u*)—LRH; *Storm* and *Calm* not associated]. Previous volumes of this edition have regularly shown H3, O21, and Y3 (all Associated with Group III) as a subfamily comprising an uncle and 2 sibling nephews (see, e.g., the schemas for *ElComp*, *ElPerf*, *ElJeal*, and *ElServe* in *DV* 2:70, 96, 107, and 124, respectively), and they evince that

---

[26]B47 was first described in an edition of the poetry by Gardner (1952), who—noting that the artifact had been cited among manuscripts of the Paradoxes and Problems by Evelyn Simpson (see Simpson, 1948, p. 145)—credited Milgate with having alerted her to its "importance for the poems" (lxxvi). Although Gardner fails to assign it membership in one of the numbered groups, not only its texts of the Satyres, but also its genealogical associations in previous volumes of this edition (see, especially, the schemas in vol. 2) indicate that it belongs in Group III, and Grierson would surely so have classified it had he known of its existence.

[27]The question marks in the foregoing formula correspond to the hatched lines on the stemmas, which denote the indeterminate proximity to the holograph of an artifact that descends directly from it.

relationship on the stemma for *Sat1* below. On the other stemmas, however, while O21 and Y3 invariably appear as siblings, their relationship to H3 varies. H3—which presents its Satyres as an incomplete, misordered, and mostly unnumbered set (see above)—derives its text of each of these poems from the LOH (though they stand—in 1, 2, 4, 3 order—at 5, ?, 3, and 4 removes, respectively, from the holograph). O21 and Y3, on the other hand, which also record the Satyres in a nonstandard order (see the discussion on p. lxxvi above), derive their texts (in 1–5 order) variously from the LOH, the LRH, the LRH, the LOH, and the LRH², and—mediated through their missing parent (ϵ^1 on the *Sat1* stemma)—these copies stand at 6, 5, 2, 3, and 2 removes from the respective originals. Partly because of the highly derivative nature of some of these copies and partly because of simple scribal incompetence, the texts of the Satyres preserved in these artifacts are extremely corrupt. In their most remote text, e.g.—that of the 112-line *Sat1*—H3 records some 40 substantive misreadings, while O21 and Y3 record 76 and 67 respectively. As corrupt as O21 and Y3 generally are, that the vast majority of their errors derive from their missing parent is evident in the genealogy of *Sat5*, whose stemma shows that parent (β^4) to descend directly from the LRH². At 2 removes from the holograph, O21 records 29 substantive blunders and Y3 records 26, but 25 of these are passed on from β^4. The only evident influence of any of these artifacts on the Satyres' seventeenth-century transmissional history appears in line 1 of *Sat3*, where O21 apparently supplies B's emendation of A's authorial "choakes" to "checks," a mistake not finally repaired until Grosart (N) recovered the authorial reading from B33 in 1872 (see Figure 10 below).

4. **The NY1-VA2 parent-child pair** [1(1)—LOH, 2(2)—LRH, 3(3)—LOH, 4(4)—LRH, 5(5)—LOH; + *Storm* and *Calm*]. NY1 was originally owned and apparently compiled by John Cave, of Lincoln College, Oxford (see Beal, *Index*, p. 253 and *CELM*), who prefaces the volume with his own 16-line poem "Vpon Mʳ Donn's Satires" (subscribed "Io. Ca. / Jun. 3. 1620") and proceeds with an independently numbered 40-page module comprising the 5 canonical Satyres, *Lit*, *Storm*, and *Calm* (for a fuller description of NY1's contents and Cave's method of compiling, see *DV* 2:lxxv–lxxvi). Deriving variously from the LOH and the LRH, the Satyres stand, respectively, at 2, 2, 1, 1, and 2 removes from the holograph on the stemmas below; and—despite their relative proximity to Donne's originals—their texts contain a considerable amount of error (NY1's LRH-derived transcription of *Sat2* evinces some 20 substantive differences from the holograph, e.g., and its LOH-derived copy of *Sat3* contains 15). Since a collector like Cave would surely have known, when he inscribed his dedicatory poem in 1620, that Donne was "Doctor," his reference to Donne as "Mʳ" likely points to his having assembled at least the major parts of his manuscript prior to Donne's ordination (*Har*, written in 1614, is the latest poem in the volume); and although his Satyres are genealogically unrelated to the existing "books," his putting the Satyres together with *Storm* and *Calm* in a discrete unit (albeit with *Lit* interpolated into the group) perhaps indicates that he had seen such a fascicle and sought to replicate it. A direct copy of NY1 written chiefly in the hand of Cave's fellow Lincolnite John Nedham and dated 1625 on its title page, VA2 adds a few further blunders to the text.

5. **Group IV: NY3** [1(1)—LRH, 2(2)—LOH, 3(3)—LOH, 4(4)—LRH, 5(5)—LRH[1]; *Storm* not associated (no *Calm*)]. Listed among the Group-III manuscripts in Grierson's initial classification, NY3 (historically known as the Westmoreland manuscript) was assigned separate, Group-IV status in Gardner's 1952 edition of the *Divine Poems* (siglum U), and sometime thereafter Alan MacColl identified its penman as Donne's friend Rowland Woodward—a credential that eventually combined with its overall textual integrity to endow the manuscript with an authority second only to that of Donne's autograph verse letter to the Lady Carey (siglum O15). NY3 has provided copy-texts for poems in every previous volume of this *Variorum*,[28] as it does here, and the soundness of its texts of the elegies prompted the suggestion that the artifact might have been transcribed "directly from Donne's own papers" (2:xci). Since we lacked stemmas for all those poems except *ElBrac*, of course, that statement necessarily held the status of only an informed opinion; in the present volume, however, where the evidence of the stemmas can be adduced, we can be certain that Woodward did not acquire his copies of the Satyres—at least not of all of them—from the author directly. As is noted at the head of this entry, he assembled a correctly numbered and ordered set of the poems deriving, respectively, from the LRH, the LOH, the LOH, the LRH, and the LRH[1], and his copies of Satyres 1, 2, and 5 do stem directly, perhaps even immediately, from the holograph; indeed, his transcription of *Sat5* is the unique surviving witness to the first revised version of the poem. On the stemmas of Satyres 3 and 4, however, NY3 stands at 2 removes from the holograph, and its texts of these poems are correspondingly less reliable. Whereas the texts of Satyres 1, 2, and 5 require only 2 substantive emendations each, that of *Sat3* must be verbally emended in 7 instances and that of the 244-line *Sat4* in 14. The details here presented suggest that during the years in which he was assembling his collection, Woodward's proximity to Donne and his access to authorial copies of the poems varied from time to time and enable a more nuanced understanding of the significance of his manuscript than has hitherto been possible.

6. **Group I: B32** [1(1)—LRH, 2(2)—LOH, 3(3)—LOH, 4(4)—LRH; *Storm* and *Calm* not associated]. **O20-SP1** [1(1)—LRH, 2(2)—LOH, 3(3)—LOH, 4(4)—LRH, 5(5)—LRH[2]; *Storm* and *Calm* not associated (*as noted above, C2 and C8 are ordinarily members of Group I, but contain the Group-II text of the Satyres and are thus listed with that group on Figure 2*)]. In Grierson's original classification, Group I included B32, C8, and O20 only, C2 and SP1 remaining unknown until their discovery in 1927 by H. J. L. Robbie, who assigned both artifacts to Group I and—refining Grierson's observation that one of the sources of A was a manuscript "identical with, or closely resembling" C8 (2:lxxxvi)—tentatively ventured that, at least in its "first part," C2 might be closer than "any existing MS." to the artifact used to set A into type (417).[29] Grierson conjectured that the "nucleus of the [Group-I] collection" (2:xc) was the "old [manuscript] book" that Donne asked to borrow from Henry Goodere in 1614

---

[28]*Variorum* texts based on NY3 include the funeral elegy *Sorrow* in vol. 6, the intermediate sequence of epigrams in vol. 8, the first 12 love elegies in vol. 2, and the Westmoreland sequence of Holy Sonnets in vol. 7.1.

[29]"An Undescribed MS. of Donne's Poems," *RES* 3:415–19.

when he faced "the necessity of printing" his poems and "addressing them to" the Earl of Somerset (see *Letters*, 196–97), somewhat puzzlingly concluding on circumstantial grounds that—"allowing for the carelessness, indifference, and misunderstandings of secretaries and copyists"—the text of such a collection "would be accurate" (2:xci). Subsequently, Gardner, though she specified no exact role for Goodere's "old book" in the process, extended this notion, stating in her 1952 *Divine Poems* (U) the "belie[f]" that the lost progenitor of Group I (equivalent to δ³ on the *Sat1* stemma) was "a copy" (U:lxiv) of the compilation Donne assembled in response to the pressure from Somerset and, correspondingly, that the Group-I artifacts "preserv[e] 'the text of the "edition" of 1614'" (U:lxvi).[30] Without directly contesting the ascription of extrinsic authority to Group I by his OUP predecessors, Wesley Milgate asserts that "[t]here is no single 'Group-I text' of the *Satires*" (Y:xliii) and plausibly posits that the archetype of Group I contained only the first 4 of these poems, the Group-II text of *Sat5* having most likely been independently added to the other 4 by the scribe of O20 (who transmitted it to SP1) and the entire Group-II set having been substituted for the Group-I set by the parent of C2 and C8 (δ⁴ on the *Sat1* stemma below). Milgate's theory that Donne circulated the Satyres in an original set and two successively revised versions will be discussed below.

The information encoded at the head of this entry shows that B32 and the O20-SP1 pair present a conventionally numbered and ordered set of Satyres 1–4 that derive, respectively, from the LRH, the LOH, the LOH, and the LRH; and the Group-I archetype (δ³ on the *Sat1* stemma) stands, respectively, at 3, 4, 3, and 3 removes from these holographs (in the case of *Sat5*, as has been noted, B32 drops out of the picture,

---

[30]This warrant of authenticity implicitly applies to the Satyres as well as to all other poems in the manuscript, even though Gardner recognizes that "the original" of C2 and C8 incorporated a "different text" (lxii) of the Satyres into its collection. In her edition of *The Elegies and The Songs and Sonnets* in 1965 (siglum X), Gardner characterizes her former "belie[f]" about the origins of Group I as a "suggest[ion]" (X:lxv), but she does not retract it in the reissue of U in 1978, even though she has in the meantime become convinced by Margaret Crum's analysis of the physical characteristics of the Group-I artifacts (Crum, 128–32) that the "copy" of Donne's collection was unlikely to have been "a single manuscript," but probably "consisted of separable parts." By 1978 Gardner has also been persuaded, perhaps in conversation with Milgate, that the Group-I archtype "contained only [the first] four Satires" (U, 1978, lxii–lxiii).

Gardner also (U:lxii) presents a global stemma for Group-I, later endorsed by both Crum and Milgate (in both Y and BB), that points to shared defects in the copies of *Goodf* preserved in C2, C8, O20, and SP1 as evidence that a lost ancestor (which she designates X2) existed between those artifacts and the "copy" of Donne's collection (X) from which both B32 and that ancestor derive (on the stemma for *Sat1* below, this ancestor would occupy a position between δ³ and O20). The stemmas included in the present volume, however, are based solely on the evidence contained in manuscripts of the Satyres, and none of these constructs exactly matches the stemma postulated by Gardner. In the case of Satyres 1–4, this discrepancy might be due to the C2-C8 parent's having substituted the Group-II text of the Satyres for that in Group I, thus removing C2 and C8 from the Group-I lineage and causing any variants that might have been introduced by X2 (if it existed) to manifest themselves for the first time in O20; in the case of *Sat5*, of course, the shape of the group is distorted by B32's failure to contain a copy of the poem. A second explanation for the above-mentioned discrepancy is implicit in Crum's suggestion that Gardner's X "may have been not one book," but a "collection of books and extra sheets" (132), which clearly enables the possibility that the genealogy of various poems or groups of poems might differ. In this connection, it might be noted that no artifact equivalent to Gardner's X2 appears among the Group-I artifacts on the stemma for *ElBrac* presented in volume 2 of this edition (see DV 2:46).

and the O20-SP1 pair appear among the Group-II artifacts).[31] The consequence of this remoteness is evident, for example, in the textual deterioration evinced in the copies of *Sat1* contained in B32, O20, and SP1, which—deriving errors successively from β^2, γ^2, and δ^3, as well as adding mistakes of their own—manifest 18, 17, and 19 corrupt substantive readings, respectively. In the case of *Sat2*, on whose stemma these artifacts appear at yet a further stage of remove, the corresponding numbers of errors are 24 (B32), 29 (O20), and 33 (SP1), and a comparable record of inaccuracy in these artifacts, paralleling that in the Group-I texts of the elegies, is detailed in the introductions and apparatuses for Satyres 3 and 4 below.[32]

Given the incompleteness of the Group-I set of Satyres and the distance-from-holograph and level of verbal corruption evinced by their texts, it is difficult to credit the notion that Donne was closely involved in the origins of Group I. It is true that these manuscripts are free of spurious items, that—in Gardner's words (U:lxiii)—they "contain no poem which can be dated with certainty after Donne's ordination in 1615," and that they provide the sense of an ending to Donne's poetic career by concluding with *Har*, an obsequy apparently written after August of 1614 in which Donne declares that his muse "hath spoke her last" (l. 258).[33] But the assembly of such a collection need not have been Donne's own project. It could easily have been accomplished by someone who knew Donne (or of Donne), who had accumulated copies of his various poetic writings over the years (or knew where to obtain them), and who—whether knowledgeable of the Donne-Somerset transaction or not—recognized Donne's "interre[ment]" of his "Muse" (*Har* 256) and entry into the priesthood as a significant transitional moment and decided to commemorate it by organizing (or making available) for private circulation a manuscript collection that would serve as the very "valediction to the world" (*Letters*, 197) that Donne had described as the purpose of the abortive "Somerset" edition and mark the conclusion of his poetic career. Such a collector would not necessarily have possessed all the poems in the latest and most uncorrupted versions (as, indeed, the compiler of δ^3 did not), but the collection would have served its intended purpose and have been of interest to others who shared an interest in Donne's overall achievement as a poet. The recent discovery that the copy of δ^3 preserved in O20 (traditionally known as the Dowden

---

[31] A further parental manuscript (γ^2 on the *Sat1* stemma) that begat both the Group-I archetype (δ^3) and F21 appears immediately above that archetype in the genealogy of Satyres 1 and 2. As noted above, F21 contains only these 2 Satyres, and while the possibility cannot absolutely be ruled out that its scribe selected only these 2 from a fuller set available in γ^2, such evidence as survives indicates that γ^2 itself contained only these 2, for no artifact corresponding to γ^2 appears on the stemmas for Satyres 3–5. The Group-I set of 4 Satyres thus appears to have been assembled by the scribe of δ^3, who obtained the text of the first 2 from γ^2.

[32] For a summary account of the corruption in both the text and sequencing of Group-I's collection of the Elegies, see DV 2:lxxiv.

[33] (a) This is the date of composition determined by Gardner, who reasons that since Donne explicitly declares *Har* to be his "last" poem and in the above-cited letter to Goodere refers to his promise to "my L. Harrington, to write nothing after that" (*Letters*, 198), it must have been composed after the completion of *Sal*, which bears the date August 1614 in the Group-I manuscripts (see U:lxiv). (b) Following the entry of *Har* by the primary scribe in C2, other copyists have inserted a few additional poems, those by Donne including *Christ*, which does not appear in the other Group-I artifacts, and second copies of *Broken* and *Mess*.

manuscript) was penned by Donne's longtime friend George Garrard indicates that such a collection could pass muster even with some who had a close relationship with Donne, although the C2-C8 parent's substitution of the Group-II set of Satyres for that available in δ³ shows that at least some collectors were more discriminating in their choice of text than was Garrard.[34]

7. Group II: C2-C8 [1(1)—LRH, 2(2)—LRH, 3(3)—LRH, 4(4)—LRH, 5(5)—LRH²; *Storm* and *Calm* not associated]. B11 [4(?)—LRH, 5(5)—LRH²; no *Storm* and *Calm*]. DT1-H4 [1(*u*)—LRH, 3(2)—LRH, 4(*u*)—LRH, 5(*u*)—LRH², 2(*u*)—LRH; *Storm* and *Calm* not associated]. B40 [3(*u*)—LRH, 4(*u*)—LRH, 5(3)—LRH², 2(*u*)—LRH, 1(*u*)—LRH; *Storm* and *Calm* not associated]. TT1 [3(*u*)—LRH, 4(*u*)—LRH, 5(3)—LRH², 2(*u*)—LRH; *Storm* and *Calm* not associated]. (*As noted above, the first 2 manuscripts listed here ordinarily belong to Group I.*) Of the Group-II manuscripts containing the Satyres, Grierson's original classification included only DT1 and H4, which he recognized as parent and child (his Group II also included CT1 and B7, a second parent-child pair from which the Satyres are absent), but he briefly noted B40's "connect[ion]" with the Group-II artifacts and—on grounds of its contents—thought it "probably older" (2:cv) than they. In her 1952 *Divine Poems*, Gardner recognizes the original 4 Group-II manuscripts and—because it contained *Ham*—speculates that their prototype (which she designates Y and locates at the head of a stemma from which descend the parent-child pairs CT1-B7 and DT1-H4) was compiled "after 1625," the year of James Hamilton's death; furthermore, she thinks it "likely" that this compiler "had access to Donne's own papers," reasoning that although it might have been "preserved among…[his] papers" (U:lxvii–lxviii), Donne was unlikely to have circulated the unperfected *Res*, which appears throughout the group. Since B40 contains no religious poems, she does not mention it, although in the 1965 *Elegies and the Songs and Sonnets* she describes the collection "preserved in" B40 as a smaller one from which the Group-II prototype (Y) "grew…by accretion" (lxviii) and—while still formally confining Group II to the CT1-B7 and DT1-H4 pairs—introduces both it and WN1, which had recently been discovered by Alan MacColl, under the Group-II rubric in her list of sigla. Adding B30 to her Group-I stemma and B40 to that for Group II, moreover, she posits a single comprehensive construct showing the descent of both groups from a single urtext labeled α (see X:lxx). In this edition Gardner reiterates the post-1625 date of compilation for Y, but drops the earlier speculation that it was based on Donne's "own papers."

Remaining silent on the questions of the date of compilation and the possible relationship of the Group-II prototype to the author's papers, Milgate in 1967 again

---

[34] The identification of Garrard as the O20 copyist was first announced by Gary A. Stringer on February 20, 2009, in a session on Digitizing Donne at the 24th annual meeting of the John Donne Society. A digital presentation detailing the similarities between known writings of Garrard and O20 is available online under the Resources tab of the *DigitalDonne* website (http://DigitalDonne.tamu.edu). Although the texts he copied were several steps removed from their respective holographs, Garrard himself was a fairly accurate scribe: of the 17 *Sat1* errors he records, 15 derive from superior manuscripts on the family tree; of his 29 *Sat2* errors, he is responsible for 5. In addition to filling out the Group-I collection of 4 Satyres by adding the fifth from Group II, he enhances the collection by moving 9 poems from their original positions in order to create a series of generically unified groups.

limits Group II to the original 4 members and repeats Gardner's description of the collection in B40 as a smaller one from which the Group-II prototype "seems to have grown by accretion," deeming its text "on the whole rather better" (Y:xliii). Relying on Gardner's descriptions of B40 and WN1, moreover, he similarly includes both with the Group-IIs on his sigla list, and—as with Group I previously—posits a global stemma for the Group-II Satyres that in many respects resembles that included here for *Sat5* (see Y:xliv and Figure 18 below). Also in 1967, Alan MacColl cites a letter Donne wrote to Sir Robert Ker in 1619 that apparently accompanied a gift of "the Poems, of which you took a promise" (*Letters*, p. 21) and declares it "likely" that these were "the poems…that make up the Group II collection" (259). In thus resurrecting Gardner's hypothesis that the Group-II archetype drew on Donne's own papers, MacColl further argues that, since Ker had commissioned *Ham*, he would certainly have had a copy to add to the collection later and that other post-1619 poems could similarly have been appended "to produce [Gardner's] Y in its final state" (259).[35]

Citing MacColl's "very plausibl[e]" argument, in 1978 Gardner again points to the presence of *Res* as proof that the Group-II prototype (her Y) drew on "Donne's own papers" and identifies Ker as its compiler, additionally approving the hypothesis that Y merged poems from the Donne-Ker papers with the smaller collection preserved in B40 (U, 1978, p. 149). Y, whose stemma remains unchanged, Gardner now thinks "cannot have reached final form" before 1623, the date she assigns to *Father*, which appears in all of the original Group-IIs. No doubt because it contains no *Divine Poems*, B40 here disappears from Gardner's sigla list, but in 1978 (siglum BB) Milgate does so include it and WN1 as well. To a full endorsement of Gardner's most recent description of the origins of Group II, Milgate adds the bibliographical information that in both CT1 and DT1 *Ham* appears as a late addition to the artifact, being separated from the main body of text by a blank page in the former and being inscribed in a second hand in the latter. Having been discovered by him in 1977, TT1 and TT2 are added to the roster of Group-II artifacts by Beal (1980), who recounts the arguments that locate the origins of Group II in authorial papers left to Ker and cautions that "[n]othing can be known for certain about any of these 'collections' of Donne's poems, or about their relationship with extant MSS" (*Index* 246).

Beal's caveat notwithstanding, some light can be shed on the foregoing arguments—at least insofar as they affect the Satyres—by attending to the information encoded at the head of this entry and that conveyed by the stemmas presented below. Variously labeled γ^3, β^5, β^5, β^4, and β^5, the Group-II archetype stands, respectively, at 2, 1, 1, 1, and 1 removes from holograph on the stemmas here presented for Satyres 1–5, and, as noted above, in each case it derives from the most recently revised holograph (i. e., from the LRH of Satyres 1–4, from the LRH² of *Sat5*)—the only such lineal progenitor of which this can be said. Curiously, however, the promise of reliability implicit in the position of these artifacts in the genealogy of the various poems is betrayed by the actual quality of their texts and by their failure to record

---

[35] MacColl (1972, 35) subsequently bolsters this argument by citing a letter from William Drummond to Ker in 1621 in which Drummond refers to "Done, who in his trauells lefte you his [poetic scrolls]" (see D. Laing, ed., *The Correspondence of Sir Robert Ker first Earl of Ancram*, Edinburgh (1875), i, p. 24).

the poems in the authorial sequence. In the case of $Sat1$, e.g., the Group-II progenitor (γ^3) adds 11 substantive errors to the 8 introduced in β^2 and passes these 19 scribal blunders on to δ^4 and δ^5, whose copyists add a few mistakes of their own, as do the penmen of the extant artifacts. In the upshot, these manuscripts evince 23 (C2), 26 (C8), 25 (B40), 22 (DT1), and 22 (H4) errors in their texts of $Sat1$. With respect to $Sat2$—whose stemma differs from that of $Sat1$ not only in the addition of TT1, but also in the placement of B40—the extant manuscripts inherit 13 errors from the group archetype (β^5) and 3 and 7, respectively, from γ^4 and γ^5, the chain of deterioration eventually resulting in 24 (C2), 26 (C8), 20 (DT1), 23 (H4), 24 (B40), and 39 (TT1) misreadings in the artifacts themselves.[36] And substantial levels of corruption in the Group-II texts of Satyres 3–5 are detailed in the textual introductions and apparatuses below. As with the elegies, moreover, whose texts in the Group-II artifacts also evince numerous misreadings (see DV 2:lxix, lxxiv–lxxv), the Group-II archetype transmits the Satyres to its descendants as an unnumbered set that bespeaks the compiler's utter ignorance of the normative authorial sequence. Indeed, as is discussed in point (f) on page lxxvi above and outlined in Figure 2, only in the C2-C8 parent, whose compiler rejected the Group-I texts of the poems in favor of a set from the Group-II lineage, is the normative ordering restored.[37] Despite its recording each of the Satyres in the most recently revised version, in short, these facts seem incompatible with the notion that the Group-II prototype consisted of (or even derived closely from) Donne's "own papers"—at least as regards the Satyres.

Finally, the information here presented provides a perspective on 3 additional propositions advanced in the editions surveyed above. First, the facts that 49 of the 50 Donne poems contained in B40 appear in DT1 (which, at 143 poems, is the fullest of the Group-IIs), that 44 of these 49 are concentrated among DT1's first 48 items, and that the texts of the individual poems in the 2 manuscripts invariably trace back to a common scribal ancestor strongly support Gardner's suggestion that the Group-II archetype incorporated the smaller collection preserved in B40.[38] Further, although

---

[36]Within Group II, the genealogies of Satyres 2, 3, and 4 are identical, the stemma for each of these poems depicting the division of the textual lineage embodied in the group archetype (β^5 on the $Sat2$ stemma) into 2 parallel strands of descent which—through yet two other missing manuscripts (γ^4 and γ^5)—lead to the (also missing) parent of C2 and C8 and to the remaining members of the group. In the case of $Sat1$, however, TT1 does not contain the poem, and the B40 text—which is entered in a different hand from that which recorded the other Satyres and separated from them by $ElBrac$ and "Sleep next society"—descends from the parent of DT1 (see footnote 20 above).

[37]The C2-C8 parent's appropriation of the Group-II text and simultaneous reimposition of the Group-I arrangement (as well as his rejection of the spurious "Sleep, next society") mark its collector as a person who possessed a particular knowledge of and regard for what Donne had finally intended for the Satyres, very likely a member of a circle of like-minded aficionados concerned with such matters (it would have been easier, after all, simply to append the Group-II text of $Sat5$ to the set of 4 from Group I—as Garrard had done). Unfortunately, according to the error-count in Satyres 1 and 2 detailed above, the texts of the individual poems promulgated by this collector are no cleaner than those of their Group-I counterparts, but he nevertheless persuaded the compilers of C2 and C8 to accept his version of the entire set, and through C2 that version eventually appeared in the first printed edition.

[38]In its current state, two leaves containing the original pages 71–74 of DT1 are missing, a lacuna entailing the loss of ll. 34–45 of $Canon$, the entirety of $LovDeit$ and $Will$, and ll. 1–30 of $ExExpost$ (the contents of the missing pages may be inferred by comparing H4, copied before the damage to DT1; the numbers here given are based on the pre-loss contents of the artifact).

B40 and DT1 are equidistant from the holograph on each of the stemmas below and (in the case of Satyres 2–5) C2 and C8 are a further step removed, the record of variation presented in the historical collations below shows B40's texts to be approximately equal in corruption to those in the other Group-II artifacts—not, as Milgate had opined, "on the whole rather better" (see the tally of errors for Satyres 1 and 2 above). And, lastly, despite its similarity to the section of the *Sat1* stemma depicting the relationship of Groups I and II, Gardner's 1965 stemma tracing the origins of both groups to a single lost urtext (α) obviously cannot pertain to the Satyres, since—as is explained in the previous section—Group-I's texts descend variously from the LOH and the LRH, while Group II's uniformly descend from the LRH.

Milgate's Theory of Donne's Revisions of the Satyres

Milgate (1967) cites the existence of "striking variant readings" within the manuscript pool that cannot be "due to accidents of transmission" (lvi) as evidence of authorial revision in the Satyres and—averring the poems to have "circulated as a set" that was "absorbed as a group into larger collections" (lvi)—identifies 2 major overhauls of the entire sequence and links each to a particular period in Donne's life. Having originally composed the first 4 Satyres at various times between 1593 and the spring of 1597, Milgate hypothesizes (see footnote 9 above), Donne revised them in conjunction with his composition of *Sat5* shortly after entering Egerton's service and presented the entire group—4 revised and 1 newly written—to the "Lord Keeper's family" (lviii) sometime in 1598. The last (and second revised) version, Milgate finally conjectures, dating from 1607 or shortly thereafter, was "prepared for the Countess of Bedford" (lix), whose acquaintance Donne had recently made and who—as Jonson declares in the above-cited epigram—"desir'd" them. According to this theory, (1) the text of the original version is contained in the "books" and, in a "progressively deteriorating" (lvii) form, in some of the Group-III manuscripts (C9, H3, H5, H6, H7, O21, Y3); (2) the text of the first revison is contained in NY3, Group I, and "possibly" SN3, B33, and HH1; and (3) the text of the final version is contained in Group II (which includes C2 and C8). In his apparatus Milgate represents the successive versions synecdochically by citations from, respectively, OQ1 and H6 (original version), NY3 and B32 (first revision), and C2, B40, and DT1 (final version), and he outlines the theory schematically in a comprehensive stemma at the close of his discussion (see Y:lxi).

Milgate is of course not the first to suggest that Donne himself altered the texts of the Satyres—as early as 1872, e.g., Grosart speculated that "fondling" (for "changeling") in *Sat1* 1 was "the author's revised word" (1:9)—and that these poems evince revision is a central premise of the present edition. From the analytical perspective here presented, however, which entails the development of a separate genealogy for each individual poem, Milgate's attempt to describe the transmissional history of the Satyres globally, at the level of the entire set, is fundamentally misguided, resulting in the inability to identify particular authorial revisions/versions reliably and, more

---

The 5 B40 poems removed to the latter parts of DT1, apparently in the interests of tightening generic grouping, are *BedfReas*, *Fever*, *Dream*, *ValWeep*, and *ConfL*. For Gardner's comparison of the contents of the 2 manuscripts see V:lxviii–lxix.

broadly, to account accurately for the poems' general transmissional history. With respect to the first of these shortcomings, for example, in his discussion of the manuscripts that preserve what he takes to be the original form of the Satyres, Milgate notes that the lying historian "Surius" in Sat4 48 is called "Sleydan" in some manuscripts and—entirely on impressionistic grounds—finds both readings to be authorial, supposing Donne to have substituted the name of "Surius" (a Catholic) for that of the original "Sleydan" (a Protestant) in order to certify his *bona fides* as a professed Anglican upon entering Egerton's household (lvii). The stemma for Sat4 presented in Figure 15, however, shows that "Surius" (in various spellings and malformations) is universally the reading throughout all branches of the genealogical tree except that "Sleydan" (or recognizable mutations thereof) appears in the descendants of γ^2 (B13, OQ1, VA1-P3) and ζ (C9-H6) and in NP2, artifacts that appear in separate genealogical lines at, respectively, 2, 5, and 5 removes from the holograph. Not all of Milgate's identifications of alternative readings as authorial are wrong, of course, but the position of these variants on the stemma shows that, whether confessionally motivated or not, the change from "Surius" to "Sleydan" cannot have been Donne's and that manuscripts containing "Sleydan" do not embody an authentic early version of the poem.[39]

Undergirding Milgate's wholistic approach to the question of revision is the proposition that "[t]he text of manuscripts containing all five Satires...is invariably homogeneous" (lvi). By this he apparently means, unexceptionably, that, apart from scribal blunders and minor interventions, every member of each of the major groups preserves the same text—that all descendants of a given parental urtext record the distinctive readings of that archetype and thus constitute an identifiable family. In order to prove that Donne had revised the Satyres as a set rather than individually, however, Milgate would need to demonstrate something rather different: that within each set all 5 poems exhibited homogeneity of version (i.e., that all the texts in the "books" stemmed from the LOH, e.g., or that each of those in Group I stemmed from the LRH). And while some collections do evince such unity, this latter proposition is far from "invariably" true; indeed, among the manuscripts in which original and revised versions of poems are intermingled are the "books" (B13, OQ1, P3, VA1), Group IV (NY3), and the Group-Is (B32, O20-SP1)—3 groups that are central to Milgate's overall theory.[40]

---

[39] ζ frequently gives evidence of having been compared with manuscripts outside its genealogical line (see, e.g., footnote 2 on p. 216 below), which seems to have happened here. That H6 interlines "Surius" as a variant to "Sleydan" indicates either that both readings stood in ζ or that the H6 scribe, following a procedure elsewhere observable, corrected his manuscript against A; the cognate C9 records "Sleydan" only. NP2 seems similarly to have obtained "Sleydan" extra-lineally, since its cognate LR1 derives from ε^3 the normative "Surius."

Milgate does not address the fact that, except for those named above, all manuscripts containing what he regards as the early version of the Satyres evince the reading "Surius."

[40] To summarize, the following artifacts do in fact evince uniformity of version in their texts (in top-to-bottom order on Figure 2): the texts in 4 of the Group III manuscripts (H5, B47-C9-H6) derive solely from the LOH; the texts in 2 manuscripts Associated with Group III (H3, HH1) derively solely from the LOH; the texts in all the Group II manuscripts (C2-C8, DT1-H4, B40-TT1) derive solely from the LRH (or LRH²); and the texts in 3 Unclassified manuscripts (H7, H8, Y2) derive solely from the LOH. On the other hand, such "homogene[ity]" is absent from the "books" (B13, OQ1, P3, VA1),

Finally, Milgate's two-stage dating of the putative revisions of the Satyres is similarly dependent upon his theory of global revision. Having concluded that NY3 and the Group-I manuscripts contain the same (intermediate) version of the text and believing there to be only a single version of Sat5, Milgate undertakes to account for the absence of Sat5 in "so authoritative a collection" as Group I. The explanation he eventually hits on involves imagining a set of circumstances under which Donne might have been moved to revise Satyres 1–4, but not Sat5, and the result is the above-described scenario thought to have played out in the early months of Donne's employment with Egerton. This 4-poem revision is then speculatively identified as the ancestor of NY3, which also incorporated the newly composed Sat5, and of the Group-I archetype, a "less accurate copy" (lviii) from which Sat5 was somehow omitted. Contravening this account, however, is the genealogical analysis detailed above and represented in Figure 18, which demonstrates that Donne revised Sat5 not only once, but twice, the 14 descendants of the LOH containing the original version and NY3 preserving the sole surviving copy of the first revision. Evidence presented above (see footnote 31) also suggests that, rather than descending as a 4-poem unit from a superior manuscript, the Group-I archetype of the Satyres (δ^3 on the Sat1 stemma) was assembled piecemeal, its compiler deriving the texts of Satyres 1 and 2 from the missing artifact that also begat F21 (γ^4 on the Sat1 stemma).[41] Milgate's further proposal that the Group-II (second revised) version of the Satyres arises from Donne's attempt to ingratiate himself with the Countess of Bedford is similarly rooted

---

which interject the revised version of Sat2 among their otherwise original-version texts; from 4 other artifacts Associated with Group III (O21-Y3, NY1-VA2), which variously intermingle LOH, LRH, and LRH² versions within their collections; from Group IV (NY3), which has 2 texts deriving from the LOH, 2 from the LRH, and 1 from the LRH¹; and from the Group-I manuscripts (B32, O20-SP1), which similarly intermingle variant versions, including (in O20-SP1) the Group-II (LRH²) version of Sat5.

Among the manuscripts that intermix original and revised versions within their sequences, NY3 and the 3 Group-Is uniquely share the pattern of derivation LRH-LOH-LOH-LRH with respect to their texts of Satyres 1–4 (Sat5 is absent from the Group-I archetype), and the general similarity of text that follows from this commonality of origin no doubt partly explains why Milgate sees all these artifacts as members of a single family. The more nuanced account of their genealogical relationships provided here, however, shows that NY3 and the Group-I archetype exist on separate genealogical branches on the stemmas for Sat1 and Sat2 and that NY3 and that archetype exist within the same lineage in the relationship of uncle to nephew on the stemmas for Sat3 and Sat4—degrees of genealogical separation that entail significant textual differences (in Sat1, e.g., NY3 diverges from the holograph in only 2 substantive readings, while the Group-I texts diverge in about 20). As is pointed out above, moreover (see footnote 31), the compiler of the Group-I archetype appears to have assembled his collection piecemeal, deriving texts of Sat1 and Sat2 from superior urtexts (γ^2 and δ^2 on the stemmas for Sat1 and Sat2) whose respective holographs of origin happen to match those in the first half of the pattern described above (LRH-LOH) and adding from within the same lineage as NY3 texts of Sat3 and Sat4 whose holographs of origin match the other half of the pattern (LOH-LRH). In light of the divergent genealogies of the Group-I Satyres, however, this replication of NY3's holograph-of-origin pattern can only be regarded as coincidental.

[41] Milgate rightly recognizes that O20-SP1 filled out the incomplete collection derived from the Group-I archetype by adding the Group-II version of Sat5, and he acknowledges that Sat5 is widely present among the manuscripts that contain the earliest version of the Satyres (i.e., the "books" and the Group-IIIs), but, owing to the alleged paucity and insignificance of variants in Sat5, is unable to "decide at what stage in the transmission it was added" (lxi).

in historical coincidence, its principal bibliographical justification consisting in the fact that within Group II the text of Sat3 evinces extensive revisions, an effort Milgate thinks might reflect both the "self-examination" (lx) that Donne undertook in response to Thomas Morton's attempt in 1607 to persuade him to "take holy orders" (lix–lx) and his desire to appeal to the "tastes of his new patroness (for the Countess was a religious woman)" (lix). These associations, of course, are purely conjectural and are dependent upon a genealogy of the Satyres that is incompatible with the history of transmission detailed above.

The question of revision aside, the notion that the Satyres circulated primarily as an authorially structured 5-poem unit finds no support in the account of their transmission presented above. While it might seem improbable that Donne himself never gave anyone a complete set of the Satyres, the only horse's-mouth evidence that he might have done so—and this is proof only by inference—is his conditional promise in the above-cited letter (see p. lxviii) to "acquaint" his friend with "all" his compositions. Rather, the overwhelming impression created by the surviving manuscript collections is of poems, whether in original or revised versions, circulating promiscuously along the channels of transmission individually or in 2- or 3-item clusters and eventually coalescing into fuller collections in the manuscripts of scribes who sometimes interlarded them with poems of other kinds and mingled them with poems of other authors and frequently had no idea of the normative sequence. Among the artifacts described above, of course, we have identified a small handful—most notably the missing parent of the OQ1, P3 and VA1 and the urtext that gave rise to C2 and C8—that reflect their compilers' positive understandings of not only the proper arrangement of the poems, but also, in the latter case, the difference between earlier and later versions of the poems, but these are scribal documents, neither assembled nor circulated by the author himself.

The Satyres in the Seventeenth-Century Prints

Having accommodated the objections of the censors by emending or expunging offensive words and lines in Satyres 1, 2, and 4 (and flagging most of the omissions with conspicuous placeholder dashes), John Marriot eventually obtained permission to include the poems in the first collected edition of Donne's Poems in 1633 (A), where, under the section title and running head "Satyres" and in the authorial arrangement, the 5 canonical Satyres appear immediately before "A Hymne to God the Father" as the next-to-last Donne poems in the edition (the volume concludes with a selection of prose letters and the "Elegies on the Authors Death"). The manuscript primarily used in setting A into type was C2,[42] which, as noted above, appears at 4

---

[42]The certainty that C2, specifically, is the Group-I manuscript used in the typesetting of A has emerged gradually over the course of this Variorum project. Although he eventually concluded that, because it "omits the last ten lines" of EdHerb and differs from the edition in other specific lections, C2 could not be the actual source of A, in the 1927 article cited above H. J. L. Robbie noted that the manuscript and the edition evinced a remarkable similarity of contents and sequencing of materials in their opening pages and observed that C2 "may be a version closer [than any other manuscript] to that used to set up the first part of 1633 (417), further opining that C2 "or a MS. from which it is derived...has been used to set up The Progresse of the Soule in 1633" (p. 418). Similarly citing the shared unique sequence of materials and, especially, headings in the artifacts' opening pages, as well as specific

removes from the LRH (or LRH[2]) on the stemmas for Satyres 1–5, respectively, and brought with it a substantial increment of error—C2's text of *Sat4*, e.g., evinces over 40 separate misreadings. Although, inevitably, he admitted a few additional errors of his own (substituting "it self death" for the normative "it selfes death" in *Sat3* 40, e.g.), A's editor generally strove to correct perceived semantic or metrical lapses in the C2 text, and in this effort he not only followed his own sense of logic and rhythm (independently changing "our land" to "the land" in *Sat2* 77, e.g., and eliding "who hath" to "who'hath" in *Sat4* 103), but also occasionally compared both DT1 (from which he seems to have obtained the hyphenated "blanck-charters" [for C2's "blanke charters"] in *Sat3* 91, e.g.) and H6 (from which he adopts, e.g., the substitution "He thrusts on more" [for C2's "Hee trusts me more"] in *Sat4* 111). Such examples as those here given, of course, are multiplied many times over in the discussions of the individual Satyres below, and the editorial approach they demonstrate is of a piece with that applied by A's editor to the poems included in previous volumes of this *Variorum* (see, e.g., DV 7.1:lxxii–lxxiii).

In the generically consolidated and reorganized second collected *Poems* (B), the *Satyres* are brought forward to a position between the *Epithalamions* and the *Letters to Severall Personages* in the middle of the volume (see Figure 3), and the noncanonical "Men write that love and reason disagree" is appended to the group as "Satyre VI." Apparently expecting no further scrutiny from the censor, moreover, B's editor restores all the material he had omitted from A (except the word "Letanye" in *Sat2* 33, which remains absent until recovered by the editor of G), replaces two emendations he had made in A's text of *Sat1* with the authorial wording (see the textual introduction to *Sat1* below), and—as noted above—accepts from O21 an emendation for the first line of *Sat3*. His most concerted editorial efforts, however, consist in a much more thorough examination of H6 than he had been able to carry out previously (for an account of H6's emergence as a source for A and B, see DV 2:lxxvii–lxxix). He does not, as the following discussions of the individual Satyres make clear, indiscriminately adopt every alternative reading available in H6, but his comparison of the artifact nevertheless results in the emendation of A's text in dozens of further instances—21

---

shared readings, we asserted the parent-child relationship of C2 and A in *The Holy Sonnets* in 2005 (see DV 7.1:lxxii, esp. fn. 11), but mitigated the claim with the recognition that a lost sibling or parent of C2 could not absolutely be ruled out as the edition's copy-text; and Gary A. Stringer elaborated this argument in "The Making of the 1633 *Poems, by J. D. with Elegies on the Authors Death*," delivered at the annual meeting of the John Donne Society in 2010. More recently, Tracy E. McLawhorn cited A's replication of C2's anomalous "Belongs" in *Prim* 26 (for the required—and otherwise universal—subjunctive form "Belong" in the clause "if halfe ten / Belong unto each woman") as concrete verbal proof that C2 specifically—not a lost parent or sibling—was A's setting text, pointing to the fact that C2's extant sibling, C8, gives the normative "Belong" and must have derived it from the lost parent (see Tracy E. McLawhorn, "A Critical Edition of Donne's 'The Indifferent,' 'Love's Usury,' 'The Will,' 'The Funerall,' 'The Primerose,' and 'The Dampe' and a Digital Edition of 'To His Mistress Going to Bed,'" Diss. Texas A&M U, 2013, p. 182). And further proof of the specific C2-A relationship appears below in line 185 of *Metem*, where the C2 scribe misrecords "All a new [2]Mantle [1]downy overspreds" (for the normative "All a new Downy Mantle ouerspreads"), attempting to clarify his mistake by affixing ordinal numbers to "Mantle" and "downy," but leading A's compositor to bungle the correction as "All downy a new mantle overspreads."

FIGURE 3: PLACEMENT OF THE SATYRES* IN THE PRINTED EDITIONS†

Siglum	Pages	Context Within Volume
A	325–49	penultimate poems in vol.; after Lam; followed by Father, prose letters, elegies on Donne
B	123–45	in midst of vol. between epithalamions and verse letters
C	123–45	in midst of vol. between epithalamions and verse letters
D	118–39	in midst of vol. between epithalamions and verse letters
E	118–39	in midst of vol. between epithalamions and verse letters
F	118–39	in midst of vol. between epithalamions and verse letters
G	118–38	in midst of vol. between epithalamions and verse letters
H	107–25	in midst of vol. between epithalamions and verse letters
I	107–31	initial Donne poems in 1st of 3 vols. (after elegies on Donne); followed by epithalamions
J	8–13	initial Donne poems in vol. (after elegies on Donne); followed by epithalamions
K	155–60	in midst of vol. between epithalamions and verse letters
M	400–25	penultimate poems in vol.; after epithalamions; followed by Latin poems
N	5–50	initial poems in 1st vol.; followed by Metem
O	153–77	in midst of 1st vol. between epithalamions and epigrams
P	175–203	penultimate poems in 2nd vol.; between Metem and epigrams
Q	145–71	in midst of vol. between epithalamions and verse letters
S	121–39	in midst of vol. between epithalamions and verse letters
T	91–108	third group of poems in vol.; between elegies and epigrams
Y††	3–25	initial poems in vol.; followed by epigrams
Z	15–37	initial Donne poems in vol. (after elegies on Donne); followed by elegies
AA	155–73	in midst of vol. between epigrams and Metem
DD	214–44	in midst of vol. between epithalamions and verse letters

*This figure pertains to Satyres 1–5 only.
†Modern editions L R U V W X BB CC do not contain the Satyres.
††Y contains Satires, Epigrams, and Verse Letters only.

in Sat4 alone—and a further intermingling of original- and revised-version readings in the texts of the Satyres.

A page-for-page resetting of B, the 1639 third edition of the Poems (C) records a few changes of spelling and punctuation in the Satyres' texts, but other than a couple of blunders reflects no verbal differences from the text of B; and in the fourth edition (D, with its 2 reissues E and F), set successively from C, the text similarly remains unchanged except for a few alterations of accidentals and a handful of further substantive alterations, none of which points to comparison with another artifact (the conjectured "gallant," he" [for the censored "Letanie"] in Sat2 33 is D–F's most notable innovation). In the Restoration edition of 1669 (G), however, set into type from F, the editor not only modernizes spelling and punctuation throughout, but also interjects the spurious "Sleep, next Society and true friendship" as "Satyre VI" (thus pushing the previously inserted "Men write that love and reason disagree" to the seventh position—see Table A) and introduces numerous verbal changes to the texts of Satyres 1–5. Some of these are blunders or independent attempts at improvement (without artifactual authority, e.g., he changes the received "subtile wittied antique youths" to "giddy-headed antick youth" in *Sat1* 62), but for others he obviously consulted one or more manuscripts (his restoration of "Letanie" at the end of *Sat2* 33, e.g., must derive from manuscript, since no previous edition had included it), and possibly A (see the discussion of G in the textual introduction to *Sat5* below). G's alterations of F's texts of the Satyres are comprehensively detailed in the individual textual introductions and apparatuses below. The authorship of the two noncanonical Satyres is discussed and their texts are reproduced in Appendix 1 elsewhere in this volume.

Table A: Spurious Satyres in the printed editions

Source	Men write that love	Sleep, next Society
B	• Satyre VI	
C	• Satyre VI	
D	• Satyre VI	
E	• Satyre VI	
F	• Satyre VI	
G	• Satyre VII	• Satyre VI
H	• Satyre VI	
I	• Satire VI	
J	• Satire VI	
K	• Satire VII	• Satire VI
M	• Satire VI	
N	• Satire VII	• Satire VI
O	• Satire VI	
P	• Satire VI	• Satire VII
Q	*unnumbered**	*unnumbered**

*Q gives both poems in an appendix of poems attributed to Donne.

The *Satyres* in the Modern Prints

Following a pattern previously noted in this *Variorum* (and similarly described by Stringer, 2011, pp. 45–46), the first 5 post-seventeenth-century editions that contain the Satyres—from Tonson (H) through Bell (I), Anderson (J), and Chalmers (K) to Lowell (M)—present a text based on G, although (except that, curiously, K imports the spurious "Sleep next society" directly from G) I–K and M derive this text through H (see Table A).[43] More precisely, I derives from H, and J derives from I, while both

---

[43]That H does not include "Sleep next society" may represent a simple oversight, but Tonson's occasional imposition of emendations from B or C indicates his awareness of an earlier edition from which this second spurious Satyre was absent and raises the possibility that he consciously rejected it. Since I, J, and M, following their usual practice, sequentially reproduce the text as transmitted through Tonson, they also fail to contain this second noncanonical Satyre. Indeed, in this connection K's inclusion of the poem is somewhat surprising, for it constitutes the only evidence so far encountered in the history of this *Variorum* edition that K consulted a source other than H. Similarly perplexing is that O, which obtains "Men write" from B, does not pick up "Sleep next society" from G; in this omission O's editors perhaps follow the previous example of M. N bases both spurious Satyres on G, but emends both toward manuscript readings, and P also prints both from G, citing the same manuscripts as N and accepting

K and M revert to H for their copies of the poems. In a text evincing further modernization of spelling and punctuation throughout, Tonson transmits to these successors most of G's innovations (the above-mentioned "giddy-headed...youth" in *Sat1* 62, e.g.) and introduces a few independent sports (reversing the normative "be naked" to "naked be" in *Sat1* 41, e.g.), but he also occasionally draws on either B or C to correct a perceived misreading (replacing G's erroneous "Jawes" with the authorial "Laws" in *Sat2* 112, e.g.). Other than K (which derives "Sleep next society" from G), M is the only artifact in the direct line of H to reflect the influence of another artifact, showing a handful of readings that appear to derive from Lowell's comparison of B (for examples, such as Lowell's substitution of "Crantz" for the received "*Grants*" in *Sat3* 49, see the individual textual introductions below).

In basing his text of Satyres 1–3 on B33, whose title-page date convinces him of its early origins (see footnote 9 above), Grosart (N) becomes the first editor since the seventeenth century to set a Donne poem into type from manuscript (he uses G as copy-text for Satyres 4 and 5),[44] and the first editor ever to print an LOH-derived text of any of these poems; and his regard for manuscripts extends to the collation of B32, B40, and H7 as well. Although he occasionally recovers such authentic readings as "barenes" in *Sat1* 39 (where all previous editions had read "barenness"), the scholarly aspirations underlying Grosart's procedure are systemically thwarted by carelessness (he prints, e.g., "cry [for his copy-text's *cries*] the flatterer" in *Sat4* 182), inaccuracy (he mistranscribes B33's "goe" at the end of *Sat3* 81 as "goo," e.g.),[45] and an unfathomable eclecticism (from H7, e.g., he imports the incomprehensible "It rides killingly" [for B33's normative "It ridlingly"] in *Sat2* 8), which entails the intermingling of readings from various manuscripts, the seventeenth-century prints, M, and H.

The Grolier Club edition (O), prepared by C. E. Norton and Mabel Burnett (James Russell Lowell's daughter), and Chambers (P) appeared on opposite sides of the Atlantic within a year of each other, and both are print-based editions (see Stringer, 2011, 46–47). The Grolier editors return to A as copy-text for the Satyres (and for all other poems that it contains), faithfully reproducing its substantives (except that they add the censored material from a later edition), but also incorporating (without recording the changes in their textual notes, which cite only substantive variants from the seventeenth-century editions) the numerous punctuational emendations that Lowell had penciled into his personal copy of M and modernizing the edition orthographically and mechanically. Accordingly, they print such of A's anomalies as "Fine," (for "Myne?") in *Sat4* 83, but also, e.g., restore A's correct "bear" in *Sat4* 43, where every prior modern edition had derived the erroneous "hear" from G. O's substitution of G's "faith" for A–F's correct "saith" in *Sat4* 35 is the sole instance in which the editors emend their copy-text toward a reading from a later edition, apparently deriving the substitution from M. Because he finds none of the seventeenth-century editions to be of "supreme authority," on the other hand, Chambers (O) sees "no choice but to

---

some—but not all—of N's emendations. Not until Grierson comprehensively analyzes the manuscript evidence are both poems ascribed to Sir John Roe and expunged from the canon.

[44]The exceptions are the individual printings of *EtRD* and *EtED* in Cullum (siglum 66), of *ElWar* in Waldron (sigla 67 and 68), and of *InLI* in Tomlins (siglum 69).

[45]Grosart's correction of the erroneous "barenness" is apparently inadvertent—see the textual introduction to *Sat1* below. Haskin (2002) calls N "the most careless edition of Donne ever printed" (181).

be eclectic" (1:v), and he acts on this conviction religiously, intermingling readings from A, B, E, G, and (very likely mediated through Grosart) H, as well as adopting a few details from B33 (also possibly following Grosart) and 1 or more unspecified manuscripts. Just within the confines of *Sat3*, to take but one example, Chambers prints A's "chokes my spleen" (for B's "checks…" [or G's "cheeks…"]) in line 1, B's "mills, rocks" (for A's "mills, & rocks") in line 107, and G's hyphenated "state-cloth" (where A–F give "statecloth") in line 48, as well as replacing the A–G solecism "lawes/…bids" in lines 56–57 with "…bid," a correction first introduced in H. And the subtitle "Of Religion," which appears beside the heading of *Sat3* in his table of contents, derives from B33. As is detailed in the individual textual introductions below, a similar hodgepodge of diversely sourced lections appears in Chambers's texts of the other 4 Satyres.

In explicit response to the perceived inadequacies of N, O, and P, especially as teaching texts, in his OUP edition of 1912 (Q) Grierson undertakes to broaden and rationalize the use of manuscript evidence, to fully record in textual notes all changes made to the copy-text, and to avoid eclecticism in the imposition of emendations (see Stringer, 2011, 47–50). And he approaches this task scientifically, locating, describing, collating, and sorting into family groups all the then-known British- and American-owned manuscripts of Donne's poems and attempting to determine their relationships to the early editions. As a result of this analysis, Grierson concludes that "taken all over," A is "far and away superior to any other single edition and…to any *single* manuscript" (2:cxv–cxvi), and, in order to proceed systematically, adopts it as the basis for all the poems it contains (including the Satyres), meticulously replicating all substantive and accidental features of its text (except, of course, that he recovers from other sources the material censored from A). But he also recognizes that A contains errors that cannot be corrected without consulting the manuscripts and, in an effort to avoid mere eclecticism, formulates a kind of proto-genealogical principle to guide him in their use: to establish "the agreement of the manuscripts whether universal or partial" and to "not[e] in the latter case the comparative value of the different groups" (2:cxvii). In instances in which the "correct reading has been preserved in only one or two manuscripts" (2:cxx) and the "agreement" principle is rendered inoperable, Grierson avers, "each case" must be considered "on its merits" (2:cxix). This is obviously a revolutionary editorial program, and it enables Grierson to posit texts whose reliability far exceeds that of any of his predecessors. Despite the scope and rigor of the approach, however, Grierson's record of distinguishing scribal and compositorial errors from legitimate authorial readings is inconsistent, partly because—as is discussed above—he is unaware of certain important manuscript witnesses that have since come to light (most notably C2), but principally because he fails to develop a truly stemmatological understanding of the relationships among the various textual artifacts. In constructing the text of *Sat4*, e.g., consulting the manuscripts enables him to restore for the first time in the printed history of the poem the authorial "they pay" (for A's innovative "shall pay") in line 106, but—as noted above—from OQ1 and VA1 (which stand, respectively, at 4 and 5 removes from the LOH on the stemma) he adopts the scribal "He speakes no [for the authorial *one*] language" in line 38, and with the sole support of O3 he reduces the normative plurals "tries /...thighes" to "trye /...thighe" in lines 205–06. In the upshot, as is detailed in the textual introduction to *Sat4* below, Grierson follows A in error in 8 instances, corrects the text received from his predecessors by restoring A's reading in 8 instances, introduces from manuscript 5 corrections to A's text, and contaminates A's text with erroneous manuscript readings in 7 instances—an almost evenly balanced record of correction and corruption. The individual textual introductions below describe a similarly mixed record of success and failure in Grierson's attempts to recover the authentic text of the other 4 Satyres.

As on the rest of Donne's poetry, Grierson's influence on the subsequent editorial history of the Satyres proves hegemonic, 4 of the 6 successors collated in this *Variorum* implementing an editorial method essentially identical to his and all adopting to varying extents his choices at specific points of textual variation. Since these editors' respective handlings of the individual Satyres are fully detailed in the textual introductions and critical apparatuses below, a brief characterization of their practices will suffice here, and in order to describe accurately how editorial approaches to these poems evolved sporadically over the 7 decades between the appearance of Q and the organization of this *Variorum* project, we shall consider these successors in straightforward chronological order.

Hayward (S) paraphrases Grierson's "agreement-of-the-manuscripts" principle ("when several good MSS. agree where the editions differ in a reading, then the reading of the MSS. is probably correct" [xxi]) and—while including only a handful of textual notes—produces a virtual reprint of Q's text of the Satyres, evincing almost all of Q's emendations of A, including, e.g., the substitution of the NY3-derived "Crantz" for A's "Crants" in *Sat3* 49. Showing S's occasional divergence from Q (and A), however, is its replacement of the revised "out-doe" in *Sat2* 32 with the original "out-swive," a "more direct" (770) reading for which Hayward credits B32, NY3, and O20.

In an edition containing a severely curtailed apparatus and aimed at "those who wish to read Donne's poetry for pleasure" (xi), Bennett (T) pointedly rejects the prevailing Griersonian paradigm,[46] declaring that "since there is no single authoritative text of any kind available to us," it is "advisable to base each poem upon whatever accessible [i.e., available in America during World War II] text has the fewest obvious errors" (xxv). Accordingly, from among manuscripts located at Harvard and the New York Public Library he selects NY3 as the base text for each of the Satyres, but regards it as only relatively more authoritative than other available choices, not only modernizing orthography and pointing (he alters NY3's punctuation of *Sat1* in some 118 instances, e.g.) and regularizing meter with numerous marks of contraction and elision, but also impressionistically emending NY3's verbals toward readings from print and other manuscripts (his text of *Sat3*, e.g., contaminates NY3's original version of the poem with 5 revised-version lections adopted from A, 1 of which A had imported from H6). Thus, although he is the first editor since Grosart to set a Satyre into print from manuscript and although (principally because NY3 contains

---

[46]Following Hayward, a one-volume redaction of Q had appeared in 1929; Hayward had updated S in 1930; Fausset had published a modernized Q (with some adversion to S) in the 1931 Everyman *Poems*; Q had been reissued in 1933; and in 1941 Hillyer had published a Random House *Complete Poetry and Selected Prose* based on the 1930 update of S (see Stringer, 2011, p. 50, and Keynes, pp. 214–15).

the original version of the poem, whereas A contains the revised) his text of *Sat3* differs from that of Grierson in some 23 readings, the eclectic construct produced by Bennett represents no real advance over the text previously established in Q. As is evident in the following discussion, Bennett's approach attracted no following, his edition constituting a methodological dead end.

Milgate (Y), whose theory of Donne's revisions of the Satyres we have discussed above, is Grierson's institutional heir at OUP and a committed disciple of his editorial approach. He thus adopts A as copy-text, generally preserving its spelling and accidentals, but emends it from manuscript according to an expanded version of the "concensus-of-the-manuscripts" and "comparative-value-of-the-different-groups" theory, in a bottom-of-page apparatus citing variant readings from manuscripts selected to represent the "main traditions of the text" (see Y:lxxi–lxxiv) and carefully specifying in his notes the differences between his texts and those of Grierson. Unsurprisingly, this similarity of method produces similarity of results, and—except that he systematically elides and/or contracts hyper-syllabic locutions in order to regularize meter[47] and in dialogic passages marks changes of speaker with quotation marks—Milgate's text closely resembles that of his predecessor. In developing his edition of *Sat1*, e.g., Grierson not only recovers the censored lines 81–82 from another source, but also imposes a further 10 verbal emendations on A's text, and Milgate follows him in all but 1 of these changes, in 2 further instances inserting from manuscript emendations that Grierson had declined. And Milgate adopts 14 of Grierson's 18 alterations of A's punctuation, including in line 102 the set of syntax-altering parentheses that Grierson had interpolated from OQ1 (see p. 20 below). A further consequence of this close adherence to Grierson's method, of course, is that Milgate's text of *Sat1* retains the same 14 scribal errors that had gone undetected in the work of his mentor (see p. 20 below), and comparable similarities obtain with respect to their editions of the other 4 Satyres.

Methodologically, Shawcross (Z), too, is of the school of Grierson, adopting A as his copy-text and—although he systematically marks elisions and contractions in an effort to regularize meter—replicating its orthography and punctuation. He recognizes, however, that A contains errors, and—guided by a personalized version of the Griersonian principle—determines to emend it when a "later version or the reading of a consensus of manuscripts seems to be closer to Donne's 'original'" (xxi), providing support for his choices in an extensive (though selective) historical collation of manuscript and print witnesses in a section of textual notes. His text of *Sat4*, to take but one example, evinces some 14 emendations of readings in A, all of which had previously appeared in Q (and all but 3 of which had appeared in Y), and these variously involve both the correction of errors existing in A and the introduction of new errors into A. In line 83, e.g., where A's compositor had erroneously set "Are not your Frenchmen neate? Fine," Shawcross restores the authorial "...Mine?" But in lines 205–06, he follows Grierson in replacing the authorial (and otherwise universal) "tries

---

[47]Citing the frequent use of elision marks and contractions in A, Milgate justifies his imposition of additional such marks as the continuation of a program of metrical regularization that A's editor had intended, but had been unable to carry out consistently. In the text of the Satyres, Milgate avers, this failure "become[s] a serious problem" (see Y:lxxii–lxxiii).

/...thighes" with the scribal "trye /...thighe," an O3 reading for which—although O3 is listed among the 159 manuscripts he has "attempted to examine and collate" (xxi)—his textual notes credit Grierson. These and numerous other examples cited in the textual introductions below give point to Shawcross's observation that, "like others before it," his text is "eclectic and somewhat subjectively based" (xxi).

Both of the final 2 editions to be discussed here—those of Smith (AA) and Patrides (DD)—walk the line between the popular and the scholarly, interspersing a few notes on the text among a fuller set of explanatory glosses; and both, though in different ways, are heavily indebted to Grierson and prior twentieth-century editors. An avowed eclecticist who aims to present "the richest and most pointed readings...that have good authority among the early versions" (14), Smith prints a thoroughly modern-ized text based principally on A, but emends toward the later seventeenth-century editions as he sees need, occasionally citing variants unspecifically in "MS" or "*some MSS*" or "*several MSS.*" Except that—uniquely among twentieth-century editors—he retains the scribal "barrennesse" that A had accepted in line 39 and follows Y in printing "Nor" (for A's "Not") in line 19 and "that" (for "who") in line 53, e.g., Smith's text of *Sat1* is a virtual reprint of Grierson's, not only retaining over a dozen scribal errors that had appeared in A, but also reproducing in lines 58 and 101–02 significant emendations of wording and punctuation that Grierson had interjected into A's revised-version text from manuscripts containing the original version of the poem (see the textual introduction to *Sat1* below).

Invoking the authority of Grierson and other "textual critics," Patrides (DD) defends his choice of A as basic copy-text for his edition on grounds that, "save for Donne's lifetime, his reputation to our own century is based on the printed versions" (2). He thus produces an old-spelling text of the poems that, like Smith's before him, occasionally refers to variants in "one MS" or "several MSS," but relies principally on the seventeenth-century prints and his twentieth-century predecessors' mediation of them. In his treatment of *Sat2*, e.g., Patrides accepts 6 of the verbal corrections that Grierson had imposed on the text of A, retains 2 of A's erroneous readings that Grierson had corrected from manuscript, rejects 1 erroneous emendation that Grier-son had independently imposed, and follows Grierson's repunctuation of A in over a dozen instances. And he reproduces all the scribal misreadings in A that Grierson had failed to identify. Patrides's occasional comparison of Z is evident in his repetition of an otherwise uniquely spurious reading in *Sat1* 61, which he supports with the same textual misinformation that Shawcross had cited.

Copy-texts Used in this Edition

However many variant forms they may have passed through as they took shape in Donne's study, stemmatological analysis of the surviving evidence shows that each of the Satyres circulated in only an original and a single revised manuscript version (or 2 revised versions, in the case of *Sat5*) in the decades prior to their print publication in 1633. As is detailed in the individual textual introductions below, the number of substantive alterations ranges from about 20 in *Sat3*, to only 1 in *Sat4*, Satyres 1 and 2 both evincing 3 authorial changes and the twice-revised *Sat5* evincing 7. Except in the case of *Sat3*, of course, none of these revisions reflects a major reconceptualization of the poem—some of the individual changes, as suggested above, may be only semi-deliberate—but they all reveal Donne's continued engagement with the poetic material and identify distinct moments of origin for separate authorial strands of transmission (see On Stemmas and Revision above). The tally of changes above might suggest that only in the case of Sat3 would the goal of enabling readers to fully appreciate both original and revised versions require printing two separate texts, but we nevertheless here present in full both the original and the revised texts of Satyres 2, 3, and 5, while presenting only a single text—that of the revised version—of Satyres 1 and 4.

The decision to print these particular texts arises from an attempt to accomplish 2 overlapping, but not entirely congruent, purposes. One is to provide users of this edition the opportunity to study the entire sequence of Satyres in its cleanest, least corrupted embodiment—that of NY3, whose provenance and use as copy-text in previous volumes of this *Variorum* are described in detail above. Although its texts of Satyres 3 and 4 are a step further removed from the holograph than those of Satyres 1, 2, and 5, there is no question that, overall, NY3 is the single soundest manuscript of these poems. Its penman Rowland Woodward is a careful, consistent, and intelligent copyist whose occasional interlinear and marginal corrections demonstrate his concentration on the task at hand, and he is seldom thrown off balance when Donne's syntax becomes knotty or his vocabulary recondite. When adjusted with the few necessary emendations, NY3 brings us as close to the details of Donne's actual writing as a scribal document is ever likely to do, and it seems desirable to print the entire run of poems in this relatively clean state.

The second purpose is to fulfill our stated policy of presenting separate texts of both original and revised versions of poems exhibiting authorial revision, which, if followed literally here, would entail printing 2 separate texts of 4 lengthy poems whose variant versions evince very few verbal differences. Of Sat3, of course, it is clearly necessary to print 2 texts, and NY3's original version is accompanied below by an edition of the revised version. Since NY3's renditions of Sat1 and Sat4 embody Donne's final intentions for those poems, however, and since the few differences between those versions and the originals are explicitly detailed in the poems' critical apparatuses, users seem unlikely to need full copies of the earlier versions, and we have not provided them. NY3's texts of Sat2 and Sat5, on the other hand, present, respectively, the original and the first-revised version of the poem, and in the interests of providing users with a quotable text of the final versions of these, we have provided a second text of each. The copy-text for these, as well as for the final version of Sat3, is DT1, whose texts are marginally cleaner than those in the other artifacts in which they appear. All emendations of both original and revised versions of the poems are discussed in the individual textual introductions below and individually itemized in each poem's apparatus.

The Critical Tradition

Not only are the Satyres among Donne's earliest known writings, but they also rank him among the first—perhaps as *the* first—to write formal verse satire in English. As noted in the Textual Introduction above, with very few exceptions scholars accept that Donne began the Satyres while a student at Lincoln's Inn and completed them after becoming secretary to Sir Thomas Egerton, dating them between 1593 and 1602, when Donne was dismissed from Egerton's service. Donne himself describes these poems in a verse letter to Rowland Woodward as "Satyrique thornes" shown "to too many" and confesses in a prose letter to an unnamed recipient in about 1600 that because of their content, to them "there belongs some feare." The Satyres are widely praised and quoted by Donne's contemporaries, including Everard Guilpin, Ben Jonson, Francis Davison, Joseph Wybarne, Thomas Freeman, and John Cave. Later in the seventeenth century the Satyres are referred to as examples of Donne's poetic skill and wit by such writers as W. Ling, Giles Oldisworth, Lucius Cary, and Sir Aston Cokayne, although in the closing years of that century Dryden takes exception to the poems on grounds that they need to be "Translated into Numbers, and English," so that they might "appear more Charming."

Primarily because of their subject matter and genre, the Satyres were generally held in high regard during the eighteenth century, a regard exhibited most notably by Alexander Pope and Thomas Parnell, who enacted Dryden's suggestion and recast, or "versify'd," several of the poems into the more metrically regular heroic couplets that characterize the poetry of the Augustan Age (see Appendix II). In various historical eras, moreover, readers repeatedly call attention to the language and style of the Satyres and persistently use such descriptors as "rough" or "rugged," "harsh," "uncouth" or "rude," "jarring," and "crabbed." Ben Jonson (1619) may very well have been speaking of the Satyres in his oft-quoted comment to William Drummond that "Done for not keeping of accent deserved hanging." A century later Warburton (1751) comments that Donne's lines "have nothing more of numbers than their being composed of a certain quantity of syllables," and Gray (1752) observes that Donne "observes no regularity in the pause, or in the feet of his verse."

It is the nineteenth century that produced some of the most colorful, and quotable, commentary on the Satyres, both to praise and to blame. In defense of the poems, Coleridge (1811) proclaimed that there was "no surer Test of a Scotch-man's Substratum" than to have him read the Satyres aloud and "if he made manly Metre of them, & strict metre,—then—why, then he wasn't a Scotchman, or his Soul was geographically slandered by his Body's first appearing there," and later, in 1836, Coleridge writes that Donne's muse "on dromedary trots." Spence (1823) reacts to the poems as one would to "unhewn stones" that come upon him with "the force and effect" of having been "flung from the hand of a giant." Landor (1836) writes of Donne's "Frost-bitten, and lumbaginous" verses that "gnarl'd and knotted, hobbled on," and Bradford (1892), in characterizing Donne's "wanton disregard of the laws of English versification," deplores that Donne splits words "to make a rhyme" and shakes "accents…over the verse from a pepper-box." In reaction to Pope's rewriting of Donne's Satyres, on the other hand, Patmore (1846) describes the results as having been achieved "in much the same style as the sailor who, having obtained a curiosity in the form of a weapon of a sword-fish, 'improved' it by scraping off, and rubbing down, all the protuberances by which it was distinguishable from any other bone."

Beyond these assessments of Donne's versification, late-nineteenth and early-twentieth century commentators focus their attentions primarily on two points:

the ways in which Donne's Satyres differ from those of his contemporaries and the classical sources that influenced Donne's work in this poetic genre. Concerning the former, the conclusions of such writers as Grosart (1872–73), Minto (1880), Bradford (1892), Gosse (1899), and Grierson (1909) are that the quality of Donne's Satyres is "masterly" and that his are "wittier" than those of Lodge, Marston, and Hall, which are characterized as "languid," "grotesque and labored," and "thin and empty." Concerning the latter point, Donne's sources, an array of writers from the late nineteenth through the twentieth centuries maintain that Donne's primary influences in the Satyres are Horace, Persius, and Juvenal, some arguing for one of these individually and others positing any two or all three in combination. The uniform opinion in these discussions is that Donne is no mere imitator, but that, instead, he reimagines the genre in terms of the lively language and realistic detail of Elizabethan London.

Among the first to read the Satyres biographically are Grierson (1921), who saw the record of Donne's early life contained in these poems, and Lindsay (1934a), who believed that they reflect "the troubled state of Donne's life" during the period of his brother's death, his questioning of Catholicism, and his attempts to find employment. While such mid-twentieth century scholars as Carey (1963), LeComte (1965) and Heath-Stubbs (1969) praise Donne for providing vivid glimpses of his life in London, the two prominent biographical issues center on the questions of his use of personae and the nature of his religious quest. Some commentators acknowledge a unique voice speaking in the Satyres and view that speaking voice as a unifying factor for the sequence. Others, however, disagree that there is a single speaker throughout the five poems, and there is considerable disagreement about whether or not the voice is that of Donne himself. Both Skelton (1960) and Hutchinson (1970), for example, believe that the poems have separate speakers, Skelton reading each as a distinct dramatic monologue and Hutchinson commenting that the distance between Donne and these personae is "not very wide." In contrast, Elliott (1976) believes the speaker to be a "Christian humanist" created by Donne; Dubrow (1979) argues that the voice of a single satirist is heard throughout the sequence, one not precisely identifiable with Donne but sharing a similar "complex character"; and Hester (1982) maintains that the five poems present a single voice whose outstanding feature is religious "zeal."

In examining the unity and structure of the sequence as a whole, the scholarship often focuses on the centrality of Sat3, not simply because it normatively occupies the middle position among the five poems, but primarily because its subject is religion. As early as 1751 Warburton notes Donne's "strong propensity to Popery" in the Satyres, but it is not until the twentieth century that the question of religion is addressed much beyond Sat3. Scholars who mention the topic in the first half of the twentieth century, such as Gardner (1948) and Grierson (1948), suggest that the poems reflect Donne's Catholic education and heritage, but Bald (1970) is the first to argue for what he describes as Donne's "unsettlement," that is, the precarious dilemma of being neither Catholic nor Protestant. In pursuing this argument, Bald rejects the notion that the Satyres were written from a Catholic point of view and thus sets the stage in the 1970s for wide-ranging approaches to the treatment of religion in the poems. They are variously read as reflecting Donne's knowledge of the "methods of meditation" (Hutchinson, 1970), as examining the "ideal of Christian charity" as a "principle for a life of social action" (Elliott, 1976), and as showing, in their "preoccup[ation] with religion" that "Jack Donne and John Donne coexisted throughout Donne's life" (Dubrow, 1979). In accordance with this shift in approach to the poems Warnke (1987) asserts that religion is a "dominant theme" in the Satyres, and Parfitt (1989) articulates the position of a great many critics when he avers that in their "ubiquity" religious allusions throughout the sequence constitute the "texture" of the Satyres. Hester (1982), in the only twentieth-century book-length study devoted exclusively to the Satyres, argues that the poems explore the problems of Christian satire, that the persona is a "zealous prophet" concerned with his duty to himself, his fellow citizens, and his God who carries out a "creative shaping (or re-shaping) of the generic, conventional, intellectual, and biographical materials" available to Donne in the 1590s.

Certainly, the Satyres' treatment of religion remains a critical concern throughout the twentieth century, but in the 1980s various commentators re-examine the poems as expressions of Donne's anxieties and concerns about his social standing and place in the world. Carey (1981) finds in the Satyres "raucously apparent" evidence that Donne's "ambitious nature" contains the "contradictory seeds" of "the wish to make his way in the world, and the wish to be integrated into it." Slights (1981) reads the poems as expressions of Donne's "doubt about his relation to society," even as he embraces a "responsibility to the world of men." Marotti (1986) interprets the poems through the "social coordinates" of Donne's "strong attraction to the very world being criticized." These analyses of the Satyres as revelatory of Donne's sense of his place in the world modulate then in the late 1980s and 1990s to examinations of the poems as acts of self-fashioning, especially by calling attention to them as rhetorical acts. Thus, Waller (1986) speaks of the "self-conscious[ly]" chosen "rhetorical pose" in terms of which Donne surveys "the more bizarre or corrupt aspects of society," and Morse (1989) argues that Donne is "as much preoccupied with his own pretensions to be a satirist as with the follies and abuses that he would criticize." Baumlin (1988, 1991) characterizes the Satyres as "self-critical explorations of their literary form" that call into question whether each poem "validates or becomes the genre by performing it and enacting its aims." Manley (1995) states that Donne "hopes to reconcile his perceptions to his imagined status in the social structure, to his dramatized roles as scholar-wit, jurist, theologian, courtier, and office-holder." Finally, for Corthell (1997) Donne's self-fashioning in the Satyres is a "textual practice which creates a range of provisional, shifting relations between the subject and ideology."

Beyond the five-poem sequence of formal verse satires, Donne's satiric poetry also includes not only *Metem*, which—despite its 520-line length—has received far less commentary than the Satyres, but also *Coryat* and *Macaron*, both of which have also received scant critical attention. One of the few poems by Donne that carries a specific date (August 16, 1601), the revised version of *Metem* was apparently finalized some six months after Robert Devereux, Second Earl of Essex, was executed for his failed revolt against Queen Elizabeth (see the textual introduction to *Metem* below). In direct contrast to the concreteness of the 1601 date, identification of the genre of *Metem* and the circumstances of its composition elicit very different, and at times diametrically opposed, views. The poem has been variously described as an unfinished epic, an allegory, an anti-epic, an epic satire, a parody of Du Bartas's *Sepmaines*, a formal paradox, and a mock-epic intentionally left as a fragment. With regard to the circumstances of its composition, scholars such as Grierson (1912), Mahood (1950), and Bald (1970) see a strong link between Donne and Essex and view the latter's execution as the event that compelled Donne to write the poem. LeComte (1965) even goes so far as to claim that Essex's tragic demise was "among the most poignant" events of Donne's life. Other scholars, however, take a decidedly different stance. Murray (1959), for example, maintains that the biographical supposition that Donne was influenced by Essex's death "hasn't much" factual support, and Milgate (1967), as another example, finds in the poem no "special reference" to Essex's execution and states that there is "no evidence" that Donne "was really close to the Earl or was much affected by his downfall."

The chronological record of interpretive commentary on *Metem* reveals similarly divergent opinions, and, as Bryan (1965) observes, the history of reactions to the poem are "as fragmented, contradictory, and generally inconclusive as the poem itself." In the seventeenth century, Jonson (1619) notes that after Donne took holy orders he "repente[d] highlie" of writing *Metem* and sought to destroy it and all his poems, and later in the century Marvell (1673)—in his prose work *The Rehearsall Transpros'd, The Second Part*—invokes Donne's conceit of the transmigration of the soul to satirize his ecclesiastical opponents. Although little mention is made of the poem in the eighteenth and early-nineteenth centuries, three notable poets speak of or notice it favorably. Pope (1753) deems it a "fine" poem and laments that Donne never completed his "noble Design"; Blake (c. 1795) uses two lines from Donne's poem as a caption for and commentary on one of his own sketches; and Coleridge (1817) singles out two stanzas of *Metem* as examples of "excellent" verse that shows the "self-impassioned" language of "poetic fervor."

In the late-nineteenth century, and well into the twentieth, the critical attitude toward *Metem* changes, and commentators almost universally express condemnation, even revulsion, for the poem. Among the earlier critics, Ward (1858) refers to *Metem* as "disgusting burlesque"; Gilfillan (1860) comments that the poem contains "too many far-fetched conceits and obscure allegories"; and Chambers (1896) opines that there are many things in the poem that "one would wish away—just as one inevitably removes a slug from a rose's heart or lily's chalice." The early-twentieth century commentators, who focus in large part on the strain of philosophical skepticism embodied in the poem, follow in the same dismissive vein. Grierson (1912) concludes that the poem is "un-Christian," that its "dominant notes" are those of "scepticism and melancholy, bitter and sardonic"; Eliot (1926) asserts that none of Donne's poems is "more difficult, more unpleasant, more disturbing, more unsatisfactory" than *Metem*; Crofts (1936) finds *Metem* to be "the most deliberately outrageous" of Donne's poems; Coffin (1937) voices surprise that in the poem Donne records some of his "bitterest statements against women" mere weeks before his marriage to Anne More; Bush (1945) calls it "a satirical extravaganza" that is "submerged in a kind of brutal sexuality"; Allen (1952) describes the poem as "the monstrous offspring of a violent 'contamine'"; and Gransden (1954) believes that although it exhibits "liveliness and technical adroitness," the poem is "indecent as well as unpatriotic."

In the latter half of the twentieth century, however, critics call for a reassessment of *Metem.* Among these are Williamson (1969), who maintains that the poem deserves a reconsideration "of its place in Donne's corpus"; Milgate (1967), who argues that the poem's attacks on tyrants and favorites of the court are "generalized and unemotional" and opines that too many commentators have missed the work's "verve and high-spirited fun"; and Snyder (1973), who reads the poem as a parody of Du Bartas's *Sepmaines* and suggests that Donne is "having fun at the expense of the literary and religious Establishment." In 1972 Gardner pronounces the poem a "brilliantly executed and coherent work which makes a powerful and sardonic point," the dedication and epistle being a part of the jest. Mueller (1972), seeing parallels with "the larger contours and substance of Ovid's epic," assesses the poem as "a transition piece" that allowed Donne to discover his "true personal and poetic direction," while Carey (1981) calls *Metem* a "masterpiece" that contains numerous "quotations which would establish the reputation of a lesser writer." Warnke (1987) insists that religion and sex, not politics, "play the principal roles" in the poem, but the critics cannot agree whether the religious perspective of the poem is "un-Christian" or "Catholic" or "anti-Protestant" or shows no religious belief at all. Finally, the single most commented-on reference in the poem is that to "the great *Soule*" mentioned in the opening line of stanza 7, and the conflicting identifications it has generated—whether as Calvin, Elizabeth Drury, Queen Elizabeth, John Knox, Robert Cecil, Luther, Mahomet, or Donne himself—serve as a microcosm of the interpretive difficulties the poem poses.

The two final pieces of indisputably canonical poetry included in this volume, *Coryat* and *Macaron*, were both published in *Coryat's Crudities* (1611) along with other mock-commendatory verses that prefaced the volume (see the separate textual introductions to the poems below). *Coryat* was quoted, paraphrased and adapted by a number of Donne's contemporaries, and scholars associate the poem, as well as the volume in which it originally appeared, with those writers with whom Donne dined at the Mitre and the Mermaid taverns. For many critics, the poem reveals much more about the limited capacities of the historical figure Thomas Coryate than it does of Donne's abilities as a poet. Beyond the consideration of the poem's style and subject, Roebuck (1996) argues that regardless of how inconsequential or facetious this piece of satiric verse may appear, we, nevertheless, "catch the shadow of Donne," who was as full of "the uncertainties of religious questions as Coryate was brashly free of doubt." The primary critical point made with regard to *Macaron* is that it is Donne's example, employing his characteristic wit, of macaronic verse, which is typically a jumble of words in English, Latin, French, Italian, and Spanish.

The commentary summarized in this volume exhibits a great diversity of opinions and critical approaches to Donne's satirical poems, and there is every reason to believe that scholars will continue searching for new ways to untangle the historical knots and to comprehend the interpretive challenges that these poems present. We hope that the compilation of commentary in this volume will enable an understanding of the historical record and, thereby, aid in the identification of new or as yet underdeveloped areas of critical inquiry.

§

The Satyres is the first print volume to be published in this edition in over a decade. In 2004, with the previous volume (*The Holy Sonnets* [2005]) nearing completion, the General Editor moved from the University of Southern Mississippi and transferred the *Variorum's* editorial headquarters to Texas A&M University, where the project remained until undertaking a further move to East Carolina University in 2011. The relocation to Texas A&M originally included plans to develop an electronic archive of Donne materials that would enhance the edition's digital dimension, but these plans immediately blossomed into an enterprise of far greater scope and importance when in December of 2004 Cushing Memorial Library and Archives acquired at auction a large cache of seventeenth-century Donne editions.[48] Coinciding with a growing emphasis on digital humanities within the university, especially as manifest in the activities of the Center for the Study of Digital Libraries (CSDL) and the University Libraries' Digital Initiatives program, this acquisition not only made readily available to the *Variorum* a wealth of essential primary materials, but also facilitated access to expert technical support and other institutional resources that, over the period of the subsequent decade, enabled us to develop *DigitalDonne: the Online Variorum* (http//:donnevariorum.tamu.edu). This electronic repository, which in 2010 the *Variorum* Advisory Board formally incorporated into the project by defining it as Volume 1 of the edition, presents a broad and expanding array of research tools and information about Donne and the *Variorum* project, including collation software, transcriptions of copies of poems used in constructing the edition, bibliographies and databases of both primary and secondary materials, concordances to various individual print and manuscript volumes and to Donne's collected poetic corpus, and digital facsimile editions of the most significant seventeenth-century printed and manuscript collections of Donne's poetry. In the spring of 2013 we reached an agreement with the recently established Initiative for Digital Humanities, Media, and Culture (IDHMC) at Texas A&M according to which the IDHMC will maintain *DigitalDonne* as an online presence in perpetuity. Our gratitude to those at A&M who have supported and facilitated this work is expressed in the section of Acknowledgments above.

Even before *The Holy Sonnets* was completed and the development of *DigitalDonne* begun in the project headquarters, work on *The Satyres* was underway, and this volume has been an object of concentrated focus by certain members of our editorial staff for the past 15 years. The original co-Volume Commentary Editors, appointed in organizational meetings in the early 1980s, were William B. Hunter, Jr., and M. Thomas Hester, who divided the commentary into segments chronologically and recruited Contributing Editors to cover the various periods. When, in 1994, Hunter withdrew from the project, the Advisory Board appointed Dennis Flynn to share duties with Hester by assuming Hunter's former role. In the upshot, Hester assumed personal responsibility for commentary on the Satyres, *Coryat*, and *Macaron* for the period 1598–1799 and, along with Flynn, coordinated the collaboration of the Contributing Editors, whose initial assignments for coverage were as follows: commentary on the

---

[48]This collection is described in Christopher L. Morrow, ed., *The Texas A&M John Donne Collection*, Texas A&M University Libraries, 2006.

Satyres, *Coryat*, and *Macaron* for the period 1800–1911—Jeffrey Johnson; commentary on the Satyres, *Coryat*, and *Macaron* for the period 1912–1967—Paul Stapleton; commentary on the Satyres, *Coryat*, and *Macaron* for the period 1968–1978—Julie Yen; and commentary on *Metem* for all periods—Brian Blackley. As the work progressed, some realignment of these assignments became necessary, especially with respect to the period 1912–1967, which included a vast number of items requiring summary, and to the years between 1979 and 2001 (the eventual cut-off date for commentary in this volume), which had initially not been specifically assigned. In this adjustment, Julie Yen took on additional responsibilities for the post-1978 period, and Anne James was added as a fifth Contributing Editor with responsibilities for helping with the more recent commentary and for filling in various gaps in coverage that became apparent as we sought to finalize the volume for publication. The single most sweeping adjustment of assignments came in 2005, however, when Jeffrey Johnson accepted appointment as a third co-Volume Commentary Editor. In that office Johnson assumed the principal responsibility for bringing the commentary portion of the volume to completion, annotating scores of items that remained to be handled (especially in the 1912–1967 period); vetting the work of all other contributors for accuracy, consistency, and bibliographical completeness; and coordinating the work of the entire team of contributors. In the final stages of the volume's preparation, Johnson—with substantial aid from Tracy McLawhorn and students working under her supervision—undertook the indexing of the volume in the project's central office, and Johnson composed the general overview of commentary included above as The Critical Tradition. For this volume, Paul Parrish continued in his long-standing role of Chief Editor of the Commentary, providing guidance, support, and an additional level of critical supervision of the work of Johnson and the other commentary editors.

The textual work, too, represents the extensive collaborative efforts of several editors. Following completion of our volume *The Elegies* (2000), Ted-Larry Pebworth was designated principal textual editor for the Satyres, and labored alone in this role for a number of years, completing the initial compilation of the set of transcriptions used in the construction of the texts (including, e.g., verifying transcriptions against original sources in the National Library of Wales, the Folger Library, and the Huntington Library) developing a preliminary theory of the textual transmission of the Satyres in the seventeenth century, selecting the principal copy-text for the Satyres (NY3) and proposing emendations of it, preparing a preliminary presentation of the noncanonical satires presented in Appendix I below, and aiding in the establishment of protocols of formatting and reportage for all texts and apparatuses in the volume. In 2006, with Pebworth in declining health and needing help to carry the work forward, we were fortunate to enlist Donald Dickson in the project as Associate General Editor and Textual Editor, his initial task being to replace Michael Salda, who had initially held the assignment of editing *Metem*; and upon completion of the volume on the Holy Sonnets, Gary Stringer joined in the textual work on the Satyres as well. From 2006 until the project's departure from Texas A&M for East Carolina University in 2011, Dickson played a major role in the textual work on the Satyres, not only carrying out additional on-site proofreading of manuscripts in the National Library of Wales, the Folger Library, and other repositories, but eventually producing editions of *Sat1*,

Sat2, *Sat5*, and *Metem*, as well as drafting textual introductions and apparatuses for our presentations of *Coryat*, *Macaron*, and the dubious "Loe her's a Man" and preparing a preliminary version of the section of "Analyses of Early Printed Copies" for all poems in the volume. With the aid of Mary Farrington, moreover, Dickson completed an initial proofreading of all the volume's textual apparatuses in the summer of 2009. In the above-noted realignment of responsibilities that began in 2006, Gary Stringer initially undertook to produce an edition of *Sat4*, but thereafter added *Sat3* to his remit, and when the *Variorum* moved to East Carolina in the summer of 2011 with the volume unfinished, it fell to Stringer to bring the entire body of textual work to completion. This further work entailed not only finalizing his own edition of *Sat3*, but also reviewing the other work in the volume for completion and consistency of approach and presentation. Further analysis carried out in the light of newly discovered information eventually dictated a fundamental revision of the work on *Metem*, and Stringer also revised and completed the existing work on *Coryat*, *Macaron*, "Loe her's a Man," and the noncanonical poems included in Appendix I, as well as preparing the editions of the eighteenth-century imitations of Donne Satyres included in Appendix II. Stringer also wrote the General Textual Introduction included above.

Others listed on the title page above as assistants in the textual work for this volume include Ernest Sullivan, who played a primary role in compiling the initial set of poem transcriptions used in editing the texts for this volume; Dennis Flynn, who aided in the completion of our collection of transcriptions of items in the Houghton Library; and Tracy McLawhorn, whose contributions to the textual work here presented began in 2008 when, as a graduate student, she composed the first version of the Historical Collation for *Sat4*, and greatly multiplied following her appointment as the project's full-time Technology Editor and Assistant Textual Editor in 2011. In that role, which also entailed typesetting the volume, McLawhorn aided in the preparation of the charts of variants in the seventeenth-century and modern prints that are included in the various textual introductions, vetted all the textual apparatuses in the volume for completeness and consistency of format, reviewed and groomed into final form the section of Analyses of Early Printed Copies that accompanies each of the poems, and—aided by Jeff Johnson, Greg Kneidel, Gary Stringer, and students working under her supervision—carried out for each poem a final, comprehensive proofreading of the textual apparatus against a raw collation of the textual sources.

JEFFREY S. JOHNSON

Principal Co-Volume Commentary Editor

GARY A. STRINGER

General Editor
and
Senior Textual Editor

TEXTS
and
APPARATUSES

THE
SATYRES

Satyre 1.

Away thou changeling motley humorist,
Leaue me, and in this standing wodden chest
Consorted with these few bookes, lett me ly
In prison, and here be coffind, when I dy.
Here are Gods conduits, graue Diuines: and here   5
Natures Secretary, the Philosopher,
And ioly Statesmen, which teach how to ty
The Sinews of a Citties mistique body.
Here gathering Chroniclers, and by them stand
Giddy fantastique Poets of each Land.   10
Shall I leaue all this constant companee
And follow headlong, wild, vncertaine thee?
First sweare by thy best loue in earnest
(If thou which Lovst all, canst loue any best)
Thou wilt not leaue me in the middle Street   15
Though some more spruce companion thou do meet.
Not though a Captane do come in thy way
Bright parcell-guilt with forty dead mens pay.
Nor though a briske perfum'd pert Courtier
Deigne with a nod thy curtesy to answer.   20
Nor come a veluet Iustice with a long
Great traine of blew-cotes 12 or 14 strong,
Shallt thou grin or fawne on him, or prepare
A Speach to court his bewteous Sone and heire.
For better or worse take me, or leaue mee,   25
To take and leaue me, is adulteree.
O Monster, superstitious Puritane
Of refind manners, yet ceremonial man,
That when thou meetst one, with inquyring eyes
Dost search, and like a needy broker prize   30
The silke and gould he weares, and to that rate
So high or low dost vaile thy formall hatt.
That wilt consort none, vntill thou haue knowen
What Lands he hath in hope, or of his owne.
As though all thy companions should make thee   35

Ioyntures, and mary thy deare companee.
Why shouldst thou, that dost not only approue
But in ranke itchy Lust desyre and loue
The nakednesse and barenesse to inioy
Of thy plump muddy whore or prostitute boy,   40
Hate vertu though she be naked and bare?
At birthe, and death our bodyes naked are:
And till our Soules be vnapparelled
Of bodyes, they from blis are banished.
Mans first blest State was naked, when by Sin   45
He lost that, yet he was clothd but in beasts skin.
And in this course attire which now I weare
With God and with the Muses I confer.
But since thou like a contrite penitent
Charitably warnd of thy sins dost repent   50
These vanities and giddinesses; Lo
I shut my chamber dore and come let's go.
But sooner may a cheape whore that hath beene
Worne by as many seuerall men in Sin
As are black feathers or musk-color hose   55
Name her childs right trew father mongst all those;
Sooner may one guesse who shall beare away
Th'infant of London, heire to an India;
And sooner may a gulling Weather-Spy
By drawing forth heauens Scheame, tell certainly   60
What fashiond hatts, or ruffs, or Suites next yeare
Our supple-witted antick Youths will weare
Then thou when thou departst from hence canst show
Whither, why, when, or with whome thou wouldst go.
But how shall I be pardond my offence   65
That thus haue sind against my conscience?
Now we are in the street: he first of all
Improuidently proud creepes to the wall
And so imprisond and hemm'd in by mee
Sells for a Litle state his Libertee.   70
Yet though he cannot skip forth now to greet
Euery fine silken painted foole we meet,
He them to him with amorous smiles allures
And grins, smacks, shruggs, and such an itch indures
As Prentices or Schooleboyes which do know   75
Of some gay sport abroade, yet dare not go.
And as fidlers stop lowest at higest Sound
So to the most braue stoopes he nighest ground.
But to a graue man he doth move no more
Then the wise politique horse would hertofore   80

Or thou O Elephant or Ape wilt do
When any names the king of Spayne to you.
Now leapes he vpright, ioggs me, and cryes do you see
Yonder well fauord Youth? Which? Yea, t'is hee
That dances so diuinely. Oh sayd I   85
Stand still, must you dance here for company?
He droopt: We went: till one which did excell
Th'Indians in drinking his Tabacco well
Mett vs: they talkd: I whisperd let vs go:
May be you smell him not; trewly I do.   90
He heares not me: but on the other side
A many colord peacock hauing spied
Leaues him and me: I for my lost Sheepe stay.
He followes, overtakes, goes in the way
Saying, him, whom I last lefte, all repute   95
For his deuise in handsomming a sute,
To iudge of Lace, pink, panes, cutt, print, or pleight,
Of all the Court to haue the best conceit.
Our dull Comedians want him: let him go.
But oh God strengthen thee, why stoopst thou so?   100
Why: he hath trauayld. Long? No: but to mee
Which vnderstand none he doth seeme to bee
Perfect French and Italian: I replide
So is the pox: he answered not but spide
More men of Sort, of parts, and qualities.   105
At last his Loue he in a window spies
And like Light dew exhald, he flings from mee,
Violently rauishd to his Lecheree.
Many weare there: he could command no more:
He quarreld, fought, bled, and turnd out of dore   110
Directly came to me, hanging the hed
And constantly awhile must keepe his bed.

Textual Introduction

Complete copies of "Satyre 1" (*Sat1*) can be found in 31 seventeenth-century manuscripts and in all 7 editions/issues of Donne's collected *Poems* printed in the seventeenth century (A–G). Short excerpts from the poem appear in Joseph Butler's eighteenth-century commonplace book (IU2) and in two issues of Samuel Sheppard's *MERLINVS ANONYMVS* (1653; sigla 33a–b). As is shown on Figure 2, *Sat1* sometimes appears in the company of 1, 2, or 3 other Satyres in the manuscripts, but it typically appears as the first of a 5-poem set, as it does in the seventeenth-century prints. Variant readings in lines 20, 45, and 55 divide the manuscripts into two distinct lines of descent, the first headed by a lost original holograph (LOH) reading "Courtesyes" (l. 20), "first best state" (l. 45), and "muske Collored hose" (l. 55) and the second from a lost revised holograph (LRH) containing the minor revisions "curtesy" (l. 20), "first blest State" (l. 45), and "musk-color hose" (l. 55). Descendents of the LOH include the three independently circulated "books" of Satyres (OQ1, P3, VA1) plus their cognate B13, the traditional Group-III manuscripts (B46, C9, H5, H6), and a few other manuscripts either Associated with Group III (H3, H7, HH1, O21, Y2, Y3) or unclassified (B33, B47, C5, H8, NP3). Descendents of the LRH include NY3 (the sole Group-IV manuscript, here used as copy-text); the traditional Group-I manuscripts (B32, C2, C8, O20, SP1), though two of them contain the Group-II text; part of the expanded Group II (B40, DT1, H4); and the unclassified F21. The stemma of *Sat1* (Figure 6) on page 40 below illustrates the exact relationships among these artifacts.

The first scribal variation in the lineage descending from the LOH appears in the postulated missing artifact β^1, which introduces the readings "departest hence" in line 63 (where the LOH reads "departst from hence") and "of parts, of qualityes" in line 105 (where the LOH reads "of parts, and qualities"). Stemming from β^1 are, on the one hand, the parent-child pair NY1 and VA2, which evince such anomalies as "sweare to me" (for the normative "sweare") in line 13 and "and for worse" (for "or worse") in line 25, and, on the other, γ^1, which trivializes the authorial "That wilt consort none untill thou haue knowne" in line 33 to "…till thou hast knowne." γ^1, as shown on the stemma, then passes this scribally altered line down the genealogical tree to its descendants, the missing cognates δ^1 and δ^2.

Perpetuating the submetrical "That wilt consort none, till thou hast knowne" in line 33, δ^1 also introduces and passes on to its descendants the sophistication "O Monstrous superstitious Puritan" (for the authorial "O Monster, superstitious Puritane") in line 27, a corruption other scribes repeat; the omission of "right" in the normative line-56 phrase "childs right true father" (yielding "Childs true father"); and "Infanta" (for the normative "Infant") in line 58, among other variants. As noted above, δ^1

gives rise to B13 and to ε^1, B13 incorporating into a larger poetical collection a cognate of the independently circulating "book" of Satyres (which also includes *Storm* and *Calm*) contained in OQ1, P3, and VA1. B13 follows δ^1 in inscribing *Sati* in the second ordinal position among its Satyres (and labeling it "Satire the second"), but deviates from the other offspring of δ^1 in recording "gyrne, [for the normative *grine*] or faune" in line 23 and the anomalous "whom I last mett" (for the normative "…last left") in line 95. In addition to misplacing the phrase "do you see" at the end of line 83 to the beginning of line 84 (an error P3 corrects independently), ε^1 reorders the poems into the standard 1–5 sequence, replaces the authorial "yonder" with "yon" in line 84, and contracts the normative "let us go" in line 89 to "letts go," reducing the line to 9 syllables. These variants pass on to OQ1—which, e.g., adds to the growing body of error "neat [for the normative *perte*] Courtier" in line 19 and reverses the normative "he was clothd" in line 46 to "was he clothde"—and to ζ^1, parent of the siblings P3 and VA1. Among the ζ^1 anomalies transmitted to P3 and VA1 are the omission of "yet" from the normative line-46 phrase "yet hee was cloth'd" (yielding "he was clothd") and the change of the normative past-tense "talkt" in line 89 to "talke" (yielding "They talke. I whisperde…"). Such differences as those in line 32 (where VA1 erroneously reads "the formall hatt," while P3 gives the normative "thy…") and 35 (where VA1 reads the normative "all thy Companions," while P3 omits "all") show that neither of these manuscripts can be the source of the other and mark them as siblings rather than parent and child.

A second branch of the β^1-γ^1 lineage is headed by δ^2, which repairs the meter of γ^1's submetrical "That wilt consorte non, till thou hast knowne" in line 33 by inserting "with" (yielding "…consort with non…").[1] δ^2 also simplifies the authorial subjunctive "thou do meet" in line 16 to the indicative "thou dost meete" and omits "yet" from the authorial "He lost that, yet he was clothd but in beasts skin" in line 46 (thus metrically regularizing the line), passing these changes on to its offspring ε^2 and ε^3. ε^2 adds to the errors accumulated in the δ^2 branch of γ^1's offspring by reversing line 37's normative "dost not only approue" to "not onlie dost approue," changing the authorial "skip forth now" to "now step forth" in line 71, and rewriting the LOH's "goes in the way" to "goes on the way" in line 94, a change also evident in the descendants of the LRH. ε^2's offspring are ζ^2 and ζ^3, the former the ancestor of the traditional Group-III manuscripts B46, H5, and the C9-H6 pair and of B47, which records a Group-III text of the Satyres. Into the corrupted text descending from ε^2, ζ^2 introduces the distinguishing readings "Births and Deathes" (for "birthe, and death") in line 42, "nighest the ground" (for "nighest ground") in line 78, and "D'yee" (for "do you") in line 83, lections passed down to η^1 and η^2 and thence to their respective offspring. η^1 corrupts the text further by, among other blunders, omitting "an" from the normative line-58 phrase "heire to an India" (yielding "Heyre to India") and pluralizing the normative "peacock" in line 92 to "Peacocks," errors transmitted to its offspring B46 and H5. Readings in such lines as 97 (where B46 reads the normative "Cut, Print" while H5

---

[1]Whether to assign genealogical priority to the 9- or to the 10-syllable rendition of line 33 is a matter of editorial judgment, and it is possible that δ^1 inadvertently dropped "with" from "consort with" rather than that δ^2 added "with" to "consort none." The basic shape of the stemma remains the same whatever the decision.

reads the anomalous "print, cutt") and 32 (where H5 reads the normative "vaile" while B46 reads the anomalous "raise") confirm the usual finding of this *Variorum* that B46 and H5 are siblings (or cousins) rather than parent and child.

From η^2, ζ^2's second direct descendant, stem B47 and θ, the parent of C9 and H6. Perhaps deliberately, the scribe of η^2 alters the normative "iollie statesmen" in line 7 to "wyly stats=men," and—among other changes—replaces the normative "Improuidently" in line 68 with "vnprouidently," passing these down to its offspring. B47 records further errors, including the mistranscription of the normative "Chroniclers" in line 9 as "Cronicles" and the omission of the first "me" in the line-25 phrase "take me, or leaue mee" (yielding "…take or leaue me"). And the scribe of θ, parent of C9 and H6, alters the normative text in numerous instances, including the reordering of "hattes, or ruffes, or suites" in line 61 as "suites or ruffes or hatts" and the insertion of "heere" into the line-13 phrase "sweare by thy best loue" (yielding "sweare heere by thy best loue"), the latter designed to impose metrical smoothness on the author's 9-syllable line (and followed in 1635 when B's editor imported "here" into the text from H6).

Stemming from ε^2 in parallel descent to ζ^2 is ζ^3, which begets the siblings H8 and NP3. Among the blunders introduced in ζ^3 and passed on to H8 and NP3 are the misreadings "Ioyntures, or [for the normative *and*] marry" in line 36 and "Thy [for the normative *These*] vanities" in line 51, the latter perhaps caused by eyeskip to or residual memory of the phrase "thy sinns" in the previous line. Divergences in lines 4—where NP3 reads the corrupt "here be confinde" (as against H8's normative "here be coffin'd")—and 58—where NP3 retains the authorial "heire" (while H8 omits the word)—show that H8 and NP3 are not copied one from the other, but descend independently from ζ^3, although the sheer quantity of textual error in NP3 suggests that one or more corrupt copyings may stand between it and the parent artifact.

The second direct descendant of δ^2, which gives rise to the final family of manuscripts in the LOH lineage, is ε^3, parent of H3 and—through the intermediary artifact ζ^4—of O21 and Y3. ε^3's most distinctive reading is the unique "Cerimonious [for the authorial *ceremonial*] man" in line 28, but it also misreads "Thirteene" for "14" in the line-22 phrase "12 or 14 strong," and "heau'ns Sceane" (for the normative "heauens Scheame") in line 60, a blunder shared by some descendents of the LRH. H3 evinces numerous anomalies, including the spurious "mystiede [for the correct *mistique*] bodie" in line 8, "poets of each band [for the authorial *land*]" in line 10, and "louest all loust anie" (for the normative "Lovst all, canst loue any") in line 14, to name but a sampling. From the extremely corrupt ζ^4 its offspring O21 and Y3 obtain such uniquely idiosyncratic readings as "patt" (for "rate") in line 31, "knowe" (for "Name") in line 56, and "shirtes" (for "Suites") in line 61. That O21 gives the anomalous "must you daunce there for Company" in line 86, where Y3 reads the correct "…dance heere…," e.g., shows that Y3 cannot be copied from O21, and O21's reading the correct "godes conduits" as against Y3's solecism "gods conduts" in line 5 shows that it is not copied from Y3; the usual finding of this *Variorum* that O21 and Y3 are siblings rather than parent and child is thus confirmed in this instance.

The evidence does not permit filiation of any of the 5 manuscripts appearing at the upper left on the stemma (Figure 6) with other artifacts or groups, but their readings in lines 20 (where all except H7 give "Courtesyes [for *curtesy*]"), 45 (where all give "best for [blest] state," though HH1 initially leaves a blank space for which a second scribe has marginally supplied the normative "best"), and 55 (where all give "muske Collored [for *musk-color*]") mark them as offspring of the LOH. Among these, the soundest are B33 and C5, which record 7 and 13 errors, respectively, while H7 records 20 corrupt readings, HH1 records 18, and the extremely corrupt Y2 records 55. It is unlikely that any of these descends immediately from the LOH, though the relative cleanness of B33 suggests that it stands fairly close to that artifact; the quantity of error in Y2, on the other hand, may represent the cumulative blunders of a succession of maladroit copyists. Here as elsewhere (see, e.g., the Textual Introduction for *Sat3* below), H7 appears to be contaminated, its recording of the LRH's "Curtesy" in line 20 perhaps being an instance of this and its recording of γ³'s "fondlinge" in line 1 certainly being so.

As stated above, the evidence indicates that Donne revisited *Sat1* at least once, effecting the minor revisions of "Courtesyes" to "curtesy" in line 20, "best" to "blest' in line 45, and "muske Collored" to "musk-color" in line 55, though whether these changes are deliberate or inadvertent is not clear. From this revised text (the LRH) stem NY3, which diverges from its source only in a couple of readings in line 23 and in a few idiosyncratic spellings (itemized below in the discussion of emendations of the copy-text), and β², which—through its offspring γ² and γ³ and 3 other now-missing intermediaries—leads eventually to the extant Group-I and Group-II manuscripts. To the authorial changes in lines 20, 40, and 55 β² adds a number of scribal alterations, including those shown in the following table:

Table 1.1: Scribal errors in β²

Line no.	LOH, LRH	β²
16	more spruce companion thou do meet	…thou dost…
32	dost vaile thy formall hatt	dost rayse…
47	course attire which now I weare	…I now weare
62	supple-witted antick Youths	subtle-witted…
63	thou when thou departst from hence canst show	…can showe
84	well fauord Youth? Which? Yea. 'tis hee	…oh tis hee
94	goes in the way	goes on the way

As is evident, these changes are all either grammatical mistakes (e.g., "dost" in line 16 [where the subjunctive "do" is required]; "can" in l. 63), trivializations ("rayse" in line 32 [a misunderstanding of Donne's "vaile"—"to lower in sign of submission or respect" (OED 2.I.b)]; "subtle-witted" in line 62), or errors of inadvertence ("I now" in line 47; "oh" in line 84 [an eyeskip to "Oh sayd I" in the following line]; "on" in line 94), and they descend to the artifacts below them on the genealogical tree. Like many scribes in the LOH lineage, moreover, the β² scribe misunderstands the rapid alternation of question and answer in line 101, recording "he hath trauelld long? no…" (for the authorial "he hath trauayld. Long? No…"), an error corrected independently in B32, but passed on to all other descendants of β² and thence into the seventeenth-century prints.

γ², the first of β²'s immediate offspring shown on the stemma, begets F21 and—through the intermediate artifact δ³—the Group-I manuscripts B32, O20, and SP1. γ² introduces the distinctive readings "xiii" (for the normative "14") in line 22, a mistake also evident in the ε¹ family of the LOH lineage; "Iointers" (for the correct "Ioyntures") in line 36, a trivialization corrected independently in SP1; "warn'd by [for the normative *of*] thy Sinns" in line 50; and "In [for the authorial *for*] his devise" in line 96, passing these anomalies on to F21 and δ³. Among F21's several blunders are "Thou wilt not leaue in the wilde Streete" (for "…leaue me in the middle Street") in line 15 and "like a needy Brother [for the normative *broker*]" in line 30. δ³ reverses the normative "now I weare" in line 47 to "I now weare" and reduces the authorial plural "giddinesses" in line 51 to the singular "Giddines," transmitting these to its descendants B32 and the O20-SP1 pair. To these accumulating errors B32 adds "inquiring lyes [for the normative *Eyes*]" in line 29 and "that [for *this*] course attire" in line 47, among others. O20 and SP1, on the other hand, differ from δ³ only in such slight details as spelling δ³'s "been" in line 53 as "bin" (thus providing a sight rhyme with "Sin" in the following line), and their relationship as parent and child must be inferred primarily from their kinship in other poems. Despite their basic similarity, the two differ, however, in several instances, including the above-mentioned line 36, where O20 gives "Iointers" as against SP1's "Ioyntures," and line 92, where SP1 reads the plural "Peacockes" as against O20's normative "Peacocke."

β²'s other immediate offspring is γ³, which leads—through δ⁴ and δ⁵, respectively—to the cognates C2 and C8 (normally members of Group I, but evincing a Group-II text of the Satyres) and to the DT1-H4 pair and B40 (part of the expanded Group II). γ³ adds the following 11 alterations to the 7 introduced in β²:

Table 1.2: γ³ alterations of the β² text

Line no.	β²	γ³
1	changeling motley humorist	fondlinge…
23	Shallt thou grin	Wilt…
27	Monster, superstitious Puritane	Monstrous…
39	nakednesse and barenesse	…Barrennes
60	heauens Scheame	…Scenes
63	departst from hence	…from me
78	to the most braue stoopes…ground	…stoopt…the ground
90	May be you smell him not	T'may bee…
97	cutt, print or pleight	Print, Cutt, and Plight
101	Why: he hath trauayld. long?	Why…travayl'd longe;

Like those introduced at the β² stage of transmission, all but one of these changes seem to arise from scribal carelessness or misunderstanding. The changes of "Shallt" to "Wilt" (l. 23), "Scheame" to "Scenes" (l. 60), "hence" to "me" (l. 63), "stoopes" to "stoopt" and "ground" to "the ground" (l. 78), and "cutt, print or" to "Print, Cutt, and" (l. 97), e.g., are trivializations or errors of inadvertence, while the replacement of "Monster" with "Monstrous" (l. 27), of "barenesse" with "Barrennes" (l. 39), and of "Why: he hath trauayld. long" with "Why…travayl'd longe" (l. 101) bespeak a failure to understand Donne's construction. Scribal idiosyncrasy may explain the substitution of "T'may be" for "May be" (l. 90). The most interesting innovation, adopted by the Grolier editors in 1895 (O) and by every twentieth-century editor except Bennett (T), is "fondling" in line 1, and it is difficult to account for. On its face, this is what Gardner called a "genuine alternative" (X, p. 124), and it is not easily explained as a scribal misreading of "changeling" or a careless mistake.[2] By adding the connotation of "foolishness," moreover, "fondling" might even be thought to increase the conceptual complexity of the line, since "changeling" and "humorist" are somewhat redundant (on the other hand, as Grierson noted [2:106], "fondling" may overlap semantically with "motley"—see the Commentary for interpretive remarks on these variants). Despite these qualifying features, however, it is finally impossible to accept "fondling" as an authorial change—because of the place at which it enters the transmissional history of the poem. As shown in the lists above, 7 variants are introduced into Donne's revised text in β² and a further 10 here in γ³, and the only one for which an authorial origin might plausibly be argued is "fondling"—all the others are either certainly or almost certainly scribal. A coherent scenario in which Donne somehow managed to interject "fondling" as the sole change into a text at least twice removed from the LRH and marred by nearly a score of accumulated scribal corruptions is impossible to imagine. A linguistically sensitive scribe, perhaps led to notice "changeling" by its prominence in the first line of the poem and wishing to eliminate the element of redundancy in "changeling" and "humorist," is the more likely agent of this change.

As noted above, γ³ begets the missing manuscripts δ⁴ and δ⁵, which in turn lead to the cognates C2 and C8 and to the parent-child pair DT1-H4 and B40. δ⁴ initi-ates and transmits to C2 and C8 the additional anomalies "Not" (for "Nor") in line 19, "wᵗʰ enquireinge lyes [for the normative *eyes*]" in line 29, and the unintelligible "him whome I last left, s'all [for the authorial *all*] repute" in line 95, the blunders in lines 19 and 95 eventually passing from C2 into the poem's first printing in A. The siblings C2 and C8 differ only in minor details: in line 65 C8 reads "myne [as against C2's *my*] offence," e.g., and in line 78 C2 gives the reversal "stoopt he the Nighest [for C8's normative *nigh'est the*] grounde." With the exceptions of "Or [for the normative *Oh*] said I" in line 85 and "pinch" (for the correct "pink") in line 97, δ⁵ reproduces γ³'s substantives accurately, its offspring differing only in some few such readings as B40's erroneous "meetst me" (for DT1's normative "meet'st one") in line 29 and B40's "him whom I last left's, all repute" (for DT1's normative "…left, all") in line 95, B40's anomaly sufficiently resembling the δ⁴ lection "…left, s'all" to suggest that this error arises in both instances from the same blunder or imperfection in γ³ and is corrected by DT1 independently.

---

[2] See "Appendix 2," *DV* 7.1:111–12 for guidelines followed in this edition to distinguish authorial from scribal manuscript variants.

Figure 4: Significant Variants in the 17ᵗʜ-Century Prints of "Satyre 1"

~ = agrees with LRH ▽ = agrees with nearest corresponding reading on left ( ) = specific source of variant c = compositor

Line no.	LRH/DV reading	A	B	C	D–F	G
1	changeling	fondling (γ³)	changeling (H6)	▽		▽
6	Natures Secretary	~	~	~	~	Is ~
7	ioly	~	wily (H6)	▽	▽	▽
13	best loue	~	~, here (H6)	▽, ▽	▽, ▽	▽, ▽
33	vntill thou	~	~	~	~	till ~
40	whore or prostitute boy	~, ~ ~	whore, prostitute ~ (H6)	▽, ▽	▽, ▽	~, ~ ~
46	yet he was clothd	~ ~	hee was ~	▽ ▽	▽ ▽	▽ ▽
53	whore that	~, who (c)	▽, ▽	▽, ▽	▽, ▽	▽, ▽
53–54	beene / Wome	~ / ~	~ / ~	~ / ~	~ / ~ out (c)	▽ / ▽
55	musk-color	~ ~	~ ~	~-coloured (c)	▽ ~ ▽	▽ ~ ▽
58	Th'infant of London, heire	The infant ~ ~, ~	The infant ~ ~, ~	▽ ▽ ▽ ▽, ▽	▽ ▽ ▽ ▽, ▽	▽ Infantry ▽ ▽, hence
60	heauens Scheame	~ Sceanes (c)	~ Scheme (?)	▽ ▽ ▽	▽ ▽ ▽	▽ ▽
62	supple-witted antick Youths	subtile wittied antique ~ (β²)	▽ ▽ ▽	▽ ▽ ▽	▽ ▽ antick	giddy-headed ▽ youth
70	his Libertee	high ~ (c)	his ~ (?)	▽ ▽	▽ ▽	▽ ▽
73	He them to him	~ then ~ ~ (c)	~ them ~ ~ (?)	▽ ▽ ▽	▽ ▽ ▽	▽ ▽ ▽
78	stoopes he nighest ground	stoopt ~ nigh'st the ~ (γ³)	stoops ▽ ▽ ▽	▽ ▽ ▽	▽ ▽ ▽	▽ ▽ ▽ ▽
81–82	ll. included	ll. om (censor)	ll. restored (?)	~	~	
92	peacock	~	~	~	~	Peacocks
95	all repute	s'all ~ (δ⁴)	all ~	▽	▽	▽ ▽
97	cutt, print, or pleight	print, cut, and plight (γ³)	▽, ▽, ▽ pleite	▽, ▽	▽ ▽, ▽, ▽	▽, ▽, ▽
100	stoopst	~	stop'st	▽	▽	~
101	Why: he hath trauayld. Long?	~, ~ ~ travailed, ~? (γ³)	▽, ▽ ▽ traveled, ▽?	▽, ▽ ▽, ▽?	~, hath he travelled, ~?	Why. He hath travelled, ~;
102	vnderstand			~	~	understood
108	Lecheree	liberty (c)	lechery (?)	▽	▽	▽ ▽
109	weare there	~	~	~	there were	▽

The Seventeenth-Century Prints

Evincing the 7 scribal errors derived from β² (in ll. 16, 32, 47, 62, 63, 84, 94), the 10 from γ³ (ll. 1, 23, 27, 39, 60, 63, 78, 90, 97, 101), and 2 from δ⁴ (ll. 19, 95), the revised text of *Sat1* first enters print in the 1633 edition of Donne's collected *Poems* (A), set into type—as are poems edited in previously published volumes of this *Variorum*—from C2. Among the aforementioned corruptions, A is linked to the C2-C8 pair by line 95's "him whome I last left, s'all repute," an unintelligible sport unique to these manuscripts and quickly replaced in B with the normative "...all repute"; and the reading that specifically cements the C2-A relationship is the shared spelling "plight" (where C8 gives "pleight") in line 97, a spelling first introduced in β² and appearing in all its descendants except SP1 and C8. Although A's embodiment of the C2 text is generally accurate, it differs not only in omitting lines 81–82, but also in changing C2's "Whore, yᵗ" to "whore, who" in line 53, "his Libertye" to "high libertie" in line 70, "He them to him...allures" to "He then..." in line 73, and "rauishd to his Lecheree" to "...his liberty" in line 108. The alteration of "them" to "then" in line 73 is likely inadvertent, and the replacement of "yᵗ" with "who" in line 53 may be as well (A exhibits no systematic preference for referring to persons with "who"), but the omission of lines 81–82, which contains a deprecating reference to the king of Spain, is surely intended to make the poem more acceptable to the government censor, as is the bowdlerization of "Lecheree" to "liberty" in line 108. Indeed, in light of this consideration, it is not unreasonable to suspect that the substitution of "high [for the authorial *his*] libertie" in line 70 bespeaks a deliberate attempt to ennoble the poem's content (see the General Textual Introduction, p. xci). Otherwise Marriott takes his usual care in proofreading the printed text, correcting initial mistakes in the typesetting of lines 29, 32, 40, 41, 50, 59, and 84 (see the Analysis of Early Printed Copies on p. 245).

The text of A undergoes careful revision in the 1635 edition (B), B's editor not only restoring lines 81–82, but also emending the text substantively in 12 other instances (see Figure 4 below). These include changing "fondling...humorist" to "changeling...humorist" in line 1; "Jolly Statesmen" to "wily Statesmen" in line 7; "sweare by thy best love in earnest" to "sweare by thy best love, here, in earnest" in line 13; "muddy whore, or prostitute boy" to "muddy whore, prostitute boy" in line 40; "yet he was cloath'd" to "he was cloath'd" in line 46; "heavens Sceanes" to "heavens Scheme" in line 60; "high libertie" to "his libertie" in line 70; "He then...allures" to "He them...allures" in line 73; "stoopt hee" to "stoops he" in line 78; "whom I last left, s'all repute" to "whom I last left, all repute" in line 95; "stoop'st" to "stop'st" in line 100, and "to his liberty" to "to his lechery" in line 108. Except for "changeling" in line 1 and "wily" in line 7, these alterations are all apparently calculated to improve meter (ll. 13, 40, 46), eliminate obvious errors (ll. 60, 78, 95, 100), or restore readings that A's editor had changed in an effort to blunt the criticism of the censor (ll. 70, 81–82, 108), and all are available in H6, the manuscript shown in previously published volumes of this *Variorum* to have supplied B with emendations for poems in other genres (see *DV* 2:lxxviii–lxxix) and undoubtedly drawn on for these changes as well ("wily" in line 7 is available in only B47, H6, and C9, e.g., and the inserted "here" in line 13 only in C9 and H6). That his intention is to provide a smooth, readable text and not necessarily to adopt every variant available is revealed in the fact that B's editor refuses a further 20 alternate readings that were available to him in H6, including "vaile [for *raise*] thy formall hatt" in line 32, "nakednesse and barenesse" (for "…barrennesse") in line 39, and "supple-witted [for *subtile wittied*] antick youths" in line 62.

The text of *Sat1* undergoes relatively few substantive changes in the subsequent seventeenth-century editions (C–G), and for only 1 of these is there any reason to suspect that the editor consulted a manuscript or prior print source. In 1639, the third edition (C) replaces A and B's "musk-colour" with "musk-coloured" in line 55; and the fourth (D and its reissues E and F) trivializes Donne's reference in lines 53–54 to "a cheape whore that hath beene / Worne by…men" to "…Worne out by…men," recasts the received "Why, he hath traveled long?" in line 101 to "Why hath he travelled long?" and reverses "Many were there" to "Many there were" in line 109. All these changes except that in line 101 carry over into the Restoration edition of 1669 (G), where G's editor—in addition to modernizing much of the spelling—further tries to make sense of the dialogue in lines 100–01 by altering "stopp'st" to "stoop'st," reversing D's "hath he" to "He hath," inserting a period after "why," and beginning a new sentence with "he" (yielding "why stoop'st thou so? / Why. He hath travelled long"). G also supplies the implied verb in line 6, giving "here / Is Natures Secretary (for "here / Natures Secretary"); reduces "untill thou have known" in line 33 to "till…"; misunderstands "who shall beare away / The infant of London, Heire to an India" in lines 57–58 as "who shall bear away / The Infantry of *London*, hence to an *India*"; rewrites "subtile wittied antique youths" in line 62 as "giddy-headed antick youth"; pluralizes the received "Peacock" in line 92 to "Peacocks"; alters "understand" to the preterite "understood" in line 102, and inadvertently drops "a" from the line-106 phrase "in a window." The one change for which G almost certainly consulted either A or a manuscript appears in line 40, where G restores the "or" that B, following H6, had dropped. In changing the authorial "plump muddy whore or prostitute boy" to "plump muddy whore, prostitute boy," of course, H6 and B regularize the meter of the line at the expense of changing its syntax, but there is nothing in their version that would have prompted G's editor to intervene had he not seen the authorial alternative in another artifact. Since the correct version of the line is available in all manuscripts except the descendants of ζ^2, it is not possible to identify G's specific source for the emendation.

The Modern Prints

Further modernizing orthography and mechanics, Tonson (H) bases his text of *Sat1* on G, not only maintaining in the stream of transmission the changes introduced by G in lines 6, 33, 40, 58, 62, 101, and 102, but also adding further changes of his own: he elides "to enjoy" to "t'enjoy" in line 39, inverts "be naked" to "naked be" in line 41, respells "pleit" in line 97 as "plait," restores the comma after "Why" and respells "travelled" as "travail'd" in line 101 (yielding "Why, he hath travail'd long;"), and supplies the omitted "a" in line 106. These changes then join others stemming from β^2 (ll. 16, 32, 47, 62, 63, 84, 94), γ^3 (ll. 23, 27, 39, 63, 90, 97), δ^4 (l. 19), A (l. 53), B (ll. 7, 13, 46), C (l. 55), and D–F (ll. 54, 109) to constitute a highly idiosyncratic text that is passed along to Tonson's later eighteenth- and earlier nineteenth-century successors Bell (I), Anderson (J), Chalmers (K), and Lowell (M), who vary this text only slightly. The specific relationships amongst these editions—that J derives from I, that K and M revert to H for their setting texts—are confirmed by readings in, e.g., lines 90 and 95 (see Figure 5).

The text of *Sat1* in the edition of Grosart (N)—the first editor since the seventeenth century to consult manuscripts (but see footnote 44 on p. xcv above)—differs significantly from any that had previously appeared in print. According the artifact "great if not absolute authority" (1:3) because of the 1593 date inscribed in a contemporary hand (see footnote 9 on p. lxvii above) on its title page, Grosart selects B33 as the copy-text for *Sat1* (and for the other two poems it contains, *Sat2* and *Sat3*); and although he consults B32, B40, H7, and "all" preceding editions of Donne (1:xii)—noting many of their variants in his textual notes—his reading text accurately presents B33's substantives except in line 3, where he misreads B33's "Consorted" as "Consoled"; in line 23, where he corrects B33's erroneous "grinne of" to "grinne or"; in line 32, where he replaces B33's "uaile" with the β² trivialization "raise"; and line 53, where he silently replaces B33's "cheap hoore that" with "...who." This adherence to B33 leads Grosart to retain such unique B33 anomalies as "little roome" (for the normative "...state") in line 70 and "dance to" (for the normative "dance here") in line 86, but also in line 39 to print, for the first time ever, the authorial "barenes" (all prior editors record the γ³ error "barrenness"), although his marginal gloss indicates that he regarded "barenes" as merely a variant spelling of "barrenness." Apart from the few blunders, emendations, and retentions of B33's eccentricities here noted, Grosart presents an authentic, original-version text of the poem.

The final two nineteenth-century editions—the Grolier Club (O) in 1895 and Chambers (P) in 1896—construct the text of *Sat1* in accordance with their usual practices. The Grolier editors return to A for copy-text and—except that they supply from a later edition the couplet omitted in A (ll. 81–82)—follow its substantives faithfully (see, for example, the readings "fondling" in the opening line, "barrenness" in line 39, "scenes" in line 60, "high" in line 70 and others cited in Figure 5). O, however, systematically modernizes spelling (e.g., printing "travelled" for "travailed" in l. 101), expands elided participles (e.g., printing "clothed" for "cloathd," in l. 46), supplies apostrophes in possessives (e.g., printing "Man's" for "Mans" in l. 45), and adds punctuation throughout; and none of these changes are recorded in the notes. Comparing A, B, E, and G, but asserting that since none of these is of "supreme authority," he has "no choice but to be eclectic," Chambers constructs a text that most resembles A, but introduces alternative readings from B ("changeling" [for "fondling"] in line 1, "wily" [for "jolly"] in line 7, "scheme" [for "Sceanes"] in line 60, "lechery" [for "liberty"] in line 108, among others) and, apparently, E (recording E's "Hath he" [for the alternative "he hath"] in line 101 to produce the question "Hath he travell'd long?"). Perhaps alerted by Grosart's prior use of the artifact, Chambers also collates B33, recording many of its variants in his notes and accepting into his reading text its correct "bareness" in line 39; and P's "musk-coloured" (for "musk-colour") may also derive from B33, although the reading is available in C–G. P's anomalous "Doth"

Figure 5: Variants in the Modern Prints of "Satyre 1"

blank column = agrees with LRH reading   ~ = agrees with LRH reading   OoV = Origin of Variant   A–G = variant appears in 17th-c. eds.

• = variant appears in modern eds.   { = to be read together

Line no.	LRH/DV reading	Variant	OoV	A–G	H	I	J	K	M	N	O	P	Q	S	T	Y	Z	AA	DD
1	changeling	fondling	γ³	A	•	•					•		•	•		•	•	•	•
3	Consoled	Consoled	N		•	•	•	•	•	•								•	
6	Natures	Is ~	G	G	•	•			•										
7	ioly	wily	H6	B–G	•	•	•	•	•			•		•					
13	loue	~ , here	H6	B–G	•	•						•							
16	do	dost	β²	A–G	•	•	•	•	•		•	•	•	•		•	•		•
19	Nor	Not	δ⁴	A–G	•	•			•								•		•
20	curtesy	Courtesyes	B33	A–G	•	•	•	•	•	•	•			•		•	•		•
23	Shallt	Wilt	γ³	A–G	•	•	•	•	•	•	•			•					
25	or	and	B33, NY3							•									
27	Monster	Monstrous	γ³	A–G	•	•	•	•	•		•	•	•	•	•	•	•		•
31	rate	race	K	A–G	•	•	•	•	•			•		•					
32	vaile	rayse	β²	A–G	•	•	•	•	•					•					
33	consort	comfort	S	G		•	•	•	•		•								
33	vntill	till	G	A–G	•	•	•	•	•										
39	barenesse	barrennes	γ³	A–G	•	•	•	•	•					•					
39	to inioy	t'enjoy	H	A–G	•	•	•	•	•	•		•							•
41	be naked	naked be	H		•	•	•	•	•			•							
45	blest	best	LOH		•	•	•	•	•			•							
46	yet he	he	H6	B–G	•	•	•	•	•	•	•	•	•	•		•	•	•	•
47	now I	I now	β²	A–G	•	•	•	•	•		•		•	•		•			
53	that	who	H6 / A ?	A–G	•	•	•	•	•	•	•	•	•	•			•		•
54	Worme	~ out	G	G	•	•	•	•	•			•		•					•
55	musk-color	~-coloured	C	C–G	•					•									
58	infant of London, heire	infantry ~ ~, hence	G	G													•		
58	infant	Infanta	B13														•		

Line no.	LRH/DV reading	Variant	OoV	A–G	H	I	J	K	M	N	O	P	Q	S	T	Y	Z	AA	DD
60	Scheame	scenes	δ⁴	A							•								
62	supple-witted	subtle ~	β²	A–F	•	•	•	•	•		•	•	•	•		•	•	•	•
62	supple-witted	giddy-headed	G	G	•	•	•	•	•		•	•	•	•		•	•	•	•
63	from hence	~ me	γ³	A–G	•	•	•	•	•	•	•	•							
63	canst	can	β²	A–G	•	•	•	•	•	•	•	•							
67	all	~,	G	G					•	•	•	•							
68	Improuidently	Unprouidently	B33												•				
70	state	roome	B33						•										
70	his	high	A	A								~ the							
73	them	then	A	A															
78	nighest	nigh'st the	γ³	A–G	•	•	•	•	•	•	•	•	•	•		•	•	•	•
84	Yea	Oh	β²	A–G	•	•	•	•	•		•	•	•	•		•	•	•	•
89	let vs	let'us	OQ1	I		•													
90	May be	It ~~	I																
90	May be	T ~~	β²	A–G	•	•	•	•	•		•	•	•	•		•	•	•	•
93	stay	stray	M						•										
94	in	on	β²	A–G	•	•	•	•	•		•	•	•						
95	lefte,	~,	I								•								
95	all	s'all	δ⁴	A															
97	cutt, print, or	print, cutt, and	γ³	A–G	•	•	•	•	•		•	•		•	•			•	•
97	pleight	plight	β²	A					•										
97	pleight	plait	H																
97	pleight	pleat	O								•		❦						
97	pleight	pleite	B	B–G								•	•						•
101	he hath	Hath he	E	D–F															
101	trauayld. Long	~, ~	β²	A–G	•	•	•	•	•	•	•		⁛	⁛					
102	vnderstand	understood	G	G	•	•	•	•			•								
109	weare there	there were	D	D–G	•	•	•	•	•		•								

(for the normative "Dost") in line 30 is anticipated in J and M, but likely represents Chambers's independent mistake.

Having analyzed the preceding editorial tradition and developed an organized inventory of the manuscript resources available for preparation of an edition (see the General Textual Introduction), Grierson (Q) chooses A as copy-text for *Sat1* (as for other poems) and follows A's wording, spelling, and punctuation. In an effort to eliminate error and present a readable text, however, Grierson not only adds the omitted lines 81 and 82, but also emends A's punctuation in about 20 instances and its wording in 10 others. Formulating a method that takes into account the "agreement of the manuscripts whether universal or partial" as well as the "comparative value of the different groups" (2:cxvii), Grierson bases some of his emendations on lections that occur widely among the manuscripts, but others rest on his own authority or that of only one or two artifacts. Thus he emends A's "barrennesse" to "bareness" in line 39, citing as his authority B13, B32, B33, H6, HH1, NY1, NY3, O20, and OQ1; "Sceanes" to "Scheme" in line 60, citing B13, B32, B33, HH1, NY1, O20, OQ1, and B–G; "high" to "his" in line 70, citing B–G and "*all* MSS."; "then" to "them" in line 73, noting that "then" appears only in A; "stoopt" to "stoops" in line 78, citing B13, B32, B33, H3, H6, O20, OQ1, and B–G; "s'all" to "all" in line 95, citing B–G and the "MSS. *generally*"; and "liberty" to "lechery" in line 108, citing B–G and "MSS." For his alteration of A's "infant" to "Infanta" in line 58, on the other hand, he cites B13, OQ1, and H6 only; and for his change of "subtile wittied" to the more typically spelled "subtile-witted" in line 62 he cites only B32 and O20. Further, in order to clarify the dialogue in A's rendition of lines 101–02—"Why, he hath travailed long? no, but to me / Which understand none, he…"—Grierson substitutes "Why? he hath travayld; Long? No; but to me / (Which understand none,) he…," attributing the changes in line 101 to B46 and the parentheses in line 102 to OQ1 (except Z and DD, all subsequent editions adopt Grierson's version of these lines). Despite his rigorous approach to the materials, Grierson's analysis does not result in a true genealogy for the poem; thus, except for the change of "barrennesse" to "barenesse" in line 39 and of "can" to "canst" in line 63, he leaves unaltered 14 scribal errors introduced at the β^2, γ^3, and δ^4 stages of the text's evolution, as well as the one—the sophistication of "that" to "who" in line 53—attributable to A itself. For several emendations (in ll. 32, 41, and 50, e.g.), Grierson specifies A's reading incorrectly, indicating that the copy he compared contained the inner forme of sheet 2T in the uncorrected state. As shown by lections in lines 58 ("Infanta"), 63 ("canst"), and elsewhere, Hayward (S) essentially reproduces Q, though he admits into his reading text the blunder "comfort [for *consort*] none" in line 33 and drops "Which?" from Q's "Yonder well favoured youth? Which? Oh, 'tis hee" in line 84.

Except Bennett (T), who follows a manuscript (see below), Grierson's approach to copy-text heavily influences subsequent twentieth-century editors of *Sat1*. Milgate (Y), Grierson's successor in the Oxford University Press series, uses A as copy-text, but—in addition to supplying from B the censored lines 81–82—emends substantives 10 times (changing "Not" to "Nor" in l. 19, "barrennesse" to "barenesse" in l. 39, "who" to "that" in l. 53, "Sceanes" to "Scheame" in l. 60, "can" to "canst" in l. 63, "high" to "his" in l. 70, "then" to "them" in l. 73, "stoopt" to "stoops" in l. 78, "s'all" to "all" in l. 95, and "liberty" to "lechery" in l. 108), as well as replacing A's "subtile wittied" in line 62 with "subtile-witted"—all changes (except those in lines 19 and 53) that had been previously imposed by Grierson. And although Milgate retains the normative "Infant" in line 58, rejecting Grierson's "Infanta," he follows Grierson in enclosing in parentheses the clause that spans lines 37–40—"(that does...prostitute boy)"—and essentially accepts Grierson's understanding of the exchange between the satirist and the fop in lines 101–02, imposing as necessary to sense the parentheses that Grierson had imported into line 102 from OQ1 and similarly allocating the parts of the dialogue: "'Why? he hath travail'd.' 'Long?' 'No, but to me' / (Which understand none) 'he doth seeme....'" In addition to marking passages of direct discourse with quotation marks (as in the foregoing example), Milgate imposes elision marks in order to regularize meter (see ll. 46, 58, 61, 69, 77, 83, 84, 89, 92, 101, 103, and 104), and he alters A's punctuation some 24 times, most notably in lines 85, 90, 98, 101, and 104 to mark ends of clauses with periods rather than semicolons. Milgate also collates multiple copies of A, differentiating corrected and uncorrected readings in his notes.

Essentially adopting the Griersonian approach, Shawcross (Z), too, bases his text for *Sat1* on A, emending it occasionally when "a consensus of manuscripts seems to be closer to Donne's 'original'" (xxi). In addition to supplying the censored lines 81–82 from a later edition, respelling A's "subtile wittied" in line 62 as "subtile-witted," and admitting the typographical blunder "Wither" (for "Whither") in line 64, Z differs verbally from A in lines 39 (reading "barenesse" for A's "barrennesse"), 58 (reading "Infanta" for "infant"), 60 (reading "Scheme" for "Sceanes"), 63 (reading "canst" for "can"), 70 (reading "his" for "high"), 73 (reading "them" for "then"), 78 (reading "stoops" for "stoopt"), 95 (reading "all" for "s'all"), and 108 (reading "lechery" for "liberty")—all changes (except the misspelling in line 64) introduced previously by Grierson. Shawcross also alters A's punctuation in 10 instances and—in an effort to regularize meter—introduces 12 marks of elision.

Smith (AA) and Patrides (DD) also follow their usual practices in establishing the text of *Sat1*. Acknowledging his deliberate eclecticism, Smith prints a modernized text that aims to present "the richest and most pointed readings...that have good authority in the early versions" (14). Except that it retains the erroneous "barrennesse" in line 39—and thus becomes the only edition other than O to do so since N recovered the correct "barenesse" from B33 (see Figure 5)—AA evinces all the emendations made by Q to the text of A, including "Infanta" (for "infant") in line 58 and the interpolated parentheses in line 102—"(Which understand none)." Further, AA accepts Q's understanding of the dialogue in lines 101–02, but appears to follow Y in punctuating the lines; and AA also likely reflects Y's influence in adopting the emendations "Nor" (for "Not") in line 19 and "that" (for "who") in line 53. Adding the omitted lines 81–82 from a later edition, Patrides adopts A as copy-text and generally follows its spelling and punctuation, but—like Grierson before him—emends A's substantive errors in lines 39, 60, 63, 70, 73, 78, 95, and 108, as well as respelling "wittied" as "witted" in line 62. DD's other verbal alteration of A—of "giddinesses" to "giddinesse" in line 51—is likely a careless mistake. Since Patrides occasionally abandons his copy-text in favor of idiosyncratic readings appearing in Grierson (see, e.g., DV 7.1:70), it is noteworthy that he accepts into his text of *Sat1* neither Grierson's "Infanta" in line 58 nor the interpolated parentheses in line 102.

Among twentieth-century editors, as noted above, Bennett (T) alone adopts a manuscript copy-text, becoming the only modern editor other than Grosart to do so. And he chooses the same artifact that we use in this *Variorum*—NY3—apparently judging it to be the "accessible text" containing "the fewest obvious errors" (xxv). Substantively, therefore, Bennett's text differs from those rooted in the print tradition in numerous instances. For example, T records 17 readings not found in Q (see Figure 5), including "changeling" (for "fondling") in line 1, "monster" (for "monstrous") in line 27, "vail" (for "raise") in line 32, "supple-witted" (for "subtile-witted") in line 62, "from hence" (for "from mee") in line 63, "nighest" (for "nigh'st the") in line 78, "Yea" (for "Oh") in line 84, and "Maybe" (for "'T may be") in line 90. Believing it "inappropriate" that Donne should suffer the "minor poet's fate of being printed only in antiquarian texts," however, Bennett changes NY3's punctuation in 118 places (including, e.g., importing into line 102 the parentheses that Q had derived from OQ1) and thoroughly modernizes its mechanics and spelling. A noteworthy consequence of this last mentioned policy is the loss of several sight rhymes created in NY3's original orthography (see. e.g., the ends of ll. 11–12, 25–26, 35–36, 83–84, 97–98, 107–08, 109–10, and 111–12).

Copy-text Used in this Edition

As is evident from the discussion above, Bennett's handling of *Sat1*—as well as of other poems—constituted an editorial dead end (see the General Textual Introduction); and our selection of NY3 as copy-text here is dictated not by Bennett's prior decision, but by the fact—as the stemma shows—that NY3 is genealogically the surviving witness closest to Donne's lost revised holograph (LRH), containing none of the errors introduced into the prints by the scribes of β^2, γ^3, and δ^4. Verbally, the text we present resembles Bennett's except in three places: in line 23 we emend NY3's "girne and fawne" to "grin or fawne" (Bennett retains "girne and..."), following the stemmatological evidence that "girne" and "and" are scribal slips on the part of Rowland Woodward; and in line 25, where Woodward overwrote "and" with "or" in the phrase "For better or worse," we record "or," while Bennett reads "and" (Bennett either did not notice the overwrite or interpreted it differently). Otherwise, we emend NY3's idiosyncratic spelling "tell" to "till" in lines 43 and 87, change the pen-slip "Whether" to the required "Whither" in line 64, and alter the manuscript's punctuation in 15 instances, all of which are explicitly cited in the apparatus. Nearly three-dozen regularizations needed to prepare a manuscript copy-text for print are also recorded in a separate section of the apparatus.

Textual Apparatus

Copy-text, poem: NY3.   **Texts collated:** B13 (ff. 50v–51v); B32 (ff. 88–89); B33 (ff. 96–97); B40 (ff. 70–72); B46 (ff. 3v–5v); B47 (ff. 97–99); C2 (ff. 15v–16v); C5 (ff. 68v–69v); C8 (ff. 1–3v); C9 (ff. 12–13v); DT1 (ff. 13–14v); F21 (ff. 1–3v); H3 (ff. 6–7); H4 (ff. 1–2v); H5 (ff. 116–17v); H6 (pp. 61–64); H7 (ff. 40–42v); H8 (*ll.* 1–60 *only*, f. 67r–v); HH1 (ff. 63–65); IU2 (*ll.* 15–22, 35–36, 41–44, 71–76 *only*, f. 60); NP3 (ff. 115–16v); NY1 (pp. 1–4 *of* Satyres *section*); NY3 (ff. [2–3]); O20 (ff. 1–2v); O21 (pp. 172–76); OQ1 (ff. 198–99v); P3 (ff. 4–5); SP1 (ff. 8–9v); VA1 (ff. 1–2v); VA2 (ff. 5–6); Y2 (pp. 1–9); Y3 (pp. 10–12); A (pp. 325–28); B (pp. 123–27); C (pp. 123–27); D (pp. 118–21); E (pp. 118–21); F (pp. 118–21); G (pp. 118–21[*misnumbered 221*]); 33a–b (*ll.* 59–62 *only*, sig. B1v).

Emendations of the copy-text: Heading: *Satyre* 1.] Satyra .1ª   Line 5 conduits,] ~∧   6 Philosopher,] ~.   23 grin] girne   *1st* or] and   25 mee,] ~∧   28 man,] ~.   40 boy,] ~∧   41 bare?] ~∧   43 till] tell   58 London,] ~∧   64 Whither] Whether   83 vpright,] ~;   84 Yea,] ~.   87 till] tell   93 stay.] ~∧   94 goes] ~,   95 him,] ~;   96 sute,] ~;   97 pleight,] ~∧   99 go.] ~∧   100 thee,] ~∧

Regularizations of the copy-text: Line 3 with] wᵗʰ   5 and] &   7 which] wᶜʰ   14 which] wᶜʰ   15 the] yᵉ   18 with] wᵗ   20 with] wᵗ   21 with] wᵗ   29 with] wᵗ   42 our] oʳ   43 our] oʳ   47 which] wᶜʰ   48 With] Wᵗ   with] wᵗ   53 that] yᵗ   64 with] wᵗ   73 with] wᵗ   75 which] wᶜʰ   78 the] yᵉ   82 the] yᵉ   84 Which] which   87 which] wᶜʰ   96 For] for   handsomming] handsoming   98 the] yᵉ   101 Long] long   102 Which] Wᶜʰ   103 French] french   105 and] &   command] cōmand   110 and] &

HISTORICAL COLLATION

Format:

Imperfections: *ink blots obscure some letters in ll. 13, 20, 21, 22 and page containing ll. 61–112 missing*   H8.

Indentations: *ll. 39, 67 ind 3 sps*　B33. *ll. 111–12 ind 2 sps*　DT1 H4 A; *l. 49 ind*　H3; *ll. 15 and 71 ind 12 sps*　IU2; *ll. 27, 28 ind 4 sps*　O21 Y3; *no ind*　Σ.

Miscellaneous: D^r: Doone: *is running head in ms.*, »(50)« *written above HE in top M*　B32; *general HE* Ihon Dunne his Satires / Anno Domini 1593 *precedes Sat1 on separate title page*　B33; *poem scribally numbered 1 in left M beside HE*　B46; *general HE* Satyrs. *precedes HE*　H5; »P.« *written to left of HE*　H6; *poem scribally attributed to I.D. in right M beside HE*　H8; *poem numbered every 5 ll. in left M*　NY1 VA2; »p. 118.« *to left of HE*　O20; *ll. 99–102 appear in the order 100, 101, 99, 102 and are scribally numbered, respectively, 2, 3, 1, 4, in left M, to correct the order*　O21 Y3; *scribal section* HE—Mr Iohn Dunnes / Satires—*in top right corner of f.* 198　OQ1; *ll. 28 and 29 entered in reverse order and correctly numbered in left M*　SP1; *ll. 81–82 silently om*　A.

Headings: Satire the second. |　B13.　**Satyre:** 1:.　B32 C2(1.st) C8(i.st) H8 O21(ye first.) VA2 A–G.　Satyra　B40.　Satyre.　B46 DT1.　Satyre 2: On the Humorist. |　B47.　Sat: i^a　C5.　Satyre.2.　C9 H6 HH1. Satire i.　F21 NY1 Y3(the first).　A Satyre of M:^{r} Iohn Donnes　H3. Satire:　H4.　Satyra Prima.　H5 H7 NY3(.1.^{a}).　Empty Fop　IU2. Iohn Donne Satyr: 1: The Humerist |　NP3.　Satyre .1^a.　O20.　Satira i^a　OQ1 SP1 Y2(prima).　Iohon Donne his Satires / The first. |　P3. Sat: 1.　VA1.　om　B33.

1 Away] ~,　H5; ~ from me　P3.　changeling] ~,　B13 HH1 NY1 SP1; fondling　B40 C2 C8 H4 A; fondling-　DT1(*var:* ›Changeling‹) H7.　humorist,] B13 B32 C2 C5 C8 H5 NY3 A–G; ~;　HH1; ~!　NP3 OQ1; ~.　SP1; ~$_\wedge$　Σ.

2 me,] ~$_\wedge$　C5 C8 H3 O21 P3 Y3; ~!　NP3; ~;　NY1; ~:　OQ1.　in] om　B46 O21.　this] thy　SP1.　standing] Same ~　B46; ~-　H7. wodden] ~-　H7.　chest] ~,　B32 C8 F21 HH1 O20 OQ1 A–G; Christe　B46.

3 Consorted] Comforted　C8 Y3; conforted;　O21.　bookes,] ~;　B13 O21; ~$_\wedge$　B46 B47 C5 C9 H3 H5 H6 H8 HH1 NY1 OQ1 P3 VA1 VA2 Y2 Y3.　ly] ~, C8; ~;　O21.

Alternate line: Wth these few books consorted lett mee ly　NP3.

4 prison,] ~$_\wedge$　C5 H3; ~;　O21 P3; ~!　OQ1.　here] there　O21 Y2.　be] om　H3(»~«) Y2.　coffind,] B32 F21 NY3 O20 A–G; confyn'd　B47 C8 O21 Y3; confinde,　NP3; coffened　P3; ~$_\wedge$　Σ.　when I] and　NP3.　dy.] ~,　B33 B47 C5 DT1 F21 H3 H4 H6 NP3 Y3; ~:　B40 H8; ~!　OQ1; ~;　A.

5 are] be　O21.　Gods] God's　H3 NY1.　conduits,] ~$_\wedge$　B33 B47 HH1 NY3; ~;　A–C.　graue] ~-　B40.　Diuines:] NY3; ~$_\wedge$　B33 H3 O21 VA1 Y3; ~;　B46 C5 OQ1 D–G; ~.　B47; ~,　Σ.　here] ~,　C8 P3.

6 Natures] Is Nature's　B46 H5 H8 NP3 G.　Secretary,] ~$_\wedge$　B33 B47 C5 C8 C9 H3 H6 NP3 NY1 O21 OQ1 VA2 Y3.　Philosopher,] ~$_\wedge$　B33 B47 C5 DT1

H3 H4 H8 NP3 VA1 Y3; ~;   B40 O21; ~:   B46 HH1 D–G; ~.   NY1 NY3 SP1
VA2 A–C; ~!   OQ1.

7 ioly] wyly   B47 C9 H6 B–G; w^c   O21; ~- SP1; w^th   Y3.   Statesmen,] ~∧
B33 H5 H8 NY1 OQ1 P3 VA2; stats=men∧   B47 H7 NP3 O21; states men,   C5;
states-men,   SP1 Y3; stats man,   Y2.   which] (~   H8 NP3; that   NY1 VA2.
ty] trye   C5.

8 a] om   H3.   Citties] Cities'   H4; ~,   HH1; Kingdomes   NP3.
mystique] Mustique→»~«   C8; mystiede   H3; ~ SP1.   body.] ~∧   B33 B47
DT1 P3 Y3; ~:   B40 H5; ~,   C8 F21 H4 H6 Y2; ~.| H3; ~;   H7 HH1 O21 A–G;
~)   H8 NP3; ~!   OQ1.

9 Here] Heer's   H7.   gathering] gath'ring   DT1 H3 H4; ~- SP1.
Chroniclers,] Chronicles∧   B33 Y3; ~;   B40 NY1 VA2; ~.   B46; Cronicles,   B47
HH1 NP3 O21; ~∧   C5 F21 VA1 Y2; Chronicles;   H8; ~!   OQ1.   them] ~,
C2.   stand] ~,   B13 B32 C8 F21 O20; ~.   O21.

10 Giddy] ~,   B40; ~;   O21.   Poets] ~,   B40.   each] rich   NP3; this   Y2.
Land.] ~:   B32 F21 H5 O20 Y2; ~∧   B33 B47 Y3; ~;   B40 H4; hand.   C9; band∧
H3(M var: »~∧«); ~!   OQ1.

11 all] of   H3.   companee] ~,   B13 C5 C8 H4 H5 HH1 O20 A–G; ~»,«
H8; ~;   O21; ~?   OQ1 P3 Y2.

12 headlong,] B13 B32 B46 C8 F21 H8 NY3 O20 SP1 Y3 A; ~;   O21; ~∧   Σ.
wild,] B13 B32 H8 NY1 NY3 O20 SP1 VA2; ~;   O21; ~∧   Σ.   vncertaine] ~,
O21; incerteine   Y3.   thee?] ~∧   B33 F21 NP3 Y3; ~;   C5 O21; ~.   P3 VA1 Y2.

13 First] ~,   B–G.   sweare] ~,   B33 OQ1; ~ here   C9 H6; ~ to me   NY1
VA2.   loue] ~,   Y2; ~, here,   B C; ~ here,   D–G.   in] **   H8; & ~   Y2.
earnest] ~,   B32 C8 H5 HH1 O20 SP1; ***nest   H8; ~.   O21.

14 (If] ∧~   B32 C5 HH1 NP3 O21 Y3.   thou] ~,   H6.   which] who   C9
H6.   Lovst] louest   B47 C5 C8 H3 HH1 NP3 NY1 O21 OQ1 P3 SP1 VA1 VA2
Y3; Lovd → ›~‹   NY3.   all,] ~∧   B33 B47 C2 C5 H8 NY1 P3 VA1 VA2 Y2 Y3;
~;   O21.   canst] can   B13 B33 F21 HH1 OQ1 Y2 Y3; om   H3 NP3.   loue]
loust   H3.   any] me   O21 Y3.   best)] ~∧   C5 NP3 Y3; ~.   HH1 O21; ~,)
SP1.

15 me] om   F21 VA2.   in the] ithe   IU2.   middle] ~-   H5 O21 SP1; om
IU2.   Street] ~,   B13 B32 B40 C2 C8 H5 HH1 O20 P3 SP1 A–G.

16 spruce] spouce → »~«   H3; ~-   H7.   companion] Companions → »~«
H3; Companion»s«   H3.   do] B13 B33 C5 HH1 NY1 NY3 OQ1 P3 SP1 VA1
VA2; dost   Σ.   meet.] ~,   B13 B32 H4 H5 O20 SP1 VA2 A–G; ~∧   B33 B46
B47 C5 C9 DT1 F21 H3 H6 H7 HH1 IU2 NP3 NY1 P3 VA1 Y3; ~;   B40; ~.|
OQ1.

17 Not] ~,   H4 SP1; No   IU2 Y2.   though a] tho'a   IU2.   Captane] ~;
O21.   way] ~,   B32 B40 C8 H5 HH1 NP3 O20 SP1; ~;   O21; ~.   VA1.

18 Bright] ~,   H4; ~· VA2.   parcell-guilt] B46 C5 H5 H7 NY1 NY3 SP1; ~∧
~,   B13 B32 B40 C2 C8 HH1 O20 Y2 A–G; ~∧ ~;   O21; ~∧ ~   Σ.   with] wi'
IU2.   dead mens] ~=~   H3 SP1 VA2; ~ means   C5.   pay.] ~,   B13 B32 B40
C2 C8 H4 O20 A; ~∧   B33 B47 C5 C9 DT1 F21 H3 H6 H7 IU2 NP3 Y3; ~;   H5
H8 O21 P3 SP1; ~:   HH1 OQ1 B–G.

19 Nor] Not   B13 B33 B47 C2 C5 C8 HH1 NP3 NY1 O21 OQ1 P3 VA1 VA2 Y3
A–G; No   Y2.   though a] ~, ~   B13; tho'a   IU2.   briske] Brissle   B46; ~,
H5; ~· H7 SP1; bright   HH1.   perfum'd] ~,   B13 H3 H5; perfumed   F21
HH1; ~· H7 SP1.   pert] om   B46; ~· H7 SP1; young   IU2; neat   OQ1 Y2.
Courtier] ~,   C8 OQ1 P3.

20 Deigne] dam'd   O21; daign'd   Y3.   nod] ~,   B32 C8 HH1 O20 OQ1 VA1
A–G.   thy] a   IU2.   curtesy] curtesies   B13 B33 B46 B47 C5 H5 H6 HH1
NY1 OQ1 P3 VA1 VA2 Y2; Curtsies→ ›courtsies‹   C9; Courtsie   IU2.
answer.] ~,   B13 C2 H4 H7; ~∧   B33 B40 B47 C5 DT1 F21 H3 IU2 NP3 P3 VA1
Y3; ~:   H5 HH1 OQ1 B–G; ~;   H8 SP1.

21 Nor] ~,   H4 H8.   come a] ~, ~   B13; om ~   F21; tho'a   IU2; comes ~
NP3; though ~   NY1 VA2; came ~   O21 Y3; (~ ~   P3 VA1.   veluet] vertues
H3; ~· H7 NP3 SP1.   Iustice] ~,   B13 B40 B47 H5 H6 HH1 NY1 VA2; ~;
O21 OQ1.   with] come   IU2.   a long] along   IU2.

22 Great] With   IU2.   of] o   IU2.   blew-cotes] ~∧ ~   B13 B32 B40 B47
C5 F21 H4 H6 NP3 O21 OQ1 P3 VA1 Y2 Y3; blewcoats   B33 B46 C9 IU2;
Blewcoats,   C2; ~·~,   C8 DT1 H8 G; ~∧ ~,   H3 HH1 A–F; *lewe∧ ~   O20.
12] ~,   B13 B32 H4 O20 SP1 A–F.   14] xiii   B32 F21 H3 IU2 O21 SP1 Y3;
~· B–F.   strong,] ~∧ B13 B32 B33 B40 B46 B47 C9 DT1 H3 H4 H6 H8 IU2
NP3 Y2 Y3; ~?   C2; ~.   C8 F21 H5 HH1 NY1 VA2; ~;   O21; ~)   P3 VA1.

23 Shallt] Wilt   B40 C2 C8 DT1 H4 Y2 A–G; Shall   H3 NP3.   thou] you
H3.   grin] gyrne,   B13; ~,   B32 B40 C2 C8 H4 H7 HH1 O20 P3 SP1 B C;
girne   B47 C5 NY3 Y3; once grimn   NP3.   or fawne on him,] and ~ ~ ~,   B32
C5 NY3 O20 SP1; of ~ ~ ~,   B33; ~ ~ ~ ~∧   B46 H3 VA1; ~ ~ ~ ~:   NP3; ~ ~ ~
~;   NY1 VA2; on him, or fawne;   O21; on him, fawen,   Y2; one him or fawne∧
Y3.   or] om   NP3.   prepare] ~.   C5; ~,   H4 HH1 OQ1.

24 Speach] ~,   C8 HH1.   bewteous] virtuous   Y2.   Sone] ~,   B13 SP1.
and] an   B46; or   Y2.   heire.] ~;   B32 O20 O21; ~∧   B33 B47 C5 H3 H6 NP3
VA1 Y3; ~?   B40 C2 C8 DT1 H4 H5 H7 OQ1 A–G; ~:   C9 F21 Y2; ~,   H8.

25 better] ~,   B13 H4 H7.   or] &   B13 B32 B33 B46 C5 H5 HH1 NY1
NY3(→ ›~‹) VA2.   worse] ~,   B13 B40 DT1 H7 HH1 SP1; for ~   C9 F21 H8
NP3 NY1 O21 VA2 Y3.   me,] ~∧   B33 C5 C8 H3 NY1 P3 VA1 VA2 Y3; om
B47 H8 NP3; ~|,   H6; ~;   O21 OQ1.   or] and → ›~‹   B33; ar   B46; and   C5;

~, C9; ~| H6.   mee,] B40 C8 H7 OQ1 P3; ~.   B32 B46 H4 O20; ~;   H5 H8 O21 SP1; ~:   A–G; ~∧   Σ.

26 take] ~,   B13 B32 B40 C2 C9 F21 H4 H7 HH1 SP1 A–G.   and] ~,   C9; |~| H6; or   Y2.   me,] B13 B32 B40 C8 F21 H5 HH1 NY3; ~∧   Σ.   is] both's   NP3; were   Y2.   adulteree.] ~;   B32 F21 O20; ~:   B40 H8; ~∧   B47 DT1 H3 H4 H6 NP3 O21 Y3; ~..   C5; ~!   OQ1.

27 Monster,] B32 F21 NY3 O20; ~∧   B33 B46 HH1 Y2; Monstrous,   C2 A–G; ~!   H5 NY1 SP1 VA2; Monstrous∧   Σ.   Puritane] ~,   F21 O20 O21 A–F.

28 refind] refyned   HH1.   manners,] ~;   B13 HH1 O21 OQ1; ~!   B40 H7; ~∧   B46 H6 NP3 VA2.   ceremonial] Cerimonious   H3 O21 Y3; ~-   SP1; ceremonicall   Y2.   man,] B32 C2 OQ1 A–G; ~.   B33 B46 HH1 NY3 SP1; ~!   H5 NY1 VA2; ~;   H8 O21; ~∧   Σ.

29 meetst] meetest   B32 C5 F21 HH1 O20 O21 SP1 Y3; meetes   B47 H7 Y2.   one,] ~∧   B33 B46 B47 C5 F21 H3 H8 NP3 O21 VA1 Y3; me∧   B40; ~;   H7 NY1 VA2; him∧   Y2.   inquyring] refin'd   O21 Y3.   eyes] lyes   B32; lyes, C2(→ ›~,‹) C8(→ »~,«); ~,   HH1 OQ1; ~;   A(unc).

30 Dost] Doest   B33 C5 OQ1 VA1; doth   HH1.   search,] ~∧   B33 B46 B47 C5 C9 H4 H6 NP3 NY1 O21 OQ1 VA1 VA2 Y2 Y3.   like] (~   H5.   a] an   Y2.   broker] ~,   B32 B40 F21 O20; ~)   H5; Brokeres   NP3; brooker   Y3.   prize] ~,   HH1 O21.

31 silke] ~,   B13 C2 DT1 H7 P3 SP1 A–F.   weares,] ~∧   B33; ~;   O21 Y2; wares, G.   rate] ~;   B13; ~,   F21 H5 HH1 OQ1 G; patt.   O21 Y3(∧).

32 high] ~,   B13 DT1 H4 H5 H7 P3 SP1.   or] and   NP3.   low] ~,   B13 B40 C2 C8 H7 HH1 P3 A–G.   dost] doest   B33 C5 H8 HH1 OQ1 VA1; dothe   H3.   vaile] rayse   B32 B40 B46 C2 C8 DT1 F21 H4 NP3 O20 SP1 A–G.   thy] the   VA1.   formall] former   Y2.   hatt.] hate∧   B32 C5 NP3 Y2; ~∧   B33 B47 DT1 H3 H4 H7 P3 VA1 Y3; ~:   B40 B46 C2(→ ›Hate‹) C8 H8 OQ1 A(cor); ~,   C9 H6 HH1; ~;   H5 SP1; hate: A(unc).

33 That] Thou   B46 B47 H6(→ ›~‹) P3.   wilt] will   H3 HH1 SP1 Y2; witt   NP3.   none,] ~∧   B33 B40 F21 NY1 P3 VA1 VA2; with ~∧   B46 C9 H7 H8 NP3; with ~,   B47 H3 H5 H6 Y3; wᶜ ~;   O21.   vntill] till   B13 B46 B47 C9 H3 H6 H8 NP3 O21 OQ1 P3 VA1 Y3 G.   thou haue] ~ hast   B13 B46 B47 C9 H3 H6 H7 H8 NP3 O21 OQ1 P3 VA1 Y2 Y3; th'hast   H5.   knowen] B46 F21 NY3 P3 VA1 Y2; knowne,   SP1; knowne   Σ.

34 Lands] lande   H3 NP3.   in] of   NP3.   hope,] ~∧   B33 B47 C9 H3 H6 NP3 NY1 P3 VA1 VA2 Y2 Y3; ~;   H5 O21 OQ1.   owne.] ~,   B13 C8 C9 H6 O21 Y2 A; ~∧   B32 B33 B47 DT1 H3 NP3 Y3; ~;   B40 H5 H7; ~:   H4 OQ1.

35 As though all] ~ thou ~   HH1; Nor hope yᵗ   IU2; ~ if ~   NY1 VA2; ~ ~ om   P3.   companions] ~,   C8 H7.   thee] the   F21 IU2.

36 loyntures,] loynters,   B13 B32 B47 C9 F21 H5 H6 HH1 O20 P3; loynters∧
B46 H3 IU2 VA1 Y3; ~∧   C5 VA2 Y2; Iointeres;   O21.   and] or   H3(*var:* »~«)
H8 NP3.   mary] B32 IU2(marie) NY3; manie   H3(→ ›monie‹ [*var:* »marry«]);
marrie   B13 B46 B47 C8 DT1 OQ1 SP1; marry   Σ.   companee.] ~∧   B33 B47
C5 F21 H3 IU2 NP3 P3 Y2 Y3; ~,   H4; ~;   O21; ~:   OQ1.

37 Why] But ~   B46.   shouldst] shouldest   B40 C5 F21 SP1 VA1.   thou,]
B32 B40 C5 C8 H3 H7 NY3 O20 SP1 B; ~;   O21; ~∧   Σ.   that] (~   B13 B46
B47 H5 H8 NP3 NY1 OQ1 P3 VA1 VA2 D–G.   dost not only] doest ~ ~   B33
C5 HH1 OQ1 VA1; not onlie dost   B46 B47 C9 H5 H6 H8(doest) NP3 O21 Y3.
approue] ~,   B32 C8 H5 H7 H8 O20 OQ1 P3 A–G.

38 ranke] ~-   NP3 SP1.   itchy] itchlie   B46; it thy   B47; itchthy   NP3;
itching   Y2.   Lust] B46 C9 H3 H5 H6 H8 HH1 NY1 NY3 O21 OQ1 SP1 VA1
VA2 Y3; best   B47; ~)   H7 NP3; ~,   Σ.   desyre] ~,   B13 B32 B40 B46 C2 DT1
H4 H5 H7 H8 O20 SP1 A–G.   loue] ~,   C2 F21 P3 D–G; ~.   C5; ~;   HH1
O21.

39 nakednesse] ~,   B13 B32 B40 B46 C8 DT1 F21 H4 H7 H8 O20 P3 SP1; naked
nest,   H3.   barenesse] barrennesse   B40 B46 B47 C2 C8 DT1 H4 H7 NP3 O21
Y2 A–G; ~,   F21; ~ → ›barenness‹   HH1.   inioy] ~,   B13 C5 C8 HH1 OQ1
P3 A–G.

40 Of] yf HH1.   thy] the   B46 B47 H7.   plump] ~-   H7 SP1; lumpe;
O21; lumpe   Y3.   muddy] ~-   H7 SP1; ~;   O21.   whore] B33 B47 C5 H3
NP3 NY1 NY3 O21 OQ1 P3 VA1 Y2 Y3; ~;   H7; ~,   Σ.   or] om   B46 B47 C9
H6 O21 Y3 B–F; and   P3 VA1 Y2.   prostitute] prostituted   P3 VA1.   boy,]
~)   B13 B46 B47 H5 H8 NY1 OQ1 P3 VA1 VA2; ~;   B32 F21 O20 B C; ~∧   B33
C2 C5 C9 DT1 H3 H4 H6 HH1 NP3 NY3 O21 Y2 Y3 A; ~:   B40; ~.   C8; ~?   H7
SP1; ~;)   D–G.

41 vertu] ~,   B32 B46 C2 C8 DT1 F21 H3 H4 H5 HH1 NY1 O20 OQ1 SP1
A–G; not ~   IU2.   she] om   IU2.   be naked] ~ ~,   B13 C2 H4 O20 SP1
A–C; om ~   B46 IU2; naked be   F21 NP3 NY1 O21 VA2 Y3; ~ nak't,   H7; ~
nak'd   P3.   and] or   IU2.   bare?] B13 B46 C9 H5 H6 HH1 NY1 OQ1 VA2
B–G; ~,   B32 B40 C2 SP1 A(*unc*); ~;   C8 F21 H7 H8 O20; ~:   P3 A(*cor*); ~∧   Σ.

42 At] "~   NY1 VA2.   birthe,] B13 B32 C2 DT1 HH1 NY3 SP1 A–G; Births∧
B46 B47 C9 H5 H6; ~;   O21; ~∧   Σ.   death] ~,   B13 C2 HH1 SP1 A–G;
Deathes   B46 B47 C9 H5 H6; dead,   O21.   are:] B40 NY3 OQ1; ~,   B13 C9
H5 H6 H7 O21; ~.   B32 C2 C8 F21 HH1 NY1 O20 SP1; ~;   H8 P3 A–G; ~∧   Σ.

43 And] "~   NY1 VA2; ~,   B–G.   till] tell   NY3.   Soules] bodies   F21.
be] are   IU2 P3.   vnapparelled] ~.   B46; ~,   C5 HH1; vn›-a‹paraled   O20;
~, → ›~‹   OQ1.

44 Of] Our   B33; From   IU2; "~   NY1 VA2.   bodyes,] ~∧   B33 HH1 IU2
NP3; ~;   H3 H7 O21.   from] of   IU2.   are] be   C9.   banished.] ~.|
B13; ~∧   B33 B47 C5 DT1 H4 IU2 NP3 O21 VA1 Y3; ~:   B40 OQ1 C–G.

45 Mans] (~ H8; "~ NY1 VA2.   first] ~, O21.   blest] best B13 B33
B47 C5 C9 H6 H7 H8 NP3 NY1 OQ1 P3 VA1 VA2 Y2 Y3; blist   C2; *om*
HH1(»best«); best, O21.   State] ~, C8 O21.   naked,] ~: B13; ~ₐ C5 H3
H7 NP3 Y2; ~; P3 VA1 D–G.   Sin] ~, H3.

46 He] "~ NY1 VA2.   that,] it; B13; ~ₐ B32 Y2; itₐ H3; it, H8 HH1
NP3 OQ1 P3 VA1; ~; O21.   yet] *om* B46 B47 C9 H3 H5 H6 H8 NP3 O21 P3
VA1 Y3 B–G.   he was] was he OQ1.   clothd] Clothed B40 B47 C5 P3;
~, B46 C2 NY1 O20; Clothed, F21 HH1 Y3; ~; O21.   but] *om* C5 NP3.
beasts] beast F21 H3; a ~ NP3; *om* P3.   skin.] ~, B13 C9 H4 H5 H8 HH1
O21 A–G; ~ₐ B33 B47 C5 DT1 F21 H3 H6 H7 NP3 VA1 Y3; ~; B40; ~.| C2;
~: OQ1.

47 this] that B32(→ »~«).   course] coarse B–G.   attire] ~, B13 B32 C2
F21 H5 O20 SP1 A–G; ~; HH1 OQ1.   now I] I now B32 B40 C2 C8 DT1
H4 H5 O20 SP1 Y2 A–G; ~, ~ VA1; ~ *om* Y3.   weare] ~, B32 F21 H5 HH1
O20 VA1 D–G.

48 God] Gods, B13; ~, B32 B40 B46 C2 DT1 H7 NP3 O20 SP1 A–G; god
B47 C5 O21 VA2 Y2 Y3; god, C8 H4; gods OQ1 P3 VA1.   Muses] ~, B40
O20.   confer.] ~.| B13 B40 H6; ~ₐ B32 B33 B47 DT1 H3 H7 NP3 VA1 Y3;
~: C5; ~, F21 H4 OQ1.

49 since] ~, SP1.   thou] ~, B46 H6.   like] (~ B46 HH1.   penitent]
~, B32 H6 OQ1 A–G; ~) HH1.

50 warnd] warned B47 F21 P3; warned, HH1 Y2; ~; O21; warm'd A(*unc*).
of] by B32 F21 O20 SP1; *om* HH1.   sins] ~, B13 B40 C2 C8 C9 H5 H6
NP3 NY1 O20 P3 A–C; sinne, B32; sinne B33; ~) B46; Sin F21.   dost]
doest B33 C5 HH1 OQ1 VA1.   repent] ~, B13 B32 C8 F21 O20 OQ1;
~. B46; ~; HH1.

51 These] Those H3; Thy H8 NP3; Th'are O21 Y3; ~, P3.   vanities] ~,
B13 B32 B40 C2 DT1 F21 H3 H4 H7 O20 SP1 A–G; ianities HH1; ~; O21.
giddinesses;] B13 B40 B46 C8 H8 NY3 Y2; Giddines, B32; ~ₐ B47 C5 H3 O21
Y3; ~. H6 VA1 VA2; ~: H7 NY1 OQ1 P3; ~! NP3; Giddiness; O20 SP1;
~, Σ.   Lo] ~, B32 DT1 F21 H8 NY1; soe B47 C2(→ ›~‹) O21 Y3; ~. VA1.

52 chamber] ~~ B46.   dore] B47 C5 NP3 NY3 OQ1 P3 Y3; ~; B46 H8 O21;
~, Σ.   come] ~, B13 B40 B47 C2 DT1 H3 H5 H6 O20 OQ1 SP1 A–G; ~:
B46 H8; ~; C9.   go.] ~ₐ B33 B47 C5 NP3 O21 Y2 Y3; ~; B40; ~, H4 A;
~: H8; ~! OQ1.

53 cheape] ~~ SP1.   whore] ~, B40 C2 C8 F21 H3 H6 HH1 SP1 A–G.
that] who C9 H6 HH1 NP3 A–G; (~ H5 H8 P3 VA1.   beene] ~, C5 C8
OQ1.

54 Worne] ~, HH1; ~ out D–G.   in] on B47; as O21.   Sin] ~, B32
B40 F21 H5 NY1 O20 OQ1 VA2 A–G; ~. C2 C5; ~; O21.

55 As] (~ O21 Y3.   are] bee O21 Y3.   black] ~- DT1.   feathers] B33
C5 NP3 NY1 NY3 OQ1 P3 VA1 Y2; ~;   O21; ~,   Σ.   or] and   NP3.
musk-color] muskcollered   B13 NY1 OQ1; ~ₐ ~   B32 F21 O20 SP1; ~ₐ Collored
B33 H3 NP3 O21 P3 VA1 Y2 Y3; Muskecollour   B40 C8; ~=colored   B46 H5 H8
VA2 C–G; ~ₐ coullerd   B47 C5 H7 HH1; ~-colourd   C9 H6.   hose] ~,   B32
C5 C8 DT1 H4 H6 HH1 O20 A–G; Clothes   H3; ~)   H5 H8 P3 VA1; ~;   O21.

56 Name] names B47; knowe O21 Y3.   childs] Childe   C5 H3(→ »~«)
VA2.   right] om   B13 C9 H6 OQ1 P3 VA1.   trew] om   B47 O21 Y2 Y3.
father] ~,   B40 B47 C2 C8 F21 H7 NY1 VA2 A–G.   mongst] amongst   B47 C9
H6 O21 OQ1 Y3; amonge   H3 P3 VA1.   all those;] ~ ~ₐ   B13 B33 B46 B47 C5
DT1 F21 H7 HH1 VA1 VA2; ~ ~.   B32 C8 H6 O20 P3; ~ ~:   C2 H8 NY1 OQ1
Y2 A–G; om ~ₐ   H3 Y3; ~ ~,   H4; althose,   NP3; om ~,   O21.

57 guesse] gueste,   B32(→ »~«) SP1; ~,   C2 C8 H5 H7 NY1 O20 O21 A–G.
away] a waye   B13 VA2; ~,   C8; a-way   H7.

58 Th'infant of] B33 B47 H5 H7 HH1 NY1 NY3 VA2; The Infanta ~   B13 H8
OQ1 P3 VA1; The Infant, in   B46; Th'Infanta ~   C9 H6; Th'Infanta'of NP3;
The Infantry ~   G; The Infant ~   Σ.   London,] ~;   B13; ~ₐ   B32 B33 B47
C5 C9 F21 H5 H6 NP3 NY3 O20 O21 OQ1 P3 VA1 Y2 Y3.   heire] theire   B47;
Th'heire H7; borne   H8; borne ~   NP3; heis   O21 Y3; hence   G.   an] om
B46 H5 VA2 Y2 G; rich   B47 H7 O21 Y3.   India;] ~ₐ   B13 B33 B47 F21 H3 H7
NP3 P3 Y3; ~.   B32 B46 C5 C8 H8 O20 VA1 Y2; ~,   C2 DT1 H4 H6 OQ1 A; ~:
NY1 VA2 B–G.

59 gulling] ~- B33 H7; om   Y2.   Weather-Spy] ~ₐ ~   B13 B33 B47 C2 C8
H3 O21 VA1 Y3 A(unc); weatherspye,   B32 O20; ~ₐ ~,   B40; weatherspie   F21;
~=~,   NY1; ~ₐ guller ~   Y2.
    Alternate line: Tell me thou subtile gulling, weather-spie,   33a–b.

60 drawing] laying Y2.   forth] but   H3.   heauens] Heau'ns   DT1 H3 H4
H7; weathers   HH1.   Scheame,] ~ₐ   B13 B46(M var: »Skeame«) B47 C5 C9
H8 P3 VA1 VA2 D–G; Scheames,   B40 SP1(M var: »Skeame«); Scenes,   C2
DT1 H4 A; Sceanes,   C8; Sceane,   H3 Y3; schæmes,   H7 Y2; om   NP3; scene;
O21.   certainly] ~,   B32 OQ1.

61 fashiond] fashione   F21 P3 VA1; fashioned   HH1 NP3 A.   hatts,] ~ₐ
B33 F21 H5 NP3 OQ1 Y2 Y3; suites,   C9 H6; ~;   O21.   ruffs,] ~ₐ   C9 F21 H5
H6 O21 OQ1 Y2 Y3; sutes,   HH1; suits,   33a–b.   or] om   Y2.   Suites] ~,
B47 NY1 O20 33a–b; hatts   C9 H6; ruffes   HH1; shirtes;   O21; shooes, → ›~‹
VA1; om   Y2; shirtes   Y3; bands,   33a–b.   yeare] ~,   B13 B32 OQ1; ~;   O21.

62 Our] or B13.   supple-witted] ~ₐ ~   B13 B47 C5 OQ1 P3 VA1 VA2;
subtle-~   B32 F21 O20; subtle, wittyed   B40 C2 C8 H5 A–F; subtle=~=   B46;
subtill-wittied   DT1; subtill, ~   H3 33a–b; subtile=wittied,   H4; ~-~-   H7; ~ₐ
~,   HH1; ~-headed   NP3; ~-~   NY1(M var: »subtile«); suppled; witty;   O21;

subtle-~, SP1; subtile, wittie Y2; suppled, witty Y3; giddy-headed G.
antick] B46 B47 C9 H4 H5 H6 NP3 NY1 NY3 P3 VA1 D–G 33a–b; antique- H7;
antique; O21; antique Σ.   Youths] youthe H3 H7 G; ~; O21.   will]
shall B46 B47 H5.   weare] ~, B13 B32 B40 DT1 F21 H4 H7 HH1 O20 P3
SP1; ~. B46 C2 C8 O21 33a–b; ~; H5 A; ~? OQ1; ~: VA2 B–G.

63 Then] Than H3.   thou] ~, B32 B40 B46 C2 C8 DT1 F21 H4 H5 HH1,
O20 SP1 Y2 A–G.   departst] departest B13 B32 B46 B47 C5 C9 H3 H5 H6
NP3 NY1 O20 OQ1 P3 VA1 VA2 Y3; deptest, O21; departs Y2.   from] om
B13 B46 B47 C9 H3 H5 H6 NP3 NY1 O21 OQ1 P3 VA1 VA2 Y3.   hence] ~,
B32 F21 H5 H7 O20 OQ1 SP1; me B40 C2 C8 DT1 H4; thence, HH1; thence
O21; mee, A–G.   canst] can B32 B33 B40 B46 C2 C8 F21 H4 H7 O20 SP1
Y2 A–G.   show] ~, B40 C8 O20 O21 SP1.

64 Whither,] Wheather, B32 B47 C5 F21 H5 H7 HH1 NP3 NY3 O20 P3 SP1
VA1 Y2; ~; O21; ~, Y3.   why,] ~; O21; ~, Y3.   when,] wheare,
B13 B33 HH1 NY1 OQ1 P3 VA1 VA2; ~; O21; ~, Y3 G.   whom] ~, B40
F21.   thou wouldst] tho'uldst B13 OQ1 VA1; ~ wouldest C5 SP1.   go.]
~, B33 B47 C5 H3 HH1 NP3 VA1 Y2 Y3; ~; B40; ~, DT1 F21 H4 OQ1.

65 But] ~, HH1 VA1.   pardond] pardoned B13 B40 B47 C2 C5 C8 DT1
H4 H5 H7 HH1 NP3 OQ1 P3 SP1 VA1.   my] myne B13 C8 C9 H6 H7 NP3
O21 OQ1 P3 SP1 VA1 Y3.   offence] ~, B13 B32 C5 C8 H4 H5 HH1 O20 O21
SP1; ~? Y2.

66 sind] sinned B47 HH1; sayd O21 Y3.   conscience?] ~. B33 C2 C5 C8
NY1 P3 VA1 VA2 Y2 A; ~, B40 B47 H3 NP3 Y3; ~, H4 O21.

67 Now] But SP1.   in the] i'th NY1 VA2.   street:] streets; B32; ~,
B33 B40 DT1 H3 H4; ~; C2 C8 H7 O20 O21 A–G; streetes, B47 HH1 NP3;
~. C9 H6 NY1 VA2; streetes, H5; ~, Y2 Y3.   all] ~, B32 C8 F21 H6.

68 Improuidently] (~ B13 H5 NP3 OQ1; Unprouidently B33 B47 C5 C9 H6
HH1 O21 Y3.   proud] B33 B47 C5 F21 NY1 NY3 O21 P3 VA2 Y3; ~) B13 H5
NP3 OQ1; ~, Σ.   to] next H3 NP3.   wall] ~, B13 B32 B40 C8 DT1 H5
H7 HH1 O20 OQ1 VA2 A; ~. B46 C2 NY1; ~: C5 P3; ~; O21 B–G.

69 imprisond] ~, B13 B32 H7 O20 OQ1 SP1 VA2 B–G; imprysoned, B40 C2
HH1 A; imprisoned B47 C8 P3 VA1 Y3.   hemm'd] hemmed HH1.   in] ~,
B40.   mee] ~, B40 C8 DT1 H5 HH1 NY1 O20 VA2.

70 Sells] sell B47.   for] (~ OQ1.   state] »roome« B33; ~, B46 H4 H5
HH1 SP1 VA1; ~) OQ1.   his] high A.   Libertee.] ~; B13 B40 H4 B–G;
~, B33 B47 H3 NP3 P3 VA1 Y2 Y3; ~: C5 DT1 H7 O21 OQ1; ~, A.

71 Yet] and B47; ~, H6.   cannot] can nott HH1 Y2; ~, O21.   skip
forth now] now step forth B46 B47 C9 H5 H6 H7 NP3 Y3; step ~ ~ HH1; now

sett foorth   O21.   greet] ~,   B13 B32 C8 P3; meete   F21.
   Alternate line: Goe & skip forth to greet   IU2.

   72 Euery] ~-   H7; Evry   IU2; ~;   O21.   fine] ~,   C8 DT1 H4; ~-   H7 SP1;
~;   O21.   silken] painted   B46 C9 H6 NY1 VA2 Y3; om   B47; ~,   C8 DT1
H4; painted,-   H7; painted;   O21.   painted] silken   B46 C9 H6 NY1 O21 VA2
Y3; om   C5; pointed   H3; silken-   H7.   foole] ~,   B32 DT1 F21 O20.   we]
you   IU2; he   O21 Y3.   meet,] ~∧   B33 B47 C9 DT1 F21 H3 H7 IU2 NP3 P3
VA1 Y2; ~;   B40 C8 H4; ~.   B46; ~:   NY1; meetes.   O21; meetes∧   Y3.

   73 He] ~,   SP1.   them] then   B46 B47 H3 A.   him] ~,   B13 B40 C8 F21.
smiles] looks   NP3.   allures] ~,   B13 B40 C8 DT1 H5 HH1 NY1 OQ1 A–G.
   Alternate line: Who Thee from me wᵗʰ am'rous smile allures   IU2.

   74 grins,] ~∧   B47 H3 IU2 P3; girne,   C5; grimms,   NP3; ~;   O21.   smacks,]
shure∧   H3; ~∧   IU2 P3 Y2; ~;   O21.   shruggs,] Shugs,   B46 Y3; shugges∧
B47; ~∧   H3 IU2 P3; shuges;   O21.   such] ~,   B32; willinge   H3.   an] and
B32(→ »-«) O20; om   F21 H3.   indures] ~,   B13 C2 C8 H5 H6 O20 A–G.

   75 Prentices] ~,   B13 B32 B40 C2 C8 DT1 F21 H4 H7 O20 P3 SP1 VA1 A.
or] and   B46 B47 C9 H6 NP3 O21 Y3.   Schooleboyes] ~,   B13 B46 C8 H4 H6
HH1 Y3 B C; schoole boyes   B32 IU2 NP3 Y2; schoole-boyes,   DT1 H5 OQ1;
Schoole=boyes   H3 H7 SP1 VA2 A; schoole boyes,   P3 VA1.   which] who
NP3.   know] ~,   B32 C2 C8.

   76 gay] play   NP3.   sport] sports   P3.   abroade,] ~∧   B32 B33 B40 B47
C5 H4 IU2 NP3 NY1 O21 VA2 Y2; ~;   HH1.   yet] &   B47; but   IU2 NY1
VA2.   go.] ~,   B32 B40 C2 H4; ~∧   B33 B47 F21 H3 IU2 NP3 O21 VA1 Y2 Y3;
~:   DT1; ~;   H5 O20; ~.| OQ1.

   77 as] att   F21.   fidlers] fidler*   O21.   stop] lowest   B46; stoope   H3;
a   Y2.   lowest] ~,   B13 B32 C2 C8 H4 H7 O20 OQ1 Y3 A–C; lowst   B33 C9
H6 Y2; stop,   B46; ~;   O21.   higest] NY3; highest,   B46; the highest   H4
OQ1; hiest   P3 Y3; highest   Σ.   Sound] ~;   B13 HH1; ~,   B40 C8 DT1 H5
O20 A–G; ~.   O21.

   78 So] ~,   HH1.   most] om   H3 OQ1 P3.   braue] ~;   B13 O21; ~,   B32
B46 B47 C2 C5 C8 H7 HH1 O20 SP1 Y2 A–G; brauest   H3 OQ1 P3.   stoopes]
stoopte   B40 C2 C8 DT1 H4 H7 Y2 A; stoopeth   HH1; ~,   VA2; stopt   Y2.
he] ~,   B40 OQ1.   nighest] nigh'st   B33 B40 B47 C8 C9 DT1 H4 H5 H6 H7
A–G; the ~   C2; neerest   HH1.   ground.] ~;   B13 O21; the ~∧   B33 B47 C8
DT1 H6; the ~;   B40 NY1; the ~.   B46 Y2 A–G; ~∧   C5 H3 NP3 VA1 Y3; yᵉ
~,   C9 H4 H7 VA2; the ~:   F21 H5; ~:   OQ1; ~,   P3.

   79 to] om   OQ1.   graue man] ~ ~,   B32 B40 B46 B47 C2 C8 DT1 H4 H5
HH1 NY1 O20 OQ1 A; ~-~   H7; ~-~,   SP1; braue ~   Y2.   doth] doeth   C5
VA1.   move] stope   Y2.   more] ~,   B32 C8 H5 HH1 O20 O21.

80 Then] Than   C–G.   the] om (→»~«) Y3.   wise] ~,   O21; ~ SP1.
politique] ~,   O21.   horse] ~,   H7 O21.   would] did   B47 O21 Y3.
hertofore] ~,   B13 B32 DT1 H5 O20 P3 SP1 A–G; ~:   B40 OQ1; ~.   C2 C8 H7;
om   NP3; ~;   NY1; here-tofore.   VA2; here to fore.   Y2.

81 *line om*   A.   thou] ~,   B46 H5 HH1 P3 VA1 VA2; then   NP3.   O] .~.
B13; an   NP3.   Elephant] B33 B47 C2 C5 C8 C9 H3 H6 NP3 NY1 NY3 O21
OQ1 VA2 Y2 Y3; ~, Σ.   Ape] ~,   B46; ox   O21 Y3.   wilt] would'st   B47
H3 O21 Y3; would   NP3; will   Y2.   do] ~,   B32 B40 C5 C8 HH1 O20 OQ1
B–G.

82 *line om*   A.   names] name   B47 H3 P3 VA1.   king] K.   B33; ~ H3.
of] ~ H3.   you.] ~∧   B33 B47 H3 H4 NP3 Y3; ~;   B40 O21 P3; ~:   HH1; ~?
OQ1.

83 he] ~,   P3.   vpright,] ~∧   B47 H6 NP3 Y3; ~;   H7 NY3; vp=right,   Y2.
ioggs] iooes →io»y«es   HH1; waggs   NP3.   me,] ~∧   B33 C5 C9 H6 HH1 SP1
VA1 Y3.   and] om   B46 B47 H5 NP3.   cryes] ~,   B32 B40 C2 C8 C9 DT1
H5 H6 HH1 NY1 O20 SP1 A–G.   do you see] om om om   B13 OQ1 VA1;
D' yee ~   B46 C9 H5 H6; ~ yee ~   B47; ~ ~ ~,   C5 C8; d' ~ ~   NP3; (~ ~ ~
VA2.

84 Yonder] doe you see ~   B13; doe yo^u see yon   OQ1 VA1; ~~~ ~~~ ~~~ yon
P3.   well fauord] ~ fauored   B32 B40 C2 O20 O21 P3 Y3 A; ~-~   B33 DT1;
welfauoured   B46 H3 HH1 OQ1 SP1; welfauor'd   B47 C8 H4 H6 NY1 VA1 VA2;
~ fashiond   C5; ~-favoured   H5 B–G.   Youth?] ~;   B33 C2 C8 O21 P3
A(*unc*); ~,   B47 C5 Y2 Y3; ~:   HH1 VA1; ~∧   NP3.   Which?] ~.   C5; ~∧
F21; why∧   NP3; ~,   O20 VA1; ~∧   O21 Y3.   Yea,] ~∧   B13 B33 B47 C5 HH1
NY1 O21 OQ1 P3 VA1 VA2 Y3; oh∧   B32 B46 C8 C9 DT1 F21 H3 H4 H6 H7
O20 SP1 Y2; oh!   B40; Oh,   C2 H5 A–G; see∧   NP3; ~.   NY3.   hee] ~.   C5;
~,   C8 SP1.

85 dances] daunceth   H5 NP3 O21 VA1 Y3.   diuinely.] ~;   B40 C2 C8 DT1
H4 H5 H7 O21 OQ1 A–G; ~,   B47 C5 F21 HH1 VA1 Y2; ~!   NP3; ~.).   VA2.
Oh] Or   B40 DT1 H4(*var:* »~«); ~,   C9 H3 H5 H6 A–C.   sayd] sayd   H7; (~
NY1.   I] ~,   B32 C5 H3 H6 O20 A–G; ~)   NY1.

86 still,] ~;   B13 NY1 SP1 VA2; ~∧   B47 C5 H3 NP3 O21 OQ1 Y3 G; ~.   H6.
must] & ~   Y2.   dance here] ~ to   B33; needs dance   H3; ~ there   O21;
heere dance   P3; ~ om   Y2.   company?] ~∧   B33 C5 NP3 O21 P3 VA1 Y3;
~,   HH1 Y2; ~.   NY1.

87 droopt:] B13 NY3 OQ1; ~∧   B33 NP3; droop'd;   B46; droop'd,   B47 D–G;
drooped,   C5 HH1; ~;   NY1 O21 SP1 VA2; ~:   OQ1; ~,   Σ.   We] he   H7
O21.   went:] C5 NY3; ~∧   B13 H4 NP3 OQ1; ~;   HH1; ~∧ on;   NY1 VA2;
wept;   O21; ~,   Σ.   till] (~ B13; tell   NY3.   one] ~,   H5; ~;   O21.

which] (~   B40 C2 C8 DT1 H4 H7 OQ1 A–G; yᵗ   C9 H3 NP3 Y2; (that   H5; (who   O21; who   VA2 Y3.   excell] ~,   C8.

88 Th'Indians] the Indians   B13 B47 C5 H3 NP3 OQ1 SP1 VA1 Y2; ~,   C2 C8 C9 A–C; Th'Indian   H7; the Indians,   HH1; yᵉ Indian   O21 P3 Y3; ~.   VA2. in] for   H3 OQ1 P3 VA1.   drinking] ~;   O21.   well] ~)   B13 B40 C2 DT1 H5 H7 O21 A–G; ~,   B32 B46 F21 HH1 O20; ~.   C5 VA1; ~,)   C8 H4; ~.) OQ1.

89 vs:] B32 H3 NP3 NY3 B–G; ~.   B13 F21 VA1; ~;   H5 H7 HH1 O20 P3 SP1 Y2; ~ₐ   Y3; ~,   Σ.   talkd:] talkt;   B13 H4 Y2; talked: B32 C5 SP1; talkt, B33 OQ1 Y3; talked;   B40 O20; talk't.   B46; ~,   B47 C9 H5 H6 H7 O21; ~;   C2 C8 DT1 NY1 A–G; talked,   F21 HH1; talkeₐ   H3 P3; talktₐ   NP3; talke.   VA1; talkt: VA2.   whisperd] ~;   B13; ~,   B32 B46 C9 H6 HH1 O20 P3 G; whispered,   B40(whisped,) B47 H5 OQ1 SP1 Y2 A–F; whisperedₐ   C2 C5 C8 H3 NP3.   let vs] let's   H3 P3 VA1; (letts   OQ1.   go:] NY3; ~,   B13 B40 H5 H7 HH1 O20 A–G; ~.   B46 SP1 VA2; ~,)   OQ1; ~ₐ   Σ.

90 May] T'may   B40 C2 C8 DT1 H4 H5 A–G; It ~   Y2.   be] ~,   C2. him] ~,   VA2.   not;] B13 HH1 NY1 NY3 VA2; ~ₐ   B47 F21 VA1 Y3; out; O21; ~,   Σ.   trewly] ~,   B47.   do.] ~:| B13; ~;   B32 B40 HH1 O20 O21 A; ~ₐ   B33 B47 F21 H3 H4 NP3 NY1 VA1 VA2 Y2 Y3; ~,   C2 OQ1 P3; ~:   H5 H7.

91 heares] heard   O21 Y3.   not me:] C5 NY3 OQ1; ~ ~;   B13 B32 H7 O20; ~ ~ₐ   H3 NP3 O21 P3 Y2 Y3; ~ ~.   NY1 VA2; me not,   VA1; ~ ~,   Σ.   but] ~,   A–G.   the other] thother   VA1.   side] ~,   C5 C8 HH1.

92 A] (~   B13.   many] ~=   OQ1 A.   colord] Coloured   B40 B46 C2 F21 H3 H5 HH1 NP3 O21 OQ1 P3 SP1 VA1 Y2 Y3 A–G.   peacock] Peacocks B40 B46 H3(→ »~«) H5 H6 H7 HH1 SP1 Y2 Y3 G; pecockes,   O21.   spied] spid'e)   B13; spide   B32 B33 B46 C2 C5 DT1 H3 H4 H7 NP3 NY1 O20 SP1 VA1 Y2 Y3; spide,   B40 C8 F21 H5 H6 O21 OQ1 A–G; spi'd.   C9.

93 him] ~,   B13 B40 B46 H7 SP1; ~;   H4 O21.   me:] C5 H5 NY3 OQ1 VA2 G; ~;   B13 B32 C2 C8 HH1 NY1 O20 SP1 A–F; ~.   H6; ~ₐ   Y3; ~,   Σ.   stay.] H6 SP1 VA1; ~,   B13 B32 B40 C8 C9 H5 O20 OQ1; ~;   A–G; ~ₐ   Σ.

94 followes,] ~ₐ   F21 H3 Y3; ~;   O21 SP1.   overtakes,] ~;   B13 O21; ~ₐ   B33 F21 Y3; ~,.   C5; over-takes,   B C.   goes] ~,   NY3 O20.   in] B13 B33 B47 C5 H3 H7 HH1 NY1(M var: »on«) NY3 OQ1 P3 VA1 VA2; on,   C2; on   Σ.   way] ~,   B32 B33 B40 C2 C5 C9 H5 HH1 O20 VA1 Y2 A–G; ~.   C8 H6 OQ1; ~.| H3; ~;   H7.

95 Saying,] ~ₐ   C5 F21 H4 O20 O21 P3 VA1 Y3; Leaueingeₐ   H3; ~;   H5 HH1; ~:   NY1 OQ1 VA2.   him,] B32 H7 O20 SP1; ~;   NY3; he;   O21; heeₐ   Y3; ~ₐ   Σ.   whom] (~   B13 P3 VA1.   lefte,] mett)   B13; ~ₐ   B33 B47 H3 H6

NP3 NY1 OQ1 Y2; left's, B40; ~; H4 O21; lost, HH1; ~) P3 VA1. all]
s'all C2 C8 A; ~- O21. repute] ~, C8 O21.

96 For] In B32 B46 F21 H3(var: »~«) H5 O20 SP1. deuise] ~, B32 B46 C2
F21 O20 A G. handsomming] hand somming B32; hand-sominge NP3.
sute,] B13 B32 B40 C2 H5 HH1 O20 O21 OQ1 A–G; ~. C8; shute_∧ NP3; ~;
NY3; ~_∧ Σ.

97 of] a H7. Lace,] ~; O21. pink,] Pinch, B32 DT1 F21 H4; pinch_∧
B40; ~_∧ C9 H6; pinkes; O21; pinckes, Y3. panes,] Pane, B46 C9 H5 H6
NP3; ~; DT1 O21. cutt, print,] ~, ~_∧ B33 B46 B47 F21 H3 NY1; print, Cutt,
B40 C2 C8 DT1 H4 H5 H7 A–C G; ~; ~, O21; ~_∧ ~, OQ1; ~_∧ ~_∧ VA2 Y3;
~_∧ om Y2; print_∧ cut, D–F. or] and B40 C2 C8 DT1 H4 A–G. pleight,]
playt_∧ B13 NY1 VA1 VA2; Plight, B32 B40 O20 A; ~_∧ B33 B47 C9 H3 H6
NY3 Y2; Pleate_∧ B46 HH1 NP3 O21 Y3; Plight_∧ C2 C5 DT1 F21 H4; plaite,
H7 P3; pleate, OQ1.

98 Court] ~, C2 C8 A; towne C9 H6; rest O21 Y3. to haue] t'~ B46.
conceit.] ~, B32 C2 C8 DT1 F21 O20 O21 P3; ~_∧ B33 B46 B47 C5 H3 H4 H6
NP3 VA1 Y2 Y3; ~; B40 C9 A–G; ~: H5.

99 Comedians] Comœdiant H3. him:] C5 H5 NP3 NY3 Y2; ~. B32 B46
NY1 O20 P3 VA2; ~_∧ H3 H7 VA1 Y3; ~; HH1 SP1; ~, Σ. him] me Y2.
go.] C5 C9 H5 H6; ~, B32 B40 C2 C8 O20 SP1; ~; A–G; ~_∧ Σ.

100 But] ~, B40 B46 H5 H6 HH1 D–G. oh] ~, C2 C8 DT1 H4 H6 O20
A–C; our H3; ~! H7 SP1. God] god B47 C5 C8 F21 H4 NY1 O21 OQ1 P3
VA1 VA2 Y2 Y3. thee,] ~; B13 Y2; ~_∧ B33 C5 H6 NP3 NY1 NY3 P3 VA1
VA2. stoopst] stopst C9 H6 VA1 B–F; sleep'st H3; stoopest HH1; stoopes
Y2. so?] ~, B32; ~_∧ B33 B46 H3 HH1 NP3 O21 P3 VA1 VA2 Y3; ~. C5
NY1.

101 Why:] NY3; ~, B32 A–C; ~? B46 C5 H5; om C8(»~«); ~; HH1; ~. G;
~_∧ Σ. he hath] om ~ C8(»~« ~); ~ had DT1 H4; hath he O21 Y3 D–F.
trauayld.] travell'd_∧ B13 B33 B40 DT1 F21 H4 NP3 O21; traueld; B46 H5;
traueld, B47; ~_∧ C2 C8 C9 H3 H6 H7 O20 OQ1 SP1 VA1; trauayled_∧ C5 A;
travelled_∧ HH1 Y2 Y3 B–G; ~; NY1 VA2; trauailed. P3. Long?] ~; B13
B40 C2 C8 DT1 H4 H7 O21 G; ~, B33 C9 H3 H6 OQ1 Y2 Y3; ~_∧ NP3; ~.
VA1. No:] NY1 NY3 VA2; ~_∧ B13 C5 C8 H4 H7 HH1 NP3 O21 P3 VA1 Y3;
~. B32 F21 O20; ~; B40 B46; ~? OQ1; ~, Σ. mee] ~, C9 H6; ~; O21.

102 Which] (~ B13 B46 OQ1 P3; Who C9 H5 H6 NP3. vnderstand]
vnderstandˢ HH1. none] C5 NY1 NY3 VA1 Y3; ~;) B13; ~) B46 OQ1 P3;
om H3(»~«); nought, H7; ~; O21; ~, Σ. doth] doeth C5; dooth C8;
om HH1. seeme] seemes HH1. bee] mee B32 O20; ~, C8.

103 Perfect] ~ of H3. French] ~, B13 B32 B47 C2 C8 DT1 F21 H7 HH1
O20 P3 SP1 A–G. and] or NP3. Italian:] C5 DT1 HH1 NY3 Y2; ~. B13

B40 H4 OQ1 VA1 B D–G; ~,   B33 B47 F21 H6 P3 Y3 C; ~∧   B46 H3; Italy;
NP3; ~;   Σ.   replide] ~,   B13 B32 H5 H6 O20 D–G; replyed   B33 DT1 HH1
OQ1 P3 VA1 Y2 Y3; replyed,   C2 C8 A–C; ~.   F21.

104 is] are   P3.   pox:] B13 C5 F21 NY3 OQ1; ~.   B40 B46 C9 H6 NY1 SP1
VA1 VA2 B–G; ~;   H4 H5 H7 O20 Y2 A; Pope,   O21; ~,   Σ.   answered]
answer'd   B13 B32 B33 B46 B47 C9 F21 H6 H7 NP3 NY1 O20 VA2 B–G.   not]
~,   B13 B32 B33 B40 B46 C2 C8 C9 DT1 F21 H5 HH1 O20 A–G; ~:   OQ1.
spide] spied   B13 C2 DT1 H3 HH1 O21 P3 VA1 VA2 Y2 Y3; spied,   C8; ~,   H7;
espied   OQ1.

105 Sort,] ~∧   B33 B47 C5 F21 H6 OQ1 Y2 Y3; Sortes,   H3.   parts,] ~∧   B33
C5 F21 H4 H5 H6 NP3 B–G; Portes,   H3; port;   O21; parte,   VA1; porte∧
Y3.   and] of   B13 B46 B47 C8 H3 NP3 NY1 O21 OQ1 P3 VA1 VA2 Y2 Y3.
qualities.] H7 HH1 NY1 NY3 SP1 VA2 B C; ~,   B13 B40 C2 C8 VA1 D–G;
~;   B32 H5 O20 A; ~:   DT1; ~∧   Σ.

106 last] ~,   B13 HH1.   Loue] ~,   B13 B32 B40 F21 O20 OQ1 SP1.   he]
~,   HH1.   a] om   G.   window] windowes   O20.   spies] ~,   B13 B32 C2
C8 C9 F21 H5 O20 A–G; ~;   B40 HH1.

107 And] ~,   C9 H6.   like] (~   H5.   Light] om   C5; nights   H7.   dew]
day   O21 Y3.   exhald,] ~;   B13 B46 C5 O21; ~∧   B47 DT1 F21 H3 H4 H7 NY1
P3 VA2 Y2; ~)   H5; exhaled,   HH1; exhaled∧   P3.   flings] flies   B13 P3.
from] om   Y2.   mee,] B32 B40 C8 HH1 NY3 O20; ~.   P3; om   Y2; ~∧   Σ.

108 Violently] (~   B46; ~,   DT1; violent   Y2.   rauishd] C2 C9 H5 H6 NY1
NY3 A; rauish't)   B46; ravished   HH1 B–G; ravisht   Σ.   to] with   HH1.
Lecheree.] ~∧   B33 B47 C5 DT1 H3 NP3 O21 VA1 Y3; ~:   B46 H5 OQ1 Y2;
~,   H4 P3; liberty;   A.

109 weare there:] B32 NY3 O20; were ~:   B13 F21 OQ1 SP1; ~ theare: C5;
were ~∧   H3 NY1 O21 P3 VA1 VA2 Y2 Y3; were ~;   H5 HH1; there were,   D–G;
were ~,   Σ.   he] but   H7.   more:] NY3; ~,   B32 B40 C8 DT1 H4 O20
SP1; ~;   H5 A–G; ~.   P3; ~∧   Σ.

110 quarreld,] quarrelled,   HH1; ~∧   NY1; ~;   O21; quarrells,   P3 VA1.
fought,] ~;   O21.   bled,] ~∧   DT1 F21 Y2; ~;   O21 A–G.   turnd] turned
F21 HH1.   dore] ~,   B40 C9 O20 Y2; ~.   C8; ~;   HH1.

111 Directly] ~,   H7.   came] comes   O21 Y3.   me,] ~∧   B13 B33 B46 B47
C9 H3 H7 NP3 O21 P3 VA1 Y3 A; ~;   B32 O20.   the] his   B47 NY1 O21
OQ1 VA2.   hed] NY3; head,   B13 B32 B40 C8 H5 HH1 O20 O21 OQ1
A–G; head.   C5; head   Σ.

112 constantly] ~,   H7.   awhile] B40 C8 F21 H4 NY3 O20 O21 SP1 VA1 Y2;
a while,   B13; a while   Σ.   his] the   NP3.   bed.] ~.| B13 C2 C8 C9 F21

H3 H5 NP3 O20 OQ1 VA1; ~:|| B33; ~.|.|.| B40; ~.|| DT1; ~| HH1;
~ ̬ O21; ~: Y3.

Subscriptions: finis secund: ID.| B13. ffinis B40 B46 O21(~.|) VA1(~.|)
Y3. |.ffinis.| H7. Finis Primæ Satyra. /I. Donne NY1
VA2(Satyræ). Finis the first Satire P3. *om* Σ.

Verbal Variants in Selected Modern Editions

Editions collated: H I J K M N O P Q S T Y Z AA DD.
Format:
Indentations: *ll. 111, 112 ind* Q S Y Z AA DD; *ll. 1, 49 67 ind* T; *ll. 49 67
ind* Y.
Headings: SATYRE I. H Q S Y Z DD. SATIRE I. I J K M N O P T.
Satire 1 AA.

1 Away] A Way H Z. changeling] fondling O Q S Y–AA DD.

3 Consorted] Consoled N.

6 Natures] Is ~ H–K M.

7 ioly] wily H–K M P.

9 Chroniclers] Chronicles N.

13 loue] ~ here H–K M P.

14 canst] can N.

16 do] N T; dost Σ.

19 Nor] T Y AA; Not Σ.

20 curtesy] Courtesyes N.

23 Shallt] N T; Wilt Σ. grin] girn T. or] and T.

25 or] and N T.

27 Monster] N T; monstrous Σ.

30 Dost] Doth J M P.

31 rate] race K.

32 vaile] T; raise Σ.

33 wilt] will P. consort] comfort S. vntill] till H–K M.

37 dost] doth J.

39 barenesse] barrenness H–K M O AA; ~ N(M *var*: barrenness). to
inioy] ~'~ H–K.

40 thy] this N.

41 be naked] naked be H–K M.

45 blest] best N.

46 yet] *om* H–K M P.   beasts] beast's H–K M–O T AA; beasts' P.

47 course] coarse I–K M O P T AA; ~ N(M *var:* coarse).   now I] N T; I now Σ.

50 sins] sinne N.

51 giddinesses] giddinesse DD.

53 that] T Y AA; who Σ.

54 Worne] Worn out H–K M.

55 musk-color] ~-coloured H–K M N P.

58 Th'infant] The Infantry H–K M; The Infanta Q S AA Z.   heire] hence H–K M.   to an] to *om* H–K M.

60 Scheame] scenes O.

62 supple-witted] N T; giddy-headed H–K M; subtile-~ Σ.   antick] antique N Q S Y Z DD.   Youths] youth H–K M.

63 Then] N(M *var:* Than) Q Y Z DD; Than Σ.   hence] N T; me Σ.   canst] can H–K M–P.

64 Whither] Whether N; Wither Z.   when] where N.

68 Improuidently] Unprouidently. N.

70 state] roome N.   his] high O P.

73 them] then O.

77 stop] stoop J K.   lowest] ~ N(M *var:* low'st); low'st Y.

78 stoopes] stooped O.   nighest] T; nigh'st the Σ.

80 Then] N Q Y Z DD; Than Σ.

84 Which] *om* S.   Yea] N T; Oh Σ.

86 here] to N(M *var:* too).

90 May be] N; It ~ ~ I J; Maybe T; 'T ~ ~ Σ.

93 stay] stray M.

94 in] N T; on Σ.

95 all] 's all O.

96 deuise] deuice   Σ.

97 cutt, print, or] N T; print, cut and   Σ.   pleight] N; plait   H–K M;
plight   Q Y Z DD; pleat   Σ.

100 stoopst] stopp'st   P.

101 he hath] Hath he   P.   trauayld. Long?] ~$_\wedge$ ~:   H; ~$_\wedge$ ~;   I–K M N;
~$_\wedge$ ~?   O P; ~; ~?   Q S.

102 vnderstand] understood   H–K M.

108 Lecheree] liberty   O.

109 weare there] there were   H–K M.

112 awhile] K M O T; a while   Σ.

Subscriptions: *none.*

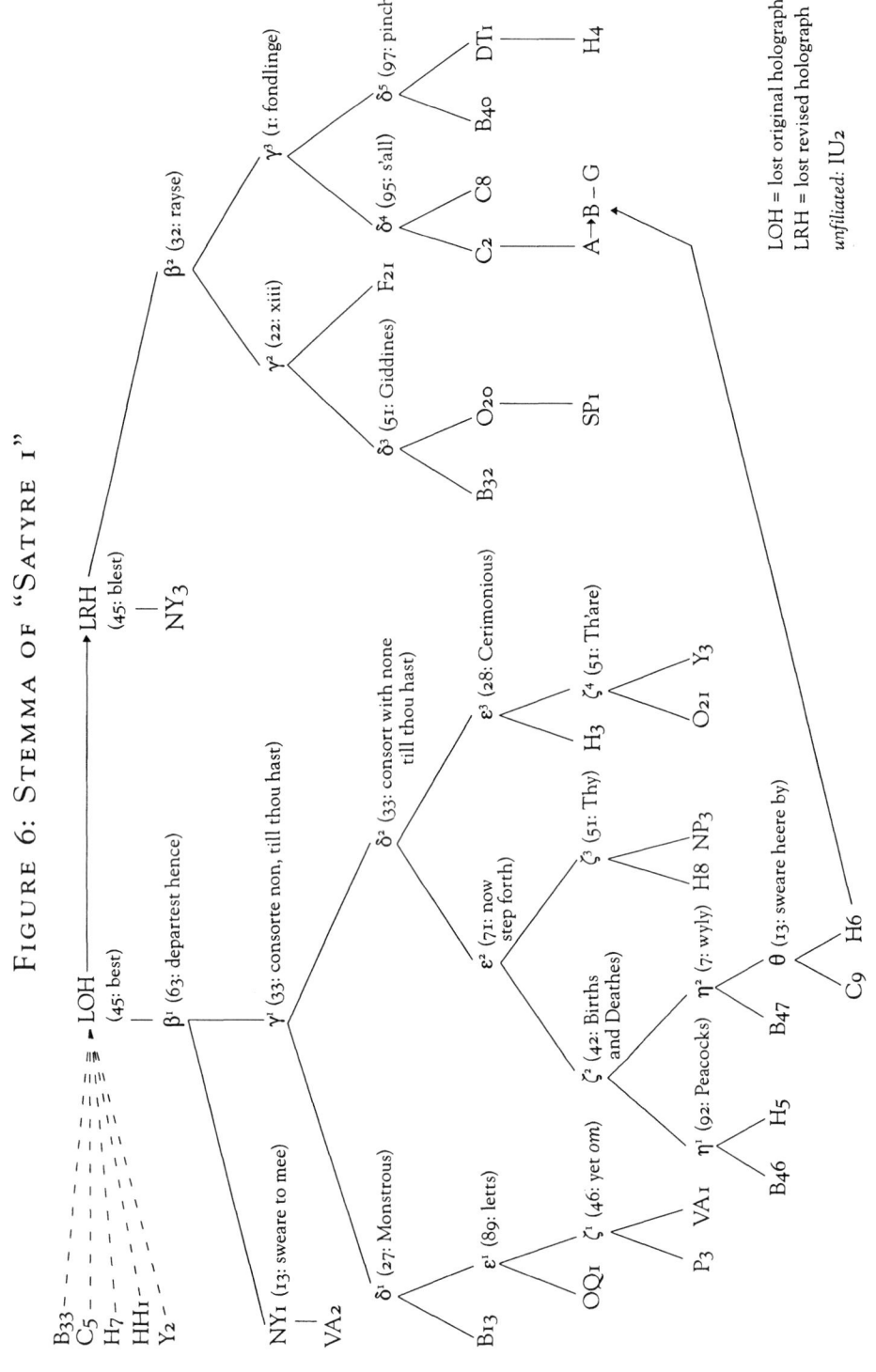

FIGURE 6: STEMMA OF "SATYRE 1"

Supporting Detail for Stemma of "Satyre 1"

LOH (B33 C5 H7 HH1 Y2 β¹)
 1 Away thou **changling** motley humorist
32 So hy or low doest **uaile** thy formall hat.
33 That wilt **consort none untill thou haue** knowne

B33: To the distinguishing readings of the LOH adds the following:
  63 Then thou when thou departst from hence **can** show
  64 Whither, why, **where,** or wth whom thou wouldst go

C5: To the distinguishing readings of the LOH adds the following:
  25 ffor better **and** worse take me and leaue mee
  27 Oh **monstrouse** superstitiouse puritan

H7: To the distinguishing readings of the LOH adds the following:
  20 Deigne wth A Nodd thy **Curtesy** to Answer,
  27 O **Monstrous** suppstitious *Puritan*
  71 Yet though he cannot **now stepp forth** to greet

HH1: To the distinguishing readings of the LOH adds the following:
  64 whether, Whie, **Where,** or wth whō y^{u} wouldst goe
  71 yet though he can nott **step fourth now** to greet

Y2: To the distinguishing readings of the LOH adds the following:
  62 our **subtile** wittie Antique youths will weare
  90 **It may** be you smell him not, truly I doe

β¹ (NY1-VA2 γ¹): To the distinguishing readings of the LOH adds the following:
  63 Then thou when thou **departest hence** can'st showe

  NY1-VA2: To the distinguishing readings of the LOH and β¹ adds the following:
    13 ffirst sweare **to mee** by thy best loue in ernest
    35 As **if** all thy companions should make thee

  γ¹ (δ¹ δ²): To the distinguishing readings of the LOH and β¹ adds the following:
    27 O **Monstrous** superstitious Purytane

    δ¹ (B13 ε¹): To the distinguishing readings of the LOH, β¹, and γ¹ adds the
    following:
      56 name her Childes <right> true father 'mongst all those
      58 The **Infanta** of London; heire to an India
      83 Now leaps hee vpright, loggs mee, & Cryes <**doe you see**>

B13: To the distinguishing readings of the LOH, β¹, γ¹, and δ¹ adds the following:
95 sayinge, him (whom I last **mett**) all repute

ε¹ (OQ1 ζ¹): To the distinguishing readings of the LOH, β¹, γ¹, and δ¹ adds the following:
25 ffor better **or** worse take me; or leaue me,
88 the Indians **for** drinckinge his Tobacco well.)

  OQ1: To the distinguishing readings of the LOH, β¹, γ¹, δ¹, and ε¹ adds the following:
  19 Not though a briske pfum'de **neat** Courtier,

  ζ¹ (P3 VA1): To the distinguishing readings of the LOH, β¹, γ¹, δ¹, and ε¹ adds the following:
  89 mett vs; they **talke** I whisper'd, letts goe

δ² (ε² ε³): To the distinguishing readings of the LOH, β¹, and γ¹ adds the following:
16 Though some more spruce Companion yᵘ **dost** meete

  ε² (ζ² ζ³): To the distinguishing readings of the LOH, β¹, γ¹, and δ² adds the following:
  71 Yet though he cannot **now step forth** to greete

  ζ² (η¹ η²): To the distinguishing readings of the LOH, β¹, γ¹, δ², and ε² adds the following:
  42 **At Births and Deathes** our Bodies naked are

    η¹ (B46 H5): To the distinguishing readings of the LOH, β¹, γ¹, δ², ε², and ζ² adds the following:
    45 Mans first **blest** state was naked, when by Sinne

    η² (B47 θ): To the distinguishing readings of the LOH, β¹, γ¹, δ², ε², and ζ² adds the following:
    7 and **wyly** stats=men wᶜʰ teach how to tie

      B47: To the distinguishing readings of the LOH, β¹, γ¹, δ², ε², ζ², and η² adds the following:
      58 th' infant of London ›theire‹ to **rich** Indya

      θ (C9 H6): To the distinguishing readings of the LOH, β¹, γ¹, δ², ε², ζ², and η² adds the following:
      58 **Th'Infanta** of London heire to an India

ζ³ (H8 NP3): To the distinguishing readings of the LOH, β¹, γ¹, δ², and ε²
adds the following:
    51 **Thy** vanityes & giddinesses; Loe,

ε³ (H3 ζ⁴): To the distinguishing readings of the LOH, β¹, γ¹, and δ² adds the
following:
    28 Of Refin'd manners, yet **Cerimonious** man

    H3: To the distinguishing readings of the LOH, β¹, γ¹, δ², and ε³ adds the
    following:
        71 Yet thoughe hee cannot **Scippe forthe nowe** to greet

    ζ⁴ (O21 Y3): To the distinguishing readings of the LOH, β¹, γ¹, δ², and ε³
    adds the following:
        51 Th'are Vanityes; and giddinesses soe

LRH (NY3 [provides copy-text for this edition]; β²)
    20 Deigne wᵗ a nod thy **curtesy** to answer.
    45 Mans first **blest** State was naked, when by Sin

β² (γ² γ³): To the distinguishing readings of the LRH adds the following:
    32 Soe high or lowe dost **rayse** thy formall hate
    62 Our **subtle-witted** Antique youthes will weare,

    γ² (δ³ F21): To the distinguishing readings of the LRH and β² adds the following:
        22 Greate trayne of Blewe Coates |xii, or **xiii** strong.

    δ³ (B32 O20 SP1): To the distinguishing readings of the LRH, β², and γ² adds
    the following:
        51 These Vanities, and **Giddines** loe,

        B32: To the distinguishing readings of the LRH, β², γ², and δ³ adds the
        following:
            29 That when thou meetest One, with inquiring **lyes**

        O20: To the distinguishing readings of the LRH, β², γ², and δ³ adds the
        following:
            36 **Iointers,** and marye thy deare Companee.
            92 A many color'd **Peacocke** having spyde

        SP1: To the distinguishing readings of the LRH, β², γ², and δ³ adds the
        following:
            36 **Iointures,** and marrie thy deare companie.
            92 A manie colorued **Peacockes** hauing spide

F2ı: To the distinguishing readings of the LRH, β^2, and γ^2 adds the following:

78 so to the most braue stoopes he nighest **the** grownd:

γ^3 (δ^4 δ^5): To the distinguishing readings of the LRH and β^2 adds the following:

1 Away thou **fondlinge** *Motley Humorist*

63 Then thou, when thou **depart'st from me** can show,

δ^4 (C2 C8): To the distinguishing readings of the LRH, β^2, and γ^3 adds the following:

95 Sayinge, him whome I last left, **s'all** repute

δ^5 (B40 DT1-H4): To the distinguishing readings of the LRH, β^2, and γ^3 adds the following:

85 That dances soe deuynelye; **Or** said I

B40: To the distinguishing readings of the LRH, β^2, γ^3, and δ^5 adds the following:

92 A manye Coloured **Peacocks** haueing spide,

DT1-H4: To the distinguishing readings of the LRH, β^2, γ^3, and δ^5 adds the following:

101 Why hee **had** trauell'd long; Noe, but to mee

Satyre 2.

Sir, Though (I thanke God for it) I do hate
Perfectly all this towne, yet ther is one State
In all ill things so excellently best
That hate towards them breeds pity towards the rest.
Though Poetry indeed be such a Sin   5
As I thinke that brings dearths and Spanyards in;
Though like the pestilence or old fashiond loue
It ridlingly catch men, and doth remoue
Neuer till it be steru'd out, yet their State
Is poore, disarm'd, like Papists, not worth hate.   10
One like a wretch which at barr iudgd as dead
Yet prompts him which stands next, and could not read
And saues his Life, giues Ideot Actors meanes
Steruing himselfe to liue by his Labord Sceanes,
As in some Organes puppets dance aboue   15
And bellows pant below which them do moue.
One would moue Loue by rhimes; but witchcrafts charmes
Bring not now their old feares, nor their old harmes.
Ramms and Slings now are seely batteree,
Pistolets are the best artilleree.   20
And they who write to Lords, rewards to gett,
Are they not like boyes singing at dores for meat?
And they who write because all write, haue still
That Scuse for wrighting and for wrighting ill.
But he is worst, who beggerly doth chaw   25
Others witts fruites, and in his rauenous maw
Rankly digested doth those things outspue
As his owne things, and they'are his owne: tis true.
For if one eate my meate, though it be knowne
The meat was myne, the excrement is his owne.   30
But these do me no harme. Nor they which vse
To outswive dildoes; and out vsure Iewes:
To out drinke the Sea: outsweare the Letanee:
Who with Sins all kinds as familiar bee
As Confessors: and for whose sinfull sake   35

Schoolemen new tenements in hell must make,
Whose strange Sins Canonists could hardly tell
In which Commandments large receite they dwell.
But these punish themselues: th'insolence
Of Coscus only breeds my great Offence,   40
Whome time, which rotts all, and makes botches poxe
And plodding on must make a calfe an oxe,
Hath made a Lawyer: which was alas of late
But a scarse Poet: Iolyer of this State
Then are new benefic'd Ministers, he throwes   45
Like Netts, or Lyme-twiggs, whersoe're he goes
His title of Barrister on euery wenche:
And wooes in Language of the Pleas and Benche.
A motion Lady; speake Coscus. I haue beene
In loue ere since tricesimo of the Queene: 50
Continuall Claimes I haue made: Iniunctions gott
To stay my Riuals Suite, that he should not
Proceede: spare me: In Hilary terme I went,
You sayd if I returnd this Sise in Lent
I should be in remitter of your grace,   55
In th'interim my letters should take place
Of affidauits. Words, Words, which would teare
The tender Labyrinth of a soft mayds eare
More, more, then ten Sclauonians scolding, more
Then when winds in our ruynd Abbeys rore.   60
When sick of Poetry, and possest with Muse
Thou wast, and mad, I hop'd: but Men which chuse
Law practise for meere gayne, bold Soule, repute
Worse then imbrotheled Strumpets prostitute.
Now like an Owllike Watchman he must walke   65
His hand still at a bill: Now he must talke
Idely like Prisoners, which whole months will sweare
That only Suretiship hath brought them there,
And to euery Sutor ly in euery thing
Like a Kings fauorit, yea like a king;   70
Like a wedge in a blocke wring to the barr
Bearing like Asses and more shameles farr
Then carted whores, ly to the graue Iudg: for
· Bastardy abounds not in Kings titles, nor
Simony and Sodomy in Churchmens Liues   75
As these things do in him, by these he thriues.
Shortly (as the Sea) he will compasse all our Land
From Scotts to Wight; from Mount to Douer Strand;
And spying heires melting with gluttonee
Satan will not ioy at their Sins as hee.   80

For as a thrifty Wench scrapes kitchin stuffe,
And barrelling the droppings and the snuffe
Of wasting candels which in 30 yeare
Relique like kept perchance buyes wedding geare,
Piece meale he getts lands: and spends as much time   85
Wringing each acre, as men pulling Prime.
In Parchments then large as his fields he drawes
Assurances, bigg as glossd ciuil Lawes:
So huge that Men in our times forwardnesse
Are fathers of the Church for wryting lesse.   90
These he wrytes not: Nor for these written payes,
Therfore spares no length: As in those first dayes
When Luther was profest, he did desyre
Short Pater Nosters, saying as a fryer
Each day his beads, but hauing lefte those lawes   95
Adds to Christs prayer, the power and glory clause.
But when he sells or changes Lands, he'impayres
His wrightings, and vnwatch'd, leaues out Ses heires
As slily as any Commentor goes by
Hard words or sense: or in diuinity   100
As Controuerters in vouchd texts leaue out
Shrewd Words which might against them cleare the doubt.
Where are those spred woods which clothd hertofore
These bought Lands? Not built; nor burnt within dore.
Where th'old Landlords troopes and almes? In great halls   105
Carthusian fasts, and fulsome Bacchanalls
Equally I hate: Meanes blesse: In rich Mens homes
I bid kill some beasts, but not Hecatomes.
None sterve, none surfet so: But oh we'allow
Good workes as good, but out of fashion now   110
Like old rich wardrobes. But my words none drawes
Within the vast reach of th'huge Statute Lawes.

Satyre 2.

Sir, though (I thanke God for it) I doe hate
Perfectly all this towne, yet there's one state
In all ill things soe excellently best
That hate towards them, breeds pittie towards the rest.
Though Poetrie indeed bee such a sinn,   5
As I thinck, that brings dearths, and Spaniards in;
Though, like the pestilence, or old fashion'd loue
It ridlingly catch men, and doth remoue
Neuer, till it bee staru'd out, yet their state
Is poore, disarm'd, like papists, not worth hate.   10
One (like a wretch, which at barr iudg'd as dead,
Yet prompts him which stands next, and could not read,
And saues his life) giues Ideott-actors meanes,
(Sterving himself) to liue by his labour'd sceanes,
As in some organs, puppetts dance aboue,   15
And bellowes pant belowe, which them doe moue.
One would moue loue by rimes; but witchcrafts charmes
Bring not nowe their old feares; nor their old harmes.
Ramms, and Slings nowe are sillie batterie,
Pistoletts are the best Artillerie.   20
And they who write to Lords, rewards to gett,
Are they not like boyes singing at dores for meate?
And they whoe write because all write, haue still
That scuse for writinge; and for writing ill.
But hee is worst, whoe beggerlie doth chawe   25
Others witts fruits, and in his rauenous mawe
Rancklie digested, doth those things out-spewe
As his owne things, and they are his owne, t'is true,
For if one eate my meate, though it bee knowne
The meat was mine, the'excrement is his owne.   30
But these doe mee noe harme; nor they which vse
To out-doe dildoes; and out-vsure Iewes;
To out-drinke the sea; out-sweare the Letanie:
Who with sinns all kinds as familiar bee
As Confessors; and for whose sinfull sake   35

Schoolemen newe tenements in hell must make,
Whose strange sins, Cannonists could hardly tell
In which commandements large receipt they dwell.
But these punish themselues; the insolence
Of Coscus, only breeds my great offence,   40
Whom time (which rotts all, and makes botches, poxe,
And plodding on, must make a calfe an oxe)
Hath made a lawyer; which was alass of late
But a scarce poett; Iollier of this state
Then are newe benefic'd Ministers, hee throwes   45
Like netts, or lyme-twiggs, wheresoe're hee goes
His title of Barrister on euery wench,
And wooes in language of the Pleas, and bench.
A Motion Lady; speake Coscus; I haue bine
In loue e'uer since tricesimo of the Queene,   50
Continuall claymes I haue made, Iniunctions gott,
To stay my Riualls sute, that hee should not
Proceed; spare mee; In Hillarie terme I went,
You said, if I return'd this sise in Lent
I should bee in Remitter of your grace;   55
In th'interim, my leters should take place
Of Affidauits: words, words which would teare
The tender Laborynth of a softe maids eare:
More, more then ten Sclauonians scolding, more
Then when windes in our ruin'd Abbeyes roare.   60
When sick with poetry, and possest with Muse
Thou was't, and madd, I hop'd; but men which choose
Lawe-practise for meere gaine, bold soule, repute
Worse then embrothel'd strumpetts prostitute.
Nowe, like an Owle-like watchman hee must walke   65
His hand still at a Bill, nowe hee must talke
Idly, like prisoners which whole mon'eths will sweare,
That onlie suretishipp hath brought them there,
And t'euerie sutor lye in euerie thinge,
Like a kings ffauourite, yea, like a Kinge;   70
Like a wedge in a block, wringe to the barre,
Bearing like Asses, and more shameless farre
Then carted whores, lye to the graue Iudge: for
Bastardie abounds not in kings titles, nor
Simony, and Sodomy in Churchmens liues,   75
As these thinges doe in him; by these hee thriues.
Shortly (as the sea) hee will compass all our land
From Scotts to wight, from mount to Douer strand,
And spyeng heires melting with luxurie,
Sathan will not ioye at their sinns, as hee.   80

For as a thrifty wench scrapes kitchin stuffe,
And barelling the droppings and the snuffe
Of wasting candles, which in thirty yeare
(Relique-like kept) perchance buyes wedding geare,
Piece-meale hee getts lands; and spends as much time   85
Wringing each acre, as men pulling prime.
In parchments then, large as his fields, hee drawes
Assurances, bigg as gloss'd Ciuill lawes,
Soe huge, that men (in our tymes forwardnes)
Are fathers of the Church for writing lesse.   90
These hee writes not, nor for these written payes,
Therefore spares noe length; as in those first dayes
When Luther was profess'd, hee did desire
Short pater nosters, sayeng as a ffryer
Each daye his beads, but hauing left those lawes   95
Adds to Christs prayer the power and glorie clause.
But when hee sells, or chaunges, lands, h' impayres
His writing, and (vnwatch'd) leaues out ses heires,
As slilye as any Commenter goes by
Hard words, or sence; or in diuinity   100
As controuerters in vouch'd texts, leaue out
Shrewd words which might against them cleare the doubt.
Where are those spread woods, which cloath'd heretofore
Those bought lands; not built; nor burnt within doore.
Where the'old Landlords troops, and almes? In great Halls   105
Carthusian fasts, and fulsome Bachanalls
Equally I hate; meanes Blesse: in ritch mens homes
I bid kill some beasts, but not hecatombs.
None sterue, none surfett soe: but (oh) wee allowe
Good workes as good, but out of fashion, nowe,   110
Like old ritch Warderobes; but my words none drawes
Within the vast reach of th' huge statute Lawes.

![] Textual Introduction

Complete copies of "Satyre 2" (*Sat2*) can be found in 34 seventeenth-century manuscripts and in all 7 seventeenth-century editions/issues of Donne's collected *Poems* (A–G). Short excerpts from the poem appear in Joseph Butler's eighteenth-century commonplace book (IU2) and in the various editions of Lucius Cary's *Discourse of INFALLIBILTY* (1651; sigla 31a–b), Samuel Sheppard's *MERLINVS ANONYMVS* (1653; sigla 33a–b), Joshua Poole's *The English PARNASSUS* (1657; sigla 44a–d), Thomas Forde's *A THEATRE OF WITS* (1661; siglum 49), and Forde's *Virtus Rediviva* (1661; sigla 50a–b). As is shown on Figure 2, *Sat2* sometimes appears in the company of 1, 2, or 3 other Satyres in the manuscripts, but it normatively appears as the second of a 5-poem set, as it does in the seventeenth-century prints. Variant readings in lines 32, 61, and 79 divide the manuscripts into two distinct lines of descent, the first headed by a lost original holograph (LOH) reading "outswive" (l. 32), "sick of Poetry" (l. 61), and "gluttony" (l. 79) and the second from a lost revised holograph (LRH) containing the revisions "out doe" (l. 32), "sick wth poetry" (l. 61), and "luxurie" (l. 79). A variant in line 104—where a slight majority of the LOH's descendants read "these bought Lands," while most of the descendants of the LRH read "those…"—may also be authorial in origin. Descendants of the LOH include the traditional Group-III manuscripts (B46, C9, H5, H6), three of the traditional Group-I manuscripts (B32, O20, SP1), three manuscripts Associated with Group III (H3, H7, HH1), eight unclassified manuscripts (B33, B47, C5, F21, NP3, SN3, SN4, Y2), and NY3—the sole Group-IV manuscript, here used as copy-text. Descendants of the LRH include the three independently circulated "books" of Satyres (OQ1, P3, VA1) plus their cognate B13 (Associated with Group III); the remaining Group-I manuscripts (C2, C8), whose texts of the Satyres read with Group-II; part of the expanded Group II (the cognates B40 and TT1 and the parent-child pair DT1-H4); a further four manuscripts Associated with Group III (the parent-child pair NY1-VA2 and the siblings O21 and Y3), and the unclassified H8. The stemma of *Sat2* (Figure 9) illustrates the exact relationships among these artifacts.

Along with three other independent branches of transmission (headed, respectively, by the postulated missing artifacts β^1, β^2 and β^3) and the six manuscripts listed at the upper left on the stemma, NY3 descends directly from the LOH; and it appears to differ from what Donne originally wrote in only two substantive particulars. The first, which consists in the omission of "not" from line 22's normative "Are they not like boyes singing at dores for meat" (yielding "Are they like…"), is likely a careless mistake, although it does regularize the line metrically. The second, an eye-skip error also evident in NP3 and the descendants of δ^2, consists in the complete omission of line 46, an omission enabled by the fact that the line can be dropped without distorting the syntax of the passage: the clause "…he throwes (l. 45)…His title of Barrister on euery wenche" (l. 47) seems complete without the intervening simile "Like Netts, or Lyme-twiggs, whersoe're he goes" (l. 46). Our emendation of these verbal errors and a few marks of punctuation is further discussed below.

The lost β¹—progenitor of the traditional Group-III manuscripts B46, C9, and H6, as well as of the unclassified B47—introduces into the line of transmission such distinctive readings as "Singers at dore" (for "boyes singing at dores") in line 22, "gets [for the normative *buyes*] weddinge geare" in line 84, and "in Halls" (for the authorial "in great halls") in line 105, and this archetype independently changes the LOH's "of" in line 61 to "with"—see the discussion below. From β¹ descend B46 and γ¹, which in turn begets B47 and δ¹, parent of the siblings C9 and H6. The product of a very careless and strongly interventionist scribe, B46 has a number of idiosyncratic read-ings, including "euerie [for *ther is one*] state" in line 2, "some found…villanouslie" (for "ill things…excellently") in line 3,[1] and "plea's in [for *and*] Bench" in line 48; and γ¹ introduces and passes to its descendants the singular "organ" (for the nor-matively plural "Organes") in line 15 and "his [for *this*] state" in line 44, the latter a trivialization also evident in the work of several other scribes. B47 is marked by such corruptions as "death remoue" (for "doth remoue") in line 8 and "witch crost [for the normative *witchcrafts*] charmes" in line 17; and δ¹ alters the authorial readings "this Sise" to "next Size" in line 54, "spares no length" to "spare no length" in line 92, and "my words none drawes / Within the vast reach of th'huge Statute Lawes" to "neere draw /…Law" in lines 111–12. As will be discussed below, for *Sat2* as for other poems in this edition (see, e.g., *DV* 2:lxxix–lxxx), δ¹'s offspring H6 seems to have supplied the editor of the 1635 *Poems* (B) with several emendations to the text received from the 1633 edition (A).

Shown to the immediate right of β¹ on the stemma as another direct descendant of the LOH is β², parent of the two Scottish manuscripts SN3 (written in the hand of William Drummond) and SN4. Unique β² readings that descend to SN3 and SN4 include the omission of "such" in line 5's normative "Poetry indeed be such a Sin" (yielding "…be a sinne"), "Bastards [for the authorial *Bastardy*] abounds not" in line 74, and the omission of "first" in the normative "those first dayes" in line 92 (yielding "those dayes"). That SN3 omits "ill" in line 3 where SN4 reads the normative "all ill thinges" shows that SN4 cannot be copied from SN3; and that SN3 reads the normative "Doores" in line 22 where SN4 reads the singular "doore" suggests—though perhaps does not prove certainly—that SN3 cannot be copied from SN4. In any case, these artifacts exhibit a sibling relationship in their texts of *Sat4* (see the discussion and stemma for that poem on pages 146 and 202 below), and there is no reason to doubt that the same relationship obtains here. Previous editors' misreading of Drummond's

---

[1] These line-2 and -3 innovations in B46 apparently represent the B46 scribe's encounter with B33, the only other contemporaneous artifact to record these readings (OJ1, in which they also appear, consists in manuscript additions to a copy of A in a modern hand—see the *CELM*), and that the B46 scribe imports only these 2 locutions from B33, as well as that he alters B33's syntax, suggests that he may be working from memory, perhaps having briefly seen (or heard) B33's rendition of the lines but having never had the artifact in his possession. For his part, the B33 scribe at some point interlines the normative readings of lines 2 and 3 above his original version (see the Historical Collation).

identification of his source text as the "b. B. coppy" is discussed in footnote 18 on page lxxiv in the General Textual Introduction above.

β^3, shown to the right of β^2 on the stemma, is marked by the readings "Rawly… these" (for the normative "Rankly…those") in line 27, "they [for the normative *these*] do me no harme" in line 31, "wrvnge" (for "wring") in line 71, and the omission of "then" in line 87—yielding "Parchments as large as" (for the normative "Parchments then large as") in the descendants of γ^2 and "parchment large as" in H7. These variants descend from β^3 to its offspring H7 (a seriously corrupt manuscript that has proved impossible to filiate in other instances—see the Textual Introduction to *Sat*3, p. 102 below) and γ^2, which introduces such unique variants as "Candle" (for the authorial "candels") in line 83 (although O2o's offspring SP1 independently expands this to the plural), "these [for the normative *those*] first dayes" in line 92, and "such words as" (for "Shrewd Words which") in line 102. This growing body of error then descends to Y2 (which adds further blunders in lines 6, 12, 16, and elsewhere—see the Historical Collation) and δ^2 (which omits line 46, committing the same eye-skip as NY3 and NP3, and records "these spied [for the normative *those spred*] woods" in line 103). δ^2 in turn produces the two offspring F21 and ε^1, the latter leading to the Group-I manuscripts B32 and the parent-child pair O2o and SP1. Independent blunders by the F21 scribe include the unintelligible "Poetry indeed by [for the correct *be*] such a Sinn" in line 5 and "death [for the correct *dearths*] & *Spaniards*" in line 6, among others; ε^1's distinctive verbal variants, passed on to its descendants, are "toward" (where other descendants of β^3 read the normative "towards") in line 4 and the substitution of "with" (for the LOH's "of") in line 61; and in lines 16, 42, 47, and elsewhere ε^1 introduces into the genealogical line differentiating punctuation as well. B32 reproduces ε^1 faithfully, and O2o diverges from ε^1 in only a handful of readings—giving, e.g., "scarce a" (for the normative "a scarse") in line 44 and "haue I" (for "I haue") in line 51. SP1, on the other hand, differs substantively from the parent O2o in lines 25, 34, 73, 83, 91, 104, and 105 (see the Historical Collation).

Although they cannot be placed more precisely than is shown, the manuscripts appearing at the upper left of the stemma (B33, C5, H3, H5, HH1, and NP3) all descend, with varying degrees of immediacy, from the LOH independently, and all share the LOH's defining "Gluttony" (as opposed to "luxurie") in line 79. All except B33 and H3, furthermore, evince "sick of [for *with*] Poetry" in line 61 as well. With respect to line 32's "outswive" / "out doe" variant, C5, H3, and H7 evince the LOH's more direct "outswive," while the scribes of B33 and HH1—each apparently operating independently—record the periphrastic "out doe" to which Donne reverts in the LRH. The copyist of NP3 writes "out sweare Dildoes," either not understanding Donne's locution or misreading his source, while the scribe of H5 gives "out-ly Lawyers," perhaps understanding the locution, but declining to record it. The artifacts listed as "unfiliated" at the lower right on the stemma include IU2, which very likely derives from print (see *DV* 2:204), although the evidence in the present instance is insufficient to enable such a determination; OJ1, which derives some of its readings from B33 (see particularly the Historical Collation for lines 2, 3, and 6), but also evinces various independent scribal adjustments of the wording; and P1, which—although it reads "rawly" in line 27 and thus apparently belongs among the descendants of β³—otherwise consists of a series of uncollatable and eccentrically spelled excerpts.

As noted above, the changes of "outswive" to "out-doe" in line 32, of "sick of Poetry" to "sick with poetry" in line 61, and of "melting with gluttonee" to "melting with luxurie" in line 79 represent Donne's slight revision of *Sat2*. And the alteration of "These bought Lands" to "Those bought lands" in line 104 may also be authorial. The change to "luxurie" substitutes a more broadly inclusive term than "gluttonee" to characterize the "melting" excesses of "heires" driven to sell off bits of their estates in order to support their general appetite for opulence. On the other hand, it seems likely that pudicity—rather than the opportunity to alliterate "dildoes" with "out doe"—prompted the change from "outswive" in line 32; and in this regard we might note that even the milder phrase proved too strong for the censor of the 1633 *Poems* (A), who additionally expunged "dildoes" from the line. According to definitions cited in the *OED*, "sick of Poetry" could mean either "tired or weary of " poetry [A.5.a] or "made ill by" [A.1.b] poetry, and since Donne clearly intends the latter in his description of Coscus's evolution from bad poet to greedy lawyer, he may have altered "of" to "with" in order to eliminate an initially unnoticed ambiguity (that four scribes in the LOH lineage made this same change independently suggests that others also saw "with" as the clearer word in this context). On the question of the author's responsibility for the "These" / "Those" variant in line 104, the bibliographical evidence yields no clear answer. The descendants of the LOH evince seven originary occurrences of "These" (in NY3, β³, B33, H3, H5, H7, and HH1) and four of "Those" (in β¹, β², C5, and NP3), a fact making it somewhat more likely that "These" was the LOH's reading and that "Those" is a scribal change—one perhaps caused by the residual influence of "those spred woods" in the previous line. Among the descendants of the LRH, on the other hand, only the parent-child pairs NY1-VA2 and DT1-H4 read "These," the remaining artifacts reading "Those." This may indicate either (a) that the LRH evinced the authorial revision of "These" to "Those," passing "Those" down to both β⁴ (among whose offspring the NY1 scribe altered "Those" to "Theise") and β⁵ (among whose offspring DT1 altered "Those" to "these"), or (b) that the LRH retained "These," but that both γ³ and β⁵ altered "These" to "Those," as four scribes in the LOH lineage had done before them. Recognizing the impossibility of exactly accounting for this "These" / "Those" crux, we have let stand the "These" appearing in NY3 (the artifact chosen as copy-text for the original version of the poem), but have emended the reading of DT1 (the copy-text for the revised version of the poem) from "These" to "Those," which we deem more likely to have been the reading of the LRH.

Incorporating the above-noted authorial changes, the revised version of the poem descends from the LRH in two genealogical strands headed, respectively, by the missing artifacts β⁴ and β⁵. As shown on the stemma, the β⁴ lineage includes nine extant manuscripts either Associated with Group III (NY1-VA2, O21-Y3, B13), "unclassified" (H8), or numbered among the "books" of Satyres that circulated as an independent collection containing also *Storm* and *Calm* (OQ1, P3, VA1). The β⁵ lineage comprises the Group-I manuscripts C2 and C8, as well as four members of the expanded Group II (DT1-H4, B40, TT1).

Among other variants β⁴ introduces and passes on to its offspring NY1 and γ³ the reversal "doe them [for the normative *them do*] mooue" in line 16 (although H8 corrupts "doe" to "doth" and the O21-Y3 siblings misread "doth not"), "witchcraft charmes" (for "witchcrafts…") in line 17, and "Sathan would [for the authorial *will*] not ioy at their sinns" in line 80. To name but three of many such anomalies, NY1 records "a state" (for "one State") in line 2, "ridingly" (for "ridlingly") in line 8, and "in hell new tenements" (for "new tenements in hell") in line 36, transmitting these to its offspring VA2. To the growing body of error γ³ adds "iudg'd is [for the normative *as*] dead" in line 11, "that state" (for "this state") in line 44, and "Ly like [for *Like*] a kinges favorite" in line 70. From γ³ stem H8—which records such misreadings as "saying (like [for the normative *as*] a *ffrier*)" in line 94 and "hard [for *voucht*] texts" in line 101—and δ³, whose distinctive variant, transmitted to all artifacts below it on the genealogical tree, is the trivialized "as bigg as glossy [for *bigg as glossd*] Civill Lawes" in line 88. δ³ then begets ε² and ε³, which lead, respectively, to the above-mentioned "books" of Satyres and to the siblings O21 and Y3. Among other blunders, ε² reduces the normative "whersoe're" in line 46 to "where ere," substitutes "Ly to the Iudges" for the normative "ly to the graue Iudg" in line 73, and misreads "these Lawes" for the normative "those lawes" in line 95, adding these to the accumulated body of error bequeathed to its offspring B13 and ζ. B13 records the scribal "singers, at meñs dores" (for the authorial "boyes singing at dores") in line 22 and the misunderstanding "hould soule repute" (for the correct "bold Soule, repute") in line 63; among ζ's numerous scribal blunders are the omission of "the" from the authorial phrase "the pestilence" in line 7 (yielding merely "pestilence"), the insertion of an extraneous "in" at the beginning of line 86 (yielding "in wringing [for the normative *Wringing*] each acre"), and the unique "Comenter goeth [for the normative *goes*] by" in line 99. OQ1 evinces the reversal "Slinges are nowe" (for "…now are") in line 19 and renders line 48 hypermetrical by uniquely inserting an extra "the" into the normative phrase "in Language of the Pleas" (recording "in the language…"), amongst other errors. OQ1's sibling η introduces and passes on to its offspring P3 and VA1 such mistakes as the omission of "their" in the normative line-18 phrase "their old harmes" (yielding "old harmes") and the ungrammatical "doe [for *doth*] those things out spew" in line 27. Among other added corruptions, both P3 and VA1 exhibit major omissions, P3 lacking the words "spred woods which clothd" in line 103 and VA1 lacking the entirety of line 42. δ³'s other offspring, the extremely corrupt ε³, records errors in over three dozen instances, including the line-14 blunder "(while himself starues)" (for the normative "Steruing himselfe") and "nott whole [for the normative *but not*] Hecatombes" in line 108. Of ε³'s two descendants, Y3 differs substantively from the parent only in line 67, but the extremely corrupt O21 manifests a further dozen errors, including those in lines 7, 10, 46, 83, and 99 (see the Historical Collation).

The last descendants of the LRH shown on the stemma comprise the strand of artifacts headed by β⁵, which—through the lost artifact γ⁴—reaches to a family comprising the Group-I siblings C2 and C8 and the Group-II parent-child pair DT1-H4 and—through the corresponding artifact γ⁵—to the siblings B40 and TT1. All these manuscripts evince the "outswive"-to-"out doe," "sick of"-to-"sick with," "gluttonee"-to-"luxurie," and "These"-to-"Those" revisions recorded in the LRH; and other variants—all of them scribal corruptions—are added successively as the text descends down the genealogical tree. β5 introduces more than a dozen such variants, including—just in the first half of the poem—"Pestelence and [for the normative *or*] olld fashioned loue" in line 7, "Ridlinglye yt" (for "It ridlingly") in line 8, "cannot [for *could not*] read" in line 12, "organ" (for "Organes") in line 15, "singers [for *boyes singing*] at doores" in line 22, "excuse" (for "scuse") in line 24, and "breeds my lust [for *great*] offence" in line 40. To these β5's offspring γ4 adds "rithmes" (for "rhimes") in line 17 (perhaps merely a variant spelling—see *OED*, "rhythm, *n.*" II. 6), and "Great [for the authorial *In great*] Halls" in line 105, illogically changing "Halls" from the site of the "Carthusian Fasts, and fullsome Bacchanalls" that the satirist hates to a third object of his hatred. And γ4's child δ4 further contaminates the text by—among other changes—"correcting" Donne's elliptical phrase "sinns all kinds" in line 34 to "sinns of all kinds," by inverting the authorial "But a scarse Poet" in line 44 to "But scarce a Poett," and by reducing the normative "Relique like kept" in line 84 to "(Reliquelye kept)"—all trivializations appearing in other manuscripts as well. Copied from δ4, the siblings C2 and C8 each add a smattering of further error: C2, e.g., alters the normative "affidauits" in line 57 to "Affedaritts," misreads "meere gayne" in line 63 as "more gayne," and misrecords the normative "vnwatch'd" in line 98 as "(vnmatch'd)"; C8 evinces such anomalies as "they that" (for "they who") in line 21, "Then anie [for *are*] newe benefic'd ministers" in line 45, and "Oule=light" (for "Owllike") in line 65. DT1, the second direct descendant of γ4, diverges from the parent in about half-a-dozen instances, recording "nor worth" (for "not worth") in line 10, "saue [for *saues*] his life" in line 13, and "hold [for *bold*] soule repute" in line 63, among others; H4 in turn departs from the parent DT1 in lines 73, recording "like [for *Then*] carted whores," and 92, recording "spares for noe length" (for "spares no length").

As shown on the stemma, the second direct offspring of β5 is the postulated γ5, parent of the siblings B40 and TT1. To the scribal changes introduced in β5, γ5 adds a further handful, including "they that [for the normative *who*] write" in line 23, the elision "T'out drinke" (for "To out drinke") in line 33, "those [for *these*] punish themselues" in line 39, and "meere gaynes" (for "...gayne") in line 63. B40's idiosyncrasies include "*Slauonians* [without a *c*]" (for the normative "Sclauonians") in line 59 and "adds to *Christ prayer*" (for the correct "...Christs...") in line 96. The more corrupt TT1 diverges from the parent in dropping "eate" from the normative "one eate my meate" in line 29 (yielding "one my meat") and "none" from the normative "my words none drawes" in line 111 (yielding "my woordes drawes"), amongst several other errors.

The Seventeenth-Century Prints

Like the other four Satyres, *Sat2* first enters print in the 1633 *Poems* (A), set into type from C2. As Figure 6 shows, A embodies over a dozen readings originating with β5, including—e.g.—"Ridlingly it" (for "It ridlingly") in line 8, "just [for *great*] offence" in line 40, and "next [for *this*] size" in line 54; and A's "rithmes" (for "rimes") in line 17 and "great hals?" (for "In great halls...") in line 105 derive from γ4. δ4 variants manifest in A include "sinnes of all kindes" (for the normative "Sins all kinds") in line 34, "scarce a" (for "a scarse") in line 44, and "Reliquely" (for "Relique like") in line 84; and A's derivation specifically from C2 is indicated by the colons following "make" (yielding "make:") in line 36 and "doubt" (yielding "doubt:") in line 102, the former unique to C2 and the latter otherwise appearing only in OQ1 and H8. Although surely not fully aware of how distant his setting text might be from Donne's holograph, A's editor clearly understood the need for some emendation and rendered the much-inflected C2 text fit for print not only by imposing the usual manuscript-to-print conventions (capitalizing the first words of lines, expanding brevigraphs and abbreviations, regularizing format, e.g.), but also by correcting a number of outright errors and by accommodating the objections of the licensing authorities. A thus rejects C2's uniquely erroneous "There are…Ministers" in line 45 in favor of the correct "Then are…," corrects C2's anomalous "Affedaritts" in line 57 to "affidavits," and replaces C2's "vnmatch'd" in line 98 with the authorial "unwatch'd," e.g.; and A omits the words "Dilldoes" in line 32 and "Letanye" in line 33, as well as withholding from print the entirety of lines 69–70 and 74–75, although the editor marks each of these instances as a deliberate deletion by replacing the offending words with dashes. In addition, as is shown on Figure 6, A independently reduces the first authorial "towards" in line 4 to "toward," the authorial "dearths" to "dearth" in line 6, and the authorial "our land" to "the land" in line 77, all three of these minor editorial (or compositorial) changes being transmitted into B–F and those in lines 6 and 77 into G and beyond.

From A Sat2 passes on into B, and the text of each of the subsequent seventeenth-century collected editions (C–G) is based on that of its immediate predecessor. Figure 6 lists 14 instances in which B alters the text of A, not only restoring all the censored material except "Letanye" in line 33 (which would remain unprinted until its inclusion in G in 1669), but also introducing a handfull of independent editorial/compositorial changes—including "or like" (for "yea like") in line 70 "Where [for *When*] Luther was profest" in line 93, and "Meane's blest" (for "meanes blesse") in line 107. And—as with the texts of the other Satyres—B emends a further few of A's readings toward H6, dropping from line 34 the extraneous "of" that A had derived from δ⁴, dropping "was" from the normative phrase "which was alas of late / But scarce a Poët" in lines 43–44 (yielding the nonsensical "which alas…Poët"), introducing H6's unique parentheses to enclose the long clause spanning lines 92–96 that compares Coscus's needlessly lengthened "Assurances" to Luther's expanded version of "Christs prayer," and changing A's obscure line-105 construction "Where's the'old landlords troops, & almes, great hals?" to H6's more intelligible "…almes? In halls…"—to name but four examples. C is a page-for-page resetting of B, but changes spelling or punctuation in half-a-dozen instances, including modernizing B's "then" to "than" in lines 60 and 64; and in reprinting the C text, D (and its reissues E and F) introduces about 40 changes of accidentals and one of substance, conjecturing the three-syllable "gallant, he" to replace the still-absent "Letanye" at the end of line 33 and provide a rhyme for "familiar be" in line 34. G, the final seventeenth-century edition, generally modernizes the spelling of the received D–F text, alters the punctuation in over two dozen instances, and independently imposes such editorial changes as "Maids soft [for *soft maids*] ear" in line 58, "Sclavonians scolding's" (for "…scolding") in line 59, "Wedding chear" (for "wedding geare") in line 84, "Maids [for *men*] pulling prime" in line 86, "the fields" (for "his fields") in line 87, and "statutes Jawes" (for "statute lawes") in line 112. Also among G's changes are several indicating the editor's sporadic consultation of one or more manuscript sources: the most notable example is his original

FIGURE 7: SIGNIFICANT VARIANTS IN THE 17TH-CENTURY PRINTS OF "SATYRE 2"

~ = agrees with LOH   ▿ = agrees with nearest corresponding reading on left   ( ) = specific source of variant   < > = word(s) omitted   c = compositor

Line no.	LOH/DV reading	A	B	C	D–F	G
4	1st towards	toward (c)	▿	▿	▿	~ (?)
4	2nd towards	~	toward (c)	▿	▿	~
6	dearths	dearth (c, H6?)	▿	▿	▿	▿
7	or	and (β5)	▿	▿	▿	~
8	It ridlingly	Ridlingly it (β5)	▿	▿	▿	▿
12	could not	cannot (β5)	▿	▿	▿	▿
14	Sterling himselfe	(~ ~) (LRH)	‸~‸ (H6?)	‸~‸	‸~‸	(~ ~)
15	Organes	Organ (β5)	▿	▿	▿	~
17	rhimes	rithmes (γ4)	▿	▿	▿	▿▿▿
22	boyes singing at dores	singers at doores (β5)	▿▿▿	▿▿▿	▿▿▿	▿▿▿
24	Scuse	excuse (β5)	~	▿	▿	▿
32	dildoes	<dildoes> (censor)	~	~	~	~
33	outsweare	to out-sweare (β5)	▿	▿	▿	▿
33	Letanee	<Letanie> (censor)	▿	▿	gallant, he	~
34	all kinds	of ~ ~ (δ4)	<of> ~ ~ (H6?)	<of> ~ ~	<of> ~ ~	<of> ~ ~
36	make,	~; (C2)	▿	▿	▿	▿
40	great	just (β5)	▿	▿	▿	▿
43	was alas	~	alas (H6)	~	~	~
44	a scarse	scarce a (δ4)	▿	▿	▿	▿
46	whersoe're	wheresoever (c)	▿	▿	▿	▿
50	ere since	ever ~ (β5)	~	▿	▿	~
54	returnd	Returne (β5)	~ (H6?)	▿	~	~
54	this	next (β5)	▿	▿	▿	▿
58	soft mayds	~	~	~	~	Maids soft (c)
59	scolding	~	~	~	~	scolding's (c)
64	then	~	~	than (c)	▿	

Line no.	LOH/DV reading	A	B	C	D–F	G
69-70	*ll. included*	*ll. om* (censor)	*ll. included*	*ll. included*	*ll. included*	*ll. included*
70	yea like	<~> <~>	or like (c)	◡ ◡	◡ ◡	◡ ◡
74-75	*ll. included*	*ll. om* (censor)	*ll. included*	*ll. included*	*ll. included*	*ll. included*
77	our Land	the ~ (c)	◡ ᷑	◡ ᷑	◡ ᷑	◡ ᷑
84	Relique like	Reliquely (δ⁴)	▽	▽	▽	▽
84	geare	᷑	᷑	᷑	᷑	chear (c)
86	men	᷑	᷑	᷑	᷑	Maids (c)
87	Parchments	parchment (β⁶)	▽	▽	▽	
87	his fields	᷑	᷑ ᷑	◡ ᷑	◡ ᷑	the ~ (c)
89	in ... forwardnesse	(~ ... ~) (β⁶)	(◡ ... ◡)	(◡ ... ◡)	(◡ ... ◡)	(~ ... forwardness)
92-96	As ... clause.	᷑ ... ᷑	(◡ ... ◡) (H6)	(◡ ... ◡)	(◡ ... ◡)	(◡ ... ◡)
93	When	◡	Where (c)	▽	▽	▽
97	Lands	land (β⁶)	▽	▽	▽	▽
102	doubt.	~: (C2)	~. (H6)	◡:	◡:	◡:
105	In great halls	great hals? (γ⁴, A)	In hals. (H6)	▽ ▽	▽ ▽	▽ ▽
107	Meanes blesse:	~ ~	mean's blest. (c)	▽ ▽:	▽ ▽:	▽ ▽:
108	but not	~ no (β⁶)	▽ ▽	▽	▽	▽
109	oh	(Oh) (γ⁴)	(▽)	(▽)	(▽)	(▽)
112	Lawes	᷑	᷑	᷑	᷑	Jawes (c)

printing of the censored "Letanie" at the end of line 33; and G's "towards…towards" (for B–F's "toward…toward") in line 4, "Organs" (for A–F's "Organ") in line 15, and "When [for B–F's *Where*] *Luther* was profest" in line 93 are further instances. Despite his recovery of this handful of authentic readings, however, the text that G's editor bequeaths to his modern successors is marred not only by the independent "improvements" noted above (in lines 58, 59, 84, 96, and 112), but also by a long string of blunders and interventions imposed by the editors and compositors of A–F and by the C2, δ⁴, γ⁴, and β⁵ scribes.

The Modern Prints

   Although he had access to either B or C (and apparently followed one of these editions in rejecting G's innovative "Jawes" in favor of the earlier "lawes" in line 112), Jacob Tonson (H), the earliest modern editor, uses G as his basic setting text, evincing such of that edition's idiosyncratic readings as "Maids soft" in line 58, "Wedding chear" in line 84, and "Maids pulling prime" in line 86 (see Figure 7). And Tonson's successors Bell (I), Anderson (J), Chalmers (K), and Lowell (M) all perpetuate the text developed by Tonson in an evolutionary pattern described elsewhere in this *Variorum*: I derives from H and gives rise to J, while K and M revert to H for their setting texts (among this group, e.g., I and J uniquely give hyphenated constructions in ll. 7, 94, and 112; see Figure 8). Whether deliberate or inadvertent, M's "Pistollers" (for "Pistolets") in line 20 is one of Lowell's occasional innovations, and his reversion to the singular "organ" (for "organs") in line 15 likely derives from B (see *DV* 2:lxxxii–lxxxiii for parallel instances of these relationships and procedures). In the absence of any evidence that Tonson ever saw a manuscript of Donne's poetry, his replacement of the received "rythmes" in line 17 with "rhymes" must be regarded as his independent modernization of an archaic spelling, and this change persisted in all subsequent editions until O, following A as copy-text, reverted to "rhythms."

   Becoming the first editor in over 200 years to print a Satyre from manuscript, Grosart (N) selects B33—a descendant of the LOH—as his basic setting text for *Sat2* (as also for *Sat1* and *Sat3*); correspondingly, his text includes such anomalous lections as "All this toune perfectly" (for the usual "Perfectly all this towne") in line 2 and "There are some found so villainously best" (for "In all ill things so excellently best") in line 3 (see Figure 8). But Grosart also collates B32, B40, and (with particular care) H7, as well as the seventeenth-century prints, and eclectically emends B33 as he sees need—e.g., N's "It rides killingly" (for the normative "Ridlingly it") in line 8 derives from H7, and its "jawes" (for "lawes") in line 112 derives from G. N's immediate successor, the Grolier Club edition (O), follows its usual practice of adopting A as copy-text, repeating A's substantives exactly (except for importing from one of the later seventeenth-century prints the material censored from A), but thoroughly modernizing spelling and revising the punctuation.

   Chambers (P), the last of the nineteenth-century editors, is an admitted eclecticist who bases his text on A, B, E, and G, but who also is influenced by Grosart to consult the occasional manuscript—his notes to *Sat2*, e.g., cite variants in B33 in particular. Accordingly, P follows A in recording "sins of all kinds"—where B–G give "sinnes all kindes"—in line 34 and "which was, alas"—where B–G give "which, (alas)"—in line 43, but also prints G's "jaws" in line 112. Interestingly, although he prints lines 69–70 and 74–75—which had been suppressed in A, but restored in B–G—Chambers adheres to A in refusing to print "Dildoes" in line 32 and "Letanie" in line 33, lections he certainly knew in both print and manuscript. Chambers also uniquely emends the singular "soul" in line 63 to "soul[s]" and inserts a comma after "strumpets" in line 64, producing the unintelligible "…bold soul[s] repute / Worse than embrothell'd strumpets, prostitute."

The first twentieth-century edition to include *Sat2* is that of Grierson (Q), which—as a matter of editorial policy—takes A as its copy-text for the poem. Grierson alters A's punctuation in nearly two dozen instances; and—having compared all available manuscripts and B–G—not only restores all the material censored from A, but also corrects its wording in 8 others (in ll. 6, 34, 44, 54, 77, 84, 87, and 105). Since Grierson did not understand the textual history of the poem stemmatologically, however, he leaves untouched the β⁵ errors in lines 7, 8, 12, 15, 22, 24, 33, 40, 54, 97, 105, and 108, as well as the γ⁴ spelling "rithmes" in line 17 and the spelling "toward" (first occurrence) introduced by A's compositor in line 4. In a notable intervention that lacks either print or manuscript support, Grierson hyphenates the normative phrase "Bearing like asses" in line 72 to "Bearing-like asses," effecting a syntactical and conceptual change that subsequently elicited a considerable amount of critical discussion (see Notes and Glosses in the commentary). As usual Hayward (S) provides a virtual reprint of Q, differing substantively from it only in printing the singular "dearth" (where Q gives "dearths") in line 6 and—on the authority of B32, O20, and NY3—"out-swive" (where Q gives the revised "out-doe") in line 32.

As for the other Satyres, Bennett (T) chooses NY3 as copy-text for *Sat2*, although he modernizes accidentals and—at the cost of several end-of-line sight rhymes—spelling, regularizes the meter both by introducing numerous elisions and—in line 39—by expanding the manuscript's elided "th' insolence" to "The insolence," and imposes quotation marks to clarify the dialogue in lines 49–57. Substantively, T adds the sub-title "The Lawyer" to the heading, emends line 34's "Sins all kinds" to "sin's all kinds," recovers the omitted line 46 from A, replaces NY3's "sick of Poetry" with A's "sick with…" in line 61, and accepts the Griersonian "Bearing-like" in line 72. Perhaps also for metrical reasons, T leaves unemended NY3's anomalous "Are they like boyes" (for the normative "…not like boyes") in line 22.

Milgate (Y), Grierson's spiritual heir and successor in the Oxford University Press series, also takes A as copy-text, producing a version of *Sat2* that differs substantively from that of his predecessor only in lines 17 (where he substitutes "rimes" for the ambiguous γ⁴ spelling "rithmes" found in A and Q), 54 (where he accepts the β⁵-A anomaly "returne" that Q had rejected), and 72 (where he rejects Q's hyphenated "Bearing-like"). In the interests of metrical regularity and readability, moreover, Milgate introduces a number of elisions, and he marks the dialogue in lines 49–57 with quotation marks; in the upshot, however, his text retains 13 errors emanating from β⁵—in lines 7, 8, 12, 15, 22, 24, 33, 40, 54 (two readings), 97, 105, and 108 (see Figure 7).

Of the final three editions collated in the present edition—Shawcross (Z), Smith (AA), and Patrides (DD)—Shawcross and Patrides follow Q and Y in using A as copy-text, while Smith, unabashedly eclectic, aspires to print "the richest and most pointed

FIGURE 8: VARIANTS IN THE MODERN PRINTS OF "SATYRE 2"

[blank] = agrees with LOH reading   ~ = agrees with LOH reading   OoV = Origin of Variant   A–G = variant appears in 17th-c. eds.

• = variant appears in modern eds.   { = to be read together   < > = word(s) omitted

Line no.	LOH/DV reading	Variant	OoV	A–G	H	I	J	K	M	N	O	P	Q	S	T	Y	Z	AA	DD
4	1st towards	toward	A	A–F	•						•	•	•	•			•	•	•
6	thinke that	ame afraid	B33							•									
6	dearths	dearth	A	A–G	•	•	•	•	•		•	•	•	•		•	•	•	•
7	or	and	β5	A–G	•	•	•	•	•	•	•	•	•	•		•	•	•	•
7	old fashiond	~	I							•					•				
8	It ridlingly	Ridlingly it	β5	A–G	•	•	•	•	•		•	•	•	•		•	•	•	•
8	It ridlingly	~ rydes killingely	H7							•									
12	could not	cannot	β5	A–G	•	•	•	•	•	•	•	•	•	•		•	•	•	•
14	by his	by's	H		•	•				•									
15	Organes	organ	β5	A–F	•	•	•	•	•	•	•	•	•	•		•	•	•	•
17	rhimes	rhythms	γ4	A–G							•	•							
20	Pistolets	Pistollers	M						•			•							
22	not	<not>	NY3	A–G	•	•	•	•	•	•	•	•	•	•	•	•	•	•	•
22	boyes singing	singers	β5	A–G	•	•	•	•	•		•	•	•	•		•	•	•	•
24	Scuse	excuse	β5	A–G	•	•	•	•	•	•	•	•	•	•		•	•	•	•
31	these	those	B33	A–G	•			om		•	•	•	•	•		•	•	•	•
32	outswive	out-doe	LRH	A–G	•	•	•	•	•	•	•	•	•	•		•	•	•	•
32	dildoes	<Dildoes>	A	A				•			•	•							
33	outsweare	t' out-swear	H		•														
33	outsweare	to ~	β5	A–G		•	•	•	•		•	•	•	•		•	•	•	•
33	Letanee	<Letanee>	A	A–C						•									
33	Letanee	gallant, he	D	D–F								•							
34	all	of ~	δ4	A						•									
37	Whose	In ~	B33			•	•	•	•		•	•	•	•		•	•	•	•
40	great	just	β5	A–G					•										•
43	was	<was>	γ1H6	B–G	•	•	•	•	•		•	•	•	•		•	•	•	•

62   ❦   TEXTS AND APPARATUSES

Line no.	LOH/DV reading	Variant	OoV	A-G	H	I	J	K	M	N	O	P	Q	S	T	Y	Z	AA	DD
44	a scarce	scarce a	δ⁴	A-G	•						•	•						•	
45	Then	Than	H	A-G	•	•	•	•	•		•	•	•	•	•			•	•
46	whersoe're	wheresoever	A	A-G								•							
54	returnd	Returne	β⁵	A												•			
54	this	next	β⁵	A-G	•						•	•		•	•	•		•	•
58	soft mayds	Maid's soft	G	G				•	•										
60	Then	Than	C	C-G								•							
61	When	Which	Z									•					•	•	•
61	of	with	LRH	A-G	•	•	•	•	•		•	•	•	•	•	•	•	•	•
63	bold	hould	H7	H7															
63	Soule	souls	H							•									
63	Soule	sole	H7	H7						•									
68	That	The	P		•							•							
69-70	ll. included	ll. om	A	A							•	•							
70	yea	or	B	B-G	•														
71	wring	wringd	B33							•									
72	Bearing like	~~	Q								•	•							
74-75	ll. included	ll. om	A	A	•							•							
77	he will	he'll	H																
77	our	the	A	A-G	•	•	•	•	•		•	•	•	•	•	•	•	•	•
79	gluttonee	luxury	LRH	A-G	•	•	•	•	•		•	•							
84	Relique like	Reliquely	δ⁴	A-G	•		•	•	•		•	•	•	•					
84	geare	chear	G	G				•	•			•							
86	men	Maids	G	G				•	•		•	•							
87	Parchments	parchment	β⁵	A-G	•	•	•	•	•		•	•							•
87	his	the	G	G								•							
91	written	writings	B33							•									
97	Lands	land	β⁶	A-G	•	•	•	•	•		•	•	•	•			•	•	•
99	As	And	G	G					•										
99	Commentor	Commentator	DD						•		•	•	•	•			•	•	•

Line no.	LOH/DV reading	Variant	OoV	A–G	H	I	J	K	M	N	O	P	Q	S	T	Y	Z	AA	DD
104	These	Those	LRH?	A–G	•	•	•	•	•		•	•	•	•		•	•	•	•
105	Where	Where's	β⁵	A	•	•	•	•	•		•	•	•	•		•	•	•	•
105	In	<In>	γ⁵	A							•								
105	great	<great>	β¹	B–G	•	•	•	•	•	•	•	•							
107	Meanes	Meane's	B	B–G	•	•	•	•	•	•	•	•							
107	blesse	blest	B	B–G	•	•	•	•	•	•	•	•							
108	not	no	β⁵	A–G	•	•	•	•			•	•	•	•		•	•	•	•
112	Statute	statute's	P							•	•								
112	Lawes	jawes	G	G						•									

readings…that have good authority in the early versions" (AA:14). Despite his basic reliance on A, Shawcross emends the text in some nine substantive instances (ll. 6, 34, 44, 54, 61, 77, 84, 87, and 105), citing support for his choices in various manuscripts and the later seventeenth-century prints, and is followed in all these emendations except those in lines 77 and 87 by Patrides. Shawcross's most curious change occurs in line 61, where—against all other witnesses—he prints the unintelligible "Which sicke with Poëtry" (for the normative "When…") and supports his choice with a spurious textual note. Both this emendation and a simplified version of the accompanying textual note also appear in Patrides (see Figure 7). Smith avoids the erroneous "Which" in line 61, but otherwise modifies A's text in all the same instances as Shawcross and adds two others, changing A's "toward them" to "towards them" in line 4 and respelling its "rithmes" as "rhymes" in line 17. As Figure 7 shows, of the 14 β^5 errors recorded in A, all three of these editions correct A's "Returne" in line 54 to "return'd," and Z and AA correct A's "parchment" in line 87 to "parchments"; the 12 remaining (in ll. 7, 8, 12, 15, 22, 24, 33, 40, 54, 97, 105, and 108) are retained in all three.

Copy-texts Used in this Edition

As noted above, *Sat2* survives in an original and a slightly revised version, and we here present emended reading texts of both. The copy-text for the original version is NY3, the surviving artifact closest to the LOH and the artifact similarly used for this purpose by Bennett in his modernized text of 1942. Of the five substantive emendations imposed by Bennett, however (see above), we have adopted only one: restoration of the omitted line 46. In addition, we have inserted the "not" uniquely omitted by NY3 in line 22 (changing "Are they like boyes singing" to the normative "Are they not like boyes singing"), expanded NY3's elided "th'insolence" to "the insolence" in line 39 (an elision otherwise found only in B32), and altered the manuscript's punctuation in 14 places where it seemed likely to mislead a reader. The copy-text for the revised version of the poem is DT1, the least corrupted surviving descendant of the LRH. Bringing this text into conformity with that lost archetype, however, requires emending it in nearly 2 dozen instances, since DT1 contains not only corrupt readings inherited from artifacts higher on the genealogical tree, but also idiosyncratic mistakes of its own. We have thus corrected the 14 previously noted β^5 errors (in lines 7, 8, 12, 15, 22, 24, 33, 40, 54 [2], 87, 97, 105, and 108); the 2 γ^4 errors (in lines 17 and 105); and the 7 verbal blunders for which the DT1 scribe is himself responsible, emending "nor" to "not" in line 10, "saue" to "saues" in line 13, "about" to "aboue" in line 15, "world" to "words" in line 57, "hold" to "bold" in line 63, "or" to "nor" in line 91, and "these" to "Those" in line 104. The remaining changes required to render DT1 readable, nearly a score of them, all involve punctuation. For both the original and the revised versions of the poem, all emendations, as well as the regularizations needed to prepare a manuscript text for print, are explicitly noted in the textual apparatus.

Textual Apparatus

Copy-texts: Original version: NY3.   Revised version: DT1.

Texts collated: B13 (ff. 51v–52v); B32 (ff. 89–90v); B33 (ff. 97v–98v); B40 (ff. 64v–66); B46 (ff. 1–3); B47 (ff. 95–97); C2 (ff. 16v–18); C5 (ff. 69v–70v); C8 (ff. 3v–6v); C9 (ff. 10–11v); DT1 (ff. 23v–25v); F21 (ff. 3v–6r); H3 (ff. 7v–9); H4 (ff. 11–12v); H5 (ff. 126–27v); H6 (pp. 57–60); H7 (ff. 43–45v); H8 (ff. 68–69v); HH1 (ff. 61–63); IU2 (*ll. 47–52, 57–58 only*, f. 60); NP3 (ff. 117–18v); NY1 (pp. 5–8); NY3 (ff. [3v–4v]); O20 (ff. 2v–4v); O21 (pp. 143–47); OJ1 (*ll. 2–3, 6, 22, 25–27, 32–34, 36, 41, 49–50, 54, 62–63, 69–70, 74–75, 77, 86, 98 only*, pp. 329–32); OQ1 (ff. 199v–200v); P3 (ff. 5v–6v); SN3 (ff. 21–23); SN4 (ff. 9–11); SP1 (ff. 10–11v); TT1 (ff. 25v–26v); VA1 (ff. 3–4v); VA2 (ff. 6v–7v); Y2 (pp. 9–16); Y3 (ff. 51v–52v); A (pp. 329–32); B (pp. 127–30); C (pp. 127–30); D (pp. 121–25); E (pp. 121–25); F (pp. 121–25); G (pp. 121[*misnumbered 221*]–24); 31a–b (*ll. 41–42 only*, p. 107); 33a–b (*ll. 5–6 only*, sig. A3; *ll. 39–48, 111–12 only*, sig. A4v; *ll. 19–20 only*, sig. A8v; *ll. 109–10 only*, sig. B8v); 44a–b (*ll. 34–36 only*, sig. 2Q7v); 44c–d (*same lines*, sig. 2Q3v); 49 (*ll. 21–22 only*, sig. D1; *ll. 23–24 only*, sig. K1v); 50a–b (*ll. 21–22 only*, sig. D1; *ll. 23–24 only*, sig. K1v).   **Not collated:** P1 (*ll. 2–4, 9–10, 20, 24–30, 32–33, 45, 47–52, 55–57, 80, 89–90 only*, f. 53r–v). .

Emendations of the copy-text, original version: Heading: *Satyre 2.*] Sat: 2.ᵃ
Line 14 Sceanes,] ~.   19 batteree,] ~ₐ   21 Lords,] ~;   gett,] ~ₐ
22 not] *om*   27 Rankly] ~ → »Rawly«   32 dildoes] ~~widdows~~ ~
36 make,] ~.   40 Offence,] ~.   42 oxe,] ~ₐ   44 But] ›~‹   46
line om; supplied from H7   53 went,] ~ₐ   63 Soule,] ~ₐ   68 there,]
~.   70 king;] ~.   73 whores,] ~ₐ   81 a] ›~‹   84 geare,] ~ₐ
88 Assurances,] ~;

Regularizations of the copy-text, original version: Line 1 Sir] Sʳ   4 the] yᵉ
6 that] yᵗ   7 the] yᵉ   11 which] wᶜʰ   12 which] wᶜʰ   16 which]
wᶜʰ   29 For] for   31 which] wᶜʰ   34 with] wᵗ   38 which
Commandments] wᶜʰ Cōmandmᵗˢ   41 which] wᶜʰ   48 wooes] woes
the] yᵉ   52 that] yᵗ   57 which] wᶜʰ   60 our] oʳ   61 with] wᵗ
62 which] wᶜʰ   67 which] wᶜʰ   77 the] yᵉ   our] oʳ   79 with] wᵗ
82 *2nd* the] yᵉ   83 which] wᶜʰ   89 our] oʳ   94 Pater Nosters] Pat.ʳ
Nost.ʳˢ   99 Commentor] Cōmentor   102 which] wᶜʰ   the] yᵉ
103 which] wᶜʰ   104 within] wᵗin

Emendations of the copy-text, revised version: Heading: *Satyre 2.*] Satyre.
Line 4 rest.] ~;   7 or] &   8 It ridlingly] ridlingly it   10 not] nor

66

hate.] ~‸   11 (like] ‸~   12 could not] cannot   13 saues] saue
15 organs] organ   aboue] about   17 rimes] rithmes   20 Artillerie.]
~,   22 boyes singing] singers   24 scuse] excuse   28 true,] ~‸
33 out-sweare] t'out-sweare   36 make,] ~‸   40 great] just
44 poett;] ~,   49 Coscus;] ~,   50 Queene,] ~‸   53 went,] ~‸
54 return'd] returne   this] next   55 grace;] ~‸   56 place] ~.
57 Affidauits:] ~,   words,] ~.   words] world   60 roare.] ~‸
62 madd,] ~‸   63 bold] hold   soule,] ~‸   64 strumpetts] ~,
prostitute.] ~,   70 Kinge;] ~.   80 hee.] ~,   84 (Relique-like] ‸~·~
87 parchments] parchment   88 bigg] ~,   91 nor] or   97 lands]
land   98 heires,] ~‸   104 Those] these   doore.] ~‸   105 Where]
Where's   In great] Great   107 hate;] ~,   108 not] noe   112
Lawes.] ‸~

Regularizations of the copy-text, revised version: *The manuscript exhibits initial
capital letters in ll. 1, 6, 11, 17, 19, 25, 38, 39, 49, 55, 56, 59, 63, 67, 68, 75,
80, 84, 87, 91, 97, 98, 99, 103, 105, 106, 107, 108, 109, and 112; all other
first-of-line capitals supplied.*   Line 1 Sir] S^r 4 That] y^t 11 which]
wch 12 which] wch and] &   16 which] wch 19 and] &   28
and] &   31 which] wch 32 and] &   34 with] wth 35 and] &
38 which] wch 41 which] wch and] &   43 which] wch 48 and]
&   52 that] y^t 57 which] wch 61 1st and 2nd with] wth and]
&   62 and] &   which] wch 67 which] wch 75 and] &   79
with] wth 83 which] wch thirty] 30.   85 and] &   89 that] y^t
102 which] wch the] ye 103 which] wch 104 within] wthin   105
and] &   107 ritch mens] ritchmens   112 Within] Wthin

HISTORICAL COLLATION

Format:
   Imperfections: *possible loss of text to trimming, ll. 62 and 67*   C5.
   Indentations: *l. 49 ind*   IU2; *l. 1 ind*   NY3 SN4; *l. 1 hanging ind*   SP1; *ll.
      111–12 ind*   Y3; *no ind*   Σ.
   Miscellaneous: *D^r: Doone: is running head in ms.*   B32; *nonscribal gloss the
      mean is best in left M at l. 107*   B46; *poem nonscribally attributed to I: D: in
      right M beside HE*   B47; ›I:D.‹ *in left M at l. 1*   DT1; »ID:« *in left M at l.
      1*   H4; »P.« *in M opposite HE*   H6; *immediately follows snippets from Sat1
      under general HE* Empty Fop   IU2; *every 5th l. numbered in arabic in left
      M*   NY1 VA2; *HE in left M*   NY3; *ms. emendations and additions in a copy
      of A*   OJ1; ›T. S.‹ *written in left M opposite HE,* ›after b. B. coppy‹ *in right
      M beside HE*   SN3; *l. 60 inserted scribally in right M*   Y2; *attributed to Dr.
      D. in right M*   31a–b; *immediately follows ElPerf 35–36 as a single item
      under the same HE*   44a–d.
Headings: Satire 3^d. | B13.   **Satyre:. 2^d**   B32 C2 C8 H8(2.) SN3(2.) A(II.)–
      G(II.).   Sat. 2da B33 NY3(2.^{a}) VA1(2:).   *Satyre*   B46 DT1 H4 O20.

Satyre 1: Agaynst Poets and Lawyers. B47. | .Satyra. Secunda. |
C5(2ᵃ) H7 VA2 Y2. Satyres. [*section HE*] C9 H6. Satire 2ᵈ: | F21
NY1(2). Another Satyre of M:ʳ Iohn Donne H3. Satyra Quinta.
H5. Satire HH1. Iohn Donne | Satyr 2. | the lawyer. | NP3.
Law Satyre O21. *Satira 2ᵃ* OQ1 SP1. The secound Satire P3.
Sat: 5 | SN4(M: »Satyre II«). Lawe Satire Y3. *Wicked. v. Forms of*
dispraising. 44a–d. *om* B40 IU2 OJ1 TT1 31a–b 33a–b.

1 Sir,] B47 C2 DT1 H5 H7 NY3 OQ1 SP1; ~; O21 A–G; ~ₐ Σ. Though]
(~ B13 NP3 OQ1 Y2; ~. B33. (I] ₐ~ B13 C5 H3 H7 NP3 OQ1 Y2. for
it)] ~ ~ₐ C5 H3 TT1; ~ ~, H7; for't) O21 Y3. do] ~ not O21 Y3.

2 Perfectly] ~, B13 B46 VA1; *om* B33 C5. towne,] ~; B13 O21 SN3
SN4; ~ₐ perfectly, B33 C5; ~: H6 H7 OQ1; ~ₐ P3 TT1; ~. VA1.
ther is one] in euery B33(*var:* ›~ ~ ~‹) OJ1; euerie B46; there's ~ B47 C2 C8
C9 DT1 H4 H5 H6 H8 O21 P3 Y2 Y3 A–G; ~ ~ in ~ H3(→ »~ ~ ~«); theirs one
NP3; ~ ~ a NY1 VA2. State] ~, C8 HH1; ~; OQ1.

3 In] There B33(*var:* ›~‹) OJ1; Hath B46. all] are B33(*var:* ›~‹) OJ1;
in't B46. ill] *om* B13 H5 OQ1 SN3 Y2; some B33(*var:* ›~‹) B46 OJ1.
things] ~, B32 B40 O20 Y2; found B33(*var:* ›~,‹) B46 OJ1; thinkes F21 NY1.
excellently] villainously B33(*var:* ›~‹) B46 OJ1. best] ~, B32 B33(*var:* ›~ₐ‹)
C2 C8 F21 H4 SP1 A–G; bleste B46 Y2; blest, H5 HH1; ~. OJ1; lest SN3.

4 That] As B33. hate] ~, B40 A. towards] toward B40 NY1 A–F;
~, C9 H6. them] that, B13 C9 H6; ~ → ›that‹ B33; ~, B40 B46 C2 DT1
HH1 O20 OQ1 Y2 A–G; it H5; ~; O21. breeds] breed, H7. towards]
in B13; toward B32 B33 H5 NY1 O20 SP1 TT1 B–F; to B46 B47 C9 H6 H7
OQ1. rest.] ~, B32 HH1 O20; ~ₐ B40 B47 F21 H3 NP3 NY1 O21 P3 TT1
VA2 Y3; ~; C2 C8 DT1 A; ~: H4 OQ1.

5 Poetry] ~, G 33a–b. indeed] ~, O21 G 33a–b. be] by F21.
such] *om* SN3 SN4. Sin] ~, B32 C8 DT1 H5 HH1 O20 OQ1 SN4 SP1 D–G
33a–b.

6 As] ~, B47 G; (~ SN3 SN4. I] I'ame B33; (~ C9 H5 H6; (I'me
OJ1. thinke] afraid B33; ~, B40 B47 C2 C8 DT1 H4 HH1 G 33a–b; feare
C5; ~), C9 H6; ~) H5 SN3 SN4; ~»,« H7; afraide) OJ1. that] *om* B33
C5 H3 NP3 OJ1 Y2 33a–b; might B46 B47 H7; ~, C9 H6, OQ1; it F21 Y3; him
→ ›it‹ O21. brings] bringe B46 B47 H7; bringeth NP3. dearths]
Dearth, B32 H3 H7 O20 SP1 A–G; death B46 F21; dearthe B47 C9 H5 H6
H8 HH1 O21 OQ1 Y3; ~, C2 C8 DT1 H4 VA1; dearth; NP3; pale dearth
Y2; the plague, 33a–b. and] *om* H3. Spanyards] ~, H7; the Dutch
33a–b. in;] DT1 H5 H8 NY3 SN4; ~, B13 C2 H4 NY1 SP1 VA2 A; ~. B33
F21 O20 SN3 33a–b; ~.| C8; ~: HH1 OQ1 B–G; ~ₐ Σ.

7 Though] ~, C9 DT1 H6. the] *om* H3 OQ1 P3 VA1. pestilence] B47
C2 C5 H3 NP3 NY1 NY3 OQ1 P3 SN3 TT1 VA2 Y3 A–C; ~; O21 Y2; ~, Σ.

or] and B40 C2 C8 DT1 H3 H4 HH1 NY1 O21 P3 SN3 SN4 TT1 VA1 VA2
A–G.   old fashiond] ~ fashioned   B40 C2 F21 H3 NY1 TT1; ~=~   B46 OQ1;
~-fashioned   C5; could fashioned   NP3.   loue] ~,   B13 B32 C8 HH1 O20
A–G; Loues   H7.

8 It ridlingly] ridlingly it   B40 C2 C8 DT1 H4 TT1 A–G; ~ ridinglie   B46 B47
C5 C9 H6(→ ›~ ~‹) NY1 SN3 SP1 VA2 Y2; The ridleinge   H3; ~ ~ ~ →
~ ›riddingly‹   H6; ~ rydes killingely,   H7; ~ riddling   H8 NP3 P3 VA1.
catch] doth ~   B47; catches   C5; catcheth   H3 H7 H8 NP3(→ ›catchest‹);
catch't   O21 Y3; cath   P3.   men,] ~∧   B46 C5 NY1 P3 TT1 VA1; ~;   C2 C8
O21 A.   doth remoue] death ~   B47; ~ ~.   C8; removes   H7.

9 Neuer] ~,   B33 B40 B46 B47 C2 C9 DT1 H4 H5 H6 SN3 SN4 A–G; ~ → ~»,«
C8.   steru'd] stau'd   B47; starued   C5 OQ1 P3; om   NY1(M: »~«).   out,] ~.
B13 H8 NY1 P3 VA2; ~;   B32 B46 C2 C8 C9 F21 HH1 O20 SN4 A–F; ~:   B40
H6; ~∧   NP3; ~!   TT1.   their] your   NP3.   State] estate   B13 H3(→ »~«)
H8 OQ1 P3 VA1.

10 poore,] ~∧   B33 C5 H7 H8 NY1 TT1 VA2 Y3; ~;   O21.   disarm'd,] ~∧
B33 H3 H7 H8 HH1 NP3 NY1 OQ1 SN3 SN4 TT1 VA1 VA2 Y3; disarmed,
C5 F21 P3; disdain'd;   O21.   Papists,] ~;   B13; ~∧   B33 B46 C5 H3 NP3 NY1
O21 P3 SP1 TT1 VA1 VA2 Y3; Papist∧   Y2.   not] nor   DT1 H4.   worth]
worthie   OQ1.   hate.] ~;   B32 H5 O20; ~,   B40 H3; ~∧   B46 B47 C2 DT1
F21 H4 NP3 P3 TT1 VA1 VA2 Y2 Y3; ~.| C9; ~:   H7 A–G.

11 One] Or   B32 F21 H5 H7 O20 P3 SP1 Y2; ~,   C2 C8 NY1(M var: »Or«)
SN4 VA2 A D–G; (~   HH1 VA1.   like] (~   B40 B46 B47 C2 C8 C9 H6 NP3
OQ1 TT1 Y3 A–G.   wretch] ~,   B40 C2 C8 DT1 H3 H8 O20 VA1 Y2 A–G; ~)
TT1 Y3.   which] (~   B13 H7; that   B46 C9 H6; om   C5.   barr] ~,   B32; a
~   H7 NP3.   iudgd] Iudged,   F21; iudged   H4 P3 TT1 VA2; ~,   OQ1 VA1;
Iudge   Y2.   as] is   B13 H3 H8 O21 OQ1 P3 VA1 Y3; om   H7 NP3.   dead]
~,   B13 C8 DT1 H5 H7 O20 OQ1 SP1 A B G.

12 Yet] (~   H8 P3.   prompts] prompes   B40 C2 HH1 VA1(,).   him] om
H3.   which] that   B46 B47 C9 H6 HH1 SN3 SN4 VA2; who   H5; om   NY1;
y^ts   Y2.   stands] stoode   H3 NP3; stand   HH1.   next,] ~∧   B33 B46 C5 C9
F21 H6 H7 NP3 NY1 O21 SN3 SN4 TT1 VA1 VA2 Y3; om   OQ1.   and] yet
H3; w^ch   H5; y^t   NY1 VA2.   could not] cannot   B40 C2 C8 DT1 H4 O21 TT1
Y3 A–G; can ~   Y2.   read] ~,   B13 B32 DT1 H4 H5 H7 HH1 O20 SP1 A
D–G; rea[trimmed]   H8.

13 And] (~   H4 O21.   saues] saue   DT1 H4.   Life,] B32 B33 C5 F21 H3
H5 NY3 SN3 SN4 VA2 Y2; ~;   O20; ~:   SP1; ~∧   TT1; ~)   Σ.   giues] geue
OQ1; (~   TT1.   Ideot Actors] ~=~   B40 B46 C2 C8 DT1 NP3; Ideots ~   B47
Y2.   meanes] ~,   B32 C5 C8 DT1 H6 H7 B–G; ~;   HH1.

14 Steruing] B33 B46 B47 C5 C9 H3 H6 H7 HH1 NY3 OQ1 SN3 SN4 TT1 Y2
B–F; while   O21; (while   Y3; (~   Σ.   himselfe] B33 B46 B47 C5 C9 H3 NY3

B–F; him selfe   H6 H7; ~,   HH1 OQ1 SN3 SN4 Y2; him selfe)   NP3 VA2;
~ starues,   O21; ~ starues)   Y3; ~)   Σ.   to liue] om om   SN3; ~ ~,   VA1.
by his] by om   B46 H5; by's   B47 H3.   Labord] laboured   B40 B46 C5 SN3
SP1 TT1 VA1.   Sceanes,] B40 DT1; ~;   B32 C9 H5; ~∧   B33 B47 F21 H3 H4
H8 HH1 NP3 O21 OQ1 P3 TT1 VA1 Y3; scaynes   SN3; scheames∧   Y2; ~.   Σ.

15 As] or ~   H5; And ~   SN3 SN4.   some] ~.   C5.   Organes] *Organ*,
B40 C2 C8 DT1 A–F; ~,   B46 H7 HH1 SP1 G; organ   B47 C9 H4 H6 TT1.
puppets] Pappittes   F21; puppies   H3.   aboue] ~,   B13 B32 B40 C8 H5 H7
HH1 O20 OQ1 SN4 SP1; about,   DT1.

16 bellows] Billowes   VA1.   pant] pantes   OQ1.   below] ~,   B13 B32 B33
B40 C2 DT1 H4 HH1 O20 SP1 VA1 A–G.   them do] doe them   B13 H3 NY1
OQ1 P3 VA1 VA2; om ~   B46; doth them   H8; doth not   O21 Y3; ~ did   SN3.
moue.] ~,   B32 B40 H8 HH1 O20 SN4; ~∧   B33 B47 C8(→ ~».«) F21 H3 H4 H6
NP3 O21 OQ1 P3 SN3 TT1 VA1 VA2 Y2 Y3; ~:   C5; ~;   H7.

17 One] on   B47; ~,   SP1.   moue] winne   O21 Y3; more   Y2.   Loue] ~,
VA2.   rhimes;] ~,   B33 B46 B47 C5 F21 H5 H6 H8 P3 SN3 SN4 SP1 VA1 Y2;
rithmes;   C2 C8 DT1 A–G; Rime,   H3; ~:   H4; rythmes,   H7 NY1(M *var*: »~«,)
VA2; ~∧   NP3 O21 TT1 Y3; rithmes∧   OQ1.   but] by   F21.   witchcrafts
charmes] B33 B40 C5 DT1 H5 HH1 NY3 TT1 A–F; witch crost ~   B47;
witch-crafts ~   C2; ~=charm»es«.   C8; witch craft ~   C9 NP3; ~, ~   H4;
witchcraft charm[*trimmed*]   H8; witchcraft-~   OQ1; witch-craft-~   VA2; ~ ~,
G; witchcraft ~   Σ.

18 Bring not] Now ~ ~   NP3.   now] om   B46 H3 OQ1 NP3 P3 VA1;.
their] there   B47 C5 O21 VA1 VA2 Y3; your   NP3.   feares,] ~∧   B33 B46 B47
O21 P3 TT1; ~;   DT1; feare,   SN3.   nor] now, ~   B46; but   SP1.   their]
om   C5 P3 VA1; they   H3 H8; your   NP3; there   VA2 Y3.   old harmes.]
~ ~∧   B33 B46 B47 F21 H7 NP3 NY1 O21 OQ1 VA1 Y2 Y3; ~ ~;   B32 H4 O20;
~ ~,   B40; ~ ~:   H5; ~=~∧   HH1.

19 Ramms] ~,   B13 C2 DT1 H7 HH1 P3 SP1 A–G; ~ now,   B46; Rimes   O21
Y3.   Slings] ~,   C9 H6 P3; songes;   O21; songs   Y3.   now are] ~, ~   B40
C9 H6 O21; om ~   B46; om ~ but   NP3; are nowe   OQ1; are now a   Y2.
seely] B32 B40 C8 F21 NY3 O20 SN4 SP1 A–C; symple   H7 Y2; silly   Σ.
batteree,] B13 B32 C2 C8 DT1 H5 H8 NY1 SN4 VA2 A–G; Batterys∧   F21 NP3;
~:   HH1; ~.   SP1; ~∧   Σ.
        Alternate line: The Canons throat is but / frail battery,   33a–b.

20 Pistolets] Pistolls   NP3 O21 Y3.   are] ~ nowe   H5 NP3 Y2; nowe ~
OQ1.   the] your   C9 H6.   artilleree.] ~,| B13; ~∧   B33 B40 B47 H3 H4
O21 OQ1 P3 TT1 Y2 Y3; ~,   DT1; Artillerys∧   F21 NP3; ~;   H5; ~:   SN3 SP1;
Artilly.   33b.

21 who] that   C8 O20 SP1 TT1.   write] ~,   C5; writ   P3.   Lords,] B32
B40 B47 C2 C8 DT1 F21 H4 H5 O20 SN3 A–G; ~;   H7 NY3; ~∧   Σ.   rewards]

reward   B47 H3 Y2.   gett,] B13 B32 B40 C8 DT1 H4 H5 HH1 SN4 A–G; ~:
OQ1; ~;   P3; ~.   49 50a–b; ~∧ Σ.

22 they] *om* NP3 OJ1.   not] but NP3; *om* NY3 OJ1.   like] ~ to OJ1.
boyes singing] singers,   B13 C8; ~, ~   B32 F21 O20; Singers   B40 B46 B47 C2
C9(M *var:* ›|~ ~.|‹) DT1 H4 H6(*var:* ›~ ~‹) TT1 A–G 49 50a–b; ~ *om* H5;
~, who sing Y2.   dores] mens ~ B13; dore   B33 B46 B47 C9 H3 H6 H8 NP3
NY1 O21 OJ1 P3 SN4 VA1 VA2 Y3; ~ singing H5; a doore   OQ1.   meat?] ~∧
B33 F21 HH1 NP3 O21 TT1 VA1 Y2 Y3; ~;   B40; ~.   B46 C5 OJ1 SN3.

23 And] *For* 49 50a–b.   they who] ~ that   B40 P3 TT1; *om* who   B47;
those ~   C5; whosoe NP3.   write] writ,   B13 Y2; ~,   B32 B46 C2 C5 C8 F21
H3 H7 H8 O20 P3 A–G 49 50a–b; wryt   VA1.   write,] writt∧   C9 H3 H6 Y2;
~∧   H7 NP3 O21 P3 TT1 Y3; ~?   OQ1; writ,   SN3; wryt;   VA1.   still] ~,   C5
H6 49 50a–b.

24 That Scuse] ~ excuse   B40 C2 C8 DT1 H4 P3 TT1 VA1 A–F 49 50a–b;
Thats 'scuse   C9 H6; ~ sauce   H3; A sence   H7; ~ same   O21 Y3; ~ sence
OQ1; ~ scape Y2; ~'excuse G.   for wrighting] NY3 P3 VA1; ~ writing B33
B47 C5 NY1 O21 OQ1 SN4 TT1 Y3; ~ writinge;   DT1; fore-wrytinge,   H7;
~ writing,   Σ.   and] ~,   HH1.   wrighting] NY3 P3; writing   Σ.   ill.]
~,   B33 B40 H4 SN3; ~∧   B47 H3 NP3 TT1 VA1 Y3; ~;   C2 F21 H8 O21 A.

25 But] And B13.   worst,] ~∧   B33 B47 C8 C9 F21 H3 H5 H6 HH1 NY1
O21 OQ1 P3 TT1 VA1 VA2 Y2 Y3; worse,   H7; worse∧   H8 NP3.   who] that
H8 NP3 SP1 Y2.   beggerly] (~)   B40 C2 A–G; beggardlie B46; (~   C8; in
his OJ1; beggery Y2.   doth] doeth C5; ravinous OJ1.   chaw] maw   OJ1.

26 Others] Other   C5 O21 Y3; ~-   H7.   witts] witte   C5; ~,   F21 H8;
~-   H7.   fruites,] ~∧   H3 H7 NP3 NY1 OJ1 P3 TT1 VA2.   and] *om*   H3
OJ1.   in his rauenous] most beggarly doth   OJ1.   maw] ~.   C8; chawe.
OJ1; ~,   SP1.

27 Rankly] Rawly   B32 B46 F21 H7 O20 SP1 Y2; ~ (M *var:* »Rawly«)   NY1;
~ → »Rawly« NY3.   digested] ~,   B13 C8 DT1 HH1 OQ1 A–G; digested,
B32 B40 C2 F21 H7; disgested   B47 H5 H6 SN3 SN4 Y2; disgected,   O20.
doth] doeth   C5; do   OJ1 P3 VA1; does   SN3.   those] these   B32 F21 H7
H8 NP3 O20 O21 SP1 TT1 VA1 Y2 Y3; the   H6(*var:* ›~‹).   things] same
H6(*var:* ›~‹); *om*   OJ1.   outspue] out spew   B13 B33 B47 C2 H5 H8 O21 OQ1
P3 TT1 VA1 VA2 Y2 Y3; out spue,   B32 C5; out=spue   B40 B46 C9 DT1 H4 H6
H7 NP3 OJ1 SN3 SN4 SP1; out=spue,   C8 A–G; out shew   H3; ~,   HH1.

28 things,] ~;   B32 B40 B46 C2 C8 C9 H6 HH1 A–G; ~∧   B33 NP3 P3 TT1
Y3; ~:   F21 NY1 OQ1 SN4 VA2.   they're] B46 B47 C9 H5 H6 H8 NY1 NY3
SN3 SN4 VA2 Y2; they are   Σ.   owne:] NY3; ~;   B32 H8 NY1 O20 OQ1 VA2;
~.   B46; ~∧   C8(→ »~,«) H3 H4 HH1 NP3 O21 P3 TT1 VA1 Y3; ~,   Σ.   tis]
its B33; *om*   O21 Y3.   true.] ~,   B13 B33 B40 C8 A–G; ~∧   B47 DT1 H3 H8

NP3 NY1 O21 P3 SN3 TT1 VA1 VA2 Y3; ~:   F21 H7 OQ1 Y2; ~;   H4 H5 H6
SN4; ~.;   HH1.

29 For] ~,   C9 H6.   one] owne   C2 VA2.   eate] *om* TT1.   meate,]
~∧ B33 B47 C8 H4 H7 NP3 NY1 SN3 TT1 VA2 Y3.   knowne] ~,   B32 C5
HH1 O20.

30 was] is   B47.   myne,] ~∧   B47 F21 H4 NP3 NY1 O21 P3 TT1 VA2 Y3; ~;
OQ1.   the excrement is] B40 C9 H4 NY3 TT1 Y3; ~ ~ *om*   B47 SN3;
~ excrements *om*   C5 H3 O21 OQ1 Y2; th' ~ ~   C2 C8 DT1 H6 HH1 A–G;
th'~ 's   H7 NY1 P3 VA2; th'~'his   SN4; thexcrements *om*   VA1; ~ excrement's
Σ.   owne.] ~, B40 F21 H4; ~∧   B47 C5 H3 NP3 O21 TT1 VA1 Y2 Y3; ~:
OQ1 A.

31 these] those   B13 B33 H3 H8 NY1 OQ1 P3 TT1 VA1 VA2; they   B32 F21
H7 O20 SP1 Y2.   harme.] H8 NY3 VA1; ~;   B13 B46 C2 C8 DT1 SN3 SN4;
~∧ B47 F21 NP3 TT1; ~:   OQ1; ~, Σ.   Nor] for F21.   they] those   C9
H6 O21 TT1 Y3.   which] who   B33; that   C9 H6.   vse] ~,   C8 HH1.

32 outswive] out doe   B13 HH1 O21 P3 TT1 VA1 VA2 Y3; outdoe   B33 H4;
out-doe   B40 C2 C8 DT1 H8 NY1 OQ1 A–G; out=swiue   B46 H6 H7 SN3 SN4
SP1; out swiue   B47 F21 H3 Y2; out-swine   C9; out-ly   H5; out sweare NP3.
dildoes;] B32 C2 C8 DT1 NY3 O20 O21 OJ1; ~:   C5; Lawyers,   H5; ~∧   NY1 P3
TT1 VA2 Y3; ———;   A; ~, Σ.   and] or   B13 B33; to   C9 H6.
out vsure] outvsure   B32 NY1 O20 SN3; ~-~   B33 B40 B46 C2 C8 C9 DT1 F21
H3 H6 H7 H8 SN4 SP1 A–G; ~-vsury   H5; ~ vsury   HH1 NP3 Y2.   lewes:] C5
HH1 NY3; ~;   B32 C2 DT1 O20 A; ~,   B40 H5 OQ1 P3 SN3 SN4 B–G; ~.   B46
C8 H8 NY1 SP1 VA2; ~.| H3; ~∧ Σ.

33 To out drinke] ~ outdrinke   B33 O20; t'~ ~   B40 B47 H7 NP3 NY1 TT1
VA2 Y2; ~ ~=~   B46 C2 C8 DT1 H8 SN4 SP1 A–G; T'~-~   C9 H5 H6.
Sea:] NY3; ~;   B32 B46 DT1 O20; ~∧   NP3 O21 TT1 VA2; ~, Σ.   outsweare]
out sweare   B13 C5 F21 HH1 NY1 O21 P3 VA1 VA2 Y2 Y3; t'out *Swear*   B40
B47 NP3 TT1; out-sweare   B46 H5 H8 SN3 SN4 SP1; t'out=sweare   C2 DT1;
t'~   C8 C9 H4 H6 H7; and ~   H3; to out-sweare   A–G.   Letanee:] DT1 NY3;
~,   B33 B40 C9 H5 H6 H8 O20 OQ1 SN4 VA2 G; ~.   B46; ~;   C2 C8 HH1;
——— A; *om*   B C; gallant, he   D–F; ~∧ Σ.

34 Who] ~,   B40 C2.   Sins] ~,   C2 HH1 SP1.   all] of ~   B46 C2 C8 H3
NP3 O21 P3 TT1 Y2 Y3 A 44a–d; ~→ ›of‹ ~   SP1.   kinds] ~,   B32 B33 F21
O20 OQ1; kinde   H3 NP3 P3 TT1.   as] *om* O21 Y3.   bee] ~,   B32 C8 H5.

35 Confessors:] B46 B47 C5 C8 NY3 O20 Y2; ~;   B13 C2 DT1 HH1 NP3 O21 A
44c–d; ~.   H8 P3 SP1; ~∧   TT1 VA1 Y3; ~, Σ.   sake] ~,   B40 C5 G 44a–d.

36 Schoolemen] ~,   B13 B40 C8 HH1 A–F; Schoole men,   C2; Schoole men
C5 H8; Schoole=men   OQ1 SN3 SN4 VA1; School   44a–b; *Pluto*   44c–d.
new tenements] ~ tormentes now   B47 H6(*var*: ›~ ~ now‹); ~ ~ now   C9; in hell
H3 H5 NP3 NY1 VA2; ~ torments   SN3.   in hell] new Tenements   H3 H5

NP3 NY1 VA2.　　make,] B32 B40 C9 O20 SN3 44a–b; ~:　C2 SN4 A–G; ~.
C5 C8 H8 HH1 NY1 NY3 SP1 44c–d; ~;　H5 OQ1; ~ₐ　Σ.
　Alternate line: Schoolemen, in hell new torments more must make.　OJ1.

37　Whose] In ~　B33; who　SN4.　　strange] stronge　B13; straying　HH1.
Sins] ~,　C2 DT1 HH1 SP1 A–F.　　Canonists] (Canonist　Y2.　　could] can
B46 B47 H7 H8 NP3 O21 Y2 Y3.　　hardly] scarcely　O21 Y3.　　tell] ~, C8 H3;
~.　O21.

38　In] (~　OQ1.　　which] what　NY1(M *var:* »~«) VA2; whose　OQ1.
Commandments] Commandment's　B46.　　receite] recite　SN3; receipts　Y2.
dwell.] ~ₐ　B13 B32 B33 B47 F21 H3 H4 NP3 O21 P3 SN3 TT1 VA1 Y3; ~,　B40
O20 VA2 Y2 G; ~:　HH1; ~)　OQ1.

39　But] for　B40 B46 B47 TT1.　　these] those　B40 H3 H7 H8 NP3 TT1 Y2.
punish] punished　SN3.　　themselues:] ~.|　B13; ~.　B32 B46 F21 H8 O20
OQ1 P3 SP1 VA1 B–G; ~ₐ　B33 TT1; ~,　B40 B47 C5 H3 H7 NY1 O21 VA2;
~;　C2 C8 C9 DT1 H5 H6 SN3 Y2 Y3 A; them selues;　HH1.　　th'insolence]
B32 F21 NY3 O20 SP1 Y2; the insolence,　C5; The insolence　Σ.
　Alternate line: But above all, the gaudy insolence　33a–b.

40　Coscus] Coccus　B13; ~,　B32 DT1 O20 B–G; Cascus　F21; Cosens　H3
NP3(Cozens); Couscus　H4(*var:* »~«); *staring* CROCUS,　33a–b.　　only] ~,
B–G; *om*　33a–b.　　breeds my] *gives me*　33a–b.　　great] iust　B40 C2 C8
DT1 H4 TT1 A–G 33a–b; harts　NY1 VA2.　　Offence,] B32 B40 C2 C9 DT1
H5 H6 O20 OQ1 Y2 A–G; ~.　B46 C5 C8 H8 NY3 SN4 SP1; ~:　HH1; ~;　NY1
VA2 33a–b; ~ₐ　Σ.

41　Whome] *As*　31a–b.　　time,] H5 H7 NY3 SP1; ~ₐ　Σ .　　which] B13
B32 B33 C5 F21 H3 H5 H7 HH1 NY1 NY3 O20 O21 SP1 Y3; *om*　31a–b; (~　Σ.
rotts] ~.　VA2; *om*　31a–b.　　all,] ~ₐ　C5 H4 HH1 NP3 NY1 O21 OQ1 P3 SN3
TT1 VA1 VA2 Y3; ~ₐ things,　OJ1; ~)　Y2; *om*　31a–b.　　and] *om*　OJ1 31a–b.
makes] make　VA1.　　botches] ~,　B32 C9 DT1 SP1 G 33a–b; bottes　B47.
poxe] ~,　B13 B32 B40 B46 C2 C5 C8 C9 DT1 H5 H8 O20 OQ1 VA2 A–G 31a–b
33a–b; yᵉ ~　B47; ~)　P3 VA1.

42　*om* VA1.　　plodding] ~,　F21; *om*　P3.　　on] ~,　B32 B40 B46 C2 C8
DT1 F21 HH1 O20 A–G 33a–b; *om*　P3.　　must] *om*　P3; will　31a–b.
make] makes at length　P3.　　calfe] ~,　B13 B32 B46 C2 O20 SP1 33a–b; ~
become　P3.　　an] ~ an　B.　　oxe,] B32 B33 H5 HH1 O20; ~ₐ　B13 F21 H3
NY1 NY3 O21 P3 Y3; ~).　B46 Y2; ~.　C5 H7 SP1; ~;　H4; ~.)　H6 33b; ~)　Σ.

43　Lawyer:] B32 F21 NY3 O20 SP1; ~.　B46; ~;　C2 C8 DT1 NP3 P3 A–G; ~ₐ
H4 H7 O21 SN3 TT1 Y3; ~,　Σ.　　which] who　C9 H6; ~,　B–F 33a–b.
was] ~,　B46 H5; *om*　B47 C9 H6 B–G 33a–b.　　alas] ~,　B46 B47 H5; a Lasse
C2 VA1; (~)　C8 H7 HH1 OQ1 Y2 B–G.　　of] a　VA1.　　late] ~,　C2 C8
33a–b.

44　a scarse] scarce a　B47 C2 C8 C9 H6 H7 O20 O21 SP1 Y3 A–G 33a–b; ~ ~

(M var: »scarse a«)   NY1; om ~   Y2.   Poet:] ~;   B13 B46 NP3 SP1 B–G;
~,   B33 B40 B47 C2 C8 C9 DT1 H4 H6 H7 HH1 OQ1 Y2 A 33a–b; ~.   C5 H8
NY1(M var: »~ₐ«) P3 VA1 VA2; ~ₐ   H3 O21 TT1 Y3.   lolyer] ~:   B32;
collier   NP3; sollicitor   TT1.   of] in   33a–b.   this] that   B13 B33 H3 H8
O21 OQ1 P3 VA1 Y3; his   B47 C9 H6 H7 NP3 NY1 VA2 Y2.   State] ~,   B46
C2 C8 HH1 A–G 33a–b; ~.   C5.

45 Then] There   C2; Than   SN3.   are] anie   C8; our   33a–b.   new
benefic'd] ~-benificed   B47; ~ benificed   C5 NY1 O21 P3 VA1 VA2 Y3;
~=benific't   H3; ~ benifited   SN3; ~-~-   SP1.   Ministers,] ~;   B32 H3 NP3
O20 O21 Y3; ~:   C5 F21 OQ1 SP1; ~ₐ   TT1 Y2; Trades-men,   33a–b.   he]
O ~   33a–b.

46 om   B32 F21 NP3 NY3 O20 SP1.   Like] (~   C9 H6 SN4.   Netts,]
~ₐ   B46 B47 C9 H5 H6 HH1 NY1 O21 OQ1 SN3 SN4 TT1 VA2 Y2 Y3.   or]
of   O21.   Lyme-twiggs,] limetwiggs,   B13 B33 B40 C5 H4 HH1 B–F; ~=~ₐ
B46 H5 NY1 SN3 SN4 VA2; ~ₐ ~ₐ   B47 H8 VA1; ~ₐ ~,   C2 C8 OQ1 P3;
limetwigges)   C9 H6; ~ₐ twigge,   H3; limetwiges ₐ   O21 TT1 Y2 Y3.
whersoe're] where ere   B13 OQ1; where so e're   B33 C2 H8; wher soere   B40 B47
SN4; where soeuer   C5; whers'ever   HH1; (where ere   P3 VA1; wheresoever
A–G.   goes] ~»,«   C8; ~,   C9 H6 HH1 A–F; ~)   P3 SN4 VA1; ~.   33a–b.

47 His] Tells   IU2; The   33a–b.   title] himself   IU2.   of] om   IU2 Y2.
Barrister] ~,   B13 C2 H5 HH1 A–G 33a–b.   on] to   IU2.   euery] eury   C9
SN3.   wenche:] NY3; ~,   B13 B32 B40 C2 C5 C8 DT1 H5 HH1 IU2 O20 SN3
SN4 SP1 A–G 33a; ~.   B46; ~;   H8; ~ₐ   Σ.

48 And] om   33a–b.   wooes] B40 B47 C5 C9 DT1 H5 H6 H8 HH1 NP3 NY1
SN3 SN4 SP1 A–G; woes   Σ.   in] ~ the   OQ1 33a–b.   of the] o'~   IU2.
Pleas] ~,   B13 B32 B40 C2 DT1 H3 H4 H7 SP1 VA1 A–C; pleyes   SN3.   and]
in B46; or   B47 H5 IU2 SN3; on   H7(var: »~«); at   O21.   Benche.] ~ₐ   B13
B33 B47 C2 H3 H4 NP3 O21 P3 TT1 VA1 Y2 Y3; ~,   B40 IU2; ~:   B46 H8 OQ1
A; ~;   33a–b.

49 A] As   IU2.   motion] ~,   C2 C8 C9 H6 H8 A; om   IU2.   Lady;] ~.
B13 H8 VA1 B C; ~ₐ   B32 F21 IU2 NP3 O20 SN3 TT1 Y2 Y3; ~:   B33 H5 H7
OQ1 SP1 D–G; ~,   B40 B47 C2 C5 C8 H3 HH1 O21 SN4 A.   speake] (~
B32 F21 NP3 O20 SN3 SP1 TT1 Y2; speakes   C5 H3; om   IU2.   Coscus.] ~)
B32 F21 O20 SN3 SP1 TT1 Y2; ~,   B33 B40 C5 DT1 H7 HH1 O21; ~;   B46 C2
C8 C9 H5 H6 SN4 A; ~ₐ   B47 H3 H4 Y3; om   IU2; cosen)   NP3; Cassus say on.
OJ1; ~:   OQ1 P3.   beene] ~,   C5 C8 IU2.

50 In] Thy   OJ1.   loue] ~,   B46 C2 C8 SN3 SN4 A; ~.   OJ1.   ere] om
B13 O21 Y3; ever   B32 B40 C2 C8 F21 H4 H5 H7 H8 O20 OQ1 P3 SP1 TT1 VA1
A–G.   since] ~,   B13.   tricesimo] 30ᵐᵒ   B13 VA1; 3ᵐᵒ   B33; 3ⁱᵐᵒ   HH1;
secundo   OJ1; 37°   OQ1; the 3ᵗʰ   P3.   of the] o'~   IU2.   Queene:] H8
NY3; ~.   B13 B46 C5 C8 C9 F21 HH1 NY1 O20 O21 SP1 D–G; Q.   B33; ~,
B40 C2 H5 H6 OQ1 SN3 SN4 A–C; ~ₐ   Σ.

51 Claimes] ~, B40 HH1; Claime O21 OQ1 Y2 Y3.   I haue] ~ ha' B46;
~ om H5; om ~ HH1; Ive IU2; haue I O20 SP1; ~ ha'ue SN4.   ˙ made:]
B32 NY3 O20; ~; B13 O21 SP1; ~₍ B47 HH1 NP3 P3 TT1 Y3; met₍ IU2; ~,
Σ.   gott] ~, C5 DT1 H4 O21.

52 stay] stop H3.   Suite,] ~; C2 O21; suites₍ H3; ~₍ H8 IU2 NP3 P3
TT1 Y3.   that he] Heavn bless IU2.   should] yᵉ IU2; shall O21 Y3.
not] ~. C5; ~, C8; Plot. IU2; ~ proceed TT1.

53 Proceede:] B47 NY3; ~; B13 B32 DT1 H5 NP3 NY1 O20 O21 SN4 SP1 VA2
G; ~. B33 B46 C9 H6 H8 P3 VA1; ~₍ H3 Y3; om TT1; ~, Σ.   me:] H5
NY3 OQ1; ~. B13 B33 C9 H6 H8 P3 VA1; ~₍ B46 B47 H3 NP3 NY1 TT1 VA2;
~, C5 F21 H7 SN3 Y3 G; ~; Σ.   Hilary terme] ~ ~; B46; ~ ~, B47; ~-~
SP1.   went,] B13 C2 C8 C9 H6 O20 OQ1 SN4 A–G; ~[gutter] H8; ~; HH1;
~₍ Σ.

54 sayd] ~, B32 B40 B46 B47 C2 C8 DT1 H4 HH1 O20 OQ1 SN4 SP1 A–G.
returnd] returne B40 C2 C8 DT1 H3 H4 TT1 Y2 A; returned C5.   this] next
B40 C2 C8 C9 DT1 H4 H6 TT1 A–G; these C5.   Sise] B13 B33 B40 B47 C2
DT1 H5 H8 HH1 NY1 NY3 O21 P3 VA1 Y3; Size, B46; Assize TT1; '~ VA2;
size Σ.   Lent] ~, B32 H5 HH1 O20 SN4 SP1 A–G; ~. C5.

55 remitter] a ~ NP3; remitte SN3.   your] the NP3.   grace,] B32 C5
H5 HH1 NY3 O20 OQ1 SN4 SP1; ~; C2 C8 H7 H8 A–G; ~. F21 SN3; ~₍ Σ.

56 In] And ~ H7.   th'interim] B33 B46 C2 C8 C9 H3 H4 H5 H6 NY1 NY3
VA2 Y2 A–G; ~, B40 DT1; the Interim, H7; the Interim Σ.   take] haue
P3.   place] ~; B46; ~: C5; ~, C8; ~. DT1 HH1.

57 affidauits.] ~₍ B13 HH1 TT1 Y3; ~; B32 C8 NP3 O20 O21 SP1; ~, B33
B40 C5 DT1 F21 H4 H7 P3 Y2; offidauitts, B46; ~: B46 OQ1 A; Affedaritts,
C2; Affidanus₍ H3; Affe=dauitts. NY1 VA2.   1st Words,] ~. DT1; ~₍ F21
OQ1 P3 SN3 TT1 VA1 Y3; ~; HH1 SP1.   2nd Words,] B32 B40 C2 C8 H6
NY3 O20 SP1 Y2 A–G; world₍ DT1; ~₍ (M var: »wor[trimmed]«) H4; om O21
Y3; ~₍ Σ.   which] that B13 H3 H8 NY1 O21 OQ1 P3 VA1 VA2 Y3.
teare] ~, SN4.
    Alternate line: Then follow affidavit words to tear IU2.

58 Labyrinth] labo'rinth F21; Laborinths O21.   soft mayds] virgins IU2;
maids softe NP3 G; ~ maydens O21 Y3; ~=~ OQ1; om ~ VA1.   eare]
~, B32 B40 H4 O20 SN3; ~. C2 C5 C8 F21 H8 HH1 NY1 SP1 VA2 A–F;
~: DT1; geere NP3.

59 More,] ~₍ B33 B47 C5 C9 F21 H6 NY1 OQ1 P3 TT1 VA2 Y3; ~; O21.
more,] B13 C2 C8 NY3 P3 SN4 A–F; om C5 H5 OQ1; ~₍ Σ.   then] than
SN3 B–F.   ten] ~, HH1.   Sclauonians] Slavonians B13 B33 B40 B47 C9
H6 SN4 VA1 Y2; Slauonian's B46; Sclauonian C5 H5 NY1 O21 VA2 Y3; ~,
C8; Slauonian H3 OQ1; Slavonians, SP1.   scolding,] scouldinges, B13 B46

H5 H8 NY1 OQ1 P3 VA2 G; ~^ B32 B47 C8 H7 SP1 TT1 Y2; scoldings.   C5; ~;
HH1 NP3 SN4; scoldinges^   O21 VA1 Y3.   more] ~, P3.

60 Then] Than   H3 SN3 C–G.   winds] winde   H3 H8; mynes   VA1.
ruynd] ruined   F21 P3.   rore.] ~^   B47 DT1 H3 H4 H7 NP3 NY1 OQ1 TT1
VA2 Y2 Y3; ~,   C2; ~;   SP1 A; were^   VA1.

61 When] Then   H5.   of] B32 C5 F21 H5 H7 HH1 NP3 NY3 SN3 SN4 Y2;
with   Σ.   Poetry,] ~^   B33 B47 C5 C8 H5 HH1 NP3 NY1 O21 OQ1 P3 SN3
TT1 VA1 VA2 Y2 Y3.   and] om NP3.   with] of C5 H7.   Muse] ~, C8
HH1; ~: Y2.

62 wast,] ~;   B13 SP1; ~^   B33 C5 F21 H3 NY1 P3 SN3 TT1 VA1 G; wert,
H8; wert^   NP3 O21 Y3; was, VA2.   and] (~ B33 B46; run   H3; but NP3.
mad,] B32 B47 C2 C5 F21 HH1 NY3 O20 SN3 SN4 Y2 A–G; made^   B46; ~.
C8; ~^ Σ.   I] (~ C9 H6; & SN3.   hop'd:] ~. B13 H8; ~;   B32 C2 DT1
F21 H3 H7 HH1 O20 SN4 SP1 A–G; ~) B33; ~, B40 B47 H4 Y2; ~.) B46 C9;
hoped,   C5; ~). H6; ~^ NP3 SN3 TT1; hope. O21 VA1 Y3; hope: P3.   but
Men which] thou then didst   B46; ~ when men   OJ1.   chuse] vse   B47;
~[trimmed] C5.

63 Law practise] ~=~   B47 DT1 NY1 OQ1 SN4 SP1; Lawes ~ H5; ~ practizes
H7.   meere] more   H3.   gayne,] ~;   B13 C2 C8 NP3 O21 Y2 A–G; gaynes,
B40; ~. B46; ~^ C5 H7 HH1 OQ1; gaynes^ TT1.   bold] hould   B13 C5
DT1 H4 H7; (~ NP3 OQ1; and   OJ1.   Soule,] B32 C9 O20; sole^ C5 H7
HH1 OJ1; soules   H5; ~) NP3 OQ1; ~^ Σ.   repute] ~, C5; ~. HH1.

64 Worse] Such ~ B46.   then] than   H3 SN3 C–G; them   P3.
imbrotheled] B32 NY3; Brotheld   B46; embreatheld   B47; inbrothelled   OQ1;
imbrothled Y2; imbrotheld Σ.   Strumpets] ~, B40 DT1 H3; Strmpests F21.
prostitute.] ~^   B13 B33 B47 H3 H4 NP3 NY1 O21 TT1 VA1 VA2 Y2; ~, B40
DT1 OQ1 SN3; ~: C5 SP1.

65 Now] ~,   B40 C2 DT1 H4 H6; Nowle   Y3.   like] (~ H8 HH1 NP3.
Owllike] C2 F21 H4 NY3 TT1 VA1 A–C; Owlelight   B13; Owelike   B32 B33
O20; Owle=lykes   C5; Oule=light   C8; Owle, like   H3; owle like   NP3 P3;
Owle-eyd   O21 Y3; owle   SN3; Owle-like   Σ.   Watchman] ~, B40 C2 C9 H6
A–C; watchmen   H3(var: »~«) P3; ~) H8 HH1; watch-man)   NP3; watch man
VA2.   he must] muste he   H3.   walke] ~, C5.

66 hand] hands   B33 HH1 SN4.   at] in   H3.   a] his   H5 P3.   bill:] ~;
B33 B47 H5 HH1 NP3 O21 OQ1 Y2; ~, B40 C2 C5 C8 DT1 H3 H4 H7 NY1 SN3
SP1 VA2 A–G; ~. H6 H8 P3 VA1; ~^ TT1 Y3.   he must] muste he   H3.
talke] ~. C5 C8.

67 Idely] ~, B32 B46 H6 OQ1 SP1; Idly   B33 C5 H4 H8 NP3 P3 SN3 Y2; Idlye,
B40 B47 C2 C8 C9 DT1 F21 H5 O20 A–G.   like] (~ OQ1.   Prisoners,] ~^
B46 B47 C5 C9 DT1 H4 OQ1 TT1 Y3; ~; NP3 O21.   which] whoe with   C5;
who   C9 H6 NP3.   whole] hole   B33; a ~ Y3.   months] mouthes   C5 H8

NY1 VA2; month   O21(moneth) Y3.   sweare] sweare[*trimmed*]   C5; ~, DT1
HH1 SP1.

68 Suretiship] suertie shipp   B13; *Surtishipp*   B40; suerti=shipp   NY1 VA2;
~, O21 B–F.   them] *om*   F21.   there,] B13 B40 C2 C8 DT1 H5 SN3 A–G;
~ₐ   B33 B47 F21 H3 H4 NP3 O21 TT1 VA1 VA2 Y2 Y3; ~)   OQ1; ~. Σ.

69 *line replaced with long dashes*   A.   to euery] t'~   DT1 H4; ~ eury   OJ1
SN3; ~ each   Y2.   Sutor] ~, C2 C8.   ly] ~, B46 NP3.   euery] eury
SN3.   thing] ~,   B13 B32 B40 C2 C5 C8 DT1 H8 HH1 O20 OQ1 SN4 B–G.

70 *line replaced with long dashes*   A.   Like] Ly ~   B13 H8 O21 OQ1 P3 VA1
Y3.   kings fauorit,] ~ ~;   B13 B46 NP3; ~ ~ₐ   B32 B47 H4 O21 P3 SN3 TT1
Y3; King ~,   C8(→ »~ ~,«); ~ ~:   H6; ~~ₐ   VA2.   yea] nay   B46 C5 OJ1;
or   B47 B–G; ~, DT1.   king;] B32 C2 C8 H5 O20 Y2; ~ₐ   B33 B47 F21 H3
H4 NP3 O21 OJ1 P3 SN3 TT1 VA1 Y3; ~,   B40 C5 NY1 OQ1; ~:   B46; ~. Σ.

71 Like] and ~   O21 Y3.   *2nd* a] *om*   H5; yᵉ   Y2.   blocke] ~, B40 B46
C2 C8 DT1 H4 H7 HH1 OQ1 A–G; blockes   H5.   wring] wrvnge   B32 B46
F21 H3 H7 O20 SP1 Y2; wringd   B33; wringed   C5; winge   VA1.   barr] ~,
C5 DT1 HH1 SP1 A–G.

72 Bearing] Brayinge   NP3.   Asses] B47 C5 C9 NY3 O21 TT1 VA1 Y3; ~;
NP3 NY1 VA2; ashes   Y2; ~, Σ.   shameles] themselves   H3(M *var*: »~«);
harmelesse   TT1.   farr] ~.   B40 C5 HH1; ~, B46; ~ → »~,«   C8.

73 Then] like   H4; Than   SN3 B–G; *om*   TT1; The   VA2.   carted
whores,] ~ ~ₐ   B32 C5 C9 H3 H6 H8 NY3 O20 SN4 VA1 VA2 Y2; ~ ~:   H5 H7;
~ howres,ₐ → »~ ~,ₐ«   HH1; ~ ~;   NY1 O21 Y3; ~~ₐ   SP1; *om* om   TT1.   ly]
~, C2 C8 A–G; bee   SP1.   graue] *om*   B13 H3 H8 OQ1 P3 VA1; ~. TT1.
Iudg:] ludges,ₐ   B13 H3; ~, B33 B47 F21 H5 H7 NY1 SN3 SN4 VA2 Y2; ~. B46
C9 H6; ~;   C2 C5 C8 H4 HH1 NP3 O21 A–G; ludges,   H8 P3 VA1; Iudges:
OQ1; ~ₐ   TT1 Y3.   for] ~ Bastardy aboundes   TT1.

74 *line replaced with long dashes*   A.   Bastardy] Bastards   SN3 SN4; *om*
TT1.   abounds] ~, H3; *om*   TT1.   not] ~, NY1 VA2.   in] *om*   NY1
VA2.   Kings] k'gs   B33; a ~   H7.   titles,] ~; B46 H4 NP3 Y2; ~ₐ   C5
OQ1 TT1 Y3.   nor] ~.   C5.

75 *line replaced with long dashes*   A.   Simony] ~, B13 B32 C2 C8 DT1 H3
H4 H8 NY1 O20 OJ1 SP1 VA2 Y2; Nor ~,   H7; Nor ~ → ›~‹   HH1.   and] nor
B46 C2 C8 H3 H7 H8 O20 O21 P3 SP1 Y2 Y3; or   TT1.   Sodomy] ~, H7.
Churchmens] Church mens   B13 B32 B47 H3 H4 O20 P3 VA1 Y2; church-mens
H5 H8 NY1 OJ1 SN4 SP1 G; Church men   F21 VA2; Churchmen   NP3.
Liues] ~, B40 C8 DT1 H8 O20 O21 SN4 SP1 B–G; Lifes   C2.

76 him,] ~; B40 B46 C2 C8 DT1 H4 NY1 SN4 VA2 A–G; ~:   H7 SP1; ~ₐ
F21 HH1 NP3 O21 TT1 Y3.   these] those   B47.   thriues.] ~; B32 H8; ~,

B33 B40 H5; ~∧ B46 B47 H3 H4 HH1 NP3 O21 OQ1 SN3 TT1 VA1 VA2 Y3; ~: H7 Y2.

77 Shortly] ~, B47 H5 SN4. (as] ∧~ B33 B40 B47 F21 H3 H5 H7 H8 HH1 NP3 O21 OJ1 P3 TT1 VA1 Y3. the] om B46 OJ1. Sea)] ~∧ B33 F21 H3 H8 HH1 NP3 O21 OJ1 P3 TT1 VA1 Y3; ~, B40 B47 H5 H7 Y2. he will] he'le B46 B47 C9 H3 H6 H8 NP3 OJ1 OQ1 P3 VA1 Y2. compasse] compa'sse SN4. our] the OQ1 VA1 Y2 A–G. Land] ~, B32 B40 C2 C8 HH1 O20 OQ1 SN4; landes H5 NP3; ~; A–G.

78 Scotts] ~, B13 C2 C8 H7 O21 A–F; Serttes H3; Scott H5. Wight;] B13 B40 C8 NY3 O21 A–F; ~∧ B33 OQ1 P3 TT1; Weight; C2; weight∧ NP3; *Weight,* NY1 VA2; ~, Σ. Mount] ~, C2 C8 F21 A; Moune H3. Douer Strand;] NY3; ~ ~, B32 B40 DT1 F21 OQ1 SN3 SN4; Douerstrand. B46; ~ ~. C2 C5 C9 H6 NY1 A–G; ~ ~∧ → ~ ~».« C8; Dovers sandes, H5; ~ stran[*trimmed*] H8; Douerstrand, O20; ~ sand∧ O21 Y2 Y3; ~-~. SP1; ~ stand∧ VA1; ~ ~∧ Σ.

79 spying] slyinge H3. heires] ~, B46 HH1 VA1; aire Y2. with] in H3 NY1 VA2; to Y2. gluttonee] Luxury B13 B40 C2 C8 H4 NY1 O21 P3 TT1 VA1 VA2 Y3; ~, B32 C5 F21 H5 H6(*var:* »luxury,«) HH1 O20 SN4; luxurie, DT1 H8 OQ1 A–G.

80 will] would B13 H7 H8 NY1 O21 OQ1 P3 VA1 VA2 Y3. at] in OQ1. their] his B40 TT1. Sins] ~, B13 B32 B40 B46 B47 C2 DT1 F21 H4 H7 O20 SN4 A–G; ~ → »~,« C8; sinne, H5. hee.] ~, B13 DT1 G; ~∧ B33 B47 H3 H4 NP3 O21 P3 SN3 TT1 VA1 VA2 Y3; ~; B40 HH1; ~: H8 OQ1 Y2.

81 as] (~ H8 HH1 P3 VA1 G. a] om O21; the Y2. thrifty] thisty H3. scrapes] scraps B47 P3 SN3. kitchin stuffe,] DT1 HH1 NY3 O20 OQ1; *Kitchinstufe∧* B40 C2 C8 NP3; ~=~∧ B46 H7 SP1; kitchinge ~. C5; kitching ~∧ F21 H3 H6 NY1 O21 Y2; ~-~, H5; kytchinstuffe, SN4; kitchinge-~∧ VA2; kitching-~, A–G; ~ ~∧ Σ.

82 om B13. barrelling] ~ all H5; ~ vp H8 NP3. droppings] ~, B32 B40 C2 F21 H4 H7 NP3 O20 SN4 SP1 A–G; drops H5. and] of H3 VA2. snuffe] ~. C5; snufs C8; ~, A–C.

83 wasting candels] B33 H4 H5 NP3 NY3 O21 TT1 VA1 Y3; ~ Candle, B32 F21 O20 Y2; ~ ~; HH1; watching ~, P3; ~-~, SP1; ~ ~, Σ. which in] within B46 C9 H5 H6; w^th ~ B47. 30] B33 C5 DT1 H4 NY3 P3 Y2; seaven H5; thirtie Σ. yeare] ~. B46 SP1; yeares B47 H3; Yeares, C5; ~, HH1 O20.

84 Relique like] B13 B33 B47 NY3 O20 TT1 VA1; (Reliquelye C2 C8 A–G; Reliquely C5 NY1 O21 SN4 VA2 Y3; ~ lie H3; Reliquelike H4 HH1; Reequelie SN3; Belgiquely Y2; ~-~ Σ. kept] ~, B13 B32 B46 B47 C9 H5 H6 HH1 NY1 O20 OQ1 VA2; ~,) B40 C8; ~) C2 DT1 A–G. buyes] gets B46 B47 C9 H6; buye C5. wedding geare,] ~ ~. B13 C8; ~ ~∧ B33 B46 F21 H4 H6 NY1 NY3 O21 TT1 Y3; ~ geares∧ B47; ~-~, C9; ~ Cheare∧ H3 NP3; ~-~: H7;

~ ~.) H8; ~ ~) HH1 P3 VA1; ~ ~: OQ1 SN3 SN4; ~ ~; SP1 A–F; weeding
cheare∧ Y2(M *var:* ›geare‹); ~ chear) G.

85 Piece meale] B13 C2 NY3 VA1 Y2; ~=~ B40 DT1 H5 H8 P3 SP1 VA2;
Peecemeale, C9; ~-~, H3; Peicemeale Σ. lands:] NY3; land; B32 O20; ~∧
B33 C5 P3 TT1 VA1 VA2; ~; C2 C8 DT1; land∧ H3 O21 Y3; land, F21 SP1
Y2; ~, Σ.

86 Wringing] In ~ H3(→ »~«) H8 NP3 OQ1 P3 VA1. acre,] ~; B13; ~∧
B33 C5 C9 H6 H8 NY1 O21 P3 TT1 Y3; *om* NP3; aire∧ SN3. as] *om* NP3.
men] *om* NP3; Maids G. pulling] ~ for B13 H7; doe ~ B47; *om* NP3;
in ~ P3. Prime.] ~.| B13; ~∧ B33 B47 H3 H4 O21 P3 SN3 TT1 VA1 Y2 Y3;
~, B40; *om* NP3; ~: OQ1.

87 Parchments] parchment B40 B47 C2 C5 C8 DT1 H4 H7 NP3 O21 SN3 SN4
TT1 Y2 Y3 A–G; parchment, C9 H6. then] ~, B13 B40 B46 B47 C2 C8 C9
DT1 H6 A–G; *om* B32 F21 H7 NP3 O20 SP1 Y2. large] ~, B13 H3; as ~,
B32 F21 Y2; as ~ C9 H5 O20 SP1. as] ~ are NP3; (~ SN3. his] *om*
C9 H6; the G. fields] ~, B32 B40 B46 C2 C9 DT1 H5 H6 O20 SN4 SP1
A–G; feild B47 O21; feild) SN3. he] de H3. drawes] ~. C8.

88 Assurances,] ~∧ B13 B33 H3 H4 H7 H8 HH1 NP3 OQ1 P3 TT1 VA1; ~;
B32 NY3 O20 SN4;. assurem^{res}: O21 Y3(assurements). bigg] as ~ B13 H3 H7
HH1 O21 OQ1 P3 VA1 Y3; ~, C2 C8 DT1 H4 Y2 A–G. glossd] glossy B13
O21 OQ1 P3 VA1 Y3; glosse C5; Glost H3 HH1; gloz'd H5; glossed Y2.
Lawes:] H7 HH1 NY3; ~, B13 B40 C2 C9 DT1 H5 H6 OQ1 A–G; ~. B32 B46
C5 F21 NY1 O20 SN4 SP1 VA2; ~.| C8; ~; P3; ~∧ Σ.

89 huge] ~, B13 B33 B40 C2 C9 DT1 H5 H6 H7 H8 SN4 SP1 A–G; ~ → »~,«
C8. that] as B46 B47 C9 H5 P3 Y2. Men] ~, C2 H6. in] (~ B40
C2 C8 DT1 H4 P3 TT1 A–G. our] *om* C5; (~ VA1. times forwardnesse]
~ ~) C2 C8 DT1 H4 P3 VA1 A–G; Tyme ~ H3; ~ ~, HH1 SN4 SP1;
~=~, OQ1.

90 the] our H3. Church] ~, B46; ~; O21. wryting] the ~ H3;
wrightinge P3 VA1. lesse.] ~; B32 H4 O20; ~∧ B33 B40 B47 F21 H3 NP3
O21 P3 SN3 TT1 VA1 Y2 Y3; ~: OQ1.

91 These] those B47 O21. he] *om* C5. wrytes] wrights P3 VA1.
not:] NY3; ~; C2 C8 O20 SP1 A–G; ~∧ H4 O21 TT1 Y3; ~, Σ. Nor] Not
B32; (for → ›or‹ DT1. these] those B47 C5 H5 O21 SP1 Y3; the H3 VA1.
written] writings B33 HH1; writer F21; writeinge H3; ~, H7. payes,] B13
B32 B40 C5 C8 DT1 H5 H7 NY3 O20 OQ1 SN3 SN4 A–G; ~. C2 HH1; ~∧ Σ.

92 Therfore] There fore VA2. spares] spare C9 H6. no] for noe
DT1(→ ›~‹) H4. length:] ~. B32 C9 H8 O20 P3 VA1(lenge); ~, B33 B40 B47
H3 H5 SN3(lenth) SN4 G(lenth); ~; C2 C8 DT1 H4 H6 NY1 SP1 VA2 A–F;
lesse, H7(*var:* »~«,); ~∧ NP3 O21 TT1 Y2 Y3. As] (~ H6 B–G. those]

these B32 F21 O20 SP1 Y2; the   H3 H7.   first] *om*   SN3 SN4.   dayes]
~.   C8 SN3.

93   When] Where   B–F.   Luther] Lucifer   H5.   profest,]   ~‸ B33 C5 H3 H8
NP3 SN3 VA2 Y3; proffessed,   B40; ~;   C2 O21; ~:   C8; profess'd,   C9 DT1 H4
H6; professed‸   TT1.   desyre] ~,   C8.

94   Short] that   H5.   Pater Nosters,] ~ ~‸   B13 C5 H4 H8 HH1 TT1;
Paternosters,   B33 H6 H7; Paternoster's,   B46; Paternosters‸   C8 VA1; ~-noster‸
H5; ~-noster,   NP3;   NY1; ~ noster‸   O21 Y3; ~-~‸   SP1.   saying] ~,
HH1.   as] (~   B13 P3 VA1; like   H3; (like   H8.   a] y^e   Y2.   fryer] ~)
B13 H8 P3 VA1; ~,.   B46; ~,   C5 C8.

95   beads,] ~:   B13 P3; ~.   B46 H8 VA1; ~;   HH1 NP3 NY1 VA2; ~‸   TT1.
but] ~,   C9.   hauing] haue   F21.   those] these   B13 H7 OQ1 VA1; his
B32 F21 O20 O21 SP1 Y2 Y3; the   NY1(M *var*: »his«) VA2.   lawes] ~,   H3
OQ1 A–G.

96   to] vnto   H8.   Christs] *Christ*   B40.   prayer,] ~;   B13; prayr‸   B33
H6; ~‸   C5 C9 DT1 F21 H4 H5 H8 NP3 O21 OQ1 P3 SN3 TT1 Y2 Y3; Prayers‸
H3(→ »~‸«).   power] ~,   B13 B32 H7 SP1; Pow'r   B33.   glory] glories   B46;
~,   O21.   clause.] clawse.   B13(claws) C2 SN4; ~,   B32 H8 O20 VA2; ~;   B33;
clawes,   B40; ~‸   B47 F21 H3 H4 H7 HH1 NY1 O21 Y2; clawese‸   C5 NP3 TT1
VA1 Y3; ~,)   H6; ~:   OQ1; *clawse*;   SN3; ~.)   B–G.

97   when] where   H3.   sells] ~,   B13 B32 B40 C2 DT1 F21 H4 O20 SN3 SP1;
~;   O21.   changes] changeth   C5 P3; ~,   DT1; engages   O21 Y3.   Lands,]
B33 H8 HH1 NY3 OQ1; ~‸   B13 C5 H3 P3 VA1 Y3; land‸   NP3 NY1 O21 SN3
TT1 VA2 Y2; land,   Σ.   he'impayres] B40 B46 C2 C8 DT1 NP3 NY1 NY3 SN4
TT1 VA2 A–G; he impayres,   C5; hee empaires   Σ.

98   wrightings,] NY3 P3 SN4; wrytinges,   B13; writing,   B40 C9 DT1 F21 H4 H6
O21; writinge‸   B46 B47 NP3 Y3; writings‸   C8 NY1 OQ1 Y2; writt,   H3;
wrighting‸   TT1; ~‸   VA1; writings,   Σ.   vnwatch'd,] ~‸   B33 H3 H4 H8
NP3 NY1 O21 OQ1 P3 SN3 SN4 SP1 VA1 VA2 Y2 Y3; (~)   B40 B46 B47 C8 C9
DT1 A–G; (vnmatch'd)   C2; unwatched,   C5; vnwatched‸   F21 HH1; vn-watcht',
H5; (vn-watch'd)   H6; vmatch'd‸   H7(*var*: »~‸«) TT1; (vnseene)   OJ1; vnmatchd‸
TT1.   out] ~,   H5 A–G.   Ses] (~   B13 H8; his   B32 C5 F21 H3 H5 H7
NP3 O20 SN3 SP1 TT1 VA2 Y2; *om*   C9; (his   O21 P3 VA1(→ ›~‹) Y3.
heires] ~)   B13 H8 O21 P3 Y3; ~,   B32 C2 C9 F21 HH1 O20 OQ1 SN3 B–G; ~.
C5 C8 SP1; ~;   H4; (~   VA1.

99   As] And   G.   slily] ~,   B40 H5; sly   C9 H6; ~;   H3; silly   Y2.
any] a   O21.   Commentor] Commentary   H3.   goes] goe   B47; go'th
H3; goeth   OQ1 P3 VA1.   by] ~,   B32 C5 A; he   Y2.

100   words] ~,   B13 B32 B40 C2 DT1 H4 H7 O20 P3 SP1 A–G; word   H5; ~;
O21.   sense:] ~,   B13 B33 B47 C9 H4 H5 H6 HH1 O21 P3 SN3; ~;   B40 C2

C5 C8 DT1 F21 H7 NP3 NY1 OQ1 VA2 A–G; ~‸ H3 Y3; sentences, Y2. or]
~, B–G. diuinity] ~. C5 SN4; ~, OQ1.

101 Controuerters] ~, B13 B40 C2 C8 A; Controuersees B33; Controuersers
B46 B47 H5 P3; Controuersors, C9 H6.   vouchd] voucht B13 B33 B47 C5 C8
F21 H5 H7 HH1 NP3 NY1 O21 OQ1 P3 VA1 VA2 Y2 Y3; harde H3 H8.
texts] ~, B40 C2 C9 DT1 H3 H4 H6 H7 A–G; text B47 NP3 P3.   leaue]
leaues B40 B47 C5 H7 P3 SN4 TT1 VA2 Y2.

102 Shrewd] Such B32 F21 O20 SP1 Y2; shrewed B47 VA1; Harde C5; ~
NY1(M var: »Such«); Shewd TT1.   Words] ~, B13 B40 C2 C8 C9 H3 H6
NY1 OQ1 SP1 A–G.   which] as B32 F21 O20 SP1 Y2.   against] om H5;
gainst SN4.   doubt.] ~‸ B33 B47 H3 H4 H6 H7 NP3 NY1 O21 P3 TT1 VA1
VA2 Y2 Y3; ~, B40 HH1; ~: C2 H8 OQ1 A.

103 Where] When B32.   those] these B32 F21 NP3 O20 SP1; the B46
Y2.   spred woods] ~ ~, B13 B40 C2 C5 C8 C9 DT1 H5 H6 H7 NY1 OQ1 Y2;
spyed ~, B32 O20(→ ›~ words,‹) SP1; spied ~ F21; spi'd ~, H3; ~∙~ H8; ~
wordes O21 Y3; om om P3; ~-words, VA2.   which] om P3.   clothd]
clothed B47 C5 F21 HH1 O21 Y3; om P3.   hertofore] ~. B46; here to fore
C2; her before H3.

104 These] B32 B33 DT1 F21 H3 H4 H5 H7 HH1 NY1 NY3 O20 VA2 Y2; those
Σ.   bought] ~ bought C8(→ »~«).   Lands?] ~‸ B13 B32 B33 P3 SP1; ~:
B47 O21 Y3; ~; C2 C8 DT1 NP3; ~, C5 F21 H4 H6 O20 SN3 SN4 Y2; ~.
VA1.   built;] DT1 NY3; ~‸ B33 B47 C9 H6 H8 NP3 O21 OQ1 P3 TT1 VA1
VA2 Y3; ~, Σ.   nor] or B46 C9 H6 NY1 VA2; ~ → ›and‹ B47; Not C2
C8 Y2.   burnt] ~, F21 O20; burn'd H8; ~ → ›burnde‹ NP3.   within]
with in C5 O21.   dore.] ~? B32 F21 O20 SN3 SP1; ~‸ B33 B47 C5 DT1 H4
H6 NP3 NY1 O21 P3 TT1 VA2 Y2 Y3; ~, B40 VA1; ~; B46; ~: C9 OQ1;
doores‸ H3(→ »~‸«) H7; doores? SN4.

105 Where] Whers B40 C2 C8 DT1 H4 H7 H8 NP3 SP1 TT1 Y2 A; With
NY1(M var: »~«) VA2.   th'old Landlords] B32 C2 DT1 F21 H7 NY3 Y2 A;
~ Land=lords B40; the old land-lords SN3 VA2; the old Land lordes SN4;
the old-~ SP1; the old ~ Σ.   troopes] ~, B13 B32 B40 C2 C8 DT1 H3 H4
H7 H8 HH1 O20 VA2 A–G; greate ~ H5; ~; O21.   and] om NP3.
almes?] ~: B33; ~‸ B40 B47 H7 NY1 O21 P3 SN3 TT1 VA2 Y3; ~, C2 C8 A;
~,? H3; om NP3; Alme.rs VA1; armes‸ Y2.   In] om C2 C8 DT1 H4 A.
great] om B40 B46 B47 C9 H6 TT1 Y2 B–G.   halls] ~, B40 HH1; ~; C2;
balls NP3; ~? NY1 A; Thralls SN3; ~. VA2.

106 Carthusian] Carthusians HH1.   fasts,] feasts, B13 C5 F21 H3 H8(→ ›~,‹)
NP3; ~‸ B33 C2 H5 H6 NY1 OQ1 P3 TT1 VA1 VA2; feast, B47; ffactes‸ O21
Y3; feasts‸ SN3 Y2.   Bacchanalls] ~. B46 C5; ~, C2 HH1; ~.| C8;
~| H4.

107 I] om OQ1.   hate:] ~, B13 B40 C2 C8(→ »~;«) C9 DT1 H3 H4 H6 HH1

NY1 OQ1 P3 SN4 VA1 VA2 A; ~‸   B46(→ »~;«) B47 NP3 O21 TT1 Y2 Y3; ~;
F21 H7; ~.   H5 B–G; heate,   SN3.   Meanes] ~ → ›meane's‹   B46; Meane's
H5 H8 B–G; meats   P3.   blesse:] ~;   B32 C2 H4 O20 P3 A; blest‸   B46(→
›best‸‹) B47(blessd) Y2; ~,   C5 F21 HH1 SN3; ~‸   C9 H6 TT1; blessed‸   H3;
best.   H5; blest,   H7; best‸   H8 NP3; blisse,   O21; ~.   SN4 VA1; blisse‸   Y3;
blest.   B–G.   rich Mens] ~=~   C8; ritchmens   DT1 O21 TT1 B C; great ~
NY1(M *var*: »~« ~) VA2.   homes] ~,   C5 B C; ~;   H8.

108 bid] hidd   C8(→ »~«).   some] om   P3.   beasts,] ~;   B13 NP3; ~‸   B33
B46 O21 P3 SN3 SP1 TT1 VA1 Y3; beast‸   F21.   but] om   NY1(M *var*: »~«)
O21 P3 VA1 VA2 Y3; vt   OQ1.   not] no   B40 C2 C8 DT1 H4 NY1 TT1 VA2
A–G; ~ whole   O21 Y3; om   OQ1.   Hecatomes.] ~‸   B13 B40 B47 C8(→
»~;«) C9 H3 H4 H6 NP3 O21 OQ1 P3 TT1 Y2 Y3; ~,   C2 H5 HH1 SN3 A–G.

109 sterve,] ~‸   B33 C5 O21 SN3 TT1 Y3; staurie,   VA1.   none] nor   H8
SN3.   surfet] ~,   B13; surget   B46; ~;   H5; surett   VA2.   so:] ~.   B13 B46
C9 H6 H8 VA1 VA2 B–G; ~;   B40 H4 H7 P3 SN4 A; ~,   B47 C2 C5 C8 H3 H5
O21 SN3 Y3; ~,:   F21; ~‸   OQ1 TT1.   But] ~,   P3.   oh] ~,   B46 P3; (~)
C2 C8 DT1 A–G; om   H3 H8 NP3; ~!   H7 SP1; (ah!)   SN3.   we'allow] B33
NY3; we allowe,   C5 A; wee allowe   Σ.
   Alternate line: Now feast the por, but O / we do allow,   33a–b.

110 workes] ~,   B13 B47 C9 H4 B–G.   as] are   TT1.   good,] ~;   B13 HH1
NP3; ~.   B46; godd,   C5 H5(God,); ~‸   NY1 O21 P3 TT1 VA2 Y3.   out]
not   B13 C5 O21 Y3; one   H3.   of] as   O21.   fashion] ~,   B40 C2 DT1
H6.   now] ~,   B40 C9 DT1 H4 HH1 SN4 SP1 VA1 A–G; ~;   C2 C8; ~.   C5
VA2 33a–b.

111 Like] ~‸   H7.   old] ~‸   H7; ~,   HH1; om   P3 VA1.   rich] ~‸   H7.
wardrobes.] ~,   B33 B47 F21 NP3 O21 VA1; ~;   B40 B46 C2 DT1 H4 A; ~:   C8
H7 H8 HH1 OQ1 Y2; ward-robs.   SN3; ~‸   TT1 Y3.   But] ~,   C2.   none]
neere   C9 H6; om   TT1.   drawes] draw   C9 H6 H7.
   Alternate line: But stay, the Barister, perchance may draw   33a–b[*draw,*].

112 Within] None ~   TT1; With in   VA2; My words ~   33a–b.   vast] lust
P3; om   33a–b.   reach] ~,   B13 HH1.   of] ~,   F21.   th'huge] B40 C2 C8
C9 DT1 H4 H5 H6 H8 NP3 NY3 SN4 A–G; huge   B46 B47 NY1 P3 TT1 VA2;
the   OQ1 Y2; the huge-   SP1; th'   33a–b; the huge   Σ.   Statute] Statutes
H8 Y2 G; ~-   SP1.   Lawes.] ~.| B13 B47 C2 C8 H3 O20 O21 OQ1 VA1 Y2;
~| B40 F21 NP3; ~..   C5; Law.| C9 H6; ~‸   DT1 Y3; Lawe.   H7 33a–b;
Jawes.   G.

Subscriptions: I.D.| B13 SN3 SN4.   *Finis*   B40 B46 DT1 H4 H7.   Finis
Secundæ Satyræ | Io: Donn.|.   NY1 VA2(Ioh:).   I:D: ffinis.| O21 Y3.
finis the Second Satire.| P3.   finis Satira 2.^d   Y2.   *Dr. D.*   31a–b.
om   Σ.

Verbal Variants in Selected Modern Editions

Editions collated: H I J K M N O P Q S T Y Z AA DD.
Format:
  Indentations: *ll. 39, 111, and 112 ind* Y; *no ind* Σ.
Headings: SATYRE II. H Q S Y Z DD.   SATIRE II. I–K M–P.   SATIRE
  II THE LAWYER T.   *Satire 2* AA.

2 ther is] there's Σ.
   Alternate line: All this toune perfectly, yet in euery state N.

3 *Alternate line:* There are some found so villanously best, N.

4 towards] toward O–Q S Z DD.   them] that N.   towards] toward N.

6 thinke that] ame afraid N.   dearths] dearth H–K M O P S.

7 or] N T; and Σ.   old fashiond] ~-~ I J N–P T.   loue] loues N.

8 It ridlingly] T; Ridlingly it Σ.
   Alternate line: It rydes killingely, catcheth men, and removes N.

12 could not] T; cannot Σ.

14 by his] by's H–K M; ~'~ Y Z.

15 Organes] organ M O–Q S Y Z AA DD.

17 rhimes] rhythms O–Q S Z DD.

20 Pistolets] Pistollers M.

22 not] *om* T.   boyes singing] N T; singers Σ.   dores] dore N.

24 That] Th' H–K; The M.   Scuse] N T; excuse Σ.

26 Others] Other's I; Others' J M–P T AA.   witts] wit's H–K M O; wits'
N P T AA.

31 these] those N.

32 To] ** K.   outswive] S T; ** K; out-do Σ.   dildoes] ** K P.
and] or N.

33 outsweare] t' out-swear H–K; to ~ M O AA; to out-sweare P Q S Y Z
DD.   Letanee] ---- P.

34 all] of ~ O P.

37 Whose] In ~ N.

40 great] N T; just Σ.

43 was] *om* H–K M.

44 a scarse] scarce a H–K M O P.   this] that N.

45 Then] N Q Y Z DD; Than Σ.

46 wheresoe're] wheresoever O Q S Z DD.

50 ere] ever O Q S Y Z AA DD.

54 returnd] return O Y.   this] N T; next Σ.

58 soft mayds] Maid's soft H–K M.

59 then] N Q Y Z DD; than Σ.   Sclauonians] Slavonians' M N.
scolding] scoldings H–J M.

60 Then] N Q Y Z DD; Than Σ.   Strumpets] strumpet's N.

61 When] Which Z DD.   of] with Σ.

63 bold] hould N.   Soule] souls H–K M; sole N; soul[s] P.

64 then] N Q Y Z DD; than Σ.

66 hand] hands N.

68 That] The P.

69 euery thing] everything P T AA.

70 yea] or H–K M O P.

71 wring] wringd N.

72 Bearing like] ~-~ Q S T.

73 Then] N(M *var*: than) Q Y Z DD; Than Σ.

74 Bastardy abounds] ~ 'bounds P; ~'~ Y Z.   Kings] ~' I–K M–O T AA;
king's P.

77 he will] he'll H–K M P.   our] the H–K M O P DD.

79 gluttonee] N T; luxury Σ.

81 kitchin stuffe] M–P T AA; kitching-stuff Σ.

84 Relique like] Reliquely H–K M O P.   geare] chear H–K M.

86 men] Maids H–K M.

87 Parchments] parchment H–K M O P DD.   his] the H–K M.

88 Assurances] Assurance K.

91 written] writings N.

94 Pater Nosters] ~-~ I J; paternosters M–P T.

97 Lands] N T; land Σ.

98 Ses] his N.

99 As] And   H–K M.   Commentor] Commentator   DD.

104 These] N T; Those   Σ.

105 Where] Where's   O Q S Y Z AA DD.   In] *om*   O.   great] *om*   H–K
M N P.

107 Meanes blesse] Mean's blest   H–K M P; ~ bles[t]   N.

108 not] T; no   Σ.

112 Statute Lawes] ~-~   I J; ~ jawes   N; statute's jawes   P.

Subscriptions: *none.*

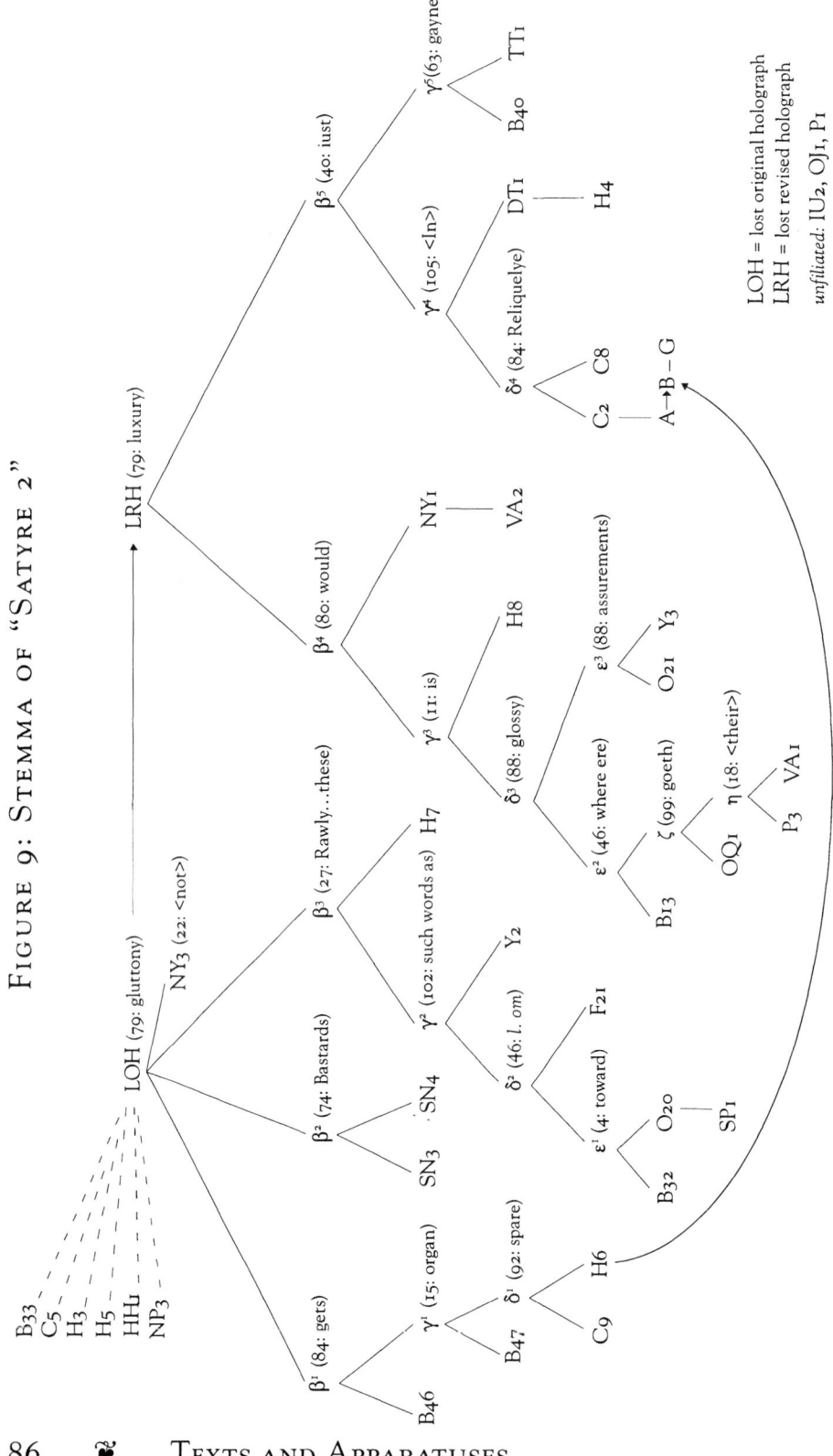

FIGURE 9: STEMMA OF "SATYRE 2"

Supporting Detail for Stemma of "Satyre 2"

LOH (B33 C5 H3 H5 HH1 NP3 NY3 β¹ β² β³)
   32 To **outswive** dildoes; and out vsure lewes:
   79 And spying heires melting wᵗ **gluttonee**

  B33: To the distinguishing readings of the LOH adds the following:
    3 **There are some found so villanously** best,

  C5: To the distinguishing readings of the LOH adds the following:
   42 And ploddinge **one** must make a Calfe an oxe.

  H3: To the distinguishing readings of the LOH adds the following:
    8 **The ridleinge catcheth** men, and dothe remoue

  H5: To the distinguishing readings of the LOH adds the following:
   78 from Scott to Wight, from Mount to **Dovers sandes,**

  HH1: To the distinguishing readings of the LOH adds the following:
    3 in all ille things so excellentlie **blest,**

  NP3: To the distinguishing readings of the LOH adds the following:
   62 Thou **wert** but madd I hopte but men wᶜʰ chuse

  NY3 (provides copy-text for this edition): To the distinguishing readings of the LOH
  adds the following:
   22 Are they <not> like boyes singing at dores for meat?

  β¹ (B46 γ¹): To the distinguishing readings of the LOH adds the following:
   22 Are they not like **Singers** at dore for meate.
   84 Relicke=like kept, perchance **gets** weddinge geare

    B46: To the distinguishing readings of the LOH and β¹ adds the following:
     3 Hath in't some founde soe **villanouslie bleste**

    γ¹ (B47 δ¹): To the distinguishing readings of the LOH and β¹ adds the following:
    15 As in some **organ** puppets dance aboue
    44 but scarce a poet, Iollier of **his** state

      B47: To the distinguishing readings of the LOH, β¹, and γ¹ adds the following:
       8 It riddingly doth catch men, and **death** remoue
      17 on would moue loue by rimes, but witch **crost** charmes

δ^1 (C9 H6): To the distinguishing readings of the LOH, β^1, and γ^1 adds the following:

54 You said if I return'd **next** 'Size in Lent

92 Therfore **spare** no length. As in those first dayes

β^2 (SN3 SN4): To the distinguishing readings of the LOH adds the following:

74 **Bastards** abounds not in kings Tytles, nor

SN3: To the distinguishing readings of the LOH and β^2 adds the following:

3 In all <ill>things so excellentlie **lest**

22 Are they not like Boyes singing at **Doores** for meat.

SN4: To the distinguishing readings of the LOH and β^2 adds the following:

3 In all **ill** thinges soe excellently **best**

22 Are they not like Boyes singing at **doore** for meate?

β^3 (γ^2 H7): To the distinguishing readings of the LOH adds the following:

27 **Rawly** disgested, Doth **these** things out-spewe

γ^2 (δ^2 Y2): To the distinguishing readings of the LOH and β^3 adds the following:

102 **such** words **as** might might against them cleare ye doubt

δ^2 (ϵ^1 F21): To the distinguishing readings of the LOH, β^3, and γ^2 adds the following:

46 *om* line

103 Where are these **spied** woodes wch clothed heretofore

ϵ^1 (B32 O20-SP1): To the distinguishing readings of the LOH, β^3, γ^2, and δ^2 adds the following:

4 That hate towards them breedes Pittie **toward** the rest,

B32: To the distinguishing readings of the LOH, β^3, γ^2, δ^2, and ϵ^1 adds the following:

75 Symony, **and** sodomy in Church mens lives

O20-SP1: To the distinguishing readings of the LOH, β^3, γ^2, δ^2, and ϵ^1 adds the following:

75 Simonye, **nor** Sodomye in Church mens liues,

F21: To the distinguishing readings of the LOH, β^3, γ^2, and δ^2 adds the following:

5 Though Poetry indeed **by** such a Sinn.

Y2: To the distinguishing readings of the LOH, β^3, and γ^2 adds the following:

105 Where's th'old Landords Troopes, & Alm's in <**great**> halls

H7: To the distinguishing readings of the LOH and β³ adds the following:
   8 It **rydes killingely, Catcheth** men, and **removes**

LRH (β⁴ β⁵)
   32 To **out:doe** Dildoes, and outvsuer Iewes.
   79 And spyinge heires melting with **luxurie**

β⁴ (NY₁-VA₂ γ³): To the distinguishing readings of the LRH adds the following:
   80 Sathan **would** not ioy at their sinns as hee.

   NY₁-VA₂: To the distinguishing readings of the LRH and β⁴ adds the following:
      8 It **ridingly** catch men and doth remooue

   γ³ (δ³ H8): To the distinguishing readings of the LRH and β⁴ adds the following:
      11 One like a wretch, wch at barre iudg'd is dead
      70 **Lye like** a *Kings ffauourite*, yea like a King.

      δ³ (ε² ε³): To the distinguishing readings of the LRH, β⁴, and γ³ adds the
      following:
         88 Assurances as bigg as **glossy** Civill Lawes,

         ε² (B13 ζ): To the distinguishing readings of the LRH, β⁴, γ³, and δ³ adds the
         following:
            46 Like netts, limetwiggs, **where ere** hee goes
            73 then carted Whores, Ly to the **<graue> Iudges**

            B13: To the distinguishing readings of the LRH, β⁴, γ³, δ³, and ε² adds
            the following:
               22 Are they not like **singers**, at mēns dores for meat?

            ζ (OQ₁ η): To the distinguishing readings of the LRH, β⁴, γ³, δ³, and ε²
            adds the following:
               99 as slylie as any Comenter **goeth** by

               OQ₁: To the distinguishing readings of the LRH, β⁴, γ³, δ³, ε², and ζ
               adds the following:
                  48 and woes in **the** language of the pleas and benche:

               η (P3 VA₁): To the distinguishing readings of the LRH, β⁴, γ³, δ³, ε²,
               and ζ adds the following:
                  18 Bringe not ther old feares, nor **<their>** old harmes

ε³ (O21 Y3): To the distinguishing readings of the LRH, β⁴, γ³, and δ³ adds
the following:
14 **while himselfe starues**, to liue by his labor'd scenes
108 I bid kille some beastes **<but>** nott **whole** Hecatombes

H8: To the distinguishing readings of the LRH, β⁴, and γ³ adds the following:
101 As Contrauerters in **hard** texts leaue out

β⁵ (γ⁴ γ⁵): To the distinguishing readings of the LRH adds the following:
40 Of Coscus onely breedes my **lust** offence,

γ⁴ (δ⁴ DT1-H4): To the distinguishing readings of the LRH and β⁵ adds the
following:
105 Wheres the'old Landlords troops, & almes? **<In>** Great Halls

δ⁴ (C2 C8): To the distinguishing readings of the LRH, β⁵, and γ⁴ adds the
following:
84 **Reliquelye** kept) perchance buyes weddinge Geare,

DT1-H4: To the distinguishing readings of the LRH, β⁵, and γ⁴ adds the
following:
10 is poore, disarm'd, like papists, **nor** worth hate

γ⁵ (B40 TT1): To the distinguishing readings of the LRH and β⁵ adds the
following:
63 Law practice for meare **gaynes**, bould soule repute

Satyre 3.

Kind pity choakes my spleene; braue scorne forbids
These teares to issue which swell my eylids.
I must not Laugh, nor weepe sins, and be wise,
May rayling then cure these worne maladyes?
Is not our Mistres fayre Religion   5
As worthy of all our Soules deuotion
As vertu was to the first blind Age?
Are not heauens ioyes as valiant to assuage
Lusts, as earths honor was to them? Alas
As we do them in meanes, shall they surpas   10
Vs in the end? And shall thy fathers Spiritt
Meete blind Philosophers in heauen, whose meritt
Of strict Life may be'imputed fayth, and heare
Thee whome he tought wayes easy and neare
To follow, damn'd? Oh if thou darest, feare this,   15
This feare great courage, and high valor is.
Darest thou ayd mutinous Dutch? Darest thou lay
Thee in Shipps, woodden Sepulchers, a pray
To Leaders rage, to Stormes, to shott, to dearthe?
Darest thou dive Seas, and dungeons of the earthe? 20
Hast thou couragious fyer to thaw the yce
Of frozen north discoueryes, and thrice
Colder then Salamanders, Like diuine
Chilldren in th'ouen, fires of Spayne and the Line,
Whose Cuntryes Limbecks to our bodyes bee   25
Canst thou for gayne beare? And must euery hee
Which cryes not Goddesse to thy Mistres, draw,
Or eate thy poysonous words? Courage of straw;
O desperate Coward, wilt thou seeme bold, and
To thye foes, and his who made thee to stand   30
Soldier in this worlds garrison, thus yeild
And for forbid warrs, leaue th'appointed field?
Know thy foes: the foule Deuill, whom thou
Striu'st to please, for hate not loue would allow
Thee fayne his whole Realme to be ridd: and as   35

The worlds all parts wither away and pas,
So the worlds selfe, thy other lou'd foe, is
In her decrepit wayne; and thou louing this
Dost loue a witherd and worne Strumpet. Last,
Flesh (it selfes death) and ioyes, which flesh can tast   40
Thou lou'st, and thy fayre goodly Soule, which doth
Giue this flesh power to tast ioy, thou dost lothe.
Seeke true Religion; Oh where? Myrius
Thinking her vnhous'd here, and fled from vs
Seekes her at Rome; There, because he doth know   45
That She was there a thousand yeares ago,
He loues her raggs so, as we here obay
The State Cloth wher the Prince sate yesterday.
Crantz to such braue Loues will not be enthralld
But loues her only, who at Geneua is calld   50
Religion, playne, simple, sullen, young,
Contemptuous, yet vnhandsome; as among
Lecherous humors, ther is one, which iudges
No wenches wholesome, but course cuntry drudges.
Graius stayes still at home here: and because   55
Some Preachers, vile ambitious bawds, and lawes
Still new, like fashions, bidd him thinke, that Shee
Which dwells with vs is only perfect, hee
Imbraceth her, whome his Godfathers will
Tender to him being tender; as wards still   60
Take such wifes as their Guardians offer, or
Pay values. Careles Phrygas doth abhor
All, because all cannot be good; as one
Knowing some women whores, dares mary none.
Graccus loues all as one, and thinkes that so   65
As women do in diuers Cuntryes go
In diuers habitts, yet are still one kind,
So doth, so is Religion; and this blind-
nes, too much light breeds. But vnmoued thou
Of force must one, and forc'd but one allow;   70
And the right; aske thy father which is Shee;
Lett him aske his; Though Truthe and falshood bee
Neare twins, yet Truth a litle elder is.
Be busy to seeke her. Beleeue me this
Hee'is not of none, nor worst which seekes the best.   75
To'adore, or scorne an Image, or protest,
May all be bad; doubt wisely; In strange way
To stand inquyring right is not to stray.
To sleepe, or run wrong, is. On a high hill
Ragged and steepe Truthe dwells; and he that will   80

Reach it, about must, and about go
And what th'hills sodainnes resists, win so.
Yet striue so, that before Age (Deaths twilight)
Thy Mind rest; for none can worke in that night.
To will implyes delay: therfore now do.   85
Hard deedes the bodyes paynes; hard knowledg too
The minds endeauors reach; and Misteryes
Are as the Sun, dazeling, yet playne to'all eyes.
Keepe the Truthe which thou hast found: Men do not stand
In so ill case here, that God hath with his hand   90
Signd kings blanc Chartres, to kill whom they hate,
Nor are they Vicars, but hangmen to fate.
Foole and wretch wilt thou let thy Soule be ty'de
To Mens Lawes, by which She shall not be tryed
At the last day? Oh will it then serve thee   95
To say a Philipp, or a Gregoree,
A Harry, or a Martin tought thee this?
Is not this excuse for meere contrarys
Equally stronge? Cannot both sides say so?
That thou mayst rightly obay power, her bounds know: 100
Those past, her nature, and name is chang'd, to be
Then humble to her is Idolatree.
As Streames are, power is: Those blest flowers which dwell
At the rough Streames calme head thrive and proue well:
But hauing lefte their rootes, and themselues giuen   105
To the Streames tyrannous rage, Alas, are driuen
Through Mills, rocks, and woods, and at last allmost
Consum'd in going, in the Sea are lost.
So perish Soules, which more chuse mens vniust
Power, from God claym'd, then God himselfe to trust.   110

Satyre 3.

Kind pittie choakes my splene, braue scorne forbidds
Those teares to issue, which swell my eye-lidds.
I must not laugh, nor weepe sinns, and bee wise,
Can railing then cure these worne maladies?
Is not our Mistress faire Religion,   5
As worthy of all our Soules deuotion
As Virtue was to the first blinded age,
Are not Heaue'ns ioyes as valiant to aswage
Lusts, as Earths honour was to them? Alass
As wee doe them in meanes, shall they surpass   10
Vs in the end? And shall thy fathers spirit
Meet blind Philosophers in heauen, whose meritt
Of strict life may bee imputed faith, and heare
Thee whom hee taught soe easie wayes, and neare,
To follow damn'd? O if thou dar'st feare this,   15
This feare, great courage, and high valour is;
Dar'st thou aide Muti'nous Dutch, and dar'st thou laye
Thee in shipps, wooden sepulchers, a praye
To leaders rage, to stormes, to shott, to dearth?
Dar'st thou diue seas, and dungeons of the earth?   20
Hast thou couragious fire to thawe the Ice
Of frozen North-discoueries, and thrice
Colder then Salamanders, like divine
Children in th'oven, fires of Spaine, and the line,
Whose countreyes Limbecks to our bodies bee,   25
Canst thou for gaine beare; and must euerie hee
Which cries not Goddesse to thy mistress, drawe,
Or eat thy poysonous words? Courage of strawe;
O desperate Coward, wilt thou seeme bold, and
To thy foes, and his (who made thee to stand   30
Sentinell in this worlds garrison) thus yeild,
And for forbidden warrs, leaue th'appointed field?
Knowe thy foe, the foule Deuill, whom thou
Striu'st to please, for hate, not loue, would allowe
Thee faine his whole realme to bee quitt; and as   35

The worlds all parts wither away and passe,
Soe the worlds selfe, thy other lou'd foe, is
In her decrepit waine, and thou louing this,
Dost loue a withered, and worne strumpett; last,
Fleash (it selfe's death) and ioyes which fleash can tast   40
Thou louest, and thy faire goodly soule, which doth
Giue this fleash power to tast ioye, thou dost loath.
Seeke true Religion, oh where? Mirreus
Thinking her vnhous'd here, and fled from vs,
Seekes her at Rome, there, because hee doth knowe   45
That shee was there a thousand yeares agoe;
Hee loues her raggs soe, as wee here obaye
The state-cloath, where the Prince sate Yesterday.
Crants to such braue loues will not bee inthrald,
But loues her only, who at Geneua is call'd   50
Religion, plaine, simple, sullen, yonge,
Contemptuous yet vnhandsome; as amonge
Leacherous humors there is one that iudges
Noe wenches wholesome, but course countrey drudges;
Graius stayes still at home here, and because   55
Some preachers, vile ambitious bawds, and lawes,
Still newe like fashions, bid him thinke that shee
Which dwells with vs, is only perfect, hee
Embraceth her, whom his godfathers will
Tender to him, being tender, as Wards still   60
Take such wiues as their Guardians offer, or
Pay valewes; careless Phrygius doth abhorr
All, because all cannot bee good; as one
Knowing some women whores, dares marry none;
Gracchus loues all as one, and thinkes that soe   65
As women doe in diuers countreyes goe
In diuers habitts, yet are still one kinde,
Soe doth, soe is religion; and this blinde-
nes too much light breeds: but vnmou'd thou
Of force must one, and forc'd but one allowe;   70
And the right; aske thy father which is shee,
Let him ask his; though truth and falshood bee
Neare twins, Yet truth a litle elder is;
Bee buisie to seek her, beleiue mee this,
Hee's not of none, nor worst, that seekes the best;   75
To adore, or scorne, an Image, or protest,
May all bee bad; doubt wiselie, in strange waye,
To stand inquireing right, is not to straye;
To sleepe, or run wronge is; on a huge hill
Cragged, and steepe truth stands, and hee that will   80

Reach hir, about must, and about goe;
And what the hills suddennes resists, winn soe;
Yet striue soe, that before age, deaths twilight,
Thy soule rest, for none can work in that night;
To will implyes delaye, therefore nowe doe,   85
Hard deeds, the bodies paines; hard knowledge too
The minds endeauors reach, and misteries
Are like the sun, dazeling, yet plaine to all eyes;
Keepe the truth which thou hast found; men do not stand
In soe ill case here, that God hath with his hand   90
Signed kings blanck-charters to kill whom they hate,
Nor are they Vickars, but hangmen to fate;
Foole, and wretch, wilt thou lett thy soule bee tyed
To mans lawes, by which shee shall not bee tryed
At the last daye? Will it then boote thee   95
To say a Phillipp, or a Gregorie,
A Harrie, or a Martin taught thee this?
Is not this excuse for meere contraries
Equallie stronge, cannot both sides say soe?
That thou maist rightly obay power, her bounds knowe;   100
Those past, her nature, and name is chang'd, to bee
Then humble to her, is idolatrie;
As streames are, power is, those blest flowers that dwell
At the rough streames calme head, thriue, and proue well;
But hauing left their rootes, and themselues giuen   105
To the streames tyrannous rage, alass are driuen
Through mills, and rocks, and woods, and at last, almost
Consum'd in going, in the sea are lost;
Soe perish soules, which more choose mens vniust
Power from God claymed, then God himself to trust.   110

Textual Introduction

Complete copies of "Satyre 3" (*Sat3*) survive in 28 manuscripts and all 7 seventeenth-century editions/issues of Donne's collected *Poems*, and the first 54 lines of what was undoubtedly once another full copy appears in a 29th manuscript (NP3). Further, brief snippets of the poem appear in B51, Joseph Butler's commonplace book (IU2), OJ1 (ms. emendations in a copy of A), and Richard Whitlock's *ZΩOTOMIA* (1654; siglum 38). Although *Sat3* appears in the company of 2 or 3 other Satyres in 3 manuscripts, it ordinarily circulated as part of a 5-poem set, and it normatively occupies the third position within that group, as it does in the seventeenth-century prints (see Figure 2). A good deal of scribal variation crept into the text as the poem circulated along the channels of transmission, and the evidence indicates that Donne himself revisited the poem to effect revisions in his discursus "Uppon Religion" (as one early copyist subtitled it). Whether these changes were dictated by dogmatic, social, or (even perhaps) political considerations is a matter for critical debate, but whatever the motives behind them, they represent the most extensive recasting of any single poem treated so far in this *Variorum*.

The stemma below traces the earlier and later versions of the text, respectively, to the lost original holograph (LOH) and a single revised holograph (LRH), which are principally distinguished by the following variants:

Table 3.1: Differences between the original and the revised versions of *Sat3*[*]

Line no..	Original Reading	Revised Reading
2	These teares	Those teares
4	May rayling	Can railing
7	blind Age	blinded age
14	wayes easy and neare	so easie wayes, and neare
17	Dutch? Darest	Dutch, and dar'st
30	who made thee	(who made thee
31	Soldier in this worlds garrison	Sentinell in this worlds garrison
32	forbid warrs	forbidden warrs
33	Know thy foes	Knowe thy foe
35	to be ridd	to bee quitt
79	high hill	huge hill
80	Ragged...Truthe dwells	Cragged...truth stands
81	Reach it	Reach hir

84	Thy Mind rest	Thy soule rest
88	as the Sun	like the sun
94	Mens Lawes	mans lawes
95	Oh will it then serve thee	Will it then boote thee
107	Mills, rocks, and woods	mills, and rocks, and woods

*The textual snippets used in Table 3.1 are derived, respectively, from the original and the revised versions of the poem printed above; their accidentals are thus those of NY3 and DT1, as emended.

Of the 19 artifacts containing the original version of the poem, 3 are members of the traditional Group III (C9, H5, H6), 6 are Associated with Group III (B13, H3, HH1, NY1, VA2, Y2), 1 is the sole member of Group IV (NY3), 3 are members of Group I (B32, O20, SP1), and 6 are unclassified (B33, NP3, H8, OQ1, P3, VA1). Six of these (shown at the upper left of the stemma) derive more or less directly from the LOH, while the remaining 13 descend through the postulated missing artifacts β^1, β^2, and β^3. Defined by the unique variants "lost [for the normative *left*] their rootes" in line 105, "To follow)" (for "To follow" [without parentheses]) in l. 15, and "(for hate not loue)" (for "for hate not loue" [without parentheses]) in line 34, β^1 begets and passes the above-cited readings on to γ^1 and H8. Reflecting a pattern of descent shared with the other 4 Satyres in this volume, γ^1 then gives rise to B13 and (through the intermediaries δ^1 and ε) to OQ1, P3, and VA1—the three manuscript "books" containing only the 5 Satyres, *Storm*, and *Calm*. γ^1's distinctive readings include "durst [for the normative *darest*] feare this" in line 15, an alteration otherwise found only in the stematically remote H4, and the trivialization "not to stay" (for the normative "not to stray") in line 78, an error also introduced by the B32, NY1, and β^4 scribes. Among H8's unique readings are the meter-regularizing "worlds first blind Age" (for "first blind Age") in line 7 and the reversal of the normative "Limbecks to our bodyes bee" to "to our bodies limbecks bee" in line 25.

γ^1's immediate descendants are the siblings B13 and δ^1, the former incorporating a cognate of the independently circulating "book" of Satyres into a larger collection of Donne's poems. B13 evinces such anomalies as "Salanders" (for "Salamanders") in line 23 and "Cuntrie is Limbeck to" (for "Cuntryes Limbecks to") in line 25, while δ^1 uniquely introduces and passes down the line of transmission "myne [for *my*] ei lyds" in line 2 and "ages twilight"—for "Age (Deaths twilight)"—in line 83, among other variants. δ^1's offspring are OQ1—which uniquely interjects the dittographic "waies waies" into the normative line-14 phrase "wayes easy" (yielding "waies waies easy") and rewrites line 46's normative "a thousand yeares" as "one thowsand yeare"—and ε, parent of the siblings P3 and VA1. To its offspring ε transmits the misreadings "braue loue" (for the authorial "braue Loues") in line 49 and the unique "which [for *who*] at Geneua is cald" in line 50. P3 and VA1's relationship as siblings rather than parent and child is confirmed in such lines as 53—where P3 records the anomalous "one who iudges" (as opposed to VA1's normative "on wch Iudges"—and 67—where P3 gives the normative "are still one kind" (as opposed to VA's anomalous "ar all still one kinde."

Shown to the immediate right of β^1 on the stemma, β^2 is the parent of the siblings

C9 and H6. As has been frequently noted in this *Variorum*, numerous alterations in the C9-H6 text evince the β² scribe's willingness to rewrite passages in the interests of "improved" logic, euphony, or—especially—meter (see, e.g., the discussion of the C9-H6 family's modifications of the text of *Sappho* in DV 2:412). Those concerns are here evident in his expansion of the normative "blind" to "blinded" in line 7 (thus adding a tenth syllable to the line), in his elisions of the authorial "thou hast" to "th'hast" in line 89 and of "with his" to "with's" in line 90, and in his unique ordering of the elements "Mills, woods, rocks" (for the authorial "Mills, rocks, and woods") in line 107. Indeed, β²'s insertion of an additional syllable into line 14 (recording "wayes so easy & neere" [for the authorial "wayes easy and neare"]) closely anticipates Donne's own subsequent revision of the line to "so easye ways & neare," and β²'s alteration of the original "Reach it, about must, and about go" in line 81 to "Reach Her, about must, and about, must goe" both anticipates Donne's eventual revision of "it" to "her" and—by insertion of the second "must"—effects a metrical regularization subsequently imported from H6 into the text of B.

Also stemming directly from the LOH is β³, head of the third major branch of the LOH lineage. β³ begets NY3 (the lone Group-IV manuscript), which here supplies the copy-text for the early version of the poem, and γ², which (through δ²) gives rise to the traditional Group-I manuscripts B32, O20, and SP1 and (through δ³) to the unclassified artifacts H3 and Y2. β³'s distinctive readings include "sin" (for the normative "sins") in the line-3 phrase "nor weepe sins," "honors were" (for the normative "honor was") in line 9, and "his [for the authorial *this*] worlds garrison" in line 31. Either mechanically or lexically, β³'s scribe also seems to have botched line 99, where neither of its offspring correctly records the authorial question "Is not this excuse for meere contrarys / Equally stronge..." (NY3 reads "...Equally strange... ," while the 5 descendants of γ² give "...Equally true..."). To these β³ anomalies NY3 adds the hypercorrection "nor" (for "not") in the normative line-3 phrase "not Laugh, nor weepe" (producing "nor Laugh, nor weepe"); maims the grammar of β³'s incorrect "honors were" in line 9 (evincing "honors was"); misreads the authorial "ambitious bawds" as "Ambitions bawds" in line 56; records the atypical "Phrygas" (for "Phrigius") in line 62, perhaps in order to regularize the line's meter; substitutes "me" for the authorial "thee" in line 97's normative "taught thee this" (yielding "tought me this"); records the idiosyncratic scribal spelling "tought" (for "taught") in both lines 14 and 97; and atypically spells "wifes" (for the normative "wiues") in line 61. Our selective emendations of these scribal deviations and those traceable to β³ are recorded in the textual apparatus.

γ², β³'s other direct descendant, adds and transmits to its offspring δ² and δ³ a number of unique scribal misreadings, including "decrepitt vaine" (for the authorial "...wayne") in line 38, "Grant" (for "Crantz") in line 49, "Grugus" (for "Graius") in line 55, and "Grattus" (for "Graccus") in line 65. δ², in turn, adds to the growing body of distinguishing readings the uniquely punctuated "...nor weepe; sin" in line 3 (where only B47, H7, H3, and Y2 have any pointing at all—and that a comma), "a thousand yeare" (for the normative "...yeares") in line 46, and "thinckes soe" (for the authorial "thinkes that so") in line 65. B32 misreads "stay" (for the normative "stray") in line 78 (an error it shares with several other artifacts), recasts the normative adjective-noun "bodyes paynes" in line 86 as object-plus-verb (giving "bodye paines"), and uniquely describes the normatively "dazeling" sun in line 88 as "dareling." O20 and its offspring SP1 adhere so closely to their ancestral predecessors that they must be distinguished as a separate strain within the γ^2-δ^2 line of descent by punctuation: in line 79, for instance, they correctly mark the end of the sentence that concludes mid line (giving "To Sleepe, or runne wrong, is. On a high hill…"), where B32 reads "…wrong, is on…" and the H3-Y2 pair read a comma ("…wrong is, on…"); uniquely within the β^2 lineage, moreover, they record a comma after "wretch" in line 93 (yielding "Foole and wretch,"), where all other descendants are without punctuation. While SP1, apparently on the basis of sense alone, corrects O20's "Nor are the Vicars" in line 92 to "…they Viccars," SP1 corrupts O20's correct "Hard deedes the bodyes paines" in line 86 to the ungrammatical "Hard deedes the bodie paines" and O20's normative "Power, from God clam'd" in line 110 to "Power, from God damn'd." δ^3, parent of H3 and Y2, adds to the accumulating body of error in line 65 (supplying "as" to repair γ^2's metrically deficient "and thinckes soe" [yielding "and thinkes as soe"]) and 88 (penning "dazelinge yet paine [for the normative *plaine*] to all eyes"), among other instances. Numerous divergences—such as H3's unique "fond blinde age" (for Y2's authorial "first blind age") in line 7 and Y2's anomalous "taught all ways easie" (for H3's normative "taught wayes easie") in line 14—show that H3 and Y2 cannot have been copied one from the other and mark them as siblings rather than parent and child.

As noted above, the 6 original-version texts of *Sat3* shown on the upper left corner of the stemma (except VA2, which is a copy of NY1) all descend independently, though perhaps not immediately, from the LOH. Including the partial manuscript NP3 (ll. 1–54 only), these artifacts all evince the array of readings that define the original text (see Table 3.1 above), with the following exceptions: in line 7 H5 substitutes "soules first" for the normative "first blind"; in line 32 NP3 expands "forbid" to "forbidden"; in line 80 B33 spells "Ruggued" (for "Ragged"); and in line 107 H5 inserts an extra "and" (recording "Milles, and Rockes, and Woodes [for the normative *Mills, rocks, and woods*]"), while the NY1-VA2 pair give "Mills & rocks, & at last," omitting "woods" altogether. These earmark readings apart, the most corrupt of these manuscripts—H5—records over 20 substantive errors, and even the cleanest—B33—records 9. While a particularly maladroit copyist might introduce a dozen—or even a score—of errors in a single act of transcription, it seems likely that the quantum of corruption embodied in some of these artifacts is the cumulative result of a series of scribal mishandlings.

Embodying the 21 authorial revisions shown in Table 3.1 above, the LRH begets— through a handful of lost intermediaries—8 further manuscripts: the siblings O21 and Y3 (Associated with Group III), the family comprising the siblings C2 and C8 (normally Group Is, but evincing the Group-II text of the Satyres) and the parent-child pair DT1 and H4 (Group II), and the cognates B40 and TT1 (Group II). The parallel descent of O21 and Y3 from a common ancestor has been demonstrated repeatedly in this *Variorum* (see, e.g., the stemma of the revised *ELBrac* text in DV 2:46), and this relationship obtains for all 5 Satyres in the present volume. In other instances, one or more other manuscripts stands between the parent manuscript and O21-Y3, and the sheer number of the unique variants passed down to O21 and Y3 suggests that β^4 may similarly incorporate errors introduced incrementally as the text descended through a series of now-lost manuscripts. No such missing artifacts can definitely be inferred from the extant data, however; β4 is thus shown on the stemma as a direct descendant of the LRH. β4 errors passed on to O21 and Y3 include uniquely labeling the poem "Satyre yᵉ Second," reading "& [for the normative *Oh*] if thou dar'st" in line 15, expanding the normative "worlds selfe" in line 37 to "world it selfe," identifying "Graius" in line 55 as "Graines," and boosting the 9 syllables in Donne's line 81 ("Reach hir, about must, and about goe") to 10 ("reach her about, must; I and about goe"), a metrical repair previously seen in several descendants of the LOH. Particular instances in which either O21 ("checks [for *choakes*]" in l. 1, e.g.) or Y3 ("*Pharigius* [for *Phrigius*]" in l. 62, e.g.) diverges from the normal reading recorded in its cognate show that neither can be copied from the other and confirm the usual relationship of these artifacts as siblings rather than parent and child.

As shown on the stemma, β5, the final direct offspring of the LRH, begets γ3 (parent of δ4 and DT1) and γ4 (parent of B40 and TT1)—all of which give a Group-II text of the Satyres. Compared to β4, β5 preserves a much cleaner text of the poem, its definitive readings being "his [for *this*] worlds garrison" in line 31, a variant also introduced in β3; the insertion of "h'is" in the line-33 phrase "the foule Deuill, whom" (yielding "the foule Deuill, h'is whom"); the unique substitution of "the" for the authorial "her" in line 47 (yielding "loues the [for *her*] raggs, soe"); the (also unique) substitution in line 57 of the ungrammatical "bids" for "bid" in the authorial "Some preachers, vile ambitious bawds, and lawes / Still newe like fashions, bid him thinke" (yielding "…bids him thinke"); and the syntax-altering trivialization of the normative "too" in line 86 to "to" (yielding "hard knowledge to / The minds endeauors reach" [for "hard knowledge too / The minds endeauors reach"]). To these alterations, γ3 adds the variant "in [for the normative *to*] the first blinded age" in line 7, omits "here" from the normative "men do not stand / In soe ill case here, that God hath with his hand" in lines 89–90 (yielding "…in soe ill case, yᵗ God…"), and trivializes "proue" to "doe" in line 104 (yielding "thriue & doe [for *proue*] well"). γ3's offspring δ4, parent of the siblings C2 and C8, reproduces and passes on to its offspring the γ3 text with little variation, although uniquely among the descendants of β5 it does number the poem as the ".3ᵈ." of the Satyres (see Figure 2) and uniquely among all artifacts in line 64 pluralizes the normative "women" to "woemens" (yielding "Knoweing some womens whores"). Similarly, the parent-child pair DT1 and H4 follow γ3 closely, deviating from it only in such particulars as reducing the normative "Loues" in line 49 to the singular "loue" (recording "Crants to such braue loue")—a lection otherwise found only in the descendants of ε and in TT1—and in redirecting the reference of the pronoun in line 94 from "soule" to "mans lawes" (producing "…to mans lawes, by wᶜʰ hee shall not bee tryed" in place of the authorial "lett thy soule bee tyed / To mans lawes, by wᶜʰ she shall not be tryed"), a scribal blunder otherwise appearing only among the descendants of the LOH. The final artifacts filiated on the stemma, B40 and TT1, derive from γ4, which records the distinctive β5 readings in lines 31, 47, and 57, but reduces β5's "h'is" in line 33 to "is" (yielding "the foule Divell is")—a lection otherwise found only in the unfiliated artifacts B47 and H7. In line 51 γ4 also uniquely gives the variant form "*Sollen*" (for the usual "sullen") in describing Genevan religion as "playne, simple, *Sollen*, younge," and further introduces the unique spellings "*Gardeans*" into the line 61-phrase "such wiues as their Guardians offer" (yielding "...*Gardeans* offer") and "indevoires" into the line-87 phrase "The minds endeauors reach" (yielding "...*indevoires* reach"). Numerous substantive divergences (e.g., B40's inscribing the correct "dearth" in line 19, where TT1 gives "death") make it certain that B40 does not derive from TT1; and such discrepant spellings as TT1's correct "Too [for B40's *to*] much light breedes" in line 69 and TT1's normative "perish [for B40's *pirrish*] soules" in line 109 suggest—if they do not prove certainly—that the maladroit copyist of TT1 has not independently corrected B40's anomalies, but has instead derived the normative readings from γ⁴. As is usual in this edition, therefore, the stemma shows B40 and TT1 as siblings rather than as parent and child.[1]

---

[1] The comprehensive stemma of the Satyres presented by Milgate (see Y:lxi) reflects his belief that NY3 and the Group-1 manuscripts (B32 and O20 are the two he mentions) embody an intermediate authorial text of the poem that stands between Donne's earliest version (preserved in the independently circulating "books" of Satyres—of which Milgate specifically names B13, OQ1, and VA1) and his latest (preserved in the Group-II manuscripts—of which Milgate specifically names C2, DT1, and B40). Further, there is evidence that might at first glance seem to imply an additional stage of authorial revision occurring between what on the main stemma in Figure 12 are designated the LOH and the LRH. In truncated form, a stemma incorporating these additional stages of revision for *Sat3* would appear as follows:

Sat3: Pseudo Stemma
(retains naming conventions of main stemma; new entries shown in brackets)

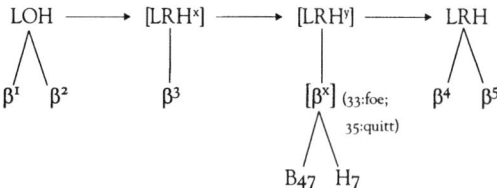

A fuller critique of Milgate's theory of the composition and transmission of the Satyres appears above in the General Textual Introduction to this volume (see pp. lxxxviii–xci). Of its possible applicability to *Sat3* we need say only that instead of representing Donne's "first thoughts" (Y:lvii), such distinctive B13-OQ1-VA1 readings as "This fear Corage [for *great courage*] & high valour is" in line 16 and "not to staye" (for "not to stray") in line 78 are scribal blunders, and their absence in the β³ genealogical line (which includes NY3 and B32) amounts merely to the avoidance of error; and since none of the defining lections of the β³ artifacts (the singular "sin" in line 3 and the plural "honors" in line 9, e.g.) carries over into the text presented in the descendants of the LOH, neither can they be described as authorial. The postulation of [LRHˣ] as shown above is thus not called for.

The situation of B47 and H7, on the other hand, is somewhat more complicated. Both these manuscripts are left unfiliated on the full stemma given in Figure 12. The two readings that most strongly appear to justify the postulation of [LRHʸ] as their progenitor are the singular "foe" in line 33 and "quitt" in line 35, two of the authorial revisions listed in Table 3.1 above. Viewed simply *per se*, of course, any instance in which "foes" had been altered to "foe" (or vice versa) would raise the immediate suspicion of a scribal slip. Except for B47 and H7, however, the plural "foes" invariably appears throughout the original line of descent while the singular "foe" invariably appears throughout the revised line, a fact indicating that something in the wording of this passage worked powerfully to

The Seventeenth-Century Prints

Evincing the authorial revisions cited in Table 3.1 as well as the above-noted scribal changes introduced in β⁵ (in ll. 31, 33, 47, 57, and 86), γ³ (in ll. 7, 90, and 104), and δ⁴ (in l. 64), *Sat3* enters print in 1633 (A) in an eclectic version based on C2, but influenced by DT1 and (in at least one crucial reading) by H6—three manuscripts shown previously in this edition to have been employed as A was being compiled and set into type (see, e.g., *DV* 2:lxxvi–lxxviii and 7.1:lxxii). The reading that specifically links A to C2 is "she" in line 94 ("by which she [i.e., "thy soule"] shall not be tryed"), where both DT1 and H6 read "hee." And this association is further evident in various instances involving punctuation (e.g., A follows C2 in failing to provide needed medial punctution in line 99 ["Equally strong cannot both sides say so?"], where DT1 records a comma ["...strong, cannot..."] and H6 a question mark ["...strong? Cannot..."]) and spelling (e.g., A records C2's atypical "unhansome" in line 52 [the only occurrence of this word in Donne's poetry], where both DT1 and H6 record the normative "vnhandsome" [with a *d*]). On the other hand, A likely adopts from DT1 the hyphenated

---

keep copyists focused on the text they were transcribing. And this intralineal uniformity lends weight to the suspicion that in B47 and H7 "foe" is authorial as well—especially since the reading occurs in conjunction with the distinctive Donnean revision "quitt" a mere two lines further on.

Against the conclusion suggested by this line of reasoning, however, are details in the textual makeup of both B47 and H7 that—were they not categorically disqualified as descendants of the LOH by the "foe"-"quitt" cruxes—would tend to associate them, respectively, with the β² and the γ² families. B47 shares a number of the distinctive β² (C9-H6) readings, including the uniquely plural "cowards" (for "coward") in line 29, "And [for the normative *He*] loues" in line 47, "Grants" (for the authorial "Crantz" in line 49), and the unique "Or [for *Oh*] will it then serve" in line 95 among others, while at the same time failing to evince such distinguishing C9-H6 lections as "the foule Deuill, he" (for the authorial "the foule Deuill, whom") in line 33, "about must & about must goe" (for the normative "about must, and about go") in line 81, and the unique "thyselfe" (for "thy Soule") in l. 93. Thus, but for "foe" and "quitt," B47 could plausibly be depicted on the main stemma as branching off the β² lineage at a point above the parent of C9 and H6, as it is on the stemmas for the other 4 Satyres. Similarly, H7 shares many distinctive lections that appear in γ²—including "Earths honours were" (for the normative "...honor was") in line 9, "Frossen Norths [for the correct *north*] Discoueryes" in line 22, and "Is not this excuse for meere Contrarys / Equallie true [for the authorial *strong*]" in line 99—but lacks others—such as the unique "decrepitt vaine" (for "decrepit wayne") in line 38, "Grugus" (for "Graius") in line 55, and "Grattus" (for "Graccus") in line 65. And this configuration of readings would locate H7 somewhere above γ² in the β³ lineage on the main stemma—if it did not record "foe" and "quitt."

Finally, although distinctive differences in such lines as 14–15 (where B47 gives the anomalous "two easie wayes, and nere / be dam̄'d" [while H7 normatively reads "...and neare / To followe, Dam̄d"]) and 64 (where H7 gives the trivialized "will marry none" [while B47 normatively reads "dares marrie none"]) show that neither can have been copied directly from the other, B47 and H7 share a number of readings in addition to "foe" and "quitt" that, were it not for their respective links to the β² and γ² lineages, would further support positioning them as cognate, if distant, descendants of [LRH¹] as postulated in the Pseudo Stemma above. These include the singular "sinn" (for "sins") in line 3, "dangers" (for the authorial "dungeons") in line 20, "the foule deuill is" (for "the foule Deuill, whom") in line 33, the unique "oh where's Mireus" (for the normative "Oh where? Myrius") in line 43, "and [for the normative *He*] loues her raggs" in line 47, and "who at Geneua's [for the uncontracted *Geneua is*] calld" in line 50. In the upshot, the most plausible way to explain the apparent contradictions presented by the foregoing evidence—that (1) these artifacts evince a cousinly relationship, while (2) at the same time tracing their respective descents up through two distinct genealogical strains within the LOH lineage

"blanck-charters" in line 91 ("Sign'd Kings blanck-charters"), where both C2 and H6 give the two words unconnected, and—among the numerous instances in which A's compositor undoubtedly followed house style or his own lights—seems occasionally to adopt DT1's punctuation (e.g., "…strumpet; last…" in line 39, where C2 records "…Strumpett, last…" and H6 "…strumpet. Last…"). The one reading that A certainly imported from H6 appears in line 81, where—with only Y2, the NY1-VA2 pair, and its own sibling C9—H6 fills out Donne's 9-syllable "Reache her, about must, and about, goe" by inserting a second "must," a metrical "repair" that results in A's "Reach her, about must and about must goe." Further, following one or the other of his alternate manuscripts, A's editor also corrects such of C2's blunders as the meaningless "Filfe" in line 37 (A gives "selfe"), the anomalous "Knoweing some woemens whores" in line 64 (A gives "Knowing some women whores"), and the trivialized "best flowers" in line 103 (A gives "blest flowers"). On the other hand, A admits several errors of its own, including "it selfe [for the normative *selfes*] death" in line 40, "thinking her unhous'd her [for the correct *here*]" in line 44, and the illogically inserted question mark after "Salamanders" in the lines 22–26 question "…and thrise / Colder than Salamanders? like divine / Children…Canst thou for gaine beare?" (this question mark persists in all the seventeenth-century editions, but among manuscripts appears in only H8).

Already compromised not only by the scribal errors accumulated in the β5 lineage, but also by the eclecticizing interventions of A's editor and by compositorial blunders, the text of *Sat3* sustains a scattering of further changes as it appears in the succeeding seventeenth-century editions/issues (B–G), several of them—as the following list shows—introduced into B from H6 after the editor had had more leisure to study the variants it offered and one, apparently, from O21.

As is shown in Figure 10, most of the 9 readings certainly or probably adopted into B from H6 seem intended to improve meter ("forbid" in l. 32, "Or will" in l. 95, the omission of "and" in l. 107) or logic ("to" in l. 7, "foes" in l. 33), and the line-7 change of "in" to "to" actually restores an authorial reading altered by the scribe of γ3. The poetic sensitivity reflected in these choices—though not in every respect consistent with Donne's own—is further reflected in the editor's refusals: of the original-version options available in H6, B declines "May" (l. 4), "Souldier" (l. 31), "ridd" (l. 35), "high" (l. 79), "Ragged…dwells" (l. 80), "mind" (l. 84), "as" (l. 88), and "serue" (l. 95), rejections suggesting that the editor recognized Donne's revisions of the poem as improvements and determined to preserve them in his own work. As detailed in the Historical Collation below, B's editor also undertakes a thoroughgoing repointing of the poem, showing particular interest in strengthening punctuation at the ends of clauses and sentences (e.g., B replaces weaker marks with periods in a full dozen instances).

In the seventeenth-century editions that follow B, significant textual variants

---

and also (3) evincing two of the defining readings of the LRH lineage—is to posit scribal contamination (i.e., to suppose that at some indeterminable point or points in the poem's transmissional history one or more copyists came into possession of disparate texts of the poem and intermingled their readings). In light of these considerations, the possibility of [LRH^y] must be rejected and B47 and H7 left unfiliated.

FIGURE 10: SIGNIFICANT VARIANTS IN THE 17TH-CENTURY PRINTS OF "SATYRE 3"

~ = agrees with LOH
✓ = agrees with nearest corresponding reading on left
( ) = specific source of variant
c = compositor

Line no.	LOH/DV Reading	A	B–C	D–F	G
1	choakes	~	checks (O21?)*	~	cheeks (c)
3	and	~	~	~	but (c)
7	to	in (γ³)	~ (H6)	✓	~
31	this	his (β⁵)	✓	✓	~ (?)
32	forbid	forbidden (LRH)	~ (H6)	~	~
33	foes	foe (LRH)	~ (H6)	~	~
33	Deuill	deuill h'is (δ⁴)	devill, he (H6)	✓, ✓	✓
40	it selfes	it selfe (c)	~~ (c or H6)	~	~
44	here	her (c)	~ (c)	✓	~
47	He	~	And (H6)	✓	~ (?)
47	her	the (β⁵)	✓	✓	✓
49	Crantz	Crants	✓	✓	Grants (?)
57	bidd	bids (β⁵)	✓	✓	✓
81	2nd must om	2nd must ins (H6)	✓	✓	it (c)
84	that	~ (LRH)	the (H6)	✓	~ (?)
86	too	to (β⁵)	✓	✓	✓
90	here ins	here om (γ³)	✓	✓	✓
94	not	~	om (c)	✓	~ (?)
95	day? Oh will	~? Will (LRH)	~? Or will (H6)	~? ✓	~? ✓
97	thee	~	~	✓	me (?)
101	is	~	~	~	are (c)
104	proue	do (γ³)	✓	✓	✓
107	rocks	& rocks (LRH)	~ (H6?)	~	~

*Although B's change of A's "chokes" to "checks" could be strictly inadvertent, that it occurs in the easily noticed line 1 of the poem and that it entails altering half the word's letters ("oke" to "eck") suggest that the change is deliberate. O21 seems the likely source of the change since it is the sole manuscript to read "checks" and since it (or a cognate) supplied some readings for the first appearance of *ElBrac* in print, in B (see *DV* 2:17, 46).

appear only in the last (G), the changes introduced in the third (C) and fourth (D and its reissues E and F) being few and minor. C is a page-for-page resetting of B and imitates its source even to the point of reproducing B's apostropheless "thappointed" in line 32 ("leave thappointed field"), deviating from it only in updating a couple of its old-fashioned spellings (respelling B's "woodden" as "wooden" in line 18, e.g.); and D–F reproduces the text of C with only a few further modernizations of spelling (e.g., changing C's "waine" in line 38 to "wane") and changes in punctuation (e.g., replacing the comma that ends line 2 in A–C ["eye-lids,"] with a period ["eye-lids."]). By contrast, as is shown in Figure 10, the editor of the Restoration edition of 1669 substantively alters the received text in some 10 instances, and some of these changes indicate his having consulted, at least cursorily, one or more manuscripts. Such changes as "but" (l. 3), "it" (l. 82), "me" (l. 97), and "are" (l. 101) apparently reflect the editor's independent effort to "correct" passages that he took to be unintelligible, clumsy, or ungrammatical, but he may have derived the authorial "not" that had been inadvertently dropped from line 94 in B (and never restored) from a manuscript, and he must have consulted another source for "Grants" in line 49—and very likely for "this" in line 31 and "that" in line 84 as well. Both "Grants" and "this" were available in the C9-H6 pair to one of which—as has been shown previously in this edition (see, e.g., DV 2:lxxxii)—G turned for emendations of other poems.

The Modern Prints

In essential respects, as Figure 11 below shows, the modern editors' respective treatments of the text of Sat3 parallel their handling of texts presented in previously published volumes of this Variorum (see, e.g., DV 7.1:lxxxiv–lxxxviii; see also Stringer, 2011, pp. 43–55). Systematically modernizing orthography and mechanics, Tonson (H) bases his text of Sat3 on G, and this text passes on to his later eighteenth- and earlier nineteenth-century successors Bell (I), Anderson (J), and Chalmers (K) with little change. Readings introduced into the print tradition in G and shared by these editions include "but [for the normative and] be wise" in line 3, "Grants" (for "Crants") in line 49, and "about it go" (for either the authorial "about go" or the received H6 reading "about must goe") in line 81, among others. Tonson also contributes a handful of lections not found in G, restoring the B–F "checks [for G's unique cheeks] my spleen" in line 1,[2] dropping "all" from the normative 11-syllable phrase "As worthy of all our Soules devotion" (yielding "As worthy of our...") in line 6, and introducing meter-regularizing elisions in lines 76, 88, and 101. That H and K print "Doubt wisely, in strange way" in line 77, while I and J give "...wisely. In..." confirms the usual finding that Chalmers (K) reverts to H for his setting text rather than deriving it successively from J, as well as showing that J is based specifically on I.

Evincing "but be wise" in line 3 and "about it go" in line 81, Lowell's 1855 Boston edition (M) also presents a text ultimately based on G, but its inclusion of Tonson's elided "name's" in line 101 shows Tonson to have been Lowell's immediate source (Lowell refuses the elisions Tonson introduced in lines 76 and 88). And though he spells it with a "z" rather than an "s," Lowell reverts to one of the earlier seventeenth-

---

[2] For Tonson's use of either B or C in constructing his text of the elegies, see DV 2:lxxxiii.

century prints for "Crantz" in line 49 (where G gives *Grants*; we have shown in previous volumes that Lowell frequently compared B).

For *Sat3*, as for *Sat1* and *Sat2*, Grosart (N) bases his edition on B33 and thus—except for Bennett (T), who 70 years later uses NY3—is the only editor ever to choose as copy-text an artifact containing the original version of the poem, printing such LOH lections as "ridd" (for "quitt") in line 35, "Raggued…dwells" (for "Cragg'd…stands") in line 80, and "mynd" (for "Soule") in line 84, as well as B33's anomalous "daungers" (for the normative "dungeons") in line 20. On the other hand, Grosart manifests his usual eclecticism in bypassing, e.g., the B33-LOH readings "May" in line 4, "high hill" in line 79, and "it" in line 81 in favor of the revisions "Can," "huge hill," and "her." Such innovative readings as "but be wyse" in line 3 and "Grants" in line 49 point to N's occasional reliance on G, and N's omission of "all" from the line 6 phrase "of all our sowles deuotion" (a meter-regularizing gesture first introduced into the print tradition by H) likely reflects the influence of M (see *DV* 7.1:lxxviii for a parallel instance of N's following M). Grosart's recording of "abought it goo" in line 81 not only provides another instance of his eclectic use of G, but also bespeaks his characteristic carelessness in transcription (B33 reads "…goe").

In accordance with the edition's guiding policy, Norton's update (O) of Lowell's 1855 edition (M) follows A as its copy-text and faithfully reproduces A's substantives, including "in [for the authorial *to*] the first blinded age" (a γ^3 error) in line 7, "Flesh (itself [for the correct *it selfes*] death)" in line 40, and (uniquely among the modern prints) the ungrammatical "laws /…bids [for *bid*] him think" in lines 56–57. On the other hand, O systematically modernizes A's language, replacing archaic spellings ("pitty" in line 1 is respelled as "pity"), dropping terminal *e*'s ("thinke" in line 57 is shortened to "think," e.g.), expanding elided participles ("unhous'd" in line 44 is changed to "unhoused," e.g.), supplying apostrophes in possessives ("leaders rage" in line 19 becomes "leader's rage"), and adding punctuation throughout. Norton's footnotes cite variants in B, C, D, F, and G, and some of his changes to A's accidentals may derive from these editions. Others—such as the spelling "Gracchus" (for A's "Graccus") in line 65 and the italicization of "*Goddess!*" in line 27—likely derive from Lowell's prior work in M. O's most curious deviation from A appears in lines 86–87, where—for the first time ever in an edition—he prints the authorial "hard knowledge too / The mind's endeavours reach" (for the received "…to / The…"). In light of Norton's determination to adhere strictly to A, this is almost certainly a mistake, but it is worth noting that "too" was available in both H3 and H7, which Norton had added to Harvard College Library by May 4, 1905, and may have had in hand while completing the work on O.

Although he silently adds from B33 the subtitle "Of Religion" to the heading "Satire iii." in his table of contents and although he mentions B33 and SN3 in his general headnote to the Satyres, Chambers (P) otherwise makes no apparent use of manuscripts in editing *Sat3*, instead constructing his text eclectically from the seventeenth-century editions and apparently drawing a few details from his eighteenth- and nineteenth-century predecessors. He accepts, for example, A's "chokes my spleen" (for B–F's "checks…" and G's "cheeks…") in line 1 and "in [for B–G's *to*] the first blinded age" in line 7, yet he rejects A's "devill h'is" in line 33 (preferring B–G's "devil, he")

FIGURE 11: VARIANTS IN THE MODERN PRINTS OF "SATYRE 3"

[blank] = agrees with LOH reading   ~ = agrees with LOH reading   OoV = Origin of Variant   A–G = variant appears in 17th-c. eds.
• = variant appears in modern eds.   ( ) = specific source of variant   { = to be read together

Line no.	LOH/DV reading	Variant	OoV	A–G	H	I	J	K	M	N	O	P	Q	S	T	Y	Z	AA	DD
1	choakes	checks	B	B–F	•	•	•	•	•			•	•	•		•	•	•	•
2	These	Those	LRH	A–G	•	•	•	•	•	•	•	•	•	•		•	•	•	•
3	and	but	G	G	•	•	•	•	•	•									
4	May	Can	LRH	A–G	•	•	•	•	•	•	•	•	•	•		•	•	•	•
6	of all	of	H	A	•	•	•	•	•	•									
7	to	in	γ³	A	•	•	•	•	•	•									
9	honor	honors	NY3					•	•			•	•				•	•	
20	dungeons	daungers	B33																
31	Soldier	Sentinell	LRH	A–G	•	•	•	•	•			•	•	•		•	•	•	•
31	this	his	β⁵	A–F															
32	forbid	forbidden	LRH	A									•	•					
33	foes	foe	LRH	A															
33	Deuill	~, he	H6	B–G	•	•	•	•	•	•	~ he's	•	•	the •			~ h'is		the •
35	ridd	quitt	LRH	A–G	•	•	•	•	•		•	•	•	•			~ h'is		~ h'is
40	it selfes	it selfe	A	A															
46	yeares	yeare	B33	B–F															
47	He	And	H6	B–F	•	•	•	•											
47	her	the	β⁸	A–G	•	•	•	•	•		•	•	•	the •			•	•	the •
49	Crantz	Grants	?	G	•	•	•	•	•		•								
53	which	that	LRH	A–G	•	•	•	•	•	•	•	•	•	•		•	•	•	•
55	Graius	Grajus	B	B–G						Grayus									
56	ambitious	Ambition's	NY3															•	
57	bidd	bids	β⁵	A–G								•			•				
61	Guardians	Gardens	B33								•						•		
62	Phrygas	Phrygius	LRH	A–G	•	•	•	•	•				•	•		•	•	•	•

Line no.	LOH/DV reading	Variant	OoV	A–G	H	I	J	K	M	N	O	P	Q	S	T	Y	Z	AA	DD
72	his	this	J	A–G	•	•	•	•	•		•	•	•	•		•	•	•	
75	which	that	LRH	A–G	•	•	•	•			•	•	•	•		•	•	•	•
77	wisely; In	~.~	I		•	•	•	•		•						•	•		•
79	high	huge	LRH	A–G	•	•	•	•	•	•	•	•	•	•		•	•	•	•
80	Ragged	Cragged	LRH	A–G	•	•	•	•				•				•			•
80	dwells	stands	LRH	A–G	•	•	•	•	•		•	•	•	•		•	•	•	•
81	it	her	LRH	A–G	•	•	•	•					•		•	•			•
81	about go	~must ~	H6	A–F															
81	about go	~it ~	G	G															
84	Mind	soul	LRH	A–G	•	•	•	•	•	•	•	•	•	•		•	•	•	•
86	too	to	β⁵	A–G		•	•	•				•				•			
88	as	like	LRH	A–G	•	•	•	•	•	•	•	•	•	•		•	•	•	•
88	to all	to all	LOH	A–G						•		•							
89	the Truthe	~'~	Z													•			
89	thou hast	~'~	Y																
90	ill case here	ill case	γ³	A–G	•		•	•	•	euell case	•	•	•	•		•	•	•	•
92	they	thy	K							• (B33)									
94	Mens	man's	LRH	A–G	•	•	•	•	•		•	•	•	•		•	•	•	•
95	Oh will	Or will	H6	B–G	•	•	•	•	•		•	•	•	•		•	•	•	•
95	Oh will	will	LRH	A															
95	serve	boote	LRH	A–G	•	•	•								•	•			
97	thee	me	G	G	•	•	•	•	•		•	•	•	•		•	•	•	•
100	rightly obay	~'~	Y													•			
101	nature, and	~,'~	Z		•	•	•	•	•		•	•	•	•		•	•	•	•
101	name is	name's	H					•								•			
103	which	that	LRH	A–G	•	•	•	•	•		•	•	•	•		•	•	•	•
104	proue	do	γ³	A–G	•	•	•	•								•			•
107	rocks	and rocks	LRH	A												•			•
107	woods, and	~,'~	Y													•			•

and A's "mills, & rockes" in line 107 (preferring B–G's "mills, rocks"). From G (or one of its followers) he derives the hyphenated "state-cloth" in line 48 (where A–F give "statecloth"), and he follows H (or, possibly, N) in emending the ungrammmatical "lawes /...bids" found in A–G in lines 56–57 to "...bid." Chambers is also the first editor to elide "Geneva is" in line 50 to "Geneva's" (a metrical adjustment later employed by Y and Z) and the last editor ever to record the corrupt line 86–87 construction "hard knowledge to / The mind's endeavours reach" (for the authorial "...too /...").

In accordance with his conviction that that A is "far and away superior to any other single edition, and...to any *single* manuscript" (2:cxvi), Grierson (Q) selects A as copy-text for *Sat3* and—with a single exception—follows its orthography meticulously, even letting stand the line-54 spelling "course country drudges" that B had altered to "coarse..." and passed on to C–G. (The exception occurs in line 49, where Q adopts from NY3 the spelling "Crantz" [A has "Crants"] on grounds that the *z* "emphasizes the Dutch character of the name" [2:114].) On the other hand, Grierson diverges from A verbally in lines 7, 33, 40, 44, 47, 57, 86, 90, and 95, as well as altering A's punctuation in some 25 instances. His changes of A's "it selfe" to "it selfes" in line 40 and "her" to "here" in line 44 repair obvious typesetting blunders, and his substitution of "bids" (for "bid") in line 57 repairs a grammatical error that began with β⁵ and perpetuated itself down the line of descent into all the seventeenth-century prints. Although he refers to "the older version of the *Satyres*" (2:114) in citing the manuscripts' "Souldier" as an alternative to A's "Sentinell" in line 31 and avers that the manuscript lections "ragged" and "rugged" (for A's "Cragg'd") in line 80 are "legimate" (2:116), Grierson does not attempt to postulate a stemma and fails to systematically distinguish alternate versions of *Sat3*. His attempts to correct A from manuscript by replacing A's "in the first blinded age" with "to..." in line 7, "Know thy foe, the foule devill h'is" with "...foes: The foule Devill" in line 33, "the ragges" with "her ragges" in line 47, "ill case" with "ill case here" in line 90, and "Will it then boot thee" with "Oh, will..." in line 95 are thus logically or aesthetically—rather than genealogically—based, and the results are mixed. The changes in lines 7, 47, and 90 succeed in restoring LRH readings that had been lost at the β⁵ and γ³ stages of the text's evolution, but those in line 33 and 95 interject readings from the original lineage into the version descending from the LRH. Grierson's retention of A's "his [for the authorial *this*] worlds garrison" in line 31 and "do [for the authorial *proue*] well" in line 104 similarly reflect an inadequate grasp of the text's transmissional history. Finally, other than the Grolier editors, who very probably blundered into the reading, Grierson is the first editor to print the correct "too" (for the received "to") at the end of line 86 and thus to clear up a syntactical problem that had disfigured the text for almost 300 years.[3] This correction has been adopted by all subsequent editors. Except that he mistakenly inserts "the" before "forbidden" in line 32 (yielding "the forbidden warres"), Hayward reproduces

---

[3]Grierson describes the "to"/"too" distinction as a mere question of spelling, but infers from their treatments of the passage that N and P had regarded "to" as a preposition. Since the seventeenth-century editions characteristically distinguish the adverb from the preposition by spelling, however, it seems likely that they, too, read "to" as a preposition and were understood so to have done by their editorial successors.

Grierson's text exactly, even to the point of adopting from NY3 the spelling "Crantz" (with a ʒ) in line 49.

Persuaded that the absence of any "single authoritative text" makes it "advisable to base each poem on whatever accessible text has the fewest obvious errors" (xxv), in 1942 Roger Bennett (T) becomes only the second editor since the seventeenth century to set *Sat3* into type from manuscript. Bennett's choice for copy-text is NY3, one of few artifacts available to him as an American scholar working during World War II and also the manuscript chosen by the present editors as copy-text for the original version of the poem. In addition to modernizing spelling and punctuation, Bennett adds from an unspecified source the subtitle "Of Religion" to the heading and emends NY3 substantively in lines 3 (changing "nor" to "not" and "sin" to "sins"), 7 (changing "blind" to "blinded"), 14 (changing "ways easy" to "so easy ways"), 17 (changing "Dutch? darest" to "Dutch, and dar'st"), 81 (changing "and about go" to "and about must go"), 99 (changing "strange" to "strong"), and 107 (changing "Mills, Rocks" to "mills and rocks"). Except for the added subtitle and the alteration of "nor" to "not" in line 3, Bennet explicitly credits all these emendations to A; and while the changes in lines 3 and 99 correct errors in NY3's transcription, those in lines 7, 14, 17, and 107 contaminate the NY3 text with readings from the revised version of the poem. As Figure 11 above shows, insertion of the second "must" in line 81 vitiates NY3's text with a reading that A had adopted from H6. The differences between T's presentation of the NY3 text and that provided in the present edition are discussed below.

Milgate (Y) is Grierson's spiritual and institutional successor in the Oxford University Press series, and he substantively reproduces the text of A as emended by Q except in lines 95 (where he refuses the "Oh" that Q had imported from the earlier version of the text) and 104 (where he rejects the γ³ trivialization "do" that Q had accepted in place of the authorial "proue"). On grounds that "Crants" in line 49 "seems to be what Donne wrote" (p. 144), Milgate also refuses the NY3 spelling "Crantz" that Grierson had preferred, but for his handling of punctuation, Milgate is deeply indebted to Grierson, diverging from his predecessor in only 4 instances. More than any previous editor, Milgate is concerned to regularize Donne's meter, imposing elisions and contractions freely throughout the couse of the poem and—along with all his editorial forerunners—adopting G's expansion of A's "Cragg'd" to "Cragged" in line 80 in order to provide the line a full 10 syllables. Representative examples of such metrical adjustments are shown in Figure 11 above.

Shawcross (Z), too, sets *Sat3* into type from A, emending it—in accordance with his usual practice—when "a later version or the reading of a consensus of manuscripts seems to be closer to Donne's 'original'" (xxi). In implementing this Griersonian approach, Z diverges verbally from A in lines 7, 33, 40, 44, 47, 57, 86, and 95—all of which are among the alterations of A that Grierson had previously imposed and all but one of which (that in l. 95) had been similarly adopted by Y. Z differs from Q and Y, however, in retaining the spurious "h'is" that A had inherited from β⁵ in line 33 (a decision that leaves the line with a full 10 syllables) and in refusing to change A's "case, that" in line 90 to the authorial "case here, that" (a decision also perhaps calculated to preserve a metrically smooth line). Shawcross does not adopt Q's thoroughgoing repunctuation of the poem, but his concern with meter leads him to impose almost all the elisions previously implemented by Milgate (see Figure 11 for examples).

Declaring himself interested in "offer[ing] the richest and most pointed readings of Donne's poems that have good authority in the early versions" (p. 14), Smith (AA)—as is his usual practice—specifies no particular copy-text for *Sat3*, but presents a modernized, eclectic text based generally on the seventeenth-century editions, most heavily on A. Accordingly, AA emends the text of A in lines 7, 33, 40, 44, 47, 57, 86, 90, 95, and 104—all but the last of these also emended by Grierson. AA differs from Q, however, in choosing B–G's "Devill, he, whom…" in line 33 (where Grierson had opted for the manuscript reading "Devill (whom…)") and B–G's "Or will…" in line 95 (where Grierson had preferred the manuscript lection "Oh, will.…" In emending A's "do well" in line 104 to the manuscript reading "prove well" in line 104, Smith's choice echoes that of Milgate before him. Although his textual notes sometimes refer to particular seventeenth-century editions, Smith treats the manuscript evidence unspecifically, citing variants only in "MS," "*some MSS*," "*several MSS*," or "*most MSS*."

In an edition that also veers away from the scholarly toward the popular, Patrides (DD) similarly fails to name specifically those few manuscripts from which he derives emendations or reports variant readings, referring instead to "a MS," "some MSS," or "several MSS." DD does, however, preserve old spelling, and specifies A, "as supplemented by" later editions, as its "basic text," verbally emending A's text of *Sat3* in lines 7, 32, 40, 44, 47, 57, 86, and 90. DD's adherence to A is manifest in its retention of A's often-abandoned "foe…h'is…" in line 33, "day? Will…" in line 95, and "do well" in line 104. And DD is the only edition since 1654 to retain A's contracted "Cragg'd" (for the expanded "Cragged") in line 80. Patrides's recording of the anomalous "the forbidden wars" (for "forbid/forbidden wars") in line 32 is likely a careless mistake, although he did have a precedent in the similar blunder of Hayward, as Figure 11 shows.

Copy-texts Used in this Edition

As copy-text for the original authorial version of *Sat3*, we have chosen NY3 (see the General Textual Introduction above). As noted previously, Bennett (T) also sets the poem into type from NY3; and while we have not imposed the emendations in lines 7, 14, 17, 81, and 107 that Bennet chose (all of which contaminate the early version of the text with readings from A), we have followed Bennet in changing "nor Laugh" to "not Laugh" and "sin" to "sins" in line 3 and "strange" to "strong" in line 99—the first on grounds that "nor" is the hypercorrection of the NY3 scribe Rowland Woodward, the second and third on grounds that "sin" and "strange" are the innovations of the β[3] scribe. Other verbal errors requiring correction include the β[3] lections "honors" (emended to the authorial "honor") in line 9 and "his" (emended to the authorial "this") in line 31, as well as Woodward's misreadings "Ambitions" (emended to the authorial "ambitious") in line 56 and "tought me" (emended to the authorial "…thee") in line 97. Woodward's idiosyncratic spellings "tought" in lines 14 and 97 and "wifes" in line 61 we have let stand. Further, we have not intervened to alter his atypical "Phrygas" (a meter-saving alternative to the normative trisyllabic "Phrygius") in line 62, nor have we expanded his unique elisions "may be'imputed" in line 13, "th'hills" in line 82, and "to'all" in line 88, which represent Woodward's formal imposition of metrical regularity on lines whose 11 syllables Donne apparently expected to fit easily into the underlying rhythmical structure of the poem. Our few alterations of NY3's punctuation are listed in the textual apparatus.

The copy-text for the revised version of the poem is DT1, generally the most reliable of the Group-II manuscripts and, in the case of *Sat3*, the least corrupt descendant of the LRH (see the General Textual Introduction above). In addition to the 20-plus authorial revisions detailed in Table 3.1 above, DT1 inherits 5 verbal errors from β⁵ and a further 3 from γ³, and the scribe of DT1 blunders twice himself. The β⁵ mis-readings include "his [for the authorial *this*] worlds garrison" in line 31, "Deuill, his, whom" (for the authorial "Deuill, whom") in line 33, "the [for the authorial *her*] raggs" in line 47, "bids [for the authorial *bid*] him thinke" in line 57, and "hard knowledge to" (for the authorial "...too") in line 86; the γ³ mistakes are "in [for the authorial *to*] the first blinded age" in line 7, the omission of "here" in the authorial phrase "soe ill case here" in line 90, and the trivialization "doe [for the authorial *proue*] well" in line 104; independently, DT1 misreads "braue loues" (for Donne's "...loue") in line 49 and "by which hee [for Donne's *shee*] shall not bee tryed" in line 94. In each of these instances, of course, we have emended up the line of transmission toward the reading of the LRH. DT1 is one of those manuscripts whose scribe seems to have "regard[ed] the line end as sufficient punctuation in itself" (see p. lvii above), and it also contains a number of intralineal errors or deficiencies in pointing. To present a readable text has thus required emending the punctuation in nearly 20 places, all of which are itemized in the textual apparatus.

Textual Apparatus

Copy-texts: Original version: NY3.   Revised version: DT1.

Texts collated: B13 (ff. 52v–53v); B32 (ff. 90v–91v); B33 (ff. 99–100v); B40 (ff. 58–59); B47 (ff. 99–100v); B51 (*ll. 12–13 only*, f. [42v]); C2 (ff. 18–19); C8 (ff. 6v–9); C9 (ff. 14–15v); DT1 (ff. 14v–16); H3 (ff. 12–13v); H4 (ff. 2v–4); H5 (ff. 128–29v); H6 (pp. 65–68); H7 (ff. 46–48v); H8 (ff. 70–71v); HH1 (ff. 65–67); IU2 (*ll. 45–48 only*, f. 60); NP3 (*ll. 1–54 only*, f. 119r–v); NY1 (pp. 9–12); NY3 (ff. [5–6]); O20 (ff. 4v–6v); O21 (pp. 177–81); OJ1 (*ll. 11, 32, 75, 77, 79, 80, 82, 95 only*, pp. 333–36); OQ1 (ff. 201–202v); P3 (ff. 7–8); SP1 (ff. 12–13v); TT1 (ff. 21–22); VA1 (ff. 5–6v); VA2 (ff. 8–9); Y2 (pp. 17–25); Y3 (pp. 12–15); A (pp. 333–36); B (pp. 131–34); C (pp. 131–34); D (pp. 125–28); E (pp. 125–28); F (pp. 125–28); G (pp. 125–28); 38 (*ll. 77b–79a only*, p. 218).

Emendations of the copy-text, original version: Line 3 not] nor   sins] sin   9 honor] honors   4 maladyes?] ~.   15 this,] ~$_\wedge$ 18 Shipps,] ~$_\wedge$ 19 dearth?] ~,   23 Salamanders,] ~;   30 thee] ~,   31 this] his   32 field?] ~.   37 selfe,] ~$_\wedge$ foe,] ~$_\wedge$ 39 Last,] ~$_\wedge$ 42 power] ~,   46 ago,] ~$_\wedge$ 51 Religion,] ~.   56 ambitious] Ambitions   57 Still] ~,   58 vs] ~,   61 offer] ›will‹ ~   70 Of force must] (M: ›Of force‹) Must   97 thee] me   99 stronge] strange   102 Then] ~,   109 chuse] ~,

Regularizations of the copy-text, original version: Heading: *Satyre 3.*] Sat: .3.ᵃ   Line 2 which] wch 5 our] o^r 6 our] o^r 13 may be'imputed] maybe'imputed   17 *2nd* Darest] darest   18 woodden] wodden   20 the] y^e 21 the] y^e 24 the] y^e 25 our] o^r 26 And] and   27 Which] W^{ch} 28 Courage] courage   37 lou'd] loud   40 which] wch 41 which] wch 53 which] wch 57 that] y^t 58 Which] W^{ch} with] w^t 65 that] y^t 68 blind-] ~=   71 the] y^e which] wch 72 and] &   73 a litle] alitle   74 Beleeue] beleeue   75 which] wch the] y^e 80 that] y^t 83 that] y^t 84 that] y^t 86 the] y^e 88 the] y^e 89 the] y^e which] wch 90 that] y^t with] w^t 94 which] wch 99 Cannot] cannot   101 and] &   104 the] y^e and] &   107 *2nd* and] &   108 the] y^e

Emendations of the copy-text, revised version: Heading: *Satyre 3.*] Satyre. 2   Line 2 eye-lidds.] ~-~$_\wedge$ 3 wise,] ~$_\wedge$ 7 to] in   19 dearth?] ~,   20 earth?] ~,   25 bee,] ~;   28 words?] ~.   31 this] his   33 Deuill,] ~, his,   39 last,] ~$_\wedge$ 40 (it] $_\wedge$~   47 her] the   raggs] ~,

soe,] ~∧   49 loues] loue   51 plaine,] ~∧   sullen,] ~∧   57 bid]
bids   69 too] to   71 right;] ~,   72 truth] ~,   77 wiselie,] ~∧
82 soe;] ~,   86 too] to   90 case here] case   94 shee] hee   101
chang'd,] ~∧   bee] ~,   104 proue] doe   108 going,] ~∧   109 1st
God] ~,

Regularizations of the copy-text, revised version: *Initial capital letters supplied in ll.*
11, 12, 24, 25, 27, 28, 30–32, 34–42, 44–48, 50–52, 56–64, 66–68, 70, 71,
73–75, 77–82, 84, 85, 87–110.   Line 2 which] w^ch   9 Alass] alass
11 And] and   15 O] o   17 and] &   26 and] &   27 Which]
w^ch   28 Courage] courage   30 and] &   39 and] &   40 which]
w^ch   41 and] &   which] w^ch   48 the] y^e   51 yonge] Yonge
58 Which] w^ch   with] w^th   65 and] &   68 blinde-] ~=   70 and]
&   71 which] w^ch   75 that] y^t   80 *1st and 2nd* and] &   83 that]
y^t   89 which] w^ch   90 that] y^t   93 and] &   94 which] w^ch
101 and] &   103 that] y^t   104 and] &   105 and] &   107 *2nd*
and 3rd and] &   109 which] w^ch   110 trust.] ~. |

Historical Collation

Format:

   Imperfections: *missing leaves causing loss of ll. 55–110*   NP3.

   Indentations: *ll. 109–10 ind*   C9 H6; *line 1 hanging ind*   H3 H7 SP1; *l. 49*
   ind   NP3; *l. 1 ind*   NY3; *no ind*   Σ.

   Miscellaneous: D^r: Doone: *is running head in ms.*   B32; *HE entered by scribe*
   who entered Satyres 1 and 2, text entered by a different scribe   B33; *entire*
   text written in right M of ms., ›131‹ *follows l. 13*   B51; *text run together*
   with that of Sat2, HE in left M   C8; *space left for missing ll. 85–88 at*
   bottom of f. 15   C9; »P.« *left of HE*   H6; *poem scribally attributed to I. D.*
   in right M beside HE   H8; *3rd of 3 Satyres snippets collectively headed*
   Empty Fop   IU2; *every 5th line numbered scribally in arabic in left M*
   NY1 VA2; »p. 125« *written left of HE*   O20; *ms. emendations and*
   variants in a copy of A   OJ1; *l. 92 inserted scribally in right M*   P3.

Headings: Satire the 4.th | B13.   **Satyre: 3.^d**   B32 C2 C8(.3.) C9(3.) H6(3.)
H8(3.) HH1(3) A(III.)–G(III.).   »Sat. 3. / Of Religion.«   B33.   A
Satire   B40.   Satyre .3. Uppon Religion. | B47.   <u>Satyre.</u> 2   DT1
O21(ye Second.).   The Fourthe Satyre   H3.   Satyre: »(3).«   H4.
Satyra Sexta.   H5.   .Satyra. Tertia.   H7 SP1(3^a) VA2.   I Donne |
Satyre: 3. | NP3.   Satire 3   NY1.   Sat: .3.^a   NY3.   Satyr.   O20.
Satira 3^a   OQ1 Y2(Tertia.).   The third Satire | P3.   *Satire*   TT1.
Sat:3:   VA1.   Satire the Second: Y3.   *om*   B51 IU2 OJ1 38.

   1 choakes] checks   O21 B–F; cheeks   G.   spleene;]   B13 B32 C2 C8 HH1
NY3 O20 P3 Y3 A–G; ~∧   NP3 TT1; ~:   SP1; ~,   Σ.   forbids] for bidds
B40; ~,   HH1.

2 These] those B40 C2 C8 C9 DT1 H4 H6 H8 O21 TT1 Y3 A–G.   issue]
~, B13 B32 B40 C8 DT1 H3 H4 H5 H7 HH1 O20 SP1 VA1 Y3 B–G; ~; O21.
swell] fitt H3.   my] myne OQ1 P3 VA1.   eylids.] Eye lidds. B32 HH1
P3; ~ₐ B33 H3 H6 NY1 TT1 VA1; ~; B40 O21; eye lidds ₐ B47 H4 OQ1
VA2 Y2 Y3; ~, C2 C9; eye-lidds ₐ DT1 H7 NP3; ey-lids. H5 SP1 D–G;
eye-lids: H8; eye-lids, A–C.

3 not] nor B13 C9 H6 HH1 NY3.   Laugh,] ~ₐ B40 B47 C8 C9 H3 H6
H8 NP3 NY1 O21 OQ1 TT1 VA2 Y2 Y3; ~. P3.   nor] & H8 Y2.
weepe] ~; B32 O20 SP1; ~, B47 H3 H7 Y2.   sins,] sin ₐ B32 B47 H3 H7
Y2; ~ₐ H6; om NP3; sin, NY3 O20 SP1; ~; O21; Surs ₐ TT1.   and] but
G.   wise,] B32 B40 H4 H5 NY3 O20 OQ1 A–G; ~»,« C8; ~; C9 HH1 P3;
~: H7 NY1 VA2; ~ₐ Σ.

4 May] cann B40 C2 C8 DT1 H4 O21 TT1 Y3 A–G.   rayling] ~, H6; ~.
VA1.   then] ~, H6.   these] all ~ NP3; those O21.   worne] wore →
»~« H4; om NP3; worme O21.   maladyes?] ~ₐ B32 H3 TT1 VA1 Y2 Y3;
~; B40 O21; ~. H6 NY3 O20 SP1; ~: NP3.

5 Is] ~'t H7(→ »~«).   Religion] ~, C8 DT1 HH1 O21 A–G; ~? P3.

6 all] om H3 H7.   deuotion] ~, B13 B32 B40 HH1 O20 O21 OQ1 A–G;
~? C8.

7 to] in C2 C8 DT1 H4 H5 Y2 A.   first] fond H3; soules ~ H5; worlds
~ H8.   blind] blinded B40 B47 C2 C8 C9 DT1 H4 H6 O21 TT1 Y3 A–G;
om H5.   Age?] ~ₐ B33 NP3 O21 TT1 VA1 Y2 Y3; ~; C2; ~, C8 DT1.

8 heauens] heau'ns DT1(Heaue'ns) H4 H5 VA1; Heauen's H3.   ioyes]
~, VA1.   assuage] ~? C8; ~, HH1.

9 Lusts,] ~ₐ B40 H7 OQ1 TT1; lust, B47 Y3; ~? C8; ~; NP3; Lust's ₐ
H3; lust; O21.   as] ~ the H3; ~' Y2.   honor] honors B32 H3 H7 NY3
O20 SP1 Y2.   was] weare B32 H3 H7 O20 SP1 Y2.   them?] ~! B33;
~, B47 Y2; ~; O21; ~ₐ TT1; ~. VA1; ~: Y3.   Alas] ~, HH1 A–G;
~! SP1; Ah lasse VA2.

10 them] ~, O20.   meanes,] ~; B13 NP3 Y3; ~ₐ H3 H7 NY1 O21 OQ1
P3 SP1 TT1 VA1 VA2 Y2.   shall] soe ~ H3.   surpas] passe H3.

11 end?] ~; B33 NP3 O21; ~, C2 Y2 Y3 A; ~ₐ TT1.   thy] the H7; our
OJ1.   Spiritt] ~, HH1.

12 heauen,] ~ₐ B13 B32 B33 B47 B51 P3 TT1 VA1 Y3; ~? C8 HH1; heau'n,
H3(heaue'n) H4; heav'n ₐ H5; ~; H7 O21.   whose] (~ H8 P3 VA1.

13 strict] strick't B40; straight H5; stickt O21.   Life] ~, B13 C2 HH1
NP3 O20 Y2.   may be'imputed] maybe'imputed NY3; ~ be imputed Σ.
fayth,] ~; B13 B51 NP3 NY1 VA2 Y2 Y3; ~ₐ B32 TT1; ~? B40 B47 H5; ~)

H8 P3 VA1.   and] *om* B51.   heare] here B40 B47 H3; *om* B51; ~ thee
H4; heere H7 SP1 TT1 VA2; ~, O21; where Y2.

14 Thee] The B33 H3; he B47; ~, C2 C8 H7 HH1 SP1 A–G; *om* H4.
whome] (~ OQ1 P3 VA1.   tought] NY3; taught, B40 H7 O20 Y3; taught;
O21; hath taught P3; taught Σ.   wayes easy] ~ ~, B13 H8 SP1 VA1; ~ ~;
B33; soe easie ways B40 C8 O21 TT1 Y3 A G; two easie wayes, B47; soe easye
wayes, C2 DT1 H4 B–F; ~ so ~ C9; ~ »so« ~ H3; ~ ›so‹ ~ H6; ~ waies ~
OQ1; all ~ (~ Y2.   neare] ~, DT1; ~) Y2.

15 To] be B47.   follow,] ~.) B13; ~‿ B32 B33 B40 DT1 H3 H4 NY1
O21 SP1 TT1 VA2 Y2 Y3; *om* B47; ~) H8 OQ1 P3 VA1; ~; NP3.
damn'd?] ~; B33 O21 Y2; ~, H3 Y3; ~. H8; damned, NP3; damned? P3
TT1; ~.? VA1.   Oh] ~, B32 H3 HH1 O20 SP1 G; & O21 Y3; Or TT1.
darest,] NY1 NY3; durst‿ B13 H4 OQ1 P3 VA1; ~‿ B40 H7 HH1 O20 SP1
TT1 VA2; darst, C2 A–G; dare, H5; dost‿ NP3; darst‿ Σ.   this,] B32
B40 C8 DT1 H8 HH1 O20 O21 SP1 VA1; ~. C2 H4 A; ~: OQ1 B–G; ~;
P3; ~‿ Σ.

16 feare] ~, DT1 H4 HH1 O20 OQ1.   great] *om* B13 B47 OQ1 P3 VA1.
courage,] ~‿ B47 C2 C8 C9 H6 NY1 OQ1 P3 TT1 VA2 Y3 B–F; ~; O21.
is.] ~; B32 B40 C2 DT1 O20 O21 A; ~, B47 H3 NP3 TT1 Y2 Y3; ~: C8
OQ1 SP1; ~, H4.

17 Darest] H3 NY3 P3 SP1; Durst OQ1; Dar'st Σ.   mutinous] mutiners
B32; Mut'inous DT1; the ~ NP3.   Dutch?] ~, B33 C2 C8 DT1 H5 NP3
O21 A; Datoh? B47; ~‿ H4 TT1 Y3; ~; HH1 Y2; ~. VA1.   Darest] H3
NY3 SP1; and darst B40 C2 C8 DT1 H4 O21 TT1 Y3 A–G; Durst OQ1;
dar'st Σ.   lay] ~, C8.

18 Thee] The B33 H3; *om* VA1.   in] midst P3.   Shipps,] B32 C2 C9
DT1 H3 H4 H6 HH1 NY1 O20 SP1 VA2; yᵉ ~‿ O21; ~', VA1; ship‿ Y2;
~‿ Σ.   woodden] (~ B13 B47 H7 H8 NP3.   Sepulchers,] ~) B13 B47
H7 H8 NP3; ~‿ B33 H3 O21 P3 TT1 VA1 Y3; ~? OQ1; ~; Y2.   pray]
prey B13 H4 H8 O21 Y3 A–G.

19 Leaders] ~ → ›leader‹ P3.   rage,] ~; O21; ~‿ OQ1 TT1.   Stormes,]
~‿ H5 TT1 Y2 Y3; ~; O21.   shott,] ~‿ NP3 NY1 TT1 Y3.   dearthe?]
death? B13 C9 H6(→ ›~?‹) HH1(→ »~?«) O20(→ ›~?‹) VA2; ~‿ B33 NP3
VA1 Y3; ~, B40 C8 DT1 H4 H5 H8 NY3; Death, H5 (→ ›~,‹); ~; O21;
death; OQ1; death‿ TT1 Y2(→ ›~‿‹).

20 Darest] B13 NY3 P3; durst OQ1; Darst Σ.   dive] diues B47.   Seas,]
~‿ B47 C9 H3 H5 H6 TT1 VA2 Y2 Y3; ~; O21.   dungeons] dangers B32
B33 B47 H3 H7 O20 SP1 Y2.   earthe?] ~‿ B33 DT1 NP3 TT1 VA1 Y2 Y3;
~; B40; ~, H5; ~. O21.

21 Hast] Darst B32; Hadst SP1.   fyer] ~, B40; side, H5.

22 north] Northes B32 H3(Northe's) H7 O20 SP1 Y2; ~- B33 C9 DT1. discoueryes,] ~; B32 NP3 O20 O21; ~ₐ B33 TT1 Y3; ~? B47 C2 C8 C9 H6 H7 HH1 NY1 VA2. and] ~, H6. thrice] ~. VA2.

23 then] than SP1 C–G. Salamanders,] Salanders, B13; ~ₐ H3 TT1; ~? H5 H7 H8 A–G; ~; HH1 NP3 NY3 O21; Salamander, VA1. Like] (~ H8 NP3.

24 in th'ouen,] B40 C2 DT1 NY3 A–G; ~ ~? C8; i'~ₐ H3; ~ the Ouen) H8 NP3; ~ th'ouens, NY1; ~ the ouen; O21; ~ the Oven∧ OQ1 P3 TT1 VA1; ~ the ouens∧ VA2; ~ the Oven, Σ. of] om B47. Spayne] ~, B13 B32 B40 C2 DT1 H3 H4 H8 O20 P3 SP1 VA1 A–G; ~? C8; ~; OQ1. and the] om NP3. Line,] B32 B40 DT1 H4 H5 NY3 O20 O21 A B; ~? C8 HH1; om NP3; ~. C; ~ₐ Σ.

25 Whose] (~ B47. Cuntryes] Cuntrie is B13; ~, B40 HH1 OQ1 SP1; ~; O21; contrey P3. Limbecks] Limbeck B13; ~, H3; om H5 H8 NP3. bee] ~, B32 B40 H5 O20 O21 A–G; ~) B47; ~? C2 NY1 VA2; ~; DT1 H4 SP1; ~: HH1; ~—— NP3; ~. VA1.

26 gayne] ~, B40. beare?] ~!, B33; ~, B47 H4 O21 Y3; ~; DT1 Y2; ~,? HH1; ~. VA1. must] ~ not NY1 VA2; for Y2. euery] enuie H3(var: »~«); euer Y2. hee] ~? C8; ~, O21.

27 Which] (~ B47. not] ~, B33 NY1 A–G; out O21. Goddesse] ~) B13; ~, B33 NY1 VA2 A–G; Gods, HH1; (~) OQ1. thy] this HH1; yʳ O21. Mistres,] ~ₐ B13 B32 C2 C8 H3 H7 H8 HH1 NY1 O20 P3 SP1 TT1 VA1 VA2 Y2 Y3; ~) B47. draw,] B13 B40 C2 DT1 H4 H5 NY3 P3 SP1 A–C; ~? HH1; ~. O21; ~ₐ Σ.

28 words?] ~; B33 Y2; ~, C2 C8 DT1 H3 H4 VA1 A; ~ₐ NP3 O21 TT1 Y3. Courage] (~ B47. straw;] DT1 NY3; ~, B32 H5 H7 HH1 O20; ~: B40; ~. C2; ~? C8; ~! C9 H6 NY1 SP1 VA2 A–G; ~ₐ Σ.

29 Coward,] ~; B13 HH1 P3; ~ₐ B33 H7 H8 O21 TT1 Y3; Cowards) B47; Cowards! C9 H6; ~: H5; ~! NP3 NY1 VA2; ~? OQ1; courage, Y2. wilt] will B47 H8; wild Y2. thou] you H8. bold,] ~; B13; ~? NP3 P3; ~ₐ O21 OQ1 TT1 VA1 Y3.

30 foes,] ~ₐ B47 C2 C8 H5 H8 NY1 O21 OQ1 TT1 VA1 VA2 Y3 A D–G; ~; NP3. his] to ~ B13; ~, C8 H5 OQ1 Y2 D–G; ~; NP3 O21; he P3. who] (~ B40 C2 C8 DT1 H4 O21 OQ1 TT1 Y3 A–G; that B47. thee] ~, B32 B33 HH1 NY3 O20. to] om H3 NY1 P3 TT1 VA2. stand] ~, O21.

31 Soldier] Sentinell B40(sentynell) C2 DT1 H4(~') TT1 A–G; Centinell C8 O21 Y3; ~, H8. this] his B32 B40 C2 C8 DT1 H3 H4 NY3 O20 SP1 TT1 A–F. worlds] worldes ~ TT1; ~. VA1. garrison,] ~) B40 C2 C8 DT1 H4 OQ1 Y3 A–G; ~ₐ H6 H8 P3 TT1 VA1; ~; H7 Y2; ~? NP3; ~,)

O21.   yeild] ~? B13 B47 H8 NY1 OQ1 P3 VA2; ~, B40 DT1 H5 HH1 O20 A–G.

32 for] om OJ1.   forbid] B13 B33 C9 H3 H5 H6 H7 HH1 NY1 NY3 OJ1 VA2 B–G; bid Y2; forbidden Σ.   warrs,] B32 B33 B40 C2 DT1 NY3 O20 OJ1 Y2 A–C; wayes, HH1; ~; O21; ~. VA1; ~^ Σ.   leaue] ~' O21; and ~ OJ1.   th'appointed] the appointed B13 B47 C9 H3 HH1 O21 OQ1 P3 TT1 VA1 Y3.   field?] ~^ B33 C2 H7 NP3 P3 TT1 Y3; ~. C8 HH1 NY3 VA1; ~, O21.

33 foes:] ~; B32 B33 H6 HH1 NY1 O20 SP1 VA2 B–F; ~; → ›foe;‹ B40; foe^ B47 C8(»,«) TT1 Y3; Foe, C2 DT1 H4 H7 A; ~^ H3 NP3 P3 VA1; ~. H8; foe; O21; ~, Y2.   Deuill,] ~^ B13 B32 B33 H5 H8 NP3 O20 O21 OQ1 P3 SP1 VA1 Y2 Y3; ~^ is, B40 B47 H7; ~^ h'is, C2 A; ~^ h'is C8; ~, he C9 H6; ~, his, DT1 H4(var: »he | he's«); ~^ is TT1; ~, he, B–F; ~^ (he, G. thou] then ~ Y2.

34 Striu'st] strivest B40 C2 C8 HH1 NP3 O20 OQ1 P3 TT1 VA1 Y3 A; then seemst H5; strives H7(→ ›~‹) Y2.   please,] ~^ B13 C8 H4 H8 P3 TT1 VA1 Y3; ~; B40 NP3; ~: A; ~) G.   for] (~ H8 OQ1 P3 VA1.   hate] ~, B13 B32 B40 C2 C8 C9 DT1 H6 H7 HH1 NP3 O20 SP1 A–G; ~; O21.   loue] ~, B13 B40 C2 C8 C9 DT1 H4 H6 H7 O21 A–G; ~) H8 OQ1 P3 VA1.   allow] ~»,« C8; ~, O20.

35 Thee] ~, O20 SP1.   fayne] ~, C8 HH1 A–G.   his] this HH1 P3. Realme] ~, B33 C2 C8 H3.   ridd:] ~, B32 H6 O20 P3 SP1 Y2; ~; B33 H5 NY1 VA2; quitt; B40 C2 C8 DT1 O21 A–G; quitt. B47 Y3; ~. C9 H8 OQ1 VA1; ~^ H3; quitt, H4 H7; ~? HH1; quitt^ TT1.

36 worlds] wolds B33.   parts] ~, HH1 VA2; ~; O21.   wither] ~, H3; whithe^r H7(→ »~«) VA2.   away] a way B13; ~, B32 B47 H5 H7 H8 HH1 O20 SP1; a way, VA2.   pas,] B40 DT1 H8 HH1 NY3 O20 O21 A–G; ~^ → »~,« C8; ~: NY1 VA2; ~^ Σ.

37 So] to B13 H5.   worlds] wolds B33; world O21 Y3.   selfe,] B32 B40 C8 DT1 H3 H4 H5 HH1 O20 SP1 A–G; Filfe, C2; it ~; O21; ytt ~, Y3; ~^ Σ.   thy] (~ B13 B47 C9 H6 H8 NP3 OQ1 P3 VA1.   lou'd] loved B40 C2 C8 P3 TT1 Y3; lord H3(var: »~«); loud H6 NY3 VA1.   foe,] B32 B40 C2 DT1 H4 O20 SP1 A–G; ~) B13 B47 C9 H6 H8 NP3 OQ1 P3 VA1; for, C8(→ »~,«); for^ Y2; ~^ Σ.   is] ~, HH1; vs Y2.

38 In] Is ~ NP3.   decrepit] decrepid B13 B33 H4 H5.   wayne;] B33 B40 H5 NY3 O21; vaine; B13 B32 O20; vaine, H3(var: »~,«) OQ1 Y2; vaine: SP1; ~^ TT1 Y3; ~, Σ.   and] om H5.   this] ~, B40 DT1 HH1 A–G.

39 Dost] Doest B33 HH1 OQ1 P3; Dust H3.   witherd] ~, B13 B33 H4 H7 H8 NP3 VA1; withered, B40 DT1 P3 SP1; wethered C2; withered H5 HH1 OQ1 TT1 Y2 A–G; withered; O21.   worne] a ~ B47; old H3.

Strumpet.] B33 C9 H6 NY1 NY3 O20 VA2 Y3; ~: B13 H8 SP1; ~, B40 B47
C2 C8 O21 OQ1; ~∧ H3 TT1; ~; Σ.   Last,] H5 HH1 A–G; ~∧ Σ.

40 om B32.   Flesh] ~, C9 H6 NP3 O20.   (it selfes] ∧~ ~ B13 C9 DT1
H6 H8 NP3 OQ1 P3 VA1 VA2; ∧is ~ B47; (~ self H3 SP1 A; ∧itselfe's
H4 NY1; ∧~ selfe, H7; (ytselfe O20; (~ selfe) Y2.   death)] ~, B13 B47
C9 H6 H8 P3 VA1 Y2; ~∧ H4 H7 OQ1; ~; NP3 NY1 VA2.   ioyes,] B13
B40 NY3 O20 SP1; ~∧ Σ.   flesh] death O21.   tast] ~, C2 H5 A–G;
cast VA1.

41 lou'st,] ~; B32 H8 NP3 O20 VA2; louest; B33 NY1 O21 A–G; lovest,
B40 C2 C8 DT1 H4 OQ1 P3; ~∧ H3 H7; louest∧ TT1 VA1 Y2 Y3.   goodly]
godlie, HH1.   Soule,] ~∧ B47 H4 NP3 NY1 OQ1 TT1 VA2 Y3; ~; O21.
doth] doeth NY1.

42 this] thy NY1 OQ1 P3 VA1 VA2.   power] powre B13 NY1; Powre,
B32 B40; ~, NY3 O20.   tast] tastes B47.   ioy,] ~∧ B13 H3 H4 H6 P3
TT1 VA1 Y2.   thou] '~ HH1.   dost] doest HH1 OQ1 P3 VA1.
lothe.] ~; B40 C2 C8 H4 O21 A; ~∧ B47 H3 H7 NP3 TT1 VA1 Y3; ~.| C9;
~, H8 G; ~: OQ1 VA2 Y2.

43 true] om H5.   Religion;] ~. B13 C2 C9 H3 H5 H8 VA1 A; ~! B33
NP3; ~∧ B47; ~, DT1 HH1 O21 P3 Y3 B–G; ~: H7 SP1; ~? OQ1.   Oh]
~. B40; ~, H3 VA1.   where?] ~∧ B13 O21 TT1 Y2 Y3; ~! B33; where's∧
B47 H7; ~, C2 C8; ~: G .   Myrius] H5 NY3; Mirius B32 H3 H6 H7 O20
SP1; Myrreus C2; Mirreus, C8; Mirius, C9; Mereus, HH1; om NP3;
Merreus O21 Y3; Morius Y2; Mireus Σ.

44 Thinking] Thinketh H3 NP3.   her] here, B47.   vnhous'd] in hausd
B47; vn-hous'd H5 SP1; vnhowsed H7 HH1 O21 P3 Y3.   here,] ~∧ B47
H3 H5 OQ1 P3 TT1 Y3; ~; O21; her, A.   vs] ~, B32 B40 C8 DT1 H4 H5
O20 A–F; ~. HH1 Y2; ~; G.

45 Seekes her] Religion seek IU2; Seeke ~ Y2.   Rome;] B32 B40 NY1
NY3 O20 O21 SP1; ~. B13; Roome; B33 VA2; Roome, C2 TT1; ~∧ IU2
NP3 P3; ~: OQ1; Roome. VA1; ~, Σ.   There,] B32 B40 C9 DT1 H6 HH1
NY3 O20 A–G; om H7 IU2 NP3; ~∧ Σ.   because] be-cause H7; ~ that
NP3.   he] wee IU2; she TT1.   doth] om IU2.   know] ~, C8 HH1.

46 That] Once NP3.   there] ~, C8; om H5.   a thousand] ~ iooo
B13; one ~ OQ1; 1000 Y2.   yeares] yeare B32 B33 OQ1 P3 SP1; a yeare
O20.   ago,] B13 B32 C2 C8 H6 H7 H8 O20 A–G; ~; B40 DT1 H4 HH1; ~:
C9 H5; ~. VA1; ~∧ Σ.

47 He] and B47 C9 H6 H7 IU2 B–F.   loues] love IU2; leaues O21.
her] the B40 C2 C8 DT1 H4 IU2 TT1 A–G.   raggs] ~; B13 H4 H8 NP3; ~,
B33 B47 C2 C8 C9 DT1 H5 HH1 OQ1 P3 VA1 Y2; ~: NY1 VA2; rage; O21;
rage, Y3.   so,] B32 B40 H7 HH1 NY3 O20 SP1 A–G; om H3; heere∧ H5;
~∧ Σ.   here] doe ~ H3; om H5.   obay] ~, C8 HH1.

48 State Cloth] ~ ~,   B13 B32 HH1 O20; ~=~   B33 B47 C9 H3 H6 H7 NP3
NY1 VA2 G; ~-~,   B40 DT1 H5 SP1; Statecloth,   C2 C8; statecloath   O21
TT1 A–F.   yesterday.] ~∧   B13 B47 H3 H7 H8 NP3 O21 P3 TT1 VA1 Y2 Y3;
~;   B40 H4; ~.| C9; ~:   OQ1.

49 Crantz] NY3; Grant   B32 H3 O20; *Grants*   B40 B47 H6 O21 TT1 G;
Grants,   C9; Morus   H5 Y2; *blank space*   H7; Crawle   HH1; [*space*]rantes
NP3; *Crates*   OQ1; *Grant,*   SP1; Crants   Σ.   such] om   NP3 TT1; much
Y2.   braue] braues   VA1.   Loues] Loue   B13 DT1 H4 P3 TT1 VA1; ~,
C8 HH1; ~ witt,   H3; ~;   O21; om   VA2.   be enthralld] ~ ~,   B32 B40 C8
DT1 H8 HH1(→ ›~ enthralled,‹) O20 O21 OQ1 A–G; b'inthrald',   H5; ~'~
H7; b'enthral'd   NY1 VA2; ~ thrawld   Y2.

50 loues] love*   H7.   only,] B13 B32 B40 C2 C8 DT1 H4 HH1 NP3 NY3
O20 SP1 A–G; ~∧   Σ.   who] which   P3 VA1.   Geneua is] Geneua's   B47
C9 H6 H7 H8 NP3 NY1 VA2.   calld] ~.   B47 C8 Y2; ~,   C2; called,   HH1.

51 Religion,] ~.   B40 NY3; ~;   H4 H8; ~:   H5; ~∧   H7 HH1 NP3 OQ1 SP1
TT1 Y2 Y3.   playne,] ~∧   B47 DT1 NP3 TT1 VA1 Y2; ~;   O21.   simple,]
~∧   NP3 TT1 Y3; ~;   O21.   sullen,] solemne,   B13 B47 C9 H6 H8 OQ1 P3
VA1; *Sollen.*   B40; ~∧   DT1; solemne∧   NP3; ~;   O21; Sollen∧   TT1;.
young,] ~∧   B13 B33 B47 H3 H4 H6 H7 NP3 O21 OQ1 P3 TT1 VA1 Y2 Y3; &
~,   HH1.

52 Contemptuous,] ~∧   B32 B33 B47 C9 DT1 H3 H7 HH1 OQ1 TT1 Y2 Y3
B–G; ~;   NY1 O20 O21.   yet] and   H5; yea   NP3.   vnhandsome;] ~,
B13 B47 H6 NP3 VA1; ~.   C2 C8 O20 A–G; ~:   C9 H7 OQ1 SP1 Y2; ~∧   H3
O21 P3 TT1 Y3.

53 humors,] ~∧   B32 C9 DT1 H3 H5 H6 H7 H8 NY1 TT1 VA1 VA2 D–F;
humorists∧   NP3; ~;   O21 Y2; ~.   B.   ther is] thers   B40 (theris) NP3;
their ~   H7.   one,] B32 B40 NY3 O20 SP1; ~∧   Σ.   which] that   B40
C2 C8 C9 DT1 H4 NP3 O21 TT1 Y2 Y3 A–G; who   B47 H5 H8 P3.   iudges]
~,   C8 HH1 O21.

54 wenches] wretches,   O21.   wholesome,] ~∧   B33 B47 C2 C9 H3 H6 H8
NP3 NY1 O21 OQ1 P3 TT1 Y3; whole-some∧   VA2.   course] curse   H3; ~-
H5; coarse   HH1 B–G; poore   O21.   cuntry] B13 B32 B33 H7 NY3 VA2;
country   Σ.   drudges.] ~∧   B13 B47 H3 H4 NP3 TT1 VA1 Y2 Y3; ~;   B40
DT1 H8; ~:   C2 C8 OQ1 A; ~.| C9; ~,   O21.

55 Graius] Grugus   B32 H3 O20 Y2; Grayus   B33 B40 C9 H6 TT1; Grayius
B47; Graines   O21 Y3; Grugus,   SP1; Grajus   B–G.   stayes] ~,   VA2.
here:] NY3; ~∧   B33 C9 H3 NY1 P3 TT1 VA1 VA2 Y2 Y3; ~;   B40; ~,   Σ.

56 Preachers,] ~∧   B13 H3 H5 H7 H8 OQ1 TT1 VA1 Y2; puacher,   HH1;
p'cher,   O21; p'cher∧   Y3.   vile] (~   B40 H3 H8 O21 OQ1 TT1; vilde   H4;
~,   H5 HH1; (vild   H7 Y3.   ambitious] ambititious,   B47; ~,   H5 Y2;

Ambitions NY3.   bawds,] ~_∧ B33 H5 NY1 O21 TT1 VA2 Y2 Y3; ~)   H3
H7 OQ1; bawes_∧ VA1.   lawes] ~, B40 C8 DT1 HH1.

57 Still] ~,   NY3.   new,] B32 B40 B47 H6 HH1 NY3 O20 P3 SP1; nowe_∧
H3(→ »~_∧«) O21 Y3; ~_∧ Σ.   fashions,] ~_∧ B13 H3 P3 SP1; ~,) B40; ~:
H7; ~) H8 O21 TT1 Y3.   bidd] bidds B40 C2 C8 DT1 H4 TT1 A–G.
him] them HH1.   thinke,] B32 B40 NY3 O20 SP1; ~_∧ Σ.   Shee] ~,
B32; ~[trimmed] H7.

58 Which] (~ B13.   dwells] dwelleth HH1.   with] ~, H3.   vs]
~, B32 B33 C2 C8 DT1 H4 HH1 NY3 O20 SP1 A–G; om H3(→ »~«).
only perfect,] ~ ~) B13; Perfect onlye, H7; ~ ~: OQ1; ~ ~_∧ P3 Y3; ~ ~;
SP1 Y2.

59 Imbraceth] B32 B47 C2 C8 NY3 O20 A–G; embraceth Σ.   her,] B32
B40 B47 C2 C8 DT1 H4 NY1 NY3 O20 SP1 VA2 A–G; ~_∧ Σ.   his] om
H7(»~«).   Godfathers] godfather B47 HH1; God-ffathers H5 VA2 Y2;
god fathers OQ1 P3.   will] ~, HH1.

60 Tender] tenderes O21 Y3.   to] vnto H3.   him] B33 B47 H8 NY3
OQ1 P3 TT1 VA1 Y2; ~, → »~;« C8; ~; O21; ~, Σ.   tender;] ~. B13
H8 OQ1 TT1 VA1; ~, B47 C2 DT1 H4 H5 H6 P3 Y3 A; ~_∧ C8 H3; ~: H7.
still] ~. C8(→ »~,«); ~, HH1.

61 Take] takes P3.   wifes] NY3; wiues, B32 O20; wayes B33; wiues Σ.
their] there B33(ther) VA1 VA2 Y3; the H3 HH1.   Guardians] Gardens
B33; ~, O21; Guardian OQ1.   offer,] ~; O21 SP1; ~_∧ OQ1 TT1.

62 values.] Valewe. B13; ~: B40; ~; DT1 H3 H4 P3 Y2; valies. HH1;
~, O21 OQ1.   Careles] om B33.   Phrygas] Phrigias B13; Prigas B33;
Phrigus H3; Phrigas HH1 NY1 VA2; Phrigius, O21 VA1; virgins Y2;
Pharigius Y3; Phrigius Σ.   doth] doeth VA1; doe Y2.

63 All,] ~_∧ B33 H3 TT1 VA1 Y2 Y3; ~; O21.   because] ~, H3.   all]
~; O21; om Y2.   cannot] can not Y2.   good;] ~. B13 P3 VA1; ~_∧
B33 H3 TT1; ~, B47 C2 C8 H5 H6 H7 NY1 OQ1 VA2 Y2 Y3 A; ~: H8 SP1.
one] ~, B47 O21 OQ1.

64 women] woemens C2 C8.   whores,] ~_∧ B13 B33 C2 H3 H7 H8 NY1
P3 SP1 TT1 VA2 Y3.   dares] dare B13 P3; will B33 H5(M var: ›doth‹) H7
VA1.   mary] B32 C9 NY3 O20 O21 TT1; marry Σ.   none.] ~_∧ B13 B47
H3 HH1 TT1 VA1 Y2 Y3; ~; B40 DT1 H4; ~, O21.

65 Graccus] B13 B33 NY1 NY3 OQ1 P3 VA1 VA2 Y3 A; Grattus B32 H3
O20 SP1; Grotus Y2; Gracchus Σ.   one,] ~; B13; ~_∧ TT1; ~. VA1.
thinkes] ~, C9 H7 O20 SP1; thinges H3.   that] om B32 O20 SP1; as H3
Y2.   so] ~, HH1 O21 OQ1; (~ P3 VA1.

66 As] (~ H8.   do] ~, HH1.   diuers] Diverse B40 H3 O21.
Cuntryes] NY3 VA2; fashons B33; Countries Σ.   go] ~. C8.

67 diuers] diuerse H3 HH1 O21.   habitts,] ~;   B13 O21; ~ₐ   B33 TT1
VA1.   are] ~ all   VA1.   kind,] B32 B40 C9 DT1 H5 H6 HH1 NY3; ~:)
H8; ~;   O21 A–G; ~:   OQ1; ~)   P3 VA1; ~ₐ   Σ.

68 So] shee P3.   doth,] ~ₐ he.   H5; ~ₐ hee, → »~,«   H7; ~ₐ   TT1; ~;
HH1 O21; doeth, VA1.   is] ~, C8; his H5.   Religion;] ~,   B13 B32
B47 H3 H5 H6 H7 H8 HH1 O20 OQ1 SP1 VA1 Y2; ~.   P3 Y3; ~ₐ   TT1.
blind-] blindnes   TT1; ~ₐ   VA1.

69 nes,] B32 B40 C8 NY3 O20 VA1; =~ₐ   H3 H8 O21 P3;   ~.   HH1; =~,
SP1; om TT1; ~ₐ   Σ.   light] lights B32 H3(→ »~«).   breeds.] ~;   B13
B40 C2 H4 O21 OQ1 A; ~,   B32 H3 O20 SP1 Y2 Y3; ~:   C8 DT1 NY1 VA2;
~ₐ   H7 TT1; blinds.   HH1.   vnmoued] vnmov'd   B33(vnmooud) B40 C2 C8
DT1 H3(→ »~«) H4 HH1 NY1 OQ1 P3 VA1 VA2; om H5; vnmould, O20
SP1.   thou] ~, O21; then   TT1.

70 force] forc'd NY1 VA2.   must] but B13 H8 NY1 OQ1 P3 VA1 VA2.
one,] ~;   B13 H4; ~ₐ   TT1.   forc'd] ~, C9 H5 H6 Y2.   but] must B13
H7 H8 NY1 OQ1 P3 VA1 VA2.   allow;] ~. B13 HH1 NY1; ~,   B33 C9 H6
H7 H8 O21; ~ₐ   B47 H3 H5 OQ1 TT1 VA1 VA2 Y2 Y3.

71 right;] ~.   B13 C9 H5 H6 H8 VA1 Y3; ~,   B32 B40 B47 C2 C8 DT1 O20
SP1 TT1; ~ₐ   H3 OQ1 Y2; ~:   H7 P3 VA2.   father] ~,   B32 O20 SP1.
Shee;] B32 NY3 O20; ~,   B40 C2 C9 DT1 H5 H6 H7 H8 HH1 O21 A–G; heeₐ
H3; ~.   SP1; ~? VA1; ~ₐ   Σ.

72 his;] C2 DT1 H4 NY3 O20 O21 A; ~,   B32 B40 H3 H7 P3 SP1 Y3; ~:
B33 C8 C9 Y2; ~ₐ   TT1; ~.   Σ.   Truthe] ~,   B13 B32 B40 C2 DT1 H4; true
Y2.   bee] ~. VA1.

73 twins,] ~:   B13 H6; ~;   C9 H4 H7; ~ₐ   H3 OQ1 TT1; tynns, VA1.
Truth] ~,   H4.   elder] older H3.   is.] ~ₐ   B13 B33 B47 H3 HH1 OQ1
TT1 Y2 Y3; ~;   B40 C2 DT1 H4 A; ~,   C8 C9 O21; ~:   H7.

74 her.] ~;   B32 H5 H7 HH1 NY1 O20 VA2 B–G; ~,   B33 B40 C2 C8 DT1
H3 H4 H8 Y2 A; ~ₐ   B47 O21 P3 TT1 Y3; ~:   OQ1.   this] ~,   B40 C2 DT1
H4 HH1 O21 A–G; ~;   O20; ~:   OQ1; ~. VA1.

75 Hee'is] B40 B47 C9 DT1 H4 H5 H6 H8 NY1 NY3 O21 VA2 Y3 A–G;
Hee is Σ.   none,] ~;   O21; menₐ   OJ1; ~ₐ OQ1 P3 TT1.   nor] or H6
H8; the OJ1.   worst] ~,   B13 B32 B33 B40 C8 C9 DT1 H5 H6 H8 O20 SP1
A–G; worse H7; ~;   O21.   which] B13 B32 B33 H3 H5 H7 NY1 NY3 O20
SP1 TT1 VA2; that Σ.   seekes] seekest O21.   best.] ~ₐ   B33 B47 H3
H7 O21 OQ1 P3 TT1 VA1 Y2 Y3; ~;   DT1 H4; ~:   H8 NY1.

76 To'adore,] B40 NY3; To adoreₐ   B32 B47 C8 H3 O20 O21 P3 TT1;
T'adoreₐ   NY1 VA2 Y3; To adore, Σ.   or] to TT1.   scorne] ~,   DT1.
an] and H7.   Image,] ~;   B13; ~ₐ NY1 TT1 Y3.   protest,] B32 B40 B47
C2 C8 C9 DT1 HH1 NY3 A–G; ~;   H6; ~ₐ   Σ.

77 May all be] ~ albee B13; ~ well ~   H5; All may ~   H8; Wee ~ ~   OJ1.
bad;] ~,   B33 H4 H8 HH1 VA1; ~.   B47 H6 P3 Y3 B–G; ~:   C9 H5 OQ1 SP1;
soe ~;   OJ1.   doubt] — ~ 38.   wisely;] ~.   B13 H6 H8 P3; ~:   B32 B40
H5 HH1 O20 VA2; ~₋   B47 DT1 H3 H4 H7 O21 TT1 Y2 Y3; ~,   C2 C8 OQ1
VA1 A–G 38.   way] ~,   DT1 H7 HH1.

78 right] ~,   B13 B32 B40 B47 C2 C8 C9 DT1 H4 H5 O20 SP1 Y2 Y3 A–G
38.   stray.] staye.   B13 B32 NY1 P3 VA2; staye₋   B33 O21 OQ1 VA1 Y3;
~;   B40 C9 DT1 H4 A–G; ~₋   B47 H3 SP1 TT1 Y2; ~,   C2 C8(→ »~;«) H5
H6 H8; staye,   HH1; ~:   38.

79 sleepe,] ~₋   B32 B47 C2 H3 H5 H7 HH1 NY1 O21 OQ1 TT1 VA2 Y2 Y3;
stop,   OJ1.   run] ~,   B40 H7 P3 VA1; to ~   OQ1.   wrong,] B32 B47 C2
C9 H5 H6 H8 NY3 O20 Y2 A–G 38; ~₋   Σ.   is.] ~₋   B32 O21 Y3; ~;   B33
C2 DT1 NY1 VA2; ~:   B40 HH1 TT1 A; ~,   B47 C8(→ »~;«) H3 H4 Y2;
~ — 38.   a] an   P3 Y2.   high] huge B40 C2 C8 DT1 H4 O21 TT1 Y3
A–G.   hill] ~.| H3; ~,   H4 H5 O21 A–G.

80 Ragged] ~,   B13 SP1; Rugged   B33(Ruggued) OQ1 P3 VA1; Cragged   B40
TT1 Y3; Cragg'd,   C2 A–F; Cragg'd   C8; cragged,   DT1 H4 O21 G.   steepe]
~,   B13 B40 B47 H5 O21 P3 A–G; ~;   Y2.   dwells] B33 HH1 NY3; ~.   B13
VA1; standes;   B40 O21; stands,   C2 C8 DT1 H4 Y3 A–G; standes₋   TT1;
~,   Σ.

81 it,] ~₋   B33 H3 H7 VA1 Y2; her,   B40 B47 C2 C8 C9 DT1 H4 H6 H8 A
G; her₋   O21 TT1 Y3 B–F.   about must,] ~ ~₋   B47 C9 P3; ~, ~₋   H3 H7;
must about₋   H5 TT1; ~ he ~,   H8; must about,   HH1; ~, ~;   O21; aboue, ~₋
Y2.   and] om   H7(»~«); I ~   O21 Y3.   about] ~,   H6; a bout   O21.
go] ~,   B13 B40 H5 H7(→ »must« ~,) H8 HH1 O20 OQ1; ~.   C2 VA1; ~;   C8
DT1 H4(→ »must« ~;); must ~,   C9 H6 NY1 VA2; must ~   Y2; must ~;   A–C;
must ~:   D–F; it ~:   G.

82 And] ~,   B47 P3.   what] wᵗʰ   O21 Y3.   th'hills] C9 H6 NY3; yᵉ Hill
H7; the   O21 Y3; the hills'   VA1; the hills   Σ.   sodainnes] H8 NY3 TT1;
sodnynes   B13; sodennes   B32 O20 SP1 Y2; suddaynes   B33 B47 C2 C8 H6
HH1 NY1 OQ1 VA1 VA2; suddennes (M var: ›suddaynesse‹)   C9; sodaine
H7(→ »~«); steepnesse   OJ1; soudainnes   P3; suddennes   Σ.   resists,] ~;
B13 H4; ~₋   B32 C8(→ »~,«) H3 HH1 TT1 VA2; resist;   O21; reiects,   Y2;
resist₋   Y3.   so.] ~₋   B13 B47 H3 H4 H7 H8 O21 P3 TT1 Y3; ~,   B33 DT1
VA1 D–G; ~;   B40 C2 H5 Y2 A; ~:   C8 OQ1 SP1.

83 striue] striues   B47 H3(→ »~«).   so,] ~₋   B33 B47 C2 C8 H3 H5 H7 H8
O21 TT1 Y2 Y3.   that] as   C9 H6 O21.   Age] ~, B47 C2 C8 C9 DT1 H4
H5 H6 HH1 O21 A–G; the ~   H7(→ »~«); ages   OQ1 P3 VA1.   (Deaths]
B13 B32 H3 H7 H8 NY3 O20 SP1 Y2; om   OQ1 P3 VA1; ₋~   Σ.   twilight)]
B13 B32 H3 H7 H8 NY3 O20 SP1 Y2; twy light₋   B33; twy=light₋   B47 C8; ~,
DT1 NY1 VA2 A–G; ~₋   Σ.

84 Thy] the   OQ1 P3 VA1.   Mind] soule   B40 C2 C8 DT1 H4 O21 TT1
Y3 A–G.   rest;] ~,   B33 B40 B47 C2 C9 DT1 H3 H6 HH1 OQ1 P3 VA2 Y3
A–G; ~: H7; ~∧ TT1 VA1; rests,   Y2.   can] om   OQ1.   in that] ~ the
B13 B32 C9 H3 H6 H7 H8 O20 OQ1 SP1 VA1 B–F; 'ith   P3; ~ om   Y2.
night.] ~∧   B33 B47 H3 OQ1 TT1 Y2 Y3; ~,   C2 H4 O21 P3 A; ~; DT1; ~:
HH1; light∧   VA1.

85 om   C9.   will] ~,   B32 C2 H5 O20 A–F.   implyes] imployes
H7(→ »~«) OQ1.   delay:] B33 HH1 NY1 NY3 O21 VA2; ~∧   TT1; ~; Y2;
~, Σ.   therfore] ~,   H6.   now] ~,   H6.   do.] B32 NY1 NY3 O20 P3
B–F; ~,   B47 C2 DT1 H8; ~: H5 H7 G; ~∧   Σ.

86 om   C9.   deedes] ~,   B13 B40 C2 C8 DT1 H4 NY1 VA2 Y2 A–G;
deades,   HH1.   the] thy   B47.   bodyes] bodye   B32 B47 H8 O21 SP1
Y3.   paynes;] ~.   B13 VA1; ~,   B32 H4 H5 H7 HH1 O20 OQ1 P3 Y2 Y3;
payne,   B47 H3 H6; payne.   H8; ~∧   TT1.   too] to   B13 B32 B40 C2 DT1
H4 H6 H8 HH1 OQ1 P3 VA1 A–G; toe → »to.«   C8; ~,   NY1 O21 VA2.

87 om   C9.   minds] minde   H3.   endeauors] ~,   NY1.   reach;] ~,
B13 B47 C2 C8 DT1 H3 H6 H7 HH1 OQ1 P3 VA1 A; ~: B33; ~∧   H4 Y2 Y3;
~. SP1 TT1.   Misteryes] ~,   B40 HH1; ~....   P3.

88 om   C9.   as] like   B40 C2 C8 DT1 H4 O21 TT1 Y3 A–G.   Sun,]
~∧   B13 C8 H4 H7 HH1 NY1 P3 SP1 TT1 VA1 VA2 Y2 Y3; ~; B33; sonn,
B40 H3; sonne∧   OQ1.   dazeling,] ~; B13; dareling,   B32; ~∧   H3 TT1;
daz'ling∧   H4 H7 P3; dazlinge,   H5 H8 VA2 A–G; dazlinge; NY1.   playne]
paine   H3(var: »~«)Y2; ~,   H6.   to'all] to all   Σ.   eyes.] ~∧   B33 H3 H4
H6 H7 HH1 O21 OQ1 TT1 Y2 Y3; ~,   B47; ~; C2 DT1 A.

89 the] ~ the   H6.   Truthe] ~,   B40 C8 SP1 VA1.   which] that   B32
H3 H7 O20 SP1 Y2.   thou hast] th'~   C9 H6.   found:] ~; B13 C2 DT1
H4 H7 NY1 SP1 VA2 A–G; ~∧   B32 HH1 TT1; ~. B33 C8 H6; ~,   B47 H3
H5 H8 O20 O21 OQ1 P3 VA1 Y2 Y3.   stand] ~,   O21.

90 ill] euell   B33.   case] ~,   C2 C8 DT1 H4 A–G; ease   P3.   here,] ~;
B13 NY1; ~∧   B40 B47 C9 H3 H6 H8 O21 P3 TT1; om   C2 C8 DT1 H4
A–G.   that] but   Y2.   hath] hat   VA1.   with his] with's   C9 H6.
hand] ~,   C8.

91 Signd] Signed   B40 C2 DT1 H4 HH1 P3 TT1 Y3; signed,   O21; Sing'd
Y2.   kings] ~,   H4 NY1.   blanc] ~=   B40 DT1 H4 H5 H7 H8 TT1 A–G;
blacke,   B47; blacke   H3(var: »~«) NY1(var: »~«) VA2.   Chartres,] B32 B40
C8 HH1 NY3 O20 VA1 VA2 Y2 Y3; Charts,   B33; Caracteres;   O21; ~∧   Σ.
whom] all   H5.   hate,] B13 B40 C2 DT1 H5 H6 H8 NY3 O20 O21 OQ1
A–G; ~. P3; ~∧   Σ.

92 they] the   B32 O20; thy   B33 O21.   Vicars,] ~; B13 O21; ~∧   B47 H3
H8 OQ1 P3 SP1 TT1 VA2 Y3.   hangmen] Hagmen   B33; Hang-men   H7;

hang men   HH1 Y3.   fate.] Fate.   B32 C2 H5 H7 O20 SP1 A–G; ~∧   B47
C9 H3 NY1 O21 TT1 VA1 Y3; ~;   DT1 H4; ~:   OQ1; hate.   P3; state∧   Y2.

93   Foole] ~,   B13 B33 B40 C9 DT1 H4 H6 H7 O21 SP1 VA1 Y2.   wretch]
~,   B13 B33 B40 C2 C8 C9 DT1 H6 HH1 O20 O21 SP1 VA1 A–G; ~;   H5;
wretched   H7(→ »~«); ~!   H8.   thy Soule] thyselfe   C9; ~ sould   H4;
~ selfe   H6.   ty'de] B32 C9 H3 H4 H6 NY3 SP1 Y3; tyed,   C8; ~,   O21;
tyed   Σ.

94   Mens] B32 B33 H3 H5 H7 HH1 NY1 NY3 O20 SP1 VA2 Y2; mans   Σ.
Lawes,] ~;   B13 O21; ~∧   B33 C9 H3 NY1 P3 TT1 VA2; ~? H7.   She] he
B13 DT1 H4 H6; we   B47 H8; thou   C9; it   H5.   shall] shalt   C9.   not]
om   B–F.   tryed] ~,   C2; ~.   C8; try'd   C9 H3 H4 H6 H7 NY1 SP1 Y3; ~?
HH1 O20; tride;   O21.

95   day?] ~.?   B13; ~;   B33; ~.   H7 OQ1 VA1; ~∧   O21 TT1; ~,   Y2 Y3.
Oh] om   B40 C2 C8 DT1 H4(→ »or«) O21 TT1 Y3 A; or   B47 C9 H6 OJ1
B–G; ~,   H5 SP1.   serve] boote   B40 C2 C8 DT1 H4 O21 TT1 Y3 A–G.
thee] the   H3; ~?   OQ1 VA1.

96   say] ~,   B40 H5.   Philipp,] Pillip,   B33; ~∧   B47 C8 C9 H7 NY1 O21
OQ1 TT1 VA2 Y2 Y3 B–G.   Gregoree,] B40 C2 C8 DT1 H5 H6 H8 NY3
OQ1 VA1 A–G; ~.   O21; Grigorie∧   P3 Y3; ~∧   Σ.

97   Harry,] B13 B32 B40 DT1 H4 H5 H6 H8 HH1 NY3 O20 SP1 VA1 A; Mary∧
O21; Henry∧   Y2; ~∧   Σ.   a] om   TT1.   Martin] ~,   B40 VA1.
tought] NY3; told   H8; taught   Σ.   thee] the   B33 H3 VA2; me,   H5; me
NY3 G.   this] ~∧   B33 O21 TT1 Y2 Y3.

98   this] thy   O21.   excuse] ~,   C8 Y3; ~;   O21.   for] ~,   HH1; fore
O21.   contrarys] ~?   B13 C8 H3; ~,   O21 A–G.

99   stronge?] ~,   B13 DT1; true?   B32 H7 O20 SP1; ~!   B33; ~∧   B40 C2 C8
A; true∧   H3; strange?   NY3; stronger?   TT1; true;   Y2; ~;   B–G.   Cannot]
can not   B33 HH1 Y2.   sides] syde   HH1.   so?] ~!   B33; ~,   C8; ~∧
O21 TT1 VA1 Y2 Y3; ~.   P3.

100   mayst] mayest   B33 C2 HH1 O21 P3 SP1 VA1 A–G.   obay] ~,   VA1.
power,] power,   B13 B40 NY1; ~;   H4 O21; ~∧   OQ1 P3 SP1 TT1 VA1 Y3.
her] om   VA1.   bounds] bonds   O21 TT1 Y3; bownes   VA1.   know:] B40
H8 NY3; ~,   B13 C8 P3; ~.   B32 H5 NY1 O20 SP1 VA2; ~;   C9 DT1 O21
OQ1 A–G; know[trimmed]   H7; ~∧   Σ.

101   Those] These   B32 H3 H7 O20 OQ1 SP1 Y2.   past,] ~∧   B33 H3 H7 H8
OQ1 P3 TT1 VA1 Y2 G; parts,   HH1.   nature,] ~∧   B47 C9 H6 H8 HH1
NY1 P3 TT1 VA2; ~;   O21.   and] her   O21 Y3.   name is] name's
B47(names) C9 H6 H8 OQ1 P3(names) VA1(nams); ~, ~ C8; ~ are   G.
chang'd,] ~∧   B33 C2 C8 DT1 H3 H4(→ »~,«) H7 SP1 TT1 Y2 Y3 A; ~:   H8

NY1 VA2; ~;   O21 B–G; changed,   P3; ~.   VA1.   be] ~,   C2 C8 DT1
A–G; ~;   O21.

102 Then] ~,   B32 NY3 O20 B–F.   humble] ~,   H4; *om* H7($\rightarrow$ »~«);
himselfe Y2.   her] ~,   B32 B40 DT1 H4 H6 O20 O21 SP1 B–F; his   VA1.
Idolatree.] ~.| B13 H3; ~;   B40 C2 C8 DT1 A; ~$_\wedge$ B47 H4 HH1 P3 TT1
VA1 Y2 Y3; ~,   O21 OQ1.

103 are,] her   B13 B47 NY1(*var*: »~$_\wedge$«) VA2; ~$_\wedge$ B32 TT1 Y3; ~;   O21.
is:] ~;   B13 C9 NY1 O21 SP1 VA2 Y2 B–G; ~,   B33 B47 C2 C8 DT1 H3 H4
H7 HH1 VA1 Y3 A; ~.   H6 OQ1 P3; ~$_\wedge$ TT1.   blest] best   C2 H3 O21
Y3.   flowers] streames   C9 H6(M *var*: »[*trimmed*]wers«); floores   H3; flowr'es
H7; flowes   O21 Y3.   which] that   B40 C2 C8 C9 DT1 H4 H6 O21 TT1 Y2
Y3 A–G.   dwell] ~,   C8 H4.

104 At] As   H3.   the rough] ~'~   D–F.   Streames] ~,   OQ1.   head]
B32 B33 H7 NY1 NY3 O20 OQ1 P3 TT1 VA1 VA2 Y2 Y3; ~, Σ.   thrive]
~,   B13 B32 C2 DT1 H4 H6 O20 SP1.   proue] do   C2 C8 DT1 H4 O21
A–G.   well:] H5 NY3; ~,   B13 C2 C9 H4 H8 OQ1 A–G; ~.   B32 C8 O20;
~;   B40 DT1 NY1 VA2; ~$_\wedge$ Σ.

105 lefte] lost   B13 H5 H8 OQ1 P3 VA1.   rootes,] ~$_\wedge$ B33 H3 H7 H8 O21
TT1 Y3.   themselues] them selues   B33 B40.   giuen] ~,   H4 O21.

106 rage,] ~;   B13; ~$_\wedge$ B33 H7 H8 O21 P3 TT1 Y3; rape$_\wedge$ Y2.   Alas,] C9
H3 H6 HH1 NY3 O20 SP1 B–G; ~!   H7; (~)   H8; *om*   OQ1 P3 VA1; (a lasse)
Y2; ~$_\wedge$ Σ.

107 Through] Trough   B33; Thorough   C9 HH1; though   O21; ~,   VA1.
Mills,] ~$_\wedge$ NY1 TT1 VA2 Y2; ~;   O21.   rocks,] and ~,   B40 C2 C8 DT1 H4
H5 NY1 O21 VA2 A; ~$_\wedge$ B47 HH1 Y2; woods,   C9 H6; and ~$_\wedge$ TT1 Y3.
and woods,] rocks,   C9 H6; *om om*   NY1 VA2; ~ ~;   O21; ~ ~$_\wedge$ SP1 TT1.
at] ~ the   C9 H6.   last] ~,   C2 C9 DT1 H4 H6 A–G.   allmost] all most
C8 Y2.

108 Consum'd] consumed,   HH1; Consumed   P3($\rightarrow$ ›~‹) TT1.   going,] ~$_\wedge$
C2 C8 DT1 H3 H4 H8 HH1 OQ1 SP1 TT1; ~;   O21.   in] are ~   H5.
Sea] seas   B32 H3 H7 O20 SP1; ~,   C2 C8 HH1.   are] *om* H5.   lost.]
tost.   B13; ~$_\wedge$ B33 B47 H3 H6 P3 TT1 VA1 Y2 Y3; ~;   C9 DT1 H4 H5 O21;
~:   H7 OQ1 A–G.

109 So] To   HH1.   perish] pirrish   B40; ~,   HH1.   Soules,] ~;   B13
O21; ~$_\wedge$ B33 B40 B47 H3 H4 H7 TT1; fooles,   OQ1.   chuse] ~,   B40 B47
NY3 O20.   mens] mans   C9 H6; men   H3 HH1 Y2.   vniust] ~,   C8.

110 Power,] B32 B40 B47 C9 H6 H8 NY3 O21 SP1 Y3 B–G; ~;   O20; ~$_\wedge$ Σ.
from] (~   H5.   God] ~,   DT1.   claym'd,] ~$_\wedge$ B33 C2; claymed,   DT1
HH1; ~)   H5; ~;   O21 P3; damn'd,   SP1; claimed$_\wedge$ TT1.   then] than   H3.
God] tried   B47.   himselfe] him selfe   B33 VA2; him selfe,   B47; ~,   C9

H6.   to] in → »~«   H7.   trust.] ~ₐ B13 C9 NY1 OQ1 TT1; ~| B33
HH1; ~.| B40 C2 C8 DT1 H3 H5 VA1; ~: H4; ~.|. O20.

Subscriptions: finis Quart. I. D.| B13.   Finis B40 H7 O21 VA1 Y3.
   I. D.| H3 H4(*om* → »~«).   Finis tertiæ Satiræ NY1 VA2(*adds* Ioh:
Donne.).   Finis the third Satyre. P3.   *om* Σ.

Verbal Variants in Selected Modern Editions

Texts collated: H I J K M N O P Q S T Y Z AA DD.
Format:
   Indentations: *l. 43 ind* T; *ll. 43, 109–10 ind* Y; *no ind* Σ.
Headings: SATYRE III. H Q S Y Z DD.   SATIRE III. I–K M–P.
   SATIRE III OF RELIGION T.   *Satire 3* AA.

1 choakes] checks H–K M.

2 These] T; Those Σ.

3 and] but H–K M N.

4 May] T; Can Σ.

6 all] *om* H–K M N.   Soules] Soul's H K M O T AA; souls' I J P.

7 to] in O P.   blind] blinded Σ.

9 honor] honors T.

13 be'imputed] H–K T Y Z; be imputed Σ.

14 wayes easy] so easie ways Σ.

17 *2nd* Darest] and ~ Σ.

18 Shipps woodden] ship's ~ H M; ships' ~ I–K AA; ~, ~ N–P T.   pray]
N; prey Σ.

19 Leaders] leader's H–K M O; . leaders' P T AA.

20 dungeons] daungers N.

23 then] N Q Y Z DD; than Σ.

28 thy] the K.

31 Soldier] N T; Centinel H–K M; Sentinel Σ.   this] his O–Q S T Y Z
AA DD.

32 forbid] forbidden O Q Y Z AA; the forbidden S DD.

33 foes] foe O DD.   Deuill] ~ (he H–K M; ~ he's O; ~ he P AA; ~
h'is Z DD.

35 ridd] N T; quit   Σ.

36 worlds] world's   H–K M–P T AA.

37 worlds] world's   H–K M–P T AA.

40 it selfes] it self's   H N; itself's   I–K M P T AA; itself   O.

43 Myrius] T; Mirreus   Σ.

46 yeares] yeare   N.

47 He] And   P.   her] the   H–K M O P.

49 Crantz] Grants   H–K N; Crants   O P Y Z AA DD.

53 which] N T; that   Σ.

54 course] coarse   I J M O P T AA.

55 Graius] Grajus   H–K; Grayus   N.

56 ambitious] Ambition's   T.

57 bidd] bids   O.

61 Guardians] Gardens   N(M *var:* ~).

62 Phrygas] T; Phrygias   K; Phrygius   Σ.

65 Graccus] Gracchus   H–K M O P AA.

66 diuers] diverse   I J.

67 diuers] diverse   I J.

72 his] this   J.

75 which] N T; that   Σ.

77 bad;] ~.   H–K M O P T; ~:   N.   wisely;] ~,   H K M Z AA DD; ~.   I J;
~;   N.

79 high] T; huge   Σ.

80 Ragged]   T; Ruggued   N; Cragged   Σ.   dwells] N T; stands   Σ.

81 it] T; her   Σ.   go] it ~   H–K M N; must ~   Σ.

82 th'hills] P T Y Z; the hills   Σ.

84 Mind] N T; Soul   Σ.

86 too] to   H–K M N P.

87 minds] Mind's   H–K M–P T AA.

88 as] T; like   Σ.   to'all] H–K T Y Z; to all   Σ.

90 ill] euell N.   here] Q S T Y AA DD; *om* Σ.

91 kings] kings' I J M–O.

92 Nor] Now J.   they] thy K; th'y N(M *var:* ~).

94 Mens] T; man's Σ.

95 Oh] N Q S T Z; *om* O Y DD; Or Σ.   serve] N T; boot Σ.

97 thee] me H–K M T.

101 name is] name's H–K M Y.

103 which] N T; that Σ.

104 proue] N T Y AA; do Σ.

107 rocks] and ~ O Q S T Y Z AA DD.

110 then] than H–K M O P S T AA.

Subscriptions: *none*.

FIGURE 12: STEMMA OF "SATYRE 3"

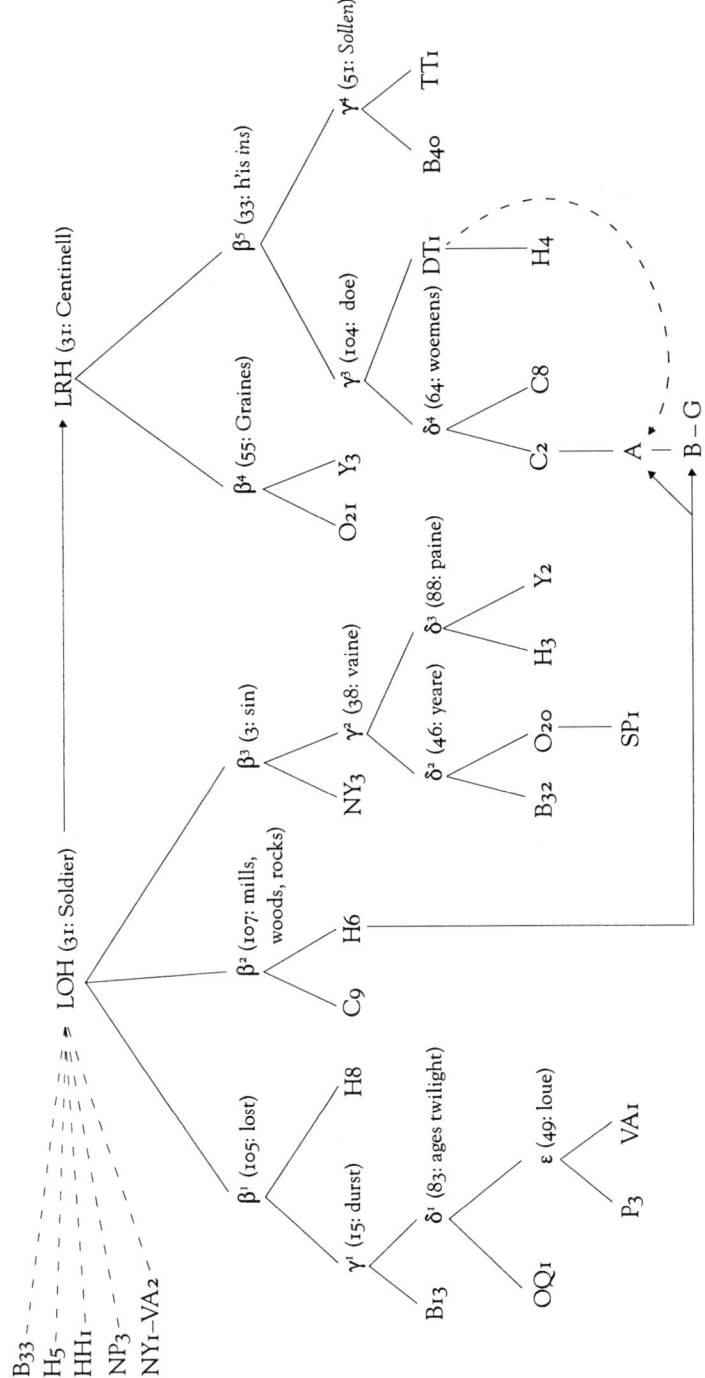

LOH = lost original holograph
LRH = lost revised holograph

unfiliated: B47, B51, H7, IU2, OJ1

Supporting Detail for Stemma of "Satyre 3"

LOH (B33 H5 HH1 NY1 NP3 β^1 β^2 β^3)

31 **Souldier** in this worlds garrison, thus yeild,

B33: To the distinguishing readings of the LOH adds the following:

36 The **wolds** all parts wither away and passe

61 Take such **wayes** as ther **Gardens** offer, or

H5: To the distinguishing readings of the LOH adds the following:

7 as vertue was **in the soules first** age?

13 of **straight** life may be imputed fayth? and heare

HH1: To the distinguishing readings of the LOH adds the following:

27 wch cryes not **Gods to this** mistres draw?

49 **Crawle** to such braue loves, Will not be enthralled,

NP3: To the distinguishing readings of the LOH adds the following:

4 May rayling then cure **all these** maladyes:

15 To follow; damned, oh if thou **dost** feare this

NY1: To the distinguishing readings of the LOH adds the following:

24 Children in **th'ouens**, fires of Spayne & the line

26 Canst thou for gayne beare? And must **not** euery Hee

β^1 (H8 γ^1): To the distinguishing readings of the LOH adds the following:

51 Religion; plaine, simple, **solemne**, yong,

105 But haueing **lost** their rootes & themselues giuen

H8: To the distinguishing readings of the LOH and β^1 adds the following:

7 As vertue was to the **worlds** first blind age?

81 Reach **her**, about **he** must, & about goe,

γ^1 (B13 δ^1): To the distinguishing readings of the LOH and β^1 adds the following:

15 To follow.) damn'd? o yf thou **durst** feare this

16 This feare *om* Corage, & high valour is.

B13: To the distinguishing readings of the LOH, β^1, and γ^1 adds the following:

23 Coulder than **Salanders**, like Dyvine

25 Whose Cuntrie **is Limbeck to** our bodies bee

δ^1 (OQ1 ϵ): To the distinguishing readings of the LOH, β^1, and γ^1 adds the following:

2 Theis teares to issue which swell **myne** ei lyds

80 **Rugged** and steep truth dwells, And he that will

83 yet stryve soe, that before **ages twilight**

OQ1: To the distinguishing readings of the LOH, β¹, γ¹, and δ¹ adds the
following:
14 thee (whom he taught **waies waies** easy and neere
17 **Durst** thou aide mutynous Dutch? **Durst** thou laie

ε (P3 VA1): To the distinguishing readings of the LOH, β¹, γ¹, and δ¹ adds
the following:
49 Crants to such braue **loue** will not bee enthral
50 but loues her onely **which** at Geneua is cald

β² (C9-H6): To the distinguishing readings of the LOH adds the following:
14 Thee whom he taught wayes **so easy** & neere
107 Through **mills, woods, rocks,** & at **the** last, almost

β³ (NY3 γ²): To the distinguishing readings of the LOH adds the following:
3 I must not Laugh, nor weepe **sin,** and be wise,
9 Lusts, as earths **honors** was to them

NY3: To the distinguishing readings of the LOH and β³ adds the following:
3 I must **nor** Laugh, nor weepe sin, and be wise,
99 Equally **strange?** cannot both sides say so?

γ² (δ² δ³): To the distinguishing readings of the LOH and β³ adds the following:
38 In her decrepitt **vaine;** and thou loving this
55 **Grugus** stayes still at home here, and because

δ² (B32 O20): To the distinguishing readings of the LOH, β³, and γ² adds the
following:
32 And for **forbidden** warrs, leaue th'appoynted fielde.
46 That she was there a thousand **yeare** agoe,

B32: To the distinguishing readings of the LOH, β³, γ², and δ² adds the
following:
17 Darst thou ayde **mutiners** Dutch? Darst thov lay
40 **line om**

O20: To the distinguishing readings of the LOH, β³, γ², and δ² adds the
following:
18 thee in Ships, wodden Sepulchers, a **Pray**
93 Foole and wretch, wilt thou lett thy Soule be tyde

δ³ (H3 Y2): To the distinguishing readings of the LOH, β³, and γ² adds the
following:

65 Grotus loues all as one, & thinkes **as** soe

88 are as yᵉ sun dazeling, yet **paine** to all eies

H3: To the distinguishing readings of the LOH, β³, γ², and δ³ adds the following:

7 As vertue was to the **fond** blinde age?

Y2: To the distinguishing readings of the LOH, β³, γ², and δ³ adds the following:

14 thee whom he taught **all** ways easie & neare

LRH (β⁴ β⁵)

31 **Centinell** in this worldes garrison,) thus yield

β⁴ (O21 Y3): To the distinguishing readings of the LRH adds the following:

47 Hee loues her **rage**, soe as wee heere obay

55 **Graines** stayes still at home heere, & because

β⁵ (γ³ γ⁴): To the distinguishing readings of the LRH adds the following:

31 sentinell in **his** worlds garrison) thus yeild,

33 Know thy Foe, the foule Devill **h'is**, whome thou

47 hee loues **the** raggs, soe as wee here obaye

γ³ (δ⁴ DT1): To the distinguishing readings of the LRH and β⁵ adds the following:

7 As vertue was **in** the first blinded Age;

90 In soe ill Case *om*, yᵗ God hath with his hand

104 At the rough streames calme head, thrive, & **do** well,

δ⁴ (C2 C8): To the distinguishing readings of the LRH, β⁵, and γ³ adds the following:

52 Contemptuous, yett vnhandsome. As amonge [C2's accidentals]

64 Knoweinge some **woemens** whores dares Marry None.

DT1: To the distinguishing readings of the LRH, β⁵, and γ³ adds the following:

49 Crants to such braue **loue** will not bee inthrald,

94 to mans lawes, by wᶜʰ **hee** shall not bee tried

γ⁴ (B40 TT1): To the distinguishing readings of the LRH and β⁵ adds the following:

33 Know thei foe; the foule Divell **is**, whom thou

51 *Religion*. playne, simple, *Sollen*. younge,

Satyre 4.

Well; I may now receaue and dy; My Sin
Indeede is greate, but I haue beene in
A Purgatory, such as feard hell is
A recreation, and scant Mapp of this.
My mind nor with prides itche, nor yet hath beene   5
Poysoned with loue to see, or to bee seene;
I had no Suite there, nor new Sute to show,
Yet went to Court; But as Glare which did go
To'a Masse in ieast, catch'd, was fayne to disburse
The hundred Marks which is the Statuts curse   10
Before he scap'd, so it pleasd my destinee
(Guilty of my Sin of going) to thinke mee
As prone to all ill, and of good as forgett-
full, as proud, lustfull, and as much in debt,
As vayne, as wittlesse, and as false as they   15
Which dwell at Court, for once going that way.
Therfore I sufferd this. Towards me did run
A thing more Strange, then on Niles slime, the Sun
Ere bredd; Or all which into Noahs Arke came;
A thing which would haue pos'd Adam to name;   20
Stranger then seauen Antiquaries Studyes,
Then Africks Monsters, Guyanas rarityes;
Stranger then Strangers; One who for a Dane
In the Danes massacre had sure beene slayne,
If he had liud then; And without helpe dyes   25
When next the Prentises 'gainst Strangers rise.
One whom the watch at noone letts scarse go by;
One to'whom th'examining Iustice sure would cry
Sir, by your Priesthood tell me what you are.
His clothes were strange, though course; and black though bare.   30
Sleeuelesse his Ierkin was, and it had beene
Veluett; but t'was now (so much ground was seene)
Become tufftaffeta; And our Chilldren shall
See it playne rash awhile, then nought at all.
This thing hath trauaild, and sayth, speakes all tongs   35

And only knowes what to all States belongs.
Made of th'accents, and best phrase of all these
He speakes one Language. If strange meats displease
Art can deceaue, or hunger force my tast.
But Pedants motley tong, Soldiers bumbast,   40
Montebancks druggtong, nor the termes of Law
Are Strong inough preparatiues, to draw
Mee, to beare this; yet I must be content
With his tong, in his tong calld Complement,
In which he can win Widows; and pay skores;   45
Make Men speake treason; cosen subtilst whores;
Outflatter fauorites; and out-ly either
Iouius; or Surius; or both together.
He names me,'and comes to me, I whisper, God,
How haue I sin'd, that thy wraths furious rod,   50
This fellow, chuseth me? He sayth, Sir,
I loue your iudgment; whom do you prefer
For the best Linguist? And I selely
Sayd, that I thought, Calepines Dictionary.
Nay, but of Men, most sweete Sir; Beza then,   55
Some Iesuits, and two reuerend men
Of our two Academyes I nam'd; There
He stopd me;' and sayd; Nay, your Apostles were
Good pretty Linguists; and so Panurge was,
Yet a poore gentleman all these may pas   60
By trauaile. Then as yf he would haue sold
His tong he praysd it, and such wonders told
That I was fayne to say; If you had liud, Sir,
Time inough to haue beene Interpreter
To Babels bricklayers, sure that tower had stood.   65
He adds; If of Court Life you knew the good
You would leaue Lonenes. I sayd, not alone
My Lonenes is; But Spartanes fashione
To teach by paynting Drunkards doth not last
Now; Aretines Pictures haue made few chast.   70
No more can Princes Courts (though ther be few
Better pictures of Vice) teach me vertu.
He like to'a high stretchd Lute String squeakd, Oh Sir,
Tis sweete to talke of Kings. At Westminster
Sayd I, the Man that keepes the Abbey tombes   75
And for his price doth, with whoeuer comes
Of all our Harryes, and our Edwards talke,
From king, to king, and all their kinne can walke,
Your eares shall heare nought but king; your eyes meet
Kings only; the way to it, is kings Street.   80

He smackd, and cryed, He'is base, Mechanique, course,
So'are all your Englishmen in their discourse;
Are not your frenchmen neat? Myne? as you see
I haue but one frenchman; looke, he followes mee.
Certes, they are neatly clothd; I of this mind ame   85
Your only wearing is this Grogerame.
Not so, Sir, I haue more; vnder this pitche
He would not fly. I chafd him. But as itche
Scratchd into smart, and as blunt Iron ground
Into an edg, hurts worse, So I, foole, found   90
Crossing hurt me. To fitt my sullennesse
He to an other key his Stile doth dresse
And asks, what newes? I tell him, of new playes.
He takes my hand, and as a Still which stayes
A Sembriefe twixt each dropp, he niggardly   95
As loth to'inrich me so, tells many a ly.
More then ten Holinsheds, and Halls, and Stowes
Of triuial household trashe he knowes; he knowes
When the Queene smild or fround; and he knowes what
A Subtile Statesman may gather of that.   100
He knowes who loues whome; and who by poyson
Hasts to an Offices reuersion.
He knows who hath sold his Land, and now doth begg
A Licence, old Iron, Shoes, bootes, or egg-
shells to transport. Shortly boyes shall not play   105
At blowpoynt, or spancounter, but they pay
Toll to some Courtier; And wiser then all vs
He knowes which Lady is not painted. Thus
He with home meats tryes me; I belch, spue, spitt,
Looke pale and sickly like a Patient, yett   110
He thrusts more; And as if he had vndertooke
To say Gallobelgicus without booke
Speakes of all States and deedes which haue been since
The Spanyards came, to'the losse of Amyens.
Like a bigg Wife at Sight of lothed meat   115
Redy to trauayle so I sigh and sweat
To heare this Maccaron talke; In vayne; for yet
Ether my humor, or his owne to fitt
He like a priuiledg'd Spy, whome nothing can
Discredit, Libells now gainst each great Man.   120
He names a price for euery Office payd;
He sayes our Warrs thriue ill, because delayd;
That Offices are entayld; and that ther are
Perpetuityes of them, lasting as farr
As the last day; And that great Officers   125

Do with the Pyrats share, and Dunkerkers.
Who wasts in meat, in Clothes, in horse he notes,
Who loues whores, who boyes, and who goates.
I more amas'd then Circes Prisoners, when
They felt themselues turne beasts, felt myselfe then   130
Becomming traytor; and mee thought I saw
One of our Gyant Statuts ope his iaw
To sucke me in for hearing him. I found
That as burnt venomd Lechers do grow sound
By giuing others their Soares, I might grow   135
Guilty and he free; Therfore I did show
All Signes of Lothing; But since I ame in
I must pay myne, and my forefathers sin
To the last farthing; Therfore to my powre
Toughly'and stubbornly'I beare this crosse; but th'howre   140
Of mercy now was come; he tryes to bring
Me to pay'a fine to scape his torturing;
And sayes, Sir, can you spare me? I sayd willingly;
Nay, Sir, can you spare me a crowne? Thankfully'I
Gaue it as ransome; but as fidlers still   145
Though they be payd to be gone, yet needs will
Thrust one more Iigg vpon you, so did hee
With his long complementall thankes vex mee.
But he is gone, thanks to his needy want
And the Prerogatiue of my Crowne; skant   150
His thanks were ended, when I which did see
All the Court filld with more strange things then hee
Ran from thence with such or more hast then one
Who feares more actions doth make from prisone.
At home in holesome Solitarines   155
My piteous Soule began the wretchednes
Of Suiters at Court to mourne. And a traunce
Like his who dream't he saw hell, did advaunce
It selfe o're me;' and such Men as he saw there
I saw at Court, and worse, and more. Low feare   160
Becomes the guilty, not th'accuser; Then
Shall I, nones Slaue, of high-borne or raysd men
Feare frownes? and, my Mistres Truth, betray thee,
To th'huffing braggart pufte Nobilitee?
No, No. Thou which since yesterday hast beene   165
Allmost about the whole world, hast thou seene
O Sun, in all thy iourney, vanity
Such as swells the bladder of our Court? I
Thinke he which made yon waxen garden, and
Transported it from Italy to stand   170

With vs at London, flouts our Court here; for
Iust such gay paynted things, which no sapp, nor
Tast haue in them, ours are; and naturall
Some of the Stocks are; their fruits bastard all.
T'is ten a clock and past: All whom the Mues   175
Baloon, Tennys, Dyett, or the Stewes
Had all the morning held, now the second
Time made ready that day, in flocks are found
In the Presence; and I; (God pardon mee.)
As fresh and sweete their apparells be, as bee   180
The fields they sold to buy them; For a King
Those hose are, cryes his flatterers; and bring
Them next weeke to the Theater to sell.
Wants reach all States; Me seemes they do as well
At Stage, as Court. All are Players. Who ere lookes   185
(For themselues dare not go) ore Cheapeside bookes
Shall find their Wardrobes Inuentory. Now
The Ladyes come; As Pyrats which did know
That ther came weake Ships fraught with Cucchianel
The men boord them; and prayse, as they thinke, well   190
Ther bewtyes; they the mens witts; both are bought.
Why good witts ne'er weare Scarlett gownes, I thought,
This cause; These men, mens witts for Speaches buy
And women buy all redds which scarlett dy.
He calld her bewty Lymetwiggs, her haire nett;   195
She feares her druggs ill layd, her hayre loose sett.
Would not Heraclitus laugh to see Macrine
From hatt to Shoo, himselfe at doore refine,
As the Presence were a Meschite; And lift
His skirts and hose, and call his clothes to shrift,   200
Making them confesse, not only mortal
Great Staines and holes in them, but venial
Feathers and dust, with which they fornicate,
And then by Durers rules survays the State
Of his each Limbe, and with Strings the odds tryes   205
Of his neck to his legg, and wast to thighs.
So in immaculate clothes, and Symmetry
Perfect as Circles, with such nicety
As a young Preacher at his first time goes
To preach, he enters; and a Lady which ows   210
Him not so much as good will, straight arrests
And vnto her protests, protests, protests,
So much, as at Rome would serve to haue throwne
Ten Cardinals into th'Inquisition,
And whisperd by Ihesu so often, that a   215

Purseuant would haue rauishd him away
For saying our Ladyes Psalter. But t'is fitt
That they each other plague, they meritt it.
But here comes Glorius that will plague them both,
Who in the other extreame only doth   220
Call a rough carelesnesse good fashione.
Whose cloke his Spurs tear, whom he spitts on
He cares not. His ill words do no harme
To him. He rusheth in; as if Arme Arme
He came to cry; and though his face be as ill   225
As theirs which in old hangings whip Christ, still
He strives to looke worse; he keepes all in aw
Ieasts like a Licenc'd foole, commands Like Law.
Tyr'd now I leaue this Place; and but pleasd so
As Men which from Iayles to'execution go,   230
Go through the great Chamber (why is it hung
With the 7 deadly Sins?); beeing among
Those Ascaparts, men bigg inough to throw
Charing Crosse for a barr, men which do know
No token of worth, but Queenes man, and Fine,   235
Liuing barrells of beefe, flagons of wine,
I shooke Like a Spyed Spy. Preachers which are
Seas of witt and arts, you can, then dare
Drowne the Sins of this Place, for for mee
Who ame a skant brooke it inough shalbee   240
To wash their Staines away; Though I yett
With Machabees Modesty the knowne meritt
Of my worke lessen; yet some Wise men shall
(I hope) esteeme my writts canonicall.

Textual Introduction

Complete copies of "Satyre 4" (*Sat4*) survive in 33 manuscripts and all 7 seventeenth-century editions/issues of Donne's collected *Poems*, and the final 42 lines of what was undoubtedly once another full copy appear in a 34th manuscript (B11). About 20 lines are excerpted in Joseph Butler's eighteenth-century commonplace book (IU2), and manuscript emendations of 3 lines are recorded in OJ1, a copy of A. Under the heading "The Fourth Satyr," moreover, H5 preserves an uncollatable prose paraphrase of lines 1–51a (ff. 111v–112), and a smattering of words and phrases drawn from about 35 lines scattered throughout the poem are contained in P1 (also not collated). Further, print snippets of the poem appear in Joseph Wybarne's *The New Age of Old Names* (1609; siglum 5) and in various issues of Samuel Sheppard's *MERLINVS ANONYMVS* (1653; sigla 33a–b) and Joshua Poole's *The English Parnassus* (1657–78; sigla 44a–d). Although *Sat4* appears alone or in the company of 1, 2, or 3 other Satyres in 8 manuscripts, it normally subsisted within a 5-poem set, and it typically occupies the 4th position within that group, as it does in the seventeenth-century prints (see Figure 2).[1]

As shown in Figure 15, the stemma for *Sat4* closely resembles those of the other 4 Satyres (see figs. 6, 9, 12, and 18). A good deal of scribal variation crept into the text as the poem circulated along the channels of manuscript transmission, but the evidence does not suggest that Donne himself revised the poem in any major way. The only change that definitely appears to be authorial occurs in line 184, where roughly half the artifacts read "mee thinkes they doe as well" as opposed to the revised "Me seemes they do as well." Accordingly, the stemma divides the artifacts into two major lines of transmission that trace their origins, respectively, to a lost original holograph (LOH) reading "methinks" and to a lost revised holograph (LRH) reading "me seems." Descendents of the LOH include the three independently circulated "books" of Satyres (plus their cognate B13), the traditional Group-III manuscripts, and a few other manuscripts either Associated with Group III or unclassified. Descendents of the LRH include NY3 (the sole Group-IV manuscript, here used as copy-text), the traditional Group-I manuscripts (though two of them contain the Group-II text), and part of the expanded Group II (CT1 and B7, normally members of Group II, lack the poem). This configuration of the artifacts largely accords with a pattern seen

---

[1]As is noted in the General Textual Introduction above (see p. lxxiv), William Drummond's headnote to the poem provides a contemporary confirmation of *Sat4*'s place in a five-poem set: "This Satyr (though it here haue the first place because no more was intended to this booke) was indeed the Authors fourth in nomber & order; he hauing wreten fiue in all to which this caution will sufficientlie direct in the rest" (SN3, f. 14v).

previously in this edition, where the Group-III manuscripts and certain unclassified artifacts contain an earlier state of the text than do the Group-Is and -IIs, which preserve its later manifestations.

A number of readings divide the LOH lineage into two major branches, which descend from lost artifacts labeled, respectively, β^1 and β^2 on the stemma. β^1 further splits into two sub-lineages, leading on the one hand to the lost artifact γ^1, on the other to γ^2. β^1 introduces and passes on to its descendants a number of scribal errors, including "in [for the authorial *of*] going" in line 12, "pretty good [for the authorial *Good pretty*] Linguists" in line 59, and the meter-destroying "wth the Dunkerkers" (for "Dunkerkers") in line 126—the distinguishing variant shown on the stemma. γ^1, which gives rise to B13 and δ^1, records further deterioration of the text, reading "He speakes no [for the authorial *one*] language" in line 38, "Sleydan [for *Surius*]" (which is further corrupted to "Snodons" in B13 and to "Steyden" in P3) in line 48, "sillylie I" (for "I seelily," which rhymes more closely with "Dictionarie" in the following line) in line 53, and "her haire ill [for the correct *loose*] set" in line 196, this last a dittographical substitution derived from "druggs ill layd'e" earlier in the line. To the accumulating errors B13 adds such further blunders as "this [for the authorial *my*] Sinn" in line 12 and "Niles shine" (for "Niles slime") in line 18. Also descended from γ^1, δ^1 introduces not only the erroneous "who fearing" (for the authorial "Who feares") in line 154 (the variant shown on the stemma), but also "recreation to and scarse mapp" (for "recreation, and scant Mapp") in line 4 and "I have but one S^r" (for "…one french-man") in line 84. OQ1, one of δ^1's immediate offspring, uniquely omits "yet" (from the phrase "nor yet hath beene") in line 5 and—also uniquely—inserts "my" before "good" in the line-13 phrase "of good as forget-" (yielding "of my good…"). ε^1, sibling of OQ1 and parent of the VA1-P3 pair, then corrupts the text still further, omitting "catch'd" from the phrase "catch'd, was fayne to disburse" in line 9 and trivializing the normative "dwell at Court" in line 16 to "liue at Court," amongst other mistakes. As is shown on the stemma, P3 and VA1 (offspring of ε^1) stand at the end of the γ^1 branch of the β^1 lineage; and readings (amongst others) in lines 13 (where VA1 gives the normative "all ill," while P3 omits "all") and 62 (where P3 gives the normative "praised it," while VA1 uniquely reads "phraisd it") show that neither can have been copied from the other and mark them as siblings rather than parent and child.

The γ^2 branch of β^1's descendents comprises all except H5 of the usual Group-III artifacts plus two unclassified manuscripts whose texts of the Satyres are associated with those of Group III in several cases. γ^2 evinces the above-specified β^1 variants in lines 12, 59, and 126, adding to them "with home meates cloyes [for the normative *tryes*] me" in line 109, "Who wasts in cloathes, in meate" (for "…in meat, in Clothes") in line 127, and "her beautyes" (for the authorial "her bewty") in line 195, amongst other errors. γ^2's immediate offspring, H8 and δ^2, record further scribal corruption: H8 uniquely gives "or [for *nor*] new sute" in line 7, encloses in parentheses the clause "wch did goe / To Masse in iest" (ll. 8–9), and erroneously reads "the *Iesus* [for *our Ladyes*] Psalter" in line 217, apparently deriving the substitution from the oath "by Iesu" mentioned in line 215. To the growing body of error δ^2 adds "motly tounges" (for "motley tong") in line 40, "p^{re}paratiues enough" (for "inough preparatiues") in line 42, and "in [for *at*] Westminster" in line 74, passing these on to its offspring B47 and ϵ^2. B47 evinces misreadings in lines 13 (recording "of all good [for *of good*]"), 169 (giving "made you [for the authorial *yon*] waxen garden"), and 240 (reading "shallowe [for the normative *scant*] brooke")—the first two of these being unique. B47's sibling ϵ^2 uniquely places parentheses around the phrase "as loath to inrich me soe" in line 96, inserts an extraneous "in" into the normative "He thrusts more" in line 111 (producing "He thrusts in more"), and intensifies line 238's description of "Preachers" as "seas of art" in line 238, recording "Great seas...." From ϵ^2 derive the Group-III manuscripts B46 and—through ζ—the siblings C9 and H6. The interventionist tendency of the B46 scribe results in such unique constructions as "I yet haue bin in" (for the normative "I haue beene in") in line 2; "noe Sute at Courte.../ But onlie thither went" (for the authorial "no Suite there.../ Yet went to Court") in line 7; and "Guyana's Monsters; Affricks rarities" (for "Then Africks Monsters, Guyanas rarityes") in line 22. A determination to "improve" Donne's text is also evident in ζ, which—as we have shown repeatedly throughout this edition—frequently alters lines to regularize meter or sharpen diction. Examples of this intention are evident in ζ's offspring C9 and H6, which—for example—evince "nor yet sute to show" (for the authorial "nor new Sute to show" in line 7; "two most reuerend" (for "most reuerend") in line 56, an addition that brings the line up to 10 syllables; and "Dunkerkers" in line 126, thus removing the extraneous "wth the" that had been mistakenly inserted before "Dunkerkers" by the β^1 scribe and restoring the line to metrical regularity. That C9 and H6 are siblings (rather than parent and child) has been demonstrated repeatedly throughout this edition (see, e.g., *DV* 2:10).

The second major branch of the LOH lineage, that headed by β^2, leads, through at least 4 now lost manuscripts, to the sibling pair O21-Y3 (Associated with Group III), H3 (Associated with Group III), H5 (Group III), and the cognates LR1 and NP2 (unclassified). Among β^2's distinguishing readings are the scribal reversal "Span-Counter or Blowe pointe" (for the authorial "blowpoynt, or spancounter") in line 106, a reversal also appearing in the later β^4 lineage, and the sophistication "of my redemptio̅" (for the normative "Of mercy") in line 141, a substitution also instituted by ϵ^1 and passed on to its offspring VA1 and P3.[2] Additionally, β^2 inserts an extraneous "a" into the phrase "gaue it as Ransome" in line 145 (producing the hypermetrical "...as a Ransome"), a trivialization also evident in all δ^2's descendants and in two artifacts from the LRH lineage. β^2's offspring γ^3 passes the above noted β^2 readings on to its offspring, the cognates O21 and Y3, adding the unique blunders "And pritie" (for the authorial "Good pretty") in line 59, "Curius" (for "Surius") in line 48, and "prize" (for "praise") in line 190, among others. Variants in such lines as 13 (where O21 omits half the line, while Y3 is complete) and 188 (where Y3 erroneously reads "by," while O21 gives the correct "my") confirm the usual finding of this *Variorum* that these artifacts are siblings deriving from a common parent rather than parent and child. γ^4, β^2's other offspring, corrupts the text still further. Its unique readings include "An [for the normative *the*] hundred Markes" in line 10, "But [for the authorial *yet*] I muste bee content" in line

_____

[2]Notably, the authorial "mercy" is also replaced by "redemption" (with or without "my") in all members of the γ^1 branch, as well as in δ^2's offspring B47, showing how strongly linked were the ideas of "beare[ing]" a "crosse" (expressed in the previous line) and "redemption" in the culture of Donne's time.

43, and "for his pennie" (for the authorial "…price") in line 76. These and other errors pass on to H3, which adds "my sin / I know [for the authorial *my syn / Indeed*] is Greate" in line 2, "our [for *the*] Prentisses" in line 26, and the unique dittographical "Some Iesuites and some [for the normative *two*] Reuerend men" in line 56. H3's sibling δ3 exhibits the accumulated body of error derived through γ4 and adds the submetrical "you shall heare" (for the normative "Your eares shall heare") in line 79, the reversal "soe often by Iesu" (for the authorial "by Iesu soe often") in line 215, and "swallowing barrels of Beere" (for the correct "lyvinge barrels of beefe") in line 236, a trivialization closely resembling the NY1-VA2 pair's "Swilling barrels of beere" in the LRH lineage. These and a score of other blunders then descend to δ3's offspring H5 and ε3, in each of which the text manifests further deterioration. For example, H5 reads "He answeares" for "hee adds" in line 66 (a sophistication also appearing in ε2's offspring B46 and in SN3 in the LRH lineage), "smerk'd" for "smackt" in line 81 (a unique error), and (also uniquely) "lost [for the normative *last*] farthinge" in line 139. H5's sibling ε3 adds the errors "and also [for *onely*] knowes" in line 36, "hee speakes a [for *one*] language" in line 38, and "not a king will balke" (for "and all their kiñ cañ walke") in line 78, among others. ε3's descendants LR1 and NP2 are marked as siblings rather than parent and child by numerous instances in which one reads normatively while the other errs: e.g., in line 13 LR1 omits "all" from the authorial phrase "to all ill," while NP2 reads the phrase correctly; and in lines 48 and 49 LR1 normatively reads "out lye either / Iouius or surius," while NP2 substitues the surname of the protestant controversialist John Sleidan for "surius." Shown at the upper left of the stemma, HH1 records the LOH's defining "mee thinkes" (though miscopying it as "mee think"), but cannot be filiated with other artifacts in the lineage.

Evincing the minor authorial change of "mee thinkes" to "Me seemes" in line 184, the lineage descending from the lost revised holograph (LRH) comprises the sole Group-IV manuscript (NY3); the 5 major Group-Is (B32, C2, C8, O20, SP1), part of the expanded Group-II family (B40, DT1, H4, TT1), and 7 other manuscripts traditionally either Associated with Group III (NY1, VA2, Y2) or unclassified (B11, O3, SN3, SN4); and the most economical stemmatic diagram of the relationships among these texts requires postulation of an additional 7 missing artifacts (see Figure 15). The lineage divides into two separate branches headed, respectively, by the lost artifacts β3 and β4. Defining readings of β3, all apparent corruptions of the LRH, include "Like to [for the normative *Like*] a bigg Wife at Sight of lothd meat" in line 115, a trivialization that requires elision of the normative "loathed" in the end of the line; the unique "so I belche [for the normative *sigh*] and sweat" in line 116, apparently a memory slip caused by the linking of "belch[ing]" and "meats" in line 109's "He with home meats tryes me; I belch, spue, and spit"; and "I'le [for *I*] leaue this Place" in the line 229, a misreading otherwise recorded only in HH1. To these alterations β3's offspring NY3 adds such further blunders as the omission of "a" in line 96's normative "tells many a ly" (yielding "tells many ly"); the unique "Shows" (for "shoes") in line 104, and "Run" [for *Ran*] from thence" in line 153. These and other aberrations are listed as "Emendations of the copy-text" in the apparatus. γ5, β3's other immediate scion, introduces "strangest" (for "strangers") in line 23; "our Court lyfe" (for the normative "Court Life") in line 66, creating an 11-syllable line; and the hyper-correct "Queenes Presence" (for the authorial "Presence") in line 199 and passes the accumulated body of error on to Y2 and δ⁴. Among other misreadings the very corrupt Y2 records "Taffata" (for the normative "tufftaffeta") in line 33, "Thus things haue traueled" (for "This thing hath trauaild") in line 35, and "gett out [for the normative *gather*] of that" in line 100. δ⁴, parent of the Group-I manuscripts B32 and O20, is a fairly accurate copy of its parent, but blunders in rendering the normative "Montebancks" in line 41 in the singular (giving "Mountebancke"), reducing line 50's "wraths furious rod" to "wrath furious rod," and omitting "such" from the phrase "and such wonders told" in line 62. Finally, at the end of its particular branch of transmission, B32 adds a few similar slips of the pen to the accumulated quantum of error, recording such misreadings as "pas'd [for *pos'd*] Adam to name" in line 20, "t'was [for the normative *T'was now*] (so much ground was seene)" in line 32, and "Maerine" (for the correct "Macrine") in line 197. δ⁴'s other offspring, O20, also exhibits a handful of further lapses, giving "will [for the authorial *would*] crye" in line 28, omitting "so" from the line-59 phrase "so panurge was," and dropping "his" from the normative "Of his each limne" in line 205, for instance. SP1 is a generally faithful copy of its parent O20, though it miscopies O20's "Tufftaffaty" as *"Taffata"* in line 33 and in line 171 misreads O20's "Wᵗʰ vs in London" as "Which is in London," the "in" in both cases being a γ⁵ deviation from the normative "at London."

Standing at the head of the second major branch of the LRH's descendants, β⁴ leads (through at least three additional now-lost artifacts) to seven additional manuscripts and to the seventeenth-century prints. β⁴ records over three dozen errors, including the meter-destroying "neither [for the normative *nor*] wᵗʰ prides itch" in line 5, the trivialized "pretious" [for the authorial *piteous*] soule" in line 156, and "where wᵗʰ [for either wᵗʰ wᶜʰ or *by* wᶜʰ] they fornicate" in line 203. To these blunders, β⁴'s immediate offspring γ⁶ adds others, inserting an extraneous "as" in the line-14 phrase "as proud, lustfull" (yielding "as proud, as lustfull"), altering "Stile doth dresse" to "stile doth addresse" in line 92, and changing "free" to "freed" in line 136, for example. δ⁵, one of γ⁶'s scions, further corrupts the β⁴ "neither" to "neithers" in line 5, records "in [for the normative *at*] Court" in line 16, and reduces "their Staines" to "yᵉ staynes" in line 241, a trivialization appearing outside this subfamily only in the lineage-1 pair O21 and Y3. C2, the most reliable of δ⁵'s offspring, appears to be a faithful copy of the parent and leads to the poem's first printing in A, as will be demonstrated below; C8, another of δ⁵'s offspring, introduces a few further mistakes, including "no" [for *new*] suite" in line 7, "to [for *of*] good as forgett= / Full" in lines 13–14, and "doe not [for *noe*] harme" in line 223. The partial manuscript B11, δ⁵'s third offspring, is written in the hand of the C8 scribe, who apparently took each of his copies directly from the parent text (rather than copying one from the other) as is evidenced by B11's agreement with C2 against C8 in some instances, and C8's agreement with C2 against B11 in others: e.g., in the above-cited line 223 B11 reads the correct "no harme" with C2 as against C8's "not harme," while in line 219 C8 and C2 correctly read the proper noun "Glorious" as against B11's adjectival "glorious." The fragment of *Sat4* in B11 is immediately followed by a full copy of *Sat5* in the same scribal hand; and the presence of these Satyres in B11, inserted into the artifact amidst works by other poets and other scribes, point to the quondam circulation of the δ[5] *Satyres* as a discrete collection, much like that preserved in OQ1, VA1, and P3.

DT1 and its offspring H4 also derive from γ[6], recording the lineal errors noted above, including the parent's extraneous "as" in the line 14, "addresse" (for "dresse") in line 92, and "freed" (for "free") in line 136. To these blunders DT1 adds (and passes on to H4) "are not yo[r] ffrenchmen neat in mee" (for the normative "...neat? Myne?") in line 83, the eyeskip omission of lines 137b–139a, and the omission of "lust" from the authorial "lust such gay paynted things" at the head of line 172 (giving "such gaye..."). That H4 is the child of DT1 has long been recognized, and that relationship is here marked by its corruption of DT1's "prides itch" to "pride itches" in line 5, "asmuch in debt" to "as farre in debt" in line 14, and "wisemen" to "wise man" in line 243.

β[4]'s other immediate offspring is γ[7], parent of B40 and TT1. In *Sat4* γ[7] bequeathes to them the many β[4] family errors mentioned above, including "neither" (for "nor") in line 5, "pretious" (for "piteous") in line 156, and "where w[th]" (for either "wth w[ch]" or "by w[ch]") in line 203. To these γ[7] adds, e.g., the trivialized "and [for the authorial *as*] wittlesse" in line 15, "agaynst" (for the required elision "gainst") in line 26's normative "When next the Prentises gainst Stranger rise" (B40 gives "prēteces," suggesting that γ[7] spelled the word with a "c," and TT1 further corrupts this to "pretences"), and "reverent [for the normative *reuerend*] men" in line 56—this latter also a mistake in the copy-text that has required emendation. Though B40 is remarkably true to γ[7], both it and TT1 add to the accumulated roster of misreadings; B40, e.g., records the slip "my [for the normative *mee*] thought" in line 131 and substitutes "those staynes" (for the normative "their staynes") in line 241; TT1 (anticipating "strange meates" later in the line) writes "strange [for the correct *one*] language" in line 38, conflates lines 78–79 (recording "ffrom *Kinge* to *Kinge* naught but *kings* you[r] eyes meet"), and drops "hose" from the line 182's "Those hose are"—to name but a few of its many blunders. Comparing this list of errors shows that B40 and TT1 each read normatively in places where the other errs and confirms the usual finding of this *Variorum* that the two derive from a common source rather than one from the other.

β[5], progenitor of the unclassified manuscripts SN3 and SN4, also descends from the LRH, passing along to its offspring the unique errors "the ground" (for "ground") in line 32, "other Iesuites" (for "Iesuits") in line 56, and "subtle courtier [for the normative *statesman*]" in line 100, among a dozen or so other misreadings. Scribally dated "anno 1594,"[3] the copy of *Sat4* in SN3 is written in the hand of William Drummond of Hawthornden, and it exhibits such a further degree of deterioration as to suggest that the β[5] text had passed through one or more corrupting stages before coming into his hands. Just within the first 66 lines, for instance, Drummond records "and [for *or*] to be seene" in line 6, "Three hundredth [for *The hundred*] Marks" in line 10, "tell me what yee [for *you*] are" in line 29, "antient [for *accent*] & best phrase" in line 37, "strong enough preparations [for *preparatiues*]" in line 42, "thy wreathes [for *wraths*] furious rod" in line 50, "Calepinus [for *Calepines*] Dictionarye" in line 54, and "He answers [for *adds*]" in line 66. SN4, on the other hand, seldom diverges from β[5], though it

---

[3] Because of line 114's mention of "the losse of Amyens," an apparent reference to an event of 1597, various commentators have doubted the accuracy of this date—see the "Date and Circumstances" section of the Commentary on *Sat4*.

does exhibit such occasional variants as "*Affrick* [for the normative *Africks*] Monsters" in line 22 and "Towne" (for Babel's "tower") in line 65. Such instances as these, in which one errs while the other reads normatively, mark SN3 and SN4 as parallel descendants of a common ancestor rather than as parent (or grandparent) and child.

The three manuscripts shown to the right of the LRH on the stemma all share the lineage's defining "Me seems" in line 184, but cannot be more precisely filiated within it. The John Cave manuscript (NY1) and its copy (VA2) place a formal title page before the section of Satyres with which they open ("Five Satires: / The Letanie: The / Storme, and / Calm / By Mr Iohn Donne"); and, while its position on the stemma indicates that it cannot derive from one of the "books" in which the Satyres circulated as a discrete collection (the descendants of δ¹), Cave must at least have seen such a collection and sought to imitate it. NY1 diverges from the LOH in over 30 instances, including the unique insertion of "great" before "antiquaries" in line 21 (yielding "great antiquaries"), the (also unique) sophistication of "Low feare" to "Pale feare" in line 160, and replacement of the generic "Purseuant" in line 216 with "Topcliffe" (the most notorious pursuivant of the age)—an identification also made by the ζ scribe, whose two offspring record the reading either marginally (H6) or as the primary reading (C9). VA2 is an almost word-perfect copy of NY1, although it does misread "prize" (for "price") in line 121 and "turnd [for NY1's normative *turne*] beasts" in line 130. Entered in Nicholas Burghe's poetical miscellany and dated "c. 1638" (Beal, *Index* 470), O3's copy of *Sat4* is chronologically and (apparently) genetically remote from the LRH. It records numerous one- and two-word errors—"map of bliss" (for the normative "Mapp of this") in line 4 and "hath breed" (for *Ere bredd*) in line 19, e.g.—and utterly mangles the author's "...You would leaue Lonenes. I sayd, not alone / My Lonenes is; But Spartanes fashion..." in lines 67–68, giving "...You would leaue Loanes and your Natiue nation / But I replied that sure the Spartane fashion...."

Whether or not it deserves Grierson's condemnation as of all manuscripts the "worst, the fullest of obvious and absurd blunders" (2:cv), H7 presents a thoroughly mongrelized text of *Sat4*. Its "he thinks" in line 184 seems a corruption of the LOH's "mee thinkes," and its "with home-meats clopes mee" in line 109 looks like a misreading of the γ² "...cloyes me"; yet it also shares with the descendants of γ⁵ the unique readings "Affrique" (for "Africks") in line 22, "Stranger, then Strangest [for *strangers*]" in line 23, and "goe [for *are*] neatly cloath'd" in line 85, while at the same time lacking the defining β³ readings "belch" (for "sigh") in line 116, "th'apparells" (for "their apparrells") in line 180, and "Ile [for I] leaue this Place" in line 229. It is shown as "unfiliated" on the stemma. P1, a series of uncollatable short snippets drawn from throughout the poem, is also not filiated.

The Seventeenth-Century Prints

Set into type from C2, *Sat4* first enters print in the 1633 *Poems* (A), its textual integrity compromised not only by the body of error accumulated in the β⁴ lineage, but also by interventions on the part of A's editor and the government licenser, who—apparently in the interests of decency—required Marriott to expunge lines 134–136a (which mention "burnt venomd Lechers") before finally authorizing publication. As charted in Figure 13, A's text differs substantively from that of the LRH (and this

~ = agrees with LRH   ∇ = agrees with nearest corresponding reading on left   ( ) = specific source of variant   c = compositor

Line no.	LRH/DV reading	A	H6	B	C	D-F	G
2	but I	~ (LRH)	~ yet ~	∇ ∇ ∇	∇ ∇ ∇	∇ ∇ ∇	∇ ∇ ∇
5	nor	neither (c; β⁴: neithers)	not	neither	∇	∇	∇	∇
8	Glare	Glaze (δ⁵)	?	∇	∇	∇	∇
12	2ⁿᵈ of	~ (LRH)	in	in	∇	∇	∇
14	lustfull	as ~ (γ⁶)	?	?	?	?	?
16	at	in (δ⁵)	?	in	∇	?	?
18	Niles	~ (c or H6; β⁴: Nilus)	?	?	∇	?	∇
19	into	~ (c or H6; δ⁵: to)	?	?	∇	?	?
22	Africks	~ (c; β⁴: Affrick)	?	?	?	?	?
35	sayth	saith (LRH)	?	?	?	?	faith
36	knowes	knoweth (β⁴)	?	knoweth	∇	∇	∇
43	beare	~ (LRH)	?	?	?	?	hear
47	and	or (β⁴)	?	or	∇	∇	∇
57	There	~ (LRH)	?	here (c)	∇	∇	∇
59	and so Panurge	and so Panirge (c; LRH: Panurge)	so Panurgus	?	?	?	so Panurgus
61	By	~ (LRH)	?	?	?	?	But
62	wonders	words (β⁴)	?	?	?	?	?
65	that	the (β⁴)	∇	∇	∇	∇	?
67, 68	Lonenes	lonelinesse (β⁴)	lonnesse	?	∇	∇	∇
69	last	~ (LRH)	tast	∇	∇	∇	?
79	king	Kings (β⁴)	?	Kings	∇	∇	?
80	kings Street	Kingstreet (C2; C8: Kings street)	kings streete	Kingsstreet	?	Kings street	∇
81	course	coarse: (c; C2: course)	?	coarse	∇	∇	∇
83	Myne	Fine (c)	Mine	∇	∇	∇	∇
84	frenchman	~ (LRH)	Sᵗ	∇	∇	∇	∇

Line no.	LRH/DV reading	A	H6	B	C	D-F	G
86	this	your (β⁴)	~	your	▽	▽	▽
90	foole	~ (LRH)	(~)	(▽)	(▽)	(▽)	(▽)
92	dresse	addresse (γ⁶)	dresse	▽	▽	▽	▽
97	and...and	or...or (β⁴)	▽...◁	▽...▽	▽...▽	▽...▽	▽...▽
99	smil'd or frownd	frown'd, or smil'd (β⁴)	▽◁ ▽◁	▽, ▽◁	▽◁, ▽◁	▽, ▽◁	▽, ▽◁
103	who hath	~' ~ (c)	~ om	~', ~	~', ~◁	~◁	~◁
104	Shoes, bootes, or	bootes, shooes, and (β⁴)	~', ~,	bootes, shooes, and	▽◁, ▽, ▽	▽◁, ▽, ▽	▽◁, ▽
106	blowpoynt, or spancounter	span-counter, or blow-point (β⁴)	blow point, or span-counter	span-counter, or blow-point	▽◁, ▽	▽◁, ▽	span counter, ▽
106	they pay	shall pay (c)	they pay	shall pay	▽	▽	▽
108	which	what (β⁴)	wᶜʰ	what	▽	▽	▽
109	tryes	tries (LRH)	cloyes	▽	▽	▽	▽
111	thrusts more	~ on ~ (H6; C2: trusts me more)	▽ ▽ ▽	▽ ▽ ▽	▽ ▽ ▽	▽ ▽ ▽	▽ ▽ ▽
111	as if he had	as if he (β⁴)	~ hee had	~ ◁ '◁	~ ▽ ◁ ▽	~ ▽◁ ▽◁	~
113	which haue	that hath (β⁴)	wᶜʰ haue	that have	▽	▽	▽
120	gainst	'gainst (c or H6; C2: agaynst)	▽	▽	▽	▽	▽
122	sayes	saith (β⁴)	~	saith	▽	▽	▽
123	2ⁿᵈ that	~ (LRH)	~	om	~	~	?
132	Statuts	Statutes (LRH)	Statutes (LRH)	Statutes	Statues	Statutes	▽
134	venomd	censored	venimd	venome	▽	▽	venomous
146	Though	~ (LRH)	~	Thou	~	~	~
152	more...then	~...~ (LRH)	~...~	~...than	~...◁	~...◁	such...as
154	doth make	doth hast (γ⁶)	makes	doth hast	▽▽	▽	▽▽
156	piteous	precious (β⁴)	~	~	~	~	~
159	o're me; 'and such	on mee, Such (β⁴)	or'e mee, and Such	o'r mee: Such	▽ ∴ ▽	▽ ∴ ▽	▽ ∴ ▽
164	th'huffing braggart	huffing, braggart (γ⁶)	the ~◁~	huffing, braggart	▽, ▽	▽, ▽	th'~◁
166	whole world	~~ (H6; γ⁶: om world)	~~	~~	~	~	~
169	yon	your (β⁴)	yond	your	▽	▽	▽

Line no.	LRH/DV reading	A	H6	B	C	D–F	G
171	Court here	Presence (β⁴)	Courtiers	▽	▽	▽	▽
178	are	~ (LRH)	?	were	▽	▽ ▽	?
182	cryes his	cry the (β⁴/c; C2: cryes yᵉ)	crye his	▽ ▽	▽	▽	crys the
182	flatterers	~ (LRH)	?	?	?	?	flatterer
183	1ˢᵗ to	~ (c; γ⁶: unto)	?	?	?	?	?
188	did	doe (γ⁶)	?	doe	▽	▽	▽
194	scarlett	scarlets (β⁴;C8: skarlett)	?	scarlets	▽	▽	▽
199	As	As if (γ⁶)	?	As if	▽	▽	▽
203	with which	wherewith (β⁴: where with)	with w.ᶜʰ	wherewith	▽	▽	▽
211	straight	he (β⁴)	strayt	he	▽	▽	▽
215	whisperd	~ (LRH)	whispers	▽	▽	▽	▽
217	saying	~ of (β⁴)	?	~ of	▽	▽	▽
222	whom	~ (LRH)	or ~	▽ ▽	▽	▽	▽
223	not	~ (LRH)	not hee	▽ ▽	▽ ▽	▽ ▽	▽ ▽
224	rusheth	~ (LRH)	?	?	rushes	▽	▽
225	came	meant (β⁴)	?	meant	?	?	?
226	still	yet ~ (β⁴)	?	?	?	?	?
230	Men which	men (c)	~ w.ᶜʰ	men	▽	▽	▽
234	which	that (β⁴)	w.ᶜʰ	that	▽	▽	▽
235–36	Fine, /Liuing	fine, /Liuing (c; β⁴: fine, Liuing)	fine, /Liuing	fine, /Liuing	◁ /◁	◁ /◁	◁ /◁,
236	beefe,	~, (LRH)	~,	~,	~,	~,	~, and
238	witt	Wits (δ⁶)	?	Wits	▽ ▽ ▽	▽ ▽ ▽	Wit
240	a skant	but a scarce (β⁴)	a scant	but a scant	▽	▽ ▽ ▽	▽ ▽ ▽
241	their	the (δ⁶)	theyr	the	▽	▽	▽
243	Wise men	wise man (β⁴)	wiseman	wise man	▽	wise men	▽

Variorum) in some 40 readings, and further variations are introduced successively as the poem is transmitted to the remaining seventeenth-century editions and issues (B–G). β⁴ readings that make their way into A include "lonelynes" (for the authorial "Lonenes") in line 67, "precious [for *piteous*] Soule" in line 156, and "he [for *straight*] arrests" in line 211; among lections deriving from γ⁶ are "addresse" (for "dresse") in line 92, "hast [for *make*] from Prison" in line 154 (apparently a memorial holdover from "more hast" in the previous line), and "huffing, braggart, puft Nobility" (for "th'huffing braggart, pufte Nobilitee") in line 164. Several variants originating with δ⁵ are also manifest in A, the proper name "Glaze" (for the authorial "Glare") in line 8 and "Seas of Wits [for the singular *witt*]" in line 238 among them; and the readings that identify C2 specifically as A's source are the singular "Kingstreet" in line 80, where C2's sibling C8 gives "Kings street," and the plural "Scarletts Dye" in line 194, where C8 records "skarlett...." Also listed in Figure 13 are a number of independent changes imposed on the C2 text by A's editor, and almost all of them are deliberate emendations intended to improve rhythm, grammar, or sense. This editor's use of elision to regularize meter, widespread throughout the volume, is illustrated by the entry for line 103 on the chart, where the manuscript's "He knows who hath sold his land, & now doth begg" is compressed to "...who'hath sold his land...," and he also normalizes rhythm by changing the forms of words ("Nilus" to "Niles" in line 18; "vnto" to "to" in line 183, e.g.) and, on occasion, by inserting words perceived to be missing (adding "whole" before "world" in C2's submetrical rendition of line 166, e.g.). A concern with the sense of the text is also evident throughout: for instance, in line 19 "to Noahs Arke came" is sharpened to "into Noahs Arke came," and C2's apparently ungrammatical "cryes yᵉ flatterers" is replaced with "cry the flatterers" in line 182. Line 111 records perhaps the most striking instance of A's determination to create sense where C2's reading is problematic. As the satirist seeks to repel the slanderous would-be courtier by looking "pale and sickly like a Patient," the courtier escalates his assault: "yet / He thrusts more" (in the language of the LRH). Apparently finding β⁴'s innovative "Hee thrusts mee more" unintelligible, the δ⁵ scribe interprets the phrase as a reference to the courtier's conveyance of confidential gossip and rewrites accordingly: "Hee trusts me more." Confronting this reading in C2, A's editor apparently finds it, too, unsatisfactory and emends to "He thrusts on more."

A's editor almost certainly derived this repair—as well as the "whole" inserted to regularize the meter of line 116 and perhaps "Niles" in line 18, "Myne?" in line 83, and lines 134–36a (which had been censored from A)—from H6, which, as we have pointed out previously (see *DV* 2:lxxviii–lxxxix, and *DV* 7.1:lxxiii), seems to have become available to him before the volume was actually printed, but too late in the production process for him to make the extensive use of it that is evident in the second edition of 1635 (B). In any case, included among the entries on Figure 13 are 21 in which B emends the text of A toward H6 readings, and these—derived from an offspring of the LOH—constitute the lion's share of the further changes that corrode, mongrelize, and (in a few cases) correct the text of the poem as it migrates through the successive seventeenth-century printings. Some H6 readings imported into B—"Glare" in line 8, "wonders" in line 62, "lonnesse" in line 67, and "piteous" in line 156, for example—actually restore authorial readings that had been lost in the evolution of the β⁴ lineage. Others—such as "Sʳ" (for the authorial "frenchman") in line 84, "cloyes" (for "tryes") in line 109, "Courtiers" (replacing β⁴'s erroneous "presence") in line 171, and "He cares not hee" (for the authorial "He cares not" in line 223—are metrical or logical sophistications imposed by the γ² (l. 109), ε² (l. 171), or ζ (ll. 84, 223) scribes in the β¹ lineage. B also introduces a handful of blunders for which the editor had no manuscript warrant—"here" (for "There") in line 57; "venome" (for the authorial "venomd," censored from A) in line 134; "Thou" (for "Though") in line 146; "were [for the authorial *are*] found" in line 178, e.g.—and a couple of these (those in line 57 and 178) persist in the subsequent seventeenth-century editions.

The third edition of 1639 (C) and the fourth of 1649 (D), reissued with altered title pages in 1650 (E) and 1654 (F), introduce few further changes into the text. C is a page-for-page resetting of B, generally differing from the parent only with respect to accidentals; and its substantive errors (it trivializes the authorial "Giant Statutes" in line 132 to "Giant Statues" and "rusheth" in line 224 to "rushes") and its corrections—it replaces B's "Thou" with "Though" in line 146 and eliminates an extraneous "have" from B's line 173—are equal in number. Somewhat surprisingly, D restores "Statutes" in line 132, but otherwise changes C's wording only in line 243, recording—perhaps unintentionally—the authorial "wise men," where C had read "wise man."

The text of the fourth edition (F) passes on into G, the Restoration edition of 1669, which—as Figure 13 shows—substantively differs from its predecessor in over a dozen instances. The effects of these final changes are mixed and not always easy to account for. Some—such as the replacement of "saith" in line 35 with "faith" and the respelling of the line-81 adjective "coarse" as "course"—result from carelessness or misunderstanding; others—such as the change of "burnt venome Leachers" to "burnt venomous Leachers" in line 134 and expansion of the line-123 phrase "there are" to "that there are" (thus effecting a parallel with "That offices are" earlier in the line)—apparently bespeak the independent efforts of G's editor to improve the sense or syntax of the poem. The most intriguing—and baffling—are those in which the editor imposes emendations that he can only have derived from manuscript. His substitution of "so Panurgus was" for the authorial "and so Panurge was" in line 59 is among these, as are his restoration of the authorial "last" in line 69, where B through F had been satisfied with "tast" (in the clause "To teach by painting drunkards, doth not last/tast"), and his recovery of the correct "To th' huffing braggart, puft Nobility" in line 164, where every previous seventeenth-century edition had perpetuated C2's erroneous "To huffing, braggart, puft Nobility." About which manuscript (or manuscripts) G consulted it is impossible to be certain—"Panurgus" was available in all descendents of β¹, H7, and the NY1-VA2 pair; "last" was ubiquitously available except in B13, B46, C9, H6, H7, LR1, NP2, OQ1, and TT1 (which record "tast"); and the definite article appears before "huffing" in all artifacts except the descendents of γ⁶. The sole surviving manuscript to evince all three of these variants, including an elided form of "the" (giving "To th' huffing…") is H8, and it is worth noting that from a family comprising H7 and H8 G's editor obtained his text of *ElProg* (see DV 2:309). If G's editor did consult H8 (or a lost cognate) in constructing his text of *Sat4*, however, he used it sporadically and obviously felt free to pick and choose among its readings, passing up, for instance, "pretty good [for the normative *Good pretty*] Linguists" in the first half of the line (l. 59) from which he obtained "Panurgus."

The Modern Prints

In essential respects, as Figure 14 shows, the modern editors' respective treatments of the text of *Sat4* parallel their handling of texts presented in previously published volumes of this *Variorum* (see, e.g., *DV* 7.1:lxxxiv–lxxxviii). Systematically modernizing orthography and mechanics, Tonson (H) bases his text of *Sat4* on G, and this text passes on to his later eighteenth- and earlier nineteenth-century successors Bell (I), Anderson (J), and Chalmers (K) with little change. Readings introduced into the print tradition in G and shared by these editions include "faith" (for the normative "saith") in line 35, "hear [for *beare*] this" in line 43, "so Panurgus" (for "and so Panurge") in line 59, and "such strange things as" (for "more strange things than") in line 152, among others. Tonson also contributes a handful of lections not found in G, including "Statues" (for the authorial "Statutes") in line 132—a reading possibly derived from C—and a contracted "to 've thrown" (for the normative "to have thrown") in line 213.[4] That H and K print "to've thrown," while I and J give "to'have thrown" confirms the previous finding of this *Variorum* that Chalmers (K) reverts to H for his setting text rather than deriving it successively from J. And the fully spelled out "have" in line 213, as well as other such instances as their inclusion of a comma after "and" in line 35 (giving "and, faith") where H and K have no punctuation show that J is based specifically on I.

Evincing the above-cited readings in lines 35, 43, 59, and 152, Lowell's 1855 Boston edition (M) also presents a text ultimately based on G, but its inclusion of variants that originate with H (such as the contraction of "Would not" to "Would n't" in line 197 and of "so often" to "so oft" in line 215) show Tonson to have been Lowell's immediate source. That he does not perpetuate, for instance, the H–K misreading "Statues" (for the authorial "Statutes") in line 131, however, indicates that Lowell consulted one of the earlier seventeenth-century prints; and we have shown in previous volumes that he frequently compared B.

Grosart, a thoroughgoing eclecticist, designates G as his copy text for *Sat4*, but collates B32 and B40, as well as H7. From H7 he adopts "strangest" (for G's normative "strangers") in line 23 (citing his source in a note), and in line 35 he prints "saith [he]" (for G's "faith"), mistakenly crediting the "he" to B32 (since B32 reads only "sayth," it seems likely that Grosart derives this lection, too, from H7, which reads "sayth he"). In previous volumes we have noted that Grosart occasionally compares M (see *DV* 7.1:lxxviii), and in this poem he apparently owes to M such variants as the elision "t' all" (for G's "to all") in line 36, the hyphenated "court-life" (for G's "Court life") in line 66, and the re-spelled "Ascaparts" (with a c, where all previous editions had recorded "Askaparts") in line 233. Regrettably, in line 41 N misprints the normative "termes of law" as "terme of law," retains G's bungled "…all these may pass. / But travail…" (for the correct "…passe / By travaile…") in lines 60–61, and carelessly mangles the grammar of G's "crys the flatter" in line 182, recording "cry the flatterer."

In accordance with the guiding policy of the edition, Norton's update (O) of Lowell's 1855 edition (M) follows A as its copy-text and, except for admitting—without acknowledgment—G's "faith" (for A's correct "saith") in line 35 and restoring the censored lines 134–36a, faithfully reproduces the substantives of A, including such

---

[4]For Tonson's use of either B or C in constructing his text of the elegies, see *DV* 2:lxxxiii.

[blank] = agrees with LRH reading
A–G = variant appears in 17th-c. eds.
~ = agrees with LRH reading
• = variant appears in modern eds.
ᵥ = agrees with nearest corresponding reading on left
{ = to be read together
OoV = Origin of Variant

Line no.	DV/LRH reading	Variant	OoV	A–G	H	I	J	K	M	N	O	P	Q	S	T	Y	Z	AA	DD
2	but	but yet	H6	B–G	•	•	•	•	•	•	•	•							
4	recreation	recreation to	OQ1								•		•	•		•			
4	scant	scarse	OQ1								•		•	•					
5	nor	neither	β⁴	A–G	•	•	•	•	•	•	•	•	•	•		•	•	•	•
8	Glare	Glaze	δ⁵	A	•									•		•			•
9	To'a	To	δ⁵	A–G	•														
12	2ⁿᵈ of	in	H6	B–F	•	•	•	•	•	•	•	•	•	•					
14	lustfull	as lustfull	Yᴬ	A	•									•		•	•	•	•
16	at	in	δ⁵	A–G	•	•	•	•											
23	Strangers	strangest	H7							•									
35	This	The	H6	B–G	•	•	•	•	•	•	•	•	•	•					
35	sayth	faith	G	G	•	•			•	~[he]	•	•							
36	knowes	knoweth	β⁴	A–G	•	•	•	•	•	•	•	•	•						
38	one	no	Y¹																
43	beare	hear	G	G	•	•	•	•	•	•	•	•	•						
47	and	or	β⁴	A–G	•	•	•	•	•	•	•	•	•	•					•
56	Some	Some other	SN3																
57	There	here	B	B–G	•	•	•	•	•	•									
59	and so Panurge	so Panurgus	G (H8?)	G					•	•	•								
61	By	But	G	G	•	•	•	•	•	•	•								
62	wonders	words	β⁴	A												•	•		
65	that	the	β⁴	A–G							•						•		
67/68	Lonenes	loneliness	β⁴	A							•								•

Line no.	DV/LRH reading	Variant	OoV	A–G	H	I	J	K	M	N	O	P	Q	S	T	Y	Z	AA	DD
69	last	tast	H6	B–F								•				•			
73	to'a	a too	NY3 (a 'to)												•		•	•	•
79	king	Kings	β⁴	A–G	•	•	•	•	•	•	•	•	•	•		•	•	•	•
80	kings Street	Kingstreet	C2	A							•						•		•
83	frenchman	Fine	A	A							•								
84	frenchman	Sir	H6	B–G	•	•	•	•	•	•	•	•	•	•		•	•	•	•
86	this	your	β⁴	A–G	•	•	•	•	•	•	•	•	•	•		•	•	•	•
90	I, foole,	I (foole)	H6	B–G	•	•	•	•	•	•	•	•	•	•	•	•	•	•	•
92	dresse	addresse	γ⁸	A							•								
95	Sembriefe	Semibrief	H																
96	me so	mee, so	δ⁵	A–G	•	•	•	•	•	•	•	•	•	•	•	•	•	•	•
97	and...and	or...or	β⁴	A–G	•	•	•	•	•	•	•	•	•	•	•	•	•	•	•
99	smild or fround	frown'd, or smil'd	β⁴	A–G	•	•	•	•	•	•	•	•	•	•	•	•	•	•	•
104	Shoes, bootes, or	bootes, shooes, and	β⁴	A–G	•	•	•	•	•	•	•	•	•	•	•	•	•	•	•
106	blowpoynt, or spancounter	span-counter, or blow-point	β⁴	A–G	•	•	•	•	•	•	•	•	•	•	•	•	•	•	•
106	they	shall	A	A–G							•								
108	which	what	β⁴	A–G	•	•	•	•	•	•	•	•	•	•	•	•	•	•	•
109	tryes	cloyes	H6	B–G	•	•	•	•	•	•	•	•	•	•		•	•		
111	thrusts more	thrusts on more	H6	A–G	•	•	•	•	•	•	•	•	•	•	•	•	•	•	•
111	as if he had	as if he	β⁴	A									˜ he'd	˜ he'd	˜ he'd	' me ˜			
111	as if he had	as he had	H6	B–G	•	•	•	•	•	•	•	•	•	•		•	•	•	
113	which	that	β⁴	A–G	•	•	•	•	•	•	•	•	•	•		•	•	•	•
113	haue	hath	β⁴	A											•				
117	this	his	NY3								•								•
117	talke; in vaine	talke in vaine	β⁴	A	•	•	•	•	•	•	•						•	•	•

Line no.	DV/LRH reading	Variant	OoV	A-G	H	I	J	K	M	N	O	P	Q	S	T	Y	Z	AA	DD
122	sayes	saith	β⁴	A-G	•	•	•	•		•	•	•	•	•		•	•	•	•
132	Statuts	Statues	C(?)		•		•	•											
133	in for hearing him.	in; for hearing him,	G	G							•			•					•
134	venomd	venome	B	B-F										•					•
134	venomd	venomous	G	G	•	•				•									
148	complementall	complimented	J				•			•									
152	more...then	such...as	G	G	•	•				•									
154	make	hast	γ⁶	A-G	•	•	•	•	•		•	•	•			•	•	•	•
156	piteous	precious	β⁴	A					•		•					•			
159	o're	on	β⁴	A	•						•	•		•		•	•		•
159	and such	Such	β⁴	A-G							•	•				•			•
164	th'huffing	huffing	γ⁴	A-F	•	•	•		•		•	•	•			•			•
169	yon	your	β⁴	A-G	•	•	•	•	•	•	•	•	•			•	•		•
170	Transported	Transplanted	NY3												•				
171	Court here	Presence	β⁴	A	•	•	•	•	•	•	•	•	•			•	•	•	•
171	Court here	Courtiers	H6	B-G					•										
178	are	were	B	B-F											•				
179	I	aye	P									•				•			
180	their	th'	NY3				•			•	•	•	•			•			•
182	cryes his flatterers	cry the flatters	A, β⁴	A			•			cry the flatterer	•								•
182	cryes his flatterers	crys the flatterer	G	G			•				•	•							
185	Players	prayers	J				•	•		•	•								
188	Ladyes come	Lady's come	H		•		•				•					•			
188	did	do	γ⁸	A-G	•		•		•	•	•	•	•			•	•	•	•
194	scarlett	scarlets	β⁴	A-G	•		•		•	•	•	•				•	•		•
197	Would not	Wouldn't	H		•		•		•	•	•	•	•			•		•	•

Line no.	DV/LRH reading	Variant	OoV	A-G	H	I	J	K	M	N	O	P	Q	S	T	Y	Z	AA	DD
199	As	As if	γ⁶	A-G	•	•	•	•	•	•	•	•	•	•		•	•	•	•
203	with which	wherewith	β⁴	A-G	•	•	•	•	•	•	•	•	•	•		•	•	•	•
204	survays	survay	β⁴	A-G	•		•	•	•	•	•	•	•	•			•	•	•
205	tryes	trye	O3	A-G	•	•		•	•	•	•	•	•	•		•	•		•
206	thighs	thighe	O3						•	•	•	•	•			•			
211	straight	he	β⁴	A-G	•	•	•	•	•	•	•	•	•	•		•	•	•	•
213	to haue	to've	H		to'have	◁'◁													
215	whisperd	whispers	H6	B-G	•	•	•	•	•	•	•	•	•	•			•		•
217	saying	saying of	β⁴	A-G	•	•	•	•	•	•	•	•		•			•		
222	whom	or whom	H6	B-G	•	•	•	•	•	•	•	•	•						•
223	not	not hee.	H6	B-G	•	•	•	•	•	•		•							
224	rusheth	rushes	C	C-G	•	•	•	•	•	•	•	•		•			•		•
225	came	meant	β⁴	A-G						•	•	•	•	•					•
226	still	yet still	β⁴	A						•	•	•	•		•		•	•	•	•
229	I	I'll	NY3																
230	which from	from	A	A-G	•	•	•	•	•	•	•	•	•	•		•	•	•	•
234	which	that	β⁴	A-G	•	•	•	•	•	•	•	•	•	•			•	•	•
235-36	Fine/ Liuing	fine/ Liuing.	G	G	•	•	•	•	•	•	•	•	•	•	•	•	•	•	•
238	witt	Wits	δ⁵	A-F							•	•							
240	a skant	but a scarce	β⁴	A							•	•		•	•				•	
240	a skant	but a scant	H6	B-G			•	•	•	•	•	•	•	•			•		•
241	their	the	δ⁵	A-G							•	•	•	•			•		•	•
241	Though	Although	H6	B-G							•	•			•					
242	knowne meritt	merit	NY3																
243	men	man	δ⁵	A-C			•	•	•	•	•	•	•	•		•	•	•	•
244	writts	witts	K					•											•

of A's misreadings as "Fine" (for "Mine?") in line 83 and "shall" (for "they") in line 106. O does, however, systematically modernize A's language, replacing archaic spellings ("chuseth" in line 51 is respelled as "chooseth"), dropping terminal *e*'s ("seene" is shortened to "seen," e.g.), expanding elided participles ("liv'd" is changed to "lived," e.g.), supplying apostrophes in possessives ("Noahs Arke" becomes "Noah's ark"), and adding punctuation throughout. Norton's footnotes cite variants in B, C, D, F, and G, and some of his changes to A's accidentals may derive from these editions. Others—such as the spelling "Afric's" (without a *k*) in line 22 and the substitution of a semicolon after "him" for A's period in line 133—likely derive from Lowell's prior work in M, as does the above-mentioned G reading "faith" (for A's "saith") in line 35.

Chambers (P), as usual, constructs his text eclectically from A, B, E, G, and H, and derives at least one reading from an uncited manuscript. From A Chambers adopts the δ⁵ lection "Glaze" (where B–G record the authorial "Glare") in line 8, but he rejects other A readings, accepting the B–G lections "but yet I have beene in" (where A gives "but I have beene in") in line 2 and "here / he stopt mee" (where A gives "There...") in lines 57–58. On occasion, Chambers adopts readings that appear only in B–F and are contradicted by both A and G: "sinne in going" (for A and G's "sin of going") in line 12 and "doth not tast" (for A and G's "doth not last") in line 69, for example. In line 35 he accepts G's innovative "faith, speaks" (where A–F record "saith, speakes"), but refuses G's restoration of the authorial "th' huffing braggart, puft Nobility" (as opposed to A–F's metrically smoother "huffing, braggart, puft Nobility") in line 164. Chamber's "semi-breve" (for A–G's "Sembriefe") in line 95 follows an expanded spelling first introduced in H, though Chambers likely derived the spelling from Grosart, the nearest ancestor to record the innovation. And in line 179 he uniquely renders "are found / In the Presence, and I" as "...and aye," transmuting the syntax of every prior edition by substituting an adverb for Donne's pronoun. In line 225, without citing a source, he records the manuscript reading "came to cry," where every prior edition had given "meant to crie."

Persuaded that A is "far and away superior to any other single edition, and...to any *single* manuscript" (2:cxvi), Grierson (Q) chooses A as copy-text for *Sat4*, but, in addition to restoring the material censored from A, emends it in nearly 60 other instances—including 26 changes in wording and substantive punctuation. A few of these changes are based on Grierson's independent sense of what is grammatically, logically, or esthetically required at given points, and others derive from the later seventeenth-century editions. The vast majority of his emendations, however, are buttressed by his citation of readings from the manuscripts, which he is the first to use extensively and methodically. Grierson's independent alterations include, for example, the cosmetic modernization of A's "grown'd" in line 89 to "ground" and the reduction of the capital "W" on line 128's "Whores" to a minuscule (giving "whores"), as well as the syntax-altering repunctuation of the line-232–33 construction "(why is it hung / With the seaven deadly sinnes) being among..." as "...sinnes?). Being among...." In imposing emendations from manuscript Grierson aspires to avoid mere eclecticism by invoking an "agreement-of-the-manuscripts" principle, interpreting this information in light of "the comparative value of the different [manuscript] groups" (cxvii), and in some instances this procedure proves fruitful: consulting the manuscripts enables Grierson, for the first time in the printed history of the poem, to restore the authorial "they pay" (for A's eyeskip error "shall pay") in line 106 and "As men which from gaoles to'execution goe" in line 230, where A had dropped the "which" and installed the corrupt "As men from gaoles...." In other instances Grierson's treatment of the manuscript evidence is difficult to understand: in line 8, for instance, he retains the proper name "Glaze" found in A, citing B32, C8, O20, and SN3, but notes that "Glare" appears in the *"rest of [the] MSS."* Similarly, he retains A's hypermetrical "addresse" in line 92, citing DT1 and H4, though he is aware that the shortened form "dresse" appears in NY3 and O20, manuscripts whose readings he prefers in other instances. Indeed, that Grierson decides deliberately to abandon the "agreement" criterion in favor of other considerations is evident in his handling of several lines, including 4, where he adopts from OQ1-VA1 "a recreation to, and scarce map" (for A's "recreation, and scant map"); 38, where he accepts the B13-OQ1 reading "no [for A's normative *one*] language"; 56, where with the sole support of SN3 he gives "some other Jesuites" (for A's normative "some Jesuites"); and 205–06, where he reduces the plurals "tries /...thighes" to "trye /...thighe," citing O3—the only artifact in the entire pre-1912 transmissional history of the poem to record those readings. Substantively, in sum, Grierson follows A in error in lines 8, 14, 80, 92, 156, 159, 171, and 240; corrects the received text by restoring A's readings in lines 2, 35, 57, 84, 109, 215, 222, and 223; imports correct readings from manuscript in lines 9, 16, 106, 154, and 230; and introduces error from manuscript in lines 4, 38, 56, 133, 205–06, and 241 (see Figure 14). As this almost evenly balanced record of correction and corruption shows, the text Grierson eventually produces is difficult to distinguish from what might be developed by a purely eclectic method. As is shown by his readings in lines 4, 56, 205–06, and elsewhere (see Figure 14), Hayward (S) presents a virtual reprint of Q (though he does restore the authorial "one language" in line 38, where Q had imported B13's "no language").

Most of his twentieth-century successors present a text highly similar to Grierson's, Bennett (T) being the lone exception (see Figure 14). Milgate (Y), Grierson's heir in the Oxford series, also adopts A as copy-text, but cites 14 verbal emendations (ll. 4, 9, 16, 62, 67–68, 69, 83, 106, 111, 113, 154, 164, 230, 238) and one spelling change (that of "Panirge" to "Panurge" in l. 59)—all except those in lines 69 and 111 imposed by Grierson before him. Milgate's replacement of A's "last" with "tast" in line 69 (for which he credits H6 and OQ1) and of A's "thrusts on" with "thrusts me" in line 111 (for which he credits B40, C2, and DT1) are among 10 instances (in ll. 4, 38, 56, 69, 111 [twice], 134, 205, 206, 226, and 241) in which his text differs from Grierson's, and these include the four mentioned above (ll. 4, 38, 56, and 205–06) for which Grierson has only dubious support among the manuscripts. A major difference between Q and Y, not detailed in the discussion above, is Y's imposition of elision marks throughout the poem in an effort to regularize Donne's meter.

Shawcross (Z), too, sets Sat4 into type from A, emending it—in accordance with his usual practice—when "a later version or the reading of a consensus of manuscripts seems to be closer to Donne's 'original'" (xxi). In implementing this Griersonian approach, Z diverges verbally from A in lines 9, 16, 38, 67–68, 83, 106, 113, 154, 164, 205–06, 226, and 230—all of which are among the alterations of A that had previously been imposed in Q and all but three of which (those in ll. 38, 205–06, and 226) had been similarly adopted by Y. These changes include replacing the compositorial

"Fine" with the authorial "Mine?" in line 83, a correction also imposed in all other editions except O, and accepting Grierson's repairs of the above-noted blunders in lines 106 and 230. Z also uniquely follows Q in accepting the B13-OQ1 lection "no [for A's authorial *one*] language" in line 38 and—except for S—is the only edition other than Q ever to admit the O3 lections "trye /…thighe" (for A's authorial "tries /…thighes") in lines 205–06. Especially in light of his abandonment of A in these latter two instances, Shawcross's preservation of A's submetrical "words told" (for the correct "wonders told") in line 62—a reading otherwise absent from the print tradition except for O—and his preservation of A's mispunctuated "So I sigh, and sweat / To heare this Makeron talke in vaine" (for the correct "…talke; in vaine;") in line 117 seem especially curious and give particular point to his acknowledgement that his text is "eclectic and somewhat subjectively based" (xxi).

Declaring himself interested in "offer[ing] the richest and most pointed readings of Donne's poems that have good authority in the early versions" (p. 14), Smith (AA)—as is his usual practice—specifies no particular copy-text for Sat4, but presents a modernized, eclectic text based generally on the seventeenth-century editions, most heavily on A. As is shown on Figure 14, AA diverges verbally from A in 14 instances (in lines 9, 16, 62, 67, 68, 83, 92, 106, 113, 154, 164, 226, 230, and 238), and the departures in lines 62, 67, 68, 83, 92, 113, 164, 226, and 238 derive from B–F or G. In lines 9, 16, 106, 154, and 230, however, AA follows Q in emending toward manuscript readings, unspecifically citing variants in "MS," "*some MSS*," or "*several MSS*."

In an edition that also veers away from the scholarly toward the popular, Patrides (DD) similarly fails to name specifically those few manuscripts from which he derives emendations or reports variant readings, referring instead to "a MS," "some MSS," or "several MSS." DD does preserve, however, old spelling and specifies A, "as supplemented by" later editions, as its "basic text," verbally emending A's text of Sat4 in lines 9, 16, 62, 67, 68, 83, 106, 113, 164, 205, 226, and 230. Most of these alterations derive from the later seventeenth-century prints, but in replacing A's "To Masse" with "To'a Masse" in line 9, "in Court" with "at Court" in line 16, "shall pay" with "they pay" in line 106, and "odds tries" with "odds trye" in line 205, DD follows Grierson in adopting manuscript readings. Especially curious is that DD does not match "trye" with a reduction of "thighes" to "thighe" in line 206, but leaves an imperfect "trye"–"thighes" rhyme. Also curious, given his acceptance of the changes in lines 9, 16, 106, and 205, is Patrides's refusal to follow Grierson in emending A's "hast from prison" to the manuscript lection "make from prison" in line 154.

Copy-text Used in this Edition

Persuaded that the absence of any "single authoritative text" makes it "advisable to base each poem on whatever accessible text has the fewest obvious errors" (xxv), in 1942 Roger Bennett (T) became the first editor in over 300 years to set Sat4 into type from manuscript. Bennett's choice for copy-text was NY3, one of few artifacts available to him as an American scholar working during World War II; and although the present editors have selected from a much broader range of artifacts than was available (or known) to Bennett, we, too, have chosen NY3, concluding that it contains the cleanest surviving text of the revised version of the poem. In addition to modernizing spelling and punctuation and imposing numerous contractions and elisions intended to smoothen Donne's meter, Bennett emends NY3 substantively in lines 56, 86, 96, 97, 115, 116, 174, 217, 232, 235–36, and 240. Of these the changes of "this Grogerame" to "your grogaram" in line 86, "and Halls, and Stowes" to "or Halls or Stows" in line 97, "saying o^r Ladyes Psalter" to "saying of Our Lady's psalter" in line 217, "…Queenes man, and Fine, / Liuing barrells of beefe" to "'Queen's man,' and fine / Living, barrels of beef" in line 235–35, and "Who ame a skant brooke" to "Which am but a scarce brook" in line 240 are without bibliographical warrant, imported from A and chosen to satisfy Bennett's personal aesthetic and/or logical preferences.[5] These, of course, we have not implemented.

Analysis of the evidence, however, has led us to adopt half-a-dozen of the emendations imposed by Bennett and to add a further 8, as shown in Table 4.1:

Table 4.1: Substantive emendations of the copy-text

Line no.	NY3 lection	Emendation	Source of NY3 error	Artifacts containing error** (listed in left-to-right order across the stemma)
*56	reuerent men	reverend men	NY3 scribe	B13 ε^1 NY3 Y2 B40 O3
73	Like to'a high stretchd	Like a to'high stretchd	NY3 scribe	HH1 NY1-VA2 NY3
*96	many ly	many a lie	NY3 scribe	NY3
*115	Like to a bigg Wife	Like a big wife	β^3 scribe	β^3 γ^7
*116	belche and sweat	sigh and sweat	β^3 scribe	β^3
117	his Maccaron talke	this Maccaron talke	NY3 scribe	VA1 δ^2 H5 NP2 HH1 NY3 DT1-H4 γ^7
153	Run from thence	Ran from thence	NY3 scribe	γ^3 HH1 NY3 Y2
170	Transplanted it	Transported it	β^3 scribe	ε^2 HH1 β^3
*174	Stocks are there; fruits bastard all	Stocks are; their fruits bastard all	NY3 scribe	*see Historical Collation*
180	th'apparells be	their apparells be	β^3 scribe	H3 HH1 NY3 B32 O20-SP1 γ^7 β^5
203	Feathers or dust	Feathers and dust	NY3 scribe	H8 HH1 NY1-VA2 NY3
229	Ile leaue	I leaue	β^3 scribe	HH1 β^3
*232	Sins?) beeing among	Sins?). Being among	NY3 scribe	*see Historical Collation*
242	the merritt	the knowne merritt	β^3 scribe	γ^3 H3 H7 HH1 β^3 γ^7 β^5

* emendation also in T
** Greek letters = error occurs in all the artifact's descendants

---

[5]Bennett credits the repunctuation in 235–36 that results in "fine / Living, barrels of beef…" to Grierson, but G was in fact the first edition to introduce a comma after "Living" and has been followed in this by all subsequent editions until the present one.

Analysis of the corpus of variants in light of the stemma for *Sat4* presented above indicates that 8 of the 14 substantive copy-text errors requiring emendation are chargeable to Donne's friend Rowland Woodward, who wrote out NY3—perhaps expressly for the library of his quondam employer Francis Fane, First Earl of Westmoreland—sometime after the death of Anne Donne in 1617 (see *DV* 7.1:lxvii–lxx). The remaining 6 were introduced by the scribe of β³ before the text came into Woodward's hands. Most of these, as the chart above shows, are errors of inadvertency or simple slips of the pen, and several of them occur in one or more artifacts outside the β³ line of descent, showing that the mistakes in question were easy for more than one scribe to make. As is indicated by the notation "*see Historical Collation*" in Table 4.1, the variant forms of lines 174 and 232 are too numerous to list on the chart, but of them we may say that the evidence supports the readings we have adopted: "Iust such gay paynted things, which no sapp, nor / Tast haue in them, ours are; and naturall / Some of the Stocks are; their fruits bastard all" in lines 172–74; and "Tyr'd now I leaue this Place; and...Go through the great Chamber (why is it hung / With the 7 deadly Sins?); beeing among / Those Ascaparts...I shooke Like a Spyed Spy" in lines 229–37. The evidence is similarly confused at line 242, where about half the extant manuscripts hypermetrically read "(with Machabees modestie) the knowne meritt," while the remainder achieve metrical smoothness by omitting "knowne"; and artifacts evincing each reading appear among the descendants of both the LOH and the LRH. This pattern of distribution suggests that "knowne," despite its addition of an extra syllable to the line, is authorial and that its absence betokens the independent decision of various scribes to regularize Donne's line. In this instance, as in all others, we have emended up the line of descent toward the inferred reading of the LRH.

For all the influence it had on its successors, T might as well never have existed, and the A-based text established by Grierson went essentially unchallenged throughout the twentieth century.[6] Figure 14 lists some 39 instances in which Q either restores or perpetuates scribal misreadings that A had derived from β⁴, γ⁶, δ⁵, or C2, as well as two (in l. 133 and ll. 235–36) introduced by the editor of G; and with the few exceptions shown in the figure, all these pass on to Q's successors. Some of these errors consist in mere inversions of word order (the change of the authorial "smild or fround" to "frown'd, or smil'd" in l. 99, e.g.) or substitution of one particle for another (replacing Donne's "which" with "that" in l. 113, e.g.), but a number of them—particularly those in lines 8, 86, 92, 96, 111, 133, 156, 169, 171, 182, 188, 203, 211, 225, 235–36, and 240—affect meaning or meter in relatively significant ways. In the Griersonian text, for instance, the scoffer who went "To'a Masse in ieast" (l. 9) is erroneously called "Glaze," whereas Donne names him "Glare" (l. 8); and the "wretchednes / Of suiters at Court" (ll. 156–57) is mourned by the speaker's "precious soule" rather than, correctly, by his "piteous soule" (l. 156). Similarly, all subsequent editors except AA follow Grierson in adopting A's meter-destroying "doth addresse" (for the authorial "doth dresse") in line 92, and every edition from Q onward has recorded A's "flouts our Presence" (for the authorial "flouts our Court here") in line 171 and the hypermetrical "but a scarce brooke" (for the correct "a skant brooke") in line 240 (this last reading is even

---

[6]Unless otherwise noted, T's readings are excluded from the following account in this paragraph.

accepted by T). Additional A-based errors perpetuated by Q include "doe know" (for the correct "did know") in line 188, "wherewith they fornicate" (for "with which they fornicate") in line 203, "he arrests" (for "straight arrests") in line 211, and "meant to crie" (for "came to cry") in line 225. The editorial errors that Grierson imports from G in lines 133 and 235–36 involve punctuation: whereas A correctly reads line 133 as "To sucke me in, for hearing him. I found...," G replaces the comma after "in" with a semicolon and removes the period after "him," yielding "To sucke me in; for hearing him I found..."; further, G repunctuates lines 235–36 to yield "No token of worth, but Queenes man, and fine / Living, barrells of beefe...," thus nonsensically establishing "fine / Living" as a parallel to "Queenes man" among the "token[s] of worth" recognized by the "Askaparts" who inhabit the "great chamber" (ll. 231–36). Donne, however, ends the clause—and line 235—with "Fine"; "Liuing" then joins with the remainder of line 236 to create an appositive for the "Askaparts"—"Liuing barrells of beefe, flagons of wine." We are pleased to be able to restore this and other authorial readings in the present text.

Textual Apparatus

Copy-text: NY3.   **Texts collated:** B11 (*ll. 203–44 only*, f. 95r–v); B13 (ff. 48–50); B32 (ff. 91v–94v); B40 (ff. 59v–62v); B46 (ff. 6–10v); B47 (ff. 100v–104v); C2 (ff. 19–22); C8 (ff. 9–15v); C9 (ff. 16–19v); DT1 (ff. 16–20); H3 (ff. 9–12); H4 (ff. 4–7v); H5 (ff. 122–25v); H6 (pp. 69–77); H7 (ff. 49–54v); H8 (ff. 72–75v); HH1 (ff. 67v–72); IU2 (*ll. 18–20, 23–27a, 29b–30, 35–36, 73, 127–28, 198, 225b–28 only*, f. 74v); LR1 (ff. 283–85v); NP2 (ff. 1–4); NY1 (pp. 13–20); NY3 (ff. [6v–9v]); O3 (pp. 40–43); O20 (ff. 6v–10v); O21 (pp. 184–93); OJ1 (*ll. 134–36a only*, p. 341); OQ1 (ff. 202v–05v); P3 (ff. [8v–11]); SN3 (ff. 15–20v); SN4 (ff. 3–8); SP1 (ff. [14–18]); TT1 (ff. 22–24); VA1 (ff. 6v–10); VA2 (ff. 9v–12); Y2 (pp. 25–42 [pp. 24–43]); Y3 (pp. 17–22); A (pp. 337–45); B (pp. 135–42); C (pp. 135–42); D (pp. 129–36); E (pp. 129–36); F (pp. 129–36); G (pp. 128–35); 5 (*ll. 18–23 only*, p. 113); 33a–b (*ll. 225–28 only*, sig. A7; *ll. 18–20, 23–27, 31, 33, 47–48, 52–54, 94, 96–97, 129–30, 138–49 only*, sigs. C3–C4); 44a–b (*ll. 129–30 only*, sig. Q6; *ll. 18–23 only*, sig. 2N4v); 44c–d (*same lines*, sigs. Q2, 2M8v).   **Not collated:** B51 (*l. 236 only*, f. 43v); P1 (*ll. 27–29, 61–62, 88–89, 143–47, 151, 153–54, 165–67, 188–90, 200–03, 225–26, 228–30, 233–34, 236–37, 242–44 only*, f. 53v).

Emendations of the copy-text: Heading: *Satyre 4.*] Sat: 4ᵃ.   Line 30 were] weare   44 Complement,] ~.   47 out-ly] outly   either] ether   56 reuerend] reuerent   58 me;'] ~';   59 was,] ~ₐ   71 Courts] ~,   (though] ₐ~   72 Vice)] ~,   73 to'a high] a to'high   77 talke,] ~ₐ   81 course,] ~ₐ   90 So I, foole] ~, ~ₐ~   92 dresse] ~.   96 a] *om*   102 to an] to'an   104 Shoes] Shows   115 Like] ~ to   lothed] lothd   116 sigh] belche   117 this] his   142 pay'a fine] pay 'afine   151 were] weare   153 Ran] Run   159 me;'] ~';   163 and,] &ₐ   Truth,] ~ₐ   170 Transported] Transplanted   174 are;] ~ₐ   their] there;   176 Baloon] Balon   178 Time] ›~‹   180 their apparells] th'apparells   192 ne'er] ne›a→e‹re   thought,] ~ₐ   199 were] weare   203 and] or   fornicate,] ~.   205 the odds] th'odds   214 th'Inquisition,] ~.   219 both,] ~.   222 on] one   225 be as] ~'~   229 I] Ile   232 Sins?);] ~?)ₐ   242 knowne] *om*

Regularizations of the copy-text: Line 5 with] wᵗ   6 with] wᵗ   8 which] wᶜʰ   10 which] wᶜʰ   13 and] &   forget-] forgett=   14 and] &   15 and] &   17 I sufferd] Isufferd   18 the] yᵉ   19 which] wᶜʰ   20 which] wᶜʰ   24 the] yᵉ   25 without] wᵗhout   26 the] yᵉ   'gainst] gainst   29 Sir] Sʳ   30 and] &   33 our] oʳ   41 the] yᵉ

164

44 With] Wth 45 which] wch 50 that] y^t 51 Sir] S^r 52
iudgment] iudgm^t 53 For] for   the] y^e 54 that] y^t 55 Sir]
S^r 57 our] o^r 63 Sir] S^r 65 that] y^t 71 ther be] therbe
73 Sir] S^r 75 that] y^t 76 with] w^t 77 1st and 2nd our] o^r 78
From] from   79 your] y^r 87 Sir] S^r I haue] Ihaue   88 But] but
94 which] wch 99 the] y^e and] &   104 egg-] egg=   108 which]
wch 109 with] w^t 112 without] w^{t}hout   113 which] wch 118
Either] Ether   122 our] o^r 123 that] y^t 125 the] y^e that] y^t
126 with] wth 131 Becomming] Bec$\overline{o}$ming   132 our] o^r 143 Sir]
S^r 144 Sir] S^r 146 to be] tobe   148 With] Wth 150 the] y^e
151 which] wch 152 the] y^e with] w^t 153 with] w^t 154 from]
fr$\overline{o}$ 156 the] y^e 159 o're] ore   165 which] wch 166 the] y^e
168 our] o^r 169 which] wch 171 With] Wth our] o^r 172
which] wch 175 the] y^e 176 the] y^e 178 made] Made   that] y^t
185 All] all   Who] who   188 which] wch 189 with] w^t 190
and] &   194 which] wch 203 with] w^t which] wch 205 with]
wth 207 Symmetry] Sym̅etry   208 with] wth 210 which] w^{ch}
217 our] o^r But] but   223 His] his   224 He] he   226 which]
wch 228 commands] c$\overline{o}$mands   230 which] wch 232 With] Wth
234 which] wch 237 which] wch 239 the] y^e 242 With] Wth

HISTORICAL COLLATION

Format:

Imperfections: *pp. containing ll. 1–202 missing* B11; *text lost to wear in right
M of f. 16* DT1; *text lost to bleedthrough and water damage throughout*
O3.

Indentations: *l. 225b ind* IU2; *l. 1 ind* NY3; *ll. 30, 93 ind* SN3; *l. 1
hanging ind* SP1; *l. 23 ind* 5; *no ind* Σ.

Miscellaneous: D^r: Doone: *is running head in ms.* B32; *ll. 143b–144a om,
143a and 144b run together as single l.* B47; *every tenth line numbered in
right M in 2nd hand* C2; *ll. 171, 180, 211 numbered in left M in 2nd
hand* C8; ›I: [missing]‹ *in right M beside HE, ll. 137b–139a om, ll. 137a
and 139b run together as single l.* DT1; *ll. 137b–139a om, ll. 137a and
139b run together as single l.,* »Two verses omitted« *in right M beside fused
ll. 137–39* H4; *every tenth line numbered in right M in 2nd hand, M gloss*
›Dr Reinolds, and Dr Andrewes‹ *keyed to two reuerend men in l. 56, M
gloss* ›The old L. chamberlaine Hunsdon‹ *keyed to his in l. 158, M gloss*
›Topcliff‹ *keyed to pursuivant in l. 216, M gloss* ›L.B.‹ *keyed to Glorious in
l. 219* H5; »P.« *to left of HE* H6; *poem scribally attributed to I. D. in
right M beside HE* H8; »Printed« *penciled in right M at l. 1, ll. 7b–8a om,
ll. 7a and 8b run together as single l.* LR1; *running HE Sat 4, every fifth l.
scribally numbered in left M, l. 20 added in right M in second hand* NY1;
HE in left M NY3 SN4; »p. 128.« *left of HE* O20; *ll. 12b–13a om, ll.*

12a–13b run together as single l., ll. 165–67 entered in the order 166, 167,
165 O21; *ms. emendations in a copy of A* OJ1; *scribal note on f. 14v*
*locates poem in a 5-poem set (see footnote on p. *** above),* ›anno 1594‹ *to*
right of HE SN3; *ll. 78b–79a om, ll. 78a–79b run together as single l., last*
3 words of l. 140 entered at the beginning of l. 141 TT1; *every fifth l.*
scribally numbered in left M VA2; *ll. 21–22 om, remaining ll. in the order*
19, 23, 20, 24 and error flagged by [*in left M, ll. 223b–224a om, ll.*
223a–224b run together as single l. Y2; *ll. 165–68 entered in the order*
166, 167, 165, 168 and numbered ›2, 3, 1, 4‹ *in left M* Y3; *ll. 134–36a*
replaced by dashes A; *entire text in italics, quoted in chapter entitled* The
Wolfe of Romulus, M *gloss* Dunne in his Satyres. *5; quoted in a prose*
paraphrase of Sat4, excerpts from ll. 18–149 included under HE A Generall
Prognostication. For the Year 1653, *excerpts from ll. 225–28 included*
under HE Februaries Observations. *33a–b; ll. 18–23 quoted under HE*
Strange., *ll. 129–30 quoted under HE* Amaz'd. *44a–d.*

Headings: M:ʳ Dunns first Satire. | B13. **Satyre:. 4.ᵗʰ** B32 C2 C8 C9(4.)
H6(4.) H8(4.) A(IIII.) B(IV.)–G(IV.). *Satyre.* B46 DT1 O20.
Satyre 4. Of the Courte. B47. Another Satyre by the same I:D: | H3.
Satire: H4. Satyra quarta. H5 H7 SP1(4ᵃ.) VA2 Y2. Satira 4ᵗᵃ
HH1 OQ1(4ᵃ). A Pill IU2. .Satyra. NP2. *Satire .4.ᵗʰ* NY1.
Sat: 4ᵃ. NY3. A Satire against yᵉ Court / wrighten by Docter Donne, In
/ Queene Elizabeths Raigne O3. Satyre. the. ffourth; O21 Y3(Satire).
The 4ᵗʰ· Satyre P3. SAT. 4 SN3 SN4 VA1. *om* B11 B40 LR1
OJ1 TT1 5 33a–b 44a–d.

1 Well;] B32 B40 NY3 O20 SN4 A–G; ~: B46 LR1; ~, C2 C8 DT1 SP1; ~.
NP2; ~ₐ Σ. I may now] may I ~ H3; now I may Y2. receaue] ~, B13
B32 B40 C2 H4 HH1 NP2 SP1 VA2 Y2 A–G. dy;] ~, B13 B47 C9 H3 H5 H6
HH1 LR1 SN3 SN4 Y3; ~. B46 H7 OQ1 VA1 B–G; ~: C8 H8 P3 SP1; ~ₐ NP2
O21 TT1 Y2. Sin] ~, HH1.

2 Indeede] in deed B47 H7 HH1 VA1; I knowe H3; in=deed OQ1.
greate,] ~. B46; ~; H4 LR1; ~ₐ O21 OQ1 TT1; ~: Y3. but I] ~ yet ~ C9
H3 H6 O3 B–G; ~ ~ H7(*var:* »yet ~«); ~ ~ yet B46. in] *om* LR1 NP2.

3 A] in ~ LR1 NP2; * O21; *om* VA1. Purgatory,] ~; B13 NY1 O3 O21
VA2; ~ₐ B40 P3 TT1; ~: LR1 Y3; ~. VA1. such] and SP1. as] a LR1.
feard hell] feared ~ B40 H3 H4; feared-~ DT1; feare as ~, LR1 NP2. is] ~,
HH1.

4 recreation,] ~; B13; ~ₐ C8 H5 LR1 SN3 TT1 Y2 Y3; ~ to, OQ1 P3 VA1.
and] or O3. scant] ~, B47; scarce H3(*var:* »~«) H5 H8 LR1 NP2 O21 OQ1
P3 VA1 Y3. Mapp] Mase Y2. this.] ~, B32 O20; ~ₐ B47 C9 H3 NP2
O21 TT1 VA1 Y2 Y3; ~; DT1; bliss O3; ~: OQ1.

5 My] (~ H7. mind] ~, B13 B32 C2 C9 H6 H7 HH1 O20 SP1 Y2 A–G.
nor] neither B40 DT1 H4 TT1 A–G; not B47 C9 H6 O3 O21 Y3; neithers C2;

neither's C8. with] *om* H3(»~«). prides] pride H3(»~«) H4. itche,]
~; B13 O21; ~∧ H3 P3 TT1; itch'es, H4. yet] *om* OQ1. beene] ~, C8.

6 Poysoned] B32 B40 DT1 H7 LR1 NY3 O3 O20 SP1 TT1 Y2; ~, HH1;
poysned LR1 SN4; poyson'd Σ. loue] ~, B40 B46 C2 DT1 H7 O3 Y3; ~;
C8. see,] ~; B13; ~∧ B47 C8 C9 H3 H6 H7 H8 LR1 NP2 NY1 O3 O21 SN3
TT1 VA2 Y2 Y3. or] nor B13 OQ1; and H7 SN3. to bee] ~' ~ B46.
seene;] B40 C9 DT1 H5 NY3 SN4; ~. B13 B46 H7 H8 HH1 NP2 NY1 OQ1 P3
SN3 SP1 VA2; ~∧ B47 H3 O3 O21 VA1 Y2 Y3; ~| TT1; ~, Σ.

7 Suite] shewt VA1. there,] at Courte. B46; ~∧ B47 TT1; at Court, H5
LR1(∧) NP2 O21 OQ1 P3 VA1 Y3. nor] or H8; *om* LR1. new] *om* B13
B46 H5 LR1 O21 OQ1 P3 VA1 Y3; no C8 NP2; yet C9 H6. Sute] *om* LR1;
shewt VA1. to] *om* LR1 VA1. show,] B13 B32 H5 NY3 O20 SN4 SP1;
shew, B40 C8 H8 HH1(→›~‹,) A–G; shew∧ B47 DT1 H3 H4 NY1 O3 OQ1 TT1
VA2 Y2; *om* LR1; ~∧ Σ.

8 Yet] But onlie B46; *om* LR1; It O21. went] thither ~, B46; *om* LR1.
to] *om* B46 LR1. Court;] ~. B13 B32 H6 H8 O20 SP1; *om* B46 LR1; ~,
B47 H3 NP2 NY1 O3 O21 P3 VA2 Y2 Y3; ~: C9; ~∧ H7 OQ1 TT1 Y2; ~,.
VA1. But] *om* B46 Y2. as] '~ B46; to Y2. Glare] Glaze B32 C2
C8 SP1 A; ~, H3 H5 HH1 VA1; G[*blank*] H7; Clare LR1 NP2 O3 P3; Glaze,
O20; gaze Y2. which] *om* B46 NY1 VA2; whoe H3; (~ H8; I Y2. go]
~, HH1; ~; Y2.

9 To'a] H5 NY3; to a B13 B32 B40 B46 B47 DT1 H4 H7 HH1 NY1 O3 O20
SN3 SN4 SP1 TT1 VA2 Y3; To Σ. Masse] mask H4 O21 Y3. ieast,] ~)
H8; ~∧ LR1 P3 TT1 VA1. catch'd,] Catch't, B13 B47 C9 H6 HH1 OQ1 SN3
SN4 VA2 Y2; catch't∧ B46 H3 H7 O21 Y3; ~∧ C8 NY1 TT1; and∧ H5 LR1
NP2; Catch∧ O3; *om* P3 VA1. was] ~, C8 Y3; ~; O21. fayne] ~,
O20. disburse] ~, C2 C8 OQ1; deburse SN3.

10 The] Three B46 HH1 SN3; An H3 H5 LR1 NP2; *om* P3; (~ VA1.
hundred] hundreth H5; 100 LR1 NP2 OQ1(C) Y2; (300 P3; hundreth SN3.
Marks] ~, B13 B32 B40 C2 C8 DT1 H5 H6 O20 O21 SP1 VA1 Y3 A–G; ~; O3.
which] (~ B46 B47 H3 H8 HH1 LR1. is] was DT1 H4 LR1; wth O3.
curse] ~, B32 C2 C9 DT1 H4 H5 HH1 O20 SN3 D–G; ~) B46 B47 H8 LR1 P3
VA1; ~. C8; ~; H6(→»~,«) A–C.

11 scap'd,] scap't: B13 B47 LR1 SP1; ~; B32 C9 DT1 O20 SN3 SN4; scap't.
B46 H3 H7; scapt; C2 C8 H5 NY1 VA2 Y3; ~: H6 NP2; ~. H8 TT1; scaped,
HH1; scapte∧ O3 P3 VA1; scapte, O21 Y2 A–G; escap'te∧ OQ1. so it] ~, ~
B46 H3; ~'~ C9 O3 A–G. pleasd] pleased C2 C8 HH1 O3 TT1.
destinee] Destinie B32 B40 B46 C2 C9 H3 H5 H7 SN3 SN4 SP1; ~, C8 H6 H8;
Destinee, O20; ~. VA1.

12 (Guilty] ∧~ C9 H3 H5 H6 H7 NP2 O21 P3 TT1 VA1. my] this B13;
om O21. Sin] *om* OQ1; ~, VA1. of] in B13 B46 B47 C9 H6 H8 P3

VA1 B–F; *om*   O21 OQ1.   going)] ~),   C2; ~,   C9 H5 H6 NP2 P3; ~‸   H3
VA1; *om*   O21; ~,)   A–G.   to] *om*   O21.   thinke] *om*   O21.   mee] ~,
B32 C8 H4 HH1 O20; *om*   O21.

13 As prone to] *om*   O21.   all] *om*   B47 H8 LR1 O21 P3.   ill,] ~;   B13
H4; ~‸   LR1 O3 OQ1 TT1 VA2; *om*   O21; ~.   VA1.   and] *om*   P3 VA1.
of] to   C8; ~(→ ›as‹)   H3.   good] ~,   B32 O20 SP1; all ~   B47; ~;   O21;
my ~   OQ1.   forgett-] ~‸   H4; forgettfull‸   TT1; forgott=   Y2.

14 full,] ~‸   B46 H3 OQ1; =~,   H8 O3 P3 SN3; *om*   TT1.   proud,] ~, as
proude,   H3; ~‸   O3 O21 TT1 Y3.   lustfull,] ~‸   B32 NY1 O3 TT1 VA2;
as ~,   C2 C8 DT1 H4 HH1 LR1 NP2 OQ1 P3 VA1 A; as ~‸   H3; and ~,   H5;
~;   O21 Y3.   as much] asmuch   DT1; ~ farre   H4.   in debt,] ~ ~‸   B40
B46 C2 C8 H3 H4 H8 LR1 O3 O21 OQ1 P3 TT1 VA1 Y2 Y3; ~ ~.   B47; ~ ~:
HH1; indebt‸   NP2.

15 vayne,] ~‸   NP2 O3 O21 TT1 VA1 Y3 G.   as] and   B40 TT1.
wittlesse,] ~‸   B46 NP2 TT1 VA2; ~;   O21.   false] ~,   H5.   they] ~,   B32
HH1 O20; ~.   O21.

16 Which] that   OQ1.   dwell] dwelt   LR1; liue   P3 VA1.   at] in   C2 C8
LR1 A–G.   Court,] ~;   B13 H8 O21; ~.   B46 C9 H6 H7 NP2; ~‸   LR1 VA1.
for] ~,   C9 H6.   way.] C2 C8 HH1 LR1 NY3 A–G; ~;   B32 H5 NY1 O20 VA2;
~,   B40 C9 DT1 H6 SN4; ~:   P3; ~‸   Σ.

17 sufferd] suffered   B13 SP1 TT1 VA1 Y2 Y3 A; suffered,   DT1.   this.] ~;
B32 H5 H7 O20 O21 SP1 A–G; ~,   C2 C8 DT1 H4 HH1 O3 OQ1 TT1; ~:   H8
Y2; ~‸   NP2.   Towards] Toward   NY1 P3 VA2.   did] ther ~   HH1.   run]
~,   H4 OQ1; come   LR1 NP2.

18 thing] ~,   B40.   Strange,] ~‸   B13 B32 B46 B47 C9 H4 H6 HH1 IU2 LR1
NY1 O20 P3 SN3 SN4 TT1 VA1 VA2.   then] than   H3 IU2 SN3 B–G 44a–d.
on] one   B40 Y3; out   B46.   Niles] Nilus   B32 B40 C2 C8 DT1 H3 H4 H7 H8
LR1 NP2 O3 O20 P3 SP1 TT1 Y2.   slime,] C2 C8 DT1 H4 H7 NY3 SN4 Y2
A–G; shine‸   B13; slimes‸   C9 H6; ~‸   Σ.   Sun] ~,   H4; sonne   LR1.
    Alternate line: a thing more strange, then e'r came to NO-/AH,   33a–b.

19 Ere] are   HH1; hath   O3.   bredd;] B13 B32 B40 B46 NY3 O20 O21 SP1;
~‸   IU2; breed;   O3; breed,   Y2; ~,   Σ.   Or] *om*   O3.   all] ~ all   O3; *om*
O21 Y3.   which] that   B46 H5; *om*   IU2.   into] vnto   B46 O3; to   C2 C8
P3 VA1; in   IU2.   Noahs] Noes   C9 H6 LR1; ~,   H7.   came;] B40 DT1 H8
NY3 SN4; ~,   B13 B32 C2 C9 H5 H6 HH1 O20 O21 OQ1 44a–d; ~.   H7 NY1 P3
SP1 VA2; y^t ~‸   IU2; ~:   A–G 5; ~‸   Σ.

20 *om*   VA2.   A] *om*   IU2.   thing] ~,   B32 C2 DT1 O20 A; *om*   IU2;
think   LR1.   which] that   B46 Y2.   haue] *om*   H7; ha   IU2.   pos'd]
pas'd   B32; posed   B40 C2 C8 DT1 H3 H4 HH1 NP2 O3 TT1 Y2 5 44a–d.
Adam] ~ himself   IU2.   name;] B40 C9 DT1 NY3 SN4; ~.   B13 H8 SN3

44a–d; ~,   B32 C2 C8 H6 O20 OQ1 SP1 A 5; ~:   H5 B–G; ~∧   Σ.
 Alternate line: and would have pos'd ADAM himself / to name.   33a–b.

 21 Stranger] ~,   HH1.   then] than   NP2 C–G 44a–d.   seauen] Seau'en
H4; 7   H5 LR1 NP2 P3; ~,   VA1; the ~   5.   Antiquaries] Antigracies   HH1;
great ~   NY1 VA2.   Studyes,] ~∧   B13 B46 B47 C9 H3 H4 H7 LR1 NP2 NY1
O3 O21 P3 TT1 VA1 VA2 Y3; ~;   H8; ~:   HH1; ~.   5 44a–d.

 22 Then] om   B46; Than   H3 SN3 C–G 44a–d.   Africks] Affrick   B13 B32
B40 C2 C8 DT1 H3 H4 H7 H8 HH1 NP2 O20 P3 SN4 TT1 VA1 Y3; Guyana's
B46; Affrique-   SP1.   Monsters,] ~;   B46 H4; monster∧   LR1; ~∧   NP2 SN3
TT1.   Guyanas] Affricks   B46; or ~   O3; then ~   P3 VA1; Guinas   44a–d.
rarityes;] B40 DT1 H5 NY3; ~.   B32 C8 SP1 44a–d; ~∧   H3 H4 H7 LR1 NP2 NY1
O3 O21 P3 TT1 VA1 VA2 Y3; ~:   H8 HH1; ~,   Σ.

 23 Stranger] ~,   H7.   then] than   H3 IU2 SN3 C–G 44a–d.   Strangers;]
strangest.   B32 O20 SP1; ~,   B47 C9 H4 H5 H6 LR1 O3 O21 OQ1 33a–b; ~.
H3 P3 SN4 5 44a–d; Strangest,   H7 Y2; ~:   HH1 Y3 G; ~∧   IU2 SN3 TT1 VA1;
strangest∧   NP2; ~; (var: »strangest«)   NY1.   One] ~,   C2 DT1 A–C; is ~
SN3; om   5 44a–d.   who] ~,   D–G; om   5 44a–d.   for] far   LR1; om   5
44a–d.   a] om   5 44a–d.   Dane] ~,   OQ1 A–G 33a–b; om   5 44a–d.

 24 In] At   O3.   massacre] ~,   B46 B47 C8 O21 Y2 Y3 33a–b.   sure beene]
bene sure   P3 VA1.   slayne,] B32 B40 C2 C8 C9 H5 H6 NY3 O20 O21 VA2 Y2
A–G; ~.   NY1; ~;   SN3; ~∧   Σ.

 25 If] om   B46 IU2.   he had] had he   B46 IU2; he   B47.   liud then;] B13
H8 NY1 NY3 SN4 VA2 A–G; lived ~;   B32 B40 C2 O20 VA1; liud ~,   C8 H5
H7 HH1 O21 Y3; liud ~:   LR1; then liud;   O3; liud ~∧   TT1; ~ ~,   Σ.
And] nay   IU2.   without] wᵗʰ out   C2 VA2; ~,   VA1; '~   D–F.   helpe] ~,
B47; doubt   IU2.   dyes] ~,   B32 B40 C2 DT1 HH1 O20 OQ1 SP1 A–G 33a–b;
~.   H6; he ~   IU2.

 26 the] our   H3; om   TT1.   Prentises] ~,   H3 HH1 33a–b.   'gainst]
against   B13 B32 B40 B46 LR1 O20 OQ1 P3 SP1 TT1 VA1 Y2.   rise.] ~,   B32
C8 HH1; ~;   B40 DT1 H4 O20 SN3; ~∧   B46 B47 H3 IU2 NP2 O3 O21 P3 TT1
VA1 Y2; ~:   H5 OQ1 Y3.

 27 One] ~,   B13 B32 B40 B46 B47 C2 H7 HH1 A–C; on   O3 33a–b; he   P3.
the] he   B40.   at] of   Y2.   noone] none   H3; ~,   H4 HH1 Y3.   letts
scarse] scarce let's   B46 O3 Y2.   by;] B40 DT1 NY3 G; ~,   B13 H5 H6 H8 HH1
O20 SN4 SP1 A–C 33a–b; ~.   C2 H4; ~,∧   OQ1; ~∧   Σ.
 Alternate line: Whome watch woud ask at noneday who He were   IU2.

 28 One] ~,   B13 B32 B47 C2 C8 O20 SP1 A–G; om   B46 O3; And   HH1; he
P3.   to'whom] LR1 NY3; to whome,   B40 C2 C8 DT1 A–F; whom   B47;
to whome   Σ.   th'examining] C8 C9 H5 H6 H7 LR1 NY1 NY3 P3 SN4 VA2;
the examning   HH1; the Examinge   O3; the examinine   VA1; the examininge
Σ.   Iustice] ~,   C2 C8 O21; Iustices   H5 NP2.   sure would] om ~   H5 NP2

P3 VA1; would sure   HH1; ~ will   O20 SP1.   cry] ~,   C2 DT1 OQ1 A–G; ~;
C8; ~.   O20.

29 Sir,] B32 B40 C2 DT1 H5 H7 NY3 O3 O20 SP1 A–G; ~∧   Σ.   Priesthood]
~,   B32 B46 C8 H5 HH1 O20 SP1 VA1; Preists=hoode   H3; preist-hood   P3.
what] who   O3 OQ1.   you] yᵉ B46 SN3.   are.] ~,   B32 O21; ~;   B40 C8
HH1; ~∧   B47 H3 H4 H7 LR1 NP2 O3 O20 P3 TT1 VA1 Y2 Y3; ~:   H8; ~?   NY1
OQ1 VA2.

30 clothes] ~,   VA1.   were] weare   NY3 O3 O20 SN4.   strange,] graue∧
B46; ~∧   B47 DT1 H4 HH1 IU2 LR1 NP2 NY1 OQ1 P3 SN3 SN4 TT1 VA2.
though] but   IU2.   course;] B40 C9 NY3; ~∧   B47 LR1 NP2 NY1 O3 SN3 TT1
Y3; curse,   H3; coarse∧   IU2; coarse;   A–G; ~,   Σ.   and] though   LR1.
black] ~;   B13; ~,   B32 B40 C2 C9 H3 H5 H8 O20 SN4 SP1 Y2 A–F.   though]
&   B47 IU2 O21 Y3; (~   H7; yet   LR1.   bare.] B32 B46 NY1 NY3 O20 VA2; ~,
B13 B40 C2 C8 H8 O21 OQ1 SN3 SN4; ~;   C9 DT1 SP1 A B; ~:   H5; ~∧   Σ.

31 Sleeuelesse] Sleeue-les   H5 NY1 VA2.   Ierkin] Ierking   O3.   was,] ~∧
H7 HH1 NP2 NY1 SN3 TT1 VA2; ~:   Y3.   and] (~   B32.   it] yet   B13.
beene] ~,   H4 HH1 O21.
      Alternate line: Whose sleevelesse jerkin was tufft-taffaty,   33a–b.

32 Veluett;] B32 C2 C8 DT1 H4 NY3 O3 O20 O21 Y3; ~∧   HH1 TT1 VA1; ~:
NP2 SP1; ~,   Σ.   but] &   O21.   t'was] was   H3 H5 O21 Y3; ~,   H6; it was
SN3 Y2.   now] *om*   B32 LR1 NP2; ~,   B40 H6 O3 O20 O21 SP1; none   HH1
Y2.   (so] ∧~   H4 TT1; (,~   HH1.   ground] the ~   SN3 SN4.   seene)] ~∧
B40 H4 TT1; sinn)   Y3.

33 Become tufftaffeta;] ~ ~,   B13 NP2 O21 P3 SN4 VA2 Y3; ~ Tufftaffitye;
B32 H5 O3 O20; ~ Tuftaffetæ;   B40; Tufftaffata become,   B47 H6; ~ Tuftaffatye;
C2 H4 H8 A–G; ~ Tuftaffetie: C8; Tufftaffata become∧   C9; ~ Tufftaffatie.   H3;
Tuff-taffata become,   H7; ~ ~∧   LR1 TT1; ~ Tuff=tafata,   NY1 OQ1; ~ Tufftafta,
SN3; ~ *Taffata*,   SP1 Y2; ~ ~.   VA1.   shall] ~,   HH1; ~ -   OQ1.

34 See it] seet   B47.   awhile,] B46 B47 H8 NY3 O20 O21 SN3 Y2 A–C;
while,   B40; ~∧   H4; a while;   HH1; a while∧   LR1 P3 SN4 TT1; a while,   Σ.
then] ~,   B13; that   H3(*var*: »~«).   all.] ~,.   B40; ~∧   B47 H3 H4 H7 LR1
NP2 O3 O21 P3 Y3; ~,   HH1 OQ1.

35 This] the   B47 C9 H6 B–G; (~   HH1; Thus   Y2.   thing] ~,   SP1; things
Y2.   hath] haue   H8 Y2; has   IU2.   trauaild,] travel'd,   B13 B46 DT1 H4
H5 H8 HH1 NP2 O3 SN3; ~∧   B47 IU2 LR1 VA2; ~;   NY1 O21; travailed∧
OQ1; trauelld∧   TT1 Y3; traueled,   Y2.   and] ~,   C9 H6.   sayth,] ~∧   B13
B40 B47 DT1 H3 H4 H7 H8 LR1 O21 P3 TT1 VA1 VA2 Y2 Y3; (faith)   B46; (~)
H5 HH1; sais∧   IU2; saieth∧   NP2 O3; faith∧ (M *var*: »~∧«)   NY1; sayeth,   SN3;
faith,   G.   speakes] he ~   H3 H7 H8 Y2; speake   O21.   tongs] ~,   B13 B40
C2 DT1 H5 HH1 SN4 B–G; ~.   B32 O20.

36 only] also   LR1 NP2.   knowes] ~,   B32 H5 O20 O21 SP1; knoweth,   B40

C8; knoweth   C2 DT1 H4 LR1 TT1 A–G.   what] *om*   B13 B47 C9 H6 H8
OQ1 P3 VA1.   States] state   B47 H4.   belongs.] what ~.   B13 C9 H8 P3; ~;
B40; ~∧   B46 C8 H3 H4 IU2 LR1 NP2 O3 TT1 Y2 Y3; what ~∧   B47 VA1; ~,
C2 DT1 O21 SN3 A; what ~,   H6 OQ1.

37 th'accents,] B40 C2 C8 DT1 H4 NY3 A–G; the accents∧   C9 H3 H6 H8 NY1
TT1 VA2 Y3; the accent∧   H5 LR1 NP2 P3 SN4; the antient∧   SN3; the accend,
VA1; the accents,   Σ.   of] yᵗ NP2.   all] *om*   B32 B46 C9 H3 H5 H6 H8
LR1 NP2 O3 O20 OQ1 P3 SN3 SN4 SP1 VA1 Y2.   these] ~,   B32 B40 C2 C8
DT1 O3 A–F; ~.   HH1 G.

38 one] no   B13 OQ1 P3 VA1; on   B40 B47; a   LR1 O3; no ›→ a‹   NP2;
strange   TT1.   Language.] ~;   B32 B46 C2 C8 H4 H5 O3 O21 A; ~,   B47 H7
OQ1 P3 VA1 G; ~:   HH1 O20 SP1 Y2; ~∧   TT1.   strange] stronge   B13.
meats] meat   B47(→ ›~‹) LR1; meales   O3.   displease] ~.   B13 G; ~,   B32 C8
DT1 H5 O20 OQ1 A–F; ~;   C2.

39 deceaue,] ~∧   LR1 NP2 NY1 TT1 VA2 Y3.   force] ~,   B32.   my] his
B46; a   O3; may   Y2.   tast.] B32 B40 B46 H6 NY3 O20 SN4; ~∧   B13 B47 H3
H4 H7 LR1 NP2 OQ1 SN3 TT1 VA1 Y2 Y3; ~;   DT1 HH1 O3; fast∧   O21; ~,   Σ.

40 Pedants] Pedant's   B46 H4; pedant   HH1; ~⁔ SP1; ~,   D–F.   motley]
mothy   C9; ~⁔ H5 H7 SP1.   tong,] NY1 NY3 SN3; tongue;   B13; tongues,
B46 B47 C9 H6; tongue.   H3; ~∧   LR1 TT1; ~;   O21; toung,   Σ.   bumbast,]
B32 C2 C9 DT1 H5 H8 NY3 O20 OQ1 P3 SN4 VA2 A–G; bum baste,   C8;
bombart∧   HH1; ~∧   Σ.

41 Montebancks] Mountbanks   B13(Mount'bancks) H8 HH1 OQ1 VA1;
Mountebancke   B32 C9 LR1 O20 SP1; mountebackes   B47; Mount-bankes   NP2;
Mountbank   P3.   druggtong,] B40 C2 H7 NY3 A–F; drugg tongue,   B13 H8
HH1 O3 OQ1 SN3 Y2; drug tounge;   B32 O20; drugs-tongue,   B46; ~∧   LR1;
drugg-tongue∧   NP2; drugs∧   P3; drugg toung: SP1; drugg tonge∧   TT1; drugge,
VA1; drugg=tounge,   Σ.   nor the] no=~   B47; ~ our   H3.   Law] ~,   B32
HH1 O20 O21 OQ1 P3 G.

42 Strong] strange   O3 P3.   inough preparatiues,] B13 B40 DT1 HH1 NY3
O20 A–C; Preparatiues enough∧   B46 B47 C9 H6 OQ1; ~ preparyatiues∧   O3; ~
preparations∧   SN3; ~ ~∧   Σ.   draw] ~.   C8; ~,   HH1; ~ ⁔ OQ1.

43 Mee,] NY3; ~;   O21; ~∧   Σ.   beare] heare   H7 LR1 G; leaue   O3.
this;] ~.   B13 NP2 VA2; ~,   B47 C2 C8 O3 O21 SN3 SN4 Y2 A–G; ~:   C9 H6
H8 LR1 NY1 P3 SP1 VA1 Y3; ~∧   TT1.   yet] But   H3 H5 LR1 NP2.
I must] must I   SN3 SN4.   content] ~,   B40 HH1 O21; ~.   OQ1.

44 his] this   H7.   tong,] NY1 NY3 SN4; tongue∧   C9 H3 H8 NP2 P3 Y2 Y3;
~∧   LR1 TT1; tongue: A–F; tongue,   Σ.   in] (~ O3; calld ~   P3.   tong]
LR1 NY3 TT1; tongue,   B13 B32 C2 C8 H7 O20 SP1 A–F; tongue's   B46; ~,
DT1 H4; tongue)   O3; tongue∧   Σ.   calld] cold   B46; cull'd   C8; *om*   P3;

called TT1.   Complement,] SN3; ~.   B32 C9 HH1 NY3 O20 SN4 SP1; ~,.
B40; ~:   C2 C8 H5 NY1 O21 OQ1 VA2 A–G; ~;   DT1; ~∧ Σ.

45 In] W^th B13 O3; (~ HH1.   win] wooe H3 P3; woe, VA1.
Widows;] B40 H4 NY3 O21; ~∧   B47 C9 H7 LR1 NP2 O3 TT1; ~, Σ.   and] or
B46; *om* P3 VA1.   skores;] B32 B40 DT1 NY3; ~,   B13 C2 C8 C9 H5 H8 OQ1
SN3 SN4 SP1 VA2 A–G; ~∧ Σ.

46 speake] ~, VA1.   treason;] B32 H3 NY3 O20 SP1; ~∧   LR1 P3 TT1 Y2; ~,
Σ.   subtilst] B13 B32 C9 H6 H7 NP2 NY3 O20 SN4 SP1; Subtle H3 P3 Y2;
subtellest HH1 NY1 OQ1 SN3 VA2; Subtliest O3; suttlest Σ.   whores;] B32
B40 DT1 NY3 SP1; ~∧   B46 B47 C9 H3 H6 LR1 NP2 NY1 O3 O21 P3 TT1 VA1
VA2 Y3; ~. O20; ~, Σ.

47 Outflatter] B46 C9 H4 NY3 O21 SN4 SP1 B–F; out feather B47; Out=flatter
C8 DT1 H5 H6 H7 H8 A G; *Who could out flatter* 33a; *Who could out-flatter*
33b; Out flatter Σ.   fauorites;] B40 NY3; ~∧   B46 LR1 O3 TT1 Y3; ~, Σ.
and] or B40 C2 C8 DT1 H4 TT1 A–G; *om* 33a–b.   out-ly] C9 H6 H8 NY1
OQ1 SN3 SN4 VA2; ~∧ ~ B13 B40 B47 C2 H3 H7 LR1 NP2 O3 P3 VA1 Y3
33a–b; onlie Y2; outlye Σ.   either] ~, C8 33a–b; ei=ther HH1; ~; G.

48 *om* B47.   Iouius;] NY3 O20 O21; ~∧   C9 H3 H8 LR1 NP2 NY1 O3 OQ1
P3 SN3 SN4 TT1 VA2 Y2 Y3; ~, (M *var*: ›Iunius,‹) H4; ~, Σ.   or] of H8;
and 33a–b.   Surius;] B40 NY3; Snodons∧ B13; Sleydan∧ C9 NP2 OQ1; ~∧
H4 LR1 O3; ~, (M *var*: ›sleidan,‹) H5; Sleydan, H6(*var*: ›~‹); *Turius*, H8; Sarius,
HH1; Curius; O21; Steyden∧ P3; Sucius, SN3 SN4; *Sucius*∧ SP1; *Lurius*∧
TT1; *Slydan*, VA1; Suvius∧ Y2; Curius, Y3; ~, Σ.   together.] ~∧ B13 H4
LR1 NP2 O3 O21 TT1 VA1 Y3; ~.l H7; ~.) HH1; ~; NY1; ~: OQ1 Y2.

49 me,'and] NY3; me∧ and B47 C9 H3 H6 LR1 NY1 O3 OQ1 P3 TT1 VA2 Y2
Y3; me, and Σ.   comes] names NP2; come SN3.   me,] ~. B13 C9 H6
P3 VA1; ~; B32 H8 NY1 O20 O21 VA2 Y2 A–G; ~∧   B46 LR1 O3 TT1; ~:
OQ1 SP1.   I] (~ B46.   whisper,] ~; B32 H6 O21; whispd, B47 NY1 VA2;
~∧ LR1 SN3 SN4 TT1 Y3; whispered: O3 OQ1.   God,] B32 B40 C2 C8 DT1
HH1 NY3 O20 P3 SN4; ~! C9 NY1 VA2 A–C; ~l. H6; (~∧ LR1; ~∧ Σ.

50 sin'd,] ~? B13; sinned, B40 C2 C8 HH1; ~∧   B46 B47 C9 DT1 H6 H7 H8
NY1 O21 P3 SN3 VA1 Y2 Y3; sinned∧ LR1 NP2 O3 TT1 VA2.   wraths] wrath
B32 O20 Y3; wreathes SN3; *wrath-* SP1.   furious] ~~ SP1.   rod,] B32 B40
H6 NY3 SN4 A–G; ~∧ Σ.

51 This] That ~ H3; (~ H8 NY1 O3 P3 VA2.   fellow,] ~∧ C8 H3 H5
HH1 LR1 NP2 O21 OQ1 SN4 SP1 TT1 VA1 Y2 Y3 A; ~) H8 NY1 O3 P3 VA2.
chuseth] choseth C2 C8 LR1 VA1; Crosseth O3; chaseth O21 Y3.   me?] ~,
B40 B47 O21; ~) B46; ~. H5 OQ1; ~; HH1 Y3 C–G; ~!) LR1; ~∧ O3 TT1;
~! SP1; ~: Y2.   sayth,] ~∧ B13 B46 C8 H3 H4 HH1 LR1 O21 SN4 Y2 Y3;
sayeth, H6 H8 NP2; sayeth∧ O3 SN3; ~: OQ1; saieth. TT1.   Sir,] B47 C2
C9 DT1 NY3 SN4 SP1 A–G; ~! NY1 VA2; ~∧ Σ.

52 loue] like   H3 H5 LR1 NP2 P3 VA1.   iudgment;] B32 C2 C8 C9 NY3
A–C; ~ₐ   B46 LR1 O3 O21 SN3 TT1; ~. H6 P3; ~,   Σ.   you]
ye SN3.   prefer] ~,   O21 A–G.
   Alternate line: whom I / thought   33a–b.

53 the] yoͬ   OQ1 P3 VA1.   Linguist?] ~;   B40 Y3; ~,   C9 H3 H6 H7 HH1
O3 SN3 VA1 Y2; ~ₐ   O21; linguistes? OQ1 TT1.   I selely] seelily I   B13 B46
P3 VA1; sillylie I,   OQ1.
   Alternate line: the best linguist, I see *Lily*   33a–b.

54 Sayd,] ~ₐ   C9 H3 H4 H6 H7 H8 HH1 LR1 NY1 O3 O21 OQ1 P3 TT1 VA1
VA2 Y2 Y3 G.   that] om   B13 H3 H7 OQ1 P3 SN3 SN4 VA1.   thought,]
B32 B40 NY3 O20 O21 SP1; though ₐ   C8 H8; ~ₐ   Σ.   Calepines] Calepinus
SN3.   Dictionary.] ~,   B40 B47 C2 C8 OQ1; ~ₐ   H3 H4 H6 HH1 LR1 NP2
O3 O21 TT1 VA1 Y2 Y3; ~:   SN3; ~;   SN4 A; ~.| SP1.
   Alternate line: answer'd / *CALEPINE*, 33a–b.

55 Nay,] B40 B46 B47 C2 C8 DT1 H4 HH1 NY3 A–G; ~ₐ   Σ.   Men,] ~?
B47 O21 SP1; ~ₐ   H4 H5 H8 HH1 LR1 NP2 NY1 O3 P3 SN4 TT1 VA1 VA2 Y2.
most] (~   H5 LR1 O3; om   Y2.   sweete] ~?   B47; ~,   H6 HH1.   Sir;] NY3;
~.   B40 C9 P3 TT1 A–G; ~?   B46 DT1 H8 NP2 NY1 VA2; ~,   C2 O20 OQ1
SN4; ~ₐ → ~»,«   C8; ~!   H4 H7; ~)   H5 LR1 O3; ~,.   H6; ~ₐ   Σ.   Beza] ~,
B13 B47 C9 H6 LR1 NY1.   then,] B32 B40 C2 C8 C9 DT1 H5 H6 NY3 O20
SN4 A–G; th**ₐ   HH1; ~ₐ   Σ.

56 Some] ~ other   SN3 SN4.   Iesuits,] ~ₐ   B46 C9 H3 H6 O3 O21 SN3
TT1; ~;   H5; Iesuists,   P3; Iesuite,   Y2.   two] ~ most   C9 H6; some   H3;
~ other   H7 H8 Y2.   reuerend] reuerent   B13 B40 LR1 NY3 O3 P3 TT1 VA1
Y2.   men] ~,   O21.

57 Academyes] ~,   B40 C2 C8 HH1 O21 Y2 Y3 A; Academie's,   H3; accademes
O3.   I] om   O21 Y3.   nam'd;] named: B13 H7 LR1; ~ₐ   B32 O3 O21 Y3;
named;   B40 TT1 A–G; ~.   B46 C9 NY1 OQ1 P3 SN4 VA2; ~,   B47 C2 O20
SN3 SP1; named,   C8 DT1 HH1; named ₐ   H3 H4 NP2 Y2; ~:   H8.   There]
~,   B40(→ ›then,‹ HH1; and ~   H5; here   B–G.

58 stopd] DT1 H3 H6 NY1 NY3 VA2; stopped   HH1; stopt   Σ.   me;] ~;ₐ
B32 B40 O20; ~ₐₐ   B46 C9 H8 LR1 NY1 O21 P3 TT1 VA2 Y3; ~'; NY3; ~,ₐ   Σ.
sayd;] B40 H8 NY3 VA1 A; ~ₐ   B13 H3 HH1 O3 O21 TT1 Y3; ~.   C9 H6; ~:
H5 LR1 NY1 VA2 B–G; ~,   Σ.   Nay,] B32 B40 C2 DT1 H3 H4 H8 HH1 NY3
O20 SN4 A–G; om   O3; ~ₐ   Σ.

59 Good pretty] pretty good   B13 B46 B47 C9 H3 H6 H7 H8 OQ1 P3 VA1; & ~
O21 Y3.   Linguists;] B40 NY1 NY3 O21 SN3 VA2 Y2; ~ₐ   B46 O3 TT1; ~:   H8
LR1; ~.   OQ1 VA1; ~?   Y3; ~,   Σ.   and] om   C9 H6 H8 O3 G.   so] om
B32 O20 SP1.   Panurge] Panargus   B13 H7; Panurgus   B46 B47 C9 H6 H8
NY1 OQ1 P3 VA1 VA2 G; Panury   HH1; Panurage   O21 Y3.   was,] B13 DT1
H8 NY1 OQ1; ~;   B40 NP2 SN4 A–G; ~.   C2 C8 O20 VA2; ~:   H5; ~ₐ   Σ.

60 Yet] But   C9 H3 H5 H6 NP2; though   LR1.   gentleman] ~,   B40 B47 C2
DT1 H3 H4 H8 HH1 LR1 P3 SN3 SP1 Y3; ~:   H7; ~.   NP2; ~;   O21 A–G;
Gentlemen   SN4; gent: Y2.   pas] ~,   B32 C8 O20; ~;   O21; ~.   Y2 G.

61 By] But   G.   trauaile.] travell.   B13 C9 H6; ~;   B32 DT1 H4 NY1 O20
SN4 SP1 VA2; travile,   C2 OQ1; ~,   C8 O21; travell;   H5 O3 SN3 Y2; ~ₐ   H7
TT1 G; ~:   HH1 LR1.   Then] ~,   C2 C8 H6 P3 A–G; That   H3(var: »~«).
yf] *om*   H3.

62 tong] B13 B40 DT1 H3 H4 LR1 NY1 NY3 SN3 SP1 TT1 VA2 Y2 Y3; ~;   O21;
~, Σ.   praysd] praised   B32(prays›e‹d) HH1 O3 O20 P3 TT1 A–G; phraisd
VA1.   it,] ~ₐ   C9 LR1 NP2 O3 TT1 VA1 Y3; that,   H3; ~;   H5.   such] *om*
B32 O20 SP1.   wonders] ~wo*d*s → ~‹   B40; words   C2 C8 DT1 H4 TT1 A;
wonder   NP2.   told] ~,   B32 B40 DT1 H5 H8 O20 B–G; ~.   B46.

63 say;] B13 B40 LR1 NY3 O20 O21; ~ₐ   B46 B47 NP2 NY1 O3 TT1 VA2; ~.
H6; ~:   H7 OQ1 P3 SP1; ~,   Σ.   If you had] Had yoʷ   H3 H5 H7 H8 LR1
NP2 P3 VA1 Y2; ~ ~'~   A–C.   liud,] H5 H6 NY3 O20 A–G; liued ₐ   B47 DT1
H4 HH1 O3 O21 TT1 Y2 Y3; lived,   C2; ~ₐ Σ.   Sir,] B32 B40 H5 H6 NY3
A–G; ~ₐ Σ.

64 inough] enought   H7.   to haue] t'~   B46 O3; 't ~   SN4; to *om*   TT1.
beene] be   TT1.   Interpreter] an ~   B13 B47 O3 VA2; ~,   DT1 HH1; an ~.
NY1; a ~   OQ1.

65 Babels] ~=   B40 SP1; Babell   OQ1.   bricklayers,] ~ₐ   B47 C2 LR1 NY1
O3; bricke layers,   H3 SN3; Bricke-layers,   H5 H8 VA2 Y2; brick-layers ₐ   H7;
Brick Layers ₐ   TT1.   sure] sur[*blot*]   B40; *om*   C9 H6.   that] B32 H5 H7
HH1 LR1 NP2 NY1 NY3 O20 SN3 SN4 SP1 VA2 Y2; the   Σ.   tower] Towne
SN4.   stood.] ~ₐ   B13 B47 H3 H4 H7 HH1 LR1 O3 O21 SN4 TT1 VA1 Y2 Y3;
~:   B32 O20 OQ1; ~,   SN3 C.

66 adds;] B40 NY3 O3; answerd ₐ   B46; ~ₐ   H3 LR1 NP2 NY1 O21 TT1 VA2
Y3; answears,   H5; ~.   OQ1 P3 VA1; answers ₐ   SN3; ~, Σ.   of] ~ our   B32
O20 SP1 Y2; oʳ   H7; ~ yᵉ   LR1 NP2 NY1 VA2.   Court Life] ~ ~,   B32 H3 H4
H7 O20 O21; Courtlife   B40 C2 C9; ~=~   C8 H5 VA2; ~·~,   SP1.   you] yee
SN3.   knew] know   B40(»~«) C8 TT1.   good] ~,   B13 B40 C8 DT1 H5
HH1 P3 SP1 A–G; ~;   B32; Good,   C2; Good   H3 SN3; Good;   O20; ~ ·
OQ1.

67 Lonenes.] ~;   B32 HH1 O20 O21; lonelinesse.   B40; lonelynes;   C2 C8 A;
lone-nesse.   C9 NP2; lonelinesse,   DT1 H4; lownesse,   H3; ~:   H5 LR1 SP1; ~,
H7 OQ1 P3 SN3 SN4 Y2 Y3 lonelines ₐ   TT1.   I] *om*   OQ1.   sayd,] ~ₐ   B32
C2 C8 DT1 H3 H4 LR1 NP2 NY1 P3 SN4 SP1 TT1 VA1 VA2 Y2 Y3; ~.   B46; ~;
O21; *om*   OQ1.   not] Sʳ ~   OQ1 P3 VA1.   alone] ~,   HH1 B–G.
    Alternate line: You would leaue Loanes and youʳ Natiue nation   O3.

68 Lonenes] lonelynes   B40 C2 C8 DT1 H4 TT1 A; lone-nesse   C9; lownesse
H3.   is;] B32 NY3 O20 SN4 SP1; ~.   B13 B46 C9 H6; ~:   B47 H5 NP2; ~ₐ

H_3 H_4 H_8 O_{21} SN_3 TT_1 VA_1 Y_2 Y_3; ~! LR_1; ~, Σ.   Spartanes] Spartan's
H_3.   fashione] ~, B_{32} B_{40} C_2 C_8 DT_1 HH_1 O_{20} O_{21} SN_3 A; ~.| H_3; ~.
NY_1 B–G.

Alternate line: But I replied that sure the Spartane fashion O_3.

69 To] (~ P_3.   by] (~ H_3; my Y_2.   paynting] ~; B_{32}; ~, C_2 C_8 DT_1
H_4 H_7 O_{20}.   Drunkards] ~, B_{13} B_{47} H_5 HH_1 LR_1 NP_2 A–C; ~; B_{46};
drunkeness) H_3; ~: O_{21}; ~) P_3 VA_1.   doth] doe H_4 H_7 NP_2 O_{21} SP_1 Y_3;
I do LR_1.   last] tast B_{13} C_9 H_6 H_7 LR_1 NP_2 TT_1 B–F; ~, B_{32} C_2 H_5 O_{20}
O_{21} G; taste; B_{46}; tast, OQ_1.

70 Now;] B_{32} B_{40} H_8 NY_1 NY_3 O_{20} VA_2 A–F; ~, B_{46} C_2 C_8 SN_4 Y_2; Nor∧
H_7; om LR_1; how∧ NP_2; And∧ O_3; ~: SP_1; ~∧ Σ.   Pictures] ~, C_8 H_7
VA_1.   haue] om O_{21}.   made] make O_{21}; ~, P_3.   few] ~ men H_5 H_7
LR_1 Y_2.   chast.] B_{40} NY_3 SN_4 SP_1 VA_1; ~∧ B_{46} B_{47} H_3 H_7 HH_1 LR_1 NP_2
O_3 OQ_1 P_3 TT_1 Y_3; ~, C_9 H_6 SN_3; ~: DT_1 H_8 Y_2; ~; Σ.

71 can] doe B_{46}; are H_3; then P_3.   Courts] ~, B_{13} C_2 C_8 DT_1 H_4 H_6
NY_3 O_{20} SN_3 SN_4 VA_1 Y_3 A–G; ~; B_{40} O_{21}.   (though] ∧~ B_{40} C_2 C_8
DT_1 H_4 H_7 NY_3 O_{21} SN_3 SN_4 TT_1 Y_3 A–G; ∧thought VA_1.   ther be]
therebe C_9 NY_3; they ~ H_3(»→ ~« ~).   few] fe* HH_1(M var: »seene«); ~)
VA_2 Y_2.

72 Better] but B_{47}; Betters H_3(→ »~«).   of] in Y_2.   Vice)] ~; B_{40}
H_4; ~, C_2 C_8 DT_1 H_7 NY_3 SN_3 SN_4 Y_3 A–G; ~.) H_6; ~), NY_1; ~∧ O_{21} TT_1
VA_1.   teach] to ~ O_3.   me] men NY_1 O_3 VA_2.   vertu.] ~; B_{32} B_{40}
C_2 C_8 Y_2 A; ~∧ B_{46} H_3 H_4 HH_1 NP_2 O_3 O_{21} OQ_1 P_3 VA_1 Y_3; ~, O_{20}; the
~∧ TT_1.

73 He] ~, B_{47} C_2 C_8 DT_1 H_4 SP_1 A–C.   like] lide H_3(var: »~«).   to'a]
to B_{46} SN_3; a B_{47} C_8 H_3 H_7 H_8 IU_2 LR_1 O_3 O_{21} P_3 SP_1 Y_3; an H_5 NP_2;
a too HH_1 NY_1 VA_2; a to' NY_3; to an OQ_1 VA_1 Y_2; to a Σ.   high] ~=
B_{46} B_{47} DT_1 H_4 H_7 H_8 HH_1 NY_1 OQ_1 SN_3 VA_2 B–G; om O_3.   stretchd]
B_{32} DT_1 H_6 H_8 NY_1 NY_3 O_3 O_{20} SN_4 SP_1; stretcht= B_{46}; stretched- B_{47};
strecht, C_8; ore-stretched' H_5; stretched HH_1; out stretcht LR_1 NP_2; stretcht
Σ.   Lute String] Lutestringe, B_{13}; ~=~ B_{46} B_{47} H_4 H_5 H_7 OQ_1 VA_2 B–G;
Lutestring C_9 H_6 HH_1 TT_1; ~ om IU_2; ~ ~, P_3 VA_1; ~ stringes SN_3.
squeakd,] DT_1 NP_2 NY_1 NY_3; squeakt∧ B_{13} O_3 O_{21} P_3 TT_1 VA_1 VA_2 Y_3; ~∧
B_{32}; Squee'sd, B_{46}; squeaks∧ B_{47} H_3; squeaks, C_9 H_6 SP_1; squeakt; H_4;
sq'ueakes; H_8; squeaked∧ HH_1; squeektout∧ IU_2; ~: LR_1; ~. O_{20}; squakt|
SN_3; cried∧ Y_2; Squeak't, Σ.   Oh] ~. B_{46}; ~, C_9 HH_1 O_{20}; om H_5 P_3.
Sir,] B_{32} B_{40} C_2 C_8 C_9 DT_1 NY_3 O_{20} A–G; ~! NY_1; ~∧ Σ.

74 Tis] Its SN_3.   sweete] ~, B_{40}.   talke] talk ~ O_3.   Kings.] ~,
B_{13} C_2 C_8 H_7 P_3; ~; B_{32} DT_1 H_4 NY_1 O_{20} SP_1 VA_2; ~∧ B_{40} B_{47} H_3 HH_1
O_3 O_{21} OQ_1 SN_3 TT_1 Y_3; ~: H_5 H_8 Y_2.   At] In B_{46} B_{47} C_9 H_6; A H_7.
Westminster] ~. B_{13} HH_1; West-Minster H_5 SP_1; westmister LR_1; ~, O_{21}
SN_3 A–G; Westminister Y_2.

75 Sayd] (~   C9 H5 H6 O3 O21 SN4 Y3.   I,] ~∧   B13 LR1 P3 SN3 TT1 VA1;
~;   B46 H4; ~)   C9 H5 H6 O3 O21 SN4 Y3; om   H3(→ »~∧«); ~:   H8.
Abbey] Abbeys   HH1; Abbot   LR1.   tombes] ~,   B32 B40 C2 C8 DT1 H5
O20 OQ1 SP1 A–G; Tomes   SN3 SN4.

76 price] ~,   B13 B46 B47 H7; pennie   H3 H5 LR1 NP2.   doth,] B13 B32
B40 DT1 H4 H5 HH1 NY3 O20 SP1; om   LR1; doeth∧   NY1 VA1; ~∧   Σ.
with] om   H3(»~«) H5 LR1 NP2; to all   O3.   whoeuer] C9 H5 NY1 NY3 O3
O21 SN4 Y3; soeuer   H7(var: »~«); whosoever   HH1; (who ever   LR1; whoe euer
Σ.   comes] ~,   B32 C2 C8 DT1 HH1 O20 O21 A–G; ~)   LR1; ~:   OQ1.

77 our] Sir → ›~‹   B40; Sir   TT1.   Harryes,] ~∧   B46 B47 C2 C8 C9 H6 H8
NP2 NY1 O3 O21 OQ1 SN3 TT1 VA2 Y3; Henries∧   H3 H5 LR1.   our] Sr →
›~‹   B40; om   NP2; of   O3; all ~   P3 VA1; Sir   TT1.   talke,] ~∧   B47 C9 H3
H4 H6 H7 NP2 NY1 NY3 O3 O20 OQ1 P3 SN3 SN4 SP1 TT1 VA1 VA2 Y2 Y3;
talks∧   LR1.

78 king,] B40 C2 H4 H7 NY3 SN4 VA1; ~∧   Σ.   king,] ~;   H7; ~∧   LR1 NY1
O3 SN3 SN4 TT1 Y3 A.   and] ore   O21 Y3; om   TT1.   all] not   LR1 NP2;
om   TT1.   their] a   LR1 NP2; or   O21; om   TT1.   kinne] ~,   HH1; king
LR1 NP2; line   O21 Y3; om   TT1.   can] will   LR1 NP2; ore   O3; om   TT1.
walke,] ~∧   B13 B47 C8 C9 H3 H4 H6 H7 O3 O21 P3 VA1 Y2 Y3; ~;   H5; balke∧
LR1 NP2; ~.   NY1 VA2; om   TT1; ~:   A–G.

79 Your] you   H5 LR1 NP2; om   TT1.   eares] om   H5 LR1 NP2 TT1.
shall] om   TT1.   heare] hire   NP2; ~,   O21; om   TT1.   nought] ~,   C2 H3
SN3 A–F; nothing   HH1.   king;] NY3 O21; ~∧   B13 B46 H3 Y3; ~,   B32 C9
H6 O20 P3 SN3 SN4 SP1 VA1; Kinges; → ~;   B40; kings∧   HH1 LR1 O3 TT1;
Kings;   A–G; kings,   Σ.   your] and ~   H3 O3.   meet] ~[trimmed]   H8; ~;
HH1; ~.| TT1.

80 Kings] Kinge   O3.   only;] B13 B40 DT1 NY3 VA2 A–G; ~:   H8; ~.   P3
VA1; ~∧   TT1 Y3; ~,   Σ.   the] & ~   LR1 NP2.   to it,] B40 C2 NY3 A; ~'~∧
B46 NY1 VA2; ~ ~∧   Σ.   is] om   B47; ~,   H5.   kings Street.] King ~,   B32;
King ~;   B40 O20; Kingstreet: B46; ~ ~∧   B47 C8(~ ~».«) H3 NP2 O21 TT1
VA1 Y3; Kingstreete.   C2 A–C; ~-~.   C9 H5 H7 NY1 SP1 VA2; king ~.   DT1;
kingestreete∧   H4 LR1; Kinge ~∧   O3; ~ ~:   OQ1 Y2; ~ ~;   SN3.

81 smackd,] smackt,   B13 DT1 H4 H7 OQ1 P3 SN3; smack't∧   B46 B47 LR1
O21 TT1 VA1 VA22 Y2 Y3; ~∧   C8(~»,«) C9 H6 NY1; smil'd∧   H3; smerkd',   H5;
smacked∧   HH1; smackes,   O3.   and] he   H5 NP2.   cryed,] B40 C2 DT1
HH1 NP2 NY3 OQ1 P3 SN3 SP1 Y2; ~;   B32 LR1 O20; cry'd∧   C8(~»,«) H3 H4
H7 NY1 Y3; cry'de;   H8; ~∧   O3 TT1; Cryd.   VA1; cry'de,   Σ.   He'is] hee is
B13 B32 HH1 O20 O21 P3 VA1 Y3; tis   H3(var: »he's«); His is   SP1.   base,] ~∧
B32 C2 LR1 O21 SN3 TT1 VA1 VA2 Y2 Y3; om   H3.   Mechanique,] ~∧   B47
C8 H3 H7 LR1 O3 TT1 VA1 Y2 Y3 G.   course,] ~∧   B46 B47 H3 H4 H6 H8
LR1 NP2 NY3 O3 O21 SN3 SN4 TT1 Y2 Y3; ~ → ~»,«   C8; ~.   NY1; ~;   SP1;
coarse∧   TT1; coarse,   A–F.

82 So'are] NY3; And so are   H8; Soe are   Σ.   all] om   B46 B47 C9 H3 H6
LR1 NP2; are   C8.   your] our   H3 H7 O21; om   Y2.   Englishmen] English
men   B13 C2 VA2 G; ~,   C8 O3; Englishe   H3 H8 OQ1 P3 VA1; english-mē
SN3.   in] all ~   H3.   their] o͏ͬ   O21.   discourse;] B40 DT1 NY3; ~ʌ   B46
B47 H3 H4 LR1 NP2 O3 TT1 Y3; ~,   C2 O21 VA1; ~.| C8; ~: :   OQ1; ~:   P3;
~.   Σ.

83 your] you   H5; yᵉ   LR1 NP2.   frenchmen] ffrench men   B13 H3 O21 P3
TT1; French-men   H5 SN4 VA2; French   H7.   neat?] ~ʌ   DT1 TT1; ~,   H3
H5 HH1 O3 SN3 Y2; ~!   LR1; ~;   O21 Y3; ~.   VA1.   Myne?] fineʌ
B40(M *var:* »~ʌ«) TT1; ~;   B46; ~ʌ   B47 C8 H5 LR1 NP2 O3 O21 P3 SN3 VA1
Y2 Y3; ~,   C2 G; in mee,   DT1 H4; om   H3; mynesʌ   H7; Myne'sʌ   H8; Muina,
HH1; Fine,   A.   as] is   SN3.   see] ~?   B40 H3 H5; ~,   C2 C8 DT1 H8
HH1 A–G; ~.   O20.

84 I] (~   O3.   but] om   Y2.   one] ~,   C9 H6; a   Y2.   frenchman;]
B40 NY3 O21; ~ʌ   B47 H7 NY1 TT1 Y3; Sʳ,   C9 H6 H8 P3 B–G; here,   H3;
French-man,   H5 VA2; nowʌ   LR1; ~)   O3; Sʳʌ   OQ1 VA1; french man,   Y2;
~,   Σ.   looke,] B32 C2 DT1 NY3 O20 P3 A–G; om   B46 O3; ~ʌ   Σ.   mee.]
~;   B32 H5 H8 O20; ~ʌ   B47 H3 H7 LR1 NP2 O3 O21 P3 SN4 TT1 VA1 Y3; ~:
OQ1 Y2; ~,   D–F.

85 Certes,] B40 HH1 NY3 VA1; Cert'sʌ   H4 LR1; ~ʌ   Σ.   they are] ~ goe
B32 H7 O20 SP1 Y2; th' ~   B46 C9 H6 H8 NY1 O3 VA2.   clothd;] B13 B32
NY3 O20 OQ1; clothed,   B47 HH1 O3; ~:   C9 H5 LR1; ~ʌ   H3 H7; ~.   H6 H8
NP2 NY1 P3 TT1 VA1 VA2 A–G; ~,   Σ.   I] ~,   C2 A–G.   mind] om
SN3.   ame] ~,   B40 C2 DT1 H5 O20 A–G; ~ʌ → ~»,«   C8.

86 Your] That ~   OQ1.   wearing is] weare ~   H3; weare-is   OQ1.   this]
yoͬ   B40 B46 C2 C8 DT1 H4 A–G; of ~   H3; the   O21 TT1 Y3.   Grogerame.]
~:   B40 C8 Y2; ~;   B46 C2 NY1 OQ1 VA2 A; ~ʌ   B47 H3 H6 LR1 O3 P3 SP1
TT1 Y3; ~,   H4 H5 O21 C–G; Grogreram.   H7; grogreamʌ   HH1; gromʌ
NP2; Grogogram.   SN4; Grogrameʌ   VA1.

87 Not] (~   O3.   so,] B40 C9 H6 NY3 O20 Y3; ~ʌ   Σ.   Sir,] ~ʌ   B46 B47
DT1 H3 H4 LR1 P3 SN3 TT1 VA1 VA2 Y2; (~)   H5; ~)   O3; ~;   O21.   I] ~.
VA1.   more;] ~,   B13 C2 OQ1 SN3; ~.   B46 C9 H5 H6 H8 NP2 P3 A–G; ~ʌ
B47 C8(~»;«) DT1 H3 H4 H7 HH1 O21 TT1 VA1 VA2 Y2 Y3; ~:   LR1 SP1.
vnder] ~ vnder   O3; (~   Y2.   pitche] ~,   DT1 HH1; ~.   VA2.

88 fly.] B46 C9 H6 H8 NP2 NY3 P3 VA1; ~ʌ   H3 H4 TT1 VA2; ~:   H5; flee,
HH1; ~!   LR1; ~;   NY1 O3 O21 SN4 A–G; ~.:   OQ1; ~,   Σ.   chafd] chaft
B13 C8 H3 OQ1 SP1 VA2; chac't   B46 B47 P3 VA1; chas'd   C9 H6 SN3; cha'fte:
H5; ~,   H7; ~;   H8; chased   HH1; chaffe   O3 Y2.   him.] H6 NY3 O20 B C;
~;   B13 B40 B46 NY1 O21 Y2 A; ~ʌ   B32 TT1 VA1 VA2 Y3; ~:   C9 SP1 D–G;
om   H5 H7 H8 LR1 NP2; ~,   Σ.   as] om   TT1.   itche] an ~   H5 H7; ~,
HH1.

89 Scratchd] Scratcht B13 B46 C9 H3 H7 LR1 OQ1 P3 SN3 TT1 VA1 VA2 Y2
Y3; scratched B40 C2 C8 HH1; Streached H4(M *var*: »Scratched«); scratch
NP2 O3. into] to H3; ~, H8. smart,] smarts, H8; ~; O21; ~∧ TT1.
and] or H3 H5 LR1 NP2 NY1 O3; or, VA2. Iron] ~, C8 OQ1. ground]
om C8; ~, HH1; ~; O21.

90 Into] Ground ~ C8. edg,] ~∧ B13 B46 C9 H3 H7 H8 HH1 LR1 NP2
NY1 O3 P3 SN3 SN4 SP1 TT1 VA1 Y2 Y3; ~; O21. worse,] ~: B13 H6 H7
H8 SP1 Y2 A–G; ~; B46; ~; H3 H5 O20 O21 P3 SN4; ~. NP2 VA1; ~∧ OQ1
TT1. So] ~, B40 H4 NY3 A–G; (~ TT1. I,] ~∧ Σ. foole,] B32 B40
C8 DT1 H4 NY3 O20 SN4 SP1; (~) C9 H5 H6 LR1 O3 OQ1 SN3 B–G; ~)
TT1; ~∧ Σ. found] ~, B32 C2 C8 HH1 O21 A–G.

91 Crossing] Crowing HH1. hurt] did ~ LR1 NP2; hurts VA1. me.]
~.| B13; ~; B32 B40 C2 C8 H3 O3 O20 O21 A; ~, B47 DT1 H4 HH1 NY1
OQ1 VA2; ~: LR1 P3; ~∧ TT1 Y2. sullennesse] ~, B32 H5 HH1 O20 SP1
A–G; sillinesse SN3.

92 an other] C8 NY1 NY3 SN3 VA2 Y2; a nother B13 O3 O21; another Σ.
key] ~, B40 C2 C8 O3 OQ1 A. Stile] ~, C2. dresse] ~; B13 H8 D–G;
~. B32 HH1 NY3 O20 SN3 SN4 B C; ~, B40(»aDresse,«) B46 H5 H7 SP1 VA2;
addresse. C2 C8 A; addresse, DT1; addresse H4 NP2; ~: OQ1.

93 And] Hee O3 OQ1. asks,] B40 B46 C2 H5 H6 LR1 NY3 A–G; ask∧
C8; askt∧ H7 O3; ~∧ Σ. newes?] ~. C9 H6 Y2; ~; H3 O3 G; ~: P3; ~,
SN3 VA1; ~∧ TT1. tell] tellinge B47. him,] NY3; *om* B47 H7(»~∧«); ~∧
Σ. of] what B46. playes.] B32 DT1 H5 H6 NY1 NY3 O20 SN4 VA2 A–C;
~, B40 C2 SN3 D–G; ~; B46 C9 H8; plagus∧ HH1; ~∧ Σ.

94 my] me by the OQ1. hand,] ~; B13 H8; ~∧ LR1 NP2 O21 SN3 TT1
Y3; ~: OQ1. and] as Y2. as] (~ B46. a] *om* SN3. Still] ~,
B13 C2 H5 SP1 A; sill NP2. stayes] ~, HH1.
    Alternate line: to take me by the hand, and 33a–b.

95 Sembriefe] sem briefe B32 DT1; ~, C2 C8 A–G; sem-breife C9; semibreife
H3 H7 NP2 NY1 O3 P3 SN3 SP1 VA2 Y2. twixt] betwixt LR1 NP2; twix
O21. each] the O21 Y3. dropp,] ~; B13 H3 H4 O3 O21; ~,) B46; note,
H5; note∧ NP2; ~∧ NY1 TT1 VA1 VA2; stoppe, P3 Y2. he] *e
C8(→ »h«e); so H5 LR1 NP2; (~ P3 VA1. niggardly] ~, B32 B40 H6 A–G;
~- NP2.

96 As] (~ B46 C9 H5 H6 Y3; ~, B–G; *om* 33a–b. loth] *om* 33a–b.
to'inrich] H5 NY1 NY3 VA2 Y3; *om* 33a–b; to enrich Σ. me] ~, B13 C2 C8
H8 NP2 OQ1 A C–G; ~) H5 P3 VA1; ~. B; *om* 33a–b. so,] B47 HH1 NY3
O20 SN3 SN4 SP1; to, B32; ~) B46 C9 Y3; *om* H5 LR1 NP2 O3 33a–b; ~),
H6; too; H7; ~; O21; too∧ Y2; ~∧ Σ. tells] ~ he H5 LR1 NP2; ~ me
O3; tell 33a–b. many] more 33a–b. a] *om* NY3 33a–b. ly.] B32 H8
HH1 NY3 O20 SN4; ~; B40; ~, C2 C8 DT1 H5 SN3 A–G; lies∧ 33a–b; ~∧ Σ.

97 More] om 33a–b.   then] than SN3 D–F.   ten] then → »~« H4.
Holinsheds,] Hollingsheads,   B32 LR1 NP2 P3 SP1 TT1 VA1; ~‸ B46 O3;
Holland sheades,   C2; Hollingsheads‸ C9 O20 OQ1; ~;   O21; Holinshade‸
SN3; *Hollings-heads*, SN4; Hollinsheeds‸ Y2; Hollinsteads‸ Y3;
HOLLEGSHEADS, 33b.   and] B13 B32 B46 B47 HH1 NY1 NY3 O3 O20 SN3
SN4 SP1 VA2 Y3; om OQ1 33a–b; or Σ.   Halls,] *Hales*, B40 DT1 H4; ~‸
B47 C8 HH1 LR1 NP2 O3 OQ1 SN3 Y2 Y3; Hales‸ TT1; om 33a–b.   and]
B13 B32 B46 B47 HH1 NY1 NY3 O3 O20 SN3 SN4 SP1 VA2 Y3; or ten   33a–b;
or Σ.   Stowes] ~, B32 B40 C2 C8 DT1 H5 O20 O21 A–G 33a–b; slows
HH1.

98 Of] a HH1.   household] house-hold H5.   trashe] ~! B46; stuffe →
›~:‹ B47; ~,   C8 DT1 H4 H7 OQ1 P3 SN3 SN4 SP1 VA1; Y3 D–G; ~. C9 H6 B
C; ~: H5 LR1; ~; H8 NY1 O21 VA2 A; teach, HH1; stuffee → ›~‹ O20;
stuffe → ›~,‹ VA1.   knowes;] B40 C2 C8 NY3 O21 A–G; ~: B13; ~. B32
O20 SP1 Y3; ~‸ LR1 NP2 O3 OQ1 SN3 TT1; ~, Σ.   he] om LR1.
knowes] ~, B40 HH1; om LR1.

99 smild] ~, B13 B32 H5 H7 H8 O20 SN4 SP1; fround, B40 C2 C8 DT1 H4
P3 A–G; frownd C9 H6 OQ1 TT1 VA1; smyled HH1; smilt O3.   fround;]
H8 NY3 O21; Smil'd; B40; smylld,   C2 C8 C9 DT1 H4 H6 OQ1 VA1 A–G;
frowned, HH1; ~‸ LR1; frownt‸ O3; smiled, P3; frawnd, SN3; smild‸ TT1;
~, Σ.   and] or H5.   he knowes] om om H5 LR1 NP2 OQ1 P3 VA1; ~ ~,
SP1 B.

100 Subtile] cuñing LR1.   Statesman] States mann B40 TT1; ~, C2 C8
HH1; States=man H3 H5 VA2 Y3 A–G; Stat-sman NP2; Stats-man, P3;
courtier SN3 SN4; statist Y2.   gather] gett Y2.   of] out ~ H3 Y2; by
LR1 O3.   that.] ~, B32 C2 H3; ~; B40 A–G; ~‸ B47 C8 H4 LR1 NP2 O3
O21 P3 TT1 VA1 Y2 Y3; ~? OQ1.

101 knowes] ~, B32 H7 SP1.   loues] ~, B40 DT1 H4 H8 HH1 VA1 Y3 G;
loueth H3; loue, LR1; ~; O21 A–F.   whome;] B13 H8 NY3 A G; who‸
B47; ~‸ LR1 NP2 O21 TT1 Y2 Y3; om O3; ~. P3; ~, Σ.   who by] how to
Y2.   poyson] ~, C2 HH1.

102 Hasts] Hast C2 HH1 Y2; hastneth OQ1 P3; Hasteneth VA1.   to an]
~'~ NY3.   Offices] Officers H3 H7 O21.   reuersion.] ~, B40 C2 C9 SN3;
~‸ B47 H3 H6 LR1 NP2 O3 OQ1 TT1 VA1 Y3; ~; C8 DT1 H4 O21 A–G; ~:
H8 SP1; in ~. Y2.

103 knows] ~, SP1.   who hath] ~ om B13 B46 B47 C9 H6 H8 O3 OQ1 P3
VA1 Y2; ~'~ DT1 A–C.   sold] ~, O21.   Land,] ~‸ C9 H7 LR1 OQ1 TT1
VA2 Y2 Y3; ~; O21.   now] who H5.   begg] ~, C2.

104 A] om LR1 NP2.   Licence,] ~‸ B46 H3 H5 LR1 O3 TT1 VA1; ~. SP1.
old] of ~ H3(→ »~«).   Iron,] ~‸ LR1 P3 TT1; ~; O21.   Shoes,] bootes,
B40 C2 DT1 H3 H4 NP2 A–G; bootes‸ B46 C8 LR1 TT1; bookes, H5; Shows,

NY3; ~∧ O21 OQ1 P3 Y3; *om* SN3 SN4.   bootes,] ~; B13; shoes∧ B40 H5
LR1 NP2 TT1; or shoes, B46; shoes, C2 C8 DT1 H3 H4 A–G; ~∧ O3 OQ1 P3;
bookes; O21; bookes∧ Y3.   or] And B40 C2 C8 DT1 H4 H5 TT1 A–G; *om*
O21.   egg-] Eggs= H3; ~∧ O20 SN3; Eggeshells∧ TT1.

105 shells] =~ H3 H8 O21 P3 SP1; ~, O20; *om* TT1.   transport.] C9 H6
NY3 P3 SN4 VA1; ~: B13 DT1 H5 H8 LR1 NP2 SP1; ~, B40 B47 OQ1 SN3 Y2;
~∧ TT1; ~; Σ.   Shortly] ~, G.

106 blowpoynt,] SpanCounter, B40 C2; blowe=pointe, B46 H8 P3 SP1;
blow=poynt∧ B47 C9 OQ1; spancounter∧ C8 O21 TT1 Y3; span-counter∧ DT1;
Span=Counter, H3 H4 H5 A–F; blow point, H6 H7 HH1; span counter∧ LR1
NP2; ~∧ NY1; blow poynte∧ O3 VA1 VA2 Y2; span counter, G.   or] on
VA1.   spancounter,] spān counter, B13 B32 OQ1 VA1; blowpoint, B40 C2
O21; Span=Counter, B46 H8 P3 SN4 SP1 VA2; span Counter. B47; blow point,
C8; span-counter∧ C9 H7 NY1; blowe-point, DT1 H5 A–G; Blowe pointe∧ H3
LR1; blowe=point∧ H4; Span countre∧ HH1 Y2; blowpoint∧ NP2 Y3; ~∧ O3;
spangecounter, SN3; blewepoint∧ TT1.   they] the B32; shall B40 TT1 Y2
A–G; ~ shall H5 NY1 VA2.

107 Courtier;] ~: B13 B46 LR1 SP1 ~, B40 C2 C8 DT1 H3 H4 H7 HH1 NP2
O3 SN3 Y2; ~. B47 C9 H6 H8 P3 SN4 VA1; ~∧ TT1; ~:) Y3.   And] ~, C9
H6.   wiser] (~ H3.   then] than H3 SN3.   vs] ~, B32 B40 C2 C9 DT1
H6 SN4 A–G; ~) H3; ~: OQ1.

108 which] what B40 C2 C8 DT1 H3 H4 H5 LR1 NP2 P3 TT1 VA1 A–G.
not] *om* P3.   painted.] ~: B13 DT1 H3; ~; B32 C2 C8 H4 H7 HH1 O3 SP1
A; ~, B47 LR1 O20 SN3 TT1 Y2; ~∧ O21 Y3.   Thus] ~, HH1 O21.

109 He] ~, H4.   home meats] ~=~ B40 B46 C2 C9 DT1 H4 H6 H7 HH1
OQ1 SN4 SP1 VA2 A; sowre ~ H3; honie ~ H5(M *var*: ›~‹ ~); ~ meat LR1;
some ~ NP2 Y2; whome ~ VA1 Y3.   tryes] cloyes B46 B47 C9 H6 H8 B–G;
tyres H3 LR1 NY1 O21 VA2 Y3; clopes H7; tried OQ1.   me;] ~: B13 H5
LR1 SP1; ~. B32 B47 C9 H3 H6 O20 VA1 B–G; ~, C2 DT1 H4 H7 HH1 NP2
O3 OQ1 P3 SN3 SN4 Y2 Y3; ~∧ TT1.   I] ~, H3.   belch,] ~; O21; ~∧
TT1.   spue,] ~; B46 O21; hem, H3; ~∧ TT1 Y2 Y3.   spitt,] ~∧ B40 B47
C9 H3 H8 HH1 NP2 NY1 O3 P3 TT1 VA1 Y2 Y3; ~; O21; ~. SP1.

110 Looke] Look't H3.   pale] ~, B13 B32 B40 DT1 H4 HH1 O20 O21 OQ1
SP1 A–G; sickly, H7.   and] Pale, H7.   sickly] ~, B32 B46 C2 C8 H6
OQ1 VA1 A–G; and H7.   Patient,] ~; B13 C9 H3 H4 H6 H7 HH1 A; ~:
H5; ~∧ LR1 VA1 Y3; ~. NP2 NY1 VA2.   yett] ~, O21 VA1.

111 thrusts] ~ me B40 DT1 H4 H7 TT1; ~ in B46 H5; trusts me C2 C8; ~ on
C9 H6 A–G; ~ me; O21; ~ mee, Y3.   more;] NY3 A–G; ~∧ H3 H8 LR1
NP2 P3 SN3 TT1 VA1; *om* O21 Y3; ~, Σ.   And] *om* B13 H5 H7 LR1 NP2
NY1 O3 OQ1 VA2 Y2; on mee, H3; ~, H6; on, H8 P3 VA1.   as] (~ C9
H6.   if] *om* B46 B47 C9 H6 HH1(»~«) B–G.   he had] ~ *om* B40 C2 C8

DT1 H4 TT1 A; ~'~   B46 NY1 SP1 VA2 B; *om* ~   O20.   vndertooke] ~,
HH1; '~   A.

112 say] ~ all   H3 NY1 VA2; read   P3 VA1.   Gallobelgicus] Gallobelligices
B13; Gallo Belgicus   B32 C2 H6 OQ1; Gallo=Belgicus   B46 DT1 H4 H5 H7 O3
SP1 Y2 A–G; Gallo=Bellgieces   H3; GallBelgicus   O20; Gallobelgius   P3;
Gallobelligus   SN3.   without] wth out   B13(wth ot) B47 C2 Y2; ~=   H3;
with-out-   VA2.   booke] ~,   B13 B40 C8 HH1 O20 OQ1 SN4 SP1 C–G;
~)   C9 H6; ~.   H5 H8 NY1 VA2; ~:   P3.

113 Speakes] speake   DT1; spake   H4.   States] ~,   B32 B40 C2 C8 DT1 H3
H4 H6 HH1 O20 SN4 SP1 Y2 A.   deedes] ~,   B40 C2 DT1 H4 H5 H7 NP2
SP1 A.   which] that   B40 C2 C8 DT1 H4 TT1 A–G.   haue] hath   B40 C2
C8 DT1 H4 A.

114 Spanyards] Spaniard   H3 O21 SN3 SN4 Y2 Y3.   came,] B32 C8 NY3 O20
A–F; ~_   Σ.   to'the] NY3; to   B13; to th'   B46 C9 VA2; toth'   NY1; to y^t
Y2; to the   Σ.   losse] Tosse   H3.   Amyens.] ~,   B40 C8 O21; ~_   B47 H3
H4 H7 HH1 NP2 P3 TT1 Y2 Y3; Amines;   O3; ~:   OQ1; Aameens_   VA1.

115 a] to ~   B32 B40 NY3 SP1 TT1 Y2; to'~   O20.   bigg Wife] ~ ~,   B32 C2
C8 HH1 O20 Y2 A–G; ~=~   NY1 O3 VA2; biggewife   OQ1.   Sight] the ~
P3 VA1.   lothed] loth'd   B32 B40 NY3 O20 OQ1 P3 SP1.   meat] ~,   B32
C2 DT1 O20 SP1 A–G; ~.   OQ1.

116 trauayle] LR1 NY1 NY3; travell;   B13 HH1 O3 O21; trauell,   B46 C9 DT1
H4 H6 Y3; travell   NP2 SN3 TT1 Y2; trauell: OQ1; ~;   SP1; ~:   A–G; ~,   Σ.
so] ~,   B32 O20.   sigh] ~,   B13 C2 DT1 H4 H6 H7 H8 OQ1 P3 A–G; belch,
B32 O20 SP1; sight   H3 LR1; belche   NY3 Y2.   sweat] ~,   B40 H7 HH1 O20
OQ1.

117 this] his   B40 B46 B47 C9 DT1 H4(→ »~«) H5 H6 HH1 NP2 NY3 TT1 VA1.
Maccaron] *Makron*   B40 SN3 TT1; Maca=roone   B46; makaroone   B47 C9 H4
H6; ~-   H5; *Macheron*   H7; mavaron   HH1; *Macron-*   SP1.   talke;] B32 H6
NY3 O20 P3 SN4 SP1; ~.   B13 H8 VA1; ~:   C9 H5; ~,   DT1 H7 HH1 O21 SN3
Y2 Y3 B–G; ~_   Σ.   vayne;] B32 B40 B46 HH1 NY3; ~:   C9 NP2 OQ1 A–G;
~.   H3 H6 H8; ~_   H7 LR1 O3 O21 P3 SN3 TT1 VA1 Y2 Y3; ~,   Σ.   for yet]
forgett   H7; ~ ~   NY1(M *var:* ~ »get«); as ~   P3 VA1 Y2;; ~ ~,   A–G.

118 my] by   Y3.   humor,] B13 B32 B40 C2 DT1 H4 HH1 NY3 O20 A–G; ~_
Σ.   fitt] ~;   B13 B40 SN3; ~,   B32 H8 HH1 O20 A–G; ~.   C2 C8.

119 He] ~,   C9 DT1 H6.   priuiledg'd] privelidged   B40 H7 HH1 P3 TT1 Y2;
priviled=ged   C2; ~ →»priuelidged‹   C8; privilidg   LR1 NP2 O3 Y3.   Spy,] ~_
C9 H4 H7 H8 LR1 NP2 OQ1 P3 TT1 VA1 VA2; ~;   O21.   whome] where
H3(*var:* »~«); (~   H7 OQ1 P3 VA1; (which   H8.   nothing] noe thinge   B13
SN3.

120 Discredit,] ~;   C2 O21; ~_   H3 LR1 NY1 TT1; ~)   H7 H8 OQ1 P3 VA1.

Libells] ~, O3.   now] ~, B46; new H3(var: »~«).   gainst] against B13
B32 B47 C2 C8 H7 H8 LR1 NP2 O20 OQ1 P3 SN3 SP1 TT1 VA1 Y2; on
H3(var: »~«).   Man.] ~, B40 OQ1 SN3; ~∧ B47 DT1 H3 H6 H7 LR1 NP2 O3
O21 P3 SN4 TT1 VA1 Y2 Y3; ~; H4; ~. . H8; ~: HH1.

121 price] prize B13(prise) H3 VA2.   Office] om C8(»~«).   payd;] B32
B40 NY3 O20 SP1 A–G; ~, B13 C2 C8 DT1 H5 H8 SN4 VA2; ~: HH1; payed∧
NP2; ~∧ Σ.

122 He] And howe H3; howe   H5 LR1 NP2; And OQ1.   sayes] ~, B32;
saith B40 C8 DT1 TT1; sayth, C2 H4 A–G; om H3 H5 LR1 NP2; ~:
OQ1.   thriue] thriues O20 P3 VA1.   ill,] ~, B13 C9 H3 H7 H8 HH1 NY1
O3 O21 OQ1 SN3 SN4 TT1 VA1 VA2; om LR1 NP2 P3.   delayd;] B40 NY3
A–G; ~, B13 B32 C8 H4 O20 O21 OQ1 SN3 SN4 VA2; ~. C9 H8 HH1 VA1;
betray'd∧ H3; th'are ~; H5; they are ~∧ LR1; they are delayed∧ NP2; delaied.
SP1; ~∧ Σ.

123 That] how ~ LR1 NP2.   Offices] officers SN3.   entayld;] NY1 NY3
VA2; ~∧ B46 LR1 NP2 O21 TT1; delayd∧ O3; intailed, B–F; intailed∧ G; ~,
Σ.   and] om O3.   that] because O3; om B–F.

124 them,] ~∧ B46 C8 C9 DT1 H3 H4 H6 H7 LR1 NY1 O3 O21 P3 SN3 SN4
TT1 VA1 VA2 Y3.   as] a LR1.   farr] ~, B13 HH1.

125 day;] ~: B13 C2 C8 Y2; ~, B32 B46 B47 H3 H5 H6 H7 NY1 O3 O20 SN3
SN4 VA2 Y3; ~∧ LR1 TT1; ~. NP2 OQ1 P3 VA1.   that] ~ the H7; the
O3.   Officers] ~, A.

126 Do] doth OQ1.   the] om VA1.   Pyrats] ~, B32.   share,] ~∧ B47
C8 C9 H5 LR1 NP2 NY1 O3 SN3 SN4 TT1 Y2 Y3.   and] ~ wᵗʰ the B13 B46
B47 H8 OQ1 P3; ~ wᵗʰ VA1.   Dunkerkers.] ~; B13 B40; Dunkerkes(→»~∧«)
B46; ~∧ B47 C2 H3 H4 HH1 LR1 NP2 O3 OQ1 SN4 TT1 VA1 Y2 Y3; ~: H5
H8; drunkers. P3; ~, SN3.

127 wasts] waste B32 H7 O20 P3 SP1.   meat,] Cloathes, B46 C9 H6 H8;
cloathes∧ B47; ~∧ HH1 IU2 NP2 NY1 OQ1 TT1 Y3; meats∧ LR1; Cloth, O21.
in] & HH1.   Clothes,] meate, B46 B47 C9 H6 H8 O21; Clothe, H3 Y3; ~∧
IU2 NP2 NY1 O3 OQ1 P3 TT1; cloth∧ LR1.   horse] ~, B13 B32 B40 B46 C9
H6 HH1 O20 O21 SN3 SN4 VA2 Y2 A–F; horses, C2 C8.   notes,] B13 B40
C8 C9 H5 H8 NY3 SN4; ~. B32 O20; ~; A–G; ~∧ Σ.

128 loues] Loueth B46 C9 H6 LR1 NP2 Y2; ~, O21.   whores,] ~∧ best, B46;
boyes, H5; ~; H7 HH1 O21; a whore∧ IU2; ~∧ LR1 TT1 Y3; ~? OQ1.
who] and H3; om IU2.   boyes,] ~∧ C9 H7 LR1 TT1 Y3; whores, H5;
a boy∧ IU2; ~; O21; ~? OQ1.   and] om B47 H7 LR1 NP2 O21 OQ1 Y3.
goates.] ~.| B13; ~, B32 HH1 O20 O21 P3; ~∧ B47 H4 LR1 NP2 O3 TT1 VA1
Y2 Y3; loue ~. C9; loues ~∧ H3 IU2; loues ~. H6; ~? OQ1.

129 I] ~, C9 H6; ~; O21.   amas'd] ~, B46 SN4; amazed HH1 NP2 O3

TT1.   then] than   SN3 B–G 44a–d; om   VA1.   Circes] ~,   H3 44a–b;
Cirtes   VA1.   Prisoners,] Poisne'es_∧   B46; poysoners_∧   B47; ~_∧   DT1 H8 HH1
LR1 NP2 NY1 O3 O21 TT1 VA1 VA2 Y3 33a–b; pris'ners,   SN4.   when] ~,
H3 VA1.

130 themselues] them selues   B40 B46 H7 HH1 LR1 O3 SN4 VA2.   turne]
turnd   B46 B47 H3 H5 H7 H8 O3 O21 OQ1 SN3 VA1 VA2 Y2; turned   HH1.
beasts,] ~:   B13; ~;   B32 O20 O21; beast,   B47; ~_∧   H7 O3 TT1 33b; beast:
LR1; beast;   Y2; ~– 44a–d.   felt] om   33a–b 44a–d.   myselfe] B32 H8 NY1
NY3 O20 OQ1 P3 SN3 SN4; om   33a–b 44a–d; my selfe   Σ.   then] ~,   B40;
om   33a–b 44a–d.

131 traytor;] B13 B32 B40 DT1 NY3 O20 O21; ~:   LR1 NY1 SP1 VA2; ~.   NP2
VA1; ~_∧   SN3 TT1 Y2; ~,   Σ.   and] ~,   B46 H6.   mee thought] my ~   B40
H3(*var:* »~«) LR1; ~ ~,   B46 H6; ~=~   C8; methought   H7 H8 O20 G; I ~
SN3.   saw] ~,   OQ1.

132 of] ~,   H7.   our] his   O21.   Gyant] ~=   B46 C9 H6 OQ1 SP1 VA2;
Giants   H7 P3 VA1 Y2.   Statuts] Statues   B13 H3 H4(→ »~«) H7 NY1(M *var:*
»~«) OQ1 O3 P3 SN3 SP1 TT1 VA2 Y2 Y3 C; ~(M *var:* »Statües«)   B40; ~,   C8;
Statues;   O21; statute VA1.   ope] open   H5.   his] her   O3 P3.   iaw]
Maw   H3; ~,   HH1 O20.

133 in] ~,   B40 B46 B47 C2 C8 DT1 Y3 A–F; ~;   H4 O21 G; Inne,   HH1; ~.
TT1.   him.] ~;   B32 B40 H5 O20; ~,   C8 H4 HH1 NY1 O3 OQ1 VA2 Y2
C–G; ~_∧   H3 O21 SN3 TT1 Y3; ~:   H8 LR1 SP1.   found] ~:   H3.

134 *line replaced with dashes*   A.   That] ~,   B47.   burnt] brunt   B40; ~-
C9 H6 SP1 VA2; burnd   O3 SN3; burlite=   OQ1; burnd-   SN4.   venomd]
venom   B47 B–F; venomdt   O3; venome,   SN3; venome=   SN4; venomous   G.
Lechers] ~,   B32 C2 H3 HH1 O20 O21.   do] did   H3 OJ1; might   H5 LR1
NP2; om   OQ1 P3 VA1.   sound] ~,   HH1 O20.

135 *line replaced with dashes*   A.   others] other   P3.   Soares,] ~;   B13 H4;
~:   B46 Y2; ~_∧   LR1 TT1 VA1.   I] soe ~   H3 H5 LR1 NY1 VA2.

136 *1st 4 words replaced with dashes*   A. Guilty] ~,   B13 B32 B40 B46 C2 C8 C9
DT1 H4 H6 HH1 O20 OJ1 OQ1 P3 SP1 B–G; ~;   O21.   he] bee   DT1
H4(»~«) Y2.   free;] ~:   B13 B32 H5 H7 HH1 LR1 O20 B–G; ~,   B40 B47 C9
H3 H6 O3 OJ1 P3 SN3 SN4 TT1 VA1 Y3; ~.   B46 NP2 OQ1; freed: C2 C8;
freed;   DT1; free'd,   H4(→ »~,«).   I did] did I   LR1 O21 Y3.   show]
~,   HH1.

137 All] The   O3.   Signes] signe   B47.   Lothing;] ~:   B13 C9 H5 LR1
O21 Y2; ~,   B40 B47 C2 C8 H7 NY1 OQ1 SN3 VA2; ~.   H3 H6 H8 NP2 P3 VA1
Y3; ~_∧   O3 TT1.   But] om   DT1 H4.   since] om   DT1 H4.   I] om   DT1
H4.   ame] om   DT1 H4.   in] ~,   B32 B40 HH1 NY1 VA2 A–G; om   DT1
H4.

138 om DT1 H4.   pay] bear   33a–b.   myne,] ~‸   H3 H8 LR1 NP2 NY1 O3
O21 P3 SN3 TT1 VA1 VA2 Y2 Y3; my own,   33a–b.   forefathers] Fore-fathers
H5 VA2 33a–b; forefather   H8; fathers   HH1.   sin] ~.   C8 HH1 NY1 VA1; ~,
H5 H8 O21 SN4 VA2; sins,   33a–b.

139 To] om   DT1 H4.   the] om   DT1 H4.   last] om   DT1 H4; lost   H5;
la*t   O3; vtmost   OQ1.   farthing;] ~.   B13 C9 H6 H8 OQ1 P3 SN4 SP1 VA1
B–G; ~:   B46 H5 HH1 LR1 NY1 O20 SN3 VA2 Y2; ~,   B47 H7 Y3; om   DT1
H4; ~‸   H3 O3 TT1.   Therfore] wherefore   H3.   powre] ~,   B40.
    Alternate line: resolv'd to pay the / last farthing,   33a–b.

140 Toughly] ~,   B13 B32 B40 DT1 H4 H7 O20 P3 SP1; Throughly   O3; roufghly
Y2.   'and] NY3; om   LR1 NP2; ‸~   Σ.   stubbornly] ~;   B32; ~,   B47 H7
O3 O20 O21 Y2 Y3; om   LR1 NP2.   'l] NY3; lle   H7(»‸~«); ‸~   Σ.   beare]
bore   O21 Y3.   this] my   C9(*var:* → ›~‹); his   H7; that   NY1; the   TT1.
crosse;] ~:   B13 H8 NY1 SP1; ~,   B46 B47 C2 C8 H4 H7 O3 OQ1; ~.   C9 H6
NP2 VA2; ~‸   LR1 SN3 TT1 VA1 Y3.   th'howre] B40 H3 H5 NY1 NY3 O3
VA2 A–G; the houre   Σ.
    Alternate line: bearing my burthen toughly, / and stubbornly, but behold after
    excessive / baiting a time   33a–b.

141 mercy] redemption   B13 B47 H7 OQ1; ~,   B32 O20; my Redemption's   H3;
my redemption   H5 LR1 NP2 O21 P3 VA1 Y3.   now] om   B13 H3 H7 O21 Y3
33a–b.   was] ~ not   B13; om   H3 OQ1 33a–b; ~ now   H7.   come;] ~:   B13
C9 C–G; ~,   B47 DT1 H3 HH1 P3 Y2 Y3; ~.   H6 H7 H8 NP2 NY1 OQ1 SN4
VA1; ~‸   LR1 O3 TT1; comd.   VA2; arrives,   33a–b.   he] om   33a–b.
tryes] cryes   SN3; om   33a–b.   to bring] om om   33a–b.

142 pay'a fine] pay ~   B46; pay a sinn   B47; pay a ~,   C2 C8 DT1 H4 SN3 SN4;
a ~   C9 H6 O3 Y3; pay a ~;   H3; pay 'afine   NY3; affine   O21; paye a ~   Σ.
to scape] ~ escape   B13 B47 OQ1 P3 VA1; t'escape   B46 H8; ~ stop   H5.   his]
this   SN3.   torturing;] B40 H8 NY3; ~.| B13; ~:   B32 HH1 O20; ~,   C2 C9
DT1 H4 H5 OQ1 SP1 VA2 A–G; ~.   H6 H7 P3 SN4; ~‸   Σ.
    Alternate line: but I must / pay a fine to scape further torture,   33a–b.

143 om HH1.   sayes,] ~‸   B46 H3 NY1 O3 O21 OQ1 P3 SN4 SP1 TT1 VA2;
sayth,   H5; ~.   H6 VA1; said‸   H7 SN3 Y2; sayd,   H8; sayth‸   LR1 NP2.
Sir,] B40 C2 C8 DT1 H3 H5 H7 NY3 O20 SP1 A–G; ~‸   Σ.   me?] ~‸   B47 H7
LR1 TT1; ~;   C2 C8 C9 A; ~,   H5 H6 NP2 O3 O21 Y3; ~.   NY1 VA1 VA2; ~:
SN3 Y2.   I] om   B47.   sayd] om   B47; ~,   C9 H6 H8 O21 A; ~:   OQ1; ~;
B–G.   willingly;] B13 NY3 SP1 A–G; ~,   B32 DT1 H4 H5 O3 SN4; ~:   B40;
om   B47; ~.   H8 P3 VA2; ~?   OQ1; ~‸   Σ.
    Alternate line: can you / spare me quoth he, willingly said I,   33a–b.

144 Nay,] B32 C2 C9 H6 NY3 A–G; om   B47; And sayes‸   HH1; ~;   O21; ~‸
Σ.   Sir,] S.ʳ   B13 B46 H8 NP2 SN3 SN4 VA1 Y2; Sʳ,   B32 C2 C8 DT1 H5
NY3 O20 SP1; Sʳ‸   B40 C9 H4 H7 HH1 LR1 NY1 O3 OQ1; om   B47; S.ʳ,   H6;
Sʳ:‸   O21 Y3; sire‸   P3; ~‸ TT1 VA2.   can you spare me] om om om om   B47.

crowne?] ~:   B13; ~,   B32 H5 SN3; ~‿   B47 HH1 LR1 TT1 Y2 Y3; ~.   C9 H6
VA1; ~;   O3 O20 O21 OQ1.   Thankfully'l] NY3 O20; thankfully I,   DT1;
thankfully, I   HH1 SN3 SN4 Y3; I thankfully   O3; thankfully,   Y2;
thankfully I   Σ.

    Alternate line: a shil-/ling quoth he most thankfully said I   33a–b.

145 Gaue it] Give ~   B32 H3 H7 O20 SP1 TT1; Gaue't   B46; ~ ~,   C2 C8
A–G; ~ *om*   LR1; I giue itt   Y2; *om om*   33a–b.   as] ~ a   B46 B47 C9 H3 H5
H6 H7 LR1 NP2 O21 SP1 Y2 Y3 33a–b; for   OQ1.   ransome,] ~.   B13 B46 C9
H3 H6 H8 P3 VA1; ~,   B40 C2 C8 DT1 H4 HH1 NP2 O3 OQ1 Y3 33a–b; ~:
B47 H7 SP1 Y2; ~‿   LR1 TT1.   fidlers] ~,   SN3 A–G 33a–b.   still] ~,   B32
C2 H6 HH1 O20 SN4 A–G; *om*   33a–b.

146 Though] Thou   B.   be] *om*   H7(»~«); are   O3.   payd] payed   NP2
NY1 33a–b; *om*   O3; ~,   Y2.   to be] ~ *om*   O3; & bid   Y2; on purpose to
have them   33a–b.   gone,] ~:   B13; ~)   B46; ~‿   H3 H4 O21 TT1 Y3; ~;
HH1; goe,   O3 Y2.   yet] ~,   O3.   needs will] need ~   B47 O3; *om* ~   H5
LR1 NP2; will needs   33a–b.

147 one] on   B47 O3 SN3 VA1; some   LR1; soone   NP2.   more Iigg] Iigg
more   B40 DT1 H4 H7 O3 O21 TT1 Y3 33a–b; ~ leggs   LR1.   vpon] on   O21
Y3.   you,] ~:   B13 B47 H8 OQ1 SP1 A–G; ~;   B32 C9 H3 H5 O20; ~.   B46
VA1; ~|.   H6; ~‿   LR1 NP2 O3 O21 P3 TT1 Y3; me,   Y2.   so] ~| H6.
did] *om*   B13 B47 OQ1 P3 VA1 33a–b.   hee] ~,   B32 O20; ~:   H7.

148 long] *om*   LR1; large   NP2.   complementall] complem^t (all   H4.
thankes] ~,   B13 HH1 SN4 SP1 Y2; ~)   H4.   vex] did ~   B13 OQ1 P3 VA1;
doth ~   B47.   mee.] ~;   B40 C2 C8; ~‿   B47 H3 H4 LR1 NP2 O3 O21 TT1
VA1 Y2 Y3; ~,   HH1; ~:   OQ1 G.

    Alternate line: with his complemental thanks / began a new to torment
    me,   33a–b.

149 he] ~'   B32.   gone,] ~;   B13 NY1 VA2; ~‿   B40 B47 H3 H7 LR1 NP2
O21 P3 SN3 TT1 VA1 Y3; ~:   C9 OQ1; ~.   H6; ~!   H8.   want] ~,   B32 B40
C8 DT1 H5 H7 HH1 NP2 P3 SN4 SP1 VA2 A–G; wants   O21 Y3.

    Alternate line: yet at length / vanish'd,   33a–b.

150 Prerogatiue] priuieledge   B47 P3 VA1; ~,   H3; perogatiue   HH1; ~;   O21;
Purgatorie   TT1.   my] many   O21.   Crowne;] ~.   B13 B46 C9 H5 H8 NP2
NY1 P3 SP1 VA1 VA2; ~,   B47 H7 OQ1 SN3 Y2 Y3; ~:   C8 HH1 LR1 A–G;
~‿   H3 O3 TT1.

151 His] Were ~   B46.   were] *om*   B46.   ended,] ~‿   B46 NY1 O21 P3
TT1 VA1 VA2 D–G; ~;   O3; ~:   OQ1.   I] ~.   B47; ~,   H5 H8 SP1 A.
which] (~   B13 B40 B47 C2 C8 DT1 H4 A–G; *om*   HH1(M *var:* »~«) OQ1 P3
VA1; (who   LR1; who   NP2.   see] ~)   C8; ~,   HH1 P3.

152 filld] filled   HH1 O3 TT1.   more] things ~   C8; such   G.   strange]
om   SP1.   things] *om*   B32 C8 O20; ~,   H8 OQ1 SP1 VA1.   then] than

SN3 B–F; as   G.   hee] ~)   B13 B40 B47 C2 C8 DT1 H4 LR1 A–G; ~,   B32
H5 H7 HH1 O20 SN3 SN4 SP1; ~[trimmed]   H8; ~.   Y2.

153 Ran] Run   HH1 NY3 O21 Y3; I run   Y2.   thence] ~,   B13 B46 B47 C2
C8 H3 O21; them   TT1.   with] wᶜʰ   B47.   such] ~,   B13 B32 C2 C8 DT1
H3 H4 O20 SN3 SN4 SP1 VA1 B–G; much   Y2.   or] om   Y2.   more] ~,
VA1.   hast] hate,   B46; ~,   B47 C2 C8 DT1 H4 NY1 OQ1 SN3 SN4 SP1 VA2
A.   then] than   H3 SN3 B–G.   one] on   B40 O3.

154 Who] yᵗ   Y2.   feares] fearing   OQ1 P3 VA1.   more] moe   O3.
actions] B40 B47 C9 H3 H7 LR1 NP2 NY1 NY3 O3 O21 OQ1 P3 TT1 VA1 VA2
Y3; ~;   Y2; ~,   Σ.   doth] om   B46 C9 H5 H6 LR1 NP2 OQ1 P3 VA1 Y2.
make] om   B13; hast   B40(ᐧ→ ~‹) C2 C8 DT1 H4 H7 A–G; makes   B46 C9 H5
H6 NP2 OQ1 Y2; hasts   LR1 P3 VA1.   prisone.] NY3 SN4; prison;   B40 DT1
A; prison₍   B47 C8 H3 H4 H8 LR1 NP2 NY1 O3 O21 TT1 VA1 Y3; Prison,   C2
VA2; prison: OQ1; ~₍   SN3 Y2; prison.   Σ.

155 At] ~,   HH1.   home] ~,   B32 B40 B46 DT1 HH1 O20 SP1; whome   Y3.
Solitarines] ~,   B32 HH1 SN4; ~.   O21.

156 My] (~   H8.   piteous] pretious   B40 C2 C8 DT1 H4 TT1 A.   Soule]
om   O3.   began] ~,   B47 LR1 NP2 A–F.

157 Suiters] suit SN3.   at] of   VA1.   Court] ~,   B32 H4; the ~   O3.
mourne.] B32 H3 NY3 O20 SP1 VA1; moane,   B46 B47 H5 H8; ~;   C2 C8 DT1
H4 HH1; ~| C9; warne,   H7; ~₍   TT1 Y3; ~:   Y2; ~,   Σ.

158 Like] (~   B46 C9 H6 H8 LR1 NP2 P3 VA1.   his] ~,   B40 B46 C2 C8 DT1
H4 SN4 A–G; him   H7(var: »~«) LR1 SP1; ~ → ›he‹   O21.   who] (~   B13;
wᶜʰ   O3.   dream't] dream'd   B13 C2 H3 H5 H7 H8 LR1 OQ1 SN3 VA1; ~,
B32 H4 O20; dreamed   P3.   saw] see   H4(var: »~«).   hell,] ~)   B13 B46 C9
H5 H6 H8 LR1 NP2 P3 VA1; ~₍   H7 NY1 O21 OQ1 TT1 VA2 Y3.   advaunce]
~:   Y3.

159 It selfe] Itselfe   C9 H4 O20 SN4; ~ om   HH1.   o're] on   B40 B47 C2 C8
DT1 H3 H4 H7 NP2 O21 TT1 Y2 Y3 A; or   SN3(var: ›ouer‹).   me;'] ~.   B46
NP2; ~;   H4 H8 O21; ~₍   LR1 TT1 Y3; ~';   NY3; more,   VA1; ~:   B–G; ~,   Σ.
and] om   C2 C8 DT1 H4 A–G.   Men] om   B46 LR1 O3; me   NP2.   he] I
P3 VA1.   there] ~,   B32 B46 C8 OQ1 SN4 SP1 A–G.

160 I saw] Sawe I   H5 LR1 NP2.   Court,] ~;   B40; ~₍   LR1 NY1 O3 O21
TT1 VA2 Y3.   worse,] ~₍   B46 B47 C8 HH1 NY1 OQ1 TT1 VA2 Y3; more,
H5; more₍   LR1 NP2.   more.] ~:   B13 OQ1; ~,   B40 B47 H3 H6(→ »~;«) H7
HH1 O3 O21 SN3 Y2 Y3; ~;   B46 C2 C8 DT1 H4 H8 P3 SN4 A–F; worse.   H5
NP2; worse: LR1; ~₍   NY1 TT1.   Low] howe   H3; Pale   NY1 VA2; ~,   O21.
feare] ~ ‑   OQ1.

161 Becomes] Benumbes   H3.   guilty,] ~₍   B47 C9 H8 NP2 OQ1 P3 TT1
VA1; ~;   O21.   th'accuser;] C9 H7 NY3 SN4; the accuser.   B13 B46 H8 OQ1

VA1; the accuser; B40 C2 C8 HH1 O20 SP1 A–F; the accusar∧ H3 O3 O21
SN3 Y3; ~, H5; ~. H6; ~: NY1 VA2; yᵉ accuser: P3 G; the Accuser, Σ.
Then] ~, H4 A–G; why should I ~, H5; why should I ~ LR1 NP2.

162 Shall] being H5; (being LR1 NP2. I,] B32 B40 C2 C8 C9 DT1 H6
HH1 NY1 NY3 O20 VA2 A–G; om H5 LR1 NP2 ~∧ Σ. nones] (~ B13 B46
B47 H7 H8 O3 O21 OQ1 P3 SN3 SP1 VA1 Y3; noe H3; mone Y2; none G.
Slaue,] ~) B13 B46 B47 H7 H8 LR1 NP2 O3 O21 OQ1 P3 SN3 SP1 VA1 Y3; ~∧
H3 HH1 TT1; slaues∧ Y2. high-borne] H5 NP2 NY3; ~∧ ~, B13 B32 B46 C2
C8 H3 H4 H8 O20 OQ1 SN4 Y2 A; highborne C9; ~-~, DT1 SP1; highborne,
H6; ~∧ ~ Σ. raysd] raysed B40 C2 C8 DT1 H4 HH1 P3 TT1. men] ~,
C2 C8 H4 SN4 Y2.

163 Feare] Fears O20. frownes?] ~, B32 C9 H3 H4 H7 NP2 O3 SN3 SN4
VA1 Y2; ~; B46 G; ~∧ H6; ~: H8 LR1; ~. HH1 O20 SP1. and,] A–G; or∧
NY1 VA2; ~∧ Σ. my] om P3. Mistres] Mʳˢ B13 B32 C2 C8 H8 HH1
LR1 O3 O20 O21 OQ1 SN4 SP1 VA1 Y2 Y3; Mʳˢ, B46; ~, B47 DT1 H5; Mrs?
H4; nomʳˢ P3. Truth,] B47 C2 C8 DT1 H5 SN4 A–G; ~∧ Σ. thee,]
B40(→»~∧«) B46 NY3 O21; mee∧ O3 OQ1; ~? P3 VA1; ~∧ Σ.

164 th'huffing] B40 C9 NY3 G; huffing C2 C8 H4; huffing, DT1 A–F; the
huffinge, H3 SN3 SN4; ~, H5 H8; the Huffing- H7; the huffinge Σ.
braggart] ~, B13 B40 B46 C2 C8 DT1 H4 H5 H8 HH1 Y2 A–G; Braggard, H3
SN3 SN4; braggard- H7; Braggard O3 VA1; braggard; O21. pufte] puffd
H8; ~- SP1; pust VA1; puffe Y3. Nobilitee?] ~. B32 B46 C2 C8 H6 O20
SP1 A; ~∧ B47 H3 H7 HH1 LR1 O3 O21 TT1 Y2 Y3; ~; H4; ~: OQ1 SN3.

165 No,] ~. B40 SN3; ~∧ C9 H5 HH1 O3 O21 OQ1 SN4 TT1 Y3. No.]
B40 C9 H6 NY3; ~; B46 H5; ~∧ H3 NY1 O21 VA2 Y3; ~! TT1; ~, Σ.
Thou] ~, C9. which] (~ B13. yesterday] ~, DT1. beene] ~) B13.

166 Allmost] om HH1. whole] om C2 C8 DT1 H3 H4 H5 LR1 NP2 SN3
SN4. world,] ~: B13; ~∧ H3 H8 OQ1 P3 TT1. thou] not H8. seene]
~? OQ1; ~, A–G.

167 O] (~ C9 H5 H6 HH1 LR1 NP2 NY1 O21 OQ1 P3 VA1 VA2 Y3. Sun,]
~∧ B13 B47 H7 H8 O3 O21 SN4 TT1 Y2 Y3; ~; B46; ~) C9 H5 H6 HH1 LR1
NP2 NY1 OQ1 P3 VA1 VA2; Sonne, H3. iourney,] ~∧ B47 C8(→ »~,«) H3
H5 H7 HH1 LR1 NY1 O3 SN3 SN4 SP1 TT1 VA1 VA2 Y3. vanity] ~, B13
B32 B46 C8 HH1 NP2 O20 SN4 A–G.

168 our] the H5 LR1 NP2 O3 O21 OQ1. Court?] ~, H7 HH1 O3; ~: H8
Y2; ~∧ TT1 VA1. I] om VA1.

169 Thinke] Thinks C2; ~, C9 H6 NP2; I ~ TT1. which] (~ H8 OQ1
P3 VA1; that O3. made] om H5 LR1 NP2. yon] NY1 NY3 OQ1 P3 SN4
VA1 VA2; you B13 B47 HH1 SN3; your B40 C2 C8 DT1 H4 TT1 A–G; yond
C9 H6; the Σ. waxen] om SN3 SN4; ~- SP1. garden,] gardens, B47;
~∧ H5 LR1 NP2 OQ1 Y3; ~; SN3. and] brought, ~ H5 LR1 NP2.

170 Transported] Transplanted   B32 B46 C9 H3 H6 H7 HH1 NY3 O20 SP1 Y2;
~   NY1(M *var*: »Transplanted«); translated P3.   it] yett O3; ~,   B–G.
Italy] ~,   C9 DT1 H4 H6 O3 SN3 SN4 B–G.   stand] ~ ~ → »Strand« B40; ~,
C8 SP1; strand   H7(→»~«); the strand   O3 Y2; ~;   O21.

171 With] Which SP1.   vs] ~, C2 C8 A–G; is SP1.   at] in B32 H3
O20 SP1 Y2.   London,] ~;   B13 O21; ~∧   H7 HH1 NY1 O20 TT1 VA1 VA2;
~) H8 OQ1 P3; ~: LR1.   flouts] followes B13; stouts B47; floates H3.
Court] presence;   B40 H4; Courtier;   B46; presence, C2 DT1 LR1 A; Presence
C8(~»,«) O21 TT1 Y3; Courtiers;   C9; Presence. H5; Courtiers. H6; presence:
NP2; courts SN3; Courtiers, B–G.   here;] B32 B47 H8 NY3 O3 O20 SP1; ~:
B13; ~∧   H3 VA2; ~,   H7 HH1 NY1 OQ1 P3 SN3 SN4 VA1 Y2; *om* Σ.

172 lust] *om* DT1(»~«) H4 Y2.   such] ~, H4.   gay] ~, H4; *om* P3.
paynted] fruits ~, H4.   things,] ~∧ B46 C9 H6 NY1 OQ1 SN3 TT1 VA2 Y3;
om H4; ~. Y2.   which] wth VA2 Y2.   no] *om* B47.   sapp,] ~∧ C8
OQ1 TT1 Y3; ~: O21 Y2.   nor] ~, C8.

173 haue] have ~ B.   them,] ~∧ B40 H5 H8 O3 OQ1 TT1; ~; LR1.
ours] are TT1.   are;] ~,   B32 B47 C2 C8 DT1 H4 H5 H7 H8 O3 O20 P3 SN3
SN4 SP1 A; ~∧   H3 O21 OQ1 VA1 Y3; ~. LR1; ~: NP2; ours∧   TT1; all∧ Y2.
and] such, Y2.   naturall] seeme ~ H5; ~. H6 OQ1 P3 SN4; some ~   H7
LR1 NP2.

174 Some] branches H5 H7 LR1 NP2.   Stocks] Stookes H3; ~; H4 O21;
stalke H5; stocke H7 LR1 NP2 OQ1; ~, HH1.   are;] Y2; ~∧ B46 DT1 H4
H5 H7 HH1 LR1 NY3 OQ1 SN3 SN4 SP1 TT1 VA2 Y3; *om* O21; ~. VA1; ~,
Σ.   their] there DT1 LR1 VA1 Y3;   there, NY1 SN3 SN4 VA2; there;
NY3.   fruits] fruite B47 NP2 O3 Y2; ~, H5 A–F.   bastard] bastards B46
B47 C9 H6 H7 O3 O21 Y2 Y3.   all.] ~; B40 O3; ~∧ B47 H3 HH1 NP2 NY1
O21 P3 TT1 VA1 VA2 Y2 Y3; ~? H4; ~.| SN3.

175 a clock] ~ ~, B13 B32 H8 O20; aclock, B40 B47; of ~ B46 HH1 O21;
O'Clocke, VA1.   past:] B40 C9 LR1 NY3 SN4; ~; B13 C2 C8 DT1 HH1 SP1
VA1 A–G; ~. B46 H6 H8 NP2; ~∧ O21 P3 TT1 Y3; ~, Σ.   whom] (~ P3
VA1.   Mues] B32 B46 B47 C9 H3 H4 HH1 LR1 NY3 OQ1 SP1 TT1 Y2 Y3;
Muse, C2; Muse NY1 O3 P3 VA1 VA2; ~, Σ.

176 Baloon,] ~∧ LR1 O21 OQ1 TT1 Y2 Y3.   Tennys,] Diett, H5; ~∧ LR1
OQ1 TT1 Y2; or ~; O21; or ~, Y3.   Dyett,] the ~, B13; dies, H3(→ »~,«);
Tennis, H5; ~∧ H7 LR1 NP2 OQ1 TT1 Y2 Y3; *dice*, H8.   or] ~ else B46
B47 C9 H6 H8; at H7; and VA1.   Stewes] ~, B32 C2 C8 O3 A; ~; O21.

177 Had] hath HH1.   morning] fore-noone H5; fornoone LR1; fore noone
NP2.   held,] ~∧ B47 C9 H6 H8 TT1; ~. H7; ~: LR1; ~) P3 VA1; ~; SP1.
now] (~ B46 B47 C9 H6 H8; nor H3(*var*: »~«).   the] (~ NP2.   second]
~) H6; Strond SN3.

178 made] that H5 NP2; of LR1.   ready] ~,   B40 H7 HH1 O3 P3 Y3 A–G;

day H5 LR1 NP2; ~; O21.   that] made H5 LR1 NP2.   day,] ~) B46
B47 C9 H6 H8; ready, H5; ~∧ H7 HH1 NY1 O3 O21 P3 SP1 TT1 VA2 Y2 Y3;
ready∧ LR1; ready) NP2.   flocks] flocke B32; ~, C2 A–C.   are] were
B–F.   found] formd H4; ~. O21.

179 Presence;] B32 H8 NY3 O20 Y3; ~∧ B46 H7 HH1 LR1 SN3 TT1; ~: SN4; ~,
Σ.   and] Am H7(var: »~«).   I;] B40 NY3; ~, DT1 H5 NY1 A D–G; ~?
H7(var: »ay«?); ~. B C; ~∧ Σ.   (God] ∧~ H3 H5 H7 H8 O3 OQ1 P3 VA1.
mee.)] NY3 Y3 A–C; ~). B32 B46 C2 C9 H6 NY1 SP1; ~:) B40; ~∧∧ H3 H7 P3
TT1 VA1; ~.∧ H5 H8; ~:∧ O3 OQ1; ~∧) Σ.

180 fresh] ~, B13 B32 DT1 H4 H7 P3 SP1 A.   and] as OQ1.   sweete] ~,
P3.   their apparells] th'~ B32 H3 NY3 O20 SN4 SP1; the ~ B40 HH1 SN3
TT1; ~ apparrell O3.   be,] ~; B13 B46 O21; are, H7; ~∧ TT1 Y3.

181 fields] ~, HH1 SP1; feild P3.   they] the VA1.   sold] ~, HH1.
them;] ~. B13 B46 C9 H6 H7 NY1 P3 VA2 B–G; ~, B47 H3 H5 HH1 O3 SN3
SN4 Y3; ~: C2 H8 LR1 NP2 OQ1 SP1 Y2; ~∧ TT1 VA1.   King] ~, HH1
O21.

182 Those] These B32 H3 H7 O20 SP1 Y2.   hose] om TT1; hooses Y2.
are,] ~; B46; ~∧ B47 H3 H7 H8 LR1 NY1 OQ1 SN3 SN4 SP1 TT1 VA1 VA2 Y3
G; one∧ P3.   cryes] cry B46 C9 H5 H6 A–F; (~ NY1 SN3 VA2; (cry O21
Y3.   his] the B40 B47 C2 C8 DT1 H4 TT1 A G; those H5 LR1 NP2.
flatterers;] B32 C2 C8 NY3 A–F; ~: B13 DT1 HH1; flatterer; B40 G; ~∧ H3 H5
LR1 NP2 VA1; ~) NY1 O21 VA2 Y3; flatteres∧ O3; flatters) SN3; flatterer∧
TT1; ~, Σ.   and] a B13; wch H3 LR1 NP2; that H5.   bring] brings
B47 Y2; doth ~ H8 OQ1 P3; doeth ~ VA1.

183 next weeke to] to the Theater B32 H3(~ ~ ~,) O20 SP1 Y2; ~ ~ vnto C2
C8 DT1 H4(→ ~ ~ »~«); ~ om vnto H5 LR1 NP2; the ~ ~ ~ O3 OQ1.   the
Theater] next weeke B32 H3 O20 SP1 Y2.   sell.] ~; B40 C2 C8 A; ~∧ B47
H8 NP2 NY1 O3 TT1 VA1 VA2 Y2 Y3; ~: C9 OQ1; ~, DT1 H3 H4.

184 Wants] ~, B40 C8; want Y2.   States;] ~: B46 H5 H8 SP1; ~. B47 LR1
NP2 NY1 SN3 VA2 B–G; ~, C2 C9 H3 H6 H7 HH1 O3 O21 OQ1 P3 VA1 Y2
Y3; ~∧ TT1.   Me seemes] ~ thinkes B13 B46 B47 C9 H3 H5 H6 LR1 NP2
O21 OQ1 P3 SP1 VA1 Y3; he thinks H7; methinkes H8; ~ think HH1;
~ seme O3.   as well] aswell B13.

185 At] As H7(var: »~«).   Stage,] ~; B13 C2; ~∧ DT1 H3 H5 HH1 LR1
NP2 NY1 O21 OQ1 SN3 TT1 VA1 VA2 Y2 Y3.   as] or HH1.   Court.]
~, B32 H3 O3 O20 P3 SN3 SP1 Y3; ~; B40 C2 C8 DT1 H4 H5 O21 SN4 A–G;
~: B46 C9 HH1 LR1 NY1 VA2 Y2; ~∧ TT1.   are] o^r H3(var: »~«) H7(var:
»~«) Y2.   Players.] B13 H6(→ »Playes.«) LR1 NY1 NY3 SP1 VA2; ~; B32 O3
O20 O21 P3 SN4 B–G; ~∧ B47 H3 NP2 TT1 VA1 Y2; Playes; C9; ~: H5;
~, Σ.   Who ere lookes] ~ om ~ B13; ~ ore ~ B32 H3(→ »whoere« ~) O21

Y2; ~ orelookes   B46 H4 O20; ~ ~ looke   B47; ~'~ ~   H5 SN4; ~ ou^(er) ~
H7(*var:* ~ »e'er« ~); ~ ~ ~[*trimmed*]   H8; ~ ~ ~,   HH1; ~ ore-~   SP1.

186 (For] ∧~   H3; ∧where   O21; (where   Y3.   themselues] them selues   B40
B47 LR1 O3 VA2 Y3; they ~   C9 H6.   dare] dares   LR1.   not] ~)   B13 C9
H6 H8 O3 OQ1 P3 VA1.   go)] *om*   B13 C9 H6 O3 OQ1 P3 VA1; ~,)   C8
SN4; ~∧   H3; ~;   O21.   ore] In   B13 B47 C9 H6 H8 OQ1 P3 VA1; on   H3
H5 LR1 NY1 O3 VA2; or   H7(→ »~«) NP2.   Cheapeside] Cheap side   B47 Y2;
cheape-side   H5 VA2.   bookes] ~,   B13 B40 C2 C8 DT1 H5 SN3 SN4 A–G;
booke   B47; ~;   HH1.

187 Wardrobes] waredrops   B13 B32 C2 C8 H3 H5 HH1 LR1 NP2 O3 O20 O21
OQ1 SN4 SP1 VA1 Y2 Y3 A; ward-robs   SN3.   Inuentory.] ~.| B13; ~;   B32
C2 C8 DT1 H4 O3 O20 SN3 SN4 A; ~,   B47 H7 Y2; ~∧   H3; ~:   H5 HH1 LR1
NP2 O21 Y3.   Now] ~,   A–G.

188 come;] B13 NY3 A; ~∧   B47 H3 H4 NY1 O21 OQ1 TT1 VA2 Y2 Y3; ~.   C9
H6 H8 P3 VA1 B–G; comes∧   O3; ~,   Σ.   As] And (~   H8; And ~   OQ1.
Pyrats] ~,   B47 C2 C8 C9 DT1 H4 H6 H7 O3 Y2 Y3 A–G; ~;   O21.   which]
that   O3.   did] doe   C2 C8 DT1 H4 H8 NP2 OQ1 TT1 A–G.   know] ~,
B32 G.

189 That] *om*   B46.   came] come   O3.   Ships] ~,   C2 DT1 VA1; vessells
LR1 NP2.   with] w^(ch)   H3.   Cucchianel] HH1 NP2 NY3 SP1 VA1 Y3;
Cutchinell   B13 B46 B47 H7 O3 O21 TT1 Y2; Cutchanell.   C2 C8; Cochenele
C9 LR1; Cutcheuell   H3; Cutchianeill: H5; Cotchenele,   H6; Cutchanell)   H8;
~.   NY1 VA2; Couchanell,   OQ1; *long dash*   P3; Cuthanell   SN3; ~,   SN4;
Cutchanell,   Σ.

190 boord] bearde   H3(*var:* »~«).   them;] B40 NY3 O21 SN4 A–G; 'em,   B13;
~∧   LR1 NP2 OQ1 TT1 VA1; ~,   Σ.   prayse,] B32 B40 C2 C8 DT1 H4 H5 NY3
O3 O20 SP1 VA1 A–F; prize∧   O21 Y3; ~∧   Σ.   as] (~   B13 B40 B46 B47 C9
H6 H7 H8 HH1 LR1 NP2 NY1 O3 OQ1 VA2 Y3 G.   they] I   TT1.   thinke,]
B32 C9 H4 H6 NY3 O20 P3 SP1 A–F; ~)   B13 B46 B47 NP2 NY1 O3 VA2 G; ~,)
B40; ~∧   Σ.   well] ~,   C8 H4 A–G; ~)   C9 H6 H7 H8 HH1 LR1 OQ1 Y3.

191 bewtyes;] B32 B40 B46 HH1 NY1 NY3 O3 O20 O21 VA2 A–G; ~.   H8 VA1;
~∧   LR1 TT1; beauty∧   NP2; ~,   Σ.   they] ~,   B13 B46 H7 VA2; or, ~   NP2.
witts;] B40 NY1 NY3 O21 VA2 A–G; ~.   C9 H6 P3 SP1 VA1; ~:   H8; Witt;
HH1; ~∧   TT1; ~,   Σ.   are] ore   B47.   bought.] ~,.   B40; taught∧   B46;
~∧   B47 H3 H7 LR1 NP2 O3 O21 P3 SP1 TT1 VA1 VA2 Y2 Y3; ~,   C8 HH1 SN3;
~;   DT1; ~:   H4 H5 OQ1.

192 witts] ~,   C8; witt   HH1.   ne'er] *om*   H4(»nere,«) LR1 NP2.   weare]
were   B40 C2 H4(→ »~«) H8 LR1 O21 SP1 VA1; wore   H3 O3.   Scarlett]
scarlets   B47.   gownes,] ~∧   B32 B47 H3 NY1 O3 O21 P3 TT1 VA2 Y2 Y3;
~.   B46 NP2; *om* LR1; gounds;   VA1.   thought,] ~∧   Σ.

193 This] ~;   O3.   cause;] B40 DT1 HH1 NY3 O20 SN4; ~.   B13 B32 B47 C9

H6 H8 OQ1 SP1 VA1 Y3; ~‸ LR1 O3 O21 TT1 VA2; ~, Σ.　　　These] those
B46 B47 C9 H6 NP2 OQ1 P3.　　　men,] ~‸ C9 H5 H6 H8 NP2 NY1 O3 O21
OQ1 P3 SN4 TT1 VA2 Y2 Y3; om　LR1 SN3 VA1.　　　witts] ~, C8 C9 H6 H8
HH1 P3; witt　OQ1 VA2.　　　for] ~ for　NP2.　　　Speaches] ~, C9 H6 O21.
buy] ~, B32 C2 C8 C9 H5 H6 H8 OQ1 SN4 A–G; ~; B40; om　O21 Y3.

194 buy] buyes H7.　　　all] ~, NP2.　　　redds] ~; B13 SN3; ~, C8 H4 O3
O20 SN4 VA1.　　　which] wth B47 H3 H8 NP2 SN3 VA1 Y3; that　O3.
scarlett] Scarletts B40 C2 DT1 H4 H7 HH1 NY1 VA2 A–G; skarled　SN3.
dy.] ~.| B13; ~‸ B47 H3 NP2 NY1 O3 P3 SN3 SP1 TT1 VA1 VA2 Y2; ~, DT1;
~; H4; Dyes‸ O21 Y3.

195 om　LR1 NP2.　　　calld] calls B13 B46 B47 C9 H5 H6 H8 O3 O21 OQ1 P3
SN3 SN4 VA1 Y3; called　HH1; call　Y2.　　　bewty] beawties B13 C9 H5 H6
H8; beauties, B46; ~, H4 O21.　　　Lymetwiggs,] lime=twiggs‸ B46; lyme
twiggs, C8 C9 P3 SN3; lyme-twiggs, DT1 H5 H7 SN4 SP1 VA2; ~‸ O3 TT1;
lime twiggs‸ Y3.　　　haire] ~, B13 B46 C8 C9 H6 H7 SP1; hayres　NY1.
nett;] C9 NY3; ~, B13 B32 B40 C8 DT1 H4 H5 H8; ~. C2 H6 HH1 A; netts‸
H3 Y2; a ~‸ O21 Y3; neet, SN3; ~: B–G; ~‸ Σ.

196 om　LR1 NP2.　　　druggs] drug's B46; Reds　H5(M var: ›~‹).　　　ill] ~,
B32.　　　layd,] ~; B13 O21; ~‸ B32 B47 NY1 TT1; plac'd, H5; layed, P3; ladie,
Y2.　　　hayre] haires B32 O20; teeth　H7.　　　loose] ill B13 H8 OQ1 P3 SN3
SN4 VA1; lose　H7.　　　sett.] ~: B46 SN4; ~‸ B47 H3 NY1 O3 O21 OQ1 P3
SP1 TT1 VA1 VA2 Y2 Y3; ~; C2 C8 A; ~, DT1 H4.

197 not] ~. Y3.　　　Heraclitus] Heraolitus H7.　　　laugh] ~, B46 C2 SN3.
Macrine] Maerine B32; ~, B40 HH1 O21 SN4 A–G.

198 hatt] ~, C2 H7 SN4 A–F; om　O3; Hate　TT1.　　　Shoo,] B32 C2 C8 DT1
H4 HH1 NY3 O20 SN4 SP1 A–G; foote, B13; shew　NY1(M var: »~«) VA2; ~;
O21; sue‸ TT1; ~‸ Σ.　　　himselfe] him self IU2; om　LR1 Y2.　　　at] as
H3(var: »~«); om　NY1(M var: »~«) VA2.　　　doore] om　NY1(M var: »~«) VA2.
refine,] B32 C2 C9 H5 H6 NY3 A–G; ~? B46 DT1 H4 H7 P3 VA1; ~: HH1;
him self ~‸ LR1 Y2; ~! NP2; ~. SN3 SP1; ~‸ Σ.

199 As] ~ if B46 C2 C8 DT1 H4 H5 H7 NP2 A–G; (~ C9 H6; (~ if LR1; Att
TT1.　　　Presence] Queenes ~ B32 H3 O20 SP1 Y2; Queens ~, H7; ~(M var:
»Queene ~«) NY1; ~; O21.　　　a] at B47.　　　Meschite;] Mosqueet, B13;
~, B40 B47 H3 O3 O20 SP1 Y2; Moschite, C2 C8 DT1 H4 A; ~) C9 H6;
Mosquite‸ H5; ~‸ H7 HH1 TT1; ~? H8 NY1(M var: »muskett«) VA2; mesquie)
LR1; Mosquite) NP2; Meschity? O21 Y3; moschit‸ OQ1; mischeife, P3;
Meshite, SN3; ~. VA1; Moschite: B–G.　　　lift] shift B47; ~, HH1; liste
SN3.

200 skirts] ~, B13 B32 B40 DT1 H4 H8 P3 SP1; shirts C8; shirtes, H3 H7;
cloake H5 LR1; cloke, NP2; shirt Y2.　　　and] aloft, H5; om　LR1 NP2.
hose,] om　H5 LR1 NP2; ~‸ NY1 OQ1 TT1 VA2 Y3.　　　call] all B47; calls

TT1.   his] the   SP1.   to] *om*   B40(»~«).   shrift,] B32 B40 C2 H5 H8 NY3
SP1 A–G; ~.   C8 HH1; ~?   LR1 NP2; shriste∧   SN3; stifte∧   TT1; ~∧ Σ.

201 confesse,] B13 B32 B47 C2 C8 DT1 H6 HH1 NY3 O20 P3 SP1 Y2; to ~∧   H7;
~∧ Σ.   not] **t C9.   only] any O21 Y3.   mortal] ~, SN4.

202 Staines] ~, B13 B32 B40 C2 C8 DT1 H4 H7 O20 O21 P3 SP1; holes H3.
holes] ~,   C2 C8 NP2 B C; staines H3; ~;   O21.   in] on B32; *om* LR1
NP2; and O21.   them,] ~;   B40 H8 A; ~∧ C8 H7 NY1 O21 SP1 TT1 VA2
Y3; *om* LR1 NP2.   but] ~ also LR1 NP2 TT1.   venial] ~, B32 O20 O21
SN3 SN4; ~.   C2 C8 SP1; sinns ~ H3.

203 Feathers] ~, B13 B40 DT1 H4 H7 SN4 SP1.   and] are B32; or H8
HH1 NY1 NY3 VA2.   dust,] ~∧ B11 C9 H4 H6 H7 H8 LR1 NY1 O3 P3 SN3
SP1 TT1 VA1 VA2 Y2 Y3; durt∧ HH1; ~;   O21.   with which] wherw^th B11
C8 DT1 H4 TT1 A–G; where wth B40 C2; *om* ~ H3(»~« ~); by ~ H5 LR1
NP2.   fornicate,] H7 O20 OQ1 SN3; ~;   B32 B40 B46 H8; ~.   C2 DT1 NP2
NY3 SN4 A; ~,;   H4; ~:   H5 B–G; ~∧ Σ.

204 And] ~, C9 H6.   then] ~, C9 H6; *om* LR1.   by] (~ B46.
Durers] Duras B13; Dureus B47 TT1; duren's H3; Dureru's H5; Diwers HH1;
dures LR1; Druries NP2; Drures O3; darers O21 Y3; Drawers Y2.   rules]
~, B11 B32 C8 C9 DT1 H6 O20 SP1; ~) B46; rule LR1 NP2 SN3 SN4 Y2; ~;
O21.   survays] suruay B11 B13 B40 C2 C8 C9 DT1 H4 H6 O21 OQ1 P3 TT1
VA1 Y2 Y3 A–G.   State] ~, B11; estate P3.

205 his] *om* B46 H8 O20 SP1.   Limbe,] ~:   H5; ~;   NY1 VA2; ~∧   TT1 Y3.
with] each O21 Y3; ye Y2.   Strings] silke ~ B46; ~, B47; stringe H5 Y3;
strength HH1; string; O21.   the] *om* B47 HH1; th' NY3 Y2; he SN3.
odds] threads, B47; odes O3.   tryes] ~, B32 B40 O20 SP1; Try O3.

206 Of] from H5 LR1 NP2.   neck] ~, B13 B40 DT1 VA1; next H3(*var:*
»~«); Legg H7 HH1; ~;   O21.   to] & B13.   legg,] ~∧ B46 TT1; wriste,
H5; necke, H7 HH1; wast∧ LR1; wast, NP2; leggs; O21; leggs, Y3.   and]
frō LR1; or O3.   wast] waste B11 B13 B46 C8 DT1 H3 OQ1 SN4 SP1 Y2
Y3 B C G; ~, B40; small H5 NP2.   to] t'his H5; ~ his H7 LR1 NP2 OQ1
P3 VA1; to's H8; ~ ye HH1; the SN3; so ~ his TT1.   thighs.] ~∧ B13 B47
H3 H6 NP2 NY1 P3 TT1 VA1 VA2 Y2 Y3; ~, B32 C9 O20 OQ1; ~; B40 DT1
H4; thyge∧ O3; ~:. SP1.

207 in] (~ B40; *om* B47.   immaculate] miaculate O3.   clothes,] ~∧
C8 C9 H3 H6 H7 HH1 LR1 NP2 NY1 O3 SN3 SN4 TT1 VA1 VA2 Y3.
Symmetry] ~. B13; ~, B40 H6 HH1 SN4; sincerity O21; sumetrie SN3;
simmeritie Y3.

208 Perfect] ~, B47.   Circles,] ~∧ B13 B46 B47 DT1 H7 H8 HH1 LR1 NP2
O21 OQ1 P3 TT1 Y3; ~; B32; ~) B40.   with] (~ B13 B46; wch H4.
such] ~ such OQ1.   nicety] ~, B11 B40 H4 H5 H7; ~. HH1 VA1; amity
LR1 NP2; imetyrie SN3.

209 As] (~ B40 H8 LR1 NP2 OQ1 TT1.   young] yonger SN3.   Preacher]
~, B13 B47 O3.   his] the B13 B46 B47 C9 H6 H7 H8 OQ1 VA1; *om* P3.
time] trym H7.

210 preach,] ~) B13 B46 B47 H8 LR1 NP2 OQ1 TT1; ~; B32 O20; ~,) B40;
~ˌ C8(»~,«) H3 SN3 VA1 Y3; ~: H7 SP1; peach; O21.   enters;] B40 H5 H7
HH1 NY3; ~. B13; ~ˌ B46 TT1 VA1; ~ˌ in LR1; eats; O21; eates, Y3; ~, Σ.
Lady] ~, H6 SP1; ladies hand LR1.   which] (~ B46 B47 P3 VA1; that ~
NP2.   ows] ~, C2.

211 Him] *om* LR1; ~, O3.   so much] somuch B11.   as] *om* HH1.
good will,] ~ ~; B13 B32; goodwill) B46; ~ ~) B47 P3 VA1; goodwill, C2 C9
H5 H6 NY1 OQ1; ~ ~ˌ H3 H8 HH1 Y3; Goodwillˌ H7 O21 TT1; Goodwill:
O20.   straight] he B11 B40 B47 C2 C8 DT1 H4 O3 TT1 A–G; hee ~ B13
H3 H5 H7 H8 LR1 NP2 NY1 OQ1 P3 VA1 VA2; *om* HH1.   arrests] ~, B11
B32 B40 C2 DT1 H5 H6 SN4 A–G.

212 her] ~, B11 NP2.   *1st* protests,] ~ˌ LR1 OQ1 SN3 TT1 Y2 Y3 A–F;
pertestesˌ O3; ~. VA1.   *2nd* protests,] ~ˌ LR1 O3 OQ1 SN3 TT1 Y2 Y3
A–F; ~. VA1.   *3rd* protests,] ~. B11 B32 B47; ~ˌ B13 B46 H3 H5 LR1 O3
O21 SN3 TT1 VA1 Y2 Y3 A–F; ~; B40 H4.

213 So much,] B13 B32 H5 NY3 SN3 SN4; Somuchˌ C8; (~ ~ˌ → ›~ ~ˌ‹ H6;
~ ~ˌ Σ.   as] *om* B46 H6(›~‹); that P3 VA1.   at] *om* B47.   Rome] ~,
B13 B32 B40 O20.   serve] well ~ B46; haue serud H6(→ ›~‹) TT1 Y2.
to haue] t'~ SN4.   throwne] ~, B32; throwen B46 P3 TT1.

214 Cardinals] ~, H4(→ »~«); Cardynall TT1.   into] in to B40.
th'Inquisition,] VA2; the Inquisition, B11 O21 SN3 D–F; the Inquisition; B13
C2 C8 SN4 A–C G; the inquisition. B32 B40 DT1 H8 O20 SP1; the Inquisition:
H4 OQ1 Y2; ~; H5; the Inquisition) → ›the Inquisition,‹ H6; ~ˌ NY1; ~.
NY3; the Inquisitionˌ Σ.

215 And] A HH1.   whisperd] whispers B13 B46 C9 H3 H6 LR1 NP2 B–G;
whispered B40 DT1 H4(→ »whisperes«) H7 HH1 O3 OQ1 TT1; whispers, B47;
whisper, O21; ~, P3 VA1.   by Ihesu] ~ ~, B11 B32 B46 B47 C2 O20 Y2
A–G; soe often B13 H5 LR1 NP2; ~ Iesus C8(→ »~ ~«) DT1 H4(→ »~ ~«); ~ ~;
O21; (~ ~) OQ1; ~ loue P3; By [*blank space*] VA1.   so often,] ~ ~ˌ B11
B46 C9 H6 H8 HH1 NY1 O3 O21 P3 TT1 VA1 VA2 Y2 Y3; By Iesu, B13 H5; by
Iesuˌ LR1; (by Iesu) NP2.   that] tha SN3; ~, VA1.   a] ~. C8.

216 Purseuant] ~(M *var:* ›Topcliffe‹) C9 H5; pursuiuant DT1 H5(M *var:*
›Topcliffe‹) NP2; Topcliff H6(*var:* ›~‹) NY1(M *var:* »~«) VA2; Topcleip H8;
Topfife O3; Topclief OQ1.   rauishd] rauisht B11 B13 C9 H3 H4 H5 H7 LR1
NP2 O3 O21 OQ1 P3 SN3 VA1 Y3; Ravished B40 C2 C8 HH1 NY1 TT1 VA2.
him] *om* P3.   away] quite ~ B13 B47 C9 H6 H8 OQ1 P3 VA1; ~, B32; ~;
H4; a way VA2.

217 our] of ~ B11 B40 C2 C8 DT1 H4 TT1 A–G; *om* C9 H6; ~ H3(→ »of«

~); the   H8.   Ladyes] Iesus   C9 H6 H8; ladie   O3.   Psalter.] ~:   B11 B13
H3 H5 LR1; ~,   B40 B47 H4 HH1 NP2 O3 SN3 VA1 Y3; ~;   C2 C8 DT1 NY1
SN4 VA2 Y2 A; ~‸   H7 TT1; Spalter;   O21; phalter.   OQ1.   But] &   B47.

218 That] for   O21.   they] the   H7(»~«); ~,   SP1.   each other plague,]
~ ~ ~;   B13 B46 O21 SP1; ~ ~ plagues‸   H3(→ ~ ~ ~ »~‸«); ~ ~ ~‸   NY1 TT1
VA2; plague each other;   OQ1; plague each other‸   P3; plague each other,   VA1.
they] yᵗ Y2.   it.] ~:| B13; ~;   B40; ~‸   B47 H3 H5 HH1 NP2 NY1 O21 TT1
VA1 Y2 Y3; ~:   H4 OQ1 P3; ~,   O3.

219 here] there   H5.   comes] come   H5 LR1 Y2.   Glorius] ~,   B32 C2 C8
DT1 HH1 O3 O20 SP1 VA1.   will] om   HH1(»~«).   them] 'em   B46.
both,] B11 B40 C2 DT1 OQ1 SN4 SP1 A–G; ~;   B32 C9 O20; ~.   NY3; ~‸   Σ.

220 Who] ~,   DT1 H4 H6 OQ1 A.   in] (~   O21 Y3.   the] an   H5 LR1;
his   NP2; om   OQ1; th'   SN4 Y2.   other] om   H5 OQ1.   extreame] ~,
B40 B46 C2 C8 C9 DT1 H4 H6 O3 A–C; ~ rudenes   H5; ~)   O21 Y3; extreames
OQ1 Y2.   only] dwells and   H3; ~,   OQ1.   doth] ~,   B32.

221 a] om   OQ1.   rough] ~·   SP1; wrought   Y2.   carelesnesse] ~;   B13; ~,
B32 B40 B47 C2 C8 H3 O20 SN4 SP1 A–G.   good] a ~   O21 Y2 Y3.
fashione.] HH1 NY3; ~,   B11 C2 C8 C9 H4 H5 OQ1 SN4 SP1; ~;   B13 B32 B40
DT1 O20 A–G; ~‸   Σ.

222 cloke] ~,   B11 B40 H7.   tear,] teares,   B13 H7 H8 LR1 OQ1 P3 VA1 Y2;
~;   B40 HH1 O20 O21 SP1 A–G; teres‸   NP2; ~‸   TT1.   whom] or ~   C9
H6 B–G; who   H7.   on] ~,   B13 B32 B40; vpon   H7 Y2; ~.   NY1.

223 not.] B47 H8 NY3 P3 VA1; ~;   B13 B40 DT1 H4 H5 NY1 O21 SP1 VA2; ~:
B46 NP2 Y2; ~‸ hee.   C9 H6 B–G; ~, → ~ »he«,   H7; ~‸   TT1; ~,   Σ.
His] And ~   B46; om   Y2.   ill] om   HH1 Y2.   words] om   Y2.   do]
can ~   O21 Y3; om   Y2.   no] not   C8; om   Y2.   harme] ~,   B11 C2 C8; ~.
B46 H7 NY1 VA2; ~;   DT1; om   Y2.

224 him.] B13 B46 H8 NY3 P3 VA1; ~‸   B11 DT1 H3 H4 H7 NY1 O21 TT1 VA2
Y2 Y3; ~;   B40 HH1 O3 A B; ~:   LR1 NP2; ~,   Σ.   He] ~,   HH1; lie   Y2.
rusheth] rushes   B32 H3 O20 SP1 C–G; rush'd   NY1; ~;   O21; rushed   VA2;
rushes,   Y2.   in;] NY3; ~‸   B11 B13 C8 H7 H8 HH1 LR1 NP2 NY1 O3 SN3
TT1 VA2 Y3; and‸   O21; om   Y2; ~,   Σ.   if] ~,   B11; though,   HH1(M var:
»~«,).   1st Arme] C9 H6 H8 LR1 NY3 O3 OQ1 P3 SN3 TT1 VA1 Y2 Y3; ~,   Σ.
2nd Arme] ~,   B32 B40 B46 C2 C8 H5 O21 SN4 VA2 A–G.

225 He] om   B47.   came] meant   B11 B40 C2 C8 DT1 H4 TT1 A–G.
cry;] ~,   B32 B46 B47 C9 H3 H5 H6 H7 O3 O20 OQ1 SN3 SP1 Y2 Y3; ~.   H8
NP2 P3 VA1; ~‸   LR1.   though his] though's   B46.   face] ~,   B11 C2.
be as] ~'~   NY3.   ill] ~,   B11 B32 C2 C8 O20.
    Alternate line: and tho his face bee ill   IU2.
    Alternate line: That linsey, woolsey face of his, as ill   33a–b.

226 theirs] ~, B40 DT1 H4 OQ1 B–G 33a–b; those   C9 H5 H6 HH1 NP2; they
H7 Y2; om   LR1.   which] who   DT1 H4 H5 LR1 NP2 O21 OQ1 33a–b.
hangings] ~,   DT1 HH1 O21; hangeinge,   H3; hanging   O3.   whip] whipt
B40 LR1 NP2 TT1; w^{th}   Y2.   Christ,] ~;   B46; ~_∧   H3 H5 HH1 NY1 O3 O21
SN3 TT1 VA1 VA2 Y3 33a–b; ~.   P3; ~:   Y2.   still] yett ~   B11 B40 C2 DT1
H4 H8 TT1 A; yett ~.   C8; ~,   H5 SN3; ~.   33a–b.

227 He] yet ~   LR1 NP2.   strives] striveth   H5.   worse;] B32 B46 NY1 NY3
O20 O21 VA2 Y3 B C; ~.   B13 B47 H8 P3 VA1; ~_∧   H3 H4 HH1 IU2 LR1 TT1;
~: SP1 Y2; ~,   Σ.   he] om   H5; &   LR1 NP2.   keepes] keepe   B47.
aw] ~,   B11 B13 B32 B40 B46 C2 C8 DT1 H5 H6 H7 H8 NY1 O20 OQ1 SN4;
~;   A–G.

   Alternate line: The knave would fain look worse, keeps all in aw,   33a–b.

228 leasts] ~,   B13 C2 DT1 H5; rests   B47; Liciencd ~   TT1.   Licenc'd]
lycen'ct   B13 H7 IU2 O21 P3 VA1; licen'd   B40 B47 C2; om   TT1; silent   Y2.
foole,] ~;   B13 SN3; fooles,   B47; ~_∧   H7 LR1 P3 TT1.   commands] & ~
NP2.   Law.] ~;   B11 B40 C2 C8 DT1 O3; ~.| B13 H7 OQ1; ~_∧   B47 H3 H4
HH1 LR1 O20 P3 TT1 VA1 Y2 Y3; a ~.   NP2; ~,   O21.

229 Tyr'd] ~,   B11 B32 C2 H6 NP2 O20 A–G; tyred   B47 HH1 P3; Try'd   Y2.
now] om   LR1 NP2.   I] Ile   B32 H3(→ »~«) HH1 NY3 O20 SP1 Y2.   Place;]
DT1 NY3 O21; ~:   HH1; ~_∧   LR1 O3 SN3 TT1; ~.   VA1; ~,   Σ.   and] ~,
C9; (~   O3; om   O21 OQ1 P3 VA1 Y3.   but] (~   B46 B47 C9 H6 H8; be ~
TT1.   pleasd] plesed   B40 HH1 LR1 O21 P3 TT1 Y3.   so] ~,   B40 DT1 HH1
OQ1 SN4 VA1.

230 As] At   H3.   Men] ~,   SP1.   which] om   A–G; which → »which«
H3 H7.   layles] layle   B13 B46 C9 H6; geole   B47; Goales   C2 H4 P3; ~,   C8
O20; Gaoles   H7 O21 A–G; goale   H8; galley   LR1; Gayles   NP2; execution
VA1(var: ›Goales‹); goailes   Y3.   to'execution] H5 H7 H8 NY1 NY3 VA2 A–G;
& execution,   B46; to execution   Σ.   go,] ~.   B11 B32 H7 HH1 NY1 O20 P3
SN4 SP1; ~;   B40 DT1 H4; ~)   B46 B47 C9 H6 H8 O3; ~_∧   H3 LR1 NP2 O21
SN3 TT1 VA1 VA2 Y3; ~:   OQ1 Y2.

231 Go] soe   B13 H3 TT1 Y2; I ~   LR1 NP2.   through] thorough   HH1.
the] that   P3.   great] gard   Y2.   Chamber] ~;   B13 HH1 LR1; ~,   B32 B40
B47 C8 DT1 H3 H4 NP2 O3 O20 O21 P3 SN3; ~.   B46 C9 H5 H6 H8 VA1; ~?
OQ1.   (why] B11 B32 C2 C8 NY1 NY3 O20 SN3 SN4 SP1 VA2 A–G; _∧~?
B46; _∧w^c   O21 Y3; _∧~   Σ.   is it] tis   B46 B47 H3 H8 O3; ~ that   H5 LR1
NP2; it is   HH1 OQ1 SN3 TT1; is om   O21.   hung] ~)   B32 O20 SP1.

232 Sins?);] ~)   B11 C2 SN3 A–C; ~?   B32 C9 DT1 H4 H6 LR1 NP2 O20 P3
SP1; ~;   B46 O21 Y2; ~.   H7 Y3; ~_∧   H8 TT1; ~?)   NY1 NY3 VA2 D–G; ~,)
SN4; ~,   Σ.   among] ~.   B11; a monge   O3.

233 Those] These   B32 H3 H8 O20 SP1 Y2.   Ascaparts,] Ascapares_∧   B47;

~‸ C9 H6 LR1 TT1 Y3; ~; H3; ~: O21; ~. P3 VA1; Ascapats, SN3; Arcaparts‸ Y2. men] (~ B46 C9 H6. throw] ~, B11 C2.

234 Charing Crosse] *Charingcrosse* B40 TT1; ~=~ B46 B47 DT1 H5 H7 SN4 VA2; ~=~, NY1 ~ ~, VA1. barr,] ~: B13 LR1; ~; B40 H5 HH1 OQ1 SN4 SP1; ~. B46 NP2 P3 VA1; ~‸ B47 H8 TT1. men] (~ H8. which] that B11 B40 C2 C8 DT1 H4 TT1 A–G. do] *om* B13. know] ~, HH1.

235 No] not O3. token] tokens H7. worth,] ~; B13; ~‸ C8 C9 H4 H6 H7 H8 NY1 O3 SN3 SN4 TT1 VA1 VA2 Y2 Y3; ~: LR1. Queenes man,] ~=~‸ B46; ~ ~‸ B47 HH1 LR1 P3 TT1 Y2; ~·~, C9; Queen's ~, H7; ~ Men, H7 O3; ~ ~; O21. and] *om* O3. Fine,] B32 B40 C8 DT1 HH1 NY3 O20; Gyne‸ SN3; ~; SN4; find‸ TT1; ~‸ Σ.

236 Liuing] swallowing H5(M *var:* ›~‹) LR1 NP2; Swilling NY1 VA2; Leauing SN3; ~, G. barrells] by barrell Y2. of] *om* Y2. beefe,] Beere, H5 NP2 NY1 VA2; beere‸ LR1; ~‸ P3 TT1 Y3. flagons] & ~ B47 H7(→ »~«) H8 O21 P3 VA1 Y3 G. wine,] B32 C2 HH1 NY3 O20; ~. B11 H5 NP2 NY1 P3 SN3 SN4 SP1 A–G; ~? B13 OQ1; ~; B40 DT1; ~) B46 C9 H6 H8; ~‸ Σ.

237 shooke] shak'd H7. Spyed] spyde B13 B46 B47 C9 H3 H5 H6 H7 H8 NP2 NY1 O3 SN4 Y2; syed O21. Spy.] ~; B11 B40 C2 C8 H3 H5 HH1 O3 SN3 SN4 A; ~.| B13; ~= B47; pye; DT1 H4(»~;«); ~, NP2; spy* O21; ~‸ TT1; ~: Y2. Preachers] ~, NP2; ~! NY1. which] (~ OQ1. are] ere ~ SN3.

238 Seas] Great ~ B46 C9 H6 LR1 NP2. witt] witts B11 C2 C8 H7 HH1 NY1 SP1 VA2 A–F; ~, B13 B40 DT1 H4 LR1 SN4; witts, B32 O20. arts,] art; B13; art, B46 C9 H5 H6 LR1 NP2 O3 SN3 SN4; arte‸ B47; ~‸ H7 TT1; ~: H8; ~; O21; ~) OQ1; ~. VA1. can,] ~; B13 H5 SP1; ~‸ B46 H3 HH1 LR1 O3 O21 OQ1 P3 TT1 VA1 Y2 Y3. then] them HH1. dare] ~, B11 A–G.

239 Drowne] To ~ B46 C9 H6. Sins] synn H7. this] ~, H3. Place,] ~: B13 H5 LR1; ~‸ B47 H3 TT1; ~; H8 HH1 NP2 NY1 O20 O21 SN4 VA2; ~? OQ1; ~. SP1 VA1. *1st* for] C8 HH1 LR1 NY1 NY3 O21 TT1 VA2 Y2 Y3; as O3; ~, Σ. *2nd* for] *om* O21 Y3. mee] ~, B11 H6 OQ1; ~; O21.

240 Who] Which B11 B40 C2 C8 DT1 H4 TT1 A–G. a] butt ~ B11 B40 C2 C8 DT1 H4 TT1 Y2 A–G. skant] scarce B11 B40 C2 C8 DT1 H4 TT1 A; shalowe B32 B46 H3 O20 SP1 Y2; shallow- H7. brooke] B47 H3 H7 H8 LR1 NY3 TT1; ~: B13; ~; B46 O21; ~, Σ. shalbee] B11 B13 B40 B46 DT1 H5 H7 NP2 NY1 NY3 O21 OQ1 SN4 VA1; shall bee, B32; shall be Σ.

241 wash] wishe O3. their] the B11 C2 C8 O21 VA1 Y3 A–G; these B40 DT1 H4; away ~ B46; those TT1. Staines] ~; B46; stayne VA1. away,] ~: B11 B13 C–G; ~, B32 H3 H4 HH1 NP2 O3 O20 SN3 SP1 Y2; *om* B46; ~‸ B47 H7 TT1 Y3; ~. C9 H6 H8 LR1 OQ1 P3 VA1; a way‸ O21; a way;

VA2.   Though] although   B46 B47 C9 H6 H8 O21 Y3 B–G; and ~   H5 O3; ~,
Y2.   I] ~,   H6.   yett] (~   B13; ~,   H6.

242 With] (~   B46 B47 C9 H6 H8 OQ1 G.   Machabees] Machabs   B13;
Machabæus   O21 Y3; Machabus   SP1.   Modesty] B32 H4 H5 H7 LR1 NY3 O3
O20 P3 TT1 VA1; ~)   B13 B46 B47 C9 H6 H8 OQ1 G; modestlie,   HH1; ~.
O21; ~, Σ.   the] haue not ~   H5 LR1 NP2.   knowne] om   B32 B40 B47
H5 HH1 LR1 NP2 NY3 O20 O21 SN3 SN4 SP1 TT1 Y2 Y3; om → »~«   H3 H7;
om Σ.   meritt] ~,   B11 HH1 O21.

243 worke] con'd   H5 Y2; Works   HH1; cou'd   LR1 NP2; ~;   O21.   lessen;]
B13 B46 H4 NY3 O3 SN4; ~:   B11 C2 C8 A–G; ~.   DT1 NY1 VA2; lesson,   H5
LR1 NP2 Y2; Lesson;   H7; ~ˏ TT1; ~, Σ.   yet] ytt   O3; that   SN3.
some] my   H7(var: »~«); suche   O3.   Wise men] wiseman   B11 B46 C8 C9
H6; ~ man   B32 B47 C2 H3 H4 O20 Y2 A–C; wisemen   DT1 H5 H7 H8 NP2
NY1 O3 OQ1 SN4 VA1; ~-man   SP1.   shall] ~,   A–G.

244 (I] ˏ~   B11 B13 B40 C2 C8 DT1 H3 H4 H5 H7 HH1 NY1 O3 TT1 VA2
A–G.   hope)] ~,   B11 C2 A–G; ~ˏ   B40 C8 DT1 H3 H4 H5 H7 HH1 NY1 O3
TT1 VA2 Y2.   esteeme] affirme   B46 B47; ~)   Y2.   writts] witts   B13 B47
LR1 NP2 O3; writt   C9 H5 H6; witt   H3 OQ1 P3 VA1 Y2; workes   NY1(M var:
ˏwordesˏ); ~,   O21 SP1; words   VA2.   canonicall.] B32 H5 H6 H8 NY3 O3 O20
O21 SN3 VA2 Y2 A–G; ~.I.   B46; ~ˏ   H4 TT1; ~:   Y3; ~.I   Σ.

Subscriptions: ID]   B13 SN3; Finis   B40 B46 H7(.) O21(I~.I) TT1 Y2 Y3; The
Satyre of the courte by Mr· Dun*e   NP2; *Finis Quartæ Satyræ Io. Donn.*   NY1
VA2; finis D. D.   O3; Finis the 4th Satyre.I   P3; I: D:I   SN4; om   Σ.

Verbal Variants in Selected Modern Editions

Editions collated: H I J K M N O P Q S T Y Z AA DD.

Format:
Indentations: *ll.* 155, 175, 229, 243, 244 *ind*   Y; *ll.* 155, 175, 229 *ind*   AA; no
ind Σ.
Headings: SATYRE IV.   H Q S Y Z DD.   SATIRE IV.   I–K
M–P.   SATIRE IV THE COURT 1597?   T.   *Satire 4*   AA.

2 but] ~ yet   H–K M N P.   I haue] I've   T.

4 recreation] ~ to   Q S Y.   scant] scarse   Q S.

5 nor] P T; neither   Σ.

7 show] shew   H J N Q S Y Z DD.

8 Glare] H–K M N T; Glaze   Σ.

9 To'a] To   H–K M–P.

12 2nd of] in   P.

13 to all] ~'~   Y Z.

14 lustfull] as ~   O Q S Y Z AA DD.

16 at] in   H–K M–P.

18 then] Q Y Z DD; than   Σ.

21 then] Q Y Z DD; than   Σ.

22 Then] Q Y Z DD; Than   Σ.   Africks] Q S Y Z DD; *Africk's*   Σ.
Guyanas] Q S Y Z DD; *Guiana's*   Σ.

23 then] Q Y Z DD; than   Σ.   Strangers] strangest   N.

24 Danes] *Dane's*   H J K M N; Danes'   I O P T AA.

33 tufftaffeta] *Tufftaffaty*   Σ.

35 This] The   H–K M N P.   trauaild] travell'd   K M O P T AA.   sayth]
faith   H–K M O P.   speakes] he ~   N.

36 knowes] T; know'th   Y; knoweth   Σ.

38 one] no   Q Z.

40 Pedants] Pedant's   H–K M–O T AA; pedants'   P.   Soldiers] Soldier's   I J
M–O T AA; Soldiers'   P.

41 Montebancks] Mountebank's   H–K M–O T AA; Mountebanks'   P.

43 beare] hear   H–K M N.

47 and] T; or   Σ.

48 or Surius] *om*   S.

53 selely] sillily   H–K M O P T AA; seellily   N Q S Y Z DD.

56 Some] ~ other   Q S.

57 There] here   H–K M N P.

59 and] *om*   H–K M N.   Panurge] Panurgus   H–K M N.

61 By] But   N.   trauaile] travel   J K O P T.

62 wonders] words   O Z.

65 that] T; the   Σ.   tower] Tow'r   H I K.

67 Lonenes] loneliness   O.

68 Lonenes] loneliness   O.   Spartanes] *Spartane's*   H–K M N P AA;
Spartans'   O T.

69 last] taste P Y.

73 to'a] a too T.

75 Abbey tombes] ~-~ I J.

79 king] T; Kings Σ.

80 kings Street] *King's-~* H–J M; King's ~ K N P T; King-~ O; Kingstreet
Q S Y Z DD; King ~ AA.

81 course] H N; coarse Σ.

83 Myne] Fine O. as] eyes J.

84 frenchman] Sir H–K M N P.

86 this] your Σ.

92 an other] another Σ. dresse] address O Q S Y Z DD.

95 Sembriefe] Semibrief H–K M N; semi-breve P AA; sem'breve T.

97 then] Q Y Z DD; than Σ. *1st* and] or Σ. *2nd* and] or Σ.

99 smild or fround] T; frown'd or smil'd Σ.

104 Shoes, bootes] T; boots, and shoes K; boots, shoos Σ. or] T; and Σ.

106 At] As H. blowpoynt] blow-point T; *span-counter* Σ. spancounter]
span-counter T; *blow-point* Σ. they] shall H–K M–P.

107 Toll] Toil K. then] N Q Y Z DD; than Σ.

108 which] T; what Σ.

109 tryes] cloys H–K M N P.

111 thrusts] T; ~ me Y; ~ on Σ. if] *om* H–K M N P. had] *om* O Y Z
AA DD.

112 Gallobelgicus] *Gallo-Belgicus* Σ.

113 which] T; that Σ. haue] hath O.

116 trauayle] travel J.

117 this] his T.

118 humor] honour K.

122 sayes] T; saith Σ.

125 As] At J.

128 who boyes, and who goates] * * * * * K.

129 amas'd] Q S Y Z DD; amazed   M O P AA; amaz'd   Σ.   then] Q Y Z DD; than   Σ.

130 myselfe] my self   H Q S Y Z DD.

132 Statuts] Statues   H–K.

134 venomd] venomous   H–K M N; venom   O–Q S Z DD; venomed   AA.

136 he] be   J.   show] shew   Q S Y Z DD.

138 forefathers] forefather's   H K; forefathers'   I J M–P T AA.

142 pay'a] Y; pay a   Σ.

148 complementall] complimented   J.

152 more] such   H–K M N.   then] as   H–K M N; than   O P S T AA.

153 Ran] Run   T.   then] Q Y Z DD; than   Σ.

154 make] haste   H–K M–P DD.

156 piteous] precious   O Q S Y Z AA DD.

158 dream't] dreamed   AA.

159 It selfe] Itself   I–K M–P T AA.   o're] on   O Q S Y Z AA DD.   and] T; om   Σ.

164 th'huffing] huffing   O P.   pufte] puff'd   K T; puffed   O P AA.

169 yon] T; your   Σ.

170 Transported] Transplanted   T.

171 Court here] T; Courtiers   H–K M N P; presence   Σ.

175 a clock] o'clock   J K M O T.

178 are] were   M.

179 I] aye   P.

180 their] th'   T; ~'   Z.

182 cryes] H–J T; cry   Σ.   his] M T; the   Σ.   flatterers] flatterer   H–J N.

184 Me seemes] Meseems   M–P T.

185 Players] prayers   J.

187 Wardrobes] wardrops   Q S Y Z DD.

188 Ladyes] Lady's   H J.   did] T; do   Σ.

194 scarlett] T; scarlets   Σ.   dy] die   H I N Q S Y Z DD.

197 Would not] Wouldn't   H–K M.

199 As] T; ~ if Σ.   Meschite] T; mosque   P; Moschite   Σ.   And] '~   Y.

203 and] or   T.   with which] T; wherewith   Σ.

204 survays] T; survey   Σ.

205 tryes] trye   Q S Z DD.

206 thighs] thighe   Q S Z.

211 straight] T; he   Σ.

213 to haue] ~'~   H–K.

215 whisperd] whispers   H–K M N P.   often] oft   H–K M.

216 Purseuant] Persuivant   H–K M O P T AA.

217 saying] K; ~ of   Σ.   Ladyes] Lady's   H–K M O P T AA; Ladies'   N.

222 whom] or ~   H–K M N P.

223 not] ~ he   H–K M N P.

224 rusheth] rushes   H–K M N.

225 came] P T; meant   Σ.

226 still] yet ~   O Y.

229 I] I'll   T.

230 which] *om*   H–K M–P.

234 which] T; that   Σ.

236 flagons] and ~   H–K M N.

238 witt] wits   M O P Z DD.

240 Who] Which   Σ.   a] but ~   Σ.   skant] scarce   O Q S T Y Z AA DD.   shalbee] shall be   Σ.

241 their] T; the   Σ.   Though] O T Y Z AA DD; Although   Σ.

242 Machabees] Machabee'   H–K; Macabee's   M–P T; Maccabees'   AA. knowne] *om*   T.

243 men] man   P Q S Y Z AA DD.

244 writts] wits   K.

Subscriptions: *none.*

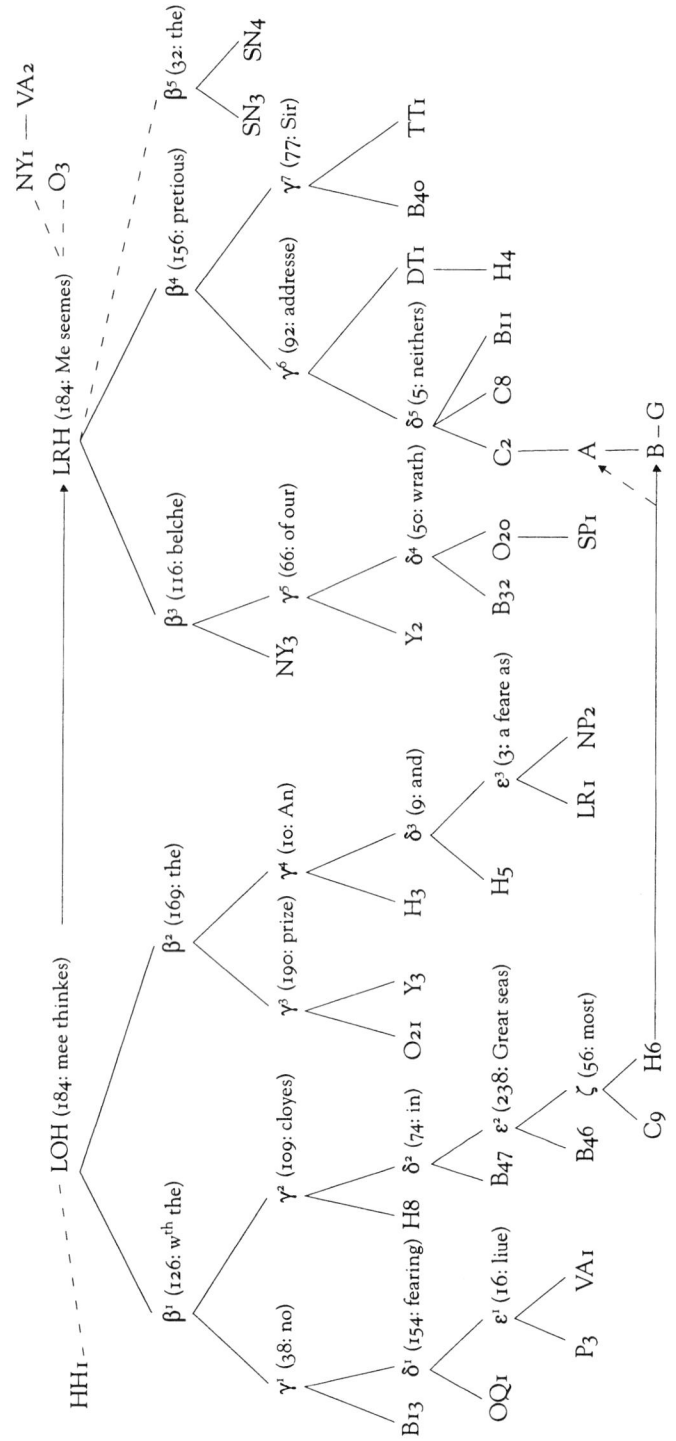

FIGURE 15: STEMMA OF "SATYRE 4"

LOH = lost original holograph
LRH = lost revised holograph
unfiliated: H7, IU2, OJ1, P1

Supporting Detail for Stemma of "Satyre 4"

LOH (HH1 β¹ β²)
   184 Wants reach all States; **mee thinkes** they doe aswell

HH1: To the distinguising readings of the LOH adds the following:
   17 Therfore I suffred this, towards mee **ther** did runn
   21 Stranger, then seauen **Antigracies** studies:

β¹ (γ¹ γ²): To the distinguising readings of the LOH adds the following:
  103 Hee knowes who [om] sold his Land, & now doth begg
  126 doe wth the Pyrats share, & **wth the** Dunkerkers;

   γ¹ (B13 δ¹): To the distinguishing readings of the LOH and β¹ adds the following:
     38 Hee speakes **no** language. If stronge meates displease.
   148 Wth his longe Complementeall thanks, **did** vex mee.

     B13: To the distinguishing readings of the LOH, β¹ and γ¹ adds the following:
     HE M:^{r} Dunns **first** Satire.|
      12 (guiltie of **this** Sinn in goeinge) to thinke mee

    δ¹ (OQ1 ε¹) : To the distinguishing readings of the LOH, β¹ and γ¹ adds the following:
      4 a recreac̄on **to** and scarse mapp of this:
   154 who **fearing** more actions makes from prison

     OQ1: To the distinguishing readings of the LOH, β¹, γ¹, and δ¹ adds the following:
      5 my mynd nor wth prydes itch, nor [om] hath ben
    13 as prone to all ill and of **my** good as forget=

     ε¹ (VA1 P3): To the distinguishing readings of the LOH, β¹, γ¹, and δ¹ adds the following:
      9 To Masse in least [om] was faine to disburse
    16 W^{ch} **liue** at Court for once goeinge that waye

γ² (H8 δ²): To the distinguishing readings of the LOH and β¹ adds the following:
  109 He with home meates **cloyes** mee; I belch, spew, spitt
  127 Who wasts **in cloathes, in meate**, in horse he notes,

   H8: To the distinguishing readings of the LOH, β¹, and γ² adds the following:
     7 I had noe suite there, **or** new sute to shew,
   37 Made of the accents & **the** best phrase of these

δ² (B47 ε²): To the distinguishing readings of the LOH, β¹, and γ² adds the following:

40 but pedants motly **tounges**, souldiers bumbast
74 tis sweete to talke of kings **in** Westminster

  B47: To the distinguishing readings of the LOH, β¹, γ², and δ² adds the following:

  93 And asks what newes? I **tellinge** of new playes
  143b–144a–d *ll. om*

  ε² (B46 ζ): To the distinguishing readings of the LOH, β¹, γ², and δ² adds the following:

  96 **(as loath to inrich me Soe)** tells many a lye
  238 **Great** seas of witt and art, you can then dare

    B46: To the distinguishing readings of the LOH, β¹, γ², δ², and ε² adds the following:

    8 **But onlie thither went,** as Glare did goe
    22 **Guyana's Monsters; Affricks rarities,**

    ζ (C9 H6): To the distinguishing readings of the LOH, β¹, γ², δ², and ε² adds the following:

    56 Some Jesuits & two **most** reuerend men
    128 Who loueth Whores, who boyes, and who **loues** Goates.

β² (γ³ γ⁴): To the distinguising readings of the LOH adds the following:
141 of **my** redemptiō was come; he tryes to bring
169 Thinke he wᶜ made **the** waxen garden, and

  γ³ (O21 Y3): To the distinguising readings of the LOH and β² adds the following:
  190 the men bord them; & **prize** as they thinke well
  193 this Cause These men mens witts for speaches, **[om]**

  γ⁴ (H3 δ³): To the distinguising readings of the LOH and β² adds the following:
  10 **An** hundred Markes (whiche is the Statutes curse
  43 Mee to beare this; **But** I muste bee content

    H3: To the distinguising readings of the LOH, β², and γ⁴ adds the following:
    1 Well **may I** nowe receiue and dye, my sinne
    2 **I know** is Greate, but **yet** I haue bin in

    δ³ (H5 ε³): To the distinguising readings of the LOH, β², and γ⁴ adds the following:
    9 to'a Masse in iest, **and** was faine to disburse
    79 **you** shall heare nought but **kinges,** your eyes meete

H5: To the distinguising readings of the LOH, β², γ⁴, and δ³ adds the following:

14 full, as proud, **and** lustfull, and as much in dett
19 e're bred, or all **that** into Noahs Arke came,

ε³ (LR1 NP2): To the distinguising readings of the LOH, β², γ⁴, and δ³ adds the following:

3 **in** a purgatory: such **a feare as** hell, is
32 veluet, but t'was [**om**] (so much ground was seene)

LRH (NY1-VA2 O3 β³ β⁴ β⁵)

184: Wants reach all states. **Me seemes** they doe as well

NY1-VA2: To the distinguising readings of the LRH adds the following:
21 Stranger then seuen **great** antiquaries studies
64 Tyme enough to haue been **an** interpʳter.

O3: To the distinguising readings of the LRH adds the following:
137 **The** signes of loathing but since I am In
140 **Throughly** and stubbornly, I beare this crosse, but th'hower

β³ (NY3 γ⁵): To the distinguising readings of the LRH adds the following:
116 Redy to trauayle so I **belche** and sweat
229 Tyr'd now **Ile** leaue this Place; and but pleasd so

NY3: To the distinguising readings of the LRH and β³ adds the following:
49 He names **me,'and** comes to me, I whisper, God,
225 He came to cry; and though his face **be'as** ill

γ⁵ (Y2 δ⁴): To the distinguising readings of the LRH and β³ adds the following:
66 He adds, if of oʳ Court life you knew yᵉ good
171 wᵗʰ vs **in** London, flouts oʳ Court here, for

Y2: To the distinguising readings of the LRH, β³, and γ⁵ adds the following:
1 Well **now I may** receiue, & die my sinne
8 yett went to Court **to gaze as I** did goe;

δ⁴ (B32 O20-SP1): To the distinguising readings of the LRH, β³, and γ⁵ adds the following:
41 **Mountebancke** drug tounge; Nor the termes of lawe,
50 Howe haue I sinn'd, that thy **wrath** furious rod,

B32: To the distinguising readings of the LRH, β³, γ⁵, and δ⁴ adds the following:
  20 A Thinge, which would haue **pas'd** Adam to name,
  178 Tyme made ready that day, in **flocke** are found

O20-SP1: To the distinguising readings of the LRH, β³, γ⁵, and δ⁴ adds the following:
  28 One, to whom the Examining Iustice sure **will** crye.
  59 Good pretty linguists, and [**om**] Panurge was.

β⁴ (γ⁶ γ⁷): To the distinguising readings of the LRH adds the following:
 156 my **pretious** soule began the wretchednes
 171 wth vs at London, flowts our **presence**, for

  γ⁶ (δ⁵ DT1-H4): To the distinguising readings of the LRH and β⁴ adds the following:
   14 Full, as proud, **as** lustfull, and as much in debt
   92 He to another key, his stile, doth **addresse**.

    δ⁵ (C2 C8 B11): To the distinguising readings of the LRH, β⁴, and γ⁶ adds the following:
     5 My minde, **neithers** with Prides Itch, nor yett hath beene
     111 Hee **trusts me more**, And as yf he vndertooke

    DT1-H4: To the distinguising readings of the LRH, β⁴, and γ⁶ adds the following:
     83 are not yor ffrenchmen neat **in mee**, as you see,
     137b-139a *ll. om*

  γ⁷ (B40 TT1): To the distinguising readings of the LRH and β⁴ adds the following:
   15 as vayne, **and** wittlesse, and as false as they
   77 of all **Sir** *Harries*, and **Sr** *Edwards* talke,

β⁵ (SN3 SN4): To the distinguising readings of the LRH adds the following:
 32 Veluett, but 'twas nowe (soe much **the** grounde was seene)
 43 mee to beare this, yet **must I** be content

Satyre 5.

Thou shalt not laugh in this leafe, Muse, nor they
Whome any pity warmes. He which did lay
Rules to make Courtiers (he beeing vnderstood
May make good Courtiers, but who Courtiers good?)
Frees from the stinge of ieasts all, who'in extreame   5
Are wretched or wicked: Of these two a theame
Charity and Liberty giue me. What is hee
Who Officers rage and Suters miseree
Can wright and ieast? If all things be in all
(As I thinke, since all which weare, are, and shall   10
Bee, be made of the same Elements,
Each thing, each thing implyes or represents)
Then Man is a World; in which Officers
Are the vast rauishing Seas, and Suters
Springs, now full, now shallow, now dry; which to   15
That which drownes them run. These selfe reasons do
Proue the World a Man; in which Officers
Are the deuowring Stomack, and Suters
Th'Excrement which they voyd. All men are dust;
How much worse are Suters who to mens Lust   20
Are made prayes. O worse then dust or wormes meat;
For they do'eat you now, whose selues wormes shall eat.
They are the Mills which grind you, yet you are
The wind which driues them; And a wastfull warr
Is fought against you, and you fight it. They   25
Adulterate Law, and you prepare their way
Like Wittalls; The'issue your owne ruine is.
Greatest, and fayrest Empresse, know you this?
Alas, no more then Thames calme head doth know
Whose Meades her armes drowne, or whose corne o'reflow.   30
You, Sir, whose righteousnesse she loues, whom I
By hauing leaue to serue ame most richly
For seruice payd, authoriz'd now, begin
To know and weede out this enormous sin.
O age of rusty Iron, some better Witt   35

Call it some worse name, yf ought equall itt.
The Iron Age that was, when Iustice was sold, now
Iniustice is sold deerer farr; Allow
All claym'd fees and dutyes, Gamesters, anone
The mony which you sweare and sweat for is gone   40
Into'other hands; So controuerted Lands
Like Angelica, scape the Striuers hands.
If Law be in the Iudges hart, and he
Haue no hart to resist Letter or fee
Wher wilt thou appeal? Power of the Courts below   45
Flow from the first maine head: And these can throw
Thee, if they suck thee in, to misery,
To fetters, halters; But if th'iniury
Steele thee to dare complayne, alas, thou goest
Against the Streame, when vpwards, when thou'art most   50
Heauy and most faynt. And in those Labors, they
'Gainst whome thou shouldst complayne, will in thy way
Become great Seas, ore which when thou shalt bee
Forc'd to make golden bridges, thou shalt see
That all thy gold was drown'd in them before.   55
All things follow their Likes; Only who haue, may haue more.
Iudges are Gods. He who made and sayd them so
Ment not Men should be forc'd to them to go
By meanes of Angells. When Supplications
We send to God, to Dominations,   60
Powers, Cherubins, and all heauens Courts, if wee
Should pay fees, as here, dayly bread would bee
Scarce to Kings; so t'is. Would it not anger
A Stoick, a Coward, yea a Martyr
To see a Purseuant come in, and call   65
All his Clothes, Copes; bookes, Primmers; and all
His Plate, Chalices; and mistake them away
And aske a fee for comming? Oh ne're may
Fayre Laws whight reuerend name be strumpeted
To warrant thefts; She is established   70
Recorder to Destiny on Earth; and Shee
Speakes fates words; and but tells vs who must bee
Rich, who poore, who in chayres, who in iayles;
She is all fayre, but yet hath foule long Nayles,
With which she scratcheth Suters. In bodyes   75
Of Men (so in Law), Nayles are th'extremityes,
So'Officers stretch to more then Law can do,
As our nayles reach what no els part comes to.
Why bar'st thou to yon Officer, foole? Hath hee
Gott those goods for which earst men bar'd to thee?   80

Foole twise, thrise; Thou'hast bought wrong, and now hungerly
Begst right. But that dole comes not till these dy.
Thou'hadst much; and Laws Vrim and Thummin try
Thou wouldst for more; and for all hast paper
Inough to clothe all the great Carraques pepper.   85
Sell that, and by that thou much more shalt leese
Then Hammon if he sold his antiquitees.
O Wretch, that thy fortunes should moralize
Æsops fables, and make tales Prophesies.
Thou art that swimming dogg whom shadows cosened   90
And diu'dst neere drowning for what vanished.

Satyre 5.

Thou shalt not laugh in this leafe Muse, nor they
Whom any pittie warmes; Hee which did laye
Rules to make Courtiers, (he being vnderstood
May make good Courtyers, but whoe, courtiers good?)
Frees from the stinge of ieasts all, whoe in extream   5
Are wretched, or wicked; of these twoe a theame,
Charitie and libertie, giue mee. What is hee
Whoe officers rage, and sutors miserie
Can write and ieast? If all things bee in all,
As I thinke, since all, which were, are, and shall   10
Bee, bee made of the same elements,
Each thing each thinge implyes, or represents,
Then man is a world, in which officers
Are the vast rauishing seas: and suters
Springs; now full, nowe shallowe, nowe drye, which to   15
That which drownes them run. These self reasons doe
Prooue the world a man; in which Officers
Are the deuouring stomack, and sutors,
The excrement, which they void. All men are dust;
Howe much worss are sutors whoe to mens lust   20
Are made prayes. O worse then dust, or wormes meate;
For they doe eate you nowe, whose selues wormes shall eate.
They are the mills which grinde you, yet you are
The winde which driues them, and a wastfull warre
Is fought against you, and you fight it; they   25
Adulterate Lawe, and you prepare their waye,
Like Wittolls; th'issue your owne ruine is.
Greatest, and fairest Empress, knowe you this?
Alass noe more then Thames calme head doth knowe
Whose meades hir armes drowne, or whose corne or'eflowe.   30
You Sir, whose righteousnes shee loues, whom I
By hauing leaue to serue, am most ritchly
For seruice paid, authoris'd nowe beginn
To knowe, and weed out this enormous sinn.
O age of rusty iron, some better witt,   35

Call it some worse name, if ought equall it:
The iron age that was, when Iustice was sould, nowe
Iniustice is sold dearer farre; allowe
All demaunds, fees, and duties, gamsters, anon
The money which you sweare and sweate for, is gone   40
Into other hands, soe controuerted lands
Scape like Angelica, the striuers hands.
If Lawe bee in the Iudges heart, and hee
Haue noe heart to resist Letter, or fee,
Where wilt thou appeale? Power of the Courts belowe   45
Flowe from the first maine head; and these can throwe
Thee, if they suck thee in, to miserie,
To fetters, halters; but if the iniurie
Steele thee to dare complaine, alass, thou go'est
Against the streame, when vpwards, when thou art most   50
Heauy, and most faint; and in those labours they
'Gainst whom thou should'st complaine, will in thy waye
Become great seas, o're which when thou shalt bee
Forc'd to make golden bridges, thou shalt see
That all thy gold was drown'd in them before;   55
All things followe their like, onely, who haue, may haue more.
Iudges are Gods; hee whoe made, and said them soe,
Meant not men should bee forc'd to them to goe
By meanes of Angells; when supplications
Wee send to god, to dominations,   60
Powers, cherubins, and all heauens Courts, if wee
Should pay fees as here, daily bread would bee
Scarce to kings; soe t'is. Would it not anger
A Stoick, a Coward, yea a Martyr
To see a Pursuiuant come in, and call   65
All his cloathes, copes; bookes, primers, and all
His plate challices, and mistake them away,
And aske a fee for comminge? Oh ne're may
Faire Lawes white reuerend name bee strumpetted
To warrant thefts: shee is established   70
Recorder to destiny on earth, and shee
Speakes Fates words, and but tells vs whoe must bee
Ritch, who poore, who in chaires, whoe in Iayles,
Shee is all faire, but yet hath fowle long nailes,
With which shee scratcheth Sutors. In Bodies   75
Of men, soe in Lawe, nailes are the extremities,
Soe officers stretch to more then Lawe can doe,
As our nailes reach what noe else part comes to.
Why bar'st thou to yon officer, foole? hath hee
Gott those goods, for which men erst bared to thee?   80

Foole, twice, thrice, thou hast bought wrong, and nowe hungerly
Begg'st right; but that dole comes not till these dye.
Thou had'st much, and Lawes vrim, and thummim trye,
Thou would'st for more, and for all, hast paper
Enough to cloathe all the great Carricks pepper.   85
Sell that, and by that thou much more shalt leese,
Then Haman, when hee sould his antiquities.
O wretch, that thy fortunes should moralize
Æsops fables, and make tales, prophecies.
Thou art that swimming dogg, whom shadowes cosened,   90
And diu'dst neare drowning, for what vanished.

Textual Introduction

Complete copies of "Satyre 5" (*Sat5*) can be found in 26 seventeenth-century manuscripts and in all 7 editions/issues of Donne's collected *Poems* (A–G), and short excerpts from the poem appear in various editions of William Basse's *A HELPE TO DISCOVRSE* (1629–82; sigla 18g–r) and in Samuel Sheppard's *MERLINVS ANONYMVS* (1653; sigla 33a–b). In addition, the Crynes copy of A (OJ1) exhibits emendations to several lines in a modern hand. As is shown in Figure 2, all manuscripts that contain *Sat5* also contain the 4 other canonical Satyres, and in these artifacts *Sat5* typically (though not invariably) appears as the final item in a 5-poem set, as it does in the seventeenth-century prints. Distinctive readings in lines 39, 42, 56, 72, 80, 87, and 91 divide these artifacts into 3 distinct lines of descent that derive, respectively, from a lost original holograph (LOH) and two slight revisions of it (LRH¹ and LRH²). Descendants of the LOH include the 3 "books" of the Satyres (OQ1, P3, VA1—all traditionally unclassified manuscripts) and their cognate B13 (Associated with Group III); a family composed of the unclassified manuscripts B47 and H8 and the Group-III artifacts C9, H5, and H6; a family comprising the parent-child pair NY1-VA2 and Y2 (all Associated with Group III); and two further manuscripts Associated with Group III that derive from the LOH independently—H7 and HH1. The sole descendant of the LRH¹ is NY3 (Group IV); and from the LRH² stem the cognates O21 and Y3 (Associated with Group III), 4 of the Group-I artifacts (C2, C8, O20, and SP1), and 4 of the Group-II artifacts (the parent-child pair DT1-H4 and the siblings B40-TT1). The unaffiliated B11, a damaged artifact containing only *Sat5* and a partial copy of *Sat4*, also springs from LRH². The stemma presented in Figure 18 illustrates the precise relationships among these artifacts.

The variants that distinguish the three holographs may be conveniently charted as follows:

Table 5.1: Distinguishing variants in the LOH, the LRH¹, and the LRH²

Line no.	LOH	LRH¹	LRH²
39	claym'd fees	claymd fees	demaunds, fees
42	Like Angelica scape	Like Angelica, scape	scape like Angelica
56	likes	Likes	like
72	tells vs	tells vs	tells *om*
80	earst men	earst men	men erst
87	if	if	when
91	Who diu'd	And diu'dst	And diu'dst

As Table 5.1 makes clear, the sole substantive change introduced at the LRH[1]/NY3 stage of the text's evolution, a change that marks the LRH[1] as a separate authorial version of the poem, is the replacement in line 91 of the LOH's "Who diu'd" with "And diu'dst" in the evolving corrupt-suitor = Aesopian-dog conceit with which the poem concludes. A further handful of revisions appear in the LRH[2] lineage, which not only perpetuates the LRH[1]'s line-91 "And diu'dst," but also alters "claymd fees" to "demaunds, fees" in line 39, "Like Angelica, scape" to "scape like Angelica" in line 42, "Likes" to "like" in line 56, "tells vs" to "tells" in line 72, "earst men" to "men erst" in line 80, and "if he sold" to "when he sold" in line 87. The LRH[2]'s omission of "vs" from the normative "Speakes fates words; and but tells vs who must bee" (yielding "…but tells who…"), of course, renders the line submetrical and is surely a blunder; and the transposition of "Like Angelica" and "scape," the reduction of "Likes" to the singular "like," and the reversal of "earst men" to "men erst" seem of little consequence and may all be inadvertent. The changes of "claymd fees" to "demaunds, fees" and of "if he sold" to "when he sold," on the other hand, apparently represent conscious choices, and the presence of all the above-noted changes in every artifact of the LRH[2] lineage leaves no doubt that all six were included in the LRH[2] and are equally the responsibility of the author (see *DV* 7.1:111–12, for the criteria used in this edition to identify authorial revisions).[1]

As shown on the stemma, the first family of artifacts descending from the LOH is headed by the postulated missing artifact β[1], progenitor of the "books" of Satyres and their cognate B13. β[1] introduces and passes on to its descendants B13 and γ[1] the variants "warnes" (for the authorial "warmes") in line 2, "prepare the [for the normative *theire*] waye" in line 26, and "Caricks [for the normative *great Caricks*] pepper" in line 85. B13, which is without surviving issue, uniquely records "rage" (for the normative "ruine") in line 27, alters "armes drowne" to "arme drownes" in

---

[1](a) In line 30, a number of manuscripts descending from the LOH evince problems in handling the clause recorded in NY3 as "Whose Meades her armes drowne," raising the question whether the ungrammatical "armes…drownes" existed in the LOH: B13 reads "drownes," but reduces "armes" to "arme," and the descendants of γ[1] all read "drowne" in the past tense (= "drownd"), as do VA2 and H8. Y2 gives "drownes," as do B47, C9, and H6, but the C9-H6 pair also normalize grammar by reducing "armes" to the singular. And it also seems possible that "armes…drownes" existed in the LRH[2]. "Drownes" appears in the offspring of both β[4] (O21 and Y3) and γ[4] (B40 and TT1), while the descendants of γ[4] all give "drowne." Either β[4] and γ[4], looking at the authorial "drowne," each independently inscribed the erroneous "drownes," or the γ[3] scribe corrected "drownes" to "drowne" on his own. We here take the position that "Meades…drowne" is Donne's phrase and conjecture that the cumulative effect of "Meades" and "armes" somehow led a number of scribes to add an "s" to "drowne."

(b) Another problematical variant appears in line 14, where the adjectives "rauishing," "raveninge," and "revenous" are ambiguously scattered throughout the manuscript corpus as modifiers of "Seas." The descendants of β[1] are divided between "ravening" and "ravenous," as are the offspring of β[3] and the unfiliated H7 and HH1, and the offspring of β[4] give "ravenous"; NY3 and all members of the β[2] and β[5] families, on the other hand, record "rauishing." Correspondingly, the online *Complete Concordance to the Poems of John Donne* shows that Donne used various derivatives of "to ravish" and "to raven" from time to time, listing 2 instances of "ravishing" (including this one), 2 of "ravish," 2 of "ravish'd," and 1 of "ravishers," as well as 4 of "ravenous" (including "ravenous maw" in *Sat2* 26). Since the lack of stemmatic and vocabular clarity on this matter makes it impossible to be certain which—if only one—of these words is Donne's, we have retained the copy-texts' "rauishing" in both reading texts and merely listed the variant readings in the Historical Collation.

line 30, omits "that" from the normative phrase "Iron Age that was" in line 37, and reverses the normative "earst men" in line 80 to "men erst." γ^1, immediate ancestor of the "books" of Satyres, substitutes "drownd" (for the normative "drowne") in line 30, "wch was" (for "that was") in line 37, and "can come to" (for the authorial "comes to") in line 78, adding these to the growing body of error. OQ1 records "the [for the normative *these*] twoe" in line 6, reverses line 28's "know you this" to "yo^u knowe this" (accusing, rather than questioning, the Queen), and misreads "better witt" as "better will" in line 35, among other lapses. To the errors inherited from β^1 and γ^1, δ^1 adds and passes down to its offspring P3 and VA1 such further blunders as "all whom [for the authorial *who*] in extreame" in line 5, the omission of "now dry" from line 15's normative "now shallow, now dry; which to" (yielding "now shallow, wch to"), "drawes" (for "drownes") in line 16, "whose corne they oureflow" (for "whose corne oreflow") in line 30, "and therfore can throw" (for "And these can throw") in line 46, and "a goulden brydge" (for "golden bridges") in line 54. Existing at the far end of the β^1 line of transmission, both P3 (ll. 10, 24, 32, and 44, e.g.) and VA1 (ll. 60, 71, 72, 77, and 83, e.g.) admit numerous further mistakes.

Shown to the right of β^1 on the stemma is β^2, which heads a line of transmission comprising the unclassified manuscripts H8 and B47 and three members of Group III—H5, C9, and H6. Distinguishing β^2 readings include "suitors y^t [for *who*]" in line 20 (although H5 records "w^{ch}" independently), "Scape like *Angelica*" (for the LOH's "Like Angelica, scape") in line 42, "their like" (for "...Likes") in line 56 (a reading unique among descendants of the LOH), "made & stilde [for the authorial *sayd*] them so" in line 57, and—apparently—"officers foote" (for "Officer, foole") in line 79.[2] To the errors acquired from β^2 H8 adds "much more" (for the normative "much worse") in line 20, "Adulterate lawes [for *Law*]" in line 26, and "thou shouldst [for *shalt*] bee" in line 53, for example. And H8's sibling γ^2 introduces several further blunders, including (1) the omission of "that was" from the normative "the Iron Age that was, when Iustice was sold" in line 37 and the corresponding insertion of "did" into line 38's normative "Iniustice is sold deerer far; Allow..." to yield the revised sentence "the Iron age when Iustice was sold.../...did allow..." and (2) "if they sucke thee, into miserie" (for the authorial "if they suck thee in, to misery") in line 47. γ^2's offspring B47 omits "iests" from line 5's normative "frees from the stinge of iests all" (although the scribe did mark this as an instance of perplexity rather than inadvertence by leaving space for the word) and records numerous careless blunders, including—just within the opening

---

[2](a) In line 56 the H6 scribe first wrote "calld," but then inserted "stil'd" above it as a variant, indicating either that "calld" was an inadvertent trivialization or, perhaps more likely, that both words were available in ε, his source text; H6's sibling C9 gives only "stil'd."

(b) Explaining how C9 and H6 can record the normative "officer, foole" in line 79, while their predecessors on the genealogical tree have the corrupt "officers foote," is a matter of conjecture. It is unlikely to the point of near impossibility that H8, B47, and H5 could all have been looking at "officer, foole" in their source texts (either β^2 [H8], γ^2 [B47], or δ^2 [H5]) and each have independently corrupted it in exactly the same way—"officers foote" almost certainly entered the lineage in β^2 and descended successively to γ^2, δ^2, and ε. If this is so, we must then conclude that as he edited his manuscript for printing (see DV 2:lxxviii–lxxix), the resourceful compiler of ε somehow encountered the authorial "officer, foole" in an ancillary source and substituted it for the "officers foote" that he had received from δ^2.

lines—"giues" (for "giue") in line 7, "offices" (for "officers") in line 8, and "Element" (for "Elements") in line 11. δ², γ²'s second offspring, is a fairly faithful copy of the parent, adding commas after "dry" in line 15, "age" in line 37, and "all" in line 84; eliding the normative "the issue" in line 27 to "th'yssue"; replacing the parentheses that normatively enclose "soe in Lawe" in line 76 with commas;[3] and altering the text substantively only in changing line 23's normative "yet you are" to "and you are." From δ² descend H5—which diverges from its parent in such substantive readings as "those [for the normative *these*] two" in line 6, "cold [for *calme*] head" in line 29, and "boxes" (for "Copes") in line 66—and ε, parent of C9 and H6. ε is a heavily edited manuscript, which—in addition to correcting δ²'s corrupt "officers foote" in line 79—imposes on the received text over 20 changes (most of which appear to be deliberate emendations), including the unique readings "stomacks" (for "Stomack") in line 18, "eate [for *doe eate*] you" in line 22, "her arme drownes" (for "her armes drowne") in line 30, "power.../ Flowes" (for "Power.../ Flow") in lines 45–46, and "shaddowes fedd [or *ledd*]" (for "shadows cosened") in line 90. These and other changes then descend to C9 and H6, the latter of which, as is discussed below, supplies several emendations to the text of B in 1635.

As shown on Figure 18, the final family descending from the LOH is headed by the missing artifact β³, which begets three manuscripts Associated with Group III—Y2 and the parent-child pair NY1 and VA2. The distinguishing readings of β³ include the plural "excrementes" (for the normative "excrement") in line 19, "w^ch [for the normative *who*] to mens lust" in line 20, and the unique readings "if rustie iron seeme" (for "of rusty Iron, some") in line 35, "escape [for *scape*] the striuers hands" in line 42, "when vpward" (for "when vpwards") in line 50, "and no^w Lawes *Vrim* and *Thummin* trye" (for "and Laws Vrim...") in line 83, and "make them [for *tales*] prophesies" in line 89. Just within the first dozen lines, Y2 records the additional corruptions "Courtier" (for the normative "Courtiers") in line 3, "may make good Courtiers, but how? Courtiers good" (for "May make good Courtiers, but who Courtiers good") in line 4, "sling [for *stinge*] of ieasts" in line 5, "each thing, each thing imploys [for *implyes*]" in line 12, and "(Angelica like)" (for "Like Angelica") in line 42. NY1, on the other hand, diverges from β³ in only three substantive particulars, misreading "warnes" (for "warmes") in line 2, "fee for his cominge" (for "fee for cominge") in line 68, and "parts come to" (for "part comes to") in line 78. NY1's child VA2 miscopies its parent in half-a-dozen instances, introducing further errors in lines 12, 19, 23, 29, 30, and 38. Sharing the distinctive LOH readings listed in Table 5.1 above (except in line 56, where H7 gives the singular "like"), H7 and HH1 clearly derive from the LOH, but cannot be filiated more precisely than is shown on the stemma.

As noted above, the lone descendant of Donne's first revision of the poem (in LRH¹) is NY3, whose text is differentiated from the earliest version by the change of the original "Who diu'd" to "And diu'dst" in line 91, a change preserved in Donne's final revision of the poem. And among surviving seventeenth-century artifacts, NY3 presents the cleanest copy of the authorial holograph from which it derives, requiring

---

[3] The evidence indicates that these parentheses existed in the LOH, and they are also present in NY3; they are replaced by commas throughout the LRH² lineage, however, Donne apparently having changed them in his final adjustments to the text.

correction of verbal errors in only two instances—in line 5, where the scribe misre-cords the plural "Stings of ieasts" for the author's "stinge...," and in line 73, where the scribe records the trivialization "who in chaynes" for the author's "...chayres." Our emendations of these blunders and certain necessary changes of the manuscript's punctuation and orthography are discussed below at the end of this introduction.

The most important changes Donne made in his final revision of the poem, one of which is a clear blunder and two of which may be inadvertent, are recorded in the postulated LRH² and are itemized in Table 5.1 above: the change of "claymd fees" to "demaunds, fees" in line 39, of "Like Angelica, scape" to "scape like Angelica" in line 42, of "Likes" to "like" in line 56, of "tells vs" to "tells" in line 72, and of "if" to "when" in line 87. From the LRH² descend β⁴ (parent of O21 and Y3) and β⁵, which—through various intermediaries—begets a further 9 manuscript copies of the poem.

An extremely corrupt artifact, β⁴ introduces and transmits to its descendants over two dozen misreadings in what it heads "Satire the Third," including the omission of "he" from the normative line-3 phrase "he beeing vnderstood" (yielding "being vnderstood"), the omission of "most" from the line-32 phrase "most richly" (yield-ing "richly"), the misreading "Thy non [O21: *now*] age" (for the authorial "The Iron Age") in line 37, "demaunders" (for "demaunds") in line 39, and the simplification of the line 83–84 clause "Thou'hadst much; and Laws Vrim and Thummin try / Thou wouldst for more" to "Thou hast much wouldst more." In addition, O21 and Y3 both record individual substantive errors, including—in O21—blunders in lines 4, 19, 30, 47, and 52 and—in Y3—blunders in lines 46 and 56.

At the head of the final major lineage shown on the stemma, β⁵ adds a further handful of errors to those introduced in the LRH², transmitting them to its descen-dants γ³ and γ⁴. These include the trivialization "warnes" (for "warmes") in line 2 (a mistake also appearing among some descendants of the LOH, but independently corrected here by β⁵'s descendant DT1), pluralization of the authorial "stinge" in line 5 to "stinges" (an error subsequently reversed to the correct "stinge" in δ³); "employes" (for "implyes") in the authorial clause "Each thing, each thing implyes" in line 12 (a corruption later corrected independently by the DT1 scribe); the plural "Excrements" (for "Excrement") in line 19, which also occurs in H7, HH1, and the NY1-VA2 pair; "these [for *those*] labors" in line 51, which otherwise appears only in H7; "the [for *thy*] way" in line 52, and "the [for *that*] swimming dog" in line 90, a trivialization otherwise appearing only in the descendants of δ¹ and in H7. Most definitively, β⁵ also records two unique readings: the reversal "sweate, & sweare" (for the authorial "sweare and sweat") in line 40 and "and tells" (for the authorial "and but tells") in line 72, the latter increasing the corruption in a line already corrupted by the LRH²'s prior omission of "vs."

To this growing body of error γ³, the first direct descendant of β⁵ shown on the stemma, adds "Ment not yᵗ Men" (for "Ment not Men") in line 58 (an addition also appearing in OQ1), the singular "Court" (for the authorial "Courts") in line 61, and the unique omission of "erst" from the revised "for which men erst bared" (yielding "for wᶜʰ men bared") in line 80. γ³'s offspring δ³ transmits these and a few further idiosyncrasies of its own to the siblings B11, C2, and C8, including "who, [with a comma]" (for the normative "who") in line 4 and "libertye, [with a comma]" (for the normative "Liberty") in line 7. Although each of these variants is shared by one or more other artifacts, two unique readings set the δ^3 family definitively apart from all others: the insertion of an extraneous "to" in the line-49 phrase "to dare complayne" (yielding "to dare to Complayne") and the misreading "lacke [for the authorial *aske*] a Fee for Comminge" in line 68, which eventually descends into A through C2 and remains in the seventeenth-century prints until corrected by G. Within the family, B11 and C8 are the product of the same scribe; and although their spelling and punctuation diverge in numerous instances, they differ substantively only in lines 35 (where C8 reads the anomalous "come [for B11's authorial *some*] better witt"), 74 (where B11 reads the anomalous "all fair, yett [for C8's normative *but yett*] hath"), and 79 (where B11 reads the normative "yon officer," while C8 mistranscribes "you officer"). C2 diverges substantively from the parent in only two instances, misrecording the singular "Ieast" (in the authorial phrase "Stinge of ieasts") in line 5 and "Meane [for *mayne*] heade" in line 46. Each of γ^3's other direct offspring—O20 and DT1—generates a bit of further error: O20—incorporating the Group-II text of Sat5 into the 4-poem set of Satyres it obtained from the Group-I prototype—uniquely misrecords "then [for *the*] Issue" in line 27, "How" (for the normative "Allow") at the end of line 38, "Buyest [for *Begst*] right" in line 82, and "when [for *whom*] shadowes coosened" in line 90 and joins various other manuscripts in misreading the normative "chayres" in line 73 as "Chaynes"; DT1 omits lines 3b–4a, uniquely inserts "and" into the normative "Like Wittalls; Th'issue your owne ruine is" (yielding "...and th'issue...") in line 27, and (also uniquely) misrecords "and howe" (for "and now") at the end of line 81. O20's child SP1 commits further blunders in 10, 11, 15, 30, and 46; H4 misrecords its parent's normative "write and ieast" as "...or ieast" in line 9 and changes "what vanished" in line 91 to "whats...."

β^5's other immediate scion, γ^4, is the parent of the final two manuscripts shown on the stemma—B40 and TT1. γ^4 uniquely entitles Sat5 "A Satire 3," alters the revised "like" in line 56 to the original "Likes," and uniquely substitutes "Stone" for the authorial "Stoick" in line 64. B40 appears to represent the parent faithfully, but TT1 is extremely corrupt, introducing further errors in lines 15, 26, 41, 44, 46, 50, 52, 61, 63, 72, and 91.

The Seventeenth-Century Prints

The text of Sat5 first enters print in the collected *Poems* of 1633 (A), set into type from C2 (for a discussion of A's parentage, see the General Textual Introduction above). A avoids the β^5 blunders "warnes" in line 2 and "stinges" in line 5, but evinces β^5's erroneous "employes" (for the correct "implyes") in line 12, "excrements" (for "Excrement") in line 19, "sweate, and sweare" (for "sweare and sweat") in line 40, "these [for *those*] labours" in line 51, "the way" (for "thy way") in line 52, "and tells who" (for "and but tells vs who") in line 72, and "the [for *that*] swimming dog" in line 90. In addition, A derives from γ^3 the hypermetrical "Ment not that men...go" (for the normative "Ment not men...go") in line 58, the singular "Court" (for "Courts") in line 61, and the truncated "men bared" (for "earst men bared" [or "men erst bared"]) in line 80; and although A independently drops the extraneous "to" from δ^3's hypermetrical "to dare to complaine" (yielding "to dare complaine") in line 49, the edition accepts δ^3's

~ = agrees with LRH1   ṽ = agrees with nearest corresponding reading on left   ( ) = specific source of variant   < > = word(s) omitted   c = compositor

Line no.	LRH1/DV reading	A	B	C	D–F	G
9	and ieast	~ ~ (LRH²/C2)	~	~	~	in ~ (c)
12	implyes	employes (β⁵)	~ (H6)	~	~	~
19	Excrement	excrements (β⁵)	▽	▽	▽	▽
26	their	~	the (H6 or c)	~	~	~
33	authoriz'd now,	~, ~, (H6 or c)	~, ~,	~, ~<	~, ~<	~, ~, (c)
35	some...Witt	Some...~ (c)	(~...~ (H6)	(~...~	(~...~	Some... ~ (c?)
36	2nd itt.	~; (c)	~;) (H6)	~;)	~;)	~; (c)
37	that was	~ ~	~	<~> ~	~	<~> ~ (c)
38	deerer farr; Allow	~; ~	~) did ~ (H6)	~) ~	~) ~	~; ~ (?)
39	claym'd fees	demands, ~ (LRH²/C2)	~ ~ (H6?)	~ ~	~ ~	~ ~
40	sweare and sweat	sweat, ~ sweare (β⁵)	▽, ~	▽, ~	▽, ~ (c)	▽, ~
42	Like Angelica, scape	Scape, like Angelica (LRH², c)	▽, ~	▽, ~	▽, ~	▽, ~ <
50	1st when	~	~	<~> (c)	~	<~> (c)
51	those	these (β⁵/C2)	▽	▽	▽	~
52	thy way	the ~ (β⁵/C2)	~ ~ (H6?)	~	~	~
56	Likes	like (LRH²/C2)	▽	▽	~	~
57	Gods. He	~; he (γ³/C2)	~; ▽	~; ~	~; ~	~; and ~ (c)
57	and sayd	~ ~	~	<~> ~	~	<~> ~ > (c)
58	Ment not Men	~ ~ that ~ (γ³/C2)	~ ~	~ ~	~	~ ~ (c)
61	Courts	Court (γ³/C2)	~	~	~	~
68	aske	lack (δ³/C2)	▽	~	~	~ (?)
72	but tells vs	<~> ~ <~> (LRH², β⁵)	<~> ~ <~> ^	<~> ~ <~>	<~> ~ <~>	<~> ~ <~>
80	earst men	<~> ~ (γ³)	~ ~ (H6?)	~	~	~
87	if he	when ~ (LRH²/C2)	~ ~ (H6?)	~	~	when ~ (?)
90	that...dogg	the...~ (β⁵/C2)	▽...	▽...	▽...	▽...
90	cosened	~	cozened	▽	~	cozeneth (c)
91	And	~ (LRH²)	Which (H6)	▽	▽	▽
91	diu'dst	div'st (DT1, c)	▽	▽	▽	▽
91	vanished	~	~	~	~	vanisheth (c)

anomalous "lacke" (for the correct "aske") in line 68. Perhaps with reference to DT1, A's editor also emends C2's anomalous "Ieast" in line 5 to the normative "jests" and C2's nonsensical "Meane heade" to "maine head" in line 46, and he independently reduces C2's normative "ye extremytyes" in line 76 to "extremities." Further, either the reading of DT1 or his own sense of the grammar of the passage leads this editor to alter C2's "div'dst" to "div'st" in line 91—thus enshrining a scribal lection that has appeared in every subsequent edition up to the present one.

Each of the second through the fifth seventeenth-century editions (B–G) is based on its immediate predecessor, though occasional instances of editorial and/or compositorial intervention are incorporated in the course of this transmission (the text's evolution through the seventeenth-century collected editions is illustrated in Figure 15). Of the above-noted misreadings that A inherits from various ancestors in the β5 line of transmission, those in lines 19, 40, 51, 72, and 90 persist in B–G, while B's editor consults H6 in order to correct "employes" in line 12, "the" in line 52, "Court" in line 61, and "men bared" in line 80 to "implyes," "thy," "Courts," and "erst men bared," respectively. Apparently also from H6, B derives "the [for the authorial *their*] way" in line 26, the syntax-changing "The iron Age *that* was, when justice was sold (now / Injustice is sold dearer) did allow…" (for "…when Iustice was sold, now / Iniustice is sold deerer farre; allow…") in lines 37–38, the original "claim'd fees" (for the revised "demands, fees") in line 39, and "Which [for *Who* or *And*] div'st" in line 91. On the other hand, B rejects meter-regularizing changes that H6 effects in lines 22 (the omission of "to"), 56 (the omission of "Only"), and 73 (the insertion of "and"), as well as overlooking (or rejecting) H6's correct "aske" in line 66. Perhaps most puzzlingly, B overlooks in H6 the "but" and "vs" that would have expanded β5's metrically deficient "and tells" to "and but tells vs" in line 72 (on B's use of H6 as a source of emendations, see, e.g., *DV* 2:lxxix–lxxx and the General Textual Introduction above).

Other than a few changes of spelling and punctuation, the *Sat5* text remains stable in C–F. On the text received from D–F, however, G's editor imposes substantive changes in lines 9, 37, 38, 50, 57, 58, 68, and 87. Of these, alteration of the received "write and jest" to "write in jest" in line 9 is an editorial trivialization, and the omissions of "that" in lines 37 and 58, of the first "when" in line 50, and of "and sayd" (with the accompanying insertion of "and" before "he") in line 57 apparently represent the editor's independent efforts to regularize meter. Further, in an attempt to clarify the poem's concluding conceit, G independently alters the rhyme words "cozened" (l. 90) and "vanished" (l. 91) to "cozeneth" and "vanisheth," aligning them with "Thou art" rather than "dog…cozened" earlier in the sentence. G's restoration of the authorial "…Injustice is sold dearer far, allow…" (replacing the B–F reading "…Injustice is sold dearer) did allow…" in line 38, its replacement of the received "lack" with the authorial "ask" in line 68, and its replacement of B–F's "if he sold" with the revised "when he sold" in line 87, on the other hand, all reflect the editor's consultation of an additional member of the LRH² lineage. Among its print predecessors, G could have derived the authorial version of line 38 and line 87's revised "when" only from A, but the authorial "ask" in line 68 had never before been printed and must necessarily have come from a manuscript. If G's editor did derive the corrections to lines 38 and 87 from A rather than from either an existing or a lost manuscript scion of the LRH², these emendations would join those cited in the Textual Introduction to *Metem* below among the rare instances in which G reflects the influence of a seventeenth-century edition prior to F.

The Modern Editions

The history of *Sat5* in the modern prints replicates that of the other four Satyres and is illustrated graphically in Figure 17: Tonson (H) sets the text into print from G, as is evident in his recording G's "write in [for *and*] jest" in line 9 and "Iron Age was [for *that was*]" in line 37 (see also readings in ll. 50 and 57); and he independently reduces G's "do eat" in line 22 to "eat," elides line 40's "for is" to "for, 's," and changes the grammatically problematical "Flow" in line 46 to "Flows." H's replacement of G's innovative "cozeneth"-"vanisheth" rime in lines 90–91 with the normative "cozened"-"vanished" apparently indicates his comparison of either B or C (see *DV* 2:lxxxiii). I (Bell) derives from H and gives rise to J (Anderson), while K (Chalmers) and M (Lowell) revert to H for their setting texts (among this group, e.g., I uniquely introduces and transmits to J an exclamation point after "Muse" in line 1 [reading "Muse!"] as well as the hyphenated "mis-take" in line 67; M and K return to the readings of G–H). Lowell's occasional practice of comparing B is not unmistakably evident in his text of *Sat5*, although his restoration of the spelling "Carrick's"—where "Charricks" (with an *h*) had been introduced in C and had remained in D–I—may point to his having consulted the earlier edition (see *DV* 2:lxxxii–lxxxiii for parallel instances of these relationships and procedures).

Although he registers readings from B32, B40, H7, and A in his notes, Grosart (N) specifies G as his copy-text; and his recording of the idiosyncratic G readings in lines 9, 37, 50, 57, and—uniquely—the "cozeneth"-"vanisheth" rime in lines 90–91 (see Figure 17) indicates his adherence to that edition. In two instances—dropping of "do" from the line-22 phrase "do eat" (= "eat") and "correction" of the received "Flow" to "Flows" in line 46—N appears to adopt readings from H, but although he says nothing of the "Flow"-to-"Flows" change, his textual note describes his omission of "do" as an independent metrical regularization. While generally modernizing spelling and punctuation (and following M in such minor details as, e.g., the enclosure in parentheses of the clause "since all.../...elements" in lines 10–11), the Grolier Club editors (O) substantively reproduce the text of A. O thus becomes the only edition since 1633 to record "employs" (for "implyes") in line 12, "Court" (for "Courts") in line 61, and "men bared" (for "erst men bared") in line 80; and among modern editions only P joins O in printing "lack [for *ask*] a fee" in line 68. Chambers's (P) is the last edition of the nineteenth century, and no poem illustrates P's admitted eclecticism more clearly than *Sat5*. At points of significant variance, as is shown in Figure 17, Chambers gives A's readings in lines 9 ("and [for *in*] jest"), 37 ("that was" [for "was"]), 57 ("he who made and said" [for "and he who made"]), 68 ("lack" [for "ask"]), and 90–91 ("cozened"-"vanished" [for "cozeneth"-"vanisheth"]). On the other hand, he follows B in lines 26 ("the [for *their*] way"), 38 ("dearer—did" [for "deerer farre"]), 52 ("thy [for *the*] way"), 80 ("erst men bared" [for "men bared"]), and 87 ("if [for *when*] he sold"). And in lines 50 and 58, respectively, he adopts from G the readings "upwards" (for "when upwards") and "Meant not [for *not that*] men...." Chambers's "Flows" (for

"Flow") in line 46 and "hungrily" (for "hungerly") in line 81 are his own independent adjustments; and although he cites no authority for the change, his expansion of the received "and tells us" in line 72 to the authorial "and but tells us" must derive from a manuscript, since it had appeared in no prior edition.

In accordance with his conclusion that A is "superior to any other single edition" (2:cxvi), Grierson (Q) selects A as his copy-text for *Sat5*; and although he replicates such of the edition's anomalous spellings as "wreched" (with no *t*) in line 6 and "scracheth" (with no *t*) in line 75, Grierson introduces meter-smoothing elisions in lines 33, 80, and 90 and modifies A's punctuation in nearly 20 places. He also—as Figure 17 indicates—abandons A's verbals in some 7 instances, giving "implies" (for "employes") in line 12, "Courts" (for "Court") in line 61, "aske" (for "lack") in line 68, "and but tells us who" (for "and tells who") in line 72, "th'extremeties" (for "extremities") in line 76, "erst men bar'd" (for "men bared") in line 80, and "what's" (for "what") in line 91. For all these changes Grierson cites the authority of later editions and/or manuscripts, and all except the acceptance of H4's anomalous "what's" in line 76 represent the correction of error. Since he fails to understand the evolution of the text genealogically, however, Grierson's adherence to A leads him to retain the β5 errors "sweat, and sweare" (for "sweare and sweat") in line 40, "these [for *those*] labours" in line 51, "the [for *thy*] way" in line 52, and "the [for y^e] swimming dog" in line 90, as well as the γ3 "Meant not that" (for "Ment not") in line 58 and the "div'st" (for "diu'dst") that A imported from DT1 in line 91.

Grierson's twentieth-century successors Hayward (S), Milgate (Y), Shawcross (Z), Smith (AA), and Patrides (ZZ) all present an A-based text as emended by Grierson except that none accepts the line-91 "what's" that Grierson had adopted from H4, and both S and DD drop "in" from the line-43 phrase "Law be in the Judges heart" (yielding "Law be the…"). Among these, S systematically modernizes "then" to "than" but otherwise imitates Q exactly, even to the point of spelling "wreched" in line 6 and "scracheth" in line 75. Milgate (Y), too, largely reproduces the punctuation and orthography of Q, but introduces numerous elisions in an effort to regularize Donne's meter; both Shawcross (Z)—who also elides a handful of constructions—and Patrides (DD) generally follow the accidentals of A. Smith (AA) provides a popularized text that follows Q's verbals (except in line 91), but modernizes spelling throughout.

In a semi-popular edition that systematically modernizes spelling and punctuation, Bennett (T) is the lone twentieth-century editor to use a manuscript copy-text, and—since he chooses NY3 for this function—the lone editor to print an earlier version of the text. He thus gives the original "claim'd fees" (for the revised "demaunds…") in line 39, "Like Angelica, scape" (for "Scape like Angelica") in line 42, "All things follow their likes [for *like*]" in line 56, "but tells us who" (for "but tells who") in line 72, and "if [for *when*] he sold" in line 87. On the other hand, he appends the explanatory "To Sir Thomas Egerton / *ca.* 1597" to the numbered heading ("Satire V"), emends NY3's "stings" in line 5 to A's "sting," corrects (without acknowledgment) NY3's erroneous "chaynes" in line 73 to "chairs," and—citing H4 for both—joins all other editions in printing "div'st [for the manuscript's *diu'dst*] near drowning" as well as joining Q and S in printing "what's [for *what*] vanished" in line 91. In two passages, Bennett's alterations of punctuation are also substantive: he moves the closing parenthesis that normatively

[blank] = agrees with LRH¹ reading ~ = agrees with LRH¹ OoV = Origin of Variant A–G = variant appears in 17th-c. eds.
. = variant appears in modern eds. ( ) = specific source of variant < > = word(s) omitted

Line no.	LRH¹/DV reading	Variant	OoV	A–G	H	I	J	K	M	N	O	P	Q	S	T	Y	Z	AA	DD
1	Muse,	~|	I			·	·												
6	wretched	wreched	A	A	·	·	·	·	·	·			·	·		wrech'd	·	·	·
9	and	in	G	G						·				·	·		·	·	·
12	implyes	employs	β⁵	A	·	·	·	·	·	·	·	·		·	·				·
19	Excrement	excrements	β⁵	A–G	·	·	·	·	·	·	·				·			·	·
20	to	no	J			·	·	·	·	·	·				·				
22	do'eat	eat	H				·		·	·	·								
24	And	<And>	K			·	·	·	·	·	·								
26	their	the	H6/B	B–G	·	·	·	·	·	·				·					
30	come	can,	J	J		·	·	·	·	·				·			·	·	·
37	that	<that>	G	G		·	·	·	·	·									
39	claym'd	demands	LRH²	A	·	·	·	·	·	·	·			·	·				·
40	sweare and sweat	sweat ~ swear	β⁵	A–G	·	·	·	·	i's	·	·			·			·	·	·
40	for is	~ 's	H	H	·	·	·	·	i's	·	·			·			·	·	·
42	Like Angelica, scape	Scape, like Angelica	LRH²	A–G	·	·	·	·	·	·	·			·			·	·	·
43	be	<be>	J				·	·			·				·				
43	in	<in>	S			·	·	·	·	·	·		·		·			·	·
46	Flow	Flows	H			·	·	·	·	·	·		·		·			·	·
50	1ˢᵗ when	<1ˢᵗ when>	G	G	·	·	·	·	·	·		·		·			·	·	·
51	those	these	β⁵	A–G	·	·	·	·	·	·		·		·			·	·	·
52	thy	the	β⁵	A	·	·		·	·	·		·		·			·	·	·
56	Likes	like	LRH²	A–G	·	·	·	·	·	·		·		·			·	·	·
57	He	and ~	G	G	·	·		·	·	·		·		·			·	·	·

Line no.	LRH¹/DV reading	Variant	OoV	A–G	H	I	J	K	M	N	O	P	Q	S	T	Y	Z	AA	DD
57	and sayd	<~> <~>	G	G	•	•	•	•	•	•	•		•	•		•	•	•	•
58	not	~ that	γ³	A–F									•	•		•	•	•	•
61	Courts	Court	γ³	A							•								
67	mistake	mis-take	I									•			• (H6?)				
68	aske	lack	δ³	A–F							•	•							
72	but tells vs	tells	LRH¹, β⁵	A–G	•	•	•	•	•	•	•								
73	chayres	chaines	K					•											
73	3ʳᵈ who	and ~	H						•	•	•								
76	so in	~ ~	Y													•			
76	th'extremityes	extremities	A	A–G	•	•	•	•	•	•	•	•							
80	earst	<earst>	γ³	A				•			•					•			
81	wrong, and	~ ~	Y								•								
81	hungerly	hungrily	P									•							
87	if	when	LRH², G	A, G	•	•	•	•	•	•	•		•	•		•	•	•	•
90	that	the	β⁵	A–G		•	•	•	•	•	•	•	•	•		•	•	•	•
90	cozeneth	cozeneth	G	G		•			•	•									
91	And	Which	H6	B–G	•	•	•	•		•									
91	diu'dst	div'st	DT1/A	A–G	•	•	•	•	•	•		divest	•	•	•		•	•	•
91	what	~'s	H4							•			•		•				
91	vanished	vanisheth	G	G															

occurs at the end of line 12 to the end of line 11 and inserts a period at the end of line 12, thus changing the author's kernel sentence "If all things be in all...Then Man is a world" to "If all things be in all...Each thing each thing implies...." In the second instance he inserts a dash after "Age" in line 37, turning "The Iron Age" into an appositive ("The Iron Age—that was when injustice was sold...") rather than a predicate nominative ("The Iron Age that was, when Iustice was sold...").

Copy-texts Used in this Edition

NY3 and DT1 provide, respectively, the copy-texts used here for the first revised and final versions of the poem. Like Bennett before us, we emend NY3's misreadings "stings" in line 6 to "stinge" and "chaynes" in line 73 to "chayres." Additionally, although we retain Rowland Woodward's idiosyncratic spellings "wright" (l. 9) and "Carraques" (l. 85), neither of which is likely to be misunderstood, we alter the ambiguous "ther" (l. 26), "Steale" (l. 49), "reuerent" (l. 69), and "till" (l. 82) to "their," "Steele," "reuerend," and "tell," respectively. These and our few clarifying adjustments of the punctuation are itemized as emendations of the copy-text in the Textual Apparatus, as are the routine regularizations needed to prepare a manuscript copy-text for print. The cosmetic regularizations necessary to ready DT1 for print are similarly noted in the apparatus, as are the alterations of punctuation (in ll. 6, 20, 30, 75, 76, and 82) necessary to producing a readable text. More significantly, however—since DT1 not only inherits one substantive error from the LRH[2] itself and commits several blunders of its own, but also evinces corrupt readings introduced in β^5 and γ^3—bringing DT1 into conformity with Donne's final version of the text requires that the poem be verbally emended in 15 of its 91 lines, as follows:

Table 5.2: Verbal emendations of the DT1 text

Line no.	Error (Source)	Emendation
3b–4a	*ll. om* (DT1)	*ll. restored*
5	stings (β^5)	stinge
19	excrements (β^5)	excrement
27	{and} th'issue (DT1)	th'issue
40	sweate, and sweare (β^5)	sweare and sweat
51	these (β^5)	those
52	the (β^5)	thy
58	y^t men (γ^3)	men
61	Court (γ^3)	Courts
72	<but> tells <vs> (β^5, LRH[2])	but tells vs
80	men <erst> bared (γ^3)	men erst bared
81	howe (DT1)	nowe
90	the (β^5)	that
91	diu'st (DT1)	diu'dst

Among the emended readings here charted, those in lines 3b–4a, 5, 27, and 81 are given in all previous editions, and the plural "Courts" (l. 61) appears in all editions except A and O. Further, all editions except A and O give a version of line 80 that includes "erst," although no prior edition has printed the revised "men erst bared" in that line; and all editions since P have recorded the correct "but tells vs" in line 72. On the other hand, "excrement" in line 19, "sweare and sweat" in line 40, "those" (l. 51), and "that" (l. 90) appear only in Bennett (T), who bases his text on the first revised version found in NY3; and among the editions produced since Grierson established A as the preferred copy-text for the poem, only Bennett has printed "thy" in line 52 and "men" in line 58. The preterite familiar form "diu'dst" in line 91—discussed more fully below—has not appeared in the reading text of any prior edition.

Two passages in the poem pose particular questions of punctuation: the sentence that begins "If all things be in all" in line 9 and ends with "Then Man is a World..." in line 13 and the "so-t'is" clause in line 63. With regard to the first, NY3's rendition of the poem uniquely encloses the entirety of lines 10–12 in parentheses, thus determining that the qualifier "As I thinke" at the head of line 10 be read as part of the construction within parentheses; the final revision recorded in DT1, however, gives no parentheses in these lines, but rather sets off the qualifying "As I thinke" with commas, leaving "As I thinke" to be read ambiguously as a modifier either of the "since-all–which-weare" clause that occupies lines 10–12 or of the "If–all-things-bee-in-all" construction that begins in line 9 and extends into line 13. Whether NY3's parentheses in lines 10–12 represent Donne's revision or a clarifying intervention on Woodward's part is uncertain, but if Donne's, they represent a middle-stage repunctuation of the passage that—either by accident or by design—did not survive in the final version of the poem. On the other hand, since DT1's punctuation of the passage typifies that of the descendants of both the LOH and the LRH², it surely reflects Donne's handling of the matter in at least one stage of the poem's evolution. Rather than intervening to reconcile a divergence on which the evidence provides no clear guidance, we have left the differing punctuations of NY3 and DT1 unemended in this passage.

NY3 sets off "so t'is" in line 63 as a discrete statement: "...if wee / Should pay fees, as here, dayly bread would bee / Scarce to Kings; so t'is." And since the evidence indicates that β¹, β², and β³ all three gave a period after "Kings," there is little doubt that this sentence-ending punctuation derives from the LOH. Similarly, the descendants of β⁴ end the clause after "Kings" (O21 with a semicolon, Y3 with a period), and all descendants of γ³ read a semicolon or a colon at this point—except DT1, which punctuates after "kings" with a comma and transmits that mark to H4. This evidence makes it fairly certain that the LRH² read a semicolon after "kings," and we have emended DT1's punctuation to reflect this belief: "...Scarce to kings; soe t'is."

Finally, two instances of problematic grammar must be mentioned. The first involves the clause "Power of the Courts belowe / Flowe..." in lines 45–46, which appears in both NY3 and DT1. This is obviously ungrammatical by modern standards, but Shakespearean precedents for such usage are cited by Grierson and Milgate (see the Notes and Glosses); and among seventeenth-century sources, only the descendants of ε "correct" "Flowe" to "Flowes." We have thus left the construction unemended in both copy-texts. The second involves the preterit familar verb form "diu'dst" in line 91. As noted above, Donne's handling of the conceit comparing the greedy suitor to the deluded dog in Aesop's fable changed between his earliest version of the poem and the second. In the first version, the opening clause identifies the suitor with the dog, and the relevant points of comparison are specified in relative clauses that describe, in the past tense, the dog's foolish behavior:

> Thou art that swimminge dogg whom shadowes cosoned
> Who diu'd neere drowninge for what vanished. (90–91)

In the revision, Donne sharpens the criticism of the suitor by changing the grammar of line 91 to make the diving "neere drowning" an action of the suitor himself:

> Thou art that swiming dogg whom shadows cosened
> And diu'dst neere drowning for what vanished.

This version, however, embodies an apparent incongruity between the present tense of "Thou art" and the past tense of "[thou] diu'dst," and among the descendants of the LRH², the scribes of β⁴, DT₁, and TT₁ normalize "diu'dst" to the present tense (either "diuest" or "diu'st"), transmitting the change to their respective descendants. Similarly, as noted above, A's editor substitutes "div'st" for C2's "div'dst," thus imposing a scribal/editorial lection that has persisted in every subsequent edition. There can be no doubt, however, that the past tense form is what Donne wrote: when the revision is first introduced in NY3, Woodward initially writes the predictable "div'st," but then attempts to impose a "d" between "v" and "s" before crossing through the whole blurry mess and writing out a new, clean "diu'dst"; and in the γ³ branch of the β⁵ lineage, all offspring of δ³ (C2, C8, and B11) and the O20-SP1 pair give the past tense, as does B40 in the γ⁴ branch. What difference this tense change might make is a matter of interpretation, but no prior edition has provided readers the opportunity to consider the question. We are pleased to do so here.

Textual Apparatus

Copy-texts: First revised version: NY3.   Final version: DT1.

Texts collated: B11 (ff. 96–98); B13 (f. 54r–v); B40 (ff. 63–64); B47 (ff. 105–06); C2 (ff. 22–23v); C8 (ff. 15v–17v); C9 (ff. 20–21v); DT1 (ff. 20–21v); H4 (ff. 7v–9); H5 (ff. 118–19); H6 (pp. 77–80); H7 (ff. 55–57); H8 (ff. 76–77); HH1 (*ll. 1–14, 19–91 only*, ff. 72–74); NY1 (pp. 21–24); NY3 (ff. [10–11]); O20 (ff. 10v–12); O21 (pp. 181–84); OJ1 (*ll. 11, 58, 66, 68, 72, 76, 91 only*, pp. 346–49); OQ1 (ff. 206–07); P3 (ff. 11v–12v); SP1 (ff. [18–19v]); TT1 (ff. 24v–25); VA1 (ff. 10–11v); VA2 (ff. 12v–13v); Y2 (pp. 43–50 [42–49]); Y3 (pp. 15–17); A (pp. 346–49); B (pp. 143–45); C (pp. 143–45); D (pp. 136–39); E (pp. 136–39); F (pp. 136–39); G (pp. 135–38); 18g–i (*ll. 3–4 only*, p. 116); 18j (*same lines*, p. 117); 18k–m (*same lines*, p. 114 [*misnumbered 221 in 18k*]); 18n–q (*same lines*, p. 109); 18r (*same lines*, p. 69); 33a–b (*ll. 35–36 only*, sig. A5v).

Emendations of the copy-text, first revised version: Line 4 good?)] ~$_\wedge$)
5 stinge] stings   9 ieast?] ~.   10 weare,] ~$_\wedge$ are,] ~$_\wedge$ 11 Elements,] ~$_\wedge$ 26 their] ther   47 misery,] ~$_\wedge$ 49 Steele] Steale   50 Streame,] ~$_\wedge$ vpwards,] ~;   53 Seas,] ~;   60 God,] ~;   Dominations,] ~$_\wedge$ 68 comming?] cōming.   69 reuerend] reuerent   73 chayres] chaynes   74 Nayles,] ~;   76 Law),] ~)$_\wedge$ th'extremityes,] ~'~$_\wedge$ 77 do,] ~$_\wedge$ 79 Officer,] ~$_\wedge$ 82 till] tell   89 fables,] ~;

Regularizations of the copy-text, first revised version: Heading: *Satyre* 5.] Sat:
5^a.   Line 2 which] wch 10 which] wch 14 the] y^e 15 which] wch 16 which] wch 17 the] y^e which] wch 19 which] wch 23 which] wch 24 which] wch 30 o'reflow] oreflow   31 Sir] S^r loues] Loues   33 authoriz'd] authorizd   39 claym'd] claymd   40 which] wch 45 the] ye 46 maine] Maine   50 the] ye 51 and] &   52 'Gainst] Gainst   53 which] wch 55 drown'd] drownd   57 He] he   68 ne're] nere   69 strumpeted] Strumpeted   75 which] wch 78 our] o^r 79 Hath] hath   80 which] wch 81 and] &   82 that] y^t 83 and] &   Thummin] Thūmin   86 and] &   87 Hammon] Hāmon   88 that] y^t 90 that] y^t

Emendations of the copy-text, final version: Heading: *Satyre* 5.] Satyre. |
Line 3b–4a he being vnderstood / May make good Courtyers,] *om* (supplied from C2)   4 good?)] ~$_\wedge$)   5 stinge] stings   6 theame,] ~;   19 excrement] excrements   20 sutors] ~?   27 th'issue] and ~'~   30

228

or'eflowe.] ~;   40 sweare and sweate] sweate, ~ sweare   51 those] these
52 thy] the   58 not] ~ y^t 61 Courts] Court   63 kings;] ~,   t'is.]
~'~,   72 but] *om*   vs] *om*   75 Sutors.] ~,   76 men,] ~;
Lawe,] ~$_\wedge$ 80 erst] *om*   81 nowe] howe   82 dye.] ~,   90 that]
the   91 diu'dst] diu'st

Regularizations of the copy-text, final version: *The manuscript exhibits initial
capital letters in ll. 1, 17, 31, 35, 43, 48, 57, 60, 79, 80, 88, and 89; all other
first-of-line capitals supplied.*   Line 2 which] wch 5 the] y^e 7 What]
what   9 If] if   10 which] wch shall] shall=   13 which] w^{ch}
15 which] wch 16 which] wch These] these   17 which] w^{ch}
19 which] wch All] all   22 you] yo^u 23 the] y^e which] w^{ch}
you] yo^u 24 which] wch and] &   25 you] yo^u you] yo^u
27 your] yor 28 and] &   31 Sir] S^r.   37 that] y^t 39 and] &
40 which] wch 45 Power] power   46 and] &   51 and] &
52 'Gainst] gainst   53 which] wch 63 Would] would   72 Fates]
ffates   75 With] wth which] wch 80 which] wch 81 and] &
82 that] y^t 83 and] &   and] &   84 and] &   86 that] y^t
that] y^t 89 and] &   91 vanished.] vanished. |

HISTORICAL COLLATION

Format:
Imperfections: *text lost to water damage in l. 76*   B11.
Indentations: *l. 1 ind*   NY3; *l. 35 ind*   33a; *no ind*   Σ.
Miscellaneous: *ll. 3b and 4a om, ll. 3a and 4b run together as a single l.*   DT1
H4; ›I: D‹ *in right M at l. 1*   DT1; »P.« *to the left of the HE*   H6; »here in
Printed copy« *in space left for om l. 83*   H7; *ll. 15–18 om and* »desunt 4
cae:« *written in left M between ll. 14 and 19*   HH1; *every 5th l. numbered
in arabic in the left M*   NY1 VA2; *HE in left M*   NY3; »p. 135 | « *to left of
HE*   O20; *ll. 13–20 scribally numbered 1–8 in left M, ll. 31–34 entered in
the order 31, 33, 32, 34 and scribally numbered 1, 3, 2, 4 in right M, ll.
83–84 garbled and conflated into a single l.*   O21; *ms. emendations and
additions in a copy of A*   OJ1; *l. 19 placed between ll. 14 and 15 and ll.
13–20 numbered in left M to correct the order, ll. 83–84 garbled and conflated
into a single l.*   Y3; *couplet among miscellaneous canonical excerpts under the
collective HE* "MICHEALMASSE TERM, Octob: 24, ends November 28,"
merged with Calm 27–28 and 31–34 as a discrete entry   33a.
Headings: Satyre 5:th B11 C2 C9(5.) H6(.5.) H8(.5.) A(V.)–G(V.). |Satire
the 5th. | B13.   A. *Satire. 3:*   B40 TT1.   Satyre 5. Of the miserie of
the poore suitors at Co^{u}rt. | B47.   *Satire 5.th*   C8(Satirr.) NY1.
Satyre. | DT1 O20.   Satire. H4.   Satyra secunda. H5.
|.Satyra Quinta. | H7 SP1(.5^a.) VA2 Y2.   Satira 5ta HH1 OQ1.
Sat: 5^a.   NY3.   *Satyre ye third.* | O21.   The 5th Satyre P3.   Sat:
5. | VA1.   Satire the Third   Y3.   *om*   OJ1 18g–r 33a–b.

1 shalt] shal G.   laugh] ~, C8.   leafe,] B11 C2 C8 C9 H6 NY3 Y3
A–G; ~∧ Σ.   Muse,] (~,) B13; (~∧) B47 H5 H7 H8 HH1 OQ1 P3 VA1
Y2; ~∧ H4 NY1 O21 TT1 VA2 Y3.   they] ~,   B11 B13; ~. | C8; ~– OQ1.

2 warmes.] warnes: B11 C2 SP1; warnes; B13 C8 O20; warnes, B40 H7;
~, B47; ~; C9 DT1 O21 A; ~: H4 H8 HH1 Y2; warnes. NY1 P3 VA1 VA2;
warnes∧ OQ1 TT1.   which] (~ OQ1.

3 Courtiers] B11 B47 C9 H6 HH1 NY1 NY3 TT1 VA1 VA2; ~;   B13; ~:
O21; Courtier Y2; ~, Σ.   (he] ∧~ B13 B40 H7 OQ1 G; om DT1(»∧~«)
H4 O21 Y3; ∧~, H5; (~, H6.   beeing] (~ B40 H5 O21 Y3; om DT1(»~«)
H4.   vnderstood] om DT1(»~,«) H4; ~) H5 O21 Y3.
    Alternate line: Those Rules well practis'd, rightly vnderstood, 18g–l
18m(*practis'd∧*) 18n–r.

4 May] om DT1(»~«) H4; *Might* 18g–r.   make] om DT1(»~«) H4.
good] om DT1(»~«) H4 P3.   Courtiers,] ~; B13 O21; om DT1(»~∧«) H4;
~∧ OQ1 TT1.   but] (~ H4; *yet* 18g–r.   who] ~, B11 C2 C8 DT1; ~?
H5; not O21; how? Y2; *few* 18g–r.   good?)] B47 C9 H6 H8 NY1 SP1 VA2
A–F; ~∧∧ B13 H7 TT1 Y3; ~,∧ H5; ~.∧ O21 18g–r; ~?∧ G; ~,) Σ.

5 Frees] ffree's B47 Y2 G; free HH1 O21 Y3.   stinge] stinges B40 DT1
H4 NY3 O20 SP1 TT1; sling Y2.   ieasts] ~; B40 O21; *blank space* B47;
least C2; ~, HH1 VA1 Y3.   all,] B11 B40 C2 C8 DT1 H5 NY3 O20; ~;
B13; ~∧ Σ.   who'in] NY3; whome in P3 VA1; whoe in Σ.

6 wretched] ~, B13 B40 DT1 H4 SP1 VA1.   wicked:] ~; B11 DT1 H4
H5 NY1 O21 SP1 VA1 VA2; ~. B13 C9 H6 H8 P3; ~, B40 B47 HH1 OQ1 Y2
Y3 G; ~∧ TT1.   these] those H5 H8; the OQ1.   theame] ~. B40; ~;
DT1; ~, O21; ~: OQ1.

7 Charity] ~, B11 B13 B40 C8 H4 H7 O20 SP1 VA1.   Liberty] ~, B11
C2 C8 DT1.   giue] giues B47 H7; ~; HH1.   me.] ~; B11 B40 C2 H5
O20 O21; ~, B47 H4 OQ1 Y2 Y3; ~: H7 SP1; om HH1; ~! TT1.

8 Officers] offices B47.   rage] C8 H5 NY3 OQ1 P3 TT1 Y2 Y3; ~; O21;
~, Σ.   miseree] ~. C8; ~, HH1 P3; ~; O21.

9 wright] HH1 NY3; write, B13 B40 C2 C8 H5 H7 H8 P3 SP1 A–F; writt,
H4; write Σ.   and] or H4(*var:* »~«); in G.   ieast?] ~, B40; ~. HH1
NY3 OQ1; ~; O20 SP1 Y2; ~∧ TT1.   *2nd* all] ~, B11 B40 C2 C8 DT1 H5
O20 A–G.

10 (As] NY3 O21 Y3; (~, C9 H6; ∧~ Σ.   thinke,] ~∧ B40 C8 SP1 TT1
Y2; ~) O21 Y3; ~. VA1.   all] ~, B11 B40 C2 C8 DT1 O20 SP1 Y2 A–G.
which] (~ OQ1; om P3.   weare,] B11 C2 O20; were∧ B13 C8 C9 H6 OQ1
TT1; ~∧ NY3; were, Σ.   are,] ~∧ C8 C9 H7 NY3 OQ1 TT1 Y3.
and] or SP1.   shall] ~= B11 B40 C2 C8 DT1 H4 H5 NY1 O20 SP1 VA2.

11 Bee,] ~; O21; ~) OQ1; =~∧ SP1; ~∧ TT1.   be] om B13 SP1.
made] ~ made OQ1.   same] selfe ~ OJ1.   Elements,] B11 B40 C2 DT1

H5 H8 HH1 O20 OQ1 P3; Element‸ B47; ~. VA1; ~: A–G; ~‸ Σ.

12 thing,] ~‸ C9 DT1 H4 H6 H8 TT1; ~; O21. thing] ~, B11 C8. implyes] employes B11 B40 C2 C8 HH1 TT1 A; ~, B13 DT1 H4 H8 NY1 VA1; employes, O20 SP1 Y2; ~; O21. or] & Y2. represents)] C9 H6 NY3; ~, B11 C2 DT1 A; ~. B13 H5 HH1 NY1 B–G; ~: B40 OQ1 SP1; ~; H8; representeth: VA2; ~‸ Σ.

13 Then] ~; OQ1. World;] B11 C2 C8 NY3 O20 A–G; ~, B13 DT1 H5 H8 HH1 OQ1 P3 SP1 VA1; ~: H7; ~‸ Σ. which] ~, H5 A–G. Officers] ~, HH1 A–G.

14 om TT1. rauishing] raveninge B13 B47 H5 H7 O21 Y3; rauenous C9 H6 H8 OQ1 P3 VA1. Seas,] ~; B11 C2 C8 H8 NY1 VA2 Y3 A–G; ~: DT1; ~‸ HH1; ~. VA1. Suters] ~, B13 HH1 O21 A–G.

15 om HH1 TT1. Springs,] ~; B11 C2 C8 DT1 O21 A–F; ~‸ B13 B47(spinges) H4 H7 P3 VA1; Spring, SP1. full,] ~‸ B47 C9 O21 P3 Y3; fall, SP1. shallow,] ~‸ C9. now] om P3 VA1. dry;] B11 C8 NY3 O20 A B; ~‸ B13 B47 H7 H8 Y2 C; ~: O21; om P3 VA1; ~, Σ. which] ~, A–G. to] too B47 Y2; (~ P3.

16 om HH1 TT1. That] ~, O20 SP1. drownes] drowneth B47; drawes H7 P3 VA1; drowne OQ1. them] ~, B47 A–G; ~) P3. run.] ~: B11 C2 C8 H5 NY1 OQ1 VA2 A–G; ~, B40 H4 H7 O20 Y2; ~; B47 SP1; ~‸ O21. selfe reasons] ~ reason B47; ~=~ OQ1.

17 om HH1 TT1. the] a Y2. World] Man H7(var: »~«) Y2; ~, OQ1. a] yᵉ Y2. Man;] ~, B40 B47 C9 H5 H6 H8 NY1 O21 OQ1 VA2 Y3 A–G; ~‸ H4 P3 VA1; World‸ H7(var: »~‸«) Y2. which] ~, OQ1 A–G. Officers] ~; O21.

18 om HH1. Stomack,] stomacks, C9 H6; ~; O21 Y3; ~‸ TT1. Suters] ~, B40 DT1.

19 Th'Excrement] H6 NY3; The excrements, B11 C2 C8 DT1 NY1 O20 SP1 A; the excrements B40 H4 HH1 TT1 VA2 Y2 B–G; The'Excremēts H7; the excrement Σ. they] the O21 VA2. voyd.] ~; B11 B40 C2 C8 H4 O20 O21 A–F; ~, B47 HH1; ~: H5 NY1 OQ1 VA2 Y2. dust;] DT1 H5 H8 HH1 NY3 O20; ~, B13 B40 C2 O21 A–G; ~: OQ1; ~. P3 SP1; ~‸ Σ.

20 worse] more C9 H7 H8; ~ (var: ›more‹) H6. Suters] B47 C9 H6 HH1 NY3 P3 TT1 VA1; ~? DT1 H4 OQ1; ~, Σ. who] yᵗ B47 C9 H6 H8 O21 Y3; wᶜʰ H5 H7 HH1 NY1 VA2 Y2. Lust] lustes B47.

21 prayes.] ~, B40 O20; ~? B47 C9 H5 HH1 NY1 O21 VA2 Y3; preyes; H4; ~; H6 H7 SP1; preyes. H8 A–F; ~: OQ1 Y2; ~‸ TT1; preys? G. O] & B47; ~, H5. then] than B–G. dust] ~, B11 B13 B40 C2 DT1 H4 H7 O20 O21 SP1 A–C. wormes meat;] DT1 NY3 SP1; wormesmeate‸ B13; wormesmeat, B40 C8; ~ ~, C2 C9 O20 O21 VA2 A–G; ~·~; H5; ~ ~. H6; ~=~, OQ1; ~ ~‸ Σ.

22 do'eat] NY3; eate   C9 H6; doe eat   Σ.   you] ~,   C9 H6 O20 SP1.
now,] ~∧   B47 H7 P3 TT1 VA1; om   O20 SP1; ~;   O21.   selues] ~,   B11.
eat.] ~;   B40 O20; ~∧   B47 C8 NY1 O21 OQ1 TT1 VA1 Y2 Y3; ~,   H4 H6 VA2.

23 the] they   H7(→ »~«) VA2.   which] that   B47.   you,] ~;   B13 H8;
~∧   H7 TT1 VA1.   yet] and   C9(&) H5 H6.   are] ~,   HH1 O21.

24 The] they   P3.   wind] windes;   O21; ~,   SP1; winds   Y3.   which]
that   B47.   driues] driue   O21 Y3.   them;] NY3 OQ1 P3 SP1 A–G; ~.
B13 Y3; ~:   C9 H8; ~∧   TT1; ~,   Σ.   a wastfull] awast full   B40; ~ wast=full
OQ1 SP1.   warr] ~,   O21.

25 Is] if   Y2.   you,] it;   O21; ~∧   TT1; ytt,   Y3.   it.] B13 C9 H6 H8
NY3 P3 VA1 Y3; ~;   B40 DT1 H4 OQ1 A–G; ~!   TT1; ~∧   Y2; ~,   Σ.
They] ~;   O21.

26 Law,] ~;   B13; ~∧   C9 NY1 P3 TT1; lawes,   H8 HH1.   their] there
B11 B47 VA2; the   B13 C9 H6 H8 HH1 O21 OQ1 P3 TT1 VA1 Y2 Y3 B–G;
ther   B40 NY3.   way] ~,   DT1 SP1 B–G; ~:   HH1; ~.   Y2.

27 Wittalls;] Wittolls,   B11 C2 C8 O20; ~.   B13 C9 H6 H8 VA1; wittolls;
B40 DT1 H4; ~:   B47 HH1 OQ1 P3 Y3; ~,   H7 NY1 VA2 A–G; Wittolles∧
SP1 TT1; Victualls∧   Y2.   The'issue] B11 C2 C8 C9 H5 H6 H7 NY3 A–G;
the yssue,   B40; and ~   DT1 H4; then Issue   O20 SP1; The issue   Σ.   your]
of their   Y2.   ruine] rage   B13.   is.] ~∧   B11 B47 C8(~».«) HH1 O20
TT1 VA1 Y2 Y3; ~;   B40 H4 A; ~:   H5 O21 OQ1.

28 Greatest,] B13 B40 DT1 H4 H7 HH1 NY3 O20 SP1; ~∧   Σ.   Empresse,]
~∧   B13 B47 H4 H7 H8 NY1 O21 OQ1 P3 TT1 VA1 VA2 Y2 Y3; ~;   O20.
know you] yoᵘ knowe   OQ1.   this?] ~∧   H7 O21 TT1 Y2 Y3; ~.   P3.

29 Alas,] B11 C2 H5 H8 HH1 NY3 A–G; ~∧   Σ.   more] ~,   B11 OQ1
SP1.   then] the   VA2; than   B C G.   Thames] Theames   H5 P3;
Theame   VA1.   calme] cold   H5.   head] ~,   B40.   doth] does   OQ1;
doeth   VA1.   know] ~,   OQ1 SP1.

30 Whose] om   B47; those   O21.   Meades] ~,   B40 H7; medowes   O20
SP1.   armes] arme   B13 C9 H6.   drowne,] drownes;   B13; drownes,
B40(Drownes,) B47 C9 H6 O21 SP1 Y2 Y3; drown'd,   H8 OQ1 P3 VA1 VA2;
~∧   NY1 G; drownes∧   TT1.   or] ore   Y2.   corne] yᵗ O21.   o'reflow.]
ore=flowe.   B11 C8 D–G; ~;   B40 DT1; ~∧   B47 H4 HH1 TT1 Y2 Y3;
ore=flow∧   H8 VA2; o'r flowe∧   NY1; ~,   O20 B; ouerflowe,   O21; oreflewe:
OQ1; they ouerflow∧   P3 VA1.

31 You,] C9 H6 NY3; ~∧   Σ.   Sir,] ~∧   B11 B47 H8 HH1 NY1 O21 OQ1
TT1 VA2 Y2 Y3.   whose] (~   B47 H5 H8.   loues,] ~∧   TT1 Y3; ~.   VA1.
whom] (~   H7 OQ1.   I] ~,   O21.

32 hauing] ~,   B11.   serue] B47 H8 NY3 O21 SP1 TT1 VA1 Y2; ~,   Σ.
most] om   O21 P3 Y3.   richly] ~,   HH1.

33 payd,] ~; B40 Y2; ~) B47 H5 H8 OQ1; ~. O21; ~‸ P3 TT1 VA1.
authoriz'd] Authorised B11 B40 C2 HH1 O20 SP1; ~, B47 C9 H5 H6 H8 OQ1
B–F; authorized, C8 Y3 A; (~ P3; ~. G. now,] H7 NY3; ~) P3; ~‸ Σ.
begin] begun H8.

34 know] ~, B11 B13 B40 C2 DT1 H4 H7 O20 SP1. out] ~, B11; ~.
H7. enormous] Enormious C9 NY1 O21 TT1 VA1 VA2 Y2 Y3. sin.] ~;
B40; ~‸ B47 H4 O21 TT1 VA1 Y2 Y3.

35 age] ~, B11; ~! H7 NY1. of] if NY1 Y2; if → ›~‹ VA2. Iron,]
~; B13; ~‸ C9 NY1 TT1 Y2 Y3 33a; ~! H5 H8 A–G; ~? H7; ~: O21.
some] come C8; (~ C9 H6 B–F 33a–b; seeme NY1 Y2; seeme → ›~‹ VA2.
better] ~, Y2. Witt] ~, B13 DT1 33a–b; will OQ1.

36 name,] ~‸ H7 H8 NY1 TT1 VA2 Y3. ought] nought H7(→ »~«);
aught P3; ~, Y2. itt.] ~; B11 B40 C8 O20 A; ~‸ B47 H4 O21 OQ1 P3
TT1 VA1 Y2 Y3; ~, C2; ~). C9 H6; ~: DT1; ~;) B–F; ~.) 33a–b.

37 The] thy O21 Y3. Iron Age] ~ ~, B40 C9 H5 H6 P3 SP1 VA1; ~-~
H7; now ~, O21; ~ ~ Age TT1; non ~ Y3. that] om B13 B47 C9 H5
H6 O21 Y3 G; wᶜʰ H7 OQ1 P3 VA1 Y2. was,] B11 B13 C2 C8 DT1 NY3
O20 P3 A–G; om B47 C9 H5 H6 O21 Y3; ~‸ Σ. when] (~ O21 Y3.
sold,] ~‸ C9 H4 H5 O21 OQ1 Y2 Y3 B–F; ~! TT1. now] (~ B47 C9 H5
H6 B–F.

38 Iniustice] Inn Iustice HH1. deerer] ~) C9 B–F. farr;] ~, B11 C2
C8 H7 Y2 G; ~. B13 H8 OQ1 P3 SP1 VA1; ~) B47 H5 H6(→ ›om‹) O21 Y3;
om C9 B–F; ~); ~: HH1; ~! TT1; fare. VA2. Allow] did ~ B47 C9 H5
H6 O21 Y3 B–F; ~ → »did« ~ H7; How O20 SP1.

39 claym'd] demaunds, B11 B40 C2 C8 DT1 H4 A; claymed H5 H8 HH1;
Clayme H7 VA1; demands O20 SP1 TT1; demaunderes, O21 Y3(‸). fees]
~, B11 B13 B40 C2 DT1 H4 NY1 O20 O21 P3 SP1 VA2 A B C(unc).
dutyes,] ~. B13 C9 H6 H7 H8 OQ1 VA1 Y3 B–F; ~; H4 H5 O21 A; ~‸ O20
SP1 TT1; ~: Y2. Gamesters,] ~‸ B13 B40 B47 H4 H7 H8 NY1 O21 OQ1
P3 TT1 VA1 VA2 Y2 Y3.

40 mony] ~, Y2. which] om H8. you] wee HH1. sweare] sweat,
B11 B40 C2 C8 DT1 H4 O20 SP1 A–C; ~, B13 H7 P3 VA1 VA2; sweat TT1
D–G. sweat] sweare B11 B40 C2 C8 DT1 H4 O20 SP1 TT1 A–G. for is]
~, ~ B11 B13 B40 C2 C8 DT1 HH1 P3 A–G; for's B47 C9 H5 H6 H7 NY1
VA2; for om Y2. gone] ~, O21.

41 Into'other] NY3; into others B47 H6 O21 OQ1 TT1 Y3; in t'others H5;
Into an others Y2; Into other Σ. hands;] ~, B11 B40 B47 C2 DT1 H4
O20 Y3; ~. B13 C8 C9 H6 H8 NY1 OQ1 P3 VA1 VA2; Lands: H7(→ »~:«);
~: SP1 Y2 A–G; ~‸ TT1. controuerted] contrauerted B13 OQ1;
controuersed O21 Y3; con– P3; [space] VA1. Lands] ~, B40 SP1;
~; O21.

42 Like] B13 H7 HH1 NY1 NY3 OQ1 P3 VA1 VA2; Scape, ~ C9 H6 A–G; scape (~ H5; (Angelica ~) Y2; Scape ~ Σ. Angelica,] B11 C2 C8 C9 DT1 H4 NY3 O20 A–F; ~) H5; ~; H6; ~Λ Σ. scape] B13 H7 HH1 NY3 OQ1 P3 VA1; escape NY1 VA2 Y2; om Σ. Striuers] striuer's H4. hands.] ~Λ B13 B47 H4 P3 TT1 VA1 Y3; ~; B40 O21; ~: Y2.

43 Law] ~, H7. hart,] ~; B11; ~Λ TT1 VA1 Y2 Y3. he] ~, HH1; ~; O21.

44 Haue] hath P3 VA1. no] nor TT1. resist] ~, VA1. Letter] ~, B11 B13 B40 C2 DT1 H4 H6 O20 OQ1 A–G; ~; O21; —— P3; letters, SP1. or] —— P3. fee] ~, B11 B40 C2 C9 DT1 H5 HH1 O20 SP1 A–G; ~. H6; ~; O21; —— P3.

45 Wher] When VA1. appeal?] ~, B47 P3 Y2; ~Λ HH1; ~; O20; ~. VA1. Power] Powre B11 B40 C2 C8 H5 NY1 VA2 A B; ~, HH1. of] if HH1. the] o' O21 Y3. Courts] Court SP1 Y2. below] ~, O21 SP1 D–G.

46 Flow] Flowes C9 H6. the] their HH1. maine head:] NY3; ~ ~; B11 B40 C8 DT1 O20; ~ ~Λ B47 NY1 TT1; Meane ~; C2; maynehead, H6; meane ~, HH1; meane ~Λ O21 Y3; ~ ~, Σ. these] those C9 H6 HH1 OQ1 Y3; therefore P3 VA1; there SP1. throw] ~ thee TT1.

47 Thee,] ~Λ B40 H4 H7 NY1 O21 OQ1 P3 SP1 VA1 VA2 Y3; The, C2; om TT1. if] ~ → ›(‹~ B40; (~ OQ1 P3 TT1 VA1. they] the O21. suck] such, HH1. thee] ~ → ›)‹~ B40; ~, B47 C9 H6; The C2; ~) TT1; om Y2. in, to] into B13 B47 C9 H5 H6 HH1 O21 TT1 Y3; ~, ~ → ~ ›)‹~ B40; ~Λ ~ H4 SP1 Y2; ~) into OQ1 P3 VA1. misery,] B11 B40 C2 C8 DT1 H7 HH1 O20 OQ1 SP1 A–G; ~) B13; ~Λ Σ.

48 To] om OQ1; As Y2. fetters,] ~Λ H4 NY1 TT1 Y2; ~; O21. halters;] ~: B11 HH1 SP1 Y2; ~. B13 C9 H6 H8 B–G; ~, B40 B47 H4 H7 OQ1 P3 Y3; ~Λ TT1 VA1. th'iniury] C9 H6 NY3; the iniurie, B11; the Iniurie. B13; ~, HH1; thy iniury O21 Y3; the iniury Σ.

49 Steele] Steale B13 H4 (→ ›~‹) NY3. thee] ~, B47; the C2. complayne,] to ~, B11 C2 C8; ~; B13 H8 O21 A; ~. OQ1 VA1; ~Λ P3 TT1. alas,] B11 B47 C2 DT1 H5 HH1 NY3 O20 A–G; ~! H7; ~Λ Σ. thou] then P3. goest] go'st B47 C9 DT1 H6 P3 VA2 D–G.

50 Streame,] ~Λ C9 H4 H6 H7 NY1 NY3 O21 P3 SP1 TT1 VA2 Y2 Y3 G. when vpwards,] ~ ~. B13 VA1; ~ ~Λ B40 OQ1 TT1; ~ ~; C9 H4 H5 NY3 O21; ~ ~, → »vpwards when,« H7; ~ ~: H8 A–F; ~ vpward; NY1 VA2; ~ vpwardΛ Y2; om ~, G. when] om TT1 Y2. thou'art] NY3; th'art H5 H7 NY1 VA2; thou are Y3; thou art Σ. most] ~. B11.

51 Heauy] ~, B11 B13 B40 C2 C8 DT1 H4 H7 O20 SP1; ~; O21. most] om C9 H6(m̶o̶s̶t̶) H7 Y2. faynt.] NY3; ~; B11 C8 DT1 H4 Y3 A–G; ~Λ NY1 O21 TT1 VA1 VA2 Y2; ~, Σ. And] ~, H6. those] these

B11(theise) B40 C2 C8 DT1 H4 H7 O20 SP1 TT1 A–G.   Labors,] B13 B40
B47 C9 H5 H6 NY3; ~∧ Σ.   they] ~,   B11 B40 C2 A–G.

52 'Gainst] ('~ H8.   whome] ~, O20.   shouldst] shouldest   B40 C2
HH1 VA1.   complayne,] ~;   B13; ~) H8; ~∧   P3 TT1.   will] bee TT1.
thy] the   B11 B40 C2 C8 DT1 H4 O20 SP1 A; yᵗ O21.

53 Seas,] ~;   NY1 NY3 O21 SP1; ~∧   TT1.   which] ~,   B11 B13 C2 C8
O20 O21 SP1 A–G.   shalt] shouldst   H8.

54 Forc'd] forced   HH1 O21 TT1 Y3.   golden] a ~ P3 VA1.   bridges,]
~∧   O21 TT1 Y3; bridge∧   P3 VA1.   shalt] shat B47.   see] ~,   B11 HH1
SP1.

55 gold] ~, H7; ~;   VA1.   drown'd] drowned HH1.   before.] ~,   B11
C2 C8; ~∧   B13 B47 H4 H5 H7 NY1 OQ1 TT1 VA1 VA2 Y2 Y3; ~;   DT1 O20
A.

56 All things] althinges O21.   their] the H7(→ »~«); there VA2 Y3.
Likes;] HH1 NY3; ~,   B13 B40 NY1 OQ1 P3 VA1 VA2 Y2; lyke∧ C2; like:
H5; like; H8; ~∧   TT1; like, Σ.   Only] ~,   B11 C2 C8 DT1 A; om C9
H6; ~. H4.   who] they Y2.   haue,] ~∧   C9 H6 H8 HH1 NY1 OQ1 TT1
VA1 VA2 Y3 G; om Y2.   may] om Y2.   more.] ~,   B40 OQ1; ~∧   B47
C8 H4 H7 H8 NY1 O21 TT1 VA1 VA2 Y2 Y3 A; ~;   O20.

57 Gods.] B13 H7 NY3 P3 VA1; ~,   B40 B47 C9 H4 H6 NY1 Y2 Y3; ~: H8;
~∧   O21 TT1; ~;   Σ.   He] and ~   G.   who] wᶜʰ OQ1 P3 VA1.
made] ~,   B11 B13 B40 C2 DT1 H4 O20 SP1.   and] om O21 Y3 G.
sayd] stild B47 C9 H5 H8; calld H6(var: ›stil'd‹); om O21 Y3 G.   so]
~,   B40 DT1 H5 O20 SP1 A–G.

58 not] ~ that B11 C2 C8 DT1 H4 O20 OJ1(~ ›that‹) OQ1 SP1 A–F; ~,
HH1.   Men] ~,   B11 C2 C8; man H4.   be forc'd] beforc't C8; ~ forced
HH1 O21.   them] ~,   B11 C2 C8 O20 SP1.   go] ~,   B11 C2 C8 A–G.

59 Angells.] ~:   B11 H5 H7 OQ1 SP1; ~,   B40 B47 C2 O21 VA2; ~;   C8
DT1 H4 HH1 NY1 O20 A; ~∧   TT1; Angles, Y2.   Supplications] ~,   B11;
supplication B–F.

60 God,] ~∧   NY1 OQ1 TT1 VA2 Y2; ~;   NY3 O21 Y3.   to] ~ to VA1.
Dominations,] ~∧   B13 B40 B47 H4 NY1 NY3 OQ1 P3 TT1 VA1 VA2 Y2 Y3.

61 Powers,] powrs, B40 H5; ~∧   O21 OQ1 P3 TT1 VA1 Y2 Y3.
Cherubins,] Cherubims, NY1; ~;   O21; ~∧   TT1 Y2.   and] om B47.   all]
om TT1.   heauens] heau'ns H6 H7.   Courts,] Court, B11 C2 C8 DT1
H4 H5 O20 SP1 Y2 A; ~,   B13 C9 H6 O21 OQ1 P3 TT1 VA1 Y3; Court∧   B47
H7; ~. HH1.   if wee] om om HH1.

62 Should] If wee ~ HH1.   fees,] B11 B13 B40 C9 H6 H8 NY3 P3 G; seed∧
HH1; ~∧   Σ.   here,] hear; B40; heare∧   H7; ~;   O21; ~! TT1; heare,
VA1; ~∧   Y3.   dayly] daly VA2 Y2.

63 Kings;] ~. B13 C9 H6 H8 NY1 P3 VA1 Y3; ~, B40 B47 DT1 H4 H7
HH1 Y2; ~: H5 SP1; ~∧ TT1.   so t'is.] B47 C9 H6 H8 NY3 P3 G; ~ ~∧
C8(→ »~ ~;«) H4 VA1 Y3; ~ ~: H5 SP1; ~ ~; H7 NY1 O20 VA2 B C; ~'~;
O21 D–F; ~ it is: OQ1; ~ it is∧ TT1; ~'~, A; ~ ~, Σ.   not] non B13.

64 Stoick,] Stone, B40; ~; O21; ~∧ OQ1; stone∧ TT1.   Coward,] ~;
B13; ~∧ NY1 OQ1 TT1 VA2.   yea] or Y2.   Martyr] ~. B11; ~, H7
HH1 A–G; ~; O21.

65 in,] ~∧ B47 H4 H7 H8 HH1 NY1 O21 TT1 VA1 VA2 Y2 Y3.

66 his] ~, H5.   Clothes,] ~∧ B11 B13 B40 C8 NY1 OQ1 P3 TT1 VA2 Y2
Y3; copes, C9 H6.   Copes;] B13 DT1 H8 NY3 A–G; clothes∧ C9 H6;
boxes, H5; om HH1(»~∧«); ~∧ TT1 VA2; ~, Σ.   bookes,] ~∧ B13 B40
B47 H4 HH1 NY1 O20 P3 TT1 VA1 Y3; & ~, C9 H6; om Y2.   Primmers;]
H8 NY3 A–G; ~∧ H7 HH1 O21 TT1 VA1 Y2; *Primmer*, SP1; ~, Σ.   and]
yea ~   OJ1.

67 His] ~, H5.   Plate,] B11 B47 C2 C9 H5 H7 NY3 SP1 A–G; ~∧ Σ.
Chalices;] NY3 A–C; ~∧ B47(Chillices) OQ1 TT1; Callices, H8; Callices∧
Y2; ~: Y3; ~, Σ.   mistake] mis-take C9 H6; take H7 OQ1 Y2; ~, H8.
away] ~, B11 B40 C2 C8 DT1 H8 HH1 OQ1 A–G; a waye B13; ~? NY1;
a way? VA2.

68 aske] lack B11 C2 C8 A–F; ~ them H7(→ »~«).   comming?] ~; B11
C2 C8 O20 O21 OQ1 A; ~. B13 NY3 VA1; ~, H7 HH1 Y2 Y3; his ~? NY1
VA2; ~∧ P3 TT1.   Oh] ~, B11 C2 H5 A; & B47; ~∧ → »~,« C8; ~!
H8; ~; B–G.   ne're] neare B11 B40 C2 C8 H7 HH1 O20 SP1 TT1; neere
B13 VA1 VA2.

69 Fayre] faires H5.   Laws] ~, H4; lawe Y2.   whight] NY3; white Σ.
reuerend] reverent B13 B40 H5 HH1(~ → ›reuerent‹) NY3 P3 TT1 VA1.
strumpeted] ~, HH1 A–G.

70 thefts;] ~: B13 C2 C8 DT1 SP1 A–G; ~. B47 C9 H6 H7 H8 OQ1 P3
VA1 Y3; ~, H4 O20; ~! H5; ~∧ HH1 TT1.   established] ~, C9 HH1.

71 to] of B13.   Destiny] ~, B11 C2 C8 A–G.   on] and VA1.
Earth;] HH1 NY3; ~∧ B47 C8(~»,«) H4 TT1 VA1 Y3; ~: Y2; ~, Σ.

72 fates] ~, HH1.   words;] NY3 O21; ~∧ TT1; ~. VA1; ~, Σ.   and]
om H7(→ »~«) Y2.   but] om B11 B40 C2 C8 DT1 H4 O20 SP1 TT1 A–G.
tells] tell H5 Y2.   vs] om B11 B40 C2 C8 DT1 H4 O20 O21 SP1 TT1 VA1
Y3 A–G.   who must bee] om om om TT1.

73 Rich,] ~∧ B47 H7 NY1 P3 VA2 Y3; Who must be ~∧ TT1.   poore,]
~; H8; ~∧ TT1.   chayres,] chaynes∧ B47; Chaynes, H7 NY3 O20 SP1
Y3; Chaines; O21; ~∧ P3 TT1 Y2.   who] & ~ C9 H6.   iayles;] B11 C8
NY3; ~, B40 DT1 H8 SP1 VA2; Goales; C2; ~. C9 H6 H7 O20 OQ1; ~:
H5 A–G; gayles∧ O21 Y3; ~∧ Σ.

74 fayre,] ~: B13; ~‸ HH1 O21 TT1 VA2.   but] *om* B11; & HH1.
foule] huge H7.   Nayles,] B11 B40 C2 C8 DT1 H5 O20 SP1 VA2 A–G;
~. H7; ~; NY3; ~‸ Σ.

75 scratcheth] ~; O21; scratches Y2; scatcheth G.   Suters.] ~; B11 C2
C8 H4 HH1 NY1 O20 O21 VA2 Y2 A; ~, B40 B47 DT1; ~: H5 H7 B–F; ~‸
TT1.   In] As ~ C9 H6.   bodyes] ~, C2; ~ of men TT1.

76 Of] *missing* B11.   Men] [*missing*]; B11; ~; B40 C2 C8 DT1 A; ~, C9
H4 H5 H6 O20 OQ1 SP1 B–G; ~. O21.   (so] B13 B47 H7 H8 HH1 NY1
NY3 P3 VA1 VA2 Y2; ‸~ Σ.   Law,] ~, B11 B40 C2 C8 C9 H5 H6 A–G;
~‸ DT1 H4 O20 SP1 TT1; lawes, O21 Y3; ~; OQ1; ~) Σ.   Nayles]
~, B40 SP1; nayes VA1.   th'extremityes,] the extremities, B11 C2 DT1
H5 OQ1; the extremyties; B40 H8; ~‸ C9 H6 H7(thextremities) NY3; the
Extremityes. O20 SP1; extremities, A; extremities. B–G; the extremeties‸ Σ.

77 So'Officers] NY3; for oficers OQ1; So officers Σ.   stretch] ~, B11;
streeche Y2.   more] ~, Y2.   then] than B13 B C G; the VA1.   do,]
B11 B40 C2 DT1 H5 HH1 OQ1 SP1 A–G; ~‸ Σ.

78 nayles] neals H7.   reach] ~, B11 B13 H5 H8 P3 SP1 VA1 Y2 Y3;
~; O21.   no] none H8.   els part] part els H5; ~ parts NY1 VA2.
comes] come NY1 VA2; can come OQ1 P3 VA1; can Y2.   to.] ~; B40;
too‸ B47 HH1 TT1 Y3; ~‸ H4 H7 VA1; ~: OQ1; ~, VA2; doe‸ Y2.

79 bar'st] C9 DT1 H4 H5 H6 H7 HH1 NY1 NY3 O21 OQ1 VA2 Y3; barest
Σ.   to] *om* H5 Y2.   yon] you C2 C8; yond C9 H6 H7 NY1 VA2.
Officer,] B11 C2 C8 C9 DT1 H6 HH1 VA2; ~? B40 SP1 A–G; officers‸ B47
H5 H8; ~; H4 O20; ~. TT1; ~‸ Σ.   foole?] ~, B11 C2 C8 Y2 A–G; ~‸
B40 TT1; foote? B47 H5 H8; ~! SP1.

80 goods] ~, B11 B13 C2 C8 DT1 H5 H8 O20 O21 OQ1 P3 SP1 VA1 Y2
A–G.   for] *om* B47.   earst men] *om* ~ B11 C2 C8 DT1 H4 HH1(→ men
»earst«) O20 SP1 A; men erst B13 B40 O21 TT1 Y3; curst ~ Y2.   bar'd]
bared B11 B40 C2 C8 DT1 H4 HH1 O20 O21 TT1 Y3 A.   to] *om* Y2.
thee?] ~‸ H7 OQ1 P3 TT1 VA1 Y2 Y3; ~: H8; ~. HH1; ~, O21.

81 Foole] ~, B11 C2 C8 DT1 H4 H7 H8 HH1 VA2 A–G; ~! SP1; fooles
Y2.   twise,] ~‸ C9 H6 HH1 NY1 OQ1 P3 VA2; two Y2.   thrise;] NY3
OQ1 P3; ~‸ H4 H7 H8 HH1 NY1 VA1 VA2 Y3; or three, Y2; ~, Σ.
Thou'hast] NY3; th'hast C9 H6; hast thou H7 Y2; thou hast Σ.   wrong,]
~‸ B47 H7 NY1 OQ1 P3 TT1 VA1 VA2 Y2.   and] *om* C9 H6 O21 Y3.
now] howe DT1 H4; more P3; *om* Y2.   hungerly] hungʳl[*trimmed*] H8;
hungʳ; buy O21 Y3(hungeʳbuie).

82 Begst] Beggest HH1 P3; Buyest O20 SP1; begs Y2.   right.] H8 NY3
VA1; ~? B40; ~, B47 C9 H6 H7 HH1 OQ1 P3 Y3 C–G; ~: H5 NY1 SP1
VA2; ~‸ TT1 Y2; ~; Σ.   that] the P3.   not] ~, O21.   till] tell
NY3.   these] thou B47; those H8. · dy.] ~; B40; ~‸ B47 C8 C9 H4 H8

HH1 O21 P3 TT1 VA1 Y2 Y3 D–F; ~,   DT1 O20; ~:   OQ1.

83 *om* H7.   Thou'hadst] NY3; thou hast   O21 Y3; thou hads   Y2; Thou hadst   Σ.   much;] HH1 NY3; ~∧   O21 P3 TT1 Y2 Y3; ~,   Σ.   and] ~ now NY1 VA2 Y2; *om*   O21 Y3.   Laws] *om*   O21 Y3.   Vrim] ~,   B11 B13 C2 DT1 H4 SP1; *om*   O21 Y3.   and Thummin] B47 C2 C8 NY1 NY3 O20 Y2; *om om*   O21 Y3 VA1; ~ *Thimym*   OQ1; ~ Thummim   Σ.   try] ~,   B11 C2 C8 DT1 SP1; ~.   B40; *om*   O21 Y3 VA1.

84 Thou] *om*   O21 Y3.   wouldst] wouldest   B40 VA1; woo'st   P3.   for] haue   H8; *om*   O21 Y3.   more;] ~,   B13 B47 C9 DT1 H4 H6 H7 H8 HH1 O20 OQ1 P3 SP1 VA1 Y2 Y3; ~∧   B40 TT1.   and] ~,   C9 H6.   all] ~,   B40 C9 DT1 H5 H6 OQ1.

85 clothe] ~,   B11 C8.   great] *om*   B13 OQ1 P3 VA1.   Carraques] NY3; Charracks   H4; Carrackes   H5 Y3; Carricks.   H7; Carrecks   HH1 O21 OQ1; Carrick   P3 TT1 VA1; Charricks   C–G; Carricks   Σ.   pepper.] ~∧   B13 B47 H4 HH1 NY1 O21 P3 TT1 VA1 VA2 Y2 Y3; ~,   B40 H7 O20; ~;   H5; ~:   OQ1.

86 that,] it,   H7; ~∧   NY1 O21 TT1 VA2 Y3.   by] buy   H7 HH1.   that] ~,   C8 H7 Y2.   thou much more shalt] ~ ~ ~ shall   B40 Y2; ~ shalt much more   B47 C9 H6 P3 VA1; much more thou shalt   H8; thowe shalt more OQ1.   leese] ~,   B11 DT1 H5 O20 SP1 A B; ~.   B40.

87 Then] the   Y3.   Hammon] Hamman,   B11; *Haman*   B40 H4 SP1 TT1; Haman,   C2 C8 DT1 HH1 O20 A; Hammond   C9 H6 H7; ~,   H5 B–G; Hammin   O21; Hamon   OQ1; *blank space*   VA1.   if] when   B11 B40 C2 C8 DT1 H4 O20 O21 SP1 TT1 Y3 A G.   sold] ~ all   H7; had ~   Y2.   antiquitees.] ~∧   H4 HH1 O20 O21 OQ1 TT1 VA1 Y2 Y3.

88 O] ~!   H7.   Wretch,] B11 C9 DT1 H6 H7 HH1 NY3 G; ~!   H5 SP1; ~∧   Σ.   fortunes] fortune   B47 H8 O21 OQ1 Y2 Y3; ~,   H7.   should] now ~   H7 Y2.   moralize] ~,   O21.

89 fables,] ~∧   NY1 OQ1 P3 TT1 VA2 Y2; ~;   NY3.   tales] ~,   B11 C2 DT1 H7 O20 SP1 A–G; them   NY1(M *var:* »~«) VA2 Y2.   Prophesies.] ~; B40 H5; ~∧   B47 C9 H4 OQ1 TT1 VA1 Y2 Y3; Prophsies. → »~«.   C8; ~!   H7 NY1 VA2; Proplicyes.   H8(M *var:* >~<.); ~,   O21.

90 art] are   P3.   that] the   B11 B40 C2 C8 DT1 H4 H7 O20 P3 SP1 TT1 VA1 A–G.   dogg] ~,   B11 B40 DT1 H5 H8 HH1 O20 Y3; ~.   O21; *om* VA1.   whom] when   O20 SP1; whose   Y2.   shadows] shadow   Y2. cosened] ~,   B11 B40 C2 DT1 H5 O20 A–C; cousen'd   C8 NY1(coson'd) O21 VA2 Y3; ledd   C9; fedd   H6; coozned,   H8; cosned   OQ1 VA1; ~.   SP1; fled Y2; cozeneth,   G.

91 And] Who   B13 B47 H5 H7 H8 HH1 NY1 OQ1 P3 VA1 VA2; Which C9 H6 B–G.   diu'dst] diu'd   B13 B47 C9 H6 H7 H8 NY1 OQ1 P3 VA1 VA2 Y2; Dived'st   B40; diuest   C8(→ »~«) O21 TT1 Y3; diu'st   DT1 H4; diu'd,

H5; dived HH1; div'st, A–F.   neere] neare B11 B40 C2 DT1 O20 SP1
A–G; nere H7 P3 Y2.   drowning] ~, B11 B40 DT1 HH1 O20 Y2 A–G;
drowndeinge, C2; ~; H4.   what] whats H4; y^t Y2.   vanished.] ~. |
B11 B13 B40 B47 C2 C8 C9 DT1 H5 NY1 O20 VA1; ~: H4 Y3; ~$_\wedge$ H7 HH1
O21; vanisheth. G.

Subscriptions: Finis. | I D. | B13.   Finis B40 H7 O21(. |) Y3.   *Finis*
   Quintæ et vltimæ Satyræ. IOHN DONNE NY1 VA2(Ioh: Donne.).
   The end of the 5th and last Satire. | P3.   finis quintæ Satiræ. | Y2.
   om Σ.

Verbal Variants in Selected Modern Editions

Editions collated: H I J K M N O P Q S T Y Z AA DD.
Format: Indentations: *ll. 28, 35, 90, 91 ind* Y; *ll. 28, 35 ind* AA; *no ind* Σ.
Headings: SATYRE V. H Q S Y Z DD.   SATIRE V. I–K M–P.
   SATIRE V TO SIR THOMAS EGERTON *ca. 1597* T.   *Satire 5* AA.

   8 Officers] Officer's H K M T; officers' I J N–P AA.   Suters] Suitor's H
K M T; suitors' I J N–P AA.

   9 wright] write Σ.   and] in H–K M N.

   12 implyes] employs O.

   19 Excrement] T; excrements Σ.

   20 to] no J.

   21 prayes] preys Σ.   then] Q Y Z DD; than Σ.   wormes] worm's H M
O T AA; worms' I–K N P.

   22 do'eat] Y; eat H–K M N; ~$_\wedge$ ~ Σ.

   24 And] *om* K.

   26 their] the H–K M N P.

   27 Wittalls] wittols M O P T AA.

   29 then] Q Y Z DD; than Σ.   Thames] Q S Y Z DD; ~' Σ.

   30 corne] can J.

   36 ought] aught M O P T AA.

   37 that] *om* H–K M N.

   38 farr] did P.

   39 claym'd] demands O Q S Y Z AA DD.

   40 sweare] T; sweat Σ.   sweat] T; swear Σ.

42 Like Angelica, scape] T; Scape, like *Angelica* Σ.   Striuers] I Q S Y Z DD; strivers' O AA; striver's Σ.

43 be] *om* J.   in] *om* S DD.   Iudges] Q S Y Z DD; Judge's Σ.

46 Flow] Flows H–K M N P.

50 *1st* when] *om* H–K M N P.

51 Heauy] ~' H Y Z.   those] T; these Σ.

52 thy] the O Q S Y Z AA DD.

56 Likes] T; like Σ.

57 He] and ~ H–K M N.   and sayd] *om* H–K M N.

58 not] ~ that O Q S Y Z AA DD.

61 heauens] Q S Y Z DD; heaven's Σ.   Courts] court O.

67 mistake] mis-take I J P T.

68 aske] lack O P.

69 Laws] Q S Y Z DD; Law's Σ.   whight] white Σ.   reuerend] rev'rend I J.

72 fates] Q S Y Z DD; Fate's Σ.   but tells vs] tells H–K M–O.

73 chayres] chains K.   *3rd* who] and ~ H–K M N.   iayles] gaols H–J P AA.

76 so in] ~'~ Y.   th'extremityes] extremities H–K M–P.

77 then] Q Y Z DD; than Σ.

80 earst] *om* O.

81 wrong, and] ~,'~ Y.   hungerly] hungrily P.

83 Laws] Law's H–K M–O AA.   Thummin] T; Thummim Σ.

85 Carraques] Charrick's H I K N; Carrick's J M O P; Carrack's T AA; Carricks Σ.

87 Then] N(M *var*: than) P Q Y Z DD; Than Σ.   Hammon] Haman O Q S Y Z AA DD.   if] P T; when Σ.   sold his] ~'s H–K.

89 Æsops] Esop's H K P; Aesop's I J M–O T AA; Esops Σ.

90 Thou art] Tou ~ K; ~'~ Q S Y Z; ~'rt AA.   that] T; the Σ. cosened] cozeneth N.

91 And] Which H–K M N.   diu'dst] divest P; div'st Σ.   what] ~'s Q S T.   vanished] vanisheth N.

Subscriptions: *none.*

FIGURE 18: STEMMA OF "SATYRE 5"

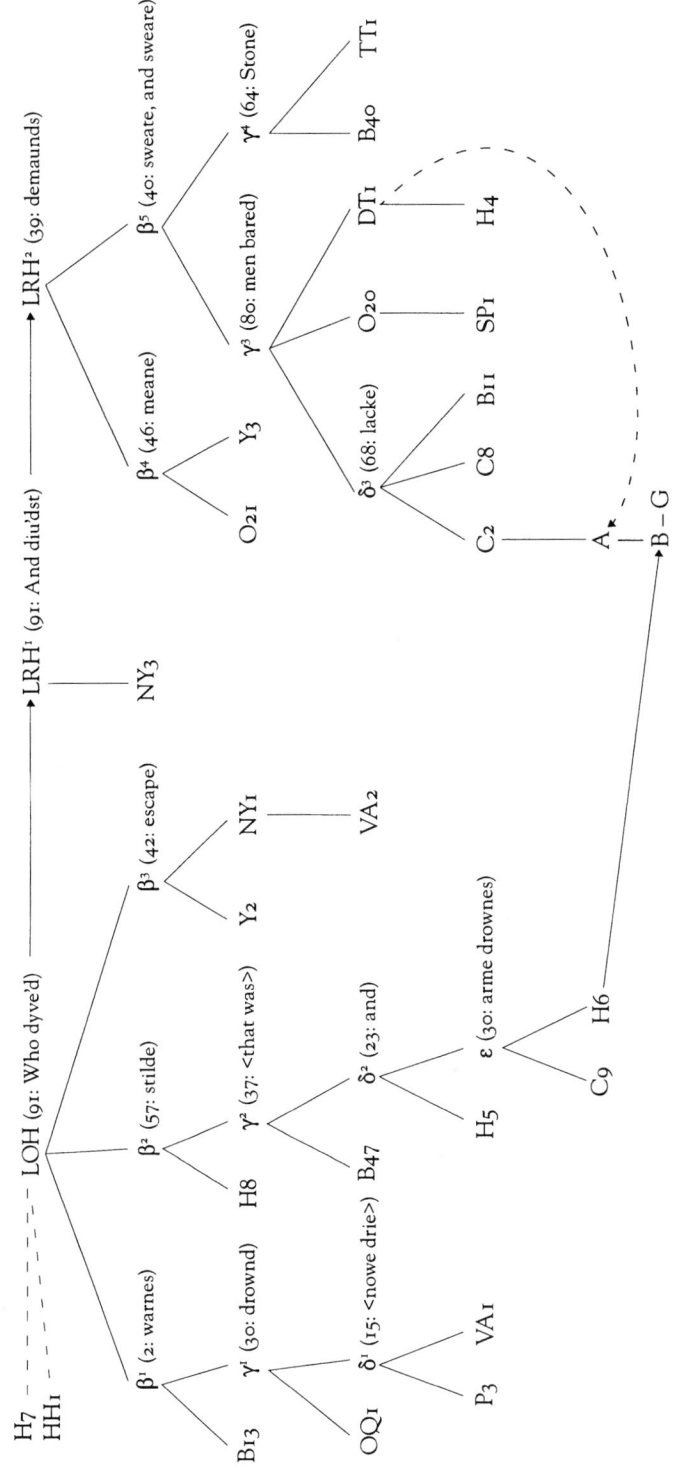

LOH = lost original holograph
LRH = lost revised holograph

unfiliated: OJ1

Supporting Detail for Stemma of "Satyre 5"

LOH (H7 HH1 β¹ β² β³)
   14 Are the vast **raveninge** Seas, And Suito^rs
   39 All **claymed** fees and dutyes, Gamsters, anon
   91 Who dyve'd nere Drowninge for what vanished

H7: To the distinguishing readings of the LOH adds the following:
   2 whom any pittie **warnes**, He wch did Lay

HH1: To the distinguishing readings of the LOH adds the following:
   12 Each thing, each thing **employes** or represents.

β¹ (B13 γ¹): To the distinguishing readings of the LOH adds the following:
   2 whome anie pittie **warnes**; Hee wch did laye

   B13: To the distinguishing readings of the LOH and β¹ adds the following:
      30 Whose meades her **arme drownes**; or whose corne oreflowe.

   γ¹ (OQ1 δ¹): To the distinguishing readings of the LOH and β¹ adds the following:
      30 Whose meades her **armes drownd**, or whose corne oreflewe:

      OQ1: To the distinguishing readings of the LOH, β¹, and γ¹ adds the following:
         86 Sell that, and by that thowe shalt <**much**> more leese

      δ¹ (P3 VA1): To the distinguishing readings of the LOH, β¹, and γ¹ adds the following:
         15 springs now full now shallow, <**now drie,**> which (to

β² (H8 γ²): To the distinguishing readings of the LOH adds the following:
   42 **scape like Angelica** the striuers hands
   57 Iudges are gods, he who made & **stild** them soe

   H8: To the distinguishing readings of the LOH and β² adds the following:
      37 The yron age **that was** when Iustice was sold, now^s

   γ² (B47 δ²): To the distinguishing readings of the LOH and β² adds the following:
      37 the Iron age <**that was**> when iustice was sold, (now

      B47: To the distinguishing readings of the LOH, β², and γ² adds the following:
         73 rich who poore, who in **chaynes** who in Iailes

      δ² (H5 ε): To the distinguishing readings of the LOH, β², and γ² adds the following:

23 They are the Mills wch grind you, **and** you are

> H5: To the distinguishing readings of the LOH, β², γ², and δ² adds the
> following:
> 61 powr's, Cherubins, and all heavens **Court**, yf we

> ε (C9 H6): To the distinguishing readings of the LOH, β², γ², and δ² adds
> the following:
> 14 Are the vast **rauenous** Seas, & Sutors
> 30 Whose meads her **arme drownes**, or whose corne ore'flow.

β³ (Y2 NY1-VA2): To the distinguishing readings of the LOH adds the following:
42 Like *Angelica* **escape** the striuers hands.

> Y2: To the distinguishing readings of the LOH and β³ adds the following:
> 80 gott thos goods, for w^{ch} **curst** men bard thee

> NY1-VA2: To the distinguishing readings of the LOH and β³ adds the following:
> 68 And aske a fee for **his** cominge? o ne'er may

LRH¹ (NY3)
91 **And diu'dst** neere drowning for what vanished.

> NY3 (provides copy-text for this edition): To the distinguishing readings of the LRH¹
> adds the following:
> 14 Are ye vast **rauishing** Seas, and Suters

LRH² (β⁴ β⁵)
39 All **demaunds**, ffees, and dutyes, Gamsters, Anon
42 scape **like Angelica** the striueres handes;

> β⁴ (O21 Y3): To the distinguishing readings of the LRH² adds the following:
> 14 are the vast **rauening** seas, & suitors,
> 46 fflow from the first **meane** head & these cañ throwe

> β⁵ (γ³ γ⁴): To the distinguishing readings of the LRH² adds the following:
> 14 Are the **ravishinge** Seas; and Suters
> 40 The Monye wch you **sweate, & sweare** for, ys gone

> > γ³ (δ³ O20-SP1 DT1-H4): To the distinguishing readings of the LRH² and β⁵ adds
> > the following:
> > 80 Gott those Goods, for w^{ch} **men bared** to Thee?

δ³ (C2 C8 B11): To the distinguishing readings of the LRH², β⁵, and γ³ adds the following:

68 And **lacke** a Fee for Comminge; oh, neare may

C2: To the distinguishing readings of the LRH², β⁵, γ³, and δ³ adds the following:

46 Flowe from the first **Meane** heade; And these can throwe

C8: To the distinguishing readings of the LRH², β⁵, γ³, and δ³ adds the following:

35 O age of rustie Iron, **come** better witt

B11: To the distinguishing readings of the LRH², β⁵, γ³, and δ³ adds the following:

74 Shee is all faire, <but> yett hath foule long nailes,

O20-SP1: To the distinguishing readings of the LRH², β⁵, and γ³ adds the following:

82 **Buyest** right; but that dole comes not till these Dye,

DT1-H4: To the distinguishing readings of the LRH², β⁵, and γ³ adds the following:

12 each thing each thinge **implyes**, or represents,

γ⁴ (B40 TT1): To the distinguishing readings of the LRH² and β⁵ adds the following:

64 **Stone**, a Coward, yea a Martir

ANALYSES OF EARLY PRINTED COPIES

(Since the Satyres appear as a continuous series of poems in all seventeenth-century editions and issues, they are treated in this analysis as a single bibliographical unit.)

Poems, by J. D., 4to, 1633 (siglum A)

Copies Collated:

> *Sat1*: CtY, DFo, L, M, MH, MiU, TxAM1.
> *Sat2*: DFo, L, M, MH, OJn, TxAM1.
> *Sat3*: CtY, DFo, L, MH, TxAM1.
> *Sat4*: CtY, DFo, M, OJn, TxAM1.
> *Sat5*: DFo, L, M, MH, OJn, TxAM1.

Relevant section: Tt3–Tt4, Vv–Xx⁴, Yy1–Yy3; 13 leaves; pp. 325–49.

Press variants:

Sheet Tt, inner forme

	Uncorrected (CtY, MH, MiU):	Corrected (L, M, DFo, TxAM1)

Tt3v (p. 326):

Sat1, l. 29	eyes;	eyes
l. 32	hate	hat
l. 40	of	Of
l. 41	bare,	bare:
l. 50	warm'd	warn'd

Tt4 (p. 327):

Sat1, l. 59	weather Spie	weather-Spie
l. 84	youth;	youth?

Miscatchings:

	Catchword:		Initial Word:	Affects:
Tt4	And	Tt4v	That	*Sat1*, l. 85
Xx1	One	Xx1v	One,	*Sat4*, l. 27
Yy2v	Begst	Yy3	Beg'st	*Sat5*, l. 82

Note: In *Sat5* 52, the apostrophe before "'Gainst" has fallen out or does not ink in the L and M copies.

§

Poems, by J. D., 8vo, 1635 (siglum B)

Copies Collated:

> Sat1: CtY, MH, TxAM.
> Sat2: CtY, MH, TxAM.
> Sat3: CtY, MH, TxAM.
> Sat4: CtY, MH, TxAM.
> Sat5: CtY, MH, TxAM.

Relevant section: I4–I8, K1–K7; 12 leaves; pp. 123–145.

Press variants: *none*.

Miscatchings:

	Catchword:		Initial Word:	Affects:
K2	One	K2v	One,	*Sat4*, l. 27
K6v	Wee	K7	We	*Sat5*, l. 60

§

Poems, by J. D., 8vo, 1639 (siglum C)

Copies Collated:

> Sat1: CtY, MH, TxAM.
> Sat2: CtY, MH, TxAM.
> Sat3: CtY, MH, TxAM.
> Sat4: CtY, MH, TxAM.
> Sat5: CtY, MH, TxAM.

Relevant section: I2–I8, K1–K5; 12 leaves; pp. 123–45.

Press variants: *none*.

Miscatchings:

	Catchword:		Initial Word:	Affects:
I8	One	I8v	One,	*Sat4*, l. 27

Notes: (1) In *Sat1* 69, the apostrophe in "imprison'd" inks only partially (MH, TxAM) or not at all (CtY).

(2) In *Sat3* 21, the "s" in "couragious" inks only partially (MH) or not at all (CtY, TxAM).

(3) In *Sat3* 24, the comma after "th'Oven" inks only partially, making it appear to be a period in *CtY*.

(4) In *Sat3* 91, the comma after "hate" has drifted to the top of the line.

(5) In *Sat4* 89, the apostrophe in "Scratch'd" does not ink in any copy.

(6) In *Sat4* 167, the tail on the comma after "journey" fails to ink in all copies except *TxAM*, where it is barely visible.

(7) In *Sat4* 229, the apostrophe in "Tyr'd" inks only partially (*CtY, TxAM*) or not at all (*MH*).

§

Poems, by J. D., 8vo, 1649, 1650, 1654 (sigla D, E, F)

Copies Collated:

    Sat1: 1649: *CtY, MH, TxAM*. 1650: *CtY, MH*. 1654: *CSmH, CtY*.
    Sat2: 1649: *CtY, MH*. 1650: *CtY, MH*. 1654: *CSmH, CtY*.
    Sat3: 1649: *CtY, MH, TxAM*. 1650: *CtY, MH*. 1654: *CSmH, CtY*.
    Sat4: 1649: *CtY, MH*. 1650: *CtY, MH*. 1654: *CSmH, CtY*.
    Sat5: 1649: *CtY, MH*. 1650: *CtY, MH*. 1654: *CSmH, CtY*.

Relevant section: I3v–I8, K1–K6; 12 leaves; pp. 118–39.

Press variants: *none*.

Miscatchings:

	Catchword:		Initial Word:	Affects:
K1	Sir	K1v	Sir,	*Sat4*, l. 29
K2	An	K2v	And	*Sat5*, l. 93

Note: Examination of multiple copies on the Lindstrand Comparator shows that the sections of 1649, 1650, and 1654 containing the Satyres are printed from a single typesetting, 1650 and 1654 being reissues of the sheets of 1649.

§

Poems, by J. D., 8vo, 1669 (siglum G)

Copies Collated:

> *Sat1*: CtY, L, *Mathews,** TxAM.
> *Sat2*: CtY, L, *Mathews*, TxAM.
> *Sat3*: CtY, L, *Mathews*, TxAM.
> *Sat4*: CtY, L, *Mathews*, TxAM.
> *Sat5*: CtY, L, *Mathews*, TxAM.

Relevant section: I3v–I8, K1–K5v; 11 leaves; pp. 118–38.

Press variants: *none*.

Miscatchings: *none*.

Misnumberings: 221 [for 121], 213 [for 123].

---

*Elkin Mathews copy, in private hands.

Infinitati Sacrum
16. Augusti. 1601.
M e t e m p s y c h o s i s
Poema Satyricon.

Epistle

Others at the Porches and Entries of their Buildings sett their
Armes, I my Picture, if any Colours can deliuer a Mind soe plaine and
flatt and through light as mine. Naturallie at a new Author I doubt
and stick and doe not Quicklie say Good. I censure much and taxe:
And this libertie costs me more then others, by how much my owne things   5
are worse then others. Yet I would not be so rebellious against my-
selfe as not to doe it, since I loue it; nor soe vniust to others as to
doe it *Sine Talione.* As long as I giue them as good hold vpon me,
they must pardon me my bitings. I forbid noe reprehender but him
that like the *Trent Counsell* forbids not Bookes but Authors,   10
damning whatsoeuer such a name hath or shall write. *None*
writes soe ill that he giues not something *Exemplarie*, to follow,
or flie. Now when I begin this booke, I haue no purpose to come into
any Mans debt; how my Stock will hold out I know not, perchance
wast, perchance increase in vse. If I doe borrow any thing of   15
Antiquitie (besides that I make accompt that I paie it to Posterity
with as much and as good) yow shall finde me still to acknowledge it
and to thanck not him onlie that hath dig'd out *Treasure* for me but
that hath lighted me a Candell to the place. All which I will bid
yow to remember (for I would haue no such Readers as I can   20
teach) is that the *Pithagorean Doctrine* doth not onlie carry
one *Soule* from Man to Man, nor Man to Beast, but indifferently
to Plants also, and therefore yow must not grudge to find the same
Soule in an Emperor, in a Posthorse, and in a Mushrome, since
noe vnredines in the Soule, but an Indisposition in the Organs workes this. And   25

therefore though this Soule could not moue when it was a Milon, yet
it may remember and now tell me, at what lasciuious Banquett it
was serue'd. And though it could not speak when it was a Spider,
yet it can remember and now tell me who vs'd it for Poison to
attaine Dignitie. Howeuer the bodies haue dul'd her other faculties,
her memorie hath euer bene her owne; Which makes me soe seriously
deliuer yow by her relation all her passages, from her first making, when
she was that Aple which Eue eat, to this Time when she is he whose life
yow shall find in the end of this booke.

30

First Songe

1.

I sing the progresse of a Deathles Soule
Whom Fate which God made, but doth not controule
Plac'd in most shapes; All tymes before the Law
Yoak'd was, and when, and since, in this I singe.
And the great WORLD in his ag'd Eueninge   5
From Infant Morne, through Manlie Noone I draw:
What the Gold *Chaldee* or Siluer *Persian* saw,
Greeke brasse or *Roman* Iron, is in this one,
A worke to outweare *Seth's* Pillars, Brick and Stone,
And (holie writts excepted) made to yeild to none.   10

2.

Thee, Eye of Heauen, this great *Soule* enuieys not;
By thy Male-force is all we haue begott;
In the first East, thou now beginst to shine
Suckst earlie balme and Iland Spices there
And wilt anon in thy loose-raind Carrere   15
At *Tagus*, Po, *Sene*, *Thames* and *Danow* dine
And see at Night thy *Westerne Land* of *Myne*,
Yet hast thou not more Nations seene then shee
That before thee, one day began to bee
And thy fraile light being quench'd, shall long long outliue thee.   20

3.

Nor holie *Ianus* in whose Soueraigne Boat
The Church and all the Monarchies did float,
That Swimming Colledge and free Hospitall
Of all Mankind, that Cage and Viuarie
Of Fowles, and Beasts, in whose Wombe, Destiny   25
Vs and our latest Nephewes did install
(For thence are all deriu'd that fill this *All*)
Didst thou in that great Steward-ship Embark
Soe diuers shapes into that floating Park
As haue bene mou'd and inform'd by this heauenly sparke.   30

4.

Great Destiny the Comissarie of God
That hast mark't out a Path and Period
For euery thing, who where we Ofspring took,
Our waies and ends seest at one instant, Thou
Knott of all Causes, Thou whose changeles Brow   35
Ne're smiles nor frownes! O vouch thou safe to looke
And shew my storie in thy eternall Booke
That (if my praier be fitt) I may vnderstand
So much my selfe, as to know with what hand
How scant or liberall this my life's *Race* is spand.   40

5.

To my *six lustres* almost now outwore,
Except thy Booke owe me soe many more,
Except my legend be free from the letts
Of steep Ambition, sleepie Pouertie,
Sprighte-quenching Sicknes, dull Captiuity,   45
Distracting Busines, and from Beauties Netts
And all that calls from this and to other whetts,
O let me not launch out, but let me saue
Th'expence of braine and spirit; that my Graue
His right and due, a whole vnwasted Man, may haue.   50

6.

But if my Daies be long and good inough,
In vaine this Sea shall enlarge or enrough
It selfe; for I will through the waue and fome
And shall in sad lone wayes, a liuely Spright,
Make my dark heauy Poeme light and light   55
For though through manie Streights and Sands I rome
I launch at paradise and saile towards home;
The Course I there began, shall here be staid
Sayles hoisted there, strook here, and Ankers lay'd
In *Thames*, which were at *Tigris* and *Euphrates* wayd.   60

7.

For this great *Soule* which here amongst vs now
Doth dwell and moues that hand and Tongue and Brow,
Which as the Moone the Sea, moues vs, to heare
Whose Storie with long Patience yow shall long
(For tis the Crowne and last Strayne of my Song)   65
This *Sowle* to whom *Luther* and *Mahomet* were
Prisons of flesh; This *Soule* which oft did teare
And mend the Wracks of th' Empire and late *Rome*
And liu'd where euery great Change did come
Had first in *Paradise*, a low but fatall Roome.   70

8.

Yet no Low Roome nor then the greatest lesse
If (as deuout and sharp men fitlie guesse)
That crosse, our Ioy and greif, where nailes did tie
That *All* which alwaies was *All* eueriewhere
Which could not Syn, and yet all Syns did beare   75
Which could not Dye, yet could not chuse but Dye,
Stood in the selfe-same roome in *Caluarie*
Where first grew the forbidden learned Tree
For on that Tree honge in Securitie
This *Soule* made by the Makers Will from pulling free.   80

9.

Prince of the Orcharde, faire as dawning Morne,
Fenc'd with the Law and ripe as soone as borne
That Aple grew, which this *Soule* did en-liue
Till the then Climing Serpent that now creepes
For that offence for which all Mankind weepes   85
Tooke it: and to her whom the first Man did wiue
(Whom and whose race only forbiddings driue)
He gaue it, she to her Husband; both did eate;
Soe perished the Eaters, and the Meat
And we (for Treason taints the blood) thence Dy and Sweat.   90

10.

Man all at once was there by Woeman slaine
And one by one we are here slayne o're againe
By them! The mother poysned the Wel-head,
The Daughters here corrupt vs Riuoletts,
No smalnes scapes, no greatnes breaks their Netts,   95
She thrust vs out, and by them we are led
Astray, from turning to whence we are fled.
Were prisoners Iudges, t'would seeme rigorous;
She Syn'd, we beare; part of our Paine is, thus
To loue them whose fault to this painful Loue yoak'd vs.   100

11.

Soe fast in vs doth this Corruption grow
That now we dare ask why we should bee soe.
Would God (disputes the Curious Rebell) make
A law, and would not haue it kept? Or can
His Creatures will crosse his? Of euery Man   105
For one shall God (and be iust) vengance take?
Who Synn'd? 'Twas not forbidden to the Snake,
Nor her, who was not then made: Nor is't writt
That Adam cropt or knew the Aple: yet
The Worme and she and he and we endure for it.   110

12.

But Snatch me Heauenly Spirit from this vaine
Reckning their Vanities; lesse is the Gaine
Then hasard still to meditate on Ill
Though with good Minde; Their resons like those Toyes
Of glassy bubles which the Gamesome Boies   115
Stretch to soe Nice a Thinnes through a Quill
That they themselues break, do themselues spill;
Arguing is Heretiques game; and exercise
As wrastlers perfects them; not liberties
Of Speach, but Silence, hands not tongues end Heresies.   120

13.

Iust in that Instant when the Serpents gripe
Broke the sleight Veynes, and tender Conduit Pipe
Through which this Soule from the Trees root did draw
Life, and growth, to this Aple fled away
This loose Soule, old, one and another Day.   125
As lightning, which one scarse dares say he saw
'Tis soe soone gone (and better proof the Law
Of Sence then Faith requires) swiftlie she flew
T'a dark and foggie Plott: Her, her fate threw
There through th'Earth's pores and in a plant howsd her anew. 130

14.

This plant thus abled to it selfe did force
A place where no place was, by natures Course;
As Ayre from water, water fleets away
From thicker bodies, by this root throngd soe,
His Spungie confines gaue him place to grow,   135
Iust as in our streets, when the people stay
To see the Prince, and haue soe filld the Way
That Wesels scarse could passe, when she comes nere
They throng and cleaue vp, and a Passage clere,
As if for that time, their round bodies flatned were.   140

15.

His right arme he Thrust out towards the East,
Westward his lefte; the'ends did themselues digest
Into ten lesser Strings, these fingers were
And as a Slumberer stretching on his bed,
This way he this, and that way Scattered   145
His other leg, which feet with Toes vpbeare;
Grew on his Midle parts, the first Day, haire
To show that in Loues busines he should still
A Dealer be, and be vsd well or ill;
His Aples kindle, his Leaues force of Conception kill.   150

16.

A Mouth but Dumbe he hath, blind Eyes, Deaf Eares
And to his Shoulders dangle subtill Haires:
A young Colossus there he stands vprighte
And as that Grownd by him were Conquered
A leauy Garland weres he on his head   155
Enchas'd with litle fruits, soe red and bright
That for them yow would call your Loues lips white;
Soe of a lone vnhaunted place possest
Did this Soules Second Inne, built by the Guest,
This Liuing buried Man, this quiet Mandrake rest.   160

17.

Noe lustfull woman came this Plant to greiue
But 'twas because there was none yet but Eue.
And she (with other purpose) kild it quite:
Her syn had now brought in Infirmities,
And soe her Cradled Child, the moist red Eyes   165
Had neuer shutt, nor slept since it saw light.
Poppie she knew, she knew the Mandrakes Might
And tore vp both and soe coold her Childs blood.
Vnuertuous Weeds might long vnuext haue stood,
But hee's short liu'd that with his Death can doe most good.   170

18.

To an vnfetter'd Soules quick nimble hast
Are falling Starrs, and harts thoughts but slow pac't:
Thinner then burnt Ayre flies this Soule, and shee
Whom fower new Comming and fower parting Suns
Had found and left the Mandrakes Tennant, runs   175
Thoughtles of Change, when her firm Destinie
Confin'd and eniayld her that seem'd soe free,
Into a Small blew Shell, the which a poore
Warme Bird orespred, and satt still euermore
Till her enclos'd Child kikt and pok't it self a Dore.   180

19.

Out crept a Sparrow, this Soules mouing Inne
On whose raw Armes stiffe Feathers now begin
As Childrens Teeth through Gummes, to break with Paine,
His flesh is Ielly yet, and his bones Threds,
All a new Downy Mantle ouerspreads.   185
A mouth he opes which would as much containe
As his late howse, and the first howre speaks plaine
And Chirps alowd for meat; Meat fitt for men
His father steales for him, and soe feeds then
One, that within a Month will beat him from his Hen.   190

20.

In this Worlds youth wise nature did make hast,
Things ripened sooner and did longer last:
Alreadie this hot Cock in Bush and Tree,
In feild and Tent oreflutters his next Henn.
He asks her Not who did soe last nor when,   195
Nor if his Sister or his Neece she be,
Nor doth she pule for his Inconstancie
If in her Sight he change, nor doth refuse
The next that Calls, both libertie doe vse,
Where Store is of both kinds, both kinds may freely chuse.   200

21.

Men till they took Lawes which made freedome lesse
Their Daughters and their Sisters did ingresse;
Till now vnlawfull, therefore ill, 'twas not.
Soe Iolly, that it can moue, this Soule is,
The bodie soe free of his Kindnesses,   205
That selfe preseruing It hath now forgott
And slackneth soe the Soules and bodies knott
Which Temperance streytens; freelie on his shee freinds
He blood and Spirit, Pith and Marrow spends,
Ill Steward of himself, Himself in three yeares ends.   210

22.

Els might he long haue liu'd; Man did not know
Of Gummy blood which doth in Holly grow
How to make birdlyme; nor how to deceiue
With feyned Calls, hid nets, or inwrapping snare
The free Inhabitants of the pliant Ayre: 215
Man to beget and Woeman to conceiue
Ask't not of Roots nor of Cock-sparrowes Leaue.
Yet chooseth he, though none of these he feares,
Pleasantlie three, then streytned twenty yeares
To liue, and to increase his race, himself outweares.   220

23.

This Cole with ouerblowing quencht and dead,
The Soule from her too Actiue Organs fledd
To'a Brook: A female fishes Sandy Roe
With the Males Ielly newly leauned was
For they had intertouch't as they did passe.   225
And one of those small bodies, fitted soe,
This Soule inform'd and abled it to Row
It self, with finny Oares which she did fitt;
Her Scales seem'd yet of Parchment, and as yett
Perchance a fish, but by noe name could yow call it.   230

24.

When goodlie like a Ship in her full Trim
A Swan soe white that yow may vnto him
Compare all whitenes, but himselfe to none,
Glided along and as he glided watch'd
And with his arched Neck this poore Fish catch'd;   235
It mou'd with State as if to look vpon
Low things it Scorn'd, and yet before that one
Could think he sought it, he had swallow'd cleare
This, and much Such, and vnblam'd deuour'd there
All but who too Swift, too great, or well arm'd were.   240

25.

Now swomme a Prison in a Prison putt
And now this Soule in double walls was shutt,
Till melted with the Swans digestiue fire
She lefte her howse, the fish, and vapourd forth.
Fate not affording bodies of more worth,   245
For her, as yet, bids her againe retire
To 'nother fish, to any new desire
Made a new Pray, for he that can to none
Resistance make, nor complaint, sure is gone;
Weaknes invites, but silence feasts Oppression.   250

26.

Pace with her Natiue streame this fish doth keep
And Iourneys with her towards the glassie deep
But oft retarded: once with a hidden Nett
Though with great Windowes: for when Need first taught
These tricks to catch food, then they were not wrought   255
As now, with Curious Gredines to lett
None scape, but few and fitt for vse to gett,
As in this Trap a rauenous Pike was tane
Who though himself distrest would faine haue slaine
This wretch, so hardlie are ill habitts left againe.   260

27.

Here by her Smalenes she two Deaths orepast,
Once Innocence scap'd, and left the oppressor fast.
The nett through swome, she keepes the liquid path
And whether she leap vp sometimes to breath
And suck in Ayre, or find it vnderneath   265
Or working Parts like Mills or Lymbecks hath
To make the water thin and Ayre-like, faith
Cares not, but safe the place she's come vnto
Where fresh with salt Waues meet, and which to doe
She knowes not, but betwene both makes a boord or two.   270

28.

So far from hiding her guests Water is
That she showes them in bigger Quantities
Then they are. Thus doubtfull of her Way
For game and not for hunger a Sea-Pye
Spi'd throughe this trayterous spectacle from high   275
The Silly fish, where it disputing lay
And to end her doubts, and her, beares her away:
Exalted she is but to the Exalters good
As are by great Ones, Men which lowly stood
Rais'd to be the Raysers Instruments and food.   280

29.

Is any kind Subiect to rape like Fish?
Ill vnto Man, they neither doe nor wish,
Fishers they kill not, nor with noise awake,
They doe not hunt nor striue to make a Pray
Of Beasts, nor their young Sonnes to beare away.   285
Fowles they pursue not, nor doe vndertake
To spoile the nests industrious Birds doe make
Yet them all these vnkind kinds feed vpon,
To kill them is an Occupacion;
And Lawes make Fasts and Lents for their Distruction.   290

30.

A suddaine stiffe land-wind in that selfe hower
To Sea-ward forc'd this Bird that did deuoure
The fish; he cares not for with ease he flies,
Fatt Gluttonies best Orator; At last
Soe long he hath flowen and hath flowen soe fast   295
That many Leagues at Sea, now tyr'd he lyes
And with his Pray, that till then languisht, Dyes;
The Soules noe longer foes, two waies did erre,
The fish I follow and keepe noe Calender
Of the other, He liues yet in some great Officer.   300

31.

Into an Embrion Fish this Sowle is throwne
And in due time throwne out againe and growne
To such vastnesse as if vnmanicled
From Greece, Morea were, and that by some
Earthquake vnrooted, loose Morea swome,   305
Or Seas from Africks bodie had seuered
And torne the hopefull Promontories head,
This fish would seeme these; And when all hopes faile
A great Ship ouersett or without Saile
Hulling, might (when this was a whelp) be like this Whale. 310

32.

At euery stroke his brasen fins doe take
More circles in the broken Sea they make
Then Canons voices when the Aire they teare.
His ribbs are Pillars, and his high arch'd Roof
Of Bark that blunts best Steele, is Thunder proof.   315
Swim in him swallowed Dolphins without feare
And feele noe Sides as if his vast Wombe were
Some Inland Sea, And euer as hee went
He spouted riuers vp, as if hee ment
To ioyne our Seas with Seas aboue the firmament.   320

33.

He hunts not Fish but as an officer
Stayes in his Court as his owne Nett and there
All Sutors of all Sorts themselues inthrall;
So on his back lies this Whale wantoning
And in his Gulf-like throat sucks euery thing   325
That passeth nere; Fish chaseth Fish and all
Flier and follower in this Whirlepoole fall.
O might not States of more Equality
Consist, and is it of necessitie
That thousand guiltles Smals to make one Great must die?   330

34.

Now drinks he vp Seas, and he eates vp flocks,
He iustles Ilands and he shakes firme Rocks.
Now in a roomefull howse, this Soule doth float
And like a Prince She sends her faculties
To all her limms, distant as Prouinces: 335
The Sun hath twentie Times both Crab and Goat
Parched since first launcht forth this liuing boat:
Tis greatest now, and to Destruction
Neerest; There's noe Pause at Perfection,
Greatnes a period hath, but hath no Station.   340

35.

Twoe litle fishes whom he neuer harm'd
Nor fed on their kind, Two not throughly arm'd
With hope that they could kill him, nor could doe
Good to themselues by his Death, (they doe not eat
His flesh, nor suck those Oyles, which thence out sweat)   345
Conspir'd against him, And it might vndoe
The plott of all that the Plotters were twoe
But that they fishes were and Could not speak.
How shall a Tirant wise strong Proiects break
If Wretches can on them the Common Anger wreak?   350

36.

The flaile-fin'd Thresher and Steelebeak'd Swordfish
Onlie attempt to doe what all doe wish:
The thresher backs him, and to beat begins.
The sluggard Whale yeilds to Oppression
And to hide himself from shame and Danger, downe   355
Begins to Sink; The Swordfish vpward spins
And gores him with his Beake; his Staffe like Fins
So weareth one, his Sword the other plies
That now a Scoffe and Pray this tirant dies
And (his owne Dole) feeds with himself all Companies.   360

37.

Who will reueng his Death? or who will Call
Those to accompt that thought and wrought his fall?
The heires of slaine kings, we see are often soe
Transported with the Ioy of what they gett
That they Reuenge and Obsequies forgett   365
Nor will against Such men the people goe
Because he is now dead, to whom they should show
Loue in that Act, some kings by vice being growne
Soe needie of Subiects Loue, that of their owne
They think they lose, if loue be to the dead Prince showne.   370

38.

This Sowle now free from Prison and passion
Hath yet a litle Indignation
That soe small hammers should so soon downe beat
Soe great a Castle, and hauing for her Howse
Got the streight Cloister of a wretched Mouse   375
(As Basest men that haue not what to eat
Nor enioy ought, doe far more hate the great
Then they who good repos'd Estates possesse)
This Soule, late taught that great things might by lesse
Be slayne, to gallant Mischeif doth her self addresse.   380

39.

Natures great Masterpece an Elephant,
The only harmles great thing; The Gyant
Of Beasts, who thought noe more had gone to make one wise
But to be iust and thankfull, loth to' offend
(Yet nature hath giuen him noe knees to bend),   385
Himself he vpprops, on himself relies
And foe to none, suspects noe Enimies,
Still sleeping stood; vext not his Phantasie
Black Dreames; like an vnbent Bow carelesly
His Sinewy Proboscies did remissly Lie,   390

40.

In which as in a Gallery, this Mouse
Walk'd and suruey'd the roomes of this vast howse
And to the Braine, the Soules bed Chamber, went
And gnawd the life Cords there; like a whole Towne
Cleane vndermin'd, the slaine beast tumbled Downe;   395
With him the Murderer dies, whom Enuy sent
To kill not saue, for onlie he that ment
To die, did euer kill a man of better Roome,
And thus he made his Foe his Pray and Tombe,
Who cares not to turne back may any whither come.   400

41.

Next hows'd this Soule a Wolues yet vnborne whelp
Till the best Midwife, nature, gaue it help
To issue, It could kill as soone as goe.
Abell, as white, and mild as his sheep were
(Who in that trade, of Church and kingdomes, there   405
Was the first Type) was still infested soe
With this wolfe, that it bred his losse and woe
And yet his Bitch, his Sentinell, attends
The flock so neere, soe well warnes and defends
That the Wolfe (hopelesse els) to corrupt her Intends.   410

42.

He took a Course which since successfully
Great Men haue often taken, to espie
The Counsells, or to break the plots of foes;
To Abels Tent he stealeth in the Dark
On whose skirts the Bitch slept; Ere she could bark   415
Attach'd her with streight gripes, yet he cald those
Embracements of Loue: to loues work he goes
Where deeds moue more then words, nor doth she show
Now much resist, nor needs he streighten soe
His Pray, for were she loose she would not bark nor goe.   420

43.

He hath engag'd her, his she wholy bides;
Who not her owne, none others Secrets hides:
If to the Flock he come, and Abel there
She faines hoarse barkings, but she biteth not,
Her faith is quite, but not her loue forgott;   425
At last a Trap, of which some euery where
Abell had plac'd, ended his Losse and feare
By the Wolfes Death, And now iust time it was
That a quick Soule should giue life to that Mas
Of Blood in Abels Bitch, and thither this did passe.   430

44.

Some haue their Wiues, their Sisters some begott
But in the liues of Emperors yow shall not
Read of a lust the which may equall this;
This Wolfe begatte himselfe and finished
What he begun aliue, when he was dead;   435
Son to himselfe and father too, he is
A ridling lust for which Scholemen would misse
A proper Name: the whelp of both these lay
In Abels Tent, and with Soft Moaba
His Sister, being young, it vsd to sport and play.   440

45.

He soone for her too harsh and Churlish grew
And Abell (the Dam dead) would vse this new
For the feild: Being of two kinds made
He as his Dam from Sheep droue Wolues away
And as his Sire he made them his owne pray.   445
Fiue yeares he liu'd, and Cousen'd with his Trade,
Then hopeles that his faults were hid, betraide
Himselfe by flight, and by all followed:
From dogs a Wolfe, from Wolues a Dog he fledd
And like a spy to both Sides false he perished.   450

46.

It quickned next a toyfull Ape, and soe
Gamesome it was, that it might freely goe
From Tent to Tent and with the Children play;
His Organs now soe like theirs he doth find
That why he cannot laugh and speak his Mind   455
He wonders much; withall most he doth stay
With Adams fifth Daughter, Syphatecia,
Doth gaze on her, and where she passeth, pas,
Gathers her fruit and tumbles on the Grasse
And wisest in that kind, the first true Louer was.   460

47.

He was the first that more desir'd to haue
One then another, first that ere did craue
Loue by mute Signes, and had noe power to speak;
First that Could make loue faces, or could doe
The Vaulters sobresalts, or vsd to wooe   465
With hoiting Gambolles, his owne bones to break
To make his Mistress merrie, Or to wreak
Her Angers on himself; Sins against kind
They easily doe, that can let feed their mind
With outward Beauty, beauty they in boies and beastes doe find.   470

48.

By this misled, too low things men haue prou'd
And too high; Beasts and Angels haue bene lou'd:
This Ape though els through-vaine, in this was wise,
He reacht at things too high, but open way
There was and he knew not she would say nay: 475
His Toies preuaile not, likelier meanes he tryes,
He gazeth on her face with teare-shot eyes
And vplifts subtilly with his russet Paw
Her kid-skin Apron without feare or Awe
Of Nature; Nature hath no Iaile though she haue law.   480

49.

First she was seely and knew not what he ment;
That vertue by his Touches chaft and spent
Succeeds an Itchy warmth, that melts her quite;
She knew not first, now cares not what he doth
And willing half and more, more then half loth   485
She neither pulls nor pushes, but outright
Now Cries and now repents; when Tethlemite,
Her brother, enters and a great Stone threw
After the Ape, who thus preuented flew;
This howse, thus battered Downe, the soule possest a new.   490

50.

And whether by this Chang, she lose or win
She Comes out next, where the Ape would haue gone in.
Adam and Eue had mingled Bloods, and now
Like Chimiques equall fires her temperate Womb
Had stewd and formd it, And part did become   495
A spungie Liuer that did richly allow
Like a free Conduit, on a high hills brow
Life-keeping Moisture, vnto euery part,
Part hardened it selfe to a thicker hart
Whose busie furnaces lifes spirits doe imparte.   500

51.

Another part became the Well of Sence,
The tender wel arm'd feeling braine, from whence
Those sinewy strings which doe our bodies tie
Are raueld out, and fast there by one end
Did this Soule Limms, these limms a Soule attend   505
And now they ioynd; keeping some qualitie
Of euery past shape, she knew Trecherie,
Rapine, Deceipt, and Lust and Ills enowe
To be a woeman; Themech she is now,
Sister and wife to Caine, Cain that first did plow.   510

52.

Who ere thou beest, that readst this Sullen writt
Which iust so much Courts thee, as thou dost it
Let me arreast thy Thoughts, Wonder with me
Why Ploughing, building, ruling and the rest
Or most of those Arts whence our liues are blest   515
By Cursed Cains Race inuented be
And blest Seth vext vs with Astronomie.
There's nothing Simplie good, nor ill alone,
Of euery qualitie Comparison
The only Measure is and Iudge Opinion.   520

Textual Introduction

Complete copies of "Metempsychosis" (*Metem*) survive in 8 contemporary manuscripts and in all 7 seventeenth-century editions/issues of Donne's collected *Poems* (A–G); and the text in one artifact, the Gosse ms. (F10), has been so extensively revised by a second scribe as to constitute a ninth witness—here designated F10(*cor*). Short excerpts from the poem appear in 4 manuscripts (AF1, B28, B51, IU2), in the 4 issues of Joshua Poole's The English PARNASSUS (1657–78; sigla 44a–d), and in the 3 issues of Marvell's THE REHEARSALL TRANSPROS'D (1673–74; sigla 54a–c). A brief introductory epistle accompanies the poem in all the major manuscripts and in the printed editions; its genealogy is described on pages 307–08 below.

Six of the primary manuscript witnesses—H6 (Group III), C2 (Group I) and the parent-child pairs CT1-B7 and DT1-H4 (all Group II)—are among the early seventeenth-century comprehensive collections of Donne's poems, while two—F10 and B29—exist as single-poem copies in composite artifacts containing works by other authors. Now in the Folger Shakespeare Library and having originally been in the collection of Sir Thomas Phillipps (1792–1872), F10 was owned in the late nineteenth century by Edmund Gosse, who in first bringing it to the attention of modern readers described it as the "earliest version" of the poem he had yet seen and—though he thought it "not very intelligently made"—conceded that among its "fifty or sixty slight variants" were "several which are distinct improvements upon the printed text, and one or two which actually clear up difficulties in the latter" (*Life and Letters* 1:140–41).[1] F10 was subsequently collated by Grierson (Q), for whom it supplied "some important emendations" (2:218); Hayward (S), who labeled it one of "the best extant MSS." of the poem (p. 252); Bennett (T), who adopted some of its readings; Milgate (Y), who found it "of great value" in correcting "the deficiencies in the large collections" (p. lxii); and Shawcross (Z), who cited it among the texts he had consulted. Neither Smith (AA) nor Patrides (DD) mentions F10 specifically, and its influence on their texts is mediated through prior editions.

B29 was discovered in the British Library in 1928 by H. J. L. Robbie, who thought it might "represent an early version of the poem" (215) and listed about 25 instances in which it deviated significantly from Grierson.[2] The following year the manuscript was noticed by Hayward (S), who, echoing Robbie's designation of it as "an early version," averred that "[i]n a few cases its readings are to be preferred to those of any

---

[1] Entitled "Dr :Donnes' Μετεμψύχωσις with Certaine select Dialogues, of Lucian, and The Tale of The Fauorite," F10 is described and discussed by Lara M. Crowley, "Cecil and the Soul: Donne's *Metempsychosis* in its Context in Folger Manuscript V.a.241," *English Manuscript Studies* 13 (2007):47–74.

[2] "Two More Undescribed MSS. of John Donne's Poems," *RES* 4:214–16.

Legend:
~ = agrees with LOH
◄ = agrees with nearest corresponding reading on left
<> = word(s) omitted
? = reading uncertain
boldfaced readings = authorial

Line no.	LOH	B29	LRH/DV reading	β	F10	γ	H6	δ	C2	ε
4	Yoak't **was**	~	~	~ vs	~	~	~	~	~	~
5	in…Euening	~…	~…	to…	◄…	◄…	◄…	◄…	◄…	◄…
9	outlast	~	outweare	◄	◄	◄	~	◄	◄	◄
10	holly **writs**	~	~	~	~ writt	~	~ writt	~	~	~
11	**Thee, eye**	~,	~,	~,	The∧ ~	~∧	(~	~∧	The∧ ~	~∧
11	**Sowle**	~	great ~	~	~	~	~	~	~	~
13	begin'st	~	~	~	~	~	~	~	beginns	~
16	**Danow**	Dano[missing]	~	~	~	~	~	~	Danon	~
27	For thence	~	~	~	~	From ~	~	~	~	~
29	diuers	~	~	~	diuerse	~	~	~	~	~
29	Park	Bark	~	~	~	~	~	~	~	~
38	praier be fitt	paper fitt	~	~	~	~	~	~	~	~
44	steepe Ambition	Sleepe ~	~	~	~	~	~	~	~	~
47	other	~	~	~	~	~	~	~	others	~
54	lone wayes	~	~	~	Loue ~	~	~	loue ~	~	~
56	**Sands & straights**	~ ~ / straig[missing]	**Streights ~ Sands**	◄ ◄	Streigth's ~ Sand's	streights ~ lands	◄ ◄	◄ ◄	◄ ◄	◄ ◄
57	and sayle	~	towards	◄	~	~	~	~	~	◄
57	toward	~	towards	◄	~	~	~	~	~	◄
58	beginne	~	began	◄	~	~	~	~	~	◄
61	this…**Sowle**	~…	~…	~…	◄…	◄…	that…	◄…	the…	◄…
61	emong	~	amongst	◄	◄	◄	◄	◄	◄	◄
64	shall longe	~	will ~	will ~	~	~ ◄	◄	◄	◄	~
65	Strayne	Chayne	~	~	~	~	~	~	~	~
67	of flesh	<~ ~>	~	~	~	~	~	~	~	~

Line no.	LOH	B29	LRH/DV reading	β	F10	γ	H6	δ	C2	ε
69	where	ʔ	ʔ	ʔ		ʔ	ʔ	ʔ	when	ʔ
69	great change	ʔ ~	ʔ	ʔ ʔ	greater ~	ʔ ʔ	ʔ ʔ	ʔ ʔ	ʔ ʔ	ʔ ʔ
70	in paradise	a ~	ʔ	ʔ	ʔ	ʔ	ʔ	ʔ	ʔ	ʔ
77	Stock't	ʔ	Stood	▾	▾	▾		▾	▾	▾
83	enliue	ʔ	ʔ	ʔ	ʔ	<~>	>~<?	<~>	<~>	<~>^
86	her	ʔ	to ~	▾	ʔ ▾	ʔ ▾	▾	ʔ	ʔ	ʔ ▾
87	whose race	ʔ	ʔ	her ~	▾	ʔ	ʔ		ʔ	ʔ	ʔ
89	eater	ʔ	eaters	▾	▾	▾		▾	▾	▾
94	corrupt yᵉ Riuulets	ʔ ~	~ vs ~	ʔ ▾	~ as Riuolett's	~ vs <~>	~ ▾ nothing letts	~ ▾ <~>	ʔ ▾ <~>	~ ▾<~>^
97	to whence	from ~	ʔ	ʔ	ʔ	ʔ	from ~	ʔ	ʔ	ʔ
99	beare	ʔ	ʔ	ʔ	ʔ	ʔ	ʔ	heare		
100	To loue them	<To> Loue ~	~ ~	ʔ ~	ʔ ~	ʔ ~~	Them to loue	~ ~	ʔ ~	ʔ ~
102	bee so	ʔ	ʔ	ʔ	doe ~	ʔ	ʔ	ʔ	ʔ	ʔ
106	shall God	ʔ ʔ	ʔ	will ~	ʔ ▾	ʔ ▾	ʔ ▾	ʔ	ʔ ʔ	ʔ ʔ
112	the gaine	ʔ	ʔ	ʔ	ʔ	their ~	ʔ ▾	ʔ ▾	ʔ	ʔ ▾
117	do...spill	ʔ ...	ʔ ...	ʔ ...	ʔ ...	ʔ ...	and ~ ...	~ ...	ʔ ...	ʔ ...
118	game	gaine	ʔ							
119	perfects	profitts	ʔ	ʔ	ʔ	perfitts	perfitt	perfitts		
126	dare scarce	ʔ	scarse dares	▾	▾	▾	dares ~	scarce dares	▾	▾
129	Pitt...fate	ʔ ...	Plott...	▾...▾	▾...▾	...fates	▾...▾	▾...▾	▾...▾	ʔ ...
130	anew								a new	
131	This Plant	ʔ	ʔ ~	The ~	ʔ ▾	ʔ ▾	ʔ ▾	ʔ ~	ʔ ▾	ʔ ▾
133	fleets	flotes	ʔ	ʔ	ʔ	ʔ		ʔ	ʔ	ʔ
136	As...when as	ʔ ...~	iust as...when	▾ ▾...▾	▾ ▾...▾	▾ ▾...▾	▾ ▾...▾	▾...▾	▾ ▾...▾	▾ ▾...▾
137	so filled is	~ ~	and haue so fild	▾ ▾ ▾	▾ ▾ ▾	and so filld	▾ ▾ vp	▾ ▾ <vp>	▾ ▾ ▾ <vp>	▾ ▾ <vp>
138	could passe	ʔ	ʔ	ʔ	can ~	ʔ	ʔ	ʔ	ʔ	ʔ
141	thrust	thrusts	ʔ	ʔ	ʔ	ʔ	▾	▾		▾
150	apples kindle	ʔ	ʔ	ʔ	ʔ	~ kind	ʔ	ʔ	ʔ	ʔ

Line no.	LOH	B29	LRH/DV reading	β	F10	γ	H6	δ	C2	ε
155	leauy	~	~	~	~	~	~	leafie	▽	▽
158	lone	~	~	~	loue	~	~	~	~	~
165	the…eyes	her…~	~…	~…	~…	~…	~…	~…	~…	~…
176	change	~	~	~	Changes	~	~	~	~	~
177	eniayld	exhal'd	~	~	~	~	~	~	~	~
180	enclos'd	~	~	~	~	enclothd	vnclothd	encloth'd	vncloth'd	encloth'd
180	pok't	~	~	?	prickt	peck'd	~	peck'd	pick'd	peck'd
183	through gummes	~ ~	~ ~	~ ~	<through> ~	~	~	~	~	~
184	bones	~	~	~	bone	~	~	~	~	~
185	mantel	matell	~	~	~	~	~	~	~	~
195	last	~	~	tast	~	~	~	~	~	~
199	doe vse	~	~	~	doth ~	~	~	~	~	~
201	till…tooke	while…~	~…	~…	~…	~…	~…	~…	~…	~…
201	freedome	~	~	~	~	~	freedoms	~	~	~
203	Till now	~	~	~	tis ~	~	~	~	~	~
207	slakeneth	slackens	~	~	~	~	~	~	~	~
214	hidd netts	~	~	~	~	his ~	~	~	~	~
214	snare	~	~	~	~	~	~	snares	▽	▽
219	pleasantlie three	blank blank	~	~	~	~	~	~	▽	~
220	his race	~ ~	~	~ ~	~	~	~	~	<~> <~>	~
222	too actiue Organes	~ ~	~	to ~	~ ~	~ ▽	~	to ~	▽	▽
225	they had	~ ~	~	~ ~	~ ~	<~>	these ▽	~ ▽	~ ▽	~ ▽
225	entertouch't	~	~	~	~	enter-touched	~-▽	~-▽	~-▽	~-▽
227	rowe	~	~	~	~	~	~	roe	▽	▽
230	cowld you	~	~	~	<yow>	you could	~ ▽	~ ~	~ ~	~ ~
232	as y^w may	~ ~	that ~	~ ▽	~ ▽	~ ▽	~ ▽	~ ~	~ ~	~ ~
240	or wel arm'd	and ~ ~	~	~	~	~	~	~	~	~
251	w^t her natiue	~ ~	~	~	~	~	~	~	~	~

Line no.	LOH	B29	LRH/DV reading	β	F10	γ	H6	δ	C2	ε
252	towerd	~	towards							
253	retarded	regarded								
260	This wretch	~	~		~, This ~					
260	habitts	haunts	~							
267	Water	~	~					weather		
269	Where fresh				When ~					
269	which to doe	~	~	what ~ ~	~					
275	this...spectacle	~...~	~...~	~...~	his... ~					
277	to end	~	~		so ends					
279	As...stood	~...	~...	~...	~...		(~...~)	~...		
280	Rais'd			It rais'd	~		Its ~	It ~		
280	instruments			instrument						
288	these...kindes	~...	~...	~...	those...	~...	~...	~...		
291	same howre		selfe ~							
296	many leagues at Sea			<many> ~	<many> ~	<many> ~	~ ~>o're past<†	<many> ~		
301	this Sowle			our ~						
305	vnrooted				onrooted					
308	This fish	The ~								
318	Inland Sea	~			Iland ~					
318	hee went	~			she ~					
319	he ment	~			she ~					
321	a fauorite		an officer							
322	Lies still at Court, and Is him selfe a nett	~~~~, ~ ~~~~	stayes in his ~ as his owne Nett and there							
323	Where Sutors	~	All ~							

†Inserted from A

Line no.	LOH	B29	LRH/DV reading	β	F10	γ	H6	δ	C2	ε
330	thousand...smalls	thousands....small	~.....	~.....	~	~.....	~.....	~.....	~.....	~.....
337	launch't forth	~	~	~	~	launch'd ~	~	~	launch'd ~	~
344	do not eate	~	~	~	~	did ~	~	~	~	~
345	outsweat	~	out streat	out streat	~	∨ ∨	out-sweate	out streat	outstreate	out streate
349	Tirant	~	~	~	~	~	~	Tyran	~	∨
351	flaile-fin'd	flatt fin'd	~	haile-~	~	~	~	~	~`~	~
355	danger	daunder	~	~	~	~	~	~	~	~
358	weareth one	~	dyes	were the ~	were ~	well ∨	∨ ∨	∨ ∨	were ∨	∨ ∨
359	Iyes	~	dyes	∨	∨	∨	∨	∨	∨	∨
368	And kiges...are	~`.....	some ~...being	~`.....	~`.....	~`.....	~`.....	~`.....	~`.....	~`.....
378	who good	whome <good>	~	~	~	~	~	~	~	~
383	who had been king but y¹ too wise	~ ~ ~ ~	who thought no more had gone to make one wise	∨ ∨ ∨ ∨	∨ ∨ ∨ ∨	<more> ∨ ∨ ∨	∨ ∨ none <∨> ∨ <gone> ∨	∨ ∨ no <∨> ∨ gone ∨ one ∨	∨ ∨ nor <∨> ∨	∨ ∨ no <∨> ∨ ∨ ∨
384	Hee was, just, thankfull	~`, ~`,	but to be iust and thankfull	∨ ∨ ∨ ∨ ∨	∨ ∨ ∨ ∨	∨ ∨ ∨ ∨	∨ him ∨ ∨ ∨ ∨	∨ ∨ ∨ ∨	∨ ∨ ∨ ∨	∨ ∨ ∨ ∨
385	Yet Nature	For ~	~	~	∨	~	~	~	~	~
394	life cordes	~	~	~	lifes ~	~	~	~	~	~
396	Murtherer	~	~ dies	~	~	∨	∨	~	~	∨
397	saue	~ ~	~	*ape	rape	scape	∨	~	∨	∨
397	ment	~ ~	~ ~	~	~	~	~	went	~	~
399	his foe	him for	~ ~	~	~	~	~	~	~	~
400	whither	whether	~	~	~	~	~	~	whether	~
402	gaue it	~ ~	~ ~	~ ~	~ him	~	~	~	~	~
405	the trade	~	that ~	~	∨	~	∨	~	∨	∨
406	infested	~	~	~	~	~	~	infected	~	~
409	Flock so neere	~ ~	~	flocks ~ well	~	~	~	~	~	~
411	way	~	course	∨	∨	∨	∨	∨	∨	∨

Line no.	LOH	B29	LRH/DV reading	β	F10	γ	H6	δ	C2	ε
415	skirt	~	**skirts**	▽	▽	▽	▽	▽	▽	▽
416	Attach'd	Attach	~	~	~	~	~	~	~	~
419	Now much resist	~ ~					Resistance ~	~ ~	Nor ~ ~	~
419	nor needs	~	~	~ ~	~ ~	~ ~	~ neede	~ ~	~ ~	~ ~
420	not barke	~	~	~	nor ~	~	nor ~	~	~	~
421	wholy	~	~	~	onlie	onely	onely	~	~	~
422	none	no	~	~	~	~	no	~	~	~
427	ended	~	~	~	~	end and	ends both	end and	~	~
431	wiues		~	~	Wifes			~		
432	life of Princes	~ ~	liues ~ Emperors	▽ ~ ▽	lifes ~ ▽	liues ~ ▽	~ ▽ ▽	~ ▽ ~	▽	~ ▽
434	begatte	~	~	begott			~	▽	▽	▽
435	begunne	~		~		began	~	~	~	~
438	A proper Name	\<proper\> ~	A proper Name	~	~	~	~	~	~	~
451	next a / toyful Ape	~ ~ / ~ ~	~ ~	~ ~ / ~ ~	wext ~ / toilefull ~	~ ~ / ~ ~	~ ~ / ~ ~	~ ~ / ~ ~	~ ~ / ~ ~	~ ~ / ~ ~
454	like theirs	~	~	~	~ them	~	~	~	~	~
456	Hee wonders, much; / W^r all most	~ ~ / ~ ~	~ ~ / ~ ~	~ ~ / ~ ~	~ ~ ~ / withall, ~	~ ~ / ~ ~	~ ~ / ~ ~	~ ~ / ~ ~	~ ~ / ~ ~	~ ~ / ~ ~
458	where...passeth	⋮	~	~...	when...	~...	~...	~...	~...	~...
459	frute	~	~	~	~	fruits	~	~	~	~
460	in that kind	~ ~	~	~...	of ~	~	~	of ~	~	~
466	hoyting...bones	hoisting...howse	~ ⋮	~...	halting...	~...	~...	~	~...	~...
468	Her angers	~ ~	~	~...	~	~ Anger	~	~	~	~
475	could say nay	~ ~	would ~ ~	~ ~	~	~	▽	▽	▽	~ ~
477	tear-shot	~ ~	~	~ ~	teare-shed	~ ~	~	~	~ ~	~ ~
478	vplifts softly	~ ~	~ subtilly	▽ ~	~	▽	~	~	▽	~ ▽
480	she haue	~	~ ~	~	~	~	~ was	~	~ hath	~ ~
484	now cares	nor ~	~ ~	~ ~	~	~	~	~	~	then ~

Line no.	LOH	B29	LRH/DV reading	β	F10	γ	H6	δ	C2	ε
485	halfe and...loth	~ ~...~	~ ~...~	~...*oth	~ then...Forth	~...blank	~...wroth	~...blank	~...blank	~...blank
488	enters	~	~	~	~	enterd	▾	▾	▾	▾
490	a new	~	~	~ ~	another	~ ~	~ ~	~ ~	~ ~	~ ~
500	Lifes spirits	Life sprights	~ ~	~ ~	~ ~	~ ~	liues ~	~ ~	~ ~	~ ~
504	there by one	~ ~ ~	~ ~ ~	~ ~ ~	thereby ~	~ ~ ~	thereby on	~ ~	~ ~	~ ~
506	ioynd	ioyne	~	~	~	~	~	~	~	~
508	enowe	~	~	~	inough	~	~	~	~	enough
510	Cain, Cain	~, <Caine>	~, ~	~, ~	~, ~	~, ~	~; to ~	~, ~	~, ~	~, ~
511-20	st om	st om	st present	st present	st present	st present	st present	st present	st present	st present
512	l. om	l. om	thou dost	~ ~	~ Courts	~ ~	~ ~	~ ~	~ ~	~ ~
515	l. om	l. om	those arts	~	~	~	~	these ~	~ ~	~ ~

other rescension" (p. 252) and adopted several of them into his reading text; and in 1942 Bennett (T), producing a text based on A, similarly accepted a handful of B29's unique readings as emendations. In his Oxford edition of 1967, Milgate (Y) pointed to "some seventy-five" unique readings in B29, but averred that "only two" of these were "certainly correct" (lxiii); on the other hand, he opined that "most" of some 20 other readings that B29 uniquely shared with F10 were "certainly right" and ventured the quasi-stemmatic conclusion that the two artifacts descended from "a common original," while the remaining manuscript copies descended from a copy in which the "readings peculiar" to B29 and F10 "were lost" (lxiii). Shawcross (Z), as with F10, lists B29 among the texts for the poem and cites a handful of its readings; also as with F10, Smith (AA) and Patrides (DD) derive their minimal knowledge of F10 from prior editors.

As shown on the stemma in Figure 22, our analysis indicates that *Metem* in fact exists in an original and a revised version, the text in B29 being the sole surviving descendant of the lost original holograph (LOH) and all other texts being descendants—through the further missing urtexts β, γ, δ, and ε—of the lost revised holograph (LRH). Neither B29 (which contains numerous errors as well as exhibiting significant physical damage at the margins of many leaves),[3] F10 (the closest descendant of the LRH), nor any other surviving artifact represents the original from which it derives with complete accuracy, and the descent of the text through the various levels on the genealogical tree traces a pattern of continuous decline. Donne's revisions of the poem, as well as stemmatologically important scribal errors, are recorded in Figure 19.[4]

Counting the added stanza 52 (ll. 511–20), Figure 19 records 28 instances of what we judge to be authorial revision, which are denoted by the paired bold-faced entries in the columns headed LOH and LRH/DV.[5] While opinions may well differ as to whether some of these changes should be attributed to Donne rather than to the copyist of β (in line 86, for instance, is the alteration of the indirect object "her" to the more obvious "to her" an authorial or a scribal change?), most would agree that such alterations as "outlast" to "out-weare" in line 9, "As in our streets, when as the people stay / To see the Prince so filled is the waye" to "iust as…when…/…and haue soe fild" in line 136–37, and "tooke a way" to "took a Course" in line 411 are the work of the author.[6] The most striking changes—certainly Donne's—occur in the latter half of the poem, where four separate passages embody alterations seemingly designed to render them less politically incendiary. Including the absence of the final stanza in the LOH/B29, these differences are displayed in Table 6.1.

---

[3] As listed on Figure 19, B29 contains errors in lines 29, 38, 44, 67, 68, 97, 118, 119, 141, 165, 177, 185, 201, 207, 219, 240, 253, 260, 308, 330, 351, 355, 378, 385, 399, 400, 416, 422, 438, 466, 484, 500, 506, and 510.

[4] Figure 19 lists only authorial changes and substantive scribal variants that bear on the establishment of copy-text and on the transmissional history of the poem in the manuscripts and seventeenth-century prints (principally A); the genealogy of the text discussed below will be explained primarily in terms of the detail recorded in this figure. A full record of substantive and semisubstantive variants in the artifacts is provided in the Textual Apparatus.

[5] See entries for lines 9, 11, 56, 57, 58, 61, 77, 86, 89, 94, 126, 129, 136–37, 232, 252, 291, 321–23, 359, 368, 383-84, 396, 405, 411, 415, 432, 475, 478, and 511–20.

[6] See DV 7.1:111–12 for the guidelines followed in this edition for identifying revisions.

Table 6.1: Major revisions in the text of *Metem*

(1) <u>Lines 321–23</u>

Original version (LOH/B29):   Hee hunts not fish, **But as a fauorite**
                                          Lies still at Court, and is him selfe a nett
                                          Where Sutors of all sorts themselus enthrall....

Revised version (LRH/F10):   He hunts not Fish **but as an officer**
                                          stayes in his Court as his owne Nett and there
                                          All Sutors of all Sorts themselues inthrall....

(2) <u>Lines 368–70</u>

Original version (LOH/B29):   **...And kīges** by vice ar growne
                                          So needy of Subjects loue, yᵗ of their owne
                                          They think they loose if loue be to yᵉ dead prince Showne....

Revised version (LRH/F10):   **...some kings** by vice being growne
                                          Soe needie of Subiects Loue, that of their owne
                                          they think they loose, if loue be to the dead Prince showen.

(3) <u>Lines 381–84</u>

Original version (LOH/B29):   ...an Elephant
                                          The onely harmles great thinge; The Giant
                                          Of Beasts, **who had beene king but yᵗ too wise**
                                          Hee was, just, thankfull, loth t'offend....

Revised version (LRH/F10):   ...an Elephant
                                          the only harmles great thing; The Gyant
                                          of Beasts, **who thought noe more had gone to make one wise**
                                          but to be iust and thankfull, loth to' offend....

(4) <u>Lines 432–33</u>

Original version (LOH/B29):   But in the life of **Princes** yʷ shall nott
                                          Read of a lust the which may equall this....

Revised version (LRH/F10):   But in the lifes of **Emperors** yow shall not
                                            read of a lust the which may equall this....

(5) <u>Lines 511–20</u>

Original version (LOH/B29):   *stanza absent*

Revised version (LRH/F10):   *stanza included*

    The latter three of these revisions—the change of the categorical "And kīges" to the qualified "some kings" in line 368, omission of explicit reference to kingship in the enumeration of the elephant's noble qualities (lines 383–84), and replacement of the locally pertinent "Princes" with the more exotic "Emperors" in line 432—apparently reflect the general sense of apprehension that Donne elsewhere associated with the circulation of his satirical writings.[7] But in the alteration of the simile in lines 321–23—which initially compares the whale to a "fauorite" who "Lies still at Court, and is him selfe a nett / Where Sutors…themselus enthrall," but in revision likens him to "an officer" who "stayes in his Court as his owne Nett and there / All Sutors …themelues enthrall"—it is difficult not to suspect a specific topical allusion; and recognition that these lines embody an authorial change will no doubt fuel further speculation on the possible political allegory encoded in this part of the poem (see the Date and Circumstances section of the Commentary on *Metem* below).

The differing forms of the heading in the various manuscripts also support the account of the text's genealogy here presented, as is shown in Table 6.2.

Table 6.2: The evolution of the heading in the manuscript copies of *Metem*

Component	B29	F10	H6	C2	CT1, B7, DT1, H4
HE	Infinitati Sacrum. (*in l. M above work*)	D:ʳ Donnes Μετεμψύχωσις. | / with/ Certaine select Dialogues,/ of/ Lucian,/ and/ The Tale of/ The Fauorite. | (*engrossed; on separate title page*)	Infinitati Sacrum/ 16. Augusti. 1601./ Metempsychosis/ Poema Satyricon/ (*centered over work*)	Infinitati Sacrum. 16.°/ Augusti 1601./ Metempsychosis./ Poema Satyricon. (*centered over work*)	(*substantively match C2, except that H4 omits the date; centered over work*)
subHE1	*none*	EPISTLE	Epistle	Epistle. |	Epistle.
epistle	*ll. 1–12a of letter*	*text of letter*	*text of letter*	*text of letter*	*text of letter*
subHE2	Poema Satiricum/ Metempsychosis	*none*	First Song	First Songe.	ffirst Songe.*
poem	*text of poem*	*text of poem*	*text of poem*	*text of poem*	*text of poem*

*Subheading "THE PROGRESSE OF THE SOULE." introduced above "*First Song.*" in A.

Among the surviving texts, as Table 6.2 makes clear, that in H6 is the earliest to include all six of the standard components of the heading—the dedication to "infinity" ("Infinitati Sacrum"), the date ("16. Augusti. 1601."), the title of the poem ("Metempsychosis"), the generic descriptor ("Poema Satyricon"), and the section labels over the introductory letter ("Epistle") and the poem ("First Song")—and since these elements recur in the artifacts below H6 on the stemma, they undoubtedly existed in γ. Given the fullness and taxonomic specificity of this heading, moreover, it seems clear that it is authorial, deriving ultimately from the LRH, and that even though it

---

[7]As noted in the General Textual Introduction above, in a letter sent to an unnamed friend in about 1600, Donne concedes that "to…[his] satyrs there belongs some feare" (LR1, 308v).

must have existed in β, the F10 scribe essentially ignored it (of the standard elements it contains only the poem title, translated into Greek) in the interests of melding the poem with the other works in his collection. B29, on the other hand, appears to exhibit an earlier, less fully developed form of the heading, placing the rubric "Infinitati Sacrum" as an introduction to the epistle and introducing the poem proper with only the generic descriptor "Poema Satiricum" and the specific title "Metempsycosis."[8]

B29 also lacks the date and—as is noted in Table 6.2—the final stanza of the poem. In initially describing B29, Robbie says nothing about the absent date, but notes that the manuscript lacks stanza 52 and suggests that this final stanza may have been a later addition to the poem (p. 215); and Hayward endorses Robbie's view of B29, though averring that the poem was composed "[i]n 1601" (p. 252). Subsequently, Milgate—without mentioning the lack of a date in B29—declares that Donne composed the poem in "August 1601" (p. xxv) and explicitly rejects Robbie's suggestion that B29 "represented the original form of the poem," describing the absent final stanza in that artifact as "missing" and attributing that absence, as well as the truncated form of the epistle, to the fact that B29 was copied from "a defective exemplar" (p. lxiii). All other twentieth-century editors implicitly accept the 1601 date of composition and, apparently, Milgate's view of B29 as well. The genealogy of the text here demonstrated and the evolving form of the heading on the work, however, support Robbie's belief that Donne added the final stanza when he revised the poem and, furthermore, point to 16 August 1601 as the date when that revision was finalized. Connecting the revisions of the poem—especially those itemized in Table 6.1—to August of 1601 seems likely to encourage the views of readers who associate the poem with events surrounding the failed Essex rebellion earlier in that year (see the Date and Circumstances section of the Commentary on *Metem* below).

As listed on Figure 19, the β scribe introduces into the stream of transmission nearly a score of additional variant readings, including those in lines 4, 5, 64, 87, 106, 131, 180, 195, 222, 269, 280, 301, 345, 397, 434, 456, and 485. Of these, "yoak't vs [for *was*]" (l. 4), "to [for *in*]...euening" (l. 5), "will [for *shall*] long" (l. 64), "her [for *whose*] race" (l. 87), "will [for *shall*] God" (l. 106), "The [for *This*] plant" (l. 131), "to [for *too*] actiue Organes" (l. 222), "what [for *which*] to do" (l. 269), "our [for *this*] Sowle" (l. 301), and "begott [for *begatte*] himselfe" (l. 434) seem simple trivializations in which a more commonplace or predictable locution is substituted for the authorial reading.[9] Others suggest blunders in the β scribe's penmanship: it seems doubtful that β clearly recorded the authorial "pok't" in line 180, for example, since β's offspring

---

[8]Beside the heading of the letter, B29 bears the accession date "16 October 1725," inscribed by Humphrey Wanley, the first keeper of the Harleian Library; and beside the heading of the poem and again at the end appears the name of one "Edward Smith," a former owner and perhaps the same "Edward Smyth" whose name appears on folio 8 of C1. While Beal dates B29 from the 1620s, the evidence indicates that the LOH from which it derives was completed at some point before 16 August 1601. Despite having ample space to continue, the copyist inexplicably breaks off the introductory Epistle in mid-sentence less than half way through ("None wrights so ill that..."). The poem itself starts on the first leaf of a gathering, though the leaf containing the Epistle is not the first leaf in its gathering, a fact suggesting that the Epistle and its heading were added at some point after inscription of the poem.

[9]The line-86 addition of "to" (= "to her") improves parallelism with the following "to her husband" (l. 88) and is thus possibly the author's.

F10 and γ record, respectively, "prickt" and "peckd"; and similar defects apparently led to the erroneous "tast" (for "last") in line 195 and the neologistic "out streat" (for "out sweat") in line 345. Moreover, it seems likely that a β blunder somehow produced an indecipherable construct ending in "ape" in line 397, since F10 records "rape" and γ gives "scape"; and in line 485 the presence of a similarly unintelligible reading ending in "th" apparently accounts for F10's conjectural "Forth" and the unfilled blank space in γ.[10] Scribal misunderstanding seems to characterize the remaining two errors in this list. In the simile spanning lines 279–80, Donne describes the hapless fish's being plucked from the sea by a "sea Pie" and then devoured as an instance of the truism that lowly "men" who are elevated by "great ones" are certain to be victimized: "As are by great ones men̄ wch lowly stood / Rais'd to bee the raisers instruments, and foode"; β interjects an "It" at the head of line 280 and reduces the plural "instruments" to the singular "instrument," thus shifting the subject of "rais'd" from "men" to, apparently, the fish ("It") and destroying the sense of the passage.

In two noteworthy instances, moreover, β alters the LRH's punctuation in ways that obscure Donne's syntax. The original version of the poem in B29 correctly records a period at the end of line 203 ("Till now unlawful, therefore ill, 'twas not."), the subject of this crabbed clause ("'t") referring to "Men['s]" alleged "ingress[ion]" of "their Daughters and their Sisters" in the era before humans "took Lawes." And the LRH must have ended line 203 with similarly strong pointing. β, however, drops the punctuation after "not," thus creating uncertainty as to whether "'twas not" belongs with the foregoing "Till now unlawful, therefore ill" or with the following "So iolly that it can moue this Sowle is…" (l. 204) and sowing a confusion in the following lines that would not be fully clarified until the appearance of Grierson's edition in 1912.[11] The second instance involves β's alteration of the punctuation in line 456,

---

[10]To the naked eye F10 appears to read the spurious "Footh," and editors from Grierson onward have so reported it. But magnification shows, resting atop the manuscript's original black ink, a blue dot almost entirely covering the bar of the capital "F" (which extends only rightward from the stem) and, in the same blue ink, a lowercase "o" covering the third letter in the word, which appears to have originally been a minuscule "r." Our interpretation of these details is that the F10 scribe originally wrote "Forth," but that a later owner or vetter overwrote the original "r" with an "o" and attempted to turn the original "F" into a "T" by blotting the "F's" crossbar, thus emending the manuscript's reading to that of A—"Tooth." The scribe's original "Forth" seems just barely plausible in light of OED definition A.1.b.—"expressing promptitude or eagerness for action."

[11]C2, copy-text text for the poem's first printing (in A), renders lines 201–04 as follows:

Men, till they tooke lawes wch made freedome lesse
Theyre daughters, and theyre Sisters did ingresse
Till now unlawful, therefore ill, t'was not
So Iolly, y^t it can moove thys Soule, is….

In setting this text into type, A's editor initially adds commas at the ends of lines 201 (="lesse,") and 202 (= "ingresse,") and—misled by the absence of pointing after "not"—attempts to make sense of the passage by raising the comma after "ill" to a semicolon (="ill;"). Dissatisfied with this result, he then stops the press to replace the comma after "Soule" with a semicolon and capitalize "is" (="Soule; Is"). In B this same editor removes the comma after "daughters" in line 202 (="daughters"), adds a comma after "now" in line 203 (="now,"), removes the semicolon he had previously inserted after "ill" (="ill"), which also renders the syntax of the line ambiguous: whereas the pointing recorded in the LRH ends the clause after "much" ("…Hee wonders, much;") and aligns "W^t all most" with the following "hee doth stay," β's removal of the semicolon after "much" and repositioning of the comma (yielding "He wonders much withall, most…") creates a vagueness that subsequently leads the γ scribe to stop the first clause after "wonders" (= "wonders;"). This restructuring—and the equivocal "much withall, most he doth stay" that follows—passes on into A–G and all subsequent editions.

β's offspring include F10 and γ, F10 being the nearest surviving descendant of the LRH and thus the copy-text followed here. Incorporating the above-discussed errors introduced in β, F10 adds further substantive blunders in lines 10, 11, 29, 54, 69, 94, 102, 138, 158, 176, 180, 183, 184, 199, 203, 230, 260, 269, 275, 277, 288, 305, 318, 319, 351, 358, 394, 397, 402, 409, 420, 421, 431, 432, 451, 454, 458, 460, 466, 477, 485, 490, 504, 508, and 512 (see Figure 19), and our emendations of these plus various necessary adjustments of the punctuation are discussed below at the end of this introduction. γ likewise records β's errors, adding to them the following further slips of the pen, trivializations, eye-skip errors, and misunderstandings: "From [for the authorial *For*] thence are all deriv'd" (l. 27), "through straights and lands [for *Sand's*]" (l. 56), "I launch…and I [for *and*] saile" (l. 57), "this Soule did blank space [for *enliue*]" (l. 83), "The Daughters here corrupt vs blank space [for *Riuolett's*]" (l. 94), "lesse is their [for *the*] gaine" (l. 112), "Arguing…perfitts [for the more usual *perfects*] them" (l. 118–19), "Her, her fates [for *fate*] threw" (l. 129), "and so [for *have so*] filld the way" (l. 137), "His Apples kind [for *kindle*]" (l. 150), "her encloth'd Child…peck'd [for *enclos'd…pok't*]" (l. 180), "the first howse [for *houre*] speakes" (l. 187), "deceive / With faynd Calls, his [for *hidd*] netts, or enwrapping Snares [for *snare*]" (l. 213–14), "For they intertouched [for *had intertouch't*]" (l. 225), "by noe name you could [for *cowld you*] call it" (l. 230), "leagues [for *many leagues*] at Sea" (l. 296), "they did [for *doe*] not eate" (l. 344), "so well the [for *so weareth*] one" (l. 358), "who thought no [for *no more*] had gone to make one wise" (l. 383), "enuy sent / To kill not scape [for *saue*]" (l. 396–97), "a trap…end and [for *ended*] his losse" (l. 426–27), "finished / What he began [for *begun*]" (ll. 434–35), "Hee wonders; much [for *wonders much;*] withall, most hee doth stay" (l. 456), "Gathers her fruits [for *fruit*]" (l. 459), "wreake / Her anger [for *angers*]" (ll. 467–68), "more then halfe blank space [for *loth*]" (l. 485), and "Her brother enterd [for *enters*]" (l. 488). Combined with those deriving from β, all these misreadings are passed on to γ's successors on the stemma.

The genealogical tree again forks at γ, one branch leading to H6, the other to δ, which in turn begets C2 and, through ε, the CT1-B7 and DT1-H4 parent-child pairs. Prepared as the copy-text for a planned edition of Donne's poetry by a highly diligent, knowledgeable, and resourceful collector-editor, H6 adds to the misreadings initiated

and strengthens to a period the semicolon appearing in the corrected form of A in line 204 (="soule. Is"):

> Men, till they tooke lawes which made freedome lesse,
> Their daughters and theyre Sisters did ingresse,
> Till now, unlawful, therefore ill t'was not
> So jolly that it can move this soule. Is….

in β and γ something over 60 further blunders, sophistications, and "improvements" of its own.[12] And while H6 does not stand in the direct line of transmission from the LRH to the first printing of the poem in A, it supplies a few emendations to the C2 setting text of that edition (see Table 6.3 below) and many more to the re-edited text of B two years later; and many of these changes are perpetuated in the poem's subsequent textual history. Among the 60 plus H6 variants cited in footnote 12, for example, those in lines 10, 16, 54, 73, 76, 99, 117, 130, 137, 267, 279, 296, 358, 383, 443, and 485 are imported—in either direct or modified form—into the text of B. These alterations are detailed in the discussion of the seventeenth-century prints below.

H6's sibling δ, as is also shown on Figure 19, adds a further 13 scribal lections to those added by β and γ, including "sad loue [for lone] wayes" (l. 54 [a misreading having previously appeared in F10]), "we heare [for beare]" (l. 99), "leafie [for leauie] garland" (l. 155), "enwrapping snares [for snare]" (l. 214), "abled it to roe [for rowe]" (l. 227), "make the weather [for water] thinn" (l. 267), "Instruments" (replacing β's "Instrument" with the authorial reading) (l. 280), "Tyran [for Tyrant]" (l. 349 [a spelling also employed by δ in l. 359]), "went [for ment] / To die" (l. 397–98), "was…infected [for infested]" (l. 406), "wonders. Much…" (for "wonders, much;") (l. 456 [δ first introduces a full stop here]), "of [for in] that kind" (l. 460), and "these [for those] arts" (l. 515). Joining those accumulated in β and γ, these corruptions then descend to δ's offspring C2 and ε.

C2, the primary setting text for the text's entry into print in A, adds 22 substantive and semisubstantive scribal changes to the above-specified accretion of error, including "The [for Thee] Eye of heaven" (l. 11), "beginns [for begin'st] to shine" (l. 13), "Danon [for Danow]" (l. 16), "to Others [for other] Whets" (l. 47), "the [for this]…Soule" (l. 61), "when [for where]…did come" (l. 69), "with [for w^{ch}]…boyes" (l. 115), "Argueing his [for is] Heretiques game" (l. 118), "hows'd her a newe [for anew]" (l. 130), "your love [for Loues] lips" (l. 157), "vncloth'd [for enclos'd] Child" (l. 180), "to encrease, himselfe [for to encrease his race, himself]" (l. 220), "Pace with [for with her] native streame" (l. 251), "an ill habitt's [for are ill habits] left" (l. 260), "when [for where] it…lay" (l. 276), "dobts [for doubts]" (l. 277) "lanch'd [for launch'd]" (l. 337), "were the [for weareth] one" (l. 358), "any whether [for whither] come" (l. 400), "Nor [for Now] much resist" (l. 419), "shee hath [for haue] Law" (l. 480), and "Tethelemite" (for "Tethlemite") (l. 487). Most of these blunders carry over directly into the print tradition, although several evoke an attempted repair on the part of A's editor, as is discussed below.

The second direct descendant of δ, as shown on the stemma, is ε, which in turn begets the CT1-B7 and DT1-H4 parent-child pairs. ε itself is a remarkably accurate copy of δ, verbally diverging from the parent in only a handful of instances (reading,

---

[12]Figure 19 notes H6 variants in lines 10, 61, 83, 94, 97, 100, 117, 119, 126, 137, 180, 225, 279, 296 (imported from A), 345, 383, 419 (2), 420, 421, 422, 427, 480, 485, 500, 504, and 510; and the Historical Collation records further H6 sports in lines 4, 16, 17, 36, 54 (2), 62, 71, 73, 76, 99, 100, 106, 111, 114, 130, 131, 159, 170, 172, 206, 224, 231, 238, 261, 267, 273, 292, 324, 342, 358, 403, 437, 443, 460, 492, 494, 516, and 520. For a description of H6 and its place in Donne's textual history, see, e.g., DV 2:lxx and lxxviii; see also the digital facsimile of the artifact, including a full bibliographical description, at DigitalDonne: The Online Variorum http://donnevariorum.tamu.edu.

for example, "No [for *Nor*] her" in line 108, "toward [for *towards*] the Glassie Deepe" in line 252, "left th'oppressor [for *the oppressor*] fast" in line 262, and "Th'heires [for *The heires*]" in line 363). The copyists of ε's offspring CT1 and DT1, however, are considerably more maladroit: CT1 introduces over 30 further substantive errors, transmitting these to its child B7, which adds 33 further blunders of his own; DT1 introduces 7 additional corrupt lections into the text inherited from ε, passing these on to H4, which corrupts the text with a further 20 scribal mistakes of its own (see the Historical Collation). The principal importance of the ε family in the poem's subsequent textual history lies in the possibility that DT1 supplied the occasional correction to the text of C2 as the editor of A sought to prepare a readable text for the poem's first appearance in print.

The Seventeenth-Century Prints

Evincing the 28 authorial revisions incorporated into the LRH (in ll. 9, 11, 56, 57, 58, 61, 77, 86, 89, 94, 126, 129, 136–37, 232, 252, 291, 321–23, 359, 368, 383–84, 396, 405, 411, 415, 432, 475, 478, 511–20), the 18 scribal errors initiated in β (ll. 4, 5, 64, 87, 106, 131, 180, 195, 222, 269, 280, 301, 345, 397, 421, 434, 456, 485), the 27 scribal errors introduced in γ (ll. 27, 56, 57, 83, 94, 112, 119, 129, 137, 150, 180, 187, 214, 225, 230, 296, 344, 358, 383, 397, 427, 435, 456, 459, 468, 485, 488), the 13 scribal errors from δ (ll. 54, 99, 155, 214, 227, 267, 280, 349, 397, 406, 456, 460, 515), and 13 scribal lections from C2 (ll. 13, 16, 47, 61, 69, 130, 180, 220, 337, 358, 419, 480, 487), the text of *Metem* first enters print in the 1633 edition of Donne's collected *Poems* (A), constituting—as it does in the parent manuscript—the first poem in the volume (on C2 as A's setting text, see footnote 42 in the General Textual Introduction).

Predictably, A does not translate the C2 text into print with photographic exactitude, recording a combination of inadvertent blunders and conscious changes numbering about 30 in all. These include—as is shown in Figure 20—insertion of the editorially confected "THE PROGRESSE OF THE SOULE" above the rubric "*First Song*," which appear together at the top of an elaborately typeset page 1 of the volume as a formal title for the poem proper. The mistakes and some of the deliberate emendations merely increase the accumulation of error in the text, of course, but other editorial changes—whether imposed independently or obtained by comparing one or more other manuscripts—actually restore authorial readings; and despite its various shortcomings the overwhelming impression created by A's handling of *Metem* is of a poem edited with intelligence, sensitivity, and industry.

A's blunders and gratuitous sophistications include "vouch-safe thou" (for the normative "vouch thou safe") in line 36, "daughters here corrupts [for *corrupt*] us" in line 94, "She thrusts (*cor*) us out" (for "...thrust...") in line 96, "see the Princesse (*cor*)" (for "...Prince") in line 137, "pick'd...a dore" (a further corruption of the C2-δ "Peck'd...") in line 180, "industruous" (for "industrious") in line 287, "at [for *as*] his owne net" in line 322, "wreched" (for "wretched") in line 375, and "nor barke" (for "not barke") in line 420; and the changes in lines 36, 180, 322, and 420 are perpetuated in subsequent editions. On the other hand, the edition repairs a number of C2's errors, changing "The Eye of heaven" to "Thee, eye of heaven" in line 11,

~ = agrees with LOH   ⌄ = agrees with nearest corresponding reading on left   ( ) = specific source of variant   < > = word(s) omitted   c = compositor

Line no.	LRH/DV reading	A	B	C	D–F	G
HE	Poema Satyricon. / First Songe	Poëma Satyricon: / THE / PROGRESSE / OF THE SOULE. / First Song.	⌄	⌄	⌄	⌄
4	Yoak'd was	~ us (β)	⌄	⌄	⌄	⌄
5	in his…Eueninge	to ~ … (β)	t'his…~ (c)	⌄….	⌄….	⌄….
7	Gold	~	cold (c)	⌄	⌄	~(A)
10	writts	~	writt (H6)	⌄	⌄	⌄
13	beginst	begins (C2)	~ (c, H6)	?	?	?
16	Danow	Danon (C2)	~ (H6)	?	?	?
27	For thence	From ~ (γ)	?	⌄	⌄	⌄
29	diuers	diverse (c)	⌄	⌄	⌄	⌄
36	vouch thou safe	vouch-safe thou (c)	vouchsafe ⌄ (c)	?	?	?
54	And shall	?	~ hold (H6)	?	?	?
54	lone wayes	love ~ (C2)	~ ~ (H6)	?	?	?
56	Sands	lands (γ)	⌄	⌄	⌄	⌄
57	saile	l ~ (γ)	~ ~ (γ)	?	?	?
59	hoisted	hoised (γ)	⌄	⌄	⌄	⌄
59	strook	stroke (γ)	⌄	⌄	⌄	⌄
61	this great Soule	the ~ ~ (C2)	~ ~ (c)	⌄	?	?
64	yow shall	~ will (β)	⌄	⌄	⌄	?
69	liu'd where	~ when (C2)	?	?	⌄	?
87	whose race	her ~ (β)	?	?	⌄	?
93	poysned	poisoned (γ)	⌄	⌄	⌄	poyson'd (c)
94	corrupt vs	corrupts ~ (c)	~ ~ (c, H6?)	?	?	?

Line no.	LRH/DV reading	A	B	C	D–F	G
94	Riuoletts	<~> (γ)	~ (F10)	?	?	?
99	beare	here (δ)	~ (H6)	?	?	?
106	shall God	will ~ (β)	~	▽	?	▽
112	Reckning	Reckoning (δ)	▽	▽	?	▽
112	Vanities	?	vanitie (c)	▽	?	▽
112	the Gaine	their ~ (γ)	~	?	?	?
114	Their resons like	~ ~	~ reason's ~ (c)	? ▽	~ ~ (c)	~ ~
117	do…spill	~…	and ~…~ (H6)	~…~	?	?
126	one…dares	~…	~…	~…	?	~…dare (c)
129	fate	fates (γ)	▽	▽	?	▽
130	Earth's pores	~~ (cor)	earth~ (A unc)	~?	earthpores (c)	~ ~ (A)
130	anew	a new (C2)	~ (c, H6)	?	?	?
131	This plant	The ~ (β)	▽	▽	?	▽
137	Prince	Princesse (cor) (c)	~ (A unc)	?	?	?
137	haue soe filld	<~> ~ fill'd (γ)	<~> ~ fill up (H6)	<~> ~	<~> ~	<~> ~
147	parts	~	part (c)	▽	▽	▽
150	kindle	kinde (γ)	~ (F10)	?	?	?
155	leauy	leafie (δ)	~	▽	▽	▽
158	a lone	~	?	?	alone (c)	?
180	enclos'd	uncloath'd (C2)	inclos'd (F10)	~	?	?
180	pok't	pick'd (C2, c)	▽	pic'd (c)	pick'd (c)	▽
185	a new Downy	downy a new (C2, c)	~~~ (c, H6)	?	?	?
195	last	tast (β)	▽	▽	?	▽
204	moue, this Soule is	move, ~ soule; ls (cor)	~ ~ (A cor, c)	~ soul. ▽ (c)	~ soul. ▽ (c)	~ : ▽ (c)
206	selfe preseruing	~	~	~	~ (c)	~
212	Holly	~	~	~	hollow (c)	~ (A)
214	hid	his (γ)	▽	▽	?	▽

Line no.	LRH/DV reading	A	B	C	D–F	G
220	his race	<~> <~> (C2)	~ ~ (H6)	~ ~	~ ~	~ ~
225	had intertouch't	<~> ~ (γ)	~ ~ (F10)	~ ~	~ ~	~ ~
227	abled	~	~	~	~	able (c) ~
227	Row	roe (δ)	~ (c, H6)	▽	~	~
230	could yow	you could (γ)	▽	▽	▽	▽
249	sure is	~	~	~ ~	is sure (c) ▽	▽
251	her Natiue streame	the ~ (c)	~ ~	~ ~	~ ~	~ ~
267	water	wether (δ)	~ (H6)	~	~	~
269	which to doe	what ~ (β)	~	▽	▽	~
273	doubtfull	~	her ~ (c)	~	~	~
280	Rais'd	It's ~ (H6)	~	~	~	~
280	Instruments	instrument (β)	▽	▽	▽	
287	industrious	industrious (c)	~ (c)	~	~	~
296	many Leagues	leagues o'er-past (c)	▽ ▽ ▽	▽ ▽ ▽	▽ ▽ ▽	o'rpast (c)
301	this Sowle	our ~ (β)	▽	▽	▽	▽
322	as…Nett	at…~ (c)	▽…▽	▽…▽	▽…▽	▽…▽
332	llands	~	~	~	lands (c)	~ (A)
337	this…boat	~…~	his…~ (c)	▽…▽	▽…▽	▽…▽
344	doe not	did ~ (γ)	▽	▽	▽	~
345	out sweat	outstreat (β)	▽	▽	▽	~
349	Tirant	Tyran (δ)	▽	▽	▽	~ (c)
358	weareth	were the (C2)	well ▽ (H6, DT1)	▽	▽	▽
359	tiran	tyran (δ)	▽	▽	▽	~ (c)
362	accompt	account (c)	▽	▽	▽	~
368	Act, some	~. Some (δ)	~. ▽	~. ▽	~. ▽	~.
383	noe more had gone	~ ~ ~ ~	none <~> had <~> (H6)	▽ <~> ▽ <~>	▽ <~> ▽ <~>	▽ <~> ▽ <~>
383	one wise	~	him ~ (H6)	~	▽	~
397	saue	scape (γ)	▽	▽	▽	▽

Line no.	LRH/DV reading	A	B	C	D–F	G
419	Now much resist	Nor ~~ (C2)	~ ~ ▽	~ ▽	~ ▽	~ ▽
420	not bark	nor ~	~	~ ▽	~ ~	~ ~ ▽
427	ended	ends all (c)	~ ▽	~ ▽	~ ▽	▽
434	begatte	begot (β)	▽	▽	▽	▽
435	What he begun	~~ began (γ)	~	~	~	~
443	kinds made	~ ~	~ thus ~ (H6)	~ ▽ ▽	~ ~	~ ~ ▽
456	wonders much; withall	~. Much with all (δ)	~. ▽ ▽	~ ▽ ▽ ▽	~ ▽ ▽ ▽	~ ▽ ▽ ▽
459	fruit	fruits (γ)	~	~.	~.	~.
460	in that kind	of ~~ (δ)	▽	▽	▽	▽
468	Angers	anger (γ)	~	~	~	~
474	too high	~ ~	~	~ ~	~ ~	to ~ (c)
479	or Awe	~ ~	~	~ ~	~ ~	of ~ (c)
480	laile	gaole (c)	▽	▽	goale (c)	▽
480	haue law	hath ~ (C2)	~	~ ~	~ ~	~ ~
484	now cares	~	nor ~ (c)	~ ~	~ ~	~ ~
485	loth	Tooth (c)	wroth (H6)	▽	▽	▽
487	Tethlemite	Tethelemite (C2)	Thelemite (c)	▽	▽	▽
488	enters	entred (γ)	▽	▽	▽	▽
493	mingled	~	~	~	~	migled (c)
503	sinewy	~	~	~	~	sinew (c)
508	enowe	~	enough (c)	▽	▽	▽

"with the Gamesome Boyes" to "which…" in line 115, "Argueinge his Heretiques game" to "Arguing is…" in line 118, "your love lips" to "your Loves lips" in line 157, "snares" to "snare" in ine 214, "dobts" to "doubts" in line 277, "any whether come" to "any whither come" in line 400, "And (Abell ye Dam dead)" to "And Abell (the dam dead)" in line 442, and "Goale" to "gaole" in line 480. And A modernizes C2's "divers" to "diverse" in line 29 and C2's "loose" to "lose" in line 491. Particularly indicative of the editor's concern with intelligibility and metrical regularity are his patches of the C2 text in lines 251, 296, 358, 427, and 485, where he inserts "the" into the defective line-251 phrase "wth native streame" (= "with the native stream"), changes "That leagues at Sea, now ty'rde he lyes" to "…leagues o'er-past at sea…" (l. 296), alters "so were the one" to "so well the one" in line 358 (a change possibly derived from DT1 or H6), changes "a Trap…End and his losse" to "a trap…ends all his losse" (l. 426–27), and addresses the β-generated problem at the end of line 485 by emending C2's "more then halfe *blank space*" to the puzzling "more then halfe Tooth."[13] Although "Tooth" is replaced by H6's "wroth" in the subsequent edition (B), the editor's repairs in 251, 296, and 427 persist in subsequent seventeenth-century editions and beyond.

If A's editor might have imposed most of the above-noted changes to C2 solely on the basis of sense, he also alters the manuscript's text in 9 lines that are not obviously in error, and in these instances he must have compared one or more other artifacts. The following chart lists these emendations and possible sources of each among extant artifacts:

Table 6.3: A's emendations of C2

Line no.	C2's reading	A's reading	Possible sources of A
83	did *blank space*	did **enlive** (*cor*)	B29, F10, H6
222	to Active	**too active**	B29, H6
260	**an** ill **habitt's** left	**are** ill **habits** left	*all artifacts*
276	**when** yt disputinge laye	**where** it disputing lay	*all artifacts*
280	**It** Rays'd, to be ye Raysers	**It's** (*cor*) rais'd, to be the Raisers	H6
280	**Instruments**	**instrument**	F10, H6, DT1, H4
383	Who thought **nor** had gone	who thought, **no more** had gone	F10
397	he y^t **went**	he that **ment**	B29, F10, H6
406	was still **infected**	was still **infested**	B29, F10, H6
515	**these** Arts	**those arts**	F10, H6

---

[13]Grierson (2:225) raised the possibility that "Tooth" was used here in some "rare adjectival sense" to mean "eager, with tooth on edge for," but rejected the possibility on the advice of Sir James Murray, who declared "We know nothing of *tooth* as an adjective in the sense *eager*.…" The possibility that Grierson's original speculation might explain A's reading finds some support in *OED* definition I. 2. a of *tooth*—"taste, liking."

Among these instances, C2's "an ill habitt's" (l. 260) and "when" (l. 276) are unique sports; theoretically, any other artifact on the stemma could thus have supplied the emendations. And since the corruptions "did *blank space*" (l. 83), "went" (l. 397), "infected" (l. 406), and "those" (l. 515) are introduced in δ, their corrections might have derived from any of δ's genealogical predecessors (B29, F10, H6). Among manuscripts previously identified in this edition as sources of A's text (see, e.g., DV 2:lxxvi–lxxix), however, only C2, DT1, and H6 contain *Metem*; and of the emendations of C2 noted here, all—with the exception of that in line 383—are available in H6. Indeed, the line-280 clause "It's rais'd, to be the Raisers instrument" (where A initially set the β-C2 lection "It…" before correcting to "It's…") is available only in H6, which must have supplied this emendation and almost certainly the others as well.[14]

In the expanded and reorganized edition of 1635 (B), *Metem*—along with the immediately following *Corona* and *Holy Sonnets* proper (this sequence derives from C2)—is moved from its position as the first poem in the volume to very near the end, where it precedes the Divine Poems and commendatory "*Elegies upon the Author*" with which the volume concludes.[15] And the text of the poem, set successively from A, undergoes a further round of painstaking revision as well. The editor introduces 12 further meter-smoothing elisions and contractions, 63 changes in punctuation, and—as is shown in Figure 20—verbal alterations in lines 7, 10, 13, 16, 54, 94, 99, 112, 114, 117, 130, 137, 147, 150, 180, 185, 220, 225, 227, 267, 273, 337, 358, 383,

---

[14]That A incorporates "enlive" as a press variant in line 83 (see Table 6.3) while omitting "Riuulets"/"Riuolett's" in line 94 (see Figure 20) also points to H6 as the edition's source for these corrections since B29 and F10 (the other possible sources) contain both readings, while H6 contains the first, but lacks the second—exactly matching the pattern of the edition. (H6 dealt with the lacuna in γ by manufacturing the implausible "Nothing letts," which A's editor either failed to notice or—more likely—rejected.) And that "enlive" appears in A only as a stop-press correction, having initially been omitted, supports the notion advanced previously in this edition (see DV 2:lxxvii–lxix) that H6 became available to A's editor only after the volume was set in type and nearing publication, too late to permit the more extensive use that he made of the artifact two years later in B. Certain other of A's defects—such as its failure to fill in C2's blank space at the end of line 485 with H6's intelligible "wroth," an emendation subsequently incorporated into B—may also be explained by a last-minute arrival of H6 on the scene, when a thorough comparison was not possible.

It should further be pointed out that although 6 of the altered C2 lections listed in Table 6.3 are available in B29 and 7 in F10 and although it required a true stoke of brilliance—or luck—for the editor independently to restore the LRH lection "who thought, no more had gone, to make one wise" in line 383 (rather than deriving it from F10—the only extant possibility), there is finally no reason to believe that A's editor compared either of these artifacts as he finalized his text. Had he done so, he would have found, e.g., the authorial lections "Riuulets" (l. 94) in both (like other descendants of γ, A leaves a blank space), "last" (l. 195) in B29 (A and F10 record "tast"), "many leagues" (l. 296) in both (A concocts "leagues o'erpast"), "out sweat" (l. 345) in B29 (A and F10 read the neologistic "outstreate"), "weareth" (l. 358) in B29 (A and F10 give "were the"), "ended" (l. 427) in both (A concocts "ends all" independently), and "loth" (l. 485) in B29 (F10 conjectures "Forth"; A interpolates "Tooth"). In preparing for print a 520-line poem from an obviously corrupt manuscript text, of course, A's editor might well have overlooked—or even seen and rejected—one or more corrections available in B29 or F10, but his evident determination to present as smooth and intelligible a text as possible makes it difficult to believe that he would have missed them all had these artifacts been available.

[15]As Marriot acknowledges in an "Errata" notice on the final page of B, the prefatory epistle to *Metem* is mistakenly left "*in the beginning of the Booke*," but should have been moved to appear on page 301 "*before the Progresse of the Soule.*"

❦   Texts and Apparatuses

443, 484, 485, 487, and 508.[16] Among the latter category the changes of A's "gold" to "cold" in line 7, of "vanities" to "vanitie" in line 112, of "reasons" to "reason's" in line 114, of "parts" to "part" in line 147, of "doubtful" to "her doubtful" in line 273, and of "this" to "his" in line 337 have no manuscript support and must reflect independent choices (or perhaps, in a couple of instances, carelessness) on the part of B's editor or compositor. As noted above, however, a number of these alternate readings were available only in H6 and certainly stem from that manuscript, including B's "hold in sad lone wayes" (for A's "shall in sad love wayes") in line 54, "and do themselves spill" (for "doe…") in line 117, "so fill up the way" (for "so fill'd…") in line 137, "who thought none had, to make him wise" (for "who thought, no more had gone, to make one wise") in line 383 (a rejection of the patch that he had contrived in A for C2's bungled line), "of two kindes thus made" (for "of two kindes made") in line 443, and "wroth" (for "Tooth") in line 485. In 12 further instances, moreover, B changes A toward readings available in H6[17]; and although several of these revisions—of "begins" to "beginst," of "downy a new" to "a new downy," e.g.—constitute obvious grammatical or syntactical repairs that any intelligent editor might well have made on his own and although each is available in either DT1, F10, or B29, it seems likely that B's editor culled them, too, from H6 as he compared A to that artifact.

The most puzzling among B's emendations of A are the insertion of the correct "Rivolets" (where A leaves a blank space) in line 94 and the changes of A's "apples kinde" to the authorial "apples kindle" in line 150, of "uncloath'd child" to the correct "inclos'd child" in line 180, of "intertouched" to the authorial "had intertouch'd" in line 225, and of "now cares not" to "nor cares not" in line 484. None of these emendations is available in H6 or any artifact below it on the genealogical tree. "Rivolets," however, was available in both B29 ("Riuulets") and F10 ("Riuolett's"), as were "kindle," "enclos'd," and "had intertouch't"; and "nor cares" was available in B29. Since it seems impossible that B's editor could independently have intuited the missing authorial reading in all these instances, the apparent conclusion is that, as he finalized his text, he obtained access to one of the manuscripts appearing above γ on the stemma. And comparison of the emendations he chose to the variants available in the artifacts we know he consulted points to F10 (or possibly the missing β) as that manuscript. The key to this understanding lies in the editor's handling of the crux in

---

[16]The elisions occur in lines 5, 8, 47, 129, 134, 171, 225, 316, 363, 384, 396, and 492. The changes in pointing occur in lines 5, 12, 34, 73 (from H6), 74, 76 (from H6), 80, 89, 99, 102, 106, 125, 150, 154, 157, 159, 193, 196, 202, 203–204 (see the discussion above), 205, 220, 235, 239, 240, 254, 257, 270, 271, 279 (from H6), 282, 295, 297, 301, 307, 311, 330, 337, 339, 341, 357, 362, 365, 371, 383, 386, 397, 403, 405, 410, 422, 433, 455, 482, 485, 486, 489, 491, 506, 507, and 517.

[17]B changes A's "holy writs" to "holy writ" in line 10, "begins" to "beginst" in line 13, "Danon" to "Danow" in line 16, "corrupts" to "corrupt" in line 94, "here" to "beare" in line 99, "anew" to "a new" in line 130, "Princesse" to "Prince" in line 137 (a reversion to the uncorrected reading of A), "downy a new" to "a new downy" in line 185, "to encrease, himselfe outweares" to "to encrease his race himselfe outweares" in line 220, "roe" to "rowe" in line 227, "wether" to "water" in line 267, and "were the one" to "well the one" in line 358. Although not directly available in H6, B's *Thelemite* (for A's four-syllabled *Tethelemite*) in line 487 may derive from H6's three-syllabled "Tethlemite"; B's change of A's "enow" to "enough" in line 508 destroys the sight-rhyme with "now" in line 509 and may bespeak the compositor's unthinking imposition of a habitual spelling.

line 485, where he replaces A's speculative "Tooth" with H6's "wroth," which he had apparently not noticed in time to incorporate it in A. The substitution of "wroth" in B, of course, shows his continuing awareness of the problem in this line and indicates his determination to find the best possible solution. At this point in the poem, B29 records the correct "loth," and it is impossible to believe that this intelligent and sensitive editor, who scrutinized and extensively adjusted the text of the poem over a period of many months, would not have preferred it to "wroth" had he known of its existence. F10, on the other hand, concocting a response to the bungled reading in β (see p. 281 above), conjectures the unlikely "Forth," which, even had he seen it, B's editor would certainly have rejected in favor of "wroth" (and, had he had access to β, he would have confronted the same unintelligible construction that led to F10's "Forth"). We thus conclude that B's editor cannot have seen B29 and that the emendations "Rivolets" (l. 94), "kindle" (l.50), "enclos'd" (l. 180), and "had intertouch'd" (l. 225) derive from F10 (or possibly β)—and, accordingly, that "nor" (l. 484), which occurs only in B29, is B's independent editorial or compositorial change.[18]

With the publication of B, the Herculean editorial labors devoted to *Metem* in Marriot's publishing house reach an end, and the text undergoes relatively little further change in the seventeenth century prints. C, a page-for-page resetting of B, introduces only a handful of changes to the punctuation (in ll. 109, 124, 315, 339, 389, and 390), and its two verbal changes are a modernization of "then" to "than" in line 462 and a

---

[18]This argument that F10 influenced B's text of *Metem* in these few instances represents our best attempt to interpret the available evidence, and it can explain, e.g., why such authorial readings as "who did so last [rather than *taste*]" in line 195 and "so weareth [rather than *were* or *well*] the one" in line 358 are not incorporated into B—they were available only in B29. But it might seem to be undercut by the editor's failure to restore "many leagues at sea" in line 296 (where he had previously concocted "leagues o'er-past…" to repair C2's metrically deficient "leagues at Sea") or "ended" in line 427 (where he had previously substituted "ends all his losse" for C2's unintelligible "End and…")—both of which *were* available in F10. One explanation of this apparent contradiction is that the textual circumstances he faced made it impossible for this editor to regard his copy-text as sacrosanct: his apparent determination to achieve intelligibility and rhythmical smoothness required him to emend C2 in numerous places—not only with readings drawn from H6 and F10, but also with independently concocted patches when no acceptable manuscript option was available. He may thus have felt that "leagues o'er-past" and "ends all" satisfied his basic criteria and seen no reason to revert to "many leagues" and "ended" simply because they appeared in a manuscript. In this connection, his retention of C2's spurious "outstreat" in line 345 (which is also recorded in F10) is among his most curious choices, for he almost certainly saw the authentic "out sweat" in H6. We can only assume that "outstreat" seemed legitimate—indeed, in context a meaning of "flow out" seems unavoidable—and note that in 1879, some 246 years after the word's first (and only other) appearance in print in this poem, it seemed similarly legitimate to Robert Browning, who adopted it in line 180 of *Net Bratts* ("I strike the rock, outstreats the life-stream at my rod!") and in a note cited Donne as his source (see OED, "outstreat"). Among modern editors who have explicitly noticed the word, Grosart (N), working before B29 and the reading "out sweat" had come to light, offers the first gloss, describing "outstreat" as an archaic form of "outstretch" that Donne deliberately misspelled in order to effect a rhyme with "eat" in line 344; and, although he cites "out sweat" in both B29 and H6, Milgate (Y) subsequently echoes Grosart's etymology. Neither Shawcross (Z), Smith (AA), nor Patrides (DD) includes a textual note on this variant, each printing the received "outstreat" and glossing it as "exude." To explain these discrepant readings as Donne's revision of the original "out sweat" to the neologistic "outstreat"—a word identical to its predecessor except in the replacement of "w" with "st"—rather than as a scribal misreading would seem to us a perversion of the evidence.

typographical transposition that alters "gaole" to "goale" in line 480. Set successively from C, the fourth edition (D and its two re-issues E and F) alters the punctation in over 30 instances (in lines 34, 63, 89, 105, 110, 113, 135, 137, 139, 149, 151, 158, 159, 205, 209, 212, 252, 279, 280, 316, 325, 330, 338, 351, 387, 408, 416, 433, 435, 511, 513, and 519), but the words in only 8. D's separation of C's "warmbird" into "warm bird" (l. 179) is a typographical correction, although its "alone" (for C's "a lone") in line 158 and "awy" (for "away") in line 277 are typographical mistakes, as is also perhaps the restoration of the authorial "reasons" (for C's "reason's") in line 114. The substitution of "hollow" for "holly" in line 212, of "is sure" for "sure is" in line 249, of "lands" for "Ilands" in line 332, and of "not bark" for "nor bark" in line 420 are compositorial errors or sophistications. Perhaps because its editor had no access to fresh manuscript material for this poem,[19] G also evinces few editorial changes, altering punctuation in 24 lines (ll. 6, 19, 138, 156, 203, 204, 207, 209, 258, 300, 311, 330, 399, 402, 417, 421, 425, 433, 449, 458, 480, 481, 512, and 520) and the wording in 11 (ll. 7, 126, 130, 212, 227, 349, 359, 474, 479, 493, and 503). Of the verbal changes, those of "dares" to "dare" (l. 126), "abled" to "able" (l. 227), "too" to "to" (l. 474), "or" to "of" (l. 479), "mingled" to "migled" (493), and "sinowy" to "sinew" (l. 503) constitute editorial or compositorial errors, and the respelling of the received "Tyran" as "Tyrant" in lines 349 and 359 is merely a modernization. G's substitutions of "gold Chaldee" (for B–F's "cold...") in line 7, of "earths pores" (for D's "earthpores") in line 130, and of "Holly" (for D's "hollow") in line 212, on the other hand, restore authorial readings and hint that G's editor sporadically compared A (the only print to read "gold" in line 7) as he finalized his text—an impression corroborated by his reimposition of a semicolon after "ill" in line 203 (= "ill;"), where B–D record no punctuation, and his corresponding repunctuation of B–F's "soul. Is" in line 204 as "soul: Is," which more closely matches A's "soule; Is."

The Modern Prints

Although in 1872 Grosart (N) bases his text of *Metem* on B7, which the British Library had acquired from the library of the Earl of Denbigh in 1851, B7's is the most corrupt version of the work ever printed or penned, and using it merely leads Grosart to increase the quantum of textual error. In a pattern demonstrated frequently in previous volumes of this *Variorum*, the efforts of the other eighteenth- or nineteenth-century editors, among whom only Chambers (P) seems ever to have seen a manuscript of the poem (Chambers cites B7 in his notes on the poem), are generally confined to picking through prior editions in search of solutions to the poem's textual problems and to modernizing spelling and punctuation in accordance with evolving linguistic norms (see Figure 21). As is shown by his reproducing such of G's erroneous readings as "dare" (l. 126), "able" (l. 227), and "sinew" (l. 503), Tonson (H) derives his text from G, but also introduces independent errors (e.g., "slack'neth not [for *so*]" in line 207) and corrections ("this [for G's *his*] living boat" in line 337), which are passed on to I, J, and K—and some to M and N as well. I's derivation fom H is evident from its repetition of H's independent errors and corrections (see the entries for ll. 57, 126,

---

[19]See DV 2:309 and the textual introduction to *Sat4* in this volume (p. 152) for instances in which G's editor imports manuscript readings into the text received from D–F.

177, 207, 227, and 503 in Figure 21), and that J derives from I is manifest in such uniquely shared readings as "'tis [for *it is*] in this one" in line 8 and "when he [for *she*] comes" in line 138 (see also entries for lines 29, 120, and 264 in Figure 21). K reverts to H for its setting text, reproducing the above-mentioned readings in G while avoiding the readings peculiar to I and J. As noted above, M (the first Lowell edition) also derives from H and shares many of H's innovative readings, including "struck" (for "strook" or "stroke") in line 59, "swam" (for "swome") in line 241, "his [for *this*] traiterous spectacle" in line 275, "a riding [for *ridling*] lust" in line 437, and "wrath" (for the received "wroth") in line 485. On the other hand, Lowell departs from H in a number of instances, occasionally substituting an independent change (recording, e.g., the unique "the others [for H's *t'others*] whets" in line 47) and occasionally consulting either A or B (e.g., M restores the authorial "abled [where G–K give *able*] it to row" in line 227—see also the entries for lines 207, 249, and 480 in Figure 21).[20]

In addition to innovatively choosing a manuscript as copy-text (B7), Grosart (N)—noting its designation by the author as "Poema Satyricon" (1:66)—is also the first editor to locate *Metem* physically beside the other Satyres, a placement otherwise effected only by Milgate (Y) and Smith (AA). Although he freely alters its punctuation and capitalization, Grosart generally replicates B7's orthography, and he draws from B7 such otherwise unprinted lections as "she comes" (for "she's come") in line 268, "It rais'd" (for the received "It's rais'd") in line 280, and "then cares" (for "now cares") in line 484 (see also the entries for lines 180, 227, 438, 477, 511, and 515 in Figure 21). On the other hand, Grosart abandons B7 in over a dozen instances, not only correcting such of the manuscript's obvious verbal blunders as "who thought no had gone to make one wise" to "who, thought none had to make him wise" in line 383 and "end, and his losse" to "ends all…" in line 427, but also—most often in an attempt to smooth out the meter—eclectically adopting various seventeenth-century print readings in places where B7's readings are perfectly intelligible (see the entries for lines 10, 36, 47, 54, 112, 114, 117, 127 273, 296, 419, and 443 in the Historical Collation and Figure 21). That N replaces B7's "reasons" in line 114 with "reason's," which was available in only B and C, points to B as his likely source for all these emendations.

In a note (1:68), Grosart refers to "the American edition" of 1855, and he apparently obtains from M the hypenated forms "then-clyming" in line 84, "high-arch'd" in line 314, and "any-whither" in line 400, as well as "thoroughly [for *throughly*] arm'd" in line 342 (see Figure 21). The Grolier Club edition (O) also includes the hyphenated "high-arched" and "any-whither," harking back to Lowell's prior effort in M, and perhaps picks up the line-114 "reason's" (for "reasons") from M as well. O's avowed policy, however, is to reproduce the wording of A, and—although they modernize spelling and freely alter the edition's punctuation—the editors correspondingly print such of A's anomalies as "sad love [for *lone*] ways" in line 54, "princess" (for "prince") in line 137, and "downy a new [for *a new downy*] mantle" in line 185 (see also, e.g., the entries for lines 13, 96, 99, 137, 180, 349, and 487 in Figure 21). Faced with A's

---

[20]Stringer, 2011, p. 47, describes Lowell's occasional borrowings from A and B.

[blank] = agrees with LRH reading ~ = agrees with LRH OoV = Origin of Variant A–G = variant appears in 17th-c. eds.
• = variant appears in modern eds. { = to be read together < > = word(s) omitted

Line no.	LRH/DV reading	Variant	OoV	A–G	H	I	J	K	M	N	O	P	Q	S	T	Y	Z	AA	DD
4	Yoak'd was	~ us	β	A–G	•	•	•	•	•	•		•	•	•	•	•	•		•
5	in his…Eueninge	to ~…~	β	A–G	•	•	•	•	•	•		•	•	•	•	•	•	•	•
6	through…Noone	though…~	H		•			•											
8	is in this one	't is ~ ~ ~	I		•	•	•		•	•									•
10	holie writts	~ writ	H6	B–G	•	•	•	•	•	•				•	•	•	•		•
10	holie writts	~ Writ's	P									•							
13	beginst to shine	begins ~ ~	C2	A							•			•					•
27	For thence	From ~	Y	A–G	•		•	•	•		•		•	•	•	•			•
29	diuers shapes	diverse ~	A	A–G	•	•	•	•	•	•	•	•	•	•	•	•	•		•
32	hast mark't	hath ~	Z		•	•	•											•	•
36	vouch thou safe	vouchsafe thou	A	A–G	•	•	•	•	•	•		•	•	•	•	•	•		•
47	to other whetts	~ others ~	C2	A–G	•	•	•	•	•	•		•	•	•	•	•	•		•
47	to other whetts	the others ~	M						•										
54	And shall	~ hold	H6	B–G	•	•	•	•	•	•		•	•	•	•	•			•
54	sad lone wayes	~ love ~	C2	A					•										
56	Streights and Sands	~ ~ lands	Y	A–G	•	•	•	•	•	•		•	•	•	•	•			•
57	saile towards home	l ~ ~ ~	Y	A–G	•					•						•			•
57	saile towards home	~ toward ~	Y	A–G	•				•	•						•			•
59	Sayles hoisted	~ hoised	Y	A–G												•			•
59	strook	stroke	Y	A–G	•				•	•		•	•	•	•	•			•
59	strook	struck	H																
61	this great Soule	the ~ ~	C2	A–G	•				•	•		•	•	•		•	•		•
64	yow shall long	~ will ~	β	A–G	•	•	•	•	•	•		•	•	•	•	•			•

Line no.	LRH/DV reading	Variant	OoV	A–G	H	I	J	K	M	N	O	P	Q	S	T	Y	Z	AA	DD
68	Wracks	wrecks	H		•	•	•	•	•		•		•	•	•		•	•	•
69	liu'd where	~ when	C2	A–G	•	•	•	•	•		•	•	•	•	•		•	•	•
69	great Change	greater ~	T												• •				
71	no Low Roome	nor ~ ~	P									•							
87	whose race	her ~	β	A–G	•	•	•	•	•	•	•	•	•	•	•	•	•	•	•
96	thrust	thrusts	A(cor)	A						•	•								
99	beare	here	δ	A							•								
106	shall God	will ~	β	A–G	•	•	•	•	•		•	•	•	•	•	•	•	•	•
112	Vanities	vanity	B	B–G	•	•	•	•	•		•	•	•				•		•
112	the Gaine	their ~	γ	A–G	•	•	•												
114	resons	reason's	B	B–C	•	•	•	•	•		•	•							
117	do...spill	and ~...˜	H6	B–G	•	•			•		•	•							
120	end Heresies	and ~	I																
126	one...dares say	~...dare ~	G	G															
129	fate	fates	Y	A–G	•	•	•	•	•		•	•	•	•	•		•	•	•
130	Earth's pores	earth-pores	A(unc)	A–F	•	•	•					•							
131	This plant	The ~	β	A–G	•	•	•	•	•		•	•	•	•	•	•	•	•	•
137	Prince	Princesse	A(cor)	A							•	•							
⎡ 137	haue soe filld	so fill up	H6	B–G	•	•	•				•	•			•		•		•
⎣ 137	haue soe filld	<haue> ~ ~	Y	A							•								
138	when she comes	~ he ~	I		•	•			•										
147	Midle parts	~ part	B	B–G	•	•		•	•		•	•					•		•
155	leauy	leafie	δ	A–G	•	•	•	lazy	•		•	•	•	•	•	•	•	•	•
157	yow would call	ye ~ ~	I		•	•	•	•											
177	eniayld	engoal'd	H	A							•	•			•				
180	enclos'd	unclothed	C2	A							•								

Line no.	LRH/DV reading	Variant	OoV	A-G	H	I	J	K	M	N	O	P	Q	S	T	Y	Z	AA	DD
180	pok't	pick'd	A	A-G	•	•	•	•	•	•	•	•	•	•			•	•	•
180	pok't	peck'd	Y												•	•			
185	a new Downy	downy a new	C2,A	A	•	•	•	•	•		•								
195	last	taste	β	A-G	•	•	•	•	•		•								
197	Inconstancie	inconstandie	AA		•	•	•	•	•										
207	slackneth soe	~ not	H		•	•	•	•	•										
214	hid nets	his ~	Y	A-G	•	•	•	•	•										
227	abled	able	G	G	•	•	•	•											
227	Row	roe	δ	A	•	•	•	•	•	•	•	•							•
230	could yow	you could	Y	A-G	•	•	•	•	•		•								
241	sworrne	swam	H	A-G	•	•	•	•	•		swum	•			•	•			•
249	sure is	is sure	D	D-G	•	•	•	•	•				•						
251	her Natiue streame	the ~~	A	A-G	•	•	•	•	•		•								
258	Trap	trip	J			•	•												
264	whether she leap	whither ~~	I		•	•	•									•			
268	she's come	shee comes	B7			•	•	•	•			•							
269	which to doe	what ~~	β	A-G	•	•	•	•	•	•	•	•	•				•	•	•
273	Thus	~ her	B	B-G	•	•	•	•		•									
275	this…spectacle	his…~	H		•	•	•	•	•	•	•	•							
275	this…spectacle	the…~	B7			•	•			•									
280	Rais'd	It's ~	H6	A-G	•	•	•	•	•	•(It ~)	•	•					•	•	•
280	Instruments	instrument	β	A-G	•	•	•	•	•		•	•					•	•	•
296	many Leagues	leagues o'erpast	A	A-G	•	•	•	•	•										•
301	this Sowle	our ~	β	A-G	•	•	•	•	•	•	•	•			•	•	•	•	•
305	vnrooted	uprooted	Y		•	•	•	•	•		•					•	•	•	•
322	as…Nett	at…~	A	A-G	•	•	•	•	•		•						•		•

Line no.	LRH/DV reading	Variant	OoV	A–G	H	I	J	K	M	N	O	P	Q	S	T	Y	Z	AA	DD
342	throughly arm'd	thoroughly ~	M		•				•	•	•	•		•	•			•	•
344	doe not eat	did ~~	Y	A–G	•	•	•	•	•	•	•	•	•	•	•	•	•	•	•
345	out sweat	outstreat	β	A–G	•	•				•	•	•		•	•	•	•	•	•
349	Tirant	tyran	δ	A–F	•						•	•		•	•				
354	yeilds	leads	J																
358	So weareth one	~ well the ~	H6, DT1	B–G	•	•	•		•	•	•	•		•	•	•	•	•	•
359	tirant	tyran	δ	A–F	•					•	•	•		•	•	•	•	•	•
362	accompt	account	A	A–G	•					•	•	•		•	•		•	•	•
377	Nor enioy ought	~ ~ aught	K					•		•	•	•							
383	noe more had gone	none had	H6	B–G								•							
383	make one wise	~ him ~	H6	B–G	•			•	•	•	•	•							
397	saue	scape	Y	A–G	•			•	•	•	•								
397	ment	went	B7		•						•								
400	any whither	~~	M		•				•	•	•								
409	warnes and defends	warms ~~	K					•	•	•	•			•	•		•	•	•
410	hopelesse els	~ self	M								•								
419	Now much resist	Nor ~~	C2	A–G	•	•	•	•	•	•	•	•	•	•	•	•	•	•	•
419	Now much resist	Nor make†	Q																
420	would not bark	~ nor ~	A	A–C	•			•			•					•	•	•	•
427	ended his Losse	ends all ~~	A	A–G	•			•		•	•	•					•	•	•
434	begatte himselfe	begot ~	β	A–G	•	•	•	•	•	•	•	•		•	•	•	•	•	•
435	What he begun	~ ~ began	Y	A–G						•	•	•	•						•
437	A ridling lust	~ riding ~	H	A–G	•			•	•	•	•	•		•	•				
438	both these lay	~ those ~	B7						•	•	•								

†"make" inserted in angle brackets

Line no.	LRH/DV reading	Variant	OoV	A–G	H	I	J	K	M	N	O	P	Q	S	T	Y	Z	AA	DD
443	of two kinds made	~ ~ thus ~	H6	B–G	•	•	•	•	•	•	•	•	•	•	•		•	•	•
456	wonders much; withall	~. Much with all	δ	A–G		•	•	•	•	•		•	•	•	•	•	•	•	•
457	Syphatecia	Siphateria	N							•									
459	Gathers her fruit	~ ~ fruits	Y	A–G	•	•	•	•	•			•	•	•	•	•		•	•
460	wisest in that kind	~ of ~ ~	δ	A–G	•	•	•	•	•	•	•	•	•	•	•	•	•	•	•
468	Her Angers	~ anger	Y	A–G	•	•	•	•	•	•	•	•	•	•	•	•	•	•	•
477	gazeth on her face	~ in ~ ~	B7							•									
480	Nature hath no laile	~ ~ ~ goal	C	C–G	•														•
480	she haue law	~ hath ~	C2	A–G	•	•	•	•	•	•	•	•	•	•	•	•	•	•	
484	now cares not	nor ~ ~	B	B–G	•	•	•	•	•		•	•							
484	now cares not	then ~ ~	B7							•									
485	more then half loth	~ ~ ~ wrath	H		•	•	•	•	•	•		•							
485	more then half loth	~ ~ ~ wroth	H6	B–G		•	•	•		•	•	•							
487	Tethlemite	*Tethlemite*	C2	A															
487	Tethlemite	*Thelemite*	B	B–G	•	•	•	•	•	•	•	•	•	•	•		•	•	•
488	Her brother enters	~ entred	Y	A–G	•					•									
490	thus battered Downe	was ~ ~	N			•	•	•		•		•							
490	possest a new	~ anew	J				•												
497	Like a free Conduit	~ ~ ~ conduct	K					•	•			•							
503	Those sinewy strings	~ sinew ~	G	G	•		•	•	•	•		•							
508	Ilis enowe	~ enough	B	B–G	•	•	•	•	•	•		•							
511	beest…readst	bee…reade	N							•									
515	Or most	And ~	N							•									
515	our liues	~ lies	Z							•									

seemingly impossible "more then halfe Tooth" in line 485, however, O adopts from B or one of the subsequent seventeenth-century editions the reading "...wroth."

The last editor to complete his work before the modern discovery of either F10 or B29, Chambers (P) produces—as is his wont—an eclectic text based primarily on the seventeenth-century prints; and although he occasionally cites variants in C and—as noted above—B7, in *Metem* he intermingles a few readings from A with a text based primarily on the heavily edited amalgam instituted in B. Among the variants listed in Figure 21, for instance, P's "Writ's" (for the alternative "writ") in line 10 derives from A, as do "shall" (for "hold") in line 54, and "vanities" (for "vanitie") in line 112; but at other points of difference Chambers chooses what he apparently regards as rhythmically or conceptually superior readings initiated in B, including "reason's" (for "reasons") in line 114, "and do...spill" (for "do...spill") in line 117, "earth-pores" (for "earth's pores") in line 130, "so fill up" (for "so fill'd") in line 137, "enclosed" (for "uncloath'd") in line 180, "Thus her, doubtful" (for "Thus doubtfull") in line 273, "none had, to make him wise" (for "no more had gone...") in line 383, and "wroth" (for "Tooth") in line 485 (see also entries for lines 147, 185, 358, 443, 484, and 487 in Figure 21). P's "nor [for *no*] low room" in line 71 is unique among printed editions; and although it matches that in H–M, P's spelling of "swam" (for A–G's "swome") in line 241 is likely an independent modernization.

Except for C2 and B29, which had not yet been brought to modern attention,[21] Grierson (Q) employs all existing manuscripts of *Metem* in the preparation of Q, although—as with other poems—he assigns them a merely supportive-corrective role in developing a text based on the poem's first printing in A. While adhering closely to A's orthography, Grierson nevertheless alters its punctuation in 89 instances,[22] and he emends its wording in 31 places, as is shown in Table 6.4.

Table 6.4: Q's verbal emendations of A

Line no.	A's Reading	Q's Reading	Authority Cited for Emendation plus (Successors that Adopt Q's Reading; Σ = all)
10	writs	writt	B–G, F10 (Σ)
13	begins	beginst	*none*; notes A's reading (Σ)
16	Danon	Danow	*none*; notes A's reading (Σ)
36	vouch-safe thou	vouch thou safe	all mss.; notes A's reading in A–G (Σ)
54	love wayes	lone ~	B–G; notes A's reading in A, Gp I, F10 (Σ)
93	poisoned	poison'd	G; notes A's reading in A–F (Σ except AA)
94	corrupts us	corrupt ~	B–G, F10; notes A's reading (Σ)

[21]H. J. L. Robbie first announced the discovery of C2 in 1927 ("An Undescribed MS. of Donne's Poems," *RES* 3:415–19), and in the following year—as is cited in note 2 above—he similarly described B29.

[22]Of these, according to his textual notes, 59 are Grierson's independent changes (credited to *Ed*), 20 derive from (or match) B, 5 derive from D–G, 1 derives explicitly from G, 2 derive from H, 1 derives from O, and 1 derives from F10. The most important of these, as noted above, is his intelligible repunctuation of the construction spanning lines 201–04.

99	we here	~ beare	B–G, F10; notes A's reading and "heare" in Gp II (Σ)
130	a new	anew	*none*; notes A's reading (Σ)
137	Princesse	Prince	B–G, F10, Gp II, A(*unc*); notes A(*cor*) reading (Σ)
137	and so fill'd	~ have ~ ~	F10; notes A's reading in A and Gp II; cites "and so fill up" in B–G (Σ except DD)
150	apples kinde	~ kindle	B–G, F10; notes A's reading in A and all other mss. (Σ)
180	uncloath'd child	inclos'd ~	B–G, F10; notes A's reading; cites "encloth'd" in Gp II and H6 (Σ except T)
185	downy a new	a new downy	B–G, F10, Gp II; notes A's reading (Σ)
214	his nets	hid ~	F10; notes A's reading in A–G and Gp II (Σ)
220	encrease	~ his race	*none*; notes A's reading (Σ)
225	intertouched	had intertouch'd	B–G, F10, H6; notes A's reading in A and Gp II (Σ)
227	roe	rowe	*none*; notes A's reading (Σ)
251	the native streame	her ~ ~	all mss.; notes A's reading in A–G (Σ)
254	need	Need	F10; notes A's reading in A–G (Σ except T, Z, AA)
267	make the wether thinne	~ ~ water ~	B–G, F10; notes A's reading in A, B7, CT1, DT1 (Σ)
287	industruous	industrious	*none*; notes A's reading (Σ)
290	fasts, & lents	Fasts, and Lents	B–G; notes A's reading (Σ except T, Z, DD)
296	leagues o'er-past at sea	many leagues ~ ~	F10; notes A's reading in A–G; notes "leagues at sea" in Gp II and H6 (Σ except DD)
316	swallowed	swallow'd	*none*; notes A's reading (Σ except AA, DD)
351	flaile-find	flaile-finn'd	*none*; notes A's reading; notes "flaile-finnd" in B and C (Σ except AA)
358	were the one	well ~ ~	*none*; notes A's reading (Σ)
419	Nor much resist	~ make* ~	*Ed*; notes A's reading in A–G; notes "Now must" in H4, "Now much" in other Gp-IIs and F10; notes "Resistance much" in H6 (*none*)
443	kindes made	~ thus ~	*none*; notes "thus" *om* in A (Σ except Y)
485	Tooth	loth*	*Ed*; notes A's reading in A and F10; notes *blank space* in Gp II, with "loath" inserted in second hand in CT1; notes "wroth" in B–G (Σ)
487	*Tethelemite*	*Tethlemite*	all mss.; notes A's reading; notes "Thelemite" in B–G (Σ)

*Enclosed in angle brackets (= <make/loth>) in Q's text to mark it as an editorial conjecture.

Grierson's reasons for most of these changes are apparent: "writs" (l. 10), "beginst" (l. 13), "Danow" (l. 16) "corrupt" (l. 94), "anew" (l. 130), "a new downy" (l. 185), "had intertouch'd" (l. 225), "rowe" (l. 227), and "industrious" (l. 287) eliminate obvious grammatical, typographical, or factual errors; "poison'd" (l. 93), "and have so fill'd" (l. 137), "swallow'd" (l. 316), "thus made" (l. 443), and "Tethlemite" (l. 487) regularize meter; "lone wayes" (l. 54), "we beare" (l. 99), "apples kindle" (l. 150), "inclos'd child" (l. 180), "encrease his race" (l. 220), "make the water thinne" (l. 267), "well the one" (l. 358), "Nor make resist" (l. 419), and "loth" (l. 485) address evident lapses in intelligibility; "Need" (l. 254), "Fasts, and Lents" (l. 290), and "flaile-finn'd" (l. 351) are apparently intended to sharpen linguistic precision. Although the readings replaced by the remaining emendations listed on the Table are not self-evidently erroneous, Grierson's examination of the manuscript evidence obviously led him to view "vouch thou safe" (l. 36), "Prince" (l. 137), "hid nets" (l. 214), "her native streame" (l. 251), and "many leagues" (l. 296) as authorial readings that had somehow never been incorporated into the seventeenth-century editions of the poem.

The information in Table 6.4 also reveals the full spectrum of Grierson's tactics for developing and authenticating the text in an editorial environment newly populated with manuscripts, although his decision not to implement a uniform notational system leaves some vagueness as to the specific authority he intends to invoke for certain of his emendations and undercuts his professed intention of "put[ting] the reader in exactly the same position…[as he was himself] at each stage in the construction of the text" (1:vii).[23] For changes that he apparently regards as self-evidently necessary (see entries for lines 13, 16, 130, 220, 227, 287, 316, 351, 358, and 443), he cites no specific support, merely noting the "incorrect" reading of A (even though each of these changes is supported in one or more manuscripts that he cites in other instances); and for three emendations in the list—"lone wayes" in line 54, the contracted "poison'd" in line 93, and the capitalized "Fasts, and Lents" in line 290—he credits print sources only, although each of these is also available in one or more manuscripts. Perhaps he also regards each of these as incontestable. For a further 9 alterations, however (those in lines 10, 94, 99, 137, 150, 180, 185, 225, and 267), he not only records the support of the prints (which begins with B in all instances except line 137, where the uncorrected state of A reads with B–G), but also buttresses it with a citation of F10 and—for lines 137, 185, and 225—of other manuscripts as well.[24] As authority for "vouch thou safe" (l. 36), "her native stream" (l. 251), and "*Tethlemite*" (l. 487), which appear in none of the editions, Grierson specifically names every manuscript of the poem, obviously regarding these as instances in which "the manuscripts *alone* give us what is obviously the correct reading" (2:cxix). And for "and have so fill'd" (l.

---

[23] A statement of Grierson's reportorial principles and goals is laid out in his "Preface" (1:vii–x).

[24] Among these 9 changes Grierson notes the support of H6 for "had intertouch'd" in line 225 and—as a later, second-hand interpolation—"inclos'd child" in line 180. He is wrong about line 225, however: like all other descendants of γ, H6 reads merely "enter-touched." Had he possessed (or been willing to credit) a full and accurate collation of H6, he might also have cited its support for "writs" (l. 10), "corrupt" (l. 94), "beare" (l. 99), "Prince" (l. 137), "a new downy" (l. 185), and "water" (l. 267). It seems unlikely that this information would in turn have prompted him to identify H6 as the source of these changes in B (as we have done above), but in his survey of manuscripts, he does acknowledge H6 as "very probabl[y]" an "influence" on B (2:xcvii).

137), "hid nets" (l. 214), "Need" (l. 254), and "many leagues" (l. 296)—constituting cases in which he judges that "the correct reading has been preserved in only one or two manuscripts" (2:cxx)—his sole cited authority is F10. Finally, completing the roster of possibilities, are the emendations "Nor make resist" in line 419 and "loth" in line 485, for neither of which he has artifactual authority (although he does note that a later hand has inserted "loath" into the blank space originally left for the word in CT1). In accordance with Grierson's own practice, these are attributed to "Ed" in Table 6.4. The emendation "Nor make resist" results from Grierson's failure to understand Donne's construction ("show / Now much resist"), a construction which he actually cites in B7, CT1, DT1, and F10; and his independent interpolation of "loth," for which he apparently received the encouragement of Sir James Murray in the exchange previously cited (see note 13 above and Q, 2:224–25), repairs (correctly) one of the most glaring flaws in the received text of the poem.

For 21 of his 31 emendations to A Grierson found a precedent in B, whose editor sought to repair various defects he had come to perceive in his initial printing of the poem in A. Similarly, as is indicated by the data enclosed in parentheses at the end of each line-entry in Table 6.4, among his 6 successor editors 21 of Grierson's emendations are universally accepted, while only 1—the conjectural "nor make resist" in line 419—is universally rejected (otherwise, the capitalized constructions in lines 254 and 290 draw the least approval, at 3 editors each). In keeping with the conclusion suggested by these similarities, moreover, all of Grierson's successors except Smith, who acknowledges adopting "no single copy text" (p. 14), also follow Grierson in declaring A as the base text for their edition of the poem. This general acceptance not only of many of Grierson's editorial choices, but also of his general approach to the editing of *Metem*, of course, results in a succession of highly similar twentieth-century texts of the poem, the principal differences among them being determined by individual editors' decisions on how closely to adhere to the copy-text, especially in light of new manuscript evidence entailed in Robbie's discoveries of C2 and B29, and on whether or not to modernize the language and punctuation.

Substantively, the editions of *Metem* most closely resembling Grierson's are those of Hayward (S), Shawcross (Z), and Patrides (DD). Indeed, S is a virtual reprint of Q except that it adopts B29's "did so last [for the received *taste*]" in line 195 (the first edition ever to print this authorial reading), rejects Grierson's "Nor make resist" in line 419 in favor of A's "Nor much resist" (a reading initiated by the scribe of C2), removes Grierson's line-485 "loth" from the realm of conjecture by citing B29, programatically modernizes "then" to "than," and changes 3 marks of punctuation. Shawcross, too, accepts "loth" in line 485 (as, indeed, does every post-Grierson editor), and—except that he records the typographical blunders "hath [for the normative *hast*] mark'd" in line 32 and "lies" (for "lives") in line 515, rejects the capitalizations in line 290, and reverts to "Nor much resist" in line 419—produces a text that is verbally identical to Grierson's, even following him in recording the scribal lection "tast" in line 195 (which Hayward had previously corrected to B29's authorial "last"). With respect to accidentals, Shawcross adheres more closely to A's punctuation than had Grierson (retaining A's pointing in some 36 instances where Grierson had changed it), but independently imposes about 20 marks of elision and contraction in order to smoothen

Donne's meter. Verbally, the edition of Metem in DD is also very much like Grierson's, differing only in Patrides's acceptance of B's "and so fill up [for Q's F10-derived *have so fill'd*] the way" in line 137, his (unannotated) replacement of Grierson's "tast" with "last" in line 195, his refusal of the capitalizations in line 290, "his retention of A's "leagues o'er-past at sea" (for Grierson's manuscript-derived "many leagues at sea") in line 296, and his reversion to "Nor much resist" in line 419. Additionally, Patrides, like Hayward, modernizes A's "then" to "than" throughout and restores A's punctuation in 36 of the nearly 90 instances in which Gierson had altered it. Among the three editions here grouped, only that of Shawcross includes detailed textual notes listing his emendations and citing the available variant readings.

The texts of Metem presented in Bennett (T) and Smith (AA) are also based on the seventeenth-century editions, T citing A as its source-text and AA eclectically offering "the richest and most pointed readings that have good authority in the early versions" (p. 14). As in S and DD, however, the textual information included in T and AA is minimal, as both editions walk the line between the scholarly and the popular. In attempting to accommodate the general reader, both modernize spelling (including signaling possessive case by the use of apostrophes), and Bennett introduces a number of contractions (changing "aged" to "ag'd" in line 5 and "moved" to "mov'd" in line 30, e.g.) intended to regularize meter. A part of Smith's approach to the task of modernizing, on the other hand, entails assuming "a readiness [on the part of the reader] to slur or elide, without the signal of an apostrophe," which results in his expansion of many forms that are contracted or elided in the seventeenth-century editions (see, e.g., his change of "Plac'd" to "Placed" in line 3 and of "t'her" to "to her" in line 86). Bennett and Smith also differ markedly in their handling of punctuation: within just the first 100 lines of the poem (which collectively present about 175 instances in which punctuation is at issue) Bennett diverges from A (and, indeed, from B–G as well) in 66 instances, while within that same span Smith—despite his refusal to designate a copy-text—retains the punctuation of the seventeenth-century editions in all but 7 instances, and in 4 of those he follows Q.

Verbally, Bennett accepts all of Grierson's emendations as listed in Table 6.4 except those in lines 180 (retaining A's "uncloth'd" where Q had accepted the "enclos'd" found in B–G and F10), 290 (retaining A's lower-cased "fasts," which Q had capitalized), and 419 (retaining "Nor much resist" in place of Q's "Nor make resist"). As is shown in Figure 21, however, in addition to its numerous modernizations (illustrated by the entries for lines 59, 241, 349, 359, and 377), T emends 7 other readings in which Q had followed A, imposing "divers" (for "diverse") in line 29, "other" (for "others") in line 47, "this great soul" (for "the...") in line 61, "greater change" (for "great change") in line 180, "peck'd" (for "pick'd") in line 180, "did so last" (for "...tast") in line 195, and "as his own net" (for "at...") in line 322. Of these changes Bennett's severely restricted apparatus notes only "others" (credited to H4), "greater" (credited to F10), and "last" (credited to B29).

Smith also adopts all of the Griersonian emendations listed in Table 6.4 except "Nor make resist" in line 419 and the contractions in lines 93, 316, and 351, which are categorically excluded by Smith's program of modernization (additional modernized forms in AA appear in lines 59, 241, 349, 359, and 377—see Figure 21). In addition to the unique blunder "inconsistancy" (for "inconstancie") in line 197, Smith further diverges from Q in recording "other [for *others*] whets" in lines 47, "the [for *their*] gain" in line 112, "her fate [for *fates*] threw" in line 129, "as [for *at*] his own net" in line 322, and "she have [for *hath*] law" in line 480. For the changes in lines 112, 129, and 322 AA provides no annotation; those in lines 47 and 480 are each attributed to A and an unnamed "MS." As noted above, Bennet shares "other" in line 47 and "as" in line 322, but among modern editions "the" (l. 112), "fate" (l. 129), and "have" (l. 480) appear solely in Smith and Milgate (Y). Since Smith fails to credit either B29 or F10—the only possible sources—for his emendations in lines 112 and 129 (although he suggests that he will name a specific manuscript "where there is some question of the authority of a reading" [p. 15]), it seems clear that he derived these emendations from Milgate's apparatus. That neither Milgate nor Smith adopts B29's "last" in line 195 supports this inference.

Among modern Donne editors, Milgate (Y) is Grierson's successor at the Clarendon Press and both institutionally and intellectually committed to Grierson's aims and methodology, declaring A as copy-text and emending it in accordance with Griersonian principles and practices. Indeed, although he differs from Grierson in introducing about two dozen marks of elision and contraction, he essentially replicates Grierson's punctuation, adopting (without acknowledgment) 83 of the 89 changes to A that Grierson had imposed. He accepts, moreover, all of Grierson's prior substantive emendations except "Nor make resist" in line 419 and "kindes thus made" in line 443, replacing both with manuscript readings. His analysis of the textual evidence, on the other hand, leads Milgate to impose a further 17 verbal emendations on the text of A, as is presented in Table 6.5.

Table 6.5: Y's verbal differences from Q and A

Line no.	Q/A Reading	Y's Reading	Authority Cited for Emendation
27	From all	For ~	B29, F10; notes "From" in A, Q, and all other mss.
47	to others whets	to'other ~	all mss. except C2; notes "others" in A, C2, and Q
57	I saile	saile	B29, F10; notes "I saile" in A, Q, and all other mss.
57	towards	toward	B29, F10; notes "towards" in A, Q, and all other mss.
61	the great soule	this ~ ~	all mss. except C2 and H6; notes "the" in A, C2, and Q and "that" in H6
112	their gaine	the ~	B29, F10; notes "their" in A, Q, and all other mss.
129	her fates	~ fate	B29, F10; notes "fates" in A, Q, and all other mss.
180	pick'd...a dore	peck'd...~ ~	C2, CT1, DT1, H6; notes "pick'd" in A, "prickt" in F10, and "pok't" in B29
305	unrooted	uprooted	*none*

322	at...net	as...~	all mss. except B29* and DT1; notes "at" in A and Q and "in" in DT1
344	did not eate	do ~ ~	B29, F10; notes "did" in A, Q, and all other mss.
419	Nor make/much resist	Now much ~	B29, CT1, DT1, F10; notes "Nor much" in A and C2, "Resistance much" in H6, and "Nor make" in Q
420	nor barke	not ~	all mss. except F10; notes "nor" in A, F10, and Q
427	ends all	ended	B29, F10; notes "End and" in C2 and CT1, "ending" in DT1, "ends all" in A and Q, and "ends both" in H6
443	kindes thus made	kindes made	*none*; notes "thus " in H6 and Q
468	Her anger	~ angers	B29, F10; notes "anger" in A, Q, and all other mss.
480	hath law	have ~	B29, CT1, DT1, F10; notes "hath" in A, C2, and Q and "was" in H6
485	loth/Tooth	loth	B29; notes *omitted* in C2, CT1, and DT1, "Tooth" in A, "Footh" in F10, and "wroth" in H6
488	brother entred	~ enters	B29, F10; notes "entred" in A, Q, and all other mss.

*Cites B29's alternate version of line (see Figure 19).

Although his adoption of "saile" in line 57 reduces an eleven-syllable line to metrical regularity and his acceptance of "loth" in line 485 fills a notable semantic gap, none of the remaining A/Q readings that Milgate emends is self-evidently erroneous, and his changes seem primarily motivated by a desire to accommodate an expanded range of textual materials comprising not only a more thorough knowledge of F10 than Grierson had had, but also the additional evidence provided by B29 and C2. And this additional information does in fact steer him toward a more sophisticated understanding of the relationships among the early artifacts[25] and, thus, to a text that more nearly realizes Grierson's goal of using the manuscripts to "get back as close as may be to what the poet wrote himself" (Q, 2:cxii).

As is shown in the rightmost column of Table 6.5, every emendation initiated by Milgate except the typographical blunder "uprooted" in line 305 is supported by manuscript evidence—including that in line 443 (the meter-destroying omission of "thus"), where Milgate follows the Griersonian practice of noting only the artifacts in which the correct reading *does not* appear. And while it is true that universal

---

[25]Milgate actually represents his understanding of the genealogy of the manuscripts with a stemma that, while not (in our view) correctly recognizing both an original and a revised authorial version of the poem, resembles that presented in Figure 22 with respect to the descendants of γ (see Y:lxii–lxiv).

manuscript support is neither cited nor available in each of these cases, the emendations Milgate imposes in line 47 ("other"), 61 ("this"), 322 ("as"), 419 ("Now"), 420 ("not"), 443 ("kinds made"), and 480 ("have") all satisfy Grierson's "agreement of the manuscripts" criterion (Q, 2:cxvii), each appearing not only in a majority of the manuscripts, but also—and more importantly—in artifacts that are dispersed up and down the full range of levels delineated in Milgate's stemma. Further, his appreciation of the hierarchical relationships among the various artifacts enables a more nuanced understanding of "the comparative value of the different groups" (Q, 2:cxvii) than had been available to Grierson and prompts Milgate's adoption of 9 emendations that appear solely in B29 and F10: "For all" (l. 27), "saile" and "toward" (l. 57), "the gaine" (l. 112), "her fate" (l. 129), "do not eate" (l. 344), "ended" (l. 427), "angers" (l. 468), and "brother enters" (l. 488). Milgate's choice of "peck'd" in line 185, which appears in all descendants of γ (see Figure 22), is apparently induced by the failure of B29 and F10 to concur in a single reading (B29 gives "pok't," F10 "prickt"); and although it appears in only B29, the correctness of "loth" (l. 485) is apparently so obvious as to compel acceptance. Curiously, the superior "last" (l. 195), which also appears in only B29, does not similarly draw Milgate's endorsement.

The Introductory Epistle

As mentioned in footnote 7 above, the transcription of the introductory epistle contained in B29 breaks off in the middle of line 12, not only making it impossible to know whether Donne altered this prose text when he revised the poem proper, but also depriving us of a strand of textual information that might have lent an added degree of certainty to the differentiation of authorial from scribal variants in the artifacts located at the upper levels of the stemma (see Figure 22). Especially in light of the fact that the epistle and the poem invariably traveled as a unit, however, the surviving evidence is sufficient to confirm the validity of the stemma not only for the poem, but also for the prose epistle, whose genealogy may be briefly described as follows.[26] From the LRH the epistle descends to β and, thence, to F10 and to γ. β records a clean copy of the text, but the appearance in both B29 and H6 of "whatsoeuer [for *what euer*]...shall write" in line 11 suggests that F10's "what euer" is a scribal trivialization; similarly, the appearance in all the descendants of γ of the more difficult "doe borrow" in line 15 implies that "doe borrow" derives from the LRH through β and points to F10's "borrow" as a further scribal blunder. Both these F10 readings have been emended in the copy-text, as has F10's erroneous "vs" (for "is") in line 21. β's other offspring, γ, introduces 3 scribal changes, sophisticating "my owne things" to "mine..." in line 5, reversing "finde me still" to "still find mee" in line 17, and omitting "to" in the line-20 phrase "bid / you to remember" (= "bid / you remember"), and each of these errors descends to H6 and to δ. H6 adds further scribal changes in lines 24, 27, 31, 32, and 33, the three most important being "Macaron" (for "Mushrome") in line 24, "can now tell" (for "now tell") in line 27, and "shee

---

[26] Although no evidence suggesting revision appears in the existing lines, the copy of the epistle in B29, as with the poem, exhibits a number of blunders, including the omissions of "and" in line 2, of "them" in line 8, and—most notably—of the clause "by how much...then others" that spans lines 5 and 6 (this clause is similarly dropped by the scribe of DT1).

whose life" (for "he…") in line 33, which subsequently affect the print history of the epistle. Incorporating the scribal changes introduced in lines 5, 17, and 20 by the γ scribe, δ repeats the trivialization of "whatsoeuer" to "what euer" previously seen in F10 and transmits all four erroneous readings down the genealogical tree. With repect to these four scribal readings, C2—most likely through inadvertence—independently restores the authorial "my" in line 5, but records γ's "still find mee" (l. 17) and "bid / you remember" (l. 20) and δ's "what euer" (l. 11), adding the unique inversion "say quicklye" (for "quickly say") in line 4 and (also uniquely) omitting "as" in the line 7–8 phrase "as to / do it" (= "to / do it"). To the corrupt readings received from γ (ll. 5, 17, 20) and δ (l. 11), ε adds the scribal "bene euer" (for "euer bene") in line 31, the same transposition previously made in H6, and transmits these mistakes to its offspring CT1 and DT1. Among blunders affecting 8 of the epistle's 34 lines (see the Historical Collation for lines 7, 8, 13, 16, 19, 25, 31, and 33), CT1's omission of the lines 7–8 clause "since I… / doe it" stands out as the most egregious; and—except that it restores "to" in line 16 where CT1 had omitted it—B7 records all these errors and adds others in lines 6, 13, 14, and 30. DT1, ε's second scion, copies the parent faithfully except for omitting the lines 5–6 clause "by how much…then others" (an omission also occuring in B29), but its child H4 adds the lines 6–7 omission "my / selfe…uniust to" to the parent's mistakes and records further blunders in lines 16, 18, 24, and 32.

Set into type from C2, the first printed edition (A) evinces the scribal errors deriving from γ ("still find me [for *finde me still*]" [l. 17] and "bid / you [for *you to*] remember" [l. 20]), δ ("what euer [for *whatsoeuer*]" [l. 11]), and C2 itself ("say quicklye [for *quickly say*]" [l. 4] and "to [for *as to*]/ do it" [ll. 7–8]), and A's compositor substitutes "will have" for "would have" in line 20. Containing these 6 errors, the epistle passes into the subsequent seventeenth-century edition (B), which further corrupts the text with 3 readings derived from H6: "Macaron" (for "Mushrome") in line 24, "can now tell" (for "now tell") in line 27, and "shee whose life" (for "he…") in line 33. C–G exhibit no further verbal changes.

Of the above-mentioned blunders in A, those in lines 11 ("what euer"), 17 ("still finde"), and 20 ("bid you") are perpetuated in every subsequent edition; "say quickly" (l. 4) appears in all except N (which follows B7's "quickly saye") and Y (which adopts "quickly say" on general manuscript authority); "to do it" (l. 7) appears in all except Y (which adopts "as to do it" on the specific authority of B29 and F10); and "will haue" (l. 20) appears in all except N (which follows B7's "would…"), Y (which derives "would" from "MSS"), and AA (which apparently obtains "would" from Y). Passed on to the modern editions through G, B's "Macaron" (l. 24), "can now tell" (l. 27), and "shee whose life" (l. 33) subsequently appear in familiar patterns: "Macaron" and "can now tell" are accepted by H–M and P; "shee whose life" is recorded in H–M and—somewhat surprisingly—T, which apparently imports it into its A-based text from H6. Except for N, which adopts B7's "she is in her" (for "she is hee") in line 33, the remaining editors follow A in each of these lines. Otherwise among the moderns, H–M drop the clause "by how much…others" that spans lines 5–6 (a blunder also made by B29 and the DT1-H4 pair), M mistranscribes "nor" as "or" in line 22, and Z inadvertently omits "to" in the line-18 phrase "and to thanke" (= "and thanke").

Copy-Text Used in this Edition

F10 here provides the copy-text for both the poem and the epistle because of extant artifacts it stands closest to Donne's revised holograph and presents the least corrupted version of the revised text. At least twice removed from the LRH, however, F10 not only records the dozen-and-a-half verbal errors introduced into the poem in β, but also—as noted above—initiates nearly 50 substantive mistakes of its own (the lines containing these scribal blunders are enumerated on pages 280–82 above). All these mistakes, of course, require correction, as do some 199 instances in which F10's punctuation (or lack thereof) is either misleading or positively obfuscatory. In the epistle the corresponding number of verbal errors is 3, the number of punctuational mistakes 20. All emendations of both words and punctuation are listed in the "Emendations of the copy-text" sections of the Textual Apparatus below.

As is shown in Figure 19, which includes an entry for every line containing a substantive error introduced in β and in F10 itself, the emendations required to restore the copy-text's readings to those of the LRH are implicit in the genealogical relationships among the manuscripts as depicted on the stemma. Since by definition it would be impossible to recognize the β scribe's alteration of any authorial revision that might have been inscribed in a *missing* parent (the LRH), all mistakes identifiable as blunders on the part of the β scribe necessarily manifest themselves as deviations from the LOH, whose readings are embodied in B29—its sole surviving offspring. Correspondingly, each of the 18 β-level errors noted in Figure 19 is here emended to the LOH/B29 reading. Among these, as Figure 21 illustrates, "Yoak'd was [for *vs*]" (l. 4), "in [for *to*]…eueninge" (l. 5), "shall [for *will*] long" (l. 64), "whose [for *her*] race" (l. 87), "shall [for *will*] God" (l. 106), "This [for *The*] plant" (l. 131), "pok't [for *pick'd* or *peck'd*]…a Dore" (l. 180), "which [for *what*] to doe" (l. 269), "Rais'd [for *It's rais'd*]…Instruments [for *instrument*]" (l. 280), "this [for *our*] Sowle" (l. 301), "thence out sweat [for *outstreat*]" (l. 345), "not saue [for *scape*]" (l. 397), "begatte [for *begot*] himselfe" (l. 434), and "wonders much; withall [for *wonders. Much with all*]" (l. 456) have appeared in no prior edition.

Of the 48 verbal blunders introduced in F10, 32 are unique to that artifact and are thus emended to the otherwise universal reading (see the entries in Figure 19 for lines 29, 69, 102, 138, 158, 176, 183, 184, 199, 203, 230, 260, 269, 275, 277[2], 288, 305, 318, 319, 394, 402, 409[2], 431, 451[2], 454, 458, 477, 490, and 512). A further 8 (in lines 10, 11, 54, 420, 421, 460, 504, and 508) are similarly identifiable as innovations of the F10 scribe, even though they are coincidentally matched in one or more artifacts located below F10 on the stemma (in H6 solely in 4 instances, in δ and its descendants in 2, in C2 solely in 1, and in ε and its descendants in 1), and are therefore emended to the normative reading of the LOH. And even though the evidence in each case is not solely stemmatological, the remaining 8 errors are also readily recognizable as F10 sports, and—with a couple of exceptions—the appropriate emendation clearly implied. We substitute the LRH's revised "vs Riuoletts" for F10's nonsensical "as Riuolett's" in line 94, the LOH's "pok't" for F10's conjectural "prickt" in line 180 (a misreading caused by the indecipherable lection in β, as noted above), the solely authorial "flaile-fin'd" for F10's solecistic "haile-find" in line 351, the solely authorial "so weareth"[27] for F10's mistaken "so were the" in line 358 ("so weareth" also baffles the γ scribe, who records "so well the"), the LOH's "saue" for F10's conjectural "rape" in line 397 (a blunder—like that in line 180—caused by β's unreadability), the LRH's "liues" for F10's idiosyncratic "lifes" in line 432, the solely authorial "hoyting" for F10's trivialized "halting" in line 466, and—like every editor since Grierson—the solely authorial "loth" for F10's conjectural "Forth" in line 485. Our restoration of authorial readings in places specifically corrupted by the F10 scribe has added "could yow" (for "you could") in line 230, "weareth" in line 358, and "wisest in [for *of*] that kind" in line 460 to the above-specified list of readings that have not previously appeared in print.

Among the above-noted emendations, the decision to replace F10's "rape" with B29's "saue" in line 397 is perhaps the most problematic, especially since every prior edition of the poem has recorded the γ scribe's "scape" at this point. The passage in question, here given in its emended form, describes the mouse's murder of the elephant and the consequent death of the murderer himself:

> …the slaine beast [the elephant] tumbled Downe;
> With him the Murderer [the mouse] dies, whom Enuy sent
> To kill not saue, for onlie he that ment
> To die, did euer kill a man of better Roome,
> And thus he made his Foe his Pray and Tombe…. (395–99)

The general import of these lines seems clear enough—that the mouse understood his assault on the elephant as a suicide mission, but that "Enuy" made him willing to accept that consequence. Although F10's "To kill not rape" in line 397 describes alternative forms of injury to a victim (to "kill" or to "rape"), in this context those alternatives would seem to make sense only if directed toward the elephant. Rather than the elephant, however, the intended victim of the actions denoted by these verbs must be the mouse himself, as is indicated in the following clause ("for onlie he that ment / To die, did euer kill a man of better Roome"), which is offered as an explanation for the mouse's behavior. The alternatives "kill" and "saue," on the other hand, do describe actions that may intelligibly refer to the mouse, although the grammar of "whom Enuy sent / To kill not saue" obscures this meaning. Believing Donne to have intended "kill" and "saue" to be understood in a passive sense—"whom Enuy sent / To [be] kill[ed] not [to be] saue[d]"—we have thus adopted the original "saue" from B29.

About half of our adjustments of F10's punctuation also derive from B29, which makes especially effective use of the colon and the semicolon and may in this respect reflect the pointing of the LOH (compare Donne's uses of these marks in the digital facsimile of *Carey* online at *DigitalDonne* (http://donnevariorum.tamu.edu). As noted above, these and all verbal emendations are specified in the apparatus below. Under a separate heading, the apparatus also lists the scores of regularizations needed to ready F10 for print—including normalization of the spelling of numerous plurals that the scribe has rendered with apostrophes before the final "s"—e.g., "Beast's" rather than "Beasts" (l. 25). Using H6 as a guide, we have also restored the heading to the revised form embodied in the LRH.

---

[27]Used in *OED* sense 2.a of *wear*: "To bear or carry (arms, also a stick or cane)."

Textual Apparatus

General heading to entire work*: *Infinitati Sacrum* 16.° *Augusti 1601*
Metempsychosis Poema Satyricon. B7 C2 CT1 DT1 H4(*date om*) H6
A–G. Infinitati Sacrum. B29(*in left M above work*). D:ʳ *Donnes'*
Μετεμψύχωσις. *with Certaine select Dialogues, of Lucian, and The Tale of The
Fauorite.* F10(*on separate title page*).

Letter

Copy-text, letter: F10. **Texts collated:** B7 (f. 92r–v); B29 (*ll. 1–12a only,* f.
154r); C2 (f. 5r–v); CT1 (pp. 201–02); DT1 (f. 106r–v); F10 (f. 2r–v);
F10(*cor*)** (f. 2r–v); H4 (f. 85r–v); H6 (pp. 89–90); A (sigs. A3–4v); B (sigs.
A5–6v); C (sigs. V3–4v *inserted between pp. 300 and 301*); D (pp. 290–92); E
(pp. 290–92); F (pp. 290–92); G (pp. 286–87).
Emendations of the copy-text, letter: Heading: *Epistle*] EPIST»L«E Line 3
mine.] ~‸ 4 Good.] ~‸ 7 it,] ~‸ it;] ~‸ 8 *Talione.*] ~, 10
Authors,] ~‸ 11 whatsoeuer] what euer write.] ~‸ 12 follow,] ~‸
13 flie.] ~‸ booke,] ~‸ 14 debt;] ~, 15 vse.] ~, doe] *om*
20 can] ~, 21 is] vs *Doctrine*] ~, 24 Posthorse,] ~‸ 24
Mushrome,] ~‸ 25 this.] ~‸ 26 Milon,] ~‸ 28 Spider,] ~‸
30 faculties,] ~‸
Regularizations of the copy-text, letter: Line 1 *Others*] Others 2 if] If
10 forbids] forbidˢ 18 dig'd] dig'd 19 which] w:ᶜʰ 25
Indisposition] Indispoc̄on 33 which] w:ᶜʰ

---

*For a diagram of the composition of the heading and the arrangement of its constituent parts with respect to the texts of the introductory epistle and the poem in the various manuscripts, see Table 6.2 above.

**As referred to in the apparatus below, the entity designated F10(*cor*) consists solely in a pattern of alterations to the original punctuation of F10 imposed by a second scribe, and this definition of F10(*cor*) occasionally produces ambiguity in the Historical Collation. In instances in which the lemma consists of the unemended F10 reading, but F10(*cor*) differs, the F10(*cor*) reading will be listed as a variant in the proper place; in instances in which the lemma consists of an emended F10 reading and the unemended F10 reading is listed as a variant, however, the absence of F10(*cor*) from the list of variants does not necessarily imply F10(*cor*)'s agreement with the lemma, since F10(*cor*) may not exist at all in that instance. Clarification of such instances is provided in the full collation of F10(*cor*) against F10 presented on the *DigitalDonne* website (http://donnevariorum.tamu.edu).

Format, letter:
Indentations: *no ind*   Σ.
Miscellaneous: *Wanley's acquisition date* 16 October 1725 *appears above the heading, ll. 1–12a only*   B29.
Headings, letter: *om*   B29.   **EPIST»L«E.**   F10;   *Epistle.*   Σ.

1 *Others*] ~,   B7.   Porches] ~,   B7 CT1 H4.

2 Armes,] ~;   C2 H6 A–G.   I] ~,   C2 A–G.   Picture,] ~; C2 CT1 DT1 A–G; ~_∧   H6.   if] (~   H6.   deliuer] delive[*missing*]   C2.   a] *missing*   C2. plaine] F10 H6; ~,   Σ.   and] *om*   B29.

3 flatt] F10 H4; ~,   Σ.   through light] ~=~   B29 H6.   mine.] ~_∧   B29 F10; ~[*missing*]   C2; ~:   H4; ~).   H6.   Naturallie] ~;   B29.   Author] ~,   A–G.   doubt] F10 H4; ~,   Σ.

4 stick] F10 H4; ~,   Σ.   and] an[*missing*]   C2.   Quicklie say] ~ ~,   B29 DT1; say quicklye,   C2 A–G.   Good.] ~,   B29; ~_∧   F10; ~;   F10(*cor*); ~:   H4. much] ~,   B7 B29 CT1 DT1 F10(*cor*).   taxe:] ~,   B7; ~;   C2 CT1 DT1 A–G; ~.   H6.

5 *last 6 words om*   B29 DT1(*words restored in a 2nd hand*) H4.   then] than B C G.   others,] ~_∧   DT1; ~.   H4.   my] mine   B7 CT1 H6.

6 *1st 4 words om*   B29 DT1(*words restored in a 2nd hand*) H4.   then] than B C G.   others.] ~;   F10(*cor*); ~:   H6.   would] could   B7.   my-] *om*   H4.

7 *line om*   H4.   *last 11 words om*   B7 CT1 H6(*words restored scribally*). selfe] ~,   B29 C2 DT1 A–G.   it,] ~_∧   CT1 F10 H6.   it;] ~,   C2 DT1 F10(*cor*); ~_∧   F10.   since I loue it; nor soe vniust to others as to] *om om om om om om om om om om om*   B7 CT1 H6(›~ ~ ~ ~ ~ ~ ~ ~ ~ ~ ‹).   others] ~,   C2 DT1 A–G.   as] *om*   C2 DT1 A–G.

8 doe it] *om om*   B7 CT1 H6(»~ ~«); ~ ~,   F10(*cor*); ~ ~;   H4.   *Talione.*] ~,   B7 F10.   them] *om*   B29.

9 they] and ~   B7.   me] *om*   H6(»~«) .   bitings.] bytinge: B29; ~;   H4.   reprehender] F10 H6; ~,   Σ.

10 that] ~,   H6.   *Counsell*] ~,   F10(*cor*) H6.   forbids] ~,   H6.   Bookes] F10 H4; ~,   Σ.   Authors,] ~.   B7 CT1 H4; ~_∧   F10.

11 whatsoeuer] B29 H6; what ever   Σ.   name] Man,   B29.   hath] ~,   B7 C2 CT1 DT1.   write.] ~:   B29; ~_∧   F10 H4.

12 writes] wrights   B29; write   G.   ill] ~,   B7 C2 A–G.   something] some thing   B7 C2 A B; some=/thing   CT1.   *Exemplarie,*] ~_∧   H4 H6.   follow,] ~_∧   F10.

13 flie.] ~, B7; ~ₐ F10; ~; F10(*cor*).   Now] ~, DT1.   booke,] ~ₐ B7
F10 H4.   to come] *om om* B7 CT1.   into] in B7; in to H4.

14 debt;] doubt; B7; ~, C2 F10 H4 A–G; ~. H6.   out] ~, B7 C2 CT1
DT1 F10(*cor*).   not,] ~. B7 C2 CT1 DT1; ~; F10(*cor*) A–G.

15 increase] ~, DT1.   vse.] ~, F10; ~; F10(*cor*) A–G; ~ₐ H6.   If I doe]
If I F10; I did not H4(M *var:* »~ ~ ~«).

16 *Antiquitie*] B7 F10; ~, Σ.   (besides] F10; ₐ~ Σ.   that] ~, C2 CT1
DT1 H4.   accompt] account, B7; Account H6 A–G.   that] *om* H4.
to] *om* CT1.   Posterity] F10 H6; ~, Σ.

17 as much] asmuch B7; ~ ~, C2 CT1 DT1 H4 B–G.   good)] ~, B7 H6;
~. C2 CT1 DT1; ~ₐ H4; ~: A–G.   finde me still] F10; still finde mee Σ.
it] F10; ~, Σ.

18 thanck] ~, H4.   onlie] ~, B7.   hath] *om* H4.   dig'd] digged B7
C2 H4 H6.   me] F10; ~, Σ.

19 me] *om* B7 CT1.   place.] ~; B7 H4.   All] ~, DT1.

20 to] F10; *om* Σ.   remember] ~, C2 A–G.   would] will A–G.
Readers] ~, H4.   can] ~, F10.

21 is] vs F10; ~, Σ.   *Pithagorean*] ~· B7.   *Doctrine*] ~, B7 CT1 DT1
F10.

22 Man] ~, DT1.   Man,] ~; DT1.   Man] ~, DT1.

23 also,] ~; B7 CT1 DT1; ~: C2 A–G; ~. H6.

24 Posthorse,] F10(*cor*) D–F; post horse, B7 CT1; ~ₐ F10; Post-horse, Σ.
in] *om* H4 H6.   Mushrome,] F10(*cor*); Mucheron. B7; ~ₐ F10; Musheron:
H4; Macaron, H6; Maceron, B(ₐ)–G; Mucheron, Σ.

25 Indisposition] ~, B7.   Organs] ~, DT1 F10(*cor*).   workes] worke B7
CT1.   this.] ~: DT1; ~ₐ F10.

26 therefore] ~, DT1 H6.   moue] ~, B7.   Milon,] F10(*cor*); ~ₐ F10;
Melon: H6; Melon, Σ.

27 remember] B7 F10 H4; ~, Σ.   now] can ~ H6 B–G.   me,] ~ₐ B7
DT1 H4 H6.   it] is B7 H4.

28 serue'd.] served. B7 H6; ~; C2 H4.   speak] ~, C2 A–G.   Spider,]
~ₐ F10 H4; ~: H6.

29 remember] F10; ~, Σ.   me] ~, C2 H6 A–G.   vs'd] used A–G.
Poison] ~, B7 CT1 DT1 H4.

30 Dignitie.] ~, B7.   Howeuer] F10 H6; How ever Σ.   her] *om* B7.
faculties,] ~ₐ F10.

31 euer bene] beene ever   B7 CT1 DT1 H4 H6.   owne;] DT1 F10 H6; ~,   Σ.
me] *om*   B7 CT1.

32 deliuer] ~,   H6.   yow] *om*   H6.   relation] ~,   DT1 F10(*cor*) H6.
passages,] F10 H6; ~_∧   Σ.   making,] ~_∧   C2 CT1 DT1 A–G.   when]
w^{ch}   H4.

33 eat,] ate,   H6.   Time] ~,   B7 CT1 DT1 H4 H6.   he] in her   B7 CT1;
~,   C2 DT1 H4 A; shee   H6; shee,   B–G.   whose] whole   B7 CT1.

34 yow shall] ~ ~ yo^w shall   H4.   booke.] ~| B7; ~.| C2 DT1; ~_∧   H4.

Verbal Variants in Selected Modern Editions

Editions Collated: H I J K M N O P Q S T Y Z AA DD.
General heading to entire work: INFINITATI SACRUM, 16 *Augusti*, 1601.
    METEMPSYCHOSIS. *Poema Satyricon.*   H Q Y Z DD.   THE
    PROGRESS OF THE SOUL. INFINITATI SACRUM, 16 AUGUSTI, 1601.
    METEMPSYCHOSIS. POEMA SATYRICON.   I–K M N O S AA.
    METEMPSYCHOSIS OR THE PROGRESS OF THE SOUL Poêma
    Satyricon *Infinitati sacrum* August 16, 1601 (A fragment)   T.
Format, letter:
    Indentations: *no ind*   H–J N Q S Y Z AA DD; *l. 1 ind*   K M O P T; *l. 13*
        ind at Now   T; *1st line overhangs*   I.
    Font: *text in italics*   H I.
Headings, letter: EPISTLE.   Σ.

4 Quicklie say] N Y; say quickly   Σ.

5 *last 6 words om*   H–K M.   then] N Q Y Z; than   Σ.

6 *1st 4 words om*   H–K M.   then] Q Y Z; than   Σ.   would] could   N.

7 as to] Y; to   Σ.

9 me] *om*   O.

11 whatsoeuer] what euer   H Q S Y Z DD; whatever   Σ.

12 writes] write   H–K M N.   something] some thing   Q S Y Z AA DD.

14 Mans] Q S Y Z DD; man's   Σ.

15 any thing] anything   O P T.

17 finde me still] still find me   Σ.

18 to] *om*   Z.

20 to] *om*   Σ.   would] N Y AA; will   Σ.

22 nor] or   M.

24 Posthorse] post horse   T; Post-horse   Σ.   Mushrome] Maceron   H–K; macaron   M P; Macheron   N; mucheron   O Q S Y Z DD.

26 Milon] Melon   Σ.

27 now] can ~   H–K M P.

30 Howeuer] How ever   H Q S Y Z DD.

33 eat] ate   I J O.   he] she   H–K M T; in her   N.

Poem

Copy-text, poem: F10.   **Texts collated:** AF1 (*ll. 94, 180, 267, 485 only,* pp. 1–27); B7 (ff. 93r–102r); B28 (*ll. 507b–09a only,* f. 114v); B29 (ff. 155r–67r); B51 (*ll. 250, 518–20 only,* f. 43); C2 (ff. 5v–12r); CT1 (pp. 203–23); DT1 (ff. 107r–15v); F10 (ff. 3r–15v); F10(*cor*) (f. 2r–v) H4 (ff. 86r–94v); H6 (pp. 91–108); IU2 (*ll. 309–20, 328–32, 334–35 only,* f. 75r); A (pp. 1–27); B (pp. 301–27); C (pp. 301–27); D (pp. 293–313); E (pp. 293–313); F (pp. 293–313); G (pp. 288–310); 44a–b (*ll. 501–04 only,* sig. S5v; *ll. 381–83 only,* sig. Y2; *ll. 231, 236 only,* sig. 2B6; *ll. 21–26, 29 only,* sig. 2H6); 44c–d (*same lines,* sigs. S1v, X6, 2B2, 2H2); 54a (*ll. 61–62, 66–69, 148–50, 193–94, 331, 318–19, 379–80, 387, 404–06, 444–46, 449–50 only,* pp. 63–67); 54b–c (*same lines,* pp. 57–61).

Emendations of the copy-text, poem: Heading: *Supplied from H6.*   Line 4 was] vs   singe.] ~∧   5 in] to   6 draw:] ~∧   7 saw,] ~∧   8 one,] ~∧   9 Pillars,] ~∧   Stone,] ~∧   10 writts] writt   none.] ~∧   11 Thee,] The∧   not;] ~∧   12 we] ~,   begott;] ~∧   17 Myne,] **Myne**∧   20 thee.] ~∧   22 float,] ~∧   25 Beasts,] Beast's∧   29 diuers] diuerse   30 sparke.] ~∧   33 thing,] ~∧   took,] ~∧   38 vnderstand] ~.   41 outwore,] outworne∧   44 Pouertie,] ~∧   45 Sicknes,] ~∧   Captiuity,] ~∧   47 whetts,] whett's∧   50 due,] ~∧   Man,] ~∧   haue.] ~∧   51 inough,] ~∧   52 vaine] ~,   54 lone] Loue   Spright,] ~∧   57 home;] ~∧   59 strook] stroke   60 wayd.] wayed∧   64 shall] will   69 great] greater   70 Roome.] ~∧   73 crosse,] ~∧   greif,] ~∧   76 Dye,] ~∧   81 Morne,] ~∧   87 whose] her   88 eate;] ~∧   90 Sweat.] ~∧   93 Wel-head,] ~∧   94 vs Riuoletts,] as Riuolett's∧   95 Netts,] Nett's∧   97 fled.] ~∧   98 prisoners] ~,   Iudges,] ~∧   rigorous;] ~∧   99 Syn'd,] ~∧   beare;] ~!   100 fault] ~,   vs.] ~∧   102 bee] doe   soe.] ~∧   104 law,] ~!   105 will] ~,   106 shall] will   107 Synn'd?] ~,   Snake,] ~∧   112 Vanities;] ~∧   125 Day.] ~∧   131 This] The   132 Course;] ~∧   134 soe,] ~∧   135 grow,] ~∧   137 filld] fild   138 could] can   141 East,] ~∧   142 lefte;] ~,   144 bed,] ~∧   145 way] ~,   this,] ~∧   146 vpbeare;] ~∧   152 Haires:] ~∧   157 white;] ~∧   158 lone] loue   159 Guest,] ~∧   160 rest.] ~∧   163 quite:] ~∧   164 Infirmities,] ~.

167 knew,] ~∧   169 stood,] ~.   172 pac't:] pac'ᵗ∧   176 Change]
Changes   180 pok't] prickt   183 through] om   Paine,] ~∧   184
bones] bone   Threds,] ~∧   191 hast,] ~∧   192 last:] ~∧   194
oreflutters] ~,   195 last] tast   when,] ~∧   196 be,] ~∧   199 doe]
doth   vse,] ~∧   200 chuse.] ~∧   202 ingresse;] ~∧   203 Till] tis
ill,] ~;   not.] ~∧   204 is,] ~.   205 Kindnesses,] ~∧   209 Spirit,]
~∧   spends,] ~∧   212 grow] ~.   214 nets,] ~∧   217 Leaue.] ~∧
218 feares,] ~∧   220 liue,] ~∧   221 dead,] ~∧   222 too] to   226
soe,] ~∧   228 fitt;] ~∧   230 yow] om   233 none,] ~∧   235
catch'd;] ~∧   239 Such,] ~∧   240 great,] ~∧   were.] ~∧   242
shutt,] ~.   244 fish,] ~∧   249 gone;] ~∧   253 retarded:] ~,   257
gett,] ~.   260 This] ~, this   wretch,] ~∧   261 orepast,] ~∧   269
Where] When   which] what   270 two.] ~∧   275 this] his   277
to end] so ends   away:] ~∧   279 Ones,] ~.   280 Rais'd] It ~
Instruments] Instrument   food.] ~∧   281 Fish?] ~,   282 wish,] ~∧
283 awake,] ~∧   288 these] those   vpon,] ~∧   290 Distruction.] ~∧
293 fish;] ~,   flies,] ~∧   297 languisht,] ~∧   298 erre,] ~∧   300
Officer.] ~∧   301 Into] ~,   this] our   305 vnrooted] onrooted
swome,] ~∧   307 head,] ~∧   308 these;] ~,   310 Hulling,] ~∧
Whale.] ~∧   313 teare.] ~∧   315 proof.] ~∧   318 Inland] Iland
hee] she   319 He] she   if] ~,   hee] she   320 firmament.] ~∧
323 inthrall;] ~∧   326 nere;] ~,   327 fall.] ~∧   330 die?] ~ |
331 flocks,] ~∧   332 Rocks.] ~∧   335 limms,] ~∧   Prouinces:] ~∧
337 boat:] ~∧   339 Neerest;] ~,   Perfection,] ~∧   343 hope] ~,
345 sweat)] streat∧   348 speak.] ~∧   350 wreak?] ~. | 351 flaile-
fin'd] haile-find   355 downe] ~.   356 Sink;] ~,   357 Beake;] ~,
Fins] ~.   358 weareth] were the   359 dies] ~.   367 show] shew
370 lose] loose   371 passion] ~,   375 Mouse] ~.   379 Soule,] ~∧
taught] ~,   381 Elephant,] ~∧   385 bend),] ~∧∧   387 none,] ~∧
Enimies,] ~∧   390 Lie,] ~∧   393 Braine,] ~∧   394 life] lifes   395
vndermin'd,] ~∧   Downe;] ~∧   397 saue] rape   401 Soule] ~,
402 Midwife,] ~∧   it] him   403 goe.] ~∧   404 Abell,] ~∧   408
Sentinell,] ~∧   409 flock] flocks   neere] well   410 Intends.] ~∧
413 foes;] ~∧   414 Tent] ~,   420 not] nor   goe.] ~∧   421
wholy] onlie   422 hides:] ~∧   424 not,] ~∧   425 forgott;] ~∧
427 plac'd,] ~∧   430 passe.] ~∧   431 Wiues] Wifes   Sisters] ~.
432 liues] lifes   433 this;] ~∧   434 begatte] begott   435 dead;] ~∧
438 Name:] ~,   440 Sister,] ~∧   play.] ~∧   443 feild:] ~,   445
pray.] ~∧   446 Trade,] ~∧   449 Wolfe,] ~∧   450 to] (~   false]
~)   451 next] wext   toyfull] toilefull   453 play;] ~∧   454 theirs]
them   456 much;] ~∧   withall] ~,   457 Syphatecia,] ~∧   458
where] when   pas,] ~∧   460 in] of   was.] ~∧   463 speak;] ~∧
466 hoiting] halting   468 himself;] ~,   473 through-vaine] ~∧ ~
wise,] ~∧   475 nay:] ~∧   476 tryes,] ~∧   477 teare-shot] teare-shed
480 Nature;] ~,   law.] ~∧   481 ment;] ~∧   483 quite;] ~∧

485 and] then   loth] Forth   487 Tethlemite,] Tethlemit$_\wedge$ 488 brother,] ~$_\wedge$ 489 flew;] ~$_\wedge$ 490 a new] another   491 lose] loose   492 in.] ~$_\wedge$ 494 Chimiques] ~,   498 part,] ~$_\wedge$ 501 Sence,] ~$_\wedge$ 504 there by] thereby   506 ioynd;] ~,   507 past shape] ~-~   Trecherie,] ~$_\wedge$ 508 Rapine,] ~$_\wedge$ Deceipt,] ~$_\wedge$ enowe] inough   509 woeman;] ~,   now,] ~$_\wedge$ 510 plow.] ~$_\wedge$ 512 dost] Courts   514 building,] ~$_\wedge$ 517 Astronomie.] ~$_\wedge$ 518 alone,] ~$_\wedge$

Regularizations of the copy-text, poem: *Initial capital letters supplied in ll. 2, 7, 12, 14, 16, 18, 19, 22, 24, 25, 32, 50, 52, 62, 64, 74, 85, 89, 97, 102, 104– 106, 108–110, 114, 115, 117, 119, 120, 122–125, 127, 128, 130, 133–138, 140, 142, 145–148, 150, 152, 154–157, 159, 160, 162, 166, 168, 172, 175– 180, 182, 184, 185, 187–190, 192, 194–200, 202–205, 207–209, 212–215, 217–220, 222, 224–230, 234, 235, 237, 240, 242–248, 252–257, 259, 262, 264, 265, 267, 272–274, 276, 282, 285, 287–289, 292, 295, 296, 300, 302– 304, 306, 307, 312, 314, 315, 317, 320, 322, 325, 326, 329, 332, 333, 335, 337, 342–348, 352, 356, 357, 359, 362, 364–368, 370, 372, 375, 377, 380, 382–385, 392, 394, 397, 398, 402, 403, 406, 409, 410, 412, 414, 419, 422, 429, 430, 433, 437–440, 443, 446–448, 450, 452–455, 457, 459, 460, 464, 466–469, 472, 474, 475, 477, 479, 480, 482, 484, 485, 487–490, 492, 494, 495, 498, 502, 504, 506, 507, 509, 515, 516, 518–520.*   Line 2 which] w:^{ch} 3 Plac'd] Plac'd   4 Yoak'd] yoak'd   5 ag'd] ag'd   7 *Chaldee*] **Chaldee**   *Persian*] **Persian**   8 *Greeke*] **Greeke**   *Roman*] **Roman**   9 *Seth's*] **Seth'^{s}**   11 *Soule*] **Soule**   16 *Tagus, Po, Sene, Thames* and *Danow*] **Tagus, Po, Sene, Thames** and **Danow**   17 *Westerne Land*] **Westerne Land**   20 quench'd] quench'd   21 *Ianus*] **Ianus**   23 Swimming] Swiṁing   25 in] In   27 deriu'd] deriu'd   *All*] **All**   30 mou'd and inform'd] mou'd and inform'd   36 Ne're] nere   40 life's] life'^{s} *Race*] **Race**   41 *six lustres*] **six lustres**   46 Netts] Nett's   47 calls] call's   56 Streights and Sands] Streigth'^{s} and Sand's   57 towards] toward^s 60 *Thames*] **Thames**   which] w^{ch} *Tigris* and *Euphrates*] **Tigris** and **Euphrates**   61 *Soule*] **Soule**   63 to] To   64 Patience] Patiene   66 *Sowle*] **Sowle**   *Luther* and *Mahomet*] **Luther** and **Mahomet**   67 *Soule*] **Soule**   which] w:^{ch} 68 *Rome*] **Rome**   69 liu'd] liu'd   70 *Paradise*] **Paradise**   74 *All*] **All**   alwaies] alwais   *All*] **All**   75 Syns] Syn's   77 selfe-same] selfe=same   *Caluarie*] **Caluarie**   80 *Soule*] **Soule**   82 Fenc'd] Fenc'd   83 *Soule*] **Soule**   90 taints] taint's   92 o're] ore   93 The] the   107 'Twas] twas   142 the] The   153 vprighte] vprihte   174 Comming] Coṁing   195 asks] ask's   220 outweares.] ~.| 241 swomme] swōme   250 Oppression.] ~.| 253 once] Once   260 againe.] ~.| 289 Occupacion] Occupaācon   291 land-wind] land=wind   292 Sea-ward] Sea=ward   310 might] miht   315 blunts] blunt's   340 Station.] ~.| 345 which] wch 350 Common] Coṁon   wreak.] ~.| 354 Oppression] Oppresson   370 showne] showen   380 addresse.] ~.| 390 remissly] remishly   417

Embracements] Embracem:^{ts} 426 which] w:^{ch} 465 wooe] woe   467
Mistress] M:^{rs} 478 with] w:th 520 Opinion.] ~. |

HISTORICAL COLLATION

Format, poem:

Imperfections: *Final stanza (ll. 511–20) missing, text lost to damage in ll.* 15, 16, 34, 35, 36, 54, 55, 56, 74, 75, 76, 95, 96, 114, 115, 156, 175, 199 B29; *l. 55 originally om and entered scribally in left M* H6.

Indentations and stanzaic pattern: *divided into 10-line sts* Σ.   *Sts unnumbered* B7 B29 CT1 F10 H4; *sts numbered in arabic* C2 DT1 H6; *sts numbered in roman* A–G.   *Last l. of each st indented two spaces* B7 C2 CT1 DT1 H4 H6 A–G.

Miscellaneous: »Edward Smith« *beside HE and following st* 51 B29; Mantle *and* downy *in l.* 185 *numerically reordered by scribe* C2; ›Mandrake‹ *in left M beside l.* 121, ›Spar^{o}[trimmed]‹ *in right M beside l.* 178, ›Mouse‹ *in left M beside l.* 374, ›wolfe‹ *in left M beside l.* 401, ›[trimmed]og‹ *in left M beside l.* 430 F10; *Lines marginally located in poem by st number* 54a–c.

Headings, poem: *ffirst Songe* B7 C2 CT1 DT1 H4 H6.   Poema Satyricum Metempsycosis B29.   *om* F10.   *Whale* IU2.   THE PROGRESSE OF THE SOULE. *First Song.* A–G.

1 Deathles] death-lesse H6.   Soule] ~, B29 F10(*cor*) A–G.

2 Whom] When B7 CT1.   Fate] fate B7 H4; ~, C2 DT1 A–G. which] wth B7; (~ H6.   made,] ~$_\wedge$ H4.   but doth not] doth but H4(M *var:* »~ ~ ~«).   controule] ~, C2 DT1 F10(*cor*) A–G; ~) H6.

3 Plac'd] Plac't B29.   shapes;] ~: B29 H4; ~. H6.   Law] ~, F10(*cor*).

4 Yoak'd] Yoak't B29.   was,] B29; vs, Σ.   when,] ~$_\wedge$ H4; then, H6.   since,] ~$_\wedge$ B7 B29.   singe.] B29 C2 A–C; ~, F10(*cor*) D–G; ~$_\wedge$ Σ.

5 WORLD] ~, B29.   in his] B29; t'~ B–G; to ~ Σ.   ag'd] F10; aged Σ.   Eueninge] ~, B7 CT1 F10(*cor*) B–G; ~; C2 A.

6 Morne,] ~$_\wedge$ H6.   through] to B7 CT1.   draw:] B29; ~. C2 A B; ~, F10(*cor*) C–G; ~$_\wedge$ Σ.

7 Gold] colde B7 B–F.   *Chaldee*] Chadee; B7 CT1(*var:* »~«); ~, C2 DT1 H4 A–G.   saw,] B29 F10(*cor*) H4 A–G; ~$_\wedge$ Σ.

8 brasse] F10; ~, Σ.   Iron, is] ~$_\wedge$ ~ H6; ~, '~ B–G.   one,] ~$_\wedge$ B7 CT1 DT1 F10 H4 H6; ~; A–G.

9 to outweare] F10; t'outlast B29; ~ out-wear G; t'~ Σ.   Pillars,] ~$_\wedge$ F10 H6.   Brick] ~, B29 CT1 DT1.   Stone,] F10(*cor*) A–G; stones B7; ~$_\wedge$ Σ.

10 (holie] ˏ~ B29 DT1.   writts] writt F10 H6 B–G.   excepted)] ~ˏ
B29.   to] om B7.   none.] ~| B7; ~ˏ CT1 F10; ~.) H4.

11 Thee,] The ˏ B7 C2 F10 H4(M var: »~ˏ«); ~ˏ CT1 DT1 H6.   Eye] (~
H6.   Heauen,] heau'n, B7 DT1; ~ˏ H4; ~) H6.   great] om B29.
not;] B29; ~, C2 F10(cor) A–G; ~ˏ Σ.

12 By thy] ~ this B7; ~'~ C2.   Male-force] ~ˏ ~ B7 B29 CT1 H6; ~ˏ ~,
C2 A–G; ~-~, DT1 H4.   we] ~, F10.   haue] B29 F10 H6 D–G; ~, Σ.
begott;] B29; ~, C2 F10(cor) A; ~. H4 B–G; ~ˏ Σ.

13 East,] ~; DT1; ~ˏ H4 H6.   beginst] beginns C2 A.   shine] ~; B29;
~, C2 H6 A–G.

14 Suckst] Suckt H4.   balme] F10 H6; ~, Σ.   there] ~, F10(cor) H6
A–G.

15 loose-raind] ~ˏ ~ B29.   Carrere] Carr[missing] B29; ~, F10(cor).

16 Po,] ~: H4.   Thames] F10; ~, Σ.   Danow] Dano[missing] B29; Danon
C2 A.   dine] missing B29; ~. C2 A; ~, B–G.

17 Night] ~, B7 CT1 F10(cor); last H6.   Myne,] ~ˏ B7 CT1 DT1 F10 H4
H6; ~: B29.

18 then] than B C.   shee] ~, B29 C2 F10(cor) A–G.

19 before thee, one day] ~ ~ˏ ~ ~ B29 DT1 H4 B–G; one day before thee H6.
bee] ~, B29 DT1 A–G; ~. F10(cor).

20 And] ~, H6.   quench'd,] quench't ˏ B29; quenched, H6.   shall] om
H4(»~«).   1st long] ~ , C2 DT1 H4 H6 A–G.   outliue] out-liue DT1 H4;
out live A–C.   thee.] ~ˏ B7 CT1 DT1 F10.

21 Noah's Ark as HE for ll. 21–26 44a–d.   holie] any B7; wholy B29.
Ianus] ~, B7 C2 CT1 DT1.   Boat] ~, B29 F10(cor).
        Alternate line: Holy Janus soveraign boat, 44a–d.

22 The] Where 44a–d.   Church] B7 F10 H4 H6; Churches 44a–d; ~, Σ.
the] om 44a–d.   float,] B29 44a–d; ~. F10(cor); ~; A–G; ~ˏ Σ.

23 Colledge] ~, B29 C2 DT1 H4 A–G 44a–d.   free Hospitall] ~ ~, B29; ~ ~.
F10(cor); ~-~ 44c–d.

24 Mankind,] ~; B7 CT1; Man kind: B29; mankindes. H4; ~ˏ 44a–d.
Cage] ~, B29 CT1 DT1 H4.   Viuarie] ~, F10(cor).

25 Fowles,] ~ˏ B7 CT1 H6 44a–d; fooles, H4.   Beasts,] ~; B29; Beast's ˏ
F10.   Wombe,] ~ˏ B7 B29 CT1 H4 H6 44a–d.   Destiny] ~, F10(cor).

26 Vs] B7 F10 H6 44a–d; ~, Σ.   install] ~, DT1; ~. F10(cor) 44a–d.

27 (For] B29 F10; ˏFrom H6; (ffrom Σ.   thence] then B7 CT1(»~«).

are] and   H4.   deriu'd] F10 H4 H6; ~,   Σ.   fill] fills   B7 CT1.   *All*)] ~.)   B29 C2; ~,)   H4; ~∧   H6.

28   Didst] Didest   B29; Did   H4.   Steward-ship] F10; Stewardship   Σ.

29   diuers] diuerse   F10 A–G.   shapes] ~,   B29.   into] in to   H4. Park] Bark,   B29; ~,   DT1 A–G.
     Alternate line: The floating park, That did all kinds and shapes imbark 44a–b 44c–d(floating-park,).

30   mou'd] mooved,   C2 CT1 A–G.   inform'd] informed   B7 CT1. heauenly] heau'nly   CT1.   sparke.] ~∧   B7 DT1 F10 H6; ~?   B29; ~:   H4.

31   Destiny] doctrine   B7; ~,   DT1 H4 H6.   Comissarie of] ~'~   DT1. God] ~,   B29 C2 F10(*cor*) A–G.

32   mark't] B29 F10 H4; mark'd   Σ.   Path] ~,   CT1 DT1 H4.   Period] ~.   H4.

33   thing,] ~;   B7 B29 CT1 DT1; ~∧   F10; ~:   H4.   who] ~,   C2 H6 A–G. where] were   B7 CT1(→»~«).   Ofspring] ofsprig   B29; of spring   CT1; of-spring   H6 A–G.   took,] ~∧   B7 CT1 DT1 F10 H4 H6.

34   Our] *missing*   B29.   waies] ~,   B7 B29 CT1 DT1 H4.   ends] ~,   B29 D–G.   instant,] ~;   B7 CT1 DT1 A; ~.   C2 A(*unc*) B–G; ~:   H4.

35   Knott] [*missing*]t B29.   Causes,] ~:   B29.   Thou] ~,   F10(*cor*). Brow] ~,   B29 F10(*cor*).

36   Ne're] *missing*   B29.   smiles] F10 A–G; ~,   Σ.   frownes!] F10; ~,   Σ. vouch thou safe] ~-~, ~   H6; vouch-safe thou   A; vouchsafe thou   B–G. looke] ~,   B29.

37   shew] showe   DT1.   storie] ~,   C2 A–G.   Booke] B7 CT1 DT1 F10; ~;   B29; ~.   Σ.

38   praier] paper   B29.   be] *om*   B29.   may vnderstand] ~ ~.   F10; ~ '~   A.

39   selfe,] ~∧   B29 H4 H6.   hand] ~,   B29 DT1 A–G.

40   scant] F10 H6; ~,   Σ.   or] howe   H4.   life's] liues   B29.   spand.] ~| B7; ~∧   CT1 DT1; ~.| F10(*cor*); ~:   H4.

41   *lustres*] ~,   B29.   now] none   B7.   outwore,] ~∧   B7 CT1 H4; out wore C2; outworne∧   F10; out-wore∧   H6; out-wore,   D–G.

42   thy] the   B7 CT1.   more,] ~∧   B7 C2 CT1 H4 H6.

43   my] the   B7.

44   steep] Sleepe,   B29.   Pouertie,] B29 F10(*cor*) A–G; ~,   Σ.

45   Sprighte-quenching] Spiritt∧ ~   B7 CT1 H6 C–G; Spirit=~   B29 DT1 H4 A

B; Spiritt=~, C2.　　　Sicknes,] ~∧　F10.　　　Captiuity,] Capacitie∧　B7; ~∧　CT1
DT1 F10 H4 H6; ~——　F10(cor).

46　Netts] ~,　F10(cor) A–G.

47　this] F10 H6; ~,　Σ.　　　to other] ~'~　B7 CT1; ~ Others　C2 A; t'others
B–G.　　　whetts,] ~∧　B7 CT1 DT1 F10 H4 H6.

48　out,] ~∧　H4.　　　saue] ~.　F10(cor).

49　braine] Baine,　B7; ~,　B29 CT1 DT1 H4.　　　spirit;] ~,　B7 B29 CT1 H6.
Graue] ~.　F10(cor).

50　right] ~,　B7 B29 CT1 DT1 F10(cor) H4.　　　due] ~∧　F10.　　　Man,] ~∧　Σ.
haue.] ~|　B7; ~.|　C2; ~∧　CT1 DT1 F10 H6; ~,　F10(cor).

51　long] ~,　C2 CT1 DT1 H4 A–G.　　　inough,] F10(cor) A–F; ~∧　Σ.

52　vaine] ~,　F10.　　　enlarge] F10 H6; ~,　Σ.　　　enrough] ~,　F10(cor).

53　It selfe;] ~ ~,　DT1; Itselfe,　H4; ~ ~.　H6.　　　waue] ~,　B7 CT1 DT1 H4
A–G.　　　fome] ~;　B29; ~,　C2 F10(cor) A B D–G.

54　shall] hold　H6(M var: »~«) B–G.　　　sad] ~,　B29.　　　lone wayes,] loue
~,　B7 C2 F10 A; loue-~,　CT1 DT1; loues ~∧　H4; ~ ~∧　H6.　　　Spright,] F10;
Spri[missing]　B29; ~∧　Σ.

55　Make] Marke　H4.　　　1st light] F10; ~,　Σ.　　　2nd light] Li[missing]　B29;
~.　C2 F10(cor) A–G.

56　though] om　H4(»~«).　　　Streights] C2 H6; Sands　B29; Streigth's　F10;
~,　Σ.　　　Sands] F10; straig[missing]　B29; landes　Σ.　　　I rome] missing　B29;
~ ~,　A–G.

57　paradise] F10 H6; ~;　F10(cor); ~,　Σ.　　　saile] B29 CT1 F10; sayles　B7; I ~
Σ.　　　towards] toward　B29.　　　home;] B29 A–G; ~.　F10(cor); ~∧　Σ.

58　Course] curse　B7.　　　began,] begiñe,　B29; ~∧　CT1 H4 H6.　　　staid] ~,
F10(cor) A–G; ~.　H4.

59　Sayles] ~,　H6.　　　hoisted] B7 B29 F10; hoysed　Σ.　　　strook] B29 H6;
stroke → ›strucke‹　H4; stroke　Σ.　　　here,] ~,　B7.

60　Thames,] ~∧　H4.　　　Tigris] C2 F10 H6 G; ~,　Σ.　　　wayd.] wayed∧　B7
F10; ~∧　CT1 DT1 H6; layde:　H4(M var: »~∧«).

61　For] ~——　54a–c.　　　this] the　C2; that　H6.　　　Soule] ~,　54a–c.
amongst] emong　B29.　　　now] ~,　B29.

62　dwell] B7 B29 F10; ~,　Σ.　　　moues] ~,　B29; moue　H6.　　　hand] F10;
tongue,　H6; ~,　Σ.　　　Tongue] F10 H4; hand,　H6; ~,　Σ.　　　Brow,] ~∧　B7
C2 CT1 DT1 H4 H6.
　　　Alternate line: Does dwell, and——　54a–c.

63 Which] ~, H6.   as] (~ H4.   Moone] ~, B7 B29 C2 CT1 DT1.
the] and B7.   Sea,] ~) H4; ~∧ D–G.   vs,] ~: B29 H4; ~; CT1
F10(cor).   heare] ~, F10(cor).

64 Storie] ~, C2 A–G.   Patience] Patiene F10.   shall] B29; will Σ.
long] ~, B29 F10(cor); ~; A–G.

65 Crowne] B29 F10; ~, Σ.   Strayne] Chaine B29.

66 This] om 54a–c.   Sowle] songe B7 CT1(→ »~«); ~, DT1 H6; om 54a–
c.   whom] which 54a–c.   Luther] ~, B7 B29 C2 CT1 H4 A B.   were]
~, B29 F10(cor).

67 Prisons] ~: B29.   of flesh;] ~ ~, B7 CT1 DT1 H4 H6 54a–c; om om
B29.   teare] ~, B29 A–G; ~. F10(cor).

68 mend] men B7 CT1(→ »~«).   Empire] F10 H6 54a–c; ~, Σ.   Rome]
Roome. B29; ~, F10(cor) A–G 54a–c.

69 liu'd] lived C2.   where] when C2 A–G 54a–c; there ~ H4.   great]
greater F10.   come] ~, B29 C2 F10(cor) A–G; ~. 54a–c.

70 in] a B29.   Paradise,] ~∧ B7 CT1 DT1 H4 H6.   low] ~, B7 C2 CT1
DT1 H4 A–G.   Roome.] ~∧ B7 CT1 DT1 F10; ~.| C2.

71 no] nor H6.   Roome] F10; ~, Σ.   nor] ~, DT1 H4.   then] the
H4(var: »than«).   greatest] ~, C2 H4 A–G.   lesse] ~, B29 F10(cor) A–G.

72 If] ~, DT1.   deuout] ~, B7 CT1 DT1 H4.   guesse)] ~∧ B7.

73 crosse,] C2 H6 A–G; ~∧ Σ.   our] (~ H6.   Ioy] F10 H6; ~, Σ.
greif,] ~∧ B29 F10.   where] (~ B–G.   tie] ~, F10(cor).

74 That] [missing]at B29.   All] F10; ~, Σ.   alwaies] om B7.   All] B29
F10 H6; ~, Σ.   eueriewhere] F10; every where, B7 B29 B–G; ~, F10(cor);
Every where Σ.

75 Which] missing B29.   Syn,] ~∧ B29.   Syns] Syn's F10.   beare] ~,
B29 F10(cor) H4; ~; A–G.

76 Which could] [missing]uld B29.   2nd Dye,] B29 F10(cor); ~) H6; ~; A;
~;) B–G; ~∧ Σ;.

77 Stood] Stock't B29.   selfe-same] F10 B–G; ~∧ ~ Σ.   Caluarie] ~,
B29 C2 A–G; ~. F10(cor).

78 grew] ~, B7.   Tree] ~: B29; ~, F10(cor) A–G.

79 Securitie] ~, B29 F10(cor).

80 Soule] ~, C2 CT1 H6 A.   made] ~, H6.   Will] ~, DT1 H4 H6.
free.] ~| B7; ~∧ CT1 H6.

81 Orcharde,] ~∧ H4.   Morne,] B29 A–G; ~∧ Σ.

82 Fenc'd] Fenc't B29.   Law] F10 H6; ~, Σ.   as soone] assoone H6.
borne] ~, B29 F10(cor).

83 grew,] ~∧ B7 B29 CT1 H4 H6.   en-liue] om B7 C2 CT1 DT1
H4(»enliue«) A(unc); enliue, AF1 B29; ~, F10(cor); enliue H6 A(cor)–G.

84 Till] Then B7 CT1.   the] ~, H6.   then] ~, H6.   Climing] ~,
H6.   Serpent] ~, B29 DT1 H6 A–G.   that] wᶜʰ H6.   now] ~, H6.
creepes] ~, F10(cor).

85 offence] ~, B29 C2 DT1 H4 A–G.   Mankind] Man kind C2.
weepes] ~. F10(cor); ~, A–G.

86 it:] F10; ~, Σ.   to her] F10; om ~, B29; ~'~ Σ.   wiue] ~, B29
F10(cor).

87 (Whom] (~, B7 CT1 DT1 H4 H6; ∧~, B29.   whose] B29; her Σ.
race] ~, B7 C2 CT1 DT1 A–G.   driue)] ~, B29.

88 it,] ~; B7 B29 CT1.   she] ~, A–G.   to her] B29 F10 H4; ~'~ Σ.
Husband;] B29 F10; ~, Σ.   eate;] A–G; ~, F10(cor); ~∧ Σ.

89 perished] perish't B29.   Eaters,] eater, B29; ~∧ H6.   Meat] ~,
F10(cor) D–G; ~: A.

90 taints] taint's F10.   Dy] ~, B7 CT1 DT1.   Sweat.] ~| B7; ~, B29;
~∧ CT1 F10 H6.

91 once] ~, B29.   slaine] ~, F10(cor) A–G.

92 2nd one] ~, B29.   we are] B29 F10 H4 H6; ~'~ Σ.   o're] ov'r C2.
againe] ~, B29 F10(cor); ~. C2.

93 them!] F10; ~; B29; ~: H4; ~∧ H6; ~. Σ.   poysned] poyson'd B7 H6
G; poysoned C2 CT1 H4 A–F; Poiso'ned DT1.   Wel-head,] ~∧ ~∧ B7 H4
H6; ~∧ ~, B29; ~-~∧ C2 CT1 DT1 F10; ~-~. F10(cor).

94 corrupt] corrupts A.   vs] ~, C2 H6 A–G; yᵉ B29; as F10; ~ → »~,«
H4.   Riuoletts,] om B7 C2 CT1 DT1(›~∧‹) H4(»~∧«) A; ~∧ B29; Riuolett's∧
F10; nothing letts H6(M var: [missing]»ulets«).

95 no] nor H6.   breaks] breake A(unc).   Netts,] ~∧ B7 CT1 DT1 H4
H6; missing B29; Nett's∧ F10; Nett's. F10(cor).

96 thrust] thrusts CT1 A(cor).   led] missing B29.

97 Astray,] ~∧ H6.   turning] ~, C2 DT1 H4 A–G.   to] from B29 H6.
fled.] ~∧ B7 CT1 DT1 F10; ~, C2 H4 A(unc).

98 prisoners] ~, F10.   Iudges,] ~∧ F10.   rigorous;] B29; ~, F10(cor)
A–G; ~∧ Σ.

99 Syn'd,] ~∧ DT1 F10 H4.   beare;] heere, B7 C2 CT1 DT1 H4(var: »~∧«)

A; ~! F10; ~, H6.   Paine] sinn, B7; paines B29; sinn CT1.   thus] ~, F10(*cor*).

100 To loue them] *om* ~ ~, B29; ~ ~ ~, C2 A–G; Them to loue H6. fault] ~, DT1 F10.   painful] payne full H6.   Loue] ~, B7.   yoak'd] yoak't B29.   vs.] ~| B7; is → »~« CT1; ~ˬ F10 H6.

101 grow] ~, B29 F10(*cor*) A–G.

102 ask] ~, B29 C2.   bee] doe F10.   soe.] ~ˬ B7 CT1 F10 H4 H6; ~, C2 B–G.

103 make] ~, F10(*cor*).

104 law,] ~! F10; ~ˬ H6.

105 will] ~, C2 F10 A–C.   Man] ~, B7 B29 F10(*cor*).

106 one] F10 H4; ~, Σ.   shall] B29; will Σ.   iust)] ~,) B C.   take?] ~ˬ DT1; ~| H4.
        Alternate line: Will God (and bee iust) for one vengeance take? H6.

107 Synn'd?] ~, F10.   Snake,] B29; ~. DT1 F10(*cor*); ~ˬ Σ.

108 Nor] No B7 CT1; Noe, DT1.   her,] ~ˬ B7 B29 CT1 DT1 H4. made:] B29 F10; ~, C2; ~ˬ H6; ~; Σ.   is't] is t C.   writt] ~, F10(*cor*).

109 cropt] ~, B7 C2 CT1 DT1 A–G.   Aple:] F10; ~, B29 D–G; ~; Σ.

110 Worme] C2 F10 A–C; ~, Σ.   she] B29 F10 H6; ~, Σ.   he] F10 H6; ~, Σ.   it.] ~| B7; ~.| C2; ~ˬ CT1 DT1.

111 me] wee B7; ~, H6.   Heauenly] heau'nly CT1 DT1.   Spirit] ~, C2 DT1 H6 A(*unc*)–G.   vaine] ~, B29 F10(*cor*); strayne H6.

112 Reckning] B29 F10 H6; Reckeninge Σ.   Vanities;] B29; ~ˬ F10; vanitie, B–G; ~, Σ.   the] B29 F10; their Σ.   Gaine] ~, B29 F10(*cor*).

113 Then] Than B C.   still] ~, B7 C2 CT1 DT1 H4 A–C.   Ill] ~, B29 F10(*cor*) A–G; ~. H4.

114 Though] [*missing*]ough B29.   Minde;] B29 F10; minds, H6; ~, Σ. resons] ~, H6; reason's B C.   like] (~ B29.   those] the B29.   Toyes] ~) B29; ~, F10(*cor*). ·

115 Of glassy] [*missing*]lassy B29.   bubles] B29 F10 H6; ~, Σ.   which] with C2 A(*unc*).   Boies] ~, F10(*cor*).

116 Nice a Thinnes] thin a nicenes H4.   Quill] ~, F10(*cor*) D–G.

117 themselues] them selues B29.   break,] ~) B29.   do] and ~ H6 B–G. themselues] them selues B29.   spill;] F10; ~: B29; ~, C2 A–G; ~ˬ Σ.

118 is] his C2.   game;] F10 B; gaine, B29; ~, Σ.   exercise] ~, B29.

119 As] (~ H6. wrastlers] ~, B29 C2 DT1 A–C. perfects] proffitts
B29; perfitts C2 CT1 DT1; perfitt H6; perfect A(unc). them;] ~, B7 CT1;
~: B29 H4; ~), H6. liberties] ~, B29.

120 Speach,] ~ₐ H4 H6. Silence,] B29 F10 H6; ~; Σ. hands] ~, B7 C2
CT1 DT1 A–G. tongues] ~, C2 DT1 A–G. Heresies.] ~ₐ B7 B29 CT1
H6; Hiresie, H4.

121 that] the B7 CT1. gripe] ~, C2 F10(cor) A.

122 Veynes,] ~ₐ H6. Conduit Pipe] ~ ~, B29 F10(cor) B–G; ~-~, A.

123 this] the B7 CT1. Soule] ~, B7. draw] ~. F10(cor).

124 Life,] ~ₐ B29 H6. growth,] F10; ~ₐ Σ. Aple] F10 H4; ~, Σ.
away] ~, B7 C–G.

125 old,] ~ₐ B29. one] ~, B7 CT1 DT1 H4. another] an other B29.
Day.] C2 F10(cor) A(unc)–G; ~; B29; ~, A(cor); ~ₐ Σ.

126 lightning,] ~ₐ B7 B29 CT1 H4. scarse dares] dare scarce B29; dares
scarse H6; ~ dare G. say] ~, C2 DT1 H4 A–G. saw] ~, A–G.

127 gone] ~, C2 DT1 A–G. proof] proofs H6.

128 Sence] ~, B7 C2 CT1 A–G. then] the DT1 H4(var: »than«); than B
C. flew] ~, F10(cor).

129 T'a] F10 B–G; To a Σ. dark] ~, CT1 DT1 H4. Plott:] F10; Pitt;
B29; ~, DT1 H4 H6; ~; Σ. Her,] ~ₐ H6. fate] B29 F10; fates Σ.

130 There] That B7; ~, H6. th'Earth's pores] F10; the Earthes powers, B7;
yᵉ Earths ~, B29; ~-~, A(cor); th'earth-~, A(unc)–C; th'earthpores, D–F;
th'Earths ~, Σ. her] ~, CT1. anew.] ~ₐ B7 B29 CT1 H6; a new. C2
A; ~.| DT1; a new, H4.

131 This] B29; The Σ. plant] ~, H6. abled] B29 F10; ~, Σ. it selfe]
ytselfe H4; her ~ H6. force] ~, F10(cor).

132 place] ~, B29 C2 DT1 A–G. was,] F10; ~ₐ B29 H6; ~; C2 A–G;
~: Σ. natures] F10 H4 A–G; Natures Σ. Course;] B29; ~, F10(cor);
~. H6; ~ₐ Σ.

133 fleets] flotes B29. away] ~, F10(cor).

134 by] and ~ H4. throngd] thronged C2 CT1 DT1 H4 A. soe,] ~ₐ Σ.

135 confines] ~, DT1. grow,] C2 F10(cor) A–C; ~: D–G; ~ₐ Σ.

136 lust] om B29; (~ H6. streets,] ~ₐ CT1 DT1 H4 H6. when] ~ as
B29.

137 Prince,] ~ₐ B29 D–F; ~ → »Princesse's« CT1; ~) H6; Princesse,

A(cor).   and] om B29.   haue] F10; om Σ.   filld] filled is   B29; ~ vp
H6; fill up   B–G.   Way] ~;   B29; ~,   C2 F10(cor).

138 could] can F10.   passe,] ~∧ B29 H4.   nere] ~.   G.

139 throng] ~,   B29 DT1 H4 D–G.   vp,] ~∧   B7.   clere,] ~∧   B7 C2 CT1
DT1 H4 H6.

140 if] ~,   C2 DT1 H4 H6 A.   time,] ~∧   B7 B29 CT1 B–G.   were.]
~∧   B7 CT1.

141 Thrust] thrusts B29.   East,] ~∧   B7 C2 CT1 DT1 F10 H4 H6.

142 Westward] West-ward   A.   his] he B7.   lefte;] ~,   B7 F10 H6.
themselues] them selues B29.   digest] ~,   F10(cor).

143 Strings,] ~;   B29.   were] ~:   B29 A–G; ~.   C2; ~,   F10(cor).

144 as] om B7.   bed,] B29; ~.   F10(cor); ~;   A–G; ~∧   Σ.

145 way] ~,   B7 F10 H6.   this,] ~∧   F10.   way] ~,   H6.   Scattered]
scatterd B29; ~,   F10(cor).

146 leg,] ~;   C2.   vpbeare;] ~,   B7; ~∧   C2 CT1 F10; vp-beare∧   DT1 H4 H6;
~.   F10(cor); up beare;   B–G.

147 Midle parts,] ~ ~∧   B29 H6; Mid-parts,   DT1 H4(var: »~-~,«); ~ part,   B–G.
Day,] ~∧   B29 H6.   haire] ~,   B29 F10(cor) A–G.

148 show] C2 F10 54a–c; ~,   A–G; shew Σ.   busines] om   H4(»~«).

149 be,] ~∧   54a–c.   vsd] ~,   C–G.   well] F10 H6 D–G 54a–c; ~,   Σ.
ill;] B29 F10; ~:   A–G; ~,   54a–c; ~∧   Σ.

150 kindle,] B29 F10 54a–c; kind∧   H6; ~;   B–G; kinde,   Σ.   Leaues] B29
F10 H6 54a–c; ~,   Σ.   kill.] ~∧   B7 CT1 H6; ~.| C2; ~| DT1.

151 Mouth] B29 F10 D–G; ~,   Σ.   Dumbe] ~,   C2 H4 A–G.   hath,] ~;
A–G.   Eares] ~,   B7 B29 C2 F10(cor) A–G.

152 Haires:] B29; ~.   F10(cor); ~;   A–G; ~∧   Σ.

153 vprighte] ~,   B29 C2 F10(cor) A–G.

154 Conquered] ~,   B29 F10(cor) B–G.

155 leauy] B29 F10 H6; leafie Σ.   head] ~;   F10(cor).

156 Enchas'd] [missing]chas't B29.   fruits,] fruicts∧   B29; fruicts,   CT1; ~∧
H6.   red] ~,   B7 C2 CT1 DT1 H4.   bright] ~,   F10(cor) G.

157 Loues] love C2.   white;] A; ~,   B29 C2 F10(cor) B–G; ~∧   Σ.

158 Soe] ~,   A–G.   a lone] ~ loue F10; alone D–G.   possest] ~,   C2
F10(cor) A–C.

159 Inne,] ~∧ H4.   the] that H6.   Guest,] B29; ~. F10(cor); ~∧ Σ.

160 Man,] ~∧ B7.   Mandrake] ~, A–G.   rest.] ~∧ B7 B29 F10 H4 H6;
~| DT1; ~.| F10(cor).

161 greiue] ~, B29 F10(cor) A–G.

162 Eue.] C2 F10; ~; B29; ~: A–G; ~∧ Σ.

163 (with] ∧~ B7 CT1.   purpose)] ~∧ B7 CT1.   quite:] B29; ~, F10(cor);
~; A–G; ~∧ Σ.

164 syn] sinnes B29.   Infirmities,] F10(cor) A–G; ~. F10; ~∧ Σ.

165 Child,] ~∧ DT1 H4 H6.   the] her B29.   moist red] ~-~ C–G.
Eyes] ~, F10(cor).

166 shutt,] ~; B7.   slept] ~, DT1 H4.   light.] F10; ~; B29; ~, C2 A–G;
~∧ Σ..

167 knew,] ~∧ F10.   Mandrakes Might] ~ ~, F10(cor); ~ ~; A–F; ~-~; G.

168 both] B29 F10 H6; ~, Σ.   Childs] cheekes B7.   blood.] F10; ~; B29
A–G; ~∧ Σ.

169 Vnuertuous] vn=vertuous H4.   Weeds] ~, B7.   vnuext] B29 F10;
vn-vext H4; vnvex'd Σ.   stood,] ~. F10; ~; A–G; ~∧ Σ.

170 short liu'd] ~ ~, B7 C2 H4 A–G; ~-~, DT1.   can] may H6.   good.]
~∧ B7 CT1 H6 G; ~.| DT1.

171 vnfetter'd] vnfettered C2.   hast] ~, B29 F10(cor).

172 Starrs,] ~∧ H6.   thoughts] B29 F10 H6; ~, Σ.   but] om H6.   slow
pac't:] ~ pac'd∧ B7 CT1; ~ pac'de. C2; ~-pac'de∧ DT1 H4; ~ ~∧ F10; ~ pac^d,
F10(cor); slowly pac'd∧ H6; ~ pac'd: A–G.

173 then] than B C.   Ayre] ~, H4.   Soule,] ~; B29.   shee] ~,
F10(cor) H6.

174 Comming] B29 F10 H6; ~, Σ.   Suns] ~, F10(cor).

175 found] B29 F10 H6; ~, Σ.   runs] runnes[missing] B29.

176 Change,] ~∧ B7 B29 CT1; Changes, F10.

177 Confin'd] F10 H6; ~, Σ.   eniayld] entayl'd B7; exhal'd B29.   her]
~, B29 A–G.   free,] F10 A–G; ~∧ Σ.

178 2nd a] was B7.

179 Warme Bird] Warmebird B C.   orespred,] or'e spred, B7 DT1 B C;
or'e-spredd, H6.   euermore] ~, A–G.

180 enclos'd] encloth'd B7 CT1 DT1 H4(var: »~«); vncloth'd C2 H6(M var:

»~«) A.   Child] chide H4(*var:* »~«).   kikt] ~, H4 A–G; kick'd, B7 CT1 DT1 H6(ʌ).   pok't] B29; pick'd A–G; peck'd, B7; prickt F10; Peck'd Σ. self] ~, B7.   Dore.] ~, B7; ~ʌ B29 CT1 DT1 H6; ~: H4.

181 Out crept] ~˗~ DT1 H4; Outcrept A–C.   Sparrow,] ~ʌ B7 CT1 H6. Inne] ~, F10(*cor*) A–G.

182 Feathers] ffathers B7 CT1.   begin] ~, A–C.

183 Teeth] ~; B29.   through] *om* F10.   Gummes,] F10 A–G; ~ʌ Σ. Paine,] C2 F10(*cor*) A–G; ~ʌ Σ.

184 yet,] ~ʌ B29.   bones] bone F10.   Threds,] B29 C2 A–G; ~ʌ Σ.

185 a new Downy Mantle] ~ ~ ~ matell B29; ~ ~ ²Mantle ¹downy C2; downy a new mantle A.   ouerspreads.] ouer spreadesʌ B7 CT1; ~, C2 A–C; ~ʌ DT1 H6.

186 opes] ~, B7 C2 CT1 DT1 A–G.   as much] asmuch B7 CT1 DT1. containe] ~, F10(*cor*).

187 howre] <u>hows</u> C2 DT1 H4(*var:* »~«) H6(→ ›~‹).   plaine] ~; F10(*cor*); ~, A–G.

188 alowd] a low'd C2.   meat;] ~. C2 A–G; ~, H6.   men] ~, F10(*cor*).

189 steales] ~ him B29.   for] from B7.

190 One,] ~ʌ B7 B29 H4 H6.   Month] ~, C2 DT1 A–G.   Hen.] ~| B7; ~.| DT1; ~: H4.

191 nature] Nature B29 CT1 DT1 H6 B C.   hast,] B29 F10(*cor*) A–G; ~ʌ Σ.

192 ripened] ripned B7 CT1 H6; ripen'd B29; ripe'ned DT1.   sooner] B29 F10 H6; ~, Σ.   last:] B29; ~, C2 F10(*cor*); ~; A–G; ~ʌ Σ.

193 Alreadie] All ready C2.   hot] whott B29.   Cock] ~, B29 54b–c; ~; 54a.   Bush] ~, H4.   Tree,] F10 B–C 54a–c; ~ʌ Σ.

194 feild] ~, B7 B29 CT1 DT1 F10(*cor*) H4.   Tent] ~, F10(*cor*) 54a. oreflutters] ore' flutters B7 B29 CT1 H4 H6; ore'-flutters DT1; ~, F10.   his] *its* 54a–c.   Henn.] F10; ~; B29; ~, C2 A–G; ~, &c. 54a–c; ~ʌ Σ.

195 Not] B29 F10 H6; ~, Σ.   last] ~, B29; tast F10; tast, Σ.   when,] ~ʌ B7 CT1 F10 H4 H6; ~; B29.

196 Sister] ~, B7 C2 CT1 DT1 H4 A.   or] nor B7.   Neece] Neipce B7 CT1 DT1.   be,] B29 F10(*cor*) A–G; ~ʌ Σ.

197 Inconstancie] ~, F10(*cor*).

198 he] shee B7.   change,] ~; B29.   refuse] ~, F10(*cor*).

199 Calls,] ~;   B7 B29(cales) CT1 A–G; ~∧   H4.   doe] doth   B7 F10.
vse,] C2 F10(cor); ~;   A–G; ~∧   Σ.

200 Where] When   B29.   kinds,] ~∧   H4 H6.   chuse.] ~∧   B7 B29 F10
H6.

201 Men] B29 F10 H4; ~,   Σ.   till] while   B29.   Lawes] ~,   B7 CT1 DT1
H4.   freedome] freedoms   H6.   lesse] ~,   B29 F10(cor) A–G.

202 Daughters] ~,   C2 CT1 DT1 H4 A.   ingresse;] B29; ~,   F10(cor) A–G;
~.   H6; ~∧   Σ.

203 Till] tis   F10.   now] ~,   B–G.   vnlawfull,] ~;   B29 H4.   ill,] ~∧
B29 B–F; ~;   F10 A G.   not.] B29 H6; ~∧   Σ.

204 Iolly,] ~∧   B29 H4 H6.   moue,] B7 CT1 F10; ~∧   Σ.   Soule] ~,   C2
DT1 A(unc); ~;   H4 A(cor); ~.   B–F; ~:   G.   is,] B29; ~–   C2; ~.   F10;
~∧   Σ.

205 bodie] ~,   H6 A–F.   of] from   B7.   Kindnesses,] ~∧   B7 C2 CT1 DT1
F10 H4.

206 selfe preseruing] ~·~   DT1 D–G; ~ procuring → ~ ›~‹   H6.   forgott] ~,
B29 F10(cor) A–G; ~?   H4.

207 slackneth] slakens   B29.   Soules] ~,   C2 DT1 A–F; ~;   H4.   knott]
~,   F10(cor) A–G.

208 streytens;] ~,   B7 C2 CT1 DT1 H4 H6.   freelie on his] ~'~'~   DT1.
freinds] freend   B29; ~,   F10(cor).

209 blood] ~,   B7 CT1 DT1 H4 A–G.   Spirit,] ~∧   C2 F10.   Pith] F10 H6
D–F; ~,   Σ.   spends,] F10(cor) A–G; ~;   B29; pends∧ → »~∧«   H4; ~∧   Σ.

210 himself,] him selfe∧   B29; ~∧   H6.   Himself] him selfe   B29.   ends.]
~∧   B7 CT1.

211 liu'd;] ~,   B7 CT1 H6; ~:   B29; ~.   DT1.

212 blood] ~,   H4 A–G.   Holly] hollow   D–F.   grow] ~.   F10; ~,   D–G.

213 birdlyme;] F10; bird=lyme;   B29; Byrd-lyme,   C2 A–G; ~,   Σ.   deceiue]
~,   F10(cor).

214 feyned] B7 F10; fain'd   Σ.   Calls,] ~∧   DT1 H4 H6.   hid] B29 F10;
his   Σ.   nets,] ~∧   B7 F10.   snare] snares   B7 C2 CT1 DT1 H4; ~,   B29.

215 pliant] ply'ant   B.   Ayre:] F10; ~.   B29 C2 A–G; ~∧   Σ.

216 beget] B7 F10 H6; ~,   Σ.   conceiue] ~,   B29 F10(cor); deceaue
H6(M var: »~«).

217 Ask't] Ask'd   B7 CT1 DT1 H4.   Roots] B29 F10 H6; ~,   Σ.

Cock-sparrowes] ~ₐ ~ B7 H4 H6; Cocksparrowes C2 CT1; ~-~, A–G.
Leaue.] B29 H4; ~: A–G; ~ₐ Σ.

218 he,] ~ₐ B7 B29 CT1.   these] those B7.   feares,] H6 A–G; ~ₐ Σ.

219 Pleasantlie three,] *om om* B29; ~ |~| H6.   twenty] |~| H6.
yeares] ~; B29; ~, F10(*cor*).

220 liue,] ~ₐ B29 F10 H6.   increase] ~, C2 A.   his race,] ~ ~ₐ AF1 B29
H6 B–G; *om om* C2 A.   himself] him selfe B29.   outweares.] ~ₐ B7
CT1; out weares, B29; out-weares, DT1 H6; ~.| F10; out=weares. H4.

221 with] wᶜʰ B7.   ouerblowing] ever blowinge B7 CT1; over bloweinge C2
H4.   quencht] quenched, B7; quench'd C2 H6 A–G; quench'd, CT1 DT1
H4.   dead,] B29 F10(*cor*) A–G; ~ₐ Σ.

222 too] to B7 C2 CT1 DT1 F10 H4.   fledd] ~, F10(*cor*); ~. H4.

223 To'a] To a B29.   Brook:] ~, B7 CT1 DT1 H4 H6(→ ›~ₐ‹); ~; B29 C2
A–G.   Roe] Rowe B7 CT1 DT1 H6; ~, F10(*cor*).

224 the] a H4.   Ielly] ~, C2 DT1 H4 A–G.   leauned] leaven'd B7 CT1;
leau'ned C2 H4 A–G; sanded H6(*var*: ~).   was] ~, B7 A–G.

225 For they] (~ these H6.   had] B29 F10 B–G; *om* Σ.   intertouch't] B29
F10; intertouched C2 A; inter-touch'd DT1; enter-touched H6; intertouch'd Σ.
passe.] F10; ~) H6; ~, A–G; ~ₐ Σ.

226 bodies,] ~ₐ B7 B29 CT1 H4 H6.   soe,] F10(*cor*) A–G; ~ₐ Σ.

227 inform'd] B29 F10; ~, Σ.   abled] able G.   Row] Roe B7 C2 CT1 A.

228 It self,] F10; Itselfe H4; ~ ~ₐ Σ.   Oares] F10 H4; ~, Σ.   fitt;] B29;
~, C2 F10(*cor*) H6 A–G; ~ₐ Σ.

229 Parchment,] ~ₐ H6.

230 fish,] ~ₐ H6.   could yow] yoᵘ could B7 C2 CT1 DT1 H4(*var*: »yoᵘ
would«) H6 A–G; ~ *om* F10.   it.] ~ₐ B7 B29 CT1 DT1; ~.| C2.

231 goodlie] ~, C2 A–G.   full] first H6.   Trim] ~, F10(*cor*) A–G.
    Alternate line: Goodly. Like a ship in her full trim. Portly. Stately.   44a–d.

232 Swan] ~, A–G.   white] ~, DT1.   that] as B29.   him] ~, F10(*cor*).

233 himselfe] him selfe C2.   none,] F10(*cor*) A–G; ~ₐ Σ.

234 along] F10; ~; B29; a long, C2; ~, Σ.   watch'd] watched B7; watch't
B29 H6; ~, C2 A–G.

235 Neck] ~, H4.   catch'd;] Catcht, B7 CT1; catch't; B29; ~. C2 A;
~ₐ DT1 F10 H4 H6; ~, F10(*cor*); ~: B–G.

236 mou'd] mooved B7.   State] F10; ~, Σ.   vpon] ~, F10(cor).
Alternate line: Mooving in state.   44a–d.

237 Scorn'd,] ~∧ B7; ~; B29.

238 he] it H6.   it,] ~: F10(cor).   swallow'd] B29 F10 H6; swallowed Σ.

239 This,] ~∧ B29 DT1 H6.   Such,] ~∧ F10.   vnblam'd] ~, B7 CT1
F10(cor) B–G; vn=blam'd C2.   deuour'd] deuoured H4.   there] ~,
F10(cor).

240 All] ~, DT1 H4 A–G.   but who] who but H4(var: ›~ ~‹).   1st too]
to B7 C2 CT1.   2nd too] to B7 C2 CT1; or DT1 H4.   great,] ~∧ F10.
or] and B29.   well arm'd] ~=~ H4; ~ armed H6 B–G.   were.] ~| B7;
~∧ B29 DT1 F10 H4 A; ~.| C2.

241 swomme] swum DT1; swam̄ H6.   1st Prison] ~, B7.   putt] ~,
F10(cor) A–G.

242 shutt,] A–G; ~. F10; ~∧ Σ.

243 digestiue] digested H4(var: »~«).   fire] ~, F10(cor) A–G.

244 howse,] B29 F10; ~∧ Σ.   fish,] ~; B29; ~∧ F10.   vapourd] vapoured
B7.   forth.] F10 H6; ~: B29; ~; A–G; ~∧ Σ.

245 worth,] F10; ~∧ Σ.

246 her,] F10; ~∧ Σ.   retire] ~, F10(cor).

247 To 'nother] F10; ~ an other B29; T'a nother C2; ~ another H4; T'another
Σ.   desire] ~, F10(cor).

248 Pray,] F10 H6; ~: B29; prey; A–G; prey, Σ.   for] ~, A–G.

249 make,] ~∧ B29 H6.   complaint,] ~∧ B29 H4.   sure is] is sure D–G.
gone;] B29 F10(cor) G; ~. DT1 H6 A–F; ~∧ Σ.

250 invites,] ~∧ H6.   feasts] feeds B7; feast's C2.   Oppression.] ~| B7;
~∧ B29 B51 CT1 H6; ~.| C2 F10.

251 her] om C2; the A–G.   streame] B29 DT1 F10 H6; ~, Σ.
keep] ~, F10(cor) A–G.

252 her] ~, B7 C2 CT1 DT1 A–C.   towards] toward B7 B29 CT1 DT1 H4.
deep] ~, F10(cor) A–G.

253 retarded:] regarded: B29; ~. H6; ~, Σ.   Nett] ~, F10(cor).

254 Windowes:] F10; ~, Σ.   for] (~ B29 H6 B–G.   taught] ~, F10(cor).

255 wrought] ~, F10(cor).

256 As now,] Anon, B7; ~ ~∧ H6.   lett] ~, F10(cor).

257 scape,] ~∧ H4; ~; H6.   few] B29 F10; ~, Σ.   vse] ~, H6.   gett,]
A; ~) B29 H6; ~. F10 H4; ~,) B–G; ~∧ Σ.

258 As] ~, A–G.   Trap] ~, G.   rauenous] rauenouous H6.   tane]
~, F10(cor) A–G.

259 Who] ~, H6 A–G.   himself] him selfe B29 H4.   distrest] F10 H6;
distres'd B29; ~, Σ.   slaine] ~, F10(cor).

260 This] ~, this F10.   wretch,] ~∧ B29 F10 H4 H6; ~; A(cor)–G.   so]
(~ H6.   are] an C2.   habitts] haunts B29; habitt's C2.   againe.] ~∧
B7 B29 CT1 H4; ~.l C2 F10; ~). H6.

261 she] the H6(M var: »~«).   orepast,] A–G; ore past∧ CT1 H6; ~∧ Σ.

262 scap'd,] scap't, B29; ~∧ H6.   the oppressor] th'oppresser B7 CT1 DT1
H4; th ~ B29; th'oppresso[rs] H6.   fast.] F10 H6; ~;   A–G; ~∧ Σ.

263 through swome,] ~-~,   B7 C2 CT1 A–G; ~-swamme, →›~-~,‹ DT1; ~ ~∧
H6.   path] ~, F10(cor) A–G.

265 suck] such → »~« DT1.   Ayre,] ~∧ B7; ~: B29.   or]
and B7.   find] finds B29.   vnderneath] ~, F10(cor) A–G.

266 like] her B7 CT1.   Mills] B29 F10 H6; ~, Σ.   hath] ~, F10(cor).

267 water] weather B7 CT1 DT1; Wæther C2; wether H4 A.   thin] B29
F10 H6; ~, Σ.   and] or B7.   Ayre-like,] airelike∧ B7 CT1 A B; ~∧ ~∧
C2 DT1 C–G; ~=~∧ H4.

268 not,] ~; B29.   she's come] shee comes B7 CT1.   vnto] ~l B7;
~, F10(cor).

269 Where] When F10.   fresh] ~, C2 A–G.   which] B29; what Σ.
doe] ~, F10(cor).

270 not,] ~∧ H4 H6.   both] ~, B29.   boord] ~, DT1.   two.] ~∧ B7
B29 CT1 F10 A; ~.l C2.

271 her] om H4(»~«).   guests] B29 F10 H6; ~, Σ.   is] ~, F10(cor) B–G.

272 showes] shewes B29 C2 H6.   Quantities] ~, F10(cor).

273 are.] ~; B29 F10(cor); ~, H4 H6.   Thus] and ~ H6; ~ her B–G.
Way] ~, F10(cor) A–G.

274 game] ~, B7 CT1 DT1 H4.   hunger] ~, DT1.   Sea-Pye] F10 H6;
~∧ ~ Σ.

275 Spi'd] Spyed C2 A–G.   this] the B7 CT1; his F10.   trayterous]
traitrous B29 H6.   spectacle] ~, B7 C2 CT1 A–G.   high] ~, F10(cor)
A–G.

276 Silly] seely A–G.   fish,] DT1 F10 H4; ~∧ Σ.   where] when C2.
lay] ~,   C2 CT1 DT1 A–G.

277 to end] B29 H4; so ends F10; t'~ Σ.   doubts,] ~∧ C2 H6 A–G.
her,] ~∧ B29 H4.   away:] B29; ~│ B7; ~, C2 F10(cor) A–G; ~∧ Σ.

278 she is] ~ ~, B29 C2 DT1 H4 H6; ~'~, A–F; she's G.   to] om B7.
the Exalters] ~'~ B29 CT1 DT1 H6.   good] ~, F10(cor) A–F; ~. G.

279 As] om B7 CT1; (~ AF1 H6 B–G.   Ones,] ~∧ B29 H6;
~. F10.   stood] ~) H6; ~. A; ~.) AF1 B C; ~,) D–G.

280 Rais'd] It ~ B7 CT1 DT1 F10 H4; It ~, C2 A(unc); Its ~ H6; It's ~,
A(cor)–C; It's rais'd D–G.   Instruments] B7 C2 CT1; ~, B29; Instrument,
DT1; Instrument Σ.   food.] ~│ B7; ~.│ C2 DT1 F10(cor); ~∧ CT1 F10 H4
H6.

281 Fish?] ~∧ B29; ~, F10; ~,? F10(cor).

282 Man,] B7 C2 F10 A; ~∧ Σ.   doe] ~, C2 CT1 DT1 H4 A–G.   wish,]
F10(cor) B–G; ~∧ B29 F10 H6; ~; H4; ~: Σ.

283 awake,] ~∧ B7 CT1 DT1 F10 H4 H6.

284 hunt] F10; ~, Σ.   Pray] B29 C2 F10; prey Σ.

285 Beasts,] ~∧ H4.   away.] B29 F10; ~; A–G; ~∧ Σ.

286 vndertake] ~, F10(cor).

287 nests] ~, B29.   make] ~. F10(cor); ~; A–G.

288 these] those F10.   vpon,] F10(cor) A–G; ~∧ Σ.

289 Occupacion;] F10; ~│ B7; ~, C2 CT1 A–G; ~∧ Σ.

290 And] As H4.   make] makes DT1 H4.   Fasts] F10 H6; ~, Σ.
Distruction.] B29 A–G; ~│ B7; ~.│ C2; ~∧ Σ.

291 land-wind] ~∧ ~ B7 H4.   selfe] same B29.   hower] ~, F10(cor).

292 Sea-ward] ~∧ ~ B7 H6.   Bird] ~, F10(cor) H6 A–G.   that] wᶜʰ H6.
deuoure] ~, F10(cor).

293 fish;] ~, B7 CT1 F10; ~∧ H4; ~. H6.   not] F10; ~; H4; ~, Σ.
flies,] F10(cor) A–G; ~∧ Σ.

294 Orator;] ~: C2 F10(cor) A–G.   last] ~, F10(cor).

295 he hath] she ~ B7 CT1; ~'~ DT1.   1st flowen] ~, B7 C2 CT1 A–G;
flowne B29; flowne, DT1 H4 H6.   2nd flowen] flowne B29 CT1 DT1 H4
H6.   fast] ~, F10(cor) B–G.

296 many] B29 F10; om Σ.   Leagues] ~ H4(»oerpassed«) H6(‹or'e past›); ~

o'er-past   A–F; ~ o'rpast   G.   Sea,] ~₍ᴧ₎   B29 DT1 H4.   tyr'd] ~,   H6.
lyes] ~,   F10(*cor*) A–G.

297 his] is   B7.   Pray,] C2 F10; ~₍ᴧ₎   B29; prey₍ᴧ₎   H6; prey,   Σ.   languisht,]
~₍ᴧ₎   B7 F10 D–G; languish'd,   DT1 H4 H6.   Dyes;] F10; ~,   B29 A; ~.   C2;
~:   B–G; ~₍ᴧ₎   Σ.

298 Soules] ~,   H6.   erre,] DT1 F10(*cor*) A–G; ~₍ᴧ₎   Σ.

299 follow] B7 F10 H6; ~,   Σ.   Calender] ~,   F10(*cor*).

300 Of] O   B7.   the other,] F10; ~'~,   B29; ~ ~;   C2 A–F; ~ ~:   G; ~'~;   Σ.
Officer.] ~₍ᴧ₎   B7 CT1 F10 H6; ~.I   C2.

301 Into] ~,   F10.   Fish] ~,   C2 A–G.   this] B29; our   Σ.   throwne]
throwen   B7; ~,   F10(*cor*) B–G.

302 time] ~,   B7.   throwne] throwen   B7.   againe] B7 F10 H4; ~,   Σ.
growne] growen   B7.

303 vastnesse] F10 H6; ~,   Σ.   vnmanicled] ~,   F10(*cor*); vn-manacled   H4.

304 Greece,] C2 F10 A–G; ~₍ᴧ₎   Σ.   were,] ~₍ᴧ₎   B29.   that] ~,   H6.
some] ~,   F10(*cor*).

305 Earthquake] Earth quake   H6.   vnrooted] onrooted   F10.   loose]
~,   B7 CT1 H4.   swome,] F10(*cor*) H4 A–G; ~₍ᴧ₎   Σ.

306 bodie had] ~? ~   B7(»~₍ᴧ₎ ~«) CT1; ~'~   DT1.   seuered] ~,   F10(*cor*).

307 head,] A; ~.   F10(*cor*); ~;   B–G; ~₍ᴧ₎   Σ.

308 This] The   B29 H4.   these;] B29; ~₍ᴧ₎   H6; ~,   Σ.   And] ~,   H6 A–C.
faile] ~,   F10(*cor*) A–G.

309 ouersett] C2 F10 H6 IU2; ~,   Σ.   or] and   H4.   Saile] ~,   F10(*cor*).

310 Hulling] ~₍ᴧ₎   B29 F10 IU2.   might] ~,   H4 H6.   (when] ₍ᴧ₎~   H6 IU2.
whelp)] ~,   H6; ~₍ᴧ₎   IU2.   this] the   IU2.   Whale.] ~₍ᴧ₎   B7 B29 CT1 DT1
F10 H4 IU2; ~.I   C2.

311 At] And   B7.   euery] ev'ry   IU2.   take] ~,   F10(*cor*) B–F; ~.   G.

313 Then] Than   IU2.   voices] ~,   B29 DT1 A–G.   teare.] B29; ~,
F10(*cor*); ~:   A–G; ~₍ᴧ₎   Σ.

314 are] and   H4(*var*: »~«).   Pillars,] ~₍ᴧ₎   IU2.   high arch'd] ~ arch't   B29
IU2; ~-~   DT1 H6.

315 Bark] ~,   B29.   Steele,] ~₍ᴧ₎   H6.   Thunder proof.] ~ ~₍ᴧ₎   B7 C2 CT1
F10; ~=~₍ᴧ₎   DT1 H4 H6; ~-~,   A–G.
       Alternate line: Is thunder proof   IU2.

316 swallowed] swallow'd   B29 H6 B–G.   Dolphins] ~,   C2 DT1 F10(*cor*) H4

A–C.　　feare] ~,　B29 F10(cor) A–G.
　　Alternate line: Within him Dolphins swim w^(th)out all fear　IU2.

317　Sides] B29 F10 IU2 D–F; ~,　Σ.　　were] ~,　F10(cor).

318　Inland] Iland　B7 F10; In-land　DT1 H4.　　Sea,] ~;　B29; ~_∧　IU2.
hee] she　F10.
　　Alternate line: —and ever as he went,　54a–c.

319　He] she̍　F10.　　vp,] ~_∧　B29 IU2.　　if] ~,　F10.　　hee] she　F10.
ment] ~,　B29 F10(cor).
　　Alternate line: He spouted rivers up—　54a–c.

320　our] the　IU2.　　*1st* Seas] ~,　B7 B29 C2 DT1 A–G.　　with] wi'　IU2.
firmament.] ~_∧　B7 CT1 DT1 F10 H4; ~.l　C2.

321　hunts] hauntes　B7.　　Fish] B7 F10; ~;　DT1; ~,　Σ.　　an officer] a
fauorite　B29; ~ ~,　F10(cor) A–G.

322　Court] F10 H4; ~,　Σ.　　as] in　DT1 H4; ~ → »at«　H6; at　A–G.
Nett] F10; ~,　Σ.　　there] ~,　F10(cor).
　　Alternate line: Lies still at Court, and is him selfe a nett　B29.

323　All] Where　B29.　　inthrall;] B29 A–G; ~,　C2 F10(cor); ~_∧　Σ.

324　So] ~,　F10(cor).　　his] the　H6(M *var:* »~«).　　wantoning] ~,　A–G.

325　Gulf-like] gulfelike　B7 C2.　　throat] ~,　B7 C2 CT1 DT1 A–C.　　thing]
~,　F10(cor).

326　nere;] B29; ~.　C2 DT1 A–G; ~,　Σ.　　*1st* Fish] ~,　C2 CT1.　　*2nd* Fish]
B29 F10 H4; ~,　Σ.　　all] ~,　F10(cor) A–G.

327　Flier] ~,　CT1 DT1 F10(cor) H4.　　follower] ~,　B29 F10(cor) A–G.
fall.] B29 F10(cor) H4; ~;　A–G; ~_∧　Σ.

328　of] o'　IU2.　　Equality] ~,　F10(cor).

329　Consist,] DT1 F10 H4; ~;　B29; ~_∧　IU2; ~?　Σ.　　necessitie] ~,　F10(cor).

330　thousand] thousands　B29.　　Smals] C2 F10 H6 IU2; small　B29; ~,　Σ.
Great] ~,　A D–F.　　die?] ~_∧　B7 IU2; ~.l　C2; ~l　F10.

331　Seas,] the ~_∧　IU2.　　he] om　IU2.　　flocks,] F10(cor) A–G; ~_∧　Σ.
　　Alternate line: Now drinks he up Seas,—　54a–c.

332　He] It　H4.　　Ilands] F10 IU2; lands　D–F; ~,　Σ.　　Rocks,] A–G;
~_∧　Σ.

333　roomefull] roome full　B7; roome-full　CT1 DT1 H4.　　howse,] F10; ~_∧
Σ.　　float] ~,　F10(cor) A–G.

334　And] om　B7.

335 limms,] ~‿ B7 F10 H6 IU2; Lambes, H4(*var:* »~«).   distant as] like distant IU2.   Prouinces:] B29; ~. F10(*cor*) A–G; ~, H4; ~‿ Σ.

336 Times] ~, B7.   Crab] ~, B7 B29 CT1 DT1 H4.   Goat] Goates B7; ~, B29 F10(*cor*).

337 Parched] F10; Parch't, B29; Parch'd, C2 CT1; Parch'd DT1 H4 H6; ~, Σ. launcht] B29 F10; launch'd Σ.   this] his B–G.   boat:] B29; ~, C2 B–G; ~. F10(*cor*) H6 A; ~‿ Σ.

338 now,] ~‿ B29 H6 D–G.

339 Neerest,] Noe rest, B7; ~, F10 H4; ~. H6.   There's] there is B29. Perfection,] C2 C–G; ~. F10(*cor*) H6 A B; ~‿ Σ.

340 hath,] ~‿ H6.   Station.] ~| B7 DT1; ~‿ B29 CT1 H4 H6; ~.| C2 F10.

341 fishes] ~: F10(*cor*); ~, B–G.   whom] (~ H6.   harm'd] ~, A–G.

342 kind,] ~; B29; ~‿ H6.   throughly] firmly H6.   arm'd] ~, F10(*cor*).

343 hope] ~, F10.   him,] ~‿ B7.

344 themselues] them selues, B29; them selues C2.   by his] ~'~ DT1 B. Death,] ~; B7 C2 CT1 DT1; ~: H4 A–G.   (they] B29 F10; ‿~ Σ.   doe] B29 F10; did Σ.   eat] ~) B29.

345 flesh,] ~‿ H6.   Oyles,] ~‿ B29 H6.   out sweat)] one streate‿ B7 CT1; outstreate, C2 A–G; ~ streat‿ DT1 F10 H4; ~ streat,) F10(*cor*); ~‿~) H6.

346 him,] ~: B29; ~. H4 H6.   vndoe] ~, F10(*cor*).

347 all] F10 H6; ~, Σ.   twoe] ~, F10(*cor*) H6 A–G; ~. H4.

348 were] F10 H6; ~, Σ.   speak.] ~‿ B7 B29 DT1 F10 H4; ~, C2 F10(*cor*).

349 Tirant] Tyran B7 C2 CT1 DT1 A–F.   break] ~, F10(*cor*) A–G; ~? H6.

350 them] ~, B7.   wreak?] ~‿ B7; ~. B29 H4; ~.| C2 F10.

351 flaile-fin'd] flatt‿ ~ B29; ~‿ ~ C2; haile-~ F10.   Thresher] F10 H6; ~, Σ.   Steelebeak'd] F10; steelback't B29; the Steele=beak'd H4; Steele-beake H6; steel-beak'd Σ.   Swordfish] CT1 F10; Sword-fish DT1 A–G; ~, F10(*cor*); sword fish Σ.

352 Onlie] ~, H6.   doe] ~; B7; ~, C2 A–G.   wish:] F10; ~. C2 DT1 A–G; ~‿ Σ.

353 him,] ~‿ H6; ~: D–G.   begins.] F10; ~, F10(*cor*); ~; A–G; ~‿ Σ.

354 Whale] ~, B29.   Oppression] ~: F10(*cor*); ~, A–G.

355 And] ~, H6.   to hide] B29 F10 H6; t'~ Σ.   himself] him selfe B29;

~, F10(cor).   shame] ~,   B7 C2 CT1 DT1 H4.   Danger,] daunder,   B29.
downe] ~.   F10.

356 Sink;] ~,   F10 H6; ~.   H4.   Swordfish] sword fish   B7 B29 C2 H4;
Sword-fish   H6 B–G.   vpward] vpwards   CT1 H4.   spins] ~,   F10(cor)
A–G.

357 Beake;] ~,   B7 C2 CT1 DT1 F10; ~ˬ   H4.   Staffe like] ~-~   B29 DT1 H4
A–G; stafflike   H6.   Fins] ~.   F10; ~,   A.

358 weareth] B29; were the   C2 F10 A; well the   Σ.   plies] ~,   F10(cor) A–G.

359 Scoffe] ~,   DT1 H4 A–G.   Pray] prey   B7 H4; ~,   C2; prey,   CT1 DT1
A–G.   tirant] Tyran   B7 C2 CT1 DT1 A–F.   dies] lyes   B29; ~.   F10; ~,
A–G.

360 Dole)] ~,)   H4.   himself] him selfe   B29.   Companies.] company,ˬ   B7;
~.| C2; ~ˬ   CT1 DT1 H4 H6.

361 Death?] ~ˬ   B29.

362 accompt] ~,   B7 C2 CT1 DT1; account,   B29 A–G; account   H6.
thought] F10 H6 B–G; ~,   Σ.   fall?] ~ˬ   B29.

363 The heires] Th'eires   B7 CT1 DT1 H4 H6.   kings,] ~ˬ   H6.   see are]
~'~   B–F.

364 Transported] ~,   F10(cor).   gett] ~,   F10(cor) A–G.

365 they] ~,   A(cor)–G.   Reuenge] ~,   B7 B29 C2 CT1 H4 A.   forgett] ~,
C2 A–G; ~.   F10(cor).

366 goe] ~,   F10(cor) H4 A–G.

367 he is] C2 F10; he's   Σ.   dead,] ~ˬ   B7 B29 CT1 H6.   show] shew   F10
H4.

368 Act,] F10 H6; ~;   B29; ~:   H4; ~.   Σ.   some] And   B29.   being] ar
B29.   growne] ~,   F10(cor).

369 owne] ~,   F10(cor).

370 lose,] A–G; loose;   B7 CT1; loose,ˬ   B29; loose,   Σ.   showne.] H4 A–G;
~| B7; ~.| C2; showen.   F10; showen.| F10(cor); ~ˬ   Σ.

371 Sowle] ~,   C2 A.   free] ~,   B29; freed   H6.   Prison] ~,   C2 DT1 H4
A–G.   passion] ~—   B29; ~,   F10 A–G.

372 Indignation] ~,   DT1; ~;   F10(cor).

373 beat] ~,   F10(cor).

374 Castle,] ~;   B29 H4; ~.   C2 CT1 DT1 A–G.

375 Cloister] ~,   B7.   Mouse] ~.   F10.

376 men] ~, B–G.   that haue not] not hauing B7.   eat] ~, F10(cor) A–G.

377 ought,] ~, H4(*var:* »aught«); ~ᴧ H6.

378 Then] They DT1; Than B–G.   they] ~, C2 A–G.   who] whome
B29.   good] *om* B29.

379 Soule,] C2 A–G; ~ᴧ Σ.   taught] ~, F10.   by] be B7 CT1(→ »~«).
  Alternate line: being late taught that great things might by less 54a–c.

380 slayne,] ~ᴧ B7.   her self] herself B7 DT1 H4 A.   addresse.] H4
A–G; ~.| DT1 F10; ~ᴧ Σ.
  Alternate line: Be slain, to gallant mischief it doth it self address: 54a–c.

381 Masterpece] F10; master peice, B7 C2; master peece B29; Maister=peice
H4; ~, H6; Master-piece, Σ.   Elephant,] CT1 F10(cor) A–G; ~ᴧ Σ.
  *Alternate line: Elephant. The stiffe-kneed carry-castle. Natures great Master-
piece.* 44a–d.

382 thing;] ~. CT1 DT1 44a–d; ~, H6.   The] *om* 44a–d.

383 Beasts,] F10 H6; ~; Σ.   thought] ~, A.   noe more] no *om* B7 CT1
DT1; nor C2; *om om* H4(»~ ~«); none H6 B–G.   had] ~, B–G.   gone]
CT1 F10; *om* H6 B–G; ~, Σ.   one] him H6 B–G   wise] ~, F10(cor)
B–G.
  Alternate line: Of Beasts, who had beene king but yᵗ too wise B29.
  Alternate line: of beasts. 44a–d.

384 iust] ~, C2 CT1 DT1 A–G; ~; H4.   thankfull,] ~ᴧ B7 H4.
to' offend] t'~ B7 CT1 DT1 B–G; ~ᴧ ~. C2; ~' ~, F10(cor); ~ᴧ ~ H4; t'~, H6;
~ᴧ ~, A.
  Alternate line: Hee was, just, thankfull, loth t'offend B29.

385 (Yet] ᴧ~ B7 C2 CT1 DT1 H4; (For B29.   nature] Nature B29 C2 CT1
DT1 H6.   bend),] ~)ᴧ B29 H6 A–G; ~ᴧᴧ Σ.

386 Himself] Him selfe B29.   vpprops,] ~ᴧ B7; vp proppes, B29 H6;
vp-propps, DT1 H4 A–G.   himself] him selfe B29 C2.   relies] ~,
F10(cor) B–G.

387 And] *Who* 54a–c.   none,] ~ᴧ F10 H6; ~; G.   Enimies,] A–G;
~| B7; ~: F10(cor); ~, &c. 54a–c; ~ᴧ Σ.

388 stood;] ~, B29 H4 H6.   vext] vex'd DT1 H4 H6.   Phantasie]
phantasies B29; ~, C2 F10(cor).

389 Dreames;] B29 F10; ~ᴧ H4; ~, Σ.   Bow] ~, B7 C2 CT1 DT1 A B.
carelesly] ~, F10(cor).

390 Proboscies] F10; Proboscis Σ.   remissly] remishly F10.   Lie,] F10(cor);
~.| C2; ~: H4 B; ~. A C–G; ~ᴧ Σ.

391 which] ~, DT1 H6.   Gallery,] DT1 F10 H4 H6; ~∧ Σ.

392 Walk'd] DT1 F10 H6 G; Walkt B29; ~, Σ.   suruey'd] ~, F10(cor).
howse] ~; F10(cor); ~, A–G.

393 Braine,] ~∧ F10 H6.   the] and H4(var: »~«).   bed Chamber,] ~ ~∧
B7; bedchamber∧ B29 H4 H6; Bedchamber. C2; ~-~∧ CT1; Bedchamber, DT1
A; ~-~, B–G.   went] ~, F10(cor) A–G.

394 gnawd] gnawed B7 C2.   life Cords] ~-~ CT1 DT1; lifes ~ F10.
there;] ~, B7 C2 CT1 DT1; ~∧ H4.   Towne] ~. H4.

395 vndermin'd,] ~∧ B7 B29 CT1 F10 H6 G.   tumbled] tumled B7.
Downe;] B29; ~. F10(cor); ~, A–G; ~∧ Σ.

396 Murderer] F10; murther B7 CT1; murth'rer B–G; Murtherer Σ.   dies,]
om B29; ~∧ A.   sent] seat H4.

397 kill] ~, B29 DT1 F10(cor) H4 A–G.   saue,] ~; B29; scape, C2 A;
rape, F10; scape; H4 B–G; scape. Σ.   for] ~, A–F.   ment] went B7
C2 CT1 DT1 H4(M var: »~«).

398 die,] ~∧ B29 H6.   Roome,] F10 A–G; ~∧ Σ.

399 his] him B29.   Foe] B7 F10; for B29; ~, Σ.   Pray] F10; prey B7
CT1 G; ~, B29 C2 F10(cor); Prey, Σ.   and] his H6(var: ›~‹).   Tombe,]
B29 F10; ~: A–G; ~∧ Σ.

400 cares] Care B7 CT1.   turne] torne B29.   back] CT1 F10 H6; ~, Σ.
whither] where B7 CT1(→ »whether«); whether B29 C2.   come.] ~∧ B7 B29
H4 H6; ~.| C2 DT1 F10(cor).

401 Next] ~, C2 A–G.   Soule] ~, F10; Mouse H4(var: »~«).   Wolues]
Wolfes B29 H6.   vnborne] vn-born CT1.   whelp] ~, A.

402 Midwife,] A–G; ~∧ Σ.   nature,] F10; ~∧ H4; Nature, A–F;
Nature∧ Σ.   it] him F10.   help] ~, A.

403 issue,] ~; B7; ~. C2 DT1 A–G; ~: CT1.   kill] ~, C2 A–G.   soone]
well H6(M var: »~«).   goe.] B29 H6; ~, C2 F10(cor) A; ~: B–G; ~∧ Σ.

404 Abell] DT1 H4 A–G; ~∧ Σ.   white,] ~∧ H6 54a–c.   were] ~,
F10(cor) A–G 54a–c.

405 (Who] (~, DT1 H6 B–G; ∧~, 54a–c.   that] the B29.   trade,] C2
F10 H6 B–G; ~∧ Σ.   Church] ~, B7 C2 CT1 DT1 A–F.   kingdomes,] ~∧
B7 B29 H4 H6 54b–c.

406 Type)] ~), B29.   infested] infected B7 C2 CT1 DT1 H4.   soe] ~,
F10(cor) A–G.
       Alternate line: was the first type— 54a–c.

407 wolfe,] ~‸ B7 C2 CT1 H6.   it] hee B29.   losse] ~, C2.   woe] ~.
B29 H4; ~, C2; ~;   A–G.

408 Bitch,] ~‸ H4.   Sentinell,] H6 D–G; ~‸ Σ.

409 flock] flocks F10.   neere,] ~‸ B7 CT1 DT1 H4; well, F10.   warnes]
~, B7 CT1 DT1 H4.   defends] ~, F10(cor) A–G.

410 That] (~ B7 CT1.   Wolfe] ~, H6 A–F.   (hopelesse] ‸~ B7 CT1
H6.   els)] ~, H6.   her] ~, C2 CT1 DT1 A.   Intends.] ~‸ B7 CT1 F10
H4; ~.| C2.

411 Course] F10 H4; way B29; ~, Σ.   since] ~, A–G.   successfully] ~,
F10(cor) A–G.

412 taken,] ~‸ B7 CT1.   espie] ~, F10(cor).

413 Counsells,] ~‸ H6.   foes;] ~, B29 F10(cor) A–G; ~‸ Σ.

414 Tent] ~, B7 F10.   stealeth] ~, B29.   Dark] ~, A–G.

415 skirts] skirt B29.   slept;] ~, B7 H6; ~: H4.   bark] brak B29;
~, A–G.

416 Attach'd] Attach B29; Attatcht H4.   those] ~, A–C.

417 Loue:] F10; ~, DT1 H4 H6 G; ~; Σ.   goes] ~, B29 F10(cor) A–G.

418 Where] When C2.   then] than B C.   words,] ~; B29 C2 A–F;
~. DT1.   she] hee H6.   show] ~, A G.

419 Now much resist,] ~ ~ ~; B29; Nor ~ ~, C2; ~ must ~, H4(var: »Nor ~
~,«); Resistance much, H6.   needs] neede H6.

420 Pray,] C2 F10; ~; B29; Prey‸ H6; preye, Σ.   for] ~, A–G.   loose]
B29 F10 H6; ~, Σ.   not] nor F10 H6 A–C.   bark] B7 F10 H6 D–G; ~, Σ.
goe.] B29 A–G; ~.| C2 DT1 F10(cor); ~‸ Σ.

421 her,] ~‸ B7 H4; ~; B29 A–G.   his] ~, C2 DT1 H4 A–G.   wholy]
onlie F10 H6.   bides;] ~‸ B7 C2 CT1 DT1 H4 H6; ~: G.

422 owne,] ~‸ H6.   none] no B29 H6.   hides:] B29; ~, A; ~. B–G;
~‸ Σ.

423 come,] ~‸ B29 H6.   there] ~, C2 A–G.

424 hoarse] horse B29.   barkings,] ~‸ B29 H6.   not,] F10(cor) A–G;
~‸ Σ.

425 quite,] ~‸ H6.   forgott;] B29; ~, C2; ~. A–F; ~: G; ~‸ Σ.

426 Trap,] ~‸ B7 H4.   where] ~, F10(cor).

427 plac'd,] placed‸ B7; plac't‸ B29; ~‸ C2 CT1 F10 H4 H6 A(unc).
ended] end, and B7 C2(‸) CT1(and → »both«); ending DT1 H4(var: »~«); ends

both   H6; ends all   A–G; end all   A(*unc*).   Losse] ~,   C2 CT1 DT1 H4 A–G.
feare] ~;   F10(*cor*); ~,   A(*cor*)–G.

428 Wolfes] wolues   B29 C2 DT1 H4 A–G.   Death,] F10 H4 H6; ~;   Σ.
was] ~,   B29.

430 passe.] ~ˌ   B7 B29 F10 H6; ~.| C2 DT1.

431 Wiues] Wifes F10.   Sisters] ~. F10.   begott] ~,   A–G.

432 liues] life   B29; lifes   F10.   Emperors] Princes   B29; ~,   H4.

433 lust] ~,   B7 DT1 H4 B–G.   this;] B29 A–G; ~ˌ   Σ.

434 begatte] B29; begott   Σ.   himselfe] B7 F10 H6; him selfe   B29; ~,   Σ.

435 begun] B29 F10; begann   Σ.   aliue,] ~;   B29; a liue,   C2; ~ˌ   H4.
dead;] F10(*cor*); ~,   A–C; ~.   D–G; ~ˌ   Σ.

436 himselfe] F10 H4 H6; him selfe,   B29; ~,   Σ.   too,] ~ˌ   B7 B29 CT1 H4
H6.   is] was   B29(*var:* ›~‹).

437 lust] B29 F10; ~,   Σ.   misse] wishe   H6(M *var:* »~«).

438 proper] om   B29.   Name:] B29; ~ˌ   B7; ~,   F10 H4 H6; ~.   Σ.   these]
those   B7.

439 with] w^ch   B7.   Moaba] ~,   B7 CT1 A–G.

440 Sister,] A–G; ~ˌ   Σ.   young,] ~ˌ   B29 H6.   sport] ~,   CT1 DT1 H4.
play.] DT1 H4 A–G; ~.| C2; ~ˌ   Σ.

441 harsh] F10 H6; ~,   Σ.   grew] ~,   B7 A–G.

442 Abell] ~,   B7; (~   C2.   (the] ˌ~   C2.

443 feild:] B29; ~ˌ   B7 H4; ~,   Σ.   made] thus ~   H6; ~,   A; thus ~,   B–G.

444 He] ~,   B7 CT1 DT1 H6 A–G.   as] and   B7 CT1.   Dam] ~,   H6
A–G.   Sheep] ~,   B7 C2 CT1 DT1.   droue] ~,   F10(*cor*); draue   H6.
Wolues] Wolfes   B29.   away] ~,   C2 F10(*cor*) A–G 54a–c.

445 Sire] ~,   C2 DT1 H4 H6 A–G.   pray.] preyˌ   B7 CT1 H4; ~ˌ   B29 F10;
preye.   DT1 A–G 54a–c; ~,   H6.

446 liu'd,] ~ˌ   B29 H6.   Cousen'd] B29 F10 H6 B; cousoned   Σ.   Trade,]
~ˌ   B7 B29 CT1 F10 H4; ~.   DT1; ~:   54a–c.

448 Himselfe] Him selfe   B29.   followed:] F10; ~,   A–G; ~ˌ   Σ.

449 dogs] ~,   A–G.   Wolfe,] ~ˌ   B29 F10 H6; Wolve;   C2; ~;   A–F.
Wolues] ~,   A–C.   he] h'   54b–c.   fledd] ~;   A–G; ~:   54a–c.

450 And] ~,   A–C.   spy] ~,   DT1 H6 54a–c.   to] (~   F10.   false] B7

C2 CT1; ~) F10; ~, Σ.   he] ~ /he   54b–c.   perished.] ~| B7; ~.| C2;
~ˏ CT1 H4.

451 quicknd] quickened   DT1; quickend   H6.   next] ~, B7 G; wext F10.
toyfull] toy-full   B7 C2 CT1 DT1; toilefull   F10.   Ape,] ~ˏ B29; ~; DT1.

452 was,] ~ˏ   H4 H6.

453 1st Tent] ~,   H4.   2nd Tent] F10 H6; ~; F10(cor); ~, Σ.   play;] ~,
F10(cor) A–G; ~ˏ Σ.

454 theirs] them   F10.   find] ~: F10(cor); ~, A–G.

455 laugh] ~, C2 CT1 DT1 H4 A.   and] nor B7.   Mind] ~; F10(cor);
~, A–G.

456 wonders] ~; B7 H6; ~, B29; ~. C2 CT1 DT1 A–G.   much;] B29;
~ˏ Σ.   withall] Wᵗ all B29; wᵗʰ all, DT1 H4 A–G; ~, Σ.

457 fifth] B29 F10; fift Σ.   Daughter,] F10; ~ˏ Σ.   Syphatecia,] C2 A–G;
~; B29; ~: F10(cor); Siphateria ˏ H4; ~ˏ Σ.

458 and] ~, A–F.   where] when F10.   passeth,] F10 A–G; ~ˏ Σ.
pas,] A–G; ~ˏ Σ.

459 fruit] F10; fruictes, B7 CT1; ~, B29; fruicts DT1; fruits, Σ.   Grasse]
~; F10(cor); ~, A–G.

460 in] B29 H6; of Σ.   kind,] ~ˏ B7 B29 CT1 H6.   was.] ~ˏ B7 CT1
F10 H4 H6; ~; B29; ~.| C2.

461 first] ~, C2.   desir'd] desired B7 CT1.   haue] ~, F10(cor).

462 One] ~, B7 CT1.   then] the B7 CT1(→ »~«); than C–G.   another,]
other, B7; an other; B29; ~; C2 CT1 DT1 A–G; ~: H4.   ere] hee B7.
craue] ~, B7 F10(cor).

463 Loue] ~, B7.   Signes,] ~ˏ H6.   speak;] ~, B7 C2 CT1 DT1; ~ˏ F10
H4 H6.

464 loue faces,] ~-~, C2 CT1 DT1.

465 sobresalts,] F10; Sumersalts, B29; Somber saltes ˏ H4; ~ˏ H6;
Sombersaltes, Σ.   wooe] ~, B7 F10(cor).

466 hoiting] hoisting B29; halting F10.   Gambolles,] Gambolds, C2 CT1
DT1; gambolds ˏ H4; ~ˏ H6.   bones] howse B29.

467 merrie,] ~ˏ B29; ~; C2 DT1 A–G; ~: F10(cor).   wreak] ~, F10(cor).

468 Her] His B7.   Angers] B29 F10; Anger, DT1; anger Σ.   himself;]
him selfe; B29; him selfe. C2; ~, F10 H4; him selfe, H6; ~. Σ.   kind]
~, F10(cor).

469 easily] easly B29.　　doe,] ~ₐ H6.

470 boies] ~,　B7 CT1 DT1 H4.　　find.] F10 A–G; ~.|　C2; ~ₐ Σ.

471 prou'd] ~,　A–G.

472 high;] ~,　B7 CT1 H4 H6; ~: B29.　　Beasts] ~,　B7 B29 CT1 DT1 H4.
Angels] ~,　B7.　　lou'd:] F10; ~.　H6; ~;　A–G; ~ₐ Σ.

473 Ape] F10 H4; ~,　Σ.　　through-vaine,] ~-~ₐ B29; ~ₐ ~,　DT1 F10;
throughvaineₐ H4.　　wise,] A–G; ~.　H4; ~ₐ Σ.

474 reacht] B29 F10; reach'd　Σ.　　high,] ~ₐ B29; ~;　F10(cor); ~.　H4.

475 was] F10; ~,　Σ.　　would] could　B29.　　nay:] B29; ~;　A–G; ~ₐ Σ.

476 not,] ~ₐ B29.　　tryes,] A–G; ~ₐ Σ.

477 on] in　B7 CT1.　　face] ~,　F10(cor).　　teare-shot] ~ₐ ~　B7; ~-shed
F10.　　eyes] ~,　F10(cor) A–G.

478 vplifts] vp lyfts　C2 A–G.　　subtilly] F10 H6; softly　B29; subtly　Σ.

479 kid-skin] kidskin　B7 C2 CT1 H6 A–G; ~ₐ ~　B29.　　Apron] ~,　B29.
or] of　G.

480 Nature;] nature,　B7 H4 G; ~,　CT1 F10 H6; ~: F10(cor); nature;　A–F.
Iaile] gaole,　C2(Goale,) A–G; ~,　DT1; gaole　H4.　　haue] hath　C2 A–G;
was　H6(M var: ›hath‹).　　law.] F10(cor) A–G; ~.|　C2; ~:　H4; ~ₐ Σ.

481 First] ~,　C2.　　seely] F10; silly　B29 A–F; silly,'　DT1; silly'　H6; silly,　Σ.
ment;] ~,　A–G; ~ₐ Σ.

482 vertue] ~,　B7 C2 CT1 A–G.　　Touches] ~,　B7 C2 CT1 DT1 A.
chaft] chas'd　B7; chaf'd,　CT1 H4; chaf'd　DT2 H6.　　spent] ~,　B7 CT1 DT1
A–G.

483 warmth,] ~:　F10(cor).　　quite;] ~,　F10(cor) H4 H6 A–G; ~ₐ Σ.

484 now] then　B7 CT1; nor　B29 B–G.　　doth] ~,　F10(cor) A–G.

485 half] ~,　B7 CT1.　　and] then　F10.　　then] they　H4(var: »than«);
than　B.　　loth] wroth　AF1 H6; om　B7 C2 CT1(»~«) DT1 H4(»wroth«);
Forth　F10; Forth → »Tooth«　F10(cor); Tooth　A; wroth,　B–G.

486 pulls] ~,　B7 B29 C2 CT1 DT1 H4.　　pushes,] ~ₐ H4.　　outright]
out right　B7 C2 CT1 DT1; ~,　F10(cor); out-right　B–G.

487 Cries] F10; ~,　Σ.　　repents;] ~,　B7 B29 CT1 H6.　　Tethlemite,]
Tethelmiteₐ B7; Tethelemiteₐ C2 A; Tethlemitₐ F10; Thelemiteₐ B–G;
~ₐ Σ.

488 brother,] A–G; ~ₐ Σ.　　enters] F10; ~,　B29; enterd　H6; entred,　Σ.

489 Ape,] ~∧ H4.   who] ~, H6 A–G.   preuented] ~, F10(cor) H6 A–C. flew;] B29; ~. H6 B–G; ~, A; ~∧ Σ.

490 howse,] B29 F10; ~∧ Σ.   battered] B7 C2 F10 H4; Batt'red DT1; batterd Σ.   Downe,] ~∧ H6.   a new.] ~ ~∧ B7 CT1 DT1; ~ ~.| C2; another. F10.

491 whether] whither H4.   Chang,] F10; ~∧ Σ.   lose] B29 A–G; loose, H4; loose Σ.   win] ~, A.

492 next,] ~∧ B7 B29 CT1 DT1 H4 H6.   the Ape] ~'~ DT1 H4 H6 B–G. in.] D–G; ~, C2 A–C; ~∧ Σ.

493 Adam] ~, B7 CT1 DT1 H4.   Eue] ~, B7 DT1.   now] ~ F10(cor).

494 Chimiques] ~, F10.   fires] B29 F10 H4; ~, Σ.   temperate] temprat B29; temperd H6.

495 stewd] ~, B7 DT1 H4; stued, B29.   it,] ~∧ B29; ~; C2; ~: A–G. become] ~, F10(cor).

496 Liuer] ~, B7 C2 CT1 DT1 A–G; ~; F10(cor).   richly] ~' H6.   allow] ~, F10(cor) A–G.

497 Conduit,] ~∧ B7 B29 CT1 DT1 H4 H6.   high hills] ~-~ DT1.   brow] ~, F10(cor) A–G.

498 Life-keeping Moisture,] ~∧ ~ ~∧ B7 CT1 H4 A; ~-~-~∧ B29; ~-~ ~∧ C2 DT1 H6 B–G.   part,] F10(cor) A–G; ~∧ Σ.

499 hardened] F10 H6; hardned Σ.   hart] ~, A–G.

500 lifes] Life B29; liues H6.   spirits] sprights B29.   imparte.] F10 A–G; ~.| C2; ~∧ Σ.

501 Brain *as HE for lines 501–04* 44a–d.   Another] An other B7 B29. Sence,] A–G; ~; F10(cor); ~∧ Σ.
  Alternate line: The Well of sence, 44a–d.

502 wel arm'd] ~-~ CT1 DT1 H4 H6 G.   braine,] ~∧ B7 C2 CT1 H6; ~: B29.   whence] ~, F10(cor) A–G.
  Alternate line: from whence 44a–d.

503 sinewy] sinew G.   strings] ~, B7 CT1 44a–d.   which] that 44a–d. tie] ~. F10(cor); ~, A–G 44a–d.

504 raueld] raueled B7 H4.   out,] ~: F10(cor).   there by] thereby F10 H6.   one] on H6.   end] ~, F10(cor) A–G 44a–b; ~; 44c–d.

505 this] a B7 CT1.   Soule] ~, B29.   Limms,] ~; B29.   attend] ~. F10(cor); ~, A–G.

506 ioynd;] ~∧ B7; ioyne∧ B29; ~. C2 DT1; ~, CT1 F10 H6 B–G; ~:
F10(cor) A.

507 past shape,] ~ ~: B29; ~ ~. DT1 H6; ~-~, F10; ~ ~; H4 B–G.
Trecherie,] F10(cor) A–G; ~∧ Σ.
    Alternate line: Shee knew treachery B28.

508 Rapine,] ~∧ B28 B29 F10.   Deceipt,] ~∧ B28 F10 H4.   Lust] B29 F10;
~, Σ.   Ills] ill B7; ~, F10(cor).   enowe] enough B7 B28 CT1 DT1 B–G;
inough F10 H4; inough. F10(cor).

509 woeman;] B29 H4; ~. B28 C2 DT1 A–G; ~, Σ.   Themech] *om* B28;
Temech B29.   she is] *om om* B28.   now,] CT1 A–G; *om* B28; ~∧ Σ.

510 Sister] ~, C2 CT1 DT1 H4.   Caine,] *om* B29.   Cain] to ~ H6.
plow.] F10(cor) A–G; ~.| C2. ~∧ Σ.

511 beest,] bee B7 CT1; ~∧ DT1 H4 H6 A–G.   readst] reade B7.   writt]
~. C2; ~, F10(cor) H4 A–C.

512 thee,] ~∧ H6; ~; G.   dost] Courts F10.   it] ~, C2 A–G; ~; H4.

513 thy] my B7 CT1.   Thoughts,] ~. CT1; ~∧ H4; ~; D–G.   me] ~,
F10(cor) A–F.

514 building,] ~∧ F10.   ruling] ~, DT1 H4 H6.   rest] ~, A–G.

515 Or] Are B7.   those] these B7 C2 CT1 DT1 H4.   Arts] ~, F10(cor)
A–G.   blest] ~. C2; ~: F10(cor); ~, A–G.

516 inuented] should ~ H6.   be] ~, C2 F10(cor) A–G.

517 vext] vex'd DT1 H4 H6.   vs] ~, C2.   Astronomie.] B–G; ~, C2 A;
~∧ Σ.

518 There's] There is B51.   good,] ~∧ CT1 H6.   nor] or B7 B51 DT1
H4.   alone,] F10(cor) A–G; ~∧ Σ.

519 qualitie] ~, C2 H4.   Comparison] ~, B51 F10(cor) A–C.

520 only] seemely H6(*var:* >~‹).   Measure] ~, H4.   is] F10; *om* H4; ~,
Σ.   Iudge] ~, B51 DT1 A–F.   Opinion.] ~| B7 H4; ~.| C2 F10; ~: DT1.

Subscriptions: ffinis.| DT1.   Finis. H4

Editions collated: H I J K M N O P Q S T Y Z AA DD.

Format, poem:

    Indentations and stanzaic pattern: *divided into 10-line sts* Σ. *Sts numbered in roman* H–J M–Q S Y Z DD; *sts numbered in arabic* T AA; *sts unnumbered* K. *Line 1 of each st ind 3 spaces* H M N; *no ind* I–K; *l. 10 of each st ind 2 spaces* O Q S Y AA DD; *ll. 1–9 of each st ind 3 spaces* T.

Headings, poem: THE PROGRESS Of the SOUL. *First* SONG. H M N O P S Y Z AA DD. THE PROGRESS OF THE SOUL. I J. FIRST SONG. K T.

  4 was] us Σ.

  5 in] to Σ.

  6 through] though H K.

  8 is] 't is I J.

 10 writts] O; Writ's P; writ Σ.

 13 beginst] begins O.

 18 then] Q Y Z DD; than Σ.

 27 For] Y; From Σ.

 29 diuers] diverse I J Q S Y Z AA DD.

 32 hast] hath Z.

 33 euery thing] everything P.

 36 vouch thou safe] vouchsafe thou H–K M–P.

 37 shew] show K M O P T AA.

 39 my selfe] H Q S Y Z DD; myself Σ.

 45 Sprighte-quenching] Spirit-~ Σ.

 46 Beauties] Q S Y Z DD; beautie's Σ.

 47 to other] t'others H–K N Z; the others M; ~ other's O; ~ others P Q S DD; t' ~ T Y AA.

 54 shall] hold H–K M N.   lone] love O.

 56 Sands] lands Σ.

 57 saile] H–K Y; I ~ Σ.   towards] t'wards I J; toward Y.

 58 staid] stayed M O AA.

59 hoisted] hoised   O–Q S T Y Z DD.   strook] struck   H–K M–P T AA; stroke   Q S Y Z DD.

60 wayd] weighed   M O AA.

61 this] N T Y; the   Σ.

64 shall] will   Σ.

68 Wracks] wrecks   H–K.

69 where] N Y; when   Σ.   great] greater   T.

71 no] nor   P.   then] N(M *var:* than); than   Σ.

87 whose] her   Σ.

93 Wel-head] wellhead   T.

96 thrust] thrusts   O.

99 beare] here   O.

105 Creatures] creature's   H K M–O; creatures'   I P T AA.

106 shall] will   Σ.

108 Nor] Not   P Q T.

112 Vanities] vanity   H–K M N.   the] Y AA; their   Σ.

113 Then] N Q Y Z DD; Than   Σ.

114 resons] reason's   H–K M–P.

117 do] and ~   H–K M N P.

120 end] and   I J.

121 Serpents] Q S Y Z DD; serpent's   Σ.

123 Trees] Q S Y Z DD; tree's   Σ.

126 dares] dare   H–K M.

128 then] than   H–K M O P S T AA; ~   N(M *var:* than).

129 fate] Y AA; fates   Σ.

130 Earth's] earth   P; earths   Q S Y Z DD.

131 This] The   Σ.

132 natures] Q S Y Z DD; nature's   Σ.

137 Prince] princess   O.   haue soe filld] so fill up   H–K M N P DD; *om* so filled   O.

138 she] he   I J.

147 parts] part   H–K M P.

148 Loues] Q S Y Z DD; love's   Σ.   show] shew   J N.

155 leauy] lazy   J; leafie   Σ.

157 yow] ye   I J.   Loues] Q S Y Z DD; love's   Σ.

159 Soules] Q S Y Z DD; soul's   Σ.

166 slept] sleept   Z.

167 Mandrakes] Q S Y Z DD; mandrake's   Σ.

168 Childs] Q S Y Z DD; child's   Σ.

171 Soules] Q S Y Z DD; soul's   Σ.

172 harts] heart's   H K M–O T AA; hearts' I P.

173 then] N(M *var*: than) Q Y Z; than   Σ.

175 Mandrakes] Q S Y Z DD; mandrake's   Σ.

177 eniayld] engoal'd   H I K; engaoled   M.

180 enclos'd] unclothed , O; uncloth'd   T.   pok't] peck'd   N T Y; pick'd   Σ.
it self] Q S Y Z DD; itself   Σ.

181 Soules] Q S Y Z DD; soul's   Σ.

183 Childrens] H Q S Y Z DD; childrens'   M; children's   Σ.

185 a new Downy] downy a new   O.

191 Worlds] Q S Y Z DD; world's   Σ.

195 last] S T DD; taste   Σ.

197 Inconstancie] inconsistancy   AA.

198 Sight] sights   N.

207 soe] not   H–K.   Soules] Q S Y Z DD; soul's   Σ.   bodies] Q S Y Z DD;
body's   Σ.

214 hid] his   H–K M–P.

219 then] than   M–P S T AA DD.

223 fishes] Q S Y Z DD; fish's   Σ.

224 Males] Q S Y Z DD; male's   Σ.

227 abled] able   H–K.   Row] roe   N.

228 It self] H Q S Y Z DD; Itself   Σ.

230 could yow] you could   Σ.

241 swomme] swam   H–K M P T AA.

243 Swans] Q S Y Z DD; Swan's Σ.

248 Pray] prey Σ.

249 sure is] is sure   H–K.

251 her] the   H–K M O P.

258 Trap] trip   J.

263 swome] swam   H–K.

264 whether] whither   I J.

268 she's come] she comes   N.

269 which] what Σ.

272 showes] shews   H–J.

273 Then] Than   H–K M–P S T AA.   Thus] ~ her   H–K M N P.

275 this] his   H–K M; the   N.

276 Silly] seely   Q S Y Z DD.

278 Exalters] Q S Y Z DD; exalter's Σ.

280 Rais'd] It ~   N; It's ~   Σ   Raysers] Q S Y Z DD; Raiser's Σ.
Instruments] instrument Σ.

284 Pray] prey Σ.

294 Gluttonies] Q S Y Z DD; gluttony's Σ.

296 many Leagues] leagues o'erpast   H–K M–P DD.

297 Pray] prey Σ.

298 Soules] soul's AA.

301 this] our Σ.

305 vnrooted] uprooted   Y.   swome] swam   H–K.

306 Africks] Q S Y Z DD; *Africk's* Σ.

307 Promontories] Q S Y Z DD; *Promontory's* Σ.

313 Then] N(M *var.* Than) Q Y Z DD; Than Σ.   Canons] J Q S Y Z DD;
cannon's   H I K M; cannons' Σ.

322 as] T Y AA; at Σ.

325 euery thing] everything   O P T.

332 iustles] jostles   I J M N P T AA.

342 throughly] thoroughly   M N.

344 doe] Y; did   Σ.

345 out sweat] outstreat   Σ.

349 Tirant] tyran   O Q S Y Z DD.

351 Thresher] thrasher   M.

353 thresher] thrasher   M.

354 yeilds] leads   J.

356 vpward] upwards   J.

358 weareth] well the   Σ.

359 Pray] prey   Σ.   tirant] tyran   O Q S Y Z DD.

362 accompt] account   Σ.

367 shew] J H; show   Σ.

369 Subiects] J Q S Y Z DD; subject's   H K; subjects'   Σ.

370 lose] loose   N(M *var*: ~).   showne] shewn   J.

377 ought] aught   K P T AA.

378 Then] N(M *var*: than) Q Y Z DD; Than   Σ.

380 her self] H; herself   Σ.

381 Natures] Q S Y Z DD; Nature's   Σ.

383 noe more had gone] none had   H–K M N P.   one] him   H–K M N P.

390 Proboscies] Proboscis   Σ.

393 Soules] Q S Y Z DD; soul's   Σ.

396 Murderer] K M O P AA; murth'rer   Σ.

397 saue] 'scape   Σ.   ment] went   N.

399 Pray] prey   Σ.

400 any whither] ~-~   M–O.

401 Wolues] Q S Y Z DD; Woolue's   N; Wolf's   Σ.

405 kingdomes] Kingdome's   N.

409 warnes] warms   K.

410 els] self   M.

414 Abels] Q S Y Z DD; *Abel's*   Σ.

417 loues] Q S Y Z DD; love's Σ.

418 then] N Q Y Z; than Σ.   show] shew H.

419 Now] Y; Nor Σ.   much] make Q.   resist] ~ N(M *var:* resistance).
nor] no J.

420 Pray] prey Σ.   not] nor O Q S T Z AA DD.

422 others] J Q S Y Z DD; others' I P; other's Σ.

424 hoarse] hoorse N(M *var:* ~).

426 euery where] everywhere M–P T.

427 ended] Y; ends all Σ.

428 Wolfes] wolve's H N; Wolves Q S Y Z DD; wolf's Σ.

430 Abels] Q S Y Z DD; *Abel's* Σ.

434 begatte] begot Σ.

435 begun] began Σ.

437 ridling] riding H–K M.

438 these] those N.

439 Abels] Q S Y Z DD; *Abel's* Σ.

443 made] O Y; thus ~ Σ.

445 pray] prey Σ.

456 wonders much; withall] ~. ~ₐ with all, Σ.

457 Adams] Q S Y Z DD; *Adam's* Σ.   Syphatecia] Siphateria N.

459 fruit] fruits Σ.

460 in] of Σ.

462 then] Q Y Z DD; than Σ.

465 Vaulters] Q S Y Z DD; vaulter's Σ.   sobresalts] sombersalts Σ.   wooe]
woe   N(M *var:* ~).

468 Angers] Y; anger Σ.

477 on] in N.

480 Iaile] goal H K; jayle N T; gaol Σ.   haue] Y AA; hath Σ.

481 seely] silly Σ.

484 now] nor H–K M P; then N.

485 then] N(M *var:* than) Q Y Z DD; than   Σ.   loth] wrath   H–K M; wroth   N–P.

487 Tethlemite] Thelemite   H–K M N P; Tethelemite   O.

488 enters] Y; entred   Σ.

490 thus] was   N.   a new] anew   J.

491 lose] loose   N(M *var:* ~).

494 Chimiques] Q S Y Z DD; chemics'   AA; Chymique's   Σ.

497 Conduit] conduct   K.   hills] Q S Y Z DD; hill's   Σ.

499 it selfe] H Q S Y Z DD; itself   Σ.

500 lifes] Q S Y Z DD; life's   Σ.

503 sinewy] sinew   H–K M.

508 enowe] enough   H–K M N.

511 beest] bee   N.   readst] reade   N.

515 Or] And   N.   liues] lies   Z.

516 Cains] Q S Y Z DD; *Cain's*   Σ.

Subscriptions: *none*

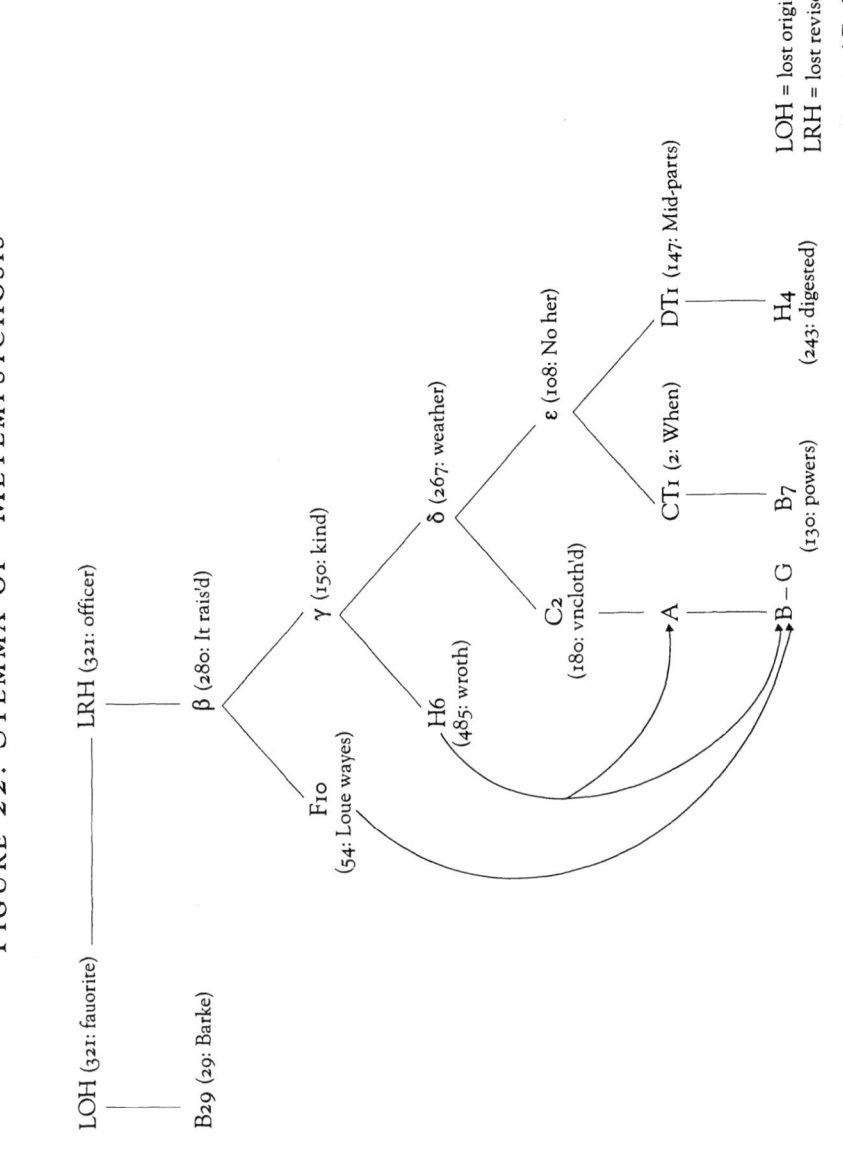

FIGURE 22: STEMMA OF "METEMPSYCHOSIS"

LOH = lost original holograph
LRH = lost revised holograph
unfiliated: AF1, B28, B51, IU2

Supporting Detail for Stemma of "Metempsychosis"

LOH (B29)
    321–22 …But **as a fauorite / Lies still at Court**…

    B29: To the distinguishing readings of the LOH adds the following:
       29 So diuers shapes, into that floating **Bark,**
       38 That (if my **paper** fitt) I may vnderstand

LRH (β)
    321–22 …but **as an officer / stayes in his Court**…

    β (F10 γ): To the distinguishing readings of the LRH adds the following:
     195 he ask's her Not who did soe **tast** nor when
     222 the Soule from her **to** Actiue Organs fledd

       F10: To the distinguishing readings of the LRH and β adds the following:
        54 And shall in sad **Loue** wayes, a liuely Spright
        69 And liu'd where euery **greater** Change did come

       γ (H6 δ): To the distinguishing readings of the LRH and β adds the following:
        27 **From** thence are all deriu'd that fill this All
        83 That Apple grew w.ch this Soule did *blank space*

         H6: To the distinguishing readings of the LRH, β, and γ adds the following:
          62 Doth dwell, and **moue** that **tongue, and hand**, and browe
          94 The daughters heere corrupt vs, **nothing letts**

         δ (C2 ε): To the distinguishing readings of the LRH, β, and γ adds the following:
          99 She sinn'd, we **here**, part of our payne is, thus
          267 To make the **Wæther** thynne, and Ayre lyke Fayth

           C2: To the distinguishing readings of the LRH, β, γ, and δ adds the following:
            69 And lived **when** every greate Change did come,
            180 Till her **vncloth'd** Child kick't & Peck'd it selfe a dore.

           ε (CT1-B7 DT1-H4): To the distinguishing readings of the LRH, β, γ, and δ adds the following:
            108 **No** her whoe was not then made; Nor is't writt
            252 And Iourneyes wth her, **toward** the Glassie Deepe

CTI-B7: To the distinguishing readings of the LRH, β, γ, δ, and ε adds
the following:
  6 ffrom infant Morne, **to** Manly noone I drawe
  27 (ffrom **then** are all deriu'd, that **fills** this All)

DTI-H4: To the distinguishing readings of the LRH, β, γ, δ, and ε adds
the following:
  128 Of sence **the** ffaith requires) swiftly shee flewe
  147 Grewe on his **Mid-parts**, the first daye, haire

ANALYSES OF EARLY PRINTED COPIES

Poems, by J. D., 4to, 1633 (siglum A)

Copies Collated: *CtY, DFo, L, M, MH, OJn, TxAM1*.

Relevant sections: A3–A4v, B–D⁴, E1–E2; 16 leaves; pp. [4] 1–27. A4v blank.

Press variants:

Sheet B, inner forme

	Uncorrected (MH)	Corrected (CtY, DFo, L, M, OJn, TxAM1)
B1v (p. 2):		
l. 13	east	East
l. 17	mine	Myne
l. 19	be	bee
B2 (p. 3):		
l. 31	commissary	Commissary
l. 34	instant.	instant;
l. 36	Ne're	Ne'r
Catchword	VII.	VI.
B3v (p. 6):		
l. 95	breake	breaks
l. 96	thrust	thrusts
l. 97	fled,	fled.
B4 (p. 7):		
l. 111	Spirit,	Spirit
l. 115	with	which
l. 119	perfect	perfects
l. 125	day.	day,
l. 130	th'earth-pores	th'earths-pores

Sheet B, outer forme

	Uncorrected (MH, TxAM1)	Corrected (CtY, DFo, L, M, OJn)
B3 (p. 5):		
l. 83	did	did enlive

B4v (p. 8):

| | l. 137 | Prince | Princesse |

Sheet C, inner forme

| | Uncorrected (*CtY, DFo, OJn*) | Corrected (*L, M, MH, TxAM1*) |

C1v (p. 10):

| | l. 187 | howre | houre |

C2 (p. 11):

| | l. 204 | soule, is | soule; Is |

C3v (p. 14):

| | l. 260 | wretch, so | wretch; So |
| | l. 260 | againe | again |

C4 (p. 15):

| | l. 280 | It | It's |

Sheet D, inner forme

| | Uncorrected (*TxAM1*) | Corrected (*CtY, DFo, L, M, MH, OJn*) |

D2 (p. 19):

| | l. 365 | they | they, |

D3v (p. 22):

	l. 427	plac'd end	plac'd, ends
	l. 427	feare	feare,
	Catchword	XLIV	XLIV.

Miscatchings:

	Catchword:		Initial Word:	Affects:
C4	XXX,	C4v	XXX.	*st* HE XXX.
D1v	XXXVI,	D2	XXXVI.	*st* HE XXXVI.

Note: In l. 503, the "i" in "bodies" does not fully ink in MH, L, and *TxAM1*.

§

Poems, by J. D., 8vo, 1635 (siglum B)

Copies Collated: CtY, MH, TxAM.

Relevant section: A5–A6, V5–V8, X^8, Y1–Y2; 16 leaves; pp. [3] 301–27.

Press variants: *none*.

Miscatchings:

	Catchword:		Initial Word:	Affects:
X3v	XXVII.	X4	XXVIII.	*st* HE XXVIII.
X5v	XXVI.	X6	XXXVI.	*st* HE XXXVI.

§

Poems, by J. D., 8vo, 1639 (siglum C)

Copies Collated: CtY, MH, TxAM.

Relevant section: V3–V8, X^8, Y1–Y2; 16 leaves; pp. 301–27.

Press variants: *none*.

Miscatchings: *none*.

Note: The apostrophe in "is t" (l. 108) on sig. V7v (p. 306) either does not ink or has dropped out of the chase.

§

Poems, by J. D., 8vo, 1649, 1650, 1654 (sigla D, E, F)

Copies Collated: 1649: CtY, MH, TxAM.   1650: CtY, MH, TxAM.   1654: CSmH, CtY.

Relevant section: V1v–V8, X1–X5; 13 leaves; pp. 290–313.

Press variants: *none*.

Miscatchings:

	Catchword:		Initial Word:	Affects:
V8	XXX.	V8v	XXIX.	*st* HE XXIX.

Notes: (1) Examination of multiple copies on the Lindstrand Comparator shows that the sections of 1649, 1650, and 1654 containing the Satyres are printed from a single typesetting, 1650 and 1654 being reissues of the sheets of 1649.

(2) During the press run, the terminal "s" in *justles* (l. 332) on sig. X1 (p. 305) deteriorated so that it does not ink well in some copies. It is barely visible in the *TxAM* copy of E and completely invisible in the *CSmH* copy of F.

(3) During the press run, commas following *resist* in l. 419, *come* in l. 423, *lust* in l. 433, and *judge* in l. 520 pulled loose from the chase; consequently, commas are missing in most of the copies collated though clearly visible in l. 419 in the MH copies of D and E, in l. 423 in the CtY copies of D and E and the MH copy of E, in l. 433 in the MH and *TxAM* copies of E, and in l. 520 in the *TxAM* copy of D.

§

Poems, by J. D., 8vo, 1669 (siglum G)

Copies Collated: *CtY, L, Mathews,** *TxAM*.

Relevant section: T7v–T8, V⁸, X1–X2v; 12 leaves; pp. 286–308.

Press variants: *none*.

Miscatchings:

	Catchword:		Initial Word:		Affects:
T7v	debt	T8	debt,		*Epistle*, l. 14
V8	XLI	V8v	XLI.		*st* HE XLI.
X1v	XLIX	X2	XLIX.		*st* HE XLIX.
X2	and	X2v	And		l. 506

Misnumberings: 191 [for 291], 307 [for 305], 308 [for 306], 309 [for 307], 310 [for 308].

---

*Elkin Mathews copy, in private hands.

Vpon Mr. *Thomas Coryats* Crudities.

Oh to what heigth will loue of greatnesse driue
    Thy leauened spirit, *Sesqui-superlatiue?*
Venice vast lake thou hadst seen, and would'st seeke than
    Some vaster thing, and foundst a Cortizan.
That inland Sea hauing discouered well,   5
    A Cellar-gulfe, where one might saile to hell
From Heydelberg, thou longdst to see; And thou
    This Booke, greater then all, producest now.
Infinite worke, which doth so farre extend,
    That none can study it to any end.   10
T'is no one thing; it is not fruite, nor roote;
    Nor poorely limited with head or foote.
If man be therefore man, because he can
    Reason, and laugh, thy booke doth halfe make man.
One halfe being made, thy modesty was such,   15
    That thou on th'other halfe wouldst neuer touch.
When wilt thou be at full, great Lunatique?
    Not till thou exceed the world? Canst thou be like
A prosperous nose-borne wenne, which sometime growes
    To be farre greater then the Mother-nose?   20
Goe then; and as to thee, when thou didst goe,
    Munster did Townes, and *Gesner* Authors show,
Mount now to *Gallo-belgicus*; Appeare
    As deepe a States-man, as a Gazettier.
Homely and familiarly, when thou commest backe,   25
    Talke of *Will* Conqueror, and *Prester Iacke.*
Goe bashfull man, lest here thou blush to looke
    Vpon the progresse of thy glorious booke.
To which both Indies sacrifices send;
    The west sent gold, which thou didst freely spend,   30
(Meaning to see'it no more) vpon the presse.
    The east sends hither her deliciousnesse;
And thy leaues must embrace what comes from thence,
    The Myrrhe, the Pepper, and the Frankinsence.

This magnifies thy leaues; But if they stoope   35
    To neighbour wares, when Merchants doe vnhoope
Voluminous barrels, if thy leaues doe then
    Conuay these wares in parcels vnto men,
If for vaste Tomes of Currans, and of Figs,
    Of Medcinall, and Aromatique twigs,   40
Thy leaues a better methode doe prouide,
    Diuide to Pounds, and Ounces subdiuide;
If they stoope lower yet, and vent our wares,
    Home-*manufactures*, to thicke popular faires,
If *omniprægnant* ther, vpon warme stals   45
    They hatch all wares for which the buyer cals,
Then thus thy leaues we iustly may commend,
    That they all kinde of matter comprehend.
Thus thou, by meanes which th'Ancients neuer tooke,
    A Pandect makest, and Vniuersall Booke.   50
The brauest Heroes, for publique good
    Scattred in diuers lands, their limmes and blood.
Worst malefactors, to whom men are prize,
    Doe publique good, cut in Anatomies;
So will thy Booke in peeces: For a Lord   55
    Which casts at Portescues, and all the board,
Prouide whole Books; Each leafe enough will be
    For friends to passe time, and keepe companie.
Can all carouse vp thee? No: thou must fit
    Measures; and fill out for the half-pinte wit.   60
Some shall wrap pils, and saue a friends life so,
    Some shall stop muskets, and so kill a foe.
Thou shalt not ease the Critiques of next age
    So much, at once their hunger to asswage.
Nor shall wit-pyrats hope to finde thee lie   65
    All in one bottome, in one Librarie.
Some leaues may paste strings there in other books,
    And so one may, which on another looks,
Pilfer, alas, a little wit from you,
    But hardly* much; And yet, I thinke this true;   *I meane from   70
As *Sybils* was, your booke is mysticall,   one page which
    For euery peece is as much worth as all.   shall paste
Therefore mine impotency I confesse;   strings in a booke.
    The healths which my braine beares, must be farre lesse;
Thy Gyant-wit o'rethrowes me, I am gone,   75
    And rather then reade all, I would reade none.

Textual Introduction

"Vpon Mr. Thomas Coryats Crudities" (Coryat) and a macaronic quatrain on the same subject (Macaron) first appeared in 1611 along with numerous other mock panegyric verses—many by friends of Donne—in one of the first travelogues published in England, Thomas Coryate's CORYATS Crudities, Hastily gobbled vp in five Moneths trauells in France, Sauoy, Italy, Rhetia commonly called the Grisons country, Heluetia alias Switzerland, some parts of high Germany, and the Netherlands; Newly digested in the hungry aire of ODCOMBE in the County of Somerset, & now dispersed to the nourishment of the trauelling Members of the Kingdome (STC 5808; siglum 6). That same year both Donne's poems were included in THE ODCOMBIAN BANQVET: Dished foorth by THOMAS THE CORIAT, and Serued in by a number of Noble Wits in prayse of his CRVDITIES and CRAMBE too (STC 5810; siglum 7), a (possibly pirated) printing of the encomiastic verses that prefaced the Crudities.[1] Although Macaron was not included in an edition of Donne's poetry until Chambers (P) incorporated it, Coryat appeared in the fourth collected edition of the Poems (D, and its reissues E and F), whence it descended to G and the subsequent modern editions; and lines 57–72 were published in Sheppard's MERLINVS ANONYMVS (siglum 33a). Except for that in AF1, a transcription of the text of G entered on blank leaves in a copy of A, no manuscript witness of the poem survives.

In both its earliest appearances in print—in the Crudities (6) and Banquet (7)—Coryat has no actual heading, but is introduced by the phrase Incipit Ioannes Donne, and the accompanying Macaron ends with the subscription Explicit Ioannes Donne, the two Latin tags thus segregating Donne's submissions from those of other authors. Deriving his text from either 6 or 7, the editor of D supplied the title "Vpon Mr. Thomas Coryats Crudities" by which the poem is now usually known and which we have adopted here. In addition to changing Donne's familiar form "wouldst" to "would" in line 3 and the past tense "longdst" to "long'st" in line 7 and adding an "s" to "sometime" in line 19 (producing "sometimes"), D introduces 3 substantive changes of greater significance—the trivializations "learned [for leauened] spirit" in line 2, "Garrettier" (for "Gazettier") in line 24, and "Tons" (for "Tomes") in line 39—and these descend to G, which adds the further substantive corruptions "hast" (for "hadst") in line 3, "hence" (for "thence") in line 33, and "as [for at] once" in line 64, as well as respelling D's "Tons" in line 39 as "Tuns."

---

[1] Separated from Coryat and Macaron by some 35 pages in the Crudities, another poem beginning "Loe her's a Man" and ascribed to "Ioannes Dones" has sometimes been attributed to Donne as well. It is presented as a dubium and its authorship discussed in a separate chapter of this volume.

In a pattern observed elsewhere in this *Variorum* (see the Textual Introduction for *Sat1*, e.g.), Tonson (H) takes his text from G, reproducing not only all but 1 of the major verbal changes which G had derived from D (in line 3 Tonson independently corrects "would" to "wouldst"), but also G's "hast" (for "hadst") in line 3, "hence" (for "thence") in line 33, "Tuns" (for D's "Tons") in line 39, and "as" (for "at") in line 64. I then follows H; J follows I (except—perhaps carelessly—respelling "Tuns" as "Tons"); and K reverts to H for its text. Also based on H, M reproduces the errors here itemized, as well as independently altering "hatch all wares" in line 46 to "thatch…," an emendation (or accident) not subsequently repeated; and Grosart (N)—though he claims to use the text of G—adopts H's text as well. The most noteworthy emendations in this whole series of editions are those introduced by Tonson in line 51, where for Donne's single word "publique" he substitues the phrase "their Countrey's" in order to provide the line a full 10 syllables, and in line 56, where the plural "Portescues" is rendered as a possessive ("Portescue's").

Below the heading of *Coryat* in Lowell's second edition (O) appears the date 1649, indicating that O's text is based on D, and—though it modernizes spelling—O does in fact substantively reproduce the text of D, including its various errors, except in lines 7 (where O independently corrects D's "long'st" to "long'dst"), 24 (where O independently—as had AF1 previously—corrects D's "Garretteir" to "gazeteer"), and 56 (where O accepts the possessive "Portescue's" introduced by H). Although for the first time since 1611 Chambers (P) retrieves *Macaron* from the *Crudities* and cites that volume's first printing of *Coryat*, he rejects (or overlooks) its authorial "leauened" (for D's "learned") in line 2 and "Tomes" (for D's "Tons") in line 39, producing (as is his wont) an eclectic text that combines not only 6's "Gazettier" in line 24, but also readings first introduced variously in D (as previously noted), G ("as" [for "at"], line 64), and H (the possessive "Portescues's" in line 56, which he accepts on grounds that the plural "casts at Portescues" is unidiomatic—see the commentary).

Also citing *Coryat*'s original appearance in 6, Grierson (Q) becomes the first editor since 1611 to print "leauened" in line 2, as well as following O and P in restoring 6's "Gazettier" in line 24. He appears not to have noticed "Tomes" in line 39, however, printing D's "Tons" and failing to mention the earlier reading in either his textual or his explanatory notes; and at other points of variance he also follows D, giving "would" (for 6's "wouldst") in line 3, "sometimes" (for 6's "sometime") in line 19, "medicinall" (for 6's "Medcinall") in line 40, and "there" (for 6's "their") in line 45, as well as following D's orthography throughout. Although he modernizes spelling, Hayward (S) otherwise reprints Q's text except in the single instance of "would'st" in line 3, where Q had retained D's "would."

Except that Bennett (T) modernizes spelling, while Milgate (Y) does not, their editions are otherwise highly similar. T adopts D's heading, but to it adds the date 1611 and—except that he updates such of 6's words as "then" to "than" and "leau's" to "leaves" throughout (in lines 33, 35, 37, 41, 47, and 67), introduces elisions and contractions in order to regularize meter (giving, e.g., "thou'dst" [for 6's "thou hadst"] in line 3), and corrects 6's "their" to "there" in line 45—prints 6's substantives exactly, including an elided "leaven'd" (for the "learned" introduced in D) in line 2, "sometime" (for D's "sometimes") in line 19, "gazeteer" (for D's "Garrettier") in line 24, and—for the first time since 1611—"Tomes" (for D's "Tons") in line 39. Y, too, evinces the heading introduced in D and cites 6 as copy-text, also (as usual) eliding and contracting various constructions in the interests of smoothing meter (6's "thou hadst" in line 3 is elided to "thou'hadst," e.g., and 6's "discouered" in line 5 is contracted to "discover'd"), but Y's text differs substantively from that of T only in line 39, where—although he cites 6's reading in his textual notes—Milgate prints "Tonnes" rather than "Tomes."

Shawcross (Z) also adopts D's heading and claims 6 as copy-text, but the accidentals of his text indicate that he actually follows 7, rather than 6. Among many details that might be cited in proof of this assertion are his alteration of every occurrence of 6's "leau's" to "leaves" except that in line 35 (where he gives "leav's"), a pattern exactly matching that of 7; his replication of 7's respelling of 6's misleading "their" in line 45 as "ther" (without the terminal e); and his replication of 7's spelling "lims" in line 52 (where 6 records "limmes"). In the interests of metrical regularity Shaw-cross, like Bennett and Milgate before him, imposes such elisions as "thou'hadst" (for "thou hadst") in line 3 and "discover'd" (for "discouered") in line 5, and he emends 7's "sometime" to "sometimes" in line 19; but he otherwise records 7's substantives accurately, including "leavened" in line 2, "Gazettier" in line 24, and "Tomes" in line 39. Except for rejecting the elisions "thou'hadst" and "Homly'and" that Z had imposed in lines 3 and 25, respectively; expanding Z's "makst" in line 50 to "mak-est"; and substituing a period after "Anatomies" (= "Anatomies.") in line 54 for the comma inserted in Z, Patrides (DD) reproduces Z's text exactly.

Finally, although he mentions that *Coryat* was first published in 6, Smith (AA) constructs, in his usual manner, a thoroughly modernized, eclectic text: with every modern editor except Bennett and Milgate, Smith emends 6's "sometime" in line 19 to "sometimes"; and in line 2 he prints the authorial "leavened" that Grierson had recovered and in line 24 the correct "gazeteer" first introduced in modern times by the Grolier editors. Though he notes the existence of 6's "Tomes" in line 39, however, he chooses the "tons" introduced in D.

Opinions on how to categorize *Coryat* generically varied among the early editors. The editor of D inserted it at the end of his section of "Funerall Elegies," where it precedes the newly discovered *Token* and a collection of prose letters, and it retained this postion among funeral elegies in G, as well as in Tonson (H) and Chalmers (K). Bell (I), Anderson (J), and Grosart (N), however, placed it with the Verse Let-ters, while Lowell (M) and the Grolier Editors (O) grouped it with the love elegies. Chambers (P) created a unique category of "Commendatory Verses" to include it and *Amic*, adding the previously neglected *Macaron* in a section of "Poems hitherto Uncollected." Following the lead of Grierson (Q), all twentieth-century editions of the complete poems (as well as Milgate's *Satires* [Y]) have grouped *Coryat* and *Macaron* in sequence at the end of the Satyres (apparently because his edition contains only "English" poems, Patrides [DD] excludes *Macaron*).

Copy-text Used in this Edition

Since no manuscripts other than the print-derived AF1 survive, the copy-text employed here is that of the first printing of the poem in the 1611 *Crudities*. In addition to correcting the printer's misleading "their" in line 45 (where we have adopted "ther" from *Banquet*) and his systematic misspelling of "leaues" as "leau's")—an irregularity also repaired throughout *Banquet* except in line 35 (see the apparatus)—we have altered the copy-text only in order to regularize an ampersand (&) in line 3 to "and." As noted above, the editor of D introduced the substantive errors "learned" (for "leauened") in line 2, "Garretteir" (for "Gazettier") in line 24, and "Tons" (for "Tomes") in line 39, and the correctness of "leauened" and "Gazettier" has appeared self-evident to all editors since the authorial lections were recovered, respectively, by Q and O. "Tomes," however, has not met with universal acceptance on the part of recent editors, going unnoted by Grierson and Hayward and being rejected—without comment—by Milgate and Smith after its recovery by Bennett. Bibliographically, it seems less likely that the compositor/editor of the *Crudities* received a manuscript from Donne that read "tonnes" (or "Tonnes") in line 39, mistook the 2 n's in the word for an m, and set the word into type as "Tomes" than that the editor/compositor of D, encountering the authorial "Tomes" in a poetic context that mentions "voluminous barrels" 2 lines previously (l. 37) and failing to understand the "Tomes"-"leaues" conceit employed in this passage, trivialized "Tomes" to "Tons." We have therefore retained the reading of the original *Crudities*.

Textual Apparatus

Copy-text: 6.   **Texts collated:** 6 (sigs. d3–d4); 7 (sigs. E2v–E3v); AF1 (pp. 440–41); D (pp. 262–64); E (pp. 262–64); F (pp. 262–64); G (pp. 260–63); 33a (*ll. 57–72 only*, sig. A2).

Emendations of the copy-text: Heading: *supplied.*   33 leaues] leau's   35 leaues] leau's   37 leaues] leau's   41 leaues] leau's   45 ther] their   47 leaues] leau's   67 leaues] leau's

Regularizations of the copy-text: 3 and] &

HISTORICAL COLLATION

Format:

Indentations: *even numbered ll. ind*   6; *1st l. ind*   AF1; *no ind*   7 D–G 33a. Font: *text in italics*   33a.

Miscellaneous: Incipit Ioannes Donne *introduces* Coryat *and* Macaron   6 7.

Headings: Upon Mr Tho: Coryat's Crudities.   AF1; *V*pon Mr. Thomas Coryats Crudities.   D–G;   *om*   6 7 33a.

1 heigth] height   AF1 D–G.

2 leauened] learned   AF1 D–G.

3 vast] *om*   AF1.   hadst] hast   AF1 G.   would'st] would   AF1 D–G. than] then   AF1; ~,   D–G.

4 Cortizan.] ~,   AF1.

5 inland] in-land   AF1 D–G.   Sea] ~,   AF1 D–G.   well,] ~ₐ   7; ~;   AF1.

6 Cellar-gulfe,] ~ₐ ~,   AF1 D–G.

7 longdst] longst   AF1 D–G.   see;] ~:   7 D–G.

8 Booke,] ~ₐ   7.   then] than   AF1 G.   all,] ~ₐ   7.   now.] ~:   AF1.

11 thing;] ~,   AF1 D–G.   fruite,] ~ₐ   AF1 D–G.   roote;] ~,   7 AF1; ~.   D–G.

12 or] and   AF1.

366

14 Reason,] ~‸   AF1 D–G.   halfe make] make half   AF1.

19 sometime] sometimes   AF1 D–G.

20 then] than   AF1 D–G.   Mother-nose?] ~‸ ~?   AF1 D–G.

21 then;] ~,   7 AF1 D–G.   thee,] ~‸   AF1 D–G.

22 Townes,] ~‸   D–G.   show,] ~;   D–G.

23 *Gallo-belgicus*;] ~·~:   7; ~·~,   AF1.

24 States-man,] Statesman‸   AF1 D–G.   Gazettier.] ~,   AF1; Garretteir.
D–G.

25 familiarly,] ~‸   AF1.   commest] com'st   7 AF1 D–G.

26 *Will*] ~.   AF1 D–G.

27 lest] least   AF1.

28 booke.] ~,   AF1 D–G.

29 send;] ~,   AF1.

30 spend,] ~.   AF1.

31 (Meaning] ‸~   AF1 D–G.   more)] ~‸   AF1 D–G.   presse.] ~,   AF1.

33 leaues] leau's   6.   thence,] hence,   AF1; hence‸   G.

34 Frankinsence.] ~,   AF1.

35 leaues;] leau's;   6; ~,   AF1.

37 barrels,] ~;   7 D–G.   leaues] leau's   6.

38 men,] ~;   7 AF1 D–G.

39 Tomes] tuns   AF1 G; Tons   D–F.   Currans,] Currants‸   AF1;
Currants,   G.

40 Medcinall,] medicinall‸   AF1 D–G.

41 leaues] leau's   6.

42 Pounds,] ounces,   AF1.   subdiuide;] sub-divide;   D–G.

43 wares,] ~‸   AF1 D–G.

44 Home-*manufactures*,] ~·~‸   AF1 D–G.

45 *omniprægnant*] omni-*prægnant*   7 AF1 D–G.   ther,] their,   6.   stals]
~,   AF1 D–G.

46 cals,] ~;   D–G.

47 leaues] leau's   6.

50 makest,] makst,   7 AFı D–G.   Booke.] ~∧   AFı.

51 Heroes,] ~∧   AFı D–G.   good] ~,   AFı D–G.

52 Scattred] Scattered   7 D–G.   diuers] diverse   AFı.   lands,] ~∧   AFı
D–G   limmes] lims   7; limbs   AFı D–G.

54 good,] ~∧   7.   Anatomies;] ~,   7 AFı.

55 peeces:] ~,   AFı; ~;   D–G.

56 board,] ~∧   AFı D–G.

57 Books;] ~,   AFı.

   Alternate line: No, one great Book, each leafe enough will be,   33a.

58 companie.] ~,   AFı.

59 No:] ~,   7 AFı D–G.

   Alternate line: All can't carowse like thee; no, thou must fit   33a.

60 Measures;] ~,   AFı 33a.   wit.] ~:   D–G.

61 so,] ~;   33a.

63 Critiques] Criticks   AFı D–G 33a.   age] ~,   33a.

64 much,] ~∧   33a.   at] as   AFı G 33a.   hunger] *hungers*   33a.
asswage.] ~:   AFı D–G.

65 lie] ~,   33a.

67 leaues] leau's   6.   there] ~,   33a.

68 *Alternate line: And so one may (which way so e'r he looks.)*   33a.

69 Pilfer,] ~∧   D–F.   alas,] ~∧   D–F.   you,] ~;   D–G.

70 much;] ~,   AFı 33a.   yet,] ~∧   7 AFı D–G 33a.   I thinke] *me thinks*
33a.   this] *tis*   33a.   true;] ~,   AFı; ~.   D–G 33a.

71 booke is] *books are*   33a.

72 as much worth] worth as much   AFı.

73 mine] my   AFı.   confesse;] ~,   AFı D–G.

74 healths] wealth   AFı.   beares,] ~∧   AFı D–G.   lesse;] ~,   AFı;
~:   D–G.

75 Gyant-wit o'rethrowes] ~∧ ~ ~   AFı; ~-~'~   D–G.   gone,] ~;   D–G.

76 then] than   AFı G.

Subscriptions: *I. D. / The end of Funerall Elegies.*   D–F.   *I.D.*   G.

Verbal Variants in Selected Modern Editions

Editions Collated:. H I J K M N O P Q S T Y Z AA DD.
Format:
>   Indentations: *ll. 21, 51, 73 ind* Y; *no ind* Σ.
>   Miscellaneous: *include* M *gloss at l. 70* Q S T Y Z AA DD.

Headings: *Upon Mr. Thomas Coryat's Crudities.* H I(Tho.) J(Tho.) K M N
>   O(Crudities. 1649.) P Q S T(Crudities. 1611.) Y Z AA DD.

1   heigth] heighth   S Y; height   Σ.

2   leauened] learned   H–K M–P.

3   Venice] *Venice'* H–K N–P T AA; Venice's   M.   hadst] hast   H–K M
N P.   would'st] would   O Q.   than] then   H–K M P S T AA.

7   longdst] long'st   H–K M N.

8   then] Q Y Z DD; than   Σ.

19   sometime] T Y; sometimes   Σ.

20   then] Q Y Z DD; than   Σ.

21   as] *om* J.

22   show] shew   J.

24   Gazettier] Garretteer   H–K M N.

33   thence] hence   H–K M N.

39   Tomes] T Z DD; Tuns   Σ.   Currans] Q S Y Z DD; Currants   Σ.

46   hatch] thatch   M.

51   publique] their Countrey's   H–K M N.

52   diuers] diverse   I J.   limmes] Y Z DD; limbs   Σ.

56   Portescues] Portescue's   H–K M–P.

58   to] *om* J.   keepe] ~ good to   J.

64   at] as   H–K M N P.

65   wit-pyrats] ~-piratos   J.

75   Thy] The   N.

76   then] N Q Y Z DD; than   Σ.

Subscriptions: *I. D.* H K.

Analyses of Early Printed Copies

CORYATS *Crudities*, 8vo, 1611 (siglum 6)

Copies Collated: C (SSS.29.17), CSmH, DFo (Copy 1), DFo (Copy 2), DFo (Copy 3).

Relevant sections: d3–d4; 2 leaves.

Press variants: *none.*

Miscatchings: *none.*

§

The Odcombian Banquet, 4to, 1611 (siglum 7)

Copies Collated: CSmH, CLU-C, WBU.

Relevant sections: E2v–E3v; 2 leaves.

Press variants: *none.*

Miscatchings: *none.*

§

Poems, by J. D., 8vo, 1649, 1650, 1654 (sigla D, E, F)

Copies Collated: 1649: CtY, MH. 1650: CtY, MH. 1654: CSmH, MH.

Relevant sections: S3v–S4v; 2 leaves; pp. 262–64.

Press variants: *none.*

Miscatchings: *none.*

Note: (1) Examination of multiple copies on the Lindstrand Comparator shows that the sections of 1649, 1650, and 1654 containing the Funerall Elegies are printed from a single typesetting, 1650 and 1654 being reissues of the sheets of 1649.

§

Poems, by J. D., 8vo, 1669 (siglum G)

Copies Collated: *CtY, L, Mathews,*[*] *TxAM.*

Relevant sections: S2v–S4; 3 leaves; pp. 260–63.

Press variants: *none.*

Miscatchings: *none.*

---

[*]Elkin Mathews copy, in private hands.

In eundem Macaronicon.

Qvot, dos *hæc*, **Linguists** perfetti, *Disticha* fairont,
  Tot cuerdos **States-men**, *hic* liure fara *tuus*.
Es *sat* a **my** l'honneur estre *hic* inteso; Car **I leaue**
L'honra, de personne nestre creduto, *tibi*.

Explicit Ioannes Donne.

A Macaronic on the Same.

As many perfect linguists as these two distichs make,
Just so many wise statesmen will this your book make.
It is enough for my honor to be herein understood; Because I leave
The honor, not to be believed by anyone, to you.

Textual Introduction

As is explained in the textual introduction to *Coryat* above, "In eundem Macaroni-con" (*Macaron*) was first published in 1611 as the second of Donne's 2 contributions to the section of encomiastic verses prefacing *Coryat's Crudities* (STC 5808; siglum 6) and its reprint *The Odcombian Banquet* (STC 5818; siglum 7), which—except for a blunder in *Banquet*'s setting of line 2—present identical texts of the poem. No manuscript witness survives. Among the seventeenth-century editions, *Coryat* was first gleaned from one of the 1611 printings for inclusion in D and appeared in the canon regularly thereafter; *Macaron*, however, was not similarly incorporated and—although printed and discussed in an 1865 exchange in *Notes and Queries* (see the commentary)—was overlooked by editors until Chambers (P) included it in a section of "Poems Hitherto Uncollected," separated by over 200 pages from the section of "Commendatory Verses" into which he had placed *Coryat*. Accepting the poem's authenticity and citing its appearance in the *Crudities*, Grierson (Q), Chambers's immediate successor, moved the poem to its original position following *Coryat*, grouping both with the Satyres. There it has remained in subsequent editions.

Although the contributions of numerous encomiasts intermingle various modern languages with Greek and Latin in the *Crudities* (Henry Peacham even writes "In the Vtopian tongue" [sig. l1]), Donne's lines constitute the most thoroughly macaronic single poem in the volume (see the commentary). Whether at Donne's behest or someone else's, the printer of the *Crudities* (which we follow here as copy-text) attempted to distinguished the various languages used in the quatrain typographically—setting the Latin words in italic type; the French, Italian, and Spanish in roman; and the English in gothic—and he succeeded in this design except in two instances, both of which we have emended: in line 1 we present the Spanish "dos" in roman rather than the original italic, and in line 3 we print "a" (which is in one of the Romance languages) in roman rather than the original gothic. The appended translation is that of Donald Dickson.

Textual Apparatus

Copy-text: 6.   **Texts collated:** 6 (sig. d4); 7 (sig. E4).
Emendations of the copy-text: 1 dos] *dos*   3 a] **a**

Historical Collation

Format:

    Indentations: *ll. 2, 4 ind*   6 7.

    Font: *text in gothic, italics, and roman*   6 7.

Headings: In eundem Macaronicon.   6 7.

  1 dos] *dos*   6 7.

  2 fara] fata   7.

  3 a] **a**   6 7.

Subscriptions: *Explicit Ioannes Donne.*   6 7.

Verbal Variants in Selected Modern Editions

Editions Collated:. P Q S T Y Z AA.

Format:

    Indentations: *ll. 2, 4 ind*   P Z; *no ind*   Σ.

    Font: *text in roman*   P; *text in gothic, italic, and roman*   Σ.

Headings: IN EUNDEM MACARONICUM.   P.   *In eundem Macaronicon.*
  Σ.

Subscriptions: *om* Z.   Explicit Joannes Donne.   Σ.

374

ANALYSES OF EARLY PRINTED COPIES

CORYATS *Crudities*, 8vo, 1611 (siglum 6)

Copies Collated: C (SSS.29.17), CSmH, DFo (Copy 1), DFo (Copy 2), DFo (Copy 3).

Relevant sections: d4; 1 leaf.

Press variants: *none*.

Miscatchings: *none*.

§

The Odcombian Banquet, 4to, 1611 (siglum 7)

Copies Collated: CSmH, CLU-C, WBU.

Relevant sections: E4; 1 leaf.

Press variants: *none*.

Miscatchings: *none*.

 # Dubium

Textual Introduction

In the 1611 CORYATS *Crudities* (STC 5808; siglum 6) Thomas Coryate included a poem beginning "Loe her's a Man" and attributed to one "Ioannes Dones," and the poem was included without change of attribution in *THE ODCOMBIAN BANQVET* (STC 5810; siglum 7), a (possibly pirated) reprint of the front matter of the *Crudities* published that same year.[1] As with *Coryat* and *Macaron*, no manuscript witness of the poem survives. Perhaps because it did not appear until some 35 pages after the *Coryat-Macaron* sequence in the *Crudities*, the first editor to connect the poem with Donne was Chambers (P), who in 1896 observed that although it "comes at a different place in the…[*Crudities*], and the name is differently spelt," he did "not doubt" that it was "by Donne" (2:297) and placed it in an appendix of "Poems Hitherto Uncollected." Subsequently, Grierson (Q), declaring that "[i]t may be by Donne, but was not printed in any [seventeenth-century] edition of his poems" (2:129), consigned the poem to a place among his notes to *Coryat* and *Macaron* and omitted it entirely from his 1929 one-volume edition of the *Poems*. In the 1914 and 1932 editions of his *Bibliography*, Keynes identified "Loe her's a Man" as Donne's, but in 1958 opined that it was "probably not by Donne" (129) and maintained that position in the 1973 4th edition. Keynes's change of mind may have been partly motivated by the argument of I. A. Shapiro, who—in a 1936 letter to the *Times Literary Supplement*—declared that "the rhythm and mood" of *Coryat* are "quite unlike, and much finer than, anything in 'Dones'' poem," but rejected Donne's authorship of the latter primarily on grounds of the spelling of the name and the separation of "Loe her's a Man" from the other Donne poems in the collection. Whatever changed Keynes's mind, Shapiro's argument did not dissuade Simpson, who—in the 1948 revision of her *A Study of the Prose Works of John Donne*—included "Loe her's a Man" among the "lines which Donne contributed" (47) to Coryate's volume. In the 1970 *Life*, on the other hand, Bald seemed to echo Shapiro, observing that "the orthography [of 'Dones'] is against" (193) the attribution. More recently, Centerwall (2003) has argued that "Loe her's a Man" was lost to the canon through an "oversight" (87) on Grierson's part and defended the authenticity of the poem. No edition since Grierson's has printed it.

---

[1]Opinion on who was behind the publication of *Banquet* is divided: Bald describes it as "a sort of preliminary puff" (192) instigated by Coryate himself prior to the publication of the *Crudities* proper; Craik (2004), on the other hand, thinks it "probably" produced "by Thomas Thorpe" (78), and Strachan (2006) speculates that "John Taylor may have been responsible."

Chambers's initial notice implies that he finds the style of "Loe her's a Man" compatible with that of Donne's other poems; and Shapiro, even though he thought the poem inferior to *Coryat*, concedes that "[w]hile there is nothing specifically characteristic of Donne in the style or language of 'Ioannes Dones's' lines to Coryate," if they are "read by themselves, there is nothing to suggest that they cannot be his." Both Simpson (47) and Centerwall (93–94) find evidence of the poem's authenticity in the fact that it shares with a prose letter attributed to Donne the Rabelaisian conceit of frozen words that become audible upon thawing,[2] and Centerwall further avers that it "uses rhetorical devices characteristic of Donne" (94). The remaining scholars cited above do not address the question of style explicitly, apparently regarding the attribution as a purely bibliographical matter involving (1) the separation of "Loe her's a Man" from *Coryat* in the volume and (2) the spelling of the author's name.

On these issues the evidence is not definitive, but seems to tilt against Donne's authorship. Plainly, Coryate gladly accepted—indeed, encouraged—multiple submissions from individual encomiasts; several besides Donne are represented by more than one poem. The beginning of each contributor's submission is marked by the Latin tag "*Incipit* [author's name]," the ending by a matching "*Explicit* [author's name]," and all of a given writer's poems are placed together between a single set of tags. Finding this method of grouping "always" to be Coryate's practice, Shapiro notes that 1 of the 8 poems contributed to the *Crudities* by Glareanus Vadianus stands apart from the other 7, but labels this instance "hardly...an exception" on grounds that the single poem is inserted in "the supplement" and concludes that "we are meant to take the contributions of "Ioannes Donne and Ioannes Dones as the work of different authors." Centerwall, on the other hand, bluntly rejects Shapiro's argument with respect to Vadianus—"an exception is an exception" (89)—and further points out that verses by both Laurence Whitaker and Ben Jonson appear in more than one place in Coryate's collection (which Centerwall defines to include not only the *Crudities*, but also *Coryats Crambe*, a subsequent work published in 1611 that prefaces certain other of Coryate's writings with a handful of commendatory verses that had been been "omitted" [sig. A2] from the *Crudities*). To Vadianus, Whitaker, and Jonson, Centerwall adds "Donne" / "Dones" as a fourth encomiast whose poems were not all grouped together.

Shapiro's explanation of this issue is the more persuasive. It is true that individual pieces of the overall contributions of Vadianus, Whitaker, and Jonson are dispersed throughout the *Crudities* (and the repetitious *Banquet*) and the *Crambe*, but Coryate's

---

[2](a) Appearing on f. 296v of LR1, the letter in question (Keynes no. 68a.6) begins "Sʳ That Loue wᶜʰ went wᵗʰ you" and dates from shortly after Essex's fall in 1599; it is transcribed by Simpson (p. 310), who attributes it to Donne and names Henry Wotton as the likely recipient (the editors of the ongoing OUP prose letters project have as yet reached no final conclusion on the identity of either the author or the addressee). (b) In a wide-ranging "meditat[ion]" (37) on Donne's uses of Rabelais, Prescott (1998, 40–43) also associates the aforementioned letter with the episode reported in *Pantagruel*, albeit hedgingly ("Whatever texts lie behind the letter's allusion to frozen words" [41]), and in a similar tentative vein links "Loe her's a Man" to Donne; in a later essay (2010) she avers that the "Dones" of the *Crudities* is "probably" Donne (173). In this regard it might be noted that "Dones" is not alone among Coryate's encomiasts in invoking Rabelais: the headnote to Laurence Whitaker's "Sonnet composé en rime a la *Marotte*" (sigs. d6r–v) describes Coryate as "cet Heroique Geant Odcombien, nomme non Pantagruel, mais Pantagrue...."

was clearly a fluid, cumulative enterprise to which various prefaces, introductions, and commentatory verses were added piecemeal as the work (which came to include the *Crambe*) lurched toward completion in the printing shop. Vadianus's stray (and final) poem in the *Crudities* appears in a so-labeled "supplement or ouerplus" of late-arriving "Panegyricks" to whose authors Coryate claims he "could not conueniently giue the repulse" without offending supporters who "most importunatly perswaded" him to include them (sig. i1). And the allocation of Whitaker's poems to separate parts of the volume is a function of the differing purposes served by each of the contributions: Whitaker's first poems (sigs. a1–a3), the initial verses in the volume, consist in a series of 29 "opening and drawing *distiches*" alphabetically keyed to and explicative of the 13 sections of an elaborate emblematic title page with which the *Crudities* is ornamented; his other poems—1 each in Greek, Latin, English, and French—are grouped on sigs. d4v–d6v among the subsequent collection of poems commendatory of the *Crudities* proper. Comprising 13 additional distiches on the title-page emblem and appearing on sigs. a3r–v, Jonson's first poems immediately follow those of Whitaker; then succeeds on sigs. b1–b3v a prose "Character of the famous *Odcombian*, or rather *Polytopian*, *Thomas the Coryate*...," ascribed to an unnamed "*charitable friend*" (sig. b1) but surely by Jonson as well (*Polytopian* is Jonson's signature word), and this leads directly to Jonson's second poetic contribution—an acrostic in praise of "...the Righ [sic] Noble Tom, Tell-Troth of his trauailes...and his *Booke*..." (sig. b4). A third Jonson poem, enclosed in the customary "*Incipit*"-"*Explicit*" tags and addressed "*To the London Reader, on the* Odcombian *writer, Polytopian* Thomas *the Traueller*," subsequently appears as the first item in the *Crambe* (sigs. A2–3), which—according to Coryate's headnote—contains "Certain Verses Written Vpon Coryats Crvdities, Which Shovld Haue been Printed with the other Panegyricke lines, but then were vpon some occasions omitted, and now communicated to the WORLD" (sig. A2). Coryate is vague about what "occasion[ed]" the omissions, but in the case of Jonson's poem, it seems at least possible that he deliberately withheld it from the *Crudities*, reckoning its function of addressing the "*Reader*" to have been fulfilled by the lengthy "Epistle to the Reader" (sigs. b2–b8) that he himself had already composed and calculating that it would be of greater value in promoting the *Crambe*.[3] Whatever the case, the circumstances here surveyed clearly indicate that the timing of submissions and the particular functions they served affected their placement within Coryate's volume(s). If "Loe her's a Man" is Donne's, its separation from *Coryat* and *Macaron* stands as the unique instance in the collection in which the dispersal of a single author's plural contributions cannot be accounted for by one or the other of these factors.

With respect to the second issue—the different spellings of the authors' names—the evidence again weighs against ascribing "Loe her's a Man" to Donne. In his "Introduction to the ensuing verses" Coryate boasts that the encomiastic poems prefacing his book constitute "*such a great multitude of Verses as no booke whatsoeuer printed in England these hundred yeares, had the like written in praise thereof*" (sig. c1v) and proudly asserts

---

[3] That the poem was not printed in the *Crudities* because Jonson had not yet composed it when the volume went to press seems unlikely in light of Coryate's explicit description of the verses of several other encomiasts in the *Crambe*—among whom Whitaker again appears—as "*made since my booke of Crudities came forth*" (sig. b2).

that they were *"composed by persons of eminent quality and marke, as well for dignity as excellencie of wit"* (sig. c1), further averring that he had read all the contributions aloud to Prince Henry before publication and had included them all at the prince's *"expresse commandement"* (sig. c1v). By 1611, of course, Donne's reputation as a poet was firmly established, and he was well known in the royal household, having, e.g., published *Pseudo-Martyr* and dedicated it to King James only a year before; and he was also well known to Coryate (who in other instances spells his name correctly) and to others who were involved in assembling material for the *Crudities*, including (especially) Jonson and Whitaker.[4] That any of these people would ignorantly have mispronounced Donne's name—which, as Shapiro notes, the "Dones" spelling would have required—is unthinkable, and for Coryate to have obscured Donne's identity deliberately would have been inconsistent with his program of self aggrandizement through celebrity endorsement. Further, given that Coryate had to focus on it specifically in order to supply the marginal glosses, "Loe her's a Man" can scarcely have slipped into the volume unnoticed; and, finally, as Dennis Flynn points out (private email), we have not a single holographic example of Donne's having spelled his own name other than "Donne" (though the s-like squiggle with which it frequently terminates may prove confusing to some modern readers—for examples, see Bald, facing page 213). In light of these considerations, it is hard not to agree with Shapiro that "we are meant to take the contributions of Ioannes Donne and Ioannes Dones as the work of different authors."

This conclusion does not obviate the above-noted arguments from style and similarity of Rabelaisian content, of course, which several critics have found compelling, and it leaves unanswered the question of who, if not Donne, "Ionnes Dones" might have been. Shapiro identifies two "similar but actually quite distinct surnames" in sixteenth- and seventeenth-century records—"Dun" (in various spellings) and "Dunch" (also variously spelled, but sometimes "Dun(ne)s" or "Don(n)es")—and refers to contemporary "records of a number of different persons, some of them quite unrelated, all bearing the name John Dun." It thus seems at least remotely possible that new bibliographical or historical evidence on the authorship of "Loe her's a Man" may yet come to light. In order to make the poem available for continued consideration, we here present a typographical facsimile of the text, including the marginal notes, as printed in the only authoritative source—the 1611 *Crudities* (siglum 6).

---

[4](a) In addition to the connection through the *Crudities*, Coryate and Donne are documentarily related in an account of those who attended a "Convivium Philosophicum" at the Mitre Tavern in September of 1611 and—in a 1615 letter from Ajmere, India, to the "Worshipfull Fraternitie of Sirenaical Gentlemen" who met regularly at the Mermaid Tavern in Bread Street—Donne was among those to whom Coryate requested that he be remembered (see Coriate, *Traueller*, p. 45; see also Shapiro, 1950, pp. 7–9, and Bald, pp. 190–95). (b) Among many, a signal example of Whitaker's central role in the production of the *Crudities* is his having listened to Coryate read the entirety of the *Crudities* aloud *"before it came to Presse"* (*Crambe*, sig. H3); Whitaker's familiarity with Donne is evident not only in their documented convival associations in the Mitre and Mermaid taverns, but also in Coryate's having specified him—in the 1615 letter from India—as one who would know where Donne was living at the time.

Incipit Ioannes Dones.

Loe her's a Man, worthy indeede to trauell;
Fat Libian plaines, strangest Chinas grauell.
For Europe well hath seene him stirre his stumpes:
Turning his double shoes to simple pumpes.
And for relation, looke he doth afford   5
Almost for euery step he tooke a word;
What had he done had he ere hug'd th'Ocean
With swimming *Drake* or famous *Magelan*?
And kis'd that *vnturn'd** *cheeke* of our old mother,
Since so our Europes world he can discouer?   10
It's not that [a] *French* which made his [b] *Gyant* see
Those vncouth Ilands where wordes frozen bee,
Till by the thaw next yeare they'r voic't againe;
Whose *Papagauts*, *Andoüilets*, and that traine
Should be such matter for a Pope to curse   15
As he would make; make! makes ten times worse,
And yet so pleasing as shall laughter moue:
And be his vaine, his gaine, his praise, his loue.
  Sit not still then, keeping fames trump vnblowne:
  But get thee *Coryate* to some land vnknowne.   20
  From whēce proclaime thy wisdom with those wōders,
  Rarer then sommers snowes, or winters thunders.
  And take this praise of that th'ast done alreadie:
  T'is pitty ere thy *flow* should haue an *eddie*.

Explicit Ioannes Dones.

* *Terra incognita.*

a *Rablais.*
b *Pantagruel.*

380

Appendix 1

Noncanonical Satires Printed in the Seventeenth-Century Editions

The two satires below—beginning, respectively, "Men write that love and reason disagree" and "Sleep, next Society and true friendship"—were implicitly ascribed to Donne by their inclusion in various manuscript compilations of his poetry, both eventually making their way into the seventeenth-century editions of the collected *Poems* (see Figure 1 in the Introduction to Volume 3 above). Included in the new material added to B from H6, "Men write" was inserted after the 5 canonical Satyres as "Satyre VI" and retained that place and number in the following four editions and issues (C–F). Under the title "A Satyricall letter, To, S.ʳ Nich. Smith," H6 also contained "Sleep, next Society," but beneath this heading the scribe had entered the admonition "Quere if Donnes or S.ʳ Tho: Rowes"; and this caveat, perhaps combined with the poem's incendiary characterization of King James in the end of the poem, apparently convinced B's editor to decline the poem. It was finally incorporated in the final seventeenth-century edition (G), however, where it was inserted among the Satyres as "Satyre VI," pushing "Men write" into the final position in the sequence as "Satyre VII." In the manuscripts, the poems bear various headings: "Men write" is called "A Satire: vpon one who was his Riuall in a widdowes Loue" in B2, but elsewhere simply "Satyre" (though ordinally numbered within several of the collections); including H6, "Sleep, next Society" is addressed to Sir Nicholas Smith in 9 of the manuscript headings, but is labeled simply "Satyre" (whether ordinally numbered or not) in the other 4. Among copies of "Men write," only H8—which includes the marginal annotation "Sr. Th: Roe" beside its heading—ascribes the poem to someone other than Donne; "Sleep, next Society," however, is tentatively linked to Sir Thomas Roe in H6 (and in its copy C9) and is directly ascribed to "I. R:" in DT1 (and its copy H4), but otherwise is explicitly (as in the case of H8) or implicitly attributed to Donne.

As noted above in the General Textual introduction, Tonson's 1719 edition of Donne poetry (H)—although generally based on G—curiously omitted "Sleep, next Society" and presented "Men write that love" as "Satire VI"; and the editions of Bell (I), and Anderson (J), which derived their text successively from H, followed Tonson in this particular. In a departure from his usual practice of replicating Tonson, however, Chalmers (K) retrieved "Sleep, next Society" from G and included both spurious satires in the order and numbering of G. Lowell's edition of 1855 (M), normally based on H, also followed H in presenting "Men write that love" as "Satire VI" and omitting "Sleep, next Society." As explained in the textual introductions to the various canonical Satyres elsewhere in this volume, Grosart (N) used B33 as the copy-text for Satyres 1–3, but reverted to G for the copy-texts of Satyres 4 and 5 and also derived from G the 2 spurious satires, presenting them in G's order and adding to "Sleep, next Society" the subtitle that he found in H7: "To S Nicholas Smith." Apparently following the precedent of Lowell (M), the Grolier Club edition (O) included only "Men write that love" as "Satire VI," while Chambers (P) included both spurious satires, "Men write that love" as "Satire VI" and "Sleep, next Society" (with the inscription to Nicholas Smyth) as "Satire VII" (see Table A on page xciv above).

Grierson (Q) rejected Donne's authorship of these two poems and determined that both were probably by Sir John Roe (1581–1608), his conclusion based on attributions and their appearance in sequences of poems known to be by Roe in authoritative manuscripts (2:cxxix–cxxxii). Presenting a fully developed critical edition of each poem based on a collation of manuscripts known to him and their treatment by prior editors, Grierson printed the two spurious Satyres, along with 7 other poems, in "Appendix B" under the heading "POEMS PROBABLY BY SIR JOHN ROE, KNT."[1] No edition of Donne's poetry since Q has included either poem in the canon, nor has Grierson's attribution of them to Roe been challenged.

In the interests of providing a historical perspective on Donne's reputation as a satirist, we here present reading texts of both "Men write" and "Sleep, next Society," basing each on its first printing in a collected edition of Donne's *Poems*. In H6, B's editor found a generally sound text of "Men write," and—though he misunderstood his copy-text in 1 instance and failed to correct 2 compositorial errors—handled it with characteristic concern for intelligibility, adding or changing about 30 marks of punctuation in order to clarify meaning or to align the manuscript text with the conventions of print (many of H6's sentences lack end punctuation, e.g.) and modernizing spelling throughout. The verbal errors include the misreading "Dry'd" (for H6's "Vrg'd") in line 17, the dittographical "some some" (for "some") in line 19, and the transposition "art rewarded" (for "rewarded art") in line 36, as well as 2 deliberate emendations: in line 18 the editor interpolates an elided "thou" in an effort to clarify meaning (changing the manuscript's "wouldst haue this" to "wouldst th'have this"); and—in an attempt to make sense of one of the poem's most difficult passages—he introduces a full stop after "allow" at the end of line 34 and changes H6's "Besides her…" at the beginning of line 35 to "Besides, here…." The result, which we have preserved in the text printed below, seems marginally more intelligible than the original "Doe what shee can, loue for nothing sheele allow / Besides her were too much gayne and m^{er}chandize." We have also left the remainder of B's text largely undisturbed, having only corrected the 3 aforementioned verbal errors in lines 17, 19, and 36; expanded "&" to "and" in line 23; and changed the punctuation in lines 28 and 33 (see the list of emendations below).

Although we have not attempted to develop a full stemma for the poem, a rough collation shows that the surviving manuscripts of "Sleep, next Society" form two distinct lines of textual transmission, which differ in over 2 dozen substantive readings. One version of the poem is preserved in 3 Group-III manuscripts (C9, H5, H6), in

---

[1] In addition to Grierson's discussion, see the account of Roe and his poetry in Ernest W. Sullivan, II, "Minor Poets of the Earlier Seventeenth Century," *Seventeenth-Century British Nondramatic Poets: First Series*, ed. M. Thomas Hester, vol. 121 (Detroit and London: Gale Research, 1992), pp. 321–23.

4 manuscripts Associated with Group III (H7, HH1, HH4,Y2), and in 2 unclassi-
fied manuscripts (B47, H8); the other appears in the Group-II artifacts B40, DT1,
and H4. It is not clear whether the alternate strains derive, respectively, from an
original and a revised holograph or whether, instead, each descends from a separate
scribally corrupted copy of a single original (is, for example, Group II's "he tells most
cunningly" in line 37 Roe's improvement over his original "…most perfectly," or is
"perfectly" a scribal trivialization of "cunningly"?); but it is clear that G derived its
text of the poem from a Group-II manuscript, and its replication of DT1's atypically
spelled "Huishers" (for "Vshers") in line 103 (which otherwise appears only in H8)
and DT1's unique "greatness [for *weaknes*] hide" in line 113 points to DT1 (or pos-
sibly a missing cognate) as that manuscript.[2] Whether or not the Group-II text of
the poem constitutes a separate authorial version, among its distinctive readings are
several that are clearly erroneous with respect to sense or meter, including, e.g., "In
which" (for the alternative "'Mongst which") in line 22, "only his skill" (for "touch
his…") in line 39, "but nere fought" (for "but so never fought") in line 41, "Winemill"
(for "Windmill") in line 42, "fathers ill" (for "father ill") in line 53, "if his Captaine"
(for "his Captayne") in line 65, "thou hadst" (for "hadst") in line 72, and "till I can"
(for "vntill I can") in line 133. Apparently on the basis of sense alone, G's editor
recognized several of these errors and attempted to correct them, changing "only" in
line 39 to "on" (yielding "on his skill"), "Winemill" in line 42 to "Windmill," and
"till I can" in line 133 to "till that I can." He allowed to stand, however, the barely
readable "In which" in line 22, the submetrical "but nere fought" in line 41, the unin-
telligible "fathers ill" in line 53, the nonsensical "if his Captaine" in line 65, and the
hypermetrical "thou hadst" in line 72. Further, he introduced on his own a handful
of verbal mistakes, including—among others—"slip" (for "skipp," which appears only
in Y2) in line 2, "thy [for *my*] dear friends" in line 4, "sound him" (for "soundly")
in line 31, "his [for *each*] Whore" in line 35, "Duel" (for "Duello") in line 39, "give
the [for *thee*] place" in line 83, and "Neither yet" (for "Neither") in line 100. And
G's editor was particularly maladroit in handling punctuation, as is shown—to look
at only the first 3 lines of the poem—by his introduction of a comma after "next" in
line 1 (= "Sleep next, Society"), his imposition of a full stop after "slip" at the end
of line 2, and his removal of the semicolon that appears in DT1 after "trouble" in
line 3 and punctuation of the end of that line with a period (= "the worlds troubles
rock me."). As with "Men write," our aim in presenting "Sleep, next Society" is to
groom the copy-text into readable shape with minimal intervention, but to do so has
required correction of the above-noted errors in DT1 for which G failed to provide
acceptable alternatives, as well as of G's independent verbal blunders and its more
egregious failures in punctuation. All these changes—as well as our repair of certain
of G's typographical lapses—are itemized below in Emendations of the copy-text.

---

[2] If, as seems likely, DT1 is the specific manuscript from which G derived "Sleep, next Society," the
editor obviously ignored the manuscript's marginal attribution of the poem to "I. R:," and he similarly
dismissed (or did not see) the caveat about the poem's authenticity that appeared in C9 and H6, to one
or the other of which he apparently had access (see *DV* 2:434). This casual attitude toward the authen-
ticity of the volume's contents likely springs from the same spirit that prompted his title-page advertise-
ment that the edition contained "*Divers Copies under his* [Donne's] *own hand, never before printed.*"

Satyre VI.

Men write that love and reason disagree,
But I ne'r saw't exprest as 'tis in thee.
Well, I may lead thee, God must make thee see,
But, thine eyes blinde too, there's no hope for thee.
Thou say'st shee's wise and witty, faire and free,   5
All these are reasons why she should scorne thee.
Thou dost protest thy love, and wouldst it shew
By matching her as she would match her foe:
And wouldst perswade her to a worse offence,
Then that whereof thou didst accuse her wench.   10
Reason there's none for thee, but thou may'st vexe
Her with example. Say, for feare her sexe
Shunne her, she needs must change; I doe not see
How reason e'r can bring that *must* to thee.
Thou art a match a Iustice to rejoyce,   15
Fit to be his, and not his daughters choyce.
Vrg'd with his threats shee'd scarcely stay with thee,
And wouldst th'have this to chuse thee, being free?
Goe then and punish some soone-gotten stuffe,
For her dead husband this hath mourn'd enough,   20
In hating thee. Thou maist one like this meet;
For spight take her, prove kinde, make thy breath sweet.
Let her see she hath cause, and to bring to thee
Honest children, let her dishonest bee.
If shee be a widow, I'll warrant her   25
Shee'll thee before her first husband preferre,
And will wish thou hadst had her maidenhead,
(Shee'll love thee so) for then thou hadst bin dead.
But thou such strong love, and weake reasons hast,
Thou must thrive there, or ever live disgrac'd.   30
Yet pause a while; and thou maist live to see
A time to come, wherein she may beg thee.
If thou'lt not pause nor change, she'll beg thee now.
Doe what she can, love for nothing shee'll allow.
Besides, here were too much gaine and merchandise,   35

And when thou rewarded art, desert dies.
Now thou hast odds of him she loves, he may doubt
Her constancy, but none can put thee out.
Againe, be thy love true, shee'll prove divine,
And in the end the good on't will be thine.   40
For, though thou must ne'r thinke of other love,
And so wilt advance her as high above
Vertue as cause above effect can bee,
'Tis vertue to be chaste, which shee'll make thee.

Copy-text: B (pp. 146–47).
Emendations of the copy-text: Line 17 Vrg'd] Dry'd   19 some] ~ some
   23 and] &   28 for] ~,   33 now.] ~,   36 rewarded art,] art rewarded,

Satyre VII.

Sleep, next Society and true friendship
Mans best contentment, doth securely skipp
His passions and the worlds troubles; rock me
O sleep, wean'd from my dear friends company,
In a cradle free from dreams or thoughts, there   5
Where poor men ly, for Kings a sleep do fear.
Here sleeps House by famous Ariosto,
By silver-tongu'd Ovid, and many moe,
Perhaps by golden-mouth'd Spencer too pardie,
(Which builded was some dozen Stories high)   10
I had repair'd, but that it was so rotten,
As sleep awak'd by Ratts from thence was gotten:
And I will build no new, for by my Will,
Thy fathers house shall be the fairest still
In Exceter. Yet, methinks, for all their Wit,   15
Those wits that say nothing, best describe it.
Without it there is no Sense, only in this
Sleep is unlike a long Parenthesis.
Not to save charges, but would I had slept
The time I spent in London, when I kept   20
Fighting and vntrussd gallants Company,
'Mongst which Natta, the new Knight, seized on me,
And offered me the experience he had bought
With great Expence. I found him throughly taught
In curing Burnes. His thing hath had more scars   25
Then Things himself; like Epps it often wars,
And still is hurt. For his Body and State
The Physick and Councel (which came too late)
'Gainst Whores and Dice he now on me bestows
Most superficially: he speaks of those   30
(I found by him) least soundly who most knows.
He swears well, speakes ill, but best of Clothes,
What fits Summer, what Winter, what the Spring.
He had Living, but now these waies come in
His whole Revenues. Where each Whore now dwells,   35

And hath dwelt, since his fathers death, he tells.
Yea he tells most cunningly each hid cause
Why Whores forsake their Bawds. To these some Laws
He knows of the Duello, and touch his Skill
The least Jot in that or these, he quarrel will,   40
Though sober, but so never fought. I know
What made his Valour undubd Windmill go
Within a Pint at most: yet for all this
(Which is most strange) Natta thinks no man is
More honest than himself. Thus men may want   45
Conscience, whilst, being brought up ignorant,
They use themselves to vice. And besides those
Illiberal Arts forenam'd, no Vicar knows,
Nor other Captain less then he. His Schools
Are Ordinaries, where civil men seem fools,   50
Or are for being there; His best bookes, Plaies,
Where, meeting godly Scenes, perhaps he praies.
His first set prayer was for his father ill
And sick, that he might dye: That had, until
The Lands were gone, he troubled God no more: 55
And then ask'd him but his Right, That the whore
Whom he had kept, might now keep him: She spent,
They left each other on even terms; she went
To Bridewel, he unto the Wars, where want
Hath made him valiant, and a Lieutenant   60
He is become: Where, as they pass apace,
He steps aside, and for his Captains place
He praies again: Tells God, he will confess
His sins, swear, drink, dice and whore thenceforth less,
On this Condition, that his Captain dye   65
And he succeed; But his Prayer did not; they
Both cashir'd came home, and he is braver now
Than his captain: all men wonder, few know how.
Can he rob? No. Cheat? No. Or doth he spend
His own? No. Fidus, he is thy dear friend,   70
That keeps him up. I would thou wert thine own,
Or thou hadst as good a friend as thou art one.
No present Want nor future hope made me
Desire (as once I did) thy friend to be:
But he had cruelly possest thee then,   75
And as our Neighbours the Low-Country men,
Being (whilst they were Loyal, with Tyranny
Opprest) broke loose, have since refus'd to be
Subject to good Kings, I found even so,
Wer't thou well rid of him, thou't have no moe.   80

Could'st thou but chuse as well as love, to none
Thou should'st be second: Turtle and Damon
Should give thee place in songs, and Lovers sick
Should make thee only Loves Hieroglyphick:
Thy Impress should be the loving Elm and Vine,   85
Where now an ancient Oak with Ivy-twine
Destroy'd, thy Symbole is. O dire Mischance,
And, O vile verse! And yet our Abraham France
Writes thus, and jests not. Good Fidus for this
Must pardon me, Satyres Bite when they kiss.   90
But as for Natta, we have since faln out:
Here on his knees, he pray'd, else we had fought.
And because God would not he should be winner,
Nor yet would have the Death of such a sinner,
At his seeking, our Quarrel is deferr'd,   95
I'l leave him at his Prayers, and as I heard,
His last, Fidus, and you and I do know,
I was his friend, and durst have been his foe,
And would be either yet; But he dares be
Neither. Sleep blots him out and takes in thee.   100
"The mind, you know is like a Table-book,
"The old unwipt, new writing never took.
Hear how the Huishers Checques, Cupbord, and Fire
I pass'd; by which Degrees young men aspire
In Court; and how that idle and she-state,   105
(When as my judgment cleer'd) my soul did hate.
How I found there (if that my trifling Pen
Durst take so hard a Task) Kings were but men,
And by their Place more noted, if they erre;
How they and their Lords unworthy men prefer;   110
And as unthrifts had rather give away
Great Summs to flatterers, than small debts pay;
So they their weaknes hide, and greatness show
By giving them that which to worth they owe:
What Treason is, and what did Essex kill,   115
Not true Treason, but Treason handled ill:
And which of them stood for their Countries good,
Or what might be the Cause of so much Blood;
He said she stunck, and men might not have said
That she was old before that she was dead.   120
His Case was hard, to do or suffer; loth
To do, he made it harder, and did both;
Too much preparing lost them all their Lives,
Like some in Plagues kill'd with preservatives.
Friends, like land-souldiers in a storm at Sea,   125

Not knowing what to do, for him did pray.
They told it all the world, where was their wit?
Cuffs putting on a sword, might have told it.
And Princes must fear Favorites more then Foes,
For still beyond Revenge Ambition goes.   130
How since Her death, with Sumpter-horse that Scot
Hath rid, who, at his coming up, had not
    A Sumpter-dog. But till that I can write
    Things worth thy Tenth reading (dear Nick) goodnight.

Copy-text: G (pp. 138–42).

Emendations and Regularizations of the copy-text: Heading: *Satyre* VII.] ~ VI.
Line 1 Sleep, next] ~∧ ~,   2 skipp] slip.   3 troubles; rock me] ~∧ ~ ~.
4 my] thy   14 still] ~.   15 Exceter] Excester   21 vntrussd] untrust
22 'Mongst] In   25 hath] had   26 Things] T[*blank space*]   28
late)] ~∧   29 Dice] ~)   bestows] ~:   30 superficially:] ~∧   those]
~.   31 (I found by him)] ∧~ ~, ~ ~,   soundly] sound him   33 what
Winter] ~ What ~   35 each] his   39 Duello] Duel   touch] on
40 these,] ~∧   41 so never] nere   42 go] ~.   46 whilst,] ~∧
49 he.] ~,   53 father ill] fathers ~,   54 sick,] ~∧   65 his] if ~
66 succeed;] ~,   68 how.] ~,   69 Or] or   73 me] ~,   81 love,]
~∧   82 Damon] damon   83 thee] the   86 Ivy-twine] ~∧ ~,   87
Destroy'd,] ~∧   Mischance,] ~?   97 last, Fidus, and] ~; and Fidus,
100 Neither.] ~∧ yet.   Sleep] sleep   102 unwipt,] ~∧   103
Cupbord,] ~∧   104 pass'd; by] ~: (~   105 Court; and] Court) And
106 hate.] ~,   111 And as unthrifts] ~, ~ ~,   113 weaknes] greatness
121 hard,] ~∧   122 both;] ~∧

Appendix 2

EIGHTEENTH-CENTURY IMITATIONS AND ADAPTATIONS OF DONNE'S SATYRES

More than any other of his poems, Donne's Satyres drew the attention of English critics and poets of the age immediately following, most of whom—if they agreed with Dryden that Donne's wit and force of thought were unmatchable—found his "Numbers" and his "Dignity of Expression" sorely wanting (see The Critical Influence of Dryden and Pope in the commentary). And this judgment prompted several writers to "translate" one or more of the poems into language conformable to current canons of taste, as well as to update the topical content of the poems with contemporary references. The most important of these adapters was Pope, who among his published Satires included not only his own versions of Satyres 2 and 4, but also a poetically updated rendition of *Sat3* by Thomas Parnell. Since the implicit critiques embodied in these poetical adaptations constitute an important part of the neoclassical response to Donne's practice as a satirist, we here present reading texts of all 3, basing each on its first appearance in print; and we also include a "versified" rendition of Donne's "Satyre I" by the cleric and poet William Mason, which—though likely composed in the 1750s—lay buried in Mason's commonplace book until its publication by Donald Low in 1965 (see Low 292–97).

Pope included his translation of both *Sat2* and *Sat4* in volume II of the 1735 edition of his *Works*, introducing them under the general heading "Satires of Dr. *John Donne*, Dean of St. Paul's," labeling them, respectively, "The Second Satire of Dr. *John Donne*" and "The Fourth Satire of Dr. *John Donne*," and inviting comparison of his translations with the originals by including italicized facing-page transcriptions of Donne's texts as printed in the edition of 1669 (G).[1] From this edition we take the text of the "Second Satire." We take Pope's rendition of *Sat4*, however, from a pamphlet of 2 years previously in which Pope printed the poem under the title "The Impertinent, or a Visit to the Court. A Satyr" and neither claimed the poem (the

---

[1]Pope's use of G (rather than the more recent H) as the basis of his translations is indicated, e.g., by his facing-page printing of the "jawes" (for "lawes") that G had introduced into the line of transmission in *Sat2* 112 and of G's correct "soul" in line 63 (where H had introduced "souls"); and Parnell's similar use of G is shown, e.g., in the facing-page printing of G's "but [for *and*] be wise" in line 3 and "all our Souls devotion" in line 6, where H omits "all" (Parnell translates this as "all our soul's devoutest flame"). It is impossible to tell whether Mason's adaptation followed G or H, but that it was one of the 2 is shown by his line 80 ("What troops to Nova Scotia ought to sail"), which renders the misconceived "Infantry of *London* hence to *India*" that G had introduced in Donne's line 58.

title page ascribes the poem merely to "an Eminent Hand") nor pointed out its basis in Donne's prior work.[2] Though it never appeared in an edition of his own works, Parnell's versification of *Sat3* saw print in Pope's edition (*Works*, Vol. II, Part II [1738]), which supplies the text presented here.

We here print these 4 adaptations in Donne's order, altering each as necessary in order to present a readable text. Having originally appeared in print, Pope's and Parnell's renditions require little editorial adjustment, as is shown in the brevity of the apparatuses with which they are accompanied. Mason's "versification" of *Sat1*, on the other hand, is unfinished, existing in what are essentially authorial foul papers, and to sort through the incompletions, cancellations, and interlined revisions in the effort to groom it into a publishable text that incorporates the author's final intentions entails considerably more intervention. In addition to imposing about 2 dozen regularizations of manuscript features, we have changed (or supplied) nearly 40 marks of punctuation and systematized the presentation of Mason's footnotes (which appear variously as footnotes or endnotes). We have also let stand readings in lines 12 ("St John") and 25 ("Nor tho") that Mason cancelled in the manuscript. The second of these is likely a simple slip of the pen that occurred in the process of revision; the former seems to represent a name that Mason intended to cancel, but for which he never found a replacement. Since both are necessary for metrical regularity, we have retained them in the reading text and noted the cancellations in the apparatus.

---

[2]Pope was an inveterate tinkerer with his texts. In further tweaking his text of "Satire 2" for the 1738 edition, e.g., he reverts from the name "Peter" he had previously used in lines 66 and 74 to Donne's original "Coscus." In revising the text of "The Impertinent" for publication as "Satire 4" in 1735, he added 14 lines between the current lines 31 and 32 and adjusted other wording throughout, including the extensive revision of what are here given as lines 72–77.

First Satire of Dr Donne Versified.

(by William Mason)

Away, fond Fop! mad motley thing begone.
Fatigued alike with thee and this vile town
I quit ye both, and henceforth swear to dwell
Here close immur'd in this small studious cell;
Here rest composd, till Lifes vain vision ends,   5
These shelves my world, these few choice books my friends.
See, here Religion marks her favrite band
Where Locke, Clarke, Warburton, and Berkley stand;
Here too obsequious Nature deigns to send
Her Secretary Newton for my friend;   10
Bold Politicians next a freeborn few
Harrington, Sidney, St John, Montesquieu;
Historians next their rightful Place assume
Theres all save Thomas Carte[3] and David Hume.
And last those chosen Bards whose tuneful toile   15
Bids Fancys roses bloom in Reasons soil.
    What? shall I leave this constant Company,
For Pride, Caprice, impertinence, and thee?
Well, for this once I will. Yet mark me, Sir,
I'll have ye under oath before I stir.   20
Swear first by your best Love, (but thats a jest,
He that loves evry one, loves no one best)
Yet swear you will not leave me in the street
For each dull Lord, or each pert fop we meet;
Nor tho D– – big Chariot passes by   25
With all in Gibbets proper Blazond high
Nor tho the silken fluttring x x come
Essencd and chaird from forth the Drawing room;
Yet still I'll hold thee strictly to thy vow
Tho x x nod an answer to thy Bow.   30
"What hard conditions? who can keep them Sir!

---

[3]Thomas Carte an Englishman as he is pleasd to let his readers know in his title page out of a pre-
sentiment that without that distiction he might from his Principles be thought a Frenchman, or some
slave of an arbitrary Monarch.

"Suppose we meet my good Lord Chancellor,
"How must I act if chance his train pass by?"
A reverent Bow with distant decency.
But nor to Him, nor all his worthy race   35
Ape G— cringe, and C—s frontless face.
What? shall each Knave, bait flattrys tempting Hooks
Because tis said they bit at Doctor x. x?
     Know, from my Soul I honestly disprove
Incontinence in friendship, as in Love.   40
Who calls me friend, must take me for his Life
For worse, and better, as he takes his wife.
     Starchly polite and formally refind
Thou Ape in person and thou Ox in mind
On Each new Lord thy impudence can gaze   45
And strait with Cox and Langfords[4] skill appraise
The Gold and silk he wears and at that rate
So high or low dost raise thy formal hat.
Thou knowst th'Estate exact of evry Person
What in fee-simple held, what in reversion,   50
If that be small hes no compeer for thee
And prudishly thou quitst his Company.
Fool! dost thou think with thy vast genius smit
He'll jointure thy dear parts and wed thy wit.
     But why scorn Virtue? one would think she'd please 55
A taste like thine so fond of Nudities
For Virtue's very naked; Nay I'll swear
The Medicean statue's not more bare.
And why this Love of Dress? At Death, and birth,
Naked we come, and Naked go to Earth;   60
And till our Souls put off this robe of Clay
Nor Bliss is theirs, nor Heavns eternal Day.
Innocence first was Adams only wear,
That lost, he borrow'd raiment from the Bear.
And I myself in this plain suit of mine   65
Sometimes hold dalliance with the willing Nine.
     But come methinks I see some sign of grace,
A Penitential Blush oerspreads thy face,
Therefore lets go. I'll try thee once for all;
And take a single saunter up the Mall.   70
Yet sooner shall Vanessas melting Heart
Maturely practis'd in the yeilding Art,
Who grants to all her Lovers all their prayrs
In buckskin Breeches or in Solitaires,

---

[4] two Auctioneers and large salesmen

Sooner shall she be able to record   75
Who gave the last sweet Prattler to her Lord
Than thou when thou departst from me can show
Whither, to whom or Wherefore thou wouldst go.
Sooner shall I who am no statesman tell
What troops to Nova Scotia ought to sail   80
And sooner *Long* thro tellescopic Eye
Poring on Saturns disk⁵ shall there descry
How long dread K x x oer learnings troop⁶ shall stand
Sage regulator of a Gown and Band.
  Yet now tis past and whatsoeer befall   85
I own most frankly I deserve it all
Who 'gainst my Conscience thus at highest Noon
Have dard appear with such a known Buffoon.
This said, we cross the Strand. Here first of all
Improvidently proud he takes the wall   90
And there confind and shoulderd up by me
Sells for some little state his Liberty.
Now tho he can't with arms expanded greet
Each skipping fop that flutters thro the street
Yet still the coxcomb Wink, the arch humbug,   95
The grinning smile, and the familiar Shrug—
All All are practisd oer with Wondrous Art,
Not Woodwards self could better play the part.
Meanwhile he inly longs to get away
Like Eaton Boys to pass their bounds at Play   100
And as for highest Notes Musicians know
To stop their strings proportionately low
So when some taller Officer he sees
He to his height adapts his low congees
But moves no more to any plain-drest friend   105
Than thou, O Chien savant! wouldst condescend
To shew thy tricks before some roguish spark
Who wantonly blasphemd thy grand Monarque.
  But now quite extacied he pulls my Coat
And crys "Nay Dearest Sir I beg you'd note   110
"Yon strait young Man of Quality; I swear
"I ne'er beheld so exquisite an air,
"In one year more Desnoyer I'll engage

---

  ⁵and surely if any thing relating either to this person or the affair he was engagd in was to be found out by Stargazing, where was it more likely to be predicted, than in the cold aspect of this dull and leaden Planet.
  ⁶the metaphor of Learnings troop is not without a peculiar propriety in this place, the great Legislator in his speeches to the Senate ex Officio, having been always fond of calling the members of it subditi and himself Princeps and Imperator.

"Makes him the finest Dancer of the Age."
Perhaps he may—and let him dance his fill   115
All I request of you is to stand still.
      Rebuk'd with this he got some paces on
Eer any shone distinguishd from the throng
But soon alass it was our happless doom
To meet a thing all powder and perfume,   120
A very nuisance to the public street,
Not A x x self more infamously sweet.
He stopt and squeesd his hand; I tip'd the wink
And said 'fore Heavn I'll not endure this stink.
Tis all in vain; however having spied   125
A goldlacd Peacock on the other side
He leaves the Civet Cat. Alone I wait
At last returnd, he thus resumes his prate.
"My friend the Peer I left beyond dispute
"Has the best fancy in a birthday suit,   130
"Others may have some taste, but he's your man
"To judge of Dresden or of Point d'Espagne,
"To place embroidry on a showy Colour,
"Then Gods! to see him cock a Kevenhuller."
Whats that to me? dost think I care a farthing.   135
Go recommend his taste at Covent Garden,
The Dull Comedians want him—Oh good-lack!
At Bow again! thoult surely break thy back.
"Nay Sir in my poor judgment I declare
"That Gentleman has quite a travelld air,   140
"Tis truly French." So is the Pox, what then.
He answers not but seeks more Gentlemen.
None comes amiss in his impartial Eye,
All All have parts and taste and Quality.
      Tir'd to the last I seize the cringing Spark   145
And drag him nolens volens from the Park,
When Fanny Murray seeing something odd
Pass by her window gave the Fop a nod.
An added smile set all his soul on fire
And thro strong vanity and some desire   150
Like liquid dew exhald away he hies,
Crosses the street and to her Lodgings flys,
Bounces up stairs and opes her chamber door
When (sad to tell!) Sᵣ Dick was there before.
Kickd Boxd and Cudgelld by the angry Knight   155
Home and to bed he steals in piteous plight
And had he gaind the Fair and lov'd his fill
He'd scarce have earnd a longer Surgeons Bill.

Copy-text: William Mason's Commonplace Book, York Minster Library, pp. 19–24.

Emendations of the copy-text: Line 21 jest,] ~ᴧ   30 Bow.] ~ᴧ   33 by?"] ~?ᴧ   36 face.] ~ᴧ   48 hat.] ~ᴧ   50 held,] ~ᴧ   reversion,] ~ᴧ   52 Company.] ~ᴧ   67 grace,] ~ᴧ   68 face,] ~ᴧ   72 Art,] ~ᴧ   74 Solitaires,] ~ᴧ   78 go.] ~ᴧ   82 fn3 to be found] so ~ ~   92 Liberty.] ~ᴧ   95 humbug,] ~ᴧ   96 Shrug—] ~ᴧ   97 Art,] ~ᴧ   106 thou,] ~ᴧ   108 Monarque.] ~ᴧ   112 air,] ~ᴧ   120 perfume,] ~ᴧ   121 street,] ~ᴧ   122 sweet.] ~ᴧ   123 hand;] ~ᴧ   125 vain;] ~ᴧ   130 suit,] ~ᴧ   132 d'Espagne,] ~ᴧ   133 Colour,] ~ᴧ   136 Garden,] ~ᴧ   138 back.] ~ᴧ   141 French."] ~ᴧ"   142 Gentlemen.] ~ᴧ   140 air,] ~ᴧ   143 Eye,] ~ᴧ   146 Park,] ~ᴧ   148 nod.] ~ᴧ   151 hies,] ~ᴧ   152 flys,] ~ᴧ   154 before.] ~ᴧ

Regularizations of the copy-text: Heading: *italics and attribution supplied*   Line 8 and] &   12 Sᵗ John] Sᵗ John   14 and] &   18 and] &   19 Yet] yet   20 I'll] Ill   25 Nor tho] Nor tho   28 and] &   29 I'll] Ill   36 and] &   44 and] &   46 fn2 and] &   47 and] &   57 I'll] Ill   69 I'll] Ill   81 *Long*] Long   84 and] &   89 Here] here   96 and] &   113 I'll] Ill   120 and] &   123 and] &   124 I'll] Ill   138 At] at   141 So] so   144 and] & and] &   152 and] &

THE SECOND SATIRE OF Dr. *JOHN DONNE.*

(by Alexander Pope)

YES; thank my stars! as early as I knew
This Town, I had the sense to hate it too:
Yet here, as ev'n in Hell, there must be still
One Giant-Vice, so excellently ill,
That all beside one pities, not abhors;   5
As who knows *Sa* * *, smiles at other whores.
    I grant that Poetry's a crying sin;
It brought (no doubt) th' *Excise* and *Army* in:
Catch'd like the Plague, or Love, the lord knows how,
But that the cure is starving, all allow.   10
Yet like the Papists, is the Poets state,
Poor and disarm'd, and hardly worth your hate.
    Here a lean Bard whose wit could never give
Himself a dinner, makes an Actor live:
The Thief condemn'd in law already dead,   15
So prompts, and saves a rogue who cannot read.
Thus as the pipes of some carv'd Organ move,
The gilded puppets dance and mount above,
Heav'd by the breath, th' inspiring bellows blow:
Th' inspiring bellows lie and pant below.   20
    One sings the Fair; but songs no longer move,
No rat is rhym'd to death, nor maid to love:
In love's, in nature's spite, the siege they hold,
And scorn the flesh, the dev'l, and all but gold.
    These write to Lords, some mean reward to get,   25
As needy beggars sing at doors for meat.
Those write because all write, and so have still
Excuse for writing and for writing ill.
    Wretched indeed! but far more wretched yet
Is he who makes his meal on others wit: 30
'Tis chang'd indeed from what it was before.
His rank digestion makes it wit no more:
Sense, past thro' him, no longer is the same,
For food digested takes another name.

I pass o'er all those Confessors and Martyrs 35
Who live like *S–tt–n*, or who die like *Charters*,
Out-cant old *Esdras*, or out-drink his heir,
Out-usure *Jews*, or *Irishmen* out-swear;
Wicked as pages, who in early years
Act sins which *Prisca's* Confessor scarce hears: 40
Ev'n those I Pardon, for whose sinful sake
Schoolmen new tenements in hell must make;
Of whose strange crimes no Canonist can tell
In what Commandment's large contents they dwell.
One, one man only breeds my just offence; 45
Whom crimes gave wealth, and wealth gave impudence:
Time, that at last, matures a clap to pox,
Whose gentle progress makes a calf an ox,
And brings all natural events to pass,
Hath made him an Attorney of an Ass. 50
No young divine, new-benefic'd, can be
More pert, more proud, more positive than he.
What further could I wish the fop to do,
But turn a wit, and scribble verses too?
Pierce the soft lab'rinth of a Lady's ear 55
With rhymes of this *per cent.* and that *per year*?
To court a wife, and spread his wily parts,
Like nets or lime-twigs, for rich widows hearts?
Call himself Barrister to ev'ry wench,
And wooe in language of the Pleas and Bench? 60
Language, which *Boreas* might to *Auster* hold,
More rough than forty *Germans* when they scold.
Curs'd be the wretch so venal and so vain;
Paltry and proud, as drabs in *Drury-lane.*
'Tis such a bounty as was never known, 65
If *Peter* deigns to help you to your *own*:
What thanks, what praise, if *Peter* but supplies!
And what a solemn face if he denies!
Grave, as when pris'ners shake the head, and swear
'Twas only Suretyship that brought 'em there. 70
His *Office* keeps your Parchment-fates entire,
He starves with cold to save them from the fire;
For you, he walks the streets thro' rain or dust,
For not in Chariots *Peter* puts his trust;
For you he sweats and labours at the laws, 75
Takes God to witness he affects your cause,
And lies to every Lord in every thing,
Like a King's Favourite—or like a King.

These are the talents that adorn them all,
From wicked *Waters* ev'n to godly ——   80
Not more of Simony beneath black gowns,
Nor more of bastardy in heirs to Crowns.
In shillings and in pence at first they deal,
And steal so little, few perceive they steal;
Till like the sea, they compass all the land,   85
From *Scots* to *Wight*, from *Mount* to *Dover* strand.
And when rank widows purchase luscious nights,
Or when a Duke to *Jansen* punts at *White's*,
Or city heir in mortgage melts away,
Satan himself feels far less joy than they.   90
Piecemeal they win this acre first, then that,
Glean on, and gather up the whole estate.
Then strongly fencing ill-got wealth by law,
Indentures, Cov'nants, Articles they draw,
Large as the fields themselves, and larger far   95
Than civil *Codes*, with all their glosses are;
So vast, our new Divines, we must confess,
Are fathers of the Church for writing less.
But let them write for you, each rogue impairs
The deeds, and dextrously omits, *ses heires:*   100
No commentator can more slily pass
O'er a learn'd, unintelligible place;
Or, in quotation, shrewd divines leave out
Those words, that would against them clear the doubt.
    So *Luther* thought the Pater noster long.   105
When doom'd to say his beads and Evensong;
But having cast his cowle, and left those laws,
Adds to Christ's prayer, the *Pow'r and Glory* clause.
    The lands are bought; but where are to be found
Those ancient woods, that shaded all the ground?   110
We see no new-built palaces aspire,
No kitchens emulate the vestal fire.
Where are those troops of Poor, that throng'd of yore
The good old landlord's hospitable door?
Well, I could wish, that still in lordly domes   115
Some beasts were kill'd, tho' not whole hecatombs;
That both extremes were banish'd from their walls,
Carthusian fasts, and fulsome *Bacchanals*;
And all mankind might that just Mean observe,
In which none e'er could surfeit, none could starve.   120
These as good works 'tis true we all allow;
But, oh! these works are not in fashion now:

Like rich old wardrobes, things extremely rare,
Extremely fine, but what no man will wear.
  Thus much I've said, I trust without offence;   125
Let no Court Sycophant pervert my sense,
Nor sly Informer watch these words to draw
Within the reach of Treason, or the Law.

Copy-text: Pope, *Works*, Vol. II, 1735, pp. 132–41.
Emendations of the copy-text: Line 57 parts,] ~.
Regularizations of the copy-text: Heading: *attribution supplied*   Line 70
  brought] broughr

THE THIRD SATIRE OF Dr. *JOHN DONNE:*
By Dr. PARNELLE.

Compassion checks my spleen, yet Scorn denies
The tears a passage thro' my swelling eyes;
To *laugh* or *weep* at sins, might idly show,
Unheedful passion, or unfruitful woe.
Satyr! arise, and try thy sharper ways,   5
If ever Satyr cur'd an old disease.
    Is not *Religion* (Heav'n-descended dame)
As worthy all our soul's devoutest flame,
As Moral Virtue in her early sway,
When the best Heathens saw by doubtful day?   10
Are not the joys, the promis'd joys above,
As great and strong to vanquish earthly love,
As earthly glory, fame, respect and show,
As all rewards their virtue found below?
Alas! Religion proper means prepares,   15
These means are ours, and must its *End* be theirs?
And shall thy Father's spirit meet the sight
Of Heathen Sages cloath'd in heavenly light,
Whose Merit of strict life, severely suited
To Reason's dictates, may be *faith* imputed?   20
Whilst thou, to whom he taught the nearer road,
Art ever banish'd from the bless'd abode.
    Oh! if thy temper such a fear can find,
This fear were valour of the noblest kind.
    Dar'st thou provoke, when rebel souls aspire,   25
Thy *Maker's* Vengeance, and thy *Monarch's* Ire?
Or live entomb'd in ships, thy leader's prey,
Spoil of the war, the famine, or the sea?
In search of *pearl*, in depth of ocean breathe,
Or live, exil'd the sun, in mines beneath?   30
Or, where in tempests icy mountains roll,
Attempt a passage by the Northern pole?
Or dar'st thou parch within the fires of *Spain*,
Or burn beneath the line, for Indian gain?

Or for some *Idol* of thy *Fancy* draw,   35
Some loose-gown'd dame; O courage made of straw!
Thus, desp'rate Coward! would'st thou bold appear,
Yet when thy God has plac'd thee Centry here,
To thy own foes, to *his*, ignobly yield,
And leave, for wars forbid, the appointed field?   40
    Know thy own foes; th' *Apostate Angel*, he
You strive to please, the foremost of the Three;
He makes the pleasures of his realm the bait,
But can *he* give for *Love*, that acts in *Hate?*
The *World*'s thy second Love, thy second Foe,   45
The *World*, whose beauties perish as they blow,
They fly, she fades herself, and at the best
You grasp a wither'd strumpet to your breast.
The *Flesh* is next, which in fruition wasts,
High flush'd with all the sensual joys it tasts,   50
While men the fair, the goodly *Soul* destroy,
From whence the *flesh* has pow'r to tast a joy.
    Seek thou Religion, primitively sound—
Well, gentle friend, but where may she be found?
    By Faith *Implicite* blind *Ignaro* led,   55
Thinks the bright Seraph from *his* Country fled,
And seeks her seat at Rome, because we know
She there was seen a thousand years ago;
And loves her Relick rags, as men obey
The *foot-cloth* where the Prince sat yesterday.   60
    These pageant Forms are whining *Obed*'s scorn,
Who seeks Religion at *Geneva* born,
A sullen thing, whose coarsness suits the crowd,
Tho' young, unhandsome; tho' unhandsome, proud:
Thus, with the wanton, some perversely judge   65
All girls unhealthy but the Country drudge.
    No foreign schemes make easy *Cæpio* roam,
The man contented takes his Church at home;
Nay should some Preachers, servile bawds of gain,
Shou'd some new Laws, which like new-fashions reign,   70
Comand his faith to count *Salvation* ty'd
To visit *his*, and visit *none* beside,
He grants Salvation centers in his own,
And grants it centers but in his *alone:*
From youth to age he grasps the proffer'd dame,   75
And *they* confer his *Faith*, who give his *Name:*
So from the Guardian's hands, the Wards who live
Enthral'd to Guardians, take the wives they give.

From all possessions careless *Airy* flies,
For, *all* professions can't be good, he cries,   80
And here a fault, and there another views,
And lives unfix'd for want of heart to chuse:
So men, who know what *some* loose girls have done,
For fear of marrying *such*, will marry *none*.

The Charms of *all*, obsequious *Courtly* strike;   85
On each he doats, on each attends alike;
And thinks, as diff'rent countrys deck the dame,
The dresses altering, and the sex the same;
So fares Religion, chang'd in outward show,
But 'tis Religion still, where'er we go: 90
This blindness springs from an excess of light,
And men embrace the *wrong* to chuse the *right*.

But *thou* of force must *one* Religion own,
And only *one*, and that the *Right* alone.
To find that *Right one*, ask thy Reverend Sire;   95
Let him of his, and him of *his* enquire;
Tho' *Truth* and *Falshood* seem as twins ally'd,
There's Eldership on *Truth's* delightful side,
Her seek with heed—who seeks the soundest *First*
Is not of *No* Religion, nor the *worst*.   100
T'*adore*, or *scorn* an Image, or *protest*,
May *all* be bad: doubt wisely for the best;
'Twere wrong to sleep, or headlong run astray;
It is not wandring, to inquire the way.

On a large mountain, at the Basis wide,   105
Steep to the top, and craggy at the side,
Sits sacred *Truth* enthron'd; and he, who means
To reach the summit, mounts with weary pains,
Winds round and round, and every turn essays
Where sudden breaks resist the shorter ways.   110

Yet labour so, that, e're faint age arrive,
Thy searching soul possess her Rest alive;
To work by twilight were to work too late,
And *Age* is twilight to the night of *fate*.
To *will* alone, is but to mean delay;   115
To work at *present* is the use of day:
For man's employ much thought and deed remain,
High *Thoughts* the *Soul*, hard *deeds* the *body* strain:
And *Myst'ries* ask believing, which to View
Like the fair *Sun*, are plain, but dazling too.   120

Be *Truth*, so found, with sacred heed possest,
Not *Kings* have pow'r to tear it from thy breast,

By no blank Charters harm they where they hate,
Nor are they *Vicars*, but the *hands* of Fate.
Ah! fool and wretch, who let'st thy soul be ty'd   125
To *human* Laws! Or must it *so* be try'd?
Or will it boot thee, at the latest day,
When Judgment sits, and Justice asks thy plea,
That *Philip* that, or *Greg'ry* taught thee this,
Or *John* or *Martin? All* may teach amiss: 130
For, every contrary in each Extream
This holds alike, and each may plead the same.
    Wou'dst thou to *Pow'r* a proper duty shew?
'Tis thy first task the bounds of pow'r to know;
The *bounds* once past, it holds the name no more,   135
Its nature alters, which it own'd before,
Nor were submission humbleness exprest,
But all a low *Idolatry* at best.
    Pow'r, from above subordinately spread,
Streams like a fountain from th'eternal head;   140
There, calm and pure the living waters flow,
But roar a Torrent or a Flood *below*;
Each flow'r, ordain'd the Margins to adorn,
Each native Beauty, from its roots is torn,
And left on Deserts, Rocks and Sands, or tost   145
All the long travel, and in Ocean lost:
So fares the soul, which more that Pow'r reveres
Man claims from God, than what in God inheres.

Copy-text: Pope, *Works*, Vol. II, Part II, 1738, pp. 151–63.

THE IMPERTINENT, OR A Visit to the COURT.
A SATYR.
By an Eminent Hand.

(by Alexander Pope)

WELL, if it be my time to quit the Stage,
Adieu to all the Follies of the Age!
I die in Charity with Fool and Knave,
Secure of Happiness beyond the Grave.
I've had my *Purgatory* here betimes,   5
And paid for all my Satires, all my Rhymes:
The Poet's Hell, its Tortures, Fiends and Flames,
To this were Trifles, Toys, and empty Names.
    With foolish *Pride* my Heart was never fir'd,
Nor the vain Itch *t'admire*, or *be admir'd*;   10
I hop'd for no *Commission* from his Grace;
I bought no *Benefice*, I begg'd no *Place*;
Had no *new Verses*, nor *new Suit* to show;
Yet went to COURT!—the Dev'l wou'd have it so.
But, as the Fool, that in reforming Days   15
Wou'd go to Mass in jest, (as Story says)
Could not but think, to pay his *Fine* was odd,
Since 'twas no form'd Design of serving God:
Such was my Fate; whom Heav'n adjudg'd as *proud*,
As prone to *Ill*, as negligent of *Good*,   20
As deep in *Debt*, without a thought to pay, ⎱
As *vain*, as *idle*, and as *false*, as they ⎬
Who *live* at *Court*, for going once that Way! ⎰
    Scarce was I enter'd, when behold! there came
A Thing which *Adam* had been pos'd to name;   25
Noah had refus'd it lodging in his Ark,
Where all the Race of *Reptiles* might embark:
A verier Monster than on *Africk*'s Shore
The Sun e'er got, or slimy *Nilus* bore,
Or *Sloane*, or *Woodward*'s wondrous Shelves contain;   30
Nay, all that lying Travellers can feign.

This Thing has *travell'd*, speaks each Language too,
And knows what's fit for ev'ry State to do;
Of whose best Phrase and courtly Accent join'd,
He forms one Tongue exotic and refin'd.   35
Talkers, I've learn'd to bear; M–*tt*––*x* I knew,
Henley himself I've heard, nay *B–dg–l* too:
The Doctor's Wormwood Style, the Hash of Tongues,
A Pedant makes; the Storm of G––*s–n*'s Lungs,
The whole Artill'ry of the Terms of War,   40
And (all those Plagues in one) the bawling Bar;
These I cou'd bear; but not a Rogue so civil,
Whose Tongue can complement you to the Devil.
A Tongue that can cheat Widows, cancel Scores,
Make *Scots* speak Treason, cozen subtlest Whores,   45
With Royal Favourites in Flatt'ry vie,
And *Oldmixon* and *Burnet* both out-lie.
    He spies me out. I whisper, gracious God!
What Sin of mine cou'd merit such a Rod?
That all the Shot of Dulness now must be   50
From this thy Blunderbuss discharg'd on me!
Well met (he cries) and happy sure for each,
For I am pleas'd to learn, and you to teach;
What *Speech* esteem you most?—"The *King's*," said I,
But the best *Words?*—"O Sir, the *Dictionary.*"   55
You miss my aim; I mean the most acute
And perfect *Speaker?*—"*Onslow*, past dispute."
But Sir, of Writers?—"*Swift*, for closer Style,
"And *Ho*—*y* for a Period of a Mile."
Why yes, 'tis granted, these indeed may pass;   60
Good common Linguists, and so *Panurge* was:
Nay troth, th'*Apostles*, (tho' perhaps too rough)
Had once a pretty Gift of Tongues enough.
Yet these were all *poor Gentlemen!* I dare
Affirm, 'twas *Travel* made them what they were.   65
    Thus others Talents having nicely shown,
He came by soft Transition to his own:
Till I cry'd out, You prove yourself so able,
Pity! you was not Druggerman at *Babel:*
For had they found a Linguist half so good,   70
I make no question but the *Tow'r* had stood.
    "Obliging Sir! I love you, I profess,
"But wish you lik'd Retreat a little less;
"Spirits like you, believe me, shou'd be seen,
"And (like *Ulysses*) visit Courts, and Men.   75
"So much *alone*, (to speak plain Truth between us)

"You'll die of Spleen"—Excuse me, *Nunquam minus*—
But as for *Courts*, forgive me if I say,
No Lessons now are taught the *Spartan* way:
Tho' in his Pictures Lust be full display'd,   80
Few are the Converts *Aretine* has made;
And tho' the Court show *Vice* exceeding clear,
None shou'd, by my Advice, learn *Virtue* there.
    At this, entranc'd, he lifts his Hands and Eyes,
Squeaks like a high-stretch'd Lutestring, and replies: 85
"Oh 'tis the sweetest of all earthly things
"To gaze on Princes, and to talk of Kings!"
Then happy Man who shows the Tombs! said I,
He dwells amidst the Royal Family;
He, ev'ry Day, from *King* to *King* can walk,   90
Of all our *Harries*, all our *Edwards* talk,
And get by speaking Truth of Monarchs dead,
What few can of the living, *Ease* and *Bread*.
"Lord! Sir, a meer *Mechanick!* strangely low,
"And coarse of Phrase—your *English* all are so.   95
"How elegant your *Frenchman?*"—Mine, d'ye mean?
I have but one, I hope the Fellow's clean.
"Oh! Sir, politely well! nay, let me dye,
"Your only wearing is your *Padua-soy*."
Not Sir, my only—I have better still,   100
And this, you see, is but my Dishabille—
Wild to get loose, his Patience I provoke,
Mistake, confound, object, at all he spoke.
But as coarse Iron, sharpen'd, mangles more,
And Itch most hurts, when anger'd to a Sore;   105
So when you plague a Fool, 'tis still the Curse,
You only make the Matter worse and worse.
    He past it o'er; put on an easy Smile
At all my Peevishness, and chang'd his Style.
He asks, "What *News?*" I tell him of new Plays.   110
New Eunuchs, Harlequins, and Operas.
He hears; and as a Still, with Simples in it,
Between each Drop it gives, stays half a Minute;
Loth to enrich me with too quick Replies,
By little, and by little, drops his Lies.   115
Meer *Houshold Trash!* of Birth-Nights, Balls and Shows,
More than ten *Holingsheds*, or *Halls*, or *Stows*.
When the *Queen* frown'd, or smil'd, he knows; and what
A subtle Minister may make of that?
Who sins with whom? who got his Pension *Rug*,   120
Or quicken'd a Reversion by a *Drug?*

Whose Place is *quarter'd out*, three Parts in four,
And whether to a Bishop, or a Whore?
Who, having lost his Credit, pawn'd his Rent,
Is therefore fit to have a *Government*?   125
Who in the *Secret*, deals in Stocks secure,
And cheats th'unknowing Widow, and the Poor?
Who makes a *Trust*, or *Charity*, a Job,
And gets an Act of Parliament to rob?
Why *Turnpikes* rose, and why no Cit, nor Clown   130
Can *gratis* see the *Country*, or the *Town*?
Shortly no Lad shall *chuck*, or Lady *vole*,
But some excising Courtier will have Toll.
He tells what Strumpet Places sells for Life,
What 'Squire his Lands, what Citizen his Wife?   135
And last (which proves him wiser still than all)
What Lady's Face is not a whited Wall?
As one of *Woodward*'s Patients, sick and sore,
I puke, I nauseate,—yet he thrusts in more;
Shows *Poland*'s Int'rests, takes the *Primate*'s part,   140
And talks *Gazettes* and *Post-Boys* o'er by heart.
Like a big Wife at sight of loathsome Meat,
Ready to cast, I yawn, I sigh, I sweat:
Then as a licens'd Spy, whom nothing can
Silence, or hurt, he libels the *Great Man*;   145
Swears every *Place entail'd* for Years to come,
In *sure Succession* to the Day of Doom:
He names the *Price* for ev'ry *Office* paid,
And says our *Wars thrive ill*, because *delay'd*;
Nay hints, 'tis by Connivance of the Court,   150
That *Spain* robs on, and *Dunkirk*'s still a Port.
Not more Amazement seiz'd on *Circe*'s Guests,
To see themselves fall endlong into Beasts,
Than mine, to find a Subject staid and wise,
Already half turn'd Traytor by surprize.   155
I felt th'Infection slide from him to me,
As in the Pox, some give it, to get free;
And quick to swallow me, methought I saw
One of our Giant *Statutes* ope its Jaw!
In that nice Moment, as another Lye   160
Stood just a-tilt, the *Minister* came by.
Away he flies. He bows, and bows again;
And close as *Umbra* joins the dirty Train.
Not *Naso*'s self more impudently near,
When half his Nose is in his Patron's Ear.   165
I blest my Stars! but still afraid to see

All the Court fill'd with stranger things than he,
Run out as fast, as one that pays his Bail
And dreads more Actions, hurries from a Jail.
    Bear me, some God! oh quickly bear me hence   170
To wholesome Solitude, the Nurse of Sense:
Here Contemplation prunes her ruffled Wings,
And the free Soul looks down to pity Kings.
Here still Reflection led on sober Thought,
Which Fancy colour'd, and a Vision wrought.   175
A *Vision* Hermits can to Hell transport,
And bring ev'n me to see the Damn'd at Court.
Not *Danté* dreaming all th'Infernal State,
Saw such a Scene of *Envy*, *Sin*, and *Hate*.
Base Fear becomes the Guilty, not the Free;   180
Suits Tyrants, Plunderers, but suits not me.
Shall I, the Terror of this sinful Town,
Care, if a livery'd Lord or smile or frown?
Who cannot flatter, and detest who can,
Tremble before a *noble Serving-Man?*   185
O my fair Mistress, *Truth!* Shall I quit thee,
For huffing, braggart, puft *Nobility?*
Thou, who since Yesterday, hast roll'd o'er all
The busy, idle Blockheads of the Ball,
Hast thou, O *Sun!* beheld an emptier fort,   190
Than such as swell this Bladder of a Court?
Now pox on those who shew a *Court in Wax!
It ought to bring all Courtiers on their backs.
Such painted Puppets, such a varnish'd Race
Of hollow Gewgaws, only Dress and Face,   195
Such waxen Noses, stately, staring things,
No wonder some Folks bow, and think them *Kings*.
    And now the *British* Youth, engaged no more
At *Fig's* or *White's*, with *Felons*, or a *Whore*,
Pay their last Duty to the *Court*, and come   200
All fresh and fragrant, to the *Drawing-Room:*
Colours as gay, and Odours as divine,
As the fair Fields they sold to look so fine.
"That's *Velvet* for a *King!*" the Flatt'rer swears;
'Tis true, for ten days hence 'twill be *King Lear's*.   205
Our Court may justly to our Stage give Rules,

---

  *A famous Show of the Court of France in Waxwork. (In 1735 Pope glosses Donne's "Waxen garden" on the facing page (l. 169) as "[a] show of the *Italian* Gardens in Waxwork, in the time of King James the First." The 1735 edition also explains the references in line 199: "Fig's, a Prize-fighter's Academy, where the young Nobility receiv'd instruction in those days; White's was a noted gaming house: it was also customary for the nobility and gentry to visit the condemned Criminals in *Newgate*.")

That helps it both to *Fool's-Coats* and to *Fools*.
And why not Players strut in Courtiers Cloaths?
For these are Actors too, as well as those:
Wants reach all States; they beg but better drest,   210
And all is *splendid Poverty* at best.
    Painted for sight, and essenc'd for the smell,
Like Frigates fraught with Spice and Cochine'l,
Sail in the *Ladies*: How each Pyrate eyes
So weak a Vessel, and so rich a Prize!   215
Top-gallant he, and she in all her Trim,
He boarding her, she striking sail to him.
"*Chere Comtesse!* you have Charms all Hearts to hit!"
And "*sweet Sir Fopling!* you have so much wit!"
Such Wits and Beauties are not prais'd for nought,   220
For both the Beauty and the Wit are *bought*.
'Twou'd burst ev'n *Heraclitus* with the Spleen,
To see those Anticks, *Fopling* and *Courtin*:
The *Presence* seems, with things so richly odd,
The Mosque of *Mahound*, or some queer *Pa-god*.   225
See them survey their Limbs by *Durer*'s Rules,
Of all Beau-kind the best proportion'd Fools!
Adjust their Cloaths, and to Confession draw
Each idle Atom, or erroneous Straw;
What Terrors wou'd distract each conscious Soul,   230
Convicted of that mortal Sin, a Hole!
Or should one Pound of Powder less bespread
The Monkey-Tail that wags behind his Head!
Thus finish'd and corrected to a hair,
They march, to prate their Hour before the Fair,   235
So first to preach a white-glov'd Chaplain goes,
With Band of Lily, and with Cheek of Rose,
Sweeter than *Sharon*, in immaculate trim,
Neatness itself impertinent in him.
Let but the Ladies smile, and they are blest;   240
Prodigious! how the Things *Protest, Protest*:
Peace, Fools! or *Gonson* will for Papists seize you,
If once he catch you at your *Jesu! Jesu!*
    Nature made ev'ry Fop to plague his Brother,
Just as one Beauty mortifies another.   245
But here's the *Captain*, that will plague you both,
Whose Air cries Arm! whose very Look's an Oath:
What tho' his Soul be Bullet, Body Buff?
Damn him, he's honest, Sir,—and that's enuff.
He spits fore-right; his haughty Chest before,   250
Like batt'ring Rams, beats open ev'ry Door;

And with a Face as red, and as awry,
As *Herod's* Hang-dogs in old Tapestry,
Scarecrow to Boys, the breeding Woman's curse;
Has yet a strange Ambition to *look worse:*   255
Confounds the Civil, keeps the Rude in awe,
Jests like a licens'd Fool, commands like Law.
Frighted, I quit the Room, but leave it so,
As Men from Jayls to Execution go;
For hung with *Deadly Sins I see the Wall,   260
And lin'd with *Giants,* deadlier than 'em all:
Each Man an †*Ascapart,* of strength to toss
For Quoits, both *Temple-Bar* and *Charing-Cross.*
Scar'd at the grizly Forms, I sweat, I fly,
And shake all o'er, like a discover'd Spy.   265
Courts are no match for Wits so weak as mine;
Charge them with Heav'n's Artill'ry, bold *Divine!*
From such alone the Great Rebukes endure,
Whose *Satyr's sacred,* and whose Rage *secure.*
'Tis mine to wash a few slight Stains; but theirs   270
To deluge Sin, and drown a Court in Tears.
Howe'er, what's now *Apocrypha,* my Wit,
In time to come, may pass for *Holy Writ.*

Copy-text: Pope, *The Impertinent,* 1733, pp. 5–16.
Emendations of the copy-text: Line 222 Spleen,] ~.
Regularizations of the copy-text: Heading: *attribution supplied*   Line 54
      King's,"] ~,ʌ   55 *Dictionary.*"] ~.ʌ   57 dispute."] ~.ʌ   59 Mile."] ~.ʌ
      96 *Frenchman?*"] ~?ʌ   110 *News?*"] ~?ʌ

---

*The Room hung with Tapestry now very antient, representing the *Seven Deadly Sins.*
†A Giant famous in divers Romances.

COMMENTARY

THE
Satyres

 # The Satyres

DATES AND CIRCUMSTANCES

Most scholars, believing that Donne began the Satyres while he was a student at Lincoln's Inn and that the last of the series was completed when Donne became secretary to Sir Thomas Egerton, date the Satyres between 1593 and 1597 or 1598. In addition, the standard critical opinion accepts Donne as among the first writers, if not the first, of formal verse satire in English.

Bayle (1697 [1736, 4:85]) comments that Donne's Satyres were written "early in the reign of James the first, though they were not published till after his death, in the year 1633." Warton (1774, 3:278) makes a similar observation.

Chalmers (1810, 5:124) states that the Satyres "must have been written very early, as [Donne] was a young man when he renounced the errors of popery."

Collier (1820, 1:152–60) presents a dialogue between Morton, Elliot, and Bourne, the last of whom seeks to establish that Donne is the first English satirist. As evidence that Donne's Satyres predate those of Hall, Lodge, and Marston, Bourne refers to a manuscript copy of Donne's "three first satires preserved in the British Museum (among the Harl. MS. No. 5110 [B33]): it is entitled 'Ihon Dunne his Satires. Anno Domini 1593'" (155), and he adds, by way of internal evidence, that "there is not a reference to any single event, or to any peculiarity of dress and custom, that does not belong to the date which the MS. bears, viz. 1593" (159). During the dialogue, Bourne also speculates, based on a letter from Donne to Goodyer and on indications in Thomas Freeman's epigrams, that a few printed copies of the Satyres, though no longer extant, had been produced circa 1614. Other commentators who suggest that Donne's Satyres are the earliest examples of the genre in English include Collier (1871), Grosart (1872–73, 1:2), an anonymous commentator writing in *TB* (1876, 350), Dowden (1890) Chambers (1896, 2:242), Furst (1896, 230–31), Thompson (1899, 505–06), Lang (1912, 284), Clive (1966, 8), Oliver (1997, 12), Post (1999, 5), Prescott (2000, 229), and Hadfield (2001, 54, 57). Among those suggesting 1593 as the probable initial date are Grosart (1872–73, 1:2), an anonymous commentator writing in *TB* (1876, 350), Gosse (1893, 237), Thompson (1899, 505–06), Guiney (1920, 14), Nethercot (1925a, 105), Payne (1926, 27), Williamson (1930, 59), Crofts (1936, 128), Cazamian (1952, 312), Smith (1952, 223), Andreasen (1963, 75), and Sullivan (1992, 220).

Jessopp (1855, x, xvii–xviii) contends that Donne penned his Satyres while a student at Lincoln's Inn (as do Rousseau and Rudenstine [1972, 56], Marotti [1986, 38], Smith [1992, 82], Patterson [1994, 146], Nutt [1999, 28], and Reid [2000, 39]), and he describes Donne as "lashing" in the Satyres "the follies and vices of his day" (x). He further asserts that the poems are important for their "poetical merit" and are "historically interesting," in as much as they "procured" for Donne "considerable celebrity" and also "introduced him to the notice of men of influence and power" (xviii).

Hazlitt (1868, 483–84) draws attention to "Harl. MS. 5110, which contains *Ihon Dunne his Satires, Anno Domini* 1593."

Grosart (1872–73, 1:2–4, 2:xxx–xxxiii) introduces the texts for the seven poems he believes constitute the Satyres, and he then comments that the internal evidence also points to an early date, concluding that "they must have been among the earliest of their author's productions of any extent, while they are certainly the most noticeable and characteristic" of Donne's verse (1:2).

An anonymous commentator writing in *TB* (1876, 337–39, 350), following his extended biography of Donne, expresses that "it seems difficult to connect a life so gentle with that of a satirist" and suggests that "his indulgence in that species of composition belongs to an early and wild period of his life" (350).

Masson (1876, 338) briefly notes that the Satyres "were produced between 1593 and 1597, that is to say from the poet's twentieth to his twenty-fourth year." Similar views are expressed by Furst (1896, 230–31), White (1935, 126n3), Tredegar (1936, 173), Gransden (1954, 101–02), Redpath (1956, xix), Harris (1960, 191), Menascè (1969, 49), Smith (1971, 469), Rousseau and Rudenstine (1972, 56), Hester (1977b, 525; 1977c, 184), Selden (1978, 59), Zunder (1982, 9), B. Smith (1991, 103, 161), and King (2000, 374).

Gosse (1893, 237–38, 245) asserts that there is little doubt that the Satyres "are wholly Elizabethan," and that totaling seven in number, they "belong to the same general category as those of Hall, Lodge, and Guilpin" (237). Oliver (1997, 11) also comments on the Elizabethan character of the Satyres.

Norton (1895, 1:239) contends that "many allusions" in the Satyres "make certain" that they were composed before the death of Queen Elizabeth and, citing Collier's discovery of the date 1593 in B33, observes that "if this date be correct, they [by which he apparently means *all* the satires] were written when Donne was not more than twenty years old."

Chambers (1896, 2:242–46) states that the Satyres, which are seven in number, "are all amongst Donne's earliest works" (242).

Furst (1896, 230–31) contends that whether or not Donne is the first English satirist is "still a mooted question." He believes the Satyres number seven and speculates that "a reading between the lines suggests that the author must have been at this period, a vigorous, fearless, mildly cynical, yet usually good humored, man of the world."

Saintsbury (1898, 279, 366) notes that "it is still very uncertain what credence is to be attached to a MS. ascription of Donne's *Satires* to a date as early as 1593" (279).

Alden (1899, 75–90, 115–16) finds the Satyres to be "the experiments of a young man" (90), and he proposes that the actual date of composition "is involved in some obscurity, and, owing to the disputed claims of priority among the various satirists of the last decade of the sixteenth century, is a matter of no little interest," explaining that "on the authority of Harleian MS. 5110 [B33]," the Satyres "are commonly referred to the year 1593." Further, he points to the talk "of a printed volume of Donne's poetry, containing the satires, which is supposed to have appeared during the author's lifetime," but concludes that "the best authority" rejects "the idea of this hypothetical and much-regretted volume" (76–77). After surveying a variety of details that offer possibilities for dating the poems from their internal evidence, he determines that "in the absence of contradictory evidence, the MS. date of 1593 may be tentatively accepted," adding that "the fourth satire dates from 1598 or thereabout" and "the fifth is probably to be placed near 1600" (82). Nilsen (1997, 140) also posits the terminus dates for *Sat4* and *Sat5* as 1598 and 1600, respectively.

Concerning the dates of the Satyres, which he numbers as seven, Gosse (1899, 1:28–45) calls attention to the 1593 date on the Harleian manuscript [B33] of the first three, and of the fourth, he writes, "although it contains interpolations which seem to belong to 1597, [it] is dated 1594 in the Hawthornden MS." He stresses the importance of knowing that "we have nearly six hundred lines of very independent and characteristic verse which we can confidently attribute to Donne's earliest manhood" (28).

Thompson (1899, 505–06) states that Donne's first poems stand in contrast to what one might expect from his education, and he notes that Donne "was a satirist before Hall, and after the languid attempt of Lodge."

Garnett and Gosse (1903, 2:272–73, 292) assert that the earliest of the English satirists is Donne, who "composed the first three of his *Satires* in 1593" (272), followed by Lodge (*Fig for Momus* 1595), then Hall (*Vigidemiarum* 1597–99), then Marston (1598), and finally Guilpin (*Skialetheia* 1598).

Grierson (1906, 155) states, without explanation, that the Satyres "may date from 1593, but the earliest unmistakable reference is to 1597."

Grierson (1909, 4:197, 205–08) claims that whether or not Donne is chronologically the first English satirist, he is, nevertheless, "the first who deserves attention, the first whose work is in the line of later development, the only one of the sixteenth century satirists whose influence is still traceable in Dryden and Pope" (197).

Schelling (1910, 319–21) comments that the actual date of the Satyres "is difficult to ascertain," even though "there seems much reason to believe several of them [were] already written by 1593." He adds that "to Donne the penning of his six or seven satires was as incidental to a career of celebrity in prose, poetry, and divinity as was the writing of *Venus and Adonis* to Shakespeare" (319).

Grierson (1912, 2:x, xiv–xvii, 100–05) contends that "the earliest date assignable" to the Satyres "is 1593, or more probably 1594–5," noting, in reference to the inscription on the back of Harleian MS. 5110, that "the handwriting is not identical with that in which the poems are transcribed, and it is impossible to say either when the poems were copied or when the title and date were affixed" (100). Grierson comments further that based on various allusions—including those to Banks' performing horse and "the Ape and the Elephant" (*Sat1* 80–81) and "ideot actors" (*Sat2* 13)—he believes that the first three Satyres "were probably written between 1594 and 1597" (103). He adds that the reference in *Sat4* to "the losse of Amyens" (l. 114) indicates that the poem "must have been written after March 1597," and notes that lines 31–33 of *Sat5* date the poem between "1598, if not earlier, and February 1601–02" by their reference to Donne's employment with Egerton, suggesting 1598–9 as the actual date of composition (104). [See the Notes and Glosses for more detailed discussions of these allusions—ed.]

Aronstein (1920, 155) points out that Donne composed his Satyres around the same time that the genre was experiencing a short, premature rebirth in France also.

Jenkins (1923, 568) dates the first four Satyres between 1593 and 1599.

Fausset (1924, 49) dates the first four Satyres in 1593–94. Ryan (1948, 8) suggests the same years.

Nethercot (1925a, 105) notes Thomas Warton's error (1774) in dating the Satyres later than Hall's and his failure to appreciate Donne's "satirical virtues."

Walker (1925, 68–69) remarks that while the publication date of the Satyres is late ("it was not till 1633 that the first five of the seven appeared"), the poems are "among the works of Donne's youth."

Elton (1932, 209) observes that the Satyres appear to predate Donne's marriage.

Woolf (1932, 21–22) notes that the targets of Donne's Satyres are indicative of his youth.

Tate (1933, 129–30), noting that the Satyres "resemble" those of Hall, Marston, and Tourneur, believes that "if we put such poets together against the background of the widespread influence of Martial, they form a school that makes intelligible not only the 'Satires' of Donne (1593) but much of that great poet's most characteristic later writing." He adds that "the satirists of the 1590's went back through Sackville to Lyndsay and Dunbar," and "the medieval sense of all-pervading mortality, of the vanity of the world, survives" in these satirists, "who continue to use the theme as a weapon of critical irony upon the vaunting romanticism of the Renaissance."

Lindsay (1934a, 577) suggests that the Satyres reflect "the troubled state of Donne's life" resulting from his brother's death, his questioning of Catholicism, and his attempt to find employment "without lessening his self-respect."

Lindsay (1934b, 636) suggests that the Satyres are the product of Donne's attempt "to become a 'normal' youth of the period" after his years of recusancy and struggle to leave the Catholic faith.

Atkins (1937, 396) believes that the 1593 date on the Harleian manuscript is suspect and asserts that the Satyres were written between 1596 and 1597.

Bennett (1939, 69) notes that Donne and Everard Guilpin were students together at the Inns of Court in the early 1590s, at the time that Donne was "probably writing" the Satyres.

Gardner (1948, 31) includes the Satyres among Donne's earliest poems and notes that they reflect Donne's "Jesuit upbringing," especially regarding "the Elizabethan policy of repression of Catholicism."

Milgate (1950, 230) comments that the date of 1593 on the first three Satyres in the Harleian manuscript is "probably that affixed, correctly or incorrectly, to the first in the MS. from which he was copying."

Sprott (1950, 344) posits that Donne was composing the Satyres in 1598.

Wilcox (1950, 193), noting the unpublished circulation of Donne's Satyres, observes generally of Elizabethan satire that "a closer observation of the sequence of productions and more precise dating would help in revealing just how and why the satire of the 1590's came about."

Baker (1952, 51) notes that while Donne may have been the first to imitate classical satire, Lodge, Hall, and Marston quickly followed.

Gransden (1954, 9–10) states that the Satyres were written during a time when Donne lived in London and prior to the "adventures" he records in *Calm* and *Storm*. Similar views are expressed by Cox (1956, 109) and Untermeyer (1959, 124–25).

Lewis (1954, 469) believes "it is doubtful whether precedence" should be given to Lodge or to Donne as the first English satirist since the former's *Fig for Momus* appeared in 1595 and the latter's first two Satyres "may well be assigned, on internal evidence, to an earlier date."

Davenport (1955, 12) states that the Satyres were circulating in manuscript from at least 1598.

Kermode (1957, 25) believes that the Satyres are contemporaneous with the Elegies.

Sutherland (1958, 31) notes that all of the Elizabethan satirists, including Donne, were young men in their twenties.

Alvarez (1961, 196) comments that Donne did not participate in "the contemporary satiric wars" but that Guilpin "plagiarized from Donne in order to join battle with Marston and Hall."

Allen (1965, 85–86) calls Donne the "originator" of Elizabethan satire and indicates that Donne's Satyres are seven in number, pointing out that three appear in a manuscript dated 1593 and stating that the others "were completed shortly after the accession of James I."

Zivley (1966, 88–89) notes that Gosse (1899) and Grierson (1912) consider the Satyres contemporaneous with the Songs and Sonets, but she observes that while the two groups of poems share some characteristics, their imagery "differs greatly," adding that the experience of the Satyres is also "microcosmic" in that "it is one of crowds and activity, through whose abundance and diversity the many possible experiences of the world are represented."

Andreasen (1967, 115, 193) asserts that the Elegies and Satyres were probably written about the same time (115) and that they are probably Donne's earliest poems (193).

Gardner (1967, 193) notes that five Satyres were printed in 1633, after being "'excepted' by the licenser in 1632," adding both that a sixth was added in 1635 but rejected by Grierson (1912) and that titles do not appear either in the manuscripts or in these early printings.

Milgate (1967), positioning his assessment primarily as an extension and refinement of the prior work of Grierson (1912), assigns *Sat1* "almost certainly" to 1593 (p. 117), *Sat2* to 1594 (p. 127), *Sat3* to "1594 or 1595" (p. 140), *Sat4* to "between March and September" of 1597 (p. 148), and *Sat5* to "probably the early part of 1598" (p. 165). Moreover, Milgate postulates that Donne revised Satyres 1–4 before presenting them, along with the newly-composed *Sat5*, to the "Lord Keeper's family" (lviii) sometime in 1598 and that he revised them a second time in 1607 or shortly thereafter for presentation to the Countess of Bedford (lix) (see the General Textual Introduction above, especially footnote 9 and the section "Milgate's Theory of the Revisions of the Satyres").

Lecocq (1969, 362, 364) notes that *Paradoxes* was written closer in time to the composition of the Satyres than to other works by Donne (362). Further, acknowledging the usefulness of the Verse Letters as a veritable commentary on the Satyres, or more exactly an explanation of the state of mind in which the poems were written, he cautions that questions about the dating of the Satyres cast doubt on the strength of conclusions drawn from attempts to read the poems in light of the Verse Letters (364).

Fischer (1971, 372) claims that the Satyres, written between 1592 and 1598, are contemporaneous with most of Donne's love lyrics.

Hebaisha (1971, 25) observes that at least four of the Satyres were circulating in manuscript before 1597–98.

Kermode (1971, 135) remarks that Donne's "youthful sympathies must have been with the persecuted Romanists," for the Satyres "contain bitter allusions to 'pursuivants', tormentors of Jesuits," noting also that "the odious Topcliffe is mentioned by name in some manuscripts."

Smith (1971, 469) states that, "with Joseph Hall's Virgidemiarum (1597)," the Satyres "are the first formal satires written in English and owe something to Roman satiric writers, especially Horace, Juvenal and Persius." He adds that Donne's Satyres, along with five of the Elegies, "were at first refused a licence for the edition of 1633," but the ban on the poems "was lifted before the volume went to press and they appeared in it," though "a few blanks" in the 1633 edition "may indicate cuts made to meet the Licenser's objections."

MacColl (1972, 34) suggests that the "C. B." who, according to Drummond in the Hawthornden MS, had a copy of the Satyres, may be Christopher Brooke, and notes that Rowland Woodward "evidently possessed a manuscript including the Satyres and the Elegies dating from before 1603."

Rousseau and Rudenstine (1972, 56) comment that the Satyres were "unpublished during Donne's lifetime" and "were at first circulated privately in manuscript and only printed in 1633, two years after the poet's death."

Shawcross (1972, 250–52, 268–69) maintains that the texts of the poems "are not definitive: a diplomatic text drawn from various printed and manuscript sources seems to be the best that can be achieved in view of the lack of authorial materials." Further, the dates of composition of the Satyres "are uncertain and debated," though he proposes probable dates for several of the poems based on internal references and notes. He also says that placing the poems between 1593 and 1598 "is to spread them over too long a period," for "it makes them incidental or even occasional poems, in the sense of being provoked by some specific reason for writing at just that time" (250–51). He concludes that "the biographical implications" of the Satyres "depend on their dates, our interpretation of them, and the way in which we see Donne involved." He reads the poems "as being written within a short time of each other," after Donne's "return from service and during his employment by Egerton, employment which held out a number of hopes of 'getting somewhere' or of 'being somebody,'" and thus he sees them "as the products of a thoughtful mind viewing some of the evils of this world; progressing from the problem of self to the problems of law courts and lawyers (which and who still thwart real justice) to the problems of religious belief to the problems of the aristocratic world of his day…to the problems which greed breeds in both the haves and the have-nots" (268–69).

Swift (1974, 47–48) wonders if Donne's poems were among the satires burned by order of the Bishop of Canterbury in 1599.

Kermode and Hollander (1973, 1045) comment that Donne wrote the Satyres "in the 1590s, a time when they were greatly in vogue," adding that "publication of satire was inhibited in 1598."

Tomashevskii (1973, 9) classifies the Satyres, along with the Verse Letters, as representative of a middle period in Donne's artistic career, adding that Donne's poems from this period intrude into the real world and explore its social customs, court and bourgeois life, and the disasters of the age.

Bellette (1975, 130) notes that Donne seems never to have regretted writing the Satyres and believes that Donne's comment to Wotton in 1600 that "to my satyrs there belongs some feare" was perhaps prompted by "the recent ban on satires and the burning of works by Marston, Davies, and Guilpin," adding that Donne "valued them to the extent of considering them worthy of careful revision as late as 1607, when they were sent to the Countess of Bedford."

Elliott (1976, 105) asserts that when Donne wrote the first of the Satyres in 1593, he may not have intended "a unified collection of formal verse satires," but evidence suggests that he was "still revising these poems for private circulation as late as 1607." Further, because Donne "prepared the subsequent satires in the 1590's and then collected them into a 'book' in the early 1600's," he "had ample opportunity to provide" the poems "with elements of formal unity and with a narrative structure," and "in so doing he had an abundance of models in both English and classical satires."

Sinha (1977, 55) states that the Satyres were composed before 1598–99 and that 1593 is "the earliest date assignable to them." He believes that the poems "belong to the period of that sudden outburst of formal satire and satirical comedy which distinguishes the last years of the sixteenth century," which resulted from several "deep currents of influence," among them the "disruptive social and economic changes of the time," leading to "the growth of an interest first in realism and then in psychology (in those days called 'anatomizing') in the early 1590s."

Partridge (1978, 36–37) argues that Donne composed the Satyres and the Elegies at about the same time but says that "there seems some doubt whether the first was in circulation by 1593."

Dubrow (1979, 76) states that although the exact dates of the Satyres "are uncertain," the poems "were definitely written during the period when the genre was flourishing in England," noting that "most scholars" date *Sat1* "somewhere between 1593 and 1595," and so it may have come before the work of Hall, who called himself "the first English satirist," as well as Lodge's *A Fig for Momus* (1595). She adds that Donne "probably returned to satire sporadically during the rest of the decade, writing the final poem in the group around 1598 or 1599."

Carey (1981, 50) notes that the Satyres were written in the 1590s, at a time when Donne was seeking chances "to satisfy his thirst for action and self-advancement."

McCabe (1981, 191) observes that the satires of many of Donne's contemporaries, such as Hall, Guilpin, and Marston, were published between 1597 and 1599 and that Donne's "were apparently circulating in manuscript at the same time."

Slights (1981, 177–78) argues that the Satyres were written in the 1590s, at a time when "troubled men took their cases of conscience to their pastors and preachers who discussed casuistical problems in sermons."

Corthell (1982, 156–57) suggests that the textual tradition of the Satyres "encourages thinking of the poems as a book marking stages in Donne's development as a poet from his years at Lincoln's Inn to his first position as secretary to Lord Keeper Egerton," noting that because the poems are "concerned with public circumstances," they "provide a unique opportunity for studying the relationship between Donne's self-presentation and his awareness of the political and social realities of the late Elizabethan period." He adds that Donne began writing the poems "at the Inns of Court, traditionally places where young men made the passage from the still largely impractical training of the universities to the world of power and influence" and where the benchers felt "some dissension concerning their function in English society" so that "there was an increase in social tension between the legal professionals and their students and the 'gentlemen' of the Inns."

Hester (1982, 3–5) argues that the Satyres "reveal much about Donne's early poetic and his concomitant moral-aesthetic perspective on late Elizabethan morals and manners." The poems are "much too sophisticated to be apprentice pieces or early experiments," he says, and "offer a unified, sequential examination of the problems of Christian satire, a creative shaping (or re-shaping) of the generic, conventional, intellectual, and biographical materials" Donne had available in the 1590s (3–4). He suggests further that the Satyres show Donne "making his (poetic) beginning by focusing on the (apocalyptic) ending," and as a result, "to appreciate fully the stances, tensions, and generic complexities essential to these five poems, we must start at the end—at the end of the sixteenth century and the climate of opinion in which they were written," for "it is there that we find the bases for the genre and the persona Donne creates" (5).

Zunder (1982, 9) argues that the Satyres "are an attempt to focus on contemporary society," noting that, "written in the last decade of the sixteenth century," they demonstrate an awareness of "contemporary change."

Shawcross (1983, 13) claims that the available evidence points to the Satyres "appearing first [in print] in a collected edition" and that they "had circulated as a group previously," enhancing Donne's reputation as a poet.

Kerins (1984, 37) believes that although the Satyres "were composed by 1598," their circulation in manuscript "seemed to have been rather tightly circumscribed for a decade." He also notes that "by 1609 evidence shows that the poems were 'widely known in manuscript,'" and that in 1610 Donne's reputation as a satirist "was at its zenith."

Parry (1985, 46) says that the Satyres and "most" of the Elegies "belong to the 1590s," and that these were the poems that "enjoyed the widest circulation in manuscript."

Patrides (1985, 213) asserts that the Satyres and Elegies "may have been written in the early 1590s," perhaps as early as 1593 and mainly in 1597–98, but "they may also have been written periodically, the third satire possibly composed as late as 1620, after Donne took orders."

Marotti (1986, 38, 127–28) argues that Donne composed the first four Satyres "before he entered government service, the first two clearly belonging to his early Inns period," and that all of these poems "are the work of a man eager to become a part of the Establishment but angry about the forms of self-abasement necessary to succeed in a world of social, economic, and political power relationships." He contends that the Satyres "were written for an audience of men similarly impatient for preferment and fond of asserting their intellectual, moral, and social autonomy," and the poems "assume common attitudes toward City and Court as well as a sophisticated knowledge of the way the social system worked," adding that "the sins and follies that Donne attacked in these poems were part of the daily life of many Inns members" (38). He concludes that along with the Elegies and *Paradoxes*, the Satyres belong "to the youthfully impudent atmosphere" Donne knew "at the Inns of Court and, by extension, to the private communications between close friends: to have allowed them to reach a wider public would have been to risk personal embarrassment and misinterpretation, dangers highlighted by the 1599 bishops' order banning satires, epigrams, and obscene and politically dangerous literature" (127–28).

Robson (1986, 87) suggests that the Satyres "belong to the years before Donne's marriage in 1601" and believes that "his beginnings as a poet may have coincided with the sudden vogue of satire in the 1590s."

Shawcross (1986, 120–21) contends that the Satyres "had been circulated in manuscript groups" before January 1615 when Donne "called in his poems for publication before his ordination," and adds that in the generic ordering in the manuscripts and in print, the five Satyres "are generally grouped together and in that order."

Rogers (1987, 169–70) believes that since the Satyres, like other early poems of Donne's, circulated in manuscript, they probably predate Hall's, noting that "from internal and other evidence" the Satyres, along with the Elegies, *Paradoxes* and "some" of the Songs and Sonets, can be dated "to the late 1590s."

Zunder (1988, 79) suggests that Satyres 1, 2, 4, and 5, following the tradition of satire in the late sixteenth century, "are responses to the economic and social changes of the sixteenth century," adding that *Sat1* and *Sat2* "are responses to the rise of capitalism," and *Sat4* and *Sat5* "to the increased power of the court and the central government, in particular to the Court of Star Chamber."

Parfitt (1989, 28) posits that in the 1590s Donne could "draw on a very old native tradition of 'complaint,'" but one "modified…by adaptation to classical Latin models more suitable to the urban sophistication such satirists wished to present."

Norbrook (1990, 9) claims that the Satyres "go beyond their Roman models by depending for much of their wit on an informed knowledge of current affairs, including an ability to criticize the inaccuracy of the available news-sheets." He adds that the "boldness" of satire in the 1590s "provoked a reaction; the intellectuals had moved a long way beyond the borders of acceptable discourse" so that "it is not surprising to find Donne oscillating so insecurely between self-assertion and self-deprecation."

Chandra (1991, 79) notes that the Satyres were the first poems that Donne wrote, and he points out that the "internal textual evidence" related to Queen Elizabeth I and to "the uncertainty of the religious situation depicted" in *Sat3* testify to their early date.

Sellin (1991, 87–88) contends that Sat3 "is likely to postdate the other four satires." See more under Sat3: Date and Circumstances.

Wheeler (1992, 120–21) states that while "Donne looked to the Roman satirists for method, manner and ideas," this influence was "negligible," adding that Donne's Satyres are "quite unique in English literature at the beginning of the 1590s" in the attention they draw "to the deeply religious element which is constantly present in all of Donne's works."

Klawitter (1994, 113–14) comments that the Satyres were written "nearly contiguous to or, as many suspect, shortly before" the writing of the Songs and Sonets. He notes that these "brash and toothy" poems are "just the kind of thing a reader would expect from a young man biding his time in Lincoln's Inn in the later years of Queen Elizabeth's reign." He adds that although the Satyres "cannot be dated precisely, their manuscript tradition is old (where they generally appear as a unit)," noting that most scholars have placed them in the early 1590s, "after Donne's undergraduate days but before he attempted soldiering in the 1596 Cadiz expedition."

Patterson (1994, 146) asserts that the Satyres "can be roughly assigned to the time when Donne was a law student in London and during his appointment as secretary to Sir Thomas Egerton, the Lord Keeper, in 1598." She adds that these poems "can do more to explain the political Donne" than any of his Songs and Sonets or sermons.

Sowerby (1994, 330) comments that "internal evidence" makes clear that Donne wrote the Satyres "before Hall (perhaps as early as 1593)," though "they were not printed until later."

Strier (1994, 231) contends that, contrary to the view of some, Donne did not so much reject previous models of poetry as change them, and that "from the beginning of his poetic career, Donne was writing a kind of antipoetry." Thus, in the 1590s, during the "sonnet boom," Donne wrote the Satyres, and while he "may not be the first writer of Horatian verse satire in English," Donne "is certainly among the first."

Pebworth (1996, 131) writes that during Donne's employment with Egerton, he "was worried about the effects that a wide circulation" of the Satyres and Elegies "might have on his reputation and his hopes for advancement in public affairs." Once "the politically dangerous final years of Elizabeth's reign were safely in the past (and after his injudicious marriage had ended his employment with Egerton)," Donne then "allowed a wider distribution" of the Satyres, "sending them to Ben Jonson, who, in turn, sent along a copy of them—accompanied by his own Epigram 94—to Lucy, Countess of Bedford." He adds that the existence of "four surviving manuscript booklets" that have only the Satyres and Storm and Calm further indicates that the Satyres "eventually circulated widely as a group among members of Donne's coteries during his lifetime."

Nutt (1999, 28, 171) notes that the Satyres are Donne's "earliest poems and exhibit clear signs of frustrated energy and ambition" (28). Like the Elegies, he thinks, the Satyres were written during the 1590s, when Donne "was either travelling and fighting abroad, or living the life of an intellectual rake at Lincoln's Inn" (171).

Blissett (2000, 101) states that Donne wrote the Satyres at an "unsettled time" in his life when he "was not embarked on anything recognizable as a literary career."

Ellrodt (2000, 310–11) believes that the "outburst" of satire in the 1590s "disclosed a mood of individual protest and discontent." He adds that at the turn of the century in England "social and literary influences" were favorable to a "greater acuity of self-awareness" that "could account for the self-assertiveness displayed" in the Satyres and in *Metem* but that does not explain the "persistent egocentricity" evident throughout Donne's writings.

King (2000, 374) considers Donne one of "the pre-eminent satirists" of the 1590s, and he adds that the "censor's original refusal to license the poems for publication" points to their "controversial character."

Reid (2000, 39) states that, "written between 1591 and 1601," the Satyres "belong to a period in Donne's life when his trouble with the world had to do with his Catholic background."

Sproxton (2000, 118) describes the Satyres, poems that demonstrate "a lively and energetic mind, driven by a fierce passion to destroy pretension," as Donne's "earliest poetry."

Sullivan (2000, 301–02) notes that the Satyres were printed in 1633 despite being denied licensing in September 1632. The Stationers' Register records the granting of permission in October 1632, he observes, the texts of the poems apparently gaining "the licenser's approval by the deletion of offensive materials," though, he adds, it "is not clear whether licensing delay or concern over their content relegated the Satyres to the very end of the volume."

Wiggins (2000, 26–29, 32) cautions against using "the autobiographical voice or content" of the Satyres "to date their composition," primarily because "their text could easily represent the reflections of a writer working ten years after the events he describes and just as ambitious as ever" (26). He believes that "the 'body'" to which Donne conceives himself to belong in the Satyres is "greater than that represented by any single polititian or political regime," namely, "the body of civil discourse formed by Castiglione," and that the figure of Egerton is himself "subsumed" and "idealized" by the context of *The Courtier*. He argues that such an approach to the Satyres explains "how Donne could go on revising" the poems "long after dismissal from Egerton's service" and how he could "feel no qualms about presenting them to the Countess of Bedford even though they constituted a reminder of his misconduct a scant six years earlier in marrying Ann More" (27). Wiggins quotes from Angel Day's *The English Secretary* (1586) to argue that Donne "records the success of the endeavor when he has the historical Egerton actually enter the poems to hire him as his spokesman" (29). As such, Wiggins asserts, Donne perceives that his task as a secretary is "to develop in himself Castiglione's disabused intelligence" (32).

Young (2000, 22) notes that "if the usual datings are reliable," the Satyres "were written more than ten years before the Holy Sonnets."

Edwards (2001, 46) suggests that Donne's grief at his brother's death in 1593 "tempted him to write bitterly 'satirique' poetry 'in skorne of all.'"

Flynn (2001, 112–13) observes that "by the fall of 1597" Donne's Epigrams, Elegies and Satyres remained his "main achievements." Acknowledging that such poetry "would not by itself have assured success for any candidate to become a member of an Elizabethan Court officer's secretariat," Flynn calls Donne's poems "extraordinary," as would have been evident to "anyone with some knowledge of Roman elegiac and satiric verse," and they may have appealed to Egerton.

Smith (2001, 169) notes that the 1633 edition of Donne's poetry "omits all or part of nine lines" of the Satyres, adding that the seventeenth-century reader of Folger Shakespeare Library STC 7045 Copy 2 has "in all instances except one…added the expunged words."

GENERAL COMMENTARY

The earliest extant comments on Donne's Satyres are by the poet himself, in two early verse epistles to Rowland Woodward and in a prose letter to his good friend, Henry Wotton. In the one poetic epistle (*RWThird* 3–6) in response to Woodward's request for some of his poems, Donne says his "muse"

> affects…now, a chast fallownesse,
> Since shee to few, yet to too many'hath showne
> How love-song weedes, and Satyrique thornes are growne
> Where seeds of better Arts, were early sown.

In the second epistle, on "thy songs perfection," Donne asserts that Woodward's poems have "halfe quench'd [the] Satirique fyres which urg'd me to have writ / In skorne of all" (*RWEnvy* 6–7).

For instance, Everard Guilpin (1598 [1974, 82–87])—to whom Donne probably composed a verse epistle (*EG*) in which he refers to his own (satiric) "spleen" (l. 11)—paraphrases *Sat1* and borrows extensively from *Sat4* in his Satire V of *Skialetheia*. Others who comment on this connection include Finkelpearl (1963, 164–67), Carroll, Introduction and Notes in Guilpin (1974), Hester (1984, 3–17), and Shelburne (1994, 140). Guilpin probably intends Donne the satirist in his allusion to "the *Prester Iohn* of wit" in his Satire I (l. 8).

In a prose letter (*c.* 1600), which accompanied a copy of his own prose *Paradoxes*, Donne writes:

> I meane to acquaint you with all myne: and to my satyrs there belongs some feare and to some elegies & these [—the prose Paradoxes—] perhaps shame. Against both which affections although I be tough enough yet I have a ridling disposition to bee ashamed of feare & afrayd of shame. Therfore I am desirous to hyde them without any over rec[k]oning of them or there maker. But they are not worth thus much words in theyre disprayse.

Whether "not worth thus much words" includes his Satyres is not clear from this letter preserved in the Burley manuscript (fol. 308v), but subsequent commentary on the Satyres illustrates that readers of Donne's poems did not have such a low opinion of them.

Davison (1602? [Transcribed from Davison's autograph in Harley MS 298, fol. 151 ff.; recorded in Nicolas, 1:xliii–xlv.]) lists under the heading "Manuscripts to get" the following: "Satyres, Elegies, Epigrams, etc. by John Don."

Jonson (1607? [1616, 796]) writes about his and Donne's patroness in a poem ("To

Lucy, Countess of Bedford, / with M. Donnes Satyres") that accompanied his gift of the Satyres to the Countess of Bedford and that describes their excellences:

> LVCY, you brightnesse of our spheare, who are
>   Life of the *Muses* day, their morning-starre!
> If workes (not th'authors) their owne grace should looke,
>   Whose poemes would not wish to be your booke?
> But these, desir'd by you, the makers ends
>   Crowne with their owne. Rare poemes ask rare friends.
> Yet, *Satyres*, since the most of mankind bee
>   Their vn-auoided subiect, fewest see:
> For none ere tooke that pleasure in sinnes sense,
>   But, when they heard it tax'd, tooke more offence.
> They, then, that liuing where the matter is bred,
>   Dare for these poemes, yet, both aske, and read,
> And like them too; must needfully, though few,
>   Be of the best: and 'mongst those, best are you.
> LVCY, you brightnesse of our spheare, who are
>   The *Muses* euening, as their morning-starre.

Wybarne (1609, 113) quotes lines from *Sat4* of Donne, whom he calls "the tenth Muse."

Davies of Hereford (1610) addresses a sonnet "*To the no less ingenious then ingenuous Mr. John Dun*" that seems to praise the Satyres:

> Dunne is the *Mouse* (they say) and thou art Dunne:
> But no dunne *Mouse* thou art; yet thou art one
> That (like a *Mouse*) in steepe high-waies does runne
> To finde foode for thy *Muse* to prey upon.
> Whose pallat is so dainty in her taste,
> That she distasts the least unsavory Bit:
> But that's unlike a Mouse; for, he will wast,
> All in his way; and oft himself with it,
> Not much unlike some Poets of our Times,
> That spoile good paper with their byting Pen,
> Like this of mine, but yet my doggrell Rimes
> Do byte at none but *Monsters* like to men:
>   *And that (I know) thy Pen hath rightly donne,*
>   *Which doing right, makes bright the Name of* Dunne.

Around 1610 (1947, 8:34), Jonson sent several epigrams to Donne praising the merits of his poems, presumably including the Satyres; for example, "To Iohn Donne" refers to Donne's "euery worke" and "earely wit" (l. 3).

The Roman Catholic controversialist Fitzherbert (1613, 107), in his response to *Pseudo-Martyr*, uses the Satyres against Donne, saying that as a controversialist Donne now has passed "*ultra crepidam*, that is to say, beyond his old occupation of making Satyres (wherein he hath some talent, and may play the foole without controle)" now that he has attempted to use his "extravagant conceytes" in religious disputation but has offered only "skambling studies."

Freeman (1614) laments the small number of the Satyres in "To John Dunne," Epigram 84, sig. K1v–K2:

> The *Storme* describ'd, hath set thy name afloate,
> Thy *Calme*, a gale of famous winde hath got:
> The *Satyres* short, too soone we them o'relooke,
> I prethee *Persius* write a bigger booke.

In the comments by Ben Jonson recorded by William Drummond of Hawthornden (1619 [1925, 1:135])—that he "esteemth John Done the first poet in the World in some things" and "that Donne wrote all his best Pieces before he was Twenty five Years of Age" [by 1597–98]—it is likely, given Jonson's neoclassical credentials and judgment, that he included the Satyres among those "best Pieces."

Cave (1620–25) commends the Satyres in his poem "Upon Mr Donns Satires. June 3. 1620" (NY1), observing, for example:

> Oh how it joys me that this quick brain'd Age
> can nere reach thee (Donn) though it should engage
> at once all its whole stock of witt to find
> out of thy well plac'd words thy more pure minde.

In the first edition of *Poems* (1633, 382–83, 398), in which Donne's five Satyres appear as the penultimate poems, followed only by *Father* and some prose letters, Walton, although distinguishing the Satyres from the poems Donne composed when "more matur'd," wonders rhetorically, "Was every sinne, / Character'd in his *Satyres*? made so foule / That some have fear'd their shapes, and kept their soule / Freer by reading verse?"—and "these at his twentieth yeare?" (382–83).

In the same volume, Arthur Wilson describes the poems as "nimble *Satyres...*/ (With nervy strength)" (398).

Daniel (c. 1640 [1959, 12]) writes of Donne that "as a Poet...all wit did soe emprove" that he "Makes Satire Sweet" (ll. 79, 82).

Ling (1640, sig. Ab4) writes of "*Dun's* profound skill, / Making good Verses live, and damning ill" (ll. 3–4).

Walton (1640, B4r–v) writes of Donne that "the recreations of his youth were Poetry, in which he was so happy, as if nature with all her varieties had been made to exercise his great wit, and high fancy" and refers to "those pieces which were carelesly scattered in his younger daies (most of them being written before the twentieth yeare of his age, [before] his penitentiall yeares, [when he] view[ed] some of those pieces loosely scattered in his youth, [and] wisht they had ben abortive." He does not, however, refer to the Satyres (or any of Donne's early poems) by name. In subsequent editions of *The Life*, Walton alters this passage to read: "his sharp wit...those pieces which were facetiously Composed and carelessly scattered" and "that hath been loosely (God knows too loosely) scattered" (1658, 75–86; 1670, 54–61; 1675, 52–59).

The anonymous author of *Vindex Anglicus* (1644, sig. 4), in a comparison of eight English poets with seven classical poets, appears to describe Donne as "our English...Juvenal."

In 1648, "G. O." (identified by Sampson [1921, 93] as the Royalist divine Giles Oldisworth [1619–1678]) entered his own annotations in a 1639 edition of Donne's

Poems, writing rhymed couplets at the heads of several of the groupings of the poems; above the Satyres, he comments, "Both bolde and rare needes must those writers bee / Who can and dare write all they hear and see!"

Cary (1651, 107, 288) quotes *Sat2* 41–42 (107) favorably and calls Donne "one of the most wittie" poets (288).

Jonson's amanuensis, Samuel Sheppard (1653, sigs. A2r–C3v), adapts and paraphrases lines from the Satyres in the preface to his satirical pamphlet.

Cokain (1658, 113) asserts to "Mr. Thomas Bancroft" that "our prime wit / (In the too few short *Satyres* he hath writ) / Renowed *Don* hath jear'd vice-lovers from their crimes."

Milton's nephew, Edward Phillips (1674, 398), briefly notes that Donne "in his youth first of all produced love poems and then satires and verse letters."

Young (1725, 2:60) includes Donne in his lament for the absence of great satire:

> Why slumbers *Pope*, who heads the tuneful train,
> Nor hears that virtue, which he loves, complain?
> Donne, Dorset, Dryden, Rochester, are dead,
> And guilt's chief foe in *Addison* is fled.

Spence (c. 1730–36 [1949, 247]), writing a history of English poetry in French, notes the many "judicious sentiments" ("sentimens judicieux") in Donne's Satyres, as well as a "puerile affectation" in trying to say "something fine" ("quelque chose de beau"). He views the poems as largely a "tissue of epigrams," ("Tissu d'Epigrammes"), the "versification," like that of Donne's contemporaries, is "very bad" ("tres mauvaise").

Spence (c. 1730–36 [1966, 1:188]) notes conversations of Pope's poetic circle concerning Donne's satirical works in remarks first published as *Spence's Anecdotes* in 1820, though widely known during the eighteenth century.

Pope (1735, [98], 131–61), in the "Advertisement" to the edition of *The First Satire of the Second Book of Horace Imitated* that was incorporated into the 1735 edition of his *Works*, cites Donne in defense of his own satirical practice (see Pope [1735] under The Critical Influence of Dryden and Pope below) ([98]). Later in the volume, Pope introduces his versifications of Donne's second and fourth satires under the section heading "Satires of Dr. *John Donne*, Dean of St. Paul's," critiquing Donne's "roughness" with an epigraph from Horace:

> *Quid vetat, ut nosmet* Lucili *scripta legentes*
> *Quaerere, num illius, num rerum dura negarit*
> *Versiculos natura magis factos, & euntes*
> *Mollis?*   Hor. [Sat. ix.56–59]

> ["What prevents us likewise, while reading the work of Lucilius, from asking whether his own nature, or the difficult nature of his material, denied him verses more polished and smooth?"]

Pope then prints (132–41) an imitation of *Sat2* entitled "The Second Satire of Dr. *John Donne*" and (142–61) a revised version of *Sat4* under the title "The Fourth Satire of Dr. *John Donne*" (see Appendix 2).

Cooper (1737, xii) writes that Donne, along with Corbet, "added Wit to Satire, and restor'd the almost forgotten Way of making Reproof it self entertaining."

An anonymous columnist in *The Champion* (1740, 2:259) identifies Donne with Pope as satirists who attacked sycophant poets.

Warburton (1751, 4:253) writes of "the *manly Wit* of Donne, which was the Character of his genius, suited best with Satire; and in this he excelled, tho' he wrote but little."

Johnson (1755–85) uses Donne's Satyres to illustrate a whole range of his definitions. See glosses of individual lines for examples. See also Atkinson (1951) and Perkins (1953) for an overview of Johnson's citations of Donne in his dictionary.

Whalley (1756, 1:xlviii) urges that "it is to the honour of Jonson's judgement" that Pope, "the greatest poet of our nation," shared "the same opinion of Donne's genius and wit; and hath preserved part of him from perishing, by putting his thoughts and satire into modern verse."

Granger (1769, 1:186–87) quotes Dryden's comment on Donne ("the greatest wit, though not the greatest poet of our nation") to support his own view that Donne's "greatest excellency was satire."

Headley (1787, xv) does not list Donne in his scale of "The Select Beauties" of English poetry, believing Donne to be solely a "Satyrical" writer, and classifying him along with Hall, Marston, and Rowlands.

Anderson (1792–95, 4:4–5) claims that in reading the Satyres Donne's contemporaries "seem to have rated [Donne's] performance beyond their just value."

Kippis (1793, 4:334–38) offers an extended footnote to his summary of Walton's *Life* (1640) that provides a fairly full summary of the critical reputation of Donne's writings from Jonson through Joseph Warton. In his commentary on the "taste" of "Dr. Warton," he urges the highest opinion of Donne as a poet but laments that "none of his poetical works are read at present, excepting his Satires" (334).

Gilfillan (1860, 1:204) concludes his overview of Donne's verse by noting that the Satyres "shew, in addition to the high ideal qualities, the rugged versification, the fantastic paradox, and the perverted taste of their author, great strength and clearness of judgment, and a deep, although somewhat jaundiced, view of human nature."

Grosart (1872–73, 1:x, xxvii–xxviii) asserts that the Satyres "carry in them an unwritten chapter of Elizabethan history" (x). He argues that the poems demonstrate Donne's "eminently *judicial* and justified" manner and approach, adding that Donne's "honest, unfearing, unsparing striking at the highest-seated wrong-doers, and a felicitous realism of word-painting" make "these first of English Satires very notable indeed." Further, he proposes that Donne is "proportioned too in his noble rage" in that "he does not treat follies and vanities as if they were vices, any more than he does vices as if they were merely follies and vanities," adding that while Donne "is pungent," he is "never in a fury."

Prior to offering several excerpts from Sat3 and Sat4, Masson (1876, 338–42) states that such epithets as "majesty" and "sublimity" appear "altogether out of place in a criticism of Donne."

Dowden (1890, 802–03) claims that Donne's Satyres are "among the poems which were not spun out of his brain, but were written, to use Wordsworth's expression, with his eye upon the object."

Norton (1895, 1:239) comments that "there is plenty of sound feeling, good sense and wit" in Donne's Satyres, "as well as of acute observation and picturesque delineation of life and character."

Furst (1896, 230–31) commends the Satyres for showing "the results of wide and exact observation," and he adds that the "unusual modes of thought are expressed with such accurate figures and such finished word-fitting that the work abounds in passages remarkable in their aptness for quotation," though the "unexpectedness of thought and the extraordinary compactness of expression" often makes it necessary to "read and reread a passage many times before its content is wholly understood and appreciated."

Saintsbury (1896, 1:xxii–xxiii), in his introduction to Chambers' edition of Donne's poems, notes that Donne's Satyres "display to the full his manly strength and shrewd sense," that "his handling of the perennial subjects of satire is far more fresh, serious, and direct than is usual with Satirists," and yet "it is not here that we find the true Donne."

In a review of Gosse (1899), an anonymous commentator writing in *The Nation* (1900, 112) calls the first four Satyres "extraordinary performances for a youth," noting that "though rugged in versification, they show as a whole remarkable breadth and keenness of observation and maturity of thought."

Chadwick (1900, 36–37), reviewing Gosse (1899), contends of Donne's Satyres that "nothing could be more unlike the characteristic Elizabethan verse," adding that, in particular *Sat4* "afforded ample illustration of that stupendous learning which was the wonder of his time," and that *Sat3* offers "some of those things which have attracted quite as many to Donne's poetry as its riot of the senses and its sexual daring."

Wendell (1904, 123) begins his assessment of Donne's poetry by noting that the Satyres are "in every sense the least palpably conventional, and so apparently the most genuine, of his time and perhaps of our language."

Concerning the total number of Satyres, Grierson (1909, 4:205) notes that while "the editions since 1669 contain seven," yet "the explicit testimony of Sir William Drummond" indicates that "Donne wrote only five."

Sinclair (1909, 179–80, 199–200) quotes *Sat1* 1–24 as "a short specimen" of the Satyres and then states, "noble lines stud every page" (199–200).

Grierson (1912, 2:x, xiv–xvii, 100–05) asserts of Donne that "it is not in the *Satyres* that this wit of his is to us most obvious," for "nothing grows so soon out of date as contemporary satire" (x). He adds that in these poems, and "notably the third," there is a "reflective, moralizing strain" that "predominates" (xiv).

MacLeane (1915, 178) describes the Satyres as "quite a novel experiment."

Aronstein (1920, 160–61) argues that in the Satyres the whole life of the times, the theater, the seasonal markets with their shows, the fashion, the local and national politics, the deplorable state of governmental affairs and theological disputes, along with the entire knowledge of the time—theology and philosophy, linguistics and literature, geography and history, the Bible, classical mythology, and medieval sagas—are freely exploited by Donne in pictures and comparisons with humor and spirit. He finds the spiritual richness of the young Donne and the power of his words to be astonishing.

Guiney (1920, 13–14) describes the Satyres as "subtle, though rough and powerful," and states that the poems "show a strife, involving some vital change," in Donne's mind.

Grierson (1921, xviii) believes that the record of Donne's early years is contained in the Satyres, which he describes as "harsh, witty, lucid, full of a young man's scorn of fools and low callings, and a young thinker's consciousness of the problems of religion in an age of divided faiths, and of justice in a corrupt world."

Fausset (1924, 52–53) suggests that the targets of Donne's Satyres are also aspects of himself.

Simpson (1924, 47, 152–58) mentions references to Rabelais in the Satyres and *Coryat*, adding that several items in "Donne's *Catalogue*" remind us of the Satyres, specifically the reference to Topcliffe in some manuscripts of *Sat4* and to Luther's changing of the Lord's Prayer in *Sat2*.

Nethercot (1925a, 130) notes that a few readers of Donne's Satyres in the Romantic period began to understand the difficulties of his poetry.

Eliot (1926, 139–40) believes of Donne that "the longer poems, and especially the Satires, contributed as much or more toward his original reputation as the short poems better known to most of us." He concedes that Donne's Satyres are "less metaphysical" than his other poems, but remarks that "the nature of satiric poetry is (or was) such that its exercise gave play to some of the faculties, which became completely developed in his metaphysical poetry," adding that Donne is not necessarily a satirist "in the modern sense," nor is the "irony and wit" in other poems "in the same sense of a satiric kind." Eliot says that "satire" has two meanings: "a verse form or genre," or "a mood or attitude."

Cogan (1929, 188) argues that because of their narrow focus on contemporary abuses, the Satyres are "inclined to be a trifle tedious to the modern reader."

Hayward (1930, 121) believes that the Satyres are "the least appreciated" of Donne's poems since they are also the "most awkwardly constructed."

Eliot (1931, 18) believes that Donne's originality is in the Songs and Sonets, Elegies, and Satyres rather than the *Sermons*.

Williamson (1932, 581) comments on the 1639 edition of Donne's *Poems*, which contain "several notes relative to the canon of Donne's verses," including references to a sixth and seventh of the Satyres, of which he asserts, "none of these poems occurs in the 1633 edition, but all appear in the 1635 edition," and "I have never been able to find Donne in these poems; they smack too much of a convention." He adds that "the original entries in the Stationers' Registers may throw some light on [the matter]" in that entries for 13 September 1632 and 31 October 1632 both refer to five satires.

Lewis (1934b, 655) argues that the Satyres attempt "not so much an acceptance of society as it was, but the provision for society of some metaphysical principles," and he adds that we should allow Donne's later works to "elucidate" his Satyres.

Lindsay (1934b, 636) disagrees with Lewis (1934b), arguing that *Sermons* and *Pseudo-Martyr* should not be used to understand the Satyres.

Crofts (1936, 129) calls the Satyres "modern," adding that Donne's poems are "full of knaves and fools and spades called spades."

Rugoff (1939, 171) comments that beggars, strumpets, and street characters affected Donne vividly and contribute to the strain of realism in his poems, especially in the Satyres.

Jonas (1940, 205–06) credits Donne as "one of those" who rescued satire "from the trammels of fable and pastoral innuendo."

Hillyer (1941, xxii, xxxii–xxxiv) describes the Satyres as "merely vituperative," arising from Donne's "own resentments," and are "not sufficiently objective as portraits of characters to emerge from the passing interest of their day." He acknowledges that the poems have a certain historical interest since they are "early satires in the five-stress couplet," but he points out that Chaucer "is clearly the first master of the satirical couplet in passages from his *Prologue*" (xxxii). He also finds the initial four Satyres, in particular, to be focused on "spheres of life in which Donne was personally involved," leading to "the unrestrained bitterness of their hyperbole" that reveals as much about Donne's "own disappointments as of the society of the time," while *Sat5*, "presumably addressed to a more detached subject—the corruption of the judiciary— nevertheless exhumes the victims of the former onslaughts and subjects them to an after-drubbing" (xxxiii).

Hardy (1942, 62–63) finds the Satyres "repellent in their savagery," but showing "the strength of a tiger," "the sincerity of a seminarist," and "the orginality of the inventor, or rebellious experimenter." She adds that to read the poems "is like being present at the opening of a play" as Donne immediately establishes a particular city-scene, while "the stage is always crowded" with the various types and characters of Elizabethan London.

Legouis (1942, 184–96) notes that while re-reading the Satyres, he "made a list of those words that resisted explanation after the OED had been anxiously consulted," and the compiled results consist "of (1) words (2) meanings that Donne might be claimed to have either originated or at least introduced into the literary language" (184–85). See Notes and Glosses of individual lines for examples.

Stein (1944a, 269–71) suggests that the "satiric spirit" which appears in all Donne's works connects him with rationalism, but that "it is in satire that we find the freest expression of ideas dangerous in their realism" (269). He emphasizes the "urbane detachment" of the Satyres and connects Donne's "melancholy" with his "satiric spirit" (270–71).

Ryan (1948, 8) states that the Satyres show Donne "to be precocious in vice as well as in learning and in mastery of words."

Danby (1950, 519–21) argues that Donne occupies the same social and literary tradition as Beaumont and Fletcher, for like them he was the "marginal beneficiary of the Great House tradition, who survived, depressed and now utterly dependent, to write subserviently under the conditions inaugurated by James" (519). The Satyres and Songs and Sonets exhibit the same stand "on truth and his own independent experience," and with a "kind of dignity which he feels due both to God and the Muse" (520). However, within ten years, Danby says, the "truth" Donne was dedicated to in the Satyres becomes "the fabrication of the compliments he there despised" in the Verse Letters and Anniversaries (521).

Milgate (1950, 230, 383) notes Heltzel's (1938) discovery that Joseph Wybarne, in *The New Age of Old Names* (1609), had used lines Sat4 18–23 to describe the Antichrist and acknowledged Donne's Satyres in the margin as his source (ed.—see Sat4 General Commentary), "a reference that would have been pointless if the Satires had not been widely known in manuscript." He adds that Francis Davison included Donne's Satyres both in a list of manuscripts which he wanted to get and in a list of "Papers Lent" and suggests that Davison "might have lent his brother an incomplete set of Satires to which he wished to make additions" (230). He concludes that the only writings of Donne's that we can be sure Davison knew about were the Satyres, Elegies, and Epigrams and that the evidence generally suggests that the poems printed before 1633, the Satyres and the Epigrams, "seem to have been most widely known to the casual reader" (383).

Ochojski (1950, 538) notes that Donne mentions over "forty Spanish and Portuguese authors" in his works, including the Satyres, and of those references "at least half of them [are] Jesuit polemicists of the Counter-Reformation."

Sprott (1950, 344) questions whether Donne revoked the Satyres in his 1 April 1627 sermon to King Charles (*Sermons* 7:408).

Leishman (1951, 118) asserts that the Satyres are "far less characteristic" of Donne's work than the Elegies.

Cazamian (1952, 364) finds that the conceits in the Songs and Sonets provide more of a focus for humor than those in the Satyres and Elegies. Nilsen (1997, 139) remarks similarly.

Cox (1956, 112) argues that the Satyres are "adaptations to contemporary life of stock Latin themes," with Sat3 standing out for its "penetrating and serious discussion of the problem of choosing between rival religious beliefs, the alternative possibilities being embodied in short satirical portraits."

Redpath (1956, xix) notes that the Satyres provide evidence about London in the 1590s but also illustrate Donne's learning.

Sutherland (1958, 33) observes that Donne's Satyres escaped the Bishops Ban because they had not been printed.

Kishimoto (1960, 61–72) writes broadly of the Satyres, noting their association with Horace and their dramatic characteristics. He says that Donne's satire is double-edged, attacking both that which is figuratively suggested (the tenor) and the figurative image itself (the vehicle), and he agrees with other commentators that the Satyres are characteristically witty.

Martz (1960, 330, 336) states that the Satyres provide "the most stiking example of a successful coordination" of the "three prime elements" operating in Donne's poetry (336), namely, "the love song, the satire, and certain religious arts" (330).

Alvarez (1961, 197) mentions a note by Francis Davison "sometime after 1608" indicating that he wished to include Donne's Satyres in his *Poetical Rhapsody*.

Andreasen (1963, 63, 69) believes that the "superficial negativeness" and "ugliness" of the Satyres are "redeemed" by their positive social values, as well as their "lightning" movement and wit (63). She notes that the first two poems contain little "praise of virtue" and are "highly visual, dramatic, and concrete" (69).

Carey (1963, 24) says that the Satyres "teem with the actualities of Elizabethan London and burn with social protest."

Gros (1964, 73) asserts that in the Satyres (as well as the Elegies and the love poems) Donne devalues women almost as much as he overestimates them.

Geraldine (1965, 116, 119) suggests that Donne is more concerned in the Satyres with the use and abuse of reason than with failures of the will (119). She suspects that the content of these poems is comparable to that of Donne's "little book of cases" of casuistry (116).

LeComte (1965, 48) observes that the Satyres provide glimpses of London life.

Esler (1966, 229–30) believes that Donne's "satirical railing" indicates that he was "probably troubled with the disease of melancholy."

Zivley (1966, 87) notes that Donne's critics have neglected the Satyres because their genre was "fleeting and imitative," and they are dissimilar to Donne's more popular poetry. She then itemizes the follies exposed by the poems.

Gardner (1967, 193) notes that the manuscripts of the Satyres show "no tradition of titles."

In a detailed linguistic analysis, Koch (1967, 81) concludes that the following features are "necessary for 'verse satire'": a "specific fundamental arrangement of topics," "culturally specific proper names as topic," and a "specific semantic type of sentence (valuative : negative)."

Heath-Stubbs (1969, 23) praises the Satyres for being "packed with thought" as well as being "vivid and dramatic in their observation of contemporary life."

The imagery in the Satyres, Lecocq (1969, 393–95, 397–98) states, always appears centrifugal in relationship to the apparent subjects, but centripetal in relationship to the fundamental themes in the poems. As such, the multitude of human activities, of which Donne paints an astonishingly detailed picture, compose a sort of universal *danse macabre* (393). He adds that the natural setting in the Satyres is reduced almost exclusively to two images, that of the river and that of the mountain, the one representing movement toward inevitable destruction and the other showing how one can find salvation (393–94). In addition, he poses the following questions with regard to the place of the Satyres in Donne's canon: are we not here within the confines of profane poetry and sacred poetry? Could satyre be a decisive stage of the progress of the soul? Since it gives us such a serious lesson, could it be this moral poetry which marks the transition between the glorification of the senses and the exaltation of divine feeling? (394–95). Further, the merger of *carpe diem* with *memento mori* becomes the dialectic of the Satyres (397). Finally, he considers how Walton's report of Donne's transformation of his own death into a dramatic spectacle reflects a theatricality that informs the composition and concerns of the Satyres (398).

Nelly (1969, 61) observes that the "realism" of the Satyres "reveals the bold, independent mind of Donne, the steely appraising eye, which if trained predominantly on the inward scene, missed no detail that passed without," adding that the poems "are full of the savagery of youthful scorn for the false fashions of London society in the 1590s."

Crinó (1970, 69) states that the Satyres are not considered Donne's best work.

Kermode (1971, 133–34) remarks that it is "doubtful," with the exception of *Sat3*, that the Satyres "play much part in anybody's thinking about Donne."

Powers (1971, 7) observes that the Satyres "were popular in manuscript."

Webber (1971, 290) argues that the topicality of the Satyres has made them less interesting to modern readers, for "Donne the political rebel, as he was in his early twenties, has never stirred our interest."

Empson (1972, 96) observes that Donne "became famous during his lifetime for poems which he refused to print," but unlike the love poems, the Satyres "could be shown round" since they "had claims to be grave and moral," and writing in this genre "was considered a respectable pastime."

MacColl (1972, 30) comments that Donne's reputation as a satirist was established by 1598 when he "had been paid the compliment of imitation by Everard Guilpin." He points out further that when Joseph Wybarne quoted from *Sat4*, "he could count on the *Satyres* being known, or at least known of," but MacColl also reminds us that the epigram Jonson wrote to accompany the copy of the Satyres he sent to Lady Bedford indicates that the poems "were not necessarily widely read."

Shawcross (1972, 272) argues that in the Satyres Donne "constitutes himself as a personal, unloyal opposition to the Establishment, angry with the world for its indifference to him, and angry with himself for his partial involvement with it."

Parker (1975, 21, 113) calls the Satyres "uncomfortable works, as they were meant to be" (21) and regards them as "obvious examples" of Donne's "pioneering spirit as far as social criticism goes" (113).

Dubrow (1976, 132) observes that Donne's Satyres "often show obvious signs of carelessness and haste" and that the "quality of his poems" in different genres "varies considerably."

Lauritsen (1976, 117–18) observes that few of Donne's poems "have inspired as much silence" as the Satyres, which he believes merit more critical attention than they have received so far.

Yoklavich (1976, 552) comments that a son of Donne's friend Mrs. Thomas Cokayne, Sir Aston Cokayne, a minor poet and playwright, praises Donne in his poem "To my learned friend Mr. Thomas Bancroft upon his Book of Satyres" published in his collection *Small Poems of Divers Sorts* (1658). After referring to Horace, Persius, Juvenal, and Ariosto, and two contemporary satirists Barclay and Wither, Cokayne calls Donne "our prime wit."

Datta (1977, 9) finds "the classical satiric stand-point" to be one of "moderation between extremes," whereas Donne's "is more absolute, more religious than moral." She points out that while his contemporary Joseph Hall's stance is that of "*In medio virtus* ('virtue is in the mean')," Donne's is "*In summo foelicitas* ('Joy is in the extreme')" symbolised by his mistress, named variously as 'vertue'" (*Sat1* 41) and "'my Mistresse Truth'" (*Sat3* 80, *Sat4* 163) "and 'law'" (*Sat5* 69); and that in *Sat2* "we are made aware only of her absence, as love and marriage are bought and sold, honour is prostituted."

Hester (1977c, 184) observes that in the Satyres, "it is apparent that the outstanding feature and in many ways the abiding concern of the speaker is with 'zeal,'" and "the initial and final concern of all five is with the concomitant hatred and charity of the satirist himself." He adds that the poems are unique for "their application and elaboration of the decorum of the biblical satirists, their accommodation of one set of principles from biblical aesthetics to the moral and spiritual dilemmas of late sixteenth-century man."

Hoover (1978, xii) believes that the Satyres "disclose a skeptical and cynical outlook."

Javitch (1978, 132) asserts that the satires of Donne and his contemporaries introduce "uncompromising anti-courtly attitudes, which only intensify with the coming of James I to the throne."

According to Selden (1978, 46), English satirists of the 1590s such as Donne "shared a common social and cultural milieu which had an important conditioning effect on their satiric writings." They were young men who had come from the universities to the Inns of Court "to study law and seek preferment at court." Their outlook was "cynical and elitist" and their reading of the classics "extensive." But such reading "did not finally determine their conception of the form and content of literary genres."

Cousins (1979, 107) contends that the Satyres offer "the most persuasive evidence that the term 'mannerism' accurately defines a moment in English literary history." The poems, he says, present Donne's "considered response, and the first unified response, to the ideas and forms of the High Renaissance styles," and "their attitudes, design, and detail find counterparts in Italian mannerist art," though the poems also exist as "quite independent creations." He explains that "the centrality of skepticism to the English mannerist style" most clearly "indicates the usefulness of the term 'mannerism,'" adding that while it "suggests a European context" for Donne, it also encourages us to "examine the singularity" of his achievements.

Corthell (1982, 156, 162) suggests of the Satyres that "because they are satires and therefore concerned with public circumstances," they offer a "unique opportunity for studying the relationship between Donne's self-presentation and his awareness of the political and social realities of the late Elizabethan period" (156). He adds that the poems "present Donne's developing awareness of the fearful relatedness of religious and secular authority and power in Elizabethan England" (162).

Miller (1982, 827–28) comments that when, in the nineteenth century, Donne's poetry "occasionally" attracted interest among the "discerning," it was for the Satyres, not the lyrics, adding that the same attitude existed in the eighteenth century, which "valued metrical euphony too highly to accept even the satires." He concludes that though Donne's lyrics are now generally preferred, the Satyres are seen as "artistically effective in their original form, although this artistry is of a different order from that of the lyrics," adding that "with images accumulated from a similarly wide range of sources," the Satyres create a "thematic center."

Kerins (1984, 35) argues that in the Satyres, Donne "writes from a tradition of secular humanism, a tradition which extolled the poet as a creator himself."

In Mann's view (1985, 538), Donne's Satyres "confront fragmentation," "expose it as a corruption of God's original design," and "offer a positive response." By presenting "ideal virtue in the figure of a woman, who must be loved," he says, the poems "focus on the process of bringing that love into action by restoring the relation of body and soul."

Parry (1985, 46–48, 50) suggests that the Satyres "are part of an outbreak of such writing" in the decade of the 1590s, when a "new naturalism swept through English verse, reacting against the more formal beauty and dignity of the poetic generation of Sidney, Spenser and Marlowe," demonstrating instead "a premium on direct, frank observation, outspoken opinions and iconoclastic attitudes, the sign of a new generation bidding for poetic power." He continues that "the fashions and morals of the Court are a favourite target," yet the poems show "no disposition to reform, only to record the bizarre fads of the day," for after all, Donne's audience "lay at Court and at the Inns of Court, where people knew and enjoyed the world he caricatured" (46–47). He asserts further that the Satyres "survive because of their documentary power for the sights and smells and intrigues of Elizabethan London," and although the themes are "trifling" (with the exception of Sat3), "the social observations are constantly referred back to religious issues or classical antecedents," providing a "background of morality" (48). He concludes that the Satyres "come from a poet caught up in the mainstream of contemporary life to a degree unmatched by any non-dramatic writer since Chaucer" (50).

According to Caracciolo-Trejo (1986, 2:11, 13), the Satyres possess an elevated tone of implicit social protest in referring to persons typical of the court as well as to bureaucrats, judges, noblemen, ladies, and servants in a detailed catalogue of moral failings (11). He adds that in these poems the dissolute libertine poet gradually gives way to the devotional poet and to the agonized believer (13).

Marotti (1986, 15–16) conjectures that the Satyres were likely gathered "into sets to be circulated in 'books' or quires." He suggests that ("at Jonson's urging") Donne "sent the five-poem version of the Satires to the Countess of Bedford," adding that "some of the manuscripts indicate that earlier sets of three or four satires might have circulated, while some of the manuscript evidence points to the circulation of the Satires along with the two verse letters to Brooke ('The Storme' and 'The Calme') and with Sir John Roe's (?) 'Sleep, next society.'"

Waller (1986, 242, 245) suggests that the Satyres reveal "some of the age's most crucial cultural contradictions," for the poems "are not merely the product of a personal crisis, even though they are insistently articulated as confusing and wounding the self." He states further that these poems "record a fascination with being thrown into experience and finding no way of examining its meaning except from within" (242). He also remarks that by the turn of the century, Donne was an MP and a private secretary to Egerton, a "rising young man confidently waiting on the fringes of the Court, his satirical poetry and verse letters those of a fashionably cynical young man on the make" (245).

Rogers (1987, 170) writes of the Satyres that "where Hall had gone through the imitation of Juvenal in a bookish way," by contrast Donne "immediately involves himself and us in the urban scene," adding that the "seriousness" of the Satyres "sometimes masks the element of play."

According to Zunder (1988, 79), the Satyres, other than Sat3, are "responses to the economic and social changes of the sixteenth century," and thus are "characteristic of the tradition of satire in the century, from Wyatt onwards," and "these changes are viewed, again characteristically, in traditional terms."

Parfitt (1989, 33) asserts of the Satyres that "the quality of the best writing" in them "suggests that Donne is imaginatively engaged," yielding a "curious blend of the witty, superior satirist figure with another which is restless and unrooted." He points out that these poems "do not concern themselves very much with women, even though satire of women is common in both the native and classical traditions," yet he adds that "it would be misleading to see this reticence as suggesting respect for the feminine, for what attention is given to women in these poems fits her into traditional male-defined roles."

Patrides (1989, 105) says that Donne's Satyres "are among his most successful productions," forming his "most perfectly orchestrated cluster of poems," and he notes further their positive impression on Pope.

Fish (1990, 235) asserts that "irony" is the "subject" of the Satyres.

Chandra (1991, 79–80) purports that the Satyres do not have many of the "qualities of metaphysical poetry," but they "give an idea of Donne's awareness of the corruptions of the age which nurtured and not only tolerated but enjoyed the conventional love poetry against which he was to declare a crusade."

B. Smith (1991, 161, 174–75, 185–86) states that the "sexual freedom" celebrated in such works as Greene's *Menaphon* (1589), Lodge's *Rosalynde* (1590), and Sidney's revised *Arcadia* (1593) is "vigorously attacked" in the Satyres (161). He argues further that in the Satyres Donne speaks of homosexual behavior in a "Christian cosmic context" (174), in which the "specific sexual target" Donne attacks is that of "a man lusting after a boy" (186).

Smuts (1991, 108) remarks that "the Elizabethan taste for Petrarchism, allegory and rhetorical artifice gave way before an emphasis on plain speech, psychological insight and vividly immediate portraits of corruption," and Donne's Satyres, along with Jonson's court poems and Roman tragedies and Bacon's essays and historiographical works, "incisively dissect the corrosive effects of luxury, ambition and power upon a ruling elite."

Norbrook (1992, 23–25) notes that the Satyres, which circulated only in manuscript, "powerfully evoke the emergence of London as a centre of political debate" (23), and he comments further that the "sceptical view of all forms of public morality and political authority" promoted in the poems "ventured on dangerous ground" (25).

Davies (1994, 2), in a discussion of the effects of reading Donne's poems, notes briefly that the Satyres and Elegies "make free with the obscene."

Griffin (1994, 11–12, 140) remarks that Donne "gives a strong impression of the climate of oppression under which a Renaissance satirist operated," explaining that "the satirist disdains the court world but is nevertheless dangerously drawn to it" (11–12). Griffin also asks, "is Donne's interlocutor merely a hanger-on, a political climber, or a spy seeking to entrap the satirist into a libelous, disloyal, or papist sentiment?" (140).

Cain (1995, 83) argues that although Donne has traditionally been regarded as a "conservative monarchist," this idea is challenged by "the anti-monarchical, subversive elements" in the Satyres.

Manley (1995, 397–98) comments that throughout the Satyres, "the attempt to reform the world through the negotiation of compromises and discriminations is thwarted by the world's erosion—through a kind of 'stream-effect'—of all moral potential."

Sawday (1995, 202) contends that Donne "moved within the enclosed circles of court wits, lawyers, and place-men," though he was "clearly not a 'court' poet," adding that the Satyres contain "matter for 'some feare'—a classic anxiety of the courtier-poet."

Slights (1996, 70, 73) comments that the Satyres "place more emphasis on the self-destructive, parasitic, and exploitative worlds of town and court than on the dangers of stagnation in private study," yet they "express both delight in privacy and fear of isolation, both a sense of duty to participate in social relations and a fear of losing personal integrity and autonomy." She adds that "although male figures predominate" in the Satyres, Donne's "satiric analysis of the moral and intellectual bankruptcy of town and court includes references to widows and whores as well as to the men who cheat them" (70). Commenting on the Satyres and the letters written during his exile at Mitcham, she concludes that Donne "consistently valued private retirement with its opportunities for study and reflection yet loathed its paralyzing dullness," noting that Donne "desired to participate actively in the world but feared entanglement in the corrupt ways of the world of business and politics" (73).

Burt (1997, 147–48, 154) remarks that Storm 49–50 "predict or echo" the Satyres, as well as the "coarser Elegies," in which "jealous husbands, dangerous news, and uncontrollable information virtually define life in modern London and at court" (148). He adds that the poem printed as Satyre Six in 1669 "sounds very little like Donne" (154).

Corthell (1997, 19, 24, 26, 53–54) argues that Donne's "satirical rendition of late Elizabethan ideology, on the one hand, and new historicist representations of the same period, on the other, are early and late stages of a long historical process of working on the relationship between the literary text and ideology," or in other words, "on the one hand, the subject is entirely contained by the ideological formations he satirizes/criticizes; on the other, satirist and critics want to reclaim a strength from their powerlessness." Thus, Donne, "like most Elizabethan verse satirists," is "obsessed with the problem of investing moral authority in a subject who speaks for a moral minority." Further, he claims, Donne's "satirical production of ideology repeatedly slides into a satirical production of the subject of satire," and "in the act of defining the object of his attack Donne discovers his own desire in the object." As a response then, Donne writes in order "to textualize the problem," and "this textual practice, emerging in a context of early modern conflicts over authority and representation, contributes to the creation of a new, literary subject of history" (19). As such, Corthell concludes, the Satyres "invite readers to identify with the authority derived from authorship and writing—to identify, that is, with either the author or the wise man who confers authority on the texts" (54).

Oliver (1997, 61, 67, 168n13, 262, 233) mentions Donne's letter, "written about 1600, possibly to Wotton" (168n13), in which Donne states, "to my satires there belongs some fear." He also alludes several times to "Donne's pulpit rejection of his satires" (262) in a 1627 sermon (7:408). He observes further that if "the remark about his best verse being the least truthful" is viewed as fact, then such a statement "would amount to an affirmation of the fictional nature" of the Elegies, Satyres, and Songs and Sonets, "all poems whose existence embarrassed him" (233).

Blissett (2000, 102–03, 110, 113–114, 118) believes "that Jonson placed the highest estimation" on the Satyres (103), adding that Jonson's "To Lucy Countesse of Bedford, with Mr Donnes Satyres" suggests that he "must have copied or caused [them] to be copied" (102). He notes further that Francis Davidson "made a note to ask Jonson or someone else for a copy" of the Satyres (102), and such copying "argues great admiration" (110). In addition, he observes that in the Satyres "the royal Presence itself does not escape judgment" (113), citing specifically Sat2 69–70, Sat3 91–92, and Sat4 74, 78–80, 181–82, and 181–85. While he explains that Sat5 is the only one to make a "complimentary address to the Queen" (114), he concludes that Donne's poems are concerned with the evils of the court, a place he identifies with the theatre, and therefore "must convey the wretchedness of suitors" (118).

King (2000, 374) summarizes the targets of the Satyres as "the fashionable excesses of Elizabethan costume, hyperbole in romantic poetry, courtly flattery and corruption in law courts."

Reid (2000, 49) states that the Satyres "have a considerable range of ways to express alienation, from sardonic and self-ironizing fun to resolving on heroic individuality."

Robbins (2000, 424–25) notes that though Jonson was a "rival seeker of patronage," he fulfilled the Countess of Bedford's wish to see the Satyres—a wish "perhaps prompted by Henry Goodyer"—and added a poem praising both the poems and the Countess.

Sproxton (2000, 121) observes that in the Satyres, as in Pseudo-Martyr, Donne "was pleased to vent his wrath against posture."

Lee (2001, 60) explains that Donne developed a new style or trend of poetry, one seen especially well in the Satyres, that reacts to intellectual idealism and shows a heightened interest in realism and in psychologically informed perspectives.

Mackenzie (2001, 79) suggests that the intention of the Satyres is "to scandalize life at court."

DONNE AS SATIRIST

Pope (1735 [98]) conjectures that despite writing Sat4 Donne was "*acceptable to the Princes and Ministers under whom*" he lived, because he was "*a Satyrist,*" not "*a Libeller,*" and "*to a true Satyrist nothing is so odious as a Libeller, for the same reason as to a man truly virtuous nothing is so hateful as a Hypocrite.*"

Cooper (1737, xii) writes that Donne, along with Corbet, "added Wit to Satire, and restor'd the almost forgotten Way of making Reproof it self entertaining."

Brown (1748, 3:333), in his essay on the history of satire, describes Donne's importance to the genre, stating:

'Twas then plain DONNE in honest vengeance 'rose,
His wit refulgent, tho' his rhyme were prose:
He 'midst an age of puns and pedants wrote
With genuine sense, and *Roman* strength of thought.

Warton (1774, 4:50) compares Donne's Satyres unfavorably to those of Hall, though stating that Donne "lived so many years later" [sic] and was "susceptible of modern refinement," especially by Pope.

Headley (1787, xv), in his scale of "The Select Beauties" of English poetry (among whom Donne is not included), classifies Donne solely as a "Satyrical" writer, along with Hall, Marston, and Rowlands.

Hallam (1839, 2:316) appends to his discussion of Hall the comment that Donne, as a satirist, has "as much obscurity as Hall" and "still more inharmonious versification, and not nearly equal vigour."

Spalding (1852, 280) notes in his brief discussion of satire that Donne's are "as obscure as Hall's, and hardly in any respect better than they, but more widely known in recent times through Pope's modernized alterations of them."

B[lond] (1861, 90) asserts that, after Hall, Donne was "the second man to write English satire proper," and in his Satyres Donne "lashed the vices of society and the Court, and literary charlatans."

Clarke (1872, 1:286) characterizes Donne as "a vigorous although rude satirist."

Grosart (1872–73, 2:xxvii–xxxi) states that in the Satyres Donne "does not simply scold and call it invective, or give nicknames, or 'report' scandals," nor does he "hold-up physical or mental infirmities to ridicule," but instead he fixes "his eye keenly on the wickedness he is roused to expose," and he does so "with a crashing destructiveness, a bearing-down *momentum* of indignation, a sad passionateness of scorn, and honest, unfearing, unsparing striking at the highest-seated wrong-doers, and a felicitious realism of word-painting" that makes these poems "very notable indeed" (xxvii). In presenting "pictures of the age, in its manners and usages and morals," the Satyres, Grosart asserts, are "inestimable." The poems are "a man's living heart pulsating with the most tragical reality of emotion," so that by comparison Hall's "look thin and empty, and painfully envious of contemporaries" (xxviii). Grosart believes that it is likely that Hall "had heard, or read at least, the first four of Donne's Satires in MS, and wrote his own in the recollection of them," so that his challenge in *Virgidemarium* for Donne to be "the *second* English Satirst" is actually a call for Donne to follow his example and "not hold in MS. his Satires" (xxx–xxxi).

In his assessment of the Satyres, Minto (1880, 852–54) describes the poems as "very different" from the "dashing, smirking, fluent imitations of the ancients which Joseph Hall put forth with a claim to be the first of English satirists." He contends that the poems "are not scholarly exercises or artistic displays," but instead "have their root in the individual feelings and thoughts of the writer" and thereby "reveal the genuine workings of his mind upon the facts that life presented to it." Finally, he believes that in these poems "the high spirits and unworldly mind of generous youth shine through," adding that "the terrible crudeness and power" of the poems is not a "churlish crudeness," but is rather the "boisterous extravagance of youth, the delight of a fresh untamed intellect in its own strength" (852–53).

Bradford (1892, 355–64) finds that Donne's Satyres are "masterly," elaborating generally that one need not "settle whether he was the first of English satirists in date," since in terms of "quality," "no other can be placed beside him in his own line," and saying more specifically that Hall is "far more conventional," Wither is "thinner, though certainly clearer," and Marston, though with a "touch of Donne's force," is nonetheless "more grotesque and labored." He concludes that while "obscurity and coarseness" will hamper the critical reception of Donne's Satyres, anyone who studies them "carefully" is "repaid" thus: "How the characters stand out! With what energy he lashes the vices and follies around him!" (362).

Saintsbury (1896, 1:xxii–xxiii) notes that the Satyres display Donne's "manly strength and shrewd sense," that Donne's handling of satiric subjects "is far more fresh, serious, and direct than is usual with Satirists," but that it is not in the Satyres that we find the "true Donne."

Alden (1899, 92) comments that Lodge's satiric verse preceded Donne's "by at least two years," adding that while Donne's work "may have been in manuscript form before the publication of the *Fig for Momus*," Lodge probably did not see the manuscript. Nilsen (1997, 65) comments similarly on Donne and Lodge.

Gosse (1899, 1:37) observes that the Satyres are not "general invectives" like those of Hall, nor "fantastic libels against individuals" like those of Marston, but are instead a "series of humorous and sardonic portraits of types," such as "the Theophrastians a little later loved to define and describe."

Thompson (1899, 505–06) notes that Donne's first poems, as Satyres, were the reverse of what one might suspect from his education, adding that they were "among the very earliest of English satires, in the formal sense of the word." Affirming the 1593 date for the Satyres, he notes that Donne "was a satirist before Hall, and after the languid attempt of Lodge."

Grierson (1909, 4:197, 205–08) contends that Donne's Satyres are both "wittier than those of his contemporaries," "weightier in their serious criticism of life, and happier in their portrayal of manners and types" (206–07). By way of example, he then provides brief overviews for each of the five poems before he adds that the Satyres "were very popular," and, judging "from the extant copies or fragments of copies, as well as from contemporary allusions," they "appear to have circulated more freely than the songs and elegies" (208).

Sinclair (1909, 180) repeats Gosse's (1899) assessment of the Satyres and concludes that Donne must have thought that "his great predecessors had never completely shaken off a timidity and monotony which had come down to them from Surrey and Gascoigne."

Brooke (1913, 187), noting that Donne was "one of the first great English satirists, and the most typical and prominent figure of a satirical age," comments that satire comes "with the Bible of truth in one hand and the sword of laughter in the other."

Symons (1916, 83) suggests that intellectual pride caused Donne "to satirise the pretensions of humanity."

Aronstein (1920, 157) argues that Donne is completely original in the content of the Satyres, which in seriousness of conviction, force and profundity of thought, spirit, and wit leave far behind the more simplistic works of Joseph Hall and, above all, Marston's ambitious ostentatiousness and pompousness.

Fausset (1924, 43–44, 49) expresses that while Hall's and Guilpin's satirical efforts were "trivial and derivative," Donne's are the earliest indications of a fundamental "attitude towards life" (43) that remained hostile to the sentimentality of contemporary poetry. He believes that although the first four Satyres inadequately demonstrate Donne's individuality, they do reveal something of his early life in London.

Eliot (1926, 142) contends that "the satirist spirit is not simple but complex" and specifies that the two qualities of Donne's satirist are, first, "an active ratiocinative intellect, interested in a variety of subjects rather than coordinated to one intent," and second, "a keen eye for common observation."

Payne (1926, 26–27, 31) believes that "almost certainly" Donne is "the orginator in England" of satiric verse (27), and he adds that in the Satyres "there is little, if any, mere personal attack, and no hysterical outcries against vice in general" (31).

Simpson (1931, 24) points out that Donne, Hall, and Marston pioneered formal verse satire in England.

Spencer (1931, 182) suggests that Donne and his contemporaries in the 1590s (notably Hall, Marston, and Guilpin) took a scornful attitude toward their world.

Tate (1933, 129–30) argues that Donne's Satyres resemble those of Hall, Marston, and Tourneur, whom taken together "form a school." He adds that the satirists of the 1590's "went back through Sackville to Lyndsay and Dunbar" in portraying a "medieval sense of all-pervading mortality, of the vanity of the world," which is used thematically "as a weapon of critical irony upon the vaunting romanticism of the Renaissance."

Lewis (1934b, 655) explains that what Donne attempts in the Satyres is less "an acceptance of society as it was," and more the "provision for society of some metaphysical principles such as those of constancy, or ideal youth," and he cautions against simplifying the way any group of Donne's poetry of the early period is treated, since "it is difficult to assess the relative importance of humanist and metaphysical attitudes."

Lindsay (1934b, 636) asserts that in the Satyres Donne hoped "to preserve his pride, his intellectual subtlety and sense of aloofness (nourished by the hard years of exclusion from the racial bond through his oppressed recusancy)," and, at the same time, "while 'deserting' the family cause, to become a 'normal' youth of the period."

Hardy (1942, 62–65) believes the Satyres to be "among the earliest" in England, and notes further that Donne's "far exceed" those of his contemporaries "in originality, boldness and harshness" (62). She finds that the references to court and courtiers "all bespeak an extravagance and a superficiality" that Donne, "whose mind was hungry for deeper matter," found "galling" (64).

Stein (1944a, 266–82) contends that "like the satirists of the first century, only more energetically," Donne revolts against the "threadbare artifices and petty affectations in contemporary literature," which for Donne include "the popular Petrarchan idolatry of women." He adds that Donne is a "recognized leader" both in the "movement against mythology" and in "rejecting the Elizabethan ideal of imitation" (267). While Stein does not question the "depth" of Donne's "moral sincerity," he notes that Donne "does not, like other Elizabethans, look into his spleen and write" (268). Further, according to Stein, Donne "has the satirist's eye for realistic details, and also the satirist's knowledge of human motives," and he asserts that many of Donne's thrusts are aimed, "not at private morals or at safe objects like gluttony, avarice, and lust," but rather "at wealth, at officers, at court, even at the legal religion." In addition, Donne's satiric spirit connects him with a "new rationalism," as characterized by a "quality of urbane detachment," by which Donne "is the spiritual relative of the great English masters, Chaucer, Shakespeare, Burns, and Byron" (269–70). Finally, he believes that it is "plain" that Donne "suffers from melancholy" and that "there is a definite connection between his melancholy and his satiric spirit" (271), adding that the "cumulated ailments" that produce Donne's bodily and spiritual melancholy "prove too powerful for the purge of satire" (282).

Stein (1946, 109, 113) argues that Donne's conception of obscurity in his Satyres "is not the same as Hall's or Marston's" (109), adding that the primary reasons for Donne's Satyres are "his desire to stimulate the fit reader and discourage the unfit" (113).

Leishman (1951, 106–07, 118) asserts that while Donne "can scarcely be regarded as the originator" of English satire, he might be viewed as "the precursor of that sudden outburst of formal satire and satirical comedy" produced by the young university and Inns of Court men (106). He adds that other than Donne's characteristic "dramatic quality" and his "tendency to indulge in mere wit for its own sake," the Satyres show little that is "clearly distinguishable" from other Elizabethan satires, especially regarding their "absence of clear outline and plan" and "a tendency to pile detail upon detail" in presenting "one damned thing after another" (118).

Cazamian (1952, 154, 362–63) draws a distinction between humor and satire, categorizing Donne (with Lodge, Hall, and Jonson) as a humorist (154). He suggests further that "moral indignation" is subordinated to "wit and fancy" in the Satyres (363).

Smith (1952, 226–27) states that Donne "exhibits the nervous and angry temper which might have made a successful satirist," but he adds that Donne's "observations do not extend far into the fabric of contemporary society."

Gransden (1954, 106–07) describes Donne as "one of the most humanistic of the great English poets, and therefore one of the least typical of satirists," adding that Donne's contemporaries "greatly admired" the Satyres, which "are amazingly mature, nimble, vigorous and effective." He concludes that if Donne had written only the Satyres, he would be regarded as "an important late Elizabethan poet," for in any literary history of English verse Donne's Satyres "would have to be described as a landmark."

Kernan (1959, 117–18) believes that the Satyres "constitute the most notable modification of the tradition" and that in them Donne "concentrates on cudgeling the fools for their ostentation, their pursuit of meaningless goals, their bad manners, and their persistent, boring attempts to talk to that humble and retiring scholar, John Donne," enabling him to create the "most consistent and ordered formal satires of the period."

Peter (1956, 133–34) calls attention to the "originality" of the Satyres and describes Donne as "a seminal agent, an individual and distinguished mind" who "did much to accelerate the sophistication" of Elizabethan satire.

Harris (1960, 191–92, 199) notes that the Satyres "analyse Donne's preoccupations with his own intellectual, social, and spiritual progress" and that Donne uses the satyr figure less than any contemporary satirist (191–92), adding that while Donne's poems reflect the same setting as Davies' epigrams, Donne's characters have more life, and the Satyres have more affinity with Donne's other work than with the works of contemporary satirists.

Skelton (1960, 204) notes that the Satyres and Elegies are "extremely colloquial" and "enlivened by an observation of contemporary manners which is vigorous, coarse, and acute" (204).

Gros (1964, 73) asserts that Donne, in his devaluation and overestimation of women in the Satyres, is in line with his contemporaries, especially the virulent satirists such as Marston.

Allen (1965, 86, 110, 113–15) notes that as a satirist Donne "had at least as great an influence" as Hall (86n5), that with Marston he shared "few similarities" (110), and that with Lodge and Hall he drew upon the Roman satirists for establishing the form, style, obscurity, and subject matter of his satiric verse (113). He also asserts that Donne's use of the heroic couplet for his Satyres "probably determined the verse form employed by most of his successors" (86).

LeComte (1965, 48) notes that with Guilpin, Hall, and Marston, Donne shared his interest in satire, which LeComte defines as "a form of social criticism" in verse.

Bross (1966, 147) notes that in the Satyres Donne is "more humorous than bitter," adding that in Donne's satirization of the courtier he concentrates on "the ridiculous" and "seems to delight in his own grotesque hyperbolic exaggeration."

Esler (1966, 229–30) believes that Donne's "satirical railing" indicates that he was "probably troubled with the disease of melancholy."

Gardner (1969, 214) notes that "by nature" Donne had "both the melancholy and the scorn of the satirist," and she adds that in the Satyres Donne shows himself as a "proud and irritable young man" who, in spite of his disappointment in the world, attempts "to school himself to patience" so that he might accept "in a religious spirit" what life may bring.

Hodgart (1969, 141–42) argues that Elizabethan satire is primarily the work of "young literary men" who were "determined moralists" and who were "voicing the discontent of a whole generation of over-educated and under-employed writers," were thus "rightly held to be subversive." He adds that while "this literature is sadly disappointing as poetry," Donne's Satyres are full of "brilliant ideas and images," but are "very hard to read aloud, and suffer from obscurity of thought." He contends that Donne's are the best of their era because they "boldly discuss topics outside the normal field of formal satire."

Lecocq (1969, 359–61, 386) points out that in the Satyres Donne seems at every moment, however light his words, to live a personal adventure so that it is always himself with whom he is concerned. His quest is for isolation, and that often puts him in opposition to the outside world; consequently, he does not orate, but utters a private dialogue (359). This perspective on the world, Lecocq thinks, originates in two personal circumstances for Donne: (1) his early financial independence, with the liberty it afforded him to bide his time and to delay making irreversible intellectual or spiritual decisions, and (2) his upbringing as a Roman Catholic, with its dangers of potential espionage and betrayal (360). As such, there is in Donne an ever-present will to submit reality to a personal analysis and to the domination of intelligence, even as his mind must, of necessity, exert itself with originality (361), though Lecocq adds that one suspects also an unhealthy need to stand alone, to go farther than anyone in irreverence and complexity (386).

Menascè (1969, 49) believes that younger poets like Donne discovered in satire not only an opportunity to rebel against pastoral and sentimental language (such as that of Spenser), but also a vehicle for criticizing corruption.

Miner (1969, 8–11, 36) contends that "the rejection of existing social conventions" is central to Donne's Satyres, pointing out that "repeatedly" in the poems "the bitter observation of the court shifts to the private response of the speaker," who "is revolted to the verge of nausea by what he sees," and who "repeatedly struggles to be alone, to scurry back to his private lodging, or to find his spiritual home" (8–9). He explains that although the Satyres are in a form that makes it "difficult to avoid writing public poetry," Donne's success is in "making them private" (10). He adds that "the revulsion from the court and the self-assessment that he was, or should be, a Catholic" provide "ample reasons" in accounting for Donne's turn to "private subjects, private attitudes, and private poetry to recapture an integrity threatened by the court from without and from religious uncertainty within" (36).

Ashley (1970, 61) asserts that while Elizabethan satire is as "experimental" as Elizabethan plays, the former "is almost always less interesting," adding that otherwise "interesting writers" are likely to become "more than usually clumsy and unattractive in this period when they undertake to write satire." He believes that Donne "was probably the best" of the Elizabethan satirists, but the Satyres "are basically 'not in it,' as the English say," with Donne's best verse, "which lies in other genres where he was a great master."

Hutchison (1970, 356, 359–60) asserts that Donne "does not draw a firm line between the demands of formal verse satire and satire which is defined as Menippean or Varronian" (356). He observes further that Donne's satiric approach is "militant and serious," adding that "one of the basic themes or lessons" of Donne's Satyres is his "plea for self-knowledge and an attack on things which delude and cheat the self" and that such self-analysis "goes hand in hand with the whole process of meditation" (359–60).

Summers (1970, 23–24) says that within the Satyres, Donne "gave the voice of his outrageous and witty young man a fully developed social and dramatic context," and that "however much he suffers from the fops and boors and fools on the street and at Court, his descriptions of them are usually delightful." He adds that in the Satyres Donne "put narrative, dialogue, argument, and rapidly and erratically moving verses to the creation of an extraordinary sense of this movement, this scene, these odd people and their odder language," explaining that "his central speaker is nearly always finely witty, but in his fearful alertness, the impatience of his responses, and the intemperance of his suffering, he often seems more of a participant than a judge of the satiric situation."

Winny (1970, 15–16) notes that the Satyres "are blunt and vigorously abusive" and adds that the "energy" in the poems is directed primarily "against a society grown corrupt and vicious."

Datta (1971, 9) notes that while "the classical satiric stand-point is one of moderation between extremes," Donne's is, by contrast, "more absolute, more religious than moral."

Hebaisha (1971, 25) argues that Donne helped to change the "tone" of English satyre from complaint to Renaissance satyre.

Sanders (1971, 33) suggests with regard to the Satyres that laughter for Donne is to be understood as "an act of participation, not of withdrawal," for the poems contain "none of that censorious complacency, making invidious exception for himself, which often makes the satirist ridiculous in ways he clearly hasn't envisaged," adding that such an approach is "a danger game for which everything is in question, nothing is sacred, and the only obligation is the obligation not to be dull."

Jensen (1972, 409) suggests that what readers of Renaissance satire value "is directly related to rhetoric and oratory, and thus subject to a decorum which offers far greater latitude than the narrow limits of satire—as a genre—would seem to permit." The wit of Renaissance satire is therefore not "fine wit, for it rarely attempts the discovery of occult resemblances," nor does it exemplify the "incisive precision that we associate, for example, with the satire of Pope." Rather, Jensen asserts, "in its exuberance and youthful self-delight, in its variety of techniques and tactics, and above all in its impulse toward the dramatic," the very best Renaissance satires, and Donne's among them, "most successfully deny by their very brilliance the boundaries of genre criticism."

Medine (1972, 49, 51–52) remarks generally that the satirist's challenge is to resolve his "basic impulses" for offering praise and blame "into an integrated poetic scheme," but Donne, "the best known and perhaps most successful satirist of the day," was able to solve this "fundamental problem" (49). He goes on to say that Donne "not only inveighs against materialism, sensuality, and self-delusion, but also recommends important religious and civic ideals," and Donne also successfully integrated his Satyres by combining "the commendation of virtue with the deprecation of vice" (51).

Rousseau and Rudenstine (1972, 56) point out that the Satyres "are extraordinarily diverse in tone as well as subject matter" and that through Donne's employment of "the witty, abusive, self-consciously theatrical speaker," he "seems to be more a writer of comedies and farces, relishing his own cleverness, than a serious moral commentator," one who "seems primarily intrigued by the prospect of fresh encounters and amusing discoveries."

Shawcross (1972, 267, 269) says that in accord with "the etymological meaning of satire," Donne's satiric practice, "unlike that of some of his contemporaries," is to fill the poems with "a full panorama of the evil Donne sees about him" (267). He expresses further that Donne concerns himself "with mankind, not with self and not with public adjustments," and that we therefore see a Donne whose "personal life is resolved enough for him to contemplate the world around him analytically," and a Donne whose "future will contain a direct means of showing his concern with mankind and a re-examination of his self as a result of the loss of security" (269).

Lewalski and Sabol (1973, 6) assert that Donne's Satyres exhibit the same characteristics found in Elizabethan verse satirists such as Marston, Hall, and Jonson and add that Donne "addresses the usual Elizabethan satirical topics: corrupt courts, foppish courtiers, bad poets, foolish religious sectaries."

Newton (1974, 428–29) believes that Donne "as poet, critic, and pioneer" in the writing of satire may have "foreseen" and "even entertained" the view of his contemporary readers who "regarded satire as an essentially anarchic genre written by self-serving and self-indulgent men." Thus, the Satyres present "the unfolding drama of Donne's exploration of the satiric character, together with the record of his discoveries" that also reveal "an intense critical interest on Donne's part in his own character as a satirist."

Raizada (1974, 100, 107–08) praises Donne as "one of the greatest Elizabethan satirists" (100) and suggests that Donne exhibits "the nervous and angry temper which is characteristic of a successful satirist," adding that "the force and originality of Donne's intellect" appear most clearly in these poems, which are "marked by an unusual energy and a richness of contemporary reference" through "piling detail upon detail" and thus exposing "vistas opening on corruption in every direction" (107–08).

Swift (1974, 44–45) comments that Donne's Satyres, which were passed from hand to hand until the first posthumous publication of his works in 1633, are the earliest imitations of classic models in England, even the first examples of formal verse satire. He suggests that as career-oriented university wit, Donne wrote primarily in order to get the attention of the court, but claims that the Satyres communicate no presentiment of the profound religiousness or the tortured consciousness of the later works, although they often take up the topic of religion, allude to biblical and theological controversy, and present themselves according to the expectations of the genre as moralistic.

Bellette (1975, 130, 132–34, 137–38) observes a "curious anomaly" when Donne's Satyres are considered in the tradition of Elizabethan verse satire: on the one hand, "the first two at least predate the satires of Lodge, Hall, and Marston," and thus Donne "cannot be accused of merely following fashion," and on the other, Donne imitates the Latin genre but not through "any direct transcription" (130). It is in the Satyres, Bellette believes, that Donne's view of the world as "irrevocably tainted" first appears, adding that we should not miss Donne's "unique" sense that worldly participation entails "a grave responsibility to one's own soul" (132). He suggests that Donne's "essential position" in the Satyres is that of a man who, "while hating perfectly the world, is prone to all its ills," of one "who will in short be judged as he is judging," and of one, though in an "obscure way," who feels "called upon to bear the responsibility" both for "his own sins" and for the "world's as well," a responsibility "borne out by some curious phrases which imply both a priestly and a Christ-like function" (137–38). As such, he concludes, Donne "has modified greatly the traditional role of satirist," seeking in his Satyres to Donne's involvement in the world of the poems "is such that distance and detachment, though in places desired and actively sought after, are not possible in ethical and religious terms" (138).

Lauritsen (1976, 129–30) suggests of the Satyres that while the first four concern themselves "ostensibly at least, with abstractions, with, that is, generalized aspects of the condition of fallen humanity," Sat5 "alone treats of a specific and at least potentially remediable evil: the bribing of the judiciary as too frequently practiced in England in the 1590's," and thus only the fifth can "aspire to be what satire is generally supposed to be: a corrective." He argues further that "the moral paradox implicit" in the Satyres is that "it is only by recognizing and accepting one's fallen state that one can begin to rise above it," yet the speaker's own "moral superiority in the earlier satires precludes that self-knowledge which is essential for the perception and correction of whatever evils are remediable in man's fallen state."

Hiller (1977, 15) notes that the Satyres lack the "calmness and urbanity" of Wyatt's, exhibiting instead thought that is "vigorous and forceful," imagery that is "arresting," and verse that is "rugged and often irregular," adding, however, that "while there is anger in the satirist's heart, there is also compassion for the weaknesses of man."

Sinha (1977, 76–77) states not only that the Satyres project "the poet's personality from the start" and bear an "unmistakable individuality of tone," but also that they are "related directly to the circumstances" of Donne's career and are "reflections of his preoccupations with his own intellectual, social, and spiritual progress." This quality, Sinha believes, distinguishes Donne from the other Renaissance satirists, but he adds that even more it is the "dramatised action" in these poems, which were "composed in nervous and frenetic images," that "sets them apart." He also notes that "the extreme unevenness" of the Satyres cannot be "minimised or ignored," and the poems also suffer "because of the relative absence of detachment on the part of the poet."

Javitch (1978, 132) asserts that the satires of Donne and his contemporaries introduce "uncompromising anti-courtly attitudes, which only intensify with the coming of James I to the throne."

Cousins (1979, 100, 102) argues that in his Satyres Donne introduces into Elizabethan literature "the role of the virtuoso as hero," and the "sophisticated, challenging quest" is realized as "an attempt to redefine our perception of experience and so reality itself." The poems stress a "calculated drama" that "partly reflects, partly creates, the manner of a man apart, a distinctive sensibility" (100). He asserts further that satiric rhetoric "has to be antithetic, since people claim to write satire because they see unacceptable contradictions in the world around them," but by contrast, Donne "uses a peculiarly subtle rhetoric of contradiction" (102).

Dubrow (1979, 76–77, 80, 83) says that a comparison of Donne with other satirists "highlights the idiosyncratic qualities in his poems and supports the conventional wisdom about his originality" (83). She asserts that juxtaposing Donne's Satyres with those of his contemporaries reveals striking stylistic differences, notably "a type of concentrated and rich language that is absent from the other satirists of the period" that results from Donne's insistence on "cramming satiric commentary into both the tenors and the vehicles of his figures" (76–77). She adds that the personae of Donne's contemporary satirists are based with little variation on the "isolated, bitter, and defiant" speaker established by Juvenal, in contrast to Donne's persona, who is "a more complex character," one voicing "peculiar contradictions and variations." She observes that Donne "gives noticeably less space to the faults of contemporary literature" than the other satirists of the period because Donne realized that his own poetry already provided "an alternative" by which he was "attempting to teach a new literary style both through precept and example." Further, while other satirists "refer only sporadically" to court life, Donne "broods on it repeatedly" probably because of his "own ambivalent relationship" to it (80). She concludes that on occasion the Satyres "fail because of their author's determination to merge very different literary traditions," namely, "the presence of Juvenalian mockery within a Horatian dialogue." Yet, when the poems succeed, it is because of Donne's "ability to explore literary conventions rather than merely rejecting them, to mold satiric traditions to his own stylistic mannerisms and ethical preoccupations" (83).

Carey (1981, 48–49) argues that Donne's "ambitious nature" contains the "contradictory seeds" of "the wish to make his way in the world, and the wish to be integrated into it" that together "inclined him to an active rather than a contemplative life," and it is "this urge for activity" that in the Satyres is "raucously apparent." He observes further that virtually all the English satirists of the time, including Donne, were "ambitious young men who deliberately gave their satires informal publication, by circulating them in manuscript, in order to bring themselves to notice." Rather than reflecting any "serious discontent with the age," the satiric verse of Donne and so many of his contemporary satirists, Carey believes, "amounted to self-advertisement within the court group, of a kind necessary for those not born into wealthy or influential families," and thus, when Donne "managed to attract the interest of his superiors, he quickly dropped satire-writing."

Slights (1981, 172, 177–78) suggests that Donne's Satyres struggle with the tension between a "revulsion from the frivolity and corruption of society" and a "sense of responsibility to the world of men," adding that Donne's "doubts about his relation to society" affirm his belief "that men must act in this imperfect world, that their salvation depends on acting in accordance with their consciences, and that conscience presupposes knowledge" (172). She adds that Donne's "casuistical habit of mind" testifies both to Donne's "psychological insight and imaginative power" and to his "independence and originality as moralist and churchman" (177).

Corthell (1982, 156) thinks that because the Satyres are "concerned with public circumstances," they "provide a unique opportunity for studying the relationship between Donne's self-presentation and his awareness of the political and social realities of the late Elizabethan period," noting that the composition of the Satyres "occupied Donne while he was studying matters controverted between Catholics and Protestants," and all five poems "are informed by Donne's perception of the public consequences of a private religious commitment."

Gallenca (1982, 321), in a comparison of Donne's Satyres and Marston's *Scourge of Villainy*, argues that although both satirists have been criticized by what some have seen as their vulgarity (and even more have seen as their obscurity), it is their violence that most surprises us. Both reveal a stark realism that seems to have been born of their disgust and colored by allegory.

Hester (1982, 3–4, 117–18, 129) argues that the Satyres are "much too sophisticated to be apprentice pieces or early experiments" and instead "disclose how, early in his career, Donne successfully met aesthetic, poetic, and moral problems and shed much light on his own opinion of his duty as Christian poet, fallen man, and religious devotee" by offering "a unified, sequential examination of the problems of Christian satire, a creative shaping (or re-shaping) of the generic, conventional, intellectual, and biographical materials available to Donne in the 1590s" (3–4). As such, these poems show that "Christian satire requires a constant process of adjustment, critical adaptation, and inventive transformation, not just of the strictures and strategies of Horace and Juvenal, but to the speaker's own condition as a fallen man in and of an inconstant world." He adds that Donne is ever the "comic poet," but the intelligence directing his comic spirit is "distinguished by the ability to perceive keenly, in himself and in all men, the false," for Donne's complementary "clear-sighted recognition of truth" is central to his poetic ability "to take a conventional form or mode and re-animate it, re-use it, revive it, yet not take out its essential strengths" (117–18). Finally, he contends that "no other satirist" goes so far as Donne in confronting "the issue of the legality of satire and the dangers of satire directly and fully" (129).

B. King (1982, 41–42) observes that the Satyres "are more urbane, somewhat less crabbed and obscure" than those of Donne's contemporaries, yet the poems "are similar to other late Elizabethan attempts to castigate vice and fashion," adding that "they work up outrage and take a shotgun approach with too many targets vaguely in sight."

Kerins (1984, 35) states that the Satyres are characterized by an "introspective method" which "authenticates the public satiric voice" in them, adding that Donne writes "from a tradition of secular humanism, a tradition which extolled the poet as a creator himself."

Stein (1984, 73–75) observes that no one other than Donne "had the sureness of hand and eye" to transplant Roman satire "into original English poems so flowering in their present that they seemed fully rooted there" (73–74), adding in particular that "nothing in the classical and native precedents quite corresponds to Donne's use of satiric spokesmen" (75).

Parry (1985, 46–48) suggests that the Satyres "are part of an outbreak" of satiric writing, "when a new naturalism swept through English verse, reacting against the more formal beauty and dignity of the poetic generation of Sidney, Spenser and Marlowe," and demonstrating instead "a premium on direct, frank observation, outspoken opinions and iconoclastic attitudes, the sign of a new generation bidding for poetic power." He continues that "the fashions and morals of the Court are a favourite target," yet in calling attention to the Court's "corrupt humours," Donne shows "no disposition to reform, only to record the bizarre fads of the day" (46–47). He asserts further that the Satyres "survive because of their documentary power for the sights and smells and intrigues of Elizabethan London," and while he describes the themes of the Satyres (with the exception of *Sat3*) as "trifling," he adds that the social observations of the poems "are constantly referred back to religious issues or classical antecedents" (48).

Toliver (1985, 95) remarks that "no Renaissance poet except Jonson points up so effectively as Donne the reinforcements that lyric and satire may gain from each other, and none is so absolute in what he expects of true dialogue," and these two related propositions "bear upon the topography of Donne's imaginative world" in that "lyric for him is often either a witty probing of relations-of-two or an enactment of communion in an enclosed place," while satire "reacts to the failure of personal relations and looks abroad to the court and the city."

Marotti (1986, 39, 209) suggests that "the usual approach to satire by way of intellectual and literary history has obscured the social coordinates of this genre in Elizabethan England." In particular, Donne and his contemporary satirists were fully aware that satire was not so much an expression of "one's devotion to moral ideals or one's condemnation of worldly vice" as it was the "literary form practiced by those whose ambitions were frustrated and who yearned to involve themselves more deeply in the social environments they pretended to scorn." Thus, "the motive of envy is habitually associated with the satiric urge," Marotti says, and "the subtext of most satiric literature, including Donne's, is the strong attraction to the very world being criticized," which is confirmed both by "the sociocultural encoding of this genre and the particular coterie context of Donne's Inns-of-Court audience" (39).

Waller (1986, 240–41) posits that the Satyres point us to "the restless confusion of the aspiring intellectuals living in London" and to "the peculiarly brittle and artificial self which, in a mixture of longing and antagonism, wishes to locate itself in that world." The poems thus create "an impression of tactile, optic shock, conveying the countless and restless movements" of an individual walking through a city, but these poems "are careful to articulate very clearly a sense of moral dedication to the appropriate public concerns of the ambitious public servant." Further, Waller asserts, the "rhetorical pose" in the Satyres involves "surveying the more bizarre or corrupt aspects of society in the light of the traditional sources of humanist wisdom" even as they "stress the evils of ambition, affirm the contemplative life over (without scorning) the active, and above all express allegiance to the traditional ideals of justice, harmony, piety, and truth which have seemingly been lost." Finally, he argues that like Marston's and Hall's work, Donne's Satyres "are radical only in their self-conscious choice of a modish rhetoric," the "fireworks" of which are "belied by the cannily, even cynically, conservative values" that are achieved by "playing a habitual game: they are competitive, aggressive, and rhetorically self-conscious because of fashion; they are episodic."

Lord (1987, 109) proposes that "until the 1630s" English satire "was typical rather than topical," yet Donne's, Marston's, and Hall's, which are imitations of Juvenal, Persius, Horace and Martial, "attracted ecclesiastical censure in spite of their concern with types rather than individuals."

Vickers (1987, 170) believes that Donne's "individual handing of inherited forms appears very early on" so that "where Hall had gone through the imitation of Juvenal in a bookish way," Donne instead "immediately involves himself and us in the urban scene."

Baumlin (1988, 364) describes Donne's Satyres "as self-conscious, self-critical explorations of their literary form," and thus the question each of the five poses is "whether the poem validates or becomes the genre by performing it and enacting its aims." According to Baumlin, critics then must ask whether or not in Donne's use of the genre his satiric language claims the power "to punish, persuade, reform," but Baumlin answers, "we shall find that it does not."

Morse (1989, 272–73) argues that Donne's "early ventures" in satire are "as much preoccupied with his own pretensions to be a satirist as with the follies and abuses that he would criticise." On the one hand, Donne "knows that he cannot offer the authoritative point of view of the well-established insider," and on the other, he "is equally well aware that his own bid for attention by the very act of writing makes him cut as dubious a figure as any swaggering gallant of the Elizabethan *beau monde*." He adds that Donne "purports not to take his role as satirist entirely seriously" so that "although he will satirise, he affects to be largely uninterested in what he is writing about and can therefore only pursue his ill-assorted role rather half-heartedly."

Parfitt (1989, 24, 27–28, 33) states that Donne's satirist occupies a role different from that of Marston or Hall in that "the persona observes but does not consider reform" (24). He argues further that although "an Elizabethan social satirist is almost committed to take account of the Court," Donne's Satyres appear "more than commonly interested" in the court. He acknowledges the apparent "contradiction" between satire of court and "the idea of the bright young man aspiring to a Court-based career," but he explains that "daring is fundamental to satire, the willingness of the satirist frankly to confront vice wherever he finds it." Yet, he notes that Donne's poems, operating as they do within classical and native literary traditions, as well as precise cultural conventions, can be seen as presenting "a finely judged approach" rather than one of "folly or envy" (27–28).

Carey (1990, xxii–xxiii) says that Donne's speaker is "serious, responsible, moralistic," and that he "deplores vice and corruption," detecting them "in practically everyone except himself." He adds that the Satyres and Elegies make evident, "through different masks, the same antagonism, superiority, and resentment" so that the poems are not to be taken "at face value" but are instead to be recognized as projecting "compensatory fantasies." He insists that the "high-mindedness" of the poems is only a pose and that the Royal Court had "a mesmeric attraction" for Inns of Court students, since it was "the sole source of the career-opportunities for which their education had fitted them" so that "by setting up as moral arbiters, they invested themselves with an authority they lacked in life."

Mackenzie (1990, 65) remarks that "the dangers of incoherence" for late Elizabethan writers "are at their most obvious in verse satire and in the urban literature which overlaps with it," which project "an image of the city as a place of atomised crowds, of figures seen with the sharpness of caricature or silhouette; a scene pullulating with energy, confusion and sharp-witted cozening." He adds that the Satyres record Donne's "engagement with this teeming world which at once exhilarates and repels him."

Norbrook (1990, 9) claims that the Satyres move not only "beyond their Roman models by depending for much of their wit on an informed knowledge of current affairs, including an ability to criticize the inaccuracy of the available news-sheets," but also "beyond the borders of acceptable discourse" so that "it is not surprising to find Donne oscillating so insecurely between self-assertion and self-deprecation."

Baumlin (1991, 78–79) contends that the Satyres "reveal an ambivalence toward language," for the satirist "condemns the words of others for their deception and abuse" while also "noting the inability of his own words to cause reform," which he contrasts with "the almost universal optimism of Renaissance critics and poets toward the form." As a result, Donne's poems appear "more startling, and more poignant" in his "critical testing of the genre's ability to carry out its aims."

B. Smith (1991, 164) comments that Foucault's notion of "'perpetual spirals of power and pleasure'" is "very much at issue" in the Satyres.

According to Guibbory (1993, 131), the Satyres "express an overwhelming sense of the degeneracy of late-sixteenth-century English society."

Griffin (1994, 11–12, 121) remarks that Donne offers a "strong impression of the climate of oppression under which a Renaissance satirist operated," explaining that "the satirist disdains the court world but is nevertheless dangerously drawn to it." He adds that "the life" of the Satyres is seen "not in their intemperate disgust but in their drama and precise observation" (11–12) and that Donne's and Hall's satyres are "marked with type figures" (121).

Klawitter (1994, 113) insists that in the Satyres there are "traces of homophobia," and it is therefore "essential" that readers participate in "a close examination of sexual intent" in these poems.

Manley (1995, 382–84, 396–97, 401–02) argues that the "early Horatian experiments" of Donne and Lodge suggest that "the formal difference of verse satire resided in its attempt to establish moral and social difference" (382), adding that "the presence of a core of moral truth or natural fact underlying appearance" encourages the satirist "to discriminate between the counterfeit and the genuine representation" (384). He also comments that Donne's Satyres "pit an anti-social moral integrity against the fear of social isolation, an attempted moral accommodation to society against a sweeping indictment of it," and in moving through "a series of moral problems and social environments," Donne hopes "to reconcile his perceptions to his imagined status in the social structure, to his dramatized roles as scholar-wit, jurist, theologian, courtier, and office-holder." As a result, Manley posits that insofar as "the simulation of virtue usurps the reality, the satirist's only truthful act must be a confession of his inability to represent a social order where the differences between true and false, feigned and counterfeit no longer matter" (396–97). He concludes that the rhetoric of the Satyres "engenders fear" because it "eliminates the possibility of compromise with the world by showing that there are no safe waters in which worldlings may glide," and as such, all of the Satyres "tend to end on a note of surprised disillusionment, as if, in the process of unfolding, they exhaust all hope in the project of selection and refinement they set out to perform" (401–02).

Biester (1997, 69, 81, 83) suggests that satire offered "young aspirants" such as Donne "a medium in which to make the transition from student to courtier not in spite of its dangerous associations, but precisely because of them" (69). He observes that in contrast to Wyatt, Gascoigne, and Ralegh, whose court satires "carried the weight of the authors' experiences," Donne "proleptically put the disillusionment before the bitter experience" (81). He states further that the Inns of Court "provided the perfect setting for mock-rebellion" in Donne's Satyres (83).

Corthell (1997, 23–24, 27–28) asserts that Donne attempts to "center" the project of satire "in the satirist," but this approach yields a "subject of satire" divided by "competing models of authority," for Donne's "confidence in his verbal power exists alongside the desire for an 'authority' derived from power" (23). By "questioning its own authority," Donne's text "opens to critique the relations between power and authority in general and succeeds as a powerful representation of a moment of historical change" (24). Corthell argues that instead of regarding the Satyres "as reflections of Donne's lifestyle and the views of the coterie," the poems should be treated "as productions of a coterie or community, whether it be professional, political, religious, or literary," and he concludes that Donne's "satirical work on various systems of self-fashioning is a textual practice which creates a range of provisional, shifting relations between the subject and ideology" (27–28).

Meakin (1998, 33–34, 48–49) discusses Donne's attitude to the Muses in the Satyres, noting relevant passages from *Sat1* 10 and *Sat2* 61–62, and concludes that "at worst" in the Satyres, Donne "is dismissive of the convention" (49).

Ellrodt (2000, 12) suggests that in the Elegies, Satyres, and love poems, as in Petrarchan sonnets contemporary with Donne, "there is often a mere posing for effect."

Reid (2000, 40–42, 46) describes Donne as a "lightweight satirist" who avoids the risks of his contemporaries as "censor of the age" (46), though he finds the Satyres "remarkable" for Donne's "observation of the world around him and his management of the satirist's role" (40). He argues that in the Satyres Donne assumes a position of "stoic aloofness from a corrupt world," yet this posture is complicated by the fact that Donne could not satirize his world "at any level of seriousness without bringing himself in" so that "the very extravagence of his scorn rebounds on the scorner" (42).

Robbins (2000, 423) notes Donne's "anxiety" about his Satyres in his letter to Wotton (1599–1600).

Sproxton (2000, 118) states that much of the Satyres' content consists of "ribald scoffing directed at his contemporaries" in which Donne "sets himself up as a moral arbiter, rebuking the lack of authority at the Inns of Court," adding that Donne "never claimed importance" for these poems.

Wiggins (2000, 18, 35) argues that the Satyres "depict Donne himself confronting impasses, resisting self-deception, becoming disabused," and "this movement accounts for their difference from all other English formal satire of the period" (18). He notes further that Donne's "unrelieved stress on the futility of poetry" differentiates Donne from fellow satirists of the time. He says that unlike Marston or Hall, Donne "never boasts of his own poetic achievement, never criticizes his fellow poets or engages in literary feuding with them, never complains about envious detractors, never sets himself up as an arbiter of literary taste, as a critic of the critics, engages in no ostentatious displays of learning, and could not care less about his reception by anything as vague and inconsequential as a reading public" because poetry is "simply not a serious enough subject to warrant so much concern" (35).

Edwards (2001, 56), alluding to Donne's reference in *Sermons* (7:408), suggests that Donne's "conscience may have troubled him" as he "looked back from a pulpit" and contemplated the writing of satires.

Fulton (2001, 73, 93) believes that the "indignation" in the Satyres "represents a movement in poetic expression that had quite conscious motives, separate from the individual conditions of Donne's biography" (73). He adds that "it is no coincidence" that Donne "remained unpublished" since he was "the most radically anti-court satirist," and leaving the Satyres in manuscript form "gave them a level of freedom over the less controlled dissemination of his published contemporaries" (93).

Lee (2001, 61–62) explains that in the Satyres Donne invites the reader into the scenes and characters found in the poems so that he operates as a director, speaking to the reader sometimes directly and individually and sometimes deeply in meditation, but always accompanying the reader to the Court and through the streets of London.

Hadfield (2001, 57, 66, 125) finds that Donne's Satyres added to the "proliferation" of this form of writing by such authors as Marston, Nashe, and Hall, which "eventually led to the banning of the genre by the church in 1599" (57). He recommends that Hall's satires "be read alongside" Donne's "experiments" in that genre

(66), adding that young poets like Donne and Spenser wrote satires "as part of their literary training" (125).

PERSONAE

Grosart (1872–73, 2:xxviii–xxx) writes of Donne's satirist that he "is pungent, yet never in a fury," and "is proportioned too in his noble rage" in that he "does not treat follies and vanities as if they were vices any more than he does vices as if they were merely follies and vanities." He adds of the speaker that, while "'weighing' the large actions condemned against the petty actors of them," he offers "a fine gentlemanliness of rebuke; contemptuous, dainty of touch, yet penetrative as a Toledo-blade" (xxviii).

Skelton (1960, 204–05, 210) states that Donne's satirists are individuals rather than abstractions and that the poems function as "dramatic monologues" (205) in which Donne's speakers embody the contradictions and complexities of the human personality.

Andreasen (1963, 60–62) posits that the persona is not Donne himself; "however much Donne's own views shimmer behind him," adding that the Satyres are unified by the speaker, who stands for "spiritual values" against the period's increasing materialism (60). Further, she says, the speaker is characterized more fully than the adversaries since he remains constant while the others change from poem to poem, and he is an "idealistic but troubled scholar" (62) whose wrath is directed at sins rather than sinners (61).

Zivley (1966, 89) characterizes the persona of the Satyres as "a thoughtful scholar," a mature observer meditating on morality.

Lecocq (1969, 359, 361) argues that the persona in the Satyres is the complete opposite of a gull, and as a figure who undeniably reacts as a cornered man (359), the persona is someone whose thirst for knowledge is a need for certainties, someone who ultimately discovers, though, the extent of the empire of illusion, of hypocrisy, and of falseness (361).

Miner (1969, 38–39) remarks that Donne's "satiric narrator" is "the plain man and his is a private voice," one who "cannot forbear imagining the nightmare world of the court, whose guards affright his memory, and whose informers or pursuivants make him shake in public like a spied spy, whose activities would cause his private life to be haled into public view." The persona, he concludes, "could not hope to lead a private life in London or at the court."

Hutchison (1970, 355) suggests that "the distance between Donne and his *personae* is not very wide" in the Satyres, and states that the personae are "best represented by a type of honest, retiring scholar who is intolerant of vice and folly, and who occasionally is provoked into *saeva indignatio* which he combines with a hortatory style in his defense of reason and traditional morality." He adds that it is "an over-simplification" to read the personae as undistinguished from one another since the speaker of a given poem "does not remain undeveloped or static within a particular work, and is readily distinguished from the *personae* of the other satires."

Summers (1970, 23–24) explains of Donne's Satyres that "his central speaker is nearly always finely witty, but in his fearful alertness, the impatience of his responses, and the intemperance of his suffering, he often seems more of a participant than a judge of the satiric situation."

Powers (1971, 81) finds that although Donne and Guilpin successfully created satirists "with superior cultural attainments and tastes," this type of persona did not "catch on" in their time.

Sanders (1971, 33–34) describes the voice of the Satyres as that of "improviser, mimic, censor or buffoon," a voice offered "in all its twists and turns as it wheedles, regales, shocks, and then tickles its audience." As such, the voice becomes "inescapably a performance," in which "the crowding of syllables suggests an impetuous improviser, and the imposition (by a whisker) of last-minute metrical order shows the improviser's mastery pitting itself successfully against the necessary formal impediment which gives zest to the performance."

Kusunose (1972, 95–115) believes that the speaker of the Satyres is closely associated with Donne himself and that in these poems Donne is more self-conscious and introverted than other satirists. In all of the Satyres, and especially in Sat3, Donne's self-interests are evident. Kusunose thinks that Donne may have abandoned the satire form later because be became increasingly aware that its form was limiting in terms of developing interests in such themes as the body and soul or sense and intellect.

Newton (1974, 429) argues that Donne's "exploration of the satiric character is not in itself 'dramatic'" in that Donne "confronts the satiric character for the most part through his own individual persona, after the manner of a lyric poet," and it is Donne's "struggle to comprehend and to contain this impulsive and turbulent character" that provides the "considerable power and interest" of these poems.

Swift (1974, 47) notes that the speaker of the Satyres, following the Roman model and derived from a unified conglomerate of materials, becomes a dramatic figure. The speaker establishes himself in the traditional manner as a *vir bonus* and a heroic moralist, as a well-educated, unsophisticated judge of character, who demands honesty and openness to take a position against the excesses of his society and for the positive norms threatened by it.

Bellette (1975, 132) insists that in the Satyres "there is no real sense of the author himself being threatened by what he portrays" and that "there is a certain unconvincingness to the stance" of the satirist inhabiting "a kind of privileged state" where he is "safe" from the "infection" of worldly involvement.

Elliott (1976, 110, 116) notes that "from a moral standpoint" the Satyres are "about the dilemma of the Christian humanist," whereas "from a literary standpoint" the poems are "about the problem of satire as a poetic form." As a result, "if the speaker is to be a satirist, he must be of a new breed," becoming "a Christian satirist," that is, "one guided by the law of charity, who teaches and gently reforms his brother." He adds that "while the speaker's external conflicts with the world and the agents of corruption provide much of the dramatic interest of the poems," what is also "central" to the Satyres are the speaker's "internal struggle and ultimate failure in his role as Christian satirist" (110). He further suggests that Donne's protagonist in the Satyres "seems to have made a mature, if perhaps temporary, adjustment to life's frustrations," adding that "whether he will be any more successful in reforming society in his new station in government" remains unanswered in these poems (116).

According to Lauritsen (1976, 119–21), the Satyres "tell us more about the satirist than the thing satirized" in that, in the case of Donne, the speaker comes to realize that "the satirist who satirizes man's fallen condition is ultimately satirizing himself" (119–20). He explains that images associated with body and soul "define the moral polarities which operate within the sensibility of the speaker," who wishes to associate himself only "with the pure and virtuous qualities of the soul," but who is increasingly dismayed to discover that "he is both body and soul, both a social being and a fallen man" (120–21).

Dubrow (1979, 80–81, 83) suggests that "the most striking point of comparison" between Donne's Satyres and those of his contemporaries "is their personas," who are, without variation, "isolated, bitter, and defiant," whereas Donne's speaker is "a more complex character" whose changes "do not form a consistent pattern" but instead "stem from Donne's complex and often contradictory responses to his genre and his subject matter" (80–81). She adds that "the presence of Juvenalian mockery within a Horatian dialogue leads to a persona that seems unnecessarily 'nasty'" (83).

According to Slights (1981, 151), when Donne's speaker is viewed "in the context of the ideas and concerns of casuistry," the reader immediately recognizes "a man struggling with doubts about how he ought to live and a satirist trying to solve the problem of how best to use language to lead others to right action." It is "this double concern" that "accounts for the voice of the satires and for their sometimes bewildering structure" and that "also helps to distinguish Donne's satires from other Elizabethan satires," whose "focus is more wholly on the objects of the satirist's scorn."

Gallenca (1982, 325–30), in a comparison of Donne's Satyres and Marston's *Scourge of Villainy*, posits that the melancholic and often hypochondriacal personae of the two poets concur in a tragic vision of broken communication with God (325–27), as seen in the trajectory of the dupe, who is drawn into the corrupt legal system, absorbed by the system, imprisoned by its machinations, and ultimately brutalized (328–29). Most importantly, however, Donne and Marston show that the dupes and those who dupe them are not opposites, for while the one applies himself with skill and deception, the other uses verbosity to conceal his basic emptiness and is torn apart by unstable moods (329–30).

Hester (1982, 4–5, 11–12) states that the poet of the Satyres, "or at least his persona," is "the figure who envisions the decay and destruction of order and value," but "this self-conscious awareness of his own fallen nature only reinforces his awareness of the precarious position at the end—at the end of the 'golden age,' at the end of the century, at the end of what many of his contemporaries insisted were 'the last dayes,'" adding that "the search for and creation of a voice appropriate to such conditions is one of the central impulses" of the Satyres (4). He argues further that "the outstanding feature and in many ways the abiding concern" of Donne's satiric speaker is "zeal," and as such "satire, or the satirist's understanding of his own duty, is always viewed as a relationship: as a duty to himself, his countrymen, and his God" (11).

B. King (1982, 41–42) argues that the Satyres "make explicit the persona of many of the lyrics, a cynical educated young man of the world, familiar with London and the Court, experienced in love, somewhat libertine, but as willing to judge others as any moralist."

Barańczak (1984, 172) asserts that the persona of the Satyres is reflected in the poetic contrasts, antitheses, and paradoxes, as if in a mirror. The persona, he adds, is internally conflicted, suspended between God and nature, pulled by the opposing urges of the body and the soul, unsure of how to live or of his place on this earth.

Kerins (1984, 55) contends that "through a scrupulous analysis of his own soul," Donne's speaker achieves "the necessary purification to comprehend the corruption of the society at large."

Stein (1984, 75) argues that there is nothing in "classical and native precedents" that is equivalent to Donne's "use of satiric spokesmen" and that Donne's speakers "are outsiders, whether angry or disengaged, or both more and less; or both and at the same time earnest seekers," and as such, "they furnish considerable and varied amusement" but are not themselves "actively amused." He adds that in preferring "a certain distance most favourable to their power of inventive observation," the satiric personae display an "aroused singlemindedness" involving "no apparent concern for what can be seen or said by means of grace, pliancy, and peripheral vision."

Sloane (1985, 177–78) notes that Donne's "various personae" in the Satyres are "not totally distinct from the speaker, even in their vices." After citing Donne's comment on satiric writing from Sermons 7:408, he argues that "to the extent that Donne points toward his own earlier, unredeemed wit, he encourages us to track the growth and development of his artistic persona."

Parfitt (1989, 23–24, 26–27) notes that Donne's satirist is "a victim rather than an hectic flogger or heated surgeon," one who "observes but does not consider reform" and whose role, even in his "restless" searching, is "individual rather than social" (23–24). He adds that while Donne's satirists "are at times hermits by inclination and yet restlessly responsive to social experience," they "seem aimless—outraged perhaps, but without thoughts of reform" (26–27).

Fish (1990, 235) contends that the Satyres "record the desperate and always failing effort of the first-person voice to distinguish himself from the variability and corruption" that he observes around him, and Fish further notes the "self-defeating gesture of these poems."

Baumlin (1991, 21, 78–79) asserts that Donne's satirist is "ostensibly" consistent throughout the Satyres, a "singular, unified voice whose identity unfolds throughout and, indeed, depends and grows in self-knowledge, much like a dramatic character." As such, the poems reveal the speaker's "own exploration of his literary form: the story told in each is of the poet learning, through insight and error, to become a Christian satirist," though Baumlin questions "whether the speaker learns to be a better satirist from one poem to the next" (21). He adds that the Satyres "reveal an ambivalence toward language: the satirist condemns the words of others for their deception and abuse, at the same time noting the inability of his own words to cause reform," and further, "accompanying this ambivalence toward language is a skepticism about the satirist's role, whether he is ever capable of accomplishing anything other than his own self-incrimination" (78–79).

Guibbory (1993, 131) finds particular qualities in each of Donne's satirists, asserting that he "embodies qualities that oppose the viciousness of society: he is constant and scholarly" (Sat1), is "devoted to God and spiritual values, earnest and searching rather than complacent" (Sat3), prefers the "'meane' to either extreme" (Sat2), is "filled with hatred for vice" (Sat2) and "vicious people in power" (Sat5) but "moved by pity for humanity" (Sat3 and Sat5), and she adds that the satirist "presents himself as virtually alone in condemning the vices of his time—as if he were the last good man in a totally corrupt society."

Hester (1994a, 205–06) suggests that Donne's speaker is "consistently defined" by having to defend, define, or declare his "devotion" amongst a "legion of adversarial readers, voyeurs, spies, and agents—without admitting or denying his violations of their patriarchal, governmental, or ecclesiastical 'Statutes.'"

Strier (1994, 231) asserts that Donne's satiric persona is likely similar to his "historical person—an intellectual struggling to maintain detachment from a compromised and engulfing political and social world."

Biester (1997, 90) cites Donne's "reflection" on the writing of satires in Sermons 7:408 as the first of readings that focus on "the speaker's self-involvement in the satirized behavior of the unnamed other in the poem."

Corthell (1997, 19) finds that Donne, "like most Elizabethan verse satirists," is "obsessed with the problem of investing moral authority in a subject who speaks for a moral minority."

Oliver (1997, 53) contends that the Satyres "present a variety of context-determined personae," noting in particular the contradiction between the speaker of Sat3 who "implies an approval of the right of Catholics (and Puritans) to practise their religion" and that of Sat4 who opens "by fiercely mocking Catholicism." He adds that we can "rationalise the contradiction and say that both personae dramatise aspects of Donne's thinking," yet he insists, "we shouldn't feel under any kind of obligation to explain what appear to be inconsistencies."

Prescott (1999, 289) suggests that, given their subsequent clerical careers, Donne and Hall were probably not "crazed with outrage," but adopted their satiric personae to "appear pathological."

Blissett (2000, 101, 115) notes that Donne's speaker "may show dislike and avoidance but he never offends: he strives precariously toward balance" (101). He proposes further that the distinctly masculine voice of the Satyres is that of "a somewhat older and graver John Donne" (115).

Prescott (2000, 229) observes that "the satirical personae, themselves not wholly in good moral health, are subtly imagined and not exempt from Donne's irony."

Reid (2000, 41–42) describes the "narrators" of the Satyres as "standoffish" and "studious figures," who, though "soberly dressed and given to solitude," are "quite unable to resist the lively inanity of the pests who seize their company." He argues further that Donne is unable "to establish a persona that speaks with satiric authority."

Wiggins (2000, 25–26, 32) proposes that readers of the Satyres "are in much the same position" as readers of the Holy Sonnets, "in that the concept of the persona" (i.e., a figure distinct from the author), which aids in "understanding the dramatic set pieces" of the Elegies and the Songs and Sonets, in the Satyres "loses its value." He argues that we cannot "pretend that the Satyres are not an autobiographical text," for the satirist's voice "is that of Egerton's secretary, or at least the voice of a young man who was seeking the opportunity to fashion himself as the confidant and spokesman of a great man like Egerton." He contends that it was Castiglione who "shaped Donne's conception of the conventions by which one could engage in self-revelation" (26), and concludes that Donne "engages in a dialogue with himself" throughout the Satyres (32).

GENRE

Although Donne provides no direct commentary on his own Satyres, he does comment on "satyre," "satyrists," or "satirical libel" in a number of *Sermons*, including 1:179 (1618), 1:215 (1616/17), 2:53 (1618), 3:112 (undated), 3:183 (undated), 4:91 (1622), 4:253 (1622), 4:317 (1623), 4:341 (1622/23), 5:192 (1621?), 5:333 (undated), 6:307 (1625), 6:316 (1625?), 7:212 (1626), 7:408 (1627), 8:65 (1627), 9:184 (1629/30), and 9:336 (undated).

Bayle (1697 [1736, 4:86]), in a discussion of Donne's Satyres, defines a satire as "an epigram on a larger scale" and epigrams as "satires in miniature," adding that "an epigram must be satyrical, and a satire epigrammatical."

Brown (1748, 3:333), in his essay on the history of satire, describes Donne's importance to the genre, stating:

'Twas then plain DONNE in honest vengeance 'rose,
His wit refulgent, tho' his rhyme were prose:
He 'midst an age of puns and pedants wrote
With genuine sense, and *Roman* strength of thought.

Aronstein (1920, 158–59) calls the Satyres, with the exception of *Sat3*, real satires in the truest sense, and he describes the form of the poems either as dramatic tales (*Sat1* and *Sat4*) or reflections, i.e., religious/literary tracts (*Sat2* and *Sat5*).

Randolph (1941, 137) states that satire shares with medieval literature "the debates between body and soul, *estrifs* between vice and virtue, allegorical presentations of the Seven Deadly Sins, and the popular Backbiter and Detraction characters from the morality plays," as well as "the broad purpose and intent of the morality play," and he lists Donne among the "many eminent churchmen" who "have served youthful apprenticeships to satire."

Bush (1952, 93) states that Elizabethan satire, including Donne's, "was the one really dull product of that golden age."

Lewis (1954, 3:469) explains that the Satyres are written "under the influence of the old blunder which connected *satira* with *satyros*."

Lecocq (1969, 365, 396) asserts that even labeling these poems as satires indicates that they defy all classification (365). He notes, however, that some of Donne's Verse Letters offer a valuable commentary on the state of mind in which the Satyres were written and show that the formal epistle can include satiric reflection. Consequently, however important its moral content, satire is itself subject to the judgment that the poetry of meditation elaborates, and the satiric genre, therefore, remains inferior to this other genre of profane poetry. He concludes that satire is a deceitful genre, even when it recommends virtue, because there is no virtue outside of religion, and religion necessarily includes virtue (396).

Miner (1969, 162) argues that satire deserves "a major historical place in Metaphysical poetry" because Donne and his contemporary satirists "nursed Metaphysical poetry" in this genre.

Ashley (1970, 61–63) argues that Elizabethan satire is "no cruder" than Elizabethan drama, though "it is almost always less interesting." He thinks that "really quite interesting writers tend to become more than usually clumsy and unattractive in this period when they undertake to write satire," and that although Donne was "probably the best of them," even the Satyres "are basically 'not in it,' as the English say, with his best work, which lies in other genres where he was a great master." Ashley criticizes Elizabethan writers for satirizing "not what they knew from life but what they read in literature," for writing "pretty imitations of classical authors" rather than "what they really felt and knew and understood," for borrowing "not only the style of men long dead but their subjects too—when all around them were fit subjects for satire" (62). Finally, he adds that Elizabethan society "kept its satirists as harmless pets, some of them dangerously fanged but all of them adequately muzzled" (63).

Jensen (1972, 409) suggests that much of what we value in Renaissance satire "is directly related to rhetoric and oratory, and thus subject to a decorum which offers far greater latitude than the narrow limits" of the genre "would seem to permit." As such, in their "exuberance and youthful self-delight," in their "variety of techniques and tactics," and especially in their "impulse toward the dramatic," the very best Renaissance satires, and Donne's among them, "most successfully deny by their very brilliance the boundaries of genre criticism."

Lewalski and Sabol (1973, 6) assert that "the impact of genre and tradition upon Donne is especially evident when he writes in such classical genres as satire and elegy."

According to Bellette (1975, 131), Donne both "initiated and departed from the norms of Roman satire as it was understood and rendered into English in the last decade of the sixteenth century." Further, Renaissance satire relies "largely on an attitude of studied detachment on the part of the author" that stems from an attitude of "*saeva indignatio* which the Elizabethans, including Donne, found so attractive in Juvenal."

Hester (1982, 3–4, 117–18) argues that the Satyres "are imitations of the Latin genre," noting in particular that "the exasperated indignation of Juvenal's 'difficile est saturam non scribere'" and "the rough asperity of Persius and the exhortative irony of Horace find their complements in the paradoxical encounters of Donne's persona with knaves and fools, as well as in his conversational style." He adds, however, that the speaker "is not simply a Juvenalian 'railer' in Elizabethan garb who modernizes the situations of Horace in the tones of Persius" and explains further that the Satyres are "much too sophisticated to be apprentice pieces or early experiments" and instead "disclose how, early in his career, Donne successfully met aesthetic, poetic, and moral problems." In this regard, Hester says, they "shed much light on his own opinion of his duty as Christian poet, fallen man, and religious devotee" by offering "a unified, sequential examination of the problems of Christian satire, a creative shaping (or re-shaping) of the generic, conventional, intellectual, and biographical materials available to Donne in the 1590s" (3–4). As such, these poems show that "Christian satire requires a constant process of adjustment, critical adaptation, and inventive transformation, not just of the strictures and strategies of Horace and Juvenal, but to the speaker's own condition as a fallen man in and of an inconstant world" (117–18).

Helgerson (1983, 123–25, 135–36) observes that for Donne and his immediate contemporaries the writing of satire "was the sign of their generation," and their satires "stood in clear opposition to the solipsism of love poetry" identified with Sidney and Spenser (123–24). He adds that as an amateur, rather than a professional, poet, Donne "played" in the Satyres a role representing "only a limited part" of his identity, "not the central ethical core" (135–36).

Toliver (1985, 95) remarks that "no Renaissance poet except Jonson points up so effectively as Donne the reinforcements that lyric and satire may gain from each other, and none is so absolute in what he expects of true dialogue," adding that for Donne "lyric and satire are the systole and diastole of his secular poetry."

Marotti (1986, 39) suggests that "the usual approach to satire by way of intellectual and literary history has obscured the social coordinates of this genre in Elizabethan England." In particular, Donne and his contemporary satirists "knew full well" that the genre "was less a way of expressing one's devotion to moral ideals or one's condemnation of worldly vice than it was the literary form practiced by those whose ambitions were frustrated and who yearned to involve themselves more deeply in the social environments they pretended to scorn." Thus, "the motive of envy is habitually associated with the satiric urge," and "the subtext of most satiric literature, including Donne's, is the strong attraction to the very world being criticized," which is confirmed both by "the sociocultural encoding of this genre and the particular coterie context of Donne's Inns-of-Court audience."

Baumlin (1988, 364, 366) describes the Satyres as "self-conscious, self-critical explorations of their literary form." As such, the question each of the five poems poses is "whether the poem validates or becomes the genre by performing it and enacting its aims." Critics then must ask whether or not in Donne's use of the genre his satiric language claims the power "to punish, persuade, reform," yet he determines "that it does not" (364). He adds that Donne "is the first to discover, and enact, the limitations of classical satire," and "what allows this discovery is the poet's radical reflection on the weakness of language, a reflection spurred on," he argues, "by the culture's refusal to grant his Catholicism authority—or grant it simply the right of utterance" (366).

Baumlin (1991, 81, 151) describes Donne as the first English writer "to discover the rhetorical as well as moral limitations" of satire, and whether or not one decides to read the Satyres as "revision or rejection of their classical models," one can be certain that Donne's "critique of the Roman satirists is subsumed within a broader critique: the problem of genre becomes a problem of rhetoric, particularly of the competing theologies of language" (81). He adds that Donne's poetry "continually confronts an anxiety of validation," which the Satyres attempt to resolve "by becoming something more (or other) than satire" (151).

Fowler (1993, 95) observes that Donne and his contemporaries "thought that satires (which they spelled 'satyres') should be rough like a satyr's pelt," which was a "false etymology" and a "false doctrine" developed "out of Renaissance Italian genre theory."

Biester (1997, 34–35) disagrees with Helgerson (1983) that "the shift from the sonnet and pastoral of Sidney and Spenser to the epigram and satire of Donne and Jonson" was unrelated to the abuses they satirized or their frustrated career aspirations, arguing instead that the generic shift, along with "the accompanying shift toward compressed and oblique style," signals "an updated version of the career paradigm typical of the earlier generation, the pattern of embracing, then rejecting, poetry."

Sherwood (1997, 69) identifies the Satyres as "one of several modes of speaking centered in the same male audience."

According to Prescott (1999, 289), "at its best (which probably means Donne), Elizabethan satire implicitly explores the unstable mentality behind its claims to cure society's ills."

Cheney and Prescott (2000, 65) label the Satyres as "experiments in the genre."

Fulton (2001, 73–74) suggests that the "freedom that Donne and his contemporaries seek, even in respect to religion, is primarily from social and especially political pressures," which are more apparent in Elizabethan satire "than in any other genre." Thus, he argues that "the full meaning" of the Satyres "cannot be experienced without reconsidering the counter-cultural group to which [Donne] belongs."

Sources, Influences, and Analogues

Dryden (1693 [1974, 4:78]) explains that Donne's "rudeness" came from his subservience to the example of classical satire:

> Wou'd not *Donn's* Satires, which abound with so much Wit, appear more Charming, if he had taken care of his Words, and of his Numbers? But he follow'd *Horace* so very close, that of necessity he must fall with him: And I may safely say it of this present Age, That if we are not so great Wits as *Donn*, yet, certainly, we are better Poets.

Brown (1748, 3:333), in his essay on the history of satire, describes Donne's importance to the genre, stating:

> 'Twas then plain DONNE in honest vengeance 'rose,
> His wit refulgent, tho' his rhyme were prose:
> He 'midst an age of puns and pedants wrote
> With genuine sense, and *Roman* strength of thought.

An anonymous piece in *The World* (1755) asserts that "every man of taste" will admire "the gaiety and good sense of Horace" as seen "in paraphrases of and translations of Donne."

Saintsbury (1887, 145–47, 150–51) suggests that the roughness of Donne's verse derives from the belief of the "ancients" that "*Satura*" should be composed in "somewhat unpolished verse" and from following the style of Persius, "the most deliberately obscure of all Latin if not of all classical poets" (151). Others who note the important influence of Persius include Chambers (1896, 2:242–46), Lang (1912, 284), Payne (1926, 30–31), Sharp (1934, 502), Crofts (1936, 129), Stein (1942, 692), Leishman (1951, 108), Morris (1953, 41), Gransden (1954, 101), Archer (1961, 147), Partridge (1978, 37), Selden (1978, 59–60), Kupersmith (1985, 150–51), Patrides (1985, 213),

Warnke (1987, 22), Sowerby (1994, 345–46), Prescott (2000, 229), and Lee (2001, 61–62).

Alden (1899, 85, 88–89) asserts in general that in Donne's Satyres "there is little of the native English element" (88). Following brief summaries of each of the Satyres, he calls attention to the "variety of satirical types," noting that "the methods of satirical narrative, of reflection, and of direct rebuke" are all "Horatian and Juvenalian elements" (85). He also asserts that Donne was "least of all men imitative" and that even when writing in a "classical form" he shuns "obvious unoriginality" (85). Consequently, Donne's style in the Satyres, though not "distinctly imitative," is more reminiscent of the style of classical satire "than any we have yet met with," especially with respect to "its compactness, its indirect method, its allusiveness" (88). Finally, he adds that the humor is "sharp and subtle" and "based largely on exaggeration," while the vices satirized show the influence of classical satire, though Donne remained "as usual untrammeled and original" (88–89). Others who note the combined influence of Horace and Juvenal include Upham (1908, 183n1), Hutchison (1970, 356), Hebaisha (1971, 29), Kermode and Hollander (1973, 1045; 1975, 739), Kermode, Fender, and Palmer (1974, 61), Kernan (1976, 117), Guilhamet (1987, 39), and Nilsen (1997, 140).

Gosse (1899, 1:28–35) asserts that the Satyres make clear what Donne learned from Persius and Juvenal (32) and that Donne, along with the other English satirists, attempted to introduce, though without conscious collusion, the Roman element of the Satura, "that 'mixture' of social scandal and moral diatribe in a picturesque sort of realistic rhetoric which Lucilius had been the first to develop into a fine art" (34). In Juvenal, he believes, Donne was charmed by "the deep knowledge of life, the universal cynic savagery, the resolute and brutal determination to haul Truth up out of her well, however roughly"; and as for Persius, he notes that the versification of Persius was in Donne's time identified as "violent and rugged," and his style thought to be "turbid and involved to an extreme degree" (35). Together, Juvenal and Persius formed in the minds of the Elizabethan satirists the ideal "of what manly satire must be" (35). Gosse also suggests that Isaac Casaubon's lectures on Persius may have sparked the sixteenth-century rediscovery of the Latin poet (29), and he further notes the "very close and very curious resemblance" between Donne's Satyres and the work of Régnier, although he then adds that the latter did not begin to write in the genre until 1598, "by which time the mushroom school of London satirists was already at the height of its vogue" (32–33). Others who note the combined influence of Juvenal and Persius include Garnett and Gosse (1903, 2:272), Eliot (1926, 141), Spencer (1931, 185), Sharp (1940, 29), Jack (1951, 1014), Baker (1952, 51), LeComte (1965, 48), Heath-Stubbs (1969, 22), Patterson (1970, 104–05), Warnke (1987, 22), Ray (1990, 284), Sowerby (1994, 345–46), and Prescott (1999, 288–89). Samarin (1972, 171–72) also notes parallels with Régnier.

Stephen (1899, 598) contends that Donne, Hall, and Marston in their satires were "showing their superiority by contempt for the world around," and following "the precedent of the Roman satirists," they all "made the curious blunder" that satire "must be rough and uncouth and obscure."

In a review of Gosse (1899), an anonymous commentator writing in The Nation

(1900, 112) objects to Gosse's suggestion of Casaubon as a possible source of influence on the English satirists, noting that though Casaubon's lectures on Persius at Geneva were given between 1590 and 1600, his edition of Persius was published in 1605. Gosse's suggestion, he implies, would require believing that the report of Casaubon's lectures was "so effective in England as to induce not only Donne, but Hall and Marston, who also wrote their satires before 1600, to adopt this poetic form."

Grierson (1909, 4:206–07) explains that the Satyres have characteristics in common with other imitations of Juvenal, Persius, and Horace in the late sixteenth century, "notably a heightened emphasis of style and a corresponding vehemence and harshness of versification." He asserts further that the classical models Donne had in view were those of Martial, Persius, and Horace. Commenting that "imitation alone will not account for Donne's pecularities" in the genre, he nonetheless identifies Horace at least as much as Persius as "Donne's teacher," and it is Horace whom Donne "believes himself to be following in adopting a verse in harmony with the unpoetic temper of his work." Others who note the combined influence of Horace and Persius include Simpson (1931, 25), White (1935, 126), Leishman (1951, 107), Redpath (1956, xix), Rousseau and Rudenstine (1972, 56), Lord (1987, 109), Patrides (1989, 105), and Post (1999, 6).

Lee (1910, 351–55) argues of the Satyres that "the uncouth metaphor, the harsh epithet, the varying pause in the line," characteristic of Donne's "rhyming decasyllables," seem "to mirror irregularities which dominate Du Bartas's or Sylvester's achievement" (353). Although he concedes that Donne does not acknowledge the influence of Du Bartas (351), he contends, nevertheless, that Donne's Satyres appear "in a garb barely distinguishable from this style of Du Bartas and Sylvester" (354).

Schelling (1910, 319–21), prior to offering very brief overviews of the Satyres, asserts that the subjects and the method of the poems "combine the narrative and reflective satire of Horace with the spirit of direct rebuke," and that while the poems are "prevailingly pessimistic in tone," they do not adopt the "Juvenalian attitude of authority to castigate vice and patronize virtue" (320).

Aronstein (1920, 157, 160–61) notes that from Horace, Persius, and Juvenal Donne learned his manner of presentation, that mixture of realistic portrayal and the sharp moral critique of life in an elevated rhetorical style (157). Yet he adds that the Satyres are permeated by a high idealism that recalls Persius, and probably Juvenal, more than the urbanity and serenity of Horace (160–61).

Hutton (1924, 151) notes that the Satyres were "perhaps the first" based on the formal Roman verse satire.

Walker (1925, 69–71) cites Hall's postscript regarding his satires, that the genre is "naturally 'both hard of conceit and harsh of style…unpleasing both to the unskilful and over-musical ear,'" and finds that "this principle was misinterpreted to mean that the lines need not obey any law of scansion at all" (69). In effect, then, the Elizabethans desert their classical models by "writing verse which was not only plain, pedestrian, low in tone, adapted to the subject, but which was not really verse at all, which defied all rule and would not scan" (70–71).

Brooks (1934, 565) cites as a model for Donne Thomas Drant's translation in *Horace His arte of Poetrie, pistles and Satyrs Englished* (1567), adding that one might believe that Donne, "intending to write satires after the Horatian model, had thought it worth while at least to glance at Drant's translation."

Lindsay (1934b, 636) insists on a strong Horatian presence in the Satyres, which demonstrates Donne's "effort to accept society for what it was."

White (1935, 126) notes the imitative quality of the Satyres, adding that they even took "material from Horace, Persius, and Juvenal, before Hall published Virgidemiarum."

Crofts (1936, 128–29) states that Donne "wrote gritty satires in a Roman vein," and he describes the Satyres as "very modern" expressions of the genre written "in the manner of Persius, full of knaves and fools and spades called spades."

Jonas (1940, 205–06) accepts Donne's kinship with the Roman satirists but argues that his poems were more than simply imitations.

Randolph (1941, 137) states that satire generally shares with medieval literature "the debates between body and soul, estrifs between vice and virtue, allegorical presentations of the Seven Deadly Sins, and the popular Backbiter and Detraction characters from the morality plays, as well as with the broad purpose and intent of the morality play." He lists Donne among the "many eminent churchmen" who "have served youthful apprenticeships to satire."

Hardy (1942, 63) claims that the Satyres "imitate Juvenal." Samarin (1972, 171) finds a similar influence.

Randolph (1942, 378) states that in grouping his Satyres, Donne follows the classical precedent of composing "clusters of satires."

Stein (1944a, 267–68) contends that there is "no important evidence" to confirm that Donne's "literary attitude is in any material way directly influenced by classical satire," yet "like the satirists of the first century, only more energetically," Donne revolts against "the threadbare artifices and petty affectations in contemporary literature," which for Donne include "the popular Petrarchan idolatry of women, and the impractical doctrine that 'all that faire is, is by nature good.'" He adds that Donne is "a recognized leader in the movement against mythology" and in the effort to reject the "Elizabethan ideal of imitation." While he does not question the "depth" of Donne's "moral sincerity," he notes that Donne "does not, like other Elizabethans, look into his spleen and write."

Stein (1946, 114) asserts that the "definite and important bond" between Donne and Persius is their "return to a more intellectual [sic] pregnant manner of writing" and their opposition "to the dangerous facility that swims on the lips," adding in a footnote that both "are revolting against a style influenced by Ovid."

Wilcox (1950, 198) notes Donne's "naturally satiric vein" and states that Donne "learned much" from the satires of Horace and Juvenal and the elegies of Ovid.

Cazamian (1952, 312) sees Donne's Satyres as an outgrowth of his earlier studies of "erratic traits in character" that contain "a moral aim."

Gransden (1954, 9–10, 101–02) states that, like the prototypical satires of Horace and Juvenal, Donne's are "urban, or rather metropolitan, in spirit and subject" (9–10), for, he adds, "one can't be urbane without being urban," and the genre "is a form of private tragi-comedy, sociably anti-social" (102). It is this metropolitan spirit that also aligns the poems "in style and technique" with Persius (101).

Lewis (1954, 3:469–70) contrasts the unrelieved "monotony of vituperation" in

Donne's Satyres to the "cheerful normality" of Horace and the "occasional grandeur" of Juvenal. Zimbardo (1998, 67) also notes the contrast of Donne's Satyres to those of Horace and Juvenal.

Sutherland (1958, 30–33) asserts that Juvenal and Persius commanded a "rather malign influence" over Donne and the other Elizabethan satirists, who wrote in an age that was "thoroughly un-Roman" (30). He notes that Donne's "metrical irregularity" and his obscurity, as he leaves the reader "staggering from one couplet to another, coming up against unexpected objects in the half-darkness and never really sure where the poet is taking him" (32–33), chiefly reflect the influence of the Roman satirists.

Kernan (1959, 117–18) notes Donne's debt to Juvenal and Horace, "particularly in the arrangement and dramatic handling of his satiric material," as well as his "insolent" manner of writing and his "coarse and rough" speech.

Erskine-Hill (1964, 15) believes that Donne saw himself according to his own interpretation of Horace, but that he also adopted "the *persona* of the satirist as hero," a synthesis of Horatian and Juvenalian characteristics.

Allen (1965, 85, 113) states that "the most cursory reading" of Donne and his contemporary satirists "reveals an astonishing lack of originality" (85), as Elizabethan poets draw upon the Roman satirists not only for form, style, obscurity, and subject matter, but even for proper names (113).

Lecocq (1969, 359, 385) asserts that any passage of the Satyres proves that in Donne the spirit of Horace undergoes a complete transformation (359). He states further that Donne chooses the inverse of euphuistic facility and Ciceronian eloquence, adding that if his style evokes Persius more than Juvenal, it is because all rhetoricians are suspect for Donne (385).

Menascè (1969, 49) states that younger poets like Donne updated for Elizabethan culture the fashion in satire much as Horace, Persius, and Juvenal had done for the Roman.

Miner (1969, 10) points out that the private quality of the Satyres "has led to some disagreement as to Donne's classical model." In particular, "the crabbed strong lines" lead many to align him and contemporary satirists with Persius, while "the embittered, personal invective" in Donne displays "kinship with Juvenal." Miner argues, however, that "the closest specific resemblance" of any Elizabethan satire is to the satire of Horace, a similarity Dryden noted "on the basis of prosody and the plain style." In addition, Miner says, Donne goes beyond "the three Roman satirists in creating a speaker who is not only incoherently bitter like that of Persius, indignant like that of Juvenal, and detached like that of Horace, but quite simply private."

Patterson (1970, 109–10) argues that the formal verse satyres of Marston, Guilpin, and Donne "match virtually word for word" the instructions regarding "the Ideas of Reproof, especially Vehemence," that "were current in Italy from about 1560 to 1590, and which were also available in Sturm's 1571 edition of Hermogenes."

Hebaisha (1971, 24, 27, 28–29) believes that in formal verse satire Donne found a classical source for "attacking society and exposing its hypocrisy and vice" (24) and that Donne captured more of the spirit of his classical models than the other Elizabethan satirists (27) since his lack of moral purpose gave his poems a lighter tone (29).

Kusunose (1972, 95–115) points to the influence of Roman satirists, especially

Horace, and the relative brevity of Donne's poems compared to those of classical predecessors.

Rousseau and Rudenstine (1972, 56) note that Donne's Satyres "reveal his lively interest in the works of the Roman satirists," adding that Donne "thoroughly transforms whatever he borrows," yet although the Satyres are "wonderfully original," they reflect his attraction to "the realism and the air of sophistication, the vivacity and the wit," of much of Roman literature.

Samarin (1972, 171–72) claims that in their questioning of court life and religious attitudes, the Satyres partially recall Agrippa d'Aubigné's "Les Tragiques."

Lewalski and Sabol (1973, 6) assert that the influence of "genre and tradition" on Donne is "especially evident" when he writes in classical genres such as satire and elegy. They note that Donne's contemporary satirists, namely, Marston, Hall, and Jonson, created many written and theatrical satires, yet in their imitations of Roman satire, their poems have a "looser structure and much more realistic detail, as well as harsh, rugged metrical effects which the Elizabethans mistakenly assumed to be common in classical satire."

Swift (1974, 45) describes the Satyres as representative of the posture of satire in their time because Donne still held to the mistaken connection between *satura* and *satyr*. This error led Donne to orient himself towards Horace, though he also engaged the *saeva indignatio* of Juvenal. He adds, however, that Donne probably fell also under the harsher and darker influence of Persius, who was widely known even before the publication of Casaubon's *Commentaries* (1605).

According to Bellette (1975, 131), Donne "at once initiated and departed from the norms of Roman satire as it was recognized in his day." Further, the Renaissance satiric manner, which relies especially on "an attitude of studied detachment on the part of the author," is "not so much an Horatian detachment," but instead "the kind of detachment that comes from holding the world at arm's length, and in revulsion declaring oneself to be no part of it," an attitude "of *saeva indignatio* which the Elizabethans, including Donne, found so attractive in Juvenal."

Elliott (1976, 105–10) states that "although English Renaissance satirists varied widely in their *personae* and in formal techniques, they all paid homage to the classical precedent of Horace, Persius, and Juvenal in collecting their satires into clusters and dividing their poems into groups or 'books' usually composed of three, five, or seven poems," adding that Juvenal's "followed a five-part structure" similar to that of Donne. Further, these Renaissance satirists "also learned from the classical tradition that satire, as a descendant of the Greek satyr-play, should be quasi-dramatic in character, held together by the experience of the Narrator-Satirist" (105–06). He also perceives in the Satyres numerous thematic echoes from the gospel of Matthew in the Sermon on the Mount (5.1–16), Christ's healing of the leper (8.1–4), the good and the bad fruit (7.16–20), the idea of idolatry (7.6), and the portrayal of hypocrites (6.16) (108–09).

Hester (1977c, 174–75) argues that Donne's satirist "is not simply a Juvenalian 'railer' in Elizabethan garb who only modernizes the situations of Horace in the tones of Persius," but rather a "'zealous' prophet," one assimilating "the view of the satirist as a Christian 'rebuker' whose earliest precedents were the Old Testament Prophets" and who "achieves a balance, an integration, to use his own words, of 'Kinde pitty' and 'brave scorn' (III, 1) not found in the Latin originals (nor in the other formal verse satires of the Renaissance)." Guibbory (1993, 131) concurs with this view of the satirist's religious zeal.

Partridge (1978, 37) observes that the Satyres present a "crotchety logic" that was "not original, but derived from Donne's reading in Spanish authors," particularly Góngora, Luis de Granada, Jorge de Montemayor, and St. John of the Cross.

Selden (1978, 59) contends that the Satyres "owe no servile debt to any classical models: their re-creation of traditional materials is too innovative to be categorised as 'Horatian' or 'Juvenalian,'" but he adds that "superficial analogies" can be drawn between Donne and Persius, for they "share a distaste for extravagantly expressed and unqualified idealism (Persius' opposition to Alexandrian refinement and Silver Latin romanticism is paralleled by Donne's rejection of Petrarchan mellifluousness), and the styles of both combine colloquial plainness (Persius' *plebeia prandia*) and philosophical or religious elevation."

Dubrow (1979, 71–72) argues that in the Satyres we discover "a blend of the Horatian and the Juvenalian," though she specifies that "in the character of his speaker, in the relationship between that speaker and the satiric antagonist, in the tone of his satiric thrusts," Donne is much closer to Juvenal than Horace, and further that Donne's satirist "is marked by a sense of his own superiority that distinguishes him sharply from Horace's" (71–72).

Hester (1981, 20) points out that while it is "generally agreed" that the Satyres are the "first 'sustained imitation of the Latin genre' in English literature," he clarifies that Donne "reinvents whatever he borrows or imitates, amplifying it to fit the imaginative strategies of his own."

Gallenca (1982, 309–11, 319) argues that Donne's Satyres and Marston's *Scourge of Villainy*, though different in style, share the same tenor and audience and the same restlessness and tendency towards speculation (309–10). They also exhibit, he thinks, a neo-Stoic focus of attention on the duality of soul and matter, as seen in the antagonism between social appearances and spiritual awakening, immediate gratification and eternal damnation. In that both writers paint a world of instability and anxiety in which the courtier is a frivolous performer (310–11), each seeks in his own way to affect a stylistic shift that will renew the world's perception of objects as declarations of one's affections and spirit (319).

According to Hester (1982, 5–6), the "exasperated indignation of Juvenal's *'difficile est saturam non scribere'*" is heard throughout the Satyres, and "the rough asperity of Persius and the exhortive irony of Horace find their complements in the paradoxical encounters of Donne's persona with knaves and fools, as well as in his conversational style." Yet, beyond these "imitations of the Latin genre," he maintains that the poems enact a "concept of satirical decorum available to the Renaissance Christian satirist, a view of the requirements of the satirist that satisfied both the general rhetorical principles of verse satire and the ethical prescriptions of late sixteenth-century England." Thus, Donne's satirist participates in an "older and more comprehensive view" of the genre, one "sanctioned by biblical example, patristic commentary, and sixteenth-century homiletic and critical opinion," which was modeled by the "first formal definition of satire in English literature" found in Thomas Drant's preface to his

1566 translation of Horace's Satires, which includes in one volume "both the Satires of Horace and the Lamentations of Jeremiah," and it is "to this view of the satirist as a 'zealous' prophet" that Donne's poems "seem most fully indebted."

Stein (1984, 73–74) observes of Donne that among those "interested in Roman elegies or satires" Donne alone had "the sureness of hand and eye to convert old models into original English poems so flowering in their present that they seemed fully rooted there." He states further that with regard to satire what Donne "most wanted was the tradition for licensed freedom of movement," adding that Donne "seems to have had a discerning eye for precedents and suggestions that would suit his own temper and purposes," including not only "the Roman examples" and "the prophets of scriptural tradition," but also the "speakers in the native tradition: Langland, Skelton, the Spenser of *Mother Hubberds Tale* and *Colin Clouts Come Home Again*, Martin Marprelate, and soon the railing figure who would become the malcontent on the stage, and that figure dear to the hearts of Englishmen well before he answered to the name of 'plain dealer.'"

Kupersmith (1985, 150–51) states that in the Satyres Donne "deliberately cultivated Persius' obscurity" by writing in "the old-fashioned 'satyr' style."

Sloane (1985, 177) notes that in the Satyres Donne's Christianity is "more prominent" than the influence of Horace, Juvenal, or Persius.

Baumlin (1986a, 105) notes that "in Donne's imitations of Persius the speaker's direct address to his reading audience (of which Egerton, in 'Satyre V,' is a conspicuous member) makes this audience aware that the satirist's concerns are its own; and as he speaks to this audience directly he tries to influence it directly." He adds that in Persius Donne found the "broad outline of a deliberative and essentially public voice whose moral exhortations, much more than laughter or rage, could best result in reform."

Baumlin (1986b, 450, 455, 466–67) contends that Donne's Satyres, along with Hall's and Marston's, test "the resources of each Roman model to enact change in contemporary society" (455), adding, however, that among his contemporaries only Donne "imitate[s] Persius successfully—to draw on his moral seriousness and tendency to philosophize, and make effective use of his structural and stylistic devices" (450). He concludes that while Hall and Marston selected Juvenal as "their preferred model," Donne found Persius the "best vehicle for his own serious Christian insights" but adds that Donne would not have been "secure" in following Persius had he not, like Hall and Marston, "tested the resources of all three Roman models" (466–67).

Waller (1986, 242) contends that when they are placed "in their literary context," the Satyres "show a particularly brilliant manipulation of a Horatian persona in a Juvenalian context, the careful observer among the frantic and bewildering randomness of experience," and the poems "produce a self simultaneously gripped by, and yet determined to discriminate among, the flurry of experiences passing by." The reader is thus "cloyed with quickly passing detail" and is "never certain whether boredom may suddenly become grippingly significant, or when trivial remarks may suddenly alter our hold on power."

Beck (1987, 25–26) points out that while satire and epistolary satire might not yet have been established, the "satiric mode" was "common in England during the late Middle Ages," and she suggests that "as poet-satirist at the court of James IV of Scotland, Dunbar can be viewed as a rather obvious predecessor of Donne." Like Juvenal in the classical tradition and Langland, Dunbar, or Wyatt among earlier British writers, Donne is "a harsh critic, or stern poet-prophet, whose critique turns into a ferocious satirical attack or judgment upon the vanities and vices of his age and of the world at large." She adds that "as an Anglo-Catholic and as a British classical poet," Donne also emulates Wyatt in "harmonizing medieval and Renaissance modes with Latin and Anglican styles so that native imagery and accentual rhythms as well as classical forms and rhetorical approaches contribute force to the satirical tirades" and "may resemble" the works of Juvenal and Persius, or of Ezekiel and Jeremiah, as well as Alexander Barclay's satiric *Eclogues*, and, "especially," William Dunbar's poetic satires.

Baumlin (1988, 366) argues that Donne is "the first to discover, and enact, the limitations of classical satire," and "what allows this discovery is the poet's radical reflection on the weakness of language, a reflection spurred on," he argues, "by the culture's refusal to grant his Catholicism authority—or grant it simply the right of utterance" (366).

According to Parfitt (1989, 33), the Satyres are not much concerned with women, "even though satire of women is common in both the native and classical traditions." He cautions, however, that "it would be misleading to see this reticence as suggesting respect for the feminine, for what attention is given to women in these poems fits her into traditional male-defined roles," and "there is no evidence of any effort to get beyond these stereotypes."

Dubrow (1990, 153) suggests of Donne that "it is no accident" that two of the Satyres imitate Horace's Satire I. ix, "a poem that depicts an encounter with a bore," even though other plot models were offered by Horace, Juvenal, and Persius, for, she explains, the Horatian account enacts Donne's "recurrent fantasy of intrusion, whether by a 'Busie old foole' of a sun, by an eavesdropper, or, most ominously, by a political spy."

Larson (1990, 134) remarks that whether Donne follows Horace, Juvenal, Martial, or all three poets in the Satyres, he nevertheless "makes them his own," for Donne's "innovations" in the genre, "dependent as he undoubtedly was on classical works," are "what prevented recognition of those sources for so many years and what make disagreements on his borrowings as common as they are."

Baumlin (1991, 22, 25–26, 28–29, 81) describes Donne as the first English writer "to discover the rhetorical as well as moral limitations" of satyre, and whether or not one decides to read the Satyres as a "revision or rejection of their classical models," one can be certain that Donne's "critique of the Roman satirists is subsumed within a broader critique: the problem of genre becomes a problem of rhetoric, particularly of the competing theologies of language" (81). As such, he argues that with Donne's Satyres one must attend to "the dynamic interplay" between "the decorum of his classical models and the demands of his unique historical circumstances" (22). He believes that Donne's "re-creation" of satiric decorum "grants him a literary authority, asserting his right to be read or heard," though it does not "guarantee him a persuasive moral authority in his own culture," and thus the Satyres "explore their own lack of authority," specifically in their "explorations of the dangers that arise when one theology (or any form of ideology) robs another of its worldview," their "self-sustaining voice," and their "enabling vocabulary" (25–26). As such, the poems "bring to a crisis this radical reflection on genre, asserting their need for formal models even as they question the moral authority and rhetorical efficacy of their precursors in this new cultural setting" (28).

Hester (1992, xii–xiii) believes that Donne's "fashionable adaptations" of Horace and Juvenal show that the satire of the period "remains a largely conservative vehicle" as it reworks this classical form within "the spirit of the medieval-Renaissance traditions of Christian humanist *imitatio*."

Wheeler (1992, 120–21) states that while Donne was attracted to the Roman satirists for "method, manner and ideas," this influence was "negligible," adding that Donne's Satyres are "quite unique" in late sixteenth-century English literature in the attention they draw "to the deeply religious element which is constantly present in all of Donne's works." Thus, affixing to the Satyres any such label as "Horatian," "Persian," or "Juvenalian" is "impossible, for Donne was all, and at the same time none."

Gorbunov (1993, 93–95) suggests that Donne wrote the Satyres, and his other poems, as though he were intentionally competing with Spenser, Marlowe, Shakespeare, and other Elizabethan poets, which in turn inspired the originality of his poetry. Gorbunov argues further that in contrast to the general Elizabethan approach to verse satire, Donne did not craft his Satyres as allegories or pastorals. Instead, Gorbunov says, like Wyatt, Donne drew from the classical Roman models of Horace, Persius, and Juvenal, though unlike Wyatt's neo-Stoic form of satire, Donne did not present his Satyres as friendly messages to an actually existing addressee (93). In addition, Gorbunov states that throughout the Satyres Donne sounds notes of disaffection with the monarch, a topic which gradually becomes the overall object of English satire in the 1590's (95).

Griffin (1994, 12) argues that Donne is generally acknowledged as "the best of the Elizabethan satirists," adding that "the idea that the satirist is a sort of satyr founders when one takes up Donne's poems," since their rhetoric is "derived more from Horace than from Juvenal," for Donne's "fawning courtiers" (Sat1 and Sat4) are "Horatian, as is the satirist's presentation of himself as foolish victim." He adds that Donne also "rejects the satirist's angry rant" and concludes that "it is Donne, among all the English imitators of Horace," who "most resembles Horace."

Strier (1994, 231) notes that Donne did not so much reject models as change them, and he sees Donne as, if not the first, at least among the first writers of "Horatian verse satire in English."

Post (1999, 5–6) argues that Donne and Jonson were alone among their contemporaries in developing "a radically different idiom" through their reading of Roman authors. Donne looked to the writings of Horace, Juvenal, and Persius for "a stylistic alternative to the musicality of court verse," and, like Hall, Donne "seems to have appreciated general differences among the models."

Ellrodt (2000, 348–49) argues that Donne and his contemporaries wished to reject imitation in favor of "self-assertion and singularity." He notes also that while Donne condemned literary theft in Sat2 25–30, he was imitated by Guilpin. Donne does not seem to have been influenced by Italian, Spanish, or French poets, Ellrodt thinks, although he apparently read them (e.g., *Sat1* 10), and while he did not, "and hardly could," acknowledge his debt to the Roman satirists and elegists, Donne repaid their literary influence "with as much and as good."

Prescott (2000, 229) notes of the Satyres that "the classicized names typical of such satire signal a revival of classical methods."

Wiggins (2000, 18, 158n6) argues that the Satyres are "autobiographical in the tradition of Horace and Ariosto" as they "depict Donne himself confronting impasses, resisting self-deception, becoming disabused" (18). He adds that although Donne "exhibits awareness of literary models" in the Satyres, "literary authority was not the major formative influence" (158n6).

UNITY AND STRUCTURE

Grierson (1921, 5) contends that the "record" of Donne's early years is "contained" in the Satyres.

Lindsay (1934b, 636) believes that the Satyres form a unified group.

Archer (1961, 144) observes that a three-part structure is common among the poems in the Songs and Sonets, Elegies, and Satyres.

Andreasen (1963, 60, 62, 74) suggests that the Satyres are unified by the speaker, who stands for "spiritual values" against the period's increasing materialism (60), as well as by their "interlocking imagery" (62). Two strands of imagery, one abstract and the other concrete, recur both in individual satyres and from one poem to another so that "imagery, drama, and dialogue" all work together to contrast spiritual with secular values (74).

Geraldine (1966, 27–28) finds *Sat3* to be "the pivot of the whole satiric sequence, giving moral and religious weight to the themes of inconstancy and opportunism which the first two satyres set forth and the last two carry forward."

Lecocq (1969, 365–68) states that in spite of their numerous marks of resemblance with the other profane works, the Satyres form a homogeneous and distinct group (365). He explains that a consideration of the subjects of the five poems (1: fickle person, 2: lawyer, 3: religion, 4: court, and 5: justice) seems to suggest a pattern of two poems about individuals and three poems about institutions. The governing principle is, however, more complex: each of the Satyres contains both portraits and general observations that target one or another institution (366). The first two focus on private morality and the last two on public morality; there is a symmetrical complementarity between *Sat1* and *Sat2*, and *Sat4* and *Sat5*. As such, he concludes that not only a double complementarity (*Sat1* and *Sat2*, *Sat4* and *Sat5*), but also a double analogy (*Sat1* and *Sat4*, *Sat2* and *Sat5*) operate in structuring and unifying the sequence (367). Within this structure, then, *Sat3*—with its focus on religion—functions as a link between private and public morality (368).

Hutchison (1970, 363) notes that in several instances Donne "pointed to the need to integrate" the powers of the soul, namely in *Sat3* "in the passages on the search for Truth" and in *Sat4* in drawing "a parallel between the introductory section of the poem, the journey to court, and the prophetic vision which results."

Sanders (1971, 39) comments that to describe the Satyres as "performances" is to say that we have an art that is "finally *inventive* rather than creative." Throughout these poems "the improvisatory feel of the rhythms" becomes "the medium through which we receive the inventive bravura." This type of "satirical activity," he says, can therefore "have no structure beyond the episodic, and no satisfactory termination except by courtesy of its hearers." Because "mere inventiveness" cannot provide "a structure with an inner necessity of its own," he believes most of the Satyres "go on too long," ending "more often with a whimper than a bang."

Sito (1971, 409), commenting on a translation of the Satyres into Polish, describes each poem as being an intellectual construct, a complete treatise.

Medine (1972, 51–52) explains that "unlike Drant [1567] and others who divided their volume into separate sections," Donne provided "particular values or norms" in each of the Satyres. He concludes that "in combining the positive and negative statements" within each poem, Donne "integrated the entire design of his collection," and thus, even though Donne "treats a wide variety of material and concerns himself with the praise of virtue and the deprecation of vice," the Satyres "stand apart from most collections of the period."

Shawcross (1972, 261–62) argues that the Satyres "pillory five universal dilemmas besetting man," proceeding from "man's relationship with himself to his control by law to his control by religious belief to his control by the artificial world of society to his succumbing to greed or its effects in others." As such, the poems "pose the constant duel between the id and the superego, the problem of change in this world, the need for a guiding philosophy of life, the pride man shows in externalities, and the avaricious nature of man," concluding that "there is no sure means out of any of these dilemmas, although the 'I' of each suggests that by recognition of their existence and their evil, man will be better able to withstand their assaults upon him."

Swift (1974, 47) describes the Satyres overall as being of medium length and beginning explosively, with a single monometric dramatic monologue, in which a speaker turns to an imploring antagonistic *adversarius*, or silently listening *nonce*, to analyze and discuss a topic. These situations, which are usually without a plot, but appropriately dramatic, complete the presentation of the topic elliptically, with breaks filled with random reflections, anecdotes, dialogues, short dramas, portraits, debates, sermons, and aphorisms.

Elliott (1976, 105–06) believes that while Donne may not have intended "to compose a unified collection," there is, nevertheless, "considerable evidence" that Donne "planned" for the Satyres "to be read as a whole, with the central position" of *Sat3* "serving to focus attention upon the ethical and religious meaning of the entire collection." In doing so, Donne "followed the conventions of narrative and formal structure which he inherited from the English and classical traditions," interweaving throughout the poems "numerous Biblical allusions, many of which he drew from the four chapters of Matthew's Gospel which recount the Sermon on the Mount," that "strengthen the structural and thematic unity" of the poems and "provide a key to the internal conflict of the speaker-protagonist whose moral development the poems trace."

Lauritsen (1976, 120) suggests that the Satyres present a "progress of self-discovery," in which the speaker moves from "that detachment which is born of a desperate need to believe that one is morally superior to the world of ordinary mortals to that moral engagement and commitment which can only come when one realizes that one is not only in the fallen world, but *of* it."

Hester (1977c, 185–88) argues that in their "five-act sequence" the Satyres "disclose the satirist's growing awareness of the nature and uses of Christian 'zeal.'" In their sequential development, the poems portray the speaker's "moral character" (*Sat1*), "aesthetic development" (*Sat2*), "spiritual awareness" (*Sat3*), and "his efforts to implement the lessons of that self-knowledge" (*Sat4* and *Sat5*) (185–86). He adds that "the dramatic portrait" of the satirist "duplicates the mythic or Christian structure of human history" in delineating a journey "from innocence" (*Sat1*), "to darkness and despair" (*Sat2*), and "finally to self-knowledge" (*Sat3*), "suffering and God-given knowledge" (*Sat4*), and "obedience" (*Sat5*) (187). As a result, the sequential structure indicates that the satirist's "self-awareness and 'zeal' are the method and 'cure' for 'these worne maladies'" (*Sat3* 4) (188).

Carey (1981, 63–64) asserts that Donne "deliberately" provided an "informal publication" of the Satyres "by circulating them in manuscript" as a means of "self-advertisement within the court group."

Slights (1981, 177) notes that only *Sat3* "closely resembles the case of conscience structurally," yet she adds that all of the Satyres "exhibit to a striking extent the casuist's double focus on self-examination and practical action." She explains that "the shifting tones and subjects" of the poems "and their unity as a group are intelligible only when we recognize that the speaker is working out his own case of conscience at the same time as he is exposing the evil around him." As a result, "by showing the incipient recluse" of *Sat1* "developing into the dedicated public servant" of *Sat5*, Donne "provides a model of a man discovering how to act according to his conscience in a perplexing situation."

Corthell (1982, 156) writes that "the textual tradition" of the Satyres, "'in nombre and order' as Donne wrote them according to Drumond of Hawthornden," encourages readers to consider the poems "as a book marking stages in Donne's development as a poet from his years at Lincoln's Inn to his first position as secretary to Lord Keeper Egerton."

Zunder (1982, 9) remarks that the structure of the Satyres has "given rise to difficulty, but each poem has in fact a clear structural coherence."

Kerins (1984, 37, 55) asserts that *Sat1* and *Sat4* are "related by the simple fact that both are variations on Horace's famous 'Bore satire' (I, 9)," and "the striking dissimilarities" of the two, he suggests, result from "the effect of a change in the character of Donne's persona" throughout the Satyres, or, said differently, the "effect of Donne's satiric plot." Further, while *Sat2* and *Sat5* "share no common source," they are "clearly related by the epistolary form in which they are composed," though they "investigate the question of law and justice from quite different perspectives." As for *Sat3*, he says, it is "the nexus which energizes the transformation from intellectual detachment to emotional involvement in an imperfect world" (37). He adds that "the progress" of Donne's Satyres "leads almost inevitably" to the conclusion that "the change from a private to a public satiric voice" throughout the sequence is "not entirely due" to the "occasional nature" of the poems (55).

Patrides (1985, 213) states of the Satyres that in their "final form" they seem to "constitute 'a unified narrative' intended to be read 'as a whole,'" adding that the poem appended to the satires, *Coryat*, is only "an appendage" and "representative of those poems which partake of the spirit of the five satires proper."

Shawcross (1986, 120–21) contends that Donne's Satyres had apparently circulated in manuscript groups before January 1615 when Donne "called in his poems for publication before his ordination," adding that the poems "have been worked into a manuscript grouping by genres and types," and that *Sat1–Sat5* "are generally grouped together and in that order in the manuscripts and in print."

Baumlin (1991, 21–22, 92, 150–51) insists that though the Satyres are "disparate poems," they are "organically and thematically unified," with each poem progressively "deepening in its understanding of the nature of satire." He grants that "thematic unities may legitimately be discovered" within the poems, but he questions "whether the speaker learns to be a better satirist from one poem to the next." Any readings, he asserts, emphasizing a "meta-narrative unity" tend "to downplay other intertextual relations—relations to the classical models, for example—realms of imitation that necessarily call into question the collection's presumed unity of voice." Instead, he reads the poems "as studies in contrast, works that explore the problems of rhetoric and Reformation theology, each returning to the problematic relation between traditional literary form and social reform" (21–22). He argues that a "dialectical interplay between decorum and *kairos* continues throughout Donne's collection of satires: a rhetoric of decorous imitation, one seeking to recreate the stylistic features (and thus invoke the linguistic presence or 'speaking image' of the model) confronts a *kairotic* recognition of change, of critical difference borne of the poet's unique political and religious circumstances" (92). Finally, he speculates if the poems demonstrate "a progressive reach beyond the realm of literary form in order to validate and enact the author's aims, with diatribe, homily, and law taking the place of spleen and satiric laughter" (151).

Hester (1991, 98), commenting on the manuscript circulation of the Satyres, observes of *Sat3* that it "*never* appears alone, never without at least two other of the satires" and then describes the grouping details.

Sellin (1991, 86–87) argues of the Satyres that "defining Donne's *liber satyrarum* as consisting of merely five pieces is arbitrary and unhistorical," that "originally the collection often incorporated a sixth satire," and thus that "any 'book of Donne's satires' that contained only five pieces would clearly be incomplete, for it would fail to encompass much of Donne's work in the genre."

Slights (1991, 94) asserts that *Sat3* "is most interesting and significant" when viewed in the context of the other Satyres, "which as a group explore the problem of how to participate in human society without compromising personal integrity."

Stringer (1991, 80, 82–83) provides a chart of the surviving seventeenth-century manuscripts of the Satyres. Delineating "their Donne Variorum sigla," "their traditional sigla," and "their historical names or library shelfmarks," the chart demonstrates how the poems circulated, with variations, as a group. He adds that "the chart also reminds us that some artifacts contain and attribute to Donne as many as six or seven satires" (80).

Kiséry (1997, 112) notes of the Satyres that no paragraphing appears "in any of the editions published before Pope's Imitations."

Oliver (1997, 53) finds evidence that the Satyres, along with *Storm* and *Calm*, "circulated together as a manuscript 'book,' and thus presented the reader with a range of voices."

Wiggins (2000, 18, 25, 27) argues that the Satyres depict Donne "confronting impasses, resisting self-deception, becoming disabused," and this understanding organizes the five poems "into a unified account of the social life of an aspirant to political prominence in late Elizabethan London" (18). Furthermore, Egerton's presence in the Satyres links them together "as five parts of the one coherent book that Donne considered himself to have created" (25). He suggests further that Donne represents Egerton ("possibly long after the fact") as "authorizing" the Satyres. Donne's continued revisions of these poems and his 1608 presentation of them to the Countess of Bedford "confirm that he regarded them as a serious, coherent work presenting him in a favorable light and setting forth his qualifications to act as the voice" of at least one, if not both, of these powerful patrons (27).

Fulton (2001, 71) traces the development of a "tradition" from Grierson (1921) to Carey (1981) that "misrepresents the unity of the original, interdependent conception" of the Satyres, which "were not individually anthologized in the manuscript editions." He argues that "their original order and narrative development suggests a unity that is threatened by the tendency to fit them individually into the various stages of Donne's career."

LANGUAGE AND STYLE

In his comments recorded by William Drummond of Hawthornden, Ben Jonson (1619 [1925, 1:133, 138]) surely had the Satyres in mind when he remarked "that Done for not keeping of accent deserved hanging" (133) and may have been speaking of the Satyres when he said to Drummond that "Done himself for not being understood would perish" (138).

Milton's nephew, Edward Phillips (1674, 398), acknowledges the "roughness" in the Satyres, but focuses attention more on the "sharpness of Wit, and gayety of Fancy" of those "brisk and Youthful Poems," which "are rather commended for the heighth of Fancy and acuteness of conceit, then for the smoothness of the Verse."

Dryden (1693 [1974, 4:78]) addresses the "rudeness" of Donne's style, asking, "Wou'd not *Donn's* Satires, which abound with so much Wit, appear more Charming, if he had taken care of his Words, and of his Numbers?" The more complete context for Dryden's comments here appears below in the General Commentary, Critical Influence of Dryden and Pope.

In a long poem comparing Donne and Pope, Harte (1730, sig. C2r) writes: "*Donne* teem'd with Wit, but all was maim'd and bruis'd, / The periods endless, and the sense confus'd."

Spence (c. 1730–36 [1949, 247]) observes that "one can find plenty of judicious sentiments" in Donne's Satyres, but avers that these sentiments "are always encumbered by a puerile affectation of seeking to say something fine," and throughout the poems, which are "nothing but a tissue of epigrams," the versification "is very bad."

Warburton (1751, 4:249) proclaims that "the manly Wit of Donne, which was the Character of his genius, suited best with Satire; and in this he excelled, tho' he wrote but little," adding that Donne's lines "have nothing more of numbers than their being composed of a certain quantity of syllables." Conceding that Donne's verse "did not want harmony," he adds that Donne "took the sermoni propiora of Horace too seriously; or rather he was content with the character his master gives of Lucilius,

Emunctae naris durus componere versus. [Hor Sat 1.4.8]
["Keen-nosed but harsh in versification."]

Birch (1752, 27) may be referring to (and is certainly including) the Satyres when he writes that Donne's "poetical works shew a prodigious fund of genius under the guise of an affected and obscure style and a most inharmonious versification."

Gray (1752? [1911, 37n1, 175]) compares Donne's versification with that of Spenser, citing the latter for "an unusual liberty in its feet," while concluding that in the Satyres Donne "observes no regularity in the pause, or in the feet of his verse, only the number of syllables is equal throughout." Donne, he surmises, "thought this rough uncouth measure suited the plain familiar style of satirical poetry" (37n1). In the same vein, in a letter to Thomas Warton, he compares the Satyres to Hall's Virgidemiae, which, he writes, are "full of spirit and poetry; as much of the first, as Dr. Donne, and far more of the latter" (175). Others who note the intentional irregularity of Donne's prosody in the Satyres include Saintsbury (1887, 150–51), Hales (1891, 1:558–60), Richter (1902, 391–415), Lang (1912, 283–84), Hamer (1930, 50), Elton (1932, 209), Stein (1946, 98–99), Wasserman (1947, 70–71), Jack (1951, 1012–14), Lewis (1954, 469–70), Kermode (1957, 25), Sutherland (1958, 32–33), Kernan (1959, 117–18), Mazzeo (1969, 160), Kermode (1971, 133–34), Smith (1971, 469), Elkin (1973, 27), Robson (1986, 87), and Shawcross (1991b, 77).

Hume (1754–62, 6:171–75) states that "when carefully inspected" the Satyres reveal "some flashes of wit and ingenuity," but they are "totally suffocated and buried in the hardest and most uncouth expression that is any where to be met with."

Granger (1769, 1:186–87) asserts that satire was Donne's "greatest excellency," but adds that in spite of his "prodigious richness of fancy" Donne's "thoughts were much debased by his versification."

Knox (1782, 167–68, 440) contends that in contrast to the "remarkably harmonious" verse of Juvenal, Donne "seems to have thought roughness of verse, as well as sentiment, a real grace" and expresses puzzlement "that a writer who did not studiously avoid a smooth versification, could have written so many lines without stumbling on a good one" (167–68). He adds that because of neglecting "the graces of composition," Donne "will therefore soon be numbered among those once celebrated writers, whose utility now consists in filling a vacancy on the upper shelf of some dusty and deserted library" (440).

Warton (1782, 264) comments that in the Satyres Donne "degraded and deformed a vast fund of sterling wit and strong sense, by the most harsh and uncouth diction."

Anderson (1792–95, 4:4–5) asserts that the Satyres "display a prodigious richness of fancy, and an elaborate minutenesse of description," adding that Donne's thoughts "are seldom natural, obvious, or just, and much debased by the carelessenesse of his versification."

The anonymous author of *The Progress of Satire: An Essay in Verse* (1798; qtd. in Shawcross [1991b, 77]) writes, "Rough Donne, in homely strains, devoid of art, / Spoke the plain truths that prove an honest heart."

Drake (1800, 2:170) states of the Satyres that if it is true that "the purport of poetry should be to please," no other author "has written with such utter neglect of the rule," for "it is scarce possible for a human ear to endure the dissonance and discord of his couplets, and even when his thoughts are clothed in the melody of Pope, they appear to me hardly worth the decoration."

Chalmers (1810, 5:124) says that Donne's "numbers, if they may be so called," are in the Satyres "certainly the most rugged and uncouth of any of our poets" and that Donne appears "either to have had no ear, or to have been utterly regardless of harmony," but then suggests that, since Donne "was certainly not ignorant or unskilled in the higher attributes of style," he must have written his poems in this manner because he was "not desirous of public fame."

Coleridge (1811 [1984, 12.2:216, 230]) comments in his marginalia, "I would ask no surer Test of a Scotch-man's *Substratum* (for the Turf-cover of Pretension & they all have) than to make him read Donne's Satires aloud. If he made manly Metre of them, & yet strict metre,—*then*—why, then he wasn't a Scotchman, or his Soul was geographically slandered by his Body's being first apparentearing there" (216). Further, in a note scribbled next to *Sat5*, he explains, "Satyrs (for in the age of Donne they took the literal meaning) were supposed to come all rough from the woods, with a rustic accent" (230). Others who note Donne's understanding of the rustic nature of satyrs include Walker (1925, 69), Kermode and Hollander (1973, 1045; 1975, 739), Raizada (1974, 100), Warnke (1987, 22), Fowler (1993, 95), Lerner (1999, 5–6), and Saunders (1999, 177, 177n30).

Drake (1817, 1:615) observes that while "among his contemporaries" Donne enjoyed "an extraordinary share of reputation," a "more refined age" and a "more chastised taste" have "very justly" relegated his poetry to "the shelf of the philologer," adding that "a total want of harmony of versification, and a total want of simplicity both in thought and expression" are Donne's "vital defects."

Sanford (1819, 4:137), describing Donne as "something of a poet," contends nonetheless that in "the highest sense of the word" one can "almost say" that there is no poetry in Donne and concludes that Donne was "more witty than learned; and more learned than poetical."

[Spence] (1823, 52), in an unsigned article, characterizes the Satyres as being "as rough and rugged as the unhewn stones that have just been blasted from their native quarry; and they must have come upon the readers at whom they were levelled, with the force and effect of the same stones flung from the hand of a giant."

Croly (1835, 2:284–85) comments that as a poet Donne was "powerful but rude: his taste was displayed in perpetual epigram, and his morality in the roughest scorn of public manners" and then adds that "as an apology for the style of his poems, it is to be remembered that they were all written before he was twenty-five."

Coleridge (1836, 1:148) penned the following lines on Donne's versification:

With Donne, whose muse on dromedary trots,
Wreathe iron pokers into true-love knots;
Rhyme's sturdy cripple, fancy's maze and clue,
Wit's forge and fire-blast, meaning's press and screw.

Landor (1836, 220), in his poem "A Satire on Satirists," writes, "Frost-bitten, and lumbaginous, when Donne, / With verses gnarl'd and knotted, hobbled on" (ll. 110–11).

In a brief biographical sketch of Donne, Cunningham (1837, 3:242) describes the Satyres as "pungent and forcible, but exceedingly rugged and uncouth in their versification."

An anonymous commentator writing in *The Penny Cyclopaedia* (1838, 9:85) asserts that the Satyres, "though written in a measure inconceivably harsh, are models of strength and energy," though he adds that generally speaking what Donne "has composed in the heroic measure is painfully uncouth and barbarous."

Prior to quoting brief passages from *Sat4* by way of illustration, Lewes (1838, 375–76) says that it may be "very readily granted" that Donne's "'poems' are not poems at all" and adds that "his poetical sins are *concetti*; ruggedness of versification, which is indeed nothing but measured prose, and very bad prose, as far as relates to style; want of consistency and harmony, nay, even truth, in his illustrations; and an almost total deficiency of imagination, or any feeling of art," though he concedes that Donne is "full of wit, subtlety, and fancy."

Hallam (1839, 2:316) appends to his discussion of Hall the comment that Donne, as a satirist, has "as much obscurity as Hall" and "still more inharmonious versification, and not nearly equal vigour" before concluding that "the roughness of these satirical poets was perhaps studiously affected; for it was not much in unison with the general tone of the age."

Craik (1845, 3:170–71), noting the stylistic contrast between Donne's Satyres and Pope's rendering of them, concludes that Donne's lines, "though they will not suit the see-saw style of reading verse,—to which he probably intended that they should be invincibly impracticable,—are not without a deep and subtle music of their own" and that "whatever harshness they have was designedly given to them, and was conceived to infuse into them an essential part of their relish."

Patmore [?] (1846, 230, 233–35) contends that Donne's "ordinary *versification* is about the very ruggedest that ever has been written," adding that "we shall not extract any particular lines to prove this assertion, since we shall make few quotations which will *not* prove it." Though he defends Donne by asserting that "even his worst versification will be pardoned, since no sacrifice of meaning is ever made to it," yet he believes that "this defect will always prevent Donne from becoming popular" (230). He provides a series of passages from *Sat3* as "a good specimen of the *average* flow (!) of Donne's verses," and then asks, who, "loving best of course the marriage of sound and meaning, would not yet prefer climbing, with Donne, these crags, where all the air is fresh and wholesome, to gliding, with Thomas Moore, over flats, from beneath the rank verdure of which arises malaria and invisible disease?" (234).

Farr (1847, xii) asserts that Donne's "great offence" is thought to be "harshness of versification," and while admitting that Donne's verse is "frequently rugged and sometimes obscure," he adds that "this once favourite writer may nevertheless be pronounced to be a true and often a delightful poet."

Carruthers (1854, 4:188), in an introductory comment to Pope's rendering of *Sat2*, notes that Donne "wrote Latin verses much smoother and more correct than his English numbers." He then mistakenly observes that Donne died in 1662, "having survived many schools of poetry and politics: he was in his eighty-ninth year," concluding that "the style of this old poet, though rugged and most unmusical, is not very antiquated in expression."

Cleveland (1854, 165–66) writes that Donne is "almost entirely forgotten" as a poet and "has not much harmony of versification," yet he asserts that Donne "exhibits much erudition, united to an exuberance of wit, and to a fancy, rich, vivid, and picturesque, though, at the same time, it must be confessed, not a little fantastical."

Jessopp (1855, x, xvii–xviii) explains that during Donne's days at Lincoln's Inn he "amused himself with occasional exercise of composition, in prose and verse, mere trifles for the most part—clever sallies flowing out from an exuberant wit," and that while this early verse is "occasionally rugged," it is "characterized by a vigour and grasp of mind which in so young a man is truly wonderful." He adds that "the very faults are those of a man who has more power than he knows how to manage, certainly not those of one who is aiming at an originality which he does not possess" (xvii–xviii).

Gilfillan (1860, 1:204) concludes his overview of Donne's verse by noting that, while demonstrating "high ideal qualities," the Satyres also show the "rugged versification, the fantastic paradox, and the perverted taste of their author, great strength and clearness of judgment, and a deep, although somewhat jaundiced, view of human nature."

B[ond] (1861, 90) compares Donne's Satyres with Hall's and notes that Donne's are "less musical, but far more vigorous and fuller of good character-painting," and he then laments the difficulty of finding passages that are "both good and unobjectionable," concluding that Donne "fell into the common vice of his time, and sometimes wrote indecently."

Craik (1861, 1:552–53), writing in general of Donne's poetry, states that "things of the most opposite kinds—the harsh and the harmonious, the graceful and the grotesque, the grave and the gay, the pious and the profane—meet and mingle in the strangest of dances." Commenting specifically on the Satyres, Craik adds that he finds "wholly unfounded" the "notion" that the harshness of the Satyres is attributable to the English language not being "sufficiently advanced" in Donne's day.

Whipple (1869, 231) describes Donne's poems, "or rather his metrical problems," as "obscure in thought, rugged in versification, and full of conceits which are intended to surprise rather than to please," adding, however, that they "still exhibit a power of intellect, both analytical and analogical, competent at once to separate the minutest and connect the remotest ideas."

Corser (1873, Part 5:223) briefly notes "the rugged and discordant diction, and inharmonious versification" of the Satyres.

MacDonald (1874, 115–16) describes Donne's verse as "harsh and unmusical beyond the worst that one would imagine fit to be called verse," and he believes that Donne's "unenviable distinction of having no rival in ruggedness of metric movement and associated sounds" is "clearly the result of indifference," especially since Donne "*can* write a lovely verse and even an exquisite stanza."

An anonymous commentator writing in *TB* (1876, 337–39) states of the Satyres that "a little ruggedness of metre, a few archaisms in spelling and expression, repel the indolent readers of the present day, who pronounce such books to be unintelligible" (337). He then admits to having followed Coleridge's suggestion in reading Donne's poems by "giving *each thought* its due proportion in the utterance" with the result that "attention to that rule has greatly smoothed out their apparent ruggedness" (338).

In his discussion of moral satire, Arnold (1877, 438–39) espouses that the satires of Donne and Hall are "too rough and harsh to have much poetical value."

Saintsbury (1887, 145–47, 150–51) asserts of the Satyres that "all alike display Donne's peculiar poetical quality—the fiery imagination shining in dark places, the magical illumination of obscure and shadowy thoughts with the lightning of fancy" (147). He proposes further that while Donne's faults as a poet "are not least seen" in the Satyres, "the force and originality of Donne's intellect are nowhere better shown" (150–51).

Schipper (1888, 204–06), using the opening sixteen lines of *Sat1* to illustrate his ideas, describes the style of the Satyres as rough and clumsy and notes the contrast with the shorter lyrics, which are more fluid. He then comments on Donne's use of rhyme in the Satyres, noting not only the scarcity of breaks in the rhyme pattern and of the use of feminine rhyme, but also a carelessness on Donne's part concerning the purity of his rhymes.

Hales (1891, 1:558–60) states that while Donne "claims notice as one of our earliest formal satirists," yet his "misspent learning," "excessive ingenuity," and "laborious wit" significantly taint "almost the whole of Donne's work" (559–60).

Bradford (1892, 355–64) states of Donne that "the essence of his poetical gift, the essence of his moral character, was effort, struggle," so that Donne was constantly "at war with the elements of style, bending them, rending them, straining them to match the sweeping tide of his thoughts and passions" (355–56). Further, he comments, "conceits are scattered over the natural movement of his writing like red knots on a white garment." He finds that Donne is "often unintelligible, wantonly so," and describes Donne as one who "flings down his ideas before you like a tangled skein; you meddle with it at your peril" (357). He affirms that Donne is "always regarded as an example of rough and jarring metre" (358), elaborating that while Donne's "peculiar excellence is not metrical," yet "the ruggedness, the force that stamps his verse is far more characteristic of his thought" (360). He agrees that "it would be foolish to deny the extreme, absurd harshness of many of Donne's lines," but also contends that Donne "had an artistic aim in the very halt of his verses," a view confirmed by the fact that the Satyres "are rougher than his lyrics and serious pieces" (358). Nevertheless, he adds that "nothing can palliate Donne's wanton disregard of the laws of English versification" (in that "words are split to make a rhyme, accents are shaken over the verse from a pepper-box," leaving the reader to think himself "adrift in chaos"), yet "it would be simplicity to confound Donne's rhythm with that of an incompetent poetaster," for he is "never commonplace, never monotonous, never tame," and "beneath his apparent carelessness there is profound skill in the variation of pauses, in the management of periods." He concludes that "when the merits of Donne's versification are considered," it would take "a bold man" to "make excuses for him," noting that perhaps no English poet "has surpassed the vigor of movement in even the harshest of his satires, though they are difficult to quote" (358–59).

Gosse (1893, 245) claims that "the violence of Donne's transposition of accent is most curiously to be observed" in the earliest Satyres and that "no poet is more difficult to read aloud." By way of illustration, he quotes Sat4 235–41, explaining that the reader must "treat the five-foot verse not as a fixed and unalterable sequence of cadences, but as a norm around which a musician weaves his variations, and the riddle is soon read," and he proceeds to offer a scansion of the lines.

Furst (1896, 230–31) states of the Satyres that their "unusual modes of thought are expressed with such accurate figures and such finished word-fitting that the work abounds in passages remarkable in their aptness for quotation," which is "limited only by the unexpectedness of thought and the extraordinary compactness of expression, making it often necessary to read and reread a passage many times before its content is wholly understood and appreciated."

Alden (1899, 83) surmises that "it seems probable" that the Satyres have given rise to the view that Donne's poetry is "metrically infelicitous," adding that the measure of the Satyres "is characterized by approximation to the common speech of conversation," thus throwing "both syllable-counting and observance of regular accent into the background." He further observes that "the style is like the metre: rugged, free and conversational in construction, and yet extremely compact, almost always vigorous, occasionally obscure either through conciseness or Latinized construction."

In a review of Gosse's edition (1899), an anonymous commentator writing in The Academy (1899, 505–06) explains that the "extreme form" of Donne's Satyres is marked by a "crabbedness of both style and metre" and depends not only on "violent ellipsis as regards sentence-structure," but also on "violent elision and wilful [sic] accentuation as regards metre." Thompson (1899, 505–06) also comments on the crabbed and violent meter of the Satyres.

In a review of Gosse's edition (1899), an anonymous commentator writing in Book Reviews (1899, 482–83) identifies Donne as "the turbulent poet of the satires" and asserts, "there will always be a small but not unimportant minority who will continue to swear by the magnificent outburst of poetry in Donne's works, while the majority simply swear at his crabbedness."

Gosse (1899, 2:333–34) builds upon his earlier work (1893) in offering a justification of Donne's "curious ruggedness" in the Satyres, explaining that because "the conventional line vexed his ear with its insipidity," Donne therefore chose to break up the line into "successive quick and slow beats" in an attempt "to develop the orchestral possibilities of English verse."

Stephen (1899, 598) contends that Donne and his contemporary satirists "had not made the simple discovery that the better our manners the more easily we can rub in a good caustic phrase."

In a review of Gosse (1899), an anonymous commentator writing in The Nation

(1900, 112) calls the first four Satyres "extraordinary performances for a youth," noting that "though rugged in versification, they show as a whole remarkable breadth and keenness of observation and maturity of thought."

Taine (1905, 1:340–41) identifies Donne as a "poignant" satirist, one whose verse is very crude, but adds that his imagination is precise and intense.

Grierson (1906, 155) describes Donne's Satyres as "the most interesting and, metrically, the most irregular of the late sixteenth-century work of this kind."

Melton (1906, 1–2, 148) examines the rhetoric of Donne's verse, beginning with the premise that Donne has been "either not understood, or not appreciated" by those who study versification and notes that it is only those who are not "too dull to catch the music of the ripples, and even the eddies, of rhythm" who will be able to appreciate "the delicacy of Donne's lighter verse, or the straight thrust of his satire" (1–2). The opening chapter of the study provides an historical overview, from Ben Jonson to the present, of the metrical side of Donne's poetry, and the second chapter consists of "an application, to the poetry of Donne, of the theory of 'secondary word-accent in English verse,' as advanced by Professor [James Wilson] Bright" (1). In the final chapter, Melton explains and illustrates in detail the rule, or "secret," of Donne's versification, that is, "when a word, a syllable, or a sound, appears in arsis, get it into thesis as quickly as possible, and *vice versa*" (148). For specific instances, see the Notes & Glosses for all the Satyres.

Saintsbury (1908, 160–61) confesses that he has been "tempted to think that Donne and others thought themselves entitled to *scazontics*—that is to say, iambic lines with spondaic or trochaic endings, such as the ancient satirists who used the metre often preferred," and yet he admits that this may not be the case and instead that Donne, "recognising the classic practice of equivalence and substitution, used it in experiment more freely than wisely, as upon the *corpus*, admittedly *vile*, of satire."

Grierson (1909, 4:206) writes that Donne's Satyres show "something like a consistent effort to eschew a couplet structure, and to give to his verse the freedom and swiftness of movement to which, when he wrote, even dramatic blank verse had hardly yet attained," admitting that "such verse is certainly not smooth or melodious," though "the effect is studied and is not inappropriate to the theme and spirit."

Schelling (1910, 319) comments that Donne's Satyres are "conversational" in being "rough, irregular, and careless of the graces of versification," yet he explains that they are "concise and compact in thought and at times obscure from the use of a Latinized construction."

Comparing Donne to Spenser, Northup (1911, 37n1) notes that in the Satyres Donne "observes no regularity in the pause, or in the feet of his verse, only the number of syllables is equal throughout." Northup surmises that Donne "thought this rough uncouth measure suited the plain familiar style of satirical poetry."

Schelling (1913, 69) comments that Donne's style is marked by a "surprising directness" that is "free from the accepted smoothness and over-indulgence in figure" of his contemporaries, and while Donne's versification can be "abrupt and harsh at times," it is "always vigorous."

In a review article, Belden (1915, 147) laments that Grierson's edition (1912) does not include a study of Donne's "highly idiosyncratic metric and verse-rhetoric."

Colvin (1915, 17–18) notes the "strong and chafing current" of Donne's verse, characterized by a "love of acrobatic thought-play and of forcing together into strained imaginative relation ideas that naturally had none."

MacLeane (1915, 178) notes the "often ragged and tuneless versification" of the Satyres.

Jackson (1917, 218) cites without explanation or example "the obscurities, the roughnesses, the grotesque conceits, the studied eccentricities that mar" Donne's verse.

Huxley (1919, 186, 189) finds in Donne's verse "a conceited subtlety of thought combined with a harshness of metre" (189), the latter "a protest against Spenserian facility" (186).

Grierson (1921, xxii–xxiv) argues that the harshness and ruggedness of Donne's verse result, on the one hand, from "the desire to startle," and on the other, from "the desire to approximate poetic to direct, unconventional, colloquial speech." Thus, the effect Donne aims at is "bending and cracking the metrical pattern to the rhetoric of direct and vehement utterance" (xxii–xxiii). Further, Donne "writes as one who *will* say what he has to say without regard to conventions of poetic diction or smooth verse," and what Donne says, as well as the metrical effects of its presentation, is "subtle and surprising" (xxiv).

Nethercot (1922, 463–67, 472–73) observes that Donne's reputation "as metrist has undergone many vicissitudes" (463) and then summarizes the views regarding Donne's poetic style from Ben Jonson to the early twentieth century, first stating that after 1900 "very few opinions can be found which condemn Donne unequivocally and unqualifiedly for his 'harshness'" and then probing the reasons for this more positive view (467). He comments that Donne "was essentially a modern poet" to the extent that "one can imagine him in complete sympathy with the realists, imagists, and *vers librists* of the last decade and a half," and he concludes, "for many years, indeed, it has been a habit to call the measure" of the Satyres "conversational," which is "not quite such a criminal offence as it was in the eighteenth century" (472–73).

Jenkins (1923, 561, 568) contrasts Donne's "intricate, obscure, and rough" (561) intellectual poetry with that of Spenser and thus considers the Satyres representative of Donne's "indifference" to and "contempt" for contemporary poetic conventions (568).

Fausset (1924, 49–50) believes that the "abrupt and rugged versification" of the first four Satyres demonstrates Donne's rebellion against "a polished style," and his "conscious experiments in a new versification" accord with "the cynical realism of his subject-matter."

Hutton (1924, 152–53) states that in the Satyres "the note is harsh" and adds that Donne's style, "if not smooth, is balanced" in that he "fits the expression to the thought."

Wells (1924, 121–22) comments that in the first four Satyres sense takes precedence over style and that these poems demonstrate little of the "radical imagery" for which Donne is known.

Bredvold (1925, 232) asserts that Donne's mind, "made of the toughest fibre," accounts for the "toughness in his style," adding that the "genuineness" of Donne's nature "shines through the crabbed verse and the tortured 'conceits.'"

Nethercot (1925b, 171) argues that Pope chooses to imitate Donne because of his "remarkable satirical ability" and his "roughness."

Walker (1925, 69–70) remarks that the Satyres "show the characteristics which mark Donne's works in general," namely, "they are weighty in thought and rich in wit, but almost intolerable in style" (69). Walker says Donne's misuse of meter "is another instance of that intellectual wilfulness which so seriously mars Donne's work," adding that "no man is great enough to be granted the right to take such liberties with his mother-tongue; and the taking of such liberties is an evidence not of greatness but of littleness" (69). He comments further that "the lines of Horace's satires, though they show occasional licences, scan," whereas "all too frequently" Donne's lines "will not scan" and are "not five-beat iambics" (70).

Eliot (1926, 145) insists that the Satyres "have that same ferocity of language which would have made us wait in St. Paul's all night to hear a two hour sermon by him; and the ferocity is in the language rather than in the experience," adding that *Sat1* is "typical" and "one of the best."

Legouis (1928, 88–90), using numerous examples from the Satyres, takes issue with Melton (1906) and Saintsbury (1908). Of the former, he states that the theory of arsis-thesis variation, which he calls "a sort of *reductio ad absurdum*" (88n2), "contains one ounce of truth to a pound of violence to language" (89n4), and of the latter that the practice of substitution is by no means unique to Donne's verse but is instead a prevalent feature throughout Elizabethan literature, including in Spenser (89–90).

Williamson (1928, 428–29) contrasts the "metrical felicity of the lyrics" with the "cacophony" of the Satyres, observing that Donne's poetry frequently reflects a conflict between intellect and verse or sense and sound, and in the Satyres "sound is sacrificed almost altogether to sense, resulting in jarring monstrosities."

Cogan (1929, 185) calls attention to Donne's "reckless disregard of the accepted standards of harmony and smoothness," noting in this context that Donne, as with other "mystics," seems "to discard all artifices which appealed merely to the senses, and to produce allurements for the intellect."

Eliot (1930, 552), noting the criticisms leveled by Ben Jonson, John Dryden and Samuel Johnson against Donne's "irregularities in versification," believes their opinions were based at least in part on the Satyres, which he characterizes as "less polished" than Donne's "best work."

Addleshaw (1931, 39–40) believes Donne's verse is "as bad as it can be" and finds it "almost intolerable," adding that while some poems, including the Satyres, contain "fine gold," others are "poor, extravagant and strained, clumsy and harsh."

Stewart (1931, 58–59) points to the Satyres as evidence of Donne experimenting "unceasingly with metre" and describes these verses as "unbearably harsh and rugged."

Woolf (1932, 24) asserts that Donne's verse is deliberately unconventional, and she suggests that Donne was fascinated by particularities to the extent that he "selects one detail and stares at it until he has reduced it to the few words that express its oddity."

Sharp (1934, 510–11, 515) believes that convention does not fully account for the harshness of Donne's Satyres or those of his contemporaries. He observes that while the deliberate harshness may appeal to some, this verse cannot be considered musical (510). He argues that Donne used elision to reduce lines to ten syllables (511), adding that Donne and his contemporaries believed harshness was advantageous in "elegiac, expository, and occasional poetry" as well as satire (515).

Wild (1935, 415) identifies the Satyres as baroque to the extent that Donne translates the work of baroque poets from other countries, writes in the same style, and shares their mental perspective (point of view).

Tredegar (1936, 173) describes the Satyres as "the most awkwardly constructed" of any poems in Donne's canon. While he notes that the "thrusts and sallies" of satyre can be "exhilirating," such harsh language "tends to distract the reader's attention from the subtle allusions."

Winters (1939, 45–46) notes that Donne's meter is "sometimes grossly incorrect" due to the "perverse misplacement of accents."

Sharp (1940, 4, 30) describes Donne's style as "marked by subtlety and ratiocination, by impassioned, direct utterance, and by a great imaginative power linked to a daring and unchecked wit," all of which "led Donne constantly into obscurity, harshness, and extravagance" (4). The harshness of Donne's satiric verse, he explains, "consists in a bold disregard for the harmonious disposition of sounds" that distinguishes Donne from the "Spenserian esthetic" (30).

Hillyer (1941, xxxii–xxxiii) asserts that in the Satyres Donne's "metrical roughness and impatient rhyming are conspicuous" and may have resulted from "experiments in Classical quantity which engaged the Elizabethan poets in their more pedantic mood," adding that "the Classical writers themselves were wont to give an appropriately jagged effect to their verse when they were writing satire." He states further that in the Satyres "we see the results of rage and haste as well as of deliberate effect" so that in reading them "one would imagine Donne to be an atrabilious hermit rather than a man eager for friendship and a job at Court." In addition, he believes that the "harshness" of Donne's technique "is justified when it is intentional," but "when it becomes mere self-indulgence, the result is a careless dissonance." He concludes that "if we grant the author's intention we must admit also its extemporary power," which he supports by claiming that when Pope "versified" the Satyres, he "took all the life out of them."

Hardy (1942, 62) finds the Satyres "repellent in their savagery, but strong with the strength of a young tiger."

Stein (1942, 682, 685–86) argues that Donne uses complex rhyme techniques not only for variety but also to create "strong austere music" (682), and he believes that Donne's "taste" for sound differs from that of some contemporaries and earlier poets and that Donne's "delight in explosive vigor" is particularly apparent in the Satyres (685–86).

Stein (1944b, 391–92, 405–06, 409) states that the Satyres are "the product of a different taste," one that "was artistically incomprehensible, and naturally harsh," noting that the "basic cause" of Donne's harshness is his "monosyllabic flexibility and characteristic avoidance of the more assertive iambic rhythms—even to the point of weakening his fifth foot and rime" (391–92). The harshness Donne creates, he adds, is "not for variety within a harmonious poem, but for a larger variation within the harmony prevalent in contemporary verse," by which Donne does not create "a new literary style" but instead adapts "for his own needs a style of recognized antiquity, though of limited acceptance" (405–06). He labels Donne "the perfecter of the harsh style" and concludes that for Donne "harshness and discords are much more than a matter of taste or convention: they are an absolute artistic necessity, reflecting the state of his soul and the world" (409).

Stein (1944c, 380–82, 390, 392–93, 395) finds that Donne's tendency to separate the syllables in a stress-shift or trochee with a pause is peculiar to his versification (380). Stress-shift in the fifth foot is one of Donne's most unusual metrical characteristics and occurs frequently in the Satyres, he notes, usually with stress-shifts in the third and/or fourth feet (381–82). While the prosodic difficulties of these poems result in a strong desire to regularize, the "ripples" created by "partly articulated syllables" imitate speech "not at its richest or most stately, but at its most intimate, most direct" (390). He argues that most of the extra syllables in the Satyres are not intended to be elided, adding that Donne extends "metrical liberty" to the foot preceding the caesura in monologue as well as conversation (392–93) and likes to bring two unstressed syllables and one stressed syllable together either in trisyllabic feet or with a stress-shift after a pause (395).

Wagner (1947, 253), citing Sat3 68–69 and Sat4 13–14, believes Donne to be the only "high-ranking" English poet who divides a word in half "at the end of a line," adding that Donne is "continually forcing one on from line to line in this manner."

Contrasting the style of Donne to that of baroque French poets such as Malherbe, Boase (1949, 168) suggests that Donne cultivates an intimate quality throughout his poetry, except perhaps in the Satyres.

Hamilton (1949, 30) states that in the Satyres Donne "aimed at a staccato roughness," and that in fact "condensation and close packing of his lines" form the "general feature of his style."

Moloney (1950, 233, 236–37) disagrees with Stein (1944c) that elision is an important element in Donne's versification (233). He tabulates the number of elisions and contractions in the Satyres in comparison with the Songs and Sonets and reports that Donne "uses proportionately two and one-half times as many elisions" in the Satyres (236). He concludes that "elision is a major and continuous practice" in Donne, that the practice is exaggerated in the Satyres, and that Donne emphasized the "fictional nature of his metrical regularity" in the Satyres with frequency "by deliberately violating the decasyllabic norm." He admits, however, that elision does not account fully for the problems of Donne's versification (237).

Jack (1951, 1016, 1020) says that the Satyres are "long outbursts, impassioned soliloquies" that do not divide into paragraphs, and Donne's "daring and trenchant imagery," which we would expect the Augustans to have considered harsh (1016), was admired by Pope (1020).

Stein (1951, 258) contends that Donne uses "imitative sound" more in the Satyres than in his other poetry but argues that Donne does not take this technique very seriously.

Bush (1952, 50) notes the "bold irregularity" of the Satyres in identifying Donne as one who "stood outside the development of balanced smoothness."

Morris (1953, 42–44, 48, 50, 110–11, 120) argues that the irregular rhythms of the Satyres are intended to replicate spoken language (42). He notes that they were composed in iambic decasyllables but that the irregularities make the original pattern almost unrecognizable, and Donne's pauses sometimes function like musical rests and must be included in the scansion (43). He argues that Donne uses sprung rhythm for "irregularity and variety," not "as a guiding metrical principle" (44). Further, the "rhythmical basis" of the Satyres is not the single line, but the "verse paragraph," and thus Donne "is not fettered by the metrical line" (48). He believes that the sensitivity of Donne's ear "shows itself wherever the poet undertakes a descriptive or a dramatic passage" (50), and the rhythm of the Satyres is also "deliberately irregular to suit the conversational tone and 'unpoetic' subject-matter" (110). He concludes that in the Satyres Donne takes "deliberate pains to use the coarsest and least poetical words and phrases which he can find," and this "excess of vulgar language" is motivated by Donne's "desire to be true to his subject-matter" (120).

Gransden (1954, 102) does not find it surprising that the Satyres are "very un-even," in that typically the reader, while being "taken by a fine and just observation, a clever example, a memorable phrase," quickly loses "the thread of the often difficult argument" and becomes "bored."

Bush (1955, 19) believes that the "harsh, cynical, sensual, private (or self-centered), and 'sceptical' strains" of Donne's verse "fell on receptive ears" in the 1920s.

Redpath (1956, xix) describes the Satyres as "unwieldy and quite witty."

Oras (1960, 18) states of Donne's pauses in the Satyres that "they occur abundantly all over the line" and are "exceptionally frequent" in the last third of the line, with the result that the tone "becomes almost that of colloquial prose."

Skelton (1960, 204) argues that Donne's roughness is individual rather than con-ventional and that the Satyres are "enlivened by an observation of contemporary manners which is vigorous, coarse, and acute."

Jones (1961, 34) states that the "light rhymes and general absence of end-stopping" in the Satyres "represent a marked extreme in English couplets," adding that "the whole rhythmic is created by an interplay" between the prose construction that Donne develops "within the verse-structure."

Bryan (1962, 173–74) notes that the Satyres are not found in any of the nineteen seventeenth-century commonplace books he examined, adding that the poems' ear-nestness and "turgid style" may have kept them from what were generally collections of lighter verse.

Stein (1962, 29–30) argues that in the Satyres simplicity is part of Donne's style.

Andreasen (1963, 63, 74) believes that in the Satyres Donne wants to "make vice repulsive to both the ear and mind" (63), adding that Donne's idealism "compensates" for his conscious "roughness" (74).

Sullens (1964, 175, 267), after undertaking "a word-by-word check of Donne's English poems against the O.E.D." (175), concludes that Donne's neologisms, includ-ing those that appear in the Satyres, are characterized by "darting, turning, untamed figurative expressions" that provide "no evidence" that Donne's purpose was "to enlarge the language," but rather indicate that Donne "merely took whatever liberty might bend a word to his thought" (267).

Allen (1965, 123) describes Donne's style as "crabbed," but adds that "his meaning is throughout fairly clear."

Geraldine (1965, 130) argues that Donne's satiric language "appeals only to the intellect" and is "less persuasive and less effective" than the language of the sermons.

Zivley (1966, 89–94) states that Donne uses images "centripetally" to emphasize the central themes of the poems (89–90). Further, Donne's use of several successive images to express the same idea limits the reader's scope of interpretation and reinforces the purpose of satyre, which is "to awaken man to an awareness of his own failings so that he can amend and correct them" (90–91). In addition, the imagery reflects all human experience, not only the activity and corruption of the Elizabethan world, and Donne often uses the same image to illustrate different subjects or uses an image within an image, which underscores the ubiquity of the faults he satirizes but can be confusing for readers (92–93). Finally, Donne's occasional use of anticlimax "serves to draw the reader away from the main stream of the poem" (93–94).

Andreasen (1967, 11, 193) points out the use dialogue in the Satyres (11) and adds further that these poems are technically Donne's most "conventional," though they are not "imitative" (193).

Roscelli (1967, 467) notes that Donne's verse was "frequently harsh" and adds that in comparison with Spenser and Milton his diction appeared "commonplace."

Alvarez (1969, 333), in describing Donne's poetry as "masculine," explains that in such poetry "the intellect counted for more than the ear" so that "the cult of harshness" also accompanies this style.

Heath-Stubbs (1969, 22–23) comments that although the Satyres are written in couplets, the form "is treated with the utmost freedom, both in the matter of run-on lines and of stress." He suggests that it was primarily the Satyres that contributed to Donne's "reputation for roughness and obscurity," a reputation that led to his poetry being "almost universally under-valued and neglected for nearly three centuries after his death," and he then praises the Satyres for being "vivid and dramatic in their observation of contemporary life."

Kermode (1969, 20–21) notes Donne's "colloquial harshness, the application of his imagery, his expression, strong argument, persistent dialectical sleight-of-hand, [and] indefatigable paradox" as the stylistic elements that distinguish Donne from his poetic predecessors.

Lecocq (1969, 362, 369, 384–87) claims that the Satyres have key affinities with *Paradoxes*, in that paradox functions not as a game, but as a dialectical method, almost a means of knowledge (362). He comments further that throughout the Satyres Donne escapes into what seem to be digressions and draws us to the periphery, if not outside, of what we believe to be the thought of Donne, who forbids us to distinguish the essential from the secondary (369). Nevertheless, he argues that readers can sense the Satyres' aesthetic unity through the tormented expression, even if the syntax is exaggeratedly complicated, and through the liveliness of intelligence, even if the wit is too subtle or too insistent (384). These aspects of style give the Satyres an irritating obscurity, which for Donne, who does not trouble himself to be understood, corresponds to a manner of being and thinking (384–85). He explains that Donne prefers asymmetrical structures, whose clumsiness invites us to verify the rigor of the reasoning, as well as a mixed assemblage of long and short sentences, simple and interwoven, light and dense, which reflect the course of a thought in the process of moving forward, while a more harmonious and balanced style would represent only the unfaithful reconstruction of a thought already dead (385–86). He concludes that the satirical style of Donne not only has the essential qualities of liveliness, color, and movement, but also refuses, more violently than in any of Donne's contemporaries, to bend to the demands of good taste; his nervous and discordant style is an image of his temperament (387).

Menascè (1969, 49–50, 54) notes the prevalence of iambic pentameter and bitter rhymes in late sixteenth-century Elizabethan satire, particularly in those of Donne (49–50). She also considers the Satyres to be the least poetic of Donne's poems. While they often defy comprehension, she says, the Satyres are noteworthy for their deliberately anti-poetic style, for their use of the cadences of everyday speech, for their crude realism in certain images, and for their clever word games (54).

Murphy (1969, 164) remarks that within the Satyres we can see "the new and different sense of the ways in which English syntax, the necessary forms of complete and intelligible utterance, might be manipulated to evoke a new awareness and refocus an old awareness of the self and the world."

Patterson (1970, 110, 172) argues that the run-on lines used by Marston and Donne in their satires "almost certainly derived from the Idea of Vehemence" (172), a subcategory of the "Ideas of Reproof" which "were current in Italy from about 1560 to 1590, and which were also available in Sturm's 1571 edition of Hermogenes" (110).

Kermode (1971, 133–34) notes that the Satyres possess the "usual energy, a rightness of contemporary observation rather splenetic, of course, in character."

Nagoya (1971, 86–88), though giving most of his attention to the Songs and Sonets, includes some of Donne's Satyres in his discussion of the dramatic nature of Donne's poems.

Powers (1971, 128–29) draws attention to Donne's use of the "asyndetic line" to create a realistically curt effect.

Sanders (1971, 33–34) states that the Satyres are "meticulously scored for the speaking voice and there is usually only one way of saying the lines," though "the difficulty is to find that one way." He acknowledges that "metrically the verse may seem a very unstable compound" and that Donne, "with a sovereign indifference to prosodic decorum," has "crammed the most slipshod of colloquial rhythms—cadences heavily slurred and elided, with anything up to four syllables in a single foot—into a pedantically finger-ticking five-beat line." But he adds that "the packed and chaotic quality that results is a working quality," lending itself "splendidly to an excitable, super-stimulated rhetoric, exceedingly emphatic stresses, and a very broad range of expressive inflexion—everything from an exasperated shriek to a lugubrious growl," which in turn "suggests an impetuous improviser," while the "imposition (by a whisker) of last-minute metrical order shows the improviser's mastery pitting itself successfully against the necessary formal impediment which gives zest to the performance."

Bullough (1972, 61) singles out Donne's use of the epigram in the Satyres for praise, noting that Donne was "an innovator in combining elements of Horace, Juvenal and Persius and in stringing together epigrammatic portraits with a strong quasi-dramatic or descriptive content."

Empson (1972, 125–26) asserts that "during his lifetime, Donne was often accused of being metrically rough," but thinks that was not Donne's intention except in the Satyres, in which he "relied on the reader to give the lines the intonation demanded by the meaning, which in itself was often strained."

Kusunose (1972, 95–115) remarks that the irregularity of Donne's meters in the Satyres has contributed to their being among the least appreciated of his works. Imperfect meters and irregular rhymes are dominant, he says, perhaps resulting from Donne's inexperience in satirical forms.

Miles (1972, 276–77) points out that if Donne is "a poet of thought and argument as his interpreters tell us, then readers should be able to receive directly the qualities of the 'prose' in the poetry itself, the recurring poetic shapes and the sense of his characteristic line of thought, the structure of his argument." She believes "a reader can easily have such a sense" because Donne is a poet "who makes plain the pattern he works with." She concludes that while the Satyres move "by hyperbole which gives a second thought to another side or another attitude," Donne also "counters the hyperbolic extremes, believing that 'means' are blessings."

Shawcross (1972, 253, 262–63, 266) explains that "the ridicule and humor" in the Satyres "lies in exaggeration, puns (some obscene), unusual rhyme or versification, and ambiguity," and "the ultimate aim is reform through awareness and disgust and pity." He suggests that "part of Donne's satiric technique in these poems rests in the prosody, part in the style," adding, on the one hand, that "the alteration of meter has such definite and appropriate effect that—at least generally—such alteration seems deliberate" (262–63), and, on the other, that "the style is low, as expected of satiric writing, for its language is low, its mode is conversational, its allusions are commonplace and of the human world rather than of the world of knowledge, its effect is not uplifting and its aims are directed toward ordinary men" (266).

Kermode and Hollander (1973, 1045) state that for Donne's Satyres "the ancient model was Horace," whose satiric verses "are colloquial in manner and have similar themes, but are not, in this sense, 'harsh.'"

Kermode, Fender, and Palmer (1974, 61) point out that Donne imitates Horace "quite correctly sometimes," but they note that Donne "employs a certain rough harshness of manner as appropriate to satire, that you don't find in Horace."

Levi (1974, 11) states that Donne's style "could not be imitated" and notes the "taut, syncopated language" of the Satyres.

Raizada (1974, 108) argues that everything in the Satyres "that might make Donne's lines come smoothly off the tongue is deliberately avoided," and thus there are accents "violently misplaced," there are extra syllables "thrust in" or "made out by a Chaucerian lengthening of the mute 'e,'" and there are some lines that "defy scansion altogether."

Gill (1975, 418) points out that when we compare Donne with his contemporary satirists, Donne's wit appears as "a showpiece of verbal skill," but we also sense that he "is in better control of his display," for the poems themselves "justify the wit and do not allow the attention that he calls to his own ingenuity to interfere with their primary purpose."

Lauritsen (1976, 118–19) argues that "the tortured verse" of the Satyres "mirrors exactly the torment not only of a mind which perceives a fallen world," but also "of a mind which is deeply uncertain of its relationship to the evils of that world, of a mind which, in short, is profoundly riddled with anxiety" so that "the tortured lines" are then "ultimately inseparable from their meaning" and serve as "an accurate reflection of the sensibility of the speaker."

Tarlinskaja (1976, 188, 190) indicates that most critics believe that the Satyres "are rife with gross distortions of the traditional iambic pentameter," that these poems "have altogether ceased to be syllabo-tonic," and that they "have created their own specific metrical canon" (188). She concludes that the poems "depart considerably from almost all the limits of the modern English nondramatic iambic pentameter," they "have already ceased to be iambic pentameters," and they can be considered "a typical transitional form" (190).

Of Donne's "astringent" Satyres, Partridge (1978, 37–39, 42–43) observes that they "often employ colloquial and metrical contractions, which the 1633 edition omitted to mark, causing some confusion in the scansion of lines." Noting that Donne was "well acquainted with the metrical principles of his age," he argues that "the types of prosodic elision current were not necessarily true contractions of speech, nor were they strictly observed in scribal orthography," and even though "extra syllables at the medial pause, or at the end of a line, were widely employed," the heart of Donne's "metrical usage was spontaneity, not rule" (37–38). He finds that "idiosyncratic shifts of stress, coupled with daring but inconsistent elision and tight control of syllables, were responsible for the crudity of his metre," insisting that "most common in Donne's metric is the deliberate imposition of a prose rhythm upon the prosodic pattern" that results in a "hesitant" style that is "crabbed" and "halting." He concludes that the Satyres "are most difficult when the expected metrical stresses are flouted by rhetorical ones" (38–39), and he argues that there seem to be "more inversions of stress in Donne's poetry than in any other poet of the sixteenth and seventeenth centuries" and that Donne "freely employed the licence of rhyming on unstressed final syllables" (43). As a result, Donne's metrical practice is "a tacit plea for liberation, not for the straight-jacket," that "through variations of stress and pause" achieves a "control of pace and emphasis" (43).

Selden (1978, 59–60) contends that "the most important poetic affinity" between Donne and Persius is their "mixed style" in that Persius "is remarkable for his deepening of the moral and perceptual ambience of satire to an extent that almost exceeds the limits of classical decorum." He concludes that satire of all periods "has exploited the possibilities of stylistic incongruity for effects of ridicule, raillery, sarcasm, bathos and irony," noting that Donne's "'mixed style' is remarkable for its intensity of perception and feeling and its total subversion of classical decorum," as well as "a sense of the interpenetration of the spiritual and the sensual, the sublime and the carnal."

Cousins (1979, 96–97, 100) argues that in the Satyres Donne "redefines elegance, affects to despise magnificence, and shares Ralegh's fascination with skepticism," and that even though Donne's "carefully wrought style defies labelling," that of "mannerist" indicates "at least its main, rather than its incidental, qualities." Further, the Satyres and Elegies "create a determinedly new style whose ideas and forms find counterparts in Italian mannerist painting," in which through "likeness, not influence," Donne "introduces into Elizabethan writing, and connects, ideas recurrent in Italian mannerist art theory." He explains that Donne "supplants heroism of the body and the will with the intellectual heroism of the virtuoso" and "also implies that the motions of the spirit design aesthetic shape," adding that Donne "develops these ideas through his fascination with skepticism." As a result, Cousins finds it "not surprising" that Donne "embodies" such ideas "in rhetorical forms which are linked to, and which are in effect counterparts to, two related mannerist forms: the *contrapposto* and the *figura serpentinata*" (96–97). He concludes that the Elegies and Satyres "suggest that there can be no more sophisticated, challenging quest than his: an attempt to redefine our perception of experience and so reality itself," and "the calculated drama" of the poems "partly reflects, partly creates, the manner of a man apart, a distinctive sensibility" (100).

Dubrow (1979, 76–79) states of the Satyres that their meter is "harsh," their imagery is "vivid and often coarse," and their tone is "forceful and strident" (76), adding that their "intensity and rapidity" result from Donne's syntax (78). She expresses her surprise in discovering that Donne's syntax "distinguishes him from the other satirists of the 1590's, rather than allying him with them," and it is the syntax that ultimately "helps to explain" why Donne's satiric verses "are far more uneven in quality than those of the other satirists of the 1590's," for "when he writes carefully enough to avoid fruitless ambiguities, his complicated grammar permits an intensity and richness of ideas and images that is virtually unmatched in the genre." Yet, she adds of Donne that "at times his sentence structure is so puzzling that a reader can barely follow it, and the results are predictably disastrous" (78–79).

Gilbert (1979, 110) asserts that because Donne wrote in the first decades of the seventeenth century, his work "shows few traces of the baroque style of poetry that became fashionable in later decades."

Carey (1981, 48–49) believes that the "very texture" of the Satyres "reflects Donne's active temper" so that "asked what they are about, we should best reply: agitation." He adds that the poems are "hives of energy" and "are remarkable less for their social insight than for their impatient physical movement," which "is apparent as much in the vehement, bludgeoning rhythms as in the way the syntax and subject matter are fractured and pushed about."

Attridge (1982, 299) remarks that the Satyres' rhythms show a "disregard of the stricter metrical rules" and "are less expressive of the control and organisation of mental experience than of vigorous spontaneity."

Bradshaw (1982, 338, 353, 356) argues that throughout the Satyres Donne "employs a particular rhythmic effect," namely, the "sustained rise," which is characterized by Donne's "revolutionary" use of increasing emphasis on the accented words of a given line (338). He believes that Donne's "radical principles" pose "a formidable challenge not merely to the prosodic assumptions of his contemporaries but also to the metrical theories of later ages" (353). Finally, because he concludes that Donne's metrical practice is "structural not accidental," he states that Donne's purpose is "to make expressive variations of stress possible" (356).

Corthell (1982, 156–57) writes that the Satyres "record the emergence of a witty self that is nothing more (or less) than a style; the major features of this style are the principle of similitude and paradox." He suggests further that "Donne's search for and maintenance of a relation to the external power of society influenced his choice of a style," and "this relation and choice at once distance us from Donne and make him seem 'our contemporary.'"

Miller (1982, 827–28) briefly comments that satire "seemed the most congenial use" for expressing Donne's "paradoxical style," and concludes that while readers prefer Donne's lyrics to his Satyres, the latter are "regarded as artistically effective in their original form, although this artistry is of a different order from that of the lyrics."

Kerins (1984, 35) posits that the Satyres are characterized by an "introspective method" which "authenticates the public satiric voice" in them.

Martines (1985, 40–41) suggests that the "'irregular and prosaic metre'" of the Satyres enables Donne "to tilt his verse towards the realism of speech," which Donne achieves through "simplicity of diction, learned words and metaphors, meters inclined towards speech rhythms, a natural enough syntax, a wealth of ironies, studied hyperbole, erudite glitter, and immediacy of tone," all of which "go to bear the accents and viewpoint of a mundane man, well educated, well connected, traveled, socially alert, disabused, and given to reflecting on amatory matters—a favorite gentlemanly pastime."

Parry (1985, 53) argues that in the Satyres and Elegies Donne's wit "takes the form of a relentless application of similes and analogies that force the subject into new associations in virtually every couplet," and as a result, the reader is "staggered by the number of odd angles and points of view that can be achieved," adding that the effect "is often of strenuous mental flailing to keep the subject moving and to meet the expectation of constant diversion that this technique sets up" with its "cracking, laugh-a-line pace."

Patrides (1985, 213) points out that the roughness of the Satyres, "in both subject and expression," affected their publication since all five, "initially refused a license, were permitted to appear only after some lines were removed."

Shawcross (1985, 207) contends that "the question of Donne's prosody is a frequent one for the literary years preceding Coleridge, but for Coleridge as well," noting that satire "provided then and apparently even today the cause for disparaging Donne's poetic ear and arguing that the received texts are suspect even in line-arrangement." As a result, he argues, "it must unendingly be pointed out that the prosody of the satires is not so rough and harsh as the popularly repeated cliché would have it."

Caracciolo-Trejo (1986, 2:13) states that throughout the Satyres Donne constantly expresses himself in libertine verbal habits that no felt conviction can turn into the conventional or hypocritical. Instead, Donne's idiomatic grasp always carries him to the edge of caricature and critique. In another sense, he argues, the Satyres possess a narrative and dramatic quality that makes them come alive even for remote readers like ourselves.

Daalder (1986, 97) takes issue with C. S. Lewis's (1954) complaint about the metrical irregularity of the Satyres and argues that Donne "appears to have believed in syllabic regularity, and we can form a reasonable notion of how we are to pronounce the lines in the light of this." Yet, he cautions, "our knowledge of his accentuation is likely to remain limited, since his syllabification can give us only limited information about it."

Evett (1986, 119–20) challenges Cousins (1979) and complains that he neglected to study the "actual structure" of the poems, adding that had Cousins done so, "he would have observed that all of them consist of strings of images, some literal, some metaphoric, sometimes completed in a phrase or so, rarely developed through more than two or three lines, sometimes obedient to some strict logical procedure but more often arbitrary, accidental, even surprising, and each image of about the same apparent importance as another." Instead of the "periodic subordination that characterizes Renaissance and mannerist art," Evett says, the Satyres are structured on the "Grotesque," which Donne achieves through "free, incessant movement from one image to the next, the images themselves being disparate, strong, exotic, surprising, often disproportionate or mangled or monstrous."

Waller (1986, 240–41, 244) posits that the Satyres "take us directly into the restless confusion of the aspiring intellectuals living in London, and in particular into the peculiarly brittle and artificial self which, in a mixture of longing and antagonism, wishes to locate itself in that world." As such, the poems create "an impression of tactile, optic shock, conveying the countless and restless movements that walking through a city involves the individual in." He argues that like Marston's and Hall's work, Donne's Satyres "are radical only in their self-conscious choice of a modish rhetoric," namely, "accents are deliberately harsh, lines dislocated, the structure of argument developed by rapid shifts rather than smoothness, details are piled up seemingly at random, and the whole held together, seemingly, only by the indignant voice of the speaker," adding that the "rhetorical fireworks" are achieved by "playing a habitual game: they are competitive, aggressive, and rhetorically self-conscious because of fashion; they are episodic" (240–41). Finally, then, the Satyres "grow from a distinctive class and cultural atmosphere" and in their "aggressiveness," they are "often blatantly masculinist, written for and addressed to self-consciously fashionable and ambitious young men" (244).

Parfitt (1989, 24, 27) notes of the Satyres that "the style of these poems is marked by rapidity: things are listed, pictures change, the focus shifts" (24), and he argues that "the quality of the best writing" in these poems indicates that Donne is "imaginatively engaged, and what emerges is a curious blend of the witty, superior satirist figure with another which is restless and unrooted" (27).

Patrides (1989, 104–05) states that the "tone and argument" of the Satyres are "summarily indicated in the comment of one speaker in particular: 'I do hate / Perfectly all this towne'" (Sat2 1–2), but he notes, "the hate is Swiftian, and rises to the level of great art," adding of the poems that their "language, images, syntax, meter are violent, tortuous, contorted, brilliantly conveying the scorching indignation, the burning hatred."

Mackenzie (1990, 54, 65) suggests that Donne's Satyres and Elegies "crackle with an intermittent energy of the grotesque but it remains a matter of extravagant physical detail, a relish for the distorted and the overblown that sometimes turns nasty" (54). He remarks that what "saves" the poems "from incoherence is, firstly, a mastery of rhetorical syntax that works beneath and through their helter-skelter detail," and secondly, "the recurrent impulse towards the ideal of a centred stability and seclusion." Both features, he argues, demonstrate Donne's "exercise of control through rhythm and syntax," pointing to a writer "whose poetic voice takes naturally to the rhythms of speech and heightens them into rhetorical address, a writer attuned to drama who will end his career as a masterful preacher" (65).

Tomlinson (1990, 29–30) believes that "it's a fairly common experience," in reading the Satyres, "to start reading one of them and only after a bit to realize consciously that this is in fact couplet verse." "Again and again," he explains, "the second line of the rhyming couplet runs straight on into the beginning of the next couplet; in fact, there is so little point to the rhymes that one feels Donne himself would have been happier using either blank verse, or, as the playwrights sometimes do, a mixture."

Chandra (1991, 82–83) contends that most of the Satyres "begin as dramatic monologues, but that is not all: there is constant action and change of situation as the poem proceeds." He goes on to point out some salient characteristics of the Satyres: "the variety of characters and incidents, a well-connected and sustained narrative, dramatisation of the situations and dialogues, metaphysical wit which links the most unrelated thoughts and things together, and 'metaphysical' argument indulged in with all show of seriousness, requiring the closest and most concentrated attention from the reader, who, although he may remain unconvinced in the end, thoroughly enjoys the ingenuity of it."

Austin (1992, 20) notes that of all of Donne's poetry, the Satyres in particular "use concrete vocabulary."

In brief analyses of each poem, Gorbunov (1993, 93–97) traces the development of the Satyres as dramatic monologues, noting that this approach to the form is unusual by Elizabethan standards.

Nilsen (1997, 140) finds Donne's writing style "vigorous, rugged, free, and conversational in tone," though also "compact, and sometimes obscure." He finds the vocabulary "concrete, intellectual, and insightful," and the development "dramatic," though the writing exhibits "some coarseness and cynicism." Finally, the "satirical types" represented in the individual poems range "from satirical narrative, to satirical reflection, to direct rebuke."

Post (1999, 5) points out that "although there had been earlier examples of courtly poetry moving in the direction of speech, most notably in the 'manly' lyrics of Sir Thomas Wyatt, who had also experimented with Horatian satire," no other poet "had so charged verse with the searching, colloquial immediacy that Donne brought to all his poetry," including the Satyres. He adds that Donne "puts in motion" the "registers of speech, not song," with "his opening utterances," and that in reading these poems we glimpse "how deeply Donne's imagination was affected by the quotidian in all its mutability, how deeply he pursued the prosaic in verse."

Blissett (2000, 104) ponders the reason for Jonson's hostility to Donne's poetry and to the Satyres specifically and suggests that the frequent irregularities of Donne's poetic style "prompt one to say" that the Satyres are "written not *in* but *against* the couplet." Rather than the usual "brightness" of the heroic couplet, Donne creates "an effect of chiaroscuro" that reflects "the mixture of gravity and levity, of the morally serious and the indecorous, of the sacred and the profane," pervading the Satyres.

Ellrodt (2000, 118–19) argues that "conversational vivacity" makes Donne's Satyres "more dramatic" than Hall's, and while this quality is occasionally found in other contemporary satyres, it cannot be explained as the influence of the theatre since "the language heard on the stage was still highly rhetorical and would hardly have suggested the colloquial tone of Donne's poems." Further, Donne seems to have been responsible for "the transfer of the satiric or epistolary mode of composition and style to the lyric."

King (2000, 374) finds that "the notoriously difficult sense and irregular prosody" of the Satyres "exemplify satirical roughness."

Knottenbelt (2000, 113, 116) observes that Dryden's comments about Donne's "rough cadence" and "deep thoughts" were directed to the Satyres (113). He adds that only a tone-deaf reader "will consistently read iambic measures into a five-footed line, especially in the fifth foot," which is instead a "trochaic inversion," which, particularly in the Satyres, is "more usually preceded by a stress-shift in the third or fourth foot" (116).

Prescott (2000, 229) finds that the "jounce and obscurity" of the Satyres "derive from the condensation and mental rapidity typical of Donne's wit."

Fulton (2001, 93) states that Donne's Satyres "are characterized by an obscurity unlike that of his other poetry."

Suhamy (2001, 401, 413), in order to counter Donne's reputation as a writer of harsh verse, draws a distinction between the concepts of meter and rhythm to demonstrate that Donne's lines are difficult to scan but show ingenuity and originality (401). He concludes that reading Donne aloud is a difficult exercise since it is necessary to respect the form and the feeling, which often pull in opposite directions, but to find the true voice of the poet, his inflections, his stops and starts, as well as his desire for metrical and rhythmic sublimation, is to identify with him, and therein to understand him (413).

RELIGION

Warburton (1751, 4:260–61) suggests that Donne has a "strong propensity to Popery, which appears from several strokes" in the Satyres.

Elwin and Courthope (1881, 3:427n1), in a prefatory note to Pope's rendering of *Sat2*, explain that Donne was "brought up as a Roman Catholic, and the first of the two Satires versified by Pope must therefore have been composed in his early youth, as it is evidently written with a predeliction for the Romish Church, the authority of which he began to question about the age of eighteen."

Aronstein (1920, 158) believes that the delay of justice, the haughty fraudulence of officials, and the corruption of lawyers display a scorn in the Satyres that is shared by English Catholics, to whom Donne belonged.

Stein (1944a, 278) points out Donne's allegiances to truth and religion despite the scepticism of the Satyres.

Gardner (1948, 31) suggests that the Satyres reflect Donne's "Jesuit upbringing in their hatred of the Elizabethan policy of repression of Catholicism."

Grierson (1948, 307) observes that the Satyres express sympathy for victims of

Catholic persecution and that *Sat3* outlines the problem of seeking truth honestly and freely.

Mahood (1950, 104) states that the Satyres are "crammed with imagery" related to the disputes between the Roman and the Reformed churches.

Harris (1960, 193) believes that Donne is motivated to write satire by "the sense of his own sin and the fear of contamination."

Andreasen (1963, 59, 75) observes that the Satyres are "a dramatization of the contrast between the sacred and the profane" (59), and in so far as they "anticipate many of the themes of his religious poetry," they indicate that there is "no great dichotomy between the rakish 'Jack Donne' and the pious Dr. Donne" (75).

Erskine-Hill (1964, 163) notes that Donne was a Catholic when the Satyres "were probably composed."

Geraldine (1966, 25–26, 34) observes that the Satyres provide the clearest illustration of Donne's focus on religion in his early poetry and concludes that the "best" of the Satyres "have literal and moral excellence, and that excellence is rounded out by the spiritual highlighting" (34).

Bald (1970, 70, 72) rejects the argument that in the Satyres Donne "writes from the point of view of a Roman Catholic," pointing out that "Donne may perhaps reveal a greater intimacy with Catholicism than other contemporary satirists, but his references to the Roman Church are, if anything, severer than those to Protestantism" (70). He argues, instead, that the evidence of the poems "suggests that Donne's immersion in controversial divinity resulted in a period of unsettlement during which neither Catholicism nor Protestantism could wholly satisfy him," and "his natural inclination to scepticism was for a time reinforced by a mood of cynicism in which he flaunted his sense of insecurity" (72).

Hutchison (1970, 360) argues that the Satyres "are not 'meditative' poems," yet Donne's "knowledge of the methods of meditation—part of his 'private' religious voice—appears to contribute to the impetus of the poems and may have influenced their occasion," adding that Donne's "provision of a concrete and vivid setting for a meditation on invisible things was as necessary as the creation of a fiction is in satire."

Morris (1970, 213) comments that "when Donne writes about religion no living prelate, priest or reformer is permitted in the poem" and that "for all their violence and allusiveness" the Satyres "are abstractions from contemporary life and their judgements of the human situation are made in ethical categories."

Kusunose (1972, 95–115) suggests that Donne's interest in religious matters sets his Satyres apart from those of others. He notes in particular *Sat3*, where Donne's concerns about the contemporary conflicts between Protestants and Catholics and about the schisms in the church of his day move his focus beyond mere satire.

Elliott (1976, 106–07) observes that the five Satyres taken together "present a probing examination of the ideal of Christian charity as a fundamental principle for a life of social action and reform," in which "the central character" is Donne's young persona "who attempts to find a satisfactory role for himself as an educated Christian in a corrupt world." Throughout his "unified narrative of an experience which was not unlike his own in the 1590's and early 1600's," Donne "raises important questions about the nature of satire itself: how might the satirist correct his society without violating the law of Christian charity himself? How may satire be an effective tool for bringing about reform?" Because, Elliott says, Donne recognized the implications of these questions "to be religious as well as social and aesthetic," the poems are permeated with "important Biblical references which alert his readers to the deeper moral implications of his persona's struggles and searching."

Hester (1977c, 184) suggests that the Satyres are unique for "their application and elaboration of the decorum of the biblical satirists, their accommodation of one set of principles from biblical aesthetics to the moral and spiritual dilemmas of late sixteenth-century man."

Selden (1978, 46) states that although the English satirists of the 1590s found models in Horace and Juvenal for themes, structural form, and "a sense of the satirist's persona," their conception of the world "was still dominated by a medieval Christian idea of moral struggle."

Dubrow (1979, 81) comments that Donne's Satyres are unique among his contemporaries in being "preoccupied with religion," and this contrast "reminds us that Jack Donne and Dr. Donne coexisted throughout John Donne's life." The religious references, in particular, "are as varied in tone and intent as their author's attitudes to religion apparently were."

Corthell (1982, 156) writes that Donne was occupied with the composition of the Satyres "while he was studying matters controverted between Catholics and Protestants," and these poems "are informed by Donne's perception of the public consequences of a private religious commitment."

Gallenca (1982, 321–22, 325–27), in a comparison of Donne's Satyres and Marston's *Scourge of Villainy*, comments that sexual indulgences illustrate for the two poets corporeal abandonment and its dire results, as putrefaction begins the process of degradation. Thus, for both satirists, sexual appetites have become signs of the Christian's dislocation (321–22). Despite their doctrinal differences, Gallenca thinks, the satiric works of Donne and Marston maintain a fundamental Christian vision emphasizing the virtues of liberty exercising self-restraint and the certainty that a person's grandeur depends on turning toward God (325–27).

Nicholl (1984, 29) believes that the "knotted and bitter mood" of the Satyres reflects Donne's unique expression of the "rich, heated tones of Elizabethan recusancy."

Shami (1984, 221) identifies "the reluctant satirist of the satires" as one of Donne's "models" of men of a "middle nature," of those who are "exemplary" because "they are struggling to rectify God's image in themselves and have accepted their adversities as part of this regenerative process."

According to Sloane (1985, 174), "Augustinianism is the major principle of Donne's poetry," revealed "most explicitly" in the Satyres and in the later divine poetry.

Caracciolo-Trejo (1986, 2:13) argues that in the Satyres the dissolute libertine poet gradually gives way to the devotional poet and to the agonized believer.

Warnke (1987, 4–5) remarks that "a dominant theme" of the Satyres is "religious": for example, the "persecution of the English Catholics" in *Sat2* and *Sat4*, and "the question of which Christian sect possesses the truth" in *Sat3*. Further, "a powerful personal drama is implied" in these poems in "the conflict between the urgent imperative to find and be loyal to religious truth on the one hand and, on the other, the powerful arguments of self-interest and, indeed, self-preservation." Thus, Donne "aspired toward success, fortune, and fame (difficult for an avowed Catholic to achieve in the England of Elizabeth)."

Baumlin (1988, 364, 366) asserts that Donne "is the first to discover, and enact, the limitations of classical satire," and "what allows this discovery is the poet's radical reflection on the weakness of language, a reflection spurred on," he argues, "by the culture's refusal to grant his Catholicism authority—or grant it simply the right of utterance" (366).

Morse (1989, 271) suggests that in the Satyres Donne "exposes the contradictions and conflicts in his mind," that is, "as a sometime Catholic he perceives himself as belonging neither with those who have kept faith with Rome nor the unruffled courtiers with whom he comes in contact." As such, the poems enact a rhetorical method in which Donne "continually ironises secular pursuits by enveloping them in religious imagery."

Parfitt (1989, 26–30) comments on the "ubiquity" of Donne's religious allusions in the Satyres, noting that they "relate specifically to Catholicism" and that they form "the texture" of these poems (26–27). He finds it impossible to believe that Donne's religious position in the 1590s "was essentially an intermediate, undetermined one" since Donne "was clearly on course for secular, Court-based employment," and thus "headed towards a loyalist position not easily maintainable by a known Catholic and not properly valid for a firm one." He adds that it might be thought that "the religious scepticism of the satires is a device to postpone commitment," for Donne "may have felt in the 1590s that the position of English Catholics was far from fixed," and thus Donne writes "neither the poems of a firm Catholic nor of a decided apostate" (29–30).

Baumlin (1990, 67) argues that Donne's fears regarding the Satyres stem "explicitly" from their "pro-Catholic polemic, putting them at odds, politically as well as doctrinally, with the Protestant Monarchy."

Carey (1990, xxii–xxiii) maintains that for a "young Catholic" such as Donne, "the isolation and antagonism of the elegies and satires expressed his reaction to the Protestant community which had victimized him" and that "the frequent obscurity of the poems also enforces the rift between Donne and society."

Baumlin (1991, 26–27, 151–52) contends that "the Reformation and its consequences" are "a thematic presence" in the Satyres. Further, he posits that the "vulnerability" of Donne's rhetoric, which relies "on the sacramental theology of Roman Catholicism and its traditional mechanisms of spiritual reform," points in these poems "to the dominant culture's (specifically, the Protestant court's) intolerance toward competing ideologies and belief-systems" (26–27). He adds that whether Donne "was Catholic or Anglican is finally moot," but that "what matters is that his writing never resolves the conflict satisfactorily." In this regard, then, Donne's "skepticism toward language and literary form, his many literary poses and his critical rewriting of models all have their origins in a mind and personality shaped by religious controversy, a controversy whose participants could cast all in doubt—particularly the stability of meaning in language, at the same time looking to language as an instrument of belief and persuasion" (151–52).

Corthell (1997, 37) comments that the Satyres "often represent the satirist as a kind of recusant," but first warns, "we ought to be cautious about interpreting this as solidarity with Catholicism," explaining that these poems "capitalize on the experience and discourse of Catholic recusancy as a particularly rich and often equivocal response to historical change and Elizabethan ideology."

Kiséry (1997, 124) says that Donne was a Catholic when he wrote the Satyres.

Oliver (1997, 10–11, 36–37, 150) comments on the "striking continuity" (11) between Donne's religious and secular verses, noting especially that the Satyres, Elegies, and Holy Sonnets share "introspection, inconsistencies, and, most importantly, use of role-play" (150). He contends, however, that the poems Donne wrote while he was residing at the Inns of Court, including the Satyres, "are of little assistance in the attempt to pin down the stages in Donne's religious progress," even though they indicate that Donne "was alive to the humorous possibilities of the beliefs and practices of both Catholics and Protestants." Yet, he explains that the poems' "uncertain attitude to Catholicism" largely confirms "the impression given by both Walton and Donne himself that what he was essentially attempting during the period of his 'irresolution' was to define himself specifically in relation to his Catholic patrimony." He concludes that it was "far more a matter of arbitrating 'between ours and the Roman Church' than of standing back from all of the Churches, indigenous and continental, and choosing the one which struck him as the most doctrinally pure," and Donne's attempt "to clarify where he stood in relation to the religion of his childhood turned out to be a lifetime's occupation" (36–37).

Blissett (2000, 120) states that when Donne wrote the Satyres he "was still a deeply troubled nominal Roman Catholic."

Reid (2000, 39–40) says that while the Satyres belong to that segment of Donne's life "when his trouble with the world had to do with his Catholic background," Donne is "evenhanded in his jibes" as he conceives his "religious predicament" with "an unusual range of international and learned reference." He concludes that Donne's "religious unease does not discharge itself in partisan animus but is suspended in a general feeling of absurdity."

Fulton (2001, 79), citing Donne's words regarding "indifferent things" in *Pseudo-Martyr*, believes that the Satyres assert "the necessity of maintaining a liberty of thought, even towards religion."

THE CRITICAL INFLUENCE OF DRYDEN AND POPE

Dryden (1668 [1971, 17:30]) explains his displeasure with the verse of John Cleveland by comparing it to Donne's Satyres: "there is this difference betwixt his Satyres and Doctor *Donns*, That the one gives us deep thoughts in common language, though rough cadence; the other gives us common thoughts in abstruse words."

Dryden (1693 [1974, 4:6–7, 78]), praising Charles, the Earl of Dorset and Middlesex, states:

> Donn alone, of all our Countrymen, had your Talent; but was not happy enough to arrive at your Versification. And were he Translated into Numbers, and English, he wou'd yet be wanting in the Dignity of Expression. That which is the prime Vertue,

THE SATYRES 🐝 505

and chief Ornament of *Virgil*, which distinguishes him from the rest of Writers, is so conspicuous in your Verses, that it casts a shadow on all your Contemporaries; we cannot be seen, or but obscurely, while you are present. You equal *Donn*, in the Variety, Multiplicity, and Choice of Thoughts; you excel him in the Manner, and the Words. I Read you both, with the same Admiration, but not with the same Delight. He affects the Metaphysicks, not only in his Satires, but in his Amorous Verses, where Nature only shou'd reign…(4:6–7).

Donne's "rudeness," he explains, came from his subservience to the example of Horace:

Wou'd not *Donn's* Satires, which abound with so much Wit, appear more Charming, if he had taken care of his Words, and of his Numbers? But he follow'd *Horace* so very close, that of necessity he must fall with him: And I may safely say it of this present Age, That if we are not so great Wits as *Donn*, yet, certainly, we are better Poets (4:78).

Others who repeat Dryden's assessment of Donne's wit, of his need to be translated metrically, and of his affecting the metaphysics include an anonymous commentator writing in *TB* (1876, 337–38), Saintsbury (1887, 147), Hales (1891, 1:558–60), Norton (1895, 1:xxiv), Furst (1896, 230–31), and Alden (1899, 75–83).

In a prose letter to William Wycherley, Pope (1706 [1956, 16]) is most likely discussing Donne's *Satyres* when he writes that "*Donne* (like one of his Successors [Wycherley]) had infinitely more Wit than he wanted Versification: for the great dealers in Wit, like those in Trade, take least Pains to set off their Goods; while the Haberdashers of small Wit, spare no Decorations or Ornaments."

Young (1725, 3) includes Donne in his lament for the absence of great satire:

Why slumbers *Pope*, who leads the tuneful Train,
Nor hears that Virtue, which He loves, complain?
Donne, Dorset, Dryden, Rochester are dead,
And Guilt's chief Foe in *Addison* is fled;
Congreve, who crown'd with Lawrels fairly won,
Sits smiling at the Goal while Others run,
He will not Write; and (more provoking still!)
Ye Gods! He will not write, and *Mævius* will.

In his poetic defense of Pope's *Dunciad*, Harte (1730, sig. C2r) writes that "vig'rous nature join'd / In one" the wit of Donne and Oldham and "center'd 'em in *Dryden's* mind."

Spence (c. 1730–36 [1966, 1:188]) notes discussions within Pope's poetic circle of Donne's satirical works, widely known during the eighteeenth century though first published as *Spence's Anecdotes* in 1820.

Pope (1733, 5–16) in an anonymous pamphlet publishes an adaptation of *Sat4* as *The Impertient, or a Visit to the Court. A Satyr*, attributing the poem on the title page to "an Eminent Hand" (see Appendix 2).

Pope (1735, [98], 131–61), in the "Advertisement" to the edition of *The First Satire of the Second Book of Horace Imitated* that was incorporated into the 1735 edition of his *Works*, cites Donne in defense of his own satirical practice:

the Example of so much greater Freedom in so eminent a Divine as Dr. Donne, seem'd a

*proof with what indignation and contempt a Christian may treat Vice or Folly, in ever so
low, or so high, a Station. Both these authors [Horace and Donne] were acceptable to the
Princes and Ministers under whom they lived. The Satires of Dr. Donne I versifyed at the
desire of the Earl of Oxford while he was Lord Treasurer, and of the Duke of Shrewsbury
who had been Secretary of State; neither of them look'd upon a Satire in Vicious Courts as
any Reflection on those they serv'd in. And indeed there is not in the world a greater error,
than that which Fools are so apt to fall into, and Knaves with good reason to incourage,
the mistaking a Satyrist for a Libeller; whereas to a true Satyrist nothing is so odious
as a Libeller, for the same reason as to a man truly virtuous nothing is so hateful as a
Hypocrite. ([98])*

Later in the volume (131), Pope introduces his versifications of Donne's second and
fourth satires under the section heading "Satires of Dr. *John Donne*, Dean of St. Paul's,"
critiquing Donne's "roughness" with an epigraph from Horace:

*Quid vetat, ut nosmet Lucili scripta legentes
Quaerere, num illius, num rerum dura negarit
Versiculos natura magis factos, & euntes
Mollis?*   Hor. [Sat. ix.56–59]

["What prevents us likewise, while reading the work of Lucilius, from asking whether
his own nature, or the difficult nature of his material, denied him verses more pol-
ished and smooth?"]

Pope then prints (132–41) "The Second Satire of Dr. *John Donne*," an imitation of
Sat2 that presents the 1669 text of Donne's poem in italics on facing pages, and he
publishes (142–61) a revised version of *Sat4* under the title "The Fourth Satire of Dr.
John Donne," similarly facing his poem with the Donne text of 1669 (see Appendix 2).

Parnell (1738, 151–63) has his "versification" of *Sat3* included in the 1738 edition
of Pope's *Works*, including (like Pope before him) the Donne text of 1669 (or 1713)
on facing pages (see Appendix 2).

An anonymous columnist in *The Champion* (1740, 2:259) identifies Donne with
Pope as satirists who attacked sycophant poets.

Mason (1747, 18) uses Pope's persona (Museaus) to praise Donne's centrality to
the satiric genre, which "dawns, tho' thou, rough Donne! hew out the line"; and later,
following Pope's example, writes an imitation of *Sat1* that begins "Away, fond Fop!
mad motley thing begone" (see Appendix 2).

Warburton (1751, 4:249) asserts of the Satyres that it is "to be lamented" that
Pope "did not give us a Paraphrase, in his manner," of *Sat3*, "the noblest work not
only of this, but perhaps of any satiric Poet," adding that Parnell's version of *Sat3* (see
Appendix 2) "will serve to shew the force of Dr Donne's genius," even though Parnell
"did not seem to understand and so was not able to express it in its original force."

Whalley (1756, 1:xlviii) urges that "it is to the honour of Jonson's judgement" that
Pope, "the greatest poet of our nation," shared "the same opinion of Donne's genius
and wit; and hath preserved part of him from perishing, by putting his thoughts and
satire into modern verse."

Granger (1769, 1:186–87) quotes Dryden's comment on Donne ("the greatest wit,
though not the greatest poet of our nation") to support his own view that Donne's

"greatest excellency was satire," adding that he had "a prodigious richness of fancy; his thoughts were much debased by his versification."

Warton (1774, 4:50) compares the Satyres unfavorably to those of Hall, stating that Donne, "though he lived so many years later, was susceptible of modern refinement, and his asperities were such as wanted and would bear the chisel" of Pope.

Warton (1782, 264) comments that the Earls of Shrewsbury and Oxford encouraged Pope "to melt down the weighty bullion" of Donne's Satyres, observing that Donne had "degraded and deformed a vast fund of sterling wit and strong sense, by the most harsh and uncouth diction."

Pope's versifications of the Satyres are the emphasis of an anonymous biographical essay (1784, 4:469–78), which suggests that once "Translated into Numbers, and English," as Dryden (1693) expressed it, Donne's poems are not inferior to any satiric verse.

According to an unsubstantiated anecdote, Johnson (c. 1785 [Hill (1897, 2:404)]), in response to the comment of a certain Mr. Crauford of Hyde Park Corner—"Do you know, Dr. Johnson, that I like Dr. Donne's original Satires better than Pope's"— observed, "Well, Sir, I can't help that."

Anderson (1792–95, 4:4–5) argues that the influence of Dryden and Pope led to the conclusion that Donne's Satyres, "which abound with so much wit, assume more dignity and appear more charming, when 'translated into numbers and English.'"

Drake (1800, 2:170) states of the Satyres that even when Donne's thoughts "are clothed in the melody of Pope," they appear "hardly worth the decoration."

Chalmers (1810, 5:124) notes that Dryden "fixed" Donne's character "with his usual judgment," and he also paraphrases Dryden's pronouncement of Donne that "if his Satires were to be translated into numbers, they would yet be wanting in dignity of expression." He adds that in comparing the originals of Donne's Satyres to Pope's translations, the reader "will probably think that Pope has made them so much his own as to throw very little light on Donne's powers" and that Pope "every where elevates the expression, and in very few instances retains a whole line."

Coleridge (1811 [1984, 12.2:216]) comments in his marginalia that "to read Dryden, Pope &c, you need only count syllables; but to read Donne you must measure *Time*, & discover the *Time* of Each word by the Sense & Passion."

Collier (1820, 1:152–60), during his presentation of a dialogue between Morton, Elliot, and Bourne, in the poetical *Decameron*, records Elliot's comment that he has "read nothing more of [Donne's] satires than what has been modernised by Pope" (153).

Spence (1823, 50–55), in an unsigned article, asserts that "general readers are probably acquainted with Donne chiefly as a writer of satires," and that as such "they know him only through the medium of Pope," which he adds, "is equivalent to knowing Homer only through the same medium." He explains further that Pope "attempted to give his readers an idea of Donne, by changing his roughness into smoothness, and polishing down his force into point," but in doing so "he altered Donne into Pope—which was a mere impertinence," for "each is admirable in his way—quite enough so to make it impossible to change either, with advantage, into a likeness of any other" (52). Others who note that the Satyres were known to many primarily through Pope's rendition of them include Jameson (1829, 2:94–95), Spalding (1852, 280), and Arnold (1877, 438–39).

Croly (1835, 2:284–85) notes that regarding Donne's Satyres, Pope "felt the necessity of softening their barbarian ruggedness, and throwing the interest of modern topics over their remote allusions."

Cunningham (1837, 240–42) quotes Dryden's comments that Donne is the greatest wit of England and that he affects the metaphysics, and he also notes of the Satyres that Pope "has translated, or rather paraphrased them into his own smooth verse" (242).

An anonymous commentator writing in *The Penny Cyclopaedia* (1838, 9:85) notes that the merits of the Satyres "were discovered by Pope, who (to use his own odd phrase) translated them into English."

Craik (1845, 3:170–71) mentions Pope's "translation" of Donne's "four [sic] Satires into modern language" and then comments that "whatever irregularity may be detected" in Donne's poems, "if they be tested by Pope's narrow gamut," yet Donne demonstrates "a wider compass, and freer and more varied flow, of melody than Pope had a taste or an ear for."

Patmore [?] (1846, 230, 233–35), in assessing Donne's Satyres, which he contends are "the best in the English language," asserts that "a satirist should never get into a passion with that which he is satirizing, and call names, as Dryden and Pope do; it is totally inconsistent with the dignity of the *judicial* position he assumes." He then commends "the gentlemanly Donne," who "resorts more often to the simple and the crushing strength of truth, than to the 'cat-o' nine-tails' of invective" (233). He expresses further displeasure with Pope, who "took it upon himself to 'improve'" some of Donne's Satyres, but he did it, Patmore says, "in much the same style as the sailor who, having obtained a curiosity in the form of a weapon of a sword-fish, 'improved' it by scraping off, and rubbing down, all the protuberances by which it was distinguishable from any other bone" (234–35). Others who note that Pope's and/or Parnell's renditions of the Satyres should be judged harshly include an anonymous commentator writing in *TB* (1876, 350), Hales (1891, 1:560), Furst (1896, 230–31), Alden (1899, 83), Stephen (1899, 613), Nethercot (1925b, 171 and note), and Nilsen (1997, 140, 154).

Carruthers (1854, 4:188), in an introductory note to Pope's rendering of *Sat2*, writes that Donne's poems "abound in sense and wit, and Dryden had suggested the modernisation of his satires."

Willmott (1854, 94), in an introductory note to Parnell's rendering of *Sat3*, explains that "Pope, instigated by the Duke of Shrewsbury and Lord Oxford, set some of Donne's harsh tunes to music" and contends that in his reworking of Donne, Pope "had a personal interest in the task, his object being to rebuke the clamour against his sarcasm, by showing that good men like Hall and Donne had publicly portrayed and exhibited vice in the boldest colours."

Jessopp (1855, x, xvii–xviii) notes that the Satyres earned "the warm praise" of Dryden, and further, "even induced Mr. Pope to 'versify' (!) them" (xviii).

Grosart (1872–73, 2:xxviii–xxx) comments that "one of the 'Curiosities of Literature'" is that "Pope and Parnell re-versified the Satires of Donne" (xxviii) and asserts that these "improvements" show Pope to be "a matchless Verser," though "no Poet in the deep sense of the much-abused word." It is not surprising, he adds, that "Parnell could not be expected to succeed where Pope failed; and he fails egregiously" (xxx).

Dixon (1880, 8), in the context of a query over a word in *Sat4* 8, comments, "I have a copy of Pope in which his paraphrase is printed along with Donne's original doggerel."

Bradford (1892, 355–64) notes that while Pope "admired" Donne's *Satyres*, he "considered it necessary to polish and practically rewrite them before presenting them to the delicate palates of his own public" (355). He asserts further that Donne's subjects "do not require the broad canvases of Dryden, nor has he Dryden's lucidity and rapidity," yet he adds that "even Dryden cannot approach him in power" and Donne makes Pope "seem dry and tame" (362).

In the context of his praise for *Sat4*, Gosse (1893, 236–38, 245) notes of this poem that "its attraction for Pope is well known" (238).

Norton (1895, 1:xxiv–xxviii), discussing the translations of Donne's *Satyres* by Pope and Parnell, writes of the former that "though his lines flow more smoothly than those of Donne, they lack the conciseness and sincerity of his original" (xxv), and concerning Parnell's reworking of *Sat3*, he states, "one of the most direct, serious, and masculine of Donne's poems, full of real emotion and the expression of sincere conviction, becomes a piece of artificial diction, feeble in substance and poor in form" so that the reworking becomes a "transmuting of gold to clay" (xxv–xxvi).

Saintsbury (1896, 1:xviii–xxiii) states in his discussion of the *Satyres* that those critics of the late seventeenth century through the eighteenth century who expressed that Donne had no poetic ear "no doubt founded their belief to a certain extent on certain words of Dryden's" (xix). In addition, during his defense of the irregularities in Donne's metrics, he concludes that "the satiric pieces in which these peculiarities are chiefly shown, which attracted the attention of Pope, and which, through his recension, became known to a much larger number of persons than the work of any other Elizabethan Satirist, have the least share of Donne's poetical interest" (xxi–xxii).

Grierson (1909, 4:197, 205–08) asserts that Donne is "the only one of the six-teenth century satirists whose influence is still traceable in Dryden and Pope," adding that Pope found in Donne "a satirist whose style and temper were closer in essential respects to his own than those of the suave and urbane Horace" (197).

Schelling (1910, 319–21, 365) calls attention to the "'variety, multiplicity, and choiceness of thought'" attributed to Donne by "the judicious Dryden" (365).

MacLeane (1915, 178) notes that the *Satyres* were "extolled by Dryden and para-phrased by Pope—two fastidious masters of metrical rhythm."

Bradford (1917, 74) notes that Pope, despite his admiration for the *Satyres*, felt compelled to "practically rewrite them" for his own audience.

Saintsbury (1921, 698), interpreting Dryden's comment that Donne "affects the metaphysics," states that Dryden opposes "metaphysics" not to "philosophy" but to "nature," adding that if "metaphysical" is used in the sense of "things that come after the natural," then it suits "all the poetry commonly called 'metaphysical,' whether it be amatory, religious, satirical, panegyric, or merely trifling," to which "philosophi-cal" applies less readily.

Nethercot (1922, 463–74) relates that Dryden's comments "were made upon

Donne's versification in only one type of his poetry—his satires, which are unquestionably the most apparently rough and irregular of all his work," adding that "for two hundred years or so the majority of readers based their verdict concerning Donne's rhythm" on these poems. He describes Pope's and Parnell's "self-styled 'versification'" of the Satyres as "the most conspicuous illustration" of the popular attitude toward Donne, as well as of "the popular approval of Pope's work," which provides "sufficient evidence of the public's opinion of Donne's metrics," for "there were few who did not hold that Pope had vastly improved the 'numbers'" (464).

Nethercot (1925b, 171 and note) believes that "Pope's acquaintance with Donne began early, although perhaps it cannot be traced so far as is the case with Cowley, or even Crashaw." He adds that although Pope claims that his "revision" of Donne was performed "'at the desire' of Oxford and Shrewbury," critics are "generally agreed that he simply took refuge under the cloak of 'so eminent a Divine as Dr. *Donne*' in prosecuting his quarrels, and cared little how his author suffered in the process." He includes in a note that Pope's choice of Donne for his own purposes illustrates "his recognition, first, of Donne's remarkable satirical ability, and second (his ostensible reason for attempting the paraphrases), of Donne's roughness."

Williamson (1930, 221, 223) notes the neoclassical interest in and imitation of the Satyres, especially by Pope (221), and quotes Dryden's comparison of Donne's Satyres with Cleveland's (223).

Watkins (1936, 80–81), noting Johnson's quotations from the Satyres in his dictionary, comments that apparently Johnson knew the poems well, despite his dismissal of them in his *Life of Pope*.

Butt (1939, xlii–xliii) argues that Pope's versification of the Satyres is not surprising since "he and his contemporaries may not have read Donne with the enthusiasm with which we read him to-day, yet certainly they read him." He suggests that Pope would probably have agreed with Dryden's assessment of the Satyres and may not have required the suggestion of Oxford and Shrewsbury to imitate them.

Jonas (1940, 205–06) suggests that Dryden should have recognized that Donne's rugged style was necessary for the communication of his ideas.

Wells (1940, 196, 292) notes modern writers' appreciation of Donne's satirical works (196), though adding that many readers forget that Donne, in addition to his lyric poetry, wrote "trenchant social satires paraphrased by Pope" (292).

Wasserman (1947, 69–71), responding to Dryden's (1693) comment, believes Donne was not eager to make his Satyres "charming." Further, he notes Donne's "intentionally halting meter" and his "enjambed couplets" before stating that Parnell often considered Donne's language "too humble and unpoetic" and his word order "too close to that of prose" (70–71).

Jack (1951, 1011) notes that Pope appreciated some passages in Donne's poems and retained them in his own versions.

Kermode (1957, 25) believes that the Satyres, except for *Sat3*, are of little interest to most readers despite Pope's attentions to them.

Erskine-Hill (1964, 14–15) suggests that Pope and his contemporaries saw Donne the way Horace saw Lucilius, that is, "they deplored his rough numbers but admired his wit and the fearlessness with which he attacked corruption in high places."

Low (1965, 292), in introducing William Mason's imitation of Sat1 (1747), observes that while Donne was "not favoured in the eighteenth century as a lyrical or religious poet," he was "admired as a satirist." The Mason imitation, he adds, is interesting in being later than those of Pope and Parnell.

Lecocq (1969, 387–88) notes that Pope, when he adapts Donne's Satyres to the taste of his time, dilutes and tones them down. Thus, whereas Donne creates an entire personal vision of the world, Pope offers the stereotypical personae of tradition.

Singh (1971, 50) acknowledges that Pope's *Satires of Dr. John Donne Versified* was well known and adds that "the practice of 'versifying' Donne's poems would seem to have been more widespread in the 1730's than is generally supposed," noting that there are "several imitations of Donne in *The Universal Spectator* of this period."

Elkin (1973, 42–43) contends that although the Augustans were aware of the earlier English satirists, they took little interest in them, with the foremost exception of Pope, primarily because Donne "took too little care of his numbers."

Partridge (1978, 36–37) argues that "because of their language and versification," the Satyres are "often regarded as the least satisfying of Donne's compositions," but they were, nevertheless, "still read a century after Donne's death." Dryden found the Satyres "crude and undignified," while Pope, in his 1735 "re-modelled versions" of Sat2 and Sat4, used "only the thematic materials," for his talent "was ill accommodated to Donne's irregular and prosaic metre," and Thomas Parnell, "Pope's protegé and Irish contemporary," "versified" Sat3.

Gilbert (1979, 110) asserts that the "plain style" of the Satyres "seem[s] far more difficult to read, and obscure in image, beside Dryden," explaining that "the subjective imagery" of Donne's style "is not very useful in argument and statement" and noting that only in Sat3 does Donne equal "Dryden's work." Further, in the Satyres, Donne "seems to struggle with his material," lacking the "clear general thought of defined ideals such as Dryden had."

Miner (1981, 103) states that Dryden was familiar with only Donne's Satyres, and he thought "his satires too much like Horace's, and in particular too harsh in style."

Miller (1982, 827–28) comments that Pope "tried to rescue Donne for the eighteenth century by the curious expedient of 'translating' his satires into verse, that is, by regularizing them," adding that "in addition to replacing Donne's strong lines and surprising caesurae with regular meter," Pope "homogenizes the works."

Weinbrot (1982, 205, 300) reads the Satyres in relation to Horace, who "was leagued with his court and its values," and Pope, who "offers a Tory and Stuart, rather than Whig and Hanoverian, genealogy," adding that the three poets "were not merely safe but encouraged under their dispensations" (205). He states further that Pope, in his imitations of Donne, "initiates his reader into Donne's world by evoking an image of the satirist as indignant enemy of vice in what is, nonetheless, a well-ordered state," and "the first part of this image is consistent with the perception of Renaissance satire," the second with "the opposition's perception of Queen Elizabeth as friend to liberty and freedom at home and enemy to tyrants abroad." He concludes that Donne's "freedom and combativeness thus remain in Pope's versifications, where they are emblems of his opposition loyalties" (300).

Baumlin (1986b, 449) comments of *Sat3* and *Sat5* in particular that "when Donne (to use Dryden's phrase) 'affects the metaphysics,'" he "does so in imitation of Persius."

Fowler (1993, 94–95) observes that "Pope's *rifacimento* of the Satyres "introduce[s] nuances and fine rhythms that the earlier poet had not thought to attempt," adding that the "roughness" Pope objected to in Donne "was not altogether the result of incompetence and negligence," for "Donne and his contemporaries thought that satires (which they spelled 'satyres') should be rough like a satyr's pelt." Such "false etymology, and false doctrine out of Renaissance Italian genre theory" was corrected by Dryden, "with his improved knowledge of the classics."

Pask (1996, 137–39) quotes Dryden's comments on the Satyres and observes that Donne's reputation as a satirist "accentuated his prosaic 'roughness' as the negative complement of a properly regulated 'poetic diction'" (138), a tendency "summarized" (139) by Pope's versifications of *Sat2* and *Sat4*. After quoting Warburton's comments in his 1751 edition of Pope, Pask concludes that Donne's "poetic reputation as a satirist and 'libertine in wit' probably precluded the recognition of his religious prestige" (139).

Kiséry (1997, 117) notes that "Dryden was the first to represent Donne as the earliest and foremost of English satirists, although one still lacking in versification and style."

Lerner (1999, 5–6, 7–8, 13) argues that if Pope had not been attracted to the Satyres "he wouldn't have bothered to rescue them" (6). While late twentieth-century readers tend to prefer Donne's "gnarled actuality" (8) to Pope's "rage for order" (7), Pope saw Donne as a "threat" to civilization and thought that "versifying was the way to control it" (8). Further, Pope's changes to the "*form*" of the poems "were so far-reaching that they turned into ideological changes" (13).

Rude (1999, 153) cites Dryden's comments in A *Discourse Concerning the Original and Progress of Satire* and adds that Donne "was highly regarded as a satirist" by the Augustans.

Reid (2000, 42–43) argues that Donne's satiric persona does not speak with the "magisterial authority" of Dryden's or Pope's.

Rude (2001, 223, 225) discovers "several references to Donne as a writer of satires" that "have gone unnoticed" (223), including lines 35–42 of Edward Young's *The Universal Passions: Satire I: to his Grace, the Duke of Dorset* (1725) and a passage from "A Literary Article" in *The Champion* (24 May 1740), in which "the author includes a selection from Pope's adaptation of *Sat4* "to debunk an unidentified poet" (225).

 *Satyre* 1.

COMMENTARY

Date and Circumstances

Grierson (1912, 2:103) explores the internal evidence from *Sat1* and concludes that "on the whole 1593 is a little too early a date" and that the poem was "probably written between 1594 and 1597." Peter (1956, 132) concurs with this range of dates.

Grierson (1929, xvii–xviii, xxv) considers that the circumstances of Donne's early life help explain the passionate "tenor" of *Sat1* and make it "more intelligible and forgivable" (xvii–xviii). Donne's "familiarity with the London of 1594–96" is evidenced in his mention of "Banks's performing horse and the performing elephant, the ape that would come over the chain for a mention of the Queen" but would sit still "for the Pope and the King of Spain" (xxv).

Hayward (1929, 120) asserts that the date of *Sat1* can be "fixed" on the basis of "allusions" to events "approximately between the years 1593–1597." He cites the evidence of the date 1593 inscribed on B34, a manuscript of *Sats1–3*. Others who refer to this date and manuscript include Milgate (1967, 117) and Craik and Craik (1986, 256).

Atkins (1934, 39) includes *Sat1* in a list of contemporary references to the Banks horse and observes that Banks and his horse are most frequently mentioned after 1595 and before 1600, when they appear to have gone abroad.

Atkins (1937, 396) notes the reference to the Banks horse in lines 79–82, adding that since the horse was on tour in Edinburgh in April 1596, Donne's use of the word "heretofore" may mean that the poem was written while the horse was out of London in 1596 or 1597.

Gransden (1954, 10) states that *Sat1* was "written about 1593." Others who note this date include Biester (1997, 89–90), Zunder (1982, 9), and Carey (1990, 420).

Milgate (1967, 117) cites allusions to celebrated animal entertainments as well as to the "heir or heiress" to the Spanish crown as evidence for dating *Sat1* in 1593, noting also Donne's customary "alertness" in observing contemporary events.

Shawcross (1967, 412) dates *Sat1* "after 1594," citing the allusion to "Banks' elephant and ape," but before 1598 and publication of Edward Guilpin's *Skialetheia*.

Warnke (1967, 106) dates *Sat1* "during the period 1593–1598," based on unspecified topical references. Smith (1971, 469) also posits this same range of dates.

Winny (1970, 12) asserts that *Sat1* was "probably written before 1594."

Everett (1972, 5; 1986, 3) comments that Donne's "most vivid evocation of London" occurs in *Sat1*, "which must be the product of his early twenties when he was still a student at Lincoln's Inn."

Shawcross (1972, 250–51) argues that *Sat1* is dated after 1594 "because of its reference to Banks' theatrical act involving an elephant and an ape" (ll. 80–81), though prior to 1598 "when Everard Guilpin published *Skialetheia*," which borrows from *Sat1*.

Patrides (1985, 34) dates *Sat1* "from the early 1590s."

Marotti (1986, 39–40) remarks that *Sat1* and *Sat2* "especially reflect the Inns-of-Court setting in which they were composed," noting further that Donne's life at Lincoln's Inn was "arranged around a regimen of study from four o'clock to ten o'clock each morning," and the "less respectable activities in which he 'took great liberty'" seem to reflect "the poet's splitting of himself" into "the scholar-moralist and the inconstant fool addicted to the fashions of Court and City." Others who note the Inns of Court context include Trevor (2000, 87), Biester (1997, 89–90), Corthell (1997, 28), and Nutt (1999, 171).

Zunder (1988, 79) suggests that *Sat1*, *Sat2*, *Sat4*, and *Sat5* are "responses to the economic and social changes of the sixteenth century, in a way that is characteristic of the tradition of satire in the century, from Wyatt onwards."

Gorbunov (1993, 93) accepts as definitive the date of 1593 for *Sat1*.

Nutt (1999, 40) suggests that at this time of his life Donne "invested enormous energy trying to gain a prominent position in the court" and that the court is at the "heart" of this poem.

Edwards (2001, 201–02) finds that *Sat1* reflects Donne's knowledge of "street life, including low life," in 1590s London.

General Commentary

Mason (1747, 18) praises Donne's centrality to the satiric genre, and sometime after 1753, in his commonplace book, writes an imitation of *Sat1* that begins, "Away, fond Fop! mad motley thing begone."

Gosse (1899, 1:37) writes of *Sat1* that the "hero" is "a gossiping, volatile society-man, with whom the poet, in his stoic simplicity, proudly contrasts himself," yet he notes that Donne "says little that we can take to be autobiographical."

Williamson (1930, 221) observes that *Sat1* contains "the first portrait of Sir Fopling Flutter who was to adorn so many pages of Restoration literature."

Woolf (1932, 22–23) equates the speaker's reading list with Donne's, observing that the speaker apparently "liked facts and arguments."

Sprott (1950, 336), citing *Sat1*, comments that Donne's habit was to write "solitary in a room full of books."

Leishman (1951, 109–10) states that the "realistic detail" in *Sat1* "predominates over mere wit" and that the poem is "much more dramatic" than other Elizabethan satires.

Cazamian (1952, 363) notes that the fop in *Sat1* is "entirely innocent of any humorous intent" but that the speaker's attitude "approaches very nearly what we now call humor," and the satirical pretext gives way to "an orgy of amusing conceits." Nilsen (1997, 141) also comments on the humor in *Sat1*.

Johnson (1953, Item 53) reads the poem as a contrast between soul and body or virtue and lust.

Sultan (1953, Q6) queries if there is an allegorical or symbolic meaning to *Sat1*.

Of *Sat1* and *Sat2*, Lewis (1954, 470) states, "it is difficult to guess how these two pieces would affect us if we did not know the author's name."

Alvarez (1961, 193) sees Everard Guilpin's imitation of *Sat1* in the fifth satyre of *Skialetheia* as "the earliest surviving evidence of Donne's influence" and questions whether it was "an act of homage" or plagiarism.

Andreasen (1963, 64) argues that *Sat1* contrasts "the constancy which adherence to virtue produces and the inconstancy which results from commitment to profane and material values."

Allen (1965, 86) states that in *Sat1* Donne "attacks a 'humourous' courtier—that is, a creature of whims."

Low (1965, 292) comments that William Mason, in imitating *Sat1*, "keeps near to Donne's text, expanding the original where he feels expansion is desirable in the light of a modified poetic idiom." Mason, like Donne, appears indignant "at being torn away from congenial reading to uncongenial company." See also Mason (1747).

Powers (1971, 59, 74–75, 153) observes that *Sat1* is unusual in having a fully depicted and private setting, which is retained by Guilpin and Marvell ("Flecknoe") in their imitations of Donne. Concerning Guilpin's adaptation, she concludes that Guilpin makes the issues clearer but "less profound and complex" (75), and she contrasts the "looser, random development" of Donne's poem with the "tightened organization" of Marvell's "Flecknoe" (153).

Everett (1972, 7–9) notes that *Sat1* seems to "drift aimlessly," which she believes is "one of its chief charms" as it "flaunts a lordly *sprezzatura*" (7). She argues that the poem is "less externalized commentary than internalized debate," and finally she suggests that the poem is about "chargeable travels" and "dear-bought experience," which was "a subject that goes deep into what moved Donne as a poet throughout his career" (8–9).

Shawcross (1972, 271) contends that Andreasen's (1963) reading of "the dilemma" of *Sat1* "as the opportunism and lechery of a young rake" is "not only circumscribed but essentially wrong."

Tomashevskii (1973, 14) argues that *Sat1* is notable for its sharp criticisms of the Puritans, those representatives of the bourgeois circles hated by Donne.

Kermode, Fender, and Palmer (1974, 62) note that *Sat1* is "conventional" in that it "very much" represents a "London street scene of the 1590's."

Marotti (1974, 167) remarks that *Sat1* is "psychomachic in character, externalizing a strong, inner conflict," thus "involving the reader in a battle that is finally broader than the poet's own personal problems."

Parker (1975, 21) notes that *Sat1* "pillories foppish lovers."

Parker and Patrick (1975, 10, 13) suggest that *Sat1* is "carefully constructed to bring out and interrelate two main themes—self-deception, exemplified by the speaker, and inconstancy, exemplified by his 'friend'" (10). They argue further that the poem "already exhibits the tension between the spirit and the flesh" as well as "the concern with constancy," themes that preoccupied Donne later in life, and conclude that Donne did not believe that constancy was really possible, since in the poem, "constancy is realizable only through self-imprisonment" (13).

Zunder (1982, 12) observes that in *Sat1* Donne is consciously speaking "as a representative of his society" and that "the remarkable sureness of the writing" results from "his sense of being basically at one with his society."

Mackinnon (1983, 681) argues that "the scholar and the fop need each other" and that the poem "subverts its apparent seriousness by making the scholar transparent in his satire: the world he affects to loathe he secretly adores," while the fop "exhibits comic resilience," and it is "this human comedy" that "makes the poem live."

Toliver (1985, 98) observes that in its dramatization of "the contrast between the integrity of the private place and the role-playing of the street," the poem's movement is "toward dispersal and centerless street wandering" so that "manners are subject to revision according to one's sidewalk opportunities."

Marotti (1986, 39–40) argues that of all the Satyres "the first two especially reflect the Inns-of-Court setting in which they were composed: Donne advertises in them his knowledge of the environment in which he and his audience lived." Remarking on Donne's description of how the "pathetic gull" imitates the behavior of "fashionable gallants and courtiers," he notes that "the boundary between self-satirization and satiric attack on the outside world is blurred," adding that "just as the satiric persona's intellectual and moral complacency is disturbed by his socially irritating association with the inconstant fool who has befriended him, so too Donne and his readers were, no doubt, morally, intellectually, and emotionally ambivalent about their own attraction to the world outside their chambers."

Waller (1986, 242) notes that *Sat1* "gives us the conventional rejection of the Court as corrupt and trivial," even though there is "a clear fascination with it as a place where the self can acquire experience and employment," adding that "the self is in fact defined" by such interaction.

Low (1990, 467) observes that "the compact between the studious speaker and his giddy tempter is described as if it were a marriage vow, a contract first sworn to, then betrayed." He also says that while Donne satirizes the relationship, he makes it "central to the poem," noting "the importance and difficulty of what has been called 'male bonding' or the building up of a support system among young male equals."

Ray (1990, 284) notes that in *Sat1* "the speaker stabs at many types of individuals, including the contemplative person, the active person, a soldier, a courtier, a judge, a flatterer, the worldly person, the lecherous person, and the fop."

Shawcross (1991a, 28) suggests that *Sat1* "takes the form of a *debat* between soul and body" in which the soul triumphs, and he adds that "most people" read the poem "as a statement of the victory of intellect and truth and the defeat of desire and temptation." But he argues that "we cannot accept the scholarly recluse of the poem as model (though some critics seem to), nor can we totally reject the drives of the worldly humorist as Donne represents him," for the poem is "ambiguous" in that "it does not involve ridicule or social reformation."

Gorbunov (1993, 94–95) states that Donne, who generally emphasizes the relationships between people and social phenomena, provides in *Sat1* precise, though grotesque, portraits of his contemporaries that recreate London's social customs as a broken system of conflicted secular and sacred values. The characters in *Sat1*, Gorbunov argues, belong to a world of imaginary, ostentatious ideals which pervert the hierarchical sense of the Great Chain of Being, a world in which the most lowly is capable of subordinating the highest.

Klawitter (1994, 124) argues that *Sat1* and *Sat4* both show "how liable one was to meet people one did not want to meet in the streets of London," and though "encounters were inevitable," he notes that "cruising does not always land one a perfect bedfellow."

Manley (1995, 397–98) comments that in *Sat1* "the scholar-satirist seeks to reclaim the soul of his worldly friend by establishing a clear and firm distinction between the motley humorist's foolish connoisseurship and the moral judgement that can separate a 'fine silken painted foole' [l. 72] from a 'grave man' [l. 79]." He adds that "the distracted survey of details" in the poem suggests that "discrimination mocks itself by becoming a connoisseurship of surface," for "the once obligatory symbolism of rank, talent, and worth has vanished."

Biester (1997, 20–21, 92–93) suggests that *Sat1* "steers a dangerous course between announcing its poet as satirist and satirizing the satirist's claim to moral superiority" (20). He notes that both *Sat1* and *Sat4* are "performances designed to arouse wonder," though the former "is sheltered in the near-holiday world of the Inns of Court" and the latter "walks abroad in the everyday world of the court." He argues further, contra Baumlin (1991—see under Personae and Religion) and Fish (1990—see under Personae), that Donne "is implicated in giddiness not *despite* his role as satirist, but *because* of it" in that Donne "hedges" by "playing both sides of his culture's ambivalence toward satire and jesting" even as he exploits "the form, writing the kind of witty poem that can attract him notice" (92–93). Thus, Donne "seems to be rehearsing" for the "even more dangerous game" he plays in *Sat4* (93).

Corthell (1997, 31) notes that the "center" of *Sat1* and "the community that would be constructed around it" are "unable to stabilize themselves." As a result, the Christian humanist is portrayed as "a hollow ego-ideal, a vapid Inns of Court wit who fashions himself against, and therefore is curiously bound to, Donne's man of the crowd," with the consequence that "the subject of satire on the world is as slight as that of the object of satire."

Nutt (1999, 33, 37, 40) finds that *Sat1* creates "a picture of a society bloated with its own success and motivated by greed" (33), and the "fashionable young men" who populate the poem are "shallow, foolish, arrogant, and so apparently intent on humour they are incapable of seeing their own folly" (37). The walk in the street "exhibits all sorts of poor behaviour," and especially the "selfish pursuits" of "courtly self-advancement or mere sexual gratification" (40).

Prescott (2000, 230) finds that Donne's "monstrous 'motley humorist' has all the vices a bustling London affords."

Robbins (2000, 423) calls the poem "an innocuous imitation of Horace, reapplied to a universally ridiculed target, the fatuous, obsequious, quarrelsome devotee of fashion."

Trevor (2000, 88) suggests that if *Sat1* "can be taken as evidence," Donne is "subject to distractions" that "prompt regret when they are fulfilled."

Wiggins (2000, 34) observes that the theme of this poem appears to be "constancy."

Edwards (2001, 201) believes that *Sat1* springs from Donne's understanding that "emotionally he is two men," both scholar and humorist.

Hadfield (2001, 57) observes that the poem's "predominant image is that of venereal disease, the punishment for the excesses of youth."

Donne as Satirist

Commenting on the first ten lines of the poem, Eliot (1926, 142–44) argues that "the indignation" in *Sat1* "is wholly faked, and in conformity with tradition" (142). He contends that "it does not matter that Donne loved the Court as much as anybody" or that "his hatred of courtiers, so far as it is sincere, is that of a man who spent a large part of his life, and wrote a great many of his letters, in courting courtiers." On the contrary, the point is that in satire Donne "found a type of poetry which could convey his random thoughts and reflections, exercise his gift for phrasing, his interest in the streets of London, his irritability and spleen" (143–44).

Gransden (1954, 104–05) describes the London society presented in *Sat1* as "the sort of rip-roaring, cut-and-thrust, allusive atmosphere in which satire normally kicks and thrives," adding that the lawyers, suitors, and courtiers Donne condemns are "conventionally derived," yet "originally and forcefully expressed."

Powers (1971, 59, 68–70, 73), reminding us that in Elizabethan satire "locations are usually merely indicated, and usually public and urban," remarks that *Sat1* "is exceptional in its private setting as well as in the fullness with which it is detailed" (59). She adds that "the whole poem is a narration to a silent Companion" (69), but the speaker "maintains the sense of the incident's immediacy" and "cast[s] the conversational exchanges between him and the humorist into direct discourse" so that the narrative acquires "the air of an action being described at the time that it is occurring—a desirable effect to those who worked within the precepts of the plain style and thus aimed at the effect of 'real' life" (70). She states further that "the view of the Satirist as a morally superior man was not generally projected by satiric poets" and that "superiority, as some of the Elizabethan satirists saw it, might be intellectual and cultural, rather than plainly moral" (73).

Sanders (1971, 35–36) comments that at times in *Sat1* "the comic exasperation of the speaker is so surely mimed and orchestrated" that the satirist's role "becomes a part of the satire." He describes "the pose of Donne's satirical stance" as "extremely elegant," and he concludes, "this poise unites him with his audience, by its amused confession of a common fallibility."

Lewalski and Sabol (1973, 6) state that *Sat1* reveals Donne's "resemblance to contemporary analogues" as well as the "heightened dramatic quality" of Horace's *Satires* 1.9.

Newton (1974, 429–31) maintains that Donne's "struggle with satiric character within himself" is evident from the beginning of *Sat1* (429). He argues that the opening lines of the poem, as well as the Satyres in general, "are 'humorous' in the sense that the Humorist himself is humorous," and he also suggests that "the main thing which differentiates Donne from the Humorist is his very energetic (and tense) effort to maintain a tight control upon what he says and does" (430–31). He concludes that Donne's "triumph" at the end of the poem is not "particularly strong," noting that *Sat1* "does not resolve the inner tension with which it began," and asking, "What about Donne (or, more accurately, the satirist in Donne)? What is his basis for 'constancy'? What is his defense against his own potential anarchy?" (431).

According to Raizada (1974, 101), *Sat1* "is much more realistic and dramatic than most Elizabethan satires which generally deal in mere description and denunciation," even though its theme may not be original.

Lein (1980, 147) suggests that Donne's early poems show a "pessimistic moral position," and citing *Sat1*, he asserts that the "essence" of the poem's action is "the sense of defilement, curiously mixed with a sense of complicity."

Eddy and Jaeckle (1981, 122) remark that in *Sat1* Donne's "satiric authority is undercut by an unresolved tension between Stoic and Christian ethics," a "specific tension" that Donne "never explores" again.

Hester (1982, 12–13, 17–19) asserts that *Sat1* "endorses the scholar's 'zealous' mockery of the humorist's inconstancy at the same time that it discloses the satirist's naive idealism and lack of self-criticism" in that the satirist "mistakes satire to be only the contemplative assertion of ideals to inconstant fools" (12–13). Hester concedes that *Sat1* is not as successful as *Sat3* and *Sat4* but maintains that as Donne's "first work" in the satiric genre it is "most instructive about his conception of the features, limitations, and duties of Christian satire." He argues that the poem is "a comic study in failure, a witty dramatization of the radical and seemingly irremediable gap between the intentions of the satirist and the obduracy of his *adversarius*" (17).

Hester (1984, 3–7) points out that Everard Guilpin's "imitative strategies" in his *Satire V* "illustrate not only his considerable debt" to Donne's *Sat1*, "but also certain ideas about the genre held by those young satirists of the 1590s, the position of Donne in that literary milieu, and how the relative merits of these two poems derive in part from their authors' responses to their literary genre" (3). He also states that while Donne's echoes of Horace emphasize the "moral legitimacy of satire," Guilpin's echoes of Donne "merely identify the poetic game being played" as opposed to "a generic problem to be solved or a moral paradox to be evaluated." As such, Guilpin's uses of Donne serve as "merely generic signposts which carry little of the symbolic import of Donne's inventive imitations of the Horatian model" (7). Parfitt (1989, 22–23) also notes the connections with Guilpin.

Kerins (1984, 41–42) believes that in *Sat1* "the two manifestations of the satirist, moralist and courtly wit, duplicate the same failure of constancy" that is evident in the relationship between the satirist and the humorist. The "moralistic censor," he suggests, "overwhelms one with the language of sin," and while the courtier-satirist "disarms one with pointed quips and elegant asides," he too is "powerless in the real world." He concludes that Donne "exposes the limits of traditional methods of satiric authentication" in *Sat1*, adding that for Donne, "the true satirist must first gain a precise awareness of his own diminished status in order finally to transcend it and to create a viable satire which speaks to both the spiritual and secular needs of a sophisticated society."

Sherwood (1984, 69) argues that Donne's "often embittered social criticism" betrays his "frustrated desire to participate in a community," and that *Sat1* "expresses that desire in revealing terms" when Donne "bandies the speaker between the lethal dangers of reclusion and the scattering whimsy of the outside world."

Toliver (1985, 95–96) remarks that Donne "measures the fickleness of 'fondling motley humorists' and others by the standard of personal loyalty and constancy," and the speaker's critique of the court and the city "rises out of what he regards as the treachery and the counterfeiting that reign abroad."

Baumlin (1991, 68–69) argues that the details of *Sat1* are "humorously exaggerated and usually more descriptive" of the satirist's "own interests, fears, and prejudices— all of which suggests that the satirist, from the beginning, is himself involved in the world and its follies."

Chandra (1991, 80) states of the wide variety of characters portrayed in *Sat1* that it would be "difficult" to find their equal in other poetry of the period and adds further that there is a "remarkable point of contrast between the tone of the fashionable poetry of the Elizabethan age and that of Donne's."

A. Smith (1991, 111–12) argues that the Satyres "deny us a secure moral vantage point," noting that in *Sat1* the poet "writes as a solitary contemplative who is dragged from his books, partly by his own virile urge, to witness the active depravities of the streets, the courts, the Court." He concludes that "the drama" of the poem "simply stages the contradictions of our natural impulses, projecting people's animal urges into civic life."

According to Guibbory (1993, 131), the Satyres "suggest contrary impulses, both outrage at this corrupt society, and a certain attraction to it," a conflict suggested in *Sat1*, "in which the scholarly speaker, introverted and virtuous, and his inconstant companion, the ambitious and comically sycophantic would-be courtier, seem to represent conflicting, contrary aspects of Donne."

Low (1993, 351) points out that women have "small place" in *Sat1*, "except as degraded and degrading impediments," adding that "far more important than women is the relationship between the two main characters."

Klawitter (1994, 115, 120–21) comments that *Sat1* "evinces more traces of Rachel than of Leah," that is, a preference for the contemplative rather than the active life, "or so he doth protest" (115). He suggests further that when Donne "effeminizes" the adversarius, he "demonstrates the kind of homophobia that male students at the Inns of Court found necessary to prove their masculinity as they jockeyed in the throes of puberty and sexual self-definition" (120).

Strier (1994, 231) observes that *Sat1* "manifests Donne's characteristic techniques— bold, colloquial address, metrical roughness, striking phrases," but primarily the poem "manifests the complex drama of the Donnean lyric, where the speaker's attitudes as well as those of his interlocutor are being interrogated."

Biester (1997, 90–93) points out that *Sat1* "winks" in "both abjuring and claiming the role of moral arbiter" found in Donne's Horatian model and adds that throughout the poem Donne "sustains [a] pattern of alternately, or even simultaneously, separating himself from the friend and identifying himself with him" (90–91). He argues further that "the other's failed repentance casts a shadow over the speaker's own," and the speaker himself is "witty but not phantastical, capable of recognizing folly for what it is" (91). He contends that Donne is "implicated in giddiness not despite his role as satirist, but because of it," and as such, "the position of the solitary railer" is a position "simply untenable for one whose ambitions lie in public service and participation in the all-too-giddy life of the court" (92).

Corthell (1997, 29–30) posits that *Sat1*, like *Sat2* and *Sat4*, "works at establishing a subject position by producing an other even as it suggests that such self-definitions are unstable, if necessary, ideological projects," and he argues that the poem reveals "the degree to which the satirist's position, even the position of Christian scholar, depends upon the presence" of the humorist.

Shawcross (2000–01, 28) notes that *Sat1* has been "judged inept" by critics who expect "a dominance of the satiric to imbalance the poem and lead to a clearly didactic moral statement."

Persona

Hughes (1968, 22–23, 25) notes that "the basic pose" of *Sat1* and *Sat2* is that of "the fresh scholar (now pretending to be a grave elder philosopher) disdaining the world of the market place and, added to it, the court" (22). He points out that in *Sat1* "the foolish lover" is "at the mercy of time" and "must move in whatever time wrinkle the narrator chooses to assign him," though by contrast the persona "controls time, bending it to his will and making it dance to his music" (25).

Korte (1969, 78–80) contends that the satirist of *Sat1* "lacks an authoritative ethos," noting that "he remains a poseur, an actor who is almost as much a 'humorist' (in the seventeenth-century sense of the word) as his foppish companion whom he satirizes." He suggests that the mask the satirist wears could be read as that of "the *vir bonus*, the 'good plain man' of classical satire who represents a norm, a rational standard," yet he adds that Donne's satirist "is not such a man, for his authoritativeness is frequently undermined by over-dramatization" (78). He suggests further that the "theatricality" of the poem "may be most clearly seen by noting the abrupt fluctuations in tone that accompany the satirist's donning of each new mask" (78–79), and concludes that *Sat1* is "a witty, clever, and subtle work" that is "flawed" because Donne's fails "to establish an authoritative ethos in his speaker" (80).

Lecocq (1969, 369–71) determines that *Sat1* 1–52 introduces the reader to an inconstant, flattering, debauched (perhaps even depraved) interlocutor and to a reclusive, bookish persona who in no way represents the perfect *vir bonus* (369–70). Indeed, he argues, Donne appears to have established an interlocutor and a persona who are equal in importance and whom Donne presents as a diptych of two contrasting portraits (370). This complex persona is himself subject to satiric criticism and is thus not excluded from the corruption depicted in the satiric universe even as he plays the educative role of the satirist (370–71). He believes, as such, that Donne understands the weakness inherent in any satirical undertaking (371).

Sicherman (1969, 38, 40) suggests that in *Sat1* "the poet endorses his speaker's mockery at the same time that he mocks, not unsympathetically, the speaker's vehemence, unmitigated as it is by self-criticism" (38). She adds that "in this comedy of an exasperated moralist and a moral idiot, the humor comes from their quick repartee and from the scholar's irritated commentary" (40).

Commenting on *Sat1*, Farmer (1970, 305) argues that the satiric genre "cultivates one of the principal devices that characterizes the lyric—namely, the interiorized *persona*," yet "satiric irony creates a distancing effect through manipulation of point of view" in such a way that "the *persona* is addressing us."

Hutchison (1970, 356–57) comments that the persona in *Sat1* is satirized early in the poem as a "slightly pretentious scholarly recluse" and then in the latter half as one who "cavorts around" fools and "fawns on others."

Powers (1971, 41, 73, 82) asserts that the satirist of *Sat1* and *Sat4* is "the embodiment of the highly cultured man," the "cultural superior of those whom he satirizes," as he "views them from the distance that intelligence, taste, and disdain for the superficial and frivolous create for him." Further, this separation situates the persona in the "awkward position" of despising offenders even as he associates with them (82).

Sanders (1971, 35–36) argues that Donne's satirist is "a Malvolio in Cheapside," whose "gravity is simply the crowning incongruity," and this "extremely elegant" pose, he explains, unites Donne with his readers "by its amused confession of a common fallibility."

Everett (1972, 8) states that "it is not difficult to recognize the younger Donne in the learned and fanciful scholar" and, noting a parallel with *TWHail* 30 in which Donne "refers to himself as 'Thy debtor, thy echo, thy foil, thy zany,'" argues that "the zany friend" of *Sat1* "is foolish mainly through his desire to be at the centre of things, a desire close to an impulse recurrent in Donne's writings."

Kermode, Fender, and Palmer (1974, 63) contend that *Sat1* provides the reader with "the sense of Donne in the London of that time," as the persona adopts what is "only a pose" of "the solid man, the student, not really affected by all this folly."

Bellette (1975, 133) notes that "for the first half of the poem the confusions of the humorist are very much those of the speaker," which Donne expresses throughout *Sat1* with "a striking confusion of values."

Parker and Patrick (1975, 13) suggest that the speaker of *Sat1* is "the primary butt and focus" of the poem as his character is "progressively revealed, first by means of his attitudes in part one and secondly by means of his responses to the events in part two."

Elliott (1976, 111–12) argues that the speaker "departs from the tone and temperament" of the Juvenalian satirist, primarily as the speaker "imitates Christ in his patience." He adds that at one point the speaker "acts the good Samaritan" and concludes that the persona is successful in maintaining "the delicate balance between his general calling as a Christian and his particular calling to be a satirist."

Lauritsen (1976, 121–23) argues that in reading *Sat1* as a "more or less conventional dramatic monologue," the poem exposes "the central and irreducible fact" that the speaker "succumbs to temptation without the visible or audible presence of a tempter," and the reasons he does so not only "lack any objective correlative whatever," but also are "diametrically opposed to his own vigorously upheld best inclinations" (121). He concludes that "the object of the speaker's contempt" in the poem "is ultimately his own fallen state and, by extension, the fallen state of man," which is the "real—if not readily apparent—subject" of the Satyres (123).

Lewis (1977, 1, 3, 10, 15–16) argues that the speaker of *Canon* is "the *adversarius*" of *Sat1*, "talking back to his friend the satirist and triumphantly announcing at the end that the situation has completely changed and that their former positions in relation to each other have altered in a way that the critic and adviser could hardly have anticipated" (1). She adds further that there are no "grounds for identifying the satirist and the *adversarius* with the body and the soul of one individual or for making a very specific correlation between the characters in the poem and John Donne himself," but instead each figure "is dominated by one aspect of his nature, a studious one by his 'spiritual-intellectual nature' and a foolish one by his 'physical-sensual nature'" (15–16).

Cousins (1979, 102–04) notes the "fine ambivalence" of *Sat1*'s persona, whose "seriousness" is "inseparable" from his "sly, unobtrusive amusement" and which contrasts with "the humor-ridden Fool who invades the scholar's quiet" and who "is incapable of ambivalence" (102–03). He concludes that the poem's shape is that of "a *contrapositum*," which "jars together two quite contradictory attitudes toward experience and values, giving precedence to neither" (103–04).

Dubrow (1979, 73, 81) argues that like his counterpart in the Horatian model for *Sat1*, Donne's persona is "guilty of the same fault, inconstancy, for which he blames his foolish companion" (73). She points out that the speaker is "also characterized by his worldliness and sophistication," and she suggests that in his "knowing acknowledgement of vice" the speaker "closely resembles Marston's persona, William Kinsayder," though adding that "what is peculiar to Donne's own satires is the fascinating—and disconcerting—blend of the secular and the religious, the worldly and the other-worldly" (81).

Eddy and Jaeckle (1981, 116–19) argue that the persona of *Sat1* "views his society's values with the same scorn that the Stoic feels for his world," noting also that the speaker experiences "the attraction of social interaction, even though entering a corrupt society may be a transgression against internal law" (116). They observe that "the same world that drives the Stoic to seclusion" also drives the persona "to the 'constant company' of his study," for he "is aware of the lack of rationality and virtue in the outside world" (117). They conclude, "the persona's ability to discriminate between virtue and foolishness stems from study and reflects the most fundamental doctrine of Stoicism, that knowledge results in virtue" (119).

Slights (1981, 153) argues that the persona "shows his eagerness to guide others to virtue when he subordinates the question of what he himself should do to the opportunity to instruct and reform his companion." As such, the poem provides "a dramatic version of the casuistical principles that apparently trivial actions," such as joining a friend for a walk, "are morally significant and that intellectual effort must precede moral action."

Corthell (1982, 158) states that in *Sat1* "the satirist's anxiety at being left alone drives home the point that his identity depends, in some paradoxical way, on the presence of this other against which he measures himself."

Gallenca (1982, 309, 314–15, 317) states that in contrast to the personae of Hall and Marston, Donne's speaker seems weak and confused often (309). However, like Marston, Donne focuses on the humorist's courting of the rich and his profligate division of his time between a prostitute and a dandy, which Donne's narrator presents as a personal disappointment (314–15). While Donne's humorist retires from society, the speaker is finally a dupe who sells his liberty and is not to be confused with the retiring satirist who expands his freedom (317).

Hester (1982, 17–19, 21–22, 31) contends that the persona's "apparent inconsistency" is his "most troublesome" characteristic (18). He argues that "the scholar is presented as an exemplary contrast to the inconstancy and foolishness of the fop (*laus et vituperatio*)," but he also points out that to over-emphasize this point "is to overlook the primary tension it develops—the tension within the speaker in his anxious search for a satiric stance that will satisfy both his private and public duties as Christian scholar" (18). He suggests that the foolishness of Donne's speaker is the same kind of foolishness that Erasmus praises in *Moriae Encomium*, "the type of foolishness that makes a man more concerned with the soul of himself and others than with what many would term rational behavior, that makes a man suffer personal pain and self-effacement in order to convince another man of the error of his ways," so in the context of sixteenth-century religious thinking, the foolishness should be understood as "precisely the duty of the Christian scholar" (18–19). He adds that "the speaker's fulfillment of this duty is exemplified further in the various roles he assumes in dealing with the 'humorist,'" which taken together make evident that the scholar "assumes those roles assumed by Christ and advocated in His parables, the roles of Christian scholarship assumed also by the earliest Christian 'scholars,' the biblical prophets," which are "actions essential to his status as Christian scholar" (21–22). He concludes that "to offer the speaker as a viable alternative to the foolishness attacked in the poem is not to suggest that he is ideal," and "his nearly exclusive reliance on the recitation of scholastic ideals in his attempt to reform the fop shows that he is not yet Donne's most effective or mature satiric spokesman" (31).

Hunter (1983, 111) suggests that the two speakers in *Sat1* may represent two sides of a single person, offering us a contrast between "a social faddist" and "someone who tries to rise above such transient values."

Kerins (1984, 38) remarks that *Sat1* "introduces us to a novel satiric persona—one clearly alien to the aggressive scourgers who strut forth in the opening lines of most Elizabethan satires." He suggests that the persona "affects the role of the wise man who has subordinated all passion," and thus, "instead of being sport to the satirist, the humorist is clearly a threat to him." He concludes that the persona's wit is "entirely defensive" and serves as the satirist's "intellectual shield in a war waged ultimately against a portion of himself that he seeks to deny."

Stein (1984, 72–73) argues that the narrator of *Sat1*, "a theatrical image of the youthful Donne," is "a large figure who can divide himself into the persona (1) who speaks the first fifty lines, (2) who then records in different voices what he sees and hears, and (3) who also speaks self-characterizing replies in dialogue," adding that "behind him is the poet who is responsible for the narrator and all else."

Baumlin (1986b, 460–61) argues that "a specifically Horatian feature" of *Sat1* is the speaker's "manner of rebuke," in which the persona "is an ironist rather than a railer, allowing the *adversarius* to condemn himself through his flighty words and frantic behavior." He also notes that "since self-deprecation is an attribute of the Horatian persona," readers should expect that "much of the irony and implied criticism" in the poem "redounds upon the satirist himself," but that "complications arise in the text's attitude toward its model, when Donne's satirist cannot laugh at his own inconstancy."

Caracciolo-Trejo (1986, 2:11–12) points out that since all at court in *Sat1* is pretense, pompous venality, and empty forms of hypocrisy, the truth from which the poetic speaker writes makes him return, sick, to his own inner reflections. He adds that since we do not know with certainty to whom *Sat1* is directed, everything in the poem makes one think of a kind of conversation of the poet with his own various personalities.

Docherty (1986, 111) observes that "the humorist (perhaps as an aspect of the speaker's divided personality, a representation or image of the persona) rushes from the poet in the street and away to his love, leaving the poet alone" during their walk in the street and suggests that "that the poet and humorist are one," especially in the complicated reflection of one another in the mirror image.

Fish (1990, 235–36) argues that the persona of *Sat1* fails "to distinguish himself from the variability and corruption" he encounters so that what the persona "pushes away or tries (in an impossible effort) to push away is himself."

Baumlin (1991, 68) comments that while the self-deprecation in *Sat1* "is an attribute of the Horatian persona," Donne's satirist finally "proves unable to laugh at his own inconstancy."

Shawcross (1991a, 30) contends that "the relater of the poem (whether 'I' or some omniscient observer) is not to be considered the poet who has written the poem," and insists that "Donne is not, emphatically not, the 'I'" of *Sat1*, "much as one wants to romanticize upon Jack Donne, the rake, and Dr. John Donne, the Dean of St. Paul's."

B. Smith (1991, 175) contends that the persona of *Sat1* is "everything the importunate visitor is not," namely, "rational," "whole," and "stable."

Gorbunov (1993, 94–95) argues that in *Sat1* Donne's use of dramatic monologue allows him to address real life in Elizabethan England directly, and it gives him a sharper vision than older English satirists. He states further that Donne, in surpassing his characters intellectually and in clearly seeing what they represent, offers in *Sat1* an attitude towards the figure of the narrator that is essentially new.

Shelburne (1994, 149–50) argues that in *Sat1* the humorist "displays exactly the kind of 'diverse,…wavering, and…changeable' mind that Cicero warns about and that indeed, Donne's speaker anticipates," yet he adds, the speaker "implicates himself" through his own inconstancy, which in turn "shifts our attention" in the poem "from the folly of the adversarius to that of the speaker," a shift signaled by the opening lines of the poem. He concludes that "the enforced constancy of the beaten adversarius" stands in "bitter contrast to the speaker's drama of self-betrayal through inconstancy."

Biester (1997, 90–91, 93) asserts that throughout *Sat1* Donne "sustains" a "pattern of alternately, or even simultaneously, separating himself from the friend and identifying himself with him," a feature comparable to "Horace's street nightmare" (90). He argues that regardless of whom the "Other" is modeled on, this "Other" is "someone like young Jack Donne" (91), someone who "is not yet ready to move from Jack to John," but one who is also "unwilling to risk presenting himself now as more

Jack than John" so that while "John Donne speaks the poem," he works to distance Jack even though he remains "unable to extinguish him" (93).

Corthell (1997, 31) observes that "the scholar's Christian humanism enables him to assume a position of moral mastery with respect to his satiric butt," yet this position "does not help him make moral decisions, nor does it prove effectual in changing the humorist."

Wiggins (2000, 32, 52, 53) describes the "studious, priggish self-deceived youth" (32) who narrates *Sat1* as "a clever observer of everyone but himself," unaware that he "is as ridiculous as the frisky companion whom he deplores" (32), and one who remains "deluded," complacent, and "bookish" (52–53).

Hadfield (2001, 57) finds that in *Sat1* Donne, under Juvenal's influence, "represents himself as a disillusioned malcontent who foolishly fails to distance himself from the excesses of a young courtier" and who thereby implicates himself "as one rather too keen on the world's fripperies and the chance of self-advancement."

Sources, Influences, and Analogues

Alden (1899, 153) comments that the opening lines of Guilpin's Satire V in *Ski-aletheia* "seems to be a paraphrase of the opening" of *Sat1*. Milgate (1967, 116–17) also notes this similarity.

Walker (1925, 70–71) states that while Donne's indebtedness to Horace is "obvious" in *Sat1*, "so is the vigour, and so is the essential originality," adding that Donne follows Horace "much more closely" in *Sat4* than in *Sat1*.

Leishman (1951, 109) notes that the "bare outline" of *Sat1* may have been suggested to Donne by Horace's *Satire* 1.9. Others who note this source in Horace include Lewalski and Sabol (1973, 91), Selden (1981, 118), Carey (1990, 420), Baumlin (1991, 67), and Prescott (2000, 229–30).

Rickey (1966, 186) notes *Sat1*'s mention of the muses in her listing of Donne's classical allusions.

Milgate (1967, 116–17) finds that though *Sat1* was "perhaps suggested" by the ninth satire of Horace's first book of satires, it is "a brilliantly original adaptation of the general methods of Roman satire."

Warnke (1967, 106) places *Sat1* "among the earliest of English formal satires based on Latin models."

Everett (1972, 7–8) states of *Sat1* that Donne learned from the Roman satirists that "satire must be, if not urbane, at least urban" and that it "must focus itself on some central civilized community." In particular, Donne "borrows Horace's device of a saunter through a peopled city" and "the sophisticated complication of Horace's dialogue formula," and from Juvenal Donne "perhaps learned that a personal relation to a great city both loved and detested was worth the expressing." He argues further that the dialogue exhibits the conventions of "the mannered and knotted burst of conversation that opens the first satire of Horace's younger imitator, Persius," adding that Donne possibly "took a hint from Persius here in that his poem is as much an internalized debate as it is a piece of reporting."

Parker and Patrick (1975, 14) suggest that *Sat1* "bears an interesting resemblance to Persius's fourth satire," itself a monologue which "focuses on the self-deception and inflated self-image of the fool Alcibiades—the 'whip' of the Stoic satirist speaker—and likewise contains a high/low motif, embodied in the aristocrat Alcibiades and the old vegetable-hawker, who are equated." They also perceive resemblances with Shakespeare's *Tro.*, itself a satire "in which the Trojans and the Greeks respectively represent the 'high' and 'low' counterparts of defective perception."

Selden (1978, 60) remarks that "like Horace's satirist, Donne's is not without some self-irony," yet adding that "unlike Horace's, the satirist's wit has a complexity of tone which implies a 'unified sensibility', in which thought and feeling are undissociated."

Dubrow (1979, 73–74, 76) points out that in *Sat1* Donne "criticizes his speaker far less than Horace laughs at his." As the poem proceeds, "it devotes an increasing amount of attention to the bore himself rather than to the persona." Donne's speaker, she continues, "expresses both the self-deprecatory wryness we find in Horace and a kind of harshness very foreign to the Latin poet," and she concludes that "Donne's blend of Horatian and Juvenalian elements" produced mixed results. When his persona "spit[s] out Juvenalian insults" within the framework of a dramatic Horatian dialogue, the cruelty makes the satirist seem "churlish." However, when he "borrows the vividly realized, precisely detailed portraits of Juvenalian satire" and puts them into the structure of a Horatian dialogue rather than the "loose, list-like structure that so often mars Juvenalian satire," his accomplishment exceeds that of Juvenal and of other imitators of Juvenal in the Renaissance (73–74). Moreover, "the rapid shifts within a single satire between quiet Horatian meditation and acerbic Juvenalian mockery make Donne's poems more lively" so that, in short, "many of the achievements of his satires, as well as some of their limitations, stem from the way he adapts classical satire" (76).

Hamilton (1979, 405) suggests that one of Donne's sources for *Sat1* could be Sir Thomas Hoby's translation of Castiglione's *The Courtier*. He notes that both texts include a situation in which a friend is "deserted for one better dressed," adding that "the parallel is strengthened by the occurrence of 'fond' at the beginning of the Castiglione paragraph, and Donne's curious use of the adjective 'fondling' in the first line of his satire."

Eddy and Jaeckle (1981, 111–14, 121) suggest that *Sat1* "borrows structural, strategic, and philosophical elements from Persius's third satire," though acknowledging that Donne "transforms them in order to intensify the theme of moral inconstancy" (111). They specify further that "the dramatic situations of the two poems are far different" (112), and they find that Donne changes his source in two ways: (1) by maintaining "the integrity of the dramatic situation throughout, never losing sight of his original two characters," and (2) by complicating "the moral decision" (114). They conclude that even though Donne may also have been influenced by the third satire of Horace's second book, which was "the model for Persius's third satire," Donne's poem "still owes more to Persius's poem" (121).

Hester (1982, 32) argues that *Sat1* "endorse[s] Horace's comic view of the satirist as idealist caught in the obdurately myopic society of man." He notes that like Horace's poem, *Sat1* is "a comic study in failure that delineates the radical and seemingly irreconcilable distance between the good intentions of the satirist as *vir bonus* and the *adversarius* as obdurate fool" so that "the speaker's recitation of Christian ideals serves finally only to place him in a precarious position where he, too, is victimized by the self-destructive adultery of the town," and "reformation by satire is left at the end of the poem as seemingly an impossible ideal."

Hunter (1983, 111) observes that *Sat1* was an "excursion in Persius's wake" that was not successful "or witty enough in English" for Donne to try imitating the classical writer's "disjoined" style again.

Baumlin (1986b, 460–62) finds that "a specifically Horatian feature" of *Sat1* is "the speaker's manner of rebuke," which in no way "approaches a direct or a bitter invective." As with his Horatian model, Donne's persona is "an ironist rather than a railer, allowing the *adversarius* to condemn himself through his flighty words and frantic behavior" (460–61). He also argues that structurally the poem "recalls Horace by its dramatic setting," adding that "throughout the satirist's address to his friend— and particularly when he makes the humorist swear not to leave him once they get out on the street," we have a "witty, conversational speech imitating Horace's *sermo pedestris*," as well as a "language highly revelatory of character" (461–62). He adds, however, that Donne "attempts far more than a rehashed version of the Horatian plot," striving instead "for an exact reversal of the dramatic situation in *Sermo* 1.9" in that Horace's "Impertinent wishes to accompany the satirist, while Donne's persona chooses to accompany the humorist," which, as a result, "makes Donne's satirist all the more culpable" (462).

Baumlin (1991, 73–74) comments that in *Sat1* Donne "turns Horace's ironies into an expression of conscience too dire for laughter," for Donne "rejects the entire ethical foundation of Horace's comic satire, redefining as sin his model's 'lesser frailties' and folly."

Wheeler (1992, 117–118) notes that in *Sat1* Donne "has caught the gay spirit of Horace's satire," though she adds that "there is no direct borrowing from Horace" and suggests that Donne also drew on Persius's third satire.

Klawitter (1994, 119) observes that apart from the rhetorical style of Horace's ninth satire, what is also echoed in *Sat1* is "the intense frustration that his narrator feels," and "this feeling of helplessness is peculiar to Donne and Horace." He says that Horace invented "the use of the dialogue form," and "the busy-body who bothers the narrator in Horace's Satire 1.9 sets an obvious tone for Donne's street-person" in both *Sat1* and *Sat4*, though he adds that "the dialogue in Juvenal's ninth satire tells us more about Donne's narrator than about the narrator's *bete noire*, the bothersome fop." He concludes that Juvenal is "more valuable" than Horace in enabling us to understand "the primary speaker in Donne."

Shelburne (1994, 149–50), comparing Donne to Thomas Drant and Everard Guilpin, who both imitate Horace, comments that Donne "confronts a similarly fashion-conscious adversarius," adding that "for Donne, as for Drant and Guilpin, the idea of friendship seems to occur naturally in the context of formal satire." He states further that the "reservations" the satirist expresses about leaving his study to join the adversarius "recall two Ciceronian passages in which Laelius urges caution in contracting friendships." He explains that "while this adversarius seems an ideal target of satire," emphasizing "only his inconstancy" misreads the satire, as the Ciceronian context indicates, since Cicero "is not concerned primarily with the inconstant friend," but rather with "cautioning those who might mistakenly adopt such men as friends," and thus, *Sat1* "dramatizes the consequences of ignoring Cicero's advice."

Biester (1997, 90–92) accepts Horaces' *Satire* 1.9 as Donne's "primary model," but finds that *Sat1* distinguishes itself from its model in three ways: while Horace's poem takes place in the street, "Donne's journey begins and ends at home"; "Horace is wandering aimlessly, but Donne's decision to leave home is deliberate"; and "Donne himself is no more secure than his friend" (91). Biester argues further that Donne does not write "with the Horatian goal of establishing norms, nor the Juvenalian goal of scourging the vicious," but instead "in the spirit of the revels, and with the goal of self-promotion" (92).

Corthell (1997, 28) observes that *Sat1* "begins by evoking the opening review of studies" in Marlowe's *Faustus*.

Blissett (2000, 116) suggests that the "fantastic flitting character" Asotus in *Cynthia's Revels* "bears some resemblance to the flibbertigibbet" of *Sat1*.

Trevor (2000, 88–89, 92, 93) cites a 1622 letter to Goodyer, in which "the 'false waies' with which Donne associates his prior 'poison' remind us of the speaker's wayward sallies" in *Sat1* (89). In addition, comparing *Cor1* 2 with the opening of *Sat1*, he finds that Donne "frequently" associates "scholarly activity with suffering and isolation" (92). Finally, a 1619 letter to Carre describes a situation in which "the scholarly self is ostensibly split," much as "the dutiful student is distinguished from" the humorist in *Sat1* (93).

Wiggins (2000, 32–33) notes that the "solemn youth" narrating *Sat1* "does not recognize that he is only the other half of one of those strange hermaphrodites made of 'study and play,'" such as those "inhabitants" of *EpLin*. Further, he proposes that a scene from Book II of *The Courtier* "could as easily be a source" of *Sat1* as Horaces' *Satire* 1.9 in that the former describes the humorist "to perfection" and "explains his behavior in a way that implicates the narrator."

Fulton (2001, 89) notes that Donne "modifies the more self-confident satiric persona of Juvenal and Persius" in *Sat1*, in which "the morally resistant voice becomes complicit in the hypocrisy of its social surroundings."

Hadfield (2001, 57) sees the influence of Juvenal in this poem, which "seeks to castigate and expose folly rather than suggest a better way of living and behaving."

Selleck (2001, 158, 173n41) suggests that the opening line of *Sat1* "expresses an almost Jonsonian discomfort with the idea of a changeable or humorous identity and a preference for more 'constant company'" (158), adding, however, that the speaker's recognition in lines 65–67 of "his own complicity in what he satirizes" (173n41) is unlike Jonson.

Unity and Structure

Aronstein (1920, 160–61) states that *Sat1*, *Sat2*, and *Sat4*, because of their shifting, multiple subjects, lack artistic unity.

Johnson (1953, Item 53) reads the poem as a dramatic monologue with four "scenes" (the study, the street, the lover's chamber, and the study).

Milgate (1967, xxiv) comments on a "looseness of structure" in *Sat1*, which Donne "does his best to overcome" by means of imagery and poetic closure.

Shawcross (1967, 397) sees the poem as a "debate" between the body and soul of the speaker over two questions: (1) whether his soul should follow his body and (2) why his body should "hate vertue." This debate takes place "indoors" (ll. 1–12), "in the street" (ll. 67–105), and "in his love's chambers" (ll. 106–110), "from which he returns home" (ll. 110–12).

Sat1, Lecocq (1969, 371–372) argues, has not only two contrasting portraits (inconstant interlocutor and persona), but also two parts that are connected and that complete one another: the dramatic opening introduction to the characters in lines 1–52 and the narrative of the walk they undertake together in lines 67–112. Connecting the two parts, and effecting the poem's shift from dramatization to narration, is the persona's side-street aside in lines 53–66. In the second part, he notes, verb tenses shift from present to past (and, in places, back again), building to a conclusion in the past tense. Because these temporal markers ultimately indicate that the whole poem—even its dramatic opening and the transitional aside—must be comprehended as having already happened, he believes that Donne fashioned *Sat1* as a trompe-l'oeil.

Powers (1971, 41, 73, 82) suggests that *Sat1* is "a typical example of the poems structured on the details of just one human figure," and this "single-character presentation" distinguishes him as "the victim" in this poem "shown in the complex of attitudes that define him as a 'humorist,'" namely, "by his lack of concern for the Satirist's taste for study, that he scorns learning; by his interest in the size of another's estate, that he is materialistic; by his unwillingness to walk other than by the wall, that he is too proud; in his valuing the company of 'euery fine silken painted fool', that he lacks perspective; in his elaborate rituals of courtesy, that he is ludicrous; and so on" (41).

Parker and Patrick (1975, 10, 14n) note that *Sat1* has "two distinct parts of approximately equal length" that are "bridged by a transition of seven couplets," the whole "being further divided into stanzas of predominantly twelve lines each." Further, they say, "the events of the second part of the poem parallel in sequence, climax, and the thematic significance of the events of the first," adding that both parts "function to reveal progressively, by means of dramatic monologue, the character of the speaker, who is the poem's primary focus" (10). They also cite Mary Claire Randolph (1942) and note that *Sat1* "exhibits the principal characteristics of formal verse satire as composed by such writers as Persius and Juvenal": (1) "a bi-partite structure, in which a 'specific vice or folly, selected for attack, was turned about on all its sides in Part A…and its opposing virtue was recommended in Part B'"; (2) "two participants, a Satirist and his *Adversarius*"; (3) "the device of monologue"; (4) "a lightly delineated background—possibly a street," providing "'a steady stream of type-figures on whom the Satirist can comment'"; (5) "spasmodic or elliptical conversation, 'frequently without either Satirist or *Adversarius* being clearly identified as the speaker'"; (6) "occasional use of a transition"; and (7) "an implied or explicit admonition to virtue or rational behavior toward which 'the whole…rhetorical procedure is pointed.'" Noting Randolph's observations that the virtue "will be the precise opposite of the vice of folly ridiculed," Parker and Patrick assert that Donne "satirizes both the vice and the putative virtue" (14n).

Sinha (1977, 59) states that *Sat1* is "bipartite in structure," noting that "while in the one a specific vice is turned about on all its sides and thoroughly exposed, its opposing virtue is recommended in the other."

Slights (1981, 156) argues that while *Sat1* "shows the influence of the casuistical tradition," its structure "is not that of a case of conscience" in that "instead of exemplifying the movement from doubt to certainty, the speaker raises a moral question, decides to act without resolving his doubts, and thus raises more questions about the relation of thought to action and the efficacy of moral instruction," and the final four lines "provide an epilogue to his dilemma."

Hester (1982, 29–30) argues of *Sat1* that "the relatively stable first half takes place in the sanctity of his study," which operates "within providential time," and "the shuttling, shifting second half of the poem takes place in the streets," where "the shifts in time are as frequent as the shifts in motive and attention by the courtiers seen there." He explains that "the contrast between the two scenes and the two characters enforces the scholar's praise of the eternal and condemnation of the temporal" in that "the scholar controls time in the poem while the fop and his townsmen are controlled by it." He notes further that "the circular movement of the poem," which "begins and ends in the scholar's study," is thus "emblematic at once of the circle of eternity and the eternal design of human history, and of the moral shape of the scholar's and the fop's conduct."

Zunder (1982, 9) argues that *Sat1* "is built on a distinction" between "the constancy of the speaker and the inconstancy of the companion." The speaker is associated with people and places that are considered to be "accepted repositories of wisdom," while the companion is associated "with appearances."

Language and Style

Addleshaw (1931, 44–45) identifies *Sat1* as the "most cacophonous" of the Satyres.

Gransden (1954, 104–05) notes that *Sat1* creates "the sort of rip-roaring, cut-and-thrust, allusive atmosphere in which satire normally kicks and thrives." He also points out that the "anecdotal, conversational passages" of *Sat1* "are the real stuff of satire," adding that "Donne's condemnations of lawyers, suitors and courtiers, though originally and forcefully expressed, are yet conventionally derived."

Milgate (1967, xxiv) observes in *Sat1*'s references to clothes "a sequence of congruent imagery through the poem" and "a sort of finality" in "a clinching epigrammatic couplet."

Alvarez (1969, 333) argues that Donne's writing is "masculine" in that it is "rigorous, independent and sane, which is the tone of the narrator" of *Sat1*, and in this "tough, witty voice," Donne was objecting to "the indignities of 'whining Poetry.'"

Korte (1969, 79–80) observes that in *Sat1* "innuendo and a careful choice of words" create comic effects which "serve to undercut the authoritative *ethos* of the satirist."

Powers (1971, 69–70, 108, 115) describes Donne's creation of immediacy in *Sat1* through the use of the historical present tense, the use of direct speech, and the omission of identifying tags (69–70), and notes further Donne's use of narration as a departure from the usual "static style" of Elizabethan satyre (108). She suggests that there are "touches of the farcical" in *Sat1* and that "the movements are exaggerated to ridiculous degrees in the description of the humorist's action," the satirist himself providing "a norm to measure them by" (115).

Erskine-Hill (1972, 274) notes that in *Sat1* "the superior wisdom of the speaker is unchallenged, except implicitly in its failure to make any impact upon ebullient folly," adding that "by virtue of this implicit challenge, a balance is struck," which lends "a degree of astringent irony to what would otherwise have been a simple union of comic perception and firm moral assurance." He concludes that *Sat1* "is a precocious, and not wholly unsuccessful, attempt to emulate the shaped narrative, the perfect control and the finely shaped balanced assurance of the Latin poem."

Everett (1972, 6–7, 9) remarks that "the dazzlingly animated opening fifty lines disclose a prospect of crowded London streets from which sharp details stand out." She notes that "this animated scene is not (as we soon learn) the real thing" but is rather the "young scholar's half-appalled and half-enchanted fantasy." She adds that the point at which the persona descends "into the London of actuality" is "signaled by an abrupt change of style," where the friend "ceases to be *thou* and becomes *he*," and the reader "ceases to stand in for that friend and becomes an onlooker." She observes that sometimes the voices of the humorist and the satirist are intertwined "to the point at which their identities are confused," even though their roles are very different from each other (6). She argues further that *Sat1* "appears to drift aimlessly," yet "one of its chief charms" is "its easy rambling movement, as of a liberated self-abandonment to whatever happens" (7).

Jensen (1972, 403–04) notes that *Sat1* displays the "tendency toward dramatic presentation" that is characteristic of Renaissance satire, namely, "a flashing, self-conscious poetic energy." He also remarks that "the crowning excellence" of the poem "emerges from Donne's management of the total performance," for he is the "playwright-director who superintends every word and gesture, every modulation of tone, every shift of light or shadow."

Newton (1974, 429–31) comments that the sentences in *Sat1* "may be so long and complex that you have difficulty following them—just as Donne himself has some trouble keeping track of the Humorist—but in the end the syntax works out—just as Donne in the end finally controls the Humorist" (430). Moreover, he says, Donne similarly "'hems in' the reader (and, one suspects, himself) by his extravagant or 'humorous' yet ultimately very tight syntax" by "darting barbs in every direction, wrapping clause within clause and satire within satire," thus extracting "an enormous energy of strict attentiveness from the reader," while seeming "to exert a correspondent energy to keep his own emotions and perceptions under control." Newton concludes about the Satyres as a whole that it is "the promise of control" that "keeps us reading these otherwise wild and nearly hysterical poems" (431).

Hiller (1977, 15) remarks that Donne's Satyres have none of Wyatt's "calmness and urbanity," adding that *Sat1* and *Sat3* are "personal meditations," in which "the thought is vigorous and forceful, the imagery arresting, the verse rugged and often irregular."

Sinha (1977, 63) notes that in *Sat1* Donne "governs point, compactness, speed, climax, contrast, surprise, and a score more of the special effects" that are "necessary for good and effective satire." He concludes that the apparent "simplicity and nonchalance" of *Sat1* is in fact "only an assumed simplicity of verbal surface beneath which there exists a skillfully evolved and delicately managed development of dialectical argument in a dramatic pattern."

Cousins (1979, 102) asserts that in *Sat1* "*contrapositum* does not fashion strikingly individual images," but instead Donne "designs" the poem "by jarring together, not fusing, irreconcilable contradictions."

Eddy and Jaeckle (1981, 113) note that Donne is like Persius in his shifting of pronouns in *Sat1*, and they point out that "until line 67, the speaker uses 'I' and 'thou,'" but from that point on, Donne "refers to the humorist as 'he.'"

Corthell (1982, 159) remarks that *Sat1* "abounds in incidental satire" and that Donne "characteristically makes the images used in his comparisons the objects of satire," thus creating an effect of "an infinite plenitude of vice and folly," each "fantastic comparison" representing "another instance of the inconstancy and unpredictability which the foppish humorist epitomizes."

Hunter (1983, 110) suggests that Donne "deliberately introduced...disorder" in the first sixty-six lines of *Sat1* because he was "consciously imitating the style of Persius," but elsewhere in his poetry there is never "anything quite so complex, quite so rhetorically forced, as these lines" probably because he realized that "Persius's style handled in this disjointed way was not well suited to English."

Kerins (1984, 39–41) notes that when the action of *Sat1* moves into the street from the study, "the tone and complexion" of the poem are "greatly changed" in that "while the scholarly cell was a world in which moral postures were assumed, the street transposes them into courtly social configurations." As a consequence, part two consists of the satirist's "witty narration of what the two encounter on their stroll," a mode very different from the "direct address" of lines 1–64. Moreover, in the first part, Kerins says, the humorist "did nothing and said nothing," becoming "merely the object upon which the satirist vented his spleen, contracted in marriage, and shrived in confession." Kerins finds part two, by contrast, to be "animated and dramatic" (39), adding that "both halves of this satire are dramatic—but in radically different ways," the first part a "dramatic monologue" and the second, a "more traditional dramatic set piece with characters clearly delineated and a great deal of action" (39–40). He also finds "an important change in the satiric angle of vision between the two parts," with the progression from a "censuring voice" that is "moralistic" in part one to a voice that is "entirely social" in part two. Similarly, the satirist's wit is "transposed into a new key," as it moves from "extended analogies and long-winded harangues" to a diminished voice characterized by "witty retorts and curt asides" (40). Kerins concludes that "the poem ends in a scene of physical mayhem reduced to imaginative order by the sheer verbal dexterity of the speaker's epigrammatic wit" (41).

Toliver (1985, 98) observes that in its dramatization of "the contrast between the integrity of the private place and the role-playing of the street," the language of *Sat1* is "slippery" and its movement is "toward dispersal and centerless street wandering."

Woodring (1994, 231) suggests that *Sat1* reveals Donne's "characteristic techniques—bold, colloquial address, metrical roughness, striking phrases," adding that "most of all, it manifests the complex drama of the Donnean lyric, where the speaker's attitudes as well as those of his interlocutor are being interrogated."

Oliver (1997, 34) notes that *Sat1*, along with the other poetry written at Lincoln's Inn, would have established Donne "as a writer of knotty, sophisticated verse."

Religion

Geraldine (1966, 26–27) highlights the theme of inconstancy in *Sat1*, arguing that while this is a moral rather than a spiritual issue, Donne consistently emphasizes the religious dimension.

Selden (1978, 61) remarks that "the scholar's books are pretentious and ridiculous," and yet "at the same time sublime," adding that Donne's "Christian and Neoplatonic touches" are "called to rational account and reduced to mock-seriousness and self-deflation."

Eddy and Jaeckle (1981, 119–20) argue that after the speaker enters the street, Donne "introduces a Christian conception of sin into the poem, thereby complicating its moral vision and illustrating the poet's uneasiness with the Stoic formulation that knowledge leads to virtue." They add, that according to Stoic doctrine, "knowledge should insure the speaker's virtue, but Donne implies that awareness of Christian truths and moral doctrines is not a guarantee against temptation."

Hester (1984, 6) points out that in *Sat1* Donne not only relies "more heavily than Guilpin on the imagery and pattern of Horace's sermon," but he is "also more concerned with the moral and social role of the satirist in a providential world." As a result, *Sat1*'s religious language, he argues, "especially the reiterated moral application of the marriage analogy" and "the consistent eschatological perspective," is "integral to his exploration of the Christian bases and limitations of satire as an agent of societal and personal reform."

Mann (1985, 538) notes that *Sat1* "places a densely contemporary portrayal of the frivolity of an inconstant fop against a firm background of religious value."

Baumlin (1991, 73–74, 76–77), noting that "the expression of personal guilt" in Donne's speaker is probably not part of the imitation of the classical source, reminds us that Donne is "a Christian satirist (and perhaps Catholic at the time of writing), a poet whose introspectiveness and sense of conscience presumably surpass the pagan and philosophically eclectic (though typically epicurean) Horace." Baumlin explains that in revising the classical model, Donne "turns Horace's ironies into an expression of conscience too dire for laughter," for Donne "rejects the entire ethical foundation of Horace's comic satire, redefining as sin his model's 'lesser frailties' and folly" (73). As such, *Sat1* describes thematically "the failure of penitence in the satirist's world, perhaps even the loss of Catholic-sacramental penance," which in turn "points to a larger failure, one of importance to the collection as a whole: the failure to find, or fashion, an efficacious rhetoric of reform." He suggests further that *Sat1* "is well placed in the collection" because it "reveals the reason classical satire (specifically Horatian satire) fails as a theology of language" (73–74). He argues finally that in one of his sermons Donne describes an issue that he had confronted in *Sat1*, namely, that "the problem of writing classical satire in a Christian culture" is that the Christian must lament "his own condition as well as the world's, since his subject—the weakness not of one man but of fallen humanity—reflects the satirist's own 'self-guiltinesse,'" and thus, "far from reforming society, his ridicule can only worsen it" (76–77).

Nutt (1999, 40) asserts that Donne's targets in *Sat1* "are all intent on selfish pursuits, whether courtly self-advancement or mere sexual gratification," and he concludes that the satirist's stance is "undilutedly Christian, if not Catholic."

NOTES AND GLOSSES

1–48 *Away...I confer.* **SLIGHTS** (1981): this section "presents an unresolved dilemma," in which "the speaker feels responsible to act as his companion's moral guide, but he also believes that involvement in such frivolous company is irresponsible abandonment of the life of simple virtue" (155). **EVERETT** (1986): "The dazzlingly animated" opening lines "disclose a prospect of crowded London streets" that "is not (as we soon learn) the real thing," but instead "only a reverie, entertained in anticipation, and we have still to descend into the London of actuality." Further, the moment of this descent "is signalled by an abrupt change of style," at which point "the addressed friend ceases to be *thou* and becomes *he*; the reader ceases to stand in for that friend and becomes an onlooker" (4).

1–16 *Away...do meet.* **SCHIPPER** (1888): in this passage, only ll. 1, 3, 7, 9, 11, 12, 15, and 16 are more or less regular, though ll. 3 and 7 barely qualify as regular, and all of the other eight lines reveal various irregularities including stress inversions, double unstressed opening syllables, slurring of the verse, and enjambment, the latter of which accounts for Donne's frequent use of caesura (204–06).

1–12 *Away...wild, vncertaine thee?* **MINER** (1969): "the private life envisioned as the alternative to the public is a life of contemplation—but of the very public world from which he recoils," and the "sources of comfort are divines, scientists, statesmen, historians, and poets. In contemporary terms, the scientific natural philosopher was a student of the retired, contemplative life, and a couple of the other comforters are ambiguous as to their public or private status. But the statesmen, even if read in books, exemplify the very world his satires attack." Further, "nothing could be more significant than the imagery he uses to describe the private world to which he retreats. The imagery is dominantly restrictive, suggestive of painful confinement and death" (39–40). **PARKER AND PATRICK** (1975): the purpose of the lines is "to establish the speaker's character and the polarity of temperament distinguishing the protagonists. The stanza opens with the speaker exhorting a companion to 'Leave mee,' a command stemming, we discover, from a seemingly valid conviction of moral and intellectual superiority." This attitude of superiority stems "from the speaker's image of himself as a spiritual purist, as exemplified by his preoccupation with 'Gods conduits' and 'grave Divines,'" and "the stanza contains a subtle pattern of ironies, inconsistencies, and contradictions which substantially undercut the validity of the speaker's assertions. There are, for example, the 'few bookes' which the speaker professes to consort with, as opposed to the battalion of Divines, statesmen, philosophers, and chroniclers that follows, not to mention a voluminous collection of poets. There is the contradiction posed by 'standing' and 'lying': the speaker will 'lye' in his 'standing' chest. There is further contradiction between 'jolly' and 'grave' and, finally, between 'giddie' and 'constant,' 'giddie' farcically annihilating the whole point of the speaker's sermon" (11). **EDDY AND JAECKLE** (1981): after the scholar's "protracted stay in the closet, he probably desires some diversion, as his images of the room as a prison and as a coffin intimate. Furthermore, the values to be found in his books are not above suspicion. The list starts appropriately enough with 'Gods conduits, grave Divines,' but by its last category, the 'Giddie fantastique Poets of each land,' the persona's choice of adjectives betrays an unrealized discontent and prepares for his later decision" (113). **MORSE** (1989): "in the act of abandoning his sager counsels for a more erratic guide Donne implies that he is probably getting in deeper than he knows and that in abandoning his role of the reclusive scholar, in order to mingle with the flamboyant company of the streets, he may consequently lose all perspective upon the world" (273).

1–10 *Away...of each Land.* **GRIERSON** (1929): these lines present a picture, "just such as Walton indicates," of a young "gallant" who like Donne is a visitor of ladies but is unable "to share his graver studies" (xxv). **SMITH** (1970): "The poet writes as a solitary contemplative who is dragged from his books, partly by his own virile urge as it appears, to witness the active depravities of public life or of Court or the Law. But the studies he leaves are no more exempt from human absurdity than the life outside and have no more absolute claim on one" (142).

1–4 *Away...when I dy.* **GRANSDEN** (1970): the passage "carries a strong note of contemptus mundi," and "there is also an echo of Martial" in the "allusion to the classical tradition of withdrawal, usually into the country" (14). **KAWASAKI** (1971): these lines "exemplify the agoraphobic use of the self-contained microcosm" and are "also slightly thanatophilous, which makes it seem all the more characteristic of the earlier Donne" (39). **CAREY** (1981): "The speech contradicts itself. Although Donne professes to want to be left in his study, he calls it a coffin and a prison. Not surprisingly he and the intruder are out among the crowds well before the end of the poem" (48). **KLAWITTER** (1994): "The room is so constraining that it is nothing more than a 'chest' or a 'prison,' something so tight that it can serve adequately as a coffin for the recluse. Surrounded by his books, which, we discover, include theology, philosophy, political science, chronicles, and poetry, but no law books, the student is content to rot, but his intruder will not leave him so" (115). **TREVOR** (2000): these lines "bear witness to the speaker's failed attempt at dismissing his visitor, but they also cast this visitor as a specter of humoral intemperance, leaving the speaker to choose between his company and the familiar, dungeon-like quality of a Donne study" (87). Although the study "resembles a prison or a tomb," it is "more like a womb," the speaker finding therein the "'constant company' of divines, philosophers, statesmen, chroniclers, and poets who nurture his intellect." Imagining "his death in such surroundings" is for the speaker imagining himself "nestled, perhaps even suffocated, under the pages of his favorite authors, or even under the volumes of notes written in his own hand" (88).

1–3 *Away...lett me ly* **PARFITT** (1989): Donne has "the satirist's dislike of the contemporary," and "this necessarily means rejection of Court and City," though Donne's "emphasis is not on administering the whip or knife." This opening is "close to Guilpin's fifth satire and it is likely that Guilpin has imitated Donne" (22–23).

1–2 *Away...wodden chest* **FISH** (1990) (reading "fondling motley humorist"): the passage displays "instability" in that "a humorist is a person of irregular behavior, 'a fantastical or whimsical person' (*OED*); a fondling is a fool, someone dazed, incapable of focusing (in an earlier manuscript Donne wrote 'changeling'); and motley is what a fool wears because a cloth 'composed of elements of diverse or varied character' (*OED*) perfectly suits one who is without a center. It also suits the traditional figure of the satirist, the writer of a random discourse who moves from one topic to another in ways that display no abiding rationale; the linking definition of satire as 'satura medlye'—a full dish of mixed fruit indiscriminately heaped up—was a standard one in the period and linked the satirist both with the court fool" and also with "the 'mirror' or recorder figure who reflects the disorder of a world without coherence and has no coherence of his own." Thus, "what the first-person voice pushes away or tries (in an impossible effort) to push away is himself; rather than saying, as he would like to, 'Get thee behind me Satan,' he is saying (in perfect self-contradiction), 'Get thee behind me me.' From the beginning he is protecting and defending an identity—a separateness from flux and surface—that he never really has" (235–36).

1 *Away...humorist,* **SMITH** (1971): "the poem leaves us to guess who Donne's companion is and what he stands for. He may be an aspect of the poet's own nature, the active man of the world in him as against the retired contemplative man his profession makes him" (469–70). [So also, Chmielewski (2001, 614).] **HESTER** (1977c): "the anger and hatred of the satirist are apparent from his opening injunction to the fop" (188). **BIESTER** (1997) (reading "fondling motley humorist") observes that Donne "takes on the persona of satirist" even as he dismisses the humorist. The "epithet 'fondling motley humorist' fits perfectly with the details of the Other that the poem goes on to provide, but it also boomerangs, serving as an apt description of the satirical jester himself, Donne's own role" (90). **BLISSETT** (2000) suggests that this line "might be addressed by Wellbred or Edward Know'ell to Matthew, by Asper to Fastidius Brisk, by Horace to Crispinus, by Criticus to any of the courtiers at Cynthia's court, or by Ben Jonson himself to a certain kind of playgoer" (111).

1 *changeling motley humorist,* **SHAWCROSS** (1967) (reading "fondling motley humorist"): "the foolishly pampered body, subject at various times to the four humours (blood, phlegm, yellow bile, black bile—happiness, indifference, anger, melancholy)" (15). **WARNKE** (1967) (reading "fondling motley humorist"): "foolish, changeable person" (106). **SMITH** (1971) (reading "fondling motley humorist"): "foolish, changeable zany" (470). [Similarly, Patrides (1985, 214).] **HILLER** (1977) (reading "fondling motley humorist"): "foolish, capricious, fantastical person. [Similarly, Hunter (1983,

110), Craik and Craik (1986, 256), Carey (1990, 420), Jones (1991, 626), and Nutt (1999, 31–32).] The humorist may represent that part of the satirist's being, his body, which is susceptible to fleshly temptations and whose continual urgings for material satisfaction are a distraction to the contemplative man" (175). **HUNTER** (1983) (noting both alternative readings ["fondling" or "changeling"]): "he is ravished by appearances and will follow wherever they lead, being willing to leave the speaker's side at any moment" in that "he follows whatever appearances he feels attractive." Further, "in modern terms the OED definition of 'humorist' as 'faddist' seems appropriate" (110). **CAREY** (1990) (reading "fondling motley humorist"): "whimsical person" (420). [So also, Chmielewski (2001, 614).]

1 *changeling* **GROSART** (1872–73) (noting "fondling" in the 1633 ed. [A]): "As 'changeling' is ambiguous, being used for fairy changelings, and as 'motley' expresses the various picked costumes of different customs which the foppish Englishman was supposed to delight in, probably 'fondling' was the author's revised word" (1:9). **GRIERSON** (1912), reading "fondling," notes "changeling" in the "majority" of the mss. and avers that both words are authorial, but thinks it "impossible to say" which is Donne's revision: "He may have changed 'fondling' (a 'fond' or foolish person) thinking that the idea was conveyed by 'motley', which, like Shakespeare's epithet 'patch', is a synecdoche from the dress of the professional fool or jester. On the other hand the idea of 'changeling' is repeated in 'humorist', which suggests changeable and fanciful....'Changeling' has of course the meaning here of 'a fickle or inconstant person', not the common sense of a person or thing or child substituted for another, as 'fonding' is not here a 'pet, favourite', as in modern usage" (2:106). **SULLENS** (1964) (reading "fondling"): this meaning of the word is not recorded in the OED (259). **BEWLEY** (1966) (reading "fondling"): "foolish person" (168). [So also, Patrides (1985, 214).] **MILGATE** (1967) (reading "fondling"): "This is the reading of Donne's final version...; the earlier reading, 'changeling' (one given to change, a fickle or inconstant person, O. E. D., sense I), was presumably rejected because its meaning is already contained in 'humorist' and 'motley'" (118). **ROUSSEAU AND RUDENSTINE** (1972) (reading "fondling"): "Fawning, ingratiating" (57). [So also, Campbell (1989, 234).]

1 *motley humorist,* **ROUSSEAU AND RUDENSTINE** (1972): "Person subject to 'humors' or fancies; 'motley' suggests someone highly changeable in mood" (57). **GORBUNOV** (1993): after Donne's introduction of this figure, it became a stock character type in English dramatic comedy.

1 *motley* **SULLENS** (1964): the OED cites Donne as the earliest source for the meaning of this word (251). **BEWLEY** (1966): "referring to the dress of a court jester" (168). [So also, Campbell (1989, 234).] **MILGATE** (1967): "varying in character or mood, changeable" (118).

1 *humorist,* **CHAMBERS** (1896): "according to Ben Jonson's favourite sense of *humour* for 'type of character,' and here especially in the deprecating sense of 'coxcomb,' 'fribble'" (2:243). [Similarly, Milgate (1967, 118), Campbell (1989, 234), and Chmielewski (2001, 614).]

2–10 *Leaue me,…of each Land.* **BALD** (1970): these lines describe Donne's "'study' in the chambers in Lincoln's Inn which, Walton says, he shared with Christopher Brooke. These studies were in reality small cells, which must have been extremely cramped, partitioned off from the larger chamber by wainscoting, and furnished with little more than a stool, a table, and a set of shelves." Interestingly, "there were poets and historians, philosophers and theologians on Donne's bookshelves, but not law books, or none that he thought worth mentioning. It is clear that his interests ranged far beyond the curriculum that he was supposedly following" (62). [Similarly, Parry (1985, 43).] **WINNY** (1970): "The list comprises divinity, natural philosophy or science, politics, history and finally poetry, whose authors Donne affects to slight while admitting the quality which makes them congenial to him" (13–14).

2–6 *Leaue me,…the Philosopher,* **CROFTS** (1936) cites these lines as evidence that Donne "saw through" the pretenses of his times (129).

2–5 *Leaue me,…graue Diuines:* **BAUMLIN** (1991): the description is notable for its "ambivalence": "if his study is a prison to him, he should *want* to escape from it. And even as he admonishes his flighty companion, his mind is far away from deeper studies, especially of the 'grave Divines' (5) with whom he keeps company." Increasingly we see the "critical relation" between Donne's text and his Horatian model, as *Sat1*—"more than a rehearsal or rehashed version of the Horatian plot"—calls for "its complete inversion, Horace's importuning stranger here becoming the poet's intimate friend. And while Horace hopes for nothing more than to be rid of his *adversarius*, Donne's speaker goes so far as to make his friend swear *not* to abandon him on the street" (69). **EDWARDS** (2001) cites these lines as evidence of Donne's "wide reading in his study," which apparently included Aristotle, statesmen, historians, and poets. The "Latin poets almost certainly included Horace, who was to some extent imitated in this 'satyre,'" while "no law books were mentioned" (43).

2–4 *Leaue me,…when I dy.* **GUSS** (1966): these lines show Donne's life "to be pure, secluded, and dedicated" (203n3). **HUGHES** (1968): "the refuge of the study," which "is a barricade against the world," the "great merit of this hermitage" being its "stability, for outside is all flux and all change" (22). **PATTERSON** (1990): these lines illustrate the "the necrophilic imagination" of Donne (53). **SLIGHTS** (1996): the passage "contrasts a life of retired privacy with the world beyond," and as such, "characterizes the private world as a prison and associates it with the grave" (70). **NUTT** (1999): "if we now examine the way Donne describes his private rooms, we will be able to see that his grasp of the dilemma is entirely human and not mere artifice," for the speaker "recognises from the start that the temptation is real" (32). **EVERETT** (2001): the poem "opens by making a harshly ironic statement of chosen isolation." Donne "sees that lonely life as a kind of death; and yet that death is also (we perceive) the life of the writing" (61).

2 *standing wodden chest* **GROSART** (1872–73) comments that "books were kept in 'chests;' but query, Is the poet not here humorously likening his little study-closet to such a chest? Cf. Marvell's 'Flecknoe,' lines 10–14" (1:9). [Similarly, Smith (1971, 470), Rousseau and Rudenstine (1972, 57), Lewalski and Sabol (1973, 91), Hiller

(1977, 175), Patrides (1985, 214), Craik and Craik (1986, 256), Campbell (1989, 234), Carey (1990, 420), and Jones (1991, 626).] **MILGATE** (1967) describes the construction of chambers at Lincoln's Inn after 1587: two members occupying each half-chamber, itself divided into a bedroom and study; Donne roomed in two of these with his friend Christopher Brooke (according to Izaak Walton) [so also, Craik and Craik (1986, 256) and Kruzhkova (1994, 153–54)]. Donne "seems to have been sensitive to the effects of closed spaces, and such a room might well appear to him like a chest 'standing' (i.e. on end)" (118).

2 *chest* **MILGATE** (1967): a good rhyme, "as the word was then pronounced" (and frequently spelled) "chist" (118). **SHAWCROSS** (1967): "room, library, compared here to the coffin of the body" (15). **SMITH** (1971): "a study, such as those for the students in Lincoln's Inn" (470). [So also, Carey (1990, 420).] **PATRIDES** (1985): "chamber for study" (214). [So also, Chmielewski [2001, 614].]

3–4 *lett me ly...when I dy.* **EVERETT** (1972): "a life that is for all its narrowness secure and sanctioned by the wisdom of those dead philosophers, historians, and poets who line the shelves of his grave-sized study" (6). **SLIGHTS** (1981): the speaker's "wish to live and die in studious isolation is ironically hyperbolic," for "the images of confinement and death express his awareness of how self-destructive total withdrawal from the human community would be." The "brief characterizations of the authors he reads" are "not entirely admiring, for authors have value through their relationship with reality outside their own minds as 'Gods conduits' or 'Natures Secretary' (ll. 5–6), as chroniclers of other men's deeds or teachers of the body politic" (152–53).

3 *Consorted* **PARKER AND PATRICK** (1975): "a consort is, in one sense, a lover, and the fact that the speaker has forsaken his 'consorts' for a new 'love' meta- phorically consummates his infidelity. This meaning of 'consort' is borne out by such sexually suggestive double entendres as 'fondling,' 'lye,' 'dye,' 'stand,' 'constant,' and 'conduits.' Also clear is the irony of the speaker's denunciation of his friend as 'thou fondling motley humorist' and 'wild uncertaine thee': The speaker is unwittingly describing himself" (12). [Similarly, Corthell (1997, 29).] **ROBBINS** (2000): the speaker portrays "himself as happily 'consorted' with books of theology, philosophy, political theory, history and poetry—though the frivolous friend who lures him out into the town may well be a recognition of another side of the real Donne" (431).

3 *bookes,* **RICHTER** (1902) cites this word to illustrate a stretching of syllables (405).

4 *In prison,...I dy.* **LEGOUIS** (1928) cites this line as an instance of "trisyllabic feet" (86).

4 *In prison,* **HESTER** (1982): the "images of imprisonment, confinement, and banishment" all "convey the scholar's view of the human condition as an imprison- ment and isolation from the source of ultimate spiritual freedom." As such, "when the scholar insists that he shall remain 'in prison' and 'from blisse [be] banished' until death, and wonders aloud how he shall be 'pardon'd [his] offence,' he is invoking the

traditional Christian metaphor for man's condition since the Fall, or, to use Aquinas' term, the 'natural' imprisonment of man's will" (25).

4 *coffind,* **JOHNSON** (1755): "To inclose in a coffin." **MILGATE** (1967): "chest," as in l. 2, often meant "coffin" (118).

5–10 *Here are…of each Land.* **LAURITSEN** (1976): "the private chamber with which the speaker identifies himself is conspicuously the domain of the soul" (122).

5–6 *Here are…the Philosopher,* **TARLINSKAJA** (1976): "the accentual uniformity" of these lines "has been seriously disturbed" (187).

5 *Here are…and here* **MELTON** (1906) cites this line as following the "rule" of Donne's verse rhetoric: "[w]hen a word, a syllable, or a sound, appears in arsis, get it into thesis as quickly as possible, and *vice versa;* having twisted, pressed, or screwed…all the meaning out of that word, take up another and carry it through the same process" (148). For other examples, see *Sat2* 16, 32, 59, 65, 79, and 82; and *Sat4* 2, 23, and 47.

5 *Gods conduits, graue Diuines:* **GRIERSON** (1929): these divines included "Thomas Aquinas and some of the older theologians," but "the majority would be modern controversialists—Spanish, French, Italian, and German," including Bellarmine's *Disputationes de Controversiis Christianae Religionis* of 1593 (xxvi). **MILGATE** (1967): "channels conveying God's Word" (118). **SANDERS** (1971): the speaker's "taste" here in "rather low metaphors" suggests "that his mind is already out in the streets though he isn't" (36).

5 *conduits,* **SMITH** (1971): "pipes, channels" (470). [So also, Patrides (1985, 214), Campbell (1989, 234), and Jones (1991, 626).]

5 *Diuines:* **CHMIELEWSKI** (2001): "theologians" (614).

6 *Natures Secretary, the Philosopher,* **RICHTER** (1902) cites this line to illustrate the occurrence of a double unstressed syllable in the middle of the verse that shows Donne's attempt to overcome the disparity between word accent and verse rhythm (401). **GRIERSON** (1912): "i.e. Aristotle. He is always 'the Philosopher' in Aquinas and the other schoolmen" (2:106). [So also, Grierson (1929, xxvi), Rousseau and Rudenstine (1972, 57), Tomashevskii (1973, 161), Patrides (1985, 214), Campbell (1989, 234), and Carey (1990, 420).] **MILGATE** (1967) adds references to John of Salisbury's *Metalogicon* (4. 7) and Suidas, who first called Aristotle "Secretary of Nature"—i.e. "one acquainted with the secrets of nature." The line should be scanned:

$$/ \quad\quad\quad\quad\quad\quad / \quad\quad\quad\quad\quad /$$
$$/ \ x \quad\quad / \ x \quad\quad x \ x \quad\quad x \ / \quad\quad x \ x$$
"Natures | Secret | 'ry, the | Philos | opher" (118).

SHAWCROSS (1967): "probably the generic meaning is intended, although Aristotle is often cited" (15). [So also, Smith (1971, 470), who adds that "a 'philosopher' might be a natural scientist or even an alchemist, who would be nature's secretary because he handled nature's secrets," Hiller (1977, 176), Craik and Craik (1986, 256), and Jones (1991, 626).]

7–10 *And ioly...each Land.* **CORTHELL** (1997) senses a "comic falling off" from the previous line. Observes that the "inclusion of poetry and exclusion of law treatises would seem to 'consort' the satirist with the 'gentlemen' of the Inns who were interested in advancement by other means than the legal profession" and notes that the poets are "hardly 'constant' company, and in any case one could argue that the satirist is one of them" (30).

7–8 *And ioly...mistique body.* **RUGOFF** (1939): an example of a small group of figures that finds in the human body "elaborate parallels to the organization of society" (177), and thus, the opposite of images finding parallels between the microcosm and the macrocosm. **SIMPSON** (1943) cites these lines as an example of Donne shifting the rhyme "awkwardly from a stressed to an unstressed syllable" (127). **KRUZHKOVA** (1994): these lines refer to a policy (similar to cosmogony) which emphasized the entirety of an object of study, likening it to the human body: a ruler as a head, etc. (154).

7–8 *ty...body.* **RICHTER** (1902) cites the rhymed words of the couplet here to illustrate level stress (409).

7 *ioly Statesmen,* **GRIERSON** (1912): Donne "probably meant 'overweeningly self-confident...full of presumptuous pride...arrogant, over-bearing' (*OED*)" (2:106). [Similarly, Milgate (1967, 118), who also cites Nashe, Works 1:116, and Carey (1990, 420).]

7 *ioly* **KERMODE** (1970): "overbearing" (97). **SMITH** (1971): "presumptuous, showy" (470). **ROUSSEAU AND RUDENSTINE** (1972): "proud, overweening" (57). **PARKER AND PATRICK** (1975): "here read as meaning 'indulging in, or fond of, conviviality and social merriment; festive; jovial (*O.E.D.* I. 4)" (13). **HILLER** (1977): "fine, excellent" (176). **PATRIDES** (1985): "presumptuous; 'wily' (acc. to 1635–69 and a few MSS)" (214). **CAMPBELL** (1989): "splendid (possibly used ironically)" (235). **JONES** (1991): "arrogant" (626).

7 *ty* **MILGATE** (1967): this rhyme with "bodie" [Milgate's spelling]—"a tenth accented syllable with an unaccented eleventh—is an example of what C. S. Lewis called 'Simpsonian' rhyme"; see P. Simpson, "The Rhyming of Stressed with Unstressed Syllables in Elizabethan Verse" (*MLR* 38 [1943]) and Donne's *Storm* 55–56 (118–19).

8 *The Sinews...mistique body.* **RICHTER** (1902) cites this line to illustrate the occurrence of a double unstressed syllable in the middle of the verse that shows Donne's attempt to overcome the disparity between word accent and verse rhythm (401). **LEGOUIS** (1928) cites this line as an instance of "trisyllabic feet" (86). **STEIN** (1942) criticizes Legouis's (1928) opinion that Donne intended the stress to fall on the last syllable (678).

8 *mistique body.* **MILGATE** (1967): as opposed to the physical body of a city ("its houses, streets, etc."), its spiritual body "is its existence as a community of persons, the 'body politic.'" This comparison "to the human body is a commonplace, as is the metaphorical use of 'sinew' as 'the main strength, or chief support' of a society"; see

Holinshed (1587) 3:1343b and Nashe, *Works* 3:271 (118). **SMITH** (1971): "the civic organism as distinct from the physical fact" (470). [So also, Craik and Craik (1986, 256) and Campbell (1989, 235).] **CHMIELEWSKI** (2001): "city as a collection of people, loyalties, and ideas, i.e., the body politic" (614).

8 *mistique* **SULLENS** (1964) notes that the *OED* cites Donne as the earliest source for this meaning of the word as it is found in *ElNat* 4 and suggests that *Sat1* should be cited as earliest (1593?) (251).

9–12 *Here gathering…wild, vncertaine thee?* **MURPHY** (1969): the word "head-long" is an adverb, and its action points to the "I" persona, but Donne also exploits "a syntactic ambiguity of 'headlong' as reinforcing the attributive adjectives of 'wild' and 'uncertaine.' This is a kind of effect dependent upon the new interest in syntactic experiment attendant upon the Senecan fashion" (165–66). **FISH** (1990): in l. 11 the speaker "vows not to leave the 'constant company' of his library; but in the previous line that company is said to include 'Giddy fantastic poets,' an acknowledgement that at once belies the claim of constancy and points once again to the giddiness (absence of stability) of the speaker, who is after all practicing poetry at this very moment." Even the syntax of l. 12 betrays him: i.e., "Who is 'headlong'—that is, madly impetuous—the motley humorist or the speaker who (at least rhetorically) disdains him? Since 'headlong' can either be an adverb modifying 'I' or an adjective modifying 'thee' it is impossible to tell, and this impossibility faithfully reflects the absence of the difference the speaker repeatedly invokes" (236).

9–10 *Here gathering…of each Land.* **JONAS** (1940): "slight verses lasted as long as weighty histories" (204).

9 *Here gathering…by them stand* **LEGOUIS** (1928) cites this line as an instance of "trisyllabic feet" (86).

9 *gathering Chroniclers,* **CAMPBELL** (1989): "historians who gather information" (35). [Similarly, Chmielewski (2001, 614).]

9 *gathering* **RICHTER** (1902) cites this word to illustrate a slurring of syllables (403). **SMITH** (1971): "scavenging" (470). [So also, Jones (1991, 626).]

9 *Chroniclers,* **JOHNSON** (1755): "A writer of chronicles; a recorder of events in order of time." **GRIERSON** (1929): these chroniclers must have included Holinshed, Stowe, Surius, and Sleidan (xxvi). **MILGATE** (1967): "chroniclers who merely gather information [so also, Patrides (1985, 214) and Craik and Craik (1986, 256)], much of it 'trivial household trash,'" as in *Sat4* 97–98 (119).

10–12 *Giddy fantastique Poets…vncertaine thee?* **WIGGINS** (2000): "bringing the list of authors, that 'constant company,' with whom he communes in his 'standing woodden chest' to a close on a comic anti-climax with the 'giddie fantastique Poets of each land,'" the narrator here "fails to recognize his resemblance to the 'headlong, wild uncertaine' companion who lures him into the street against his better judgment" (33).

10 *Giddy fantastique Poets of each Land.* **GRIERSON** (1912): in a letter to Buckingham, who was in Spain, Donne says that his library "is filled with Spanish

books 'from the mistress of my youth, Poetry, to the wife of mine age, Divinity.'" Further, this line "points to the fact, which Donne was probably tempted later to obscure a little, that this first prolonged visit to the Continent had been made before he settled in London in 1592, and probably without the permission of the Government" (2:106). **GRIERSON** (1929): in addition to Spanish poets, there were "doubtless also Latin, Italian, French, and English" (xxvi). **STEIN** (1944c) notes the stress-shift in the first foot (378). **MILGATE** (1967): "the poets come last," which accords with "Bacon's division of learning" (*Advancement of Learning*, 2:4). It is "fruitless" to speculate which poets are meant (119). **BIESTER** (1997): Donne "implicitly joins this giddy company" by writing the poem, "but he insists that his friend repent his own 'giddinesses' before they hit the street." Donne's "own repentance, then—his own escape from giddiness—would be to relinquish the role of satirist altogether, a move he cannot make without abandoning the goal of displaying himself as wit." Thus, Donne "preempts the charge that might be brought against him—in his case, the charge that he is 'fantastical'—by leveling it against himself. It is a brilliant hedge, since it allows him to proceed with the business of self-display" (90). **ELLRODT** (2000): when Donne "speaks lightly" of poets here, it is "the pose expected from a gentleman who will never condescend to print" (350).

10 *Giddy fantastique* **SYMONS** (1916): the phrase shows Donne's contempt for contemporary poetry and his desire to be completely original (94). [Similarly, Woolf (1932, 23).] **CRAIK AND CRAIK** (1986): "wild imaginative. Even the poets are constant (l. 11) in contrast to his visitor (l. 12)" (256). **CAMPBELL** (1989): "capricious fanciful" (235).

10 *Giddy* **SMITH** (1971): "light, capricious" (470). [So also, Parker and Patrick (1975, 13).]

10 *fantastique* **SMITH** (1971): "dealing in unrealities; extravagant" (470).

11–12 *Shall I leaue...wild, vncertaine thee?* **HUGHES** (1968) answers: "Of course, he does," noting that the speaker "shuts the door on his strained-after image (compounded of scholarship, asceticism, and a thirst for quiet) and follows the fledgling courtier." Observes that "Donne in the poem follows the Donne out of the poem" and that "the personality Donne wants to be confronts the personality he might be, as though he recognized that he was a secret sharer of the enemy's position," and thus a "personality begins to separate itself from its creator, and even to look on its creator as the adversary" (22). **ELLIOTT** (1976): "As his companion tries to entice him to leave his study, this scholar strikes the pose of the isolated malcontent who mocks the folly of the world from the safety of his library" (110). **SLIGHTS** (1981): here is "the satirist's problem in its broadest terms: Should he become responsibly involved in human society, or should he detach himself from the corruptions of worldly affairs? Since Donne is writing poetry rather than prose casuistry, he does not pose a formal case of conscience but creates a dramatic situation from which the moral problem gradually emerges," namely, "the satirist cannot simply dismiss his friend" because "he has responsibilities to the busy world of men outside the solitude of the study" (151–52). **HARTWIG** (1995): the "adjectives attributed to the 'thee' who wishes to go out are markedly the attributes of the horse that needs taming and controlling. Given the traditional associations of the rider/trainer of horses as the soul and the horse as the body, the situation is one that undoubtedly has occurred before. Because the speaker/soul knows the resistance of an untrained horse/body to discipline and realizes the necessity to repeat disciplinary lessons, he proceeds to require promises from his companion before accompanying him into the streets" (262–63). NUTT (1999): Donne's "grasp of the dilemma is entirely human and not mere artifice." The satirist "goes on to prick his companion with all the penetration of a needle-sharp pen," for he "recognises from the start that the temptation is real, however severely he castigates him for being weak and shallow" (32).

12 *And follow…wild, vncertaine thee?* GRIERSON (1912): the word "wild" "is possibly an adverb here, going with 'follow'. The use of 'headlong' as an adjective with persons was not common," yet Donne's line is "ambiguous," and "the subsequent description of the humorist would justify the adjective" (2:107). [Similarly, Biester (1997, 91).]

12 *headlong, wild,* MILGATE (1967): the comma "indicates that 'headlong' is an adverb," though it might be read as an adjective modifying "humorist ('thee')"; but the latter meaning seems already implied by "wild uncertaine" (119).

13–26 *First sweare…me, is adulteree.* POWERS (1971) believes that the speaker's evident familiarity with the humorist's foibles makes him guilty of moral weakness in agreeing to leave the study (82–83). BAUMLIN (1991): "the poet neither recognizes nor admits his personal involvement," but instead "with an air of complete self-righteousness, he utters warnings against three possible rivals for the Humorist's companionship, a captain, a courtier, and a justice," and, in doing so, highlights that "language and clothing alike reflect one's spiritual state." Revealingly, the poet himself "wears 'course attire' [l. 47] and, *perhaps* proudly, calls attention to it, his humble clothes proclaiming his difference from the typical courtier and his repudiation of such vain display" (69–70). NUTT (1999): the "three types, soldier, courtier, judge, which Donne uses to illustrate his companion's tendency to wander," ultimately offer the companion "the same thing, preferment." With regard to the "'Captaine' and 'Justice' that gain is even more obviously equated with money" (33).

13–18 *First sweare…dead mens pay.* USHERWOOD AND USHERWOOD (1984): the passage refers to Donne's "experiences in 1596," when he joined Essex's expedition to Cadiz, where he was "surrounded by hardened veterans eager to wreak death and destruction in a Catholic country" and where he learned "the harsh side of military life. Their pay covered necessities, provided that captains were honest, which Donne doubted. Too many made a profit by drawing the pay of men no longer answering their names at roll-call" (1226).

13–15 *First sweare…Thou wilt not leaue me* PARKER AND PATRICK (1975): this command "is the reverse of his initial command: 'Leave mee,'" and provides "a more ludicrous example of the inconstancy demonstrated by the inconsistencies of stanza 1" (11).

13–14 *First sweare...best)* **BIESTER** (1997) remarks that "the sarcasm seems hypocritical" from the author of *Ind* (91). **NUTT** (1999): Donne "knows that even if he wins the assurance, it will mean little" (33).

13–14 *earnest...best)* **RICHTER** (1902) cites the rhymed words of the couplet here to illustrate level stress (409).

13 *First sweare...in earnest* **LEGOUIS** (1928): "Supposing 'earnest' to be normally accented, the line would be, not one, but two syllables short; however, that word rhymes with 'best' [l. 14], and Donne probably wanted his reader to shift the stress to the last syllable" (86). **STEIN** (1942) disagrees with Legouis (1928) that Donne intended the stress to be shifted to the last syllable (678). **STEIN** (1944c) cites this line as an example of stress-shift in the fifth foot (382). **MILGATE** (1967): the line "lacks a syllable, unless the 'r' in 'earnest' is syllabic, and the word is a trisyllable" (119). **WIGGINS** (2000): with "the oath which he makes his companion swear," Donne is "pointedly implicating an earlier self in the self-deceived discourse" of the narrator of *Sat1* (33).

13 *loue in earnest* **PATRIDES** (1985): "'love, here, in earnest' (acc. to 1635–69)" (214).

13 *earnest* **GROSART** (1872–73) explains of the meter here that "even when first written, in e | arnest | would be harsh; but it would be far more harsh at a later date, when pronunciation was more slurring, and when this license of increasing the syllables of a word had greatly gone out" (1:9–10). **SMITH** (1971): "Pronounced as three syllables" (470). [So also, Campbell (1989, 235).]

15 *middle Street* **GROSART** (1872–73): "middle of the street: Latinate, *in media via*" (1:10). [So also, Milgate (1967, 119), Craik and Craik (1986, 256), and Jones (1991, 626).]

16 *spruce* **JOHNSON** (1755) defines as "Nice; trim; neat without elegance." **MILGATE** (1967): this begins a "train of imagery from clothing" that runs through the "gilt armour and lace of the captain" (l. 18), the "velvet garb of the justice" (l. 21), and the "coats of servants" (l. 22) (120).

18 *Bright...dead mens pay.* **CRAIK AND CRAIK** (1986): "shining in gold or silver lace bought with the pay of forty dead men whose names he fraudulently keeps on the payroll" (256).

18 *parcell-guilt* **GROSART** (1872–73): "part-gilded" (1:10). [So also, Milgate (1967, 120), Smith (1971, 470), Rousseau and Rudenstine (1972, 58), Patrides (1985, 214), Carey (1990, 420), and Jones (1991, 626).] **MILGATE** (1967) refers to Thomas Dekker, *News from Hell* (1606), sig. E1v (119–20). **WARNKE** (1967): "clad in armor" (107). **SMITH** (1971): "figuratively with money or literally with showy armour," or "partly guilty" (470). [So also, Hiller (1977, 176) and Campbell (1989, 235).]

18 *forty dead mens pay.* **GROSART** (1872–73): "'dead names' are names which carry no service, the phrase being adopted from the very common custom of carrying

dead men's names on the companies' muster-rolls, and thereby drawing pay in excess of the true numbers" (1:10). [Similarly, Bewley (1966, 168), Kermode (1970, 97), Smith (1971, 470), Rousseau and Rudenstine (1972, 58), Hiller (1977, 176), Patrides (1985, 214), Campbell (1989, 235), and Carey (1990, 420).] MILGATE (1967) says that this practice was allowed "as a recognized perquisite" [so also, Warnke (1967, 107)]; on the abuse of "forging muster rolls," refers to Matthew Sutcliffe, *The Practice, Proceedings, and Laws of Arms* (1593), p. 320. Notes that "forty 'dead pays' would, of course, be grossly excessive" and that references to this abuse are frequent, for "the swindle was too profitable to be quickly stamped out," according to *OED* "dead pay," extending from 1565 to 1663 (119).

19–20 *Nor though…to answer.* PARFITT (1989): one of the "striking" and "recurring concerns" is the Court, "which is returned to naggingly as the example of corruption, condescension and folly" (24).

19 *pert* PATRIDES (1985) (reading "piert"): "pert, dapper" (214). [So also, Chmielewski (2001, 614).] NUTT (1999) (reading "piert"): "an alternative spelling of 'pert' which carried much more negative weight for Donne's age than for ours where it often implied a boldness and audacity which was inappropriate. The word carries none of the connotations of 'cuteness' it has today" (33).

20 *Deigne…to answer.* LEGOUIS (1928): "'courtesie' (in the meaning of 'curtsy') is probably dissyllabic, and 'answer' is accented on the second syllable to rhyme with 'courtier' [l. 19] (reckoned as three syllables)" (86).

20 *curtesy* MILGATE (1967) (reading "courtesie"): pronounced as spelled "Courtsies" in H6, this word "suggests that the line is properly syllabic:

```
    /     x     x  /    x   /      x  x́   /  x
Deigne with │ a nod, │ thy court │ 'sie to │ answer" (120).
```

21–24 *Nor come…and heire.* CAREY (1990): "Courting the son and heir of a great lawyer, in hope of personal advantage," is presented "as a peculiarly disgusting kind of self-abasement," suggesting that *Sat1* (like the other Satyres) "ostensibly engaged in condemnation," but actually projected "unacknowledged desires and ambitions" (xxiii). BATES (1992): the passage "suggests that, in its flattering mode, courting epitomizes fraudulence and dissimulation" (31). WIGGINS (2000): in large measure Donne owed "his introduction into the Lord Keeper's service to his friendship with Thomas Egerton, Junior, with whom he sailed to Cadiz and went on the Islands Expedition." As such, "Thomas Egerton, Senior, and other members of Donne's coterie reading Satyre I would have enjoyed a laugh at Donne's expense (a laugh allowed them by Donne, of course) and recognized the poem as depicting the secretary at a stage of development preceding his achievement of that disabused self-awareness which was an essential qualification for his post" (33).

21–22 *Nor come…14 strong,* FLYNN (2001) cites these lines as an instance of Donne's interest in "judicial abuse," and adds that "this Horatian gibe was directed at Elizabethan types but came short of suggesting that the entire administration of the law and the judicial system were corrupt" (114).

22 *blew-cotes* GROSART (1872–73): "the livery of the lower retainers and servitors, and in especial of those in and from the country" (1:10). [Similarly, Bewley (1966, 169), Milgate (1967, 120), Shawcross (1967, 15), Kermode (1970, 97), Rousseau and Rudenstine (1972, 58), Lewalski and Sabol (1973, 91), Hiller (1977, 176), Patrides (1985, 214), Craik and Craik (1986, 256), Campbell (1989, 235), Carey (1990, 420), Jones (1991, 626), and Chmielewski (2001, 614).] MILGATE (1967) refers to OED "blue," II.5.c, and "blue coat," 2., and notes that twelve or fourteen in a retinue "probably in double file, would show extravagance and ostentation." SMITH (1971): "servants wore blue coats; but so did minor officials of the law, such as beadles" (471).

23–24 *Shallt thou…and heire.* PARKER AND PATRICK (1975): the "final irony is the speaker's admonition to his friend against preparing a speech to court the Justice's 'beautious sonne and heire,' for the whole of stanza 2 comprises the speaker's attempt to 'court' his friend's fidelity within the above-mentioned love context" (11).

23 *Shallt thou…or prepare* LEGOUIS (1928) cites this as one of four lines in the poem (cf. ll. 25, 57, and 103) "consisting each of ten syllables, neither more nor less and which refuse to fall, not only into five iambs, but even into five feet, be they iambs, trochees, pyrrhics, or spondees" (87–88).

23 *Shallt* GROSART (1872–73) reading "Shalt" but noting that the reading is "usually 'Wilt,'" claims "'Thou shalt swear thou wilt not,' is the better English; but 'shalt' expresses the repetition of the oath to him" (1:10).

24 *A Speach…and heire.* STEIN (1944c) cites this line as an example of stress-shift in the first three feet (383). MILGATE (1967): "impressed by the judge's splendour," the humorist "will think of cultivating his son and heir as a way into high society, or as a source of wealth" (see *Sat2* 79: "melting with luxurie"), "or as a potential ward"—all grounds for the heir to seem "beauteous" (120).

25–26 *For better…is adulteree.* LECOCQ (1969): these lines reveal the speaker's feminine jealousy of his inconstant interlocutor (369). MURPHY (1969): the couplet is "a dazzling display of Elizabethan dramatic wit. The endless playing on 'or' and 'and,' applying the phraseology of the marriage service to a casual association of friends with its witty reversals of expected meaning, is a stock in trade of Tudor rhetoric. The bravado of the sexual innuendo is, of course, unmistakably a sign of the new sophistication of the Inns of Court Wits for whom Donne seems to have set the tone. It was calculated to shock. But exploiting syntax to play on drawing 'headlong' into 'wild' and 'uncertaine' pithily isolates unity and diversity in states of being" (166). SANDERS (1971) calls attention to the "thundering stresses" that reveal the "staring exasperation of the speaker" (34). HESTER (1982): "the speaker 'consorts' with the fool in the same earnestness with which he approached his studies, offering him a relationship based on love—and sanctified by Love—in place of the adulterous companionship of whores and faithless courtiers, a relationship correspondent to his own consorting with God" (21). KERINS (1984): by "invoking the idea of marriage,"

Donne both "defines his satirist's defensiveness" and "initiates a subtle descent into physicality" (38–39). **CRAIK AND CRAIK** (1986): "a humorous application of the words of the marriage service" (256). **HARTWIG** (1995): "the requirement of fidelity couched in terms of the marriage vow, suggest[s] that the soul is aware from past experience that the body probably cannot keep a vow of fidelity, but that it is necessary to require a commitment anyway" (263). **NUTT** (1999): "In a witty parody of the marriage vows, Donne demands that his friend eschew all…temptations and remain with him" (33).

25 *For better…or leaue mee,* **RICHTER** (1902) cites this line to illustrate level stress (395–96). **LEGOUIS** (1928): see note for l. 23. **STEIN** (1944b) states that the harshness of this line "may well be interpreted as the result of carelessness or a lapse in technical skill," classifying this line among "the truly worst" (401). **STEIN** (1944c) notes that reading the end of the line as two unstressed syllables followed by two stressed makes it comprehensible (387). **PARKER AND PATRICK** (1975): these "reversals further demonstrate the speaker's inconstancy, as well as his illusory morality" in that the comment "is rendered in a love context, but is now pushed to its most ludicrous extreme," suggesting "a marriage vow." Moreover, the "concept of adultery is simultaneously introduced, subtly emphasizing the marriage motif, and is equated, for the benefit of the wayward friend, with inconstancy" (12). [Similarly, Corthell (1997, 29–30).]

25 *or worse* **GROSART** (1872–73) reading the phrase as "and worse" but noting that it is "usually 'or'" instead of "and," [so also, Patrides (1985, 215)] explains "when you are impressing on one the conditions, as Donne is here, the 'or' is the more emphatic—remember you take me for better or for worse; that is, for worse when the worse comes. 'Or' probably our author's later word" (1:10).

26 *To take and leaue me,* **MILGATE** (1967): "The comma after 'take' in 1633 (and in several manuscripts) brings out the sense: 'to take me, and after that to leave me'" (120).

27–36 *O Monster,…thy deare companee.* **LEGOUIS** (1942): "the humorist who breaks in upon Donne's meditations is no *Puritan* in the ecclesiastical sense of the noun" presented in the *OED*, but "on the other hand the moral sense, first recorded in 1592 (Greene, *Repentance*) does not apply here at all," for "the intruder" is not "'extremely strict, precise, or scrupulous in religion or morals.'" Yet, "we are distinctly told (ll. 29–36) in what his puritanism does consist," namely, "he is socially exclusive," that is, "a snob." Further, "another explanation would consist in constructing *of refined manners* with *puritan,* by ignoring the comma," and as such, Donne "would then have anticipated by nearly three hundred years the only instance in the *OED*" for "'puritans of economic principle,'" and "his meaning would be: 'precisian, rigorist, as regards manners.'" Thus, "if this interpretation is adopted the *yet* before *ceremoniall* would not imply opposition," but "practically, 'always'" (187–88). **HUNTER** (1983): here "an unexpected change takes place: the person addressed is now inconsistently called puritanical, one who judges not by appearance alone but by the wealth which such appearance implies." Furthermore, "such a calculating response is utterly foreign to that of the humorist, both earlier as 'wild uncertaine thee' (line 12), and in the subsequent part of the poem when he makes advances to the outward appearances of everyone whom he meets in the street," and "this being true, one must read (and perhaps print) this section as a long interruption" (110).

27–32 *O Monster,...thy formall hatt.* BRENNAN (1988): "Like any other aspiring courtier, the ambitious writer was expected to keep a sharp eye out for prospective patrons, calculating from whom he might gain the most advantage. He needed to be able to form a rapid assessment of a great noble's wealth, influence and possible response to an unsolicited approach. The young John Donne, already weary of court life, savagely mocked this kind of blatant opportunism" (2).

27–28 *superstitious Puritane ... yet ceremonial man,* ROUSSEAU AND RUDENSTINE (1972): "An excessively fastidious person. The 'humorist' is presented as someone characterized by contradictions—he is a kind of puritan, yet is also 'superstitious' ('Roman Catholic') and 'ceremoniall'" (58). [Similarly, Craik and Craik (1986, 257) and Carey (1990, 420).] NUTT (1999): Donne "chastises" his companion for hypocrisy, "for being puritanical in his readiness to condemn others, yet wholly enslaved to the petty rituals of social practice" (34).

27–28 *superstitious Puritane / Of refind manners,* SMITH (1971): "punctilious purist of courtly etiquette (like Osric in *Hamlet*)" (471). CAREY (1990): "A joke: the 'humourist' is like a Puritan in punctilious conduct, but addicted to ceremony, which Puritans condemned" (420).

27 *O Monster, superstitious Puritane* GRIERSON (1912): "The 'Monster' of the MSS. is of course *not* due to the substitution of the noun for the adjective, but is simply an older form of the adjective. [Similarly, Milgate (1967, 120).] Compare 'O wonder Vanedermast', Greene's *Friar Bacon and Friar Bungay*" (2:107).

27 *superstitious Puritane* HILLER (1977): "over-scrupulous purist" (176). [So also, Patrides (1985, 215), Campbell (1989, 235), and Jones (1991, 626).]

27 *superstitious* MILGATE (1967): "punctilious, over-scrupulous"; see *OED* 3 (120). ROUSSEAU AND RUDENSTINE (1972): "also a term applied pejoratively to Roman Catholics" (58).

27 *Puritane* GROSART (1872–73) explains, "I remove the usual comma (,) after Puritan," for Donne "does not call him a Puritan, but a Puritan of manners; where Puritan is used metaphorically, or for the sake of the paradoxical point, instead of Purist" (1:10). RUGOFF (1939) calls attention to Donne's contempt for extreme religious positions such as Puritanism, adding that the image is used simply as a "symbol of the contemptible" (92). MILGATE (1967): "one who is, or affects to be, or is accounted extremely strict, precise, or scrupulous in religion or morals"; see *OED* 2 (120).

28 *Of refind manners, yet ceremonial man,* STEIN (1944c) cites this line as an example of an extra syllable before the caesura (394). MILGATE (1967): "addicted to ceremony or ritual, precise in observance of forms of politeness"; see *OED*, adj.

2. The humorist is "a 'monstrous' Puritan in his excessive scrupulosity over refined manners, and yet even more in being 'a ceremonial man,'" since ceremonies were abhorrent to Puritans" [so also, Smith (1971, 471) and Chmielewski (2001, 614)]. The line has eleven syllables; "the light second syllable of 'manners,' coming before a marked medial pause, is treated as if it were an extra light syllable at the end of a line:

x /   x   /   x   x   /   x /   x   /

Of re | fin'd man | ners, ‖ yet cer | emon | iall man."

For other examples, see *Sat2* 43; *Sat4* 22, 65, 185, 210; *Sat5* 39, 40, 59; *Metem* 150, 371, 374; *Merc* 5; *TWHail* 1, 16; *ILRoll* 6; *HWKiss* 20; and *BedfWrit* 59 (120–21).

28 *refind* **KERMODE** (1970): "reformed" (97).

28 *yet ceremonial man*, **HILLER** (1977): "nevertheless a lover of ceremony" (176).

28 *ceremonial* **JOHNSON** (1755): "Formal; observant of old forms."

29–40 *That when thou...or prostitute boy*, **MILGATE** (1967) says that there is no intrinsic connection here "between obsequiousness and lechery." Instead, they are "brought together under the general heading of man's sin" by "sleight of hand" (xxiv).

29–32 *That when thou...thy formall hatt*. **ALDEN** (1899) compares these lines to Juvenal III.140ff. (85). [So also, Milgate (1967, 121).] **SLIGHTS** (1981): the speaker's "vivid caricatures...illustrate the need to discriminate between superficial and substantial worth," and "the witty malice with which he compares his friend's calculation of social worth with the practised appraisal of a seedy pawnbroker hits off precisely the confusion of value with cost in both" (153–54).

30 *broker* **MILGATE** (1967): "pawnbroker or second-hand clothes dealer" (121). [So also, Smith (1971, 471), Patrides (1985, 215), Campbell (1989, 235), Carey (1990, 420), and Jones (1991, 627).]

30 *prize* **GROSART** (1872–73) (reading "prise"): "price or set at value" (1:10). **MILGATE** (1967): "appraise" (121). [So also, Smith (1971, 471), Patrides (1985, 215), Campbell (1989, 235), and Jones (1991, 627).] **SHAWCROSS** (1967): "apprise" (15). [So also, Hiller (1977, 177).]

31 *silke and gould* **MILGATE** (1967): emblematic of "extravagance and ostenta-tion in dress," as evidenced by "two centuries" of statutory limitations on "wearing of cloth of gold (one kind of which consisted of gold thread sewn with silk), crimson cloth, velvet, etc."; see M. C. Linthicum, *Costume in the Drama of Shakespeare and His Contemporaries*, p. 144 (121).

31 *rate* **CHMIELEWSKI** (2001): "value" (614).

32 *vaile thy formall hatt*. **CRAIK AND CRAIK** (1986) (reading "raise thy formall hat"): "raise your hat according to due form" (257).

32 *vaile* **GROSART** (1872–73) (reading "raise"): "Stephens' MS. 'vaile'=(nautical) to lower, not the flag, as some writers have said, but the topsails, in token of submis-sion or courteous recognition of authority, the vessel being thus placed at the mercy

of the other. [Similarly, Milgate (1967, 121)]. Hence it was applied metaphorically to any such act. We have the word 'vail' used as above in Marlowe (T. the Great, ii. 1), '…shall vail to us.' So too Hall (Satires, book iii. v.), 'his bonnet *vail'd*.' Probably *'vail'* was our author's variation, set aside on observing the word 'high'" (1:10–11). MILGATE (1967) (reading "raise"): "For the adjustment of this courtesy to the wealth or rank of the person greeted, compare Massinger's *Emperor of the East* (1632), I. ii. 187–92" (121). PATRIDES (1985) (reading "raise"): "'vaile', i.e. doff (acc. to several MSS)" (215).

32 *formall* MILGATE (1967): "rigorously observant of forms, precise, ceremonious"; see *OED* A.8 (121).

32 *hatt.* HILLER (1977): "'hate' (1633)" (177).

33–34 *That wilt…of his owne.* NUTT (1999) finds the humorist "incapable of kindness" except when "he sees the chance for personal gain" (34).

33 *consort* MILGATE (1967): "accompany"; see *OED* I (121).

33 *none,* PATRIDES (1985): "'with none' (acc. to some MSS)" (215).

33 *vntill* MELTON (1906) cites this word to illustrate secondary accent in the prefix "vn-" (87, 95).

34–36 *What Lands…deare companee.* NUTT (1999): the "superstitious puritan" (l. 27) is "incapable of kindness, 'That wilt consort none', unless he sees the chance for personal gain by inheriting their property or property they themselves hope to inherit," and "the logical conclusion of this attitude has the friend's 'companions' all formally leaving their property to him, mimicking the property rights of marriage" (34).

34 *hath in hope,* CHMIELEWSKI (2001): "expectations of inheriting" (614).

35–36 *As though…deare companee.* STEIN (1942) notes that the stress-shift in the last foot of l. 35 results in a feminine ending which is rhymed with a masculine (681). This stress-shift, along with the one in the first foot of the following line, "marches" the rhythm into the following line (684). NUTT (1999): these lines present the "logical conclusion" of the humorist's attitude in the two previous lines, which has his "'companions' all formally leaving their property to him, mimicking the property rights of marriage." Donne "build[s] on the previous accusation about adultery here" and also "turns the criticism into another opportunity for wit where 'deare' is a pun, intimate and expensive" (34).

35 *As though…make thee* STEIN (1944c) cites this line as an example of stress-shift in the fifth foot (382).

35 *companions* RICHTER (1902) questions if "ion" is to be read here as bisyllabic or monosyllabic (404).

36 *Ioyntures,* MILGATE (1967): "a jointure" (quoting *OED* 4), "'strictly speaking, signifies a joint estate, limited to both husband and wife,' though often extended to mean the sole estate of a wife" [similarly, Smith (1971, 471), Rousseau and Rudenstine

(1972, 58), Hiller (1977, 177), Patrides (1985, 215), Campbell (1989, 235), Carey (1990, 420), and Kruzhkova (1994, 155)]. "Donne's usage is strict, as befitted a student of Lincoln's Inn" (121). **SHAWCROSS** (1967): "deeds of co-ownership of an estate, as that given by a wife as dowry" (16). **CHMIELEWSKI** (2001): "joint-tenants" (614).

37–48 *Why shouldst…I confer.* **LEISHMAN** (1951) notes the similarities between this argument, in which Donne deliberately confuses the metaphorical and literal meanings of "naked," and Berni's argument praising debt in *capitolo* (109–10). **CHANDRA** (1991): "There is nothing in common between the nudity of the body and the nudity of the soul: and it may be hard to be convinced that the coarser and ruder the dress, the nearer is man to the blessed state; but the argument proceeds with such a convincing playfulness that we fall in humour with it, and have no choice but to concede, although for the time being alone" (81).

37–47 *Why shouldst…now I weare* **HESTER** (1982): the speaker's "exhortation to his presumptive companion follows another picture of the vanity and clothing of the fool as a form of adultery," and "his exhortation is phrased in terms of the original, present, and final clothing of man." As such, Donne's scholar "envisions luxurious apparel…as a proud flaunting of the very sign of a man's sin and as an adulterous cupidity which disregards the divine order at work in the world, a view substantiated by his depiction of man's natural and unnatural imprisonments in the world," and "thus, the fool's preferences for gaudy clothing, earthly honors, and the company of whores are seen to be the ways he misuses his freedom and chooses to clothe and imprison himself further in sin" (24–25).

37–41 *Why shouldst…naked and bare?* **STEIN** (1944b): in these lines, "part of the harshness is due to the unexpected shock of startling associations" (398–99). **ROY AND KAPOOR** (1969): Donne "satirizes London society for its love of pleasure and indulgence as inspired by the Renaissance," the "satirical comment upon such a state of affairs" emerging from Donne's "concern for virtue." The "intensity" of the lines "does not lie in the apparent obscurity or coarseness of the examples given within brackets but in Donne's realistic criticism of the way of life and his concern for virtue" (98). **EDDY AND JAECKEL** (1981): "the fool's behavior evokes the severity of justice. Unable to be merciful to the point of indulgence, the Stoic persona speaks scornfully of his companion's actions," the "Stoic objectivity toward fellow man, a mixture of justice and mercy," enabling the scholar "in one breath to complain of a fop's smell and in another to stay for his lost sheep" (118–19). **HUNTER** (1983) notes that the speaker "castigates the humorist again, now for his preference for the nudity of sexuality over the 'natural' nudity of virtue, birth, death, and Eden, concluding that God clothed Adam and Eve with skins, which the speaker accepts for himself ('this course attire,' line 47)." Suggests that "leather is indeed a more permanent clothing than cloth but evidently at the moment not fashionable" and points out that "the rhythms of the lines are consciously roughened" (110). **MANN** (1985): the passage "concentrates on the discipline of 'course attire' which can bring the body back into the service of the soul to 'conferre' with God and with the Muses. The speaker first establishes an opposition between body and soul but also stresses their relation. What is needed is acceptance of the body and then discipline which brings body and soul into relation, not simply escape from the body. The ultimate union of body and soul, a point of reference of essential importance for Donne throughout his works, is adumbrated here in the figure of naked 'vertue' as contrasted with the figure of the naked whore (body without soul)" (538). **BREDBECK** (1991): Donne "invokes sodomy not as a specific condemnation of male-male eroticism but as part of a larger attack on undifferentiated debauchery in which 'prostitute boy' and 'plumpe muddy whore' are equivalent—though prurient—terms" (16). **SHERWOOD** (1997) observes that here, "and repeatedly in the letters to Lucy Bedford," virtue is characterized as feminine (71). **MEAKIN** (1998) believes that Donne's "references to male homosexuality or bestiality as we would categorize them today are, without exception, unambiguously negative" and suggests that "the discrepancy among manuscripts and editions in the spelling of the word, 'barenesse' in line 39 is...pertinent here. Is the word 'bareness' or 'barrenness'?" (117). **NUTT** (1999): "Having clearly put his companion's failings on public display, Donne takes a bold step and asks the central question of the whole satire" as "he sets up a strident antithesis, with virtue on one side and his companion (and all he represents) on the other" (34).

37 *Why shouldst...only approue* **RICHTER** (1902) cites this line to illustrate level stress (395–96).

38–48 *But in...I confer.* **ANDREASEN** (1963): "Virtue is simple, bare, and unchanging; it is achieved by conferring with God and with the Muses, reflected in a contemplative life and coarse clothing. But the young rake, however much he may enjoy nakedness at some moments, is as fickle and inconstant as the fashions which he follows" (65).

38 *ranke* **MILGATE** (1967) quotes *OED*, 13—"lustful, licentious"—and 14—"gross, loathsome" (122). [So also, Hiller (1977, 177) and Patrides (1985, 215).]

38 *itchy* **TREDEGAR** (1936): an example of Donne's "unhesitating use of a word unpleasant, unpoetic, but realistic" (170). **MILGATE** (1967): "from 'itch,' an uneasy or restless desire or hankering" (122). [So also, Patrides (1985, 215).]

39 *barenesse* **GRIERSON** (1912), in reaction to the 1633 reading ("barrenness"), states, "'bareness' is the correct reading" (2:107). **HILLER** (1977): "'barrenness' (1633)" (177).

40 *Of thy...prostitute boy,* **LEGOUIS** (1928) cites this line as an instance of "trisyllabic feet" (86).

40 *plump* **SMITH** (1971): "coarse, dull; fat" (471).

40 *muddy* **GROSART** (1872–73) says he has not seen the word "so applied, but it is stronger than the nearest synonym 'filthy'" (1:11). **MILGATE** (1967): "morally impure, 'dirty'"; see OED 7—"with some reference, perhaps, to her complexion" (122). **SMITH** (1971): "foul, gross" (471). [So also, Hiller (1977, 177), Patrides (1985, 215), Campbell (1989, 235), and Jones (1991, 627).] **CHMIELEWSKI** (2001): "cloudy" (614).

41 *Hate vertu...and bare?* **GORBUNOV** (1993): the "naked" virtue here refers to

unchanging spiritual and moral values that always remained for Donne an indispensible condition of the search for the true and strict interpretation of a phenomenon (94).

42–48 *At birthe,…I confer*. **HARRIS** (1960): in these lines, the speaker "absorbs the satyr figure" (191). **SINHA** (1977): these lines indicate, on the one hand, that "their roughness of style may be regarded as just an acceptance of a popular convention: of the current popular notion, arising from the long persisting lexicographical error which confused the English 'satyre' with the Greek *satyros* and ignored its connection with the Latin *satura*, that satire should be loose-jointed, rudely devised, and obscurely and harshly worded," but on the other hand, "there is a possibility" that the roughness "resulted from the dictates" of Donne's "own temper" (56–57). **DOCHERTY** (1986): "Here even nakedness becomes understood in terms of clothing. For nakedness turns out to be not real nudity at all, but a clothing of the soul in bestial skin. The skin, then, as surface or material of the body is itself a representation or image of the soul." There is also a "fundamental confusion of the notion of personal identity in these lines": "course attire" is possibly "the clothing of the scholar, worn by the speaker," but it may also refer to "the bestial skin of the soul of the speaker, the speaker's breath, which is to be revealed in instants of birth and death. To that extent it is, punningly, a 'corps' attire, the body itself" (112). **FORTIER** (1991): "This account of the poet's relation to the Muses is in the context of a contrast between the poet's cloistered existence and the active, somewhat bawdy life of his friend (or double), the motley humourist." In addition, "it is important to note the connection made between our fallenness and our conferring with the Muses, for it is only in a fallen man, a man separated into the ego and the Other, that the Muse comes into being. The Muse, the Other, is part of our fallen nature and therefore, at the same time as she comes bearing gifts, she is ineradicably a part of our discontent, part of our loss, and nothing she can give can ever completely satisfy" (94–95). **LEE** (2001) states that these lines show Donne's purpose in the poem (61).

42–44 *At birthe,…are banished*. **TOLIVER** (1985): the speaker's "'wild uncertaine' friend calculates the worth of each passerby according to the cut of his cloth, though for the speaker himself virtue alone gives satisfaction" (99).

42 *At birthe,…naked are:* **MILGATE** (1967) quotes Job 1.21 (122). **CORTHELL** (1997): the speaker's "detailed knowledge of the world he claims to abhor" contradicts "such worn pieties" as this line (30).

43–48 *And till…I confer*. **ELLIOTT** (1976): "Since he must wear Adam's 'beast skin' anyway, as a poet he will don the beast's robe of the satirist" (111).

43–44 *And till…are banished*. **SHAWCROSS** (1967): "The soul's bliss when divested of the body is contrasted by implication with the body's bliss when naked in intercourse" (397). **KRUZHKOVA** (1994) notes that the same image is found in *ElBed* 33–35, and quotes the lines in Russian (155).

43–44 *vnapparelled…banished*. **RICHTER** (1902) cites these words to illustrate syllabic stretching with past participles (405).

43 *And till…vnapparelled* **STEIN** (1942) notes Donne's use of the dramatic

technique of lightening the last foot of the line by concluding with a polysyllabic word (683).

43 *vnapparelled* **JOHNSON** (1755): "Not dressed; not cloathed." **MILGATE** (1967): "undressed, from the verb 'unapparrell,'" used in *Har* 12 and metaphorically inherent in *Sermons* 6:87 (122). **SMITH** (1971): "Pronounced as five syllables" (471).

44 *banished.* **SMITH** (1971): "Pronounced as three syllables" (471).

45–48 *Mans first...I confer.* **LAURITSEN** (1976): the speaker "perceives the irrevocable and inescapable nature of his bond to his companion just before he succumbs...to his outwardly invisible and inaudible entreaties and plunges with him into the inferno of the street"; the bond that "links the speaker with his companion, soul with body, is the bond of original sin" (122–23). **ZUNDER** (1982): the presence in sixteenth-century England of "conspicuous expenditure—of an increasing prosperity—was not incidental" but was "symptomatic of changes taking place in English society," and "it was part of the long transition from feudalism to capitalism" (11). **NUTT** (1999): "nakedness is in fact a 'blest state' which was undone by Adam and Eve's original sin." Despite his "coarse attire," Donne "is able to communicate 'With God, and with the Muses', we presume by his reading and by prayer. What necessity is there, Donne implies, for anything richer or better; for the gaudiness and excess of the court?'" (35).

45–46 *Mans first...in beasts skin.* **STEIN** (1942) notes the feminine/masculine rhyme caused by the stress-shift in the final foot (681). **PATRIDES** (1985): "as related in Genesis 3.21" (215). [So also, Craik and Craik (1986, 257), Campbell (1989, 236), and Carey (1990, 420).]

45 *blest* **GROSART** (1872–73) (reading "best"): "'Blest' is stronger, as implying the state before the Fall. Man's first state might have been 'best' without being 'blest.'" (1:11). [Similarly, Milgate (1967, 122)].

46 *He lost that,...beasts skin.* **GROSART** (1872–73): the line is "a foot too long, showing either that the transcriber had by an error written y^t as that and yet, or that it was taken from a copy where the author had doubted of his word, and accidentally left both" (1:11). **MILGATE** (1967) quotes Gen. 2.25. "In the state of innocence man was naked. When he lost that he was still clothed only in the skins of beasts. Hence all we need, or are entitled to wear, is 'course attire'" (122). **WOODS** (1984) describes the line as being "mostly iambic pentameter," yet adds that it "cannot be scanned even with great allowance for elision:

    x /   x / x x   /   / x /   x
Hee lost that, yet hee was cloath'd but in beasts skin."

Notes that while an "elision of 'hee was' would rectify the syllabification," no such changes "will render the line iambic" (252). **CAREY** (1990) cites Gen. 3.21 (420).

46 *yet* **PATRIDES** (1985): "(omitted acc. to 1635–69 and a few MSS)" (215).

46 *beasts skin.* **ELLIOTT** (1976): "Donne clearly associates the *satyre* clothed in beast skin of the Greek drama with the satirist" (111).

47–48 *And in this...I confer.* **GUSS** (1966): these lines counteract the argument that Donne "conjoins libertinism with satiric melancholy" (203n3).

47 *this course attire* **SMITH** (1971): "the garb of a scholar or contemplative" (471). [So also, Hiller (1977, 177).] **HESTER** (1982): "The scholar's emblematic defense of his 'course attire' is framed by a picture of the ubiquity of extreme apparel in all stations of Elizabethan society and by his metaphoric view of apparel as either an act of love or a form of imprisonment" (23). **CORTHELL** (1997): the passage suggests "the rough and ready 'satyr' of Elizabethan satire, so there may be an attempt—parallel to the opposition between his clothing and the humorist's—to distinguish satire from 'giddie' poetry" (172n28).

47 *course* **WARNKE** (1967): "coarse" (107). [So also, Patrides (1985, 215).]

47 *attire* **JOHNSON** (1755): "Clothes; dress; habit."

48 *With God and with the Muses I confer.* **COFFIN** (1937): this line indicates Donne's main sources of inspiration. The "muse" is "his earthly mistress" and "religion" his "heavenly" (57). **DANBY** (1950): this line epitomizes the "independence" and "dignity" of the Elizabethan courtier (520).

49–66 *But since...against my conscience?* **SELDEN** (1978): the section is "framed by religious metaphors," and "within the frame is a large empty space, functionless as argument or narrative." In addition, "the two framing sentences and the long inner sentence each begin with 'But'. Within the frame are three illustrative analogies each beginning with 'sooner'. Embedded in the first analogy is a simile," and "the analogies are richly interlinked. The first analogy is structured in three elements: analogy's subject + simile + analogy's predicate. The first element ('cheape whore') is linked by contrast to the second analogy ('Heire to'an India', i.e. to great wealth); the second element ('feathers' and 'hose') is linked by association with the third analogy ('hats', 'ruffes', 'suits'); the third element (bastard with no father) is linked by contrast to the second analogy ('Infant of London'). There is, finally, a fourth linkage—between the first element ('Worne...in sinne') and both parts of the frame ('warn'd of thy sinnes' and 'That thus have sinn'd'). The interweaving of the paragraph's imagery is not merely a piece of rococo artistry but a baroque mixing of styles" (62–63). **SLIGHTS** (1981): the speaker's "ambivalence marks the pivotal second section...where he decides to act. He speaks of penitence and sin in an exasperated but amused voice, for he knows that his lecture is falling on deaf ears and that, while he should not go, neither should he stay" (155). **BAUMLIN** (1991): these "vignettes, intended as social criticism, serve only to whet his friend's desire for such influential companionship. Though the reader recognizes the criticism in the speaker's words, the Humorist sees only the glitter and the prospects for pleasure. The poet's claim that his words have brought repentance to his friend is therefore either thoroughly naive or thinly veiled sarcasm" (71–72).

49–52 *But since...let's go.* **CORTHELL** (1997): the quotation marks provided by

Milgate in his edition (1967) "give us no help in assigning the last speech to the humorist or the satirist, but each possibility seems to work as well as the alternative" (30).

50 *Charitably warnd of thy sins dost repent* **RICHTER** (1902) cites this line to illustrate the occurrence of a double, or extra, syllable in the opening foot that should be collapsed to form a single foot (400–01). **LEGOUIS** (1928) cites this line as an instance of "trisyllabic feet" (86). **STEIN** (1944b) states that the harshness of this line "may well be interpreted as the result of carelessness or a lapse in technical skill," classifying this line among "the truly worst" (401).

50 *warnd* **HILLER** (1977): "'warmed' (1633)" (177). [So also, Patrides (1985, 215).]

50 *sins* **GROSART** (1872–73) (reading "sinne"): "Usually 'sins:' and as penitents as a rule confess their sins, not their sin, and as previously Donne has charged him with no one sin in particular, but with several sins, the plural was doubtless our author's revised word." (1:11).

51 *giddinesses;* **JOHNSON** (1755): "Frolick; wantonness of life."

52–64 *I shut...thou wouldst go.* **KLAWITTER** (1994): "the narrator is dubious about his guide's intentions," for "a whore can better name her bastard's father than can the guide explain where he is planning to take the narrator. A meteorologist may better predict street fashion than can the guide tell the poor narrator his destination" (115–16).

52 *I shut...let's go.* **FISH** (1990): the "claim of difference [between the 'I' and the 'thee' of the poem] is further (and fatally) undermined when the speaker without any explanation decides that he will follow along after all," and "the distance between 'leave me' and 'don't leave' has been traveled in only fifteen lines," and thus the "stutter rhythm of push away/embrace is now instantiated in the poem's narrative as the now indistinguishable pair prepares to exit together" (236).

53–64 *But sooner...thou wouldst go.* **SLIGHTS** (1981): "His friend cannot be trusted because he is nonrational. He does not think about or understand the motives, consequences, or moral nature of his actions. The word of a man who does not think is worthless, regardless of how sincerely the promise is given" (154). **NUTT** (1999) divides this passage into "three examples followed by a conclusion." In the first example of the whore, the "wit depends on the usage of 'Worne' to apply to the clothes and to her use by men, and of course there is the extra sense of something being worn out, which adds to the superior moral tone adopted throughout the poem." In the second example concerning "some unspecified rich London heiress," "'India' is used typically by Donne because of its excess. The "final example of impossible guesses" is "a charlatan who studies the weather to tell the future" (36). This section of the poem then is "a self-mocking recognition of Donne's stupidity in giving in, since the companion immediately shows no sign of either purpose or calm," and Donne is "left stunned by his friend's childish excitability" (40).

53–62 *But sooner...Youths will weare* **ALDEN** (1899) notes that these lines "suggest the similar incidental irony in Juvenal X.219ff." (85). [Similarly, Milgate (1967, 122).] **HESTER** (1982): "This description of matters of considerable spiritual, even divine, significance—the naming of children and the unity of the family, the question of royal succession, and the 'heavens Scheame'—in terms of clothing imagery, the realization that issues rightly reliant on divine guidance have become as superficial as fashions, shows the concern the scholar feels is appropriate towards the adulterous inconstancy typified by the 'motley humorist'" (23–24).

53–56 *But sooner…mongst all those;* **RUGOFF** (1939): the "frankness" and "vigor" of this analogy contributes to the realism of the satire (171).

53–55 *a cheape whore…musk-color hose* **NUTT** (1999): "a whore, so experienced, she has been employed as often as people wear black feathers or musk-coloured (reddish brown) tights to hide the fact that they are dirty" (36).

54–55 *Worne by…musk-color hose* **RUGOFF** (1939): Donne's "interest in the fashion, quality, and condition of clothes reflects something of the life he led as a free-living youth-about-town and, later, as pensioner among courtly patrons." The Elizabethans were "notorious for their adventurous spirit in clothing-fashions," and in these lines, Donne writes "knowingly" of an "empty-headed London dandy" and of whores (120).

54 *by* **PATRIDES** (1985): "'out by' (acc. to 1650–69)" (216).

55 *black feathers or musk-color hose* **SMITH** (1971): "fashions of the day. Musk is a reddish brown or dark purple colour" (417). [Similarly, Hiller (1977, 177), Patrides (1985, 216), Craik and Craik (1986, 257), Campbell (1989, 236), and Carey (1990, 421).]

55 *black feathers* **MILGATE** (1967): "fashionable among gallants around 1593"; see Sir John Davies's *Epigrams*, no. 47 and no. 48 (122).

55 *musk-color* **SULLENS** (1964): Donne's usage of this word is earlier than the earliest sourced cited by *OED* (183–84). **MILGATE** (1967): "apparently a dark shade of brown, does not appear in Royal Wardrobe accounts until the Stuart period"; see M. C. Linthicum, *Costume in the Drama of Shakespeare and his Contemporaries* (1936), p. 14 (123).

57–58 *away…India;* **RICHTER** (1902) cites the couplet here to illustrate impure rhyme (410).

57 *Sooner may…beare away* **RICHTER** (1902) cites this line to illustrate a metrical inversion from iambic to trochaic in the first three feet (395). **LEGOUIS** (1928): see note for l. 23. **STEIN** (1942) notes that the rhythm carries over to the next line as a result of the stress-shift in the third foot (684). [Similarly, Stein (1944c, 383).]

57 *beare away* **MILGATE** (1967): "as a prize; 'win' as ward, or as wife" (123).

58 *Th'infant…to an India;* **GROSART** (1872–73): "Some lost local allusion, corresponding with the 'Child of Hale,' near Liverpool=a giant" (1:11). **NORTON** (1895) acknowledges that he "cannot explain this verse, or the emendation of it in

the edition of 1669, which seems to be rather an attempt to remove a corruption or an obscurity, than a true various reading" (1:240). GRIERSON (1912) (reading "Infanta"): "It is not necessary to suppose a reference to any person in particular. The allusion is in the first place to the wealth of the city, and the greed of patricians and courtiers to profit by that wealth" (2:108), and the phrase "contains possibly, besides its obvious meaning, an allusion to the fact that since 1587 the Infanta of Spain had become in official Catholic circles heir to the English throne" (2:102). [Similarly, Kermode (1970, 98), Smith (1971, 472), Rousseau and Rudenstine (1972, 59), Lewalski and Sabol (1973, 92), Hiller (1977, 178), Craik and Craik (1986, 257), Campbell (1989, 236), Carey (1990, 421), Jones (1991, 627), Kruzhkova (1994, 155), and Nutt (1999, 36).] LEGOUIS (1928) (reading "Infanta") cites this line as an instance of "trisyllabic feet" (86). SMITH (1971) (reading "Infanta"): "Strictly, the Infanta is the eldest daughter of the king and queen of Spain who is not heir to the throne, just as the Infante is the second son and not the heir. But the word was popularly used to mean any young daughter of a noble house and here may just refer to the best marriage-prospect then going in London." No "particular person whom Donne might have had in mind" has been suggested by anyone (472).

58 Th'infant of London, HAYWARD (1950) (reading "Infanta"): "no particular heiress is intended" (99). BEWLEY (1966) (reading "Infanta"): "general reference to the daughters and heiresses of rich London merchants" (170). MILGATE (1967): referring "not primarily to any particular person," but to "the wealthiest heiress (still a minor, and probably a ward) you can think of among the families of the merchant princes of the City"; see John Chamberlain's joking reference to "the Infanta Norreys" in *Letters*, 1:258. Further, Infant (or Infante) "can mean either a princess or prince of Spain" [so also, Patrides (1985, 216)], "and it is possible that Donne himself" used this spelling, which appears in some artifacts, "to make the satiric effect more general by including male heirs" who could "be profitable as wards" (as in l. 24). Thus, Grierson (1912) may well be right "in seeing a secondary reference to the claim of the Infanta of Spain to the throne of England"; see the 1588 bull of Sixtus V confirming the deposition of Elizabeth and naming Philip II as King of England. Roman Catholics recognized the Infanta as heir to the English crown (123). SHAWCROSS (1967) (reading "Infanta"): "the Infanta (princess) of Spain had been advanced as the Roman Catholic heir of the English throne since 1587" (397). WARNKE (1967) (reading "Infanta"): "This may be a specific reference to some wealthy heiress" (108). PATRIDES (1985): "*infant* (acc. to 1633–54 and most MSS): the 'Infante', a princess or prince of Spain; also read as 'Infanta' (acc. to some MSS and most modern editors) and even 'Infantry'! (acc. to 1669)" (216). CHMIELEWSKI (2001) (reading "Infanta"): "an eldest daughter and heir, and thus a good marriage prospect; specifically a Spanish princess, and perhaps an indirect reference to Queen Elizabeth's recent courtship by Phillip II of Spain" (614).

58 heire to an India; SMITH (1971): "stands to inherit vast wealth" (472).

58 India; MILGATE (1967): "vast wealth" [so also, Patrides (1985, 216)]; see Thomas Middleton, *Anything for a Quiet Life*, 4:2, 70–71 (123).

59–64 *And sooner...thou wouldst go.* RUGOFF (1939): the "frankness" and "vigor" of this analogy contributes to the poem's realism (171).

59 *a gulling Weather-Spy* SHAWCROSS (1967): "a deceitful weather forecaster," or "a fraudulent astrologer" (16). [So also, Smith (1971, 472), Rousseau and Rudenstine (1972, 59), Hiller (1977, 178), Patrides (1985, 216), Craik and Craik (1986, 257), Campbell (1989, 236), Jones (1991, 627), and Nutt (1999, 36).]

59 *gulling* BEWLEY (1966): "cheating" (170). [So also, Warnke (1967, 108).] MILGATE (1967) adds "deceptive" (123). CHMIELEWSKI (2001): "deceiving" (614).

59 *Weather-Spy* JOHNSON (1755): "A star-gazer; an astrologer; one that foretels the weather." SULLENS (1964): the *OED* cites Donne as the earliest source for the meaning of this word (257). BEWLEY (1966): "astrologer" (170). [So also, Chmielewski (2001, 614).] MILGATE (1967): "weather prophet" (123). [So also, Chmielewski (2001, 614).]

60–62 *By drawing...will weare* STEIN (1942) observes that placing the caesura near the end of the line starts a new rhythm that flows into the next line (683).

60 *drawing forth heauens Scheame,* GRIERSON (1912): "In preparing his 'theme' or horoscope the astrologer had five principal things to consider, (1) the heavenly mansions, (2) the signs of the zodiac, (3) the planets, (4) the aspects and configurations, (5) the fixed stars. With this end in view the astrologer divided the heavens into twelve parts, called mansions, to which he related the positions occupied at the same moment by the stars in each of them ('drawing the horoscope'). There were several methods of doing this. That of Ptolemy consisted in dividing the zodiac into twelve equal parts. This was called the equal manner. To represent the mansions the astrologers constructed twelve triangles between two squares placed one within the other. Each of the twelve mansions thus formed had a different name, and determined different aspects of the life and fortune of the subject of the horoscope. From the first was foretold the general character of his life, his health, his habits, morals. The second indicated his wealth; and so on. The different signs of the zodiac and the planets, in like manner, had each its special influence" (2:108–09).

60 *heauens Scheame,* MILGATE (1967): "a diagram showing the relative positions, either real or apparent, of the heavenly bodies" [so also, Smith (1971, 472), Rousseau and Rudenstine (1972, 59), Hiller (1977, 178), and Campbell (1989, 236)]. "The astrologer divided the scheme of the heavens into twelve 'mansions,' and from the relative positions of the heavenly bodies in each mansion, from the signs of the Zodiac and the 'aspects' of the planets, he arrived at his predictions"; see "scheme," *OED* 2, and *ElBrac* 59–61 (123).

60 *heauens* RICHTER (1902) cites this word to illustrate a slurring of syllables (403).

60 *Scheame,* SULLENS (1964): Donne's usage of this meaning of the word is earlier than the earliest source cited by *OED* (231).

61–62 *What fashiond…will weare* **BIESTER** (1997): "No one who has seen Donne's melancholy pose…in the Lothian portrait—probably painted in 1595, after the poem was written—can avoid smirking" when Donne offers this question, so that his "indictment of melancholy must be read asquint" (91–92).

61 *ruffs,* **JOHNSON** (1755): "A puckered linen ornament, formerly worn about the neck." **NUTT** (1999): "an elaborate lace collar familiar in the portraiture of the period" (36).

61 *Suites* **MILGATE** (1967): "a matching ensemble of doublet, hose, coat, jerkin, mandilion or cloak"; see Linthicum, p. 212 (123).

62 *supple-witted* **JOHNSON** (1755) reads as "giddy-headed" and defines as "without thought or caution; without steadiness or constancy." **GRIERSON** (1912) (reading "subtile-witted"): "There is something to be said for the 'supple-witted' of H51 and some other MSS. 'Subtle-witted' means 'fantastic, ingenious'; 'supple-witted' means 'variable'. Like Fastidious Brisk in *Every Man out of his Humour,* they have a fresh fashion in suits every day. 'When men are willing to prefer their friends, we heare them often give these testimonies of a man; He hath good parts, and you need not be ashamed to speak for him; he understands the world, he knowes how things passe, and he hath a discreet, a supple, and an appliable disposition, and hee may make a fit instrument for all your purposes, and you need not be afraid to speake for him.' *Sermons* 80. 74. 750. A 'supple disposition' is one that changes easily to adapt itself to circumstances" (2:109). **MILGATE** (1967) reads "subtile-witted" but notes that in the alternative reading "supple" means "compliant" (123). **HILLER** (1977) (reading "subtle-witted"): "'subtle wittied' (1633)" (178). **PATRIDES** (1985): "*subtile-witted* (acc. to some MSS): 'subtile wittied' (acc. to 1633–54 and a few MSS) or 'supple-witted' (acc. to some MSS) or 'giddy-headed' (acc. to 1669)" (216). **CRAIK AND CRAIK** (1986) (reading "subtile-witted"): "fine-witted (with word-play: (1) ingenious; (2) thin)" (257).

62 *antick Youths* **MILGATE** (1967) (reading "antique"): "fantastics," who are "ironically credited with discriminating and penetrating intellects in their pursuit of fashions"; see Lucio in Shakespeare's MM (123).

62 *antick* **JOHNSON** (1755) (reading "antique"): "Odd; wild; antick." **WARNKE** (1967) (reading "antique"): "antic" (108). **SMITH** (1971): "fantastic" (472). [So also, Hiller (1977, 178), Patrides (1985, 216), Campbell (1989, 236), and Jones (1991, 627).] **ROUSSEAU AND RUDENSTINE** (1972) (reading "antique"): "Antic, bizarre" (59).

63 *Then* **PATRIDES** (1985): "than" (216).

63 *departst from hence* **CORTHELL** (1997) notes Milgate's preference for "depart'st from mee" over "from hence," adding that Milgate's reading "*is* better," though "only if the speaker of 'Come, lets goe' is the humorist, since then the satirist's leaving would be in doubt until the lines (65–66) on his conscience" (172n30).

65–66 *But how…against my conscience?* **MILGATE** (1967), "for the idea," cites

Sat4 11–16 (124). **EDDY AND JAECKLE** (1981): "if the humorist represents the body and if the decision to leave the morally safe study is the capitulation of the soul to the lower desires, then the soul must assume full responsibility for the actions of the body on the street" (115–16). **SLIGHTS** (1981): "Since he knows the futility of trying to teach virtue to someone unwilling to think, his decision to go is contrary to his own best judgment. He is guilty of inconsistent, nonrational behavior—ironically the very things he condemns so scathingly" (154–55). **HUNTER** (1983): a "perplexing couplet which must be another aside that the persona addresses to himself," for "in what way has he thus sinned?" (110). **FISH** (1990): "if by conscience he means an inner integrity—an identity that holds itself aloof against all external temptations and assaults—then conscience is what he has not had ever since his first words revealed a mind divided against itself. Ironically, that mind is now unified (if that is the right word) when it accepts (certainly not the right word) its implication in the giddy and the variable, and ventures out into the world to encounter other versions of himself, others who, like him, are 'many-colored' and forever on the move" (237).

66 *sind against my conscience?* **EDDY AND JAECKLE** (1981): because of this phrase, "we know that this sin is done in full knowledge and that it represents a fall from grace," his sin thus "not only a denial of reason in favor of the bodily appetites," but also "an offense against God" (120–21). **STRIER** (1993): here Donne "played lightly with the idea that the unpardonable 'offense' is to sin against one's own conscience" (306). **BIESTER** (1997): this confession occurs after the humorist has both repented and "immediately reverted to his 'giddy' behavior." While "the other's failed repentance casts a shadow over the speaker's own," nevertheless "the confession stands, marking Donne's speaker as witty but not phantastical, capable of recognizing folly for what it is" (91).

66 *conscience?* **MILGATE** (1967): "a trisyllable" (124).

67–108 *Now we are...to his Lecheree.* **SLIGHTS** (1981): this section "is not directly concerned with analysis of the satirist's dilemma but narrates the consequences of his decision. The giddy young man fulfills his predictions. Images of motion chart his unstable progress," and "the satirist describes this cavorting in language that fixes its value precisely, but in action, he restricts himself to witty but largely unregarded jokes at his companion's ignorance and excesses. His images express feelings both of responsibility and of futility" (155–56).

67–78 *Now we are...nighest ground.* **KLAWITTER** (1994): "If we already feel sorry for the victim, we feel even more so when we are thrust with him out of cloistered gentility into the turmoil which follows." The guide's "only mistake" in the street is "taking the protected position: next to the wall he avoids being jostled in the street proper and avoids being hit by offal flying from windows overhead, but he is at the narrator's mercy and cannot exercise the 'libertie' he would like to 'skip forth' to greet 'every fine silken painted foole we meet'" (116–17).

67–70 *Now we are...his Libertee.* **MILGATE** (1967): the humorist furtively takes the place of honor, "the wall side, given in politeness to one's superior"; see "Nashe's gibe at Gabriel Harvey" (*Works* 3:76). The alternative position, nearer to the street, is "the more hazardous, involving the risks of mire underfoot and of refuse thrown from the windows above." The humorist shows care "for his clothes as well as for his dignity," but he acts "improvidently" because his action impedes "his freedom of movement in catching the eye of courtiers, etc." (124). **WARNKE** (1967): "it was customary for the person of higher social rank to 'take to the wall,' that is, to walk as far as possible from the muddy center of the street" [so also, Kermode (1970, 98), Smith (1971, 472), Rousseau and Rudenstine (1972, 59), Hiller (1977, 178), Patrides (1985, 216), Craik and Craik (1986, 257), Campbell (1989, 236), Carey (1990, 421), and Chmielewski (2001, 614).] "The speaker's companion is trying to assert his superiority" (108). **HESTER** (1982): "The full import of the fop's moral myopia is conveyed by the scholar's description of the fool's initial act once they are in the street," and the scholar's "interpretation of the actions of the fool as those of one 'first of all / Improvidently proud' affirms his own view of the necessity of Providence." As such, the dandy's "foolishness" is "not just that he misunderstands the legitimate ends of his use of freedom, but that he is unaware of its source" (25–26). **BIESTER** (1997): the companion "takes to the wall, like a shadow," an act that "gains him status, but at the expense of his 'libertie': just as the speaker began the poem 'in prison' in his small room at Lincoln's Inn, so his *semblable* is now 'imprison'd, and hem'd in by mee' (69–70). Symmetry in Donne is no accident, and his 'shadow' is more a reflection than an Other" (92).

67–68 *Now we are…to the wall* **NORTON** (1895): "Taking the wall side, which politeness assigns to the superior person. Nash, in his attack on Gabriel Harvey, the friend of Spenser, says he made 'no bones of taking the wall of Sir Philip Sidney, in his black Venetian velvet'" (1:240). **NUTT** (1999): "the present tense takes us into the confusion with him. Addressing his companion as 'He' furthers our complicity with the poet and encourages us to enjoy the satire" (37).

68 *Improuidently proud creepes to the wall* **STEIN** (1944c) (reading a comma after "proud") notes the stress-shift after the caesura (378). **SHAWCROSS** (1967) quotes the proverb, "The weakest goeth to the wall" (397). **KRUZHKOVA** (1994): to be closer to the wall was considered a privilege, leading to the expression "to take the wall of somebody"—to take a more honorable position (155).

68 *Improuidently* **JOHNSON** (1755): "Without forethought; without care." **SULLENS** (1964): the *OED* cites Donne as the earliest source for this word (195).

69 *And so…by mee* **STEIN** (1944c) (reading a comma after "imprisond") cites this line as an example of stress-shift after a pause (379).

70 *state* **GROSART** (1872–73) (reading "roome"): "1633 and usually 'state;' also 'high' for 'his.' We have here, in the variations of 'roome' and 'state,' one proof among many that the ordinary text gives the author's own revision of the earlier form as represented by the MS. of 1593. The fellow takes the wall-side as the more honourable, and is thereby closed-in more than Donne, who is on the outside. Hence Donne wrote, 'he sells his liberty for a little room,' using 'room' in the sense of state or station, as he uses it in Progress of the Soul, xl. line 8; but on revision he saw that the word was here so ambiguous that at first sight it expressed the contrary, so he altered

it to 'state'" (1:12). **SMITH** (1971): "status, prestige" (472). [So also, Rousseau and Rudenstine (1972, 59), Hiller (1977, 178), Patrides (1985, 216), Campbell (1989, 236), and Chmielewski (2001, 614).]

70 *his* **HILLER** (1977): "'high' (1633)" (178). **PATRIDES** (1985): "(acc. to 1635–69 and all MSS): 'high' (acc. to 1633)" (216).

70 *Libertee.* **KLAWITTER** (1994): the word is "no doubt a deliberate pun" and "must be appreciated as both 'freedom' and 'suburb'" since Donne would have been "only too familiar with the 'liberties' of London as the playhouses he loved to frequent" (116–17).

71–76 *Yet though...dare not go.* **RAIZADA** (1974): the poet "ridicules the superficial fool who judges everyone by the amount of finery he wears upon his body and does not realize that man was naked in the state of innocence" (101).

71 *skip forth now* **PATRIDES** (1985): "'now step forth' (acc. to a few MSS)" (216).

72 *Euery fine...we meet,* **KLAWITTER** (1994): "if we need any reminder that the men of the day wore cosmetics," this line indicates "they did, and our obsequious guide is so taken with the painted dandies that he stoops lower and lower to greet them, depending upon their rank, the greatest bringing him closest to the ground" (116–17).

72 *Euery* **RICHTER** (1902) cites this word to illustrate a slurring of syllables (403).

72 *silken* **SULLENS** (1964): Donne's use of this meaning of the word is earlier than the earliest source cited by the *OED* (232).

73–76 *He them...dare not go.* **STEIN** (1951): the reader is required to perform the actions described, but "dare" is the only word that "really penetrates far below the surface of the fop's personality" (259).

73 *He them...smiles allures* **LEGOUIS** (1928) cites this line as an instance of "trisyllabic feet" (86).

73 *them* **HILLER** (1977): "'then' (1633)" (178). **PATRIDES** (1985): "(acc. to 1635 and the MSS): 'then' (acc. to 1633)" (217).

73 *with amorous smiles allures* **B. SMITH** (1991): "The guide's way with the people he meets has a distinctly sexual edge" (175).

73 *amorous* **RICHTER** (1902) cites this word to illustrate a slurring of syllables (403).

74 *smacks,* **SULLENS** (1964): Donne's use of this meaning of the word is earlier than the earliest source cited by the *OED* (234). **MILGATE** (1967): "his lips, as a sign of relish or anticipation" (124). [So also, Craik and Craik (1986, 257) and Carey (1990, 421).]

74 *shruggs,* JOHNSON (1755): "To express horror or dissatisfaction by motion of the shoulders or whole body."

74 *itch* MILGATE (1967): "hankering" (124).

75–76 *As Prentices,…dare not go.* RUGOFF (1939): Donne's images taken from the family are "limited" and leave Donne "unmoved" imaginatively (170–71). NUTT (1999): "the companion's impatience is compared to apprentices or schoolboys who are trapped in their place of work, knowing there is some exciting activity they are missing outside" (37).

75 *Schooleboyes* JOHNSON (1755): "A boy that is in his rudiments at school."

77–78 *And as fidlers…nighest ground.* MORRIS (1953): the words "lowest," "most," "highest," and "nigh'st" are "all connected by assonance" and are also "doubly drawn to their opposites in meaning by position and vowel-assonance" (60). NUTT (1999): "as a violinist has to stop the string at the lowest position on the fingerboard to reach the highest note, so his friend bends lowest to the grandest people they meet" (38).

77 *And as fidlers…higest Sound* RICHTER (1902) cites this line to illustrate a metrical inversion from iambic to trochaic in the first two feet (395). STEIN (1944c) (reading a comma after "lowest") cites this line as an example both of stress-shift in the first foot carrying over to the second (382) and of an extra syllable before the caesura (394). MILGATE (1967) quotes Sidney's *Arcadia* in *Poems* (1962), ed. Ringler, p. 81 (124). SHAWCROSS (1967): "a fiddler bends over as he fingers high notes" (397). PATRIDES (1985): "Since a viol de gamba is held upright, the stops for high notes are literally positioned lowest" (217). [So also, Craik and Craik (1986, 257) and Campbell (1989, 236).]

77 *stop lowest* SMITH (1971): "stop the string at the lowest fret" (472). [So also, Hiller (1977, 178) and Chmielewski (2001, 614).]

77 *stop* SULLENS (1964): Donne's use of this meaning of the word is earlier than the earliest source cited by the *OED* (235).

78–79 *most braue…graue man* ROUSSEAU AND RUDENSTINE (1972): "Finely dressed," and contrasting with "grave" ["graue"] (l. 79), the latter meaning "not only serious or sober, but also plainly or simply dressed" (59).

78 *So to…ground.* SHAWCROSS (1967): "he is the most subservient to the most superior people" (397).

78 *most braue* MILGATE (1967): "finely dressed, resplendent" (124). [So also, Smith (1971, 472), Hiller (1977, 178), Patrides (1985, 217), and Jones (1991, 628).] NUTT (1999): the description "does not imply physical or moral courage here, but something akin to brashness or showiness" (38).

78 *stoopes* HILLER (1977): "'stooped' (1633)" (178).

79–82 *But…king of Spayne to you.* NORTON (1895): "The horse was named Morocco, and Hall in his *Satires*, book iv, sat. 2, couples the mention of him, as here, with that of an elephant, as if there had been one exhibited about the same time" (1:241). **ATKINS** (1934) quotes a description of Banks' horse from R. Chambers' "Domestic Annals of Scotland" (1596): "By a sign given him, he would beck for the King of Scots and for Queen Elizabeth, and when ye spoke of the King of Spain, would both bite and strike at you" (40). [Similarly, Smith (1971, 472), Rousseau and Rudenstine (1972, 59), Lewalski and Sabol (1973, 93), Hiller (1977, 179), Freeman (1978, 128), Craik and Craik (1986, 257), and Carey (1990, 421).] **HARTWIG** (1995): Donne's reference here "is more than an isolated topical allusion," for it "enhances the reading of the 'motley humorist' and speaker's contest as 'a debate' between the body and soul because the horse and rider are traditionally associated with body and soul in discussions of their natures" (262–63). **NUTT** (1999): Donne's "friend seems incapable of even noticing those Donne regards with some respect." Consequently, Donne "compares him to a performing horse, immobile unless instructed to move, and to elephants and apes which would respond to the King of Spain's name with the same incomprehension as any other. At a time when explorers were just beginning to return from America and the East, not only with tales of strange beasts and sights, but with the real things, exhibitions of exotic animals (and peoples) were very popular in Elizabethan London" (38).

79 *graue man* **ZUNDER** (1982): Donne places this person "against the companion and the other characters as a positive figure combining rank with personal worth, and age. And, throughout the poem, he implicitly affirms the traditional values violated by the companion" (11). **WIGGINS** (2000): this person, "ignored by the speaker's superficial companion in favor of more fashionable passersby, suggests Egerton" (25).

79 *graue* **SHAWCROSS** (1967): "soberly dressed" (17).

80–85 *Then the wise…dances so diuinely.* **PARKER AND PATRICK** (1975): "The animal figures are immediately followed by a dancing youth, whom the humorist joins in dancing, and a reeking tobacco smoker, with whom the humorist briefly confers," the speaker thus equating "the behavior of the humorist and his low companions with the animals" (12).

80–82 *Then the wise…king of Spayne to you.* **HESTER** (1982): the humorist's "actions are 'falls' and moral suicide is substantiated by the scholar's comparison of the fop's gestures to specific animals." While "these allusions are to animals that actually performed in London in the early 1590s," they also show in the context of the poem that "the fool's 'stoops' violate the orderly Chain of Being." As such, "instead of distinguishing him from the animals, by illustrating his intellectual superiority, the clothing of the fool and his attitude towards the clothing of others illustrate his inferiority to 'the wise politique' animals to which he is compared." Thus, "the scholar objects not to any faults latent in the animals themselves, but only to the fool's likeness or dissimilarity to creatures below his own ordained station." Consequently, the comparisons show that "even the horse, the elephant, and the ape are more sensible than the fool" in that "the animals to which the scholar compares the fool identify the precise virtues that the fool lacks." As an example, the elephant is "pictured in emblem books as a reminder of the necessity of man's humility," and "the contrast between the fool's constant bowing before 'the most brave' and the elephant's refusal to bow upon hearing the name of the villainous 'King of Spaine' emphasizes emblematically the fop's misplaced devotion." Similarly, "the horse is a symbol of loyal service," and "certainly, no quality is more evident in the fool than disloyalty—unless it is his propensity to ape the manners and dress of an affected courtier." The ape, as perhaps the "most frequent subject from the animal world appearing in emblem books," usually serves "as a reminder of man's specific place in the divine design and man's ability to imitate the creativity of God through moral recreation of himself. Considered the most intelligent and the most like man himself, the ape is seen as emblematic of man's imaginative and creative powers, his propensity for imitation, his powers of creation that render him most God-like" (26–28). **KRUZHKOVA** (1994): such contemptuous name-calling, addressed to Spanish monarchs or Roman popes, existed in 1592 as an innocent, if buffoonish, entertainment amongst patriotic Londoners (155).

80–81 *the wise politique…Elephant or Ape* **GRIERSON** (1929): these topical references show Donne's "familiarity with the London of 1594–96" (xxv). **CAREY** (1990): "Well-known performing animals in Donne's London, trained to bow at Queen Elizabeth's name but not the King of Spain's" (421). [So also, Chmielewski (2001, 614).]

80 *Then the wise…hertofore* **LEGOUIS** (1928) cites this line as an instance of "trisyllabic feet" (86).

80 *Then* **PATRIDES** (1985): "than" (217).

80 *the wise politique horse* **GROSART** (1872–73): "Banks' horse Morocco (a horse alluded to by almost every writer of the day)" (1:12). [So also, Grierson (1929, xxv), Hayward (1950, 100), Milgate (1967, 124), Shawcross (1967, 17), Smith (1971, 472), Patrides (1985, 217), and Campbell (1989, 237).] **MILGATE** (1967) cites and summarizes other allusions to this animal, collected by S. H. Atkins (*N&Q*, 21 July 1934), and quotes Nashe's *The Unfortunate Traveller* (*Works*, 2:230) (124).

80 *politique* **MILGATE** (1967): "sagacious, diplomatic" (124).

81–82 *O Elephant or Ape…king of Spayne to you.* **GROSART** (1872–73): "This couplet not in 1633" (1:12). **MILGATE** (1967): "The wise politique editor of 1633 omitted these two lines, perhaps fearing that they would give offence, by recalling the King's journey to Spain in 1623 as a prospective suitor of the Infanta. The lines were added in 1635, probably from O'F (which similarly reads 'ô')" (125). [Similarly, Patrides (1985, 217).]

81 *O Elephant or Ape* **GRIERSON** (1912): "the Ape and Elephant seem to have been animals actually performing, or exhibited, in London about 1594" (2:101). [So also, Hayward (1950, 100), Warnke (1967, 108), Smith (1971, 473), and Patrides (1985, 217).] **GRIERSON** (1929): the performing ape "would come over the chain for a mention of the Queen" but would sit still "for the Pope and the King of Spain" (xxv). **MILGATE** (1967), on the elephant, cites Sir John Davies' epigram no. 47,

"In Dacum" and Jonson's *Every Man out of his Humour* 4:6, 60–61. Quotes Joseph Hall, *Virgidemiarum* 4:2, 93–95; William Basse, *Poetical Works* (1893), p. 336; and Sir Thomas Browne, *Vulgar Errors* 3:1. Notes that Donne is "the only writer to refer to this response by the elephant to the name of the King of Spain." As for the ape, this "was also well known"; quotes Jonson, *Bartholomew Fair* in *Works*, 6:13 and cites Nashe, *Works* 3:37 (125). [So also, Smith (1971, 473).] SHAWCROSS (1967): Banks added these to his act from 1594 (17).

83–112 *Now leapes...keepe his bed.* SINHA (1977): "The conversation begins abruptly and continues eliptically, broken and interrupted here and there, throughout the whole elaborate, studied rhetorical apparatus. Here it would be useful to remember that classical satire, as it was descended from oral genres, was still in Augustan Rome designed to be recited in public arcade or forum and was probably energetically dramatised as the speaker gave his lines" (62).

83–104 *Now leapes...So is the pox:* LEISHMAN (1951) cites these lines as evidence that *Sat1* is "much more dramatic than most Elizabethan satires" (110). EVERETT (1986): "the voices of the two friends intertwine to the point at which their identities are confused, despite the fact that their roles are in theory so far apart" (4). CORTHELL (1997) cites these lines as evidence of the "weak witticisms" that the speaker uses to support his "moral superiority." They "lack the moral punch we might expect after the buildup in the first half of the poem" and function chiefly "to reinforce the scholar-satirist's superiority and detachment, not to exercise charity or to instruct the humorist" (31).

83–98 *Now leapes...the best conceit.* POST (1999): this passage "is meant to convey the city's seaminess: its smells, its licentiousness, its strange sights, including the silly sartorial habits of a stray fop," and is also intended "to convey the poet's extraordinary agility, not just in his momentary asides and triumphs over his boorish companion, but in his thorough flouting of poetic convention: in the interpolated 'dance' of dialogue" (7).

83–93 *Now leapes...Leaues him and me:* KLAWITTER (1994): "In this segment of the satire the drama is quite visual: the guide sees a young man and preciously notes him as 'hee that dances so divinely.' This is mincing language, and there seems little doubt that Donne thus effeminizes the guide who, as if the chatter were not enough, breaks out in a dance right on the street much to the surprise and chagrin of the student-narrator" (117–18).

83–87 *Now leapes...We went:* BRADFORD (1917) cites these lines to illustrate Donne's comic use of dialogue (87). STEIN (1951) notes that the fop's speech illustrates his character (258). STEIN (1962) cites these lines as an example of Donne creating a scene by using sound in a way that is "suggestive and interpretative" rather than imitative (39–40). HARTWIG (1995): "The horse rearing, as in 'Now leaps he upright,' is bound to 'jogg' the rider, if we follow through with the associations of the body/soul = horse/rider reading of the poem." Training a horse as Banks trained Morocco is "a tedious, repetitive labor," and "essential to this kind of training is the endless patience and persistence of the trainer to repeat reward and punishment in the face of the horse's resistance to obedience." Nonetheless, the horse, once trained, is "totally reliable to do what the trainer asks it to do." Similarly, the soul "has spent many hours training the body to obey its commands, and in this passage, which is an actual present dialogue between the 'I' and the 'you,' this training manifests itself in the obedience of the 'You' to the command and shaming technique of the 'I'" (265–66).

83–86 *Now leapes…here for company?* POWERS (1971) cites these lines as evidence of Donne's use of farce in the Satyres (115). KERINS (1984): "Donne's satirist now becomes a courtly sophisticate, deflating the folly of his energetic companion with the easy grace of a languid quip." At this point, "the action and most of the dialogue belong to the humorist," and "the wit is epigrammatic." The humorist exhibits "his follies both in words and actions only to be disarmed by a nonchalant retort, the kind of casual elegance which defines both speaker and gull" (40). NUTT (1999): the reader is "encouraged to see with Donne's eyes as his friend 'leaps' with excitement on spotting a young man apparently renowned for his dancing. The use of dialogue here, and elsewhere in the poem, reinforces our sense of immediacy and complicity with the poet. It is as though Donne is speaking directly to us, an invisible third, as he walks along with his frantic companion" (38).

83 *Now leapes he vpright, ioggs me, and cryes do you see* LEGOUIS (1928) cites this line as an instance of "trisyllabic feet" (86). MORRIS (1953) cites this line as an example of a non-decasyllabic line (43).

83 *ioggs* JOHNSON (1755): "To push; to shake by a sudden impulse; to give notice by a sudden push." MILGATE (1967): "nudges" (125).

85–86 *Oh sayd I…here for company?* FISH (1990): "The fiction that it is not he but his fickle companion who refuses to stand still is rhetorically maintained by the distinction of pronouns" (237).

86 *Stand still,…for company?* ALLEN (1965): "his embodied Humour is urged not to dance in the street" (110n110).

87–105 *We went:…and qualities.* BAUMLIN (1991): "Yielding to the courtier's own 'clothed' and hypocritical language, Donne's speaker, like Horace, now attempts to beat the Humorist at his own game of ironizing and wordplay," such that the poet's words "have become offensive weapons, bristling with punning sarcasm. Significantly, though, they have no effect on the Humorist" (75).

87–90 *He droopt:…trewly I do.* NUTT (1999) notes that although Donne "condemns" the smoker, his "words fall on deaf ears, other than ours" (38).

87–89 *till one…Mett vs:* KERMODE, FENDER, AND PALMER (1974): "There were many attacks on tobacco in the period, not least because it was very expensive. It cost threepence for a little pipe if you went in [and] bought it at a tobacconist's," and thus, "it was a piece of conspicuous consumption which was much deplored and soon James I wrote a pamphlet against it. This is again very modish. Tobacco had only come in about twenty years earlier and the fashion is being attacked" (62–63).

87 *He droopt: We went:* COUSINS (1979): as illustrated here, "the second half of

the poem is a series of epigrams. The scholar parades his gift for improvised belittlement, even briefly sketching its success in reducing the Fool," each encounter being "presented in a crisp, self-contained epigram which raises the scholar as it depresses the Fool" (103).

88 *drinking his Tabacco* **GROSART** (1872–73): "the common phrase for smoking" (1:13). [So also, Bewley (1966, 170), Hiller (1977, 179), Craik and Craik (1986, 257), and Carey (1990, 421).] **NORTON** (1895) notes, as a contemporary example, Ben Jonson's *Every Man in his Humour* (3.2) (1:241). **LEGOUIS** (1942): this instance predates the earliest mention in the *OED*, "sense 5 = 'draw in or inhale,' first recorded in 1598 (B. Jonson, *Ev. Man in Hum.*)" (185). [So also, Sullens (1964, 212).] **MILGATE** (1967) observes that "there are only two references definitely earlier than Donne's here to tobacco prepared for smoking (1588, 1589). 'Drink' is the usual word" (125). [So also, Carey (1990, 421).] **SMITH** (1971) "Tobacco was introduced into England in 1565 but not smoked until Raleigh acquired an Indian pipe in 1586. Its proper use was for years a matter of avant-garde dispute, and writers speak more often of drinking tobacco than of smoking it" (473). **PATRIDES** (1985): "thought at the time to be intended for drinking, not smoking" (217). **CAMPBELL** (1989): "before the smoking of tobacco became fashionable, it was used (like tea leaves) for making a hot drink" (237). [So also, Chmielewski (2001, 614).] **KLAWITTER** (1994): "only two references to tobacco used for smoking purposes are earlier than Donne's, so we can surmise that the practice was new and thus appropriate for the environs of the Inns where social experimentation would be common. 'Drinking' tobacco was the ordinary phraseology, but its effect was as much external as internal since the poor narrator lets us know how offensive the smoker smelled" (117–18).

89 *I whisperd let vs go:* **GRIERSON** (1912) (reading "let'us" for "let vs"): "Donne's use of colloquial slurrings must be constantly kept in view when reading especially his satires. They are not always indicated in the editions: but note l. 52" (2:109).

90 *smell* **GROSART** (1872–73): "the frequent allusions to this in Elizabethan times are very extraordinary," and he then cites Marston's *Antonio and Mellida* (II.i.55–58) (1:13).

92 *many colord* **JOHNSON** (1755): "Having many colours." **SULLENS** (1964): Donne's use of this word is earlier than the earliest sourced cited by the *OED* (183).

93 *Sheepe* **PARKER AND PATRICK** (1975): "emphasizes the speaker's spiritual preoccupation, again expressed in priestly terms. 'Sheep' functions ironically as well, for the speaker follows the humorist like a sheep; the sheep should, of course, be following the shepherd" (12). **BLISSETT** (2000): Donne's speaker "combines exasperation with responsible care" for his "lost sheep" (111).

95–98 *Saying,...the best conceit.* **CRAIK AND CRAIK** (1986): "The last-encountered man is reputed to have the best judgement (conceit) of any courtier in his inventiveness (device) as to lace, decorative holes (pink), strips (panes), ruff-crimpings (print), slashes (cut) and pleats, by way of beautifying (handsoming) an outfit (suit)" (257).

95 *all repute* CHMIELEWSKI (2001): "everyone esteems" (614).

95 *all* HILLER (1977): "'s'all' (1633)" (179).

95 *repute* MILGATE (1967): "esteem, value" (125). [So also, Shawcross (1967, 17) and Patrides (1985, 217).] HILLER (1977): "consider" (179).

96 *deuise* MILGATE (1967): "faculty of devising, inventiveness, ingenuity" (125). SMITH (1971): "invention" (473). [So also, Patrides (1985, 217), Campbell (1989, 237), and Chmielewski (2001, 614).] ROUSSEAU AND RUDENSTINE (1972): "Ingenuity" (60). HILLER (1977): "resourcefulness" (179).

96 *handsomming* JOHNSON (1755): "To render elegant or neat." MILGATE (1967) refers to *OED*, v. "handsome," meaning "to make handsome, or becoming, to beautify or adorn" (125). [So also, Shawcross (1967, 17), Smith (1971, 473), Hiller (1977, 179), Patrides (1985, 217), Campbell (1989, 237), and Jones (1991, 628).]

96 *sute,* JOHNSON (1755): "Cloaths made one part to answer another."

97 *To iudge...or pleight,* MORRIS (1953) cites this line as an example of "an 'overloading' of the line with stressed syllables" (47).

97 *pink, panes, cutt, print, or pleight,* ROUSSEAU AND RUDENSTINE (1972): "'pinke': decorative eyelet on a garment; 'panes': strips of cloth joined to make a single piece; 'print': shaped pattern of neck-ruff pleats; 'plight': pleat" (60).

97 *pink, panes, cutt, print,* GROSART (1872–73): the word "pink" equals "eyelet-holes"; the word "panes" equals "slits or openings, through which the net lining was seen or pulled out"; and "the instances are common which prove that 'in print' meant in regular or apple-pie order." But the word as used here, and "its cognate use as meaning impressions of various kinds, and some of the examples where it is used in speaking of ruffs," suggest that it "meant such frilling or crimping as is done with an Italian iron." When, for example, "Bp. Earle, in his *Microcosmography,* speaks of the preference of the Puritan dame for small Geneva print," he intends not so much the "regularity" as "the small and formal frilling they wore, in opposition to the large crimpings of people of fashion." Since "regularity was an essential in ruffs, and could only be attained by a machine 'print' or impression," the "general sense of exactness and precision is more likely to have been taken from such printing than from the regularity of type over manuscript" (1:13). [Similarly, Milgate (1967, 125), who quotes Jonson, *Cynthia's Revels,* 5:4.298, and W. C. Linthicum, *Costume in the Drama of Shakespeare and his Contemporaries* (1936), pp. 153–54, Smith (1971, 473), Hiller (1977, 179), Patrides (1985, 218), Campbell (1989, 237), Carey (1990, 421), and Jones (1991, 628).]

97 *pink,* SHAWCROSS (1967): "an ornamental, somewhat scalloped pattern" (17).

97 *panes,* JOHNSON (1755): "A piece mixed in variegated works with other

pieces." **MILGATE** (1967): "strips of cloth [so also, Shawcross (1967, 17) and Patrides (1985, 218)] joined to make one cloth, sometimes with lace or other trimming material inserted in the seams; or strips of the same cloth distinguished by colour or separated by lines of trimming; or strips made by slashing a garment lengthwise to expose fine lining or an undergarment: used often in sleeves and breeches"; see W. C. Linthicum, *Costume in the Drama of Shakespeare and his Contemporaries* (1936), pp. 172 and 205 (125–26). [So also, Smith (1971, 473).] **CAREY** (1990): "panels" (421).

97 *cutt,* **MILGATE** (1967) quotes *OED* III. 16: "fashionable shape," or, "more probably, 'slash, incision into the edge of a garment for ornament' (*O.E.D.* IV. 19)," as in *Ado,* 3.4.19 (126). **SMITH** (1971): "a slash" (473). [So also, Hiller (1977, 179) and Campbell (1989, 237).]

97 *print,* **MILGATE** (1967): "Applied to the exact crimping, goffering, or set of the 'plaits' or pleats of the neck-ruffs then worn; used also of other pleated garments. 'To maintain a "spruce ruff" or one "starched in print" the wearer must carry his head straight and avoid damp' (Linthicum, p. 160)" (126).

97 *pleight,* **MILGATE** (1967): "pleat, either of ruffs, or of other garments, such as French breeches"; see W. C. Linthicum, *Costume in the Drama of Shakespeare and his Contemporaries* (1936), p. 205 (126). **SHAWCROSS** (1967) adds, "condition (of the clothes)" (17). [So also, Patrides (1985, 218).]

98 *Court* **PATRIDES** (1985): "'towne' (acc. to a MS)" (218).

98 *to haue the best conceit.* **MILGATE** (1967): "to have the best notion of judgement" in matters of "style in those days of various and swiftly changing fashions"; see the opening speech in George Chapman, *All Fools,* 5:2 (126).

98 *conceit.* **SMITH** (1971): "idea, conception" (473). [So also, Patrides (1985, 218), Campbell (1989, 237), and Jones (1991, 628).] **HILLER** (1977): "judgment" (179). [So also, Chmielewski (2001, 614).]

99 *Our dull…let him go.* **WIGGINS** (2000): the narrator "is completely unaware that his own poetic discourse resembles nothing so much as stage comedy and, in fact, derives its strength from the resemblance" (34).

99 *Our dull Comedians want him:* **MILGATE** (1967): this "sartorial expert would be a godsend to actors"; see *Sat4* 180–85, "where courtiers sell their cast-off Court clothes to the Theatre" (126). [Similarly, Rousseau and Rudenstine (1972, 60).] **HILLER** (1977): "i.e. they need him for their repertoire" (179). **CRAIK AND CRAIK** (1986): "Our actors need him to brighten up their wardrobe" (257).

99 *dull Comedians* **SMITH** (1971): "comic actors who relied on outlandish clothes for laughs" (473). [So also, Patrides (1985, 218) and Campbell (1989, 237).]

99 *Comedians* **SHAWCROSS** (1967): "those interested only in the amusing, unserious, make-believe side of life" (17). **CHMIELEWSKI** (2001): "comic actors; unwanted clothes of courtiers were a source of costumes for the theater" (614).

100–04 *But oh…So is the pox:* **GROSART** (1872–73): "I find a difficulty in the allocation of the different parts of the dialogue. 'I reply'd' shows that 'he doth seem...Italian' is spoken by the Macaron. Hence I take it that 'Why?' is most probably the absent and unattending exclamation of the same, who is intent on his courtesy to the stranger; 'He hath travelled long?' the query of Donne; the 'No, but' part of the Macaron's answer, 'No, but he doth seem,' &c.; while the phrase 'to me...none' is Donne's parenthetical clause, meaning [said he] to me, which understood none of these things, or as humorously explanatory of his pretended blunder—So is the pox—[said he] to me, which understood not his affected lingo" (1:13–14). GRIERSON (1912): "I divide the speeches thus:—

> Donne. Why stoop'st thou so?
> Companion. Why? He hath travail'd.
> Donne. Long?
> Companion. No: but to me (*Donne interpolates* 'which understand none')
>   he doth seem to be
>   Perfect French and Italian.
> Donne. So is the Pox.

...But it seems to me that these words have no point unless regarded as a sarcastic comment interpolated by Donne, perhaps *sotto voce*. 'To you, who understand neither French nor Italian, he may seem perfect French and Italian—but to no one else.' Probably an eclectic attire was the only evidence of travel observable in the person in question" (2:109–10). [So also, Milgate (1967, 126).] ALVAREZ (1961) cites these lines as evidence of the "rigorous, independent and sane" masculinity of the voice in which Donne objected to contemporary poetry (124). SANDERS (1971): "The mimicry is not directed merely at the satiric butts, but also at the satirist whose fat, phlegmatic complacency is elegantly caught in that last 'knock-down' retort. The raconteur is unconsciously dramatising himself—as in the earlier spluttering tirade against the inconstancy of the 'humorist'" (34).

100 *But oh...stoopst thou so?* CRAIK AND CRAIK (1986): "Donne ironically pretends to think that his companion is doubled up with pain" (257).

100 *But oh God strengthen thee,* HESTER (1977c): "the scholar's patience is often tested to the point of outrage and disgust with the fop's sins" (188).

100 *stoopst* MILGATE (1967): the humorist, "as in l. 78, is bowing obsequiously, forgetting again the injunction of the satirist (ll. 49–51); hence, 'God strengthen thee'" (126). SMITH (1971): "bow and scrape" (473). PATRIDES (1985): "'stopp'st' (acc. to 1635–54)" (218).

101–04 *Why:...So is the pox:* KERMODE, FENDER, AND PALMER (1974): "The fop rushes off and bows deeply to someone who has travelled," which was thought "a great joke," since people left, especially for France and Italy, and returned with "all sorts of outlandish un-English habits and were much derided for doing so" (63). NUTT (1999): there is a notable "subtlety" in the "poet-reader relationship" here, as Donne "interjects his own aside" in order "to point out that his companion speaks neither language." The poets assumes that readers have "followed him so closely in this journey, imagined and satirical, that we are absolutely of his mind when he finally turns on his companion with the rebuke, 'So is the Poxe'; which not only reminds us of the moral superiority he has claimed all along, but of our own mortality" (39).

101 *Why: he hath trauayld. Long? No: but to mee* **PATRIDES** (1985): "The line's punctuation is erratic in both the MSS and the editions" (218).

101 *trauayld.* **ROUSSEAU AND RUDENSTINE** (1972): "Traveled" (60).

102 *Which vnderstand none* **HAYWARD** (1950): "presumably" an aside, "by the poet interrupting his companion's answer to the enquiry 'Long?'" (101). **MILGATE** (1967) adds that "[e]very satirist and epigrammatist of the period inveighs against the aping of continental fashions by Englishmen, especially by returned travelers," and quotes Portia in *MV* 1.2.65–68. Suggests that the humorist's clothing is "probably the only evidence of his acquaintance—if any—with France and Italy" and cites "An Affected Traveller" in *The Overburian Characters* (1936), ed. Paylor, p. 11 (126–27). **CRAIK AND CRAIK** (1986): "The companion's naive parenthesis unconsciously proclaims his inability to judge. Some critics take the parenthesis to be the satirical narrator's" (257).

103 *Perfect French...I replide* **LEGOUIS** (1928): see note for l. 23. **STEIN** (1944c) notes the stress-shift before a pause, which he considers to be one of Donne's more "peculiar and individual traits" (379).

103 *Perfect French and Italian:* **CHMIELEWSKI** (2001): "the most fashionable" (614).

104 05 *So is...and qualities.* **NUTT** (1999): at this point "the companion is both silenced and alienated" (39).

104 *pox:* **SHAWCROSS** (1967): "syphilis" (18). [So also, Chmielewski (2001, 614).] **SMITH** (1971) adds, "often called the French or Italian disease and assumed to be native to those countries" (474). [So also, Rousseau and Rudenstine (1972, 60), Kermode, Fender, and Palmer (1974, 63), Patrides (1985, 218), Craik and Craik (1986, 257), Campbell (1989, 237), and Nutt (1999, 39).]

105 *More men...and qualities.* **CRAIK AND CRAIK** (1986): "more men distinguished for position, talents and merits" (257).

105 *of Sort, of parts,* **MILGATE** (1967): "of rank and talents" (127). [So also, Patrides (1985, 218) and Jones (1991, 628).]

105 *of Sort,* **LEGOUIS** (1942): this instance predates the earliest mention in the OED, "sense 2b = 'of (high) quality or rank,' first recorded in 1603" in MM (185). [So also, Sullens (1964, 234).]

106–12 *At last...keepe his bed.* **BAUMLIN** (1991): the poet here "enacts his final reversal of the Horatian plot, resolution coming not by the boor's departure but by his return. Equally significant is the satirist's return to the theme of constancy. In accompanying his friend, the poet himself chose to leave the 'constant company' of his books; now, in the wake of the satirist's own inconstant choice, it is the Humorist

576 ❦ COMMENTARY

who must 'constantly a while...keepe his bed'" (76). **REID** (2000): "For all the hard words, the lively motions of the writing make the pest more a young blade than the butt of satiric condemnation" (41).

106–08 *At last...to his Lecheree.* **SELDEN** (1978): in this passage, "the carnal force of the last line (unleashed in the savage thrusts of the three stresses) is intensified by the expansive and mocking lyricism of the previous line: the gallant's mortal weakness is both absurd and tragic and yet neither absolutely" (61). **NUTT** (1999): when the humorist "at last encounters his lover in a window," it is "the final signal to depart from Donne, who has all along been merely a convenience" (39).

106–07 *At last...from mee,* **MILGATE** (1967) quotes Edward Guilpin's imitation in *Skialethia*, Sat. V, sig. D7ᵛ (127).

106 *Loue he in a window spies* **CHMIELEWSKI** (2001): "a prostitute" (614).

107–10 *And like...out of dore* **MILGATE** (1967): an image with a typically "neat brevity and a humorous satiric exaggeration," in which the fop "whisks away" from his companion (xx). See Henry Parrot's *Cures for the Itch* (1626), sig B3ᵛ (127).

107 *like Light dew exhald,* **HENINGER** (1960): the line provides "a witty meteorological image, noteworthy for its incisiveness," in which the "silly lover" is "irresistibly drawn up to the woman like a shapeless, senseless vapor exhaled by the sun" (201). [Similarly, Hiller (1977, 180).]

107 *Light dew* **SHAWCROSS** (1967): "erotic perspiration" (18).

107 *flings* **MILGATE** (1967): "dashes, rushes away. He evaporates like dew drawn off swiftly by the bright sun (his mistress)" (127).

108 *Lecheree.* **GROSART** (1872–73) notes the reading "liberty" in 1633 (1:14). [So also, Hiller (1977, 180).]. **PATRIDES** (1985): "(acc. to 1635–69 and all MSS): 'liberty' (acc. to 1633)" (218).

109–12 *Many...keepe his bed.* **LECOCQ** (1969): this conclusion—which is not one—plunges us into confusion. We are less deceived by the poverty of the pun on "constantly" than intrigued by the entire expression "constantly a while." It is only there, indeed, that we become conscious of what the use of certain preterits had obscurely announced: the speech and the monologue, like the walk, belonged in the past. The poem was fashioned as a trompe-l'oeil (371–72).

109–10 *Many...turnd out of dore* **PARRY** (1985): "In real life we only have to remember the fatal quarrels in which Marlowe and Jonson became involved, the ambushes around Court, the ease with which people found themselves in prison, the prevalence of shattering illnesses, and the general beggarly and brutal environment, to understand why there is so much abrasiveness in Donne" (52).

109 *Many* **SHAWCROSS** (1967): "others awaiting their turn with the whore" (18). [So also, Rousseau and Rudenstine (1972, 60) and Chmielewski (2001, 614).]

109 *weare there:* **PATRIDES** (1985): "'there were' (acc. to 1650–69)" (218).

109 *he could command no more:* **MILGATE** (1967): his mistress "entertaining others," he is "no longer in 'sole command'" (127). **SHAWCROSS** (1967): neither "further intercourse" nor "further sexual vigor" (18).

109 *command* **SMITH** (1971): "have her at his disposal" (474). [So also, Patrides (1985, 218), Craik and Craik (1986, 258), Campbell (1989, 237), and Chmielewski (2001, 614).]

110–12 *He quarreld,...keepe his bed.* **KERINS** (1984): "This final image of brawling sensualists is a perfect antithesis of the opening scene of sterile contemplation. Neither scene affords its protagonist true satisfaction and thus both satirist and humorist are ultimately unfaithful to their respective vows." In addition, "the iterative imagery unites them in a marriage of which neither can be proud. They are reflections of each other in that they both pursue unrealizable ideals of fulfillment: one in cerebral meditation untested by experience, the other in social conquests unredeemed by spiritual values" (41). **FISH** (1990): the humorist "comes home, where he lives, to the speaker, and he comes 'directly,' as if by instinct, and as he comes he shares with the speaker the pronoun 'me'—is it 'comes to me while hanging his head' or 'comes me who am hanging my head'? The attribution of 'constancy' is mocked not only by the immediate qualification of 'a while,' but by everything that has transpired in a poem where inconstancy rules and most spectacularly rules the voice who would thrust it from him" (237).

110 *turnd out of dore* **ROUSSEAU AND RUDENSTINE** (1972): "The 'humorist' is beaten in his effort to claim exclusive possession of his mistress" (60).

111–12 *Directly came...keepe his bed.* **SHAWCROSS** (1967): "Indicating exhaustion from his previous activities" (397). **KLAWITTER** (1994): the guide "must keep to his bed because he has...caught the pox as indicated by his dysfunctional member, 'hanging the head.'" Thus, "Donne's fop has been humiliated, and his detumescence is of considerable interest to Donne's narrator, not only because it indicates the narrator's delight at his own superiority (he is not the one with the inability to perform) but also because it reveals the homophobic narrator's suppressed fascination with another man's penis" (118–19). **NUTT** (1999): "Donne has the final word, and in the last few lines projects events forward to the aftermath in which his companion ends up crawling back to him" (39).

111 *came to me, hanging the hed* **HESTER** (1977c): "The fop's moral blindness and adultery are mocked throughout the poem, but this last scene illustrates that the satirist maintains an attitude of Erasmian charity for the fop as a man who endangers his own soul by his immorality" (188). **CORTHELL** (1997): "the satirist's ineffectuality is reemphasized when his unfaithful mock marriage partner returns to his control, 'hanging the head,' only because of a physical beating by rival johns" (31).

111 *hanging the hed* **SHAWCROSS** (1972): "Finally body sees 'his love' in a window, she apparently beckoning him to join the many others awaiting her services. Sexually spent, and unable to attain more time with 'his love' even by fighting, the

body returns to the soul 'hanging the head' (with its obvious double entendre)" (254). **HILLER** (1977): "The phrase has sexual reference" (180).

112 *constantly awhile must keepe his bed.* **MILGATE** (1967): "A parting shot" as the humorist "is at last constant in something (if only for a while)" (127). **SMITH** (1971): "the 'motly humourist' of the streets himself finishes up in a course of retired constancy" (474). **KLAWITTER** (1994): the final line "does not mean the adversarius goes to the narrator's home because the line specifies he goes to his own bed" (236).

112 *constantly* **CRAIK AND CRAIK** (1986): "Compare 1. 11" (258).

 # Satyre 2.

COMMENTARY

Date and Circumstances

Grierson (1912, 2:103) explores the internal evidence from *Sat2* and concludes that "on the whole 1593 is a little too early a date" and that the poem was "probably written between 1594 and 1597." Peter (1956, 132) concurs with this range of dates.

Jenkins (1923, 568) dates this poem to 1594 or 1595. Others who posit this range of dates include Cobb (1956b, Item 8), Zunder (1982, 12), and Prescott (2000, 230).

Hayward (1929, 120) asserts that the date of *Sat2* can be "fixed" on the basis of "allusions" to events "approximately between the years 1593–1597." He cites the evidence of the date 1593 inscribed on B34, a manuscript of *Sats1–3*. Others who concur with this range of dates based on topical allusions include Milgate (1967, 117), Warnke (1967, 106), Smith (1971, 469), and Shawcross (1972, 250–51).

Grierson (1929, xxv) observes that both *Sat2* and Sir John Davies in his "Gulling Sonnets," composed in 1594, direct satire "against the same person, a lawyer who had turned poet and published in 1594 *Zepheria*, a series of sonnets full of legal terms and long, harsh words." Others who note this comparison with Davies include Milgate (1967, 127), Shawcross (1967, 412), and Carey (1990, 423).

Grierson (1930, 190) argues that Donne would not have written this poem when he was employed by Egerton.

Harrison (1937, 412) notes that the reference to the "Sclavonian scolding" (57–60) dates the poem to sometime after July 23, 1597, "when the Ambassador from Poland was so foolish as to rebuke Queen Elizabeth in public audience." Shawcross (1967, 412) refers to this same incident.

Louthan (1951, 97) believes the poem to have been written while Donne was in transition between Catholicism and Anglicanism since the attitudes expressed "are critical of both faiths."

LeComte (1965, 25) dates this poem to 1593–94, noting that Donne's sympathy with the prosecuted in lines 9–10 may have been occasioned by the death of his brother Henry.

Milgate (1967, 127–28) finds "no specific evidence" to date *Sat2*, but thinks it likely that its composition was "prompted, in some degree," by the publication of the *Zepheria* sonnets (127), which "might have circulated earlier in manuscript." Additional evidence is the date inscribed by William Drummond of Hawthornden on SN 2067, the manuscript containing his transcriptions of *Sat2* and *Sat4*: "the date which he wrote against the latter, 1594, is impossible for that poem and may have been attached to the wrong satire" (128).

Shawcross (1967, 412) thinks a date of 1594 possible but asserts that *Sat2* must have been composed "before November 1598, not yet Elizabeth's quadrigesimus," and points to line 50.

Marotti (1974, 164) writes that Donne composed his Satyres and Verse Letters "for close friends who shared his intellectual and moral assumptions—men like Christopher Brooke," to whom Donne addressed *Sat2* and *Storm* and *Calm*.

Hester (1977b, 525–27) agrees with modern editors that *Sat2* was written in early 1594 but contends that Henry Donne's death "at the hands of the state," and not the sonnet sequence *Zepheria*, was the "major impetus" behind the poem. He contends that the poem focuses on the notion that abuses of the law have become so common that indeed the law has become the enemy, and that the impetus for the view is the enforcement of the statute that "led to the imprisonment and death of Donne's younger brother Henry in late May of 1593" (525). Noting that we have no records of Donne's reaction to his brother's death, he suggests that *Sat2*, "typical [as] it is of Donne's careful and oblique approaches to controversial issues—is his expression of hatred for the corrupt machinations of the law" (526). He also points out that "one other coincidence sustains such a proposition—the sudden change in tone and subject" of the Satyres "after late 1593" (526–27).

Partridge (1978, 39) states that *Sat2* was composed around 1594, noting that the poem "pillories incompetent poetry and the abuse of law, with which Elizabethans were familiar from Stubbes's *Anatomy of Abuses* (1583)."

Lein (1980, 130), observes that *Sat2* was written before Donne was employed by Egerton and "probably soon after his brother died as a result of the official persecution of missionary priests" and during the time Donne was "closeted with Beza and Bellarmine as well as studying law," and argues that the poem "begs for consideration if only to evaluate Donne's efforts to measure his experience during that early, vital period."

Hunter (1982, 6) agrees with the argument that *Sat2* was written in 1593 and offers support for the theory by pointing out that lines 13 and 14 refer to the poet Robert Greene. Observing that Donne had taken Greene's side in his quarrel with Gabriel Harvey, that *Groats-worth of Witte* was published shortly after Greene's death in 1592, and that the responses to the work by Thomas Nashe and Henry Chettle had appeared by the end of the year, he suggests that the poem's "reference to Greene is further evidence to support that date and to emphasize the currency of Donne's satire."

Patrides (1985, 34) dates *Sat2* "from the early 1590s."

Marotti (1986, 38) follows Grierson (1912) and postulates that Christopher Brooke, Donne's "closest friend at Lincoln's Inn," may also have been "the addressee" of *Sat2*.

Corthell (1987, 25–30; 1997, 31–37) comments that *Sat2*, a poem usually associated with Donne's Lincoln's Inn period, gives us a revealing picture of not only the contemporary Inns of Court environment but also "his self-presentation as a satirist" (25). In those days, the "coterie of wits" to which Donne belonged considered themselves "students of civility," or "gentlemen," and was "especially anxious to cultivate courtly postures and activities that would set them apart from the lawyers and law students," a professional group that was considered socially inferior as well as threatening to the traditional order of things. Since the young gentlemen regarded the Inns of Court "as a kind of liminal place where they could make the passage from parental control to the larger social circle where they would assume their occupational identities," and where they learned the courtly codes of behavior and language in order to secure advancement in the Elizabethan system of patronage and preferment, the social conflict between the two groups of young men who came of age at the Inns was essentially "a conflict between two systems of advancement: professionals like Coscus used the legal system, while the amateur gentlemen sought connections with the Court" (25–26).

Carey (1990, 423) observes that "the lawyer-poet Coscus has not been identified."

General Commentary

Cary (1651, 107, 288) quotes *Sat2* 41–42 favorably (107) and calls Donne "one of the most wittie" poets (288).

Bayle (1697 [1736, 4:85]) may be referring to *Sat2* when he writes of "one of Donne's juvenile performances,…a lively satirical piece, on the literature of the times."

Pope (1735, 132–41) prints "The Second Satire of Dr. *John Donne*," an imitation of *Sat2* that presents the 1669 text of Donne's poem in italics on facing pages.

Gosse (1899, 1:38) describes *Sat2*, in general, as "an attack on the Lawyer, as a type," and adds that it is "by no means an attractive or lucid composition."

Bradford (1917, 81) cites various passages from *Sat2* to demonstrate the "vigor of movement" found throughout the Satyres.

Aronstein (1920, 158) states that the attack in *Sat2* on the poets of the age, especially Donne's rejection of most contemporary poetry, outdoes even Ben Jonson's own opposition to the poetry of the times.

Grierson (1929, xvii–xviii) considers that the circumstances of Donne's early life help explain the passionate "tenor" of *Sat2* and make it "more intelligible and forgivable."

Hillyer (1941, xxii, xxxii–xxxiv) observes that *Sat2* "opens with an attack on poetasters, reminding one in matter if not in manner of Pope's *Epistle to Dr. Arbuthnot*, but it shifts its grounds to bombard the lawyers" (xxxii).

Louthan (1951, 81, 94–97, 99–101) describes *Sat2* as an "atypical" example of Donne's use of the "dialectical mode" (81). Despite his own use of technical language in his love lyrics, he notes, Donne ridicules Coscus' pompous and unconvincing use of legal terminology in courtship (99), adding that poetic "incantation" rather than "dialectic" is less effective than money for either seduction or "political aggrandizement" (100). He questions why Donne combines the lawyer and the poet in Coscus and concludes that it provides continuity to the poem (99–100). He observes, finally, that the speaker does not advocate returning to the past, but instead for a mean between past and present (101).

Of *Sat1* and *Sat2*, Lewis (1954, 470) ponders, "it is difficult to guess how these two pieces would affect us if we did not know the author's name," adding that *Sat2* "would not, perhaps, be much read save by specialists."

Andreasen (1963, 67) notes that the offence of fraud satirized in *Sat2* is more serious than the follies of *Sat1*.

Milgate (1967, xxiv, xx, 128) considers *Sat2* to "fall apart badly" (xxiv), but he points also to "how much wit and humour—how much sheer fun" are found in *Sat2* (xx). The poem is "not concerned with a specific poet, with a type of poet, or even with poetry in general," but Donne uses the figure of Coscus "to give some appearance of unity to his satire of the abuse of poetry, and, more important, of the abuse of law" (128).

Comparing this poem unfavorably to *Sat1*, Hughes (1968, 26) points out that *Sat2* lacks the more successful poem's "controlled chaos" and "stunning juggling of time for symbolic effect" and concludes that this is the "tamest" of the Satyres.

Nelly (1969, 84) notes that in *Sat2*, Donne's satirist "rail[s] against extremes such as 'Carthusian fasts, and fulsom Bachanalls'" and declares his own preference in the phrase "meanes blesse."

Powers (1971, 177–79) states that *Sat2* "includes an Arcadian theme" (177) in which "the Arcadian ideal of the comfortable, secure (but not luxurious or easy) rural life" is jeopardized by the lawyer-figure who "becomes ominously ruinous to the very structure of English economic and social life" (179).

Smith (1971, 474) suggests that the target in *Sat2* is "a bad poet who becomes a worse lawyer and then viciously misuses the law to enrich himself."

Shawcross (1972, 256) argues that Donne's main theme in *Sat2* is "change, change which has brought corruption and decay and disutility through opportunists, imitators, and venal hypocrites." In the society that Donne describes, time "rots all things and develops minor illness (botches) into wasting disease (syphilis)," and "the law, so fear-inducing and difficult of correction by the people, has been perverted into an instrument of the few to swindle the many."

According to Raizada (1974, 101), the targets of *Sat2* are "the extravagances of love poetry and the sins of lawyers," adding that this poem is "much less individual and characteristic and much closer to the general run of Elizabethan satires."

Parker (1975, 21) notes that in *Sat2* Donne focuses his attention on "'poor disarm'd Papists, not worth hate', on poets, men of the theatre, libertines and petty crooks."

Lauritsen (1976, 123–24) contends that the subject of *Sat2* is the "matter of the perversion of the world, whether this be in law, theology, or poetry." He notes that the speaker "exclud[es] himself from the action of the poem altogether," and he builds his case against Coscus carefully to ensure that "we understand precisely how far removed he is from Coscus' immoral offenses."

Hester (1977c, 188) notes that unlike *Sat1*, which centers on the satirist's "charity and stewardship," the emphasis of *Sat2* is on "the satirist's hatred."

Williams (1977, 111, 117–18) suggests that "the history of confusion about the poem's precise aim or subject may indicate that Pope's incentive to its alteration should not be considered merely a concern to give it new 'numbers' or a higher stylistic gloss" (118). He argues that given the substantive changes that Pope made, the eighteenth century poet probably shared the view of some more recent critics that the poem is "in conflict with itself." He also points out that there are many different critical views on the central theme of *Sat2*, and the differences are mirrored in the various titles that the poem appears under in the manuscripts (117).

Partridge (1978, 39) notes that Coscus is "a lawyer-poet, reminiscent of those at

Lincoln's Inn," and that the poem "pillories incompetent poetry and the abuse of law, with which Elizabethans were familiar."

Lein (1980, 130–31) remarks that *Sat2* has not received the attention that it deserves because "a derogatory critical tradition" (130) has told us that "it is feeble-minded and perhaps best forgotten." He insists that the poem is "a major creative effort, a vigorous attempt on Donne's part to weld together his disparate worlds of law, love, poetry, and religion, and that it embodies a striking statement of his moral imagination." Conceding that the poem may be different from Donne's other Satyres, he maintains that "it is hardly inferior to them; and it is worth some effort to plumb its unique character and to define its energy and artistry more accurately."

Zunder (1982, 12) notes that *Sat2* centers on the figure of "Coscus as lawyer," and he finds that Donne's "criticism of contemporary poetry—virtually the dismissal of contemporary poetry (lines 5–30)—is secondary," adding that "the direction" and "emphasis" of the poem is "on wealth."

Patrides (1985, 34) finds the tone of the poem, "summarily indicated" in its opening lines, to be "hate" that is "Swiftian," rising to "the level of great art."

Toliver (1985, 100) observes that the speaker of *Sat2* "considers both poets and lawyers in the context of language," adding that the poem's "concern with language is another side of society's failure to commit itself to open, recognizable truths."

According to Caracciolo-Trejo (1986, 2:12), the satirical critique in *Sat2*, centered as it is on the ritualistic fashion of the law, that is, on a system more interested in forms than in law, concludes on a note of dismay and impotence.

Low (1990, 468; 1993, 35) points out that in *Sat2* Donne "pits poetry against law," and "these two professions represent kinds of writing and ways of advancing in life and love."

Gorbunov (1993, 95) says that the bribability of officers in *Sat2* can be understood by considering centuries of sanctified values in English culture. Moreover, Gorbunov argues, Donne explores in the conduct of the money-hungry lawyer Coscus the cultural behavior that finally infringes on the traditional foundations of life.

Scodel (1993, 481) notes that toward the end of *Sat2*, Donne "celebrat[es] a mean of country hospitality and attack[s] the extremes of bacchanalian excess and monk-like fasts," but the passage only "escapes rather than confronts the poem's urban universe of hack poets and corrupt lawyers, figures all too close and threatening to the urban satirist."

Corthell (1997, 32, 35, 37) states that the "social critique" of *Sat2* participates in "the semiotics of the Inns of Court," and the tension between "the serious law students" and "the students of civility" increased as "professionals" such as Coscus opted for the legal system and "the amateur gentlemen" operated within the Court (32). He argues further that even though lawyers have always been targets of satire, "Renaissance attacks on them displayed a new anxiety" among those like Donne who, feeling "acutely the effects of being knocked loose of traditional moorings," perceived lawyers as "the emerging order that was replacing the old agrarian society" (35). He adds that the poem focuses primarily on "change," "power," and the "disturbing linkages between aspects of both" (37).

Wiggins (2000, 14, 34) finds that *Sat2* "bears (perhaps anguished) witness" to Donne's recognition that although poets were "innocuous, vulnerable, rather pathetic—but cheerfully deluded—individuals with never enough money in their pockets," poetry was "his principal means of demonstrating his social qualification" (14). The poem is Donne's "only extended disquisition on poetry and on its social uses," though "its pessimism is chilling," and Donne does not display "the exalted claims of Sidney's *Apology for Poetry* or Jonson's aspirations to political influence through laureateship." As Donne portrays it, poetry "is pitiable, not hateful," for "it has no power to injure others," and poets themselves are "innocuous—self-indulgent for the most part, self-destructive at worst" (34).

Edwards (2001, 44) notes Donne's "contempt" for greedy lawyers who could only court women with "legal jargon" and "lies" by which they are enabled "to accumulate estates." He believes that Donne was ahead of his contemporaries in expressing such attitudes and that Donne "had a particular lawyer-poet in mind."

Donne as Satirist

Leishman (1951, 110) suggests that *Sat2* is "much less individual" than *Sat1* and "much closer to the general run" of other Elizabethan satyres.

Milgate (1967, xix–xx) points in *Sat2* to a method in Donne's "ironic or illustrative allusion to things not strictly relevant to the main subject of satire," where often "the allusion is introduced as an image," thereby increasing "the fullness" of the world he satirizes (xix), and Donne uses this device with more "frequency and resource" than any of his contemporaries. He thus brings "a proper degree of disgust" to his "denunciation of images of corruption." Milgate cites Lewis (1954, 469–70), whose list of such images "out of their context" merely tends "to exaggerate the frequency with which they occur, and to falsify the actual effect of such things in their place in the poem, where they are usually given a more subtle and complex satiric bite by the wit and humour of the treatment" (xx).

Piper (1969, 59–62, 208–09) compares Donne to Marston and notes that the two poets share the practice of using epigrams that is common among Renaissance satirists, but in *Sat2* we can see a "tremendously extended thrust of thought": it takes the speaker more than forty lines to resolve the social ills mentioned in the first four lines (59–60). He also observes that Donne's wit is "much wider ranging, much more pointed in its articulation, in short, much more demanding than Marston's." To follow his wit, the reader must be familiar with contemporary ideas (such as benefit of clergy laws, the tradition of courtly love, the concept of confession, prejudices against Spaniards and Papists) as well as the "brass" to absorb the shock of harsh terms like "excrement," "Dildoes," and "poxe." As such, he thinks, Donne must have envisioned "an extremely narrow audience," in particular, "a few of the wittiest and most elegantly cynical young fellows at the Inns of Court" (60). He adds, however, that Donne is "persistently aware" of his audience: the poem beginning with an addressee in the word "Sir," "always smacks of talk—even if it is the snappy talk bandied between unbearably clever young dandies" (60–61). He concludes that Donne's Satyres showcase his "remarkable wit and vigor, probably, better than any other of his couplet poems," and they illustrate that the poet "responded to virtually every aspect of the heroic couplet which his age had discovered" (208–09).

Roy and Kapoor (1969, 98) note that in *Sat2* Donne jibes at "those unscrupulous persons who take up the profession of law only to cheat others and to fill their personal coffer," and that "this greed of gain and self-aggrandizement at the cost of others appears offensive to the moral sense of an artist like Donne" because he had studied to be a lawyer himself.

Hebaisha (1971, 30) suggests that *Sat2* illustrates Donne's "interest in the poetics of his time." He notes that "the passage where Coscus the late lawyer courts his lady with legal terms is an attack upon the exaggerated conceits of the Elizabethan sonneteer," and thus the poem can be seen as an example of Donne "attacking what he considers a dead poetic tradition." He adds that Donne's "attack on would-be poets is found in abundance in Latin and Elizabethan satirists" and contends that in the Satyres, Donne "was never original in his choice of theme."

Powers (1971, 57, 62) argues that *Sat2* is "a reflection on the evils that lawyers do" (57) and finds that the Companion serves "no other ostensible function than that of an attentive auditor to what is, essentially, the Satirist's monologue" (62). She also notes that the auditor's role is psychologically important in that "his presence provides a target (in this type of satire) for the Satirist's remarks," and thereby "the reader is both distanced from the action (which does not technically involve him anyway) and at the same time is a spectator as it goes on before his eyes" (62).

Erskine-Hill (1972, 274) thinks that *Sat2* is "one of the less successful" among the five Satyres. Commenting on Donne's satirical targets, "the abuse of poetry, law, and finally property," which are "united in the figure of Coscus in a largely formal sense," he notes that "the union does not seem a source of dramatic or poetic life."

Newton (1974, 431–34) argues that in *Sat2* Donne "self-consciously, and a bit self-righteously, accepts responsibility for the satiric character and calls upon no Humorist to shoulder part of the blame," but nonetheless, Donne "also tries to evade responsibility by dissipating most of his hate into 'pitty'" (431). He adds that "the greatest object of a satirist's hate can easily become the self," for the satirist "has first himself to blame that he sees the world as ugly, blind, and diseased" (431–32). In the poem's "repulsive introduction," the use of "quasi-medical imagery," not uncommon in Elizabethan satire, suggests that everything in society is in "irremediable decay," an idea that Coscus brings to the satirist's mind, provoking him, "in simile after reckless simile, to denounce the rottenness of all things in his society, even of the church and of the state" (432–33). He concludes that Donne, discovering that the enemy of society resembles himself, "breaks out in extraordinarily violent language, language which itself attacks the fabric of society, and leaves him only with the power of his hate" so that in the poem's conclusion "it is little wonder that he should deny the dangerous lawlessness of what he has said" (434).

According to Raizada (1974, 101), the target of *Sat2* is "the extravagances of love poetry and the sins of lawyers," and as such, "it is much less individual and characteristic and much closer to the general run of Elizabethan satires."

Partridge (1978, 39) observes that Coscus is "a lawyer-poet, reminiscent of those at Lincoln's Inn," and that the poem "pillories incompetent poetry and the abuse of law, with which Elizabethans were familiar."

Hester (1979, 138–39, 147–48, 157) argues that *Sat2* should be seen "as an ironic apologia for satire that is unified by the satirist's concern with public and private perversions of language and the presumptuous abuse of the Word" (138). In the poem, Coscus is represented as "a sort of Uncreating Word that is both the perpetuator and product of a mechanical, materialistic prostitution of the word of man and God" (138). Further, he notes that the poem contains eight examples of the lawyer's "insolence," which all focus on his "abuse of language," and his "numerous transgressions" reveal "the range of such abuses throughout the Elizabethan world and their spiritual significance as perversions of the 'words' which God has given to man" (138–39). He adds that through the speaker's "condemnation of all poetry and his association of his own poetry with disease, defenseless soldiers, and materialistic 'beggars,'" the speaker thus "inverts the traditional roles of satirist as doctor, moral soldier and disinterested commentator on mankind's follies" (147). However, by suggesting that "society's moral depravity produces and victimizes poets" and "by forcing the reader to struggle with the harshness, obscurity and parodic techniques of his poem," the satirist, Hester argues, initiates "the first step toward recovery of language" through "the experience of reading the poem" (147–48).

Lein (1980, 148, 150) suggests that the society represented in Sat2 is "past redemption" (148), and he argues that Sat2's "profound despair and psychological uncertainties" provide the reader with "unique insights into the early moral world of the poet" (150). He adds that Sat2 "is the most important formal mastering of classical verse satire in English Renaissance poetry," displaying "a thorough mastery of the mode, its metaphoric style, and its principal structural manipulations," and the poem thus "represents a significant early effort by Donne to combine his various talents in large, coherent structures" (150).

Slights (1981, 156–60) observes that in Sat2 the speaker addresses himself "sternly to a 'bold soule,'" acknowledging that his friend's posture as poet has been ridiculous but warning that taking up the law for selfish motives is even more despicable," and that in analyzing "the question of occupational choice," the satirist "indirectly struggles with personal doubts about his responsibility as a poet" (156–57). She suggests that the satire is "double-edged": the speaker's "tongue-in-cheek exaggerations effectively mock Puritan charges that poetry is socially harmful, but his contempt is for poets, not their attackers," and thus, "the butt of the satirist's ridicule is not a type of poetry so much as a type of poet" (157–58). She adds that "both poetasters and corrupt lawyers pervert language from its proper end of truth, but bad poets, however greedy, harm only themselves" (158). She concludes that "obviously Coscus is not an attack on a particular individual but a portrait of all who live for success rather than service" (159).

Hester (1982, 12–13, 33–35, 39–42, 53) asserts that in Sat2 Donne articulates "his development of a moral satirical criterion, based on his recognition that some sins deserve pity and others only hatred" so that the satirist "turns melancholically to sarcastic self-criticism because no discernible results are realized by his 'Good workes'" (12–13). He notes that "despite his vituperative tone," the satirist "does not assume the role of satyr-satirist raging at the shapes of evil surrounding him" (33), and that "rather than making one last charitable effort to instigate reform," he instead "distances himself from his satirical adversaries by way of irony and sarcasm."

While the speaker "dramatizes an alternative to these vices" by "providing a moral contrast to the pernicious abuse of words he sees throughout his country," the problem of satire "in the larger arena of social-moral man" and "the place of the zealous satirist in society" remain "unsettled" (34). Since he finds himself "cast into the role of advisor (or scourge) to a world of decaying communication," Donne's speaker, Hester says, turns into an "ironist, like the ancient satirist" (35). As such, the satirist's "distinction between the pitiful character of the poets' offences and the menacing enormity of the lawyers' is central to his argument," and poets are thus shown to be "not so much the major culprits of linguistic abuse as its victims," both through the "abandonment of their vatic function" and through "the town's acceptance of the ethos of the lawyers" (39).

He notes further that the poem's "association of poetry with recent calamities in England" acknowledges "the current failure of poetry to realize its civilizing and moral capabilities" in that those who "would move Love by rimes" are "impotent" because of "the moral failures of society," and therefore "it is not any innate 'sinfulness' in poetry that dooms poets to ineffectiveness but the moral depravity of the times" (41). In short, the "defiant sarcasm" at the poem's close suggests that the satirist "has not resolved those doubts about his role as satirist," although it does present the criteria for the Christian satirist by its display of "his charity for sinners and his hatred for their sins as well as his possession of the two essentials of successful oratory—good character and eloquence." Hester believes that *Sat2* should be read "as an initial apologia" for satire and for "the central concerns of many of Donne's later works" (53).

Corthell (1987, 25–31) finds that *Sat2* participates in the social conflict between the professional lawyers and gentlemen amateurs "as the satirist works to gain the rhetorical upper hand over Coscus" by using the language of courtesy literature, which would have been a natural resource for Elizabethan satirists because "it comprised the period's most extensive and coherent system of thinking about self-presentation." He suggests that courtesy literature, in addition to upholding the status quo, could also "be manipulated to undermine the established order" (26).

He comments further that Donne's "ironic ridicule of the poets" in *Sat2* "traces a classic maneuver of courtly self-promotion." He points out that Donne attacks Coscus "by comparing and contrasting the lawyer's self-interested diligence with the prodigality and versifying fashionable in the circle of gentlemen with whom Donne associated at the Inns of Court," a "rhetorical strategy" on which his contention that "Coscus is the chief of sinners" depends. But Coscus' sins are actually not particularly unique, and it is in fact his success that evokes the indignation of the satirist, "who aligns himself with figures of powerlessness and dispossession—poets, papists, 'ruin'd Abbeyes,' bilked heirs, old landlords." Thus, "by another familiar gesture of courtly self-definition," Coscus's success, Corthell suggests, "is contrasted with the satirist's self-acknowledged disconnectedness, which silently testifies to his moral superiority" (28). He argues that Donne uses Coscus "to focus his anxieties about participation in a changing society." Donne could have chosen to become a lawyer, which would "have placed him at the cutting edge of early modern culture," but instead chose "to cultivate the traditional role of prodigal poet as a prelude to a responsible occupation at court." Driven by an overwhelming sense of ambition, Donne simultaneously despised as well as envied the successful Coscus, "who played the game of advancement by improvising on the old rules" (29). Corthell concludes that "locating" the Satyres "within the social conditions and discursive practices of the late sixteenth century" helps us to understand why for Donne "it was difficult not to write satire" (30).

Baumlin (1991, 84–85) contends that even as *Sat2* "invokes Juvenal's stylistic decorum or *prepon*," aspects of "*kairos*—of changed circumstances, to which the poet must respond if his words are to achieve their aims—insinuate themselves, testing the model's adequacy in this new cultural setting." Citing changes in contemporary society, such as enclosures of public land, dissolution of monasteries, and the growing prominence of the English Church, he notes that "the complexities of contemporary power structures, whether legal, political, or religious, place the Juvenalian satirist in an untenable rhetorical situation, speaking to a strange and unreceptive, indeed untouchable and irredeemable audience." In the world described in *Sat2*, the satirist as poet becomes "in this new age 'disarm'd,' incapable of reforming or in any way influencing his world," for poetry "has become powerless."

Patterson (1994, 150) reads *Sat2* as Donne's "manifesto for the satiric program, as a writerly exposé of a crisis in Law in the most comprehensive sense." She argues that "in its focus on the textual nature of malfeasance, the complicity in systemic corruption of writing and the intelligence that drives it," the poem helps us to understand Donne's "political poetics" as well as do the other satires.

Corthell (1997, 31–33, 35–37) points out that because in *Sat2* the relationship between the satirist and "the satirized other" is more complicated than the one between the scholar and the humorist in *Sat1*, Coscus' successes "generate indignation, an anger that seems connected to a threat to the dignity of the satirist." The threat results in not only "a satiric counterattack on Coscus," but also "a subversive representation of the discourse of power" (31–32). He contends that Donne's satirical portrait of Coscus "reproduces a typical early modern attitude toward lawyers and the law." But even though lawyers have always been targets of satire, "Renaissance attacks on them displayed a new anxiety" because "to men like Donne, who felt acutely the effects of being knocked loose of traditional moorings, the lawyer took on special importance in his role as a shaper of the emerging order that was replacing the old agrarian society" (36–37).

Persona

Louthan (1951, 97) cautions against assuming that in *Sat2* Donne is speaking in his own person.

Hughes (1968, 22) suggests that the "basic pose" in both *Sat1* and *Sat2* is that of "the fresh scholar (now pretending to be a grave elder philosopher) disdaining the world of the market place" and "the court."

Elliott (1976, 112) observes that the persona in *Sat2* encounters "serious obstacles" in his role as a "Christian satirist," and although the speaker insists that he is right in attacking his targets, "his frustration has begun to resolve into another, more serious sin—despair."

Hester (1977a, 27–28) notes that like Horace's speaker, Donne's satirist "evokes the same rich complexity in his ambiguous and saucy conclusion," noting on the one hand, the satirist's "melancholic and ironic admission that his satire is ineffective," and on the other, that he "cannot be prosecuted" since he "has simply told the truth about present conditions in England." Consequently, the fact that his attempts to reform society are ineffective "reflects poorly not on the efforts of the satirist but on the perverse character of national morality." He concludes that Sat2 recalls the classical poet's argument that that "satire which is good poetry is legal as poetry and as social criticism," but Donne's satirist also introduces the idea that "the abuse of language and law is so widespread that the civilizing force of the words of poetry and law have become largely ineffective." Nevertheless, "the abuse or disregard or the truthful potential of language" from which England suffers in turn provides the satirist "with his strongest defense for continuing to write satire."

Hester (1979, 139–40) says that Donne's persona as "ironist," serves as an "advisor to a world of decaying communication," and concedes that "his own efforts to stir reformation are inconsequentially 'out of fashion' in order to confirm the menacing implications of his own satirical thrusts." Hester also points out that the satirist's "hyperbolic mimicry of the *misomusoi* 'poet-haters' intimates that poets are not the present enemies of the state but only victims of the disease by which men like Coscus 'thrive.'" In short, Donne's persona draws our attention to "the disregard of his own poetry," thereby "ironically validat[ing] his claim that the current abuse of word and Word which 'breeds [his] just offence' is the ultimate enemy of English morality and civilization."

Slights (1981, 159) comments that the speaker in both Sat1 and Sat2 "is more concerned with showing the moral dangers inherent in practical decisions than with resolving doubts or discovering an innocent course of action" (159).

Hester (1982, 39–40) argues that viewing the satirist as a "minister and scourge" is "ironically suggested by the associations of poetry with calamities that the authoritative *Book of Homilies*, the medical authorities of the day, and the weekly sermons taught were brought in because of God's anger with the community." Thus, when the poem is read according to "the techniques of an apologia," Donne "has merely allowed his persona to voice sarcastically the objections to poetry that Horace's legalistic Trebatious, Juvenal's pragmatic interlocutor, and Persius's effeminate monitor supplied in the Latin defenses."

Kerins (1984, 42–43) states that the speaker of Sat2 "has great difficulty in locating anyone worthy of his 'just offence,'" but he ultimately discovers a "fit adversary" in Coscus, "a terrible poet newly turned lawyer." He asserts further that "after the narrator dispatches with epigrammatic sting a parade of poetical wretches, the central theme of this poem begins to emerge—the satirist's concern about his own vulnerable status."

Fowler (1987, 94–95) notes that Donne's persona in the Satyres may remind us of Horace's speakers, "but no recent poet had kept up a dramatic voice so believable, so forceful, with such spontaneous and superior vitality" (94). He argues that Sat2 "is actable monologue—even, in places, dialogue," but he also cautions "not to confuse the voice with Donne's own," because the poet "takes up several incompatible roles," and while he "has poetic feeling to a high degree, the same cannot quite be said of his sincerity" (95).

Fish (1990, 237–38) espouses that Sat2 presents the persona in "the spectacle of a self-divided being continuing to claim a spurious independence," and thus, "the speaker's relationship to the world he scorns" is as "precarious" as Donne's, for the poem does not authorize us to allow the poet "to stand outside the predicament of" the persona.

Corthell (1997, 31) notes that "the bond between the satirist and the satirized other is here more conflicted than that between the scholar and humorist" in *Sat1*.

Wiggins (2000, 32, 34, 148) finds that the narrator of *Sat2* is the same figure as in *Sat1*, with the exception that "he has matured so much and so suddenly (as youths often do) that it takes a reader's breath away," (32), and as such, he "leaves us no room to see around him, to ironize him" in that he recognizes himself as "a giddy, fantastic poet" whose character "may accord no better with the gravity which he so admires than his former companion's infatuation with stylish clothes" (34). He adds that "the voice of the grave man who tugs Donne's sleeve and forces him to examine himself" is "the voice that we must imagine filling the space" between *Sat1* and *Sat2* (148).

Sources, Influences, and Analogues

Aronstein (1920, 160) describes the portrait of the machinations of Coscus as similar to the satire of Rabelais.

Lindsay (1934a, 577) suggests that Donne's concern with moderation in the poem indicates that he had read Horace, Drant's translation of Horace, and Martial.

Leishman (1951, 111) observes that the "exhaustive and contemptuous detail" of the simile at lines 81–86 compares with passages in Jonson's comedies.

Louthan (1951, 133) doubts that Donne's "hierarchy of poetasters" is intended as literary criticism.

Peter (1956, 134–36) notes that in *Sat2* Donne "willingly eschews the privilege of moral rebuke" and turns instead, in imitation of Juvenal, "directly to the concrete case, one that is obnoxious to him personally" (135). He believes that Donne's attitude to law is "Roman" and that Donne's "contempt for Court life can be related, not only to Wyatt, but to Juvenal's attitude towards degenerate patricians also" (136).

Rickey (1966, 186) notes the references in *Sat2* to "Coscus, Carthusian fasts, and Bachanalls" in her listing of Donne's classical allusions.

Milgate (1967, xix, 127–28) sees one source of *Sat2* in the use by "Roman satirists" of "ironic or illustrative allusion to things not strictly relevant to the main subject of satire" (xix). A different source for this poem, as a subject of satire, are the "forty poems in *Zepheria*" (published in 1594), "mostly feeble efforts in the 'Petrarchan' style," featuring "atrocious new coinages" drawn from legal terminology (127–28). Carey (1990, 423) also notes the legal terminology.

Warnke (1967, 106) puts *Sat2* "among the earliest of English formal satires based on Latin models."

Lecocq (1969, 373) suggests that, in the amorous missives by Coscus, Donne employs a style like that which Sir John Davies parodies in his *Gulling Sonnets* and which Donne encountered in the first sonnets of Barnes' *Parthenophil and Parthenope* or in certain poems of *Zepheria*.

Piper (1969, 122) suggests that Rochester's "My Lord All-Pride" may have been inspired by *Sat2*'s famous lines on plagiarists but points out that Donne's language is "more trenchant, more intensely reasoned, and more demanding." Rochester's re-working of Donne's image, he thinks, is "more accessible to general attention, more showy," and he argues that Rochester represents a "halfway point" between Donne, who in his poem excluded society in general, and Pope, who in his revision of the poem "politely invited society at large to consider every step, every term, and every figure in his."

Hebaisha (1971, 30) believes that Donne is attacking the "exaggerated conceits of the Elizabethan sonneteer."

Swift (1974, 47) finds in *Sat2* a weakened form of the conventional two-part structure, which in the case of Donne's poem satirizes first London and then poetry, and finally the very old literary motif of the smarmy lawyer (as represented by Juvenal VII) in connection with the similarly related topic of the squandered inheritance (Juvenal VIII) and the contrasts between city and county (Juvenal III, LX).

Hester (1977a, 23–25, 28–29) observes that *Sat2*, like the first poem in Horace's second book of *Satires*, follows "the scheme of a conventional satirical *apologia*" (23), but he also notes that Donne changes the dialogue in Horace's poem into a "monologue or dramatic epistle," adds a "parody of the Platonic-Puritan contentions about the dangerous nature and effects of 'lying' poets," and introduces the notion that "the widespread disregard for the potential truth-bearing capabilities of language has brought about the regrettable state of poetry" (23–24). He expresses further that "Horace's fools" become "Juvenalian knaves," but Donne's speaker's approach "remains Horatian," explaining that while "the objects of his scorn may be more at home in one of Juvenal's streets which overflow with obscenity" than "in one of Horace's urbane dramatized conversations," the satirist "still retains the approach of Horace" (24–25). Hester concludes that Donne's "central satiric techniques" in *Sat2* are borrowed from Horace, though Donne "modifies the degree of irony with which the satirist is equipped, focuses more fully and seriously on the personal condition of the speaker and adds a psychological complexity, religious dimension, and verbal ambiguity not present in his Latin model" (28). While he suggests that Donne's "more somber mood and acrimonious tone" could be attributed to the poet's experience as an English recusant and the death of his younger brother who was prosecuted for helping a Jesuit priest, he argues that the Horatian echoes take the poem "beyond an autobiographical perspective" to focus on the conventions of satire and, thereby, add credibility to the notion that a nation's response to satire is "a significant barometer of its moral health" (28–29).

Hester (1979, 141, 143, 157) points out that Donne follows the Roman satirists in constructing a three-part argument, which begins with "the satirist's expression of misgivings and essential, personal imperatives about the writing of satire," continues with "an examination of the literary or legal practices of the day," and ends with "either concessions about future satire, the affectation of differing forms of ironic modesty, or a final ambiguous disparagement of the poet's own works." He contends that Donne uses this strategy to expose a problem that he shared with the Roman poets: "the dangers to the spiritual health of the nation inherent in the abuse of lan-guage," but he adapts their work to fit Christian principles (141). He argues further that *Sat2* "can be read as an initial statement of the attitudes and central concerns of many of Donne's later poems," noting that the speaker's concern with the abuses of language "is identical to the dismay with cramped, superficial and abusive attitudes towards love and the language of love" that we hear in the Songs and Sonets, *Metem*, *Ignatius*, and the Anniversaries (157).

Lein (1980, 131–33, 142, 146–47, 149) concedes that the portrait of Coscus is meant to target a contemporary but argues that in *Sat2* Donne "wished even more to experiment with the form of classical satire" (131–32). He notes that "inept poets and lawyers were familiar subjects in classical satire, as was the larger theme of the poverty of literary men," and he points out that the poem "imitates the formal design of many Latin satires: a prologue introducing speaker, secondary target, and environment, followed by the primary satiric portrait." While many critics "deplore" this two-part division in the poem, this structure, Lein observes, "is found in all the major Roman satirists" (132). He also comments that while the tone of the poem's opening lines "embodies a Juvenalian virulence," its epistolary form recalls Persius' *Satire VI* which combines satire and Horatian epistle and he thus argues that "the poem is a highly wrought imitation" (132–33). He adds, however, that Donne transcends his sources "in his combination of topic and in his metaphoric structure, and these elements reveal his technical brilliance and thematic originality." Based on a consideration of *Sat2*'s structure and "some striking allusions and verbal echoes," he concludes that Donne's poem is a "radical imitation of Juvenal's *Satire VII*" (142), and he remarks that the poem's final lines which promote the ideal of moderation through food images can be traced to Persius' *Satire VI* and Horace's *Epistles* II.2 (149). He also sees a similar relationship between *Sat2* and a number of Donne's other works, noting that aspects of "the moral construction" of the poem "suggest its importance for an understanding of Donne's imaginative development" in that the poem's "conceptualizations of the world as Hell and Purgatory" are elaborated in such poems as *Sat4*, *ElPart*, *Metem*, and the Anniversaries (146–47).

Gallenca (1982, 318) points out that the actions of Coscus should remind readers of the perverse and sterile union of the dandy and the prostitute in *Sat1* and recall similar travesties of oath and bond by Crispus and Publius in Marston.

Hester (1982, 34, 36, 38) notes that "on one level, as suggested by the name of the satirist's central target (Coscus)," *Sat2* is "a conventional attack on corrupt lawyers, a common type in verse satire from as early as Horace's fifth satire of *Book II* and Juvenal's tenth satire" (34); and that "the classical expressions most relevant to Donne's poem are the satirical *apologiae* of the Roman verse satirists, those programmatic defenses by Horace (*Satire II. i*), Juvenal (*Satire I*), and Persius (*Satire I*) that judge Roman civilization by the caliber of its law and letters while relying on a traditional scheme and strategy" (36). He suggests that Donne uses more mimicry and parody than his classical models but focuses on the same problem they targeted, and concludes that the result in *Sat2* "is an even stronger defense" than Donne found in his Latin models, "a defense that gains aesthetic authority by its glances at and specific echoes of the Roman satiric triumvirate and moral authority by the speaker's demonstration of the vatic character of his genre" (36). Thus, Donne's poem goes beyond an attack on the abuse of words by poets and lawyers to paint "a picture of the chaos and sterility the land of England suffers" because of this kind of immoral behavior (38).

Baumlin (1985, 32–33) argues that it is easy to miss the "decorum" of *Sat2* because its "verbal borrowings" from the Roman satirists are not obvious. Although the poem includes " thematic allusions to Horace," Juvenal is Donne's main source in terms of its persona, style, satiric method, and "especially in its concern for exposing the 'tragical vices' of men." But rather than imitating a particular poem of Juvenal's, Donne chooses to reproduce the "decorum" of the classical poet: Donne "draws upon Juvenal's Renaissance reputation as the *vir iratus*, the fierce and bitter satirist." Pointing out that the word "hate" is used four times in *Sat2* and only once in the other four Satyres, he suggests that this word defines for Donne the persona of the Juvenalian satirist, and comments that *Sat2* has a "typical" Juvenalian persona who remains aloof from the city and its vices that he observes and "does not participate in dramatic action."

Baumlin (1986b, 466–67) contends that *Sat2* "tests—and rejects—Juvenal: the speaker's 'hate' and 'just offense' erupt in a bitter invective against the criminal Coscus, and yet his words cannot bring such a man to justice—he has learned that crime demands the retribution of law, in the place of which Juvenalian invection is ineffectual."

Baumlin (1991, 28, 82, 92) argues that *Sat1*, *Sat2*, and *Sat4* "explore the vulnerability of the poet's present circumstances obliquely through their own explicit criticisms of the classical models" (28). He also notes that although Donne's persona maintains that his indignation is "just," we should not forget "the ambivalence with which Renaissance critics read Juvenal, an ambivalence that subtly pervades Donne's own critical reinterpretation of this model" (82). He concludes that the "*kairos*" of *Sat2*, "the acknowledgment of cultural change that leads Juvenal to fail as an effective model for satire," leads to the recognition that satire has to redeem two things before its purpose can be achieved: "human nature" and "human discourse," and while *Sat2* succeeds in redeeming neither, it "surpasses its classical model by asserting that language and genre alike have fallen in need of redemption," for to write "classical satire in the poet's changed circumstances without this recognition would be a naive exercise in imitation, an exercise in decorum without *kairos*" (92).

Wheeler (1992, 118) suggests that the reference to the "plight of poets" found throughout *Sat2* recalls Juvenal's seventh satire.

Gorbunov (1993, 95) notes that the key themes in *Sat2* and *Sat5*—the bribability, falsity, and the chicanery and greed of judges—appear for the first time in English literature in these poems and, further, soon became common concerns in the urban comedies of Ben Jonson and Thomas Middleton.

Wiggins (2000, 16–17, 107) finds the same "high-handed contempt of writers" in *Sat2* as in the young Donne's letters to Wotton (16), and he adds that *Noct* "represents the most heightened instance of a detachment from poetry" that first appears in *Sat2* (107).

Unity and Structure

Aronstein (1920, 160–61) states that *Sat1*, *Sat2*, and *Sat4*, because of their shifting, multiple subjects, lack artistic unity.

Hillyer (1941, xxii, xxxii–xxxiv) comments briefly that *Sat2* "as a whole exhibits a lack of unified construction" (xxxii).

Erskine-Hill (1964, 162) notes the "miscellaneous" composition of this satire.

Hughes (1968, 25) suggests that *Sat2* could be considered a "companion piece" to *Sat1* in that the two poems are of equal length; the persona that Donne adopts in each poem is the same, "rich in years, wisdom, and grace"; and the targets of both "have a curious resemblance to the Donne outside the poems." In fact, the first two Satyres are, he notes, "directed against Donne himself" and are "ironically suicidal" (25).

According to Lecocq (1969, 372–73), *Sat2* has a three-part structure: an introductory portrait of the persona's hatred and the state of poetry (1–30), a transition (31–38), and the satire of Coscus's insolence (39–112).

Powers (1971, 62) asserts that the satirist's silent auditor in *Sat2* and *Sat4* is structurally important, since he provides a target, other than the reader, for the satire.

Kerins (1984, 54–55) comments that both *Sat2* and *Sat5* "are in the form of the satiric epistle," adding that while *Sat2* "is addressed to a presumably fictitious 'Sir,'" *Sat5* "is addressed to Sir Thomas Egerton, Lord Keeper of the Great Seal." He adds that *Sat5* "is concerned with a concrete contemporary issue—the abuses of a graft-ridden legal system, specifically the Star Chamber fees," and thus "the manifest fiction" of *Sat2* is "reduced to an 'authoriz'd, satiric inquiry, one in which Donne himself was currently engaged." He concludes that although *Sat2* "is the most topical" of the Satyres, "it is also the most generalized."

Baumlin (1991, 92) contends that *Sat2* is comparable to *Sat1* in its "criticism of Horace" in that it "invokes the stylistic decorum of its Juvenalian model," and in this poem Donne "rejects the model's method of rebuke, repudiating any claim to effect change in a world where both man and language have suffered a fall." What *Sat2* accomplishes, however, is to prepare for the recovery of "the persuasive power traditionally ascribed" to satire "by revealing the extent of language's decay." He concludes that the "dialectical interplay between decorum and *kairos* continues throughout Donne's collection of satires: a rhetoric of decorous imitation, one seeking to recreate the stylistic features (and thus invoke the linguistic presence or 'speaking image' of the model) confronts a kairotic recognition of change, of critical difference borne of the poet's unique political and religious circumstances."

Shawcross (2000–01, 28) suggests that "recognizing the form, genre, and mode of Renaissance" verse satire "should lead to rereadings and reevaluations" of poems such as *Sat2*, which, he adds, "is not bifurcated into two topics."

Language and Style

Rhys (1924, 313) introduces Pope's version of *Sat2* with the observation that while Donne's style is "rugged and most unmusical," it is "not very antiquated in expression."

Rugoff (1939, 76) draws attention to the grasp of legal terminology which enables Donne to ridicule its misuse.

Benham (1941, 471) cites *Sat2* as evidence that Donne "was nauseated by the conventional current poetry."

Louthan (1951, 98, 137–38) contends that that linguistic "obscurity" and "extremely abrupt transitions" make this poem difficult (98). He suggests that while this poem is "obscure by design" (137), this was not Donne's normal practice but an attempt to dissociate certain poems, including this one, from his personal life.

Erskine-Hill (1964, 162) calls attention to "the often needlessly rough numbers" of the poem and its "cryptic strokes of wit."

Bross (1966, 133, 137) states with regard to Sat2 and Sat4 that Pope was not put off by Donne's "shocking and grotesque metaphors and similes," nor did he "water down" Donne's "coarse or ribald language" (133). He argues that Donne's style is characterized by "exploding capsules," that is, "compressed, economical, contracted statements" that follow one after another in quick succession (137).

Milgate (1967, xix–xxi) says that "ironic or illustrative allusion to things not strictly relevant to the main subject of satire" is a frequent stylistic device in Sat2, often "introduced as an image." Donne's originality in using this device, "found occasionally in the Roman satirists," is in "almost invariably making the minor term of the image, or the thing to which reference is made, itself an object of satire or an emblem of corruption" (xix), and Milgate notes that Donne uses this device with more "frequency and resource" than any of his contemporaries. Moreover, Donne's images achieve "at once a neat brevity and a humorous satiric exaggeration, whether pictorial" or "more subtly" through witty comparisons (xx–xxi).

Hughes (1968, 26) remarks that "the roll call of fools" in Sat2 is "full and boisterous: rhymesters, theatrical poets, plagiarists, poetasters, shysters, libertines," but he also notes that the poem is "merely a compendium, an assembling of leftover victims" from Sat1.

Lecocq (1969, 372) claims that although Sat2 opens with the salutation "Sir," the remaider of the poem has little, if anything, to do with an epistolary spirit or style.

Piper (1969, 61–62, 122) notes that Donne made "illuminating use of the couplet's definitive and emphatic qualities"—to "define separate epigrams," which then suggested parallel relationships, and to define "rhetorical antitheses," albeit often in a "syntactically slanted and metrically crabbed manner." But he also observes that Donne "has used the couplet only incidentally." He notes that Donne also uses enjambment and couplet stops, concludes major thoughts in the middle of a line, and sometimes inserts "metrically fragmentary interpolations—solicitous, witty, exclamatory—which pervade and obstruct the metrical flow"—all of which suggest that Donne's "satiric utterance is always referential, always relevant" (61). Donne may appear to be arrogant, he concludes, but that is "not because he is too selfishly devoted to his own satiric perceptions to concern himself with an audience, but because he is too willing to confine his full satiric impact to an audience which extensively shares his feelings and knowledge along with his intellectual penetration and range, with an audience, that is to say, which excludes us" (61–62).

Erskine-Hill (1972, 274) observes that the mood in the poem is one of "somewhat hectoring indignation," noting that "there is some effectiveness in the change of Coscus from a figure of mere ridicule to one of menace" and concluding that the poem "abounds in strokes of vigorous and mordant wit."

In the context of discussing Sat2, Shawcross (1972, 263–64) remarks that what Jonson objected to in Donne's metrical rhythm "was apparently the very frequent use of trochees and spondees and pyrrhics," but he suggests that "what Donne gains by his practice is an enhancement of the naturalness afforded by language and idea, plus an unavoidable emphasis on the words and ideas that are important," as well as "an ambiguity on occasion which is significant for the context."

Swift (1974, 46–47) asserts that *Sat2* remains interesting in spite of its overlapping strong lines which often go emphatically against the rules, adding that the sense of the lines is made clear by Donne's well-known sensibility for the rhythm of his dialectically-structured arguments.

Sinha (1977, 63) finds that *Sat2* is not as dramatic as *Sat1*, noting, "there is only a thesis to be argued," which the satirist "expounds" in a manner that is "discursive, anecdotal, and elusive: concrete examples, presented with the maximum of colourful and realistic detail, mingle with passages of generalization, but the ebullience and liveliness" of *Sat1* "are missing."

Williams (1977, 117) remarks that the concluding lines of *Sat2* "seem cramped, hurried, abrupt."

Partridge (1978, 40) praises the linguistic achievements of *Sat2* and remarks that "few readers" of the Satyres "appreciate the movement" of Donne's verse "within the line, or from one line to the next." He notes that "the directness of language is surprising," for "little grammatical complexity endangers the sense," and the poem is not "garnished unduly with schemes of words." Directing our attention to the connection between the language and the meaning of the poem, he observes that the interplay of various aural effects "blends merrily" with the "repetition of words and more," thereby emphasizing "Donne's exasperation at those who misapply legal language in their courtships."

Dubrow (1979, 77) observes that Donne sometimes "achieves a Chinese-box effect of image within image by including yet another simile, and yet more satire, within the vehicle," noting an example from *Sat2*, in which Donne "compares the way a man acquires land to the way a woman saves for her wedding—and then in turn compares her thrift to a form of religious devotion."

Lein (1980, 147–48) remarks that Donne's description of "the extremity of vice" is made stronger by "a significant stylistic feature—the heavy use of negative comparatives and superlatives," and he counts more than twenty instances of this literary device and suggests that they "powerfully reinforce the metaphoric patterns of increasing degeneracy."

Kerins (1984, 42, 44) observes that *Sat2* "begins unmistakably with the voice of the courtly wit." The satirist adopts the pose of "the jaded courtier smug in his elegant superiority," and Kerins suggests that "the poised composure of the opening lines and the epistolary form in which they are contained" define the world of this poem as one of "courtly sophistication" (42). But he adds that the poem ends on an "elegiac" note: while "new men like Coscus" destroy "traditional aristocratic values," the satirist can only watch helplessly as he "eloquently assesses the state of the world and demonstrates the insufficiency of his courtly perspective" (44).

Baumlin (1985, 35–37, 39–40) notes that Coscus's "grotesqueness" is described in humorous terms, and "the effects are typically Horatian." However, the consequences of Coscus' crime are serious and "the tragic implications of his actions ultimately demand a style that rises above the low comic to a manner of expression more serious and grand," which results in a style that, "like the subject matter," mixes "the serious and the ludicrous, the base and the high tragic"—a "stylistic hallmar[k] of the Juve-nalian satirist" (35). In his imitation of Juvenal, however, Donne introduces greater depth into the concerns of satire by going beyond the initial targets of bad poetry and bad lawyers and focusing on the more serious matter of "the abuse and weakness of language." Donne's satirist recognizes the "weakened powers of a fallen language" and "can point out only the futility of his own language to do good" (36–37). He suggests further that when Donne uses Horace and Juvenal, he copies their "stylistic features" but rejects "their linguistic optimism, their methods of rebuke, and any as-sertion of ability to effect change in a world where both man and his language have suffered a fall." Consequently, Donne's imitation of Juvenal leads to a "failed" satire, one "aware of its incapacity to reform." Compelled to deny "efficacy to the language of the Juvenalian satirist," Donne transforms Sat2 "into a self-consuming artifact" (39). He concludes that Sat2 illustrates "the ways *kairos* can undermine decorum," in the manner that poems which "call into question the validity or efficacy of their own form tend, ultimately, not so much to surpass as to destroy or reject their models"; in short, "they tend, simply, to deconstruct" (39–40).

Hamburger and Schuenke (1985, 17) point to the specialized jargon of judicial legalese in Sat2 as an example of the bold innovation of language found throughout Donne's poetry.

Corthell (1987, 27) finds that in Sat2 Donne's rhetoric is "primarily conservative," noting that "the love poets pitied by Donne rely upon the magical, incantatory power of langauge," but "opposed to this mystification of poetic language" we find Coscus's "affected metaphysical style which reduces poetry to the level of a legal 'motion' (49)."

Corthell (1997, 32–33) notes that in Sat2 the satirist "works to gain the rhetorical upper hand over Coscus" by means of the "'tropes of courtesy' classified and analyzed by Frank Whigham" [*Ambition and Privilege: The Social Tropes of Elizabethan Courtesy Theory* (Berkeley and Los Angeles: University of California Press, 1984)].

Oliver (1997, 34) notes that Sat2, along with the other poetry written at Lincoln's Inn, would have established Donne "as a writer of knotty, sophisticated verse."

Notes and Glosses

1–24 *Sir,...for wrighting ill.* **MILGATE** (1967): in these lines, the "sly but admira-bly sustained caricature," using "comparisons and allusions," is "easy to miss." Donne's images "often achieve at once a neat brevity and a humorous satiric exaggeration" (xx).

1–10 *Sir,...not worth hate.* **DOCHERTY** (1986): "In an emotion of hatred the hated object can become less hated, and even pitied instead, when placed alongside some other extremely 'ill' thing," and "here, the primary object of hatred is poetry itself; but this becomes less hated when compared with the rhetoric of the law. The cure for poetry is outlined as another form of hunger, a cathartic purgation or starva-tion, like the cure for material disease such as the plague," and "just as the body must be starved for its health, so likewise poetry has to be starved out" (242). **MORSE** (1989): Donne "humorously alludes to the Puritan claim that the poor harvests of the 1590s and the Spanish Armada of 1588 were God's punishment on England for her sins," suggesting that, perhaps for Puritans, there can be no greater sin than "that of being a poet." Donne thus casts himself as a sinner, but, "like the Papists, not worth the hate." Donne asks "not to be hated as a poet" and also asks "not to be hated as a Papist." In desiring attention as a poet, he also asks "to remain unnoticed." His satire can thus be "the more abusive because it is to be discounted in advance," for its "strenuousness is only a mock strenuousness," only "vitriol and water." It demonstrates its "superficiality even when it is written from the heart" (273).

1–4 *Sir, … towards the rest.* ROUSSEAU AND RUDENSTINE (1972) paraphrase as "All ill things have one state in which they are quintessentially bad; when they achieve this condition, they are so hateful as to make their other states seem merely pitiful." Add that Donne "may also be punning on state as denoting an occupation or class (estate) of society—in this case, the occupations of poetry and the law" (60). HESTER (1979): "Like the Latin defenses, Donne's *apologia* begins with an analysis of the character of satire, its moral bases and restrictions" (143). The "most surprising note here," one that has "most disturbed modern readers," is the "parenthetical comment by the satirist." It is not intended as "a parody of Christian teaching but, in accordance with the distinction between venial and mortal sins, conforms to Christian teaching about the correct and necessary uses of hatred." In terms of the "larger strategies," it also "serves to establish from the outset the uniqueness of the satirist's moral stance through the definition of his vision as a gift of God" and affirms that "even the assent to folly and crime by 'all this towne' cannot obviate the need for and value of the satirist's moral perspective," a view reiterated in the poem's conclusion (143–44).

1–2 *Sir, … all this towne,* GRANSDEN (1954): "The satirist must appear as a *poseur,* taking up an attitude of moral and intellectual superiority," which requires "a large vocabulary, a short range (i.e., a few choice spirits among whom to circulate one's efforts) and the rhetorician's rather than the lyric poet's technique" (102). SANDERS (1971): Donne was "salutarily aware that being a satirist had dangerous affinities with being a fop—the fop whose voice we hear exquisitely mimicked" in these lines (37). HESTER (1977c): as announced here the "stress" of the poem "is on the satirist's hatred" (188). CAREY (1981): the satirist's "hate is a way of drawing attention to himself," and "while he rips open society's sores, he can project himself as not only more honest and upright than the rest of mankind but as cleverer, full of smart answers, altogether outstandingly able" (49). HESTER (1982): Donne's speaker "never goes so far as to endorse Juvenal's view that man's irrationality has reached a degree that makes reformation impossible," for here "total degradation is yet only a threat." Further, "in terms of the paradigm of satire-as-zeal," *Sat2* "dramatically isolates the anger or 'brave scorn' of the prophetic dialectic, in order to evaluate its applicability in a moral climate that threatens the viability of satire itself" (33). KERINS (1984): the poem "begins unmistakably with the voice of the courtly wit," and "here the satirist plays the jaded courtier smug in his elegant superiority. The poised composure of the opening lines and the epistolary form in which they are contained stand in stark contrast to the passionate exclamation" that opens *Sat1* (42). PARRY (1985): this opening "is no preliminary to escape, but rather to an enthusiastic involvement in the crowd of bad poets and fancy lawyers he professes to despise" (47). **CLAMPITT** (1988): what causes Donne's "gorge to rise is a bad poet who is also a lawyer—the stereotypical creep, still revoltingly alive and identifiable notwithstanding the Elizabethan attire. That the author is himself a poet and a lawyer only adds to the scathing force of the indictment" (7). **FISH** (1990): "Here the speaker begins by firmly distinguishing himself from the town which he does 'hate / Perfectly' (1–2). The perfection of his hatred and the distance it implies are compromised, however, when he specifies it more precisely: he hates those who wield words, and he hates especially poets, and among poets he hates those who have transferred their verbal arts to the public sphere in order to manipulate the law" (237). **CORTHELL** (1997): "the satirist claims to 'hate / Perfectly all this towne,'" but "within the space of nine lines we read that poets, like Papists, are 'not worth hate'" (37). **POST** (1999) notes the "colloquial immediacy" of Donne's opening lines, adding that the "registers of speech, not song, are what the poet puts in motion with his opening utterances" (5).

1 *Sir,* **GRIERSON** (1912): a note in SN 2067 prefixed to this poem indicates that it "is taken from 'C. B.'s copy', i.e. Christopher Brooke's," and it is "quite possible" that *Sat2* "was addressed to him" (2:111). **MILGATE** (1967), citing Grierson's (1912) suggestion that "the poem is addressed to Christopher Brooke," objects that the evidence in SN 2067 is "very weak" (128–29). **LECOCQ** (1969) suggests that the "Sir" here may be Chancellor Egerton (375). **WIGGINS** (2000): "the use of the appelation 'Sir' to designate Egerton" in *Sat5* 31 "links Egerton" (25) to the addressee here, and in contrast to *Sat4*, Donne uses "Sir" here "to establish a solidarity with the grave man and to exalt himself thereby" (54).

2–4 *yet ther is one...towards the rest.* **MILGATE** (1967): all evil things "occur in one form that is so essentially evil that our hatred for this enables us to view the less heinous forms of the vice with pity" (128). There is "a perfect or quintessential state of everything in which it is 'best' or purest; in this sense, evil ('ill') itself can take a form which is 'best' and 'excellent'" (129). **LECOCQ** (1969): the use of the word "state" and the plurals that follow indicate that all the men of the law are targeted through Coscus. It is the abusive, fraudulent, and criminal enrichment of an entire professional category that is denounced; it is the scandal of transgression of the law and rights by those who, instead of serving them, help themselves in order to commit with impunity an abuse of power (374–75).

2–3 *one State...excellently best* **SHAWCROSS** (1972): "the one state is not the state of love," for Donne "is using the vehicle of love pleaders and their function in poetry to satirize the court pleader and his fiction," and the name Coscus "epitomizes this" since the subject of the poem "is lawyers and the law courts, not poetic amorists" (271). **NEWTON** (1974): Donne "self-consciously, and a bit self-righteously, accepts responsibility for the satiric character and calls upon no Humorist to shoulder part of the blame," and "at the same time, he also tries to evade responsibility by dissipating most of his hate into 'pitty.'" Moreover, the pity Donne refers to here is "largely but a reflex of a greater hate" (431).

2 *Perfectly...one State* **STEIN** (1944c) cites this line as an example of first foot

stress-shift (378), and of a stress-shift joining a stressed syllable with two unstressed ones (397).

2 *Perfectly* **SMITH** (1971): "thoroughly" (474).

2 *one State* **GROSART** (1872–73): "one position in this town, viz. that which he satirises, the state of Coscus" (1:18). **SHAWCROSS** (1967): "the court of law, particularly the lawyer's part in its operation" (18).

2 *State* **ROUSSEAU AND RUDENSTINE** (1972): "Condition, state of being." (60).

3 *excellently best* **SMITH** (1971): "most nearly perfect in evil" (474).

4 *hate...towards the rest.* **SMITH** (1971): "other things by comparison are so much less evil that one pities rather than hates them" (474).

4 *them* **MILGATE** (1967): "ill things" when they are in an "excellently best" state (129).

4 *pity* **MILGATE** (1967) cites *Sat3* 1–4, where pity modifies the satirist's "scorn, anger, or hatred" (129). [So also, Patrides (1985, 219).]

5–22 *Though Poetry...for meat?* **ELLRODT** (2000): in speaking "contemptuously of poetry" here, Donne "obviously takes the pose expected from a gentleman who will never condescend to print" (350).

5–10 *Though Poetry...not worth hate.* **WHITLOCK** (1960): "The irony here seems shot through with understandable tenderness. The presenting of his mother must have made a strong impression on the young Donne, for it was certainly not brought about by any untoward action by her. It was a case, like so many others, of a quiet, peaceful person being mistreated only for her beliefs. This cannot be said of the later imprisonment of his brother, Henry, at least not to the same degree" (383). **LEIN** (1980): "The conjunction of verse and pestilence here links the prologue and main satire still more closely, for the poem's opening movement from poetry to law is a symbolic presentation of the process of Time, both in terms of growth and in terms of progressive disease." As such, "the town is sick and evil," and some have "merely advanced in the illness more than others." It is thus "within this context of universal malaise and rampant vice that variations on the central experience emerge" (134–35). **DIPASQUALE** (1993): "poverty-stricken rhymers" are associated here with "both Catholicism and the maladies of Petrarchan desire; their self-defeating 'sinne' weakens England and makes it vulnerable to the extravagant fashions and ultra-Catholic aggressions of Spain, while they themselves are afflicted with the plague-like disease of 'old fashion'd love': pitiable and impotent, they suffer its 'Ridlingly' paradoxical symptom of icy fire, fever and chills" (82).

5–8 *Though Poetry...catch men,* **HESTER** (1982): although the "association of poetry with recent calamities in England" acknowledges the "current failure of poetry to realize its civilizing and moral capabilities," it is primarily an "ironic strategy that discloses the ultimate harm the insolence of Coscus portends." A "view of the satirist as minister and scourge is ironically suggested by the associations of poetry with calamities" that, according to the "authoritative *Book of Homilies*, the medical authorities of the day, and the weekly sermons," were a result of "God's anger with the community—and supports the satirist's initial view of himself as an agent or benefice of God's ire. Satire *can* be associated with dearths, famines, the Spaniards, and the plague since it too arises from God's anger or that of God's agent" (39–40).

5–6 *Though Poetry...and Spanyards in;* ROUSSEAU AND RUDENSTINE (1972): the passage "alludes ironically to the Puritan charge that poetry is conducive to moral decay, and brings punishment from God in the forms of recurring famines and threats of foreign invasion" (61). FREER (1996): Donne "repeatedly alludes to the influx of Spanish gold," here "writing in the persona of a starving poet" (500).

6–9 *brings dearths...steru'd out,* HESTER (1977a): "Donne's satirist suggests that the widespread disregard for the potential truth-bearing capabilities of language has brought about the regrettable state of poetry" (24).

6 *As I thinke...Spanyards in;* MILGATE (1967): the line "echoes, and gives precision to, the common Puritan charge that poetry, the nurse of idleness and effeminacy, takes men from fruitful labour and is the enemy of the military virtues"; see Gosson's *School of Abuse* (1579) (129).

6 *dearths* MILGATE (1967): "There had been a time of great scarcity in 1586, and another was developing in 1594 (lasting into 1598); each coincided with signs of a growing threat from Spain" (129). SHAWCROSS (1967): "costliness (and famine)" (18). [So also, Smith (1971, 474) and Patrides (1985, 219).]

6 *Spanyards* SHAWCROSS (1967): "passionate avowers of their love" (18).

7–9 *Though like...steru'd out,* MILGATE (1967): poetry, plague, and (according to Petrarchan tradition) love "can be cured only by starving out the ailment." Starving poets are familiar in classical, Renaissance, and Augustan poetry. On plague, see Walter Bruel, *Praxis Medicinae* (1585) as translated by "J. A." (1632), pp. 406–07. As for love, "loss of appetite was one of the symptoms," but if "still in the sanguine stage," love could be treated by spare diet, reducing "the amount of blood in the body" and thus reducing desire; see MM 4:3, 150–53 and Burton, *Anatomy of Melancholy*, part. 3, sect. 2, memb. 5, subsect. 1 (129). SMITH (1971): "men catch poetry mysteriously, as they catch the plague or caught love in old romances" (474).

7–8 *like the pestilence...catch men,* LEIN (1980): these lines on "the tenacious hold of poetry" directly adapt "Juvenal's *'nam si discedas, laqueo tenet ambitiosi / [consuetudo mali, tenet insanabile multos] / scribendi cacoethes et aegro in corde senescit'* (VII. 50–52; 'For if you would give it up, the itch for writing and making a name holds you fast as with a noose, and becomes inveterate in your distempered brain,' *Juvenal and Persius*, ed. G. G. Ramsay, Loeb Classical Library, rev. ed., Cambridge, Mass., 1940, pp. 140–41)." Further, Donne's "ideas of poetry as 'Pestilence' and of Coscus as a 'mad' poet both derive from these lines" (142).

7 *Though like...old fashiond loue* RICHTER (1902) uses this line to illustrate the

occurrence of a double unstressed syllable in the middle of the verse that shows Donne's attempt to overcome the disparity between word accent and verse rhythm (401).

7 *pestilence* SHAWCROSS (1967): "the plague" (18). [So also, Patrides (1985, 219).]

7 *old fashiond loue* SHAWCROSS (1967): "true and sincere love" (18).

8 *It ridlingly...doth remoue* STEIN (1944c) (reading "Ridlingly it catch men") cites this line as an example of stress-shift in the first three feet (383).

8 *ridlingly catch men,* HESTER (1977a): Donne's satirist offers a sarcastic glance at the survival of a belief in "the incantatory powers" of satire (23). MCGRATH (1980): Donne's "complaint against the abuses of poetry is founded in a recognition that poetry might deceptively and 'ridlingly...catch men'" (73).

8 *ridlingly* JOHNSON (1755): "In the manner of a riddle," a riddle being "an enigma; a puzzling question; a dark problem." OED (1914) cites this as the earliest use of the adverbial form. ROUSSEAU AND RUDENSTINE (1972): "Inexplicably" (61). CHMIELEWSKI (2001): "mysteriously, without obvious cause" (614).

8 *catch* SHAWCROSS (1967): "entangle, charm" (18).

9–10 *yet their State...not worth hate.* NORTON (1895): "'Their' has no antecedent; it refers to 'the poets' understood" (1:241). [So also, Milgate (1967, 129).] NEWTON (1974): "Like the 'hate' of the first line," the self-hate here "is dissipated by the double means of pity and projection" (432).

9–10 *their State...like Papists,* ROUSSEAU AND RUDENSTINE (1972): this passage "alludes to legal restrictions imposed in England upon Catholics in the 1580's" (61). HESTER (1982): this passage "alludes to the specific statute that had recently led to the arrest and suspicious death of Donne's younger brother (for harboring a Jesuit priest)" and also suggests that "the sharp attack on legal procedures that propels the poem probably had specific biographical origins, and that the impetus of the poem was not, as has been assumed, the group of anonymous sonnets, *Zepheria*, which appeared in 1592" (40). OLIVER (1997): in this allusion, it is difficult to know whether the speaker "is being contemptuous or sympathetic" (36). STEVENS (2001): Donne speaks here, as he does in *Pseudo*, to the Catholics' "condition or state within a state" (63).

9 *steru'd out,* SHAWCROSS (1967): "destroyed (particularly by famine or cold)" (18). SMITH (1971): "starvation cures a man of the itch to earn his living by poetry, as it supposedly cures the plague and love" (474).

9 *their* MILGATE (1967): "the poets'" (129).

10 *Is poore,...not worth hate.* RUGOFF (1939) cites this line as an example of Donne's images drawn from the great religious controversy of his time, adding that this extremist position is used as a "symbol of the contemptible" (92). BAUMLIN (1991) suggests the possibility of a "serious argument" that is "woven as if into the underside of the poem, an argument that Papists are not worth hate, that there are

people and practices and attitudes at court far more insidious and dangerous to the nation" (88). **CORTHELL** (1997): Donne relates changing social conditions "by analogy to the Reformation," and this line "marks the attack on poetry as a Puritan discourse" (35). **DIPASQUALE** (1999): here Donne "explicitly paralleled the two practices—that of the poet and that of the Catholic" (229). [Similarly, Edwards (2001, 53).] **WIGGINS** (2000): "apart from preparing the reader" for *Sat3* and "offering a suggestion as to Donne's religious position in the mid-1590s, the comparison of poets to papists" here "deepens the impasse with which Donne confronts his judge" (39–40).

10 *poore, disarm'd, like Papists,* **MILGATE** (1967) cites *Statutes of the Realm* 4: 707, where by "statute 27° Eliz. c. 2. (1584–5)" Jesuits and other priests were banished for refusing the oath of supremacy and laity were fined or imprisoned for "not disclosing to a J. P. or other officer the presence of a priest in the kingdom"; cites also Robert Southwell's *An Humble Supplication to Her Majesty* (1591), ed. Bald (1953), pp. 1, 40ff. and notes that Donne's brother died in 1593 "as a result of his violation of the statute referred to" (130). **SMITH** (1971): "Roman Catholics were so discriminated against in late sixteenth-century England that—Donne implies—there was no point in persecuting them since they could not injure the State" (475). **PATRIDES** (1985) notes that Roman Catholics were "relentlessly persecuted under Elizabeth I" (219).

11–43 *One…made a Lawyer:* **ELWIN AND COURTHOPE** (1881): Donne's "design is to blacken the character of the attorney by comparing his crimes with others which are allowed to be heinous, but which the poet says have in them something of humanity," and this argument "flows naturally on in Donne's colloquial style to its proper climax" (3:428n1).

11–16 *One…do moue.* **RUGOFF** (1939): Donne's only direct comment on the theatre in these years is a "contemptuous" one, and unless we interpret these lines to refer only to hack playwrights and inferior actors, these comments are not easy to reconcile with the information that Donne was a "great frequenter of Playes" (106). [So also, Ellrodt (2000, 119).] **HARRIS** (1962): Donne associated the theatre "with folly and idleness, and often also with shame and degradation" (262). **BAUMLIN** (1991): "the actors become puppets prompted by the dramatist's panting 'wind.' The speaker condemns them all, then, for having divorced the heart from the tongue: the playwright does not speak for himself, nor do his actors speak their own thoughts" (85). **WIGGINS** (2000): these are "perhaps the most memorable" lines of the poem as "the image of the convict reciting his neck verse crystallizes Donne's view of the relation of poets and lawyers, of poetry and power," for "it is the lawyer, after all, who passes judgment on the neck verse, who decrees life or death for the poet, and it is the poet who must cope with the legal system, not the lawyer who must adjust himself to poetic fictions" (35–36).

11–14 *One…Labord Sceanes,* **RUGOFF** (1939): "a contemptuous comment on playwrights is made absolutely withering by a courtroom simile," and these lines make "strikingly vivid use" of the custom of pleading "benefit of clergy" (78). **BROSS** (1966): Donne "intends to compare the two total situations (the salvation of an illiterate by a condemned man, vs. the support of an actor by a starved poet's work).

For the strict grammarian, the zealous semanticist, the statement of comparison should actually compare the two actions themselves, but Donne's sentence really makes its statement of comparison about only the two persons involved—the starved playwright and the condemned man. By means of a relative clause tacked to the compared noun, 'wretch,' Donne haphazardly implies, but does not make, a comparison between the two situations taken as wholes" (141). PIPER (1969) (reading parentheses surrounding "like...Life"): the "suspensive material" that "introduces the elements of a double analogy (poet-wretch; actor-illiterate) runs two and one-half lines. The couplet break, which separates the prompting of the illiterate from his salvation, gives this as yet unrelated material a dramatic emphasis—if one can catch and enjoy it. The application of this analogy, which is squeezed into the last line and one-half of the passage, is also dramatically suspended by the splintering of the predicate, 'gives...meanes...to live,' and, especially, by line-end emphasis on the quite empty term 'meanes': it thus bursts forth only in the last half-line of the passage." As such, "the point of this passage, the irony of a poet's starving to death while giving actors the means of life, is hard to grasp" (208–09). ROUSSEAU AND RUDENSTINE (1972): "starving playwrights provide ignorant actors with materials to make a living, just as a condemned prisoner may help a more ignorant person (who cannot read the court's Latin) to escape punishment" (61). LEIN (1980): this passage "portrays a deathly environment which somehow manages to generate further life, but life lacking all value, purpose, and meaning. The portrait of the world which Donne offers us insists that there is a relentless erosion of value. At the same time it maintains that all existence is but a form of death in life and that within temporality itself there is no redemptive value" (149). DOCHERTY (1986): the "cure for poetry, the starvation of the poet, is dependent, paradoxically, on the poetry being repeated, rehearsed or read," for as others "repeat the words of the poet, the poet is starved out and thus, it seems, cured." The poet is here judged "through the activity of 'prompting' or bringing others into life and public speech or a kind of confession" (243). PATTERSON (1994) (reading parentheses surrounding "like...Life"): "the primary theme of bad Law enters surreptitiously, in parenthesis. It also enters ambiguously; for though the comparison between poverty-stricken playwright and condemned criminal sounds contemptuous at the level of epithet ('wretch,' 'idiot'), at the narrative level it points to a natural generosity among the underprivileged, along with the ingenuity that allows them to exploit the absurd and the obsolete in the judicial system (the benefit of clergy and the use of a rudimentary literacy—the 'neck-verse'—to claim it)" (148).

11–13 *like a wretch...saues his Life,* BEWLEY (1966): "a prisoner subject to the capital penalty" who prompts "an illiterate prisoner in court" and saves his life (clerics "having at least minor orders" were "exempted from the punishment of death for certain offenses" if they could "read the opening lines of Psalm 51") (172). [So also, Milgate (1967, 130), who cites Thomas Platter's *Travels in England* (1599) and Donne's *Sermons* 1:232, Shawcross (1967, 18), Warnke (1967, 110), Smith (1971, 475), Patrides (1985, 219), Docherty (1986, 243), Carey (1990, 423), Kruzhkova (1994, 157), and Chmielewski (2001, 614–15).]

11 *One...as dead* **STEIN** (1944b): the "harsh consonants" of this line "are apparently from carelessness or lack of interest" (403).

11 *One* **SHAWCROSS** (1967): "a playwright" (18). [So also, Chmielewski (2001, 614).]

11 *at barr iudgd as dead* **SMITH** (1971): "condemned to death at the Bar" (475).

12 *prompts* **CAREY** (1990): "Helps his illiterate neighbour to read the 'neck-verse' and claim benefit of clergy" (423).

13–16 *giues Ideot Actors...do moue.* **HESTER** (1981): "in the larger rhetoric of the poem, the poets or poetasters described here escape the satirist's harsher rebuke only because their pathetic inadequacy renders them less a threat to the nation than more powerful abusers of words such as the meretricious lawyer Coscus" (20). The "'Organ' simile is original with Donne," but "the figure of the poet as 'bellows' or, more specifically, the poetaster as 'bellows' is not," for Donne's image "amplifies the opening image in satirical *apologiae* by Horace [Satire I.iv.19–21] and Persius [Satire V]." The bellows of Horace and Persius could not be "organ bellows," but their portraits of the poetaster as "hot-air expirant is identical to the derisive point of Donne's image: the 'poore' poet 'labor[s]' (*laborantis*) 'as' (*imitare*) 'bellows' (*follibus, folle*) 'pant' (*anhelanti*)." Donne's figure both reveals the "literal dependency of the 'ideot actors' on the artist," and, "like its classical analogues," it "suggests that such poetasters merit their anonymity and poverty because of the insubstantiality and hollowness of their laborious efforts" (21).

13–14 *giues Ideot Actors...Labord Sceanes,* **HUNTER** (1982): when Donne "sympathizes with starving poets who help others to success," he may have been thinking of Robert Greene (6).

13 *Ideot* **MILGATE** (1967): etymologically, "one without special knowledge," hence "ignorant" or "uneducated" (130). **SMITH** (1971): "ignorant" (475) [so also, Patrides (1985, 219)]; see *ElNat* 1 and *Image* 26 (219).

14 *Steruing himselfe* **SHAWCROSS** (1967): "although killing himself by deprivation for his act" (19).

14 *to liue by his Labord Sceanes,* **CORTHELL** (1997) notes the satirist's "patronizing attitude toward the professional playwright" as evidence of his "disinterested amateur stance," which is "part of a larger courtly strategy of privileging amateurism and recreation over professionalism and industry" (34).

15–17 *As in some...witchcrafts charmes* **MELTON** (1906) uses these lines to illustrate an "arsis-thesis variation of repeated sounds, syllables, and words" (142, 146).

15–16 *As in some...do moue.* **W. L. of LEICESTER** (1772) cites these lines to illustrate "the old organ" that had "moving figures" on it (565). **GRIERSON** (1912) says that "Marlowe and his fellows" are "the bellows which set the actor-puppets in motion" (2:110). **HAYWARD** (1950): "An oblique allusion to contemporary dramatic poets" (102). **MILGATE** (1967): "ideot actors" are "inspired by the overworked playwright" (xxi). See J. B. Leishman's collection of "images by which poets and playwrights assert the dependence of actors upon them" (in *Parnassus Plays* [1949], pp. 344–45), of which this "is the most original and wittily accurate." Some sixteenth-century Continental organs had "puppets or figures" attached, "actuated or 'inspired' by air from the bellows which labored ('pant') away unseen"; see E. J. Hopkins and E. F. Rimbault, *The Organ; its History and Construction*, 2nd ed. (1870), pp. 87–88; and C. Sachs, *History of Musical Instruments* (1940), p. 308. Such adornments on English organs came much later; see *Archaeologia* 35 (1853):332; W. Ludham, *Gentleman's Magazine* 42 (1772):565n; and W. L. Sumner, *The Organ*, 2nd ed. (1955), p. 110 (130).

15–16 *As in some...pant below* **ROUSSEAU AND RUDENSTINE** (1972): "Marionettes hung on the organ and moved by wind from the bellows" (61).

15 *puppets* **SHAWCROSS** (1967): "the hands and feet of the organist" (19).

16 *And bellows...do moue.* **MELTON** (1906): see note for *Sat1* 5.

16 *moue.* **ROUSSEAU AND RUDENSTINE** (1972): "Animate, inspire" (61).

17–24 *One would...wrighting ill.* **BAUMLIN** (1991): "there is no truth in the love poet," for the "charm-like sound of his verses" prevails over their "empty sense." Furthermore, if the love poet "elevates manner over meaning," there is "no meaning at all" to be found in the "language of those 'who write, because all write,' and 'have still / That excuse for writing, and for writing ill' (23–24), the fourfold repetition of 'writing' and 'write' turning composition into a mindless moving of pen across paper" (85).

17–20 *One would...best artilleree.* **KERINS** (1984): these lines "epitomize the worldly satirist. In a universe governed by wit and its corollary, social preeminence, sophistication is all. The 'Pistolets' pun illustrates this kind of urbanity: as well as being handguns, pistolets are also Spanish coins. Thus these lines pretend an interest in military innovation while, more important, they coolly observe that in Love's war money is more efficient than the 'seely' verses of love-struck poets. In a moral framework the satirist may decry this situation; in a courtly one he dismisses it with a pun" (42–43). **DOCHERTY** (1986) cites a manuscript variant that provides "greater clarity to the concealed pun." Says that the emendation "makes more apparent the pun on 'ram/rhyme', giving what may in fact appear to be more coherent: 'Rams [rhimes] and songs now are silly battery, / Pistolets are the best artillery'." Believes that this makes "doubly significant" the pun on the word "rhime," "suggesting a reading or version in which the power of rhyme does, despite the first two lines quoted, have the historically real power of the 'ram'" (196). **MAROTTI** (1986): Donne "objected to those who slavishly followed the literary fashions of the day, including the courtly practice of composing Petrarchan lyrics. The man who 'would move Love by rimes' (17) is foolish because he is not aggressive enough" (41).

17–18 *One would...old harmes.* **SMITH** (1971): "trying to win love by poems is now as old-fashioned and superstitious as trying to harm people by spells" (475). [So also, Chmielewski (2001, 615).] **LEIN** (1980): in these lines, "the aesthetic loss is quietly communicated," and "the single word 'charms' evokes all the ritual, beauty, daring, and mystery which no longer exist." The lines also reveal the "strain of lost nobility" (136). **DIPASQUALE** (1993): the speaker "mocks every kind of poet from the professional playwright to the dilettante lyricist." Donne here "plays upon a popular Reformation theme," one associating "the Catholic past with a now defunct magic. The writer of feeble Petrarchan pleas finds himself thwarted in the pursuit of sex because he trusts in the poetic equivalent of 'hocus-pocus'; his superstitious mumblings make no impression on the women of the satirist's reformed and enlightened age" (82). **CORTHELL** (1997): "the love poets pitied by Donne rely upon the magical, incantatory power of language" (33), and this "devaluation of poetry" includes satyre (173n38).

17–18 *witchcrafts charmes...old harmes.* **SMITH** (1971): "trying to win love by poems is now as old-fashioned and superstitious as trying to harm people by spells" (475). **HESTER** (1982): the satirist's "ironic denigration of poetry continues with the allusion to the old Irish belief that the 'riddles' of satire have magical powers of life and death over its victims." It is not clear as to whether or not the satirist "would support such a theory about satire," but "the syntax of his admission, with its superbly ironic rhyme, reveals that he views this change in the opinion of satire as another instance of the general loss suffered by his countrymen." The speaker "undercut[s] the validity of this lore by suggesting that the 'harmes' resulting from such 'charmes' must have been merely psychological, but even the admission emphasizes that this change is another instance of the loss of faith in the powers of language, and hence a decrease in the satirist's effectiveness with the people" (40).

17 *One would...witchcrafts charmes* **STEIN** (1944c) (reading "rithmes" rather than "rhimes") cites this line as an example of Donne allowing an extra syllable before the caesura (394). **MORRIS** (1953) (reading "rithmes" rather than "rhimes") notes that the word "but" in this line functions as an "outride," or a "hanger," a means for introducing "an extra half-foot into a line without affecting the metrical count," adding that "the outride must always immediately follow a stress, and is theoretically followed by a slight pause" (46).

17 *moue Loue* **SMITH** (1971): "provoke or cause love" (475). [So also, Patrides (1985, 219).]

17 *rhimes;* **MILGATE** (1967): "incantations or spells" (130).

17 *witchcrafts charmes* **MILGATE** (1967), on witches, cites Reginald Scot's *The Discovery of Witchcraft* (1584) and quotes George Giffard's *A Dialogue concerning Witches and Witchcrafts* (1593) in *Shakespeare Association Facsimiles,* (1931) 1:sigs. A2v–A3. On the "increasing tendency to ascribe the witches' conception of their powers to delusion," cites L. Babb, *The Elizabethan Malady* (1951), pp. 54ff. (131).

18–19 *Bring not...seely batteree,* **STEIN** (1944c) cites these lines as an example of stress-shift carrying over from the first foot to the second (383).

19–20 *Ramms...best artilleree.* **GRIERSON** (1912): "Money is as much more effective than poetry in love as fire-arms are than rams and slings in war" (2:110). **MILGATE** (1967): "Battering rams and slings are pitiable (*seely*) weapons of assault nowadays," compared to pistols; on "controversy over the relative virtues" of the long-bow and guns, see K. Muir in *Shakespeare Quarterly* 10 (1959):137; and Humfrey Barwick, *A Brief Discourse concerning the Force and Effect of All Manual Weapons of Fire and the Disability of the Long-Bow* (?1594), sig. A4r. "In love's war, charms and spells, and old-fashioned ways of wooing are weak weapons compared with money" (131). **LEIN** (1980): "Women, like walled towns under siege, are no longer won by force, by manly courage and dedicated perseverance, but by appealing to base desires which corrupt all honor. The whole quality of love thus becomes sullied by money" (136). **HESTER** (1982): the poet "relies on the wrong weapons in his wars of love," for "when compared to 'Pistolets,' the 'rimes' of the lyricists are as pitiable in the wars of love as archaic martial weapons would be in the wars of nations. It is only gold, as the pun on 'Pistolets' (a Spanish coin) affirms, that has any power today." Further, "the Spanish 'Artillerie' that poses the greatest threat to English civilization has already been brought in, not by the silly poets but through the invasion of naked appetite and aggressive materialism which now advance through the land" (41).

19 *Ramms...seely batteree*, **RICHTER** (1902) uses this line to illustrate a metrical inversion from iambic to trochaic in the first two feet (395).

19 *Ramms* **SMITH** (1971): "battering rams" (475). [So also, Patrides (1985, 219).]

19 *seely batteree*, **SMITH** (1971): "feeble and ineffectual weapons of assault" (475). [So also, Patrides (1985, 219).]

19 *seely* **SHAWCROSS** (1967): "feeble" (19). [So also, Chmielewski (2001, 615).] **WARNKE** (1967): "silly, in its obsolete sense as ineffective, futile" (110). **KERMODE** (1970): "foolish" (100). **ROUSSEAU AND RUDENSTINE** (1972): "Weak, pitiful" (61). **GRIGSON** (1980): "useless" (19).

20 *Pistolets...best artilleree*. **SHAWCROSS** (1972): "The involved pun suggests, first, that little guns, rather than rams and slings, are today the best ordnance, that they subtly will devastate the opponent; second, that Spanish money will 'move Love' best in the eternal war of love; and third, that punning proves the most successful art" (254–55).

20 *Pistolets* **GROSART** (1872–73): "A pun = (Spanish) money, and from French small pistols" (1:19). [Similarly, Bewley (1966, 172), Shawcross (1967, 19), Kermode (1970, 100), Smith (1971, 475), Rousseau and Rudenstine (1972, 61), Grigson (1980, 19), Patrides (1985, 219), Carey (1990, 423), and Chmielewski (2001, 615).] **LOUTHAN** (1951): the pun here establishes the theme that "money is the best artillery for political aggrandizement, seduction, what have you" (100). **MILGATE** (1967): "The most effective weapon against foreign countries is gold that buys information, corrupts officers of state, and foments rebellion"; see *ElBrac* 31–32 [so also, Patrides (1985, 219)] and Gardner, *The Elegies and the Songs and Sonnets*, p. 115, where this poem is dated "c. 1593-4" (131). **SMITH** (1971) adds that "Women are now won by bullets"; cites *ElWar* 38 (475).

21–28 *And they...his owne things*, **JENKINS** (1923): in these lines, Donne is "making war upon" the other poets of his own era by rejecting their ideals and versification (568–69).

21–22 *And they…for meat?* **FORDE** (1661) cites these lines on the topic of professional poets (sig. C8b). **DOCHERTY** (1986): "these lines establish an analogy between the kind of writing that this poem actually is and the activity of prayerful communication" (244). **MAROTTI** (1986): here Donne expresses "an aversion to various forms of poetry, an attitude consistent with the harshly unpoetic stance of the formal satirist," and he mocks "not only hack playwrights and plagiarists, but also those who wrote complimentary verse to beg for money" (40–41). **LOW** (1993): Donne laments poetry being reduced "to mere writing for hire, writing for fashion, or plain theft. None of these disorders is simply literary; instead they illustrate how society determines, and in bad times deforms, the writing of poetry. About the second failing, writing for fashion, Donne is relatively mild. As a weakness of the financially secure, it more amuses than concerns him directly. About the first, writing for money, he is harsher. He was too near being forced into that humiliating position himself" (35–36). **KLAUSE** (1994): like other poets, Donne had to "invent hyperbolic compliments which he knew were meretricious, no matter how extensively they were associated with grander themes, how subtly they were qualified with demurrals or hints of resentment, or how truly they were in some limited way deserved. Before he found himself an epideictic poet, he had belittled that role" (184–85). [Similarly, Robbins (2000, 431).] **WIGGINS** (2000): Donne acknowledges that as a poet he may seek patronage, but he "insists that this corruption of language is nothing to Coscus's tyranny over words in the writing of contracts" (34–35). **FLYNN** (2001): Donne here "took aim at the patronage system," particularly "suitors' degrading use of poems as a means to advancement," even though he "himself did apply for work, most likely using his writings and/or his reputation for them as credentials" (114).

21 *they who write to Lords,* **SMITH** (1971): "poets who dedicate their writings to noble patrons" (475). **DIPASQUALE** (1999): Donne "confronts his own uneasiness with being one of those poets" who write for patrons (237).

22 *Are they…for meat?* **STEIN** (1944c) cites this line as an example of stress-shift in the first three feet (383).

22 *like boyes singing at dores* **GROSART** (1872–73): "1633, and usually, 'like singers at doores.' Indifferent, except that 'boys' introduces an unnecessary distraction, without adding to the thought" (1:19–20).

23–30 *And they who…his owne.* **SULLIVAN** (1989) notes that Donne's readership included "poets, dramatists, biographers, musicians, translators, compilers of verse miscellanies—the literate elite," and states in reference to these lines, "amusingly, Donne did not care much for such reader/writers" (2).

23 *And they who write because all write,* **WHEELER** (1992): the line "is an echo of the first satire of Juvenal, where a similar complaint is made in the opening lines" (119).

23 *because all write,* **CHMIELEWSKI** (2001): "it is fashionable" (615).

25-31 *But he...no harme.* **ALBRIGHT** (1985): "To speak the language of satire tends to reduce the satirist's own speech to excrement" (137).

25-30 *But he...his owne.* **GROSART** (1872-73) conjectures that if "Rumours of Hall's intended 'Vergidemiarum...toothless satyrs'" reached Donne, then the "'praise' of the Anatomie's prefixed poems may have been a kind of *solatium* for the earlier 'stolen march,'" the knowledge of which could explain the continued anonymity of that "praise." Regardless, adds that "even so soon as 1593," Donne "regarded some one as in some way thieving on his manor" (2:xxxi). **ALDEN** (1899) responds to Grosart (1872-73), stating, "there is no internal evidence, in Hall's satires, of the author's familiarity with those of Donne; and I see no necessity for believing that any existed" (115-16). **WHITE** (1935): "Material properly disgested is like food properly digested: it furnishes the writer with the creative energy necessary for the production of something new, individual. Imperfect digestion of food leads to vomiting, just as the imperfect assimilation of sources produces literary refuse" (127). **ANDREASEN** (1963): Donne succeeds in making vice "vividly repulsive" through the "ugliness" of this passage (63). **MILGATE** (1967) quotes a similar passage in John Marston's *The Scourge of Villainy* 11:74ff., in *Poems*, ed. A. Davenport (1961), pp. 169-70. Says that Marston might have known Donne's Satyres "in manuscript through his friend Guilpin, who imitated them as early as 1598" (131-32). **LEIN** (1980) suggests that the "symbolic movement from meat to excrement, nourishment to waste, contains exact analogical parallels to the primary experience of the poem" and that the "interjected 'beggarly'" further "evokes all that sense of lost nobility, or eroded personal value" seen earlier in the poem. Argues that the lines clarify "even more how the poem operates—as a series of interrelated analogies, all conceived in relation to an overriding sense of universal degeneration," but finds that the "excremental metaphor exposes new implications for the poet himself," for the "universal infection has reached the poet's inner world," such that "[e]ven the 'fruits' of his own vigorous creative spirit are succumbing to the rotting process of reality." Concludes that the speaker's "disgust determines the violence of his imagery" (138-39). **DOCHERTY** (1986): "The reader is the one who is made sick here; for it is the reader who is now in the position of the pitiful poet. Starvation of poetry is prescribed and its replacement by some more 'original' discourse of affirmation or negation" (244). **BAUMLIN** (1991): "Even as it condemns the servile imitator the passage itself parodies Seneca's discussion of imitation, which observes that 'the food we have eaten, as long as it retains its original quality and floats in our stomachs as an undiluted mass, is a burden; but it passes into tissue and blood only when it has been changed from its original form. So it is with the food which nourishes our higher nature,—we should see to it that whatever we have absorbed should not be allowed to remain unchanged, or it will be no part of us. We must digest it; otherwise it will merely enter the memory and not the reasoning power.' In Donne's version, the product of imitation becomes not nourishment or 'sinew' but excrement—a devastating if scurrilous attack on the theft of another's words." The result is multiple levels of irony: "the poet, imitating Juvenal, here imitates Seneca on the subject of imitation, in order to ridicule others who imitate the poet himself," and thus this "tour de force" of necessity "becomes an implicit criticism of the satirist's own writing. Can the satirist, himself an imitative poet, escape the charge he has just levelled against others? If poetry is harmless, meaningless, powerless in contemporary society, how can the satirist's own words—the very satire he composes—claim in any way to be authentic or efficacious? By casting doubt on the powers of his medium, the poet necessarily weakens his own words as instruments of reform" (86). **WHEELER** (1992): the metaphor here was "probably taken from Persius" (119). **LOW** (1993): Donne saves his harshest criticism for literary theft "because it involves competition among men vying for place and therefore strikes nearest to home." As such, "the anxiety revealed here is that of a man whose wit, his only negotiable asset in the struggle for patronage, may be appropriated by others as hungry as himself. But the crisis is more than personal. The old poetic community, in which the practice of *imitatio* and the communal sharing of tradition depended on common cultural assumptions—which, the imagery implies, were in turn cradled in the certainties of the old religion—has died. Imitation, which should be constructive and communal (in the ancient *topos*, like bees gathering nectar and converting it into honey) has become a savage war of individuals, who steal food from one another and turn it into excrement" (36). **MEAKIN** (1998): this passage presents Donne "at his most derisive on the abuses of poetry, and so the absence of a Muse may be significant in that he does not associate her with the kind of bodily degradation—prostitution, defecation—evident in the epigrams and satires of Harington, Davies, Hall, and others," and he thus appears to be "dismissive of the convention" (49). **SAUNDERS** (1999): this "extraordinary passage figure[s] failed poetic creativity in unmistakably anal terms," Donne's imagery evincing an "investment in orality at least equal to his investment in anality as a figure for the process of poetic production: the 'maw' that 'chaws' and 'spues' is as significant as the digestive system that defecates." It may also be significant that "five of these six lines are enjambed, as if to suggest mimetically something of the breathlessness associated with rapid, gluttonous eating, and also the uncontrolled 'splurge' effect of poetry that is spewed forth in an undifferentiated mass" (175–76). **WIGGINS** (2000): Donne condemns poetic imitation in a letter, "whose reference to Dante's *Inferno* indicates a focus on poetic authorities, not those in other branches of learning." [Wiggins does not provide any documentation for this letter—eds.]. Donne "concedes that real power rests with Lord Chancellors, not with poets, and since it is to their authority that one must submit despite one's own judgment, one should not add false authorities" (37–38).

25–28 *who beggerly…his owne things,* **NEWTON** (1974): the "plagiarist" is one of the other "odious characters" in the poem, and Donne's "hate for him makes Donne himself spew out the most disgusting image thus far" (432). **GREENE** (1982): Donne is an "iconoclast" whose "jokes tend to betray respect," and here he "turned back the hoary Senecan image of digestion upon itself" (44).

25 *chaw* **SHAWCROSS** (1967): "chew" (19). [So also, Smith (1971, 475) and Patrides (1985, 220).]

26 *Others witts fruites,* **SMITH** (1971): "the fruits of the wits of others, other writers' works" (475).

27 *Rankly* **MILGATE** (1967): "grossly, coarsely," [so also, Patrides (1985, 220)],

with a "suggestion of luxuriance and rottenness" (132). SHAWCROSS (1967): "inadequately" (19).

27 *digested* PATRIDES (1985): "'disgested' (acc. to some MSS)" (220).

31–38 *But these…they dwell.* HORNE (1983) suggests that the lines apply to "only one writer," Thomas Nashe, who "was notorious for his bohemianism and frequenting of taverns, as were many of his fellows." Notes that what "really pins down the reference is Donne's mention of 'Dildoes,'" pointing out that in "contemporary sources, the *Choise of Valentines* is often spoken of simply as 'Tom Nashe his Dildo', showing that this was the 'strange sinne' of the poem which excited most comment" (414–15).

31 *these do me no harme.* HESTER (1982): "by 'mee' he intimates that these poets cannot after all efface the power of his own 'Good workes as good.' They are signs and victims of national decay as much as perpetuators of any unhealthy attitude towards language" (41).

31 *these* MILGATE (1967): "helpless poets (ll. 5–10), whether they are playwrights (ll. 11–16), wooers (ll. 16–20), flatterers for a fee (ll. 21–22), fashionable scribblers (ll. 23–24), or plagiarists (ll. 25–30)" (128).

31–32 *vse / To* MILGATE (1967): "make it a practice or habit" (132). SMITH (1971): "habitually" (475).

32 *outswive* and *out vsure* MELTON (1906) (reading the first word as "out-doe") uses the first word to illustrate secondary accent in compounds (87, 88) (for both words, see note for *Sat1* 5) (162).

32 *outswive dildoes;* SMITH (1971) (reading "outdo"): "dildoes were artificial phalluses and to outdo—or outswive—them might in the poet's view be a prodigious feat indeed" (476).

32 *outswive* LEGOUIS (1942) (reading "out-doe"): this instance predates the earliest mention in the *OED*, "sense 2 = 'excel, surpass,' first recorded in 1607 (Shaks, *Cor.*)" (186). [So also, Sullens (1964, 226).] MILGATE (1967) (reading "out-doe"): "out-copulate" (132). PATRIDES (1985) notes the alternative readings "out-doe" and "out-swive" and says that "both words mean 'out-copulate'" (220).

32 *dildoes;* LEGOUIS (1942): this instance predates the earliest mention in the *OED*, "first recorded in 1610 (B. Jonson, *The Alchemist*) and in a vaguer sense" (185). [So also, Sullens (1964, 179).] MILGATE (1967): "artificial phalluses"; see *ElAnag* 53 (132). [So also, Shawcross (1967, 19), Warnke (1967, 110), Rousseau and Rudenstine (1972, 61), Patrides (1985, 220), and Carey (1990, 423).] PATRIDES (1985): "the word was displaced in 1633 by a dash" (220). [Similarly, Carey (1990, 423).] SULLIVAN (2000): the word was replaced by "a horizontal line" (302) in the 1633 edition, but "filled in" (304) by Marriot in 1635. SMITH (2001): in a copy of the 1633 edition (Folger Shakespeare Library STC 7045 Copy 2), a seventeenth-century reader has restored the censored word by "(brazenly)" writing "'Dildoes' in the margin" (169).

32 *out vsure* LEGOUIS (1942): the *OED* uses "Pope's imitation of Donne's satires" to illustrate this word, even though the verb is found in Donne's "original," and thus, the date of its first use "should be altered from 1735 to *c.* 1597" (186–87). [Similarly, Sullens (1964, 184).]

33 *To out drinke...the Letanee:* STEIN (1944b) (reading "To out-drinke the sea, to out-sweare the Letanie") states that the elisions in this line "may prevent the reader from recognizing the scansion immediately" (394).

33 *To out drinke the Sea:* LEGOUIS (1942) notes that "the definition of *outdrink* in *OED* is twofold: 'a. To drink (anything out or up, drink dry). b. To outdo in drinking, drink more than.'" Believes that "the existence of a rests solely on Donne's use of the term," adding that if this is so, then this definition "should disappear altogether: *To outdrinke the sea* means, not 'to drink the sea out, completely,'" but "'to drink more than the sea does'; the force of *out-* is exactly the same as in the three other verbs" (195). As such, Donne "alludes to the fact that the sea constantly drinks in all the rivers" (196). [Similarly, Milgate (1967, 132).] SULLENS (1964): the *OED* cites Donne as the earliest source for this word (197).

33 *outsweare the Letanee:* GROSART (1872–73): "the allusion is doubtless to the old Roman Litany with its long catalogue of saints, as if he should say, Swear by all these" (2:xiin1). SMITH (1971): "take God's name in oaths more than the Litany invokes it in supplication" (476). ROUSSEAU AND RUDENSTINE (1972): "Opponents of the English litany condemned its frequent invocations of God as swearing" (61).

33 *outsweare* GROSART (1872–73) notes that the reading is usually "to outsweare," although his edition drops the "to": "The elision of the 'to' requires the '*or* outusure' to be '*and*;' and, indeed, even with 'to,' the 'and' is preferable; not that he means that each does all, but he lumps these different classes in one as doing him no harm" (1:20).

33 *Letanee:* GROSART (1872–73): "1633 leaves blank" (1:20). GRIERSON (1912): "'Letanie,' the reading of all the MSS., is indicated by a dash in 1633 and is omitted without any indication by 1635–39. In 1649–50 the blank was supplied, probably conjecturally, by 'the gallant'. It was not till 1669 that 'Letanie' was inserted" (2:110). [So also, Milgate (1967, 132), Patrides (1985, 220), and Sullivan (2000, 302, 304–05).] CHMIELEWSKI (2001): "Litany, where God's name is repeatedly invoked" (615). SMITH (2001): this is the only one of the nine censored lines in the Satyres (1633) where the seventeenth-century reader of the Folger Shakespeare Library STC 7045 Copy 2 has not replaced the missing word. This suggests that the reader "read and copied the additions from an earlier printed edition, probably before 1650, because if he had access to the 1650, 1654, or 1669 editions, he might have added 'gallant,' he' or 'Letanie' as he had emended the other passages" (169–70). An alternative interpretation could be that the reader was "morally offended by this single word and refused to add the words into his volume" (170n27).

34–38 *Who with...they dwell.* BAUMLIN (1991): in the spirit of *Ignatius*, the poet here "ridicules the Scholastic dogma that reformers sought to dismantle. And yet the poet is equally critical of Protestant abuses, and the Canonist's confusion over the application of theological law reflects on all the combatants in the Reformation controversy" (89).

34 *Sins all kinds* **MILGATE** (1967): "Sins" is a "possessive plural"—i.e., "sins"—"'all the varieties of every sin,' familiar to priests who hear them uttered in the confessional" (132).

34 *all* **PATRIDES** (1985): "(acc. to 1635–69 and most MSS): 'of all' (acc. to 1633 and a few MSS)" (220).

35 *Confessors:* **SHAWCROSS** (1967): "priests who hear others' confessions" (19). [So also, Chmielewski (2001, 615).]

36–38 *Schoolemen...they dwell.* **MILGATE** (1967): new sins "require new classifications, and hence new places of punishment in Hell"; see the doctrine "that all those convicted of a particular sin were consigned to the same region of Hell," as in Dante's *Inferno* and in *The Golden Legend*, ed. F. S. Ellis (1900), 6:109ff. (132). [So also, Shawcross (1967, 19).] [Similarly, Rousseau and Rudenstine (1972, 61) and Patrides (1985, 220).]

36 *Schoolemen...must make,* **COFFIN** (1937) cites this line and states that Donne's skepticism sometimes found support in scholasticism (52).

36 *Schoolemen* **MILGATE** (1967): "a satiric glance at the arrogance of the Schoolmen as they (and not God himself) 'make' these places" in Hell; see *Essays*, p. 27 (132). **SHAWCROSS** (1967): "the Scholastics who classified and disputed philosophic arguments on the basis of fine distinctions" (19). **SMITH** (1971) "Aristotelean theologians, who subtly categorized sins and their punishment" (476). **CHMIELEWSKI** (2001): "Scholastic theologians, who classified sins and assigned them each a specific place in Hell" (615).

37–38 *Whose strange...they dwell.* **SMITH** (1971): "The sins they claim are so strange that canon lawyers, schooled in the task, would have the greatest difficulty in deciding just which ample commandment of the ten actually covers them" (476).

37 *strange* **MILGATE** (1967): "new outlandish" (132).

37 *Canonists* **MILGATE** (1967): "canon-lawyers" (132). [So also, Shawcross (1967, 19), Warnke (1967, 110), Rousseau and Rudenstine (1972, 61), Patrides (1985, 220), and Carey (1990, 423).] **SMITH** (1971): "legal theologians, who judge issues by reference to ecclesiastical law" (476). **CHMIELEWSKI** (2001): "those who study canon (religious) law" (615).

38 *Commandments* **SHAWCROSS** (1967): "of the area controlled by one of the Ten Commandments" (19).

38 *large receite* **MILGATE** (1967): "broad scope" (133). **SHAWCROSS** (1967): "broadly inclusive domain; place to receive the sinners" (19).

38 *receite* **SMITH** (1971): "receptacle, accommodation, scope" (476). **ROUSSEAU AND RUDENSTINE** (1972): "Area of jurisdiction" (61). **PATRIDES** (1985): "receptacle, region" (220).

39–45 *th'insolence…benefic'd Ministers,* **HALL** (1991): "Coscus's 'insolence' is defeated by Donne's own contempt for one whom only 'Time…Hath made a Lawyer' and who has all the complacency of 'new benefic'd ministers'" (165).

39–44 *th'insolence…a scarse Poet:* **NEWTON** (1974): "this repulsive introduction hints at what is bothering Donne throughout this *Satyre.* While using the quasi-medical imagery which is conventional in Elizabethan satire, it includes the implicit assumption (which becomes explicit in *Satyre* V) that all things are in irremediable decay. At the heart of the satirist's soul, perhaps, is this notion; and anger erupts when some vicious fool reminds him of it" (432–33). **LEIN** (1980): these "bitter lines on Time represent the argument around which the poem's designs revolve" and "clarify the structural role of Coscus. He and his career are symbolic counters for Donne's vision of universal decay. Coscus' 'growth' within the poem from poet to lawyer, the surface movement which seems to account for the curiously indirect opening, structurally validates the poem's vision of Time, for Coscus' career demonstrates that in time men become deformed and plunge into greater and greater venality and beastliness. The progressive verb 'plodding on,' with its nuances of purposeless motion, of innate and unredeemable brutishness, reinforces the intensely negative tone of the poem's full opening" (134).

39 *But these…th'insolence* **STEIN** (1944c) notes this line as an example of stress-shift after a pause (379).

39 *But these punish themselues:* **ANDREASEN** (1967): the "curmudgeonly scholar" who narrates the poem sees that sins carry their own punishments (115). **MILGATE** (1967): "All manner of other evil-doers" (apart from poets) (128).

39 *punish* **MELTON** (1906) uses this word to illustrate secondary accent in the suffix "-ish" (87, 97).

39 *insolence* **LECOCQ** (1969): in its Latin sense, the word means "excess"; it denotes extravagance or arrogance (373). [So also, Smith (1971, 476).]

40–62 *Of Coscus…I hop'd:* **MILGATE** (1967): Coscus was worst of all evil-doers (ll. 31–39) "when he wrote poetry; but even then he was not beyond hope" (128).

40–58 *Of Coscus…mayds eare* **GRIERSON** (1912) says that it would be "interesting if we could identify the lawyer-poet, Coscus" and adds that Donne, like Sir John Davies in *Gullinge Sonnets,* probably had mainly in mind an anonymous series of sonnets, *Zepheria,* the style of which "exactly fits Donne's description" in ll. 57–58, yet "we do not know who the author of *Zepheria* was, so cannot tell how far Donne is portraying an individual in what follows. It can hardly be [John] Hoskins or [Sir Richard] Martin, unless *Zepheria* itself was intended to be a burlesque, which is possible. Quite possibly Donne has taken the author of *Zepheria* simply as a type of the young lawyer who writes bad poetry; and in the rest of the poem portrays the same type when he has abandoned poetry and devoted himself to 'Law practice for mere gain' [l. 63], extorting money and lands from Catholics or suspected Catholics, drawing cozening conveyances" (2:103).

40 *Coscus* SHAWCROSS (1967): "a name perhaps chosen because it was used by the anonymous author of the vapid sonnet sequence *Zepheria* (1594); often used in contemporary poetry for a court pleader" (19; 1972, 255). [So also, Rousseau and Rudenstine (1972, 62).] KERINS (1984): "this comical type was familiar to the wits from the anonymous sonnet sequence, *Zepheria* (1594), wherein a poet importunes his lady in convoluted legal conceits—a work mocked in Sir John Davies's *Gullinge Sonnets*" (60). CAREY (1990), acknowledging the publication of *Zepheria*, says that Coscus "has not been identified" (423). KRUZHKOVA (1994) identifies this as a Latin name indicating the connection of Donne's Satyres to their classical Roman sources (158). CHMIELEWSKI (2001): "a name sometimes given to flatterers at Court" (615).

40 *great Offence,* MILGATE (1967) (reading "just offence") glosses as "the offence I justly feel" [so also, Smith (1971, 476)] and suggests that this is probably Donne's own revision. Believes that the earlier reading "great" is "weak, being less energetic than 'hate Perfectly' (ll. 1–2)" (133). LEIN (1980) (reading "just offence"): Donne "undoubtedly revised the passage to 'just' in order to reinforce, ironically, the justice of his indignation at a lawyer, and hence to fortify his own moral position" (148).

40 *great* GROSART (1872–73): "Here 'my offence' is the offence to me or in my eyes; and therefore 'just' is far stronger than 'great'" (1:20). PATRIDES (1985) (reading "just") notes the readings "'great' (acc. to most MSS) or 'harts' (acc. to a MS)" (220).

41–42 *Whome time,…an oxe,* MILGATE (1950): these lines are misquoted in *Sir Lucius Cary…His Discourse of Infallibility…*(1651), and "Dr. D" is printed in the margin of the text (382). HESTER (1982) (reading the lines as within parentheses): "As a reminder of the mortality of man (time 'rots all': *tempus edax rerum*), this parenthesis supports the satirist's earlier remarks about the eventual punishment for all malefactors; but, in addition, by identifying the thoroughly temporal manner and motive of Coscus' activities, the interpolated clause offers a microcosmic simile for his growth from a sinful but essentially foolish poetaster into a national enemy. Coscus-the-poet was like a calf and a blister, harmless in themselves, still manageable; but as a lawyer he has become a cumbersome, dangerous animal and a social disease because of the size of his hunger and the extent of his contagiousness" (44). WIGGINS (2000): Coscus has "plodded on at the Inns of Court" and only "time" has "made him a lawyer" (38).

41 *makes botches poxe* MILGATE (1967): "makes pimples, as they develop, reveal themselves as the effects of serious disease" (133). SHAWCROSS (1967): "makes syphilis from pustules" (20). [So also, Rousseau and Rudenstine (1972, 62) and Patrides (1985, 220).]

41 *botches poxe* CHMIELEWSKI (2001): "syphilitic rashes" (615).

41 *botches* JOHNSON (1755): "A swelling, or eruptive discoloration of the skin." SMITH (1971): "boils or rashes" (476).

41 *poxe* SMITH (1971): "eruptive skin diseases; syphilis" (476).

42 *And plodding…a calfe an oxe,* MILGATE (1967) quotes *The Return from Parnassus,* Part 2, ll. 1664–65, and Jonson, *Poetaster* 1.2.120ff. (133).

42 *plodding* HESTER (1982): "*Plodding* or mere diligence through the performance of large quantities of moots was one way of gaining admission to the bar" (145).

43–44 *a Lawyer:…a scarse Poet:* GRIERSON (1929): the lines are "directed against the same person" as were Sir John Davies' "Gulling Sonnets," that person being "a lawyer who had turned poet and published in 1594 *Zepheria,* a series of sonnets full of legal terms and long, harsh words" (xxv).

43 *Hath made…of late* MILGATE (1967): a line of eleven syllables, the light second syllable of "Lawyer," coming before a marked medial pause, treated as if it were an extra light syllable at the end of a line; see note on *Sat1* 28, which lists other examples.

44 *But a scarse…this State* GROSART (1872–73) asks, "Could Sir John Davies be intended?" (1:20). GRIERSON (1912): "Donne uses 'scarce' thus as an adjective again" in *Sat4* 4 and 240, and "by 'jollier of this state' he means 'prouder of this state', using the word as in 'jolly statesmen', l. 7" (2:111).

44 *But a scarse Poet:* MILGATE (1967): not "that Coscus is scarcely a poet, but that he is a bad one"; see the Italian usage of John Florio in *A World of Words* (1598) and *Sat4* 4 and 240 (133). SMITH (1971): "scarcely a poct; a feeble poet" (476). GRIGSON (1980): "something of a poet" (20).

44 *a scarse* SULLENS (1964): "Scarce as an adj. does not have this meaning" in *OED.* "The sense of the adv. as given under B. 1. and 2. is nearer to Donne's meaning" (264). PATRIDES (1985): "(acc. to most MSS): feeble; 'scarce a' (acc. to 1633–69 and some MSS)" (220).

44 *Iolyer of this State* MILGATE (1967): "prouder of this (new) position in life. For 'jolly' in this sense, cf. 'Satire I', l. 7" (133). SMITH (1971): "more puffed-up with his new status as a lawyer" (476).

44 *Iolyer* BEWLEY (1966): "prouder of" (173). [So also, Patrides (1985, 220).] GRIGSON (1980): "more stuck up, grander" (20).

44 *this* PATRIDES (1985): "'that' (acc. to some MSS) or 'his' (ditto)" (220).

45–57 *Then are…Of affidauits.* RUGOFF (1939): as Donne "ridicules such a penchant for legal phraseology," he "shows the technical grasp we might have expected," and the terms are handled "familiarly if to absurd effect" (76).

45–49 *he throwes…A motion Lady;* ALLEN (1965): the lover described here "woos in language of the Pleas and Courts" (110n110).

45–47 *he throwes…euery wenche:* **HESTER** (1982): these lines evoke "the commonplace bird-lime image of man's sinfulness," an interpretation "reinforced by the pejorative description of the poet-barrister's title as the product of 'plodding' mortality, the advance form of a disease, and basically animalistic" (43).

45–46 *he throwes / Like Netts, or Lyme-twiggs,* **MILGATE** (1967): "Properly speaking, only the 'nets' are 'throwne'" (133). **SMITH** (1971): "devices for snaring birds" (476). [So also, Rousseau and Rudenstine (1972, 62) and Patrides (1985, 221).]

45 *Then* **PATRIDES** (1985): "than" (221).

45 *new benefic'd Ministers,* **LEIN** (1980): the "sense of profane monetary concern" is "the burden intended by Donne's comparison" here, in which "ministers who rejoice in their worldly placement instead of their calling pervert their station as much as Coscus does his" (137). **BAUMLIN** (1991): "The comparison, seemingly innocent, points to the Elizabethan court's attempt to assume religious as well as temporal authority" (89–90).

45 *benefic'd* **PATRIDES** (1985): "given ecclesiastical preference such as a rectory" (221).

45 *Ministers,* **SHAWCROSS** (1967): "those receiving church preference in the form of a rectory or perpetual curacy" (20).

45 *throwes* **SULLENS** (1964): Donne's usage of this meaning of the word is earlier than the earliest source cited by *OED* (239).

46 *Lyme-twiggs,* **MILGATE** (1967): "twigs smeared with bird-lime (a sticky substance made from hollybark) for catching small birds" (133). [So also, Chmielewski (2001, 615).] **SHAWCROSS** (1967): "snares" (20).

47 *wenche:* **SHAWCROSS** (1967): "usually signifying a whore" (20).

48–60 *And wooes…Abbeys rore.* **LOW** (1993): "The new world brings with it more direct and selfish forms of writing and courtship. Coscus, the representative of new man—once a poet, now a lawyer—makes love in legal language. Why not, if the only aim of writing is to serve self-interest?" As such, "the clear implication of Donne's image is that the social fabric, the religious and cultural architecture, within which love poetry once subsisted, has been ruthlessly dismantled by its enemies, leaving Donne and his contemporaries to inhabit the bare ruins" (36–37).

48–57 *in Language of…Of affidauits.* **WARNKE** (1967): "These lines abound in technical legal terms" (111).

48–49 *And wooes…A motion Lady;* **CORTHELL** (1997): "Coscus's defection from the ranks of the poets is aggravated by his pathetic attempts to continue as a poet writing in a strained 'metaphysical' style," and this "affected" style "reduces poetry to the level of a legal 'motion'" (33–34).

48 *And wooes…and Benche.* **ROUSSEAU AND RUDENSTINE** (1972): "i.e., makes love in legal language" (62).

48 *Language of the Pleas and Benche*. **MILGATE** (1967): "All the legal terms in Coscus's wooing precisely describe the actions by which one would claim possession of a contested piece of land" (133).

48 *Pleas and Benche*. **BEWLEY** (1966): "Court of Common Pleas and Court of Queen's Bench" (173). [So also, Milgate (1967, 133), Shawcross (1967, 20), and Smith (1971, 221).] **SHAWCROSS** (1967) adds that the Queen's Bench was the "highest court of common law, attended by the Queen" (20). [So also, Patrides (1985, 221).]

49–57 *I haue beene...Of affidauits*. **LOUTHAN** (1951) notes the unusual presence of dialogue in these lines (98). **COBB** (1956b): Coscus has conducted his romance according to the steps of a property claim, and these legal terms are used deliberately rather than randomly (Item 8). **SMITH** (1971) notes that "[l]egal wooing in verse had a fashion in the 1590s and there are many instances and burlesques of it." Points to and quotes from *Zepheria* (1594) whose "unknown poet" is "barbarously like Donne's Coscus" (476–77). **ROUSSEAU AND RUDENSTINE** (1972): these lines "constitute Coscus' plea to his lady" (62).

49–53 *A motion....spare me:* **GROSART** (1872–73): "this being the lady's exclamation, as before, and meaning 'allow me to leave'" (1:20).

49–50 *I haue beene...the Queene:* **LEIN** (1980): "Coscus' tedious complaints testify that despite his efforts a rival has gained ground with his mistress. His affair has waned, a fact Donne intensifies by making Coscus insist on dates" (141).

49 *A motion...I haue beene* **STEIN** (1944c) cites this line as an example of Donne adding "an extra feminine ending in the foot preceding the cesura" (393).

49 *A motion Lady; speake Coscus.* **MILGATE** (1967): Coscus makes "an application for a rule or order of the court, permitting the case to proceed. The judge (i.e. the lady) grants it ('Speake')" (133). [So also, Shawcross (1967, 20), Smith (1971, 477), and Patrides (1985, 221).]

50 *tricesimo of the Queene:* **ALDEN** (1899) notes that the date of this reference "would be appropriate at any time after 1588" (78). **BEWLEY** (1966): "the thirtieth year of the Queen's reign" (173). [So also, Milgate (1967, 133), Shawcross (1967, 20), Smith (1971, 477), Rousseau and Rudenstine (1972, 62), Grigson (1980, 20), Patrides (1985, 221), and Chmielewski (2001, 615).]

51–53 *Continuall Claimes...Proceede:* **MILGATE** (1967): "Coscus has pressed his suit during the last six years whenever the lady has let him approach 'nigh' enough" (133–34).

51 *Continuall Claimes* **MILGATE** (1967): claims "formally reiterated within statutory intervals," so that they "might not be deemed to be abandoned"; see John Rastell, *An Exposition of Certain Difficult and Obscure Words, and Terms of the Laws* (1595) (133). [So also, Smith (1971, 477) and Patrides (1985, 221).]

51 *Iniunctions* **MILGATE** (1967): "Judicial processes" issued by Chancery "to 'stay' proceedings of the Common Law courts if the suit was unjust or had been brought

on insufficient grounds (e.g. to harass the defendant), also to compel restitution to an injured party. The lady has from time to time admitted that she has been unjust to Coscus, and has ceased to listen to the pleas (both unfair and frivolous) made by his rival" (134). [So also, Smith (1971, 477) and Patrides (1985, 221).]

53 *spare me:* MILGATE (1967): "excuse me, allow me to go"; see *Sat4* 143 (134).

53 *Hilary terme* BEWLEY (1966): "the term from January 11 to January 31 in which the superior English courts were in session" (173). MILGATE (1967): "kept at Westminster from 23 January to 12 February. [So also, Patrides (1985, 221) and Chmielewski (2001, 615).] Coscus has returned to the attach well within the year and a day allowed by law for the making of his claim" (134). SHAWCROSS (1967): "January session of the Westminster courts" (20). SMITH (1971): "the first term of the English legal year, running from early January to early April" (477). [Similarly, Rousseau and Rudenstine (1972, 62).]

54–55 *You sayd…your grace,* NORTON (1895): "Legal phraseology signifying 'I should be replaced in possession of your grace'" (1:241). MILGATE (1967): his "present claim on the lady is based on her invitation to 'returne'; but the more valid claim is that his love for her has antedated that of his rival—his right is that of first possession" (134). SHAWCROSS (1967): "Coscus has left his Lady to attend court from January to around March" (20).

54 *this Sise* SMITH (1971) (reading "next 'size"): "next assize" (477).

54 *this* PATRIDES (1985) reads as "next" but notes: "'this' (acc. to several MSS)" (221).

54 *Sise* JOHNSON (1755): "[contracted from *assize.*]", and assize is "an assembly of knights and other substantial men, with the bailiff or justice, in a certain place, and at a certain time." BEWLEY (1966): "assize"—i.e., "the periodical sessions of the judges of the English superior courts" (173). [So also, Milgate (1967, 134), Shawcross (1967, 20), Kermode (1970, 101), Smith (1971, 477), Rousseau and Rudenstine (1972, 62), Grigson (1980, 20), Patrides (1985, 221), and Chmielewski (2001, 615).]

55–57 *I should…Of affidauits.* MILGATE (1967): "while he has been absent (in the 'interim' of his pleadings)," Coscus "has used the only other means possible to win his case—by sworn statements (affidavits) in his love-letters" (134). SHAWCROSS (1967): "I should regain possession of you by dint of having had first possession, antedating my rival's claim" (20).

55 *in remitter of your grace,* SMITH (1971): "entitled to her grace retrospectively, by his former claim rather than the later one" (477). [Similarly, Rousseau and Rudenstine (1972, 62) and Patrides (1985, 221).]

55 *remitter* JOHNSON (1755): "In common law, a restitution of one that hath two titles to lands or tenements, and is seized of them by his latter title, unto his title that is more ancient, in case where the latter is defective." LEGOUIS (1942): this instance predates the earliest mention in the *OED*, "sense 2 = 'restoration to rights or privileges, or to a previous state,' first recorded in 1623 (in *Crt and Times*

Jas I)." The *OED* "passes by the construction *in remitter of*, which is Donne's" (186). [So also, Sullens (1964, 230).] **MILGATE** (1967) quotes Rastell, *An Exposition of Certain Difficult and ObscureWords, and Terms of the Laws* (1595): "when a man hath two titles to anie land, and he commeth to the lande by the last title, yet he shall bee judged in by force of his elder title, and that shall bee saide to him a remitter"; quotes "A Meere Common Lawyer," *The Overburian Characters*, ed. W. J. Paylor, p. 31 (134). **PATRIDES** (1985): "retrospectively entitled to" (221). **CHMIELEWSKI** (2001): "a claim based on having had a prior claim, i.e., prior to his rival's (l. 52)" (615).

56–57 *should take place / Of affidauits.* **SMITH** (1971): "serve as sworn statements in his absence" (477). [So also, Patrides (1985, 221).]

56 *In th'interim* **RICHTER** (1902) uses this phrase to illustrate a slurring of syllables (403).

57–64 *Words, Words,…Strumpets prostitute.* **BAUMLIN** (1985): the imagery is by turns "elevated," "outlandishly humorous," "trivial," and eventually "obscene." But though the images "are mixed in tone, the phrasing is vigorous throughout, at times impassioned. The hammer-like effect of the figure epizeuxis ('Words, words…More, more…') lends grandeur to the expression, a grandiloquence which certainly conflicts with but is not lost in the ridiculousness of the subject matter; anaphora and ploche ('Now…hee must walke…now he must talke,' or the twice-repeated 'lye' of later lines) are rhetorical schemes which add vehemence to the satirist's invective" and "keep our attention focused on Coscus's deceitful words and actions" (34–35).

57 60 *Words, Words,…our ruynd Abbeys rore.* **LECOCQ** (1969): the image of the ruined abbeys is not introduced without a reason in a context where it is a question of bad poetry; it underlines a single turn of mind, for it is men like Coscus who ended up possessing the ecclesiastical holdings confiscated in the time of Henry VIII, and who have let the ruins multiply in order to satisfy their egoism and their appetite for wealth (373). [Similarly, Hester (1979, 151).] **HESTER** (1977a): the satirist "equates the lawyer's perversions of the language of the law with abuse of the Word" (24). **LEIN** (1980): "Even a wooing calls forth from the poet a vision of disintegration—of winds ceaselessly wearing down the edifices of the past, a malevolent erosion made emotionally oppressive by the speaker's insistence on the wind's 'rore.' Time, whether in the shape of sea or wind, inexorably erodes our reality. And coupled with the poet's agony at that devastation, we find once more his overriding sense of lost value, here compressed so that love and religion coalesce. Love and beauty (delicately communicated by the phrase, 'The tender labyrinth of a soft maids eare'), and, by transfer, the values of both in religion, all fall prey to relentless forces. The juxtaposition of 'maid' and 'ruin'd Abbeyes,' furthermore, conjures up at once the earlier association of women with conquered towns and reveals again how closely interrelated these manifestations of decay are for Donne" (139). **CORTHELL** (1982): Coscus is "linked to a historical process which began with the dissolution of the monasteries, and his compassing of 'all our land' becomes a stage in that process" (161). **TOLIVER** (1985): "The speaker is not amused [by] Coscus's plague of legal terms" that "cor-

rupts" his "language of courtship." Further, "it is difficult to gauge the decibels of ten tongue-lashing Slavs, but the effect is that of Babel" (100–01). **CORTHELL** (1997): "After something like a Polish joke, the evocation of the ruined abbeys is particularly striking. It suggests a link between Coscus and a historical process that began with the dissolution of the monasteries so that his compassing of 'all our land' becomes a stage in that long sequence of events" (36).

57–58 *Words, Words,...mayds eare* **RUGOFF** (1939) notes Donne's grasp of legal language even as he ridicules it (76). **MORRIS** (1953) cites these lines as an example of "the repetition of single words or phrases to produce accumulative or auditory effects, or both" (71). **CAREY** (1981): "That nothing sharper than a word would be required to fracture the ear's membranes, confirms for us the delicacy of the structure; and the suggestion of something within the body being torn acts—like the probe-and-wound simile—acutely on our senses" (145). **WHEELER** (1992) says that Persius was "no doubt" the model for these lines, which "are reminiscent of the interlocutor's warning, '*Sed quid opus teneeras mordaci radere vero / auriculas?*'" (119). **WIGGINS** (2000): the words "which Coscus uses to seduce his mistress, sound sinister. In a precise, systematic way, they turn the mistress into a commodity, into a piece of land to be seized by the shrewdest, richest lawyer" (39).

57 *affidauits*. **JOHNSON** (1755): "A declaration upon oath." **LEGOUIS** (1942): this instance predates the earliest mention in the *OED*, "first recorded in 1622 (Malynes, *Anc. Law-Merch.*)" (185).

57 *Words, Words,* **BAUMLIN** (1991): Coscus's "wooing" is "like that of the love poet," which "is empty of meaning" (87).

58 *The tender...mayds eare* **GROSART** (1872–73): "the maid was not soft to him; but the inner labyrinth of the ear is most delicate, and one beauty of a woman's outer ear is its softness; and Donne thus speaks in the revised form of the whole organ as tender" (1:21). **WILLIAMS** (1977): "Donne's pun on 'ear' (i.e., the vagina)" (115).

58 *Labyrinth* **JOHNSON** (1755): "A maze; a place formed with inextricable windings." **SULLENS** (1964): Donne's usage of this meaning of the word is earlier than the earliest source cited by *OED* (221).

59–60 *More, more,...Abbeys rore.* **MELTON** (1906): "At that time *than* was spelled and pronounced *then* [so also, Patrides (1985, 221)]. Furthermore, we have here the *a*-sound in *Sclav-*, and possibly in *–beys*, varying with the similar sound in *áb-*; and the *o*-sound in Sclavón-, *scóld* and *óur* varying with the similar sound in *more* and *roar*, while *ru-* is sufficiently near to be classed with these; and a sound in *–ians* and *–ing* varying with a similar sound in *than, ten, when, winds, in,* and *–in'd,* leaving, in twenty syllables, only two sounds *ru-* and *–beys,* without decided variants; and yet, with all this, the lines possess a rhythm that is absolutely bewitching" (111). Also, for l. 59, see note for *Sat1* 5.

59 *ten Sclauonians scolding,* **ROUSSEAU AND RUDENSTINE** (1972): "Alluding to the (reputedly) raucous sound of Slavic speech" (62). **HESTER** (1982): "The Sclavonian simile recalls, again, the 'barbarism' that English homilists,

pamphleteers, and officials identified with the Spanish threat" (145). **PATRIDES** (1985): "Slavs brawling in their cacophonous languages" (221).

59 *Sclauonians* **SULLENS** (1964): Donne's usage of this meaning of the word is earlier than the earliest source cited by *OED* (234). **BEWLEY** (1966): "Germans" (173). **MILGATE** (1967): "Sclavonia, or Slavonia, was, strictly speaking, the tract of country between the rivers Slav and Drau"; see Ortelius, *Theatrum Orbis Terrarum* (1592), maps 87, 88. The name is "loosely applied, however, to regions in or near the old Roman province of Dalmatia"; see Munster, *Cosmographia* (1572), p. 1067. "When 'Sclavonian' is not merely a term of abuse (as in Nashe, *Works*, 3:109; Henry Parrot, *Laquei Ridiculosi*, 1613, sig. A3), it seems to mean chiefly 'one who speaks an outlandish, barbarous tongue'"; see Middleton, *Works*, 4:226, 228 (134). **SHAWCROSS** (1967): "referring to the rapid, harsh sound of Slavonic speech" (20). Possibly dating the poem by reference to an "event of July 23, 1597" (412). **SMITH** (1971): "Slavs, whose language, not being understood, was a by-word for noisy outlandishness" (477). [So also, Chmielewski (2001, 615).] **CAREY** (1990): "Slavs; speakers of barbarous tongues" (424).

59 *scolding,* **SMITH** (1971): "brawling" (477).

60 *Then when...Abbeys rore.* **ELWIN AND COURTHOPE** (1881): "a reflection on the destruction of the Monasteries" (3:429n3). **MELTON** (1906) cites this line as an example of Donne's ear for rhythm (126). **STEIN** (1944c) cites this line as an example of an extension of stress-shift from the first to the second foot (383). **ELLRODT** (2000): the line "vividly reproduces the noise heard" (201).

60 *Then* **PATRIDES** (1985): "than" (221).

60 *our ruynd Abbeys* **ROUSSEAU AND RUDENSTINE** (1972): "Abbey churches in decay since the dissolution of the monasteries" (62).

60 *ruynd Abbeys* **BEWLEY** (1966): "English monasteries were despoiled under Henry VIII" (173). **MILGATE** (1967) quotes *Ham* 23–24 (134).

61–64 *When sick...Strumpets prostitute.* **SLIGHTS** (1981): the speaker "now replies sternly to a 'bold soule,' acknowledging that his friend's posture as poet has been ridiculous but warning that taking up the law for selfish motives is even more despicable." Although he "considers directly only what his audience ought to do," he also "analyzes the question of occupational choice" and "indirectly struggles with personal doubts about his responsibility as a poet" (156–57). **KERINS** (1984): "Editors usually read this 'bold soule' (l. 63) as someone other than Coscus, the addressee of the preceding two lines. In effect they are saying that Donne begins this sentence apostrophizing Coscus and ends it apostrophizing someone else. It seems much more likely that the satirist, enraged at Coscus's 'insolence,' continues to address him here as 'bold soule.' Coscus as poet was harmless, since poets were 'poore,' 'disarm'd,' and 'not worth hate.' But now with Coscus in the halls of justice for 'meere gaine,' the satirist realizes he is indeed formidable, armed with the very best artillery, 'Pistolets'" (43–44). **LOW** (1985): from Donne's "jaundiced imagination, neither poetry nor law emerges unscathed." Further, "not to be ambitious is madness; to be ambitious is worse. Donne's lawyer, who had done what Donne himself patently both hopes and fears to do, has for his ultimate goal the ownership of land" (76–77). **FORTIER** (1991): "the quiet life with the Muse is contrasted favourably with an active life of debauchery and dishonour. But this is hardly to say something very positive about the Muse. Poetry is a sickness, a possession, a madness" (95).

61–62 *When sick...I hop'd:* **CORTHELL** (1997): "Coscus's abandonment of poetry for the law is an important element in Donne's satire, which turns on the problem of writing and its relationship to life." The satirist may have hoped that Coscus would "return from the prodigal episode of poetic madness to the prosaic world of work" (33).

61 *When* **PATRIDES** (1985) reads as "Which" but notes: "'When' (acc. to 1654 and some MSS) or 'Then' (acc. to a MS)" (221).

61 *possest with Muse* **MILGATE** (1967) cites Plato's *Ion*, 533–34 and *Phaedrus*, 245 (135).

61 *Muse* **LEGOUIS** (1942): Donne's use of this word "without either possessive adjective" or "the definite article" is "at least unusual and harsh." Such a use of the word may be "mere bad grammar," but Donne may be using it as "an equivalent to 'inspiration,'" and if the latter, then "both sense and construction should have been recorded in the *OED*" (188). [So also, Milgate (1967, 135).] **SULLENS** (1964): "The meaning here is close to O.E.D. 2a, but Donne's line suggests a generalized muse, the meaning being that of the impulse to create poetry" (263). **SHAWCROSS** (1967): "both contemplation and poetic inspiration" (20).

62–64 *but Men...Strumpets prostitute.* **RUGOFF** (1939) notes the "frankness" and "vigor" of these images taken from street characters and describes Donne in these lines "administering what is apparently the ultimate in insults" (171). **FLYNN** (2001): Donne presents these men "as typical of the legal profession" (114).

62–63 *but Men...bold Soule, repute* **GRIERSON** (1912): "The 'bold soule' addressed, and invoked to esteem such worthless people aright, is the 'Sir' (whoever that may be) to whom the whole poem is addressed. A note in *HN* prefixed to this poem says that it is taken from 'C. B.'s copy', i.e. Christopher Brooke's. It is quite possible that this *Satyre*, like *The Storme*, was addressed to him" (2:111).

62–63 *Men which...for meere gayne,* **BALD** (1970): "In retrospect the years at Lincoln's Inn seemed to Donne to have been largely wasted. A certain unworldliness, tinged perhaps with youthful snobbery, characterized his attitude during these years. The majority of his contemporaries, though studying the law, had no thought of making it their profession," and thus Donne was "contemptuous" of unscrupulous lawyers (78–79). **MAROTTI** (1986): "The target of the attack is a lawyer-poet whose verse is a crass parody of true poetry, but whose real crime is his naked greed, which poses an economic threat to social superiors with whom both Donne and his readers wanted to identify," and while "fantasizing that this man will use his legal maneuvers to increase his real-estate holdings," the speaker "treats land as the gentleman's natural possession that should not fall into the hands of ruthless middle-class entrepreneurs" (40).

62 *mad,* SHAWCROSS (1967): "carried away with desire" (20). CHMIELEWSKI (2001): "inspired" (615).

63 *meere* PATRIDES (1985): "'more' (acc. to a MS)" (221).

63 *bold Soule,* MILGATE (1967): "A parenthesis, addressed to the poet's own soul, or to the 'Sir' of l. 1" (135). [So also, Smith (1971, 477).]

63 *repute* JOHNSON (1755): "To hold; to account; to think." MILGATE (1967): "An imperative: 'estimate'" (135). SHAWCROSS (1967): "are esteemed" (20). ROUSSEAU AND RUDENSTINE (1972): "Consider, judge to be (imperative form)" (62). PATRIDES (1985): "should be esteemed to be" (221).

63–64 *repute | Worse then* SMITH (1971): "Think of them as worse than" (477).

64 *Worse then...Strumpets prostitute.* SMITH (1971): "more corrupt than embrothelled strumpets" (477).

64 *then* PATRIDES (1985): "than" (221).

64 *imbrotheled* JOHNSON (1755): "To enclose in a brothel." SULLENS (1964): the OED cites Donne as the earliest source for this word (194). MILGATE (1967): a neologism possibly "stimulated" by the "atrocious new coinages" found in *Zepheria* (1594) (128).

64 *Strumpets* SHAWCROSS (1967): "strumpets who" (20).

65–76 *Now like...he thriues.* GRIERSON (1912) says that the "subject of the long sentence is 'He' (l. 65), and the infinitives throughout are complements to 'must,'" acknowledging that this is "the only method" that enables him to "construe the passage, and it carries with it the assumption that 'bearing like' should be connected by a hyphen to form an adjective." Adds that "certainly it is 'he', Coscus, who is 'more shameless, &c.,' not his victims," who are "the 'bearing-like asses', the patient Catholics or suspected Catholics whom he wrings to the bar and forces to disgorge fines" (2:112). WILLIAMSON (1940) disputes that the verb "wring" is transitive, arguing that it changes Donne's meaning, and adding that Donne extends the comparison of Coscus to the "prisoners" as he "becomes shameless enough to lie like a lawyer" (38–39). BEWLEY (1966): "difficult and not very satisfactory," this passage turns from "satirizing Coscus, the lawyer-poet in his role of verse-maker," to considering him "in his professional character," one who might today be called "an ambulance-chaser" (174). MANLEY (1995): the "strutting and talking" of Coscus "leads by association upward and across the comparable counterfeitings which together found a whole society" (388–89). ROBBINS (2000): although the poem's "generalized target, the swindling professional lawyer, was despised by the gentry and hated by many more," Donne "chooses risky analogies for his lying" and for his comparison of "squalid law-practice" to "royal bastardy and churchmen's corruption." The fact that "the reigning monarch was a queen, not a king would be no defence, since Elizabeth was notorious for her sometimes disastrously misjudged favouritism. Even more seriously, Donne went directly against the compulsory Oath of Allegiance in implicitly echoing the pope's decree that Henry VIII's divorce from Catherine of Aragon was invalid and Elizabeth consequently illegitimate" (423).

65–70 *Now like…like a king;* **CORTHELL** (1982): "Here the dazzling comparisons explode into subversive analogies" so that Donne "tries to narrow his focus to the figure of Coscus," yet "he is brought up short by the identification of Coscus with the center of power itself." The "difference between the comparison in line 65 and those in line 70 is perhaps the difference between Horace and Juvenal" and "leads Donne into meditation on the political order instead of the blame and praise proper to the satirist" (159–60).

65 *Now like…must walke* **MELTON** (1906): See note for *Sat1* 5. **LOUTHAN** (1951) observes that Coscus is always looking for someone to injure financially (102).

65 *like an Owllike Watchman* **BEWLEY** (1966): "he walks the streets looking for anything to make capital of" (174).

65 *Owllike* **SULLENS** (1964): Donne's usage of this word is earlier than the earliest sourced cited by OED (184). **MILGATE** (1967): "wakeful at night" (135).

65 *he* **MILGATE** (1967): Coscus, who "reached the 'excellently best' or purest form of evil, putting himself beyond the bounds both of pity and of hope, when he chose to practice law only for gain, by every shabby trick. The rest of the poem deals with this evil, for which only hatred can be felt" (128).

66–68 *Now he must…brought them there,* **HESTER** (1982): Coscus "arrives at the court talking idly, claiming that only the debts of others have brought him there, posing as a helper of the poor, when he actually seeks only personal profits" (46).

66–67 *talke / Idely* **BEWLEY** (1966): "in a manner void of worth or usefulness," as a prisoner who "must conceal rather than reveal his meaning" (174). **SMITH** (1971): "speak deliberately beside the point, to play for time or confuse the issue" (477).

66 *His hand…must talke* **MORRIS** (1953) cites this line as an example of "a reversed foot at the beginning of a line, followed by one in the middle of the line after a pause" (45). He also states that the line is bound "closer together" through its "interior rhyme" (56).

66 *His hand still at* **SMITH** (1971): "(a) clutching; (b) signing, putting his hand to" (477).

66 *still at a bill:* **SHAWCROSS** (1967): "still looking out for money" (21). **ROUSSEAU AND RUDENSTINE** (1972): "Perpetually holding a bill (legal document, as well as a watchman's weapon or halberd)" (62).

66 *at* **MILGATE** (1967): "holding" (135).

66 *bill:* **BEWLEY** (1966): "probably a pun," since a "bill" was "not only a written statement of a legal case, but a halberd carried by a watchman" (174). [So also, Milgate (1967, 135), who quotes Chapman, *An Humorous Day's Mirth,* 7:80–81, Grigson (1980, 20), Patrides (1985, 222), and Carey (1990, 424).] **SMITH** (1971):

"(a) a watchman's halberd; (b) a legal statement or petition; (c) an order to pay" (477). **CHMIELEWSKI** (2001): "an account; a watchman's halberd (a weapon that is a combination of spear and ax)" (615).

67–68 *Idely...them there,* **RUGOFF** (1939): the images, related to the legal profession, are "based as much on observation of human nature as on an interest in technical niceties" (77). **KRUZHKOVA** (1994): these lines speak of the most respectable reason for which a person could appear in prison, namely, to be charged for someone else's debt (158).

68 *only Suretiship...them there,* **BEWLEY** (1966): putting "a false face on his own practices," he does "as prisoners do who say they have been held liable for the default or crime of another" (174).

68 *Suretiship* **JOHNSON** (1755): "The office of a surety or bondsman; the act of being bound for another." **MILGATE** (1967): "responsibility taken by one person on behalf of another, as for payment of a debt" (*OED*). "This is a respectable reason for being sent to prison (since one is brought there by another's default and one's own generosity), and is too good a lie to give up easily (it is maintained for 'whole months')" (135). [So also, Carey (1990, 424).] **SHAWCROSS** (1967): "having become liable for payment of the debt of another, who has defaulted" (21). **KERMODE** (1970): "standing bail for another" (101). [Similarly, Smith (1971, 478), Rousseau and Rudenstine (1972, 62), Patrides (1985, 222), and Chmielewski (2001, 615).]

69–78 *And to euery...Douer Strand;* **MINER** (1969): "What seems at the outset a conventional satire of a conventional satiric diction, the lawyer, turns by clever use of that more directive figure, the simile, to a condemnation of a considerable sweep of creatures: courtiers, kings, asses, whores, kings again, and divines. The inviolability of clergy and the *arcana imperii* are rent away like flimsy veils to reveal an ugliness beneath. It would be difficult to exaggerate the daring and the subversive innuendo that the court of Elizabeth I would associate with the attribution of bastardy to king's titles," and thus "the force behind the lines is enormous," generating in "outrage and hatred. Surprisingly, the end of the passage, with its image of the sea in flood, does not bring the nausea that it might, but a lyricism manqué" (164–65).

69–76 *And to euery...do in him,* **HUGHES** (1968): in these lines, Donne "comes closer to the throne, and the polite ignoring of the Queen doesn't do much to temper the imprudence of the lines" (27).

69–70 *And to euery...like a king;* **RUGOFF** (1939): these lines "cast reflection openly on royal worth" (153). **LOUTHAN** (1951) emphasizes the erotic aspects of these lines (102–03). **HAUBLEIN** (1979): "The king appears as a corrupt traitor, who may be susceptible to other vices. He may attract worthless favorites who resemble him and thus be subject to the same scathing attacks which Donne levels at the Court elsewhere" (97). [Similarly, Corthell (1997, 32).] **PATRIDES** (1985): "Censored, these lines were represented in 1633 by dashes" (222). [So also, Sullivan (2000, 302).] **LOW** (1993): Donne "plays on the familiar similarities between the various forms of 'courting,' whether in love, in law, or in politics," in which "sexual love is reduced to a subordinate but fully congruent place in a universally grim, treacherous, self-seeking society, a society that lacks true community in its legal and political relationships as in its writings, since the chief concern of its members is personal gain. The social bonds break down, feudalism gives place to a proto-Darwinian market economy, and love, like other social relationships, is commodified" (37). **CAIN** (1995): Donne employs "the apparently gratuitous simile" in order "to illuminate the corrupt lawyer," which "reflects Donne's 'anti-absolutist' attitude" (85).

70 *Like a...a king;* **ELWIN AND COURTHOPE** (1881) comment, as a note to Pope's rendition of *Sat2*, "this line, with two or three others in the Satire, is transferred unaltered from Donne" (3:430n2). **MELTON** (1906) uses this line not only to draw a metrical comparison with Wyatt's "Description," l. 9 (191), but also to illustrate "when trisyllabic words, or three monosyllabic words are repeated with an intervening number of syllables" (203). **STEIN** (1944c) cites this line as an example of stress-shift after the caesura (378) and as an example of stress-shift carrying over from the first foot to the second (383). **MILGATE** (1967): "A touch of Juvenal's loftier and more daring manner"; see *Sat4* 72–75. "It seemed too risky to the editor of 1633, who omitted ll. 69–70" (135).

70 *Like* **PATRIDES** (1985): "'Lye like' (acc. to a MS)" (222).

70 *yea* **PATRIDES** (1985): "(acc. to most MSS): 'or' (acc. to 1635–69)" (222).

71–76 *Like a wedge...do in him,* **SHAWCROSS** (1972): Coscus "is like the lower die of an anvil as used in Roman coinage ('a wedge'); he must press against the upper die ('the bar'), producing identical coins ('Bearing like Asses'). That is, the lawyer acquires money over and over again by twisting testimony as he pleads at the bar of law. In this he shows himself to be an ass and two-faced (since the ass pictured Janus, the two-faced god). And he must lie to the grave judge more shamelessly than do whores rounded up and transported to court in a cart. (As whores, the embrotheled strumpets of line 64, lawyers also 'wring' to a different—obscene—kind of 'bar,' bearing their posteriors which are similar to whores'. The nouns of lines 74–75 iterate their being strumpets, 'bastardy'; their being greedy, 'simony'; and their baring of their posteriors, 'sodomy')" (255–56). [Similarly, Patrides (1985, 222).]

71–73 *Like a wedge...the graue Iudg:* **GRIERSON** (1930) defends his reading of these lines against Sisson's (1930a) objections (see notes to ll. 71–72), arguing that "bar" could not be intended to refer to the lawyer. Believes that his reading is consistent with Donne's description of the lawyer's self-serving practices in the second part of the poem (190). **SISSON** (1930b) acknowledges the evidence for "bearing" in the manuscripts and early editions but still believes Donne could have intended "braieing." Provides evidence that coming to the bar could refer to the lawyer as well as the prisoner and insists that "Asses" must be plural (214). **LOUTHAN** (1951) paraphrases these lines to demonstrate that they describe simony "accomplished with the aid of sodomy" (103). **COBB** (1956a): the word "wedge" means "ingot," since Donne used this meaning several times in his sermons and often used images related to coinage. In this case, the meaning is that the lawyer strains his words to make his case acceptable just as an ingot must be shaped to the mold or "blocke" (Item

40). **HAGOPIAN** (1958) argues that Donne never formed compounds from like + a verb, adding that there are two "reasonable" ways to read the original lines: (1) Coscus "rings" to the Bar "as asses do, and more shamelessly than whores he tells falsehoods to the judge", or (2) "Coscus carries a posterior similar to those of whores, and more shamelessly than they he lies prone before the judge." Favors the second reading as it seems more characteristic of Donne and argues for the restoration of the original punctuation (256). **LEIN** (1980): the lines are "perversely ambiguous," but "the connotations of coinage are intended and crucial. The moral power of the analogy, in fact, rests directly on the blunt identification of Coscus with coinage, for by this maneuver Coscus becomes an incarnation of yet another of the forces which defile the world of the poem. The key phrase, in addition, associates the actions of Coscus clearly with prostitution and anality." Further, the "acme" of Coscus' "maturation into bestiality comes when Donne attributes sodomy to him. The 'Bearing like Asses' passage and the line on 'Symonie 'and Sodomy' thus contain a telling union of the motifs of sexuality, bestiality, and money, implications we are also intended to apply to the shameless whores" (137–38).

71–72 *Like a wedge...shameles farr* **HALL** (1957): the "asses" refers to a Roman coin, in which case the lawyer adapts his conscience to the case as the asses are imprinted by the hammer. In addition, "he" is the subject of "wring," and Donne's comparison of one lawyer with "plural objects" may suggest that the lawyer is "many-faced" (Item 24). **MABBOTT** (1957): in later Roman coining, the "wedge" was the lower die and the "bar" the upper. The obverse of the Roman as in the Republic was the two-faced Janus, and the pun also means that lawyers make themselves look more ridiculous by pushing close to the bar (Item 19).

71–72 *Like a wedge...like Asses* **BELDEN** (1915) says that this "unintelligible" passage "is given a meaning by hyphenating 'bearing like'—'Bearing-like Asses' = the patient Catholic gentry whom Coscus hales into court to pay fines for their recusancy." Asserts that "bearing-like" is a "preposterously un-English" and "un-Donnian coinage" (142). **SISSON** (1930a) disputes Grierson's (1912) addition of the hyphen in "bearing-like" (see notes to ll. 65–76), suggesting that Donne intended "braieing" instead of "bearing" and that "wring" should be intransitive. Says that the passage would then mean that "the lawyers force their way through the packed crowd to the Bar, braying like asses" (142). **COBB** (1956a) believes that "wedge" does not mean "a triangular piece of metal used for splitting wood but means *ingot*," and Donne is indicating that "just as the ingot must shape itself to the mold ('blocke') so the dishonest lawyer must strain the purport of his words ('wring' them) to make his case acceptable to the court ('barre')." Notes that if this interpretation is followed, "'Bearing' modifies the 'hee' of line 65." Adds that there is "the possibility that Donne is using the Norman French word *Asses*, a conjunction or concurrence; an acquiescence" and that "'like' is an adjective synonymous with *similar*." Concludes that we would then have "a sustained figure: like the ingot in its mold, the dishonest lawyer must shape his words to fit the pattern required by the court; and in so doing 'hee' is enduring a forced acquiescence, like that endured by the ingot. For him, the forcing agent is the 'barre'; for the ingot, it is the 'blocke'" (Item 40). **MILGATE** (1967): "Coscus must work his way laboriously to the counsellors' bar (through the crowded court) like a wedge through a block of wood, pressing on with the dogged stupidity characteristic of asses [so also, Smith (1971, 478) and Rousseau and Rudenstine (1972, 62)], and (a practiced liar, ll. 69–70) he must lie to the judge." On the "crowded condition of the courts," see Chapman, *All Fools*, 2.1.324ff. (135). The lines "seem to give a striking picture" of Coscus's "insensitive, arrogant, and unprincipled behaviour when it comes to the straightforward, as distinct from the more secret and shady, practice of the law" (289). **WARNKE** (1967): "this obscure passage probably means that the poet-turned-lawyer specializes in bringing suspected Catholics to trial" (111). **PATRIDES** (1985): "The numismatic image concerns an ingot shaped in a mould (*blocke*)" (222).

71 *Like a wedge...to the barr* **CORTHELL** (1997): Coscus's "practice of law is marked by dull persistence" (34).

71 *wedge* **SHAWCROSS** (1967): "the lower die of an anvil used in Roman coinage" (21). [So also, Patrides (1985, 222).]

71 *wring to the barr* **GROSART** (1872–73): "I do not know the carrier's or ostler's phrase 'wring to the bar,' but I take it that 'bar' has here the double sense of bar and bar of a court of justice; that 'wring' is used in a combination of its senses of twist and pinch" (1:21).

71 *wring* **GROSART** (1872–73) (reading "wringd") lists as alternate readings "wrung" and the usual "wring"; explains "I do not know the carrier's or ostler's phrase 'wring to the bar,' but I take it that 'bar' has here the double sense of bar and bar of a court of justice; that 'wring' is used in a combination of its senses of twist and pinch; and that the meaning is, that he twists close up to the bar, and squeezes as close as a wedge in wood the bearing-like Asses his clients, and to the judge lies, &c" (1:21). **MILGATE** (1967): "writhe, labour, contend" (*OED*); see Chamberlain, *Letters*, 1:318 (135). **CAREY** (1990): "force a way through the crowd in court" (424). **CHMIELEWSKI** (2001): "strive or struggle" (615).

71 *barr* **SHAWCROSS** (1967): "the upper die against which the wedge presses. 'Wring' is an infinitive following 'he must,' l. 66 (21). [So also, Patrides (1985, 222).]

72–75 *Bearing...Churchmens Liues* **HESTER** (1982): "That Coscus' legal activities are illegitimate extensions of the sexual appetite motivating his seductions is made clear by the satirist's repeated insistence that the lawyer always 'lyes'" (73), and "his lies are merely an expansion of the sexual appetite he exhibited as a poet, as suggested by the homosexual implications of the comparison of the 'Sodomy' by which he thrives to that which 'abounds...in Churchmens lives' (74–75), by the comparison of his lies to the male prostitution used to gain royal preferment, and by the insistence that his bearing in the courtroom is 'more shameless farre / Then [that of] carted whores' (72–73)." Further, such metaphors "equate Coscus' mendacity with violations of the major vessels of social stability: sex and generation, money and coining, health and religion" (44–45).

72–73 *Bearing like...graue Iudg:* **RUGOFF** (1939): "adding insult to injury," Donne "describes the work of the lawyers as sordid, and does so in imagery drawn from the characteristics of common prisoners" (77–78).

72–73 *Bearing like…carted whores*, **MILGATE** (1967): in describing Coscus, this "hovers between words and images expressing the characteristics now of the individual, now of the class" (135). **SHAWCROSS** (1967) says that the "coins which are produced (born) are all similar (like). The point is that lawyers, since they are like wedges, must press at the bar of law (extort information and thence payment by twisting testimony), and thus they show themselves to be asses and two-faced." Suggests Donne's awareness that the coin "had been extremely debased (from 12 oz. to ½ oz.)" and adds that Donne intended "the pun 'baring posteriors similar' to those of the 'carted whores,' which emphasizes the meaning of 'twist' for 'wring'" (397).

72 *Bearing like Asses* **MORRIS** (1953) states that this phrase "is rhythmically much more effective than would be 'like bearing asses'" (68).

72 *Bearing like* **KERMODE** (1970): "patient" (101).

72 *Bearing* **MILGATE** (1967): "pressing, moving with persistence" (135). The word is a "participle of an intransitive verb describing Coscus's motion" (289).

72 *Asses* **SHAWCROSS** (1967): "Roman coins, the obverse of which usually pictured Janus, the two-faced god" (21). **PATRIDES** (1985): "plural of the Roman bronze coin *as*" (222).

72 *more shameles* **MILGATE** (1967) quotes Lynn Thorndike's translation of a passage on lawyers from *Liber de Similitudinibus et Exemplis* in *Speculum* 32 (1957):791 (135).

73–76 *for…do in him*, **LEIN** (1980): the "moral force" of this passage on kings "lies in its attack on the highest social level. Royalty itself is seen as nothing more than a degenerate flowering, a burden showing how completely Donne saw the world stripped of true nobility" (141).

73 *Then* **PATRIDES** (1985): "than" (221).

73 *carted whores*, **MILGATE** (1967): "convicted prostitutes were taken from the court in a cart to Bridewell, where they were whipped naked in public (*O.E.D.*, 'cart,' vb. 2)" (136). [Similarly, Warnke (1967, 111), Smith (1971, 478), Rousseau and Rudenstine (1972, 62), Patrides (1985, 222), and Chmielewski (2001, 615).] **SHAWCROSS** (1967): "those rounded up and brought before a judge" (21).

73 *graue Iudg:* **SHAWCROSS** (1967): "one who is severe in his punishment" (21).

74–80 *Bastardy abounds…as hee.* **LAURITSEN** (1976): "Like Satan, Coscus subverts the Word to his own ends. But, wonders the speaker, does the poet, a fallen and fallible man, do this too?" (125).

74–76 *Bastardy abounds…do in him*, **SHAWCROSS** (1967): "'Bastardy' because he is like a strumpet (l. 64), 'symonie' because he looks out for money (l. 66), and

'Sodomy' because of 'bearing like asses' (l. 72)" (397). **PARFITT** (1989): these religious references "fit into traditional categories of anti-clericalism" (26).

74–75 *Bastardy abounds...Churchmens Liues* **STEIN** (1944c) cites these lines as the only examples by Donne of an extra syllable following a stressed syllable because of the force of attraction (397). **PATRIDES** (1985): "Censored, these lines were represented in 1633 by dashes" (222). [So also, Sullivan (2000, 302).]

74 *Bastardy abounds* **RICHTER** (1902) (reading "Bastardy'abounds") uses this phrase to illustrate a slurring of syllables (402–03).

74 *Kings titles,* **SMITH** (1971): "lines of descent, their claim to the throne, which might be founded in legitimate descent but usually is not" (478).

75 *Simony...Churchmens Liues* **CORTHELL** (1997): if Grierson's (1912) interpretation of ll. 71–73 is correct (see note for ll. 65–76), then this line "would seem calculated to obfuscate any clear identification with Romanists" (37).

75 *Simony and Sodomy* **RICHTER** (1902) (reading "Symonie'and Sodomy") uses this phrase to illustrate a slurring of syllables (402–03).

75 *Simony* **LOUTHAN** (1951): the word could refer to bribery in a non-ecclesiastical context (103). **MILGATE** (1967): "Traffic in church livings was sufficiently prevalent to warrant legislation, Stat. 31 Eliz., cap. 6, 4–5"; see Stubbes, *Anatomy of Abuses* (1583), Part II, sigs L3–6, to the effect that "ways were found of evading the law" (136).

75 *Sodomy* **MILGATE** (1967): "a stock charge" of Protestants against monastic orders, "especially in recounting 'revelations' during the dispossession of the monasteries by Henry VIII"; see Burton, *Anatomy of Melancholy*, part. 3, sect. 2, memb. 5, subsect. 5, on "Bale's catalogue of sodomites, at the visitation of abbeys" (136).

76–78 *by these...to Douer Strand;* **LEIN** (1980): "The comparison seems inept, too extreme for a single individual; but the reasons for its creation are clear. It is an analogy manifesting progressive decay" (139).

76 *these things* **LOUTHAN** (1951): the phrase refers to Coscus' activities (102).

76 *him,* **CHMIELEWSKI** (2001): "Coscus" (615).

77–78 *Shortly...to Douer Strand;* **MILGATE** (1967): "He will gain possession of all Britain, from Scotland to the Isle of Wight, from Mount St. Michael (Land's End, Cornwall) [so also, Smith (1971, 478) and Carey (1990, 424)] to Dover shore: i.e. the length and breadth of the land" (136). [So also, Shawcross (1967, 397), Rousseau and Rudenstine (1972, 63), and Patrides (1985, 222).] **SLIGHTS** (1981): Coscus's "destructiveness is not confined to individuals or even to families," for the "greed he embodies threatens the whole country," and "since Coscus does not live in these ill-gotten estates, he does not fulfill the landlord's traditional responsibilities of economic and moral protection and support. The woods disappear from the countryside without returning in the form of new construction or hospitable fires in the manor house" (158–59). **LOW** (1985): "Donne's lawyer, who had done what Donne himself patently both hopes and fears to do, has for his ultimate goal the ownership of land," which was for Donne "something so desirable that it was sinful even to think about it. Land meant security, as the landless Donne knew, even before his disgrace put that security forever beyond his grasp" (77). BAUMLIN (1991): "Encompassing all of England in the compass points of these four lands, such elevated, expansive language contrasts with the scurrilous humor of previous lines, and yet this very contrast is a hallmark of Juvenalian satire, whose style mixes the serious and the ludicrous, the base and the high tragic" (84).

77 *compasse* MILGATE (1967): "to seize, lay hold of"; see *OED*, "compass," vb. IV. 9; see *Sermons*, 6:190 (136). SMITH (1971): "encompass, get into his own possession" (478). [So also, Patrides (1985, 222).]

78 *Mount* GROSART (1872–73): "Mount St. Michael, Land's End, Cornwall. He seems to omit all the Irish Channel coast as not compassed by a sea" (1:21). [So also, Kermode (1970, 102), Smith (1971, 478), and Carey (1990, 424).]

79–86 *And spying...pulling Prime.* LEIN (1980): "Whatever else we make of these lines, we are forced to note that they expressly concern both dissolution and temporality," the "central action of 'wasting candles'" providing "a major manifestation of disintegrating life forces. But Donne intensifies his picture of dissolving substances with the term 'droppings,' a nuance which immediately associates the basic action with the earlier passage on meat and excrement. The total metaphoric action involves a vision of aristocratic wealth dissolving, losing all substance and value, while out of the leavings, Coscus, like a servant (and more important, like the earlier poets), makes his fortune and reputation." However, the "chief significance" of the passage is found in "its direct expression of the relationship between time and the wasting and also of the distasteful servility of the entire process, an element heightened by the implicit contrast between light and nobility, on the one hand, and servant droppings on the other" (140).

79–85 *And spying...he getts lands:* CORTHELL (1997): "The figure of ironic deprecation is part of a larger courtly strategy of privileging amateurism and recreation over professionalism and industry. The satirists' disinterested amateur stance is implicit in his patronizing attitude" (27). As such, Donne "sharpens his attack on Coscus" by "contrasting the lawyer's self-interested diligence to the prodigality and versifying fashionable in the circle of gentlemen with whom Donne associated at the Inns of Court" (34). Further, "by another familiar gesture of courtly self-definition, Coscus's success, attributed to his moral failure, is contrasted with the satirist's self-acknowledged disconnectedness, which silently testifies to his moral superiority" and also "better qualifies him to exercise the power that has been usurped by Coscus)" (35).

79 *And spying heires melting with gluttonee* MELTON (1906) cites this line to draw a metrical comparison with Wyatt's "Charging of his loue," l. 10 (189). See also note for *Sat1* 5. SMITH (1971) (reading "gluttonee" as "luxury"): "spying out heirs who are dwindling away with debauchery (and whose early deaths may thus leave their inheritance open to legal chicanery and pocket-lining)" (478). LEIN (1980) (reading "gluttonee" as "luxurie"): "The verb 'melting' carries on the central

action of dissolution, while the world 'heires' presents the full context as one of the dissolution of nobility. The word 'luxurie' contributes the association of sexuality, a combination strengthened by the pun in 'heires' which also contributes the idea of wealth. In Donne's time, 'luxurie' commonly denoted lechery, an association going back to the concept of *luxuria*" (138).

79 *melting* **SULLENS** (1964): "This O.E.D. meaning is given only under transitive uses, while Donne's use is intransitive" (262).

79 *gluttonee* **GROSART** (1872–73), noting the usual reading "luxurie," states: "As between 'gluttony' and 'luxury' the latter is by far the more general, and therefore the more appropriate term; for heirs were not supposed to get rid of their estates by mere gluttony, a vice of older age, but by debauchery generally; and the especial sense in which luxury was frequently then used, and which the mere mention of the word would bring up, agrees best with the word 'melting,' whether applied to their estates or to themselves: 'lean as a rake' is an old saying." (1:21). **MILGATE** (1967) (reading "luxurie") quotes Middleton, *A Trick to Catch the Old One*, 1.1.3–4 (136). **ROUSSEAU AND RUDENSTINE** (1972) (reading "luxurie"): "Sensual pleasures" (63). **PATRIDES** (1985)(reading "luxurie"): "lust; 'gluttonie' (acc. to a few MSS)" (222).

80 *Satan… as hee*. **STEIN** (1944c) cites this line as an example of stress-shift in the first three feet (383). **LEIN** (1980): "The corruption of Coscus, who excels in sin, eclipsing everyone else in his depraved actions, is staggering." Donne "identifies Coscus directly with all the great sins—pride, prostitution, adultery, idleness, hypocrisy, simony, fraud," and thus is one who "even outstrips Satan" (144–45).

81–102 *For as…cleare the doubt*. **SANDERS** (1971): "These innocent/malicious comparisons of course are aimed partly at eternal devious, comfort-loving, egocentric human nature—the same the world over, in kitchen wenches and Protestant reformers, legal foxes and biblical expositors. But the breathless multiplication of unpredictable simile gives us a quite extraordinarily dense and populous world—a kind of milling, intellectual fairground in which all but the most agile are likely to perish in the crush" (38–39).

81–86 *For as…pulling Prime*. **MILGATE** (1967) the lines exemplify Donne's "frequent use of a device found occasionally in the Roman satirists, very rarely in the English—the use of ironic or illustrative allusion to things not strictly relevant to the main subject of satire," often (as here) "introduced as an image," in which "the minor term of the image, or the thing to which reference is made," is "itself an object of satire or an emblem of corruption" (xix). A series of images—candles of poor quality, poor servants, as well as the "decay of moral sense in a community that allows both," stashed relics, and "obsessive gambling"—are "all used to illustrate and sharpen the attack on legal malpractice in the land-grabbing frauds of the time." But in this process, these practices themselves "also suffer satiric disparagement" (xx). **SINHA** (1977): "The avarice of the lawyer comes in for special attention and there is exhaustive and contemptuous detail in the simile in lines 81–86 reminiscent of Ben Jonson's practice" (66). **KERINS** (1984): "The vulgarity of single-mindedness is lost on Coscus, the new man of the late Renaissance, upwardly mobile and oblivious to morality and to traditional courtly decorum." In particular, "the first simile dismisses Coscus as a nonentity by equating him with a kitchen wench. This defensive scorn is undercut, however, in the next simile, showing what true 'men' are doing in the meantime: while the courtiers are playing parlor games like primero, Coscus is slowly devouring their lands" (44).

81–85 *For as… he getts lands:* **DUBROW** (1979): Donne "achieves a Chinese-box effect of image within image by including yet another simile, and yet more satire, within the vehicle," and in this "extraordinarily complex passage," he "compares the way a man acquires land to the way a woman saves for her wedding—and then in turn compares her thrift to a form of religious devotion" (77). **REID** (2000): "in its heartless way," this passage presents "an unforgettable shot of a servant's life" (40).

81–84 *For as a…wedding geare,* **RUGOFF** (1939): "There are not many figures of this truly homely kind in Donne" (120).

81 *kitchin stuffe,* **JOHNSON** (1755) reads as "kitchenstuff" and defines as "the fat of meat scummed off the pot, or gathered out of the dripping-pan."

82 *And barrelling…the snuffe* **MELTON** (1906) uses this line to draw a metrical comparison with Wyatt's "To his unkind loue," l. 7 (189). See also note for *Sat1* 5.

82 *barrelling* **SMITH** (1971): "storing up" (478). [So also, Patrides (1985, 222).]

82 *droppings* **JOHNSON** (1755): "That which falls in drops." **GROSART** (1872–73): "drippings [from roast meat]" (1:21).

82 *snuffe* **GROSART** (1872–73): "the derivation of the word, and its use in the present passage, show that it meant the 'droppings from a candle, the result of gut-tering; inclusive, probably, of the candle-end embedded in the outspread mass.' It was probably from the candle-end thus forming one with the true snuff, and becoming a part of the kitchen-maid's prerogative, that 'snuff' came, in a secondary sense, to mean a candle-end nearly burnt out" (1:21–22). [Similarly, Rousseau and Rudenstine (1972, 63).] **MILGATE** (1967): "candle-end"; see Stubbes, *The Second Part of the Anatomy of Abuses* (1583), sig. G7v (136). **SHAWCROSS** (1967): "the charred material of a candlewick" (21). **PATRIDES** (1985) refers to *Image* 24 (222).

83 *yeare* **MILGATE** (1967): "the Old English uninflected plural *géar*" (136).

84 *Relique like kept* **MILGATE** (1967): "The kitchen-maid treasures her hoard as if it were a sacred relic; it does, in a way, like a relic, contribute to her future bliss" (136). [So also, Shawcross (1967, 21).]

84 *Relique like* **JOHNSON** (1755) reads as "Relickly" and defines as "in the man-ner of relicks," a relic being "that which is kept in memory of another, with a kind of religious veneration." **SULLENS** (1964): the *OED* cites Donne as the earliest source for this word (199). **PATRIDES** (1985): "(acc. to most MSS): 'Reliquely' (acc. to 1633–69 and a few MSS)" (222).

84 *wedding geare,* SULLENS (1964): a word combination that the *OED* does not record (207).

84 *geare,* PATRIDES (1985): "'chear' (acc. to 1669)" (222).

85–102 *Piece meale...cleare the doubt.* PATTERSON (1994): "The corrupt lawyer, Coscus, is described as accumulating land by sharp practice, deliberately producing flawed legal documents so that he may later profit from his own errors." The implication is that "assurances, or title deeds to property, have grown so complicated that they can be deployed to cheat those whom they should protect," and Donne "equates fraudulent legal writing to textual scholarship which avoids precisely the 'hard words' that most need glossing, or the dishonest theological controversy which, when citing the text of Scripture, leaves out those intractable passages which cannot be brought into line with the position being argued. But what makes this broader conception possible is the huge territory that 'law' covered, virtually synonymous with 'society,' or 'the system,' but a system without coherence. Common law, civil law, canon law; all three were competing for jurisdiction in Elizabethan England, a situation creative at least of relativism, at worst of cynicism" (148–49).

85–90 *Piece meale...wryting lesse.* MANLEY (1995): "By analogy with revisions in the canonical texts by protestant theologians, Coscus' rewriting of the social landscape effectively prevents traditionally 'vouch't Texts' from being heard" (398).

85–86 *Piece meale...pulling Prime.* LOUTHAN (1951) sees a contrast between greed ("wringing") and devotion ("ringing" church bells) (100). PARTRIDGE (1978): the passage "recalls the courtiers' gambling recreation of *primero,* a game that resembled modern poker." Although the "rhyme-words here are mostly strong monosyllables, Donne does not invoke monosyllabic lines to excess; he tends rather to halt the rhythm by juxtaposing stressed syllables" (40). [So also, Corthell (1997, 34).] LEIN (1980): in this passage, "we have symbols of idealized wealth being fragmented into baser pieces (the gold ingot and candles provide analogical examples)." The "structural importance of the verb 'teare' to describe Coscus' wooing now becomes clearer" as that "wooing contains the motif of piecemeal destruction which underlies so much of the imagery." Moreover, "wringing" reminds us of the previous image of coin-making so that the couplet is "fully intended to bind imaginatively two major passages defining the nature of the world's disintegration and its profound identification with making money" (140–41).

85 *Piece meale* HESTER (1982): "With a poet as fond of word play as Donne it is not impossible that 'Peecemeale,' immediately following the phrases 'Relique-like' and 'wedding gear,' is an ironic allusion to the Eucharist" (145–46).

86 *Wringing* GROSART (1872–73): "twisting out, extorting" (1:22). [So also, Smith (1971, 478).] MILGATE (1967): "wresting (from the self-indulgent heirs)" (137). [So also, Patrides (1985, 223).]

86 *men* PATRIDES (1985): "'Maids' (acc. to 1669)" (223).

86 *pulling Prime.* GROSART (1872–73): "'Prime,' in primero, is a winning hand of

different suits [with probably certain limitations as to the numbers of the cards, since there were different primes], different to and of lower value than a flush or hand of [four] cards of the same suit. The game is now unknown, but from such notices as we have, it would seem that one could stand on their hands, or, as in écarté and other games, discard and take in others (see Nares, *s.v.*). From the words of our text, the fresh cards were not dealt by the dealer, but 'pulled' by the player at hazard, and the delays of maidish indecision can be readily understood; albeit, as above, the Stephens' MS. substitutes 'men' for 'maids'—the latter probably our author's later correction" (1:22). [Similarly, Bewley (1966, 174), Kermode (1970, 102), Smith (1971, 478), Rousseau and Rudenstine (1972, 63), Carey (1990, 424), and Chmielewski (2001, 615).] MILGATE (1967): "Coscus takes no longer getting money out of each acre than a gamester does in pulling out a winning card." [So also, Warnke (1967, 112).] The game is "a sort of poker much played by courtiers for high stakes"; see Nares's *Glossary* (1888), 2:687ff. and *Archaeologia* 8:131–32, 148ff. Further, "'prime' was the winning hand consisting of different suits; to 'pull for prime' was to draw for a card or cards which might make the player prime" (137). SHAWCROSS (1967): "acquiring the best in quality, the larger part; from pulling the winning card in a popular card game" (21). [So also, Patrides (1985, 223).]

86 *pulling* SULLENS (1964): the *OED* cites Donne as the earliest source for the meaning of this word (252).

87–102 *In Parchments…cleare the doubt.* BAUMLIN (1991): the poet's "broader target" here "has become the abuses of…'Schoolmen' or, rather, of polemicists on either side of the Reformation controversy," and "the advent of such controversy has, in this 'times forwardness,' opened a floodgate of theological language, exemplified by Luther's (initially Erasmus's) emendation of so sacred a text as the Lord's Prayer. And if Reformation theology changes the words one prays, how might it change the meaning and effect of those words? Who are the 'Commenter[s]' and 'controverters' the poet inveighs against (on both sides, one assumes)?" (90–91).

87–96 *In Parchments…glory clause.* LEISHMAN (1951) compares these lines with a passage from Dryden to show that while Donne here uses the similes to illustrate his subject, he often seems to subordinate the idea to the illustration (111–12). HESTER (1982): the "sheer bulk" of the lawyer's writing, which is "here derided through puns as a perverse form of phallic hyperbole and corrupt procreation," is of "little concern" to Coscus for "he does not have to copy them nor pay to have them copied," and "verbosity is not an obstacle to Coscus because he has left the law in his unscrupulous dealings" (45–46). WIGGINS (2000): "for Coscus, entering the legal profession has been what leaving the monastery was for Luther. Having become a lawyer, Coscus is no longer subject to the law, just as Luther was no longer required to tell his beads when he ceased to be a friar." Like Luther, Coscus "adds the 'power and glory clause' in the form of the many provisos he attaches to his titles and assurances" (40).

87–88 *In Parchments…ciuil Lawes:* STEIN (1944c) cites these lines as examples of stress-shift after a pause (379). CORTHELL (1987): "Coscus's legal writings, more than his legalistic poems, are the objects of Donne's satire. Unlike the powerless rhymes of the Petrarchists, the writs of Coscus are changing English society by redistributing the land. They imitate both their author's voraciousness and the objects of his desire" (27; 1997, 34).

87 *his* GROSART (1872–73): "seeing the fields when the parchments were drawn were not 'his,' but the heir's" (1:22).

87 *drawes* MILGATE (1967): "draws up" (137). [So also, Patrides (1985, 223).]

88 *Assurances,* BEWLEY (1966): "legal evidence of the conveyance of land or property" (174). MILGATE (1967): "documents securing the title to property" (137). SHAWCROSS (1967): "pledges (of land)" (21). [So also, Rousseau and Rudenstine (1972, 63).] SMITH (1971): "deeds of conveyance" (478). [So also, Patrides (1985, 223).]

88 *glossd ciuil Lawes:* MILGATE (1967): "In Coscus's hands they become as large as the whole body of Civil Law with Commentary"; see Stubbes, *Anatomy of Abuses,* Part II (1583), sig. E7v (137). [So also, Smith (1971, 478), Rousseau and Rudenstine (1972, 63), and Patrides (1985, 223).]

88 *glossd* JOHNSON (1755): "To explain by comment."

89 *in our times forwardnesse* MILGATE (1967): "in these advanced days" (137). [So also, Smith (1971, 478) and Patrides (1985, 223).]

90 *fathers of the Church* MILGATE (1967): "The Fathers are notoriously bulky writers" (137). [So also, Smith (1971, 479) and Chmielewski (2001, 615).] ROUSSEAU AND RUDENSTINE (1972): "Learned, venerable churchmen, especially Biblical commentators" (63).

91–96 *These he…glory clause.* SHAWCROSS (1972) notes "the intermixture of standard iambic lines with lines containing variety in feet" and adds, "the reversed foot which begins line 91 is finally reversed again with a symmetrical pattern of a spondee, a pyrrhic, and a spondee in between; the reversed feet of line 92 are continued over a strong medial pause but then reversed by what appears (but is not) a pyrrhic; lines 93–95 are regular; and line 96 also begins with a reversed foot but the spondee that follows allows the brief passage to end regularly. The 'feel' of the passage is of common speech, but the important words for the point being made—like 'writes,' 'written,' 'length,' 'Addes,' 'Christs prayer'—are stressed partially by an iambic pattern, partially by alterations in the metric. What Donne gains by his practice is an enhancement of the naturalness afforded by language and idea, plus an unavoidable emphasis on the words and ideas that are important," as well as "an ambiguity on occasion which is significant for the context" (263–64).

91–92 *These he…no length:* STEIN (1944c) cites these lines as an example of stress-shift in the first three feet (383). SMITH (1971): "not having to write these himself or pay a scribe to write them, he finds it to his legal advantage to make the documents unreadably long" (479).

91 *These he… written payes,* STEIN (1946): this line "may possibly be read with-

out stress-shifts" (99). **ROUSSEAU AND RUDENSTINE** (1972): "i.e., he neither writes them himself, nor pays the clerks who write them for him" (63).

91 *wrytes not:* **HESTER** (1982): Coscus's "final legal maneuvers—he 'writes not' (91), 'spares no length' (92), and 'leave[s] out' (101)—figure the essence of him and his words: they are absence, negation, privation, 'sinne…in-deed,' or, in Augustine's words, '*Dictum, factum, concupitum, contra legem…; Forma peccati, deformitas*'" (47).

92 *Therfore spares…first dayes* **RICHTER** (1902) uses this line to illustrate a metrical inversion from iambic to trochaic in the first three feet (395).

93–96 *When Luther…glory clause.* **GROSART** (1872–73): "close of the Lord's Prayer, 'for Thine is the Kingdom and the Power and the Glory'" (1:22). **ELWIN AND COURTHOPE** (1881): "when this Satire was written Donne had evidently a leaning towards the unreformed Church," and "his Catholic tendencies and his hatred of the monied interest that rose out of the spoliation of the monasteries made his satire peculiarly acceptable to Pope" (3:431–32n1). **NORTON** (1895): "'The power and glory clause' of the Lord's Prayer is not to be found in the Vulgate, but was added by Luther in his translation of the New Testament" (1:241). [So also, Bewley (1966, 174), Warnke (1967, 112), and Kruzhkova (1994, 158).] **GRIERSON** (1912): the phrase "was taken by Erasmus (1516) from all the Greek codices, though he does not regard it as genuine. Thence it passed into Luther's (1521) and most Reformed versions" (2:112). [Similarly, Erskine-Hill (1964, 165), Milgate (1967, 137), Smith (1971, 479), Rousseau and Rudenstine (1972, 63), Elliott (1976, 109), Patrides (1985, 223), and Carey (1990, 424).] **ERSKINE-HILL** (1964): Donne distinguishes here between "Luther the monk" and "Luther the theologian" (165). **MILGATE** (1967) quotes the gibe at Luther in *Courtier's Library*, ed. Simpson (1930), p. 33 and, more respectful, *Essays*, p. 9 (137). **HESTER** (1982): "The 'Power and glory' phrase is highly ironic, of course; and although its saucy use here may accuse Luther of a 'personal laziness,' its major effect is to render the charge against Coscus doubly damning by the contrast between the power and glory the lawyer seeks through defrauding clients and the power and glory Luther demanded to be paid to God in daily prayer. Actually, the simile is quite precise in its reiteration of Coscus' 'Shrewd' manipulations of legal words as analogous to perversion of the Word: Luther at prayer altered a document of the Law, omitting from the *Pater noster* acknowledgment of the eternality of the Father's justice and mercy (for ever and ever); Coscus in private ('unwatch'd') alters documents of the law, omitting from testaments the phrase ('*ses heires*') that enforces the father's undying love for his children" (46). **OLIVER** (1997) comments on Donne's "disrespectful vignette" of Luther, seen "firstly as a hard-pressed, or lazy, Catholic friar saying his rosary, then as the rigorous—and ambitious—reformer he later became" (36).

93–94 *When Luther…Short Pater Nosters,* **CROLY** (1835): here Donne exhibits "the propensity to sneer at the Reformation, which marked the unsettled nature of Donne's opinions in early life." Donne "had written a satirical 'Catalogue of Rare Books,' one of which is named, 'M. Lutherus de abbreviatione Orationis Dominicæ,' with reference to his omission of the doxology," a satire "in imitation of Rabelais' 'Catalogue of the Library of St. Victor'" (2:293n).

93 *was profest*, **SMITH** (1971): "had taken the vows of a religious order" (479). [So also, Rousseau and Rudenstine (1972, 63) and Chmielewski (2001, 615).]

94 *Short Pater Nosters*, **SHAWCROSS** (1967): "the prayer 'Our Father which art in heaven' (Luke 11:2–4), repeated often in the rosary" (22). [So also, Patrides (1985, 223).]

95 *lawes* **CHMIELEWSKI** (2001): "those first monastic vows (l. 93)" (615).

96 *the power and glory clause.* **SHAWCROSS** (1967): "the phrase added to the 'Our Father' by Protestants: 'For thine is the Kingdom and the Power and the Glory, Forever and ever'" (22). [So also, Kermode (1970, 102), Patrides (1985, 223), and Chmielewski (2001, 615).]

97–102 *he'impayres ...cleare the doubt.* **BALD** (1970): into these lines "creeps a note of impatience, almost of cynicism, at the methods of the religious controversialists on both sides" (70–71). **TOLIVER** (1985): "in a noisy world people seek the most noticeable way to sally forth and the most imposing speech. Meanwhile, the good works for which lawyers should be trained go undone, and connections between the private soul and private works are broken. The results Donne finds equivalent to misreadings of biblical texts" (101).

97 *changes* **SMITH** (1971): "exchanges" (479).

97 *impayres* **SMITH** (1971): "abbreviates, so as to diminish his own legal obligation" (479).

98 *vnwatch'd,* **SMITH** (1971): "if one does not keep a sharp eye on him" (479).

98 *Ses heires* **SHAWCROSS** (1967): so that "the land will not devolve upon the heirs of the purchaser but will default to the lawyer" (22). [So also, Smith (1971, 479), Rousseau and Rudenstine (1972, 63), and Patrides (1985, 223).] **CHMIELEWSKI** (2001): "his heirs" (615).

99 *any Commentor* **SMITH** (1971): "commentators upon difficult authors (such authors as Donne) notoriously sidestep passages they cannot make sense of" (479). **CORTHELL** (1997): Coscus's technique "could have been learned from reading biblical commentaries" (34–35). **CHMIELEWSKI** (2001): "a writer on religious controversy" (615).

99 *Commentor* **JOHNSON** (1755): "One that writes comments; an explainer; an annotator."

99 *goes by* **SHAWCROSS** (1967): "avoids, passes over" (22). **PATRIDES** (1985): "bypasses" (223). **CHMIELEWSKI** (2001): "passes by, ignores" (615).

100 *Hard words or sense:* **SMITH** (1971): "harsh conditions and penalizing clauses in a legal document, which the trickster craftily conceals" (479).

101 *Controuerters* **SULLENS** (1964): the *OED* cites Donne as the earliest source for this word (191). **MILGATE** (1967): a neologism possibly "stimulated" by the "atrocious new coinages" found in *Zepheria* (1594) (128); "controversialists" (137). [So also, Smith (1971, 479) and Patrides (1985, 223).]

101 *vouchd texts* **SMITH** (1971): "texts cited as authoritative" (479). **ROUSSEAU AND RUDENSTINE** (1972): "Texts used as evidence in a theological dispute" (63). **CAREY** (1990): "Biblical passages cited by controversialists to support arguments" (424).

101 *vouchd* **SULLENS** (1964): Donne's usage of this word is earlier than the earliest sourced cited by *OED* (190). **MILGATE** (1967): "brought forth as evidence or confirmation. Strictly speaking it is the theological arguments that are vouched *for* by the texts" (137). **PATRIDES** (1985): "said to be authoritative" (223). **CHMIELEWSKI** (2001): "authorized" (615).

102 *Shrewd* **SMITH** (1971): "awkward, or difficult to get round; sharp" (479). **ROUSSEAU AND RUDENSTINE** (1972): "embarrassing or damaging— evidence that counts against one" (63).

102 *which might against them cleare the doubt.* **SMITH** (1971): "which might settle the controversy in favour of their opponents" (479). [So also, Chmielewski (2001, 616).]

103–12 *Where are...Statute Lawes.* **MANLEY** (1995): "Unlike Horace, who has no trouble maintaining his faith in satire against the warnings of the lawyer Trebatius, the urbane satirist who began Donne's satire with a superior contempt for the town becomes by the end a dispossessed plaintiff lamenting the loss of traditional moral ground," and "the ambiguous syntax also suggests that his word lacks the power to prosecute, that its impotence in the face of the law's power makes it not worth persecuting" (398–99).

103–11 *Where are...rich wardrobes.* **ROUSSEAU AND RUDENSTINE** (1972): "This forceful compression of moral energy—the sharp accusations and expressions of helplessness—reveals a poet who is deeply concerned with 'good workes,' and one whose discoveries are frequently shocking and perplexing as well as intriguing and entertaining" (56–57). **ZUNDER** (1982): the "growth of a land market, and the commercialization of agriculture, were features of the English economy in the sixteenth century, as was the movement of capital from town to country," for England was "a predominantly agricultural society. And lawyers were among those accumulating wealth and buying land. Donne's employer, Egerton, was one of them." In the portrait of Coscus, a "new element is seen to establish itself in the countryside: an element perceived as alien to old humane traditions, motivated by a concern, not for mutual obligation, but for private gain" (13–14).

103–05 *Where are...and almes?* **STEIN** (1944c) notes that the first four feet in the line are stress-shifted (384). **HESTER** (1982): "Caring as little for the land as they do for the law, men such as Coscus treat it as a mere object to be possessed, the more the better. These new landlords have let the woods rot, have disbanded the attendants and servants maintained by the old landlords, and have abandoned the 'old fashion'd' giving of alms," and "this transition by the satirist from Coscus-as-lawyer to Coscus-as-landlord discloses the awful power over words and with words that man possesses" (47–48). **CORTHELL** (1987): "Against the new order that is almost literally being written by Coscus, the satirist opposes a naturalized traditional order that is a commonplace of sixteenth-century satire" (28).

103–04 *Where are…within dore.* **MILGATE** (1967): "The woods are cut down, not for building or firewood needed on the estate, but for quick profit" [similarly, Smith (1971, 479–80) and Chmielewski (2001, 616)]; see Middleton, *Michaelmas Term*, 2.3.372–74 (137–38). **SHAWCROSS** (1967): "the woods have not been used for building or for warmth, but let rot" (22). The point is "not only that they should be put to use, but that lands should be used as in the past and not owned by so few mere landlords as now, as the succeeding lines show" (397). [So also, Smith (1971, 479–80) and Carey (1990, 424).] **LEIN** (1980): "Even the landscape exhibits the effects of a destructive process. And that process, again, is expressed in terms suggesting a lost rich beauty, though there is a greater sense, in these last lines, of the willful destruction of beauty," an idea that is "a commonplace in sixteenth-century satire" (136).

103 *spred woods* **LOUTHAN** (1951): the phrase refers both to the woods which were "widespread" and to the timber which is now "distributed like the rest of the Catholic wealth" (101). **HESTER** (1982): "The barren woodlands merely mirror the uncreating words of Coscus, which have been stripped of their proper spirit of justice and charity. And 'Time,' which 'hath made a lawyer' of Coscus, now threatens to make a sterile wasteland of the nation because of the uncharitable, fraudulent, irresponsible actions of such Englishmen. The rottenness of the woods reflects not just the effects of the enclosure movement but the permeation of the nation by the spiritual blight manifested in the infectious abuse of word and Word typified by the mendacious lawyer-landlord" (48–49).

104 *Not built; nor burnt within dore.* **CAREY** (1990): the "woods have not been used for estate purposes but sold to profit the lawyers" (424).

105–12 *In great halls…Statute Lawes.* **SLOANE** (1985): "The speaker argues that the true source of blessedness, the impulse to observe 'meanes' (and avoid extremes), is within, not without, enforced by laws. Indeed 'Good workes' are now out of fashion, in our observance of externally imposed laws—the very laws, we assume, that are in fashion (like legalistic poetry) and that produce such vapid pettifoggers as Coscus" (175).

105–09 *In great halls…surfet so:* **BROSS** (1966): Donne has "smothered the reader in a tangle of generals and particulars. The elliptical precept, 'Mean's blest,' is hardly perceived as the rule because it is lost between two illustrations of its violation" (134–35). **HESTER** (1982): "Words are food, too, and can be images of the spiritual food of the Word. Coscus' bacchanalian verbosity, on the other hand, is finally and merely a 'Carthusian fast' spiritually. Only physical and spiritual starvation result from the spread of his verbal antifeasts of words." As such, this "final exhortation" evokes a "significant image of the satirist," for his plea is "literally" for "a community feast, a ceremony...of charity and brotherhood." What he further urges is "the reestablishment of the Christian spirit of community, a national participation or celebration of the Feast of Love to counter the antifeast of Coscus' deformed words. This vision, the Renaissance urged, was especially the responsibility of the poet, the poet as the moderator or, in Augustine's term for the Word, the mediator. The 'beast' of Coscus' Uncreating Word can be vanquished, after all, by the country's return to meaningful, charitable communion. The unreality of Coscus' words can be displaced by the reestablishment of a sense of community that images the example of the Word and His loving sacrifice: 'Blessed are those who are invited to the marriage feast of the Lamb'" (Rev. 19.9) (49).

105–08 *In great halls...not Hecatomes.* POWERS (1971) notes "the Arcadian theme and its implicit connection with a former period, the Golden Age," adding that the theme was "common enough in the English Renaissance, and sometimes (as it may be here) was linked with the contemporary socio-economic changes that were bringing landed gentry to the city, with such effects on the country life as the Satirist here deplores" (179).

105–07 *Where th'old...Meanes blesse:* DATTA (1971): "In this *Satyre* only does Donne appeal to the mean, but notably it is in contrast to ascetic and orgiastic religion" (9). POWERS (1971): these lines show Donne developing the idea of the satirist as a balanced and reasonable man (91). NEWTON (1974): "Coscus epitomizes the universal decay which the similes imply, and he is a causer of that decay. It is Coscus who corrupts the law, encourages prodigal heirs, and breaks up the estates of the old hospitable lords." In addition and "unexpectedly," there emerges "a principle by which hate may be controlled and perhaps even eliminated: 'meancs blesse,'" and thus, Donne can now "direct his hate equally, toward the excesses which Coscus helps young prodigals to and toward the mean penury which ensues" (433).

105 *Where* MILGATE (1967) (reading "Where's") cites *ElBrac* 31–32, one of "several other examples in Donne's verse of this idiomatic use of a singular verb with a plural subject following" (138).

105 *troopes and almes?* MILGATE (1967): "crowds of relatives, guests, and servants in the young man's father's day, before the slick lawyer wrested the estate away, and the charity once dispensed to the needy by the master of the great house"; see Juvenal, *Sat.* 1:92 and Hall, *Vergidemiarium* 5:2, "Housekeeping's dead," with the notes in Davenport's edition of Hall's *Poems;* see *The Servingman's Comfort* (1598), Shakespeare Association Facs. 3 (1931), G4v and sigs. H2v–H4 (138). SMITH (1971): "the throngs of people to whom the great estates gave a centre and employment; and the charity dispensed by the head of the house" (480). PATRIDES (1985): "the old landlord's employees and beneficiaries" (223).

105 *troopes* ROUSSEAU AND RUDENSTINE (1972): "Retainers and guests, symbolic here of a vanished era of generous hospitality and conviviality" (64).

105 *almes?* SHAWCROSS (1967): "charities (from the landlord)" (22).

105 *great halls* SMITH (1971): "great houses; the dining halls of those houses" (480).

106 *Carthusian fasts,* MILGATE (1967): "The Carthusians were an order of monks founded by St. Bruno in 1086, noted for the severity of their rule"; see *Sermons* 2:297–98 (138). [So also, Shawcross (1967, 22), Patrides (1985, 223), and Chmielewski (2001, 616).] SMITH (1971): "extreme austerity of fare" (480). [Similarly, Rousseau and Rudenstine (1972, 64).]

106 *fulsome* MILGATE (1967): "cloyingly or disgustingly excessive" (138).

106 *Bacchanalls* MILGATE (1967): "licentious orgies, like those thought to characterize the ancient *Bacchanalia,* held in honour of Bacchus, god of wine" (138). [So also, Smith (1971, 480).]

107–09 *Meanes blesse:…surfet so:* SLIGHTS (1981): "The satirist would substitute for parasitic greed and fashionable ostentation an ideal of moderation and social responsibility," yet "the whole town is corrupt, and good works are 'out of fashion now'" (159).

107 *Meanes blesse:* GROSART (1872–73): "'Mean's bless,' means then, as now, meant riches, possessions, but never the mean or middle. 'Mean' is here the middle between waste and avarice," and Donne "explains the means [as] a mean corresponding to one's station" (1:22). ALDEN (1899) points to Horace, Satire 2 of Book II., ll. 88–125; Juvenal XI.; and Persius VI (86). GRIERSON (1912): "in all things means (i.e. middle ways, moderate measures) bring blessings," and "see O.E.D., which quotes for the plural in this sense: 'Tempering goodly well Their contrary dislikes with loved means.' Spenser, *Hymns.* In the singular Bacon has, 'But to speake in a Meane.' *Of Adversitie*" (2:113). [So also, Milgate (1967, 138), Smith (1971, 480), and Carey (1990, 424).] STEIN (1962): Donne seeks rather than exemplifies the mean (163). MILGATE (1967) cites *OED,* "means"; Plato, *Republic* 10:619a, *Laws* 3:691c, etc.; and Aristotle, *Eth. Nic.* 2:6, 1107a, 2–3; *Eth.* 2:7, and *Pol.* 4:11, 3 (138). HESTER (1977a) says that Elizabethan culture "counsels moderation," yet "even here there is wry modification of the Horatian dictum, conveyed in this case by the pun on 'mean' as 'lowly' and 'immoral' and by the suggestion that only the 'meanest' of actions finds the blessing of his materialistic society" (30; 1982, 52). ELLRODT (1980): the phrase demonstrates that Donne "truly sought the via media" (170). BLISSETT (2000) describes this phrase as "surely the most condensed, not to say crabbed, statement of the Horatian ideal of *aurea mediocritas*" (111).

107 *Meanes* KERMODE (1970): "middle ways" (102). ROUSSEAU AND RUDENSTINE (1972): "Moderation; the mean between extremes" (64).

107 *blesse:* PATRIDES (1985): "'blest' (acc. to 1635–69 and a few MS)" (224).

108 *Hecatomes.* JOHNSON (1755): "A sacrifice of an hundred cattle." MILGATE (1967): "a great public sacrifice, properly of 'a hundred oxen,' loosely of 'a great number of victims'" (138). SHAWCROSS (1967): "great slaughters" (22).

[Similarly, Smith (1971, 480), Rousseau and Rudenstine (1972, 64), and Patrides (1985, 224).]

109–12 *But oh...Statute Lawes.* **LECOCQ** (1969): this conclusion is strange, bringing an abrupt change of tone. Suited more for eclogue or elegy, these lines are ambiguous, as they set "workes" and "words" in opposition (373). **MURPHY** (1969) says that "the syntactic ambiguity" here serves the "satiric turn in that the sentence by a simple violation of concord that admits of 'my words' as subject, 'drawes' as indicative verb, and 'none' as object," forms in this passage "a true anatomy of true crimes." Adds that such an instance of syntactic exploitation "makes especially vivid Donne's double judgment upon the lawyers and their willful abuse of language" in that "[g]enuine criminals pass through the interstices; simple and honest men or those wicked only to their own hurt are entrapped and destroyed" (166). **NEWTON** (1974): Donne "concludes with an evasive maneuver which suggests that he has not really said anything serious at all. He denies the real, and frightening, implications of his hate," which is conveyed "in extraordinarily violent language, language which itself attacks the fabric of society, and leaves him only with the power of his hate" (433–34). **HESTER** (1977a): Donne concludes "in the manner of the classical *apologia*," and "the intimation that his satire is a 'Good worke' repeats Horace's *bona carmina*." Both Donne and Horace "insist that the legality of satire must be determined by the truthfulness of its vision," for "the issue at stake" is "the legal status of satire" and both poets "suggest that neither the ancient *tabulae* nor the 'huge state lawes' are violated by them." Further, "the ambiguous reference to 'none' in Donne's line (as a reference to himself as well as to those malefactors who go unpunished in spite of his revelation of their misdeeds) recalls Trebatius' admission that the satirist frees himself from legal culpability if his verse is *bona carmina*." Consequently, Donne's "echo of the Latin poem, like Horace's references to Lucilius, provides ancient authority from the canon of satire for his own efforts to support his own claims about his mission," yet Donne's satirist "finds religious sanction for his efforts, playing on the doctrinal controversy about the efficacy of good works by suggesting that the Anglican society, having discarded this doctrine from its salvation theology, disregards the meritorious character of such acts as well" (26–27). **KERINS** (1984): "The sparkling analogy linking 'Good workes' with 'old rich wardrops' [as he reads the phrase—ed.] both admitted as 'good' but currently unfashionable is a perfect epitome of the secular, courtly viewpoint. Beyond the witty play on the Thirty-nine Articles, the equation of fashionable attire with moral actions serves to underline the superficial nature of the satirist's world." As such, "'Good workes' may indeed by praiseworthy, but fortunately for his own safety, they are 'out of fashion now'" (44). **TOLIVER** (1985): "Mere words even of a more open and rational sort are helpless to guarantee a social contract in these confusions of the city and the court" (101). **BAUMLIN** (1991): "Juvenalian invective, the satirist here concludes, cannot compel reform, no matter how self-righteous or indignant or zealous the speaker's pose; his harsh language may attempt to shame criminal individuals like Coscus, may attempt, in the manner of Juvenal, to 'punish' them with words, yet it cannot bring them to justice. The poet's words, in short, are too weak." In fact, "the satirist's own safety demands that his words fail: should they be read as anything more than an exercise in imitation—as anything more than mere 'poetry'—they would themselves be deemed 'worth hate' by the likes of Coscus, imperiling, we would presume, the poet himself" (87–88). **HESTER** (1994a): "the play on the Protestant doctrinal erasure of Good Works, the sarcastic variation on the conventional sumptuary trope, and the saucy alliterative equation of 'Good workes' and 'my words' can be read as commonplaces of the sort of hectoring highjinks and moralistic claims of the genre, a version of the adolescent hyperbole familiar to Inns of Court satire." In addition, "as a reminder of the cruelty of Tudor legal enforcement techniques, most notably the (supposedly illegal) Topcliffean inquisitions implemented to enforce the prolix statutes against Roman Catholics, 'drawes' offers less a playful than a fearfully anxious perspective on the role of the religious critic and outsider," and the verb "also hints at one of the central methods of the government's secret police—the reliance on pursuivant spies and agents provocateurs to entrap anyone who, 'Like [the] old rich' ancient nobility…, still confessed a doctrine of 'Good workes' instead of allowing the new soteriology by which the 'wardrop' (wardrobe) of Christ's blood covers the totally depraved sinner from the infinite reach of divine Law" (204).

109–11 *But oh…rich wardrobes.* **HESTER** (1977c): these lines demonstrate that the satirist's "inability to overturn the widespread disregard of words and the Word, and to charitably reform the 'bold soule' (63) Coscus, results in his charity being ultimately displaced by disgust and hatred" (189). **CORTHELL** (1997): "one of the changes resulting from Coscus's refashioning of the community is compared to one of the chief points controverted by reformers and Catholics" (36). **WIGGINS** (2000) observes that in a 1585 Parliamentary address the Queen offered a comparison "identical" to Donne's when she said, "I see many over-bold with God Almighty, making too many subtle scannings of his blessed will, as lawyers do with human testaments" (40).

109–10 *we'allow…fashion now* **SMITH** (1971): "we concede that good works are good but disregard them because they are not now in fashion" (480). [So also, Rousseau and Rudenstine (1972, 64).] **ELLIOTT** (1976): the speaker, "[s]till preaching the Christian philosophy that the law is useless when lacking a spirit of charity," asserts that "legislation alone is ineffective against corruption," for "[o]nly good will and good works can reform such wickedness" (112).

109 *oh* **MILGATE** (1967): "a sigh, as the satirist contemplates the melancholy fact" (138).

110 *Good workes* **LOUTHAN** (1951): the double meaning here includes behavior as proof of Christian life and "charitable projects." The speaker does not commit himself to Catholicism but does reject the materialism of the Reformation (101). **MILGATE** (1967): "We are condescending enough to admit the desirability of good actions; unfortunately they are not in fashion"; Article XI of the Thirty-nine Articles set forth as Church of England doctrine that "we are justified before God by Faith only (*Gal.* 2:16); but Article II 'allows' that Good Works which are the fruit of Faith are 'pleasing and acceptable to God'" (138). **PATRIDES** (1985): "Anglicans like Donne regarded 'faith' and 'good works' as alike indispensable to man's salvation;

but, they claimed, Catholics down-played the former, and Calvinists like the extreme ones of Amsterdam the latter"; see *Will* 19–21 (224).

111–12 *But my words…Statute Lawes.* MILGATE (1967): "A final hit at the times. Lawyers and lawsuits abound, legislators swell the statute-books to enormous proportions; but no one can accuse the satirist of an offence against any law"; see *Sat4* 131–34 (139). SMITH (1971): "no one can bring the satirist's charges within the scope of Acts of Parliament, even though those laws now encroach so far upon one's liberty to speak and act" (480). ROUSSEAU AND RUDENSTINE (1972): "i.e., lawyers and religious writers may conceal or tamper with the truth in their works (lines 89–102), but no one can demonstrate any similar 'illegal' or untruthful modifications in Donne's outspoken writings" (64). HESTER (1977b): "the use of 'vast' and 'huge' as pejoratives reiterates the antagonistic view central to the entire poem of the 'statute laws' which had proved fatal to his brother. His own recent personal tragedy is the crucial contributory factor to Donne's angry, 'fearful' attitude" (527). HESTER (1977c): the "final declaration is hedged with irony," for "the fact that he cannot be brought to court for libel enforces the truthfulness of his depiction of the corrupt lawyers at the same time that it mocks the current disregard of the nation for the truthful potentials of language and law." Nonetheless, the "emphasis of the satirist's conclusion is on his own hatred of those who threaten the spiritual and linguistic bases of English civilization" (189). LEIN (1980): like "theological texts which could clear up a difficulty," the words of the poet will be "neglected or ignored," and "the subsequent sense of the futility of all human effort perfectly reinforces the nihilism of the poem's central vision" so that "the most he can do is rage, thus maintaining his self-respect, and then lament his loss" (150). CORTHELL (1982): these lines are a "riddle" in that "the poem does wish to speak authoritatively, but at the same time it tries, like a paradox, to escape being called an ill thing by being nothing" (160). PATTERSON (1984): these lines strive for "a piece of self-reassurance," and "the implication is that satire is a safe mode of self-expression so long as it remains private and unpublished, a perception shortly to be substantiated by the Bishops' Order of 1599 which forbade the publication of satire" (92). MAROTTI (1986): "the satirist's ethical posture and his social status are portrayed in this poem as precarious. His moral outrage is compromised by his envious resentment of the very man he criticizes." The poem reflects "the vulnerability of the Inns gentlemen who scorned the less-dignified kinds of legal and business careers available to them, but who felt unrewarded or rejected by the corrupt, but more socially prestigious, courtly establishment" (40). CAREY (1990): "This satire infringes no law, despite the current spate of legislation" (424). PATTERSON (1994): the initial two treason acts during Elizabeth's reign "specifically included words along with overt acts in the definition of treason; four other parliamentary statutes in the sessions of 1571 and 1572 were intended to deal with the new threat posed by the Jesuits and by Elizabeth's excommunication and to further extend the definition of treason." A new act in 1585 "covered the mere presence in the realm of a Jesuit or newly trained seminary priest or the act of receiving a traitor into one's house" (149–50). HESTER (2000) compares these lines to the conclusion of *Bait*, suggesting that the "'fishe' that is 'wiser farre' than Donne" in *Bait* 27–28 "may well be the Donne who not only did not participate in the literary debate of Marlowe and Raleigh but also did not circulate this poem beyond his circle of manuscript readers" or "reveal himself to be a recusant 'fish' by responding publicly to Marlowe's 'bait'" (40). **WIGGINS** (2000): the "immediately preceding twenty-five lines of the poem, which describe Coscus seizing estates by twisting the language of contracts, suggest rather strongly that 'drawes' is singular only in form and by contact with 'none,' and that 'words' is its actual subject. Donne would then be saying that his words as a poet endanger no one, in the way that Coscus's legal jargon does." An alternate interpretation "(not requiring that the singular 'drawes' not really be singular) would have Donne saying that no one—like Coscus's scribe or clerk—sets down Donne's words or draws them out, at his behest, in such a way as to place those of whom he writes within the jeopardy of vaguely written, and hence far-reaching, laws" (36). **CHMIELEWSKI** (2001): "his words (this poem) are still safely beyond the far-reaching statutes against various kinds of speech, as well as the lawyers who bring such suits" (616).

111 *old rich wardrobes*. **SMITH** (1971): "luxurious stocks of clothes of a bygone day, still good in their substance but not now the fashion" (480).

111 *wardrobes*. **MILGATE** (1967): seems to refer to "an old-fashioned wardrobe containing valuable things now unusable because fashions have changed, just as the treasury of good works can no longer be displayed or 'worn' in public" (138–39).

112 *th'huge Statute Lawes*. **HESTER** (1994a): "a reference to the Statute against Recusants," which "had led to the martyrdom of Donne's younger brother" (204).

112 *Statute* **SULLENS** (1964): Donne's usage of this meaning of the word is earlier than the earliest source cited by *OED* (235).

 *Satyre 3.*

COMMENTARY

Date and Circumstances

Grierson (1912, 2:103) states that *Sat3* provides "no datable references" (Ochojski [1950, 542] concurs that no date can be determined from the poem's details), that the "tone" of the poem "reflects the years in which Donne was loosening himself from the Catholic Church," and that it was "probably written between 1594 and 1597." Others who concur with this range of dates include Williamson (1930, 16–17), who describes this period as one of "greatest distress" for Donne when "scepticism was creeping into England with Montaigne," Mahood (1950, 102), Peter (1956, 132), Milgate (1967, 139), Jackson (1970, 29), and Shaw (1981, 37).

Grierson (1929, xvii–xviii, xxvi) considers that the circumstances of Donne's early life help explain the passionate "tenor" of *Sat3* and make it "more intelligible and forgivable" (xvii–xviii). He finds that *Sat3* reveals "the trend" of Donne's "thought on religious controversies, the line of escape by which he made his way to conformity."

Hayward (1929, 120) asserts that the date of *Sat3* can be "fixed" on the basis of "allusions" to events "approximately between the years 1593–1597." He cites the evidence of the date 1593 inscribed on B34, a manuscript of *Sats1–3*. Milgate (1967, 117) notes this same dated manuscript.

Bennett (1934, 26) dates the poem between 1593 and 1595.

Battenhouse (1942, 217–18) states that the martyrdom of Donne's brother Henry (August 1593) "precedes by only a year the probable date" of *Sat3* and that at about this time Donne "was reading deeply in the writings of Cardinal Bellarmine, and he was undertaking a systematic examination of the points in divinity being controverted between the Roman and the reformed churches." Others who note the context of Donne's brother and of Donne's study in religion include Leishman (1951, 29–30), Nelly (1969, 15), Jaffe (1977, 95), and Carey (1990, 424–25).

Hardy (1942, 65–66) states that *Sat3* was written in 1593 or 1594, which was an "exceedingly dangerous" time for Donne because "Elizabeth was still on the throne," because of "the Acts against Popish recusants and Jesuits," because of his brother's imprisonment, and because Donne himself "still had his way to make."

Stein (1944a, 278) notes the "personal significance" to Donne of *Sat3*'s subject matter.

Gardner (1948, 31) notes that *Sat3* was written "not much later than 1593."

Husain (1948, 50) believes that *Sat3* was "written as early as 1594." Empson (1993, 81) concurs with this date.

Kermode (1957, 28) states that *Sat3* must have been written in the 1590s.

Mueller (1962, 12) argues for 1593 as the probable date of *Sat3*.

Sloan (1965, 24) argues that *Sat3* was written "soon after 1593," adding that the poem reacts to "a scene of religious and political turmoil controlled into tense order by the magnificent but tyrannical Queen."

Bewley (1966, xxviii, 176) dates *Sat3* during Donne's years at Lincoln's Inn, "although it may be as late as 1597" (xxviii), adding that if lines 17–19 draw on "his experience in the Azores expedition," as he had in *Storm* and *Calm*, this would suggest a date of 1597 (176). Others who concur with this date include Zuberi (1966, 149) and Melchiori (1983, 179).

Andreasen (1967, 10) argues that since *Sat3* was contemporaneous with "much of the cynical and apparently amoral love poetry," it defies the neat compartmentalization of Donne's life proposed by biographical criticism.

Milgate (1967, lix–lx, 139–40) argues that *Sat3* was "heavily revised" after Donne met Lucy Harrington, countess of Bedford, late in 1607 and cites a parallel passage in *Letters*, p. 29 (lix–lx). But dating the poem in its original version is difficult, he thinks, because its topical references are ambiguous. It would be "most unlikely" that Donne "would, or could, have written" as he does in *Sat3* "had he still been a convinced Roman Catholic," Milgate argues, and he cites Walton's estimate that Donne became a Protestant while attending the Inns of Court, supporting this story with a variety of biographical and documentary evidence and noting that *Sat3* implies a "background of earnest inquiry." Since its reference to the "fires of Spaine" may better be interpreted as "anticipatory excitement" leading to participation in the Cadiz (139) and Islands expeditions than to recollecting the results of these events, he concludes by dating the poem precisely in "1594 or 1595" (140). Carey (1990, 424) concurs with the comments regarding Donne's religious position and the poem's dates.

Shawcross (1967, 412) dates *Sat3* "1597?–1598?"

Warnke (1967, 106) dates *Sat3* "during the period 1593–1598."

Martz (1969, 31) notes that *Sat3* was written "in those years when Donne was a young law student, and just before he departed (in 1596 and 1597) to participate in those two military voyages." Klause (1993, 338, 354) also notes Donne's study at the Inns of Court.

Nelly (1969, 15), asserting that *Sat3* was written in 1593, when Donne was only twenty-one years old, "marvel[s] at the maturity and the balance of mind which it reveals."

Crinò (1970, 69) gives a date of 1593 for *Sat3*, at a time when Donne was still a Catholic.

Hebaisha (1971, 32) believes this poem to have been written after 1596 when Donne had recovered from the death of his brother, since he appears to be "much more personally involved" than in the previous Satyres.

Slights (1972, 100) believes that *Sat3* "was probably written in the 1590's" and thereby "anticipates the attitudes and form characteristic of later Anglican casuists."

Kermode and Hollander (1973, 1045) suggest that *Sat3* "probably belongs to 1595."

Broadbent (1974, 106) believes that Donne wrote *Sat3* "c.1594 while himself turning from catholic to protestant." Others who describe this period as one of religious transition include Craik and Craik (1986, 258), Mallet (1990, 19), and Empson (1993, 81).

Kermode, Fender, and Palmer (1974, 55–56, 64) contend that the pressure Donne felt to depart from the Catholic faith provides an explanation for why Donne, "a bright young man of twenty-two, in 1594," would have written *Sat3* (55).

Partridge (1978, 41) believes that *Sat3* was written around 1597, when "Donne had already withdrawn his loyalty to the Catholic faith."

Sellin (1978, 15) points out that arguments dating *Sat3* between 1592–96 "have long involved dangerous circularity, and originally sprang from mistaken evaluation of manuscript evidence." He argues that "new facts suggest a later genesis," noting Donne's allusion "to a polar expedition that he could not have learned of before 1598–1602 at the earliest," as well as a "similarity between a famous conceit in the poem and a Dutch medallion of 1619," and concludes that *Sat3* "dates from the 1620's, not the 1590's."

Sellin (1980, 275, 281–84, 292–94, 297–98, 302–04) asserts that the date of *Sat3* "has depended almost exclusively on speculative argument regarding Donne's spiritual biography rather than on historical or bibliographical facts" (275). He remarks that the structure and content of *Sat3* "reflect the military and political situation in early 1620" more directly and fully than during an earlier date, and as such the poem is tied more to Donne's concerns related to the Synod of Dort and to the Thirty Years' War than to "hesitation between, or skepticism toward, the Anglican and Catholic faiths during the 1590s" (294). He adds that one could be certain that *Sat3* antedates 1620 "if one could positively assign any of the surviving manuscripts containing the poem to an early date," but he espouses that "nearly all of the pertinent manuscripts are later than 1620," noting that no one "has dared to date them earlier on the basis of handwriting or of paper, watermarks, or similarly objective bibliographical criteria" (298). Finally, he states, "several of the earliest and most authoritative manuscripts" containing *Sat3* include poems "which clearly establish that they could not have been copied earlier than the period 1614–1620" (298).

Carey (1981, 46) writes that *Sat3* is "roughly datable in 1595."

Zunder (1982, 14) contends that *Sat3* was likely written in 1594–95 and stands as "a response to the religious changes of the century." The difficulty addressed in the poem "comes with the question of particular ecclesiastical allegiance," he suggests, and though Donne's Catholic upbringing "no doubt posed the question to him with especial acuteness," Zunder finds him "expressing a characteristic quandary" of his day. Carey (1990, xxii) expresses similar views about the religious context.

Melchiori (1983, 182) posits that in *Sat3* the frequency of echoes from Shakespeare's *R2* suggests that Donne must have seen the play no later than 1595–96.

Kerins (1984, 59), in response to Sellin's (1980) dating of *Sat3* in 1620, asserts that he finds that date "untenable." He explains that "the Dort medallion presented to Donne, on which Sellin bases much of his argument, depicts a temple, not a female allegorical figure of 'Truth'" and that the mistress motif permeating *Sat3* continues in *Sat4* "with the climactic appeal to 'Mistresse Truth' (l. 163), and is echoed in the symbolic depiction of the queen" in *Sat5* 28–30.

Patrides (1985, 34, 213) dates *Sat3* with the other Satyres "from the early 1590s" (34), though he notes it may "have been written as late as 1620, after Donne took orders" (213).

Willmott (1985, 60) asserts that *Sat3* is unique because it conveys Donne's "fierce insistence that truth can, and must, be found," an insistence that can be attributed to the fact that the poem was written between 1593 and 1598 when Donne was moving away from the Roman Catholic Church to the Church of England. The poem betrays the poet's own uncertainties, Willmott suggests, though "the mood at the end of the poem seems one of Protestantism, but not of final commitment."

Marotti (1986, 41) observes that in *Sat3*'s "refusal to adopt a stance of faithful Catholicism," the poem "constitutes a necessary gesture in preparation for the pursuit of a courtly career," though "in its skeptical, even iconoclastic attitudes," *Sat3* becomes "the kind of dangerous statement whose disclosure outside his coterie Donne feared."

Van Emden (1986, 50) thinks that *Sat3* was penned "in the early 1590s when Donne was still a Catholic" and is daring in its "Catholic bias."

Zunder (1988, 79–80) contends that Donne likely wrote *Sat3* in 1594 or 1595, "at the juncture between leaving the Inns of Court and seeking the patronage of Essex," at a time that "belongs to a moment of transition in his life."

Guibbory (1990, 825) writes that while the date of *Sat3* is uncertain, "the anxiety about royal power (figured as female and identified with the watery female element) would seem to place the poem in the company of those clearly written during the reign of Elizabeth."

Hester (1991, 98) observes that in the manuscripts *Sat3* "*never* appears alone, never without at least two other" of the Satyres, and "often with other poems composed during the last decade of Elizabeth's reign." He also points out the verbal borrowing from *Sat3* in Ben Jonson's 1611 "Ode. To Sir William Sydney."

Sellin (1991, 85, 87–88) contends that the tendency in some late twentieth-century critics to persist in reading *Sat3* as part of a unified whole reveals an attachment to "a subject-matter poetics" which is "primitive, to say the least" (85). He states further that the evidence for dating *Sat3* does not necessarily confirm that it was composed at about the same time as the other four Satyres, "let alone that it was the third in order of composition." He asserts that "arguments for early dating are purely conjectural, resting largely on association in the so-called 'satire manuscripts' with other poems presumed to be early" and that "even arguments dating the actual physical manuscripts earlier than the end of the second decade of the seventeenth century tend to involve dangerous circularities rather than bibliographical facts." He contends further that what little internal evidence there is suggests that the poem is "likely to postdate" the other Satyres and that if scholars insist on linking *Sat3* with the other four, then they "should at least do so with full awareness that it postdates them by up to several years and that it could never have been the third satire in order of composition" (87–88).

Scodel (1993, 481) is convinced that Donne wrote the poem during a transitional period of personal crisis around 1596, when he had left the Catholic faith but had not yet joined the English church, and suggests that Donne's use of the mean was the way "a religious deviant in an England that punished nonconformity" justified his choice.

Strier (1993, 285) notes that Sat3 was written in the mid-1590s, "early in the period of Donne's suspension of commitment," and that the poem's "ultimate import is to stand as a defense of such suspension."

Oliver (1997, 51–52) notes that although there has been a tendency to "fuse" the speaker of Sat3 with "Walton's nineteen-year-old Donne," the poem "gives no access, or at least only indirect access, to the poet's thinking at the time of writing," when he was in his "early twenties."

Nutt (1999, 121, 138) senses that at the time of writing Sat3 Donne was "undergoing a crisis of faith himself, desperately trying to resolve the clash between his ambitions and his inherited faith," and while Donne "was eager for a position of influence and power," such opportunities for him as a Catholic "were firmly denied him" (121). Further, he says, Donne was also "only 21 and presumably knee-deep in 'profane mistresses'" (138).

Knottenbelt (2000, 119) dates Sat3 "between 1603 and 1607."

Prescott (2000, 230) notes that Sat3, "on the difficult necessity of eventually deciding which is Christ's true bride among the several aspirants to that role," is "harder to date" than the other Satyres.

Wiggins (2000, 41, 160n27) proposes that scholars who argue that Sat3 "was written long after" the other Satyres "may only be paying tribute to the success of a young John Donne's impersonation" (41), namely, of an older man, an Egerton.

Donoghue (2001, xxvi) dates Sat3 as "an early poem, probably written when his apostasy was new."

Edwards (2001, 48–49, 160) states that this poem was "probably written in the 1590s" (160), noting that in late 1593, when Donne "seems to have plunged into theological study" after his brother's death (48), "doubt wisely" was "the principle which governed his private thoughts" and "no doubt he kept private" this poem (49).

Fulton (2001, 71–73, 75, 78–80) asserts that Sat3 "has been so often considered in relation to its author's biography that the poem suffers from not being understood within the larger context of Elizabethan satire" (71). He disagrees with Marotti's (1986) attempt "to fit the poem within his vision of Donne's poetry as serving courtly ambitions" (72) and cautions that while the "religious tension" in Sat3 "seems particularly suited to Donne's personal struggle," the poem "also reflects a struggle within English society to come to terms with the many philosophical untenabilities and social horrors of the last seventy years of religious history" (78). He argues that the poem supports neither Bald's (1970) depiction of Donne as an "'unyielding Catholic'" (79) in the 1590s nor Carey's (1981) reading that sees it as "negotiating or asserting Donne's apostasy" (79) in the aftermath of his brother's death. As such, Sat3 "does not indicate a broken resignation, nor does it express sacrifice to political exigency," but instead, "it speaks against such actions" (80).

General Commentary (Religion)

Jonson (1610) alludes to *Sat3* in his "Ode: To Sir William Sydney on his Birth-Day" when advising Sydney that "he doth lacke / Of going backe / Little, whose will / Doth urge him to runne wrong, or to stand still" (*The Forest*, ll. 27–30).

An anonymous emblem poem, once thought to be by Goodyer (*The Mirrovr of Maiestie*, 1618), seems indebted to Donne's hill of Truth emblem in *Sat3*.

In his defence of English conservatism, Whitlock (1654, 313) refers to and cites *Sat3*.

Parnell (c. 1714 [cited in Warburton (1751, 4:253)]) "versified" *Sat3* 1–16, 79–89.

Cunningham (1837, 3:240–42), in a brief biographical sketch, mentions Donne's shift from "the religion of his family" to "his espousing the doctrines of the reformed church" and then quotes *Sat3* 93–102 as an emphatic recording of Donne's "conviction of the right and duty of private judgment in matters of faith" (241).

Minto (1880, 852–54), in the midst of his discussion of *Sat3* and prior to quoting ll. 77–81, asserts that Donne "ridicules with mirthful mockery the light grounds on which men take up with religious creeds, and vindicates the right of inquiry in a strain which shows that he reserved his own judgment under the persuasions of his Roman Catholic tutors" (852).

Hare and Hare (1889, 2–3) quote *Sat3* 5–7 and 10–11, making the point that "the threatenings of Christianity are material and tangible."

Dowden (1890, 802–03) states that *Sat3* is "the most remarkable" of the Satyres but one "which hardly deserves that name," adding that it is "rather a hortatory poem addressed to those who fail as Christians to stand with their loins girt and their lamps burning."

Gosse (1899, 1:38–39) characterizes *Sat3* as "a diatribe against the extravagance and hypocrisy of the Religious Man," and he adds that this poem, in which "the theologian in Donne makes his first appearance," becomes "a sermon—the first that its author preached from any pulpit."

Courthope (1903, 3:149–51) explains that in *Sat3* a "mixture of strong religious instinct and philosophic skepticism appears in its simplest form" and then concludes of Donne's character, after quoting ll. 77–84, that "on this principle he himself seems to have proceeded" (150–51).

Grierson (1912, 2:x, xiv–xvii, 100–05), commenting on *Sat3*, writes of Donne's religious conversion that "it would be as absurd, in the face of a poem like this and of all that we know of Donne's subsequent life, to call it a conversion in the full sense of the term, a changed conviction, as to dub it an apostasy prompted by purely political considerations" (xvi). Noting, however, that "the latter predominated," he goes on to explain the difficulties facing the English Catholic in the reign of Elizabeth whose choices were to live "cut off rigorously from the main life of the nation, with every avenue of honourable ambition closed to him" or to live "the starved, suspected life of a recusant" (xvi). He then posits that Donne escaped this dilemma, "not by any opportune change of conviction, or by any insincere profession, but by the way of intellectual emancipation," in which Donne comes to the conclusion "that whichever be the true Church it is not by any painful quest of truth, and through the attainment of conviction, that most people have accepted the Church to which they may belong" (xvi–xvii). He then adds that by the time he wrote *Sat3* Donne had not yet reached the conclusion "that the Church of England offered a reasonable *via media*" (xvii).

For Aronstein (1920, 160–61), *Sat3* represents the apogee of Donne's satirical art, even though the poem is not really a satire but rather a poetic engagement of the poet with himself on the topics of religion and the religious. He adds that the power and profundity, the originality and freedom of spirit Donne demonstrates in the poem are astounding, especially amidst the sectarian discord and fanaticism of the time. He concludes that seldom has the position of basic religious seekers been portrayed as free from blind belief in authority, and as such, the poem bears the stamp of a brilliant personality and is, like everything truly great, exceptional in its own way.

Fausset (1924, 54–55) suggests that *Sat3* reflects Donne's own religious struggles at a time when "a sullen agnosticism seemed the only possible attitude."

Bredvold (1925, 209–10) observes that Donne "speaks with scorn of those feeble, hesitating spirits who adhere to any sect without studying and thinking the problem through for themselves." He finds that "one cannot escape the obligation of making a choice," though "unceasing labor is necessary," and that Donne is confident that truth can be found, "provided one goes back far enough to the original sources and cultivates an open mind."

Sencourt (1925, 63–64, 67) argues that *Sat3* was written before Donne's love poetry. He summarizes the poem to show that although Donne distrusts organized religion, he does not question the need for religion (64), suggesting that, as in his later works, Donne was concerned about attacking the Roman Catholic Church while claiming to be Catholic (67).

Walker (1925, 71) notes that in *Sat3* Donne "shows a noble disposition, a noble love of truth," which is "difficult to discover and manifold of aspect" in assessing the various sectarian positions.

Payne (1926, 34) states that Donne's "attitude toward religion" in *Sat3* provides the "gravity of purpose to justify it and to give dignity to its exposures."

Grierson (1929, xxv–xxviii) believes that *Sat3* demonstrates that Donne "had studied the religious controversies of the day" (xxvii) and indicates "the trend" of Donne's thought on religious controversies, "the line of escape by which he made his way to conformity" (xxvi). Though Donne's position was "difficult" and his way of escape is "interesting," it is a position "easy to misrepresent by a critic who has no sympathy with or understanding of the complexities of the human heart" (xxvii). It was by means of the intellectual inquiry urged throughout *Sat3* that Donne "detached himself from Catholicism rather than by any change of heart," and Grierson conjectures that "King James and circumstances" made Donne "against his will a controversialist" (xxviii).

Elliott (1931, 341–42) argues that Donne's religious ideas in this poem are similar to those of the middle phase of his life (1600–1615), in which "his Christianity was nominal" and he was "very critical of popular Christian tendencies." Donne was concerned that controversy caused people to accept doctrines out of "weariness," Elliott thinks, and his work "satirized 'those who write for religion without it'" and, above all, those who regarded Christianity as displacing the morality of the ancients."

Sparrow (1931, 149) asserts that Sat3 reveals that Donne "was as far from being at heart a Roman Catholic as he was from being at heart a sceptic."

Doggett (1934, 277) sees evidence in Sat3 that Donne "inclined to anti-probabilism" in the 1590s.

Hughes (1934, 82) opines that Donne's "defense of liberty of conscience" should "be even better known than it is," adding that the important part of Donne's argument is not so much the necessity of the search for truth but the idea that humankind must regain a truth that has been lost over time.

Lindsday (1934a, 577) insists that Donne's perspective in Sat3 "is humanist rather than orthodox."

Jordan (1936, 40–43) cites Donne's portraits of the churches in Sat3 as evidence of his belief that no church monopolized truth (40), and he situates Donne with "the moderates who subscribed to no party rather than with the main stream of Anglican theory" (43).

Battenhouse (1942, 217–18) contends that Sat3 "directs its jibes at all men who choose their religion uncritically," and he believes that the poem "is the more re- markable" because of Donne's Catholic heritage, his Romanist tutors Ellis and Jasper Heywood, and the martyrdom of his brother Henry. He adds, however, that "the facts of the Donne family hardly prepare us for the tolerant spirit which breathes in John's poem" and that in fact what is particularly striking is the author's "concilia- tory spirit."

Hardy (1942, 63–68) believes that Sat3 provides a "clue" to Donne's "mental un- rest and his attitude to religious matters" when he was "loosening himself from the Catholic church and authority" (63). She senses in the poem Donne's "perplexity" in his suspicion of "intolerance" and his dread for the limitations "of any one creed, as the falcon dreads the wires of a cage." Donne's longing "for Truth and Unity" and his pleas "for a recognition of the fundamental values underlying" sectarian factions manifest his "preoccupation with spiritual light and his sense of the insufficiency of reason as an aid to its appreciation" (66–67). She concludes that in Sat3 "Jack Donne the libertine, anticipates John Donne the great divine" (68).

Moloney (1944, 140–41) states that Sat3 presents the "earliest manifestation" of Donne's "tortuous religious course," that is, Donne's "wavering and uncertainty" between "his outward rejection of the claims of Rome" and "his patent confession of his inability to find a sense of security elsewhere."

Stein (1944a, 268, 278–79) describes Sat3 as offering "a remarkable doctrine in the history of religious tolerance," and adds of Donne, "nor does he change his basic attitude after finally joining the Anglican Church." He argues that "rationalism may contribute to Donne's religious melancholy" although "he never completely loses faith in reason" (268). He states further that "when we remember Donne's own efforts to 'seeke true religion,'" the theme of Sat3 "takes on a personal significance," for Donne "cannot make a choice for any of the trivial reasons he ascribes to his fools," and thus his efforts "are not made without cost," but "he must pay in 'expense of spirit' for the stubborn independence that will not accept religion on the say-so of a godfather, and that will not succumb like the normal soul" (278–79).

Wagner (1947, 256) quotes Donne's injunction in line 43 (which he mistakenly attributes to *Sat4*—eds.) and questions where Donne sought religion.

Gardner (1948, 31) believes that *Sat3* shows that Donne "had broken with the Roman Church" and reflects "a serious, candid mind, free of cynicism."

Grierson (1948, 307, 310) suggests that *Sat3* advocates following the religion of one's fathers and that Donne must have acquiesced to joining the religion of his country-men before he entered Egerton's service (307), noting that Donne reacts against the dissenters for creating schism (310).

Husain (1948, 52–54) argues that *Sat3* employs "not the language of scepticism but of an earnest inquirer after truth, who has embarked on that odyssey of the spirit, the search for a 'true religion,'" and as such Donne shows his distrust of "the principles on which he thought the Roman Catholic as well as the Reformed Churches were based" (53).

Mahood (1950, 103) sees in *Sat3* evidence of Donne's own struggles "to reorientate himself in matters of faith."

Ochojski (1950, 542) comments that Donne's tone of tolerance toward all religions, including Catholicism, is contrary to official English policy.

Leishman (1951, 29–30, 38, 112–13) suggests that the limitations to Donne's pros-pects imposed by his Catholicism as well as "the sufferings of his own family" would have caused Donne to reconsider his religious affiliation (29–30). He adds that Donne's interest in religion at this time was "sincere" whereas later it became more worldly (38) so that in *Sat3* Donne "*is* inspired by his subject in itself," even though he finds it "strange" that for Donne saving truth consists of a mingling "of facts and ideas, of truths of religion and truths of history" (112–13).

Gardner (1952, xvii–xix) argues that *Sat3* establishes "the root of Donne's religious development" (xix) by showing him to be someone "to whom the idea of God not only is self-evident, but brings with it a sense of absolute obligation" (xvii). As such, the argument of the poem "rests on two assumptions: that the search for 'true Religion' is the primary duty of a moral being, and that truth exists and can be known." She states further that by the time Donne wrote the poem he had "moved away from the Roman position," that the poem is directed "against the insufficient reasons for which men adhere" to differing confessions, and that the poem contains no trace of "philosophic scepticism" (xviii).

Legouis (1952, 99) asserts that when Leishman (1951) says that *Sat3* dramatizes Donne's search for religion among the diverse churches, he seems to be using the word to mean "moving" or even "emotional" or perhaps even "imaginative," adding that by this usage, any narrative, whether in verse or prose, is "dramatic."

Smith (1952, 224–25) states that the effect of *Sat3* resides in its extended conceit, "that the love of God is visible in Elizabethan society only as one of several kinds of 'lecherous humours.'"

Gransden (1954, 102–03) believes that the religious subject matter of *Sat3* "seems wholly to have engaged Donne's personal feelings," adding that Donne's "interest in religion was certainly not a professional one," but rather "a reasoned and reasonable protest again[st] extremism and schism."

Lewis (1954, 547) identifies Sat3 as one of those poems whose content is "so interesting" that the reader is "apt to overrate" it as a poem.

Cox (1956, 112) observes that Sat3 "stands out for its penetrating and serious discussion of the problem of choosing between rival religious beliefs, the alternative possibilities being embodied in short satirical portraits."

Kermode (1957, 28–29, 37) finds the poem's "brisk impatience" appropriate for satire but unexpected in a "deliberative poem about religion," adding that the poem is concerned with the search for religion, not the result (28–29). He states further that even the young Donne found "the language of passionate exploration and rebuke appropriate to religious themes" (37).

Adams (1958, 11–12) asserts that in Sat3 Donne "strongly denigrates the idea of accepting any religious position on the basis of someone else's authority." He comments further on Donne's "unresolvedness or irresolution" for determining the one true religion, though he acknowledges that Donne "recognizes the need for decision."

Sowton (1960, 185) notes that Sat3 "chiefly attacks false attitudes to religion" and speaks to the necessity both to find one's own truth and to accept that it may not be truth for others.

Mueller (1962, 150–51) cites the descriptions of Catholicism and Calvinism in this poem as evidence that Donne saw the Church of England as an attempt to return to the ways of the primitive church by pruning away "the superfluities accrued by the Roman Church."

Andreasen (1963, 69) comments that, unlike the other Satyres, Sat3 is "a soliloquy conducted in meditative isolation."

Bennett (1964, 26, 136) states that in Sat3 Donne "considers the relative claims of nonconformity, Anglicanism and Roman Catholicism" (26) and that his "religious temperament" does not permit him to "content himself with the transient and the manifold" (136).

Sloan (1965, 24) asserts that in Sat3 Donne's thesis "is not pro-Catholic, nor pro-Puritan, nor pro-Anglican," but instead Donne urges that in matters of religion one should "follow the dictates" of conscience, which "must be shaped by a firm conviction arrived at through reason" and "tempered by tradition."

Woodhouse (1965, 56) cites Sat3 as evidence that Donne's early religious interests were mainly intellectual and that his questioning of the locus of religious authority was to be expected given his family background.

Geraldine (1966, 27–29) notes that Sat3 begins and concludes with the possibility of damnation and refers to "the last end of man" (27) at least nine times. Donne's four counsels ("feare this," "knowe thy foes," "Seeke true religion," and "keepe the truth that thou hast found") show him to be stirred to more eloquence by "mental apathy" than "outright malice or passion" (28), adding that Donne equates seeking truth with seeking God and that the poem finally concerns itself with the condition of the soul (29).

Andreasen (1967, 20) states that even in this youthful poem, Donne saw "his Protean intellectual metamorphoses" as a means of attaining truth.

Milgate (1967, xxiv, 140) says Sat3 seems in most respects "superior to the rest" of Donne's Satyres, its aesthetic unity "saved by the happy chance that the possible sources of truth in religion are limited to three," and "there is, moreover, a limited area of subject-matter to be treated, and a consistent particular theme dominates the whole" (xxiv). *Sat3* is an attack on "the paltry attitude of men to the finding of a religious faith, in contrast to the courage and energy they display in other concerns" (140).

Williamson (1967, 44, 51–52, 81–82) notes that Donne "began to question both love and religion" (44) even in his early work, citing *Sat3* and *LovDeity*. He suggests that the "search for true religion" in *Sat3* is "the most obvious example" (51) of Donne's advocacy of courageous seeking, adding that Donne did not deny the flesh or the world but his need for variety made it difficult for him to complete the search advocated in the poem.

Jackson (1968, 40, 43–44) insists that it is helpful to approach *Sat3* "by beginning with certain distinctions between visible and invisible, or revealed and hidden" (40), asserting first that "to ascribe any great importance to a church invisible and separate from the public community was far from ordinary medieval doctrine," and then asking, "in the actual situation in England during Donne's lifetime how was a Catholic to adhere to a visible church in fact? Where was the Catholic Church visible?" (44).

Heath-Stubbs (1969, 24) argues that *Sat3* "has considerable subtlety of thought as well as personal feeling" as it "expresses the scepticism and doubts about the conflicting claims of different forms of Christianity" Donne contemplated "in the period between his abandonment of the Roman Catholic allegiance of his family and his taking Anglican orders."

Lecocq (1969, 378) points to the finale of *Sat3* as confirmation that the five Satyres collectively assert that the fundamental choice of a religion is not disconnected from the stance Donne takes concerning the power held by humans, and bowing before this power in admiration is nothing less than idolatry.

Miner (1969, 34) believes that Donne had a "real attachment to Catholicism," arguing that "the evidence, not that he was a communicating Catholic, but that he suspected he should be," can be found in *Sat3*.

Moore (1969, 41–43, 49) suggests that any attempt at a full understanding of *Sat3* "must also be an attempt to understand Donne's religious beliefs at the time he wrote the poem" (41). He argues that the poem "is not about one man's uncertainty as to which church to join," but instead "a general plea for all men to re-examine their religious views" (43), a plea that "uses the uncertainty it has produced as the impetus for the search" (49).

Nelly (1969, 154) cites *Sat3* as an example of Donne's "dialectical method" that is characterized by "a deeply personal search for truth" and a "passionate analysis of reality," both physical and metaphysical, that realizes "its dénouement only in the ultimate, synthesizing Cause of reality, the very Ground of our Being, the Creator Himself."

Bewley (1970, 15, 27) notes that one suspects that T. S. Eliot "as a devout High Churchman is a little outraged by a note of latitudinarianism" in *Sat3* (15). He claims further that *Sat3* "is not so much an examination of the representative claims of the Roman, Anglican, and Genevan Churches as a statement of the necessity for conducting such an examination" and that, "characteristically, Donne arrives at no conclusion except that man must search unceasingly for the truth," even as "he gives us some unforgettable pictures of types of Elizabethan Christians" (27).

Jackson (1970, 29–30, 34, 82, 152–53) asserts that at the time of writing Sat3 Donne had "no church" (82) other than "some kind of invisible religion" (29). Yet, he claims that the poem clearly reveals Donne's "interest in the revealed or visible forms of religious life and his dissatisfaction with invisible religion as a perpetual life condition" (29). He explains that even though the poem insists that "the soul must somehow discover a deeper and more direct access to the original and invisible source of power," yet Donne also "does not give up hope of discovering 'true religion' according to some visible channel" (34). In short, he concludes, Donne expresses throughout Sat3 that "the inner experience had to have its outward expression" (153).

Kermode (1970, xix) points out that Sat3, which examines the "relation between wise doubt and certainty," stands out as "a deliberative poem about the choice of religion."

Michener (1970, 64) states that in Sat3 Donne "glorifies the intellectual quest regardless of its ultimate achievements."

Winny (1970, 9) argues that Sat3 "proves the concern" that Donne shared with a "great body" of his contemporaries regarding their assurance that "the religion authorized by the Queen was spiritually superior to the others, or that catholicism and true allegiance were incompatible."

Hebaisha (1971, 34) espouses that Donne must have been a Protestant at the time of writing Sat3 because a Catholic is not permitted to question his religion.

Powers (1971, 26) suggests that Donne's injunction to seek religious truth for oneself reflected the contemporary emphasis on gaining knowledge through experience.

Baker-Smith (1972, 405, 431) writes of Donne that "vigilance was to be the price of spiritual health," and as such, in Sat3 readers "encounter an important aspect of the poet's mind" (405). He sees a "clear unity" in Donne's "vigilant critique of pseudo-religion," and comparing Sat3 with HSShow, he argues that they both express "responsible discrimination in religious matters" (431).

Bullough (1972, 63) states that Sat3 "confirms that the poet had turned his back on Catholicism without giving himself to any other sect," the poem asking "where true religion is to be found" and rejecting "the absolute claims of all the quarreling sects."

Given its focus on religious questions, Samarin (1972, 171) finds Sat3 to be singularly serious among Donne's Satyres. He says that Donne champions a position of religious tolerance and attempts to protect adherents of the Catholic faith from excessive attacks.

Slights (1972, 95–101) argues that Sat3 raises the problem of "where in the actual world is true religion to be found?" and that Donne's casuist approach is "to concentrate, not on solutions to the problem, but on methods of resolving it," which will require "an honest, strenuous, personal search for the truth" (95–96). She states that while Donne "admits that the problem of choosing among existing churches is real and difficult," he "denies that its complexity absolves his questioner from the responsibility of choice" (99). She concludes that Donne does not separate "the speculative from the practical understanding," but instead "conceives of the conscience as rational activity based on knowledge and stresses the inviolability and ultimate responsibility of the individual conscience" (100).

Kermode and Hollander (1973, 1017–18, 1045) state that Donne's "choice of the English church as nearest to the true primitive and catholic was no doubt made possible by the labors of Hooker and other apologists." They add that in holding to the English *via media*, Donne's "chosen church avoided the errors of Rome, but maintained its contact with the ancient learning and forms," and Donne also "rejected the extreme Calvinists with detestation, but, like them, knew his Augustine" (1017–18). Noting that the poem may have been written in 1595, they argue that Donne probably saw himself as a Protestant "from about the turn of the century." They praise the poem for "the impassioned immediacy of its religious argument" and remind us that while Donne was writing the Elegies, he was also "profoundly concerned to use his mind and poetic powers on what seemed to him the greatest single issue, that of the true religion" (1045).

Lewalski and Sabol (1973, 6) note that *Sat3* "reflects something of Donne's own religious uncertainties."

Broadbent (1974, 105) characterizes "the conflict" in *Sat3* as that "between God and Caesar, spiritual and temporal power, exemplified in the need to choose 'a religion' from among Roman catholic (international, right wing), Anglican (national, liberal), and the protestant left wing exemplified in Calvinism."

Kermode, Fender, and Palmer (1974, 56, 63) contend that "it would have been impossible" for a person such as Donne "not to have taken a profound interest in religion" (56), concluding that the "very extraordinary" *Sat3* is a "passionate meditation" focusing "on the necessity to choose a religion, with all the difficulties that are in the way of choice and coming from a man of extremely sceptical temperament" (63).

Raizada (1974, 103) points out that in *Sat3* Donne "is opposed to dogma or parochial set of beliefs and makes a plea for true religion, virtue and truth."

Parker (1975, 21) links the expression of contempt for various Christian sects in *Sat3* to Donne's own growing sense of scepticism.

Elliott (1976, 112–13) argues that in the narrative situation of *Sat3* the speaker seeks the comfort of true religion and that it is in this narrative interlude, which "functions as does a soliloquy in drama," that the speaker "tempers himself with faith to withstand the greater trials which await him in the very den of iniquity, the court."

Lauritsen (1976, 125–26) observes that initially *Sat3* seems to be "a positive statement about man's quest for true religion," but argues that when we take into account the speaker's "rigid expectations of himself and the world and his inflexible conception of himself as not only apart from the world but morally superior to it," the poem turns into "the least satirical" as well as the "darkest" of all the Satyres.

Hester (1977c, 186, 190) posits that *Sat3*, which is "central in position and importance," functions both "as meditation and satire simultaneously" and "dramatizes the satirist's self-confirmation of the religious basis of his satire" (186). He adds that the satirist's "'zealous' meditation on the need for religion at the present time" is motivated by "the surety of damnation" for those who do not trust in God (190).

Hiller (1977, 15) finds that *Sat3* "does not quietly expound a philosophy already resolved upon but rather dramatizes the poet's attempts to formulate one," adding that "it is as if Donne is working out his own salvation as he writes." He argues that while the satirist feels anger, "there is also compassion for the weaknesses of man" so that "the 'railing'" of Sat3 "is tempered with reason and good sense."

Sinha (1977, 66) maintains that Sat3 "is aimed against those who refuse to make the effort to find truth in religion, or make the search wrongly on narrow sectarian lines."

Hester (1978a, 35–36, 38, 54–55) points out the critical focus on the structure of Sat3 and the reformative capabilities in satiric poetry and argues that "both issues are resolved by an analysis of the pattern of satirical and exhortative portraits and the Christian psychology which the satirist evolves in the poem" (35). He contends further that Sat3 illustrates that "the complete integration of the faculties of the rational soul and their exercise both privately and publicly" are "the moral responsibility of man" (38). Finally, he asserts that for Donne's satirist "the 'cure' for which he searches and the mode of discovery itself are one" and that satire and religion, which are united in this poem, "demand recognition of one's position in the providential universe as a fallen man, recognition of the need for hatred of sins and love of sinners, and the regeneration of the mind which is the only 'cure' for misdevotion" (55).

Partridge (1978, 43) contends that in Sat3 "the implications for the state of Donne's religious convictions at the time are significant" in that while Donne "accepted the Christian religion and the supreme power of God as axiomatic," he was, nevertheless, "confused and distressed by man's *demarche* from Christianity's essential ideals."

Cousins (1979, 104) sees a connection between the religious questioning in Sat3 and the sense of skepticism that pervades his later work.

Hester (1980b, 87, 90–92, 95–97) asserts that Sat3's satirist "ridicules five types of sectarian illogicality and irrationality" and that in denouncing "contemporary parochialists for their failures" the ridicule in the poem "is not a reaction to the practices of their chosen denominations," but instead "an exposure of the lack of understanding on which these types base their choices" (87). He then focuses specifically on the character of Phrygius, who is not, he argues, "in the technical sense of the word, an atheist but an 'atheistic' Separatist, most likely a Barrowist," noting that "either allusion—to Separatism or to Barrowism—is more likely in Donne's ironic portrait than the age's more general, and hence more slippery, malediction 'atheism'" (95–97).

Sellin (1980, 288–89, 303–04) says that Sat3 "does anything but assure success in attaining to the religious knowledge that brings salvation" and that "finding the truth in religion is not guaranteed simply because the task has been attempted, even thought the attempt is mandatory for all mankind" (288–89). Reading the poem in the context of the Synod of Dort, he surmises that scholarly analyses of Donne's "personal, idiosyncratic" religious expression that is often attributed to Donne's "Anglicanism" in Sat3 "may very well be characteristic of sister Protestant churches of the period too," adding that Donne's "relationship to Calvinism and foreign churches abroad would have to be considered in a context quite different from what present scholarship generally envisions" (303–04).

Carey (1981, 12, 14–16) labels Sat3 "the great, crucial poem of Donne's early manhood" (12) and argues that the poem aims "to make out that choosing a religion is a purely intellectual business, as unemotional as mountaineering" and that Donne "needed to convince himself of this, in order to allay his personal turmoil" (14–15).

Mann (1981, 290) contends that in *Sat3* "perverse attitudes towards religion are equated with perverse attitudes towards women."

Richmond (1981, 226) notes that *Sat3* includes a "skeptical tone and moderate outlook," and the poem is "equally capable of censuring both slavish Catholic devotion to an unreformed church and naive Protestant iconoclasm."

Slights (1981, 161–65) observes that for the young man of *Sat3* "the complexities and contradictions of institutionalized religion are apparently leading him to cynicism, accompanied, perhaps, by a swaggering bravura" (161). She argues further that after Donne "has demonstrated the folly of choosing any, none, or all of the major existing churches on the basis of inadequate authority," he "discusses how the dilemma can be resolved," and in doing so, proposes not a solution but "a method for discovering one" (162). She believes that for Donne, "to decide a moral problem on the basis of probabilism" leads only "to logical chaos" (165), and, thus, in particular, "instead of separating thought from action, the speculative from the practical understanding, Donne conceives of the operation of the conscience or moral reason as action" (163).

Corthell (1982, 166) comments that in *Sat3* there are "parallels between Donne's verbal maneuvers and the equivocations of a priest before a commissioner" and that while such parallels "do not prove Donne to be a Catholic," they do highlight Donne's "predicament and method by drawing our attention to patterns of argument and self-presentation which emerge when the individual addresses the relation between the absolute claims of secular power and personal religious obligation in the sixteenth century."

Gallenca (1982, 328) contends that in *Sat3* and *Sat4* Donne expresses a fear of accusations of slander and libel, underscored by frequent fears about Roman Catholicism, which could well explain his detestation of infidelity. All of these agonies are disguised expressions of a fear of damnation, secretly linked to a possible change of religion.

J. King (1982, 280) notes that in *Sat3* Donne "uses the transition from one generation to the next as a metaphor for religious reform."

Miller (1982, 828) argues that *Sat3* uses "related images to picture men as engaging in a kind of courtship of the truth" and thus "provides a defense of moderation and of a common ground between the competing churches of the post-Reformation world." Arguing that the poem was written "in the period of Donne's transition from the Roman Catholic Church to the Anglican," he states that *Sat3* rejects each of the established churches and "calls on men to put their trust in God and not in those who unjustly claim authority from God for churches of their own devising."

Smith (1982, 27) suggests that in *Sat3* "there is no doubt that Donne's intricate management of his intellectual middle course opens him to misunderstanding" primarily because he is "particularly subtle in his way of sifting from opposite extremes what seems reasonable in them."

Briggs (1983, 87–88) expresses that even though Donne probably converted to the English Church "fairly early in his career," *Sat3* is "strongly opposed to the acceptance of 'any local religion' merely because it is imposed by the state," and the poem "is filled with bitterness and contempt for religious hatred and wars" that "seem merely to provide opportunities for aggression that conveniently divert men's attention from their true spiritual state."

Kantra (1984, 93–94, 105) asserts that Donne's "search for religious truth" is like "mundane courtship" (94), adding that "religious satire and religious sociology" have "generic similarities" (105).

Kerins (1984, 46) suggests that *Sat3* "should be read as a 'dialogue of one,' an introspective analysis of the presuppositions from which spring both the secular and religious angles of vision," the foundations of which must be "fully dissected" before "a viable satiric vision" can be realized.

McKevlin (1984, 11–12) states that *Sat3* does not voice "the grumbling of an embittered sceptic who despairs of finding truth," but instead "a protest against the blind following of religious institutions" and "the apathy of those who will make no search at all." He comments that Donne's insistence that "the intellect itself is capable of knowing truth" suggests that "the individual and God can achieve union not through the dogmas of religious creeds but through the intellectual investigation of reality where ontological truth corresponds to the truth in the Divine Mind."

Sherwood (1984, 199) notes that in *Sat3* "there is the incomplete search for a 'true religion' (43), the injunction to 'doubt wisely' (77) in a progress spiraling upward ('about must goe') to Truth on a 'huge hill' (79–81)."

Steadman (1984, 14) remarks that Donne is "preoccupied" in *Sat3* with the question of true religion and the "judicious use of doubt as a means of discovering it."

Mann (1985, 539) argues that *Sat3* "fully embodies the figure of an ideal woman, 'Truth,' and identifies her as a biblical type."

Parfitt (1985, 44) notes in reference to *Sat3* that Donne "ended his life as Dean of St Paul's in the Anglican communion, having by his own account found it difficult to balance the claims of Catholicism, Puritanism, and moderate Anglicanism."

Parry (1985, 48–49) states that in *Sat3* Donne writes as "an uncommitted man" who is "aware that there are many tenable positions between Romanism and Calvinism." While Donne "accepts the conventional wisdom that there must be one true Church," he is given to philosophical scepticism "because of the inadequate quality of information available," even though the English church and state were especially intolerant of skepticism. He also notes that Donne's presentation of the various European churches as female figures "should not be seen as a cynical view, because the female personification of 'Religio' was a commonplace in prints at the time." Finally, he thinks that Donne's reliance on "individual inquiry" in the question of religion "indicates he has already parted from the Catholic position."

Patrides (1985, 35) calls *Sat3* "an idealistic soliloquy on the spiritual values which the narrator sees everywhere perverted."

Citing the speaker's quest for truth in *Sat3*, Toliver (1985, 101) argues that the search for a church personally preoccupied Donne for many of his later years, and the truth that Donne was looking for was not the kind that "attaches to incidents and occasions, to axioms, or even to the postulates of science and credos, but truth absolute, centered, universal."

Willmott (1985, 60) asserts that *Sat3* is unique because it conveys Donne's "fierce insistence that truth can, and must, be found," an insistence that can be attributed to the fact that the poem was written in the period when Donne was moving away from the Roman Catholic Church to the Church of England (between 1593 and 1598), and it betrays the poet's own uncertainties, as, for example, "the mood at the end of the poem seems one of Protestantism, but not of final commitment."

Caracciolo-Trejo (1986, 2:12) believes that Sat3 shows Donne to be a man who was always ahead of his time, namely by proposing that truth is something personal and inconvertible and by portraying religious conflict in its personal and existential dimension.

Gilman (1986a, 118) finds it "intriguing" that as Donne "broods on the hard and lonely climb around the obstacles of competing churches," his imagination fastens on the iconoclastic controversy.

Klause (1986, 419) maintains that Donne's assertion that truth is "unambiguous" and "'elder' (however slightly) than falsehood" comes more directly from the poet himself than the "arch commentary" in Metem, which was probably written not long after Sat3.

Marotti (1986, 43) posits that "the intellectual and religious idealism" of Sat3 "had dangerous implications" since Donne's placement of "Mistress Truth at the moral center of the world" in turn "ideologically displaced the idealized Queen Elizabeth, who had herself appropriated some of the features of an older Catholic Mariolatry to enhance her power" so that Donne might well fear the poem's transmission "beyond its restricted readership."

Van Emden (1986, 50) thinks that Sat3 was penned "in the early 1590s when Donne was still a Catholic" and is daring in its "Catholic bias."

Waller (1986, 245; 1993, 231) sees in Sat3 "contradictions and insecurities" that point to Donne's "religious anxieties as he moved out of his family Catholicism."

Comparing Sat2 and Sat3, Clampitt (1988, 7) suggests that the latter states more directly what is hinted at in the former, "a protracted wrestling" in the speaker about different approaches to the search for the true church.

Weimann (1988, 87) finds that Sat3 achieves its authority in the anti-authoritarian ideology of searching, investigating, and experimenting.

Zunder (1988, 79–80, 84) argues that Sat3 is Donne's response to "the rise of Protestantism" (79). He notes that the poem begins with a review of "typical and dynamic" contemporary activities in England in the mid-1590s, from aiding the Low Countries in the war against Spain to developing imperial and capitalist enterprises, but is still grounded in four "traditional points of reference: of the devil, the world and the flesh, and the soul," which shows that Donne still had confidence in the "fundamental certainties of the dominant view." He maintains that Donne's questions about "which church to belong to" represent "a typical quandary of the time," even though his background as a Catholic in a Protestant society would have made the problem particularly difficult. Further, he finds that Donne's representation of various churches as women reflects a life-long habit of seeing things in sexual terms, and he also finds in the ending of the poem ideas that were current in France at the time: religious toleration and the right of the people to resist "unlawful authority" (80). But even as he asserts that Sat3 "stands as a landmark in the growth of religious toleration and liberty of conscience in England," he also detects some inconsistency in the poem, remarking that Donne's religious tolerance "conflicts with the earlier insistence on the idea that there is one true church to be found by the persistent seeker," and this contradiction, he concludes, "is something specific to England in the 1590s" (84).

Canfield (1989, 155) asserts that in Sat3 "Christianity's primitive anti-imperial demo-cratic thrust, co-opted by feudalism, still manages to survive in dialectical tension."

Parfitt (1989, 58–59) comments that in Sat3 Donne "seems to advocate a pragmatic fidelity to the version of Christianity prevailing where you happen to live," though he does so "with a complexity and tentativeness which leave the famous passage on Truth effectively unresolved."

Baumlin (1990, 68–69) remarks that Sat3 "flaunts the poet's recusancy," contending that the poem's "exhortation to seek true religion" becomes "an invective against the political enforcement of conscience, an argument, admittedly oblique, for religious tolerance, and thus an argument against contemporary court policies."

Norbrook (1990, 10) posits that when Donne did finally choose a church, "one of his reasons for doing so was to gain wealth and power," yet he argues that Donne's career cannot be considered a "linear movement towards power" and that he never did become a part of the establishment; the "dialectical movement" of Sat3, he suggests, offers us a better description of the trajectory of Donne's career.

Ray (1990, 278, 284) notes of Sat3 that "one manuscript adds to the title 'Of Religion' and another adds 'Upon Religion,'" further commenting that "a recurring problem to Donne and others of his time was how one is to determine what religion, in the midst of many churches and factions, is indeed the true religion" (278).

Stanwood (1990, 77) observes that while Sat3 allows us to follow Donne's "troubled mind at work," it also illustrates many of the religious problems of the Renaissance and Donne's engagement with them.

Baumlin (1991, 57–58, 120, 122, 136–37) asserts that in Sat3 Donne "restates the Pyrrhonist arguments that fuel the religious controversies of his age: the problem of interpretation, the insufficiency of reason and, above all, the partial truth of language" (57–58). He suggests further that "doubt can be therapeutic" for Donne, who "turns to it as to an antidote for false belief," yet he questions whether Sat3 "ever moves beyond doubt, ever offers more than the via negativa of skepticism" (136). He adds that "of course, all is not doubt and denial," for "there are implicit assertions lurking in this otherwise antidogmatic poem, arguments for religious tolerance and, deeply hidden, for Catholic fideism," though he urges that Donne's "major target is once again more political than theological" (137).

Chandra (1991, 231–32) asserts that in the middle of Sat3 Donne "finds himself bewildered" and suggests that "to express anxiety in these terms over the uncertainty in the matter of faith shows that despite the averred profligacies of his youthful life, Donne was not unconcerned with religion."

Hester (1991, 97, 99–101) points out that Sat3 "appropriates the terms and lexicon of current religion controversy" in such a way that Donne "figures contemporary English worship as a nominalist worship of names and symbols, remarkable for its absence of Presence" (97), adding that the poem "might just figure forth 'truly' the 'mistress' who had displaced Christ's Bride, at least in the imperial propaganda of late Elizabethan Court poetry" (100). He concludes that "as an Elizabethan manuscript satire," Sat3 reveals "more about the difficulty and the danger (spiritual and physical) that confronted Donne in his search for the 'Presence' of God in Elizabethan England" than about which sect he finally chooses, thereby offering "a glimpse into the psychological dynamics that animate in equally equivocal textures his elegies, lyrics, and even his holy sonnets" (101).

Mahler (1991, 45) describes Sat3 as a type of subjective, individualized speech about religion, one which approaches the subject without superceding it, which searches for the truth without claiming truth's power, and which gives substance to the religious word without, however, demanding the need for recognition above and beyond the individual.

Schoenfeldt (1991, 255) notes that in Sat3 Donne "converts religious choice into a question of sexual predilection."

Slights (1991, 91–92) suggests that "in the revisionist version of Donne's career," Sat3 becomes "less a defense of the individual conscience than a report of a liminal state in a young man's development when he is rebelliously rejecting the persecuted religion of his family yet unwilling to submit to the religion of the broader society." She believes that the poem "shows us very little about its author's religious beliefs and nothing at all about his allegiance to any institutionalized church" so that instead of raising "questions of religious doctrine," the poem "is concerned with the reciprocal relationship between religion and other human activities."

Singh (1992, 36) comments that the speaker in Sat3 insists on the necessity of making a personal decision about the true church but at the same time maintains "an open-ended and inquiring outlook which refuses to allow temporal or spiritual authority to dictate faith to him" so that "honest doubt" is "more valuable than unthinking acceptance."

Smith (1992, 81) observes that the "drift" of Donne's argument in Sat3 is that the divides of Christian sectarianism lead individuals "to conclude that any worldly cause must be more worthy of their devotion than the pursuit of a true Christian life." Further, he says, Donne's measured deliberations throughout the poem show his "characteristic" mode of reasoning.

DiPasquale (1993, 77–78) maintains that Sat3's "parallel between Catholicism and Petrarchism points to a related analogy in Donne's love poetry" in that "their discourses of desire uphold a creed of non-fulfillment, assert the efficacy of erotic relics and sacraments, and proclaim invalid any love doctrine that challenges the orthodoxy of frustration."

Empson (1993, 81–82, 126–27) points out that "the police state which uses torture to impose a doctrine was very familiar in the sixteenth-century," adding that "the whole climax" of Sat3's argument "is against all popes or princes who do this wicked thing." He comments further that while the poem is often regarded "as a commonplace bit of Anglican liberalism," such a poem "was not usual, or safe, then, and the licensers still doubted whether to publish" the Satyres even after Donne's death (81–82). Further, reacting to Hughes' (1934) argument that Sat3 presents Donne's "defence of liberty of conscience," Empson states that the poem cannot be "twisted into an attack on this clumsy attempt at moderation, as apart from an attack on religious persecution in general" (126–27).

Gorbunov (1993, 96) contextualizes *Sat3* in terms of Donne's Catholic heritage, his family's experiences with religious persecution, and his ultimate conversion to Protestantism, noting that the poem concerns a moment of sharp spiritual crisis. It reveals, he argues, that Donne's attitude towards the Reformation is of an especially personal character, differing strongly from the patriotic view of Sidney and Spenser. He concludes that Donne's position of wise skepticism, one in which Donne never doubts the basis of Christian dogma, is nonetheless radical for his time.

Scodel (1993, 480–82, 501) insists that Donne's "spiritual and independent engagement with ancient philosophy and literature gave him a vital critical distance from his culture's dominant habits of mind" and argues that in *Sat3*, Donne rejects the *via media* of the Anglican church in favor of "a mean of skeptical inquiry" between various Christian sects "to enlarge the sphere of individual freedom" (480). Convinced that Donne wrote the poem during a transitional period of personal crisis around 1596, when he had left the Catholic faith but had not yet joined the English church, he suggests that Donne's use of the mean was the way "a religious deviant in an England that punished nonconformity" justified his choice (481). Ultimately, he finds that the scepticism in the poem is kept in check, noting that "while Donne questions the validity of any given ecclesiastical and political formation, he does not doubt God's ultimate benevolence and man's eventual ability to find his proper place in the world" (501).

Strier (1993, 284–85) describes *Sat3* as a radical poem and, while contending that "such a view is not anachronistic," concedes that the poem is not consistent in its radicalism but points out that "its radicalism is its deepest and poetically most distinguished strain." He believes Donne's biography provides "the proper context" for reading *Sat3* and asserts that he is "implicitly rejecting the claim, made throughout this century by various scholars," that the Satyres are "fundamentally Roman Catholic in point of view and sensibility."

Davies (1994, 19–21) posits that if the "I" and "thou" of *Sat3* are both read as Donne, then "some of the manic quality of this poem, together with the dead-ends it offers, comes into focus," especially the pressures to "break faith with his family" or to "break faith with his own life's ambitions and autonomy." He believes Donne to be a "self-condemning apostate" whose options are "to return to the True Church, which he cannot and will not do; to live in the body and the moment, like 'thou' of the early passages; or to take the arduous and solitary path of the interrogative soul through a landscape composed all of questionings" (20).

Griffin (1994, 11) remarks that Donne's topic of true religion in *Sat3* is "too serious for mere laughter or railing" and that "indeed, his declaration of hatred seems almost a perfunctory gesture."

Hester (1994a, 208, 211–12), commenting on the religious tolerance in *Sat3* that other critics have remarked on, contends that it is "actually only an equal scorn for various shapes of intellectual and spiritual laziness or stupidity." What is truly striking about the poem on religion, he argues, is its discovery that "true religion" is nowhere to be found in Elizabethan England, specifying that "the major thrust of the argument is that the terms of religious controversy have become rather political than confessional," as the satire ends with an extended metaphor about power (208). Further, he asserts that "read in the lexical arena of the late Elizabethan sectarian wars," the poem inscribes "the major themes, texts, allusions, and attitudes of the Recusant position" in its evocation of "the tropes and polemical strokes of English Catholic critiques of the state of religion in Elizabethan England" (211–12).

Klause (1994, 183–84) observes that in Sat3 Donne "would like to avoid a dependence on fallible 'persons' in so important an inquiry (which will lead finally to a personal God), but he cannot," and thus "despite his resistance, personal models and heroes were for him a deep necessity."

Kruzhkova (1994, 158) notes in relation to Sat3 that Donne came from a Catholic family and received a Catholic religious education, adding that Catholicism was severely persecuted at this time in England and was considered barely less than treasonous. He states that because the pursuit of any sort of career as a Catholic was impossible, Donne likely was impelled to convert to Anglicanism.

Strier (1994, 231–32) argues that Sat3 has as its subject matter "the central concern of sixteenth-century Europe, the division of the Church into competing churches," adding that the poem shows the importance that the young Donne placed on "the integrity of the individual conscience," for he was "not about to accept anything on authority."

Brown (1995, 54–57) asserts that personal responsibility for "one's own faith, understanding, and moral choices" is the central concern of Sat3, noting that the poem "explores criteria by which the perplexed conscience adjudicates conflicting authorities, and it advances a process of inquiry similar to that of Protestant casuistry" (54–55). She finds that Donne's characters "choose their religion for insufficient reasons, but when all the reasons are combined, they form a more valid basis for judgment," adding that Donne's purpose "is not to discredit the religious alternatives that he represents," but rather "to criticize inadequate standards for moral choice" (56).

Patterson (1995, 228) notes in passing "the idealistic skepticism" of Sat3, "with its demands that each man determine and keep his own Truth."

Scodel (1995, 45) claims that Sat3 transforms "both Aristotelian ethics and Pyrrhonist skepticism" and thus "spurns the English church's self-description in order to advocate a skeptical inquiry as the true religious mean," even as it rejects "any of the rival, state-sponsored Christian denominations."

Corthell (1997, 38–40, 47) argues that Sat3 "rehearses the vexed question of self-fashioning in Renaissance culture," suggesting that the truth-seeker looks "very much like an individual, an autonomous self even," yet he also finds that the speaker's autonomy is complicated by "a true psychoanalytic ambivalence," by his "lack of wholeness" or "a desire of the Other," which, in the context of the poem, is true religion. He notes further that "the search for true religion is represented through a masculine discourse of desire," which is "complete with oedipal inflection" (39), in which each religious position is figured in terms of a type of woman. He explains that these male responses to the female figures can be interpreted as "strategies of denying lack," and "in the terms of Donne's allegory, this failure to acknowledge one's lack (i.e., lack of the truth) results in a flawed religious choice" (40). Sat3, he concludes, "attacks shallow historicizations of religion and then works equally hard to imagine a way of rescuing 'true religion' from history," and even though the poem fails to solve the problem, it succeeds in creating a powerful "practice of writing" (47).

Oliver (1997, 51, 54, 61, 63) argues that *Sat3* contains Donne's "most sustained and direct poetic treatment of the subject of religion" and that "the radicalism" of the poem "must have seemed a completely fresh departure" from Donne's previous poetic output (51). He insists that the poem is "entirely at odds with its age in its lack of concern, ultimately, with doctrine," noting that the speaker "talks of truth rather than doctrine, religion rather than church," and "seems only intermittently interested in locating the truth within a specific Christian body" (61). He states further that *Sat3* is "ahead of its time in its stress on the need to find the truth for oneself" (61) and concludes that when read in the context of the Elizabethan religious settlement, the poem is "deeply disloyal, not to say treacherous" (63).

Patterson (1997, 30, 35n40) notes that because Locke owned a 1654 edition of Donne's poems, he "would certainly have read" *Sat3*, which "allows us to posit a direct influence" (35n40) on Locke's "ironic conclusion, in his *Letter concerning toleration*, that religion cannot be mandated by the state" (30).

Prescott (1997, 47) reminds us that the "domestic comedy" of *Sat3* has "eternal consequences."

Johnson (1999, 38) notes that "one of the most significant, and possibly the most visible, of Donne's religious struggles derives from his understanding of the Church" and that in *Sat3* "many critics have analyzed his religious conflicts in ways that tend to isolate and overemphasize the issue of his sectarian allegiance."

Nutt (1999, 123) argues that in writing *Sat3* Donne was "far from" the "Protestant despair" that some critics attribute to him, which he believes is "self-evident when we consider the image of God" Donne presents in the poem.

Haskin (2000, 317–18) notes that the first of Coleridge's "grounds for recommending the perusal of our elder writers," written in the front of the *Reliquiae Baxterianae* "about 1820," applies "as conspicuously to his reading of Donne's sermons and satires as it does to the works of the writers he mentions by name," a point implicit in Coleridge's annotation on *Sat3*, "which shows how intimately linked Donne and Milton were in his reading experience."

For King (2000, 374), the poem "anatomises the failures of those who decline to undertake" the quest for religious truth or who "unite with 'false' churches."

Prescott (2000, 230) finds that in *Sat3* Donne insists, "with remarkable courage," on "recalling his upbringing in a Catholic family subject to prosecution" and that "mere power, whether in Rome, Geneva, Germany, or England, cannot offer sufficient guidance to the individual soul."

Reid (2000, 46–48) sees in *Sat3* a "moral intelligence at work" that "brings out a surprisingly solid person" (48). He argues that the poem satirizes "misplaced courage and various sorts of churchmanship," but it serves primarily as an "Erasmian" expression of the Christian life, as "a moral reflection" of "the war of virtue with vice." He suggests, then, that the father Donne may represent in the poem is John Donne senior, an Erasmian-type Christian "who lived a life of heartfelt piety issuing in practical goodness" rather than a Catholic "in the heroic tradition of his mother's family." He adds that if this assumption is correct, then Donne is not "shuffling into apostasy" but is instead "looking for a sane and central religious tradition" (46–47).

Robbins (2000, 424) states that the poem "interrogates the various brands of Christianity on offer in western Europe."

Trevor (2000, 91) finds the speaker's resolve to "Seeke true religion" indicative of dissatisfaction with "his own display of Christian belief."

Wiggins (2000, 29, 46) argues that the "craven counsel to impersonate the master," urged by Angel Day's *The English Secretary*, was "used by Donne and transformed into a strategy for producing" in *Sat3* "one of the most subtle and daring statements about religion in a Renaissance despotism that comes down to us from the Elizabethan period" (29). In addition, the acknowledged problem in *Sat3* is that religion "should amount to more than a posture," yet "the existence of penalties" leaves "even the loyal adherent of the Settlement in doubt as to whether attendance at services is a matter of conviction or convention."

Edwards (2001, 70, 160–62) notes that Donne "mocked the Church of England" (70), and yet is "in earnest about religion" (162) while rejecting Catholicism, Calvinism, Puritanism, and Erastianism. He adds that Donne does not clarify whether he is referring to his father or his stepfather in ll. 14–15 and 71–72, but he "does not refer to his mother who was the religious enthusiast and martyr in the family" (160).

Fulton (2001, 73, 78–79, 101–02, 102n60) argues that the imperative to "seek true religion" represents "not only a thematic exploration of the problem of maintaining truth" in the Satyres, but also "a problem endemic to the genre of Elizabethan satire as a whole." He cautions against using "our knowledge of Donne's future conversion and even his temporally vague retrospective narratives" in *Pseudo* to construct Donne's religious position, since "we simply do not know where he stood" when writing *Sat3*, adding that "where he would stand is inconsequential" (78–79). Further, he concurs with Empson (1993) and Strier (1993) in seeing the poem "as an early instance of 'liberalism,'" (102n60), noting that Milton and Spinoza furthered Donne's "arguments concerning the kind of knowledge possible in a free state" (101), particularly "in their works on toleration" (102), *Areopagitica* and *A Theologico-political Treatise and A Political Treatise*.

Hadfield (2001, 57) reads *Sat3*'s attacks against "the variety of religious faiths and divisions as ways of obscuring, not revealing, the word of God."

Donne as Satirist

Lewis (1934a, 604) espouses that Donne's insistence in *Sat3* upon sceptical methods of approaching truth is often "taken as evidence of a humanist attitude," but he argues instead that at this "early stage" of his life Donne's was "only a modified sceptical and discursive approach" so that his attitude is not one of "humanist open-mindedness," but instead one that is "vividly personal."

Stein (1944a, 268) argues of *Sat3* that Donne's "independent intellect makes free use of some of the challenging methods and attitudes of skepticism" and that Donne "does not attack the mind," but "the misdirected use of the mind," adding that Donne's scepticism "is used as an instrument to further tolerance and to eliminate much of the prejudice that blocks the approaches to truth."

Hodgart (1969, 142) states that Donne is satirical in *Sat3* "only insofar as he writes frankly and rudely of Calvinists, Anglicans and Romans."

Lecocq (1969, 376) argues that Donne invokes the term "railing" at the beginning of *Sat3* to suggest that he did not consider his satire of great value and to minimize the offensiveness of what will become, in a long attempt at persuasion, a call to civil and religious disobedience.

Moore (1969, 41–43) finds that the satire of *Sat3* "is not directed against authority and its tendency toward persecution, but toward the individual and his too easy acceptance of authority in order to avoid facing the awesome demands of a constant and active religious faith" (41). As a result, the poem insists that there is no sure way to Truth and that success "will come only through an effort which gains its impetus from the desperation of the seeker's uncertainty" (42).

Hutchison (1970, 361–62) suggests that in *Sat3* Donne "uses spiritual combat as a means of involving his audience and at the same time warns them that the effort will not be easily made," but can only be achieved "by means of an individual confrontation with vice which involves not only the persona but the satirist and reader." He finds that compared to other satirists of the period, Donne "lays emphasis on this deliberate confrontation with vice so that it could be vigorously resisted and refuted," and the poem contains "none of the subordination of philosophy and theology to the depiction of actual vice, nor of the moral ambiguity which characterizes much of the formal verse written in the 'satyr' tradition."

Summers (1970, 24) argues that *Sat3* "creates the speech of a man torn between tears and laughter, outraged by the usual confusion of mortal and immortal values and convinced of the necessity of seeking 'true religion,'" and the poem "ends with an attack on the wisdom, justice, and safety of anyone's mindlessly following an established religion," a position that "could hardly have been spoken with impunity before a monarch of the time."

Slights (1972, 95–101) argues that approaching *Sat3* "as a dramatization of a case of conscience enriches our reading of the poem and explains features which have puzzled modern readers" (100). She finds that "the attitude toward human authority" Donne presents in *Sat3* parallels that of the Anglican casuists in their consideration of "the problem of the relationship of the individual conscience to civil law" (97). Further, she points out that in the poem "human rulers have legitimate authority, but the individual conscience is the final judge" so that "to transfer the responsibility of choice to civil or ecclesiastical authority is morally and intellectually corrupt" (98). She adds that in addressing the dilemma "of discovering the true church as a particular man's personal problem of conscience while simultaneously showing it to be an instance of a universal moral question," Donne's tone "is most personal at the beginning of the poem where he reacts emotionally and attacks personally the superficiality of his fictive audience" (99).

Miller and Berrey (1974, 42–44) argue that in *Sat3* Donne is "as far removed as Marston and Hall from the older tradition of estate-satire, which attempted to discover and heal the wounds of the body politic" (42). They add that in *Sat3* Donne "is more consistent, in thought and style, than most of the 'new' satires of his contemporaries" and that his ethical scheme "provided him with a persona more useful and sound than the 'satyr' satirist" (43). They conclude that though Donne's pity and scorn "cancel each other out, and though he refuses to 'rail' with indignation," Donne's feelings are, nevertheless, "controlled, not exhausted: he moves from incredulous outrage, to witty contempt, to urgent gravity" so that "before Dryden, perhaps only Donne recaptured the unity of Roman verse satire, which drew from several disciplines and displayed stylistic variety, but maintained equilibrium" (43–44).

Newton (1974, 434–35) suggests that *Sat3* is written "from a position of a tensed yet curiously irresolute balance" and "attempts to ask more seriously and directly just where—for the satirist in this world—some foundation for constancy can be found." In this poem, he argues, Donne "seeks (in good satiric tradition) a 'cure,' through 'railing,'" and "for the first time, Donne directly admits that he is a satirist."

According to Bellette (1975, 136–38), the dilemma Donne offers is that "one must encounter the world, know all its subtleties, recognize one's own involvement in it through the common fall, yet strive to remain free of its contagion." As a method for approaching this dilemma, he argues that *Sat3* "is more concerned with establishing the correct frame of mind in which to meet the foe than with setting out a list of practical instructions" (136). As such, he argues that Donne "modified greatly" the traditional role of the satirist, adding that Donne's "true originality lies in those elements which have been singled out here for their abandonment of these purposes," so that "to take upon oneself in penance rather that to condemn or seek to extirpate is the attitude which Donne seems to adopt toward the sins he describes." He claims further that "not even in the vivid pictures" depicted within the Satyres is there "an 'improving' intention," for "such intentions, wearisomely proclaimed by almost every Elizabethan satirist, are disavowed" in *Sat3* (138).

Hiller (1977, 15) finds that *Sat3* "does not quietly expound a philosophy already resolved upon," but instead "dramatizes the poet's attempts to formulate one," adding that "it is as if Donne is working out his own salvation as he writes." He argues that while the satirist expresses "anger," there is also "compassion for the weaknesses of man" so that "the 'railing'" of *Sat3* "is tempered with reason and good sense."

Dubrow (1979, 81–83), in her discussion of *Sat3*, notes that "what is omitted from the satires is no less interesting than what is included" and that "the other satirists of the 1590's, like the satirists of all ages, are intensely self-conscious about their experimental and highly controversial genre," and thus they "include long defenses of satire in their prefaces and incorporate frequent references to its virtues within the satires themselves" (81–82). By contrast, Donne's Satyres "contain no such theoretical apologia," and in fact Donne "fails to defend that genre—and, indeed, sometimes chooses to criticize it," which in itself shows that he was "more optimistic about the health of literature in England" (82) than were his fellow satirists.

Corthell (1982, 170) points out that the "correspondence between railer and seeker" by which Donne generates "the special force" of *Sat3* explains why Donne chose satire "as the vehicle for his first major religious poem, a poem which has its eye on the relations between the individual and authority."

Hester (1982, 55–58) observes that in *Sat3* the satirist realizes "his duty as a Christian 'Sentinell'" (31) so that "his considerations of current abuses provide the fullest defense so far of the central principle of verse satire—*laus et vituperatio*" (55–56). He adds that the poem embodies a form of railing "borrowed from Juvenal but accommodated to Christian principles" that the satirist employs throughout the poem "as he follows each satirical portrait of a current mental failure with charitable instruction for overcoming that limitation" (58).

Stein (1984, 81) argues that "the accepted necessity of seeking" that is promoted in *Sat3* "shows the mark" of "a conscientious reformist, an individual who is intent on discriminating between good and bad in his own reason and motives."

Waller (1986, 241) asserts that *Sat3* "is valuable because it seems to use satiric means to non-satiric ends, and provides a valuable commentary on both the fashion for verse satire and on some of the contradictions of the age upon which Donne was brooding, yet trying to accommodate."

Norbrook (1990, 10) contends that the satirist of *Sat3* is "a critical intellectual who has set aside all traditional religious prejudices and institutional loyalties," and yet is one who has not found "the correct position in the via media either." He notes further that the poem's "brusque imperatives reveal Donne's uneasy awareness that the critical audience to which it is addressed as yet scarcely exists."

Baumlin (1991, 121–22, 131–32) observes that Donne is "no less a satirist for seeking to persuade and for obscuring his politically dangerous persuasions behind a cloak of difficult, allusive language and a thoroughgoing skepticism" (121–22). Donne's abandonment of "Juvenal's *saeva indignatio* and Horace's *sermo* style" and his adoption of "the protreptic zeal and the obscure, abstruse, extravagant diatribe style of Persius," he says, turns "into an expression of Catholic-Pyrrhonist skepticism even as he turns the model's penchant for obscurity into a deliberate strategy of masking and indirection" (132).

A. Smith (1991, 109) notes that *Sat3*, in which "the searching play" of Donne's mind "persistently works to try a present case in a wider context of men's motives and understanding," confronts the reader "with a bizarre medley of moral questions," and as such, the poem's movement "amounts to a sifting of the relative claims on our devotion such as commonly distract us from our absolute obligations to seek the truth."

Davies (1994, 19–21) observes that "there was a sense in which Donne was uniquely at home in the sphere of 'doubt'" and that "the emotional complexity of this 'new' position of scepticism" appears in *Sat3* as "a highly charged, violently indignant voice denounces the religious errors of his time, which it enumerates and scourges one by one" (19–20). Thus, he states, "the tongue of the speaker is a frenzied whiplash doling out correction in literally all directions" (20).

Corthell (1997, 38) believes that *Sat3* "rehearses the vexed question of self-fashioning in Renaissance culture," and he suggests that the truth-seeker looks "very much like an individual, an autonomous self even."

Wiggins (2000, 50–52) suggests that *Sat3* "represents an extraordinary act of self-abnegation" as Donne permits an "idealized" Egerton to speak as "the authority figure" (50). He also reminds us that it "was a courtier that Donne sought to be," and in this poem "the zealous secretary" seeks to fashion himself "as a great man's mirror" (51–52).

Persona

Mueller (1962, 12) identifies the speaker of *Sat3* as Donne.

Stein (1962, 177) notes Donne's "authentic" and "skeptical" voice in the poem.

Andreasen (1963, 69) states that *Sat3* is the only one of the Satyres that is a soliloquy and adds that the speaker counsels "his own better self" in this poem.

Sloan (1965, 14–16, 19), reacting to Andreasen (1963), argues that *Sat3* should be read as an oration rather than as a soliloquy, and as such, the persona is to be seen as attempting "to persuade a real audience" rather than simply himself (16). He characterizes the audience as "lusty" and "youthful" men "eager for adventure and romance," an audience "whose fathers had taught them to break with tradition" and "to whom courage and valor must be expressed in terms of action, battle, and dueling" (19).

Jackson (1968, 40–42), in answer to the question he poses concerning *Sat3*, "Who speaks in his poem, and to whom is it addressed?" (40), posits that Donne, because he is speaking to himself, is both speaker and auditor. "In such a view," he explains, "the auditor, whose voice is largely, perhaps entirely, unheard," represents the "image of the poet," and the speaker then represents "the self-reflexive center who is able to generate, direct, see, or speak to such images" (40).

Roberts (1968, 106–08, 114–15) says that the speaker of *Sat3* "is alone" and that the opening lines establish a tone that "forces" from the speaker, who is "totally paralyzed by his contradictory thoughts and emotions," the "most agonizing protests" (106–07). Roberts argues that "although in one sense the speaker is no closer to finding the true religion at the end of the poem than he was at the beginning" (114), nonetheless he "comes to realize many significant aspects of his problem: 1) the absurdity of accepting uncritically the authority of another in matters of religion; 2) the equal absurdity of abandoning the immensely important quest all together in utter despair and confusion; 3) the courage and asceticism that are needed to face the ultimate mysteries of life boldly; 4) the futility of expending one's energies in the pursuit of worldly achievements while avoiding the crucial questions of life; 5) that Truth can be had only by God's enlightening and illuminating the mind of man, after man has made the valiant effort to prepare himself for this revelation" (114–15).

Lecocq (1969, 396) notes that in *Sat3* the persona speaks to himself and not to some young man whose conscience he pretends to guide.

Hutchison (1970, 356) argues that in *Sat3* the persona "dominates and is above the scene," and as such the moral tone is "persistent and explicit."

Jackson (1970, 30–32) states that the relationship between the speaker and auditor "parallels the relationship of soul to flesh and represents the traditional medieval debate between body and soul," though he adds that in Donne's expression of this debate "one voice is silent—the flesh, the external and visible self." He concludes that the "possibility" for reconciling "the visibility of actually existing men" with "the hidden power of God" is "adumbrated by the ambivalence and unity in the person addressed."

Powers (1971, 181–83) comments that *Sat3*'s satirist "addresses his auditor directly," as a "'real' individual," a young man whose courage and daring leads him "to challenge rivals to duels, but not to face the idea that he has been taught 'too easie wayes' in the duties of religion" (181). She adds that the speaker expresses "his warmest personal interests" in constructing his argument so that religious truth "becomes personified as a spiritual mistress, for whom one searches like an explorer" (181–82).

Slights (1972, 94) believes that in *Sat3* Donne "assumes the persona of a casuist advising a young man whose confusion over the complexities and contradictions of institutionalized religion is apparently leading to cynicism, accompanied, perhaps, with a swaggering bravura."

Lauritsen (1976, 125–26) comments that given the persona's "rigid expectations of himself and the world and his inflexible conception of himself as not only apart from the world but morally superior to it," *Sat3* becomes "the least satirical" and "the darkest" of the Satyres, in so far as "the speaker's world view and, with it, his self-esteem begin seriously to break down."

Sellin (1980, 293) espouses that Donne's speaker "seems neither to be so uncertain of religious truth as apostles of an early date seem to believe, nor to be admonishing himself and his own way of life," but "instead appears to be addressing a hypothetical young gentleman adventurer who has cultivated all the admirable virtues necessary to undertake brave deeds of knight-errantry," even though he has "neglected the most essential principles" of a "religious commitment and the courage to adhere to one's conscience despite the demands of any secular authority."

Shaw (1981, 37) notes that the speaker of *Sat3* "is caught between the necessity of seeking 'true religion' and an inability to accept the authority of any existing church to instruct him," for, in effect, maintaining "an independent position demands a far greater degree of self-confidence than the speaker," who is "anything but sanguine about his uncommitted status," can possibly "muster."

Kerins (1984, 48) contends that the "reformed satirist" of *Sat3* "is unique in that he finds himself part of a complex fallen world struggling toward an ideal of Truth," and that "in making this bold attempt," the speaker "neither denies his own frailty nor does he blunt the reality of moral viewpoint," but instead "chooses to trust in a personal relationship with God available to all and to use his God-given powers in the process of seeking out Truth."

Stein (1984, 81) argues that although the speaker of *Sat3* "does not declare his identity," yet "trusted readers (like Wotton) would certainly have recognized the autobiographical resemblances to the serious young man who could not ask his own father about truth and, unlike Wotton, did not have a settled religious faith to carry forth and bring home, but had to seek."

Baumlin (1986b, 466–67) describes the persona of *Sat3* and *Sat5* as "a preacher, persuading and teaching his audience rather than ridiculing or punishing," adding that "Persius is the model for these poems, both of which rely heavily on this Roman's moral gravity and protreptic zeal."

Mahler (1991, 41–42) explains that in *Sat3* the speaker finds himself from the start in a paradoxical situation, one which hinders his thoroughly understood actions as a satirist; he feels compassion as well as anger towards the world, and the compassion prevents a sudden release of anger, while the anger prevents the free flow of tears.

Singh (1992, 36) comments that the speaker in *Sat3* insists on the necessity of making a personal decision about the true church, but at the same time maintains "an open-ended and inquiring outlook which refuses to allow temporal or spiritual authority to dictate faith to him, and which sees honest doubt as being more valuable than unthinking acceptance."

Davies (1994, 19–20) maintains that the "highly charged, violently indignant voice" of Sat3 "denounces the religious errors of his time, which it enumerates and scourges one by one," in "a frenzied whiplash doling out correction in literally all directions."

Oliver (1997, 52–54, 159, 236) argues that Donne's original audience might not "have automatically identified speaker with writer" (52). He cautions against a biographical interpretation of the poem that identifies Donne's religious position with that of the speaker, since "external evidence suggests that the real-life Donne was in some respects less like the poem's speaker and more like its implied audience" (53). While the speaker is a "serious young man," his implied listener "is more like the speakers of the other satires" (53). Thus, "if a figure resembling the poet" appears in Sat3, "it is as implied addressee rather than as speaker." He concludes that the voice used by the speaker "is one of Donne's supreme achievements in the poem," as it "evokes a specific audience early on through the use of the familiar thou/thee" (54).

Nutt (1999, 119) comments that Sat3 "opens firmly in the first person," shifting to the second in line 11, yet "the tone does not shift into one of distanced address," so that the questions raised in the poem "are primarily a matter of intense concern for Donne" as he disputes "primarily with himself."

Wiggins (2000, 41–42, 48, 50, 53) finds that in this poem Donne "moves inside the grave man's mind and speaks for, not to, him" so that Donne "impersonates an Egerton." Consequently, the voice we hear in Sat3 seems "much older" than that of the other Satyres, "more stern and austere," and the poem seems "to be the product of a much later period in Donne's life" (41). While the "authority figure" represented in Sat3 is "idealized," his words are "credible" (42) in their "poignant, even bitter," comments projecting "the voice of a father acknowledging the death of paternal authority by its own hand" (48). He concludes that Donne "served Egerton" either "as a flattering mirror or as an accurate—and therefore honestly complimentary—one" (53).

Genre

Aronstein (1920, 160–61) asserts that Sat3 is not really a satire, but rather a poetic engagement of the poet with himself on the topics of religion and the religious.

Martz (1960, 338) asserts that Sat3 "belongs to no single genre" in that the poem stands as "a unique and perfectly Donneian blending of love-song weeds, satiric thorns, and those better arts sown early in his life."

Sloan (1965, 14–16) associates Sat3 with the classical oration.

Roberts (1968, 106) remarks that Sat3 "stands apart from" the other Satyres "in the seriousness of its tone, in its subject matter, and in its basic technique." While he notes that "there is actually more satire" in Sat3 "than meets the eye on first reading," he adds that the poem is "satiric only in part."

Inglis (1969, 42) points out that satire was a genre employed by many Elizabethan poets, often "addressed to a friend" and taking the "form of a homily on moral behaviour, generally with asides on contemporary abuses," adding that Sat3 "is probably the best known of its kind."

Erskine-Hill (1972, 275–76) states that *Sat3* "may merit (though not altogether for the same reasons) the term 'Tragical Satyre' which Dryden was later to apply to Juvenal."

Slights (1972, 85–86) comments that even though critics generally recognize the significance of *Sat3* as an early poetic expression of Donne's religious ideas, "the implicit dramatic situation which is largely responsible for the imaginative vitality of the poem has never been explained." In particular, she argues that "the usual view" of the poem as a "satiric meditation" does not "account convincingly for its tone or its logical development," which can only be properly explained when the poem is approached as "a dramatization of a case of conscience," in which "the speaker of the poem is a casuist trying to deal with the problems of a doubting conscience."

Sinha (1977, 66–67) asserts that *Sat3* is "not a satire in the ordinary sense," but rather "an epistle on the subject of finding the true religion," in which Donne is "inspired by a subject that affected him, perhaps, more vividly than the subjects" of the other Satyres.

Sellin (1980, 297), remarking that "it is not wholly beyond doubt" that *Sat3* is a satire, questions the extent to which the similarities between *Sat3* and such poems as *Cross* and certain elegies "(which some Donne manuscripts entitle satires)," epigrams, and verse letters challenge critics' assumptions about the poem's genre.

Carey (1981, 12) argues that most of *Sat3* is "not a satire at all," but is instead "a self-lacerating record of that moment which comes in the lives of almost all thinking people," that is, when the beliefs of one's youth "come into conflict with the scepticism of the mature intellect."

Hester (1982, 71) contends that restricting one's reading of *Sat3* "to either the devotional or the rhetorical aspects of the satirist's voice is to overlook its most significant characteristic—its union of private and public discourse, its concomitant meditative and satirical stance." In particular, he argues that the poem "dramatizes the internal process on which man's active life must be based," and "as a satire spoken to a general Elizabethan audience, its ridicule of fallacious and inadequate mental efforts is the dynamic actualization of the speaker's private conclusions."

Parry (1985, 48) states that *Sat3* "falls among" the Satyres because "much of it is given over to an account of the various fashions that prevail in religion, and to wry reflections" that individuals willingly engage in "all sorts of brave or foolhardy ventures" and yet remain indifferent to the "infinitely more important challenge of eternal life or death."

Mallet (1990, 19) comments first that a satire "is generally defined as a piece of writing in which vices or follies are held up to ridicule" and then adds that only the first part of *Sat3* "is satirical in this sense."

Baumlin (1991, 120) remarks that *Sat3* "avoids both the raging, Juvenalian invective and the self-deprecating humor of Horace," and yet, he asks, in what sense can the poem "even be called a formal satire?" and "[h]ow can the poet write of religious tolerance without implicating himself and the readers he seeks to persuade?" He contends that Donne's "political exigencies render his actual aim and subject literally unspeakable" so that because the poem is "incapable of announcing what it wishes to persuade," it becomes instead an essay "in skepticism and negative argument."

Hester (1991, 98–99) believes that a letter accompanying ten of Donne's *Paradoxes* suggests that "these are late Elizabethan manuscript satires—a generic coding slighted" if *Sat3* is read "solely as meditation, oration, case of conscience, verse epistle, personal apologia, public panegyric, or unequivocal revelation of where precisely Donne himself stood 'inquiring right' (78) in the Counter-Reformation wars of truth."

Mahler (1991, 41–42) states that *Sat3* evades the usual expectations of genre through its strict establishment of the *dispositio* under the rubric of the sermon-type *genus deliberativum*, which is typified by the presence of the two functions of deliberative speech: persuasion and exhortation.

Of *Sat3*, Sellin (1991, 85–87) questions, "first, how do we know the poem is a satire?", adding that "if the poem were written in Latin iambics, the identification would be immediate," but the English equivalent of pentameter rhymed couplets "provides no adequate litmus test to distinguish satire from the Elegies, the Anniversaries, or a number of the Divine Poems, not to speak of other generic types" (85–86). He comments further that "the traditional title" also "provides no adequate guide to genre" because "we cannot be sure that the titles we have are Donne's," and that the Roman or Romanized Greek names in the poem are more closely aligned "not with the other satires or the elegies but with the epigrams" (86). He also questions the "argument, the mimetic posture, the plotting, even the style" of *Sat3*, wondering if "these elements unite it with the other satires," and finally insists that "defining Donne's *liber satyrarum* as consisting of merely five pieces is arbitrary and unhistorical" (86).

Slights (1991, 92) wonders why, "if the problem of finding true religion grew out of Donne's intensely personal religious struggle," he treated the problem "in a satire, a genre associated with social criticism," and then responds that "one plausible answer" is that Donne "saw religious faith as unavoidably involved in the social, the political, and the economic as well as in the narrowly spiritual."

Oliver (1997, 183) asserts that "the sharing of assumption" is necessary "for the proper functioning" of satyre, and thus *Sat3* is unsuccessful as a satyre since "the ebb and flow of the poem generates too much uncertainty."

Fulton (2001, 73, 76, 80) argues that the imperative to "seek true religion" represents "a problem endemic to the genre of Elizabethan satire as a whole" (73). He adds that *Sat3* "operates distinctly as a generic expression, both in style and in its focus on power and knowledge" (76) and that its "aspirations toward intellectual freedom" situate the poem "in the heart of the satiric mode of the 1590s" (80).

Sources, Influences, and Analogues

Simpson (1924, 5–6) notes that *Sat3* anticipates passages in *Essays* and *Sermons*, making untenable the traditional divisions between Donne's prose and poetry and between periods in his life, for Donne was seeking truth at all stages of his life.

Hughes (1934, 82) compares Donne's belief in the power of truth in "both knowledge and behavior" with Milton's in *Areopagitica*.

Leavis (1935, 239) feels that the achievement of *Sat3* is not representative of his other literary achievements.

Baker (1952, 118) asserts that in *Sat3*, *HSShow*, and *Essays* Donne "repeatedly urges a *sensus communis* to make possible religious unity, or at least toleration for unessential doctrinal differences."

Gardner (1952, 123) finds no parallel between *Sat3* and *HSShow*, for the subject of the former is "the problem of authority," whereas that of the latter is "what is the mark of the Church of Christ?"

Duncan (1959, 171) suggests that Donne's injunction to "doubt wisely" in *Sat3*, the final lines of *Metem* (518–20), and his concern with the "new Philosophy" in *FirAn* 205 have caused modern readers to think of Donne as a sceptic since they have assumed "that in the seventeenth century, as in the twentieth, science bred skepticism and relativism."

Martz (1960, 337) explains that the first two-thirds of *Sat3* is dominated by a "satiric tone of 'railing,'" though this tone is "not like the public railing of the Roman satirists."

Rickey (1966, 186) lists "the salamander and Phrygius" as classical allusions in this poem.

Milgate (1967, xxiii, 140) thinks Donne interprets in *Sat3* "the supposed obscurity and harshness of Persius and Juvenal as an opportunity for testing out the language to the full" (xxiii). The central idea of the poem, he says, is seen, though "more crudely stated," in Donne's "early prose composition, Problem 5," which he quotes (140).

Warnke (1967, 106) puts *Sat3* "among the earliest of English formal satires based on Latin models."

Williamson (1967, 53) notes that Donne blames Luther rather than Calvin for attempting to bind the soul to human laws, both in this satyre and in *Metem*, and adds that Donne's reference to "our Mistresse faire Religion" "anticipates the connection of sacred and profane love" in the Holy Sonnets.

Lecocq (1969, 396) points out that Donne presents in *HSShow* the same theme he presents in *Sat3*, one of wooing and wedding religion as if she were a spouse.

Baker-Smith (1972, 431) argues that "when Donne's writings are placed in relation to his vigilant critique of pseudo-religion they demonstrate a clear unity," especially with *HSShow*. In response to the criticism that "the two poems raise different questions: the problem of authority in the satire, the marks of the Church in the sonnet," he explains that "if one sees them as expressions of responsible discrimination in religious matters," then "the difference fades."

Slights (1972, 85, 87–88, 91, 93–94, 100) argues that "through the voice of a casuist" Donne analyzes in *Sat3* "the problem of religious truth as a personal moral dilemma in which right action depends on rational thought," and yet, she states, instead of offering "an authoritative solution to the specific problem," Donne "explains the theoretical basis of casuistry and provides a model of the process by which a man may *stand inquiring right* and thereby save his soul" (85). She also points out that in the seventeenth century there developed "a body of Anglican casuistical literature," which "exhibits simultaneous reliance on and distrust of Roman Catholic casuistry," and that "this Anglican case divinity is remarkably similar to Donne's attitude towards problems of conscience and to the ideas and form dramatized" in *Sat3* (88) as it wrestles with "the tension between individual conscience and ecclesiastical authority" (91). Finally, she points out that in contrast to "the personal quality" of *HSShow*, *Sat3* "has seemed to some readers strangely unimpassioned," yet the speaker of the poem, in his casuistical role, "is not acting out his own spiritual struggle, but advising another man confronting a moral problem" (100).

Ansari (1974, 139) notes that *Sat3* is written "after the manner" of Persius and that instead of regarding it as a "mere satire" it would be more productive to view it as "an exploratory inquiry into truth," one that "is not equivalent to straying but to a careful, unbiased and pragmatic approach to experience."

Gill (1974, 53–54) points out that in *Vertues Encomium: or, the Image of Honour* (1614) Richard Niccols includes an epigram that echoes the description of the hill of Truth in *Sat3*. Quoting the epigram, he notes that both Donne and Niccols emphasize "repeated effort or patient industry" rather than "the pleasures at the top of the hill" or "the thorns barring the way."

Miller and Berrey (1974, 36) insist that "the fundamental question" raised by the speaker in *Sat3* "is concerned with the same central issue about the four cardinal virtues that is also found in the works of Ficino, More, and Erasmus: the relationship between virtue conceived naturally according to pagan philosophy and supernatural virtue springing from grace infused by God through Christ."

Partridge (1978, 41) espouses that "the moralistic tone of the poem is directed against casual and irresponsible religious affiliations, and anticipates the kind of thinking that kindles the mature letters to friends and patrons."

Frye (1980, 47) suggests that Donne's image of truth standing on top of a hill is a "human vision of recreation" that is reminiscent of Dante's *Purgatorio* as well as Yeats's "Sailing to Byzantium."

Sellin (1980, 292–94) reads *Sat3* in the context of the Synod of Dort and the Thirty Years' War, and as a result, believes that the poem "looks forward to another poem of remarkably similar vein soon to follow, and also concerned with events in Bohemia," *HSShow* (293–94).

Shawcross (1980, 59) believes that in Plutarch's *Moralia*, "the index entry *Virtutis in philosophia profectus* leads us to the essay on *Progress in Virtue*," where one finds that Plutarch's "words on progress," written in 43 BC, sheds light on Donne's image of the hill of truth.

Mann (1981, 290) posits that *Sat3*'s "dry review and rejection of doctrinal extremes in the evaluation of women and marriage" is echoed in a later sermon (*Sermons* 3:242), and she adds that the explicit analogy between woman and religion in *Sat3* is "implied" in the Songs and Sonets, especially *Commun*.

Hester (1982, 56–57, 59–60) argues that the major satiric strategy of *Sat3*, "the alternation of 'pitty' and 'scorn' towards pathetic and ignoble examples of misdevotion," is comparable "to Juvenal's attack on the vanity of human prayers in *Satire* X" (56). He claims that just as Juvenal "concluded with a metaphoric *exemplum imitandum*," which intimates, in particular, "how man can move beyond the tragedy and mockery of this world," so Donne's speaker "concludes with a metaphoric plea for humble devotion." He adds further that Donne's speaker also imitates Juvenal's in "exhibiting the same alternating stances" between scorn and laughter, by which the speaker achieves "an exemplary contrast to the examples of misdevotion he attacks through the meditative ordering of his own mental faculties" (57). Both satirists in turn then "actualize the *mens sana*, the humility and right reason, prerequisite for devotion, in their demonstrations of the imminent and perpetual destructivenss of human misdevotion" so that the similarities between *Juvenal* X and *Sat3* suggest that Donne's poem "might well be an attempt to convert the Latin satire on the vanity of ambitious human prayers into a vehicle of Christian meditation" (57). On a separate but thematically related matter, he argues that the satirist "directs his assault at the imprudence of the valiant adventurers," who commit "all their energies to merely physical action," demonstrating the failure of these adventurers "to use their memory correctly, in accordance with the claims of Cicero, Aquinas, Augustine, and Bernard that the healthy exercise of this faculty is essential to achieving prudence" (59).

Melchiori (1983, 182) notes that *Sat3* contains a frequency of echoes from *R2*.

Baumlin (1986a, 92, 94–95, 104) argues that *Sat3* avoids both "the raging, Juvenalian style" and "the jesting, self-deprecatory manner of Horace" and that in doing so Donne "has led some of the poem's best critics to question its conformity to the classical genre." He explains that although abandoning "Juvenal's *saeva indignatio* and Horace's *sermo* style," Donne captures "the protreptic zeal and the diatribe style" of Persius (92). He believes that the "moral seriousness" of Persian diatribe "does provide an appropriate vehicle for Christian subject matter" (94) through its "complex rhetorical form" that includes such "typical stylistic and structural devices" as "paradox, hyperbole, catachresis and other forms of 'violent' metaphor; *prosopopoeia* and an impassioned, second-person address; rhetorical questions and such schemes as *subjectio* and *ante occupatio*; and, above all, monologistic dialogue, with its abrupt transitions in both speaker and argument" (95).

Baumlin (1986b, 449, 466–67) describes the persona of *Sat3* and *Sat5* as "a preacher, persuading and teaching his audience rather than ridiculing or punishing," adding that "Persius is the model for these poems, both of which rely heavily on this Roman's moral gravity and protreptic zeal." He argues that in contrast to Hall and Marston, who chose Juvenal as their model, Donne "found in Persian satire the best vehicle for his own serious Christian insights," though Donne was not fully "secure in this choice" until he had "tested the resources of all three Roman models" (466–67).

Gilman (1986a, 117) conjectures that the figure of Truth may be based either on the "personified *Veritas* described in Ripa's *Iconologia*," which appears as "an indominable nude, her sun and palm leaf and open book in her hand, her foot planted on the globe," or on "the many Renaissance versions of *Cebes' Tablet*," in which "philosophical mountaineers are shown clambering past Fortune, Opinion, and other distracting women toward the chaste figures of Truth and Felicity on the summit."

Ray (1990, 278, 284) notes of *Sat3* that "a recurring problem" for Donne is "how one is to determine what religion, in the midst of many churches and factions, is indeed the true religion" and that this problem "similarly appears" in *HSShow* (278).

Baumlin (1991, 121–22, 125–27, 131–32), repeating much of his earlier argument (1986a), urges that "Persius uses diatribe in the stoic manner, as a vehicle for cognitive (and hence moral) certitude," whereas Donne acts "more the role of cynic or skeptic" and transforms "diatribe into a vehicle for doubt." This "intrusion of skepticism," he explains, "thus denies one of the most prominent features of Persian satire: its confidence in a singular, consistent ethical foundation" (132).

Sellin (1991, 88) argues that Donne's poem that most resembles Sat3 is Cross, for both "involve religious subject matter, something quite unusual in satire"; both "eschew narrative or dialogue, consisting instead of purely dramatic monologue"; and both exhibit a structure in which they "begin dramatically as though in response to a remark uttered by another before the poem begins," then involve a "complication originating in consideration in cursu of the response of an addressee," and finally "depict an ethos of respectful benevolence correcting an object of earnest spiritual concern."

Masselink (1992, 95–97) argues that in both Sat3 and HSShow Donne "rejects extremes," adding that "in neither does he identify any earthly church as housing true religion." She comments further that Donne's "advice" in the satire to "doubt wisely" (77) and his "catalog of questions" in HSShow express "just such doubt as to where the true church is to be found," concluding that Donne is "willing to eschew individuals—the Phillips or Gregorys, the Harrys or Martins," yet "what he defends remains unspecified," as he "champions in these poems" the Church universal "defended in the sermons" (95–96).

Scodel (1993, 482, 486–87) argues that while the satiric portraits of how not to seek true religion provided in Sat3 have "Juvenalian models," the careful arrangement of these portraits "recalls Horatian depictions of opposite deviations from the mean rather than Juvenal's looser mode of progression" (486–87). He comments further that among Donne's own work the early paradoxes bear "the most fruitful parallels" to Sat3 (482).

Strier (1993, 306) believes that Biathanatos and its assertion about the role of conscience offers us the "best guide" to the poem.

Scodel (1995, 46, 50, 54–56) suggests that Sat3 "is one of three poems in which Donne imitates Horatian satire by invoking the mean," and yet, he warns, unlike Horace, Donne "does not treat the mean as an unproblematic norm," in that Donne "repeatedly transforms the mean in order to make it applicable to his search for 'true religion' in a dangerous and bewildering world of secular temptations and rival religious sects" (46). He believes that the mean position promoted in the poem is based on the scepticism of the Pyrrhonists, who were labeled not only "inquirers" and "seekers" because they "professed to search ceaselessly for the truth," but also "doubters" because they "doubted all dogmatic claims" (54).

Corthell (1997, 38) states that Sat3 "rehearses the vexed question of self-fashioning in Renaissance culture," and he suggests that the truth-seeker looks "very much like an individual, an autonomous self even," and that this individual shows up in other familiar Donnean scenes, such as Flea, in which "a defiant rejection of certain cultural codes and structures is juxtaposed with an ingenious clearing of space for a 'private' experience" that "in turn, finally opens on to an attempted but never entirely successful resolution."

Oliver (1997, 51, 64–65, 113, 164, 175) contrasts the "recognisably contemporary world of naval expeditions and religious dissent" evoked by this poem with the "literary and artificial" constructions of Gascoigne and Lodge (51). In terms of religion, the "closest parallels" to the satire are found "in texts written from firmly within the embattled Catholic minority, particularly Robert Southwell's An Humble Supplication to Her Majesty" (64). He observes that Donne's "eschatological interest" in Sat3 is echoed in *Lit, Corona*, and many of the Divine Poems (113). He also compares the "premium on investigative thinking as the route to the truth" (164) at the beginning of *Biathanatos* with *Sat3* (164), and he also notes that *Pseudo* presents "the antithesis of the argument" expressed in *Sat3*, in which "civil and religious authority are boldly pried apart from each other so that royal jurisdiction in matters of religion can be looked at with a critical eye" (175).

Patterson (1997, 30) notes that the scepticism of *Sat3* appears "with amusement and something like detachment to the issue of the Cross as supreme image and as still forbidden in the English church" in a sermon of January 1630 (*Sermons* 9:161).

Prescott (1997, 47–48) observes that Donne "hardly needed Rabelais to see that an inability to identify true religion can be figured as a failure to locate Christ's true bride," but Donne's reference to Panurge "gains texture" by juxtaposing *Sat3*'s sexual imagery with "Rabelais's demonstration of how timorous narcissism can congeal the spirit." Regardless of Donne's religious allegiance at the time, she says, "and however he read Rabelais's religion—Lutheran, Evangelical, or simply blasphemous," Donne surely recognized "a telling example of how those in power need not force conscience" (48). Further, she observes that Panurge's inability to commit to a wife resembles the speaker of *Sat3*'s unwillingness to make a religious decision, and she adds that "*this* domestic comedy has eternal consequences" (47). She notes that Donne, in "daring" to condemn "those who love a particular sect because some theologian or government tells them to," could have found a relevant example in Rabelais since Pantagruel does not force Panurge to make a choice but "joins him on his voyage to resolve his dilemma" (98), adding that neither Donne nor Panurge arrive at a final answer.

Meakin (1998, 87) uses Donne's injunction to "doubt wisely" (l. 77) in cautioning readers to formulate "the right sorts of questions," particularly regarding *Sappho*.

DiPasquale (1999, 160) compares Mirreus's idolatry in expressing reverence to the Pope with that of the lover in *Fun*, who "deals with frustration precisely as does the Catholic" of *Sat3*.

Hodgson (1999, 105) finds that *HSShow* is a poem that "parallels" *Sat3*, but the sonnet "focuses much more explicitly on a spiritual marriage to God and the Church."

Nutt (1999, 140) contrasts the "apotheosis of the intellect" in this poem with *HSBatter*, in which "'Reason' is the barrier to unity with God."

Wiggins (2000, 18, 43–46, 50) notes that in both *Sat3* and *Noct* Donne used *The Courtier* "as a standard for measuring the regime's capacity to comprehend and appreciate individuals like himself" (18). Wiggins also explores the relationship between *Sat3* and a (1589?) letter that Francis Bacon—"like Donne, filling a secretarial role for a member of the Privy Council"—wrote touching on "Elizabeth's policy in 'ecclesiastical causes' for the signature of Sir Francis Walsingham" (43). In the letter, Bacon "wrestles" with the primary matter of *Sat3*, "the conflicting imperatives of the state and the individual conscience," but Donne, "projecting himself in a poem," is more free "to speak openly of an impasse which Bacon (though as disabused as any statesman of his time) is forced to obfuscate" (45). *Sat3* then "represents the healing discourse necessitated by exercises of the sort that Bacon and other English secretaries engaged in" (46), and the "healing utterance" offered by the speaker "is generated by the same code governing the debates of Castiglione's courtiers: salvation lies in the disabused awareness of stalemate" (50).

Young (2000, 61) remarks that "the perplexity of the speaker" in *Sat3*, who finds that "none of the current conceptions of the Church is satisfactory," recalls the poetry of Henry Vaughan.

Fulton (2001, 75–76, 78, 79, 99–100, 106) notes that *Sat3* shares with Persius's first satire "a dialogue of unlabelled voices, which could either be between himself and an imaginary friend, or merely internal" (75). He remarks further that Donne's satirical treatment of religion is reminiscent of Marston's second satire in *The Scourge of Vilianie* and Guilpin's first satire. He believes further that Lucio's phrase in MM, "grace is grace, despite of all controversy" (1.2.24–25), "represents a similar concern for the problems of multiple belief systems, or even 'religions'" (78), and he compares Guildenstern's "holy and religious fear" (*Ham.* 3.3.8–10) to "the ironic criticism" of *Sat3* and *Sat4* (99). In addition, Fulton argues that *Sat3* urges the same point as Donne's later religious writing, namely, "the necessity of hard-won knowledge over false allegiance" (79), and he concludes that *Sat3*'s "treatment of the problem of obtaining religious knowledge under political pressure is part of a wider satiric criticism of socially and politically legitimated systems of belief" (106).

Kneidel (2001, 241) recognizes that in Donne's 1629 sermon on Paul's conversion (9:161–62), which echoes *Sat3*, Paul's "prudent adaptability" serves as a model for Donne "to express his changable and changing religious beliefs."

Sequence and Unity

Andreasen (1963, 64) notes the centrality of this poem "in both position and theme" and adds that this poem has organic unity in comparison with the previous two. Patrides (1985, 34–35) also notes the importance of the poem's middle position among the five Satyres.

Milgate (1967, xxiv) states that *Sat3*'s aesthetic unity is "saved by the happy chance that the possible sources of truth in religion are limited to three," a fact that is "neatly reflected in the triple structure of the whole poem," adding that there is "a limited area of subject-matter to be treated, and a consistent particular theme dominates the whole."

Medine (1972, 52) argues that "by showing that morality requires awareness, knowledge, and responsible action," *Sat3* "implies all the virtues praised" in the Satyres, namely, "the constancy and intellectual commitment" of *Sat1*; "the temperance" of *Sat2*; and "the moral sensitivity" of *Sat4*. Moreover, the "quest" described in *Sat3* "anticipates exactly" the reference to Sir Thomas Egerton in *Sat5*, where Donne addresses Egerton "in the midst of the indictment of society." In *Sat3* Egerton is seen as a "realization of the ideal" that "truth involves knowledge translated into responsible action" (51–52).

Hester (1977c, 193) espouses that the structure of the speaker's "progress in self-knowledge" throughout the Satyres and his "final achievement of a working, divinely-qualified balance between his hatred and charity" finally provide, as seen in *Sat3*, "a dramatization of the satirist's understanding of and conformity to the 'decorum' of the earliest Christian reformers."

Slights (1981, 160–61) argues that "the general neglect of the relation" of *Sat3* to the others and the "failure to understand" the "dramatic context" of *Sat3* "has obscured its imaginative vitality," contending that the poem is "central to the sequence thematically as well as numerically" so that, in particular, "the general themes of detachment and involvement and sin and virtue are particularized in a specific problem of doubt."

Hester (1982, 13, 15, 54) asserts that *Sat3*, which is "central in position and importance" in the Satyres as a whole, "dramatizes the satirist's self-confirmation of the religious basis" in his satiric enterprise (13), adding that the question posed in *Sat3* of whether or not "'railing' can 'cure these worne maladies'" is "central" to all of the Satyres (15).

Mann (1985, 539) believes that *Sat3* "reverses the degenerative cycle" of the other Satyres, which "describe contemporary experience as a process of degeneration, as a type of the biblical age from Creation to the Flood," and that, as a result of its "positive affirmations," *Sat3* "assumes a central, normative place" in the sequence.

Parry (1985, 48) states that among the Satyres, *Sat3* "alone has a steady intellectual development, an argument to unfold and a serious conclusion."

Baumlin (1986a, 99) argues that, despite the shared "dramatic, Horatian ironies" of *Sat1* and *Sat4*, the opening lines of *Sat3* have posed an intervening question about the "moral efficacy" of formal satire as a method "of achieving social change."

Sellin (1991, 85, 87, 89) contends that reading *Sat3* "as part of a greater entity betrays commitment on the part of most commentators to a subject-matter poetics," and that in the late twentieth century such an approach "is primitive, to say the least" (85). He points out that *Sat3* "is not always present in manuscript collections of the satires," that it "does not always bear the number three," and that it does not "invariably occur in the third position" (87). As such, he argues, "we cannot be absolutely sure from printed or manuscript evidence" that *Sat3* "was the third in order or that it was composed as part of the suite of satires with which we connect it" (87), and thus scholars should treat *Sat3* "as an independent entity, not as a part of a larger whole" (89).

Slights (1991, 94) comments that *Sat3* is "most interesting and significant" when read in the context of the other verse Satyres, which together "explore the problem of how to participate in human society without compromising personal integrity," particularly in the ways in which *Sat3* "complicates and disrupts any attempt to see in Donne a dramatic conversion from alienation and moral isolation to absorption within an absolutist power structure."

Stringer (1991, 80–81) explains that *Sat3* "appears in twenty-nine manuscripts and in all seven seventeenth-century editions/issues of Donne's collected poems," and he includes a chart detailing the manuscripts by their Donne Variorum sigla, their "traditional" sigla, "their historical names or library shelfmarks," "the location of the poem," and finally, "the poem's ordinal position among satires within each artifact." He concludes that scholars "will eventually come to see" *Sat3* as a "progressing 'work' constituted over the course of time by several participating 'versions,'" and any interpretive constructions must "necessarily take into account the structural and thematic implications of the poem's evolutionary nature."

Corthell (1997, 37) notes that the "interrelationship of power, change, and the subject is more fully and clearly manifested" in *Sat3* as "the problem of historicism" than in *Sat2*.

Blissett (2000, 102) observes that the "roster of devotées" in *Sat3* is exceptional, noting that usually "Donne's persons are one-on-one, even when in crowds."

Wiggins (2000, 40–41, 48, 51, 57) shows that the "step from poetry" in *Sat2* to religion in *Sat3* is "less abrupt than at first it seems" in that "the metaphor of religion" used in both poems forms a link "so firm as to constitute one piece of evidence that Donne considered his 'book of satires' to be a coherent single work in five parts" (40–41). He argues that while *Sat2* "deflates its author's ego," *Sat3* presents "the disabused apprentice statesman" summoning "all his courage to make a truly destabilizing gesture" by daring "to open the question of a state religion's influence on individual conscience" (41). Further, in "a fascinating drama of reversals," the speaker of *Sat3* answers "the very same charge that he had leveled" against the speaker of *Sat1* (48). In addition, in his "passage" from *Sat2* to *Sat3*, Donne "traded the mimetic tradition in poetry of poems imitating poems for a social mimesis in which selves constitute themselves by impersonating other selves in a manner equally as conscious as the poetic" (51). He adds that *Sat4* expresses "revulsion at the mental operation of the secretary which Donne performed" in *Sat3*, noting, however, that "the general issue of integrity is the same" in *Sat4* as in *Sat3* (57).

Fulton (2001, 74) observes that *Sat3*'s "personal nature, where 'I' and 'thou' seem to refer to the same person, and the imperatives seem self-applied, carries forward an internal voice created in the earlier satires," and especially *Sat1*.

Structure and Method

Adams (1958, 11–13) asserts that *Sat3* is "a completely unified poem, structurally." In addition to being "about one subject" and being "spoken by a single 'voice,'" the poem presents to the reader "a single cycle from the importance of religion to the need for finding true religion back to the importance of religion" (11–12). Even though he describes *Sat3* as "indeterminate or unresolved," he believes the poem succeeds in that its irresolution results from Donne's "structurally conceived" intention (13).

Geraldine (1965, 116) believes that Donne addresses three kinds of "intellectual bankruptcy" in this poem: 1) *inconsideratio* (lack of awareness); 2) *ignoratia* ("culpable ignorance"); and, 3) deliberately misguiding another, and assigns the opening 40 lines to the first kind, lines 53–89 to the second, and the remainder of the poem to the third.

Sloan (1965, 17–23) delineates that *Sat3*, when viewed through the lens of traditional rhetorical principles, is structured as follows: entrance (ll. 1–4), narration (ll. 5–42), and proof (ll. 43–110). However, he also argues that according to the Ramists, who "favored their own 'natural method' over traditional arrangement," the poem has a four-part structure: "an entrance, to gain the good will of the audience," "the argument that religion is 'worthy of all our Soules devotion,'" "the argument concerning where religion should be sought," and "the argument concerning how religion should be sought" (23).

Milgate (1967, xxiv, 140) finds a "triple structure" in *Sat3*, reflecting three "possible sources of truth in religion" (xxiv). The poem's triple structure includes three "movements": (1) an attempt to rail against "the weakness and cowardice of men in respect of religion" in lines 1–43; (2) the properly "satirical" part of the poem in lines 43–69, dealing with "the trivial reasons why men adopt a form of religion"; and finally (3) an "exhortation to an active pursuit of a personal faith," written in the "grave and forceful style of Donne's verse letters to his men friends" (140).

Roberts (1968, 107) observes that "after a brief introduction, comprising the first four lines," *Sat3* divides "into three easily recognizable sections or movements: Part I (ll. 5–42), Part II (ll. 43–88), and Part III (ll. 89–110)."

According to Lecocq (1969, 376–77), *Sat3* is structured in four movements: an introductory portrait of the interlocutor, focused on his health and his experiences; a survey, using the conceit of wooing and wedding, of the various possible religions from which the interlocutor can choose; an assertion of the quest for truth; and a discourse on human power structures and individual choice in matters of faith.

Smith (1970, 140, 143) argues that the movement of *Sat3* "amounts to a sceptical weighing of relative claims on one's devotion, in respect of the search for a possible truth" (140), and he adds that Donne "writes as a solitary contemplative who is dragged from his books, partly by his own virile urge as it appears, to witness the active depravities of public life or of Court or the Law"; however, "the studies he leaves are no more exempt from human absurdity than the life outside and have no more absolute claim on one" (143).

Shawcross (1972, 268) argues that the organization and structure of *Sat3*, which he describes as "as a triple structure within a limited area of subject matter," should not "be a basis for finding fault" with the other Satyres. As "a delimited case of conscience," *Sat3* "*should* be more closely argued, *should* be organized, *should* adhere closely to the theme," whereas similar demands need not be made of the other Satyres.

Lewalski and Sabol (1973, 6) describe *Sat3* as "a hybrid form," the first part of which presents "a serious satire both of those who ignore or scorn religion and of various type characters who represent faulty sectarian religious attitudes," while the second provides "a moral essay urging (without satiric or comic overtones) the search for true religion through honest doubting investigation."

Miller and Berrey (1974, 27–29, 37–38) assert that *Sat3* "has logical and psychological unity, a sense of thought progression" and that "the primary reason for the clarity and integrity" of the poem is that it is "carefully structured according to the framework of the cardinal virtues, one of the most basic and persistent moral patterns in Western ethical thought" (27–28). They explain that "after a preface on the satirist himself and on the contrast between nature and grace (ll. 1–15)," *Sat3* is divided into the following four parts: "the first major section depicts the irrational 'courage' of irreligious adventurers (ll. 16–32); the second, the irrational pursuit of religion by analogy with extravagant amorists (ll. 43–69); the third, the rational effort to achieve religious truth (ll. 69–88); the last, the unjust claims of civil power over the religious conscience of the individual (ll. 89–110)" (37).

Slights (1981, 161) argues that in assuming "the voice and method of a casuist" in *Sat3*, Donne subordinates ironic wit to rational discourse and "logical analysis replaces dramatic contrast as a structural principle."

Mallet (1990, 19) specifies that the argument of *Sat3* "falls into three sections: a condemnation of those who fail to seek for religious truth (lines 1–42); encouragement to seek 'true religion' despite the doubts and conflicts of an age of religious controversy (lines 43–87); and a warning that it is better to risk persecution for disobeying the secular authorities, than to risk damnation by betraying the truth reached by the efforts of the individual conscience."

Norbrook (1990, 10) concedes that Donne was often motivated by his desire for wealth and power in his career decisions, but maintains that "the dialectical movement" of *Sat3* shows something other "than a linear movement towards power," adding that in the court, Donne "never really did gain a secure foothold."

Sellin (1991, 88) argues that *Sat3* and *Cross* both exhibit a structure in which they "begin dramatically as though in response to a remark uttered by another before the poem begins," then involve a "complication originating in consideration *in cursu* of the response of an addressee," and finally "depict an ethos of respectful benevolence correcting an object of earnest spiritual concern."

Smith (1992, 81) explains that the opening lines of *Sat3* "confront us with a bizarre medley of moral questions" and "the movement" of the remainder of the poem "amounts to a sifting of the relative claims on our devotion that commonly distract us from our absolute obligation to seek the truth."

Corthell (1997, 38, 40) traces the arc of the argument in *Sat3* as it moves from a meditation on authority, through an analysis of different religious positions, to an ambivalent conclusion about the nature of power, and argues that the poem is structured like a "good new historicist essay." He concludes that the poem is both "constituted" and "divided" by "the erotically construed search for what is lacking—true religion—and by a set of relationships to power" (40).

Language and Style

Coleridge (1811 [1984, 12.2:225–26, 228]) reveals his admiration for Donne's poetry in two marginal notes on *Sat3*. In the first he writes, "if you would teach a Scholar in the highest form, how to *read*, take Donne, and of Donne this Satire. When he has learnt to read Donne, with all the force & meaning which are involved in the Words—then send him to Milton—& he will stalk on, like a Master, *enjoying* his Walk" (225–26); and in the second, "Knotty, double-jointed Giant! Cramp of Strength!" (228).

Chadwick (1900, 36–37), within a review of Gosse (1899), asserts that in lines 79–84 of *Sat3* we find "one of those splendid figures which illuminate the tortuous darkness of Donne's most serious and difficult verse," and he concludes that "the metre does not necessitate the proper reading in such lines as these, and if Donne, knowing what he meant, and preferring quantity to accent, could read them musically, the secret of his art is hidden from us," adding that Gosse "has done little to make it opener than it has been heretofore."

Leavis (1935, 238) notes the dramatic qualities of *Sat3*.

Legouis (1952, 99), to illustrate the dramatic quality of Donne's poetry, points to *Sat3*.

Gransden (1954, 102–03) argues that only *Sat3* "seems wholly to have engaged Donne's personal feelings" and that "the strong, yet extraordinarily expressive blank verse is forced, by his poetic will, to become in its sounds and movement the meaning which, in lesser poets, blank verse merely clothes" (102–03). He further states that the "modernity" of the controversy in *Sat3* "between God's word and its differing interpreters" makes this "the most readable and interesting" of the Satyres, adding that the poem's "homogeneity," "lucidity," and "objectivity," as well as its "lack of sensationalism," make the poem "far less Juvenalian, far less of a 'farrago,'" than *Sat1* and *Sat2*, "which run much more to type" (104).

Kermode (1957, 28, 37) finds the poem's "brisk impatience" appropriate for satire but unexpected in a "deliberative poem about religion" (28), adding that even the young Donne found "the language of passionate exploration and rebuke appropriate to religious themes" (37).

Martz (1960, 338) explains that the satiric base of *Sat3* is created by "the coarse language, the rough meter, the tone of fierce contempt."

Milgate (1967, xxiii) finds Donne in *Sat3* testing "language to the full, to achieve density and compactness as well as energy and vigour." He believes that Donne tries out even "what seemed to be viable of the current attempts to Latinize English," and he points to lines 69–71, in which Donne uses the couplet "with a sensitiveness to rhetorical utterance and a freedom (not to say a licence) which dramatists did not attempt in blank verse until later."

Roberts (1968, 106, 108–09) states that "there is a distinction between the serious and the solemn" and that in reading Donne, and *Sat3* in particular, one must understand that when Donne "is most serious, he can be playful and witty; and when he is most solemn, he can be most artificial and insincere" (106). He comments further that the contrast in the first half of the poem between secular courage and spiritual courage "re-enforces the idea of frustration and confusion" and that the "images of strenuous human activity" that predominate in the first half "contrast effectively" in the second half "with the serene and calm images of Truth and God," adding that much of the imagery "is clearly sexual" (108–09).

Lecocq (1969, 378) finds the final movement of *Sat3* to be moving and lyrical, an intriguing accompaniment to the poem's overall logical argumentation that suggests that Donne is addressing not only his friend but himself as well.

Menascè (1969, 51) states that in language and style *Sat3* is almost a sermon.

Kermode (1970, xix) points out that *Sat3* examines the "relation between wise doubt and certainty," and although the poem "is stylistically rugged" in imitation of Renaissance satire, it stands out as "a deliberative poem about the choice of religion."

Smith (1970, 140) comments that the opening of *Sat3* "moves abruptly through a series of seemingly disparate considerations" and that such movement "amounts to a sceptical weighing of relative claims on one's devotion" in the "search for a possible truth."

Kermode (1971, 136) notes that the poem is "odd" in "the brisk impatience of its manner, an exasperated harshness proper to satire but strange in a deliberative poem about religion."

Powers (1971, 48–49, 181–83) remarks that Donne ignores "the restraints of the single line, splitting the grammatical units, and letting not only parts but even split words run over to the next line," and that in doing so Donne's primary concern "seems to have been to give the surge of speech rhythms," which he intended "to be strongly felt" (48–49). In addition, he comments on the use of first names for "the representatives of contemporary religions" and asserts that through this choice Donne "converted the several realms of experience" expressed in the poem "into the terminology (and conceptual form) of the one that is most familiar and meaningful to the young man the Satirist is addressing" (182–83).

Erskine-Hill (1972, 275–76) notes that in the opening lines of Sat3 "the alternative attitudes of laughter or tears conflict with and check one another" and that the poem, in "the confusion of conflicting claims with which the seeker after 'true religion' must contend," thereby "calls each attitude into play at different points."

Miller and Berrey (1974, 38–39, 41–42) argue that "variations in diction and imagery" confirm that Donne "consciously based" Sat3 on "the pattern of the cardinal virtues," namely, fortitude, temperance, prudence, and justice (38–39). They also note that the imagery in the latter half of the poem "differs sharply" from that of the first half in that "it shifts from the hectic world of adventurers and amorists to a landscape dominated by the hill of Truth, the stream of power, and a flower preserved by a right relation to the headwaters of the stream" (41). They explain that the final lines are "less tightly knit" because Donne combines questions, imperatives, and declarative analogies (42).

Raizada (1974, 103) points out that Sat3's imagery is "largely sexual," and underlying the poem "is a picture of the amorous inclinations of the Elizabethan gallant" and thus for the various religious sects, Donne presents "characters who have eccentric sexual preferences."

Elliott (1976, 105) observes that because Sat3 is "more personal and subdued in tone and because its even clarity contrasts with the roughness and obscurity" of the other Satyres, critics have more readily treated the poem separately.

Hester (1976, 100–01) argues that in Sat3 79–84, "the spiraling motion of the pilgrim's mind, which contrasts with "the rectilinear movement of the adventurers and amorists" offers "the most significant feature of Donne's image" and that, in particular, "the circularity of the progress around the hill in combination with the gradual rectilinear movement up it by the pilgrim reproduces that spiral motion which ancient, medieval, and Renaissance philosophy alike delineated as emblematic of the motions of the rational soul of man."

Hiller (1977, 15) notes that Sat1 and Sat3 are "personal meditations," in which "the thought is vigorous and forceful, the imagery arresting, the verse rugged and often irregular." Sat3 in particular, he says, "does not quietly expound a philosophy already resolved upon" but instead "dramatizes the poet's attempts to formulate one," adding that "it is as if Donne is working out his own salvation as he writes."

Sinha (1977, 66–67) remarks that the wit in Sat3, "seen in the imagery which is largely sexual," becomes "transformed by a genuine passion and an eager mind at work, the last of which makes the poem intensely dramatic," adding that the "undoubted feeling of sincerity" in the poem is "penetrated by an intense hunger for truth."

Hester (1978a, 54) argues that in Sat3 "the spiral motion of the pilgrim up and around the hill" is "enforced by both the diction and syntax of Donne's image" so that as "a satire spoken to a general Elizabethan audience," the poem dramatizes "the internal process on which man's active life must be based."

Carey (1981, 13) espouses that "no one before Donne had written English verse in which the pressures of passionate speech could be retained with such unhindered power."

Bradshaw (1982, 338–40, 352–54, 356–58) asserts that in Sat3 "the metrical complication corresponds with the concentration of intense thought and feeling" (340) so that "the sustained rises are perfectly adapted to express emotional and intellectual stress—the struggle to apprehend and control violent emotion, and the effortful process of difficult thought" (352). He believes that it is "difficult to exaggerate the originality and importance of Donne's achievement in this poem" (352–53), remarking that "the extraordinary rhythmic command necessarily depends upon Donne's pressing the iambic pentameter to its limits while keeping within those limits" (354) and that Donne could not have produced such stylistic effects in Sat3 "without a grasp on the distinction between lexical accent and metrical ictus" (356).

Corthell (1982, 165) contends, with respect to Sat3, that the intellectual "endeavor" of "defining individual responsibility in an authoritarian system" cries out "for quibbles and paradoxes" in a manner that suggests that Donne was "influenced by the style of political argument used by an oppressed religious minority."

Stein (1984, 81–82) remarks that Sat3 is "often personal in its language" in that "some of the answers are presented as near and easy, and the speaker sympathetically tries to encourage other seekers" (81).

Baumlin (1986a, 92, 96–98, 104), noting Donne's "contempt for slavish imitators," asserts that in Sat3 Donne's "re-creation of a Persian voice avoids close verbal imitation" (92) by instead echoing Persius in "the distinctive tone of native homily and complaint" (97). Yet, he insists that "Persius evidently taught Donne much about concise expression and complexity of syntax, rigorous argumentation, abrupt transitions in thought, hyperbolic and catechretical imagery, the drama and forcefulness of second-person address" (104).

Van Emden (1986, 50–51) observes that the movement of Sat3 "echoes the meaning" and that "the rhythmical patterns vary a good deal" as Donne stresses the physical effort of the pilgrim, "so that the total effect is not of a flowing, dexterous verse form like that, for instance, of Pope," but rather "it is harsh and demanding, as befits a poem revealing something of the struggles of a young Elizabethan Catholic who wanted fame and fortune, but not at the expense of truth."

Warnke (1987, 23) argues that the "intense evocation of the necessary religious quest and the psychological obstacles" of Sat3 make it "surely the most powerful and dramatic" of the Satyres, adding that in the poem "wit is used most purposefully—rather than, as so often in the young Donne, for its own sake alone."

Mallet (1990, 19) notes that although some critics have suggested that Donne "learned his poetic skills from the example of the London theatres," there are parts of Sat3 in which "the verse is handled with a freedom and assurance that was not to be heard on the stage until the end of the 1590s."

Tomlinson (1990, 29–30) argues that Sat3 shares "the decasyllabic rhyming couplets that became much more popular in the long reign of Dryden, Pope and Johnson," adding that that "inert, technical fact is about all Donne's couplets share with any of the later verse."

Watts (1990, 15–16) believes that, as in *Sat3*, Donne's "most effective moments occur when the strenuous style coincides with a strenuous imagined activity," stating, by analogy, "if you like modern jazz, you should like Donne's rhythms, for, having established the basic metre" of iambic pentameter, he "likes to challenge it with powerfully varied counter-rhythms." He adds that Donne "preferred to dramatise spontaneity and struggle by using the rhymes as resistances to be overcome" and that the enjambment frequently "seems to force the sense through the unavailing barrier provided by the rhyme."

Baumlin (1991, 120–21, 126–27, 130) comments that readers describe *Sat3* "as the most forceful and most confident" of the Satyres, yet the opening lines "reveal the poet's continued anxiety over the form and function" of satire (120–21). He adds that "in contrast to Hall's or Marston's confident programmatic assertions of the power of their literary form," *Sat3* exhibits a "very tentativeness of such language" (121). Finally, he states, "since the poem's more controversial arguments are concealed within such tortuously complex syntax and ambiguous, equivocal language," Donne "may simply be responding to the stylistic decorum of his Persian model," but it is more likely that Donne "finds in obscurity a political safeguard—and political expediency is assumed to be a cause of Persius's own stylistic obscurity" (130).

Sellin (1991, 86, 88) finds *Sat3* "less irregular, as it were less shaggy, than the other so-called satyr poems," which he believes "suggests differentiation from" the other Satyres (86). Further, he describes *Sat3* as "purely dramatic," in contrast to *Sat1*, *Sat2*, and *Sat4*, which he states "are all narrative in manner of presentation," and thus, "the relationship between the 'I' and the audience" in *Sat3* is "utterly different" from that in the other Satyres.

Stringer (1991, 80), in response to Sellin's (1991) assertion of the regularity of meter in *Sat3*, contends that "no one up to now has collected the data that would justify any but the most cautious of pronouncements about the meter of any of the satires."

Frontain (1995, 5) suggests that in *Sat3* Donne imagines the speaker's search for the true Church "in a witty reversal of the terms of the Petrarchan conceit of woman as an angelic or redemptive force deserving to be worshiped," and by "importing Spenserian allegory into formal verse satire," Donne embodies the Church as "a woman besought by the male lover/believer."

Corthell (1997, 42) recognizes that Donne's hill of truth "is encircled by paradoxes and problems," including those "on force, the riddle of truth and falsehood (ll. 72–73), the regressive interrogations of fathers (ll. 71–72), and the puzzling lines on 'hard knowledge' and 'mysteries…dazling, yet plaine to'all eyes' (ll. 87–88)."

Nutt (1999, 117–18, 121) quotes Coleridge's comment on learning to read from this poem, suggesting that in *Sat3* Coleridge "found a rich combination of sound and feeling, thought and structure" (117). Nutt states that the opening fifteen lines demonstrate "how firmly rhyme is subordinate to sense" in that we "almost fail to notice" Donne's rhyming couplets "because his frequent enjambment disguises them so effectively" (118). Further, he finds *Sat3* "full of emotion and passion," a poem "firmly under control: something Coleridge would have admired enormously" (121).

Fulton (2001, 75) notes that in *Sat3* Donne "uses the first person singular only once," adding that "in a more public manner" than the other Satyres, Donne "frequently uses the plural 'we' or 'our' to signify the public realm of Britain."

NOTES AND GLOSSES

1–43 *Kind pity…Seeke true Religion*; **MILGATE** (1967): "Since the pity and scornful laughter proper to a satirist are mutually destructive, a cure of the weakness and cowardice of men in respect of religion might be effected by railing" (140). **SCODEL** (1995): Donne "first seeks a mean of proper emotional response as he confronts mankind's sinful neglect of religion and then boldly transforms the Aristotelian mean of courage in order to advocate brave spiritual battle against sin" (46). **REID** (2000) states that these lines illustrate "the contorted, ingenious manner that is the vice of Donne's style" (46).

1–15 *Kind pity…damn'd?* **DAALDER** (1986): "no assumption about English in Donne's time can straighten out" the accentual roughness of these lines, and "we are not entitled to believe that we can systematically infer his accentuation in speech from his practice in verse" (99). **MAHLER** (1991): instead of confronting an object in an aggressive manner from the beginning, the speaker holds back and asks questions. With that, the question is immediately established on the grounds of the satirical speaker building his supposedly healing criticism. If the norm of *virtus* was valued as a basic virtue by the Roman satirists, then belief would have to be the corresponding Christian analog. The question of religion as legitimization of satirical speech is evident in the reflexive nature of *Sat3* and provides it with a fundamentally meditative characteristic; if only true belief could lead to a release, true bravery presents itself as the appropriate search for the truth, which does not, however, want to be taken over from others as a complete concept, but must, rather, be discovered individually (42).

1–9 *Kind pity…to them?* **MOORE** (1969): the poem begins with Donne "describing his own state of mind and posing a series of questions," the "balanced division in Donne's mind" being caused by "the state of the world or, more specifically, by man's lack of devotion to 'faire Religion.' The poet's response of both anger and pity is appropriate, because the cause of man's lack of devotion is a stupidity that deserves scorn, but the result—damnation—is too serious to be anything but pitied. As a result, the poet is paralyzed. He cannot devote himself entirely to either anger or sorrow" (43).

1–7 *Kind pity…blind Age?* **RAY** (1990): "The speaker (Donne?) begins with conflicting emotions: 'pity' prevents his 'spleen' (considered to be the seat of scorn within one) from venting itself, while 'scorn' prevents his tears (evidence of 'pity') from flowing. He cannot, then, either laugh scornfully or weep pitifully: neither of these is the 'wise' way. He will attempt to purge his emotions and convey his satire by 'railing,' bitterly and harshly scolding or criticizing the maladies he perceives ('worn' because of existing a long time)." Further, Donne's "question in ll. 5–7 implies that those of the 'first blinded age,' of pre-Christian times that did not have the light of Christian truth, were devoted to their ideal of virtue even more than Christians are to the Christian religion" (278).

1–4 *Kind pity…worne maladyes?* CAZAMIAN (1952): these lines indicate the "state of repression under which Donne writes" (363). ROBERTS (1968): these lines "establish a tone of despair which is indicated by the various paradoxical contrasts that suggest desire and urgency for action on the one hand and yet an inability to act and frustration on the other that forces from the speaker the most agonizing protests" (107). [Similarly, Lecocq (1969, 375), who also questions if railing can teach one the proper way to choose a religion.] ELLIOTT (1976): "the speaker has retreated to the seclusion of his study to meditate upon his ambivalent feelings toward the city of men and upon the seeming ineffectiveness of satire as a cure for evil" (112). HESTER (1978a): "The thrust of his announcement is that he must not 'laugh' only at the sins of his countrymen nor 'weepe' only for their condition. Rather, because these 'maladies' are 'worne,' that is, habitual and therefore not easily displaced, he must both disclose the idiocy of such practices (through ridicule—'brave scorn') and explain the need for and acceptability of healthy alternatives (through charitable exhortation—'Kinde pitty') in order to 'be wise.' In this sense, his oxymoronic urgings do not render him impotent as a satirist, but dictate the form and method his 'railing' must assume. In this context, the word 'railing' takes on several connotations. If it means the angry ridicule of the ancient satirists, then it is a pejorative term; but if 'railing' means the combination of *laus et vituperatio*—in this case, the Christian attitude of charity for sinners and hatred for their sins—then it can posit a 'cure' for the present age. It is precisely such a form of 'railing' that the satirist employs throughout the poem, in fact, as he follows each satirical portrait of a current mental failure with charitable instruction as to how that limitation can be overcome. His opening lines satisfy the 'Question' section of a typical meditation, then, by examining 'What [he] thinke[s] and should thinke' as a Christian satirist" (38–39). CAREY (1981): Donne "seeks relief in anger, denouncing the pastimes (sex, squabbling, adventure) on which young men like himself fritter away their energies" (12). CORTHELL (1982): "the satirist seems momentarily unable to define even his relation to the satirized" (162). BAUMLIN (1986a): "The satirist begins, suggestively, by denying the splenetic outbursts of hate and 'just offense' that characterize the Juvenalian persona of 'Satyre II': pity now 'chokes' his spleen. At the same time he declares that he 'must not laugh' at sins in the manner of a Horace. The satirist, in short, has discovered how difficult it is to find an appropriate response toward 'sinnes': any of the reactions conventionally associated with the classical satirists would conflict with his own 'kindness,' his 'bravery,' or his 'wisdom.'" Yet, "the reference to 'cure' may surprise, for the word marks the first time in Donne's collection of satires that his speaker even alludes to the possibility of reform through this literary genre" (100). STRIER (1993): opening "in a state of puzzled yet highly stylized self-contemplation," the speaker exists "in a state of anxiety and bafflement," stressing "both his emotionality and his baffled state." The speaker's emotions "interfere with one another," and "we are thrown suddenly and uncomfortably not just into the speaker's mind but into his internal bodily processes. 'Spleen' was a term with a range of reference that was simultaneously and ambiguously psychological and physiological." Further, "the opening sentence ends with the speaker considering a response that is different from both laughing and weeping, and presumably (but not assuredly) compatible with 'wisdom,'" and Donne's "complex and conflicted proem to the satire seems to end (fitly) by questioning the efficacy of a mode that it was about to adopt. Neither we nor the poet are sure that there is a satiric mode able both to 'cure these worne maladies' and to enable the speaker to 'be wise'" (286–88). [Similarly, Wiggins (2000, 46).] **FULTON** (2001): the opening lines "derive power from the very fact that they undermine the confidence of the satiric mode that gives them expression" and "announce a kind of skepticism of and freedom from even this system of thought" (81).

1–3 *Kind pity...be wise,* **HEBAISHA** (1971) calls this "a lament" on the death of Donne's brother (33). **HESTER** (1977c): the satirist's "meditation on the dynamic use of the three powers of the rational soul begins with lines that read like a paraphrase of [Thomas] Becon's definition of the 'zeal' of the Prophets [in the seventh homily of the *Book of Homilies*]" (189). **KERINS** (1984): "The assumption of moral rectitude and the display of courtly wit are perhaps the two most basic authenticating devices of traditional satire," and the poem "opens with an explicit denial of those satiric formulas." Thus, "Donne affirms that the pursuit of wisdom denies the easy answers provided by either satiric mode," so that "the use of 'Kinde' engages the satirist's awareness of his involvement in mankind," and "brave scorn" "underlines his public role as a satiric poet in a sophisticated society" (45). **TREVOR** (2000): "contrary to what Donne claims in his 1622 letter to Goodyer," he is "well aware of the spleen" (91).

1–2 *Kind pity...my eylids.* **RICHTER** (1902) cites the rhymed words of the couplet here to illustrate level stress (409). **STEIN** (1942) observes the feminine/masculine rhyme caused by the stress-shift in the last foot (681). **SMITH** (1970): the opening lines move "abruptly through a series of seemingly disparate considerations," it being Donne's "characteristic mode to call in a diversity of circumstances, weighing this area of concern against that, so as to see a claim or an experience relative to other human affairs" (140). **SMITH** (1971): the satirist "turns now to an evidence of human folly which equally evokes his derisive anger and his fellow-feeling of pity, so that the two impulses frustrate each other" (480). [So also, Singh (1992, 39) and Scodel (1993, 481).] **JAFFE** (1977): the poem "opens with a kind of chiasmus," in which "pity relates to tears, scorn relates to spleen, and the emotions clearly conflict. If he had felt pity alone, he might have succeeded in the tragic mode of satire, or he might not have tried his hand at satire at all. If he had felt scorn without pity, he might have found laughing satire congenial or, again, he might have dismissed the abusers of relition as too trivial to write about. But the speaker feels both emotions; and the conflict, especially as expressed in the closed pattern of a chiasmus, seems to imply a stasis in the speaker's mind, a recognition that no solution is available" (95). [Similarly, Blissett (2000, 112).] **MALLET** (1990): "the 'sins' he is about to consider demand his pity for those who are his fellow human beings, but they also provoke his contempt, so that the two impulses check each other" (19). **EDWARDS** (2001): these lines "may be interpreted as a display of self-satisfied and patronizing contempt for those whom he is about to denounce" (200).

1 *Kind pity...scorne forbids* **NUTT** (1999): "The harsh consonants of the first line, 'Kinde', 'chokes' and 'scorn', and the abrupt caesura after 'spleene' before the poem has even begun, are all indicative of anger" (117). **FULTON** (2001): this line "echoes (or

informs) the language" of *Sat3* as it indicates that Donne and Guilpin "had already developed between them a vocabulary for discussing satire," and thus, the line both "connotes a generic mode" and "speaks an insider language" (83–84). **SUHAMY** (2001): the two extra accents on the first and the seventh syllables provoke a heaviness in the spondee not deprived of expressivity, but not threatening the iambic rhythm, since the even syllables are filled with accents. After all, by its nature, poetic diction is more regular, more hammered out than ordinary speech; the overabundant accents which create clusters of spondees here do not provoke a return to prose nor an anticipation of free verse (410–11).

1 *Kind pity choakes my spleene;* **MILGATE** (1967): "the pity 'natural' to a well-disposed man (which chokes with grief the satirist's scornful laughter)" (140). **BAKER** (1975): "Natural (kind) compassion tempers my ridicule and laughter" (72).

1 *Kind pity* **ENRIGHT** (1997): "fellow-feeling" (96).

1 *choakes* **PATRIDES** (1985): "'checks' (acc. to 1635–54)" (224).

1 *spleene;* **JOHNSON** (1755): "Anger; spite; ill-humour." [So also, Rudrum, Black, and Nelson (2000, 120).] **GROSART** (1872–73): "from the context (line 3), it would seem to mean splenetic laughter" (1:27). [So also, Milgate (1967, 140), quoting Persius, *Sat.* 1:11–12 and citing Hall, *Virgidemiarum* 4:1, 74; Rousseau and Rudenstine (1972, 64); Kermode and Hollander (1973, 1045; 1975, 739); Broadbent (1974, 106); Patrides (1985, 224); Willmott (1985, 61); Carey (1990, 425); Jones (1991, 629); and Singh (1992, 39).] **BEWLEY** (1966): "thought to be the seat of melancholy" (175). [So also, Clements (1966, 59), who adds that it was also the seat of "mirth," Hiller (1977, 180), Patrides (1985, 224), Hieatt (1987, 236), Enright (1997, 96), Nutt (1999, 118), Blissett (2000, 112), Chmielewski (2001, 616), and Fulton (2001, 80–81).] **SHAWCROSS** (1967): "the seat of anger and ridicule" (22). **FULTON** (2001): by using this term, Donne "orients himself in the convention of a satirist defending his voice against conflicting internal and external voices," as Persius does in his first satire (80). Donne's only other use of the word occurs in *EG* 11–12, which probably predates *Sat3* (83).

1 *braue scorne* **MILGATE** (1967): "a 'fine show' of scorn (demanded of the satirist)" (140). **KERMODE AND HOLLANDER** (1973): "the flaunting scorn of the satirist" (1045).

1 *braue* **SHAWCROSS** (1967): "superior" (22).

2 *These teares…my eylids.* **RICHTER** (1902) uses this line to illustrate level stress (395–96).

3–7 *I must…blind Age?* **GRANSDEN** (1970): "The use of classical models by Christian writers inevitably involved them in confusions which could not always be reconciled. The replacement of pagan philosophy by the Christian faith could make even the best classical models seem morally deficient" (14).

3–4 *I must…worne maladyes?* **JAFFE** (1977): "Without answering the question, the poet simply plunges into the subject as if he cannot help himself. Offering no substantive transition, he moves from one rhetorical question about his satire to further unanswered questions about religion" (95).

3 *I must...be wise,* SMITH (1971): "the wise course is neither to laugh at sins nor to weep over them" (481). [So also, Kermode and Hollander (1973, 1045), Willmott (1985, 61), Mallet (1990, 19), Singh (1992, 39), and Enright (1997, 96).] ROUSSEAU AND RUDENSTINE (1972): "i.e., I must nonetheless be wise" (64). WHEELER (1992): Donne "refers to the two possible attitudes toward sin," one based on "'the plaintive Prophete Ieremie'" and another based on "'the pleasant poet Horace.'" For the confluence of these two attitudes, "Democritus of Abdera was referred to as the laughing philosopher, while Heraclitus of Ephesos was conventionally the weeping philosopher. Donne believes that even Heraclitus would laugh to see the pretentious Macrine" (119–20). SCODEL (1993): Donne's "rejection of laughter and weeping sounds Stoic. Seneca argues that the wise man should 'calmly' accept human faults without either laughing or weeping because he should not trouble himself with others' misfortunes. Seeking passionless detachment from the foolish world, the Stoics advised suppressing the emotions rather than bringing them to the mean, as Aristotle recommended," and "like many of his contemporaries, Donne the satirist is more Aristotelian than Stoic regarding the emotions. He does not seek Stoic impassivity. Though he wants to avoid the extremes of laughter or weeping, he does not suggest that his 'pitty' and 'scorn' are themselves improper" (482).

3 *Laugh,* MILGATE (1967): "laugh to scorn"; see *OED*, vb. 5 (140). [So also, Jones (1991, 629).]

3 *weepe* MILGATE (1967): "lament with tears"; see *OED*, vb. II. 6 (140). [So also, Baker (1975, 72), Hiller (1977, 180), and Jones (1991, 629).]

4 *May rayling...worne maladyes?* STEIN (1944b): the line exemplifies a characteristically Donnean harshness in its "insistent repetition" of a vowel sound, a "relentless hunting a sound to death" (404). SCODEL (1993): this line "fully reveals that Donne seeks not Stoic detachment but rather an efficacious and therefore morally justifiable expression of emotion. 'Railing' recalls Juvenal's most familiar stance, the angry abuse that stems from indignation. Yet Donne does not simply vent his rage in a Juvenalian outburst; instead he weighs the propriety of giving expression to his anger. His sense that expressing rage might be the best response to sin runs counter to Stoic but not to Aristotelian norms. Seneca argues that both Heraclitus's weeping and Democritus's laughter are better responses to folly than anger, the most violent emotion; Aristotle, by contrast, argues that there is a mean of virtuous anger" (482–83). CORTHELL (1997): the "beneficent aspect of railing is always accompanied by a dark potential for inflicting injury or causing disorder," so "the railer is at risk" since his "free speech might be read as sedition" (40–41). FULTON (2001): in this line, Donne "shifts subtly" to a concern for wisdom, "which should have been covered by the self-confident satiric mode ('brave scorn') that he struggles to maintain in the first two lines, but, it seems, is not." Further, "whether wisdom may be found in either state or mode of expression is an uncertainty that continues in the question" of this line (81).

4 *rayling* LECOCQ (1969): this word simply designates the spirit of satire. Writers

of the end of the sixteenth century employ it because it is a pejorative term, and satire passes for a low and despicable genre. It is their way of saying that they know that this genre is disdained, and to deflect, when they cultivate it, the sarcasms of their detractors (376). **SMITH** (1971): "abusing, inveighing against them" (481). [So also, Kermode and Hollander (1973, 1045), Willmott (1985, 61), Craik and Craik (1986, 258), Mallet (1990, 19), and Singh (1992, 39).]

4 *worne maladyes?* **FULTON** (2001): According to "the generic conventions within which Donne tightly operates, 'worn maladies' would imply social ailments—worn, as if ineffectually treated by other forms of discourse" (81).

4 *worne* **MILGATE** (1967): "stale and hackneyed" (140). **SMITH** (1971): "long-standing; ingrained" (481). [So also, Kermode and Hollander (1973, 1045), Patrides (1985, 224), Craik and Craik (1986, 258), Lloyd-Evans (1989, 295), Mallet (1990, 19), Jones (1991, 629), and Singh (1992, 39).]

5–43 *Is not…Oh where?* **MINER** (1969): "To Donne, born a Catholic in a Protestant country of rival Establishment and reform factions, the crisis of conscience was in no small measure a question of defining religion aright" (151).

5–42 *Is not…dost lothe.* **SLIGHTS** (1991): "This auditor has been taught that devoting himself to the world, the flesh, and the devil is to court damnation and that he must seek salvation through the church God has instituted. The satirist's rhetorical questions aren't meant to provide a startlingly new system of values or to condemn the life of a soldier and courtly gallant as inherently sinful, but to jolt his auditor from apathy. He challenges the young man to recognize the discrepancy between his religion and the activities and attitudes that actually make up his life." These lines "situate religion logically and chronologically within a social context, identifying it as the communal, traditional faith of the Christian and establishing its supreme importance over other objects of devotion offered by contemporary society" (92).

5–22 *Is not…north discoueryes,* **POWERS** (1971): these lines demonstate the satirist's method of posing "jabbing rhetorical questions" which demand to be answered (80).

5–20 *Is not…the earthe?* **BAUMLIN** (1986a): the "goal" of this section is "to make its audience aware of the enormity of the situation, aware of the pointlessness of all human actions when spiritual needs are neglected. To accomplish this, Donne's speaker turns to a favorite device of the Persian diatribist, a series of rhetorical questions or *percontationes*" (96).

5–15 *Is not…To follow, damn'd?* **SHAWCROSS** (1972): the poem "makes clear both man's retreat from religion and also his confusion. No longer does 'our Mistresse faire Religion' receive our soul's devotion: we will not now join our father's spirit in heaven, where he has met the faithful, blind philosophers of the age before God's enlightenment, for we shall be damned" (256). **KERMODE, FENDER, AND PALMER** (1974): the speaker asks, "shouldn't religion be as important to us as virtue was in the age before the Incarnation, the blinded age, the age of the pagan philosophers? Shouldn't the joys of heaven, of which we have assurance, be as strong to us, control our passions, as the desire for earthly honour did in the pagan world?" (64). [Similarly, Willmott (1985, 61).]

5–9 *Is not...to them?* **MINER** (1969) cites these lines as an instance in which the poem takes a "lyric and affirmative" turn (162). **SINHA** (1977): we discover that, "surprisingly," most of the poem is "an extended sexual conceit," and *Sat3* "affects us through this. Underlying the satire is a picture of the amorous proclivities of the Elizabethan gallant" (67). **HESTER** (1978a): "The delineation of the present age as the second 'blinded age' and the comparison of the eternal rewards of 'devotion' with the temporal rewards of 'vertue' are commonplace to Christian satire, of course; the most significant phrase here is 'all our Soules devotion.' It denotes, on the one hand, the satirist's concern with the soul of every man and, on the other, his realization that devotion entails the exercise of 'all' of each man's soul, that is, all his rational faculties" (39–40).

5–7 *Is not...blind Age?* **SPARROW** (1931): this passage is "not asked in the spirit of a rhetorical question" (146). **SLIGHTS** (1972): "What horrible irony, he laments, if pagan philosophers should be saved on the basis of a good life directed by reason unaided by revelation, while you throw away the chance of salvation" (95). [Similarly, Hieatt (1987, 236).] **KERINS** (1984) identifies these lines as "the symbolic center," in which Donne "links the moral realm with the secular: 'faire Religion' is 'our Mistresse'—the language of the two satiric viewpoints coalesces" (45–46). **STRIER** (1993): these lines are "meant to be sarcastic, perhaps a form of 'railing,'" yet they emerge "as more baffled than biting as Donne reveals that the sins or 'maladies' with which the poem is here concerned are failures in spiritual commitment" (288).

5 *Mistres fayre Religion* **COFFIN** (1937): the phrase corresponds to the unnamed mistresses in the Songs and Sonets as an object of Donne's "courtship" [similarly, Nutt (1999, 118)], and the line is comparable to *Sat4* 163 in that Donne identifies truth with religion at this point in his life (57). **SINGH** (1992): "The search for a true church will be described in the poem in terms of a man's search for a good woman. The use of sexual metaphors to characterize religious pursuits is characteristic of Donne, but it receives sanction from the Bible where the Church is described as the Bride of Christ" (39). **CORTHELL** (1997): Donne's "admission of desire into the poem by means of the witty figure of 'our Mistresse faire Religion' can be interpreted as a destabilizing move with respect to subjectification" (40). **FULTON** (2001): "the rather sudden jump" to this figure "momentarily" brings together the elegiac and satiric modes (85).

5 *Religion* **RICHTER** (1902) questions if "ion" is to be read here as bisyllabic or monosyllabic (404).

6 *worthy* **STEIN** (1944c): an example of an elided "y" ending before a word beginning with a vowel (390).

6 *all our Soules deuotion* **MILLER AND BERREY** (1974): "not merely 'the single souls of each of us' but rather 'the whole soul, all the soul of each of us'?" (40).

6 *all* **GROSART** (1872–73): the word "is usually and properly dropped, as it throws

the accents all wrong; and as in the previous line we have 'Relig|ion|,' so we must have 'devo|tion|,' not de|votion|'" (1:27).

7 *As vertu…blind Age?* **SMITH** (1971): "the early pagan philosophers, who lived perforce in blind ignorance of Christ and true religion, none the less gave their devotion to the abstract idea of virtue" (481).

7 *vertu* **GROSART** (1872–73): "virtus, valour" (1:27). **BROADBENT** (1974): "classical ethics as opposed to Christian religion" (106).

7 *to* **PATRIDES** (1985): "(acc. to 1635–69 and most MSS): 'in' (acc. to 1633 and a few MSS)" (224).

7 *the first blind Age?* **KENNER** (1964): "the heyday of Greece and Rome, before the Christian revelation was vouchsafed" (42). [So also, Rousseau and Rudenstine (1972, 64), Kermode and Hollander (1973, 1045), Hiller (1977, 180), Craik and Craik (1986, 258), Lloyd-Evans (1989, 299), Mallet (1990, 19), Singh (1992, 39), Enright (1997, 96), Nutt (1999, 118), and Rudrum, Black, and Nelson (2000, 120).] **BEWLEY** (1966): "Although antiquity did not possess the light of Christian revelation, many of the pagans led noble and heroic lives. Earthly honor inspired them to virtue as the hope of salvation inspired a later age" (175). [So also, Chmielewski (2001, 616).] **CLEMENTS** (1966): "Pagan antiquity" (59). **PATRIDES** (1985): "the pre-Christian era" (224).

7 *blind* **MILGATE** (1967): "denied the light of revelation" [so also, Shawcross (1967, 23), Baker (1975, 72), Patrides (1985, 224), Carey (1990, 425), and Jones (1991, 629)]; see *Sermons* 9:85 and Browne, *Hydriotaphia*, 4, on "the virtuous heathen" (140).

8–15 *Are not…To follow, damn'd?* **LEAVIS** (1935): Donne uses the rhyming couplet structure to control tone, leading up to the emphatic "damn'd" in l. 15, and the use of "assuage" creates a "lagging deliberation of stress upon 'lusts'" (238–39). **STEIN** (1962): this passage reproduces "the exact inflections of an earnest, reasoning voice," as metrical stress is placed on the most emphatic words and that weight is given to key words without disturbing the rhythm (28). Donne here "is thinking *in* metered language" (29), yet the passage is marked by its simplicity of style (30). **DONOGHUE** (2001), noting Leavis (1935), draws the implication that Donne's "peculiar force in English poetry consists in his developing," in passages such as this, "a style that is at one with the verse that Marlowe and Shakespeare devised for the theater" (xxii).

8–9 *Are not…to them?* **NORTON** (1895): "i.e., to those who lived in the first blinded age" (1:242). **MALLET** (1990): "can the promise of bliss in heaven not calm our desires, as the hope of honour on earth calmed those of the pagan philosophers?" (19). [So also, Ray (1990, 278) and Singh (1992, 39).] **STRIER** (1993): "The test of 'devotion' is, apparently, moral—its ability, as the enjambment insists, to 'assuage / Lusts,' to lead persons to suppress or (better) redirect their appetites and passions" (288).

8 *Are not…to assuage* **RICHTER** (1902) uses this line to illustrate the occurrence of a double, or extra, syllable in the opening foot that should be collapsed to form a single foot (400–01).

8 *valiant* **SHAWCROSS** (1967): "strong" (23). [So also, Smith (1971, 481), Rousseau

and Rudenstine (1972, 64), Patrides (1985, 224), Lloyd-Evans (1989, 295), Jones (1991, 629), and Enright (1997, 96).]

9–15 *Alas…To follow, damn'd?* **HIEATT** (1987): "Those ancient philosophers, blind as they were, may have the saving faith imputed to them by Christ because they lived so virtuously; but we, having the benefit of Christ's clear and easy-to-follow commands, may be damned for taking other paths" (236).

9–10 *them?* and *them* **KENNER** (1964): "the great pagans" (42). [Similarly, Patrides (1985, 224), Craik and Craik (1986, 258), Lloyd-Evans (1989, 299), Carey (1990, 425), and Enright (1997, 96).] **MILGATE** (1967): "those who lived in the 'first blinded age,' whose spur to virtue was fame on earth" (141). **SHAWCROSS** (1967): "the worthies of pagan antiquity (the 'blinde Philosophers' of l. 12)" (23). **HILLER** (1977): "i.e. pagans, who devoted themselves to the virtue of earthly fame" (180).

9 *as earths honor was to them?* **SHAWCROSS** (1967): "rather than salvation is for us" (23). **KERMODE** (1970): "to the pagans of the 'first blinded age'" (103). [So also, Smith (1971, 481), Rousseau and Rudenstine (1972, 64), and Kermode and Hollander (1973, 1045).]

9 *honor was* **PATRIDES** (1985): "'honours were' (acc. to some MSS)" (224).

10–15 *As we…To follow, damn'd?* **BAKER-SMITH** (1972): "the opposition is between the Christians who are saved by faith—to whom virtue is a consequence rather than a cause of salvation—and the sages of antiquity whose ethical discipline may be accepted in lieu of faith" (405–06). [Similarly, Ray (1990, 278–79).] **NUTT** (1999): it "seems to baffle" Donne "to think that ancient philosophers might confront his own father in heaven with their own beliefs equally accounted as faith, and be able to witness his own soul damned in spite of his father's caring instruction" (118).

10–11 *As we…the end?* **SMITH** (1971): "as we surpass the pagans in the means of getting to heaven (for we have the revelation of Christ in the New Testament) may they not surpass us in that end itself, and get there while we go to hell?" (481). [So also, Lloyd-Evans (1989, 299), Mallet (1990, 19), and Singh (1992, 39).]

10 *As we do them in meanes,* **WARNKE** (1967): "We surpass the ancients in means because we have the revealed truth of the Christian religion" (113).

10 *meanes,* **ROUSSEAU AND RUDENSTINE** (1972): "Christian means to salvation and true glory" (64). [So also, Craik and Craik (1986, 258) and Enright (1997, 96).]

11–15 *thy fathers…feare this,* **KERMODE** (1971): "The main theme is simply the importance of having a religion; without that one is worse off than 'blind (i.e. pagan) philosophers'" (136). **CAREY** (1981): Donne is "chiefly concerned in this part of the poem with moral conduct rather than the choice of true religion," but the "lack of consistency between the assumption that there are 'easie wayes' to salvation available from one's father, and the insistence (in the hill of Truth passage) that salvation depends on 'hard knowledge' which the individual must win for himself, is glaring. Put side by side the excerpts reveal the conflict between adult independence and fidelity to inherited beliefs, from which all the heat and impatience of the poem evolve. The phrase 'thy fathers spirit' has a particular resonance because we associate it with the Ghost's speech in *Hamlet* ('I am thy father's spirit'), which it's hard to keep out of our heads. Perhaps we shouldn't try to, for an early version of *Hamlet* had been acted by 1589, and Donne may be echoing it. Was he also thinking of his own father (dead, like old Hamlet, and speedily replaced by a stepfather)? As he had been barely four when his father died, his memory of him must have been hazy at best. But that would not necessarily make it less poignant," for it is unlikely that in *Sat3*, "when Donne writes about religion and fathers, he does so without any thought of his own father, whose religion he is about to abandon. His father had been a Catholic, and the 'easie wayes and near' he taught were those of Rome." Since Donne "assumes that his father is in heaven" and since *Sat3* is "adamant that there is only one true religion which leads to heaven, the argument of the poem would appear to be over before it has begun. There is no need to start labouring up Truth's hill; Catholicism must be right" (13–14). [Similarly, Docherty (1986, 126).] **MARTZ** (1985): these lines, "with their ironic use of the Calvinist doctrine of imputed righteousness," express "the central issue of Donne's entire career" (9). **YOUNG** (1987): "In raising the theme of the virtuous heathen—a lively topic in the Middle Ages and among Renaissance humanists—Donne simply stands Calvinism on its head: instead of Christ's righteousness imputed to a man on the basis of his faith, Donne speculates that virtuous pagans might have faith imputed to them on the basis of righteousness." And thus "the severe Calvinist version of grace is subverted by a witty turn growing out of a moderate Erasmian attitude amidst the horrors of sixteenth-century religious strife" (32–33). **BAUMLIN** (1991): "the pagan's 'merit' (a thin disguise, perhaps, for the Catholic 'good works'?) is anathema to the Protestant, who asserts 'justification by faith' alone; but more important, the poet has from the beginning made all argument for one religion moot. Salvation belongs to the virtuous and faithful, while a member of the 'right' church, when espoused for the wrong reasons, remains spiritually endangered" (129).

11–13 *thy fathers...imputed fayth*, **BAUMLIN** (1986a): the passage "points clearly to the value Donne's speaker places on the strictness and the discipline of the moral philosophy his model [Persius] espouses" (96). **WIGGINS** (2000): Donne's "use of the father figure" here "dramatically implicates the grave man himself in the historical developments leading to the impasse his words reveal." The speaker seems to forget that "his secretary's father and step-father were Catholics and that—if he *is* Egerton—his own father was a Catholic." The "grave man intends with his words only to register a commonplace criticism of the times: sons of Christian fathers are leading lives less Christian than pagan philosophers. However, his generalization about fathers taken within the specific context of his times betrays the issue he is evading." Thus, the "speaker must bring himself—or be brought—to realize that the time has long gone by, in late Elizabethan England, when an appeal to the general principles of Christianity is enough to overcome profound spiritual malaise" (47).

11–12 *Vs in...whose meritt* **RICHTER** (1902) cites the rhymed words of the couplet here as an example of feminine rhyme (411).

11 *thy fathers Spiritt* LECOCQ (1969): this reference offers a potential nod to Thomas Egerton as the identity of the interlocutor (376). [See also, l. 71].

11 *end?* CRAIK AND CRAIK (1986): "salvation" (258).

11 *thy* BROADBENT (1974): "talking to himself (in any case split between pity and scorn). Perhaps his father, up in heaven after death, will meet classical philosophers who were so virtuous that their their virtue was counted as faith; while the Christian son is sent to hell" (106).

12–15 *Meete...To follow, damn'd?* STRIER (1993): "The 'blinde Philosophers' are unequivocally 'in heaven,' not in limbo or in Purgatory. They seem, in fact, more solidly and substantially there than does 'thy fathers spirit.' A puzzle is how the philosophers got to be 'in heaven.' They did so, it seems, on strictly Catholic grounds, through, as the line-break suggests, 'merit.' The explication of 'merit' as 'strict life' is a highly moralistic and Pelagian view, but fully intelligible in a philosophical context, and fully in keeping with the stress in the poem on the capacity of 'devotion' to 'asswage / Lusts.' Yet the situation is not so straightforward. It turns out that salvation is by faith, after all, and Donne is speculating or postulating that 'merit / Of strict life may be'imputed faith.' This is a startlingly un-Lutheran use of the key Lutheran concepts of 'imputation' and faith, since the force of the notion of 'imputed' righteousness was precisely to oppose the philosophical, classical, and 'common sense' idea of achieved, actual righteousness." And "Donne's elaboration on 'easie wayes,'" which are "a chimera," "produces the weak enjambment and redundancy of 'and neare / To follow'" (289–90).

12–13 *whose meritt...be'imputed fayth,* MILGATE (1967): "The Scriptures seem to allow the possibility of salvation to men of virtue who have not heard of Christ" [so also, Warnke (1967, 113), Smith (1971, 481), Rousseau and Rudenstine (1972, 64), Kermode and Hollander (1973, 1046), Baker (1975, 72), Craik and Craik (1986, 258), Mallet (1990, 20), and Singh (1992, 39–40)]. See Acts 17.30; Rom. 2.14–15; Burton, *Anatomy of Melancholy*, part. 3, sect. 4, memb. 2, subsect. 6; and Browne, *Religio Medici*, 1:4. See also, *Sermons* 4:119. Luther "taught that Justification was granted by God to men in response to the disposition of faith alone (*sola fides*), and that it brought with it the imputation to the sinner of the merits of Christ." Donne "impudently" uses Luther's concepts "to suggest what would have horrified Luther: that men can be saved by their own 'merit of strict life' and that this can be imputed to them as justifying faith" (141).

12 *blind Philosophers* CLEMENTS (1966): "Pagan philosophers" (59). [So also, Smith (1971, 481), Lloyd-Evans (1989, 299), and Jones (1991, 629).]

12 *blind* MILGATE (1967) points to l. 7 (141). [So also, Enright (1997, 96).] HILLER (1977): "i.e. pagan" (180).

13 *may be'imputed fayth,* STEIN (1944c) cites "be" in this line as an example of an elided "e" ending before a word beginning with a vowel (390). ENRIGHT (1997): "a cautious suggestion that a virtuous life might compensate for the absence of Christian faith" (96).

13 *may be* **PATRIDES** (1985): "the caution is well advised, for the possibility of counting one's decent life ('good works') in lieu of faith would be anathema to most Protestants"; see *Will* 19–20 (225).

13 *imputed fayth,* **BEWLEY** (1966): "faith vicariously ascribed to men of virtue who had no access to Divine Revelation" (176). **CLEMENTS** (1966): "accounted as" faith (59). **CAREY** (1990): "Credited to them as faith, so earning salvation—an un-Protestant idea, which would have scandalized Luther and Calvin" (425).

14–15 *wayes easy and neare / To follow,* **SINGH** (1992): "i.e. follow the Christian way" (40).

14 *Thee…and neare* **STEIN** (1944c): an example of first foot stress-shift (378) as well as of stress-shift before a pause (381).

14 *wayes easy and neare* **WILLMOTT** (1985): "refers to the Catholic notion that one can achieve personal salvation through good deeds" (60). **MALLET** (1990): "such easy and direct ways" (20).

14 *neare* **GROSART** (1872–73): "at hand, therefore not troublesome or laborious" (1:27). [So also, Smith (1971, 481), Lloyd-Evans (1989, 296), and Enright (1997, 96).]

15–42 *Oh if…dost lothe.* **SCODEL** (1993): Donne's "list of various kinds of 'desperate coward' underscores their extremism. Reversing conventional depictions of military men as boldly active and lovers as meekly passive in order to emphasize the mad excesses of both, Donne opens with a soldier who entombs himself in 'ships woodden Sepulchers,' thus making himself a 'prey,' and ends with a gallant amorist who attacks others with sword or 'poysonous words.'" Further, "the imagery of hot and cold used to describe the middle figures, the explorers and buccaneers, also emphasizes their extremism, which ancient and Renaissance texts often describe in terms of the contraries of hot and cold." As Donne proceeds, he "boldly revises the Aristotelian mean of courage. Aristotle argues that the courageous man has the proper amount of fear and can therefore face death in battle, the most terrifying thing. Donne christian-izes the ancient philosopher's formulation by suggesting that 'great courage' demands a proper fear of damnation" and that "the truly courageous man dares to confront and combat the most terrifying things, damnation and the 'foes' of God, the infernal triad of the devil, world, and flesh that the poet proceeds to describe" (484–85).

15–20 *Oh if…the earthe?* **HESTER** (1978a): "The fact that Elizabethans did ac-complish all these heroic deeds might, from one context of values, suggest a paean to their tremendous daring and accomplishment. But the ambiguity of that repeated verb 'dars't' (the implication that it means 'how can you dare' as well as 'have you dared') and the imagery of death and suicide which dominates these lines support the satirist's exasperated conclusion that such acts of physical prowess are actually 'courage of straw,' a rashness that leads to physical and, more important, spiritual suicide. The *memento mori* tone focuses on the mortality of man: his ships are mere 'Sepulchers,' his body cannot withstand long the assault of the elements of the world, his own words are 'poysonous,' and his physical existence is the constant 'prey / To leaders rage, to stormes, to shot, to dearth'" (42–43).

15–16 *Oh if…valor is.* **MOORE** (1969): "To dare has a sense of activity. It means both to have courage and to venture. Under ideal circumstances the possibility of eternal damnation should automatically provoke a response of fear, but in fallen times damnation is forgotten, and a conscious effort is required to face it and the fear it causes" (44). **STRIER** (1993): "Courage becomes the central theme," as Donne calls for "true daring which, paradoxically, and in good Aristotelian fashion, involves proper fear. Yet Donne admires the military and navigational daring, even the foolhardiness, of his generation" (290). **NUTT** (1999) questions to whom the "witty, emphatic, spiritual call to arms or challenge" is directed (118).

15 *feare this,* **GERALDINE** (1965): the first in a series of four imperatives, this one recognizing the value of moral and spiritual warfare over physical (117). **ROUSSEAU AND RUDENSTINE** (1972): "i.e., fear the possibility of such damnation" (64).

16 *This feare…valor is.* **WILLMOTT** (1985): "Paradoxically the acceptance of the fear of damnation implies spiritual courage" (61). **RAY** (1990): this line "insists that this fear of not gaining salvation, even though the means of doing so are easily at hand, is the greatest fear that takes the greatest courage to face and the one that the individual should consider above all others" (278–79). **WIGGINS** (2000): the "father speaker" here "begins his admonition with a useful message: the only thing to fear…is failing to be afraid of what is truly frightening" (47).

17–28 *Darest…Courage of straw;* **MOORE** (1969): Donne "shows how meaningless conventional courage is with respect to the essential religious questions of salvation," listing "the adventurous things that men do for the sake of exploration, war, trade, and love" and then contrasting them to "man's true duty." The "normal courage" portrayed here "is really little more than a willingness to undergo physical hardships and danger. True courage, however, requires vigilance and commitment. The truly brave man is not an adventurer, but a sentinel who knows his duty and remains at his post. Deeds which man normally associates with courage are, in fact, only distractions which tempt him to leave his appointed post" (44). [So also, Ray (1990, 279–80), Corthell (1997, 40), and Nutt (1999, 119).]

17–26 *Darest…gayne beare?* **BURT** (1997) questions why Donne "expound[s] at length the hazards of foreign travel, when his larger argument requires only that the true field of valor be shown to be religion, the war with the Devil," and notes that these "explorations and contests (all but one of his examples involves a boat) are what has proven the unworth of the Great World," for it is "on the sea that the need for human beings to turn inward has recently been shown" (157).

17–22 *Darest…north discoueryes,* **EVANS** (1978): Donne "would have experienced on [his] expeditions something of the roughness of life at sea in Elizabethan vessels, and something of the spirit of adventure which still animated ordinary sailors and nobleman adventurers alike; in this way he saw the world," and "the expeditions with Essex, for instance, have furnished him with this image" (31). [Similarly, Nutt (1999, 119).]

17–19 *Darest…to dearthe?* **BEWLEY** (1966): "These lines suggest that Donne may have been drawing on his experience in the Azores expedition," as he had also done in *Storm* and *Calm*, so that the date for the poem may be 1597 (176). **CAREY** (1990): "within three or four years of writing" *Sat3*, Donne engaged in just such "rash, hot-blooded, and woefully unspiritual escapades" as are listed here, suggesting that *Sat3* (like the other Satyres) "ostensibly engaged in condemnation," but actually projected "unacknowledged desires and ambitions" (xxiii).

17–18 *Darest…a pray* **STEIN** (1942) notes the rapidity at the beginning of the line caused by beginning the line with two light syllables (685). **STEIN** (1944c) shows that Donne uses two light syllables in succession in l. 18 after the runover in l. 17 "to quicken the beginning of the second line" (387).

17 *Darest…thou lay* **RICHTER** (1902) cites this line to illustrate the occurrence of a double unstressed syllable in the middle of the verse that shows Donne's attempt to overcome the disparity between word accent and verse rhythm (401).

17 *Darest thou ayd mutinous Dutch?* **ALDEN** (1899): the allusion here "might belong to any date after 1580" (78). **GRIERSON** (1921): "To the Catholic Donne the Dutch are still mutineers" (235). **BEWLEY** (1966): "The Protestant Dutch had revolted against their Spanish Catholic rulers" (176). **MILGATE** (1967) notes that the Dutch revolt, since 1586, had been given English "ayd" [so also, Shawcross (1967, 397), Smith (1971, 481), Rousseau and Rudenstine (1972, 64), Kermode and Hollander (1973, 1046), Broadbent (1974, 106), Hiller (1977, 181), Patrides (1985, 225), Willmott (1985, 61), Craik and Craik (1986, 258), Hieatt (1987, 236), Lloyd-Evans (1989, 299), Carey (1990, 415), Mallet (1990, 20), Singh (1992, 40), Enright (1997, 96), Rudrum, Black, and Nelson (2000, 120), and Chmielewski (2001, 616)]. Demurs at Grierson's (1921) suggestion of Donne's Catholic disdain for the mutineers, since "the average Englishman" did not support the Dutch with "much lively sympathy," and points to *ElWar* 5–6 (141). **SELLIN** (1980): "Some may think that the phrase 'mutinous Dutch' dates the poem in the 1590s, on the ground that the adjective 'mutinous' was relevant to the Dutch in those years but could not apply to the lawful government that signally honored Donne in 1619. Donne's adjective is technically correct whether one speaks of 1596 or 1622, for that is exactly what the Dutch were from their abjuration of Philip of Spain until 1648, when Spain formally recognized their right to independence" (304).

18–19 *a pray…to dearthe?* **ROUSSEAU AND RUDENSTINE** (1972): "Perhaps an allusion to Donne's own experience on the Islands Expedition (1597)" (65). **HESTER** (1982): "The *memento mori* tone focuses on the mortality of man: his ships are mere 'Sepulchers,' his body cannot withstand long the assault of the elements, his own words are 'poysonous,' and his physical existence is the constant 'prey / To leaders rage, to stormes, to shot, to dearth'" (61).

18 *Shipps, woodden Sepulchers,* **WILLMOTT** (1985): "Life on board is so hazardous that the ship is compared to a wooden coffin" (61).

18 *Sepulchers,* **MILGATE** (1967) quotes *Storm* 45 and *ElWar* 26–27 (141).

18 *pray* **WILLMOTT** (1985): "victim" (61).

19 *Leaders rage,* **GRIERSON** (1912): "This phrase might tempt one to date the poem after the Cadiz expedition and Islands voyage, in both of which 'leaders' rage', i.e. the quarrels of Howard and Essex, and of Essex and Raleigh, militated against success; but it is too little to build upon. Donne may mean simply the arbitrary exercise of arbitrary power on the part of leaders" (2:114). [Similarly, Milgate (1967, 141–42), quoting Shakespeare, *Jn.* 2.1.265 and *Sat5* 8; Melchiori (1983, 179); and Mallet (1990, 20).]

19 *dearthe?* **WILLMOTT** (1985): "scarcity of food" (61). **MALLET** (1990): "famine, shortage of supplies" (20).

20 *dive Seas,* **LEGOUIS** (1942): "sense 7 = 'to dive into,'" predates the earliest *OED* listing, that "first recorded in 1615 (Chapman, *Odyss.*)" (186). [So also, Sullens (1964, 211).]

20 *dungeons* **MILGATE** (1967): "mines, or caves" (142). [So also, Kermode and Hollander (1973, 1046), Baker (1975, 72), Craik and Craik (1986, 258), and Singh (1992, 40).]

21–26 *Hast thou...gayne beare?* **SELLIN** (1980): "every one of the ingredients that make up Donne's famous expression occurs in the Barents narrative [of the Dutch explorer's third voyage in 1596–97]: new and sensational discoveries in the far north; inhospitable wastes of ice and snow; fascinating horrors of winter in the polar regions; stirring instances of spirit, courage, and resourcefulness in the face of disaster; and ironic oppositions of fire and ice, heat and cold, life and death" (280–81).

21–22 *Hast thou...north discoueryes,* **MASOOD-UL-HASAN** (1958): "There is the realistic sense of cold in 'the icy Poles' and a sense of wonder and courage in discovering the passage to the alluring East" (29). **ROUSSEAU AND RUDENSTINE** (1972): "There were numerous attempts in the Renaissance to discover a northwest passsage to the Indies" (65). **MELCHIORI** (1983): these lines may refer to the discovery of New Zembla (or New Semlia) by the Dutchman William Barentz in 1596, and in 1600, Shakespeare refers to Dutch shipping in *TN* (3.2.26–28) (179).

22–26 *and thrice...for gayne beare?* **MORRIS** (1953) paraphrases: "and canst thou, thrise colder than Salamanders, like the divine children in the oven, bear for gain the fires of Spain and the line, whose countries are alembics to our bodies?" (69).

22–25 *and thrice...bodyes bee* **HIEATT** (1987): "For personal profit, do you endure (as though you were ever-cold, fire-proof salamanders, or Shadrach, Meshach, and Abednego, surviving the fiery furnace of Daniel 1 and 3) the heat of southern climes and the equator, which desiccates our bodies as stills evaporate fluids?" (236).

22–24 *Of frozen...the Line,* **RUGOFF** (1939) points out various uses of the image of the salamander, popularly supposed to be capable of living indefinitely in fire, noting that here it is a fitting emblem of the physical life of sailors at the equator (210–11). **STEIN** (1942): placing the caesura at the end of the line starts a new rhythm that carries into the next line (683).

22 *frozen north discoueryes,* **MILGATE** (1967): "Attempts to find a north-west passage to the Pacific were made by the Cabots (in and after 1497), Martin Frobisher

(1576–8), John Davis (in each of the three years 1585–7), and most recently by the Dutchman, Barents (1594)" (142). [So also, Smith (1971, 481), Kermode and Hollander (1973, 1046), Patrides (1985, 225), Willmott (1985, 61), Craik and Craik (1986, 258), Lloyd-Evans (1989, 229), Mallet (1990, 20), Singh (1992, 40), and Enright (1997, 96).]

23–24 *diuine / Chilldren in th'ouen*, **GROSART** (1872–73): "Cf. Daniel iii.19–25," which equates to "the heats of the tropics and the artillery of Spain, that claimed those seas and countries" (1:27). [Similarly, Bewley (1966, 176), Clements (1966, 59), Milgate (1967, 142), citing *Calm* 28 and quoting T. Bastard, *Chrestoleros* [1598], 4:23, l. 8, Shawcross (1967, 23), Smith (1971, 482), Rousseau and Rudenstine (1972, 65), Kermode and Hollander (1973, 1046), Baker (1975, 72), Hiller (1977, 181), Patrides (1985, 225), Willmott (1985, 61), Craik and Craik (1986, 258), Lloyd-Evans (1989, 299), Carey (1990, 425), Mallet (1990, 20), Singh (1992, 40), Enright (1997, 96), Nutt (1999, 119), Rudrum, Black, and Nelson (2000, 120), and Chmielewski (2001, 616).] **HESTER** (1978a): "The irony is that the three children of Daniel 3.11–30 were thrown into the fires because they refused to accept a false religion, specifically to worship the 'golden image'; Donne's adventurers, on the other hand, seem to worship gold ('gaine') and dare the fires of the equator in order to worship their goddess" (43).

23 *then* **PATRIDES** (1985): "than" (225).

23 *Salamanders,* **BEWLEY** (1966): "lizardlike creatures believed able to exist in fire" (176). [So also, Shawcross (1967, 23), Smith (1971, 481), Rousseau and Rudenstine (1972, 65), Kermode and Hollander (1973, 1046), Broadbent (1974, 106), Baker (1975, 72), Hiller (1977, 181), Patrides (1985, 225), Willmott (1985, 61), Craik and Craik (1986, 258), Lloyd-Evans (1989, 299), Mallet (1990, 20), Jones (1991, 629), Singh (1992, 40), Enright (1997, 96), and Nutt (1999, 119).] **CLEMENTS** (1966): "able to survive fire because they are cold-blooded" (59). [So also, Milgate (1967, 142), citing Aristotle, *Hist. Animal.* V. 19, 552b and Pliny, *Nat. Hist.* X. 86, and Chmielewski (2001, 616).]

24 *Chilldren…and the Line,* **STEIN** (1944b): the "harsh consonants" in this line "are apparently from carelessness or lack of interest" (403).

24 *th'ouen,* **RICHTER** (1902) cites this phrase to illustrate a slurring of syllables (403).

24 *fires of Spayne and the Line,* **CLEMENTS** (1966): "The Inquisition and the equator" [so also, Bewley (1966, 176), Smith (1971, 482), Rousseau and Rudenstine (1972, 65), Kermode and Hollander (1973, 1046), Broadbent (1974, 106), Baker (1975, 72), Hiller (1977, 181), Patrides (1985, 225), Willmott (1985, 61), Craik and Craik (1986, 258), Lloyd-Evans (1989, 299), Mallet (1990, 20), Singh (1992, 40), Enright (1997, 96), and Chmielewski (2001, 616)]; these are objects of "beare," l. 26 (59). **MILGATE** (1967): "the tropical heat of the regions of the Spanish main and the equatorial line," with a possible allusion to the Inquisition as "a danger attendant on being taken prisoner" (142). [So also, Shawcross (1967, 23).]

24 *the Line,* **KENNER** (1964): "the equator" (42). [So also, Jones (1991, 629).]

25 *Limbecks to our bodyes* **KENNER** (1964): "vessels in which substances are dis-

tilled by heat" (42). [So also, Bewley (1966, 176) and Clements (1966, 59).] **MILGATE** (1967): "alembics [so also, Shawcross (1967, 23), Warnke (1967, 113), Patrides (1985, 225), Carey (1990, 425), and Chmielewski (2001, 616)] or stills. Our bodies sweat in these climes, in a process like distillation" (142). [So also, Rousseau and Rudenstine (1972, 65), Kermode and Hollander (1973, 1046), Baker (1975, 72), Hiller (1977, 181), Willmott (1985, 62), Craik and Craik (1986, 259), Mallet (1990, 20), Jones (1991, 629), Singh (1992, 40), Enright (1997, 96), and Rudrum, Black, and Nelson (2000, 121).] **WARNKE** (1967): "The conceit refers wittily to both the hot climate of Spain and the burning of Protestants there as heretics" (113). [So also, Smith (1971, 482).]

25 *Limbecks* **JOHNSON** (1755): "A still."

26–28 *must euery...Courage of straw;* **WILLMOTT** (1985): "Must every man who does not address your mistress as 'Goddess!' either draw his sword to defend himself or swallow your insults? Such courage is a sham (by comparison with the true courage of lines 15–16)" (62). [Similarly, Mallet (1990, 20).]

26 *for gayne beare?* **SMITH** (1971): "endure hardships for mere monetary gain" (482). [Similarly, Broadbent (1974, 106), Willmott (1985, 62), and Enright (1997, 96).]

27–28 *Which...poysonous words?* **SMITH** (1971): "must every man who does not hail one's mistress as a goddess either draw his sword and fight or suffer any insults one chooses to thrust down his throat?" (482). [So also, Craik and Craik (1986, 259) and Singh (1992, 40).] **STRIER** (1993): "This is obviously meant to be an image of spurious, misapplied valor, but the imagistic context complicates this intention. The only mistress previously mentioned in the poem is 'our Mistresse faire Religion.' The connection suggests that perhaps violent defense of this Mistress against every other is 'courage of straw' as well. Perhaps 'faire Religion' is not to be defended by the sword, and perhaps other 'mistresses' are fair—like virtue, for instance, or other, non-Christian religions" (290–91).

27–28 *draw, / Or eate thy poysonous words?* **MILGATE** (1967): "fight a duel with you or swallow your insults" (142). [So also, Hieatt (1987, 236).]

27 *draw,* **CLEMENTS** (1966): "i.e., draw his sword" (59). [So also, Patrides (1985, 225), Enright (1997, 96), and Chmielewski (2001, 616).] **HILLER** (1977): "i.e. fight a duel" (181).

28–31 *Or eate...thus yeild* **NUTT** (1999): Donne continues "the same belligerent metaphor" to "locate and acclaim true courage" as he did to dismiss false courage, and here he "employs rhythm again to signal the significance of the idea" (119).

28 *Or eate...of straw;* **MOLONEY** (1950): this line is almost unrecognizable as decasyllabic due to its multiple elisions (236).

28 *eate thy poysonous words?* **LLOYD-EVANS** (1989): "swallow sickening insults" (300).

28 *Courage of straw;* **LEGOUIS** (1942): this phrase "does not appear in the *OED*,"

and "the nearest approach" is that of "'man of straw,' with its primary meaning: 'a counterfeit, sham, dummy; similarly, a face of straw, etc.'" (188–89).

28 *of straw;* **MILGATE** (1967) quotes *OED* 7, implying something "of trifling value or importance," but notes that the words "seeme bold" in effect "shift the primary meaning to sense 2. e, 'counterfeit, sham, dummy,' as in the phrase 'man of straw'" (142). **CRAIK AND CRAIK** (1986): "worthless" (259).

29–35 *O desperate...to be ridd:* **HAMER** (1930): "The whole passage is so un-rhythmical that any scansion can only be tentative" (50).

29–32 *O desperate...appointed field?* **HESTER** (1982): "the warriors who only 'dare' the perils of the world 'leave th'appointed field' of God's service by eschewing, in St. Bernard's words, 'that which we knowe.' They fail to use their memory" (60).

29 *O desperate...seeme bold,* **SCODEL** (1993): "the poet berates as a 'desperate coward,' a 'thou' who represents both himself and his fellow men," and the satire's "oxymoronic 'desperate coward'" is thus a "new version of Aristotle's rash man. Although Aristotle contrasts rashness and cowardice as excess and defect on either side of courage, his detailed analysis of the rash man breaks down the distinction between these extremes by arguing that rash men are generally 'rash cowards,'" and Donne's "'desperate' coward' similarly collapses the distinction between the two extremes: he 'seem[s] bold' in recklessly fighting in 'forbidden warres' but is afraid to fight the spiritual battle 'appointed' by God" (483–84).

29 *desperate* **CRAIK AND CRAIK** (1986): "in a state of despair; ready for damnation" (259).

29 *Coward,* **RICHTER** (1902) cites this word to illustrate a slurring of syllables (403).

30, 33 *foes* and *foes:* **HILLER** (1977): "viz. the Devil, the world, and the flesh" (181). [So also, Craik and Craik (1986, 259), Singh (1992, 40), and Enright (1997, 96).]

30–32 *who made...appointed field?* **GRIERSON** (1912): Donne "considers the rashness of those whom he refers to as a degree of, an approach to, suicide. To expose ourselves to these perils we abandon the moral warfare to which we are appointed" (2:114). **HIEATT** (1987): "As a soldier of Christ will you leave the field of battle ap-pointed by him for the sake of the wrong wars?" (236). [Similarly, Singh (1992, 40).]

30–31 *stand / Soldier in his worlds garrison,* **HESTER** (1978a) (reading "Sentinell"): "The truly brave man, the satirist reflects, is the Christian 'Sentinell,' the man who recalls his origin in God and his eventual judgment by Him and therefore weds his purpose to God's and remains steadfast to His 'garrison'" (43). **SCODEL** (1993): "The image conflates Saint Paul's Christian soldier, who 'stands' firm against his spiritual foes (Eph. 6:11–17), and a classical topos based on an influential mistranslation of a passage in Plato's *Phaedo.* Refusing to commit suicide, Socrates argues that man dwells in a 'prison' (*phroura*) that he has no right to leave until God bids him to do so; ancient and Renaissance readers often gave *phroura* the contextually implausible meaning of 'garrison'" (485–86).

30 *his* **MILGATE** (1967): "God's" (142). [So also, Shawcross (1967, 23), Smith (1971, 482), Rousseau and Rudenstine (1972, 65), Kermode and Hollander (1973, 1046), Broadbent (1974, 106), Patrides (1985, 225), Willmott (1985, 62), Craik and Craik (1986, 259), Mallet (1990, 20), and Chmielewski (2001, 616).]

31 *Soldier* **HESTER** (1991) (reading "Sentinell"): "a term Donne used in his Latin epigrams to denote the Catholic crusade" (97). **STRINGER** (1991): "eight manuscripts, all the seventeenth-century prints, and Q, Y, and Z read 'Sentinell' for the 'Soldier' given in NY3 and nineteen other manuscripts," and thus, "we may well suspect that Donne's change was prompted by the evolving climate of religious tension, rather than by pure aesthetics (indeed, 'Sentinall,' the later choice, renders the line hypermetric)" (81).

31 *this* **HILLER** (1977): "i.e. God's" (181).

32 *And for...th'appointed field?* **STEIN** (1944b): the elisions in this line "produce rhythms and combinations of consonants that cannot be justified" (402).

32 *forbid warrs,* **MILGATE** (1967): "Contention with one's fellows in battle, love, or exploration 'for gaine' is, in the moral sphere, forbidden because sinful" (142–43). **SMITH** (1971): "wars whose ends are worldly and not holy" (482). [So also, Hiller (1977, 181), Lloyd-Evans (1989, 300), Mallet (1990, 20), and Enright (1997, 96).]

32 *forbid* **CHMIELEWSKI** (2001): "worldly battles with aims or goals not in the defense of true religion" (616).

32 *th'appointed field?* **SMITH** (1971): "the moral battlefield of this world, in which Christians are God's soldiers" (482). [So also, Willmott (1985, 62), Lloyd-Evans (1989, 300), and Mallet (1990, 20).]

33–42 *the foule Deuill,...dost lothe.* **GRIERSON** (1912): Donne "has three foes in view—the devil, the world, and the flesh" (2:114). [So also, Rousseau and Rudenstine (1972, 65), Lewalski and Sabol (1973, 95), and Hieatt (1987, 237).] **MELCHIORI** (1983) notes that these lines draw on the discussion of the formula for baptism in the *Book of Common Prayer*, stating that Donne repeated this imagery often and directing readers to *HSScene* and *HSShe* as examples (180). **FERRY** (1997) supposes, "for a moment," that the word "Realme" "refers to the earth rather than hell," stating that the lines would make sense, "for the Devil would only be releasing one from life on earth." Believes, however, that "if it is granted that Realme refers to the earth, then to be quit must mean 'to be free from the earth' or 'to die,' and as such it modifies the direct object of *would allow*, that is, *Thee*." Suggests that the "lines mean something like this: 'Acting out of hate, not love, the Devil would willingly allow you to be free from the earth.'" Notes that "[f]or those who serve the Devil there is an obvious catch-22," for the Devil, like God, "will free his servants from this world, but for very different reasons and to very different ends" (223–24). **NUTT** (1999): in this "lengthy, complex sentence," Donne "rails at himself (and us) for being preoccupied with earthly things at the expense of his eternal soul" (120).

33–41 *Know...Thou lou'st,* **HESTER** (1982): "the emphasis is on what man should remember about his origin and end: the realm of hell that awaits the devil's lovers, the eventual end of a world of which 'all parts wither away and passe' (36), and the immortal source of 'joyes' for all men, the soul. The recollection of these crucial facts about man's condition in the spectrum of eternal time provides, then, an exhortative directive and viable alternative to the adventurers' imprudent, spiritual amnesia" (62).

33–35 *the foule Deuill,...to be ridd:* **MILGATE** (1967) (reading "quit" rather than "ridd"): a "tangled" sentence: "The foul Devil, whom you strive to please, would be only too willing, out of hate not love, to grant you the whole of his kingdom of Hell to satisfy you" [so also, Rousseau and Rudenstine (1972, 65), Kermode and Hollander (1973, 1046; 1975, 740), Baker (1975, 72), Willmott (1985, 62), Craik and Craik (1986, 259), Hieatt (1987, 237), and Mallet (1990, 20)]. The words "to be quit" might mean "to be rid of your importunity," or "in full discharge of what he owes you" (143). **DANIELS** (1981): "the admonished reader is enamored of these evils. He is said to love the strumpet world and the decaying flesh, and good parallelism would require that the initial item in the series stress the fact that he loves the Devil. Indeed, that import of the first item is alluded to in the second, where the world is referred to as 'thy other lov'd foe,' the first loved foe necessarily being the Devil." Such a reading "meets the need for parallelism of idea, requires no syntactical gymnastics, and harmonizes with Christian tradition" (15–16).

33–34 *Know...would allow* **PATRIDES** (1985) notes that the lines "read variously in the MSS and the editions" (226).

33 *Know...whom thou* **STEIN** (1944c): an example of a nine-syllable line with a stress-shift (377). **MOLONEY** (1950): this line is almost unrecognizable as decasyllabic due to its multiple elisions (236). **MORRIS** (1953) states that the primary pause in this line "counts in the scansion in the same way as a rest does in music" (43).

33 *Know thy foes:* **GERALDINE** (1965): the second in a series of four imperatives denounces "short-sighted allegiances" and introduces "the old triumvirate" (117). **MILGATE** (1967) quotes Burton, *Anatomy of Melancholy,* part. 2, sect. 3, memb. 2, and notes that Donne deals with "The foule Devill" (ll. 33–35), the world (ll. 36–39), and "last, Flesh" (ll. 39–42) (143).

33 *foes:* **KENNER** (1964): "the world, the flesh, and the devil" (43).

34–35 *Striu'st...to be ridd:* **SMITH** (1971): "the devil would willingly give you for your service his whole kingdom of hell, to be rid of it, though out of hate not love" (482). [So also, Hiller (1977, 181), Lloyd-Evans (1989, 300), and Singh (1992, 40).]

35 *fayne his whole Realme to be ridd:* **GRIERSON** (1912): "Whether we read 'quit' or 'rid,'" the phrase "seems to mean 'to be free of his whole Realm'—an unparalleled use of either adjective" (2:114). [Similarly, Bewley (1966, 176) and Rudrum, Black, and Nelson (2000, 121).] **BROADBENT** (1974): "gladly let you possess his whole realm (i.e. the world)" (106). **SINGH** (1992): "Obscure. It may mean that the devil will give you his kingdom to be rid of your importunities" (40).

35 *fayne* **ENRIGHT** (1997): "gladly" (96). [So also, Chmielewski (2001, 616).]

35 *his* SHAWCROSS (1967): "God's" (23). [So also, Patrides (1985, 225).]

35 *to be ridd:* CLEMENTS (1966) (reading "quit"): "To be rid of you" (59). CAREY (1990) (reading "quit"): "As quittance (reward) for your soul" (425). ENRIGHT (1997) (reading "quit"): "in return" (96).

35 *ridd:* GROSART (1872–73) says that the more frequent reading "quitt" is "apparently used in a sense not attributed to it in dictionaries. To be free of, that is, to be free as a naturalized subject to go through and enjoy his realm. If Johnson's second meaning were altered to—[make us] set free, it would include this, and probably be more correct. Donne, however, omits 'of,' just as his contemporaries used other verbs without a preposition" (1:28). GRIERSON (1912): "Whether we read 'quit' or 'rid' the construction is difficult. The phrase seems to mean 'to be free of his whole Realm'— an unparalleled use of either adjective" (2:114). KERMODE (1970) (reading "quit"): "free" (104). [So also, Lewalski and Sabol (1973, 95).] RUDRUM, BLACK, AND NELSON (2000) (reading "quit"): the word "has the sense of being in exchange for something, *OED v* quit 11c" (121).

36–39 *The worlds...worne Strumpet.* MORSE (1989): Donne "warns against the dangers of worldliness" (267).

36–38 *The worlds...decrepit wayne;* PATRIDES (1985) cites *FirAn* 1ff. (226). CRAIK AND CRAIK (1986): "all earthly things are perishable, and the earth itself is nearing its end" (259).

36 *The worlds all parts wither away* MILGATE (1967) quotes *Sermons* 9:185 (143).

36 *The worlds all parts* GRIERSON (1912): "Here 'all' means 'every'" (2:114). [So also, Broadbent (1974, 106), Willmott (1985, 62), and Mallet (1990, 20).] CLEMENTS (1966): "All the parts of the world" (59).

37–38 *worlds selfe,...decrepit wayne;* ROUSSEAU AND RUDENSTINE (1972): "It was a common contemporary belief that the physical world was entering its final stages of decay" (65). [So also, Lloyd-Evans (1989, 300) and Mallet (1990, 20).]

37 *thy other lou'd foe,* WILLMOTT (1985): "another paradox; the newly baptised Christian promises to renounce the devil, the world and the flesh (i.e. the three 'foes' which Donne is examining here), but although failure to renounce them will lead to damnation Donne finds them attractive" (62). CHMIELEWSKI (2001): "the temptations of the world" (616).

38–39 *In her...worne Strumpet.* RUGOFF (1939) comments on the "frankness" and "vigor" of this analogy to describe those pursuing worldly things (171).

38 *her decrepit wayne;* BEWLEY (1966): "It was widely believed that the world was in her last age" (176). [So also, Milgate (1967, 143), adding reference to *FirAn* and Victor Harris, *All Coherence Gone* (1949), Smith (1971, 482), Kermode and Hollander (1973, 1046), Broadbent (1974, 106), Willmott (1985, 62), Mallet (1990, 20), and Singh (1992, 40).] CLEMENTS (1966): "decline" (59). [So also, Patrides (1985, 226).]

38 *wayne;* SULLENS (1964): Donne's usage of this meaning of the word is earlier

than the earliest source cited by *OED* (243). **PATRIDES** (1985): "wane, decline" (226). [So also, Enright (1997, 96).]

39 *Dost loue…worne Strumpet.* **NUTT** (1999): behind this image lies the idea that in Donne's time the "notion that the world was likely to end soon was a common one amongst theologians" (120).

39 *Strumpet.* **WILLMOTT** (1985): "prostitute" (62).

39 *Last,* **MALLET** (1990): "finally" (21).

40–42 *Flesh…dost lothe.* **JACKSON** (1968): "The speaker here acts in sympathy with the soul, and directs his voice to the auditor whose affections are fastened upon the flesh, so that the discourse from speaker to auditor parallels the relationship of soul to flesh, and represents therefore the traditional medieval debate between body and soul. In Donne's debate, however, one voice is silent—the flesh, the external and visible self. Taken in this way, the soul seems to say to the body, 'you love yourself, when you should love me because I am the one who gives you the very power to love.' Or to switch to the parallel terms of speaker and auditor, Donne's most inner voice says to the outer image of himself, 'See how much I love you, that I give you my life power; why don't you love me?' Yet even though the flesh is accused and is silent, the speaker understands that external power of himself well enough to know that he gives that other part the power to love; he both speaks to it and understands it; the two are in some communication. Consequently, the distinction between them, though real and uncomfortable, is not ultimate" (41). **KERMODE, FENDER, AND PALMER** (1974): "You ruin, or stain, the soul, which moves the body, for the sake of bodily pleasure. What you should be doing instead of yielding to these foes is seeking true religion" (65). **OSMOND** (1990): Donne uses "'flesh' that is 'it selfes death' primarily in a figurative sense; but the 'flesh' through which the power to taste joy is exercised, must be primarily the physical body. It is from this identical terminology but changed meaning that the paradox arises. Flesh is loved to the exclusion of that power which enables it to be lovable. But the 'flesh' that is loved is only in part and verbally the same as the 'flesh' through which the powers of the soul can be exercised" (136). **STRIER** (1993): "This is not a normal argument against 'the flesh' (a phrase which Donne does not use). It is not, in fact, despite the interjected parenthesis, an argument against 'flesh' at all. 'Joyes which flesh can taste' are never rejected or devalued. They cannot be, since the argument for the amiability of the soul is precisely that it is what enables flesh 'to taste joy.' The plea is not to renounce 'joyes which flesh can taste' but rather to have a proper philosophical understanding of them, to see them, in good Aristotelian fashion, as ontologically dependent on the 'fair goodly soule.' The soul should get credit for the body's joys," and "the argument is radically humanist and philosophical; we have come a long way from renunciation. The point is to love the soul, not to loathe the body" (291–92).

40 *Flesh…can tast* **SINGH** (1992): "Flesh itself is mortal, and the joys of the flesh bring on death" (40).

40 *Flesh (it selfes death)* **MILGATE** (1967): "The joys of the flesh bring destruction

to the flesh—as in gluttony, drunkenness, lechery; even the exercise of the functions of the body impairs it" (143). [So also, Smith (1971, 482), Kermode and Hollander (1973, 1046), Willmott (1985, 62), and Mallet (1990, 21).]

40 (it selfes death) **CRAIK AND CRAIK** (1986): "self-destroying (through self-indulgence)" (259).

40 (it selfes **HILLER** (1977): "'itself' (1633)" (182). **PATRIDES** (1985): "(acc. to 1635–69 and most MSS): 'it selfe' (acc. to 1633 and a few MSS)" (226).

41–42 thy fayre...to tast ioy, **MATSUURA** (1953): Donne's use of the term "soul" sometimes includes not only the rational but also the vegetative and sensitive souls (47). **WILLMOTT** (1985): "The soul animates the body" (62).

41–42 Soule, which...this flesh power **MILGATE** (1967) refers to Ecst 50ff. and Metem 131 (143).

42 Giue...dost lothe. **STEIN** (1946): this line "may possibly be read without stress-shifts" (99).

43–87 Seeke...endeauors reach; **SLIGHTS** (1991): "Searching for 'true religion' (43) in these bewildering conditions is a strenuous task that the speaker shares with his audience. He doesn't sneer contemptuously at others from the isolated splendor of certainty. He doesn't claim to have made it to the top of the high hill where truth stands. The only superiority he claims is that of knowing how to go about looking for truth. His mastery of 'the mindes indeavours' (87) is procedural rather than substantive; that is, human rationality consists not of getting it right, in the sense of coming out with the correct answer, but in thinking correctly" (93).

43–74 Seeke...seeke her. **NELLY** (1969): "Whether Donne in these disturbed times did not wish to adhere to any particular church, preferring 'God Himselfe to trust'; or whether his vision did indeed go beyond petty differences of sects to a greater truth which transcended, yet included them all; or whether, and this seems the most likely supposition, he is here crying out against the extremes which destroy—the extreme of martyrdom which, in his experience, seemed the exorbitant price one must now pay for adhering to the Roman Church, and the extreme of irresponsibility which prompted so many to accept uncritically, almost blindly, the tenets of any sect which could serve their cause" (15).

43–71 Myrius...the right; **MOORE** (1969): "the five bad examples mentioned in these lines represent not typical Catholics, Calvinists, and Anglicans, but fools who choose their religious positions for the same irrational reasons that other fools choose (or refuse to choose) wives." Thus, "Donne is not dissociating himself from these religious types; he is warning the reader to dissociate himself from them. Each of these foolish individuals is clearly wrong, but this is not necessarily an indictment of the institutions which they have chosen. Mirreus, Crants, Graius, Phrygius, and Graccus are not true representatives of the possible responses to the question 'Which church, if any, should one accept as the one true church?' Rather, they are men who have found various ways to avoid the challenge 'feare this.' Instead of fearing and seeking, they have fastened upon one simple perception as though it were the saving truth. The result is that, because of their simple-minded confidence in one perception, they cease fearing and seeking in a world where true religion cannot be located with any degree of certainty is to give up all chance of actually finding it." Further, "Mirreus, Crants, and Graius have not erred in being Catholics, Calvinists, or Anglicans but, rather, in believing that one can choose a church through superficial means and be absolutely certain that it represents true religion. Donne is not saying that all Catholics, Calvinists, and Anglicans are fools, but that anyone who rests all his efforts toward salvation in a belief that a certain institution represents true religion is a fool." One has to "choose a church," and it must be "the right," but "the emphasis of the satire is not so much on the specific choice as on the state of mind that the individual maintains as and after he makes his decision" (45–46). **LAURITSEN** (1976): "the speaker, carried away by his smugly satiric spirit, proceeds systematically to eliminate all available possibilities." Further, "instead of the Mistresses Truth and Faire Religion who are supposed to reside at the summit of that 'huge hill,' what the satirist discovers and presents for our delectation and consideration is a group of distinctly worldly wenches, varying in appeal from the threadbare and shop-worn beauties of Rome to the 'course country drudges' of Geneva. The selection, then, is not only unappetizing, but impossible. There is nothing to choose between them" (126).

43–70 *Myrius…one allow;* **BAKER-SMITH** (1972): "The five characters portrayed have all failed to base their religious position on an objective assessment of evidence," their criteria being "simply inadequate." The "straightforward cases" are "Mirreus the papist" and "Crants the sectarian," but Graius is someone who adopts Anglicanism "for the wrong reasons," and Phrygius and Graccus both "show the dangers of scepticism and indifference, though in opposing directions." Donne here seems to be "less concerned, at this stage at least, with the public stance adopted than with the process of enquiry behind it," which makes Graius's "bogus Anglicanism" (since it is "passively accepted") "particularly interesting." In addition, Donne seems always to have "laid stress on personal responsibility in religious affiliation," for when he "ceased to be a papist and became an Anglican it is unlikely that he thought of it as a 'conversion': it was simply a purer realisation of his Christian conviction, and advance in self-awareness" (406–07). **ROUSSEAU AND RUDENSTINE** (1972): "Mirreus is presented as a Roman Catholic," Crants "as a Calvinist," Graius "as an Anglican," Phrygius "as one who rejects all religious sects," and Graccus "as one who sees little difference among various sects" (65). [Similarly, Hiller (1977, 182), Hieatt (1987, 237), Ray (1990, 280–81), and Rudrum, Black, and Nelson (2000, 121).] **SLIGHTS** (1972): "Acting as probabilists," Mirreus and Crantz "decide the form of their religion on the basis of inadequate external authority. Graius, like the docile boy who accepts whatever woman his legal guardian chooses for him, simply thinks whatever the established authorities 'bid him thinke.' Like the shallow cynics of Jacobean comedy who believe that all women are cuckolders and hence refuse to marry an honest woman, Phrygius foolishly cuts himself off from the possibility of discovering the true church because some Christian sects must be in error. Graccus, with similar lack of discrimination and intellectual laziness, arrives at the opposite conclusion that all are equally right. Applying the 'they're all the same in the dark' approach to religion, he decides that because the Church of England, the church of Rome, and the church of Geneva are all churches, there is nothing to choose among them" (95). **SLIGHTS** (1991): Donne "aims barbs at political, economic, and ecclesiastical sins and stupidities—at men who 'obey / The statecloth where the Prince sate yesterday' (47–48), at the institution of wardship, and at preachers who are 'vile ambitious bauds' (56). These satiric thrusts at contemporary social ills don't imply that the tawdry circumstances of ordinary life are irrelevant to true religion. On the contrary, their force is to show that the search for religious truth necessarily is conducted with the same imperfect mental processes that people use in their amatory and domestic lives" (93).

43–69 *Myrius...much light breeds.* **BEWLEY** (1966): the "proper names Donne assigns to types of Elizabethan Christians are fictitious" (177). **MILGATE** (1967) finds this "the properly 'satirical' part of the poem," dealing with "the trivial reasons why men adopt a form of religion" (140). Notes that the point in these lines is that "the search for true religion (and salvation) will fail, wherever it is directed, if it is prosecuted with superficial, irresponsible, or cowardly motives" (143). Says that the names themselves have "little special appropriateness" (143–44). **CHMIELEWSKI** (2001) notes simply that "the significance of the various religious adherents' names throughout is a matter of debate" (616).

43–68 *Myrius...so is Religion;* **BAUMLIN** (1990): "Comparing the fanatical adherent of each religion to a suitor of some 'wench,' the satirist reduces religious difference—and contemporary politics—to domestic comedy. Alluding to Rome's historical abuse of ceremonial authority, Mirreus loves the Roman Church's 'ragges so, as wee here obey / The Statecloth where the prince sate yesterday,'" and "thus an ostensibly religious attack turns against the English Crown, the abuse of ceremony simply shifting from the Roman Pope to the English prince. Monarchy has created its own cult and its own idols, the King (or Queen) becoming a second Pope" (70). **CORTHELL** (1997): in addition to being "related to a type of woman," each "religious position" is "more significantly" associated with "an inadequate male response to women," and "these male responses, are, psychoanalytically speaking, strategies of denying lack. In the terms of Donne's allegory, this failure to acknowledge one's lack (i.e., lack of the truth) results in a flawed religious choice" (40). **NUTT** (1999): "always in command of structure," Donne "pursues the same pattern" for each seeker in which "their particular belief is described, then castigated via an analogy which exposes their shallow thinking" (120). **BLISSETT** (2000) compares Donne's "procession of vividly conceived figures characterized by the description of their mistresses, false religions" to Jonson's presentations of his characters in *Every Man Out* and *Cynthia's Revels* (112).

43–62 *Myrius...Pay values.* **SCODEL** (1993): the attachments of Mirreus and Crants "to the 'ragges' of a 'thousand yeares agoe'" and "to a 'yong' religion" call to mind "the contrast between what the Elizabethan prayer book describes as those 'addicted to their old customs' and those 'so newfangled that they would innovate all things.'" But by "comparing Mirrheus's fondness for Roman 'ragges' with Englishmen's fawning at a monarch's 'statecloth'" and "Crants's love for Genevan 'plaine' simplicity to a 'lecherous' preference for 'country drudges,'" Donne "associates deviations from the English church's supposed mean with two extremes of English social life." Moreover,

Graius "does not avoid extremes by staying 'at home'" but "instead mixes them through a perverse embrace of contraries. Impressionable and subservient, he obeys corrupt elders, preachers who act simultaneously like 'Godfathers' and 'bauds,' and laws 'Still new like fashions,'" and these religious statutes "are as young as Crants's church and as devoid of substance as Mirrheus's rags" (487).

43–59 *Myrius…Imbraceth her,* **HESTER** (1982): the "satirist's diction" suggests that "these religious amorists suffer from failures or abuse of the understanding in their reliance on their sensitive souls alone." Thus, "their 'errours in the understanding,' which Donne identified in his sermons as the cause of religious errors, correspond to that abuse of reason Augustine called *scientia*, knowledge only of this world, in contrast to *sapientia*, knowledge of the next world as well. Trying to recognize the Bride of Christ by her clothes, temporary housings, friends, or appearances, these amatory sectarians fail to use their understanding, strive to satisfy only their own emotional needs, and conclude the search for Truth by adoring or hating mere signs" (63).

43–54 *Myrius…cuntry drudges.* **WALKER** (1925) points to "evidence elsewhere," such as *Will* 19–21, that Donne "loved neither of these extremes" of Mirreus and Crantz (71). **SLIGHTS** (1972): the Roman Catholic Mirreus, who "indulges his taste for external religious trappings and bases his ecclesiastical allegiance solely on tradition," and the Calvinist Crantz, who "scorns tradition and chooses his church for the absence of any ceremony or ritual without scriptural sanction," together show that Donne "mocks the Roman Catholic and Puritan treatment of indifferent things" (97).

43–52 *Seeke…yet vnhandsome;* **PAYNE** (1926): "This gibe at the expense of Rome indicates that Donne is by no means disposed to accept Papal authority, while the very appropriate description of the Calvinistic doctrine, then comparatively 'young,' shows how its harsh exclusiveness repels him" (36). **ROSTON** (1974): although Donne's speaker scoffs at the "squabbling sectarianism of Christianity, dismissing the monopolistic claims of each set in turn," he does so "to justify his own temporary waivering between these sects before making that choice which, he maintains, must inevitably be made before life ends" (47).

43–48 *Myrius…sate yesterday.* **DIPASQUALE** (1993): Mirreus's mistress "is not much of a seductress," her lover "having trouble tracking her down." Mirreus's "pursuit of an evasive mistress has distinctly Petrarchan overtones," for his beloved "has, like Daphne, 'fled' the place in which her beauties might have been profaned," and "like Petrarch, he fetishizes his lady's apparel and adores an absent presence" (77–78). Further, "Mirreus and his coreligionists call the Pope Christ's vicar and revere him as the regent of the King who has 'to heaven…gone,'" committing "idolatry in adoring the Sacrament, for in doing so they 'worshippe the giftes in steede of the giuer himselfe'" (83). **STRIER** (1993) notes that Mirreus, the Catholic, "is an Englishman—by birth presumably a Protestant—who leaves 'here' and seeks 'true religion' at Rome" but that "what makes this choice irrational," it is clearly implied, is that "truth is no longer 'there.'" He believes further that "there is a suggestion of menstrual rags in the picture of Mirreus's misplaced devotion to an imagined Roman female" and that there is thus "a continuity from Rome to England in the imagery of unsavory devotion to objects associated with the lower body ('where the Prince sate')—a misogynist connection that is even tighter if 'the Prince' in question is, as it was, Queen Elizabeth" (293). **OLIVER** (1997): Mirreus, the "representative Catholic," has "an essentially superficial notion of religion, as well as a surplus of deference," yet "no criticism of Mirreus's actual beliefs is voiced," for the "flaws are all in Mirreus's attitude, his antiquarian tastes and love of ceremony ('rags' are ceremonial trappings)." Moreover, Mirreus "'seeks' a religion, in accordance with the speaker's central injunction to 'Seek true religion,'" and thus he "is unlike the poem's other named characters, who cannot be said to undertake any sort of search or research." Donne implies that Catholicism "would have been an acceptable choice if Mirreus had had better motives for its selection" (54–55).

43–46 *Myrius…yeares ago,* **KERMODE, FENDER, AND PALMER** (1974) note that Swift "uses the anagram Mreo for the Church of Rome and that, Latinized, would be Mirreus," which is "probably where that name comes from." Point out that "nobody is quite clear" on what the other names mean (65). **HESTER** (1982): Mirreus "worships authority more than Truth and looks to Rome 'because hee doth know / That shee was there a thousand yeares agoe'" and is "satisfied with this tropological view of tradition, this partial, temporal truth" (63).

43–44 *Seeke true…from vs* **RICHTER** (1902) cites the rhymed words of the couplet here to illustrate level stress (409).

43 *Seeke true Religion; Oh where?* **MOORE** (1969): "this command is the logical and proper response to the conditions described in the first forty-two lines of the satire," asking the listener "to put aside his worldly concerns and focus his attention on spiritual matters. However, in a diseased world, such a command is not easy to obey, as the question which immediately follows it suggests: 'O where?' This question reflects the central religious problem of Donne's time, namely, which of the existing Christian churches was really the one true church?" (44–45). **MARTZ** (1991) thinks that the "pain" arises, not from "a sense of apostasy from the old religion in which Donne was reared," but from "a sense of insecurity amid the warring doctrines of the day which Donne so well satirizes in his search for truth" (21). **CORTHELL** (1997): Donne's question epitomizes his "historicist dilemma," as he seeks "valid methods of arriving at a reliable historical account of true religion" (38). **NUTT** (1999): the caesura turns the assertion before the question "into a forceful statement of intent" which "is in effect the central idea of the entire satire," and the "perplexity it gives rise to is instantly captured by the rhetorical, 'O where?'" (120).

43 *Seeke true Religion;* **GERALDINE** (1965): the third and most important in a series of four imparatives; this one advocates a "particularized search" (117). **MILGATE** (1967) quotes *Letters,* p. 100 (143). **JACKSON** (1970): "this true religion means the external expression" (31). **BRODSKY** (1982): "The persuasive power of this literal command is heightened by the extended image patterns that precede it. As concise a semantic and syntactic unit as can be found in Donne's poetry, it unequivocally affirms the significance of the subject it invokes," and it "emerges as the single alternative to endeavors described figuratively, and defined appositely, as false" (841). **STRIER** (1993): "This is the speaker's message to his pleasure-loving and desperately adventur-

ous generation. Such a message would seem unexceptionable, but in the context of late sixteenth-century Europe, it is odd. For most Europeans in this period, religion was not something to be sought; it was something given, something into which one was born. It was not an object of intellectual quest. The injunction requires a highly unusual detachment from existing commitments—a detachment like Donne's own in the mid-1590s" (292).

43 *Religion;* **RICHTER** (1902) questions if "ion" is to be read here as bisyllabic or monosyllabic (404). **MELTON** (1906) calls it "an unfortunate selection" for Richter (1902) to use this word as an example of both "einsilbig" (monosyllabic) and "Zweisilbig" (bisyllabic) (52).

43 *Myrius* **GROSART** (1872–73): "probably Myrrheus = perfumed with myrrh" (1:28). [Similarly, Milgate (1967, 143–44), Kermode (1970, 104), Smith (1971, 482), Kermode and Hollander (1973, 1046), Broadbent (1974, 106), Willmott (1985, 62), Craik and Craik (1986, 259), Mallet (1990, 21), Singh (1992, 41), Scodel (1993, 487), Corthell (1997, 50), Enright (1997, 96), and Chmielewski (2001, 616).] **SHAWCROSS** (1967): "Roman Catholic" (24). [So also, Warnke (1967, 114), Patrides (1985, 226), and Donoghue (2001, xxv).]

44 *vnhous'd here,* **JOHNSON** (1755): "To drive from the habitation." **BEWLEY** (1966) notes "in England." [So also, Shawcross (1967, 24), Smith (1971, 482), Hiller (1977, 182), Patrides (1985, 226), Craik and Craik (1986, 259), and Mallet (1990, 21).] Adds, "where the Catholic Church was illegal" (177).

45 *Seekes her...doth know* **STEIN** (1944c): an example of stress-shift after the caesura (378).

45 *Rome;* **GROSART** (1872–73) (using the spelling "Roome"): "the old pronunciation still occasionally met with, as by Earl Russell" (1:28).

47–48 *He loues...sate yesterday.* **CORTHELL** (1982): the "problem of authority and obedience intrudes as soon as Donne turns to the question of where 'true religion' might be found," and the "debunking of Mirreus' position" seems to generate "a new problem even as it appears to answer the Catholic appeal to papal authority" in that "if the analogy denies the ultimacy of papal power, it also raises the question of the basis of royal power. Is obedience to this power a sort of idolatry, as the lines seem to imply? Donne comes dangerously close to answering in the affirmative" (163–64; 1997, 41). **BAUMLIN** (1991): the lines allude to "Rome's historical abuse of ceremonial authority," yet "an ostensibly religious attack turns against the English Crown, the abuse of ceremony simply shifting from Pope to prince. Monarchy has created its own cult and its own idols, the King (or Queen) becoming a second Pope" (127–28). **DIPASQUALE** (1999): "the speaker's comparison of Mirreus's reverence to that which 'wee here' give to the monarch's 'statecloth' points up the ironic parallel Donne perceives between the alleged Mariolatry of Roman Catholics and the cult of the Virgin Queen" (295–96). **WIGGINS** (2000): the equation Donne makes between the statecloth and the rags "confirms his admission that laws sanctioned by the Queen's prerogative can have a powerfully mesmerizing quality" (48).

47–48 *obay...sate yesterday.* **CLEMENTS** (1966): "We do obeisance to the cloth over the throne" (60). **MILGATE** (1967): "The state-cloth was the canopy over the chair of state." [So also, Smith (1971, 483), Kermode and Hollander (1973, 1046), Willmott (1985, 62), Craik and Craik (1986, 259), Hieatt (1987, 237), Carey (1990, 425), and Mallet (1990, 21).] See Fynes Moryson, *Itinerary* (ed. 1907–08), 4:253; Donne's letter to Magdalen Herbert in Walton, *Lives* (1956), p. 335; and Simpson, *Essays*, p. 6 (144).

47 *He* **PATRIDES** (1985): "'And' (acc. to 1635–54)" (226).

47 *her* **PATRIDES** (1985): "(acc. to most MSS): 'the' (acc. to 1633–69 and a few MSS)" (226).

47 *raggs* **MILGATE** (1967): "ceremonial trappings" of religion, which "was once to be found beneath them" (144). **SMITH** (1971): "the few shreds of the original truth that Rome retains; the ostentatious trappings that Rome substitutes for truth and worship" (483). [Similarly, Kermode and Hollander (1973, 1046), Hiller (1977, 182), Patrides (1985, 226), Willmott (1985, 62), Craik and Craik (1986, 259), Mallet (1990, 21), Singh (1992, 41), Enright (1997, 96), and Wiggins (2000, 48).]

47 *as* **BAKER** (1975): "i.e., in the same way that" (72).

47 *obay* **BAKER** (1975): "Do obeisance to" (72). [So also, Hiller (1977, 182).]

48 *State Cloth* **ROUSSEAU AND RUDENSTINE** (1972): "Rich cloth or canopy spread over a throne or chair of state" (65). [So also, Broadbent (1974, 106), Baker (1975, 72), Hiller (1977, 182), Patrides (1985, 226), Lloyd-Evans (1989, 296), Singh (1992, 41), Enright (1997, 96), and Rudrum, Black, and Nelson (2000, 121).]

49–62 *Crantz...Pay values.* **OLIVER** (1997): "the figures of Crants and Graius constitute a powerful two-pronged attack on the doctrine of the Church of England and the strong-arm tactics used to enforce it—a critique which stands after Donne himself has become an apologist for the Church of England" (57).

49–54 *Crantz...cuntry drudges.* **SOWTON** (1960): Donne shared "the common Anglican opinion" that "in external matters such as form, ritual, and Church government, the Puritans were completely over-reformed" (188). **OLIVER** (1997): the "Calvinist" Crants is "a smugly sanctimonious man" who "devotes himself to a faith which the speaker presents as uncompromisingly unattractive." While "the adjectives start inoffensively enough," they "quickly turn nasty, and there's a sneer in the idea of a faith so human in construction that the best that can be said of it is that it is 'called religion'." The simile that follows not only is deflating for Crants and "his motives" but also "demeans Calvinism itself" in that "by suggesting that Calvinists prefer crudity to refinement, the simile casts doubt on their identification of the plainness of their religion with that of primitive Christianity before its purity was sullied by unnecessary additions" (55).

49–52 *Crantz...yet vnhandsome;* **DANIELS** (1970): Petrarchism gives us "the first completely reasonable explanation" of "the description of Crants' mistress." The difficulty with "a common-sense reading of the passage is that all the adjectives ('plaine, simple, sullen, young, / Contemptuous,...unhansome') are derogatory. With this parallelism, then, why are the final two adjectives joined by *yet* instead of *and?* One toys with the possibility that *yet* may be understood as 'even'; but why should *unhansome* be thus singled out as more uncomplimentary than any of the other adjectives? The solution lies in the Petrarchan allusion contained in the phrase 'Contemptuous, yet unhansome.' The lady of the Petrarchan tradition is beautiful and disdainful. But Crants' lady is paradoxical: she is disdainful without the beauty to warrant it" (item 52).

49 *Crantz* **GROSART** (1872–73): it is "curious" that such a name "should intervene between the classical-sounding names Mirreus, Graius, and Phrygius. Can it be from Gränze or Grenze, boundary or limit, in allusion to the puritanic limits within which they withdrew themselves, and placed between themselves and others?" (1:28). **GRIERSON** (1912): Donne "has in view the 'schismatics of Amsterdam' (*The Will*) and their followers" (2:114). **MILGATE** (1967) finds "no need" to limit this to Dutch associations (*pace* Grierson [1912]) (144). **SHAWCROSS** (1967): "Calvinist" (24). [So also, Warnke (1967, 114), Kermode (1970, 104), Kermode and Hollander (1973, 1046), Broadbent (1974, 106), Kermode, Fender, and Palmer (1974, 65), Patrides (1985, 226), Singh (1992, 41), Scodel (1993, 487), Enright (1997, 96), and Donoghue (2001, xxv).] **SMITH** (1971): "a garland or wreath. Possibly the only point here is the German or Dutch associations of the name" (483). [Similarly, Willmott (1985, 62), Craik and Craik (1986, 259), and Mallet (1990, 21).] **PATRIDES** (1985): "'Grants' (acc. to a few MSS) or 'Crantz' or 'Crates' or 'Morus' (acc. to individual MSS)" (226). **CHMIELEWSKI** (2001): "suggesting a Dutch or German (?)" (616).

49 *braue* **CLEMENTS** (1966): "Splendid" (60). [So also, Smith (1971, 483), Kermode and Hollander (1973, 1046), Hiller (1977, 182), Willmott (1985, 62), Hieatt (1987, 237), Lloyd-Evans (1989, 296), Mallet (1990, 21), Jones (1991, 630), and Enright (1997, 96).]

49 *enthralld* **SMITH** (1971): "enslaved" (483). [So also, Willmott (1985, 62), Mallet (1990, 21), and Jones (1991, 630).]

50 *But loues…calld* **COLERIDGE** (1811 [1984]) scans the line as such:

x / x / x / x /
[But loves | her on]ly, who't | Gene | va's call'd | (12.2:226).

STEIN (1944c) notes the extra syllable before the caesura (394).

50 *Geneua* **SMITH** (1971): "the home of Calvin and the most rigorous Puritanism" (483). [Similarly, Rousseau and Rudenstine (1972, 65), Kermode and Hollander (1973, 1046), Patrides (1985, 226), Willmott (1985, 63), Carey (1990, 425), Mallet (1990, 21), Singh (1992, 41), Enright (1997, 96), Rudrum, Black, and Nelson (2000, 121), Chmielewski (2001, 616), and Donoghue (2001, xxv).]

51–52 *Playne,…yet vnhandsome;* **MILGATE** (1967) cites a contrast between "the 'brave' religion of Rome and the 'plaine' religion of Geneva" at "several places in the *Sermons*" and quotes 6:284 (144). **SINGH** (1992): these lines refer to "the austerity" of Calvin's doctrine (41). [So also, Klause (1994, 186).] **NICHOLL** (1992): these lines show the opposition between "the Puritan faction now in the ascendant" and "the

forbidden, atmospheric aura of Catholicism" (95). **SPROXTON** (2000): this descrip-
tion "is hardly an endearing characterisation of the Reformed faith; one would not
guess from it that Donne, the man, as opposed to the poet/persona, is being lured
towards it" (119).

51 *Religion,* **MILGATE** (1967): "Four syllables" (144).

51 *sullen,* **GROSART** (1872–73): "unsocial" (1:28). **MILGATE** (1967): "drab,
dismal" (144). **SMITH** (1971): "obstinate; dismal" (483). [So also, Patrides (1985,
226), Lloyd-Evans (1989, 296), Jones (1991, 630), and Enright (1997, 97).] **HILLER**
(1977): "sombre" (182).

51 *young,* **MALLET** (1990): "the Protestant churches belonged to the sixteenth
century whereas the Church of Rome claimed to go back to Christ's disciple, St
Peter" (21).

52–54 *as among…cuntry drudges.* **CHANDRA** (1991): Donne's simile here may
show "his irreverent attitude towards religion," but if there is irreverence, it is "directed
not against religion so much as against confusion and corruption in it which leave
the truly religious spirit in a state of uncertainty" (232).

52 *Contemptuous,* **STEIN** (1944c): an example of an elided "w" sound before a
vowel (390).

53–54 *iudges…cuntry drudges.* **HESTER** (1978a): Crants is "illogical, depicted as
comparable to a masochistic whoremonger who is 'inthrall'd' (49) by only the ugliest
of women" (46; 1982, 63).

53 *Lecherous humors,* **MILGATE** (1967): "the whims of the lecher" (144). **SMITH**
(1971): "tastes in lechery" (483). [So also, Rousseau and Rudenstine (1972, 66), Kermode
and Hollander (1973, 1047), Hiller (1977, 182), Willmott (1985, 63), Mallet (1990,
21), and Singh (1992, 41).] **PATRIDES** (1985): "the four 'humours' (blood, phlegm,
black bile, yellow bile)," according to "the old physiology, determined one's health
and disposition" (227 and 336).

53 *humors,* **PATRIDES** (1985): "dispositions" (227). [So also, Enright (1997,
97).] **CRAIK AND CRAIK** (1986): "fancies" (259).

54 *wholesome,* **MALLET** (1990): "attractive" (21).

54 *course* **PATRIDES** (1985): "coarse" (227).

54 *drudges.* **MALLET** (1990): "working girls" (21).

55–62 *Graius…Pay values.* **PAYNE** (1926): "The Church of England was evidently
too artificial a compromise to suit" Donne (36). **BAUMLIN** (1986a): "The abuse of
temporal power in forcing religious conformity" receives "implicit criticism in the vi-
gnette on 'Graius' and the personified Anglican Church" (99). **BAUMLIN** (1991): "In
place of one's father (who would, presumably, speak the truth of religion), 'Godfathers'
impose the Anglican service upon Graius," thereby "usurping the place of rightful
parental authority," and thus, "compared to the choices of the other suitors, which are

at least made in freedom, Graius's is a shotgun wedding. The threat of persecution, of prosecution, of legal and economic pressure compels his choice" (128). **STRIER** (1993): this is "the first true instance in the poem of 'railing,' [in] the Juvenalian mode," for here Donne "has contempt for the whole system of state-enforced religion," and he has "equal or perhaps greater contempt for the individual who allows his thought to be controlled by this machinery." As such, "this may be the contempt of the 'recusant,' who refused to attend his parish-church," but it may not be just "the contempt of the Catholic recusant" (294). **HESTER** (1994b) observes that Donne "describes the absence of clear thinking typical of (some) English Reform Protestants by reference to the powerful Court of Wards." Finds that these "English sectarian amorists," like "foolish adventurers who seek mere 'gaine' in their suicidal treks across the globe," are committed to "'seek' the bride of Christ but 'allow' political ideology to govern their search." Notes that Graius is representative of such "idolatrie" and that the "triple-entendres on 'still'" point to a "deadly form of foolish consistency," suggesting that the bride of Christ "has been replaced in English Reformed worship by a sort of self-serving cult of Elizabeth." Focuses on three dimensions of the "Court of Wards simile": (1) it recalls a "familiar English Catholic complaint" that the "the penal fines for recusancy" were "merely political," especially as they were administered by Cecil's Court of Wards, and were "often viewed by Englishmen of all sects" as "violations of the Magna Carta itself"; (2) for Donne, the "machinations of the Court of Wards" were "personally relevant" in that John and Henry Donne "had twice barely escaped (in 1576 and 1590)" the "vast reach" of the Court, and it is likely that their mother's "hasty remarriages to two Catholics after being widowed" were an attempt "to escape the grasp of England's 'Godfather'—and his influence on the character of her children's instruction in the 'valewes' of education in the Protestant view of Christ's bride"; and (3) there is evidence that Donne and his family "took an active role in resisting the use of politics to control the future of English 'Soules'" (130–33). **OLIVER** (1997): the description of Graius "undermines both his loyalty to the Church of England and the practices used to enforce the Elizabethan settlement." Donne creates "a multi-layered attack" on Graius, who "doesn't possess the vision or stamina to examine a range of options," instead following "the 'easy ways and near'" (l. 14) of the Church of England and doing "what preachers and lawmakers tell him to do out of fear and idleness." The preachers "act from questionable motives (they are 'vile ambitious bawds')," and "the laws regulating attendance at services and the fines levied on recusants are clearly human constructions." Finally, "the preachers and laws are responsible for deluding Graius into thinking that he is a member of the 'only perfect' church" (56).

55–61 *Graius…Guardians offer,* **ROBERTS** (1968): "Graius, totally unreflective and immature in his responses, is persuaded partly by his godfather's unauthoritative assurance that true religion can best be found at home" (109).

55–59 *Graius…Imbraceth her,* **KERMODE, FENDER, AND PALMER** (1974): "even the Church of England is not right simply because it happens to be on the spot" (66). **CORTHELL** (1997): the attack on Graius makes a "demystifying statement with respect to the union of church and state" similar to the treatment of Mirreus in ll. 47–48 (41).

55 *Graius* MILGATE (1967) glosses as "a Greek" and observes that there is no "particular point in the choice of this name" (144). [So also, Smith (1971, 483) and Chmielewski (2001, 616).] SHAWCROSS (1967): "adherent of the English or Anglican church" (24). [So also, Warnke (1967, 114), Kermode (1970, 104), Patrides (1985, 226), and Donoghue (2001, xxv).] KERMODE AND HOLLANDER (1973): "Greek; perhaps because the Greeks worshipped 'an unknown God'—Acts 17:23—and sought novelty" (1047). [Similarly, Craik and Craik (1986, 259), Mallet (1990, 21), Singh (1992, 41), and Enright (1997, 97).] BROADBENT (1974): "means a Greek, which suggests venal" (106). WILLMOTT (1985): "'Greek' was a term sometimes used for a trickster or cheat and perhaps implies intellectual dishonesty in accepting the doctrines of the Church of England unquestioningly" (63). SCODEL (1993): this name is "enigmatic" and is "probably intended to make the Englishman's allegiance to his national church seem literally alien. It also recalls Juvenal's Satire 3, which depicts the typical Greek as an empty sycophant who not only does whatever his patron commands but also derives his opinions and even his facial expressions from his patron" (487–88). KRUZHKOVA (1994): the name possibly refers to an adherent of the Greek church while simultaneously attacking the intolerance of the Anglican church (159).

56–57 *lawes / Still new, like fashions,* SMITH (1971): "devotion in England under Elizabeth was regulated by a multiplicity of laws, which were meant to uphold the Anglican settlement" (483). [So also, Kermode and Hollander (1973, 1047), Hiller (1977, 182), Mallet (1990, 21), and Singh (1992, 41).] STRIER (1993) says that if the reference to "new lawes" is taken literally, then "the most likely reference would be the activities of the 1593 Parliament," and "what this Parliament did was to extend the anti-Catholic legislation of 1581 to the Puritans, who were punished more harshly than Catholics under its provisions." Notes further that in the mid-1590s, "recusants" could refer to either Catholics or Protestants, "although the 'new lawes' and 'ambitious' preachers at the time were primarily anti-Puritan." Concludes that Donne "is speaking for 'recusants' of all kinds" (295). CORTHELL (1997): Donne's "response to historicism seems much less assured than Hooker's" as "change in the laws is suspect" (44). ROBBINS (2000): Donne reveals his impartiality by "coming out vehemently against the teaching and law of Elizabethan England" (424). EDWARDS (2001) notes that "as recently as 1558, under Queen Mary, the laws had enforced Roman Catholicism" (70).

56 *ambitious bawds,* MILGATE (1967): "bawds" because "they procure adherents, or prostitute their office, by making false claims for the English Church (i.e. that it is the only perfect Church), in order to curry favour with, and win promotion from, high officers in Church and State" (144). [So also, Smith (1971, 483), Kermode and Hollander (1973, 1047), Willmott (1985, 63), Mallet (1990, 21), Singh (1992, 41), and Chmielewski (2001, 616).]

56 *lawes* ROUSSEAU AND RUDENSTINE (1972): "Laws aimed at compelling compliance with the doctrines of the English Church. Persons who failed to attend their parish churches, for example, were fined" (66).

57 *Still new, like fashions,* **MILGATE** (1967): "A comment on the rapid succession of laws regulating beliefs, ceremonies, and penalties for recusancy, etc., that marked the growth of the English Church" (144).

57 *Still new,* **BAKER** (1975): "Continually changing" (72).

57 *bidd* **PATRIDES** (1985): "(acc. to the MSS): 'bids' (acc. to 1633–69)" (227).

58 *Which dwells...perfect, hee* **RICHTER** (1902) cites this line to illustrate enjambment (408).

58 *is only perfect,* **SMITH** (1971): "is alone perfect" (483). [Similarly, Kermode and Hollander (1973, 1047), Hiller (1977, 182), Willmott (1985, 63), Mallet (1990, 21), and Enright (1997, 97).]

59–62 *his Godfathers...Pay values.* **WIGGINS** (2000): the comparison here "not only contains none of the respect of his former reference to fathers, but constitutes as clear an acknowledgment as possible of the establishment's ability to force consciences" (48).

59 *Imbraceth her,...Godfathers will* **STEIN** (1944c): an example of fourth foot stress-shift after a pause (384).

59 *Imbraceth* **MALLET** (1990): "embraces, chooses" (21).

59 *Godfathers* **SMITH** (1971): "(a) sponsors at baptism; (b) spiritual guides—'fathers in God' (among whom might be those who make the laws that bind him)" (483). [So also, Willmott (1985, 63), Craik and Craik (1986, 259), Mallet (1990, 21), and Singh (1992, 41).]

60–62 *wards still...Pay values.* **SMITH** (1971): "pay the fine imposed upon wards who refused a marriage which their guardians had arranged for them. The Act of Uniformity of 1559 imposed fines upon people who did not attend their parish church" (483). [Similarly, Rousseau and Rudenstine (1972, 66), Kermode and Hollander (1973, 1047), Lewalski and Sabol (1973, 96), Broadbent (1974, 106), Baker (1975, 72), Hiller (1977, 183), Patrides (1985, 227), Willmott (1985, 63), Craik and Craik (1986, 259), Hieatt (1987, 237), Lloyd-Evans (1989, 300), Mallet (1990, 21), Singh (1992, 41), and Enright (1997, 97).]

60 *Tender to him being tender;* **MILGATE** (1967): "word-play heightens the contempt: 'offer to him while he is of tender years and insufficient judgement'" (144). **KERMODE AND HOLLANDER** (1973): "offer to him in his infancy" (1047). [So also, Hiller (1977, 183), Craik and Craik (1986, 259), Lloyd-Evans (1989, 297), and Singh (1992, 41).] **MELCHIORI** (1983) notes a parallel use of "tender" in a speech by Percy (Hotspur) in *R2* (2.3.41–42): "I tender you my service, / Such as it is, being tender, raw and young" (181).

60 *Tender to him* **SMITH** (1971): "offer him" (483). [So also, Willmott (1985, 63), Mallet (1990, 21), and Enright (1997, 97).] **PATRIDES** (1985): "present to him" (227).

60 *being tender;* **SMITH** (1971): "because he is young, weak, impressionable" (483).

[So also, Baker (1975, 72), Willmott (1985, 63), Mallet (1990, 21), Jones (1991, 630), and Enright (1997, 97).]

60 *wards* **RICHTER** (1902) cites this word to illustrate a stretching of syllables (405).

61–62 *Take such…Pay values.* **HESTER** (1978a): Graius's "'values' do, of course, 'Pay' because of his mental sloth, for, like the other amorists, he values only what he can see, realize, or compute easily" (46).

61 *or* **MELTON** (1906) cites this as an example of "'insignificant' words stressed to meet the exigencies of rhythm and meaning" (65, 76).

62–69 *Careles Phrygas…light breeds.* **BREDVOLD** (1925): Donne shows "scorn" here for those who fail to seek truth, which he insists is knowable, through study and thought (209–10). **LEAVIS** (1935): the rational voice of the first three lines contrasts with the "rakish levity" of the last two and illustrates the "mimetic flexibility" of the poem (239; 1936, 13–14). **SCODEL** (1993) (reading "Phygrius"): to the extent that Graccus and Phrygius "have genuine reasons for their views, they approach what Donne will reveal as the proper stance," but they "reason themselves into opposite extremes," for Phrygius "is spiritually deficient in joining 'none' while Graccus is excessive in regarding 'all' sects as valid" (488). The source of the names of Phrygius and Graccus, "an attack on Roman 'effeminacy' in Juvenal's Satire 2," clarifies Donne's "attitude toward their positions." Juvenal concludes "a thirty-five-line section inveighing against men who shamefully participate in rituals traditionally restricted to women by comparing such ceremonies to the Phrygian rites of Cybele, at the climax of which men castrate themselves, and proceeds in the next twenty-six lines to mock the marriage of the once-virile transvestite Gracchus: 'Why wait any longer,' Juvenal rhetorically asks, 'when it were time in Phrygian fashion to lop off the superfluous flesh? Gracchus…who is now arraying himself in the flounces and trailing habits and veil of a bride once carried the nodding shields of Mars!' Juvenal attacks the Phrygian rites and the Gracchian transvestite marriage as random examples of 'effeminacy' without pursing the relationship between such diverse ways of losing one's 'manhood.'" The name Phrygius is also particularly apt "as an indictment of one who fears religious commitment. Both pagan and patristic writers describe Phrygian eunuchs as, in Ovid's words, 'nor man nor woman.' Donne uses the name to construct a conceptual pun on a word not present in his text, 'neuter,' which in both Latin and Renaissance English had not only its modern meaning but also that of 'taking neither one side nor the other' (*OED*, 2)," Donne's "implicit pun" reinforcing "the link between religious abstention and a deficiency of 'manliness'" (492–93). **KRUZHKOVA** (1994): Phrygius and Graccus exemplify two different types of religious free-thinking (159).

62–64 *Careles Phrygas…mary none.* **MILGATE** (1967) quotes *Sermons* 9:75 and Burton, *Anatomy of Melancholy*, part. 3, sect. 4, memb. 2, subsect. 1 (145). **HESTER** (1980b) (reading "Phygrius"): Phrygius is usually described as an atheist, a "sound annotation" if "All" is taken as "a punning reference to God (rather than to all churches)." Phrygius "has decided only that he 'knows' of no true Church," since "all have been infected, the simile suggests, by descent from the Whore of Babylon." At a time when men "tortured, hanged, and burned each other for doctrinal differences, Phrygius could be termed an 'atheist,'" but he is not necessarily an atheist "in the strictest technical or 'modern' sense of the word," for Phrygius "does not deny the existence of God, but only that any of the current churches descends unblemished from the vicarage of St. Peter" (88–89). **HESTER** (1982) (reading "Phygrius"): it is difficult to determine "which or if Donne had a particular sect in mind in the creation of Phrygius," a difficulty "complicated by the attitudes towards the other religious sects in the age (as well as by the rapid proliferation of sects at the end of the century and the large number that were merely subspecies of each other)" (120–21). Given Donne's attention to "contemporary religious foolishness," he may have had "a specific target in mind" in portraying Phrygius. The English sect "closest in spirit and word to the 'reasoning' of Phrygius is the Seekers," but as a sect they are "simply too late a candidate for Donne's satire." Some of their beliefs, however, predated their existence as a sect. One of the founders of the Seekers—Thomas Legate—was previously a member of a sect—the Barrowists—"whose beliefs and existence correspond with the imagery and date of Donne's wry portrait." The Barrowists were, along with the Brownists, a sect that "especially alarmed the Establishment at the turn of the century." One can find "in the tenets and current estimation" of the Barrowists "consistent parallels with Donne's portrait of Phrygius" (122–23). **SCODEL** (1993) (reading "Phygrius"): "Phrygius is 'careless' primarily in the sense of 'heedless' or 'reckless.' He responds to the diversity of churches and the evident impurity of some with a rash decision to have 'none.' His 'abhorre[nce]' implied dread as much as hatred, however, and he is not only rash but also cowardly in giving up the search for 'true religion' out of excessive fear," and he "rashly denies himself the possibility of finding salvation within a true church because he is overly afraid of the possibility of being damned by the choice of a false one" (488–89). **STRIER** (1993) (reading "Phygrius"): Phrygius seems initially "to be making a logical mistake," for "it does not follow from the premise that all 'cannot be good' that all must be bad." Moreover, when Donne "shifts to the erotic analogy and activates the pun on 'abhorre,' the situation becomes more complicated," as the "context shifts from attitudes to behavior." In particular, "Phrygius is a skeptic, and here the erotic and the epistemological are strongly bound," and thus "it is important to see that Phrygius is not what, in philosophical terms, would be called a negative dogmatist." His position, therefore, "is not that all women/churches are bad," and in a religious context, "this means that he is not a Separatist, one who thought all existing churches false—that is, impure, tainted" (295–96). **PRESCOTT** (1997) (reading "Phygrius"): the name of Phrygius "recalls the cult of Cybele and her attendant eunuchs." In fact, "in his comments on Panurge's dilemma (The Third Book 48), Gargantua mentions with distaste a group of 'moles'—which critics usually take to mean monks—that 'abhor' marriage," but Donne "hardly needed Rabelais to see that an inability to identify true religion can be figured as a failure to locate Christ's true bride" (47–48).

62 *Pay values.* **GROSART** (1872–73): "A curious law, of which I can find no record = pay a fine" (1:28). [So also, Kermode (1970, 104), Grigson (1980, 21), Carey (1990, 425), and Jones (1991, 630).]

62 *values*. **OED** (1916–20): the earliest recorded use of the meaning of the word as "that amount of some commodity, medium of exchange, etc., which is considered equivalent for something else; a fair or adequate equivalent or return" (I.1.c)—specifically related to *valour* in the obsolete sense of "the value of the marriage" (3d). **KENNER** (1964): "sums paid their guardians by wards who refused arranged marriages: here compared to the fine a recusant paid for not attending his parish church" (43). [So also, Clements (1966, 60), Nutt (1999, 120–21), and Rudrum, Black, and Nelson (2000, 121).] **BEWLEY** (1966): "fines" (177). [So also, Carey (1990, 425).] **MILGATE** (1967): "Graius accepts the English Church because his godfathers (the legislators, as well as his actual sponsors at baptism) so decide; then (like a ward refusing a pre-arranged marriage) he must pay a fine (under the Act of Uniformity, 1559) if he refuses to attend his parish church" (144–45). [So also, Shawcross (1967, 397), Patrides (1985, 227), and Chmielewski (2001, 616).]

62 *Careles Phrygas* **CRAIK AND CRAIK** (1986): "the free-thinker, careless because indifferent to religion. Phryges (Greek), freemen, was the original name for the inhabitants of what became known as Phrygia in Asia Minor" (259–60). **SCODEL** (1993): "The philosophical resonance of the epithet 'careless' reveals the self-defeating nature of Phrygius's stance," for Phrygius "represents both a kind of Skepticism and a kind of Epicureanism, which the erotic analogy links as parallel and equally vain attempts to attain tranquility by suppressing the desire for knowledge, whether cognitive or erotic. Responding to the epistemological uncertainty caused by the diversity of philosophical sects, the ancient Skeptics sought tranquility by eschewing all doctrines; Phrygius responds to the diversity of religious sects by avoiding all churches. Epicureans sought tranquility by avoiding pain and pleasures that could cause pain, such as erotic love; they consequently did not marry. Donne's erotic analogy suggests that, like the Epicureans, Phrygius seeks to avert possible pain by refusing to marry a (spiritual) mistress." In addition, Donne's epithet "associates Phrygius's spiritual deficiency with an Epicurean avoidance of love," for as with its "counterpart *cura* in Latin poetry, 'care' in English Renaissance poetry can refer to a loved object, love itself, or the anxieties and pains of love," and "being 'careless' thus can connote being without love and its attendant pains." Nevertheless, "his rejection of a specifically spiritual object of desire is itself true to Epicurean principles, for the Epicureans spurned traditional religion, just as they spurned erotic attachment, as a threat to tranquility" (489–90). **STRIER** (1993): Phrygius is "the only one of the figures to have an epithet," and while the epithet first seems "inappropriate," because "if anything, Phrygius would seem to be overly careful," he is "'careless' because he is free from care—*secura*," which is "the ataraxia of the ancient skeptics" (297).

62 *Careles* **SMITH** (1971): "caring for none of the alternatives open to him; free" (483). [So also, Patrides (1985, 227), Lloyd-Evans (1989, 297), and Mallet (1990, 22).]

62 *Phrygas* **MILGATE** (1967) cannot "see any particular point in the choice of this name" (144). **SHAWCROSS** (1967): "rejector of all creeds" (24). [So also, Kermode and Hollander (1973, 1047) and Donoghue (2001, xxv).] **WARNKE** (1967): "the freethinker, or, to use the term common in Donne's day, libertine" (114). **KERMODE** (1970): "'atheist' in Elizabethan sense" (104). **SMITH** (1971): "a Phrygian. Possibly

Donne alludes to the multiplicity of gods which confronted the ancient Phrygians as a consequence of their subjection to several different peoples in turn" (483–84). [So also, Broadbent (1974, 106), Willmott (1985, 63), Mallet (1990, 22), Singh (1992, 41), and Chmielewski (2001, 616).] **PATRIDES** (1985): "the separatist" (226), "'careless' in that, as a separatist sectarian, he cares for no one else" (227). **ENRIGHT** (1997): "i.e. a nonconformist" (97).

63 *All,...as one* **STEIN** (1944c): an example of stress-shift before a pause (381).

65–71 *Graccus...the right;* **CAREY** (1981): although Donne "is busily shuffling off his Faith, the conviction that there is one 'right' church which alone certifies salvation is part of his Catholic upbringing. No church would ever mean so much to him again, and consequently when he abandoned Catholicism he lost an irreplaceable absolute" (15–16).

65–69 *Graccus...light breeds.* **COLERIDGE** (1811): "a fine instance of free, vehement, verse-disguising Verse. Read it as it ought to be read; and no Ear will be offended" (1984, 12.2:227). **KERMODE, FENDER, AND PALMER** (1974): Graccus is "a sort of Neo-Platonist who thought of all religions as belonging to the same category," a "kind of early Deist" (66). **NOVARR** (1980): Donne attacks Graccus "for his indifference and his self-indulgence, for a lack of discrimination caused by the cavalier profligacy of his affection." Donne "had no use for a self-serving, indiscriminatory latitudinarianism, though tolerance and latitude, as well as a quintessential purity, are implied in the Church Universal he envisions in 'Show me deare Christ'" (136). **SCODEL** (1993): Graccus "is described as a religious libertine: loving all sects, like all women, equally much and therefore equally little. Like Phrygius, he is both excessive and deficient: by 'too much light,' by seeking to be too enlightened or by blithely accepting the supposed 'light' of all denominations, Graccus falls into 'blindness,' the inability to distinguish the light of 'true religion.' Since 'breeds' activates the latent sense of 'light' as 'wanton, unchaste' (*OED*, 14b), the claim that 'too much light breeds' Graccus's 'blindness' recalls the Renaissance commonplace that sexual excess causes blindness and thereby suggests a physical analogue for Graccus's combination of spiritual excess and defect." An additional pun "reinforces Graccus's self-serving suppression of crucial distinctions. Aristotle defines virtues and vices as *hexeis*, normally translated into Latin as *habitus* and in Renaissance English as 'habits,'" and "the pun on 'habits' undercuts Graccus's love of all churches; while the dressing of a church or woman may not matter, their 'divers habits' in the sense of divergent dispositions define them as good or bad" (491–92). Further, Donne's "allusion to the Juvenalian Gracchus is also suggestive. Since classical and Renaissance thinkers often treated a male's excessive interest in women as a loss of 'manhood,' there is a general appropriateness in Donne's implicit comparison of his libertine" to Juvenal's "would-be woman." As such, Donne's "allusion to Roman cross-dressing undercuts his Graccus's 'blind,' self-indulgent confidence that he knows what 'kind' actually lies hidden beneath the surface 'habitus' of diverse religious denominations" (494). **STRIER** (1993): "What is striking about Graccus's view is how sensible it is," involving "neither a false premise," "nor any obviously false reasoning." There "must be something wrong with Graccus's view," yet Donne's "comment on it is ambiguous. In a violent enjambment, Donne states of Graccus's position that 'this blind- / nesse too much light breeds,'" the enjambment appearing "to establish, for a moment, 'blind' as a noun in itself." This reading possibly suggests that Graccus's view "is a pretext, some sort of hypocritical concealment, but this oblique suggestion is left entirely undeveloped. In the actual context of the poem, what the unusual mid-word line-break does is to connect Graccus, at least momentarily, with the other 'blind' figures in the poem, the 'Philosophers,' whom Donne, like Erasmus, placed in heaven. This association is appropriate, given Graccus's religious view, but it cuts against the moral condemnation of him," and "the condemnation of Graccus remains perfunctory, abstract, and deeply ambiguous" (298–99).

65 *Graccus* **MILGATE** (1967): "the Gracchi were champions of democracy; there may be some faint appropriateness in giving the name to one who finds religions (as they did men) 'of equal worth'" (145). [Similarly, Smith (1971, 484), Kermode and Hollander (1973, 1047), Willmott (1985, 63), Craik and Craik (1986, 260), Mallet (1990, 22), Singh (1992, 41), and Chmielewski (2001, 616).] **SHAWCROSS** (1967): "eclectic who considers all basically alike" (24). [So also, Donoghue (2001, xxvi).] **WARNKE** (1967): "the so-called Erastian, who believed in the principle that the religion of the monarch should determine the religion of the country" (114). [So also, Patrides (1985, 226–27).] **KERMODE** (1970): "comparative religionist of the Neo-Platonic sort" (105). **ENRIGHT** (1997): "i.e. a liberal or latitudinarian" (97).

65 *all as one,* **MILGATE** (1967): "all alike" (145). **SMITH** (1971): "every one of them equally" (484). [So also, Baker (1975, 72), Willmott (1985, 63), and Mallet (1990, 22).]

66–69 *As women…light breeds.* **MORRIS** (1953) cites these lines as an example of "over-reaving," which is used to create a "rhythmical continuity" as "the rhythm moves with the meaning" from line to line with "no break in the syntax" (48). **POWERS** (1971): these lines illustrate Donne's tendency to ignore "the restraints of the single line" in the interests of imitating speech (48). **GROVE** (1984): "sexual habits vary, and notoriously so with foreigners. Yet the verse no sooner lets sex rear its head, than it respectabilizes the (apparent) false-start." There is a "neat fold over the line-end, for decorum's sake," in ll. 66–67, a decorum "immediately given up" in the next phrases. With "that split rhyme-word, 'blind- / nesse'," the eye is perhaps "left for a second in the dark (more so with the word's second half, as it happens; so what should clarify perplexity, deepens it for an instant). Does light breed blindness?—that would be strange enough; but what if blindness, as the verse suggests, itself breeds too much light?" (59).

66–68 *As women…so is Religion;* **GRANSDEN** (1954): "Characteristically English in spirit, the poem rejects any absolute, permanently 'true' form of religion in favour of an empirical, relative approach," and "such broadmindedness and open-mindedness is a clear indication of Donne's natural dislike of all intractable claims to unique truth" (103). **ROY AND KAPOOR** (1969): Donne "does not believe in the rigid contraries of the controversialists, for he can understand the significance of relative approach even to religion" (104).

66 *diuers Cuntryes* **SMITH** (1971): "various countries" (484). [So also, Willmott (1985, 63) and Enright (1997, 97).]

67 *diuers habitts,* **SMITH** (1971): "various costumes" (484). [So also, Rousseau and Rudenstine (1972, 66), Willmott (1985, 63), Mallet (1990, 22), Singh (1992, 41), and Enright (1997, 97).]

67 *one kind,* **SMITH** (1971): "of one nature of species" (484). [So also, Mallet (1990, 22).] **WILLMOTT** (1985): "i.e., they are all women" (63).

68–85 *So doth,...now do.* **KNOTTENBELT** (2000): while "the choice of imagery is as abstract as the truth that is being conveyed," the "thought, as much as an abstract idea, indeed Truth itself, is nonetheless as concrete, physically, as the body or living matter" (119).

68–79 *and this...wrong, is.* **GERALDINE** (1965): the images of light and blindness emphasize that Graccus is urged to reform his reason rather than his will (118).

68–69 *this blind- / nes, too much light breeds.* **STEIN** (1946): "When to unexpected grammar and verbal compression the author adds subtle imagery, the labor of the reader is further increased," in that the reader comes to realize that "too much 'light' is as dazzling to the mind as to the eye" (101–02). **MILGATE** (1967): "Too much light causes this blindness." Finding truth in every religion, "Graccus is blinded to true religion when he actually comes across it"; see Jonson, *Volpone* 5.2.23 and *A Tale of a Tub,* 1:1, 56–57 (145). [Similarly, Smith (1971, 484), Kermode and Hollander (1973, 1047), Hiller (1977, 183), Willmott (1985, 63), Craik and Craik (1986, 260), Hieatt (1987, 237), Mallet (1990, 22), Singh (1992, 41), and Enright (1997, 97).] **WILLIAMSON** (1967): this same paradox appears in *Lit* 62, but the paradox only leads here to the doubts of ll. 72–82 (52). [So also, Oliver (1997, 96).] **HESTER** (1982): the blindness of the five religious types "merits" the satirist's ridicule "not because of the practices of their specific sects but because of the lack of understanding underlying their individual choices. All five seem to have progressed beyond the moral cowardice of the adventurers—their having adopted religious stances connotes their awareness of the 'worth' (or, in this case, the practical, political necessity) of religious devotion; but the fact that they rest smugly in the particular interpretation of devotion that they find most satisfying personally" thereby reveals that "their aims are temporal 'gaine' also" (63).

68–69 *blind- / nes,* **MILGATE** (1967) cites other examples of "violent enjambment" in *Sat4* 13–14 and 104–05 (145).

68 *So doth, so is Religion;* **SMITH** (1971): "religion may go in a variety of garbs from country to country but is essentially one and the same" (484). [So also, Mallet (1990, 22).]

69–110 *But vnmoued...to trust.* **MILGATE** (1967): this "last section of the poem is in the grave and forceful style of Donne's verse letters to his men friends—an exhortation to an active pursuit of a personal faith" (140).

69–84 *But vnmoued...that night.* **PAYNE** (1926): these lines "combine dignity and strength, the latter rather enhanced than lessened by the metrical abruptness" (38).

69–79 *But vnmoued...wrong, is.* **RAY** (1990): Donne "tells the 'you' that, in contrast to the five types just outlined, the individual must take the matter of religion much more seriously. One must not be influenced by ('unmoved') such insubstantial and ridiculous reasons and pressures as the five types are in choosing something as important as the true religion that will offer salvation for the soul. 'Of force' (i.e., by necessity) there is only one right one, and the individual must use all possible means to search it out. Lines 71–75 argue that one must go back to the roots of the true church by examining all the opinions of previous humans. Even if one has to go back to examine the truth existing before the Fall to achieve the 'best' religion, one should do so, since falsehood began to corrupt truth even when Adam and Eve fell in disobeying God. The act of searching in itself is of great value, because it means that one is not an atheist ('of non,' of no religion) and that one is not of the 'worst' religion. One may discover through a close examination and discrimination of religions that to 'adore' (like Roman Catholics) or to 'scorn an image' (like the extreme anti-Catholic Protestants such as the Calvinists and Puritans) or simply to 'protest' (like Protestants generally) may all be bad: i.e., one must search and examine to be sure, rather than simply to facilely accept any one way of worship as true and good (ll. 76–77). Lines 77–79 use the analogy of someone on a strange road ('in strange way'): if he ponders the alternatives carefully, he is not straying; but, if he 'sleeps' intellectually and acts without thinking and takes the wrong turn, then he is straying" (281–82).

69–75 *But vnmoued...the best.* **COLERIDGE** (1811): "Here's Brama's Hydraulic Packing-Engline! [sic] a *scrouge* of Sense!" (1984, 12.2:227). **GROVE** (1984): "Whatever writing like this does, it doesn't 'flow'. It postures, hectors, manipulates, so as to leave us no clear way out," and so "wherever we turn, we are confronted by an insistent, almost quarrelsome presence, so that reader and poem between them tussle for the upper hand, until we are brought to feel Truth not as an immobilized authority passed down to us, but as something to be struggled for and wondered at with unresting skepticism" (60).

69–74 *vnmoued thou...seeke her.* **DOCHERTY** (1986): these lines present "the notion that verifiable identity, authentic individual essence, is maintained through the regulation of history in the form of faithful repetition or representation." The problem, though, is that "such representation is impossible," for "not only did Donne 'betray' the faith of his father and familial heritage, he also wrote a large number of poems which either argue that this kind of betrayal is fundamentally constitutive of fidelity to 'reality' or truth, or which demonstrate that faithful representation is saturated by hypocrisy, infidelities, betrayals or transformations of reality" (125–26).

69–73 *vnmoued thou...elder is.* **LEISHMAN** (1934) relates these lines to Donne's study of the Church fathers (10). **ROBERTS** (1968): in these lines "the tone of the poem drastically shifts from the bantering and rather heavy-handed satire of the preceding portraits to a serious presentation of the essential dilemma or problem of the poem—the necessity of choosing the true religion and the resultant frustration that such a demand puts on the sincere seeker who refuses to settle quickly for a compromise and who is willing to exercise spiritual courage in the quest." Moreover, Donne "in no sense takes a relativistic attitude toward truth in religion," for "the speaker clearly recognizes that truth is absolute—that one and only one religion must be right and that one is obliged to find it, but apparently from the preceding review of contesting Christian sects he has decided that no single existing one contains this absolute, simple, full truth" (109–10). **DOCHERTY** (1987): "To find the truth, Donne advises some degree of conformity to past or traditional models; more correctly, he suggests that we can learn something of the truth from our familial heritage. This is of special interest in Donne's own case, for it is precisely such a heritage, that of the family of the (Thomas) Mores, which he betrayed in his apostasy" (96).

69–72 *But vnmoued…aske his*; **MILGATE** (1967) hears in these lines evidence of "what seemed to be viable of the current attempts to Latinize English" (xxiii). **MINER** (1969): Donne's response to the question where one would find true religion is "an oblique answer, one he found difficult to hold to," and "the significant element is the biblical echo: 'Remember the days of old, consider the years of many generations: ask thy father, and he will shew thee; thy elders, and they will tell thee' (Deuteronomy 32:7). [So also, Smith (1971, 484), Kermode and Hollander (1973, 1047), Hiller (1977, 183), Willmott (1985, 63–64), Lloyd-Evans (1989, 300), Mallet (1990, 22), Singh (1992, 41), and Enright (1997, 97).] To Donne personally, with his father, the injunction surely meant an acknowledgement of Catholicism as 'the right' religion" (35).

69–71 *vnmoued thou…the right*; **GRIERSON** (1912): "a stable judgement compels us to acknowledge religion, and that there can be only one. This being so, the next question is, Which is the true one? As to that, we cannot do better than consult our fathers" (2:115). **SELLIN** (1980): these lines express "exactly what the Synod of Dort attempted to do—and has been condemned by Remonstrant sympathizers for its efforts ever since" (286). **KERINS** (1984): "Man's spiritual needs impel him toward a religion, and embracing one as 'the right,' he is compelled to disavow all others. Similarly, man's physical needs urge him to take a wife, and once accepting her, he is constrained to disavow all other mistresses" (47). **STEIN** (1984): "The goal of salvation is understood to be certain, the external enemies are clearly describable, the defense of doubt is plain and dignified, but the process of attaining the goal, by seeking, doubting, striving, keeping, is less clear in itself than in its necessary conflict with the forces that would deflect it. There are abrupt turns, and open unnegotiated places in the discourse, and these are further perplexed by the varying degrees to which the speaker himself seems to enter and act in what he says, not assuming an unmoved station or formal mask for presenting the issues, but expressing the doubts, hopes, and convictions with a sense of personal urgency" (82). **ZUNDER** (1988): Donne "affirms the dominant assumption that there is only one, universal Church" (80). **CORTHELL** (1997): the lines "make it clear that the subject of desire is also a subject of power, another division in the poem, roughly symmetrical to the 'kind pitty' and 'brave scorn' of its opening line," and thus Donne's "quest is both eroticized and politicized" (40). **OLIVER** (1997): it is uncertain as to "what the speaker means by 'right'." Although it appears that he "is counseling searching for a church that makes absolute claims for its doctrine and authority," this position "contradicts the impression" given earlier. In fact, "a clue to the answer to this lies in the poem's complete lack of interest in specific religious doctrines, one of its less contemporary features" (57–58). **WIGGINS** (2000): in these lines "the voice of the Privy Councillor, speaking to Englishmen out of the whirlwind of the council chamber, comes through at its sternest." Donne provides "the most concise statement in Elizabethan literature of the vexing dilemma posed by the doctrine of *cuius regio eius religio*, the doctrine that the regime dictates and is coterminous with its church." (42). Here the poem confronts the "impasse" between the needs of the state and the individual conscience, and as such, this passage "sums up the description of spiritual malaise in the preceding twenty-five lines and opens the way, with the abruptness of a leap of faith, to an affirmation of the Settlement" (48).

69–70 *But vnmoued…one allow;* **BRADSHAW** (1982): the "very strenuous movement of the verse registers this sense of strain" between the divine injunction to choose a Church, the individual's will in exercising choice, and the State's forced choice (340). **WILLMOTT** (1985): "Whether you are left to make up your own mind ('unmoved' by others) or whether you are put under pressure ('forced') you must of necessity ('of force') choose one and only ('but') one" (63). **BAUMLIN** (1991): it is "temporal authority that ushers in intolerance. 'Unmoved' (69), as the satirist states, one must through force of reason choose a way of faith; when 'forc'd,' as one is by the Crown, one must choose 'but one' (70), which is of course the 'middle way' or *via media* of Anglicanism. Yet the word 'forc'd' alerts readers to the real obstacle, which is the arbitrary violence of 'mans lawes'" (140). **SAUNDERS** (1999) notes that Bradshaw (1982) proves these lines to be "regularly iambic" by distinguishing between lexical and metrical stresses (178–79).

69 *too much light* **CHMIELEWSKI** (2001): "which itself obscures true religion" (616).

69 *vnmoued* **MILGATE** (1967): "unswayed (by such frivolous considerations as move Phrygius and Graccus)" (145). **SMITH** (1971): "not swayed by other motives than the search for the one right religion" (484). [So also, Mallet (1990, 22) and Enright (1997, 97).]

70 *Of force…one allow;* **MILGATE** (1967): "Man must, of necessity, approve and follow one form of religion and, if forced, must approve as true one and one only." That is, "one cannot be religious without 'having a religion,'" and "in the last resort one must give one's allegiance to one religion and only to one" (145). [Similarly, Smith (1971, 484), Lloyd-Evans (1989, 300), and Mallet (1990, 22).] **HESTER** (1982): "In one sense, his words prescribe the necessity of choosing 'the right' religion, that one is obliged to find, or to quest lovingly and absolutely after, the one absolute Truth. At the same time, his advice ridicules contemporary religious intolerance by which one is 'forc'd [to] allow' the wisdom of a particular sect whether one is 'mov'd,' stirred, or convinced by its doctrine or not" (66).

70 *Of force* **HILLER** (1977): "of necessity" (183). [So also, Patrides (1985, 227), Craik and Craik (1986, 260), and Enright (1997, 97).]

70 *forc'd* **MILGATE** (1967): "probably includes the notion of being 'forc'd' by the

law to declare oneself" (145). **PATRIDES** (1985): "when compelled to choose" (227). [So also, Craik and Craik (1986, 260) and Enright (1997, 97).]

70 *allow*; **JONES** (1991): "approve" (630).

71–84 *ask thy…that night.* **GUIBBORY** (1993): "The emphasis is on seeking, on process. Discovery is difficult yet necessary, and a sceptical mind plays an important part" (128–29).

71–79 *ask thy…wrong, is.* **MAHLER** (1991): the true seeker has to protect himself from preestablished courage with true bravery, protect himself from the temptation of the devil, the world, and the flesh, which only lead one away from the right path, as well as the preformed paths, whose promises of salvation are not to be trusted: Catholicism, Calvinism, the way of the English Church, or even the model of Atheism, that is to say, an unreflective tolerance. Truth is not to be found anywhere here. It isn't found in the blind acceptance of supposed truths of any others, but rather only in an active give and take with those whose authority lies in the fact that they have already been searching for a long time (43).

71–75 *ask thy…the best.* **ZUNDER** (1988): the Church "is susceptible of rational, in fact historical, inquiry" (80).

71–73 *ask thy…elder is.* **ROBERTS** (1968): these lines "may at first appear like a manifest contradiction to the speaker's repeated insistence that one must not accept a religious position on the basis of someone else's authority," but there is in fact "no contradiction." Donne says that "*if* it were possible to ask one's father and he were to ask his, and so forth back to the dawn of Christianity"—and never does he "suggest that truth in religion can be found outside Christianity"—he "would find the answers to his questions," but this approach, "essentially the Catholic approach of historicity," is "not possible." Donne is here "not recommending a definite methodology for the finding of truth in religion," but rather is "stating in explicit terms his conviction that such a truth did exist at one particular time in history and that the present Christian sects are all merely poor or impartial representations of it. In one sense one might call this approach essentially Platonic, in that all present forms of religion are mere shadows of the immense reality that they attempt to reflect" (110). **BRODSKY** (1982): "The heuristic fiction of the precedence of 'truth' over 'falsehood' is presented here with precise and elegant effect. Logically, however, it implies a disturbing ratio of inquiry: knowledge of truth will increase in proportion to its distance from its present pursuit. The problem of deception, or at least, of inadequate definition, is also involved here, since whatever is offered as prior knowledge may appear, by the criterion of precedence, to be true" (842). **CRAIK AND CRAIK** (1986): "The idea is to return to primitive Christianity" (260). **BAUMLIN** (1991): "what, at least to Catholic opponents, is the Protestant but a prodigal son who has abandoned the ways of elder generations, an upstart fashioning a religion without his father's blessing? The allusions throughout to father-figures, to those with the wisdom and authority to save their sons, become further arguments for maintaining Roman practices of worship." Thus, "tradition once again, the refuge of Catholic fideism, urges the free acceptance of the Old Church's teachings, an acceptance prepared for by Pyrrhonist doubts over man's ability to discover for himself a sufficient and infallible rule of faith" (140). **OLIVER** (1997): "it's not clear whether the second half of the quotation deals with the possibility (a strong one in a period of religious change and controversy) that one's father and grandfather may give different answers, or is merely rationalising appealing to one's elders rather than one's peers. If the lines do constitute an appeal to the authority of antiquity, a worrying inconsistency" emerges by comparing earlier sections of the poem, and "the real disadvantage of the appeal to antiquity" is that "Catholics and Calvinists could make it with equal passion" (59–60).

71–72 *aske thy...aske his;* **LECOCQ** (1969): Donne lets us understand that one can find truth in looking not in oneself, but outside oneself (396). **KERMODE, FENDER, AND PALMER** (1974): Donne "suggests, as everyone did at this time, that you do a little historical research, for what we are looking for, of course, is the true primitive Catholic Church" (66). **HIEATT** (1987): "Inquire into the historical record until you find true Christianity" (238). **HESTER** (1994a): the biblical citation to Deut. 32.7 "would remind some readers that Recusant writers...never tired of urging that the 'incestuous' daughter of Anne Boleyn might have considerable difficulty in determining the identity of her father, a difficulty she was rumored to share with her mother, whose father might have been Henry VIII also" (210). **ELLRODT** (2000): even when Donne "boldy [sic] invited an individual quest for the true Chruch, he presented it as a quest for an authentic tradition" (29). **WIGGINS** (2000): this "mention of fathers is more positive" than the previous one, but "it swiftly moves beyond those actual fathers whose spirit will be met in heaven and seeks paternal authority in grandfathers and, by extension, in more distant ancestors" (48).

71 *the right;* **WILLMOTT** (1985): "The right choice is vital. The torments of hell (the punishment for the wrong choice) were horrifyingly real to Donne and his contemporaries" (63–64). **HIEATT** (1987): "the right religion" (238).

71 *aske thy father which is Shee;* **MILGATE** (1967) quotes Deut. 32.7 [so also, Melchiori (1983, 181) and Barańczak (1984, 172)] and Jer. 6.16. Donne "seems to be taking the Protestant point of view, that the primitive purity of the Church must be restored; but, as he well knew, all parties in religious disputes of the time appealed to such texts, and the Roman was called 'the old religion'"; see Dryden, *The Hind and the Panther,* 2:164–67 (145). **LECOCQ** (1969): this reference to a father offers a potential nod to Thomas Egerton as the identity of the interlocutor (376). [See also, l. 11]. **SMITH** (1971): Donne appeals "to the primitive state of the Church, and then of mankind altogether; he assumes that we fall further and further short of this state as time runs on" (484). **NUTT** (1999): Donne's statement here "is especially poignant when we recall that his natural father died when he was three, and the fate of his soul must have perturbed Donne immensely during this spiritual crisis" (121). **WIGGINS** (2000): this appeal "is identical to the appeal implicit in the first proposition that Elizabeth required her Catholic bishops to debate at Westminster in 1559." Elizabeth "sought to revise once and for all and silence Catholic discourse on the subject of forefathers, just as the grave man" in this poem "revises his own understanding of paternal authority. His earlier invocation of fathers to be met in heaven, he realizes (at the prompting of his youthful listeners) is perilously close to such invocations, for

example, as that of Bishop Scot of Chester, who spoke against the Settlement in the parliament of 1559." The "crucial realization" of the grave man, however, "is that he and his Christian forefathers did indeed live in blindness—albeit a papist blindness, and not the pagan blindness of those 'blinde Philosophers'—and that one cannot so simply invoke paternal authority as he did earlier in his discourse" (48–49).

71 *father* BAUMLIN (1991): "Paradoxically, doubt can prepare for one's embrace of authority as a solution to the lack of knowledge; where reason cannot lead, faith—in established practice, in the tradition and beliefs of one's 'father'—thereby becomes one's best support and guide" (57–58).

72–84 *Though Truthe…that night.* SPROXTON (2000): the passage "seems to be a personal insight" in which "we have evidence of Donne's determination to face honestly the conundrum of faith." While Donne's "perspective is overtly impartial, it is clear that, like Erasmus, he trusted the human mind to identify truth when it is discovered," a "confidence he would have derived from his Catholic upbringing" (119–20).

72–82 *Though Truthe…win so.* WILLIAMSON (1967): these lines articulate Donne's "gospel of doubt" (52).

72–79 *Though Truthe…wrong, is.* MORRIS (1953): an example of Donne's enjoyment of "ingenious argument" (20). BALD (1970): "the rejection of all the commonly accepted reasons for religious belief does not involve the abandonment of the search for truth. Donne may know that he knows nothing, but this is only the beginning of the quest, the urgency of which is beyond denial" (71–72).

72–73 *Though Truthe…elder is.* ALLEN (1945b): the "usual authority" cited for the statement is Tertullian, and "in his 'Adversus Praxen' [Opera, 1906, 229] we find what is probably the first version of this notion" (55). KERMODE, FENDER, AND PALMER (1974): "Heresy is almost as old as truth," which "would explain a great deal of [Donne's] reading in Divinity" (66). GUIBBORY (1986): "As a consequence of his belief in original perfection, Donne thinks that the farther one goes back, the closer one gets to truth and purity" (78). STRIER (1993): "This is confusing, and hardly reassuring. Are they twins or not? And 'a little elder' does not seem like a very strong or immediately apprehensible matter; it seems an awfully small difference on which to base the entire status of truth" (301). COLLINSON (2000): in the light of this statement, "what we regard as Donne's apostasy was also a kind of fulfilment and denouement" (40).

73 *a litle elder is.* KERMODE AND HOLLANDER (1973): "the need is to get back to the facts of the true primitive church; heresy is almost but not quite as old" (1047).

73 *elder* PATRIDES (1985): "because it pre-existed the 'falshood' ushered in by the Fall of Man" (227).

74–89 *Be busy…hast found:* ROBERTS (1968): these lines comprise "the thematic center of the poem," in which Donne "proposes not a final answer to his dilemma but a methodology for seeking the truth," suggesting that "like the ancient philosophers (l. 12 cf.) man's primary obligation is to seek the truth with his whole mind and strength, that he must have integrity of conscience and intellect in the search." As a consequence, Donne indicates that "the only means at man's disposal are essentially negative, purgative ones—that is, a demanding intellectual and even physical asceticism that will sufficiently purify his powers to receive the 'dazling' mysteries 'like the Sunne,' which God alone can extend to man" (110–11). In contemporary English, "the words *hill* and *mountain* are relative terms associated with altitudinal differences, but before the eighteenth century, as clearly reflected in the Authorized Version of the Bible, the Hebrew terms *gib'a* and *har* (*hill* and *mountain* respectively) were interchangeable in the Renaissance" so that "we are justified in reading *hill* as *mountain*, especially since Donne specifically calls it a 'huge hill.'" The mountain then "is a symbol of the difficulties and obstacles that must be surmounted in order to achieve realization, but more importantly, the use of mountains in Scripture as the scenes of theophanies, where God reveals Himself to man, is primary in the understanding of the poem" (112–13). **DAVIES** (1994): "The unparalleled sublimity of this awesome vision derives from magnificence of imagery combined with raw power of articulation: the reader stands dwarfed. The dramatic hill which so disempowers us with the conviction of the puniness of our capacities is created by sublime fiat of Donne's overbearing intelligence." Further, "the double 'must' achieves an initial status of apparent independence from its auxiliary function, by ellipsis, as if there were an urgent verb to must. All confirms the speaker's credentials as one who knows this journey well and has acquired the qualifications to issue this summons as a result of the throes of his own arduous ascent towards a personal truth. The hectoring voice is majestic in its certainties, a punchy speaking-voice impatient of (though assenting to) metrical control. And yet, just as its subject is momentous labour through indirection, so also its message is calculatingly oblique. An apocalyptic tone, impelled by violently spontaneous rhythms, hurries the reader from rock to rock of the track of his argument." In addition, "the passage has a Protestant emphasis on the sacred importance of the personal pilgrimage, governed by the inner light of God's Grace," though "its emphasis on active labour ('none can worke in that night…hard knowledge…the minds indeavours') implies the Catholic doctrine of works. Open receptivity to the Divine Light is not emphasized but rather the programme of ratiocination and study by which Donne accomplished his own shift from Catholic to Anglican" (21–22).

74–82 *Beleeue me this…win so.* **GRIERSON** (1929): "It was along this line of intellectual inquiry that Donne detached himself from Catholicism rather than by any change of heart" (xxviii).

74–79 *Be busy…wrong, is.* **MOORE** (1969): the passage "assumes that there is no sure, unmistakable way to true religion" and "emphasizes the need to find the right way and the danger of refusing to face the problem or of making the wrong choice, but it offers no hints as to which way the seeker should go. The image is of a man, lost in a foreign land. This is, of course, the exact position of a seeker for true religion in a diseased world" (46). **BAKER-SMITH** (1972): "The compression of statement and the urgent rhythms point to the poet's engagement here. External standards, represented by the attitudes towards 'an image', are shown to be inadequate precisely because they set up inadequate criteria," and "to be indifferent to these labels or to confuse them with the core of religion, is to miss the point" (408). **CATHCART** (1975): Donne's scepticism is "of a special kind: it is colored by a moral as well as an epistemological anxiety, and, as the speaker seeks truth and as he finds it difficult and sometimes impossible to find, we sense submerged beneath his gaiety the truth that one must be virtuous" (50). **LAURITSEN** (1976): "the quest itself, rather than the end of the quest, has become, in this fallen world, the only attainable objective." Thus, "convinced at first that he could, with every expectation of final success, seek the realm of pure spirit, the splendid isolation of the hilltop, the speaker instead discovers—to his great unease, we may be sure—that he must be always seeking, climbing, and never reaching" (126–27).

74–78 *Be busy…to stray.* **SCODEL** (1993): these lines "use the vocabulary of Pyrrhonist Skepticism." Variously called "inquirers" and "seekers," Pyrrhonists "professed to search ceaselessly for the truth and 'doubters,'" primarily "because they doubted all dogmatic claims. There is a crucial difference, however, between Phrygius's skeptical position and the one that Donne recommends," that is, Donne "signifies his rejection of the very goal of classical tranquility, which was associated with otium rather than negotium, ease rather than business" (495–96).

74–75 *Be busy…the best.* **MORRIS** (1953) cites these lines as an example of "assonance, vowel-chiming and variation within the consonantal framework, alliteration" (58–59).

75–88 *Hee's not…to'all eyes.* **STEIN** (1942) notes the "quick and abrupt" style of this passage, likening it to an "anti-Ciceronian curt style" (695).

75–84 *Hee's not…that night.* **WALKER** (1925) says that Donne loves "the search for truth," which for him "is more than the attainment," for "there is more faith in honest doubt than in half the creeds." Notes that the search "is itself a religion," and the search leads Donne "to a recognition that there is good in all religions" (71).

75–77 *Hee's not…be bad;* **WILLMOTT** (1985): "The man who is actively seeking the best church (and who is therefore not closely attached to any church) should not be thought of as having no religion or an inferior one. To be a Roman Catholic ('To adore…an image'), to scorn Catholic rituals ('scorn an image') and to be a Protestant ('to protest') may all be wrong" (64).

75 *Hee's not…the best.* **BEWLEY** (1966): "The very act of seeking for the one true religion is in itself a kind of religion, and not the worst kind" (178). **SMITH** (1971): "he is not of no religion or the worst religion who seeks the best religion" (484). [So also, Kermode and Hollander (1973, 1047), Patrides (1985, 227), Mallet (1990, 22), and Enright (1997, 97).] **CRAIK AND CRAIK** (1986): "The implied word is 'religion'" (260). **SCODEL** (1993): through "his litotes," Donne "asserts that to persevere in the skeptical search for the true church is already to belong, in some sense, to the community of true believers. Such a claim reveals how much Donne wishes to avoid Phrygius's spiritual isolation" (496). **CORTHELL** (1997): "a nearly

impenetrable tongue-twister" (42). **NUTT** (1999): Donne speaks here "with considerable tolerance" (121).

75 *not of none, nor worst* **CLEMENTS** (1966): "Not of no faith, nor the worst faith" (60). [So also, Patrides (1985, 227) and Chmielewski (2001, 616).] **STRIER** (1993): "it is not clear what it means to say that such a figure is 'not of none.' The point of the line seems precisely to defend the earnest seeker who is 'of none.' Or perhaps there is a church of seekers" (301–02).

75 *none,* **HILLER** (1977): "i.e. no religion" (183).

75 *best.* **MILGATE** (1967): "best religion" (146).

76–84 *To adore, ... that night.* **WALKER** (1925): the search for Truth leads Donne "to a recognition that there is good in all religions, and that the Truth, full and final, is very hard to find" (71). **BLOOM AND BLOOM** (1979): "The soul or core of Donne's satire is his injunction to 'doubt wisely,' a call for rational examination; it is an important stage in his religious development. Roman Catholicism lay behind him and his highest authority at the moment (about 1594–95) resided in conscience. He did not direct his 'doubts' against formal religion; they indicated neither skepticism nor uncertainty. Rather he made them his means of skirting impediments before his progress toward the 'Truths' of the primitive church" (171). **CORTHELL** (1982): these lines form "a locus classicus in Donne criticism" and are "an equivoque," in which "from one angle Donne appears to be saying that in spite of force one must allow but one true religion. From another, the lines yield precisely the opposite meaning: might is right; one will be forced to allow one religion—the right one." Further, Donne's "clever use of negatives and the subjunctive mood in the central passage on truth" and "the problem of 'hard knowledge' and 'mysteries'" emphasize that he "rises to his defense of the individual conscience by means of paradoxy and equivocation. This is not to deny the intellectual heroism of the poem; rather, it is to define the character of that heroism more precisely," as Donne "is quibbling to establish a place for inquiry within the absolute prerogatives of power" (164–65).

76–82 *To adore, ... win so.* **LYND** (1920): these lines demonstrate that Donne's "rationalist tolerance" resulted from "ardent doubt, not from ardent faith" (437). **SPROTT** (1950): these lines characterize Donne's "sceptical method" (338). **MARTZ** (1969): "In this famous passage, indispensable to an understanding of Donne, one feels the strain of thought bending the lines out of the couplet form, as though the rhymes were obstacles to overcome. The whole of the Renaissance, the Reformation, and the Counter-Reformation are pressing in upon that poem, demanding one answer to their manifold problems. That God exists, that Truth exists, Donne never doubts; but where these absolutes are to be found on earth, Donne does not know" (31). **BRODSKY** (1982): "A blank image named within a visual context, it appears with unexpected and decisive power within the poem, as if itself were suddenly sighted by the satirist with surprise." Further, "the formidable effect of the passage is not reduced by the consideration that its directness and simplicity of diction are strikingly uncharacteristic of Donne," though "whatever the degree of specific reference or influence to which it owes, Donne's representation of truth is primarily a rewriting of well-known, traditional images" (842–43). **GROVE** (1984): "what stays with one" is "not Donne's image of 'Truth', or even the laborious, circling, reaching motions by which men strive to win her, so much as the haunting realization of what unknown paths one is (right at this moment) in" (60).

76–79 *To'adore,…wrong, is.* **NELLY** (1969): these lines represent Donne's "plea for the 'via media,'" and "doubt wisely" can be "regarded as Donne's life-long motto" (15–16). **J. KING** (1982): Donne's speaker "doubts that he will ever recover truth within the material objects of this world. But he identifies the increasingly difficult process of the quest with the object of desire" (158). **ZUNDER** (1982): the "position" the speaker articulates is one of "reserved judgment," and the proposed "solution" to "the contemporary difficulties of belief is a positive scepticism." Thus, "what the lines amount to is an insight into the positive nature of inquiry. In the last years of the sixteenth century, this is a radical position to hold, and a radical proposal to make" (15; 1988, 81). **SCODEL** (1993): these lines "recapitulate the satire's movement from a triad consisting of the major churches' positions to one consisting of two extremes and the authentic mean of skeptical inquiry," in which Donne "signifies that his 'middle way' is on an unexplored road that each man must find for himself. The exhortation to 'stand inquiring right' appropriately recalls the Christian of the first verse paragraph who adheres to the mean by 'stand[ing] / Sentinell,'" Donne contrasting "his skeptical mean with the two extremes of 'sleep,' that is, shirking the quest for true religion, and 'runn[ing]e' wrong,' that is, recklessy embracing a particular church or all churches. While Donne's warning against spiritual sleep echoes Pauline admonitions like 'Let us not sleep, as do others' (1 Thess. 5:6), his warning against running recalls classical and humanist attacks on rash behavior that misses the mean" (496–97).

76–78 *To'adore,…not to stray.* **PARRY** (1985): "Donne pauses in his poem to enjoy the luxury of a sceptical reflection" (49).

76–77 *To'adore,…doubt wisely;* **SLIGHTS** (1991): the lines say "less about images than about adoring, scorning, and protesting," for "the procedure Donne's speaker recommends is to 'doubt wisely' (77), a formulation in which 'wisely' is as important as 'doubt'" (93). **STRIER** (1993): "In *propria persona* Donne presents the possibility that 'all' the major religious possibilities in Europe may 'be bad.' He does not say merely that any of them may be bad but that it is possible that they all may be," and thus, "the message of the poem becomes that of Socrates (surely one of the 'blind Philosophers in heaven'), the great proponent of therapeutic skepticism" (302). **CORTHELL** (1997): "the railer urges in the pivotal section of the poem a process of private inquiry that will eventually result in what we might call an authentic form of religious commitment. What is truly daring here is the suggestion that there may be a religious position outside of those currently accepted," and "this possibility ('May all be bad') is difficult to reconcile with the earlier assertion of the necessity ('must,' l. 70) of choosing 'one' religion." The question is whether Donne is "really saying established religions 'May all be bad,' or just that certain practices of those confessions are so" (41–42). **OLIVER** (1997): "The enquirer after truth as envisaged in the poem must, logically, be free not only to eschew the English Church but also all the other existing branches of Christendom. This explains why the Catholic/Protestant axis becomes inadequate"

(58). PATTERSON (1997) calls this the poem's "crucial sentence" which "locates religious indecision squarely within the iconoclastic debate" (14).

76 *To'adore,...or protest,* GRIERSON (1912) compares the passage to Sir Thomas Browne, *Religio Medici,* section 3 and Donne's letter to "H. R." (*Letters,* p. 29) (2:115–16). SMITH (1971): "to be a Roman Catholic, or an anti-Catholic, or a Protestant" (484). [So also, Craik and Craik (1986, 260), Mallet (1990, 22), and Chmielewski (2001, 616).] ROUSSEAU AND RUDENSTINE (1972): "to choose the middle way of the Anglican ('Protestant') Church, avoiding the extremes of 'adoring' and 'scorning'" (66). [So also, Hieatt (1987, 238).]

76 *adore, or scorne* ENRIGHT (1997): "worship like Catholics, spurn like anti-Catholics" (97).

76 *adore,* PATRIDES (1985): "like Catholics" (227).

76 *scorne an Image,* PATRIDES (1985): "like all anti-Catholics" (227).

76 *protest,* LEGOUIS (1942): "verb, sense 7 = 'remonstrate,'" predates the earliest *OED* listing, that "first recorded in 1608 (Armin, *Nest Ninn.*)" (186). [So also, Sullens (1964, 227).] MILGATE (1967): "be a Protestant" (146). [So also, Kermode and Hollander (1973, 1047), Baker (1975, 72), Hiller (1977, 183), Patrides (1985, 227), Carey (1990, 425), Enright (1997, 97), and Rudrum, Black, and Nelson (2000, 121).] MARTZ (2001): Donne uses the term "with strict etymological, legal, and historic accuracy to designate the Lutherans," for "to adore an image is Roman, to scorn an image is Genevan, to *protest* is to be a Lutheran, that is, to live somewhere between the two extremes" (22).

77–102 *doubt wisely;...is Idolatree.* MINER (1969): "religion in its civil 'power' must be distinguished in its proper degree, beyond which submission to the civil powers of religion is, as Donne defines it, 'idolatrie'" (151).

77–88 *In strange way...to'all eyes.* MEDINE (1972): the action identified here, "symbolic of all human endeavors," points to "a quest of universal significance." But "opposed to the rigidly doctrinaire sects of contemporary Christianity satirized earlier," this endeavor "is personal and private, depending entirely on the individual's understanding and persistence," and "this statement of the ideal extends beyond the individual satire in which it appears to each of the others as well" (51–52).

77–85 *doubt wisely;...now do.* MACAULAY (1931): in this passage Donne presents "almost for the first time in poetry the spirit of earnest and enquiring scepticism" (89). BAUMLIN (1991): "Doubt, from the Latin *dubitare,* suggests a state of critical reflection that wavers between alternatives. Yet the passage as a whole, speaking of the 'way' and the path toward truth, invites a second meaning of *dubitare* into the play of signification: that is, to hesitate, delay, 'stand still.' Indeed, 'To stand, inquiring right' reinforces this sense of physical as well as cognitive hesitation, of the *refusal* to act (and in acting 'runne wrong'). Where in this 'strange way' are we left, therefore, if not in a state of suspended judgment regarding both choice and action? The passage recognizes the delay and ends by urging the reader to 'do' something. But do what?"

Consequently, the passage "enacts in this syntactic and semantic ambiguity the very problem it addresses: the problem of choosing and acting in the midst of cognitive uncertainty. And if one is to 'inquire right,' of what or whom shall one make the inquiry?" As a result, fideism "is the only viable choice, and it is one born of 'wise doubt'" (138–39).

77–82 *doubt wisely; ... win so.* ROGERS (1987): "the search for a truth transcending sectarian difference, perfectly adapting verse-movement to meaning" (170).

77–81 *doubt wisely; ... go* SAUNDERS (1983): "The Renaissance man, even if given to a particular political or religious dogma, tends to be essentially sceptical. Donne was their voice" (ix).

77–79 *doubt wisely; ... wrong, is.* WHITLOCK (1654) writes "Dr. Donne" in the margin of his text here and glosses: "that Inimitable Poets Rule is true in all mending of our Intellectualls" (218). DOWDEN (1890): "In this passage we have unquestionably a personal confession, a vindication of Donne's own attitude in inquiry and doubt, addressed by himself to himself" (803). HUSAIN (1948) notes that Donne echoes St. Thomas Aquinas, who expressed an almost identical view in his commentary on Aristotle's *Metaphysics*, and quotes a section from Aquinas's work—e.g., "Any one who seeks after truth must begin by doubting stoutly, because the finding of truth is nothing else but the solving of doubt..." (58). STEIN (1962) cites these lines to illustrate Donne's mastery of "public paradoxes and antinomies" (168). JACKSON (1968): "This right inquiry and wise doubt are best understood by seeing how they parallel the better-known seventeenth-century concept of right reason, in which the psychic stance indicated by the noun 'reason' is commended so long as it moves in the direction secretly shown by the conscience" (42; 1970, 33). BELLETTE (1975): "it is significant that in a poem whose essential subject matter is belief, so much emphasis should be placed on necessary action. But what we are actually to do on the 'appointed field,' what our virtuous actions are to consist of, is not spelled out by Donne, whose reluctance to prescribe rules of appropriate conduct is particularly evident here" (136). SELLIN (1980): Donne's exhortation "squares well with the events at the synod [of Dort], for in its own opinion the orthodox party did 'stand' inquiring 'right,' did its best to 'doubt wisely,' whereas the Remonstrants (i.e., the Arminian party)—though probably 'not of none, nor worst' since they did not 'sleepe' but sought 'the best'—obviously ran 'wrong' in the eyes of their orthodox brethren, of the English and other foreign divines at Dort, and of Donne's very own sovereign" (286). WILLMOTT (1985): "To stop and ask the way on an unfamiliar road ('in strange way') is to avoid going wrong, but to make no effort ('sleep') or to set off without being sure of the way is to go wrong" (64). STRIER (1993) finds that the passage "rests uneasily on two conflicting contrasts: right and wrong, on the one hand, and sleeping versus running on the other," adding further that the punctuation "suggests that the contrast is between sleeping and running wrong, but semantically (with some help from the syntax) the contrast is between sleeping and running" (302). GRIFFIN (1994): "doubt for Donne is not an end in itself, and he firmly rejects any Pyrrhonist suspension of belief. The point, in the end, is to make a good choice. Herein Donne differs from the skeptical Lucianic tradition and reminds us that, for all their commitment to inquiry, to the free play of irony and the skeptical intellect, most satirists are at the same time roused by a sense of urgency about moral ugliness or its idiocy, by the sense that something must be done or at least said" (48). **OLIVER** (1997): Donne distinguishes doubt from "mere idleness and stasis," and consequently, "the recommendation to employ doubt does not prevent" this poem from being "a religious poem" (61). **DONOGHUE** (2001): "Doubt wisely, he advises, but keep the argument going"; see *Paradoxes*, p. 27 (xxvi).

77–78 *doubt wisely;…inquyring right* **FULTON** (2001) notes that just as Donne advises his readers to "doubt wisely" and "stand inquiring right," so Horace "adjures that 'you' act wisely, or 'right': '*tu si modo recte / dispensare*' (Satire I.2, 74–5)" (75).

77–78 *In strange way / To stand inquyring right* **MALLET** (1990): "to pause when one is lost to consider which is the right road" (22).

77 *May all…In strange way* **MILGATE** (1967) quotes *Sermons* 5:38 (146).

77 *May all be bad;* **SMITH** (1971): "easy certainties may be vicious in themselves in a situation where the truth is not simple or easily come by" (484).

77 *doubt wisely; In strange way* **BRADSHAW** (1982): "no sensitive reader will want to say, or hear, 'WISEly IN strange WAY.' '-ly' is obviously very light indeed, and 'in' is light too, but relatively stronger within the foot. In the next foot, 'strange' is evidently more strongly stressed than 'in' was, while 'way' takes additional emphasis as a rime-word and is stronger still. So, within the two feet, which are both iambs, we have a cumulative progression or sustained rise. Earlier in the same line, that crucial word 'doubt' had to be stressed at least as strongly as 'bad,' in the previous foot." Thus, "the stress on 'doubt' may be as strong as that on 'bad' or still stronger, but cannot be weaker without obscuring the emphases required to carry the sense" (338–39).

77 *doubt wisely;* **GRANSDEN** (1954): these two words "support the sense of the famous 'truth' passage, which from a Catholic point of view is heretical enough" (103). **HUTCHISON** (1970): the phrase means "rejecting facile cynicism in an active search for truth—which, once perceived by the understanding, is firmly grasped by the will" (359). **HELLEGERS** (1991): the phrase offers "an admission of the poet's suspicion of authority and an acknowledgement of the mystery, inexhaustibility, and inescapability of metaphor, which Donne's poetry—characterized by paradox, wit, and irony—embodies," and it is also "a methodological imperative which, in Donne's estimation, must inform a Protestant theology of language; it is an argument for the endless construction and deconstruction of both text and self in the impossible—but necessary—quest for the divine on earth" (10). **SLIGHTS** (1991): "doubting wisely is, if not quite a communal process, at least an interpersonal one. Donne doesn't offer a complete epistemology laying out the grounds of assent, but he does recommend as a method of inquiry the circuitous route of human discourse" (93–94). **OLIVER** (1997): the injunction "begs two questions: about what sort of doubts are envisaged, and about how long one may legitimately entertain them" (60).

77 *In strange way* **MILGATE** (1967): "on an unfamiliar road" (146). [So also, Kermode and Hollander (1973, 1047), Craik and Craik (1986, 260), and Hieatt (1987,

238).] **CORTHELL** (1997): in this phrase Donne marks "the place of a new subject of history" (37).

79–79 *To stand...wrong, is.* **NUTT** (1999): Donne's "Catholic upbringing would ironically have driven home" this idea (121).

78 *To stand...to stray.* **MILGATE** (1967) quotes *Sermons* 6:69 (146). **NEWTON** (1974): this is one of the lines that "reduce" the search for Truth "to a comparatively passive cerebration" (437).

78 *stray.* **PATRIDES** (1985): "'stay' (acc. to some MSS)" (228).

79–108 *On a high hill...are lost.* **TUVE** (1947) cites this passage as an example of "the quick, incomplete similitude used to support a position with swift effectiveness" (371–72).

79–89 *On a high hill...hast found:* **SPARROW** (1931) believes that this is "not the language of the religious sceptic" (147). **JORDAN** (1936) cites these lines as evidence of Donne's refusal to take an easy path in choosing a religious affiliation (39–40). **LEAVIS** (1936) contrasts these lines with ll. 152–62 of "Lycidas" in order to demonstrate the difference between Donne's and Milton's use of English, namely, Donne's use of words that enact their meanings (55–57). **RUGOFF** (1939): these lines show Donne taking a position "somewhere between heaven and earth," the "topography" of Donne's verse from which he observed the firmament above and the broadest aspects of the world beneath (196). **MAHOOD** (1950): these lines foreshadow the "arduous endeavour" of Donne's own career (89). **TURNELL** (1950): "The slow labouring lines and the sinewy rhythms wonderfully convey the immense effort that must be made to reach truth" (262). **JACKSON** (1968): the speaker clearly indicates that "the attitude of uncertainty was not be to used to justify permanent postponement of the risk of ascent," for while "one may stand skeptical while he is young," and perhaps "should do so when the path is hard to see or difficult to ascend safely," yet "all of this earlier contemplation is for the sake of the final effort." The speaker suggests that it is "more important to make an attempt at the top" than it is "to wait until you can be absolutely sure to make it" (43). **LECOCQ** (1969): the image of the mountain, unique to the Satyres in its appearance here, is one of two natural images at the heart of Donne's satiric message; the other image is that of the river [see ll. 103–10]. Unlike the river, the mountain becomes a didactic, as opposed to a lyrical, image, which shows us how one can find salvation and that it is at the price of the winding, painful effort of ascending the hill that salvation is merited (394). **MOORE** (1969) (reading "huge" rather than "high" and "cragged" rather than "Ragged"): the adjectives describing the hill—"huge," "cragged," and "steep,"—"emphasize the effort that is required to climb the hill rather than how visible it is." Even though "the activity of the search is described in terms of a laborious physical effort," the search is "primarily a mental one." The image is appropriate because here "mental activity does not consist of weighing several alternatives and then coming to a decision," but instead "of maintaining a constant search for the truth which will succeed, if it is to succeed at all, by suddenly breaking through all difficulties as though they had been removed" (47). **CATHCART** (1975): "The image of a person traveling around a mountain on a circular path, with each revolution coming closer and closer to the truth, is precisely illustrative of Donne's method in his poetry" (130). **HESTER** (1976) (reading "huge" rather than "high" and "Cragged" rather than "Ragged"): "Both the syntax and diction of Donne's emblem enforce the spiral motion of the pilgrim up and around the hill. The alternation of short phrases ('on a huge hill'—'Cragged, and steep'—'and hee that will') around the strong spondee 'Truth stands' connote the circular path of the seeker. These are reinforced by the explicit description in the following line, which repeats that struggling, uneven alternation of rhymes ('Reach her'—'about must'—'and about must goe')," and which creates a "vivid metrical presentation of the circular shape of the eternal hill and the circling of it by the rational soul in the pursuit of Truth itself. The circularity of the hill described in these lines is then combined with the view of it horizontally in the next line: 'And what th'hills suddennes resists'—'winne so,' in which the long introductory clause describing in long rhythms the height of the hill is offset by the short, imperative 'winne so.' It is the combination of these two lines that produces the most significant effect and meaning of the image. The circularity of the progress around the hill in combination with the gradual rectilinear movement up it by the pilgrim reproduces that spiral motion which ancient, medieval, and Renaissance philosophy alike delineated as emblematic of the motions of the rational soul of man" (100–01). **SELLIN** (1980) describes the "golden medallion" given to Donne when he visited The Hague in December 1619. Notes that the medallion commemorated the Synod of Dort and takes as "its motto the opening of Psalm 125, 'Erunt ut Mons Sion,'" portraying "a high mountain surrounded with clouds and assaulted by four diagonal winds, blowing strongly." Observes that pilgrims climbed up its "steep slope" along "a narrow path winding tortuously among rocky crags toward a round temple on the summit" and that Jehovah, "[h]idden in his effulgence," "surmounted the scene and irradiated it with the light of heaven." Suggests that the resemblance between the image in these lines and the image on the medal is "most remarkable, closer than any parallels hitherto suggested," and "the fact that at least three important manuscripts— Westmoreland, British Museum Harleian 4955, and Queen's College 216—read 'it' rather than 'her' is what really should make one extremely wary of jumping to the conclusion that Donne intended only a female personification to stand for truth in his expression" (283–85). **SHAWCROSS** (1980): "The index entry 'Virtutis in philosophia profectus' leads us to the essay on 'Progress in Virtue'": "the very ancient elucidation of progress found in Hesiod, which sets forthe that the way is no longer uphill, nor very steep, but easy and smooth and readily accomplished" (59). **CAREY** (1981): Donne "transposes the traditional image of the hill of Truth into his own strenuously mimetic rhythms," but these lines create a "rather awkward relationship with what Donne says elsewhere in the poem." While Donne indeed is "chiefly concerned in this part of the poem with moral conduct rather than the choice of true religion," the "lack of consistency between the assumption that there are 'easie wayes' to salvation available from one's father, and the insistence (in the hill of Truth passage) that salvation depends on 'hard knowledge' which the individual must win for himself, is glaring" (13–14). **SHAW** (1981): the lines "testify to a humanist faith that truth can be determined by reason and embraced by an act of will, but they show none of the exhilaration that might be expected to accompany such a pronounce-ment" and "betray instead an apprehensive view of the dangers besetting such a search" (37–38). **LOW** (1985): "this passage, though justly famous, is not really typi-cal of Donne's thinking, and, although it advocates labor in the search for truth, it is scarcely optimistic" (84). **MANN** (1985): "The specific truth Donne evokes is an individual faith, but the only norm he provides is the painful, difficult experience. The effort in time, which demands a total concentration of human powers, is every-thing. But the search involves everyone." Donne sees the truth as "available histori-cally": it is "in history" and "simultaneously is transcendent and universal." Thus, Truth "is personal but available to all and so objective," and it is "individual and corporate, a perfect ideal realized only imperfectly and through effort and pain, in imitation of crucifixion" (540). **PARRY** (1985): Donne "can imagine the endeavour even if he cannot envisage the Truth—but he insists there is a truth to be found. The journey, he explains, has to be in time, and into history, a return to to 'the streames calme head', the origins of Christianity in its primitive days. And the jour-ney is severe, with no certainty of success, yet the intelligent man has a double duty to make it, to God and his soul; otherwise what could a man say to God at the close of time, the one event Donne was sure of, the Last Judgement?" (49). **TOLIVER** (1985): "The image of this free-standing, exalted truth Donne stations in a privileged position in a passage that has been rightly recognized as crucial to him. He delays the phrase 'Truth stands' syntactically and plants it unqualified and sturdy in the center of the line, where it is readily visible from all regions. Ostensibly, he means such a truth to be theological and doctrinal, but it can just as well be personal and serve the functions of the poet's centering myth" (102). **BAUMLIN** (1986a): the "figures of repetition" here "imitate verbally the indirections of the ascent," and "the determination necessary for this search is expressed, once more almost mimetically, in the verbal repetition: 'And what the'hills suddennes resists, winne so; / Yet strive so.'" The section overall "is not easy to grasp on first reading, with its short, Senecan phrasing, its zeugmatic clauses, and its hyperbaton or avoidance of natural word order, all of which contribute to the brevity and concentration of thought," and although it "evokes the Persian style in its concision, it generally avoids its model's penchant for obscurity." In this "justly praised passage," Donne "speaks not with Persius's 'crab-bedness' but with his concentration, seriousness, and persuasive vigor," while also speaking with Persius's "symbolism." Although Donne "could have drawn on a num-ber of sources for his Hill of Truth, there are obvious parallels in theme and imagery between this allegory and Persius's own 'steep path,'" and "one can say at the very least that Persius suggested to Donne the appropriateness of serious emblem and symbol in satire" (98–99). **GILMAN** (1986a): "Proclaimed so firmly as the goal of our ascent toward true religion, 'she' may seem about to take shape as the kind of personified *Veritas* described in Ripa's *Iconologia*. Such a figure—an indomitable nude, her sun and palm leaf and open book in hand, her foot planted on the globe—would convincingly replace the procession of ragged and sullen mistresses who had earlier in the poem embodied the choice of available religions. Or again she might be drawn in the style of the many Renaissance versions of *Cebes' Tablet*; where, in the text and often in accompanying illustrations, philosophical mountaineers are shown clambering past Fortune, Opinion, and other distracting women toward the chaste figures of Truth and Felicity on the summit" (117). **MAHLER** (1991) suggests that Truth, because the pilgrim has been searching for it for a long time, becomes not the attainable goal of the search, but rather is imagined in this life as an incomplete process of searching (43–44). **STRIER** (1993) (reading "huge" rather than "high" and "cragged" rather than "Ragged"): the image "is not as conventional as it seems, and, like the 'truth as elder' trope, not as reassuring as it is commonly taken to be." In particular, the verse "gives us not only the stresses on 'huge,' 'cragged,' and 'steep,' but the powerful evocation of repetitive circularity—'about must, and about must.'" Consequently, there is "no sense of progress in this line, only of effort," and "[p]oetically, the next line is an afterthought," coming "as an addition, after a full stop," its "own structure" being "anti-climactic." Moreover, the words "winne so" are "weak and flat," as the "energy of the line goes into the hill's resistance." As a result, the "imagination of effort and resistance here is much more powerful than the imagination of success" (303). **GRIFFIN** (1994): the aim of the image is "to urge the reader toward rigorous inquiry" (47). **SEMLER** (1998): Carew's poem to George Sandys (ll. 23–28) "exhibits traits of [the] Donnean serpentine syntax" found here. **ELLRODT** (2000): the "quest for truth" advocated here converges with "the quest for reality" for Donne "when he discovered that he would never embrace truth in its wholeness before a coincidence of the mind and its objects was achieved in the divine mind" (43). **REID** (2000): the uses of enjambment "to convey the effort or ascent" and of rhymes coupling "unstressed with stressed syllables" creates a "crepuscular effect" (48).

79–82 *On a high hill...win so.* **BENNETT** (1934): these lines indicate Donne's "religious temperament" and his desire for unity and permanence (111). **LINDSAY** (1934a) speculates that a source for Donne's image of Truth may be St. Augustine *Confessions* X. [xxvi.] 37. It is further possible that Donne is thinking of "some lines from *Phaedrus*" ("Periculosum est credere et non credere; / ergo exploranda est veritas..."); however, "the only definite influences seem Horace and Montaigne" (577). **SCHOLDERER** (1934) (reading "huge hill") points to "a beautiful Italian medal of 1504," "the reverse of which represents just such 'a huge hill' as Donne speaks of, with a man bearing a burden 'going about it and about' up a spiral road," on the top of which stands the allegorical figure of Fame. Notes that the legend "consists of a line of Ovid (slightly altered) describing the splendid failure of Phaethon...Quod si non tenuit magnis tamen excidit ausis...," and argues that there is "no gainsaying the affinities of this piece with Donne's lines" (589). **COFFIN** (1937): Donne "views with despair verging upon contempt" those who believe that "natural knowledge" can bring heaven to them (182). **LEDERER** (1946): "The Mirrour of Maiestie (London, 1618; reprinted by H. Green for the Holbein Society of Manchester with a part of Minerva Britanna, 1870) is ascribed to Sir Henry Goodyer, an intimate friend of Donne. The lines of emblem 28: 'Th' ascending path that up to wisedome leades / Is rough, uneven, steepe: and he that treades / Therein, must many a tedious Danger meet,...til he come at last / Up to Her gate,...' are obviously a paraphrase of Donne's" (183n2). **BAKER** (1952) cites these lines as early evidence of Donne's view that truth must be acquired actively rather than merely accepted (159). **BEWLEY** (1952) contrasts the "energy" of these lines with the final lines of HSShow which have a "studied conventionality" (646). **MORRIS** (1953) notes the use of a physical metaphor to describe a mental or spiritual process (30). Also cites these lines as an example of "the repetition of single words or phrases to produce accumulative or auditory effects" (71). **GRANSDEN** (1954): "in these slow, majestic lines truth stands out as naked as the successive Anglo-Saxon syllables which compose the lines. There is a pause, obviously, after 'truth stands', emphasizing the eternal 'thereness' of this bare and celestial mountain." In the phrasing that follows, "the curious trick of rhythm induced by the position, *vis-à-vis* the iambic stresses of the metric norm, of 'about must, and about must goe', carries with it an uncanny suggestion of the baffled seeker after truth; no less brilliant is the way in which 'will', by its emphatic position at the end of the line, is forced to take all the emphasis of meaning which it must have." Finally, "'the hill's suddennes resist' speeds us up with a jerk, so that we feel the traveller being brought up short by that sheer mountain-side, the verbal barrier 'resists'" (102–03). [Similarly, Cox, (1956, 101), Forrest (1968, 102–04), Leavis (1968, 236–37), Roy and Kapoor (1969, 104), Ostriker (1970, 130), Winny (1970, 103–04), Partridge (1971, 235), Kermode, Fender, and Palmer (1974, 66), Raizada (1974, 105), Thompson (1978, 56), Doudna (1980, 6), Tebeaux (1981, 35), Willmott (1985, 64), and Ray (1990, 282).] **DUNCAN** (1959): these lines affirm Donne's belief that truth "*does* stand," and unlike modern skeptics, Donne "did not wonder whether to believe, but what to believe" (171). **WEBBER** (1963): these lines illustrate Donne's use of symbol (141–42). **BEWLEY** (1966) finds here the "energetic quality of Donne's thinking" in the lines' "strenuous rhythm"; they "dramatize the labor and effort exerted by the poet in his search" (xxviii). **MILGATE** (1967): Donne in this passage worked in an ancient tradition. Its "remote origins" are found in Hesiod, *Works and Days*, ll. 286–92, and "The *Tablet* of Kebes," in *Theophrastus, Herodas and Kebes*, trans. R.T Clark (1909), xv–xviii, pp. 131–33; see also Xenophon, *Memorabilia* (Loeb ed.), p. 95 and *Sermons* 9:181 (290). Further, see Persius, *Sat.* 3:56–57, 5:34–35; and Hallett Smith, *Elizabethan Poetry* (1952), pp. 293ff. Early modern work in the same tradition was frequent; it "had become commonplace, and it is impossible to point to a precise source." See Henri Estienne, *L'Introduction au traitè de la conformitè des merveilles anciennes avec les modernes* (1566), as translated in R. C[arew], *A World of Wonders* (1607), p. 58; Palingenius' *Zodiac of Life* (c. 1535–36), trans. Googe (1560–65), ed. of 1576 (1947); and Thomas Drant's introduction to *Horace His Art of Poetry* (1567), quoted in H. Brooks, "Donne and Drant," *TLS* (1934), p. 565 (291). Older possible sources also include Lucretius, *De Rerum Natura* 2, paraphrased by Bacon in the essay "Of Truth" and in *Device on the Queen's Day* (1595), in Spedding's *Life*, 1:378–80; and Augustine's *Confessions* X (xxvi), 37. Two passages that might have been influenced by *Sat3* are: Emblem 28 (p. 55) in *The Mirror of Majesty* (1618) and Jonson's *Forest*, 13: 27–30 (in *Works*, 7:121). See also, V. Scholderer in *TLS* (1934), p. 589 and *Sermons* 8:54 (290–92). **ROUSSEAU AND RUDENSTINE** (1972): "Despite the bewildering process of defining and evaluating alternatives, the poet finally achieves an extraordinary clarity and complexity of moral vision. Characteristically, for Donne, that vision is less a 'solution' to the speaker's original dilemma than an invitation to still further and more difficult explorations" (57). **SHAWCROSS** (1972) finds in this image "the mythical, magical mountain of Hesiod, of Zion, of Shakespeare's Belmonte, and of Mann." Adds that these lines, "instancing the long, circuitous route up the mountainside," are "fraught with back-sliding, with precipitous falls, with sore feet and broken bones. But implied also is the constant moving upward, if not quite always forward" (257). **MILLER AND BERREY** (1974) comment that the image "is static, massive, almost emblematic, rich in traditional associations" (41), noting a parallel to Dante, *Inferno*, Canto I, ll. 13–18, 28–30, 77–78. **NEWTON** (1974): these lines "force upon the reader a mental reenactment of the search" that enacts "an inner focusing of the mind's eye, a cure for blindness" (435–36). **HOLLOWAY** (1977): the detail in the lines is "characteristically distinctive," yet there is a "sense of harsh difficulty to be overcome by resolute effort," expressing "uncertainty, bafflement, isolation and near-despair" (18). **OUSBY** (1977) cites Seneca's letter to Lucilius (Letter 84, Annaei Senecae, *Ad Lvcilivm Epistvlae Morales*), arguing that "it is possible that Donne knew this passage" and that "we should list the passage from Seneca as yet another analogue to Donne's striking lines" (144–45). **COUSINS** (1979): Donne "speaks of the movement of the soul," and he has "shaped his image very shrewdly," adapting "an emblematic tradition of the soul's uphill search for Virtue and Wisdom." Donne's image, "through its torturous, labored movement," enacts "the idea that the search for truth is by nature winding and hard" as the "unenlightened soul proceeds obliquely and with difficulty. Donne's contemporaries emphasize exactly this indirect movement in his art when describing his poems as labyrinthine and Donne himself as an English Persius or Seneca" (104–05). **RICHARDS** (1980): while Donne "could have learnt all he needed to know about steep and craggy hills from direct experience," he may, nevertheless, "have had a literary hill in mind, not only because of possible phrase echoes, but because of the process of allegorization." In particular, Whitney's emblems provide "a treatment of the Hercules at the crossroads motif: '*Biuium virtutis & vitij*,'" in which "Hercules is shown at the crossroads of an Italianate cityscape." Further, while Hercules "seeks honour" and Donne's pilgrims "seek God's truth," both stress "the difficulty and the necessity for fortitude." In addition, Whitney "probably offered Donne a starting place for his image, but Donne perhaps returns, in his mind, as Bunyan did when he used traditional emblems, to the reality of hills of which he had experience. Donne also makes an implicit witty reference, that his truth is on one hill: it is not on the seven of Rome or the none of Geneva" (161). **SELLIN** (1980): "Although Spenser (*The Faerie Queene*, Book I, Canto x, Sts. 46–47) is concerned rather with contemplation in relationship to 'mercy' and the City of God than with the problem of truth that Donne embraces, his description of the hill 'both steepe and hy' on which the hermit Contemplation dwells (*not* the 'highest Mount' resembling Sinae, the Mount of Olives, and Helicon, to which the hermit then leads the Knight of the Red Crosse for a view of the new Jerusalem)" appears to be "a closer parallel to both the Dort medal and Donne's conceit than any suggested in Donne scholarship so far" (310). **ZUNDER** (1982): the "sureness of the writing" in this passage "is not the sureness of somebody who feels himself to be basically at one with his society, a society with generally accepted assumptions, but the sureness of someone discovering, under the pressure of personal and immediate circumstances, a new attitude, in this case a positive scepticism, which is able to restore equilibrium to life at a time when earlier convictions have been thoroughly unsettled" (14–15). **STEADMAN** (1984):

Donne "exhorts his audience to a dangerous feat of epistemological mountaineering, but nevertheless offers little practical advice beyond caution and a skeptical traverse," and the image "appears to be a variant of the well-known mountain-climbing metaphor exploited by both classical and Renaissance authors," some variants emphasizing the "delights of the prospect rather than the hazards of the climb," while others "stress the difficulties and labors of the ascent as well as the ultimate reward," but Donne emphasizes "the dangers and difficulties of ascent" (2–3). GUIBBORY (1986): Donne "suggests that one needs to rise higher to see into the past since we have fallen lower with time." This explains why in Sat3 Donne "follows the suggestion that man go farther back into the past to find truth." He "has not changed his mind within these few lines about how one gets to truth," but instead the "two images of going deeper into the past and ascending the hill are quite complementary, once we recognize that truth exists in a past that is also the highest point in time" (78–79). ZUNDER (1988): these lines are "a classic expression of the difficulty of reaching the truth," a passage Donne "took great care over, as the many revisions in the manuscripts suggest." Because Truth, "though difficult to reach," is "nevertheless, attainable," there is "no ultimate scepticism in the poem" (81). MORSE (1989): the lines present "no abstract, universal metaphor but a vindication of his own situation: Donne hoped that his circuitous path from Catholicism to the Church of England, far from damning him, might nevertheless enable him to attain salvation, in the face of any doubtful auspices and despite the gloomy prognosis. The pursuit of truth became a personal and private pilgrimage in which redemption would be won not through affiliation to one Church or another but through the intensity of his own commitment to it" (274–75). MOSELEY (1989) suggests that Donne's source here is the *Tabula Cebetis*, a familiar image often used like an emblem on title pages in the seventeenth century (24). PATRIDES (1989) recalls "Satan's ascent toward light in *Paradise Lost*: 'So hee with difficulty and labour hard / Moved on, with difficulty and labour hee' (II. 1021–22)" (105). ROEBUCK (1989): the "strength of Donne's visual imagination" is achieved "not in the study of landforms, landscapes, views and the like," but instead "in the woodcuts and, especially, the copper engravings of printed books, maps and cartes." The image here probably derives from "one or another of the woodcuts found, not uncommonly, on the title pages of learned works in the mathematical sciences which depict a female form (Sophia or Philosophy, or perhaps Fortune) atop an allegorically conceived hill into which a steep winding path is set." There is a "particularly striking example" on the title page of John Dee's *The Perfect Arte of Navigation* (London, 1577) (41). BAUMLIN (1991) quotes *Sermons* 8.54 as a gloss on this image: "Though our naturall reason, and humane arts, serve to carry us to the hill, to the entrance of the mysteries of Religion, yet to possesse us of the hill it selfe, and to come to such a Knowledge of the mysteries of Religion, as must save us, we must leave our naturall reason, and humane Arts at the bottome of the hill, and climb up only by the light, and strength of faith" (138). DAVIES (1994): Donne's "mountain of Truth bears disturbing resemblance to the traditional Catholic symbol of the mountain of Purgatory," and his "pilgrimage, fraught with stress and effort," seems "penitential." Purgatory then, "a concept jettisoned with his renunciation of Catholicism," is "transferred from the afterlife into the time-zone in which any progress must be made now, traverse and athwart the forbidding contour of the mountain, in the brief remaining span" (23). **WORDSWORTH POETRY LIBRARY** (1994): in 1593, Donne's brother died in prison and about the same time Donne seems to have "renounced" Catholicism. Although removing "a barrier to his ambitions," Donne's actions should not be regarded "simply as an opportunistic move." These lines confirm that for Donne "faith and creed were matters of the most profound seriousness." (v). **OLIVER** (1997): in the poem, the truth is "wherever a person locates it, provided that they conduct a proper search," and "because truth is where individuals locate it, Donne's hill of Truth is, for all its cragged steepness, a rather nebulous landmark, entirely lacking the definition of James I's 'steep hill' upon whose top 'the true visible Church' is to be found (James I 1619, p. 15)" (58). **STEVENS** (2001): Donne "makes it clear that it is not obedience or custom but unmediated individual labor that will find truth" (68).

79 *To sleepe, or run wrong, is.* **STEIN** (1944c) cites the passage as an example that can be read either with two unstressed syllables followed by two stressed or by allowing a stress-shift on "or" (387). **SMITH** (1971): "being indifferent or unreflectingly taking a wrong course is, in fact, to stray, whereas to inquire or doubt may not be" (484). **MALLET** (1990): "to give up the search, or to choose too hastily, is certainly the way to go wrong in the end" (22).

79 *sleepe,* **ENRIGHT** (1997): "do nothing" (97).

79 *run wrong,* **ENRIGHT** (1997): "take the wrong path" (97).

79 *high hill* **SHAWCROSS** (1967) notes that Hesiod's Hill of Virtue (*Works and Days,* 287) is the "holy hill of Zion" and also cites Ps. 2:6 (397).

80–85 *he that will…now do.* **NUTT** (1999): employing "arduous rhythm in line 81 to match the labour of the task," Donne "sees that task as an entirely intellectual one," while "the urgency and immense importance he gives the task is further underscored" in l. 85, "where the weight of the rhythm falls heavily on the final command" (122).

80–82 *he that will…win so.* **FORREST** (1968): the word "will" is "not just the sign of the future tense," combining as it does the "two meanings 'desires' and 'is firmly resolved,'" and thus, the word "is stressed; it is followed by the pause or hesitation at the end of the line which permits a slight lingering on the final /l/; and then in the next line it is followed by a stress in 'reach' where we expect an unstressed syllable. The kinesthetic imitation of strained effort is underway in the lingering stress of 'will'; it gathers momentum in the immediately following stress of 'reach'—since, despite the hesitation at the end of the previous line, the overall effect is one of a run-on line in which the meaning does not break but continues into the word 'reach.' The kinesthetic imitation then becomes dramatic in the words 'about must, and about must goe'; and it finally reaches a climax in the three thumping stresses which end the next line." Moreover, "the drama involved in this use of the word 'about' is an interesting example of the imitative powers of words." Thus, the "intensification of the stress is important in the production of the kinesthetic effect of the passage. The word has at its end the tautest stopped consonant in English; and the physical quality inherent in the action which produces the sound is brought prominently into play by the context: 'about must and about must.' These five successive words ending with alveolar stops, together with augmented stresses on the two abouts, encourage a reading involving a series of muscular lurches which continue a considerable speech tension into 'go'" (103–04).

80–81 *and he…go* **LEAVIS** (1968): in these lines "the most notable effect of effort, equally inviting the description 'image', is not got by metaphor," for "here the line-end imposes on the reader as he passes from the 'will' to the 'Reach' an analogical enactment of the reaching." This might be called "a metaphorical enactment," though this would not usually "be called metaphor." What is important is that it "provides the most obvious local illustration of a pervasive action of the verse—or action in the reader as he follows the verse: as he takes the meaning, re-creates the organization, responds to the play of the sense-movement against the verse structure, makes the succession of efforts necessary to pronounce the organized words, he performs in various modes a continuous analogical enactment" (236–37). **BAKER-SMITH** (1972): no where else in Donne's writings are we "more poignantly aware of man's role as viator, travelling towards a future perfection" (408–09).

80 *Ragged* **JOHNSON** (1755) (reading "Cragged"), mistakenly attributing the reference to Crashaw in his dictionary, defines the word as "full of inequalities and prominences." **GRIERSON** (1912): "The three epithets, 'cragged', 'ragged', and 'rugged', found in the MSS., are all legitimate and appropriate," though the "second has the support of the best MSS" (2:116). **MALLET** (1990) (reading "Cragged"): "steep, rugged" (22). **STRINGER** (1991), noting "the variants 'Cragg'd/Cragged' for Westmoreland's 'Ragged'," states that "this 'Ragged'/'Cragged' variant is merely one datum in a pattern of authorial revision that can be incontrovertibly demonstrated" (81).

81–82 *about must,…win so.* **HIEATT** (1987): "must circle around the hill in a spiral to overcome its steepness" (238).

81 *Reach* **BAKER** (1975): "Achieve" (73).

81 *about must, and about go* **SYPHER** (1955): "This circling examination occurred in a world thrown off center, wanting repose and safety" (104). **SHAWCROSS** (1967): "Must wind his way up around the hill, reaching the summit of truth indirectly" (25). **JACKSON** (1970): "The way to go seeking the path consists of an indirect, circuitous, roundabout, or back-and-forth motion, somewhat like the winding serpentine ascent of Bernini's columns for the baldacchino in Saint Peter's cathedral, for example" (34). **SMITH** (1971): "this way and that, round about" (485). [So also, Mallet (1990, 22), Singh (1992, 42), and Enright (1997, 97).] **PATRIDES** (1985): the ascent is not "easy," a "narrow path fraught with obstacles, witness the laborious punctuation and the repetition"; see Milton's *Paradise Lost*, 2:1021–22 (35).

81 *about* **BROADBENT** (1974): "zigzag" (106).

82 *And what…win so.* **MILGATE** (1967): "And by this means gain what the unexpected abruptness of the hill prevents (you from obtaining)": in other words, "when the climber comes to a sudden towering crag, he must contour it" (146). [Similarly,

Smith (1971, 485), Kermode and Hollander (1973, 1047), Baker (1975, 73), and Hiller (1977, 183).]

82 *the'hills sodainnes resists,* **GRANSDEN** (1954): the line "speeds us up with a jerk, so that we feel the traveller being brought up short by that sheer mountain-side, that verbal barrier 'resists'" (103).

82 *sodainnes* **OED** (1914–19): the first recorded use of the meaning of "Steepness, abruptness" (4). [So also, Sullens (1964, 256), Broadbent (1974, 106), Mallet (1990, 22), and Enright (1997, 97).]

82 *win so.* **GUINESS** (1986): the phrasing creates "an exact equivalent" for "'slamming on the brakes at full speed,'" and when read "with conviction," the effect "is almost that of a rush of blood to the head" (147).

83 *Yet striue so,…(Deaths twilight)* **STEIN** (1944c) cites this line as an example of two unstressed syllables followed by two stressed, which occurs frequently enough that it must be deliberate (387). **SMITH** (2001): the seventeenth-century compiler of a personal index to the 1633 edition of Donne's poems (Folger Shakespeare Library STC 7045 Copy 2) has indexed this "metaphorical epithet" under "Age" (169).

83 *Age* **OED** (1882–88): "old age" (6).

83 *(Deaths twilight)* **SINGH** (1992): "Twilight is the period just before darkness falls; old age is therefore the twilight of death" (42).

83 *twilight)* **MELTON** (1906) cites this word to illustrate secondary accent in compounds (87). **SULLENS** (1964): Donne's use of this meaning of the word is earlier than the earliest source cited by *OED* (240).

84 *Thy Mind…that night.* **MILGATE** (1967) (reading "Soule") quotes John 9.4 [so also, Shawcross (1967, 25), Smith (1971, 485), Rousseau and Rudenstine (1972, 66), Kermode and Hollander (1973, 1047), Partridge (1978, 157), Patrides (1985, 228), Craik and Craik (1986, 260), Lloyd-Evans (1989, 300), Mallet (1990, 22), Singh (1992, 42), and Enright (1997, 97)]. Claims "the change of 'mind' to 'Soule' in revision was made in the light of a distinction which Donne draws in a letter of the Mitcham period: 'though our souls would goe to one end, Heaven, and all our bodies must go to one end, the earth: yet our third part, the minde, which is our naturall guide here, chooses to every man a severall way' (*Letters*, p. 72)" (146).

84 *rest;* **MALLET** (1990): "make its final choice" (22).

84 *none can worke in that night.* **STRIER** (1993): "The reference seems to be more to Catallus's everlasting night than to the apocalyptic context of the gospel. Protestantism made this classical view available to the Christian by insisting that 'none can worke' after death—that is, by eliminating Purgatory from the cosmos" (304).

84 *that* **PATRIDES** (1985): "'the' (acc. to 1635–54)" (228).

84 *night.* **WILLMOTT** (1985): "death" (64).

85–88 *To will…to'all eyes.* **MOORE** (1969): the entire passage "stresses the need for man to act," the "positive feature of the search" being not that "it offers a sure way for man to find true religion, but that it focuses all of his energy" on a search that "prevents him from placing his hopes on a way that claims a certainty it does not have" (47). **TREVOR** (2000): Donne "does not so neatly distinguish" between the religious and the intellectual life (91).

85–87 *To will…endeauors reach;* **GRIERSON** (1912): "The order of the words, and the condensed force given to 'reach' produce a somewhat harsh effect" (2:116). **STEIN** (1946): "the unexpected grammatical structure, with the three objects preceding the subject and single verb, is further complicated by the fact that the verb 'doe' seems at first reading to take the objects in the second line" (101). **BELLETTE** (1975): "These strenuous lines at the centre of the poem, with their emphasis on the difficulty that the individual soul must encounter in its search for truth, are a long way removed from the earlier 'easie wayes and neare / To follow.' One senses Donne's wish to believe in easy and near ways, rather than have to face the 'strange way,' the rough landscape of mountains, rocks, and torrents which dominates the last third of the poem" (136).

85 *To will…now do.* **WILLMOTT** (1985): "To have good intentions ('to will') implies that you are delaying; therefore get to work immediately" (64). **STRIER** (1993): "carpe diem feeling dominates the line" so that "intention and resolution will not suffice" as Donne "insists on action" (304). **PRESCOTT** (1998) cites this line as an example of Donne's frequent "allusions to sex and adultery" in the Satyres (97).

85 *To will implyes delay:* **CRAIK AND CRAIK** (1986): "When one is determining to do a thing, one is not doing it" (260).

85 *To will* **MALLET** (1990): "to be going to, to consider this as a task for the future" (22). [So also, Enright (1997, 97).]

85 *now do.* **GROSART** (1872–73): "as it were reduplicate it" (1:29). **SMITH** (1971): "now actively begin your efforts to find truth" (485).

86–88 *Hard deedes…to'all eyes.* **HUTCHISON** (1970): "One aspect of the pursuit of self-knowledge through meditation is the emphasis placed on spiritual combat. It was necessary to wage continual warfare against oneself; to employ all one's strength in eradicating each vicious inclination, however trivial. The relationship between this practice and the militant tone of satire is clear, and Donne uses spiritual combat as a means of involving his audience and at the same time warns them that the effort will not be easily made," for "'Hard knowledge' is attained not simply by acknowledging general moral *exempla*, but by means of an individual confrontation with vice which involves not only the persona but the satirist and reader" (361). **DATTA** (1971): satire is here "at the hither side of Donne's acceptance of a variant of the ascetic ideal. The fragments of broken Christendom are imperfect brides, but Truth is a bride worthy of being striven for" (9). **TOLIVER** (1985): "Pursuit finds its most formidable barriers not on the steep hill, however, where one might be inspired to win most where the way is hardest, but in its human byways where kings, vicars, and men of law set the rules" (102). **NUTT** (1999): Donne uses "the verb 'reach,' directly with 'The minde's indeavours,'" but forces it "to work by association with the previous phrase about pain and the body. It is the kind of economic, compressed use of language which baffles many readers but it is also quintessentially poetic" (122). The "next image is far less obtuse, although knowing that for Catholics the word 'mysteries' has a very particular meaning adds greatly to our appreciation of it." For Donne "religious mystery" was "something so intimately connected with God that it was unknowable by mankind," and "what we should appreciate is that at this point in the poem Donne clearly dismisses anything unknowable." This is the one moment in the satire when we can most "hear his youthful mind warring with the faith of his birth." (123).

86–87 *Hard deedes...endeauors reach;* CLEMENTS (1966): "Difficult deeds are accomplished by the body's pains; difficult knowledge is attained by the mind's endeavors" (61). KERINS (1984): "The intellectual travail through which one must seek truth is no less arduous than those activities deemed courageous by society" (47). TREVOR (2000): the distinction between truth and the search for it "reflects the intimate relationship Donne maintains between study and devotion; the latter, while strengthened by the former, is not dependent upon it" (92).

86 *Hard deedes...knowledg too* COLERIDGE (1811): "i.e. The body's pains reach hard deeds; & likewise so do the mind's Endeavors reach hard Knowlege [sic]" (1984, 12.2:228). [So also, Smith (1971, 485), Kermode and Hollander (1973, 1047), Lewalski and Sabol (1973, 96), Willmott (1985, 64), Craik and Craik (1986, 260), Hieatt (1987, 238), Mallet (1990, 22), and Singh (1992, 42).]

86 *Hard deedes the bodyes paynes;* ENRIGHT (1997): "through the body's pains hard deeds are achieved ('reached')" (97).

86 *hard knowledg* WILLMOTT (1985): the phrase suggests the Protestant attitude that "man must depend on himself and God and not on an intermediary body such as the Church of Rome claimed to be" (60).

87–88 *and Misteryes...to'all eyes.* MILGATE (1967) quotes *Sermons* 3:356 (147). SMITH (1971): "the fact that there are central truths that our minds cannot grasp—religious mysteries—need not stop us seeking truth, for we can plainly see that the truth is there and aim towards it" (485). [So also, Kermode and Hollander (1973, 1048) and Mallet (1990, 22).] SELLIN (1980): "To the orthodox Calvinists it was the mysterious hand of Jehovah that through the tortuous political processes leading to the synod [of Dort] that had forced the Reformed unwillingly to make the climb at Dort, miraculously preserved His chosen in the right way, as Psalm 125 promised He would, and had brought them intact to their goal, upheld not by their own toilings and intentions but by His hidden grace, to the manifestation of His glory." Thus, on the Dort medals, "Jehovah hovers over the scene, invisible behind a cloud inscribed with the tetragrammaton, yet his radiance is everywhere apparent and animates all," a detail closely associated with Donne's lines, and "it is precisely at this point that the poem touches on the central allegorical signification that the medal had officially been designed to commemorate: namely, the truth of the doctrine of the perseverance of the saints, the fifth (and last) of the disputed articles that the synod reasserted" (286–87). WILLMOTT (1985): "The associations of the sun image are complex (light = life and goodness; kingship; Jesus who is the light of the world and the Son of God who rose from the dead), but here it is clearly set against the image of 'night' (line 84) with its suggestion of confusion as well as death" (64). **BAUMLIN** (1991) asks, "what problems of interpretation lurk in such oxymora? Shedding its light on the world (and thereby enabling human sight), the sun itself nonetheless 'dazzles' when observed directly, mesmerizing and confounding the sense—shrouding itself in the very light that makes all else 'plaine to'all eyes,'" and as a consequence of "this Pyrrhonist proposition, theological controversy is itself rendered moot: blinded, we are incapable of comprehending, let alone communicating, the mysteries of faith and God's grace" (137). **STRIER** (1993): the enjambment here "creates an ambiguity." Initially, "taking 'and mysteries' as continuous with the previous lines, it seems that 'the mindes indeavours' can reach mysteries as well as 'hard knowledge,'" but the line following "denies this possibility," for the passage seems to imply "that 'mysteries' are unequivocally there, that the existence of these mysteries cannot be denied." However, "what is the relationship between the 'dazling' of this sun and the 'blind- / nesse' of Graccus and the pagan philosophers? The relationship between 'the mindes indeavours' and 'mysteries' is left radically unclear. Perhaps Donne is suggesting that there are two different realms, one in which 'the mindes indeavours' can work appropriately—the realm of empirical truth and of diverse opinions—and the realm of incontrovertible, non-empirical truths that are 'plaine to'all eyes,' including those of the philosophers" (304–05).

87 *minds endeauors* **MILLER AND BERREY** (1974): the phrase is "expressed in a succinct, curt style reminiscent of the new Senecanism, especially if contrasted with the contorted syntax of the rash buccaneers" (41).

87 *Misteryes* **SINGH** (1992): "The central truths of religion" (42).

88 *Are as…to'all eyes.* **LECOCQ** (1969): the image here corresponds to that in *RWThird* 19–21: "Seeke wee then our selves in our selves; for as / Men force the Sunne with much more force to passe, / By gathering his beames with a christall glasse" (396n106). **CORTHELL** (1997) argues that "woman, truth, and the Lacanian Other can overlap in a manner pertinent to Donne's quest for true religion," and Donne's "turns from the straight allegory of 'our Mistresse' to the female truth to the paradoxical 'Sunne, dazling, yet plaine to'all eyes' (l. 88) foreground this process of mystification" (174n55).

88 *the Sun,* **ZUNDER** (1988): the image of the sun expresses "a moment of democratic openness" (82).

89–110 *Keepe…to trust.* **PARTRIDGE** (1978): "Primary stresses are seen to vary from two to six, the heavily loaded lines being 89, 100, 104 and 110, because here the poet contrasts the power of God to man-made law. For Donne it is quite feasible to have four adjacent stressed syllables, as l. 104 shows." Lines 100 and 103 are "especially weighted, by length, aphoristic content and clinching verbs at the end of the line." Further, eight of the eleven couplets "are enjambed syntactically, enhancing the vehemence and impetuosity of Donne's convictions. The scope of the rhythmical modulations, beginning with the trochaic down-beat of the opening feet of l. 89, is clear evidence of Donne's desire for freedom. There are as many as twenty-three internal pauses in this passage, though three of the lines have no medial rest for the voice," and often "a pause is found in the middle of a foot" (42–43). ZUNDER (1982): the poem here makes "a distinction between allegiance to the state and allegiance to truth" that imposes "a limitation on the power of the state, excluding from it jurisdiction in matters of belief," a "radical conclusion to reach" at the end of the sixteenth century (15–16). [Similarly, Ray (1990, 282–83).] ZUNDER (1988): there is "a sense of exhilaration in the last section of the poem," and "a sense of defiance, as Donne proceeds to set limitations to royal power in matters of belief," for "the truth is one thing; the law, another," and the law "can justify complete opposites, both Catholic and Protestant" (82). [Similarly, Oliver (1997, 64).]

89–102 *Keepe...is Idolatree.* LECOCQ (1969): this passage is one of the highest achievements of satirical poetry of all time. Only a prince of wit can show himself in such a supremely disrespectful way, and these lines alone justify the form of all the satyre of Donne (377–78).

89–97 *Keepe...thee this?* STEIN (1942): these lines illustrate the "low pitched but emphatic tones" in the Satyres. Individual syllables are "rigidly" separated by "unyielding combinations of consonants, or by the emphatic rhythm of a series of stress-shifts" (687).

89–92 *Keepe...to fate.* MILGATE (1967): "God has not given earthly kings a signed warrant to kill, the names of victims being filled in at the king's will," and kings "who do kill 'whom they hate' for differing from them are not the responsible agents of Fate, but her hangmen" (147). MINER (1969): these lines are "a reference to Elizabeth's use of pursuivants, those unscrupulous and cruel ferrets of Catholics," and there is also a "biblical allusion: 'hold fast that which is good' (I Thessalonians 5:21). Such steadfastness could only argue holding to Catholic 'truth'—if Donne could convince himself that he had found it" (35). CORTHELL (1982): "Without denying the chain of command, Donne cleverly shifts the focus from the question of divine rights to the ambivalent status of the king (vicar or hangman) in the order of things; the lines plead for a responsible exercise of power" (168–69). [Similarly, Mallet (1990, 22).] STRIER (1993): Donne's "worry in this poem is not about the tyranny of kings and princes—which he, like Luther, seems to take for granted—but rather about the tendency of the individual to allow external authorities to dictate to the conscience" (307). CAIN (1995): these lines reflect Donne's "anti-absolutist" attitude (85). OLIVER (1997): the poem's "radical force is seen in all its nakedness" in this section, "which distinguishes between human and divine power," and "although this is a logical development of the stress on the individual's freedom in religion, the directness of the attack on the misuse of power is still breathtaking in its courage" (63). ELLRODT (2000) remarks on Donne's audacity in asserting "the right of the individual to keep the truth he had found in despite of all authority" (310). FULTON (2001) remarks on the "hortatory" nature of these lines, stating that the images of power and knowledge here epitomize "the genre's preoccupation with the problem of maintaining, let alone representing, truth under power" (102). Disagrees with Strier (1993) that Donne is in agreement with Luther, arguing that the lines indicate "a fundamental rejection of both Protestant and Catholic views on secular authority—or at least, the more orthodox views that monarchs are invested with a divine, even infallible authority" (103).

89–90 *stand | In so ill case* **SCODEL** (1993): Donne denies that "temporal rulers can dictate the religious choices of their subjects," arguing that there is "no legitimate authority" other than God "in spiritual matters," for "rulers deserve obedience only in temporal affairs" (499).

89 *Keepe...do not stand* **STEIN** (1946) notes "the difference an alternate scansion can make" (99):

/ x / x x (x) / / x x /
Keepe the truth which thou hast found; men do not stand

/ x / x / (x) x / x x /
Keepe the truth which thou hast found; men do not stand

89 *Keepe...hast found:* **GRANSDEN** (1954): this injunction "lays a thoroughly Protestant onus on the individual to make up his own mind" (103). **GERALDINE** (1965) notes that this is the last in a series of four imperatives (117). **MILGATE** (1967) quotes 2 Tim. 1.14 and *Sermons* 5:124 (147). **MINER** (1969): "the general biblical injunction, 'Hold fast that which is good,' becomes far more personal" in this line, for "the individual is assumed to be right (if he can find his way through wise doubting to truth), and social notions are thought utterly wrong" (9). **NEWTON** (1974): "The notion that there *is* a goal, that truth does 'stand' and that it can be found and kept, is necessary to make us begin and keep up the search, but no end to the search can be foreseen" (437). **STRIER** (1993): "This advice precisely recapitulates the central ambiguity of this section of the poem. On one reading of the line, the aim is to keep that part or aspect of the objective truth that you have managed to recognize;" "on the other reading, you are to keep what has impressed you as the truth." Thus, "the first reading asserts the primacy of truth; the second asserts the primacy of conscience—even over truth. The poem hesitates between these views, but it is important to see that the second is a genuine historical possibility. Luther meant to equate rather than to distinguish truth and conscience at Worms" (305). **BROWN** (1995): Christians are "responsible for protecting the resolutions of conscience and reason" (57). **OLIVER** (1997): it may be at this point that the speaker "stopped talking about being damned for failing to search for the truth, and turned his attention to the subject of being damned for failing to hold on to what one knows to be the truth" (65). **YOUNG** (2000): in Donne's mind "there was space within the English church" for someone holding such views (32).

90–92 *God hath...to fate.* **GERALDINE** (1966): the "idea of vicarage carries through now to the end of the poem and is given a new figure in the image of the uprooted plant" (28). **HESTER** (1978a): "The application of Psalm 82 and the legal terms here recall the eternal 'charter' or covenant which man has with God, but the emphasis of the lines is that the covenant God 'hath with his hand' made with man is one of love—love of Him and of one's neighbors" (52).

90 *In so...his hand* **STEIN** (1942): the combination of two unstressed syllables followed by a stressed syllable attracts an extra syllable (688n28).

90 *In so ill case* **MILGATE** (1967): "such evil circumstances" (147). **SMITH** (1971): "in such an evil condition here on earth, or in matters of the salvation of one's soul" (485). [So also, Kermode and Hollander (1973, 1048), Willmott (1985, 64), Lloyd-Evans (1989, 297), and Enright (1997, 97).]

90 *case* **CHMIELEWSKI** (2001): "condition" (617).

90 *here,* **MILGATE** (1967): "on earth" [so also, Craik and Craik (1986, 260)]; or (as suggested by J. C. Maxwell to Milgate) "in religion" or "in matters of the soul" (147).

91–92 *Signd kings...to fate.* **GROSART** (1872–73): "sign'd blank charters [to] kings, &c; nor are such kings as kill those who differ from them vicars of Fate or Providence, but her hangmen" (1:29). [So also, Kermode, Fender, and Palmer (1974, 66) and Singh (1992, 42).] **HAUBLEIN** (1979): Donne here "concedes to kings only the role of fate's executioners, royal Abhorsons, whose laws are fallible and whose authority is inferior." Donne's "attitude toward kings" appears to arrange from "devout respect for the body politic, whose pattern is God himself, to attacks on the king's excesses against society to devastating satire of the royal tyrant" (98).

91 *Signd kings blanc Chartres,* **SMITH** (1971): "given kings a free hand and moral right" (485). [So also, Enright (1997, 97) and Chmielewski (2001, 617).] **MELCHIORI** (1983) notes that king's blank charters appear in *R2* (1.4.48): "Our substitutes at home shall have blank charters" (182). **EDWARDS** (2001) contrasts Donne's assertion here with his assumption in *Pseudo* that "the 'Law of Nature' gave King James an obvious right to demand this oath from his subjects" (81).

91 *blanc Chartres,* **OED** (1882–88): in the reign of Richard II, "a document given to the agents of the crown," empowering them "to fill it up as they pleased; hence figurative [for] liberty to do as one likes" (10). [Similarly, Milgate (1967, 147), Kermode (1970, 105), Rousseau and Rudenstine (1972, 67), Kermode and Hollander (1973, 1048), Broadbent (1974, 106), Willmott (1985, 64), Craik and Craik (1986, 260), Hieatt (1987, 238), Lloyd-Evans (1989, 297), and Rudrum, Black, and Nelson (2000, 122)).] **MATSUURA** (1953): a "cynical" use of the term (102).

92 *Nor...to fate.* **STEIN** (1944c): an example of stress-shift after a pause (379). **ALLEN** (1950): the line echoes Luther's *Von weltlicher Oberkeit*, which was available to Donne in Latin; the expression was perhaps "a common one or perhaps Luther and Donne had protestant minds that thought in the same way" (103). **MILGATE** (1967): "Kings who do kill 'whom they hate' for differing from them are not the responsible agents of Fate, but her hangmen" (147). **HILLER** (1977): "Nor are they the viceregents, but the instruments, of fate" (184). [So also, Willmott (1985, 65) and Singh (1992, 42).] **MELCHIORI** (1983) finds in this line an echo of *R2* (1.2.37–38): "God's substitute, / His deputy anointed in his sight" (182). **NUTT** (1999): if we "assign the pronoun 'they' thoughtfully," it "might explain why Donne in a later letter expressed some anxiety about his *Satyres* being widely read" (123). **CHMIELEWSKI** (2001):

"not proxies (vicars) but servants or assistants (hangmen), i.e., kings do not decide one's destiny, but merely help carry out what was already ordained" (617).

92 *Vicars*, **SMITH** (1971): "proxies. Kings do not take over the function of Fate but are merely Fate's instruments; they cannot kill anyone whom God has not marked for martyrdom" (485). [So also, Kermode and Hollander (1973, 1048), Broadbent (1974, 106), Craik and Craik (1986, 260), Carey (1990, 425), Jones (1991, 631), Enright (1997, 97), and Rudrum, Black, and Nelson (2000, 122).]

92 *hangmen to* **PATRIDES** (1985): "executors of any orders from" (228). [So also, Enright (1997, 97).]

92 *hangmen* **JOHNSON** (1755): "The publick executioneer."

93–110 *Foole...to trust.* **GRANSDEN** (1954): "in the peroration, the laws of God and the laws of man are sharply contrasted to the discomfiture of the latter which, Donne suggests, are the canon of most dogmatic religionists" (103–04). **SLIGHTS** (1991): "The poem ends by warning that failure to resist the coercion of conscience by political or ecclesiastical authority is the soul-destroying idolatry of preferring man's law to God's" (94).

93–102 *Foole...is Idolatree.* **BULLOUGH** (1972): "For the first time Donne goes behind legalities and considers the foundations of faith, which are to be found only in God himself and (presumably) in His word 'at the stream's calm head'" (63).

93–99 *Foole...say so?* **CAREY** (1981): for Donne, "the normal reasons for espousing Catholicism or Protestantism are pathetically inadequate. People display a senseless preference for antiquity or novelty, or they accept what their godparents tell them, or they give up trying to choose and become apathetic. Instead of thinking things out for themselves, they submit to the authority either of the Pope or, if they are Protestants, of the English monarch" (12). **BAUMLIN** (1990): "The contrast between Roman and Protestant kings (Philip of Spain and Henry VIII) proves equally poignant, pointing once again to the arbitrariness of power" (72–73).

93–97 *Foole...thee this?* **CLIVE** (1966): Donne had no personal religious doubts but enjoyed proposing abstract and unanswerable questions (8). **ROBERTS** (1968): "in these lines there is a cancelling out of authority by the four representatives of secular and religious power: Philip cancels out Harry and Gregory cancels out Martin—leaving man once more with his own conscience and his own decision" (114). [Similarly, Morse (1989, 273–74).] **MAROTTI** (1986): in these lines, Donne rejects "the Elizabethan Oath of Allegiance, placing man's responsibility to his conscience and obedience to the laws of God above submission to a merely human law" (42). **MAHLER** (1991) urges that the continuous search for Truth results in an authority that lodges itself within; the person who searches for the true, yet is in constant doubt, is only answerable to him or herself and consequently does not need to bow to any worldly authority (44).

93–95 *Foole...last day?* **MARTZ** (1960): these lines are, "simultaneously," the "public exhortations of the satirist" and "the intimate self-addresses of one who knows how to practice the religious art of seeking himself in himself": in "this hovering between the public and the meditative voice lies the essential art of the poem" (338). **MILGATE** (1967) quotes Augustine in Migne *P. L.* 43:315 and Christopher Goodman, *How Superior Powers ought to be Obeyed* (1558), Facsimile Text Society (1931), p. 46 and C. H. McIlwain's Introduction (147–48). **STRIER** (1993) finds here "real contempt" for "'mans lawes' in the realm of the soul," and sees an emphasis, as in *Biathanatos*, on "the soul's inherent freedom, on its proper refusal to be 'tyed,' its special standing" (307). **OLIVER** (1997): "it is those who fail to pursue the truth who will go to hell, not those unfortunate enough to believe the wrong thing"; however, "if hell is now reserved for those who are guilty of not searching for the truth, it seems a harsh sentence for those unfitted by temperament, upbringing, education and so on to conduct a proper search" (59). **ROBBINS** (2000) identifies here Donne's vehement reaction to "the teaching and law of Elizabethan England" (424).

93–94 *let thy Soule be ty'de / To Mens Lawes,* **MALLET** (1990): "allow your choice of religion to be made for you by man-made laws" (22). **STRIER** (1993): The enjambment exists "for a moment as a question in itself," for "the soul can only be 'tyed / To mans laws' if, foolishly and wretchedly, it allows itself to be so" (307). **FULTON** (2001): Donne "suggests that religion enforced by law cannot be real faith, since conscience must act freely on its own accord" (77).

93 *Foole...be ty'de* **RICHTER** (1902) cites this line to illustrate a metrical inversion from iambic to trochaic in the first two feet (395). **STEIN** (1944c): an example of stress-shift in the first four feet (384).

93 *Foole and wretch* **DAVIES** (1994): "The insult is thrust out from the page at our eyes as we (fools and wretches) read. But our act of reading subverts the intended trajectory of the rebuke. It ricochets back as we identify our own 'I' with the poem's 'I', to redirect 'foole and wretch' elsewhere" (23).

93 *Soule* **PATRIDES** (1985): "'selfe' (acc. to a MS)" (228).

94 *She* **BROADBENT** (1974): "the soul" (106).

94 *not* **PATRIDES** (1985): "(omitted acc. to 1635–54)" (228).

95–110 *Oh will...to trust.* **BROWN** (1995): Donne "urges his readers not to consign their souls to human authorities. God alone can insure salvation." Donne does not disavow "consulting human authority or obeying legitimate rulers," but insteads asserts "the superior value of God's commandments," contending "that only He has jurisdiction over the soul." Thus, "just as God's truth should be the source of our judgments, so His power is our source of authority," and to "stray from the source, Donne warns, is to become lost" (57).

95–99 *Oh will...say so?* **BROADBENT** (1974): "at the Last Judgment will it save you to say you were only following King Philip II of Spain and Pope Gregory XIII (defenders of Roman catholicism), Henry VIII (Anglican reformation), Martin Luther?" (106). **CORTHELL** (1982): "Man's laws all have an equal claim to truth, and Donne carefully balances temporal and spiritual leaders of Protestant and Catholic persuasions" (169). **HESTER** (1982): "The satirist's emphasis on the direction of the will by eternal standards is continued in his final rhetorical question, in which he strips King Philip, Pope Gregory, King Henry VIII, and Martin Luther of their temporal authority in order to view them as they shall be examined on 'the last day,'" for "Kings, popes, and reformers, Protestant and Catholic alike, are only men in God's eyes. To appraise Truth only by their standards or to trust solely in their apparent power is no excuse for willfully failing to defend the truth that has been revealed to or achieved by one. Committing oneself exclusively to sectarian and international struggles amounts to the assignment of one's will to 'mere contraries,' to struggles that are mere temporal battles and contrary to the interest of one's soul" (68). **PARFITT** (1989): Donne "seems to advocate a pragmatic fidelity to the version of Christianity prevailing where you happen to live, but this is done with a complexity and tentativeness which leave the famous passage on Truth effectively unresolved" (59). **STRIER** (1993): "In his attack on spiritual subservience, Donne is careful to include all forms of authority in his purview—Catholic as well as Protestant, religious as well as secular," and "the survey of conflicting possibilities leads Donne back to the epistemological realm," though "this is only momentary," for his emphasis remains on the "individual's relation to authority" (307).

95–97 *Oh will…thee this?* **KLAUSE** (1994): Donne wishes "to avoid a dependence on fallible 'persons' in so important an inquiry (which will lead finally to a personal God [110]), but he cannot; he cannot find truth only among 'things.' Despite his resistance, personal models and heroes were for him a deep necessity" (184). **OLIVER** (1997): all the names on this list "are continental religious leaders except for Henry VIII, who is invoked in mock-friendly fashion by his nickname—a cavalier gesture in keeping with the poem's view of royal power as something essentially subjective" (64).

95 *the last day?* **PATRIDES** (1985): "the Last Judgement" (228). [So also, Willmott (1985, 65), Singh (1992, 42), Enright (1997, 97), and Chmielewski (2001, 617).]

95 *will it* **PATRIDES** (1985): "(acc. to 1633 and some MSS): 'Or will it' (acc. to 1635–69) or 'Oh will it' (acc. to many MSS and all modern editors)" (228).

95 *serve thee* **SMITH** (1971) (reading "boot thee"): "do you any good" (485). [So also, Willmott (1985, 65), Mallet (1990, 22), and Singh (1992, 42).]

95 *serve* **GROSART** (1872–73), noting the alternate reading "boot," says "as between 'boot' and 'serue,' the former is=benefit, and signifies something added, as in booty; and as the plea of the just is the added merits of Christ, 'boot' may be reckoned preferable" (1:29). **CLEMENTS** (1966) (reading "boot"): "Profit" (61). [So also, Baker (1975, 73), Patrides (1985, 228), and Chmielewski (2001, 617).]

96–97 *Philipp,…or a Martin* **GROSART** (1872–73): "Philip [Melancthon], Gregory [the Great, or Gregory of Nazianzen], Harry [the Eighth], Martin [Luther]" (1:29). **GRIERSON** (1912): "surely Philip of Spain is balanced against Harry of England, one defender of the faith against another, as Gregory against Luther. What Gregory is meant we cannot say, but probably Donne had in view Gregory XIII or Gregory XIV, post-Reformation Popes," for "Satire does not deal in Ancient History. The choice is between Catholic and Protestant Princes and Popes" (2:117). [Similarly,

Kenner (1964, 44), Bewley (1966, 178), Clements (1966, 61), Milgate (1967, 148), Shawcross (1967, 397), Warnke (1967, 115), Kermode (1970, 105), Smith (1971, 486), Rousseau and Rudenstine (1972, 67), Kermode and Hollander (1973, 1048), Lewalski and Sabol (1973, 97), Baker (1975, 73), Hiller (1977, 184), Grigson (1980, 22), Patrides (1985, 228), Craik and Craik (1986, 260), Hieatt (1987, 238), Lloyd-Evans (1989, 300), Carey (1990, 425), Mallet (1990, 22), Ray (1990, 282–83), Singh (1992, 42), Kruzhkova (1994, 159–60), Enright (1997, 97), Rudrum, Black, and Nelson (2000, 122), and Chmielewski (2001, 617).] **NUTT** (1999): Donne "binds the poem firmly into the religious controversy of his age" by listing these names, "their connection being that claiming them as fathers of your faith on the last day will gain you nothing" (123–24).

96 *Philipp,* **WILLMOTT** (1985): "Philip II of Spain, the champion of the Roman Catholic Counter-Reformation. He was married to the Catholic Mary I of England (Elizabeth I's half-sister and predecessor). He made use of the Inquisition in trying to control his rebellious Dutch subjects and was responsible for the Armada (1588) not long before this poem was written" (65).

96 *Gregoree,* **NORTON** (1895): "Pope Gregory VII" (1:242). **WILLMOTT** (1985): "There are plenty to choose from! Perhaps Donne has in mind the Pope of his child-hood, Gregory XIII, who worked with Philip II to resist the Protestant reformation, or Gregory VII who had excommunicated and deposed the Holy Roman Emperor Henry IV. (The excommunication of Elizabeth I in 1570 legitimised Catholic plots against her life.)" (65). **HESTER** (1994a): "the choice of Pope Gregory XIII as the representative of the Catholic position in the penultimate section of the poem where religious advisors are stripped of their earthly titles is curious, for it was Pope Pius V who excommunicated Elizabeth; Pope Gregory XIII managed to mitigate that papal Bull considerably" (211).

97 *Martin* **WILLMOTT** (1985): "Martin Luther, an Augustinian monk and professor of theology, was the first great inspirer of the Reformation. One of his principal theories was that of 'justification by faith' and not just by good deeds as Roman Catholics argued" (65).

97 *thee* **PATRIDES** (1985): "'me' (acc. to 1669 and a few MSS)" (228).

98–100 *Is not...bounds know:* **STEIN** (1962): these lines show how Donne uses traditional "paradoxes and antinomies" to cast "ironic reflections...on human affairs" (168).

98–99 *Is not...say so?* **LECOCQ** (1969): these lines reassert Donne's fascination with paradox (378). **SMITH** (1971): "does not the same excuse that one must perforce obey authority hold equally for directly opposite religious factions, who cannot both be right?" (486). **KERMODE, FENDER, AND PALMER** (1974): "There was a doctrine that people would have liked to impose at the time which said that a person's religion should be the religion of his region. They didn't want everybody involved in these religious controversies, so you should take the religion of your King. This is what is being contested here; you must not obey power when it becomes tyranny" (67). **WILLMOTT** (1985): "This excuse (ie. hiding behind the authority of one of the leaders named in the previous two lines) is equally convincing (or rather by implication unconvincing) for people whose beliefs are completely opposed ('mere' means absolute or downright)" (65). **SCODEL** (1993): "The Pyrrhonist suspends belief by opposing every dogmatic argument with a contradictory argument of apparently 'equal strength,' pitting arguments from authority against one another. Donne adapts this skeptical method to argue that the individual must not relinquish true religion by accepting either of the extreme 'contraries' espoused by opposing (pseudo-) authorities" (498–99).

98–99 *Is not…Equally strong?* **MALLET** (1990): "will this excuse not serve equally well for opposite religious groups?" (22).

98 *Is not…meere contrarys* **MORRIS** (1953) cites this line as an example of "three or more reversed feet" following one another (45).

98 *meere contrarys* **BROADBENT** (1974): "sheer opposites. They can't all be right" (106). [So also, Craik and Craik (1986, 260).]

98 *meere* **MILGATE** (1967): "absolute, complete" (147). [So also, Kermode and Hollander (1973, 1048), Baker (1975, 73), Hiller (1977, 184), Patrides (1985, 229), and Enright (1997, 97).]

99 *strong?* **PATRIDES** (1985): "'true' or 'strange' (acc. to individual MSS)" (229).

100–10 *That thou…to trust.* **SELLIN** (1980): although Remonstrants are usually thought of as "victims of orthodox tyranny, Remonstrant magistrates in the Province of Utrecht and several of the major cities in Holland, such as Rotterdam and The Hague, interfered mightily with the rights of the orthodox to worship as they pleased when the Arminians held power in the years before 1618." Thus, "the victors at Dort chose as their motto Psalm 125 in order to attribute their deliverance to the Lord, who does not allow the 'rod of the wicked' to 'rest upon the lot of the righteous' forever, lest 'the righteous put forth their hands unto iniquity.'" In the light of "the political context of the [Dort] medal, the sentiment expressed is one very like what we find in Donne's closing lines (100–110) about the limits of secular authority in matters of religion" (286). **BRODSKY** (1982): the central conceit of these lines is "power," and the poem's "rushing cadence is again brought to a sudden halt and an earthly scene presented, its figural status underscored by an explicit exposition of the conceit's basic simile." Moreover, "the effect of the scenes described by the simile also lies in their crossing of emblematic qualities with images of nature." Further, "the poet's argument here is comparably persuasive," yet "the logical patterning of its imagery entails a strange semantic turn." In particular, the natural image of the "blest flowers" is "forced, by the pattern upon which it is constructed, to perform in a most unnatural manner" in that "although it remains unclear if these 'flowers' are directly endowed with volition, they are at the very least disturbingly capable of motion—not a displacement of petals ascribable to other causes, but an independent leave-taking of 'their roots.'" Finally, the image provides "a coherent pattern of imagery" that "refers to two opposing meanings: one of a natural state of power, the other of a nature with a power of its own." While the "logical structure of the conceit is consistent," the meanings of "power" in this context "cannot be," and thus, "the falsity, or failure, of the conceit" would be "tantamount to a forced, or weak, convergence of the two; its truth, which it cannot image or by logical argument 'win,' would lie in the tenacity of resistance between them" (843–45). MAROTTI (1986) suggests of these lines that "under the guise of speaking about all kinds of legal coercion of one's conscience, whether from Catholic or Protestant sources, Donne seems to have directed his fire at the contemporary requirement that all Englishmen, including Roman Catholics, take the Oath. The issue is put finally in terms of the qualified obedience to secular power," and Donne "not only stated that subscribing to the oath of Allegiance was an act of idolatry, but that the power that demanded such compliance was 'tyrannous,' a dangerous term to use in this context, since it charged the (basically moderate) Elizabeth with the unjust or excessive use of power in the treatment of Catholic subjects" (42–43). GUIBBORY (1990): these lines "articulate both fear of and resistance to royal power, as the speaker, identifying himself with the 'blessed flowers' and unjust monarchs with tyrannous streams, rejects idolatrous submission to earthly rulers and hopes to find ultimate (though not necessarily earthly) safety by dwelling at the calm head (God, the source of all power)" (825). [Similarly, Ray (1990, 283).] CORTHELL (1997): the image is "a misrepresentation, a pathetic fallacy, since flowers do not 'dwell' or 'leave' anywhere," but the image "seems to work on behalf of theories of passive resistance to tyranny which are at least as old as Tyndale; 'blest flowers' would here convey a Reformed understanding of the individual's conscience." Further, "there is even the hint of a meaning of 'election' here, the elect being those 'blest' who 'thrive and do well.' In either case, the point to be emphasized is that the fixed relation of the flowers contradicts the agency and mobility of the subject as truth seeker. If individual conscience 'dwells' in some fixed relation to absolute power, then how can individual conscience also be invoked as the justification for seeking the correct relationship to ultimate power—that is, true religion?" Thus, the closing passage seems to be "a mystification rather than an explanation" (45–46).

100–08 *That thou...are lost.* SHAWCROSS (1972): one "should trust God himself" and rebuff "the religious proselyters, the schismatics, and the bigots: religion is personal; it is seeking after God's truth; it is hard deeds and body's pains" (258). ZUNDER (1988): the "powerful" river image "narrows the idea of limited monarchy to exclude from it jurisdiction in matters of faith," and "at a time when the dominant view took it for granted that rulers decided their subjects' religion," such a view "is a revolutionary stand to take" (83). BAUMLIN (1990): "The Crown has overstepped the bounds of its authority, much as a swollen river breaks out of its banks, sweeping all away with it; indeed the Crown has become this river, refusing to respect the 'bounds' (100) between temporal authority and the individual conscience" (73).

100–02 *That thou...is Idolatree.* SLIGHTS (1972): this conceit "explains forcefully the theory of power behind the casuistical principle that to obey an unjust human law instead of the law of God is to court damnation. Like the stream which becomes more tumultuous as it descends from its calm source to the sea, the exercise of power becomes less perfect as it descends from God, the source of all power" (98–99). MALLET (1990): "it was widely agreed throughout the sixteenth century that the secular authorities were entitled to require a certain measure of obedience, but that there was a limit to what could be demanded; to exceed that limit was to change a proper authority into tyranny" (22). **SCODEL** (1993): Donne "claims that excess turns virtuous obedience into sinful 'idolatry.'" He does not, however, "spell out the objective change in the nature of 'power' when rulers exceed their 'bounds'—the transformation of legitimate authority into tyranny—but instead focuses on the subjective consequences for the ruled—the change in the 'nature and name' of a subject's obedience" (499). **STRIER** (1993): in these lines, the issue is not "right belief but right obedience; religious truth may be extremely difficult to attain, but this truth about 'power,' worldly power, the conscientious individual must 'know,'" and "the essential thing to know about 'power' is 'her bounds.' Right obedience knows these bounds; it is limited," and as such, Donne invokes "the great Protestant bugaboo, 'idolatry,' in a context which includes over-obedience to secular as well as religious powers, princes as well as popes" (308). **HESTER** (1994a): these lines speak to "the precise objections of the English Catholics to the Protestant substitution of the Virgin Queen for the Virgin Mary and the political term 'traitor' for the religious term 'blasphemer' or 'idolater.'" Thus, "in response to charges against the 'idolatrie' of the Mass, the 'adultery' of Mariology, and the 'treason' of their recusancy," English Catholics "responded that the true 'nature' of idolatry is the substitution of the spiritual by the political: 'so perish soules'" (208–09). **OLIVER** (1997): although the poem's "named monarchs are male, it is appropriate that power should be seen as feminine" since religion "has been constructed as feminine, and submission to abused power is said to be a perversion of true religion" (64).

100 *That thou…bounds know:* **BAUMLIN** (1986a): the poem "turns almost militant in its exhortation to scrutinize the rights and powers of temporal authority" (99).

100 *rightly obay* **RICHTER** (1902) cites this phrase to illustrate a slurring of syllables (402–03).

100 *power,* **SINGH** (1992): "Power of kings" (42).

100 *bounds* **WILLMOTT** (1985): "the limits of secular authority. For the basis of Christian teaching on this see Luke 20. 21–6" (65).

101–02 *Those past,…is Idolatree.* **STEIN** (1942): placing the caesura near the end of the line starts a new rhythm that carries into the next line (683). **WILLMOTT** (1985): "Power become tyranny once it goes beyond those limits. To obey the state in matters of religion is to make an idol of the state" (65).

101 *Those past,* **SHAWCROSS** (1967): "once her bounds are passed" (25). [So also, Smith (1971, 486), Jones (1991, 631), Singh (1992, 42), and Chmielewski (2001, 617).] **BROADBENT** (1974): "The doctrine of civil obedience versus spiritual integrity was based on 'Render unto Caesar the things that are Caesar's [even if he is a bad ruler] and unto God the things that are Gods,' Luke 20" (106).

101 *nature, and name is chang'd,* **KERMODE AND HOLLANDER** (1973): "to tyranny" (1048).

102 *humble* **RICHTER** (1902) cites this word to illustrate a stretching of syllables (405).

103–10 *As Streames...to trust.* **STEIN** (1946) notes that the "unmistakably allegorical" elements in this passage add to Donne's obscurity (108). **ANDREASEN** (1963): these lines express the "underlying attitude toward secular and spiritual matters" that permeates all of the Satyres, as leaving the heights of truth for secular pursuits leads to drowning "in the sea of iniquity" (71). **ROBERTS** (1968): Donne "metaphorically delineates the catastrophe of power," and "the emphasis of the last line suggests that it is from God alone that man will receive the ultimate answers, not from any secular or religious institution or persons" (114). [Similarly, Mallet (1990, 22), Chandra (1991, 233), and Oliver (1997, 64).] **LECOCQ** (1969): the image of the river functions as a symbol that—along with its use in *Sat2* and *Sat5*—contains all the satiric vision of Donne (393–94). In its dramatization of the idea that one cannot go back upstream, the river imagery suggests a real obsession, or even an observed and lived reality, on the part of Donne (394). **MOORE** (1969): "The relationship between the flowers and stream is not a simple one. The flowers depend upon the stream for support and nourishment; yet if they submit themselves entirely to the stream, they will be destroyed." Nonetheless, "the image is appropriate because it does not oppose man's power to god's, but puts them in a relationship which is beneficial to the individual who recognizes his need for both and is utterly destructive to the one who believes he can depend solely on the power of men" (48). [Similarly, Sloane (1981, 88), Willmott (1985, 65–66), Guibbory (1986, 80), and Singh (1992, 42).] **NEWTON** (1974): "To insist on striving for a goal which you cannot believe attainable is to risk drowning in a sea of despair. The result, for Donne, is a reflexive pulling back from the very heroic endeavor he urges," and "the final passage of the poem suggests to our kinesthetic sense that the best we can do is keep from drowning" (437). **HESTER** (1978a): "This exhortative warning, the satirist's meditative 'stirring of the affections' and directive to the will, is provided by his metaphoric description of 'Soules' as 'blest flowers.' A colloquy addressed to himself and his audience, it urges recognition of the 'desperate' foolishness of men who resign their wills to the imperial and ecclesiastical tyrants of the world" (52–53). **DOUDNA** (1980): Donne here directs "an attack on those who hold their religious beliefs simply in conformity to custom or to the political authority in power," and "comments on the relationship of the citizen to the source of religious and political authority" (6). **CORTHELL** (1982): the image "suggests the divine origin of all power, even as Donne insists upon the 'unjust' nature of man's power when it appeals to this original authority in matters of religion." While Donne "improvises within an absolutist context," his "focus on the individual succeeds in keeping the paradoxical nature of human power in the background" (169–70). **HESTER** (1982): "Part of the complexity of this passage resides in its function both as a laudatory description of the attributes of divine Power and as a satirical warning about the practices of temporal power." The passage functions then "as a description of the power of this world and its bounds, its limitations, and its failures," and "the metaphor defends the God-ordained order of the world, criticizes the unjust use of power and its abuse for the benefit of one's friends and supporters, and denounces any form of secular or religious tyranny" (69–70). **SALE** (1984): "Crudely put, the dark truth is this: acts that seem natural and easy can also be self-destructive and contrary to God's will; worse, at the time we perform these acts it may seem there was nothing we could have done about it" (48). **CRAIK AND CRAIK** (1986): "The 'calm' weather corresponds to legitimate authority, the 'rough' to the tyrannous abuse of power" (260). **MORSE** (1989): we see here both "the enunciation of a moral principle" and "a flash of Donne's own bitterness at his experience of having been caught between the Jesuits on one side and the Elizabethan State on the other" (274). **MAHLER** (1991) points out that individuals searching for the truth in *Sat3* find their support in God, who is no longer comprehensible by means of worldly things and who must be found by the subject according to its own responsibility. Notes that the final image of the stream of power, which becomes more and more dangerous and powerful the further it is removed from its source, serves as the emblem of this discovery process (44). **SCODEL** (1993): Donne's "strikingly unnatural image of flowers, which normally have no power of self-motion, willfully leaving 'their roots' suggests that persons who submit to tyranny perversely abandon and exceed their natural human capacities and dispositions. The initial positive image of the 'blest flowers' that 'thrive' at the 'calme head' implies that human beings can be nurtured rather than destroyed by worldly authority simply by remaining in their natural place, aware of the proper minimum and maximum 'bounds' of their obedience. Donne thus envisions both the objective inevitability of tyrannic excess and the subjective freedom of individuals, who can flourish by recognizing only legitimate rule or (conversely) can destroy themselves by accepting tyranny." Further, "instead of using the concept of the mean to defend the church and state of the Elizabethan settlement, Donne uses it to promote individuals' independence—but not isolation—as they seek and preserve the truth. In such an active, masculinist poem, it is striking that Donne ends with the passive and—according to Renaissance connotations of gender—feminized image of souls as flowers" (500–01). **STRIER** (1993): mentioning "power" and "bounds" appears "to have given Donne his river image," and "from the history of this image in political discourse, we would expect a discussion of how the 'stream' of power gets troubled or swollen. But, for the special purposes of his poem, Donne has started at the wrong end. He wants to continue the discussion of power, but the poem is less interested in the way that power becomes abusive than in how the individual is to act once it has become so" (309–10). **MANLEY** (1995): "The world is governed by a perilous stream-effect, whereby souls are uprooted, brought to the turmoil of the surface, swept along and 'consum'd in going'" (399). **NUTT** (1999) finds this image "curiously earthbound" since Donne has located "the bounds of power" previously "in heaven and not on earth." This conclusion, however, "is clear and consistent with the satire's central drive and intellectual concern," reminding us that the genre "was viewed as a potentially dangerous form" and that the poem presents a "challenge to kingly authority" (124). **FULTON** (2001) argues that "the vision of the stream" is "a stream of secular rather than divine power" and suggests that "calme head" be read "precisely as Donne uses it" in *Sat5*, "as the source of the monarch's power." Says that "Blessed" describes "a superficial condition of thriving," or "the flowers' seeming, rather than true condition, since they thrive near the source of power, but, as Donne writes, they have left their roots" as a result of "their proximity to the calm head." Notes further that "the

flowers have chosen a power unjustly claimed, and as a consequence lose their souls,"
and that the word "'Unjust' belongs not simply to power, implying there could be just
power claimed from God, but rather that 'Power from God' as the poem has argued,
is unjustly claimed." Cites a similar metaphor in the opening of George Chapman's
Bussy D'Ambois (ll. 82–84), which is "so similar, in fact, that one wonders if Chapman
had read Donne" (104).

103–09 *As Streames...So perish Soules,* WARBURTON (1751): in "this noble
similitude," souls that are not "passive," but "wilfully prefer human Authority to
divine," are "the object of [Donne's] satire" (4:249).

103–08 *As Streames...are lost.* MASOOD-UL-HASAN (1958): for Donne, "a
river, in general, supplied him the metaphor for selfish and thankless men of Power in
the world." Here, the river has "not only the idea of ingratitutde at its root but it was
also suggestive of deceit, treachery and hypocrisy" (28). STEIN (1984): "The 'blest
flowers' are the happy souls that dwell in true religion," who are "more like souls in
the heavenly paradise than the striving souls with whom Donne appears to identify
his own seeking. If the rough stream symbolizes no other connexion with the 'worlds
sea' than the 'tyrannous rage' of human power, then God and the 'blest flowers' can
dwell only at the calm source; just power derived from God cannot venture into the
secular stream, and the good have no place to go in the living world, and no good to
do for themselves or others. They are released from the human necessity (and choice)
of acting" (84). AUSTIN (1992): "the vocabulary is of a kind associated with poetry:
nature and lyric-type words" (20). MASSELINK (1992): "not only does this passage
echo the claim in the sermon of 1620 that 'all without the Arke [of the church] is sea'
(3:524), it also sounds very much like Donne's warning in one of the first sermons he
preached: 'the Devil labours to Devoure.... Those who are without the pale, without
the Church, and those that are Rebellious and refractary within it, these he may
devoure without any resistance' (1:165)" (96–97). OLIVER (1997): the image is "an
unexpected addition to the hilly landscape evoked earlier" and "condemns both the
abuser of power, who is a tyrant, and those who know the truth yet desert it" (65).

103–05 *Those blest flowers...their rootes,* WIGGINS (2000): Donne "makes the
same point with an architectural metaphor" in *Essays*, stating that the Church of
England "has kept 'still the foundation and corner-stone' of the Christian religion
'Christe Jesus' and has abandoned 'the spacious and specious super-edifications which
the Church of Rome had built thereupon'" (1855, 125) (49).

103–04 *As Streames...proue well:* MORRIS (1953) cites these lines as an example
of Donne using sprung rhythm not as a guiding principle, but instead "as a means for
producing irregularity and variety" (44).

103 *Those blest flowers which dwell* CORTHELL (1982) believes it important "to
note the difference between the 'blest flowers that dwell' and the dynamic climber
of the hill of truth who stands 'in strange way,' occupying a no-man's-land where
conventional social relations are suspended." Finds that the "'strange way' is a place
for marking the passage from a false set of relations to authority—those characterized
by Mirreus, Crants, Graius, Phrygius, and Graccus—to the new relation exemplified

by the 'blest flowers'" (170). **HESTER** (1982): the metaphor "counsels humility," and "this metaphor of souls as flowers, a colloquy to [the satirist] himself and his audience, urges recognition of the foolishness of men who resign their wills to the imperial and ecclesiastical tyrants of this world" (69). **STRIER** (1993): the image "takes its place with the other images in the poem of virtuous immobility," and in fact "the deepest positive image in the poem is not of motion but of stasis," and thus, "the flowers are 'blest' through consciously remaining 'At the rough streames calme head,'" thereby maintaining "their direct and unmediated relation to the divine source" (310).

104 *At the rough Streames calme head* **SMITH** (1971): "the ultimate source of earthly power is God himself, and those who root themselves around the source itself prosper" (486).

105–10 *But hauing…to trust.* **STRIER** (1993): the "figures who are in motion" in this passage are "not autonomously and diligently proceeding, though in circles, but being driven. Donne is now the Lucretian sage, watching from his secure height," and "there seem to be only two possibilities in this world: absolute self-containment and absolute other-dependence. The one is calm and 'blessed,' the other tumultuous and fatal," and thus "the Lucretian image is Donne's way of conveying an inner-worldly and naturalistic version of losing one's soul" (311). [Similarly, Wiggins (2000, 50).]

105–06 *But hauing…are driuen* **RICHTER** (1902) cites the rhymed words of the couplet here to illustrate feminine rhyme (411). **STEIN** (1942): beginning the line with two light syllables creates an effect of rapidity (685).

105–06 *themselues giuen / To the Streames tyrannous rage,* **SMITH** (1971): "yielding themselves not to God's power but to the will of earthly tyrants, which is the more violent and arbitrary the further it moves from God" (486). **SLIGHTS** (1972): "The man who obeys an unjust human law entrusts his soul to the 'tyrannous rage' of human authority instead of to his conscience, the voice of God in him" (99).

105 *lefte* **PATRIDES** (1985): "'lost' (acc. to a few MSS)" (229).

106 *the Streames tyrannous rage,* **HESTER** (1994a): "the Elizabethan satirist endorses the central Recusant distinction between confessional and political truths by characterizing current power as 'the streames tyrannous rage.' This application of the precise terms of Machiavelli's figuration of Dame Fortune as *fiumi rovinosi* (*Il Principe*, ch. 25), itself a revison of Dante's *Inferno* vii.64f., would seem to endorse once again the repeated Recusant descriptions of Elizabeth and her ministers (especially Cecil) as Machiavels" (211).

107 *Through Mills,…last allmost* **STEIN** (1944c) notes the speed and flexibility given to the rhythm by the extra syllable before the caesura (396).

107 *Mills,* **LLOYD-EVANS** (1989): "watermills" (297).

109–10 *So perish…to trust.* **JACKSON** (1968), in relation to the "several variants of the visible church" found earlier in the poem, asks, "Is God's power truly to be found in any one of these particular figures? That question is answered explicitly in the final couplet of the poem" (41–42). **ROY AND KAPOOR** (1969): Donne "would pin his faith upon God and is not with those who turn their interpretation of the faith into a creed and thus the condemnation" (103). **BAKER-SMITH** (1972): the final couplet "contains the germ of his case against the Papacy in *Pseudomartyr*, but it equally well applies to any human assumption of divine authority" (410). **HESTER** (1982): "Justice is the inner rule of the reason of the soul, the ordination of the will by the dictates of the reason. Thus, the satirist's evaluation of the current habits of men in the realm of justice, of the willful manipulation or willing submission of their wills to 'mens unjust / Power' (109–10), provides a rational and practical guide for men to avoid those subversions of the will that amount to spiritual self-betrayal" (67–68). **TEAGUE** (1987): "There is something of despair in this leap into the arms of God at the end of a poem so systematically hostile to any kind of affirmed certainty" (32). **ZUNDER** (1988): "the poem concludes with a warning which is also an assertion that freedom of conscience is divinely sanctioned" (83). **HESTER** (1991): the final couplet "provides the final generic *laus* to balance the poem's general vituperation," offering "a crisp epigrammatic reminder" that "the previous 108 lines of the poem have served primarily as a dramatic absence of 'true religion' in late Elizabethan Protestant England" (98). **STRIER** (1993): "Grammatically, as a continuation of the previous narrative, this couplet is descriptive; in tone, however, and in its relative syntactic independence (reinforced by its couplet status), it sounds like a grimly prophetic command or prayer," in which Donne's "focus remains on the will, on what persons 'chuse.'" Further, "this poem cannot imagine benign earthly power," for "power, in the poem, means power to bind or 'tie' the soul" (311–12). **OLIVER** (1997): this final couplet, "inextricably linked by its opening word to the stream/monarch analogy, refuses to allow itself to be taken as referring" both to "failing to search for the truth" and "failing to hold on to what one knows to be the truth." There is a "startling" similarity, in both "sentiment and language," to Christopher Goodman's *How Superior Powers Ought to be Obeyed of their Subjects* (65). The final couplet also "balances two sorts of guilt against each other, that of the willfully misled and that of the misleaders—though it takes the opportunity to insinuate a new criticism of the latter: that their abuse of power is compounded by their claim to have divine backing" (67). **FULTON** (2001) compares the "criticism of divine right" in Claudius's defence (*Ham.* 4.5.124) with Donne's "sentiment" here (101).

109 *So perish Soules,…mens vniust* **STEIN** (1942) cites the feminine/masculine rhyme resulting from the stress-shift in the fifth foot (681).

109 *more chuse* **ENRIGHT** (1997): "rather choose" (97).

110 *then* **PATRIDES** (1985): "than" (229).

110 *God himselfe to trust.* **HESTER** (1982): the line "announces that reasonable and just conclusion by which man can achieve both justice in the world and justice in his soul." Once more, "the internal and external, the private and public actions of man are seen to be inevitably yoked: to act justly to achieve devotion in the world, one must attain and maintain an internal justice among the rational faculties" (68). **HESTER** (1991): in "response to the *riduculae imitationes* uncovered by the poem's satirical anatomy," this passage "offers a textual presentation of an imitative

alternative to the world of 'force' and false models: 'God him*selfe* to trust'—or—'God him*selfe* to trust'—or—'*God* him*selfe* to *trust*.' Typical of the rigorous precision of Donne's cadences in all his texts, the response to the age's emphasis on 'Power' by the accents on 'God,' 'selfe,' and 'trust' presents (actually re-presents) the trinitarian emphasis throughout the poem on the re-creation of the *imago dei* in the rational soul's three functions, while at the same time undercutting the masculinity of the rational self before the Father. Thus, through the identification of God as 'him' and the simultaneous identification of the insignificance of the man as an *unaccented* 'him' Donne identifies the femininity of all believers before the Bridegroom's eternal 'Power.'" Further, "the tenseless grammatical form of the poem's *last clause* might best figure forth Donne's own position and his own advice in late Elizabethan England," in which "the 'merit' he finds 'worthy' of 'indeavour' in such a world, he satirically concludes, is 'to trust'—to trust himself to trust only God himself." Such "a final directive" might sound like "a Calvinian admission of incapacity," but in fact it is "the *threat* to free will that animates the 'perswasive force' of the poem *as satire*" (100–01). **WIGGINS** (2000): "It is no accident" that the final line "begins with the word 'power,' and, of course, that power is spelled out in the Acts of Supremacy and Uniformity and in those various statutes, 'new like fashions,' enacted in support of the Church of England" (49–50).

Satyre 4.

COMMENTARY

Date and Circumstances

Grosart (1872–73, 1:41–42) points to the phrase "the losse of Amyens" (l. 114) as evidence that the poem must have been written after the Spanish took Amiens on March 11, 1597. Since the recovery of Amiens by the French in September 1597 is not mentioned in the poem, he reasons that the poem must have been written before that event. (Others who comment on the context of Amiens include Chambers [1896, 2:244], Grierson [1912, 2:104], Grierson [1929, xxix], Hayward [1930, 120], Atkins [1937, 396], Ellrodt [1960a, 455], Milgate [1967, 148], Blissett [2000, 100, 110], and Prescott [2000, 230].) Further evidence of this date of composition, Grosart says, is the evident vogue of satires at about this time.

Norton (1895, 1:244) suggests that lines 113–14 "perhaps" refer to the invasion of France in 1594, after Henry IV "had declared war with Philip II," and notes further that Spain "took Amiens in March, 1595, and this may possibly" suggest the date of Sat4 as "the summer of that year, for Amiens was retaken by the French in September."

Alden (1899, 76, 78–79) observes that in the Hawthornden manuscript Sat4 is dated 1594 (76), but he thinks this date must be wrong, not only because of the mention of "the losse of Amyens" (l. 114) in 1597 but because the poem also makes mention of "Gallo-Belgicus" (l. 112), a newspaper that (according to Grosart, 1872–73 [1:41] and Chambers, 1896 [2:247]) began publication in 1598 [ed.—actually in 1588]. Alden thus dates Sat4 in 1597 or 1598.

Gosse (1899, 41) notes the contradiction between the dating of Sat4 as 1594 in the Hawthornden manuscript and the poem's reference to "the losse of Amyens" (l. 114) in 1597, but concludes that Sat4's "looseness of texture" suggests "it was originally composed in 1594 and extended a few years later."

Grierson (1909, 238) thinks Sat4 dates from 1597 or "the years immediately following" because in these years Donne worked for Lord Keeper Egerton, and the poem bears "the mark of the budding statesman." Others who comment on the associations with Egerton include Ochojski (1950, 542) and Rogers (1993, 652).

Grierson's (1912, 2:104) dating of Sat4 rests solely on l. 114 of the poem ("the losse of Amyens"), which he states "shows that the poem must have been written after March 1597, probably between that date and September, when Amiens was re-taken by Henry IV."

Hardy (1942, 64) states that Donne wrote Sat4 because he was galled by "the extravagance and superficiality" of the Elizabethan court and courtiers and because his "mind was hungry for deeper matter."

Milgate (1967, 148) finds "no indication" that the reference to "the losse of Amyens" (l. 114) was "a later insertion, and there is no manuscript copy of the poem without it." He dates *Sat4* accordingly between March and September 1597, probably "in the earlier part of that period, before [Donne] set off on the Islands expedition in July."

Bald (1970, 86) asserts that *Sat4* is "the only poem that can certainly be assigned to the months after the Cadiz expedition," as its mention of "the losse of Amyens" (l. 114) indicates "fairly precisely."

Erskine-Hill (1972, 282–83) thinks that we "come up against a fact of Donne's biography" in *Sat4* when we recognize "the fearful attitude towards the law" in the poem, and that here Donne reflects the "experience of being a Catholic in a Protestant state."

Shawcross (1972, 251–252) dates the poem after 1595 because of the "possible allusion" in line 22 to Raleigh's Guiana expedition. Shawcross denies that *Sat4*'s failure to mention the recapture of Amiens by the French necessarily means the poem must have been written before September 1597, and he goes on to base a possibly later date for the poem on the sound of what he calls the poem's "ring of rejection" of the lifestyle of a courtier.

Dubrow (1979, 80) finds that Donne focuses on the royal court in *Sat4* because of his "fascination with the public world" and "his own ambivalent relationship to the court" during the time he was writing the Satyres. Behind his "bitter condemnation," she suggests, "may well lie an attraction to the court of which Donne himself was not proud. The gentleman protests too much."

Wall (1985, 23–25) claims that Donne's argument focuses specifically on "the Anglican (not the Roman Catholic) Feast of the Purification of Saint Mary the Virgin, celebrated annually, like the Catholic feast, on February 2," which he believes, makes possible a more exact dating for *Sat4* and "heightens still further the irony of the speaker's religious allusions" (24–25).

Marotti (1986, 102, 105) thinks that *Sat4* is "rooted" in Donne's "search for courtly employment in the late nineties" (102). He points out that by the time he wrote *Sat4*, Donne was "no longer quite the courtly novice he was in his earlier Lincoln's Inn days." In this poem, the satirist's "aversion to suitorship, to its proper language of compliment, and to the corruptions of the system of patronage and preferment" are more those of a participant than of an outsider, signaling "a close interest in the workings of the Court" maintained by a participant who, "despite his other feelings, wanted to succeed there."

Sullivan (1993, 12) notes that the previously "uncollected printings" of Donne's verse "establish a *terminus ad quem*" for *Sat4* of 1609.

Wiggins (2000, 6) agrees with Marotti (1986) that in *Sat4* the satirist's "dismissive remarks about courtiers" should be taken "with a healthy skepticism." He maintains that these remarks, "concentrated" in *Sat4*, are supported only by "scattered" references in the rest of Donne's secular poems and should not have "induced some readers to conclude that Donne scorned the Court." In fact, Wiggins says, he scorned only "maladroit, would-be courtiers" and by censuring these "was only establishing his own superior credentials for a role at court."

General Commentary

Pope (1733, 5–16) in an anonymous pamphlet publishes an adaptation of Sat4 as *The Impertinent, or a Visit to the Court. A Satyr,* attributing the poem on the title page to "an Eminent Hand" (see Appendix 2).

An anonymous writer in *The Universal Spectator and Weekly Journal* (1734) publishes an imitation/borrowing of Sat4.

Pope (1735, [98]) thinks Sat4 exemplifies great "*Freedom in so eminent a Divine as Dr.* Donne" and proves "*with what indignation and contempt a Christian may treat Vice or Folly, in ever so low, or so high, a Station.*" He adds that, despite writing Sat4, Donne was "*acceptable to the* Princes *and* Ministers *under whom*" he lived, because he was "*a* Satyrist," not "*a* Libeller," and "*to a true* Satyrist *nothing is so odious as a* Libeller, *for the same reason as to a man* truly virtuous *nothing is so hateful as a* Hypocrite."

Spence (1823, 52) judges that, though "general readers" know Donne mainly as a satirist and mainly through "the medium of Pope," this is equivalent to knowing Homer through Pope, whose "brilliant and refined" attempt to render Donne's Sat4, "by changing his roughness into smoothness, and polishing down his force into point," is in fact merely an "impertinence" that "altered Donne into Pope."

Patmore [?] (1846, 21) complains that Pope's attempt to "improve" Sat4 is like the effort of a "sailor, who, having obtained a curiosity in the form of the weapon of a sword-fish, 'improved' it by scraping off and rubbing down all the protuberances by which it was distinguishable from any other bone."

Dowden (1890, 802) describes Sat4 as "a lively picture of the needy court suitor assuming courtier's airs" who, being "dismissed with the gift of a crown-piece," appears "a figure half-piteous, half-grotesque."

Gosse (1893, 238) calls Sat4 "the best written" of Donne's Satyres and "the best essay in this class of poetry" before the flourishing of Dryden.

Chadwick (1900, 36) thinks Sat4 affords "ample illustration" of Donne's "stupendous learning which was the wonder of his time, and may well be of ours."

Grierson (1909, 238) finds Sat4 "long and somewhat over-elaborated," considering it deals with "the fashions and follies of court-life at the end of queen Elizabeth's reign."

Simpson (1924, 319) notes that Sat4 was transcribed on folio 283 of the Burley manuscript, which also contains the accompanying marginal note, "Well, I may now receive, & die."

Lewis (1934b, 655) contends that Sat4, among the Satyres generally, is "a form of critical poetry" that exhibits "metaphysical principles" that "assume paramount importance and serve to modify, if they do not determine, the attitude of the poet."

Heltzel (1938, 421–22) notes Joseph Wybarne's quotation from lines 18–23 of Sat4 in his *New Age of Old Names* (1609) to demonstrate "the incredibility of the legend of Antichrist."

For Hardy (1942, 64–65), hanging over Sat4 is "something of the weight and lavishness of the ornate, and often tasteless, tombs of the period." She compares the satirist's view of various court spectacles Donne describes as like "the eye of a falcon hovering so high above the crowded plain that it appears no more than a pasture." Donne's mind in *Sat4*, she observes, seems both "rapacious" and at the same time "discerning."

Leishman (1951, 114–15) notes that *Sat4* is the "longest" of Donne's Satyres, "the roughest in versification, and, on the whole, the least interesting, the nearest to the common run." Moreover, the poem has "no clear plan or dominant idea" and contains detail "piled upon detail." Though "individual lines are often striking, they do not co-operate to produce a whole," he believes, but *Sat4* does "disprove the notion" that Donne "seems to have been little affected by visual impressions." Raizada (1974, 105–06) also comments on Donne's imagery in the poem.

Carey (1959, 177) notes Clement Paman's "The Taverne" as an imitation of *Sat4* and finds Paman's dialogue comparable to Donne's.

Harris (1960, 192) thinks *Sat4* "recreates a conventional scene with new force."

Milgate (1967, xxiv) finds that despite a "clinching epigrammatic couplet" in the end, *Sat4* "fall[s] apart badly."

Hughes (1968, 50, 52–53) deems *Sat4* one of the last among Donne's "utterances of the self-conscious renegade," differing from what followed as the Lothian portrait differs from the Isaac Oliver miniature, the difference "between a man partly hidden in shadow and a man fully revealed." In *Sat4*, this mask of the renegade is "most carefully adjusted," and it is "the most insistently renegade" of the Satyres (50). However, despite the "analogy which he throws over the entire satire," comparing the Israelites under Antiochus to the English "Catholic minority," Hughes finds it "difficult to take any of this more seriously than the first two satires," because "Donne was no Savonarola," and because there is "more high comedy than moral outrage in the poem." Donne engaged here in "interesting and effective experimentation," but the experiment would not be repeated because "the personality of a prophet, even a burlesque prophet, is not one which Donne chose to adopt for any length of time" (52–53).

In *Sat4*, Lecocq (1969, 379) considers the courtier, even in his capacity as a suspected police informant, to be too stupid to be truly disquieting.

Roy and Kapoor (1969, 99) comment that Donne's Satyres tend to present the "contemporary life" of his society, and they argue that in *Sat4* Donne suggests that those at the court "seem to be excused of decency, for as he enters the court he has to face the looks that lack all enchantment and rather betray hostility."

Bald (1970, 86) judges *Sat4* to be "the longest and most brilliant" of Donne's Satyres.

Hutchison (1970, 356) states that in *Sat4*, and "especially" *Sat1*, "the scene is stressed and the personae are drawn into it, although naturally they still provide the commentary on events."

Sanders (1971, 36) describes *Sat4* as "240-odd lines" marked by "passionately denouncing that bladder swollen with vanity, the Court," and followed by "a hot flush of modest sanctimony," an "exquisite little coda (better than the rest of the poem put together)," the concluding disclaimer (ll. 237–44) in which "the tongue moves with visible relish around the inside of the cheek."

Erskine-Hill (1972, 273, 286, 292–93, 303–04, 306–07) quotes Donne's letter to

Henry Wotton, which states, "To my satyrs there belongs some feare," and comments that this "is a good, though not total, summary of the spirit" of Sat4 (273). He sees the situation in the poem as "consistently dramatic," a situation affording neither the satirist nor "at this time perhaps, in real life" Donne himself the "security of the mere commentator: the wise man who can just laugh." The poem expresses "exuberant comedy" in a "dialogue with fear" (286), and in the poem's conclusion, Erskine-Hill finds a "confident and powerful judgment upon the court, vehement and energetic ridicule" but notes that this is "only one side of the satirist's human response." Equally, if not more "emphasized," is fear, either "low" fear or fear "justified and religious," mingled with "wit, hyperbole and exaggeration" (292).

Erskine-Hill dissents from the general view of Sanders (1971) that Sat4 (like Donne's other Satyres) by its nature cannot be more than "episodic" and that consequently it goes on too long (292–93). He is especially admiring of Sat4's conclusion, its "Christian vision of the damned at court," illustrating one of many points in the poem at which Pope, in his "versification," had "simply regularised away the careful inflexions of the speaking voice" (303). What Pope "took to be the wit" of Sat4 is actually "a vital and pervasive intelligence, seizing upon relationships through trenchant and concrete expression, often coloured by a sardonically comic exaggeration: the blood in the body of the poem" (304).

Finally, he finds in Sat4 an "impressive human complexity" in the way it "uses and changes Horace," in its "synthesis of classical and Christian," and in its "tension between laughter and tears, or, more precisely, between mockery and fear, each reined in and checked so that one does not outrun the other." The poem, Erskine-Hill concludes, is "far from being a shapeless and over-long denunciation," but "possesses an expressive unifying structure" (306). It is "admirable in its courage and independence: in being so intimately of its time yet so bravely against it, with all the intelligence, misgiving, principle and skill which that took" (307).

Jensen (1972, 405) asserts that in Sat4 "Renaissance satire appears at its brilliant best: playing directly to the reader's responses, making vivid and particular instances of folly which in lesser poems are mere items in a catalogue, presenting the infectious idiocies of the contemporary scene with a vitality that remains persuasive."

Shawcross (1972, 267–68) thinks that those who find Sat4 "overlong" should consider "the etymological meaning of satire: the filled-to-brimming pot, the container replete with all matter of ingredients." He points out that the poem's critique of "the courtier and the court cannot be confined in their pervasive influence to just an image or two," adding that "a demand for organization and structure" lies behind criticism of the poem's length.

Messenger (1974, 10) describes the persona of Sat4 as "a slightly naïve vir bonus" who defines his moral character in comparison to the bore and in recognition of bearing some of the corrupting influence of the court.

Parker (1975, 21) identifies the subject matter of Sat4 as "the court and the proud, lustful, bankrupt, vain, witless, false men who dwell about it."

Hester (1977c, 192) judges Sat4 as the poem that "most fully delineates" Donne's satirist "as a norm by which corrupt 'art' and manners of the courtiers can be judged."

The poem is "dominated by images of imitation, emulation, and artistic and moral models," and the satirist's "aesthetic principles reinforce his exemplary actions."

Selden (1978, 65) calls Sat4 "idiosyncratic (and therefore inimitable)" as a "Horatian experiment," although it did "make available a number of conventions which contributed to the formation of a native pattern of formal verse satire."

Dubrow (1979, 75–76) finds the "blend of Horatian and Juvenalian elements" in Sat4 "unsuccessful" because Donne "failed to recognize the problem" posed by a dialogue (such as Juvenal does not attempt) in which Juvenalian insults are "spit out" directly in the face of a companion. While Donne demonstrates "wonderful ability to establish a lively dramatic situation," the insults his "companion" must bear are "all the more cruel" because he is "a vividly realized person, not a mere satiric type." On the other hand, Dubrow thinks, while the poems of Juvenal and his "Renaissance followers" are "often boringly monochromatic," Donne's "more lively" satirist combines the "vividly realized, precisely detailed portraits" of Juvenal with a "framework of Horatian dialogue," avoiding a "loose, list-like structure" and enabling "shifts" between "quiet Horatian meditation" and "acerbic Juvenalian mockery."

Gallenca (1982, 320) proposes that in Sat4 Donne senses that eternity penetrates time, while the courtier evolves in a time that rejects eternity. For Donne, the worldly life seems a discontinuous line, and this reality wounds him because impermanence is a malady of soul and feeling.

Hester (1982, 73, 75, 94) thinks that the "nearly exclusive critical attention" given to Sat3 has had the "regrettable" effect that Sat4 has received "only scant critical attention." The poem "tests and expands the view of satire-as-religion" in Sat3, Hester believes, with the result that satire is presented here as not only a "form of Christian devotion" but a "celebration of and participation in the unfolding of the Word" (73). Sat4 deserves "acclaim" for its "structural and imagistic design," incorporating the "witty portraits" and "penetrating ridicule" of the best satire, and in particular for its renovation of the "ubiquitous bore of Horatian satire" as "a Renaissance malcontent traveler, sinister spy, and agent provocateur" embodying "the court's disregard for meaningful gesture and expression." But the "major achievement" of Sat4 for Hester is its accommodation and, indeed, its embodiment of verse satire's "rhetorical requirements" and the "moral injunctions of Christian ethics." This poem is Donne's "fullest and most audacious" adaptation of classical satirical techniques to Christian ones (75).

As such, Sat4 also constitutes, according to Hester, Donne's "boldest appraisal" of Tudor religion's "intolerance," portraying the satirist as "a traitor, a spy, victim, or outsider" and frequently comparing his "pain, fear, or conviction" to those of a recusant Catholic. In this way, the poem "exploits the cruel ironies underlying what Frances Yates called Protestant England's 'claim to have restored a golden age of imperial religion.'" Sat4 ridicules Elizabethan England's "salacious libellers, blasphemous courtiers, and vulgar politicians," whose "social and legal liberty" has been permitted to "travesty the rites, rituals, and devotional practices for which sincere believers might end up on Tyburn Hill" (94).

Kerins (1984, 48) believes that Sat4 is important in its genre because its "veneer of witty conceits" covers an "essential" concern with the "expiation of the satirist's own sense of guilt," a "precarious balancing of humor and ultimate concern."

Caracciolo-Trejo (1986, 2:13) praises *Sat4* as a rich poem that illustrates, like a great fresco, the life of the court and, above all, the demimonde of aspirants who are constantly left behind.

Marotti (1986, 102–03, 105–06, 111) calls *Sat4* the "longest and most pessimistic" of Donne's Satyres, "a poem whose intensity of criticism of the courtly world is probably a function of the frustration of his ambition" (102). It is a poem that "dramatizes the process of the breakdown of critical and moral distance" in the satirist who has "involved himself in the Court" (103). A "satiric stance of distanced criticism" here "breaks down," Marotti argues, and the satirist "finds, to his horror, that he has internalized the world he has sought to flee," a development representing Donne's own "ambivalence about his own courtiership" (105–06). Donne "dissociates himself from courtly practices and language," in part "to proclaim his independence and autonomy," in part "to express frustration and disillusionment," Marotti adding that Donne "assumed a readership whose attitudes and awareness were similar to his" (111).

Baumlin (1988, 367, 380) asserts that *Sat4*, "through self-conscious skepticism" towards "its form and function," is "a deliberately failed poem" in that it is "incapable of enacting the aims of the genre because it discovers, in the process of its own composition, the weakness of its language." One "symptom of this weakness" is the satirist's "inability to defend himself" against the "onslaught" of "the more powerful rhetoric" of the courtier, and another is Donne's "reliance upon a Roman Catholic vocabulary for guilt, punishment, and reform" (367). Baumlin thinks *Sat4* "less a critical revision than a repudiation" of the classical satiric tradition (380).

Fish (1990, 240–41), aligning Donne with the speaker of *Sat4*, asserts of Donne that "the entire poem constitutes *his* sign of loathing, *his* declaration of distance from the world he delineates and from the voice he projects."

Lewis (1990, 103) comments that *Sat4* is "remarkably like a scene from a play."

Sullivan (1993, 6–7) lists *Sat4* 18–23 among the six poems that were "published in part in Donne's lifetime" and concludes that "there was more of Donne's printed poetry with a larger circulation, a more general readership (as opposed to members of Donne's inner circle who had access to his manuscripts), and a greater potential influence during his lifetime than previously believed."

Klawitter (1994, 124) suggests that like *Sat1*, *Sat4* also shows us how difficult it was to avoid people one did not want to see in the crowded streets of London.

Price (1996, 66, 71) argues that the persona of *Sat4*, "whose guardedness approaches paranoia" (71), is to be understood as an accomplished dissembler because of his status as a recusant, which "itself enables him to out-dissemble the dissembling bore" (66).

Biester (1997, 21) notes that both *Sat4* and *Sat1* "are performances designed to arouse wonder," though the persona in the former "walks abroad in the everyday world of the court" and in the latter "is sheltered in the near-holiday world of the Inns of Court."

Nilsen (1997, 141) states that the poem is "about the wretchedness of the court and affectations of dress and speech."

Blissett (2000, 110, 112) comments that "for all the fierce energy" of *Sat4*'s persona, he is "not aggressive," but instead "endures all things as a mortification" (110). He notes further that Donne calls the bore a "thing" four times (ll. 18, 20, 35, 152) and describes him as "strange" six times (ll. 18, 21, 23, 30, 38, 152), adding that the bore "is menacing in his attentions" and is either "a disguised priest or an agent provocateur, dangerous as either" (112).

Prescott (2000, 230) finds that this "anti-court" satire "adopts Horace's tiresome companion, but with darker urgency as the stroll through London becomes in effect a descent to Hell." This companion, "a seedy and curious wanderer, has a diabolical look" and may be a government spy.

Robbins (2000, 424) notes that Sat4 "depicts treacherous machination at court," where a double agent attempts to involve the speaker "in treasonous talk."

Wiggins (2000, 6, 50–51) agrees with Marotti (1986) that in Sat4 Donne's satirist, by censuring courtiers, "was only establishing his own superior credentials for a role at court." Donne's "dismissive remarks about courtiers" should be taken "with a healthy skepticism" (6), for the poem's "anxious—at moments, frenzied—tone and its phantasmagoric parade of disturbing images" record "a malaise inseparable from" the "social mimesis" that being a courtier induced (51).

Hadfield (2001, 57) suggests that Sat4 and Sat1 attempt "to castigate and expose folly rather than suggest a better way of living and behaving."

Sources, Influences, and Analogues

Paman (1638 [2002, 177]), imitating Sat4 in a satire of his own, observes that "happy Donne & Horace, you h'd but one / Deuill haunted you, but me a legion" (ll. 3–4).

Alden (1899, 86, 88) finds that the "account of the bore" in Sat4 "instantly suggests that of Horace" in the ninth satire of his first book of satires, while the bore's "gossip" recalls Juvenal VI, 402–12. Many later commentators have also cited Horace 1.9.

Gosse (1899, 41) notes that Sat4 is "furbished forth with an extraordinary array of learned allusions," illustrating "how wide and curious" was Donne's reading. He specifies references to Ambrogio Calepino, Laurentius Surius, Paolo Giovio, Pietro Aretino, Théodore Beza, François Rabelais, Dante Alighieri, and Albrecht Dürer. Hughes (1968, 51) also comments on the breadth of Donne's allusions.

Grierson (1909, 238) observes that "like all Donne's types," the Horatian bore in Sat4 is "drawn from the life, and with the same amplification of detail and satiric point" to be found in Pope's imitations of Horace.

Grierson (1912, 2:117–18), pointing in particular to a similarity between the opening of Sat4 and the opening of Mathurin Régnier's imitation of the ninth satire of Horace's first book of satires, adds that Donne "follows a quite independent line" from Horace, whose "theme is at bottom a contrast between his own friendship with Maecenas" and the vulgar pushing of the interlocutor. Donne, on the other hand, makes his encounter "the occasion for a general picture of the hangers-on at Court," while "a more veiled thread running through the poem is an attack on the ways and tricks of informers" on Catholics and "intelligencers." Others who comment on Régnier's imitation include Geraldine (1966, 29), Erskine-Hill (1972, 276), and Slights (1981, 167–68). McCabe (2001, 82–83) also comments on Donne's references to informers.

Simpson (1924, 52) calls the poem "an adaptation of Horace's theme to Donne's own time and circumstances" rather than a translation.

Walker (1925, 70–71) comments that Donne's indebtedness to Horace is "obvious," but so is Donne's "vigour" and "essential originality," adding that Donne imitates Horace "much more closely" in *Sat4* than in *Sat1*.

Lewis (1934b, 655) contends of the Satyres generally that as "a form of critical poetry" they exhibit "metaphysical principles" that "assume paramount importance and serve to modify, if they do not determine, the attitude of the poet," and he refers to *Sat4*, which is "inspired by Horace's satire 1.9," as a particular example.

Ellrodt (1960b, 2:197) points out that *Sat4*'s apparent allusion (in ll. 157–59) to Dante's *Inferno* presents the satirist as having "dreamt" his encounter, whereas Dante makes no mention of dreaming.

Harris (1960, 192) notes that Donne gives Horace's bore more sinister possibilities as "the monster of a court hanger-on."

Rudd (1963, 208), citing the widely acknowledged analogue between *Sat4* and the ninth satire of Horace's first book of satires, locates two additional uses of Horatian material in *Sat4* (see Notes and Glosses at ll. 73–80 and 220–21), as well as allusions to Juvenal (see Notes and Glosses at ll. 103–05 and 197) and Cicero (see Notes and Glosses at ll. 67–68). Although such allusions may seem "trivial," nevertheless, their "cumulative effect" confirms Donne's "close acquaintance" with Latin authors and provides "a *starting-point* for a fruitful comparative discussion." Lecocq (1969, 359) also notes Donne's familiarity with Latin authors.

Erskine-Hill (1964, 15–16) comments that the poem "is broadly based" on Horace 1.9 but that Donne continues beyond Horace and rises "to a loftier and more Juvenalian level," adding that in the first half of the poem, Donne transforms "the Horatian comedy of situation into comedy of brilliant conversational repartee."

Geraldine (1966, 29, 36) finds originality in *Sat4*'s "careful stretching" of material from the ninth satire of Horace's first book of satires "until it covers the whole poem." Donne's use of Horace here is "the sinewy thread" that his "brain lets fall to unify the elements of the poem and bind the poetic justice with its type in the divine ordinance" (29). Concerning the satirist's dream (ll. 155ff.), she says that it "echoes" not only Dante's *Inferno* but Cicero's "Dream of Scipio," commenting that it "keeps the reader conscious of things *sub specie aeternitatis*" and also foreshadows the dream of the speaker in *Ignatius* (30). She adds that when Pope "recast the satire and left out something of the sacramental framework," he lost "more than the spiritual sense: he lost the best of the poetic energy" (36).

Rickey (1966, 186) notes "the Spartans, Caesar's histories, Circe, the Sun, and Heraclitus" in her listing of Donne's classical allusions in this poem.

Gamberini (1967, 48) observes that the figure of the satirist's interlocutor in *Sat4* suggests numerous analogies with Donne's "Character of a Scot at the First Sight" and still more with the "Character of a Dunce."

Milgate (1967, 149) distinguishes the relatively simple character presented by Horace from the complexity of *Sat4*'s "bore": "a composite figure, with traits of several stock characters in the comedy and satire of the day."

Hughes (1968, 52–53) comments that Donne's allusion to 2 Maccabees at the end of *Sat4* "sharpens the force of the analogy which he throws over" the poem. Through this analogy, "Elizabeth's court is imaged as the court of Antiochus, wherein the sanctuary of God's chosen people is defiled." In this way, the English Catholic minority "is identified with the Israelites, who ultimately rose from their humiliation and resanctified the holy places." Finally, Sat4 "looks ahead not to Bunyan but to Dryden, not to a serious equation between revelation and society but to a mock epic equation."

Erskine-Hill (1972, 277–78, 280, 284–87) finds that the "Horatian echoes" in Sat4 "are signs from Donne to his readers" that acknowledge Horace's satire "as a text to be remembered" whether he follows Horace or deviates from that original. Donne, he notes, follows Horace in certain common features of the two poems, including the satirists' public encounters by strangers, "intrusive and tactless" talkers, who "will not be shaken off" and who cause the satirists "to sweat with exasperation," seeking "to get rid of" their unwelcome companions, and, at the same time, recognizing these similarities makes clearer the significant differences in method between the two poems (277–78). Erskine-Hall identifies also "two Characters of Talkers in Theophrastus," sometimes cited as sources for Horace, as possible influences on Sat4. He notes that through his "early friend" Henry Wotton, Donne probably knew about Isaac Casaubon's work on his 1598 edition of Theophrastus, adding that Donne published an "explicitly Theophrastian" character in the 1622 edition of Sir Thomas Overbury's *A Wife* (280). He also finds an analogue within Donne's oeuvre in his "Paradox X: That a Wise Man is Known by Much Laughing," whose connection to Sat4 "is not to be doubted" (284–85). Other influences he identifies are John Skelton's "Bouge of Court" (Elliott [1976, 113]); Thomas Wyatt's First Satire; Collingbourne's plea in *The Mirror for Magistrates* (1563); and Thomas Drant's *Medicinable Morall* (1566) (286–87).

Hester (1977c, 191–92) points out the influences on Sat4 both of 2 Maccabees and of the "libels" of Pietro Aretino. Moreover, he holds that only the "first third" of Sat4 is "an adaptation" of Horace 1.9, and Donne's "imitation" is thus "transformed into a meditative analysis of the function of the satirist as moral critic and fallen human."

Dubrow (1979, 74) finds that in Sat4 the satirist's "effective and cruel rebuffs" of the courtier "remind us far more of Juvenal's bitterness than of Horace's tolerance."

Hester (1982, 74, 77, 87, 91–92, 130–33) compares the intermingling of fact and fiction in Sidney's *Astrophel and Stella* to the way that Donne in Sat4 "subtly weaves controversial and dangerous aspects of his own recusancy" into his examination of "the rhetorical and moral bases of Christian satire" (74). He adds that in Sat4 the satirist's "description of his encounter" constitutes "a tacit criticism of the conversational method of the Horatian satiric stance," for adopting Horace's "ironic urbanity and witty repartee" in effect prolongs and accentuates the satirist's "discomfort and susceptibility to more severe harm." Sat4 thus raises the issue of "satire as an act of imitation," with Horace proving "a precarious model for the Christian satirist at court" (77).

Concerning the "quite significant" influence of 2 Maccabees in the closing lines of the poem, Hester observes that as Sat4 adapts Horace's Latin, so 2 Maccabees adapts the Greek of Jason of Cyrene, and the focus is fixed on the defilement of the sanctity of the Jewish temple at Jerusalem, that is, "how priests betrayed the nation," adopting "strange forms of worship," and how "heroic leaders" such as Eleazar "opposed the adoption of foreign ways and ousted the informants and traitors from the Temple." Thus, according to Hester, Sat4 and 2 Maccabees share a concern with "traitors, martyrs, defiled meat, the sanctity of the nation, foreign manners and habits, and the dangers and rewards of opposing such illegitimate forms of action" (91). He points to further influence of sacred texts on *Sat4* in the poem's opening "*nunc dimittis*," whose source is the canticle of Simeon (Luke 2.29–32), recognizing the child Jesus in the temple at Jerusalem (92).

He further suggests that the "strategic and imagistic model" for *Sat4* is the third satire of Juvenal, who "provides a classical precedent for Donne's portrait of the artist as a spiritual fugitive from the egregious absurdities that threaten to refashion and uncreate the national character" (132–33). Finally, the last section of *Sat4* recalls "the imagery, themes, and dangerous satirical stance" of *Sat3*, especially in Donne's description of the court as "a theatrical parody of national values and the portrait of the speaker as a patriotic expatriate alienated by his convictions about the moral and ethical foundations of his civilization" (130).

Hester (1984, 3–4, 7–8, 15) notes that the imitation of *Sat4* in the fifth satire of Everard Guilpin's *Skialethia* illustrates not only certain ideas about satire as viewed by the young satirists of the 1590s, but also the "position of Donne" among them (3), including the importance of "conspicuous imitation" in their conception of the genre. In particular, Hester says, in the "last scene" of Guilpin's poem he adapts Donne's "final scene" (4), and indeed throughout Guilpin's poem "elusive allusion" to *Sat4* is evident in "turns of phrase," in "certain persistent metaphors," in "particular details given to character-types," and in "the intrusion of a level of religious language" recalling "the precise wording" of *Sat4* (7).

Hester comments further that the shift in *Sat4*'s final scene from Horace to Juvenal's third satire is particularly significant as a model "for imagery, theme, and characterization of his speaker," although in certain details even the Horatian opening section of *Sat4* "reveals a considerable debt" to Juvenal's "diatribe against the meretricious 'strangers' who dominate Roman culture." But the shift to Juvenal as a major model after *Sat4* 154 is, according to Hester, "most important to Donne's dramatic evaluation of the role of the satirist," signaling "discovery of the inadequacy and dangers" of Horace's "conversational method" for dealing with "the more severe forms of vanity, blasphemy, and criminality which dominate the Court" and call instead for "the more severe satirical methods of Juvenal" (8). Guilpin's poem, in the ways it imitates *Sat4*, participates in and expresses recognition of Donne's achievement both in reviving classical verse satire "within a particular social and literary context" and in recreating it (15).

Kerins (1984, 49, 60) finds that the "humor of Horace's discomfiture" in *Sat4* is "darkened" by the satirist's concern from the start and throughout the poem with "a Final Judgment" (49). Also indicating a contrast between "the ideal society posited in Horace's poem" and "the real, imperfect world" of Donne's is the fact that whereas Horace "escapes his garrulous companion by *refusing* to assist him," Donne's satirist must pay "a Ransome" to escape (60).

Baumlin (1986b, 460, 466–67) explains that the "hypocritical use of polite conversation," an undercurrent in Horace, becomes a "thematic focus" in *Sat4*. Neither the satirist nor the courtier "can understand the other, because each constantly—and at times deliberately—confuses figurative with literal meanings of the other's words" (460). Baumlin asserts further that the poem "criticizes its Roman models," as Donne's "initially Horatian voice renounces satirical laughter, finding that ridicule does not teach temperance," and "even the Juvenalian manner of the poem's second half is repudiated, since the speaker admits that immorality and intemperance demand 'Preachers' for reform" (466–67).

Baumlin (1988, 378–79) finds Donne relying not on the classical, Horatian model, but instead the medieval English model of complaint in Langland's *Piers Plowman* and the Italian model of spiritual progress in Dante's *Divina Commedia*.

Scodel (1993, 481) argues that the passage satirizing a court fop and a *miles gloriosus* does not confront the "real dangers" of the court, that is, "its oppressive power, spies, and capacity for contaminating all who encounter it," and the passage can be read as an allusion to "Horace's secure stance, evoking a stable moral vision unavailable to Donne and incapable of explaining the most powerful evil forces of his world."

Griffin (1994, 46–47) contends that "when read in the context of a tradition of moral inquiry," *Sat4* "is not simply an attack" on the court, but instead "offers us a satirist who reports on the spectacle of pride and vain display he has beheld at court." He comments further that *Sat4* borrows its situation from Horace's Satire 1.9, in which the satirist meets at court "one who flatters, gossips, and finally begs a crown," and thus, "presenting himself comically as discomfited victim, the satirist finally escapes and flees to the safety of his home," adding, however, that "the poem does not (as in Horace) end there." Instead, he says, Donne "turns our attention more firmly to the satirist himself and implicitly sets the poem's moral problem: Why does an honest and sensible man willingly descend into a den of corruption and flattery?" For Griffin, *Sat4* "offers no clear answer (the satirist himself does not seem to know), but it encourages our speculations." He concludes of the satirist "that going to court is a means of maintaining his moral bearings or reaffirming his standards and confirming the crucial difference between 'them' and 'me.'"

Price (1996, 70) compares the "process of crime, trial, and punishment" in *Sat4* with *Paradoxes*, "That women ought to paint," which uses a similar analogy.

Corthell (1997, 49) finds that *Sat4*'s picture of the royal court, "a dystopian version of Castiglione's Urbino, is a place to be afraid." He parallels it to the versions of the court found in "such works as Marston's Antonio plays or Chapman's *Bussy*."

Kiséry (1997, 115) notes that *Sat4* provided Pope with "a fortunate pretext for imitation, that is, for an indirect Horatian self-fashioning."

Prescott (1997, 44–46; 1998, 95–96) notes that the speaker meets at court "a walking piece of *panourgia*: a loquacious braggart, seedily dressed despite his francophile taste, a seducer of widows, a gossip and moocher," one who is even worse because "he is probably an informer on the lookout for Catholics" (44). In contrast to Rabelais's Panurge, Donne's *panourgos* "uncomfortably resembles the Father of Lies (also a wanderer up and down the earth)" (45). Donne, Prescott thinks, may be recalling "Panurge's first meeting with Pantagruel" since "he too explores how language relates to charity, whether that lacking in the *panourgos* who afflicts his narrator or that which the narrator owes even this talkative wretch" (46).

Prescott (1999, 288–89) finds that Donne "avoids Horatian *urbanitas*" even when he adapts Horace for *Sat4* (288–89).

Blissett (2000, 112, 116, 119) compares *Sat4* with Jonson's *Poetaster* III.1, which also derives from Horace's Satire 1.9, and finds Donne "much more darkly serious than either, and concerning himself not with the ordinary life of the city but with the special case of the court" (112). He also notes that the character of Amorphus in *Cynthia's Revels* resembles the "'Thing'" of *Sat4* (116), but determines that the "calm judious conclusion" of Jonson's *Cynthia's Revels* is "quite unlike the severity" of *Sat4* (119).

Wiggins (2000, 50–52) thinks that the anxiety and doubt expressed by the satirist in *Sat4* are traceable to the perplexities of the Elizabethan secretary (as portrayed by Angel Day), precariously poised in danger of ending up not merely as a "great man's alter ego" but as a "great man's despicable shadow" (50–51). He disagrees with the observation of Dubrow (1979) that Donne's loathing for his interlocutor is "an awkward hybrid," a confusion of "Juvenalian diatribe with the urbane, conversational tone of Horace," and instead argues that Donne was "too subtle a craftsman to commit such a blunder." The "taunting tone" and, at the same time, the "fascination" of the satirist toward the interlocutor is, Wiggins argues, comparable to "the bearing of Dostoevsky's Raskolnikov toward his double and evil angel, the corrupt Count Svidrigaylov" (52).

Fulton (2001, 83, 85–89, 97–98) asserts that *Sat4* "responds to" the early satires of Everard Guilpin, arguing that Donne and Guilpin shared in an "inquiry of satire's generic powers and limitations," for Donne's part evident in his expressed "distrust of mimetic representation in art and poetry" (85–86). Instead of representation, *Sat4* "suggests the possibilities of a satiric form" with a "clashing, non-mimetic stance," as in the dream sequence of *Sat4* (ll. 155ff.), which seems skeptically "to embody an experimental freedom of expression" (86–87). While other critics "usually assume" that Guilpin's satires imitate Donne's, Fulton maintains that *Sat4* itself responds to Guilpin's first satire, alluding to Aretino and using "language and imagery" similar to Guilpin's. Moreover, in Donne's reference to tapestries at court (ll. 231–32), he "subtly criticizes Guilpin," whose seven satires focus on the seven deadly sins (87–88). *Sat4* expresses a relative lack of confidence about the "efficacy" of the satiric mode of "shocking exposure" in Donne's view that "too much exposure to the bad leads to the satirist's own contamination" (89).

In another vein, Fulton compares *Sat4*'s "deconsecration of sovereignty" to the similarly satiric attitude found in *Hamlet* (96). He goes on to cite Montaigne on the problem of the royal court in the sixteenth century, "epistemologically disabled by the very power structure it hoped to serve," unable "to think otherwise than favorably" of the crown or to use language in a way that could be trusted. This "false language created out of a dependent's relation to power describes an essential tension" of *Sat4*, where the satirist, "like Hamlet and Horatio," has "a better grasp of the truth" about the court than do others, who "cannot see" and who, in fact, "speak a false language because of their proximity to the court" (97). *Hamlet* dramatizes, as does *Sat4*, the satirist moving "through a morally corrupt and unseeing court" (98).

Sequence and Unity

Gosse (1899, 1:41) observes that *Sat4* is "more than twice as long" as *Sat1*, *Sat2*, or *Sat3*, a fact indicating, he conjectures, that not only was *Sat4* "enlarged and patched," it was "furbished forth with an extraordinary array of learned allusions."

Leishman (1951, 114) describes *Sat4* as the "least interesting" of the Satyres, arguing that it lacks unity.

Andreasen (1963, 64, 71), presenting *Sat4* as part of a sequence, finds it "closely related" to *Sat1* (64). In *Sat4* the satirist "descends" from the heavenly hill of truth in *Sat3* "to consider again the purgatory which is secular life and to chastise the folly of secular desires and accomplishments" at court (71).

Powers (1971, 73–74) notes that Donne's persona is "a strong and complex one" in *Sat1* and *Sat4*, adding that Donne's "idea of Satirist-as-cultural-superior" was adapted by Guilpin and Marvell.

Erskine-Hill (1972, 276, 292) judges that, more than the "broad resemblance" to *Sat1*, *Sat4* has a "much closer relation" to the ninth satire of Horace's first book of satires (276). In another vein, he thinks that *Sat4*'s mingling of "fear" with "wit, hyperbole and exaggeration" is the development of the "antitheses of laughter and tears" appearing at the opening of *Sat3* (292).

Jensen (1972, 405–06), comparing *Sat4* to *Sat1*, finds that it "makes use of similar dramatic effects and even a roughly similar situation," but "its framework affords greater opportunity" to establish "both the speaker's character and the relation between him and his audience." *Sat4* "begins after the events it reports," and "in its opening lines we witness no clash between antithetical personalities" as in *Sat1*. If "the scholar" in *Sat1* is "an actor in a drama," the satirist in *Sat4* is "an actor who is also a comedian, drawn irresistibly to play jokes on the unsuspecting bore." In *Sat4*, accordingly, the reader not only identifies with a "good man whose views he supports against the fickle idiot who thinks only of fashion," but also feels "the pleasure of watching" the satirist make comedy and the further pleasure of "a species of dramatic irony."

Medine (1972, 51) points out that in *Sat4*, as in *Sat1* and *Sat2* and unlike *Sat3* and *Sat5*, "the reactions of the personae imply visible alternatives to the viciousness embodied in the satirized figures."

Shawcross (1972, 265) finds that among the five Satyres there is "some movement" in *Sat4* towards "spatial development."

Newton (1974, 438, 441) argues that in *Sat4* the satirist is for the first time "assured that satire is necessary," but he still finds it "difficult" to explain, without either the "Humorist" of *Sat1* or Coscus of *Sat2*, why he "should find himself in a setting that calls for satire." He is nevertheless "forced to endure whatever he encounters," trapped at court "inexplicably," and worse, "he must face what he has never directly faced" in the two earlier poems: "his own consanguinity with the Bore who afflicts him" (438). In the first four Satyres, Newton says, the satirist's uncertain character, "a burden like original sin," cannot find certain truth; constancy in *Sat1* "is a joke"; in *Sat2* "it disappears ambiguously"; in *Sat3* it seems both "necessary to be sought after and at the same time necessarily unattainable"; but in *Sat4* the satirist "comes to terms at last with the satiric character and the uncertainty it entails" (441).

Bellette (1975, 131, 134–35) does not find the five Satyres "effectively unified by any common, specific subject or method" and holds that "no justice is done, ultimately, when a group of poems is forced into a common mould in the interest of some non-poetic conception of neatness or consistency." He focuses on "the presence of the poet himself in the scene he depicts" and suggests that in *Sat1*, *Sat3*, and *Sat4* (but not in *Sat2* and *Sat5*) this element is developed, along with "the personal, moral issue which arises from this presence" (131). *Sat4*, though a "more somber" poem than *Sat1*, develops "in greater detail" a common "theme"—"the possible consequences of the slackened will in a world where men seek to pull each other down"—and both poems evidence a kind of "guilt by association and acquiescence" (134–35).

Elliott (1976, 113) contends that the closing lines of *Sat3* prepare the satirist "to withstand the greater trials" of *Sat4*, "in the very den of iniquity, the court." In *Sat4*, the reader "startles" into a "deeper awareness of human weakness," and the "question of what happened to his resolutions" in *Sat3* is "answered by the speaker's subsequent account of his exploits at court."

Lauritsen (1976, 119–20, 127–28) thinks that the first four Satyres "depend upon dramatic irony, upon our perception of the speaker's unconscious or preconscious relationship to his subject" (119). In addition, the "progress" of the Satyres is one of "self-discovery," and towards the end of *Sat4*, the satirist "achieves full self-knowledge" (120), in which he frees himself "for his ridicule of the fallen and faded fop," who resembles "the mindless man-of-the-street" in *Sat1* and whose "interest in linguistics" and "the Babylonian confusion of tongues" he speaks in "are not essentially different from Coscus'" in *Sat2*.

Hester (1977c, 185–86, 191–92) finds that *Sat4* and *Sat5* are "efforts to implement the lessons" of self-knowledge gained in the first three of the sequence (185). *Sat4* "chronicles the continuation of the satirist's education, his acquisition of God-given knowledge, his understanding of his fallen inclinations and God's active Wrath, and his attempts to implement that knowledge at the Presence Chamber" (186). The satirist's "zealous" attitude, as in the earlier Satyres, frames his reflections in confronting at the court "malcontent travelers" and "pretentious fops" (191), and the presentation of these experiences provides "the fullest exercise of the satirist's duty to his 'Mistress Truth' so far in the sequence" (192).

Selden (1978, 64) likens *Sat4*'s satirist to the "scholar-satirist" of *Sat1*, "embroiled in sin merely by being in the vicinity of the Elizabethan Vanity Fair" and "reduced thereby to the level of the objects of his satire."

Cousins (1979, 105–06) states that *Sat4* "recreates the persona and the bore" of *Sat1* in a "specifically political context." The "sudden contradiction" in *Sat1*'s speaker "is a tactic to subvert the reader's judgment," but in *Sat4* an "inner division" of the persona "defines our angle of perspective on the courtly world," revealing "a telescoping image of moral disorder."

Dubrow (1979, 74, 80) understands *Sat4* to be "far more distant" than *Sat1* from Horace, their classical model (74). At the same time, all the Satyres are dominated by issues of court life, especially *Sat4* and *Sat5*, which "dissect that world at length" (80).

Slights (1981, 167, 171–72) points to *Sat4* as a return "to the framework" of *Sat1*, "focusing directly on the satirist's case of conscience" (167), which he resolves amidst "the debased values of the courtly world" after "having formulated" his duty in *Sat3*: "to search for truth" despite "the deceptions and difficulties of the fallen world" and to follow his conscience despite "coercive human power." Concluding in "wholesome solitarinesse" (his "necessary and natural habitat"), the satirist is still "no more convinced of the efficacy of poetry to effect reformation" than he was in *Sat2*, but he is "confident that he can escape corruption and provide insight into reality" (171). In the first four Satyres, Slights argues, he has struggled with "the tension between his revulsion from the frivolity and corruption of society and his sense of responsibility to the world of men," and he considers the struggle to be less "a *debat*, weighing the comparative advantages of the contemplative versus the active life," than "a case of conscience, a question of where his duty lies" (172).

Corthell (1982, 170–71) finds that, whereas *Sat3* "stressed the curative potential of railing," *Sat4* "is pervaded by the fear of physical and spiritual punishment." In the sequence, *Sat3* "introduced the notion of fear" and "made it into a paradox" (ll. 11–16), and the "fear of damnation" is "associated with a figure of authority ('thy fathers spirit')" in *Sat3*, whereas in *Sat4* it "is found to coincide with fear of authority."

Hester (1982, 73–77, 85–86) states that *Sat4* "provides a fuller view of Donne's opinion of the genre" than *Sat3* (73) in that the "largely *private* stance of the previous poem" expands into an "examination of the *public* role of the satirist." He finds here also "a much stronger critique of the Elizabethan Establishment than the cryptic derision of the Anglican doctrine of justification and severity toward papists" in *Sat2* and a "bolder stance than the implicit plea for religious tolerance" in *Sat3* (74). *Sat4* is "the longest, the most complex, the most comprehensive" of the Satyres (75), he notes, expanding the "pattern" of the first three poems, as the "meditative evaluations" of the satirist's "encounters with fops, lawyers, and religious fakes" lead to "renewed action" (76). In contrast to *Sat1*, *Sat4* "offers a tacit criticism of the conversational method" of Horace, since here "the satirist's adoption of the ironic urbanity and witty repartee of the classical satirist" prolongs and accentuates his "discomfort and susceptibility to more severe harm." Whereas in *Sat1* the Horatian approach "led to nothing worse than comic betrayal by the fop's inconstancy," in "the malicious atmosphere of the Presence Chamber" it "proves totally inadequate and potentially dangerous" (77), and whereas in *Sat3* a "paradigm of zeal as satire" is a "private model" and an "exemplary pattern" for the satirist, in *Sat4* this "exemplary conduct" is reiterated "as an image of the Word" and "energized by the mysterious workings of the Word." Further, Hester argues, zeal is "figured" as "a response to and fulfillment of the grace of God" and is "more fully examined" than in *Sat2*, where the satirist concluded that he could not "legally be prosecuted," or *Sat3*, where he "engaged the moral laws of satire as devotion." Both "legalism and contemplation" are shown in *Sat4* to be "inadequate responses" to the "Crossings" of the "eternal into human time" (85–86).

Zunder (1982, 16–17) compares the impoverished courtier of *Sat4* to Coscus in *Sat2*: as Coscus, though he acquires land, maintains no household or hospitality, so the courtier "is forced to live by his wits" and "ends by asking the speaker for money." Moreover, like *Sat2*, *Sat4* ends "with what amounts to a plea" for official action "to correct the abuses laid bare." Both poems are written, "consciously, from a traditional position of independent criticism," with a "traditional concern for truth" akin to that seen also in *Sat1* and *Sat3*.

Hester (1984, 7, 13) finds that the "aggressive adversarius" of *Sat4* is "much more dangerous" than "the foolishness encountered" in *Sat1* (7). In fact, this development characterizes the Satyres as a group, moving from the "designation" of poetry as "sin" (in *Sat1* and *Sat2*) to the "declamation" in *Sat4* that the genre is worthy of being considered "Canonicall" by "some wise man" (13).

Kerins (1984, 37, 48–49, 51–52, 60) tries to "strengthen" the case that *Sat4* is part of a "unified structure" by exploring its relation to *Sat1* based on the fact that both are "variations" on the "Bore" in the ninth satire of Horace's first book of satires, and the perception that "dissimilarities between" them are "the effect of a change in the character of Donne's persona," or, "in other words, the effect of Donne's satiric plot" (37). Paralleling *Sat1* in source, form, and theme, *Sat4* nevertheless demonstrates "a profound change in the character" of the satirist, a change growing from his experience in *Sat3* of "engagement in an imperfect world." Consequently, unlike the "posturings of the moralist" in *Sat1*, the words of *Sat4*'s satirist show "no illusions about his involvement in mankind" or his "cavalier involvement" in the corruption of the court (48–49). *Sat1* and *Sat4* both "contrast opposite environments: one public, the street or the court, and one private, the satirist's own chamber"; but while *Sat1* moves outward from the cell to the street, *Sat4* "reverses the direction, ultimately climaxing in the inner dream vision of the court as hell," which forms "perhaps" the climax of the Satyres. The "inward movement" of *Sat4* transcends "the superficial terrain" of *Sat1*, Kerins asserts, and "symbolizes the interpenetration" of ideal and real—"a fusion embodied in this reformed, self-conscious satirist" (51–52). However, the unity of the Satyres "does not imply that Donne originally planned them as a single artistic creation," for although "each poem may be complete in itself," each may have suggested "new possibilities in satiric technique and new refinements in satiric vision." *Sat4* (like *Sat5*), at any rate, shows, according to Kerins, "more than accidental relationships" with earlier Satyres, indicating that "by this point at least" Donne was "conscious of some form of overall artistic design" (60).

Marotti (1986, 102, 105) argues that Donne in *Sat4* "fell back on the persona" of *Sat1* and *Sat2* in dramatizing the satirist's "nightmarish experience" at court (102). He notes that the closing lines of *Sat4* are "a statement that unites this work with the previous satiric poems," and that accordingly the "scholar-moralist persona" of *Sat1*, *Sat2*, and *Sat4* is "consistent" with the same "anticourtly attitudes" (105).

Baumlin (1991, 96, 100, 122) notes that, although *Sat3* "openly attacks court policies, defending the rights of private conscience against coercive judicial authority," *Sat4* "finds the satirist himself under siege, his personal beliefs placing him in immediate danger" (96). Moreover, although in *Sat1* the satirist stands "in guilty recognition of his own sinfulness," in *Sat4* his guilt becomes "an explicit and central theme: as preparation for receiving the final sacrament, the satirist begins his confession" (100). Finally, he says, *Sat2* and *Sat4* share "themes of linguistic skepticism" (122).

Strier (1993, 286) points to the satirist's "detailed knowledge of Catholic institutional and intellectual structures" in *Sat2*, arguing that in *Sat4* the satirist seems "a Catholic in a Protestant state," yet "what is most striking" about the two poems, as well as about *Sat3*, is "their independence from *any* established religious position."

Hester (1994a, 205) observes that whereas in concluding *Sat2* the satirist implies that he is not a spy and could only unjustly be so charged under Elizabethan statute, near the end of *Sat4* he "saucily confesses that he *is* a spy" (in l. 237), "a spy for the Truth," evincing fully the grounds of his later admission of fear connected to the

Satyres, in a letter to Henry Wotton (Burley ms., f. 309). Even though at the end of *Sat4* Donne "disparages the 'merit' of his work," applying as in *Sat2* "another lexical synecdoche for Christian soteriology," he recognizes "the precarious position in which his satire (and his religion) have placed him."

Corthell (1997, 48–50) asserts that the closing lines of *Sat4* "confess" the "truth" of *Sat2*'s "secret" confidence (ll. 111–12) in the legal invulnerability of the satirist. The "wise man" addressed here may be Sir Thomas Egerton, "who is directly addressed" in *Sat5* (48). The satirist in *Sat4*, like the scholar/satirist of *Sat1*, "seems unable to account for his own behavior and therefore undermines any claim to moral authority and autonomy" (49). Even "more vigorously" than the satirists of *Sat1* and *Sat2*, the satirist here, in line 23, "begins the work of self-definition by a xenophobic representation of the satiric other as an alien being" (50).

Wiggins (2000, 52–54, 57) states that the satirist of *Sat4* is aware that his interlocutor ("unlike the buffoon" of *Sat1*) is "a real threat" and, in contrast, reacts "with a frenzied volley of insults designed to ward off a peculiarly insidious evil spirit." This satirist has "shed the complacency of the bookish satirist" in *Sat1*, a "self-styled contemplative spirit," experiencing instead "the anguish of self-scrutiny in the domain of political action, where no one's hands are clean and one has to genuinely worry about being drained of subjective autonomy" (52–53). Different also, according to Wiggins, is the use in *Sat4* of the title "Sir," used in the opening line of *Sat2* to address the "grave man" (the Egerton figure who appears throughout the Satyres), in which it established "a solidarity with the grave man," thereby to "exalt" the satirist. But in *Sat4* "the tables are turned" and the title is directed at the satirist "as a sign of complicity, by a person who represents everything loathsome in public life" (54). Nevertheless, the "general issue of integrity" in *Sat4* is the same as in *Sat3*, Wiggins concludes, expressed as "revulsion at the mental operation of the secretary" performed in *Sat3* (57).

Flynn (2001, 114) finds that *Sat4*, like *Sat2*, traces "encompassing greed and corruption to their cause in the Tudor statutes stamping out Catholicism" from England.

Fulton (2001, 89–90) argues that in *Sat4* Donne "modifies the more self-confident satiric persona of Juvenal and Persius" found in *Sat1*, "where the morally resistant voice becomes complicit in the hypocrisy of its social surroundings" (89). Moreover, *Sat4*'s references to anti-Catholic statutes extend the "self-betrayal" in *Sat3* to "terms that deal more with the court's power over moral autonomy and vision."

Structure and Method

Aronstein (1920, 160–61) states that *Sat1*, *Sat2*, and *Sat4*, because of their shifting, multiple subjects, lack artistic unity.

Bamborough (1952, 170) notes that the courtier ridiculed in *Sat4* "has elements of the malcontent, the traveller, the politician, the intelligencer, and a hint of the Jesuit."

Andreasen (1963, 71–72) describes *Sat4* as "a recollection in tranquility" by a satirist who has "escaped" the temptations of the court, and the "antagonist" is a "threadbare young courtier," personifying "characteristics of the Gallicized or Italianate Englishman." In their "extremely humorous" dialogue, the satirist mocks the courtier's "egoism," and the courtier "is too obtuse and self-centered to understand" (71). This "clever" method offers "dual views of court life, that of the admiring inside-dopester and that of the revolted man of honor," both of which "disgust" (72).

Geraldine (1966, 29–31) comments that Donne's use of Horace is a unifying element in Sat4 and notes that the "covering imagery of sin, atonement, crucifixion" in the poem is "neither symbol nor allegory," but it performs "the same good service such symbols would." Going to court here "is not compared to, or made the symbol for, the 'cross' of life's vicissitudes: it *is* the cross" (31).

Zivley (1966, 90–92) states that the variety and quantity of imagery in Sat4 may appear "less poetic, less aesthetic, less witty, and less imaginative" than what Donne "conveys in his metaphysical conceits," but the "centripetal technique" employed in the Satyres "is just as effective for its purpose as the centrifugal conceit is for its," the purpose of satire being "to awaken man to an awareness of his own failings so that he can amend and correct them." Instead of "ever-widening emotional experiences," the imagery of Sat4, Zivley says, reveals the satirist's "lesson so clearly that the reader cannot possibly fail to learn it," while at the same time avoiding a didacticism that "would antagonize" (90–91). At the same time, such imagery "may even occasionally be the result of Donne's letting his mind toy with similarities rather than concentrating" on the "total effect of the poem" (92).

According to Hughes (1968, 52), the "device" of including a Biblical analogy at the end of Sat4 is "a brilliant stroke," affording "allegorical proportions" to what had otherwise been "a more or less anticipated diatribe."

Powers (1971, 62) asserts that the satirist's silent auditor in Sat2 and Sat4 is structurally important, since he provides a target, other than the reader, for the satire.

Erskine-Hill (1972, 277–84, 286, 288–90, 292–93) begins with the general principle that Donne's Horatian model is relevant to Sat4, both when he does and when he does not follow that model (277). Donne's "method is different," he asserts, for in contrast to Horace's concision and "expressive brevity," Sat4 is "copious and exuberant," a "fertile amplification of Horace." Moreover, in Anglicizing his Roman model, Donne's satirist "introduces fundamental changes" that go beyond "country and time." The dialogue takes place not along a mere street but at the royal court, and thus, Horace's "Talker" here becomes a courtier (or a would-be courtier, "conversant with the centre of power"), and Sat4 drops entirely "what might well seem the heart of Horace's poem," the relationship to Maecenas. Not only has Sat4 no parallel relationship, Erskine-Hill notes, but in fact the position of the satirist is "almost reversed" in that far from "secure in the good opinion" of an "influential" grandee, he is instead "the conscious outsider" (279).

The "most important" change Donne makes, however, is in "the treatment of the law." Horace presents Roman law as the resource and guarantee of his satirist's well-being (280), but Sat4, Erskine-Hill observes, introduces English law (in ll. 8–11) as a threat to the satirist, a threat that becomes more dangerous when the courtier's confidentiality "libels the conduct of the government." Throughout Sat4, English law, centered at court, inspires a "sense of fundamental insecurity" in the satirist as "an enemy rather than a friend," a striking "reversal" of the situation Horace presented (282). As such, Sat4 "urges upon us" the experience of one who fears "an unjust force in the law and operations of the established state" (283). Erskine-Hill points out other departures from Horace that include: the escape of Donne's satirist from court by paying the courtier "Ransome" (l. 145) and his subsequent psychological conflict (284), and the "satirist's heroic dedication of himself to Truth despite the consequences" (288). Finally, he says, the closing lines of Sat4 mark "the completion of an expressive structure" that "dramatizes a double-exposure to the court, divided by a passage of self-communing" that "regenerates" the satirist's "moral strength," and the satirist's "tone" at the end is "one of controlled understatement" (292–93).

Jensen (1972, 405–06) remarks that the satirist's description of the courtier (ll. 18–48) creates "for the total poem" several effects, including completion of the speaker's "portrait," establishing "in a rather firm way our identification with him" as "an actor who is also a comedian, drawn irresistibly to play jokes on the unsuspecting bore." The ensuing dialogue between satirist and courtier produces two effects: (1) "the sheer pleasure of watching the speaker perform" with wit and "an assurance that marks at once" his "moral superiority and his comic style"; and (2) a closeness between the reader and the speaker, "as he shares his frustration and horror; for what emerges most clearly from the encounter is the recognition that to such wit the bore remains oblivious, that the round of court activities continues."

Shawcross (1972, 265, 268) says that Sat4 is a dialogue spoken by one person, "an undefined anyone," who quotes others (268).

Newton (1974, 437–40) thinks that Sat4's satirist, in contrast to his Horatian model, at first "seems to enter the satiric scene more by choice than by compulsion" and is "victimized" by "his own sense of guilty entrapment, which is all the more threatening because its causes seem to be inexplicable" (437). The satirist's condition, "like the condition of original sin," seems "inexplicable but inevitable," as he is forced to "endure whatever he encounters" while at court, and, "worse, he must face the frightful possibility" that he belongs there (438). Yet, with the trance, the satirist "no longer merely subjects himself to the satiric scene; he discovers it from within and thus acknowledges that the vision itself is his own" (439). Thus, Newton observes, in the end, the satirist seems "no longer afflicted" with "self-disgust and despair," for his concern is mainly "how the public will respond to his satire" and what the relation is "between satiric truth and the public world" (440).

Although Zaki (1974, 124) finds fault with the structure of Sat4, he does see in it "two distinct sections dealing, respectively, with an actual and a visionary visit to the court."

Bellette (1975, 134–35) states that the opening of Sat4 (ll. 1–16) "lays heavy emphasis on the idea of a sin committed" (i.e., the satirist's having been to court), and the satirist shows "a curious inability to resist" the courtier's "libellous tirade," in response to which "his own condescensions and witticisms" are "scarcely to be distinguished" from the courtier's. In recollecting these things, the satirist is appalled not by (l. 131) "the man himself, nor the list of sins and vices he retails," but by the "self-betrayal he has permitted to occur," as he feels himself "Becoming Traytor." Thus, Bellette finds Sat4 to be "as much interior drama as external observation," and in the end, the satirist asks forgiveness for "his own presence and participation" in the horror; his figure is a "diminished" one, "whose punishment and death have been alluded to in the opening lines of the poem without our fully realizing why."

Elliott (1976, 113–15) finds, instead of the satirist's "restored faith" after his "resolutions" in Sat3, a "surprising turn" towards frustration and near loss of faith in Sat4, illustrating "the dangers of presumption and self-righteousness" for "those who suppose faith alone will shield them from temptation" (113). The satirist is "humbled" by his "experience at court," emerging from his trance at home "with renewed compassion" for "wicked courtiers." He concludes that the satirist realizes that "he can have little effect upon the corruption of the world" and thus leaves the field to preachers, and the closing reference to Maccabees is "an apology" for the satirist's "own harsh and sometimes blasphemous language" (114–15).

Hester (1977c, 185, 191) notes that in Sat4 the satirist's "awareness of his own precarious position in the providential scheme and of the duty he owes to his 'Mistress Truth'" provides "tacit condemnation" and "a worthwhile option to the hellish self-ignorance and disruptive libels he encounters" at court (185). The satirist's "zealous" attitude frames his reflections in confronting at the court "malcontent travelers" and "pretentious fops" (191).

Dubrow (1979, 74–76, 80) finds the satirist in Sat4 "distant" from his classical model. Whereas Horace begins his poem by "gently mocking his own absent-mindedness," Donne's satirist "refers briefly to his own fault in going to court," but his "hyperbolic playfulness undermines this admission of guilt." Donne "introduces his narration" of the encounter with the courtier in "a long and biting description of the bore," whereas Horace only briefly characterizes his satiric antagonist (74). Though Horace's speaker does "eventually insult his companion," Dubrow notes, he does so "only late in the poem, when he seems driven beyond endurance," and even then "his retort is gentler and more humorous than the barbs" of the satirist in Sat4. Further, the "dialogue form in Horace implies certain values absent" from Sat4, which "adopts the form but not the substance from Horace," whose poem includes "a genuine give-and-take" between the two Romans, "an exchange that includes and at times centers on the speaker's wry acceptance of his own limitations." In contrast, Dubrow thinks, in Sat4 we seldom see any "humility," but instead, "Juvenalian mockery and disdain" are "far more typical"; we are "invited to admire" the satirist's "clever rebuffs, not condemn or question them" (75). She argues that Donne's method in Sat4 differs from his fellow-Elizabethan satirists (76) in that he "gives noticeably less space to the faults of contemporary literature" than do such poets as Hall, Marston, and Guilpin, and instead the royal court, "to which other satirists refer only sporadically," is the dominant concern of Sat4, as also of Sat5, and Donne's other Satyres also "allude to it frequently" (80).

Hester (1982, 73–78, 81–90) looks at both the method behind the satirist's aims in Sat4 and the resulting narrative structure. On one level, he sees Sat4 recounting the satirist's "two visits to the court" (73), showing how "those experiences clarified for him both his precarious position as a fallen man" and his "fearful duty as a Christian satirist who is obliged to confront and expose" the court, even if "risking the charge of treason." Beyond this literal level, Sat4 also signifies for Hester the spiritual significance of the "meditative" satirist's situation, through his "typological interpretations of his adventures at court." He describes the court as a "corporealized travesty of religious rites and emblems," in its "daily routine" a "hellish prefiguration" of the punishment awaiting sinners. As such, the satirist's own role is a "potentially traitorous fulfillment of his duty" to truth, a "daring" response to the "unfolding of the Word in the world." In recounting "the satirist's confrontation with pursuivant trickery" and the "self-serving debasements of religious gestures at court," Donne "identifies the satirist's own imitation of Christian types and antetypes as an exemplary contrast to the pernicious forms of imitation that dominate the Presence Chamber" (74). The threat of being termed treasonous cannot "intimidate him into abandoning" his commitment to truth. His situation as "political and religious outsider" is thus, according to Hester, "recast in terms of the central dictum of Christian humanism—*imitatio christi*." *Sat4*'s achievement then is to have "satisfied both the rhetorical requirements of verse satire and the moral injunctions of Christian ethics" (75).

On another level, Hester finds *Sat4*'s narrative to be complicated, framed "as a traditional *meditatio mortis*" in five sections: introduction (ll. 1–4) and conclusion (ll. 237–44), "spoken from the dramatic present moment"; and "three central sections of retrospective analysis, which recount and evaluate the satirist's adventures" (75). The first of these (ll. 5–154) is "a dramatic critique of his first visit to the court, an adaption/modification of Horace." The second (ll. 155–74) is "an analysis of the Dantean trance into which he fell" when he returned home from court. The third central section (ll. 175–237) is "a description of his second visit to court," in its final eight lines "the fullest estimate of his experiences and what they taught him about his role as satirist." The introduction and conclusion explicate "the significance of this pattern," and the poem's structure is presented then "as a form of meditative action," as "the satirist's meditation" proves to be "a verbal extension and enactment of his role as devotee" of truth and participates "in the divine immanence" (76). Thus, *Sat4* first "offers a tacit criticism of the conversational method of the Horatian satiric stance," which "proves a precarious model for the Christian satirist at court" (77). This tension is felt throughout the "central stages and passages" of the Mass of the Presentation, which "reverberate throughout" *Sat4* (89) and are faithfully seen in the satirist's "moral application of the stages and canticles of the Presentation Mass to his own experiences" (90).

Zunder (1982, 16–17) reads *Sat4* as a characterization of the court in terms of "social values" such as poverty, affectation, and rootlessness. However, he believes that the poem is not "hostile to the court as an institution, despite the strength of feeling against the court apparent in it," for the poem expresses "hope that the vanities of the court may be reformed" and is written, "consciously, from a traditional position of independent criticism."

Hester (1984, 13–15) argues that in *Sat4* Donne "aims not just to illustrate his virtuosity in the daring new genres of the younger generation, but to analyze and display his moral earnestness and civic potential" as a Christian humanist (13–14). Donne presents verse satire "as a metaphor of his own 're-creation'" and thus "remetaphorizes" it as "ethical reformation (personal and civic)" (14). *Sat4*, Hester suggests, "transforms the grammar" of satire into ethical terms, not simply reviving "classical verse satire within a particular social and literary context," but recreating it (15).

Kerins (1984, 49–52) agrees with Erskine-Hill (1972) that *Sat4*'s dialogue between satirist and courtier is a "dialogue of deliberate cross-purpose." The satirist "shows his intellectual superiority," but his satire "is rendered impotent by the baseness of his companion's sensibility," for "if the victim feels no pain, the efficacy of the satirist is entirely dissipated." With the satirist's escape from the courtier, Kerins notes, Sat4 "rises to its climax," departing from its Horatian model (49–50). Given Donne's "sensitivity to the complications original sin imposes on the satiric poet," Sat4 "cannot end with a simple retreat, for the vices the satirist must confront are not only those of the corrupt world but also of the corrupt self." The onset of the satirist's trance is then not only "the climactic moment" of the poem but perhaps of the Satyres as a whole, as the "intellectual sanctuary of the meditative life is invaded by a horrific vision striking terror into the heart of the satirist" (51). Kerins concludes that the satirist's "invocation of 'Mistresse Truth'" now "strengthens him to fulfill his task of recreating imaginatively the vicious court in the compass of a controlled satiric frame" (52).

Albright (1985, 135–36) maintains that "two somewhat opposed tendencies" govern satire: "the analogical and the excrementitious." Of these Sat4 utilizes the first, showing "a remarkable fascination, on the technical level and on the level of imagery, with detailed analogies of human life" to the extent that the satirist "erects a scale model of the scene he wishes to mock" and "claims that the larger world is exactly like his diminutive and shriveled caricature."

Baumlin (1986b, 460, 465–66) notes the "hypocritical use of polite conversation" as a "thematic focus" in Sat4. Neither the satirist nor the courtier "can understand the other, because each constantly—and at times deliberately—confuses figurative with literal meanings of the other's words," and "polite discourse" ceases to be "meaningful communication." But Sat4 departs from its Horatian model here, Baumlin says, because perceived ironies in Horace become "the breakdown of polite discourse as meaningful communication" (460). Moreover, Sat4's moral complexity is something Horace never attains; its "formulation of personal guilt" is "far more serious than Horace's wry admission of fallibility," becoming in Donne's poem "an expression of conscience too dire for laughter" (465). Thus, Sat4 actually "criticizes its Roman models" in that the satirist's "initially Horatian voice renounces satirical laughter, finding that ridicule does not teach temperance." Further, in the second half of the poem, the "Juvenalian manner" is "repudiated, since the speaker admits that immorality and intemperance demand 'Preachers' for reform" (466).

Docherty (1986, 170–71) thinks that the "real comparison" in Sat4 is between "the poet and the unnamed king who bore the hurt of the cross, Christ." This recognition does not "deny the playful humor of the satire" but rather "deepens" the poem "in the comic revelation of a serious theological impulse behind the aesthetic play." The poem, for Docherty, "becomes an elaborate euphemism for the moment of vocation, the rejection of courtly life in favour of another kind of king." Accordingly, the opening and closing lines of Sat4 "become doubly charged," the former "could, quite conceivably," be "a translation of Christ's moment of resignation" in Gethsemane and the latter an establishment of the poem as "canonized or sacred text: Scripture."

Baumlin (1988, 367–69, 380–85) states that Sat4, "through self-conscious skepticism" towards "its form and function," is "a deliberately failed poem" in that it is "incapable of enacting the aims of the genre because it discovers, in the process of its own composition, the weakness of its language." A "symptom of this weakness" is the satirist's "inability to defend himself" against the "onslaught" of "the more powerful rhetoric" of the courtier. Another symptom of weakness, Baumlin asserts, is his "reliance upon a Roman Catholic vocabulary for guilt, punishment, and reform" (367). *Sat4*'s "pro-Catholic polemics" are problematic for its "attempt at Christian satire" because the primary audience for the poem, Elizabeth's court, "would surely define 'Christian' satire as the antithesis, if not indeed the repudiation of, Roman Catholicism." Catholic allusions in the poem in fact "weaken the poet's language and authority before a Protestant audience," but this is one of the "intended effects," replicating the way Catholic sacraments are "denied efficacy in Elizabeth's Protestant England." Thus, *Sat4* turns "from formal satire into an allegory on the perilous status of the loyalist Catholic at a Protestant court" (368).

Baumlin also thinks that *Sat4*, beneath its wit, voices a "more serious self-scrutiny and self-condemnation" than is evident in its Horatian model. The encounter with an "impertinent social climber" in Horace is refashioned, and the satirist's encounter in *Sat4* becomes not merely bad luck but "destinie," bearing "a full burden of guilt." At the opening of the poem, Baumlin notes, the satirist expresses his guilty sharing in the court's "weaknesses and viciousness" in a passage that becomes not only "a structuring principle" for *Sat4* as a whole, but also "literally a public confession of his culpability." This initial declaration of his "cultural difference" from his classical model "imposes a set of values that necessarily conflict with the conventional strategies of this pagan form" (369). But this divergence from the classical model, Baumlin argues, again complicates *Sat4*'s "authoritativeness within the poet's culture" since Donne's "pagan model provides little authority and small moral weight to the satirist writing in Protestant England." Among Elizabethan satirists, only Donne "seems fully aware" that the Romans were not "timeless and ideal models for moral reform," and only Donne seems aware "that imitation succeeds only through a kairotic, critical revision of the classical models" (380). For Baumlin, *Sat4* suggests that "the Christian must find in his own cultural and native tradition the techniques and attitudes that will not subvert charity—but will necessarily subvert the classical methods of ridicule and *ad hominem* attack" (381).

Moreover, Baumlin points out, in *Sat4* Donne, even after diverging radically from his Horatian model, "continues to show skepticism toward the authoritativeness" of his *Satyres* (381). Until such authorization occurs, however, "there is no one either to grant the poem moral authority or the poet temporal power to initiate reform." In this context, the standard of canonicity mentioned, 2 Maccabees, is a text "*denied authority by Protestants*," a choice emphasizing "that the authority, and therefore the efficacy," of *Sat4* "remains in doubt." Consequently, the "unresolvable tensions" between classical and Christian in the poem are less impossible than the tensions between Protestant and Catholic (382). Agreeing with Corthell (1982), Baumlin believes that as a satirist who "denies his satire authority, undermining the strength of his own words," Donne in *Sat4* "has failed to find in the decorum of his Horatian model the *kairos* or the *literary* 'authority' that would grant his words a corresponding 'religious and political authority.'" Donne's "private religious commitment" not only destabilizes the poet's relationship "with political authority" but denies "reformative power to the language and the genre" (383–84). He concludes that Donne, in rejecting the Horatian model, "fully satisfies neither the classical nor the Christian requirements of moral suasion and ultimately shows only the impossibility of Christianizing this pagan form" (385).

Baumlin (1991, 100) argues that the opening of Sat4, in departing from its Horatian model, "turns the poet's personal guilt into an explicit and central theme," and thus, "as preparation for receiving the final sacrament, the satirist begins his confession (in fact, the satire itself becomes an act of contrition)."

Price (1996, 64–66) argues that the speaker's encounter with the bore in Sat4 consists of two types of dialogue. In the first, which "resembles interrogation, a rhetorical situation appropriate for a pursuivant and recusant," the bore "pesters" the speaker with a series of questions, to which the speaker replies "evasively and ironically" (64). The second kind of dialogue consists of the bore's "ramblings and descriptions of the affective responses they elicit," and Donne stresses the bore's "ability to generate an affective response" by showing that he can both "outsmart people who make it their business (literally) to outsmart others ('subtlest whores')" and also "liberate words whose treasonous intent compels men to imprison them behind the toughest safeguards" (65). Thus, Price says, Donne "depicts not only two rhetorical situations faced by recusants but also some of the strategies of rhetorical dissimulation for outsmarting them," as the speaker "prevails, proving himself a better dissembler than even this arch-dissembler" (66).

Corthell (1997, 49–51) asserts that Sat4 represents power as "insidious and decentered, resembling Foucault's formulation" (in his History of Sexuality). A "dystopian version of Castiglione's Urbino," the court is "a place in which to be afraid," and the satirist's opening comparison of going to court and going "To'a Masse in jest" calls into question his own motive for attending the court. Corthell concludes that "the analogy points to a division in the subject—he was only joking but he was 'guilty,'" and also divided by this analogy then is the reader, "placed on the side of the Statute." Thus Sat4 "is radical not so much by virtue of its attacks on court corruption" (although the "force" of those attacks is not to be "minimized") as it is by "its representation of the discontinuous, contingent, and constructed identity of the satirist" (49).

Moreover, Corthell notes, the courtier antagonist of Sat4 is given "a xenophobic representation" as "an alien being." Here, "there seems to be a duplicity" that would both "condemn and save" the court "in the same breath." By "characterizing the courtier's satiric speeches as libels, the satirist invests the poem with what might be called 'plausible deniability.'" The coterie readers of the poem would then "be expected to read through this politic device to get at the truth about bribes and entailed offices" at court. In this way, Corthell suggests, the satirist is able to address his readers as "they have styled themselves"—as "aspiring courtiers," apt to use "the figure of the libellous court fly" as "a convenient humanist explanation" for the problem of the court. Corthell finds "most striking" about Sat4 the satirist's "failure to achieve a stable humanist identity or social center" (50).

Kiséry (1997, 111–12) notes that Sat4 was not broken into paragraphs "in any of the editions published before Pope's Imitations."

Wiggins (2000, 52–53, 57–58) observes that the satirist in Sat4 realizes that "his interlocutor represents dreadful potentialities in himself," and therefore "reacts" with a "frenzied volley of insults designed to ward off a peculiarly insidious evil spirit."

The satirist's comparing the courtier to "victims of English xenophobia and religious intolerance" makes it hard "to work up resentment" towards him, and instead, "one hears a note of hysteria in Donne himself," usually "sympathetic" towards "victims of persecution" (52–53). Accordingly, says Wiggins, in the middle of the poem, the satirist "has fled from court and rebukes himself for his cowardice," and he talks himself into "a return visit to the court" because he fears "his own motives," possibly motives of "self-interest, not service." Wiggins notes the satirist's anguish in finding himself "mirrored in the 'privileg'd spie' who so annoys him" and asks rhetorically: if the "spy has no doubt that he and Donne are alike," what evidence "does Donne have that they are not?" (57).

Wiggins believes that the concluding reference to 2 Maccabees signifies that, while Donne can know his satire "to have merit in the abstract as poetic fiction," nevertheless it "will not have served its purpose" unless Lord Keeper Egerton or some such officer at court "acknowledges that he has spoken well" and "authorizes him to speak in the future." Such release from the "impasse" has to come "from without." Only history itself "can draw one out of the looking glass of morbid self-doubt and crippling self-consciousness," and if the satirist can be "hired on those terms by those who make history," his poems may not end up "belied by history" (58).

Fulton (2001, 89–91, 96–98, 100) comments that Sat4 "describes a courtly encounter" in which "too much exposure to the bad leads to the satirist's own contamination." Here Donne "modifies the more self-confident satiric persona of Juvenal and Persius," varying in this method from his practice in the earlier Satyres, "where the morally resistant voice becomes complicit in the hypocrisy of its social surroundings." In Sat4, Fulton says, it is the satirist's "self-contamination" that makes him vulnerable to the "legal nemesis" of the Elizabethan treason statute (89). Simply by going to court, he has become susceptible to "the court's power over moral autonomy and vision" (90). Fulton also compares Sat4's "deconsecration of sovereignty" to the similarly satiric attitude found in Hamlet (96), and he goes on to cite Montaigne on the problem of the royal court in the sixteenth century, "epistemologically disabled by the very power structure it hoped to serve," unable "to think otherwise than favorably" of the crown or to use language in a way that could be trusted (97).

Shawcross (2000–01, 28) notes that Sat4, "while long, is not disorganized."

Language and Style

[Spence] (1823, 52) states that Sat4 is "as rough and rugged as the unhewn stones that have just been blasted from their native quarry," adding that, like Donne's other Satyres, it "must have come upon the readers at whom they were leveled, with the force and effect of the same stones flung from the hand of a giant." The poem is "nearly the perfection of this kind of writing."

Alden (1899, 85) claims that the "attitude toward life" in Sat4 is "uniformly pessimistic" and the "atmosphere" is "somewhat severe and unamiable," without "formal and artificial assumption of authority to castigate, as in so many of the imitative satirists."

Gosse (1899, 1:41–42) believes that Sat4 illustrates Donne's "aggressive realism, his determination to substitute for classical and romantic metaphors images drawn from life, science, and speculation of his own day." The poem, he says, is "particularly rich" in such details and is "singularly, if tantalisingly, interesting to us" as written while poets such as Spenser, Greene, and Shakespeare were writing so differently.

Leishman (1951, 108, 114–15) states that in Sat4 (as in Sat5) the "harshness of which Dryden and others accused Donne" was "deliberately cultivated" and is "much more apparent" than in Sat1, Sat2, and Sat3 (108). Sat4 is "the roughest in versification" of the Satyres, with "no clear plan or dominant idea" and contains detail "piled upon detail." Though "individual lines are often striking, they do not co-operate to produce a whole," but Sat4 does "disprove the notion" that Donne "seems to have been little affected by visual impressions" (114–15).

Regarding the dialogue in Sat4, Lewis (1954, 547) wonders "what Donne could have supposed it would gain by being printed as verse."

Erskine-Hill (1964, 16) refers to Donne's "outrageous verbal wit" in this poem.

LeComte (1965, 48) claims that Sat4 can be considered as verse "largely by courtesy of the printer."

Bross (1966, 133, 137) states with regard to Sat2 and Sat4 that Pope was not put off by Donne's "shocking and grotesque metaphors and similes," nor did he "water down" Donne's "coarse or ribald language" (133). He argues that Donne's style is characterized by "exploding capsules," that is, "compressed, economical, contracted statements" that follow one after another in quick succession (137).

Zivley (1966, 90–92, 94) remarks that Sat4's imagery is "centripetal," conveying "one basic idea" by "using two or three or even many similes and metaphors, one after another, each of which underscores" the same meaning. The effect is not to widen the reader's "aesthetic experiences and interpretations," she suggests, but to force a reader "to learn exactly the lesson or see precisely the characteristic" Donne intends (90). She also points to the "wide realm of experience" reflected in Sat4's imagery (91), arguing that it evidences the "multiplicity of Elizabethan activities and enthusiasms and their attendant corruptions" as well as "basic human traits" that are "central to human experience." This range of imagery is "so various" and "numerous" that it "may indeed distract the reader, making it difficult for him to follow the main flow of ideas." Such imagery may at times result from Donne's "letting his mind toy with similarities rather than concentrating" on the "total effect of the poem" (92). She adds that the "very brilliance and frequent occurrence" of the imagery "reveals a feeling of great activity, manifold interests, and exciting happenings" that "must have been inherent in the renaissance spirit of Elizabethan England" (94).

Winny (1970, 16–17) calls Sat4, like Donne's other Satyres, "blunt and vigorously abusive," noting that "most of its energy is directed against a society grown corrupt and vicious," which gives the poem its "disturbed manner."

Powers (1971, 108) calls attention to Donne's use of narration in this poem in contrast with the more typical style of Elizabethan satire.

Shawcross (1972, 258, 263) finds that the satiric tone of Sat4 is set by "extreme enjambing," "odd end-of-line words," hyphenations at the ends of lines, "wrenched rhymes," and "altered metrices" (258). The poem, he thinks, apparently includes deliberately "defective and hypermetric lines" despite the attempts of certain manuscript copyists to "correct" them. Some "feminine endings occur, some final syllables being catalectic, some really being accented for rhyme although normally unstressed."

Such "prosodic anomalies" provide "a more conversational, normal expression," says Shawcross, for "the lines, read normally, do not artificially end-stop." These "run-on constructions" are "typical" of the Satyres, and as one reads Sat4, "any sense of defective or excessive syllables disappears" (263).

Messenger (1974, 10–11) believes not only that the style of Sat4 is characterized by "knotty syntax," by "dense accretions of learned references," and by "nearly formless ramblings through a wide and various scene," but also that the tone is "impassioned—agonized, disgusted, frightened, outraged."

Zaki (1974, 124) comments that Sat4 is "the roughest and longest" of the Satyres.

Prior to his stylistic analysis of Sat4, McFarland (1977, 396, 403) suggests that Donne's "distortion of syntax and his semantic play" make "his figures of repetition more striking than those of his contemporaries" (396), and he concludes that repetition is only one element of "Donne's complex style" and that the stylistic rhetoric Donne uses in Sat4 is "neither haphazard nor mechanical" (403).

Dubrow (1979, 76–77) suggests that the "immediate impression" of Sat4, like that of the other Satyres, is that it is "stylistically" similar to other satire of the 1590s. She characterizes their meter as "harsh," their imagery "vivid and often coarse," and their tone "forceful and strident." Nevertheless, she argues, Sat4 exhibits "a type of concentrated and rich language that is absent from the other satirists of the period." Like Donne's other Satyres, Sat4 contains "far more ideas and images," seems "full to the point of overflowing," and moves "more rapidly from point to point" than do the poems of other satirists. Distinctively, Donne, she concludes, crams "satiric commentary into both the tenors and the vehicles of his figures."

Hester (1982, 75, 82–84, 86–87, 89) finds in Sat4 "unity complicated by diverse strands of imagery" (75). Thus the satirist, as someone "supposedly devoted to the charitable use of language for God's glory," is "most repulsed" by the courtier's "malicious and self-serving abuses of language." The "allusions to food, art, soldiers, and medicine—traditional figures for the therapeutic power of satire"—here "reiterate" that the satirist must be content with the courtier's "satanic tongue" because it is "the verbal equivalent of his own abuse of his role as a satirist" (82). On the other hand, Hester notes, imagery conveying the Passion of Christ (ll. 140–50) reinforces "the satirist's portrait of the venality that dominates the Presence Chamber" and provides "another derisive comment on the mercenary intentions of the government's enforcement of recusant penal laws" (83). Such "crucifixion imagery" also conveys the satirist's "recognition that his mortal culpability has already been atoned for by Christ's Passion," and the satirist's "association of his suffering with that of Christ" acknowledges "both his debt to the Old Covenant and his fulfillment through the New Covenant" (84). After the satirist's vision, Hester suggests, the description of his return to court is "controlled" by imagery of "the world as play, the world as God's theatre, religious ceremony as play, human history as the unfolding of God's drama, and, most significant, man's duty as *imitatio christi*" (86–87), adding that throughout the poem, "verbal echoes of the Presentation Mass are evident" (89).

Kerins (1984, 49–51) notes that in Sat4 the courtier is termed a "traveler," and "his language is satirized as a motley farrago of various tongues." Although the satirist "claims to see through this jargon," the courtier's "language of 'complement' is eminently effective in society," a danger "to be reckoned with" (49). Having "steeled himself against the insidious jargon of this court butterfly," language "with which one could 'Make men speake treason,'" the satirist, Kerins observes, "becomes mesmerized by the 'pictures of vice' painted by the courtier" (50). Subsequently, in his vision of hell, the "climactic" moment of the poem, the satirist's "anxiety" and "growing insecurity concerning his own spiritual condition" is deepened by "the movement of the verse" (51).

Albright (1985, 135–36) maintains that Sat4 shows "a remarkable fascination, on the technical level and on the level of imagery, with detailed analogies of human life," as illustrated in those moments when the satirist "erects a scale model of the scene he wishes to mock" and "claims that the larger world is exactly like his diminutive and shriveled caricature."

Baumlin (1986b, 460) finds that, in his conversation with the courtier, the satirist in Sat4 "uses wit and verbal equivocation as offensive weapons," but "neither character can understand the other, because each constantly—and at times deliberately—confuses figurative with literal meanings," demonstrating "the breakdown of polite discourse as meaningful communication." Accordingly, the satirist's "words and actions" become "as open to scrutiny as those of his *adversarius*."

Docherty (1986, 168–71) points to "a lengthy example of antonomasia" in Sat4, the satirist's inability "to name the anonymous creature who comes to plague him," yet the courtier turns the tables and "performs the act of nomination upon" the satirist, a "purgatorial visitation by the unnamed stranger" that, the satirist says, is punishment for his "sin of going" (l. 12) to court (168). Docherty finds that Sat4 "becomes an elaborate euphemism for the moment of vocation, the rejection of courtly life in favour of another kind of king" (170). Thus, "the basic strategy of Donnean antonomasia" in Sat4 is "a contrived *imitatio Christi*, by which he manages to suggest that he is in a position analogous to, if not more strictly identified as, Christ" (171).

Baumlin (1988, 366–74, 378, 384, 386) claims that Sat4's imitation of Horace "reveals an ambivalence toward language" inasmuch as "the words of others" are condemned "for their deception and abuse," while the satirist finds the "inability of his own words to cause reform" (364). Baumlin says that Sat4 also "reflects the age's crises both of faith and of discourse," as, for example, the satirist addresses "an audience that denies" the authority of his "implicitly espoused Catholicism"—denies even his "right of speech." The poem thus becomes "a self-critical exploration of its language and genre and, most poignantly, of its inability to compel reform," relying as it does "upon a Roman Catholic vocabulary for guilt, punishment, and reform" (367). Sat4 depends "on the linguistic theology of Catholicism," he says, but its "Catholic allusions serve to destabilize the value system and the language of the poem" (368). He explains that the "familiar, conversational tone" of the poem's opening counterbalances the "sophisticated rhetorical artistry of ironizing and wordplay" characteristic of Horace (369). But Donne's "Horatian satirist" is a Catholic among Protestants who is "denied any mechanism of reform" not only by the power structures, but also "by the language (the linguistic theology, as it were) of the court" (370). Baumlin finds that the satirist's subsequent inability to name the courtier, another "subtle revision of Horace," not only heightens the "humor" in the description of the courtier, it "shows up the weakness of language to penetrate beyond appearances to the falsehood and corruption within, to defend itself against the moral depravity" concealed by the courtier's "motley dress and behavior." The courtier is not "fixed and controlled" by language, but rather, he places the satirist under his "linguistic control" (371). *Sat4* thus, according to Baumlin, "explores the dress, behavior, and dangerous verbal onslaughts" of the courtier, who can literally live off his tongue, showing that "language itself"—not merely the courtier's language but the satirist's—"has become the chief focus" of the poem. In the end, the language of Donne's satirist "destabilizes Horatian satire as a vehicle of moral instruction" and "denies reformative power to the language and genre" (384). On the contrary, language, Baumlin concludes, "concretized as food" early in the poem, "may poison as well as nourish," but transforming language "into food and taste" cannot "guarantee that one gains nourishment," as the satirist demonstrates (386).

Hall (1991, 165) calls *Sat4* a "contest between a linguistic swordsman and a linguistic mountebank, whose 'tongue' is nothing but courtly 'compliment'" (l. 44).

Blissett (2000, 104) states that the deliberate irregularity in *Sat4* "encourages the reader to adopt (especially in reading aloud) a tense, staccato, emphatic delivery, so that even when regular the lines sound irregular."

Religion and Politics

Grierson (1912, 2:117) points out "a veiled thread running through" *Sat4*, "an attack on the ways and tricks of informers." Although Donne "does not state his position too clearly," he is "always" exhibiting "links" that associate him with "the persecuted Catholic minority." Hardy (1942, 42) and Hunt (1954, 172) also comment on Donne's ties to the Roman Catholics.

Crofts (1936, 129–30) states of *Sat4* and *Sat5* that Donne realized that "the glare and glitter" of court "culminated in a blaze of diamonds and that formidable old fairy," Elizabeth I, whom he believes Donne "had seen through," for after all the Queen "was a woman, and he had seen through women."

Hillyer (1941, xxii) reads *Sat4* as Donne's private response to the public contest for office and glory, in which "Robert Devereux stumbled to his ruin amid the snares laid by Robert Cecil." In *Sat4* Donne's "fierce contempt for courtiers" is expressed as "an apologia to himself" for his failings in "a contest" in which he "never actively engaged."

Ochojski (1950, 542) finds a "deep contempt" for "pursuivants" in the poem.

Bamborough (1952, 170) finds in the courtier of *Sat4* "elements of the malcontent, the traveller, the politician, the intelligencer, and a hint of the Jesuit as well."

Andreasen (1963, 71) contends that the speaker in *Sat4* "descends" from the heights of truth in *Sat3* to reconsider the purgatory of "secular life."

Geraldine (1966, 29–31) observes the way in which the equation of the court visit with penance that Donne introduces in the first four lines stretches "until it covers the whole poem." She adds that even the reminder of mortality in lines 75–78, the recollection "of those who whipped Christ," and reflections on clothing lead him into religious ideas, so that "even in the sophisticated courts of London the poet sees the affairs of this world as leverage to the gates of heaven—or of hell" (31).

Hughes (1968, 50) thinks that while in all the Satyres Donne "plays the outsider," in *Sat4* this "mask of the renegade is most carefully adjusted," as in this poem he "plays his most dangerous game, that of the recusant," for the "insulation" between him and the world is "Roman Catholicism." *Sat4* is the "most insistently renegade" of the Satyres, Hughes argues, and though it is unlikely that Donne was "literally a Papist as late as 1597," it is "all the more revealing to find him brazenly parading as a Catholic in this poem."

Miner (1969, 34) points to a sense in *Sat4* that "the outer world has oppressed or threatened" Donne's "private inner world almost to the point of destruction," suggesting "a deep, obsessive fear" based on the fact that Donne "had real attachment to Catholicism."

Bald (1970, 70) cautions that while in *Sat4* Donne "may perhaps reveal a greater intimacy with Catholicism than other contemporary satirists," nevertheless "his references to the Roman Church are, if anything, severer than those to Protestantism."

Erskine-Hill (1972, 280, 282–83, 286) points to "a marked political aspect" in the "conversation" of the courtier in *Sat4* (280), which together with the satirist's "fearful attitude towards the law" may suggest not only "a fact of Donne's biography" but "a more general response to the time." He adds that the courtier "may not be altogether what he seems," for there is a "hint" that he is "an intelligencer, and there the matter is left, most disturbingly" (286). In addition, he estimates that while Donne was "still a Catholic in 1591," he was no longer by the Cadiz expedition of 1596. While *Sat4* "has many Catholic references," they are "not all pro-Catholic and, whether pro or con, are often balanced by Protestant references," and the poem overall "urges upon us the experience of fearing an unjust force in the law and operations of the established state" (283).

Elliott (1976, 113) asserts that in *Sat4* Donne "startles his reader into a deeper awareness of human weakness" in that he "lets the speaker frustrate himself again and nearly lose his religion in the process," and it is "through this surprising turn" that Donne "stresses the dangers of presumption and self-righteousness which await those who suppose that faith alone will shield them from temptation."

Corthell (1982, 174) finds that at the end of *Sat4* the satirist "has been obsessed with religious controversy" and "predictably frames his dilemma in terms of Catholic and Protestant debates on scriptural authority and authenticity."

Gallenca (1982, 328) contends that in *Sat3* and *Sat4* Donne expresses a fear of accusations of slander and libel, underscored by frequent fears about Roman Catholicism, which could well explain his detestation of infidelity. All of these agonies are disguised expressions of a fear of damnation, Gallenca thinks, secretly linked to a possible change of religion.

Hester (1982, 74–75, 79, 83, 91, 94–95) declares *Sat4* to be Donne's "boldest commentary on his own situation in the 1590s," the "predicament of the Catholic in Elizabethan England." *Sat4* "subtly weaves" Donne's "recusancy" into his examination of "the rhetorical and moral bases of Christian satire" so that the satirist, "largely through incriminatory comparisons of Anglican hypocrisy and Catholic devotion," mounts a "much stronger critique" of the established religion than in the earlier Satyres. *Sat4*, says Hester, "applies the central contention of the recusant apologists—that they were being persecuted for religion and not for treason," and the satirist's "confrontation with pursuivant trickery and self-serving debasements of religious gestures in the court" serves as a contrast to his own "imitation of Christian types and antetypes" (74). Further, the "menacing" possibility that the satirist "might even end up on Tyburn Hill" cannot distract him "from his dedication to the imitation of Christ's passion and sacrifice." Thus, Sat4, Hester says, not only is Donne's "fullest exploration of the duties and dangers of satire" but also provides a "provocative appraisal" of Donne's circumstances as a Catholic (75). Finally, the "issues of religious politics and the politics of religion" raised in Sat4 are "more than aesthetic concerns" for Donne, whose family tree included several examples of persecuted Catholics. Hester argues that Donne's preoccupation with this heritage of family suffering "indicts the hypocrisy and injustice of a system that persecutes and destroys sincere devotees of a politically illegal religion" as it "tolerates and even fosters perversities" of truly "devotional stances for which any devout recusant would be imprisoned, tortured, or killed." Nevertheless, Hester concludes, the satirist "does not champion Catholic devotion" over "Anglican devotion," for Sat4 is "Christian satire," not "pro-Catholic polemic" (95).

Bradbury (1985, 107) calls attention to the seriousness of the charges against the courtiers satirized in Sat4, reminding us of "the great disillusionment with the courtly ideal prevalent in the 1590s, and the threat that this anticourtly reaction presented to those people whose political, social, and educational ideals had been linked to the myth of the perfect courtier."

Wall (1985, 23–25, 28–29) states that Donne's "strategy of attack" in Sat4 is to "draw an implicit comparison between the real conduct of courtly life and Christian teaching about social responsibility," and thus, Donne "uses religious allusions to establish a normative stance from which to judge the behavior of the court" (23–24). Wall's argument focuses specifically on "the Anglican (not the Roman Catholic) Feast of the Purification of Saint Mary the Virgin, celebrated annually, like the Catholic feast, on February 2," which he believes, "heightens still further the irony of the speaker's religious allusions while it enables us to date the composition of this Satyre more precisely" (24–25). These allusions to "Anglican worship," he explains, "are at once a commentary on the extent of courtly corruption and a source for the direction of Donne's response to that corruption," adding that "the courage exhibited in his honest depiction of that court's corruption, especially in light of his contrast between Anglican society, becomes itself a means of purification, not only for the speaker but also for those who would learn from him how to regard that court in a way that would lead to its purification as well" (28–29). Wall concludes that Donne's "choice of the Anglican rite for the purification as an allusory frame for his description of the court carries power precisely because of its familiarity to those who could change things at the court and its power to heighten the sense of how far that court actually was from what it claimed to be," though he notes that the evidence provided in Sat4 "is insufficient to define Donne's own religious position in 1597" (29–30).

Marotti (1986, 103–05) describes Sat4 as portraying court "favor and disfavor, amorous intrigues, the ruthless ambition of would-be officeholders and the importunity of spendthrift aristocrats and gentlemen who looked to licenses and monopolies to rescue them economically," which are "all parts of the same corrupt system centered in royal patronage" and associated with "flattery, gossip, and libel" (103). Such criticism, whether true or false, is dangerous for the satirist to hear; the courtier expresses attitudes of the "activist war faction" at court, Marotti notes, with whom Donne's "soldiership at this time associated him." The satirist expresses "a fear of moral, political, and social contagion from such a man" (104), and the satirist's "imaginary passage" out of the court "from the royal Presence Chamber" is a reminder that the court "was not simply an arena for harmless foolishness but a politically perilous place as well" (105).

Baumlin (1988, 367–70) sees *Sat4* as a poem in which "a Loyalist Catholic poet speaks to a Protestant court," but he denies that the Catholic "predicament" is the poem's "major thesis" (367), arguing instead that the "Catholic allusions" in the poem are "so *flaunted* in the text that they can only weaken the poet's language and authority before a Protestant audience," which is one of the "intended effects" (368).

Baumlin (1990, 67–68) asserts that *Sat4* makes "continual reference" to "anti-Catholic legislation enacted from 1581–1606," adding that such allusions are "even more significant" if Donne is presenting himself "as one whose religion would keep him from court, under penalty of law."

Fish (1990, 238–39) contends that the speaker in *Sat4* "plays with the dangers of displaying Catholic sympathies in a way that cannot be separated from the danger" Donne himself "risks in presenting such a speaker."

May (1991, 200) notes that in *Sat4* Donne describes the Elizabethan court as a "godless place."

Scodel (1993, 481) argues that the passage satirizing a court fop and a *miles gloriosus* does not confront the "real dangers" of the court, that is, "its oppressive power, spies, and capacity for contaminating all who encounter it," and the passage can be read as an allusion to "Horace's secure stance, evoking a stable moral vision unavailable to Donne and incapable of explaining the most powerful evil forces of his world."

Strier (1993, 286) points to the satirist's "detailed knowledge of Catholic institutional and intellectual structures" in *Sat2*, arguing that in *Sat4* the satirist seems "a Catholic in a Protestant state," yet "what is most striking" about the two poems, as well as about *Sat3*, is "their independence from *any* established religious position."

Griffin (1994, 46–47) contends that "when read in the context of a tradition of moral inquiry," *Sat4* "is not simply an attack on the world of the court," but instead presents a satirist "who reports on the spectacle of pride and vain display he has beheld at court." He comments further that *Sat4* borrows its situation from Horace's Satire 1.9, in which the satirist meets at court "one who flatters, gossips, and finally begs a crown," and thus, "presenting himself comically as discomfited victim, the satirist finally escapes and flees to the safety of his home," adding, however, that "the poem does not (as in Horace) end there." Instead, Donne "turns our attention more firmly to the satirist himself and implicitly sets the poem's moral problem: Why does an honest and sensible man willingly descend into a den of corruption and flattery?" Griffin adds that "the poem offers no clear answer (the satirist himself does not seem to know), but it encourages our speculations," concluding of the satirist "that going to court is a means of maintaining his moral bearings or reaffirming his standards and confirming the crucial difference between 'them' and 'me.'"

Price (1996, 52, 62) suggests that Donne's "involvement in the Catholic underground" provided him "with exposure to if not training in lifestyle and rhetorical dissimulation" that he depicts in *Sat4* (52). He comments further that Donne "foregrounds a Catholic subtext by impregnating" the poem "with references to religious activity," as well as to "the entire process by which government authorities outlawed, captured, interrogated, tortured, and executed recusant traitors," and he argues that Donne's "method of distributing these references illustrates the dissimulator's method of scattering subversive references rather than concentrating them" (62).

Flynn (2001, 114) contends that in both *Sat2* and *Sat4* Donne "traced encompassing greed and corruption to their cause in the Tudor statutes stamping out Catholicism."

NOTES AND GLOSSES

1–16 *Well;…going that way.* **PATTERSON** (1970) says that it is "surely more than a coincidence that effects like these (which suddenly appeared in England in the 1590's) should follow instructions for writing under the Ideas of Reproof, instructions which were current in Italy from about 1560 to 1590, and which were also available in Sturm's 1571 edition of Hermogenes." Notes that "under the headings of Asperity, Vigor, and especially of Vehemence, English poets could find descriptions of *high* styles of Reproof, already associated with the elevation they admired in Juvenal and Persius, and, in addition, already partly assimilated to the problems of the vernacular languages" (110). **BAUMLIN** (1988): in the opening lines, "ironically or no," the satirist speaks "not merely as a Christian but as a Catholic, particularly in his allusion to the sacrament of extreme unction" (369). His witty "equation" of court experiences with a purgatory "worse than the tortures of a Protestant hell" suggests (beyond "blasphemy") that he, "if not court society, may be reformed." Yet he speaks in a context where Catholicism "has been denied meaning and efficacy" by a Protestant "temporal power." Catholicism in the poem is "too dangerous a subject even to jest about" and "can only bring danger" to the satirist, "not reform to court society" (370). **LERNER** (1999): Donne "introduces an account of the corruption and eccentricities of court by announcing what a stupid ass he was to go there" (6).

1–8 *Well;…went to Court;* **MINER** (1969): the lines remind us that "the integrity of the individual provides the authority for satire of society" (8–9). **SELDEN** (1978): this "most un-Horatian" opening, focused on "mock-religious confession," may have been suggested by the "mock-heroic touches" present in Horatian satire (63). **DOCHERTY** (1986): this opening "could, quite conceivably, be a translation of Christ's moment of resignation, a moment which is itself a kind of scene of recognition or of vocation in Gethsemane" (171).

1–4 *Well;…Mapp of this.* **GRIERSON** (1912) finds that these lines "resemble the opening of Régnier's imitation of Horace's satire," though he identifies "no further resemblance" (2:117–18). **PETER** (1956): such verse "can hardly be written off as traditional or neo-classical: what strikes us at once is its originality" (133). **ELLRODT** (1960b): reacting to a sense of moral outrage, these lines express personal injury or resentment (2:289). **HARRIS** (1960): as much as "the spectacle of the world's sin," what moves Donne to write satire is "the sense of his own sin and the fear of contamination" (193). GERALDINE (1966): though Grierson cites Régnier's Horace for "this initial statement of the idea," nevertheless "the careful stretching of the analogy until it covers the whole poem is surely Donne's own" (29). MILGATE (1967) says that "similarity (confined to these lines)" to Régnier's imitation of Horace "is almost certainly accidental," noting that Régnier's work did not appear in print until 1608 and 1613 (149). SHAWCROSS (1972): the metrics of these lines set "a satiric tone" with their "extreme enjambing" and "such odd end-of-line words as 'in' and 'is'" (258). OLIVER (1997) finds here a joke about purgatory "at the expense of Catholicism" by "a speaker whose ostensible subject is something other than the belief in question" (55–56), and the speaker's "frivolous tone" suggests "a piece of bluff as far as his creator is concerned" (113).

1–4 *My Sin...Mapp of this.* SMITH (1971): the speaker "accounts himself thoroughly shriven by the purgatory he has been through" (485). [Similarly, MacKenzie (2001, 79), who adds, "this is a vitriolic riposte to a world that Donne himself had once so desperately desired").]

1–3 *Well;...A Purgatory,* MCFARLAND (1977): "Since a new sentence or clause does not begin the 'Indeed,' this is not a case of true anadiplosis but a case in which sound alone is involved schematically." Moreover, "epanalepsis ('Indeed...in'), involving the syllable rather than the word, combines with the anadiplosis for emphasis." In these lines, however, "the enjambment tends to deprive the figure of any formal or formalizing function" (398).

1 *receaue* GROSART (1872–73): "the Holy Communion" (1:39). [So also, Milgate (1967, 149), Hughes (1968, 50), and Carey (1990, 427).] BEWLEY (1966): "the Sacrament of Extreme Unction" (179). [So also, Shawcross (1967, 26), Smith (1971, 485), Grigson (1980, 23), and Oliver (1997, 36).]

2 *Indeede...beene in* MELTON (1906): the line exemplifies Donne's tendency to begin and end a line with the same sound or syllable (151). [See also note to *Sat1 5.*] STEIN (1944c): the line illustrates omission of a syllable "after the cesura," one of Donne's "devices for metrical modulation" (377).

2 *in* LERNER (1999) notes the "rhyming on a totally unimportant word" (7).

3–4 *A Purgatory,...Mapp of this.* WARTON (1797) calls attention to Donne's "licentious expression" here (4:278). WALL (1985): in this image, Donne "uses 'Purgatorie' to describe both the state of things at Court (it is worse than 'fear'd hell') and the hope he sees in the possibility that conditions at court can still be beneficial both for his speaker and the court itself (it is not in a final state like 'fear'd hell' but, like Purgatory, can be a place in which the very sufferings it inflicts can be purifying rather than damning. Since the word 'Purgatory' did not disappear from the vocabulary of Anglicans after the Reformation, Donne's use of it here does not place him definitively in either religious camp or anywhere in between" (30). LERNER (1999): "the tortured knottiness of the syntax" here makes Purgatory worse than Hell (7).

3 *Purgatory,* BEWLEY (1966): "the court" (179). [So also, Shawcross (1967, 26)

and Jensen (1972, 405).] **HUGHES** (1968): Donne "accepts the doctrine of Purgatory, in flat violation of Protestant doctrine" (50).

4 *A recreation,…Mapp of this.* **STEIN** (1944c): elision of an extra syllable (added to procure "emphasis") in a "trisyllabic foot" is one of Donne's devices for varying the metrical line (396). **SMITH** (1971): "the hell we fear is just a pleasant entertainment compared to the torment he has lately endured, and a poor shadow of it" (486).

4 *recreation,* **MILGATE** (1967) (reading "recreation to"): although only two mss. include the "to," "the sense…requires it, since Donne's point is not that Hell is a duplicate of his trials at the hands of the bore but that Hell affords the less punishment (an idea conveyed also by 'map'). Hell does not 're-create' the anguish, but is by comparison 'a diversion, an enjoyment'. The dropping of 'to' is the kind of error that could be made frequently and independently in manuscript copies." (149).

4 *scant Mapp* **HUNT** (1954): Donne "regularly thinks of a map as a scanty and inadequate picture of the world which it represents" (101); see *TWHence* and *Devotions* (241).

4 *scant* **GRIERSON** (1912) (reading "scarse"): "Donne's use of 'scarse', like his use of 'Macaron' in this poem, is probably an Italianism; in Italian 'scarso' means 'wanting, scanty, poor'" (2:118).

5–8 *My mind…went to Court;* **COUSINS** (1979): the poem's "most important lines trace, in a winding design, a moment of introspection," in which "convoluted syntax, quibbles, and contraries" act out "a mind's search for its own motives" (105). **CORTHELL** (1982): "confusing syntax complicates Donne's protestations of a free and uncorrupted mind, gratuitously raising the question of his motives in going to Court" (171). **HESTER** (1982) refers to *Sermons* 5:316–17 on "sins of omission" (79). **CORTHELL** (1997): "The tortured syntax figures a satirist who does not know his own motives" (49).

5–6 *My mind…to bee seene;* **STEIN** (1946): in this couplet, Donne's ellipsis, involving the grammatical structure, achieves "marked" compression (101). **ELLRODT** (1960b) questions whether we should believe the satirist's overly peremptory claim (2:289–90).

5 *My mind…yet hath beene* **STEIN** (1944c): as commonly do Elizabethan dramatists, Donne here admits an extra syllable, "an extra feminine ending in the foot preceding the cesura," an "extension of metrical liberty" that is "most frequent" in the Satyres (394). **SHAWCROSS** (1972): the line seems "hypermetric," but Donne's "alteration of meter" has "definite and appropriate effect" (263).

6–10 *Poysoned with…the Statuts curse* **JONES** (1961): in this passage, Donne's "technique is masterly. By using the conjunction 'then' as the rhyme-word he gives it a weight which it could not be given in prose construction, and thus gives fine emphasis to its function of logical consequence; by using a light rhyme-word he maintains a momentum so that, after the break between the pentameter cadences, the rhythm swoops down on 'Shall I, nones slave,' strengthening remarkably by its very movement the indignation" that "follows clearly" from the rhyme word (33–34).

6 *Poysoned with…to bee seene;* **STEIN** (1944c): "stress-shift" in the first foot of the line is one of Donne's chief devices for varying the metrical line (378). **MILGATE** (1967) cites Ovid, *Ars Amatoria* 1.99 and *ElNat* 22 (149).

7–8 *I had no…went to Court;* **POWERS** (1971): these lines begin the satirist's narrative to a silent companion (57).

7 *no Suite there, nor new Sute to show,* **PETER** (1956): Donne here does not scruple "to use a pun or quibble" in order "to tease his readers into close attention to what he is saying" (134). **MILGATE** (1967): "the pun equates in importance (as courtiers do) a petition to the Queen and the clothes worn by the petitioner" (149). **SHAWCROSS** (1967): "Neither a plea to make at Court to satisfy my pride nor a suit of clothes to show off" (26). **SMITH** (1971): "no petition…nor new costume" (486). **MAROTTI** (1986): this line provides evidence that Donne's presence at court was "rooted" in a "deliberate search for courtly employment" (102).

7 *Suite* **JOHNSON** (1755): "[From *To Sue.*] A petition; an address of entreaty."

8–11 *But as Glare…he scap'd,* **WARNKE** (1967) (reading "Glaze"): Glaze "was fined for attending a clandestine Mass, even though he had done so only as a joke" (116). **HUGHES** (1968): "jabs at the statute which penalizes anyone attending a Catholic mass" (50). **ERSKINE-HILL** (1972) (reading "Glaze"): although the "sardonic humour" of this focus on Glaze recalls the "list of ecclesiastically misled" in *Sat3*, "Donne himself is here, though only by analogy, made to seem vulnerable to the law"; see *Sat4* 129–34 (281). **BAUMLIN** (1988) (reading "Glaze"): the punishment of Glaze "shows that such alternatives to the court's beliefs as Catholicism are too dangerous even to jest about" (370). **CORTHELL** (1997): "the comparison foregrounds the question of motive," pointing "to a division in the subject" and also dividing the reader "against the satirist" and "on the side of the Statutes" (49).

8–10 *But as Glare…the Statuts curse* **DIXON** (1880) asks if any reader can "kindly tell me whether the word 'glare'" appears in *Sat4* 8, adding that he has "a copy of Pope in which his paraphrase is printed along with Donne's original doggerel" (8). **JESSOPP** (1880) responds to Dixon (1880), asking, "But what can Mr. Dixon mean by talking of 'Donne's original doggerel'?" (190). **K.P.D.E.** (1880) responds to Dixon (1880), stating, "*Glare* is the correct reading. As it is printed with a capital G, I assume that it is a proper name; probably that of some one, well known in Donne's time, who had gone to mass in jest and had been found out and punished for it" (191). **SOLLY** (1880) responds to Dixon (1880), writing that the edition of 1635 altered the word "from *Glaze* to *Glare*," and further that "it is plain that Donne spoke of some one who was accused under the statute of Elizabeth, cap. 1, 1580, which enacts that whosoever shall officiate at mass shall forfeit 200 marks, and be imprisoned for a year; and that whosoever shall willingly be present at mass shall forfeit 100 marks, and also be subject to imprisonment." Says that "[t]his somebody is designated *Glaze* or *Glare*, but whether either of these was a real name is doubtful," adding that it "is always *Glare*, and not *glare*, and generally is printed in a peculiar type, to show that it is a proper name." Comments that "*Two* hundred is evidently a misprint for *the* hundred," and that "Glare did not officiate, he was only 'willingly present'" (190). **PRICE** (1996): the lines refer to "a provision of the Act Against Reconciliation With Rome (1581)" (62).

8–9 *But as Glare…To'a Masse* **STEIN** (1942) finds that "stress shifts in the fourth foot" give "increased impetus" to enjambment, producing (as he says they do here) "two unstressed syllables coming together" (684).

8 *Yet went…which did go* **STEIN** (1944c): "stress-shift" after the caesura is one of Donne's chief devices for varying the metrical line (384).

8 *Yet went to Court;* **ERSKINE-HILL** (1972): after "a long preamble of explosive exasperation," this "half line" sets the scene (278–79).

8 *Glare* **BEWLEY** (1966) (reading "Glaze"): "a fictitious name" (179). **SHAWCROSS** (1967) (reading "Glaze"): his "name indicates his transparent superficiality" (26).

9–10 *disburse* and *curse* **LERNER** (1999): with these rhymed words, Donne "draws attention to what matters about the enforcement of religious orthodoxy" (7).

9–10 *was fayne to disburse / The hundred Marks* **STEIN** (1942) finds that "stress shifts in the fourth foot" give "increased impetus" to enjambment, producing (as he says they do here) "two unstressed syllables coming together" (684).

9 *catch'd,* **SMITH** (1971): "arrested for participating in a prohibited ceremony" (486).

10 *The hundred Marks…the Statuts curse* **CHAMBERS** (1896): "A statute passed in 1580 prescribed a penalty of an hundred marks for being present at mass, two hundred for officiating" (2:243). [Similarly, Carey (1990, 427) and Kruzhkova (1994, 160).] **MILGATE** (1967) adds that the statute was "23º Eliz. C. 1, sect. iii"; that the penalty for presiding at mass included "a year in prison"; that a mark (originally a weight of 8 oz.) was valued at the weight of silver, "20 pennies to the ounce," or 13s. 4d.; and that "there was no separate coin of this value" (149–50). [Similarly, Shawcross (1967, 26) and Gransden (1970, 171).] **SMITH** (1971) comments that "a hundred marks represented something over £65 at the value of the day" (486).

10 *curse* **GROSART** (1872–73): "fine or penalty" (1:39).

11–17 *so it pleasd…I sufferd this.* **BELLETTE** (1975): this passage provides a hint of "the future preacher and dean, and of a way of resolving the problem of living responsibly and knowingly in the world which has little to do with the conventional role of satirist." Donne "will in short be judged as he is judging" (137). **SELDEN** (1978): "The sheer force of self-recrimination and the accumulation of self-debasement compel the reader to transmute the mock-serious into the problematic and the melancholy" (64). **BLISSETT** (2000): these lines portray Donne's "entirely negative" judgment of the court (112).

11–14 *so it pleasd…full, as proud,* **STEIN** (1942): these lines exemplify how Donne "cultivates pliable rhythms that sometimes border on looseness." Here the effect comes from "employing many elisions, and some of these constantly threaten to become extra syllables"; from "the frequent combination of two unstressed syllables, either after a stress-shift or in a pyrrhic-spondee unit"; and, "finally, there are the actual extra syllables which are attracted into the rhythm by these other devices" (688).

11 *my destinee* **LAURITSEN** (1976): "Puzzled and deeply troubled by the irrationality and apparent purposelessness of his own behavior, the speaker retreats hastily from the crucial issue by sloughing off the burden of personal responsibility and by seeking quickly to displace his unwanted and unaccustomed guilt onto something he calls his 'destinie'" (127).

12 *(Guilty of...) to thinke mee* **RICHTER** (1902) cites this line to illustrate level stress (395–96).

12 *(Guilty of my Sin of going)* **SMITH** (1971): "he must expect to suffer for all the sins that being a courtier comprehends, and his punishment is to endure the conversation of a courtier" (486).

13–16 *As prone...dwell at Court,* **CAREY** (1981): "thwarted ambition" bred Donne's anger at the court, and he "spent the next twenty years straining every nerve to get a foothold in it"; his "hate is a way of drawing attention to himself" (63).

13–14 *as forgett- / full, as proud,* **STEIN** (1942) finds that "stress shift in the fifth foot, especially by attraction," gives "the strongest momentum of all" to enjambment, here effected by beginning a line with "an extra syllable" (685). **SHAWCROSS** (1972): "breaking of a word between two lines" manifests "trenchant wit" (258).

13 *As prone...good as forgett-* **RICHTER** (1902) cites this line to illustrate the occurrence of a double unstressed syllable in the middle of the verse that shows Donne's attempt to overcome the disparity between word accent and verse rhythm (401). **STEIN** (1944c): "stress-shift" after the caesura is one of Donne's chief devices for varying the metrical line (384).

13 *As prone to all ill,* **STEIN** (1944c): here the third syllable is an "extra syllable by attraction" (396).

15 *wittlesse,* **JOHNSON** (1755): "Wanting understanding."

16 *dwell* **MILGATE** (1967): "are continually in attendance at. The satirist suffers the same penalty as regular *habitués*, though (like Glaze) he erred by making only one feckless visit" (150).

17–154 *Towards me...from prisone.* **PRICE** (1996): the speaker's first visit to the court is framed "as a parallel to the experience of a man named Glaze who went to Mass, got caught, and had to pay the fine." While "part of the satire's humor derives from the hyperbole inherent in comparing something so trivial as suffering the conversation of a bore to something so grave as incurring punishment for recusancy," this "comparison also calls attention to the punishment of recusancy as a subject in and of itself" (61). In addition, Donne "ranges beyond the penalty to elaborate upon the agent delivering the penalty and the speaker suffering it" (64).

17–148 *Towards me...vex mee.* **ALDEN** (1899) notes that "the account of the bore" here "instantly" suggests that of Horace's *Satire* 1.9, and "the gossip of the same character" recalls Juvenal VI. 402–412 (86).

17–44 *Towards me...calld Complement,* **ELLRODT** (1960b): the product of an "amateur" at the Inns of Court; though it is an expression of wit, this characterization is no less objective and acute than those of Elizabethan professional writers (2:31–32).

17–29 *Towards me...what you are.* **COHEN** (1963): Donne "overwhelms a miserable courtier with such copious and fantastic abuse that the man is forgotten in the exuberance of the poet's invention" (263). **CORTHELL** (1982): "The character is first described as an alien being, but the terms of the description reveal as much about the satirist as they do about the bore": the satirist's "xenophobia" is itself a main "object of satire" (172).

17 *Towards me did run* **RUDD** (1963): Donne's phrasing recalls Horace's *"accurrit"* in line 3 of his Satire 1.9 [so also, Milgate (1967, 149), Erskine-Hill (1972, 276), and Baumlin (1988, 370)], but in *Sat4*, "the words lead to an outlandish (and, of course, quite un-Horatian) description of the bore" (208). **GRANSDEN** (1970): "Here Donne begins his imitation of Horace" (171).

18–150 *A thing more...of my Crowne;* **DOWDEN** (1890): the passage presents "a lively picture of the needy courtier suitor assuming courtier's airs, and in the end thankful to be dismissed with the gift of a crown-piece, a figure half-piteous, halfgrotesque" (802). **JENSEN** (1972): as "a comic butt," the courtier offers the speaker "rich opportunities for his wit" (406).

18–26 *A thing more...Strangers rise.* **ERSKINE-HILL** (1972): the passage "introduces no fewer than nine comparisons to convey his strangeness" (279); this "exuberant amplification" conjures up "more fantastic shapes" than the "wise," though "less complicated," humor of Donne's tenth Paradox (284–85). **JENSEN** (1972): the passage "fills in certain lines in the portrait of the speaker" and "establishes in a rather firm way our identification with him" (405).

18–23 *A thing more...then Strangers;* **WYBARNE** (1609): these lines express the coming of "Antichrist" and are comparable to passages in Homer, Virgil, and Spenser (112–13). **HUGHES** (1968): the passage "shows disgust for all the strangers who have been washed into England by the tides of Continental religious persecution" (50–51).

18–19 *more Strange,...Ere bredd;* **GROSART** (1872–73): "from the same source" that Shakespeare used in *Ant.*, "perhaps Pliny"; cf. *ED* 2: "Begets strange creatures on Niles durty slime" (1:39). **MILGATE** (1967) cites Pliny, *Nat. Hist.* 9.84 and *ED* 1–2 (150). **WARNKE** (1967): "the ancient belief that the snakes and other reptiles of Egypt were bred by the action of the sun on the mud of the Nile" (116). [So also, Smith (1971, 486).] **GRANSDEN** (1970) refers to Ovid, *Metamorphoses*, 1:422–37, and Spenser, *The Faerie Queene*, 1.1:21 (171).

18 *thing* **SULLENS** (1964): Donne's use of this meaning of the word is earlier than the earliest source cited by *OED* (238).

19 *all which into Noahs Arke came;* **MILGATE** (1967): it was thought that, as well as "ordinary creatures," the occupants of the Ark in Gen. 6.19–20 and 7.8–9 must have included "the more exotic denizens of the world of 'natural history': basilisk, amphisboena, leocrocuta, etc."; see Benedict Pererius Valentinus, *Comment. Et Disput. in Genesim* (1601), 457ff., and Drayton, *Noah's Flood*, ll. 456ff. (150).

19 *Noahs* **MELTON** (1906): pronounced as one syllable (190).

20 *would haue pos'd Adam to name;* **MILGATE** (1967): when Adam "named every living creature" (Gen. 2.19–20), he was able to do so, according to early commentators, because he perceived "their true natures" (150). **BAUMLIN** (1988): "the boor's lack of a name" is a "subtle revision of Horace" that not only "sharpens the humor of the description" but also "shows up the weakness of language to penetrate beyond appearances to the falsehood and corruption within" (371).

20 *A thing,...to name;* **DOCHERTY** (1986): here and throughout the opening section, *Sat4* is "overtly concerned with nomination" (168).

20 *pos'd* **SULLENS** (1964): Donne's use of this meaning of the word is cited by *OED* as the earliest source (252). **BEWLEY** (1966): "puzzled" (179). [So also, Shawcross (1967, 26).] **SMITH** (1971): "nonplussed" (486).

20 *Adam* **MELTON** (1906): the word exemplifies Donne's use of "unusual (?)" accent in proper names (86, 91).

21 *seauen Antiquaries Studyes,* **GRIERSON** (1912): given the "revival of antiquarian studies" in the reign of Elizabeth, Donne may refer to "some such society in its early stages" as Oldys mentions in his *Life of Raleigh*, p. 317. Donne's "more than one hit at Antiquaries" includes also *Antiq* and *Sat5* (2:118).

21 *seauen* **MILGATE** (1967): "like 'ten,' l. 97, this means simply, 'several'" (150). **SMITH** (1971): "many" (486).

21 *Studyes,* **SHAWCROSS** (1972): "Odd final stress for rhyme" (263).

22 *Africks Monsters,* **GRIERSON** (1912): "Africa was famous as the land of monsters" (2:118). **MILGATE** (1967): "These were thought to be as prodigious in number as in their natures: lyonsbane, crocute, cerast, anthropophages, blemmys, and many more"; see *The Excellent and Pleasant Work of J. Solinus* (1587), trans. A. Golding facsimile ed. (1955,) ch. 39ff., and Jonson's *Every Man Out of His Humour* 3.6.176–78 (150).

22 *Guyanas rarityes;* **GRIERSON** (1912) refers to Raleigh's *The Discoverie of the Large, Rich and Bewtiful Empire of Guiana* (1596) and to Shakespeare's *Oth.* (2:118). **MILGATE** (1967): "Raleigh sent Capt. Jacob Whiddon on the earliest English expedition to Guiana in 1594, but for an account of the 'rarities' Englishmen had to await Raleigh's story of his own voyage (1595)"; see Joseph Wybarne, *The New Age of Old Names* (1609), 113 (150). **SHAWCROSS** (1967): "Perhaps with reference to Raleigh's exploration of Guiana in 1595" (397). **BALD** (1970): "shows that Donne had followed with interest Raleigh's explorations" (86). **SMITH** (1971): Raleigh's

descriptions included "strange people, such as the Amazons and Anthropophagi, as well as monstrous animals" (486). [So also, Carey (1990, 427).]

23 *Stranger then…for a Dane* MELTON (1906): the line exemplifies Donne's tendency to begin and end a line with the same sound or syllable (151). [See also notes to *Sat4 2 and Sat1 5*.]

23 *Stranger then Strangers;* GRIERSON (1912): the line refers to "the unpopularity in London of the numerous strangers whom wars and religious persecution had collected in England"; in 1593, for example, "a bill was promoted in Parliament *against aliens selling foreign wares among us by retail,* which Raleigh supported" (2:118–19).

23 *Strangers;* MILGATE (1967): "foreigners" (150). [So also, Shawcross (1967, 27) and Smith (1971, 486).] WARNKE (1967): "the numerous foreigners who were living in London in the 1590s and whose unpopularity with the natives is referred to in lines 25–26" (117).

24 *Danes massacre* GROSART (1872–73): "Ethelred made peace with and paid tribute to the invading Danes, and ordered a massacre of them on St. Brice's-day, 13th November 1002" (1:39). NORTON (1895): "The tradition of this atrocious massacre, which occurred on November 13, 1002, still survived in the popular memory. When Queen Elizabeth was entertained at Kenilworth, the people of Coventry begged to be allowed 'to renew their old storied show' of the slaughter of the Danes 'to move some mirth to her Majesty.' 'The thing is grounded in story, and for pastime wont to be played in our city yearly.' *Laneham's Letters,* 1575" (1:242). BEWLEY (1966): "Ethelred the Unready ordered a massacre of all the Danes in England in 1001" (179). MILGATE (1967): Ethelred massacred the Danes (because he was weary "of buying them off"), an incident recorded not only by chroniclers but "also, perhaps by the name of the London church, St. Clement Danes"; see Stow, *Survey of London,* ii. 96, 372–73. During a 1567 progress to Kenilworth, men of Coventry asked the queen "that they might revive their old 'storial sheaw,' the massacre of the Danes"; see *Captain Cox, his Ballads and Books* (1871), 26–27 (150–51). SHAWCROSS (1967): "William the Conqueror's rout of the Danes from northeastern England" (397). SMITH (1971): "The Danish settlers were massacred throughout England in the year 1012 at the order of King Ethelred" (487). [So also, Carey (1990, 427) and Kruzhkova (1994, 161).]

25–26 *And without…Strangers rise.* SHAWCROSS (1967): "one who would be killed, if he had no help to block such action, whenever native would-be politicians began to move into influential court positions held by foreigners" (27).

26 *When next…Strangers rise.* GROSART (1872–73): "Londoners from jealousies of trade rose against foreigners on what was called afterwards Evil May-day 1517" (1:39). [So also, Milgate (1967, 151).] GRIERSON (1912) cites from Strype's *Annals* and Birch's *Life of Raleigh* illustrations from the 1590s of "the unpopularity in London of the numerous strangers whom wars and religious persecution had collected in England" (2:118–19). MILGATE (1967): "English merchants and retailers continued to be resentful against foreign traders who set up competitive businesses until and beyond the date" of *Sat4*; "threats and libels had been published" in 1593. See Stow, *Annals*

(1601), 848–51, and Strype, *Annals of the Reformation* (1924), 4:234–36, 296–301 (151). [Similarly, Kruzhkova (1994, 161–62).] GRANSDEN (1970): "London apprentices rioted against foreigners on several occasions" (171). SMITH (1971): "The London apprentices took the lead in expressing the City's hostility to foreign traders, and were always threatening a renewal of the riots of the previous reign" (487).

26 *'gainst* RICHTER (1902) uses this word to illustrate syncopy, or shortening (404).

26 *Strangers* BEWLEY (1966): "foreign craftsmen" (179).

27–29 *One whom...what you are.* SMITH (1971): "the Justice to whom the noonday watch brings him for examination would think him a Jesuit or seminarist in disguise, and as such, liable to execution" (487).

27 *One whom...scarse go by;* SHAWCROSS (1967): "one who would scarcely be admitted by sentinels even at noon (when his actions could be easily observed and, if suspicious, easily thwarted)" (27). PRICE (1996): one of several references in the poem to the surveillance of recusants (see also, ll. 215–17 and 237) (63).

27 *at noone* MILGATE (1967): "even in full daylight" (151).

28–29 *One to'whom...what you are.* ELLRODT (1960b) notes that Donne reserves his sharpest arrows for those avid inquisitors who despoiled the recusants (2:285). MILGATE (1967): "A series of proclamations (especially those of 1581, 1585, and 1591) branded Jesuits and seminary priests as traitors, under penalty of death if they entered the Queen's dominions. Some did enter, in disguise, and some of these were detected and executed"; see Strype, *Annals* (1824), 4:83–84 and Fynes Moryson, *Itinerary* (1907), 1:422 and 2:115 (151). [Similarly, Shawcross (1967, 27).] HUGHES (1968): the passage "throws a bitter glance at the priest-hunting magistrate" (51).

28 *One to'whom...sure would cry* STEIN (1944b): the line exemplifies how Donne's "elisions too often produce rhythms and combinations of consonants that cannot be justified." Here, the second, fourth, and sixth syllables are "extra syllables"; if we "swallow" them, "as if they were not present, the line becomes hopelessly mechanical," but "if we pronounce all three, the iambic structure is lost" (402).

28 *examining* SULLENS (1964): Donne's usage of this word is earlier than the earliest *OED* date (180). PRICE (1996): Donne's use of this word refers to "the formal interrogation, particularly under torture, by which the examiner attempted to extract information from the accused" (63).

29 *by your Priesthood* GRIERSON (1912): "Donne's companion looks so strange that he runs the risk of arrest as a seminary priest," required by legislation of the 1580s "to leave the kingdom within forty days under the capital penalty of treason" (2:119–20). BEWLEY (1966): "the Justice would mistake him for a Jesuit in disguise" (180). KRUZHKOVA (1994): Jesuits and Catholic priests who illegally entered England were executed as spies (162).

30–33 *His clothes...Become tufftaffeta;* **WOOLF** (1932): these lines demonstrate Donne's determination to record his vivid impressions of "actual things" (23).

30 *bare.* **MILGATE** (1967): "bare of ornament, or threadbare" (151).

31 *Sleeuelesse* **JOHNSON** (1755): "Wanting sleeves; having no sleeves."

31 *Ierkin* **MILGATE** (1967) quotes Linthicum, 202: "a short coat with a collar, sometimes sleeveless, but usually sleeved" (151).

32 *ground* **SMITH** (1971): "the fabric itself" (487).

33–34 *tufftaffeta;...nought at all.* **GROSART** (1872–73) (reading "Tufftaffaty"): "these silk stuffs" were "cheaper than velvet." Tufftaffaty "had some fluffiness"; rash "was rasé or smooth" (1:39). **NORTON** (1895) (reading "Tufftaffaty"): "Tufftaffaty was a taffeta [so also, Bewley (1966, 180)], a fabric of silk or linen, woven with a pile like velvet in tufts or spots; when the nap was worn off it would be like 'plain rash,' an inferior smooth stuff" (1:243). **SHAWCROSS** (1967): "it will continue to be worn down, and later generations will see it as rash and then not at all" (27).

33 *tufftaffeta;* **JOHNSON** (1755): "A villous kind of silk." **MILGATE** (1967): "tufted taffeta," which was "a thin, fine silk cloth, which could be woven with stripes or spots raised above the 'ground'"; see Linthicum, 124 (151). **SHAWCROSS** (1967): "a thin glossy silk" (27). **SMITH** (1971): "taffeta with a pile arranged in tufts" (487). [So also, Carey (1990, 427).] **GRIGSON** (1980): "taffeta with a tufted nap" (23).

34 *playne rash* **BEWLEY** (1966): "a thin, smooth silk" (180). **MILGATE** (1967): "a twilled fabric of silk, as here, or of wool"; see Linthicum, 85–86 (151). [So also, Carey (1990, 427).] **SHAWCROSS** (1967): "a smooth silk fabric" (27). **SMITH** (1971): "smooth fabric—silk, serge, or worsted" (487). [So also, Grigson (1980, 23).]

35–44 *This thing...With his tong,* **DOCHERTY** (1986): "a strange displacement occurs," as the "tongue of the beggar becomes that of the poet, now cast in the role of supplicant" (141). **BAUMLIN** (1988): the satirist's multiple uses of the word "tongue" (in ll. 35, 40, 41, and 44) constitute a figure of speech called *"anaclasis,"* in which the word "becomes at the same time the capacity of speech, a synecdoche for language itself, and a symbol of flattery and deception." The courtier's "artfully (i.e. deceptively) prepared feast" of language "awakens" and "deceives" the hearer's taste, "which now becomes a metonymy for intellect," a development in which the satirist dramatizes "the familiar Platonic argument against the flatteries of rhetoric" (372).

35–38 *This thing...one Language.* **ELLRODT** (1960b): without descending to invective, these lines are distinctly xenophobic (2:82). **RUDD** (1963): the episode springs from Horace's *"docti sumus"* in l. 7 of his Satire 1.9, but *Sat4* "expands it into an account of the fellow's grotesque, polyglot speech" (208).

35 *sayth,* **GRIERSON** (1912): "The 'saith' is a harshly interpolated 'so he says'" (2:120). [Similarly, Bewley (1966, 180) and Milgate (1967, 151).]

36 *only knowes...States belongs.* **SMITH** (1971): "he alone understands the several conditions of men and of politics everywhere" (487).

36 *knowes* **RICHTER** (1902) (reading "knoweth") uses this word to illustrate a stretching of syllables (405).

36 *what to all States belongs.* **ELLRODT** (1960b): the passage refers to Donne's concern with politics and statecraft as a secretary or prospective secretary to Lord Keeper Egerton (2:33).

37 *of th'accents,* **RICHTER** (1902) uses this phrase to illustrate a slurring of syllables (403).

37 *th'accents,* **SMITH** (1971): "stress falls on the second syllable" (487).

37–38 *Made of…one Language.* **GRIERSON** (1912) (reading "no language"): "Donne's companion, in affecting the accents and best phrases of all languages, spoke none" (2:120).

38–44 *If strange meats…With his tong,* **HESTER** (1982): "allusions to food, art, soldiers, and medicine," all references to "the therapeutic power of satire," in effect confirm that "the bore's satanic tongue" is "the verbal equivalent of his own abuse of his role as a satirist" (82). **BAUMLIN** (1988): "the figure anaclasis—'tongue' repeated with different shades of meaning—adds more than wit: it evaluates the boor's use of language by concretizing its effects" (372).

38 *speakes one Language.* **MILGATE** (1967): "as men did before the confusion of tongues"; see Gen. 11.1–9 (151). **SMITH** (1971): "he speaks none of the languages he affects to know but only one language made up of scraps of each of them" (487). **BAUMLIN** (1988), referring to the textual variants "no language" and "one language," suggests that "the reader should keep both variants in mind, reading 'no' as a palimpsest beneath the word 'one'" (371).

39–40 *my tast.…bumbast,* **RICHTER** (1902) uses the rhymed words of the couplet here to illustrate level stress (409). **STEIN** (1942): an example of Donne's "chief prosodic innovation," the frequent use of "stress-shift in the fifth foot," in which a feminine rhyme "is invariably matched with a masculine" (681).

39 *Art* **MILGATE** (1967): "the cook's skill" (152).

40 *Pedants motley tong,* **MILGATE** (1967): "learned jargon that mixes together English, Latin, and Greek terms" (152).

40 *motley* **SULLENS** (1964): Donne's use of this meaning of the word is earlier than the earliest source cited by *OED* (225). **SHAWCROSS** (1967): "confusing because of a pedant's diverse and complex knowledge" (27).

40 *Soldiers bumbast,* **MILGATE** (1967): "the bragging jargon of soldiers, stuffed with camp slang and scraps of foreign tongues picked up on campaigns" (152). [So also, Shawcross (1967, 27).]

40 *bumbast,* **JOHNSON** (1755): "Fustian; big words, without meaning." **GROSART** (1872–73): "bombast." From French; cf. Thomas Wright's *Dictionary of Obsolete and*

Provincial English (1:39). **MILGATE** (1967): "mixed scraps of cotton or other material used to pad out clothing, particularly 'slops' or breeches" (152).

41 *Montebancks druggtong,* **BEWLEY** (1966): "jargon in which quacks advertised their medicine" (180). [So also, Milgate (1967, 152), who refers to Jonson, *Volpone* 2.5.2–5, Shawcross (1967, 27), Gransden (1970, 171), and Smith (1971, 487).]

41 *druggtong,* **LEGOUIS** (1942): possibly both "the mountebank's tongue will praise drugs" and "it acts as a drug on the hearers." This is a combination of words that *OED* does not record (189). [So also, Sullens (1964, 204).] **GRIGSON** (1980): "smooth talk" (24).

41 *termes of Law* **MILGATE** (1967): "a jargon of Law-French and Latin and formal English phrasing often satirized"; see the character Tangle in Middleton's *The Phoenix* (152). **SMITH** (1971): "legal jargon" (487).

42 *preparatiues,* **MILGATE** (1967): "medically, the means by which the system is prepared to endure a course of treatment; also used of drinks before a meal, appetizers" (152). **SHAWCROSS** (1967): "medicinals used to make him taut enough to endure this experience" (27).

44 *With his tong,...calld Complement,* **MELTON** (1906): the line illustrates Donne's tendency to use arsis-thesis variation of the same phrase ("his tongue") in the interior of the line (190).

44 *Complement,* **MILGATE** (1967): "accomplishment; that is, fine conversation and polished behaviour" (152). [So also, Gransden (1970, 171).] **SMITH** (1971): "the jargon of courtly address" (487). **GRIGSON** (1980): "in its two meanings of accomplishment and flattery" (24).

45–47 *he can win...Outflatter fauorites;* **NEWTON** (1974): "Like Donne, the Bore is a master of language" (438).

45 *win Widows;* **MILGATE** (1967): "This way of improving one's fortunes was common, and references to it are numerous and frank"; see Middleton, *The Widow* 1.2.1–4 and Chamberlain, *Letters,* 1:32–33, 476 (152). **SMITH** (1971): "presumably rich and gullible widows" (487).

45 *skores;* **JOHNSON** (1755): "Debt imputed." **SHAWCROSS** (1967): "accounts, monetary reckonings" (27). [So also, Smith (1971, 487).]

46 *Make Men speake treason;* **ELLRODT** (1960b): words that manifest Donne's early animosity towards the Jesuits (1.1:149). **WARNKE** (1967): the passage "suggests that the grotesque creature who is the object of this satire is a professional informer, one who tries to trick his victims into saying something suspiciously pro-Catholic, or otherwise treasonable" (117).

46 *cosen subtilst whores;* **MILGATE** (1967): "The bore's 'complement' enables him to cheat even these practiced cheaters"; see Greene's "coney-catching" pamphlets (152).

46 *cosen* **SMITH** (1971): "cheat" (487).

47 *Outflatter...out-ly either* **MELTON** (1906): the line illustrates Donne's tendency to use arsis-thesis variation of the same sound or syllable in the interior of the line (162). [See also note to *Sat1* 5.] **MILGATE** (1967) refers to *Sat2* 32–33 (152). **SHAWCROSS** (1972): a line with a feminine ending that is "catalectic" (263).

47 *Outflatter* **LEGOUIS** (1942): Donne's use of this word is cited by *OED* as the earliest source (184–85). [So also, Sullens (1964, 197).]

47 *out-ly* **LEGOUIS** (1942): Donne's use of this word is cited by *OED* as the earliest source (184–85). [So also, Sullens (1964, 197).]

48 *Iouius;...both together.* **SHAWCROSS** (1972): see note to l. 47.

48 *Iouius; or Surius;* **BEWLEY** (1966): "Catholic historians" (180). [So also, Grigson (1980, 24).] **HUGHES** (1968): "casual allusions to the champions on both sides of the Catholic-Protestant controversy" (51). **GRANSDEN** (1970): "Sixteenth-century Catholic historians whose accuracy was impugned by Protestants" (171). [So also, Carey (1990, 427).] **SMITH** (1971): "Counter-Reformation historians and hagiologists, whose rendering of the religious upheavals of the earlier sixteenth century outraged Protestants" (488). **KRUZHKOVA** (1994): continental historians with strongly pronounced anti-Reformation leanings (162).

48 *Iouius;* **GROSART** (1872–73): "Paulus Jovius, an Italian who wrote a History of his own times (1483, 1552)" (1:40). [So also, Chambers (1896, 2:243), Grierson (1912, 2:120), Shawcross (1967, 27), and Empson (1993, 160–61).] **NORTON** (1895): "The *Historia sui Temporis* of Jovius, or Paolo Giovio (1483–1552), the well-known Bishop of Nocera, was not distinguished for its veracity" (1:243). [Similarly, Milgate (1967, 152), who also refers to W. F. Staton, "Roger Ascham's Theory of History Writing," *SP* 56 (1959).] **ALDEN** (1899) thinks this a "distinct use of the *personal type-names*, the Latin form of which is the only departure from English local color" in the Satyres (88).

48 *Surius;* **NORTON** (1895): "Laurentius Surius (1522–78) of Lubeck, a Carthusian monk, compiled many untrustworthy books" (1:243). **CHAMBERS** (1896): "German ecclesiastical historian. His chief work was a *Vitae Sanctorum* (1570–). He was accused, it would appear unfairly, by Protestant writers, of inventing legends" (2:243). [So also, Milgate (1967, 152) and Shawcross (1967, 27), who adds that Surius was a Carthusian.] **ALDEN** (1899) thinks this a "distinct use of the *personal type-names*, the Latin form of which is the only departure from English local color" in the Satyres (88). **GRIERSON** (1912) notes the manuscript variant "Sleydan" for "Surius," a reference to the Protestant historian John Sleidan, whose work was controverted by Laurentius Surius; he conjectures that Donne's "first sneer was at the Protestant historian and that he thought it safer later to substitute the Catholic Surius" (2:120). [Similarly, Empson (1993, 160–61).] **MILGATE** (1967), building on Grierson (1912), says that Donne bracketed "a Protestant with a Roman Catholic historian to emphasize the versatility of the bore (and of historians) in lying." Revising the satire for Egerton, Donne "would have thought it more prudent to substitute the name of another Roman Catholic historian" (153).

49–57 *He names me,...I nam'd;* **CORTHELL** (1997): "The shift in power relations at being named by the courtier seems to be registered in the satirist's extremely cautious reply," balancing Beza against "some Jesuites" (50).

49–51 *God,...chuseth me?* PETER (1956): Donne's "flippant treatment of the old theme of retribution" shows "the yawning gap between his own attitudes and those of Complaint" (135).

49 *He names me,...whisper, God,* STEIN (1944c): as commonly do Elizabethan dramatists, Donne here admits an extra syllable, "an extra feminine ending in the foot preceding the cesura," an "extension of metrical liberty" that is "most frequent" in the Satyres (393). DOCHERTY (1986): "At the moment of nomination, when the poet is addressed, he whispers, or breathes out, the minimal word, 'go'" in "its extended form, as 'God'" (169). BAUMLIN (1988): not named by language, "the boor has language, and therefore all appearances and 'truths,' under his own control" (371).

50 *furious* SULLENS (1964): this meaning of the word is not recorded by *OED* (259).

50 *rod,* MILGATE (1967): "'this fellow,' who is, as it were, the scourge of God" (153). [So also, Smith (1971, 488).] SHAWCROSS (1967) refers to Lam. 3.1 and Rev. 19.15 (397–98).

51–87 *He sayth,...I haue more;* ELLRODT (1960b): Donne derives his technique of dialogue from Roman satire rather than the Elizabethan theater, himself indicating the answers and objections of a mute interlocutor (2:191).

51–65 *He sayth,...tower had stood.* ERSKINE-HILL (1972) compares Donne's "account of the Courtier-Talker's parade of linguistic accomplishment" to line 7 in Horace's Satire 1.9 and to Jonson's *Poetaster*, 3.1.23–28 (277).

51 *This fellow,...Sir,* RICHTER (1902) uses this line to illustrate the absence of an unstressed syllable in the interior of the line (400).

51 *sayth,* MILGATE (1967): "two syllables" (153).

53–54 *And I selely / Sayd, that* STEIN (1942): Donne's enjambment "places the cesura near the end of his line, where the start of a new rhythm, propelled by grammatical or rhetorical sense, will carry over" (683).

53 *the best Linguist?* SMITH (1971): "the speaker means the man who knows most languages; the poet willfully takes him to mean the most learned lexicographer or philologist" (488).

53 *selely* MILGATE (1967): "naively" (153). SHAWCROSS (1967): "weakly" (28). GRANSDEN (1970): "Foolishly" (171). SMITH (1971): "innocently" (488).

54 *Calepines Dictionary.* GROSART (1872–73): "A polyglot dictionary by Ambrogio Calepino, an Italian philologist, who died November 30th, 1511" (1:40). CHAMBERS (1896) adds that the "fullest edition (Basle, 1590) is in eleven tongues" (2:243). [Similarly, Grierson (1912, 2:120), Bewley (1966, 180), Milgate (1967,

153), Shawcross (1967, 28), Warnke (1967, 117), Gransden (1970, 171), Smith (1971, 488), Carey (1990, 427), and Kruzhkova (1994, 162).]

55–57 *Beza then,…I nam'd;* HUGHES (1968): Donne here "speaks as a man steeped in the theological literature of the Renaissance" (51).

55 *Beza* CHAMBERS (1896): "learned Calvinist theologian" who "translated the New Testament into Latin, and wrote an *Histoire Ecclesiastique des Eglises Reformées de France* (1580)" (2:243–44). [Similarly, Carey (1990, 427) and Kruzhkova (1994, 162).] BEWLEY (1966): "Theodore Beza (1519–1605), a French Calvinist theologian" who is "called a Jesuit here because of the casuistry of his writings" (180). [So also, Shawcross (1967, 28).] MILGATE (1967) adds that two of Beza's tracts "were at some time in Donne's library" and refers to Keynes, *Bibliography*, 210 (153). SMITH (1971) notes that Beza "wrote copiously in Latin and French" (488). GRIGSON (1980): "Protestant historian and scholar" (24). PRESCOTT (1997): "the Genevan leader, so learned in Latin, Greek, and Hebrew, had in 1588 published a congratulatory poem on the Armada in eight different languages" (46).

56–57 *two reuerend men / Of our two Academyes* SIMPSON (1944) points to the Dobell MS., "now in Harvard College Library (Nor. 4506)," that "offers an explanation" in a marginal note that "supplies the names 'Dr Reinolds and Dr Andrewes.'" Identifies the former as John Reynolds (1549–1607), who was "Reader in Greek at Corpus Christi College, Oxford, from 1572/3 to 1578," and who became "Dean of Lincoln in 1593, and President of Corpus Christi College in 1598." Believes the latter to be Lancelot Andrewes, "Master of Pembroke College, Cambridge, from 1589 to 1605," and later "Bishop of Chichester, Ely, and Winchester in turn" (224). [Similarly, Milgate (1967, 153), Shawcross (1967, 398), Gransden (1970, 171), Smith (1971, 488), and McCabe (2001, 82).]

56 *Some Iesuits,* GRIERSON (1912) notes the manuscript variant "Some other Jesuites" and thinks this "condensed and sudden stroke at Beza" would be characteristic of the Satyres, in which Donne's "veiled Catholic prejudices have to be constantly borne in mind" (2:121).

57 *two Academyes* GROSART (1872–73) queries, "the Universities (of Oxford and Cambridge)?" (1:40). [Similarly, Bewley (1966, 180), Shawcross (1967, 28), and Smith (1971, 488).] MILGATE (1967): the "main accent in 'Academies' falls on the third syllable"; see *Lit* 109 (154).

58–61 *Nay, your…By trauaile.* PRESCOTT (1997, 46): Donne recalls here from Rabelais "Panurge's first meeting with Pantagruel and the many tongues in which he overflows with words and need," and thus "the comedy lies partly in the theologically suspect assumption that Apostolic glossolalia (Acts 2) is obtainable by travel, although the apostles certainly got around, and in his apparent belief that Panurge is real enough to emulate. But nobody can surpass Panurge as a linguist, not so long as he speaks such good Utopian, Lanternish, and Antipodean, tongues that even Satan would be hard-pressed to learn by travel or travail."

58–59 *your Apostles…pretty Linguists;* ERSKINE-HILL (1972): the passage "invites sardonic ridicule, but a tremendous undercurrent of indignation is felt at the same time" (285). **BAUMLIN** (1988): there is here a pun on the "Holy Spirit's 'gift of tongues' to the Apostles" (373). **KRUZHKOVA** (1994): see Acts 2.4 ("And they were all filled with the Holy Ghost, and began to speak with other tongues, as the Spirit gave them utterance") (162).

58 *He stopd me;' and sayd;* **STEIN** (1944c): elisions of extra syllables formed by "words ending in *e, ee, y* before words beginning with a vowel" are among Donne's devices for varying the metrical line (389).

58 *Apostles* **MILGATE** (1967): "A reference to the Gift of Tongues at Pentecost, Acts ii. 4, 6 ('every man heard them speak in his own language')" (154).

59 *Linguists;* **BEWLEY** (1966): "referring to the gift of tongues conferred on the Apostles at Pentecost" (181). [So also, Milgate (1967, 154), who cites Acts 2.4, 6, Shawcross (1967, 28), and Smith (1971, 488).]

59 *Panurge* **GROSART** (1872–73): "of Rabelais' immortality" (1:40). [So also, Chambers (1896, 2:244), who identifies Rabelais's *History of Gargantua and Pantagruel*, Warnke (1967, 118), and Carey (1990, 427).] **GRIERSON** (1912) specifies the first encounter of Pantagruel and the multilingual Panurge (*Gargantua et Pantagruel* 2.9) (2:121). [So also, Kruzhkova (1994, 162).] **BEWLEY** (1966) stresses Panurge's capacity to speak "in many languages" (181). [So also, Milgate (1967, 154) and Smith (1971, 488).] **SHAWCROSS** (1967): "the roguish, cowardly, and libertine favorite of Pantagruel" (28). **GRANSDEN** (1970): "Comic character in Rabelais noted for his resourcefulness" (171).

60 *pas* **MILGATE** (1967): "surpass" (154).

61–65 *Then as yf...tower had stood.* **BAUMLIN** (1988): the satirist "here feigns agreement with and wryly praises the boor's vaunted skill in language" (373).

61–62 *as yf he would...he praysd it,* **GROSART** (1872–73) indentifies this as "a proverbial saying" and points to Shakespeare's Sonnet 21 (1:40). **MILGATE** (1967) also notes the "[p]roverbial" character and cites Morris Tilley, *A Dictionary of the Proverbs in England in the Sixteenth and Seventeenth Century* (1950), p. 546; and Horace, *Epistles* 2.2.11 (154).

61 *By trauaile.* **MILGATE** (1967): "by travel and by toil" (154). **SHAWCROSS** (1967): "punning on 'travel' and 'work'" (28).

61 *sold* **GROSART** (1872–73): cf. Shakespeare *Son.* 21 and *Tro.* 4.1 (1:40).

62 *His tong...wonders told* **SHAWCROSS** (1972) (probably reading "words told"): the line seems "defective," but Donne's "alteration of meter" has "definite and appropriate effect" (262).

63–65 *I was fayne...tower had stood.* **ERSKINE-HILL** (1972): "magnificent repartee"; the "comic extravagance of this conception also sizes up the Courtier effectively in Biblical terms" as not "altogether a creature to be dismissed with a laugh" (285). **BAUMLIN** (1988): the juxtaposing of the court with the Tower of Babel here "becomes an almost typological identification," linking "two monuments of human pride" (374).

63 *fayne* **FERRY** (1997) cites this line as one of four instances in which Donne uses this word as an adjective "followed immediately by an infinitive" (225).

63 *Sir,* **WIGGINS** (2000): this usage is "sarcastic" (54).

64 *Time inough…Interpreter* **MORRIS** (1953) cites this line as an example of Donne's counterpointing of the iambic pentameter line by means of a "double reversal" of the metrical feet (45).

64 *inough* **MELTON** (1906): a word Donne would not repeat in arsis-thesis variation, though he did use it, as here, with the first syllable in arsis (173).

65 *Babels bricklayers,* **SMITH** (1971): "God confounded the language of the builders of the city and tower of Babel so that they could not understand one another and abandoned the enterprise" (488).

65 *bricklayers,* **JOHNSON** (1755): "A man whose trade is to build with bricks; a brick mason."

65 *tower* **MILGATE** (1967): "of Babel"; see l. 38 (154).

66–68 *He adds;…Lonenes is;* **ERSKINE-HILL** (1972): Donne has "almost reversed the positions" of his interlocutors, compared to those of the ninth satire in Horace's first book of satires, where Horace's "moral and social situation is guaranteed," whereas in *Sat4*, the "Talker is the one to be, or at least pretend to be, thoroughly conversant with the centre of power, the court, while Donne is the conscious outsider" (279–80). [Similarly, Baumlin (1988, 374).] **FULTON** (2001): "there is good in court life, and you just have to know where to find it"; a "second, philosophical sense" of the lines is that "one can know the good *and* be a part of court" (86).

67–72 *not alone…teach me vertu.* **FULTON** (2001): "The passage expresses a distrust of mimetic representation in art and poetry" (86).

67–68 *not alone / My Lonenes is;* **RUDD** (1963): the passage "alludes" to "a saying of Scipio's recorded by Cicero on the authority of Cato" in *De Officiis* 3.1 [so also, Smith (1971, 489)] and *De Republica* 1.17.27 (208). [So also, Milgate (1967, 154), who in addition to citing both sources also says that this is the "wholesome solitarinesse" of l. 155.] **GUSS** (1966) argues that these lines show Donne's "life to be pure, secluded, and dedicated" (203n3). **SHAWCROSS** (1967): "His aloneness is not unique; it is rigorously followed by others" (28). **ERSKINE-HILL** (1972): the passage alludes to "Cicero on the retirement of Scipio Africanus" (288). **CAREY** (1990): "An allusion to Cato's saying, recorded by Cicero, that he was 'never less alone than when alone'" (427).

67 *leaue Lonenes.* **MILGATE** (1967): "'stop keeping to yourself.' Since the satirist goes on to say that this alone-ness is not loneliness, I attribute the reading of 1633 and manuscripts with the same version to an easily made error" (154).

67 *Lonenes.* JOHNSON (1755): "Solitude; dislike of company." GROSART (1872–73): "loneliness" (1:40).

68 *Spartanes fashione* GROSART (1872–73): "Lycurgus made prohibitory laws against commerce, and forbad traveling, that the Spartan polity and simplicity might continue unaltered" (1:40). BEWLEY (1966): "the Spartans taught virtue by pointing to the effect of its opposite" (181). MILGATE (1967): "According to Plutarch (*Lycurgus*, 28.4) the Spartans would make helots drunk and bring them into their messes to disgust the young men with drunkenness" (154). [So also, Smith (1971, 489), Carey (1990, 427), and Kruzhkova (1994, 162).]

69–70 *To teach…made few chast.* PETER (1956): Donne conveys no "flattering illusions" that satire "might influence a reader" to change his way of life (133). SHAWCROSS (1967): "what is learned from observing vice does not maintain moral fiber" (28). FULTON (2001): "Spartan paintings and the other forms of representation here resemble the discursive mode of satire: of showing the bad, and castigating vice through a churlish depiction of it" (86).

69 *last* MILGATE (1967) (reading "tast"): "keep its relish"; i.e., "this method of teaching is no longer relished, or acceptable" and so is ineffective (154). [So also, Carey (1990, 427).] FULTON (2001) thinks that the variant "tast" makes less sense than "last" in the 1633 edition (86).

70–72 *Aretines Pictures…teach me vertu.* BELLETTE (1975): the passage "points to the futility of seeking to improve through the mere depicting of vice" (138). EL-GABALAWY (1976): the allusion "should be taken with a grain of salt" from the person who wrote *ElBed* and who "obviously had a strong stomach for erotic literature" (96). BLISSETT (2000) cites these lines as evidence of Donne's negative attitude toward the court (113).

70 *Aretines Pictures* GROSART (1872–73): "Aretine's verses would have been more correct. The designs were after paintings by Giulio Romano, for which he was exiled from Rome and lost the Pope's favour. Pietro Aretino, an Italian satirist, a man as profligate in life and writings as those he satirized, wrote verses to accompany the designs" (1:40). CHAMBERS (1896): "sixteen obscene designs by Giulio Romano, engraved by Raimondi, for which Aretino wrote sixteen *Sonnetti lussuriosi*" (2:244). [So also, Grierson (1912, 2:122), Rugoff (1939, 57), Milgate (1967, 154–55), Smith (1971, 489), Carey (1990, 427), Kruzhkova (1994, 162), and Semler (1998, 47).] ELLRODT (1960b): among the Italian poets Donne had read (including Dante, Petrarch, and Ariosto), Aretino may have made the liveliest impression on his imagination, although here (as in a letter to Henry Wotton [Simpson, *Prose Works*, 316–17]) he disapproves of the "pictures" as immoral, however relished by dissolute English juveniles (2:214). SHAWCROSS (1967): Aretino's "sonnets satirized the lascivious paintings of Giulio Romano" (28). GRANSDEN (1970): "notorious for his outspokenness and much admired by Elizabethan satirists," Aretino wrote "erotic poems" that were "illustrated by Giulio Romano, but the illustrations do not survive" (171). EDWARDS (1972) notes that Donne's allusion to "'Aretino's postures'" antedates that in Ben Jonson's *Volpone* (633).

71–72 *be few…teach me vertu.* **STEIN** (1942): an example of Donne's "chief prosodic innovation," the frequent use of "stress-shift in the fifth foot," in which a feminine rhyme "is invariably matched with a masculine" (681).

72 *Better pictures…teach me vertu.* **STEIN** (1944c): "stress-shift" after a pause is one of Donne's chief devices for varying the metrical line (384); this is one of many "more energetic" examples, in which "by attraction," stress-shifts "carry through to the end of the line" (385).

73–80 *He like…is kings Street.* **WOOLF** (1932): these lines demonstrate Donne's desire to record actual speech (23–24). **ELLRODT** (1960b): Donne's sarcastic disdain, an irony not found in Spenser's complaint but common among Donne's generation, spares royalty not at all (2:18). **RUDD** (1963): this "elaborate play on 'Kings'" may have been prompted by Horace's puns on the name "*Rex*" (*Satires* 1.7) (208).

73–74 *He like…talke of Kings.* **MELTON** (1906): from such "representative" examples of his verse, "unsurpassable for beauty and delicacy," it would be "more difficult to prove that Donne was not *all* ear, than that he had *no* ear" (126–27). **STEIN** (1951): the sound in these lines "is less imitative than suggestive and interpretive" (258). **HOLLANDER** (1961): "The fawning sycophant under attack answers the Poet's doubts as to the heuristic value of supposed courtly values" (301). **RUDD** (1963) sees an echo of Horace's character Tigellius, who "would talk grandiloquently of 'reges atque tetrarchas'" (*Satires* 1.3.12) (208). **POWERS** (1971) notes an element of farce in this description of the courtier (115).

73–74 *Oh Sir,…At Westminster* **SHAWCROSS** (1972): see note to lines 13–14.

73 *to'a high stretchd Lute String* **RUDD** (1963): a reminiscence of the chanting of Tigellius Horace's *Satires* 1.3.1–8 (208).

74–80 *talke of Kings….is kings Street.* **EMPSON** (1972): "*king* is incessantly repeated, as if he dislikes to admit that he is being ruled by a queen" (144). **DOCHERTY** (1986): "if there is a real 'king' or kin of kings in the poem," it is "the poet himself" (169).

74 *Westminster* **MELTON** (1906): the word exemplifies Donne's use of secondary accent in proper names (86 and 90).

75–80 *the Man…is kings Street.* **BROSS** (1966): Donne's "irony lies in the fact that both things compared are about the same to him but quite different to the courtier. He deflates the pompous courtier by noting that, overlooking the courtier's sham, courtier and guide both talk of kings. Donne's tirade repeating 'kings! kings! kings!' gives the reader great fun in seeing the courtier justly smothered in an avalanche of his favorite word" (148–49). **CRUTTWELL** (1977) notes the focus on London here, asserting that "every reference in these lines demands an erudite footnote," and adding that even "contemporary readers" must have needed "a remarkably alert and inquisitive knowledgeableness about local and contemporary events" (27).

75 *the Man…Abbey tombes* **CHAMBERS** (1896) quotes Sir John Davies' *Epigram 30, On Dacus:* "He first taught him that keeps the monuments / At Westminster his

formal tale to say" (2:244). [So also, Grierson (1912, 2:122).] **MILGATE** (1967): "He was apparently something of a 'character' in London at the time" (155).

77–80 *Of all…is kings Street.* **WARTON** (1797) calls this "a vile conceit" (4:287).

78–83 *From king,…frenchmen neat?* **MELTON** (1906): the passage illustrates Donne's tendency to use arsis-thesis variation of the same sound or syllable in the interior of the line (152–53).

78–80 *From king,…is kings Street.* **MCFARLAND** (1977): Donne's "technique" here "is 'overkill,' to exaggerate the topic introduced by the noisome companion. But the gossip misses the similarity between himself and the caretaker whom he describes, in terms ironically appropriate to himself" in l. 81 (402). **BLISSETT** (2000): "the clangorous word 'King' tolls as often as 'thing,' or the unnerving 'strange'" throughout the poem (113).

78 *walke,* **GROSART** (1872–73): "can walk from, &c." (1:40).

79 *Your eares…your eyes meet* **STEIN** (1944c): "stress-shift" after a pause is one of Donne's chief devices for varying the metrical line (384).

80 *kings Street.* **NORTON** (1895): "King Street originally ran from Charing Cross to the King's palace at Westminster" (1:243). [So also, Grierson (1912, 2:122), Hayward (1950, 111), Milgate (1967, 155), and Shawcross (1967, 29).] **GRIERSON** (1912): "It was for long the only way to Westminster from the north" (2:122). **MILGATE** (1967) refers to Stow, *Survey of London,* 2:102, 374 (155). [So also, Smith (1971, 489).]

81–87 *He smackd,…I haue more;* **BAUMLIN** (1988): "*astiesmus,* a typically Horatian figure." The satirist "willfully misunderstands the boor's words and equivocates upon them, taking 'your' in a personal rather than general sense" (375).

81 *smackd,* **GROSART** (1872–73) admits to being unaware of "a similar use of this word," which "seems to mean, made some interjectional sound of contempt; such is the original of chut, tut, tush, etc." (1:40). **SULLENS** (1964): Donne's use of the word with this meaning is earlier than the earliest source cited by *OED* (234). **MILGATE** (1967): "his lips" (155). **SHAWCROSS** (1967): "made a sharp, loud noise with his mouth" (29). **SMITH** (1971): "clapped his hands" (489).

81 *Mechanique,* **LEGOUIS** (1942): a meaning of this word that Donne may have "either originated or at least introduced into the literary language" (186). [So also, Sullens (1964, 224).] **MILGATE** (1967): "vulgar, low (like one 'engaging in a manual occupation')" (155). [So also, Shawcross (1967, 29), Smith (1971, 489), and Grigson (1980, 25).]

83–87 *Are not your…I haue more;* **GROSART** (1872–73) first divides these "uncertain" lines of dialogue into four speeches: (1) by the satirist's interlocutor, who begins, "Are not your…"; (2) by the satirist, who answers, "Mine? as you see…"; (3) by the interlocutor, who continues, "I,' of this minde…"; and (4) by the satirist, who answers, "Not so Sir…" (1:40). Later proposes to swap these assignments, so that (1) the satirist begins, "Are not your…"; (2) the interlocutor answers, "Mine? as you see…";

(3) the satirist continues, "I,' of this minde…"; and (4) the interlocutor answers, "Not so Sir…" (1:40–41). **CHAMBERS** (1896), simply using quotation marks, divides the passage into three speeches (1) by the interlocutor, "Are not your…"; (2) by the satirist, "Certes, they are…"; (3) by the interlocutor, "Not so, Sir…" (2:193). **GRIERSON** (1912) asserts, "the joke turns on Donne's pretending to misunderstand the bore's colloquial, but rather affected, indefinite use of 'your,'" applying it to himself. Divides the dialogue into four speeches: (1) the interlocutor begins, "Are not your…"; (2) the satirist answers, "Mine? as you see…"; (3) the interlocutor ("ignoring this impertinence") continues, "Certes, they are…"; and (4) the satirist answers, "Not so Sir…" (2:122). [So also, Bewley (1966, 181) and Milgate (1967, 17).] **SMITH** (1971): "the poet again wilfully misunderstands, taking as possessive the fashionable idiom 'your' which at most indicates a typical case" (489). **JENSEN** (1972): there is "sheer pleasure" in the speaker's retorts, which also "bring the reader closer" to the speaker's "frustration and horror," a recognition that "to such wit the bore remains oblivious" (406).

83–86 *Are not your…this Grogerame.* **ELLRODT** (1960b): without descending to invective, these lines are distinctly xenophobic (2:82).

83 *Are not your…as you see* **STEIN** (1944c): "stress-shift" before a pause is one of Donne's chief devices for varying the metrical line (379). **MILGATE** (1967): "The bore uses the indefinite 'your' (meaning roughly, 'which is within your knowledge'); the satirist pretends to misunderstand, and refers it to himself ('Mine')" (155).

83 *neat?* **GROSART** (1872–73): "nice, exact"; also "clean, spotless" (1:40). [So also, Milgate (1967, 155).]

83 *Myne?* **GRIERSON** (1912): "That Donne had a French servant appears from one of his letters: 'therefore I onely send you this Letter…and my promise to distribute your other Letters, according to your addresses, as fast as my Monsieur can doe it'" (*Letters* 201) (2:122). [So also, Bewley (1966, 181), Milgate (1967, 155), and Smith (1971, 489).]

84–85 *I haue but…this mind ame* **STEIN** (1944b): the elisions in these lines "may prevent the reader from recognizing the scansion immediately" (394).

84 *one frenchman;* **SHAWCROSS** (1967): "apparently a French servant" (29).

84 *he followes mee.* **CAREY** (1990): "deliberately misunderstanding the courtier's affected use of 'your' as a kind of indefinite article, points to his French servant" (427).

85 *Certes,* **SHAWCROSS** (1967): "certainly" (29).

86 *Grogerame.* **JOHNSON** (1755): "Stuff woven with large woof and rough pile." **GROSART** (1872–73): "Fr. gros-grain = silk of a large or coarse thread" (1:41). **SULLENS** (1964): Donne's use of the word with this meaning is earlier than the earliest source cited by *OED* (218). **BEWLEY** (1966): "grogram, a cloth of silk, wool, and mohair" (181). [So also, Shawcross (1967, 29).] **MILGATE** (1967) quotes Linthicum, pp. 77–78: "the name of a taffeta weave with 'gros grains' or cords in the warp," the cloth being of silk, worsted, or hair. The bore is "referring to French grogaram, which was of silk" (155). [So also, Gransden (1970, 171), Smith (1971, 489),

and Carey (1990, 427).] GRIGSON (1980): "coarse unfashionable fabric of gummed mohair and wool" (25).

87–88 *vnder this...would not fly.* GROSART (1872–73): "under this height to which I soared to swoop, he my quarry would not rise, but kept himself enmewed, or in court" (1:41). MILGATE (1967): "The satirist's quarry will not fly under the pitch, i.e. the bore will not place himself in a position to be swooped upon with further ridicule" (155). GRANSDEN (1970): "the satirist is the hawk but his prey eludes him" (171). SMITH (1971): "he would not pitch his speech lower than this highflown style" (489).

87 *I haue more;* MILGATE (1967): "The bore has said, 'Grogaram is the only fabric one can really wear.' The satirist again pretends to misunderstand, and replies, 'You are wrong in thinking one grogaram suit is all I have to wear'" (155). [Similarly, Smith (1971, 489).]

87 *pitche* GROSART (1872–73): "the height to which a hawk soars" (1:41). [So also, Bewley (1966, 181), Milgate (1967, 155), Shawcross (1967, 29), and Gransden (1970, 171).]

88 *chafd* GROSART (1872–73) (reading "chaff'd"): i.e., "chaf'd," since "there is no example of the use of 'chaff'd' in those days in our present slang sense" (1:41). MILGATE (1967): "teased, provoked. But the satirist finds that this 'crossing' of his companion is more irritating to himself" (155).

91–108 *To fitt my...is not painted.* ELLRODT (1960b): the traveler who values only what is strange was for the Renaissance a new object of satire; the wittiest of many tireless reprises and retouchings is this of *Sat4* (2:149).

91 *Crossing* SMITH (1971): "running counter to his meaning, crossing him" (489). DOCHERTY (1986): "the beggar himself becomes a kind of cross, which the poet has, purgatorially, to bear" (170)

91 *sullennesse* JOHNSON (1755): "Gloominess; moroseness; sluggish anger; malignity; intractability." RUDD (1963): "an echo of Horace's sullen ass—*iniquae mentis asellus*"—in *Satires* 1.9.20 (208). [So also, Erskine-Hill (1972, 276).]

92 *He to an other* STEIN (1944c): elisions of extra syllables formed by words with a "W-sound before a vowel" are among Donne's devices for varying the metrical line (389–90).

93 *I tell him, of new playes.* WOOLF (1932): this line refers to Donne's youthful attendance at the theater (23).

94–95 *as a Still...twixt each dropp,* ELLRODT (1960b): a typically simple allusion to apparatus for distillation in poems of the 1590s, in contrast to more complex alchemical notions appearing in later, religious poems (2:386).

94 *He takes my hand,* RUDD (1963): just as "the poet is seized by the hand" in *Satires* 1.9.4 (208). [So also, Erskine-Hill (1972, 276).]

94 *Still* SHAWCROSS (1967): "a device for distilling liquids by drops" (29). [So also, Smith (1971, 489).]

95 *Sembriefe* JOHNSON (1755) reads as "semibref" and defines as "a note in music relating to time, and is the last in augmentation. It is commonly called the master-note, or measure-note, or time-note, as being of a certain determinate measure or length of time by itself; and all the other notes of augmentation and dimution are adjusted to its value." SULLENS (1964): Donne's use of the word with this meaning is earlier than the earliest source cited by *OED* (232). BEWLEY (1966): "a half-note" (182). MILGATE (1967): pause "for the duration of a semibreve, or 'whole note' in music" (156). [So also, Warnke (1967, 119).] SHAWCROSS (1967): "an interval of time (half a breve) equal to a musical measure" (29).

97–102 *More then...Offices reuersion.* MCFARLAND (1977): in this passage, "the anadiplosis in the second line forces itself upon the reader because, instead of moving the line to an end-stop and then beginning the text line with 'He knowes,' which would be more in keeping with the advice of textbook rhetoric, Donne breaks the line near the end, starts a new clause, and then quickly enjambs. The effect is to draw an extra degree of attention to the repeated element and thus to stress the message that the antagonist is a know-it-all. Subsequently, 'he knowes' is reiterated and acts as anaphora, though somewhat more loosely than examples in most rhetorical manuals suggest." Further, in the fifth line of this passage, Donne "uses polyptoton effectively. Love and death join around the objective case 'whom' which is set off not only from 'who by poyson' but also from 'who loves,' so that the line does not read according to expectation; that is, 'who loves whom.' The inference is that the love is not mutual. The lover is one item and the beloved is another, and the twain shall not unite across the barrier of punctuation" (402).

97–100 *More then...gather of that.* ERSKINE-HILL (1972): in giving "the conversation of his Talker a marked political aspect," Donne may be "reaching behind Horace to the two Characters of Talkers in Theophrastus"; see *The Characters of Theophrastus* (1909), pp. 164–65, and Donne's "True Character of a Dunce" (280).

97 *Holinsheds,...Stowes* GROSART (1872–73): Raphael Holinshed, Edward Hall, and John Stowe (1:41). GRIERSON (1912), quoting Nashe's *Pierce Penniless*, notes how "these old chroniclers" were renowned for mingling "trifling events" with their historical accounts (2:122). [So also, Smith (1971, 489) and Carey (1990, 427).] SHAWCROSS (1967): "authors of long chronicles of England, that frequently report unhistorical anecdotes" (29). WARNKE (1967): "sixteenth-century English chroniclers" (119). [So also, Gransden (1970, 171).]

98–100 *Of triuial...gather of that.* ELLRODT (1960b): Donne's sarcastic disdain, an irony not found in Spenser's complaint but common among Donne's generation, spares royalty not at all (2:18). MILGATE (1967) refers to Nashe, *Works*, 1:194 (156). ERSKINE-HILL (1972): these things, "in the atmosphere of this poem," are "not altogether 'triviall houshold trash'" (285). CORTHELL (1997): "when presented with the evidence of vice at Court, he impugns the honesty of the messenger" (50).

98 *trashe* JOHNSON (1755): "Any thing worthless; dross; dregs."

100 A *Subtile Statesman* ELLRODT (1960b): the phrase describes Donne's concern with politics and statecraft as a secretary or prospective secretary to Lord Keeper Egerton (2:33). MILGATE (1967) refers to Donne's letter in Gosse, *Life and Letters* 2:46 (156).

101–07 *He knowes…some Courtier;* ERSKINE-HILL (1972): "so clearly a satire on court corruption that we are not surprised to notice the tones of Donne eventually taking over"; his "outrageous *enjambement* expresses the very acme of incredulous contempt—but whether for court gossip, or court abuse, it is hard to say." In these lines, it might seem merely that Donne "recklessly takes over the Courtier's conversation as a vehicle for his satire on the court," but the subjects mentioned "point unmistakably ahead to the passage in which, 'like a privileg'd spie,' he libels the whole government, and terrifies his listener at the implications of the situation" (285).

101 *He knowes…who by poyson* STEIN (1944c): the passage illustrates omission of a syllable "after the cesura," one of Donne's "devices for metrical modulation" (377); this is one of many "more energetic" examples, in which "by attraction," stress-shifts "carry through to the end of the line" (385). MILGATE (1967) quotes Juvenal's sixth (401–402) and tenth (220–24) satires, as well as Martial, *Epigrams* 3.63.3–12 (156). SHAWCROSS (1972): a line with a feminine ending that is "accented for rhyme although normally unstressed" (263).

102 *reuersion.* LEGOUIS (1942): a meaning of this word that Donne may have "either originated or at least introduced into the literary language" (185). [So also, Sullens (1964, 230).] MILGATE (1967): "the right of succession, usually on the death of the original grantee, to an office or estate. Here it is the date of succession that is 'hastened'" (156). [So also, Smith (1971, 490).]

103–08 *He knows…is not painted.* NEWTON (1974): "like Donne, the Bore can be a satirist" (438).

103–07 *He knows…some Courtier;* REID (2000): this passages exhibits the "true satirical poet's appetite for rancid detail" (40).

103–05 *and now doth…to transport.* FAUSSET (1924): these lines demonstrate Donne's "impertinent nonconformity" to current poetic conventions (51). MORRIS (1953) cites this passage as an example of Donne using "split rhyme as a means of closer over-reaving while keeping the rhyme intact" (49–50). RUDD (1963): based on ll. 31–32 of Juvenal's third satire (208). KRUZHKOVA (1994): the practice of nobles seeking to acquire every possible license, payoff, and monopoly was prolific in Queen Elizabeth's court and thus became the desired purpose of noblemen who dreamed of riches (163).

103 *sold his Land,* MILGATE (1967) refers to ll. 180–81 below and to *Sat2* 103–04 (156).

104–05 *egg- / shells* SHAWCROSS (1972): see note to ll. 13–14.

104 *A Licence,…or egg-* SHAWCROSS (1972): see note to l. 62.

104 *Licence,* MILGATE (1967): "The granting of licences, patents, and monopolies to those trading in various kinds of merchandise was common practice" and "a lucrative source of income to the courtiers responsible for granting such privileges (some of whom received 'toll,' l. 107, from the successful applicant)" (156). [So also, Smith (1971, 490) and Carey (1990, 427).]

104 *Iron,* SHAWCROSS (1972): "may be two syllables," illustrating that Donne's "alteration of meter" has "definite and appropriate effect" (262–63).

105 *shells to transport.…shall not play* STEIN (1944c): "stress-shift" after the caesura is one of Donne's chief devices for varying the metrical line (384).

105 *transport.* LEGOUIS (1942): this is a meaning of the word that *OED* does not record (189). MILGATE (1967): "both 'import' (as in l. 170 below) and 'export'" (156). [So also, Smith (1971, 490).]

106–07 *but they pay / Toll to some Courtier;* JACK (1951) considers the violent enjambment "apparently motiveless" (1012).

106 *blowpoynt, or spancounter,* WARNKE (1967): "children's games" (119). CAREY (1990): "Games rather like marbles, played with counters and the 'points' (tags) that fastened hose to doublet" (428).

106 *blowpoynt,* JOHNSON (1755): "A child's play." GROSART (1872–83) refers to the supposition that this is "the same as dust-point" and cites Weber, who "vaguely surmises that it has to do with blowing dust out of a hole," and Nares, who "as vaguely" says "it resembles push-pin." Concludes that nothing definite can be said except that the game "was a rustic or schoolboys' or pages' gambling game" (1:41). [Similarly, Chambers (1896, 2:244).] BEWLEY (1966): "a game in which arrows were blown through a tube at a target" (182). [So also, Shawcross (1967, 30).] MILGATE (1967) notes that "the 'points' here (as in 'pick-point' and 'venter-point') were the tags or laces by which hose was fastened to the doublet." Refers to J. B. Leishman, *The Three Parnassus Plays* (1949), p. 289 (157). [Similarly, Smith (1971, 490).]

106 *spancounter,* JOHNSON (1755): "A play at which money is thrown within a span or mark." GROSART (1872–73) quotes J. Strutt, *Sports and Pastimes of the People of England* (1801), describing this game as played by throwing a counter which the opponent wins "if he can throw another so as to hit it or lie within a span of it"; however, Grosart rather thinks it a game played by boys who, "directly or by rebound, endeavour to play their button or marble into a hole" (1:41). [Similarly, Chambers (1896, 2: 244) and Milgate (1967, 156).] BEWLEY (1966): "a game whose object was to throw counters so near to each other that the distance could be spanned by the hand" (182). [So also, Shawcross (1967, 29–30).] SMITH (1971): "a variant of marbles" (490).

107 *Toll to some…then all vs* STEIN (1944c): as commonly do Elizabethan dramatists, Donne here admits an extra syllable, "an extra feminine ending in the foot preceding the cesura," an "extension of metrical liberty" that is "most frequent" in the Satyres (394).

108 *which Lady is not painted.* **SHAWCROSS** (1967): "suggesting that the lady's red complexion comes from disease rather than cosmetics" (30).

109–17 *I belch,…talke; In vayne;* **POWERS** (1971) describes the satirist's response to the courtier here as farcical (115–16).

109–10 *spitt,…yett* **SHAWCROSS** (1972): see note to ll. 13–14.

109 *home meats* **LEGOUIS** (1942): a combination of words that *OED* does not record (190–91). [So also, Sullens (1964, 204).] **MILGATE** (1967) refers to *OED*, "home," B.3: "trivial gossip 'relating to one's country or nation'" (157). **SHAWCROSS** (1967): "homely titbits" (30). **SMITH** (1971): "domestic gossip" (490).

109 *belch,* **MILGATE** (1967): "The metaphor of not being able to 'stomach' the bore's talk is carried on from l. 38" (157).

111 *He thrusts…if he had vndertooke* **STEIN** (1944c): elisions of extra syllables formed by "light vowels in unstressed places" are among Donne's devices for varying the metrical line (389).

112 *To say…without booke* **STEIN** (1944c): "stress-shift" after a pause is one of Donne's chief devices for varying the metrical line (384).

112 *Gallobelgicus* **GROSART** (1872–73): *Mercurius Gallo-Belgicus,* "an annual and then bi-annual register of news, first published at Cologne in 1598;" cf. *Merc* (1:41). [So also, Chambers (1896, 2:244), Bewley (1966, 182), Warnke (1967, 119), Gransden (1970, 171), Smith (1971, 490), Grigson (1980, 25), and Carey (1990, 427).] **ALDEN** (1899) corrects Grosart's dating, noting that *Mercurius Gallo-Belgicus* was published as early as 1588 (78). Adds in a note that "the first editor, Michael von Isselt, died in 1597; and his successor took charge of the volume for 1598, a fact which perhaps may have given rise to the error" (78–79n2). **MILGATE** (1967) comments that Michael von Isselt was the publisher and that the *Mercurius* "was very popular," although its "information (often mere gossip) was not always reliable, and its Latin was far from elegant" [similarly, Shawcross (1967, 30)] and points to Jonson, *Poetaster,* 5.3.553 (157). **SHAWCROSS** (1972) dates the poem after 1594 because the *Mercurius* "began to be published in that year" (251).

113–14 *since / The Spanyards came,* **GROSART** (1872–73): probably "the year of the Armada (1588)" (1:41). [So also, Chambers (1896, 2:244), Bewley (1966, 182), Gransden (1970, 171), and Smith (1971, 490).] **NORTON** (1895) thinks that this may refer to Spain's invasion of France in 1594, "after Henry IV. had declared war with Philip II." Notes that Spain "took Amiens in March, 1595, and this may possibly indicate the date of this satire as the summer of that year, for Amiens was retaken by the French in September" (1:244). **MILGATE** (1967) adds that "the bore's information begins at the same time as the *Mercurius* (1588) and it seems as if he had learnt that periodical off by heart ('without booke')" (157).

113 *Speakes of all States* **ELLRODT** (1960b): the passage refers to Donne's concern with politics and statecraft as a secretary or prospective secretary to Lord Keeper Egerton (2:33).

114 *The Spanyards...losse of Amyens.* **STEIN** (1944c): in this line, an extra syllable gives "increased speed and flexibility to the rhythm" (396). **CAREY** (1990): "From Armada year, 1588, to March 1597 when the Spaniards took Amiens" (428).

114 *losse of Amyens.* **GROSART** (1872–73): the Spanish "surprised Amiens 11th March 1597." Since the recovery of Amiens by the French in September 1597 is not mentioned in the poem, "it is not improbable that the Satire was written between those dates, or at all events in that year" (1:41). [So also, Chambers (1896, 2:244), Grierson (1912, 2:104), Grierson (1929, xxix), Hayward (1930, 120), Smith (1971, 490), and Shawcross (1972, 251).]

115–16 *Like a bigg...to trauayle* **MILGATE** (1967): "Like a pregnant woman shocked into labour by the sight of food of a kind that she (in that condition) hates" (157). **SHAWCROSS** (1967): "Even the sight of food nauseates a pregnant woman ready to give birth, and she is repelled when her husband approaches her for intercourse; the point is the speaker must accept the inevitable" (30).

115 *a bigg Wife* **RUGOFF** (1939) notes that Donne is not awed by the process of birth, nor does he speculate much on it, but pregancy, figured vividly here, comes close to being an exception (182–83). **SMITH** (1971): "a pregnant woman" (490).

115 *lothed meat* **BAUMLIN** (1988): "both food and penis to the already burdened woman" (376).

116 *I sigh and sweat* **RUDD** (1963): as Donne sweats, so does Horace in his *Satires* 1.9.10–11 (208). [So also, Erskine-Hill (1972, 276).]

117 *Maccaron* **GROSART** (1872–73) cites Nares and Todd, stating that "persons of a certain age remember the word *maccaroni*" as "a first-rate coxcomb, or puppy, or the now temporary appellation 'dandy'"; refers to "R. B.'s [query, Richard Brome's?] Elegy on Donne," where the word is used in "the sense of an affected busy-body"; and cites John Florio (a "Maccarone, a gull, a lubby [looby], a loggar-head that can doe nothing but eat Maccaroni") and Vaugon ("a man 'sciminuto [foolish or stupid] e di poco intelletto"). Also states that the word occurs in the Preface to *Metem* (1:42). **NORTON** (1895): "In Torriano's Italian dictionary, 1698, 'macaroni' is defined 'by met., a looby, one that can do nothing but loll and eat'; hence, a fopling, a conceited pretender" (1:244). **CHAMBERS** (1896): "a fop, and especially one whose manners and speech were marked by foreign influences. In the same way, 'macaronic' verse is a medley of various languages"; see *Macaron*, which derives from either "the Italian food *macaroni*, as we might speak of a frog-eater, or from *maccarone* or *maccherone*, a fool" (2:240–41, 244). **GRIERSON** (1912): "the earliest instance of this Italian word used in English" (according to *OED*); this usage is "a proof of Donne's Italian travels" and attracted particular attention in one of the Elegies on Donne and absurdly in post-1633 editions of *Metem*, where "mucheron" in the prefatory epistle was changed to "maceron" (2:123). **MILGATE** (1967) quotes entries from Florio, *Queen Anna's New World of Words* (1611), "Maccarone," and *OED* "macaroon," 3, adding that "in another sense the word could mean 'fop, dandy,' especially one whose manner or speech showed foreign affectations" (157). **SHAWCROSS** (1967): "one who affects foreign ways; a

fop; one who talks in confused foreign tongues" (30). **WARNKE** (1967): "dandy" (119). **GRANSDEN** (1970): "buffoon" (171). **SMITH** (1971): "foolish fop" (490).

119–20 *He like…great Man.* **MCCABE** (2001): Donne is "careful to attribute the worst accusations against prominent persons not to the first-person narrator, but to an unidentified scandal-monger" (82).

119 *priuiledg'd Spy,* **MILGATE** (1967): "An informer can say anything without danger, in attempting to trap others into indiscretions" (157). [So also, Smith (1971, 490).] **HESTER** (1994a): implicates the reader too as one "intent on uncovering the illegal, ill-advised, or illegitimate 'ciphers'" of Donne's "religious, political, and amatory confessions" (206). **HESTER** (2000): "one of the central analogies" of Donne's early verse, including the Satyres, is that "the true 'lover' is constantly beset by the snares, anglings, lures, and tricks" of spies (36).

120 *Discredit,* **JOHNSON** (1755): "To disgrace; to bring reproach upon; to shame; to make less reputable or honourable."

120 *Libells* **JOHNSON** (1755): "To spread defamation; generally written or printed." **MILGATE** (1967): on Donne's "hatred of libels and calumny," see *Sermons* 4:54; *Letters* (1651), pp. 89–91; and *SecAn* 331–34 (157).

122 *He sayes…because delayd;* **MATSUURA** (1953) notes Donne's discontent with the State's tardiness in "prosecuting wars, such as with Spain" (147). **MAROTTI** (1986): the antagonist expresses one of the "typical attitudes" of "the activist war faction in Elizabethan England" (104).

122 *thriue* **SULLENS** (1964): Donne's usage of this meaning of the word is earlier than the earliest source cited by *OED* (238).

122 *delayd;* **SMITH** (1971): "impeded by political connivance and corruption" (490).

123–24 *Offices are…Perpetuityes of them,* **SMITH** (1971): "the line of succession to the chief offices of state has been settled in perpetuity" (491).

123 *entayld;* **MILGATE** (1967): "An entail was, strictly, a settlement of an estate so that it could not be bequeathed at pleasure. Here the idea is that succession to offices has been secured into the distant future" (157). **SHAWCROSS** (1967): "aside from the obscene pun, inalienable settling of such offices on a specific family" (30). **CAREY** (1990): "already allocated to future holders" (428).

124 *Perpetuityes* **GRIERSON** (1912): "inalienable rights" in real property; see *Manningham's Diary,* April 22, 1602. Donne's "companion declares that such inalienable rights are being established in offices" as well as in property (2:123). [Similarly, Warnke (1967, 119).] **MILGATE** (1967) adds a reference to *Sermons* 4:189 (158).

125 *last day;* **SHAWCROSS** (1967): "Judgment Day" (30).

125 *great Officers* **SMITH** (1971): "high authorities" (491).

126 *Dunkerkers.* **GROSART** (1872–73): "the buccaneers of the English seas." [So

also, Chambers (1896, 2:244).] **NORTON** (1895): "Dunkirk was long the nest of the freebooters who were the terror of honest commerce, preying indiscriminately on that of all nations. Their cruelties were excessive, and as a rule they neither gave nor took quarter" (1:244). **BEWLEY** (1966): "Dunkirk was then used as a base by pirates" (183). [So also, Shawcross (1967, 30), Smith (1971, 491), Carey (1990, 428), and Kruzhkova (1994, 164).] **MILGATE** (1967) refers to Nashe, *Works*, 3:171 and S. D'Ewes, *Journals of all the Parliaments* (1682), pp. 665–66; adds that he knows "of no evidence that officers of state were in league with" the Dunkirk pirates (158). **GRIGSON** (1980): "privateersmen operating from Dunkirk" (26).

127–28 *Who wasts…who goates.* **B. SMITH** (1991): "Whores, boys, goats: Donne's order is eloquent. It traces a classical decline of civilization, a Christian slippage down the chain of being" (176). **KISÉRY** (1997) notes "the undesirable discontinuity" in this passage (114).

128–31 *Who loues…Becomming traytor;* **BELLETTE** (1975): the speaker "feels himself to be part of the debasement" (134).

128 *Who loues…who goates.* **PETER** (1956): "Martial peeps out quite frankly" in this line (134). **MILGATE** (1967) refers to Marston, *Scourge of Villainy*, 3.29–50 (158). **SHAWCROSS** (1972): see note to l. 62.

129–39 *I more amas'd…the last farthing;* **SELDEN** (1978): "The rapid displacement of images and metaphors by one another serves to enhance the impression of the satirist's overwhelming mental torment" (64). **CORTHELL** (1982): "the old Adam and the old religion must both be expiated," the passage urging "a coincidence between the satirist's fear of moral pollution and his fear of the 'Giant Statutes'" (173). **HESTER** (1984): the satirist discovers that his interlocutor "is an agent or former agent attempting to get the speaker to commit an incriminating indiscretion" (10). **ALBRIGHT** (1985): "Under the spell of satirical contagion, Donne pretends to worry that his victim's loathsomeness will turn the satirist himself into a swine" (137).

129–36 *I more amas'd…he free;* **BROSS** (1966): "Here Donne's speaker makes the shocking discovery that merely by hearing the court sycophant's words he is about to become a traitor. He thinks of two situations to compare with his present predicament: (1) Circe turning men into beast, and (2) a victim of venereal disease transferring it to a healthy person in order to be cured of it. But the wit of the passage is weakened by Donne's separation of these two comparisons" (135).

129–30 *Circes Prisoners,…turne beasts,* **RUGOFF** (1939): Donne alludes to Odysseus' story, but not "in a way suggesting a really stimulated imagination" (99). **MILGATE** (1967) refers to *Odyssey* 10.203ff. (158). [So also, Carey (1990, 428).] **SHAWCROSS** (1967): "Ulysses's men were turned into swine" (30). **ELLIOTT** (1976) refers to Matt. 8.32, suggesting that this passage is Donne's "most complex allusion to Matthew's gospel," yoking together "classical and Biblical imagery" (109).

130–33 *felt myselfe…To sucke me in* **ELLIOTT** (1976): the passage refers to Skelton's "The Bowge of Court" (115). **MAROTTI** (1986): "hearing (both true and false) gossip" about "various evils of the Court" constitutes a worrisome danger for the speaker (103–04). **PRICE** (1996): Donne "could be citing any number of laws enacted between the 1570s and 1590s that progressively narrowed the definition of treason to encompass practically any offense against the government" (62).

130 *They felt…myselfe then* **MELTON** (1906): the line illustrates Donne's tendency to use arsis-thesis variation of similar phrases ("felt themselves" and "felt my selfe") in the interior of the line (192).

131–48 *Becomming traytor;…thankes vex mee.* **GRIERSON** (1912): "I should be convicted of treason; he would go free as a spy who had spoken only to draw me out" (2:123). **HARRIS** (1960): the lines recreate "a conventional scene with new force"; based on Horace's Satire 1.9, they transpose a "bore" into a "monster of a court hanger-on, a libellous creature, and as Grierson suggested [1912] probably an 'intelligencer.'" The satirist's response to this threat particularizes rather than typifies a literary "character" (192). **MILGATE** (1967): "The satirist feels himself falling under the sway of 'complement' (cf. l. 46 above), and fears that he might be led on to say things that make him liable to punishment, under provisions of one of the many statutes dealing with treason; he might then (ll. 135–36) become guilty, and the man who infected him might remain free" (158).

132 *Gyant Statuts* **GROSART** (1872–73) notes the reading "statue" in H7 and thinks "a pun is probably intended, and allusion made to the London Gog and Magog" (1:42). **SHAWCROSS** (1967): "an authoritative decree (as if from God)" (30); "the lines suggest the erroneous, obsolete meaning of 'statue,'" and "such pronouncers are but unthinking semblances of men" (398). **SMITH** (1971): "the statutory enactments against treason, which were both comprehensive and menacing" (491). **PRESCOTT** (1998): the statutes are "like the crueler Pantagruel, perhaps, or the pilgrim-swallowing Gargantua" found in Rabelais (96).

133 *To sucke me in* **GRIERSON** (1912) refers to "accounts of trials of suspected traitors" and argues on this evidence that "Donne's companion is not merely a bore, but a spy, or at any rate is ready to turn informer to earn a crown or two" (2:123). [So also, Warnke (1967, 120).]

134–36 *That as…he free;* **SULLIVAN** (2000): in the 1633 edition, "horizontal lines replace a grotesque parody of the King's touch" (302), the present lines being restored by Marriot in 1635 (304).

134–35 *as burnt venomd…their Soares,* **GROSART** (1872–73): "A belief which still causes crime and disease: crime because the belief is that the innocent sufferer should, whether male or female, be a virgin" (1:42). **MILGATE** (1967): "The superstition that a person afflicted with venereal disease ('burnt') could free himself of it by infecting someone else seems to have been an old wives' tale, unsupported (so far as I can determine) by medical opinion" [so also, Smith (1971, 491)]; see Shakespeare, *Tim.*, 4.3.63–64, and Beaumont and Fletcher, *The Custom of the Country*, 3.2.182 (158). **ELLIOTT** (1976) refers to Matt. 8.17, Christ's healing of the leper (110).

134 *venomd* **MILGATE** (1967): "infected" (158).

134 *Lechers* **SHAWCROSS** (1967): "lewd persons who burn as a result of their disease" (31).

136 *free;* **LEGOUIS** (1942): a meaning of this word that Donne may have "either originated or at least introduced into the literary language" (185). [So also, Sullens (1964, 211).] **MILGATE** (1967): "guiltless" (158).

137–40 *But since I...beare this crosse;* **BELLETTE** (1975): "at that point where he feels most infected," he alludes to "the role of bearer at sins" (138).

137–39 *But since I...the last farthing;* **GERALDINE** (1966): "this commonplace misery of boredom is presented in terms of the cross" (29–30).

137 *in* **MILGATE** (1967): "involved" (158).

138–39 *forefathers sin / To the last* **STEIN** (1942) finds that "stress shift in the fifth foot, especially by attraction," gives "the strongest momentum of all" to enjambment, here effected by "beginning a line with two light syllables" (685).

138 *forefathers sin* **MILGATE** (1967): "His own sins can hardly have deserved so much punishment; he must be paying for his forefather's sins as well" (158).

139 *To the last farthing;* **STEIN** (1944d): the "hammer blows" of the third and fourth heavy syllables, following on the light first and second, provide obvious emphasis (299).

139 *to my powre* **MILGATE** (1967): "to the limits of my endurance" (158). [So also, Shawcross (1967, 31).] **SMITH** (1971): "to the limit of my power" (491).

140 *Toughly...but th'howre* **MOLONEY** (1950) notes that multiple elisions render this line virtually unrecognizable as decasyllabic (236). **MORRIS** (1953) cites this as an example of Donne introducing "extra syllables into a decasyllabic line, which are absorbed into the metre and form dactyls or paeons" (46). **SHAWCROSS** (1972): see note to l. 5.

140 *Toughly'and stubbornly* **STEIN** (1944c): "Though the eye accept, the ear will refuse elisions" in cases such as this, where "combinations, though unmarked by apostrophes, are sometimes elidable" (392).

141–42 *he tryes to bring / Me to pay* **STEIN** (1942) finds that "stress shift in the fifth foot, especially by attraction," gives "the strongest momentum of all" to enjambment, here effected by beginning a line with "an extra syllable" (685).

142 *Me to pay...his torturing;* **STEIN** (1944c): in this line, an extra syllable gives "increased speed and flexibility to the rhythm" (396).

143–45 *And sayes,...as ransome;* **ERSKINE-HILL** (1972): "by comparison with Horace this is a most anti-climactic ending to the encounter, but it is right, for two reasons": (1) as "a derisive comment on the Courtier's earlier invitation" to "enjoy 'the good' of court life" and (2) because by it the satirist prepares "for a different kind of climax after the encounter is over" (284). Further, the "somewhat anti-climactic passing of money" does not dispel "the exasperation and fear" to which the encounter had given rise, nor the "general sense of danger with which the writing of poetry about the court had so often been associated in sixteenth- and late fifteenth-century England." See *The Complete Poems of John Skelton* (1931), p. 41 and *The Collected Poems of Sir Thomas Wyatt* (1949), pp. 185–87 (286–87). BAUMLIN (1988): "as in Horace, so here the satirist is finally saved only by the boor's own penury." But Donne's speaker, "like Horace's, gets the worst of it, for his urbanity. The Horatian *sermo*, as Donne here interprets it, results in word games and hypocrisies of which the satirist is as guilty as his *adversarius*" (376–77).

143–44 *And sayes, . . . Thankfully'I* MELTON (1906): the only example, in all Donne's approximately "seven thousand heroic lines," of an Alexandrine couplet (143).

143 *And sayes, . . . willingly;* SHAWCROSS (1972): see note to l. 5.

143 *spare me?* MILGATE (1967): as in *Sat2* 53, the satirist takes "spare me" to mean "excuse me" or "allow me to leave" (158). [So also, Smith (1971, 491).]

144 *Nay, . . . Thankfully'I* MOLONEY (1950) notes that multiple elisions render this line virtually unrecognizable as decasyllabic (236).

145 *ransome;* HESTER (1982): This payment of "Ransome" provides a "derisive comment on the mercenary intentions of the government's enforcement of the re-cusant penal laws." Having likened his going to court and "attendance at an illegal Mass," the satirist presents his "torture" in the presence of the courtier, like threats to English Catholics, as "actually intended only to encourage his contributing to the court's treasury" (83).

147 *Iigg* JOHNSON (1755): "A light careless dance, or tune."

148 *complementall* GRIERSON (1912) quotes *LXXX Sermons* 18.176: "We have a word now denizened and brought into familiar use among us, Complement; and for the most part, in an ill sense; so it is when the heart of the speaker doth not answer to his tongue" (2:123). LEGOUIS (1942): a word Donne may have "either origi-nated or at least introduced into the literary language" (185). [So also, Sullens (1964, 178).] BEWLEY (1966): "flattering but void of sincerity" (183). SHAWCROSS (1967): "ceremonious and insincere" (31). SMITH (1971): "full of courtly compliment" (491).

150–54 *skant . . . make from prisone.* ERSKINE-HILL (1972) compares to Horace's *Satires* 1.9.77–78, where similarly "the scene fills with a crowd as the poet makes his escape" (277).

150 *Prerogatiue* MILGATE (1967): "the special right of the sovereign (i.e. of the Crown); but the bore has gone off with the special privilege of having the satirist's crown piece" (158). SMITH (1971): "(a) the special power of the poet's money has bought the man off; (b) the poet exercises his sovereign choice in getting rid of him" (491).

150 *Crowne;* DOCHERTY (1986): the pun "makes of Donne the unnamed, untitled (and perhaps now uncrowned) king in the poem" (170).

150 *skant* BEWLEY (1966): "scarcely" (183). [So also, Milgate (1967, 158) and Shawcross (1967, 31).] SMITH (1971): "hardly" (491).

153–54 *then one...from prisone.* STEIN (1942): an example of Donne's frequent "riming of masculine and feminine endings" (680).

153 *Ran from thence...then one* STEIN (1944c): "stress-shift by attraction," in the second, third, and fourth feet, after initial "stress-shift," is one of Donne's chief devices for varying the metrical line (384).

154 *make* MILGATE (1967): "The construction is 'doth make haste': 'with such haste as, or more haste than, a man makes' to get away from prison" (158).

155–74 *At home...bastard all.* ERSKINE-HILL (1972): these lines are "another example of the eager self-anticipation, with which, at the beginning of the poem, Donne described the manner and matter of the Courtier's speech before he gave his opening remark" (289).

155–63 *At home...Feare frownes?* CARACCIOLO-TREJO (1986): the experience of the satirist here is similar to that of Góngora, who returned to his Córdoba in order to rediscover his interior life (2:13).

155–59 *At home...It selfe o're me;'* SELDEN (1978): "having escaped the clutches of the bore, he shifts his point of view from a Horatian one to that of the medieval dream-vision" (63).

155–57 *At home...Court to mourne.* MAROTTI (1986): the passage expresses Donne's "aversion to the role of the importunate courtier seeking advancement" (104). [Similarly, Blissett (2000, 113).]

155 *At home in holesome Solitarines* ELLRODT (1960b): the only occurrence of solitude in Donne's early poems, though it is evoked as a possibility in *Sat1* 1–12 (1.2:178). MINER (1969): "proof of the degree to which private poetry came in [Donne's] case from a desire to retreat to private integrity"; although *Sat4* to this point "purports to recount what was seen on a visit to court (ll. 1–154), it is the remainder, which is a vision seen 'in wholesome solitarinesse,' that is the more fearsome" (34). Further, the "perversion of values and the universality of threat" enter even into "the private world of the speaker," so that the "prime refuge of lyric affirmation, the private self, is perverted into nightmare" (165). ERSKINE-HILL (1972): this line, "prepared for" by the remark about the satirist's "lonenesse" (in ll. 67–68), "comes with immense relief after the almost intolerable pressure of the court encounter." In the satirist's retirement, "the moral and religious realities triumph over the temporal ones," giving rise to "the satirist's heroic dedication of himself to Truth despite the consequences, the emotion of which is utterly different from anything to be found in Horace" (288).

155 *holesome* B. SMITH (1991): "an advised choice of words" that "suggests not only 'salutary' and 'salubrious,' but *whol*eness, completeness, being all of a piece" (178).

155 *Solitarines* JOHNSON (1755): "Solitude; forbearance of company; habitual retirement."

156–68 *My piteous Soule...of our Court?* **ALDEN** (1899) thinks that the "attitude toward life," in these lines as throughout the Satyres, is "uniformly pessimistic" (85). **WINNY** (1970): "A settled rhythm is never allowed to establish itself in these lines, whose jerky movement strengthens the impression of the speaker's impatience and disgust" (16–17). **ERSKINE-HILL** (1972): a "simultaneous awareness" of the "danger" and the "challenge" of court life "powers Donne's passage of soliloquy" (287).

156–57 *the wretchednes / Of Suiters* **STEIN** (1942) contends that Donne learned from Marlowe's plays this technique of enjambment by "ending a line with a polysyllabic word in order to lighten the last foot" (682–83).

156 *My piteous Soule* **ELLRODT** (1960b) (reading "precious" soul): there is no doubt that his cherished soul is "precious" to him (2:289).

157–59 *a traunce...It selfe o're me;'* **ELLRODT** (1960b) observes that Donne's vision is conventional but, unlike medieval and Renaissance forerunners, satirical and burlesque, not to be taken seriously, and notes the similarity of *Inferno* 2.127–30 and the "Dantesque" ending of *Ignatius*, suggesting a deliberate parody (2:165). Adds that *Sat4*'s allusion to Dante is rather inexact, reflecting haste or misunderstanding: neither the descent into hell nor the ascents through Purgatory and Paradise are presented as dreams. Comments that Donne in a letter (Simpson, *Prose Works*, 314) confuses the *Purgatorio* and the *Paradiso*, suggesting that Donne's understanding of Dante was imprecise and superficial (2:197). **GERALDINE** (1966): "The little dream has echoes both of Scipio and Dante" (30). **LECOCQ** (1969): the reference here to two different times invites us to consider that the mental vision is superimposed on lived experience, on the spectacle contemplated in real time. The truth reconstructed by the imagination comes thus to be confused with that which imagination has discovered. The reader will henceforth be in an intermediate domain between the imaginary and the real, where all will lean toward the symbolic (380). **NEWTON** (1974): "what at the beginning of the poem has been described as 'A Purgatorie'" is now "seen to be an interior vision" and "a hell that is Donne's own" (439). **BELLETTE** (1975): this is not "the world observed from a safe distance, but a world which knocks on one's door, which runs towards one in the street, grasps one's hand, and finally invades the privacy of one's 'precious soule' in solitude" (135). **BAUMLIN** (1988): the reference to Dante is "poignant," as the speaker's "spiritual progress" brings him to "an apocalyptic vision of hell-on-earth, and yet there is no beatific vision to follow" (379). **FULTON** (2001): given the speaker's "skepticism" about conventional representation in satire, this dream "seems to embody an experimental freedom of expression" and "a satiric form of representation that has a clashing, non-mimetic stance" (86–87).

157 *Suiters* **JOHNSON** (1755): "One that sues; a petitioner; a suppliant."

158 *who dream't he saw hell,* **GROSART** (1872–73): "Dante" (1:42). [So also, Hayward (1950, 113), Bewley (1966, 184), Shawcross (1967, 31), Warnke (1967, 120), Gransden (1970, 171), Smith (1971, 491), Carey (1990, 428), and Meakin (1998, 107).] **NORTON** (1895): "This reference to Dante is worth noting, for Dante was not so well known at this time in England as the later Italian poets" (1:244). **MILGATE** (1967) refers to *Inferno* 1.11, 25, adding that Donne's "references to Dante are among

the earliest in England" and that "his copy of *L'Amoroso Convivio* is in the Bodleian Library" (159). **GRANSDEN** (1970) refers readers back to "the opening lines of the poem" (171). **ERSKINE-HILL** (1972): with the allusion to Dante, the "mind returns again to the experience" of encountering the courtier, "this time fully mastering it" and "suffusing it with an infernal hue"; see *Catalogus Librorum Aulicorum*, p. 52 (288).

159–68 *such Men as…of our Court?* **BLISSETT** (2000): "For all its stylistic audacities, such a passage as this of Donne's is eminently speakable, its matter forcefully advanced," recalling Dante (105).

159–60 *such Men as…worse, and more.* **ERSKINE-HILL** (1972): the poem's "mode of sardonic exaggeration should not persuade us to pass over lightly" the "boldness and plainness" of this declaration (288). **MAROTTI** (1986): Donne "resented" having to "relinquish many of his pretensions to intellectual and social independence" in seeking patronage (104).

160–64 *Low feare…pufte Nobilitee?* **ERSKINE-HILL** (1964) finds these lines "particularly heroic in feeling and dramatic in expression" (169). **ZUNDER** (1982): these lines "make clear the intimidating effect the court could have in discouraging criticism," especially for "one such as Donne of middle-or lower-class origin" (17). **WIGGINS** (2000): "Donne is talking himself into a return visit to court" (57). **FULTON** (2001): "dangerously unquestioning obedience and 'fear' of power is not just endemic to the structure itself, but officially and religiously sanctioned" (100–01).

160 *I saw at…Low feare* **KERINS** (1984): "the measured pauses and assonance" of the line are the "climactic moment of the satire," in which, though the satirist "realizes that his anxiety should beset sinners rather than their satiric accuser, the movement of the verse deepens his growing insecurity concerning his own spiritual condition" (51).

161–63 *Then…Feare frownes?* **LEWIS** (1934b): Donne's "metaphysical principles" are more in evidence here than his "humanist values." It is Donne's "assumption of this same metaphysical apparatus" that accounts for the difference between Donne and Horace that is "most clearly evident" in these lines (655).

161–62 *th'accuser; Then…raysd men* **STEIN** (1942): an example of Donne's "chief prosodic innovation," the frequent use of "stress-shift in the fifth foot," in which a feminine rhyme "is invariably matched with a masculine" (681).

161 *Becomes* **SMITH** (1971): "befits" (492).

162 *high-borne or raysd* **MILGATE** (1967): "born to, or elevated to, noble rank" (159).

162 *raysd* **SULLENS** (1964): Donne's use of this meaning of the word is earlier than the earliest source cited by *OED* (228). **SMITH** (1971): "men raised to noble rank, not born into it" (492).

163 *Feare frownes?…betray thee,* **COFFIN** (1937) compares this line with *Sat3* 5 to suggest that Donne identifies truth with religion at this point in his life (57). **STEIN**

(1944c): "stress-shift" after the caesura is one of Donne's chief devices for varying the metrical line (384).

163 *my Mistres Truth, betray thee,* ELLIOTT (1976) refers to Matt. 5.27–31 (109).

163 *my Mistres Truth,* ELLRODT (1960b): the phrase expresses the impulse in Donne's generation to penetrate beneath society's illusions (2:1).

164 *th'huffing braggart pufte Nobilitee?* GRIERSON (1912) refers to Sylvester, *Du Bartas,* 1:2 (2:124). MILGATE (1967): "'Huffing' has the suggestion of bullying arrogance"; see Burton, *Anatomy of Melancholy* 2.3.2 (159). [So also, Shawcross (1967, 31).]

164 *huffing* LEGOUIS (1942): a meaning of this word that Donne may have "either originated or at least introduced into the literary language" (185). [So also, Sullens (1964, 219).]

164 *braggart* JOHNSON (1755): "Boastful; vainly ostentatious." GROSART (1872–73): "Two classes here correspond to the other two of l. 162, high-born and raised men" (1:42).

166–74 *hast thou seene...bastard all.* ALBRIGHT (1985): the wax garden, "so helpful for derision of the court," is also "a paradigm for the whole analogical mode of satire" (136).

166–68 *hast thou seene...of our Court?* HILLYER (1941): Donne's "private answer to hopes so unacknowledged as scarcely to be called frustrate," an "apologia to himself for failure in a contest in which he never actively engaged" (xxii).

168–73 *I...ours are;* MORRIS (1953) cites this passage as an example of Donne achieving "rhythmical continuity" through "over-reaving" (48–49).

168–73 *our Court? I...Tast haue* STEIN (1942): in these lines, Donne's enjambment combines "an extreme weakening of the last foot" with the placement of "the cesura near the end of his line, where the start of a new rhythm, propelled by grammatical or rhetorical sense, will carry over," a technique that "apparently anticipates by several years the familiar style of Jacobean blank verse" (683).

168 *swells the bladder* MILGATE (1967): "puffs up, like a balloon (l. 176)" (159). SHAWCROSS (1967): "indicating its emptiness and lack of usefulness" (31).

169 *waxen garden,* GROSART (1872–73): "the now common waxwork exhibitions" (1:43). GRIERSON (1912): "the artificial gardens in wax exhibited apparently by Italian puppet or 'motion' exhibitors"; see Drayton, *Heroicall Epistles* (1597) (2:124). [Similarly, Milgate (1967, 159), Shawcross (1967, 32), Warnke (1967, 121), Gransden (1970, 171), and Carey (1990, 428).] SMITH (1971): "the lines suggest that an artificial garden of wax, made in Italy, was exhibited in London; but nothing is known of it" (492). KRUZHKOVA (1994): a costly Italian plaything made from wax figurines (164).

169 *and* MELTON (1906): "Donne's verse, like Shakespeare's, and like the prose of Coleridge, shows 'insignificant' words stressed to meet the exigencies of rhythm and meaning" (65, 68).

170 *Transported* **MILGATE** (1967): "imported (cf. l. 105 above, and note)" (159).

171 *flouts* **MILGATE** (1967): "insults, defies, mocks (by being too close a resemblance)" (159). [So also, Smith (1971, 492).] **GRANSDEN** (1970): "parodies" (171).

171 *our Court* **SMITH** (1971) (reading "our Presence"): "(a) our Royal Court or the people who attend the Queen there; (b) our demeanour" (492).

171 *Court* **MILGATE** (1967) (reading "Presence"): "can mean the chamber itself whether the monarch is present or not, as in ll. 179 and 199 below, or, as here, the assemblage of courtiers before the Queen in state or waiting for her arrival." The word "makes (by a pun) the point that the Court is, like the Italian gardens, all show"; see Paul Hentzner's travel diary in Moryson's, *Itinerary* (1889), pp. 46–49 (159). **GRANSDEN** (1970) (reading "Presence"): "the ceremonial attendance by the court on the monarch" (171). **CAREY** (1990) (reading "Presence"): "the presence chamber at court" (428).

171 *for* **MELTON** (1906): an example of Donne using an "insignificant" word in a stressed position "to meet the exigencies of rhythm and meaning" (65, 73).

172–74 *lust such gay…bastard all.* **ELLIOTT** (1976) refers to Matt. 7.16–20 (110n10).

173 *ours* **SHAWCROSS** (1967): "persons of rank" (32).

173 *naturall* **SHAWCROSS** (1967): "a synonym for 'bastard'" (32).

174 *Stocks* **MILGATE** (1967): "Some courtiers are of noble 'stock,' others are not 'naturally' noble but are, as it were, grafted on to the 'stock' of nobility (cf. l. 162 above, 'high borne' or 'rais'd men'); all are, however, illegitimate, impure, non-descript when it comes to a question of moral worth" (159). **SHAWCROSS** (1967): "main stems of a plant" (32). **SMITH** (1971): "(a) tree trunks or stems; (b) lines of descent" (492).

174 *fruits* **MILGATE** (1967) refers to Matt. 7.20 and 12.33 (160). **SMITH** (1971): "issues, actions" (492).

175–85 *T'is ten a clock…All are Players.* **SMITH** (1970): "shows us the grain of the times as no formal chronicler could, by its immediate enactment of a mind exuberantly caught up in the life of the streets, courts, chambers"; but "this is art not casual observation" (138).

175 *ten a clock.* **RUDD** (1963): "10 a.m. is chosen to indicate the time" also in Horace's *Satires* 1.8.35 (208). **MILGATE** (1967) refers to *Courtier's Library*, p. 41; *Overburian Characters*, ed. Paylor, p. 7; and Juvenal's satires 1:127 (160). **ERSKINE-HILL** (1972): though this "returns us to the court," it is probably not a "strict literal" return but a "continuation" of the satirist's Dantesque trance "which has been so crucial to Donne's satiric resolve" (289).

175 *Mues* **LEGOUIS** (1942): "riding-schools," a meaning of this word earlier than the earliest that *OED* records (191). [So also, Sullens (1964, 250).] **BEWLEY** (1966):

"stables" (184). [So also, Milgate (1967, 160), Shawcross (1967, 32), Warnke (1967, 121), Smith (1971, 492), and Carey (1990, 428).]

176 *Baloon,...or the Stewes* **STEIN** (1944c): a "nine-syllable line," which is "not one of the chief devices for metrical modulation" in the Satyres (376). **SHAWCROSS** (1972): see note to l. 62.

176 *Baloon,* **GROSART** (1872–73): "Probably the ancient *follis*, and, except in one respect, the modern football; a game in which a football ball [sic] was struck with the arm, armed with a wooden bracer, described, as in Italy, in the form of a shield studded with wooden points" (1:43). [So also, Warnke (1967, 121).] **GRIERSON** (1912): "A game played with a large wind-ball or football struck to and fro with the arm or foot" (2:124). [So also, Grigson (1980, 27).] **HAYWARD** (1950): "A form of medicine ball" (114). **MILGATE** (1967) refers to Strutt, *Sports and Pastimes* (1903), pp. 90–91 (160). **GRANSDEN** (1970): "the game of 'pallone'"; see *Shakespeare's England*, 2:462 (171). **SMITH** (1971): "a game like handball" (492). **CAREY** (1990): "A kind of volley-ball" (428).

176 *Tennys,* **MILGATE** (1967) refers to Strutt, *Sports and Pastimes* (1903), p. 87 (160).

176 *Dyett,* **GROSART** (1872–73): "the restrictions in diet consequent on visiting the place of resort next mentioned" (1:43). **BEWLEY** (1966): "eating" (184). [So also, Shawcross (1967, 32).] **MILGATE** (1967): the "bloods" prepared for "their sexual pleasures by eating aphrodisiac foods"; see Middleton, *A Trick to Catch the Old One*, 3.1.93–94. While Donne may be referring "to dieting before a visit to the stews, it is much more likely that the 'Dyet' in question was intended as a cure for disease contracted in the stews," such as in A. Schmidt, *Shakespeare Lexicon*, "diet," and *Tim.* 4.3.87 (160). **SMITH** (1971): "(a) a council of state; (b) a course of aphrodisiacal food in preparation for a visit to the brothel, or of curative food in consequence of recent visits" (492).

176 *Stewes* **BEWLEY** (1966): "brothels" (184). [So also, Shawcross (1967, 32) and Smith (1971, 492).] **MILGATE** (1967) refers to Hall, *Virgidemiarum* 4.1:94–95 (160).

177–79 *Had all...In the Presence;* **MORRIS** (1953): in this passage "the unstressed rhyme syllable is followed by a stressed syllable at the beginning of the next line, and the metrical flow is unbroken" (49).

177–78 *the second...are found* **STEIN** (1942): an example of Donne's "chief prosodic innovation," the frequent use of "stress-shift in the fifth foot," in which a feminine rhyme "is invariably matched with a masculine" (681).

177–78 *the second / Time made ready* **STEIN** (1942) finds that "stress shift in the fifth foot, especially by attraction" gives "the strongest momentum of all" to enjambment, and when this (as here) is "followed by a stress-shift in the first foot of the succeeding line," Donne achieves "the unusual effect of a runover which does not run, or skip, or swoop, but marches with steady emphasis" (684).

177 *Had all...now the second* **STEIN** (1944c): this is one of many "more energetic"

examples, in which "by attraction" after a pause, stress-shifts "carry through to the end of the line" (385). **SHAWCROSS** (1972): see note to l. 101.

178–79 *Time made ready...(God pardon mee.)* **STEIN** (1944c): "stress-shift by attraction" in the second foot, after initial "stress-shift," is one of Donne's "very frequent" devices for varying the metrical line (383).

178 *made ready* **MILGATE** (1967): "dressed" (160). **SMITH** (1971): "costumed" (492).

179 *Presence;* **BEWLEY** (1966): "the Queen's presence" (184). **SHAWCROSS** (1967): "the assembly of the court, in the presence of the nobility" (32). **GRIGSON** (1980): "the royal chamber of presence" (27).

179 *and I;* **MILGATE** (1967): "I was there too" (160).

179 *(God pardon mee.)* **GRIERSON** (1912): "that he too should be found in the 'Presence' again, after what he has already seen of Court life," as though "Dante, who had seen Hell and escaped, should return thither" (2:124).

180–87 *As fresh...Inuentory.* **KRUZHKOVA** (1994): costumes worn by the actors of Elizabethan theatre were not merely theatrical but were, quite often, gifts from courtiers. The actors were very proud of these costumes, and they served as one of the main attractions for spectators (164).

180–81 *As fresh,...to buy them;* **ERSKINE-HILL** (1964): a commonplace analogy of Elizabethan satire (170).

181 *The fields they sold* **MILGATE** (1967): "A variation of the idea of wearing manors, or lands, upon one's back"; see Tilley, *Dictionary of Proverbs*, L452, W61, and Burton, *Anatomy of Melancholy*, 3.2.2.3 (160).

182–86 *and bring...Cheapside bookes* **SHAWCROSS** (1972): "the clothes are sold next week and new ones purchased secondhand in Cheapside" (259–60).

183 *Them next...to sell.* **SHAWCROSS** (1972): see note to l. 62.

183 *Theater* **SHAWCROSS** (1972): "may be three syllables," illustrating that Donne's "alteration of meter" has "definite and appropriate effect" (262–63).

184–85 *Me seemes...All are Players.* **MASOOD-UL-HASAN** (1958): "A courtier's life seemed to be as hollow and unreal as the actor's strutting on the boards" (52).

184 *Wants reach all States;* **MILGATE** (1967): "men of every rank or condition can feel the pinch" (160). [So also, Shawcross (1967, 32) and Smith (1971, 492).]

185–87 *Who ere lookes...Inuentory.* **GROSART** (1872–73) queries whether "this means that their apparel was, like stage-apparel, hired; or that, like the latter, it might be found in others' books, because not paid for, and therefore not really their own" (1:43).

185 *All are Players.* **ERSKINE-HILL** (1972): the metaphor is "a limiting judge-

ment, lacking the philosophical resonance" it has in More's *Utopia*, in *AYL*, or in *Mac* (290). **MAROTTI** (1986): courtiers engage in "elaborate forms of self-display" (104).

186 *(For themselues...) ore Cheapeside bookes* **NORTON** (1895): "They dare not go because of the debts they owe to the haberdashers, silk-mercers, linen-drapers, and hosiers, whose shops lined Cheapside" (1:245). [Similarly, Milgate (1967, 160).]

186 *Cheapeside bookes* **PETER** (1956): Donne's "own interest is not in the mere documentation of abuses"; for "details we must go elsewhere" than *Sat4* (133–34). **BEWLEY** (1966): "account books of secondhand clothes dealers whose shops were in Cheapside" (184). [So also, Shawcross (1967, 32).] **SMITH** (1971): "the ledgers of the Cheapside tailors from whom these courtiers have had their clothes on account, and whom they thus dare not go near for fear of being dunned for payment" (493). [So also, Carey (1990, 428).]

186 *Cheapeside* **WARNKE** (1967): "a market district of London" (121).

187–228 *Now...commands Like Law.* **ELLRODT** (1960b): the product of an "amateur" at the Inns of Court, though it is an expression of wit, this characterization is no less objective and acute than those of Elizabethan professional writers (2:31–32).

187–91 *Now...both are bought.* **BROSS** (1966): "The comparison is striking: Fops, seeing ladies approach, assess their charms and attempt to gain some kind of entrance; pirates, seeing rich vessels draw near, board them. Yet, the men seem not to have ceased being pirates when they are seen praising the ladies. This is not what pirates do. The metaphoric world is interrupted by the actual world. The bubble has burst; the metaphor is dropped mid-way through the sentence." As such, "the actual and the figurative jar—the reader is jerked violently from the realm of metaphoric to that of literal truth" (140–41).

187 *Inuentory.* **JOHNSON** (1755): "An account or catalogue of moveables."

188–91 *The Ladyes come;...both are bought.* **PORTER** (1971): Donne's "punctuation and syntax" are "marvellous" and "dramatic in the extreme" but somewhat "out of focus" (37).

188–90 *As Pyrats...men boord them;* **GRIERSON** (1912): the "painted faces" of the ladies "suggest the comparison"; while there was a known attack by English pirates on a Venetian ship, "school Histories" say more about "Turkish and Moorish pirates" than about the piracy of "English merchant ships, not always confining themselves to the ships of nations at war with their country" (2:124). **ERSKINE-HILL** (1964) calls Donne's imagery here "ingeniously perceptive" (170). **SHAWCROSS** (1972): the ladies are "weak ships painted red (symbol of prostitution and the Whore of Babylon, as well as of despair), and the men, like pirates, board them, one group praising the other for beauty or wit" (260). **MAROTTI** (1986): "polite relationships between men and women in such a world are cynically artificial" (104).

188 *Pyrats* **SHAWCROSS** (1967): "pirate ships (a common image for a prostitute)" (32).

189 *Cucchianel* GROSART (1872–73): "cochineal" (1:43). [So also, Grierson (1912, 2:124), Hayward (1929, 771), Rugoff (1939, 146), and Warnke (1967, 121).] **BEWLEY** (1966): "a scarlet dye" (185). **MILGATE** (1967): "dried bodies of the female of the *coccus cacti* insect (found in Mexico and Peru) used for making scarlet dye." It was very valuable and was "classed with gold and spices," hence being "of great interest to 'Pirats'"; see Webster, *The Devil's Law Case*, 4.2.154 (160–61). **SHAWCROSS** (1967): "cochineal, a red or purple coloring agent from Central America" (32). **SMITH** (1971): "brought from South America" and "used for making scarlet dye, and highly prized. Evidently the court ladies are highly rouged" (493). **CAREY** (1990): "An expensive cargo prized by privateers preying on the Spanish South American fleet" (428).

190–96 *The men boord...loose sett.* **REID** (2000): "The narrator includes himself in this ridiculous picture of smart talk at court. Simply by recording what he thought at the time, the narrator makes himself part of the emptiness he describes, so pleased with his own wit that he cannot leave it out of the story" (41).

190–91 *The men boord...both are bought.* **STEIN** (1946): in this couplet, "any attempt to ignore the metrical variations is in danger of arbitrarily spoiling the meaning" (99). **MORRIS** (1953) cites this couplet as an example of "the omission of whole phrases, or the substitution of simple words for phrases," so that we are to understand that "both the women's beauties and the men's wits are bought" (67).

190 *The men boord...they thinke, well* **STEIN** (1944c): "stress-shift" after a pause is one of Donne's chief devices for varying the metrical line (379), although in this case, "one may perhaps scan by admitting a stress-shift in the first of the light syllables" (387).

190 *boord* **MILGATE** (1967): "accost. Donne brings out (by the words 'As Pirats') the metaphor latent in this common expression" (161).

190 *as they thinke, well* **STEIN** (1944d): "cumulative emphasis" is achieved here, where "the third syllable is stressed more than either of the first two, and the fourth more than the third" (299).

191 *bought.* **SHAWCROSS** (1967): "bribed, hoodwinked" (32).

192–94 *Why good witts...scarlett dy.* **MILGATE** (1967): "The reason why clever men do not wear scarlet gowns is that the lords buy their brains to provide them with speeches (for which the true authors get no credit), and the ladies buy up for cosmetics all the red dyes which are needed for dying scarlet" (161). [Similarly, Smith (1971, 493).] **BAUMLIN** (1988): "courtly language resembles ostentatious dress as both a commodity (an object to be bought and sold at profit) and a covering (a means of deception and superficial self-display)" (378).

192 *Why good witts...I thought,* **SHAWCROSS** (1972): "one must decide whether 'good' is stressed, whether 'wits' or 'ne'r' is stressed, and, if the former, whether 'weare' is to carry stress and thus sarcasm" (264).

192 *good witts...Scarlett gownes,* **GROSART** (1872–73) queries whether this refers to "the Lord Mayor and Aldermen of London" (referring to *Citizen* 55–56), or "is it a hit at the scarlet-gowned doctors of the universities?" (1:43).

192 *Scarlett gownes,* **LEGOUIS** (1942): a combination of words not recorded by *OED*, though related to "scarlet day," an occasion "in university or civic life observed by the public wearing of state or official robes of scarlet" (192). [So also, Milgate (1967, 161).] **SHAWCROSS** (1967): "the usual dress of lawyers" (32).

194 *women buy…scarlett dy.* **SHAWCROSS** (1967): "Referring to the woman arrayed in purple and scarlet color known as the whore of Babylon"; see Rev. 17.4 (32).

195–96 *He calld…loose sett.* **RUGOFF** (1939) explains the idea of using lime to catch birds, noting that unlike images referring to nets and snares (likely Biblical), this metaphor probably harks back to the actual fowling practice, and observing that Donne uses both "limetwigs" and "nets" as metaphors, even though he apparently mocks the speech of a "typical court gallant" in these lines (126).

195 *her bewty Lymetwiggs, her haire nett;* **MILGATE** (1967): "the compliments are very trite; both refer to methods of trapping small birds" (161). **SMITH** (1971): "traps for birds, a bathetic compliment" (493).

195 *Lymetwiggs,* **RUGOFF** (1939): "harks back to actual fowling practice. Casting bird-lime serves to describe…women who expose their bodies and paint themselves" (126). **SHAWCROSS** (1967): "snares" (32).

196 *druggs ill layd,* **MILGATE** (1967): "cosmetics badly applied" (161). [So also, Gransden (1970, 171) and Smith (1971, 493).]

196 *her hayre loose sett.* **HARDY** (1942): "a phrase curiously modern" (65).

197–206 *Would not…wast to thighs.* **ELLRODT** (1987): the truth of Donne's description is graphic and astonishing (3).

197–203 *Would not…they fornicate,* **ELLRODT** (1960b): this portrait of a courtier is true to life; though it be crankier than Heraclitus, the reader smiles nonetheless, and Donne's wit has not gone out of fashion (2:32). **KERINS** (1984): "on one level, Macrine is a stylish fop, but Donne takes pains to intimate the deeper moral dimensions of his obsessive fastidiousness" (52).

197 *Would not…Macrine* **RUDD** (1963): possibly adapted from Juvenal's Satire 10:30–36 (208). **SHAWCROSS** (1972): see note to l. 5. **SCODEL** (1995): Donne here "adopts the Democritean attitude" (47).

197 *Heraclitus* **CHAMBERS** (1896): "known as the 'weeping philosopher,' from his habitual gravity" (2:244). [So also, Carey (1990, 428).] **BEWLEY** (1966): "known as the 'Dark' or 'Weeping' philosopher" (185). [So also, Milgate (1967, 161), who adds, "even he would laugh."] **SHAWCROSS** (1967): "the weeping philosopher, who laughed because he believed that all things carried in themselves their opposites, and thus that nothing was permanent" (33). [So also, Smith (1971, 493).] **GRANSDEN** (1970) refers to Juvenal, 10:28–30 (171). **ERSKINE-HILL** (1972) refers to *Sat3*, to the tenth of Donne's *Paradoxes*, and to the preface of Drant's translation of Horace (290).

197 *Macrine* **BEWLEY** (1966): "an imaginary name" (185). [So also, Shawcross (1967, 33).] **MILGATE** (1967) refers to Persius 2:1, "addressed (respectfully) to Plotius

Macrinus" (161). [So also, Gransden (1970, 171), who adds that Donne, Hall, and Marston "all borrow 'type' names from classical verse-satire," and Kruzhkova (1994, 164).] **GRIGSON** (1980): "Macrinus, mentioned in Persius' *Satires*" (28). **CAREY** (1990): "No specific courtier seems intended here" (428).

198–99 *himselfe at doore…Meschite;* **GROSART** (1872–73): "the preening, &c. takes place outside, or at the door, before entering the presence, *i.e.* in this case the presence chamber" (1:44). **MILGATE** (1967): "Macrine's tidying of his attire is like the removal of one's shoes before entering a mosque" (161). [Similarly, Kruzhkova (1994, 164).] **ERSKINE-HILL** (1972): linked to "the infernal comparison" at ll. 157–58, these lines not only seem to say that the Court is like hell but also, in their "grotesque/fantastic" quality, are "consonant" with that earlier "trancelike effect" (289).

198 *refine,* **SULLENS** (1964): this meaning of the word is not recorded by *OED* (264). **MILGATE** (1967): "make fine again" (161). **SMITH** (1971): "make elegant" (493).

199–200 *As the…to shrift,* **MILGATE** (1967): "He lifts the skirt of his cloak to examine his hose; then he pulls up his hose to remove wrinkles" (161). [Similarly, Smith (1971, 493).]

199 *As the…And lift* **SHAWCROSS** (1972): see note to l. 5.

199 *Presence* **GROSART** (1872–73): "The word was also used for the presence-chamber," regardless of whether or not the royal "presence" was there. Ben Jonson used the word as such "very often," as well as Shakespeare, *Shr.* 4.3, *R2* 1.3, *2H4* 4.4 and Massinger, *The Bashful Lover* 1.1 and 2.1 (1:44). **FULTON** (2001): the word "conveys a sarcastically mystical quality, as if this presence contained powers imparted from above." The allusion to Islam expresses "a religious affiliation to power that infers the customarily unfavorable comparison to the Turks" (91).

199 *Meschite;* **GROSART** (1872–73) cites Cole's Dictionary and Du Cange: "a Turkish church" and "*templum Mahumetanorum*" respectively (1:44). [So also, Gransden (1970, 171).] **NORTON** (1895): "an obsolete form of mosque, here used as equivalent to 'a sacred place'" (1:245). [So also, Hayward (1950, 114).] **SULLENS** (1964): Donne's usage of this word is cited by *OED* as the earliest source (196). **SHAWCROSS** (1967): "mosque. Donne compares Macrine's entering court to a Mohammedan's entering a mosque" (33). [So also, Smith (1971, 493) and Carey (1990, 428).] **WARNKE** (1967): "Moscovite" (121). **GRIGSON** (1980): "mesquite, mosque" (28).

200 *call his clothes to shrift,* **MILGATE** (1967): "summon to confession" (161).

200 *shrift,* **BEWLEY** (1966): "confession" (185). [So also, Shawcross (1967, 33) and Smith (1971, 493).]

201–03 *Making them…they fornicate,* **RUGOFF** (1939): the passage illustrates Donne's "somewhat irreverent tendency to apply religious images to arrantly profane ideas" (90).

201–02 *mortal…but venial* **RICHTER** (1902) states that the rhyme here consists of the similarity of unstressed syllables (410). **STEIN** (1942): an example of Donne's frequent "riming of masculine and feminine endings" (680). **MILGATE** (1967): "the theological distinction between 'deadly' sins (cf. l. 232 below) and excusable or pardonable sins. The holes and stains are 'mortall' because irreparable; the feathers and dust can be removed without damage to the fabric, and are only minor faults" (161). **SHAWCROSS** (1967): "Mortal sins which stain or damage the soul are contrasted with venial sins like vanity and turmoil; also referring to sexual implements and snuff" (33).

201–02 *mortal / Great Staines* **STEIN** (1942) finds that "stress shift in the fifth foot, especially by attraction" gives "the strongest momentum of all" to enjambment, here effected by "the bringing of two unstressed syllables into close proximity, at the end of one line and at the beginning of the next" (684).

201 *Making them...only mortal* **STEIN** (1944c): "initial truncation" combined with a feminine ending is one of Donne's chief devices for varying the metrical line, albeit not foremost in the Satyres (377). **SHAWCROSS** (1972): see note to l. 101.

201 *confesse,* **MELTON** (1906): exemplifies Donne's use of secondary accent on Latin prefixes, "which may serve for ictus whenever the verse requires it" (86, 93). **SULLENS** (1964): Donne's use of this meaning of the word is earlier than the earliest source cited by *OED* (211).

202 *venial* **SMITH** (1971): "pardonable or reparable sins, such as their 'fornication' with feathers and dust which can be amended by brushing them down" (493).

203 *with which they fornicate,* **MILGATE** (1967): "i.e. the feathers and dust cling close to the fabric" (161).

203 *fornicate,* **SULLENS** (1964): this meaning of the word is not recorded by *OED* (259).

204–09 *And then by...first time goes* **CUNNAR** (1990): for Donne, "faiths eyes" do not apprehend God in the same manner that "the physical eye sees a framed picture on the wall," so that "the illusory realism of physical sight and its representation through perspective will not allow for the vision of God: 'For, in this world, our bodily eyes do not see bodies, they see but colours and dimensions'" [*Sermons* 7:344] (325).

204–06 *And then by...to thighs.* **HOGAN** (1977): "The brevity of this almost casual comment is a trifle deceiving, for it suggests a familiarity with the artist's work beyond a casual acquaintance with one or more of his pictures. Even though in a cryptic manner, Donne makes Dürer's concept integral to his own poetic purpose. Moreover, the passage indicates that Donne must have been acquainted with such works as Dürer's 'About the Art of Measurement' (*Underweysung der messing*, Nurnberg, 1525) or his 'About the Principles of Proportion.' Among the illustrations in the former is 'A man drawing a recumbent woman, in foreshortening through a frame with a network of squares on to a paper also with squares, in order to be able to reduce or enlarge proportionally.' The latter includes drawings almost identical to the directions set forth in Donne's phrasing, certainly providing support for the accuracy of the poet's visual memory, for it seems unlikely that he would have had a drawing before him as he wrote" (35–36). **WIGGINS** (2000): "Durer's rules for achieving perspective are ridiculed," an attitude that "accord[s] well with Lomazzo's and Hilliard's rejection of them" (65).

205 *Durers rules* **GROSART** (1872–73): "The great engraver, like Hogarth later, wrote a treatise on the proportions of the human frame" (1:44). [So also, Gransden (1970, 171).] **NORTON** (1895): "in his famous book *De symmetria partium humanorum corporum*" (1:245). [So also, Semler (1998, 46–47), who adds that the reference may also be to "the widely dispersed *Elementia geometrica*."] **CHAMBERS** (1896): his "*Treatise on Proportion* was published posthumously in 1528" (2:244). [So also, Smith (1971, 493), Carey (1990, 428), and Kruzhkova (1994, 164).] **MILGATE** (1967) adds that "half the book consists of diagrams of male and female figures with elaborate proportions of parts of the body to other parts and to the whole, repeated endlessly." Notes that these are "the proportions ('odds') Macrine tests ('tries'), with pieces of string as a means of measurement" (161). **SHAWCROSS** (1967): "Durer's concepts of the human body's proportions" (33). [So also, Warnke (1967, 122).]

205–06 *Of his each…to thighs.* **GRIERSON** (1912) (reading "trye" and "thighe"): "If we retain 'tryes', then we should also, with several MSS., read (l. 204) 'survayes'; and if 'thighes' be correct we should expect 'legges'. The regular construction keeps the infinitive throughout, 'refine', 'lift', 'call', 'survay', 'trye'. If we suppose that Donne shifted the construction as he got away from the governing verb, the change would naturally begin with 'survayes'" (2:125).

205 *Of his each…the odds tryes* **STEIN** (1944c): "stress-shift" after the caesura is one of Donne's chief devices for varying the metrical line (384).

205 *the odds tryes* **SHAWCROSS** (1967): "measure the proportions" (33). [So also, Smith (1971, 493).]

207 *immaculate* **LEGOUIS** (1942): Donne's use of this meaning of the word is earlier than the earliest source cited by *OED* (187). [So also, Sullens (1964, 220).]

208–10 *with such nicety…To preach,* **RUGOFF** (1939): the passage illustrates Donne's "somewhat irreverent tendency to apply religious images to arrantly profane ideas" (90).

208 *Perfect as Circles,* **ELLRODT** (1960b): a scholastic, theological rather than a scientific notion; in poems of the 1590s, Donne's interest in theology is more common than his later interest in science (2:385). **MILGATE** (1967): "The circle was universally regarded as a symbol of eternity, of God, of perfection" (161).

208 *nicety* **SHAWCROSS** (1967): "excessive elegance" (33).

210–18 *he enters;…they meritt it.* **CROFTS** (1936): these lines indicate that Donne had experience with actual courtiers (129).

210–12 *enters; and a Lady…protests, protests,* **MAROTTI** (1986): the passage "reduces the verbal transactions of courtly amorousness to mere gibberish" (105).

210 *To preach,…Lady which ows* **STEIN** (1944c): as commonly do Elizabethan

dramatists, Donne here admits an extra syllable, "an extra feminine ending in the foot preceding the cesura," an "extension of metrical liberty" that is "most frequent" in the Satyres (394).

211 *arrests* **SMITH** (1971): "buttonholes" (493).

212–17 *And vnto her...Ladyes Psalter.* **LEISHMAN** (1951): amidst "no clear plan or dominant idea" in *Sat4*, these lines are "an example of the kind of plum one may expect to find: one spruce creature approaches a woman who scarcely knows him" (114–15). **CORTHELL** (1997): "as if to balance the controversial allusiveness of the poem," these allusions make the point that "both courtship and religion are practiced at considerable risk to the subject of power" (48).

212–14 *And vnto her...th'Inquisition,* **BEWLEY** (1966): "The allusion to Protestants here is developed in the figure of the ten cardinals" (185).

212 *protests, protests, protests,* **MELTON** (1906): this phrase illustrates Donne's tendency not to use arsis-thesis variation with certain repetitions (204). **MILGATE** (1967): the word is "used in its original sense of 'makes protestation,' with a pun on its religious sense of being a 'Protestant'"; see "Herrick's promise to be Anthea's 'Protestant'." Further, "the absence of punctuation suggests the compulsive bore in action" (161–62). **SHAWCROSS** (1967): "In answer to her protests he protests that there should be no protests against his actions. He is, of course, a Protestant" (33). **SMITH** (1971): "protests his love" (494). **MCFARLAND** (1977): "the repetition would seem to be a simple reiteration of a verb for vehemence (hence, epizeuxis)," but "the recurrence should be read as noun-verb-noun (hence, continguous polyptoton); that is, 'unto her protests he protests his protests'" (403).

212 *protests,* **SHAWCROSS** (1972): "according to meaning" this is an "odd final stress for rhyme" (263).

213–14 *would serve to haue throwne / Ten Cardinals* **STEIN** (1942) finds that "stress shifts in the fourth foot" give "increased impetus" to enjambment, producing (as he says they do here) "two unstressed syllables coming together" (684).

213 *So much, as...to haue throwne* **STEIN** (1944b): the line is an "admittedly extreme" example of difficult scansion, "a series of stress-shifts, by attraction, in the first four feet"; because of its "monosyllabic opening," the first stress-shift is not "clearly marked," and the "sense of the line is not immediately apparent." Instead, "the tongue gets ahead of the brain, an occurrence not infrequent in reading Donne; and this inevitably produces a sort of friction, irritation, or harshness." In such a line, "the rhythm is hopelessly blocked unless it finds the right channel. The reader, blundering through, finds it impossible not to stress 'serve,' and that may lead him to attempt an elision in 'to have,' which adds the final touch of confusion" (393–94).

213–14 *at Rome...Ten Cardinals* **SMITH** (1971): "such a deal of protestation as would suffice to have ten Cardinals condemned as Protestants" (494).

214 *Ten Cardinals into th'Inquisition,* **STEIN** (1944b): the phrase is difficult to scan because "the reader has trouble in knowing whether the line has two elisions,

one, or none. To attempt both elisions makes the line almost unmouthable; yet the reader cannot discover this until the first elidable syllable ('Cardinalls') is past. Actually there are no elisions and the line is an alexandrine, but most readers must be patient to find this out" (394).

214 *Ten Cardinals* MILGATE (1967): "Even Cardinals, if they 'protested' as much as Macrine, would be condemned as heretics" (162). See l. 21 and note above.

214 *Inquisition,* SHAWCROSS (1967): "the inquiry into heresy" (33).

215–17 *And whisperd…Ladyes Psalter.* MILGATE (1967): "If Macrine's protestations would bring him into danger in Rome, the oath by which he frequently supports them would make him suspected, in England, of being a Roman Catholic" (162). HUGHES (1968): "a palpable hit on those paid informers who sought out recusants" (51). PRICE (1996): see note to l. 27.

215–16 *And whisperd…him away* ELLRODT (1960b): Donne reserves his sharpest arrows for those avid inquisitors who despoiled the recusants (2:285).

215–16 *so often, that a / Purseuant* STEIN (1942): in these lines, Donne's enjambment combines "an extreme weakening of the last foot" with the placement of "the cesura near the end of his line, where the start of a new rhythm, propelled by grammatical or rhetorical sense, will carry over," a technique that "apparently anticipates by several years the familiar style of Jacobean blank verse" (683).

215 *by Ihesu* SMITH (1971): "the courtier's oath 'by Jesu' would lay him under suspicion" in England, "as his protesting would, for the opposite reason, in Rome" (494).

215 *a* MELTON (1906): "Donne's verse, like Shakespeare's, and like the prose of Coleridge, shows 'insignificant' words stressed to meet the exigencies of rhythm and meaning" (65–66). SHAWCROSS (1972): see note to ll. 13–14.

216 *Purseuant* GRIERSON (1912) notes the manuscript variant "Topcliffe" as "a very interesting clue to the Catholic point of view" of the Satyres; refers to *DNB* and Meyer, *Die Katholische Kirche unter Elisabeth* (1910) (2:125). [Similarly, Robbins (2000, 424) and McCabe (2001, 82).] BEWLEY (1966): "an officer employed to find out and arrest Catholics" (185). [So also, Warnke (1967, 122), Gransden (1970, 171), and Carey (1990, 428).] MILGATE (1967) refers to *Sat5* 65. Adds that Richard Topcliffe (1532–1604) was "one of the most cruel and most hated of the informers against Roman Catholics. He tortured Southwell and investigated Nashe. Donne mentions him in the second item in *The Courtier's Library.* Though he was hated by many Protestants as much as by Catholics, disrespectful references to him might have been risky; and in revising his Satires, probably as a new servant of a higher officer of state, Donne changed his text to give a more general satiric reference" (162).

217 *For saying…But t'is fitt* SHAWCROSS (1972): see note to l. 5.

217 *saying* SHAWCROSS (1967): "reciting (the psalms of the Virgin Mary)" (33).

217 *our Ladyes Psalter.* LEGOUIS (1942): mistaking "Our Ladies psalter" for the "Jesus psalter," which repeats "Jesu" 150 times (192–93). MILGATE (1967): "It would

be rash to suppose, with Legouis, that Donne has mistaken the Lady's Psalter for the Jesus Psalter. In Protestant England the Rosary would have contained enough 'vain repetitions' of the name of Jesus to make the point here" (162).

219–28 *But here comes…commands Like Law.* ERSKINE-HILL (1972) refers to the tenth of Donne's *Paradoxes*, finding that "Glorius, by comparison to the summarized satiric *type* in the Paradox, is a dramatic presence" (291). KERINS (1984): the "antithesis" of Macrine, who "sins in making the social graces his religion," Glorius "is worse in his contempt for all decorum and, by analogy, all Christianity" (53). PATTERSON (1997): Glorius, "whose name tells all, is described as a bully" (14).

219 *Glorius* ALDEN (1899) thinks this a "distinct use of the *personal type-names*, the Latin form of which is the only departure from English local color" in the Satyres (88). MILGATE (1967) refers "for the type" to Nashe, *Works*, 1:361 (162). SHAWCROSS (1967): "a made-up name" (33).

220–21 *Who…good fashione.* RUDD (1963): the expression comes from *est huic diversum vitio vitium prope maius / asperitas agrestis et inconcinna gravisque* in Horace's *Epistles* 1.18.5–6 (208). SMITH (1971): "calls nothing else good fashion but a rough carelessness" (494).

220 *in the other extreame* MILGATE (1967): "as a complete contrast (to Macrine)" (162). SCODEL (1995): the passage uses the "mean-extremes polarity to treat issues or characters peripheral to the central issues that he confronts" (46). Neither of the passages on Macrine or Glorius addresses "the real dangers of court life depicted in the satire—its oppressive power, spies, and capacity for contaminating all who encounter it" (71).

220 *extreame* MELTON (1906): the word exemplifies Donne's use of secondary accent on Latin prefixes, "which may serve for ictus whenever the verse requires it" (86, 93).

221–22 *good fashione.…he spitts on* STEIN (1942): an example of Donne's "chief prosodic innovation," the frequent use of "stress-shift in the fifth foot," in which a feminine rhyme "is invariably matched with a masculine" (682).

221 *rough carelesnesse* SCODEL (1995): "reckless unconcern for others" (72).

222–23 *Whose cloke…do no harme* STEIN (1944c): omission of a syllable after a pause in the line is one of Donne's most daring devices for varying the metrical pattern, here an experiment in consecutive lines (377–78).

222 *Whose cloke…spitts on* SHAWCROSS (1972): see note to l. 62.

222 *Whose cloke his Spurs tear,* MILGATE (1967): "Cloaks long enough to be torn by spurs were an affectation of returned travellers and their apes"; wearing such cloaks "at Court would have been an indecorum," and "even at the Middle Temple (*Calendar of Records*, i, p. xxxvii) the wearing of cloaks was forbidden in church, buttery, and hall, and spurs might not be worn in the City unless the wearer was riding out of town"; see Nashe, *Works*, 2:300 (163).

223–24 *His ill words...To him.* **GROSART** (1872–73): "Very colloquial and careless construction. His ill words are the ill words of the sufferer" (1:44).

223 *He cares...no harme* **SHAWCROSS** (1972): see note to l. 62.

224–27 *He rusheth in;...to looke worse;* **LEWES** (1838): in this "very expressive" image, one sees "the rustling arras, and on it worked the figures of men, the malignity of whose faces, tells us how a strong feeling in the worker's mind has risen into art, which is but its realization" (375–76).

225–27 *and though...to looke worse;* **LEISHMAN** (1951): a "realistic" simile, "sufficient in itself to disprove the notion" that Donne "seems to have been little affected by visual impressions" (115). **HARRIS** (1960) notes the individuality of this "court bully" (192). **ERSKINE-HILL** (1964) notes the contrast with "the sweet, immaculate chaplain" and the "very sinister moral and religious light" in which this figure is depicted (171). **LECOMTE** (1965): the description of "hangings" fits "a Bosch now in the Prado" (27). **ERSKINE-HILL** (1972): linked to "the infernal comparison" at ll. 157–58, these lines not only seem to say that the Court is like hell but also, in their "grotesque/fantastic" quality, are "consonant" with that earlier "trancelike effect" (289). **ELLIOTT** (1976) refers to Matt. 6.16 (110). **KRUZHKOVA** (1994): seven Flemish tapestries, each emblazoned with a different deadly sin, hung in Hampton Court where, in earlier times, guards would have likely stood (164). **PATTERSON** (1997): this passage "drags sacred art back into the territory of social satire as if such art were now an anachronism (as well as being merely in service to metaphor)" (14).

226 *in old hangings whip Christ,* **BEWLEY** (1966): "tapestries on which the flagellation is pictured" (186). [So also, Shawcross (1967, 34) and Smith (1971, 494).] **MILGATE** (1967) refers to William Fennor's imitation of the passage in *The Compter's Commonwealth* (1617) (163). **HUGHES** (1968): "medieval iconography makes a brief appearance" (51). [So also, Gransden (1970, 171).]

228 *Licenc'd* **LEGOUIS** (1942): Donne's use of this word is cited by the *OED* as the earliest source (184–85). [So also, Sullens (1964, 195).]

229–37 *Tyr'd...Like a Spyed Spy.* **DUBROW** (1979): "complicated grammar permits an intensity and richness of ideas and images that is virtually unmatched in the genre" (79).

229–30 *Tyr'd...to'execution go,* **ELLRODT** (1960b): reacting to a sense of moral outrage, these lines express personal injury or resentment (2:289). **HARRIS** (1960): the lines particularize condemned men rather than typify them as a literary "characters" (192).

230–31 *As Men...great Chamber* **MCFARLAND** (1977): "The use of the conventional pattern of anadiplosis here, which has the effect of simple epizeuxis, adds little wit to the passage" (403).

230 *As Men...to'execution go,* **WARTON** (1797) states of this line that Donne "left his numbers so *much more rugged* and *disgusting*, than many of his contemporaries" (4:304).

231–32 *hung / With the 7 deadly Sins?*); **BUTT** (1939): these lines refer to some "early sixteenth-century Flemish tapestries bought by Wolsey" in 1522, now in the Great Watching Chamber at Hampton Court. Since Donne and Pope both locate these outside the Presence Chamber, there is the possibility "that these tapestries hung in the same position in late Elizabethan and Georgian days" (48). [So also, Milgate (1967, 163) and Smith (1971, 494).] **SHAWCROSS** (1967): "a tapestry picturing pride, covetousness, lust, anger, gluttony, envy, and sloth" (34). **HUGHES** (1968): see note to l. 226. **BLISSETT** (2000): Jonson's mention of wall hangings in *Cynthia's Revels* III.1.77 might have made Donne "smile in recollection" since both passages present details "of similar effect" (118).

231 *Go through…(why is it hung* **STEIN** (1944d): the pause and stress-shift in lines such as this one are a "phenomenon which is both physical and psychological" (298).

231 *the great Chamber* **BEWLEY** (1966): "the public audience chamber" (186). [So also, Shawcross (1967, 34).] **MILGATE** (1967): "Those leaving Court passed from the Presence Chamber into the Great Chamber (chiefly a place of assembly) and thence through the Guard Chamber (past 'Those Askaparts,' l. 233)" (163).

233–34 *Those Ascaparts,…for a barr,* **RUGOFF** (1939) cites this as one of only a few images from sports, in this case wrestling (127).

233–34 *to throw…for a bar,* **GROSART** (1872–73) conjectures "a test of strength" prevalent among the royal guards, referring to Bishop Corbet's poem to Lord Mordant, where, using similar terms, "he satirically describes his going to Court at Windsor" (1:44). **GRIERSON** (1912) refers to Nashe's *Have With You to Saffron Walden* (McKerrow, iii, p. 36) (2:125). **BEWLEY** (1966): "throwing an iron bar was a test of strength" (186). [So also, Shawcross (1967, 34).] **MILGATE** (1967) adds that Charing Cross, removed in 1647 by order of Parliament, "was apparently of imposing size" (163). **SMITH** (1971): "Throwing the bar was a sport much like tossing the caber. But the yeomen warders carried a halberd or bar, and to throw the bay may simply have been to manage this weapon" (494).

233 *Ascaparts,* **NORTON** (1895): "the renowned giant vanquished by Sir Bevis of Hampton" (1:245). [So also, Chambers (1896, 2:44), who also cites Michael Drayton, *Polyolbion*, Book 2, Shawcross (1967, 34), Gransden (1970, 171), Smith (1971, 494), Grigson (1980, 28), Carey (1990, 428), and Kruzhkova (1994, 164).] **BEWLEY** (1966): "the reference is to the height of the Queen's guard" (186). [So also, Smith (1971, 494).] **WARNKE** (1967): "a giant in medieval romance" (122). **MINER** (1969): "his imagination creates of the guards at Court great giants" (34).

234–36 *men which…of wine,* **CROFTS** (1936): Donne recognized that the yeomen of the guard represented "the royal power and majesty" of the Queen (129). **WARNKE** (1967): suggesting their "familiar appellation as 'beefeaters'" (122).

234–35 *men which…Queenes man,* **MCFARLAND** (1977): here Donne "embodies a type of antanaclasis in his anadiplosis" (403).

234 *Charing Crosse...which do know* STEIN (1944c): "stress-shift" after the caesura is one of Donne's chief devices for varying the metrical line (378).

234 *Charing Crosse* SMITH (1971): "the cross set up by Edward I" (494).

235–41 *No token...Staines away;* MELTON (1906): "difficult to read aloud," this passage "may excusably defy a novice" but is best read by treating "the five-foot verse not as a fixed and unalterable sequence of cadencies, but as a norm around which a musician weaves his variations" (48). Further, these lines contain arsis-thesis variation in stressed and unstressed repetitions of "-en" ("-on"), "of," and "spied" ("spy") (174).

235–36 *Queenes man,...of wine,* NORTON (1895): "The Beef-eaters—the popular appellation of the yeomen of the guard in the royal household, as well as of the warders of the Tower. This guard was established at the accession of Henry VII. in 1485" (1:246). GRIERSON (1912) notes the name "beefeaters" as giving rise to the jest and refers to Cowley's *Loves Riddle*, III, i and to Nashe. Further cites Grosart, 1:102 and McKerrow, 1:269 (2:125).

235 *No token of worth,* MILGATE (1967): "no sign of merit (but to be called 'Queen's men,' to enjoy fine living, etc.)" (163–64).

235 *Queenes man,* LEGOUIS (1942): a combination of words that OED does not record, although its analogue "King's man" is recorded (194). [So also, Sullens (1964, 205) and Milgate (1967, 164).]

236–41 *Liuing barrells...Though I yett* MORRIS (1953): "The passage starts with a strongly counterpointed line (three reversed feet), followed by one in Sprung Rhythm containing two syncopated feet (spyed Spie); then follows a straightforward iambic pentameter, which at first gives the illusion of counterpoint, since the usual initial unstressed syllable is missing. The fifth line with its one-syllable foot is sprung, and the sixth is again an ordinary iambic pentameter" (44).

236 *Liuing barrells...of wine,* HARDY (1942): "those amazing monumental men, the Queen's guard of Welshmen" (65). SMITH (1971): "the guard—the original beef-eaters—resemble the viands they consume in vast quantities" (495).

236 *barrells* MILGATE (1967): "belly and loins," also suggesting "vast quantities"; see OED 8 (164).

236 *beefe,* MILGATE (1967): "The name 'beefeater' was given to the Yeomen of the Guard, who (since 1485) guarded the Royal Houses and the Tower of London. References to their appetites are frequent"; see Corbett, *Poems*, p. 28 (164).

237–44 *I shooke Like...writts canonicall.* SHAWCROSS (1972): "of eight lines three are regular, three are defective, and two are hypermetric." Moreover, "five lines are strongly enjambed, and two others require their succeeding lines to complete their verbs" (263).

237–44 *Preachers which are...writts canonicall.* LECOCQ (1969): the admission of his fear in crossing the guards' room is not lacking in humor; the hyperbole of the metaphor could very well be here a mark of irony because it seems to replicate the preface of Hooker to the *Laws of Ecclesiastical Polity* and to say to the men of the church that since you claim to monopolize the right to criticism, what remains for you but to denounce the sins of the direst consequences? (381). **SANDERS** (1971): "an exquisite little coda (better than the rest of the poem put together)," in which he is "suddenly overtaken by a hot flush of modest sanctimony"; here, at the end of the poem, his "tongue moves with visible relish around the inside of the cheek, ending on the quizzical mockery of that unmistakably interrogative 'Canonicall.'" There is "a sureness of touch here, and a humanity" that Donne "of course couldn't sustain" (36–37). **ERSKINE-HILL** (1972): Sanders misses how "complex" *Sat4* has been; "something more than the boyish 'hot flush of modest sanctimony,'" the poem's conclusion "marks the completion of an expressive structure" (292–93). **SLIGHTS** (1981): "Only preachers can change men's fallen wills, but perhaps the poet can help to supply their erected wits with a guide to truth" (172). **CORTHELL** (1982): "obsessed with religious controversy," the satirist "predictably frames his dilemma in terms of Catholic and Protestant debates on scriptural authority and authenticity" (174). **BAUMLIN** (1988): the passage "implicitly raises the question, then, Can classical satire *ever* be 'Canonicall'?" (379).

237–41 *Preachers which are…their Staines away;* **TUVE** (1947) calls attention to the "intellectually pleasing subtleties" in this passage, namely, "the harsh wrenching of the rhythm and the homely mocking contrast in the double similitude" (186).

237–38 *I shooke Like…then dare* **SHAWCROSS** (1972): see note to ll. 13–14.

237–38 *Preachers which are…witt and arts,* **PETER** (1956): as a satirist, Donne defers to preachers any effort "to reform his contemporaries" (133).

237 *I shooke Like a Spyed Spy.* **MINER** (1969): "the suffering of fear, almost of terrors, both of the anti-Catholic court and of himself," to which "his reaction is physical" (33–34). **MAROTTI** (1986): the court is "not merely an arena for harmless foolishness but a politically perilous place" (105). **PRICE** (1996): see note to l. 27. **HESTER** (2000): see note to l. 119.

237 *Spyed* **SULLENS** (1964): Donne's usage of this word is cited by *OED* as the earliest source (201). **MILGATE** (1967): "detected" (164). [So also, Smith (1971, 495).]

238–39 *Seas of witt…for for mee* **STEIN** (1944c): two examples of the "nine-syllable line"—"not one of the chief devices for metrical modulation" in the Satyres (376–77).

238 *Seas of witt…then dare* **SHAWCROSS** (1972): see note to l. 62.

238 *you can, then dare* **MILGATE** (1967): "you have the ability and skill, then dare to use them" (164). **SMITH** (1971): "you have the power, then have the courage to use it against the Court too" (495).

239–41 *Drowne the Sins…Staines away;* **MCFARLAND** (1977): "The figures employed in these lines, polyptoton and contiguous antanaclasis, add to the force with which the speaker concludes in the hope that 'some wise man' will 'esteeme my writs Canonicall'" (403).

239 *Drowne the Sins...for for mee* **SHAWCROSS** (1972): see note to l. 62.

239 *Drowne the Sins* **SMITH** (1971): "as God drowned the sinful world at the Flood" (495).

240 *Who ame...shalbee* **SHAWCROSS** (1972): see note to l. 5.

240 *skant* **GRIERSON** (1912) (reading "scarce"): "scanty" (2:126). [So also, Milgate (1967, 164).] **SULLENS** (1964) (reading "scarce"): this meaning of the word is not recorded by *OED* (264). **SHAWCROSS** (1967) (reading "scarce"): "meager" (34). [So also, Smith (1971, 495).]

241–44 *Though I yett...writts canonicall.* **ELLIOTT** (1976): "an apology for his own harsh and sometimes blasphemous language" in the Satyres and "a key" to his "moral intent" (115). **KERINS** (1984): "the satirist's own assessment of the limitations of authority and a scrupulous evaluation of his own 'merit'" (53–54). **DOCHERTY** (1986): "the poem closes, establishing its own, if not the poet's canonization" (171). **MAROTTI** (1986): this passage "unites this work with the previous satiric poems" and their similarly "anticourtly attitudes" (105).

241–42 *I yett...meritt* **RICHTER** (1902) uses the rhymed words of the couplet here to illustrate level stress (409).

241 *To wash...Though I yett* **SHAWCROSS** (1972): see note to l. 62.

242–43 *Machabees Modesty...worke lessen;* **GROSART** (1872–73) quotes 2 Macc. 15.38–39: "And if I *have done* well, and as is fitting the story, it is that which I have desired: but if it slenderly and meanly, it is that which I could attain unto.... And here shall be an end" (1:44). [So also, Chambers (1896, 2:244), Grierson (1912, 2:126), Shawcross (1967, 34), Warnke (1967, 123), Hughes (1968, 51–52), Smith (1971, 495), and Kruzhkova (1994, 164).] **MILGATE** (1967) adds that "the books of *Maccabees* are believed by Protestants to be apocryphal, i.e., not 'canonical' or fully authoritative," and thus the satirist "hopes that someone with the necessary wisdom will recognize that his work (because it tells the truth) can be fully believed" (164). [So also, Gransden (1970, 171) and Carey (1990, 428).] **SHAWCROSS** (1972): "I too will here conclude my account. If it has been well and pointedly written, that is what I wanted; but if it is poor, mediocre work, that was all I could do" (260).

242 *With Machabees...the knowne meritt* **STEIN** (1944c): "stress-shift" in the fifth foot is one of Donne's chief devices for varying the metrical line (382). **SHAWCROSS** (1972): see note to line 5.

242 *Machabees* **ERSKINE-HILL** (1964) finds a hint of Donne's Catholicism in his allusion to an apocryphal book (171). **GRIGSON** (1980): "of the Books of Maccabees only *Maccabees* 1 and 2 were included in the canon of the Bible by the Council of Trent" (29). [Similarly, Kruzhkova (1994, 165).] **HESTER** (1982): as *Sat4* adapts Horace, 2 Macc. adapts the account by Jason of Cyrene of "certain conflicts between the Jewish nation and foreign defilers" (91).

242 *Modesty* **SHAWCROSS** (1972): "may be only two syllables" (263).

243–44 *yet some Wise men…writts canonicall.* **SHAWCROSS** (1972): "This does not mean that the canon will be followed and mankind reformed, rather he hopes his satires will at least be recognized as proposing true doctrine for the world of moral men" (262).

243 *some Wise men* **CORTHELL** (1982): "not simply a perceptive and sympathetic reader but one who indeed has the power to make Donne's work canonical—a prospective patron or employer," such as Sir Thomas Egerton (175). **BAUMLIN** (1990): this "would smooth somewhat the tensions between the poet's disclaimer of authority and his critique of court," if it is, in fact, "intended as a flattering allusion to Egerton" (76). **CORTHELL** (1997): if this refers to Egerton, "directly addressed" in *Sat5*, then the Satyres may "gesture beyond themselves *as texts* toward that 'history' that is not a text" (48). **WIGGINS** (2000): if this refers to the Lord Keeper, "then Egerton could be said to be referred to or else strongly suggested in all the satires and to be specifically designated as their legitimating authority" (25).

244 *writts canonicall.* **BEWLEY** (1966): "not apocryphal; belonging to the true scriptural canon" (186). **SHAWCROSS** (1967): "vestment, doctrine" (34). **LECOCQ** (1969): the poem ends in a play on words: Donne indicates that his work will be judged canonical since it will have the effect of a cannonball. Thus, the serious and the jovial are mingled up to the very last word of this poem (381). **SMITH** (1971): "(a) orthodox; falling within the accepted canon as Maccabees does not, or falling within the law; (b) authoritative, because what they say is true; (c) meriting approval (or reward) by the accepted canons of judgement" (495).

 Satyre 5.

COMMENTARY

Date and Circumstances

Grosart (1872–73, 1:49–50) suggests that "the great Carrick's pepper" (l. 85) was a reference to an event of 1602–03, when an English sea captain, James Lancaster, sent home pepper and other spices captured from "*a Portuguese carrack*." Chambers (1896, 2:242, 245) also notes the capture of the Portuguese ship by Lancaster.

Norton (1895, 1:246–47) points out that the address to the Lord Keeper of the Great Seal, Thomas Egerton, beginning in line 31, fixes the date of *Sat5* during Donne's employment by Egerton, which (he supposes) began in 1596 and ended in 1600. (Alden [1899, 79–80] and Lecocq [1969, 382] also date the poem to the beginning of Donne's employment with Egerton.) Norton explains that Egerton was named Lord Keeper in 1596, and because of his "unquestioned" integrity, he received the Queen's authority, either "express or implied," to "introduce reforms into the practice of the courts, to prevent delays as well as the sale of justice, and to check the extortions of officials."

Gosse (1899, 1:43) dates the poem "a little earlier" than Lancaster's capture of the Portuguese ship because lines 28–34 refer not only to the period of Donne's employment by the Lord Keeper, but also to "the bribing of judges," which Egerton was then "attempting to root out."

Grierson (1909, 238) dates *Sat5* in 1597, "or the years immediately following" and finds in the poem "the mark of the budding statesman."

Grierson (1912, 2:104–05) explains that the Portuguese ship captured in 1602–03 is the wrong ship, the phrase "the Great Carrick" never having been used about it, but that an earlier prize, "the *Madre de Dios*…belonging to the crown of Portugal," was in fact called "the Great Carrick" after its capture by Sir Walter Raleigh in 1592 and on account of "the Privy Council's disposition of the pepper contained in its cargo hold." In addition, line 31 "rules out a date before 1597 or after 1602," and thus he dates the poem in 1598 or 1599, (Leishman [1951, 106–07] and Reid [2000, 39] concur in the date for *Sat5*) observing its "note of enthusiasm," as of "one who had just entered on a service of which he is proud," and suggesting that the poem's "occasion" was likely Egerton's "endeavour to curtail the fees claim'd by the Clerk of the Star Chamber." Hayward (1929, 120), Milgate (1967, 165), and Empson (1972, 147) also note the same political occasion for the poem.

Grierson (1929, xxxi) comments that Donne probably had conformed to the Church of England on entering Egerton's service.

LeComte (1965, 61) suggests that Donne was "basking" in the satisfaction of his position with Egerton when he wrote Sat5.

Gamberini (1967, 47) finds Sat5 an exception among the Satyres, written after the first four, while Donne was serving Lord Keeper Egerton, and showing an odd transformation of the earlier, elegant, disillusioned youth suddenly adopting a business-like rhetoric—no more than a veneer—for the purposes of satire on the court and of gaining approval from his employer. There is a false note not only in this appeal to Egerton, he says, but in the young man's attitude toward the officialdom of what he calls an "age of rusty iron."

Milgate (1967, xxiv, lviii, 165) suggests that Donne wrote Sat5 "to please his patron" (xxiv), while at this time also preparing a copy of the first four Satyres for Egerton (lviii), and that all of this occurred in connection with "some specific reforming activities of Egerton at the time" (165).

Bald (1970, 100–01) states that Sat5 "records some of Donne's impressions" as a secretary "with a large share of the business that passed through the Lord Keeper's hands," the poem being concerned with "the exactions levied on suitors by the lawyers and officials of the court, not merely in the Star Chamber and in the law courts generally, but also in the Chancery and other offices to which those who had obtained royal grants had to go to get their grants validated." (Hester [1982, 98–99] and Kerins [1984, 55] also note the extended contexts for the legal levies.) Bald admits that, disappointingly, "there is no clue to Donne's secretarial activities" among Egerton's papers.

Shawcross (1972, 252) dates Sat5 during Donne's service for Egerton partly because the poem has "the ring of rejection" of the lifestyle of a courtier.

Hester (1978b, 350) finds that the poem is not "merely an attempt to impress his new employer with his ingenuity," but is primarily a critique of the "perversions of eternal Law endemic to the corruptions" that Egerton was investigating at the time.

Dubrow (1979, 80) urges that Donne focuses on the royal court in Sat5 because of his "fascination with the public world" and "his own ambivalent relationship to the court during the years in which he was writing the satires." Behind his "bitter condemnation may well lie an attraction to the court of which Donne himself was not proud," though she adds, "the gentleman protests too much."

Marotti (1981, 215) asserts that in writing Sat5, Donne "was able, while secure in Egerton's service, to view social and political scrambling with some equanimity and confidence."

Flynn (1983, 335) questions the assumption by Bald (1970) that Donne's duties as Egerton's secretary required him to have access to the legal business of the Lord Keeper. Sat5's references to legal work, he asserts, "are general and insufficient to indicate Donne's close involvement in any specific work at Egerton's direction."

Kerins (1984, 54–55) suggests that Donne's appointment as Egerton's secretary speaks to Sat5's concern with "a concrete contemporary issue—the abuses of a graft-ridden legal system, specifically the Star Chamber fees—an issue which Donne's employer had been recently commissioned to investigate." He argues that Sat5 is both "the most topical" of the Satyres and "also the most generalized," and thus "the satirist's public character allows him to analyze dispassionately the relationship between ideal justice and the adulteration effected by these corrupt officers and suitors."

Marotti (1986, 116–18, 123) contends that Donne's position as the Lord Keeper's secretary affects "the matter and manner" of Sat5. The satirist criticizes "contemporary social ills, naming particularly the abuses of the legal system Elizabeth had charged Egerton to investigate and reform," and addressing both "Queen and minister in a way that carefully advertised his own position in the political hierarchy." Although Donne discusses "the abusive legal-fee charging of court officers," Marotti suggests, his description of suitors and officers "applied to political transactions in general" (116). Donne, he argues, wrote "to the audience of friends he felt most comfortable addressing in the 1590s, men he knew from the Inns of Court and from his succeeding social experience" (118). Moreover, although Sat5 manifests Donne's "conflicts and ambivalences" about his position at court, nevertheless the poem "expresses trust in benevolent authorities within the Establishment" (123).

Baumlin (1990, 69, 74–75, 79) asserts that Sat5, in attempting "to retract the treasonous political attack" of Sat3, is "an apostate poet's hasty—and expedient—revision" of abandoned Catholic opinions (69), "little more than a piece of self-serving flattery, a patronizing of the poet's new employer." Given his appointment as Egerton's secretary, Donne felt "the need to rewrite" his earlier, "embarrassing" and "potentially dangerous," efforts as a satirist. He contends that Donne's "apostasy," whether it was caused by his brother's death through association with the Jesuits or whether he had simply determined that he would "conform to the Anglican articles of faith," was complete by the time he wrote Sat5, if not sincerely then "in all outward show" (74–75). But his relationship to authority, Baumlin concludes, could not be "without its uneasiness," its "ambivalences," its "recognition of the deep compromises" that had made him "the apostate secretary to an apostate official" (79).

Baumlin (1991, 26) avers that Sat5 is "tantamount to an act of apostasy" that "explicitly repudiates the poet's earlier Romanist views."

Sullivan (1993, 12–13) notes that the previously "uncollected printings" of Donne's verse "establish a *terminus ad quem*" for Sat5 of 1629.

Manley (1995, 400) observes that "not even the attainment of office under the Lord Keeper Egerton in 1597 was sufficient to accommodate Donne's satiric vision to the realities of power," but on the contrary, Sat5 is Donne's "most corrosive penetration to the heartless center of the social order."

Prescott (2000, 230) offers a possible date of 1598 for the poem.

Edwards (2001, 53) claims that Donne "probably showed" Sat5 to Lord Keeper Egerton, making him "a delighted employer."

Flynn (2001, 107, 112, 119–20) thinks the composition of Sat5 was one of Donne's first acts after taking office as secretary to Lord Keeper Egerton (107). Donne's desire to work for Egerton, rather than for either the Essex or Cecil factions at court, Flynn asserts, reflects "a characteristic political discretion," a value "the two men shared" (112). While Donne may have shown Sat5 to Egerton, the "daring" of the poem makes one doubt that Egerton ever showed it to the Queen (119–20).

General Commentary

Grierson (1909, 238) calls *Sat5* "a descant on the familiar theme of Spenser's laments, the miseries of suitors." Nilsen (1997, 141) also notes the echo of this theme.

Walker (1925, 72) states that the poem, beyond its legal specifics dealing with court officers and suitors, "broadens out into greater generality and condemns the satirist's own age without measure," and as such, "illustrates Donne's habitual pessimism."

Hardy (1942, 64) finds that over *Sat5* (as over Donne's other Satyres) hangs the unpleasant burden of "the weight and lavishness of the ornate, and often tasteless, tombs of the period."

Leishman (1951, 117–18) insists that the legal abuses Donne satirizes in the poem are "merely a topic for the display of his wit," which is itself "marred by the deliberately achieved harshness of the verse," exemplifying Donne's "tendency to indulge in mere wit for its own sake."

Smith (1952, 226) judges *Sat5* "the least brilliant" of the Satyres.

Harris (1960, 201) finds that *Sat5*, though deriving from "a particular impulse and occasion," nevertheless reaches "a universal image far more powerful than [Joseph] Hall's invocation of the ideal," and "a contemporary frame of reference more precise than [John] Marston's."

Bewley (1966, 187) comments on the cultivated roughness characteristic of English satire in the 1590s and feels that in *Sat5* "the manner is carried so far that it becomes an irritant." At some points, the obscurity of the poem "seems to spring less from design than from lack of control over the lines."

Geraldine (1966, 31) thinks *Sat5* "shriller and less satisfying than the other satires."

Milgate (1967, xxi, xxiv, 165) states that in *Sat5* Donne's "humorous touch" falters, "deserting him altogether" (xxi); the poem "seems to keep going at all only by a series of spasmodic efforts," as if Donne "had reached the limits of what he could achieve in this style" and was writing only "to please his patron." *Sat5* is "a rather pathetic attempt" to come up to the standard of earlier Satyres, he says, but thankfully, Donne "did not stretch out his material over greater length" (xxiv). He finds it the "weakest" of the Satyres, with "the air of a rather hastily-put-together occasional piece," as evident in its "gnomic" and "rather trite" lines (e.g., ll. 9–13, 19, 56), which fall short of the "power and originality" of the earlier Satyres. Even its "tones of homily and complaint," he asserts, "are too often heard to permit the achievement of a forceful and cumulative satiric effect" (165).

Hughes (1968, 28, 50) thinks *Sat5* to be "perhaps the bitterest" of the Satyres (28) and among Donne's writings the last of the "utterances of the self-conscious renegade," differing from what followed as the "Lothian portrait" differs from the "Isaac Oliver portrait," the difference "between a man partly hidden in shadow and a man fully revealed" (50).

Lecocq (1969, 382–83) states that *Sat5*, although related to *Sat2*, goes beyond merely repeating the technique of the earlier poem to refine and complicate it by critiquing fools and evildoers according to the demands of "Charity and liberty" (6–7). He adds that no other Elizabethan has more succinctly satirized their age than Donne has in focusing upon these two words.

Miner (1969, 32–33) sees *Sat5* as unique because it names specific people, such as Egerton and the Queen herself, but finds it particularly remarkable in the fact that it heaps scorn "not so much upon the great, who exploit suitors, as upon the suitors themselves, who do not realize the vanity of efforts which only undo them." He finds this satiric approach by Donne, "just as he was himself getting on," understandable since "the court was something Donne had experienced and which in spite of its attractions threw him back on his own resources of integrity"; indeed, he asserts, "here is one reason why he became a private poet."

Bald (1970, 100) concludes that *Sat5* gives an account of Donne's experiences as Egerton's secretary and says that what sets it apart from the others is that "the poet is no longer a mere spectator, but a participant in the issues of which he writes." Here we can detect a new sense of indignation, for "in the place of witty observation of individual affectations there is a strong, even a shocked, perception of moral corruption."

Smith (1970, 143) finds that *Sat5* "dramatizes a moral detachment," prompting "amused derision at men's pretensions" and "a disturbed diagnosis of corruptness." It offers a "vision of a civic jungle where our only weapon is a wary guardedness, founded ultimately in a cool recognition of the relativeness of human claims altogether in respect of the dust to which we must all come."

Hebaisha (1971, 29) claims that *Sat5* exemplifies—along with the other Satyres—a "detachment from moral purpose," a "flippancy and lightness, a certain urbanity," and a "civilized attitude that makes [Donne's] satires nearer in spirit to classical formal satire than those of his contemporaries."

Powers (1971, 38, 77) notes Donne's references to broad groups, such as "Officers, Judges, and 'Suiters'" (38), and sees Donne's reference to "pitty" as evidence of the possibility for various moods in Elizabethan satire (77).

Empson (1972, 147) asserts that in *Sat5* Donne labors "to support some proposed change of law, and displays philosophic breadth," but he adds that the "moral" of the poem is "that you will be ruined if you go to law" and concludes, "this is sad stuff."

Samarin (1972, 171) states that the focus on lawyers in *Sat5* suggests Donne's relations and acquaintances within that circle of society.

Shawcross (1972, 260, 267–68) argues that *Sat5* "has lost some of the spleen of the others and is almost pervaded with pity," commenting that the "misery of those who must beg for sustenance is too great for jest" (260). Readers who have thought the poem less successful among Donne's Satyres "because of the lack of humor in it" fail, he says, to "recognize that the evil exposed is deeper, emboldened by the fabric of man's impoverished life and hopes of extrication through financial improvement." Some cause for such criticism might be the apparent absence of an auditor in the poem, he surmises, "for the 'I' reflectively addresses his muse as well as the suitors who fall prey to officers," a "reflectiveness" that "reduces the sense of directness and on-the-spot conversation" (267–68).

Raizada (1974, 106) observes that *Sat5* is notable only for its bold satire of "the corruption and inefficiency of law courts," "the bribing of officials," and "the misery of suitors."

Parker (1975, 21) states that in *Sat5* Donne focuses his attention on the law, "bitterly attacking its weakness, its slowness, its injustices, and going so far as to accuse the Queen herself of ignorance of its workings."

Lauritsen (1976, 129) suggests that the "vision" of *Sat5* is a "growing awareness of self as co-partner in the corrupt world" as it presents a "potentially remediable evil: the bribing of the judiciary as too frequently practiced in England in the 1590's." Thus, *Sat5*'s homiletic and compassionate tone is an "essentially anti-satiric sentiment," a discovery that "the inherent wretchedness and wickedness of mankind are not fit objects for satiric sport."

Hester (1978b, 347–51, 361–62) considers *Sat5* "a poem much more carefully organized and illustrative of Donne's opinion of the satiric genre than readers have claimed" (347). Here the satirist is "confident that he is now morally and legally 'authoriz'd' (l. 33) to attack the moral ignorance of the Court" (348), and he does so, Hester argues, in a manner that is "judicious" and "meditative" (350), proceeding not spasmodically but in accord with "devotional, homiletic, and rhetorical principles" (351). *Sat5* not only "reveals Donne at his most 'metaphysical' in his conflation of erudite and commonplace phrases and texts," but it is also "one of Donne's most allusive poems, revealing the poet's wide reading and humanistic interests." He further emphasizes that the poem's wide-ranging citations suggest a major concern with "instruction" and with clarifying "the spiritual condition of a man faulty in understanding." While addressing "a fool" may be a weakness of the poem, he acknowledges, nevertheless the "pattern of exegeses" expresses "concern" and "tolerant charity" for the suitor at Court, who is after all a member of the audience to whom the speaker appeals. Consequently, he concludes, "the care with which the satirist presents his explications of the condition of justice in England evinces his faith in the ability of man's reason to begin the recovery of values even in the midst of a confused moral atmosphere," and "the satirist's own homiletic-devotional procedures dramatize for the suitor and the reader the method and means of regeneration" (361–62).

Carey (1981, 69) finds *Sat5* "a more respectful performance" than his other and earlier Satyres, confirming that Queen Elizabeth "is in no way to blame for the corruption rampant in her realm." Nevertheless, Donne "cannot suppress his indignation at the government agents who persecute Catholicism," he notes, and while it "would have been more tactful for Donne to have kept his Catholic resentment out of sight," this feeling "was liable to surface whenever he wrote poetry."

Slights (1981, 176–77) observes that *Sat5*'s "reflectiveness and absence of humor has provoked a largely negative critical response," and "the unifying context of the speaker's case of conscience has been ignored." However, in this poem, Donne "does not rest content with teaching virtue by presenting images of vice—even by presenting vice revealed in all its ugliness," but in addition "analyzes acutely the operation of the contemporary judicial system and the motives and consequences of individual action in those circumstances."

Corthell (1982, 175) remarks that "satirists rarely experience such an opportunity," as *Sat5* implies, "to translate their vision into action," yet among Donne's Satyres, *Sat5* is "the most pessimistic."

Hester (1982, 98–99, 103) calls *Sat5* "the most occasional" of the Satyres through its involvement with specific secretarial work under Lord Keeper Egerton's direction;

but despite this topicality it is not "hastily constructed," although a "flattering portrait" of Donne's new employer Egerton "as a figure of 'righteousnes' (31) is central to its strategy" (98–99). *Sat5* is "cast simultaneously as meditation and as oration" in that "its outer frame is meditative," its "inner frame," "forensic or oratorical" (103).

Kerins (1984, 54–55) suggests that, as *Sat4* "refashioned the perspective" of *Sat1*, *Sat5* "reinvestigates the themes of Law and Justice" from *Sat2*, adding that both *Sat2* and *Sat5* are "in the form of the satiric epistle." He argues that in *Sat5* Donne's "prime concern is not the venality of corrupt officers but rather a lack of correspondence between the reality of the present judicial system and the ideal upon which it is based." Thus, although *Sat5* is the "most topical" of the Satyres, "it is also the most generalized," and the speaker analyzes "dispassionately" the contrast "between ideal justice and the adulteration effected by these corrupt officers and suitors."

Albright (1985, 250) says that *Sat 5* (like "most poems by Donne") should be read "in a spirit of intellectual delirium," because here, as elsewhere, Donne "continually uses the language of logic, of analogy" only as "a game in which the mind delights in the reeling sensation it feels as it gropes for logical relations amid a pervasive alogicality. The imagination is always moving faster than reason, which keeps struggling for syllogistic design as it falls further and further behind."

Toliver (1985, 104) comments that *Sat5* is "less concerned with language and manners than the other satires," but it "is equally bitter about this corruption of the courtly system and the part of the social contract that should guarantee privacy and property but does not."

Baumlin (1986a, 92, 102), citing Lauritsen (1976) and Elliott (1976), notes that *Sat5* has seemed "problematic in its use of genre and convention" (92). He disputes the contention by Milgate (1967) that "tones of homily and complaint" in the poem diminish its satiric effect, retorting that "homiletic tones blend naturally with the broader diatribe elements of the poem" (102).

In his discussion of *Sat5*, Caracciolo-Trejo (1986, 2:13) claims that an aroma of bitterness infuses those experiences and those hard years of Donne's youth that he must have suffered while soliciting for positions he would never attain.

Marotti (1986, 123) contends that *Sat5* "expresses trust in benevolent authorities within the Establishment."

Baumlin (1990, 74–75, 77–79, 82) questions the "sincerity" of *Sat5* because beyond being "little more than a piece of self-serving flattery, a patronizing of the poet's new employer," the poem's "self-interested expediency" extends to both political inconstancy and "apostasy" (74–75). The poem makes an implicit claim, he says, "to transcend its limitations as literature by becoming a proclamation against political and legal corruption," something "other than mere rebuke or even persuasion—to become something other than satire" (77–78). He argues further that in *Sat5* Donne is "ambivalent in spite of himself" as he "falls short" in attempting "to praise and exhort Egerton, to exculpate Elizabeth, and to apologize for English law." He concedes that *Sat5* "does not fail entirely," for its "solution to the problem of political authority," a "thoroughly Christian" one, is "not so much to claim power for its own proclamations as to assert the role of charity in all actions" (79). The poem deals ostensibly with "abuses of the law," but its "metalinguistic subject" is actually "the charitable *interpretation* of law" (82).

Ray (1990, 284) briefly notes that *Sat5* "portrays the meanness of both legal suitors and figures in authority."

Sullivan (1993, 6–7) lists *Sat5* 3–4 among the six poems that were "published in part during his [Donne's] lifetime" and concludes that "there was more of Donne's printed poetry with a larger circulation, a more general readership (as opposed to members of Donne's inner circle who had access to his manuscripts), and a greater potential influence during his lifetime than previously believed" (7).

Patterson (1994, 146–47) describes *Sat5* as "the most clearly Elizabethan" of all of Donne's Satyres. It is "addressed both to the queen herself" and "to an unnamed justicer who is surely Egerton," and the poem "is pitched at authorized bribery, that aspect of the patronage system which requires all access to the law to be mediated by state officials, so that the legal world is divided into two populations, officers and their suitors," the former of whom "adulterate the law," while the latter "are complicit in its adulteration by paying the fees demanded of them."

Manley (1995, 400) contends that "not even the attainment of office under the Lord Keeper Egerton in 1597 was sufficient to accommodate Donne's satiric vision to the realities of power," but on the contrary, the poem is Donne's "most corrosive penetration to the heartless center of the social order." He explains that "jests and tears both prove inadequate to this exploration, which opens not with conversational banter but with a solitary apostrophe to the Muse," and "the motifs of the satire—the 'wrech'd'-ness of 'Suiters misery,' and the 'wicked'-ness of 'Officers rage'—are not so much Horatian extremes as poles in a cycle of social competition."

Reid (2000, 46) states that the closest Donne comes "to censor of the age" is in *Sat5*, which he describes as "the most earnest and the least serious" of the Satyres.

Robbins (2000, 423) notes that there are manuscript versions of *Sat5* both "with and without possibly original proper names."

Wiggins (2000, 58–59) finds *Sat5* "less a poem than a history," an example of "history as poetry" that "sets the other satires in perspective" and "renders them comprehensible."

Flynn (2001, 107–08) calls *Sat5* Donne's "most daring" Satyre, a "junior staff member's whistleblowing attack from within on the involvement of Court officers and their suitors in a corrupt system of justice."

Sources, Influences, and Analogues

Alden (1899, 85, 88) notes that Donne in *Sat5* as elsewhere "was least of all men imitative"; even in using the genre of classical satire, he "avoids obvious unoriginality" (85). He also argues that there is "little of the native English element" in *Sat5* where, even though the attack on "the oppressions practiced by legal officers" resembles "much of early English satire," the satirist speaks "as an individual, not as a representative of the people." This "note of individual pessimism" connects *Sat5* to the tradition of Roman satire, Alden says, and, moreover, its "compactness, its indirect method, its allusiveness are all of the classical sort" (88).

Grierson (1909, 238) finds *Sat5* "a descant on the familiar theme of Spenser's laments, the miseries of suitors."

Rickey (1966, 186) includes "the Muses, the iron age, Destiny, Fate, and Aesop" in her listing of the classical references in this poem.

Elliott (1976, 108–10) claims that there are "verbal echoes" and "thematic parallels" in *Sat5* from Christ's Sermon on the Mount (Matt. 5–7), specifying the phrase "O Age of rusty iron!" in line 35 matched with Matthew's concern about overindulgence in material things; Donne's reference in line 26 to officers who "Adulterate law" matched with the theme of adultery in Matthew; and the drownings in lines 29–30 and 90–91, said to echo the drowning of swine "in the chapter immediately following the Sermon on the Mount."

Hester (1978b, 349, 351–53) finds that *Sat5* takes the form of "a judicial oration," following Thomas Wilson's scheme in *The Arte of Rhetorique* (349). Within this framework, the poem cites and applies various "Renaissance and classical" sources as guides for court suitors (including Castiglione, Paracelsus, Juvenal, Ariosto, and Aesop), each clarified by biblical "texts or tenets." First among these, Hester says, is Castiglione's book of "Rules to make Courtiers," cited at the poem's start (in accord with Wilson's principles) to "get the good will" of courtiers here being addressed; the satirist "gains a willing audience (and satisfies those who most need his instruction, for 'who Courtiers good?') by tolerantly agreeing to conform to their book of behavior." He notes that Donne's jesting litotes ironically accepts Castiglione's liberal prescription (ll. 5–6) freeing courtiers "from the sting of jests" because they are already extremely "wrech'd or wicked." *Sat5* goes on to follow Castiglione's letter, if not his spirit, Hester asserts, satirizing courtiers in Christian "Charity and liberty" but not laughing at them. The satirist's "apparent willingness to adhere literally to the code of those he attacks" adds to the poem's "ironic deflations of the Italian humanist's prescriptions" (351–52).

Similarly, he contends, *Sat5*'s "assertion of the universal principle of accommodation" in lines 9–12, based on Paracelsus's *Coelum Philosophorum*, accedes to the wisdom of another preceptor highly regarded at court. Without necessarily believing the teaching of Paracelsus, the satirist "assents to it, using another form of 'wisdom' in his own defense of truth and prosecution of 'enormous sinne,'" and showing himself reasonably to be "a judicious exegete," willing to accept doctrines used at court in order to accommodate a hearing for his own satiric purposes. Two analogies in lines 13–19, applying Paracelsus's text to satire on the court, Hester notes, "delineate the 'raging' fraudulence of the officers and the suicidal incontinence of the suitors." Here the satirist not only ridicules "the stupidity of the suitors for participating in such a corrupt system," but also underlines the justice of their suffering, since even in "the most corrupt system" justice can be found (353).

Dubrow (1979, 81–82), quoting lines 1–6, thinks *Sat5* typically contrasts with the practice of Donne's contemporary satirists in incorporating no prefatory "defense of satire" or reference to its virtues in "theoretical apologia," but instead tends to question or undercut the genre.

Hester (1980a, 106–07) finds a "defense of satire" in *Sat5*, pointing to lines 7–9 as an allusion to and an accommodation of Horace's *Satires* 1.1.23–24. Whereas Horace asks why laughter may not accompany telling truth in satire ("*ridentem dicere verum*"), implicitly censuring his predecessor Lucilius for the use in satire of jocularity without truth, Donne's satirist "finds the stance of Horace inadequate" under Elizabethan conditions—an "Age of rusty iron" (l. 37) he calls it, alluding to Juvenal—and asserts that telling truth in satire under these conditions requires an end to jesting.

Slights (1981, 176) argues that *Sat5* both shares and departs from the practice of casuists, such as William Perkins, in regard to the question of taking grievances to court, but that Donne "conducts his examination from a satirical, not a casuistical perspective." She adds, "while the casuist attempts to resolve doubts and quiet troubled consciences," the satirist attempts to "overcome dangerous complacency by creating doubt," yet despite these differences, "their ultimate goals and their assumptions about human action are the same."

Hester (1982, 99–105, 107–08, 116) points out that Donne's appointment as secretary to Lord Keeper Egerton provided him with "an opportunity denied his Latin models, all of whom, even Horace, in spite of his association with Augustus and Maecenas," were outsiders confined to working not directly as reformers but as satirists through their poems and readers (99). Yet the "situation and strategy" of *Sat5* are similar to those of Juvenal's thirteenth satire, which rebukes the Roman grandee Calvinus for initiating a breach-of-trust lawsuit after a friend defrauded him.

Hester attributes "part of the brilliance" of *Sat5* to "its expansion and accommodation of the dicta and approach of the Roman satire into a Christian theodicy while enforcing the ancient prescription, *nosce teipsum*" (102). Another feature common to both Juvenal's and Donne's poems, Hester says, is a questioning by each satirist concerning the proper role of indignant laughter in satire (103). He also finds in *Sat5* an analogue to Horace, in that Donne's satirist, "through Egerton's authority," combines the attributes of both Horace's satirist and Trebatius, the Roman magistrate who discusses administration with the satirist (104). He adds that the "locus classicus" of Donne's method in *Sat5* is St. Augustine's "definition of the doctrine of accommodation" in *De Doctrina Christiana* (105), applied ironically in the satirist's opening citation of Baldassare Castiglione's rules for courtiers (107). Beyond this "topical reference to Castiglione" lies the "authoritative formula" of Horace, "*ridentum dicere verum*" (108). Finally, he notes, the last lines of *Sat5* borrow from Aesop with a side glance at Horace (116).

Zunder (1982, 18) finds that in *Sat5* the "traditional, hierarchical system, centred on the monarch," is "implicitly affirmed," and that its image of monarchy's "life-fulfilling qualities" is reminiscent of Shakespeare's image of monarchy.

Baumlin (1986a, 92–94, 100–02, 104–05) contends that *Sat5* abandons both Juvenal's "*saeva indignatio*" and Horace's "*sermo* style" and instead adopts "the protreptic zeal and the diatribe style" of Persius (92). This imitation of Persius gives a "Christian significance" to the "Stoic model's themes," utilizing "elements of rhetoric" as well as "similarities in persona and relationship to audience" (93). Although Donne does not speak as a Stoic in *Sat5*, Baumlin says, the "moral seriousness" of the Stoic model offers "an appropriate vehicle for Christian subject matter" (94). As Persius, in his own fifth satire, addressed his mentor, Cornutus, so Donne addresses his patron, Lord Keeper Thomas Egerton, attempting "to effect social change" through "direct address to a specific audience" (100). In the "serious, homiletic tone" of *Sat5*, "indignation and particularly laughter" are supplanted by "pitty," not necessarily "an attribute readers would readily associate with Persian satire, although it is a typically Stoic attitude toward the 'insanity' of human sinfulness and error" (101). Departing from the practice of Horace and Juvenal, Donne discovered in Persius, Baumlin believes, "the broad outline of a deliberative and essentially public voice whose moral exhortations, much more than laughter or rage, could best result in reform" (105).

Baumlin (1986b, 465–67) finds that the "outright rejection of laughter" in the opening lines of *Sat5*, as in those of *Sat3*, effects at the outset a Christianizing attitude in relation to the ethical relativism and humor of Horatian satire (465). He describes the persona of *Sat3* and *Sat5* as "a preacher, persuading and teaching his audience rather than ridiculing or punishing," and he explains that Persius is the "model" for *Sat3* and *Sat5*, "both of which rely heavily on this Roman's moral gravity and protreptic zeal." He argues that while Juvenal was the "preferred model" for Hall and Marston, Donne "found in Persian satire the best vehicle for his own serious Christian insights—but could not have been secure in this choice had not he, like Hall and Marston, tested the resources of all three Roman models" (466–67).

Baumlin (1990, 80) points to the satirist's ultimate rejection of classical influence in *Sat5*, where he tempers "liberty" with "Charity" and "explicitly renounces the ridicule of classical satire." The Christian virtue of charity—"the very antithesis" of ridicule and invective—here replaces zeal and "righteous indignation" with "humility and an attitude of toleration."

Baumlin (1991, 26, 150) finds that *Sat5*'s repudiation of Donne's earlier Catholic views also mitigates the force of his classical models, "and for the same reason, their inability to assert a persuasive or self-validating moral authority" (26). In *Sat5*, then, Donne's satire attempts to transform itself "into something other than classical imitation—to transform itself, in a word, into proclamation and law" (150).

Gorbunov (1993, 95) notes that the key themes in *Sat2* and *Sat5*—the bribability, falsity, and chicanery and greed of judges—appear for the first time in English literature in these poems and, further, soon became common concerns in the urban comedies of Ben Jonson and Thomas Middleton.

Corthell (1997, 53) draws a contrast and a parallel between *Sat5*'s reference to "the first maine head" (l. 46) and the comparison in Psalm 82 of "earthly and divine justice." Both writers "attack corruption in the courts of kings," he says, but in Donne's poem, "the fall of princes is ascribed to the workings of a system of bribery in God's court" (ll. 59–63). *Sat5*'s "revisionist production of the psalmist's analogy" yields "both a bitter protest against Renaissance monarchy and a radical interrogation consonant with other late Elizabethan challenges to providentialist belief."

Wiggins (2000, 5, 31–32, 59) not only thinks *Sat5*'s reference to Castiglione in lines 2–6 shows that Donne "shared" the generally high opinion of *The Courtier* at the Elizabethan court (5), he also contends that in writing *Sat5* Donne cannot have been "an alienated radical" because he invokes Castiglione "as a moral authority" for whom Donne demonstrates "respect." Moreover, beyond his respect for *The Courtier*, Donne "recognizes that to diminish Castiglione's moral judgment would be to detract from the imposing difficulty of Egerton's commission" to reform the Court. On the contrary, Donne "acknowledges Castiglione to be Elizabethan society's authority on the subject of enlightened, disabused discourse on the contradictions of public life" (31). In *Sat5*, Wiggins asserts, "the Queen, the Privy Councillor, and the secretary are fused within a discourse whose rules are laid down by Castiglione." The poem, moreover, "is an exceptionally complex dialogue like that which one experiences in *The Courtier*" (32). In the end, Wiggins concludes, *Sat5* shows that the Elizabethan regime has "passed the test represented by Castiglione's discourse," that is, "York House lives up to the standard set in Urbino, where critical discourse and self-reflection take place," and "this is why Donne introduces Castiglione and Egerton in the same breath" (59).

Edwards (2001, 53) says that whereas Juvenal "ended his satire attacking lawyers with a lament that nothing could be done," *Sat5* expresses pleasure that Queen Elizabeth "was now willing for the abuses to be brought to her attention, and that Egerton was the ideal reformer."

Flynn (2001, 115–16), comparing *Sat5*'s satirist to the satirist who addresses Calvinus in Juvenal's thirteenth satire, maintains that Donne's poem directs its attention to "pretentiously aggrieved suitors" in the royal court and courts of law, the "foremost" of whom was Robert Devereux, second earl of Essex, whose faction was "pitted against the holders of higher office," the faction led by William Cecil, baron of Burghley and his son Sir Robert Cecil. Donne tells the Essexians, as Juvenal told Calvinus, that they should drop their "protestations of wronged honor," which only seek to "replace one unjust regime with another."

Sequence and Unity

Hillyer (1941, xxxiii) understands *Sat5*'s distinction in a sequence of five Satyres as being "addressed to a more detached subject—the corruption of the judiciary." Nevertheless, the poem "exhumes the victims of the former onslaughts and subjects them to an after-drubbing."

Ellrodt (1960b, 2:53) finds that the satirical cynicism of Donne's early poetry, including the earlier Satyres, fades in *Sat5* and other poems written after his employment by Lord Keeper Egerton; criticism of the social order in *Sat5* is limited to indignation over the persecution of Catholics.

Harris (1960, 201) thinks *Sat2*'s "sport" with "legal language" and "identifiable personalities" advances "with new gravity" in *Sat5*.

Andreasen (1963, 64, 73–74), presenting *Sat5* as part of a sequence, finds it "closely related" to *Sat2* (64), particularly in its concern with the theme of the law, although focused not on lawyers who deceive their clients but on officers who take advantage of suitors, adding that the poem regards "this perversion of the law as the prostitution of a worthy ideal." *Sat5* is linked to all the previous Satyres "through a pervasive use of stream and sea imagery" (73), she notes, and, moreover, *Sat5* shares with the first four poems "the customary contrast between the righteous ideal, and the way in which it has been perverted by man's greed for material wealth and power" (74).

Bewley (1966, 187) finds *Sat5* "metrically the roughest, rhythmically the harshest" of the Satyres.

Gamberini (1967, 47) finds *Sat5* an exception among the Satyres, written after the first four, while Donne was serving Lord Keeper Egerton, and showing an odd transformation of the earlier, elegant, disillusioned youth suddenly adopting a business-like rhetoric—no more than a veneer—for the purposes of satire on the court and of gaining approval from his employer.

Milgate (1967, xxiv, lvii–lviii) thinks that *Sat5* demonstrates that in the first four Satyres Donne felt he had "drained the genre of any virtues it might have had"; moreover, he "certainly seems to have said all that he had to say, and had reached the limits of what he could achieve in this style" (xxiv). It is also possible, he conjectures, that Donne found "occasion," when presenting *Sat5* to Lord Keeper Egerton, to make certain revisions to the first four Satyres (lvii–lviii). Baumlin (1990, 84) also thinks that Donne's employment might have led to rewriting the earlier Satyres.

Hughes (1968, 53–54) finds that "similarities" in *Sat4* and *Sat5* (e.g., the "image of the raped court," the outrage with informers, and the use of the Hebrew Scriptures for closing analogies) "encourage the notion that they were written quite close to one another." Nevertheless, the satirist in *Sat5* is "quite different" from "earlier versions," he notes, as, though still an "outcast," he is now "an active participant in the battle against folly." Also varying from earlier Satyres is the "tone of the invective," suggesting that Donne "was emboldened by his service with Egerton to think of himself as an active reformer."

Lecocq (1969, 382) reads *Sat5* as a verse epistle offering council to Egerton and believes, as a result, that the poem obliges us to envisage in an entirely serious way the content not only of *Sat5*, but of the entire collection, which thereby becomes a form of political action.

Medine (1972, 51–52) finds that in each of the five Satyres Donne "advanced particular values or norms." In *Sat1*, *Sat2*, and *Sat4*, "the reactions of the personae imply viable alternatives to the viciousness embodied in the satirized figures," whereas in *Sat3* and *Sat5*, "the ideal is made direct and explicit." In *Sat3* and *Sat5* likewise, "praise and blame are integrated" and the poems are built around "contrasts and oppositions" (51). In *Sat5*, Lord Keeper Egerton is presented "as a realization of the ideal urged" in *Sat3*, "where the speaker explains that truth involves knowledge translated into responsible action." After *Sat3* has shown "the necessarily private and individual nature of moral action," *Sat5* "represents the ideal in terms of one [i.e., Egerton] knowing and acting as an individual" (52).

Newton (1974, 440–41) maintains that in *Sat5* "the two major themes" of all the Satyres "paradoxically converge": (1) "the character of the satirist—anarchic, destructive, iconoclastic" and (2) "the necessary search for 'constancy' and security." In the first four Satyres, he observes, the satirist's uncertain character, "a burden like original sin," cannot find certain truth; constancy in *Sat1* "is a joke"; in *Sat2* "it disappears ambiguously"; in *Sat3* it seems both "necessary to be sought after and at the same time necessarily unattainable"; and in *Sat4* Donne "comes to terms at last with the satiric character and the uncertainty it entails." *Sat5*, finally, "shows us that the satirist's uncertainty is the condition of all society," and thus in line 4, the question of who can make courtiers good "tunnels under the moral foundation of satire itself." Accordingly, Newton concludes, *Sat5*'s satirist attempts "to steer a course" between the "Kinde pitty" and "brave scorne" of *Sat3* and to eschew "railing."

Bellette (1975, 131) does not find the five Satyres "effectively unified by any common, specific subject or method" and holds that "no justice is done, ultimately, when a group of poems is forced into a common mould in the interest of some non-poetic conception of neatness or consistency." He focuses on "one element, of a personal and religious nature," and suggests that in *Sat2* and *Sat5* this element is "largely absent," and thus those two poems are of a "narrower scope" and are "less interesting" than the other Satyres, which include "the presence of the poet himself in the scene he depicts," as well as "the personal, moral issue which arises from this presence."

Elliott (1976, 115–16) thinks that in the opening of *Sat5* "the speaker has abandoned the role of satirist, for he now has too much pity for both the wicked and their victims to laugh at them." Yet the unity of the Satyres is preserved, Elliott believes, by his expressed intention to "continue to attack corruption from within the system as secretary to one of the Queen's most honorable officials." At the close of the sequence, the "young protagonist seems to have made a mature, if perhaps temporary, adjustment to life's frustrations."

For Lauritsen (1976, 119–20, 129), the first four Satyres "depend upon dramatic irony, upon our perception of the speaker's unconscious or preconscious relationship to his subject" (119). In the final irony of the Satyres, however, the speaker in *Sat5* comes to see that what he satirizes in the fallen world is, ultimately, himself, and the progress of the Satyres is then a "progress of self-discovery." Gradually having achieved "full self-knowledge" and "a new recognition of his own relationship to the world about him," the speaker in *Sat5*, according to Lauritsen, has progressed "from detachment to engagement, from that detachment which is born of a desperate need to believe that one is morally superior to the world of ordinary mortals to that moral engagement and commitment which can only come when one realizes that one is not only in the fallen world, but of it" (120). This vision of co-partnership in the corrupt world makes *Sat5* "at once a summary of its predecessors and an anomaly." Lauritsen finds that while the other Satyres address "generalized aspects of the condition of fallen humanity—with lust, perversion of the Word, false religion, the vanity and vacuity of courtiers, with, in short, sin"—*Sat5* is "unique" among the Satyres as the only poem in which the speaker "does not begin with a conscious and generally explicit presupposition of his moral superiority to the rest of mankind," for only *Sat5* is "predicated upon and pleads for pity and compassion." Amidst "the persistence and universality of original sin," *Sat5* alone "can aspire to be what satire is generally supposed to be: a corrective" (129).

Hester (1977c, 187) sees the satirist having overcome in *Sat5* "the lack of self-knowledge about himself and his vocation which he suffered" in earlier Satyres. His return to court in *Sat5* is a repeated manifestation of obedience, following his earlier return to court at the end of *Sat4*. The sequence of Satyres eventuates in this obedience, Hester concludes, after journeying from innocence through despair, self-knowledge, suffering, and "God-given knowledge."

Hester (1978b, 347–48, 351, 362) argues that although at the end of *Sat4* the satirist relinquishes "the sinful condition at the heart of the nation" as matter for preachers to focus on, nevertheless he returns to the subject in *Sat5*, using a method similar to that of *Sat1*, in which the "reclusive satirist attempted to reform a London fop by reciting

Christian maxims about the spiritual condition of man." In *Sat5*, Hester says, he more forcefully addresses a courtier complaining about injustice at court, not merely citing Christian maxims that are unrealized ideals of behavior but providing "a full exegesis of each text he cites," accommodating each text to the courtier's situation "in order to illustrate the spiritual consequences" of his "continued participation" in courtly corruption (347). *Sat5*'s satirist thus maintains "the disgust which nearly dominates" the first four Satyres (347–48). As he admitted ironically in the opening of *Sat2* that poetry may be (as philistines call it) a sin, so in *Sat5* the satirist begins by allowing the court its claims through admitting the prescriptions of Baldassare Castiglione's *The Courtier* (351). Hester goes on to conclude that the speaker of *Sat5*, considered in relation to the speakers of the other Satyres, "emerges as a model for the reformation of all 'gamsters' lacking in self-knowledge" (362).

Cousins (1979, 106) thinks *Sat5* "implies" that all five Satyres are "a unity," forming "an anatomy of a society," beginning "at its lowest point, with the Fool," and ending "at its apex, with the Queen herself."

Dubrow (1979, 80) likens *Sat5* to *Sat4* in that they both "dissect" the world of the court "at length," whereas the first three Satyres merely "allude to it frequently."

Marotti (1981, 214–15) observes that *Sat5* differs from the first four Satyres, "whose anticourtly sentiments mark them as the work of a social and political outsider." The satirist no longer views "government and the Court" as a "nightmarish, corrupt world." Instead, notes Marotti, these appear, "with their symptomatically exploitative relationships of officer and suitors, as an environment presided over by a benevolent monarch interested in effective reforms," an appearance about which "Donne knew better."

Slights (1981, 172–73, 176–77) points out that *Sat5* begins with a "firm announcement of purpose" rather than a question because the satirist "has resolved his case of conscience" in *Sat4*. In the first four Satyres, she says, his concerns have been "whether he ought to direct his attention to worldly affairs and the related question of *how* he should fulfill his responsibility to guide men to virtue." But he has learned successively that "good advice" is futile; that ridicule does not lead men to introspection but merely exposes sin and folly in others; and that each man must be able to "stand inquiring right" to make his own decision and choose virtue. In *Sat5*, then, his task is "to tell the truth, not just by persuading men to hate evil or by identifying certain actions as evil, but by communicating a habit of mind that enables men to discover truth in their particular circumstances" (172–73). Slights observes that *Sat5*'s "echoes" of the other Satyres have been seen as "mere repetitions" rather than as "significant indications of the dramatic and thematic structures" of all five Satyres as a group, or perhaps "the unifying context of the speaker's case of conscience" throughout the Satyres has been ignored. Slights believes that by showing "the incipient recluse" of *Sat1* "developing into the dedicated public servant" of *Sat5*, Donne "provides a model of a man discovering how to act according to his conscience in a perplexing situation" (176–77).

Corthell (1982, 175), reading the sequence of Saytres, thinks that by the end of *Sat4*, the satirist has tried to "transcend" an "estrangement from power" and recognizes that "the achievement of religious or moral probity" is "only half the struggle," for it is also necessary to deal with social and political forces that "produce laws and canons." In

Sat5, Corthell argues, the satirist has attained "a positive relation to power" and can thus be "engaged in the admirable work of reforming the Elizabethan judiciary."

Hester (1982, 13–14, 98–99, 103–04) maintains that *Sat5*, "similar in situation" to *Sat1*, nevertheless "discloses the triumph of the satirist over his previous lack of knowledge about self and vocation," replacing "the recitation of abstract ideals with 'accommodated' maxims that instruct a complaining suitor in the need for self-knowledge." The satirist is "bolder and more confident than in any of the first four poems" (13–14), Hester asserts, further commenting that *Sat5* extends *Sat4*'s "attack on the blasphemous perversions of the court into an assault against the legal corruptions it perpetuates," but with this significant difference: in *Sat4*, as in the three previous Satyres, "the satirist spoke as an outsider" whose "complaints could be dismissed as the jealous ravings of a malcontent." In *Sat5*, however, "he speaks as an insider who has the means, the opportunity, and the place to activate reform." Appointment to the Lord Keeper's staff, notes Hester, provides also the occasion "for solving the problematic view of satire" presented in the first four Satyres (98–99). The satirist's appointment by Egerton provides an advance not only over the satirist's stance in *Sat3* and *Sat4* but also beyond "the strategies of both Latin satire and the imitations of Donne's contemporaries." Egerton's authority provides the satirist "with the capacity to realize on a national scale, to actualize in the fallen world, that reform that has been central to all his poems" (103–04).

Zunder (1982, 18) contends that *Sat5* "stems to some extent from" *Sat4*'s discussion of the "wretchednes /Of Suiters" (ll. 156–57).

Kerins (1984, 37, 48, 54–55, 60) reflects that though *Sat2* and *Sat5* "share no common source," they are related by their "epistolary form," and both "investigate the question of law and justice from quite different perspectives" (37). Related to *Sat2* in source, form, and theme, *Sat5* nevertheless demonstrates "a profound change in the character" of the satirist (48). In the latter poem, Kerins says, the "satiric voice takes on a public character actively engaged," quite different from the "courtly perspective of elegant disdain which revealed its moral bankruptcy" in *Sat2*. "Charity and liberty," not mockery, inspire the "satiric inquiry" in *Sat5*, notes Kerins, and *Sat2* and *Sat5* differ also in "the opposite fictional plane on which each operates": whereas *Sat2* focused on Coscus, "a literary creation," *Sat5* is concerned with a real, contemporary issue, one that Donne's employer "had been recently commissioned to investigate." But this occasional quality of *Sat5* is not for Kerins the only cause of the development "from a private to a public satiric voice," a development that is inevitable given the "progress" of the Satyres as a whole (54–55). The content of *Sat5* shows a "more than accidental" relation to the earlier poems, he concludes, and Donne was "conscious of some form of overall artistic design" in the Satyres as a whole (60).

Baumlin (1986a, 92, 101–03) thinks that *Sat5*, if "less popular" than *Sat3*, is "no less problematic in its use of genre and convention." Both poems stress "persuasion over vituperation and meditative self-reflection, in which the poet speaks as a homilist or rhetor" (92). Moreover, he says, *Sat3*'s "opening disavowal of spleen and laughter" is related to the "similar, if more concise denial" in the opening of *Sat5* (101). Both poems try to engage their "reading audience personally," using an "impassioned, second-person address." Further, Baumlin observes, *Sat5* reuses "many of the rhetorical techniques" seen in *Sat3*, among them "elaborate image and symbol in the creation of argument" (102). He concludes that both poems deal with "the relationship between the individual and temporal power," as well as with abuse of power; and both in this connection use imagery of powerful rivers (103).

Baumlin (1986b, 465–66) finds the "outright rejection of laughter" in the opening lines of *Sat5*, as in those of *Sat3*, effects at the outset a Christianizing attitude in relation to the ethical relativism and humor of Horatian satire. He adds that in *Sat5*, following through on *Sat4*'s appeal for "Preachers" to deal with the iniquity of the court, the satirist himself acts "as just such a preacher, persuading and teaching" rather than "ridiculing or punishing."

Guibbory (1986, 80) notes *Sat3*'s concluding use of water imagery to illustrate the perils of separation from God, the "source or head" of all power, and says that accordingly in *Sat5* 45–55, the suitor who is "already downstream" may not be able to "return to the head." As "earthly powers were compared to streams" in *Sat3*, she says, so in *Sat5* "courts are a stream that can 'sucke thee in.'"

Marotti (1986, 116, 118) finds no substantial unity or sequential relationship between *Sat5* and the earlier Satyres, except for the fact of Donne's employment, which put his satirical writing on a new footing. His employment, Marotti says, "affected the matter and manner" of *Sat5*, in that it is not "the work of a political outsider" (116). However, although *Sat5* aims for "a somewhat more magisterial tone" than he takes in *Sat1*, *Sat2*, or *Sat4*, Donne's "conflicts and ambivalences about the Court and the Establishment come through strongly in this poem" (118).

Baumlin (1990, 69, 74–77) sees *Sat5* as a retraction of the "treasonous political attack" of *Sat3* (69). The opening of *Sat5* "echoes" the final image of *Sat3*, "seemingly taking up" where *Sat3* left off. The satirist here again "inveighs against those who abuse power (which, like a stream, engulfs and drowns those who court its favors)," but Baumlin suggests that *Sat5* does not go on to continue *Sat3*'s "attack on the English monarchy" (74) because much had occurred between the composing of the two poems. According to Baumlin, the satirist is no longer "fearful or overtly resentful of the burdens his Catholic background initially placed" on his advancement at court, but, instead, has reconciled himself outwardly, "perhaps even in his heart," conforming to "the Anglican articles of faith." Recusancy statutes are no longer (as they were in *Sat4*) a threat to him, Baumlin notes, and he is no longer an outsider at court, finding "an immediate audience and authority for his words" as secretary to Lord Keeper Egerton. His "earlier political attacks" on the court have thus become "suddenly embarrassing as well as potentially dangerous" (75). The speaker's criticisms of "the court's anti-Catholic policy" in *Sat4*, and especially his "most critical and potentially treasonous" attacks on Elizabethan religious policy in *Sat3*, demand "revision," says Baumlin, which he offers in *Sat5* "by exculpating the Queen, exhorting Egerton, and, above all, exempting English law." Whereas in *Sat4* the satirist hated and feared the "Giant statutes," threats to life, liberty, and property, in *Sat5* he writes of "Faire lawes white reverend name" (76–77).

Baumlin (1991, 150–51) rejects the interpretations of Lauritsen (1976) and Hester (1982) and concludes that *Sat5*, at the end of Donne's sequence of Satyres, comes as neither the culmination of a psychological progress of the soul's development nor the transformation of a program of satire into a program of legal reform. Instead, the poem constitutes a generic transformation of the sequence of Satyres, in order "to validate and enact the author's aims," with "diatribe, homily, and law taking the place of spleen and satiric laughter."

Corthell (1997, 51–52, 54) finds that Sat5 begins "on a less ambivalent note" than Sat3, "to which the opening lines seem to allude." But as in Sat3 so here a "'calme head' is imagined as somehow detached from the river's flow" in lines 29–30 (51–52). Sat5's "authorized" servant of the "Empresse," like the subjects of all five Satyres, thus illustrates a "distance between self and other" that "just as repeatedly breaks down" (54).

Prescott (2000, 230) calls Sat5 "a more perfunctory performance" than the earlier Satyres.

Shawcross (2000–2001, 28) notes that Sat5 "may be less successful and less satiric" than the other Satyres because "the displacement between the poet and the poem is lessened."

Wiggins (2000, 25, 58–59) sees Sat5 as "the dramatic climax" of the Satyres' development, revealing that Lord Keeper Thomas Egerton is the person heralded by the satirist's reference, in the closing of Sat4, to a "wise man" who will "esteem my writs Canonical"—a reference that links Sat5 to the "Sir" addressed in Sat2, also a reference to Egerton. "As much as any other single feature," Egerton's presence in the poems "fuses" the Satyres together, Wiggins says, as "five parts of the one coherent book" (25). Contrasting to the earlier Satyres, which are "poetry historicized," Sat5 is "history as poetry," in which "the historical Egerton has hired a secretary and authorized him to speak in full awareness of his secretary's critical, disabused insights into the regime." Thus, according to Wiggins, Sat5 places the Satyres "in perspective" and "renders them comprehensible," bringing the drama of the sequence "to a happy conclusion" (58–59).

Flynn (2001, 115) says that Sat5 follows Sat4's tale of moral peril (about a courtier satirist's mere visit to court) with the diatribe of a satirist who is a servant of the Lord Keeper, addressing his analysis of the moral problem at court "with disarming frankness" to Egerton and to Queen Elizabeth.

Fulton (2001, 104–05) notes the use of the phrase "calme head" in both Sat3 and Sat5, arguing that in both cases the satirist locates in the source of a river "the source of the monarch's power."

Structure and Method

Andreasen (1963, 73–74) states that Sat5's satirist "speaks to a young man who has fruitlessly bribed corrupt officials and who quietly listens to the angry tirade." The young man has himself "stripped others of their wealth" and "has now been stripped of his own by the judge," but the satirist's "anger" is less with the "young man" than with court "officers" at whom most of the satire, after the opening lines, is directed.

Zivley (1966, 92) asserts that in Sat5, as in the other Satyres, the distracting variety and quantity of the imagery may sometimes result from Donne's "letting his mind toy with similarities" instead of "concentrating" on the "total effect of the poem."

Lecocq (1969, 383–84) traces the plan of Sat5 as follows: an introduction explains the union of fops (plantiffs) and evildoers (representatives of law); the next part offers a portrait of the queen as source of all power and responsibility; a new introduction explores the metaphors of the iron age (with justice for sale) and the rusted iron age (with injustice for sale); and a turn back to the plaintiffs brings the poem to a bitter conclusion in an abrupt finale, in which all vestiges of justice and the golden age are gone and all men are thus drowned.

Medine (1972, 52) notes that *Sat5* first illustrates "the pervasive corruption of society's basic institution (the courts of law)" and then "represents the ideal in terms of one knowing and acting as an individual."

Shawcross (1972, 266), although sensing a "personal touch" in lines 28–34 (addressed to Lord Keeper Egerton and Queen Elizabeth), finds that "even these lines are generalized." The "sin" in *Sat5* "has its gestation in governmental hierarc[h]ies and laws, although its inception lies in man."

According to Newton (1974, 440–44), the two major themes of *Sat5* are (1) "the character of the satirist—anarchic, destructive, iconoclastic" and (2) "the necessary search for 'constancy' and security" (440). In "one of the most fanciful passages" of the Satyres (ll. 9–19), he says, the satirist "sets out to construct" a comprehensive, "metaphysical" picture of the evil "inherent in the nature of the world" as he sees it, a picture that Queen Elizabeth (who "is England") cannot know because she herself is "an unwitting and indeed a natural agent of destruction, like the innocent Thames." The satirist is thus "stuck in a dilemma: the invocation of Elizabeth makes it impossible for him to write satire without committing either treason or blasphemy," a dilemma that forces him to "lower his gaze" from "monarchical divinity" to "mere human agency" in lines 31–34 (441–42). But, Newton concludes, his subsequent reference to the "first maine head" (l. 46) puts him again "only a short step from secular complaint to indictment of the divine," so that once again the satirist "skirts the edge of blasphemy" (442–43).

Elliott (1976, 115) finds that in the opening of *Sat5* the satirist "has abandoned the role of satirist," having "too much pity" to laugh at either the wicked or their victims. Instead, he becomes "a more moderate reformer" albeit without betraying his "ideals." In the new role of secretary to Egerton, he "has the opportunity to redress the wrongs of the wicked lawyers by instructing and assisting their victims."

Hester (1977c, 185, 187) sees in *Sat5* "a moral responsibility in direct contrast" to the greed of officers and the "self-destructive capitulations" of suitors (185), noting that through his public service to the Queen's Lord Keeper and privately, "through the testing of his own moral assurance," the satirist instructs "without rationalizations" about his limitations and without "self-doubts" (187).

Hester (1978b, 347–51, 361–62) further defines the method of *Sat5* as not "merely citing an ideal of behavior and then lamenting" a failure to achieve it, but instead citing texts and providing "a full exegesis of each text he cites" (347). Having available to him "the wisdom of the ancients and the Scriptures," the satirist is thus "no longer compelled to interrupt his attacks with ironic or sarcastic admissions" about his own ineffectuality. Instead, Hester says, he offers his audience of courtiers "a supreme form of Christian love—the exegesis of Scriptural and even pre-Christian texts for their edification and reformation" (348–49). Explication and application of central texts help the suitor at court to understand "his relation to the dynamic character of Justice that remains in the world in spite of the petty and selfish injustices of the present legal system." According to Hester, the satirist thus conflates "the techniques of Protestant devotion and homiletics" by referring to a "popular or classical text," accommodating the text to present conditions, and then clarifying its significance with a biblical text or Christian tenet. The poem, Hester asserts, "assumes the form of a classical oration" (349) and expands on mere legal "manipulations" of court officers and suitors, creating "a judicious, meditative analysis of the eternal Law on which law is founded" (350).

He outlines the seven-part structure of the poem: the satirist's introductory statement of "his own emotional stance and his satirical charge" (ll. 1–9); a consideration of "the methodology" the satirist will follow and the "specific political and moral conditions in England" that require his satire (ll. 9–27); an "unusually" lengthy "proposition" (ll. 28–34) announcing the satirist's objective, "To know and weede out this enormous sinne"; an explication of the "general condition of justice and law in England" (ll. 35–42); a "confirmation" of this condition, considering "the character of contemporary judges and officers against whom" a suitor complains (ll. 43–63); a "confutation" that "discloses the suitor's complicity" in his own misery (ll. 63–78); and a "peroration" providing a summary in "direct address" to the suitor himself (ll. 79–91). The poem, "in presenting the legal ramifications of the suitor's case," thus follows "sound judicial principles, moving from the general to the particular" (350–51). This pattern in Sat5—"reliance on biblical texts to clarify and modify classical or humanistic texts"— suggests that "the satirist's major concern is with instruction" (361). At the end of the poem, Hester concludes, the only "unanswered question" is whether instruction can aid humans to "recognize and rely on the Words of Justice" (362).

Dubrow (1979, 76, 80) finds that differences from fellow Elizabethan satirists define Donne's method in Sat5 (76), specifying that Donne "gives noticeably less space to the faults of contemporary literature" than do such poets as Hall, Marston, and Guilpin. Instead, the royal court, "to which other satirists refer only sporadically," is the dominant concern of Sat5 as also of Sat4, while Donne's other Satyres also "allude to it frequently." But the "most striking" difference between Sat5 and the poems of contemporary satirists, she thinks, lies in the poem's persona. Most Elizabethan satiric personae are modeled "closely" on Juvenal, an "isolated, bitter, and defiant" personality. But Donne's satirist is "more complex," with "peculiar contradictions and variations in his voice" (80).

Slights (1981, 172–75, 176) asserts that in Sat5 the satirist "accepts the risks of involvement and assumes the responsibility of the satirist." Although he admits doubt "about the possibility of effecting reformation," he holds to the "moral nature of what he is doing" and "identifies himself as a poet," she argues, dealing with the suffering of "wretched victims" at the hands of "rapacious officers of the law" (172). In the "first section" of the poem, he resolves a question of whether to "direct his attention to worldly affairs" or to "guide men to virtue" by telling the truth, "communicating a habit of mind that enables men to discover truth in their particular circumstances." The "short, second section of the poem" puts the satirist's decision to involve himself at court in "a specific historical context" and "a particular time and place," the court of Elizabeth I (173). In the "longest section" of the poem, Slights goes on to note, the satirist addresses the "enormous sinne" woven into the life of the court, where "the system works to the advantage of the wealthy," even though "human law is ordained by God to apply His will to particular situations." The victims of this system he charges with "ultimate responsibility for the corruption of the system that victimizes them" (174–75). She believes that in Sat5, "the satirist's function is the opposite of the casuist's," for the satirist attempts not "to resolve doubts and quite troubled consciences," but "to overcome dangerous complacency by creating doubt." Nevertheless, like a casuist, Slights concludes, Donne's satirist "tries to create in his readers a habit of mind at once intensely committed to virtuous action and intellectually disinterested," forming men's consciences "by overcoming their reluctance to think and their tendency to try to evade moral responsibility" (176).

Hester (1982, 99, 102–06) holds that the biographical context of Sat5 reinforces its "central theme," a "personal example of the exegesis of law and Law that the satirist counsels can lead to the self-knowledge necessary for spiritual survival" (99). Addressed directly to the Lord Keeper, the poem does not merely "advise an outraged victim of legal fraudulence"; instead it counsels "the most powerful legal figure in the land" on the use of his power to "initiate reform of the legal and spiritual abuses within Elizabeth's courts" (102–03). Framed "as an oration" to the Lord Keeper, the structurally complex poem is, to Hester, simultaneously "a meditation on the satirist's role now that he is no longer a legal outsider" (103). Significantly, Egerton is viewed as someone who "has gained power because of his righteousness," which the satirist names as the source of the Lord Keeper's authority, and this fact means that Egerton "can deny the satirist's explication of the current legal predicament and of his own duty" only if he will deny that "he is indeed righteous" (104). According to Hester, the argument of the poem, then, is that the righteous man "will *enact* the process of satire in his own life." In general, and in this particular situation, satire is the "correct conduct." The "specific activity" the satirist engages in in Sat5, "the methodology he enacts and recommends for Egerton's enforcement," is the accommodation of texts— "the application of various 'wise' texts to one's situation in order to understand the spiritual consequences thereof"—and Sat5 "provides both a literal and a metaphorical application of this technique" (105–06).

Albright (1985, 250) calls Donne's method in Sat 5 "extremely lyrical," a quality accounting for the great difficulty in reading what has been termed "metaphysical poetry." He locates the satirist's statement of method in lines 9–16 (see more in notes to these lines) and concludes that Sat5 "uses the language of logic, of analogy" only as "a game in which the mind delights in the reeling sensation it feels as it gropes for logical relations amid a pervasive alogicality." He suggests that the "imagination is always moving faster than reason, which keeps struggling for syllogistic design as it falls further and further behind."

Baumlin (1986a, 92, 102, 104–05) states that Donne's method in Sat5 stresses "persuasion over vituperation and meditative self-reflection," the poet speaking "as homilist or rhetor." This method is not only compatible with satire, it "imitates a specific kind of rhetoric," namely, "the protreptic zeal and diatribe style" of Persius (92). Addressing Egerton, the satirist "discovers a means by which his words can truly influence his world" (102). Creating "a more Christian form of satire" than the "ridicule and invective" targeting individuals in the mode of Horace, Baumlin asserts, Donne's use of the method of Persius "makes his audience aware that the satirist's concerns are its own," and he can thus influence it directly (104–05).

Baumlin (1990, 69, 77–79, 81) finds, with Hester (1982), that the satirist not only speaks "as an insider" but that *Sat5* "claims to transcend" its limitations as literature, becoming an official "proclamation addressed directly to Egerton." *Sat5* "attempts, in a word, to become something other than mere rebuke or even persuasion—to become something other than satire" (77–78). He also sides with Corthell (1982) in arguing that the satirist's attitude toward the royal court is "ambivalent in spite of himself, incapable of complete identification with the powers he here courts and tries to assume for his own poetic voice." Donne tries to "identify with the established authority," he notes, an effort marked by "uneasiness" and "recognition of the deep compromises that brought him to this position of influence" (79), from which he would apply "charity and liberty to contemporary legal abuses" (81).

Wiggins (2000, 25–26, 31) finds in *Sat5*'s reference to Egerton "a mingled sense of wonder" and "retrospective illumination," both elevating the legitimacy of this poem and evoking "the coherence" of all the Satyres (25). The "concept of the persona," Wiggins says, so useful in understanding other poems, "loses its value" in relation to *Sat5* and the other Satyres. The historical and autobiographical content of these poems makes it "useless for us, with our limited knowledge, to pretend" that they are not "autobiographical poems." Donne here develops "his self-image in a detached, purposeful manner," Wiggins suggests, along lines laid out by conventions available to "young office seekers of his time." These conventions "by which one could engage in self-revelation" were shaped for Donne by Castiglione's *Il Cortegiano* (26). With his reference to Castiglione early on, Donne places Lord Keeper Egerton in the context "of that formidable ethical impasse which bedevils" all courtiers: "How to be an officer and a suitor, and hence a courtier, and retain one's integrity in the game?" (31).

Language and Style

Alden (1899, 85, 88) claims that the "attitude toward life" in *Sat5* is "uniformly pessimistic." The "atmosphere" is "somewhat severe and unamiable," without "formal and artificial assumption of authority to castigate, as in so many of the imitative satirists" (85). He adds that the style of *Sat5*, though not "distinctly imitative," more nearly resembles that of "classical satire" than Donne's other Satyres, namely in "its compactness, its indirect method, its allusiveness" (88).

Gosse (1899, 1:43) describes *Sat5* as "a very bad poem" with a "terrible rattle of redundant feet in verse that is hard to explain and impossible to justify," although he also finds in it the occasional "splendid phrase, which illuminates the dark mass."

Stein (1944b, 400–02, 404) suggests that in *Sat5* as elsewhere (he discusses *ElProg* 1–6), Donne's poetry "takes an evident pleasure in cultivating loose rhythms," making use for this purpose of elision and combinations of two or more unstressed syllables. He finds Donne sometimes "guilty" of verse that is so loosely structured that it "becomes merely prose," yet he "cannot avoid the impression" that Donne does this "intentionally, either for experiment or for mere playful destructiveness" (400). He adds that another kind of characteristic harshness occurs in Donne's "insistent repetition of words and sounds," a "relentless hunting a sound to death" (404).

Leishman (1951, 108, 117) states that in *Sat5* (as in *Sat4*) the "harshness of which Dryden and others accused Donne" was "deliberately cultivated" and is "much more apparent" than in *Sat1*, *Sat2*, and *Sat3* (108); moreover, in *Sat5* "such enjoyment as the mere play of wit affords is marred by the deliberately achieved harshness of the verse" (117).

Harris (1960, 201) thinks it amiss to "complain of Donne's scansion" or "roughness," or to "rejoice" that later verse satirists avoided such flaws. We should instead remember that Donne and the other early satirists "were trying their tongues as well as their teeth," and that Donne "in a strangely assorted company" was revealing "a new physiognomy."

Bewley (1966, 187) finds *Sat5* "metrically the roughest, rhythmically the harshest" of the Satyres.

Zivley (1966, 91–92) points to the "wide realm of experience" reflected in *Sat5*'s imagery, arguing that it evidences the "multiplicity of Elizabethan activities and enthusiasms and their attendant corruptions" as well as "basic human traits" that are "central to human experience." This range of imagery is "so various" and "numerous" that it may well "distract the reader," making it challenging "to follow the main flow of ideas."

Milgate (1967, xxiv) finds a "sequence of congruent imagery" in *Sat5*, involving "bridges and water," but despite this and the poem's "clinching epigrammatic couplet," *Sat5* "seems to keep going at all only by a series of spasmodic efforts."

Shawcross (1972, 262–65) recalls Ben Jonson's reported criticism of Donne's meter but suggests that, in *Sat5* and the other Satyres, "the alteration of meter has such definite and appropriate effect that—at least generally—such alteration seems deliberate" (262). These "prosodic anomalies" lead to "a more conversational, normal expression, for the lines, read normally, do not artificially end-stop" (263). He locates in *Sat5* "a higher number and thus percentage of hypermetric lines" than in the other Satyres, but thinks it "not justified" to conclude that this is "evidence of a flagging of ability or of interest" in *Sat5* because in each of these lines "prosodic disruption" is "nullified" by "a combination of enjambment and rhythm within the line." He finds that these lines resemble lines later written by Milton, "an embryonic drawing out of the sense from one verse into another" (264–65).

Slights (1981, 173, 175) thinks that Donne's imagery in the first section of *Sat5* "expresses compassion for loss and suffering" on the part of suitors, as well as "contempt for the evil and stupidity that cause them." But its "main force" is to explain the "mutually dependent relationship of exploiters and exploited" (173). The language towards the end of *Sat5*, she notes, "is harsh," confronting the "feckless" suitor with his "effectively perverting the law and spreading evil when he bribes officials and acquiesces in the corruption around him." But she concludes that the satirist's "anger is suffused with pity" (175).

Baumlin (1986a, 103–04) finds throughout *Sat5* a "tendency toward abstraction and conceitedness." He qualifies criticism of the poem's display of wit (citing Leishman [1951]), noting that this judgment "wrongly implies a lack of sincerity or commitment

on the part of the satirist" and asserting that there is "a peculiarly Donnean wit" in
Sat5, with its "analogies between macro- and microcosm, between bodies of water,
bodies politic, and human bodies," as in lines 9–16 (103). "Hyperbaton and figures
of repetition" make for "a tightly woven and complex argument," but, he says, "more
important than the syntax is the abstruse and 'metaphysical' nature of the argument."
The poem is "so obviously Donnean" to Baumlin because he has "transformed his
model into a truly English and personal voice." While Donne "adopts whatever there
is of value in a style like Persius's," he rejects "idiosyncratic elements" such as "crab-
bedness" or "obscurity." What Donne does adopt, says Baumlin, is "the protreptic
zeal, the homiletic tone, and the emphasis on reform through persuasion rather than
through laughter or personal attack."

Marotti (1986, 117–18) identifies in *Sat5* "a curious use of pronouns" that suggests
that the satirist is unable to separate himself or his readers from "the vexed condition
of suitorship." In describing the officer-suitor relationship (ll. 13–27), Donne "switches
from the third to the second person," he notes, and the second person pronoun in
these lines can refer to the suitors, but it also can refer to the "speaker's audience and
the poet's readers as well." It can also mean "one," a meaning that "would include the
speaker himself" (117). Marotti believes that Donne wrote this poem for Inns of Court
men and could address them familiarly in the second person, or even "switch to the
first-person-plural form that includes them both," as in lines 59–63 (118).

Baumlin (1990, 82) claims that *Sat5* "explores the relations among discursive
language, religious liberty, and 'lawful' action, between 'charitable reading' and the
reform of contemporary legal practices." The poem's "metalinguistic subject," accord-
ing to Baumlin, is how to interpret law, what constitutes crime, what truly merits
prosecution and punishment, and what deserves pity.

Religion and Politics

Grierson (1929, xxxi) suggests that though Donne probably had conformed to the
Church of England on entering Egerton's service, *Sat5* shows that his "sympathies
were still a good deal with his Catholic friends."

Crofts (1936, 129–30) states of *Sat4* and *Sat5* that Donne realized that "the glare
and glitter" of court "culminated in a blaze of diamonds and that formidable old fairy,"
Queen Elizabeth, whom he believes Donne "had seen through," for after all the Queen
"was a woman, and he had seen through women."

Lecocq (1969, 382), reading *Sat5* as a verse epistle to Egerton, believes that the
poem obliges us to envisage in an entirely serious way the content not only of *Sat5*,
but of the entire collection, which thereby becomes a form of political action.

Medine (1972, 52) states that *Sat5*, "in the midst of the indictment of society,"
holds up Lord Keeper Thomas Egerton as a political "realization of the ideal," as one
beginning to know about corruption at court and moving in the Queen's service to
deal with it through responsible action.

Hester (1978b, 349, 355) contends "in the dramatic moment of the poem, Donne's
exegete assumes the role of a legal prosecutor who cites precedents from the spiritual
Law to delineate the crimes—legal and spiritual—of which the judges, officers, and
suitors are guilty" (349). Further, he says, the satirist is "torn" between idealizing Queen

Elizabeth conventionally and "accusing her of criminal neglect," between insisting that suitors at court "solicit their own misery" and "intimating" that the Queen by ignoring effects of her policy has "contributed to their misery." Her knowing "no more than Thames calme head doth know" shows her to be, though "Greatest and fairest" of all temporal powers, "still less than ideal." The satirist salvages some esteem for the Queen, according to Hester, because she has appointed Egerton to office, and, indeed, "most of the satirist's praise is reserved for the Lord Keeper as an embodiment of righteousness" (355).

Slights (1981, 173–74) sees Sat5's reference to Queen Elizabeth as the satirist's commitment beyond "abstract, philosophical" thinking to "specific action in a particular time and place." Notwithstanding that the Queen's "ignorance" of the corruption in her government is "unavoidable," the satirist "asserts the significance of the individual conscience and its efficacy in changing the system," serving not only his "Mistresse Truth" but the Queen, through her Lord Keeper.

Hester (1982, 103–04, 116) finds that Egerton, a figure of authority "invested with the legal power of the queen because of his 'righteousness,'" is (as the satirist's employer) "the activating principle of the satiric process, the means by which satire-as-idea becomes satire-in-action." Through Egerton's authority, Hester says, "Christian satire becomes the administration of law" (103–04). At the same time, Egerton is "merely an historical metaphor" for the actual bodying forth of the "satirical process." Politically, the poem's "charge to the lord keeper, suitor, and reader" is that they "counsel, recognize, respond to, and rely upon the Words of Justice" (116).

Zunder (1982, 18) finds in Sat5 "no criticism of institutions" but merely an "exhortation to reform abuse," noting that the monarchy, specifically, is "exempted from blame," and the "traditional, hierarchical system, centred on the monarch," is "implicitly affirmed." The image of the monarchy, Zunder says, with its "life-fulfilling qualities," is reminiscent of Shakespeare's image of monarchy.

Kerins (1984, 56), citing Hester (1978b), demurs at the notion that in Sat5 the satirist's "difficulty" with Queen Elizabeth is that she is "less than ideal." Instead, he argues, the satirist means to say that precisely because "she is idealized," she is "isolated from the corruption that flows beneath her." Because the queen is conventionally conceived as ideal, Kerins thinks, Egerton is "a necessary mediate figure" who can be "authoriz'd" to "weed out this enormous sinne" (l. 34).

Marotti (1986, 118) contends that in Sat5's discussion of the relations between suitors and officers as oppressed and oppressors, Donne "writes as a peer-group representative" who has "found the sort of position of service he and his fellows sought." He thinks that "it is clear with which party" Donne and his audience identified.

Baumlin (1990, 69, 74–77, 82) argues that Sat5, "an apostate poet's hasty—and expedient—revision of his earlier recusant satire," attempts "to retract the treasonous political attack" of Sat3 (69). No longer "fearful or overtly resentful of the burdens" of being Catholic, the satirist has completed his "apostasy." This development has been "spurred on, perhaps, by his repulsion at his own brother's death through dealings with Jesuits"; alternatively, Baumlin suggests, "the poet had by now simply reconciled himself" and would "conform to the Anglican articles of faith." He no longer speaks as "an alien at or indeed enemy of the court," and must have had to sacrifice "his conscience" (75). However, the satirist has not become "an apologist for Elizabeth's religious policies," Baumlin argues, for "concern over the plight of Catholics remains," although (as in earlier Satyres) his "allusions to Reformation controversy refuse to espouse one side explicitly" (76). The satirist "restates his support if not for the Catholics' faith, then at least for their rights and economic welfare," and he maintains "his early stance against religious persecution" (77). Baumlin concludes that although Sat5 "may publicly announce the poet's own apostasy and identification with Royal power," the speaker remains sympathetic toward Catholics and their "perilous political circumstances," and still attempts "to protect the rights of conscience, placing charity above the blind and prejudicial application of law" (82).

Baumlin (1991, 148–49) argues that the political aim of Sat5 is "to assert the role Christian charity and liberty should play in English secular law," and in doing so Donne imitates Augustine "in wedding libertas to caritas." Thus, when Donne "asserts that 'Charity and liberty' provide the 'theame'" of the poem, there is "full resonance" in the terms "satirica libertas" so that beyond merely railing or rebuking, Donne "claims a liberty of Christian conscience that law—when used 'lawfully'—should preserve rather than deny." Further, he says, the poem "explores the relations among discursive language, religious liberty, and 'lawful' action, between 'charitable reading' and the reform of contemporary legal practices" to the extent that the poem "seeks to reappraise (in a sense, to reread) the actions of 'Officers' and 'Suiters' (l. 8) in order to free the innocent of blame, to look beyond the folly to the wretchedness of victims, and to give 'charitable warning' to those who, for their own profit, abuse 'Faire lawes white reverend name' (69)."

Freer (1996, 505) notes that the abuses Donne describes in Sat5 would have been known to him from attending the Inns of Court and seeing "the convoluted financial maneuvers of lawyers and suitors in Chancery and the Star Chamber."

Corthell (1997, 52) thinks that Sat5's "move to exculpate" Queen Elizabeth in relation to court abuses employs "a mystification" that is "commonly found in Elizabethan Catholic writing against persecution," a tactic comparable to exculpations of President Reagan in relation to the "Iran/Contra affair."

Flynn (2001, 115–19) finds that Donne's analysis of the royal court in Sat5 "describes a systemic and pervasive corruption," including the facts "that the Queen presided over this evil and that the Lord Keeper, the nation's chief legal officer, was functioning amidst overwhelming defilement." Although Sat5 "implausibly" characterizes Egerton as one who before his appointment did not "know" about the corruption, and also acquits the Queen of knowledge or responsibility, Flynn says, the satirist "with audacity exposes to the Queen and her Lord Keeper the iniquitous organization and rationale of their own government" (115). The fundamental injustice involves the sale of "controverted lands," formerly properties of the Church of England, "first put on the market by Tudor confiscations," for control of which suitors and officers of the court engage in legal actions, an "evergrowing volume of litigation," in which "hypocritical, grasping, and unjust claims by suitors are thwarted by corrupt officers of the law in the service of the Crown" (116). This "factional imbroglio" of Tudor government in the 1590s, according to Flynn, leads to the paradox that the monarchy, "despite having enriched itself by despoiling the church, is unable to support itself." The "grotesque system" is fueled by its origins in "the depredations set in motion by Tudor religious reform." Suitors striving to hold onto church properties are bedeviled by officers who confiscate their ill-gotten lands and goods and "aske a fee for coming" (117). Flynn concludes that in Donne's portrayal the "officers" are the Cecil faction, the "suitors" the Essexians, and the satirist aligns himself politically apart from either faction, with the Queen and the Lord Keeper (118–19).

Notes and Glosses

1–9 *Thou shalt not...and ieast?* **PATTERSON** (1970): in these lines, Donne "rejects laughter" as a means for elevating the genre through a "nonhumorous approach" (101–02). **DUBROW** (1979): these lines typically contrast with the practice of Donne's contemporary satirists in incorporating no prefatory "defense of satire" or reference to its virtues in "theoretical apologia," but instead tend to question or undercut the genre (81–82). **HESTER** (1980a) finds a "defense of satire" in these lines, an allusion to and an accommodation of Horace's *Satires* 1.1.23–24 in the first satire of his first book of satires. Whereas Horace asks why laughter may not accompany telling truth in satire ("*ridentem dicere verum*"), implicitly censuring his predecessor Lucilius for the use in satire of jocularity without truth, Donne's satirist "finds the stance of Horace inadequate" under Elizabethan conditions, an "Age of rusty iron" (l. 37) as he calls it, alluding to Juvenal, and asserts that telling truth in satire under these conditions requires an end to jesting (106–07). **BAUMLIN** (1986b): the "outright rejection of laughter" in these opening lines, as in those of *Sat3*, effects at the outset "a Christianizing attitude" in relation to the "ethical relativism and humor" of Horatian satire (465).

1–2 *laugh...pity* **MILGATE** (1967) refers to the opening of *Sat3* (165). [So also, Corthell (1997, 51).]

1 *leafe*, **BEWLEY** (1966): "page" (187).

1 *Muse*, **FORTIER** (1991) finds here a "sense of distance and disaffection" between the satirist and his muse: "the Muse is callous, incapable of the proper emphatic response, at odds with the poet's will. There may be a begrudging acceptance that the Muse plays a part in the poet's work, but there is no affection, no gratitude felt by the poet. The Muse is not an ideal figure, a goddess or a mentor, she is hardly even an equal" (95).

2–6 *He...wretched or wicked*: **GROSART** (1872–73) identifies him as "Count Baldassar Castiglione," author of *Il Cortegiano* (1:48). [So also, Chambers (1896, 2:245) and Carey (1990, 431).] **NORTON** (1895): "Castiglione, in his famous book *Il Cortegiano*, the courtier's manual in the sixteenth century, twice lays down the rule that neither the wretched nor the wicked are to be made the subject of jests,—for to jest at the one is cruelty, at the other is vanity. See Book ii, §§ 46, 83" (1:246). [So also, Milgate (1967, 165).] **HESTER** (1978b) notes the view of Dain A. Trafton (in "Structure and Meaning in *The Courtier*," *ELR* 2 [1972], 291) that this ruling out of jests deals with the merest forms of courtiership and suggests "such an ironic view of Castiglione's advice is conveyed by Donne's poem, also" (364). **WIGGINS** (2000): the reference to Castiglione "as the maker of good courtiers but not necessarily as making courtiers good" joins this "master of the art of impasse" together with Egerton "at the moment of Egerton's definitive entrance into Donne's poetic universe" (30).

2 *lay* **MILGATE** (1967): "lay down" (165).

3–4 *(hee beeing…Courtiers good?)* **NEWTON** (1974): in this parenthesis, the satirist "sums up the tension Donne is dealing with" in that he both suggests "a viable moral standard" and undermines it. "The question tunnels under the moral foundations of satire itself. Who *can* make courtiers good?" (441). **HESTER** (1978b): this "caustic parenthesis" suggests that the satirist's "emphasis ultimately is on understanding," since "the problem of the courtiers is not that they do now know the rules of justice in the realm, but that they have not 'understood' or refuse to acknowledge the consequences of applying the letter of the law while denying its spirit" (352).

3 *Rules to make…beeing vnderstood* **STEIN** (1944c): "stress-shift" in the first foot of the line is one of Donne's chief devices for varying the metrical line (378).

5–6 *Frees from the…or wicked:* **HESTER** (1978b): "the litotes here is marvelous, for like the courtiers who pervert the spirit of the law (and the Law) while answering to its letter, the satirist 'perverts' the courteous intention of their own code by allowing that he will in no way 'jest' at the suitors and officers" (351–52).

5 *Frees from the…in extreame* **STEIN** (1944c): elisions of extra syllables formed by "light vowels in unstressed places" are among Donne's devices for varying the metrical line (389).

6 *Are wretched…two a theame* **SHAWCROSS** (1972): a "hypermetric line" (263).

6 *wretched or wicked:* **MILGATE** (1967): "The wretched are those involved in lawsuits ('Suitors misery', l. 8), the wicked the unscrupulous 'Officers' of the courts" (165).

6 *wretched* **SHAWCROSS** (1972): "one syllable" (263).

6 *theame* **SHAWCROSS** (1967): "object of 'give,' whose subject is 'Charity' and 'liberty'" (35).

7–27 *What is hee…owne ruine is.* **HARRIS** (1960): Donne's ability to turn the topical references to Egerton's Star Chamber reforms into "a universal image" makes his work "more powerful than Hall's invocation of the ideal," with "a contemporary frame of reference more precise than Marston's" (201).

7–9 *What is hee…and ieast?* **HESTER** (1978b) sees in this "final gibe" a "sarcastic retort" to Castiglione's "rigid formality" in *Il Cortegiano*, a retort that "only validates further the satirist's apparent willingness to adhere literally to the code of those he attacks" (352).

7 *Charity and Liberty…What is hee* **STEIN** (1944b): the line exemplifies a char-

acteristically Donnean harshness in its "insistent repetition" of a vowel sound, a "relentless hunting a sound to death" (404).

7 *Charity and Liberty* **SMITH** (1971): "charity to pity the wretched and liberty to accuse the wicked" (496). **HESTER** (1978b): this plea for "the foundations of Christian morality" is brought to explicate the "Rules" (l. 3) of Castiglione, ironically applied "to the satirist's situation" (351). **BAUMLIN** (1986a): "dual virtues that determine the satirist's attitude toward his dual subject, 'Officers rage, and Suiters misery.'" Liberty is "no doubt a fusion of Christian liberty and the *satirica libertas* claimed by poets in this genre." Perhaps surprisingly, charity, "the preeminently Christian virtue, here becomes an equally important quality of the satirist as well as a motivating force throughout the poem" (101). **WIGGINS** (2000): "we discover very shortly that the 'liberty' to which Donne refers here was granted to him by Egerton, in whose service he now finds himself" (30).

8 *Who Officers…Suters miseree* **BEWLEY** (1966): by "Officers" Donne means "officials administering the courts, judges, clerks, etc."; by "Suiters" he means "plaintiffs in legal suits" (187). **SHAWCROSS** (1967): "Those in authority, the officers, create wretchedness by limiting liberty and those who plead suits, both entreaters for justice of a right or claim and the needy, evoke charity for their misery" (398). **SMITH** (1971): "high officials of state or the law; and those who petition them for justice or favours" (496). **FLYNN** (2001): in Donne's portrayal, "the Cecilians are officers, controlling the Court and the courts; the Essexians (whom the satirist addresses throughout most of the poem) are suitors, struggling to keep their share of spoils with which the Tudor Crown has created new nobility like the Devereux Earls" (117–18).

8 *rage,* **MILGATE** (1967): "violent or savage behaviour"; see *Sat3* 19 (165).

9–27 *If all things…owne ruine is.* **KERINS** (1984): "macrocosmic and microcosmic analogies" here illustrate the inevitable relationship between "corruption in the self and corruption in the society" (55–56).

9–23 *If all things…yet you are* **MELTON** (1906) identifies in these lines arsis-thesis variation in stressed and unstressed repetitions of "all," "shall" (in "*shall*" and "*shallow*"), "things," "be," "in," "which," "are," "and," "-ing" (in "ravish*ing*" and "Spring*s*"), and "now." In accord with this pattern, Melton conjectures in l. 11 "be made [*each*]" in arsis to vary with "'each' twice in thesis in the next line" (174).

9–17 *If all things…World a Man;* **LAURITSEN** (1976): the speaker here insists upon "the interdependence and essential oneness of humanity, especially of a fallen humanity." Both officers and suitors, "victims and victimizers are the same. We are bound together in this fallen world, and if we can rise at all, we can only rise together" (130). **COUSINS** (1979): the "labyrinthine argument makes its way through contradictions and illusions," a fine example of Donne's "mannerist rhetoric." But its "paradoxes" are rather "skeptical 'alarums to truth'" than truth itself (106–07).

9–16 *If all things…drownes them run.* **LEISHMAN** (1951) complains that in these lines "such enjoyment as the mere play of wit affords is marred by the deliberately achieved harshness of the verse" (117). **EMPSON** (1972) comments that, feeling "he was doing hackwork" when he wrote *Sat5* "to please his new employer," Donne "labours" in these lines and "displays philosophic breadth" by introducing the notion of man as a microcosm; "the moral is (very truly no doubt) that you will be ruined if you go to law." Explains that this "sad stuff" Donne may have regarded as "a commonplace," even though this seems his earliest mention of it, years before "the retirement after his marriage" (146–47). **NEWTON** (1974): this is "one of the most fanciful passages of the Satyres, where he sets out to construct a more complete and consistent, indeed a 'metaphysical,' portrayal of what he sees" (441). **ALBRIGHT** (1985): in these lines, "the heaven of language, a state of superequivalence where things slip and slide like figures of speech and all words rhyme." In this "liquefied" realm, "any hope for finding logical relations among its parts has drowned in the general thaw." In a "lyric assault against denotation," Donne's method is "a constant multiplication of terms," in which "no metaphor is allowed to settle, to stabilize into reasonableness, no predicate is allowed to fix, weigh down the poem's subject, for the poet touches on one only to cast it aside, to bound forward eagerly into further acts of predication" (250).

9–15 *If all things…now dry;* **MAZZEO** (1957): "Astrology—another branch of Renaissance natural philosophy based on the microcosm-macrocosm analogy—was also important in alchemical processes in so far as the proportions of the limbeck could bring astral powers into play" (107).

9–13 *If all things…is a World;* **MILGATE** (1967): these "gnomic lines are rather trite" (165). **STEIN** (1946): the "compression" of "abstract thought" in these lines "demands most from the reader and yet is very slow to expand." There is "not much occasion" for "this kind of obscurity" in satire, but "the strong reflective tendency in Donne, though usually translated into realistic terms, occasionally remains abstract" (103). **HAWKES** (2001): these lines offer "a typical endorsement" of "the theory of correspondence between the microcosm and the macrocosm" (151).

9–12 *If all things…or represents)* **SLOAN** (1963) suggests that Donne was either jesting here or justifying his tendency to make "logical seizures" on the mind by his comparisons (35).

9–11 *If all things…same Elements,* **WAGNER** (1947): these lines illustrate the complementary ideas of "transcending" and of "unity" in Donne's life and work (257). **BOURNE** (1947) contests Wagner's (1947) interpretation of these lines, claiming that he takes them out of context (461). **MORRIS** (1953) cites these lines as an example of "pure Sprung Rhythm" (43).

9 *If all things be in all* **GRIERSON** (1912) quotes Paracelsus, *Coelum Philosophorum: The First Canon, Concerning the Nature and Properties of Mercury:* "All things are concealed in all. One of them all is the concealer of the rest—their corporeal vessel, external, visible and movable" (2:126). [So also, Hester (1978b, 351).] **MILGATE** (1967) quotes *The French Academy* (1594), 2:18–19: "Of this matter which contained all the elements, and which God made the mother of all things, and capable of all formes, every bodie is compounded" (165). **SMITH** (1971): "if every part of the natural creation reproduces in little the constitution of the whole" (496). **NEWTON** (1974) thinks "the evil the satirist sees is only natural" in that it is "inherent in the nature

of the world" and "the propensity to *see* it is inherent in the nature of the satirist" (442). **BAUMLIN** (1986a) sees this passage as evidence supporting the criticism of Leishman (1951) that the subject of *Sat5* is merely an occasion for "display" of Donne's "wit." Argues that Leishman "wrongly implies a lack of sincerity or commitment on the part of the satirist," but he is correct in noting "the presence of a peculiarly Donnean wit in the poem" (103).

10–12 *As I thinke,…or represents*) **STEIN** (1946): enjambment and parenthesis in these lines are examples of Donne's "exacting demands," and increase the "strain on the reader" (100).

10 *As I thinke,…and shall* **RICHTER** (1902) cites this line to illustrate level stress (395–96).

11 *Bee, be made of the same Elements,* **COLERIDGE** (1811) thinks this "an impracticable Line," conjecturing that Donne may have written "'all' after the 2nd be" (228). **RICHTER** (1902) cites this line to illustrate the absence of an opening syllable (399).

11 *the same Elements,* **MILGATE** (1967) refers to *Sermons* 9:173 and *Letters* 96 (166).

12 *Each thing,…or represents*) **NEWTON** (1974): this line serves as a principle for considering the corruption of the royal court, namely, "what appears destructive is merely natural" (442). **HELLEGERS** (1991): this principle illustrates Donne's "profound suspicion of claims of disinterested interpretation." *Sat5* and Donne's other poems "read like rhetorical battlefields on which the speaker attempts to draw competing accounts into question, casting doubt on alternative representations of the world, moral action, and self" (10).

13–22 *Then Man is…wormes shall eat.* **BRENNAN** (1988): in these lines, Donne creates "a relentless downward spiral of depression," describing "the vicissitudes and degradation of preferment-hunting at the royal court" (16–17).

13–19 *Then Man is…which they voyd.* **MILGATE** (1967) finds here "equivoques on both 'man' and 'world'": man as "'mankind' (human beings collectively), compared to the natural world (in which Officers are seas, etc.)," and "'individual man,' whose body is compared to the 'world of men' or body-politic (in which Officers are stomachs, etc.)." Further, there is then "a double logical fallacy in Donne's 'proof' that 'man is the world' and that, consequently, 'the world is man'" (166). **HESTER** (1978b): these two "micro-macrocosm analogies," delineating the "'raging' fraudulence of the officers and the suicidal incontinence of the suitors," are brought to amplify the text of Paracelsus (cited in l. 9) and disclose that the principle "the satirist applied to his own function is applicable to the situation of the suitor he addresses" (353).

13–16 *Then Man is…drownes them run.* **RUGOFF** (1939): "a prelude to that dramatic declaration" in ll. 45–55 "that there can be no appeal" for the poor suitor confronted with "sundry, almost random difficulties" Donne associates with rivers and seas, providing "a dark picture of the judicial process" that confirms what we know about Donne's "attitude toward Elizabethan courts of law." At the same time, it confirms that he was "only moderately sensitive to the subtler aspects and the changing beauties of English river and stream" (205–06). STEIN (1944b): "the collapse of the iambic structure helps accentuate the ridicule" intended by the satirist. This "harshness," however, "may well be interpreted as the result of carelessness or a lapse in technical skill" (401). STEIN (1946): an example of obscure imagery using "allegory" in addition to Donne's "so-called 'metaphysical' qualities" (108). BAUMLIN (1991): here *Sat5* "echoes" the final image of *Sat3*, "seemingly taking up" where the earlier poem leaves off (141).

13–14 *Man is a World; . . . vast rauishing Seas,* RUGOFF (1939): the passage refers to similar uses of "man" as a microcosm in *Mark* l.1, and in *Devotions*, Meditation 8 (44).

13 *Man* SMITH (1971): "the human race" (496).

14–16 *Are the vast . . . them run.* RUGOFF (1939): in these lines, Donne identifies high court officers "as treacherous and corrupt," using imagery taken from phenomena of rivers and streams (205).

15 *now full, now shallow, now dry;* SHAWCROSS (1972): "a steady decline from bad to worse" (261).

16–22 *These selfe . . . wormes shall eat.* LECOCQ (1969) cites these lines to confirm his assertion that the Satyres figure forth a type of universal *danse macabre* in which even the most innocent of human beings are destined, because they have in themselves some corruption, to sink into the general putrefaction (393).

16 *selfe* BEWLEY (1966): "same" (188). [So also, Milgate (1967, 166) and Smith (1971, 496).]

17–19 *a Man; in which . . . Th'Excrement* RUGOFF (1939): an example of Donne's "elaborate parallels" between the human body and "the organization of society"—the "reverse" of images that parallel "man's body, the microcosm" to "the macrocosm of the universe." See also *FunEl* 21–25, *Devotions*, Meditation 12, and *Sat1* 7–8 (177).

17–18 *a Man; in which Officers / Are the deuowring* STEIN (1942) finds that "stress shifts" are a technique of enjambment when "two unstressed syllables" occur (as he says they do here) "as late as the third foot" of the line (684).

17 *Proue the World . . . which Officers* RICHTER (1902) cites this line to illustrate a metrical inversion from iambic to trochaic in the first three feet (395). STEIN (1944c): "stress-shift by attraction," in the second and third feet, after initial "stress-shift," is one of Donne's chief devices for varying the metrical line (383).

18 *Are the deuowring . . . and Suters* STEIN (1944c): "stress-shift" in the fifth foot is one of Donne's chief devices for varying the metrical line (382).

19–27 *All men are . . . owne ruine is.* HESTER (1978b): this "exposition" of Gen. 3.19 is brought to explicate the "Paracelsan doctrine of correspondences" mentioned in l. 9 (351, 354). MAROTTI (1986): in these lines, amidst "metaphoric definitions of the officer-suitor relationship," the satirist "switches from the third to the second person." The "you" of this passage are the "Suiters," but they are also "the speaker's audience and the poet's readers." Moreover, the word "you" here "carries the sense of 'one,' which would include the speaker himself" (117).

19–23 *Th'Excrement…yet you are* **MELTON** (1906) identifies in these lines arsisthesis variation in stressed and unstressed repetitions of "men," "dust," "worms," "eat," and "you" (174).

19 *Th'Excrement…men are dust*; **MILGATE** (1967): this "gnomic" line is "rather trite" (165).

19 *Excrement* **MILGATE** (1967): "because all the substance has been taken from them by rapacious officials" (166).

20 *How much worse…to mens Lust* **STEIN** (1944c): "stress-shift by attraction," in the second, third, and fourth feet, after initial "stress-shift," is one of Donne's chief devices for varying the metrical line (384). **MORRIS** (1953): in this line, "the counterpoint is carried as far as it will go" (45).

20 *Lust* **MILGATE** (1967): "greed" (166).

21–22 *Are made prayes…wormes shall eat.* **STEIN** (1942) thinks this couplet is an example of Donne's frequent "riming of masculine and feminine endings" (680). **SMITH** (1970) finds that this passage offers "a vision of a civic jungle" in a "cool recognition of the relativeness of human claims altogether in respect of the dust to which we must all come" (143).

21 *Are made prayes….or wormes meat*; **STEIN** (1944c): "initial truncation" combined with "a feminine ending" is one of Donne's chief devices for varying the metrical line, albeit not foremost in the Satyres (377).

21 *wormes meat*; **MILGATE** (1967) cites Morris Tilley, *A Dictionary of the Proverbs in England in the Sixteenth and Seventeenth Century* (1950), M253 (166).

22 *For…wormes shall eat.* **GROSART** (1872–73): the addition of "do" makes the line "unrhythmical"; Donne may have intended "to make some such alteration as 'whom' for 'whose selves'" (1:49). **STEIN** (1944c): elision of an extra syllable (added to procure "emphasis") in a "trisyllabic foot" is one of Donne's devices for varying the metrical line (396).

23–27 *They are the…owne ruine is.* **POWERS** (1971): these lines demonstrate "the tug between meaning and formal structure" in the Satyres, in which the speech rhythms work against the poetic structure (48–49). **SLIGHTS** (1981): "the suitors he addresses are both victims and perpetrators of injustice" (173). **FLYNN** (2001): this "syndrome is replicated in the relations between the dominant political factions of the 1590s. In this framework, the Cecilians are officers, controlling the Court and the courts; the Essexians (whom the satirist addresses throughout most of the poem) are suitors, struggling to keep their share of spoils with which the Tudor Crown has created new nobility like the Devereux Earls" (117–18).

23 *They* **COLERIDGE** (1984): "i.e. Suiters [sic]" (12.2:229).

23 *Mills* **SULLENS** (1964): Donne's use of this meaning of the word is earlier than the earliest *OED* date (224).

24–27 *a wastfull...owne ruine is.* **BALD** (1970): "the suitors, though their misery is an object for pity, are not blameless" (101).

24 *wastfull* **SMITH** (1971): "destructive; consuming; useless" (496).

24 *warr* **SHAWCROSS** (1967): "referring secondarily to the war with Spain in 1588 and afterward" (398).

25–27 *They / Adulterate...Like Wittalls;* **NEWTON** (1974): "Evil and perversion have the same compulsive natural unnaturalness of a man who longs to be a cuckold." A wittol "may deny he loves his horns, but the compulsion of his nature drives him to seek and even cherish them" (442).

25–26 *They / Adulterate Law,* **SMITH** (1971): "great officers falsify law by prostituting it to their interests, when its true duty is the protection of their suitors" (496). **ELLIOTT** (1976) finds here an echo of the Sermon on the Mount in Matt. 6.25 (109).

25 *and you fight it.* **SMITH** (1971): "suitors fight against themselves by sustaining the people who destroy them" (496).

26 *Adulterate* **MILGATE** (1967): "falsify by admixture of baser ingredients (greed, cruelty, lack of scruple)" (166).

27 *Wittalls,* **BEWLEY** (1966): "knowing, complaisant cuckolds" (188). [So also, Milgate (1967, 166), Shawcross (1967, 35), and Smith (1971, 496).] **GRIGSON** (1980): "fools" (30). **CORTHELL** (1997): a pun on "'wittail,' meaning 'victual,'" perhaps "picking up on the comparison of suiters to food" in l. 22 (51).

27 *The'issue* **RICHTER** (1902) cites this phrase to illustrate a slurring of syllables (403). **MILGATE** (1967): "result (with a play on 'children', i.e. of the adulterous relationship in which the wittol acquiesces)" (166). **SMITH** (1971): "outcome; children illicitly begotten, who ruin their legal father by devouring his goods or inheriting what would otherwise be his" (496).

28–34 *Greatest, and...enormous sin.* **LECOMTE** (1965) thinks Donne is "basking" in these lines as throughout *Sat5* (61). **BALD** (1970): "The Queen does not know, and cannot be expected to know, of the abuses committed in her name, and Egerton is only beginning to learn of their extent" (101). **SHAWCROSS** (1972): these lines are generalized, with "no direct, no personal touches," the satirist speaking of "a prevalent evil" (266). "The seeming direct addresses to Elizabeth and Egerton are not, of course, actually being spoken to them" (268). **MAROTTI** (1981) thinks Donne in these lines addresses the Queen and Lord Keeper "in a way that carefully advertised his own position in the political hierarchy" (214). **CORTHELL** (1982) believes these lines to be the "central passage of the poem," in which the "complexity" of the satirist's "stance," expressed also through a "shifting tone" and "curiously meditative sections" of *Sat5*, alerts us "to the fact that Donne's new position is not one of identification with power." Nevertheless, through this "rhetoric of courtship," he "maintains his relation to power" (177–78). ZUNDER (1982) finds here "no criticism of institutions in themselves," although "it is probably Egerton who is addressed." In particular, the monarchy "is exempted from blame." Though "ambivalent," the river imagery is reminiscent of "Duncan's words to Macbeth" in *Mac.* 1.4.28–29 (18). MAROTTI (1986): in view of the switch from third to second person six lines earlier, this address to Elizabeth and Egerton "seems like a way of establishing the speaker's (and author's) own position of authority and security, a gesture, on Donne's part, of separating himself from the abject misery of both courtly and judicial suitorship" (117). CORTHELL (1997): here the "speaking subject of the poem is hard to locate with any syntactical precision," although these lines are "explicitly dedicated to doing so." The "missing" (or "displaced"—see l. 32) preposition "by" is "needed" in l. 31 "to complete the chain of command from Elizabeth to Egerton to Donne." Probably "exigencies of meter" caused this result, though other examples of such "gaps" occur in the Satyres (51–52).

28–30 *Greatest, and…whose corne o'reflow.* ELLRODT (1960b) contrasts the caution in these lines, which Donne wrote after becoming secretary to the Lord Keeper, to his unsparing censures of royalty elsewhere in the Satyres (2:18). HUGHES (1968): here the satirist "laments the grinding abuses of the law, and nearly obliges the aging Queen to accept the responsibility" (28). [Similarly, Cain (1998, 56).] NEWTON (1974): these lines push "to the limit" the consequences of the royal court's "natural perversity." Queen Elizabeth "is England, and if the land is corrupt then she herself is an unwitting and indeed a natural agent of destruction, like the innocent Thames." The satirist is "stuck in a dilemma: the invocation of Elizabeth makes it impossible for him to write satire without committing either treason or blasphemy" (442). COUSINS (1979): in the "winding way of Donne's method" this "water imagery" neither asserts nor denies but argues with a "coolly false reasoning" that "persuades with a skeptical indirectness." The "defense" of Queen Elizabeth is "cunningly flawed," a "deliberate illusion," and an "'alarum' to truth," putting "an efficient cause next to a certain result," but leaving "the reader to determine their relationship." The passage "clearly marks the ending of the English High Renaissance" (107). FULTON (2001): the river imagery here suggests "a serious disjuncture between royal prerogative and its unwitting consequences" (105).

28 *Empresse,* BEWLEY (1966): "Queen Elizabeth" (188). [So also, Shawcross (1967, 35), Warnke (1967, 124), and Smith (1971, 496).] BLISSETT (2000): "a complimentary address to the Queen" (114).

29–30 *Alas,…whose corne o'reflow.* CROFTS (1936): these lines reveal Donne's lack of faith in the queen and in women more generally (130).

29 *calme head* MILGATE (1967): Queen Elizabeth is the "serene source" of power, "unaware of, and not responsible for, the abuses of those far from the source of power (whose activities are symbolized by flood or turbulence in the lower reaches of the river)." Note Jonson's use of this image in the Prologue to *The Sad Shepherd,* ll. 24–25 (166). BAUMLIN (1990) points out that while *Sat3* vaguely mentions a "calme head," *Sat5* "explicitly identifies" this "calme head" with Queen Elizabeth (76).

31–34 *You, Sir,...enormous sin.* **ALDEN** (1899) reads these lines as posing a difficulty for the dating of this poem offered by Grosart (1872–73) and his understanding of the allusion to "Carricks Pepper" (l. 85). Explains further that "from 1596 to 1600...Donne was secretary to Lord Ellesmere," being "discharged" in 1600 because of "his clandestine marriage," so that a satire including an address to the Lord Chancellor would not be dated "later than 1600" (80). **NEWTON** (1974) paraphrases, "You Sir, whose righteousness is loved by Elizabeth (who richly pays me by allowing me to serve her), are given authority, and you now are beginning to recognize and weed out this enormous sin." Acknowledging that these lines make only "tenuous sense," suggests that this is "perhaps indicative of Donne's difficulties at this point." Believes that the passage is "virtually impossible" to read "without getting the impression that it is Donne, not Egerton," who now begins, yet "alternatively," "beginne" might be read as an "imperative," for "whatever one finally makes of the syntax, its effect is to blur the distinction between Egerton and Donne" (442–43). [Similarly, Baumlin (1986a, 102).] **HESTER** (1982): it is "the satirist (in his poem) as well as the lord keeper (in his investigation) who is 'authoriz'd,' both by his position on Egerton's staff and by his moral-aesthetic education chronicled in the first four *Satyres*" (103). **BAUMLIN** (1986a): these lines, addressed to Egerton, "may be read as a statement of fact, that Egerton has begun the process of social and legal change; but within the argument of the poem one may easily read them as an imperative statement, an exhortation to Egerton that he undertake such action." Here, "in its address to Donne's patron, the Persian mask" blends "thoroughly and inseparably with Donne's own 'public' voice" (102). The result is also a more "Christian form of satire," akin to that recommended by Lorenzo Gambara, "written with the greatest sincerity, but without violating charity" (104). **BLISSETT** (2000): the Queen is "too exalted" to deal with court corruption "except through a just deputy and agent" (114). **FLYNN** (2001) argues that here the satirist assimilates "his own service for Egerton to Egerton's for the Queen," incorporating "three persons in one shared, satiric enterprise" (107).

31–33 *whom I...payd, authoriz'd* **SMITH** (1971): "the privilege of serving a righteous man in itself richly repays the poet's labours and justifies his attack on injustices" (496). **CORTHELL** (1982) thinks the relative pronoun "whom," referring to Egerton, "lacks the preposition 'by' to attach itself securely to 'I'" in l. 31, finding a "missing link in Donne's confident appeal to a chain of authority reaching from Elizabeth, to Egerton, to Donne," making for the "curious" fact that "the address to Egerton is syntactically confusing." Suggests that the problem may be calculated, or "merely the exigencies of meter," and, if calculated, Donne "may be putting some distance between himself and Egerton" (183).

31 *You, Sir,* **GROSART** (1872–73) identifies him as "Probably Lord Chancellor Ellesmere—a biographic fact" (1:49). **GRIERSON** (1912) says that Donne was in Egerton's employ from 1598 to 1602. Adds that Egerton since 1597 had been "busy with the reform of some of the abuses connected with the Clerkship of the Star Chamber, and this is probably what Donne has in view" in *Sat5*. On Egerton's concerns, also quotes Spedding, *Life and Letters of Francis Bacon*, ii, 56 (2:126). **MILGATE** (1967) cites Jonson's phrase, "justest Lord" in *Underwood*, xxxi (166). **SHAWCROSS** (1967):

"Sir Thomas Egerton…had conducted various prosecutions between 1581 and 1592" (35). **SMITH** (1971) admits that "possibly" this is Egerton, since he "stood for justice and legal reform in the last years of the Queen's reign, and under James I became Lord Chancellor" (496). **MEDINE** (1972) thinks that here Egerton is presented "as a realization of the ideal" offered in *Sat3*, "where the speaker explains that truth involves knowledge translated into responsible action." Notes that after *Sat3* has shown "the necessarily private and individual nature of moral action," *Sat5* "represents the ideal in terms of one [i.e., Egerton] knowing and acting as an individual" (52). **WIGGINS** (2000): after being alluded to at the end of *Sat4*, Egerton is "finally identified" in *Sat5*, and the reader "feels a mingled sense of wonder" and "retrospective illumination," both elevating the legitimacy of this poem and evoking "the coherence" of all the Satyres (25). Egerton enters the poem as "the grave man who will make courtiers good—who will take up where Castiglione left off" (31).

31 *righteousnesse* **HESTER** (1982): "since Egerton does embody righteousness, the very righteousness that is the source of his power as lord keeper, then he can deny the satirist's explication of the current legal predicament and of his own duty as lord keeper only by denying that he is indeed righteous" (104). **EDWARDS** (2001): "like many others," Donne seems to have had "genuine admiration for Egerton" (53). **FLYNN** (2001) sees Egerton's "righteousnes" as his discreet abstinence from faction in Elizabethan politics, the basis on which the Queen "authoriz'd" him to assume office (111). Notes that *Sat5* describes Egerton's "righteousnes" but "implausibly characterizes" him, "a Court officer for more than a quarter of a century," as someone unaware of the "enormous sinne" at Court before he accepted the position of Lord Keeper (115).

32–33 *ame most richly / For seruice payd*, **STEIN** (1942) finds that "stress shift in the fifth foot, especially by attraction," gives "the strongest momentum of all" to enjambment, here effected by "the bringing of two unstressed syllables into close proximity, at the end of one line and at the beginning of the next" (684).

32 *By hauing leaue…most richly* **STEIN** (1944c): "stress-shift" in the fifth foot is one of Donne's chief devices for varying the metrical line (385). **SHAWCROSS** (1972): the final syllable of the feminine ending is "accented for rhyme although normally unstressed" (263).

33 *For seruice…now, begin* **STEIN** (1944c): "stress-shift" after the caesura is one of Donne's chief devices for varying the metrical line (378).

33 *authoriz'd* **MELTON** (1906) identifies a stress on the second syllable of this word and asserts that it represents Donne's frequent use of "unusual accents" (100–01). [So also, Milgate (1967, 166).] **NEWTON** (1974): "The 'authorized' person seems to be 'I,'" but the effect of the syntax is "to blur the distinction between Egerton and Donne" (442–43). **HESTER** (1978b): "the ambiguous antecedent to the word 'authorized' suggests that it is the satirist also who '*now* beginne[s]' in the following presentation of proofs to make public through his poem and to make clear to the suitor he addresses the causes for this 'enormous sinne'" (355). **KERINS** (1984), citing Newton (1974) and Hester (1978b), observes that the "oft noted ambiguity" of this word "serves to link

Egerton's royal commission of purging the Star Chamber's abuses with the satirist's own inquiry" into "this enormous sinne" (56). [Similarly, Wiggins (2000, 31).]

33 *now, begin* SMITH (1971): he enjoins the start of "a campaign against the legal corruptions which the poem exposes" (497).

34 *enormous sin.* HARDY (1942) thinks this corruption includes not only court officers' fees and the bribing of judges but the business of monopolies (76–77). MAROTTI (1986): the "sinne" here discussed is "the abusive legal-fee charging of court officers," but the kind of relationship described "applied to political transactions in general" (116).

35–63 *O age…so t'is.* STEIN (1942) calls attention to the "loose style" of this passage (695), and in a footnote comments on "the curt bits," further noting that Donne, "like many of the prose writers, finds it natural to combine both styles" (695n65).

35–38 *O age…sold deerer farr;* ALDEN (1899) says these lines especially exemplify the uniform "pessimism" of the Satyres (85), and identifies "th'iron Age" as a reference to "Juvenal XIII, 28ff." (88). [Similarly, Simpson (1924, 53).] COFFIN (1937) notes the bitterness of these lines and concludes that Donne's scorn is "no longer tempered by 'kinde pitty'" (58). SMITH (1952) finds in these lines "a reminiscence of Juvenal" and comments that Donne here "exhibits the nervous and angry temper which might have made a successful satirist," but that Donne, "too impressed with the degeneration of the world to make much of an art of satirizing it," deals mainly with "city and court types," lacking "the general impulse which motivated English satire in the native tradition" (226–27). BEWLEY (1966) glosses the four ages of the world: Golden, Silver, Bronze, and finally Iron, "degenerate and corrupt, in which the seventeenth century saw itself as living" (188). HESTER (1978b) notes that Juvenal's "most severe pejorative for his own age must be modified" to accommodate "the waning of the Elizabethan period," bearing out *Sat5*'s "description of the head of government as indifferent and far from the activities of justice (or injustice) in the realm, much as Astraea (with whom Elizabeth was often compared) forsook the world because of human corruption" (355–56).

35 *O age…better Witt* STEIN (1944c): elision of the extra syllable formed by a feminine ending in the foot preceding caesura is one of Donne's devices for varying the metrical line (394).

35 *age of rusty Iron,* MILGATE (1967): "The next step was usually rather the Leaden Age than the age of 'rusty iron'"; cf. *FirAn* 425–26; Juvenal, *Satire* 13, l. 28 and *Satire* 6, l. 23; and Stubbes, *Anatomy of Abuses*, Part II, 1583, B2v (166). NEWTON (1974) thinks this the "most conventional of Donne's satiric exclamations," suggesting that "he has at last appropriated to himself a comfortable public voice" (443). ELLIOTT (1976) cites the Sermon on the Mount in Matt. 6.25 (108). HESTER (1978b): "Juvenal's epithet" is brought to prove the satirist's case in his "curious apotheosis of Elizabeth and praise of Egerton" in ll. 28–34 (351).

36 *yf ought equall itt.* MILGATE (1967): "if another suitable metaphor or phrase could be found to which it is equivalent" (166).

37–41 *The Iron Age…Into'other hands;* **GRIERSON** (1912) paraphrases: "'*That*', says Donne (the italics give emphasis), 'was the iron age when justice was sold. Now' (in this 'age of rusty iron') 'injustice is sold dearer. Once you have allowed all the demands made on you, you find, suitors (and suitors are gamblers), that the money you toiled for has passed into other hands, the lands for which you urged your rival claims has escaped you, as Angelica escaped while Ferrau and Rinaldo fought for her.'" Notes Alden's (1899) linking of "the iron Age" to Juvenal and also glosses "strivers hands" with reference to Chaucer's "Knightes Tale, ll. 319 ff." (2:126–27). **SMITH** (1971): "suitors are gamblers with the law who will find that by the time they have allowed for all the demands, fees and duties that a lawsuit entails, they themselves have nothing left for their efforts (Dickens made the same point in *Bleak House* over two hundred and fifty years later)" (497).

37 *The Iron Age…sold, now* **COLERIDGE** (1811) (reading 1669's "The iron Age was, when justice was sold, now") notes that Donne "sometimes makes a dissylable of liquid monos.—s͞o͞old, fier, c͞a͞er, wier, for sold, fire, care, wire. But rather throw a very strong emphasis on 'Justice', & you will find the Line read" (229).

37 *Iron Age* **SHAWCROSS** (1967): "ironically, the forsaken world at the opening of the bronze age by Astraea, goddess of justice, because of human corruption" (35).

38–41 *Allow / All…other hands;* **STEIN** (1946): "to" omitted before "gamsters" in these lines exemplifies Donne's use of ellipsis, "rather puzzling until one realizes" that a word has been omitted (101).

39 *All claym'd fees…Gamesters, anone* **STEIN** (1944c) (reading "All demands, fees"): elision of extra syllables caused by "attraction" (i.e., when two unstressed syllables' coming together may draw "an extra unstressed syllable into the rhythm") is among Donne's devices for varying the metric line (397). **SHAWCROSS** (1972) (reading "All demands, fees"): a "hypermetric line" (263), and the "strong medial pause," following "two briefer pauses," means that "the unaccented and extra syllable immediately before it has only the effect of an easing-off such as feminine lines yield" (265).

39 *claym'd fees* **MILGATE** (1967) (reading "demands, fees") cites Spedding, *Letters and Life of Francis Bacon*, ii. 56 (167).

39 *Gamesters,* **LEGOUIS** (1942): "if we adopt Grierson's explanation that 'suitors are gamblers' in a metaphorical sense, then this instance should precede, under sense 3 fig." in the *OED*, "the quotation dated 1645 (Bp. Hall, *Remedy Discontents*)" (186). [So also, Sullens (1964, 217).] **MILGATE** (1967): "gamblers." See Burton, *Anatomy of Melancholy*, part. 2, sect. 3, memb. 7 (167). [So also, Carey (1990, 431).]

40–41 *The mony…other hands;* **FREER** (1996) notes the "punning allusion to the practice of 'sweating' coins" by placing "gold coins in a leather bag and shaking them, thus giving the coins the appearance of only normal wear while leaving a deposit of gold dust in the bag" (506).

40–41 *is gone / Into'other* **STEIN** (1942) finds that "stress shift in the fifth foot, especially by attraction," gives "the strongest momentum of all" to enjambment, here effected by beginning a line with "an extra syllable" (685).

40 *The mony...is gone* SHAWCROSS (1972): a "hypermetric line" (263).

40 *you* MAROTTI (1986): "refers to the 'gamsters' being apostrophized" (117).

40 *sweare...for* MILGATE (1967): "about which you take oaths in the law-courts" (167). SMITH (1971): "take oaths for (which will imperil your soul if they are perjured)" (497).

41–42 *So controuerted...the Striuers hands.* SAINTSBURY (1896) calls these lines a "charming touch at once so literary and so natural" (1:xxii–xxiii). HESTER (1978b): reference to Ariosto amplifies the application of Juvenal's epithet (l. 35) to the satirist's case in his "curious apotheosis of Elizabeth and praise of Egerton" in ll. 29–34 (351).

41 *Into'other hands*; STEIN (1944c): elision of extra syllables caused by "attraction" (i.e., two unstressed syllables' coming together may draw "an extra unstressed syllable into the rhythm") is among Donne's devices for varying the metric line (397).

41 *controuerted Lands* FLYNN (2001): former properties of the Church of England, "first put on the market by Tudor confiscations" (116).

41 *controuerted* LEGOUIS (1942): predates the earliest OED listing of the word, that "first recorded in 1605 (T. Sparke, *Brotherly Perswas.*)" (185). [So also, Sullens (1964, 178).] MILGATE (1967): "disputed, of which the title is in dispute" (167). [So also, Smith (1971, 497).]

42 *Angelica,* GROSART (1872–73) identifies her as "St. Angelica" (1:49). NORTON (1895): "'The fairest of her sex, Angelica,' as Milton (*Par. Reg.*, iii, 341) calls her, escapes, in the first canto of the *Orlando Furioso*, from the hands of Rinaldo and Ferrau, in the second from those of Rinaldo and Sacripante" (1:247). [So also, Chambers (1896, 2:245), Bewley (1966, 188), Milgate (1967, 167), Warnke (1967, 124), Smith (1971, 497), and Grigson (1980, 30).] RUGOFF (1939): "candied garden stalks," "a delicacy once familiar, now rare" (122). ELLRODT (1960b) comments that Ariosto is one of only four Italian men of letters to whom Donne alludes (the others being Dante, Petrarch, and Aretino) and that it is not surprising an Elizabethan would have read *Orlando Furioso*, a poem related in genre to *Metem* (2:213–14). SHAWCROSS (1967): "daughter of Gallaphrone, king of Cathay, whose fortress Albracca was beseiged by Agrican, king of Tartary, among others seeking Angelica's hand," as cited in Boiardo, *Orlando Innamorato*, 1:10.26 (36). CAREY (1990): Angelica escapes "while rival suitors fight for her" as "disputed estates" vanish "in legal fees" (431).

43–45 *If Law be...thou appeal?* HESTER (1978b): these lines summarize "the central issue" of *Sat5* and its "satiric strategy." Here, "the satirist's appeal is to traditional interpretations of man and law," accommodating them "to current conditions," in an effort to "instill knowledge of his spiritual potential and moral responsibilities" in a "wrech'd" suitor (348). Ps. 40 also clarifies here Juvenal's epithet in l. 35 (351), namely, "David's admonition" in Ps. 40.8 "confirms the satirist's claim that it is the suitors who bring about their own misery" (356). MAROTTI (1986): the singular pronouns "thou" and "thee" in this passage "seem to be directed at the reader (as well as functioning, perhaps, partly, as self-address)" (117).

43–44 *If Law be...or fee* **RICHTER** (1902) cites these lines to illustrate enjambment (408).

43 *If Law be...Iudges hart,* **SMITH** (1971): "if law is merely the judge's personal inclination" (497).

44 *Haue no hart...or fee* **STEIN** (1944c): "stress-shift" after a pause is one of Donne's chief devices for varying the metrical line (379).

44 *Letter or fee* **MILGATE** (1967): "a letter from a person of influence, or a bribe, which might corrupt the judge" (167). [So also, Smith (1971, 497) and Carey (1990, 431).]

45–53 *Power of the Courts...Become great Seas,* **HESTER** (1978b): the "full context" of Ps. 40.8, alluded to by the satirist in l. 43, is amplified at length in these lines (356). **CORTHELL** (1982) finds that "the analogy of power has led Donne into blasphemy, for it is difficult not to read these lines as an indictment of the source of power itself" (176). **BAUMLIN** (1986a) cites *Sat3* 103–09, observing that here the satirist "expands and makes more abstract the analogy," and turns the "relationship between suitors and officers into an elaborate conceit readers would not hesitate to call 'metaphysical'" (103). **GUIBBORY** (1986): in these lines (which echo *Sat3*'s concluding use of water imagery to illustrate the perils of separation from God, the "source or head" of all power), the suitor who is "already downstream" may not be able to "return to the head." As "earthly powers were compared to streams" in *Sat3*, so in *Sat5* "courts are a stream that can 'sucke thee in.'" Moreover, the attempt to go upstream through court appeals may encounter "great seas" over which a suitor must make "golden bridges" in the form of bribes (80). **FLYNN** (2001): "suitors and officers engage in legal actions" over former Church properties in an "ever growing volume of litigation once stimulated and now controlled by the royal Court" (116).

45–47 *Power of the Courts...thee in, to misery,* **ANDREASEN** (1963): it is "God's Law" that "dwells at the stream's head; officials who abuse the power delegated to them by God suck in and drown those who appeal to the law" (73). **CORTHELL** (1997) draws a contrast and a parallel between *Sat5*'s reference to "the first maine head" in l. 46 and the comparison in Ps. 82 of "earthly and divine justice" (53). **FULTON** (2001): this imagery of the stream "reflects powerfully on the earlier construction" in ll. 28–30; "the river begins as a metaphor that merely drowns meads, and then becomes entwined with the actual conditions, as the 'maine head,' formerly not directly implicated, becomes the source of the problem" (105).

45 *Wher wilt thou...Courts below* **STEIN** (1944c): elision of the extra syllable formed by a "W-sound before a vowel" is one of Donne's devices for varying the metrical line (390).

45 *wilt thou appeal?* **RICHTER** (1902) cites this phrase to illustrate a slurring of syllables (402–03).

45 *the Courts below* **SMITH** (1971): "magistrates' courts and the like, whose

power draws from the courts above them and ultimately from the central judiciary, so that if the source is tainted one has no appeal from the corruptions of the lower branches" (497).

46 *Flow* GRIERSON (1912) notes a similar use of plural verbs with singular subjects in Shakespeare's *H5* 5.2.18, and *Lr.* 3.5.4 (2:127). MILGATE (1967) contends that the use of the plural form of the verb "is normal usage," citing *Lr.* 3.6.4–5 (167).

46 *first maine head:* MILGATE (1967): "the Queen," the image being an extension of l. 29 (167). NEWTON (1974): "any doubt about the identity" of this person "is removed by the insistent recollection of the water imagery previously used to describe Elizabeth" (443).

46 *these* MILGATE (1967): "'the Courts below' the Queen" (167).

48–51 *But if…most faynt.* COLERIDGE (1811): "one feels oneself yielding to the Stream after vain efforts, in these fine Lines" (229).

50 *when vpwards,* GROSART (1872–73): "when [thou goest] upwards" (1:49). MILGATE (1967): "when you try to appeal to higher authority," in that because power flows to the courts from above, to appeal is to swim against the stream, particularly difficult when one is "heavy" (sad) and "faint" (exhausted by previous efforts) (167). SMITH (1971): "when swimming upstream means also moving upwards, complaining from the lesser to the greater" (497).

52 *Gainst* RICHTER (1902) cites this word to illustrate syncopy, or shortening (404).

53 *Become great Seas,* SHAWCROSS (1967): "become important officers of the state" (36).

54–55 *Forc'd to make…them before.* MILGATE (1967): "As a bridge enables you to pass beyond the water it crosses, money will persuade the Court officers to get your complaint beyond them and have it heard; but all you will discover is that these same officers ('seas') have appropriated ('drown'd') all the money you have already spent in fees; you have nothing left to pay (?bribe) them with" (167).

54 *Forc'd to make golden bridges,* SMITH (1971): "compelled to get over by bribes" (497).

54 *golden bridges,* CHAMBERS (1896): "An euphemism for money paid to an adversary, to secure an advantage, by giving him an excuse to retreat" (2:245).

56–58 *All things follow…them to go* STEIN (1944c): elision of extra syllables caused by "attraction" (i.e., two unstressed syllables' coming together may draw "an extra unstressed syllable into the rhythm") is among Donne's devices for varying the metric line (397).

56 *All things…haue more.* RICHTER (1902) cites this line to illustrate a metrical oddity which he calls strange or unfitting verse ("fremde Verse") (400). MILGATE (1967) thinks this "gnomic" line is "rather trite" (165) and calls it a "perversion" of

Matt. 25.29, also pointing out that it is "an alexandrine" (168). [Similarly, Carey (1990, 431).] **SHAWCROSS** (1972): a "hypermetric line" (263). **HESTER** (1978b): "a conflation of Paracelsus and Matt. 25:29" (351), reaffirming "ironically the legal dilemma in which the suitors have placed themselves." The "duty of every man" set forth in the Gospel "has been perverted into a purely scientific, economic principle. By participating in such a system of injustice," the suitors "perpetuate" a violation of "justice, liberty, and charity as Christ delineated them" (356).

57–63 *Iudges...Scarce to Kings*; **LEISHMAN** (1951) complains that almost the whole point of these lines "turns on the exploitation of the double meaning of the word angel" (117). **ANDREASEN** (1963) finds here Donne's "customary contrast between the righteous ideal, and the way it has been perverted by man's greed for material wealth and power" (74). **ZUNDER** (1982): these lines illustrate how "the wit of the poem is very astringent," while its "values, and natural points of reference, are traditional, and unquestioned" (18–19). **BAUMLIN** (1990): though in *Sat5* "concern over the plight of Catholics remains," nevertheless "allusions to Reformation controversy refuse to espouse one side explicitly." Here the satirist's comparison of "political bribery to the intercession of angels and saints" indirectly "ridicules Catholic theology" (76). **BAUMLIN** (1991) adds that here in *Sat5* the Catholic doctrine of intercession is "explicitly criticized" and "becomes an obstacle rather than a bridge to salvation" (95). **CORTHELL** (1997): "a system of bribery in God's court." *Sat5*'s "revisionist production" of an analogy used in Ps. 82 yields "both a bitter protest against Renaissance monarchy and a radical interrogation consonant with other late Elizabethan challenges to providentialist belief" (53). **FLYNN** (2001): the "factional embroglio of Tudor government in the 1590s" keeps raising the cost of doing business, even for the Crown, so that "the Tudor monarchy, despite having enriched itself by despoiling the Church, is unable to support itself" (117).

57–62 *Iudges...as here*, **MATSUURA** (1953) cites these lines to argue that Donne's mentions of particular angelic orders are sometimes guided by their associations and rhymes (28).

57 *Iudges...sayd them so* **SHAWCROSS** (1972): a "hypermetric line" (263).

57 *Iudges are Gods*. **GROSART** (1872–73) cites Ps. 82.1, 2, and 6 (1:49). [So also, Smith (1971, 497), Hester (1978b, 351), and Carey (1990, 431).] **MILGATE** (1967) cites *Sermons* 1:233 (168).

57 *sayd them so* **SMITH** (1971): "declared them so" (498).

59–60 *By meanes...to Dominations*, **RICHTER** (1902) states that the rhyme here consists of the similarity of unstressed syllables (410).

59–60 *When Supplications / We send to God*, **STEIN** (1942) contends that Donne learned from Marlowe's plays this technique of enjambment by "ending a line with a polysyllabic word in order to lighten the last foot" (682–83).

59 *By meanes of...Supplications* **STEIN** (1944c): elision of the extra syllable

formed by a feminine ending in the foot preceding caesura is one of Donne's devices for varying the metrical line (394). **SHAWCROSS** (1972): a "hypermetric line" (263).

59 *Angells.* **GROSART** (1872–73): "coins so called = bribes" (1:49). [So also, Matsuura (1953, 28).] **MILGATE** (1967): "bribery"; the angel or angel-noble, worth about 10 shillings, was "a gold coin, so called from the device of the archangel Michael killing the dragon which it bore" (168). [Similarly, Warnke (1967, 124), Smith (1971, 498), and Carey (1990, 431).]

60–61 *Dominations, / Powers, Cherubins,* **GROSART** (1872–73): "Names in the angelic hierarchy" (1:49). **MATSUURA** (1953): the choice of "particular Angelic Orders" here appears based on "the associative values of their names," which "go in harmony with supplications," or it may be based on "the consideration of metre or rhyme" (28). **MILGATE** (1967) sees a pun on "angels" as "irresistible," citing *Sermons* 5:258. Listing the orders of angels—Seraphim, Cherubim, Thrones; Dominations, Principalities, Powers; Virtues, Archangels, Angels—holds that Donne's "choice of the three named here is due rather to convenience of rhyme and metre than to the sharper wit" of *ElBrac* 78 (168).

61 *heauens Courts,* **GRIERSON** (1912) quotes *Letters* 102: "so the Roman profession seems to exhale, and refine our wills from earthly Drugs, and Lees, more then the Reformed, and so seems to bring us nearer heaven, but then that carries heaven farther from us, by making us pass so many Courts, and Offices of Saints in this life, in all our petitions" (2:127).

62–63 *Should pay fees, … Would it not anger* **STEIN** (1942) says these lines rhyme the weak syllables of feminine endings, something that "almost never occurs" in Donne's verse, but cites also *Sat5* 84–85 (680). **SHAWCROSS** (1972): the final syllables of the feminine endings are "accented for rhyme although normally unstressed" (263).

62 *pay fees,* **MILGATE** (1967): "If we had to pay fees for petitions in our prayers as we have in petitioning earthly courts, even kings would lack the 'daily bread' they pray for in repeating the Lord's Prayer" (168). [So also, Hester (1978b, 351).]

63–91 *Would it not…vanished.* **COLERIDGE** (1811) thinks these lines difficult to scan, but is not inclined to alter them. Argues that in "the age of Donne" people "took the literal meaning" of the word "Satyrs" and thought they "were supposed to come all rough from the woods, with a rustic accent" (230).

63–68 *Would it not…for comming?* **COLERIDGE** (1811) thinks the text "suspicious" in these lines (230). **STEIN** (1944b): "the collapse of the iambic structure helps accentuate the ridicule" intended by the satirist. This "harshness," however, "may well be interpreted as the result of carelessness or a lapse in technical skill" (401–02). **ELLRODT** (1960b) thinks these lines, compared to Donne's critique of the social order in the earlier Satyres and other poems, express a fading cynicism (2:53). Adds that written after Donne became secretary to Lord Keeper Egerton, they and the rest of *Sat5*, along with *Metem*, are among the last satirical lines Donne wrote; his muse could not muster new satires during the long, subsequent period of his unemployment (2:285). **BAUMLIN** (1990): taking clothes, books, and plate means "the very vocabulary of Catholicism comes under assault"; this is "an outrage against language as well as charity" (77). **ROBBINS** (2000): here Donne denounces "false accusations and extortion perpetrated by the government's enforcers" (424). **FLYNN** (2001): a "grotesque system is ever fuelled by its origin: the depredations set in motion by Tudor religious reform." Suitors having gained "control of former abbeys and made chapels into dining halls" are "bedeviled by an inexorable engine of injustice," their ill-gotten properties "unjustly confiscated by officers who charge each victim a fee to cover their costs of operation" (117).

63–64 *Scarce to Kings;...a Martyr* **RICHTER** (1902) states that the rhyme here consists of the similarity of unstressed syllables (410). **STEIN** (1942): an unusual example of rhyming only weak syllables (680).

63 *Scarce to Kings;...Would it not anger* **STEIN** (1944c): "initial truncation" combined with a feminine ending is one of Donne's chief devices for varying the metrical line, albeit not foremost in the Satyres (377).

63 *so t'is.* **MILGATE** (1967): "so things are" (168). [So also, Smith (1971, 498) and Carey (1990, 431).] **NEWTON** (1974): with this "decisive" assertion, the satirist "once again skirts the edge of blasphemy," speaking now "with the voice not of a private Humorist but of a public censor" (443–44). **CORTHELL** (1982) agrees with Newton (1974) and comments that "the analogy of power has led Donne into blasphemy, for it is difficult not to read these lines as an indictment of the source of power itself" (176, 183).

64 *A Stoick, a Coward, yea a Martyr* **MILGATE** (1967): "These three would be the least likely to feel anger, the Stoic because he believed that one should be unmoved by circumstance or by passion, the coward because of his timidity, and the martyr because of his willingness (and power) to suffer without complaint for his beliefs" (168). **NEWTON** (1974): this "uneasy sequence" suggests that "the public censor's voice can never be definitive and that it is always subject to corrosion from within," a corrosion that "seems inevitable because of what the satirist perceives without" (444).

65–68 *To see...for comming?* **GRIERSON** (1912) quotes *LXXX Sermons* 52.525 (2:128). **MILGATE** (1967): "The finding of missals and of vestments and utensils required for Mass was crucial evidence in the conviction of Roman Catholics under the statutes dealing with recusancy and the banishment of priests," as cited in Robert Southwell, *An Humble Supplication* (1953), 43–44; Robert Parsons, *The Judgement of a Catholic Englishman* (1608), 43; and William Barlow's *Answer* (1609) to Parsons's book, 351–52 (169). **SMITH** (1971): "Pursuivants rooting out Roman Catholics looked for the evidence of Catholic observances, such as vestments, liturgical utensils, and manuals of devotion. The legalized witch-hunt laid anyone who owned old books or plate open to blackmail and the loss of their possessions, sometimes at the hands of frauds posing as pursuivants" (498). **CAREY** (1981): although it would have been "more tactful for Donne to have kept his Catholic resentment out of sight," it was "liable to surface whenever he wrote poetry" (69). **OLIVER** (1997): in these lines, the satirist sides "openly with Catholics, but only for a moment." Despite "all the humorous incongruity" here, "there is no mistaking the anger that flares out against the absurdly suspicious priest-taker," in a passage describing "a scene of the kind which took place in Henry Donne's rooms in 1593" (36–37).

65–66 *To see…and all* **STEIN** (1944c): an example of a "daring" truncation after a pause (377–78).

65 *Purseuant* **BEWLEY** (1966): "officer whose duty it was to arrest Catholics" (189). **MILGATE** (1967) cites *Sat4* 216 (168). [So also, Carey (1990, 431).]

65 *call* **GROSART** (1872–73): "call over, and therefore taken an inventory of" (1:49). **SMITH** (1971): "name as prohibited instruments" (498).

66 *All his Clothes,…and all* **STEIN** (1944c): truncation after a pause in the line is one of Donne's most daring devices for varying the metrical pattern (378). **STEIN** (1944d) adds that, beginning and ending this line with the same word, Donne "may be following rhetorician methods" (295).

66 *Clothes,* **RICHTER** (1902) cites this word to illustrate a stretching of syllables (405).

66 *Copes;* **SHAWCROSS** (1967): "capelike vestments of ecclesiastical officers" (36).

66 *Primmers;* **MILGATE** (1967): "The Roman Catholic Primer was a prayer-book for the use of the laity, at first mainly a translation copy of parts of the Breviary and Manual" (169). **SHAWCROSS** (1967): "prayer books" (36).

67 *His Plate, Chalices;…them away* **SHAWCROSS** (1972): a "hypermetric line" (263).

67 *mistake* **GROSART** (1872–73): "take them wrongly or without right"; refers to "Essays in Divinity, part iii. (p. 77, ed. 1855)" (1:49). **OED** (1904–08): "To take wrongfully, wrongly, or in error." [So also, Milgate (1967, 169) and Smith (1971, 498).]

68–80 *Oh ne're…bar'd to thee?* **CORTHELL** (1997): "reverence and loathing combine in an image that idealizes and then trashes the law." This image has "particular force" considered in relation to the poem's "earlier identification of suiters and excrement (l. 19)" and to the next line's "quibble on 'baring.'" Here the "strumpeting" of the law "is given a more specific, sodomitical representation" (52–53).

68–73 *Oh ne're…who in iayles;* **PETER** (1956): the satirist's "very attitude to Law is Roman," and "the respect with which he speaks of it is plain" (136). **ANDREASEN** (1963) says the satirist "knows too well" that the name of the law "has been strumpeted already" (73). **NEWTON** (1974): when, "through a paean to law," the satirist himself tries "to make courtiers good," his effort is "doomed, and the pure stream quickly curdles once again into troubled eddies" (444).

68–72 *Oh ne're…fates words;* **HARDY** (1942): "Here is enthusiasm, pride in his work and respect for his employer" (77).

68 *aske a fee* **MILGATE** (1967) cites *Sermons* 5:370 (169).

69–71 *be strumpeted…Recorder to Destiny* **STEIN** (1942) contends that Donne learned from Marlowe's plays this technique of enjambment, here in successive lines "ending a line with a polysyllabic word in order to lighten the last foot" (682–83).

69–70 *strumpeted* and *established* RICHTER (1902) cites these two words to illustrate syllabic stretching with past participles (405).

69 *whight* MILGATE (1967): "pure, innocent of wrong" (169). [So also, Ellrodt (2000, 203).]

69 *strumpeted* OED (1914–19): "To bring to the condition of a strumpet." SULLENS (1964): Donne's use of this meaning of the word is cited by OED as the earliest source (255).

70 *warrant* SULLENS (1964): Donne's use of this meaning of the word is earlier than the earliest OED date (243).

71–73 *Recorder to...who in iayles*; MILGATE (1967): there is no "parallel for this view of the Law as Recorder of Fate," but "the conception is not inappropriate if we take Fate, or Destiny, as 'the Commissary of God'" (*Metem* 31). As "'positive', that is man-made, law should be in accord with 'natural law', so the judgements of the law should record the decrees of Fate" (169). ZUNDER (1982): although this imagery is "individual," without a known parallel, yet it expresses a "traditional world-view, ordered and unified" and "intact." Moreover, the "idea of law, constituting the positive position from which the poem is written," corresponds "in its positive function" to *Sat3*'s passage on doubt and truth in ll. 76–82. The "comparative lack of force" of the passage in *Sat5* "is plainly significant," implying "a weakening of traditional ideas" resulting from "changes of the sixteenth century in England, and a need, in a new situation, to find new sources of meaning in life" (19).

71 *Recorder to...and Shee* COLERIDGE (1811) conjectures Donne wrote "Record" (230). SHAWCROSS (1972): a "hypermetric line" (263).

71 *Destiny on* SHAWCROSS (1972) questions whether there is "some elision in 'Destiny on,' either 'Dest'ny on' or 'Des ti ny'on'" (263).

72 *Speakes fates...who must bee* COLERIDGE (1811) conjectures Donne wrote "Speaketh" and "telleth" (230). RICHTER (1902) uses this line to illustrate the absence either of an opening syllable (399) or of an unstressed syllable in the interior of the line (400). MELTON (1906) rejects "but" and "us" in this line because "*but, us, and must*" are "all in thesis so near together, and without a similar sound in arsis"—a practice that "would not be like Donne" (175).

72 *but* LEGOUIS (1942) suggests "that Donne made his *but* to bear, not on the verb, but on the subject, though understood here and last expressed at the end of the preceding line? *only she tells us*, which, for all practical purposes, is equivalent to 'she alone': surely a definition of the law more in accordance with the trend of the argument" (194–95).

73 *Rich,...who in iayles*; COLERIDGE (1811) conjectures Donne wrote "Rich and who poore, in chairs who, who in jayles" (230).

73 *chayres*, **MILGATE** (1967): "chairs of State, or high offices" (169). [So also, Smith (1971, 498).] **WARNKE** (1967): "the reference is to sedan-chairs" (125).

74 *foule long Nayles*, **MILGATE** (1967): "the only blemish on the Law's beauty," the nails are only the "extremities" of the body and can be pared (169). [So also, Newton (1974, 444).]

75 *With which she...In bodyes* **STEIN** (1944c): "stress-shift" in the fifth foot is one of Donne's chief devices for varying the metrical line (382). **SHAWCROSS** (1972): the final syllable of the feminine ending is "accented for rhyme although normally unstressed" (263).

76 *Of Men...th'extremityes*, **STEIN** (1944c): elisions of extra syllables formed by "light vowels in unstressed places" are among Donne's devices for varying the metrical line (389). **SHAWCROSS** (1972): a "hypermetric line," although "so'in" may be elided (263).

76 *Of Men (so in Law)*, **RICHTER** (1902) cites this phrase to illustrate a slurring of syllables (402–03).

77–78 *So'Officers...part comes to.* **HARRIS** (1960): these lines portray the "ceaseless activity" of the world of the Satyres (192). **FLYNN** (2001): "Here officers of the Court such as the Cecils and Egerton himself are defined as the Queen's excremental tools in their rapacious scraping to maintain the heartless momentum of royal policy" (119).

78–79 *As our nayles...to yon Officer*, **SHAWCROSS** (1967): "Our nails can reach to scratch our posteriors. The next line (besides meaning doffing one's hat) makes obscene reference to officers" (37). **SHAWCROSS** (1972) adds that here, following through on the "foule long nailes" metaphor, Donne is "obscenely making his point" (261).

79–89 *Why bar'st thou...Prophesies.* **SHAWCROSS** (1972) finds these lines, even if avoiding jest, "particularly contemptuous" of "fools, who have brought on their misery" (260).

79–84 *Why bar'st thou...for more;* **KERINS** (1984): "The suitor who has gained by 'wrong' now finds himself a victim of this false image of Justice permeating the law courts." In the end, the "irony" is that "only now" he seeks "an ideal Justice which he has heretofore gleefully succeeded in perverting" (57–58).

79–80 *Why bar'st thou...bar'd to thee?* **ANDREASEN** (1963): "Having stripped others of their wealth, the young man has now been stripped of his own by the judge" (73).

79 *bar'st* **GROSART** (1872–73): "uncoverest" (1:49). **LEGOUIS** (1942): OED "does not record the intransitive, or absolute, use of the verb *bare*," and "of course Donne means: 'barest thy head'" (195). **SULLENS** (1964): this meaning of the word is not recorded in OED (258). [So also, Milgate (1967, 169).] **SMITH** (1971): "take your hat off, bare your head" (498). [So also, Carey (1990, 431).]

80 *Gott those…bar'd to thee?* STEIN (1944c): "stress-shift by attraction" in the second foot, after initial "stress-shift," is one of Donne's "very frequent" devices for varying the metrical line (383).

80 *bar'd* SULLENS (1964): this meaning of the word is not recorded in *OED* (258).

81–83 *Foole twise,…Thummin try* RICHTER (1902) cites these lines to illustrate rhyme breaking, the opposite of enjambment (409).

81–82 *and now hungerly / Begst right.* STEIN (1942) contends that Donne learned from Marlowe's plays this technique of enjambment by "ending a line with a polysyllabic word in order to lighten the last foot" (682–83).

81 *Foole twise,…hungerly* SHAWCROSS (1972): a "hypermetric line" (263) that "does not pull us up short as an anomaly" because, immediately before, in l. 79, "the line has broken into two" with the last three syllables attaching themselves to l. 80, "whereas l. 81 enjambs with the first foot" of l. 82, "after which again there is a strong break" (265).

81 *bought wrong,* MILGATE (1967): "bought injustice" (169).

82 *right.* MILGATE (1967): "justice" (169).

82 *dole* MILGATE (1967): "portion or lot in life, destiny" (*OED*, sb. 3, 4) or "distribution of gifts" (*OED*, 5), "boon" (169). SMITH (1971): "good fortune; just share" (498). HESTER (1978b) cites Micah 2.4 (351) and further notes that the satirist's allusion to prophecy of the Day of Judgment suggests that the suitors will receive a "dole" (grievance) as their "dole" (justice), summarizing "the satirist's paradoxical view of the operations of Justice amidst injustice" (358–59).

82 *these* MILGATE (1967): "law-officers" (169). SMITH (1971): "corrupt officers of the law" (498). CAREY (1990): "legal officials" (431).

83–84 *Thou'hadst…wouldst for more;* MILGATE (1967): "You had much (but have lost it); you would test the Urim and Thummim of the Law in the hope of gaining (or re-gaining) more (than you now have; or, than you had at first, before legal redress was made)" (169).

83 *Thou'hadst…Thummin try* STEIN (1944c): elision of the extra syllable formed by a feminine ending in the foot preceding caesura is one of Donne's devices for varying the metrical line (394). SHAWCROSS (1972): a "hypermetric line" (263).

83 *Vrim and Thummin* LEGOUIS (1942): predates the earliest *OED* listing of the figurative use of the phrase, that "first recorded in 1618 (Bp. Hall, *Contempl., N.T.*)" (186). [So also, Sullens (1964, 241).] MILGATE (1967): "Intensive plurals of Hebrew *ur* = 'light', and *tom* = 'perfection'; hence the 'clarity and integrity' of the Law"; cf. Deut. 33.8 (169). Further, the "nature of the gems" is not known, as cited in Num. 27.21 [so also, Hester (1978b, 359).] and 1 Sam. 14.41ff. They were used for divination, according to R. J. Beck, "Urim and Thummim," *N&Q* 4 (1957). As such, "the suggestion here might be that Law is a kind of oracle, revealing the decrees of Fate" (170). SHAWCROSS (1967): "jewels in Aaron's breastplate," as cited in Exod. 28.30

[so also, Hester (1978b, 359)], "considered mediums for the revelation of God's will" (37). **SMITH** (1971): "certain mysterious objects worn by the Jewish High Priest which empowered him to speak as the will of Jehovah," as cited in Deut. 33.8. Further, "the Hebrew words mean 'doctrine and truth' or 'light and integrity'" (498). **HESTER** (1978b) cites also 1 Sam. 7.7, commenting that all the Hebrew verses cited show "that the gems were considered authoritative and oracular means of divining God's purposes, some sort of dice," used by Jewish priests in judicial proceedings (359). **CAREY** (1990): "Hebrew: 'lights' and 'perfections,'" as cited in Exod. 28.30 (431).

84–85 *Thou wouldst...Carraques pepper.* **STEIN** (1942): these lines rhyme the weak syllables of feminine endings, something that "almost never occurs" in Donne's verse, but see also *Sat5* 63–64 (680). **BEWLEY** (1966): "You have enough legal writs to package the cargo of pepper in a carrack, i.e., a great merchant vessel" (190). **SHAWCROSS** (1972): the final syllables of the feminine endings are "accented for rhyme although normally unstressed" (263).

84 *Thou wouldst...hast paper* **STEIN** (1944c): "stress-shift" after the caesura is one of Donne's chief devices for varying the metrical line (384).

84 *Thou wouldst for more;* **SHAWCROSS** (1967): "Thou wouldst put the Urim and Thummim of the law to proof for more" (37).

84 *paper* **MILGATE** (1967): "legal documents" (as in *Sat2* 87–90)—"enough to wrap a whole cargo of pepper"; cf. *Coryat* 33–34. Further, the line scans "with a defective medial foot after a pause" (170). **SMITH** (1971): the suitor "is furnished with vast quantities of documents" concerning the goods he attempts to recover (498).

85 *Inough to clothe...Carraques pepper.* **STEIN** (1944c): "stress-shift" after a pause is one of Donne's chief devices for varying the metrical line (379). **STEIN** (1944d) adds that the pause and stress-shift in lines such as this one are a "phenomenon which is both physical and psychological" (298).

85 *clothe* **MILGATE** (1967): "The wrapping of pepper and other spices in paper (cones) was an ancient practice also," as cited in Horace, *Epistula* 2:1, ll. 267–70; Martial, 3:2, l. 4; and Catullus, 95, l. 7 (170). **SMITH** (1971): "wrap in small twists, as pepper was commonly sold" (498).

85 *Carraques pepper.* **GROSART** (1872–73): "carrick or large merchantship's cargo of pepper," a reference to an event of 1602 or 1603, when an English sea captain, James Lancaster, sent home pepper and other spices captured from "*a Portuguese carrack.*" Though the word "'carrack' may have been occasionally applied to English vessels, it was properly and generally applied to any large merchant vessels of Spanish, Portuguese, or Italian build" (1:49–50). [So also, Chambers (1896, 2:242, 245).] **NORTON** (1895): "The carrick was a vessel with a capacious hold fitted for fighting as well as for burden" (1:247). **GRIERSON** (1912) explains that the Portuguese ship captured in 1602–03 is the wrong ship, the phrase "the Great Carrick" never having been used about it, but that an earlier prize, "the *Madre de Dios*...belonging to the crown of Portugal," was in fact called "the Great Carrick" after its capture by Sir Walter Raleigh in 1592, followed later in that year by the Privy Council's disposition of the pepper contained

in its cargo hold (2:104). [So also, Milgate (1967, 170), Smith (1971, 498–99), Grigson (1980, 31), and Carey (1990, 431).]

86–87 *Sell that,…his antiquitees.* **MILGATE** (1967) raises the possibility that "Haman" refers to an Elizabethan antiquary. Paraphrases, "sell your paper and you will lose more than Haman did when he sold his old rubbish," adding that probably "Haman got much less than he had paid for his 'treasures'; the wretched suitor will do even worse when for all he has paid out he gets only the price of the paper" (170). **HESTER** (1978b) thinks *Sat5*'s reference to Haman's "Antiquities" provides "a final concatenation of many of the major images of the poem" (365).

86 *Sell that,…more shalt leese* **SMITH** (1971): "if the suitor sells the documents for their value as paper, that is all that he will get out of his going to law" (499). **HESTER** (1978b): the satirist's "final biblical allusion," to Haman's futile contrivances, reveals that the suitor's gain from legal pursuits is "worth no more than wrapping paper," nothing but "rubbish"—"an ironic inversion of the Christian paradox of man's gaining most (salvation) by possessing least (earthly goods)" (359–60).

86 *leese* **GRIGSON** (1980): "lose" (31). [So also, Carey (1990, 431).]

87 *Then Hammon…his antiquitees.* **STEIN** (1944c): elisions of extra syllables formed by "light vowels in unstressed places" are among Donne's devices for varying the metrical line (389).

87 *Hammon* **CHAMBERS** (1896) refers to *Antiq* (2:245). **BEWLEY** (1966): "the Grand Vizier to Ahasuerus in the Book of Esther," although Donne's "exact reference" is not clear (190). **MILGATE** (1967) notes the variant manuscript spellings—Haman, Hammon, and Hammond—adding that in *Antiq* the spelling is "Hammon"; but finds "no one with a name resembling these among the members of Elizabethan society of antiquaries" as listed in *Archaeologia*, 1 (1770), or by William Oldys in his "Life of Raleigh," prefixed to Raleigh's *Works* (1829), 1:317 (170). **SHAWCROSS** (1967): as cited in Esth. 3.8, "Haman sought to exterminate the Jews because 'their laws are diverse from all people; neither keep they the king's laws.'" Haman "offered to pay 'ten thousand talents of silver to the hands of those that have the charge of the business, to bring it into the king's treasuries.' But Haman himself was hanged" (398). **SMITH** (1971): the naming of Haman suggests "his collection is so much junk" (499). **HESTER** (1978b): "the traitorous priest who sold his own treasures in order to pay off the assassin but who ended up being hanged on the gallows he had erected for the faithful Mordecai" (360). **CAREY** (1990): "not the biblical Haman but an unidentified antiquary ('Hammond' in some MSS) whose collection apparently fetched little" (431).

88–91 *O Wretch,…vanished.* **LECOCQ** (1969): compare these lines to Juvenal, XIII, 28 sqq. (384n66). **NEWTON** (1974): no "paring of the nails" is "even remotely implied" in these concluding lines. Instead, "we see only a vision of fools who will never learn and ills that will never be corrected" (444). **HESTER** (1978b): this conclusion "not only clarifies the causes for the suitor's misery" but "illustrates how any man within such a system can avoid becoming the 'moral' of a pagan 'tale'" (348–49). This final allusion is a classical not a Christian text, warning not only that "men who desert the path of righteousness and the reliance on God" risk God's wrath, but also that "by trying Providence" the suitor goes "beyond even Christian understanding" (360).

88–89 *fortunes should moralize / Æsops fables,* **STEIN** (1942) finds that "stress shifts" are a technique of enjambment when "two unstressed syllables" occur "as late as the third foot" of the line (684). **MORRIS** (1953): these lines illustrate Donne's "deliberate irregularity and roughness," thereby elevating sense over sound (41).

88 *O Wretch,…moralize* **STEIN** (1944c): "stress-shift" after a pause is one of Donne's chief devices for varying the metrical line (384).

88 *that* **MILGATE** (1967): "in that. You are wretched in that your experiences provide an illustration, or a moral, of one of Aesop's fables, and turn his tale into a prophecy of your own fate" (170).

88 *moralize* **SMITH** (1971): "afford the moral for" (499).

89 *make tales Prophesies.* **SMITH** (1971): "make Aesop's fables a prophecy of your fortunes" (499).

90–91 *that swimming dogg…vanished.* **RUGOFF** (1939): an example of Donne's imagery of shadows that carries this interest "almost into the realm of fantasy," as seen also in *HuntUn* 65–66 (198–99). **GRANSDEN** (1954) thinks that Donne, "naturally a creature of moods and circumstances," must often "in moments of exasperation, disappointment and disillusion" have "apostrophized himself" with these lines (74).

90 *Thou art…cosened* **SHAWCROSS** (1972): a "hypermetric line" (263). **HARDY** (1942): the image suggests about the wretched suitor that same inability "to escape into another category," "to invent another sphere of relationship," and "to distinguish fact from that which fact suggests, or reality from the image" as can be seen in the speakers of various poems by Donne, including *Dissol* and *Metem* (249).

90 *that swimming dogg* **BEWLEY** (1966): "the swimming dog lost his bone when he grabbed for the other dog's bone he saw reflected in the water" (190). [So also, Smith 1971, 499).] **MILGATE** (1967) refers to the Latin version of *Phaedrus* in *Der Lateinische Aesop des Romulus,* ed. G. Thiele (1910), 1:4, p. 23 (170): "In snapping at the meat held in the mouth of its reflected image the dog loses the real meat. The moral of the fable is '*amittit merito proprium qui alienum adpetit*'; victims of legal officers in Donne's poem, however, lose their substance, not in grabbing at someone else's property, but in pursuing a chimera (justice)" (171). [So also, Carey (1990, 431).] **SHAWCROSS** (1967): "Aesop's tale of 'The Dog and The Shadow' ('the Dog Carrying Meat'), which moralizes on greediness" (90). **SHAWCROSS** (1972): the suitors' "greed, which has brought on their plight, has become proverbial" (261).

90 *cosened* **SMITH** (1971): "Pronounced as three syllables" (499).

91 *And diu'dst…vanished.* **GRIERSON** (1912) says the "right reading of this line" has to be either the reading he prints ("And div'st, neare drowning, for what's vanished.") or the reading (found in other sources) "And div'd neare drowning, for

what vanished." Grierson explains: "The first refers to the suitor. He, like the dog, dives for what *has* vanished; goes to law for what is irrecoverable. The second reading would refer to the dog and continue the illustration: 'Thou art the dog whom shadows cozened and who div'd for what vanish'd.' The ambiguity accounts for the vacillation of the MSS. and editions. The reading of 1669 is a conjectural emendation. The 'div'd'st' of some MSS. is an endeavour to get an agreement of tenses after 'what's' had become 'what'" (2:128).

91 *vanished.* SMITH (1971): "Pronounced as three syllables" (499).

 *Metempsychosis*

COMMENTARY

Date and Circumstances

Dated "16. *Augusti* 1601," *Metem* is one of very few Donne poems that carries a precise calendrical designation. If this date indicates the poem's completion, then Donne finished writing it some six months after Robert Devereux, Second Earl of Essex, was executed for his failed revolt against Queen Elizabeth, and four months prior to secretly marrying Anne More.

Norton (1895, 1:250) notes that *Metem* is dated 1601, "when Donne, born in 1573, was 28 years old."

Grierson (1909, 4:214) writes of *Metem*, "there can be little doubt that the mood of mind which found expression in this sombre poem" was the result of the Earl of Essex's execution on 25 February 1601.

Grierson (1912, 1:xxxi) sees significance in the biographical and psychological setting of the poem, linking it to Essex's death as an immediate result. He writes that Donne began to "compose clandestinely" during the summer that followed Essex's execution and finished it on August 16.

Aronstein (1916, 361) reads *Metem* as a commentary on Elizabeth and Essex and the subsequent execution of Essex.

Coffin (1937, 50, 221) voices some surprise that in *Metem* Donne "releases some of his bitterest statements against women" and yet married Ann More barely three weeks before Christmas of the same year (50). He notes that the "arraignment of women" in the work, as in others, has "associations in time at least, with the prevalent Elizabethan and Jacobean outbursts against the sex," but still "cannot be condoned or condemned" as simply a characteristic of the time (221).

Bennett (1942, 603–04) presents evidence that while Donne "was intimate with some of Essex's followers," such as Sir Henry Wotton and Sir William Cornwallis, the younger, it does not follow that Donne was another of the men "who placed all their hopes in the Earl of Essex."

Bush (1945, 131) is unwilling, despite a variety of circumstantial connections between Donne and Essex, to make a positive connection between Essex's execution and *Metem*. Further, he indicates some surprise that Donne would be writing a poem containing such "brutal sexuality" that "mingled gloating and loathing upon a succession of animal couplings" even as he contemplated marriage to Ann More.

Mahood (1950, 105) surmises that while Essex was being tried, Donne "must have drawn a melancholy comparison between the Earl's present condition and the figure he had cut five years previously" when sailing for Cadiz.

Hunt (1954, 167) comments that Essex was a "headstrong idealist" who represented to the intellectuals of the era "the good old English moral virtues which were going by default in the increasing sycophancy and degeneracy of the court." Such an opinion, he thinks, might well have launched the attacks Donne makes in *Metem*.

Murray (1959, 143) disputes the biographical supposition that Donne was influenced by Essex's death, claiming that the position "hasn't much" factual support.

Nicolson (1960, 103–04) argues that the contrast between *Metem*, with its satire of Elizabeth and women, and *SecAn*, Donne's "supreme tribute to Elizabeth and his 'apologia,'" was partly due to his marriage. Also a factor was Donne's contact and correspondence with Magdalen Herbert, the Countess of Huntingdon, and the Countess of Bedford, "all of whom he had reason to admire."

Rowe (1964, 34) suggests, first, that the August 16 date on the poem coincides with Donne's birthday and, second, that the line "To my *six lustres* almost now outwore" (41) indicates that Donne was nearly thirty years old.

LeComte (1965, 69) views the execution of Essex as "among the most poignant" events of Donne's life and as the single event that compelled him to write *Metem*.

Milgate (1967, xxxii) states that in *Metem* there seems not to be "any special reference to the execution of Essex," and there is "no evidence" that Donne "was really close to the Earl or was much affected by his downfall." He notes that accusations of tyrants, favorites of the court or its officers within the work are "generalized and unemotional" and suggests that too many critics have missed the "verve and high-spirited fun" in the poem, leading them into misrepresenting the poem's relationship to Donne's personal life, adding that, if anything, Donne "can be accused of not having taken his poem seriously enough." Further, Milgate considers the poem to have been completed before Ann More came to London some two and a half months after the work's August 16 date. Only at that time, he believes, did the romance "ripen" into the love that led to their illicit marriage. The bitterness against women in the poem, he states, is no more earnest than the satire of courtiers, and Donne was on the verge of "becoming enslaved to one of the former," and with a seat in Parliament in the offing for October 1, was becoming "an increasingly successful example of the latter."

Bald (1970, 80) makes a strong connection between Donne and Essex, focusing on friendships Donne had with Henry Wotton and Henry Cuffe.

Gardner (1972, 1587) asserts that the date of *Metem* is part of the dedication, not the preface, in order to argue that the date indicates when the poem was ready to be circulated among readers. Therefore, she places composition in the months prior to August 16.

Van Wyck Smith (1973, 146–47) asserts that Donne was far more inclined toward Ralegh than Essex, due to similar religious attitudes and family relations (Nicholas Throckmorton, Ralegh's brother-in-law, was married to Donne's sister [ed.—sister-in-law]). But whether Donne followed Ralegh or Essex, he would have opposed Cecil. As such, he believes that there is sufficient evidence to suggest that in 1601 Donne "shared the resentment of Ralegh and many others against Cecil," thus also having ample motivation to write a political satire against Court and Queen.

Carey (1981, 64–65) argues for a strong link between Donne and Essex, asserting that the ambitious Donne secured a personal introduction to the Earl, "probably through his college friend Henry Wotton."

Hughes (1982, 15, 37) states that *Metem* "does indeed have a connection with Essex," a connection that is "unflattering" and "dangerous." It is unflattering because Essex is represented by the ape that seduces Siphatecia, who represents Elizabeth; and it is dangerous because the stanzas relating this prurient episode are "ironically sympathetic" to Essex (15). Further, he says, Tethlemite represents "the leader of the anti-Essex party," Sir Robert Cecil, who kills the ape upon discovering the bestial intercourse (37).

Klause (1986, 437) asserts that in keeping with the skeptical thought and moral relativism of a likely source, Montaigne, the dating of *Metem* is "important as marking a transient mental present." As such, he assumes that the date given on the poem indicates when Donne began recording his thoughts.

Reid (2000, 46) believes *Metem* to be Donne's final satiric work and speculates that it is "plausible" that because of his marriage to Ann More, Donne "lost his satirical detachment and insouciance, however sardonic, and that he could no longer represent himself in his favorite satirical guise as a young man dismayed by the ways of the world."

General Commentary

As recorded by William Drummond of Hawthornden, Jonson (1619, 1:136) comments that "the Conceit of Dones transformation" in *Metem* was that

> he sought the soule of that Aple which Eva pulled, and therafter made it the soule of a Bitch, then of a sheewolf & so of a woman. his generall purpose was to have brought in all the bodies of the Hereticks from ye soule of Cain & at last left it in ye body of Calvin. of this he never wrotte but one sheet, & now since he was made Doctor repenteth highlie & seeketh to destroy all his poems.

G[iles] O[ldisworth] (c. 1648), writing annotations in the margins and blank spaces throughout a copy of the 1639 edition of Donne's poems, includes these lines of verse on the blank half page following the "Epistle" prefacing *Metem*:

> The sum of this booke you shall find to bee
> More sin, then Soule keeping some qualitye
> Of every vile beast, full of Treacherye
> Rapine, Deceipt, & Lust, & ills enough
> To be a Woman, Mother of mischiefe, Eve;

and just before the poem itself, on the opening page, he pens these lines:

> Knowledg of evil, proness to controll
> All good this is the progress of Eves Soule.

Further, he collates his copy with the edition of 1633, correctly identifies the full names of some of the persons addressed only by initials, and occasionally marks the metrical fluctuations of lines.

Marvell (1673 [1971, 176–77]), responding to criticism of his theological work *The*

Rehearsal Transpros'd in *The Rehearsall Transpros'd The Second Part*, uses *Metem* to satirize his ecclesiastical opponents. He comments that the poem has "hitherto puzzled all its Readers," provides a brief summary of the various bodies the soul inhabits, and concludes by stating,

> After this Soul had passed thorow so many Brutes, & been hunted from post to pillar, its last receptacle was in the humane nature, and it housed it self in a female Conception, which after it came to years of consent, was Married to *Cain* by the name of *Themech*. This was the sum of that witty fable of Doctor *Donne's*.

Spence (c. 1730–36 [1966, 1:188]) records Alexander Pope's comment that *Metem* is Donne's "best" poetry along with the Epistles and Satyres.

Warburton (1751, 4:247) refers to *Metem* as a "fine" poem and adds of Donne, "Poetry never lost more than by his not pursuing and finishing that noble Design; of which he has only given us the Introduction."

Hurd (1776, 1:98) comments that in writing *Metem* Donne's "good sense brought him out into the freer spaces of nature and open day-light."

Blake (c. 1795, 160), using *Metem* 35–36 as the legend for a sketch of a bearded man with legs crossed and wrists fettered, includes the following lines underneath the figure:

> Whose changeless brow
> Neer smiles nor frowns
> > > Donne

The lines also include an apostrophe, "Great Destiny the commissary of God."

Coleridge (1817 [1907, 65]), in *Biographia Literaria*, singles out stanzas two and four of *Metem*, calling them "excellent" verse showing the "self-impassioned" language of "poetic fervor."

De Quincey (1828 [1896, 10:101]), writing in *Blackwood's Magazine*, commends *Metem*, stating that "few writers have shown a more extraordinary compass of powers than Donne; for he combined—what no other man has ever done—the last sublimation of dialectical subtlety and address with the most impassioned majesty."

Wood (1829 [1883, 1:175]) recalls a visit in January 1829 when Coleridge read poetry to his company:

> He had been seized with a fit of enthusiasm for Donne's poetry, which I think somewhat unaccountable. There was great strength, however, in some passages which he read. One stanza or rather division of his poem, on the 'Progress of the Soul,' struck me very much; it was, I think, the fourth, in which he addresses Destiny as the 'Knot of Causes.' The rest of the poem seemed the effusion of a man very drunk or very mad.

Lewes (1838, 377) contends that *Metem* was not written by Donne. Citing marginalia from an individual identified only as "the friend" (ed.—actually Leigh Hunt), he writes:

> 'Metempsychosis,' is considered by the friend, before alluded to, to be spurious. 'From the versification of this poem,' says he on a most niggardly margin, 'I do not believe it to be Donne's. It has the tone and measure of a later age, and might have been

written by Sedley or Buckingham. Somebody has ignorantly attributed it to Donne, from meeting with similar opinions in some of his poems; but Donne has always the weight and imagery of old plate in him, compared with this smoother metal.' With this we entirely agree—Long live marginalia!

Patmore [?] (1846, 229), in a general discussion of Donne's poetry, groups *Metem* with the Divine Poems, rather than with the Satyres, and adds of this work, "here, as everywhere, splendid thoughts and splendid words abound."

Ward (1858 [1956, 324–25]), in editing his collection of Pope's poems, comments that *Metem* "is a disgusting burlesque on the Pythagorean doctrine of metempsychosis."

Gilfillan (1860, 1:203) espouses of *Metem* that it has "too many far-fetched conceits and obscure allegories, although redeemed, we admit, by some very precious thoughts."

Grosart (1872–73, 1:66) comments briefly on *Metem*, stating, "there are things in it one would wish away—just as one inevitably removes a slug from a rose's heart or lily's chalice." He notes further that the poem's heading, "Poema Satyricon," is reason to grant greater lenience for any offenses in the poem, adding, without specifying which stanzas, that "the offence is limited to two out of fifty-two stanzas."

Browning (1878 [2003, 14:182]) quotes *Metem* 338–40 in the first, third, and fifth lines of the following passage from his "The Two Poets of Croisic":

He's greatest now and to de-struc-ti-on
Nearest. Attend the solemn word I quote,
O Paul! There's no pause at per-fec-ti-on.
Thus knolls thy knell the Doctor's bronzed throat!
Greatness a period hath, no sta-ti-on!
Better and truer verse none ever wrote
(Despite the antique outstretched a-i-on)
Than thou, revered and magisterial Donne! (905–13).

Disraeli (1880, 351–52) refers to *Metem* as an example of the Elizabethan era, when "Philosophy introduced itself into poetry, and wit became the substitute for passion." He states further that the poem is "the most creative and eccentric in the language," but one "which must be reserved for the few."

Minto (1880, 859–60, 862) asserts of Donne's writing of *Metem* that "no other satirist ever expounded his design in such a strain of impassioned sublimity" (860). He comments further that had *Metem* been completed, it "would have been an achievement worthy of" Donne's "extraordinary powers" (862). Within the poem, he sees "a dim and fantastic foreshadowing of the modern doctrine of evolution" (859), with every inhabited body in the soul's journey "made to yield some sarcastic lesson for the times, some political or social maxim" (862).

Dowden (1890, 808) comments on *Metem* that "though the poem could never have been popular, it would have afforded, like the Scotchman's haggis, 'a hantle of miscellawneous feeding' for those with an appetite for the strange dishes set before them by Donne."

Saintsbury (1896, 1:xxiii–xxiv) describes *Metem* as "interesting" and "curious," noting especially the "comparison with Prior's *Alma*, which it of necessity suggests, and probably suggested." On the whole, the poem seems to him "uncertain in aim, unaccomplished in execution. But what things are in it!" He goes on to cite some passages from the work and avers that the "same miraculous pregnancy of thought runs through the whole" despite its never having attained "full and complete delivery in artistic form."

According to Gosse (1899, 1:131–32, 138), the preface to Metem is a "curious tirade" of "most fantastic and even giddy import," where "sarcasm stalks unabashed" and in which Donne "flings himself forth upon the glittering and elastic strands of his fancy" (131–32). He describes "the puerility of the central idea" as "extraordinary," explaining that it "may help us to understand why, with gifts of intellectual appreciation and keen refinement," Donne "never contrived to reach the first rank among men of letters," and he finds that this central idea of the poem, "if there is any thought at all," is "the bare satiric one, too cheap to be so magnificently extended and embroidered" (138).

Grierson (1912, 2:xx) states of Metem that "on the whole one must confess it is a failure" since some of its episodes "seem pointless as well as disgusting." As such, the "least attractive side of Donne's mind" is more visible here than in any other of his works, that part of his wit which is "more fatal to his claim to be a poet than too subtle ingenuity or misplaced erudition," that is, the "vein of sheer ugliness" that makes the poem "repulsive."

Eliot (1926, 149) asserts that none of Donne's poems is "more difficult, more unpleasant, more disturbing, more unsatisfactory, or contains more startling lines" than Metem, and he adds, "I simply confess myself incapable of understanding this rebus: and no critic that I have perused has given me the slightest help."

Payne (1926, 71–72, 85–86) states that the "impudent sarcasm of the first sentence" of the preface to Metem "rouses one's ire, even at a distance of three centuries" in that it gives the impression that Donne, "in the course of his connexion with great State affairs, had forgotten that he was not plenipotentiary but secretary" (71–72). Yet, he acknowledges that the poem shows that Donne was "seriously occupied by the scientific activities of the time" (72). In addition, he adds, first, that satire of women is one of the "principal threads" of Metem, showing some of Donne's "distaste for women" and, then, that the work makes obvious that Donne's "religious faith and his belief in woman had suffered shipwreck" (85–86). He concludes that the poem "leaves us with an impression of energy, sometimes of power," but the "urge of hidden thought" in the verse "never gains expression" as it struggles "against a tide of pessimism and ugliness" (86).

Lamb (1935, 421) praises not only the double use of the word "light" in Metem 55 but also the poem's "ingenious" preface.

Crofts (1936, 132–33) remarks that Metem is "the most deliberately outrageous" of Donne's poems, describing the work as one "which would certainly have landed him in jail" if it had circulated before Queen Elizabeth's death. He believes the poem to be Donne's "magnum opus" in design, in that Donne "was going to make an end," "to smite once and smite no more," by demolishing and sweeping away "all the sentimental pasteboard and puppetry of the Elizabethan era" in "a great act of liberation." He concludes that the poem "stands among Donne's works like a huge and mutilated inscription."

Bush (1945, 130–31) insists that the "matter" of *Metem* demonstrates that it was "hardly intended for print." Further, he states that the poem as a whole "is much less effective than the parts," and the text remains "a satirical extravaganza" that is "submerged in a kind of brutal sexuality." He finds that the "serious" point of the work, on the relativity of good and evil, is "plainly stated" in the concluding stanza, though the idea "has not been worked out," and as such, the poem remains clearly "another product of Jack Donne's conventional libertine naturalism."

Allen (1952, 84, 89, 91) describes *Metem*, which he believes was "doomed to fail" (84), as "the monstrous offspring of a violent 'contamine'" (89) and as "a garland of recondite allusiveness that halts the reader" (91). He states that had Donne "brought such a poem to a successful conclusion," he "would have been a greater poet than Homer" (91).

Janson (1952, 272–73, 275, 283) focuses on the biblical and zoological lore in *Metem*, even providing the "archetype" of the "ape-rape" theme, a fable in which a woman deported to an island populated by apes had two children by an ape before being rescued by Portugese sailors (275). He commends Donne for his "wealth of esoteric learning" and argues that a more complete study of the poem's sources would surely lead to "a revision of the generally unfavourable judgment" offered against the poem, which he acknowledges as one of Donne's "most ambitious achievements" (272–73). He concludes that to interpret the poem, as some critics have, "as a 'sardonic satire' on women" does not do justice "to the range and complexity" of Donne's "intention" (283).

Gransden (1954, 116–18) insists that *Metem* is a "curious poem" on a "bizarre theme" (118), for which "Dr. Donne would have had ample reason to repent (it is indecent as well as unpatriotic)" (116). But he also admits that the poem is Donne's "most fantastic piece of speculation" with "liveliness and technical adroitness" which hold "our interest in a 'tour de force,'" though adding that "perhaps the courting of so lengthy a conceit upon so arcane a theme is nowadays an acquired taste" (116–17).

Murray (1959, 141), noting that *Metem* has "received scant attention and less approval," states that the poem is "neither very good nor of much literary importance," its main value being that it was written during "an important chapter in Donne's intellectual life."

Williamson (1961, 19) notes that *Metem* has been regarded by modern critics as one of Donne's "worst exhibitions of wit."

Williamson (1963, 185) calls *Metem* the first of Donne's "ambitious poems" in which he introduced "the progress of the soul as the formal conceit."

LeComte (1965, 73–75) reads *Metem* in general as a "midway point" for Donne and as a "work of manifold interest, being partly secular and even political in its anchorage, partly spiritual" (75). In particular, he describes the last stanza as an "arrogant, impudently far from simple view of human nature and history" written by Jack Donne and stanza five, which "takes stock of past and future with supernatural insight," as a "getting ready for Dean Donne" (73–74). He contends, however, that the poem proves little about Donne the man, for the poem is "much clearer on what he is against than what he is for" (75).

Williamson (1969, 250) notes that despite the neglect "by scholars and by poets,"

Metem deserves "some consideration of its place in Donne's corpus" and that "in itself and in its relation to his other work, its importance challenges such indifference and justifies our refusal to be intimidated by this 'sullen writ.'" He asserts that Donne satirically treats the same theme as Milton's *Paradise Lost*, the soul's progress extending from Eden to Calvary, and states that the "final threat" of the poem's "concluding postscript" has been "more successful" than Donne "could have desired."

Bald (1970, 123–24) argues that *Metem*, which he calls Donne's "most disappointing work," is "conceived in the epic tradition of the Renaissance," but instead of offering serious moralizing, Donne provides "terse and savage satire directed at court and public life" through the activities of the animals.

Thomas (1971, 112, 121) notes that *Metem* has been generally regarded as "highly original though unsuccessful" and of "doubtful taste" (112), but he adds that while the poem is "so frequently dismissed as Donne's errant orphan," it is marked with "originality and complexity," by "mock seriousness," and by Donne's "love of dramatic argument" (121).

Gardner (1972, 1587) argues that Donne planned all along for *Metem* to be "a political satire disguised as the beginning of a mock-epic." She insists that the elaborate dedication and cryptic epistle are part of the jest, not a serious outline for the work, and that as such, the poem is a "brilliantly executed and coherent work which makes a powerful and sardonic point."

Mueller (1972, 109, 115, 137) suggests that twentieth-century critics have greatly undervalued *Metem* as Donne's "principal poetic blunder," since no one "can be brought to admire what he does not understand" (109). She believes that in this poem Donne serves more as historian than satirist, providing significant metamorphoses from the universal to the individual, with parallels of "epic design" that reflect "the larger contours and substance of Ovid's epic" (115). She concludes that the poem is "a transition piece" that allowed Donne to discover his "true personal and poetic direction," and she determines that the work is "well placed" at the beginning of Donne's poems in the 1633 edition (137).

Seymour-Smith (1972, 2) describes *Metem* as "a piercingly intelligent comic and satirical fragment" that is "vital" to understanding Donne's "humourous, unhappy, sceptical position in the months prior to his materially disastrous marriage." He concludes that it is impossible to say exactly what Donne's intention was in composing the poem, but that it is clearly directed against public life.

Snyder (1973, 392, 396, 407) notes *Metem*'s more favorable reception among "earlier men of letters" (citing Pope, Coleridge, Browning, and De Quincey) and observes that little has been said of its mixture of "epic and satire, morality and libertinism, learning and lasciviousness" (392). She argues that the poem is a parody of Du Bartas' divine epic, *Sepmaines* (1578), and read as such, it "acquires a sharper focus and its peculiarities begin to form a pattern" that make sense of *Metem*'s "puzzling incompleteness" (396). She concludes that most critics have taken "too seriously" the poem's "high-spirited, cynical parody," in which Donne is "having fun at the expense of the literary and religious Establishment" (407).

Van Wyck Smith (1973, 17, 141, 148), supporting Gardner's (1972) view that *Metem* is complete in itself as a political mock allegory, adds that its purpose was to satirize

Robert Cecil. Donne's "baffling changes of tone" are part of the satiric jest, such as the epic beginning being followed by reverent stanzas on the Cross that shift into "grotesque naturalism" and misogyny, which do not result from lack of control, but from Donne's anticipating "some of the techniques of *MacFlecknoe* and *The Dunciad*" (17).

Carey (1981, 149–50) states that judged by Donne's "grasp of the organic world" *Metem* is certainly his "masterpiece," noting that the work "is so rich a poem that quotations which would establish the reputation of a lesser writer can be picked out from all over it."

Wentersdorf (1982, 71, 89) argues that "probably all of the emblematic stations" in which the soul finds itself in *Metem* have "erotic connotations," and thus the world view as presented in the poem is "taken from the standpoint of the Gnostic and Hermetic philosophers" (71). He concludes that Donne set out to show that through the actions of one soul, "a shaper both of imperial destinies and of religious revolutions," the whole of history is being consistently controlled by erotic forces (89).

Caracciolo-Trejo (1986, 2:13) sees *Metem* as an ironic text—a game that permits the author to display his ingenuity in affirming the precarious spiritual condition of humankind. But the poem is also a reflection of the human situation, that of being condemned to corruption, yet still striving for the permanence denied by original sin.

Warnke (1987, 7, 23–24) insists that religion and sex, not politics, "play the principal roles" in *Metem* (7). Like Carey (1981), he directs attention to the more than usual "use of sensuous and descriptive imagery" in the work and quotes the stanza in which Siphatecia and the ape have their tryst as indicative of "the poem as a whole" (23–24).

Characterizing *Metem* as "part parody of Pythagorean philosophy and part beast fable," B. Smith (1991, 174) asserts that the poem "wittily sketched" Renaissance views of homosexuality in a "cosmic context."

Corthell (1997, 148) observes that *Metem* is an example of the "equivocal construction of the self" as it offers "disclaimers of seriousness" in delivering its less than sincere narrative of the soul.

Skepticism

Grierson (1912, 2:xiv, xvii–xviii) believes that the "reflective, moralizing strain" of *Metem* is "un-Christian," and that in the poem Donne's wit becomes an "instrument of a criticism of life, grave or satiric, melancholy or stoical" (2:xiv). He argues further that "scepticism and melancholy, bitter and sardonic" are the "dominant notes" in this "strange and sombre explosion of spleen" (2:xvii–xviii).

Bredvold (1923, 471, 475–76, 500, 502) comments that the "most striking characteristic" of Donne's early poems is their skepticism (471) and adds of *Metem* that "somewhere" Donne came in contact with and was "profoundly impressed by" skeptical and relativist philosophy (475–76). He provides a detailed discussion of the tradition of the Law of Nature, *Jus naturale*, the fundamental political and social ethics from the Stoics and Cicero to the Renaissance, and concludes that skepticism in ethics was a "definite tradition" among certain groups in seventeenth century England (500) and that Donne should be understood as "more clearly a man of his own time, a typical Renaissance skeptic" (502).

Bredvold (1925, 198) espouses that Donne's source for *Metem* was either the recently revived Greek philosophy of Sextus Empiricus appearing in Montaigne or Sextus Empiricus's own writings.

Eliot (1926, 150) believes that the "tendency" of *Metem* is "plain"—"toward intellectual anarchy"—and he concludes, "I can only offer it to any deep psychologist who may be interested."

Williamson (1934, 288) notes the skepticism of *Metem* by pointing out that the final lines of the work suggest either Hamlet's "there is nothing either good or bad, but thinking makes it so" (2.2.249–50) or Nashe's comment, "So that our opinion (as *Sextus Empiricus* affirmeth) giues the name of good or ill to euery thing" ("Preface to Sidney's *Astrophel and Stella*").

Husain (1938, 56), as a parallel to the skepticism he finds in *Metem*, notes that Marston in *What You Will* also declares, "all that exists / Take valuation from opinion" (1.1.18–19).

Moloney (1944, 108–09) explains that in the final lines of *Metem* there is an extensive reshaping, "distinctly traceable in Donne," of the ethical landscape "between mediaeval certainty and Hobbes's doubt."

Stein (1944a, 277) states that the last three lines of *Metem* contain Donne's "most famous" statement of his skepticism.

Wendell (1948, 480) argues that for Donne knowledge concerns itself with absolutes, but opinion is "a middle station, between ignorance and knowledge." Therefore, for Donne to say that the only measure and judge is opinion is a "necessary state of mind" that does not reveal "an extreme scepticism."

Grierson (1949, 38) remarks that Donne's skepticism was not the "rationalist, dogmatic skepticism of the later deists and sceptics" but was the "profounder, temperamental and spiritual" skepticism that tortures the soul with the inherent contradictions in all endeavors. It is a skepticism that laments the "inextricable interweaving of good and evil."

Mahood (1950, 106) argues that by the end of *Metem* there is "no faith in man left" and that the skepticism apparent in several episodes and especially the final stanza "suggests little faith in anything else."

Rowe (1964, 190) asserts that the ending of *Metem* is a "commendation of relativist ethics."

Milgate (1967, 191) argues that by 1601 Donne was no libertine, but was by the standards of his day middle-aged and burdened by heavy responsibilities. As such, the discontent expressed in *Metem* is "at once more orthodox and more mature" than has been thought.

Hughes (1968, 78) states that the apparent expression of faith in libertinism and "revocation of universal law" in *Metem* "is only half true" in that Donne admits "lawlessness," but he does so "without espousing it."

Seymour-Smith (1972, 2, 32) reads *Metem* as "a piercingly intelligent comic and satirical fragment" that is "vital" for an understanding of Donne's "humourous, unhappy, sceptical position in the months prior to his materially disastrous marriage" (2). He suggests that most readers take the work too seriously, stating that it is an "ambivalent comic poem, by an undecided man" (32).

Klause (1986, 437) asserts that the likely source for the skeptical thought and moral relativism found in *Metem* is Montaigne.

Genre

Saintsbury (1896, 1:xxiii–xxiv) comments that he is "not so sure" of *Metem* "as some writers have been," for while a "miraculous pregnancy of thought runs through the whole," the poem remains "uncertain in aim, unaccomplished in execution" and never achieves "full and complete delivery in artistic form."

Gosse (1899, 1:138–39) asserts that "if there is any thought at all" in *Metem* it is "the bare satiric one, too cheap to be so magnificently extended and embroidered," and written by a poet who "had little dramatic and positively no epic talent."

Upham (1908, 396) finds parallels between *Metem* and Du Bartas's *Sepmaines*. Lee (1910, 351–53) and Snyder (1973, 392) also identify similarities in the works.

Allen (1952, 88–90) sees in the work indications of an awkward combination of satire and epic Spenserian allegory, noting that there is "no pattern for such a poem, which is perhaps a way of saying it could not succeed" (90).

Janson (1952, 272–73, 275, 283) praises the "wealth of esoteric learning" in *Metem* (272–72), drawing particular attention to Donne's use of biblical and zoological lore (275), and he concludes that "to interpret the entire project as a 'sardonic satire' on women hardly does justice to the range and complexity of the poet's intention as revealed by the existing portions" (283).

Murray (1959, 141–42, 144, 146) analyzes *Metem* as an allegory of the Fall based on the writings of Philo (141–42), from whom Donne drew various symbols, as well as the names of Adam's children (144). He insists that the "essential" feature of the poem "is not the process of metempsychosis itself but the allegorical meaning of the apple's soul which undergoes it" (146).

Bryan (1965, 123) analyzes *Metem* in terms of *translatio emperii* and *translatio studii*, concepts which embody "an idea of human history as a westward movement of empire and civilization," but its incompleteness denies the culmination of the design.

Guss (1966, 196) states that Donne seemed to write more "as courtier than 'vates,'" and to be simply careless of genre."

Milgate (1967, xxvi–xxviii, xxxi) describes *Metem* as "a kind of anti-epic with incidental, but continual, satiric content," noting Donne's use of epic decorum, of *descriptio* and *translatio*, of mock-grandeur in the opening stanzas, and of the epic hero, the "deathlesse" soul whose adventures in the bodies of beasts are told (xxvi–xxvii). He adds, however, that the combination of epic sweep and satiric intent led Donne into a "parody of a grand Renaissance design that could never have been carried out" (xxviii). He explains that the "satiric expression" and the "mock-heroic elevation" are "not everywhere well sustained," but no other poem by Donne "illustrates better the power of natural description" (xxxi).

Hughes (1968, 74) reads *Metem* as an allegory of the war between Seth and Cain, ultimately drawn from Augustine's *City of God*. The conflict between the two kingdoms in Donne's work is rather one-sided, however, since only Cain's "pedigree is sketched out."

Williamson (1969, 250–52) identifies *Metem* as an "epic satire" that treats the same theme as Milton's *Paradise Lost* (250). He adds that Donne's poem states its central theme of heresy as a paradox that asks, "why can good and ill come out of their opposites?" (251–52).

Bald (1970, 124) sees Metem as "conceived in the epic tradition of the Renaissance," but instead of offering serious moralizing, Donne provides "terse and savage satire directed at court and public life" through the activities of the animals.

Gardner (1972, 1587) agrees with Milgate (1967) and argues that Donne planned all along to create "a political satire disguised as the beginning of a mock-epic." She insists that the elaborate dedication and cryptic epistle are part of the jest, not a serious outline for the work, and as such, the poem is a "brilliantly executed and coherent work which makes a powerful and sardonic point."

Mueller (1972, 115, 123, 137) finds in Metem parallels of "epic design" that reflect "the larger contours and substance of Ovid's epic" (115), and she states that the transmigration of souls idea stems from a long speech by Pythagoras to Numa in *Metamorphoses* (123). She argues that like Augustine, Donne adopted "an intensely subjective approach to experience, one which shifted emphasis from the metaphysics of the universe to the morality and the spirituality of the self" (137).

Snyder (1973, 396) argues that Metem is a parody of the first part of Du Bartas's *Sepmaines, La Sepmaine*, which tells of the seven days of creation "elaborated with metaphysical lore and Plinian natural philosophy to show the intricate perfections of God's plan." She adds that Du Bartas's conservative and orthodox viewpoint, raising questionable points of divinity and then "retreating into unquestioning faith," seems just the sort of target that Donne would enjoy debunking.

Corthell (1981, 97–98, 109–10) notes that recent studies of the genre and sources of Metem have revised "earlier judgements of the work as an ill-conceived poetic failure" (97). He views the poem as an exercise in "formal paradox," one established on the "master paradox of progress and degeneration." As a "revisionist history of the fall," Eve's eating of the apple becomes "a process whereby man evolves into a microcosm of wickedness" (109–10).

Hughes (1982, 18, 22, 37–38) states that Metem is a complete anti-epic, but the "world's soul," an "objective idea of unreason," is passing through the sequence of inhabitants, not just one soul (18). Further, he asserts that each of the beings, from the mandrake to Themech, represents one of England's Tudor monarchs and concludes that the poem is "a work of political propaganda designed beneath its surface cover to define reality by naming the Tudor monarchy as the villain" (37–38).

Klause (1986, 418, 431, 443), noting that all of the other attempts to define Metem's generic form are "checked and defeated" and are "alluded to rather than embodied," posits that Metem parallels Montaigne's *Essais* (418) and that Donne was "relating the poem to a literary genre that had been newly invented" (431). He concludes, however, that there is a "momentous difference," despite his elaboration of their similarities, "between Donne's *satura* and what Montaigne had called (3.13.532) his *fricassee*" (443).

Marotti (1986, 128) argues that the comment in the preface of Metem, "I would have no Readers as I can teach," indicates that Donne was addressing a distinct coterie who would not be bothered by the poem's mix of "epic and satiric genres" and who would have "appreciated" the poem "as a metapoetic discourse on its own ironically presented materials."

B. Smith (1991, 174) characterizes *Metem* as "part parody of Pythagorean philosophy and part beast fable."

Unity and Structure

Warburton (1753, 4:247) states of *Metem* that "Poetry never lost more" than by Donne "not pursuing and finishing that noble Design; of which he has only given us the Introduction."

Hurd (1776, 1:98) calls *Metem* Donne's "great work" and notes parenthetically that "we have only the beginning."

Minto (1880, 860, 862) states of Donne that "no other satirist ever expounded his design in such a strain of impassioned sublimity" (860). He adds that had *Metem* been completed it "would have been an achievement worthy" of Donne's "extraordinary powers," but since Donne lacked "the gift of perseverance," the "fragment" is a perfect representation of him "in the extent as well as in the limitation of his powers" (862).

Gosse (1899, 1:138) observes that at the end of *Metem* "we have not yet advanced out of sight of the Garden of Eden, and at this rate of progress it would have taken millions of verses to bring us safely down to Queen Elizabeth." He adds that Donne sensed the "inherent weakness" of his plan and abandoned it.

Eliot (1926, 149) refers to *Metem* as an "apparently unfinished" work.

Crofts (1936, 133) believes *Metem* to be Donne's "*magnum opus*" in design by which he attempted "to demolish—to sweep away—all the sentimental pasteboard and puppetry of the Elizabethan era" in a "great act of liberation." In its unfinished state, which he finds to be characteristic of "most literary enterprises of this kind," the poem stands among Donne's works "like a huge and mutilated inscription."

Of *Metem*, Allen (1952, 90–91, 93) calls the poem "a garland of recondite allusiveness that halts the reader" (91) and also refers to it as a history, "a philosophic synonym of 'progress'" that tells of humankind's gradual descent from a better state (93). He adds further that Donne's "poetic vehicle" was "so badly made and so hopelessly overloaded" that the poem "collapsed in the first furlong" (93).

Janson (1952, 272–73) states that "even as a fragment," *Metem* "must be acknowledged as one of Donne's most ambitious achievements, comparable only to the two 'Anniversaries.'"

Murray (1959, 155) asserts that *Metem*'s greatest point of interest lay in the fact that it was "unfinished," an effort in which Donne sought "a terminology, a manageable body of ideas and images in which to fix his physical, emotional, and intellectual experience," but which merely resulted in "a blind alley."

Bryan (1965, 120–21) observes that reactions to *Metem* "by three centuries of readers are as fragmented, contradictory, and generally inconclusive as the poem itself," adding that the poem's "ironic thrusts" and "precise strategy" are "shrouded by its incompleteness."

Gardner (1972, 1587) asserts that *Metem* is not a fragment and argues that the preface, far from being an outline for an intended epic poem, is an integral part of the satiric mock-epic design of the poem. She urges that the overlapping life spans of Cain's wife and Cain, Calvin and Luther, and Luther and Elizabeth, as well as the sheer tedium and monotony of chronicling the history of human evil, make the plan impossible to execute, but that Donne was completely aware of these difficulties and made the preface and the exaggerated dedication part of the joke. As such, the work is "an elaborate fiction" disguised as the first canto of an epic, with a grandiose dedication and a "parody of an explanatory epistle."

Snyder (1973, 396) argues that *Metem* is to be read as a parody of Du Bartas's divine epic, *Sepmaines* (1578), and as such, the poem "acquires a sharper focus and its peculiarities begin to form a pattern" that make sense of its "puzzling incompleteness."

Van Wyck Smith (1973, 17, 141, 148) explains that Gardner's (1972) reading of *Metem* not only unifies the poem but shows that "many of the poem's so-called failings are perhaps part of its design" (17) and argues that as a completed political mock-allegory, the poem satirizes Robert Cecil. He suggests further that the narrative operates on two different planes: (1) "a history of the growth of havoc from Genesis to Donne's own time," and (2) "a series of brief beast satires, some referring directly to Cecil, others only glancing at him" (148).

Frontain (1995, 8) asserts that "incompletion is an essential feature" of *Metem*.

Language and Style

Warburton (1753, 4:247) refers to *Metem* as a "fine" poem and adds that Donne's verse "did not want harmony."

De Quincey (1828 [1896, 10:101]), writing in *Blackwood's Magazine*, commends *Metem*, stating that "few writers have shown a more extraordinary compass of powers than Donne" and that "massy diamonds compose the very substance" of the poem, in which the thoughts and descriptions "have the fervent and gloomy sublimity of Ezekiel or Aeschylus, whilst a diamond dust of rhetorical brilliancies is strewed over the whole of his occasional verses."

Gilfillan (1860, 1:203), referring to De Quincey (1828), writes that if readers can "admire" Donne's account "of Abel and his bitch, or see any resemblance to the severe and simple grandeur of Aeschylus and Ezekiel in the description of the soul informing a body," then he "shall say no more." He concludes that "the ingenious nonsense which abounds in the middle and the close" of the poem is significantly inferior to "the dark, but magnificent stanzas" that open it.

Gosse (1899, 1:139–40) states that while *Metem* may not contain any "massy diamonds," yet there is "no question that diamond dust is sprinkled broadcast over the stanzas of this grotesque poem." In addition, Donne's language, "although frequently hard and abrupt," he states, is "genuine and lucid English" and occasionally with "brilliant intrepidity" darts "into the very central shrine of imaginative expression."

Payne (1926, 84–86) asserts that in *Metem* may be found "many brilliant things" (84), but the poem suffers from the "fault" of "a lack of taste, a deficient sense of beauty" (86). He believes that the poem's "majestic" plan and "touches of grandeur" (84–85) point to the "hidden thought" that "never gains expression" and that struggles against "a tide of pessimism and ugliness" (86).

Gransden (1954, 116–17) describes *Metem* as "indecent as well as unpatriotic," but he also believes that the poem is Donne's "most fantastic piece of speculation" with "liveliness and technical adroitness" which hold "our interest in a 'tour de force.'" He concludes that "perhaps the courting of so lengthy a conceit upon so arcane a theme is nowadays an acquired taste."

Milgate (1967, xxxi–xxxii) asserts that the "satiric expression" and the "mock-heroic elevation" of Metem are "not everywhere well sustained," but adds that no poem of Donne's "illustrates better the power of natural description." Pointing to "the grotesque fun and the sardonic humour" of the poem, he argues that Donne's failure was in not taking the poem "seriously enough as a poetic work."

Carey (1981, 149–51) contends that Metem, which he calls Donne's "masterpiece," is "so rich a poem that quotations which would establish the reputation of a lesser writer can be picked out from all over it" (149–50). He draws particular attention to the "physicality" of words that "land on the page like lumps of raw meat," the sensitive passages that give the reader "the jumpy, touched-to-the-quick feel" that comes from watching filmed surgical operations (150–51).

Caracciolo-Trejo (1986, 2:13) states that Metem never assumes a cosmic solemnity, but rather maintains a light tone that expresses an almost amused didactic demonstration.

Religion and Politics

Patmore [?] (1846, 235) groups Metem with the Divine Poems, not with the Satyres, and comments that in the poem "splendid thoughts and splendid words abound" (235).

Gosse (1899, 1:140) thinks that the tone and character of Metem are "un-Christian," and he argues that at the time of writing the poem that Donne had lost his traditional faith in the Catholic Church and that "no light had come to him" yet from the Church of England.

Grierson (1912, 2:xiv, xviii) comments without explanation that Metem is "written from a Catholic standpoint" on the theme of heresy, with Elizabeth, not Calvin, as the great heretic of the present (2:xviii). He adds that a "reflective, moralizing strain predominates" in the poem, "especially at the beginning and the end" (2:xiv).

Payne (1926, 85–86) comments that at the time of writing Metem Donne had "no religious belief," but also adds that his outlook was "more or less Catholic." He states that the poem makes obvious that Donne's "religious faith and his belief in woman had suffered shipwreck."

Crofts (1936, 132–33) interprets Metem, which he calls "the most deliberately outrageous" of all Donne's poems," as a vicious attack on Queen Elizabeth that "would certainly" have landed Donne in jail if it had circulated before the Queen's death. He argues that Donne's intention was "to demolish" and "sweep away," and thereby liberate himself from, "all the sentimental pasteboard and puppetry of the Elizabethan era." Pointing to the first sentence of the preface, he concludes that "the liberation may not be completed, but the statue to the liberator is up."

Mahood (1950, 106) argues that by the time of writing Metem Donne's "disillusioned frame of mind prevented his submission to either Rome or Canterbury," but he sees the poem as being "strongly anti-Protestant."

Hunt (1954, 172) states that publicly Donne had "stripped off the Romish rags" before writing *Metem*, but privately, in this poem unintended for publication, Donne was "willing to show himself clear as still a Catholic, and proudly so, in his emotional attachments" and bitter against the Crown which viewed Catholicism as "moral degradation and treason of mind."

Williamson (1961, 19) asserts that *Metem* presents a satiric version of the Fall.

Chitanand (1963, 66) comments that *Metem* is primarily "a satire on the Queen," specifically due to Elizabeth's persecution of Catholics.

Williamson (1963, 185) identifies *Metem* as "the first" of Donne's "ambitious poems" (185) in which he introduced "Pythagorean change or mutability" as "the formal conceit" (188).

Rowe (1964, 221) comments that Donne's "habitually contemplative nature" and his "deeply personal religion" combine in *Metem* to establish him as "a prophet, with intensely proleptic powers, at the heart of whose verse was an insight into religious realism as the creature's return to his Creator."

LeComte (1965, 75) reads *Metem* in general as a "midway point" for Donne and as a "work of manifold interest, being partly secular and even political in its anchorage, partly spiritual."

Bewley (1966, xxx–xxxi) contends that Donne was not so much converted to the English Church as he was "converted away from" the Catholic, and that in *Metem* Donne shows that he may be "still deeply, if secretly, with the Ancient Church." He states further that by 1601 Donne "was almost certainly a professed Anglican," since his official position with Egerton, who had prosecuted the Jesuit martyr Edmund Campion, allowed no affection for Rome. Accordingly, the poem shows that Donne's "transition to Anglicanism was not an easy one."

Milgate (1967, xxxii) states that there appears to be no "special reference to the execution of Essex" in *Metem* and that there is "no evidence" that Donne was either "close to the Earl" or "much affected by his downfall." Also, accusations against tyrants, favorites of the court or its officers within the work are "generalized and unemotional." In fact, he suggests, too many critics have missed the "verve and high-spirited fun" in the poem, leading them to misrepresent the poem's relationship to Donne's personal life, Milgate finding no demonstration in the poem of Donne's Roman Catholic leanings.

Hughes (1968, 68) states that in general *Metem* represents "a philosophical paradox, Donne's first extended analysis of world-deep ambiguity" and the struggle to understand why good and evil are so intertwined (68).

Williamson (1969, 250) points out that in *Metem* Donne satirically treats the same theme as Milton's *Paradise Lost*, the soul's progress extending from Eden to Calvary.

Thomas (1971, 112–13, 121) notes that the soul's journey in *Metem* parallels the ascending chain of life in Gen. 1.20–30, except for the early appearance of the sparrow. As the soul rises, he argues, "the allegorical qualities of the sins are inversely ordered," illustrating "orderly degradation" (113). The poem, which is "so frequently dismissed as Donne's errant orphan," is marked with Donne's "originality and complexity, his mock seriousness, and his love of dramatic argument" (121).

Carey (1981, 148) states that the choice of Calvin and Elizabeth as the "soule" of

Metem "could hardly have failed to make the poem anti-Protestant," and he urges this point as "further proof of Donne's lingering Catholic affiliations."

Corthell (1981, 109–10) argues that *Metem* is to be read as a "revisionist history of the fall," in which Eve's eating of the apple becomes "a process whereby man evolves into a microcosm of wickedness." In fact, he views the poem as an exercise in "formal paradox," one established on the "master paradox of progress and degeneration." Accordingly, if Donne spurs the reader to find counterarguments to his heretical view of humankind's decline, he has achieved his "paradoxical purpose."

Hughes (1982, 22, 37–38) asserts that each of the beings in *Metem*, from the mandrake to Themech, represents one of England's Tudor monarchs; i.e., Henry IV is the mandrake, Henry V is the sparrow, etc. (22), and concludes that the poem is "a work of political propaganda designed beneath its surface cover to define reality by naming the Tudor monarchy as the villain" (37–38).

Marotti (1986, 128–30, 132) claims that the "immediate political context"—where Donne is addressing a coterie audience "politically and intellectually sympathetic" (128)—is "crucial" to understanding the poem, the "thematic center" of which is not the immorality of the world or the Court, but "the shared political dissatisfaction of poet and audience" (129–30). Indeed, Marotti believes that even the work's sexual aggression becomes "a metaphor for political power," and he sees the satirization of Petrarchan and Neoplatonic love conventions in the account of the "toyful Ape" (451), whom Donne calls the "first true lover" (460), as unmasking the self-serving motives behind the fashionable amorous language and behavior of the Elizabethan Court (132).

Martz (1991, 17) resists thinking that Donne is opposed to Elizabeth in *Metem*, finding it "inconceivable" that as Secretary to Egerton and "well embarked on a secular career" he could have "contemplated even private circulation of a satire against Queen Elizabeth." He avers that "the only solution could be that Donne had in mind some compliment to the Queen's virtue, creating for her a symbolical and redeeming role similar to that played by the soul of Elizabeth Drury" in *SecAn*.

Edwards (2001, 59, 340) declares that *Metem* is "the nearest that Donne came to atheism" (59), but adds that since the poem also speaks of "Great Destiny" and "Infinity," it indicates that Donne "never disbelieved" (340).

"great *Soule*"

In the preface to *Metem*, Donne states, "shee is hee, whose life you shall find in the end of this booke," and the individual referred to here is universally assumed to be the same as the "great *Soule*" (61), though scholars have felt compelled to elucidate the ambiguity found in these lines.

Jonson (1619, 1:136), in his conversations with William Drummond of Hawthornden, believes that Donne's intent in *Metem* was to have the soul left "in ye body of Calvin" at the end of the poem.

Grosart (1872–73, 1:69), believing that the original versions of *FirAn* and *SecAn* antedate *Metem*, argues that the "great *Soule*" of *Metem* 62 originally referred to an "ideal woman" who was intended to "contrast with the more earthly type" described in *Metem* and whose life was to be celebrated in the Anniversaries. When Elizabeth

Drury died in 1610, Grosart asserts, Donne rewrote the Anniverseries and "transferred to her what he intended for that other."

Chambers (1896, 2:241) states that in the lines regarding the "great *Soule*," it "looks as if Donne meant a compliment to [Queen] Elizabeth."

In response to the "great *Soule*" reference, Gosse (1899, 1:135) notes, "it now becomes certain" that Queen Elizabeth, "the great tyrannical persecutor of the Catholics," was to be the final recipient of the soul.

Grierson (1912, 2:xviii) states that the "great *Soule*" passage "clearly indicates" that "the great heretic" is "not Calvin but Queen Elizabeth."

Payne (1926, 85) proposes that the soul in *Metem* was to come to rest in the "arch-heretic John Knox," but adds that the referent in line 61 is "undoubtedly" Queen Elizabeth.

Milgate (1967, xxvi, xxvin3) insists that any person who could fit the description of the "great *Soule*" in lines 61–63 "is ruled out by the fact that his life overlapped that of Luther" (xxvi), including, he adds, in response to Gosse (1899), the person of Queen Elizabeth (xxvin3).

Van Wyck Smith (1973, 141, 143–44) argues that while the "great *Soule*" refers to Queen Elizabeth, the subsequent lines describe a political figure behind the throne, one that fits "exactly" with Robert Cecil, Secretary of State at the time Donne was writing *Metem* (143). Cecil, he notes, "popularly known as Robertus Diabolus or Monsieur Bossu, physically weak and hunchbacked," was "an obvious butt for satire" (144), as evidenced by two other "beast satires" directed at members of the Cecil family, Spenser' s *Mother Hubberd's Tale* and Richard Niccols's *Beggar's Ape* (141).

Warnke (1987, 23) urges that Queen Elizabeth is the final incarnation of the soul.

Martz (1991, 16–17) notes a "bitter jest" in *Metem*'s preface, stating that "*hee* is the author himself." He reads the report of the soul (as a melon served at a "lascivious banquet" and as a spider "used for poison to attaine dignitie") as not merely an example by way of explanation, but actions of the soul. Thus, only if Donne were the current body inhabited by the soul could it report of these actions to him. Nevertheless, he asks, with regard to the lines following the reference to the "great *Soule*," "what then shall we make of the rest of the stanza, which seems to relate this soul to Luther and Mahomet?"

Notes and Glosses

Heading. Infinitati Sacrum WARNKE (1967): "sacred to infinity" (130). SMITH (1971): the transmigration cycle is endless and the work is "unfinished or unfinishable"; also, Donne suggests that regardless of the soul's progress through various bodies, the same conduct will emerge (503). SEYMOUR-SMITH (1972): consistent with the "generally fantastic tone," the work is dedicated to "'the infinite'" (240). CRAIK AND CRAIK (1986): the soul is deathless, and the poem is to be immortal (260–61).

Heading. Metempsychosis MILGATE (1967): the theory allowing movement of a soul into "the bodies of plants, birds, fish, animals, women, and men, as each of its previous bodies dies" (xxv). **SMITH** (1971): "transmigration of the soul," which is attributed to the Pythagoreans (503).

Heading. Poema Satyricon **SMITH** (1971): a satiric poem (503). **WENTERSDORF** (1982): "The late-Latin word 'satyricus' or 'saturicus' means of or like woodland satyrs (cf. Pliny, Hist. nat. XIX.xix.50, 'saturica signa' is 'statues of satyrs')" and may mean "'strong in sexual desire, lascivious' and 'stimulating sexual desire' (cf. Caelius Aurelianus, Acutae Passiones III.xviii.175, 'medicamina…satyrica'). 'Satyricus' is a variant of 'satiricus,' and thus may mean satirical," and as such, the subtitle means "'a poem about sexuality,' with a quibble on 'poetic satire'" (89).

Epistle. 2 *I my Picture,* **CHAMBERS** (1896): The poem appears first in the 1633 quarto, which possibly was issued with copies of Donne's portrait of 1591 by Marshall (2:240). **SEYMOUR-SMITH** (1972): indicates a proposed frontispiece (240). **CRAIK AND CRAIK** (1986): not an actual portrait, but "by an account of my purpose" (260).

3–8 *Naturallie…*Sine Talione. **PAYNE** (1926): recognized for criticizing others' work, the poet provides "a poem on which they may take their revenge, if they can," and in particular challenges them to find plagiarism or lack of originality (72).

3 *through light* **GOSSE** (1899): "Here sarcasm stalks unabashed, for Queen Elizabeth possessed no subject whose mind was less translucent, flat or plain, than that of Donne" (1:131). **MILGATE** (1967): "translucent," as the word is used in *FunEl* 61 (172). **CRAIK AND CRAIK** (1986): a pun meaning transparent or "thoroughly frivolous (compare through-vain, l. 473)" (261).

4 *stick* **MILGATE** (1967): "hesitate" (172).

4 *taxe:* **SHAWCROSS** (1967): "accuse" (309). [Similarly, Smith (1971, 503), Seymour-Smith (1972, 240), and Craik and Craik (1986, 261).]

8 Sine Talione. **MILGATE** (1967): "without punishment in kind, by the *lex talionis* (an eye for an eye, etc.)," taken from Martial, XII, lxiii, 10 (172). [Similarly, Shawcross (1967, 309).]

10 Trent Counsell **MILGATE** (1967): "a malicious deduction" from the Council's decisions that no text on sacred topics was to be published anonymously and that "an Index of prohibited books was to be prepared" (172). **SEYMOUR-SMITH** (1972): the deduction seems "to stem from common sense and a shrewd awareness of the nature of censors and committees" (240).

13–19 *Now when…to the place.* **WHITE** (1935): "Three classical concepts stand out in this passage: literature is a mine, from which all writers may dig treasure; the writer who transforms what he takes from his predecessors into 'as much and as good' is not in debt to his sources, for he has added to the treasure which posterity will have at its disposal in turn; borrowed matter is to be thankfully acknowledged, not ungratefully purloined by stealth" (127–28).

13–14 *Now when…any Mans debt;* **GOSSE** (1899): "He will borrow nothing, either from the classics or from the poets of his own day; the only person to whom he will be indebted shall be an unnamed scholar, who from some obscure Rabbinical or Spanish source has digged out the treasure of the odd subject he chooses" (1:131–32).

20–21 (*for I...can / teach*) **SEYMOUR-SMITH** (1972): "for the sophisticated only" (240).

21 Pithagorean Doctrine, **SHAWCROSS** (1967): the theory on the transmigration of the soul; Pythagoras believed also that "a pure life released the soul from any kind of body, which was otherwise its tomb or prison" (309).

24 *Mushrome* **GROSART** (1872–73) (reading "maceron") notes that Nares states that people "of a certain age" recall "maccaroni" having been used "in the sense of a first-rate coxcomb, or puppy, or the now temporary appellation 'dandy.'" Adds from Florio, "'a gull, a lubby [looby], a loggar-head that can doe nothing but eat Maccaroni,'" and from Vaugon, a man described as "'scimunito [foolish or stupid] e di poco intelletto'" (1:42). **NORTON** (1895) (reading "mucheron") footnotes it as "maceron," the French name "for what Gerhard in his 'Herbal' called Candy Alexander, or Thorough-bored parsley (Smyrnium creticum)." Adds that he cannot find maceron used in English and believes Donne wrote mushroom, which fits the idea (1:249). **CHAMBERS** (1896) (reading "macaron") notes that "a Maceron, Makeron, or Macaroon" was a common term in the seventeenth and eighteenth centuries for "a fop," and the derivation may be "from the Italian food macaroni, as we might speak of a frog-eater, or from maccarone or maccherone, a fool" (2:16). [Similarly, Grierson (1912, 2:217–18).] **HARRIS** (1902) argues that "Mucheron, i.e., mushroom, is undoubtedly the correct reading" and "maceron" a misprint. Cites Burton's *Anatomy of Melancholy* on metempsychosis, in which the soul inhabits a horse, a man, and a sponge, the latter "used as equivalent to fungus, with which it is cognate," and notes that in the epistle the order is similar, but reversed (284).

25 *noe vnredines in the Soule*, **MILGATE** (1967): the soul is capable of using all three of its faculties in a human, but the capacity of the available body (plant or animal) determines ("workes") "the kind of life it will lead" (173).

27 *and now* **SMITH** (1971): "and can now" (503).

29 *who vs'd it for Poison* **GOSSE** (1899): "It may remember not the time when it was a spider, yet recollect the vivid moment when a secret hand dropped it as poison into a cup of wine" (1:132). **SMITH** (1971): spiders were considered capable of changing food to poison inside their bodies (see *Twick* 6) (503).

30 *Dignitie.* **SMITH** (1971): "rank, office" (503).

31 *her memorie...her owne;* **SEYMOUR-SMITH** (1972): the soul has memory of its whole history (240).

32 *her relation* **SMITH** (1971): "her telling" (504).

32 *making,* **SMITH** (1971): "making headway, what was done; success" (504). **CRAIK AND CRAIK** (1986): "her creation" (261).

33 *Aple* MILGATE (1967): some supposed the fruit of the Tree of Knowledge (Gen. 2.17, 3.3) to be a fig or pomegranate. Most commentators follow Browne (*Vulgar Errors*, vii. l): "'curiosity fruitlesly enquireth'" (173).

33 *eat,* MILGATE (1967): ate (173).

First Songe. 1 *I sing…Soule* GOSSE (1899): "The poet begins, in the approved epic manner, by announcing to us his subject" (1:133). MILGATE (1967): "ritual phrase" of epic form along with other traditional gestures stating main action and addressing the muse (xxvi-ii), also a possible "mock- epic" opening (173). PATRIDES (1985): the epic characteristics are reinforced by the modified Spenserian stanza Donne uses (405).

2 *Fate…controule* MILGATE (1967) notes inconsistency with l. 31 in which Destiny is God's "Commissary" (173). SHAWCROSS (1967) points out the soul's free will; "God foresees but does not decree" (310).

3–4 *before the Law / Yoak'd was,* MILGATE (1967) (reading as "Yoak'd us,"): "The law given to Moses in the Commandments and by him to the Israelites" (173). SHAWCROSS (1967) (reading as "Yoak'd us,"): "before conduct or custom bound us" (310). PATRIDES (1985) delineates three periods of history in Donne's time: "the one 'before the law' given to Moses atop Mt. Sinai; the one during the law; and the one 'since' the law (i.e. the Christian era)" (405).

5 *ag'd Eueninge* MILGATE (1967): "'The world is now growne into his last age, wherein sects, schismes, and errors doo spread, and sinne and iniquitie aboundeth' (Charles Gibbon, *The Remedy of Reason*, 1589, A2v)." Also, see *Sat3* 36–38 (173). SEYMOUR-SMITH (1972): Donne "certainly enjoyed" the idea, "whether he believed it or not, that the world was in decay" (241). [Similarly, Patrides (1985, 405).]

6 *Morne,* SULLENS (1964): Donne's use of this meaning of the word is earlier than the earliest source cited by *OED* (223).

6 *Manlie* SULLENS (1964): Donne's use of this meaning of the word is earlier than the earliest source cited by *OED* (223).

7–8 *Gold* Chaldee…Roman *Iron,* MILGATE (1967): "the Four Monarchies (Babylon, Persia, Greece, Rome);" see l. 22, *BoulRec* 24, and *Sermons* 7:139. Each monarchy is aligned with "a stage in the general deterioration of the world from the Golden to the Iron ages," as in *Sat5* 35. Also, see Dan. 2.31–40 (173). [Similarly, Shawcross (1967, 310).] CRAIK AND CRAIK (1986) note the description of the ages in Ovid's *Metamorphoses*, 1:89–150, adding, "The Golden Age was one of innocence and plenty; the Iron Age is one of violence and competitive greed" (261).

8 *this one,* CRAIK AND CRAIK (1986): "this work" (261).

9 Seth's *Pillars,* GROSART (1872–73): "mythical antediluvian memorials" (1:90). NORTON (1895): "Seth, the son of Adam, left children who imitated his virtues. 'They were the discoverers of the wisdom which relates to the heavenly bodies and their order, and that their inventions might not be lost, they made two pillars, the one of brick, the other of stone, and inscribed their discoveries on them

both, that in case the pillar of brick should be destroyed by the flood, the pillar of stone might remain and exhibit those discoveries to mankind…Now this remains in the land of Syriad to this day.' Josephus, *Antiquities of the Jews*, Whiston's translation, book i, ch.2, §3" (1:249). **SEYMOUR-SMITH** (1972): this boast sets "the generally mocking tone" (241).

11–20 *Thee,…thee.* **COLERIDGE** (1817 [1907]): "We find no difficulty in admitting as excellent, and admitting the legitimate language of poetic fervor self-impassioned, Donne's apostrophe to the sun" in these lines (65).

11–12 *Thee,…begott;* **SHAWCROSS** (1967): "Alchemists believed the sun generated both animate and inanimate matter" (311).

11 *Eye of Heauen,* **GOSSE** (1899): Donne "addresses the sun, as he did long afterwards in his great sonnet to Lord Doncaster, celebrating the fecundity of its 'hot masculine flame,' its 'male force,' which first drew out the island spices in the far, dim chambers of the East" (1:133). **MILGATE** (1967) notes also *ED* 1–2 (173).

12 *Male-* **OED** (1882–1920) cites Donne as the earliest source for this meaning of the word.

16 *Tagus,…Danow* **SHAWCROSS** (1967): "rivers of Spain, Italy, France (the Seine), England, and Central Europe (the Danube)" (311).

16 *Danow* **MILGATE** (1967): "From Lat. 'Danuvius', collateral with 'Danubius', the (upper) Danube river" (174).

17 *Westerne Land of* Myne, **COLERIDGE** (1836), in a volume of Chalmers's *The Works of the English Poets*, marginally notes the play on the word "Myne" here and in *SunRis* 17, adding, "the use of the word 'mine' specifically for mines of gold, silver, or precious stones, is, I believe, peculiar to Donne" (1:148). **GROSART** (1872–73): "query = gold (mines)?" (1:90). **MILGATE** (1967): "America and the West Indies, usually coupled with the Eastern land of spices," as in *Coryat* 29 and *SunRis* 17 (174). [Similarly, Shawcross (1967), 311).]

19 *before thee,…to bee* **MILGATE** (1967): "The creation of plants (Gen. i. 11–13), and hence of the vegetal souls (as Pico della Mirandola says, *Heptaplus*, I. iv), took place on the third day; the sun was made on the fourth (Gen. i. 14–19)" (174). **SHAWCROSS** (1967): "Since this soul existed before the creation of the earth, it existed before God created light out of chaos. It existed in Satan and the other fallen angels" (311).

21 *holie* Ianus **G[ILES] O[LDISWORTH]** (1648): "Noah" (94). **GROSART** (1872–73): "There was but one Janus in ancient mythology, and Donne could hardly fail to remember this. Janus too, in the Latin mythology, was a particularly 'holy' god, and named before Jupiter as the beginner of all things, and the oldest of the gods in Italy. Then Donne clearly adopts the belief that Janus was Noah. He was led to use Janus, first, because his theme of Metempsychosis is a pagan one; and secondly, because the mention of the sun led up to it, Janus being the sun-divinity under another name" (1:90). **NORTON** (1895): "Sir Thomas Browne, in his *Enquiries into Vulgar and*

Common Errors, vi, 6, says, 'Janus, whom Annius of Viterbo and the chorographers of Italy do make to be the same with Noah.'" Annius of Viterbo (1432–1502) affirmed that Noah "'ob beneficium inventae vitis et vini dignatus est cognomento Jani, quod Arameis sonat vitifer et vinifer,' and the early culture of Italy was ascribed to him" (1:250). [Similarly, Grierson (1912, 2:219–20), who adds that "no mention of the ark as a link occurs," but there was a ship that "figured on the copper coins distributed at Rome on New Year's day, which was sacred to Janus."] **MILGATE** (1967): "'We call *Noah, Janus*, because hee had two faces, in this respect, That hee looked into the former, and onto the later world, he saw the times before, and after the flood,'" (*Sermons*, 8:112). In addition, "Noah is 'holy' because he 'found grace in the eyes of the Lord' (Gen. vi. 8); because, according to Annius of Viterbo's book, vii, fº. lvii, he was the first to exercise the priestly function (offering 'sacrificia et holocausta'); and because he was the type of the clergy (e.g. St. Augustine, Migne, *P.L.* xxxvii. 1731: 'Noe significat rectores Ecclesiae')" (174). **SHAWCROSS** (1967): "the two-faced God who controlled doors and thus the beginnings of things. The creations listed are thus ambivalent of good and evil"; cf. st. 52 (311).

21 Ianus **SULLENS** (1964): the *OED* "does not mention the application of this name to Noah" (261).

21 *Soueraigne Boat* **G[ILES] O[LDISWORTH]** (1648): "the Arke" (302). **SMITH** (1971): "all-saving" (505).

22 *The Church...Monarchies* **MILGATE** (1967): "because all living men were on the Ark, and hence (prospectively) all their descendants. The Ark was a type of the Church (e.g. St. Augustine, Migne, *P.L.* xxxiii.847)" (174).

23 *Colledge* **SULLENS** (1964): the *OED* cites Donne as the earliest source for this meaning of the word (244). **MILGATE** (1967): "In another work by Annius of Viterbo, *Berosi...Antiquitatum Italiae ac Totius Orbis Libri quinque* (Antwerp, 1552), we read (pp. 77–78) that Noah taught religion, astronomy, etc.: 'Noa, iam antea edoctos Theologiam et sacros ritus, coepit eos erudire humanam sapientiam', etc." (174). **SHAWCROSS** (1967): "both institution incorporating all knowledge and a prison" (311). **SMITH** (1971): "(a) company, society; (b) centre of learning in which Noah passed on the wisdom of the times before the Flood" (505).

23 *Hospitall* **MILGATE** (1967): "refuge, place of lodging" (*OED* 5) (174). **SHAWCROSS** (1967): "both institution of refuge from ills and house of prostitution" (311).

24 *Viuarie* **SULLENS** (1964): the *OED* cites Donne as the earliest source for this word (203). **MILGATE** (1967): "vivarium, a place artificially prepared for keeping animals and birds" (174). **SHAWCROSS** (1967): "place of birth" (311).

26 *latest Nephewes* **GROSART** (1872–73): "descendants" (1:90). [So also, Milgate (1967, 174) and Seymour-Smith (1972, 241).]

26 *install* **SULLENS** (1964): Donne's use of this meaning of the word is earlier than the earliest source cited by *OED* (220).

27 *thence* **MILGATE** (1967): "the Ark, and those in it" (174).

27 *this* All) **MILGATE** (1967): "the world (orbis totus)" (174). [So also, Shawcross (1967, 311).]

29 *Park* **MILGATE** (1967): see *EpEliz* 20–21 (174). **SHAWCROSS** (1967): "an enclosed area stocked with game" (311).

30 *inform'd* **SHAWCROSS** (1967): "given form and reason" (311). **SMITH** (1971): "occupied by the 'deathless soul' whose transmigrations the poem describes" (505).

30 *heauenly sparke.* **MILGATE** (1967): "the soul whose adventures are described in the poem. It was to enter more types of body than the Ark itself contained (cf. 'most shapes', l. 3)" (175).

31 *Great…God* **GROSART** (1872–73) says that Donne probably had in mind "those commissaries of the army who had the mustering of the men, and to all and everything being properly accoutred; for at the date it is less likely that he would choose an ecclesiastical metaphor, viz. the Bishop's commissary, 'who exercises ecclesiastical jurisdiction in those parts of the diocese so far remote from the see, that the chancellor cannot call the subjects thereof to the bishop's principal consistory without too much trouble' (Dyche's *Dict.* s.v.)." Notes that the "same thought" appears in *FunEl* 96 (1:90–91). **GARROD** (1946): see *HWNews* 10–11, "rugged Fate, God's Commissary" (122). **MILGATE** (1967): "Ultimately the action of Fate or Destiny lies in the will of God and his Providence; but seen 'in the world of change and becoming, accidents and events are ascribed to Destiny'" [from a letter to Wotton]. Also, "in saying that God does not 'control' Fate (l. 2), Donne seems to be referring to the visible world of change in which the action of Providence is not obvious, but can only be inferred. 'God is not Destiny; Then there could be no reward, nor punishment: but God is not Fortune neither, for then there were no Providence'" (*Sermons*, 9:303) (175). **SEYMOUR-SMITH** (1972): "deputy" (241).

31 *Comissarie* **SULLENS** (1964): the *OED* cites Donne as the earliest source for this meaning of the word (245).

33 *where we Ofspring took,* **SMITH** (1971): "where our actions have consequences that we cannot see or control" (505). **CRAIK AND CRAIK** (1986): "at the instant of our conception" (262).

33 *took,* **SEYMOUR-SMITH** (1972): "derived" (241).

35 *Knott of all Causes,* **SHAWCROSS** (1967): "intricately intertwined cord. A cause, according to Peter Ramus, was that by which a thing (object or idea or occurrence) existed" (312). **SMITH** (1971): "resolver of all actions or purposes" (505).

40 *spand.* **SHAWCROSS** (1967): "limited. The distance that the hand could stretch was considered nine inches, called a span" (312).

41–50 *To my…may haue.* **GOSSE** (1899): "Being nearly thirty years of age, Donne is not inclined, unless the book of destiny promises him at least thirty more, with a fair prospect of health and wealth and bodily comfort, to adventure in arduous, intellectual enterprise. If he is going to continue the distracting life he has endured hitherto, without respite from illness and business, the ennuis of love and the frets of ambition, the game is positively not worth the candle; he will retire from the intolerable struggle, and will go down quietly to his grave, when his time comes, 'a whole, unwasted man.' This is what he fancies he would prefer—a quiet life, without events, where there should be no 'expense of spirit,' and rest should come early to him" (1:134).

41 six lustres **NORTON** (1895): "The poem is dated 1601, when Donne, born in 1573, was 28 years old" (1:250). **MILGATE** (1967) glosses as "thirty years (of age), a 'lustre' being a 'period of five years,'" and notes that Donne "was born between 24 January and 19 June 1572, and would have been twenty-nine years and some (at most, seven) months old in August 1601." Cites I. A. Shapiro, "Donne's Birthdate," *NQ* 197 (1952): 310–13 (175).

42 *Except* **SEYMOUR-SMITH** (1972): "unless" (241).

43 *letts* **MILGATE** (1967): "hindrances" (175).

45 *Sprighte-quenching* **SULLENS** (1964): a word combination that the *OED* does not record (206). **MILGATE** (1967) (reading "Spirit-quenching") notes that "The 'spirit' destroyed by sickness is (as in l. 49) the refined and vitalizing part of the blood, by means of which the soul is able to act upon and through the organs of the body." See *Ecst* 61–62. Further, "'Spirit' is here a monosyllable," as shown by the alternative spelling "Sprighte-quenching" (175).

46 *Distracting* **SULLENS** (1964): Donne's use of this word is earlier than the earliest sourced cited by *OED* (179).

46 *Netts* **SHAWCROSS** (1967): "entrapments" (312). **WARNKE** (1967): "obstacles" (133).

47 *calls from this* **SMITH** (1971): "lures him from the business of writing the poem" (505).

47 *to other whetts,* **MILGATE** (1967): "any other pursuit" (175). [So also, Seymour-Smith (1972, 241).]

48 *launch out,* **CRAIK AND CRAIK** (1986): "set to work," the metaphor continuing in the next stanza (262).

49 *Th'expence* **SMITH** (1971): "the expenditure" (505).

52 *this Sea* **MILGATE** (1967): "the labour of writing this poem, on which he has 'embarked'" (175).

52 *enrough* **SULLENS** (1964): the *OED* cites Donne as the earliest source for this word (193).

54 *lone* **SULLENS** (1964): Donne's use of this meaning of the word is earlier than the earliest source cited by *OED* (222).

55 *light and light* **LAMB** (1824), in a letter dated 24 March, notes, "the two senses

of 'light' are opposed to different opposites" ([1935, 2:421]). **MILGATE** (1967): the two senses are opposed to "darke" and to "heavy" (175). **SHAWCROSS** (1967): "'light' as opposed to 'darke' (thus, illuminating), and as opposed to 'heavy' (thus, humorous as a 'poema satyricon' was supposed to be)" (312). **CRAIK AND CRAIK** (1986): "make my obscure difficult poem easy to understand and pleasant to read" (262).

56 *Streights* **MILGATE** (1967): "(a) narrow sea-passages, the geographical extent of the soul's wanderings, and (b) difficulties (in composing the poem)" (175).

57 *I launch...home;* **MILGATE** (1967): "'I begin my poem in Eden and bring its story to England at the end' (cf. l. 60)" (175). [So also, Smith (1971, 505).]

59 *hoisted* **MILGATE** (1967): "set. Cf.: 'as soone as they hoysed their sailes'; 'from his hoysing saile here, to his striking sayle there,'" (*Sermons*, 6:305; 9:68) (175). [Similarly, Seymour-Smith (1972, 242).]

60 *at* Tigris *and* Euphrates **MILGATE** (1967): Donne "follows the accepted belief that Paradise was in Mesopotamia" (176).

60 *wayd.* **SHAWCROSS** (1967): "weighed; that is, the anchor of his ship of life was raised in the cradle of civilization to sail the sea of life" (313).

61 *this great* Soule See Commentary under "great *Soule*."

65 *Crowne* **SHAWCROSS** (1967): "high point" (313).

66 *Mahomet* **MILGATE** (1967): pronounced with two syllables here and in *ElBed* 21 (176). [So also, Seymour-Smith (1972, 242).]

67 *Prisons of flesh;* **MILGATE** (1967): "For the idea of the soul as being imprisoned in the body, cf. Plato, *Phaedo* 82" and *Ecst* 68 (176).

68 *Wracks* **SMITH** (1971): "injuries, ruins" (506).

68 *th' Empire and late* Rome **MILGATE** (1967): "the Roman Empire (or possibly the Holy Roman Empire, or both) and Rome in recent times. The latter phrase might refer to the turbulent history of the Papal States in the century or two just passed, or, more probably, to the 'ruins' wrought by the Reformation" (176). [Similarly, Smith (1971, 506).]

70 *a low but fatall Roome.* **MILGATE** (1967): "The place ('roome') occupied by the soul in Eden was 'low' because only on the vegetable plane of being; it was 'fatall' because the apple was doomed to be plucked, because the plucking brought death into the world, and hence because it was 'fateful' to mankind" (176).

71–80 *Yet...free.* **NORTON** (1895) acknowledges that he does not know where Donne "found the fancy that the cross was planted where the tree of knowledge of good and evil had stood," but adds that "among the numerous theories as to the site of Paradise there was one, at least as old as the fourth century, that it had occupied the spot which afterwards became the site of Jerusalem." Cites "the 47th question of the *Quaestiones ad Antiochum*, ascribed to St. Athanasius, and printed (as spurious) in the Benedictine edition of his works, Paris, 1698" (1:251). **ALLEN** (1945a) points out the allusion in *Sickness* 21–22, stating, "the relationship between Adam's tree and Christ's cross (involving the legend of Seth's visit to Eden and the story of the tree that grew out of Adam's dead mouth and eventually was made into the cross) is known to most students of English Literature." Believes this identification results "from a cross-breeding of the story of the tree that grew from Adam's mouth and a persistent legend that Adam's grave became the locus of the Cross." Notes that the earliest reference to the second story comes from Origen: "Adam is buried in Calvary; hence as all died in Adam, all shall again be resurrected in Christ" (398–99). **GARROD** (1946) points to "the selfe same roome" in l. 77 (122). **GARDNER** (1952), responding to Allen (1945a), states, "the one place where Adam could not possibly have been buried is Paradise, since he was expelled from there after the Fall" (135). Continues, "we cannot take Donne to mean that the Forbidden Tree and the Cross stood on the same spot; for in a previous stanza (VI) he declares that he 'launches at paradise' and weighs anchor 'at Tigrys and Euphrates', thus placing Paradise again in Mesopotamia." Adds that Allen "goes on to say that the soul whose history he is about to relate" resides in a "low," and perhaps "fatall," "roome" (136–37). Responding that "roome" means "position," suggests that the soul was not in a "low roome," for although "it inhabited an apple, that apple hung on a tree that stood by the tree of life 'in the midst of the garden', that is, in the position of highest honour. It was the first of all trees to stand in this 'roome'. But when the Cross was raised on Calvary, it 'stood in the selfe same roome'; for 'devout and sharpe men' had held from Tertullian onwards that Calvary was the centre of the habitable globe: 'hic medium terrae,'" and "Christian sentiment has always linked the two trees: the 'lignum perditionis' and the 'lignum salvationis.'" Concludes that Donne here "makes a new and ingenious connexion of his own: both 'stood in the selfe same roome', for they were both 'in medio'" (137).

72 *sharp* **SHAWCROSS** (1967): "sagacious" (313).

73–76 *That crosse,…but Dye*, **SMITH** (1984): "the only vivid and emotive word in the passage is 'nailes,' but nails do not 'tye,' they pierce. Christ is mentioned not as a person but merely as an abstraction, and we are urged to remember that while the nails confine him he cannot really be confined, nor can he really die" (516).

74–76 *That All…but Dye*, **MILGATE** (1967): "used with only a change of tense" in *Cor2* 2–4 (176).

78 *forbidden learned Tree* **MILGATE** (1967): "the Tree of Knowledge (learning) of Good and Evil; eating its fruit was 'forbidden' to Adam." See Gen. 2.17 (176).

78 *learned* **SULLENS** (1964): this meaning of the word is not recorded by the *OED* (262).

79 *Securitie* **MILGATE** (1967): "perfect safety, one would have thought, since God had willed that it should not be plucked (and hence it was 'fenc'd with the law', l. 82)" (176).

80 *pulling free.* **SHAWCROSS** (1967): "modifying 'will' and meaning the free will of God (without exertion or coercion)" (313). **SMITH** (1971): "exempt from plucking" (506). [So also, Craik and Craik (1986, 262).]

81–120 *Prince…end Heresies*. **PAYNE** (1926): "These stanzas show us at once three of the principal threads of this remarkable poem—satire of women, scepticism in religion, and preoccupation with death" (78).

81–100 *Prince…yoak'd vs*. **SHAWCROSS** (1967): these stanzas "on the fall of Adam and Eve recall the introduction of Sin, Death, and Labor into the world" (313).

81–90 *Prince…and Sweat*. **SEYMOUR-SMITH** (1972) sees the entire stanza as "a neat and orthodox statement of the doctrine of the fall: Satan, once upright but made to crawl for his offence, gave the apple to Eve, who gave it to Adam; they were then expelled (made mortal), and corrupted us so that we suffer for the sinfulness that is in us" (242).

82 *the Law* **SMITH** (1971): "God's edict forbidding Adam and Eve to pluck the fruit" (506).

82 *ripe as soone as borne* **MILGATE** (1967): "The plants in Eden bore ripe fruits since they were edible by man and woman three days after the plants were created. 'In paradise, the fruits were ripe, the first minute' (*Sermons*, vi. 172); 'not unripe but at their prime, to be perfectly ready for the immediate use and enjoyment of the animals' (Philo Judaeus, *De Plantatione*, xiii; *Works*, translated by F. H. Colson and G. H. Whitaker, Loeb ed., i. 33)" (176–77).

84 *the then…now creepes* **MILGATE** (1967): "The curse upon Satan, the serpent of Gen. iii. 14, for having tempted Eve was 'upon thy belly shalt thou go'. This suggested that before the Fall the serpent 'went' in another fashion: cf. Basil, *De Paradiso*, iii.7 (Migne, *P.G.* xxx. 67), 'erectus celsusque in pedes incedens.'" In addition, "Josephus seems to have originated the idea that God bereft the serpent 'of feet and made him crawl and wriggle along the ground' (*Jewish Antiquities*, i. 50, translated by H. St. J. Thackeray and R. Marcus, iv. 25)" cf. *Sermons*, 10:184 (177).

87 *only forbiddings driue*) **SMITH** (1971): "one can get them to do something only by forbidding them to do it" (506).

89 *Meat* **SHAWCROSS** (1967): "both the apple containing this soul and flesh itself" (314).

90 *Treason taints the blood*) **GROSART** (1872–73): "a legal reference or simile; for 'the descendants of one attainted of treason cannot be heirs to him, and if he be male, his posterity is thereby degraded; nor can this corruption of blood be taken away but by act of Parliament or writ of error' (Dyche, s.v. attainted)" (1:91). [Similarly, Milgate (1967, 177).]

90 *Dy* **MILGATE** (1967): "'because all sinne is deriv'd upon us, by "generation," and so implyed, and involv'd in "originall sinne"' (*Sermons* 6:192), and the wages of sin is death" (177).

90 *Sweat*. **MILGATE** (1967): cf. Gen. 3.19: "In the sweat of thy face shalt thou eat bread" (177).

91–94 *Man…Riuoletts,* **DUBROW** (1990): this passage "emphasizes Eve's responsibility for the fall in terms that are not likely to cheer a prospective bridegroom" (154–55).

91–93 *Man…By them!* **GARROD** (1946): see *FirAn* 106–07 (122). **MILGATE** (1967): see *FirAn* 105–07, 180. "Women now 'kill' men, or hasten their death, by provoking coition; see ll. 206–10. The orthodox view was that it was the man's sin that brought about the Fall (I Cor. xv. 21–22); but Ecclus. xxv. 24 says: 'Of the woman came the beginning of sin, and through her we all die'" (177). **SHAWCROSS** (1967) notes that in addition to its appearance in a several Songs and Sonets, "this idea was common in religion and supplied men with reasons for their failures in life" (314). **WARNKE** (1967): as in many of the Songs and Sonets, Donne here "plays on the colloquial meaning of dying as experiencing sexual climax" (135).

93 *The mother* **SEYMOUR-SMITH** (1972): "Eve" (242).

93 *poysned the Wel-head,* **MILGATE** (1967) cites *Sermons,* 9:247: "The devill…so surprised us all, as to take mankinde all in one lump, in a corner, in Adams loynes, and poysoned us all there in the fountain" (177). **TURNER** (1987): Donne's *FirAn* and the Nethersole wedding sermon share with *Metem* the "outrageous proposition" that "'the first wedding was our funeral,' since Eve slew her husband, and since her daughters continue to kill us 'delightfully' by sexual depletion" (169).

94 *Riuoletts,* **MILGATE** (1967): "The rivulets flowing from the spring, or well-head, of humanity—Adam—are 'us' men, his descendants" (177).

97 *turning* **MILGATE** (1967): "returning (to paradise)" (177). **SHAWCROSS** (1967): "a satiric double pun: though women have led men into sin, they do not allow them to detour them from the path of life, which is their means for salvation, and by sexual intercourse ('turning' in bed), which is man's solace" (314).

98–100 *Were…yoak'd vs.* **GROSART** (1872–73): Donne refers here to "the sentence pronounced," which would "seem rigorous, viz. this one, that for her sin we bear punishment; and then says part, not of our 'sin,' but of the result of the sin—part of the 'pain,' poena, or punishment inflicted on us—is to love, &c." (1:91). **MILGATE** (1967): "If the situation were reversed, and we prisoners of God's justice could ourselves pass judgement, we should deem it harsh that we should bear the penalty of Eve's sin. This is a cautious statement, tending to 'atheism'. Estienne, speaking of atheists, tells of an Italian lord who, among his 'fearfull blasphemies' 'was not ashamed to say, that God dealt unjustly when he condemned mankind for a peece of an apple' (translated in *A World of Wonders,* 1607, by R. Carew, p. 73)" (177–78). **SEYMOUR-SMITH** (1972): "This is an attack, very playful, on God—or simplistic religion—as well as on women" (242).

99 *Paine* **MILGATE** (1967), noting that two manuscripts "paraphrase" this word as "'sinn,'" says "the 'paine' is *poena,* the penalty for sin" (178).

101–10 *Soe fast…for it.* **MILGATE** (1967): "These speculations about the justice of God in relation to Adam, Eve, the Serpent, and to mankind in general are traditional, descending mostly from rabbinical sources. They are set out in full, for example, in

Pererius's *Comment. et Disput. in Genesim*, 1601, vi. 283–96. The 'curious' (ingeniously argumentative) rebel who entertained them would not be very daring; even so, Donne says that these questionings are due to the 'corruption' of man, and are characteristic of 'heretiques' (l. 118)" (178).

101–02 *Soe fast...bee soe.* **SEYMOUR-SMITH** (1972): "This is bitterly ironic; its target is, as above, simplistic or tyrannical religiosity" (242).

103 *Curious Rebell)* **SHAWCROSS** (1967): "he who questions whether God allows salvation to man; apparently a Calvinist, who believed in the doctrine of the elect and the reality of man's depravity" (314). **SMITH** (1971): "improperly inquisitive; sophistical" (507).

105–06 *Of euery...take?* **SEYMOUR-SMITH** (1972) paraphrases as "Can God justly revenge himself on all men for the sake of one man's transgression?" but questions whether Donne, "in listing this and other traditional rabbinical speculations, was entirely serious." Believes that Donne's criticism here is "directed at the capacity of the 'Genesis' myth to explain the difficulties of humanity" (242).

106 *For one* **MILGATE** (1967): "for the offence of one" (178).

107–09 *'Twas not...the Aple:* **MILGATE** (1967) notes that in Gen. 2 "God's command not to eat of the Tree is given to Adam alone, apparently before the creation of Eve," but in Gen. 3 it is clear that "Eve and the Serpent were well aware of the prohibition." Points out that "the Bible does not say that Adam actually picked the apple" or that "he knew which tree it came from" (178).

110 *Worme* **GROSART** (1872–73): "the Serpent" (1:91).

111–20 *But Snatch...end Heresies.* **SEYMOUR-SMITH** (1972): "Considering Donne's own highly speculative nature, we cannot take this entirely at its face value: there is some more irony, if rueful, here," for Donne's "own family was 'heretic': his uncle Jasper Heywood, a Jesuit, was imprisoned in the Tower and was lucky not to have been executed—he died abroad; his brother Henry died of the plague in Newgate, where he was awaiting trial for harbouring a Roman Catholic priest, who was hanged, drawn and quartered" (243).

111–12 *vaine / Reckning* **MILGATE** (1967): "fruitless enumeration of" (178).

112–14 *lesse is...good Minde;* **MILGATE** (1967): "To think about evil, though with good intentions, always involves a danger greater than the possible benefits produced by such speculations" (178).

113 *Then* **PATRIDES** (1985): "than" (410).

114–17 *like those...themselues spill;* **GRIERSON** (1912): "What Donne says is that the reasons or arguments of those who answer sceptics, like bubbles which break themselves, injure their authors, the apologists. The verse wants a syllable—not a unique phenomenon in Donne's satires; but if one is to be supplied 'so' would give the sense better than 'and'" (2:220). **HAYWARD** (1929) cites *Sermons*, 7:294: those who "become none, but vanish into nothing, as boy's bubbles…by an overblowing become nothing" (776). [So also, Milgate (1967, 178).]

114 *Toyes* SHAWCROSS (1967): "small, showy objects designed for diversion rather than utility" (315).

117 *That they…themselues spill;* MILGATE (1967): "The line has only nine syllables"; see *Sat3* 38 note (178).

118 *Arguing is Heretiques game;* CAREY (1981): the line shows Donne "struggling to suppress reason and cling to faith long before the notion of taking Anglican orders occurred to him" (243).

119–20 *not liberties…end Heresies.* SHAWCROSS (1967): "That is, heresies are bred by talk; they are ended by silence and works" (315). CRAIK AND CRAIK (1986): "Donne here argues that heresies cannot be eradicated by argument but must be suppressed by law" (262).

119 *As wrastlers* MILGATE (1967): "as in the case of wrestlers" (178).

119 *perfects them;* MILGATE (1967): "in their heresy" (178).

121 *the Serpents gripe* MILGATE (1967): "Cf. ll. 84–86. Eve, according to Scripture, 'took of the fruit' (V. 'tulit de fructu'). Some authorities thought that she did not, as in *Paradise Lost*, herself pluck the fruit, but that she took it from the serpent, the actual plucker" (178). SEYMOUR-SMITH (1972): "grip" (243).

124–25 *fled away…another Day.* CRAIK AND CRAIK (1986): "this freed soul, two days old, fled away" (263).

124 *Life, and growth,* MILGATE (1967): "the qualities of the 'vegetal' faculty of the soul" (178).

125 *old, one and another Day.* MILGATE (1967): "two days old, but fully mature (cf. l. 82)" (178).

127–28 *better proof…Faith requires)* MILGATE (1967): "Faith, by its nature, accepts without 'scientific' proof, or proof to the senses; but the senses themselves are easily deceived, and we require proof that our perceptions are accurate" (178).

128 *then* PATRIDES (1985): "than" (410).

129 *dark and foggie Plott:* GRIERSON (1912): "The word 'foggie' has here the in English obsolete, in Scotch and perhaps other dialects, still known meaning of 'marshy', 'boggy'. The *O.E.D.* quotes, 'He that is fallen into a depe foggy well and sticketh fast in it,' Coverdale, *Bk. Death*, I. xl. 160; 'The foggy fens in the next county,' Fuller, *Worthies*" (2:220). MILGATE (1967): "'Mandrage groweth willingly in darke and shadowie places' (Dodoens, *Herbal*, 1578, pp. 437–8)" (178–79). SHAWCROSS (1967): "'spungie' (l. 135)" (179).

130 *th'Earth's pores* GROSART (1872–73): "The thought is: As the water of a spring runs into the ocean, and thence filters back through the secret ways or veins

of the earth to reappear as another spring, so this returned soul, infused into the seed, came up with the plant through the earth's 'pores'" (1:91–92). **MILGATE** (1967): "The earth was supposed to have pores like those in the human skin. 'And when the pores of the earth open, then by heate of the Sunne, this serpent "Vipera" awaketh and commeth out of his den' (*Batman upon Bartholome*, 1582, f. 386r)" (179).

130 *plant* **GROSART** (1872–73) suggests that the reference is to a mandrake, whose roots occasionally "present a very grotesque resemblance to the human figure." Notes further that "the most established virtue of the mandrake was a narcotic, and it is said to have been used as a 'pain-killer,' as chloroform is now, in surgical operations" and was also thought "to be cooling, and locally an absorbent, and a remedy for inflamed eyes (ll. 165–68)." Points out that legends "link to it the love-charms of Circe, and it comes up in St. Augustine and other Fathers and medieval Preachers to 'point a moral,' if not 'adorn a tale.'" Concludes that Donne "works all manner of odd folk-lore into his descriptions, fresh probably from Holland's 'Pliny,' and the like" (1:92). **NORTON** (1895): "The description of the mandrake conforms to the popular superstition. Rough woodcuts of the male and female mandrake may be seen in the *Ortus Sanitatis*, Venice, 1511, accompanied with an account of their operations and qualities" (1:251). **CHAMBERS** (1896): "The 'mandragora,' or mandrake, partly from its name, partly from the shape of its forked root, was looked upon as a link between the animal or human and vegetable worlds. It was supposed to shriek when it was torn up out of the earth" (1:222). [Similarly, Gosse (1899, 1:136), Redpath (1956, 119), and Shawcross (1967, 315).] **GRIERSON** (1912) quotes from Sir Thomas Browne's *Pseudodoxia Epidemica* (1646): "Many Molas and false conceptions there are of Mandrakes, the first from great Antiquity conceiveth the root thereof resembleth the shape of Man which is a conceit not to be made out by ordinary inspection, or any other eyes, than such as regarding the clouds, behold them in shapes conformable to pre-apprehensions" (2:221). **ALLEN** (1959): "The ancients had various notions about the mandragora; but when they reckoned up its uses to man, they valued it mainly as an aphrodisiac and a soporific." As suggested by the Greek *Physiologus*, the elephant "must first eat of the mandrake when he wishes to beget young. To this end the elephant leads his mate to the neighborhood of Eden where this plant grows. First she eats; then he. The two elephants, the Greek text continues, are symbols of Adam and Eve who fell through eating the mandrake" (394–95). **SEYMOUR-SMITH** (1972): "Because its root often forked into two and took the appearance of a little man, it was endowed with life," and "in fact it is poisonous, like most so-called aphrodisiacs, whose action is to inflame the sexual membranes. In l. 148 Donne refers to these aphrodisiac properties, and playfully makes the mandrake into a pubically hairy little lover on its own account. Like the poppy, it was also a soporific" (243).

131 *thus abled* **MILGATE** (1967): "The soul 'is made a slave to this body, by comming to it; It must act, but what this body will give it leave to act, according to the Organs, which this body affords it' (*Sermons*, vi. 75); but without the body the soul 'could nothing doe,'" *Air* 7–8 (179). **SMITH** (1971): "given strength" (507). **SEYMOUR-SMITH** (1972): "enabled. Now that this plant (the mandrake) has obtained a soul, it can act as it desires" (243).

134 *thicker* **SHAWCROSS** (1967): "denser, having a higher density" (315).

134 *throngd* **GROSART** (1872–73): "The construction is, The spungy confines [being] thronged so or thrust about by this root" (1:92). **MILGATE** (1967): "squeezed. The plant pressed the thinner water out of the boggy soil" (179). **SEYMOUR-SMITH** (1972): "The mandrake pushed the water away from itself in order to gain a denser medium in which to grow" (243).

137 *Prince,* **GRIERSON** (1912): "The title of 'Prince' was indeed applicable to a female sovereign. The *O.E.D.* gives: 'Yea the Prince…as she hath most of yearely Revenewes…so should she have most losse by this dearth,' W. Stafford, 1581; 'Cleopatra, prince of Nile,' Willobie, *Avisa,* 1594; 'Another most mighty prince, Mary Queene of Scots,' Camden (Holland), 1610" (2:221). [Similarly, Warnke (1967, 136).] **MILGATE** (1967): see *HuntMan* 44, and *MHPaper* 11 (179).

140 *flatned* **SULLENS** (1964): the OED cites Donne as the earliest source for this word (193).

142 *digest* **MILGATE** (1967): "divide" (179).

147 *his Midle parts,* **MILGATE** (1967): "Donne is fancifully developing the supposed resemblance of the mandrake to a man, consisting in 'a bifurcation or division of the Root into two parts, which some are content to call Thighs' (Browne, *Vulgar Errors,* ii. 6)" (179).

148 *Loues busines* **MILGATE** (1967): "By a play on words Donne attributes to the mandrake the capacity for sexual adventures which was, in fact, possessed by those who used the mandrake as aphrodisiac or to procure abortions (l. 150)" (179).

149 *A Dealer* **SHAWCROSS** (1967): "an agent, referring to the belief that mandrakes could help in the begetting of children. Hair, of course, shows virility" (316).

150 *His Aples…kill.* **GROSART** (1872–73): "his apples 'kindle' force of conception, or are aphrodisiac; his leaves [having the opposite effect] kill force of conception, or are anaphrodisiac" (1:92). [So also, Smith (1971, 507) and Seymour-Smith (1972, 243).] **MILGATE** (1967): "The aphrodisiac qualities of the fruit of the plant are frequently mentioned, e.g. by Burton, *Anatomy,* part. 3, sect. 2, memb. 2, subsect. 5," and "Browne relates from Dioscorides (cf. Matthiolus in *Dioscoridem,* 1558, p. 535) the belief that 'the grains of the apples of Mandrakes mundifie the Matrix, and applied with Sulphur, stop the fluxes of women', adding 'that the juice…procures abortion' (*Vulgar Errors,* vii. 7); but not specifically the juice of the leaves" (179). **SHAWCROSS** (1967): "The round fruits of the mandrake were used as an aphrodisiac and the leaves as a narcotic and soporific" (316).

152 *subtill* **SHAWCROSS** (1967): "fine" (316).

153 *Colossus* **SULLENS** (1964): Donne's use of this meaning of the word is earlier than the earliest source cited by OED (210). **SHAWCROSS** (1967): "referring to the huge statue of Apollo that dominated the harbor at Rhodes" (316).

156 *Enchas'd* **SHAWCROSS** (1967): "ornamented" (316). [So also, Patrides (1985, 411).]

156 *red and bright* **GROSART** (1872–73): "Whether Donne drew from some of the knaveries spoken of by Parkinson, we cannot tell; but the fruit is described by the latter in his first book of the 'Paradisus' as pale red, and in his *Theat. Botan.* as 'yellow as gold, and the bignesse of a reasonable pippin.' Bartholomew also calls it yellow" (1:92). **MILGATE** (1967): "The fruit of the male mandrake is usually described as bright golden yellow in colour ('luteo colore croci', Dioscorides, *Pedacii*, 1529, p. 14)" (179).

158 *lone* **SULLENS** (1964): see note to l. 54.

159–60 *built by...buried Man,* **GRIERSON** (1912): "the man buried alive is the 'soul's second inn', the mandrake" (2:221).

159 *Guest,* **MILGATE** (1967) identifies as "the soul itself, that built its own 'Inne' to sojourn (not dwell) in." Notes that in *Ignatius* (p. 5), Donne "translates the poem attributed to the dying Hadrian ('Animula vagula', etc.): 'My wandring sportful Soule, / Ghest, and Companion of my body'" (179–80).

160 *Man,* **HAYWARD** (1929) cites a sermon of Donne: "this living dead man, this dead and buried man" (*Sermons* [10:69]) (776).

161–70 *Noe lustfull...most good.* **GOSSE** (1899): "Eve disturbs the Soul in this 'lone, unhaunted place,' for, sin having come into the world, her child is vexed with fever, and she seeks in waste places for a herb to restore it to health. In her search she is led to the mandrake and the poppy" (1:136). **SEYMOUR-SMITH** (1972): "Eve tore up this mandrake, in order to quieten the proverbially weeping Cain" (243).

163 *other purpose)* **SHAWCROSS** (1967): "to use as an opiate, as explained in the following lines" (317).

165 *Cradled Child, the moist red Eyes* **MILGATE** (1967): "The child was Cain, whose name was often (wrongly) translated as 'lamentation', 'constant weeping' (as in Rabanus Maurus, *De Universo*, II. i; Migne, *P. L.* cxi. 32)" (180).

165 *Cradled* **SULLENS** (1964): the *OED* cites Donne as the earliest source for this word (191).

167 *Poppie...Mandrakes Might* **MILGATE** (1967): "Poppy and mandragora were well-known soporifics," and "they were also good for inflamed eyes. Dodoens says that juice from the roots of a fresh mandrake is good in 'medicines, that do mitigate the paynes of the Eyes', and that opium with vinegar 'is good to be layde to the disease, called *Erysipelas*, or Wild fire, and all other inflammations' (*Herbal*, 1578, pp. 438, 433)" (180).

169 *Vnuertuous* **MILGATE** (1967): "not having medicinal 'virtues'" (180). **SHAWCROSS** (1967): "lacking in extraordinary abilities" (317).

169 *vnuext* **GOSSE** (1899): Donne "reflects that these plants were the first to

die because of their virtues; had they been base weeds they might have lived long" (1:136). **SHAWCROSS** (1967): "uninjured, untouched" (317).

171–80 *To an...a Dore.* **SEYMOUR-SMITH** (1972): "The soul, after four days as inhabitant of the mandrake, enters a sparrow's egg. The sparrow was a symbol of lechery. The soul has now gained the faculty of movement" (243).

171–73 *To an...this Soule,* **GROSART** (1872–73) notes that this idea is "expanded" in *SecAn* 185ff. (1:92).

171 *vnfetter'd* **SULLENS** (1964): the *OED* cites Donne as the earliest source for this word (202).

173 *burnt Ayre* **SHAWCROSS** (1967): "smoke" (317).

175 *Tennant,* **SHAWCROSS** (1967): "tenancy, abode" (317).

176 *firm Destinie* **MILGATE** (1967): Donne "insists throughout that the sub-rational souls are at the command of Fate; cf. ll. 245–7, 301, as earlier, l. 129" (180).

177 *eniayld* **SULLENS** (1964): the *OED* cites Donne as the earliest source for this word (192).

180 *Till...a Dore.* **GROSART** (1872–73) says that this calls to mind "the slang phrase, 'Does your mother know you're out?'" (1:93).

181 *Out crept* **SULLENS** (1964): a word combination that the *OED* does not record (205).

181 *mouing* **MILGATE** (1967): "The new body gives scope to the 'sensible' faculty of the soul, adding the power of motion to those of life and growth (l. 124)" (180).

182–83 *stiffe Feathers...with Paine,* **CAREY** (1981): Donne got the idea of comparing cutting teeth and growing feathers from Plato's *Phaedrus* (149–50).

184 *Ielly* **SULLENS** (1964): the *OED* cites Donne as the earliest source for this meaning of the word (249).

184 *Threds,* **SHAWCROSS** (1967): "thin and weak like threads" (317).

185 *All* **MILGATE** (1967): "the bird's whole body" (180).

188 *Meat fitt for men* **MILGATE** (1967): "The sparrow's conduct, after being fed, is also 'fit' for men. The innuendo seems to involve a play on I Cor. iii. 1–3: 'I have fed you with milk, and not with meat:...are ye not carnal, and walk as men?'" (180). **CRAIK AND CRAIK** (1986): "corn, bread, etc." (263).

191–92 *In this...longer last:* **MILGATE** (1967): "Compare Drayton, *Noah's Flood,* ll. 26–30" (180).

193 *hot Cock* **MILGATE** (1967): "The sparrow was proverbially lecherous. Cf. Pliny, *Nat. Hist.* x. 52, and Tilley S715: 'as lustful as Sparrows'" (180).

194 *oreflutters* SULLENS (1964): the *OED* cites Donne as the earliest source for this word (197).

194 *next* MILGATE (1967): "nearest" (180).

197 *pule* SHAWCROSS (1967): "moan" (318). SMITH (1971): "whine" (508).

198 *change,* SMITH (1971): "transfer his sexual allegiance" (508).

200 *Where...chuse.* GROSART (1872–73): "This thought is freely used in the Elegies" (1:93).

200 *Where Store is of both kinds,* SMITH (1971): "where both male and female offer an abundance of sexual opportunity" (508).

201–10 *Men...yeares ends.* SEYMOUR-SMITH (1972): "The problem of why incest is morally 'wrong' has puzzled and fascinated men since antiquity. The most convincing anthropological reason is that marriage between close kin would have led to impossible divisions of, and therefore disputes over, authority. Donne is being baldly ironic (in the face of authoritarian 'horror') in l. 203: he is drawing characteristic attention to an unsolved problem" (243–44).

201–03 *Men...'twas not.* MILGATE (1967): "For other expressions of this 'naturalism,'" see *Relic* 30, *ConfL* 5–8, and *ElChange* 10ff. "The main ancient source was Ovid, *Metamorphoses,* x. 320 ff., often linked, as here, with the problems of peopling the earth when only the children of Adam were living to accomplish it. Cf. Beza, *Tractatio De Polygamia,* 1568 (a copy of which was in Donne's library), pp. 4–5: 'mundi initio...necesse etiam fuerit...sorore a fratre duci', etc.; similarly Annius of Viterbo, *Berosi...antiquitatum...libri quinque,* 1552, p. 44: 'Commiscebantur matribus, filabus, sororibus, et masculis, brutis.' The same material appears in Lydgate's 'Chaucer's Flower of Courtesy' (*Minor Poems,* ed. H. N. MacCracken, E.E.T.S., o.s. 192, p. 421), ll. 64–70; Gower, *Confessio Amantis,* viii. 68–70 ('it was no Sinne / The Sostor forto take hire brother, / Whan that ther was of chois non other'); and Drayton, *Noah's Flood,* ll. 99–100" (180–81).

202 *ingresse;* SULLENS (1964): the *OED* cites Donne as the earliest source for this meaning of the word (249). MILGATE (1967): "enter (carnally), O.E.D. 2 (this being the only instance quoted)" (181).

203 *Till now...'twas not.* GROSART (1872–73): "'Till now [till they have taken laws] 'twas unlawful, therefore ['twas not] ill or evil.' All this is parenthetical or digressional. Then Donne returns from his digression to his 'sparrow,' and says, 'So jolly is this body that it can move this soul (or bear it along to sympathise with its lust); so free [it is] of kindness ['his' being used as ='its,' and 'kindness' in a punning sense of acts of kind] that, &c." (1:93).

204 *Iolly,* GROSART (1872–73): see *Sat1* 7. "The two senses in which this word is used seem to have arisen from a fusing into one of two similar-sounding words—one from the French 'joli,' the other from the root 'joy,' or from a using of the more foreign 'joli' as a quasi 'joy- ly'" (1:93). MILGATE (1967): "over-confident"

(181). **SHAWCROSS** (1967): "joyous" (318). **SMITH** (1971): "sprightly; bold; lustful" (508).

205 *The bodie…Kindnesses*, **GROSART** (1872–73): Donne "returns from his digression to his 'sparrow,' and says, 'So jolly is the body that it can move this soul (or bear it along to sympathise with its lust); so free [is it] of kindness ['his' being used as = 'its,' and 'kindness' in a punning sense of acts of kind] that, &c." (1:93). **GRIERSON** (1912), emending the received punctuation and rejecting Grosart's interpretation on grounds that "Donne was far too learned an Aristotelian and Scholastic to make the body move the soul, or feel jolly on its own account," paraphrases: "The soul is so glad to be at last able to move (having been imprisoned hitherto in plants which have the soul of growth, not of locomotion or sense), and the body is so free of its kindnesses to the soul, that it, the sparrow, forgets the duty of self-preservation" (2:221–22).

205 *The bodie soe free* **CRAIK AND CRAIK** (1986): "the verb 'is' must be supplied" (263).

205 *free of* **SMITH** (1971): "lavish with" (413).

206–10 *That selfe preseruing…yeares ends.* **GOSSE** (1899): "The little cocksparrow has a brilliant existence, but might have sheltered the Soul longer if it had garnered its forces better; it is a spendthrift of its vital energy, and dies of exhaustion" (1:137). **MILGATE** (1967): "Browne expresses the common belief that 'immoderate salacity, and almost unparallel'd excess of venery…is supposed to shorten the lives of Cocks, Partridges, and Sparrowes' (*Vulgar Errors*, iii. 9). It is the 'Sparrow that neglects his life for love' (Palatine 'Epithalamion', l. 7); but this is only a special case of the general rule that 'Wee kill our selves to propagate our kinde,'" *FirAn* 110. Also, see *Fare* 24–25 (181). **SHAWCROSS** (1967): "Popular was the belief that sexual intercourse shortened one's life" (318). [So also, Warnke (1967, 138) and Seymour-Smith (1972, 244).]

206 *selfe preseruing* **SULLENS** (1964): Donne's use of this word is earlier than the earliest sourced cited by the *OED* (187).

207 *slackneth* **SULLENS** (1964): Donne's use of this meaning of the word is earlier than the earliest source cited by the *OED* (233).

207 *knott* **MILGATE** (1967): "the spirits that tie together the soul and body, and are exhausted by venery." See "That subtile knot, which makes us man," *Ecst* 64 (181). **SHAWCROSS** (1967): "interrelationship" (318).

208 *streytens;* **SULLENS** (1964): Donne's use of this meaning of the word is earlier than the earliest source cited by the *OED* (236). **MILGATE** (1967): "makes firmer" (181). [Similarly, Smith (1971, 508) and Seymour-Smith (1972, 244).] **SHAWCROSS** (1967): "corrects (punningly, to its knotted form again); reforms (by setting it on its proper course); confines and restricts ('straitens')" (318).

209 *Spirit,* **MILGATE** (1967): see note to l. 45 (181). **SEYMOUR-SMITH** (1972): "a pun involving the meaning 'semen'" (244).

210 *three yeares* GROSART (1872–73): "Pliny records a belief that the cock-sparrow only lived a year, the hen longer. Bartholomew states, contrary to Donne, that 'the cock is very jealous of his wife, and fighteth oft for her, as Aristotle saith'" (1:93). MILGATE (1967): "One year is usually given as the life-span of cock-sparrows (from Pliny, *Nat. Hist.* x. 52), though Riolanus says two (*Physiologia*, v. xxvii, *Opera Omnis*, 1610, p. 310). Donne says three years perhaps because in those days things 'did longer last' (l. 192)" (181).

211–15 *Els...pliant Ayre:* SEYMOUR-SMITH (1972): "Had this sparrow not exhausted himself with venery, he might have lived a long life: mankind at this stage of history had not learned the various ways of ensnaring birds" (244).

212 *Gummy blood* GROSART (1872–73): "It would seem that bird-lime was formerly extracted from holly" (1:93). SHAWCROSS (1967): "viscous sap" (318).

213 *birdlyme;* MILGATE (1967): "made of the sticky sap ('gummie blood') of the holly." See *Sat2* 46, and note (181).

214 *inwrapping* SULLENS (1964): Donne's use of this word is earlier than the earliest sourced cited by the *OED* (179).

215 *pliant* MILGATE (1967): "yielding" (181).

216–17 *Man...Leaue.* SEYMOUR-SMITH (1972) notes that because roots or sparrows were not used as aphrodisiacs, "the sparrow was safe from capture for these purposes" (244).

217 *Ask't...Leaue.* GROSART (1872–73): "The sparrow, when eaten, was supposed from its nature to be provocative, like the roots of the mandrake, eringoes, and potatoes. Its gall was alleged to have the same effect, and its dung powdered in wine, and specially its brains and eggs" (1:93). MILGATE (1967): "Certain roots (e.g. of mandrakes, potatoes) and the flesh, eggs, and dung of sparrows, when eaten, were supposed to be aphrodisiac or to aid conception" (181). CRAIK AND CRAIK (1986): "'Ten dozen of sparrows' and 'potato-roots' are among the ingredients of an 'elixir' in Massinger's *A New Way to Pay Old Debts*, II. ii. 17–24" (263).

218 *these* MILGATE (1967): "bird-lime, feigned calls, nets, snares (ll. 213–14)" (181).

219 *streytned* SULLENS (1964): see note to l. 208. MILGATE (1967): "restricted, confined" (181). SHAWCROSS (1967): "punning on the meanings lying prone and stiff, being reformed, and being restricted" (318). SMITH (1971): "in privation" (508). SEYMOUR-SMITH (1972): "sexually temperate, with a pun involving the meaning of the word at line 208, above" (244).

221 *This Cole* SHAWCROSS (1967): "the sparrow, fierily passionate" (319).

224 *Ielly* SULLENS (1964): see note to l. 184.

224 *leauned* SHAWCROSS (1967): "impregnated" (319). PATRIDES (1985): "leavened" (414).

225 *intertouch't* SULLENS (1964): the *OED* cites Donne as the earliest source for

this word (195). **CAREY** (1981): a "fussy verb to invent," it represents the "ultimate convergence of male and female, even in fish" (269–70).

226 *fitted* **SULLENS** (1964): Donne's use of this word is earlier than the earliest sourced cited by the *OED* (180–81).

227 *inform'd* **GROSART** (1872–73): "gave it form" (1:93). [So also, Milgate (1967, 181).]

227 *abled* **MILGATE** (1967): see note to l. 131 (181).

228 *finny* **SULLENS** (1964): Donne's use of this meaning of the word is earlier than the earliest source cited by the *OED* (215).

228 *she did fitt;* **MILGATE** (1967): "The soul works with and through the body to frame it according to its nature; cf. l. 159" (181).

229 *of Parchment,* **SHAWCROSS** (1967): "imaginary; of living matter but not vibrant" (319).

231–37 *When goodlie…it Scorn'd,* **FARMER** (1767) cites these lines "as the source for Milton's lines in *Paradise Lost* IV, 602–4" (qtd. in Shawcross [1991b, 77]).

237 *Scorn'd,* **MILGATE** (1967): "The swan, according to Rabanus Maurus (Migne, *P. L.* cxii. 894), is an allegory of Pride (*superbia*)" (181).

239 *much Such,* **SHAWCROSS** (1967): "many similar fishes" (319).

239 *vnblam'd* **SHAWCROSS** (1967): "unsinning, blameless" (319).

241 *a Prison in a Prison* **SMITH** (1971): "the fish imprisoned the soul and the swan the fish" (508).

243 *digestiue fire* **MILGATE** (1967): "The digestive process is usually spoken of in terms of heat. Burton speaks of the stomach as 'the kitchen, as it were, of the first concoction' (*Anatomy*, part I, sect. I, memb. 2, subsect. 4)" (181). **SEYMOUR-SMITH** (1972): "This is a polite way of saying that the soul was excreted by the swan, whose digestive processes had broken the fish down" (244).

244 *vapourd* **MILGATE** (1967): "A familiar word in Donne's work to describe the soul's leaving the body," as in *Expir* 2 (182).

249 *gone;* **SMITH** (1971): "lost, as an easy prey" (508).

251–60 *Pace…left againe.* **SEYMOUR-SMITH** (1972): "The pike swims through the primitive net which its owner, Adam, has constructed" (244).

253 *retarded:* **SULLENS** (1964): Donne's use of this word is earlier than the earliest sourced cited by the *OED* (187).

254–55 *when Need…catch food,* **MILGATE** (1967): "Cf. Origen, *Contra Celsum*, iv. 76 (Migne, *P. G.* xi. 1147): 'ea causa hominem creasse indifentem, ut penuria ipsa cogeretur artes invenire'. The proverbial form, 'Necessity is the mother of invention', derives ultimately from Aeschlyus, *Prometheus Bound*, l. 514, in its Latin form, 'Artis magistra necessitas'" (182).

254 *Windowes:* **MILGATE** (1967): see *Bait* 20: "'strangling snare, or windowie net'" (182). **SHAWCROSS** (1967): "openings (of the net)" (320).

256 *Curious* **MILGATE** (1967): "ingenious" (182).

257–58 *None…was tane* **GRIERSON** (1912) paraphrases, "The nets were not wrought, as now, to let none scape, but were wrought to get few and those fit for use; as, for example, a ravenous pike, &c" (2:222).

258 *As* **GROSART** (1872–73): "so" (1:93). **NORTON** (1895): "likewise" (1:252).

258 *tane* **SHAWCROSS** (1967): "taken" (320).

259–60 *Who…This wretch,* **MILGATE** (1967): "The ferocity of the pike (*lupus marinus*) is always emphasized" (182).

260 *hardlie* **SMITH** (1971): "with difficulty" (509).

261 *two Deaths* **MILGATE** (1967): "being killed by the pike, or by the owner of the net (presumably Adam)" (182).

262 *Once* **MILGATE** (1967): "for once" (182).

264–68 *And whether…Cares not,* **GRIERSON** (1912): "the manner in which fishes breathe is a matter about which faith is indifferent. Each man may hold what theory he chooses. There is not much obvious relevance in this remark, but Donne has already in this poem touched on the difference between faith and knowledge," and "a vein of restless scepticism runs through the whole" (2:222). **MILGATE** (1967): "The controversy over the manner in which a fish breathes began in Plato's *Timaeus*, 92 b, and in Aristotle, *De Respiratione*, ii–iii, x, xix; it was unsettled in Donne's day, and there are many discussions, e.g. in Rondeletius, *De Piscibus Marinis*, 1554, pp. 96–105, and Cardan, *De Rerum Varietate*, vii. 37 (edition of 1557, pp. 216–21)." Faith cares not "because this is a dispute on the level of knowledge and the senses" (182). **SEYMOUR-SMITH** (1972): "Donne is being ironic at the expense of a type of faith that can ignore facts" (244). **CRAIK AND CRAIK** (1986): "is not an article of faith (and so can be left to speculation)" (263).

264–67 *And whether…and Ayre-like, faith* **MAZZEO** (1957): "there is a curious speculation on the process of respiration in a fish and one of the two explanations Donne gives of this phenomenon is that the fish converts the element of water into the element of air by a process similar to distillation" (111).

266 *working Parts…Lymbecks* **SHAWCROSS** (1967): "fins, such as on water wheels, or a system of retorts (like gills) for mixing and distilling liquid" (320).

266 *Lymbecks* **GROSART** (1872–73): "alembic: said to mean properly the head fitted on to a flask or other distilling vessel. Gesner's *Jewell of Health*, translated by Baker, fol. 23; but used by the same author and others to mean the distilling vessel generally" (1:93). [Similarly, Chambers (1896, 1:228).]

267 *thin* SHAWCROSS (1967): "less dense and resistant" (320).

270 *makes a boord or two.* NORTON (1895): "a nautical phrase equivalent to 'makes a tack or two,' 'swims this way and that'" (1:252). [So also, Milgate (1967, 182).]

271–73 *So far...they are.* SEYMOUR-SMITH (1972): "refers to the phenomenon of refraction" (244).

274 *For game and not for hunger* SEYMOUR-SMITH (1972): "For sport, and not because it is hungry" (244).

274 *Sea-Pye* MILGATE (1967): "the oyster-catcher, a bird of the sea-shore" (182). SHAWCROSS (1967): "(*Haematopus ostralegus*)" (320).

275 *trayterous spectacle* MILGATE (1967): "'a means of seeing' (*O.E.D.* II. 5); window, or mirror" (182). SEYMOUR-SMITH (1972): "'deceitful mirror', i.e. what the bird sees is an illusion, see ll. 271–3: the pike was really smaller" (244).

276 *Silly* MILGATE (1967): "foolish, harmless, pitiable" (182).

276 *disputing* MILGATE (1967): "arguing with itself, hesitating" (182). SEYMOUR-SMITH (1972): "which way to go (which 'boord' to make)" (244).

278–80 *Exalted...food.* SEYMOUR-SMITH (1972) paraphrases as "She is exalted (raised on high), but for the good of the one who raised her." Notes that this is an "apt comment on Kings, Queens, Princes—and their favourites" (244).

280 *Rais'd to be...and food.* GRIERSON (1912) says the line is "to be taken as an aphorism" and paraphrases it as "to be exalted is often to become the instrument and prey of him who has exalted you" (2:222).

280 *Instruments* SHAWCROSS (1967): "helper" (321).

281–90 *Is any...Distruction.* PAYNE (1926): Donne's "preoccupation with the unfairness of life, so evident throughout the poem, finds vent in a stanza which might have irked his great biographer" (80). EVETT (1986): the stanza, "on the hard lot of fish," is a "noetic-realist insert" in Donne's "fully articulated renascence grotesquerie" (128).

281 *kind* SHAWCROSS (1967): "species" (321).

281 *rape* SHAWCROSS (1967): "seizure and plunder" (321).

290 *And Lawes...Distruction.* GROSART (1872–73): "In Elizabeth's reign fish-days were enacted, not as religious fast-days, but to encourage the fish-trade and our breed of seamen" (1:94). NORTON (1895): "During the reign of Elizabeth the change in the national religion and the consequent diminution of fasts and fish-days led to the decline of the fishing industry: some fishermen turned pirates, others ceased to follow the sea. In 1564 an act was passed for the maintenance of the navy, one of the clauses of which, enacted with intent to encourage seamanship, was that Wednesdays and Saturdays through the year should be fish-days on which it should not be lawful to eat flesh, under penalty of three pounds or imprisonment for three months. See

Statutes of the Realm, 5 Eliz. c. 5; cf. also *Acts of Privy Council*, New Series, vol. vii, 1558–1570. London, 1893" (1:252). [Similarly, Shawcross (1967, 321) and Milgate (1967, 182), who adds that "a more general reference" also applies "to fasts ordained by the Church, including the forty days of Lent."] SEYMOUR-SMITH (1972): "The hapless fish here may well stand for people in general, subject to the whims and fancies of the powerful: the answer to the famous question of l. 281 may well be: 'mankind'" (245).

290 *Lents* SHAWCROSS (1967): "referring to the period of forty fast days before Easter" (321).

291 *selfe* SMITH (1971): "same" (509).

293 *cares not* MILGATE (1967): "although a shore-bird" (182).

294 *best Orator;* MILGATE (1967): "A loose phrase, meaning, perhaps, that the bird proclaims gluttony by its indifference to the danger of being blown out to sea" (182). SMITH (1971): "advocate, representative" (509). SEYMOUR-SMITH (1972): "the bird is a most apt advertisement for gluttony: heedless of consequences, it destroys itself" (245). CRAIK AND CRAIK (1986): "Because his latest meal has given him strength he is an argument in favour of gluttony" (263).

298 *Soules noe longer foes,* MILGATE (1967): "Enmity is felt in the soul, in its sensible faculty (cf. Burton, *Anatomy*, part. 1, sect. 1, memb. 2, subsect. 8), but (sect. 2, memb. 3, subsect. 1) the real cause of passions lies in the 'bad humours' of the body. Hence, despite ll. 506–8 below, the enmity of these two 'sensible' souls ceased when they entered new bodies. Cf. l. 371" (183). SMITH (1971): "the soul's former foes who are so no longer" (509). SEYMOUR-SMITH (1972): "The soul of the oyster-catcher would of course have been an enemy of the soul, whose progress this poem traces, in the seized pike; but as soon as these souls leave their respective bodies (which are, as predator and preyed upon, enemies) they cease from enmity" (245).

298 *two waies did erre,* SHAWCROSS (1967): "by gluttony and by sloth" (321).

298 *erre,* GROSART (1872–73): "go, wander away" (1:94).

299 *follow* SULLENS (1964): Donne's use of this meaning of the word is earlier than the earliest source cited by the OED (216).

300 *liues* MILGATE (1967): "i.e. as a creature preying on others 'for game and not for hunger' (l. 274)" (183).

300 *Officer.* SHAWCROSS (1967): "governmental official" (321). SMITH (1971): "some great state official still typically embodies the bird's nature as the best advocate of gluttony, who seizes small fry for more sport when he is not hungry" (509). [So also, Craik and Craik (1986, 263).]

302 *throwne out* MILGATE (1967): "as a complete creature (It had been 'thrown in' as a pure soul)" (183). SMITH (1971): "put forth, extended" (509). CRAIK AND CRAIK (1986): "delivered (whales are viviparous)" (263).

303 *vastnesse* **SULLENS** (1964): Donne's use of this meaning of the word is earlier than the earliest source cited by the OED (242).

304 *Morea* **MILGATE** (1967): "Morea was a name for the Peloponnesus, which Donne here imagines as separated across the Isthmus of Corinth and from the sea-bed, 'swimming' like an island. [So also, Shawcross (1967, 321).] The idea of floating islands was a commonplace (cf. Pliny, *Nat. Hist.* ii. 96). For the comparison of a mighty fish to such an island cf. *Paradise Lost*, i. 200 ff. and vii. 412–15. Bartholomew says that bushes grow on the whale's back 'so that that great Fish seemeth an Ilande' (*Batman upon Bartholome*, 1582, f. 200v)" (183).

306 *seuered* **SMITH** (1971): "Pronounced as three syllables" (509).

307 *hopefull Promontories head,* **MILGATE** (1967): "tip of the Cape of Good Hope; 'Caput' (head, cape) 'Bonae Spei.' For the use of the adjective, compare 'learned tree', l. 78" (183). **CRAIK AND CRAIK** (1986): "The Cape of Good Hope has a mountain (Table Mountain) upon it" (263).

307 *hopefull* **SULLENS** (1964): "no O.E.D. definition fits this play on words" (260).

308 *when all hopes faile* **GRIERSON** (1912): plays "with the idea of 'the hopefull Promontory', or Cape of Good Hope" (2:222). **MILGATE** (1967): "of giving an adequate image of the whale" (183).

309–10 *without Saile / Hulling* **GROSART** (1872–73): "making a vessel like a (mere) hull, by taking in all or almost all sail. This is done either in calms or when a ship is lying to in a storm" (1:94). **MILGATE** (1967): "Fynes Moryson writes (*Itinerary*, edition of 1907, ii. 106): 'the windes were so contrary, as wee were forced to strike sayles, and lie at hull (that is, tossed to and fro by the waves)'" (183). **SHAWCROSS** (1967): "striking the side of the ship" (322). **CRAIK AND CRAIK** (1986): "The (young) whale is compared to a ship in a storm ('when all hopes fail'), capsized ('overset') or floating dismasted" (263).

309 *ouersett* **MILGATE** (1967): "capsized" (183).

311–20 *At euery...firmament.* **PATMORE** (1846): "Here is a description of Leviathan in the style of Milton, who made him 'swim the ocean stream'" (235). **GOSSE** (1899): Donne "outdoes himself in the preposterous description of this monster, which seems to be copied from a print in some fabulous book of voyages," and stands as "an example of style misapplied" (1:137).

311 *stroke* **SULLENS** (1964): Donne's use of this meaning of the word is earlier than the earliest source cited by the OED (236).

313 *Then* **PATRIDES** (1985): "than" (418).

315 *Bark* **GROSART** (1872–73): "skin." See ElJeal 4 ("sere barke") (1:94). **SHAWCROSS** (1967): "tough outer skin" (322).

320 *Seas aboue the firmament.* **MILGATE** (1967): see Gen. 1.7, 9. "The location of these waters caused great perplexity among commentators. Aquinas discusses the

two possibilities (S. T., *Ia pars*, q. lxviii, art. 2): either they were situated above the 'firmament' of fixed stars, or (like the 'sphere' of water in the Ptolemaic system) in the upper air. In either case Donne's hyperbole holds" (183).

321–22 *He hunts…owne Nett* GRIERSON (1912) cites the following passages from the *Sermons*: "A confidence in their owne strengths, a sacrificing to their own Nets, an attributing of their securitie to their own wisdome or power, may also retard the cause of God" (4:191); "And though some of the Fathers pared somewhat too neare the quick in this point, yet it was not as in the Romane Church, to lay snares, and spread nets for gain" (7:377); and "The Holy Spirit, the Spirit of comfort comes to him" (i.e., "the courtier"), "but hee will die in his old religion, which is to sacrifice to his owne Nets, by which his portion is plenteous" (3:236). Notes that the net image is "probably derived" from Jer. 5.26: "For among my people are found wicked men; they lay wait as he that setteth snares; they set a trap, they catch men." Also compares Ps. 10.9: "he lieth in wait to catch the poor: he doth catch the poor when he draweth him into his net" (2:223). MILGATE (1967): "The officer needs only to stay where he can be found to act as a snare for those who come to seek his favours" (183).

323 *inthrall;* SEYMOUR-SMITH (1972): "enslave" (245).

324 *wantoning* MILGATE (1967): "taking his pleasure, like Leviathan" in Ps. 104.26 (183).

325–30 *And in…must die?* SEYMOUR-SMITH (1972): "The whale is clearly compared to the state (rather than, I think, to an individual prince). Cf. the trope underlying Hobbes's *Leviathan*" (245).

327 *Flier and follower* SMITH (1971): "pursued and pursuer" (510).

328 *States* SMITH (1971): "conditions of people; realms" (510).

333 *roomefull* SULLENS (1964): the *OED* cites Donne as the earliest source for this word (200). SMITH (1971): "roomy" (510). [So also, Seymour-Smith (1972, 245).]

334 *And like a Prince* MILGATE (1967) cites *Sermons*, 8:117: "My soule may be King, that is, reside principally in my heart, or in my braine, but it neglects not the remoter parts of my body." Notes that the "orthodox belief was that the soul was equally in all parts of the body: 'Nam singulis sui corporis particulis tota [anima] praesto est, cum tota sentit in singulis…ubique tanta est, quia ubique tota est' (St. Augustine, Migne, P. L. xlii. 185). Cf. Aristotle, *De Anima*, 411b; Aquinas, S.T., *Ia pars*, q. lxxvi, art. 8; Franciscus Georgius, *Problemata*, 1574, f. 78a; etc." (184). SMITH (1971): see *Ecst* 65–68 (510).

336–37 *The Sun…Parched* MILGATE (1967): "twenty years have passed. In the Zodiac (a belt of the celestial sphere extending eight or nine degrees on each side of the ecliptic, within which the apparent movements of the heavenly bodies were supposed to take place) the Crab (Cancer) and the Goat (Capricornus) are chosen here as being two divisions furthest apart; they are in fact the solstitial positions of the sun, which passes through all divisions once a year" (184).

338–40 *Tis greatest...no Station.* **BROWNING** (1878) quotes and praises these three lines in stanza 114 of "The Two Poets of Croisic" ([2003, 14:182]).

339 *There's noe...Perfection,* **SMITH** (1971): "human affairs do not stay still; having reached perfection one cannot arrest the movement there" (510).

340 *period* **SMITH** (1971): "a time when it is at its height; an end" (510).

340 *Station.* **MILGATE** (1967): "permanent resting-place (O.E.D. 1. 1–3). A man can be great for a time but cannot remain so" (184).

342–43 *not throughly...kill him,* **SMITH** (1971): "not wholly fortified by the hope of killing the vastly bigger fish" (510).

345 *thence* **MILGATE** (1967): "from the torn flesh" (184).

345 *out sweat)* **GROSART** (1872–73) (reading "outstreat"): "For the sake of the rhyme straight or straught, the past forms of stretch, is brought down to 'streat.' The sense is—nor suck those oils which [were] thence outstretched or outdrawn, or (if we take the verb not in a passive sense, but as neuter-reflective) which thence stretched [themselves] out, or exuded, or poured out" (1:94). **SULLENS** (1964) (reading "outstreat") notes that the OED cites Donne as the earliest source for this word (197). **MILGATE** (1967) (reading "outstreat"): "'outstretch', used...loosely for 'exude'. Whale oil was still rather a mystery. See Browne's account of the whale cast up in Norfolk, *Vulgar Errors,* iii. 26" (184).

346–47 *it might...were twoe* **SMITH** (1971): "the fact that there were two plotters might have wrecked the plot altogether because in the normal way of human affairs they would seek to betray one another" (510). **SEYMOUR-SMITH** (1972): "an apt illustration of Donne's cynical mood" (245).

349–50 *How shall...wreak?* **SMITH** (1971): "how may a despotic ruler hope to thwart shrewd and powerful plots against him when miserable wretches can so easily revenge the petty grievances of the common people upon him!" (510).

349 *Proiects* **MILGATE** (1967): "plots, schemes" (184).

350 *them* **CRAIK AND CRAIK** (1986): "tyrants" (264).

351–60 *The flaile-fin'd...Companies.* **NORTON** (1895): "In Spenser's *Visions of the World's Vanitie* there is a description of the killing of the whale by the sword-fish," which "may have afforded the suggestion" of this stanza (1:252).

351 *flaile-fin'd* **SULLENS** (1964): the OED cites Donne as the earliest source for the meaning of this word (247).

351 *Thresher* **MILGATE** (1967): "'thrasher', the sea-fox or fox-shark, 'so called from the very long upper division of the tail with which it lashes an enemy' (O.E.D.)" (184). **SHAWCROSS** (1967): "a shark which rounds up fish by flailing its great tail" (323).

351 *Steelebeak'd* **SULLENS** (1964): a word combination that the OED does not record (206).

353–59 *The thresher…tirant dies* **MILGATE** (1967) notes that the "essential detail of this battle is given by Bartholomew (*Batman upon Bartholome*, Book xiii, 1582, f. 200v)," but quotes the "livelier statement" from "'Newes from the Barmudas', 1613 (in *Tracts and Other Papers…*, ed. P. Force, 1844, iii. 3. 22): 'Likewise there commeth in two other Fishes with them, but such, as the Whale had rather bee without their company; one is called a Sword-fish, the other a Threasher: the Sword-fish swimmes under the Whale, and pricketh him upward; the Threasher keepeth above him, and with a mightie great thing like unto a flaile, hee so bangeth the Whale, that hee will roare as though it thundered, and doth give him such blowes, with his weapon, that you would thinke it to be a cracke of great shot.'" Points to Spenser, *Visions of the World's Vanity*, ll. 62ff., and "earlier, of a different 'exemplum,' l. 28: 'So by the small the great is oft diseased'" (184).

353 *backs him*, **CRAIK AND CRAIK** (1986): "gets behind the whale" (264).

353 *to beat* **SMITH** (1971): "to lash the whale with its tail" (511).

359 *Scoffe* **SULLENS** (1964): Donne's use of this meaning of the word is earlier than the earliest source cited by the *OED* (231).

360 *(his owne Dole)* **GROSART** (1872–73) glosses as "share, portion: from the verb to 'deal'" and cites Hall (*Satires*, b. iv. s. ii.): "more than is some hungry gallant's 'dole'" (1:94). **MILGATE** (1967): "portion, thing distributed; he is himself what he distributes as dole" (184). **SMITH** (1971): "(a) he distributes rewards or alms still as a great being should, but the alms now is his own substance; (b) he is his own grief, no one else mourns for him" (511).

366–68 *Nor will…that Act,* **MILGATE** (1967): "Their love for the dead king should make them act against his slayers (but he cannot now reward their loyalty)" (185). **SMITH** (1971): "there is no point now…because he is dead and cannot appreciate the gesture" (511).

369–70 *that of…they lose,* **SMITH** (1971): "they think that love shown for a dead ruler diminishes the love which they themselves should have from their subjects" (511).

371 *and passion* **MILGATE** (1967): "The soul is subject to the effects of passion only while it is imprisoned in the body. Cf. note to l. 298" (185). **SEYMOUR-SMITH** (1972): "When Donne says that the soul, having got into a mouse, still has some small indignation, he is making fun of the convolutions of theology. This soul is playfully permitted some 'human feelings'" (245–46).

375 *streight Cloister* **MILGATE** (1967): "narrow confines. 'Cloister', *O.E.D.* 1" (185).

375 *Mouse* **MILGATE** (1967): "Pouring scorn on the idea of metempsychosis, Antonius Brunus (*Entelechia*, 1597, of which Donne owned a copy) points out the absurdity of the idea that the same soul could be in great and little creatures: 'ut ex homine in elephantum, ex elephanto in culicem, aut formicam immigrare cogamur' (p. 137)" (185).

379–80 *late taught…Be slayne,* **MILGATE** (1967): "An example of the soul's ability to remember what occurred in a previous incarnation, and to 'keep some quality' (ll. 506–7), usually evil, of the life she formerly led" (185).

381–400 *Natures…whither come.* **GRIERSON** (1912) cites *Sermons*, 10:134: regardless of how natural creatures "differ in bignesse, yet they have some proportion to one another, we consider that some very little creatures, contemptible in themselves, are yet called enemies to great creatures, as the Mouse is to the Elephant." Notes also *Devotions* (p. 62), "How great an Elephant, how small a mouse destroys" (2:223).

382 *harmles* **MILGATE** (1967): "So Pliny, *Nat. Hist.* viii. 7, 'nec nisi lacessiti nocent', etc. Topsell, *History of Four-footed Beasts*, 1607, following the traditional lore as found in Gesner, enlarges on the elephant's fidelity, love of flowers and of beautiful women, chastity, modesty, and tractability; 'Their love and concord with all mankind is most notorious' (p. 208)" (185).

383–84 *who thought…to be iust* **GROSART** (1872–73): "the elephant did not seek to be intellectually or cunningly wise after the world's wisdom, and like a tyrant, great one, or statesman, but sought to be morally wise and good" (1:94).

385 *(Yet nature…to bend)*, **GROSART** (1872–73) admits to not knowing "the originator of this belief, for Pliny, and Bartholomew following him, make him able to kneel" (1:94). **NORTON** (1895): "'There generally passes as opinion that it [the elephant] hath no joints, and this absurdity is seconded with another, that, being unable to lie down, it sleepeth against a tree…which conceit is not the daughter of later times, but is an old and grey-headed error, even in the days of Aristotle.' Sir Thomas Browne, *Vulgar and Common Errors*, iii, 1" (1:253). **MILGATE** (1967): "Aristotle states the theory only to refute it (*De incessu animalium*, 709a, 712a), and Pliny (viii. 1), Bartholomew, and Topsell (p. 196) say the elephant can kneel. The idea was, however, irresistible and turns up with wearisome frequency (as in Rowley, *All's Lost by Lust*, 1633, C3v: 'Stubborn as an elephant's leg, no bending in her')" (185). **SMITH** (1971): "The point here is their innocence, in that they have not learned to crawl to great men for advancement" (511). **SEYMOUR-SMITH** (1972): "it is unlikely that Donne himself believed this, which was better known, amongst writers, as a fallacy than as a fact" (246).

386 *Himself he vpprops*, **MILGATE** (1967): "Topsell says that after they grow old elephants do not lie down or strain their legs 'by reason of their great weight, but take their rest leaning to a tree' (p. 196)" (185).

386 *vpprops*, **SULLENS** (1964): a word combination that the *OED* does not record (207).

388 *vext* **MILGATE** (1967): "The subject of the verb is 'dreames': no horrible dreams troubled his fancy" (185).

388 *Phantasie* **SMITH** (1971): "imagination" (511).

390 *remissly* **MILGATE** (1967): "both 'carelesly' (l. 389), and 'slack'" (185).

391–95 *In which…tumbled Downe;* **GROSART** (1872–73): "'Of all other living creatures, they [elephants] cannot abide a mouse or rat, and if they perceiue that their provender lying in the manger tast or scent never so little of them, they refuse it and will not touch it' (Holland's *Pliny*, book viii c. 11)" (1:94). **NORTON** (1895): "In Spenser's *Visions of the World's Vanitie* there is a description of the killing…of the elephant by the creeping of an ant, 'a silly worm,' into his nostrils, which may have afforded the suggestion" of this episode (1:252). **MILGATE** (1967): "Though the elephant's fear of rodents was a commonplace (from Pliny, *Nat. Hist.* viii. 10) nothing is heard of the ability of the mouse to kill the elephant by gnawing its brain until Elizabethan times. The source of the idea seems to have been a study of the spices and simples of India by a Portugese physician, Garcia de Orta, published in *Goa* (1563). A Latin translation by Charles de l'Escluze (Clusius) published in 1567, *Aromatum, et simplicium aliquot medicamentorum apud indos nascentium Historia*, became very popular." The elephant's "carelessness (l. 389) lies in its not having knotted its trunk. Cf. *Locrine* (published 1595), v. i. 83–84: 'Have you not seene a mightie elephant / Slaine by the biting of a silly mouse?'" (185–86).

393 *the Soules bed Chamber*, **MILGATE** (1967): "It was disputed whether the seat of the soul was the heart, brain, liver, or blood" (see *Sermons*, 1:192, 4:294). Donne "selects the brain here, as more satisfactorily explaining the destruction of the elephant" (186).

394 *life Cords* **SMITH** (1971): "All the body's nerves and sinews were assumed to emanate from the controlling brain" (see *Fun* 9–11) (511).

398 *Roome*, **GROSART** (1872–73): "station or state" (1:95). [Similarly, Norton (1895, 1:253), Milgate (1967, 186), and Seymour-Smith (1972, 246).]

399 *Tombe*, **SULLENS** (1964): Donne's use of this meaning of the word is earlier than the earliest source cited by the *OED* (239).

400 *Who cares…whither come.* **SMITH** (1971): "a desperado who has no care for his own life may accomplish anything" (512).

400 *any whither* **SHAWCROSS** (1967): "to any place" (324).

403 *It could…as goe.* **GROSART** (1872–73) says that he does not know "where Donne got this idea. Bartholomew says, 'the wolfe whelpeth blind whelpes'" (1:95).

405–06 (*Who in…first Type*) **GRIERSON** (1912): "The trade is the shepherd's; in it Abel is type both of Church and Kingdom, Emperor and Pope" (2:223). **MILGATE** (1967): as the "first shepherd" (Gen. 4.2), Abel is "the earliest 'type' of the Church; cf. Peter Lombard, Migne, *P.L.* cxci. 1121 ('Ecclesia…cuius primitiae fuit sanctus Abel'), Augustine, *P.L.* xxxvii. 1589, and Ambrose, *P.L.* xiv. 318. He is also the desirable type of a king: 'refert praeterea imaginem quandam regalis administrationis & gubernationis: talem enim decet esse regem erga sibi subditos, qualiter pastor gregem suum regit' (Pererius, *Comment. et Disput. in Genesim*, 1601, vii, p. 330 b)" (186). **SHAWCROSS** (1967): "the second son of Adam and Eve, 'a keeper of sheep,' who was slain by his older brother Cain, 'a tiller of the ground,' because the Lord respected Abel and his offering. He is 'the first type' because he was martyred for his proper tending of his flock, as Jesus was" (325). **SEYMOUR-SMITH** (1972): Donne's "use of the word 'trade' is not complimentary" (246).

406 *still* **MILGATE** (1967): "continually" (186).

407 *wolfe,* **SHAWCROSS** (1967): "the context suggests the wolf that does not enter by the door to catch and scatter the sheep" (John 10.1–18) (325).

416 *Attach'd* **SHAWCROSS** (1967): "also implying 'attacked'" (325).

416 *gripes,* **SHAWCROSS** (1967): "grips, clasps" (325).

418 *show* **SHAWCROSS** (1967): "(resistance)" (325).

419–20 *nor needs…nor goe.* **SEYMOUR-SMITH** (1972): "because she is enjoying it" (246).

419 *Now much resist,* **GRIERSON** (1912) (reading "Nor <make> resist"): "the O.E.D. cites from Lodge, *Forbonius and Priscilla* (1585), 'I make no resist in this my loving torment', and other examples dated 1608 and 1630. Donne is fond of verbal nouns retaining the form of the verb unchanged" (2:223). [So also, Milgate (1967, 186).] **SEYMOUR-SMITH** (1972): "The meaning is: 'nor does the sheep-dog now show much resistance'" (246).

419 *streighten* **MILGATE** (1967): "confine, restrict the movements of, 'coerce'" (186).

420 *were* **MILGATE** (1967): "even were (she free)" (186).

421 *engag'd* **SULLENS** (1964): Donne's use of this meaning of the word is earlier than the earliest source cited by the *OED* (213). **MILGATE** (1967): "won over, persuaded; or possibly, 'entered into love's combat' (as one engages an enemy)" (186). [So also, Smith (1971, 512).] **SEYMOUR-SMITH** (1972): "(i) bound by obligation; (ii) fascinated; (iii) won over; (iv) entangled" (246).

424 *faines* **PATRIDES** (1985): "feigns" (423).

428–30 *And now…did passe.* **ALLEN** (1943): "The theory of conception at this time was very simple. The male and female sperms were drawn from the purest blood in the sanguinary mass. Riolanus writes, 'Semen fit ex pinguiore & puriore sanguinis'; Vicary states, 'this sparme that commeth both of man and woman, is made & gathered of the most best and purest drops of blood in all the body.' After the blood of the parents is mingled concoction takes place in the womb," and "'as the Renet and mylke make the cheese, so doth the sparme of man and woman make the generation of the Embreon.'" Further, "after concoction took place, the foetus began to develop according to the schedule" Donne mentions in *Metem* st. 50 (334–35). **MILGATE** (1967): Donne's "account of the formation of the embryo here and in ll. 494ff. is that commonly accepted, and is orthodox in every detail. Cf. *Batman upon Bartholome,* 1582, vi. 4, and Thomas Vicary, *The Anatomy of the Body of Man* (1548, as re-issued 1577, ed. F. J. and P. Furnivall, *E.E.T.S.,* Extra Ser. liii, 1888)" (186).

429–30 *that Mas / Of Blood* **MILGATE** (1967): Donne "telescopes the [gestation] process here, since the soul was thought normally to enter the body only when 'al the other members be perfectly shapen' (Vicary)" (186). **SEYMOUR-SMITH** (1972): "The wolf has impregnated the sheep-dog bitch, and so the soul leaves the trapped and slain wolf and enters into its own unborn progeny" (246).

429 *quick* **GROSART** (1872–73): "living. See Mr. W. Aldis Wright's *Bible Word-Book*, s.v." (1:95).

431 *Some haue…some begott* **MILGATE** (1967): "By marrying their daughters in the first case, and having sexual relations with their mothers in the second. Cf. note to ll. 201–3; of the second case Oedipus is the best-known example" (186). **CRAIK AND CRAIK** (1986): "By marrying their daughters they have (previously) begotten their wives; by having sexual relations with their mothers they have (subsequently) begotten their sisters" (264).

432–40 *But in…play.* **SEYMOUR-SMITH** (1972): this "delightful passage should not be taken too seriously," for "the mocking tone is unmistakable" (246).

432 *the liues of Emperors* **MILGATE** (1967): "Presumably a reference to Suetonius, 'Lives of the Caesars', especially Nero and Domitian" (187).

434–36 *This Wolfe…and father too,* **FLYNN** (1987): the wolf's death and subsequent embodiment in its own offspring suggests the Secretary of State succession from William to Robert Cecil, "ever more corrupt and dominant Councilors of the Queen" (165).

434–35 *This Wolfe…was dead;* **SHAWCROSS** (1967): "That is, since the soul within the wolf passes into the offspring of the wolf and Abel's dog, it is as if the wolf has begotten himself, is his own father and his own son, begins to live at the moment he dies" (326).

434 *begatte himselfe* **PATRIDES** (1985): "i.e. his lust was passed to his offspring" (423).

436–38 *he is…Name:* **MILGATE** (1967): "The reincarnation of the father's soul in the son makes this creature, as it were, the personification of lust—a lust which is 'puzzling', 'enigmatic', and which is a sin that the Schoolmen could not classify" (see *Sat2* 35–38) (187). **SMITH** (1971): "a form of sexual perversity that finds excitement in an enigma" (512). [Similarly, Craik and Craik (1986, 265).]

437 *ridling* **SULLENS** (1964): the *OED* cites Donne as the earliest source for the meaning of this word (252).

437 *Scholemen* **SHAWCROSS** (1967): "those medieval academicians who disputed minor differences among things, attempting to classify them into specific categories" (326).

438 *both these* **MILGATE** (1967): "Abel's bitch and the wolf" (187).

439 *Moaba* **CHAMBERS** (1896) says that he does not know "where Donne got" or if he "invented this name, together with the Siphatecia of l. 457, the Thelemite of

l. 487, and the Themech of l. 509" (2:241). **GRIERSON** (1912) says that "'Moaba', 'Siphatecia' (l. 457), 'Tethlemite' (l. 487), and 'Themech' (l. 509) are not creatures of Donne's invention, but derived from his multifarious learning," but also acknowledges the difficulty of detecting the "immediate source from which he drew." Finds that the "ultimate source of all these additions to the Biblical narrative and persons was the activity of the Jewish intellect and imagination in the interval between the time at which the Old Testament closes and the dispersion under Titus and Vespasian, the desire of the Jews in Palestine and Alexandria to 'round off the Biblical narrative, fill up the lacunae, answer all the questions of the inquiring mind of the ancient reader.'" Cites and quotes from a number of medieval and later works, including the *Chronicle of Jerahmeel*, that convey traditional Hebraic notions (2:223–24). **MILGATE** (1967) also cites the *Chronicle of Jerahmeel*, describing it as "a fourteenth century work, preserving with great accuracy a text which, translated into Greek about a thousand years earlier and then into Latin, appeared in a work falsely attributed to Philo Judaeus; it was abstracted in the compilation of Annius of Viterbo mentioned in the note on l. 21 above, and published in full (among genuine works by Philo) in *Philonis Judaei Alexandrini. Libri Antiquitatum...*, 1527, edited by Budaeus." Says that Donne "seems to have supplemented the pseudo-Philo from another source, or to have used a version of the work which had itself been supplemented" (187). **SHAWCROSS** (1967): "Moab was the son of Lot and his eldest daughter. Donne uses a feminine form of the name to indicate Moab's incestuous birth" (326). **SEYMOUR-SMITH** (1972): "Donne is drawing attention to the fact that all the earliest unions, even as recorded in scripture, were incestuous. Theologians had given attention to the problems raised by this, but without humor" (246).

443 *For...kinds made* **MILGATE** (1967): "a syllable is dropped after the medial pause" (187).

446 *Cousen'd* **MILGATE** (1967): "cheated" (187). [So also, Smith (1971, 513).] **SHAWCROSS** (1967): "deceived Abel by protecting the sheep" (326).

447 *hopeles...were hid,* **SMITH** (1971): "having no hope of keeping up the deceit" (513).

448 *followed:* **SMITH** (1971): "Pronounced as three syllables" (513).

449 *From dogs...he fledd* **SEYMOUR-SMITH** (1972): "To the dogs he was a wolf, to the wolves he was a dog" (246).

450 *perished.* **SMITH** (1971): "Pronounced as three syllables" (513).

451 *It* **SEYMOUR-SMITH** (1972): "the soul" (247).

451 *quickned* **SHAWCROSS** (1967): "enlivened, gave life to" (326).

451 *toyfull Ape,* **JANSON** (1952): the ape was "kept as a pet by the descendants of Adam. The simian gradually realises his quasi-human status, falls in love with Adam's fifth daughter, Siphatecia, and is about to seduce her when her brother, Tethlemite, drives him off with a stone" (273). Since Donne "imputes a quasi-human feeling of love to the simian, we are tempted to assume that he was familiar with the fourteenth

century 'exemplum' of the ape and the poor girl, the only previous instance, so far as we know, of this particular feature. Surely the admirer of Siphatecia, 'the first true lover,' cannot be explained solely on the basis of the crudely sexual apes-who-lead-maids-in-hell, or of the 'Martin ape' who, in an English play of 1589, attempted to violate the Lady Divinity on-stage" (274–75). Further, "Donne's ape resembles men not only because 'his organs…so like theirs hee doth finde' but also in his impulse to sin, to 'reach at things too high,' so that his attempted seduction of Siphatecia becomes the simian equivalent of the Fall of Man. In fact his only animal quality is that he 'cannot laugh, and speake his minde.' Here Donne voices a startlingly 'modern' thought, which anticipates the eighteenth century notion, held by Pope, Monboddo, and others that anthropoid apes are 'mute philosophers.' While the first specimen of an anthropoid ape to reach Western Europe did not arrive until about forty years after the date of 'The Progresse of the Soule,' there are occasional references to man-like simians in the accounts of Elizabethan travellers, as well as in the zoological writings of the period," and "however that may be, with the seventeenth century our motif became part of the literature of adventure and exploration. Presented as a true experience in some remote corner of the world, the story gained a new flavour of authenticity, until it was eventually accepted as one of the established facts of natural history. The archetype of this version of the 'rape-ape' theme appears to be a tale from Francesco Maria Guazzo's *Compendium Maleficarum* (Milan, 1608) concerning a woman who was deported to an island populated by apes. One of them led her into a cave, brought her fruit, and finally raped her. She had two children by him before she was rescued" (275). **MILGATE** (1967): "Topsell takes from Gesner a brief account (*The History of four-footed Beasts*, 1607, p. 10) of a kind of 'Munkey' very like a man: 'he loveth women and children dearly, like other of his own kind, and is so venerious, that he will attempt to ravish women'. The description, he says, 'was taken forth of the booke of the description of the holy Land'; more directly, it comes from Cardan, *De Subtilitate*, x (edition of 1560, p. 323). The baboon was said to have similar traits; cf. Aelian, *Nat. Animal.* vii. 19, xv. 14" (187–88). **SHAWCROSS** (1967): "amorous and sportive" (326).

452 *Gamesome* **SMITH** (1971): "playful" (513).

454 *Organs* **SHAWCROSS** (1967): "bodily parts" (327).

455–56 *cannot laugh…He wonders* **MILGATE** (1967) points to *Coryat* 13–14: "If man be therefore man, because he can / Reason, and laugh" and notes that Aristotle "says that man is 'the only animal that laughs' (*De Partibus Animalium*, 673a) and that reason distinguishes man from the lower animals (*Magna Moralia*, 1189a); hence laughter and speech, or laughter and reason, are often coupled as the distinguishing marks of man." Argues that the phrase "He wonders" (l. 456) "suggests a power of reasoning in the ape which, strictly speaking, it could not possess" (188).

459 *tumbles* **CRAIK AND CRAIK** (1986): "performs 'somersaults' (l. 465)" (265).

460 *true Louer* **MILGATE** (1967): "of the conventional sort, adopting the fashionable poses of the 'true lover'" (188). **SEYMOUR-SMITH** (1972): "There is of

course considerable satirical point in Donne's making of this first (and wisest) 'true', i.e. conventionally love-sick—and 'romantic'—lover into an ape" (247).

461 *He was...more desir'd* **MILGATE** (1967): "by contrast with the more usual practice (cf. ll. 195–203) [incest] before the coming of the law" (188). **SEYMOUR-SMITH** (1972): "cynically defines romantic love: the first creature to experience sexual preference was this absurd ape, who in this stanza is pictured as a fashionable Elizabethan lover—who is thus, by implication, condemned as incapable of speech, i.e. inarticulate" (247).

462 *another,* **GROSART** (1872–73) argues against the alternate reading "the other," which would "limit him to two, as though he were Isaac, whereas he is speaking of such community as exists among the sparrows" (1:95).

465 *Vaulters sobresalts,* **GROSART** (1872–73) (reading as "sombersalts"): "From other writings it appears that the lovers of Elizabeth's days used to woo their mistresses with, and vaunt their feats of activity on, the vaulting horse. Sombersalts means any such feats of leaping, not summersets merely as now understood. Cf. Cotgrave. Mercury [describing Hedon, a court gallant] '...He courts ladies with how many great horse he hath rid that morning, or how oft he hath done the whole or half the pommado [vaulting the wooden horse] in a seven-night before: and sometimes ventures so far upon the virtue of his pomander, that he dares tell 'em how many shirts he has sweat at tennis that week' (Cynthia's Revels, act ii. sc. 1)" (1:95). **MILGATE** (1967): see *H5* 5.2.138ff. (188).

465 *sobresalts,* **SULLENS** (1964) (reading "somersaults") notes that the *OED* cites Donne as the earliest source for the meaning of this word (254).

466 *hoiting* **GROSART** (1872–73) believes the word derives from "hoi," a term "used by swineherds" for "a stupid lumpish fellow" and for one who is "riotous, like one who cries hoi" (1:95). **CHAMBERS** (1896): "rioting; expressing noisy mirth" (2:241). **BEWLEY** (1966): "romping" (257). **MILGATE** (1967): "Bartholomew was apparently the first to say that the ape can be taught 'to leape and play in divers manner wise' (*Batman upon Bartholome*, 1582, f. 380r; cf. Janson, *Apes and Ape Lore...*, p. 82)" (188).

467–68 *to wreak...on himself;* **MILGATE** (1967): "In Jonson's *Cynthia's Revels*, IV. i. 205ff., Phantasie would see how Love in a man 'could varie outward, by letting this gallant expresse himselfe in dumbe gaze;...a fourth, with stabbing himselfe, and drinking healths, or writing languishing letters in his bloud'. Some more striking response to the lady's scorn might, however, be meant, e.g. suicide" (188).

468 *kind* **SMITH** (1971): "one's own nature; human nature altogether" (513).

469–72 *They easily...haue bene lou'd:* **B. SMITH** (1991): Donne here equates homosexuality with bestiality, providing "the cosmic context in which the Renaissance viewed homosexuality" (174). Being mute, the ape woos by "his looks alone," prompting Donne's "moral reflection": the "alliterative pairing" of "boys & beasts" shows that "to act on homosexual desire is to lower one's status in the great chain of being" (174).

470 *outward Beauty,* **MILGATE** (1967): "Despite the surface cynicism of the poem, the central conviction of Donne's mature love-poetry remains firm." Cf. *Under* 13–16 (188). **SEYMOUR-SMITH** (1972): "he is finding the shallow and the superficial ridiculous, not love; but there may be some real reservation about the whole notion of 'romantic love'" (247).

471 *prou'd* **SMITH** (1971): "tried, experienced" (513). [So also, Craik and Craik (1986, 265).]

472 *Beasts and Angels* **MILGATE** (1967): "Burton's list remains unsurpassed, *Anatomy,* part. 3, sect. 2, membs. 1–2" (188).

473 *through-vaine,* **SULLENS** (1964): a word combination that the OED does not record (207). **MILGATE** (1967): "thoroughly vain" (188). [Similarly, Shawcross (1967, 327) and Seymour-Smith (1972, 247).]

476 *Toies* **SHAWCROSS** (1967): "amorous antics" (327).

477 *teare-shot* **SULLENS** (1964): Donne's use of this meaning of the word is earlier than the earliest source cited by the OED (238).

478 *russet* **CAREY** (1981): "finely suggesting the furred gentleness, as well as the colour, of the animal's hand" (175).

479 *kid-skin* **SULLENS** (1964): Donne's use of this word is earlier than the earliest sourced cited by the OED (181).

480 *Nature hath...haue law.* **MILGATE** (1967): Donne "refers here to the 'libertine' conception of the Law of Nature, interpreted to mean that to live under that Law was to be free of the restraints and punishments ('gaole') imposed by the Laws of God and man. Cf. Lucretius, *De rerum natura,* v. 958–61." Donne "is not here expressing any opinion for or against the notion; he is characteristically pointing to a paradox—that under this 'Law' (of nature), even violators of this Law (by 'unnatural' conduct, e.g. 'Sinnes against kinde') incur no penalty and suffer no restraint" (189). **SEYMOUR-SMITH** (1972): Donne "merely blandly and pleasedly draws attention to this paradox, as he does to others equally disturbing to conformist minds" (247). **CRAIK AND CRAIK** (1986): see *Relic* 29–30 (265).

481 *seely* **GROSART** (1872–73): "innocent, as shown by the succeeding words, 'that virtue'" (1:95). **SHAWCROSS** (1967): "lacking in understanding" (327).

482 *That vertue...spent* **GROSART** (1872–73): "There is here the common and reprehensible omission of a preposition; reprehensible, because it is required to show that the construction is inverted=an itchy warmth succeeds [to] that virtue of innocence" (1:95–96).

482 *That vertue* **SHAWCROSS** (1967): "temperance, which would have created cold resistance" (327). **SEYMOUR-SMITH** (1972): "innocence" (247).

482 *by his...and spent* **SEYMOUR-SMITH** (1972): "the ape pleases her by masturbating her: she only knows that she likes this" (247).

482 *chaft* SHAWCROSS (1967): "implies excitation and warmth due to rubbing" (327).

483 *Succeeds an Itchy warmth,* MILGATE (1967): "a nagging desire follows (and overcomes 'that vertue', innocence)." For "itchie," see *Sat1* 38 and note (189).

483 *melts* CAREY (1981): "In the context of love, melting also suggested the oozing of the female sexual parts when excited," and "melting girls occur also in" *Ind* 2, "where we pick up intonations of a bored, affluent woman luxuriously liquefying"; and also in *ValName* (175).

486 *pulls nor pushes,* SHAWCROSS (1967): "that is, toward nor away from her" (328).

486 *outright* SMITH (1971): "openly" (514).

487 *Tethlemite,* See notes to "Moaba," l. 439.

489 *preuented* SHAWCROSS (1967): "frustrated, forestalled" (328).

489 *flew;* CRAIK AND CRAIK (1986): "who was fleeing, having been thwarted by Tethlemite's arrival" (265).

492 *She Comes out next, where* MILGATE (1967): "i.e. from a human body" (328). SHAWCROSS (1967): "That is, the soul is given birth by Siphatecia, becoming Themach (l. 509)" (328). SMITH (1971): "from that part of a woman's body; not Siphatecia's body, in fact, but Eve's" (514).

493–95 *Adam and Eue…and formd it,* MAZZEO (1957): "The growth of the fetus in the womb was thought to be controlled by certain occult kinds of heat present in the human body. These human generative fires had to be of just the right intensity" (112). MASOOD-UL-HUSAN (1958): "Donne used the word 'womb' frequently and visualised it as something very much like the chemists' pot" (16).

493 *mingled Bloods,* MILGATE (1967): "This is the usual theory of coition; cf. Aristotle, *De Generatione Animalium,* i. xix. 726b, and note to ll. 429–30 above" (189).

494 *Chimiques equall fires* MILGATE (1967): "The analogy between human generation and the preparation of the 'philosophers' stone' by alchemists ('Chimiques') is very common," and "a constant temperature ('equall fire') was desirable for both processes. In generation, says *The French Academy,* 1594, ii. Ch. 71, p. 395, 'the heate of the Matrix warmeth all this matter as it were in a little fornace'" (189). SHAWCROSS (1967): "uniform and unvarying fires by which the alchemist hoped to produce an elixir. The mixture of materials, properly combined, was discussed in male and female terms; the alembic was often identified with the womb" (328).

496 *spungie Liuer* MILGATE (1967): "The liver was thought to be 'spongy' because it controlled most of the moisture of the body, the blood being 'engendered' there" (189).

499 *hardened…thicker hart* ALLEN (1943) quotes from Pareus, on his theory of organ formation in the fetus: "duquel en cette seconde ampoulle se forme le coeur, qui est de substance charneuse, solide & espesse, ainsi qu'il appartient au membre

le plus chaud de tous les autres" ["from which a second organ is formed, made of a fleshy substance, solid and thick, as it belongs to the most vigorous member of all the others"] (335). **PATRIDES** (1985): "thicker than the liver" (426). **CRAIK AND CRAIK** (1986): "i.e. than the other organs" (265).

500 *spirits* **MILGATE** (1967): see note to l. 45 (189).

502 *wel arm'd* **MILGATE** (1967): "being protected by the hair, the skin, the flesh, the skull, the 'dura mater' and the 'pia mater' (cf. T. Vicary, *Anatomy*, E.E.T.S., 1888, p. 25)" (189). **CRAIK AND CRAIK** (1986): "i.e. by the skull, considered as a headpiece" (265).

503 *sinewy strings* **MILGATE** (1967): "'And the braine is chiefe foundation of the sinewes: for it is the well of wilfull moving & feeling. For all sinewes spring and come out of the braine' (*Batman upon Bartholome*, 1582, f. 66r). 'Sinewes' meant both sinews and nerves; hence 'moving and feeling'" (189). **SMITH** (1971): see note to l. 394 (514). **CRAIK AND CRAIK** (1986): see *Fun* 9–11 (265).

504–05 *fast there…Soule attend* **MILGATE** (1967): Donne "says that the soul joins the body when the limbs are completely formed (the orthodox opinion; contrast ll. 429–30, and note). The seat of the soul is here made the brain (consistently with l. 393; see note). Hence the soul is 'fast' at the end of the spinal cord and (apparently) radiates out to all parts of the body with the sinews and nerves" (189). **SMITH** (1971): "the soul waits at the controlling centre in the brain for the sinews to link it with the limbs, as the limbs await the vital link with the soul" (514).

505 *attend* **SMITH** (1971): "await" (514).

506–07 *some qualitie…past shape,* **SMITH** (1971): "some part of the character of every being the soul had already inhabited" (514).

508 *enowe* **SMITH** (1971): "enough" (514).

509 *Themech* See notes for "Moaba," l. 439.

510 *that first did plow.* **MILGATE** (1967): "'Cain was a tiller of the ground'" (Gen. 4.2) (189).

511–20 *Who…Opinion.* **NORTON** (1895): "The conclusion of the poem seems to have little connection with what precedes. It introduces a train of thought unrelated to the main theme. The inventions of cursed Cain's race are told in Genesis iv, 20–22, but the invention of astronomy by blest Seth rests only on ancient Jewish tradition" (1:253). **GOSSE** (1899): "The poet evidently felt the inherent weakness of his scheme, and here abandoned it, drawing the threads loosely together in a final stanza when he says that his 'sullen' poem is written to please himself and not other people, and declares that there is no such thing as positive good or positive evil, but all is a question of relative values, and to be judged by the average of public opinion" (1:138). **GRIERSON** (1909): "The mood in which the poem was conceived had passed, or the poet felt his inventive power unequal to the task," closing the poem "abruptly with a stanza of more than Byronic scepticism and scorn" (4:215). **HAYWARD** (1929):

in B29, "which seems to be an early version of 'The Progresse of the Soule,' the last stanza is omitted." It was probably "added later as a kind of makeshift conclusion when Donne realised that the poem would never be finished" (252). LECOMTE (1965): "One manuscript lacks the concluding stanza, indicating, as we should have surmised anyway, that that 'sullen,' arrogant, impudently far from simple view of human nature and history was just tacked on, anything to write 'finis' to a monstrosity" (73).

511–12 *Who...dost it* CLOUGH (1920) sees an allusion to these lines in Butler's *Hudibras* ll. 649–50: "As we find in sullen writs, / And cross-grained works of modern wits" (115).

511 *Sullen* GROSART (1872–73): "unsociable." See *Sat3* 51 (1:96). MILGATE (1967): "drab, gloomy" (189). SMITH (1971): "sombre; unaccommodating" (515).

512 *Which iust...dost it* STEIN (1946): in this line Donne "expressed his attitude perfectly when he described one of his poems" (112). MILGATE (1967): "The tone of the Epistle returns ('I would have no such readers as I can teach', etc.): 'you will find my poem just as congenial to you as you are sympathetic to it'" (189–90). SEYMOUR-SMITH (1972): "e.g. if you find it 'pointless as well as disgusting' (Grierson's phrase) you will not enjoy it, and it will puzzle and dismay you" (248).

514 *Ploughing, building, ruling* FLYNN (1987): the activities of Robert Cecil around 1601 include the following: he had worked in Parliament "for maintenance of tillage," in opposition to Ralegh's enclosure program; he had built Cecil House and was active in enough construction to be called the "master builder"; and had become the sole power behind Elizabeth's throne (165).

516 *Cursed Cains Race* WILLIAMS (1948): "Why were the arts and crafts developed by the line of Cain, the unregenerate and reprobate who had been cut off?" Pererius offers the explanation "that the arts would have undoubtedly arisen in the state of innocence anyway, and that they were probably as much in use among the descendents of Seth as among those of Cain," and Calvin states that "Moses specially mentions the arts and skill invented by the line of Cain so that we may realize that, though they were cut off from grace, still they were not void of all good, but 'were indued with giftes not to be despised'" (145–46). MILGATE (1967): "Cain, the first murderer, is cursed in Gen. iv. 11–15, made to be 'a fugitive and vagabond in the earth', and marked by God lest anyone should kill him and end his punishment. He is the type of the persecutor of the Church (Augustine, Migne, *P. L.* xli. 456). His 'race' (Gen. iv. 17–22) included Jabal, ruler of tents and raiser of cattle ('ruling', l. 514); Jubal, 'father of all such as handle the harp and organ' ('arts', l. 515); and Tubal-Cain, 'an instructor of every artificer in brass and iron' ('building'). In this line, and at least once in l. 510, the word 'Cain' seems to be dissyllabic" (190). [Similarly, Shawcross (1967, 329), who adds that Donne "ponders the paradox of blest things coming from evil, and evil things coming from good," noting that "Cain's race has achieved cultural prominence by having been denied success with natural things," and Seymour-Smith (1972, 248).] HUGHES (1968): "It is Augustine's puzzle, with which he concludes his eighteenth book, the good things that accompany the damned city" (72–73).

517 *blest Seth…Astronomie.* **WILLIAMS** (1948): Donne "sourly" indicates that "Seth, or sometimes Enoch, set up two pillars, one of stone and the other of brass, on which he wrote the history of the creation and an account of the sciences. These pillars outlasted the flood and form one link in the transmission of the antediluvian history to Moses. Also, from them Abraham learned astronomy and the sciences" (146). **MILGATE** (1967): "Seth was regarded as 'blest' for several reasons. In Gen. iv. 25–26 Eve looks upon him as successor to the murdered Abel, whose character he shared. He succeeds Abel as the type of Christ: 'Seth quippe, ut quidam putant, interpretatur "resurrectio", qui est Christus' (Rabanus Maurus, *Comment. in Genesim*, II. ii, Migne, *P.L.* cvii. 509). Cain and his race are the children of the world, but Seth and his children are the children of Light, and the 'sons of God' in Gen. vi. 2, 4 (cf. D. C. Allen, 'Milton and the Sons of God', *M.L.N.* lxi, 1946). For Seth as the discoverer of 'Astronomie' the usual reference given (in many places) is the passage from Josephus quoted in the note to l. 9 above. DuBartas shows Adam teaching astronomy to Seth (*Divine Weeks and Works*, Second Week, First Day, trans. Sylvester, 1605, p. 376). Cf. Suidas, *Historica*, edition of 1581, col. 849: 'Deum enim, Sethum illius aetatis homines appellabant, eo quod et Hebraicis literas, et stellarum appellationes invenisset, ob insignis eius pietatis admirationem' etc. The terms 'Astronomie' and 'Astrologie' both are indifferently taken & used by the learned for one and the selfesame Arte' (Sir Christopher Heydon, *A Defence of Judicial Astrology*, 1603, p. 2; he cites Josephus to 'prove' that Adam and Seth 'did addict themselves unto it', pp. 74, 305). It was astrology, with its predictions and horoscopes that Seth introduced to 'vex' mankind" (190). **SHAWCROSS** (1967): "Astronomy is ill because, like the Tower of Babel, it seeks to reach and understand heaven itself: it presumes upon God. Seth's race has brought confusion and distress by trying to dissect God's gifts of nature" (329).

518–20 *There's nothing…Iudge Opinion.* **MILGATE** (1967) paraphrases as "Comparison is the only means of measuring every quality, opinion the only basis of judging it." Adds, "Donne's thought here is quite in agreement with his mature opinions. Of Opinion he says that it is 'a middle station, betweene ignorance, and knowledge; for knowledge excludes all doubting, all hesitation; opinion does not so; but opinion excludes indifferency, and equanimity' (*Sermons*, vi. 317). This world is (in terms of the previous note) relative in its nature, and one cannot 'judge' without doubting and hesitation; it is 'opinion', not 'knowledge', on which judgement must rely" (191).

518 *Simplie* **WENDELL** (1948): the final stanza has "usually been taken as an example of the extreme scepticism which attracted Donne," but "a clue to a different interpretation is to be found in the use of the word 'simply,' in which Donne is obviously making the common distinction between simples and compounds, between that which is simple, complete, with no contrarieties in its nature, and compounds, which are made up of these contrarieties. Hence it is obvious that in this sense only God, who alone implies perfection, is good; all else, the good and evil of this world, is only relatively good or evil, of a mixed nature, partaking to a degree of both qualities." Such an interpretation "is supported by a significant passage" from *Sermons* (6:231): "That nothing is Essentially good, but God…and then upon this consideration too, That

this Essentiall goodnesse of God is so diffusive, so spreading, as that there is nothing in the world that doth not participate of that goodnesse.... So that now both these propositions are true, First, That there is nothing in this world good, and then this also, That there is nothing ill," and "since man must thus be concerned with relative values, opinion is, he says, the proper faculty of judgement" (480). **MILGATE** (1967): "This is the mode of Donne's assertion in the poem also, where he uses one of the most familiar examples of the 'mixed' nature of earthly things—the paradoxical nature of the 'benefits' to mankind of Cain and Seth in relation to their respective characters; the illustration is in keeping with the other material in the poem, and might, indeed, have been intended to come more fully into the next Canto, had there been one" (191).

Vpon Mr. Thomas Coryats *Crudities*.

COMMENTARY

Date and Circumstances

Grosart (1873, 2:xlii, 93–96), allegedly printing *Coryat* from the 1669 edition (see the textual introduction to *Coryat*), avers that the poem "originally" appeared in "The Odcombian Banquet" in 1611 (93) and deems the poem "mere banter" (xlii).

Lowell ([Norton] 1895, 1:232–33) observes that *Coryat* was "first printed among the multitude of satirically panegyric verses prefixed to Coryat's so-called *Crudities*" (232) and asserts that Prince Henry accepted the dedication of the volume on condition that the "'free and merry jests,' as Coryat good-humoredly calls them, should be printed in the place of the commendatory verses which it was then the fashion to prefix to all sorts of books" (233).

Chambers (1896, 2:226–27), asserting that *Coryat* was "[f]irst added to the [collected] *Poems*" in 1650 (the poem actually appeared in the first issue of the fourth edition, in 1649—*ed*.), states that the poem was originally printed among the "burlesque" (226) commendatory verses that Ben Jonson had "edited to the number of about 60" (226) for inclusion in the 1611 *Crudities* and was reprinted in *Banquet* that same year.

Grierson (1912, 2:128–30) also notes that Donne's verses first appeared in 1611, published "with a mass of witty and scurrilous verses by all of the 'wits' of the day, prefixed to Coryats *Crudities*" (128). Others who also indicate this date and these circumstances include Shawcross (1967, 414), Warnke (1967, 106), Smith (1971, 500), and Patrides (1985, 245).

Wilson (1945, 55) cites *Coryat* among Donne's works published before 1633.

Bewley (1966, 191) calls Thomas Coryate "an eccentric English traveler" whose account of his travels (1611) had the full title *Coryats Crudities Hastily gobbled up in five Moneths travels*. He notes that at "Prince Henry's command" some notable poets and wits, among them Jonson, Chapman, Drayton, and Donne, "wrote mock-commendatory verses to be prefaced to the volume." Others who comment on these circumstances include Milgate (1967, 1920), Warnke (1967, 126), and Chmielewski (2001, 620).

Smith (1971, 500), citing Coryate's dates as 1577(?)–1617 and calling him "a learned eccentric," describes the *Crudities* as "a diverting account of a European journey he made in 1608" that also includes "mock-panegyrics which were printed with the book as prefatory commendations," such as Donne's poem that "alludes closely to episodes in the book."

Sullivan (1993, 12) notes that the previously "uncollected printings" of Donne's verse "establish a *terminus ad quem*" for *Coryat* of 1611.

Pebworth (1996, 130) points out that *Coryat* was one of Donne's poems which was published rather than restricted to a coterie readership, making it "immediately available to wide audiences."

Flynn (2000, 336) comments that Donne's "not so dangerously satirical" verses were written shortly after *Biathanatos*, *Pseudo*, and *Ignatius*.

General Commentary

Taylor, "the Water Poet" (1612, 17–19), contributor to the joke about *Coryats Crudities*, published a series of epigrams in which he comments one at a time on the mock-commendatory poems to Coryate. A long epigram headed "Iohannes Donne" takes up Donne's poem "Upon Mr Thomas Coryats Crudities" and embroiders it.

Sheppard (1653, A2r–C3v) quotes, adapts, and paraphrases lines from *Coryat* in the preliminary material of his satirical pamphlet.

During the conversations he records between Morton, Elliot, and Bourne, Collier (1820, 1:158) includes Bourne's comment that Donne's name "appears among the satirical eulogisers of Coryate and his Crudities in 1611."

Grosart (1872–73, 2:96) explains the placement of this poem in his edition with the verse letters, noting, "these commendatory verses (burlesquely), like those of Ben Jonson and others, do not belong properly to the Verse-letters," yet "they find as appropriate a place in this division as anywhere."

Within the context of discussing the travels Donne may have undertaken to the Continent during his youth, Gosse (1899, 1:56–57, 278–79) describes *Coryat* and *Macaron* as "two scornful epistles full" of Donne's "own peculiar wit and magic," noting further that these poems "might have been written by a man who had never strayed out of London city" (57). In reference to Coryate himself, he thinks that Donne was "amused by this preposterous being" and thus "wrote several copies of 'commendatory' (or rather ironical) verses to be prefixed with those of many other writers to the *Crudities*" (279).

Grierson (1912, 2:xi) states that in its way *Coryat* is "a masterpiece of insult veiled as compliment, but it is a rather boyish and barbarous way." In a similar manner, Alvarez (1961, 197) comments on the tone.

Simpson (1924, 47) mentions references to Rabelais in the Satyres and *Coryat*.

Alvarez (1961, 197) comments that Coryate "was associated with the dinners at the Mitre and Mermaid, which Donne also attended."

Strachan (1962, 126, 139, 275) states that even though *Coryat* provides "undeniably harsh comment" (126) and epitomizes "the cutting scorn of the wits" (275), the "cruelty" of Donne's poem "did not sour Coryate's admiration for him" (139).

Rickey (1966, 186) notes the references to "Caesar's histories, and the Sybils" in her listing of Donne's classical allusions found in this poem.

Milgate (1967, xxi) thinks Donne's "humorous touch" falters in *Coryat*, "becoming rather juvenile."

Patrides (1985, 213) calls *Coryat* "but an appendage," merely partaking of the spirit of the five Satyres.

Ray (1986, 464–65) comments that *Coryat* appears to be a "potent" influence on two poems in *Death in a New Dress: Or Sportive Funeral Elegies* (1656) by S. F.: "On the Death of the most Renowned Poet, Mr. Martin Parker" and "On the Gentlewoman that so often travail'd up Holborn-Hill upon her Bum."

Scarry (1988, 77) observes that in *Coryat* "the surfaces of the pages take on the temperature of the living substance they contain."

Chandra (1991, 83–84) argues that *Coryat* "is generally dismissed as of least interest even as an example of satirical verse," but it "reveals certain aspects of Donne's mind," noting in particular that Donne appears to have been "offended" with Coryate as a result of "his pretentiousness," that the "undigested material" of Donne's poem reflects that Coryate "was scatter-brained and lacked the capacity to associate his various observations with each other," and that Donne had doubts about Coryate's "honesty and veracity, and suspected him to be guilty of exaggeration and invention and altogether false reporting."

Sullivan (1993, 5–7) lists *Coryat* among the 25 different poems that were "published in their entirety" before Donne's death (5), and concludes that "there was more of Donne's printed poetry with a larger circulation, a more general readership (as opposed to members of Donne's inner circle who had access to his manuscripts), and a greater potential influence during his lifetime than previously believed" (7).

Roebuck (1996, 146–49) argues that this poem is "a document, however inscrutable," written during Donne's "anguished searching for a securely grounded religious position" (146). The poem, he acknowledges, at first appears to be only "high spirited and/ or cruel" (147), as Donne's description of the progress of Coryate's book "is taken up in an extended conceit of the dismemberment of the gigantic body of the book into its constituent leaves, with whimsical anticipation of their fates." Although Donne conducts his argument "with much wit and panache" (147), Roebuck argues that "behind this puzzling, and perhaps inconsequential, poem in seemingly facetious vein, we catch the shadow of Donne," as full of "the uncertainties of religious questions as Coryate was brashly free of doubt" (149).

Spurr (1996, 196–97) cites a letter to Wesley Milgate from Frank Kerins (5 February 1974) in which Kerins notes that "'the commendatory poems composed by Donne and the London Wits for Coryate's *Crudities*'" (196) were pirated by Thomas Thorpe, who published them in the *Odcombian Banquet*, thus reducing sales of Coryate's work.

Prescott (1997, 42) discovers that one poem on Coryate that "does not mention Rabelais is by 'Joannes Donne'; another, which does is by 'Joannes Dones,'" and she asks, "Who is 'Dones'? Is he Donne with a typo?", and then concludes, "the poems are separated by many pages, but that is no proof either way."

Shawcross (2000–01, 28) argues that a "differentiation of generic and modal" consideration indicates that *Coryat* is "satiric but not a verse satire, even though it is written in heroic couplets: here we have wit and humor and an object of attack."

Notes and Glosses

Heading. Incipit Ioannes Donne. Vpon Mr. Thomas Coryats Crudities. **CHAMBERS** (1896) says of Coryate that he was the "son of the Rev. George Coryate of Odcombe in Somerset, born *circ.* 1577" and was "a sort of buffoon on James the First's court." Notes that he began his (mainly walking) tour in 1608, going "through France, Italy, and Germany," and covering 1,975 miles. Comments that Coryate "determined to publish his diary, and applied to wits and poets for commendatory verses," but in fact, the majority of responses turned out to be "burlesque." Points out that about 60 poems were edited by Ben Jonson and "published with the Diary as *Coryat's Crudities* in 1611," noting further that the "commendatory verses were reprinted by themselves," also in 1611, as *The Odcombian Banquet* (2:226). **GRIERSON** (1912): Coryate was "an eccentric and a favourite butt of the wits, but was not without ability as well as enterprise. In 1612 he set out on a journey through the East which took him to Constantinople, Jerusalem, Armenia, Mesopotamia, Persia, and India. In his letters to the wits at home he sends greetings to, among others, Christopher Brooke, John Hoskins (as 'Mr. Equinoctial Pasticrust of the Middle Temple'), Ben Jonson, George Garrat, and 'M. John Donne, the author of two most elegant Latine Bookes, *Pseudomartyr* and *Ignatius Conclave.*' He died at Surat in 1617" (2:128).

2 *leauened spirit,* **GRIERSON** (1912): "It is leaven which raises bread. A 'leavened spirit' is one easily puffed up by the 'love of greatness'" (2:128–29). [Similarly, Bewley (1966, 191), Milgate (1967, 192), Smith (1971, 500), and Patrides (1985, 245).] **SHAWCROSS** (1967): "raised, inflated" (37).

2 *Sesqui-superlatiue?* **SULLENS** (1964): the *OED* cites Donne as the earliest source for this word (201). **BEWLEY** (1966): "one-and-a-half times over superlative" (191). [So also, Milgate (1967, 192), Shawcross (1967, 37), Smith (1971, 500), Patrides (1985, 245), and Chmielewski (2001, 620).] **ROEBUCK** (1996): "This is the sole occurrence of the element 'sesqui-' in Donne's poetry" (148).

3 *Venice vast lake* **MILGATE** (1967): "the Venetian Lagoon"; see *Crudities,* 1:303–04 (192). [So also, Smith (1971, 500), Patrides (1985, 245), and Chmielewski (2001, 620).]

3 *than* **MILGATE** (1967): "then" (192). [So also, Patrides (1985, 245).]

4 *Some vaster thing…a Cortizan.* **BEWLEY** (1966): "Coryate devoted attention in his book to the Venetian courtesans" (191). [So also, Milgate (1967, 192) and Smith (1971, 500), who adds, "An obscene innuendo."]

5 *inland Sea* **SHAWCROSS** (1967): "apparently the Mediterranean, but also the courtesan's genital parts" (38).

5 *discouered* **SHAWCROSS** (1967): "puns on acquiring first-hand knowledge of, exploring, and unclothing" (398).

5 *well,* **SHAWCROSS** (1967): "seems to pun on the adverb and the noun, as a deep fountain" (398).

6–8 *A Cellar-gulfe,...producest now.* **ROEBUCK** (1996): "Coryate makes no explicit mention of Hell in his description of Heidelberg" (147). He "describes his descent into the labyrinthine wine cellars and then to a 'wonderful vast roome' where he saw the 'monstrous miracle,' 'so monstrously strange a thing' the greatest wine barrel in the world. Possibly reading this awestruck description of the cavernous setting and of the barrel, the 'superlative moles [bulk],' and of Babylon, put Donne in mind of his own description of the inward and secret places as he passes by the suburbs of Hell in *Ignatius*, and may have suggested 'Sesqui-superlative' of line 2" (147–48).

6–7 *A Cellar-gulfe,...From Heydelberg,* **MILGATE** (1967): "in this sea of wine one could in a double sense sail to Hell through drunkenness" (192).

6 *A Cellar-gulfe,* **SULLENS** (1964): a word combination that the *OED* does not record (204). **MILGATE** (1967): "the Great Tun of Heidelberg (which held as much liquid, Donne implies, as the Gulf of Venice)"; see *Crudities*, 2: 218 (192). [So also, Chmielewski (2001, 620).] **SMITH** (1971): "the Great Tun of Heidelberg," which in Coryate's thinking "held some 28,000 gallons of wine." Donne's aim is to indicate that Coryate "has made a rake's progress in gulfs in passing from Venice to her courtesans, thence to this sea of wine, and may now sail to hell in drink" (500). [Similarly, Patrides (1985, 245).]

7 *Heydelberg,* **SHAWCROSS** (1967): "the German university town, known for homosexuality among students" (38).

8 *then* **PATRIDES** (1985): "than" (245).

8 *producest* **SULLENS** (1964): Donne's use of this meaning of the word is earlier than the earliest source cited by *OED* (227).

9–16 *Infinite worke,...wouldst neuer touch.* **BALD** (1970) notes that there is "a note of extravagant chaffing" running through all of the verses to Coryate, citing Donne as one who "showered mock-praises upon the Crudities" (192).

10 *study it to any end.* **SMITH** (1971): "(a) find a proper ending in it; (b) finish it; (c) read it with profit" (500).

10 *to any end.* **MILGATE** (1967): "(1) because it is endless, 'infinite'; (2) 'to any good purpose'" (193).

12 *poorely* **SULLENS** (1964): Donne's use of this meaning of the word is earlier than the earliest source cited by *OED* (227).

12 *head or foote.* **SHAWCROSS** (1967): "beginning or end" (38). [So also, Chmielewski (2001, 620).]

13–14 *If man...make man.* **MELTON** (1906) cites these lines to illustrate when Donne "does not give his words, syllables, and sounds arsis-thesis variation" (201). **WIGGINS** (1945): the satire in these lines is based on the citation in logic books of "reason" as "a logical *difference* of man" and "aptness to laugh" as "a special *property* of man" (45). **MILGATE** (1967) quotes *Sermons*, 1:226, and cites *Metem* 455 (192).

14–16 *thy booke doth…wouldst neuer touch.* **SMITH** (1971): "it makes people laugh, though it does not call for a use of reason having no reason in it" (500).

14 *halfe make man.* **MILGATE** (1967): "by merely arousing laughter" (193). [So also, Patrides (1985, 245).] **SHAWCROSS** (1967): "it makes him laugh. Man is a full man because he already has reason to realize the book's idiocy" (38).

15–16 *One halfe…neuer touch.* **CHMIELEWSKI** (2001): "the humor being put in, the reason was then left out" (620).

17 *When wilt…great Lunatique?* **MILGATE** (1967): "When will you have written at the greatest length of which you are capable?" (193).

17 *full,* **CHMIELEWSKI** (2001): "complete, or like the full moon (punning on 'Lunatique'), compared to the earth (l. 18)" (620).

17 *great Lunatique?* **GRIERSON** (1912): "i.e. probably 'great humourist,' whose moods and whims are governed by the changeful moon" (2:129). [So also, Milgate (1967, 193) and Smith (1971, 500–01).] **SHAWCROSS** (1967): "punning on the full-ness of the moon, which is a bit more than a fourth of the size of earth" (38). **SMITH** (1971) notes, a "moon-like being, who is still waxing and may write at still greater length when he is at full" (500–01). **PATRIDES** (1985) refers to *WomCon* 14 (245).

19 *prosperous* **SHAWCROSS** (1967): "well filled, big" (38). [So also, Patrides (1985, 245).]

19 *nose-borne* **SULLENS** (1964): a word combination that the *OED* does not record (205).

19 *wenne,* **MILGATE** (1967): "swelling" (193). [So also, Patrides (1985, 245).] **CHMIELEWSKI** (2001): "a cyst" (620).

20 *then* **PATRIDES** (1985): "than" (245).

20 *Mother-nose?* **SULLENS** (1964): a word combination that the *OED* does not record (205). **MILGATE** (1967): "i.e. the world (which will be smaller than the extent of Coryate's travels, and smaller also than his books)" (193).

22 Munster…*Authors show,* **BEWLEY** (1966): "Coryate was a tourist traveling with guidebooks in hand" (192). **MILGATE** (1967): Donne's "jest is very unfair," both to the variousness of Coryate's "authorities" and to "his energy and skill in using them" (193). **WARNKE** (1967): "encyclopedic authorities of the Renaissance" (126).

22 *Munster* **CHAMBERS** (1896): "Sebastian Munster (1489–1552), a German Reformer, author of the *Cosmographia* (1544), a standard treatise on geography" (2:226). [Similarly, Grierson (1912, 2:129), Bewley (1966, 192), Shawcross (1967, 38), Patrides (1985, 246), and Chmielewski (2001, 620).] **MILGATE** (1967) adds a quotation paying tribute to Munster's scholarship from Coryate's "Epistle Dedicatory" (193). [Similarly, Smith (1971, 501).]

22 *Gesner* **CHAMBERS** (1896): "Konrad von Gesner, of Zurich (1516–1565), author of the *Historia Animalium* (1551–1558)" (2:226). [So also, Milgate (1967,

193).] **GRIERSON** (1912): "The *Bibliotheca Universalis, siue Catalogus Omnium Scriptorum in Linguis Latina, Graeca, et Hebraica*, 1545, by Conrad von Gesner of Zurich (1516–1565)" (2:129). [So also, Bewley (1966, 192), Shawcross (1967, 38), Smith (1971, 501), Patrides (1985, 246), and Chmielewski (2001, 620).]

23–24 *Mount now...a Gazettier.* **MILGATE** (1967): "*Mercurio Gallo-Belgicus* will inform him on politics and current affairs. But in his Introductory Essay on travel Coryate emphasizes the importance of traveling in foreign countries in the formation of a statesman's character" (193).

23 *Gallo-belgicus;* **GROSART** (1872–73): "a yearly, and then half-yearly, political register" (2:96). **GRIERSON** (1912): "a journal or register of news started at Cologne in 1598. The first volume consisted of 659 pages and was entitled: *Mercurius Gallo-Belgicus; sive rerum in Gallia et Belgia potissimum: Hispania quoque, Italia, Anglia, Germania, Polonia, vicinisque locis ab anno 1588 usque ad Martium anni praesentis 1594 gestarum, nuncius.* In the seventeenth century it was published half-yearly and ornamented with maps. Its Latin was not unimpeachable, nor its news always trustworthy" (2:60, referenced from 2:129). [So also, Bewley (1966, 192), Warnke (1967, 126), and Chmielewski (2001, 620).] **MILGATE** (1967) refers to *Sat4* 112 (193). [So also, Shawcross (1967, 38).] **PATRIDES** (1985) refers to *Merc* (246).

24 *deepe* **MILGATE** (1967): "profound" (193).

24 *States-man,* **MILGATE** (1967): "statesman" (193).

24 *Gazettier.* **GROSART** (1872–73) (reading "Garreteer") glosses as "garret hack, with probably a sort of punning reference to gazetteer" (2:96). **SULLENS** (1964): the *OED* cites Donne as the earliest source for this word (194). **MILGATE** (1967): "a writer in a gazette, a retailer of news" (193). **SMITH** (1971): "a journalist, one who writes in a gazette of the kind said to have been first devised in Venice in the sixteenth century" (501). **ROEBUCK** (1996) notes that the word is "rare indeed" and that the *OED* "gives this as the first instance, although the word *Gazett*, a Venetian coin of small value, arrives with Jonson's *Volpone* (1605)." Comments that Donne used the word only once earlier, in *Ignatius*, and that his "descent into facetious printed verse" in *Coryat* and his "imaginative descent into the facetious Hell of *Ignatius his Conclave* seem to be underwritten by the same set of concerns and marked by curious similarities of language." Suggests that these are "readily called forth by the scenes from *Crudities* such as the descent into the labyrinthine wine cellar and the sight of the superlative barrel" and that they may also be encouraged by Coryate's "projected tour of the East" (148–49).

26 *Will Conqueror,* **MILGATE** (1967) thinks this mention signifies that the "news" in Coryate's subsequent work will be "stale" (193).

26 *Will* **PATRIDES** (1985): "William, who was crowned king of England in 1066" (246).

26 *Prester Iacke.* **CHAMBERS** (1896): "or, Prester John, the mythical king of a Christian country believed from the twelfth to the fourteenth century to exist in

Central Asia, and afterwards in Abyssinia" (2:226–27). [So also, Bewley (1966, 192), Milgate (1967, 193), who adds, "here...used to suggest that the 'news' in Coryate's next work would be imaginary," Shawcross (1967, 38), and Patrides (1985, 246).] **SULLENS** (1964): a word combination that the *OED* does not record (205). **WARNKE** (1967): "legendary ruler of Ethiopia" (126). [So also, Smith (1971, 501) and Chmielewski (2001, 620), who adds, "mentioned in Munster's *Cosmographia*."]

27–28 *Goe bashfull...thy glorious booke.* **ROEBUCK** (1996): "At first perusal, the poem does not seem to be other than high spirited and/or cruel. It plays with obvious and friendly irony on Coryate's quite amazingly self-assured account of his travels" (147).

28 *progresse* **SHAWCROSS** (1967): "The book is likened to the sun in its progress across the skies" (398).

29 *both Indies* **MILGATE** (1967) quotes *SunRis* 17 and cites *Metem* 17 (193). [So also, Smith (1971, 501) and Patrides (1985, 246).] **CHMIELEWSKI** (2001): "West India was known for its gold, and East for its spices and perfumes" (620).

30–34 *The west...the Frankinsence.* **SHAWCROSS** (1967): "The gold of the Biblical triad offered to the Christ child is, of course, here obtained from the West Indies; the addition of pepper (apparently the 'spicy' matter) indicates that the book is 'blessed' with all the offerings it needs for a prosperous life" (398).

30–31 *spend, / (Meaning...the presse.* **MILGATE** (1967): "in printing so huge a book" (193).

30 *The west...freely spend,* **ROEBUCK** (1996): the passage "seems to refer to Coryate's putting up his estates as insurance against his travel, from which he made enough to pay for publication. The west here is Somerset, but it carries also the sense of West Indies gold from the previous line." There is no apparent reason for Donne "to invoke Catholic gold and Jesuit subterfuge in the case of Coryate, but if that is what can be construed from the lines, we may see Donne distracted from his facetious Johannes Factus role by his continuous musing on the politics of religion" (148).

31 *vpon the presse.* **SMITH** (1971): "on getting his vast tome into print; though without any prospect of recovering the money he spent on it" (501). **PATRIDES** (1985): "on the publication of Coryate's book" (246). **CHMIELEWSKI** (2001): "spent in the cost of printing so large a book" (620).

32–38 *The east...vnto men,* **EMPEROR** (1928): this passage "bears a certain resemblance to the lines in which Catullus predicts a like fate for a bad poet; see *Carmen* xcv, 7–8: 'At Volusi annales Paduam morientur ad ipsam / Et laxas scombris saepe dabunt tunicas.' ['But the annals of Volusius will pass away at Padua itself / And often they will provide loose tunics for the mackerel.']" (40).

32–35 *The east...magnifies thy leaues;* **MILGATE** (1967): "The leaves of the book might be used to wrap rich spices" (194). [So also, Smith (1971, 501).]

33–44 *And thy leaues...popular faires,* **ROEBUCK** (1996): the "progress" of Coryate's book, "at first imaged as the movement of the sun, is taken up in an extended conceit of the dismemberment of the gigantic body of the book into its constituent leaves, with whimsical anticipation of their fates. The use of these leaves in Coryate's intended travels to the East seems to point to the inevitable choice in his future writings of embracing either the higher matter of 'The Myrrhe, the Pepper, and the Frankinsence' (34), or lower things. They, the leaves, may 'stoope' (35) to become wrappings for 'Currans...Figs...Medicinall, and Aromatique twigs' (39–40). The gifts of the wise men to the Christ-child and Mary (Mt. 2:11) seem suggested here, gold having been named four lines before, but also witheld [sic] by the interpolation of 'Peppers,' a word which does not occur in the English Bible. If higher matters are rejected and Coryate's leaves 'stoope lower yet' (43) toward the mundane, his pages will be used by merchants as wrapping material for 'Home manufactures, to thicke popular faires' (44), as score cards by aristocratic gamblers, and for paper to use in binding other books. The scattered body parts of heroes do public good, but malefactors are cut up for demonstrations of anatomy" (147).

33 *And thy leaues...from thence,* **MILGATE** (1967) cites *Sat5* 85 for "this ancient jest" (193).

33 *leaues* **PATRIDES** (1985): "pages" (246).

33 *embrace* **CHMIELEWSKI** (2001): "be used to wrap" (620).

35 *magnifies* **MILGATE** (1967): "dignifies" (193). **SMITH** (1971): "makes them more splendid and important" (501). [So also, Chmielewski (2001, 620).]

35–48 *But if they...comprehend.* **MILGATE** (1967): a culminating "jest": "Coryate's book can be said to 'cover' ('comprehend') or include every kind of 'matter': i.e. (1) all subjects, and (2) all sorts of goods or physical material" (194).

36–42 *To neighbour...Ounces subdiuide;* **MILGATE** (1967): the leaves of the book might also be used to wrap "small quantities of commoner merchandise" (194).

36 *neighbour* **SMITH** (1971): "adjacent" (501). [So also, Patrides (1985, 246).]

36 *wares,* **SHAWCROSS** (1967): "referring to the use of the paper in the book as wrapping for various objects. Since the book is so 'traveled' and so 'learned,' Donne uses an image showing its possible ubiquity and vast knowledge" (39). [So also, Patrides [1985, 246].]

36 *vnhoope* **SULLENS** (1964): the *OED* cites Donne as the earliest source for this word (202).

37–48 *Voluminous barrels,...matter comprehend.* **SCARRY** (1988): Donne "designates the bound volume as a 'voluminous barrel,' full of wares from the east; he then begins to unbind the book, and now envisions each dismembered page as wrapped around a parcel of currants or figs, 'Medicinall and Aromatique twigs,' that fill the stalls of the fairs and marketplace." Further, "the matter in question here is not yet the human body; though that will enter later in the poem. But even here the paper packets of vegetable matter are on the verge of life: they have become 'warm' with handling and are described as being about 'to hatch.' The fact that Donne calls the pages 'leaves' underscores the continuity between them and their vegetable content. By extension, it also asserts a broader continuity between language and the material realm it seeks to represent" (76).

37 *Voluminous* SULLENS (1964): Donne's use of this word is earlier than the earliest sourced cited by the *OED* (190).

41 *a better methode* MILGATE (1967): "i.e. of handling and selling; the barrels and tons of merchandise are broken down into handy packages" (194). [So also, Smith (1971, 501) and Chmielewski (2001, 620).]

43–44 *If they stoope...popular faires,* MILGATE (1967): the leaves may be used "more humbly still" than for common merchandise, for "home-made sweets, etc., sold on stalls at village fairs" (194).

43 *vent* MILGATE (1967): "vend, sell" [so also, Smith (1971, 501), Patrides (1985, 246), and Chmielewski (2001, 620)]; see *OED*, vb. 3. 1 (194).

44 *Home*-manufactures, SMITH (1971): "home-made confectioneries" (501). PATRIDES (1985): "home-made items" (246).

44 manufactures, SULLENS (1964): the *OED* cites Donne as the earliest source for this meaning of the word (250).

44 *thicke* MILGATE (1967): "crowded" [so also, Smith (1971, 501) and Patrides (1985, 246)]; see *OED* II. 4 (194).

45–46 omnipraegnant...*the buyer cals,* MILGATE (1967): "as they lie in the heat, the leaves might be said to engender ('hatch') all the kinds of goods that people buy" (194). [So also, Smith (1971, 501).]

45 omnipraegnant MILGATE (1967) cites *Metem* 494–95 (194). PATRIDES (1985): "since the book's pages will in a sense 'hatch' (46) the items the people buy" (247).

48 *That they...matter comprehend.* BEWLEY (1966): "because used as wrapping paper for various merchandise" (192).

48 *all kinde of matter comprehend.* SMITH (1971): "the book will be in this literal way a universal compendium of matter" (501).

50 *Pandect* CHAMBERS (1896): "The *Pandectae* or *Digesta* is the elaborate code of Roman common law, compiled from the decisions and opinions of *jurisconsulti,* under the superintendence of the Emperor Justinian, in the sixth century A.D." (2:227). [So also, Milgate (1967, 194) and Chmielewski (2001, 620).] BEWLEY (1966): "a treatise covering the whole of a subject" (192). SHAWCROSS (1967): "a complete digest" (39). [So also, Warnke (1967, 127), Smith (1971, 501), and Patrides (1985, 247).]

50 *Vniuersall Booke.* MILGATE (1967): "like Munster's *Cosmographia Universalis* and Gesner's *Bibliotheca Universalis,*" l. 22 (194). [So also, Patrides (1985, 247).]

51–55 *The brauest...in peeces:* HIRSCH (1991): "What becomes of the idea of a unified self when its representative form is shown to be decomposing into separate pieces? The anatomized 'peeces' of Coryate's text are scattered for public good: some tissues will serve as pill wrappers," while "others will be used as backing in the spine of other books, and part of the book, 'as *Sybils* was,' might be lost to the wind" (70).

51 *Heroes,* **MILGATE** (1967): "three syllables" (194). **KLAUSE** (1994): Donne "was not given to hero worship" (181), and this is the only instance in which he uses this word.

53 *Worst malefactors,…are prize,* **MILGATE** (1967): "To murderers men are as ships to pirates or to an enemy, a 'prize' to be robbed and destroyed" (194.)

53 *prize,* **MILGATE** (1967): "prey, victims" (194). [So also, Smith (1971, 501), Patrides (1985, 247), and Chmielewski (2001, 620.)]

54 *Doe publique…Anatomies;* **MILGATE** (1967) quotes an Act of Henry VIII, cap. xlii (1540), stating that annually London barbers and surgeons "shall have the right in perpetuity" to anatomize four executed felons to advance the "science or facultie of surgery" (194).

54 *cut in Anatomies;* **SHAWCROSS** (1967): "when their corpses are dissected for scientific research" (39). [So also, Smith (1971, 502), Patrides (1985, 246–47), and Chmielewski (2001, 620).]

54 *Anatomies;* **BEWLEY** (1966): "bodies of executed criminals can be of public use in dissection laboratories of schools" (193). **MILGATE** (1967) suspects "an allusion to the yearly anatomy lecture given 'publicly' before students"; cites *LovExch* 42 and Gardner, *Elegies etc.,* p. 169 (194).

55–58 *For a Lord…keepe companie.* **GROSART** (1872–73) (reading "Portescue's" in l. 56): "I do not understand the allusion or allusions here. Perhaps that in ll. 55–8 refers to the custom spoken of by Harington on Playe (as quoted by Nares): 'Whear lords and great men have been disposed to play deepe play, and not having money about them, have cut cardes insteede of counters, with asserverance (on theyr honors) to pay for every peece of carde so lost a *portegue.*' The Portescue, Portaque, or Portugnese, was the great crusado of that country, worth. 3*l*. 12*s*." (2:96). [Similarly, Bewley (1966, 193), Milgate (1967, 194), and Warnke (1967, 127).]

55–57 *For a Lord…whole Books;* **SMITH** (1971): "Coryate's pages will provide whole books of counters for lords and the whole school of gamesters who play for high stakes. (A gold portague was worth over 4 pounds.)" (502).

56 *casts at* **MILGATE** (1967): possibly "casts the dice towards (winning) the coins" (195).

56 *Portescues,* **CHAMBERS** (1896) (reading "Portescue's") thinks "one would expect to find this the name of some keeper of a gambling-house." Questions Grosart's identification of a reference to a Portuguese coin here on grounds that in that case the text should be "*for* Portescues" (2:227). **GRIERSON** (1912): "'Portescue' is not given as a form of 'Portague' by the *O.E.D.,* but a false etymology connecting it with 'escus',

crowns, may have produced it" (2:129). [So also, Bewley (1966, 193) and Warnke (1967, 127).] **MILGATE** (1967): "the great crusado of Portugal" [so also, Shawcross (1967, 39) and Patrides (1985, 247)], a coin worth more than £4; see *OED*, which lists "portegue," "portaque," and "portuguese," though not "portescue" (195). **CHMIELEWSKI** (2001): "used by Lords in gaming" (620).

57 *Prouide whole Books;* **SHAWCROSS** (1967): "(rather than just leaves) for a lord who will throw money away gambling, or for a shipload of sailors" (39).

57–58 *Each leafe enough…keepe companie.* **SMITH** (1971): "one leaf will suffice for counters when friends play cards for pastime and company" (502).

58 *keepe companie.* **MILGATE** (1967): words that "call up a picture of good companions drinking heartily to Coryate's health" (195).

59–60 *Can all…half-pinte wit.* **MILGATE** (1967): "No, you cannot drink bumpers to Coryate; you must limit the amount ('fit measures') to the capacity of the man you are toasting, and fill the tankards only to the half-pint mark, to match Coryate's wit" (195).

59–60 *fit / Measures;* **SMITH** (1971): "fit the quantity of drink to the occasion" (502).

59 *carouse vp thee?* **SHAWCROSS** (1967): "drink deeply of" (39). [So also, Patrides (1985, 247) and Chmielewski (2001, 620).] **SMITH** (1971): "drink your health" (502).

59 *thee?* **MILGATE** (1967): "Coryate" (195).

59 *thou* **MILGATE** (1967): "refers to each of the friends" (195).

59 *fit* **PATRIDES** (1985): "limit, in accordance with one's capacity to drink" (247).

60 *fill out for the half-pinte wit.* **SMITH** (1971): "fill the glasses only so far as will meet the half-pint of wit they are toasting" (502).

61–62 *Some shall wrap…kill a foe.* **BALD** (1970): "Even when dismembered by shopkeepers for wrapping-paper, the book will still do good" (193).

61 *Some* **CHMIELEWSKI** (2001): "of the pages" (620).

62 *stop muskets,* **SMITH** (1971): "Early cartridges were just charges of powder wrapped in paper" (502).

62 *stop* **SHAWCROSS** (1967): "fill up, be placed inside the barrel of" (39).

63–64 *shalt not ease…to asswage.* **MILGATE** (1967): "The critics of the next generation will not have the convenience of being able to read your book all at once to satisfy their eager curiosity ('hunger'), because the leaves are scattered and the book is in pieces" (195). **SHAWCROSS** (1967): "even if future critics don't want to read any more of your book, they shall not be satisfied by reading any of it" (40).

64 *at once their hunger to asswage.* **SMITH** (1971): "to satisfy at one go their hunger

to read you (they will instead have the trouble of running around reading him in fragments, a bit here and a bit there)" (502).

65–66 *Nor shall...one Librarie.* **MILGATE** (1967): "the treasure of the *Crudities* will not be available to the plagiarist in any one library" (195).

65 *wit-pyrats* **SULLENS** (1964): a word combination that the *OED* does not record (207). **MILGATE** (1967): "The metaphor is of pirates attacking a ship ('bottome') laden with wealth" (195). **SMITH** (1971): "thieves of others' wit, plagiarizing hacks" (502). [So also, Patrides (1985, 247).] **CHMIELEWSKI** (2001): "plagerizers of your witty language" (620).

65 *pyrats* **SULLENS** (1964): Donne's use of this meaning of the word is earlier than the earliest source cited by *OED* (226).

66 *in one bottome,* **SMITH** (1971): "in one ship, as it were, which a wit-pirate might capture intact. Literally, in one book" (502).

67–70 *Some leaues...thinke this true;* **MILGATE** (1967): "Paper was pasted over the strings used to tie the quires of a book together, usually on the spine and at front and back to conceal the strings as they entered the boards (cardboard covers). Leaves of the Crudities will be used for this purpose, so that in reading another author a plagiarist might come across a page of Coryate and be able to steal (but, alas, only a little) from his work" (195).

67 *paste strings there in other books,* **SHAWCROSS** (1967): "may be used as a backing in the spine of a book" (40). [So also, Smith (1971, 502) and Patrides (1985, 247).]

68 *which on another looks,* **SMITH** (1971): "who is reading a work by somebody else, pasted up with scraps of Coryate's book" (502).

70 *But hardly* much;* **DONNE** (1611), in a marginal note in the 1611 volume of *The Odcombian Banquet*, says, "I meane from one page which shall paste strings in a booke." **SMITH** (1971): "he will be hard put to it to get much wit out of Coryate's book in any case" (502).

71–72 *As Sybils was,...worth as all.* **MILGATE** (1967): "The Cumaean Sybil came to the palace of Tarquin II with nine volumes (the 'Sybilline books'), which she offered at a high price. When Tarquin refused, she burnt three, and offered the other six for the same price; when the Roman king again refused, she burnt three more, and Tarquin bought the last three for the price originally asked for the nine." [Similarly, Chambers (1896, 1:226, 2:227) and Patrides (1985, 248).] "Coryate's book is as mysterious, each fragment being worth as much as the whole (i.e. nothing)" [so also, Smith (1971, 502)]; see Aulus Gellius, *Noctes Atticae,* 1:19; Dionysius of Halicarnassus, *Roman Antiquities,* 4:lxii, 1–4; and Munster, *Cosmographia* (1572), p. 208 (195).

71 *Sybils* **SHAWCROSS** (1967): "the book of a prophetess who attended the oracle at Delphi" (40). [So also, Chmielewski (2001, 621).]

73–74 *mine impotency...be farre lesse;* **SMITH** (1971): "he is impotent to honour

Coryate's book as it deserves for his brain will not bear such heady draughts of compliment as are in order" (502–03).

74 *healths* **MILGATE** (1967): "complimentary emotions (as expressed in drinking another's health). Donne is powerless to express so great an admiration" (195). [So also, Smith (1971, 503), Patrides (1985, 248), and Chmielewski (2001, 621).]

75 *Thy Gyant-wit o'rethrowes me,* **SMITH** (1971): "he cannot cope with the sheer bulk of Coryate's display of wit" (503).

76 *then* **PATRIDES** (1985): "than" (248).

In eundem Macaronicon.

COMMENTARY

General Commentary

Cpl. (1865, 84–85), printing *Macaron*, notes that it was "amongst the farrago of fun and nonsense dished up by the wits of the day," and then queries, "will anybody 'give me a construe?'"

In response to Cpl. (1865), R. S. Q. (1865, 145) offers first a literal translation:

> As many perfect linguists as these two distichs make,
> So many prudent statesmen will this book of yours produce.
> (Meaning obviously none at all.)
> To me the honour is sufficient of being understood; for I leave
> To you the honour of being believed by no one.

He then begs the reader's pardon for the following paraphrase:

> Could these my couplets one sound linguist breed,
> Then to true statesmanship your book might lead.
> If I'm but understood, I aim no higher:
> Be yours the honour to be deemed a liar!

By way of commentary, the writer notes that "the verses by Donne do not appear to come strictly within the class of Macaronics," which are typically "a ludicrous jumble of English, Latin, French, Italian, and Spanish words." The author further notes that "for a perfect appreciation" of Donne's sentiment "it is necessary to keep in view Coryat's introductory essay, 'On Travel in general,' in which he urges the importance of visiting foreign countries towards the formation of a statesman's character."

Within the context of discussing the travels Donne may have undertaken to the Continent during his youth, Gosse (1899, 1:56–57) describes *Coryat* and *Macaron* as "two scornful epistles full" of Donne's "own peculiar wit and magic," noting further that these poems "might have been written by a man who had never strayed out of London city." See more under General Commentary on *Coryat*.

Strachan (1962, 139, 275) states that even though *Macaron* epitomizes "the cutting scorn of the wits" (275), the "cruelty" of Donne's poem "did not sour Coryate's admiration for him" (139).

Milgate (1967) defines *Macaronicon*, or "macaronic" verse, as "a form in which, strictly speaking vernacular words are inserted into a Latin context (with Latin inflexions and constructions), and the verse is made to scan. More loosely, as here, it is verse in which two or more languages are mingled" (196).

Shawcross (1967) adds that this "burlesque" verse form gives Latin words in "italics, English in small capitals, and romance languages in roman type" (40).

Sullivan (1993, 12) notes that the previously "uncollected printings" of Donne's verse "establish a *terminus ad quem*" for *Macaron* of 1611.

Roebuck (1996, 144) writes that "not surprisingly" *Macaron* "deters the modern reader" and that in this poem and in *Coryat*, Donne "seems cheerfully to have descended" into print (144).

Notes and Glosses

Heading. In eundem Macaronicon. **SMITH** (1971): "in the macaronic manner. Macaronic verses are strictly a mixture of the vernacular and Latin in which the vernacular words take Latin forms; but the term can mean any poem written in a jumble of languages" (503).

1–4 Qvot, *dos…creduto*, tibi. **SMITH** (1971): "your book will make as many prudent statesmen as these two distichs make perfect linguists. To me the honour of being understood in this is sufficient; for I leave to you the honour of being believed by no one" (503).

2 *cuerdos* States-men, hic *liure fara* tuus. **SHAWCROSS** (1967): "if you can understand Coryate, you'll be in a good position to write a learned treatise" (40).

WORKS CITED

Adams, Robert M. 1958. *Strains of Discord: Studies in Literary Openness.* Ithaca: Cornell University Press.

Addleshaw, S. 1931. "A Famous Dean: Dr. John Donne of St. Paul's." *Church Quarterly Review* 113:38–54.

Albright, Daniel. 1985. *Lyricality in English Literature.* Lincoln and London: University of Nebraska Press.

Alden, Raymond MacDonald. 1899. *The Rise of Formal Satire in England under Classical Influence.* Series in Philosophy, Literature and Archaeology, vol. 7, no. 2. Philadelphia: University of Pennsylvania Press.

Allen, Don Cameron. 1943. "John Donne's Knowledge of Renaissance Medicine." *JEGP* 42:322–42.

———. 1945a. "John Donne's 'Paradise and Calvarie.'" *MLN* 60:398–400.

———. 1945b. "Two Annotations on Donne's Verse." *MLN* 60:54–55.

———. 1950. "Three Notes on Donne's Poetry with a Side Glance at Othello." *MLN* 65:102–06.

———. 1952. "The Double Journey of John Donne." In *A Tribute to George Coffin Taylor,* ed. Arnold Williams, 83–99. Chapel Hill: University of North Carolina Press.

———. 1959. "Donne on the Mandrake." *MLN* 74:393–97.

Allen, Morse S. 1965. *The Satire of John Marston.* New York: Haskell House.

Alvarez, A. 1961. *The School of Donne.* London: Chatto and Windus.

———. 1969. "The Game of Wit and the Corruption of Style." In *The Metaphysical Poets: Key Essays on Metaphysical Poetry and the Major Metaphysical Poets,* ed. Frank Kermode, 331–43. Greenwich, CT: Fawcett Publications.

Anderson, Robert. 1792–95. *A complete edition of the poets of Great Britain.* Vol. 4. Edinburgh: for John and Arthur Arch, and for Bell and Bradfute and I. Mundell and Co.

Andreasen, N. J. C. 1963. "Theme and Structure in Donne's Satyres." *SEL* 3:59–75.

———. 1967. *John Donne: Conservative Revolutionary.* Princeton: Princeton University Press.

Anonymous. 1618. *The Mirrovr of Maiestie: Or, The Badges of Honovr Conceitedly Emblazoned: With Emblemes Annexed, Poetically Vnfolded.* London: Printed by *William Iones,* dwelling in Red-crosse-streete.

———. 1644. *Vindex Anglicvs; or, the perfections of the English language defended and asserted.* STC V461. [Oxford]: [H. Hall].

———. 1734. "The Oxonian's Trip to the Drawing Room." *The Universal Spectator and Weekly Journal* 2 Feb. (no. cclxxviii).

———. 1740. "A Literary Article." *The Champion* (24 May) 2:259.

———. 1755. [Untitled.] *The World* 14 Aug. (no. cxxxvii).

———. 1784. *A new and general biographical dictionary.* 12 Vols. London: for W. Strahan, T. Payne and Son, J. Rivington and Sons, and others.

———. 1798. *The Progress of Satire: An Essay in Verse.* London: Printed for J. Bell [see Shaw-cross (1991b)].

———. 1838. *The Penny Cyclopaedia of the Society for the Diffusion of Useful Knowledge.* 27 vols. London: C. Knight.

———. 1876. "The First of the English Satirists." *TB* 47:337–50.

———. 1899. [Review of *The Life and Letters of John Donne* by Edmund Gosse.] *Ac* 57:505–06.

———. 1899. [Review of *The Life and Letters of John Donne* by Edmund Gosse.] *BookR* 7:482–83.

———. 1900. "Gosse's Life of Donne—I." *The Nation* 70 (8 Feb.):111–13.

Ansari, A. A. 1974. "Two Modes of Utterance in Donne's Divine Poems." In *Essays on John Donne: A Quarter Centenary Tribute,* ed. Asloob Ahmad Ansari, 139–56. Aligarh, India: Aligarh Muslim University.

Arber, Edward. 1877. *A Transcript of the Registers of the Company of Stationers of London: 1554–1640 A. D.* Vol. 4. London: Privately printed.

Archer, Stanley. 1961. "Meditation and the Structure of Donne's 'Holy Sonnets.'" *ELH* 28:137–47.

Arnold, Thomas. 1877. *A Manual of English Literature.* London: Longmans, Green & Co.

Aronstein, Philipp. 1916. "John Donne and Francis Bacon: Eine Beitragzum Kampf der Welt-anschauungen im zeitalter der Renaissance in England." *EnglStud* 49:360–76.

———. 1920. "John Donne." *Anglia* 44:115–213.

Ashley, Leonard R. N. 1970. "'To Touch Any Private Person Displeasantly': Satire in Eliza-bethan England." *SNL* 8:57–65.

Atkins, Sidney H. 1934. "Mr. Banks and His Horse." *N&Q* 167:39–41.

———. 1937. "Donne's Satires." *TLS* 22 May:396.

Atkinson, A. D. 1951. "Donne Quotations in Johnson's Dictionary." *N&Q* 196:387–88.

Attridge, Derek. 1982. *The Rhythms of English Poetry.* London and New York: Longman.

Austin, Frances. 1992. *The Language of the Metaphysical Poets.* New York: St. Martin's Press.

Baker, Herschel. 1952. *The Wars of Truth: Studies in the Decay of Christian Humanism in the Earlier Seventeenth Century.* Cambridge: Harvard University Press.

———. 1975. *The Later Renaissance in England: Nondramatic Verse and Prose, 1600–1660.* Boston: Houghton Mifflin.

Baker-Smith, Dominic. 1972. "John Donne's Critique of True Religion." In *John Donne: Essays in Celebration,* ed. A. J. Smith, 404–32. London: Methuen.

Bald, R. C. 1970. *John Donne: A Life.* New York and London: Oxford University Press.

Bamborough, J. B. 1952. *The Little World of Man.* London: Longmans, Green.

Barańczak, Stanisław. 1984. *John Donne: Wiersze wybrane wybór, przekład, posłowie i opracowanie.* Kraków: Wydawnictwo Literackie.

Bates, Catherine. 1992. *The Rhetoric of Courtship in Elizabethan Language and Literature.* Cam-bridge and New York: Cambridge University Press.

Battenhouse, Roy W. 1942. "The Grounds of Religious Toleration in the Thought of John Donne." *Church History* 11:217–48.

Baumlin, James S. 1985. "Donne as Imitative Poet: The Evidence of 'Satyre II.'" *EIRC* 11:29–42.

———. 1986a. "Donne's Christian Diatribes: Persius and the Rhetorical Persona of 'Satyre III' and 'Satyre V.'" In *The Eagle and the Dove: Reassessing John Donne,* ed. Claude J. Summers and Ted-Larry Pebworth, 92–105. Columbia: University of Missouri Press.

———. 1986b. "Generic Contexts of Elizabethan Satire: Rhetoric, Poetic Theory, and Imitation." In *Renaissance Genres: Essays on Theory, History, and Interpretation*, ed. Barbara Lewalski, 444–67. Cambridge and London: Harvard University Press.

———. 1988. "Donne's 'Satyre IV': The Failure of Language and Genre." *TSLL* 30:363–87.

———. 1990. "From Recusancy to Apostasy: Donne's 'Satyre III' and 'Satyre V.'" *EIRC* 16:67–85.

———. 1991. *John Donne and the Rhetorics of Renaissance Discourse*. Columbia: University of Missouri Press.

Bayle, Pierre. 1697. *Dictionaire historique et critique*. London: J. Roberts and Paul Vaillant. [Trans. as *A general dictionary, historical and critical*, 1736.]

Beal, Peter, comp. 1980. *Index of English Literary Manuscripts*. 2 vols. London: Mansell.

———. 2005–. *Catalogue of English Literary Manuscripts 1450–1700 (CELM)* <www.celm. org.uk>.

Beck, Joyce Short. 1987. "John Donne and William Dunbar: Poet-Satirists of the British Court." *Medieval Perspectives* 2:25–37.

Belden, H. M. 1915. "Reviews and Notes." *JEGP* 14:135–47.

Bellette, A. F. 1975. "The Originality of Donne's Satires." *UTQ* 44:130–40.

Benham, Allen R. 1941. "The Myth of John Donne the Rake." *PQ* 20:465–73.

Bennett, Joan. 1934. *Four Metaphysical Poets: Donne, Herbert, Vaughan, Crashaw*. Cambridge: Cambridge University Press.

———. 1964. *Five Metaphysical Poets: Donne, Herbert, Vaughan, Crashaw, Marvell*. Cambridge: Cambridge University Press.

Bennett, R. E. 1939. "John Donne and Everard Gilpin." *RES* 15:66–72.

———. 1942. "John Donne and the Earl of Essex." *MLQ* 3:603–04.

Bewley, Marius. 1952. "Religious Cynicism in Donne's Poetry." *KR* 14:619–46.

———. 1966. *John Donne, Selected Poetry*. Signet Classics. New York: New American Library.

———. 1970. *Masks & Mirrors: Essays in Criticism*. New York: Atheneum.

Biester, James. 1997. *Lyric Wonder: Rhetoric and Wit in Renaissance English Poetry*. Ithaca and London: Cornell University Press.

Birch, Thomas. 1752. *The life of the most reverend Dr John Tillotson*. London: for J. and R. Tonson and S. Draper, R. Ware, and others.

Blake, William. c. 1795. In *The Note-Book of William Blake called the Rossetti Manuscript*, ed. Geoffrey Keynes, 160. New York: Cooper Square Publishers, 1970.

Blissett, William. 2000. "'The Strangest Pageant, fashion'd Like a Court': John Donne and Ben Jonson to 1600—Parallel Lives." In *Wrestling with God: Literature and Theology in the English Renaissance: Essays to Honour Paul Grant Stanwood*, ed. Mary Ellen Henley and W. Speed Hill with the assistance of R. G. Siemens, 99–121. Vancouver: Henley.

Bloom, Edward A., and Lillian D. Bloom. 1979. *Satire's Persuasive Voice*. Ithaca and London: Cornell University Press.

B[ond], R[ichard] W. 1861. "Donne the Metaphysician." *TB* 3:78–91.

Boase, Alan M. 1949. "Poètes Anglais et Français de l'Epoque Baroque." *RSH* 55–56:155–84.

Bourne, Raymund. 1947. "John Donne and the Spiritual Life." *PoetryR* 38:460–61.

Bradbury, Nancy Mason. 1985. "Speaker and Structure in Donne's *Satyre IV*." *SEL* 25:87–107.

Bradford, Gamaliel. 1892. "The Poetry of Donne." *AR* 18:350–67.

———. 1917. "The Poetry of Donne." In *A Naturalist of Souls: Studies in Psychography*, 63–96. New York: Dodd, Mead.

Bradshaw, Graham. 1982. "Donne's Challenge to the Prosodists." *EIC* 32:338–60.

Bredbeck, Gregory W. 1991. *Sodomy and Interpretation: Marlowe to Milton*. Ithaca: Cornell University Press.

Bredvold, Louis I. 1923. "The Naturalism of Donne in Relation to Some Renaissance Traditions." *JEGP* 22:471–502.

———. 1925. "The Religious Thought of Donne in Relation to Medieval and Later Traditions." In *Studies in Shakespeare, Milton and Donne*, 191–232. University of Michigan Publications, Language and Literature, 1. New York and London: Macmillan.

Brennan, Michael. 1988. *Literary Patronage in the English Renaissance: The Pembroke Family*. London and New York: Routledge.

Briggs, Julia. 1983. *This Stage-Play World: English Literature and Its Backgrounds, 1580–1625*. Oxford and New York: Oxford University Press.

Broadbent, John, ed. 1974. *Poets of the 17th Century*. Signet Classics, Vol. 1. New York: Signet.

Brodsky, Claudia. 1982. "Donne: The Imaging of the Logical Conceit." *ELH* 49:829–48.

Brooke, Rupert. 1913. "John Donne." *Poetry and Drama* 1:185–88.

Brooks, Harold. 1934. "Donne and Drant." *TLS* 16 August:565.

———. 1949. "The 'Imitation' in English Poetry, Especially in Formal Satire, Before the Age of Pope." *RES* 98:124–40.

Bross, Addison C. 1966. "Alexander Pope's Revisions of John Donne's *Satyres*." *XUS* 5:133–52.

Brown, John. 1748. "An Essay on Satire." In *A collection of poems. By severall hands*, ed. Robert Dodsley, 333. Vol. 3. London: for R. and J. Dodsley.

Brown, Meg Lota. 1995. *Donne and the Politics of Conscience in Early Modern England*. Leiden: E. J. Brill.

Browning, Robert. 1878. "Two Poets of Croisic." In *The Complete Works of Robert Browning*, ed. Roma A. King, 14:127–209. 16 vols. Athens: Ohio University Press, 2003.

Bryan, Robert A. 1962. "John Donne's Poems in Seventeenth-Century Commonplace Books." *ES* 43:170–74.

———. 1965. "Translatio Concepts in Donne's 'The Progresse of the Soule.'" In *All These to Teach: Essays in Honor of C. A. Robertson*, ed. Robert A. Bryan, et al., 120–29. Gainesville: University of Florida Press.

Bullough, Geoffrey. 1972. "Donne: The Man of Law." In *Just So Much Honor: Essays Commemorating the Four-Hundredth Anniversary of the Birth of Donne*, edited by Peter Amadeus Fiore, 57–94. University Park and London: Pennsylvania State University Press.

Burt, Stephen. 1997. "Donne the Sea Man." *JDJ* 16:137–83.

Bush, Douglas. 1945. *English Literature in the Earlier Seventeenth Century, 1600–1660*. Oxford: Clarendon Press.

———. 1952. *English Poetry: The Main Currents from Chaucer to the Present*. New York: Oxford University Press.

———. 1955. "Seventeenth-Century Poets and the Twentieth Century." *Annual Bulletin of the Modern Humanities Research Association* 27:16–28.

Butt, John, ed. 1939. *Alexander Pope: Imitations of Horace*. London: Methuen.

Cain, Tom. 1995. "Donne and the Prince D'Amour." *JDJ* 14:83–111.

———. 1998. "'Satyres, That Girde and Fart at the Time': *Poetaster* and the Essex Rebellion." In *Refashioning Ben Jonson: Gender, Politics and the Jonsonian Canon*, ed. Julie Sanders with Kate Chedgzoy and Susan Wiseman, 48–70. Houndmills, Basingstoke, Hampshire: Macmillan.

Campbell, Gordon, ed. 1989. *The Renaissance 1550–1660*. Macmillan Anthologies of English Literature, Vol. 2. Gen. eds. A. Norman Jeffares and Michael Alexander. Houndsmills, Basingstoke, Hampshire and London: Macmillan Education Ltd.

Canfield, J. Douglas. 1989. *Word as Bond in English Literature from the Middle Ages to the Restoration*. Philadelphia: University of Pennsylvania Press.

Caracciolo-Trejo, Enrique. 1986. "Traducción e introducción." In *Poesía completa—edición bilingüe*, ed. Enrique Caracciolo-Trejo, 2:11–18. 2 vols. Barcelona: Ediciones 29.

Carey, John. 1959. "Clement Paman." *TLS* 27 March:177.

———. 1963. "John Donne." *Time & Tide* 44:24, 36.

———. 1981. *John Donne: Life, Mind and Art*. London and Boston: Faber and Faber. New ed. 1990.

———, ed. 1990. *John Donne*. Oxford and New York: Oxford University Press.

Carruthers, Robert, ed. 1854. *The Poetical Works of Alexander Pope*. 4 vols. London: Nathaniel Cooke.

Cary, Lucius [Viscount Falkland]. 1651. *Sir Lucius Cary, … his discourse of infallibility*. STC F317. London: Gartrude Dawson for Iohn Hardesty.

Cathcart, Dwight. 1975. *Doubting Conscience: Donne and the Poetry of Moral Argument*. Ann Arbor: University of Michigan Press.

Cave, John. c. 1620–25. "John Cave Manuscript." New York Public Library, Arents Collection.

Cazamian, Louis. 1952. *The Development of English Humor*. 2 parts. Durham, NC: Duke University Press.

Centerwall, Brandon S. 2003. "'Loe her's a Man, worthy indeede to travell': Donne's Panegyric upon Coryats Crudities." *JDJ* 22:77–94.

Chadwick, John White. 1900. "John Donne, Poet and Preacher." *NewW* 9:31–48.

Chalmers, Alexander, ed. 1810. *The Works of the English Poets, from Chaucer to Cowper*. 21 vols. London: J. Johnson.

Chambers, E. K., ed. 1896. *The Poems of John Donne*. With an Introduction by George Saintsbury. 2 vols. London: Lawrence & Bullen; New York: Charles Scribner's Sons.

Chandra, Naresh. 1991. *John Donne and Metaphysical Poetry*. Delhi: Doaba House.

Cheney, Patrick, and Anne Lake Prescott, eds. 2000. *Approaches to Teaching Shorter Elizabethan Poetry*. Approaches to Teaching World Literature, 65. New York: MLA.

Chitanand, T. P. 1963. "Donne's Progesse of the Soule." *IJES* 4:48–68.

Chmielewski, Walt T. 2001. "Notes for Satyres and Coryat." In *The Complete Poetry and Selected Prose of John Donne*, ed. Charles M. Coffin, 614–21. New York: Modern Library.

Clampitt, Amy. 1988. *The Essential Donne*. Selected and with an Introduction by Amy Clampitt. New York: The Ecco Press.

Clarke, Charles Cowden, ed. 1872. *The Poetical Works of Alexander Pope*. 2 vols. London: Cassell, Petter, and Galpin.

Clements, A. L., ed. 1966. *John Donne's Poetry: Authoritative Texts, Criticism*. New York: Norton.

Cleveland, Charles D. 1854. *A Compendium of English Literature, Chronologically Arranged, from Sir John Mandeville to William Cowper*. Philadelphia: E. C. & J. Biddle.

Clive, Mary. 1966. *Jack and the Doctor*. London: Macmillan; New York: St. Martin's Press.

Clough, Benjamin C. 1920. "Notes on the Metaphysical Poets." *MLN* 35:115–17.

Cobb, Lucille S. 1956a. "Donne's 'Satyre II,' 71–72." *Expl* 14:Item 40.

———. 1956b. "Donne's 'Satyre II,' 49–57." *Expl* 15:Item 8.

Coffin, Charles Monroe. 1937. *John Donne and the New Philosophy*. Morningside Heights, NY: Columbia University Press.

Cogan, Isabel. 1929. "John Donne: Poet and Metaphysician." *PoetryR* 20:183–94.

Cohen, J. M. 1963. "Satire." In *The Concise Encyclopedia of English and American Poets and Poetry*, ed. Stephen Spender and Donald Hall, 263–64. New York: Hawthorn Books. Rev. ed. 281–82. London: Hutchinson, 1970.

Cokain, Sir Aston. 1658. *Small poems of diverse sorts*. STC C4898. London: Wil. Godbid.

Coleridge, Samuel Taylor. 1811. *Marginalia II. Camden to Hutton*. In *The Collected Works of Samuel Taylor Coleridge*, ed. George Whalley. Vol. 12. Princeton: Princeton University Press, 1984.

———. 1817. *Biographia Literaria*, ed. John Shawcross. London: Oxford University Press, 1907.

———. 1836. *The Literary Remains of Samuel Taylor Coleridge*, ed. Henry Nelson Coleridge. 4 vols. London: W. Pickering.

Collier, J. Payne. 1820. *The Poetical Decameron, or Ten Conversations on English Poets and Poetry*. 2 vols. Edinburgh: Archibald Constable & Co.

Collier, William Francis. 1871. *A History of English Literature in a Series of Biographical Sketches*. Toronto: James Campbell & Son.

Collinson, Patrick. 2000. "English Reformations." In *A Companion to English Renaissance Literature and Culture*, ed. Michael Hattaway, 27–43. Oxford: Blackwell.

Colvin, Sir Sidney. 1915. "On Concentration and Suggestion in Poetry." *English Association Pamphlets* 32:17–19.

Cooper, Elizabeth, ed. 1737. *The Muses Library; or, A series of English poetry, from the Saxons, to the reign of King Charles II*. London: for J. Wilcox in the Strand; T. Green at Charing Cross; J. Brindley in New-Bond.

Coriate, Thomas. 1616. *Traueller for the English Wits: Greeting. From the Court of the Great Mogvl, Resident at the Towne of Asmere, in Easterne India*. Printed by W. Iaggard and Henry Fetherston.

Corser, Thomas. 1873. *Collectanea Anglo-Poetica: or, a Bibliographical and Descriptive Catalogue of a Portion of a Collection of Early English Poetry, with Occasional Extracts and Remarks Biographical and Critical. Part 5: Remains Historical & Literary connected with the Palatine Counties of Lancaster and Chester*. Manchester: Printed by Charles Simms for the Chetham Society.

Corthell, Ronald J. 1981. "Donne's *Metempsychosis*: An 'Alarum to Truth.'" *SEL* 21.1:97–110.

———. 1982. "Style and Self in Donne's Satires." *TSLL* 24:155–83.

———. 1987. "'Coscus onely breeds my just offence': A Note on Donne's 'Satire II' and the Inns of Court." *JDJ* 6:25–31.

———. 1997. *Ideology and Desire in Renaissance Poetry: The Subject of Donne*. Detroit: Wayne State University Press.

Coryat, Thomas. 1611. *Coryats Crambe, or His Colwort Twise Sodden, And Now serued in with other Macaronicke dishes, as the second course to his Crudities*. London: Printed by William Stansby.

———. 1611. *The Odcombian Banquet: dished foorth by Thomas the Coriat, and serued in by a number of noble wits in prayse of his Crudities and Crambe, too*. London: Imprinted [by George Eld] for Thomas Thorp.

Courthope, William John. 1903. *A History of English Poetry*. Vol.3. London: Macmillan.

Cousins, A. D. 1979. "The Coming of Mannerism: The Later Ralegh and the Early Donne." *ELR* 9:86–107.

Cox, R. G. 1956. "The Poems of John Donne." In *From Donne to Marvell*, ed. Boris Ford, 98–115. The Pelican Guide to English Literature 3. Baltimore: Penguin.

Cpl. 1865. "Latin Puzzle." *N&Q* 3rd ser. 7:84–85.

Craik, George L. 1845. *Sketches of the History of Literature and Learning in England*. 4 vols. London: Charles Knight.

————. 1861. *A Compendious History of English Literature, and of the English Language, from the Norman Conquest*. 2 vols. London: Charles Griffin.

Craik, Katherine A. 2004. "Reading *Coryats Crudities* (1611)." *SEL* 44.1:77–96.

Craik, T. W., and R. J. Craik, eds. 1986. *John Donne: Selected Poetry and Prose*. London and New York: Methuen.

Crinò, Annamaria. 1970. *La Satira Inglese*. Problemi ed orientamenti critici di lingue e letterature germaniche. Saggi e richerche, no. 5. Verona: Libreria Universitaria Editrice.

Crofts, J. E. V. 1936. "John Donne." *E&S* 22:128–43.

Croly, George, ed. 1835. *The Works of Alexander Pope*. 4 vols. London: A. J. Valpy.

Crum, Margaret. 1961. "Notes on the Physical Characteristics of some Manuscripts of the Poems of Donne and Henry King." *Library* 16:121–23.

Cruttwell, Patrick. 1977. "The Metaphysical Poets and their Readers." *HAB* 28:20–42.

Cunnar, Eugene R. 1990. "Illusion and Spiritual Perception in Donne's Poetry." In *Aesthetic Illusion: Theoretical and Historical Approaches*, ed. Frederick Burwick and Walter Pape, 324–36. Berlin and New York: Walter de Gruyter.

Cunningham, George Godfrey. 1837. *Lives of Eminent and Illustrious Englishmen*. Vol. 3. Glasgow: A. Fullarton.

Daalder, J[oost]. 1986. "The Prosodic Significance of Donne's 'Accidentals.'" *Parergon: Bulletin of the Australian and New Zealand Association for Medieval and Renaissance Studies* n.s. 4:87–101.

Danby, John F. 1950. "Jacobean Absolutists: The Placing of Beaumont and Fletcher." *Cambridge Journal* 3:515–40. Rpt. as "Beaumont and Fletcher: Jacobean Absolutists" in *Poets on Fortune's Hill: Studies in Sidney, Shakespeare, Beaumont and Fletcher*. London: Faber and Faber, 1952.

Daniel, George. c. 1640. *A vindication of poesie*. In *The Selected Poems of George Daniel of Beswick, 1616–1657*, ed. Thomas B. Stroup. Lexington: University of Kentucky Press, 1959.

Daniels, Edgar F. 1970. "Donne's Satire III, 52." *Expl* 28:Item 52.

————. 1981. "Donne's Satire III, 33–35." *Expl* 40:15–16.

Datta, Kitty. 1971. "Love and Asceticism in Donne's Poetry: The Divine Analogy." *The Jadaupur Journal of Comparative Literature* 9:73–97.

————. 1977. "Love and Asceticism in Donne's Poetry: The Divine Analogy." *CritQ* 19:5–25.

Davenport, A. 1955. "An Early Reference to John Donne." *N&Q* 200:12.

Davies, John, of Hereford. 1610. *The scourge of folly*. STC 6341. London: E. A[llde] for R. Redmer.

Davies, Stevie, ed. 1994. *John Donne*. Plymouth, Eng.: Northcote House, with British Council.

Davison, Francis. 1608. *A Poetical Rapsody, containing diverse sonnets, odes … .* STC 6373. London: V. S[immes] for J. Baily.

De Quincey, Thomas. 1828. *The Collected Writings of Thomas De Quincey*, ed. David Masson. 14 vols. Edinburgh: David and Charles Black, 1896.

DiPasquale, Theresa M. 1993. "Donne's Catholic Petrarchans: The Babylonian Captivity of Desire." In *Renaissance Discourses of Desire*, ed. Claude J. Summers and Ted-Larry Pebworth, 77–92. Columbia: University of Missouri Press.

————. 1999. *Literature and Sacrament: The Sacred and the Secular in John Donne*. Pittsburgh: Duquesne University Press.

Disraeli, Isaac. 1880. *Amenities of Literature*, ed. B. Disraeli. New York: Greenwood Press.

Dixon, J. 1880. "Donne's 'Satires.'" *N&Q* 6th ser. 2:8.

Docherty, Thomas. 1986. *John Donne Undone*. New York: Methuen.

―――. 1987. "Donne's Praise of Folly." In *Post-Structuralist Readings of English Poetry*, ed. Richard Machine and Christopher Norris, 85–104. Cambridge and New York: Cambridge University Press.

Doggett, Frank A. 1934. "Donne's Platonism." *SR* 42:274–92.

Donoghue, Denis. 2001. "Introduction." In *The Complete Poetry and Selected Prose of John Donne*, ed. Charles M. Coffin, v–xxxii. New York: Modern Library.

Doudna, Martin K. 1980. "Echoes of Milton, Donne, and Carlyle in 'Civil Disobedience.'" *Thoreau Journal Quarterly* 23:5–7.

Dowden, Edward. 1890. "The Poetry of John Donne." *FR* n.s. 47:791–808.

Drake, Nathan. 1800. *Literary Hours; or sketches critical and narrative.* Vol. 2. Sudbury, Eng.: for T. Cadell and W. Davies.

―――. 1817. *Shakspeare [sic] and His Times.* 2 vols. London: for T. Cadell and W. Davies.

Dryden, John. 1668. *An Essay of Dramatick Poesie.* In *The Works of John Dryden*, ed. Edward Niles Hooker, H. T. Swedenberg, and Vinton A. Dearing, 3–81. Vol. 17. Berkeley: University of California Press, 1971.

―――. 1693. *Discourse Concerning the Original and Progress of Satire.* In *The Works of John Dryden*, ed. Edward Niles Hooker, H. T. Swedenberg, and Vinton A. Dearing, 3–90. Vol. 4. Berkeley: University of California Press, 1974.

Dubrow, Heather. 1976. "Donne's 'Epithalamion made at Lincolnes Inne': An Alternative Interpretation." *SEL* 16:131–43.

―――. 1979. "'No man is an island': Donne's Satires and Satiric Traditions." *SEL* 19:71–83.

―――. 1990. *A Happier Eden: The Politics of Marriage in the Stuart Epithalamium.* Ithaca and London: Cornell University Press.

[Dubrow] Ousby, Heather. See Ousby, Heather Dubrow.

Duncan, Joseph E. 1959. *The Revival of Metaphysical Poetry: The History of a Style, 1800 to the Present.* Minneapolis: University of Minnesota Press.

E., K. P. D. 1880. "Donne's 'Satires.'" *N&Q* 6th ser. 2:191.

Eckhardt, Joshua, and Daniel Starza Smith, eds. 2014. *Manuscript Miscellanies in Early Modern England*, Material Readings in Early Modern Culture. Farnham/Burlington, VT: Ashgate.

Eddy, Yvonne Shikany and Daniel P. Jaeckle. 1981. "Donne's 'Satyre I': The Influence of Persius's 'Satire III.'" *SEL* 21:111–22.

Edwards, Anthony. 1972. "Libertine Literature." *TLS* 2 June:633.

Edwards, David L. 2001. *John Donne: Man of Flesh and Spirit.* London: Continuum.

El-Gabalawy, Saad. 1976. "Aretino's Pornography and Renaissance Satire." *BRMMLA* 30:87–99.

Eliot, Thomas Stearns. 1926. ["Donne's Longer Poems."] In *The Varieties of Metaphysical Poetry: The Clark Lectures at Trinity College, Cambridge, 1926, and the Turnbull Lectures at the Johns Hopkins University, 1933*, ed. Ronald Schuchard, 139–59. New York: Harcourt Brace, 1994.

―――. 1930. "The Devotional Poets of the Seventeenth Century: Donne, Herbert, Crashaw." *The Listener* 3:552–53.

―――. 1931. "Donne in Our Time." In *A Garland for John Donne, 1631–1931*, ed. Theodore Spencer, 3–19. Cambridge: Harvard University Press; London: Humphrey Milford, Oxford University Press.

Elkin, P. K. 1973. *The Augustan Defense of Satire.* Oxford: Clarendon Press.

Elliott, Emory. 1976. "The Narrative and Allusive Unity of Donne's *Satyres*." *JEGP* 75:105–16.

Elliott, G. R. 1931. "John Donne: The Middle Phase." *Bookm* (New York) 73:337–46.

Ellrodt, Robert. 1960a. "Chronologie des Poemes de Donne." EA 13.4:455–56.

———. 1960b. *L'inspiration personelle et l'esprit du temps chez les poètes métaphysiques anglais*. 2 vols. in 3. Paris: José Corti.

———. 1980. "Angels and the Poetic Imagination from Donne to Traherne." In *English Renaissance Studies Presented to Dame Helen Gardner in Honour of Her Seventieth Birthday*, ed. John Carey, 164–79. Oxford: Clarendon Press.

———. 1987. "Poésie et vérité chez John Donne." EA 40:1–14.

———. 2000. *Seven Metaphysical Poets: A Structural Study of the Unchanging Self*. Oxford: Oxford University Press.

Elton, Oliver. 1932. "Poetry, 1600–1660." In *The English Muse: A Sketch*, 202–31. London: G. Bell and Sons.

Elwin, Whitwell, and William John Courthope, eds. 1881. *The Works of Alexander Pope*. 10 vols. London: John Murray.

Emperor, John Bernard. 1928. *The Catullian Influence in English Lyric Poetry, circa 1600–1650*. University of Missouri Studies, Vol. 3, No. 3. Columbia: University of Missouri Press.

Empson, William. 1972. "Rescuing Donne." In *Just So Much Honor: Essays Commemorating the Four-Hundredth Anniversary of the Birth of John Donne*, ed. Peter Amadeus Fiore, 95–148. University Park and London: Pennsylvania State University Press.

———. 1993. *William Empson: Essays on Renaissance Literature*, ed. John Haffenden. Vol. I: "Donne and the New Philosophy." New York: Cambridge University Press.

Enright, D. J., ed. 1997. *John Donne*. Everyman's Poetry. London: Dent. Rpt. 1999, 2000.

Erskine-Hill, H. H., ed. 1964. *Pope: Horatian Satires and Epistles*. [London]: Oxford University Press.

———. 1972. "Courtiers out of Horace." In *John Donne: Essays in Celebration*, ed. A. J. Smith, 273–307. London: Methuen.

Esler, Anthony. 1966. *The Aspiring Mind of the Elizabethan Younger Generation*. Durham, NC: Duke University Press.

Evans, Gillian. 1978. *The Age of the Metaphysicals*. London: Blackie.

Everett, Barbara. 1972. *Donne: A London Poet*. Chatterton Lecture on an English Poet. London: Oxford University Press. Rpt. in PBA 58 (1974):245–73.

———. 1986. *Poets in Their Time: Essays on English Poetry from Donne to Larkin*. Boston: Faber & Faber.

———. 2001. "Donne and Secrecy." EIC 51:51–67.

Evett, David. 1986. "Donne's Poems and the Five Styles of Renascence Art." *JDJ* 5:101–31.

Farmer, Norman K., Jr. 1970. "A Theory of Genre for Seventeenth-Century Poetry." *Genre* 3.4:293–317.

Farmer, Richard. 1767. *An Essay on the Learning of Shakespeare…The Second Edition, with Large Additions*. Cambridge: Printed by J. Archdeacon, Printer to the University, for J. Woodyer (see Shawcross [1991b]).

Farr, Edward, ed. 1847. *Select Poetry, Chiefly Sacred, of the Reign of James the First*. Cambridge: Cambridge University Press.

Fausset, Hugh I'Anson. 1924. *John Donne: A Study in Discord*. London: Jonathan Cape. Rpt. New York: Russell and Russell, 1967.

Fennor, William. 1617. *The compters common-Wealth, or a voyage made to an infernall island long since discovered by many captains, gentlemen, merchants*. STC 10781. London: E. Griffin for G. Gibbes.

Ferry, Leonard D. G. 1997. "'Till busy hands / Blot out the text': *Realme* in *Satyre III*." *JDJ* 16:221–27.

Finkelpearl, P. J. 1963. "Donne and Everard Gilpin: Additions, Corrections, and Conjectures." *RES* 14:164–67.

Fischer, Hermann. 1971. *Englische Barockgedichte*. Herstellung. Stuttgart: Philipp Reclam Jun.

Fish, Stanley. 1990. "Masculine Persuasive Force: Donne and Verbal Power." In *Soliciting Interpretation: Literary Theory and Seventeenth-Century English Poetry*, ed. Elizabeth D. Harvey and Katharine Eisaman Maus, 223–52. Chicago: University of Chicago Press.

Fitzherbert, Thomas. 1613. *A supplement to the Discussion of M. D. Barlowes Answere To the Judgment of a catholike English man. By the way is briefly censured J. Dunnes Pseudo-martyr*. STC 11021. [St. Omer]: English College Press.

Flynn, Dennis. 1983. "John Donne in the Ellesmere Manuscripts." *HLQ* 46:333–36.

———. 1987. "Donne's *Ignatius His Conclave* and Other Libels on Robert Cecil." *JDJ* 6.2:163–83.

———. 2000. "Donne's Politics, 'Desperate Ambition,' and Meeting Paolo Sarpi in Venice." *JEGP* 99:334–55.

———. 2001. "Donne's Most Daring Satyre: 'richly For service paid, authoriz'd.'" *JDJ* 20:107–20.

Forde, Thomas. 1661. *A theatre of wits*. STC F1548A. London: R. & W. Leybourn for Thomas Basset.

Forrest, William Craig. 1968. "The Kinesthetic Feel of Literature." *BuR* 16:91–106.

Fortier, Mark. 1991. "The Muse in Donne and Jonson: A Post-Lacanian Study." *MLS* 21.4:90–104.

Fowler, Alistair. 1987. *A History of English Literature*. Cambridge: Harvard University Press.

———. 1993. "Genre and Tradition." In *The Cambridge Companion to English Poetry: Donne to Marvell*, ed. Thomas N. Corns, 80–100. Cambridge: Cambridge University Press.

Freeman, Arthur. 1978. *Elizabeth's Misfits: Brief Lives of English Eccentrics, Exploiters, Rogues, and Failures 1580–1660*. Foreword by Nicolas Barker. New York and London: Garland Publishing Inc.

Freeman, Thomas. 1614. *Runne, And a great Cast. The Second Bowle*. Published with *Rubbe, And A great Cast*. Epigrams. STC 11370. London: [N. Okes] sold by [L. Lisle].

Freer, Coburn. 1996. "John Donne and Elizabethan Economic Theory." *Criticism* 38: 497–520.

Frontain, Raymond-Jean. 1995. "'Make all this All': The Religious Operations of John Donne's Imagination." In *John Donne's Religious Imagination: Essays in Honor of John T. Shawcross*, ed. Raymond-Jean Frontain and Frances M. Malpezzi, 1–27. Conway, AR: University of Central Arkansas Press.

Frye, Northrop. 1980. *Creation and Recreation*. Toronto, Buffalo and London: University of Toronto Press.

Fulton, Thomas. 2001. "Hamlet's Inky Cloak and Donne's *Satyres*." *JDJ* 20:71–106.

Furst, Clyde Bowman. 1896. "The Life and Poetry of Dr. John Donne, Dean of St. Paul's." *Cit* 2:229–37.

Gallenca, Christiane. 1982. "La Satire Formelle." In *La Dupe Elisabethaine ou L'Homme Trompe*, 309–30. Etudes Anglaises 83. Paris: Didier.

Gamberini, Spartaco. 1967. *Saggio su John Donne*. Genova: Istituto di Lingua e Letteratura Inglese e Anglo-Americana dell' Università di Genova.

Gardner, Helen. 1948. "John Donne: An Elizabethan Master of Contemporary British Poetry." *British Africa Monthly* 15:31–32.

———, ed. 1952. *John Donne: The Divine Poems*. Oxford: Clarendon Press. Rev. ed. 1978.

———. 1967. "The Titles of Donne's Poems." In *Friendship's Garland: Essays Presented to Mario Praz on His Seventieth Birthday*, ed. Vittorio Gabrieli, 189–207. Vol. 1. Roma: Edizioni di Storia e Letteratura.

———. 1969. "The Religious Poetry of John Donne." In *The Metaphysical Poets: Key Essays on Metaphysical Poetry and the Major Metaphysical Poets*, ed. Frank Kermode, 203–24. Greenwich, CT: Fawcett Publications.

———. 1972. "The 'Metempsychosis' of John Donne." *TLS* 29 Dec:1587–88.

Garnett, Richard, and Edmund Gosse. 1903. *English Literature: An Illustrated Record*. 4 vols. London: William Heinemann.

Garrod, H. W., ed. 1946. *John Donne: Poetry and Prose with Izaac Walton's Life*. Oxford: Clarendon Press.

Geraldine, Sister M. 1965. "John Donne and the Mindes Indeavours." *SEL* 5:115–31.

———. 1966. "Donne's *Notitia*: The Evidence of the *Satires*." *UTQ* 36:24–36.

Gilbert, A. J. 1979. *Literary Language from Chaucer to Johnson*. London: Macmillan.

Gilfillan, George. 1860. *Specimens with Memoirs of the Less-Known British Poets*. 3 vols. Edinburgh: James Nichol.

Gill, R. B. 1974. "Another Reference to Donne's 'Satire III,' ll. 79–82." *ANQ* 13:53–54.

———. 1975. "A Purchase of Glory: The Persona of Late Elizabethan Satire." *SP* 72:408–18.

Gilman, Ernest B. 1986a. *Iconoclasm and Poetry in the English Reformation: Down Went Dagon*. Chicago and London: University of Chicago Press.

———. 1986b. "'To Adore, or Scorne an Image': Donne and the Iconoclastic Controversy." *JDJ* 5:63–100. Rev. as ch. 5 in *Iconoclasm and Poetry in the English Reformation: Down Went Dagon*.

Gorbunov, A. N. 1993. *Dzhon Donn i angliiskata poezia XVI–XVII vekov*. Moscow: Izdvo Moskovskogo Universiteta.

Gosse, Edmund. 1893. "The Poetry of John Donne." *NewR* 9:236–47.

———. 1899. *The Life and Letters of John Donne, Dean of St. Paul's*. 2 vols. London: William Heinemann.

Granger, James. 1769. *A biographical history of England, from Egbert the Great to the Revolution*. 4 Vols. London: for T. Davies.

Gransden, K. W., ed. 1954. *John Donne*. Hamden, CT: Archon Books. Rev. ed. 1969.

———, ed. 1970. *Tudor Verse Satire*. Athlone Renaissance Library, ed. G. Bullough and C. A. Meyer. London: Athlone Press.

Gray, Thomas. 1752? "Observations on English Meter." In *Essays and Criticisms by Thomas Gray*, ed. Clark Sutherland Northup. Boston: D. C. Heath, 1911.

Greene, Thomas M. 1982. *The Light in Troy: Imitation and Discovery in Renaissance Poetry*. Elizabethan Club Series. New Haven: Yale University Press.

Grierson, Herbert J. C. 1906. *The First Half of the Seventeenth Century*. Periods of European Literature, ed. George E. B. Saintsbury. Vol. 7. Edinburgh and London: W. Blackwood and Sons.

———. 1909. "John Donne." In *The Cambridge History of English Literature*, ed. A. W. Ward and A. R. Waller, 4:225–56. Cambridge: Cambridge University Press.

———, ed. 1912. *The Poems of John Donne*. 2 vols. Oxford: Clarendon Press.

———, ed. 1921. *Metaphysical Lyrics & Poems of the Seventeenth Century: Donne to Butler*. Oxford: Clarendon Press.

———, ed. 1929. *The Poems of John Donne*. Oxford: Oxford University Press.

———. 1930. "Donne's Satyres, II., ll. 71–3." *TLS* 6 March:190.

———. 1948. "John Donne and the 'Via Media.'" *MLR* 43:305–14.

———. 1949. *Criticism and Creation*. London: Chatto and Windus.

Griffin, Dustin. 1994. *Satire: A Critical Reintroduction*. Lexington: University Press of Kentucky.

Grigson, Geoffrey, ed. 1980. *The Oxford Book of Satirical Verse*. New York: Oxford University Press.

Gros, Leon-Gabriel. 1964. *Vie et Oeuvres de John Donne: Evenements Litterarires, Artistiques et Historiques*. Paris: Editions Seghers.

Grosart, Alexander B., ed. 1872–73. *The Complete Poems of John Donne, D. D.* 2 vols. The Fuller Worthies' Library. London: Printed for Private Circulation by Robson and Sons.

Grove, Robin. 1984. "Nature Methodiz'd." CR 26:52–68.

Guibbory, Achsah. 1986. "John Donne: The Idea of Decay." In *The Map of Time: Seventeenth-Century English Literature and Ideas of Pattern in History*, 69–104. Urbana and Chicago: University of Illinois Press.

———. 1990. "'Oh, Let Mee not Serve so': The Politics of Love in Donne's Elegies." *ELH* 57:811–33.

———. 1993. "John Donne." In *The Cambridge Companion to English Poetry: Donne to Marvell*, ed. Thomas N. Corns, 123–147. Cambridge: Cambridge University Press.

Guilhamet, Leon. 1987. *Satire and the Transformation of Genre*. Philadelphia: University of Pennsylvania Press.

Guilpin, Everard. 1598. *Skialetheia. Or, a shadow of truth, in certain epigrams and satyres*. STC 12504. London: J. R[oberts] for N. Ling. Ed. D. Allen Carroll. Chapel Hill: University of North Carolina Press, 1974.

Guiness, Gerald. 1986. "Playing for Life in Donne's Elegies, Songs and Sonnets." In *Auctor Ludens: Essays on Play in Literature*, ed. Gerald Guiness and Andrew Hurley, 137–55. Philadelphia and Amsterdam: John Benjamins.

Guiney, Louise I. 1920. "Donne as a Lost Catholic Poet." *The Month* 136:13–19.

Guss, Donald L. 1966. *John Donne, Petrarchist: Italianate Conceits and Love Theory in The Songs and Sonets*. Detroit: Wayne State University Press.

Hadfield, Andrew. 2001. *The English Renaissance 1500–1620*. Blackwell Guides to Literature. Oxford: Blackwell.

Haffenden, John, ed. 1993. *William Empson: Essays on Renaissance Literature*. Vol. I: "Donne and the New Philosophy." New York: Cambridge University Press.

Hagopian, John V. 1958. "A Difficult Crux in Donne's *Satyre II*." *MLN* 73:255–57.

Hales, John W. 1891. "John Donne." In *The English Poets*, ed. Thomas Humphry Ward, 1:558–60. London: Macmillan.

Hall, Anne Drury. 1991. *Ceremony and Civility in English Renaissance Prose*. University Park: Pennsylvania State University Press.

Hall, Vernon. 1957. "Donne's 'Satyre II,' 71–72." *Expl* 15.4:Item 24.

Hallam, Henry. 1839. *Introduction to the Literature of Europe*. 4 vols. London: John Murray.

Hamburger, Maik, and Christa Schuenke, eds. 1985. *John Donne: Zwar ist auch Dichtung Sünde: Gedichte englische und deutsch*. Reclams Universal-Bibliothek, Band 944. Leipzig: Philipp Reclam Jun.

Hamer, Enid. 1930. *The Metres of English Poetry*. London: Methuen.

Hamilton, G. Rostrevor. 1949. "The Tell-Tale Article." In *The Tell-Tale Article: A Critical Approach to Modern Poetry*, 3–59. London: William Heinemann.

Hamilton, R. W. 1979. "Donne and Castiglione." *N&Q* n.s. 26:405–06.

Hardy, Evelyn. 1942. *Donne: A Spirit in Conflict*. London: Constable.

Hare, Julius Charles, and Augustus William Hare. 1889. *Guesses at Truth by Two Brothers*. London: Macmillan.

Harris, Bernard. 1960. "IX. Men like Satyrs." In *Elizabethan Poetry*, 175–201. Stratford-upon-Avon Studies, 3. London: Edward Arnold.

Harris, C. S. 1902. "'Maceron': 'Mucheron.'" *N&Q* 9:284.

Harris, Victor. 1962. "John Donne and the Theatre." *PQ* 41:257–69.

Harrison, G. B. 1937. "Donne's Satires." *TLS* 29 May:412.

Harte, Walter. 1730. *An Essay on Satire, Particularly on the Dunciad.* London: for Lawton Gilliver at Homer's Head, against St. Dunstan's Church, in Fleetstreet.

Hartwig, Joan. 1995. "Donne's Horse and Rider as Body and Soul." In *John Donne's Religious Imagination: Essays in Honor of John T. Shawcross,* ed. Raymond-Jean Frontain and Frances M. Malpezzi, 262–84. Conway, AR: University of Central Arkansas Press.

Haskin, Dayton. 2000. "Coleridge's Marginalia on the Seventeenth-Century Divines and the Perusal of Our Elder Writers." *JDJ* 19:311–37.

———. 2002. "No Edition is an Island: The Place of the Nineteenth-Century American Editions within the History of Editing Donne's Poems." *TEXTiats* 14:169–207.

Haublein, Ernst. 1979. "King Imagery in the Poetry of John Donne." *Anglia* 97:94–115.

Hawkes, David. 2001. *Idols of the Marketplace: Idolatry and Commodity Fetishism in English Literature, 1580–1680.* New York: Palgrave.

Hayward, John, ed. 1929. *John Donne: Complete Poetry and Selected Prose.* New York: Random House. Rpt. with corrections and additions, 1930.

———. 1950. *John Donne: A Selection of His Poetry.* London: Penguin Books.

Hazlitt, W. Carew. 1868. "John Donne: Poems by him in an Early Ms." *NQR* 4th ser. 2:483–84.

Headley, Henry. 1787. *Select Beauties of Ancient English Poetry.* London: for T. Cadell.

Heath-Stubbs, John. 1969. "The Jacobeans." In *The Verse Satire,* 22–23. London: Oxford University Press.

Hebaisha, Hoda. 1971. *John Donne: The Man and His Poetry. With an Anthology of Representative Poems.* Cairo: Anglo-Egyptian Bookshop.

Helgerson, Richard. 1983. *Self-Crowned Laureates: Spenser, Jonson, Milton, and the Literary System.* Berkeley: University of California Press.

Hellegers, Desiree E. 1991. "The Politics of Redemption: Science, Conscience, and the Crisis of Authority in John Donne's 'Anniversaries.'" *New Orleans Review* 18:9–18.

———. 2000. *Handmaid to Divinity: Natural Philosophy, Poetry, and Gender in Seventeenth-Century England.* Norman, OK: University of Oklahoma Press.

Heltzel, Virgil B. 1938. "An Early Use of Donne's Fourth Satire." *MLN* 53:421–22.

Heninger, S. K., Jr. 1960. *A Handbook of Renaissance Meteorology, with Particular Reference to Elizabethan and Jacobean Literature.* Durham, NC: Duke University Press.

Hester, M. Thomas. 1976. "John Donne's 'Hill of truth.'" *ELN* 14:100–05.

———. 1977a. "The 'Bona Carmina' of Donne and Horace." In *Renaissance Papers 1976,* ed. Dennis G. Donovan and A. Leigh DeNeef, 21–30. Durham, NC: Southeastern Renaissance Conference.

———. 1977b. "Henry Donne, John Donne, and the Date of 'Satyre II.'" *N&Q* n.s. 24:524–27.

———. 1977c. "'Zeal' as Satire: The Decorum of Donne's Satyres." *Genre* 10:173–94.

———. 1978a. "'All our Soules Devotion': Satire as Religion in Donne's *Satyre III*." *SEL* 18:35–55.

———. 1978b. "The Satirist as Exegete: John Donne's *Satyre V*." *TSLL* 20:347–66.

———. 1979. "Donne's *Apologia*." *PLL* 15:137–58.

———. 1980a. "Another Allusion to Horace in Donne." *ANQ* 18:106–08.

———. 1980b. "'Carelesse Phrygius': Donne's Separatist Sectarian." In *A Fair Day in the Affections: Literary Essays in Honor of Robert B. White, Jr.,* ed. Jack D. Durant and M. Thomas Hester, 87–97. Raleigh, NC: Winston Press.

———. 1981. "Poetasters as 'Bellows': Donne's Inventive Imitation." *ELN* 19:20–21.

———. 1982. *Kind Pitty and Brave Scorn: John Donne's Satyres.* Durham, NC: Duke University Press.

————. 1984. "'All are players': Guilpin and 'Prester Iohn' Donne." *SoAR* 49:3–17.

————. 1991. "Genre, Grammar, and Gender in Donne's *Satyre III*." *JDJ* 10:97–102.

————. 1992. "Introduction." In *Dictionary of Literary Biography*, Vol. 121: Seventeenth-Century British Nondramatic Poets, ed. M. Thomas Hester, ix–xxii. Detroit: Gale Research Inc.

————. 1994a. "'Ask thy father': ReReading Donne's *Satyre III*." *Ben Jonson Journal* 1:201–18.

————. 1994b. "Donne and the Court of Wards." *ANQ* 7:130–33.

————, ed. 1996. *John Donne's "desire of more": The Subject of Anne More Donne in His Poetry*. Newark: University of Delaware Press; London: Associated University Presses.

————. 2000. "'Like a spyed Spie': Donne's Baiting of Marlowe." In *Literary Circles and Cultural Communities in Renaissance England*, ed. Claude J. Summers and Ted-Larry Pebworth, 24–43. Columbia: University of Missouri Press.

Hieatt, Kent, ed. 1987. "The Sixteenth and Seventeenth Centuries." In *Poetry in English: An Anthology*, ed. M. L. Rosenthal, 126–327. New York and Oxford: Oxford University Press.

Hill, George Birkbeck Norman, ed. 1897. *Johnsonian Miscellanies*. Oxford: Clarendon Press.

Hiller, Geoffrey G., ed. 1977. *Poems of the Elizabethan Age: An Anthology*. London: Methuen.

Hillyer, Robert Silliman. 1941. "Introduction." In *The Complete Poetry and Selected Prose of John Donne & the Complete Poetry of William Blake*, xv–lv. New York: Modern Library.

Hirsch, David A. Hedrich. 1991. "Donne's Atomies and Anatomies: Deconstructed Bodies and the Resurrection of Atomic Theory." *SEL* 31:69–94.

Hodgart, Matthew. 1969. *Satire*. New York and Toronto: McGraw-Hill.

Hodgson, Elizabeth M. A. 1999. *Gender and the Sacred Self in John Donne*. Newark: University of Delaware Press; London: Associated University Press.

Hogan, Patrick G., Jr. 1977. "The Iconographic Background of the First Verse of Donne's 'A Valediction Forbidding Mourning.'" In *New Essays on Donne*, ed. Gary A. Stringer, 26–44. Salzburg Studies in English Literature, Elizabethan & Renaissance Studies, ed. James Hogg, no. 57. Salzburg: Institut für Englische Sprache und Literatur, Universität Salzburg.

Hollander, John. 1961. *The Untuning of the Sky: Ideas of Music in English Poetry, 1500–1700*. Princeton: Princeton University Press. Rpt. 1993.

Holloway, John. 1977. *Poetry, Insight and the Self, 1120–1920*. London and Boston: Routledge.

Hoover, L. Elaine. 1978. *John Donne and Francisco de Quevedo: Poets of Love and Death*. Chapel Hill: University of North Carolina Press.

Horne, R. C. 1983. "An Allusion to Nashe's *Choise of Valentines* in Donne's Second Satire." *N&Q* 30:414–15.

Hughes, Kenneth James. 1982. "Donne's 'Metempsychosis' and the Objective Idea of Unreason." *CIEFLB* 18:15–39.

Hughes, Merritt Y. 1934. "Kidnapping Donne." *UCPES* 4:61–89.

Hughes, Richard E. 1968. *The Progress of the Soul: The Interior Career of John Donne*. New York: William Morrow.

Hume, David. 1754–62. *The History of England: from the Invasion of Julius Caesar to the Revolution in 1688*. Edinburgh: by Hamilton, Balfour, and Neill.

Hunt, Clay. 1954. *Donne's Poetry: Essays in Literary Analysis*. New Haven: Yale University Press; London: Geoffrey Cumberlege, Oxford University Press.

Hunter, William B. 1982. "John Donne and Robert Greene." *ANQ* 21:6–7.

————. 1983. "Difficulties in the Interpretation of John Donne's *Satyre I*." *SCB* 43:109–11.

Hurd, Richard, ed. 1776. *Q. Horatii Flacci epistolae ad Pisones, et Augustum: with an English Commentary and notes: to which are added critical dissertations*. Vol. 1. London: W. Bowyer and J. Nichols, for T. Cadell and J. Woodyer.

Husain, Itrat. 1938. *The Dogmatic and Mystical Theology of John Donne*. New York: MacMillan.

———. 1948. *The Mystical Element in the Metaphysical Poets of the Seventeenth Century*. Edinburgh: Oliver and Boyd.

Hutchison, Alexander N. 1970. "Constant Company: John Donne and his Satiric Personae." *Discourse* 13:354–63.

Hutton, W. H. 1924. "John Donne, Poet and Preacher." *Th* (London) 9:149–65.

Huxley, Aldous. 1919. "Ben Jonson." *LMer* 1:184–91.

Inglis, Fred. 1969. *The Elizabethan Poets: The Making of English Poetry from Wyatt to Ben Jonson*. London: Evans Brothers.

Jack, Ian. 1951. "Pope and 'The Weighty Bullion of Dr. Donne's Satires.'" *PMLA* 66:1009–22.

Jackson, George. 1917. "The Bookshelf by the Fire: V. John Donne." *Expository Times* 28:216–20.

Jackson, Robert S. 1968. "'Doubt Wisely': John Donne's Christian Skepticism." *Cithara* 8:39–46.

———. 1970. *John Donne's Christian Vocation*. Evanston: Northwestern University Press.

Jaffe, Nora Crow. 1977. *The Poet Swift*. Hanover, NH: University Press of New England.

Jameson, Anna Brownell. 1829. *The Loves of the Poets*. 2 vols. London: Coburn.

Janson, H. W. 1952. *Apes and Ape Lore in the Middle Ages and the Renaissance*. London: Warburg Institute.

Javitch, Daniel. 1978. *Poetry and Courtliness in Renaissance England*. Princeton: Princeton University Press.

Jenkins, Raymond. 1923. "Drayton's Relation to the School of Donne, as Revealed in the *Shepheards Sirena*." *PMLA* 38:557–87.

Jensen, Ejner. 1972. "The Wit of Renaissance Satire." *PQ* 51:394–409.

Jessopp, Augustus. 1855. "Some Notice of the Author and His Writings." In *Essays in Divinity by John Donne, D.D.*, ix–lxxiv. London: J. Tupling.

———. 1880. "Donne's 'Satires.'" *N&Q* 6th ser. 2:190.

Johnson, Jeffrey. 1999. *The Theology of John Donne*. Cambridge: D. S. Brewer.

Johnson, S. F. 1953. "Donne's Satires, I." *Expl* 11.8:Item 53.

Johnson, Samuel. 1755–85. *A Dictionary of the English Language*. London: W. Strahan, for J. and P. Knapton; T. and T. Longman; C. Hitch and L. Hawes; A. Millar; and R. and J. Dodsley.

Jonas, Leah. 1940. "John Donne." In *The Divine Science: The Aesthetic of Some Representative Seventeenth-Century English Poets*, 201–10. Columbia University Studies in English and Comparative Literature, 151. New York: Columbia University Press.

Jones, Emrys, ed. 1991. *The New Oxford Book of Sixteenth Century Verse*. Oxford and New York: Oxford University Press.

Jones, Evan. 1961. "Verse, Prose and Pope: A Form of Sensibility." *Melbourne Critical Review* 4:30–40.

Jonson, Ben. 1607? *Ben Jonson*, ed. C. H. Herford, Percy Simpson, and Evelyn Simpson. 11 vols. Oxford: Clarendon Press, 1925–52.

———. 1610. *Ben Jonson*, ed. C. H. Herford, Percy Simpson, and Evelyn Simpson.

———. 1616. *The Workes of Beniamin Jonson*. STC 14751. London: William Stansby.

———. 1619. "Conversations with William Drummond of Hawthornden." In *Ben Jonson*, ed. C. H. Herford, Percy Simpson and Evelyn Simpson.

Jordan, William K. 1936. "The Dominant Groups, 1603–1625. Development of Governmental and Anglican Thought with Respect to Religious Dissent." In *The Development of Religious Toleration in England from the Accession of James I to the Convention of the Long Parliament (1603–1640)*, 2:17–114. Cambridge: Harvard University Press.

Kantra, Robert A. 1984. *All Things Vain: Religious Satirists and Their Art*. University Park: Pennsylvania State University Press.

Kawasaki, Toshihiko. 1971. "Donne's Microcosm." In *Seventeenth-Century Imagery: Essays on Uses of Figurative Language from Donne to Farquhar*, ed. Earl Miner, 25–43. Berkeley, Los Angeles, and London: University of California Press.

Kenner, Hugh, ed. 1964. *Seventeenth Century Poetry: The Schools of Donne and Jonson*. New York: Holt, Rinehart and Winston.

Kerins, Frank. 1984. "The 'Businesse' of Satire: John Donne and the Reformation of the Satirist." *TSLL* 26:34–60.

Kermode, Frank. 1957. *John Donne*. Writers and their Works, no. 86. London: Longmans, Green. Rpt. 1961, 1964, 1968.

———, ed. 1969. "Introduction." In *The Metaphysical Poets: Key Essays on Metaphysical Poetry and the Major Metaphysical Poets*, 11–34. Greenwich, CT: Fawcett Publications.

———. 1970. *The Poems of John Donne*. New York: Heritage Press.

———. 1971. "John Donne." In *Shakespeare, Spenser, Donne: Renaissance Essays*, 116–48. New York: Viking Press.

Kermode, Frank, and John Hollander, eds. 1973. *The Oxford Anthology of English Literature*. Vol. I. New York: Oxford University Press. Reissued in a separate volume as *The Literature of Renaissance England*. New York: Oxford University Press.

Kermode, Frank, Stephen Fender, and Kenneth Palmer, eds. 1974. *English Renaissance Literature: Introductory Lectures*. London: Graymills.

Kernan, Alvin. 1959. *The Cankered Muse: Satire of the English Renaissance*. New Haven: Yale University Press.

King, Bruce. 1982. "Donne and Jonson." In *Seventeenth-Century English Literature*, 40–61. New York: Schocken Books.

King, John N. 1982. *English Reformation Literature: The Tudor Origins of the Protestant Tradition*. Princeton: Princeton University Press.

———. 2000. "Traditions of Complaint and Satire." In *A Companion to English Renaissance Literature and Culture*, ed. Michael Hattaway, 367–77. Oxford: Blackwell.

Kippis, Andrew. 1793. *Biographia Britannica; or, the lives of the most eminent persons who have flourished in Great Britain and Ireland, from the earliest times*. Vol. 4. London: for W. and A. Strahan; for C. Barthust, W. Strahan, J. Rivington and Sons, and others.

Kiséry, András. 1997. "'He to another key his style doth dress': Pope's Imitations of Donne." *Hungarian Journal of English and American Studies* 3:107–30.

Kishimoto, Yoshitaka. 1960. "Donne no Satyres—Sono Hyogen ni tsuite" (Donne's Satyres—On Their Expression). *Kiyo* (Kokugo/Kokubun) (Bungakubu, Baika Joshi Daigaku), no. 7 (December): 61–72.

Klause, John. 1986. "The Montaigneity of Donne's *Metempsychosis*." In *Renaissance Genres: Essays on Theory, History, and Interpretation*, ed. Barbara Kiefer Lewalski, 418–43. Harvard English Studies, 14. Cambridge and London: Harvard University Press.

———. 1993. "The Two Occasions of Donne's 'Lamentations of Jeremy.'" *MP* 90:337–59.

———. 1994. "Hope's Gambit: The Jesuitical, Protestant, Skeptical Origins of Donne's Heroic Ideal." *SP* 91:181–215.

Klawitter, George. 1994. *The Enigmatic Narrator: The Voicing of Same-Sex Love in the Poetry of John Donne*. New York: Peter Lang.

Kneidel, Gregory. 2001. "John Donne's *Via Pauli*." *JEGP* 100:224–46.

Knottenbelt, E. M. 2000. "What was John Donne Hearing? A Study in Sound Sense." In *Contextualized Stylistics: In Honour of Peter Verdonk*, ed. Tony Bex, Michael Burke and Peter Stockwell, 113–29. Amsterdam: Rodopi.

Knox, Vicesimus. 1782. *Essays moral and literary.* London: for Charles Dilly.

Koch, Walter A. 1967. "Linguistic Analysis of a Satire." *Linguistics* 33:68–81.

Korte, Donald M. 1969. "John Donne's 'Satyres' and a Matter of Rhetoric." *HAB* 20:78–81.

Kruzhkova, G., ed. 1994. *Dzhon Donn: Izbrannoe iz ego elegii, pesen i sonetov, satir, epitalam, i poslanii: s dobavieniem graviur, portretov, not i drugikh illustatsii, a takzhe s predisoviem i kommentariiami perevodchika.* Moscow: Moskovskii Rabochii.

Kupersmith, William. 1985. *Roman Satirists in Seventeenth-Century England.* Lincoln and London: University of Nebraska Press.

Kusunose, Toshihiko. 1972. "The Satires ni okeru John Donne" (John Donne in The Satires). *Ronko:* Eibei Bungaku Gogaku Kenkyu 21: 95–115.

L., W., of Leicester. 1772. "A Short Account of the several sorts of Organs used for Church Service." *The Gentleman's Magazine* 42:565.

Lamb, Charles. 1935. *The Letters of Charles Lamb,* ed. Edward V. Lucas. 3 vols. London: J. M. Dent.

Landor, Walter Savage. 1836. *A Satire on Satirists.* London: Saunders & Otley.

Lang, Andrew. 1912. "Late Elizabethan and Jacobean Poets." In *History of English Literature from "Beowulf" to Swinburne,* 283–302. London: Longmans, Green. Rpt. 1929.

Larson, Deborah Aldrich. 1990. *John Donne and Twentieth-Century Criticism.* Rutherford, NJ: Fairleigh Dickinson University Press.

Lauritsen, John R. 1976. "Donne's *Satyres:* The Drama of Self-Discovery." *SEL* 16:117–30.

Leavis, F. R. 1935. "English Poetry in the Seventeenth Century." *Scrutiny* 4:236–56.

———. 1936. *Revaluation: Tradition and Development in English Poetry.* London: Chatto and Windus.

———. 1968. "Imagery and Movement: F. R. Leavis (1945): Notes in the Analysis of Poetry (ii)." In *A Selection from Scrutiny,* comp. F. R. Leavis, 1:231–48. Cambridge: Cambridge University Press.

Lecocq, Louis. 1969. "John Donne." In *La Satire en Angleterre de 1588 à 1603,* 358–98. Études anglaises, 32. Paris: Librairie Marcel Didier.

LeComte, Edward. 1965. *Grace to a Witty Sinner: A Life of Donne.* New York: Walker.

Lederer, Josef. 1946. "John Donne and the Emblematic Practice." *RES* 22:182–200.

Lee, Sangyup. 2001. "John Donne: From Romantic Idealism to Psychological Realism." *Milton Studies in Korea* 11:59–93.

Lee, Sidney. 1910. *The French Renaissance in England.* Oxford: Clarendon Press.

Legouis, Pierre. 1928. *Donne the Craftsman: An Essay upon the Structure of the Songs and Sonnets.* Paris: H. Didier. Rpt. New York: Russell & Russell, 1962.

———. 1942. "Some Lexicological Notes and Queries on Donne's *Satires.*" *Studia Neophilologica* 14:184–96.

———. 1952. "L'État présent des controverses sur la poésie de Donne." *EA* 5:97–106.

Lein, Clayton D. 1980. "Theme and Structure in Donne's *Satyre II.*" *CL* 32:130–50.

Leishman, J. B. 1934. *The Metaphysical Poets: Donne, Herbert, Vaughan, Traherne.* Oxford: Clarendon Press.

———. 1951. *The Monarch of Wit: An Analytical and Comparative Study of the Poetry of John Donne.* London: Hutchinson University Library.

Lerner, Laurence. 1999. "What can we do with a poem?" *ESA* 42:1–20.

Levi, Peter, ed. 1974. *Pope: Selections.* Harmondsworth and Baltimore: Penguin.

Lewalski, Barbara Kiefer, and Andrew J. Sabol, eds. 1973. *Major Poets of the Earlier Seventeenth Century: Donne, Herbert, Vaughan, Crashaw, Jonson, Herrick, Marvell.* New York: Odyssey Press.

Lewes, George Henry. 1838. "Retrospective Reviews." *NM* 9:373–78.

Lewis, C. S. 1954. *English Literature in the Sixteenth Century Excluding Drama*. The Oxford History of English Literature, ed. F. P. Wilson and Bonamy Dobrée. Vol 3. Oxford: Clarendon Press.

Lewis, David. 1990. "Drama in Donne and Herbert." In *Critical Essays on the Metaphysical Poets*, ed. Linda Cookson and Bryan Loughrey, 98–109. Longman Literature Guides. Essex, UK: Longman House.

Lewis, E. Glyn. 1934a. "Donne's Third Satyre." *TLS* 6 September:604.

———. 1934b. "Donne's Third Satyre." *TLS* 27 September:655.

Lewis, Marjorie D. 1977. "The *Adversarius* Talks Back: 'The Canonization' and *Satire I*." In *New Essays on Donne*, ed. Gary A. Stringer, 1–25. Salzburg Studies in English Literature, Elizabethan & Renaissance Studies, ed. James Hogg, no. 57. Salzburg: Institut für Englische Sprache und Literatur, Universität Salzburg.

Lindsay, Jack. 1934a. "Donne and Drant." *TLS* 23 August:577.

———. 1934b. "Donne's Third Satyre." *TLS* 20 September:636.

Ling., W. 1640. "To his Friend the Author." In *The Fancies Theatre*, ed. John Tatham. STC 23704. London: John Norton for Richard Best.

Lloyd-Evans, Barbara, ed. 1989. *Five Hundred Years of English Poetry: Chaucer to Arnold*. New York: Peter Bedrick Books.

Lord, George de Forest. 1987. *Classical Presences in Seventeenth-Century English Poetry*. New Haven and London: Yale University Press.

Louthan, Doniphan. 1951. *The Poetry of John Donne: A Study in Explication*. New York: Bookman Associates.

Low, Anthony. 1985. *The Georgic Revolution*. Princeton: Princeton University Press.

———. 1990. "Donne and the Reinvention of Love." *ELR* 20:465–86.

———. 1993. *The Reinvention of Love: Poetry, Politics, and Culture from Sidney to Milton*. New York: Cambridge University Press.

Low, Donald A. 1965. "An Eighteenth-Century Imitation of Donne's First Satire." *RES* n.s. 16:291–98.

Lynd, Robert. 1920. "John Donne." *LMer* 1:435–47. Rpt. in *The Art of Letters*, 29–48. London: F. T. Unwin, 1920.

Mabbott, Thomas O. 1957. "Donne's 'Satyre II,' 71–72." *Expl* 16.3:Item 19.

Macaulay, Rose. 1931. "Anglican and Puritan." In *Some Religious Elements in English Literature*, 84–126. London: Hogarth Press.

MacColl, Alan. 1967. "The New Edition of Donne's Love Poems." *EIC* 17:258–63.

———. 1972. "The Circulation of Donne's Poems in Manuscript." In *John Donne: Essays in Celebration*, ed. A. J. Smith, 28–46. London: Methuen.

MacDonald, George. 1874. *England's Antiphon*. London: Macmillan.

MacKenzie, Clayton G. 2001. *Emblem and Icon in John Donne's Poetry and Prose*. Renaissance and Baroque: Studies and Texts, 30. New York: Peter Lang.

Mackenzie, Donald. 1990. *The Metaphysical Poets*. London: Macmillan.

Mackinnon, Lachlan. 1983. "Zealously Meditating." *TLS* 24 June:681.

MacLeane, Douglas. 1915. "Donne." *The Saturday Review* (London) 21 August:178–79.

Mahler, Andreas. 1991. "Profanierung des Sakralen—Sakralisierung des Profranen. Beobachtungen zur Entsubstantialisierung des religiösen Diskurses in der frühen Neuzeit." In *Deutsche Shakespeare-Gesellschaft West Jahrbuch*, ed. Werner Habicht, 24–45. Bochum: Ferdinand Kamp.

Mahood, M. M. 1950. *Poetry and Humanism*. Hew Haven: Yale University Press.

Mallet, Phillip, ed. 1990. *John Donne: Selected Poems: Notes*. York Notes, gen. eds. A. N. Jeffares and Suheil Bushrui. Harlow, UK: Longman Group, 1983. Seventh impression 1990.

Manley, Lawrence. 1995. *Literature and Culture in Early Modern London*. Cambridge: Cambridge University Press.

Mann, Lindsay A. 1981. "Radical Consistency: A Reading of Donne's 'Communitie.'" *UTQ* 50:284–99.

———. 1985. "Sacred and Profane Love in Donne." *DR* 65:534–50.

Marotti, Arthur F. 1974. "Donne and 'The Extasie.'" In *The Rhetoric of Renaissance Poetry: From Wyatt to Milton*, ed. Thomas O. Sloan and Raymond B. Waddington, 140–73. Los Angeles: University of California Press.

———. 1981. "John Donne and the Rewards of Patronage." In *Patronage in the Renaissance*, ed. Guy Fitch Lytle and Stephen Orgel, 207–34. Princeton: Princeton University Press.

———. 1986. *John Donne, Coterie Poet*. Madison: University of Wisconsin Press.

Martines, Lauro. 1985. *Society and History in English Renaissance Verse*. New York: Basil Blackwell.

Martz, Louis. 1960. "John Donne: The Meditative Voice." *MR* 1:326–42.

———. 1969. *The Wit of Love: Donne, Carew, Crashaw, Marvell*. Notre Dame: University of Notre Dame Press.

———. 1985. "English Religious Poetry, From Renaissance to Baroque." *EIRC* 11:1–28.

———. 1991. *From Renaissance to Baroque: Essays on Literature and Art*. Columbia: University of Missouri Press.

———. 2001. "Donne, Herbert, and the Worm of Controversy." In *Wrestling with God: Literature and Theology in the English Renaissance: Essays to Honour Paul Grant Stanwood*, ed. Mary Ellen Henley and W. Speed Hill with the assistance of R. G. Siemens, 11–25, 275–77. Vancouver: Henley.

Marvell, Andrew. 1673. *The Rehearsal Transpros'd, and The Rehearsal Transpros'd, The Second Part*, ed. D. I. B. Smith. Oxford: Clarendon Press, 1971.

Mason, William. 1747. MUSÆUS: A MONODY to the Memory of Mr. POPE, in Imitation of Milton's Lycidas. London: for R. Dodsley.

Masood-Ul-Hasan. 1958. *Donne's Imagery*. Aligarh, India: Aligarh Muslim University.

Masselink, Noralyn. 1992. "A Matter of Interpretation: Example and Donne's Role as Preacher and as Poet." *JDJ* 11:85–98.

Masson, Rosaline Orme. 1876. *Three Centuries of English Poetry, Being Selections from Chaucer to Herrick*. London: Macmillan.

Matsuura, Kaichi. 1953. *A Study of Donne's Imagery: A Revelation of his Outlook on the World and his Vision of a Universal Christian Monarchy*. Tokyo: Kenkyusha.

May, Steven W. 1991. *The Elizabethan Courtier Poets: The Poems and Their Contexts*. Columbia: University of Missouri Press.

Mazzeo, Joseph A. 1957. "Notes on John Donne's Alchemical Imagery." *Is* 48:103–23.

———. 1969. "Modern Theories of Metaphysical Poetry." In *The Metaphysical Poets: Key Essays on Metaphysical Poetry and the Major Metaphysical Poets*, ed. Frank Kermode, 158–76. Greenwich, CT: Fawcett Publications.

McCabe, Richard A. 1981. "Elizabethan Satire and the Bishops' Ban of 1599." *YES* 11:188–93.

———. 2001. "'Right Puisante and Terrible Priests': The Role of the Anglican Church in Elizabethan State Censorship." In *Literature and Censorship in Renaissance England*, ed. Andrew Hadfield, 75–94. Houndmills, Basingstoke, Hampshire: Palgrave.

McFarland, Ronald E. 1977. "Figures of Repetition in John Donne's Poetry." *Style* 11:391–406.

McGrath, Lynette. 1980. "John Donne's Apology for Poetry." *SEL* 20:73–89.

McKevlin, Dennis J. 1984. *A Lecture in Love's Philosophy: Donne's Vision of the World of Human Love in the Songs and Sonets*. New York and London: University Press of America.

Meakin, H. L. 1998. *John Donne's Articulations of the Feminine*. Oxford and New York: Clarendon Press.

Medine, Peter E. 1972. "Praise and Blame in Renaissance Verse Satire." *PCP* 7:49–53.

Melchiori, Giorgio, ed. 1983. *John Donne: Liriche sacre e profane—Anatomia del mondo—Duello della Morte*. Biblioteca Mondadori. Milano: Arnoldo Mondadori Editore.

Melton, Wightman Fletcher. 1906. *The Rhetoric of John Donne's Verse*. Baltimore: J. H. Furst.

Menascè, Esther. 1969. *Introduzione alla poesia di John Donne*. Milano: La Goliardica.

Messenger, Ann P. 1974. "'Adam Pos'd': Metaphysical and Augustan Satire." *WCR* 8.4:10–11.

Michener, Richard. 1970. "The Great Chain." *BSUF* 11:60–71.

Miles, Josephine. 1972. "Ifs, Ands, Buts for the Reader of Donne." In *Just So Much Honor: Essays Commemorating the Four-Hundredth Anniversary of the Birth of John Donne*, ed. Peter Amadeus Fiore, 273–91. University Park and London: Pennsylvania State University Press.

Milgate, Wesley. 1950. "The Early References to John Donne." *N&Q* 195:229–31, 246–47, 290–92, 381–83.

———, ed. 1967. *The Satires, Epigrams, and Verse Letters*. Oxford: Clarendon Press.

Miller, Clarence H., and Caryl K. Berrey. 1974. "The Structure of Integrity: The Cardinal Virtues in John Donne's 'Satyre III.'" *Costerus* n.s. 1:27–45.

Miller, Edmund. 1982. "John Donne." In *Critical Survey of Poetry: English Language Series*, ed. Frank N. Magill, 2:821–38. Englewood Cliffs, NJ: Salem Press.

Miner, Earl. 1969. *The Metaphysical Mode from Donne to Cowley*. Princeton: Princeton University Press.

———. 1981. "The Restoration: Age of Faith, Age of Satire." In *Poetry and Drama 1570–1700: Essays in Honour of Harold F. Brooks*, ed. Antony Coleman and Antony Hammond, 90–109. London and New York: Methuen.

Minto, William. 1880. "John Donne." *NC* 7:845–63.

Moloney, Michael Francis. 1944. *John Donne: His Flight from Mediaevalism*. Illinois Studies in Language and Literature, 29, nos. 2–3. Urbana: University of Illinois Press.

———. 1950. "Donne's Metrical Practice." *PMLA* 65:232–39.

Moore, Thomas V. 1969. "Donne's Use of Uncertainty as a Vital Force in *Satyre III*." *MP* 67:41–49.

Moorman, Charles. 1989. "One Hundred Years of Editing the Canterbury Tales." *ChauR* 24:99–114.

Morris, Brian. 1970. "Satire from Donne to Marvell." In *Metaphysical Poetry*, ed. Malcolm Bradbury and David Palmer, 211–35. Stratford-upon-Avon Studies, 11. London: Edward Arnold; New York: St. Martin's Press.

Morris, David. 1953. *The Poetry of Gerard Manley Hopkins and T. S. Eliot in the Light of the Donne Tradition: A Comparative Study*. Schweizer Anglistische Arbeiten, 33 Band. Bern: Francke.

Morse, David. 1989. *England's Time of Crisis: From Shakespeare to Milton: A Cultural History*. New York: St. Martin's Press.

Moseley, Charles. 1989. *A Century of Emblems: An Introductory Anthology*. Brookfield, VT: Gower Publishing.

Mueller, Janel M. 1972. "Donne's Epic Venture in 'Metempsychosis.'" *MP* 70:109–37.

Mueller, William R. 1962. *John Donne: Preacher*. Princeton: Princeton University Press.

Murphy, John. 1969. "The Young Donne and the Senecan Amble." *BRMMLA* 23:163–67.

Murray, W. A. 1959. "What was the Soul of the Apple?" *RES* 10:141–55.

Nagoya, Yasuhiko. 1971. "Donne no Shi no Engeiki-teki Seikaku" (The Dramatic Nature of Donne's Poems. *Kiyo* (Gengo/Bungaku) (Gaikikugogakubu, Aichi Kenritsu Daigaku) 6 (December): 85–109.

Nares, Robert. 1822. *A Glossary; or, Collection of Words, Phrases, Names, and Allusions to Customs, Proverbs, & etc.* London: Robert Triphook. A new edition by James O. Halliwell and Thomas Wright. 2 vols. London: John Russell Smith, 1872.

Nelly, Una. 1969. *The Poet Donne: A Study in His Dialectic Method.* Cork, Ireland: Cork University Press.

Nethercot, Arthur H. 1922. "The Reputation of John Donne as Metrist." *SR* 30:463–74.

———. 1925a. "The Reputation of the 'Metaphysical Poets' during the Age of Johnson and the 'Romantic Revival.'" *SP* 22:81–132.

———. 1925b. "The Reputation of the 'Metaphysical Poets' during the Age of Pope." *PQ* 4:161–79.

Newton, Richard C. 1974. "Donne the Satirist." *TSLL* 16:427–45.

Nicholl, Charles. 1984. *A Cup of News: The Life of Thomas Nashe.* London: Routledge and Kegan Paul.

———. 1992. *The Reckoning: The Murder of Christopher Marlowe.* Chicago: University of Chicago Press.

Nicolas, Nicholas H., ed. 1826. *The Poetical Rhapsody: To Which Are Added, Several Other Pieces, by Francis Davison, With Memoirs and Notes.* London: William Puckering.

Nicolson, Marjorie Hope. 1960. *The Breaking of the Circle.* New York: Columbia University Press.

Nilsen, Don L. F. 1997. *Humor in British Literature from the Middle Ages to the Restoration: A Reference Guide.* Westport, CT: Greenwood Press.

Norbrook, David. 1990. "The Monarchy of Wit and the Republic of Letters: Donne's Politics." In *Soliciting Interpretation: Literary Theory and Seventeenth-Century English Poetry,* ed. Elizabeth D. Harvey and Katharine Eisaman Maus, 3–36. Chicago: University of Chicago Press.

———. 1992. "Introduction." In *The Penguin Book of Renaissance Verse 1509–1659,* ed. H. R. Woudhuysen. London: Penguin.

Northup, Clark Sutherland, ed. 1911. *Essays and Criticisms by Thomas Gray.* Boston: D. C. Heath.

Norton, Charles Eliot. 1895. "Preface, Introduction and Notes." In *The Poems of John Donne.* From the Text of the Edition of 1633. Rev. by James Russell Lowell. 2 vols. New York: Grolier Club.

Novarr, David. 1980. *The Disinterred Muse: Donne's Texts and Contexts.* Ithaca and London: Cornell University Press.

Nutt, Joe. 1999. *John Donne: The Poems.* New York: St. Martin's Press.

Ochojski, Paul M. 1950. "Did John Donne Repent his Apostasy?" *ABR* 1:535–48.

[OED]. 1882–1920. *A New English Dictionary on Historical Principles,* ed. James A. H. Murray et al. 125 fascicles. Corrected and reissued as *The Oxford English Dictionary.* 12 vols. and supplement. Oxford: Clarendon Press, 1933.

O[ldisworth]., G[iles]. 1648. Annotations on a copy of the 1639 *Poems.* See Sampson, John.

Oliver, Paul M. 1997. *Donne's Religious Writing: A Discourse of Feigned Devotion.* London and New York: Longman.

Oras, Ants. 1960. "Shakespeare, Ben Jonson, and Donne." In *Pause Patterns in Elizabethan and Jacobean Drama: An Experiment in Prosody,* 13–19. University of Florida Monographs, No. 3. Gainesville: University of Florida Press.

Osborn, James M. 1949. "The First History of English Poetry." In *Pope and His Contemporaries,* ed. James L. Clifford and Louis A. Landa, 230–50. Oxford: Clarendon Press.

Osmond, Rosalie. 1990. *Mutual Accusation: Seventeenth-Century Body and Soul Dialogues in their Literary and Theological Context*. Toronto and Buffalo: University of Toronto Press.

Ostriker, Alicia. 1970. "The Lyric, Part I. The Poetry." In *English Poetry and Prose, 1540–1674*, ed. Christopher Ricks, 91–106. New York: Peter Bedrick Books. Rpt. by Sphere Books in 1970 and 1986.

Ousby, Heather Dubrow. 1977. "A Senecan Analogue to Donne's 'Huge Hill.'" *N&Q* n.s. 24:144–45.

Paman, Clement. 1638. *Poems of that most neglected divine, Clement Paman*. Yorkshire, Eng.: The Foundling Press, 2002.

Parfitt, George. 1985. *English Poetry of the Seventeenth Century*. London and New York: Longman.

———. 1989. *John Donne: A Literary Life*. New York: St. Martin's Press.

Parker, Barbara L., and J. Max Patrick. 1975. "Two Hollow Men: The Pretentious Wooer and the Wayward Bridegroom of Donne's 'Satyre I.'" *SCN* 33:10–14.

Parker, Derek. 1975. *John Donne and His World*. London: Thames and Hudson.

Parry, Graham. 1985. *Seventeenth-Century Poetry: The Social Context*. London: Hutchinson.

Partridge, A. C. 1971. *The Language of Renaissance Poetry*. London: André Deutsch.

———. 1978. *John Donne: Language and Style*. London: André Deutsch.

Pask, Kevin. 1996. *The Emergence of the English Author: Scripting the Life of the Poet in Early Modern England*. Cambridge: Cambridge University Press.

[Patmore, Coventry?]. 1846. "Gallery of Poets. No. I: John Donne." *LEM* I:228–36. Rpt. in *Discussions of John Donne*, ed. Frank Kermode, 18–22. Boston: Heath, 1960.

Patrides, C. A., ed. 1985. *The Complete English Poems of John Donne*. London: Dent.

———. 1989. *Figures in a Renaissance Context*, ed. Claude J. Summers and Ted-Larry Pebworth. Ann Arbor: University of Michigan Press.

Patterson, Annabel M. 1970. *Hermogenes and the Renaissance: Seven Ideas of Style*. Princeton: Princeton University Press.

———. 1984. *Censorship and Interpretation: The Conditions of Writing and Reading in Early Modern England*. Madison: University of Wisconsin Press.

———. 1990. "All Donne." In *Soliciting Interpretation: Literary Theory and Seventeenth-Century English Poetry*, ed. Elizabeth D. Harvey and Katharine Eisaman Maus, 37–67. Chicago: University of Chicago Press.

———. 1994. "*Quod oportet* versus *quod convenit*: John Donne, Kingsman?" In *Critical Essays on John Donne*, ed. Arthur Marotti, 141–79. New York: G. K. Hall.

———. 1995. "Afterword." *JDJ* 14:219–30.

———. 1997. "Donne in Shadows: Pictures and Politics." *JDJ* 16:1–35.

Payne, Frank Walter. 1926. *John Donne and His Poetry*. Poetry and Life Series, No. 35. London: George G. Harrap. Rpt. New York: AMS Press, 1971.

Pebworth, Ted-Larry. 1996. "The Early Audiences of Donne's Poetic Performances." *JDJ* 15:127–39.

Perkins, D. 1953. "Johnson on Wit and Metaphysical Poetry." *ELH* 20:200–17.

Peter, John. 1956. *Complaint and Satire in Early English Literature*. Oxford: Clarendon Press.

Phillips, Edward. 1674. *Theatrum Poetarum*. In *Sacrarum profanarumque phrasium poeticarum Thesaurus recens perpolitus et numerosior factus*, ed. Johann Buchler. London: Typis Thomæ Newcombe, 1679.

Piper, William Bowman. 1969. *The Heroic Couplet*. Cleveland: The Press of Case Western Reserve University.

Pope, Alexander. 1706. *The Correspondence of Alexander Pope*, ed. George Sherburn. Oxford: Clarendon Press, 1956.

———. 1733. *The Impertinent, or a Visit to the Court. A Satyr. By an Eminent Hand.* London: Printed for John Wileord, behind the *Chapter-house* near St. *Paul's.*

———. 1735. *The Works of Alexander Pope, Esq; Vol. II. Containing his Epistles and Satires.* London: Printed for L. Gilliver.

———. 1738. *The Works of Alexander Pope, Esq; Vol. II. Part II. Containing all such Pieces of this Author as were written since the former Volumes, and never before publish'd in Octavo.* London: Printed for R. Dodsley, and sold by T. Cooper in *Pater-noster-Row.*

Porter, Peter, ed. 1971. *A Choice of Pope's Verse.* London: Faber and Faber.

Post, Jonathan F. S. 1999. *English Lyric Poetry: The Early Seventeenth Century.* London and New York: Routledge.

Powers, Doris C. 1971. *English Formal Satire: Elizabethan to Augustan.* The Hague and Paris: Mouton.

Prescott, Anne Lake. 1997. "Donne's Rabelais." *JDJ* 16:37–57.

———. 1998. *Imagining Rabelais in Renaissance England.* New Haven: Yale University Press.

———. 1999. "Humour and Satire in the Renaissance." In *The Cambridge History of Literary Criticism,* ed. Glyn P. Norton, 3:284–91. Cambridge: Cambridge University Press.

———. 2000. "The evolution of Tudor satire." In *The Cambridge Companion to English Literature 1500–1600,* ed. Arthur F. Kinney, 220–40. Cambridge: Cambridge University Press.

———. 2011. "Menippean Donne." In *The Oxford Handbook of John Donne,* ed. Jeanne Shami, Dennis Flynn, and M. Thomas Hester, 158–79. Oxford: Oxford University Press.

Price, Michael W. 1996. "'Offending without Witnes': Recusancy, Equivocation, and Face-Painting in John Donne's Early Life and Writings." *EIRC* 22:51–81.

Q., R. S. 1865. "Latin Puzzle." *N&Q* 3rd ser. 7:145.

Raizada, Harith. 1974. "Donne as a Satirist." In *Essays on John Donne: A Quarter Centenary Tribute,* ed. Asloob Ahmad Ansari, 100–16. Aligarh, India: Aligarh Muslim University.

Randolph, Mary C. 1941. "The Medical Concept in English Renaissance Satiric Theory: Its Possible Relationships and Implications." *SP* 38:125–57.

———. 1942. "The Structural Design of the Formal Verse Satire." *PQ* 21:368–84.

Ray, Robert H. 1986. "Unrecorded Seventeenth-Century Allusions to Donne." *N&Q* n.s. 33:464–65.

———. 1990. *A John Donne Companion.* New York and London: Garland Publishing.

Redpath, Theodore. 1956. *The Songs and Sonets of John Donne. An Editio minor* with Introduction and Explanatory Notes by Theodore Redpath. London: Methuen.

Reid, David. 2000. *The Metaphysical Poets.* Harlow, Eng.: Longman.

Rhys, Ernest, ed. 1924. *Pope: Poems, Epistles and Satires.* London and Toronto: Dent.

Richards, Bernard. 1980. "Whitney's Influence on Shakespeare's Sonnets 111 and 112, and on Donne's Third Satire." *N&Q* n.s. 27:160–61.

Richmond, Hugh. 1981. *Puritans and Libertines: Anglo-French Literary Relations in the Reformation.* Berkeley, Los Angeles, and London: University of California Press.

Richter, Rudolph. 1902. "Der Vers bei Dr. John Donne." In *Beiträge zur neueren Philologie. Fetschrift für Jakob Schipper,* 391–415. Wien and Leipzig: Wilhelm Braumüller.

Rickey, Mary Ellen. 1966. *Utmost Art: Complexity in the Verse of George Herbert.* Lexington: University of Kentucky Press.

Robbins, Robin. 2000. "Poets, Friends and Patrons: Donne and his Circle; Ben and his Tribe." In *A Companion to English Renaissance Literature and Culture,* ed. Michael Hattaway, 419–41. Oxford: Blackwell.

Roberts, John R. 1968. "Donne's *Satyre III* Reconsidered." *CLAJ* 12:105–15.

———, ed. 1973. *John Donne: An Annotated Bibliography of Modern Criticism, 1912–1967.* Columbia: University of Missouri Press.

————, ed. 1982. *John Donne: An Annotated Bibliography of Modern Criticism, 1968–1978.* Columbia: University of Missouri Press.

————, ed. 2004. *John Donne: An Annotated Bibliography of Modern Criticism, 1979–1995.* Pittsburgh: Duquesne University Press.

————, ed. 2013. *John Donne: An Annotated Bibliography of Modern Criticism, 1996–2008. DigitalDonne: The Online Variorum.*

Robson, W. W. 1986. *A Prologue to English Literature.* London: B. T. Batsford.

Roebuck, Graham. 1989. "Donne's Visual Imagination and Compasses." *JDJ* 8:37–56.

————. 1996. "*Johannes Factus* and the Anvil of the Wits." *JDJ* 15:141–52.

Rogers, Pat, ed. 1987. *The Oxford Illustrated History of English Literature.* New York: Oxford University Press.

————, ed. 1993. *Alexander Pope.* Oxford: Oxford University Press.

Roscelli, William John. 1967. "The Metaphysical Milton (1625–1631)." *TSLL* 8:463–84.

Roston, Murray. 1974. *The Soul of Wit: A Study of John Donne.* Oxford: Clarendon Press.

Rousseau, George S., and Neil L. Rudenstine, eds. 1972. *English Poetic Satire: Wyatt to Byron.* New York: Holt, Rinehart and Winston.

Rowe, Frederick A. 1964. *I Launch at Paradise: A Consideration of John Donne, Poet and Preacher.* London: Epworth Press.

Roy, V. K., and R. C. Kapoor. 1969. *John Donne and Metaphysical Poetry.* With a foreword by Vikramaditya Rai. Delhi: Doaba House.

Rudd, Nial. 1963. "Donne and Horace." *TLS* 22 March:208.

Rude, Donald W. 1999. "John Donne in *The Female Tatler*: A Forgotten Eighteenth-Century Appreciation." *JDJ* 18:153–66.

————. 2001. "Some Unreported Seventeenth- and Eighteenth-Century Allusions to John Donne." *JDJ* 20:219–28.

Rudrum, Alan, Joseph Black, and Holly Faith Nelson, eds. 2000. *The Broadview Anthology of Seventeenth-Century Verse and Prose.* Broadview Anthologies of English Literature. Peterborough, ON and Orchard Park, NY: Broadview Press.

Rugoff, Milton Allan. 1939. *Donne's Imagery: A Study in Creative Sources.* New York: Corporate.

Ryan, John K. 1948. "The Reputation of St. Thomas Aquinas among English Protestant Thinkers of the Seventeenth Century." *The New Scholasticism* 22:1–33.

Saintsbury, George. 1887. *A History of Elizabethan Literature.* London: Macmillan.

————. 1896. "Introduction. John Donne." In *The Poems of John Donne*, ed. E. K. Chambers, 1:xi–xxxiii. London: George Routledge & Sons.

————. 1898. *A Short History of English Literature.* London: Macmillan.

————. 1908. *A History of English Prosody from the Twelfth Century to the Present Day.* 3 vols. London: Macmillan.

————. 1921. "The Metaphysical Poets." *TLS* 27 October:698.

Sale, Roger. 1984. *Literary Inheritance.* Amherst: University of Massachusetts Press.

Samarin, R. M. 1972. "Tragedija Dzona Donna" (The Tragedy of John Donne). *Voprosy Literatury* 17.3: 162–73

Sampson, John. 1921. "A Contemporary Light upon John Donne." *Essays and Studies by Members of the English Association* 7:82–107.

Sanders, Wilbur. 1971. *John Donne's Poetry.* Cambridge: Cambridge University Press.

Sanford, Ezekiel. 1819. *The Works of the British Poets.* Vol. 4. Philadelphia: Mitchell, Ames, and White.

Saunders, Ben. 1999. "Prosodic Pleasures and Metrical Fantasies: Donne's 'Irregularity.'" *YJC* 12:171–87.

Saunders, J. W. 1983. *A Biographical Dictionary of Renaissance Poets and Dramatists, 1520–1650*. Totowa, NJ: Barnes & Noble.

Sawday, Jonathan. 1995. *The Body Emblazoned: Dissection and the Human Body in Renaissance Culture*. London and New York: Routledge.

Scarry, Elaine. 1988. "Donne: 'But Yet the Body Is his Booke.'" In *Literature and Body: Essays on Populations and Persons*, ed. Elaine Scarry, 70–105. Selected Papers from the English Institute 1986. New Series 12. Baltimore and London: The Johns Hopkins University Press.

Schelling, Felix. 1910. *English Literature during the Lifetime of Shakespeare*. New York: Henry Holt & Co.

———. 1913. "Lyrical Poetry in the England of the Tudors." In *The English Lyric*, 31–72. Boston: Houghton Mifflin.

Schipper, Jakob. 1888. "Der *heroic verse* John Donnes." In *Neuenglische Metrik* 2:204–07. Bonn: Verlag von Emil Strauss.

Schoenfeldt, Michael C. 1991. *Prayer and Power: George Herbert and Renaissance Courtship*. Chicago: University of Chicago Press.

Scholderer, V. 1934. "Donne and Drant." *TLS* 30 August:589.

Scodel, Joshua. 1993. "The Medium Is the Message: Donne's 'Satire 3,' 'To Sir Henry Wotton' (Sir, more than kisses), and the Ideologies of the Mean." *MP* 90:479–511.

———. 1995. "John Donne and the Religious Politics of the Mean." In *John Donne's Religious Imagination: Essays in Honor of John T. Shawcross*, ed. Raymond-Jean Frontain and Frances M. Malpezzi, 45–80. Conway, AR: University of Central Arkansas Press.

Selden, Raman. 1978. "The Elizabethan Satyr-Satirist." In *English Verse Satire 1590–1765*, 45–72. London: George Allen & Unwin.

———. 1981. "Oldham's Versions of the Classics." In *Poetry and Drama 1570–1700: Essays in Honour of Harold F. Brooks*, ed. Antony Coleman and Antony Hammond, 110–35. London and New York: Methuen.

Selleck, Nancy. 2001. "Donne's Body." *SEL* 41:149–74.

Sellin, Paul R. 1978. "The Date of John Donne's 'Satyre III.'" *SCN* 36:15.

———. 1980. "The Proper Dating of John Donne's 'Satyre III.'" *HLQ* 43:275–312.

———. 1991. "*Satyre III* No Satire: Postulates for Group Discussion." *JDJ* 10:85–89.

Semler, L. E. 1998. *The English Mannerist Poets and the Visual Arts*. Madison, NJ: Fairleigh Dickinson University Press; London: Associated University Presses.

Sencourt, Robert [Robert Esmonde Gordon George]. 1925. *Outflying Philosophy: A Literary Study of the Religious Element in the Poems and Letters of John Donne*. London: Simpkin, Marshall. Rpt. New York: Haskell House, 1966.

Seymour-Smith, Martin, ed. 1972. *Longer Elizabethan Poems*. New York: Barnes & Noble.

Shami, Jeanne. 1984. "Anatomy and Progress: The Drama of Conversion in Donne's Men of a 'Middle Nature.'" *UTQ* 53:221–35.

Shami, Jeanne, Dennis Flynn, and M. Thomas Hester, eds. 2011. *The Oxford Handbook of John Donne*. New York: Oxford University Press.

Shapiro, I. A. 1936. "A Donne Poem." *TLS* 1 February:96.

———. 1950. "The 'Mermaid Club.'" *MLR* 45:6–17.

Sharp, Robert Lathrop. 1934. "Some Light on Metaphysical Obscurity and Roughness." *SP* 31:497–518.

———. 1940. *From Donne to Dryden: The Revolt Against Metaphysical Poetry*. Chapel Hill: University of North Carolina Press.

Shaw, Robert B. 1981. *The Call of God: The Theme of Vocation in the Poetry of Donne and Herbert*. Cambridge, MA: Cowley Publications.

Shawcross, John T., ed. 1967. *The Complete Poetry of John Donne*. Anchor Seventeenth Century Series. Garden City, NY: Doubleday.

———. 1972. "All Attest His Writs Canonical: The Texts, Meaning and Evaluation of Donne's Satires." In *Just So Much Honor: Essays Commemorating the Four-Hundredth Anniversary of the Birth of John Donne*, ed. Peter Amadeus Fiore, 245–72. University Park and London: Pennsylvania State University Press.

———. 1980. "The Book Index: Plutarch's Moralia and John Donne." *JRMMRA* 1:53–62.

———. 1983. "A Text of John Donne's Poems: Unsatisfactory Compromise." *JDJ* 2:1–19.

———. 1985. "Opulence and Iron Pokers: Coleridge and Donne." *JDJ* 4:201–24.

———. 1986. "The Arrangement and Order of John Donne's Poems." In *Poems in their Place: The Intertexuality and Order of Poetic Collections*, ed. Neil Fraistate, 119–63. Chapel Hill: University of North Carolina Press.

———. 1991a. *Intentionality and the New Traditionalism: Some Liminal Means to Literary Revisionism*. University Park: Pennsylvania State University Press.

———. 1991b. "Some Further Early Allusions to Donne." *JDJ* 10:75–78.

———. 2000–01. "Verse Satire: Its Form, Genre, and Mode." *Connotations* 10:18–30.

Shelburne, Steven. 1994. "The Epistolary Ethos of Formal Satire." *TSLL* 36:135–65.

Sheppard, Samuel [Raphael Desmus]. 1653. *Merlinus Anonymus. An Almanacke, And No Almanack, A Kalendar, and no Kalendar. An Ephemeris (between jest, and earnest) for the year 1653*. STC A1588. London: by F.N.

Sherwood, Terry G. 1984. *Fulfilling the Circle: A Study of John Donne's Thought*. Toronto and London: University of Toronto Press.

———. 1997. "'Ego videbo': Donne and the Vocational Self." *JDJ* 16:59–113.

Sicherman, Carol Marks. 1969. "The Mocking Voices of Donne and Marvell." *BuR* 17:32–46.

Simpson, Evelyn M. 1924. *A Study of the Prose Works of John Donne*. Oxford: Oxford University Press. 2nd ed. 1948.

———. 1931. "Donne's 'Paradoxes and Problems.'" In *A Garland for John Donne, 1631–1931*, ed. Theodore Spencer, 21–49. Cambridge: Harvard University Press; London: Humphrey Milford, Oxford University Press.

———. 1944. "Notes on Donne." *RES* 20:224–27.

Simpson, Percy. 1943. "The Rhyming of Stressed and Unstressed Syllables in Elizabethan Verse." *MLR* 38:127–29.

Sinclair, William MacDonald. 1909. "John Donne: Poet and Preacher." *Essays by Divers Hands: Being the Transactions of the Royal Society of Literature of the United Kingdom*, 29.2:179–202. London: Oxford University Press.

Singh, Brijraj. 1971. "Two Hitherto Unrecorded Imitations of Donne in the Eighteenth Century." *N&Q* n.s. 18:50.

———, ed. 1992. *Five Seventeenth-Century Poets: Donne, Herbert, Crashaw, Vaughan, Marvell*. Delhi: Oxford University Press.

Sinha, V[inode] N[arain]. 1977. *John Donne: A Study of His Dramatic Imagination*. New Delhi: K. K. Bhargawa at The Caxton Press.

Sisson, Charles. 1930a. "The Oxford Donne." *TLS* 20 February:142.

———. 1930b. "Donne's Satyres, II., ll. 71–73." *TLS* 13 March:214.

Sito, Jerzy S., et al. 1971. *Poeci jezka angielskiego*. Warsaw: Państwowy Instytut Wydawniczy.

Skelton, Robin. 1960. "The Poetry of John Donne." In *Elizabethan Poetry*, ed. John Russell Brown and Bernard Harris, 203–20. Stratford-upon-Avon Studies, 2. New York: St. Martin's.

Slights, Camille. 1972. "'To Stand Inquiring Right': The Casuistry of Donne's 'Satyre III.'" *SEL* 12:85–101.

————. 1981. *The Casuistical Tradition in Shakespeare, Donne, Herbert, and Milton*. Princeton: Princeton University Press.

————. 1991. "Participating Wisely in *Satyre III*." *JDJ* 10:91–95.

————. 1996. "A Pattern of Love: Representations of Anne Donne." In *John Donne's "desire of more": The Subject of Anne More Donne in His Poetry*, ed. M. Thomas Hester, 66–88. Newark: University of Delaware Press; London: Associated University Presses.

Sloan, Thomas O. 1963. "The Rhetoric in the Poetry of John Donne." *SEL* 3:31–44.

————. 1965. "The Persona as Rhetor: An Interpretation of Donne's *Satyre III*." *QJS* 51:14–27.

————. 1985. *Donne, Milton, and the End of Humanist Rhetoric*. Berkeley: University of California Press.

Sloane, Mary Cole. 1981. *The Visual in Metaphysical Poetry*. Atlantic Highlands, NJ: Humanities Press.

Smith, A. J. 1970. "The Poetry of John Donne." In *English Poetry and Prose, 1540–1674*, ed. Christopher Ricks, 137–69. New York: Sphere Books. Rpt. 1986; Peter Bedrick Books, 1987.

————, ed. 1971. *John Donne: The Complete English Poems*. New York and London: Penguin.

————, ed. 1975. *John Donne: The Critical Heritage*. London and Boston: Routledge & Kegan Paul.

————. 1982. "No Man Is a Contradiction." *JDJ* 1:21–38.

————. 1991. *Metaphysical Wit*. Cambridge and New York: Cambridge University Press.

————. 1992. "John Donne." In *Dictionary of Literary Biography*, Vol. 121: Seventeenth-Century British Nondramatic Poets, ed. M. Thomas Hester, 77–96. Detroit: Gale Research Inc.

Smith, Bruce R. 1991. *Homosexual Desire in Shakespeare's England: A Cultural Poetics*. Chicago and London: University of Chicago Press.

Smith, Hallett. 1952. *Elizabethan Poetry: A Study in Conventions, Meaning, and Expression*. Cambridge: Harvard University Press.

Smith, Julia J. 1984. "Donne and the Crucifixion." *MLR* 79:513–25.

Smith, Nathanial B. 2001. "The Apparition of a Seventeenth-Century Donne Reader: A Hand-Written Index to *Poems, by J.D.* (1633)." *JDJ* 20:161–99.

Smuts, Malcolm. 1991. "Cultural Diversity and Cultural Change at the Court of James I." In *The Mental World of the Jacobean Court*, ed. Linda Levy Peck, 99–112. Cambridge and New York: Cambridge University Press.

Snyder, Susan. 1973. "Donne and DuBartas: 'The Progresse of the Soule' as Parody." *SP* 70:392–407.

Solly, Edward. 1880. "Donne's 'Satires.'" *N&Q* 6th ser., 2:190.

Sowerby, Robin. 1994. *The Classical Legacy in Renaissance Poetry*. London and New York: Longman.

Sowton, Ian. 1960. "Religious Opinion in the Prose Letters of John Donne." *Canadian Journal of Theology* 6:179–90.

Spalding, William. 1852. *The History of English Literature*. Edinburgh: Oliver & Boyd.

Sparrow, John. 1931. "Donne's Religious Development." *Th* (London) 22:144–54.

Spence, Joseph. c. 1730–36. *Anecdotes*, ed. James M. Osborn. 2 vols. Oxford: Oxford University Press, 1966.

————. c. 1730–36. *History of English Poetry*. See Osborn, James M.

[Spence, Joseph]. 1823. "Donne's Poems." *RR* 8:31–55.

Spencer, Theodore. 1931. "Donne and His Age." In *A Garland for John Donne, 1631–1931*, ed. Theodore Spencer, 177–202. Cambridge: Harvard University Press; London: Humphrey Milford, Oxford University Press.

Sprott, S. Ernest. 1950. "The Legend of Jack Donne the Libertine." *UTQ* 19:335–53.

Sproxton, Judy. 2000. *The Idiom of Love: Love Poetry from the Early Sonnets to the Seventeenth Century*. London: Duckworth.

Spurr, Barry. 1996. "The John Donne Papers of Wesley Milgate." *JDJ* 15:189–210.

Stanwood, P. G. 1990. "On Altering the Present to Fit the Past." In *Approaches to Teaching the Metaphysical Poets*, ed. Sidney Gottlieb, 75–80. New York: MLA.

Steadman, John M. 1984. *The Hill and the Labyrinth: Discourse and Certitude in Milton and His Near-Contemporaries*. Berkeley: University of California Press.

Stein, Arnold. 1942. "Donne and the Couplet." *PMLA* 57:676–96.

———. 1944a. "Donne and the Satiric Spirit." *ELH* 11:266–82.

———. 1944b. "Donne's Harshness and the Elizabethan Tradition." *SP* 41:390–409.

———. 1944c. "Donne's Prosody." *PMLA* 59:373–97.

———. 1944d. "Meter and Meaning in Donne's Verse." *SR* 52:288–301.

———. 1946. "Donne's Obscurity and the Elizabethan Tradition." *ELH* 13:98–118.

———. 1951. "Structures of Sound in Donne's Verse." *KR* 13:20–36, 256–78.

———. 1962. *John Donne's Lyrics: The Eloquence of Action*. Minneapolis: University of Minnesota Press.

———. 1984. "Voices of the Satirist: John Donne." *YES* 14:72–92. Rpt. in *English Satire and Satiric Tradition*, ed. Claude Rawson, 72–92. New York: Blackwell.

Stephen, Sir Leslie. 1899. "John Donne." *NR* 34:595–613.

Stevens, Paul. 2001. "Donne's Catholicism and the Innovation of the Modern Nation State." *JDJ* 20:53–70.

Stewart, Jean. 1931. "The Late Renaissance." In *Poetry in France and England*, 45–65. London: Leonard and Virginia Woolf at the Hogarth Press.

Strachan, Michael. 1962. *The Life and Adventures of Thomas Coryate*. London: Oxford University Press.

———. 2004. "Coryate, Thomas (1577?–1617)." *Oxford Dictionary of National Biography*. Ed. H. C. G. Matthew and Brian Harrison. Oxford: Oxford University Press. Online ed. Ed. Lawrence Goldman. Oct. 2006.

Strier, Richard. 1993. "Radical Donne: 'Satire III.'" *ELH* 60:283–322.

———. 1994. "Lyric Poetry from Donne to Philips." In *The Columbia History of British Poetry*, ed. Carl Woodring and James Shapiro, 229–53. New York: Columbia University Press.

Stringer, Gary A. 1991. "*Satyre III* Colloquium: Stringer, Sellin, Slights, Hester." *JDJ* 10:79–83.

———. 2011. "Editing Donne's poetry: from John Marriot to the Donne *Variorum*." In *The Oxford Handbook of John Donne*, ed. Jeanne Shami, Dennis Flynn, and M. Thomas Hester, 43–55. Oxford: Oxford University Press.

Suhamy, Henri. 2001. "Un cas pendable? La versification de John Donne." *EA* 54:401–13.

Sullens, Zay Rusk. 1964. "Neologisms in Donne's English Poems." *AION-SG* 7:175–271.

Sullivan, Ernest W., II. 1989. "Who Was Reading/Writing Donne Verse in the Seventeenth-Century?" *JDJ* 8:1–16.

———. 1993. *The Influence of John Donne: His Uncollected Seventeenth-Century Printed Verse*. Columbia: University of Missouri Press.

———. 2000. "*Poems, by J. D.*: Donne's Corpus and His Bawdy, Too." *JDJ* 19:299–309.

Sullivan, J. P. 1992. "Satire." In *The Legacy of Rome: A New Appraisal*, ed. Richard Jenkyns, 215–42. New York: Oxford University Press.

Sultan, Stanley. 1953. "Donne's Satires, I." *Expl* 11.5:Question 6.

Summers, Joseph. 1970. *The Heirs of Donne and Jonson*. London: Chatto & Windus.

Sutherland, James. 1958. *English Satire*. Cambridge: Cambridge University Press.

Swift, Astrid, ed. 1974. "John Donne." In *Die englische Satire*, 41–48. Uni-Taschenbücher, 381. Heidelberg: Quelle & Meyer.

Symons, Arthur. 1916. "John Donne." In *Figures of Several Centuries*, 80–108. London: Constable and Co.

Sypher, Wylie. 1955. *Four Stages of Renaissance Style: Transformations in Art and Literature 1400–1700*. Garden City, NY: Doubleday & Co.

Taine, Hippolyte Adolphe. 1905. *Histoire de la Littérature Anglaise*. 2 vols. Paris: Librairie Hachette.

Tarlinskaja, Marina. 1976. *English Verse: Theory and History*. The Hague and Paris: Mouton.

Tate, Allen. 1932. "A Note on Donne." *The New Republic* 70:212–13.

———. 1933. "A Note on Elizabethan Satire." *The New Republic* 74:128–30.

Taylor, John. 1612. *Laugh, and be fat. [:or, a commentary vpon the Odcombyan blanket]* [sic]. London.

Teague, Anthony. 1987. "Suffering, Trust and Hope in English Renaissance Literature." *The Renaissance Bulletin* 14:13–44.

Tebeaux, Elizabeth. 1981. "Donne and Hooker on the Nature of Man: The Diverging 'Middle Way.'" *Restoration Quarterly* 24:29–44.

Thomas, John A. 1971. "John Donne's *The Progress of the Soule*: A Re-Evaluation." BRMMLA 25:112–21.

Thompson, Francis. 1899. "Reviews. Mr. Gosse's Life of Donne." Ac 4 November:505–06.

Thompson, Sister M. Geraldine. 1978. "'Writs Canonicall': The High Word and the Humble in the Sermons of John Donne." In *Familiar Colloquy: Essays Presented to Arthur Edward Barker*, edited by Patricia Bruckmann, 55–67. Ontario: Oberon Press.

Toliver, Harold. 1985. "Donne's Silhouettes and Absences." In *Lyric Provinces in the English Renaissance*, 95–121. Columbus: Ohio State University Press.

Tomashevskii, B., ed. 1973. *Dzhon Donn—Stikhotovoreniia*. Leningrad: "Khudozhestvennaia literatura" Leningradskroe otdelenie.

Tomlinson, T. B. 1990. "Donne's Poetry and Belief in 17th-Century England." CR 30:25–39.

Tredegar, Viscount. 1936. "John Donne—Lover and Priest." In *Essays by Divers Hands: Being the Transactions of the Royal Society of Literature of the United Kingdom*, 15:161–202. London: Oxford University Press.

Trevor, Douglas. 2000. "John Donne and Scholarly Melancholy." SEL 40:81–102.

Turnell, Martin. 1950. "John Donne and the Quest for Unity." *Nineteenth Century and After* 147:262–74.

Turner, James Grantham. 1987. *One Flesh: Paradisal Marriage and Sexual Relations in the Age of Milton*. Oxford: Clarendon Press.

Tuve, Rosemond. 1947. *Elizabethan and Metaphysical Imagery: Renaissance Poetic and Twentieth-Century Critics*. Chicago: University of Chicago Press.

Untermeyer, Louis. 1959. "The Metaphysical Man: John Donne." In *Lives of the Poets: The Story of One Thousand Years of English and American Poetry*, 122–36. New York: Simon & Shuster.

Upham, Alfred Horatio. 1908. *The French Influence in English Literature from the Accession of Elizabeth to the Restoration*. New York: Columbia University Press.

Usherwood, Stephen, and Elizabeth Usherwood. 1984. "Donne at the Taking of Cadiz." *Country Life* 175 (3 May):1226–27.

Van Emden, Joan. 1986. *The Metaphysical Poets*. Macmillan Master Guides. London: Macmillan Education.

Van Wyck Smith, M. 1973. "John Donne's 'Metempsychosis.'" RES n.s. 24:17–25, 141–52.

Vickers, Brian. 1987. "The Seventeenth Century, 1603–1674." In *The Oxford Illustrated History of English Literature*, ed. Pat Rogers, 160–213. Oxford and New York: Oxford University Press.

Wagner, G. A. 1947. "John Donne and the Spiritual Life." *PoetryR* 38:253–58.

Walker, Hugh. 1925. "Elizabethan and Jacobean Verse Satire." In *English Satire and Satirists*, 57–90. London: J. M. Dent & Sons; New York: E. P. Dutton. Rpt. New York: Octagon Books, 1965.

Wall, John N., Jr. 1985. "Donne's *Satyre IV* and the Feast of the Purification of Saint Mary the Virgin." *ELN* 23:23–31.

Waller, Gary. 1986. *English Poetry of the Sixteenth Century*. London and New York: Longman. Rpt. 1993.

Walton, Izaak. 1640. "The Life and Death of Dr. Donne, Late Deane of St Paules London." In *LXXX Sermons preached by that learned and reverend divine, John Donne, Dr of Divinity, Late Deane of the Cathedrall Church of S. Pauls London*. London: Richard Marriott. The "Life" was reissued, with some changes, in 1658, 1670, and 1675.

Warburton, William, ed. 1751. *The Works of Alexander Pope, Esq.* 9 Vols. Dublin: printed for George Faulkner, A. Moore, and A. Bradley.

Ward, Adolphus William, ed. 1858. *The Poetical Works of Pope*. Cambridge: Globe Press, 1956.

Warnke, Frank, ed. 1967. *John Donne: Poetry and Prose*. Modern Library College Editions. New York: Modern Library.

———. 1987. *John Donne*. Boston: Twayne Publishers.

Warton, Joseph. 1782. *Essay on the Writings and Genius of Alexander Pope*. London: for J. Dodsley.

———. 1797. *The Works of Alexander Pope, esq.* 9 vols. London: for B. Law, J. Johnson, C. Dilly *et al*.

Warton, Thomas. 1774. *The History of English Poetry from the Close of the Eleventh to the Commencement of the Eighteenth Century*. 4 vols. London: Printed for J. Dodsley. Rpt. 1778, 1781, and 1790.

Wasserman, Earl R. 1947. *Elizabethan Poetry in the Eighteenth Century*. Illinois Studies in Language and Literature, 32, no. 3. Urbana: University of Illinois Press.

Watkins, W. B. C. 1936. "Spenser to the Restoration (1579–1660)." In *Johnson and English Poetry before 1660*, ed. G. H. Gerould, 58–84. Princeton Studies in English, No. 13. Princeton: Princeton University Press.

Watts, Cedric. 1990. "The Conceit of the Conceit." In *Critical Essays on Metaphysical Poets*, ed. Linda Cookson and Bryan Loughrey, 9–19. Longman Literature Guides. Essex, UK: Longman House.

Webber, Joan. 1963. *Contrary Music: The Prose Style of John Donne*. Madison: University of Wisconsin Press.

———. 1971. "Stylistics: A Bridging of Life and Art in Seventeenth-Century Studies." *NLH* 2:283–96.

Weimann, Robert. 1988. *Shakespeare und die Macht der Mimesis: Autoritat und Reprasentation im elisabethanischen Theatre*. Berlin: Weimar.

Weinbrot, Howard D. 1982. *Alexander Pope and the Traditions of Formal Verse Satire*. Princeton: Princeton University Press.

Wells, Henry W. 1924. *Poetic Imagery: Illustrated from Elizabethan Literature*. New York: Columbia University Press.

———. 1940. *New Poets from Old: A Study of Literary Genetics*. New York: Columbia University Press.

Wendell, Barrett. 1904. *The Temper of the Seventeenth Century in English Literature*. London: Macmillan.

Wendell, John P. 1948. "Two Cruxes in the Poetry of John Donne." *MLN* 63:477–81.

Wentersdorf, Karl P. 1982. "Symbol and Meaning in Donne's *Metempsychosis* or *Progresse of the Soule*." *SEL* 22:69–90.

Whalley, Peter. 1756. "Life of Benjamin Jonson." In *The Works of Ben Jonson*. 7 Vols. London: D. Midwinter, W. Innys, J. Richarson, and others.

Wheeler, Angela J. 1992. *English Verse Satire from Donne to Dryden: Imitation of Classical Models*. Heidelberg: Carl Winter Universitatsverlag.

Whipple, Edwin P. 1869. *The Literature of the Age of Elizabeth*. Boston: Fields, Osgood.

White, Harold Ogden. 1935. "The Theory of Imitation from Jonson Onward." In *Plagiarism and Imitation during the English Renaissance: A Study in Critical Distinctions*, 120–202. Cambridge: Harvard University Press.

Whitlock, Baird W. 1960. "The Family of John Donne, 1588–1591." *N&Q* n.s. 7:380–86.

Whitlock, Richard. 1654. Ζωοτομια; *or observations on the present manners of the English*. STC W2030. London: Tho[mas] Roycroft for Humphrey Moseley.

Wiggins, Elizabeth Lewis. 1945. "Logic in the Poetry of John Donne." *SP* 42:41–60.

Wiggins, Peter De Sa. 2000. *Donne, Castiglione, and the Poetry of Courtliness*. Bloomington and Indianapolis: Indiana University Press.

Wilcox, John. 1950. "Informal Publication of Late Sixteenth-Century Verse Satire." *HLQ* 13:191–200.

Wild, Friedrich. 1935. "Zum Problem des Barocks in der englischen Dichtung." *Anglia* 59: 414–22.

Williams, Arnold. 1948. *The Common Expositor*. Chapel Hill: University of North Carolina Press.

Williams, Aubrey L. 1977. "What Pope Did to Donne." In *A Provision of Human Nature: Essays on Fielding and Others in Honor of Miriam Austin Locke*, ed. Donald Kay, 111–19. Tuscaloosa: University of Alabama Press.

Williamson, George. 1928. "The Nature of the Donne Tradition." *SP* 25:416–38.

———. 1930. *The Donne Tradition: A Study in English Poetry from Donne to the Death of Cowley*. Cambridge: Harvard University Press.

———. 1932. "The Donne Canon." *TLS* 18 August:581.

———. 1934. "The Libertine Donne." *PQ* 13:276–91.

———. 1940. "Textual Difficulties in the Interpretation of Donne's Poetry." *MP* 38:37–72. Rpt. in *Seventeenth-Century Contexts*. London: Faber, 1960.

———. 1961. *The Proper Wit of Poetry*. Chicago: University of Chicago Press.

———. 1963. "The Design of Donne's Anniversaries." *MP* 60:183–91.

———. 1967. *Six Metaphysical Poets: A Reader's Guide*. New York: Farrar, Straus and Giroux.

———. 1969. "Donne's Satirical 'Progresse of the Soule.'" *ELH* 36:250–65.

Willmott, Richard, ed. 1985. *Four Metaphysical Poets: An Anthology of Poetry by Donne, Herbert, Marvell, and Vaughan*. Cambridge: Cambridge University Press.

Willmott, Robert Aris, ed. 1854. "The Poetical Works of Thomas Parnell." In *The Poetical Works of Thomas Gray, Thomas Parnell, William Collins, Matthew Green, and Thomas Warton*, 1–108. London: George Routledge.

Wilson, F. P. 1945. *Elizabethan and Jacobean*. Oxford: Clarendon Press.

Winny, James. 1970. *A Preface to Donne*. London and New York: Longman.

Winters, Yvor. 1939. "The Sixteenth Century Lyric in England: A Critical and Historical Reinterpretation." *Poetry* 54:35–51.

Wood, William Page (Baron Hatherly). 1829. *A Memoir of the Right Hon. William Page Wood, Baron Hatherly*, ed. W. R. W. Stephens. 2 vols. London: R. Bentley, 1883.

Woodhouse, A. S. P. 1965. "The Seventeenth Century: Donne and His Successors." In *The Poet and His Faith: Religion and Poetry in England from Spenser to Eliot and Auden*, 42–89. Chicago and London: University of Chicago Press.

Woodring, Carl, ed. 1994. *The Columbia History of British Poetry*. New York: Columbia University Press.

Woods, Susanne. 1984. *Natural Emphasis: English Versification from Chaucer to Dryden*. San Marino, CA: The Huntington Library.

Woolf, Virginia. 1932. "Donne after Three Centuries." In *The Second Common Reader*, 20–37. London: Leonard and Virginia Woolf at the Hogarth Press; New York: Harcourt, Brace.

Wordsworth Poetry Library. 1994. *The Works of John Donne*. Ware, Hertfordshire, UK: Wordsworth Editions.

Wybarne, Joseph. 1609. *The new age of old names*. STC 26055. London: [J. Windet] for W. Barret & H. Featherstone.

Yoklavich, John M. 1976. "Sir Aston Cokayne Praises Donne's 'Satyres' (1658)." *N&Q* n.s. 23:552.

Young, Edward. 1725. *The Universal Passion: Satire I. To His Grace the Duke of Dorset*. London: Printed for J. Roberts.

Young, R. V. 1987. "Donne's Holy Sonnets and the Theology of Grace." In *"Bright Shootes of Everlastingnesse": The Seventeenth-Century Religious Lyric*, ed. Claude J. Summers and Ted-Larry Pebworth, 20–39. Columbia: University of Missouri Press.

———. 2000. *Doctrine and Devotion in Seventeenth-Century Poetry: Studies in Donne, Herbert, Crashaw, and Vaughan*. Cambridge: D. S. Brewer.

Zaki, Jafar. 1974. "Pope's adaptations of Donne's Satires." In *Essays on John Donne: A Quarter Centenary Tribute*, ed. Asloob Ahmad Ansari, 117–38. Aligarh, India: Aligarh Muslim University.

Zimbardo, Rose A. 1998. *At Zero Point: Discourse, Culture, and Satire in Restoration England*. Lexington: University of Kentucky Press.

Zivley, Sherry. 1966. "Imagery in John Donne's Satyres." *SEL* 6:87–95.

Zuberi, Itrat-Husain. 1966. "John Donne's Concept of Toleration in Church and State." *UWR* 1:147–58.

Zunder, William. 1982. *The Poetry of John Donne: Literature and Culture in the Elizabethan and Jacobean Period*. Totowa, NJ: Barnes & Noble; Sussex, Eng.: Harvester Press.

———. 1988. "The Poetry of John Donne: Literature, History, Ideology." In *Jacobean Poetry and Prose: Rhetoric, Representation, and the Popular Imagination*, ed. Clive Bloom, 78–95. New York: St. Martin's Press.

Index of Authors Cited in the Commentary

Collinson, Patrick, 740
Colvin, Sir Sidney, 488
Cooper, Elizabeth, 431, 442
Corser, Thomas, 484
Corthell, Ronald J., 423, 438, 441, 452, 456, 462,
    478, 497–98, 503–05, 515, 518, 522, 524,
    527, 530, 534, 541, 543, 550, 556, 558–59,
    563, 570, 578, 581–82, 584, 588–89, 591,
    598, 600, 604, 606, 608, 619, 622–23, 625,
    627, 628, 631, 633–34, 637, 638–39, 641,
    643, 647–48, 664, 670–71, 674–75, 684,
    687–88, 690, 693–94, 696, 699, 701, 707,
    719, 721–22, 726–27, 736, 742–44, 748,
    760–61, 765, 769, 771, 773–74, 788, 792,
    794, 800, 801, 807, 812–13, 816, 823–24, 833,
    839, 856, 862, 864, 870, 875, 879–80, 882,
    886, 890, 891, 898–900, 905, 907, 909–10,
    926, 929, 934
Courthope, William John, 655
Cousins, A. D., 438, 451, 496–97, 499, 524, 534,
    571–72, 663, 753, 791, 812, 879, 893, 899
Cox, R. G., 420, 435, 659, 752
Cpl., 991
Craik, George L., 483–84, 509
Craik, T. W. and R. J. Craik, 514, 539, 541–42, 544,
    545, 547, 549, 550, 551, 552, 557, 560–62, 563,
    565–68, 572–76, 578, 579, 652, 700, 702–03,
    705, 708–11, 712, 713–14, 715, 717, 722–24,
    725, 727–28, 731, 733–34, 737, 738, 742,
    745, 747, 757, 758, 759, 763–64, 767–68, 772,
    935–38, 941–43, 944, 948, 952, 954–55, 957,
    959–60, 962–63, 967, 969, 971–73
Crinò, Annamaria, 437, 651
Crofts, J. E. V., 416, 434, 466, 469, 540, 806, 855,
    860, 888, 899, 923, 930, 932
Croly, George, 482, 509, 640–41
Cruttwell, Patrick, 829
Cunnar, Eugene R., 854
Cunningham, George Godfrey, 483, 509, 655

Daalder, J[oost], 498, 695
Danby, John F., 434–35, 558
Daniel, George, 429
Daniels, Edgar F., 714, 723–24
Datta, Kitty, 437, 448, 644, 758
Davenport, A., 420, 611
Davies, John, of Hereford, 428
Davies, Stevie, 440, 669, 675, 678, 741, 754–55,
    765
Davison, Francis, 427
De Quincey, Thomas, 921, 925, 931
DiPasquale, Theresa M., 601, 604, 608, 610, 668,
    685, 720, 722
Disraeli, Isaac, 922

Dixon, J., 510, 813
Docherty, Thomas, 526, 556, 598, 605, 607,
    610–11, 704, 735–36, 799, 805, 810, 817, 820,
    824, 829, 832, 842, 863
Doggett, Frank A., 657
Donne, John, 427, 463, 989
Donoghue, Denis, 654, 702, 722, 724, 727, 731,
    733, 747
Doudna, Martin K., 752, 771
Dowden, Edward, 416, 431–32, 655, 746, 779,
    816, 922
Drake, Nathan, 482, 508
Dryden, John, 431, 466, 480, 505–13
Dubrow, Heather, 422, 437, 451, 460, 472, 474,
    497, 503, 524, 528, 597, 636, 674, 778, 782,
    786, 789, 791, 797, 804, 859, 866, 873, 879,
    884, 891, 945–46
Duncan, Joseph E., 681, 752

Eddy, Yvonne Shikany and Daniel P. Jaeckle, 520,
    524, 528, 534–35, 537, 554, 564
Edwards, Anthony, 828
Edwards, David L., 426, 457, 515, 519, 540,
    585, 604, 654, 672, 697, 727, 763, 867, 876,
    901, 934
El-Gabalawy, Saad, 828
Eliot, Thomas Stearns, 433, 445, 467, 489, 519,
    923, 927, 930
Elkin, P. K., 481, 512
Elliott, Emory, 422, 459–60, 471, 477, 502–03,
    523, 545, 556, 558, 589, 640, 647, 662, 692,
    696, 786, 791, 797, 807, 839–40, 846–47, 859,
    863, 871, 873, 878, 883, 898, 902
Elliott, G. R., 656
Ellrodt, Robert, 425–26, 457, 475–76, 500–01,
    545, 601, 604, 624, 645, 739, 751, 761, 777,
    785, 810, 812, 816, 819–22, 824, 828–29,
    831–34, 836, 843–44, 846, 850, 852, 855,
    857, 859, 876, 899, 904, 908, 911
Elton, Oliver, 419, 481
Elwin, Whitwell and William John Courthope,
    501, 604, 624, 629, 640
Emperor, John Bernard, 984
Empson, William, 437, 494–95, 651–52, 668, 672,
    823, 829, 865, 869, 893–94
Enright, D. J., 698, 699, 702–03, 705, 706, 708,
    710–13, 714–15, 716, 722–25, 727–29, 732–33,
    734, 736–38, 742, 745, 755, 756–58, 759,
    763–64, 766–68, 775
Erskine-Hill, H. H., 470, 502, 511, 533, 586,
    595–96, 640, 679, 692, 778, 780–81, 784,
    785–86, 790, 795–96, 798, 803, 807, 813–14,
    816, 824–27, 832, 833–34, 837, 841–45, 847,
    849–50, 852–53, 858–59, 862–63

Esler, Anthony, 436, 447
Evans, Gillian, 707
Everett, Barbara, 514–16, 523, 527, 533, 536, 540–41, 570
Evett, David, 499, 958

Farmer, Norman K., Jr., 523
Farmer, Richard, 956
Farr, Edward, 484
Fausset, Hugh I'Anson, 419, 433, 444–45, 488, 656, 834
Ferry, Leonard D. G., 713, 827
Finkelpearl, P. J., 427
Fischer, Hermann, 421
Fish, Stanley, 440, 461, 518, 526, 538, 544, 559, 564, 571, 578, 590–91, 600, 783, 809
Fitzherbert, Thomas, 428
Flynn, Dennis, 426–27, 548–49, 610, 625, 794, 810, 866–67, 872, 876, 882, 890–91, 893, 897, 900–01, 904–05, 907, 909, 912, 967, 974, 978
Forde, Thomas, 610
Forrest, William Craig, 752, 755–56
Fortier, Mark, 556, 625, 891
Fowler, Alistair, 465–66, 482, 513, 590
Freeman, Arthur, 568
Freeman, Thomas, 429
Freer, Coburn, 602, 890, 903
Frontain, Raymond-Jean, 694, 931
Frye, Northrop, 682
Fulton, Thomas, 457, 466, 480, 501, 505, 530, 654, 672, 680, 686, 688, 694–95, 697–701, 747, 761–62, 765, 772–73, 775, 789, 794, 802, 827–28, 844–45, 853, 882, 899, 905
Furst, Clyde Bowman, 416, 417, 432, 486, 506, 509

Gallenca, Christiane, 452, 460, 472, 503, 524–25, 593, 664, 782, 807
Gamberini, Spartaco, 785, 866, 876–77
Gardner, Helen, 419–20, 436, 447, 501, 609, 650, 658, 681, 919, 925, 929–31, 944, 987
Garnett, Richard and Edmund Gosse, 418, 467
Garrod, H. W., 941, 944, 946
Geraldine, Sister M., 436, 476, 493, 502, 535, 659, 688, 707, 714, 721, 734, 762, 784, 785, 795, 806, 811, 841, 844, 868
Gilbert, A. J., 497, 512
Gilfillan, George, 431, 484, 922, 931
Gill, R. B., 495, 682
Gilman, Ernest B., 666, 683, 750–51
Gorbunov, A. N., 475, 500, 515, 517–18, 526, 539, 555–56, 584, 594, 669, 875
Gosse, Edmund, 416, 417, 418, 420, 432, 444,

467, 468, 486, 510, 515, 582, 655, 690, 777, 779, 784, 789, 802–03, 865, 886, 923, 928, 930–32, 935–39, 941–42, 949, 951–52, 954, 960, 973, 978, 991
Granger, James, 431, 481, 507–08
Gransden, K. W., 417, 420, 446, 466, 469, 492, 514, 519, 532, 537, 599, 658, 690–91, 698, 733, 747, 752, 757, 762, 764, 814, 816, 819, 822, 823–24, 825, 826, 828, 831, 832, 833, 836, 838, 844, 845, 846, 847–48, 852, 853, 855, 857, 859–60, 863, 916, 924, 931–32
Gray, Thomas, 481
Greene, Thomas M., 612
Grierson, Herbert J. C., 418–19, 420, 432–33, 444, 468, 476, 480, 487–88, 501–02, 510, 514, 537, 539, 542–46, 551, 555, 561–63, 569, 572, 575, 580, 581, 582, 600, 606, 608, 614, 616–18, 625–26, 629, 630, 633, 640, 645, 650, 655–56, 658, 708–09, 712–15, 724, 736, 741, 745, 756, 758, 766, 777, 779, 784, 806, 810, 811, 812, 817–21, 823, 824, 825–26, 828, 830–31, 833, 837–38, 840, 842, 846, 848–50, 851, 855, 857, 860–61, 863, 865, 868, 873, 888, 894, 900, 903, 906, 908–09, 914–18, 923, 926–27, 932, 935, 937, 940, 947–51, 954, 957–58, 960–61, 964–66, 968, 973, 974, 977–78, 980, 982–83, 987–88
Griffin, Dustin, 440, 455–56, 475, 669, 746–47, 751, 788, 809
Grigson, Geoffrey, 609, 618, 620–21, 627, 730, 767, 811, 820, 822, 823, 825, 830, 832, 836, 839, 848, 849, 853, 860, 863, 898, 904, 915
Gros, Leon-Gabriel, 436, 447
Grosart, Alexander B., 416, 417, 431, 443, 458, 509–10, 539–40, 547–53, 555, 557, 559–60, 565–66, 569, 572–75, 577, 601, 609–11, 614, 617–18, 620, 623, 631, 634–40, 645, 698, 701–02, 706, 710, 715, 722, 724–25, 730, 758, 763, 766, 777, 811, 814, 816, 818, 820–26, 828, 830–33, 835–38, 840, 844, 846, 848–49, 851, 853, 855, 859–60, 861, 863, 865, 891, 897, 900, 904, 906–08, 910, 912, 914, 922, 934–35, 937–41, 945–60, 962–65, 967, 970–71, 974, 977–78, 983, 987
Grove, Robin, 733, 735, 744
Guibbory, Achsah, 455, 461–62, 472, 521, 653, 738, 740, 754, 769, 771, 881, 905
Guilhamet, Leon, 467
Guilpin, Everard, 427
Guiness, Gerald, 757
Guiney, Louise I., 416, 433
Guss, Donald L., 540, 558, 827, 928

Johnson, S. F., **516**, **530**

Johnson, Samuel, **431**, 508, **542**, 544, 547, 552, 557–59, 562–63, 565, 567, 571–74, 603, 618, 621, 623, 626, 628, 636, 639, 641, 645, 698, 711, 722, 756, 764, 813, 815, 820–22, 827–28, 831–35, 838, 842–44, 846, 850

Jonas, Leah, **434**, **469**, **511**, **544**

Jones, Emrys, 539, 541–42, **543**, 544, 547, 549, 551–52, 555, 561–63, 567, 573–74, 576, 698–700, 702–03, 705, 710–11, 724–25, 729–30, **738**, 764, 770

Jones, Evan, **492**, 812–13

Jonson, Ben, **427–29**, **480**, **655**, **920**, **934**

Jordan, William K., **657**, **748**

Kantra, Robert A., **665**

Kawasaki, Toshihiko, **537**

Kenner, Hugh, 702–03, 710–11, 714, 731, 767

Kerins, Frank, **423**, **438**, **453**, **461**, **478**, **498**, **520**, **525**, **534**, 549–50, **571**, **578**, **590**, **595**, **597**, **599**, **607**, **617**, **624**, 635–36, **646**, **652**, **665**, **677**, **697**, **701**, **736**, **759**, **782**, **787**, **793**, 798–99, 804–05, **845**, **852**, **858**, **863**, 866–67, **871**, **880**, **889**, **893**, 901–02, **912**, 979

Kermode, Frank, **420–21**, **437**, **481**, 493–94, **511**, **543**, 548–49, **552**, 561, 565, **609**, 621, 628, 632, 634, 638, 641, 645, 651, 659, **661**, 691, **703**, 715, 722, 724, 727, 730, **731**, **733**, 763, 767

Kermode, Frank and John Hollander, **422**, **467**, **482**, **495**, **651**, **662**, **698**, 699–700, 702–03, 705, 708–11, 713–15, 717, 722–25, **727–28**, 731, 733–34, 736, **740**, 742, 745, 747, 757, 759, 763–64, 767–68, 770

Kermode, Frank, Stephen Fender, and Kenneth Palmer, **467**, **495**, **516**, **523**, **571**, **575**, 576, 652, **662**, 700–01, **716**, **721**, **724**, **726**, **732**, 739–40, 752, 763, **767**

Kernan, Alvin, **446**, **467**, **470**, **481**

Keynes, Geoffrey, **825**

King, Bruce, **453**, **460–61**

King, John N., **417**, **426**, **442**, **501**, **664**, **671**, **744**

Kippis, Andrew, **431**

Kiséry, András, **480**, **505**, **513**, **788**, **801**, **839**

Kishimoto, Yoshitaka, **435**

Klause, John, **610**, **651**, **666**, **670**, **724**, **766**, **920**, 928–29, **987**

Klawitter, George, **425**, **456**, **518**, **521**, **529**, **537**, **559**, **564**, **566**, **570**, **572**, 578–79, **783**

Kneidel, Gregory, **686**

Knottenbelt, E. M., **501**, **654**, **734**

Knox, Vicesimus, **481**

Koch, Walter A., **436**

Korte, Donald M., **522**, **532**

K.P.D.E., **813**

Kruzhkova, G., 541, **543**, 554, 556, 561, **565**, 569, 605, **617**, **628**, 640, **670**, 727, 729, 767, 814, 818, 819, 823, 825, 826, 828, 834, 839, 846, 849, 853, 855, 859, 860, 863

Kupersmith, William, 466, **473**

Kusunose, Toshihiko, **459**, 470–71, **495**, **502**

L., W., of Leicester, **606**

Lacan, Jacques, 760

Lamb, Charles, **923**, **942–43**

Landor, Walter Savage, **483**

Lang, Andrew, 416, 466, **481**

Larson, Deborah Aldrich, **474**

Lauritsen, John R., **437**, **450**, **460**, **477–78**, **495–96**, **523**, **542**, **557**, **583**, **632**, **662**, **677**, **718**, **742**, **791**, **815**, **870**, **871**, **878**, **881**, **893**

Leavis, F. R., 680, 690, 702, 729, 748, 752, 756

Lecocq, Louis, **420–21**, **436**, **447**, **458**, **463–64**, **470**, **476**, 493–94, **512**, **522**, **531**, **549**, **577**, **591**, 595–96, **600**, **616**, **622**, **646**, **660**, **673**, **676**, **681**, **689**, **691**, **696**, 699–700, **705**, **739**, **748**, 760–61, **767**, **771**, **780**, **785**, **844**, 861–62, 864, 865, **868**, **877**, 882–83, **888**, **896**, **915**

LeComte, Edward, **436**, **447**, **467**, **580**, **803**, **859**, 866, 898, 919, 924, 933, 974

Lederer, Josef, **751**

Lee, Sangyup, **442**, **457**, **467**, **556**

Lee, Sidney, **468**, 928

Legouis, Pierre, **434**, **489**, **541**, 543–44, 547–50, 555, 559–61, **566**, 569, 571–72, **576**, 613–14, 621–23, 625, **658**, 690, **709**, 711–12, 745, 822–23, 830, 834–36, 841–42, 846–47, **852**, 855, 857, 858, 859, 861, 903–04, 911–13

Lein, Clayton D., **520**, **581**, **584**, **587**, **593**, **597**, 601–02, 605, 607–09, **611**, 616–17, 619–20, **622**, **630**, 632–35, **637**, **643**, **648**

Leishman, J. B., **435**, **446**, 466, **468**, **515**, **527**, **554**, **570**, **585**, **591**, **607**, **638**, **650**, **658**, **735**, **780**, **790**, **803**, **835**, **856**, **859**, **865**, **868**, **887**, **893**, **895**, **907**

Lerner, Laurence, **482**, **513**, 810–11, **814**

Levi, Peter, **495**

Lewalski, Barbara Kiefer and Andrew J. Sabol, **449**, **464**, **471**, **519**, **527**, **540**, **549**, **561**, **568**, **662**, **689**, **713**, **715**, **728**, **759**, **767**

Lewes, George Henry, **483**, 859, 921–22

Lewis, C. S., **420**, **463**, 469–70, **481**, **498**, **516**, **543**, **582**, **585**, **659**, **803**

Lewis, David, **783**

Lewis, E. Glyn, **433**, **445**, **672**, **779**, **785**, **845**

Lewis, Marjorie D., 523–24

Lindsay, Jack, **419**, **433**, **445**, **469**, **476**, **591**, **657**, **751**

Ling, W., **429**

Murphy, John, 494, 544, 549, 646
Murray, W. A., 919, 924, 928, 930

Nagoya, Yasuhiko, 494
Nelly, Una, 436, 583, 650, 651, 660, 717, 744
Nethercot, Arthur H., 416, 419, 433, 488–89, 509, 510–11
Newton, Richard C., 449–50, 459, 519–20, 533, 586, 600, 603, 612, 616, 644, 646, 674, 748, 753, 762, 771, 790, 796, 822, 834, 844, 877, 883, 892, 894–95, 898–902, 906, 909–10, 912, 915
Nicholl, Charles, 503, 724–25
Nicolas, Nicholas H., 427
Nicolson, Marjorie Hope, 919
Nilsen, Don L. F., 418, 435, 444, 467, 500, 509, 515, 783, 868
Norbrook, David, 424, 440, 455, 667, 675, 690
Northup, Clark Sutherland, 487
Norton, Charles Eliot, 417, 432, 506, 510, 560–61, 565, 567–68, 572, 603, 621, 640, 702, 767, 777, 818, 820, 823, 830, 836–37, 839, 844, 850, 853, 855, 860–61, 865, 891, 904, 914, 918, 937–40, 942–43, 949, 957–59, 962, 964–65, 973
Novarr, David, 732
Nutt, Joe, 416, 425, 515, 518, 536, 539, 540, 546–48, 550–51, 553, 555, 557, 559–60, 561–62, 563, 565, 567–68, 571, 575–78, 654, 671, 678, 685, 694, 697, 698, 701–02, 703, 707, 710, 711, 713, 716, 719, 721, 731, 739, 743, 748, 755, 758–59, 763, 767, 772

Ochojski, Paul M., 435, 650, 658, 777, 806
O[ldisworth]., G[iles], 429–30, 920, 939–40
Oliver, Paul M., 416, 417, 441, 462, 480, 505, 535, 598, 603, 640, 654, 671, 678, 680, 684–85, 721, 723, 726, 734, 736–37, 739, 744–45, 747, 755, 761–62, 765–66, 770, 771, 773, 775, 811, 909–10
Oras, Ants, 492
Osmond, Rosalie, 716
Ostriker, Alicia, 752
Ousby, Heather Dubrow, 753

Paman, Clement, 784
Parfitt, George, 424, 440, 454–55, 461, 474, 499, 504, 520, 538, 548, 633, 665, 667, 766
Parker, Barbara L. and J. Max Patrick, 516–17, 523, 527–28, 531–32, 536–37, 541, 543, 545, 546, 549–50, 568, 572
Parker, Derek, 437, 516, 583, 662, 781, 869–70
Parnell, Thomas, 507, 655

Parry, Graham, 423, 439, 453, 498, 540, 577, 599–600, 665, 679, 687, 744, 750
Partridge, A. C., 422, 466, 472, 496, 512, 581, 583–84, 586, 597, 637, 652, 663, 682, 752, 757, 760–61
Pask, Kevin, 513
[Patmore, Coventry?], 483, 509, 779, 922, 932, 960
Patrides, C. A., 423, 440, 466, 468, 479, 498–99, 515, 538–39, 541, 542, 543, 544, 547–48, 549–52, 553, 554–55, 557, 558–59, 560–61, 562, 563, 565, 566–67, 569, 572, 573, 574–77, 578, 581, 584, 601–03, 604, 605–06, 608–09, 612, 613, 614, 615–19, 620, 621–22, 623, 624–26, 627, 628–29, 631–33, 634, 635–37, 638–40, 641–42, 644–45, 646, 647–48, 653, 665, 686, 698, 700, 702–03, 706, 708, 710, 711, 713, 714–17, 722, 723–25, 727, 728, 731, 732, 733, 737, 738, 740, 742–43, 745, 748, 754, 756–57, 764–68, 774–75, 938, 947–48, 951, 955, 960, 966–67, 973, 977, 978, 980, 981–86, 987, 988, 989, 990
Patterson, Annabel M., 416, 425, 467, 470, 494, 540, 589, 605, 637, 648, 670–71, 685, 745, 810, 858–59, 872, 891
Payne, Frank Walter, 416, 445, 466, 656, 720, 725, 734, 923, 931–32, 935–36, 945, 958
Pebworth, Ted-Larry, 425, 978
Perkins, D., 431
Peter, John, 446, 514, 580, 591, 650, 810, 813, 824, 828, 839, 850, 862, 910
Phillips, Edward, 430, 480
Piper, William Bowman, 585, 591–92, 596, 605
Pope, Alexander, 430, 442, 505–13, 582, 779, 921, 925
Porter, Peter, 850
Post, Jonathan F. S., 416, 468, 475, 500, 570, 600
Powers, Doris C., 437, 459, 494, 516, 519, 523, 531–33, 546, 571, 583, 586, 595, 644, 661, 676–77, 691–92, 700, 733, 790, 795, 803, 813, 829, 836, 869, 897
Prescott, Anne Lake, 416, 462, 466, 467, 476, 501, 518, 527, 580, 654, 671, 685, 730, 758, 777, 784, 788, 825, 840, 867, 882, 979
Price, Michael W., 783, 788, 801, 809–10, 814–15, 819, 840, 857, 862

Q., R. S., 991

Raizada, Harith, 450, 482, 495, 520, 566, 583, 586, 662, 692, 752, 780, 869
Randolph, Mary C., 463, 469, 531
Ray, Robert H., 467, 517, 667, 683, 695, 702–03, 707, 718, 735, 752, 761, 767, 769, 872, 979

Index of Writers and Historical Figures Cited in the Commentary

Index of Other Poems and Works of Donne Cited in the Commentary

Index of Titles

Index of First Lines

(For poems presented in multiple versions, the line listed is that of the poem's first appearance, and the multiple page numbers refer to the poem's various appearances.)

ABOUT THE EDITORS

Brian Blackley is Teaching Associate Professor of English at North Carolina State University where he teaches courses in Sixteenth and Seventeenth Century Literature and Shakespeare. He has served as Managing Editor of the *John Donne Journal* since 1994, and has published on Donne, William Basse, and Shakespeare.

Donald R. Dickson is Professor of English at Texas A&M University. He is the author of *The Fountain of Living Waters: The Typology of the Waters of Life in Herbert, Vaughan, and Traherne* (1987) and *The Tessera of Antilia: Utopian Brotherhoods & Secret Societies in the Early Seventeenth Century* (1998) and the editor of Thomas and Rebecca Vaughan's *Aqua Vitæ: Non Vitis: Or, The radical Humiditie of Nature: Mechanically, and Magically dissected By the Conduct of Fire, and Ferment* (2001) and *John Donne's Poetry* (2007). A past chair of the MLA Committee on Scholarly Editions, he has been awarded fellowships by the American Council on Education (2000), the Alexander von Humboldt Foundation (1992–1993), and the National Endowment for the Humanities (1983). He is an editor of the Oxford University Press edition of the prose letters of John Donne and the Oxford edition of *The Works of Henry Vaughan* (forthcoming).

Dennis Flynn is retired Professor of English at Bentley University. He is author of *John Donne and the Ancient Catholic Nobility* and has published several essays on Donne. He is a member of the *Donne Variorum* advisory board, the editorial board of the *John Donne Journal*, and the editorial board of *English Literary Renaissance*. He is general editor of the Oxford University Press edition of the prose letters of Donne (work in progress).

M. Thomas Hester is retired Alumni Distinguished Professor of English at North Carolina State University. He has published widely on Renaissance literature, most recently as co-editor, with Dennis Flynn and Jeanne Shami, of *The Oxford Handbook of John Donne* and is the founding editor of *John Donne Journal*. He joined the *Donne Variorum* advisory board in 1982 and assumed the role of co-Volume Commentary Editor of *The Satyres* at that time.

Anne James teaches English at the University of Regina, Saskatchewan, Canada. She is an assistant editor of the Oxford University Press edition of Donne's prose letters and the *Variorum* edition of the verse letters and is embarking on a collaborative project to create a database of early modern sermon manuscripts.

Jeffrey S. Johnson is Professor of English at East Carolina University. He is the author of *The Theology of John Donne*, and he co-edited with Eugene Cunnar the collection titled *Discovering and (Re)Covering the Seventeenth Century Religious Lyric*. He has also published a number of essays on Donne and his contemporaries, including the published version of "Donne, imperfect" that he delivered as his address on becoming president of the John Donne Society in 2008. He serves on the advisory board of the *Donne Variorum*, on the executive board of the *John Donne Society*, and on the editorial board of the *John Donne Journal*.

Tracy E. McLawhorn is technology editor and assistant textual editor of the *Variorum*. She received her Ph. D. from Texas A&M University. Her dissertation, directed by Gary A. Stringer, presents a critical edition of 6 of Donne's Songs and Sonets. This work will be incorporated into the *Variorum's* edition of the Songs and Sonets.

Paul A. Parrish is Regents Professor of English Emeritus at Texas A&M University, where he taught courses on Renaissance and early modern literature for 37 years. He is the author of *Richard Crashaw* and has published articles on Donne, Crashaw, Milton, Ralph Ellison, and other Renaissance and modern writers. A former executive director and past president of the South Central Modern Language Association and a past president of the John Donne Society, he has served the *Donne Variorum* as Chief Editor of the Commentary since 1996.

Ted-Larry Pebworth is William E. Stirton Professor in the Humanities and Professor Emeritus of English at the University of Michigan-Dearborn. He is author of *Owen Felltham*; co-author of *Ben Jonson*; and co-editor of *The Poems of Owen Felltham* and *Selected Poems of Ben Jonson* and of collections of essays on Herbert, on Jonson and the Sons of Ben, on Donne, on the seventeenth-century religious lyric, on poetry and politics in the seventeenth century, on Marvell, on Renaissance discourses of desire, and on representing women in the Renaissance. He is a past president of the John Donne Society.

Paul J. Stapleton holds a Ph. D. in Comparative Literature from the University of North Carolina at Chapel Hill, where he is currently a lecturer. He carried out his work on the commentary on the Satyres under the tutelage of Robert V. Young and M. Thomas Hester while an M.A. student at N.C. State. He has published essays on Bede, Alcuin of York, the Jesuit Robert Bellarmine, John Donne, John Milton, and sixteenth-century religious controversy. His dissertation treats the varied cultural responses to the image of the cross in Elizabethan England.

Gary A. Stringer is Professor of English Emeritus at the University of Southern Mississippi, where he taught from 1972 until 2004. From 2004 until 2011 he was Visiting

Professor of English at Texas A&M University, and in 2011 assumed a three-year appointment as David Julian and Virginia Suther Whichard Distinguished Professor in the Humanities at East Carolina University, retiring in 2014. A past president of the South Central Modern Language Association and the John Donne Society, he founded the *Donne Variorum* project in 1981 and has served the edition as general editor and senior textual editor for over 30 years.

Ernest W. Sullivan, II, is Edward S. Diggs Professor Emeritus of English at Virginia Tech. He is editor of *Biathanatos by John Donne*; of *The First and Second Dalhousie Manuscripts: Poems and Prose by John Donne and Others*; and of *The Harmony of the Muses*, as well as co-editor of *Puzzles in Paper* and *Lord Jim, A Tale* by Joseph Conrad. He is author of *The Influence of John Donne: His Uncollected Seventeenth-Century Printed Verse*. Sullivan is also the general textual editor of the Collected works of Abraham Cowley. He is a past president of the John Donne Society.

Julie W. Yen is Professor and Vice Chair of the English Department at California State University, Sacramento, where she teaches courses on Shakespeare, Milton, Renaissance literature and Asian American literature. She has published essays on Donne, Richard Barnfield, and Aurelian Townshend.

DESIGNER: Sharon L. Sklar
TYPESETTER: Tracy E. McLawhorn
PRINTER AND BINDER: Sheridan Books
TYPEFACE: Goudy Old Style